TV Heaven

Jim Sangster

and

Paul Condon

Collins

HarperCollins*Publishers*
77–85 Fulham Palace Road
Hammersmith
London W6 8JB

www.collins.co.uk

Collins is a registered trademark of
HarperCollins*Publishers*

First published in 2005

10 09 08 07 06 05

10 9 8 7 6 5 4 3 2 1

A catalogue record for this book is available from the British Library

Commissioning editor – Helen Brocklehurst
Managing editor – Emma Callery
Editor – Kate Parker
Indexes – Rosi Callery, Sean Callery, Rachel Pearson, Suzy Rowe
Internal design – Sara Soskolne
Cover design – Sarah Christie
Picture research – Cat Green
Editorial assistant – Julia Koppitz

Set in Fresco by Rowland Phototypesetting Ltd,
Bury St Edmunds, Suffolk
Printed and bound in Great Britain by
William Clowes Ltd, Beccles, Suffolk

TV Heaven

Contents

Welcome to Our World

'The answer to life's problems aren't at the bottom of a bottle, they're on TV!'

Homer Simpson

Designed to be viewed in the home, television is the easiest-to-enjoy form of art around: we love the fact that it has comfier seating than most theatres, and the distractions of popcorn and other people's mobile phones are at least minimised. We also love how it can afford to take its time setting up situations and characters, with instalments spanning months, even years, rather than a box-office-friendly timeslot; compare the film *Goodfellas*, at 2 hours 30 minutes, with the (to date) five series of *The Sopranos* at 60+ hours and counting. It can also be more immediate – the early days of telly were live, remember; and some drama shows – *Coronation Street*, ER and *The Bill* among them – have flirted with the live format even as recently as 2003, just to prove that they still can. We treat certain reality TV shows like guilty pleasures: the two best nights of the TV year come from *Big Brother*, when they herd a group of egoist wannabes into a house (presumably to give society at large a rest) and then emotionally torture them for three months until the two least-hateful are left. It's a voyeuristic, hedonistic dream, like the last days of the Roman Empire with all the fun of bloodthirsty audiences and the leonine paparazzi, but without the volcanoes and with the possibility that the odd Christian might actually win. We are unashamedly passionate about television. Echoing the spirit of a certain Paul Whitehouse character from *The Fast Show*, we're tempted to declare, 'In't TV brilliant?!' When television sets first became widely available in the UK (which for the sake of argument we're taking as the months prior to the coronation of Queen Elizabeth II), TV was not thought of as in any way important; it certainly wasn't art, despite the admirable values it inherited from the BBC's first top man, Lord Reith, to 'educate, inform and entertain'. The technology of the early 1950s wasn't equipped to preserve broadcasts either; while the great purge of the archives in the 1970s was responsible for the loss of a horrific number of shows, it was the simple inability to record these programmes that accounts for their absence today.

Whereas we can now record last night's *Coronation Street* onto a home DVD recorder, the only way to preserve a live broadcast was to get a film camera and point it at a TV screen. For some TV shows, even this option was too expensive so the alternative was to take photographs of the broadcast (the work of a wonderful man called John Cura employing this 'telesnap' method accounts for some of the only surviving visual records of early episodes of *Doctor Who*, for example). In short, like a stage play, if you missed a broadcast, that was it. No Saturday 'omnibus', no satellite or cable 'Gold' channel, just your next-door neighbour's excited summary over the garden fence the next day. And it was like that pretty much up until 1980, when the first home video recorders began to take root. That was when broadcasters slowly realised that the domestic video market could be a veritable goldmine and rushed to their archives only to find many of them bare.

Television as a medium has come full circle in its 50 years of regular broadcasts. Now we have five terrestrial channels, up to 100 or more cable channels and internet broadcasts (such as the 24-hour live 'feeds' for shows like *Big Brother*). The remote control unit has given rise to the phenomenon of 'serial channel surfers'- glass-eyed alpha males whose purpose in life is to ensure anyone else in the room gets to see no more than five seconds of any programme at a time. Thanks to the technology available from the BBC, if you miss the 7.30 p.m. showing of *EastEnders* on Monday, you can watch the BBC Three repeat or the Sunday omnibus back on BBC One, or, if you're patient, as part of the ongoing repeats on UK Gold and UK Gold+1. And, as of 2005, you'll be able to download it via the BBC's media player and watch it as many times as you like within a seven-day window. It's saturation that gives new meaning to the phrase 'unmissable TV'. But then, as TV addicts, we don't for a second think this is necessarily a bad thing.

There are already a number of guides to television available, either grouped by genre (TV Detectives; TV Sci-Fi, etc.) or else in the form of listings of as many shows as the authors can find. But to date, there hasn't been a collection of critical analysis on the scale that this book attempts. Having spent the last 20 years avidly watching TV shows of the past, we feel in a very good position to understand why.

If you're reading this, then we can immediately guess two things; first, you like television (a given) and, second, you've already had a skim through the book for some of your favourites – in which case this introduction might also serve as an apology.

A staggeringly dedicated group of TV archivists called Kaleidoscope has spent over a decade compiling listings of every single programme ever made within the British Isles. The results of their research are available in the form of five or more telephone-directory-sized volumes. Obviously, our own guide will, by necessity, have some omissions. Some shows will be reduced to footnotes in history (the only reference in this book to the 1970 science fiction series *The Adventures of Don Quick*, which starred top British actor Ian Hendry, is the one you've just read), whereas others might be given a significant amount of coverage because we think they significantly influential, left the biggest impression upon the minds of the viewers or are simply shows we believe exemplify the genre better than others.

We are both products of the 1970s. We've never known a time where there were fewer than three channels or where colour TV wasn't the norm. Even though we watch 1950s and '60s dramas just as happily as the latest multi-million-dollar, all-star American import, we'll always be viewing those older shows as treasured relics rather than genuine modern competitors.

It has to be said, some shows that had our nation gripped at the time of first broadcast are almost unwatchable now. But it's equally true to say there are some modern shows that pale when compared with productions made 30 years ago. While we're always sensitive to the production methods and pressures each show endured, we also have to be aware that for many there will be little or no chance to see the bulk of these any time soon. We don't think it would be fair, for example, to declare *The Grove Family* as the best soap opera ever made, partly because so little of it exists, and partly because, sadly, that would be a whopping great lie. So this is, if you will, a fairly subjective guide through the ages.

Telly Text (or 'How to Use this Book')

This book is divided into listings for each programme. We've selected 100 shows to receive the full in-depth treatment, while there are more than 800 others to dip into as and when you fancy. We've focused more on drama and comedy than factual programming, but the very nature of the modern broadcaster's obsession with reality TV has led to a curious fusion of genres. Now we're more likely to be discussing the drama or comedy of ten members of the public in a house in Ealing than the residents and staff of an Edwardian town house – unless that house is also the setting for a reality TV experiment. Though they may well be entertaining, documentary programming as a rule tends to lean more on those Reithian BBC values we mentioned earlier. But there have been a number of significant crossovers, such as David Attenborough's *Life on Earth* and Michael Palin's travelogue shows, or the marvellous technological innovations of the *Walking with Dinosaurs* series, achievements we duly note in this book.

In this digital age, more and more shows are finding their feet on minority satellite channels first. For us, though, it's terrestrial broadcasts that count, so unless it's enjoyed broadcast on one of the five main channels in the UK in something other than late-night regional variation slots, you won't find it here. This means the tragic loss of 'unique' BSB drama *Jupiter Moon* and American imports like *War of the Worlds* (which was shown sporadically as a schedule filler in some ITV regions). Thanks to Channel Five's well-timed repeats, though, this means we can include the priceless *Prisoner: Cell Block H* (although even without Five's repeats, we'd have cheated to make sure it got in – no scruples, us).

We decided early on that we didn't want this to be simply a list of episode titles; for one thing, shows like *Z Cars* would take up more space than we could spare just listing that kind of information. We're also restricted in terms of the amount of actors we can afford to credit for long-running soaps with a high cast turn-over, although we've tried to include as many significant cast members as possible. Likewise, writers are occasionally restricted to the most significant contributors rather than exhaustive, completist lists, and the 'broadcast' sections include original runs only, rather than repeats.

To keep things simple, we've stuck to an alphabetical listing. We considered dividing entries according to genre, but there were several reasons why this seemed unhelpful to the reader, and less valid for a book of this kind. First, many programmes are cross-genre: for example *Captain Scarlet and the Mysterons* may star puppets, but we don't consider it to be in the same bracket as *Stingray*, despite the common factor of Gerry Anderson. Secondly, industry norms (such as the department of the production company making the programme) have often curiously affected a show's genre. For example, *Doctor Who* is a programme for children (whenever Mary Whitehouse attacked it, she always expressed concerns about what it was doing to children) and was shown in a child-friendly slot, but because the children's department didn't make it, it was classed as a drama and got a drama budget. And it's common knowledge that the main reason why *The Young Ones* boasted a guest band each week was purely to milk the bigger budget provided by light entertainment compared to that offered by comedy, but it doesn't sit comfortably with *The Black and White Minstrel Show* or *The Generation Game*. So, alphabetical it is then.

For each of the television programmes we're covering in this book, you'll find two main sections – one detailing the facts and figures behind the show, and then our own viewpoint, setting the programme in question into its historical context.

Title

As you've probably already spotted, programmes are listed in this book in alphabetical order. For shows with titles beginning with 'A' or 'The', discard that particular word from the alphabetisation, so you'll find *The Saint* alongside the other S-entries rather than with the Ts. We use the British titles for programmes rather than the title used in its country of origin. For instance, although viewers in Australia know what *Prisoner* is, we in Britain knew that same prison-based soap opera as *Prisoner: Cell Block H*, a change in title designed to enable UK viewers to differentiate the show from the classic 1960s surreal fantasy show starring Patrick McGoohan. Similarly, although Raymond Burr's second big starring role was in the series *Ironside*, here in the UK the programme was known as *A Man Called Ironside* instead – hence you'll find the programme listed in the Ms rather than in the Is.

Genre

On the line following the title we summarise the type of programme we're talking about. Everybody knows that *Coronation Street* is a soap opera and that *Only Fools and Horses* is a sitcom, but such a distinct and easy categorisation isn't always possible. Some programmes changed their nature over the course of time – for instance, *The Avengers* began in its first season as a detective series; by the time of its second and third seasons with Honor Blackman as Cathy Gale, it had evolved into an action/adventure show, and with the arrival of Emma Peel, the programme abandoned its original gritty roots, featuring killer robots, lethal plants from outer space and body-swap equipment, becoming an out-and-out fantasy show. Therefore we've listed the genre of *The Avengers* as Detective/Action-Adventure/Fantasy. Other programmes are also listed with multiple genres as and when appropriate.

Production companies and channel of transmission

Many programmes are made by different companies from the channel on which they are transmitted; we therefore list the production companies responsible for them, and the channels that they were originally broadcast on. For programmes that originated in other countries, both the original channel of broadcast in their country of origin and the UK channel they were shown on are listed. More information about selected broadcasters is included in the book's Glossary and in the 'History of TV' section.

Episode duration

Many programmes had a uniform duration for their episodes; others varied their episode lengths quite radically. Programmes with a variety of episode lengths are listed on a sliding scale, whereas if a show's episode length only varied with occasional special episodes, that is noted too. If times are separated with a slash mark, signifies a programme this was only ever shown in episodes of those two specific lengths.

We've listed wherever possible the duration of programmes on commercial channels like ITV and Channel 4 with the adverts cut out – for example, an episode of *Bad Girls* is listed in the schedules as running for 60 minutes, whereas, in fact, there's only about

45 minutes of actual programme with the other 15 minutes taken up with adverts and trailers.

Broadcast dates

We've tried our best to track down precise dates of transmission for as many of the programmes as possible – at the very least, we've noted the years for the first and last transmissions. If we only have a vague idea of a date, it's prefixed with a 'c.' to indicate our best guess from our source materials. One particular area of contention comes with ITV programmes. For many years, programmes were not 'networked' at the same time across all of the ITV regions – Granada might show a particular programme on a different time and day from ATV, for example. We've therefore tried to list the date of the first transmission anywhere in the UK rather than just the listings for one ITV region. For programmes originally shown abroad, the transmission dates of their country of origin are shown. We also list the dates of special 'reunion' or 'revival' episodes of programmes, but we don't separate out individual Christmas specials if they fall within the original first and last transmission dates of a programme.

Cast list

The main players in each television programme are shown here. There are some subtle differences, however:

- 'Cast' means the entire line-up of the show, i.e. everyone who ever appeared.
- 'Principal cast' is used for programmes such as soap operas, which have starred literally hundreds of cast members over the years. Here we have listed regular performers who have had a long-lasting or important impact on the show's ongoing plotlines.
- A 'regular' cast member is someone who has appeared in a block of episodes or in the majority of episodes.
- A 'recurring' cast member might have been in a significant number of episodes but not necessarily on what we might call a regular basis. For instance, a character might have appeared in the first year of a soap opera, then disappeared for 20 years, then returned for a while.
- Where character names are separated by a comma, this indicates different roles played by the same actor. A slash between names indicates the same character going by a different name.

Creator(s)

Many programmes were the brainchild of one or more specific individuals; we use this space to sing the praises of these creative geniuses.

Producer(s)/writer(s)

Taking the lead from the movie industry, it's often the producer's vision that gets the show made in the first place. You can often tell what kind of a show to expect by taking note of whether it's made by, say, Gerard Glaister (such as *Secret Army, Howards' Way*) or Glen A. Larson (*Battlestar Galactica, Knight Rider*). We also keep track of the person or people responsible for writing the scripts.

Other areas covered

Television is crammed full of memorable and not-so-memorable theme tunes. Everyone can identify those of *Coronation Street, Hawaii Five-O* or *Star Trek* and now you can even have a theme song as your ringtone. We've tried to find references for the people responsible for the theme music as well as include little snippets of pertinent trivia, such as which of them got into the pop charts.

You'll also find that some entries have additional trivia. We've also included specialist websites for some shows, which offer a little more background information.

In the body of the commentary, shows listed in ***bold italics*** are discussed in their own entry within the book.

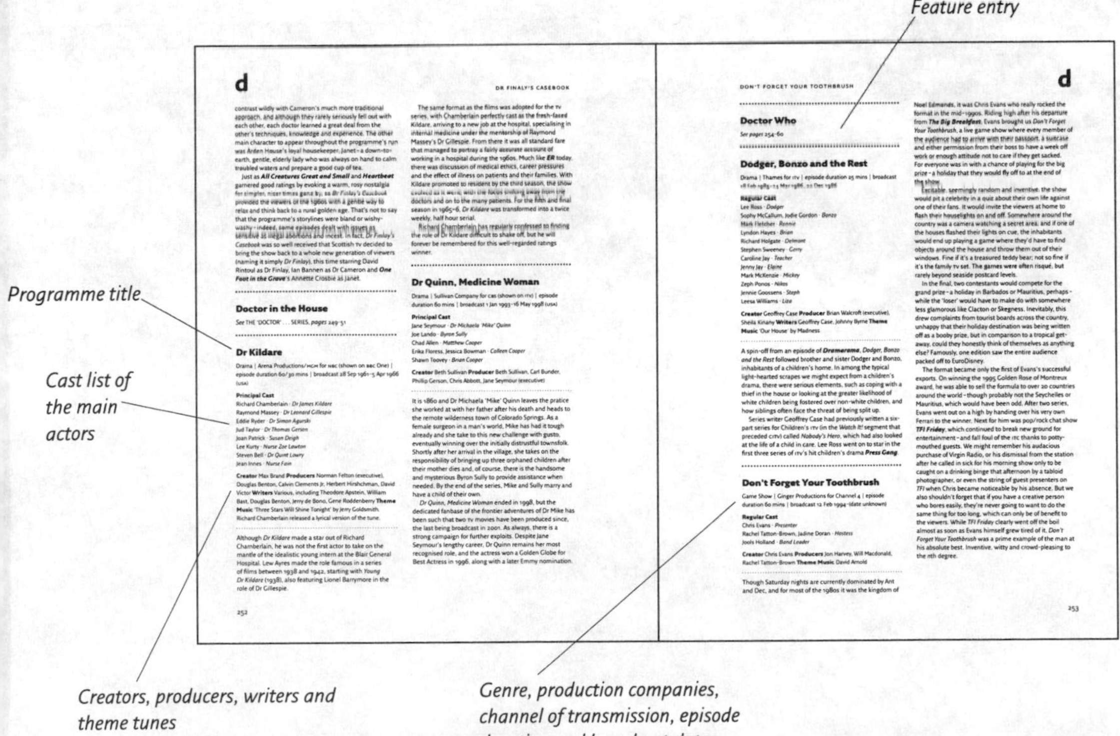

The History of TV

The roots of television in Britain – and, in fact, the world – can be found in the birth of radio and the BBC. Originally, 'BBC' stood for the 'British Broadcasting Company'. It was founded in 1922, the result of a consortium of companies to encourage the British people to use and buy into radio technology. During the General Strike of 1926, a group of politicians led by Winston Churchill called for the BBC to be brought under state control. Thankfully, the then-prime minister Stanley Baldwin was persuaded not to take such action by the BBC's general manager, John Reith. Reith believed the BBC had a duty to 'educate, inform and entertain' without fear of political influence, and these 'Reithian values' remain at the core of public service broadcasting in Britain even today. The General Strike was good for the BBC, though, as the public began to rely on its evening news broadcasts more and more. In 1927, on receipt of its royal charter, the company became the British Broadcasting Corporation.

The birth of television

The history of television has a particularly murky beginning. When asked who invented the goggle box, most people– certainly most Trivial Pursuit players – will answer 'John Logie Baird'. That particular claim is disputed by Marconi, whose rival format was the one the world eventually adopted. But even before Marconi and Baird began stag rutting for supremacy of the cathode ray tube, a number of other gentlemen contributed to the great debate. Various inventors showed their workings across the globe to suggest that they had cracked the problem of transmitting pictures in a manner similar to

Marconi's wireless telegraph, though some really only amounted to flashing lights and not much else. In 1930, a Utah farmer by the name of Philo Taylor Farnsworth patented an 'electron scanning tube' – or cathode ray tube – that he'd invented a few years before. Though John Logie Baird had successfully demonstrated his own television system at Selfridges in London in 1925, Farnsworth had been able to prove that he first outlined his ideas to his high school teacher in 1920 when he was just 14 years old. Logie Baird therefore gets the credit for inventing a mechanical television machine and Farnsworth the credit for the first all-electronic TV. There was another pretender to the throne in the form of Vladimir Kosma Zworykin. But he was born in Russia and no way was an American patent office going to let him beat their own wunderkind.

Working with an old friend, Guy 'Mephy' Robertson, and a consortium of interested parties consisting of a research engineer from the BBC and London cinema proprietor Will Day, John Logie Baird successfully transmitted rather shadowy pictures by mechanical means. In January 1924, he made his first public demonstration of the device. Baird gave his original television apparatus to the South Kensington Science Museum in 1926, and within just ten years Britain claimed the prize of the world's first transmission of 'high-definition television pictures' (a distinction coined to invalidate a German attempt by a few hundred lines of picture). The exact format for British TV wouldn't be settled on immediately though: both Baird and the Marconi company had ideas as to which format to go along with, and it was only a devastating fire at Baird's Crystal Palace centre that left the way wide open for Marconi to become the sole provider of the UK's 405-line technology, which it did on 6 February 1937. It remained the standard format for British TV until the launch of BBC Two in 1964.

Leslie Mitchell was Britain's first TV announcer when he presented the launch night of BBC television from Alexandra Palace on 26 August 1936. It was a modest affair, only broadcast to people at the Olympia Radio Show, but it was a start, and just a few months later, Alexander Palace was again the site from which the BBC launched the full TV service . . . in London, at least.

Almost all of television's great 'firsts' occurred when few people were watching, even within the small catchment area of London. On 9 December 1936, Britain's first TV cookery presentation was made as Moira Meighn showed viewers how to prepare a meal that could be cooked in just 15 minutes using just one ring on an electric stove. On 19 January the following year, the BBC broadcast the first play specially written for television – J. Bissell Thomas's *The Underground Murder Mystery*, set in Tottenham Court Road underground station. Just 400 TV sets were able to transmit it . By the end of 1937, that figure would be 2000, bolstered by the first ever sports commentary on TV – Harry Mallin reporting on an amateur England vs Ireland boxing tournament (4 February) – the live broadcast of the coronation of King George VI (12 May), the first transmission of footage from Wimbledon (21 June), the Lord Mayor's Show (9 September) and the Remembrance service from the Cenotaph (11 November).

The following year saw the first transmissions of the Oxford and Cambridge boat race (2 April), the FA Cup final (30 April), in which Preston North End beat Huddersfield Town, and Trooping the Colour (9 June). The first television serial, *Ann and Harold*, began on 12 July 1938, the first of a five-part comedy based on the radio series by Louis Goodrich and starring Ann Todd and William Hutchinson. It was all going so well until Hitler went and spoiled things. With all BBC studios and transmitters converting to wartime conditions, BBC television ceased transmission partway through a Mickey Mouse cartoon, 'Mickey's Gala Première'. Two days later, Britain and France declared war on Germany. By the time it came off the air, BBC television had an audience of around 20–25,000 households.

On 7 June 1946, the BBC recommenced transmissions from Alexandra Palace, cheekily beginning with the same cartoon that had been so rudely interrupted seven years earlier. On 7 December that year, the erection of a transmitter in Sutton Coldfield to serve the Midlands took TV outside of London for the first time. The first programme specifically aimed at children arrived on 9 June in a slot called, simply, *For the Children*, presented by Jan Bussell, and featured the Hogarth Circus, a puppet show that eventually starred a small mule called Muffin (Muffin got his own series on 20 October).

Amazingly, it took 18 months from the restoration of the television service for BBC bosses to cotton on to the fact that people might actually want to watch news programmes. *Newsreel*, the first regular television news programme, ran from 5 January 1948 until 2 January 1954. At this time, though, no presenters as we know them today were used – instead, film clips of important news stories were shown in much the same way as the well-established newsreels shown in cinemas. And on 29 July 1949, the Beeb broadcast its first ever TV weather forecast – although it took until 11 January 1954 for weather forecasters themselves to appear on camera (George Cowling was the first, broadcasting from the BBC's Lime Grove studios). Before then, we were simply treated to dignified and clipped-voiced commentary describing the meteorological happenings and an occasional disembodied hand appearing on-screen to point out wind speeds, isobars and the like.

Arrival of ITV

With the BBC proving conclusively that television did indeed have a future in the UK of the post-war years, it wasn't long until the idea of a second channel was mooted. The new channel, Independent Television (ITV), was to be set up along similar lines to the commercial channels already operating in countries like the USA – specifically, it would carry advertising as a method of generating the revenue it needed to survive rather than receiving any government or public funding. On 30 July 1954, the government established the Independent Television Authority (ITA), a distinct organisation set up to supervise the creation of the ITV network.

One of the principal differences between ITV and the BBC was in the regional focus that ITV was founded upon. Each area of the

UK was to have its own local ITV station, a policy that was deemed to be more cost-effective and less risky than establishing one huge national company. Each region would create its own programming as well as taking its pick of the output from the other regions. After more than a year's planning, the first ITV region to begin broadcasting (at 7.15 p.m. on 22 September 1955) was Associated-Rediffusion, which covered the London area on weekdays only. Weekend broadcasts for the London area were handled by ATV (Associated Television), a company that would also (somewhat confusingly) broadcast on weekdays in the Midlands region – although they didn't begin transmissions from Birmingham until 17 February 1956. ABC took over responsibilities for weekend broadcasting in the Midlands and the North, while Granada became the North's weekday franchise holder and other smaller areas were catered for by Grampian, Scottish, Border, Tyne Tees, Anglia, Ulster, Westward and Teledu Cymru, which took until 1962 to reach maximum coverage of the British Isles.

Of all of the ITV regions, Granada was the last survivor. By the early 2000s, it controlled half of the ITV network, the rest being run by Carlton, a company that took over from Thames in 1991. Regional television had been slowly phased out through the 1990s with more centrally controlled scheduling, which enabled shows like ***Emmerdale*** to be fully networked. On 7 October 2003, the government approved the merger of Granada and Carlton and the creation of a single ITV company for England and Wales. After 50 years, the principles that had inspired the regional policy of ITV were abandoned.

BBC Two, 625-line TV and colour

With America broadcasting on both a 525-line system and in colour, the British government recognised the need for an improvement to the national television system. In 1960, research began into quite how a new TV system might be handled and it was decided that the best way to go about it would be to establish a third channel – BBC Two, which would run on a picture of 625 lines and eventually take up colour in advance of the existing BBC channel and ITV. However, the new system would also require new aerials and – frustratingly – new TV sets. To enable engineers to tune televisions to the new channel, the BBC created and broadcast a test card, a screen pf various patterns, accompanied by a high-pitched whine.

On 20 April 1964, BBC TV was renamed BBC One. At the same time, BBC Two was scheduled to begin transmission, using a much clearer and sharper broadcast system utilising 625 lines of picture information (rather than the established 405 lines used by ITV and BBC One). However, a huge power failure in West London knocked out BBC Television Centre and took BBC Two off air on its launch night. BBC Two finally managed to scramble its way on air the following morning at 11.00 a.m. The first programme shown on the fledgling channel was the inaugural edition of ***Play School***.

The channel initially adopted a stripped-and-stranded approach with each night of the week taken up with specific themes – Tuesday was high-brow educational programmes, Wednesday was for repeats. The 'Seven Faces of the Week' idea, as it was known, was not a success, though, and was gradually phased out. BBC Two, however, was seen as innovative and willing to go in directions the other channels often couldn't. One direction it hadn't planned on going in was pushing the boundaries of bad language. While the first actual swearword on television occurred in an edition of ***Steptoe and Son*** (the word being 'bloody'), the dreaded F-word reared its head on 13 November 1965, during an edition of BBC Two's late-night satirical debate programme *BBC3* (ah, the prescience!). Critic Kenneth Tynan observed: 'I doubt if there are any rational people to whom the word "fuck" would be particularly diabolical, revolting or totally forbidden'. Tynan subsequently became infamous for that critical remark.

BBC Two finally begin its first regular colour broadcasts on 1 July 1967 with highlights of Wimbledon. With technology moving at such a fast rate, the Beeb was reluctant to invest in colour TV cameras in case they quickly became obsolete. Therefore the earliest colour broadcasts were designed to bring maximum coverage at minimum expense. One early beneficiary of the policy was snooker game show ***Pot Black***, which was created specifically with colour in mind.

Day time, breakfast time, all the time

Early in 1972, the government lifted its restrictions on the number of hours that television was permitted to be broadcast. As a direct result, ITV soon began scheduling more programmes in the day time, including such gems as *Paint along with Nancy, Farmhouse Kitchen,* ***Rainbow*** and a rural soap opera called ***Emmerdale Farm***. Although the BBC followed suit with its lunchtime programme ***Pebble Mill at One***, both its channels would flip to the test card in the late afternoon and through the night until the early 1980s. The most famous of all test cards, by the way, was known as 'Test Card F', depicting an eight-year-old girl (Carol Hersee, daughter of BBC engineer George Hersee) playing noughts and crosses with a toy clown.

Test Card F's airtime was cut back from 17 January 1983 when BBC One launched its first early morning service. Hosted by Frank Bough and Selina Scott, *Breakfast Time* ran from 6.30 a.m. until 9.30 a.m. each weekday morning. ITV followed suit a few weeks later with new franchise holder TV-AM, which reached screens on 1 February 1983. TV-AM's main weekday programme was *Good Morning Britain*, and its initial presentation line-up – dubbed 'the famous five'– consisted of David Frost, Robert Kee, Michael Parkinson, Angela Rippon and Esther Rantzen. With ratings struggling to pick up, TV-AM took a desperate measure and hired a puppet rodent to host the children's slot. Irreverent, egotistical and genuinely funny, Roland Rat is widely believed to have single-handedly turned the fortunes of TV-AM around. By 1985, the rat had won his own prime-time Saturday evening show on the BBC.

It wouldn't be until 27 October 1986 that the BBC would run a full day-time schedule, with the morning hours filled with chat shows like ***Kilroy*** and viewer feedback show *Open Air* and imports such as Australian soap opera ***Neighbours***. At the same time, the midday news was re-branded and rescheduled as *The One O'Clock News*.

ITV got closer to breaking the 24-hour barrier in 1987 when it began its nighttime service, showing Australian soap ***Prisoner: Cell Block H***, American imports like sci-fi action series *War of the Worlds* or the new ***Twilight Zone*** (and when they ran out, a dodgy US-UK co-produced ghost story anthology called *Worlds Beyond*), *America's Top 40* with Casey Kasem and chat show *Donohue*, along with home-grown stuff like *The James Whale Show* and *The Hitman and Her* (a pop show recorded in a real nightclub with pop god Pete Waterman and the very bubbly presenter Michaela Strachan). Annoyingly, each region had its own schedule, meaning not all of the above were shown in every part of the country. The year 1987 also marked the point where ITV ditched its morning schools and colleges strand, handing it over to Channel 4. In its place came *The Time, The Place* and ***This Morning***, a lively chat show hosted by Richard Madeley and his wife Judy Finnigan. With its morning now filling up nicely, Channel 4 finally launched its own breakfast show, the extremely classy *Channel 4 Daily*, a news-magazine show consisting of regular segments shown at the same point around the hour. The programme ran until 25 September 1992, when it was dropped to make room for ***The Big Breakfast***. It eventually went 24-hour on 6 January 1997, with BBC One following suit on 8 November 1997 (the same night saw the final broadcast of the national anthem at closedown on BBC One – a traditional part of broadcasting since the very early days of radio).

Channel 4, S4C and Five

Channel 4 is actually two channels (though for simplicity we refer to just the one throughout this book). Sianel Pedwar Cymru (S4C) covers the Welsh regions and carries Welsh-language programming as well as much of the output from Channel 4. It launched on 1 November 1982, a day ahead of Channel 4, which covers the rest of the UK. The first programme shown on this radical, controversial network designed to push back the boundaries of programming was quiz show ***Countdown***, hosted by Richard Whitely. Other highlights that night included the Liverpudlian soap ***Brookside*** and, from the ***Comic Strip*** alternative comedy circuit, 'Five Go Mad in Dorset'. ***Brookside*** grabbed the headlines – but for all the wrong reasons and soon the press was referring to 'Channel Swore', carefully ignoring 4's loftier productions like *Nicholas Nickleby* and *Walter*, the story of a mentally disabled man played by Ian McKellen. Over the years, the channel has brought us such delights as innovative music programme ***The Tube*** and lowest common denominator ***The Word***, banned or sexually explicit films marked with a red triangle, some highly innovative cinema thanks to Film Four, and the beginning of the reality TV explosion with ***Big Brother***.

On 30 March 1997, Britain gained another terrestrial channel – Channel 5. Now, in the age of satellite and cable, the launch of yet another new channel left many of us cold. What was its purpose? What did it hope to offer that we didn't get elsewhere? And why did we have to retune our TVs to get it? Some were left waiting for the answer as poor signalling meant certain areas wouldn't be able to receive the channel for some time. What it actually offered was seemingly a steady stream of documentaries about sex and Nazis – sometimes both at the same time. In 2002, Channel 5 rebranded itself as 'five', though that didn't improve its reputation (comedian Harry Hill even took to referring to the channel as 'Channel fünf'.

Multi-channel Britain

Satellite TV arrived in the UK in the mid–1980s, with Superchannel, but that was still very much a niche market, broadcasting from Europe. It wasn't until 5 February 1988, when Rupert Murdoch's Sky launched the UK's first satellite television service, that multi-channel TV became accessible to all – provided they didn't mind a big white dish hanging off the side of their house. Initially, the service included four channels – Sky Channel, Eurosport, Sky Movies and Sky News – although other European channels were available.

Two years later, Sky met its first UK rival with British Satellite Broadcasting (BSB). Launching over a year behind schedule, on 29 April 1990, BSB promised 'five-channel TV' and distinctive square aerials, or 'Squarials'. Of the five channels, Galaxy offered a mix of classic repeats of ***Doctor Who*** and ***Steptoe*** alongside original programming – something Sky were still not providing while music channel the Power Station gave Manchester DJ Chris Evans his first TV break, hosting the *Power Up* breakfast slot. 'Now' screened documentaries, lifestyle shows and classical music programmes, while the Movie and Sports channels were pretty much as they sounded. BSB Movie Channel and Sky Movies entered a bidding war, tying up all the latest blockbusters as well as a few classic films too. Sadly, despite having possibly the stronger broadcast signal and highest-quality picture ever seen on British TV, after just nine months BSB's subscriptions were so low that a merger with Sky (which, to be fair, was also struggling) was unavoidable. On 2 November 1990, Sky and BSB formally merged to form British Sky Broadcasting. By 8 April 1991, all of BSB's channels had been replaced or amalgamated into new Sky ones. Now, Sky's line-up consisted of entertainment channel Sky One, which continued to show the best and the rest of American imports, Sky News, encrypted subscription channels Sky Movies and the Movie Channel (which later became Sky Premier), Sky Sports plus MTV Europe (replacing the Power Station), and Eurosport.

Now TV addicts only had to choose one service, it was a lot easier for people to make their choice. It also meant that other channels began to arrive as consumer confidence in multi-channel TV began to rise. On 1 November 1992, a joint venture between the BBC and Thames produced UK Gold, a selection of some of the best of each channel. Effectively picking up where BSB's Galaxy had left off, it began a (to date) 14-year rotation of shows like *Doctor Who* and ***The Bill***. Exactly five years later, UKTV launched, creating three new channels alongside UK Gold – UK Horizons, UK Style and UK Arena (which, by 2004, also included UKTV History, Documentary, Food and Bright Ideas).

Thames aside, the rest of ITV's contributions to multi-channel broadcasting began on 1 October 1996 when the largest of the ITV regions, Granada, worked with Sky to create Granada Sky Broadcasting, a four-channel service of Granada Plus (similar to UK Gold), Granada Men and Motors, Granada Good Life and Granada Talk TV. ITV and the BBC continued to add to the available number of channels: BBC News 24 arrived on 9 November 1997, the BBC's first new UK channel since the launch of BBC Two in 1964; 23 September 1998 saw the launch of BBC Choice and BBC Parliament; with ITV's OnDigital service in November 1998 (a month after Sky launched their own digital satellite subscription), viewers were treated to a team-up between Granada and Carlton, by then the two biggest stakeholders in ITV, ITV2 being unveiled the same month. The ITV News Channel joined the OnDigital line-up in August 2000, with ITV Sports following in August 2001.

And so to the final push – so far. With digital TV on the increase, through satellite and cable subscriptions, Channel 4 got in on the act with E4, an entertainment channel that managed to keep shows like ***Friends*** and ***ER*** away from Sky while also offering extensive extra coverage of ***Big Brother*** for nearly three months of the year. The rebranding of OnDigital to ITV Digital was accompanied by a memorable ad campaign featuring comedian Johnny Vegas and a knitted monkey. Sadly, it wasn't enough to save the service as ITV Digital closed on 1 May 2002. In October the same year, a consortium headed by the BBC rescued the service as part of Freeview, a no-subscription service requiring a one-off purchase of a set-top box that then provided channels for free. At the time of writing, Freeview includes E4, CBBC and CBeebies, BBC Three (which replaced BBC Choice from February 2003), BBC Four, ITV2 and ITV3 among others. BBC Three became the Beeb's first-trial for comedy with shows like ***Little Britain, Two Pints of Lager and a Packet of Crisps*** and ***Monkey Dust*** all premiering there before a move to one of the terrestrial channels.

As of 2005, there are over 100 channels available to satellite and cable subscribers, with many of them also available through Freeview. As a result, terrestrial channels can no longer command the kind of audiences they once did, with even the major soaps broadcasting to only half the audience they did in the 1980s. With digital channels existing solely to provide another chance to see all your favourites, and others dedicated to giving us an early preview of new ones, TV is no longer the place the nation comes to to talk to itself. Or if it is, it now has far too many voices being aired at once to make any message wholly discernible.

The A–Z of TV

A for Andromeda

Science Fiction | BBC TV | episode duration 45 mins | broadcast 3 Oct 1961–2 Aug 1962

Regular Cast
Julie Christie · *Christine/Andromeda*
Susan Hampshire · *Andromeda*
Mary Morris · *Professor Madeleine Dawnay*
Peter Halliday · *Dr John Fleming*
Frank Windsor · *Dennis Bridger*
Patricia Kneale · *Judy Adamson*
Esmond Knight · *Professor Reinhart*
Geoffrey Lewis · *Dr Geers*
Noel Johnson · *J. M. Osborne*
Jack May · *Major Quadring*
John Hollis · *Kaufman*

Creators/Writers John Elliot, Fred Hoyle **Producers** Michael Hayes, Norman James

In the futuristic world of 1970, a group of scientists discover a mysterious signal being transmitted through space. Deciphering the signal, they realise that the message is, in fact, a series of instructions for how to construct a super-computer that has been travelling through space for centuries. Once built, it soon becomes clear that the computer has an agenda all of its own. It provides the scientists with the information for them to construct a life-form from scratch – but the life-form that's created is a near-replica of one of their own team, a young woman who recently committed suicide in the computer room – possibly driven to it by the computer itself. The replica, named Andromeda, appears to be linked to – even controlled by – the computer, until she slowly begins to discover human emotions. But can this constructed woman ever be fully human?

Picking up where ***Quatermass*** left off, *A for Andromeda* came from a story outline by astronomer Fred Hoyle. It made a star of Julie Christie, though, like most early live television, little of it survives in the archives.

A sequel – *The Andromeda Breakthrough* – made just nine months later, continued the story. With Julie Christie on the verge of international stardom, the BBC refused to pay a retainer of £300 to ensure Christie would be available for the second series, so Susan Hampshire became Andromeda. Christie went on to become one of the faces of the 1960s.

Abigail's Party

Comedy Drama | BBC One | episode duration 100 mins | broadcast 1 Nov 1977

Cast
Alison Steadman · *Beverly*
Tim Stern · *Laurence*
Janine Duvitski · *Angela*
John Salthouse · *Tony*
Harriet Reynolds · *Susan*

Producer Margaret Matheson **Writer** Mike Leigh

First shown as part of the BBC's *Play for Today* series, *Abigail's Party* so perfectly defines the true horror of suburban middle-class social climbing that it has rightfully been acclaimed as one of the true TV greats: in fact, it came 11th in the British Film Institute's survey for the greatest 100 TV programmes of all time. Writer/director Mike Leigh, who had already made a name for himself with 1976's ***Nuts in May***, refined his razor-sharp wit and social commentary with this piece of blistering satire.

While youngster Abigail and her friends hold a party next door, their parents assemble in Beverly's house to share wine, conversation and a pleasant evening. However, the monstrous lack of tact and social skills from their hostess leads to a cringe-making evening of olives, kaftans, rattan furniture and the music of Demis Roussos. Based upon the Hampstead Theatre Production, *Abigail's Party* is notable for a star-making performance from the magnificent Alison Steadman as Beverly and an early TV appearance for future ***Bill*** actor John Salthouse.

Absolutely Fabulous

See pages 24–6

Ace of Wands

Children's Fantasy Drama | Thames for ITV | episode duration 25 mins | broadcast 29 Jul 1970–29 Nov 1972

Regular Cast
Michael MacKenzie · *Tarot*
Judy Loe · *Lillian 'Lulli' Palmer*
Tony Selby · *Sam Maxted*
Donald Layne-Smith · *Mr Sebastian Sweet*
Petra Markham · *Mikki Diamond*
Roy Holder · *Chas Diamond*
Fred Owl/Fred II · *Ozymandias the Owl*

Creator Trevor Preston (with Pamela Lonsdale) **Producers** Pamela Lonsdale, John Russell **Writers** Trevor Preston, William Emms, Don Houghton, Pamela Lonsdale, P. J. Hammond, Michael Winder, Victor Pemberton, Maggie Allen **Theme Music** 'Tarot' by Andrew Bown, with lyrics by Trevor Preston. One of the great misheard lyrics of 1970s telly, with many hearing 'Tarot cards, Tarot phenomenon'; the actual lyrics are 'Tarot cards, Tarot the diamond man, Tarot guards with mystic hands'. It's a theme very much of its time, similar to ***Rainbow*** and ***Magpie*** in aping the sound of the musical *Hair* and other Age of Aquarius-style folk tunes.

Continued on page 27

Absolutely Fabulous

Jennifer Saunders (Eddy) and Joanna Lumley (Patsy), two women behaving badly.

In late 1992, the BBC launched a new sitcom that was to take the world by storm. However, on the basis that viewers weren't quite prepared for the demon about to be unleashed, the programme was tucked it away on BBC Two, where it was hoped it wouldn't offend too many people. Thankfully, this was the right decision, and *Absolutely Fabulous* became one of the most successful, popular, offensive sitcoms of all time, either winning (or being nominated for) the BAFTA for Best Comedy Series with each new season.

Although *AbFab* (as it is often abbreviated) has sometimes been accused of being little more than a female copy of ***Men Behaving Badly*** (a sitcom first screened nine months earlier), its roots extend much further back. The ***French and Saunders*** sketch show had featured a scenario with a fashionable, glamorous, lazy, pushy mother (played by Saunders) and a responsible, conscientious daughter (played by French). Realising that there was potential in exploring this concept further, Saunders went away and wrote scripts for a full six-part sitcom that expanded the short sketch into a complete world of mayhem and anarchy. The mum now had a name – Edina Monsoon, or 'Eddy' to her friends – and a job, running her own PR company. There were many rumours when *AbFab* began that the character of Edina was in fact based on famous international

PR guru Lynne Franks. Unlike Franks, Edina is a hopeless failure at running her PR business, and has even less success at organising her own life. She constantly flits from one latest fad to the next, be it trendy diets, fashionable clothing, or the latest in New Age holistic therapies and treatments.

Edina's daughter, Saffron (played in the series by ***Press Gang*** star Julia Sawalha), tries her best to rebel against her mother's excesses by behaving in an exceptionally conservative and repressed fashion. Constantly disappointed by Eddy's behaviour, Saffy is far more likely to be found scraping her drunken mother up off the floor than having a drink of 'shandy booze' herself. Her only source of comfort in trying to cope with the madness of Eddy is her grandmother. Played to utter perfection by the legendary June Whitfield, Mother appears at first sight to be a slightly dotty old lady who doesn't quite register all the things that her off-the-rails daughter is getting up to (and has been up to since the 1960s). However, Mother is far more astute than she lets on, ready to let rip with horrifically wounding bon mots whenever she feels she can hide behind her 'old lady' veneer. It takes some time before the viewer realises that doing your own thing and abandoning your children to their own devices is not exclusive to one Monsoon generation. Adding to Eddy's woes is her incompetent PA, Bubble (full name never disclosed – the implication is that she's so dim she has forgotten her proper name at some point in the dim and distant past). Bubble's level of inefficiency is so monumental that she fails to grasp even the basic rudiments of office work – such as when to arrive, what her job's supposed to be ('come in . . . *get paid* . . .'), and the purpose of a fax machine. Infamously on one occasion, she purchases a small puppy when mishearing Eddy's instruction to get herself a 'laptop'.

However, the true genius of *AbFab* lies in the creation of the character of Eddy's best friend, Patsy, and the casting of Joanna Lumley in that role. Ever since the mid-1970s, when she stepped into the limelight as Purdey in ***The New Avengers***, Joanna Lumley was synonymous with sophisticated upper-class roles (she'd also been a Bond girl and posh totty for Ken Barlow in ***Coronation Street*** as well as David McCallum's very glamorous companion in ***Sapphire and Steel***). About a year prior to *AbFab*, Lumley had appeared as a guest on the *Ruby Wax Show*, in which she portrayed herself as a hopeless drunken drug-addled Z-list celebrity. Ramping up the outrageousness of that particular performance into the character of Patsy, Lumley and Saunders created a unique sitcom monster – a woman whose appetite for men, booze and drugs is countered by the fact that she's never eaten any solid food since 1974.

Over the course of the series, we follow Eddy and Patsy's ever more desperate attempts to hang on to their youth and maintain their debauched lifestyles. From cosmetic face peels to Botox-style 'Parallox' injections, through to personal flotation tanks and fitness regimes, Eddy's ambition to be 'thin and gorgeous' is never quite realised. Similarly, Patsy's attempts to be seen with the 'in-crowd' lead her to drag Eddy to Marilyn Manson concerts (while

Sitcom
Saunders & French Productions for BBC Two/One
Episode Duration: 30 mins plus 5 × 45-min specials
Broadcast: 12 Nov 1992–present

Regular Cast
Jennifer Saunders · *Edina 'Eddy' Monsoon*
Joanna Lumley · *Patsy Stone*
Julia Sawalha · *Saffron 'Saffy' Monsoon*
Jane Horrocks · *Bubble/Katy Grin*
June Whitfield · *Mrs June Monsoon/Mother/Gran*
Christopher Malcolm · *Justin*
Naoko Mori · *Sarah*
Eleanor Bron · *Patsy's Mother*
Kathy Burke · *Magda*
Helen Lederer · *Catriona*
Harriet Thorpe · *Fleur*
Mo Gaffney · *Bo*
Christopher Ryan · *Marshall*
Gary Beadle · *Oliver*
Adrian Edmondson · *Hamish*
Kate O'Mara · *Jackie*
Marianne Faithfull · *God*
Tilly Blackwood · *Lady Candida de Denison-Bender*
Felix Dexter · *John Johnston*
Emma Bunton · *Herself*
Lulu · *Herself*
Josh Hamilton · *Serge Monsoon*

Creator Jennifer Saunders, from an original sketch by Dawn French and Jennifer Saunders

Producers Jon Plowman, Janice Thomas, Jonathan Paul Llewellyn

Writers Jennifer Saunders, Sue Perkins

Theme Music 'This Wheel's on Fire' by Bob Dylan and Rick Danko, sung by Julie Driscoll and Adrian Edmondson

TRIVIA

When her intended American remake of *AbFab* fell through, comedy legend Roseanne invited Jennifer Saunders and Joanna Lumley to re-create their characters in an episode of her own hugely successful sitcom. Patsy and Eddy appeared in the episode 'Satan Darling' on 29 October 1996. Coincidentally, Mo Gaffney appeared in the same episode, though not as *AbFab*'s Bo.

high on a cocktail of Rohypnol and poppers, just in case she gets lucky), gatecrash openings of nightclubs, and eventually get stopped at customs with a suspicious pack of white powder in her toiletry bag. Patsy's indignation at being held by customs turns to impotent fury when the tests on the powder come back negative – not only has she been sold a duff batch of coke, she's horrified to discover that she played ping-pong with Saffron while sober and actually enjoyed it.

Although the first two seasons of *AbFab* were undoubtedly the funniest and most innovative, the popularity of the series continued to grow and grow until it was transferred in 1995 to the more mainstream BBC One for the third season. Deciding to end on a high, Saunders wrote a final two-part special, 'The Last Shout', which appeared in November 1996 and saw Saffy falling for a totally unsuitable young man and very nearly marrying him . . . and that was very nearly that.

Fast-forward four years, and *AbFab* had become a huge, cult success right around the globe. In particular, the gay community took the programme to heart, worshipping Patsy and Eddy as icons of bad taste, excess and refusal to accept responsibility for any of their actions. Saunders had attempted to try something new by creating a comedy special called *Mirrorball*. Set in the world of out-of-work aspiring actresses, the pilot was a reasonable success and starred all of the regular *AbFab* actresses playing (slightly) new characters. However, when Saunders attempted to write an entire series of *Mirrorball*, she claimed that the dialogue kept reverting back to Patsy and Eddy rather than the new characters Jackie and Viv. So Saunders did the decent thing and brought TV's worst-behaved duo back for another full series in 2001. Although not as well received by critics as previous series, this fourth season of the programme none the less attracted some of its highest-ever ratings. A Christmas special in 2002 featured Patsy and Eddy heading off to New York to a reunion with her long-missing son, Serge (who turns out to be gay, but sadly just as dull and boring as Saffy), and a co-production deal with American network Oxygen funded a fifth series in late 2003. To date, the final episode of *AbFab* was transmitted on Christmas Day 2004 and saw the long-suffering Saffy finally lose patience with her mother and throw her out of the family home. But we know she'll be back, as unrepentant and fabulous as ever.

Ramping up the outrageousness of that particular performance into the character of Patsy, Lumley and Saunders created a unique sitcom monster.

On Trevor Preston's cv, in between episodes of ***Callan*** and ***The Sweeney***, and gritty South London gangster series like ***Out*** and ***Fox***, lies *Ace of Wands*, the story of a talented young magician with genuine paranormal abilities. The rather sexless magician with his collection of embroidered jumpsuits, paisley cravats and counter-culture lifestyle seemed at odds with the kind of characters played by Dennis Waterman or Ray Winstone in Preston's other work. But *Ace of Wands* also stood out from the usual low-budget videotaped serial that was served up for kids at this point in time.

From the opening titles, with pentagram, psychedelia and very groovy theme tune, this was clearly a show aimed at the same audience ***Doctor Who*** was attracting, only pre-teatime (aside from Trevor Preston, some stories were written by *Doctor Who* contributors William Emms, Don Houghton and Victor Pemberton, with others from P. J. Hammond, who later created the barmy ***Sapphire and Steel***). Like *Doctor Who*, each story was divided into episodes of three or four parts, with actors like Russell Hunter (as Mr Stab) and Brian Wilde (Henry Peacock) joining the cast as the kind of villains one might expect to see in Batman, had the caped crusader grown up in Greenwich rather than Gotham. Unlike ***The Tomorrow People*** (its successor in the 4.45–5.15 p.m. slot), *Ace of Wands* rarely stooped to daft farce, maintaining an air of menace throughout. Even with over-the-top characters like Mama Doc, the threat of being turned into a doll that can still bleed like a human was chilling stuff.

Starring as Tarot was Michael MacKenzie, a young actor with little experience in front of the TV cameras. While his understated delivery meant that he avoided some of the theatrical excesses that some actors would have given the part, it did also leave him looking a little flat and lacking in charisma compared with some of the guest performers, who often descended to undisciplined hamming as if addressing the rear stalls in a panto (something that many otherwise respectable *Doctor Who* guests also suffered from). Accompanying Mackenzie in the first two series were Tony Selby as ex-con Sam and the marvellous Judy Loe (in one of her first TV roles) as Lulli, who assisted Tarot with his act onstage and whose latent psychic powers often came in handy during their investigations. The team received occasional help from Mr Sweet, owner of a specialist bookshop (no, not that kind), whose list of contacts often proved very useful.

Acting as adviser to the series for scenes involving conjuring was noted magician Ali Bongo, who also helped build some of the props necessary for plot points. Camera trickery was also used, with blue screen (also known as CSO, colour separation overlay, or 'chroma-key') used to create some of the illusions. Scenes involving psychic links between Tarot and other characters would feature a close-up on Mackenzie's eyes, for which the actor would wear black contact lenses.

Selby and Loe left the series after its second year, as did series producer Pamela Lonsdale, who went on to develop ***Rainbow***, again for Thames. For the final year, Tarot met Mikki Diamond (Petra Markham), a journalist who, like Lulli, was trying to develop her psychic powers. Accompanying Mikki was her brother, Chas, a photographer with a habit for getting into trouble and ignoring Tarot's warnings not to interfere.

With a lack of both storage space and foresight on the part of Thames, *Ace of Wands* is another show to be missing from the archives, with only episodes from its third and final year surviving to this day. The last episode ended on a cliffhanger that was unfortunately left unresolved. While that was the last TV appearance for Tarot and his friends (aside from limited repeats in the 1970s), one character managed to escape the series for two further outings. Mr Stabs, a villain from series two adventure 'Seven Serpents, Sulphur and Salt', was resurrected for an episode of the children's anthology series *Shadows* called 'Dutch Schlitz's Shoes' (shown 8 October 1975), where he was again played by Russell Hunter, while in the second series of ***Dramarama***, another anthology for kids, the eponymous 'Mr Stabs' was played by David Jason (2 July 1984). Both stories were written by Trevor Preston and produced by Pamela Lonsdale.

Adam Adamant Lives!

Science Fiction/Adventure | BBC One | episode duration 50 mins | broadcast 23 Jun 1966–25 Mar 1967

Regular Cast
Gerald Harper · *Adam Adamant*
Juliet Harmer · *Georgina Jones*
Jack May · *William E. Simms*
Peter Ducrow · *The Face*

Creators Sydney Newman, Brian Clemens, Donald Cotton, Richard Harris **Producer** Verity Lambert **Writers** Tony Williamson, Terence Frisby, Robert Banks Stewart, Brian Clemens, Richard Harris, Jon Penington, Vince Powell, Harry Driver, Dick Sharples, Derek and Donald Ford, Ian Stuart Black, Richard Waring, James MacTaggart **Theme Music** Hal Shaper, David Lee; sung by Kathy Kirby. A sub-James Bondian effort, hugely camp and melodramatic yet infectious, this has lines like 'Bold as a knight in white armour/Cold as a shot from a gun'.

At the dawn of the 20th century, handsome swashbuckling adventurer Adam Llewellyn De Vere Adamant is led by a duplicitous woman into a trap set by his masked mortal enemy – The Face. Tired of Adamant's constant interfering in his nefarious plots, The Face freezes Adamant in suspended animation inside a block of ice, condemning him to eternal sleep and the name Adam Adamant to legend.

Sixty-five years later, a coffin is found deep beneath a building site. Inside lies the very-much-alive Adam Adamant, who is rushed to hospital to thaw out. When Adam finally awakes, he is bewildered and unnerved by the London of the swinging 1960s and takes refuge in the

apartment of Georgina Jones, a DJ in a nightclub who – thanks to the Adam Adamant stories her grandfather used to tell her – just happens to be a huge fan of his. While Adam tries to exclude Ms Jones from his escapades, he finds she somehow always manages to worm her way into the thick of things, which usually means he has to then go and rescue her. An addition to the team comes in the form of William E. Simms, a grave-voiced former Punch-and-Judy performer whom Adam employs as his butler. Fond of excruciating limericks and rhyming couplets, Simms can be relied on to fish his employer and Ms Jones out of trouble whenever necessary.

Having struck gold once with ***The Avengers*** and again with ***Doctor Who***, TV maverick Sydney Newman came up with the idea of taking the popular Victorian adventurer Sexton Blake and bringing him into the 1960s. When he discovered that the rights to Sexton Blake were not available, a new character was created, who rejoiced under many names – including Dick Daring, Magnus Hawke and Damon Kane – before Adam Adamant was selected. Though the intention had been to ape the success of the very stylish *Avengers* (many of the series' writers had previously worked on that show, and a couple of episodes share ideas analogous to ones in *The Avengers*), the two shows ended up quite dissimilar. Recorded mainly on videotape with a few filmed sequences thrown in, *Adam Adamant Lives!* couldn't match the glossy and expensive look of Steed and Mrs Peel's weekly romps, and the central relationship between Adamant and Ms Jones was nowhere near as sexy or as liberated. We can blame Adamant's Victorian values for his dismissal of Georgina in almost every episode, but it's unfortunate that the writers didn't try to fight against that by making her less of a damsel in distress and more of an equal partner.

Adam Adamant Lives! does possess enough unique qualities to have an identity of its own, with the three central leads providing a charmingly quirky government-backed crime fighting agency. Furthermore, the show managed to attract some decent guest stars, including John Le Mesurier, Patrick Troughton, Nigel Stock and T. P. McKenna. In the second series, Adam's enemy, The Face, is revealed to have also been in suspended animation. Thawed out shortly before Adam's official 100th birthday, he is at the centre of the majority of the latter's cases that year. One of the few annoying aspects of the series is the continual repetition of the rather marvellous slow-motion sequence from episode one, showing Adam falling through a door. Repeated ad nauseum in almost every single subsequent episode, it rather undermines the impact of the original sequence.

With a significant dip in ratings for the second series, Sydney Newman decided to pull the plug. It became another victim of the archive purges of the 1970s, and, despite the discovery of odd episodes over the years, 12 of the 29 episodes remain missing, possibly for ever. As a result of this, the show is not well remembered – few people saw any connection to it when Mike Myers began making the *Austin Powers* movies in 1997, despite the inclusion of the familiar-sounding concept of two mortal enemies placing themselves in suspended animation to continue their battles in another time. Yeah, baby, yeah!

The Addams Family

Sitcom | Filmways Pictures for ABC (shown on ITV) | episode duration 25 mins | broadcast 18 Sep 1964–8 Apr 1966, plus reunion special 30 Oct 1977

Regular Cast

John Astin · *Gomez Addams*
Carolyn Jones · *Morticia Addams*
Jackie Coogan · *Uncle Fester Frump*
Ted Cassidy · *Lurch/Thing*
Blossom Rock · *Grandmama Addams*
Ken Weatherwax · *Pugsley Addams*
Lisa Loring · *Wednesday Addams*
Felix Silla · *Cousin Itt*
Anthony Magro · *Voice of Cousin Itt*

Creators Charles Addams, David Levy **Producers** David Levy (executive), Herb Brower (associate), Nat Perrin **Writers** John Bradford, Jameson Brewer, Hannibal Coons, Jay Dratler, Keith Fowler, Bill Freedman, Ben Gershman, Jerry Gottler, George Haight, Carol Henning, Lou Huston, Seaman Jacobs, Ed James, Phil Leslie, Bill Lutz, Charles R. Marion, Sloan Nibley, Nat Perrin, Mitch Persons, Rick Richard, Leo Rifkin, Ed Ring, Leo Salkin, Elroy Schwartz, Jerry Seelen, Henry Sharp, Gene Thompson, Paul Tuckahoe, Arthur Weingarten, Harry Winkler, Preston Wood **Theme Music** One of the most catchy themes ever, courtesy of Vic Mizzy. Anyone humming the first few bars – 'Ba-ba-ba-dum' – is almost guaranteed to have everyone around them joining in with the 'click click'. The lyrics ('They're creepy and they're kooky/Mysterious and spooky') were sung by Mizzy with his music editor Dave Kahn, while the 'neat, sweet, petite' was delivered by Ted Cassidy.

The Addams Family and ***The Munsters*** debuted on American TV at roughly the same time, having been in development simultaneously. But whereas *The Munsters* was about a dopey dad and his odd family, *The Addams Family* had the edge, being genuinely unsettling, very creepy and consequently much funnier. A lot of this can be attributed to the show's creator, New York cartoonist Charles Addams, whose morbid but witty strips had been a regular feature of the *New Yorker* since 1932. His comic panels looked at all aspects of life and death, but by far his most popular ones concerned a nameless family who lived in a huge mansion. Door-to-door salesmen would call on the off chance of selling a vacuum cleaner only to catch a glimpse of the terrifying exhibits visible behind the lady of the house, a Goth-clad siren with an impossible wasp-like figure. In some frames, the woman's husband would join her, a ghoulish figure who might be a businessman or a gangster, and their macabre children, who would be clinging to their favourite toys, an octopus or a spare length of rope in the shape of the noose. They appeared to

have a butler and a house full of elderly relatives on day release from the latest Universal horror flick. In time, they became known simply as The Addams Family.

The family members themselves remained nameless until 1964 when TV producer Dave Levy approached Charles Addams for the rights to develop his characters into TV stars. Levy had already been responsible for a number of hit shows, including ***Bonanza*** and ***Dr Kildare***, and was sure Addams's cartoons would be his next smash success. Levy met with Addams just twice before the TV version went before the cameras. Addams's only input was to come up with names for his characters. The husband became Gomez, the wife Morticia, the daughter Wednesday and the son Pubert – until concerns over the first syllable necessitated a change to Pugsley. With the characters established, the format fell to veteran comic writer Nat Perrin to flesh out. Perrin's work with the Marx Brothers might well have been an influence on the TV Gomez, brought to life by John Astin. It could have been wildly different – Astin was originally approached to play the butler, Lurch. Caroline Jones beat hundreds of other actresses for the part of Morticia, while former child star Jackie Coogan was so desperate to play Uncle Fester he shaved his head, created his own costume and played his audition in the high-pitched whine he felt the character should have. Apparently, all other applicants were sent home. Completing the adult cast were Blossom Rock as Grandmama and six-feet-nine giant Ted Cassidy as the taciturn, sallow-faced butler, Lurch. Cassidy also supplied the helpful disembodied hand known as 'Thing', which was seen popping out of boxes around the home.

The Addams's home was, if anything, even more bizarre than the Gothic, austere setting from the drawings that inspired it. A bell rope shaped like a noose hangs from the ceiling, a samurai warrior stands guard at the foot of a huge staircase and the children seemed to have an impressive collection of 'STOP' signs in their rooms, which no doubt accounted for the terrifying number of rail crashes we heard over the two-year run. All around are dismembered or stuffed animals, including a moose head on one wall, a swordfish peering out of another (complete with a human leg in its mouth), a two-headed Galapagos tortoise frozen in mid-stroll and a growling grizzly bear looms imposingly in the hallway (actually a stuffed polar bear dirtied down). Not all of the animals were dead; a fully-grown lion called Kitty Kat was allowed to explore the house at his leisure, while other pets included Wednesday's tarantula, Fester's alligator, Pugsley's octopus and the family vulture, Zelda.

Despite such ghoulish surroundings, this family was a perennially happy one. Unlike other TV couples, Gomez and Morticia never argued – in fact, they were the single most amorous and passionate lovers ever witnessed on network TV, whether sparring with rapiers, or exchanging sweet nothings in French and Spanish. The children were encouraged to explore their individuality, and as a consequence they were impeccably polite and respectful. They were also unique in that they never seemed to need television – it would have only got in the way of their other activities.

The competition with *The Munsters* resulted in an audience split that worried their respective broadcasters. Both shows were cancelled within weeks of each other. Luckily, they both found a home in syndication, where perpetual reruns allowed them to find fans anew. A cartoon version of *The Addams Family* came in the 1970s after the characters made guest appearances in ***Scooby Doo***. Jackie Coogan and Ted Cassidy voiced their own characters, while Pugsley was played by a very young Jodie Foster. Most of the cast (apart from Blossom Rock) returned for a reunion special in 1977, though fans generally wish they hadn't. The script came from George Tibbles, former writer on *The Munsters*, which served only to illustrate the wide gulf between the two one-time rivals. In 1991, director Barry Sonenfeld brought us a film version of the Addamses, which was much closer to the source cartoons than the TV series. Starring Raul Julia as Gomez, Angelica Huston as Morticia, and Christopher Lloyd as Fester, it spawned a successful sequel, *Addams Family Values*, and a very disappointing straight-to-video movie, *Addams Family Reunion*, with a different production team and largely different cast. The success of the movies led to a revival TV show in 1988, the same year that *The Munsters Today* came to American screens. Like its predecessor, *The New Addams Family* lasted just two seasons.

Adrian Mole: The Cappuccino Years

Sitcom | Tiger Aspect/Little Dancer for BBC One | episode duration 30 mins | broadcast 2 Feb–9 Mar 2001

Regular Cast

Stephen Mangan · *Adrian Mole*
Alison Steadman · *Pauline Mole*
Helen Baxendale · *Dr Pandora Braithwaite*
Alun Armstrong · *George Mole*
Zoë Wanamaker · *Tania Braithwaite*
James Hazeldine · *Ivan Braithwaite*
Roderic Culver · *Nigel*
Harry Tomes · *William Mole*
Melissa Batchelor · *Rosie Mole*

Creator/Writer Sue Townsend **Producers** Sue Townsend, Geoffrey Perkins, Lucy Richer, Greg Brenman, Sarah Smith

The Secret Diary of Adrian Mole, Aged 13¾ had proven to be an enormous success, both as a book and a TV adaptation. However, both it and its follow-up, *The Growing Pains of Adrian Mole*, were very much products of the early 1980s, satirically railing against the Conservative government of the time. With Adrian being a life-long socialist, the landslide victory of New Labour in 1997 provided a perfect backdrop to a new story, in which Adrian's eager devotees could see how much he had grown and changed since being a frustrated teenager.

The answer, quite simply, was not much: he was still living a life of vague discontent, working as an offal chef in a trendy restaurant. His long-term muse, Pandora, was one of Blair's Babes, an ambitious political animal with a career and social circle that far outshone anything Adrian could aspire to. *The Cappuccino Years* cleverly reflected a malaise that seems to be affecting men in their early thirties – that all of the hopes, promises and expectations of childhood never really seem to amount to much. Sadly, the TV version of *The Cappuccino Years* failed to grab the imagination of either critics or viewers in the way the original adaptation had done years before.

The Adventure Game

Game Show | BBC Two | episode duration 30–45 mins | broadcast 24 May 1980–18 Feb 1986

Regular Cast
Ian Messiter, Kenny Baker · *The Rangdo*
Moira Stuart · *Darong*
Christopher Leaver · *Gandor*
Charmian Gradwell · *Gnoard*
Lesley Judd · *The Mole*
Patrick Dowling · *Host*
Bill Homewood · *Ron Gad*
Sarah Lam · *Angord*

Creators Patrick Dowling, Ian Oliver **Producers** Patrick Dowling, Ian Oliver, Christopher Tandy **Theme Music** The series boasted two completely different theme tunes. For the first, third, fourth and fifth seasons, a jaunty piece of acoustic guitar music was used – Ferdinando Carulli's *Duo in G*, performed by John Williams and Julian Bream. For the second season, a brass band arrangement of a section from Grieg's *Norwegian Dances* was used – a version that had been used as stock music by the BBC since a 1950s adaptation of ***The Railway Children***.

The Argonds of the planet Arg are a mischievous race of shape-changing dragons that sometimes take on human form. Led by the Great Rangdo of Arg, the Argonds love nothing better than to kidnap unsuspecting humans and force them to play their fiendish games, many of which involve severely lateral thinking . . .

The Adventure Game really was a unique television experience. Inspired by an early text-based mainframe computer game, *Dungeons and Dragons*, and Douglas Adams's radio comedy *The Hitchhiker's Guide to the Galaxy*, the series was created by Patrick Dowling and Ian Oliver as an educational teatime children's programme to replace Dowling's ***Vision On***. Most people aged 30 or above will remember at least a few of the elements, such as the plastic currency – Drogna – which combined shapes and colours to denote value: the number of sides of each shape were added to the colours, which came in the order of the mnemonic 'Richard Of York Gave Battle' – Red (1), Orange (2), Yellow (3), and so on. Understanding the currency was often vital to the solution of some puzzles, including the Drogna Game, which involved working out the safe route across a series of floor tiles denoting types of Drogna. Some of the trials the humans faced appeared in the form of a room full of objects that all combined to open a door or help the players retrieve an essential object. Occasionally, one of the contestants found herself trapped in pitch darkness and would have to be guided to safety by the voices of her friends, who could see her via night-vision cameras.

The most popular game, though, was the one that concluded each edition – the Vortex. A variation on the board game Fox and Hens, each contestant would take it in turns to cross a white lattice spread over open space. From the other side, the Rangdo operated the Vortex, a shimmering column visible only to Argonds (and the viewers). As each contestant took their turn, they had to guess where the Vortex might have moved to. If they'd been lucky enough to win something useful in a previous game, like a cheese roll, they could throw that onto the next point to test whether the vortex was in front of them. If they were unlucky enough to step onto the same position as the Vortex, they were evaporated and forced to walk back home to Earth.

In the first series, His Highness the Rangdo of Arg (who insists on being greeted with 'Gronda gronda Rangdo') took the appearance of a middle-aged man in a velvet smoking jacket, though for later editions he appeared as an aspidistra quivering with rage or a spitting teapot. His loyal subjects included Darong, who chose to greet the humans in the form of TV newsreader Moira Stuart; Gandor, whose human form usually resembled a deaf old butler with a shock of white hair; Gnoard, the Rangdo's niece, who presented TV broadcasts on Arg-o-Vision and careered around the puzzle rooms on roller-skates; and a curious character called Ron Gad who insisted on speaking backwards ('!Doog yrev' '?nodrap') with a vaguely Australian accent (for this reason he's often misidentified as being played by Bryan Brown). Over the course of four series, we also met the Red Salamander of Drazil – Arg's reigning Drogna Game champion – and Dogran, a small furry creature who guided players through a computer-based maze that looks suspiciously like an old BBC Micro game. The Argonds would often try to help the players through the different games if they were really struggling, or they'd just show them the solution so they could move them on to the next round.

The contestants would invariably be two people that the viewers might recognise off the telly, like one of the ***Multi-Coloured Swap Shop*** team or Janet Fielding from ***Doctor Who***, and a third person who was a member of the public – usually a university lecturer or research scientist. In the second series, matters were complicated somewhat by the addition of a fourth contestant left behind after a previous game, who the players would have to free. That the new addition was the adorable ***Blue Peter*** presenter Lesley Judd inevitably hid the fact that she was a mole, planted by the Argonds to deceive, distract and misdirect her fellow humans. The single best player was probably Graeme Garden, who seemed to sail through each puzzle

with staggering ease and was only caught out when his team-mates mistakenly thought he was the Mole. After all, nobody likes a smart arse.

A TV show almost guaranteed to get pub conversations instantly animated, *The Adventure Game* has occasionally been repeated on cable/satellite channel Challenge, though sadly not every episode exists in the archives on broadcast quality – four of them were accidentally wiped and exist only as off-air VHS recordings. The show's original producers, Patrick Dowling and Ian Oliver, had both emigrated by the time the series came to a close, but their work inspired another BBC Bristol team to come up with a reworking of the concept, *Now Get Out of That*, which pitched two teams against each other in similarly lateral puzzles. Although unconnected, the formats are often confused in people's minds with another brain-stretching activity game show, ***The Crystal Maze***.

The Adventures of Black Beauty

Children's Adventure | LWT/Talbot Television/Fremantle for ITV | episode duration 25 mins | broadcast 17 Sep 1972–10 Mar 1974, 1 Sep–15 Dec 1990

Regular Cast

William Lucas · *Dr James Gordon*
Judi Bowker · *Vicky Gordon*
Stacy Dorning · *Jenny Gordon*
Roderick Shaw · *Kevin Gordon*
Charlotte Mitchell · *Amy Winthrop*
Tony Maiden · *Albert*
Michael Culver · *Squire Armstrong*
Stephen Garlick · *Ned Lewis*
John Nettleton · *Collins*
Black Jet · *Black Beauty*

Producers Paul Knight (executive), Sidney Cole **Writers** Ted Willis, Victor Pemberton, Richard Carpenter, David Butler, Lindsay Galloway, John Kane, David Hopkins, from the book by Anna Sewell **Theme Music** 'Galloping Home', written and arranged by Denis King, is one of those theme tunes that's probably even better remembered than the show it featured in.

In the late 19th century, Dr Gordon and his family move from the hustle and bustle of London to live on an expansive country estate called Five Oaks. Dr Gordon's daughter Vicky discovers a wounded black stallion and nurses it back to health – soon the bond of mutual affection between Beauty and the Gordon family is unbreakable. Less fond of the Gordons are the tight-knit local community, who view the new family with a combination of suspicion and even occasional hostility.

A quality production, all shot on glossy colour film (mostly on location in and around Stockers Farm, Rickmansworth) and showcasing the lush English countryside to great effect, *The Adventures of Black Beauty*, based on Anna Sewell's classic children's book, was perhaps the definitive 1970s family adventure series. It ran for two seasons and 52 episodes, with even the change of young leading actress between the two seasons barely causing a flicker. When Judi Bowker left to pursue a career in the movies, Stacey Dorning was introduced as younger sister Jenny Gordon, who had apparently been at school in London for the duration of the first 26 episodes. No explanation is given as to where Vicky has disappeared, however – you'd imagine that Beauty would have done whatever he could to track down his missing owner!

A follow-up series, *The New Adventures of Black Beauty*, was transmitted in 1994 and featured William Lucas and Stacey Dorning reprising their original roles. This time episodes were filmed and set in the even more beautiful countryside of New Zealand.

Adventures of Champion

See CHAMPION THE WONDER HORSE

The Adventures of Parsley

Animation | FimFair for BBC One | episode duration 5 mins | broadcast 1970

Cast

Gordon Rollings · *Narrator*

Parsley the Lion is children's TV's very own ***Frasier***, granted his own spin-off series of 26 episodes after a successful run in ***The Herbs***. The experience might have gone to his head, though, as this series dispensed with the old garden wall introduction in favour of Parsley doing a fair imitation of the old MGM lion. Accompanied by his friend, the excitable Dill the Dog, Parsley finds himself getting into scrapes as before, with regular guest appearances from many of the original Herbs.

Gordon Rollings again provided a reassuring narration track, though a major difference here was that Parsley himself speaks, as opposed to just shaking his head and reacting to events around him as he'd previously done.

The Adventures of Rin Tin Tin

Western | Screen Gems for ABC (shown on ITV) | episode duration 25 mins | broadcast 15 Oct 1954–8 May 1959 (USA)

Cast

Lee Aaker · *Rusty*
James Brown · *Lieutenant Ripley 'Rip' Masters*
Joe Sawyer · *Sergeant Aloysius 'Biff' O'Hara*
Rand Brooks · *Corporal Randy Boone*
Tommy Farrell · *Corporal Thad Carson*
Hal Hopper · *Corporal Clark*
John Hoyt · *Colonel Barker*
Syd Saylor · *Clem Pritikin*
Les Tremayne · *Major Stone*

Producers Herbert B. Leonard (executive), Frederick Briskin **Writers** Various, including Lee Berg, Jennings Cobb, Roy Erwin, Douglas Heyes, Hugh King, John O'Dea, Samuel Roeca, Jerry Thomas **Theme Music** Hal Hopper

The film star whose films saved Warner Bros from bankruptcy came to television in the 1950s. Great-grand-pup of the original Rin Tin Tin, this one was a serious challenger to *Lassie* for biggest dog on the block. The set-up concerned Rusty, a young boy and his dog Rin Tin Tin, sole survivors of an Apache assault on a wagon train. Rescued by the cavalry, Rin Tin Tin was given the rank of private to enable him to stay on the base. Henceforth, whenever anyone shouted, 'Yo ho, Rinty,' he'd leap into action and save the day. In the UK, the series formed part of ITV's onslaught against the BBC.

The Adventures of Robin Hood

Action-Adventure | ITC/Sapphire Films/Yeoman Films for ITV | episode duration 30 mins | broadcast 26 Sep 1955–12 Nov 1960

Principal Cast

Richard Greene · *Robin Hood*
Bernadette O'Farrell, Patricia Driscoll · *Maid Marian Fitzwalter*
Alan Wheatley · *Sheriff of Nottingham*
Alexander Gauge · *Friar Tuck*
Archie Duncan, Rufus Cruikshank · *Little John*
Brian Alexis · *Will Scarlet*
Paul Eddington, Ronald Howard · *Will Scarlett*
Victor Woolf · *Derwent*
Simone Lovell · *Joan*
Donald Pleasence, Hubert Gregg, Brian Haines · *Prince John*
Peter Asher · *Prince Arthur*
Jonathan Bailey · *Prince Arthur*
Richard Coleman · *Alan-a-Dale*
Jill Esmond · *Queen Eleanor*
Ian Hunter · *Sir Richard*
Richard O'Sullivan · *Prince Arthur*

Producers Hannah Weinstein (executive), Sidney Cole **Writers** Various, including Eric Heath, Anne Rodney, John Dyson, Paul Symonds, Ralph Smart, Neil R. Collins, Milton S. Schlesinger, Michael Connor, James Carhartt, Nicholas Winter, Leslie Poynton, Oliver Skene, Leon Griffiths, Philip Bolsover, Louis Marks, Jan Read, Arthur Dales, Raymond Bowers **Theme Music** Written by Carl Sigman, sung by Dick James. James released the song as a single in 1956, but Gary Miller got his version out a week earlier and got it to No. 10 in the UK singles charts (James's version peaked at 14). Even people who weren't around at the time remember the tune: 'Robin Hood, Robin Hood, riding through the glen. . .'

Long before Michael Praed took on the mantle of ***Robin of Sherwood***, the BBC attempted a drama serial based on the legends of Robin Hood, starring future ***Doctor Who*** Patrick Troughton (broadcast 17 Mar–21 Apr 1953). But it was a slightly more lavish production two years later that established Robin as a genuine TV hero – this time on ITV. Taking his lead from Errol Flynn's film incarnation, Richard Greene's Robin of Loxley took on Donald Pleasence's evil Prince John and Alan Wheatley's slimy Sheriff in battles set in Sherwood Forest (though filmed among fake trees in a studio in Walton-on-Thames) and with a full compliment of 'Merrie Men'.

A popular series for ITV, then still in its infancy, it was also Lew Grade's first major success at ITC. It spawned a spate of similar swashbuckling serials, including ***Ivanhoe***, *Sir Lancelot* and *William Tell*.

Trivia

Monty Python's Flying Circus famously mocked the show's theme song in a sketch that swapped the name 'Robin Hood' for 'Dennis Moore', with hilarious consequences.

The Adventures of Robinson Crusoe

Adventure | Franco-London Films (shown on BBC One) | episode duration 25 mins | broadcast 12 Oct–30 Dec 1965

Cast

Robert Hoffmann · *Robinson Crusoe*
Fabian Cevallos · *Friday*
Robert Dalban · *Captain Darrik*
Alain Nobis · *Notary*
Lucas Andrieux · *Kasr*
Erich Bludau · *Robinson's Father*
Paul Chevalier · *Blinder*
Jacques Dynam · *Bush*
Jane Marken · *Jenny*
Oskar von Schab · *Jeremias B. Wooseley*
Claudia Berg · *Wooseley's Niece*

Producers Claire Monis (executive), Henry Deutschmeister **Writers** Jean-Paul Carriere, Pierre Reynal, Jacques Somet, from the novel *The Life and Strange and Surprising Adventures of Robinson Crusoe* by Daniel Defoe **Theme Music** Robert Mellin and Gian-Piero Reverberi. Did a piece of music ever convey the image of crashing waves so effortlessly? The soaring theme has since been used in adverts for beans and chocolates, and The Art of Noise covered it for their 1989 album *Below the Waste*.

Sailing from Brazil to Africa, the good ship *Esmerelda* is torn apart in a terrifying storm off the coast of South America. Robinson Crusoe, a passenger aboard the ship, finds himself cast ashore on a deserted island. As he remembers his childhood and other events from his past, he tries to build a new life for himself on the island, salvaging items from the shipwreck and fashioning crude tools to help him build a boat. Crusoe is not alone in the region, as he discovers when he rescues a young man from cannibals and later encounters a band of mutineers . . .

Daniel Defoe's novel was written in 1721, inspired by the real-life experience of Alexander Selcraig (aka Alexander Selkirk). Luis Buñuel made a film version of the tale in 1954, for which Dan O'Herlihy received a Best Actor nomination at the Oscars. But for many, it's the 13-part TV series starring Austrian actor Robert Hoffmann that left the strongest impression. Filmed in the Canary Islands by Anglo-French production company Franco-London Films, the series was exported to the USA, where it was dubbed into English, before being screened in 1965 as part of the BBC's children's programming. It was repeated year after year during summer holidays until around 1982 when, as per their contract (a small item many people forget), the BBC finally destroyed their prints, unaware that they'd owned one of the few surviving copies. Luckily one complete set was later found in a French film vault and the series has since been made available on home video.

The Adventures of Rupert Bear

Children's Puppet Drama | ATV for ITV | episode duration 11 mins | broadcast 28 Oct 1970–24 Aug 1977

Regular Cast

Judy Bennett · *Narrator*

Creator Mary Tourtel **Producers** Mary Turner and John Read **Writers** Anna Standon, Jill Fenson, from various Rupert Bear annuals **Theme Music** 'Rupert', written by Peter Callendar (as Ron Roker) and Len Beadle, sung by Jackie Lee. The song would peak at No. 14 in the UK singles charts.

The popular character from the *Daily Express* newspaper strips finally came to television in 1970. While there have been many animated series since, the one that our generation remember best is this string-puppet series with its sunny little theme tune courtesy of Jackie Lee. 'There's a million stories to be told about the things that he's done,' Jackie sang, and while it never got quite as far as a million, *The Adventures of Rupert Bear* racked up over 150 episodes in four years (156 to be precise).

Rupert dates back to 1920, when Lord Beaverbrook, then owner of the *Express*, suggested that the paper should run a comic strip of some kind to compete with the paper's rivals. One of the editors on the paper, Henry Tourtel, recommended his wife, a noted illustrator and writer. Mary Tourtel then developed Rupert for the first of thousands of stories, 'The Adventures of a Little, Lost Bear', which consisted of just two panels with a short caption and made its first appearance on 8 November 1920. Tourtel continued to write and draw Rupert's escapades until 1935 when poor eyesight caused her to retire. However, the *Daily Express* was not about to let go of a hot property like Rupert Bear and promptly hired Alfred Bestall as her replacement. Bestall himself retired eventually . . . 30 years later in 1965.

The Adventures of Rupert Bear came to TV thanks to producers Mary Turner and John Read. Turner sculpted Rupert's head by basing it on the more three-dimensional look that the bear sported on the front covers of the annuals, rather than on the flatter appearance that it had in the strips themselves. Each episode began with a shot of a mother reading a Rupert story to her young child as the camera panned down, past the bed, to a Rupert doll propped up against the closet. Narrator Judy Bennett would tell the viewers what the story was this week (an old hat, a jack-in-the-box, maybe a Chinese lantern), then each of the supporting cast would be introduced in the opening titles: Rupert's parents, Mr and Mrs Bear; Bill Badger (an absolutely uncanny look-alike for Tony Blackburn); PC Growler; Pong Ping the Pekinese dog and Podgy Pig; the terrifying beetroot-headed Raggety; and finally Edward Trunk the elephant. Then an overhead shot of Nutwood would slowly zoom in towards Rupert's house to herald the beginning of another thrilling tale . . .

Among the puppeteers was Christine Glanville, who had worked on many of Gerry Anderson's classic series, including ***Thunderbirds*** and ***Captain Scarlet***. This might account for the introduction of Rupert's flying chariot, a little device that had the handy side-effect of allowing Rupert to get from one place to another without having to walk (using vehicles to eliminate unconvincing walking sequences was a trademark of Anderson's puppet productions).

Production on the series finally ended in 1974. With later cell-animated series coming thick and fast even today, it's not surprising that this original series now languishes in a vault somewhere – or what's left of it at least, as only 90 or so of the 156 episodes have survived (worse, only 74 of those are in colour). Still, Jackie Lee's theme tune has emerged as a cult classic over the years, which is something, and Rupert continues to have adventures within the pages of the *Daily Express*, where it all started over 80 years ago.

The Adventures of Sherlock Holmes

Crime Drama | Granada for ITV | episode duration 50 mins | broadcast 24 Apr 1984–11 Apr 1994

Regular Cast

Jeremy Brett · *Sherlock Holmes*
David Burke, Edward Hardwicke · *Dr John Watson*
Rosalie Williams · *Mrs Hudson*
Eric Porter · *Professor Moriarty*
Colin Jeavons · *Inspector Lestrade*
Denis Lill · *Inspector Bradstreet*
Charles Gray · *Mycroft Holmes*

Producers John Hawkesworth, Michael Cox, Stuart Doughty, June Wyndham-Davies, Rebecca Eaton **Writers** Alexander Baron, Anthony Skene, Jeremy Paul, Alan Plater, Alfred Shaughnessy, Paul Finney, Bill Craig, Derek Marlowe, Richard Harris, John Hawkesworth, Trevor Bowen, T. R. Bowen, John Kane, Gary

Hopkins, Robin Chapman, from the stories of Sir Arthur Conan Doyle **Theme Music** Patrick Gowers

For commentary, see SHERLOCK HOLMES , *pages* 664–7

The Adventures of Superboy

See SUPERBOY *for credits and* ADVENTURES OF SUPERMAN *for commentary*

Adventures of Superman

Action-Adventure | Motion Pictures for Television | episode duration 30 mins | broadcast 19 Sep 1952–28 Apr 1958 (USA)

Principal Cast

George Reeves · *Superman/Clark Kent*
Phyllis Coates, Noel Neill · *Lois Lane*
Jack Larson · *Jimmy Olsen*
John Hamilton · *Perry White*
Robert Shayne · *Inspector Bill Henderson*
Bill Kennedy · *Announcer*

Producers Bob Maxwell, Bernard Luber, Whitney Ellsworth **Writers** Various, including Richard Fielding, Ben Peter Freeman, Dick Hamilton, Roy Hamilton, David Chantler, Jackson Gillis, Leroy H. Zehren, Peggy Chantler, Robert Leslie Bellem, Wilton Schiller, Whitney Ellsworth, based on characters created by Joe Shuster and Jerry Siegel **Theme Music** *The Superman March* by Leo Klatzkin

The last survivor of the planet Krypton, little Kal-El is adopted by farmer Jonathan Kent and his wife Martha and named Clark (after Martha's maiden name). Clark soon discovers that the different gravity and atmosphere of Earth have left him with amazing powers that he realises can be used for good. He creates an alter ego – Superman – and leaves his silver-haired mom and pop and girlfriend Lana Lang to move to the big city, Metropolis. Here he becomes a reporter for the *Daily Planet* under the editorship of Perry White, working alongside journalist Lois Lane. And that's when his adventures really begin. With his distinctive athlete's red and blue costume, sporting a bold 'S' shield on his chest and a long red cape, Clark is transformed into the protector of Truth, Justice and the American Way.

The character of Superman first appeared in 1938 on the front cover of the first edition of *Action Comics*.The first of what we now call 'superheroes', Superman was of average build – fairly athletic but nothing special; hence he could easily hide his superpowers and dramatic costume behind the plain suits and glasses of newspaperman Clark. In the 1940s, his creators, Jerry Siegel and Joe Shuster, decided to expand upon his past history by telling the story of Superboy and Clark Kent's life back in Smallville, while in the 1950s we learned that fragments of Superman's home planet had fallen to Earth as a mineral called kryptonite, which, when found in its green form, has a frightening effect upon Superman, making him weak and helpless. That decade also saw the comic book version of the character morph into the heavily muscled figure familiar to modern audiences.

The grand-daddy of superhero comic giant DC (Detective Comics), *Superman* first came to the big screen in 1941–3 in a series of cartoons from Paramount Pictures and Fleischer Studios, voiced by Clayton 'Bud' Collyer. Next came the 1948 and 1950 movie serials from Columbia Studios. In the style of the earlier Buster Crabbe *Flash Gordon* serials, Kirk Alyn (as Superman), starred in 30 episodes spread across two stories, battling the Spiderwoman and later his arch-enemy, Lex Luthor.

The first TV version of *Superman* came in 1951, with George Reeves – a square-jawed actor who'd made his movie debut in the very first scene of *Gone with the Wind* (1938) – in the lead role. In his late thirties when the series began, Reeves was perhaps a little old to play the man of steel, but his conviction and confidence made his the definitive portrayal for a generation. Phyllis Coates played Lois Lane for the first series, but for the other three the part was played by Noel Neill – who'd previously been Lois Lane in the Kirk Alyn serials (Neill also appeared in the 1977 *Superman – the Movie*). *Adventures of Superman* was introduced to viewers thus: 'Faster than a speeding bullet. More powerful than a locomotive. Able to leap tall buildings in a single bound. Look! Up in the sky. It's a bird. It's a plane. It's Superman!' The series started right at the beginning with baby Kal-El's journey to Earth and his rescue from the burning wreckage of his spaceship by the Kents.

The stories themselves tended to be closer to those of a cop show than a comic book; TV budgets being what they were, the producers generally had the money for just the one superbeing. The first two series were made in black and white, the remaining four seasons in colour, with a grand total of 104 episodes.

In 1958, George Reeves died, the exact cause of his death a mystery that remains unsolved to this day. Some say it was suicide, others the result of horseplay over a loaded gun, still more claim it was somehow gangster-related. All we can be sure of is that it brought to an end one of the most successful superhero adaptations of all time.

In the 1960s, Superman became an animated hero once again with a series of cartoons from Filmation. Voiced by Clayton 'Bud' Collyer, as he'd been for the 1940s cartoons, *The New Adventures of Superman* aired from September 1966, while the character also teamed up with other DC heroes for *The Superman-Aquaman Hour of Adventure* and *The Batman-Superman Hour* cartoons (1966–9) and *SuperFriends* (1973–86). Meanwhile, on the big screen, Christopher Reeve starred as Superman in four movies (1977–87), making us all 'believe a man can fly'. The films were produced by father-and-son team Alexander and Ilya Salkind, who in 1988 came up with a TV series to exploit their rights to the character. *Superboy* starred John Haymes Newton as the teen version of the popular hero, cast because of his facial similarity to a young Christopher

Reeve. Comic book fans might not have liked the way in which the series abandoned any pretence of being part of the wider Superman universe, with stories set in the present rather than back in the 1950s or even 1960s. But *Superboy* tapped into a new audience when the attractive leads appeared in teen magazines across America. Incidentally, Superboy and his girlfriend Lana Lang attended Shuster University's Siegel School of Journalism, the names being a tribute to the creators of the Superman character.

Sadly, a pay wrangle between Newton and the Salkinds led to Superboy being recast for its second series and Gerard Christopher donning the tights in what was renamed *The Adventures of Superboy*. Christopher was a long-term fan of the character and even contributed a few scripts to the show. Annoyingly, Warner Bros filed a lawsuit against the Salkinds who, they claimed, had rights only to the film series of *Superman*; the TV rights remained with Warner. As a consequence, the Salkinds' *Superboy* finished after four series and has never been seen again.

Warner Bros finally came up with their own TV version with a difference in 1993 – a year after *The Adventures of Superboy* ended. Pitched more as a romantic adventure, ***Lois and Clark: The New Adventures of Superman*** was, as with most modern drama series, more about the relationships between the characters than in previous versions. Lois finds herself torn between the dependable but dull Clark and the exciting but never-present Superman, a dilemma exploited by multi-billionaire Lex Luthor who begins to court Lois for his bride. Eventually Lois figures out that a pair of glasses can't hide the fact that her colleague looks identical to Superman and the two begin the relationship that was always denied their predecessors. An interesting element of continuity is that Lois's mother was played by Phyllis Coates, who had played Lois Lane for George Reeves' first TV series.

Another animated series came in 1996, inspired by the success of Warner Bros' rather stylised *Batman* cartoons. *Superman: The Animated Series* featured the voices of Tim Daly as Clark/Superman and Dana Delaney as Lois in a simply gorgeous mix of 1940s and modern styling. In the States, the series ran as a companion to *Batman: The Animated Series*, and the two shows shared both crew and guest cast. *Superman: The Animated Series* ran from 6 September 1996 until 12 February 2000 and incorporated many villains and heroes from the wider DC universe.

And so to the most recent television adaptation of *Superman*. *Smallville* (the UK had to suffer a suffix to the title – ***Smallville: Superman – The Early Years*** – because it was feared nobody would know what the title referred to) combined the attractive, ensemble-style cast of ***Dawson's Creek*** with the mystery of ***The X Files*** to create an innovative approach to a familiar tale. Newcomers to the whole Superman story are watching for the budding romance between Clark and Lana Lang – in this interpretation of the Superman story, Clark is a teenager only just beginning to identify his special powers (Kryptonian strength standing as a metaphor for puberty and sexual awakening). For long-term fans, it's dripping with irony – in these teen years, Lex Luthor is Clark's best friend and has no idea (at first) of Clark's special powers nor of the debilitating effect the mineral kryptonite has upon him.

Former ***Dukes of Hazzard*** star John Schneider plays Pa Kent while Clark's mom is Annette O'Toole, the actress who played Lana Lang in *Superman III*. *Smallville* is chock-full of references to both Superman's history and that of other DC characters, which the casual viewer might miss but the serious fan can just lap up. Christopher Reeve appeared in two episodes (before his death in 2004) as Dr Virgil Swann, a character who helps Clark discover his true origins as a son of Krypton. Superman's biological father, Jor-El, even makes an appearance or 17, played by Terence Stamp, who was one of the Kryptonian villains in *Superman II*.

Website

www.supermanhomepage.com – everything you never realised you always wanted to know about Superman in all his manifestations

The Adventures of Twizzle

Children's Puppetry | AP/Banty Books/Associated Rediffusion for ITV | episode duration 13 mins | broadcast 13 Nov 1957–10 Jun 1959

Regular Cast

Nancy Nevinson, Denise Bryer · *Character Voices*

Creator/Producer/Writer Roberta Leigh **Theme Music** Leslie Clair

The rather twee stories of a doll whose only skill was being able to stretch his arms a long way would probably be long forgotten (indeed, only one of the 52 original episodes still survives) were it not for the fact that the show marked the first in a long line of puppet adventures made by Gerry Anderson. He was working as a director-for-hire, commissioned by Roberta Leigh to adapt her stories about a doll that escapes from a toy shop, but it was here that Gerry learned the basics – and also here that he would nurture frustrations about the limitations of marionettes that would inspire him to buck against using them. Anderson particularly disliked that fact that it was impossible to achieve any sense of realism when the puppets were required to move, which is why so many of his subsequent productions – ***Stingray*** and ***Thunderbirds*** among them – made extensive and creative use of vehicles.

Another person playing second fiddle (excuse the pun) to a lesser talent was conductor Barry Gray, arranging the music of Leslie Clair. Gray would be responsible for the 'Anderson sound' (including the world-famous *Thunderbirds* march) for decades to come, while voice artist Denise Bryer also began a long collaboration with Anderson here. Her final role was possibly her greatest, that of Zelda the robotic witch in ***Terrahawks*** (1983–6).

After Henry

Sitcom | Thames Television for ITV | episode duration 30 mins | broadcast 4 Jan 1988–24 Aug 1992

Regular Cast
Prunella Scales · *Sarah France*
Joan Sanderson · *Eleanor Prescott*
Janine Wood · *Clare France*
Jonathan Newth · *Russell Bryant*
Peggy Ann Wood · *Vera Poling*

Creator/Writer Simon Brett **Producers** John Howard-Davies (executive) Peter Frazer-Jones, Bill Shepherd

Three generations of women attempt to come to terms with the death of husband, father and son. Sarah France is the mother literally in the middle of two generations of women, getting through life without her much-missed husband, Dr Henry France. Living in the basement is her no-nonsense, mature daughter Clare, her busybody mother Eleanor taking up residence in the too-close-for-comfort granny flat above. Sarah's one refuge is Bygone Books, where she works with sympathetic shop owner and confidant Russell Bryant.

This gentle generation gap comedy transferred to the small screen after four successful series on BBC Radio 4, with both Scales and Sanderson reprising their roles (although Benjamin Whitrow and ***EastEnder*** Gerry Cowper played Russell and Clare respectively for radio). Simon Brett would go on to sow *Rosemary and Thyme* for ITV, and sadly, sitcom veteran Joan Sanderson (perhaps most famous as the aurally challenged battleaxe of a guest in ***Fawlty Towers***) passed away following the recording of *After Henry*'s fourth season in 1992.

Agatha Christie: Marple

Crime Drama | Granada/Agatha Christie Ltd/WGBH Boston for ITV | episode duration 90 mins | broadcast 12 Dec 2004–present

Regular Cast
Geraldine McEwan · *Jane Marple*

Producers Damien Timmer, Michele Buck, Phil Clymer, Rebecca Eaton (executive), Matthew Read **Writers** Kevin Elyot, Stephen Churchett, Stewart Harcourt, from the stories by Agatha Christie **Theme Music** Dominik Scherrer

For commentary, see MISS MARPLE

Agatha Christie's Partners in Crime

Crime Drama | LWT for ITV | episode duration 50 mins | broadcast 9 Oct 1983–14 Jan 1984

Cast
James Warwick · *Tommy Beresford*
Francesca Annis · *Tuppence Beresford*

Producers Tony Wharmby (executive), Ron Fry (associate), Jack Williams **Theme Music** Joseph Horowitz

During the late 1960s and early 1970s, TV adaptations of Agatha Christie seemed to be the kiss of death. Even after the author's own demise in 1975, there was wariness about trying to translate her work to the screen without it becoming pedestrian or a parody. When Albert Finney starred as Poirot in the film version of *Murder on the Orient Express* in 1974, interest became piqued but it took Peter Ustinov's two Poirot movies – *Death on the Nile* (1978) and *Evil Under the Sun* (1982) – to make the vital breakthrough. From that moment on, the small screen has never looked back. Indeed, movie audiences have remained virtually bereft thanks to television's subsequent monopolising of Christie.

ITV took the first major plunge; in 1980, Tony Wharmby directed *Why Didn't They Ask Evans?* one of Christie's better non-Poirot/non-Marple adventures, shown over three nights. Among the cast were James Warwick and Francesca Annis. The same production team followed this up a year later with *The Seven Dials Mystery* (again featuring an appearance from Warwick), but it wasn't until 1982 that, almost as if creating a series of pilots, the team hit real success. *The Secret Adversary* reunited Warwick and Annis, this time as Christie's third-stringers Tommy and Tuppence Beresford, who set up a detective agency in London following World War One (in the original books, the characters age, whereas in the TV show, obviously, they don't). *The Secret Adversary* was such a hit that ITV immediately commissioned a ten-part series of hour-long episodes, *Partners in Crime*. Ironically, by creating the hour-long, one-story-per-episode format, the public who had wallowed in the multi-night TV film dramas didn't stick around, which was a shame because, although not helped by especially demanding scripts, both Annis and Warwick were terribly engaging and likeable as the Beresfords.

Partners in Crime might not have set the world alight, but there's no denying the influence of it and of LWT's three previous TV movies. The BBC swiftly answered back, first with a lavish production of *Spider's Web* (adapting a Christie stage play, not a book), starring Penelope Keith. Then of course came ***Miss Marple*** with Joan Hickson in the lead role (Hickson having already cropped up in *Why Didn't They Ask Evans?* as well as a couple of Christie adaptations in the early 1960s). ITV themselves created *The Agatha Christie Hour*, pulling together some of Christie's short stories, and featuring semi-regular characters such as Parker Pyne, Ariadne Oliver and even Poirot's secretary, Miss Lemon. In 2004, ITV took on Miss Marple with its own adaptations (billed as ***Agatha Christie: Marple***), this time starring the delightfully mischievous Geraldine McEwan.

Agatha Christie's Poirot

Crime Drama | ITV | episode duration 45–90 mins | broadcast 8 Jan 1989–16 Mar 1996, 2 Jan 2000–present

Regular Cast
David Suchet · *Hercule Poirot*
Hugh Fraser · *Captain Arthur Hastings*
Philip Jackson · *Chief Inspector James Japp*
Pauline Moran · *Miss Felicity Lemon*

Producers Nick Elliot, Linda Agran, Damien Timmer, Delia Fine, Michelle Buck, Nick Elliot, Phil Clymer, Sarah Wilson (executive), Kris Slava (supervising), Brian Eastman, Margaret Mitchell, Dominic Fulford, Christopher Hall, Donald Toma **Writers** Clive Exton, Bill Craig, Douglas Watkinson, Kevin Elyot, David Pirie, Nick Dear, Russell Murray, Michael Baker, Stephen Wakelam, David Reid, David Renwick, Anthony Horowitz, Andrew Marshall, Rod Beachem, T. R. Bowen, William Humble, Douglas Watkinson, from the original stories by Agatha Christie **Theme Music** Christopher Gunning composed a very memorable, nostalgia-tinged theme tune, reminiscent of melodies from the 1930s.

The world's most famous Belgian (with the possible exceptions of Tin Tin, Jean-Claude Van Damme and Audrey Hepburn) arrived on television in 1989 with the first in an ongoing series of adaptations of Agatha Christie's stories about moustachioed master detective Hercule Poirot. Poirot had already been seen in movie adaptations such as *Murder on the Orient Express* (1974, starring Albert Finney) and *Evil Under the Sun* (1982, starring Peter Ustinov). For TV, established actor David Suchet (brother of ITN newsreader John Suchet), with his perfectly waxed moustache and dapper demeanour, created a definitive interpretation of the role that was admired by dedicated Christie fans in just the same way that Joan Hickson's Miss Marple and Jeremy Brett's Sherlock Holmes were revered by their devotees.

In the London of the 1930s, investigator Hercule Poirot is called in to deduce the facts behind a number of terrible crimes. Poirot's eager confidant and assistant is louche ladies' man Captain Hastings; together with secretary Miss Lemon they are a team to put fear into the hearts of criminals. Helping (and occasionally hindering) Poirot is Scotland Yard stalwart Inspector Japp, a man always willing to jump to the wrong conclusion on the flimsiest of evidence. Polished and expensive-looking (particularly the feature-length episodes broadcast since 1996), *Poirot* benefited from the adaptation talents of some of the finest modern TV screenwriters, including David Renwick (***One Foot in the Grave***), Andrew Marshall (***2 Point 4 Children***) and Anthony Horowitz (***Robin of Sherwood*** and ***Foyle's War***). Despite occasional absences from the screen, David Suchet is as keen as ever to complete TV dramatisations of all of Christie's Poirot stories. So as long as ratings for the series remain high, it seems that there'll be life in the old Belgian yet.

Agony

Sitcom | LWT for ITV/BBC One | episode duration 25–30 mins | broadcast 11 Mar 1979–1 Mar 1981, 31 Aug–12 Oct 1995

Regular Cast
Maureen Lipman · *Jane Lucas*
Simon Williams · *Laurence Lucas*
Maria Charles · *Bea Fisher*
Diana Weston · *Val Dunn*
Peter Denyer · *Michael*
Jeremy Bulloch · *Rob Illingworth*
Jan Holden · *Diana*
Peter Blake · *Andy Evol*
Robert Austin · *Junior Truscombe*
Mona Bruce · *Bessie Basham*
Robert Gillespie · *Mr Mince*
Bill Nighy · *Vincent Fish*
Josephine Welcome · *Indira Patel*
Niall Buggy · *Richard*
Sacha Grunpeter · *Michael*
David Harewood · *Daniel*
Doon Mackichan · *Debra*
Robert Whitson · *Will Brewer*
Sergio Corvino · *Thaddeus*

Creators Anna Raeburn and Len Richmond **Producers** John Reardon (original series), Al Mitchell (executive), Tony Humphreys (associate), Humphrey Barclay, Christopher Skala **Writers** Anna Raeburn, Len Richmond, Stan Hey, Andrew Nickolds, Carl Gorham, Michael Hatt, Amanda Swift **Theme Music** Graham Field

Inspired in part by the experiences of real-life agony aunt Anna Raeburn, *Agony*'s Jane Lucas is a wife and mother who solves other people's problems, through her radio phone-in shows for Happening Radio and her column in *Person* magazine, while simultaneously struggling to address the problems in her own life.

This series, which helped establish Maureen Lipman in British households as a real comic talent, was a genuine groundbreaker. After years of ITV comedies that were content simply to play within the traditions of working men's clubs, such as ***On the Buses, Love Thy Neighbour*** and ***Mind Your Language***, *Agony* was refreshingly honest about life without being preachy or smug. The self-deprecating Jewish humour provided much of the laughs, especially from scene-stealing Maria Charles as Jane's mother Bea, although each member of the ensemble played their part. Simon Williams left behind the stiff upper lip of James Bellamy in ***Upstairs, Downstairs*** to play another self-centred character, Jane's husband Laurence, a psychiatrist who doesn't quite *understand* people. Peter Blake was Andy, Jane's insufferably vain colleague at the radio station (a part not too dissimilar to Kirk, the character he would play in ***Dear John*** in 1986); Jeremy Bulloch (famous among science fiction fans as the original Boba

Fett in the *Star Wars* films) played Jane's neighbour, Rob, while Peter Denyer played his boyfriend, Michael. The depiction of a gay relationship was a first for British television, where their arguments and tempestuous relationship provided the source of the comedy, rather than just the fact that they were gay. When Michael commits suicide in the final episode, it's a deeply tragic loss (Denyer, who had played one of the wayward youths in ***Please Sir!***, would join Peter Blake in the cast of *Dear John* as Ralph Dring, the most boring man in the world).

Agony ended after three series. The concept was exported to the States in 1985 as a short-lived vehicle for Lucy Arnaz, daughter of Lucille Ball and Desi Arnaz. Maureen Lipman starred in a series of adverts for British Telecom as Beatie (BT – geddit?), a Jewish mother and grandmother whose escapades reminded the nation that 'it's good to talk' and that 'if you've got an "ology" you're a scientist'. She returned to the life of Jane Lucas in 1995. *Agony Again* jumped channels to BBC One, this time showing Jane as the presenter of a TV chat show, *Lucas Live*. Jane's personal life is just as convoluted as ever, with her mother trying to reunite her with her ex-husband, despite Jane's new relationship with a social worker called Daniel. Her son Michael, named after her former neighbour, has revealed that he too is gay, while her new colleagues on television are no less self-obsessed and frustrating as the ones at the magazine used to be.

Agony Again stretched to just seven episodes, but it was one of the better attempts in the mid-1990s to revive past comedy glories: *The Legacy of Reginald Perrin* struggled without Leonard Rossiter, *Grace and Favour* tried and failed to capture the laughs of ***Are You Being Served?*** and the return of ***The Liver Birds*** left viewers more confused than nostalgic.

Ain't Misbehavin'

Sitcom | BBC One | episode duration 30 mins | broadcast 20 Mar 1994–14 Feb 1995

Regular Cast

Peter Davison · *Clive Quigley*
Lesley Manville, Karen Drury · *Melissa Quigley*
John Duttine · *Dave Drysdale*
Nicola Pagett · *Sonia Drysdale*

Creator/Writer Roy Clarke **Producers** James Gilbert (executive), Tony Dow **Theme Music** 'Ain't Misbehavin'' by Fats Waller, sung by Paul Jones

Peter Davison foreshadows his down-at-heel turn as David Braithwaite in ***At Home with the Braithwaites*** with this similar performance as the hen-pecked Clive Quigley. Poor Clive joins forces with the far stronger-minded Sonia Drysdale, a local hairdresser, as they carry out various campaigns to put a dampener on the cheeky affair between their respective spouses.

Davison, whose career was going through something of a fallow period in the mid-1990s, shines in Roy Clarke's Yorkshire-based comedy of errors, but, although the experienced cast are trying incredibly hard to make the material fizz, it never quite achieves the effervescent heights of Clarke's best work (such as ***Last of the Summer Wine*** and ***Keeping Up Appearances***). *Ain't Misbehavin'* remains, however, an interesting diversion in the careers of a major comedy writer and top-flight TV actor.

Airport

Documentary/Reality TV| BBC One | episode duration 30 mins | broadcast 2 May 1996–present

Regular Cast

John Nettles · *Narrator 1996–2004*
Liza Tarbuck · *Narrator 2005–present*

Producers Jeremy Mills, Clare Paterson, Edwina Vardey (executive), Michael Houldey, David Russell (series), Fiona Mellon-Grant, Cassie Phillips, Bridget Sneyd **Theme Music** Hal Lindes, Cherry Lodge

Life at the busiest airport in the world can be just as frustrating for the staff as well as the passengers. With a fly-on-the-wall view, cameras follow the many staff members who populate the 24-hour world of Heathrow Airport. It's amazing just how exciting delayed luggage can be, not to mention the numerous suspect packages, irate customers, drug smugglers and newly arrived superstars.

Airport has an important place in the development of modern British television, being one of the earliest examples of the emerging trend for reality-based docu-soap programming that exploded onto our screens in the mid-1990s. John Nettles abandons Jersey and Midsomer to present with his cosily dour tones what started out as a truly fascinating account of life throughout the airport. As the series progressed, the mechanics of the work in hand took a backseat to the increasingly soapy life of the personalities encountered, with the likes of bespectacled Aeroflot supervisor Jeremy Spake becoming seemingly more important than the work itself. Spake departed the series in 1999 having developed into the first true reality-TV star, going on to present *City Hospital* and appear on *Holiday* and *The Toughest Job in the World*, among others.

A 2001 spin-off switched the action to Miami Airport, and various Christmas specials have expanded the format further. Predictably, perhaps, ITV unleashed rival series *Airline* in 1998, which has also focused primarily upon members of the airport staff, in this case of Britannia Airlines and subsequently budget service Easyjet.

Airwolf

Action-Adventure | Belisarius Productions/Universal for CBS/USA Network (shown on ITV) | episode duration 50 mins | broadcast 22 Jan 1984–7 Aug 1987 (USA)

Regular Cast
Jan-Michael Vincent · *Stringfellow Hawke*
Ernest Borgnine · *Dominic Santini*
Alex Cord · *Michael Coldsmith Briggs III/'Archangel'*
Jean Bruce Scott · *Caitlin O'Shannessy*
Deborah Pratt · *Marella*
Barry Van Dyke · *St John Hawke*
Michele Scarabelli · *Jo Santini*
Geraint Wyn Davies · *Major Mike Rivers*
Anthony Sherwood · *Jason Locke*

Creator Donald P. Bellisario **Producers** Arthur L. Annecharico, Bernard L. Kowalski, Donald P. Bellisario (executive), Alan Godfrey, Alan J. Levi, Burton Armus, Clyde Ware, Jonathan Goodwill, Lester William Berke, Rick Kelbaugh, Robert Janes **Writers** Various, including Donald P. Bellisario, Burton Armus, Nicholas Corea, T. S. Cook, Westbrook Claridge, Sutton Roley, Rick Kelbaugh, Edward J. Lakso **Theme Music** Sylvester Levay

One of a number of American action series based upon a vehicle, *Airwolf* starred Jan-Michael Vincent and Ernest Borgnine as the crew of a super-powered helicopter. This is stolen by its creator, Dr Moffet (David Hemmings), only for a government organisation called 'the Firm' to hire the craft's original test pilot, Stringfellow Hawke, to steal it back again. Hawke agrees to do so if the Firm helps find his brother, missing in action in Vietnam for the last 14 years. Accompanied by his best friend, Dominic Santini, Hawke recovers *Airwolf*, only to become trapped by the Firm, represented by Archangel, into taking part in the odd mercy mission in return for help in locating his brother.

After the initial run of episodes, the series depended far too much on recycling footage of the helicopter from previous episodes, and for the final season almost the entire cast were replaced. Shown on ITV in the UK, *Airwolf* still has an ardent following, although it has suffered from being one of many very formulaic action shows made at around the same time, such as ***Knight Rider***, *Blue Thunder* and ***Street Hawk***.

Alas Smith and Jones

Comedy | BBC Two | episode duration 30 mins | broadcast 31 Jan 1984–26 Nov 1987, 16 Nov 1989–14 Oct 1998 (*Smith and Jones*)

Cast
Mel Smith, Griff Rhys Jones

Producers Martin Shardlow, Jimmy Mulville, John Kilby, Jamie Rix **Writers** Various, including Mel Smith, Griff Rhys Jones, Clive Anderson, Andy Hamilton, Simon Bell, Jimmy Mulville, Rory McGrath, Colin Bostock-Smith, Mark Cullen, Rob Grant, Doug Naylor, Guy Jenkin, Andrew Hastings, Jack Docherty, Moray Hunter, Pete McCarthy, Roger Planer, Paul Smith, Abi Grant, Nick Wilton **Theme Music** Peter Brewis, with songs by Philip Pope

Mel Smith (the podgy one) and Griff Rhys Jones had been part of the ***Not the Nine O'Clock News*** team before branching off on their own to create one of the very best comedy partnerships since ***The Two Ronnies*** went into permanent rerun. As with *Not the Nine O'Clock News*, their sketches and comic observations were very much of the time, commenting on social and cultural trends rather than specific events (recorded some months before transmission they couldn't really have been expected to comment on that week's news in advance).

In among the sketches was a hugely popular strand known as 'head-to-head' in which Mel and Griff would conduct a conversation in profile, seemingly powered only through stream of consciousness (though in reality very carefully scripted). It was the only part of the show in which there were clearly defined roles, Mel as the seemingly experienced and knowledgeable one, Griff as the idiot whose daft questions revealed just how ignorant Mel actually was. For the rest of the time, the pair refused to adopt permanent 'straight man/fool' relationships like other comic duos, with the power shifting from character to character and depending on the situation.

Taking its name from the 1970s western series *Alias Smith and Jones*, *Alas*... surprisingly only ran for four series. After that came *Smith and Jones in Small Doses*, four self-contained comedy plays, while from 1989 onwards their show was called simply *Smith and Jones*.

Trivia
Mel Smith and Griff Rhys Jones made a brief appearance at ***Live Aid*** as policemen investigating complaints about the noise – from Belgium – before introducing the unquestionable highlight of the day, Queen. Slightly less impressively, they also appeared in the sci-fi comedy film *Morons from Outer Space* (1985) alongside ***Auf Wiedersehen, Pet***'s Jimmy Nail and Paul Bown from ***Watching***. The duo have also had great successes in other fields, Griff Rhys Jones as a TV presenter, Mel Smith as a film director, notably the film version of *Mr Bean* (1997).

Albion Market

Soap | Granada for ITV | episode duration 30 mins | broadcast 30 Aug 1985–24 Aug 1986

Regular Cast
Various, including:
John Michie · *Tony Fraser*
David Hargreaves · *Derek Owen*
Noreen Kershaw · *Lynne Harrison*
Jonathan Barlow · *Roy Harrison*
Sally Baxter · *Lisa O'Shea*

Bernard Spear · *Morris Ransome*
Carol Kaye · *Miriam Ransome*
Alistair Walker · *Duane Rigg*
Peter Benson · *Larry Rigg*
Valerie Lilley · *Brenda Rigg*
Burt Caesar · *Phil Smith*
Dev Sagoo · *Raju Sharma*
Paul Bhattacharjee · *Jaz Sharma*
Phillip Tan · *Lam Quoc Hoa*
Pik-Sen Lim · *Ly Nhu Chan*
Anthony Booth · *Ted Pilkington*
Helen Shapiro · *Viv Harker*

Producer Bill Podmore (executive) **Theme Music** Bill Connor

Created as a response to the BBC's recently launched ***EastEnders*** and with the express intention of boosting ITV's weekend ratings, *Albion Market* was intended as a brand new jewel in ITV's 'soap' crown and was launched with a fanfare of publicity and a rumoured £3m budget. Broadcast on Friday and Sunday nights, *Albion Market* concerned the working woes and personal problems of a group of stall-holders in a covered market in Manchester. Accurately reflecting the multi-cultural nature of most modern cities, regular characters came from West Indian, Pakistani, Jewish and Vietnamese communities.

The large set was constructed by Granada TV in an empty warehouse next door to their existing studios, a few hundred yards away from where ***Coronation Street*** still resides. Realising that the programme was not making much of an impact on the ratings, producers introduced a couple of star names – 1960s singing star Helen Shapiro and former ***Till Death Us Do Part*** actor Tony Booth (who would of course go on to become father-in-law to Prime Minister Tony Blair). Unfortunately for everyone involved, the audience just didn't take to this programme and it was cancelled after one year and 100 episodes.

ALF

Sitcom | Alien Productions for NBC (shown on ITV) | episode duration 25 mins | broadcast 22 Sep 1986–24 Mar 1990, 17 Feb 1996

Regular Cast

Max Wright · *Willie Tanner*
Anne Schedeen · *Kate Tanner*
Andrea Elson · *Lynn Tanner*
Benji Gregory · *Brian Tanner*
John LaMotta · *Trevor Ochmonek*
Liz Sheridan · *Raquel Ochmonek*
Josh Blake · *Jake Ochmonek*
J. M. J. Bullock · *Neal Tanner*
Paul Fusco · *Voice of Gordon 'ALF' Shumway*

Creators Paul Fusco and Tom Patchett **Producers** Tom Patchett, Bernie Brillstein (executive), Steve Cioffi (associate), Paul Fusco, Thad Mumford, Laurie Gelman **Writers** Tom Patchett, Paul Fusco, Bob Bendetson, Howard Bendetson, Donald Todd, Laurie Gelman, Stephen Sustarsic, Steve Pepoon, Lisa A. Bannick, Al Jean, Michael Reiss, Victor Fresco **Theme Music** Alf Clausen

Gordon Shumway, a refugee from the planet Melmac, crash-lands his spaceship into the garage of a normal American family called the Tanners. Soon afterwards the military come looking for him and despite their surprise at Gordon's appearance – a cross between an anteater and a well-groomed dog – the Tanners decide to harbour him from the authorities. They give him a new home, and father of the house, Willie, decides to nickname him – 'ALF' – short for Alien Life Form.

An inspired combination of *My Favourite Martian* and *ET: The Extra-Terrestrial* (1982) with a little vaudeville comedy thrown in, ALF was a big star back in the States, where he held down a prime-time weekday slot for four years, appeared on *Hollywood Squares* (the American equivalent of the UK's ***Celebrity Squares***) and featured in a series of commercials for a telecommunications company. But the programme wasn't really treated with the respect it deserved when it came to the UK, shoved in the Saturday early-evening slot usually reserved for kids' shows like ***Metal Mickey***. We loved ALF for his wisecracks, which his human family never really appreciated. Whether it was mistaking his crayon box for a tube of nuclear waste, terrorising the family cat (the feline species being a favoured delicacy on his home planet) or crooning his way through a popular tune, ALF was the cause of much stress and amusement for the Tanners. Particularly exasperated was Willie, whom ALF always somehow managed (though rarely deliberately) to ensure maintained a pained expression. Similar in approach to ***Mork & Mindy***, *ALF* gave the writers the chance to satirise American lifestyles through the eyes of an alien.

The fourth series ended on something of a cliffhanger, with ALF kidnapped by the Alien Task Force. The producers had hoped to continue the series with a switch of networks, but this ultimately never materialised. It took six years for the story to be concluded with a TV movie in which ALF was shown to be living the life of luxury in a protective compound run by the Alien Task Force. During the run of the television series, two animated series were created. The first, also called *ALF*, was set back on the planet Melmac before ALF's departure for Earth, while the second, *ALF Tales*, retold classic fairy tales with ALF and his fellow Melmacian friends playing all the roles. In 2004, *ALF* returned to American screens in *ALF's Hit Talk Show*, in which he chats irreverently with celebs.

Alfred Hitchcock Presents/The Alfred Hitchcock Hour

Anthology | Shamley Productions/Universal for CBS/NBC/Michael Sloan Productions for NBC (shown on ITV) | episode duration

30/60 mins | broadcast 2 Oct 1955–10 May 1965, 5 May 1985–22 Jul 1989

Creator/Presenter Alfred Hitchcock **Producers** Alfred Hitchcock, Joan Harrison, Norman Lloyd (producers for original series), Christopher Crowe, Michael Sloan (executive producers for 1985 series), Gordon Cornell Layne (associate), Alan Barnette, Barbara Laffey, David Levinson, Andrew Mirisch, Jon Slan, Susan Whittaker **Writers** Various, including Francis Cockrell, Harold Swanton, Robert C. Dennis, Marian Cockrell, Ray Bradbury, Victor Wolfson, Stirling Silliphant, Sarett Rudley, James P. Cavanagh, Bernard C. Schoenfeld, Joel Murcott, Roald Dahl, William Fay, Fredric Brown, Halsted Welles, Evan Hunter, Bill S. Ballinger, Robert Bloch, Henry Slesar, John Collier, Richard Levinson, Bryce Walton **Theme Music** A segment from 'Funeral March of a Marionette' by Charles Gounod

In 1955, filmmaker Alfred Hitchcock was approached by MCA with a mind to producing a television show under the name *Alfred Hitchcock Presents*. A number of similar series already existed at the time, including *Suspense*, *Pepsi-Cola Playhouse* and *Kraft Television Theater*. Hitchcock had been looking to make an anthology series ever since 1940 when he'd adapted his own film *The Lodger* (1926) for radio. In signing up for his own television show, Hitchcock would not only provide a regular, high-profile means to promote his cinematic works, but would also sign one of the most lucrative contracts in the television industry, receiving just short of $130,000 for minimal involvement. Additionally, he would retain the rights to each show after initial broadcast.

Hitchcock created a new company for the project, Shamley Productions (named after his old home in England), headed by his former assistant, Joan Harrison, who would also act as executive producer of the show. She was joined by Norman Lloyd, a former actor who had worked with Hitchcock on *Saboteur* (1942) and *Spellbound* (1945), and had since become a director himself. He became associate producer and joined Hitchcock as one of the regular directors (Lloyd would also return to acting, starring in the popular medical drama ***St Elsewhere***).

Each programme would begin with the distinctive graphic of a Hitchcock caricature, designed by Hitchcock himself, and would feature a prologue and epilogue delivered direct to camera by Hitchcock and scripted by the playwright James Allardice. Allardice managed to capture perfectly the playfully lugubrious persona that Hitchcock had cultivated over the years, allowing him to share a world view as twisted as that of Charles Addams's celebrated cartoons in *The New Yorker*. Each introduction would see Hitchcock either in an electric chair, wearing a noose or in some other unusual situation, while waxing lyrical about some morbid notion of his that had a loose connection with the story that would follow. Often as not, these presentations were merely an opportunity for Hitchcock to goad the sponsors, something unheard of at the time. He introduced one advert break by saying: 'Our story tonight is about a man called Perry. It follows after a minute called "Tedious".' The clear implication was that Hitchcock, like his audience, resented advertising, even though he acknowledged its necessity.

Such an irreverent attitude won the audiences over and soon *Alfred Hitchcock Presents* had become one of the most popular television shows ever. It managed to attract many top-notch performers, such as Charles Bronson, Walter Matthau, Steve McQueen and Joanne Woodward, as well as giving directors like Robert Altman and William Friedkin their first big break. It also gained critical acclaim, winning two Emmys and gaining 17 Emmy nominations over its record-breaking ten-year run.

The format changed slightly over the years, moving to NBC in 1960 and becoming *The Alfred Hitchcock Hour* in 1962. It ran for a further three seasons, with increasingly less involvement from Hitchcock as time went on. Eventually, Hitchcock tired of the format and the show came to a suitably unnatural conclusion in the summer of 1965 with an episode entitled 'Off Season'.

In 1985, five years after the great director had died, *Alfred Hitchcock Presents* was resurrected through a combination of 'colourised' footage from Hitchcock's original presentations and new colour episodes. Some were remakes of the original stories, some new tales in a similar vein. Though it hit the screens at the same time as a number of other anthology shows, including Steven Spielberg's ***Amazing Stories*** and the revival of ***The Twilight Zone***, Alfred Hitchcock won out in the end, running for four years.

All Creatures Great and Small

Drama | BBC One | episode duration 50 mins, plus 90-min specials | broadcast 8 Jan 1978–24 Dec 1990

Regular Cast

Christopher Timothy · *James Herriot*
Robert Hardy · *Siegfried Farnon*
Peter Davison · *Tristan Farnon*
Carol Drinkwater, Lynda Bellingham · *Helen Alderson/Herriot*
John McGlynn · *Calum Buchanan*
Mary Hignett · *Mrs Hall – housekeeper*
James Grout · *Granville Bennett*
Pamela Salem · *Zoe Bennett*
Margaretta Scott · *Mrs Pumphrey*
Teddy Turner · *Hodgekin*
Judy Wilson · *Mrs Greenlaw – housekeeper*
Fred Feast · *Geoff Mallock*
Andrea Gibb · *Deirdre McEwan/Buchanan*
Jean Heywood · *Mrs Alton – housekeeper*
Rebecca Smith, Alison Lewis · *Rosie Herriot*
Oliver Wilson, Paul Lyon · *Jimmy Herriot*

Producer Bill Sellars **Writers** James Herriot, Brian Clark, Brian Finch, Johnny Byrne, Anthony Steven, from the series of books by James Herriot (real name Alf Wright) **Theme Music** Johnny Pearson

Already hugely popular with the British public, the novels of Yorkshire-based vet James Herriot were used as the inspiration for this long-running saga that was a fixture in the TV schedules for more than a decade. Tapping into two of the key British obsessions – nostalgia and cute animals – it's hardly surprising that *All Creatures Great and Small* was such a success. The books were dramatised for television as a result of feature film adaptations of *All Creatures* and *It Shouldn't Happen to a Vet* (1974 and 1976, starring Anthony Hopkins as Siegfried and Simon Ward/John Alderton as the naïve young James Herriot). When the series came to BBC One in 1978, it was an immediate hit with viewers, who were transfixed by the 1930s setting, gentle stories and character-driven, soap-like plotlines. Fifteen years later, ITV would use the same formula to create its own long-running nostalgia-fest ***Heartbeat***.

Young vet James Herriot arrives in the Yorkshire Dales town of Darrowby to take up his new post in Siegfried Farnon's veterinary practice. James finds Siegfried somewhat intimidating at first, but discovers an ally in Siegfried's less driven younger brother, Tristan, who's also a partner in the practice. Life in the Dales suits James very well – especially when he falls in love with and marries local girl Helen. The young vet's misadventures in dealing with the truculent locals were a delight to watch, especially when having to put up with yet another gruff farmer unsure of the new 'vet'nry' or pander to the ludicrous spinster Miss Pumphrey with her pampered pooch Tricky-Woo. Some viewers even tuned in hoping to see another incident of James or Tristan having to perform some vile gynaecological procedure on a pregnant cow or a sick horse – most of which were filmed without the aid of any stunt limbs, with actors Christopher Timothy and Peter Davison genuinely having to insert their arms up animals' unmentionable parts. It's one way to stop biting your nails . . .

After three seasons, the programme came to a natural end when James Herriot's original stories ran out. With war with Germany looming, James and Tristan joined the army and our two young heroes headed off into an uncertain future. The BBC had no plans to revive *All Creatures* and, just a few years later, launched another vet-based series called ***One by One***. However, audience demand is a powerful force, and after two very successful Christmas episodes in 1983 and 1985, *All Creatures Great and Small* returned full time to BBC One in 1988 with 'Oxo mum' Lynda Bellingham cast as the new Helen. While the series had been off air, Peter Davison had been performing as the nation's favourite time traveller in ***Doctor Who*** and was busy recording programmes like ***A Very Peculiar Practice*** and *Campion*, so Tristan's role in the show was significantly reduced. Replacing him in Siegfried's practice was young Scottish vet Calum Buchanan, a man with a keen interest in what 1980s audiences might know as 'green issues'. After a highly creditable 90 episodes of antics at Skeldale House, the programme eventually came to an end – a much-loved and much-appreciated traditional British drama series.

All Gas and Gaiters

Sitcom | BBC One | episode duration 30 mins | broadcast 17 May 1966, 31 Jan 1967–17 Jun 1971

Regular Cast

Robertson Hare · *The Archdeacon*
William Mervyn · *The Bishop*
Derek Nimmo · *Reverend Mervyn Noote*
John Barron, Ernest Clark · *The Dean*
Joan Sanderson · *Mrs Pugh-Critchley*

Creators/Writers Pauline Devaney, Edwin Apps **Producers** Stuart Allen, John Howard Davies

Beginning life as 'The Bishop Rides Again', a one-off pilot episode from the *Comedy Playhouse*, *All Gas and Gaiters* was a gentle, rolling ecclesiastical comedy written by husband-and-wife team Devaney and Apps. Set in St Ogg's Cathedral, episodes revolved around the happy-go-lucky bishop, his doddery old archdeacon and their young, wide-eyed assistant, Noote. Together, the three reprobates do whatever they can to try and ensure that life at St Ogg's is as stress-free as possible. However, they're constantly thwarted in their efforts to enjoy a quiet life by the dean of the cathedral, a rules-obsessed man who keeps reminding them of their duties and forcing them to get involved in boring things like church business.

Perhaps best remembered for providing the first outing for Derek Nimmo's 'television cleric', *All Gas and Gaiters* is perhaps more enjoyable than the later shows ***Oh Brother!*** and *Oh Father!* – largely because the supporting cast are so strong, in particular Robertson Hare as the naughty, boozing archdeacon. Furthermore, the satirical humour about the church in general was rather more pointed here, and more widely appreciated as viewers tended to have had more experience of meeting local priests and bishops than the closeted monks who were the subjects of the later shows.

All in the Family

Sitcom | Bud Yorkin/Norman Lear/Tandem Productions for CBS (shown on BBC One/Two) | episode duration 30 mins | broadcast 12 Jan 1971–4 Apr 1983 (USA)

Regular Cast

Carroll O'Connor · *Archie Bunker*
Jean Stapleton · *Edith Bunker*
Sally Struthers · *Gloria Stivic*
Rob Reiner · *Mike Stivic*
Mike Evans · *Lionel Jefferson*
Isabel Sanford · *Louise Jefferson*
Mel Stewart · *Henry Jefferson*

Sherman Hemsley · *George Jefferson*
Betty Garrett · *Irene Lorenzo*
Vincent Gardenia · *Frank Lorenzo*
Danielle Brisebois · *Stephanie Mills*

Creators/Writers Johnny Speight, Norman Lear, Bud Yorkin **Producers** Norman Lear, Hal Kanter, Heywood Kling, Mort Lachman, Don Nicholl (executive), Lou Derman, Brigit Jensen, Milt Josefberg **Theme Music** 'Those were the Days', by Charles Strouse, formed the opening theme and was, coincidentally, the title of the series' two unaired pilot episodes. Performed by Carroll O'Connor and Jean Stapleton, singing in character, it was a bittersweet if raucous slice of nostalgia ('. . . and you knew where you were then/Girls were girls and men were men/Mister, we could use a guy like Herbie Hoover again'). The closing theme, 'Remembering You', was by Roger Kellaway.

Archie Bunker is a loud-mouthed, opinionated and thoroughly unlikeable New York bigot who expounds upon the biting issues of the day to anyone who will listen, namely his long-suffering wife Edith (otherwise known as 'Dingbat') and daughter Gloria. Gloria has disappointed Daddy Bunker by marrying a Polish-descended sociology student, Mike, who earns himself the distinguished moniker of 'Meathead'.

Sounds familiar? The similarity of the Bunker household to that of ***Till Death Us Do Part***'s Garnett residence is entirely deliberate. In the late 1960s, Beryl Vertue, who had been acting as agent for the likes of Spike Milligan, Eric Sykes, Galton and Simpson, Tony Hancock and Johnny Speight, left her company, Associated London Films, and went to work for producer Robert Stigwood. It was for Stigwood that she would pioneer the concept of stripping down sitcom formats and selling them to Europe and America. Speight's Warren Mitchell-starring ratings buster duly became *All in the Family*, and would dominate US television for over ten years, with five years at the top of the ratings. Vertue's other notable success across the Atlantic saw ***Steptoe and Son*** become *Sanford and Son*, although sadly, later experiments with ***Men Behaving Badly*** and ***Coupling*** would fare less well.

The format was developed for the US market by notable comedy producer Norman Lear, and Carroll O'Connor, who would later star in the TV version of *In the Heat of the Night*, was perfectly cast as Bunker – so much so, in fact, you have to wonder what Alf Garnett would have made of him. In 1979, *All in the Family* was renamed *Archie Bunker's Place* after the departure of Sally Struthers and Rob Reiner – now better known as the director of films such as *This is Spinal Tap* (1984) and *When Harry Met Sally* (1985). The gap was filled by the arrival of Danielle Brisebois as the niece Stephanie. A weary Jean Stapleton was written out in 1979 when Edith died of a stroke, and by 1983 *All in the Family* would be no more, but Bunker's legacy and his effect on the sitcom art form is still felt today. One can't help but feel that Archie would have been proud.

'Allo, 'Allo!

See pages 44–5

Ally McBeal

Comedy Drama | David E. Kelley Productions for Fox (shown on Channel 4) | episode duration 50 mins | broadcast 8 Sep 1997–20 May 2002

Regular Cast
Calista Flockhart · *Ally McBeal*
Gil Bellows · *Billy Thomas*
Courtney Thorne-Smith · *Georgia Thomas*
Greg Germann · *Richard Fish*
Lisa Nicole Carson · *Renee Raddick*
Peter MacNicol · *John Cage*
Jane Krakowski · *Elaine Vassal*
Portia de Rossi · *Morgan 'Nelle' Porter*
Lucy Liu · *Ling Woo*
James LeGros · *Mark Albert*
Regina Hall · *Corretta Lipp*
Julianne Nicholson · *Jenny Shaw*
Tracey Ullman · *Dr Tracey Clark*
James Marsden · *Glenn Foy*
Josh Hopkins · *Raymond Milbury*
Hayden Panettiere · *Maddie Harrington*
Robert Downey Jr · *Larry Paul*
Albert Hall · *Judge Seymour Walsh*
Dyan Cannon · *Jennifer 'Whipper' Cone*
Jon Bon Jovi · *Victor Morrison*
Vonda Shepard · *Herself*
Steve and Eric Cohen · *The Dancing Twins*

Creator David E. Kelley **Producers** David E. Kelley, Bill D'Elia, Jeffrey Kramer, Alice West, Jonathan Pontell (executive), Roseann M. Bonora-Keris, Shea Farrell, Kim Hamberg, Pam Jackson (associate), Roberto Benabib, Constance M. Burge (consultant) Robert Breech, Peter J. Burrell, Peter Politanoff, Gary M. Strangis, Steve Robin, Mike Listo, Pamela Wisne **Writers** David E. Kelley, Constance M. Burge, Roberto Benabib, Cindy Lichtman, Peter MacNicol **Theme Music** 'Searching My Soul' by Vonda Shepard

Young lawyer Ally McBeal comes to work for her old college friend Richard Fish after instigating a sexual harassment case against her previous employers. Under Fish's leadership, Cage & Fish is unconventional to say the least. All bathrooms are unisex (apparently to help men and women 'breed familiarity' – though not to help them literally breed) and the company philosophy is more about making as much money as possible than adherence to any belief in the law. Ally's new life at the firm is complicated by her past when she learns that Billy, her childhood sweetheart and one true love, is working for the firm and is happily married to Georgia, who to Ally's disappointment is beautiful, successful and sickeningly likeable.

Continued on page 46

'Allo, 'Allo!

Edith (Carmen Silvera), René (Gordon Kaye) and Yvette (Vicki Michelle).

When you think of the horrors of war, the atrocities committed by participants on all sides and the inevitable loss of life and subsequent heartbreak, then the whole idea of building a sitcom around one of the darkest periods in human history seems doomed to failure at best, a hideously inappropriate exercise in tastelessness at worst. It's therefore testament to the skills of everyone concerned with *'Allo, 'Allo!* that not only is it almost hysterically funny at times, but that it rarely strays into territory that feels disrespectful or tacky. In fact, rather than mocking any specific nationality or group of people concerned with World War Two, *'Allo, 'Allo!* is a send-up of the BBC One drama series ***Secret Army***. The parody of *Secret Army* is so astonishingly accurate that for most members of the public, *'Allo, 'Allo!* has all but obliterated the memory of the original series, which is quite honestly a crying shame.

In the northern French village of Nouvion, café proprietor René Artois would like nothing better than to live a quiet life. Unfortunately for him, life is about as complex as it can get. The occupying German forces like to frequent his café – but so do the leaders of the local Resistance. Contentedly enjoying the fragrant company of his two waitresses, René also has to pretend that he's happily married in order to keep the peace with his tone-deaf chanteuse wife, Edith. Oh, and life would be so much easier if he could just get rid of a pair of crashed British airmen, who seem completely incapable of finding their way back home . . .

Sitcom juggernauts Jeremy Lloyd and David Croft (behind such hits as ***Are You Being Served?***, ***It Ain't Half Hot Mum***, *Come Back Mrs Noah* and ***Hi-De-Hi!***) created a scenario in which every group of participants in the war was equally ridiculed – the French were money-grabbing or randy, the Germans humourless and incompetent, the Italians proud and cowardly, and then there were the insular and so-thick-it-hurts British. Plotlines revolved around the attempts by René and the Resistance to get the British airmen back home, René's manic attempts to avoid being shot by either the Germans or the Communist resistance, or the perpetual hiding/

recovery of the *Fallen Madonna with the Big Boobies* by Van Clomp. Unlike practically every other sitcom before or since, each episode followed on from the previous one in an ongoing storyline, with some storylines stretching from one season to another. Thankfully, René was always on hand at the start of each episode to explain what had gone on before, directly addressing the viewers with the same kind of self-aware breaking of the wall between cast and viewers as Frankie Howerd had employed 15 years earlier in ***Up Pompeii!***

At times, the plots became so convoluted and twisted that even the expositional dialogue was a joy in itself. On one occasion, René reluctantly finds himself involved in a plot to kill local German general Von Klinkerhoffen, the Resistance having planted dynamite inside a special cake, with a fuse rigged to a candle on the top. Captain Geering reacts with shock, having already planned to bump off his superior with a soluble pill of arsenic hidden inside René's till: 'You do not need to kill the General – we have already arranged to kill the General! Do you not see? That if you kill him with the pill from the till by making with it the drug in the jug, you need not light the candle with the handle on the gateau from the chateau.'

It wasn't just the use of wordplay that was clever – the way in which people spoke English was inspired, too. The vast majority of the characters spoke in English but with an easily identifiable French or German accent in order to show their country of origin. The only exception to this rule was the British, who spoke in a clipped upper-class English accent that showed they were apart from everyone else. Crabtree's mangled attempts to speak French properly resulted in confusion all round for everyone (a typical joke about how rubbish the British usually are at foreign languages), and the only truly bilingual character was the determined (obsessed?) 'Michelle of ze Resistance', who was able to switch from plummy tones to Gallic twang without a moment's hesitation – often to great comic effect.

Perhaps the greatest legacy of *'Allo, 'Allo!* is its repertoire of classic catchphrases. From the captain's inability to complete the customary 'Heil Hitler' (instead just uttering ''tler!' – like Corporal Jones in ***Dad's Army***, always half a sentence behind everyone else) to Michelle's promise to 'say theengs only waaahnce' and René's perpetual efforts to bluff his way out of being found in a compromising situation by calling his wife a 'stupid woman' before making up some kind of feeble excuse. Loathed by most critics at the time and dismissed as little more than a cheap and tasteless *Carry On* clone, *'Allo, 'Allo!* was adored by audiences and lasted for over nine series. With the aim of selling the series to the American market, the fifth season of *'Allo, 'Allo!* lasted for an astonighing 26 weeks. In the end, however, the American networks were one of the few TV markets not to buy the series, which despite all the odds proved popular right across Europe.

After 85 episodes, the Allies liberated Nouvion and the Germans were rounded up. In the final ten minutes, the story jumped many years forward, where we discovered the final fate of the regular characters. After years and years of promising to leave his wife, René finally manages it. When Edith asks him what he is up to, he replies: 'You stupid woman – what does it look like I am doing? I am eloping!'

Comedy
BBC One
Episode Duration: 55 × 30 mins, 26 × 25 mins, 3 × 45 mins, 1 × 35 mins
Broadcast: 30 Dec 1982, 7 Sep 1984–14 Dec 1992, 17 Aug 1994 (tenth-anniversary special)

Regular Cast
Gordon Kaye · *René François Artois*
Carmen Silvera · *Edith Melba Artois*
Vicki Michelle · *Yvette Carte-Blanche*
Francesca Gonshaw · *Maria*
Sue Hodge · *Mimi La Bonque*
Kirsten Cooke · *Michelle Dubois*
Richard Marner · *Colonel Von Strohm*
Sam Kelly · *Captain Hans Geering*
Guy Siner · *Lieutenant Hubert Gruber*
Kim Hartman · *Private Helga Geerhart*
Richard Gibson, David Janson · *Herr Otto Flick*
John Louis Mansi · *Herr Bobby Cecil Englebert Von Smallhausen*
Hilary Minster · *General Erich Von Klinkerhoffen*
Kenneth Connor · *Monsieur Alphonse*
Arthur Bostrom · *Officer Crabtree*
Jack Haig · *Monsieur Roger Leclerc*
Derek Royle, Robin Parkinson · *Monsieur Ernest Leclerc*
Rose Hill · *'Mama'/Madame Fanny La Fan*
Gavin Richards, Roger Kitter · *Captain Alberto Bertorelli*
John D. Collins · *Fairfax*
Nicholas Frankau · *Carstairs*

Creators David Croft and Jeremy Lloyd
Producers David Croft, Mike Stephens, John B. Hobbs
Writers Jeremy Lloyd, David Croft, Paul Adam, John Chapman, Ian Davidson, Ronald Wolfe, Ronald Chesney
Theme Music David Croft, Roy Moore

TRIVIA

'Allo, 'Allo! made international stars of its cast, most of whom (with the exception of former *Carry On* star Kenneth Connor) had only been seen in supporting or guest roles in other comedy series. Testament to the series' popularity was the success of a number of stage adaptations, in the West End, Australia and around the UK.

Ally McBeal was hailed as a TV phenomenon when it first hit TV screens in 1997. Calista Flockhart's fashions, notably her micro-skirts and distinctive sheep-covered pyjamas, became the hottest items around, with catalogues falling over themselves to offer their eager customers the 'McBeal look'. Although framed within the various cases of a Bostonian legal firm, it was really more about the interaction of the sexes, theories about masculinity and femininity and the insecurities that stem from both sides.

The show's popularity was partly thanks to consistently superb writing by David E. Kelly (who also created the medical drama *Chicago Hope*), great one-liners – often from Richard Fish, the creator of the philosophical movement known as 'Fishism' – and moral dilemmas that were worked out like a moving, talking version of consequences, with viewers often left uncertain as to which side of the fence the characters had come down on.

What also helped make the show so instantly different was the gimmick of re-creating Ally's every fantasy and daydream, whether that be making love with her ex-boyfriend in a giant cup of frothy cappuccino, watching the office gossip's head inflate and explode, or having her heart shot through with hundreds of arrows at the news that her ex is now happily married. It was the kind of imagery reserved for cartoons, with characters being struck by anvils or bowling balls only to recover their composure seconds later. This had the unsettling effect of making us unsure of what was real or imaginary, so that some of the biggest shocks came when, for example, Ally delivered an energetic karate kick to a boorish man only to realise that she really had kicked him out cold – and a lawsuit inevitably followed.

One of the most enduring of all images was the sight of an apparition nicknamed Mr Huggy – a dancing baby that acted as a symbol of Ally's desire to have a child (foreshadowing the arrival of her long-lost daughter Maddie in the final year). Mr Huggy grew to prominence in the mid-1990s thanks to massive circulation via the internet. He was a computer-generated baby (created by Ron Lussier) that danced energetically to Blue Swede's version of B. J. Thomas's 'Hooked on a Feeling' ('Ooga chaka!'). When David Kelly received a video file of the freakish infant in his email, he decided to incorporate it into the show. The dancing baby soon took its place next to bopping sunflowers and singing trout in novelty gift shops around the world.

Another neat narrative trick came in the form of Vonda Shepard, who appeared in most episodes as a bar-room singer with a paranormal knack of singing whichever song would be most painfully ironic for that week's escapades. Shepard's prominence in the series led to her fronting a couple of successful albums under the banner of *Ally McBeal* soundtracks ('from and inspired by . . .') and a few more in her own name. An amazing talent, she nevertheless had the unfortunate effect of opening up the British consciousness to the genre of Country-lite music that allowed singers like LeAnne Rhymes, Shania Twain and Faith Hill to enter the charts over here. Unforgivable!

The introduction of new, increasingly eccentric characters throughout the series helped keep it interesting, although some of them (specifically that of Jon Bon Jovi) felt a little too much like stunt casting. Press speculation regarding Calista Flockhart and rumours of anorexia dogged the show, while the shock departure of Gil Bellows when his character Billy was suddenly killed off left Ally floundering with a succession of love interests that never quite made the mark. The one notable exception, Robert Downey Jr, was a hugely popular addition to the show in its fourth season, but his personal drug addiction and arrests led to him being dropped from the programme. In the end, after five years, David Kelley chose to bring his show to a close, largely to prevent the executives at Fox from having to do it for him. Its place as the Number One 'chick' show was usurped by ***Sex and the City*** (which started a year after *Ally McBeal*), especially in the UK where Channel 4 began to promote it as *Ally*'s natural successor.

By its close, *Ally McBeal* had racked up a staggering amount of awards: 27 Emmy nominations and seven wins (including Outstanding Supporting Actor in a Comedy Series for Peter MacNicol), while at the Golden Globes the show won Best Comedy Series in 1998, 1999 and 2000, gave Calista Flockhart Best Performance by an Actress in a TV Series in 1998 and collected a further seven nominations.

Amazing Stories

Anthology | Amblin/Universal for NBC (shown on BBC One) | episode duration 25/50 mins | broadcast 29 Sep 1985–10 Apr 1987

Regular Cast

Ray Walston · *Narrator*

Creator Steven Spielberg **Producers** Steven Spielberg, Kathleen Kennedy, Frank Marshall (executive), Cheryl Bloch, Skip Lusk, Stephen Semel, Steve Starkey (associate), Joshua Brand, John Falsey, David E. Vogel **Writers** Various, including Steven Spielberg, Mick Garris, Joshua Brand, John Falsey, Earl Pomerantz, Gail Parent, Kevin Parent, Lowell Ganz, Babaloo Mandell, Richard Matheson, Brad Bird, Frank Deese, Paul Bartel, Tom McLoughlin **Theme Music** John Williams

Steven Spielberg's career as a director began with Rod Serling's anthology follow-up to ***The Twilight Zone***, *Night Gallery*, and with a few episodes of ***Columbo***. By the 1980s, he was arguably the most powerful filmmaker in the Western world, with hits like *Jaws* (1975), *Close Encounters of the Third Kind* (1977), *Raiders of the Lost Ark* (1981) and *ET: The Extra-Terrestrial* (1982). In 1985 he approached Sid Sheinberg, then head of MCA, with the idea of doing an anthology series and managed to secure a two-year deal with NBC to produce over 40 episodes regardless of ratings success or failure, a move unprecedented in television history. What is even more unusual is that anthology shows had all but died off at the tail end of the 1960s after

Alfred Hitchcock Presents, The Outer Limits and, of course, *The Twilight Zone* had glutted the market with their one-off teleplays about the weird and not-so wonderful. In the 1980s, HBO's *The Hitchhiker* had enjoyed limited success, due in no small part to its regular slice of nudity, while George Romero's *Tales from the Crypt* went down the horror route with similar results.

For *Amazing Stories* (named after a 1950s pulp fiction magazine), Spielberg set about assembling the best directors and writers he could find to create his vision of self-contained stories from across all genres, including Martin Scorsese, Joe Dante, Robert Zemeckis and a young newcomer called Tim Burton. The cast lists were equally impressive: Kevin Costner and Kiefer Sutherland showed up for a one-hour special, directed by Spielberg himself, set aboard a severely damaged World War Two plane; in 'Fine Tuning' sitcom-loving aliens kidnap Milton Berle to take back home; Sondra Locke, Harvey Keitel and Beau Bridges guest starred in an episode about a haunted painter directed by Clint Eastwood; Hayley Mills played a mother tormented by a Dr Seuss-inspired 'Greibble' after she makes the mistake of throwing out her son's comic books; and Patrick Swayze foreshadowed Steven King's *The Green Mile* when he played a death-row convict who can heal the sick. The funniest episode of the lot, 'Mummy-Daddy', subverted the horror genre by featuring an expectant father-to-be stuntman dashing to be by the side of his wife, only to face hostility from pitchfork-wielding locals when he forgets that he's wearing a mummy costume from a horror movie he's making.

The problem was, like queuing for buses, audiences had waited years for a decent anthology to come along only for a glut of them to appear at once. The same year that *Amazing Stories* hit the screen, a revival of *Alfred Hitchcock Presents* episodes (complete with 'colourised' introductions from the Master of Suspense's original episodes) debuted on NBC. On CBS *The Twilight Zone* was also brought back from the TV graveyard alongside *George Burns' Comedy Week*, and ABC were ramping up their revival of *The Outer Limits* as either a movie or a television show.

To create a buzz for the series and maintain an air of surprise, Spielberg had requested that none of the storylines would be released to the press in advance, and no footage would be broadcast in trailers for the programme ahead of its transmission. But instead of creating a 'buzz', it received a backlash, with the press lining up to knock Spielberg's latest project down. Still, it was ahead of the competition in the Nielson ratings at least. In their first month, *Amazing Stories* averaged 22nd, *Alfred Hitchcock Presents* 32nd, *The Twilight Zone* 39th and *George Burns' Comedy Week* 59th. Spielberg's anthology show lasted for two series, and in the UK was not well treated by the BBC, who tended to use it as schedule filler on Sunday afternoons.

. . . And Mother Makes Three/Five

Sitcom | LWT for ITV | episode duration 25 mins | broadcast 27 Apr 1971–27 Jun 1973 (*. . . And Mother Makes Three*), 1 May 1974–11 Feb 1976 (*. . . And Mother Makes Five*)

Principal Cast

Wendy Craig · *Sally Harrison*
Robin Davies · *Simon Harrison*
David Parfitt · *Peter Harrison*
Valerie Lush · *Auntie Flo*
George Selway · *Mr Campbell*
Richard Coleman · *David Redway*
Miriam Mann, Maxine Gordon · *Jane Redway*
David Parfitt · *Peter Redway*
Charlotte Mitchell · *Monica Spencer*
Tony Britton · *Joss Spencer*
Patricia Routledge · *Mrs Fletcher*

Creator Richard Waring **Producer** Peter Frazer-Jones **Writers** Richard Waring, Peter Buchanan, Peter Robinson, Jonathan Marr (a pseudonym for Wendy Craig), Brian Cooke, Johnnie Mortimer **Theme Music** Johnny Hawkesworth

Widow Sally Harrison is left to bring her two young sons Simon and Peter up on her own. In order to make ends meet, Sally takes a job working as a receptionist to nice vet Mr Campbell. In the meantime, she tries to deal with unwelcome yet friendly advice and interference from Auntie Flo, while all the time putting up with two demanding and slightly bratty young kids. After three seasons of standard sitcom misadventures, Sally meets a soulmate – widower and father-of-one David Redway – and they get married. Suddenly the family expands from three to five, and so the title of the series changes accordingly. Another four seasons of episodes then followed, with very little aside from the title of the programme having changed, Sally still remaining harassed and worn out by the simple trials of having to run an even larger household.

It's hardly surprising that . . . *And Mother Makes Three* felt similar to the BBC sitcom ***Not in Front of the Children*** – not only did it boast the same star, Wendy Craig, playing a very similar part, it was created by the same writer, Richard Waring. All in all, both incarnations of *And Mother* were warm and accessible comedy shows, benefiting from a charismatic central performance from Wendy Craig. After starring in such a traditional sitcom format, the appearance of super-mum Craig in the subversive domestic setting of ***Butterflies*** must have come as quite a shock to many viewers.

Andy Pandy

See pages 48–9

Andy Pandy

Andy Pandy and Teddy.

Puppets were the biggest stars of the embryonic British television service, first with ***Muffin the Mule***, and later with the ***Flower Pot Men*** and Roberta Leigh's Pelham Puppet adventures, until the more sophisticated productions of Gerry Anderson took puppetry to a new level. From 1950, the King of Strings was *Andy Pandy*, a snub-nosed clown puppet famed for his blue-and-white stripy romper suit. With his best friend Teddy and the rag doll Looby Loo, Andy has entertained generations of children for over 50 years.

There really wasn't much to these episodes. In the first few editions, Andy played on his own, with his hobbyhorse or on the stairs inside his house. A few episodes in, we got to meet the other occupants of the house, Teddy and Looby Loo. Andy and Teddy might play on the seesaw, sit in the huge toy train, play with other toys or just perform routine tasks like raking the soil in the garden. Gladys Whitred would sing a tenuously related song a couple of times (once to introduce the song, a second time to encourage the kiddies to join in). Then, while Andy and Teddy went off to do something else, Looby Loo would wake up, dancing forlornly (never included in the boys' games, Looby only came alive when Andy and Teddy were out of the room) or complaining because there were biscuit crumbs in her bed – the dirty girl. Finally, there might be time to meet a few new friends, such as a flock of tiny chicks, a rabbit or a kitten – real live animals that rarely seemed fazed by the wooden string puppets.

Andy Pandy was created by Freda Lingstrom, BBC head of Children's Television, and writer Maria Bird, who would later bring

Children's Puppetry/Animation
Westerham Arts Films for BBC TV/Cosgrove Hall for BBC One
Episode Duration: 15 mins
Broadcast: 11 Jul 1950– 30 Mar 1970

Voice Cast
Vera McKechnie, Tom Conti · *Narrator*
Gladys Whitred, Valerie Cardnell · *Singers*

Creators/Writers Freda Lingstrom and Maria Bird

Theme Music Maria Bird, including the closing song 'Time to Go Home'

children the puppet soap opera ***The Woodentops***. Although one of the biggest names from the days of *Watch with Mother*, the original *Andy Pandy* episodes went out within an earlier version of the slot. Children's television, which had included such megastars as *Muffin the Mule*, had been known by the banner title *For the Children* since 1946. In 1950, *Andy Pandy* spearheaded the new title, *For the very Young*, and two years later the young viewers were introduced to two other luminaries of early junior programming, Bill and Ben, aka the ***Flower Pot Men***. The *Watch with Mother* title was created in 1953, by which time all 26 of the original *Andy Pandy* episodes had been repeated numerous times (thanks to the decision to film the episodes rather than try to perform them live as *Muffin the Mule* had been).

While older children were entertained by the thrilling adventures served up by Gerry Anderson, there was still a place for simpler stories for the very young, which ensured *Andy Pandy* always had a place in the *Watch with Mother* slot. By the late 1960s the original film prints had worn thin so 13 new colour episodes were commissioned. These were also repeated in an endless loop for much of the 1970s, by which time new stars had emerged, like ***Bagpuss***, ***Fingerbobs*** and *Mary, Mungo and Midge*. *Andy Pandy* enjoyed a brief resurgence in popularity thanks to the release of a BBC home video compilation of *Watch with Mother* in 1986, entertaining the grandkids of the children who watched the original series.

From 1950, the King of Strings was *Andy Pandy*, a snub-nosed puppet famed for his blue-and-white stripy romper suit.

The coming of the new millennium brought about a revival of many old and much-loved programmes to TV, including *Noddy*, *Bill and Ben* and, of course, *Andy Pandy*, whose stringless adventures were created using stop-motion animation by Cosgrove Hall. Teddy and a less passive Looby were joined by a draught excluder called Hissy Missy and a toy dog called Tiffo, among others.

Angel

Fantasy/Action-Adventure | Mutant Enemy/Sandollar/Greenwolf/Kuzui Enterprises for 20th Century Fox and WB (shown on Sky One, Channel 4 and Channel 5) | episode duration 45 mins | broadcast 5 Oct 1999–19 May 2004 (USA)

Regular Cast

David Boreanaz · *Angel*
Charisma Carpenter · *Cordelia Chase*
Glenn Quinn · Doyle
Christian Kane · *Lindsey McDonald*
Sarah Michelle Gellar · *Buffy Summers*
Elisabeth Rohm · *Detective Kate Lockley*
James Marsters · *Spike*
Alexis Denisof · *Wesley Wyndam-Price*
Julie Benz · *Darla*
Stephanie Romanov · *Lilah Morgan*
Eliza Dushku · *Faith*
J. August Richards · *Charles Gunn*
Sam Anderson · *Holland Manners*
Andy Hallett · *Lorne the Host*
Juliet Landau · *Drusilla*
Mercedes McNab · *Harmony Kendall*
Amy Acker · *Winifred 'Fred' Burkle*
Mark Lutz · *The Grusalugg*
Keith Szarabajka · *Daniel Holtz*
David Denman · *Skip the Demon*
Daniel Dae Kim · *Gavin Park*
Matthew James · *Merl*
Jack Conley · *Sahjahn*
John Rubinstein · *Linwood Murrow*
Vincent Kartheiser · *Connor*
Laurel Holloman · *Justine Cooper*
Alexa Davalos · *Gwen Raiden*
Vladimir Kulich · *The Beast*
Gina Torres · *Jasmine*
Jonathan Woodward · *Knox*
Sarah Thompson · *Eve*
Tom Lenk · *Andrew Wells*
Dennis Christopher · *Cyvus Vail*
Mark Colson · *Izzy*
Adam Baldwin · *Marcus Hamilton*

Creators Joss Whedon and David Greenwalt **Producers** Joss Whedon, Fran Rubel Kuzui, Kaz Kuzui, David Greenwalt, Gail Berman, Tim Minear, Jeffrey Bell, David Fury, Sandy Gallin, David Simkins (executive), Steven S. DeKnight, Ben Edlund (supervising), Howard Gordon, Marti Noxon, Jim Kouf (consulting), James A. Contner, Gareth Davies, Kelly A. Manners, Shawn Ryan, Skip Schoolnik, Tracey Stern, R. D. Price **Writers** Joss Whedon, David Greenwalt, David Fury, Douglas Petrie, Jane Espenson, Tim Minear, Tracey Stern, Jeannine Renshaw, Howard Gordon, Marti Noxon, Jim Kouf, Garry Campbell, Shawn Ryan, Mere Smith, Jeffrey Bell, Scott Murphy, David M Goodman, Steven S DeKnight, Elizabeth Craft, Sarah Fain, Ben Edlund, Drew Goddard, Brent Fletcher **Theme Music** The band Darling Violetta composed the mournful strings-led title music.

During the second season of ***Buffy the Vampire Slayer***, creator/producer Joss Whedon began to realise that actor David Boreanaz – who was playing Buffy's love interest, vampire-with-a-soul Angel – was an actor who had a big enough screen presence and fan base to carry his own series. Consequently, at the end of *Buffy*'s traumatic third year, the tragic lovebirds realise that they will never be able to be together – not least because she's mortal and he isn't. Unable to carry on living so near and yet so far from the woman he loves, Angel decides to leave Sunnydale for the rather more Stygian depths of Los Angeles. Thus, one of the most popular and successful spin-off series ever was born.

Arriving in LA, Angel soon teams up with a half-demon called Doyle, who regularly receives visions from 'The Powers That Be' of terrible events that will soon come to pass. Angel and Doyle set off to protect the innocent and help the helpless. Soon they are joined by Sunnydale's very own queen bitch, Cordelia Chase, who's down on her luck and trying, unsuccessfully, to become an actress. Angel quickly realises that there is a massive power for evil lurking in the City of Angels – not a demon, not a monster, but an organisation of corrupt lawyers, Wolfram and Hart, who *control* the demons, monsters and vampires. Beginning as a 'monster-of-the-week' show, *Angel* soon changed into a darker and more adult version of *Buffy the Vampire Slayer*, boasting ongoing plotlines that spanned many episodes. Underlining the grittier nature of this show, one of the main regulars was killed off early in the programme's run, just to unsettle viewers. As *Angel* developed, other characters joined the team – streetwise gang member Gunn, prissy Englishman (and *Buffy* alumnus) Wesley Wyndam-Price, hyper-intelligent yet fragile Fred, and Lorne, the green-skinned host of a demon karaoke bar. Angel was even for a while assisted by his own son, Connor, born from an unnatural coupling with beautiful vampire Darla.

For a lot of viewers, *Angel* was easily the equal of its 'parent' show – in fact, there were times that the quality of the writing and acting in *Angel* more than surpassed that on display in *Buffy*. As such, *Angel* developed a cult following just as rabidly loyal. Many *Buffy* fans switched over to watch *Angel* when their own beloved show was cancelled in 2003 (not least because of the transfer to *Angel* of the fans' favourite character, bleach-blond vampire and Billy Idol lookalike, Spike). Sadly, and surprisingly, after just one year of successfully surviving on its own merits, *Angel* was cancelled by the WB network in favour of an ultimately unrealised resurrection of 1960s vampire soap opera *Dark Shadows*.

Angels

Serial Drama | BBC One | episode duration 50/25 mins | broadcast 1 Sep 1975–22 Dec 1983

Principal Cast
Clare Clifford · *Shirley Brent*
Karan David · *Sita Patel*
Julie Dawn Cole · *Jo Longhurst*
Lesley Dunlop · *Ruth Fullman*
Fiona Fullerton · *Patricia Rutherford*
Erin Geraghty · *Maureen Morahan*
Shirley Cheriton · *Kathy Betts*
Kathryn Apanowicz · *Rose Butchins*
Pauline Quirke · *Vicky Smith*
Joanna Munro · *Anna Newcross*
Angela Bruce · *Sandra Ling*
Judith Jacob · *Beverley Slater*
Sarah Lam · *Linda Mo*
Sharon Rosita · *Fleur Frost*
Julia Williams · *Tracey Willoughby*

Creator Paula Milne **Producers** Ron Craddock, Ben Rea, Julia Smith **Writers** Various, including Glenn Chandler, Tony Holland, Jane Hollowood, Ginnie Hole **Theme Music** Alan Parker

For the student nurses at St Angela's Hospital in Battersea, life is never easy. Living away from home for the first time brings its own trials and problems. Some turn to the bottle, others to romance, in order to deal with their stressful jobs. The initial six lead characters included Irish girl Maureen, Ugandan Sita, party girl Jo and posh Patricia.

Angels was created by Paula Milne and began as a weekly drama series. Stylistically, it fell somewhere in-between the 'cosy' world of the soapy ITV series *General Hospital* and the much more hard-hitting ***Casualty***, which would follow some three years after *Angels'* finale, although it did achieve a greater sense of realism than many of its predecessors.

St James' Hospital in Balham, South London, doubled for St Angela's in many of the exterior sequences. From 1979, the programme changed into a twice-weekly early evening drama and became one of several shows that would, in effect, 'test out' the future ***EastEnders*** timeslot, to see if audiences would tune in for the week's second addition. As cast members moved on, the series saw changes in characters as new nurses joined the more experienced staff, and the action transferred in September 1981 to the more modern and better-equipped Heath Green Hospital in Birmingham (thereby somewhat diminishing the pun at the heart of the title of the series!).

Many of the cast members went on to much bigger success in a variety of roles – Pauline Quirke became one of the ***Birds of a Feather***, Fiona Fullerton joined Roger Moore as a Bond Girl, and Lesley Dunlop became a regular in both ***May to December*** and *Where the Heart Is*. Shirley Cheriton, Judith Jacob and Kathryn Apanowicz would move from St Angela's to Walford, joining the early cast of *EastEnders*.

Animal Hospital

Factual | BBC One | episode duration 30 mins | broadcast 29 Aug 1994–23 Dec 2003

Regular Cast
Rolf Harris · *Host*
Lynda Bryans, Steve Knight, Mairi McHaffie, Shauna Lowry, Rhodri Williams, Christa Hart, Edwina Silver, Jamie Darling · *Presenters*
David Grant, John Mead, Tessa Bailey, Adam Tjolle · *Vets*

Producers Lorraine Heggessey, Sarah Hargreaves, Jane Aldous, Claire Sillery (executive), Tina Fletcher (series), Deidre Harkin

Rolf Harris found a new career for himself when *Animal Hospital Live* broadcast a series of twice-daily reports for five days from London's Harmsworth Memorial Hospital in 1994. Viewer response to the work of this RSPCA-funded animal centre, and the plight of some of the animals attended to by the vets, was so great that the BBC were quick to commission a Christmas Day follow-up, with another week of programming scheduled very early in the New Year of 1995. With *Animal Hospital*, the BBC found one of the huge successes of its factual programming output that translated into ratings gold.

Each week, avuncular Rolf would stand at the shoulder of chief vet David Grant, among others, to observe the parade of sickly animals coming through the hospital's doors. These ranged from the outrageously cute to tear-inducingly heartbreaking, and some of the patients became celebrities in their own right.

With two series a year, this gave *Animal Hospital* the scope for moving further afield, with the first series of the year showcasing other animal hospitals, but returning to Harmsworth for the autumn run. From 1999, the show would focus on Harmsworth's close relative in Putney, but for the final years it returned to the familiar location of Harmsworth. Coming to a natural end in 2003, a series of clips shows ran throughout summer 2004.

Animal Magic

Children's Factual Entertainment | BBC TV/BBC One | episode duration 30 mins | broadcast 13 Apr 1962–20 Apr 1984

Regular Cast
Johnny Morris, Tony Soper, Gerald Durrell, Keith Shackleton, Terry Nutkins · *Presenters*

Creator Pat Beech **Producers** Winwood Reade, Jeffrey Boswell, Douglas Thomas, George Inger, Mike Beynon, John Downer
Theme Music 'Las Vegas' by Laurie Johnson; a soaring calypso arrangement in the 1960s was replaced by a ballroom dancing electric organ and 'wahwah' guitar in the 1980s.

Having made a name for himself as a storyteller on children's TV shows (as the Hot Chestnut man), in 1962

Johnny Morris was asked to front a new kind of nature programme for the BBC's natural history unit in Bristol that would combine animals with magic (you can see where they got the name from).

A natural performer, Morris was cast as a zookeeper at Bristol Zoo, interacting with the animals in filmed sequences while dubbing on appropriate character voices afterwards. We say 'appropriate' as Morris's voices always sounded exactly how we imagined a hungry hippo, a mischievous chimp or a bored lion might sound, but for some naturalists Morris's antics were the worst kind of anthropomorphism – projecting human behaviour traits upon animals and depicting them as something they're not. Sadly (for the naturalists at least) the kids loved Morris and his funny voices and the series lasted until just after its 22nd birthday. Johnny's sidekicks did, however, go on to other things. Gerald Durrell, already a noted novelist (e.g. *My Family and Other Animals*, published in 1956), established the Jersey Wildlife Preservation Trust (renamed after his death the Durrell Wildlife Preservation Trust), a zoo dedicated to breeding species on the verge of extinction. Tony Soper moved on to host another natural history series for the BBC, *Wildtrack*. Following *Animal Magic*'s demise, Terry Nutkins joined the team of presenters working on *The Really Wild Show*, the replacement CBBC wildlife series that, at the time of writing, is still running on the Beeb.

Anne of Green Gables

Drama | BBC TV/BBC One | episode duration 55 mins | broadcast 16 Sep–21 Oct 1952, 20 Feb–19 Mar 1972 (*Anne of Green Gables*), 26 Jan–2 Mar 1975 (*Anne of Avonlea*)

Regular Cast

Kim Braden · *Anne Shirley*
Barbara Hamilton · *Marilla Cuthbert*
Elliott Sullivan · *Matthew Cuthbert*
Avis Bunnage, Madge Ryan · *Rachel Lynde*
Jan Francis · *Diana Barry*
Robin Halstead, Christopher Blake · *Gilbert Blythe*

Writers *Anne of Green Gables* adapted by Julia Jones and *Anne of Avonlea* adapted by Elaine Morgan, from the novels by Lucy Maud Montgomery **Producer** John McRae

The BBC first adapted *Anne of Green Gables* in 1952 as a live broadcast over six weeks. But it's their 1972 version, followed by *Anne of Avonlea* in 1975, that survives in the archives.

Young Anne Shirley is sent, initially by mistake, to the small farm Green Gables to be fostered by Matthew and Marilla Cuthbert in Canada during the early years of the 20th century. Although they wanted a boy to help around the farm, Anne becomes the apple of their eye as she grows up against the quietly rural backdrop, forming a close friendship with local girl Diana Barry, and finding an adversary in the form of Gilbert Blythe. Despite taunts and insults, Blythe would become a close companion in *Anne of Avonlea* (and recast with Christopher Blake) when the BBC chose to adapt the sequel three years later in 1975 for the cosy Sunday afternoon drama slot.

Kim Braden, who starred as Anne in both 1970s serials, was the daughter of Bernard Braden and Barbara Kelly and would follow her career in America, appearing in television and movie versions of ***Star Trek: The Next Generation***. Other young faces of note in these well-made adaptations are future 'plonker' Nicholas Lyndhurst as Davy Keith in *Avonlea*, and, as 'just a good friend' to Anne, another actor to benefit from the work of John Sullivan, Jan Francis.

The Canadian Broadcasting Company (CBC) produced a beautiful version in 1985, which was followed by *Anne of Green Gables: The Sequel* (1987), a spin-off series, *Road to Avonlea* (1989), and *Anne of Green Gables: The Continuing Story* (2000). A rather ugly animated version surfaced in 2001–2.

Ant and Dec's Saturday Night Takeaway

Variety | Thames Television for ITV | episode duration 45–70 mins | broadcast 16 Apr 2002–present

Regular Cast

Anthony McPartlin, Declan Donnelly · *Hosts*
James Pallister · *Little Ant*
Dylan McKenna-Redshaw · *Little Dec*
Jeremy Beadle · *Himself*
Kirsty Gallacher · *Host ('Ant vs Dec' segment, 2005)*

Writer James Bachman **Producers** Anthony McPartlin, Declan Donnelly (executive), Alex Dundas (associate), Georgie Hurford-Jones, James Sunderland

After the lukewarm reception to the cheeky Geordie duo's first attempt to bring the humour of ***SM:TVLive*** to a prime-time audience in *Ant and Dec Unzipped*, Ant and Dec (as it's now impossible to refer to them as anything but the gestalt organism they have become) shrewdly went away to have a think about their next move. That time out brought them back to the same early Saturday night timeslot, but with the bigger, bouncier and altogether better *Saturday Night Takeaway*.

The format is an unashamedly traditional knees-up and is cut from the same cloth as the light entertainment shows that both the BBC and ITV were broadcasting in the golden Seventies. The main draw of the show is 'Grab the Ads', the climactic game-show section where a member of the audience plays for items advertised during a particular ITV1 show that week. Other strands over the series' run have included 'Jim Didn't Fix It' (disgruntled Jimmy Saville correspondents have their childhood wishes fixed by Ant and Dec), 'What's Next' (a wholly unrehearsed sequence where the hosts have no idea what they will be doing) and the popular 'Undercover' (a celebrity prank sequence, shamelessly cribbed from ***Noel's House Party***). The damp squib of the first series was 'Banged Up With Beadle', seeing a member of the public literally incarcerated with Jeremy Beadle for a whole week in a fort in the middle of the Solent to perform a ludicrous task. (The hoped-for reality TV spin-off never happened.)

Without doubt, the big hit of *Saturday Night Takeaway* are Little Ant and Dec. Two young lads, now minor stars in their own right, head off to interview major stars and ask the cheeky questions adults would never get away with. Bruce Willis, apparently, was not amused.

A potent ratings winner for ITV1, the shine was wiped off the Geordie star somewhat in 2005 when the BBC pitched an old favourite into the battle for audience supremacy. The return of ***Doctor Who*** went head to head with Ant and Dec and won – but only just. It seems there is enough of a family audience to go round if you can produce entertaining, colourful television of high quality.

Antiques Roadshow

Factual | BBC One | episode duration 45 mins | broadcast 18 Jan 1979–present

Regular Cast
Arthur Negus, Bruce Parker, Hugh Scully, Angela Rippon, Michael Aspel · *Presenters*

Producers Various, including Christopher Lewis (executive) Liz Baker, Robin Drake, Michele Burgess, Stephen Potter **Theme Music** Paul Reade

A charmingly wonderful TV veteran, *Antiques Roadshow* travels up hill and down dale, to cities, villages, church halls, community centres and libraries. Local residents raid attics and cellars to find that piece of furniture, painting, vase or assorted knick-knack, and let a noted expert give it the benefit of their critical eye. Of course, the history of the item is fascinating, but what everybody wants to know is: how much is it worth?

Former *Nationwide* stalwart Hugh Scully presented *Antiques Roadshow* for a mammoth 20 years, during which time it became a phenomenal ratings success. Scully was forced to hang up the magnifying glass in 2000 (after he launched his own profit-making antiques website, thereby conflicting with BBC editorial policy), stepping aside for Michael Aspel, whose grip on the big red ***This is your Life*** book was growing more tenuous by the year. Some startling finds and small fortunes have been made over the years, and some of the experts have found themselves acquiring something of a celebrity status. It's as comforting as tea and crumpets in front of the fire, and the effect *Roadshow* has had on broadcasting can be seen reflected in the likes of *Bargain Hunt* and *Cash in the Attic*. Amazingly for such a British series, the exact format of *Antiques Roadshow* has been duplicated on the American PBS network.

The Aphrodite Inheritance

Drama | BBC/Cyprus Broadcasting Corporation for BBC One | episode duration 50 mins | broadcast 3 Jan–21 Feb 1979

Principal Cast
Peter McEnery · *David Collier*
Alexandra Bastedo · *Helene*
Brian Blessed · *Basileos*
Stefan Gryff · *Charalambos*
Tony Doyle · *Martin Preece*
William Wilde · *Eric Morrison*
Costas Demetriou · *Antonio*
Carmen Gómez · *Maria*
Barry Halliday · *Barry Collier*
Karl Held · *Travis*
Godfrey James · *Inspector Dimas*
Ray Jewers · *Olsen*
Paul Maxwell · *Hellman*
Nicos Shiafkalis · *Nicos*
Tom Watson · *Wyndham*
George Zenios · *Professor Stylianou*

Creator/Writer Michael J. Bird **Producer** Andrew Osborn **Theme Music** George Kotsonis

For commentary, see WHO PAYS THE FERRYMAN?

The Appleyards

Children's Soap Opera | BBC TV | episode duration 20 mins | broadcast 2 Oct 1952–20 Apr 1957, 24 Dec 1960

Cast
Frederick Piper, Douglas Muir · *Mr Appleyard*
Constance Fraser · *Mrs Appleyard*
Maureen Davis, Tessa Clarke, Sylvia Bidmead · *Janet Appleyard*
David Edwards · *John Appleyard*
Derek Rowe · *Tommy Appleyard*
Patricia Wilson, Carol Olver, Pat Fryer · *Margaret Appleyard*
Ronnie Grant · *Robert Dickens*
John Garley · *Joe the Milkman*
Douglas Hurn · *Mr Wheeler*
Julie Webb, Erica Houen · *Sally Wheeler*
Barbara Brown · *Hazel*
C. B. Poultney · *Mr Spiller*

Creator/Writer Philip Burton **Producers** Kevin Sheldon, Naomi Capon **Theme Music** A jolly piece of stock music called 'Looking Around' by Colin Smith (aka Lloyd Thomas)

Despite the fact that *The Appleyards* began broadcasting a full 18 months ahead of ***The Grove Family***, it's the Groves who are remembered as Britain's first soap opera family. Three factors combine in their favour: first, *The Grove Family* was aired all year round; secondly, their series was shown in a grown-up slot instead of *Children's Hour*; and thirdly at least two episodes of *The Groves* exist in the BBC archives, whereas no-one ever thought that *The Appleyards*, being a live TV show for kids, would need to be remembered.

The series was shown at about 4.30–5.00 p.m. in two-week cycles every other Thursday. The structure of the Appleyard family was actually very similar to that of the Groves: mum, dad, four kids (two teens, two younger, two boys, two girls) all living in the home counties and being terribly nice to each other. Like ***Billy Bunter***, each episode was performed and broadcast twice, once on Thursday and again on Sunday, with both performances going out live. In some ways, *The Appleyards* foreshadowed ***The Simpsons*** in that, irrespective of the fact that it spanned eight seasons and 160 episodes, time never seemed to move on for the family (actually, that really is the only similarity – the Appleyards would never have tolerated the kind of beastly mischief that Bart makes his parents endure). The only betraying factor was that when the younger children got older they were replaced, poor mites.

The Appleyards disappeared from the TV just two months before *The Groves* went the same way, although a reunion special, 'Christmas with the Appleyards', was shown in 1960.

Are You Being Served?

Sitcom | BBC One | episode duration 30 mins | broadcast 8 Sep 1972, 21 Mar 1973–1 Apr 1985

Regular Cast

John Inman · *Mr Wilberforce Clayborne Humphries*
Mollie Sugden · *Mrs Mary Elizabeth 'Betty' Slocombe*
Frank Thornton · *Captain Stephen Peacock*
Wendy Richard · *Miss Shirley Brahms*
Nicholas Smith · *Mr Cuthbert Rumbold*
Trevor Bannister · *Mr James (aka Dick) Lucas*
Arthur Brough · *Mr Ernest Grainger*
Harold Bennett · *Young Mr Grace*
Larry Martyn · *Mr Mash*
Arthur English · *Mr Beverley Harmon*
James Hayter · *Mr Percival Tebbs*
Alfie Bass · *Mr Harry Goldberg*
Mike Berry · *Mr Bert Spooner*
Kenneth Waller · *Old Mr Grace*
Milo Sperber · *Mr Grossman*
Benny Lee · *Mr Klein*
Stephanie Gathercole, Debbie Linden · *Rumbold's Secretary*
Penny Irving · *Miss Bakewell*
Moira Foot · *Miss Thorpe*
Vivienne Johnson · Young *Mr Grace's Nurse*
Candy Davis · *Miss Belfridge*
Diana King, Diane Lambert · *Mrs Peacock*

Creators Jeremy Lloyd and David Croft **Producers** David Croft, Martin Shardlow, Bob Spiers, Harold Snoad **Writers** Jeremy Lloyd, David Croft, Michael Knowles, John Chapman **Theme Music** Ronnie Hazlehurst composed the theme tune with its memorable cash-register sounds. The lyrics were written by series co-creator David Croft, and the female voice announcing the floors of Grace Brothers department store was Stephanie Gathercole, a regular in the first season as Mr Rumbold's secretary. All together now: 'Ground floor perfumery, stationery and leather goods, wigs and haberdashery, kitchenware and food – going up!'

The high-water mark of TV innuendo and smuttery, *Are You Being Served?* was thought up by Jeremy Lloyd, who sent his idea for a department store comedy series to BBC staff producer David Croft (who also produced and co-wrote ***Dad's Army***). Together they created a sitcom that endured for 13 years and (an eyebrow-raisingly appropriate) 69 smut-filled episodes.

Grace Brothers department store is a somewhat old-fashioned establishment, where rules, regulations and the correct way of doing things are still paramount. Head of ladies' fashions is the bouffant-haired Mrs Slocombe, a woman with an intimidating presence and ever-changing hair colour. Her main preoccupation in life is the well-being of her 'pussy', a poor creature that's always getting wet and needing to be dried off. Mrs Slocombe's assistant is the nearly glamorous Miss Brahms, a surly young woman who spends most of her time fending off amorous advances from staff and public alike. In charge of the men's department (in the first few series) is the elderly and rather stern Mr Grainger. Reporting to him are leering and lustful Mr Lucas and the astoundingly camp Mr Humphries, a mummy's boy who is never more than a few minutes away from cooing 'I'm free!' across the department and pouncing on a new customer, tape-measure in hand. In charge of the whole shop floor is former army man Captain Peacock, an arrogant and rather stupid fellow obsessed with asserting his authority whenever and wherever possible. Captain Peacock reports up to the store's manager, Mr Rumbold, a fussy dolt with the most memorable pair of ears ever seen in retail management. Every now and again, one of the two decrepit Grace brothers themselves are to be seen venturing down onto the shop floor to examine their empire, either the ancient and dithering Young Mr Grace (complete with dolly-bird nurse) or the even older and dodderier Old Mr Grace.

And thus the staff of Grace Brothers would engage in an endless round of petty bickering, industrial disputes, stresses caused by the introduction of new product ranges, and other assorted business-related traumas and disasters. Although several of the supporting characters came and went as the series progressed, it was the five main players (Mr Humphries, Mrs Slocombe, Miss Brahms, Captain Peacock and Mr Rumbold) that stayed with the programme from beginning to end. *Are You Being Served?* became a surprise hit in the USA when it was transmitted on the PBS network from the early 1980s. Just like practically every other 1970s sitcom, the staff of Grace Brothers graduated to a cinema film in 1977, in which they all went on holiday together to Spain's Costa Plonka – sadly, it's a dire, dire film with little of the joy of the TV show. Even after the doors of Grace Brothers closed in 1985, that wasn't the end of the story. In 1992, the five main cast members reunited for two seasons of a sequel series, *Grace and Favour*, broadcast from 10 January 1992 to 8 February 1993. In this new series, the Grace Brothers' staff relocate to a country house called Millstone Manor, which they decide to convert into a posh hotel. Despite the change in venue, the comedy remained steadfastly the same, with every possible double-entendre centring on Mr Humphries' sexuality and Mrs Slocombe's pussy squeezed out of the script.

Armchair Thriller

Anthology | Thames/Southern for ITV | episode duration 25 mins | broadcast 21 Feb 1978–10 Apr 1980

Creator Andrew Brown **Producers** Andrew Brown, Jacqueline Davis, Brenda Ennis **Writers** John Bowen, Ray Jenkins, Julia Jones, Philip Mackie, Michael Ashe, Tom Clenaghan, Troy Kennedy Martin, David Hopkins (from the novels of Patricia Highsmith), Antonia Fraser, Derry Quinn, Desmond Corey **Theme Music** Andy Mackay, formerly of Roxy Music

ITV once had a long tradition of 'Armchair' dramas dating back to *Armchair Theatre*, which had run on the network on and off since 1956. Early 'Armchair' episodes were broadcast live until November 1958 when production of a science fiction story called 'Underground' was thrown into disarray when one of the actors, Gareth Jones, died halfway through the broadcast. Soon after, the episodes began to be pre-recorded. A 1967 episode, 'A Magnum for Schneider', led to the series ***Callan***, while an offshoot of the format, *Armchair Cinema*, contained 'Regan', the first episode of iconoclastic police drama ***The Sweeney***. Thames TV took on the project after the 1968 reshuffle of ITV franchises, but by 1974 there was a slow move away from the anthology format. The last came in the form of *Armchair Thriller*, a series of four- and six-part dramas often based on existing thriller novels.

Set against the familiar London skyline of the Thames logo, but shot at night, *Armchair Thriller* would begin with a dustsheet-covered armchair and a spooky shadow growing larger until we realised that the shadow itself was about to sit down on the chair. As the music ended with a dramatic flourish, the shadow's hands splayed out in shock. The title sequence alone was enough to mentally scar any children allowed to stay up late to watch it.

Out of 11 serials and 54 episodes, only one continues to stir hazy memories – 'As Quiet as a Nun'. Starring Maria Aitken as journalist Jemima Shore, the story involved a death at Jemima's old convent school and the terrifying manifestations of the Black Nun, a faceless being dressed in a habit seen in a rocking chair at the top of a dark tower. This six-part serial led to a full series, *Jemima Shore Investigates*, this time starring Patricia Hodge.

With the close of this series in 1980, ITV had produced over 450 'Armchair' editions. While ***Tales of the Unexpected*** and ***Hammer House of Horror*** would jostle for positions in the ITV schedules for a few years more, the anthology format was growing out of fashion in Britain, just as it was about to enjoy a revival in the USA, with ***Alfred Hitchcock Presents, Amazing Stories*** and the new ***Twilight Zone*** just around the corner.

The Army Game

Sitcom | Granada Television for ITV | episode duration 30 mins | broadcast 19 Jun 1957–20 Jun 1961

Regular Cast
William Hartnell · *Sergeant-Major Percy Bullimore*
Michael Medwin · *Corporal Springer*
Alfie Bass · *Private 'Bootsie' Bisley*
Norman Rossington · *Private 'Cupcake' Cook*
Charles Hawtrey · *Private 'Professor' Hatchett*
Bernard Bresslaw · *Private 'Popeye' Popplewell*
Bill Fraser · *Sergeant-Major Claude Snudge*
Geoffrey Sumner · *Major Upshot-Bagley*
Bernard Hunter · *Captain Pilsworthy*
Ted Lune · *Private Leonard Bone*
Harry Fowler · *Corporal 'Flogger' Hoskins*
Frank Williams · *Captain Pocket*
C. B. Poulter · *Major Geoffrey Duckworth*
Mario Fabrizi · *Lance Corporal 'Moosh' Merryweather*
Harry Towb · *Private Dooley*
Robert Desmond · *Private Baker*
Dick Emery · *Private 'Chubby' Catchpole*

Creator Sid Colin **Producers** Peter Eton, Milo Lewis, Max Morgan-Witts, Eric Fawcett **Writers** Various, including Sid Colin, Lew Schwarz, David Climie, Larry Stephens, Maurice Wiltshire, Marty Feldman, Barry Took, David Cumming, Derek Collyer, John Antrobus, Talbot Rothwell, Stanley Mars, Brad Ashton, Sid Nelson **Theme Music** Pat Napier; sung by Leslie Fyson and members of the cast

The successor to World War Two conscription, Britain's National Service Act became law in 1948, ensuring that every man of 18 years or over served in the armed forces for 18 months (later increased to two years). Now credited with teaching a generation the values of discipline and respect for authority, for some soldiers it gave them the change to see the world – Germany, Africa, Hong Kong – but for a few it represented one long dodge from having to find proper work. Drawing upon his own experiences in the RAF, writer Sid Colin came up with the idea of a comedy series following the exploits of a group of army recruits, the residents of Hut 29, Nether Hopping Surplus Ordnance Depot in Staffordshire.

Though the BBC had begun screening the American comedy ***The Phil Silvers Show*** a couple of months before *The Army Game* was first shown, a more likely influence on Colin was the feature film *Private's Progress* (1956). Common to both productions was William Hartnell, who played *The Army Game*'s Sergeant-Major Percy Bullimore,

an explosive, gruff man with no patience for tomfoolery. The privates themselves, led by Corporal Springer (and later 'Flogger' Hoskins), were a mixed bag of shirkers, scroungers and loafers, trying any and every trick they could think of to escape the drudgery of army life. The original batch included such characters as 'Cupcake' Cook, a Scouser whose mother used to send him food parcels; 'Bootsie' Bisley, so called because for most of his army career he'd been able to convince his superiors that he should be 'excused boots'; 'Professor' Hatchett (played by Charles Hawtrey), a delicate soul whose favourite pastime was knitting; and the educationally stunted 'Popeye' Popplewell, whose oft-repeated outcry 'I only arsked' became a national catchphrase and the title of a 1958 spin-off movie.

Initially, *The Army Game* was broadcast live, on a fortnightly basis, in rotation with *The Caroll Levis Variety Show*. Such was the public response that it eventually won its own weekly slot. Cast changes dented the popularity of later series, even though some of the newcomers included Bill Fraser as Sergeant-Major Claude Snudge (who stepped in to replace William Hartnell) and a young Dick Emery as Private 'Chubby' Catchpole (it was here that Emery began saying 'Hello honky-tonk', a catchphrase that stayed with him throughout his career). But with National Service officially ending on 31 December 1960, *The Army Game* began to look increasingly dated, and it was eventually brought to a close after an impressive 157 episodes.

Following *The Army Game*, Charles Hawtrey and Bernard Bresslaw made the break into movies thanks to the *Carry On* series that began with *Carry On Sergeant* (1958), which had also starred William Hartnell and Norman Rossington. Frank Williams (Captain Pocket) went on to star in another long-running military comedy series, as the vicar in ***Dad's Army***. Two of *The Army Game*'s stars had already been demobbed in advance of the final episode. On 23 September 1960, Alfie Bass and Bill Fraser had taken their characters and launched them in their own show, *Bootsie and Snudge*. Created by Barry Took and Marty Feldman and written by many of the same writers as *The Army Game*, *Bootsie and Snudge* ran for four series and 104 episodes, including a revival in 1974. Meanwhile, at 53, William Hartnell was beyond average army retirement age and was unlikely to continue his long association with fierce military characters. Indeed, after this point Hartnell took on only one other significant TV role. Luckily, it was the role of a lifetime – the title part in ***Doctor Who***.

Around the World in 80 Days

Documentary | BBC One | episode duration 50–60 mins | broadcast 11 Oct 1989–present

Cast

Michael Palin · *Presenter*

Creator/Producer Clem Vallance **Theme Music** Paddy Kingsland

Sending a Python every direction possible around the planet isn't quite as random an idea as it might sound. As a member of the ***Monty Python*** team, Michael Palin presented his fair share of spoof documentary segments (including one where the team visited an island populated solely by look-alikes of travelogue presenter Alan Whicker).

In 1980, Palin was asked to present an edition of *Great Railway Journeys of the World* ('Confessions of a Train Spotter', 27 Nov 1980), travelling from London Euston up to the Kyle of Lochalsh in the west of Scotland. Though many other personalities had contributed to the series – including Ludovic Kennedy and historian Michael Wood – it was Michael that the BBC turned to for an ambitious travel documentary that would follow the route of Phileas Fogg, the lead character from Jules Verne's novel *Around the World in 80 Days*.

Michael Palin began his travels on 25 September 1988 (from the Reform Club in London) accompanied by a cameraman and photographer and with a promise to deliver enough material for six 50-minute documentaries and a tie-in book. It's a credit to the Beeb that on Palin's return, scant hours ahead of the 80-day deadline, they saw how much material he'd amassed and granted the series a seventh episode. The series proved a great success and subsequent travels have taken Michael on a vertical journey from *Pole to Pole*, *Full Circle* around the globe, on a *Hemingway Adventure*, across the *Sahara* and up the *Himalaya*.

Michael Palin is possibly the perfect travelling companion – especially as he does all the work and we get to watch from the comfort of our own homes. He's unflinchingly polite, even when faced with the unfathomable bureaucracy that greets many cross-border travellers, attentive enough to draw us to fascinating landmarks and examples of local culture, and even though he's one-sixth of the most famous comedy troupe to come out of the halls of Britain's universities, it's still surprising to discover that even the Dalai Lama knows his face.

Palin has evolved from, as he puts it, 'a silly man to a silly traveller'. In 2005, when taking a momentary rest while he decided where to go next, he was forced to deny press rumours that he'd hung up his travelling boots for good: 'I have absolutely no intention of hanging up my boots,' he wrote on his website. 'Though I may well discard the current pair, for reasons of hygiene, they will instantly be replaced so that I can continue what I enjoy so much – the process of seeing and learning about the world.'

Website

Relive Michael's adventures through his site: www.palinstravels.co.uk

Arthur's Hailey's Hotel

See HOTEL

As Time Goes By

Comedy | DL Taffner Ltd/Theatre of Comedy for BBC | episode duration 30 mins | broadcast 12 Jan 1992–4 Aug 2002

Regular Cast
Judi Dench · *Jean Pargetter/Hardcastle*
Geoffrey Palmer · *Lionel Hardcastle*
Moira Brooker · *Judith Pargetter/Deacon*
Philip Bretherton · *Alistair Deacon*
Jenny Funnell · *Sandy*
Frank Middlemass · *Rocky Hardcastle*
Joan Sims · *Madge Hardcastle*

Writer Bob Larbey, based on an original idea by Colin Bostock-Smith **Producers** Philip Jones, John Reynolds, Don Taffner (executive), Sydney Lotterby, J. Clive Hedges
Theme Music 'As Time Goes By' by Herman Hupfield, performed by Joe Fagin

Nurse Jean Pargetter and army officer Lionel Hardcastle first met in 1953 in Hyde Park, leading to a three-month love affair. The pair lost touch when Lionel was posted unexpectedly to Korea and the letter he wrote to Jean explaining where he was never got through. For 38 years, each thought the other had broken the relationship off. The pair are reunited, for better or worse, when a divorced Lionel employs Jean's secretarial agency to type up his book. Jean, now widowed, lives with her erratic daughter Judith, who Lionel's suave publisher takes a shine to. Can Jean and Lionel pick up where they left off, or has too much time gone by?

As Time Goes by is sitcom royalty. Writer Bob Larbey co-penned ***The Good Life***, among others, and director/producer Sydney Lotterby had a hand in the success of ***Porridge*** and ***Open All Hours***. Geoffrey Palmer's CV is riddled with quality comedy, from ***The Fall and Rise of Reginald Perrin*** to ***Butterflies***, and the pre-Bond Judi Dench adds a consummate touch of class. The success of the series is based on no one thing – it never goes out of its way to startle you, but is as comfortable as an old pair of slippers.

By series four, Lionel and Jean bow to the inevitable and finally marry, and the series continued until 2002, with the format being adapted as a Radio 2 comedy, featuring many of the original cast, which would run for three seasons. The first episode of the radio version employed a flashback sequence to Jean and Lionel's younger days, not seen in the TV original.

Though the series has come to a close, fans around the world still hope that there's enough room for the odd Christmas special or two . . .

The Ascent of Man

Documentary | BBC Two | episode duration 50 mins | broadcast 5 May–28 Jul 1973

Presenter/Writer Dr Jacob Bronowski **Producers** Adrian Malone, Dick Gilling

While Kenneth Clark's ***Civilisation*** examined humankind's evolution through the history of art and architecture, Jacob Bronowski's 13-part *Ascent of Man* followed our growth through scientific discoveries and inventions. Bronowski's journey began in the birthplace of civilisation, the Great Rift Valley of East Africa, and travelled across the globe to Cambridge University and the discovery of DNA. He looked at the origins of war and its effect upon social evolution; traced the development of chemistry, medicine and the awareness of self; followed Copernicus and Galileo, and man's first examination of the universe and the sub-atomic particles that constitute it. Bronowski noted too how, while most animals learn to adapt to their surroundings, human beings simply change their surroundings to suit their own needs.

In the final episode, 'The Long Childhood', Bronowski theorised that while Western culture perceives itself as the high point of evolution, the creativity and intellectual development of children today is actually being stunted by modern technology. It was an astounding claim to have made more than 20 years before teenagers began to rely on the internet as their sole, often unreliable source of knowledge.

Commissioned after the success of *Civilisation, The Ascent of Man* took four years to make, leaving Dr Bronowski literally exhausted after its completion. He died of a heart attack within a year of the series being broadcast.

Ask Aspel

Factual | BBC One | episode duration 15–25 mins | broadcast 9 Oct 1970–21 Jul 1981

Regular Cast
Michael Aspel · *Host*

Producers Granville Jenkins, Iain Johnstone, Frances Whitaker, Will Wyatt

Forget news presenting, ***Crackerjack, This is Your Life, Antiques Roadshow*** and cameos in ***The Goodies*** – Michael Aspel was intended to serve just one purpose. This popular long-running comment and request show was more than just a replacement for *Junior Points of View* – Aspel presided, god-like, over this programme that provided an opportunity for a pre-video generation to see clips of popular children's shows, past and present. In other words, TV gold. Children didn't tune in to hear Aspel read out the letters of comment, or see occasional guest stars (unless they happened to be Tom Baker), it was to feast their eyes on what, at the time, were lost gems of tea-time telly.

The show ended in 1981, soon to be replaced by the slicker antics of Phillip Schofield's *Take Two*, but Aspel to this day recalls how letters would arrive that began 'Dear Ask', assuming that to be the poor chap's name.

Ask the Family

Quiz Show | BBC One/Two | episode duration 25 mins | broadcast 12 Jun 1967–22 Oct 1984, 4 Apr 2005–present

Presenters

Robert Robinson, Alan Titchmarsh, Richard McCourt (aka Dick), Dominic Wood (aka Dom)

Creator Cecil Korer **Producers** Patricia Owtram, Linda McCarthy, Cecil Korer, Rosalind Gold, Robert Toner, David Taylor, Mark Patterson **Theme Music** 'Sun Ride' by John Leach

They didn't come much more middle class than this: an early evening quiz involving two families – mum, dad, two kids – competing against each other to solve various rounds of cryptic, lateral or just generally obscure puzzles. Some rounds would be for 'the children', some for 'mother and eldest child' or 'father and youngest child' or variations of the same, while the puzzles themselves always included one round of objects shown in extreme close-up, slowly pulling back to reveal what it was (at home we'd all join in: 'Cheese grater! Bicycle! Dead fly! Nan's teeth! . . . oh, it was the inside of a watch . . .').

The avuncular Robert Robinson presided over proceedings for more than 17 years until the great purges of the mid-1980s saw its removal from the schedules.

The year 1999 saw a brief revival with Alan Titchmarsh on cable channel UK Gold, later repeated on 'proper' telly, but it was the 2005 version that grabbed the headlines as Richard McCourt and Dominic Wood – aka children's TV presenters 'Dick and Dom' – brought their own rather messy approach to the show, with the rather staid proceedings binned in favour of cake-eating competitions. Patricia Owtram, producer of the very first series, expressed her displeasure in a letter to the *Daily Telegraph*: 'I was appalled that, in a programme in which small girls took part, there were so many jokes about willies and so much sexy cuddling between a presenter and an over-excited mother. I sound like a Grumpy Old Producer. I probably am.'

At Home with the Braithwaites

Comedy Drama | Yorkshire for ITV | episode duration 50 mins | broadcast 20 Jan 2000–9 Apr 2003

Recurring Cast

Amanda Redman · *Alison Braithwaite*
Peter Davison · *David Braithwaite*
Lynda Bellingham · *Pauline Farnell*
Sylvia Syms · *Marion Riley*
Julie Graham · *Megan Hartnoll*
Kevin Doyle · *Mike Hartnoll*
Sarah Smart · *Virginia Braithwaite*
Sarah Churm · *Sarah Braithwaite*
Keeley Fawcett · *Charlotte Braithwaite*
Judy Holt · *Elaine Fishwick*
Jonathan Le Billon · *Kieran*
Garry Cooper · *Colin Skidmore*
Corrine Coward · *Moira*
Charles Dale · *McGuire*
Ben Douglas · *Jordan Fishwick*
Hazel Douglas · *Audrey*
Ray Stevenson · *Graham Braithwaite*
Elizabeth Rider · *Helen Braithwaite*
Olive Pendleton · *Mrs Braithwaite*
Kulvinder Ghir · *Manjit Mathura*
Emily Glennister · *Emily Braithwaite*
Nicholas Lane · *Tim*
Rachel Leskovac · *Ciara Pickering*
Simon Molloy · *Mr Garside*
Sadie Pickering · *Verity*
Alun Raglan · *Daniel Wolfenden*
Neil Stuke · *Keith Kershaw*

Creator Sally Wainwright **Producers** Carolyn Reynolds (executive), Sally Wainwright (associate), Kieran Roberts, Hugh Warren **Writers** Sally Wainwright, Jonathan Harvey, Sarah Daniels **Theme Music** Written by The Egg

Alison Braithwaite is a wife and mother living in Leeds. Her husband's conducting an affair that he can't quite bring himself to end, her daughters are going through those difficult teen years – Virginia discovering her sexuality thanks to an affair with their next-door neighbour Megan, Sarah getting herself into trouble with her boyfriend, and Charlotte suffering bullying at school. Alison's just turned 40 when a Euro Lottery ticket that Alison's youngest daughter bought for her comes up trumps to the tune of £38 million. With so many secrets in the family, one more can't hurt, can it?

Having worked on ***Coronation Street*** and ***Emmerdale***, writer Sally Wainwright created a thrill-a-minute series with *At Home with the Braithwaites*, packing in more revelations each episode than most soaps run through in a month. Over the space of four series, the family experiences divorce, pregnancies, battles with the tabloids, a damehood for Alison and much, much more. The series quickly became a major player in the ITV schedules; something the network recognised, recommissioning the show to the surprise of many (including the cast). Though the story has probably come to a close – with a huge wedding and Alison pursued by three potential suitors – it's possible we haven't seen the last of the Braithwaites . . .

The A-Team

Action-Adventure | Stephen J. Cannell Productions/Universal for NBC (shown on ITV) | episode duration 50 mins | broadcast 23 Jan 1983–8 Mar 1987

Regular Cast
George Peppard · *Colonel John 'Hannibal' Smith*
Mr T · *Sergeant Bosco Albert 'BA' Baracus*
Tim Dunigan, Dirk Benedict · *Lieutenant Templeton 'Faceman' Peck*
Dwight Schultz · *Captain H. M. 'Howling Mad' Murdock*
Melinda Culea · *Amy Amanda Allen*
William Lucking · *Colonel Lynch*
Lance LeGault · *Colonel Roderick Decker*
Marla Heasley · *Tawnia Baker*
Robert Vaughn · *General Hunt Stockwell*
Eddie Velez · *Frankie 'Dishpan' Santana*
Judy Ledford · *Carla*
Charles Napier · *Colonel Briggs*
Carl Franklin · *Captain Crane*

Creators Stephen J. Cannell and Frank Lupo **Producers** Stephen J. Cannell, Frank Lupo (executive), Steve Beers, Rob Bowman, Alan Cassidy, Gary Winter (associate), John Ashley, Patrick Hasburgh, Jo Swerling Jr **Writers** Various, including Frank Lupo, Stephen J. Cannell, Patrick Hasburgh, Babs Greyhosky, Richard Christian Matheson, Thomas Szolski, Stephen Katz, Mark Jones, Steven L. Sears, Bill Nuss **Theme Music** Mike Post; a theme guaranteed to get a coachload of blokes to sing along to

When *The A-Team* was first aired in the UK, it met with a divided response among young schoolboy viewers: those whose who loved it for the action sequences, the explosions and the funny characters; and fans of ***Doctor Who***, who hated it because it led to the temporary cancellation of their favourite series when scheduling clashed. 'The scripts are rubbish,' they'd moan, but no-one could hear them over the sound of yet another jeep being blown up by Hannibal and his gang.

One of the first major films to tackle the subject of the Vietnam War came right at the beginning of the conflict. *The Green Berets* (1968) was a jingoistic western relocated to the Vietnamese jungle and starring John Wayne. Its confidence in the certainty of an American victory was sadly let down by reality. Vietnam War films of the 1970s were respectful of the subject matter and of America's mood at the time, starring emotionally shattered characters like Travis Bickle in *Taxi Driver* (1976) and the paraplegic Luke Martin in *Coming Home* (1978). But Sylvester Stallone changed all that with Rambo, the monosyllabic killing machine in *First Blood* (1982). He may well have been a Vietnam vet, but he could mow down his adversaries like skittles and nothing would get in his way. Such an approach provided a cathartic sigh of relief for the American male, desperate to return to the days of the invincible American hero.

The A-Team reached television screens a year after *First Blood* had packed cinemas. It took the rewriting of the Vietnam legacy a step further to create four characters who, though highly skilled in their respective fields, were not hampered by emotional fragility like Rambo. Sure, one of them was crazy, but in an endearing way, like a funny uncle who you only see at Christmas and weddings. The war wasn't their primary motivation either, but rather the desire of three of the gang – Hannibal, Face and 'BA' Baracus – to clear their names after they had been ordered by their commanding officer to rob the Bank of Hanoi, but were then accused of looting after their superior was killed and no-one else could support their claims of innocence. With no other choice, the men broke out of prison, returned to LA and sought out their old pilot, Murdock, whom they found languishing in an asylum after a breakdown. Despite the assertion to the contrary at the beginning of every episode, the motley foursome blatantly *did* commit a crime; it's just that they were obeying orders. Like the Watergate intruders. Or Mengele.

At the start of the TV series, 'The A-Team' are little more than an American urban myth, but when journalist Amy Allen learns that one of her colleagues has been kidnapped by Mexican bandits, she decides to send a message to them to see if they are as good as their legends suggest. Pah – they're better, of course! Leader of the pack Hannibal has a talent for disguise and a love of cigars. 'Face' is a smooth con-man with a talent for seduction, though his vanity causes him to duck out of fights whenever possible. The same couldn't be said for BA, 'Bad Attitude', Baracus, a real brawler with a love of bling (and lots of it), though he is hampered somewhat by his fear of flying ('Ah ain't gettin' on no plane,' he regularly declares. He'd also begin to say, 'Ah pity tha fool that tries to get me on that–' just before his friends drug him and bundle him aboard). And finally, the crack/cracked pilot Murdock, known to friends as 'Howling Mad', and not because of his temper. Amy joins the boys in their adventures, no doubt impressed by their ability to build a fully working tank out of household objects (a tiresome skill inherited by another macho American hero, MacGyver, in the programme of that name), but she provides little more than a bit of glamour to help the show hit the required demographics. Indeed, though her role was filled in later series by Tawnia Baker and Frankie Santana, no-one was really convinced that the female characters were ever really 'proper' A-Teamers.

Every show needs their villains, and in addition to the thug-of-the-week characters there was Colonel Lynch, Colonel Decker and General Fulbright, the military men assigned to track down and capture the A-Team but who never quite get there in time (although by the conclusion of the fourth series, Fulbright has lost his zeal). In the final series, the A-Team are actually captured to face court martial and execution. The man who eventually brings them in is General Hunt Stockwell, played (in a rather smart bit of casting) by former ***Man from U.N.C.L.E.*** star Robert Vaughn. Stockwell manages to turn the situation

to his advantage and for the remainder of the series the A-Team work for him on a series of missions.

The A-Team was an odd series to pitch at children. With action figures and lunch boxes lined up in toy shops across the globe, it's worrying to consider the amount of bullets sprayed indiscriminately in every episode, and the number of cars blown up with such force that they flip three times before they hit the ground. Again and again, questions were asked about the suitability of that kind of show for younger viewers. Still, over on BBC One, Doctor Who (at least until he was temporarily cancelled) was facing cybernetic beings who could crush a man's hands to a bloody pulp and a cannibal space cook who munched on dead rats. At least with *The A-Team* you could eat your dinner at the same time . . .

Trivia

The part of Face was played by Tim Dunigan for the two-part pilot episode, but Dunigan was dropped in favour of first-choice Dirk Benedict (straight from playing Starbuck in ***Battlestar Galactica***, as a clip in the title sequence jokily reminded us) for the remainder of the series.

With Mr T having so many connections to the wrestling world, it's not surprising that a few of his friends made guest appearances, including Hulk Hogan and British-born Daveyboy Smith – aka the British Bulldog. However, a 1986 episode, 'Cowboy George', featured a hilarious guest appearance by Boy George, possibly the least appropriate example of stunt casting ever.

An Audience With . . .

Light Entertainment | LWT for TV/Channel 4 | episode duration 50–90 mins | broadcast 26 Dec 1980–present

Producers Various, including David Bell, Nicholas Barrett, John Kaye Cooper (executive) Lorna Dickinson, Richard Drewett, Helen Fraser, David G. Hillier

A hardy perennial of the independent television light entertainment output, *An Audience With* . . . provides a showcase for, well, anybody who can safely come under the umbrella of 'entertainer'. A star of choice is selected to headline their own one-person show, singing a few songs, telling a few jokes and taking 'spontaneous' questions from the invited celebrity studio audience, with a few joining the star on stage for the odd turn.

The format was launched on Boxing Day 1980, allowing Dame Edna Everage, alter-ego of Australian comedian Barry Humphries, to throw the glitter around the stage, and the format has provided the backbone to the Saturday night schedules from time to time ever since.

Curiously, though, *An Audience With* . . . transferred to Channel 4 in 1983, starting with a 90-minute appointment with Kenneth Williams, and there it would stay until 1988. Bob Monkhouse, who headlined his own show in 1994, joked that LWT must have booked the studio audience before it booked him.

Among other stars accepting the accolade of their own *Audience With* . . . Ken Dodd and Freddie Star returned twice, with Dudley Moore, Mel Brooks, Joan Rivers, Billy Connolly, Peter Ustinov, Victoria Wood, the Bee Gees, the Spice Girls, Warren Mitchell (as Alf Garnett), Tom Jones and Kylie Minogue all providing memorable outings. In 1992, to celebrate his 40th anniversary, Sooty was the subject of *An Audience With*. . . (broadcast on Children's ITV), and Joe Pasquale, fresh from the success of winning ***I'm a Celebrity . . . Get Me Out of Here***, took a slot in 2005.

Auf Wiedersehen, Pet

Comedy Drama | WitzEnd/Central for ITV, Ziji Productions for BBC One | episode duration 50–60 mins, plus specials | broadcast 11 Nov 1983–16 May 1986, 28 Apr 2002–29 Dec 2004

Principal Cast

Tim Healy · *Dennis Patterson*
Kevin Whately · *Neville Hope*
Jimmy Nail · *Leonard Jeffrey 'Oz' Osborne*
Timothy Spall · *Barry Taylor*
Gary Holton · *Wayne Winston Norris*
Pat Roach · *Brian 'Bomber' Busbridge*
Christopher Fairbank · *Albert Arthur Moxey*
Julia Tobin · *Brenda Hope*
Michael Sheard · *Herr Grunwald*
Caroline Hutchinson · *Vera Patterson*
Peter Birch · *Herr Ulrich*
Brigitte Kahn · *Dagmar*
Bill Paterson · *Ally Fraser*
Ray Knight · *Barman*
Lesley St John · *Vicki*
Catherine Whately · *Debbie Hope*
Noel Clarke · *Wyman Ian Norris*
Bill Nighy · *Jeffrey Grainger*
Mark Stobbart · *Rod Osborne*
Michael Angelis · *Mickey Startup*
Val McLane · *Norma*
James Booth · *Kenny Ames*
Emily Bruni · *Sarah*
Georgina Lightning · *Lainie Proudfoot*

Creator Franc Roddam **Producers** Franc Roddam, Allan McKeown (executive), Peter Millhouse (associate), Roger Bamford, Nick Goding, Martin McKeand, Chrissy Skinns, Joy Spink **Writers** Dick Clement, Ian La Frenais, Stan Hey, Bernie Cooper, Francis Megahy **Theme Music** For the original series, the opening tune was 'Breaking Away', while the end theme was 'That's Living Alright' (a No. 3 hit in the singles charts in 1984), both by Joe Fagin. Joe Fagin returned for the second series with 'Get It Right' and 'Back With the Boys Again'. For the BBC series, Mark Knopfler wrote 'Why Aye Man'.

While, in the early 1980s, ***Boys from the Blackstuff*** portrayed working men reacting to being unemployed and unemployable, by the middle of the decade *Auf Wiedersehen, Pet* was showing a gang of men 'getting on their bike' and heading off to foreign climes to find work. For some, like newly married Neville, old-timer Bomber and soon-to-be-divorced Dennis, the hardship of being separated from loved ones was only just made up for by the knowledge that they could at least earn enough money to support the families they'd left behind. For Oz and Wayne it was an opportunity to earn enough money to keep themselves entertained (boorish and obnoxious from the start, Oz hadn't even told his wife he was leaving the country).

The gang first assemble in Düsseldorf where a hut on a building site provides their basic accommodation. There, Neville ends up with an unwanted tattoo after just one drunken night, finds himself wrongly accused of a violent attack on a local girl (the real culprit was her boyfriend who attacked her in a jealous rage after the gentlemanly Neville escorted her home one evening) and hailed a hero after preventing a German digger from accidentally detonating an unexploded bomb left over from the war. Bomber's flirtatious teenage daughter travels out to see for herself the squalor her father has subjected himself to in order to keep his family fed. Scouser Moxey spends most of his time off sick with round after round of colds, while Cockney Wayne pursues every last single woman Düsseldorf has to offer. Brummie Barry fancies himself as something of an intellectual, having read books on many subjects and retained a few details along the way. Sadly, his pals think him a bit tedious and instead look to Dennis for leadership. And Oz manages to upset half of Germany with his loud mouth and racist attitudes (constantly moaning about the Germans and how they bombed his granny).

The role of Oz made an overnight star of former bricklayer Jimmy Nail, who surprised viewers in the second series by unveiling an appealing singing voice. He went on to record Rose Royce's 'Love Don't Live Here Any More' in the 1980s and scored a No. 1 hit – 'Ain't No Doubt' in 1992 – before creating and starring in the TV shows ***Spender*** and *Crocodile Shoes* and becoming Britain's biggest country-music recording artist of the 1990s.

When the German government decide that foreign workers should pay VAT, the gang disband, only to be reunited a few years down the line, first to help Barry renovate his dream home for his bride-to-be and later for a couple of jobs for big-shot gangster Ally Fraser that take the Magnificent Seven to Spain.

The premature death of Gary Holton (Wayne) left a cloud over the second series, although clever editing and a stand-in double helped ensure his character appeared in every episode. Sixteen years later, thanks to a collaboration between series creator Franc Roddam and Jimmy Nail, the gang were reunited for two more series, this time for the BBC. The surviving friends assemble for the funeral of Oz only to learn it was a ruse on Oz's part to get them all together to help him with a project he's working on with a disgraced former MP he met while in prison. Callous and tactless he remains, but much has changed in Oz's life since they all last met. His stretch in prison left him a reformed man. Almost.

In came Wyman, a black youth who brings news of Wayne's death. He also reveals that he is Wayne's illegitimate son and has tracked down the old friends in order to find out about the father he never knew. As Oz struggles to understand how Wayne's son could be black (and naturally causes offence along the way), he learns that his own errant son, Rod, also has a surprise for him – he's a gay Dusty Springfield impersonator . . .

Shortly after transmission of the fourth series in 2004, actor Pat Roach (Bomber) died after a long struggle with cancer. Two special episodes shown on 28 and 29 December 2004 marked the final end for the hugely popular series, with all concerned recognising that with yet another member of the gang having passed away they would feel uncomfortable continuing without them.

Website

The 'Original Auf Wiedersehen Pet Website': www.aufpet.com

The Avengers

See pages 62–6

The Avengers

Diana Rigg and Patrick Macnee, the epitome of Sixties cool.

In much the same way that ***The Simpsons*** tapped into a rich vein of post-modernism and nostalgia prevalent in the 1990s, ***Dynasty*** encapsulated the greedy and amoral 1980s and ***The Good Life*** highlighted the fears of a nation apparently falling apart in the 1970s, there's one programme whose very name evokes the most swinging decade of all, the 1960s. From the post-war austerity and gloom of the first series through to the psychedelic, high-gloss transatlantic adventures of the final run, *The Avengers* isn't just a nine-year-long examination of the changing style of television, it's also an accurate reflection of the changing face of British society.

The Avengers began in 1961, the same year that the world toyed with Armageddon when the Cuban Missile Crisis brought the USA and USSR to the brink of war. Back in Britain, still recovering from the social and economic impact of World War Two, people were starting to question whether or not the optimistic view of the future postulated throughout the 1950s would ever come to pass. Into this atmosphere of uncertainty came a television programme about a single act of random violence and the impact it had on one individual. In the first episode, 'Hot Snow', we meet young enthusiastic GP Dr David Keel, played by Ian Hendry. Keel's life is torn apart when his girlfriend Peggy is murdered by a gang of heroin smugglers. Desperate to 'avenge' his fiancée's death, Keel meets a mysterious figure by the name of John Steed, who claims to be working for a secret government ministry. Together, the doctor and the spy track down Peggy's killers and then go on to solve a series of typical spy-/police-style plots: defecting scientists, diamond smugglers, missing radioactive isotopes, etc. The first series had been specifically created by ABC's head of drama, Sydney Newman, to provide a vehicle for the popular talents of Ian Hendry after the success of his earlier series *Police Surgeon*, so it came as a huge shock when, after the first run of 26 episodes, Hendry decided to leave the series to pursue a movie career. It might have been understandable had *The Avengers* been cancelled then and there. Thankfully, ABC decided to cast another lead and carry on.

Detective/Action-Adventure/Fantasy
ABC/ABC (USA) for ITV
Episode Duration: 50 mins
Broadcast: 7 Jan 1961–21 May 1969

Regular Cast
Patrick Macnee · *John Steed*
Ian Hendry · *Dr David Keel*
Ingrid Hafner · *Carol Wilson*
Douglas Muir · *'One-Ten'*
Jon Rollason · *Dr Martin King*
Julie Stevens · *Venus Smith*
Honor Blackman · *Cathy Gale*
Diana Rigg · *Emma Peel*
Linda Thorson · *Tara King*
Patrick Newell · *Mother*
Rhonda Parker · *Rhonda*

Creators Sydney Newman and Leonard White

Producers Leonard White, John Bryce, Julian Wintle, Albert Fennell, Brian Clemens, Gordon L. T. Scott

Writers Various, including Brian Clemens, Dennis Spooner, Roger Marshall, Terrance Dicks, Peter Ling, John Gilbert, John Lucarotti, Malcolm Hulke, Robert Banks Stewart, Tony Williamson, Philip Levene, Gordon Flemyng, Terry Nation, Leigh Vance, Richard Harris, Jeremy Burnham, Tony Williamson

Theme Music For the videotaped early seasons, each episode was introduced by a modern jazz piece composed by Johnny Dankworth. From series four onwards, it was the more well-known theme by Laurie Johnson, including a slight rearrangement for the final Tara King episodes involving a lengthy drum solo before the familiar brass section blares into form.

Many scripts had already been written for the second series with Ian Hendry's Dr Keel in mind. With Patrick Macnee now elevated to star of the show, three of Keel's scripts were filmed with a short-term new medical character brought in, Dr Martin King. Another six episodes had already been written in which innocent nightclub singer Venus Smith paired up with Steed. However, the remaining episodes fell to a new character, someone who would revolutionise the portrayal of women on television and who would single-handedly kick-start the feminist movement on British TV. The character's name was Cathy Gale – the actress the legendary Honor Blackman. In hindsight, it's impossible to overestimate how much of a shock it must have been for viewers to see an emancipated, powerful and utterly sexy woman acting as an equal partner to a spy in an action-adventure series. Before Cathy Gale, women in such programmes were invariably damsels in distress needing to be rescued. After Cathy, things could never be the same again.

This new direction for *The Avengers* saw many more episodes set in foreign locations (all of them realised in a small studio in London – naturally!) and the advent of larger-than-life characters. Storylines involving petty crime were abandoned, and the programme was reformatted with John Steed – now regularly wearing his trademark bowler hat – leading his new civilian partner, Mrs Gale (widow of a white African farmer, and used to handling both guns and heavy machinery) into solving yet more threats against the UK. By the time of the third series in 1964, these spy stories had begun to include the occasional plotline that verged on the surreal or fantastic – episodes such as 'Build a Better Mousetrap' featured Cathy joining a motorcycle gang in order to find out if a pair of elderly women (who claim to be witches) living in a watermill might have anything to do with power failures at a nearby atomic research centre. Another important factor in the success of *The Avengers* were the fight sequences, and in particular Cathy's involvement in them. Mrs Gale quickly abandoned her reliance on firearms and took up judo, a skill that would see her flinging hulking stunt men around *The Avengers*' sets twice per episode on average. On one particularly memorable occasion, Honor slightly mistimed one of her moves and managed to knock former wrestler Jackie Pallow unconscious. For this reason alone, by simply rewriting the rulebook about the power balance between men and women as portrayed on screen, *The Avengers* is undoubtedly one of the most important television programmes ever made.

By early 1964, *The Avengers* was reaching new levels of success and popularity. The series was about to switch from the cheaper studio/location filming model to the much more expensive all-on-film method, and to the delight of the production team, the programme had been pre-sold to the American network ABC, which was keen to capitalise on the Beatles-inspired fashion for all things British. So it came as a huge surprise and a massive blow to the team when Honor Blackman declined to renew her contract and return for the glossy, new-look fourth series. Blackman had been offered the role of Pussy Galore in the James Bond film *Goldfinger* (1964) – setting a precedent for *Avengers* cast members to appear in the movie adventures of 007. Initially cast as new character Emma Peel (the intention being that she would have Man or 'M' appeal) was statuesque actress Elizabeth Shepherd. However, after only one and a half episodes had been recorded, Shepherd was sacked for allegedly not being able to handle the more comedic aspects of the role (she went on to star in an obscure cult series called ***The Corridor People*** for Granada). Her replacement was stunning, auburn-haired Diana Rigg, and instantaneously the on-screen chemistry between Rigg and Macnee created a sexual tension that crackled across the TV set.

In hindsight, it's impossible to overestimate how much of a shock it must have been for viewers to see an emancipated, powerful and utterly sexy woman acting as an equal partner to a spy in an action-adventure series.

From October 1965, viewers across the globe revelled in the weird and wacky adventures of Steed and Mrs Peel (like Mrs Gale, also a widow – this time of experimental pilot Peter Peel). A new, upbeat theme tune (composed by Laurie Johnson) and a concerted effort to play up the distinctive 'Englishness' of the programme ensured that *The Avengers* became a bigger hit than ever before. From killer robotic automatons called Cybernauts, through to a deadly marriage bureau and a carnivorous plant from outer space, plots got sillier and sillier and audiences revelled in it. One particular episode, 'A Touch of Brimstone', pushed the boundaries of what was acceptable in the programme to an entirely new level. Far from the standard *Avengers* fare of leather 'kinky boots', 'A Touch of Brimstone' saw Mrs Peel dressed as the Queen of Sin (complete with knee-high boots, skimpy leotard, spiked dog-collar and live snake) in a modern-day revival of the infamous Hellfire Club. When Mrs Peel is whipped by villain Cartney (a lip-lickingly lascivious portrayal by guest star Peter '*Jason King*' Wyngarde), the American network twitched with embarrassment and decided not to transmit it. This of course didn't stop executives of the same network allegedly screening this episode at their annual conventions for many years afterwards.

The fifth series burst forth into glorious colour just as the Sixties reached their peak in 1967 with the 'summer of love'. This batch of episodes are regarded by many fans of *The Avengers* as the peak of the series, the point at which the perfect balance between storylines that made sense and outrageous over-the-top characters and plots walked the narrowest of fine lines. The success of the TV show ***Batman*** was parodied in 'The Winged Avenger', Steed and Mrs Peel were brain-swapped into the bodies of agents for a foreign power, Basil and Lola, in 'Who's Who???' and Ronnie Barker played Cheshire, the evil genius behind the Philanthropic Union for the Rescue, Relief and Recuperation of Cats – PURRR – in the overwhelmingly bonkers

'The Hidden Tiger'. Other guest stars lined up by the dozen to take part in all this good-hearted nonsense, from Peter Bowles and Warren Mitchell through to Ron Moody, Peter Cushing, Christopher Lee and even a youthful Penelope Keith. A further short series of eight additional episodes were transmitted at the end of 1967 and would see Diana Rigg opting to quit the show.

The fifth series is regarded by many fans of *The Avengers* as the peak of the series – the perfect balance between storylines that made sense and outrageous over-the-top characters and plots.

The launch of the seventh series would be blighted by troubles both in front of and behind the camera. Voices had been raised in concern at ABC at the increase in wacky storylines, leading to the replacement of producers Albert Fennell and Brian Clemens with Cathy Gale-era producer John Bryce. Bryce cast inexperienced 20-year-old Canadian actress Linda Thorson as new *Avengers* girl Tara King, trainee agent No. 69 (subtle!). However, this sudden change in behind-the-scenes personnel resulted in some completely unworkable and untransmittable episodes and both Fennell and Clemens were rushed back to take the helm. Diana Rigg was persuaded to return to film a handover episode, in which Tara is introduced and Emma receives the joyful news that her late husband survived his plane crash in the Amazon. As Emma leaves Steed's apartment for the last time, she kisses him softly on the lips and warns him to 'watch out for diabolical masterminds'. Passing Tara on the staircase, Emma gives her some invaluable advice – 'he likes his tea stirred anti-clockwise' – before driving off with her husband, who in long shot looks exactly like Steed.

The seventh series of episodes contains many more 'mixed' adventures, some of which are as good as ever before, some of which simply don't work. At the time, it seemed as though much of the blame for this lack of success was laid at the feet of Linda Thorson. This is largely unjustified – Thorson's Tara King is in fact a delightful change of style from the two previous *Avengers* women, presenting a young, naïve trainee spy who's completely infatuated with the older Steed and his abilities. The lack of faith that the production team seemed to exhibit towards Tara's character is highlighted in the fact that in several episodes she is given practically nothing to do. In others, her role as supplier of exposition is palmed off to replacement characters or to 'Mother', the wheelchair-bound (and previously never mentioned) head of Steed's department. Indicative of the lack of faith the writers had in Tara is the fact that far too often both Steed and Mother refuse to believe or trust her – in 'Who Was That Man I Saw You With?', they accept the possibility that she might be a traitor far too readily. 'The Curious Case of the Countless Clues' even revolves around the notion that Steed might have a genuine motive to kill Tara.

We would argue that any lack of confidence in this season is more likely to be the fault of the writers, and in particular that of replacement script editor Terry Nation. Responsible for the Daleks in ***Doctor Who*** and later the creator of both ***Survivors*** and ***Blake's 7***, renowned writer Nation never seemed to understand the importance of strong female characters in *Avengers* storytelling. Episodes veered from the truly ghastly *Maltese Falcon* send-up 'Legacy of Death' to the oddball-for-the-sake-of-it 'Thingumajig'. Still, at least this series boasted such classic episodes as 'The Morning After', which sees a deserted London being held to ransom via nuclear bomb, the ***Prisoner***-esque 'Wish You Were Here' and perhaps the most gloriously stupid episode ever, 'Look – (stop me if you've heard this one) – But There Were These Two Fellers . . .' Guest stars in that particular episode – which features members of a vaudeville retirement home murdering property developers for daring to knock down their old theatres – included John Cleese as the man responsible for maintaining a record of every single British clown's make-up on an egg (you can guess what happens to them all, can't you?); Bernard Cribbins as a rubbish joke-writer (' "Bradley Marler?" "Well if I'm not, I'm having a great time with his wife . . ." '); and Jimmy Jewel as one of a pair of killer clowns with a neat line in asphyxiant custard pies.

Despite the fact that the series was still a huge hit in the UK, the ratings in America plummeted due to being scheduled at the same time as the massively popular ***Rowan and Martin's Laugh-In***. When the American network pulled its funding, *The Avengers* was cancelled. With the final season having been such a struggle, nobody at ABC was pushing too hard for it to continue. After 161 episodes, the series finished with Steed and Tara blasting off into space in a homemade rocket that Steed had constructed in his back garden, much to Mother's dismay: 'They're unchaparoned up there!' Once again mirroring real-life events, Steed's journey into space was transmitted just two months before Neil Armstrong's 'giant leap' for mankind.

Having spanned almost an entire decade, *The Avengers'* time was finally over. When it returned to British screens in the form of ***The New Avengers***, the adventures took place in an altogether different and much more cynical world.

Babylon 5

See pages 68–9

Bad Girls

Drama/Soap | Shed Productions for ITV | episode duration 50 mins | broadcast 1 Jun 1999–present

Regular Cast
Jack Ellis · *Officer Jim Fenner*
Linda Henry · *Yvonne Atkins*
Debra Stephenson · *Shell Dockley*
Simone Lahbib · *Wing Governor Helen Stewart*
Mandana Jones · *Nikki Wade*
Helen Fraser · *Officer Sylvia Hollamby*
Victoria Alcock · *Julie Saunders*
Kika Mirylees · *Julie Johnston*
Alicia Eyo · *Denny Blood*
Sharon Duncan-Brewster · *Crystal Gordon*
Lara Cazalet · *Zandra Plackett*
Jane Lowe · *Monica Lindsay*
Joanne Frogatt · *Rachel Hicks*
Joe Shaw · *Officer Dominic McAllister*
Luisa Bradshaw-White · *Officer Lorna Rose*
Roland Oliver · *Governor Simon Stubberfield*
Claire King · *Wing Governor Karen Betts*
Isabelle Amyes · *Barbara Hunt*
Tracey Wilkinson · *Officer Di Barker*
Lindsey Fawcett · *Shaz Wiley*
Nathan Constance · *Josh Mitchell*
Philip McGough · *Dr Malcolm Nicholson*
Kim Oliver · *Buki Lester*
Victoria Bush · *Tina Purvis*
Kerry Norton · *Maxi Purvis*
Pauline Campbell · *Al Mackenzie*
Kate O'Mara · *Virginia O'Kane*
Paul Opacic · *Officer Mark Waddle*
Lisa Turner · *Officer Gina Rossi*
Michael Higgs · *Dr Thomas Waugh*
James Gaddas · *Governor Neil Grayling*
Nicole Faraday · *Snowball Merriman*
Kellie Bright · *Cassie Tyler*
Siobhan McCarthy · *Roisin Connor*
Michael Elwyn · *Reverend Henry Mills*
Alex King · *Richie Atkins*
Stephanie Beacham · *Phyl Oswyn*
Amanda Barrie · *Bev Tull*
Jennifer Ness · *Kris Yates*
Charlotte Lucas · *Officer Selena Geeson*
Tristan Sturrock · *Officer Colin Hedges*
Dannielle Brent · *Natalie Buxton*
Antonia Okonma · *Darlene Cake*
Eva Pope · *Wing Governor Frances Myers*
Zoe Lucker · *Tanya Turner*
Rebecca Hazlewood · *Arun Parmar*
Nicola Stapleton · *Janine Nebeski*
Liz May Brice · *Pat Kerrigan*
Colette O'Neil · *Sister Thomas More*

Creators Maureen Chadwick, Eileen Gallagher, Ann McManus **Producers** Brian Park, Claire Phillips, David Crean, Cameron Roach **Writers** Various, including Maureen Chadwick, Eileen Gallagher, Ann McManus, Martin Allen, Di Burrows, Jaime Caruana, Jaden Clark, Helen Eatock, Phil Ford, Tom Higgins, Jayne Hollinson, Tim Hyndman, Liz Lake, Nick Malmholt, Jane Marlow, Paul Mousley, Jo O'Keefe, Louise Page, Guy Picot, Mark Wadlow **Theme Music** Cath Gotts, Michael Walton

Inside HMP Larkhall, life is never easy for the 'bad girls' who find themselves on the wrong side of the bars. For one thing, they have to put up with the lascivious and violent urges of corrupt warder Jim Fenner and the constant sneering of 'jobsworth' Sylvia 'Bodybag' Hollamby. For another, they have to survive the constant power struggles and in-fighting between the inmates – support the wrong side, and the most appalling punishments can be meted out.

It's hard to imagine that any television series could ever be described as a less subtle version of ***Prisoner: Cell Block H***, but that is exactly what *Bad Girls* has now become. For its first couple of seasons, it managed to maintain a remote semblance of reality, but thankfully for all connoisseurs of joyfully trashy television, the series has now decided to revel in its over-the-top plotlines, outrageous characters and plausibility-stretching scenarios. In particular, the actions of panto villain warder Jim Fenner – a man directly responsible for murder, rape, assaults and blackmail (and that's just on a good day) – have to be seen to be believed. At the end of the sixth season, it seemed as though Fenner had at last received his just desserts and been thrown into jail himself, although as most viewers know, it's hard to keep a good villain down.

Some of the prisoners were almost as despicable as Fenner himself, though. The two most popular (according to an ITV2 poll of viewers) were psychotic Shell Dockley and harsh-but-fair gangster's wife Yvonne Atkins, both women able to take care of themselves and deal with any problems with ruthless efficiency. Other friendlier inmates included the sweet best friends 'the two Julies' and the glamorous, middle-aged 'Costa cons', Phyl and Bev (played by ex-***Colbys*** star Stephanie Beacham and ***Coronation Street*** graduate Amanda Barrie). By far and away the most glamorous prisoner ever to set foot in the prison was of course Tanya Turner, one of ITV's ***Footballers' Wives***, sent to prison for cocaine possession (in one of the very few instances of one character moving from one television series to another, completely unrelated, one).

Nobody could ever seriously claim that *Bad Girls* is high art, but it does what it sets out to do extremely well and with a great deal of tongue-in-cheek style and verve.

Continued on page 70

Babylon 5

The Babylon 5 space station, the 'last, best hope for peace' in the 23rd century.

In the year 2257, Earth has just recovered from a massive intergalactic war with the alien Minbari race. Just as the Minbari were about to conquer Earth, they mysteriously surrendered (for a reason only explained in the third series) and volunteered to help establish a vast interstellar space station dedicated to the promotion of peace between all planets and races. Babylon 5 – the fifth such station, following the sabotage or disappearance of the previous four – was staffed by humans and acted like an intergalactic United Nations, welcoming ambassadors from dozens of civilisations in an attempt to iron out their problems on neutral territory. Some five miles long, the station was home to over 250,000 people and harboured its own gardens, open spaces, and even an undercity of undesirable drifters, smugglers and criminals.

Babylon 5's overarching plotline was worked out prior to the first episode being recorded. Series creator J. Michael Straczynski (who also wrote the vast majority of the 110 episodes) constructed an epic story of interstellar politics, war and intrigue that played out in real time – with each season moving the storyline along by one year in future history. During the course of the series, the heroic crew of Babylon 5 had to face (among many other things!): the trauma of the assassination of the Earth President and his replacement by a despotic new President; being caught in the middle of a war between the imperialistic Centauri and the primitive yet proud reptilian Narn; and infiltration by the sinister telepathic police the Psi-Corps. Unbelievably, as the story progressed into the third season, all of the plotlines that had at first appeared to have little to do with one another suddenly began to link together. Events reached a peak in the fourth series as the 'good guys' finally had to battle the Shadows, the ancient alien race that had been responsible for manipulating the evolution of many of the younger races since the dawn of history. Not only that; the end of the season saw the crew of Babylon 5 mounting an all-out raid on their home planet of Earth in an attempt to overthrow the corrupt regime of President Clark. The fifth and final season seemed almost like an afterthought, a lengthy

Science Fiction
Babylonian Productions for Warner Bros/TNT (shown on Channel 4)
Episode Duration: 45 mins, plus 4 × 90-min specials
Broadcast: 22 Feb 1993–3 Jan 1998

Regular Cast
Bruce Boxleitner · *Captain John Sheridan*
Michael O'Hare · *Commander Jeffrey Sinclair*
Jerry Doyle · *Michael Garibaldi*
Claudia Christian · *Susan Ivanova*
Richard Biggs · *Dr Stephen Franklin*
Peter Jurasik · *Centauri Ambassador Londo Mollari*
Mira Furlan · *Minbari Ambassador Delenn*
Andreas Katsulas · *Narn Ambassador G'Kar*
Bill Mumy · *Lennier*
Stephen Furst · *Vir*
Andrea Thompson · *Talia Winters*
Patricia Tallman · *Lyta Alexander*
Jeff Conaway · *Zack Allen*
Jason Carter · *Marcus Cole*
Tracy Scoggins · *Capt. Elizabeth Lochley*
Caitlin Brown, Mary Kay Adams · *Na'Toth*
Ardwright Chamberlain · *voice of Vorlon Ambassador Kosh*
Robert Rusler · *Keffer*
Ed Wasser · *Mr Morden*
Walter Koenig · *Bester*

Creator J. Michael Straczynski

Producers J. Michael Straczynski (plus others)

Writers J. Michael Stracynzski, J. Michael Stracaynski, Larry DiTillio, D. C. Fontana, David Gerrold, Marc Scott Zicree, Kathryn M. Drennan, Christy Marx, Scott Frost, Peter David, Harlan Ellison, Neil Gaiman

Theme Music Christopher Franke

epilogue to the main body of the novel. This was unfortunately a result of worries by the production team that a fifth season would never be commissioned and pre-emptive action that moved some of the storylines originally planned for the final season back into the fourth.

Despite the plotlines of *Babylon 5* being carefully crafted in advance, changes had to be written into the story to accommodate the departure of various characters – not least of which was the leading man of the first season, Commander Jeffrey Sinclair (played by Michael O'Hare). Many of Sinclair's future character developments had to be switched rapidly to the new captain of the space station, John Sheridan. Other ongoing plotlines would unfold over several years – one of which seeing the hinted-at lesbian relationship between second-in-command Susan Ivanova and station telepath Talia Winters come to fruition, only to be cruelly torn asunder when Talia's latent programming as a double-agent asserted itself. Although some viewers might express weary dismay at another example of Hollywood homophobia, it's worth remembering that portraying any kind of gay relationship in a fantasy or escapist TV series had rarely been attempted prior to *Babylon 5*.

Several of the regular cast had seen previous service in TV sci-fi shows, notably Bill Mumy, who had been ***Lost in Space*** as the young Will Robinson in the 1960s, and Walter Koenig, who abandoned his position on the original Starship Enterprise to become sinister Psi-Corps officer Bester.

Babylon 5 drew to a conclusion in 1998 with a final episode called 'Sleeping in Light', set 20 years after the rest of the series and revealing the final fates of many of the regular characters – most notably inter-species lovebirds John Sheridan and Delenn (magnificently portrayed by former *Scarecrow and Mrs King* star Bruce Boxleitner and award-winning Yugoslavian actress Mira Furlan). However, this was not the end of the story. A short-lived spin-off series called *Crusade* (starring former *Midnight Caller* Gary Cole) followed on the next year, telling the story of a desperate search for a vaccine to a virus released by followers of the evil Shadows.

Babylon 5 rewarded its regular viewers with an unfolding, complex and sophisticated plotline more akin to 'serious' political drama than ***Star Trek***-style shoot-'em-ups or adventure stories. At the time of writing, creator Stracyzinski is hoping to get a cinematic version of the series into production – although how the uniquely epic storytelling of the TV show will translate into a two-hour film that will appeal to newcomers is anyone's guess.

Website
www.badgirls.co.uk is the programme's official site, giving you more background on the characters and storylines of HMP Larkhall.

Bagpuss

Animation | BBC One | episode duration 15 mins | broadcast 12 Feb–7 May 1974

Regular Cast
Oliver Postgate · *Narrator, Bagpuss, Professor Yaffle, The Mice*
John Faulkner · *Gabriel*
Sandra Kerr · *Madeleine*
Emily Firmin · *Emily*

Creator/Producers Oliver Postgate and Peter Firmin **Writer** Oliver Postgate

Children of the 1970s – and indeed all child viewers since then – owe a huge amount to Oliver Postgate and Peter Firmin. Each show is so crammed full of love and sheer benevolence that it takes a hard heart not to be charmed. Next to ***Clangers***, *Bagpuss* is the best known of their output (it came fourth in a Channel 4 poll of Britain's best-loved children's telly).

Bagpuss is an old cloth cat, property of Emily, a young girl who has somehow become the proprietress of a shop – Bagpuss & Co. – that doesn't actually sell anything as it's more of an altruistic lost property office. Whenever Emily finds an object, she brings it to the shop and wakes up Bagpuss with her magical rhyme: 'Bagpuss, dear Bagpuss/Old fat furry cat-puss/Wake up and look at this thing that I bring/Wake up, be bright/Be golden and light/Bagpuss, O hear what I sing.' And of course, when Bagpuss wakes up, his friends wake up too: Madeleine, the matriarchal rag doll who sings songs with Gabriel, a banjo-playing toad; Professor Yaffle, a cynical, crotchety old book-end carved into the shape of a woodpecker; and the inhabitants of a magical 'Mouse Organ', Charliemouse, Eddiemouse, Janiemouse, Jenniemouse, Lizziemouse and Williemouse. The toys discuss what the purpose of the object might be – a decorative cushion, an inside-out house, a Mouse Mill – then the mice would tart it up a bit while singing in the round 'We will fix it, we will mend it . . .'

Like the Von Trapp chateau, Emily's shop is regularly filled with music; Gabriel and Madeleine provide a varied set of original and traditional folk songs, helped out by the high-pitched choral mice, who'd sing ditties like 'Row, Row, Row your Boat', using a pink ballet shoe as a canoe.

Gabriel and Madeleine would also tell stories of old myths associated with the object, aided by Bagpuss, who would create pictures in his mind for everyone to see. The mice would join in by loading rolls of music into their marvellous mechanical mouse organ, the perfect accompaniment to the mending, fixing and stitching that kept the mice busy. Eventually, the mystery of the object would be solved and it would be placed in the window to wait for its owner. His work done, Bagpuss would give a huge yawn and settle down to sleep, along with his friends.

The most oft-quoted scene comes from 'The Mouse Mill', in which butterbeans and breadcrumbs are purportedly the main ingredients in Charliemouse's production of chocolate biscuits (at least they are until Professor Yaffle ventures behind the mill and discovers the truth). Charliemouse's confession is a wonder to behold – he caves in without any coercion at all. The Sweeney would have been proud . . .

The production has been the source of jokes for many a stand-up comedian in a student union bar (yes, we know it looks as if Emily is actually a kleptomaniac), but that doesn't really diminish its magic. The sight of Professor Yaffle enchanted by a ballerina is enough to make anyone misty-eyed, as is the show's final message, that you might be 'baggy and a bit loose at the seam', but somebody loves you.

Trivia
Apparently, Bagpuss's distinctive pink fur was a happy accident; Peter Firmin had originally ordered marmalade-coloured material, but was so taken with the idea of a pink cat that he kept it. Emily, seen only in the photographs in the opening and closing titles, is not a real Victorian girl but the daughter of Peter Firmin – and the shop was actually the rear entrance to Firmin's house.
A 'yaffle' is a small, green breed of woodpecker.

Website
www.smallfilms.co.uk/bagpuss/people.htm is the official *Bagpuss* website, giving you more biographical detail on the cuddly stars of this most beloved of TV shows.

Ballykissangel

Comedy/Drama | Ballykea/World Productions for BBC One | episode duration 50 mins | broadcast 11 Feb 1996–15 Apr 2001

Regular Cast
Stephen Tompkinson · *Father Peter Clifford*
Dervla Kirwan · *Assumpta Fitzgerald*
Tony Doyle · *Brian Quigley*
Niall Toibin · *Father MacAnally*
Don Wycherley · *Father Aidan O'Connell*
Robert Taylor · *Father Vincent Sheahan*
Peter Hanly · *Ambrose Egan*
Tina Kellegher · *Niamh Quigley/Egan*
Catherine Cusack · *Frankie Sullivan*
Susannah Doyle · *Avril Burke*
Lorcan Cranitch · *Sean Dillon*
Victoria Smurfit · *Orla O'Connell*
Frankie McCafferty · *Donal Docherty*
Joe Savino · *Liam Coghlan*
Deirdre Donnelly · *Siobhan Mehigan*
Gary Whelan · *Brendan Kearney*

Peter Caffrey · *Padraig O'Kelly*
Aine Ni Mhuiri · *Kathleen Hendley*
Paul Ronan · *Edso Dowling*
Marion O'Dwyer · *Oonagh Dooley*
Owen Roe · *Paul Dooley*
Ciaran Owens · *Dermot Dooley*
Katie Cullen · *Grainne Dooley*
Birdy Sweeney · *Eamonn Byrne*
Mick Lally · *Louis Dargan*
Colin Farrell · *Danny Byrne*
Kate McEnery · *Emma Dillon*
Stephen Brennan · *Enda Sullivan*
John Cleere · *Kevin*
Bosco Hogan · *Dr Michael Ryan*
Allan Barry · *Superintendent Foley*
Doreen Keogh · *Imelda Egan*
James Ellis · *Uncle Minto*

Creator Kieran Prendiville **Producers** Robert Cooper, Tony Garnett, Conor Harrington, Alan Moloney (executive), Christopher Griffin, Chris Clough, Joy Lale, David Shanks **Writers** Kieran Prendiville, John Forte, Niall Leonard, Jo O'Keefe, Rio Fanning, Barry Devlin, Felicity Hayes McCoy, Robert Jones, Ted Gannon, Tim Loane, Jimmy Doyle, Mark Holloway, Terry Hodgkinson, Declan Croghan, Paul Coates, Mick Martin, Stuart Blackburn, John Flanagan, Andy McCulloch, Ursula Aspitt de Bran **Theme Music** Shaun Davey

After four years of getting pounded in the Sunday night ratings by the cosy nostalgia of ***Heartbeat***, BBC bosses decided to launch their own family-friendly, Sabbath-day drama set in picturesque countryside. And what better than to make a Sunday night drama based on the adventures of an English priest living in Ireland? The planning behind the format was very well thought out, and *Ballykissangel* became one of the BBC's most popular shows of the late 1990s.

Newly ordained Catholic priest Father Peter Clifford arrives in the remote Irish town of Ballykissangel to join the parish of Father MacAnally. Father Peter soon discovers that his progressive and modern attitudes towards life and the Church bring him into conflict with the traditionalists in the local community. However, he finds an ally in Assumpta Fitzgerald, the landlady of the local pub, Fitzgerald's Bar. Assumpta is young, beautiful, headstrong and an atheist, and soon their mutual attraction is evident for all to see. For three years, viewers thrilled at the will-they, won't-they storyline, the charisma and all-round good-heartedness of the two leads adding an extra frisson to the traditional tale of forbidden love. Father Peter and Assumpta were such popular characters that they even made a brief cameo appearance in an episode of Irish ecclesiastical comedy series ***Father Ted***.

Unfortunately, neither Stephen Tomkinson nor Dervla Kirwan wanted to continue in *Ballykissangel* in the long term, so the romance had to end tragically. Assumpta is electrocuted in a terrible accident and dies in Peter's arms. Unable to bear living in Ballykissangel any longer, Father Peter moves away to a new parish. His replacement was ex-monk Father Aidan O'Connell (who lasted for two seasons), followed by rugged Aussie Father Vincent Sheahan (who appeared in the final series only). *Ballykissangel* also concentrated on developing the characters of its supporting cast, the most memorable of whom was the town's wheeler-dealer Brian Quigley (played to perfection by Tony Doyle). Sadly Tony Doyle died suddenly just before the sixth season was about to begin filming. Without Doyle, the drive to make more episodes simply wasn't there any longer. Indeed, some people argued that the show hadn't really been the same since the departure of Peter and Assumpta.

Ballykissangel was filmed in the small County Wicklow village of Avoca, which became an overnight tourist mecca for eager *BallyK* fans from the UK and the USA (where it became a surprise hit on the PBS network). It was created by ex-***That's Life!*** presenter Kieran Prendiville, who had spent many happy holidays in Ireland as a child – often close to the town of Ballykissane. We wonder where he got the idea for the title of his programme from?

The Banana Splits

Children's Comedy | Hanna-Barbera for NBC (shown on BBC One) | episode duration 50 mins | broadcast 7 Sep 1968–29 Nov 1969

Cast

Paul Winchell · *Voice of Fleegle*
Don Messick · *Voice of Snorky**
Daws Butler · *Voice of Bingo*
Allan Melvin · *Voice of Drooper*
Jeffrey Brock · *Fleegle*
Daniel Owen · *Drooper*
Terence Henry · *Bingo*
Robert Towers · *Snorky*

*Snorky never actually spoke but merely honked, and though Don Messick was credited as providing the honks, he's since denied any involvement.

Creators William Hanna and Joseph Barbera, Sid and Marty Kroft **Producers** William Hanna and Joseph Barbera **Writers** Jack Hanrahan, Jimmie Young, Ellis Kadison, Anthony Spinner **Theme Music** Ritchie Adams and Mark Barkan gave us one of the easiest theme songs to remember the words to: 'Tra la la, la la la la', etc.

The Hanna-Barbera machine kept on rolling with this very much 'of its time' experiment in combining live TV mania with animated serials. Part *Rowan and Martin's Laugh-In*, part ***The Monkees***, ***The Banana Splits*** (or *The Banana Splits Adventure Hour*, as it was in the States) cast a saggy-eared beagle (called Fleegle), an elephant (Snorky), a gorilla (Bingo) and a lion (Drooper) as the furry members of a pop band. The gang hung out in a club-house that looked like a cartoon had been pulled into a three-dimensional world and it provided a cluttered racetrack for the gang to whizz around on their buggies, mime to songs, be invaded by

'Sour Grapes' messenger girls or just go ape whenever anyone said the phrase 'Hold the bus!' Very few of the happenings made any sense, but then it was the 1960s – what did?

The anthropomorphic anarchy was interspersed with cartoons and serials from elsewhere in the Hanna-Barbera stable: *The Arabian Knights, The Three Musketeers, The Hillbilly Bears* and *Micro Venture*, as well as a live-action serial, *Danger Island*, which featured future ***Airwolf*** star Jan Michael Vincent. In the UK, the series was shown on Saturday mornings from 1970 and in the 1990s as filler material on ***The Big Breakfast***.

Website

The Cartoon-o-rama fan site at http://members.aol.com/PaulEC1/splits.html features some great nostalgic glimpses into the world of the Splits.

Bananaman

Animation | 101/Bananaman Productions for BBC One | episode duration 5 mins | broadcast 3 Oct 1983–15 Apr 1986

Principal Voice Cast

Tim Brooke-Taylor · *Narrator, King Zorg of the Nurks, Aunty, Appleman*
Graeme Garden · *Bananaman, General Blight*
Bill Oddie · *Eric, Crow, Chief O'Reilly, Henry the Nerk, Dr Gloom, The Weatherman*
Jill Shilling · *Fiona, Samantha, Mother Nerk*

Creators Steve Bright and John Geering **Producer** Trevor Bond **Writer** Bernard Kaye **Theme Music** David Cooke

At 29 Acacia Road lives a schoolboy called Eric. His puny frame hides an amazing secret, for whenever he eats a banana he transforms into a superhero – Bananaman – with the power of flight and the strength of ten men ('ten *big* men'), though what he gains in super-powers he has to sacrifice in IQ. Battling such villains as Dr Gloom, the Nurks and the Weatherman, Bananaman relies upon his trusty friends Crow and police chief O'Reilly to save the day.

A TV adaptation of the adventures of the star of DC Thompson's *Nutty* comic in 40 five-minute episodes, *Bananaman* was aided in its achievement of cult status by a reunion of ***The Goodies***, Graeme Garden, Bill Oddie and Tim Brooke-Taylor. Producer Trevor Bond later brought us animated adventures of *Beano* stars Dennis the Menace and his dog Gnasher.

Band of Brothers

Drama | DreamWorks SKG/DreamWorks Television/Home Box Office/Playtone/BBC for HBO (shown on BBC Two) | episode duration 60 mins | broadcast 9 Sep–4 Nov 2001 (USA)

Cast

Damian Lewis · *Major Richard D. Winters*
Donnie Wahlberg · *2nd Lieutenant C. Carwood Lipton*
Ron Livingston · *Captain Lewis Nixon*
Matthew Settle · *Captain Ronald Speirs*
Rick Warden · *1st Lieutenant Harry Welsh*
Frank John Hughes · *Sergeant William 'Wild Bill' Guarnere*
Scott Grimes · *Sergeant 1st Class Donald Malarkey*
Neal McDonough · *1st Lieutenant Lynn 'Buck' Compton*
Rick Gomez · *Sergeant George Luz*
Eion Bailey · *Private David Kenyon Webster*
James Madio · *Sergeant Frank Perconte*
David Schwimmer · *Lieutenant Herbert Sobel*

Producers Stephen Spielberg, Tom Hanks, Stephen E. Ambrose (executive) **Writers** Erik Jendresen, Tom Hanks, John Orlof, E. Max Frye, Graham Yost, Bruce C. McKenna, Erik Bork, from the book by Stephen E. Ambrose **Theme Music** Robert Elhai, Michael Kamen

Publicised almost as a sequel to Stephen Spielberg's *Saving Private Ryan* (1998), the director and his *Private Ryan* headliner Tom Hanks co-produced this lavish, $125 million 10-part mini series. The link with *Saving Private Ryan* is apt, as it was filmed with the same considerations of accuracy, bleached-out vintage style of film stock, and brutal, unforgiving depictions of wartime violence.

From its formation and boot camp training, through the horrors of D-Day and beyond, the series follows the wartime experiences of Easy Company, a part of the 506th Regiment of the US Army's 101st Airborne Division, under the command of Captain (subsequently Major) Richard Winters. The company makes its way through war-torn Europe, fallen comrades being replaced without ceremony, finding themselves in an eventual attack on Hitler's fortress in Bavaria. In the final analysis, as the surviving members of the company are shipped off home or to Japan, their experiences, the horrors these men have witnessed, only amount to a few lines on a service record.

Band of Brothers is a truly stunning feat of televisual brilliance, and it's easy to see why HBO provided one of the biggest budgets ever assigned to a television project, especially considering the pedigree of the producers. Hanks (who also found a part for his son Colin in the series) was particularly passionate, believing the veterans of World War Two to be 'the greatest generation'. Once the scripts were completed, Spielberg and Hanks (the latter stepping behind the camera to direct episode five) ensured that the surviving members of Easy Company read the scripts to pass comment on their authenticity.

One week after the final episode was transmitted in America, *We Stand Alone Together – The Men of Easy Company*, reunited the surviving veterans for a special commemorative programme. Stephen Ambrose, author of the original book, passed away on 13 Oct 2002.

Band of Gold

Drama | Granada for ITV | episode duration 50 mins | broadcast 12 Mar 1995–3 Nov 1997

Regular Cast

Geraldine James · *Rose Garrity*
Cathy Tyson · *Carol Johnson*
Barbara Dickson · *Anita Braithwaite*
Samantha Morton · *Tracy Richards*
David Schofield · *Inspector/DCI Newall*
Tony Doyle · *George Ferguson*
Richard Moore · *Curly*
Rachel Davies · *Joyce Webster*
Lena Headey · *Colette*
Darren Tighe · *Smiley*
David Bradley · *Alf Black*
Janet Dibley · *Paula Graham*
Kern Falconer · *Inspector Henryson*
Vanessa Acquah · *Amanda Smeaton*
Mark Addy · *DC Sherrington*
Judy Browne · *DS Kershaw*
Janet Dibley · *Paula Graham*
Kern Falconer · *Inspector Henryson*
Sue Cleaver · *Jan*
Rachel Davies · *Joyce Webster*
Tony Capstick · *Councillor Baker*
Anita Carey · *Glennis Minkin*
Ruth Gemmell · *Gina Dickson*
Jamie Lee Hampson · *Michelle Dixon*
Louisa Millwood-Haigh · *Laura Richards*
Naomi Radcliffe · *Sarah*
Meera Syal · *Anne Denver*
Malcolm Hebden · *Mr Lidgit*
Derek Hicks · *DC Jameson*
Katie Hodgson · *Joanne Dixon*
Susan Jameson · *Kathleen Ferguson*
Bruce Jones · *Brian*
Ray Stevenson · *Steve Dickson*
Colin Salmon · *Raymond*
Jayne Ashbourne · *Lisa*
Ifran Meredith · *Charlie*

Creator Kay Mellor **Producers** Sally Head (executive), Tony Dennis **Writers** Kay Mellor, Mark Davies Markham, Catherine Johnson **Theme Music** 'Love Hurts', originally written by Boudleaux Bryant, performed by Barbara Dickson

The world of prostitution is not one likely to have the members of MediaWatch rushing to tune in, but over three series Kay Mellor introduced us to four women with very different motivations for 'walking the lanes' in an, at times, distressing series that was part-thriller part melodrama. Tracy offers herself for money to fund her drug addiction; Anita is hard-faced and self-serving, but often painfully stupid, something her manipulative married boyfriend often tries to exploit; Carol loves to shock her neighbours with her comings and goings; and Rose, who looks after the girls while always hoping to turn straight one day.

The murder of one of the prostitutes, a young mother trying to pay off loan sharks, leaves the women shaken and unsettled. A few of the women join together around Joyce, who provides the inspiration for the women to turn straight and leave the lanes behind by setting up a cleaning business called 'Scrubbit'. But one by one, the women begin to stray back, urged on by Anita's former boyfriend and pimp, the vile George Ferguson, who wants to break Scrubbit and the women in revenge for being sent to prison. But when another series of murders sees both George and one of the women's regular punters murdered, the spotlight of suspicion falls once again on the women.

A final series, retitled *Gold*, saw Rose becoming an outreach worker for social services to help other women off the streets. Carol, meanwhile, having discovered she's the beneficiary of her murdered punter's will, has to adjust to her new-found wealth – and her ownership of a chicken factory. This final series, in which Kay Mellor was joined by other writers, could possibly have been one return too many, though the strong characters and quick dialogue was almost as bold and brassy as ever.

Bar Mitzvah Boy

Drama | BBC One | duration 75 mins | broadcast 14 Sep 1976

Cast

Jeremy Steyn · *Eliot Green*
Maria Charles · *Rita Green*
Bernard Spear · *Victor Green*
Adrienne Posta · *Lesley Green*
Jonathan Lynn · *Harold*
Cyril Shaps · *Grandad Wax*
Jack Lynn · *Rabbi Sherman*
Pamela Manson · *Sylvia*
Sabina Michael · *Salon Customer*
Harry Landis · *Solly*
Harold Reese · *Synagogue Warden*
Robert Putt · *Caretaker*
Kim Clifford · *Denise*
Mark Herman · *Squidge*

Writer Jack Rosenthal **Producer** Graeme McDonald

This coming of age drama from the perspective of a Jewish boy approaching his impending bar mitzvah won Jack Rosenthal a BAFTA award (one of many), and formed part of the 1976 output of the BBC's much-missed *Play for Today* strand.

Eliot Green lives with his typically Jewish family in Willesden, northwest London, suffering a crisis of conscience in the run-up to his coming of age ceremony. His dad is a stoic cabby, his mother a nervy coiffured matriarch, his granddad a died-in-the-wool Yiddish traditionalist and his sister a sympathetic ally with a drippy

boyfriend. By the time the big day arrives, the family has wound Eliot and each other up so much that the lad simply walks out of the synagogue. If the likes of his dad and granddad are supposed to be role models, then he's decided he'd rather not be a man.

There's a clear biographical slant to Rosenthal's ever-brilliant writing, the writer's own Jewish background ensuring the piece never descends into overt stereotype. There are some great one-liners, and the climactic departure of Eliot at the crucial moment, leaving a dumbfoundedly embarrassed family, is priceless. In 1978, Rosenthal adapted his script into a musical, and it ran in both London and New York, but failed to attract a large audience. *Bar Mitzvah Boy* has a lighter touch than much of the output of *Play for Today*, but contrasted against some heavier work, this is exactly what the format was made for.

Barbapapa

Animation | Polyscope/LBS Communications (shown on BBC One) | episode duration 5 mins | broadcast 17 Jan–25 Mar 1975

Voice Cast

Alan Swift · *Narrator*
Ann Costello, Alexander Marshall · *Character Voices*

Creators/Writers Talus Taylor, Annette Tison **Theme Music** Harrie Geelen, Joop Stokkermans – 'I wanna be like Barbapapa . . .'

American mathematician Talus Taylor met French architect Annette Tison in the wonderfully romantic setting of a Parisian café, and from here possibly the most bizarrely imaginative children's book and TV character was born.

Barbapapa – a word cribbed from the French word for 'candy floss' (*barbe à papa*, also meaning 'father's beard') – is essentially an amorphous pink blob. He can mould himself into any shape he desires, which must please the slinkily black but no less bendy Barbamama no end. Yes, BP has a soulmate, and together they are parents to a collection of Barbababies. Among their offspring you'll find the feminist Barbalib (orange blob), Barbabeau (black furry blob), Barbabravo (red blob) and Barbabelle (sexy purple blob). And that's it. The Barbas bend and bounce their way through various adventures.

The character of Barbapapa first appeared in an eponymously titled book in 1970, and many more books would be written by the husband-and-wife team of Taylor and Tison (they are still married today), right up until 1984 with *Barbapapa: Mystery of the Amusement Park*.

This Netherlands-produced cartoon came to the BBC in 1975 and proved incredibly popular, spawning spin-off annuals and books. Thirty years later, *Barbapapa* still has a fanbase, fuelled by the still-in-print books and the new run of cartoons produced in the early 1990s by the Japanese owners of the character.

Website

For some *Barbapapa* fun, check out www.naughtykitty.org/barbapapa.html

The Barchester Chronicles

Drama | BBC Two | episode duration 50 mins | broadcast 10 Nov 1982–22 Dec 1982

Cast

Donald Pleasence · *Reverend Septimus Harding*
Nigel Hawthorne · *Dr Grantly*
Angela Pleasence · *Susan Grantly*
David Gwillim · *John Bold*
Janet Maw · *Eleanor Harding/Bold*
John Ringham · *Finney*
Joseph O'Connor · *Bunce*
Alan Rickman · *Reverend Obadiah Slope*

Producer Jonathan Powell **Writer** Alan Plater, from the novels ***The Warden*** and ***Barchester Towers*** by Anthony Trollope **Theme Music** Derek Bourgeois

Following on form the BBC's lavish adaptation of Anthony Trollope's ***Palliser*** novels in the mid-1970s, *The Barchester Chronicles* brought us an utterly charming adaptation of another Trollope series, *The Warden* and *Barchester Towers* (1855 and 1857 respectively). Donald Pleasence put in a superb turn as the Reverend Septimus Harding, the gentle mannered warden of Hiram's Hospital in the town of Barchester, nestling in the picturesque county of Barcetshire. Despite being essentially a nice bloke, the Reverend is living a rather nice life from the profits being creamed off from the hospital. Harding's secret is betrayed by local doctor, John Bold, and the Reverend eventually backs down, despite pressure to fight the accusations by local supporters. The second half of the story focuses on the competition to replace the local bishop (and friend of Harding) and more sleepy manipulations from a locale that could rival Albert Square for skulduggery and deceit.

Arthur Lowe was originally cast as the Reverend Harding, but he sadly passed away shortly before *The Barchester Chronicles* went into production; Donald Pleasence therefore took on the lead role. Pleasence's own daughter Angela was cast as the local doctor's offspring. Worth noting is an early appearance from Alan Rickman as the Reverend Obadiah Slope.

Barnaby

Animation | Q3 London for BBC One | episode duration 10 mins | broadcast 4 Apr–28 Jun 1973

Voice Cast

Colin Jeavons, Charles Collingwood, Gwendoline Owen, Percy Edwards · *Various Characters*

Creator Albert Barillé, based on the *Colargol* books by Olga Pouchine **Producers** Albert Barillé (original version), Michael Grafton-Robinson (UK version) **Writers** Tadeusz Wilkosz, Dariusz Zawilski, Albert Barillé, Marian Kielbaszczak **Theme Music** Original music composed by Mireille, with Colin Jeavons singing the British version of the theme: 'Barnaby the Bear's my name/Never call me Jack or James . . .'

While Disney, Hanna-Barbera and Warner Bros tend to hog the limelight in the animation industry, real animation connoisseurs favour Eastern European artists. Although produced in France, like ***The Magic Roundabout***, the lovable Barnaby (or Colargol, as he was known to the French) was brought to life by Polish animator Tadeusz Wilkosz.

Barnaby starts out as a rather poor student, arriving late for school and singing terribly. But when he meets the King of the Birds, he is given a magic whistle that prompts him to sing properly. He later gets lost in the woods and is taken in by Mr Pimoulu's circus troupe, becoming their marvellously talented 'singing bear'. Mr Pimoulu's circus also stars Sara the seal, Ricky and Dicky the drum-playing monkeys, trapeze-performing cats and Mrs Pimoulu the ticket collector, who also performs on the high wire.

Shown within the *Watch with Mother* timeslot in the 1970s, only the first 13 of over 50 episodes were translated for the UK market, which means we Brits missed out on Barnaby's trip to the moon and his travels around the world. How cruel those TV executives were!

Trivia

In Canada, Barnaby is known as Jeremy.

Website

Visit http://members.lycos.co.uk/crystaltipps/barnaby/bindex.html for some lovely pictures of Barnaby and his circus friends in all their glory.

The Basil Brush Show

See pages 76–7

Batman

Action-Adventure | Greenway/20th Century Fox for ABC (shown on ITV) | episode duration 25 mins | broadcast 12 Jan 1966–14 Mar 1968 (USA)

Regular Cast

Adam West · *Bruce Wayne/Batman*
Burt Ward · *Dick Grayson/Robin*
Alan Napier · *Alfred Pennyworth*
Madge Blake · *Aunt Harriet Cooper*
James Hamilton · *Police Commissioner Gordon*
Stafford Repp · *Police Chief O'Hara*
Yvonne Craig · *Barbara Gordon/Batgirl*
David Lewis · *Warden Crichton*
William Dozier · *Narrator*

Special Guest Villains

Frank Gorshin · *The Riddler*
Burgess Meredith · *The Penguin*
Cesar Romero · *The Joker*
George Sanders, Otto Preminger, Eli Wallach · *Doctor Schimmell/Mr Freeze*
Anne Baxter · *Zelda, Olga – Queen of the Cossacks*
David Wayne · *Jervis Tetch – the Mad Hatter*
Malachi Throne · *False-Face*
Julie Newmar, Eartha Kitt · *Catwoman*
Victor Buono · *King Tut*
Roddy McDowall · *The Bookworm*
Art Carney · *The Archer*
Van Johnson · *The Minstrel*
Shelley Winters · *Ma Parker*
Walter Slezak · *The Clock King*
Vincent Price · *Egghead*
Liberace · *Chandell/Fingers/Harry*
Carolyn Jones · *Marsha – Queen of Diamonds*
Cliff Robertson · *Shame*
Maurice Evans · *The Puzzler*
Michael Rennie · *The Sandman*
Roger C. Carmel · *Colonel Gumm*
Tallulah Bankhead · *Black Widow*
Joan Collins · *Loreli Circe/The Siren*
Milton Berle · *Louie the Lilac*
Rudy Vallee · *Lord Marmaduke Fogg*
Glynis Johns · *Lady Penelope Peasoup*
Barbara Rush · *Nora Clavicle*
Howard Duff · *Cabala*
Ida Lupino · *Cassandra Spellcraft/Doctor Cassandra*
Zsa Zsa Gabor · *Minerva*

Creator Bob Kane **Producers** William Dozier (executive), Howie Horwitz **Writers** Lorenzo Semple, Robert Dozier, Max Hodge, Fred DeGorter, Charles Hoffman, Stephen Kandel, Stanley Ralph Ross, Lee Orgel, John Cardwell, Jack Paritz, Bob Rodgers, Francis Cockrell, Marian Cockrell, Robert C. Dennis, Earl Barret, Rik Vollaerts, Sheldon Stark, Henry Slesar, Bill Finger, Charles Sinclair, Stanford Sherman, Jay Thompson, Fred DeGorter, Ellis St Joseph, William P. D'Angelo, Leo Townsend, Pauline Townsend **Theme Music** Neal Hefti – 'Dinna dinna dinna dinna BATMAN!' Prince gave a brief nod to the series' hugely iconic theme tune in his music for Tim Burton's 1989 feature film.

One of the few comic book heroes to successfully translate to the small screen, *Batman*'s success was down to two things: executive producer William Dozier remembered that a superhero is only super when pitted against super villains, not portrayed simply as a detective in a strange suit, like so many before; and despite the often farcical situations they found themselves in, the leads played each and every daft joke with utter conviction as if this could be the end of Gotham City. Never mind that some of the guest

Continued on page 78

The Basil Brush Show

'Mr Roy' and Basil Brush.

Who could possibly consider fox hunting a sport after growing up with Basil Brush as a TV hero? The animal responsible for 50 per cent of all jelly baby intake of the 1970s (***Doctor Who***'s Tom Baker looked after the rest), Basil was an essential part of BBC One's Saturday line-up for over a decade until a dispute over a change in timeslot saw him ousted.

Basil was created by Peter Firmin, the genius who also built ***Bagpuss*** and the ***Clangers*** for Oliver Postgate, but it was the vocal talents of BBC floor manager Ivan Owen that really brought him to life, with his *bon viveur* approach, always 'on' entertainer personality and borderline high-camp delivery. Basil's first TV role was playing second fiddle to a hedgehog called Spike McPike on a forgotten children's show on ITV called *The Three Scampis*. Basil's 'owner' on the show, Howard Williams, whose path would cross with Basil's again a few years later, played Bert Scampi.

By 1967, Basil was a regular guest of TV Magician David Nixon, first on *Now for Nixon* and later on *The Nixon Line*. But it was with his own *Basil Brush Show* that the silver-tongued fox made his mark. Realising that he worked best with a human to play off, Basil was given former ***Likely Lads*** star Rodney Bewes to spar with, before working his way through a succession of other straight men, all known by Basil as 'Mister': Derek Fowlds, who was 'Mr Derek' (and later the put-upon Bernard Wooley in ***Yes, Minister***); Roy North, 'Mr Roy', who left Basil's side in 1977 to front Granada's pop show *Get it Together* on ITV; and 'Mr Howard', Howard Williams.

Astoundingly, Basil's show appeared to have a budget akin to a peak-time grown-up variety show, with leggy dancers, pop acts timing their performances to give their latest records a push and ***Morecambe and Wise***-esque comedy skits. All the while, Basil's poor co-star would be trying to bring a touch of maturity to proceedings while Basil kept cracking jokes and making the most painful of puns, always accompanied by his catchphrase 'Boom boom!' Quick-witted and, despite the puns, genuinely funny, Basil was quite a handful and it wasn't unusual for his human friend to lose patience, grab him by the snout and tell him to shut up. Violence to foxes should never be encouraged, but each time it happened Basil deftly defused the tension with a sarcastic, 'OoOOOOoooh!' that sent the audience into hysterics.

A genuine superstar, the merchandising potential was huge, with soft toys, lunch boxes and even a rather tasty 'talking Basil' operated by pulling a string to let out a blast of his raucous laughter or witty one-liners. He also released two albums, both called *Boom Boom! It's Basil Brush* (1970 and 1977), containing songs from the TV show. He was a friend to the rich and famous, calling in on then-Prime Minister Jim Callaghan and visiting Buckingham Palace, and for a time it looked like there was no stopping him. But when Ivan Owen suggested to the BBC that Basil should get his own chat show in a later slot, the show was instead dropped.

Basil managed to keep his paw in, joining Stu Francis for the twilight years of ***Crackerjack***, presenting schools programme *Let's Read with Basil Brush* and hosting a gag show, *Basil's Joke Machine*, for ITV. But for all intents and purposes, he was no longer a star. So when Entertainment Rights PLC announced on 14 August 2000 that they were bringing Basil back to TV, many of his old fans were sceptical, especially when news reached us that Ivan Owen, his voice for so many years, had died after a long battle with cancer.

It was with a great sigh of relief that we finally saw the new Basil. He looked younger than ever (courtesy of a make-over using Peter Firmin's original designs) and while Owen was clearly not in control any more, his unnamed replacement did an impressive job of re-creating the wit and the talent for improvisation (although check the credits for a clue: a 'Michael Windsor' is listed as Basil's 'fitness instructor'!). The new show was a shift in format for Basil, a sitcom where Basil is the houseguest of Uncle Steven, a would-be-magician and his young niece and nephew Dave and Molly. Having met this new Basil in the fur, so to speak, we can confirm he's as wily as ever. Long may he continue – Boom! Boom!

Quick-witted and, despite the puns, genuinely funny, Basil was quite a handful and it wasn't unusual for his human friend to lose patience, grab him by the snout and tell him to shut up.

Children's Puppetry Entertainment/Sitcom
BBC One
Episode Duration: 25 mins
Broadcast: 14 June 1968–27 December 1980, 21 Sep 2002–present

Regular Cast
Ivan Owen · *Voice of Basil Brush*
Rodney Bewes · *Presenter*
Derek Fowlds · *Mr Derek*
Roy North · *Mr Roy*
Howard Williams · *Mr Howard*
Billy Boyle · *Mr Billy*
Christopher Pizzey · *Steven*
Michael Hayes · *Dave*
Georgina Leonidas · *Molly*
Ajay Chabra · *Anil*

Creators Ivan Owen and Peter Firmin

Producers Johnny Downes, Robin Nash, Brian Penders, Paul Ciani

Writers George Martin, Colin Bostock-Smith, Peter Robinson, John Morley

villains went beyond camp (Liberace as a crook called 'Fingers'? Zza Zsa Gabor as Minerva? Oscar winner Anne Baxter as two different villainesses?), Adam West and Burt Ward never shied away from the very real dangers of exploding jack-in-the-boxes, deadly giant pies or a room full of suffocating party balloons. It must have been difficult not to simply stand and giggle with glee, especially considering they also had the coolest car in the world – the turbo-charged Batmobile, a customised 1955 Ford Lincoln Futura with bat fins and red, go-faster stripes courtesy of George Barris, the 'Kustom Car King'. Stuff James Bond's Aston Martin; even before any of us could drive, that was the car we all wanted.

The character of Batman first appeared in 1939, in issue 27 of *Detective Comics* (the publication that spawned the entire *DC* range, including *Superman*, *The Flash* and *Wonder Woman*, among dozens of other characters). Creator Bob Kane was inspired by Douglas Fairbanks Senior's portrayal of Zorro to come up with an 'Acro-bat man' who fought crime (hence the old-fashioned gym suit that formed Batman's costume). Like Zorro, Batman had a secret identity – millionaire playboy Bruce Wayne, who began his life of crime fighting after witnessing the murder of his parents by a gangster called Joe Chill. A year later, Kane introduced a sidekick for Batman in the form of orphaned trapeze artist Dick Grayson – aka Robin, the Boy Wonder. The Dynamic Duo was formed – as were allegations that a wealthy adult male adopting an athletic teenage boy as his 'ward' must have something dubious in mind, a theory everyone involved in the characters' development has strenuously denied. Besides, it was probably all a cover to hide Alfred the Butler's own nocturnal pursuits. Why else would he be so handy with a needle and thread that he could knock up those exciting costumes for the master and his young friend? Batman's first live action appearance came in 1943 with a formulaic serial in the *Flash Gordon* vein, starring Lewis Wilson with Douglas Croft as Robin. Wilson made an impressive-looking superhero, let down by a rather loose-fitting and saggy-looking costume. A second serial in 1949 starred Robert Lowery and John Duncan. If Wilson had suffered from baggy clothing, the same couldn't have been said for Lowery, who more than filled the costume and could probably have done with a girdle to keep his tummy in. After such unimpressive efforts, the 1960s TV version didn't have to try that hard to do better.

The original plan was for the colourful TV series to consist of hour-long episodes, akin to most other action shows at the time. However, the decision was eventually taken to split these into two, with alternate episodes ending on a thrilling cliffhanger in which Batman and Robin would face death and destruction thanks to a trap or monstrous contraption left for them by that week's villain. Much lighter than the strips that had inspired them, the episodes took on a gleeful pantomime aspect, with puns galore, Robin's exclamations ('Holy haberdashery, Batman!'), consecutive episode titles that, when placed side by side, would form rhyming couplets ('The Joker is Wild'/'Batman is Riled'; 'The Penguin Goes Straight'/'Not Yet, He Ain't'; 'Catwoman Goes to College'/'Batman Displays His Knowledge' . . .) and guest stars popping out of windows while Batman and his friend climbed up the side of buildings provided laughs for the grown-ups that passed over the heads of younger viewers. The most iconic element, though,was the use of on-screen graphics that aped the sound effect bubbles from comic books: 'BLAM!', 'ZONK!' and of course 'KERPOW!'

Though there had been a criminal hierarchy of sorts within the comic books, it was the TV show that established the top four: former movie idol Cesar Romero slipped effortlessly into the pancake make-up and loud suits of criminal genius the Joker; acting heavyweight Burgess Meredith went for the rotund, chain-smoking Penguin; versatile performer Frank Gorshin became the Riddler, a character that hadn't made much of an impact in the comic books until he transformed the role into a major adversary; and the stunning Julie Newmar took on the role of Catwoman (though, due to Newmar's other commitments, it was Eartha Kitt who played the part for the third and final series).

The first series was originally to have started with a feature-length movie, but with concerns over the ratings for some of their other shows, ABC decided to rush *Batman* the series into production and delay the film until after the series was completed. *Batman – the Movie* (1966) pitted the Dynamic Duo against their top four adversaries, the Penguin, the Riddler, the Joker and Catwoman (played on this one occasion by Lee Meriwether), who join forces as the United Underworld. Playing to the series' strengths, the film pushed the boundaries of comic potential with such gems as Batman's fortuitous decision to pack shark-repellent spray into his utility belt and a scene where Batman tries to dispose of a bomb while surrounded by innocent victims whose mere presence hinders him to hilarious effect.

There were also a few characters who were developed for the TV show: while the comics had presented Mr Zero, the TV version was Mr Freeze; Victor Buono made several appearances as King Tut, a former history professor who begins to believe he was the reincarnation of an Egyptian monarch after an unfortunate bump on the head; Vincent Price starred as Egghead, a man with the right assets for a Batman villain – a fondness for puns that shaped his entire modus operandi; two-time Oscar winner Shelley Winters as Ma Parker, a thinly veiled twist on the legendary real-life gangster Ma Baker (immortalised by the Boney M song and later played by Winters in the 1970 film *Bloody Mama*); and the list goes on. The series was also able to react to developments in the comic books. When Batgirl was created for the strips in 1966, the character was rushed into the mix for the third series, portrayed by Yvonne Craig. But sadly by then the joys of *Batman* had begun to wane. With ratings dipping, ABC felt they couldn't justify such an expensive show any more and canned it. When an offer was made by rival network NBC to revive the show, it came just too late as the sets had all been destroyed.

West and Ward reprised their characters in animated series in the 1970s and 1980s, including *The New Adventures of Batman* (which introduced the Scrappy Doo-like Batmite) and *Superfriends*, which brought together some of the *DC* greats. But the reworking of the Batman imagery by Tim Burton's gothic, serious and utterly majestic film brought all that to an end. *Batman: The Animated Series* took its lead from Burton's film in mirroring the more serious tones of recent graphic novels rather than the more excitable 1960s efforts. While Burton made another, even darker and bloodier film (the superlative *Batman Returns*, 1992), *The Animated Series* ran until 1995 (shown in the UK as part of the Saturday morning children's show *What's Up Doc?*). But while Burton, a self-confessed comic book junkie, pitched his film just right, when Joel Schumacher took on two subsequent films in the franchise, *Batman Forever* (1995) and *Batman & Robin* (1997), he struggled to avoid sliding back into the brightly coloured campery that audiences knew from the past. For him, the temptation of the sheer joy of the 1966 TV show was just too great and as a consequence the film series was put on hold until the terrible memory of *Batman & Robin* had faded. Eight years later, *Batman Begins* (2005) once again aimed itself more at the vision of the Bat that Tim Burton had worked towards. Holy revitalised movie franchise, Batman!

Website
www.adamwest.com is the place to visit if you like your websites full of BIFF! KAPOW! action.

Battle of the Planets

Animation | Gallerie International/Sandy Frank Film Syndication/ Tatsunoko (shown on BBC One) | episode duration 25 mins | broadcast c.1 Sep 1978–c. 1979

Voice Cast
Casey Kasem · *Mark*
Ronnie Schell · *Jason*
Janet Waldo · *Princess, Susan*
Alan Young · *Keyop, Z-Zark-Z, Tiny*
Alan Dinehart · *Tiny Harper, Security Chief Anderson, President Kane*
Keye Luke · *Zoltar, Colonel Cronus, The Spirit*
William Woodson · *Announcer*
David Joliffe, Alan Oppenheimer · *Additional Voices*

Producers Jameson Brewer (executive), David E. Hanson
Writers Jameson Brewer, Peter B. Germano, Jace Paritz, Helen Sosin, Richard Shaw, Howard Post, William Bloom, Harry Winkler, Muriel Germano, Kevin Coates, Sid Morse
Theme Music Hoyt S. Curtin

It's possibly to do with residual prejudice left over from World War Two, but the Japanese cultural exchange was a long time coming. As children, our first experience of Japanese entertainment was watching the excitable but poorly scripted adventures of *Marine Boy*, a round-faced lad who lived underwater and battled a different robotic animal each week. It was a schedule filler, and we knew it. But then the BBC bought in a new animated action-adventure series called *Battle of the Planets* that had in its cast the man who's played ***Scooby Doo***'s best mate and the woman who voiced Penelope Pitstop. But ***Wacky Races*** it was not.

The planets in question were Earth and Spectra, with the camp horned villain Zoltar leading the Spectra attack and the five members of G-Force (each of whom sported costumes based on birds) acting as Earth's last defence against Zoltar's armies of robotic monsters. Mark was G-Force's leader who wore a costume based around an eagle; the rest of the team were Jason (the condor), Princess (the swan), Tiny (whose chubby frame put a little strain on the belt of his owl costume) and Keyop, a little fella who spouted half-sentences broken up by tweets and hoots (and whose costume was supposed to be a swallow, but looked more like a duck). Watching over them from the Neptune command centre were Z-Zark-Z and the mechanical canine 1-Rover-1, Star Wars-style robots that were added to the series courtesy of its American adaptors to get around some of the edits that had to be made to the more graphic elements of the original Japanese episodes.

Battle of the Planets came from re-edited footage from a Japanese show called *Science Ninja Team Gatchaman*, which we can now identify as fairly typical of Manga-style comics and anime movies. There were the wide-eyed androgynous humans, a flamboyant villain, loads of machines that looked like animals (the heroes flew around in an aircraft that could turn into a fiery phoenix), and there was a little fetish attraction too, thigh-length boots and shots of Princess's knickers as she flipped in mid-air.

Looking back at the episodes though, *Battle of the Planets* is disappointingly repetitive, with long segments recycled from the title sequence and each time the G-force gang got together to form that Phoenix. But the series at least opened our horizons to the entertainment coming out of the Far East. *Mighty Morphin' Power Rangers* once again took existing Japanese footage, recast the lead roles and re-edited the episodes to create whole new stories. Meanwhile, anime has risen in popularity thanks to feature films like *Ghost in the Shell* (1995) and *Akira* (1988). Finally, we get to see the horrific violence and overt sexual imagery that mark Anime as clearly not suitable for kids.

Trivia
Confusingly, the same *Gatchaman* footage was used to create another show in the late 1980s – *G-Force: Guardians of Space*. Many fans of *Battle of the Planets* have been left utterly baffled when catching episodes that appear to star the same characters but with different names and voices. In the mid-1990s, episodes of *Gatchaman* were edited together to create yet another show, called *Eagle Riders*.

Website
Julieann Adolf runs a really good *Battle of the Planets* site that also carries information on the other shows created out of *Gatchaman* – www.akdreamer.com/botp/ – while

probably the best site about the original Japanese series can be found at www.vacuform.com/Gatchaman/.

Battlestar Galactica

Science Fiction | Glen A. Larson/Universal TV for ABC (shown on ITV/Sky One) | episode duration 50 mins | broadcast 17 Sep 1978–29 Apr 1979, 27 Jan–4 May 1980, 8 Dec 2003–present (USA)

Regular Cast (original series)
Lorne Greene · *Commander Adama*
Richard Hatch · *Captain Apollo*
Dirk Benedict · *Lieutenant Starbuck*
Herb Jefferson Jr · *Lieutenant Boomer*
John Colicos · *Count Baltar*
Maren Jensen · *Lieutenant Athena*
Noah Hathaway · *Boxey*
Laurette Spang · *Cassiopeia*
Tony Swartz · *Flight Sergeant Jolly*
Anne Lockhart · *Sheba*
Terry Carter · *Colonel Tigh*
Ed Begley Jr · *Ensign Greenbean*
David Greenan · *Omega*
Jonathan Harris · *Lucifer*
Janet Louise Johnson · *Lieutenant Brie*
George Murdock · *Dr Salik*
Sarah Rush · *Flight CorporalRigel*
Felix Silla · *Lucifer*
Patrick Macnee · *Imperious Leader*
Kent McCord · *Captain Troy*
Barry Van Dyke · *Lieutenant Dillon*
Robyn Douglass · *Jamie Hamilton*
Richard Lynch · *Xavier*
Robbie Rist, James Patrick Stuart · *Dr Zee*
Allan Miller · *Colonel Sydell*

Regular Cast (new series)
Edward James Olmos · *Commander William 'Husker' Adama*
Mary McDonnell · *President Laura Roslin*
Katee Sackhoff · *Lieutenant Kara 'Starbuck' Thrace*
Jamie Bamber · *Captain Lee 'Apollo' Adama*
James Callis · *Doctor Gaius Baltar*
Tricia Helfer · *Number Six*
Grace Park · *Lieutenant Sharon 'Boomer' Valerii*
Michael Hogan · *Colonel Saul Tigh*
Tahmoh Penikett · *Lieutenant Karl 'Helo' Agathon*

Creator Glen A. Larson **Producers** Glen A. Larson (executive), Winrich Kolbe (associate), Leslie Stevens, Donald P. Bellisario, John Dykstra, David J. O'Connell, Michael Sloan **Writers** Various, including Donald P. Bellisario, Jim Carlson, Glen A. Larson, Frank Lupo, Terrence McDonnell, Ken Pettus, Michael Sloan, Allan Cole, Jeff Freilich **Theme Music** Stu Phillips

The effects of *Star Wars* upon popular culture can be seen in the amount of science fiction-based programmes that arrived on our screens post-1977. Biggest of the lot was *Battlestar Galactica*, a series set among the stars that mixed the histories of the Greeks, Jews and Romans together to form a backstory for a group of colonial humans locked in a battle with the robotic Cylon warriors and their Imperious Leader. When the Cylons use a Trojan horse trick to invade, Commander Adama takes charge of the Battlestar *Galactica* and leads a convoy of smaller ships away from the carnage in search of a lost tribe believed to have settled on a planet called 'Earth'. During their travels, Adama's son Apollo and his best friend Starbuck frequently go on scouting missions in their Viper craft looking for help in their battles against the Cylons, despite the fact that many planets have already been enslaved, and their own race has been betrayed by the self-serving Baltar.

A hugely expensive programme (budgeted at $1 million per episode), *Battlestar Galactica* was cancelled after just one series. Such was the enthusiastic response from the audience, though, that it was brought back as the short-lived *Galactica 1980*, a much cheaper series, in which the Galactica refugees had now reached Earth and were continuing their battles with the Cylons in the backwoods of Los Angeles. Despite only running for the equivalent of 34 episodes, the series left its mark, mainly thanks to the bold designs and distinctive voices of the Cylons (even if they did sound to British viewers like robotic sitcom star Metal Mickey).

The 2003 series was more than just a remake. Taking many fans of the original programme by surprise, this new *Battlestar Galactica* was more influenced by the ongoing story arcs, politics and conspiracy theories of shows like ***Babylon 5*** and ***The X Files***, with the Cylons now appearing in both metallic trooper form and as human clones – sleeper agents who have no idea that they're Cylons until they're activated. Starring ***Miami Vice***'s Edward James Olmos as Adama and Mary McDonnell as President Laura Roslin, the regular characters were re-imagined as much as the rest of the series, with both Starbuck and Boomer receiving a gender swap. At the time of writing, this new vision has only been shown on Sky One in the UK, but at the risk of upsetting traditionalists, it's vastly superior to the original series.

Website
There's an excellent fan site for the new series of *Battlestar Galactica* at www.patrickdavie.com/xenu/.

Baywatch

Soap | The Baywatch Company/Tower 12/Tower 18 for NBC (shown on ITV/Sky One) | episode duration 50 mins, plus specials | broadcast 23 Apr 1989, 22 Sep 1989–19 May 2001, 28 Feb 2003 (USA)

Regular Cast
David Hasselhoff · *Lieutenant/Captain Mitch Buchannon*
Michael Newman · *Michael 'Newmie' Newman*
Michael Bergin · *Jack 'JD' Darius*
Brooke Burns · *Jessica 'Jessie' Owens*

Jason Brooks · *Sean Monroe*
Brandy Ledford · *Dawn Masterton*
Simmone Mackinnon · *Allie Reese*
Stacy Kamano · *Kekoa Tanaka*
Krista Allen · *Jenna Avid*
Jason Mamoa · *Jason*
BonnieJill Laflin · *Tina*
Kala'i Miller · *Kai*
Jeremy Jackson · *Hobie Buchannon*
Gregory J. Barnett · *Greg Barnett*
Gregory Alan Williams · *Sergeant Garner Ellerbee*
John Allen Nelson · *John D. Cort*
Parker Stevenson · *Craig Pomeroy*
Erika Eleniak · *Shauni McClain*
Billy Warlock · *Eddie Kramer*
Richard Jaeckel · *Lieutenant Ben Edwards*
Pamela Anderson · *Casey Jean 'CJ' Parker*
Alexandra Paul · *Lieutenant Stephanie Holden*
David Charvet · *Matthew 'Matt' Brody*
Yasmine Bleeth · *Caroline Holden*
Jaason Simmons · *Logan Fowler*
David Chokachi · *Cody Madison*
Gena Lee Nolin · *Neely Capshaw*
José Solano · *Manuel 'Manny' Gutierrez*
Monte Markham · *Captain Don Thorpe*
Shawn Weatherly · *Jill Riley*
Peter Phelps · *Trevor Cole*
Holly Gagnier · *Gina Pomeroy*
Brandon Call · *Hobie Buchannon*
Tom McTigue · *Harvey Miller*
Nicole Eggert · *Roberta 'Summer' Quinn*
Kelly Slater · *Jimmy Slade*
Donna D'Errico · *Donna Marco*
Nancy Valen · *Captain Samantha 'Sam' Thomas*
Carmen Electra · *Leilani 'Lani' McKensie*
Kelly Packard · *April Giminski*
Angelica Bridges · *Lieutenant Taylor Walsh*
Traci Bingham · *Jordan Tate*
Marliece Andrada · *Skylar 'Sky' Bergman*
Mitzi Kapture · *Captain Alexis 'Alex' Ryker*
Jennifer Campbell · *Neely Capshaw Buchannon*
Wendie Malick · *Gayle Buchannon*
Pamela Bach · *Kate 'Kay' Morgan*
Michael McManus · *Sid Wilson*
Vanessa Angel · *Megan*
Buzz Belmondo · *Guido Torzini*
Susan Anton · *Jackie Quinn*
Ashley Gorrell · *Joey Jennings*
Vincent Van Patten · *Tom – sky surfer*
Jeff Altman · *Ed Symes*
Erin Gray · *Chief Johnson*
Ingrid Walters · *Sheryl Whalen*
Annalise Braakensiek · *Jeri*
Pat Morita · *Mr Tanaka*

Creators Gregory J. Bonann, Douglas Schwartz, Michael Berk **Producers** Various, including Kevin L. Beggs, Michael Berk, Gregory J. Bonann, Douglas Schwartz, Ernie Wallengren, Robert Silberling, David Hasselhoff, David Braff, Maurice Hurley, D. Howard Grigsby, Frank South (executive) **Writers** Various, including Gregory J. Bonann, Michael Berk, Douglas Schwartz, Terry Erwin, William Rabkin, Lee Goldberg, William A. Schwartz, David Braff, Deborah Bonann Schwartz, Kimmer Ringwald, Tanquil Lisa Collins, Maurice Hurley, Frank South **Theme Music** This series had a lot of different themes. Kim Carnes's 'Above the Waterline' appeared on the pilot movie, but was replaced by Peter Cetera's 'Save Me' for the series (although in the UK quite a number of initial episodes from the first series had the Carnes theme). From series three onwards, Jim Jamison sang the opening theme 'I'm Always Here' by Kevin Savigar and Todd Cerney, while David Hasselhoff sang the end theme, 'Current of Love'. The last *Baywatch* closing theme, 'I Believe', was written by B. A. Robertson and John Lewis Parker and performed by David Hasselhoff and Laura Branigan.

When Greg Bonann came up with an idea for a series based around his own experiences as a lifeguard for Los Angeles County, it could have ended up as a mini series or a sitcom when he first decided to pitch it. That it ended up as one of America's most lucrative exports was largely down to his sister marrying TV producer Doug Schwartz, who helped him hone the idea to a stunningly TV-friendly format: sun, sea and sexy bodies running in slow motion.

A pilot movie entitled *Baywatch: Panic at Malibu Pier* was screen in April 1989 – it attracted high enough ratings for NBC to put a television series into fast turnaround. Despite respectable viewing figures and the shock death-by-shark of one of the lead characters, the feeling that the series wouldn't sustain the action led to NBC dropping it after just one season. Major cuts in the budget, strong overseas sales and a change in production philosophy (every scene shot would be used, reducing drastically the amount of footage needing to be edited) led to the show being recommissioned. Star David Hasselhoff found he had a battle on his hands getting the scriptwriters to provide emotional storylines when everyone else knew that what viewers were tuning in for was the exposed flesh. Though the writers conceded to Hasselhoff's desires, the addition of buxom blonde actress Pamela Anderson in series three wasn't done to increase the dramatic tension.

With series six came a late-night spin-off series, *Baywatch Nights*, more of a detective story with steamy plotlines than its family-friendly sister show. *Baywatch* itself became racier too, one reason why ITV shunted it into a later timeslot in the UK before dispensing with it altogether (the final three seasons were only shown on Sky One). All in all, *Baywatch* racked up 242 episodes (including the pilot movie) over 11 seasons, while *Baywatch Nights* offered another 44 episodes. Despite Hasselhoff's noble intentions, however, it will always be remembered for its bodies beautiful rather than for its 'dramatic' scripts.

Website

www.baywatch.com is the programme's official website, giving you easy access for all your Hasselhoff and Pammy needs.

Beauty and the Beast

Fantasy | Republic Pictures for CBS (shown on ITV) | episode duration 50 mins | broadcast 25 Sep 87–4 Aug 90 (USA)

Regular Cast

Linda Hamilton · *Catherine Chandler*
Ron Perlman · *Vincent*
Roy Dotrice · *Father Jacob Wells*
Jay Acovone · *Joe Maxwell*
Ren Woods · *Edie*
Jo Anderson · *Diana Bennett*
Edward Albert · *Elliot Burch*
Stephen McHattie · *Gabriel*
Ellen Geer · *Mary*
Armin Shimerman · *Pascal*
David Greenlee · *Mouse*
Zachary Rosencrantz · *Zach*
Cory Danziger · *Kipper*
Ritch Brinkley · *William*
Lewis Smith · *Mark*
Philip Waller · *Geoffrey*
Tony Jay · *Paracelcus*
Marcie Leeds · *Samantha*

Creator Ron Koslow **Producers** Paul Junger Witt, Ron Koslow, Stephen Kurzfeld, Tony Thomas (executive), Howard Gordon, Lynn Guthrie **Writers** Various, including Ron Koslow, George R. R. Martin, David E. Peckinpah, Howard Gordon, Alex Gansa, P. K. Simonds Jr **Theme Music** Lee Holdridge

This American series took the classic fairy tale of the princess and the monster and set it in the present, creating a romantic thriller around it. Beauty in this case is wealthy lawyer Catherine Chandler, the victim of a brutal assault on the streets of New York. Catherine is rescued by a shadowy figure called Vincent, who lives in the catacombs deep beneath the city. So begins a love story of sorts, with Catherine and the lion-faced Vincent sharing tender moments while protecting the weak and needy – Catherine through her position at the district attorney's office, Vincent as a vigilante of the night.

When Linda Hamilton chose to leave the show before the third series to reboot her film career (beginning with *Terminator 2*, 1991), Catherine was killed off, although she left Vincent a son. From there, *Beauty and the Beast* became more about Vincent's vigilante activities and the romance that had captivated viewers on late-night ITV was lost.

Website

There's a nicely maintained fan site for all followers of Vincent and Catherine's tragic love story at http://www.geocities.com/shern_43537/.

The Beiderbecke Affair

Comedy Drama | Granada for ITV | episode duration 45 mins | broadcast 6 Jan 1985–18 Dec 1988

Regular Cast

James Bolam · *Trevor Chaplin*
Barbara Flynn · *Jill Swinborne*
Terence Rigby · *Big Al*
Danny Schiller · *Little Norm*
Dudley Sutton · *Mr Carter*
Keith Smith · *Mr Wheeler*
Dominic Jephcott · *DS Hobson*
Stephen Tomlin, George Costigan · *DC Ben*
Sean Scanlan · *DC Joe*
Keith Marsh · *Harry*
Colin Blakely · *Chief Superintendent Forrest*
Ian Bleasdale · *Reverend Booth*
James Grout · *McAllister, Helen of Tadcaster's Father*
Sue Jenkins · *Janey, the 'Beautiful Platinum Blonde'*
Malcolm Storry · *Peterson*
Deborah Langley · *Akela*
Robert Longden · *Pitt the Planner*
Jason Lumsden · *Bradley*
George Malpas · *Lol*
Beryl Reid · *Sylvia*
Robert Longden · *Mr Pitt*
David Battley · *John the Barman*
Peter Martin · *Charlie the Gravedigger*
Bill Wallis · *Pronk*
Judy Brooke · *Yvonne Fairweather*

Producers David Cunliffe, Keith Richardson (executive), Alan W. Gibson, Michael Glynn **Writer** Alan Plater **Theme Music** Frank Ricotti

The unlikely subject of this series is a set of long-playing records of the great jazz musician, Leon 'Bix' Beiderbecke – or rather their absence, as woodwork teacher Trevor Chaplin is duped by a dazzlingly attractive platinum-blonde door-to-door saleswoman into ordering a set of four LPs to raise money for the Cub Scouts. But when the records arrive, they're not the ones he ordered – Mozart, Cinema Organ, George Formby and a teach-yourself-Spanish album.

Trevor's lady-friend and fellow teacher Jill Swinborne has decided to stand for election as a conservation candidate for the local council. While helping Jill deliver leaflets for her campaign, Trevor begins to look for the platinum blonde, but his enquiries unearth more than he bargained for – including a conspiracy and expose of police corruption.

The Beiderbecke Tapes brought the great jazz man into the lives of Trevor and Jill once again as a set of tapes of Bix Beiderbecke are revealed to contain a recording of a conversation about nuclear waste being dumped. This time, their investigations take them far afield – to Amsterdam and Scotland. A third and final series (*The*

Beiderbecke Connection) brought Jill and Trevor (along with a baby and a Russian refugee) to yet another connection to Beiderbecke.

A gentle mystery, *The Beiderbecke Affair* and its sequels came from the pen of Alan Plater, sparkling with witty dialogue and eccentric characters – albeit at a pace that's perhaps a tad *too* gentle for modern viewers.

Belle and Sebastian

Childrens' Drama | RTF/Gaumont Television Paris (shown on BBC One) | episode duration 25 mins | broadcast 26 Sep 1965–c.1970 (France)

Cast
Mehdi · *Sebastian*
Edmond Beauchamp · *Cesar*
Jean Michel Audin · *Guillaume*
Dominique Blondeau · *Jean*
Paloma Matta · *Angelina*
Helene Dieudonne · *Celestine*
Morice Poli · *Norbert*
Claude Giraud · *Pierre Marechal*
Louise Marleau · *Sylvia*

Producers Etienne Laroche (executive), Hélène Gagarine **Writer** Cécile Aubry **Theme Music** François Rauber, Daniel White, David White

Here was a rip-roaring European children's TV drama that happily filled summer holiday slots in the UK. Young gypsy boy Sebastian is brought up on the Pyrenees farm of the elderly Cesar, alongside his grandchildren, Jean and Angelina. The children get into the usual scrapes, and then tales of a wild white dog roaming the hills start to filter down to the village. The villagers are a superstitious lot and are wary of the beast, but Sebastian uses his wily charms to bring the dog under control and names it Belle. Cue 13 episodes of fabulous adventures. The exploits of *Belle and Sebastian* proved so popular, that a second, 13-part run of this French series arrived on UK screens the following year, under the banner *Belle, Sebastian and the Horses*.

A fondly remembered piece of European hokum, French film star Cecile Aubry provided the scripts for the series from his novels (and directed episodes), and also happened to be the father of the series' star, Mehdi. A third season of the series was produced, *Sébastien et la Marie-Morgane*, but it never arrived in the UK. The programme also lent its name to a moderately successful pop group.

The Benny Hill Show

Comedy | Thames for ITV | episode duration 50 mins | broadcast 19 Nov 1969–1 May 1989

Regular Cast
Benny Hill, Henry McGee, Bob Todd, Jack Wright, Nicholas Parsons, Sue Upton, Louise English, Jenny Lee-Wright, Bella Emberg, Ken Sedd, Anna Dawson, Roger Finch, Eddie Buchanan, Lorraine Doyle, Patricia Hayes

Creator/Writer Benny Hill **Producers** John Robins, David Bell, Keith Beckett, Peter Frazer-Jones, Mark Stuart, Ronald Fouracre, Dennis Kirkland **Theme Music** The most famous UK TV theme tune around the globe, Boots Randolph's 'Yakety Sax', was used for both the opening credits sequence and for the final speeded-up chase sequence that continued over the closing credits of each edition.

There are very few British TV programmes that manage to become popular in the USA. The most famous British comedian ever in America is a man whose programmes are now virtually forgotten and deliberately ignored by many. Alfred Hill was born on 21 January 1924 in Southampton and fell in love with old-style variety and vaudeville during his childhood. Assuming the stage name Benny Hill after his favourite comic Jack Benny, he made his first television appearance very soon after the recommencement of broadcasting after World War Two on 23 March 1949, in a programme called *Music-Hall*. Hill was a comedian made for and by television. His style of comedy owed much to the traditional saucy-seaside-postcard humour made popular in cinemas by the *Carry On* films, although his comedy sketches by their very nature had none of the plotlines or characterisation that made the inherent sexism of the *Carry On* films much less 'full on' and hence less offensive.

Having appeared in a range of other programmes throughout the early 1950s, Hill finally got his own show on BBC TV on 15 March 1955. He stayed with the corporation for 13 years, writing and starring in 32 sketch shows over that period, in addition to 19 episodes of 25-minute, sitcom-style individual comedy plays. So it initially came as something of a surprise when Hill switched to Thames TV in late 1969, yet Thames was to become his natural home, a television company that admired his populist approach and supported his work without reservation. Hill made 58 hour-long specials for Thames, the vast majority of which were transmitted on Wednesday nights at 8.00 p.m. as and when they were ready for broadcast (rather than during specific seasons, as is the norm with most other programmes). Hill had a number of semi-regular characters who would pop up every now and again, including Chow Mein the Chinaman (!) and his most famous persona, the perpetually dim Fred Scuttle. He'd also parody other television programmes in his work – something that many people forget when they more readily recall all those busty, scantily clad young ladies being pursued in speeded-up motion by a leering Benny.

Benny Hill's programmes were hacked into neat half-hour editions and sold to American TV stations from 1979. Just as Hill's star was in the ascendant in the USA, it

began to go into decline over here. The arrival of alternative comedians had brought into focus the somewhat dubious nature of portraying women merely as sex objects; as complaints against Hill's style of 'naughty' comedy grew, viewing figures began to fall. The programme was finally dropped in 1989 when Thames decided not to renew Hill's contract. Some three years later, Hill died from a heart attack at the age of 68, a stupendously wealthy man due to his transatlantic success. Although it's unlikely that Hill's programmes will ever be re-evaluated and embraced by modern viewers in the same way as the *Carry On* films, it's none the less a shame that the material he produced that is genuinely amusing and inoffensive is lumped together with the rest of his output.

Trivia

Benny Hill scored the Christmas No. 1 in 1971 with 'Ernie, the Fastest Milkman in the West'. Spending 17 weeks in the British singles charts, it was also No. 1 in Australia.

Website

There's a great fan site for Benny's antics at www.vgernet.net/tpelkey/bennyhill/.

Benson

Sitcom | Columbia Pictures/Witt/Thomas Productions for ABC (shown on ITV) | episode duration 25 mins | broadcast 13 Sep 1979–30 Aug 1986 (USA)

Regular Cast

Robert Guillaume · *Benson DuBois*
James Noble · *Governor Gene Gatling*
Missy Gold · *Katie Gatling*
Inga Swenson · *Gretchen Kraus*
Rene Auberjonois · *Clayton Endicott III*
Ethan Phillips · *Pete Downey*
Caroline McWilliams · *Marcy Hill*
Lewis J. Stadlen · *John Taylor*
Didi Conn · *Denise Stevens Downey*
Bob Fraser · *Leonard Tyler*
Donna LaBrie · *Diane Hartford*
Jerry Seinfeld · *Frankie*

Creators Susan Harris, Paul Junger Witt, Tony Thomas **Producers** Paul Junger Witt, Tony Thomas, John Rich (executive), Rob Dames, Bob Fraser, Tom Reeder, Don Richetta, Tom Whedon, Susan Harris **Writers** Various, including Susan Harris, Tom Reeder, Bob Colleary, Rick McCurdy, Jeff Levin, Kathy Speer, Bob Fraser, Rich Reinhart, Tom Whedon, Rob Dames, Barry Fanaro, Winifred Hervey **Theme Music** George Aliceson Tipton

Having escaped the insanity of the Tate household (see ***Soap***), Benson DuBois is now working for Jessica Tate's widowed cousin Gene Gatling, the meek and befuddled governor of an unnamed state. Initially employed as the head of the Governor's household, Benson is promoted to the role of Governor's budget director and eventually is elected to the position of Deputy Governor. In the final series, Benson decides to stand for election against his friend and boss, causing strain to their friendship. As the series draws to a close, Benson and Gene anxiously await the results of the election...

From the talented pen of Susan Harris – the woman behind *Soap* and ***The Golden Girls*** – *Benson* was a charming, witty sitcom, providing a much-deserved star vehicle for Robert Guillaume. Amazingly, this spin-off series lasted for seven seasons – three years longer than the show that spawned it, *Soap*. At the heart of this series' success was, of course, a witty and charismatic performance from Robert Guillaume as Benson, an acid-tongued and sardonic man who refused to take even the slightest amount of rubbish from anyone. Matching Benson in the verbal sparring was German housekeeper Gretchen (bellowed catchphrase: 'I hear you!') and snide speech writer, Clayton Endicott III (played by future ***Star Trek: Deep Space Nine*** star Rene Auberjonois).

Benson was nominated for many awards over its long life, with co-stars Inga Swenson and Rene Auberjonois being singled out for particular praise. Robert Guillaume eventually won the Emmy award for Lead Actor in a Comedy Series in 1985. Notable cast members to watch out for include Didi Conn (the loveable Frenchie in the smash musical *Grease* (1978)), Ethan Phillips (ship's cook Neelix in ***Star Trek: Voyager***) and a very young Jerry Seinfeld, America's favourite sitcom star of the 1990s.

Bergerac

Crime Drama | BBC/Seven Network Australia (shown on BBC One) | episode duration 50 mins | broadcast 18 Oct 1981–26 Dec 1991

Regular Cast

John Nettles · *DS Jim Bergerac*
Terence Alexander · *Charlie Hungerford*
Sean Arnold · *Chief Inspector Barney Crozier*
Louise Jameson · *Susan Young*
Deborah Grant · *Deborah Bergerac*
Mela White · *Diamante Lil*
Celia Imrie · *Marianne Bellshade*
Lindsay Heath · *Kim Bergerac*
Geoffrey Leesley · *DC Terry Wilson*
Annette Badland · *Charlotte*
Cécile Paoli · *Francine Leland*
Tony Melody · *Chief*
Geoffrey Davies · *Roger Dubree*
Nancy Mansfield · *Peggy Masters*
Jolyon Baker · *DC Barry Goddard*
John Telfer · *DC Willy Pettit*
David Kershaw · *DC Ben Lomas*
Jonathan Adams · *Dr Lejeune*
Thérèse Liotard · *Danielle Aubry*
Michael Mellinger · *Albert Leufroid*

Roger Sloman · *Inspector Victor Deffand*
Charmaine Parsons · *Ellie*
Liza Goddard · *Philippa Vale*

Creator Robert Banks Stewart **Producers** Robert Banks Stewart, George Gallaccio, Jonathan Alwyn, Juliet Grimm **Writers** Bob Baker, Robert Banks Stewart, Rod Beacham, Alistair Bell, Chris Boucher, Philip Broadley, John Brown, Jeremy Burnham, Andrew Caine, Jeffrey Caine, Brian Clemens, Tessa Coleman, John Collee, Bill Craig, David Crane, Leslie Darbon, Roger Davenport, Terence Feely, Brian Finch, John Fletcher, Tony Hoare, Robert Holmes, Graham Hurley, Terry Jones, John Kershaw, Nick McCarthy, Tony McNabb, Peter Miller, John Milne, Gerry O'Hara, Edwin Pearce, Christopher Russell, Dennis Spooner, Edmund Ward, Paul Wheeler, Cyril Williams **Theme Music** George Fenton composed a lovely melody that incorporated a stereotypically French accordion to great effect.

Sometimes success can unexpectedly come from what seems like a disaster. In this particular instance, it was the decision by Trevor Eve to quit his role as Eddie Shoestring that ushered in one of the BBC's most successful police series of the 1980s. Producer Robert Banks Stewart felt that he still had lots of ideas for ***Shoestring*** that were worthy of seeing the light of day, so rather than binning them, he came up with a new TV series that could incorporate these unused concepts. That programme was *Bergerac*.

Bergerac was set on the Channel Island of Jersey, a tax haven where the wealthy can enjoy their money in a lavish lifestyle. With Jersey located just 14 miles off the coast of France, the programme revelled in portraying a way of life and a community that were decidedly continental in their outlook. Jim Bergerac is a police detective working for the Bureau des Etrangers, the division of the Jersey Police specifically set up to deal with crimes involving non-Jersey residents. However, Jim isn't exactly the cream of the crime-fighting crop. A recovering alcoholic with a limp, he's looked upon initially with suspicion, distrust and pity by his superiors and colleagues. As time goes by, however, Jim's natural flair for crime solving wins through, showing how invaluable he is to law enforcement on Jersey. In particular, Chief Inspector Crozier comes to rely upon Jim's insight and ability to get to the root of a particularly tricky case.

Jim's private life was never simple, either. Divorced from his somewhat snooty wife Deborah, he still maintains a strong friendship with his former father-in-law Charlie Hungerford, a Jersey-based businessman who seems to be permanently involved in one kind of dodgy deal or another. Indeed, many of Jim's investigations lead him to Charlie's door, where it's more by good luck than pure innocence that he manages to avoid being arrested. Attempting to move on from his failed marriage, Jim began relationships with tourist bureau assistant Francine Leland and then classy lawyer Marianne Bellshade (Celia Imrie, before she became Miss Babs of *Acorn Antiques*) – sadly neither of them worked out. Jim's longest-running romantic interest was bright, charming estate agent Susan Young (an underwritten role brought to life by ex-***Tenko*** star Louise Jameson) – naturally enough, this being a long-running detective series, Susan ended up murdered and dumped in the sea. Then there was beautiful ice maiden Philippa Vale – simultaneously potential girlfriend and, as an accomplished jewel thief, possible master criminal. Actress Liza Goddard – taking time off from being a team captain in long-running, charades-based game show ***Give Us a Clue*** – made Philippa the most popular recurring character in the series.

For nine seasons, *Bergerac* provided solid entertainment and a reliable presence in the BBC schedules. Finally, with Jim having left the Channel Islands to live with his new girlfriend Danielle in Provence, the series came to an end after a creditable 87 episodes. *Bergerac* was never the most challenging of programmes, but it nevertheless provided a pleasurable diversion for viewers who liked watching John Nettles driving around Jersey in a vintage red Triumph, consequently driving up tourism to the island too. A win-win situation all round!

Between the Lines

Crime Drama | BBC/Island World for BBC One | episode duration 50 mins | broadcast 4 Sep 1992–21 Dec 1994

Regular Cast

Neil Pearson · *Superintendent Tony Clark*
Tom Georgeson · *Harry Naylor*
Siobhan Redmond · *Maureen 'Mo' Connell*
Tony Doyle · *Chief Superintendent John Deakin*
Lynda Steadman · *Sue Clark*
Lesley Vickerage · *WPC Jenny Dean*
David Lyon · *Commander Brian Huxtable*
John Shrapnel · *Trevor Dunning*
Jaye Griffiths · *Molly Cope*
Jerome Flynn · *DS Eddie Hargreaves*
Robin Lermitte · *Superintendent/Chief Superintendent David Graves*
Elaine Donnelly · *Joyce Naylor*
Hugh Ross · *Commander Sullivan*
Francesca Annis · *Angela Berridge*

Creator J. C. Wilsher **Producers** Tony Garnett (executive), Peter Norris, Joy Lale **Writers** J. C. Wilsher, Russell Lewis, Steve Trafford, Michael Russell, Rob Heyland, Ray Brennan, Ron Rose, Nicholas Martin, Julian Jones, Steve Griffiths, Simon Andrew Stirling, Gordon Hann, Dusty Hughes **Theme Music** Colin Towns

When George Dixon plodded his beat in the 1950s and 1960s, viewers might have accepted that there could be one or two crooked policemen (okay, just one then), believing that the vast majority were noble upholders of the law. By the time of ***The Sweeney*** in the 1970s, we knew that there were coppers who bent the rules, but so long as they pinched villains along the way, we were happy to cheer them on. By the 1990s, however, complaints about racism, sexism and violence in the police force had

become numerous. Trying to find a new angle for the already glutted police genre, *Between the Lines* asked the question 'Who polices the police?' by transferring ambitious career copper Tony Clark into the Complaints Investigation Bureau. There, he reports to Chief Superintendent John Deakin and works alongside Mo Connell and Harry Naylor, although Deakin is forced to resign after he is revealed to have been involved in a series of cover-ups.

There's a wonderful irony about Clark being asked to pass judgement on others, as his own private life is chaotic to say the least. At the start of the series he's married but with a mistress, Jenny Dean, a young WPC (the numerous sex scenes and exposed flesh in the first series led it to be dubbed 'Between the Loins' or 'Between the Sheets'). But when his attempts to end the affair coincide with Jenny facing a disciplinary charge, she commits suicide.

Despite his private indiscretions, Clark is sensible enough to ensure his dedication to his professional life is unquestionable, even when some cases become moves in a political rather than moral game. Episodes were self-contained, with cases generally closing by the end, but there were also ongoing stories that combined the police work with more soap-styled plots, such as the investigation into Deakin in series one, Tony's infidelities, and the terminal illness of Harry's wife in the second series.

The third series of *Between the Lines* moved the three main leads into a security firm, headed by their disgraced former boss, Deakin. The shift in tone made the series the kind of generic detective fodder the previous two series had successfully avoided being. It was a mistake pretty much acknowledged in the final episode, in which Tony Clarke and Harry Naylor appeared to be blown up on board a boat.

Trivia

The series was renamed *Inside the Line* for Canadian broadcast.

Website

For fans of Between The Lines star Neil Pearson, there's a good fan site at http://members.fortunecity.com/pesto/neilp.htm.

Beverly Hills 90210

Drama | Spelling Television/Torand Productions for the Fox Network (shown on ITV1/Sky One) | episode duration 45 mins | broadcast 4 Oct 1990–17 May 2000 (USA)

Cast

Jason Priestley · *Brandon Walsh*
James Eckhouse · *Jim Walsh*
Shannen Doherty · *Brenda Walsh*
Carol Potter · *Cindy Walsh*
Jennie Garth · *Kelly Taylor*
Ian Ziering · *Steve Sanders*
Luke Perry · *Dylan McKay*
Gabrielle Carteris · *Andrea Zuckerman-Vasquez*
Brian Austin Green · *David Silver*
Tori Spelling · *Donna Martin Silver*
Joe E. Tata · *Nat Bussichio*
Tiffani-Amber Thiessen · *Valerie Malone*

Creator Darren Star **Producers** Aaron Spelling, Darren Star, Jason Priestley, Charles Rosin (executive) **Writers** Various, including Darren Star, Amy Spies, Charles Rosin, Karen Rosin, Steve Wasserman, Jessica Klein, Jonathan Roberts, Chip Johannessen, Lana Freistat Melman, Ken Stringer, Larry Mollin, Richard Gollance, Meredith Stiehm, Phil Savath, John Eisendrath, John Whelpley, Laurie McCarthy, Michael Cassutt, Elle Triedman, Doug Steinberg, Tyler Bensinger, Gretchen J. Berg, Aaron Harberts, Matt Dearborn **Theme Music** John E. Davis

The comfortably well-off but reasonably down-to-earth Walsh family move into the affluent and desirable 90210 zip code of Beverly Hills, the province of the rich, the famous and the screwed up. Twins Brandon and Brenda attend the local high school where the students drive convertibles and stock up on various issues. Quickly making friends with a tightly knit group, the series follows these youngsters through the trials of high school, college and on into the real world, providing a showcase for issues of the day – drugs, teen pregnancy, loyalty, family tragedies and personal crises.

Created by ***Sex and the City***'s Darren Star, *Beverly Hills, 90210* was basically ***Grange Hill*** with money. The series ran for ten years, seeing cast members come and g o – all of who were amusingly a good five to ten years too old to still be in High School. Original star Shannen Doherty departed after four seasons, but would later re-team with Aaron Spelling on the teen witch drama *Charmed* (which she would also leave after a short time). Spelling happily cast his own daughter, Tori, in a key role, and many of the young cast would direct episodes, with Jason Priestley becoming executive producer in 1997.

Beverly Hills, 90210 developed a massive cult audience among teenagers, and each episode would carry a list of helpline numbers, highlighting the various issues covered that week. The show proved popular enough for an adult aimed spin-off, *Melrose Place*, to hit screens in 1992 on Sky One (which would run until 1999), a show that was no less affluent and aspirational.

The Beverly Hillbillies

Sitcom | Filmways for CBS (shown on ITV) | episode duration 25 mins | broadcast 26 Sep 1962–23 Mar 1971 (USA)

Regular Cast

Buddy Ebsen · *Jed Clampett*
Irene Ryan · *Daisy Mae Moses 'Granny Clampett'*
Donna Douglas · *Elly May Clampett*
Max Baer Jr · *Jethro Bodine*
Nancy Kulp · *Jane Hathaway*

Raymond Bailey · *Milburn Drysdale*
Harriet E. MacGibbon · *Mrs Margaret Drysdale*
Bea Benaderet · *Cousin Pearl Bodine*

Creator Paul Henning **Producers** Martin Ransohoff, Al Simon (executive), Herb Brower, Joseph Depew, Mark Tuttle (associate), Buddy Atkinson, Paul Henning **Writers** Various, including Paul Henning, Mark Tuttle, Ronny Pearlman, Buddy Atkinson, Deborah Haber, Dick Wesson **Theme Music** 'The Ballad of Jed Clampett' by Paul Henning, sung by Jerry Scoggins and performed by legendary bluegrass musicians Lester Flatt and Earl Scruggs. The full-length version includes an additional verse that begins, 'Ol' Jed bought a mansion. Lawdy it was swank/Next door neighbor was pres'dent of the bank . . .'

One of the highest-rated television shows in US history, *The Beverly Hillbillies* stayed on the top of the ratings right up until its cancellation after nine years and 274 episodes. Even then, it was only taken off the air because the type of audience it attracted wasn't the 'right' demographic for advertisers. Each week, the chirpy and unforgettable title song reminded viewers of how the impoverished Clampett family from the Ozark Mountains suddenly became multi-millionaires. When kindly widower father Jed is 'shootin' for some food', he accidentally hits an underground reservoir of pure crude oil – 'black gold . . . Texas tea.' Suddenly wealthy, thanks to the OK Oil Company buying their land (to the tune of $25m), the Clampetts hop into their rickety old charabanc and relocate to the palm trees, limousines and 'ce-ment ponds' (swimming pools) of Beverly Hills in Los Angeles.

Whereas Jed does his best to settle in to his expansive 35-bedroom mansion, the rest of his family find their new lifestyle more difficult to adjust to. Granny (Jed's mother-in-law) is constantly grumpy and wants to up sticks and head back to the country, where she can indulge her passion for good home country cookin' (southern-fried muskrat and other assorted vile concoctions). Jed's glamorous tomboy of a daughter, Elly May, and Desperate Dan wannabe nephew, Jethro, complete the family. Looking after the Clampetts is Milburn Drysdale from the Commerce Bank where their $25m is being stored. Determined to keep an eye on his wealthy clients, Drysdale persuades Jed to buy the Beverly Hills mansion next door to his own – much to the disgust of his snooty social-climbing wife Margaret. Drysdale's PA, the ever-suffering spinster Jane Hathaway, often ends up explaining the quirks and intricacies of modern LA life to the innocent and naïve country bumpkins.

More than 40 years since its first transmission, *The Beverly Hillbillies* is still a charming, entertaining and very, *very* funny programme – especially the first hundred or so episodes, which were filmed in black and white. Created as a vehicle for Buddy Ebsen, who had played a similar role in the movie *Breakfast at Tiffany's* (1961), Ebsen was adamant that his character should never be portrayed as stupid, merely naïve. This, of course, led to the creation of the character of Jethro, who *was* stupid. Buddy Ebsen and Irene Ryan made a marvellous double-act as the heads of the family, with Nancy Culp's Miss Hathaway a particular joy to behold with her unrequited passion for dim farmboy Jethro. A one-off reunion special was made in 1981, followed by a moderately successful feature film in 1993.

Trivia
Cousin Pearl Bodine – Jethro's mother – was played by Bea Benaderet. Her voice would become even more famous when she later provided vocals for the sexiest cartoon neighbour in history, Betty Rubble in ***The Flintstones***.

Bewitched

Sitcom | Ashmont/Screen Gems/Sidney Sheldon Productions for ABC (shown on BBC One) | episode duration 25 mins | broadcast 17 Sep 1964–25 Mar 1972 (USA)

Regular Cast
Elizabeth Montgomery · *Samantha Stephens*
Dick York, Dick Sargent · *Darrin Stephens*
Agnes Moorehead · *Endora*
David White · *Larry Tate*
Maurice Evans · *Maurice*
Alice Pearce, Sandra Gould · *Gladys Kravitz*
George Tobias · *Abner Kravitz*
Irene Vernon, Kasey Rogers · *Louise Tate*
Marion Lorne · *Aunt Clara*
Paul Lynde · *Uncle Arthur*
Pandora Spocks · *Serena*
Erin Murphy, Diane Murphy · *Tabitha Stephens*
Bernard Fox · *Dr Bombay*
Alice Ghostley · *Esmeralda*
Greg Lawrence, David Lawrence · *Adam Stephens*

Note: Pandora Spocks, credited as playing Samantha's cousin Serena, was actually Elizabeth Montgomery. Although this might appear blindingly obvious, many viewers were convinced it was a different actress.

Creator Sol Saks **Producers** Harry Ackerman (executive), Jerry Briskin, Ernest Losso, Richard Michaels (associate), Danny Arnold, William Asher, Jerry Davis, William Froug **Writers** Sol Saks, Barbara Avedon, Jerry Davis, Bernard Slade, Paul David, Fred Freeman, Lawrence J. Cohen, Richard Baer, Ruth Brooks Flippen, Paul Wayne, Howard Leeds, John L. Greene, James Henerson, David V. Robison, Ed Jurist, Robert Riley Crutcher, Michael Morris, Rick Mittleman, Lila Garrett, Jerry Mayer, Bernie Kahn, Peggy Chantler Dick, Douglas Dick **Theme Music** Howard Greenfield and Jack Keller, accompanied by an animated title sequence courtesy of Hanna-Barbera. Greenfield and Keller also wrote lyrics to the tune, though these were never used on the show itself ('Bewitched, bewitched, you've got me in your spell./Bewitched, bewitched, you know your craft so well . . .').

Thanks to regular repeats on Channel 4, a whole new generation of viewers has discovered the magical adventures of Samantha Stephens, nose-twitching star of classic American sitcom *Bewitched*. Originally running for eight years (with the first two series made in black and white), *Bewitched* had a similar set-up to classic films *I Married A Witch* (1942) and *Bell, Book and Candle* (1958), documenting the life of ordinary man Darrin, who discovers on his wedding day that wife-to-be Samantha comes from a family of witches and warlocks. Determined to break up this 'mixed marriage', Samantha's disappointed and vindictive mother Endora does everything she can to undermine her son-in-law and try to convince her daughter that she's done the wrong thing by marrying him. Often Endora uses magic to embarrass or humiliate Darrin in front of his money-obsessed employer Larry Tate.

Some modern critics have praised *Bewitched* for subtly poking fun at racism with its jokey criticism of Endora's resistance to 'mixed marriages' – however, the solidly white middle-class cast makes it hard to believe that either producers or audiences at the time picked up on any such message.

When original Darrin, Dick York, had to quit the series owing to back problems, his replacement, Dick Sargent (who had been the original choice for Darrin but unable to take up the part), managed to deliver a near-identical performance. Some viewers never even spotted the change-over (probably because of the small size of TV screens in the 1960s!), and debates still rage today about which Darrin was better. Sitcom ***Roseanne*** later made a poignant reference to the changing face of Darrin when eldest daughter Becky was recast (the new Becky shocked her family by saying she always preferred the second Darrin).

After 254 episodes and two children (written in to incorporate Montgomery's real-life pregnancies), the series came to a close, with Endora trying and failing to test her son-in-law's fidelity – Samantha and Darrin ended the last episode just as in love as they'd been nine years earlier. In 1977, a short-lived spin-off series, ***Tabitha***, was launched, telling the adventures of Samantha and Darrin's eldest daughter, who had inherited her mother's habit of nose-twitching bewitchery. Starring Lisa Hartman – who would later join the regular cast of ***Knots Landing*** – and Robert Urich (***Soap***, *Spenser: for Hire*) as her love interest, Tabitha was now suddenly old enough to be working behind the scenes of TV station KXLA in California, despite the fact that she was only 'born' in *Bewitched* in 1966, 11 years earlier. In 2005, Nicole Kidman and Will Ferrell starred in a *Bewitched* feature film with a post-modern twist on the old story. Film producer Ferrell casts young actress Kidman as the lead in his movie remake of the old TV show *Bewitched*, little realising that his star is, in fact, a good witch in real life as well. . .

Big Break

Quiz Show | BBC One | episode duration 30 mins | broadcast 30 Apr 1991–9 Oct 2002

Voice cast
Jim Davidson · *Host*
John Virgo · *Referee*

Creator/Writer Terry Mardell **Producers** John Burrows, David Taylor **Original Music** 'The Snooker Song', written by Mike Batt, sung by Captain Sensible ('I'm famed for my aim, so you'd better believe I'm right/I'm gonna be snookering you, snookering you tonight.').

Jim Davidson, dropping the vulgar shortcomings of his stand-up comedy to enter full-on family mode, presides over this snooker-based quiz show, alongside comedy foil and fellow panto collaborator (and ex-Snooker champ) John Virgo. Members of the public are twinned with a snooker star of the day (some more well known than others) to answer general knowledge questions and win seconds on the clock. Their 'celebrity' partner would then attempt to pot as many balls as possible in the time available, thus whittling down the contestants from three to one for the final frame, with each ball potted corresponding to a prize.

Big Break was a bizarre hit for the BBC, showing that the nation's appetite for both snooker and quiz shows had not diminished (although a previous fusing, *Pot the Question*, was a flop). Jim Davidson makes a remarkably pleasant host, though he's clearly no Bob Monkhouse, and John Virgo's trick shot segment was a regular highlight. Teen players from the world of snooker were showcased in *Big Break: Stars of the Future*.

The Big Breakfast

See pages 90–2

Big Brother

See pages 93–7

The Bill

See pages 98–101

Bill and Ben

See FLOWER POT MEN, *pages* 314–15

Billy Bunter of Greyfriars School

Comedy | BBC TV| episode duration 30 mins | broadcast 19 Feb 1953–22 Jul 1961

Regular Cast
Gerald Campion · *Billy Bunter*
Kynaston Reeves, Jack Melford · *Mr Quelch*
Anthony Valentine, Julian Yardley · *Harry Wharton*
Brian Roper, Peter Greenspan · *Bob Cherry*
Laurence Harrington, Michael E. Briant,
Jonathan Margetts · *Frank Nugent*
Barry Barnett, Brian Tipping · *Hurree Singh*
David Coote, Melvyn Baker · *Johnny Bull*
Peter Scott, Ian Hobbs · *Horace Coker*
Maurice Colbourne · *Dr Locke*
Paul Whitsun-Jones · *Mr Bunter*
Christopher Hodge · *Gosling*
Melvyn Hayes, Glyn Dearman, Agaric Cotter · *Boys*

Creator/Writer Frank Richards **Producers** David Goddard, Joy Harington, Pharic Maclaren, Shaun Sutton, Clive Parkhurst **Theme Music** An extract from *Sea Songs* by Vaughan Williams, played over caricatures of the cast by Tony Hart. Later episodes suffered a ghastly electric organ arrangement that was not at all in keeping with the tone of the show.

The star of the *Magnet* magazine since 1908, 'Billy Bunter' became shorthand for anyone who is fat, greedy and lazy – before political correctness would claim that ridiculing someone for being overweight just wasn't on. Bunter was created by author Frank Richards (a pseudonym for the hugely prolific Charles Harold St John Hamilton), who also adapted his own stories for the TV version. But it's fair to say it was Gerald Campion who was responsible for bringing the 'Fat Owl of the Reform' to life. Aged 29 and married with children when he took on the part, Campion wore a padded suit to bulk him up and a pair of black pince-nez to complete the Bunter look.

Billy Bunter was a student at Greyfriars public school, housed in the Reform dormitory, which was presided over by strict disciplinarian Mr Quelch. Being exceptionally shoddy at everything except gluttony and lying, Bunter spent most of his school life thinking up excuses for why his lines were late (usually falling back on the two standbys, that one of the other boys had used his papers to light a fire with, or that a huge gust of wind had whisked them away), though no-one was ever convinced, despite desperate pleading on his part. If any of the other boys received a food parcel, the odds were that Bunter would find his way to stealing it – and then instantly deny he was anywhere nearby. He would often be heard to exclaim, 'Oh crikey!' or 'Yahroo!' and 'You beast!' and when he wasn't scoffing pie or oranges, he'd be boasting about life back at Bunter Court, the ancestral home of the Bunters (which, sadly, was merely an invention of his overactive imagination).

Considering how self-serving and plain annoying he was, for some reason the other boys, including Harry Wharton, Bob Cherry and Frank Nugent, tolerated him more than they perhaps should have. When Bunter's father found himself on the verge of bankruptcy, the 'Famous Five' helped Billy swat for the scholarship exam, while a later episode saw Billy on the verge of expulsion for one crime he hadn't actually committed, and the boys rallied round to protect him and prove his innocence. Perhaps it was because Billy was actually quite fun to have around, for all his failings.

Frank Richards's original stories were pretty enlightened for his times, tackling social issues like bullying (in the form of school thug Horace Coker) or racism. On this matter, Richards introduced an Indian student to his stories – Hurree Jamset Ram Singh – who was seen to be a studious, hard-working child and an impressive cricketer. Sadly, this element didn't exactly translate to the small screen as the boys cast as Singh were in fact Caucasians blacked up.

Each episode would be broadcast from Lime Grove studios and performed twice each Saturday, first at 5.40 p.m. for the kids, and then again at 8.00 for the grown-ups. This resulted in over 50 individual episodes being transmitted over eight years, with future stars such as David Hemmings, Michael Crawford, Melvyn Hayes and even John Osborne donning the Greyfriars uniform. Model shots of the school were included to allow performers time to change costumes or reach other parts of the sets, and the opening and closing titles included cartoon sketches by artist Tony Hart. Greyfriars finally closed its gates after the death of Frank Richards in 1961. Finding himself typecast, Gerald Campion gradually withdrew from acting to become a successful restaurateur. He died in 2002, aged 81.

The Bionic Woman

Action-Adventure | Harve Bennett Productions/Universal for ABC/NBC (shown on ITV) | episode duration 50 mins | broadcast 21 Jan 1976–13 May 1978 (USA)

Regular Cast
Lindsay Wagner · *Jaime Sommers*
Richard Anderson · *Oscar Goldman*
Martin E. Brooks · *Dr Rudy Wells*
Sam Chew Jr · *Mark Russell*
Jennifer Darling · *Peggy Callahan*
Ford Rainey · *Jim Elgin*
Martha Scott · *Helen Elgin*
Christopher Stone · *Chris Williams*
Braken · *'Max' Maximillion the bionic dog*

Creators Kenneth Johnson and Harve Bennett, inspired by Martin Caidin's novel *Cyborg* **Producers** Harve Bennett, Lionel E. Siegel (executive), Arnold F. Turner, Craig Schiller, David G. Phinney (associate), Kenneth Johnson, James D. Parriott, Arthur Rowe, Ralph Sariego, Nancy Malone, Joseph D'Agosta **Writers** Kenneth Johnson, James D. Parriott, Philip DeGuere Jr, Sue Milburn, Wilton Denmark, Arthur Rowe, Stephen Kandel, Mann Rubin, Bruce Shelly, Kenneth Johnson, Justin Edgerton, Robert L. McCullough, Daniel Kibbie, Herman Groves, William Schwartz, Ellen Wittman, Joseph A. Viola, Tom August, Helen August, Robert A. Urso, Rudolph Borchert, Connor Everts, Jim Carlson, Terrence McDonnell, David Ketchum, Anthony DiMarco,
Continued on page 103

The Big Breakfast

Chris Evans and Gaby Roslin surrounded by the Big Breakfast production crew.

Channel 4's first attempt at breakfast telly was actually quite nifty. More rigidly structured than its competitors, *The Channel 4 Daily* managed to avoid the cosiness of BBC One's *Breakfast Time* and the tabloid flavour of TVAM's *Good Morning Britain* (and later GMTV) by presenting its audience with a stylish, slick programme a bit like a broadsheet's Sunday colour supplement but available every week day. Unfortunately, hardly anyone was watching. Cue an anarchic breakfast programme that for a time was *the* show to watch over your cornflakes. *The Big Breakfast* was very canny in the way it reacted to Breakfast TV as a concept. It rescued the energetic and ambitious Chris Evans from the embers of BSB's *Power Station*, elevated Gaby Roslin from Saturday morning kiddyvision and had husband-and-wife team Bob Geldof and Paula Yates in separate slots doing interviews that covered both ends of the 'depth spectrum'. Hitting the streets and knocking on doors was comic Mark Lamarr and looking in from ITN was Peter Smith. We knew he was the newsreader – he was the only one who wore a tie.

Broadcast live from 7 'til 9 from the Lock-Keepers Cottages in Bow, East London, *The Big Breakfast* was a colourful assault on the senses. The cottages themselves had been converted into one huge house. The kitchen was handy for interviewing large groups like the Family of the Week, while the stairs provided a grand entrance for the day's Fantastically Good-looking Man – a builder or fireman who would be ogled and wolf whistled by female crew members. Upstairs, we'd find the bedroom, where Paula Yates set the trend for intimate and often saucy chats with international stars. (It was here that Paula Yates first connected with the rock star Michael Hutchence, an interview that infamously led to the break-up of her marriage to Geldof. It was also the beginning of a deeply tragic chapter in Yates' life, which ended in Hutchence's suicide, the discovery that her father was actually legendary presenter Hughie Greene and not Jess Yates, and her own suicide in 2000.) The

Entertainment
Planet 24 Productions for Channel 4
Episode Duration: 90 mins
Broadcast: 28 Sep 1992–29 Mar 2002

Cast
Chris Evans, Gaby Roslin, Paula Yates, Bob Geldof, Mark Lamarr, Kim Wilde, Mark Little, Keith Chegwin, Paul Ross, Paul O'Grady (as Lily Savage), Zoë Ball, Vanessa Feltz, Rick Adams, Sharron Davies, Denise Van Outen, Johnny Vaughan, Kelly Brook, Jenny McCarthy, Liza Tarbuck, Paul Tonkinson, Amanda Byram, Sara Cox, Gail Porter, Donna Air, Lisa Rogers, Richard Orford, Richard Bacon, Ed Hall, Dermot O'Leary, Mike McClean, Melanie Sykes · *Regular Presenters*
Peter Smith, Saxon Bains, Phil Gayle, Bridget Nzekoo, Jasmine Lowson, Simon Fielder, Angela Rippon, John Craven, Ruth England, Carol Barnes, Jemma Woodman · *News and Weather*
Wayne Hemingway, Ben 'The Boffin' Keyworth, Jody Bunting, Mark Bright, Neil Ruddock, Eddie Canter, Jon Sandys · *Experts*

Producers Charlie Parsons (executive), Duncan Gray (executive), Ed Forsdick (executive), Ben Rigden (executive), Chris Heath (associate), Paul Moore (associate), Richard Ackerman, Paul Connolly, Andy Harries, Andrew Higgie, Tim Lovejoy, Anna Reid, Asif Zubairy

Theme Music Grant Buckerfield

bathroom was inhabited by childlike, but very witty, alien puppets Zig and Zag, who had already been stars of Irish TV station RTE. The garden, dominated by a gigantic gnome, would be used for energetic games like 'Court with your Pants Down' (where celebs would try to whack a tennis ball over a net with an increasing amount of underpants pulled over their ankles) or 'Get your Knobbly Nuts Out' (which involved a blindfolded player being guided across a swimming pool by a phone-in contestant to locate oversized nut clusters with a giant spoon). And leading towards each ad break would be a trivia question that prompted the presenters to remind us: 'Don't phone – it's just for fun.'

The show became a big hit and soon it was fetching in over 1.5 million viewers; for a time it even overshadowed its rivals on ITV and BBC One. Its informal approach to the rules of broadcasting saw the crew becoming almost as famous as the presenters themselves. Chats with Dave the floor manager, 'Cable Basher', 'Carpet Monster', 'Sexy Linton', 'Sturdy Girl' and the rest became a regular part of the production, aping the trend for Zoo TV that was on the rise.

Just a couple of years in, Chris Evans was tempted away to develop his own shows (including the groundbreaking ***Don't Forget your Toothbrush*** and ***TFI Friday***). Replaced by former ***Neighbours*** star Mark Little, the show continued with its addictive mix of light-hearted banter and games. When Gaby Roslin eventually chose to move on, Zöe Ball was brought in, again with the intention of providing continuity with what had gone before. But in 1996, four years into a successful run, the *BB* fortunes began to change. A restyling of the house into an open-plan villa and a completely new presenting crew left viewers with a rather sleepy Sharron Davies, geeky Rick Adams and unenthusiastic Richard Orford. The change was disastrous and the show began haemorrhaging viewers.

Two things saved *BB* from cancellation back in 1997. First, Denise Van Outen – a bubbly blonde Essex girl who'd been hired as an eye-in-the-sky traffic reporter – was brought in to the house to work alongside Richard Orford, who himself had been moved into the house after Rick Adams' sudden departure. Second, to cover for Orford's holiday one week, the producers hired chat-show host and presenter of Channel 4's *Movie Watch* Johnny Vaughan. Vaughan was soon brought in full-time as Denise's co-presenter and the Golden Era of *The Big Breakfast* began. The arrival of Vaughan saw a shift in focus for the show, with features designed to pander to Vaughan's often ranty style, his fascination with trivia ('Vital Statistics') and his jingoistic love of bulldogs and British pride. Vaughan and Van Outen managed to eclipse even Evans and Roslin as morning TV's perfect couple.

The Big Breakfast rescued the energetic and ambitious Chris Evans from the embers of BSB's _Power Station_.

Denise Van Outen and Johnny Vaughan shared a crackling chemistry and a talent for spontaneity. Sadly, Outen's replacement,

19-year-old Kelly Brook, lacked everything Denise had boasted, except looks. Inexperienced in the art of TV presentation and clearly lacking the support she needed, Brook left after just six months to be replaced by Vaughan's old friend Liza Tarbuck, before Van Outen was eventually wooed back again to see out Johnny Vaughan's final months on the show.

The Big Brekkie never recovered from the loss of Vaughan and Van Outen. Presenters came and went, few of them displaying the ability to wake up a nation when they themselves appeared half asleep, and by the time Mike 'Squeaky' McClean inherited the poisoned chalice, the viewing figures had slumped once again – a shame as McClean was clearly perfectly suited to the format. Fearing the worst, Channel 4 decided to cut their losses and give *The Big Breakfast* notice. As execs viewed pilots for a replacement, *BB* became predominantly a clips show of its former glories. Still, *BB* got the last word. On their last live show, they erected their huge garden gnome in front of Channel 4's offices, with a hand forming an insolent V-sign where its fishing rod had been.

Quickly dubbed 'RI:Sible' by critics, Channel 4 were astounded when it failed to reach even the lows of *BB*'s final years.

The Big Breakfast replacement was *RI:SE*, a magazine show created by Sky. Quickly dubbed 'RI:Sible' by critics, Channel 4 were astounded when it failed to reach even the lows of *BB*'s final years (some reports suggest that according to official viewing figures literally no-one was watching it at some points). It desperately tried to save itself by becoming more 'Big Breakfasty', ditching all the original presenters and bringing on Channel 4 spare Iain Lee and *Big Brother 3* winner Kate Lawler, but this pale imitation quickly nose dived and was eventually scrapped, mourned by no-one.

The Big Breakfast is fondly remembered by its viewers and most of the presenters emerged unscathed. Gaby Roslin continues to co-host the BBC's annual *Children in Need* appeal with Terry Wogan and remains a popular TV personality. Johnny Vaughan bagged his own BBC One chat show and in 2004 was reunited with Denise (fresh from her successful run on Broadway in *Chicago*) for their self-titled BBC One gameshow. Liza Tarbuck juggles a successful career as actress and presenter. Even Kelly Brook has done well; having left the UK to appear in episodes of American drama *Smallville*, she emerged as one of the top 'ladmag' pin-ups, her *BB* past politely ignored.

Big Brother

Davina McCall welcomes Big Brother 2's fourth-placed contestant, Jade Goody.

There are many who still pretend not to get *Big Brother*, despite six years in which to try. For the most part, this is more intellectual snobbery on their part than any complexity in the game itself. Put simply, the appeal of *Big Brother* is people-watching – without ever being caught staring. Each year since 2000, groups of ten or more eager hopefuls have been incarcerated in a purpose-built house-cum-TV studio for up to three months in the hope of avoiding eviction and ultimately winning the grand prize. Through the process of nominations (either by the housemates themselves or, in later years, through the outcome of tasks set each week), a selection of housemates is put forward to the public vote as to who stays and who gets booted out to the cheers (or otherwise) of crowds of fans.

Based on a Dutch-developed format that had already begun to take the world by storm before we Brits got sight of it, *Big Brother* is a true TV phenomenon. Not only does it galvanise and polarise audiences more than almost every regular sporting event, it has revolutionised the concept of audience interaction and inevitably shattered traditional broadcast scheduling in a way that at the time of writing seems unlikely ever to be repaired. This is a show that has managed to dominate British culture to an extent that not one magazine, periodical or newspaper in the last few years has managed to avoid it completely. Not bad for a show some insist they 'don't get'.

The format has evolved only slightly over the years. The first season was heralded as a social experiment, with psychologists offering interpretations and explanations for the events. While the psychology show continues to feature, its importance as a justifier has been reduced somewhat; people don't watch *BB* to learn about human behaviour any more, they watch it for the fights, of which there have been many.

Reality TV
Endemol/Bazal for Channel 4
Episode Duration: 30-60 mins
Broadcast: 18 Jul 2000-present

Cast
Marcus Bentley · *Narrator*
Davina McCall · *Presenter, eviction nights*
Dermot O'Leary · *Presenter Big Brother's Little Brother*
Anjula Mutanda, Sandra Scott, Geoffrey Beattie, Peter Collett, Linda Papadopoulos, Sonia Sharp, Gareth Smith, Honey Langcaster-James · *Psychologists*
Craig Phillips, Brian Dowling, Kate Lawler, Cameron Stout, Nadia Almada, Anthony Hutton · *Winners*
Anna Nolan, Darren Ramsey, Melanie Hill, Claire Strutton, Thomas McDermott, Nichola Holt, Nicholas Bateman, Caroline O'Shea, Andrew Davidson, Sada Walkington · *Series 1 Contestants*
Helen Adams, Dean O'Loughlin, Elizabeth Woodcock, Paul Clarke, Josh Rafter, Amma Antwi-Agyei, Paul 'Bubble' Ferguson, Narinder Kaur, Stuart Hosking, Lisa Penny Ellis · *Series 2 Contestants*
Jonny Regan, Alex Sibley, Jade Goody, Tim Culley, 'PJ' Ellis, Adele Roberts, Sophie Pritchard, Spencer Smith, Lee Davey, Sandy Cumming, Alison Hammond, Lynne Moncrieff, Sunita Sharma · *Series 3 Contestants*
Ray Shah, Scott Turner, Steph Coldicutt, Nush Nowak, Lisa Jeynes, Gos Gosal, Tania do Nascimento, Gaetano Kagwa, Jon Tickle, Federico Martone, Sissy Rooney, Justine Sellman, Anouska Golebiewski · *Series 4 Contestants*
Jason Cowan, Daniel Bryan, Shell Jubin, Stuart Wilson, Michelle Bass, Victor Ebuwa, Ahmed Aghil, Becki Seddiki, Marco Sabba, Vanessa Nimmo, Emma Greenwood, 'Kitten' Pinder · *Series 5 Contestants*
Eugene Sully, Makosi Musambasi, Kinga Karolczak, Craig Coates, Derek Laud, Orlaith McAllister, Kemal Shahin, Kieron 'Science' Harvey, Vanessa Layton-McIntosh, Maxwell Ward, Saskia Howard-Clarke, Roberto Conte, Sam Heuston, Lesley Sanderson, Mary O'Leary · *Series 6 Contestants*
Jack Dee, Mark Owen, Mark 'Bez' Berry · *Celebrity BB Winners*
Claire Sweeney, Keith Duffy, Vanessa Feltz, Anthea Turner, Chris Eubank · *Celebrity BB1 Contestants*
Les Dennis, Sue Perkins, Melinda

In year one, the biggest event was when public school-educated Nick Bateman was discovered to have broken the rules after weeks of running a sly tactical campaign against his competitors. Nick's skulduggery was eventually exposed by dyslexic Liverpudlian builder Craig, who impressed everyone with his calm, mature approach to what was, in this game, a serious breech of trust. It turned 'Nasty Nick' into Public Enemy Number One and Craig into a national hero. It also turned many latecomers into *BB* addicts.

But it was in year two that things began to get explosive. Businessman Stuart found himself at the heart of two separate ferocious rows with fellow housemates early on, but it was Irish air steward Brian Dowling who proved to be the most argumentative. Brian's quick wit and naturally funny persona tended to win people over and ultimately he became the show's second winner ahead of Welsh beautician Helen, famed for her naïve charm and a dippy romance with contestant Paul (the one who professed to having lived his life like a professional rock star).

The third year saw *Big Brother* stir things up significantly. With a new house and increased number of housemates, Evil *BB* reared his head for the first time by dividing the house into 'rich' and 'poor' sides based on the outcome of various challenges. For one contestant the experience proved too much: former soldier Sandy hotfooted it over the rooftops and escaped, following lawyer Sunita, who had quit shortly after the start of the show. Never before had a *BB* house seen such bitching and sniping. Bodybuilder Adele seemed to be attempting a 'Nasty Nick'-style tactic of picking off her opponents one by one (and when she left, the furious boos left the remaining housemates baffled as to what she could have done to deserve such a reaction). Moaning model Alex complained about peeing in the shower, not getting fair rations and . . . generally everything else. PJ and Jade almost managed to win a tabloid reward for being the first players to 'do it' while in the house, though they insisted afterwards that nothing happened. Though Kate Lawler emerged as the winner, it was Jade who has maintained the highest profile. Easily influenced by both Adele and Alex, Jade managed to fight with almost everyone in the house, struggled to grasp the concept of a place called 'East Angula' (prompting Spencer to ask, politely, if she'd been 'taking stupid pills') and finally being encouraged to lose disgracefully in a strip-drinking game that left her clutching her wares and screeching in embarrassment.

Big Brother 4 proved to be something of a disappointment with most of the housemates far too aware of the cameras and playing it safe in order to stay in the house for as long as possible. The only real event that year was when Cameron, a Christian from Orkney, was sent in secret to visit the *BB* Africa house, while their representative Gaetano took his place for a week. Poor Gaetano probably couldn't believe how dull things were in Britain. Though Cameron eventually won, few people could work out how. It really should have been Jon Tickle, the self-confessed 'most boring man in Britain', which would have been appropriate.

The non-event of *BB4* had serious repercussions for the show with many people wondering if the reality TV bubble had finally burst. *BB5* was plotted to generate conflict from the beginning. The house was redesigned to create a feeling of claustrophobia, only one large bedroom was provided and the bathroom was exposed to the garden by one glass wall. The contestants were clearly selected to irritate and aggravate each other: an asylum-seeking Muslim who expressed strong homophobic beliefs and a honking, shrill, effeminate gay man; a lesbian anarchist and a body-building former soldier; a South African fitness enthusiast and a chain-smoking transsexual.

While that did increase the conflict levels dramatically (and made *BB5* the most instantly watchable series to date), *Big Brother* made a catastrophic error of judgement that, for some, took the concept of 'Evil Big Bro' too far. The first two people to be voted out by the public were not actually evicted but relocated to an adjoining bedsit, which contained plasma screens allowing them to see events within the house. Having been given a privileged insight into the gameplans of the other contestants, the pair were eventually allowed back into the house, to the delight of some and the disgust of others. 'Day 20', as it was later known, erupted into a terrifying display of anger and emotion, caused initially by a food fight that enraged some of the housemates and led to a furious row. As the fighting escalated, viewers watching on E4 could hear screams and tables being turned over, which immediately led them to believe that a full-scale fight was taking place (in truth it was mainly raised voices, though for the record it was Nadia, not Jason, who flipped the table over, and Emma who started throwing the foil serving plates at Victor). Eventually, *Big Brother* realised he had to take control. Security guards were sent in to separate the housemates, Emma was removed from the house and others were sent to different parts of the house to cool off.

People don't watch *BB* to learn about human behaviour any more, they watch it for the fights, of which there have been many.

Though *Big Brother* assured viewers that everyone was okay, the sight of Shell doubled-up, vomiting with fear on the night made it hard for us to believe that the fight hadn't affected some of the housemates more than others. The lively Jason retreated from all non-compulsory activities, earning the name 'The Incredible Sulk', though it was possible to understand his mental processes, recognising that losing his temper could have cost him the game (as indeed it did). Singer and hairdresser Dan Bryan tried valiantly to help people through the next few days and, in so doing, showed the nation that he was possibly the most intelligent, rational contestant the show had ever had. Meanwhile, Portuguese transsexual Nadia suffered horrific mood swings because of lack of cigarettes. Her difficulty with the English language and shrieking laugh turned her into an unintentional comic turn, and while her often selfish outbursts must have been hell to live with, we got to

Messenger, Anne Diamond, Goldie · *Celebrity BB2 Contestants*
James 'Kenzie' Mackenzie, Brigitte Nielsen, Jeremy Edwards, Caprice Bourret, Lisa I'Anson, John McCririck, Jackie Stallone, Germaine Greer · *Celebrity BB3 Contestants*
Paul Brennan · *Teen BB Winner*
Caroline Cloke, Shaneen Dawkins, Jade Dyer, Tracey Fowler, Tommy Wright, James Kelly, Hasan Shah · *Teen BB Contestants*

Creator John De Mol

Producers Various, including Phil Edgar Jones, Ben Adler, Kate Brown, Paul Couesiant, Conrad Green, Ruth Wrigley

Theme Music Paul Oakenfold and Andy Gray. Released on CD during the first series in 2000, the *Big Brother* theme reached No. 4 in the UK singles chart, with Oakenfold and Gray performing under the name ElementFour.

see a person trying to come to terms with the fact that she was being accepted as a real woman for the first time in her life. Her emotional incomprehension at being voted the winner was second only to Jason's disbelief that he hadn't been. Truly, this was the most action-packed and tumultuous of journeys for all of them.

In between regular series we've been treated to special celebrity editions for charity. Highlight of the first *Celebrity Big Brother*, which for the only time was a co-production between Channel 4 and the BBC in aid of ***Comic Relief***, was the moment when Vanessa Feltz began scrawling words like 'rejection' across a table-top and refusing to obey the voice of *Big Brother*. Deadpan comedian Jack Dee won the game, mainly for a rather impressive escape attempt. Sadly, a follow-up *Celebrity* series was less action-packed as the chosen contestants were all too aware of how to play the game. A houseful of people being nice to each other does not make enthralling television. So, as in series five, the third *Celebrity BB* brought together a mix of volatile people who were much more likely to create drama. Against all odds, the rather sadistic decision to add Brigitte Nielson's ex-mother-in-law Jackie Stallone as a late entrant led to the pair reconciling 20-year-old differences, rather than the catfight everyone had hoped for. In fact, the only real cause of friction was the wilfully obnoxious John McCririck, who sulked his way through an entire week and entertained us with his outlandish views on women in society while bagging the title of single laziest *BB* contestant ever.

Pretty much every channel now has some kind of reality programming, replacing many of the fly-on-the-wall documentaries that remained from a previous fad.

A special edition over Christmas and New Year 2004/5 brought housemates from previous series to a *BB*-like house to train for a one-off live pantomime performance that, thanks to a script from Jonathan Harvey, turned out to be surprisingly good. However, the most interesting variation turned out to be *Teen Big Brother – The Experiment*. Unlike other series, *Teen BB* was not shown live but pre-recorded in the summer of 2003 and shown the following October. Eight contestants, all 18 years old, spent ten days in the house and experienced the pains of nominations and evictions, decided entirely by the housemates. The eventual winner was selected by consensus – Paul, a gay hairdresser from Belfast won a holiday around the world rather than the traditional wodge of cash. But the series was remembered for another thing entirely – the first time a couple had full sex within the *BB* walls. The incident, between Tommy and Jade, caused outrage, but it also reminded us that there's no power in the universe as strong as teenage hormones.

Germaine Greer's decision to leave *Celebrity BB3* after just six days led to her writing a column for *The Times* in which she labelled *Big Brother* as a bully. We might say that no-one should attempt an experience like *Big Brother* if they don't know what they're getting into (yes you, Jackie Stallone), but Greer does have a good point to make. By once again allowing a housemate to view video footage of nominations and footage of other housemates, they're giving them a privilege that's guaranteed to upset them and lead to conflict. And though we agree that John McCririck's tantrum over his missing Diet Coke was hysterical, *BB*'s decision to secretly give all of the other housemates the fizzy beverage in the diary room was bullying. As *BB* continues, we hope the producers will spend more time thinking up interesting trials and tasks, and less time prodding the contestants with psychological sticks and treating some of them 'more equally' than others. Otherwise, this glorious TV concept might end up turning into another Orwellian dystopia – *Animal Farm* . . . although it could be argued Rebecca Loos' activities on Channel 5's *The Farm* already beat them to that!

Big Brother is set to continue for at least another few years, but its effect upon British broadcasting cannot be underestimated. ITV has struck gold with their own celebrity reality show ***I'm a Celebrity ... Get Me Out of Here!***, while the BBC, having originally turned down the chance to host *Big Brother*, developed *Fame Academy*, a hybrid of *BB* and ITV's hugely successful ***Pop Idol***. Pretty much every channel available now has some kind of reality programming, replacing many of the fly-on-the-wall documentaries that remained from a previous broadcasting fad. Whether or not this has damaged TV is another matter. Producing a solid reality show seems to be the answer for many broadcasters struggling to fill their digital/cable channels as it allows them to strip support shows throughout the week with 'live' footage, discussion programmes and repeats of the main editions. But that's less to do with *Big Brother* and more to do with us still in the very early stages of becoming a 'Digital Britain'. What it does mean for television is that it remains the place where the country talks to itself, where we exchange ideas, meet people we might never get the opportunity to and, if we're honest, it gives us the chance to feel a little superior about anyone who'd be willing to expose themselves to the nation in such an unflattering and unsympathetic way, so that we don't have to.

***Big Brother* is set to continue for at least another few years, but its effect upon British broadcasting cannot be underestimated.**

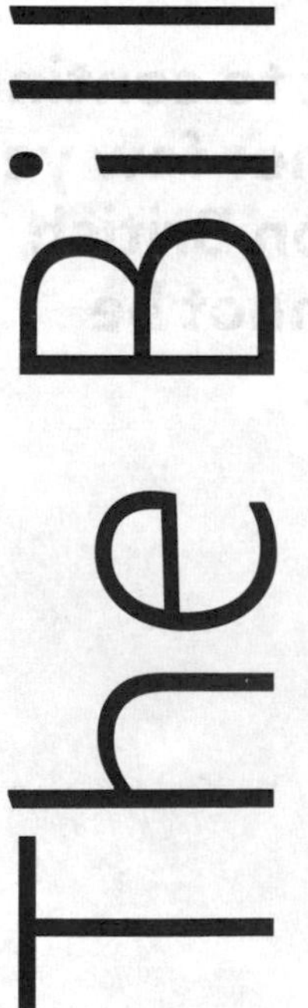

Trudie Goodwin (WPC June Ackland), Eric Richard (Sergeant Bob Cryer) and John Salthouse (DI Roy Galloway).

The inspiration for *The Bill* came partly from writer Geoff McQueen's dire financial situation and partly from a fly-on-the-wall documentary series about the Thames Valley police force. *The Bill* began as *Woodentop*, a one-off play screened as part of Thames' *Storyboard* series of potential pilots (also included in the series was the first episode of *Lytton's Diary*, starring Peter Bowles). It introduced young rookie police constable Jim Carver in his first day at Sun Hill Police Station in South London. Although he was in the care of WPC June Ackland (being 'puppy-walked', as they put it), Jim gets himself into trouble almost straight away when he clips a teenage hooligan around the ear. Sergeant Wilding manages to sort the problem out by speaking to the teenager's father, a man of old-school principles who luckily agrees with Carver's actions. Director Peter Cregeen (who had previously worked on ***Z Cars*** and ***Juliet Bravo***) chose to make the show on videotape rather than film, unlike other Thames-produced dramas such as ***The Sweeney*** and ***Minder***. He also mimicked the fly-on-the-wall style (similar to American cop show ***Hill Street Blues*** which had been shown in the UK in early 1981), with the handheld cameras following the police officers from behind into each scene.

Just a couple of months after it was aired, *Woodentop* was commissioned for a series of 12 episodes (though due to industrial action the 12th episode was not completed) and was renamed *The Bill*. There were a number of slight changes from *Woodentop* to the first episode of the series. Peter Dean's Desk Sergeant Wilding became Eric Richards' Sergeant Bob Cryer, who inherited Wilding's catchphrase 'Superstars' in reference to egotistical detectives (Peter Dean headed off to Albert Square to play Pete Beale in ***EastEnders***). DI Galloway originally appeared in the form of Robert Pugh, who played the part with a West Midlands accent. For the series, he was played by Londoner John Salthouse. PC 'Taffy' Morgan became 'Taffy' Edwards for no apparent reason.

The series showed all sides of police work, with an even split between the patrol work of the young PCs, under the care of sergeants Cryer, Penny and Peters, and the detectives, headed by the fiery DI Galloway. Each episode would tackle three or four cases, some of which would turn out to be connected, and not all of them would necessarily be resolved by close of play.

The Bill has survived, like all good long-running series, by playing with and subverting its archetypes. The ambitious wide-boy represented by Dave Litten evolved into PCs Quinnan and Taviner; the scruffy detective of Tosh Lines became the Hawaiian-shirted Ken Drummond. Then there are the shady, ultimately untrustworthy rotten apples like PCs Ramsey, Santini and Kent, and the eager WPC who wants to be accepted on her own terms, who spans from June Ackland to Kerry Young.

But inevitably there have been some characters who have stood out over the years. Reg Hollis appeared in the first episode of the series, although his character was mentioned in *Woodentop* as being on the wrong side of the gas works to be within radio contact. A creation of the massively underrated Jeff Stewart, Hollis is often dismissed as a buffoon – and indeed many an episode places him firmly in the slapstick role. But as viewers we also get to see moments when his fussy attention to detail or compassionate treatment of victims yields results other officers fail to achieve. As Police Federation rep, he's both an asset and a right pain as he provides helpful advice to his fellow officers on the one hand, but also resorts to careless gossip and rumouring on the other.

The incredibly popular Frank Burnside, played by Christopher Ellison, was introduced in three episodes of the first series (although back then he was known as 'Tommy' Burnside). Burnside returned in 1988 as a detective inspector, stepping into the shoes of DI Galloway, and became a permanent fixture until 1993. A clear descendent of *The Sweeney*'s Jack Regan, Burnside was brash and not afraid to manipulate others to get results. With a savage smile that rarely reached his steel-cold eyes, he was always one to watch out for. Viewers loved him for his flippant sense of humour and believable tough-guy approach that never sat very easily with modern styles of policing. Though he and Bob Cryer locked horns on many occasions, they respected each other as possibly the last old-fashioned coppers still around. His work with the Regional Crime Squad brought back to Sun Hill in 1998 until 2000 when he left to head a special police team in the National Crime Squad.

After three series, Thames decided to turn *The Bill* into a twice-weekly half-hour serial, with production all year round, like a soap opera. The essential difference between this series and a soap was that stories never delved into the private lives of the police and no

Crime Drama/Soap
Thames for ITV
Episode Duration: 50/30/90 mins
Broadcast: 16 Aug 1983, 16 Oct 1984–present

Regular Cast

Various, including:
John Salthouse · *DI Roy Galloway*
Eric Richard · *Sergeant Bob Cryer*
Mark Wingett · *PC/DC Jim Carver*
Colin Blumenau · *PC Francis 'Taffy' Edwards*
Trudie Goodwin · *WPC/Sergeant June Ackland*
Gary Olsen · *PC Dave Litten*
Roger Leach · *Sergeant Tom Penny*
Peter Ellis · *Chief Superintendent Charles Brownlow*
Nula Conwell · *WPC/WDC Viv Martella*
Jeff Stewart · *PC Reg Hollis*
Robert Hudson · *PC Tony 'Yorkie' Smith*
Ashley Gunstock · *PC Robin Frank*
Larry Dann · *Sergeant Alec Peters*
Jon Iles · *DC Mike Dashwood*
Tony Scannell · *DS Ted Roach*
Ralph Brown · *PC Pete Muswell*
Ronnie Cush · *PC Abe Lyttleton*
Chris Walker · *PC Nick Shaw*
Simon Slater · *Inspector Brian Kite*
Mark Powley · *PC Ken Melvin*
Sonesh Sira · *PC Danesh Patel*
Graham Cole · *PC Tony Stamp*
Barbara Thorn · *Inspector Christine Frazer*
Eamonn Walker · *PC Malcolm Haynes*
Ben Roberts · *Chief Inspector/Acting Superintendent Derek Conway*
Nick Reding · *PC Pete Ramsey*
Christopher Ellison · *DI/DCI Frank Burnside*
Kelly Lawrence · *WPC Claire Brind*
Kevin Lloyd · *DC Alfred 'Tosh' Lines*
Andrew Mackintosh · *DS Alistair Greig*
Vikki Gee Dare · *WPC Suzanne Ford*
Huw Higginson · *PC George Garfield*
Lynne Miller · *WPC Cathy Marshall*
Mark Haddigan · *PC Timothy Able*
Chris Humphreys · *PC Richard Turnham*
Seeta Indrani · *WPC Norika Datta*
Andrew Paul · *PC Dave Quinnan*
Colin Alldridge · *PC Phil Young*
Colin Tarrant · *Inspector Andrew Monroe*
Jonathan Dow · *PC Barry Stringer*
Clive Wood · *DCI Gordon Wray*
Tom Butcher · *PC Steve Loxton*
Nick Stringer · *PC Ron Smollett*
Natasha Williams · *WPC Delia French*
Roland Oliver · *Sergeant Joseph Corrie*
Carolyn Pickles · *DCI Kim Reid*
Sam Miller · *Sergeant John Maitland*

TRIVIA

There have been three spin-off series of *The Bill* so far. Frank Burnside bagged his own show in 2000, while 2001's *Beech is Back* took a side step from the main show to follow the activities of bent copper Don Beech. Finally, on 3 May 2003, the heavily ***CSI***-influenced *MIT: Murder Investigation Team* began with an investigation into the unexpected murder of Sergeant Matt Boyden, which viewers had witnessed earlier that week in *The Bill*. It starred former *EastEnder* Lindsey Coulson as DC Rosie MacManus.

scenes took place without an officer present, to maintain the idea that viewers would only see cases from the point of view of the investigating officers. As before, each episode dealt with just one or two cases that were invariably wrapped up by the closing credits, though one exception to this was the ongoing Canley Fields investigation into a series of child murders, an investigation that spanned two months. The case was eventually cracked by relative newcomer PC Dave Quinnan and arresting officer Sergeant Penny. In 1993, *The Bill* followed ***Emmerdale*** and ***Coronation Street*** by adding a third episode to its production schedule, a decision that for many fans felt like overkill. In 1998, with concerns over ratings, producers took the brave decision to drop to one or two 60-minute episodes a week, a rate they've largely stuck to ever since.

In the dangerous world of policing, we expect there to be casualties. The last of the original hour-long episodes ended on a cliffhanger as Sergeant Tom Penny was shot. Though he survived, the ongoing half-hour series occasionally came back to Penny's inability to cope with the attack – popping medication and trying to contain alcoholism – making him an abrupt and unpredictable colleague to work alongside. Penny emerged as a hero of the Canley Fields investigation, but he was finally kicked out of the force when stopped and arrested for drink-driving. Fellow sergeant Alec Peters was stabbed by a drug addict and similarly found the return to work difficult, eventually taking a desk job.

Other officers would find themselves spending time in local hospital St Hughes, but in the first decade of *The Bill* just four officers actually died: in 1989, highly unpopular officer PC Pete Ramsey was shot dead while pushing DC 'Tosh' Lines to safety; a year later, PC Ken Melvin was killed while guarding a vehicle that was fitted with a bomb; PC Phil Young committed suicide in 1991 after a period of depression, during which he had attacked fellow officer Norika Datta; and Viv Martella was shot by armed robbers in 1993. As guns become a bigger problem for officers on the streets, we might expect these statistics to rise slightly, although actually, prior to 2000, only four more officers left Sun Hill feet first: DS Jo Morgan was accidentally shot by a gang targeting June Ackland for revenge; WPC Cathy Marshall lost her footing and drowned in the Thames while on pursuit of a suspected criminal along the docklands; Eddie Santini was shot by gangsters just hours after being acquitted of manslaughter; and DS John Boulton was killed by a blow to the head by fellow CID officer Don Beech during a fight. However, 2002 alone saw ten Sun Hill regulars killed, seven as

The Bill has survived by playing with and subverting its archetypes. The ambitious wide-boy evolved into PCs Quinnan and Taviner; the scruffy detective became the Hawaiian-shirted Ken Drummond.

a result of a petrol bomb that devastated the station and one as the victim of a serial killer. It marked the start of a particularly sensationalist period for the series in which a startlingly high number of departing characters would just be killed off and almost none of the original cast would remain. By 2005, Jim Carver and June Ackland were the sole survivors from *Woodentop* – and Jim's future was looking very uncertain indeed. Such changes had the double effect of alienating many long-time viewers while simultaneously attracting new ones with its soap-opera approach.

Moving with the times, Sun Hill has shown a more optimistic view of an integrated police force than one might find credible. Racism among officers was only briefly touched upon back when PC Gary McCann joined the station and nowadays there are rarely any displays of the 'Old Boys Club' that dogs Jane Tennyson in ***Prime Suspect***. Indeed, by 2002, Sun Hill's female officers appeared to outnumber their male colleagues, with a baffling amount of airtime dedicated to the wedding of two officers rather than police work. Attitudes to homosexual officers have also relaxed, with at least one out gay character in the regular cast since the arrival of Sergeant Craig Gilmore in 2001.

It's fair to say that the concept of *The Bill* depicting a believable impression of modern policing has long been abandoned. Sun Hill officers spend much more time investigating each other ('mad' Cathy Bradford, psychotic Gabriel Kent), or their own families, than they ever did previously, as shown by a laughable number of episodes in 2004 that involved the children of either Sergeant Sheelagh Murphy or DI Sam Nixon. However, there was a time in the late 1990s when the change in viewing patterns among the British public hit *The Bill* hard. With plummeting ratings indicating that the series wouldn't survive, the shift in tone from police drama to soap, instigated by former ***Brookside*** producer Paul Marquess, was what ultimately saved it. Though ***Taggart*** began transmission a few months earlier, *The Bill*'s year-round production cycle now means it holds the record for the longest-running police drama in TV history, supplanting previous holder ***Dixon of Dock Green***. Showing brave recognition of the production strains that were suffered by the *Z Cars* cast and crew, *The Bill* team celebrated their 20th anniversary in October 2003 by performing an episode live. In March 2004, ITV revealed that it had renewed *The Bill* for enough episodes to take it up to 2010, a very public display of confidence in the show.

Tony O'Callaghan · *Sergeant/Acting Inspector Matt Boyden*
Louise Harrison · *WPC Donna Harris*
Simon Rouse · *DCI Jack Meadows*
Tom Cotcher · *DC Alan Woods*
Lisa Geoghan · *PC Polly Page*
Clive Wedderburn · *PC Gary McCann*
Philip Whitchurch · *Chief Inspector Philip Cato*
Liz Crowther · *Sergeant Jane Kendall*
Stephen Beckett · *PC Mike Jarvis*
Kerry Peers · *WPC/WDC Suzi Croft*
Mary Jo Randle · *WDC/WDS Jo Morgan*
Martin Marquez · *DS Danny Pearce*
Robert Perkins · *Sergeant Ray Steele*
Gary Whelan · *DI Harry Haines*
Jaye Griffiths · *DI Sally Johnson*
Iain Fletcher · *DC Rod Skase*
Carl Brincat · *PC Adam Bostock*
Shaun Scott · *DS/DI Chris Deakin*
Billy Murray · *DS Don Beech*
Alan Westaway · *PC Nick Slater*
Andrea Mason · *WPC Debbie Keane*
Mark Spalding · *Chief Inspector Paul Stritch*
Russell Boulter · *DS John Boulton*
Ray Ashcroft · *DS/Acting DI Geoff Daly*
Libby Davison · *DC Liz Rawton*
Lolita Chakrabarti · *WPC Jamila Blake*
Gregory Donaldson · *DC Tom Proctor*
Scott Neal · *PC Luke Ashton*
Matthew Crompton · *PC Sam Harker*
Michael Higgs · *PC Eddie Santini*
Samantha Robson · *PC Vicky Hagen*
Joy Brook · *DC Kerry Holmes*

It's fair to say that the concept of *The Bill* depicting a believable impression of modern policing has long been abandoned. Sun Hill officers spend much more time investigating each other or their own families, than they ever did previously.

George Rossi · *DC Duncan Lennox*
Jane Wall · *PC Di Worrell*
Karl Collins · *DC Danny Glaze*
Suzanne Maddock · *PC Cass Rickman*
Alex Walkinshaw · *PC/Sergeant Dale 'Smithy' Smith*
Clara Salaman · *DS Claire Stanton*
René Zagger · *PC Nick Klein*
Chris Simmons · *DC Mickey Webb*
Ben Peyton · *PC Ben Hayward*
Holly Davidson · *PC Roz Clarke*
Steven Hartley · *Superintendent Tom Chandler*
Ged Simmons · *DI Alex Cullen*
Raji James · *DS Vik Singh*
Natalie Roles · *DS Debbie McAllister*
Tania Emery · *DC Kate Spears*
Gary Grant · *DC Paul Riley*
Hywel Simons · *Sergeant Craig Gilmore*
Paul Usher · *PC Des Taviner*
Connie Hyde · *PC Cathy Bradford*
Diane Parish · *DC Eva Sharpe*
Ciaran Griffiths · *PC/Acting DC Gary Best*
Russell Floyd · *DC Ken Drummond*
Roberta Taylor · *Inspector Gina Gold*
Pal Aron · *DC Brandon Kane*
Beth Cordingly · *PC Kerry Young/Ashton*
Scott Maslen · *DS Phil Hunter*
Moya Brady · *Roberta 'Robbie' Cryer*
Lisa Maxwell · *DS Samantha Nixon*
Jane Danson · *PC Gemma Osbourne*
Cyril Nri · *Superintendent Adam Okaro*
Nicola Alexis · *PC Ruby Buxton*
Daniel MacPherson · *PC Cameron Tait*
Bernie Nolan · *Sergeant Sheelagh Murphy*
Kim Tiddy · *PC Honey Harman*
Rae Baker · *DC Juliet Becker*
Thusitha Jayasundera · *DC/DS Ramani De Costa*
Todd Carty · *PC Gabriel Kent*
Luke Hamill · *Dean McVerry*
Brian Bovell · *DC Rob Thatcher*
Michele Austin · *PC/Acting Sergeant Yvonne Hemmingway*
Vickie Gates · *Marilyn Chambers*
Bruce Byron · *DC Terry Perkins*
Andrew Lancel · *DI Neil Manson*
Natalie J. Robb · *PC Andrea Dunbar*
Ofo Uhiara · *PC Lance Powell*
James Lloyd · *PC Steve Hunter*
Wendy Kweh · *DC Suzie Sim*
John Bowler · *PC Roger Valentine*
Myfanwy Waring · *PC Amber Johannsen*
Seema Bowri · *PC Leela Kapoor*
Sally Rogers · *DC Jo Masters*
Tim Steed · *PCSO Colin Fairfax*
Chris Jarvis · *PC Dan Casper*

Creator Geoff McQueen

Producers Richard Bramall, Pippa Brill, Michael Chapman, Chris Clough, Tom Cotter, Peter Cregeen, Mike Dormer, Brenda Ennis, Michael Ferguson, Richard Handford, Tim Key, Caroline Levy, Lachlan MacKinnon, Paul Marquess, Susan Mather, Geraint Morris, Jamie Nuttgens, Chris Parr, Claire Phillips, Pat Sandys, Lloyd Shirley, Michael Simpson, Lis Steele, Baz Taylor, Tony Virgo, Donna Wiffen, Peter Wolfes, Rachel Wright

Writers Various, including Geoff McQueen, Barry Appleton, Andy Armitage, Chris Boucher, Edward Canfor-Dumas, Brendan J. Cassin, Stephen Churchett, Kevin Clarke, Neil Clarke, Jaden Clark, Cris Cole, Len Collin, Shirley Cooklin, Ben Cooper, Barbara Coy, Graeme Curry, Clive Dawson, Eric Deacon, Candy Denman, Harry Duffin, Pat Dunlop, Arthur Ellis, Gregory Evans, Peter Gibbs, Mark Greig, Steve Griffiths, David Halliwell, P. J. Hammond, Patrick Harkins, Terry Hodgkinson, Mark Holloway, Gerry Huxham, Julian Jones, Chris Jury, John Kershaw, Roger Leach, Russell Lewis, Matthew Leys, Garry Lyons, Joanne Maguire, Stephen McAteer, Simon McCleave, Nicholas McInnery, Neil McKay, Arthur McKenzie, Chris McWaters, Robin Mukherjee, Tony Mulholland, Christopher Penfold, Kieran Prendiville, Jonathan Rich, Jake Riddell, Christopher Russell, Kevin Scouler, Simon Sharkey, Martyn Wade, Don Webb, J. C. Wilsher, Matthew Wingett, Kate Wood

Theme Music 'Overdrive' by Charlie Morgan and Andy Pask. For the first three series of hour-long episodes, the theme music consisted of a bass line and percussion that evoked the rhythm of the police officers walking their beat. From the beginning of the half-hour series onwards, an additional treble line was added, originally a rock guitar riff that was later replaced by a brass section. The original closing titles showed the feet of two officers, one male pair, one female, slowly walking away from the cameras. This motif was dropped in 1988, partly due to changes in the way the ITV network handled end credits sequences. As of 2005, the end credits roll across a preview of the next episode.

Steven E. de Souza, Bruce Lansbury, Michael Sloan, Brock Choy, Norman Morrill **Theme Music** Jerry Fielding

A 1975 episode of ***The Six Million Dollar Man*** introduced us to Steve Austin's fiancée, a tennis player by the name of Jaime Sommers. When she is critically injured in a parachute jump (tragically mirroring/copying Steve's own horrific accident), Steve begs Oscar Goldman to sanction bionic implants to save her life. Along with a bionic arm and legs, Jaime is fitted with a bionic ear, but sadly her body rejects the implants and she dies.

What bionics couldn't save, the needs of a network could. Realising the potential for Jaime, she was swiftly resurrected for further appearances in *The Six Million Dollar Man* prior to being awarded her own series, *The Bionic Woman*, which began transmission soon after. Rather than dying, Jaime had been resuscitated using new cryogenic technology. A brain clot was also removed that unfortunately left her without any memories prior to the accident. She begins a new life as a schoolteacher, occasionally working as an agent for Oscar Goldman's organisation, the Office of Scientific Intelligence.

Two successful seasons on the ABC network ended with the show jumping over to NBC for its final year. As a consequence, Richard Anderson (as Oscar Goldman, who also starred alongside Lee Majors in *The Six Million Dollar Man*) became the first actor to play the same lead character on two different shows on different networks at the same time. Like *The Six Million Dollar Man*, *The Bionic Woman* began fairly straight-faced but ended with rather fantastical storylines involving aliens (the effect of *Star Wars* taking hold of every show with even the most tenuous science fiction credentials at this time). Jaime Sommers even found herself with a bionic dog called Max(imillion).

The adventures of both Steve Austin and Jaime Sommers came to an end in spring 1978 with ratings taking a bit of a dive. In the 1980s, the two series were merged into one for three TV movies that ended in 1994 with the marriage of Steve and Jaime, destined to live 'Bionic Ever After'.

Trivia

Predictably, Lyndsay Wagner found herself immortalised as a Jaime Sommers doll, part of one of the hottest toy ranges of the late 1970s. See the entry on ***The Six Million Dollar Man*** for the details.

Bird of Prey

Drama | BBC One | episode duration 50 mins | broadcast: 22 Apr 1982–27 Sep 1984

Regular Cast

Richard Griffiths · *Henry Armstrong Jay*
Carole Nimmons · *Anne Jay*
Nigel Davenport · *Charles Bridgnorth*
Jeremy Child · *Tony Hendersly*
Richard Ireson · *DS Vine*
Trevor Martin · *Chambers*
Roger Sloman · *Harry Tomkins*
Guido Adorni · *Mario*
Eddie Mineo · *Dino*
Ann Pennington · *Rochelle Halliday*
Christopher Logue · *Hugo Jardine*
Jim Broadbent · *DS Stanley Richardson*
Nicolas Chagrin · *Louis Vacheron*
Sally Faulkner · *Hannah Brent*
Richard Ireson · *Eric Vine*
Alexander John · *Potter*
Trevor Martin · *Trevor Chambers*
Mandy Rice-Davies · *Julia Falconer*
Hugh Fraser · *Kellner*
Lee Montague · *Roche*
Bob Peck · *Malcolm Greggory, MP*
Joan Blackham · *Kaye Grggory*
Jan Holden · *Mrs Lucas*
Timothy Bateson · *Mr Jorry*
Ronald Curram · *Mr Adrian*
Terence Rigby · *Duggan*
Heather Tobias · *Halston*
Michael Cashman · *Reeves*

Creator/Writer Ron Hutchinson **Producers** Michael Wearing, Bernard Krichefski **Theme Music** Fans of electropop will love David Greenslade's synthesised intro and incidental music, which at the time would have evoked German band Kraftwerk, though nowadays is more reminiscent of a rather clunky polyphonic ringtone.

Civil servants are rarely called upon to be heroes, and Henry Jay is the least likely hero of them all. But a report that he's compiled on security systems threatens to expose high-level corruption that extends to the British government and triggers alarm in certain quarters, including a sinister organisation called 'Le Pouvoir'. Soon Henry is forced to go on the run, leaving a trail of death and destruction in his wake as agents of Le Pouvoir try to catch him and destroy him and his files.

Providing the first real leading role for Richard Griffiths (who later starred in *Pie in the Sky* and played the horrible Uncle Vernon in the *Harry Potter* films), *Bird of Prey* is as much renowned for its intricate conspiracy plots as its opening titles, computer game simulations depicting crudely drawn assassins in bowler hats (for series one) and a bowler-wearing pig being chased through a maze by a wolf (series two). '*Bird of Prey* has dragged the thriller into the age of microtechnology,' wrote the *Radio Times*, and while the sight of Amstrads and BBC Micro graphics might appear comical to viewers used to broadband, MP3s and internet banking, there are some terrifyingly perceptive elements of 1980s technology that are still of concern today. At one point, for instance, Henry tells his wife about how the banks are encouraging people to rely more on plastic than real cash, as each credit card transaction creates data that can be tracked, something

he believes has worrying consequences for issues like data protection . . .

The first series concluded with Henry creating a 'Trojan horse' within the Civil Service mainframe that requires him to input a password on the 15th of every month. If he misses the deadline, copies of his file will be distributed to every governmental computer in the country – thereby ensuring his survival. By the start of the second series, though, Henry's code is about to be cracked and his life is in danger once again. As before, the body count is quite impressive (a pre-***EastEnders*** Michael Cashman is killed off rather gruesomely in the climax to the first episode), while each of the remaining episodes concludes with another round of assassination that serves only to draw the net in tighter around Henry and his wife Anne. Sadly, the final episode fumbles slightly with a confusing mix of flashbacks and slightly too economical editing that doesn't really supply the emotional release we probably deserve after eight episodes of Henry being rather reserved and unimposing in the face of world-shattering events. No wonder his wife takes to drink.

Birds of a Feather

Sitcom | Alomo Productions/SelecTV for BBC One | episode duration 30/50 mins, plus 1 × 60 mins, plus 1 × 75 min special | broadcast 16 Oct 1989–24 Dec 1994, 26 May 1997–24 Dec 1998

Regular Cast

Pauline Quirke · *Sharon Theodopolopoudos*
Linda Robson · *Tracey Stubbs*
Lesley Joseph · *Dorien Green*
David Cardy, Peter Polycarpou · *Chris Theodopolopoudos*
Alun Lewis, Douglas McFerran · *Darryl Stubbs*
Simon Nash, Matthew Savage · *Garth Stubbs*
Nickolas Grace, Stephen Greif · *Marcus Green*

Creators Laurence Marks, Maurice Gran **Producers** Claire Hinson, Allan McKeown, Michael Pilsworth (executive), Laurence Marks, Maurice Gran, Esta Charkham, Tony Charles, Charlie Hanson, Candida Julian-Jones, Nic Phillips **Writers** Laurence Marks, Maurice Gran, Geoff Deane, Sue Teddern, Peter Tilbury, Miles Tredinnick **Theme Music** 'What'll I Do' by Irving Berlin, sung by Pauline Quirke and Linda Robson

Few British sitcoms have lasted as long or been as hugely popular with the public as *Birds of a Feather*, which over the course of nine seasons notched up an impressive 101 episodes. Real-life long-term friends Pauline Quirke and Linda Robson played sisters Sharon and Tracey. Initially, both sisters had very different lifestyles – Sharon living in squalor in a high-rise flat, Tracey living the good life in a posh mansion in Chigwell, Essex. At the start of the series, the girls are shocked to discover that their husbands, Chris and Darryl, have been caught red-handed by the police in the process of committing an armed robbery. With their husbands sent to prison, Sharon decides to leave her flat and move in with Tracey and son Garth. The other main character in the series (and, to be honest, the main reason why most people watched) was Tracey's next-door neighbour, middle-aged man-eater Dorien Green. Played with more than a touch of over-the-top camp relish by the inimitable Lesley Joseph, Dorien's outrageous antics never failed to amuse – in one particularly memorable incident, her karaoke performance of Madonna's 'Like A Virgin' imprinting itself indelibly upon the mind of everyone who saw it.

Created by Laurence Marks and Maurice Gran – the writing partners behind such massive hits as ***Shine on Harvey Moon***, *Holding the Fort*, ***The New Statesman*** and ***Goodnight Sweetheart*** – scripts for *Birds of a Feather* played to the strengths of the three main actors. Initially dealing with the problems facing the two sisters now they were on their own, the stories gradually shifted to affairs of the heart, concerns over Tracey's son Garth, and, of course, Dorien's adulterous antics. A three-year break after the broadcast of the sixth series looked as though it spelt the end of the *Birds*. However, the show returned in 1997 with some major changes to the format. Chris and Darryl were released from prison and returned home – a happy reunion for Tracey, less so for Sharon. Predictably, though, the boys soon committed another crime and were put back inside again. Rapidly running out of money, the sisters were forced to sell the expensive house in Chigwell and buy a much more modest home. Similarly shocked was Dorien, who discovered to her horror that she wasn't the only one in her marriage to be unfaithful. The series finally drew to a close on Christmas Eve 1998, with Sharon festively giving birth in a stable in Ireland.

Like many British sitcoms, the format for *Birds* was sold to the US. Comedienne and chat-show host Rosie O'Donnell and former child star of ***Little House on the Prairie*** Melissa Gilbert played sisters Lorraine and Rochelle in the Fox network's *Stand by your Man*. Like most attempts to rework a British comedy series for the American market, it was quickly cancelled – in this case, after just eight episodes. Having previously worked together on various kids programmes such as *You Must Be Joking!* and *Pauline's Quirkes* and, of course, on Marks and Gran's previous hit *Shine on Harvey Moon*, Robson and Quirke maintained their professional relationship post-*Birds* by appearing in *Jobs for the Girls* (BBC One, 1995, five episodes), a factual series in which they were trained by experts to perform difficult jobs such as opera singer and Crufts dog trainer.

A Bit of Fry and Laurie

Comedy | BBC One/Two | episode duration 30–35 mins | broadcast 26 Dec 1986, 13 Jan 1989–2 April 1995

Main Cast

Stephen Fry, Hugh Laurie

Producers Roger Ordish, Jon Plowman, Kevin Bishop **Writers** Stephen Fry, Hugh Laurie **Theme Music** Simon Brint, Philip Pope and Hugh Laurie

Cambridge University alumni Stephen Fry and Hugh Laurie first met in the early 1980s while they were studying at that most renowned of higher education institutions. Brought together by mutual friend Emma Thompson, the pair soon discovered that they shared a similar sense of humour and rapidly found themselves making a name for themselves when guesting in programmes as diverse as ***The Young Ones*** and ***Saturday Live***. Fry and Laurie's uniquely witty and intellectual humour led to a one-off BBC One Christmas special in 1986. However, despite the show being a big success, it took three years for the ongoing sketch show to re-appear, this time on BBC Two, where the boys produced 25 episodes of higher-than-usual-brow sketch comedy over the course of four seasons.

At the same time as they were tickling the nation's funny-bones on the BBC, Fry and Laurie tried their hands at the tricky genre of the comedy-drama on ITV, starring in the marvellous ***Jeeves and Wooster***. The unfortunate upshot of their success was that both men were soon so in demand from other programmes, movies and later even American TV shows that their on-screen partnership sadly seems to be a thing of the past. Thankfully, Stephen and Hugh remain the closest of friends (despite Hugh's semi-permanent residency in the USA), so perhaps a future reunion isn't completely off the cards.

The Black Adder

Sitcom | BBC/Seven Network Australia for BBC One | episode duration 30–35 mins | broadcast 15 Jun–20 Jul 1983

Principal Cast
Rowan Atkinson · *Edmund the Duke of Edinburgh*
Brian Blessed · *King Richard IV*
Elspet Gray · *The Queen*
Tony Robinson · *Baldrick*
Tim McInnerny · *Percy*
Robert East · *Harry the Prince of Wales*
Peter Cook · *Richard III*
Peter Benson · *Henry VII*
David Nunn · *Messenger*
Alex Norton · *McAngus the Duke of Argyll*
Miriam Margolyes · *Princess Maria of Spain*
Jim Broadbent · *Don Speekingleesh the Interpreter*
Frank Finlay · *The Witchsmeller*
Valentine Dyall · *Lord Angus*
Stephen Frost, Mark Arden · *Guards*
Rik Mayall · *Mad Gerald*
Patrick Malahide · *Guy de Glastonbury*
Patrick Allen · *The Hawk*

Creators John Lloyd and Rowan Atkinson **Producer** John Lloyd **Writers** Richard Curtis, Rowan Atkinson with additional material by William Shakespeare **Theme Music** Howard Goodall

For commentary, see THE BLACKADDER SERIES, *pages 110–16*

The Black and White Minstrel Show

Musical Variety | BBC TV | episode duration 50 mins | broadcast 14 Jun 1958–21 Jul 1978

Regular Cast
George Mitchell · *Conductor*
Dai Francis, John Boulter, Tony Mercer, Peter Kaye, Andy Cole, Benny Garcia, Les Rawlings, Ted Darling, Bob Hunter, Karl Scott, Les Want, Edward Darling, Peter Benfield, Stephen Clark, Chris Connah, Alan Forrester, Frank Lee White, Frank McFadden, Peter Mitchley, Steve Reed, Peter Sutherland, Rob Wimbow · *The Mitchell Minstrels*
Margo Henderson, Penny Nicholls, Sheila Bernette, Margaret Savage, Elspeth Hands, Jane Marlow, Dorothy Ogden, Penny Jewkes, Kay Matthews, Delia Wicks, Gaye Collins, Dorothy Barsham, Margaret Haworth, Sandy Lawrence, Gayna Martine, Julie Morgan · *The Television Toppers*
Leslie Crowther, George Chisholm's Jazzers, Stan Stennett, Valerie Brooks, the Monarchs, Eric Morecambe and Ernie Wise, Peter Glaze, Don Maclean, Lenny Henry, Pam Ayres, Keith Harris, the Don Lusher Quartet, the Clem Vickery Vellum Stompers, the Grumbleweeds · *Hosts/Guest Entertainers*

Creator George Inns **Producers** George Inns, Ernest Maxin, Brian Whitehouse

When we come across a programme that was clearly motivated by a desire to entertain and that starred performers of undeniable talent, we naturally want to slip into evangelical mode and preach to the unconverted. But there's a significant barrier to this approach when we reach a show that at one time was one of Britain's favourites but which is now a dirty word.

During World War Two, a former accountant called George Mitchell put together a choir known as the Swing Group, made up of soldiers and ATS girls. After the war, BBC radio producer Charles Chilton hired Mitchell's choir, by now known as the Mitchell Singers, to feature on two programmes, *Cabin in the Cotton* and *Gentlemen Be Seated*, focusing on American Gospel and 'Negro' music. For this, Chilton and Mitchell researched the history of the minstrel of the 19th century and assembled a songbook of 'Negro' tunes for the latter's ensemble of eight men and eight women to perform.

By the mid-1950s, the Mitchell Singers were appearing on television on shows like *The Festival of British Popular Songs* and *The George Mitchell Glee Club*, in which the performers wore everyday clothes or dressed up as sailors or policemen, in effect transferring the kinds of song-and-dance routines Gene Kelly was making in American movies to a British setting. It was a producer for BBC television called George Inns who came up with the idea of bringing the minstrels to television and realised that the Mitchell Singers would be the perfect vehicle. After a number of TV specials (beginning with *The 1957 Television Minstrels*, broadcast on 2 September 1957), the Mitchell Singers were given their own series. With immaculate harmonies and intricate, energetic choreography, *The Black and White Minstrel Show* quickly became a big hit with the British public, who had never seen anything like it before. By the early 1960s, George Mitchell *Minstrel* albums filled three of the top five places in the British album charts.

Of course, in the 1950s Britain was nowhere near as multi-cultural as it is today and was, in many respects, what we'd now identify as racist. To the average white Briton, the influx of Afro-Caribbean immigrants in the 1950s was something new but not thought to be anything permanent, while no connection was made between the genuine black faces involved in the Notting Hill riots of 1958 and the blacked-up ones that appeared on Saturday night TV. Even the white British viewers who did make the connection to the slave minstrels of the American Deep South regarded the show as non-political light entertainment as inoffensive as Civil War reconstructions. Few had any idea that many of the most successful minstrels were in fact white men who had effectively stolen their music and stage acts from Mississippi black performers. What *The Black and White Minstrel Show* represented – for the vast majority of viewers for most of its 20-year run – was old-fashioned variety; songs parents might remember being sung by Al Jolson. We might be tempted to think that the blindness to racism inherent in the format was limited to insular Britain, but that's not exactly supported by the fact that the first ever International Television Contest in 1961 awarded the series the Golden Rose of Montreux.

The Minstrels were not without their critics, however. As early as 1963, ***That Was The Week That Was*** satirised the show's political naïvety – motivated by recent news of racial violence in America's Deep South – with its own minstrel song about 'them uppity niggers'. On 18 May 1967, the Campaign Against Racial Discrimination petitioned the BBC to ban the series, but their complaints were dismissed as being over-sensitive (a letter from the assistant to the BBC director general advised the protesters 'in your own best interests, for Heaven's sake shut up'). In November 1968, American soul singer Diana Ross refused to rehearse for the Royal Variety Performance unless the Minstrels were removed from the hall.

On 3 December 1967, the show was broadcast in colour. The following year, Charles Chilton came up with a TV special designed to address some of the criticism aimed at the show. *Masquerade* presented George Mitchell's singers without their make-up (but with Zorro-like eye masks) and performing Latin-American carnival songs. The special attracted only a fraction of the viewers, however. Still, the regular shows continued with the Minstrels singing their usual songs – 'Yankee Doodle Dandee', 'Dem Golden Slippers' and 'Camptown Races' – alongside those of Cole Porter, Irving Berlin and Noël Coward. Trying to avoid constantly causing offence, the singers even branched out a little, crooning Mexican ballads and songs about 'Red Indians' . . .

In 1975, in yet another concession to the pressure to use genuine Afro-Caribbean performers, the 17-year-old winner of ITV's talent show ***New Faces***, Lenny Henry, made an appearance. Aware of the controversy surrounding the show, Henry also realised that he was yet to reach the enviable position where he could do much about it. Still, he was one of the only genuine black participants on the programme – not that others didn't try their best to get through the auditions. Other surprising appearances over the years include such performers as Morecambe and Wise, Leslie Crowther (simultaneously starring on the children's show ***Crackerjack***), Keith Harris and his menagerie (Orville the Duck and Cuddles the sniffing monkey) . . . and Pam Ayres, the nation's favourite winsome poet.

While it was easy to defend the programme when it was getting ratings of 14 million viewers, by the end of the 1970s *The Black and White Minstrel Show* was attracting less than half that. In 1978, BBC One controller Bill Cotton decided the show had outlived its usefulness and decided not to renew it for another series. Unfortunately, no-one thought to tell the Minstrels themselves. When the BBC celebrated its 50th birthday in 1986, *The Black and White Minstrel Show* was notable by its absence. Called to defend the decision on the BBC's daytime discussion programme *Open Air*, Bill Cotton was unrepentant, despite the protests from Dai Francis, one of the original Minstrels, and a viewer who couldn't see what all the fuss was about.

Only 80 or so episodes remain in the archives, which considering the unlikelihood of a whole episode ever being repeated or released on DVD, is possibly a blessing in disguise. But it's also important not to forget that for over 30 years on TV and radio, the Minstrels were an important – and popular – part of British broadcasting.

Trivia

Controversial American director Spike Lee's film *Bamboozled* (2000) starred Damon Wayans as Pierre Delacroix, a black TV producer who decides to revive the minstrels of old in a bid to shock his superiors, but instead creates a smash hit.

Black Books

Sitcom | Assembly Productions for Channel 4 | episode duration 30 mins | broadcast 29 Sep 2000–15 Apr 2004

Regular Cast

Dylan Moran · *Bernard Black*
Bill Bailey · *Manny Bianco*
Tamsin Greig · *Fran*

Creators Dylan Moran, Graham Linehan **Producers** William Burdett-Coutts (executive), Julian Meers, Nira Park **Writers** Dylan

Moran, Graham Linehan, Kevin Cecil, Andy Riley, Arthur Mathews **Theme Music** Jonathan Whitehead

Bernard Black would be the perfect owner of a second-hand book shop if it weren't for a few minor details: his rampant alcoholism, his complete lack of interest in making any kind of profit from his business, the foul way in which he behaves towards his customers and his employee Manny, and of course his utter hatred of books. Instead, Bernard's far happier opening yet another bottle of plonk with his friend Fran, the up-tight, slightly neurotic woman who runs the trinket shop next door. Manny joins them after accidentally ingesting a copy of *The Little Book of Calm* and discovering a laid-back side to himself and a love for literature. They're attributes that come in handy when he's left to look after Bernard's accounts and run the shop while its owner is incapacitated once again. The arrangement suits all, though, and usually leads to a combination of increased profit for Bernard and all kinds of extremely surreal encounters and occurrences.

Irish stand-up comedian Dylan Moran portrays Bernard Black as a sympathetic kind of monster – his behaviour is indefensible, but the audience can emphasise with his view that the world can be a terrible, terrible place and that it's much better to approach most problems after at least a couple of bottles of red wine. Moran gets quality support from Tamsin Greig, as the decidedly oddball Fran, and Bill Bailey – showing that he's a talented comic actor as well as a musical comedian. Scripts were provided by a variety of talented writers, including series star Dylan Moran and ***Father Ted*** alumni Graham Linehan and Arthur Mathews – a fact that's clearly visible in the bonkers storylines and situations that the characters often find themselves in. Three seasons of *Black Books* have so far been produced, with the first and third seasons picking up BAFTA awards for best comedy series.

Blackadder II

Sitcom | BBC/Seven Network Australia for BBC One | episode duration 30 mins | broadcast 9 Jan–20 Feb 1986

Principal Cast

Rowan Atkinson · *Lord Edmund Blackadder*
Tony Robinson · *Baldrick*
Tim McInnerny · *Lord Percy Percy*
Stephen Fry · *Lord Melchett*
Miranda Richardson · *Queen Elizabeth I*
Patsy Byrne · *Nursie*
Rik Mayall · *Lord Flashheart*
Gabrielle Glaister · *'Bob'/Kate*
Holly de Jong · *Lady Farrow*
Tom Baker · *Captain Rum*
Simon Jones · *Sir Walter Raleigh*
Miriam Margolyes · *Lady Whiteadder*
Ronald Lacey · *Bishop of Bath and Wells*
Hugh Laurie · *Prince Ludwig*

Creators John Lloyd, Rowan Atkinson **Producer** John Lloyd **Writers** Richard Curtis, Ben Elton **Theme Music** Howard Goodall, with the strangled counter-tenor vocals of the end theme provided by Jeremy Jackman. The opening titles mocked those for ***I, Claudius*** with an unruly snake slithering across a chequered floor and refusing to stay in shot.

For commentary, see THE BLACKADDER SERIES, *pages* 110–16

Blackadder the Third

Sitcom | BBC/Seven Network Australia for BBC One | episode duration 30 mins | broadcast 17 Sep–22 Oct 1987

Principal Cast

Rowan Atkinson · *Edmund Blackadder Esq.*
Tony Robinson · *Sodoff Baldrick*
Hugh Laurie · *Prince George*
Helen Atkinson-Wood · *Mrs Miggins*
Robbie Coltrane · *Dr Samuel Johnson*
Lee Cornes · *Shelley*
Steve Steen · *Byron*
Jim Sweeney · *Coleridge*
Tim McInnerny · *Lord Topper*
Nigel Planer · *Lord Smedley*
Chris Barrie · *Mr Ambassasor the Revolutionary*
Mr Hugh Paddick · *Keanrick*
Kenneth Connor · *Mossop*
Ben Elton · *Anarchist*
Miranda Richardson · *Amy Hardwood/The Shadow*
Warren Clarke · *Mr Hardwood*
Stephen Fry · *The Duke of Wellington*

Creators John Lloyd, Rowan Atkinson **Producer** John Lloyd **Writers** Richard Curtis, Ben Elton **Theme Music** Howard Goodall reworked his *Blackadder* theme into a harpsichord-style madrigal. And very nice it is too, although the opening titles it accompanied were strangely similar to those for ***Keeping Up Appearances***.

For commentary, see THE BLACKADDER SERIES, *pages* 110–16

Blackadder Goes Forth

Sitcom | BBC/Seven Network Australia for BBC One | episode duration 30 mins | broadcast 28 Sep–2 Nov 1989

Regular Cast

Rowan Atkinson · *Captain Edmund Blackadder*
Tony Robinson · *Private S. Baldrick*
Stephen Fry · *General Sir Anthony Cecil Hogmanay Melchett*
Hugh Laurie · *Lieutenant the Honourable George Colhurst St Barleigh*
Tim McInnerny · *Captain Kevin Darling*
Gabrielle Glaister · *Driver Bob Parkhurst*

Rik Mayall · *Squadron Leader Lord Flashheart*
Adrian Edmonson · *Baron von Richtoven*
Miranda Richardson · *Nurse Mary*
Geoffrey Palmer · *Field Marshall Dougie Haig*

Creators John Lloyd, Rowan Atkinson | **Producer** John Lloyd | **Writers** Richard Curtis, Ben Elton | **Theme Music** Howard Goodall; played by the Band of the 3rd Battalion of the Royal Anglian Regiment

For commentary, see THE BLACKADDER SERIES, *pages* 110–16

Blackadder's Christmas Carol

Sitcom | BBC/Seven Network Australia for BBC One | duration 50 mins | broadcast 23 Dec 1988

Cast
Rowan Atkinson · *Ebenezer Blackadder, other Blackadders*
Tony Robinson · *Baldricks*
Robbie Coltrane · *Spirit of Christmas*
Miriam Margolyes · *Queen Victoria*
Jim Broadbent · *Prince Albert*
Miranda Richardson · *Queen Elizabeth I, Asphyxia XIX*
Stephen Fry · *Lord Melchett, Lord Frondo*
Hugh Laurie · *Prince George, Lord Pigmot*
Patsy Byrne · *Nursie*
Dennis Lill · *Beadle*
Pauline Melville · *Mrs Scratchit*
Philip Pope · *Lord Nelson*
Nicola Bryant · *Millicent*
Ramsay Gilderdale · *Ralph*
David Barber, Erkan Mustafa, David Nunn · *Enormous Orphans*

Creators John Lloyd, Rowan Atkinson **Producer** John Lloyd **Writers** Richard Curtis, Ben Elton from the Christmas book by Charles Dickens **Theme Music** Howard Goodall composed a *Christmas Carol*-style, lyrical interpretation of his original tune, complete with lyrics: 'Blackadder, Blackadder, he's sickeningly good/Blackadder, Blackadder, as nice as Christmas pud.'

For commentary, see THE BLACKADDER SERIES, *pages* 110–16

The Blackadder series

See pages 110–16

The Blackness

Children's Science Fiction | Associated Rediffusion for ITV | episode duration 25 mins | broadcast 17 Jan–21 Feb 1961

Principal Cast
Kevin Stoney · *David Owens*
Rosalie Westwater · *Anne Owens*
Diarmid Cammell · *Donald Owens*
Shandra Walden · *Mary Owens*
John Sharplin · *'Patch'/Commander Eager*
Ralph Nossek · *McGhee the Hermit*
Hamish Roughead · *Jim the Coastguard*
Dervis Ward · *The Stranger/Submarine Commander*
Barry Wilsher · *Lieutenant May RN*

Creators/Writers Howard Williams, Barry Pevan **Producer** Jim Pople

The Owens family inherit a remote island off the coast of Scotland, 'but when they arrive to take up residence, someone – or something – appears to resent their presence.' So trumpeted the TV Times to introduce this now-forgotten sci-fi adventure, back in the days when TV was black and white and aliens were made of cardboard and string – which is possibly why the aliens here had the uncanny knack to block out sunlight (barely necessary in Scotland) and plunge our heroes into darkness. Simple, effective and much cheaper than paying for latex.

Of course, it was all down the young Owens children to save the day, and over the course of the six episodes, young Donald and Mary encounter severed radio connections, glowing lights, foreign submarines, piercing alien sounds and a mysterious tramp with burnt hands. By the final episode, nearly everyone they've met has turned out to be someone else, and they more than likely decide to holiday down south the following year.

Frustratingly, after such an enticing build-up, no episodes survive of this serial.

Blake's 7

See pages 117–19

Blankety Blank

Quiz Show | BBC/Grundy Productions (shown on BBC One/ITV) | episode duration 25–30 mins | broadcast 18 Jan 1979–12 Mar 1990, 26 Dec 1997–28 Dec 1999, 2001–2002

Cast
Terry Wogan · *Host (1979–83)*
Les Dawson · *Host (1984–90)*
Paul O'Grady/Lily Savage · *Host (1998–2002)*

Creator/Writer Based on the US game show, *The Match Game* **Producers** Stanley Appel, Alan Boyd, Dean Jones, Marcus Plantin **Theme Music** Ronnie Hazlehurst

Cheap, tacky and utterly brilliant, *Blankety Blank* is quiz show alchemy – nobody knows how it's done, many have tried to ape it and failed miserably. Two contestants come up with their own word missing from a sentence, hoping to match the same word with as many of the six celebrity guests as possible. Celebrity guests would be the strictly B-list variety, with a pretty young woman in the bottom left-hand seat (Lorraine Chase, Aimi MacDonald, for example), a veteran matriarch figure (Beryl Reid, Mollie Sugden) in the middle of the top row, and an anarchic comedian (Kenny Everett, Freddie Starr) in the middle of the bottom row.

As a game show, *Blankety Blank* is pretty lame, but from Ronnie Hazlehurst's insidious theme music that puts the words Blankety Blank to effortless use, to the host's gurning to the camera, you can't help but be entertained. Terry Wogan looked after the first few years, the host who was always better than the material (purely for comedic effect), with the dour Les Dawson taking over the final years of the original run. Dawson was perfectly suited, his face telling you that this was as good as it got. A revival in the late '90s had Paul O'Grady's Lily Savage character as the host, which quickly transferred to ITV for a short-lived run.

As much a comedy as it was a game show, *Blankety Blank*, with famously cheap prizes and the legendary chequebook and pen (rivaled only by the ***Crackerjack*** pen), is a much-missed relic from a golden era of television gone by. Surely there's a place somewhere in the TV schedules for another presenter's long wand-shaped microphone to be cruelly abused by a celebrity guest?

Bless Me, Father

Sitcom | LWT | episode duration 25 mins | broadcast 24 Sep 1978–16 Aug 1981

Cast

Arthur Lowe · *Father Charles Clement Duddleswell*
Daniel Abineri · *Father Neil Boyd*
Sheila Keith · *Mother Stephen*
Gabrielle Daye · *Mrs Pring*
Derek Francis · *Bishop O'Reilly*
Patrick McAlinney · *Dr Daley*
David Ryall · *Billy Buzzle*

Creator/Writer Peter de Rosa **Producer** David Askey

A 1950s' set comedy starring Arthur Lowe as Irish priest Father Duddleswell, taking care of the parish of St Jude's. Working alongside the clumsy priest is young Father Neil Boyd, who generally ensures that Father D. keeps out of trouble – mostly. There are comedy housekeepers and nuns who Duddleswell frequently clashes with, but the humour is gentle and usually revolves around a misunderstanding at the village fete of collection box.

Occupying territory usually reserved for Derek Nimmo (***Oh Brother!*** and ***All Gas and Gaiters***), *Bless Me, Father* resided in a comfy Sunday evening slot and was made all the better by the easy presence of ***Dad's Army***'s beloved Arthur Lowe. The series was written by Peter de Rosa, who based the scripts on the novels he wrote under the pen name of Neil Boyd. Daniel Abineri, who played the fresh-faced curate, is the son of ***Survivors*** actor John Abineri.

Bless This House

Sitcom | Thames Production for ITV | episode duration 25 mins | broadcast 2 Feb 1971–22 Apr 1976

Regular Cast

Sidney James · *Sid Abbot*
Diana Coupland · *Jean Abbot*
Robin Stewart · *Mike Abbot*
Sally Geeson · *Sally Abbot*
Patsy Rowlands · *Betty*
Anthony Jackson · *Trevor*

Creators Vince Powell and Harry Driver **Producer** William G. Stewart **Writers** Vince Powell, Harry Driver, Carla Lane, Myra Taylor, Dave Freeman, Jon Watkins, Bernie Sharp, David Cumming, Derek Collyer, Adele Rose, Mike Sharland, Brian C. Cummings, Lawrie Wyman, George Evans **Theme Music** Geoff Love – yes, as in 'Geoff Love and his Orchestra', the man responsible for a hundred lift-muzak versions of pop classics

Like most fathers of a 'normal' family, Sid Abbot can sometimes find life a little bit stressful. Yes, he's got a pretty good job as a travelling salesman and a loving and supporting wife, Jean. On the other hand, his two teenage children cause him no end of worry – his son Mike is a hippy layabout, and as to what his daughter Sally gets up to . . . well, it's enough to give any father sleepless nights. Still, at least he's got his friend and neighbour Trevor to have a moan with, although Lord knows what Trevor's wife Betty has to gossip with Jean about. They're always nattering, every hour of the day – typical women!

Just as ***The Good Life*** was the BBC's definitive 1970s sitcom, so *Bless This House* became the archetypal ITV sitcom of the same period, providing a safe and cosy representation of a typical working-class family living in south London (in Putney, with Sid's favourite pub, the Horse and Hounds, sitting close to Clapham Common). As the sexual revolution of the 1960s developed into the new society of the 1970s, the entirely understandable worries and concerns felt by parents in most families were clearly reflected in the caring, if at times overbearing, father played by Sid James. Created by ***Love Thy Neighbour***'s Vince Powell and Harry Driver, *Bless This House* was much less controversial, possibly due to the fact that producer William G. Stewart (later to become famous in his own right when presenting game show *Fifteen to One*) recruited a number of other writers to bring additional perspectives to the show. Chief among them was a young woman called Carla Lane, who was simultaneously writing a show for the BBC called ***The Liver Birds***. Her writing skills added significantly to the authentic representation of typical family life in the early 1970s. Of course, it was the exceptionally strong performances by Sid James and Diana

Continued on page 120

The Blackadder series

Blackadder (The Third) and Baldrick.

Historians the world over will tell you that the single most representative and useful book on the subject of history is *1066 And All That* by W. C. Sellar and R. J. Yeatman. Published in 1930, its cover claimed to contain 'All the History you can remember . . . including 103 Good Things, 5 Bad Kings and 2 Genuine Dates'. Events were divided into 'Good Things' and 'Bad Things', kings and queens likewise, and even though most of the actual 'facts' were apocryphal or at best wildly inaccurate, it was infinitely easier to remember than the truth. One particular event apparently involved George III (who was insane) hearing the news that Americans never drank afternoon tea. Inviting them all to a compulsory tea party in Boston resulted in the Americans pouring the tea into Boston Harbour: 'and went on pouring things into Boston Harbour until they were quite Independent, thus causing the United States'. Definitely not a Good Thing. Hugely popular at the time, many people mistook the work as a parody of poorly written school essays. Indeed, when the BBC began making television (most definitely a Good Thing), they decided to adapt the book into a comedy. Broadcast on 31 January 1939, it led to the outbreak of World War Two (a Bad Thing, though it later inspired some Good Things, like ***Secret Army*** and ***Danger UXB***).

1066 And All That's loose grip on the facts found an ideal stablemate in the entire *Blackadder* series. When, in *Blackadder Goes Forth*, Baldrick is called upon to summarise the causes of the Great War and can only remember that it involved 'a bloke called Archie Duke [who] shot an ostrich 'cos he was hungry'. The first series made free with the works of William Shakespeare (notably in the first episode with liberal quotes and reworkings from *Richard III* and *Macbeth*), while the premise of Blackadder's other appearances through history played with the whole idea of history being written by the winning side. Unfortunately, it's a side he's rarely ever on.

As far as the public were concerned, the first hint of something special on the horizon came when Rowan Atkinson made an appearance on Terry Wogan's peak-time, thrice-weekly chat show and revealed that his curious pudding-bowl haircut was not in fact a

See* THE BLACK ADDER, BLACKADDER II, BLACKADDER THE THIRD, BLACKADDER GOES FORTH *and* BLACKADDER'S CHRISTMAS CAROL *for broadcast details and individual credits

bold fashion statement but the image for his new character, an ambitious forgotten figure from the past. We soon got to discover what he'd been working on. Having pretty much stolen the show from his colleagues on BBC Two's early 1980s satire ***Not the Nine O'Clock News***, Rowan Atkinson and the show's producer John Lloyd had decided to collaborate on a starring vehicle for Atkinson. Though the sitcom format would have been ideal, in the early 1980s John Cleese's ***Fawlty Towers*** stood as an intimidating monolith in the eyes of anyone hoping to avoid the ***Terry and June***-style domestic setting of traditional situation comedies. Fear of being instantly saddled with the 'not as good as *Fawlty*' label, Atkinson and Lloyd, together with writer Richard Curtis, chose to set their series in the past. Thus the character of Edmund Blackadder was born.

Their first (pilot) episode opened against the backdrop of war with Spain and the threat of Turkish invasion, some 400 vague years ago. As the king and his son Harry discuss battle strategies, the queen looks forward to the celebrations that are in preparation for her forthcoming birthday, with the responsibility of organising the entertainment falling upon the shoulders of her other son, Edmund. Aided by his two servants, the clod-headed Percy and the wily Baldrick, Edmund plots to use his mother's old love letters to the father of Scottish hero McAngus and prove that his brother is illegitimate so that he can take Harry's place as heir to the throne. Unfortunately, Edmund has miscalculated – it is he who's the bastard, not Henry.

In this nascent incarnation, Edmund was a curious hybrid of the weaselling slug of the first series and the cocky lord of the second. The king was played by John Savident, who'd later join the cast of ***Coronation Street*** as Fred Elliot, while Robert Bathurst was Edmund's brother, Henry. Most startling of all, though, was portrayal of Baldrick not by Tony Robinson but Philip Fox. Though it succeeded in convincing the powers that be to fund a full series, the pilot itself was shelved, never to be broadcast, though its story was incorporated into *The Black Adder*'s second episode, 'Born to be King'.

The first transmitted run of *The Black Adder* placed the birth of Edmund Blackadder firmly in the time of the Wars of the Roses. Dastardly Richard III (you know, the one with the hump) didn't in fact murder those two little princes in the tower – they both survived, and one of them grew up to be ever-shouty Brian Blessed (aka Richard IV). Richard has two sons – noble, intelligent, all round goody-goody Harry, and the loathsome, slimy good-for-nothing Edmund. Edmund's lack of intelligence is matched only by his cowardice, snivelling plotting and general incompetence. Luckily for Edmund, though, he has two colleagues whose stupidity and bungling make him look positively Machiavellian by comparison, Percy and Baldrick. Together, they plot to win the throne by overthrowing Richard, bumping off Harry and generally being rather horrid. Edmund decides that he needs a suitably villainous nickname to reinforce his scoundrel-like behaviour, and after briefly toying with 'the Black Vegetable', he soon adopts the moniker the Black Adder, a name to make his enemies tremble (with laughter, most likely). Astoundingly, in this first series, Baldrick does occasionally show signs of intelligence – although that's like comparing the relative intellectual capabilities of one root vegetable with another.

The Black Adder was a big risk for the BBC's comedy department. With production values on a par with a period costume drama and extensive location filming in and around Alnwick Castle in Northumberland, this was not a cheap series to make (and indeed the funding came partly from the Australian Seven Network). The disappointing ratings and lukewarm critical response led new controller of BBC One Michael Grade to make the not particularly difficult decision that it was simply too expensive to recommission. *The Black Adder* was no more. Unfortunately, it was a decision made even easier by the fact that the entire cast had been killed off in the final episode, courtesy of a gruesome piece of torture equipment and poisoned wine. Who could possibly survive that?

While natural selection would sensibly decree that each generation of Blackadders and Baldricks is killed off at a fairly young age, studies have shown that against all the odds, their bloodlines somehow survived. This unnatural perpetuation of their genes goes against all evidence shown in the first and subsequent series, however, and calls into question a horrific alternate possibility – that somehow, somewhere, Baldrick had sex with something other than a turnip. We shudder to think . . .

Having invested a great deal of time and effort in the production of *The Black Adder*, John Lloyd and Rowan Atkinson were very reluctant to let the show wither and die without having another crack at making it a success. Michael Grade was reluctant to bring the show back, considering that the first series hadn't set the ratings alight and had also been the most expensive comedy series ever made at that point in time. For *Blackadder II*, Atkinson stepped aside to allow Ben Elton to join Curtis as co-writer, the budget was slashed to the more realistic, sitcom size that it really ought to have been from the beginning and somehow the line of Blackadder was saved.

Interviewed on ***Wogan*** on the night of the transmission of the first episode of *Black Adder II*, Rowan Atkinson confirmed to viewers that the new run of shows would have more jokes in them (Ben Elton bringing forth Blackadder's fondness for protracted similes) and that Michael Grade had only agreed to bring the programme back if all of that expensive location filming was left out. In fact, *Blackadder II* had just two main sets, and was recorded almost entirely in the studio – a cost-saving exercise that forced writers Curtis and Elton into writing scripts that were less self-indulgent and much more character-focused than before.

In the England of 1560, Edmund Blackadder is a much more formidable man than his ancestor. Although he is no longer royalty, he is one of the favourites at the court of the Virgin Queen. Edmund now has a scheming brain to match his villainous goatee beard, but sadly, while the Blackadder line improves with every generation, the same cannot be said for the plankton-minded Lord Percy and Edmund's loyal servant Baldrick, whom sadly fate has chosen to *de*volve. Blackadder spends much of his time trying to curry favour with Queen Elizabeth while simultaneously trying to avoid being beheaded. Edmund's chief adversary is Lord Melchett, obsequious adviser to the queen, and another man just a click of the fingers away from execution. Indeed, the only person seemingly safe from the capricious whims of the queen is udder-fixated Nursie (real name Bernard), a woman whose grip on reality can only charitably be described as 'loose'.

Having avoided the Basil Fawlty route during the first season in making Blackadder a cretin, it's with some relief that the writers realised John Cleese didn't have the copyright on intelligent men frustrated by fate and the stupidity of those around him. This gave the series two instant bonuses – the opportunity for Blackadder to indulge in withering put-downs and fits of sudden violence (largely aimed at poor unsuspecting Baldrick), which in turn gave the audience the chance to finally empathise with the lead character. Add in the undoubted comic genius of Stephen Fry and (especially) Miranda Richardson as the fruitiest Queen Elizabeth ever seen on screen, and the fortunes of the distinctly average first year of Blackadder's reign suddenly changed. When Blackadder and the entire royal court are massacred once again – this time by the sinister German spy/impressionist Prince Ludwig – there were no doubts that they would find a way to be reborn again . . .

In *Blackadder the Third*, Edmund Blackadder is indeed reincarnated – only this time, he's no longer a prince or a nobleman but merely the butler to the Prince Regent, 'thick as a whale omelette' and the future George IV. Equally stupid, but less important, is Blackadder's under-servant, smelly-but-dim Baldrick (whom we discover has a first name – Sodoff). When he's not putting up with Prince George's bizarre behaviour and obsession with socks, Blackadder can often be found visiting Mrs Miggins' Pie Shoppe, a nearby hangout with inedible food and a strangely cheerful proprietor.

Maintaining the astonishingly high standard of *Blackadder II*, *Blackadder the Third* moves the storyline on to a Regency age familiar to fans of Jane Austen's novels – indeed, episode titles provided a parody on the style of many of Austen's books: 'Amy and Amiability', 'Sense and Senility', etc. With previous series regulars Tim McInnerny, Stephen Fry and Miranda Richardson unable to commit to a full season, the arrival of Hugh Laurie as Prince George (a descendent of Prince Ludwig the German assassin from *Blackadder II*, perhaps?) provides a more than adequate supply of total and utter stupidity that creates a perfect foil to Blackadder's machinations and plotting. Thankfully, Fry, Richardson and McInnerny returned in guest roles, with Fry's self-important Duke of Wellington clearly foreshadowing the similarly pompous General Melchett in *Blackadder Goes Forth*.

There's a more acute sense of playing with and distorting history than before (we're back to *1066 And All That*). In 'Dish and Dishonesty', Blackadder exploits the corrupt political system to take a rotten borough in an election. When Prime Minister William Pitt informs him his brother intends to stand against him, Blackadder scoffs: 'And which Pitt would this be? Pitt the Toddler? Pitt the Embryo? Pitt the Glint in the Milkman's Eye?' And England's first lexicographer, Dr Johnson, makes an appearance in 'Ink and Incapability' (despite this being a whopping historical inaccuracy – Johnson lived and died before the events of *Blackadder the Third* are supposed to have taken place), having only recently completed his magnum opus – the dictionary that contains every word in the English language – Johnson learns from the loquacious Blackadder that he might have missed a few, including 'contrafibularities', 'compunctuous', 'pericumbobulation' and 'interfrastically'. Despite the much smaller regular cast and the greater fascination with literary references than even the first series risked, *Blackadder the Third* was hugely popular with critics and public alike (winning a BAFTA for Best Comedy Series). And this time, hardly anyone survived in the last episode. Hurrah! Blackadder and Baldrick didn't expire in the last episode, though poor George was not so lucky.

On 5 February 1988, the *Blackadder* team joined their fellow funny professionals for the bi-annual ***Comic Relief*** telethon for a 15-minute sketch entitled 'Blackadder: The Cavalier Years'. It revealed that a Blackadder had been instrumental in prolonging the life, for however briefly, of King Charles I (played by Stephen Fry with a wittily accurate impersonation of our current Prince Charles). Rather predictably for a charity sketch – and despite being penned by Curtis and Elton – it wasn't a patch on pretty much everything else broadcast under the *Blackadder* banner.

Blackadder was back on form, however, with an exceptionally entertaining festive special (broadcast in between *Blackadder the Third* and *Blackadder Goes Forth*) that took the famous Dickens story of Scrooge and gave it a memorable twist. Ebenezer Blackadder is the nicest man in the whole of London, a generous soul who's so happy to be overly generous with his money and time that he has nothing left of his own. Then, one Christmas Eve, Blackadder is visited by the Spirit of Christmas, doing his 'usual round' of hauntings. Realising what an all-round good egg Blackadder is, the Spirit offers him the chance to see what some of his ancestors were like, as a bit of a cautionary tale. However, Blackadder is enthralled when he sees just how vile and bounder-esque his predecessors in the courts of Queen Elizabeth and Prince George where. He's even more exited when he gets a glimpse of 'Christmas Future', one in which his descendant conquers alien races before sweeping Queen Asphyxia XIX off her feet and marrying her, all by simply being ruthless and unpleasant. Blackadder's entire outlook on life changes and from Christmas morning he starts being utterly selfish and vile to all and sundry – including Queen Victoria and Prince Albert.

Blackadder's Christmas Carol was an ideal antidote to all of the syrupy goodwill that tends to clog up the airwaves over the festive season. It offered both a welcome return of old favourites such as Queenie and Nursie as well as a hilarious sci-fi pastiche full of over-inflated, jargon-filled dialogue. Sadly, it's not repeated very often on television. Thankfully it is available on DVD to enjoy again and again, if only to spot Roland Browning from ***Grange Hill*** as one of the enormous orphans and former ***Doctor Who*** assistant Nicola Bryant as Blackadder's intensely irritating niece, Millicent.

In 1989, the foul spawn of the Blackadder and Baldrick families resurfaced for one final series, *Blackadder Goes Forth*, causing havoc as usual among their contemporaries and more hilarity for viewers. Edmund is now a career soldier, a man who has worked his way through the ranks of the army to the position of captain, a role that enables him to put his feet up and shout at the more junior ranks. Or *enabled* him to do that – the sudden outbreak of World War One sees an indignant Blackadder stuck in the middle of the trenches with his dim batman Baldrick and an even stupider toff called George for company. Blackadder does everything he can to try and keep him and his colleagues as far away from the firing lines as he can. However, the seriously demented and bloodthirsty General Melchett seems perfectly happy to send as many soldiers as possible to an early grave.

Placing the series right in the middle of one of the bloodiest conflicts in British history was an exceptionally brave move, but one that paid off in spades. Just as ***M*A*S*H**** had shown that war and comedy aren't automatically mutually exclusive bedfellows, so *Blackadder Goes Forth* proved that the wit and slapstick present in a Curtis/Elton script is thrown into even sharper relief when contrasted against the genuine horror of trench warfare. Rowan Atkinson's world-weary delivery of the rich dialogue was a joy to behold, and it was a treat to have Tim McInnerny back as a regular character – this time as the slimy and sycophantic Captain Darling, General Melchett's assistant. In fact, *Blackadder Goes Forth* was so good that not only did it win a BAFTA award for Best Comedy Series in 1990, Rowan Atkinson also picked up a Best Light Entertainment Performance BAFTA too.

While World War Two had been a source for insightful comedy ever since Neville Chamberlain held aloft that fateful piece of paper with the claim that he had won 'peace in our time', the sheer scale of lives lost in the earlier conflict had quite understandably deterred many from extracting any humour from it. It's this particular choice of era for Blackadder to resurface in that led to the series being so well regarded. The situation in the trenches *was* ridiculously tragic, with no one sure why they were there aside from a sense of duty that somehow empowered men at the beginning of the 20th century in a way that it no longer did at its end. This Blackadder represents our own view of the war – all too aware of the sacrifices made in the name of strategy. His cynicism and nihilism came to the fore here, trapped as he was in a trench with two men still convinced there was bravery to be had from being mowed down without ever knowing why. Yet for once Edmund doesn't condemn them – he knows that they, like him, have already been condemned by the very men who sent them there in the first place. It's only in his understanding of the probable outcome that his late-20th-century attitude deserts him. All he sees are circumstances he cannot escape.

TRIVIA
Over 6.5 million people visited the Millennium Dome in its single year of operation, with a vast majority of them undoubtedly enjoying Blackadder's latest exploits. Everyone who decided not to attend the controversial attraction had to wait until 1 October 2000 to catch *Blackadder: Back And Forth* on Sky One, or until 21 April 2002 when it finally showed up on BBC One.

The final episode plays upon our own expectations. It's a trench in World War One in a series that twice before has slaughtered virtually all the characters in the final act. But it's only in that final episode that the series subtly shifts gear from being uproariously funny to heartbreakingly tragic in the blink of an eye. With mounting horror as we realise that Melchett's mad schemes are so potty that there's no way out for Edmund and his compatriots this time. Even feigning insanity won't work – as Edmund points out, who'd notice another lunatic in the middle of that war? There's a brief respite when the men suddenly begin to believe that the war could be over, and it's only when Darling details the span of the war – '1914 to 1917' – that both he and we realise their war is over, but not in the way anyone would have wanted it to be. The laughter that comes with this revelation is hollow. It's the recognition of a joke too cruel, but delivered 70 years after the event itself we can see it's completely without malice.

The final images, showing our lead characters going 'over the top' and into a hail of machine gun fire, fade to show us a field of blood-red poppies with the *Blackadder* theme played in on a solitary piano in an echoing room. That Curtis, Elton, Atkinson and the rest of the gang decided to end the series with a final two minutes that are deliberately laugh-free elevated the episode from being merely brilliant to important.

Despite rumours of a fifth series of *Blackadder* regularly doing the rounds (with the suggestion that the next run would be set in the 1950s and would feature a rock and roll band called the Blackadder Five), that was the last most of us saw of Edmund and Baldrick. In 1999, bosses at the Millennium Dome in Greenwich decided to bring Edmund and his friends back, in a one-off, 45-minute special, *Blackadder: Back and Forth*, that would initially only be screened at the attraction. The plotline involved a present-day Blackadder boasting to his dinner-party guests (Melchett, Darling, George et al.) about his new invention – a time machine. Although his invention is of course merely a 'cunning plan' to divest his guests of a considerable amount of cash, Blackadder is shocked to discover that Baldrick, of all people, has actually succeeded in building a working time machine. Together our two heroes dash back and forth throughout British history, meeting all sorts of famous characters on the way. All of the *Blackadder* repertory company were reunited in their familiar as possible roles, with extra guest appearances from supermodel Kate Moss (as Maid Marian) and Colin Firth (as Shakespeare).

The BBC's 2004 poll to determine Britain's Best Sitcom resulted in a 'first runner-up' prize for *Blackadder* (or, to put it another way, it came second). Considering the winner's trophy was engraved with caricatures of Blackadder and Del Boy from ***Only Fools and Horses***, the outcome seemed predetermined to some. But then the result was typical of *Blackadder* as a whole: to overcome obstacles galore only to fail at the final hurdle. We'd be happy to consider it a moral victory for Edmund, though; at least *Blackadder* ended leaving us wanting more . . .

Blake's 7

Third season cast members (L–R) Stephen Pacey, Michael Keating, Jacqueline Pearce, Paul Darrow, Jan Chappell, Josette Simon.

In the late 1970s, science fiction suddenly became a hugely popular genre – thanks in no small part to the release of the film *Star Wars* (1977). Little did they know it, in the months building up to *Star Wars*' arrival in cinemas, the BBC was preparing a new series that would ride the waves of this upsurge in popularity.

When BBC executives began to search for a replacement series for the soon-to-be-defunct *Softly, Softly*, they approached many different writers for suggestions. One of these writers was Terry Nation – the man who originally created the Daleks for ***Doctor Who***, and who had been responsible for writing episodes of adventure series such as *The Persuaders!*, ***Department S*** and ***The Avengers***. Nation had recently created a post-apocalyptic environmental series, ***Survivors***, for the BBC, and the time seemed right for his next project. However, at the 'pitching' meeting, Nation's ideas were all rejected by Ronnie Marsh, head of BBC Drama Series. Thinking on his feet, Nation is alleged to have come up with an idea off the top of his head for 'The Dirty Dozen in Space' – an idea quickly pounced upon by Marsh and his team.

Blake's 7 reached TV screens in January 1978, the same week that *Star Wars* opened in UK cinemas; the time was perfect for a new science fiction adventure series aimed at a slightly older audience than the still massively popular *Doctor Who*. Audiences lapped the series up, averaging at 9 million for the show's entire run – despite often being scheduled opposite ratings juggernaut ***Coronation Street***. However, despite this huge popular success, *Blake's 7* was often mocked and derided by contemporary critics for its cardboard sets and equally cardboard characters. In hindsight, such criticism seems to have some basis in fact. The budget for *Blake's 7* could never be charitably described as 'generous', leading to occasional 'special' effects that verged on the risible. Furthermore, some of the lead characters never developed much beyond ciphers, spouting deadpan dialogue in front of shocking blue-screen back-projections.

But when *Blake's 7* worked, it was marvellously entertaining drama. The series begins on the earth of the far future, where it

Science Fiction/Telefantasy
BBC One
Episode Duration: 50 mins
Broadcast: 2 Jan 1978–21 Dec 1981

Regular Cast
Gareth Thomas · *Blake*
Paul Darrow · *Avon*
Michael Keating · *Vila*
Sally Knyvette · *Jenna*
Jan Chappell · *Cally*
David Jackson · *Gan*
Peter Tuddenham · *Voice of Zen, Orac and Slave*
Jacqueline Pearce · *Servalan*
Stephen Greif, Brian Croucher · *Travis*
Josette Simon · *Dayna*
Steven Pacey · *Tarrant*
Glynis Barber · *Soolin*

Creator Terry Nation

Producers David Maloney, Vere Lorrimer

Writers Various, including Terry Nation, Chris Boucher, Robert Holmes, Allan Prior, Roger Parkes, Tanith Lee

Theme Music Dudley Simpson

seems that life exists in an organised idyll. Affairs on Earth and its colony worlds are run by the all-powerful Federation, a brutal government with a democratic veneer but a distinctly nasty underbelly that crushes any organised opposition. One man discovers the Federation's true nature when he is invited to join a resistance movement; shortly afterwards, all of the rebels are brutally gunned down by Federation troops. The man – Roj Blake – soon discovers that he used to be the leader of a resistance cell, but that the Federation caught him and erased his memory of the incident. Blake is again arrested and exiled to a prison planet on trumped-up charges of child abuse. On the journey to the prison planet Cygnus Alpha, Blake becomes reluctant friends with some of his fellow criminals – smuggler Jenna, thief Vila, dangerously violent Gan and sardonic computer expert Avon.

Soon afterwards, the prison transport ship docks with a vast alien spacecraft drifting abandoned in space. Blake and his team manage to wrest control of the ship – which they name the *Liberator* – and begin their quest to fight back against the corrupt Federation. Joining Blake's crew (and bringing the number up to seven) are alien telepath Cally and the Liberator's computer, Zen. Throughout the series, the rebels would often battle two principal agents of the Federation: the leather-clad thuggish Travis, and the elegant yet deadly Supreme Commander Servalan – the only woman in space with cocktail gowns shorter than her brutally cropped hair.

How *Blake's 7* differed from other science fiction sagas was the way in which no character was ever safe from meeting a shocking and sudden demise. Shortly after the smart-alec portable computer Orac joined the team, the burly Gan perished in an ill-fated attempt to destroy the Federation's main computer control centre. By the end of the second season, not only was Travis dead, but the whole galaxy was under attack by a race of hostile aliens, forcing the *Liberator* crew and the Federation to join forces to repel the invaders.

Behind the camera, there were major changes at the end of season two as well. Gareth Thomas declined to return for a third year to reprise his role as Blake, and Sally Knyvette also chose to depart, the characters of Blake and Jenna separating from the rest of the Seven and seemingly lost for ever. The increasingly popular character of Avon, as played by on a knife edge between camp and brutality by the inestimable Paul Darrow, was the natural successor as leader of the *Liberator*'s crew, developing a wonderful double-act with the perpetually terrified Vila. New to the crew over the final two years of *Blake's 7* were warrior Dayna, outlaw Tarrant and gunslinger Soolin (an early role for ***Dempsey and Makepeace***'s Glynis Barber).

The very best episodes of *Blake's 7* probably come in the third series, during which the battle of wits between Avon and Servalan becomes the primary focus of the show. Cast and crew were all led to believe that this third series would be the end for the show, and indeed the shock ending of the season consisted of a hologram of Blake leading the Seven into a trap and the *Liberator* being destroyed, seemingly with the evil Servalan on board. It therefore came as quite a surprise to the actors watching the episode at home to hear the

BBC continuity announcer proclaim that the series would 'be back next year' – primarily due to the huge ratings success it had enjoyed.

The series did indeed return for a fourth and final run in late 1981, but the budgetary cuts and changes to the series do show somewhat. The impressively designed *Liberator* was replaced by the shabby, run-down freighter *Scorpio*, complete with obsequious on-board computer, Slave. Plotlines became distinctly camper, relying upon science fiction clichés that had tended to be avoided in previous years.

However, the final ever episode, entitled 'Blake', was a staggeringly apocalyptic and memorable piece of TV drama. Gareth Thomas returned as Blake, scarred and world-weary, and once again trying to organise another rebellion against the corrupt Federation. Avon brings the crew of the *Scorpio* to Blake's new base, with the aim of possibly uniting their two bands of rebels. However, unbeknown to them all, Blake has been betrayed by one of his followers, and they have all walked straight into a Federation trap. In a short and brutal shoot-out, Blake and his band are all gunned down by Federation troops. By the end, only Avon is left standing, smiling grimly over the bloody corpse of his former friend and leader, surrounded on all sides by heavily armed troopers. As the end credits roll, the sound of gunfire is heard . . .

Rarely has any popular television show ever ended in such a nihilistic and downbeat way – and screening it four days before Christmas was a brave move indeed.

Urban myths claim that the suicide rate in the UK shot up following the broadcast of the final episode of *Blake's 7*, and if that is indeed true, it's hardly surprising. Rarely has any popular television show ever ended in such a nihilistic and downbeat way – and screening it four days before Christmas was a brave move indeed. Despite the fact that *Blake's 7* is perhaps unfairly remembered primarily for its dodgy effects, viewers who avidly followed the exploits of the intergalactic outlaws will always have a special place in their affections for this, a very British science fiction series.

Coupland that helped to make the scripts come alive. *Bless This House* was still performing very well in the ratings when *Carry On* icon Sid James died suddenly of a heart attack in 1976, bringing to an end (after 65 episodes) a much-loved and well-remembered series.

Blind Date

Game Show | London Weekend Television/Granada for ITV | episode duration 45 mins | broadcast 30 Nov 1985–31 May 2003

Regular Cast
Cilla Black · *Presenter*
Graham Skidmore · *Announcer*

Producers Michael Hurll (executive), Gill Stribling-Wright, Isobel Hatton, Colman Hutchinson, Chris O'Dell, Martyn Redman, Kevin Roast, Michael Longmire, Thelma McGough **Theme Music** Laurie Holloway

A long-running Saturday teatime entertainment show that tapped into and reinforced the British public's obsession with 'ordinary' people. Perennially popular host Cilla Black presented the show for 18 years, providing just the right amount of interest in the contestants who showed up for a weekly bout of innuendo, humiliation and – just possibly – the chance of romance.

Taking its inspiration from the American *Dating Game*, each week, two 'rounds' of *Blind Date* would be played, in which three contestants would do their best to impress a member of the opposite sex through the best use of *Carry On*-style double entendres, flirting and verbal dexterity. The picker would have three opportunities to ask a question to the three potential lovebirds hidden behind a screen. Once the three questions had been asked, hostess Cilla would call upon the disembodied voice of 'Our Graham' to summarise the contestants' responses and give the bewildered picker a better idea of who they should choose. Normally, the baying and cheering of the studio audience was a contributing factor in the picker's decision, with the crowd often encouraging a match with the least suitable candidate, just for the mischievous joy of watching the outcome. Once the picker had made their choice, Cilla would introduce them to 'the ones you turned down' – often a moment of sheer *schadenfreude* when the picker realised to their horror that they'd rejected the most attractive person they'd ever met in their entire life in favour of the candidate who came out with the best chat-up lines.

Eventually, picker and pickee would be united on stage as the screen was slid back, often with hilarious consequences. Cilla would then offer the 'happy couple' a number of envelopes from which to randomly choose the destination for their prize – a romantic holiday for the two of them (plus accompanying film crew – in the first few years of the show, the winners only had to put up with a photographer following their footsteps). Rumours abound, though, that there wasn't actually a random element to the holiday, and that every one of the envelopes contained the same destination. Cilla then packed the romantic couple off to enjoy their prize, on the strict understanding that they would 'come back next week and tell us all about it!' The rest of the programme would then feature the post-mortem interview of the previous week's two couples, showing video footage of their blind date before reuniting the couple in the studio to hear what they really felt about each other. For many viewers, this was their favourite part of the programme, with couples that seemed ideally suited to each other not pulling any punches as they laid into each other about each others' deficiencies.

There was a wide range of different contestants who signed up for the *Blind Date* treatment over the years. The very first contestant was Oxford University graduate Paul Fox; in later years 'golden oldies' took part to prove that love wasn't strictly the preserve of the young; and a handful of future celebrities graced the studio, including actress Amanda Holden (in 1990), CBBC presenter Ortis Deeley (in 1995) and GMTV presenter Jenni Falconer (in 1994). Things didn't always go smoothly though. In 1998, one poor contestant was left jilted at the airport when his date was so unimpressed with him that she decided not to bother. The camera crew followed him all the way to Africa where he had a great holiday on his own. Another scandal occurred when *Daily Star* reporter Nicola Gill was unmasked as a journalist by Cilla in the 'post-mortem' chat. Thankfully, the course of true love did run smooth for three couples during the course of the programme's run – Cilla had to go and buy herself a 'new 'at' for the weddings of Sue Middleton and Alex Tatham (1991), Lillian Morris and David Fenson (1994), and Anna Azonwanna and Paul Pratt (1998).

As *Blind Date* entered the 21st century, Saturday night ratings were on a distinct downward curve, and some new ideas were added to the show to try and spice it up a bit. The 'Ditch or Date' twist allowed the picker to reject their first choice and opt for another contestant (an incredibly cruel cheat of the format that not many people liked) and predictably enough, celebrities were wheeled in to take part, including C-listers such as Tara Palmer-Tomkinson and ***Big Brother*** cleanliness freak Alex Sibley. In the end, it became clear to everyone involved that *Blind Date* was becoming a little bit stale, and in an amazing move Cilla Black announced on air (during a live special) that she'd be quitting the show. It was the end of an era, and despite ITV's protestations that *Blind Date* would return with a new presenter, that was the last we saw of the show. The network tried to revive the format with a spin on the same kind of material called *Love on a Saturday Night*, presented by *Big Brother* hostess Davina McCall (having previously done similar duties on Channel 4 dating show *Street Mate*). Unfortunately, it didn't grab the viewers and, at the time of writing, Cupid's arrow seems to be conspicuous by its absence from the ITV schedules.

Blockbusters

Quiz Show | Central for ITV/BBC Two/Sky One | episode duration 25 mins | broadcast 1983–1993, 1994–5, 1997, 2000

Cast

Bob Holness, Michael Aspel, Liza Tarbuck · *Presenters*

Creator Mark Goodson **Producers** Bob Cousins, Terry Steel, Graham C. Williams, Tony Wolfe **Theme Music** Ed Welch

Are two heads better than one? That was the mission behind *Blockbusters* in which three sixth-formers, two together, one alone, would compete to answer questions and make a line of connected hexagonal tiles from one side of the games board to the other – the duo connecting blue tiles horizontally, the solo player trying to turn the tiles white via the slightly shorter vertical route. Each tile would contain a letter, which would prompt quizmaster Bob Holness to ask, for example, 'What H was a king famous for having six wives?' One of the contestants would buzz in, and if they'd correctly answered 'Henry', they'd light up the tile in their colour and win the chance to decide which tile's question they wanted to attempt. Much hilarity (although, we imagine, not for Holness) would ensue if the contestant said, 'I'd like a P, please Bob,' or occasionally 'I want U . . .'.

The player/team who won the best out of three would go on to face the Gold Run, in which the game board would be filled with tiles containing groups of initials rather than single letters, so the clue might be 'DD' and the question 'Which pop band sang songs including "Planet Earth" and "Is there Something I should Know"?' If a contestant/pair won five games in a row (later reduced to three), they'd win a big prize, like a dream holiday, but be forced to bow out of the competition.

The *Blockbusters* studio was adorned with mock marble carvings (actually polystyrene). Zeus took pride of place and others included representations of Tutankhamun, Abraham Lincoln, William Shakespeare, John Wayne, Bob Geldof and Daley Thompson. After a few seasons, the studio audience began to perform a kind of hand-jive to go along with the end theme music that eventually appeared on-screen.

Dropped by ITV in the year of its tenth anniversary, *Blockbusters* originated from an American quiz show by the same name, and has since appeared on satellite channel Sky One (first presented by Holness once more, later by Lisa Tarbuck) and on BBC Two, presented by Michael Aspel.

Trivia

Bob Holness played James Bond in radio adaptations in the 1950s, the first actor *ever* to portray the suave spy. Despite popular myth, he did *not* play the saxophone on Gerry Rafferty's song 'Baker Street' (that was Rafael Ravenscroft), though this hasn't prevented him from laughing along with the joke and at times playfully perpetuating it.

Blood Money

Drama | BBC One | episode duration 50 mins | broadcast 6 Sep–11 Oct 1981 (*Blood Money*), 12 Jan–16 Feb 1983 (*Skorpion*), 12 Sep–31 Oct 1984 (*Cold Warrior*)

Cast

Michael Denison · *Captain Aubrey Percival*
Bernard Hepton · *DCS Meadows*
Grant Ashley Warnock · *Viscount Rupert Fitzcharles*
Juliet Hammond-Hill · *Irene Kohl*
Stephen Yardley · *James Drew*
Gary Whelan · *Danny Connors*
Cavan Kendall · *Charles Vivian*
Terry Forrestal · *Gaunt*
Dean Harris · *Sergeant Danny Quirk*
Daniel Hill · *Inspector Clark*
Jack McKenzie · *DI Perry*
Anna Mottram · *Sergeant Barratt*
Terrence Hardiman · *Chief Superintendent Franks*
Mary Wimbush · *Agatha*
Tom Chadbon · *Dr Ormiston*
Ian Cullen · *Inspector Hallisay*
Lucy Fleming · *Jo*
David Swift · *Sir William Logie*
Stephen Greif · *Dr Mohammed Riffi*
Tracey Childs · *Sophy Fitzgerald*

Creator Arden Winch **Producer** Gerard Glaister **Writers** Arden Winch, John Brason, David Reid, Murray Smith **Theme Music** Simon May

Looking at the canon of work that forms the career of the late Gerard Glaister, *Blood Money* and its sequels seem at odds with him normal oeuvre. Most of Glaister's work follows the familiar routines of families (either literal or metaphorical) being put through the wringer. And more often than not, it is possible to trace the genesis of each series in a predecessor: just as ***Secret Army*** came out of ***Colditz*** and later melded into *The Fourth Arm* and ***Kessler***, or as ***The Brothers*** begat *Buccaneer*, then ***Howards' Way***, which in itself spawned *Trainer*. *Blood Money*, as a contemporary police thriller, seems the exception to the rule. At a push, it would be possible to see that Dennison's abrupt, cold Captain Percival, whose ties and origins are never truly explained, could have an antecedent in Marius Goring's John Hardy, the eponymous forensic scientist employed by everyone and anyone in Glaister's 1968 series *The Expert*.

Where *Blood Money* differs from Glaister's traditional cosy Sunday early evening fare is in its subject matter. No boardroom battles or boats, horses or aeroplanes here – this is a political caper, with a group of terrorists kidnapping a schoolboy viscount and holding him hostage. Whether they truly intend keeping him alive once they've been paid off is something no one knows – not even the kidnappers. And an unsavoury gang they are, with

Stephen Yardley as the thuggish, trigger-happy psycho, Gary Whelan as the slightly sensitive 'are we doing the right thing' wet, Cavan Kendall as the bookish media-savvy driver, and led by the Bader Meinhoff-like Juliet Hammond-Hill. And if that wasn't enough *Secret Army* co-stars to contend with, the producers chucked in Albert himself, Bernard Hepton, as the unfortunate policeman hauled in to attempt a rescue and forced to cede to Percival's less-than-scrupulous methods. The final episode brought howls of outrage from viewers as the four kidnappers were massacred in a bloodthirsty gun battle that left you wondering who the real villains were.

A year later, Denison was back as Percival in *Skorpion*. Alongside another former *Secret Army* actor, this time Terrence Hardiman, playing the policeman Chief Superintendent Franks, Percival tries to investigate corruption and gun running within the government. Less violent but a lot darker in feel, where it seemed everyone was on the side of the devils, *Skorpion* ultimately spawned an eight-part series of individual stories under the umbrella title *Cold Warrior*. Michael Denison was now joined by two assistants, the feisty Lucy Fleming and police hard man Dean Harris (who had played the same character in *Blood Money*). Parallels with John Steed and his ***New Avengers*** aside, *Cold Warrior* actually brought everything to an end rather mundanely as Percival was watered down to make him more likeable, a possible result of Arden Winch's lack of involvement.

Blott on the Landscape

Comedy Drama | BBC One | episode duration 50 mins | broadcast 6 Feb–13 Mar 1985

Regular Cast

Geraldine James · *Lady Maud Lynchwood*
George Cole · *Sir Giles Lynchwood*
David Suchet · *Blott*
Simon Cadell · *Dundridge*
Julia McKenzie · *Mrs Forthby*
Geoffrey Bayldon · *Ganglion*
John Welsh · *Lord Leakham*
Paul Brooke · *Hoskins*
Geoffrey Chater · *Minister*
Christopher Benjamin · *Chief Constable*
Jimmy Nail · *Edwards*
Brian Coburn · *Hefty*
Mary Healey · *Mrs Wynn*
Matyelok Gibbs, Sylvia Barter · *The Miss Percivals*
John Rapley · *Colonel Chapman*
Esmond Knight · *Sir Francis Puckerington*
Clare Grogan · *Hotel Receptionist*
John Junkin · *Waiter*
William Simons · *Jackson*

Producers Evgeny Gridneff, Brian Eastman **Writer** Malcolm Bradbury, from the novel by Tom Sharpe **Theme Music** Written by David Mackay, with Viv Fisher performing the human brass band sounds

Lady Maud and Sir Giles Lynchwood live is isolated splendour in their beautiful mansion deep in the English countryside. However, all is not well in their marriage – Maud desperately wants an heir to carry on the family line before she's too old, but Giles is far more interested in spending time hatching schemes in Westminster or being entertained by his tame hooker Mrs Forthby. When relations irrevocably break down, Giles is horrified when Maud threatens to kick him, penniless, out of her ancestral family home. Giles then hatches a plan – persuade his friends in government to build a bypass right through the family home, and pocket 50 per cent of the value of the compulsory purchase of the mansion. However, Maud won't hear of this, and mobilises the local community to fight back against the plans. Maud's chief lieutenant is her butler/gardener/family retainer, Blott – a foreigner with a mysterious past and an uncanny ability for mimicking other people's voices.

Based upon the best-selling novel by Tom Sharpe, *Blott on the Landscape* was a six-part romp through the soiled knicker-drawer of the minor aristocracy. A marvellous pair of character performances from Geraldine James and George Cole as the warring Lynchwoods form the core of the programme, with ***Hi-De-Hi!***'s Simon Cadell playing Dundridge, the government troubleshooter sent to make a decision on the bypass as a bewildered charisma-vacuum cast adrift on a sea of Machiavellian double-dealing and outright skulduggery. Another comedy actor totally subverting her established image was the previously prim and proper Julia McKenzie (still on people's minds from her leading role in ITV sitcom hit *Fresh Fields*), utterly traumatising a nation as the slightly-past-her-best prostitute who services George Cole with a little S&M. In fact, it's only David Suchet's bizarre Blott that doesn't quite ring true, with many lines of his dialogue completely incomprehensible thanks to an accent that deliberately darts from one end of the continent to the other.

Shot all on shiny, cheap-looking videotape, *Blott on the Landscape* sadly doesn't look as though much money was spent on it – and ideally, it could have done with losing an episode or two in order to keep the gags flowing fast and the audience transfixed. However, there are still more than a few scenes in the TV version that match the twisted brilliance of Sharpe's original novel. These include the tumultuous riot between Lady Maud's supporters and the police in a traditional English market town square (which sees the entire town centre laid to waste), and the moment when blundering Dundridge comes face to face with the king of the beasts following Lady Maud's decision to turn her house into a Longleat-style attraction. Two years later, producer Brian Eastman and writer Malcolm Bradbury reunited to film another of Tom Sharpe's novels, ***Porterhouse Blue*** – this time for Channel 4.

Blue Peter

See pages 124–7

The Blue Planet

Documentary | BBC One | episode duration 50 mins | broadcast 12 Sep–31 Oct 2001

Cast

David Attenborough · *Narrator*

Creator Alistair Fothergill **Producers** Alistair Fothergill, Andrew Byatt, Martha Holmes **Theme Music** George Fenton

Alistair Fothergill relinquished his position as head of the BBC's Natural History Unit to undertake the most extensive and daring exploration of our planet's oceans ever to be committed to camera. Eight beautifully shot films (the BAFTA-winning cinematography crew deserve a blue whale-sized back slap for their efforts) go sometimes more than a mile beneath the surface of the oceans to capture never before seen creatures in their natural habitat, alongside familiar species in often alarmingly dramatic moments.

Filmed at a cost of £7 million, this is truly a shining sapphire jewel in the BBC's natural history crown, and showcases exactly why the Corporation is still the best in the world at depicting our natural world. The patience and skill on show in bringing these sometimes beautiful, sometimes grotesque creatures to the screen is breathtaking. David Attenborough's narration (of which he wrote segments) provides that final seal of quality that an undertaking of this nature requires.

After the transmission of each film, a ten-minute supplementary programme, *Making Waves*, explained how some of the sequences in that episode were achieved. Aside from a BAFTA for cinematography, the team also scooped the same award at the 2002 Emmy awards, and George Fenton also scooped a BAFTA and Emmy for his evocative score.

Bo' Selecta!

Comedy | TalkBack/Bellyache Productions for Channel 4 | episode duration 25 mins, plus 50-min specials | broadcast 6 Sep 2002–present

Regular Cast

Leigh Francis · *Avid Merrion, Other Characters*
Craig Phillips · *The Craig*
Patsy Kensit · *Pats*
Ozzy Rezat · *Ozzy from Downstairs*

Creator Leigh Francis **Producers** Phil Clarke, Peter Fincham (executive), Spencer Millman **Writers** Leigh Francis, Spencer Millman **Theme Music** Earshot Music

When we look back at some of the most highly regarded impressionists of the past, we often come away thinking that they'd have been considerably less impressive had it not been for their make-up artists and costume designers. As Mike Yarwood used to end his act with '. . . and this is me', he wasn't telling us anything we didn't know. Kenny Everett played with this idea when he gave us an impression of Rod Stewart that had less to do with any genuine resemblance and everything to do with his inflatable backside (Everett took this a stage further by having a turbaned Indian character attempt the same act). It's a joke that both depth-charges and exposes the weaknesses in any impressionist's repertoire. For all his skill at vocal trickery, Alistair McGowan isn't David Beckham; he's Alistair McGowan doing Beckham. Meanwhile his impression of ***EastEnders***' Dot Cotton in the style of Albert Steptoe tells us more about the heritage of Dot as a character than a straight repetition of her lines with a few punchlines ever would.

The point of *Bo' Selecta!*, as we see it, is not to show us what celebrities are like, or even to mimic them for a cheap laugh. No, it's to destroy utterly the cult of celebrity. That may seem strange to state given that Leigh Francis's central character, Avid Merrion, is completely obsessed by celebrities. But his adoration has no value; he loves everyone, from the world's greatest-ever pop star to the most anonymous member of a generic boy band.

Having made his mark during sketches either side of the ads during ***Big Brother*** 2, Avid began appearing at every celebrity event from film premieres to autograph queues. By his third series of *Bo' Selecta!* he'd become a bona fide celeb with his own Channel 4 chat show ('. . . and I'm not even fully gay!'). But look at him: he plays up the fact that his Transylvanian accent leaves him with worryingly dodgy English pronunciation, even when launching a fund-raising single for which one of the benefactors will be the charity Focus (which Avid says as if it's a type of German plane from World War One); he wears a neck brace at all times (the result of an encounter with a very angry Liza Tarbuck, allegedly!), leading unsuspecting celebs to express concern – and if that doesn't get them, discussing his mother will ('She is dead. But I didn't bury her in the ground with worms and shit. She is in my wardrobe. I spray her with Lynx and surround her with pine tree fresheners so she smells like an endangered animal.'). This stream-of-consciousness delivery makes him a deadly host and very few escape with their dignity intact.

Avid is just one of the ways Leigh Francis has managed to wage his war against celebrity while remaining virtually anonymous. His other characters are realised through grotesque rubber masks and all wear glasses. These include Mel B, formerly of the Spice Girls, who bears a terrifying resemblance to ***Bullseye***'s Jim Bowen; R&B singer Craig David (whose song 'Re-Rewind' contained the 'Bo' Selecta!' hook that provided the series with its title), who's portrayed as a Yorkshireman with his own pet kestrel

Continued on page 128

Blue Peter

Peter Duncan, Simon Groom and Sarah Greene welcome a viewer to the studio.

Blue Peter's position in TV history can be illustrated by how many other programmes have cribbed from it and mocked it. ***How!*** and ***Magpie*** were unashamedly 'inspired' by it, The *Monty Python* team took a swipe at its optimism in trying to solve world issues, ***Not the Nine O'Clock News***'s Mel Smith and Rowan Atkinson ridiculed the naffness of homemade toys and everyone at some point seems to have used the old standby '. . . and here's one we made earlier.' Over 25 pets, more than 30 presenters, countless pieces of silver foil, wool and other recyclable items and a jaunty theme tune have worked together for nearly half a century to make *Blue Peter* an essential part of a child's TV upbringing.

It was the idea of producer John Hunter Blair, who identified a gap in the audience between the *Watch with Mother* diversions for pre-schoolers and the evening's entertainment for the grown-ups. Along with his secretary Gilly Riley, Hunter Blair drafted a 15-minute weekly magazine format that (according to the *Radio Times* at least) boasted regular features on 'toys, model railways, stories and cartoons'. Christened '*Blue Peter*' after the flag that's raised on a ship as it's about to set sail, it would become the very embodiment of that BBC mission statement to inform, educate and entertain.

Though many candidates were interviewed for the task of presenting the show, the job went to actor Christopher Trace after Hunter Blair learned they shared a passion for model railways. Cast as his glamorous assistant was TV presenter and former Miss Great Britain Leila Williams. Joining the team was artist Tony Hart, who drew and narrated his own cartoon strip starring Packi the Elephant (short for Pachiderm, not actually a racial slur, though still inadvisable). When Leila Williams left in 1962, she was initially replaced by Anita West, but she too left after just six months, concerned that her impending divorce from musician Ray Ellington would damage the show. Having previously been beaten to the job by Ward, Valerie Singleton joined Chris Trace in September that year. Singleton would stay with *Blue Peter* for just shy of a decade.

Children's Magazine
BBC One
Episode Duration: 15–25 mins
Broadcast: 16 Oct 1958–present

Regular Cast
Christopher Trace, Leila Williams, Anita West, Valerie Singleton, Sandra Michaels, John Noakes, Peter Purves, Lesley Judd, Percy Thrower, Simon Groom, Tina Heath, Sarah Greene, Christopher Wenner, Peter Duncan, Janet Ellis, Michael Sundin, Caron Keating, Mark Curry, Yvette Fielding, John Leslie, Diane-Louise Jordan, Anthea Turner, Tim Vincent, Stuart Miles, Katy Hill, Romana D'Annunzio, Richard Bacon, Konnie Huq, Simon Thomas, Matt Baker, Liz Barker, Zoe Salmon, Gethin Jones · *Presenters*
Percy Thrower, Margaret Parnell, George Cansdale, Peggy Spencer and many others · *Experts*

Note Sandra Michaels, at the time presenter of *Junior Points of View*, stepped in for two editions while Val Singleton was on holiday and was given her presenter *Blue Peter* badge by Christopher Trace. Peter Duncan actually did two tours of duty, first from 11 September 1980 to 18 June 1984, then after the sudden departure of Michael Sundin, Duncan returned on 9 September 1985 and stayed until 27 November 1986. He was also one of a number of past presenters to return to the show as a guest presenter for the 40th anniversary editions.

Creator John Hunter Blair (with Gilly Riley)

Producers John Hunter Blair, Clive Parkhurst, Edward Barnes, Bridget Caldwell, Richard Marson (series producers), Biddy Baxter, Lewis Bronze, Steve Hocking, Oliver MacFarlane (editors)

Theme Music 'Barnacle Bill' by Ashworth Hope. Sidney Torch's original arrangement lasted until 1979 when Mike Oldfield rearranged it and got it into the singles charts, peaking at No. 19.

It usually comes as a great surprise to some that John Hunter Blair even existed. After all, didn't Biddy Baxter create it all? Well, not quite, but arriving in 1962 as the show's first editor, she was responsible for giving the show a format that has pretty much survived for 40 years. In 1963, she commissioned Tony Hart to create the distinctive BP icon, a stylised galleon that would feature on the much-sought-after *Blue Peter* badge awarded to viewers who send in good ideas (and get them free entry into hundreds of attractions around the UK).

Blue Peter went twice weekly from September 1964, with editions on Mondays and Thursdays. This put a strain on the team and led to the introduction of a third presenter, John Noakes. Eternally cheery, often recklessly gung-ho about taking part in tasks that would have lawyers in fits today, he was the show's first 'Action Man' (after leaving *Blue Peter* in 1978, he got his own white-knuckle show, *Go With Noakes*). He famously scaled Nelson's Column to give it a bit of a brush, and he was also the first civilian in Britain to join the RAF in a five-mile-high free-fall. Noakesie joined the show just in time for another of Baxter's mad ideas, the summer expeditions to other parts of the world like Kenya and Russia. The first *BP* expedition sadly inadvertently led to Chris Trace's departure after he was discovered to have been behaving in a highly inappropriate fashion with a young woman he met in Norway. What could potentially have been a disaster miraculously ended up serendipitous when Trace's position on the banquette was taken by Peter Purves. Paired with Noakes, Purves was the first modern presenter, willing to give it a go but always with a slight air of disdain, memories of his time as an actor still fresh (something that the production team were never afraid to exploit: whenever they were short of an item they'd simply trot out a clip of Purves from his days on ***Doctor Who***).

One of the most famous incidents in the studio took place in July 1969 when a young elephant called Lulu voided her bowels and bladder all over Pete and Johnny's feet. Without question, this is the most-requested clip of over 40 years of *BP* history. This was just one time when the maxim about not working with animals would apply to *BP* a thousand-fold, whether it's taking a lion for a walk, washing the pets or trying to conduct an interview with a zookeeper as a baby gorilla tries to whip off your bra.

Pets were brought into the format both as an educational tool to show kids how to care for their pets and as a concession to those children who lived in flats or just couldn't afford a pet. The first – and indeed second – of these was Petra, a mongrel puppy (not an Alsatian, as Chris Trace explained in one edition when they were looking for a 'husband' for her!) who had joined the show in Christmas 1964, but (it was revealed some 20 years later) died after just one appearance. A look-alike was quickly found and she became presenter Christopher Trace's screen buddy. Petra's death in 1977 made the headlines and left a nation in mourning (she's commemorated by a bronze bust in the grounds of BBC TV Centre). Petra's puppy Patch arrived in 1965 and became the first dog to look after John Noakes, the other being the quite insane collie Shep, who accompanied John for seven years and became probably the best-known of all of the *Blue Peter* pets. Farmer's son Simon Groom was paired with Labrador Goldie to provide the producers with an opportunity to feature the Guide Dogs for the Blind appeal, something they'd return to with two of Goldie's pups, Prince and Bonnie. In the 1990s, Goldie was joined by Mabel, who the team rescued from an RSPCA home. Cats also got a look-in, with Jason, Jack and Jill, Willow, Kari and Oke and Smudge and Paisley. And, of course, there were a number of tortoises, including poor Fred, who was later discovered to be a Freda, and George, who died in 2004, aged 83.

Creating playthings out of old detergent bottles and cardboard boxes might sound like something we did during rationing, but these items continue to be surprisingly popular. Whether it's making an impressively detailed proscenium theatre for cut-out *Doctor Who* characters or even a miniature Tracey Island, *Blue Peter* has been on hand with 'sticky-backed plastic' (sheets of coloured sticky plastic – not merely a non-brand name for sticky tape) to reassure children that their parents don't have to bankrupt themselves to allow them to have a decent playset. Central to this for at least 20 years was former viewer Margaret Parnell, who was eventually hired by the producers to come up with inventive but cheap ideas. The 'makes' often played a part in breaking down traditional gender roles, particularly when cookery was involved. Val shows us how to make Dalek-shaped cakes (for some reason, *Blue Peter* and *Doctor Who* have remained inextricably linked over the years, and indeed its current producer was at one time a writer for the official *Doctor Who* magazine) while pretty much everyone else fails utterly to flip a pancake. Perhaps doing more harm to the gender campaign than good was Mark Curry, whose ineptitude in the kitchen had previously been evident on *The Saturday Picture Show*. His genuine surprise each and every time the ingredients ended up all over his face was probably why they hired him.

The famous *Blue Peter* garden was introduced in 1974 for the benefit of those many viewers living in homes without a garden. It was an ingenious idea as it presented the team with regular features, including how different plants can thrive under different weather conditions and even how to make a bird-feeder. To help with the project, they brought in British television's first 'celebrity' gardener, Percy Thrower. Thrower first appeared on the BBC's *Gardening Club* in 1956 before presenting the BBC Two show ***Gardener's World*** from its first episode in 1968 until 1976, when he was unfortunately sacked for a 'conflict of interest' after appearing in a weed killer commercial on ITV.

Thrower's finished garden was unveiled on the show on 21 March 1974, accompanied by the regular presenters, who at the time were Peter Purves, John Noakes and Lesley Judd. In 1979, the garden was redesigned – again by Percy Thrower – to look like an Italian sunken garden, complete with fish pond and small benches for the presenters to sit on while introducing items. Sadly, the garden was partly vandalised shortly before completion, causing a lot of distress to Percy, the presenters and the viewers. But although the damage was repaired, worse was to come when in November 1983 the show began with shots of a devastated garden. Children across the land watched in horror, wondering what kind of freak weather might have caused such destruction. It was left to Janet Ellis to confirm that vandals had once again broken into the *Blue Peter* compound at Television Centre and run amok. An expensive ornamental sundial had been tipped over and smashed; plants had been ripped up and strewn across the garden; an urn had been thrown into the pond and, worse, the vandals had poured oil into the water.

While the team all leapt in to repair the damage, for Percy Thrower it was all too much and, in a memorable scene, with tears in his eyes, he forgot himself for a moment and declared that, in his opinion, the kind of people who could do such a thing must have been 'mentally ill'. No one would admonish the man for his temporary political incorrectness. A nation was emotionally scarred that day. (In 2000, footballer Les Ferdinand boasted that he had been a member of the gang who trashed the *Blue Peter* garden. Having misjudged just how the public might react to such an admission, though, he later recanted the claim.)

The series' real low point must undoubtedly be the sacking of Richard Bacon after being exposed by a tabloid newspaper as a user of cocaine. Realising that the story had made the main news and that it would be seen by the children who make up their audience, Controller of Children's programming Lorraine Heggesey, took the unprecedented step of recording an apology to the viewers, explaining that Bacon had 'not only let himself and the team down but also let all of you down'. That this all happened just three days after the show's 40th anniversary was unfortunate. But it was also a reminder that presenters of children's TV shows must never be seen to be adults, something they'd managed to keep a secret from their audience for years (amazing considering other tabloid news stories about Peter Duncan's appearance in a 'very blue' erotic film in the 1970s, Michael Sundin's outing as gay and a fair number of extra-marital affairs over the decades). Bacon served out his rehabilitation on Channel 4's ***Big Breakfast***.

Blue Peter has always worked on the assumption that its target audience was the kind of child who wants to be educated and informed more than just entertained. Features on history or literature might have contributed to the impression that it was for middle-class children with middle-class values, while cynics will always point to the worthiness of its annual charity campaign involving the recycling of tin foil and wool or the organisation of bring-and-buy sales. But in an era where children's TV seems content to throw gunge about in the name of entertainment, there's a lot to be said for such lofty values as catering to a viewer who wants to learn something new and relishes the chance to make a difference to the world around us.

(Kes) and a bladder complaint; Michael Jackson, a curious amalgam of the shamed king of pop and the foul-mouthed Eddie Murphy (although describing one specific *Bo' Selecta!* character as foul-mouthed is a little like singling out one of Snow White's dwarves and calling him short); Davina McCall, presenter of the *Big Brother* live eviction shows, issuing careful reminders not to say 'fuck or bugger'; and the Bear, a cub who lives up a tree on Hampstead Heath and suffers from involuntary priapic euphoria. This little fella's not an overt parody of one celebrity but he is growing more and more like a bad-tempered Ronnie Corbett.

If any of this sounds critical of Avid Merrion or his alter ego, Leigh Francis, let us assure you it's nothing of the kind. Each series of *Bo' Selecta!* has had us in stitches. Even the rubbish 2004 Christmas special starring the Bear.

Trivia

Leigh Francis was helped on his way to stardom by Davina McCall. And we always thought she was such a nice girl. *Bo' Selecta!* has twice made an assault on the UK singles charts, firstly with 'Proper Chrimbo' in 2003 and then a year later with a cover of the Sonny and Cher classic 'I Got You Babe' alongside Davina McCall and Patsy Kensit.

Bob the Builder

Animation | HOT Animation/HIT Entertainment for BBC One | episode duration 10 mins | broadcast 12 Apr 1999–present

Voice Cast

Neil Morrissey · *Bob, Lofty, Farmer Pickles*
Kate Harbour · *Wendy, Dizzy, Mrs Potts*
Rob Rackstraw · *Scoop, Muck, Roley, Travis, Spud*

Creator Keith Chapman **Producers** Kate Fawkes, Theresa Plummer-Andrews (executive), Jackie Cockle **Writers** Chris Trengrove, Jimmy Hibbert, Lee Pressman, Ross Hastings, Sarah Ball **Theme Music** 'Can We Fix It', written by Mike Joyce, performed by Neil Morrissey. The song became Britain's 886th No. 1 in December 2000, with drunken Christmas revellers singing the chorus: 'Bob the Builder – Can we fix it?/Bob the Builder – Yes, we can!'

The stop-motion hero of the 21st century, Bob energised the sales of toy tool kits and shaped the ambitions of many a young boy and girl to work in the construction industry. Bob and his friend Wendy go to work every day alongside sentient construction vehicles like Scoop the bright yellow digger and Dizzy the cement mixer.

Bob isn't the only one with clever vehicles – Farmer Pickles has his tractor called Travis (though he also has a mischievous scarecrow called Spud – the less said about him the better), and none of the other townsfolk ever seem fazed by the sight of humans communicating with their cars and trucks. Why ever would they?

The series is thought to promote positive social interaction for kids, teaching them the value of cooperation and compromise – and how to build a house! Always desperate for a story, some journalists decided that with his hard hat and checked shirts, Bob could be a gay icon – a thought not supported by the gay community, apparently, having tried to distance themselves from the Village People stereotypes for years. This didn't prevent Elton John from making a guest vocal performance in a feature-length special episode, 'A Christmas to Remember', alongside Noddy Holder, Chris Evans and Alison Steadman.

Trivia

A year after his first No. 1 single, Bob scored a second, this time a version of Lou Bega's dance hit 'Mambo No. 5' with the lyrics reworked to be more pertinent to construction work than picking up girls.

Bob's Full House

Game Show | BBC One | episode duration 25–35 mins | broadcast 1 Sep 1984–27 Jan 1990

Cast

Bob Monkhouse · *Host*
Cindy Milo · *Hostess*

Creators Terry Mardell, David Moore **Producers** Various, including Geoff Miles, John Bishop **Theme Music** John Mealing

The door was always open for the audience of *Bob's Full House*, and we were happy to come in our droves. Game show God Bob Monkhouse (we really were not worthy of his talents) looked after the balls in this simple but effective skit on bingo, a similarly successful twist on the way ***Big Break*** had turned snooker into a game show (Terry Mardell devised both programmes). Four contestants played through three separate games, answering questions to light up the squares on their bingo cards. Four Corners was fairly self-explanatory, before the Monkhouse Mastercard had the contestants attempting to light up their middle line. Finally, it was an all on scramble to light the entire card in Full House, allowing the winner to go on to the Gold Card for the chance to win a holiday. If a player answered a question incorrectly, they were 'wallied' and missed a turn.

Bob's Full House obeyed many rules of the successful game show – a slick host who could sell coal to Geordies, an insidiously simple game with variations, decent prizes, and the ubiquitous revolving bit in the middle. Monkhouse was always sympathetic and would blatantly help players along if they were lagging. Much of Monkhouse's script was ad-libbed on the spot, with his cue cards simply scribbled with 'Joke' for when the comic had to insert a quickly thought up one-liner. So, in Bob's words, 'In bingo lingo clickety clicks, it's time to take your pick of the six!' Inspired!

Bod

Animation | Bodfilms for BBC One | episode duration 15 mins | broadcast 23 Dec 1975–18 Mar 1976

Voice Cast

John Le Mesurier, Maggie Henderson · *Narrators*

Creators/Writers Joanne and Michael Cole **Producer** David Yates **Theme Music** Derek Griffiths

Androgyny was cool in the 1970s. David Bowie, Marc Bolan and Suzi Quatro played with gender in their on-stage personas, ***Some Mothers Do 'Ave 'Em***'s Frank Spencer was married with a kid but was still the campest thing on TV outside of Grace Brothers department store or a British Army concert troupe. And even children's TV wasn't free from this liberating influence, as evidenced by a small bald boy in a dress whose adventures kept toddlers captivated.

Bod first appeared in book form in 1962 before finding his way onto television for his own 13-part series. His simple, geometrical design made him easier for nursery school teachers to draw on the windows compared with other pre-school heroes; his friends and relations had their own jazz-themed walk-on music and names that were as memorable as they were descriptive: Farmer Barleymow, PC Copper, Frank the Postman . . . Aunt Flo? Well, maybe not quite as memorable in her case . . .

Bod's adventures would last just five minutes, so to pad the episode out attentions would shift to Alberto Frog and his Amazing Animal Orchestra in which the kids would learn about different instruments. At the end of this segment, someone would always reward Alberto for his help by giving him a milkshake, while the other animals would take a guess at which flavour he would go for. 'I bet it's chocolate,' the hippos might say. They were inevitably wrong, however, because lime (the chosen flavour) was apparently an option – unlike in the real world where lime milkshakes are conspicuous by their absence. Finally, Maggie Henderson would voice a quick game of Snap – 'One Barleymow . . . Two Barleymow. That makes Snap!' – before Bod would turn around and go home. Simple, effective, and utterly unforgettable to anyone who watched it as a child – just as good kids' programming should be.

Bonanza

Western | NBC (shown on ITV) | episode duration 50 mins | broadcast 12 Sep 1959–23 Jan 1973, 20 Apr 1988, 28 Nov 1993, 15 Jan 1995

Regular Cast

Lorne Greene · *Ben Cartwright*
Pernell Roberts · *Adam Cartwright*
Dan Blocker · *Eric 'Hoss' Cartwright*
Michael Landon · *Joseph 'Little Joe' Cartwright*
Mitch Vogel · *Jamie Hunter Cartwright*
David Canary · *'Candy' Canaday*
Tim Matheson · *Griff King*
Harry Holcombe · *Doc Martin*
Bing Russell · *Deputy Clem Foster*
Ray Teal · *Sheriff Roy Coffee*
Victor Sen Yung · *Hop Sing*

Creator David Dortort **Producers** David Dortort (executive), John Hawkins, James W. Lane, Thomas Thompson (associate), Robert Blees, Richard Collins **Writers** Various, including David Dortort, Gene L. Coon, Thomas Thompson, Carey Wilber, Robert E. Thompson, Leonard Heideman, Anthony Lawrence, John Furia, Ward Hawkins, William R. Cox, Denne Bart Petitclerc, John Hawkins, Frank Chase, Robert Sabaroff, Norman Lessing, Don Ingalls, Michael Landon, Frank Cleaver, Preston Wood, Alex Sharp, Lois Hire, Warren Douglas, Robert V. Barron, Robert Sabaroff, Ken Pettus, Leon Benson, Don Mullavy, Jo Pagano, Murray Golden, Suzanne Clauser, Paul Schneider, Walter Black, Joel Murcott, B. W. Sandefur, Jack B. Sowards, Stanley Roberts, Arthur Heinemann **Theme Music** Ray Evans and Jay Livingston

Bonanza combined good old-fashioned family values with the great American western to make a TV show that lasted 14 years, creating stars of Lorne Greene and Michael Landon. Set in the 19th century on the Ponderosa ranch, it was the tale of a man widowed three times with sons from each marriage: Adam, the quiet, thoughtful one; Hoss, the giant with a soft centre whose Norwegian mother was killed by Indians (his name was apparently Norwegian for good luck); and Little Joe, rash and hot-tempered. They might argue and fight occasionally, but the brothers were tight and always backed each other up in a crisis. Their pa, Ben Cartwright, was a respected figure in nearby Virginia City and their home offered an open door and hearty welcome to many a weary traveller.

Though *Gunsmoke* ran for longer in the USA, it was *Bonanza* that won the hearts of millions of British viewers – the show kick-started a trend for houses to be named 'Ponderosa' – and helped ITV win the ratings battle for years. But after the death of Dan Blocker, the lovable Hoss, the series suffered a further blow when its network shuffled it around the schedules before cancelling it mid-season. The inevitable reunions and revivals followed, including a short run of movies with an entirely new cast, but including the son of the late Michael Landon.

Boon

Comedy Drama | Central for ITV | episode duration 50 mins | broadcast 14 Jan 1986–1 Dec 1992, 1 May 1995

Regular Cast

Michael Elphick · *Ken Boon*
David Daker · *Harry Crawford*
Neil Morrissey · *Rocky Cassidy*
Rachel Davies · *Doreen Evans*
Lesley-Anne Sharpe · *Debbie Yates*
Amanda Burton · *Margaret Daly*

Elizabeth Carling · *Laura Marsh*
Saskia Wickham · *Alex Wilton*
Brigit Forsyth · *Helen Yeldham*
Mark Benton · *Charlie Hardiman*
Barbara Durkin · *Glynis*
Joan Scott · *Ethel Allard*
Teddie Thompson · *Linda*
Gordon Warnecke · *Hanif Kurtha*

Creators Jim Hill and Bill Stair **Producers** Ted Childs, William Smethurst (executive), Kenny McBain, Esta Charkman, Michele Buck, Simon Lewis **Writers** Various, including Jim Hill, Bill Stair, Anthony Minghella, Guy Meredith, Paul Wheeler, Douglas Watkinson, John Flanagan, Andrew McCulloch, Geoff McQueen, Anthony Horowitz, Billy Hamon, Matthew Bardsley, Tony McHale, Kieran Prendiville, Richard LeParmentier, Paddy Fletcher, Nick Whitby, Jane Hollowood, Peter Mann, Andy De La Tour, Veronica Henry, Bernard Dempsey, Kevin Sperring, Peter Palliser, Mark Skeet, Helen Slavin, Tony Jordan **Theme Music** 'Hi Ho Silver', sung by Jim Diamond, which got to No. 5 in the UK singles charts

A western transplanted to the modern-day British Midlands (first Birmingham, then Nottingham, when production company Central shifted recording of the series to their other base), with motorbikes instead of horses, Michael Elphick starred as the soft-hearted Ken Boon who is invalided out of the Fire Service because of smoke inhalation and forced to look for work wherever he can get it. Jim Hill and Bill Stair came up with the idea of an odd-job man who decides to offer his services under the banner of 'Anything Legal Considered' (which was also their working title for the series). Inspired by old TV Westerns, they chose the name 'Boon' after Richard Boone, who'd starred in *Have Gun – Will Travel* in the late 1950s.

Ken Boon's best friend was Harry Crawford, like himself an ex-fireman, but one with more entrepreneurial drive – though not much business acumen as most of his ideas led to failure. While Harry tries his hand as a hotelier, Ken sets himself up as a courier (head of the 'Texas Rangers') atop his prized red and silver BSA 650 motorbike, 'White Lightning'. Later he becomes a freelance investigator, which puts him in positions where his sympathies often lie with his targets more often than his clients. Helping as best he can is dopey biker Rocky and initially Debbie Yates, the first in a run of secretaries for the firm.

Playing on the lovable romantic character that he'd created for the BBC sitcom ***Three Up, Two Down***, Michael Elphick decided to take a very risky decision when he accepted a part in ***EastEnders.*** He turned up as Charlie Slater's brother Harry, the uncle who had abused Kat Slater as a child and unknowingly fathered Zoe. It was a memorably harrowing yet sensitive performance that came just a few months before Elphick's death in September 2002. Boon, of course, became a launching pad for the career of another lovable performer, with Rocky Cassidy providing Neil Morrissey with his first big screen role.

The Borrowers

Children's Drama | Working Title for BBC One | episode duration 30 mins | broadcast 18 Nov 1992–19 Dec 1993

Cast
Ian Holm · *Pod Clock*
Penelope Wilton · *Homily Clock*
Rebecca Callard · *Arietty Clock*
Paul Cross · *George*
Daniel Newman · *Spiller*
Siân Phillips · *Mrs Driver*
David Ryall · *Crampfurl*
Tony Haygarth · *Mildeye*
Stanley Lebor · *Uncle Hendreary*
Pamela Cundell · *Aunt Lupy*
Victoria Donovan · *Eggletina*

Producers Tim Bevan, Walt deFaria (executive), Grainne Marmion (producer), Fiona Morham (line producer) **Writer** Richard Carpenter, from the novels by Mary Norton **Theme Music** Howard Goodall

Life is hard for Pod Clock. He has a wife, Homily, and young daughter, Arietty, to look after. He tirelessly provides for them with whatever is to hand, often putting himself in great danger to 'borrow' the things his family needs. The Clock family also happen to be just 15cm (6in) tall and live in mouse-sized holes in the nooks and crannies of old English houses. One day, Pod takes Arietty on an adventure that changes their lives in awful ways and brings the Borrowers to the attention of the big people, including Mrs Driver and her cats and dogs.

Mary Norton's four *Borrowers* books, The *Borrowers, The Borrowers Afield, The Borrowers Afloat* and *The Borrowers Aloft* were adapted across two six-part series, starring the then husband and wife pairing of Ian Holm and Penelope Wilton, along with Rebecca Callard, daughter of ***Coronation Street***'s queen of the mini-skirt, Beverly Callard.

The series captured a wonderful period detail in both script, thanks to the experienced Richard Carpenter (***Robin of Sherwood, Catweazle***), and the beautiful sets. The special effects also did a creditable job of miniaturising the diminutive Borrowers, and this remains a well-remembered segment of Sunday afternoon children's drama. Hallmark produced a US version of *The Borrowers* in 1973, starring Eddie Albert as Pod, and Jim Broadbent took the lead role in a 1997 Hollywood movie, also produced by Working Title.

Boss Cat

See TOP CAT

Bottom

Sitcom | BBC Two | episode duration 30 mins | broadcast 17 Sep 1991–10 Feb 1995, 10 Apr 1995

Regular Cast
Rik Mayall · *Richard Richard*
Adrian Edmondson · *Eddie Elizabeth Hitler*
Christopher Ryan · *Dave Hedgehog*
Steve O'Donnell · *Spudgun*
Lee Cornes · *Dick Head*

Creators/Writers Adrian Edmondson and Rik Mayall
Producers Jon Plowman (executive), Ed Bye **Theme Music** Chips Moman

When the *Radio Times* announced 'the return of ***The Young Ones***', more than a few fans of the original anarchic punk comedy would have been disappointed to learn that *Bottom* was nothing of the sort, even though it starred Ade Edmondson and Rik Mayall and featured occasional guest appearances by Chris Ryan. Bottom was closer to Edmondson and Mayall's stage act, the Dangerous Brothers, with lots of shouting and violence but with added filth.

Richie Richard and Eddie Hitler share a run-down flat that would probably fall down if they cleaned it. Most of the appliances in their kitchen could be described by ***Watchdog***'s Lynn Faulds Wood as 'a potential death trap', while their understanding of personal hygiene is limited at best. Lecherous Richie longs to 'do sex' with a woman, and while Eddie wouldn't be averse to some female company (particularly if the lady was Kim Basinger), he's equally content to get drunk and sleep where he falls.

The working title was *Your Bottom*, mainly for the schoolboy giggles it would provoke when someone mentioned that they'd seen Your Bottom. This sums up the whole approach to the series, gleefully apolitical and without an agenda – the nearest the show ever got to making a point was when Eddie was bashing Richie's head repeatedly with a door and turned to the audience to note that people blame TV for the rise in violence, yet they don't even have a TV set.

In 1997, the boys put *Bottom* on the big screen with *Guest House Paradiso*, a hit-and-miss farce. They've had more success in their live shows, which were also released on home video. *Bottom* still has the power to make us flinch in agony as Eddie and Richie do unspeakable things to each other, even though they always bounce back like a Looney Tunes character. It took barely an entire episode for us to realise that *Bottom* outclasses ***The Young Ones*** on almost every level.

Trivia
The final episode of the third series was followed by a special that had been postponed from a previous run because it involved Eddie and Rich on Wimbledon Common; its original scheduled transmission sadly coincided with a murder that took place there.

Bouquet of Barbed Wire

Drama | LWT | episode duration 50 mins | broadcast 9 Jan–20 Feb 1976 (*Bouquet of Barbed Wire*), 7 Jan–18 Feb 1977 (*Another Bouquet*)

Principal Cast
Frank Finlay · *Peter Manson*
Susan Penhaligon · *Prue Manson/Sorenson*
James Aubrey · *Gavin Sorenson*
Sheila Allen · *Cassie Manson*
Deborah Grant · *Sarah Francis*

Producers Rex Firkin (executive), Tony Wharmby (producer)
Writer Andrea Newman **Theme Music** Dennis Farnon

Peter Manson lives in the relative comfort of Surrey with his wife, Cassie, and beautiful daughter, Prue. Prue is so much the apple of her father's eye that Peter is consumed with jealousy and lust when she marries American Gavin Sorenson. Cue lots of sexual tension, infidelity galore (even Peter's wife is at it), and the central storyline of incest between father and daughter that smoulders and eventually tears the family apart. Prue dies following childbirth, but that didn't stop production of *Another Bouquet* the following year with more of the same. This time Cassie is jumping into bed with Gavin (as well as the surgeon who saves Peter's life), while Peter develops a fixation for Gavin's new girlfriend. If you blink, you'll miss just who is bedding who, so it pays to keep up.

A busy, energetic piece of television from Andrea Newman, who adapted the script from her own novel. A nation was gripped and the tabloids went mad, and *Bouquet of Barbed Wire* can arguably take the blame for beginning the trend of increasingly spicing up our television more and more.

The Box of Delights

Fantasy | BBC/Lella Productions for BBC One | episode duration 25 mins | broadcast 21 Nov–24 Dec 1984

Principal Cast
Devin Stanfield · *Kay Harker*
Patrick Troughton · *Cole Hawlings*
Robert Stephens · *Abner Brown*
Patricia Quinn · *Sylvia Daisy Pouncer*
Geoffrey Larder · *Foxy-Faced Charles*
Jonathan Stevens · *Chubby Joe*
Carol Frazer · *Caroline Louisa*
Crispin Mair · *Peter*
Joanna Dukes · *Maria*
Heidi Burton · *Jemima*
Flora Page · *Susan*
John Horsley · *Bishop of Tatchester*
Bill Wallis · *Rat*
Glyn Baker · *Herne the Hunter*

Anne Dyson · *The Old Lady*
Helen Fraser · *Ellen*
James Grout · *Inspector*
Simon Barry · *Mouse*
Paul Wilce · *Alf*
Philip Locke · *Arnold of Todi*
Charles Pemberton · *Chief Constable*
Johnny Casino · *Old Jim*
Len Edwards · *Railway Porter*
Stewart Harwood · *Pirate Rat*

Producer Paul Stone **Writer** Alan Seymour, from the novel by John Masefield **Theme Music** 'The Carol Symphony' by John Hely Hutchinson, arranged by Roger Limb, which is an intricate reworking of 'The First Noel'

For some, *The Box of Delights* surpasses even ***The Lion, the Witch and the Wardrobe*** as the ultimate winter's tale. John Masefield's fantasy introduced us to Kay, a boy whose chance (or perhaps fated) encounter with Cole Hawlings, a Punch-and-Judy man, takes him into a world where almost anything is possible. Hawlings claims to have been on the run from a terrifying enemy for centuries and has only managed to stay one step ahead thanks to a small, silver box, which the old man says contains 'such delights . . .'.

Kay agrees to take care of the box and soon he too becomes the target of the sinister Abner Brown, the lascivious Sylvia Pouncer and their pack of wolves. Aided by a group of children, Kay's journeys shrink him small enough to ride on a toy boat and transform him into fish, fowl and stag.

The series had one of the most lavish budgets ever for a children's serial – £1 million – most of which was spent on animated sequences that are probably lacking in sophistication for audiences dependent on the computer-generated photo-realism of *Harry Potter* and the like. But for the rest of us, it's like having all your Christmas cards burst into life. The campaign to make it law to watch *The Box of Delights* every Christmas begins here.

Boys from the Blackstuff

Drama | BBC One | episode duration 60–100 mins | broadcast 2 Jan 1980, 10 Oct–7 Nov 1982

Cast

Michael Angelis · *Chrissie Todd*
Bernard Hill · *Yosser Hughes*
Tom Georgeson · *Dixie Dean*
Alan Igbon · *Loggo Lomond*
Gary Bleasdale · *Kevin Dean*
Peter Kerrigan · *George Malone*
David Calder · *McKenna*
Edward Peel · *Clerk of Works*
Janine Duvitski · *Student*
Alan Lake · *Dominic*
Sean Lynch · *Brendan*
Lois Baxter · *Masseuse*
David Ross · *Donald Moss*
David Neilson · *Lawton*
Gilly Coman · *DoE Clerk*
Shay Gorman · *Malloy*
Chris Darwin · *Snowy Malone*
Vince Earl · *Jimmy Johnson*
Tamana Bleasdale · *Anne Marie Hughes*
Jamie Bleasdale · *Dustin Hughes*
Timothy Bleasdale · *Jason Hughes*
Eileen O'Brien · *Freda Dean*
Tony Haygarth · *Aitch*
Paul Barber · *Scotty*
David Fleeshman · *DoE Assistant Manager*
Cheryl Leigh · *Jackie Mills*
Julie Walters · *Angie Todd*
Jean Boht · *Miss Sutcliffe*
Jean Warren · *Maureen Hughes*
James Ellis · *Wino*
Noreen Kershaw · *Doctor*
Struan Rodger · *Father Dan*
Peter Christian · *Moey*
Dona Croll · *Hospital Patient*
Ricky Tomlinson · *Hospital Doctor*
Tony Scoggo · *Ritchy Malone*
John Carr · *John Malone*
Jean Heywood · *Mrs Malone*
Suzanne Harrison · *Clare Todd*
Clare Kelly · *Justine Todd*
Sam Kelly · *Pub Manager*
Iggy Navarro · *'Shake Hands'*

Creator/Writer Alan Bleasdale **Producer** Michael Wearing **Theme Music** Ilona Sekacz

A *Play for Today* called *The Black Stuff* introduced viewers to the hot-tempered Yosser, self-serving Loggo, gentle animal lover Chrissie, old guard socialist George, foreman Dixie (a nickname inspired by the legendary footballer and Evertonian hero Dixie Dean) and Dixie's randy but inexperienced teenage son Kev. Sent to lay tarmac on a building site in Middlesborough by dodgy contractor McKenna, the men are instantly faced with interference from the Scouse-hating site manager. But while Dixie tries to appease the site manager's many criticisms and Kev experiences the delights of a bored housewife, the rest of the gang flit off to 'do a foreigner', taking a job on the side for the promise of more money. Perhaps predictably, their new employers, a pair of dubious Irishmen, cheat them out of their life savings. Worse, McKenna sacks them all, including Dixie and Kev, for allowing Yosser and the others to leave the building site in the first place. As the gang return to Liverpool, with Yosser shell-shocked by his own gullibility, Loggo decides to leave the gang to look for work in the Shetlands.

The BBC believed that there was more mileage in these characters so Alan Bleasdale began to work on a six-part follow-up. For various 'political' reasons, one of the episodes, about McKenna, was dropped from the series and reworked as another *Play for Today*, *The Muscle Machine* (13 January 1981), in which Pete Postlethwaite played a different building contractor, Danny Duggan.

The now five-part series was finally aired towards the end of 1982, following on from *The Black Stuff* with all of the 'boys' signing on for benefits while also doing the odd job. Chrissie and Loggo accept an offer of unskilled labour on a building site from Mr Malloy, though the job is ruined by Yosser demanding to be taken on and then head-butting Malloy when he criticises Yosser's shoddy work. But the day ends in tragedy when a Department of Employment raid on the site sends the men into flight, only for one of the gang – George's young son Snowy – to fall to his death from the top of one of the buildings. The irony that the site is for a new DoE building escapes no-one.

Throughout the series, there's strong continuity with the events of the first play. Dixie remains bitter over losing the Middlesborough job and refuses to work with any of his old crew. Instead he moonlights as a night-shift security guard on the docks, where pilfering is rife and turning a blind eye to organised crime is the only safe option. With the Department of Social Security keeping around-the-clock surveillance on suspected benefit cheats, the strain on Dixie, Chrissie and their respective families takes its toll. But for Yosser the pressures are greater still: his wife has left him with three young children to support. Like the others, he struggles to find work and resorts to begging anyone he meets to 'gizza job'. Unlike his old colleagues, though, Yosser is incapable of work, his bravado in claiming 'I can do that' fails to match his very limited abilities, and mounting problems make an already impulsive and violent man completely psychotic. When his children and finally his home are taken from him, Yosser is left to roam the streets of Liverpool a wretched and broken man.

Though 'Yosser's Story' shows us just how low a man can get, it's also far and away the funniest of Alan Bleasdale's scripts, albeit a form of humour blacker than the tarmac the boys used to lay. In a scene involving Liverpool CF players Graeme Souness and Sammy Lee Yosser, Yosser plonks himself next to Souness with the words: 'You look like me . . . and ***Magnum***.' Later, at his wits' end, Yosser goes to see a priest. 'I'm desperate, Father,' he sobs, prompting the priest to take pity on him: 'Daniel . . . call me Dan.' 'I'm desperate, Dan.' As the realisation of his involuntary reference to the *Beano* sinks in, it seems heartless to laugh, but we do it anyway, just as we roar when the social worker takes the Hughes children into care only to be butted in the face by Yosser's angelic-looking little girl.

The final episode, 'George's Last Stand', looks at the last days of a forgotten great. Though it's been hinted at and mentioned in passing in previous episodes, it's in the series finale that we learn of George's past as a hugely influential and respected trade union leader. This story is told by Ricky Tomlinson – here playing George's doctor, who fights back his tears before meeting the wife of this once great man. Coming from Tomlinson's lips the doctor's eulogy to the history of Liverpool industry, its decline represented by the poor health of George, rings all the more true and impassioned (like Peter Kerrigan, Tomlinson was a real-life trade unionist who fought for his beliefs and paid the consequences). Even in this episode, Bleasdale manages to squeeze a little comedy into the tragedy, with Chrissie and Loggo escaping George's funeral to a pub filled with unique characters: a pot man who takes glasses when they're only half drained and calls time in the middle of the afternoon after having his drink spiked; a whistling former waiter still done up in his penguin tux; a terrified barman struggling to keep his nerves in check (Sam Kelly); and 'Shake Hands', a huge, threatening bald-headed brawler who insists on challenging people to shake his hands so he can crush them and then buy him a drink (when he tries the trick on Yosser he finds himself knocked out by a swift head butt).

Despite its Liverpool setting, not all of the cast were bona fide Scousers. Julie Walters, here playing Michael Angelis's wife, is from Birmingham, while Bernard Hill, like Alan Igbon, is from Manchester (though that hasn't stopped Hill being accepted as an honorary Scouser in Liverpool and playing other Liverpudlian roles, including Shirley Valentine's husband and John Lennon). However, the rest of the cast served as a veritable Who's Who of Liverpool's thriving theatre scene: Andrew Schofield, Tony Haygarth and Tom Georgeson, all of whom later starred in Bleasdale's ***Scully***; Gilly Coman also appeared in *Scully* before 'goin' modellin'' as Aveline in ***Bread***; Tony Scoggo and Peter Christian later joined the cast of ***Brookside***; and Dixie's son Kev, Gary Bleasdale, played one of Harry Enfield's 'Scousers', the recurring sketch that gave anyone attempting a bad Liverpool accent the chance to say 'Ey, caaalm down' and get away with it.

The series won a BAFTA for Bernard Hill (with a nomination for Julie Walters) and a Royal Television Society Award for Bleasdale, establishing him as one of Britain's premier documentarian dramatists. With the drama cited by many as a damning indictment of Margaret Thatcher's Britain in the early 1980s, Bleasdale asserts that he actually wrote most of the episodes before the Iron Lady came to power. Liverpool's dock front has since converted into novelty shops, restaurants and top-of-the-range apartments owned by footballers and poseurs, and famously played host to the first years of ITV's ***This Morning***. However, many of the resentments that fuelled *Blackstuff* still remain.

Trivia

Alan Bleasdale's children appeared as Yosser's kids, his second cousin played Dixie's son, Kev, and some of his other relatives acted as advisers on the initial play.

The Brady Bunch

Sitcom | Paramount Television/Redwood Productions for ABC (shown on ITV) | episode duration 30 mins | broadcast 26 Sep 1969–31 Aug 1974 (USA)

Cast
Robert Reed · *Michael 'Mike' Brady*
Florence Henderson · *Carol Tyler-Martin-Brady*
Ann B. Davis · *Alice Nelson*
Maureen McCormick · *Marcia Brady*
Eve Plumb · *Jan Brady*
Susan Olsen · *Cynthia 'Cindy' Brady*
Barry Williams · *Gregory 'Greg' Brady*
Christopher Knight · *Peter Brady*
Mike Lookinland · *Robert 'Bobby' Brady*

Creator Sherwood Schwartz **Producers** Sherwood Schwartz (executive), David M. Whorf (associate), Howard Leeds, Lloyd J. Schwartz **Writers** Sherwood Schwartz, Arnold Peyser, Martin Ragaway, Larry Rhine, Tam Spiva, Skip Webster, Harry Winkler **Theme Music** Frank De Vol, Sherwood Schwartz

Widowed architect Mike Brady marries the similarly widowed Carol Martin, combining their two families of three boys and three girls to become one big, happy, average American middle-class family. The ensuing series followed the family adjusting to living together, and focused mainly on the six children (Greg, Peter, Bobby, Marcia, Jan and Cindy) growing up, experiencing puberty and that all-important battle for the bathroom in ever-thickening layers of saccharine sweetness. Timely assistance usually came from long-serving housekeeper, Alice.

The Brady Bunch is something of a cornerstone of pop culture in America, having been around in some form from1969 to the Millennium. It has much the same resonance in the us as *Gilligan's Island*, and it comes as no surprise that both series were created by Sherwood Schwartz. From the theme song and iconic grid title sequence, a sense of optimism and all round American goodness pervades. Between 1969 and 1974, 117 episodes were produced, and there have been innumerable TV specials and cast reunions ever since. In 1981, the family were back in *The Brady Brides*, the story now focusing on the married lives of Marcia and Jan. Just when you thought it was safe to go back in the lounge, the entire clan were unleashed again as the 1990s brought *The Bradys* back to TV, but the changes in culture found a hardened family in contrast to the happy times of the 1970s. Other spin offs included the animated series, *The Brady Kids*, and *The Brady Bunch Hour*, being the family's own variety show.

In 1995, Gary Cole and Shelley Long took starring roles in a clever and extremely funny movie version of the series, where the family are stuck in a 1970s time warp of their own choosing, completely oblivious to the 1990s values and behaviour going on around them. *A Very Brady Sequel* followed in 1996, while a 2002 TV movie had the big screen cast ending up in the White House as Mike Brady becomes President of the United States!

Brass

Sitcom | Granada for Channel 4 | episode duration 25 mins | broadcast 21 Feb 1983–20 Aug 1984, 23 Apr–28 May 1990

Regular Cast
Timothy West · *Bradley Hardacre*
Caroline Blakiston · *Lady Patience Hardacre*
Barbara Ewing · *Agnes Fairchild*
Geoffrey Hinsliff, Geoffrey Hutchings · *George Fairchild*
David Ashton · *Dr McDuff*
Robert Reynolds, Patrick Pearson · *Austin Hardacre*
James Saxon · *Morris Hardacre*
Gary Cady · *Matthew Fairchild*
Shaun Scott · *Jack Fairchild*
Gail Harrison · *Isobel Hardacre*
Emily Morgan · *Charlotte Hardacre*
Bill Monks · *Job Lott*
John Pickles · *Hattersley*
Philip Bird · *Henri LeCoq*
Thomas Hannay Matthews · *Paxo*

Producers Bill Podmore, Gareth Jones, Mark Robson **Writers** John Stevenson, Julian Roach **Theme Music** Kenyon Emrys-Roberts

Bradley Hardacre is a self-made man to whom the phrase 'where there's muck, there's brass' has been a lifelong motto. Married to the titled alcoholic Lady Patience, he has spawned four foul children: Isobel (nymphomaniac redhead), Charlotte (hand-wringing, do-gooding liberal), Austin (ambitious crawler) and Morris (gay as a goose and a teddy-bear fanatic). Hardacre lives with his family in a posh mansion and generally treats the people who work for him with the utmost contempt, thinking of them as chattels to be used and cast aside whenever it suits him.

At the bottom of the hill (literally and metaphorically), in a tiny terraced house, live the Fairchilds, a family of poor workers who toil away every day to line the pockets of Bradley Hardacre. Head of the family George is a dim-witted fool who actually feels grateful to Hardacre for treating him like a slave; on the other hand, his wife Agnes is a passionate feminist who despises Hardacre and everything he stands for, the result of which is that Hardacre lusts after her with a barely concealed passion. The Fairchilds have children too: eldest son Jack, who leads his fellow workers in acts of rebellion against their cruel master, and younger son Matthew who longs to write poetry and may have more in common with Morris Hardacre than he realises . . .

Channel 4's sublime satire of life in a northern town in the 1930s combined the power struggles and family battles of ***Dallas*** with the 'It's grim oop North' historical portrayal of northern England from ***When the Boat Comes In***, dusted with a liberal sprinkling of ***Brideshead Revisited*** (beastly privileged family with gay toff son who carries a teddy bear everywhere he goes), all served up as a laughter-track-free deadpan farce. With over-the-top performances from its entire cast (most notably Timothy West as the heartless bounder Bradley Hardacre), *Brass* played with all of the conventions of serious period dramas and mercilessly twisted them to fit the format of a soap opera, complete with pregnant pauses, cliffhanger endings, shock revelations ('You mean . . . ?' 'Yes – that's *exactly* what I mean!'), double-dealings and infidelity. All 32 episodes were written by the same two authors, John Stevenson and Julian Roach, thereby creating an internal continuity for characters and storylines that would rival even the best-plotted of soaps.

Brass Eye

Comedy | Talkback Productions for Channel 4 | episode duration 25–30 mins | broadcast 29 Jan–5 Mar 1997, 26 Jul 2001

Regular Cast
Chris Morris, Peter Baynham, Bill Cashmore, Hugh Dennis, Doon Mackichan, Claire Skinner, Mark Heap, Kevin Eldon, Amelia Bullmore, Julia Davis, David Cann, Simon Pegg, Paul Mark Elliot

Creator Chris Morris **Producers** Chris Morris, Caroline Leddy, Duncan Gray, Phil Clarke **Writers** Chris Morris, Peter Baynham, Graham Linehan, Arthur Mathews, Jane Bussmann, David Quantick, Shane Allen, Charlie Brooker, Phil Clarke, James Sezchuan **Theme Music** Jonathan Whitehead and Chris Morris

Three years after the success of ***The Day Today*** on the BBC, Chris Morris created another series that parodied the conventions of serious, newsworthy television. However, unlike *The Day Today*'s emasculation of news programmes, *Brass Eye* was a merciless massacre of the TV documentary series pioneered in the 1960s by shows like *World In Action* (indeed, *Brass Eye*'s logo was a send-up of the famous man-and-globe logo associated with *World in Action* for many years). One of the principal targets for Morris' satire on this occasion was the phenomenon of the celebrity 'rent-a-quote' – stars who would agree to be filmed on camera either in support of or campaigning against something, normally with little or no idea of what they are talking about.

In one episode of the series, Morris conducted a series of interviews with celebrities and politicians to ask for their opinion about a new drug that was apparently sweeping the streets of the UK – Cake. Everyone from Bernard Manning to Conservative MP David Amess were filmed by *Brass Eye* demanding that something should be done to sort out this new menace destroying the minds of our youth – Amess even went so far as to demand in Parliament what the government was going to do about the increased amount of Cake available to buy on our city streets. Of course, there was no such drug as Cake – it had been cooked up by Morris simply to see how many people would fall over themselves to appear on TV spouting off about a fictional problem. Morris' point had clearly been made – don't believe the opinions of people you see on TV simply because someone has given them the chance to air their views.

However the controversy over the Cake episode was nothing compared to the one-off Paedophilia Special, a programme assembled by Morris as a devastating counterattack against the air of hysteria within the UK about paedophiles that had been whipped up by sensationalist tabloid newspaper coverage. On this occasion, celebrities were positively falling over themselves to rant and rail against paedophiles, reading out scripts that made absolutely no sense. Indeed, as Phil Collins happily proclaimed, he was talking 'Nonce Sense'. Typically enough, the tabloid newspapers that had led the scaremongering were the first to criticise the *Brass Eye* special, calling it disgusting and (ironically) wheeling out their own celebrity spokespeople to express that outrage. When they howled in dismay that *Brass Eye* was making a joke out of paedophilia, they predictably missed the point entirely – it wasn't making fun out of such a sensitive subject, it was making fun out of the hypocritical press and media's handling of the subject (in the very same issues that decried Morris' Paedophile Special appeared articles counting down the days until singer Charlotte Church was 'legal'). It wasn't just the papers that were angry with *Brass Eye* though. Culture Secretary Harriet Harman was quick to criticise Channel 4's judgement in allowing such a programme to be transmitted, but had to quickly retract her comments when it was revealed she had spoken out before she'd even seen the programme in question – not exactly the wisest thing for a Culture Secretary to have done.

In truth, there are moments in all seven episodes of *Brass Eye* that are genuinely shocking and indeed borderline offensive, just as there are several occasions when the viewer might begin to believe that Morris and his colleagues think they're being funnier and cleverer than they actually are. However, *Brass Eye* is a towering achievement in TV comedy, and its message is unlikely to be blunted.

Bread

Sitcom | BBC One | episode duration 30 mins | broadcast 1 May 1986–3 Nov 1991

Regular Cast
Jean Boht · *'Ma' Nelly Boswell*
Peter Howitt, Graham Bickley · *Joey Boswell*
Jonathon Morris · *Adrian Boswell*
Victor McGuire · *Jack Boswell*
Gilly Coman, Melanie Hill · *Aveline Boswell*
Nick Conway · *Billy Boswell*
Kenneth Waller · *Grandad Boswell*
Ronald Forfar · *Freddie Boswell*
Caroline Milmoe, Hilary Crowson · *Julie*

Pamela Power · *Martina the DHSS Woman*
Giles Watling · *Oswald*
Bryan Murray · *Shifty*
Rita Tushingham · *Celia Higgins*
Eileen Pollock · *Lilo Lil*
Charlie Lawson · *Yizzel*
Simon Rouse · *Yizzel's Mate*
Deborah Grant · *Leonora Campbell*
Joanna Phillips-Lane · *Roxy*
Peter Byrne · *Derek*
J. G. Devlin · *Father Dooley*
Sharon Byatt · *Irenee*
Jenny Jay · *Carmen*

Creator/Writer Carla Lane **Producers** Robin Nash, John B. Hobbs **Theme Music** 'Home', written by David Mackay and Carla Lane, sung by 'the Cast'

There are two periods of the 20th century where Liverpool seems to have been a major force in popular culture. The 1960s is the more obvious with the Beatles spearheading Liverpool's domination of the musical world, at the very end of which, when even the Fab Four had called it quits, Carla Lane began work on ***The Liver Birds***, the story of two swinging 'it' girls living in a flat in the centre of the city. The beginning of the 1980s marked a renaissance for Merseyside: the home football teams were European champions; writers like Willy Russell, Alan Bleasdale and Jimmy McGovern hit the big time; television brought us ***Boys from the Blackstuff***, *One Summer* and ***Brookside***; Willy Russell's *Educating Rita* (1983) wowed the critics on stage and at the flicks; while Frank Clarke looked like he was about to make it big on the silver screen after the success of his film *Letter to Brezhnev* (1985), which starred his incomparable sister Margi; and the charts rang to tunes from Echo and the Bunnymen, Frankie Goes to Hollywood, The Teardrop Explodes and A Flock of Seagulls. Despite mass unemployment, entertainment gave Scousers something to be proud of. And then Carla Lane gave them *Bread*.

Having spent much of the late 1970s and early 1980s writing about the lives of middle-class women in ***Butterflies***, *Solo* and *The Mistress*, Lane returned to a portrayal of the working-class Liverpudlian background that had proved such a success in *The Liver Birds*, this time with a huge Irish Catholic family, the Boswells (reusing the same surname as Elisabeth Estensen's character from that earlier show). Nelly Boswell is the domineering matriarch, a housewife with a gob the size of the Mersey Tunnel and a fiercely protective attitude towards her brood. Eldest son Joey is a cool, leather-clad vintage car-driving peacock, giving guidance to his younger siblings and generally providing the calm and level head that Boswells traditionally lack. Adrian fancies himself as the intellectual and poet of the family, reeling from the shock of having been made redundant from his job as an accountant (his real name is Jimmy, but he thinks Adrian's more appropriate for a sensitive soul like him!) and now 'hangin' by a thread' to life. Next son Jack is the charming, smart Alec who buys and sells any old tat he can get into the back of his van; sole daughter Aveline is always heading off to photographic shoots (or as she puts it, 'goin' modellin''), hoping that one day she'll get the big break but which will almost certainly never come; and baby of the brood Billy is a dreamer who's head over heels in love with Julie who lives over the road. Cluttering up the place is the messy family dog by the delightful name of Mongy.

Ma Boswell and her five children live in one small terraced house in the Dingle, the same district of south Liverpool that housed the Boys from the Blackstuff, in a steep side-road that tilts down towards the River Mersey. In the house next door lives Grandad, a crotchety old man who's perpetually whining about the late arrival of his breakfast, dinner or tea (prepared by Ma and brought to him on a tray by one of the kids). Conspicuous by his absence is the father of the family, Freddie. Nelly is disgusted by her husband, because he's abandoned the family home to wallow in the ample charms of 'that tart' Lilo Lill (Nelly's rather descriptive nickname for her love rival). Freddie is torn between love for his wife and family and the desire to no longer be tied down to anyone or anything. Completing the collection of regular characters is the family's nemesis, Martina the woman from the Department for Health and Social Security. The encounters between Martina and the Boswells (usually Joey, but occasionally some of the other kids) were often the most eagerly awaited moments in each episode, with the acidic DHSS woman getting ever more cynical and frustrated at the latest claim for benefits that the Boswells were making.

When *Bread* first began, critics were incredibly unkind towards the programme, arguing that not only was it old-fashioned and rather hammy, but that it was a much more blatant and obvious comedy series than the subtle work that Lane had become known for in the late 1970s. Others criticised her for pandering to stereotypes of typical 'thieving Scousers' – something that many in Liverpool felt was an unwelcome attack from one of their own at a time when the city was at its lowest ebb (as if the defamation of a large proportion of Liverpool's population wasn't enough, two of the Boswell boys were in fact identifiably from Manchester – an unforgivable casting decision considering how distinctive the Scouse accent is). However, despite these criticisms, *Bread* was a major hit for the BBC, particularly the first four seasons (before several of the Boswell children received head transplants). One of the core reasons for this was the clever way in which Lane created an ongoing narrative for all of the characters. Each episode needed to be watched in sequence to get the full gist of the ongoing storylines, much in the same way that a drama series does. In a way, *Bread* was actually more akin to a family drama series with jokes thrown in rather than a full-blown sitcom. Often the moments of sadness and melancholy thrown into the series provided a sharp counterpoint to the laughs; in the very best of ways, Lane was never afraid of holding back on the belly laughs when the story she was telling required it.

As the series progressed, new characters joined the fold, including Aveline's vicar husband Oswald, Irish cousin Shifty (a post-***Irish RM***, pre-*Brookside* Bryan Murray), Shifty's ex-girlfriend Celia (a semi-autobiographical character based on Lane's own experiences of being a Liverpudlian writer, portrayed by 1960s film star Rita Tushingham), and the local heavy, Yizzel (as in 'yiz'll find out'), played by future ***Coronation Street*** star Charlie Lawson. After 74 episodes of Scouse comedy, Carla Lane finally called it a day for the adventures of the Boswell family, closing the lid of the porcelain chicken stuffed full of fivers and tenners for the very last time.

While Carla Lane had been a considerable success in the 1970s, it could be argued that the Boswells outstayed their welcome on prime-time telly, damaging Lane's stock as a writer in the process. Her follow-up, *Luv*, boasted strong performances from Sue Johnston and Michael Angelis, but the mix of marital infidelity, issue-led characters and domestic guilt felt too much like a step backwards after her former TV triumphs.

Brideshead Revisited

Drama | Granada for ITV | episode duration 50 mins | broadcast 12 Oct–22 Dec 1981

Principal Cast

Jeremy Irons · *Charles Ryder*
Anthony Andrews · *Sebastian Flyte*
Phoebe Nicholls · *Cordelia Flyte*
Diana Quick · *Julia Flyte*
Simon Jones · *Lord Brideshead / 'Bridey'*
Claire Bloom · *Lady Marchmain*
Nickolas Grace · *Anthony Blanche*
John Gielgud · *Edward Ryder*
Laurence Olivier · *Lord Marchmain*
Stéphane Audran · *Cara*
Jane Asher · *Celia Mulcaster/Ryder*
Michael Gough · *Dr Grant*
John Le Mesurier · *Father Mowbray*
Bill Owen · *Lunt*
Mona Washbourne · *Nanny Hawkins*
Jonathan Coy · *Kurt*

Producer Derek Granger **Writer** John Mortimer, from the novel by Evelyn Waugh **Theme Music** Geoffrey Burgon

During World War Two, disillusioned captain Charles Ryder arrives with his regiment to new temporary billets in the grounds of a stately home, Brideshead Castle, on the Marchmain estate. It's a place he knows well; as a youth he spent many happy years as a guest of the former inhabitants – a Catholic family, the aristocratic Flytes – and his friendship with their youngest son, Sebastian. While at Oxford University, Sebastian had disgraced himself by vomiting through the open ground-floor window to Charles's room. By means of apology, Sebastain took it upon himself to adopt Charles as his companion (along with a moth-eaten teddy bear called Aloysious) and introduce him to a life outside his own, loveless family, a life of decadent jollity. It's this relationship between Charles and Sebastian that raises questions of whether their friendship was merely platonic love or sexual, a matter on which Waugh's novel doesn't elaborate and Mortimer's script offers just tactful suggestion.

When Sebastian flees to Morocco after being sent down from Oxford for alcohol-fuelled debauchery, he and Charles temporarily part company. Charles moves to France to become a painter and marries the charming Celia. But slowly he becomes drawn back into the lives of the Flytes, finding Sebastian seriously ill in a Moroccan hospital and later commencing an affair with Sebastian's sister, Julia. But after her errant father Lord Marchmain returns to Brideshead to die, Julia rediscovers her Catholicism and brings the affair to an end.

Granada bought the rights to adapt Evelyn Waugh's novel in 1977 and original director Michael Lindsay-Hogg had begun filming in Malta when a strike at ITV brought the production to a standstill. Three months later, Waugh aficionado Charles Sturridge was hired to complete the mammoth task of directing what became the most expensive filmed series made for British television up to that time. The planned six hours of TV became 13 as Sturridge and the cast pushed for a faithful re-creation of Waugh's book that included as many of the sub-plots as possible. Boasting some of the biggest names in British drama, including both Laurence Olivier and John Gielgud, it also made stars of its younger cast members, stage actress Diana Quick, Jeremy Irons (who had appeared in the final episode of the BBC's 1974 adaptation of ***The Pallisers*** as Anthony Andrews' friend) and Nickolas Grace – as the outrageous stuttering queen Anthony Blanche – as well as confirming Anthony Andrews as Britain's favourite toff (a role he'd been building upon in series such as ***Upstairs, Downstairs*** and ***Danger UXB***).

Scant months after it was broadcast for the first time, *Brideshead Revisited* won three BAFTAS – Best Drama Series, Best Film Sound, and Best Actor for Anthony Andrews – along with nominations in six other categories, including one for Geoffrey Burgon's melancholy music. In the States, it received two Golden Globe Awards and an Emmy. The series also inspired a boom in British tourism thanks to viewers falling in love with Castle Howard, the Yorkshire estate used for the exterior shots of Brideshead, and Tatton Park in Cheshire, where many of the interiors had been filmed for the series. Alongside Granada's other great drama of the time, ***The Jewel in the Crown***, *Brideshead Revisited* is now regarded as an example of the very best of British television, even if the original plan to convey rather short text of Waugh's novel in six hours rather than 13 might have made it a touch more accessible to modern audiences.

The Brittas Empire

Comedy | BBC One | episode duration 30 mins | broadcast 3 Jan 1991–24 Feb 1997

Regular Cast
Chris Barrie · *Gordon Brittas*
Pippa Haywood · *Helen Brittas*
Harriet Thorpe · *Carole*
Michael Burns · *Colin*
Russell Porter · *Tim*
Tim Marriott · *Gavin*
Judy Flynn · *Julie*
Julia St John · *Laura*
Jill Greenacre · *Linda*

Creators Richard Fegen, Andrew Norriss **Producer** Mike Stephens **Writers** Richard Fegen, Andrew Norriss, Tony Millan, Mike Walling, Terry Kyan, Paul Smith, Ian Davidson, Peter Vincent **Theme Music** Frank Renton

One of the surprise hits of the 1990s, *The Brittas Empire* could never be accused of being innovative or challenging stereotypes. Nevertheless, its darker-than-usual look at the twisted nature of middle England was hugely popular, running for seven series. Perhaps this popularity was down to the ever-increasing obsession in the Nineties about health and fitness – certainly, a sitcom located within a health centre was an inevitability sooner or later.

Chris Barrie starred as Gordon Brittas, a man with more spreadsheets than sense, an archetypal middle manager who's spent so long on personal development courses that he's lost any grip on reality. Brittas manages the Leisure Centre in Whitbury New Town, where his persistently anal-retentive nature and irritating nasal whine results in customers deserting the facility in droves. Brittas's long-suffering staff included scabrous handyman Colin, gay couple Tim and Gavin, homeless receptionist Carole (who kept her baby in a drawer behind her desk) and his perpetually crabby secretary Julie. Pottiest of all though was Brittas's wife Helen, a woman popping tranquillisers and decidedly close to a breakdown as a result of her constant exposure to her husband's odd ways.

One of the first 'traditional' sitcoms to utilise surreal and over-the-top situations, particular weird highlights of *The Brittas Empire* included the time when a group of Baptist Christians were accidentally wiped when an electrical device was dropped into the swimming pool during one of their ceremonies, and the occasion when Gordon managed to decapitate a desperate gunman with a chainsaw as part of a botched rescue attempt. Even when Brittas was unexpectedly promoted to the position of European Minister for Sport, it didn't keep him away from the Leisure Centre for long.

The Brittas Empire perhaps overstayed its welcome by a couple of years (after creator/writers Fegen and Norriss quit the series), but it still managed to pull in the viewers after 51 episodes. In the summer of 1997, Chris Barrie, Pippa Haywood and Michael Burns re-created their characters, along with real-life doctor Mark Porter, in *Get Fit with Brittas*, a series of six ten-minute programmes looking at how to achieve that healthier lifestyle. *Get Fit with Brittas* also featured appearances from June Whitfield, Leslie Ash, Nicholas Parsons and Lesley Joseph.

Brookside

See pages 140–5

The Brothers

Drama | BBC One | episode duration 50 mins | broadcast 10 Mar 1972–19 Dec 1976

Regular Cast
Jean Anderson · *Mary Hammond*
Glyn Owen, Patrick O'Connell · *Edward Hammond*
Richard Easton · *Brian Hammond*
Robin Chadwick · *David Hammond*
Jennifer Wilson · *Jennifer Kingsley/Hammond*
Hilary Tindall · *Anne Hammond*
Nicola Moloney, Annabelle Lanyon, Debbie Farrington · *Carol Hammond*
Gabrielle Drake · *Jill Hammond*
Julia Goodman · *Barbara Kingsley/Trent*
Derek Benfield · *Bill Riley*
Mark McManus · *Harry Carter*
Anna Fox · *Pamela Graham*
Jonathan Newth · *Nicholas Fox*
Claire Nielson · *Nancy Lincoln*
Gillian McCutcheon · *Julie Lane*
Murray Hayne · *Martin Farrell*
Colin Baker · *Paul Merroney*
Carole Mowlam · *Clare Miller*
Margaret Ashcroft · *Gwen Riley*
Kate O'Mara · *Jane Maxwell*
Mike Pratt · *Don Stacey*
Liza Goddard · *April Winter/Merroney*
Sarah Grazebrook · *Marion*
Carleton Hobbs · *Sir Neville Henniswode*

Creators/Writers N. J. Crisp and Gerard Glaister
Producers Gerard Glaister, Ken Riddington, Bill Sellars
Theme Music Dudley Simpson

In 1958, the BBC were in need of a replacement for the popular domestic serial ***The Grove Family*** and commissioned producer Gerard Glaister to develop *Starr & Co.*, an industrial saga of the struggles of a family business. *Starr & Co.* lasted less than a year, but it clearly appealed to Glaister, who returned to the setting again in his career. In 1972, he and writer N. J. Crisp concocted *The Brothers*, revolving around a haulage business owned and run by the

Hammond family. When the 70-year-old proprietor of the company, Roger Hammond dies, his family assemble to hear the reading of the will, with everyone expecting the company to go to eldest son, Ted, as he's the only one who stuck around to keep it running. But Roger has left some surprises for his brood, as he instead leaves equal shares to all three of his sons, with an additional share going to his secretary, long-time mistress and mother of his love-child.

In trapping the brothers to work together, Roger ensures the business's survival, for a time, but inevitably the brothers bicker and disagree about the direction the company should go in. The power struggles were never quite on the scale of ***Dallas***, but the series still managed to provide everything we'd now expect from a soap. It killed off a much-loved character – Jill Hammond, played by Gabrielle Drake – seemingly just because it could; it had the scandal of Robert Hammond's secret daughter, and of course its own collection of bitches and bastards. The business eventually falls under the spell of Paul Merroney, an ambitious man from the City whose plans to drag the old-fashioned business into Europe made the character (and actor Colin Baker) the most hated man in Britain. Merroney's main sparring partner in later episodes was the catty Kate O'Mara as the head of an aviation company; the two would continue their on-screen rivalry in the 1980s when O'Mara was cast as an evil time traveller opposite Baker in ***Doctor Who***.

Producer Bill Sellars would later bring us ***Triangle***, which also starred Kate O'Mara, while Glyn Owen (the first of two actors to play the eldest Hammond brother) headed the cast of ***Howards' Way***, yet another serial about a family business to be produced by Gerard Glaister (who had already shown an interest in maritime activities through some of the plots of *The Brothers*).

Brush Strokes

Sitcom | BBC One | episode duration 30 mins | broadcast 1 Sep 1986–7 Apr 1991

Regular Cast
Karl Howman · *Jacko*
Gary Waldhorn · *Lionel Bainbridge*
Elizabeth Counsell · *Veronica Bainbridge*
Kim Thompson, Erika Hoffman · *Lesley Bainbridge*
Mike Walling · *Eric*
Nicky Croydon · *Jean*
Howard Lew Lewis · *Elmo Putney*
Jackie Lye · *Sandra*

Creators/Writers John Esmonde, Bob Larbey **Producers** Sydney Lotterby, John B. Hobbs, Mandie Fletcher, Harold Snoad
Theme Music 'Because of You' was written and performed by 'Come on Eileen' chart-toppers Dexy's Midnight Runners during their gypsy phase. It reached No. 13 in the UK singles charts in November 1986.

The Good Life writers John Esmonde and Bob Larbey returned to BBC One with the misadventures in life and love of a cheeky young painter and decorator. Jacko lives with his sister Jean and her husband Eric in Motspur Park, south London. Together Jacko and Eric work for Lionel Bainbridge's modest painting and decorating agency. Jacko spends much of his time trying to avoid getting into trouble with Lionel, something that's made more difficult when Jacko ends up bedding Lionel's snooty daughter Lesley. Often finding himself in trouble for his dalliances with the opposite sex, Jacko isn't actually a 'jack-the-lad' in the traditional sense – he's not one to love them then leave them, instead finding himself falling deeply in love on a semi-regular basis, only to be repeatedly disappointed. When he's relaxing away from work or women, Jacko often finds himself having a drink in his favourite local pub, the White Hart, run by hulking dullard Elmo. In later seasons, Elmo comes into a significant sum of money and buys his own ghastly, tasteless wine bar, much to Jacko's chagrin. When Lionel dies of a heart attack, his wife Veronica takes over the running of the business, much to Jacko's relief, as he can use his cheeky charm on her to get his own way – or at least *some* of the time he can.

It was that exact charm that made *Brush Strokes* such a huge hit – Karl Howman as Jacko was one of the great leading men in situation comedy, a bloke whom men wanted to be and women adored. In particular, Jacko's banter was both well realised and very believable, a testament to the quality of Esmonde and Larbey's scripts.

Trivia
Actor Mike Walling branched out into co-scripting his own short-lived sitcom – the satirical ***A Small Problem***.

Buck Rogers in the 25th Century

Science Fiction | John Mantley/Glen A. Larson/Universal for NBC (shown on ITV) | episode duration 50 mins | broadcast 20 Sep 1979–16 Apr 1981

Regular Cast
Gil Gerard · *Captain William 'Buck' Rogers*
Erin Gray · *Colonel Wilma Deering*
Tim O'Connor · *Dr Huer*
Felix Silla · *Twiki*
Mel Blanc, Bob Elyea · *Voice of Twiki*
Wilfrid Hyde-White · *Dr Goodfellow*
Eric Server · *Dr Theopolis*
Pamela Hensley · *Princess Ardala*
Henry Silva, Michael Ansara · *Kane*
Thom Christopher · *Hawk*
Jay Garner · *Admiral Efrem Asimov*
Jeff David · *Crichton*
Paul Carr · *Lieutenant Devlin*
William Conrad · *Narrator*
Continued on page 146

Brookside

From L–R: Damon, Barry, Karen, Sheila and Bobby – The Grants.

The ageing *Brookside* might well represent the most serious case of Alzheimer's disease ever contracted by a television programme. Sharp, aggressive, witty and poignant at its inception, by the end it had lost its identity and forgotten both its roots and its audience. It was painful to see only a glimmer of what it had been, leaving its once-loyal audience cheated but relieved when the suffering was finally over.

Right from the beginning, *Brookside* did things its own way. Phil Redmond, creator of ***Grange Hill*** won the bid to make Channel 4's first ongoing drama series after cornering its chief exec, Jeremy Isaacs, and asking him if he felt the channel would be prepared to risk broadcasting teen swearing in a prime slot. Redmond put together a proposal that displayed an acute business sense, suggesting that his company buy real houses for the show, with the idea that they'd work out cheaper than renting studio space, and that should the programme fold, he'd be able to sell the homes off at a profit. Redmond's desire to make the series as realistic as possible even extended to setting it in a real location – Brookside Close, one of a number of newly built housing projects on Lord Derby's estate in Croxteth. Redmond's company, Mersey TV, bought up an entire close, using six houses for the characters' homes with the rest designated as production offices, make-up rooms and a canteen. Three of the houses were given garages that would be used to store equipment.

First shown on a Tuesday evening in November 1982, *Brookside* looked and sounded unlike any other television show. This was partly because the houses themselves hadn't been soundproofed, so they tended to add a slight echo to the dialogue. But mainly it was because most of the actors spoke in natural, flat Scouse tones. There was little that was theatrical about any of the *Brookside* residents, many of whom were acting on TV for the first time. Most of the juvenile leads were recruited from the Liverpool youth theatres, while Ricky Tomlinson, who played trade unionist Bobby Grant, had been a real union activist, one half of the 'Shrewsbury two' who had served a two-year prison sentence for organising flying pickets during the national builders strike of 1972. Tomlinson had also worked in northwest clubs as a compère, musician and stand-up comedian, and many of his fellow performers would show up over time, including Tony Scoggo, who played Bobby's best friend Matty, and Bill Dean, who arrived towards the end of the soap's first year as 'miserable bugger' Harry Cross (Harry's wife Edna was played by Betty Alberge, who'd played Florrie Lindley in the very first episode of ***Coronation Street***).

Right from the start, the show looked at the social issues that had attracted Redmond to it in the first place. The middle-class Collins family move to the close because they can't afford to live in their big country house any longer after Paul Collins is made redundant. In the Grant household across the way, unionist Bobby fears pay cuts and a possible strike while his eldest son Barry tries to make a living doing property renovations with materials stolen from a builders merchant where his friend works. Younger son Damon and his friends have been found responsible for graffiti that greets the Collinses on their arrival, despite Barry's attempts to defend him ('Our Damon only spells "bollocks" with one "l" ') and middle child, daughter Karen, finds herself trapped with period pains because her Catholic mother won't authorise her to go on the pill, for fear it will tempt her to promiscuity.

While the political content was stronger than any soap had attempted before, *Brookside* attracted the attention of the press because of the use of swearing that had won Redmond the commission in the first place. In truth, it was nothing stronger than a few liberal uses of the word 'piss' but it helped gain the fledgling television station the nickname 'Channel Swore'. Redmond conceded that the swearing possibly wasn't as essential to realism as he'd previously argued, and improvements to the technical side of the production were made. But *Brookside* lost none of its bite; in fact it continued to tackle specific subjects of interest that remained untouched by other soaps for years. Gordon Collins became soap's first openly gay character, which opened the door for exploring obvious topics such as queer bashing and prejudice, while also portraying the compassionate side of the gay community, such as when Gordon decides to volunteer for the gay helpline switchboard. Fortunately, however, not every gay character was weighted down with being a sole representative for gay issues: the glorious Lance Powell was one of *Brookie*'s last great creations, with a superb performance by Mickey Poppins.

A later story involving Beth Jordache and Margaret Clemens whipped the tabloids into a frenzy over British telly's first lesbian snog (and made actress Anna Friel one of the top pin-ups for lads' mags that year). Bobby Grant's union activities looked at the full implications for strikers and their families (and later, with Billy Corkhill, on strike-breaking 'scabs' too), but also brought him into contact with a man who wanted to claim unfair dismissal because of his HIV-positive status – the first AIDS storyline on British television. Unemployment was also a major source of drama, such as when

Soap
Mersey TV for Channel 4
Episode Duration: 30 mins, plus 60-min specials
Broadcast: 2 Nov 1982–4 Nov 2003

Regular Cast

Doreen Sloane · *Annabelle Collins*
Jim Wiggins · *Paul Collins*
Katrin Cartlidge, Maggie Saunders · *Lucy Collins*
Nigel Crowley, Mark Burgess · *Gordon Collins*
Ricky Tomlinson · *Bobby Grant*
Sue Johnston · *Sheila Grant/Corkhill*
Paul Usher · *Barry Grant*
Simon O'Brien · *Damon Grant*
Shelagh O'Hara · *Karen Grant*
Rob Spendlove · *Roger Huntingdon*
Amanda Burton · *Heather Haversham/Huntingdon/Black*
Daniel Webb · *Gavin Taylor*
Alexandra Pigg · *Petra Taylor*
Tracey Jay · *Michelle Jones*
Anna Keaveney · *Marie Jackson*
Cliff Howells · *George Jackson*
Allan Patterson · *Gary Jackson*
Steven Patterson · *'Little George' Jackson*
Tony Scoggo · *Matty Nolan*
Ann Haydn-Edwards · *Teresa Nolan*
Brian Regan · *Terry Sullivan*
Doc O'Brien · *George Williams*
Dicken Ashworth · *Alan Partridge*
Dinah May · *Samantha Partridge*
Bill Dean · *Harry Cross*
Betty Alberge · *Edna Cross*
Stuart Organ · *Kevin Cross*
Ray Dunbobbin · *Ralph Hardwicke*
Michael Starke · *Thomas 'Sinbad' Sweeney*
Malcolm Tierney · *Tommy McArdle*
William Maxwell · *Jack Sullivan*
David Easter · *Pat Hancock*
Sheila Grier · *Sandra Maghie*
Sharon Rosita · *Kate Moses*
Alan Rothwell · *Nicholas Black*
Ian Hendry · *Davy Jones*
John McArdle · *Billy Corkhill*
Kate Fitzgerald · *Doreen Corkhill*
Jason Hope · *Rod Corkhill*
Justine Kerrigan · *Tracy Corkhill*
Dean Sullivan · *Jimmy Corkhill*
Gladys Ambrose · *Julia Brogan*
Joanne Black · *Kirsty Brown*
Stifyn Parri · *Christopher Duncan*
Shirley Stelfox · *Madge Richmond*
Margaret Clifton · *Mona Harvey/Fallon*
Steven Pinner · *Jonathan Gordon-Davies*
Jane Cunliffe · *Laura Wright/Gordon-Davies*
Gillian Kearney · *Debbie McGrath*
Sean McKee · *Jamie Henderson*

Annie Miles · *Sue Harper/Sullivan*
Peter Christian · *Frank Rogers*
Eithne Browne · *Chrissy Rogers*
Rachael Lindsay · *Sammy Rogers/Daniels*
Kevin Carson, Stephen Walters · *Geoff 'Growler' Rogers*
Debbie Reynolds, Diane Burke · *Katie Rogers*
Noreen Kershaw · *Kathy Roach*
Michelle Byatt · *Nikki White*
Jennifer Calvert · *Cheryl Boyanowsky*
Gillian Kearney · *Debbie McGrath*
Arthur Kelly · *Geoff Wright*
Renny Krupinski · *Sizzler*
Vincent Maguire · *Brian Lawrence*
James Mawdsley · *Brian 'Bumper' Humphries*
Tricia Penrose · *Emma Reid*
Sunetra Sarker · *Nisha Batra*
Jenny Hesketh · *Louise Mitchell*
Tom Mannion · *James Markham*
Danny McCall · *Owen Daniels*
Claire Robinson · *Ronnie Williams*
Vince Earl · *Ron Dixon*
Irene Marot · *'D-D' Dixon*
Paul Byatt · *Mike Dixon*
Alexandra Fletcher · *Jacqui Dixon/Farnham*
Gerard Bostock, Mark Lennock · *Tony Dixon*
Clive Moore · *Derek O'Farrell*
Allan Surtees · *Cyril Dixon*
Steven Pinder · *Max Farnham*
Gabrielle Glaister · *Patricia Farnham*
Karen Drury · *Susannah Morrisey/Farnham*
Sue Jenkins · *Jackie Corkhill*
Claire Sweeney · *Lindsey Corkhill/Stanlow/Phelan*
George Christopher · *'Little Jimmy' Corkhill Jr*
Louis Emerick · *Mick Johnson*
Naomi Kamanga, Carla Jarrett · *Gemma Johnson*
Leeon Sawyer, Steven Cole · *Leo Johnson*
Francis Johnson · *Ellis Johnson*
Suzanne Packer · *Josie Johnson/Brooks*
Julie Peasgood · *Fran Pearson*
Geoffrey Leesley · *John Harrison*
Angela Morant · *Barbara Harrison*
Robert Beck · *Peter Harrison*
Pauline Daniels · *Maria Benson*
Nicola Stephenson · *Margaret Clemence*
Paula Frances · *Diana Spence/Corkhill*
Vickie Gates · *Leanne Powell*
Kirk Smith · *Keith Rooney*
Marcia Ashton · *Jean Crosbie*
John Burgess · *David 'Bing' Crosbie*
Jodie Hanson · *Marianne Dwyer*
Mary Healey · *Ruth Sweeney*
Kenneth MacDonald · *George Webb*

Damon Grant experiences the crushing sense of defeat when he fails to be taken on after the completion of his YTS scheme. And while Carla Lane's sitcom ***Bread*** showed Scousers as thieves and scroungers all, neither did *Brookside* shy away from portraying the realities of doing what you can while living on the poverty line, with Barry Grant and his mate Terry Sullivan taking on less-than-legal jobs to make ends meet, including working for local gangster Tommy McArdle.

Drugs, too, were a recurring theme, first with a girlfriend of Barry's who showed the hopeless and degrading side of being a junkie. Later, Heather Haversham marries architect Nick Black only to learn that he is a heroin addict. But *Brookside*'s commitment to its characters was best exemplified by the story of Jimmy Corkhill (in a marvellous performance by Dean Sullivan), who invests in a drug ring only to be lumbered with cocaine that he can't shift. In time he becomes a user and progresses to heroin. Stoned while driving, he causes a crash that kills neighbour Frank Rogers and teenager Tony Dixon, son of Jimmy's long-time rival Ron Dixon. We follow Jimmy through his waves of guilt, his time in prison for petty robberies to feed his habit, his rehabilitation and attempts to build his life back, as well as bouts of depression that are almost certainly related to narcotic dementia.

But as much as *Brookside* wore its politics on its sleeve, for some reason it also shied away from tackling too much. Both Ricky Tomlinson and writer Jimmy McGovern left the soap in frustration over its reluctance to look at the miners' strike and the Hillsborough football disaster respectively (McGovern went on to create ***Cracker***, which featured a Hillsborough story, and later wrote a drama about the ***Hillsborough*** tragedy that led to a campaign demanding for the inquest into the deaths of 96 Liverpool supporters to be reopened). Slowly, *Brookside* grew out of touch with the audience it had mirrored so closely in the beginning. The turning point was the 1994 'body under the patio' story, initially an examination of domestic violence, with Trevor Jordache's attacks on his wife Mandy and his sexual advances towards their daughters Beth and Rachel. During a violent struggle, Mandy stabs Trevor with a carving knife and she and Beth bury his body in the garden to prevent young Rachel from discovering the truth. Eventually the family are forced to flee to Ireland, aided by local window cleaner Sinbad, who had discovered the truth about Trevor and helped Mandy build a patio over his shallow grave. The story took a fascinating twist as it next looked at the probable outcome for women accused of murdering husbands after years of domestic abuse: Beth and Mandy were both sentenced to prison, prompting a campaign by women's groups to get them freed.

The Jordache saga was a ratings grabber, helped in part by channel executives allowing the soap to schedule an entire week of episodes. But it also marked the point where *Brookside* stopped reflecting modern life and started to chase sensationalist headlines with increasingly ludicrous plots. The mistake in the way they handled the aftermath of the Jordache family's ordeal was in not giving viewers enough time to get their breath back. *Brookside*'s writers were already being pushed into thinking about which great taboo they could tackle next – and incest between a brother and sister came out on top. That the couple concerned could have been models didn't harm the ratings, but it did damage credibility a little. That's not to say that the Close had never been blessed with attractive residents – far from it. But Heather Haversham, the Grant brothers and Beth Jordache were all good-looking in a way that felt attainable to the viewers, rather than being untouchable Adonises and Aphrodites. The arrival of the incestuous Simpsons marked the first instance of casting in the style of ***Hollyoaks***: actors being chosen for their exceptional looks rather than resembling the kind of people one might expect to see on a suburban Liverpool estate. The rules had changed.

All TV programmes have to move on and evolve, but it did feel as if *Brookside* had lost its way quite dramatically, what with murders, explosions, unconvincing gangster storylines (including an ongoing one that saw Jimmy's daughter Lindsay become the Ma Baker of the Northwest). Each new family came with a built-in 'past', like the Banks family, who moved to the Close just as their youngest son was released from a detention centre for joyriding, or the Musgroves, with their alcoholic father and splintered parentage. So it was a relief when a family arrived in 2000 with no 'baggage', no skeletons in the closet, just a decent divorced father of three and his second wife (played by former pop star Bernie Nolan). The Murray family were allowed to bed in, develop over time – with an involving discussion about IVF treatment – and let the viewers get to know them. In 2001, the youngest son, Anthony, began to suffer abuse at the hands of school bully Imelda Clough. When Anthony eventually stood up for himself, he accidentally killeds Imelda and, terrified, he ran off, leaving her body. A murder hunt was announced and the terrified Anthony eventually confessed all to his parents just as his father was arrested for the murder. The story showcased the amazing talent of young Raymond Quinn as Anthony and had been planned as a return to basics for the now ailing soap. Tragically for the programme, just as the story was reaching its conclusion, real-life events took over: the murders of two schoolgirls in the village of Soham left a nation in mourning. Channel 4 rightly perceived it inappropriate for them to be promoting the *Brookside* story at such a sensitive time, even though it had been recorded months earlier and bore only the most superficial resemblance to events at Soham. Due to circumstances way beyond the control of anyone, *Brookside*'s big chance had gone. Still, the soap was preparing to relaunch itself as a contender in time for its 20th anniversary with a superbly orchestrated helicopter crash that echoed the plane crash that had so invigorated *Emmerdale*. But instead of heralding a new beginning, it was the show's death knell. Just a few weeks later, Channel 4 announced that the soap would be losing its prime-time slot, and eventually it became clear to all that *Brookside*'s 21st birthday would coincide almost to the day with its final episode.

The final weeks of the programme proved fascinating viewing as the producers made use of their 'graveyard' timeslot (10.30 p.m.) to

TRIVIA

Though *Coronation Street*'s Leonard Swindley went off to his own spin-off series called *Turn Out the Lights* in 1967, *Brookside* is generally credited with the idea of the 'soap bubble', a series that takes a small group of characters and follows their exploits away from the main series. *Damon and Debbie* was a three-part series shown on 4–18 November 1987 in which Damon Grant and his girlfriend decide to run away only for Damon to be stabbed by yobs. In the first episode of *Brookside* shown in the week after the conclusion to this first 'bubble', Damon's family are informed of his death. The following year, Thames TV's *The English Programme*, for schools and colleges, featured a two-part story called 'South', in which Tracy Corkhill and her boyfriend Jamie escape to London. The programme was famous for one thing – a cringe-worthy cameo by Morrissey of The Smiths. Mersey TV was also responsible for two video-only productions, *The Lost Weekend* in 1997, in which we find out what happened when Barry Grant turned vigilante to rescue Lindsay Corkhill from gangsters, and *Unfinished Business*, released after the series ended, which concerns Steve Murray and Tinhead O'Leary getting revenge on the drug dealer who was responsible for the death of Tim's young bride Emily the previous year. Though Phil Redmond hoped that it would lead to further *Brookside* videos, this was officially the final end for the *Brookie* residents.

Long-term fans will remember that Brookside Close seemed to have its very own TV programmes, which included *The Magic Rabbits* and the long-running soap opera *Meadowcroft Park*, a name that had been a working title for *Brookside*. Footage for *Meadowcroft Park* came from projects created by local schools as part of a Mersey TV educational initiative.

Kazia Pelka · *Anna Wolska*
Sharon Power · *Lyn Matthews/Rogers*
Susie Ann Watkins · *Joe Halsall*
Sarah White · *Bev McLoughlin/Gonzales/Dixon*
Adam McCoy, Jack McMullen · *Josh McLoughlin/Dixon*
Sandra Maitland · *Mandy Jordache*
Anna Friel · *Beth Jordache*
Tiffany Chapman · *Rachel Jordache/Wright/Dixon*
Bryan Murray · *Trevor Jordache*
Gillian Hanna · *Brenna Jordache*
Ken Campbell · *Oscar Dean*
Jonathan Caplan · *Brian Kennedy*
Angela Walsh · *Carol Salter*
Stephen Dwyer · *Garry Salter*
Paul Barber · *Greg Salter*

introduce the single most repugnant character in soap history. We'd had the sadistic Trevor Jordache, the suave Tommy McArdle and the satanic Simon. Now it was time for a drug-dealing thug who made Damon Grant's foul-mouthed friends sound like choir boys. Jack Michaelson (his name was a corruption of that of the man who brought the axe down on the Close) turned the air bluer than ever and made sickening viewing for the few still watching. But Phil Redmond had a stunning reward for those loyal viewers who could stomach this vile creation, as, in the final double-length episode, Barry Grant returns to persuade the male residents of the Close – protected by the police's awareness of the Jack Michaelson's position in the drug scene, and by cast-iron alibis that the residents provided themselves – to organise a lynch mob and rid themselves of Michaelson once and for all. Thus *Brookside* delivered its final jaw-dropping plot, and all this before the mid-point ad break, the second half focusing on the departure of the final residents as the Close is sold for redevelopment. The last two surviving characters, young Nicky Shadwick and Jimmy Corkhill, transported us back to the early days, where characters talked about politics and subjects that meant something to the audience. Listening to Jimmy rant against TV executives working in London and making mindless 'entertainment' that had nothing to do with the lives of average people, we cheered him on one last time as he spoke for us all. The credits rolled only to finish with a cheeky blast of the original ***Grange Hill*** theme, to remind us of a certain show Phil Redmond had created, and of which he was now back in control.

The credits rolled only to finish with a blast of the original *Grange Hill* theme, to remind us of a certain show Phil Redmond had created, and of which he was now back in control.

The tragedy is that *Brookside* did need to end when it did. It seemed incapable of delivering the original promise of a meaningful weekly drama, having sacrificed its principles in favour of the glamour of celebrity stars. But then, Britain itself had changed, with politics as a whole less visible and an audience less driven and raging. Its legacy remains in the tighter writing of *Coronation Street* and the issue-led drama of ***EastEnders***. On the plus side, Jimmy McGovern is one of Britain's top TV writers, and Ricky Tomlinson one of our most popular down-to-earth actors. Familiar *Brookside* faces have popped up on other shows like ***The Bill*** or – graveyard for the soap scarred – ***Family Affairs***. Meanwhile, Phil Redmond's Mersey TV continues to deliver *Hollyoaks, Grange Hill* and now *The Courtroom*, a reworking of the old daytime drama series ***Crown Court***.

Mary Tamm · *Penny Crosbie*
Tina Malone · *Moe McGee*
Paul Broughton · *Eddie Banks*
Susan Twist · *Rosie Banks*
Stephen Donald · *Carl Banks*
Matthew Lewney · *Lee Banks*
Andrea Marshall · *Sarah Banks*
María Francis · *Chris Myers*
Lee Hartney · *Simon Howe*
Judith Barker · *Audrey Manners*
Kate Beckett · *Jenny Swift*
Andrew Fillis · *Gary Stanlow*
Samuel Kane · *Peter Phelan*
Richard Norton · *Shane Cochrane*
Gordon Warnecke · *Dil Palmar*
Philip Olivier · *Timothy 'Tinhead' O'Leary*
Carol Connor · *Carmel O'Leary*
Elizabeth Lovelady · *Melanie O'Leary*
Simon Paul · *Ben O'Leary*
Michael J. Jackson · *Ollie Simpson*
Lesley Nightingale · *Beryl 'Bel' Simpson*
Helen Grace · *Georgia Simpson*
John Sandford · *Nat Simpson*
Andrew Butler · *Daniel 'Danny' Simpson*
Ken Sharrock · *'JC' Bradley*
Faith Brown · *Anne Bradley*
Sarah Withe · *Jules Bradley/Simpson*
Georgia Reece · *Eleanor Kitson*
Lisa Faulkner · *Louise Hope*
Eileen O'Brien · *Gladys Charlton*
Beverley Hills · *Elaine Davies/Johnson*
Heather Tomlinson · *Tanya Davies*
Ebony Gray · *Cassie Charlton*
Philip Dowd · *Christian Wright*
Jackie Downey · *Fee Phelan*
Gerard Kelly · *Callum Finnegan*
Jack Mythen · *Wills Corkhill*
Mark Moraghan · *Greg Shadwick*
Bernadette Foley · *Margi Shadwick*
Vincent Price · *Jason Shadwick*
Jennifer Ellison · *Emily Shadwick/O'Leary*
Suzanne Collins · *Nikki Shadwick*
Marji Campi · *Jessie Shadwick/Hilton*
Dan Mullane · *Joey Musgrove*
Barbara Drennan · *Niamh Musgrove*
Christian Ealey · *Matt Musgrove*
Natalie Earl · *Kelly Musgrove*
Sam Hudson · *Ryan Musgrove*
Jason Kavanagh · *Luke Musgrove*
Megan Munro · *Leah Musgrove*
Barbara Hatwell · *Anthea Brindley/Dixon*
Leon Lopez · *Jerome Johnson*
Cheryl Mackie · *Megan Brindley*
Hayley Smitton · *Sharon Bridges*
Heather Tomlinson · *Tanya Davies*
Debra Beaumont · *Deborah Lawson*
Kenneth Cope · *Ray Hilton*
Timothy Deenihan · *Dr Darren Roebuck*
Patricia Potter · *Victoria Seagram Wilcox*
Dugald Bruce Lockhart · *Mark Wilcox*
Lucinda Curtis · *Carolyn Roebuck*
Marcus Hutton · *Nathan Cuddington*
Alexandra Westcourt · *Shelly Bower*
Neil Caple · *Martin 'Marty' Murray*
Bernie Nolan · *Diane Murray*
Steven Fletcher · *Steven 'Steve' Murray*
Katy Lamont · *Adele Murray*
Raymond Quinn · *Anthony 'Tony' Murray*
Glynn Pritchard · *Christy Murray*
Helen Sheals · *Jan Murray*
Meg Johnson · *Brigid McKenna*
Suzette Llewellyn · *Yvonne 'Vonnie' Johnson*
Greg Pateras · *Clint Moffat*
Mickey Poppins · *Lance Powell*
Simon Chadwick · *Dave Burns*
Billie Clements · *Imelda Clough*
Anne-Marie Davies · *Katrina Evans*
Kris Mocherri · *Ali Gordon*
Jessica Noon · *Kirsty Gordon*
David Lyon · *Stuart Gordon*
John Burton · *Alan Gordon*
Annette Ekblom · *Debbie Gordon*
Lynsey McCaffrey · *Ruth Gordon Smith*
Barry Sloane · *Sean Smith*
Callum Gablin · *Luke Smith*
Paul Duckworth · *Jack Michaelson*

Creator Phil Redmond

Producers Phil Redmond, Stuart Doughty, Nicholas Prosser, Mal Young, Ric Mellis, Sue Sutton Mayo, Jon East, Paul Marquess, Nicky Higgins, David Andrews, David Hanson,

Writers Various, including Joe Ainsworth, Maurice Bessman, Alan Boulter, Roy Boulter, Judith Clucas, Frank Cottrell Boyce, Peter Cox, Chris Curry, Shaun Duggan, John Godber, Neil Jones, Jimmy McGovern, Colin McKeown, Carmel Morgan, Phil Redmond, Gareth Roberts, John Oakden, Susan Pleat, Andy Lynch, Kathleen Potter, Nick Saltrese, Allan Swift, Helen J. Wilson, Valerie Windsor, Barry Woodward

Theme Music Steve Wright and Dave Roylance. The theme was originally supposed to represent a helicopter flying from Liverpool's city centre out to the Brookside estate (as was shown in the show's various title sequences over the years). Sadly, it was always a bit too 'synth' to pull this off.

Creator Glen A. Larson, based on the Universal serials, which were inspired by Dick Calkins's comic strip **Producers** Glen A. Larson (executive), Medora Heilbron, Tim King, David G. Phinney (associate), Bruce Lansbury, Leslie Stevens, Richard Caffey, Calvin Clements Jr, Jock Gaynor, John Mantley, David J. O'Connell, John G. Stephens **Writers** Glen A. Larson, Leslie Stevens, Steve Greenberg, Aubrey Solomon, Cory Applebaum, Anne Collins, Alan Brennert, David Bennett Carren, Richard Fontana, D. C. Fontana, Cory Applebaum, Patrick Hobby, Michael Bryant, Kathleen Barnes, David Wise, Marty Pasko, John Gaynor, Dick Nelson, Chris Bunch, Allan Cole, Jaron Summers, Craig Buck, Robert W. Gilmer, William Mageean, David Chomsky, Norman Hudis, Robert Mitchell, Esther Mitchell, Paul Schneider, Margaret Schneider, Francis Moss, Calvin Clements, Stephen McPherson, William Keys **Theme Music** Stu Phillips

Updating the classic comic book strips (first seen in 1929) and the 1939 Buster Crabbe serial, *Buck Rogers in the 25th Century* could also be said to have ignored the Warner Brothers Daffy Duck spoofs *Duck Dodgers*, had it not been for the presence of Mel Blanc's voice in the cast list. This TV show saw NASA astronaut William 'Buck' Rogers shot into space and accidentally frozen by his life support systems, returning to Earth 500 years later.

For the remake, Buck awakes to find Earth at war with the Draconian empire. Viewers loved the sexy Wilma Deering and the cute 'bideebideebidee' android Twiki (voiced by Mel Blanc, and physically played by Felix Silla who had been Cousin Itt in ***The Addams Family***) who accompanied Buck on numerous adventures to battle scary aliens and voluptuous space amazons. Sadly, the second series suffered a change in approach so drastic one might almost have expected Fred Freiberger to have been involved (see ***Star Trek*** and ***Space 1999***). The camp humour increased and the dramatic content all but disappeared, despite the presence of stern-faced birdman Hawk. Cancelled mid-season after 11 episodes, it still proved to be a rather less po-faced alternative to ***Battlestar Galactica*** and on its transmission in the UK, where it was shown across most of the regions, it managed to do what Daleks, Cybermen and all manner of other monsters had failed to do by obliterating ***Doctor Who*** in the ratings and sending him scuttling from his traditional Saturday slot into mid-week.

The Buddha of Suburbia

Drama | BBC Two | episode duration 65 mins | broadcast 3 Nov 1993–24 Nov 1993

Cast

Naveen Andrews · *Karim Amir*
Roshan Seth · *Harron Amir*
Brenda Blethyn · *Margaret Amir*
Susan Fleetwood · *Eva Kay*
Steven Mackintosh · *Charlie Kay*
Nisha Nayar · *Jamila*
Harish Patel · *Changez*
John McEnery · *Uncle Ted*
Janet Dale · *Auntie Jean*
Badi Uzzaman · *Anwar*
Surendra Kochar · *Jeeta*
David Bamber · *Shadwell*
Jemma Redgrave · *Eleanor*

Producers Anna Kalnars (associate), Kevin Loader **Writers** Hanif Kureishi, Roger Michell, from the novel by Hanif Kureishi **Theme Music** David Bowie

Karim is the son of an Indian father and English mother and he experiences all the problems of growing up in a mixed-race family during 1970s Britain, a society that is becoming increasingly intolerant and racist. Karim's father is having an affair with a woman called Eva while he is supposed to be giving lessons on spiritualism, and Karim is becoming ever more sexually experimental with Eva's son, Charlie, as well as long-term Indian friend, Jamila. Karim eventually finds himself with an acting career and embarking on a relationship with fellow performer Eleanor, while Charlie ends up as a punk rock star. As the story progresses, so too does the decade.

Hanif Kureishi adapted the script for *The Buddha of Suburbia* from his own novel, along with Roger Michell, who also served as director, and, although feted by the critics, failed to win any major awards at that year's BAFTAS aside from a nod for Best Design. The real success of the series, performances aside, is the depiction of the 1970s as the photography captures the varying social stratas of the decade more successfully than most other dramas attempting to capture the decade. David Bowie provided an evocative original score for the series, with the theme song performing respectably in the charts. Star Naveen Andrews has since gone on to a successful career across the pond, landing a role in a darling of the 2004/2005 US television season, *Lost*. Steven Mackintosh would go on to portray a particularly nasty villain called 'The Street' in the fifth ***Prime Suspect*** investigation, in addition to a long and varied career in low budget independent movies.

Budgie

Drama | LWT for ITV | episode duration 50 mins | broadcast 9 Apr 1971–14 Jul 1972

Principal Cast

Adam Faith · *Ronald 'Budgie' Bird*
Iain Cuthbertson · *Charles Endell*
Lynn Dalby · *Hazel Fletcher*
Georgina Hale · *Jean*
June Lewis · *Mrs Endell*
George Tovey · *Jack Bird*
Margaret Nolan · *Inga*

Rio Fanning · *Grogan*
John Rhys-Davies · *Laughing Spam Fritter*

Creator Keith Waterhouse **Producers** Rex Firkin (executive), Verity Lambert **Writers** Keith Waterhouse, Willis Hall, Douglas Livingstone **Theme Music** 'The Loner', a Standard Music library piece written by Nick Harrison and, for the second series, 'Nobody's Fool', written by Ray Davies and performed by Cold Turkey

Adam Faith had been a pop star before he turned to acting, with two No. 1 singles (including 'What Do You Want?') and 20 other top 40 hits. However, by the end of the 1960s, he was a full-time actor. *Budgie* provided him with his first TV starring role, playing a former jailbird trying to make a living on the outside. The only person who is willing to give him work is Mr Charles Endell, a Soho 'businessman' who looks to Budgie to take the rap from the police for his own misdoings.

Though Budgie had many dreams of how to get rich quick, he never quite managed to turn any of them into a reality. He was what some might call a born loser. But his charm and naturally optimistic disposition won him a legion of fans, many of whom were too young to remember him as a pop heartthrob.

Budgie ran for just two series of 13 episodes each. A spin-off series starring Iain Cuthbertson as *Charles Endell, Esq* was made for transmission in 1979 but delayed due to the ITV strike and not shown until 1980. Adam Faith struck gold once more in 1992 starring opposite Zoë Wanamaker in the BBC One romantic comedy *Love Hurts*. His death in 2003 (at the age of 63) came as a shock to his many fans.

Buffy the Vampire Slayer

See pages 148–51

Bugs

Science Fiction | Carnival Films for BBC One | episode duration 50 mins | broadcast 1 Apr 1995–28 Aug 1999

Regular Cast
Jesse Birdsall · *Nicholas Beckett*
Jaye Griffiths · *Roslyn 'Ros' Henderson*
Craig McLachlan, Stephen Houghton · *Ed Russell*
Jan Harvey · *Jan*
Paula Hunt · *Alex Jordan*
Tom Felton · *James*
Michael Grandage · *Channing Harding*
Tim Post · *Jack Ball*

Creator Brian Clemens **Producers** Caroline Oulton, Tony Dennis (executive), Peter Hider, Brian Eastman, Stuart Doughty **Writers** Brian Clemens, Duncan Gould, Stephen Gallagher, Gregory Evans, Alan Whiting, Colin Brake, Miles Millar, Alfred Gough, Frank DePalma, Bruno Heller, Alison Leathart, Calvin Clements Jr, Clive Hopkins, Terry Borst, Alex Stewart, Christopher King, Stuart Doughty **Theme Music** Gavin and Simon Greenaway

Framed for a murder he didn't commit, government agent Nick Beckett turns to an organisation called Gizmos to clear his name. Prim, cool Ros Henderson and brash Ed Russell use the latest technological wizardry to prove Nick's innocence and recruit him to their cause.

Featuring an attractive cast choc-a-bloc full of ex-soap stars, *Bugs* was brought to our screens by Brian Clemens, the man who gave us ***The Professionals*** and some of the best episodes of ***The Avengers***. Whether it was *The Avengers* for the 1990s, or just another attempt by the BBC to make ***Doctor Who*** without *actually* making *Doctor Who*, *Bugs* was never a major ratings smash, but its clever use of cliffhangers and a little will-they-won't-they between Ros and Nick kept it on our screens for four years. The final episode tried the cliffhanger trick again – with Ros and Nick kidnapped by an unseen assailant – but for once it failed to tempt the Beeb into commissioning a fifth season.

Bullseye

Game Show | ATV/Central, in association with Chatsworth Television, for ITV | episode duration 25 mins | broadcast 1981–95

Regular Cast
Jim Bowen, Tony Green · *Presenter*

Creators Andrew Wood, Norman Vaughan **Producers** Peter Holmans, Bob Cousins **Theme Music** John Patrick

'You can't beat a bit of Bully,' chirped host Jim Bowen each week, and for nearly 15 years Sunday teatime viewers agreed with him. The idea of combining the distinctly unglamorous 'sport' darts with a pub-style general knowledge quiz was unpretentious, safe and aimed at a middle-aged, working-class audience that seemed rarely served by standard quiz-show fare like ***Mastermind*** or ***The Krypton Factor***. With programme mascot Bully the Bull proudly bursting into a pub during the animated opening title sequence, it's clear what target market the producers were aiming for! Animated graphics of Bully would often appear in the bottom right-hand corner of the screen, most memorably covering his eyes when the final round gamble didn't pay off, or reading a dictionary to check contestants' spelling during word-game questions.

Over the course of three rounds, three teams of two contestants (one a darts player, one good at answering questions) would compete against each other. In the first round, the darts player would try to achieve the highest score possible, throwing at a standard darts board. If his or

Continued on page 152

Buffy the Vampire Slayer

Buffy Summers (Sarah Michelle Gellar).

Every now and again, a TV show comes along that's been inspired by a hit movie. It's almost unheard of, however, for a TV show to be inspired by a *flop* movie that was hated by practically everyone who saw it. *Buffy the Vampire Slayer* is therefore almost unique among long-running TV shows, having been resurrected from the stone-cold corpse of a film few people had seen and even fewer people liked.

The TV series is a direct continuation from the feature film, in which a Californian teenage girl called Buffy Summers (played in the film by Kristy Swanson) discovers to her horror that she is in fact 'The Slayer', the one girl in the whole of the world who has been chosen to receive special powers that will aid humanity in its battle against the forces of evil. The start of the series sees Buffy – now played by former child actress Sarah Michelle Gellar – relocate to the small Californian town of Sunnydale with her mother Joyce. Arriving in a new town and new school is never easy for anybody, but Buffy makes good friends in the form of school geeks Willow and Xander, much to the disgust of 'it girl' Cordelia Chase. Buffy soon discovers that the school's English librarian Mr Giles is, in fact, her 'Watcher', a member

Telefantasy
Mutant Enemy Productions for WB/UPN, BBC Two/Sky One
Episode Duration: 45 mins
Broadcast: 10 Mar 1997–20 May 2003 (USA)

Regular Cast
Sarah Michelle Gellar · *Buffy Summers*
Alyson Hannigan · *Willow Rosenberg*
Nicholas Brendon · *Xander Harris*
Anthony Stewart Head · *Rupert Giles*
Charisma Carpenter · *Cordelia Chase*
David Boreanaz · *Angel*
Seth Green · *Daniel 'Oz' Osbourne*
James Marsters · *Spike*
Marc Blucas · *Riley Finn*
Emma Caulfield · *Anya Jenkins*
Michelle Trachtenberg · *Dawn Summers*
Amber Benson · *Tara Maclay*
Kristine Sutherland · *Joyce Summers*
Julie Benz · *Darla*
Mercedes McNab · *Harmony Kendall*
Mark Metcalf · *The Master*
Robia La Morte · *Jenny Calendar*
Armin Shimerman · *Principal Snyder*
Juliet Landau · *Drusilla*
Danny Strong · *Jonathan Levinson*
Robin Sachs · *Ethan Rayne*
Eliza Dushku · *Faith*
Harry Groener · *Mayor Richard Wilkins III*
Alexis Denisof · *Wesley Wyndam-Price*
Lindsay Crouse · *Professor Maggie Walsh*
Leonard Roberts · *Forrest Gates*
Bailey Chase · *Graham Miller*
Andy Umberger · *D'Hoffryn*
George Hertzberg · *Adam*
Sharon Ferguson · *The First Slayer*
Clare Kramer · *Glory*
Charlie Weber · *Ben*
Abraham Benrubi · *Olaf the Troll*
Harris Yulin · *Quentin Travers*
Adam Busch · *Warren Meers*
Joel Grey · *Doc*
Tom Lenk · *Andrew Wells*
Kali Rocha · *Halfrek*
DB Woodside · *Principal Robin Wood*
Iyari Limon · *Kennedy*
Indigo · *Rona*
Sarah Hagan · *Amanda*
Clara Bryant · *Molly*
Felicia Day · *Vi*
Nathan Fillion · *Caleb*

of a secret order established to protect, guide and train each Slayer so she can perform her vampire fighting duties to the best of her ability. Initially resistant to take up the calling she never volunteered for in the first place, Buffy's natural sense of duty comes into play when an ancient and immensely powerful vampire called The Master is resurrected. Together with her Watcher, her friends, and the brooding presence of a vampire-with-a-soul called Angel, Buffy fights back against an assorted variety of demons, monsters and other nasties.

At the end of the first series, *Buffy the Vampire Slayer* had established a nice formula – a few kung-fu style fight sequences, a liberal smattering of smart-alec comments, a hip college-rock soundtrack, and you've got another successful teen programme like ***Dawson's Creek*** or ***Beverly Hills 90210*** – but with a supernatural element. However, what happened over the course of the second season would set *Buffy the Vampire Slayer* apart from all of the rest of the teen drama fare. In brief, it took risks with its characters and storylines that would have been daring for a soap or ongoing drama, but which were jaw dropping for the sci-fi/fantasy genre which traditionally told one-off stories each week or rarely referred to past continuity. One of *Buffy*'s great strengths is its impeccable sense of its own past, without ever alienating any recent converts to the show. *Buffy* took weeks, sometimes whole years or even longer, to develop ongoing stories.

On a superficial reading, the two-part story 'Innocence' and 'Surprise' was the upsetting story of an ancient curse and its effects on Buffy's new boyfriend, the friendly vampire Angel. This curse meant that whenever Angel enjoyed a moment of true happiness, his soul would be removed and he would revert to being a fearsome demonic killer. On the night of Buffy's 17th birthday, she loses her virginity to her boyfriend – scant minutes after, Angel's soul is ripped from him and he becomes the snarling monster Angelus. Making the heroine's boyfriend the main villain of the series is a marvellous twist and it's also a marvellous metaphor for the hopes and fears facing all teenage girls. Is my boyfriend the right one? Should I give it up for him? Will he turn into a monster the moment he sleeps with me? *Buffy the Vampire Slayer* manages to portray a beautifully layered metaphor for the entire experience of growing up in modern day America. In one episode, the fear of loneliness and being an outsider at school leads one girl to literally become invisible. When Buffy finally decides to 'come out' to her mother about the fact that she's the Slayer, the response is the hilariously appropriate, 'Have you tried not being a Slayer?'

At the heart of *Buffy*'s success must surely be the work of series creator and writer Joss Whedon. Whedon's film screenwriting credits included *Toy Story* (1995), *Alien Resurrection* (1997) and a script polish on *Speed* (1994) – the slick confident style he developed in those films is transparent throughout the whole of *Buffy*. As the programme's 'showrunner', Whedon had a tight control on the development of the whole series, devising ongoing storylines, introducing new regular characters, and generally steering things in the right direction. A fan

Creator Joss Whedon

Producers Various, including Joss Whedon, Fran Rubel Kuzui, Kaz Kuzui, David Solomon, Howard Gordon, David Greenwalt, Marti Noxon, Jane Espenson, David Fury, Doug Petrie, Gail Berman

Writers Various, including Joss Whedon, David Greenwalt, Rob Des Hotel, Dean Batali, Marti Noxon, David Fury, Jane Espenson, Doug Petrie, Tracey Forbes, Rebecca Rand Kirshner, Steven S. DeKnight, Drew Z. Greenberg, Drew Goddard

Theme Music Nerf Herder

of genre films and TV shows, Whedon often said he felt cheated by watching many of them – why, for example, did the young blonde girl always run down dead-end alleyways when being chased by a monster? Creating *Buffy* was his response to these clichéd conventions – Whedon and his staff always tried whenever possible never to conform to these clichés and to surprise their viewers.

Never afraid to try new approaches, Whedon wrote and directed several episodes of *Buffy* that received particular acclaim. Season four's 'Hush' features the arrival in Sunnydale of a group of sinister demons called The Gentlemen. With permanent metallic grins and a creepy method of travelling while floating a foot above the ground, The Gentlemen managed to steal the voices of everyone in the town. The result was an episode of television with no dialogue whatsoever for almost 30 minutes. Not only was this a bold experiment in itself, it also mirrored beautifully the problems Buffy was currently experiencing, in being unable to communicate with those around her. When Buffy finally defeats The Gentlemen by screaming at them, the post-modern subversion of the traditional feminine role in horror films is clearly displayed. Of course, this being Buffy, once she 'finds her voice' and kills the monsters, she finds she still can't talk to those she loves. This episode gained an Emmy nomination for Best Writing in a Drama Series.

Throughout its seven seasons and 144 episodes, *Buffy the Vampire Slayer* constantly challenged the audience's expectations and pushed back the boundaries of what was expected within a genre programme. When Buffy's best friend Willow slowly realised her true sexuality, the programme never pandered to gratuitousness by portraying a glamorous 'lipstick lesbian' relationship. Instead, the tenderness of Willow and Tara's faltering steps together provided one of the most heart-warming relationships seen in the series. When (inevitably) the programme received complaints for daring to portray any kind of gay relationship, Whedon's on-line response showed that not only his heart but also his head was in the right place. Acknowledging that many viewers found a specific element of Willow's character objectionable, Whedon posted a long and somewhat rambling 'apology' on line that finished with a heavily ironic promise – that the fact that Willow was *Jewish* would never be mentioned again . . .

One of Buffy's great strengths is its impeccable sense of its own past, without ever alienating any recent converts to the show. *Buffy* took weeks, sometimes whole years or even longer, to develop ongoing stories.

After five years and 100 episodes, *Buffy the Vampire Slayer* came to an end in two very different ways. First of all, original US network WB decided not to order any more episodes – as a consequence, the final two years switched channel to UPN. Second, Buffy herself died and was buried, following her self-sacrifice to save the world from the glamorous hell-god Glory. Being a fantasy series, death would never hold a good Slayer back, and Buffy was resurrected at the start of the next series. Always fond of plumbing emotional depths, viewers discovered that Buffy had actually gone to heaven, so it was hardly surprising when she got more than a little bit depressed about being back here in a world full of death, monsters and whiny younger sisters. Another rule-breaking episode appeared in this series, 'Once More With Feeling' – the *Buffy* musical. With a score reminiscent of many West End hits (all written by the supernaturally multi-talented Whedon, of course), the regular cast got to sing and dance their way through the usual mayhem and carnage, courtesy (in story terms) of a musical demon.

In contrast to the musical episode, the earlier 'The Body' is one of the starkest and most understated episodes of television ever broadcast. When Buffy discovers her mother lying dead on her living room sofa, we travel with her on an unbearably accurate portrayal of the immediate aftermath of bereavement. For once, Buffy can do nothing to save someone she cares about, and anybody who has ever lost a loved one shares her pain in this carefully crafted masterpiece of subtlety. For almost the whole episode, there are no monsters, no spells, nothing except a raw examination of what it feels like to suffer a loss. It's breathtaking television that needs to be seen by anyone who appreciates quality drama.

Eventually, after seven years, *Buffy* drew to a close, largely due to the desire by series star Gellar to branch out into different, more challenging, roles on the big screen – her first being that of ghost hunter Daphne in *Scooby Doo* (2002) – and also because the entire production team were exhausted thanks to a hectic schedule working on this show, spin-off series ***Angel*** and science fiction show *Firefly* at the same time. *Buffy* was, in effect, a soap opera hidden within a horror show – by couching fantastic elements in a language more familiar to most viewers, it attracted a brand new audience to genre programming and revitalised this most neglected of niche programme sectors. For a programme about the dead rising from beyond the grave, that seems more than a little appropriate.

her partner successfully answered a general knowledge question, they would swap the points scored for pounds. The two highest-scoring teams then went through to a second round, with a specially modified dartboard segmented into categories such as showbiz, literature, sport, etc. The 'clever' half of the partnership would then nominate a category for their dart thrower to aim for: should the dart land in the correct category, a bonus would be scored. Whichever category the dart landed in, a question would then be asked with cash to be won accordingly. At the end of this round, once again the lowest-scoring team would be eliminated, with the winners moving on to play 'Bully's Prize Board'. This board was largely black with eight thin red segments and a red bullseye. For every dart that hit a red segment, the contestants would take home a nominated prize. 'Keep out of the black and in the red – nothing in this game for two in a bed,' became Jim's best-known catchphrase.

Unfortunately, all of these prizes appeared as though they'd come straight out of a Littlewoods catalogue – a blender for Mum, a new lawnmower for Dad, perhaps a tricycle for the kids. Hitting the bullseye itself would result in a slightly bigger prize, such as a hi-fi system or a new telly. Taking a leaf out of the Bruce Forsyth Bumper Book of Presenting, Jim Bowen kept the show moving along courtesy of catchphrases repeated at regular intervals, and like the chequebook and pen awarded in ***Blankety Blank***, the bendy Bully, darts and commemorative tankard (a goblet for the lady contestants) presented to the losers are probably worth more nowadays for collectors on eBay than any of the original prizes.

Once the winning team had got their hands on as many of the glamorous prizes as they could, they faced a final terrible choice; should they gamble their barbeque set and swing-ball against the chance of winning an as yet unknown, much bigger prize? Inevitably, they did have a go at winning the top prize – all they had to do was to score 101 with six darts. For the winners, there were smiles all round. Those who failed to score 101 (at least half of everyone who tried) would still be shown the prize that they'd lost – 'Let's see what you would 'ave won!' Along with traditional game-show prizes of motor cars and foreign holidays, the producers somehow thought that a speed boat would be a suitable prize for contestants more at home in a Wigan pub than in the south of France. Owing to the unique nature of the pairs of contestants in *Bullseye* (most of them two blokes who happened to be mates from their local pub darts team), prizes that might have been perfectly acceptable to a married couple (the norm on most game shows at the time) became, for this show, completely inappropriate. As a result, many people at home took great joy in shouting at the telly: 'How on earth do you split a fitted kitchen or a speedboat between two people?!'

And to add insult to injury, the normally jaunty theme tune would be played in a minor key when the final gamble was lost – a moment of utter cruelty and bathos that still ranks today (in a world of reality TV embarrassment and humiliation that's much more 'in your face') as one of the nastiest format twists ever seen on television. And *that's* why so many people loved their weekly bit of *Bully*.

Butterflies

Sitcom | BBC Two/One | episode duration 30 mins | broadcast 10 Nov 1978–19 Oct 1983

Regular Cast

Wendy Craig · *Ria Parkinson*
Geoffrey Palmer · *Ben Parkinson*
Nicholas Lyndhurst · *Adam Parkinson*
Andrew Hall · *Russell Parkinson*
Bruce Montague · *Leonard Dunn*
Michael Ripper · *Thomas*
Joyce Windsor · *Ruby*

Creator/Writer Carla Lane **Producers** Sydney Lotterby, Gareth Gwenlan **Theme Music** 'Love is Like a Butterfly' was originally a hit for country and western legend Dolly Parton – it reached No. 1 in the USA but wasn't actually released as a single over here. Clare Torry sang the vocals on this cover version arranged by Ronnie Hazelhurst. Another piece of music was used to great effect to underpin Ria's cogitations – the mournful *Adagio in C* by Albinoni.

Carla Lane's *Butterflies* was a definite departure from her earlier work such as ***The Liver Birds*** or ***Bless This House***, turning away from the concept of a comedy show that tried to squeeze as many jokes as possible into half an hour, and instead focusing on a storyline that actually said something about life. By creating a show that concentrated just as much on the 'sit' as on the 'com', Carla Lane attracted huge critical acclaim and kick-started a genre of melancholy humour and 'comedy dramas' that persists to this day.

Having made her name in traditional comedies like ***And Mother Makes Three***, Wendy Craig was perhaps an obvious choice to play yet another sitcom mother. However, it was Carla Lane's primary objective to undermine that stereotypical view of what a mother is, how she should behave, and what she wants out of life. By placing challenging lines in the mouth of 'everywoman' Wendy Craig, Lane enabled every female viewer to empathise with her plight. Craig plays Ria Parkinson, a bored and frustrated housewife with two nearly grown-up children, married to steadfast and reliable dentist Ben. Life for Ria is becoming increasingly desperate – she finds she can no longer communicate effectively with Ben, who'd rather spend his time catching butterflies than sorting out their relationship problems. Her two sons, Russell and Adam, continually bicker with each other and no longer really need her, treating the family house as more of a hotel than a home. Furthermore, she's always been useless on the domestic side of things, being unable to cook anything that even approaches edibility, and having to rely upon a surly (scene-stealing) cleaner called Ruby to keep the house neat and tidy.

Then, one day Ria meets attractive middle-aged businessman Leonard Dunn. Ria is flattered by Leonard's attention and begins to look forward to their 'chance' encounters and planned meetings feeding the ducks in the park. Although viewers get to hear Ria's unvocalised thoughts and emotions, we too share her confusion and mixed feelings about her life. We can see that Ria is largely undervalued and unappreciated by her family, but at the same time we know that deep down there's still a great deal of love there for her to enjoy. But what about Leonard? Could she make a life with him? Or has time and life now passed her completely by?

Over four seasons and 28 episodes, viewers followed Ria's dilemmas, until in the last episode she stopped her meetings with Leonard and returned to her family, unsure whether or not she'd made the right decision. It wasn't until 17 years had passed that we discovered what had happened to Ria – on 17 November 2000, a ***Comic Relief*** sketch brought together almost the whole of the original *Butterflies* cast. We found out that Ria and Ben's marriage had indeed survived, and that she'd recently become a grandmother. Reunited with Leonard for one last time, she confirmed that she'd been glad she met him, but was also happy that their relationship was never anything other than platonic. Once again written by Carla Lane, this special provided the perfect coda to a delightful, if occasionally maudlin, series.

Button Moon

Children's Puppetry | Thames for ITV | episode duration 10 mins | broadcast 1981–1987

Regular Cast
Robin Parkinson · *Narrator*

Creators Ian Allen and John Thirtle of Playboard Puppets **Producer** Charles Warren **Writer** Ian Allen **Theme Music** Former-husband and wife Peter Davison and Sandra Dickinson, who sang 'We're off to Button Moon' in the opening titles and 'We've been to Button Moon' in the closing titles. Genius.

Button Moon was an environmentally sound idea, with all of the characters and settings either made from household items or looked suspiciously like they were (Mr Spoon's rocket ship had markings suspiciously similar to those of a certain well-known brand of baked beans). Mr Spoon, his wife and their daughter Tina lived at Cardboard Box House, Treacle Street. Nearby live Tina's friend Eggbert and his mummy Vanilla, the military Captain Large, Small Bottle and naughty Little Bottle, Rag Doll and Freddie Teddy, Benny Bin and Betty Bucket, and many other strange and inventive beings. Heaven help them if they ever discover fire. . .

Mr Spoon and his daughter Tina make regular trips in their rocket ('Blast off!') across Blanket Sky to the yellow attraction of Button Moon. In reality, it was a group of very creative puppeteers, dressed in black and performing against a black velvety backdrop.

Byker Grove

Children's Drama | Zenith North for BBC One | episode duration 25 mins | broadcast 8 Nov 1989–present

Regular Cast
Lucy Walsh · *Julie Warner*
Caspar Berry · *Martin 'Gill' Gillespie*
Declan Donnelly · *Duncan*
Jill Halfpenny · *Nicola Dobson*
Sally McQuillan · *Donna Bell*
Neil Shearer · *Andrew 'Cas' Pearson*
Craig Grieveson · *Ian Webster*
Brett Adams · *Noddy*
Nicola Bell · *Debbie Dobson*
Ant McPartlin · *Peter 'PJ' Jenkins*
Michelle Charles · *Marilyn 'Charley' Charlton*
Nicola Ewart · *Jemma Dobson*
Victoria Taylor · *Angel O'Hagan*
Lyndsey Todd · *Chrissie Van Den Berg*
Donna Air · *Charlie*
Stephen Carr · *Barney Hardy*
Luke Dale · *Frew*
Gemma Graham · *Amanda Bewick*
Grant Adams · *Ed*
Kerry Ann Christiansen · *Flora*
Claire Graham · *Anna Turnbull*
Joanne Mcintosh · *Brigid O'Hagan*
Andrew Smith · *Alfie Turnbull*

Creators Adele Rose **Producers** Ian Squires (executive), Matthew Robinson, Helen Gregory, Edward Pugh **Writers** Various

Created by ***Coronation Street*** scriptwriter Adele Rose to fill in the gaps in the CBBC schedule when ***Grange Hill*** wasn't on, *Byker Grove* has since eclipsed its stable-mate to become the BBC's most popular ongoing children's drama series. Initially following the story of Julie Warner, a Londoner forced to move with her family to the Northeast, the show revolved around a youth centre in Byker and the kids Julie met there. Eventually the programme had no need for its 'outsider guide' and focused solely on the Geordie kids.

The series quickly caught on to the need for social issues that had driven *Grange Hill*. A strong moral centre ran through the programme, always quick to show the repercussions of criminal and thoughtless activity – notably during a paint-balling day where PJ was shot in the face and blinded. The series drew criticism for including the topic of homosexuality when Noddy struggled to control his feelings for his friend Gary and kissed him at the cinema.

Byker Grove provided a starting block for a number of Newcastle-born actors and presenters, including Donna

Air, Charlie Hunnam (***Queer as Folk***), Jill Halfpenny (*Coronation Street*, ***EastEnders***, *Strictly Come Dancing* (see ***Come Dancing***)) and of course Ant McPartlin and Declan Donnelly, who as their characters PJ and Duncan scored 12 Top 20 hits between 1994 and 1997, including 'Let's Get Ready to Rhumble'. As themselves, Ant and Dec are currently Britain's top light entertainers thanks to shows such as ***SM:TV Live, I'm a Celebrity . . . Get Me Out of Here*** and ***Ant and Dec's Saturday Night Takeaway***.

Cadfael

Crime Drama | Central for ITV | episode duration 75 mins | broadcast 29 May 1994–28 Dec 1998

Regular Cast
Derek Jacobi · *Brother Cadfael*
Sean Pertwee, Eoin McCarthy, Anthony Green · *Hugh Beringar*
Peter Copley · *Abbot Herribert*
Terrence Hardiman · *Abbot Radulfus*
Michael Culver · *Prior Robert*
Julian Firth · *Brother Jerome*
Mark Charnock · *Brother Oswin*
Albie Woodington · *Sergeant Will Warden*

Producers Ted Childs (executive), Stephen Smallwood **Writers** Russell Lewis, Paul Pender, Christopher Russell, Ben Rostul, Richard Stoneman, from the novels by Edith Pargeter (writing as Ellis Peters) **Theme Music** Colin Towns

He had been servant to a wool merchant as a child and fought in the Crusades, witnessing the fall of Jerusalem. He once captained a fishing boat, even unknowingly fathered a son, but at the age of 40, Cadfael ap Meilyr ap Dafydd became a Benedictine monk living in the Abbey of St Peter and St Paul in Shrewsbury. His knowledge of plants and herbs proves invaluable as a minister to the sick, but it's his keen mind that provides his greatest skill, as a detective. He observes all, breaking down information methodically. In a pile of 100 dead bodies, only his eyes could pick out two who were murdered and placed among the corpses to conceal their true end.

Among the glut of rural detectives that filled the TV schedules of the 1990s, Cadfael's gimmick was to live in a time long before pathologists and forensic science. Thirteen of the 20 *Cadfael* novels were adapted for television, beginning with Edith Pargeter's second tale, the appropriately titled 'One Corpse Too Many'. Filmed in Budapest to recreate medieval Shropshire, the series was littered with familiar faces, including Terrence Hardiman and Michael Culver, both late of ***Secret Army***, guest stars like Roy Barraclough and Peter Baldwin from ***Coronation Street***, Anna Friel, Julian Glover, Sean Pertwee and of course starring Derek Jacobi, whose experiences on ***I, Claudius*** prepared him for similarly bloody despatches here.

Cagney and Lacey

See pages 156–7

Call My Bluff

Quiz Show | BBC Two/One | episode duration 30 mins | broadcast 17 Oct 1965–22 Dec 1988, 23 Jun 1997–present

Regular Cast
Robin Ray, Joe Melia, Peter Wheeler, Robert Robinson, Nicholas Parsons, Bob Holness, Fiona Bruce, Alan Coren · *Hosts*
Frank Muir, Robert Morley, Patrick Campbell, Arthur Marshall, Sandi Toksvig, Rod Liddle, Alan Coren · *Team Captains*

Creators Mark Goodson, Bill Todman **Producers** T. Leslie Jackson, Bryan Sears, Johnny Downes

Call My Bluff is the classic panel game show that preceded the tightly scripted nature of modern fare such as ***Have I Got News For You?*** and *So They Think It's All Over*. Two teams of three celebrities discuss the meaning of unusual words and attempt to outfox each other as to which is the true meaning, overlooked by a usually erudite and benign chairman. The bluff, or otherwise, is revealed by the high tech opening of a beige envelope.

A staple of the BBC Two schedules pretty much since the channel began broadcasting, the original run of this intelligent, witty show (in keeping with the slightly more intellectual remit of the second BBC channel) ran for over 23 years, outlasting its US counterpart by about 22 and a half years. Originally, *Call My Bluff* was something of a cross pollination, being based on a segment of the American radio show *Says You!*, which in turn was based on the British radio quiz *My Word!* A variation of the theme came with a 1969 American game show *Liar's Club*, hosted by ***The Twilight Zone***'s Rod Serling and involving celebrities lying about the purpose of archaic objects.

Robin Ray oversaw the early editions of *Call My Bluff*, with Robert Morley and Frank Muir as team captains, but the classic line-up came in the 1970s, with Frank Muir pitted against Patrick Campbell, and then, later, Arthur Marshall, under the watchful eye of Robert Robinson. After an absence of nine years, *Call My Bluff* returned to TV in 1997, now on BBC One, under the chairmanship of Bob Holness. Newsreader with sex appeal Fiona Bruce would take over in 2003, in a revamp of the series that appalled many viewers by ditching the much-loved team captain Sandi Toksvig.

Callan

See pages 158–60

Camberwick Green

Animation | Gordon Murray Puppets for BBC One | episode duration 15 mins | broadcast 3 Jan–28 Mar 1966

Voice Cast
Brian Cant

Creator/Producer Gordon Murray **Writers** Gordon Murray, Alison Prince **Theme Music** 'The Music Box' by Freddie Phillips: 'Here is a box, a musical box, wound up and ready to play . . .'

Continued on page 161

Cagney and Lacey

Christine Cagney (Sharon Gless) and Mary Beth Lacey (Tyne Daly).

Mary Beth Lacey and Christine Cagney are two police detectives working at the 14th Precinct in New York City. Together, they solve all manner of crimes while simultaneously juggling the challenges they face in their private lives. Mary Beth is married to construction worker Harvey and they have two sons – Harv Jr and Michael. Christine is far more career-minded than her partner, having followed in her father Charlie's footsteps by joining the police force. Constantly battling against a propensity for alcoholism, and reeling from one unsuccessful relationship to another, Christine often finds herself batting off light-hearted advances from her colleagues – notably notorious hairy-chested womaniser Victor Isbecki. Isbecki's partner is serious, dedicated – and black – family man Mark Petrie. Completing the line-up of regular characters is elderly and kindly Paul La Guardia, moustachioed Desk Sergeant Coleman, and leading the whole team the portly form of grumpy Lieutenant Samuels. Often, Mary Beth and Christine find themselves in the women's bathroom, putting the world to rights or simply just discussing the facts behind the latest crime they're working on.

Before *Cagney and Lacey*, the idea of a cop 'buddy' show starring two women simply had never been contemplated in American TV. The creation of the show, by producer Barney Rosenzweig and writing partners Barbara Avedon and Barbara Corday, would not only challenge ever pre-conceived idea about the nature of cop shows, it would also introduce a whole new demographic to corporations buying advertising space in such programmes – namely women. Initially conceived as a comedy film and titled *Newman and Redford* (the two stars of famous Western 'buddy' movie *Butch Cassidy and the Sundance Kid* (1969)), the idea didn't get much support from the US networks. Eventually, reshaped as a drama and renamed *Cagney and Lacey*, a pilot film starring ***M*A*S*H***'s Loretta Swit and Tyne Daly (recently seen as Clint Eastwood's feisty partner in the 1976 'Dirty Harry' film *The Enforcer*) was commissioned by CBS. The unexpected success of the pilot led to a short run of six episodes being made for the following season. However, with Swit unable to reprise her role, the part of Christine Cagney went to striking actress Meg Foster.

Ratings for this first short series weren't spectacular, so the network – concerned about accusations of producing an overly feminist (or even, heaven forbid, lesbian-friendly) series – planned not to make any more. However, as the programme was receiving both critical acclaim from women's groups and was selling well overseas, CBS decided to give it another go. The concession this time was that the programme and the two principal characters would be 'softened', to remove any possible 'lesbian reading' and to thereby make the programme more appealing to advertisers. A direct result of this 'butching-down' process was the replacement (from series two onwards) of Meg Foster with the blonder, more obviously glamorous Sharon Gless as Cagney number three. At the same time, the programme's focus shifted from just covering police procedures to dealing with the life and loves of the two officers. Audiences – particularly women – loved seeing police work from their perspective for the very first time. Despite this, ratings were still not massive, and CBS cancelled the show once again. A huge letter-writing campaign from members of the public around the world – combined with success at the Emmy Awards – encouraged the network to once again bring it back.

Never afraid of shying away from controversial plotlines, *Cagney and Lacey* dealt with subjects as diverse as cancer, Christine's rape, the difficult decision on Mary Beth's part on whether to quit the force or not when she falls pregnant (she didn't, and the baby was named Alice Christine), alcoholism and even the cocaine addiction of Christine's police officer boyfriend Dory McKenna. Emmys flew thick and fast, bagging Outstanding Drama Series in both 1985 and 1986. Even more spectacular was the fact that both stars were nominated for the Best Actress Emmy Award in every single one of the six years that the series was in production. On the two occasions that four-time-winner Tyne Daly failed to pick up the gong, her colleague Sharon Gless took the honours.

Cagney and Lacey finally came to an end in 1988. However, Gless and Daly were reunited several times during the 1990s in a series of irregular (and increasingly dopey) reunion telemovies. After the success of *Cagney and Lacey*, Sharon Gless took the lead role in short-lived legal drama *The Trials of Rosie O'Neill*. *Cagney* producer Barney Rosenzweig, who by then was Gless's husband, had created this role for her. In the early 2000s, in a career move of pure irony, Gless – who had been employed in *Cagney and Lacey* in an 'anti-lesbian' move by the network – joined the cast of the highly successful US version of ***Queer As Folk***. Tyne Daly plays the mother in the ongoing US family drama series *Judging Amy*.

Crime Drama
Filmways Pictures/Orion Television for CBS (shown on BBC One)
Episode Duration: 50 mins
Broadcast: 8 Oct 1981, 25 Mar 1982–16 May 1986, Nov 1994, 25 Oct 1995, 2 May 1995, 29 Jan 1996 (USA)

Regular Cast
Tyne Daly · *Detective Mary Beth Lacey*
Loretta Swit, Meg Foster, Sharon Gless · *Detective Christine Cagney*
Al Waxman · *Lieutenant Bert Samuels*
Martin Kove · *Detective Victor Isbecki*
Carl Lumbly · *Detective Mark Petrie*
Ronald Hunter, John Karlen · *Harvey Lacey*
Sidney Clute · *Detective Paul LaGuardia*
Harvey Atkin · *Desk Sergeant Ronald Coleman*
Dick O'Neill · *Charlie Cagney*
Tony La Torre · *Harvey Lacey Jr*
Troy Slaten · *Michael Lacey*
Dana Bardolph, Paige Bardolph, Michelle Sepe · *Alice Lacey*
Michael Fairman · *DI Knelman*
Barry Primus · *Sergeant Dory McKenna*
Stephen Macht · *David Keeler*
Robert Hegyes · *Detective Manny Esposito*
Jason Bernard · *DI Marquette*
Dan Shor · *Detective Jonah Newman*
Paul Mantee · *Detective Al Corassa*

Creators Barbara Avedon, Barbara Corday, Barney Rosenzweig

Producers Barney Rosenzweig, Shelley List (executive), Abe Milrad, Ken Wales, P. K. Knelman (associate), Jonathan Estrin, Liz Coe, Peter Lefcourt, Richard M. Rosenbloom, Harry R. Sherman, Ralph Singleton

Writers Various, including Frank Abatemarco, Barbara Avedon, Deborah R. Baron, Steve Brown, Barbara Corday, Barbara Corday, Sharon Elizabeth Doyle, Terry Louise Fisher, Kathryn Ford, Patricia Green, Allison Hock, Georgia Jeffries, Paul Ehrmann, Peter Lefcourt, Michael Piller, Donna Powers, Wayne Powers, Frederick Rappaport, Del Reisman, Barney Rosenzweig, April Smith, Aubrey Solomon, Frank South

Theme Music Bill Conti

Callan

Callan (Edward Woodward) keeps a tight hold on Lonely (Russell Hunter).

A light bulb swings in a gloomy room, casting light across a brick wall. In the shadows, a man squints in the glare of the light. Suddenly a gunshot rings out and the bulb shatters, leaving smoke to smoulder up from the broken filament. Another shot and a photo of the man is pierced with a bullet.

As the above description of the title sequence might suggest, *Callan* was in a class of its own. Edward Woodward starred as David Callan, a reluctant employee of Her Majesty's Security Service assigned to a secret section with a very special remit. Callan is an assassin, tasked with removing individuals perceived to pose a serious risk to national security, whether that be illegal weapons smuggling, passing secrets to the Russians or simply knowing too much to be allowed to slip through the net. The job brings Callan into contact with people who, in different circumstances, might be considered likeable, which is why, unlike other operatives in the Section, he must be 100 per cent convinced that his target truly deserves to die before he'll do the job. For Callan, there's no such thing as 'job satisfaction' – there's simply disappointment in the inevitability of human nature to produce monsters.

Invariably dressed in a brown-grey suit and matching raincoat, Callan is ashen-faced, his hair receding and speckled with grey, his waistline developing a slight middle-aged spread. In other words, he is ordinary, able to blend into his surroundings and become instantly forgettable if necessary. He's polite, charming almost, with a grim sense of humour and a belief in the absolutes of right and wrong, a distinct disadvantage in a world of greys. It's just a shame he has such a peculiar talent for killing.

We first encountered Callan in an episode of *Armchair Theatre* called 'A Magnum for Schneider' in which Callan, having left the world of espionage to work as an office clerk, is coerced into taking on another job by his former boss, Hunter. The target is a man called Schneider (Joseph Furst), who Hunter claims is an arms trader. Callan learns that he has something in common with Schneider – they are both model soldier enthusiasts – and it is this connection that allows him to investigate Schneider at close hand. However, Callan also has to deal with the suspicion, later confirmed, that Hunter has set a trap for him, having despatched his lackey Toby Meres (Peter Bowles) to frame Callan for murder. But Callan manages to turn the situation and leaves Meres with the body of Schneider . . .

The success of 'A Magnum for Schneider' led to the commissioning of a series of seven episodes. The first is a virtual rerun of 'A Magnum for Schneider' with Callan investigating a suspected Nazi war criminal, once again with the oily Toby Meres snapping at his heels (for the series, Bowles was replaced by Anthony Valentine). The entrapment of Callan by Hunter is played out once again, with Hunter deliberately revealing to Callan that his personnel file has been placed inside a red folder – the system Hunter uses to show which people are thought to be too dangerous to be allowed to live. Hence Callan is persuaded to return to work for the section – on a strictly freelance basis.

At the beginning of series two, we learn that Hunter is merely the codename of the head of the section and so as the series progresses we meet various replacement Hunters. The first (Michael Goodliffe) is a breezy civil servant who brings Callan back into the section full time and whom Callan considers to be out of his depth; even when an assassin threatens Hunter's life, he continues to react with mild bemusement and displays little awareness of the gravity of his position. However, another replacement (Derek Bond) enjoys a mutual respect with Callan. They're both fully aware of the risks they have to take, but this Hunter at least plays fair and, as a consequence, Callan almost regards him as a friend. In a cruel twist, the final episode of the second series sees Callan shoot Hunter after being brainwashed by enemy agents into believing him to be an arch traitor. Callan is shot by Toby Meres but too late to save Hunter. Viewers were left uncertain as to whether Callan himself had survived. Legend has it that graffiti was seen at the time proclaiming 'Callan lives!' and a few rumblings were heard at Number 10, as it was prime minister Harold Wilson's favourite show. Whether that influenced the decision to continue the series we don't know.

The black and white episodes had been made by ITV franchise-holder ATV, but Thames took over the show in 1970, this time in colour. In 'Where Else Could I Go?' we rejoin Callan just a few months after the traumatic events of the previous episode. Callan has been in hospital recuperating when he is visited by James Cross, the Section's replacement for Meres, who has transferred to New York. Cross brings with him a message from the new Hunter – they want Callan back in the Section ASAP. Impetuous, over-confident and incapable of following Callan's orders, Cross turns out to be more a liability than an asset. In 'Summoned to Appear', it's Cross's carelessness that results in an innocent man falling under the wheels of a moving train, leaving Callan, identified by police as a witness to the incident, forced to give (false) evidence at the inquest.

Outside the Section, Callan has only one regular acquaintance, a small-time crook called Lonely, so called because of the stench that

Crime Drama
ATV/Thames for ITV
Episode Duration: 50 mins
Broadcast: 4 Feb 1967, 8 Jul 1967–24 May 1972, 2 Sep 1981

Regular Cast
Edward Woodward · *David Callan*
Russell Hunter · *Lonely*
Ronald Radd, Michael Goodliffe, Derek Bond, William Squire · *Hunter*
Peter Bowles/Anthony Valentine · *Toby Meres*
Lisa Langdon · *Liz Marsh – Hunter's Secretary*
Patrick Mower · *James Cross*
Clifford Rose · *Dr Snell*
Harry Towb · *Judd*

Creator James Mitchell (with Terence Feely)

Producers Terence Feely, John Kershaw (associate), Lloyd Shirley (executive), Leonard White, Reginald Collin, Leonard Lewis

Writers James Mitchell, Robert Banks Stewart, Ray Jenkins, Hugh D'Allenger, Trevor Preston, William Emms, Michael Winder, Bill Craig, John Kershaw, Peter Hill, George Markstein

Theme Music 'Girl in the Dark' by Jack Trombey, a bluesy bass tune that was also used as incidental music in the episodes

follows him around. Through this relationship we learn that Callan did time in Wormwood Scrubs, which is where he and Lonely met. A meek man, humble to the point of being really irritating, Lonely is Callan's stooge, employed to acquire weaponry, perform break-ins and tail suspects. Lonely has no idea of Callan's true profession, assuming him to be a major player in London's criminal underworld. Though Callan rarely treats him with anything but distain, there's a strong bond between the men. Meres makes the mistake of underestimating this friendship when he savagely beats Lonely for information (Lonely's pitiful response to Callan as he is taken to hospital – 'Y' should've got here sooner, Mr Callan' – makes difficult viewing). While Callan is forced to spend a prolonged period in hospital after the shooting of Hunter, Lonely fears he's been abandoned and goes back to his life of crime. Callan returns just in time to arrange for the new Hunter to bail his friend out. Thanks to a sympathetic performance by Russell Hunter, Lonely was one of TV's greatest creations, a genuine one-off.

One of the best episodes of series three, 'A Village Called "G" ', involved the disappearance of Liz, Hunter's secretary, a character who appears in almost every episode but usually says little more than 'Mr Callan is here to see you, sir'. It transpires that Lisa has been taking secret firing lessons from the Section firearms expert, Mr Judd, and files pertaining to Sabovski (Joseph Furst again), believed to have been responsible for the massacre of an entire European village. Lisa was the only survivor of the massacre, and having now traced the man responsible, she has decided to kill him. But Sabovski has other ideas . . .

The final, fourth, series introduced yet another Hunter – Callan himself, albeit temporarily. He manages to abuse his position of power just long enough to secure Lonely a job as driver for the Section's communication vehicle, a taxi kitted out with surveillance equipment (it's only then that Lonely learns of Callan's true career). But when Cross is shot dead (in 'If He Can, So Could I', to allow Patrick Mower to join *Special Branch*), Callan is held responsible and his predecessor returns to the Section. Callan's final mission, spanning three episodes, involves a British spy called Richmond (T. P. McKenna) attempting to defect. Callan disobeys Hunter's orders and shoots the man, an act of defiance that marks his departure from both the Section and the series.

A feature film was released in 1974, effectively a remake of 'A Magnum for Schneider', with Eric Porter as Hunter. Callan's final TV appearance came in 1981 with a one-off play, *Wet Job* (a slang term for execution), which reunited Callan with Lonely for one final mission. In 1985, Edward Woodward headed to Los Angeles to star in ***The Equalizer***, a mind-numbingly disappointing action series in which Woodward plays Robert McCall, a private detective who offers his services to avenge victims who have been let down by official channels. Luckily, Channel 4 had, by this time, acquired the rights to rescreen the colour episodes of *Callan*, allowing viewers to see Woodward at his peak.

For commentary, see THE TRUMPTONSHIRE TRILOGY, *pages* 776–9

The Camomile Lawn

Drama | Zed Productions for Channel 4 | episode duration 60 mins | broadcast 5–26 Mar 1992

Cast
Felicity Kendal · *Helena Cuthbertson*
Paul Eddington · *Richard Cuthbertson*
Oliver Cotton · *Max Erstweiler*
Jennifer Ehle · *Calypso*
Rosemary Harris · *Older Calypso*
Tara Fitzgerald · *Polly*
Virginia McKenna · *Older Polly*
Rebecca Hall · *Sophy*
Claire Bloom · *Older Sophy*
Toby Stephens · *Oliver*
Richard Johnson · *Older Oliver*
Nicholas Le Prevost · *Hector, Hamish*
Ben Walden · *Walter*

Producers Sophie Balhetchet, Glenn Wilhide **Writer** Ken Taylor, from the novel by Mary Wesley

A year before World War Two blights the planet, five cousins, Calypso, Oliver, Walter, Polly and Sophy, gather for one last holiday at the home of their Uncle Richard and Aunt Helena, their final days of childhood innocence played out on the camomile lawn of the Cornish house. The story progresses across the years as we see the cousins grow into adults, loving and losing along the way. The narrative is peppered with flash forwards to 1984 as the cousins, now older, but not necessarily wiser, gather for a funeral, once more on the camomile lawn of their aunt and uncle, where family secrets, kept for decades, are finally revealed.

Sir Peter Hall's debut as a TV director sticks very closely to the original novel by Mary Wesley, and the veteran theatre director cast his own daughter, Rebecca, in the role of Sophy. Another quirk of casting would have a pre-***Pride and Prejudice*** Jennifer Ehle playing the younger Calypso, with her own mother, Rosemary Harris (who later played Aunt May in the 2002/4 *Spider-Man* movies), taking the role of the elder. The series was nominated for Best Drama Serial at the 1993 BAFTA TV Awards.

Candid Camera

Comedy | ABC for ITV | episode duration 60 mins | broadcast 1960–1967, 1974

Cast
Bob Monkhouse · *Host*
Jonathan Routh · *Joker*

Creator Allen Funt

The public's demand to see ordinary people made to look like idiots has never really gone away, and before ***You've Been Framed*** and ***Game for a Laugh*** came *Candid Camera*. ABC brought the series over from the US, where it had been created by Allen Funt, and installed Bob Monkhouse as the host. Funt developed the series from his own US radio show, *Candid Microphone*, placing members of the public – on microphone, naturally – in compromising and bizarre situations. The jump to television was a no-brainer in 1949, although it would still be called *Candid Microphone* until 1953, when the more familiar *Camera* title was adopted.

In the UK version, Monkhouse would present video clips of practical joker Jonathan Routh out and about, setting up gullible members of the public with a variety of gags. The gag was brought to an end with Routh uttering the famous words, 'Smile, you're on *Candid Camera*!'

The series lasted until 1967, when Monkhouse left to hit the bullseye with *The Golden Shot*, while Jonathan Routh eventually left the entertainment business to become an artist. The pursuit of public humiliation has since been taken up by the likes of Jeremy Beadle across various shows.

Captain Caveman and the Teen Angels

Animation | Hanna-Barbera for NBC (shown on BBC One) | episode duration 25 mins | broadcast 10 Sep 1977–21 Jun 1980 (USA)

Voice Cast
Mel Blanc · *Captain Caveman*
Marilyn Schreffler · *Brenda Chance*
Laurel Page · *Taffy Dare*
Vernee Watson · *Dee Dee Sykes*

Creators Joe Ruby and Ken Spears **Producers** Joseph Barbera, William Hanna and Iwao Takamoto **Writer** Jeffrey Scott **Theme Music** Hoyt Curtin. For some reason, the end theme was a hoedown country piece, complete with Jewish harp.

First seen in the USA as part of *Scooby's All-Star Laff-A-Lympics*, Captain Caveman was a hirsute hero with a difference. Frozen in a block of ice for thousands of years, he awoke in modern-day America thanks to the intervention of three foxy chicks, Brenda, Taffy and Dee Dee. They signed 'Cavey' up as the mascot for their mystery-solving gang, the Teen Angels, unmasking criminals and beating villains thanks to Cavey's multi-functional club, which produced helicopters and other useful gadgets that even managed to work, most of the time.

Captain Caveman's own series, retaining the services of the Teen Angels but free of Scooby Doo and his chums, came three years later in 1980. It was effectively a reworking of Scooby Doo's Mystery Inc., but with three

Daphnes and no great dane, just one very shaggy man with a strong pair of lungs (calling out his name: 'Cap-tain CAAAAVE-MAAAAAAAN'), courtesy of Warner Bros voice artist Mel Blanc.

Since the end of the series, *Captain Caveman* has been linked to ***The Flintstones*** in a few of their 1980s revival shows, where we finally got to discover Cavey's secret identity – a prehistoric newsman called Chester working alongside Betty and Wilma.

Captain Pugwash

Animation | BBC One/Five | episode duration 5 mins (1957–75)/10 mins (1998) | broadcast 22 Oct 1957–c.1958, 1974–11 Jul 1975, c.1998

Cast

Peter Hawkins · *Original Narrator and Character Voices*
James Saxon · *Narrator and Character Voices (1998 series)*

Creator/Producer John Ryan **Theme Music** Johnny Pearson performed a rendition of the Trumpet Hornpipe

A rather sweet and romanticised depiction of the cutthroat business of piracy on the high seas, Captain Pugwash introduced us to the crew of the *Black Pig*, led by the eponymous potbellied captain, and their many and various encounters with Cutthroat Jake's *The Flying Dustbin*.

Originally created by John Ryan for the comic *Eagle* in 1950, Captain Pugwash finally found his way onto television in 1957. Rather than using cell animation, the characters and sets were brought to life through 'flat puppets' – two-dimensional cardboard cutouts – with sliding sections added to make the mouths and eyes move. Character voices and narration for the original black and white series and the 1970s colour episodes came from versatile vocal artiste Peter Hawkins, the man who also gave us Bill and Ben, the original Daleks and the Family Ness.

In 1991, a report in a national newspaper revealed that the series had contained elements of adult humour that had so far remained undetected. The story was completely untrue and retractions soon followed, but it's fair to say that the incident can be blamed on the entirely innocent vocal characterisations of Peter Hawkins. By voicing Captain Pugwash with a clipped, nasal accent, the name of his second in command, Master Mate, suddenly took on a more onanistic interpretation. This then led to the completely apocryphal addition of 'Seaman Stains' and 'Roger, the Cabin Boy' to the crew. In fact, the cabin boy's name was Tom and the only possible rudeness was that one of Pugwash's crew was called 'Willy'. This urban myth has helped maintain Pugwash's place in the public's collective consciousness, despite John Ryan successfully obtaining damages from the newspaper in question.

The year 1998 saw an expensive revival in 26 episodes created using modern computer-based animation. At the risk of sounding like a Flat-Earthing Luddite, it lacked the charms of the originals and the late James Saxon (***Brass***) was a pale substitute for Hawkins' original voice-work.

Captain Scarlet and the Mysterons

See pages 164–6

Captain Zep – Space Detective

Children's Quiz Show/Drama | BBC One | episode duration 25 mins | broadcast 5 Jan 1983–13 Apr 1984

Cast

Paul Greenwood, Richard Morant · *Captain Zep*
Ben Ellison · *Jason Brown*
Harriet Keevil · *Professor Spiro*
Tracey Childs · *Professor Vana*

Creator Dick Hills **Producer** Christopher Pilkington **Writers** Dick Hills, Colin Bennett **Theme Music** 'Captain Zep' by the Spacewalkers

In the year 2095 at the SOLVE ('Space Office of Law Verification and Enquiry') Academy, the universe's greatest detective, Captain Zep, has been booked to deliver some video lectures on some of his toughest cases. SOLVE's principal, Jason Brown, was once a young rookie assigned to Zep's crew alongside Professor Spiro (and later Professor Vana), so Brown uses the lectures to test his young trainee space detectives (members of the studio audience) on their powers of observation. Each week, they watch a video reconstruction of the investigation and when all the clues have been revealed, they're asked questions on the case before the real culprit is unveiled. The only problem is that in Captain Zep's beat, all the suspects are aliens. . .

Often used as a point of comparison for any programme deemed to have embarrassing special effects, *Captain Zep* looked like a staggeringly cheap sci-fi series but was really a very inventive quiz, despite the rubbish prizes (the best anyone could hope for was a Captain Zep badge). While the studio audience was very real, the alien worlds and creatures the team met in their videos were constructed via blue-screen to enable the actors to be filmed alongside very simplistic animation, with just a handful of rather well-done model shots of Zep's spaceship to balance the special effects out a bit.

Carrie's War (1974)

Children's Drama | BBC One | episode duration 25 mins | broadcast 28 Jan–25 Feb 1974

Cast

Juliet Waley, Shirley Dixon · *Carrie Willow*
Andrew Tinney · *Nick Willow*
Tim Coward · *Albert Sandwich*

Avril Elgar · *Lou Evans*
Aubrey Richards · *Samuel Evans*
Rosalie Crutchley · *Hepzibah*
Matthew Guinness · *Mr Johnny*
Patsy Smart · *Mrs Gotobed*
Valerie Georgeson · *Miss Fasackerly*

Producers Anna Home (executive) **Writer** Marilyn Fox, from the novel by Nina Bawden

For commentary, see CARRIE'S WAR (2004)

Carrie's War (2004)

Children's Drama | BBC One | duration 90 mins | broadcast 1 Jan 2004

Principal Cast
Keeley Fawcett · *Carrie Willow*
Jack Stanley · *Nick Willow*
Karen Meagher · *Mrs Watkins*
Eddie Cooper · *Albert Sandwich*
Lesley Sharp · *'Aunty Lou' Evans*
Alun Armstrong · *Mr Samuel Evans*
Robert Page · *Minister*
Pauline Quirke · *Hepzibah Green*

Producers Simon Curtis, Matthew Robinson (executive), Dawn Walters (associate) Bill Boyes **Writer** Michael Crompton, from the novel by Nina Bawden **Theme Music** Nick Bicât

Carrie Willow and her younger brother Nick are evacuated from London during the Blitz to a small Welsh mining town. They are billeted above the grocer's shop with the domineering Mr Evans and his timid sister, Lou. Evans' other sister, Mrs Gotobed, and her wise housekeeper, Hepzibah, seem to have some hold over the grocer. Carrie and Nick adapt to life in the small community, but what events does Carrie set into motion that she will only be able to put to rest many years in the future?

Carrie's War is a well-remembered piece from an atmospheric era of children's drama. Director Paul Stone, who would oversee much of the BBC's later adaptations of ***The Chronicles of Narnia***, imbues this period adventure with atmosphere and substance, working from Nina Bawden's book, which was published in 1973. The BBC produced a further adaptation in 2004, featuring Pauline Quirke as Hepzibah and Alun Armstrong as Evans.

Casanova (1971)

Drama | BBC One | episode duration 60 mins | broadcast 13 Sep–29 Oct 1973

Cast
Frank Finlay · *Giovanni Casanova*
Norman Rossington · *Lorenzo/Mr Hart*
Christine Noonan · *Barberina*
Zienia Merton · *Christina*
Victor Baring · *Messer Grande*
George Benson · *Uncle*
Geoffrey Wincott · *Senator Bragadin*
David Swift · *Valenglart*
Ania Marson · *Anne Roman-Coupier*
Patrick Newell · *Schalon*
Elaine Donnelly · *Helena*
Lyn Yeldham · *Genoveffa*
Frederick Peisley · *Capitani*
Hugh Portnow · *Pantalone*
Rowan Wylie · *Colombina*

Producers Mark Shivas **Writer** Dennis Potter, from the diaries of Giacomo Casanova

For commentary, see CASANOVA (2005)

Casanova (2005)

Drama | Red Productions/BBC Wales/Granada for BBC Three/Two | episode duration 60 mins | broadcast 27 Mar–10 Apr 2005 (BBC Three)

Cast
David Tennant, Peter O'Toole · *Giacomo Casanova*
Rose Byrne · *Edith*
Laura Fraser · *Henriette*
Shaun Parkes · *Rocco*
Nina Sosanya · *Bellino*
Rupert Penry-Jones · *Grimani*
Matt Lucas · *Villars*
Clare Higgins · *Cook*

Producers Nicola Schindler, Jane Tranter, Russell T. Davies **Writer** Russell T. Davies, from the diaries of Giacomo Casanova **Theme Music** Murray Gold

Here are two distinctly different accounts of the life of the great lover, ***Casanova***, penned by two dramatists who have dominated their respective eras of work. Dennis Potter put his name to the 1971 version, which starred Frank Finlay as the eponymous cad, reviewing the events of his life from the perspective of a prison cell at the age of 73 years. For 1971, there is much nudity, coarse language and a rather frank approach to sex, which placed Potter into conflict with moral watchdog Mary Whitehouse, who was not best pleased by what she saw. Potter claimed in his defence that the series did, in fact, possess high moral values.

Russell T. Davies's version had been in varying levels of production for nearly five years, pitched first as a project for Channel 4 before following Davies to the BBC after he agreed to resurrect another hero for the corporation, ***Doctor Who***. Davies deliberately approached the material from a less salacious direction to Potter, focusing on Casanova's achievements outside of the bedroom as well

Continued on page 167

Captain Scarlet and the Mysterons

Captain Scarlet takes control as Captain Blue looks on.

In the year 2168, the security of Earth is looked after by Spectrum, an organisation run from Cloudbase, a huge airstrip-cum-control station that hovers high up in the Earth's atmosphere. When a Spectrum mission to Mars stumbles across a hidden alien complex, a harmless video camera is mistaken for a weapon and the crew open fire, destroying the city. Their act of unprovoked aggression results in the deaths of the crew, including Captain Black, and their bodies are possessed by the Mysterons, invisible aliens capable of 'retro-metabolism' – the ability to re-create and control any person or thing that they have destroyed. Using Captain Black as their agent, the Mysterons declare war on Earth and take control of another Spectrum officer, Captain Scarlet. But when a roof-top shoot-out sees the Mysteronised Scarlet fall hundreds of feet to his death, the Spectrum medics are amazed when he survives the fall. Now free of the Mysteron influence, Captain Scarlet becomes indestructible – Spectrum's greatest asset in the fight against alien terrorism.

It's a natural reaction to want to protect your precious child from any of the nastiness that life can throw at a person until absolutely the last possible moment. In dealing with the fundamentals of death on a grand scale, *Captain Scarlet* put itself up as something for parents to be worried about, to raise awkward questions like 'What does "dying" mean?', 'Why can't I play on the garage roof?' and 'Is Captain Scarlet related to Jesus?' It's just not the kind of programme that any parent would be thinking of when looking for something to keep little Johnny out of mischief. Inconveniently, it's also exactly the kind of thing that would do the trick.

Thunderbirds might well be Gerry Anderson's most popular creation, but with *Captain Scarlet and the Mysterons* Anderson became a rule-breaker of the highest order, and we love him for it. The hardware alone was a work of genius, with cars that are driven backwards via a reverse-image monitor (inspired by a real life news report that Anderson had read, which suggested rear-facing seats to be safer than the traditional forward-facing ones), the dart-like Angel Interceptors, all piloted by a truly international bevy of beautiful women, and the innovative moon buggy that hops its way across the lunar landscape. We might allow a note of cynicism here though. *Thunderbirds* had already shown the potential of multiple vehicles in the toy stores. Like many of its stable-mates, *Captain Scarlet* was exploited in comic strip and miniature toy form, as well as being used to promote breakfast cereals and ice lollies. But the fears of many of the ITV franchise holders meant that the show never really gripped its audience like *Thunderbirds* had done. Even when BBC Two repeated it years later (in heavily edited form), the resulting toy drive failed to take off like those for its big-headed cousins had done.

The first of three series to feature realistically proportioned puppets, *Captain Scarlet* was also much gloomier in tone: characters died, regularly and bloodily (puppets bleed!) in set pieces so gleefully violent that they would have been cut from any live-action show for being too sadistic. Garage mechanics crushed to death by hydraulic jacks; a whole passenger aircraft blown to pieces; cars engulfed in flames; and sufficient other 'killings' to sate the bloodlust of your average morbid teen. Except your average morbid teen probably won't be watching a show for kids any more – more fool him. For the first time, Anderson's characters are seen to suffer. Their faces contort in agony and every week our hero lies in a bloody heap; indestructible he may be, but he can still feel pain – he still bleeds.

The darkness is everywhere. In ***Stingray*** and *Thunderbirds*, plots revolved around heroic rescues and 100 per cent success; with the war of nerves central to *Captain Scarlet*, the best our heroes could ever hope for was damage limitation. Targets were missed, victories fumbled, losses a calculated risk. With the stakes this high, one of the few bad points came in the form of Colonel White's often desperate attempts to frame even Spectrum's most humiliating defeats as a step forward in the long game, which seemed misjudged and more than a little trite.

In tackling the issue of terrorism, Gerry Anderson was being incredibly perceptive. Terrorism was nothing new – the first airplane hijacking took place in the 1930s. But it seems oddly prophetic that the campaigns of the alien Mysterons should end just a month before the first ever airline hijacking by Arab terrorists. On 22 July 1968, members of the Popular Front for the Liberation of Palestine took control of an El Al flight, holding its passengers hostage and demanding that the plane be redirected to Algiers. In doing so, they made political terrorism big news. It's staggering therefore that at

Children's Puppet Drama
ITC/Century 21 for ITV
Episode Duration: 25 mins
Broadcast: 29 Sep 1967–16 Apr 1968

Regular Voice Cast
Francis Matthews · *Captain Scarlet*
Edward Bishop · *Captain Blue*
Donald Grey · *Colonel White, Captain Black, Voice of the Mysterons*
Sylvia Anderson · *Melody Angel*
Gary Files · *Captain Magenta*
Cy Grant · *Lieutenant Green*
Janna Hill · *Symphony Angel*
Paul Maxwell · *Captain Grey*
Liz Morgan · *Destiny Angel, Rhapsody Angel*
Lian-Shin · *Harmony Angel*
Charles Tingwell · *Dr Fawn*
Jeremy Wilkin · *Captain Ochre*

Creators Gerry and Sylvia Anderson

Producers Gerry Anderson (executive), John Read (associate), Reg Hill

Writers Gerry and Sylvia Anderson, Tony Barwick, Peter Curran and David Williams, Richard Conway and Stephen J. Mattick, Ralph Hart, Shane Rimmer, Bryan Cooper, Alan Pattillo, Bill Hedley, Leo Eaton, David Lee

Theme Music Composed and directed by Barry Gray. The opening music is atmospheric chord changes until the final crescendo and timpani section that became the motif of the show. It was also used in transitions between scenes. (TV personality Chris Evans used the music to great effect on his 1994 show ***Don't Forget Your Toothbrush***, alternating between two cameras in time to the seven beat 'bam bam bam badadadam'.) The end theme was a cheesy, upbeat song, 'Captain Scarlet', performed by The Spectrum, which appeared in both instrumental and vocal versions. This was how we know that 'He's the one who knows the Mysteron game – the things they plan'.

the same time as airplane hijacks became a distressingly regular occurrence in the Middle East, and IRA bombings in London, Gerry Anderson was explaining the effects of terrorism to kids, even down to having an aggressor who, it could be argued, has a genuine cause for complaint.

For all its machismo and pretend maturity, *Captain Scarlet and the Mysterons* is fortunately very much for kids, albeit for slightly older children than ***Fireball XL5*** was aimed at. Warnings at the beginning of some later episodes remind us that while Captain Scarlet is indestructible, we are not. Trying to imitate him would therefore be a rather silly thing to do, even if we could find the dynamite. The plotting is rarely complex and almost always ends in a big explosion. The characters are, if anything, even more simplistic than in *Stingray*, with personalities shaped more by country of origin than anything they do or say. Captain Scarlet is himself a difficult hero to believe in. He's indestructible, so he'll survive no matter what they throw at him, which should mean that there's zero tension in anything he takes on. Luckily there are plenty of other Spectrum agents and high profile world leaders that are not so blessed. This is therefore a show where it's not so much will he succeed but how much devastation will be left at the end (clue: LOTS!).

With *Captain Scarlet and the Mysterons* Anderson became a rule-breaker of the highest order, and we love him for it.

In his earlier productions, Anderson had often kept a few character puppets aside for 'guest' roles, but here it really felt like there was a repertory theatre. Fans discuss the many appearances of the 'Robert Mitchum' puppet that is one of the recurring 'actors' in the series (it's a game you can play with ***Joe 90*** and *The Secret Service* too – 'Didn't he play General Tiempo?').

Despite the superficial differences and lack of overt humour, *Captain Scarlet* is still very much a typical Gerry Anderson production. It continued other traditions set down by its predecessors in having both a dream episode (the superlative 'Attack on Cloudbase', which would be a contender for the best episode in any Anderson production were it not for its unsatisfying resolution) and a disappointing amount of flashback compilations (one such compilation episode has a hidden reward as we get to see that Robert Mitchum puppet playing three different characters in clips from previous episodes).

But in truth, *Captain Scarlet*'s only fault was in treating its young audience as if they have the critical faculties to distinguish between what's real and what's make-believe – like adults, in fact. Teenage boys don't want character progression and subtlety, they want violence, gore, explosions, especially when they know it's not real – everything that *Captain Scarlet* offered in its sophisticated puppetry and extremely detailed model work. And while these boys relish every second, their dads will be cringing and squirming at the sight of a puppet with blood on his face. How cool is that?

as in. The energetic tale is told from much the same viewpoint as the elderly Casanova (O'Toole) recounts his life to a serving girl in the castle where he serves as librarian. Davies's future *Doctor Who* David Tennant practically auditions for his Time Lord role as the energetic, younger Casanova, meeting grotesques along the way. Running through the narrative is Casanova's decade-spanning love affair with Henriette and the feud it creates with her husband, the slimy Grimani (Rupert Penry-Jones of ***Spooks***). Premiering on BBC Three, *Casanova* achieved record ratings for a first run drama on the digital channel.

Castaway 2000

Reality TV/Documentary | Lion Television for BBC One | episode duration various | broadcast 18 Jan 2000–21 Jan 2001

Cast

Ben Fogle, Toby Waterman, Tammy Huff, Philly Page, Sandra Colbeck, Ray Bowyer, Peter Jowers, Sheila Jowers, Padraig Nallan, Tanya Cheadle, Ron Copsey, Patrick Murphy, Gwyneth Murphy, Liz Cathrine · *Castaways*

Producers Jeremy Mills, Colin Cameron (executive), Chris Kelly

Here was bold undertaking by the BBC to place 36 people – men, women and children – ranging in age from three to 58, on the remote island of Taransay in the bleak Outer Hebrides. Over 4500 people applied for this back-to-basics career break, all willing to remain on the island for a 12-month period. Basic shelters were provided, along with communal showers, compost toilets and an annual budget of just £50,000 with which to purchase supplies that were delivered fortnightly. A schoolhouse was also renovated to allow basic schooling to take place for the children.

Throughout the Millennium year, the BBC broadcast periodical updates on the progress of the islanders, chronicling the tensions, the highs, the lows and the trials of slaughtering animals for meat and successfully growing vegetables. A few islanders fell by the wayside and returned to the mainland throughout the year, but most stuck with it, and former *Tatler* picture editor Ben Fogle became something of a heartthrob, and now has a successful career as a TV presenter.

Castaway 2000 was a departure for producer Chris Kelly, who had previously presented the ITV film show *Clapperboard* and ***Food and Drink*** for the BBC. As a producer, he had overseen a series of ***Soldier, Soldier*** and had created ***El CID***, but *Castaway* would see him take on a project with both feet firmly in reality. Along with Jeremy Mills and Colin Cameron, Kelly was nominated for a BAFTA innovation award in 2001.

Casualty

See pages 168–72

Catchphrase

Game Show | TVS/Meridian/Action Time/Carlton for ITV | episode duration 30 mins | broadcast 1986–present

Cast

Roy Walker, Nick Weir, Mark Curry · *Hosts*
Nick Jackson, Charles Foster · *Announcers*

Creator Steve Radosh **Producers** John Kaye Cooper, Stephen Leahy (executive), Royston Mayoh, Patricia Pearson

Catchphrase is a truly great game show format that obeys the rule (certainly for its most popular, ratings grabbing period) of marrying a superb presenter to a simple format and thus perform quiz show alchemy.

Irish stand-up comic Roy Walker, who was well known to audiences from stints on the outmoded *The Comedians*, might have seemed an odd choice to helm this light entertainment show, but his gentle manner with the contestants and his quick turn of catchphrase (no pun intended) proved to be a hit.

Two contestants go head to head, answering questions to win the chance to reveal a small square of a much bigger cartoon picture, often featuring the show's robotic mascot, Chip. The object of the game is to correctly identify the phrase depicted in the picture, the quicker you do it, the more cash you win. Walker passes comments on the contestants' efforts, with a timely placed 'It's good, but it's not right!', or 'See what you say and say what you see!', pop cultural phrases that soon entered the modern lexicon.

Catchphrase occupied a cosy Saturday teatime slot for much of its run and Roy Walker quickly became a popular household name until he left the show behind in 2000 to be replaced by Nick Weir. Weir's most famous contribution to the series was in breaking his foot during recording of his first episodes when running down the stairs. He presented further episodes on crutches. Sadly, it just wasn't the same, and the show's best days were clearly behind it. In recent times, *Catchphrase* transferred to a daytime slot under the watchful eye of former ***Blue Peter*** presenter Mark Curry.

In the first episode of ***Peter Kay's Phoenix Nights*** in 2001, Roy Walker guest starred as himself, making an appearance to re-open the newly refurbished Phoenix Club at the behest of Brian Potter, thus confirming *Catchphrase* and Walker's cult status.

Cathy Come Home

Drama | BBC Two | duration 75 mins | broadcast 16 Nov 1966

Cast

Carol White · *Cathy Ward*
Ray Brooks · *Reg Ward*
Winifred Dennis · *Mrs Ward*

Continued on page 173

Casualty/Holby City

Duffy (Cathy Shipton) and Megan (Brenda Fricker).

When the hugely popular and successful ***Juliet Bravo*** came to an end, the BBC began looking around for a new long-running series to take its place in the Saturday night schedules. After having briefly toyed with the idea of creating a medical series set in a quaint rural cottage hospital, the decision was made to go with a different setting – the casualty department of an inner-city hospital during the busy night shift. Youthful series creators Jeremy Brock and Paul Unwin were paired with veteran producer Geraint Morris (who had worked on ***The Onedin Line***, *Softly, Softly* and ***The Bill***) in the hope that the combination of enthusiasm with experience would create a winning formula.

Casualty began in a very low-key way, following the staff of Holby City Hospital's accident and emergency department as they arrive for their regular work on the night shift. The main 'audience identification' character in the first series was male nurse Charlie Fairhead, a man devoted to his job but getting increasingly fed up with the lack of resources available to the NHS. Other characters that quickly became very popular with viewers included Irish 'earth mother' Megan Roach, bubbly young nurse Lisa 'Duffy' Duffin, and the department's crusty consultant Ewart Plimmer. Holby itself originally occupied a space on the British map roughly where Bristol is, so Duffy and other members of staff sported strong Avonian accents. The cast's accents, along with Duffy's obsession with astrology, were gradually phased out as Holby's location became harder to pin down.

As the first series progressed, *Casualty*'s producers came under fire from two primary sources. First, the Conservative Party strongly objected to the political stance taken by many of the characters in the series, believing that the programme amounted to little more than a party political broadcast for Labour. Secondly, nursing unions complained about the way in which *Casualty* portrayed members of their profession – specifically the amount of smoking which characters were seen to be doing. This combination of complaints very nearly spelled the end for the fledgling programme, but luckily pre-production on the second series had already progressed too far for it to be cancelled without enormous expense and embarrassment for all concerned. *Casualty* had in effect taken just one season to completely rewrite the rulebook for medical dramas on television. Viewers were initially shocked to see a protrayal of doctors and nurses as fallible human beings, but very soon the truthful depiction of rounded, three-dimensional characters was winning ever-increasing audiences.

The second series saw ratings climb and complaints fall, and despite an announcement from BBC management that this series would be the last, the show was reprieved. A series of memorable storylines concentrating on the regular characters undoubtedly helped to boost viewing figures. The programme's first female paramedic (then just referred to as lowly 'ambulance drivers'!), Sandra Mute, was stabbed in the back of her ambulance by a drunk patient and died shortly afterwards in the casualty ward. Similarly, Ewart's shock death from a heart attack early in the third series came right out of the blue. In *Casualty*, life insurance policies for the staff seem to be a must . . .

One of the great guilty pleasures in watching *Casualty* has to be in playing '*Casualty* bingo' – the habit of watching all of the new guest characters at the start of each episode and trying to guess which ones will end up in A&E, with which specific complaints and whether or not they'll croak by the end of the episode. This fun game was mainly inspired by a rather predictable patch during the early 1990s after the insistence by producers that every negligent or stupid action should have a clear consequence – indeed, some writers were even told to rewrite instances where people had ended up in hospital as a result of bizarre acts of random chance. For some, this period of the show was best known as 'Causality'. Luckily, later producers realised this rather moralistic approach was neither realistic nor particularly enjoyable for those viewers wanting more of an element of surprise.

By the time of the fourth and fifth seasons, *Casualty* had really begun to hit its stride. In terms of viewing figures, the programme was more popular than it had ever been, with 13 million regularly tuning in for their weekly dose of bloodshed and mayhem on those long autumn nights. The show did face a major worry, though, when actress Brenda Fricker – heart and soul of the show as motherly Megan Roach – won an Oscar for her role in the movie *My Left Foot* (1989) and chose to quit the programme for the lure of the silver screen. Duffy was promoted to replace her as the 'sensible older nurse' figure, and despite ominous warnings from fans and critics alike, the series survived perfectly well without dear old Megan. New characters joining around this time included the first of a long series of cold, aloof consultants whose job it was to sneer at the junior staff

Drama
BBC One
Episode Duration: 50 mins
Broadcast: 6 Sep 1986–present (*Casualty*), 12 Jan 1999–present (*Holby City*)

***Casualty* Regular Cast**

Derek Thompson · *Charlie Fairhead*
Bernard Gallagher · *Ewart Plimmer*
Cathy Shipton · *Lisa 'Duffy' Duffin*
Brenda Fricker · *Megan Roach*
Julia Watson · *Baz Samuels/Hayes/Fairhead*
George Harris · *Clive King*
Lisa Bowerman · *Sandra Mute*
Robert Pugh · *Andrew Ponting*
Debbie Roza · *Susie Mercier*
Christopher Rozycki · *Kuba Trzcinski*
Nigel Anthony · *Ted Roach*
Maureen O'Brien · *Elizabeth Straker*
Helena Little · *Mary Tomlinson*
Eddie Nestor · *Cyril James*
Ella Wilder · *Shirley Franklin*
Geoffrey Leesley · *Keith Cotterill*
Susan Franklyn · *Valerie Sinclair*
Paul Lacoux · *David Rowe*
Carol Leader · *Sadie Tomkins*
William Gaminara, Philip Bretherton · *Andrew Bower*
Tam Hoskyns · *Lucy Perry*
Belinda Davison · *Alex Spencer*
Ian Bleasdale · *Josh Griffiths*
Vivienne McKone · *Julie Stevens*
Robson Green · *Jimmy Powell*
Nigel Le Vaillant · *Julian Chapman*
Mamta Kaash · *Beth Ramanee*
Patrick Robinson · *Martin Ashford*
Eamon Boland · *Tony Walker*
Caroline Webster · *Jane Scott*
Adie Allen · *Kelly Liddle*
Anne Kristen · *Norma Sullivan*
Maria Friedman · *Trish Baynes*
Maureen Beattie · *Sandra Nicholl*
Joanna Foster · *Kate Miller*
Jason Riddington · *Rob Khalefa*
Emma Bird · *Maxine Price*
Robert Daws · *Simon Eastman*
Clive Mantle · *Mike Barratt*
Suzanna Hamilton · *Karen Goodliffe*
Doña Croll · *Adele Beckford*
Christopher Guard · *Ken Hodges*
Naoko Mori · *Mie Nishi-Kawa*
Steven O'Donnell · *Frankie Drummer*
Tara Moran · *Mary Skillett*
Brendan O'Hea · *Brian Crawford*
David Ryall · *Tom Harley*
Jane Gurnett · *Rachel Longworth*
Sorcha Cusack · *Kate Wilson*
Stephen Brand · *Adam Cooke*
Jason Merrells · *Matt Hawley*

Lisa Coleman · *Jude Korcanik*
Sue Devaney · *Liz Harker*
Craig Kelly · *Daniel Perryman*
Lizzy McInnerny · *Laura Milburn/Ashford*
Robert Duncan · *Peter Hayes*
Gray O'Brien · *Richard McCaig*
Ganiat Kasumu · *Gloria Hammond*
Jonathan Kerrigan · *Sam Colloby*
Vas Blackwood · *David Sinclair*
Peter Guinness · *Elliot Matthews*
Rebecca Lacey · *George Woodman*
Paterson Joseph · *Mark Grace*
Claire Goose · *Tina Seabrook*
Rebecca Wheatley · *Amy Howard*
Vincenzo Pellegrino · *'Sunny' Sunderland*
Barbara Marten · *Eve Montgomery*
Robert Gwilym · *Max Gallagher*
Gerald Kyd · *Sean Maddox*
Jan Anderson · *Chloe Hill*
Pal Aron · *Adam Osman*
Donna Alexander · *Penny Hutchens*
Sandra Huggett · *Holly Miles*
Kwame Kwei-Armah · *Finn Newton*
Michelle Butterly · *Melanie Dyson*
Ronnie McCann · *Barney Woolfe*
Ian Kelsey · *Patrick Spiller*
Adjoa Andoh · *Colette Kierney/Griffiths*
Zita Sattar · *Anna Paul*
Will Mellor · *Jack Vincent*
Dan Rymer · *Dillon Cahill*
Kelly Harrison · *Nikki Marshall*
Martina Laird · *Comfort Jones/Newton*
Christine Stephen-Daly · *Lara Stone*
Judy Loe · *Jan Goddard*
Lee Warburton · *Tony Vincent*
Fiona Gillies · *Philippa Kinross*
Christopher Colquhoun · *Simon Kaminski*
Loo Brealey · *Roxanne Bird*
Frank Windsor · *Kenneth Samuels*
Liam Hess · *Louis Fairhead*
Simon MacCorkindale · *Harry Harper*
Holly Davidson · *Tally Harper*
Russell Boulter · *Ryan Johnson*
Orlando Seale, Sebastian Dunn · *Merlin Jameson*
Sarah Manners · *Bex Reynolds*
Matthew Wait · *Luke Warren*
Maxwell Caulfield · *Jim Brodie*
Suzanne Packer · *Tess Bateman*
Leanne Wilson · *Claire Guildford*
James Redmond · *'Abs' Denham*
Rebekah Gibbs · *Nina Farr*
Elizabeth Carling · *Selena Manning/Donovan*
Georgina Bouzova · *Ellen Zitek/Denham*
Luke Bailey · *Sam Bateman*
Elyes Gabel · *'Guppy' Sandhu*
Will Thorp · *'Woody' Joyner*

while making viewers' pulses race. Julian Chapman (played with an almost perpetual sneer by Nigel Le Vaillant, later to be star of *Dangerfield*) was just at home tearing a strip off an inexperienced nurse as he was conducting open heart surgery in CRASH or battling for extra funding from the Holby board. Series five also began the tradition of providing major 'stunts' as ratings-boosting crowd-pleasers. From riots on the football terraces through to a memorable cliffhanger when a gun-toting schizophrenic (played by Kenneth Cranham) shoots Charlie in the chest, the scene was now set for a *Casualty* that regularly did everything it could to up the ante with its drama and explosive set-pieces.

The following year, a major 'event' episode that had been planned and filmed for months, featuring the crash of a plane landing at Holby airport, had to be cancelled when it was suddenly realised that the intended broadcast date of that particular episode would coincide with the third anniversary of the Lockerbie disaster. Naturally enough, although the circumstances of the fictional crash were about as far removed as could be imagined from the deliberate bombing of the Lockerbie flight, the episode was sensibly postponed for several months. *Casualty* was at this stage being screened in a post-watershed slot of 9.30 p.m. on Friday nights. This enabled the programme to cover subject matter that would have been totally inappropriate in a family-friendly Saturday evening slot. Surprisingly though, the later transmission time did nothing to damage ratings, with some episodes attracting over 15 million viewers. BBC One controller Jonathan Powell was keen to capitalise on this success by turning *Casualty* into a regular twice-weekly 30-minute programme, akin to the already hugely successful ***EastEnders***. Although plans for converting *Casualty* into a soap were quite far advanced, the decision was eventually taken from on high that a better option would be to double the length of the show's season, so that it would now be broadcast for approximately half of the year. BBC One's new soap would instead be a glitzy, sunny portrait of the ex-pat community – ***Eldorado***. In hindsight, it seems that keeping *Casualty* as a drama series was a very lucky (or very wise) decision indeed.

Despite being a hugely popular programme with both BBC management and viewers, *Casualty* faced its biggest ever moment of crisis just one year later. The final episode of the seventh series, 'Boiling Point', saw the programme getting its highest-ever viewing figures, as 17 million people tuned in to the most powerful episode of *Casualty* yet made. Viewers watched with a growing sense of unease as the cosy familiarity of the programme they loved was brutally whipped away from them by scenes of violence, anarchy and rioting that never once shied away from showing the true pain and cost of that brutality. When the rioting mob arrived at Holby City's casualty department itself, viewers watched in horror as the thugs stole an ambulance and petrol-bombed it right in front of the familiar reception area, before setting fire to the hospital's basement. The resulting explosion and fire wiped out the entire department, killing several patients and apparently the show's young heart-throb doctor, Rob Khalefa. The timing of the broadcast of

'Boiling Point' was very unfortunate for the *Casualty* team, coming just a few weeks after the country was shocked to its core by the killing – by two young boys – of toddler Jamie Bulger. Spurred on by a pre-publicity campaign that alerted viewers to the episode's controversial content, Mary Whitehouse's National Viewers and Listeners Association spearheaded a concerted attack on BBC bosses for allowing this episode to be transmitted. Although only 700 people out of the 17 million watching made any sort of protest direct to the BBC, new BBC One controller Alan Yentob apologised to viewers and gave a metaphorical slap to the production team, saying they 'got it wrong' on this occasion. Ever since that moment, *Casualty* has never quite been the same.

The mid-1990s marked the biggest shake-up of characters in the show's history, with only the ever-reliable Charlie now left from the original line-up. Although specific characters would often come and go (and some would return, with both Duffy and Charlie's first love, Baz, coming back and then leaving again), the stock characters would often remain. Receptionists would have to be either older dragons (such as the unforgettable Norma) or young, chirpy carefree characters soon worn down by the routine of it all (Matt Hawley, played by ***Cutting It***'s Jason Merrells). Young nurses would inevitably fall for other members of the team, older nurses would be the 'solid gold' heart of the department (blue-eyed Scot Sandra or Megan replacement Kate, for instance), and every now and again something horrific would happen to one of the regulars (such as the death in a house fire of paramedic Josh's entire family). Chuck in at least one major disaster each season, such as a train crash, a motorway pile-up or a bomb in a shopping centre, and you've got a recipe for continued success.

In 1999, increased demand from BBC executives and viewers hungry for more of their favourite characters resulted in the occurrence of two distinct events. First of all, *Casualty* began a year-on-year increase in the number of episodes being made: 28 in 1999, up to 36 in 2001 and eventually up to a practically year-round 46 by 2004. Secondly, it was decided that one major BBC medical drama series simply wasn't enough, and in January 1999 *Holby City* was launched, running concurrently with its sister show. Rather than dealing with the 'sharp end' of medical problems in the accident and emergency department, the new series would be set in the surgical wards of the very same hospital and would shift slightly away from the 'patient-of-the-week' focus of *Casualty* to the lives and loves of the medical staff. Beginning with a fairly standard nine-part first season, *Holby* soon earned its wings as one of the mainstays of the BBC One schedule. By 2000, it was already being transmitted for 30 weeks of the year: since 9 October 2001, *Holby City* has been shown virtually every single week, in the same 8.00 p.m. timeslot every Tuesday night.

Ever since both programmes switched to virtual year-round transmission, they have both suffered from a similar problem – that any pretence of realism or credibility in terms of ongoing characterisation has unfortunately gone right out of the window. For

Creators Jeremy Brock, Paul Unwin

Producers Geraint Morris, Foz Allan, Sophie Anwar, Tim Bradley, Pippa Brill, Jeremy Brock, Diana Brookes, Edwina Craze, David Crean, Michael Ferguson, Fiona Francombe, Lowri Glain, Richard Handford, Sally Haynes, Corinne Hollingworth, Tim Holloway, Sue Howells, Alexei de Keyser, Chris Le Grys, Steve Lightfoot, Laura Mackie, Peter Norris, Alex Perrin, Bronagh Taggart, Paul Unwin, Mervyn Watson, Rachel Wright, Jonathan Young, Mal Young

Writers Many dozens, including Jeremy Brock, Paul Unwin, Simon Ashdown, David Ashton, Tony Basgallop, Peter Bowker, Joe Broughton, Paul Cornell, Wally K. Daly, Clive Dawson, Julie Dixon, Greg Evans, Lisa Evans, Lilie Ferrari, Emma Frost, Rob Gittins, Steve Griffiths, Billy Hamon, Jim Hill, Jackie Holborough, Andrew Holden, Ginnie Hole, Chris Jury, David Lane, Chris Lang, Steve Lightfoot, Barbara Machin, Paul Marx, Lise Mayer, Stephen McAteer, Tony McHale, Stuart Morris, Simon Moss, Robin Mukherjee, Rona Munro, Chris Murray, Jim O'Hanlon, Christopher Penfold, Ashley Pharoah, Margaret Phelan, Jeff Povey, Barry Purchese, Nick Saltrese, Robert Scott-Fraser, Manjit Singh, Sam Snape, Julian Spilsbury, Keith Temple, Richard Vincent, Don Webb, Sam Wheats, Julie White, Patrick Wilde, Susan Wilkins, James Wood, Colin Wyatt, Stephen Wyatt

Theme Music Ken Freeman provided the theme tune based upon the howl of an ambulance siren.

See* HOLBY CITY *for individual credits

example, in 2004 alone, four regular *Casualty* characters left the A&E department in a coffin: Simon Kaminski after a air crash on the way to his wedding; Charlie's ex-wife Baz died from her injuries after a car accident caused by their son Louis; paramedic Fin Newton was murdered off-screen by a disgruntled patient; and Jim Brodie died doing a passable impersonation of Gene Hackman in *The Poseidon Adventure* (1972) during two crossover episodes, 'Casualty@Holby City', transmitted over the Christmas season. Two further characters, receptionist Tally and paramedic Nikki, barely escaped with their lives from two near-death encounters and almost certainly fled *Holby* thanking their lucky stars for such a narrow escape. Scarcely a week now goes by without some major disaster or devastating emotional blow rippling through both programmes.

The aforementioned 'Casualty@Holby City' special, gripping and spectacular though it was, epitomised everything that was both brilliant yet ludicrous about the two programmes. A huge petrol tanker, driven by a young man rushing to get to A&E in time for the birth of his child, collides with an ambulance carrying his pregnant wife and careers straight into one of the wards of the hospital. She gives birth, but the skin colour of the child puts paid to any chance of him being the father. He survives just long enough to cuddle another baby (conveniently thrust into his dying arms to ensure he expires with a smile on his face) before suddenly all of the escaped petrol catches light and the hospital once again goes up in flames. Several cast members from both programmes are trapped inside the burning building and spend the second episode trying to escape from the inferno while dealing with a patient with Lassa fever and a boy who can't leave his protective oxygen bubble because of a diminished immune system. Simultaneously, receptionist Bex is kidnapped by a junkie posing as a drug company rep, and pregnant midwife Rosie is speared through her abdomen by a piece of metal.

The aforementioned 'Casualty@Holby City' special, gripping and spectacular though it was, epitomised everything that was both brilliant yet ludicrous about the two programmes.

The fact that mercifully only two series regulars perished in this little piece of Armageddon is undoubtedly more likely to be a result of contract negotiations and the need to beat ITV1 in the festive ratings battle than to carefully measured plotting and the requirements of character development. If both shows are to survive, less of a focus on outrageous and implausible incidents and character development is necessary. Hilarious, over-the-top antics from the scriptwriters and producers are all very well, but surely no programme can sustain such a level of unreality for very long before audiences tire of the sheer silliness of it all.

Wally Patch · *Grandad*
Adrienne Frame · *Eileen*
Emmett Hennessy · *Johnny*
Geoffrey Palmer · *Property Agent*
Gabrielle Hamilton · *Welfare Officer*
Phyllis Hickson · *Mrs Alley*
Frank Veasey · *Mr Hodge*
Barry Jackson · *Rent Collector*
James Benton · *Man at Eviction*
Ruth Kettlewell · *Judge*
John Baddeley · *Housing Officer*
Kathleen Broadhurst · *Landlady*
Ralph Lawton · *Health Inspector*
Gladys Dawson · *Mrs Penfold*
Ron Pember · *Mr Jones*

Producer Tony Garnett **Writers** Jeremy Sandford, Ken Loach

Both the BBC and ITV once had a rich collection of outlets for one-off plays. Serials such as *Armchair Theatre, Play for Today, Screen One* and *Screen Two* provided us with a weekly dose of drama, comedy or melodrama, often highlighting important social issues and creating the odd classic along the way. Widely recognised as one of the single most important dramas of the 1960s was *Cathy Come Home*, Ken Loach's documentary-style drama, which was first shown as a *Wednesday Play*. Centred on the plight of a young couple who become homeless, the production led to debates in Parliament and directly inspired the formation of Shelter, a charity set up to identify people living on or below the breadline and prevent them from falling victim to circumstance as the fictional Cathy did.

The play was filmed on location, and with actors either new to the screen or at least without the baggage of 'stardom', Ken Loach's style made it easier for viewers to regard the play as a fly-on-the-wall documentary. Writer Jeremy Sandford later wrote a BAFTA-winning *Play for Today*, ***Edna, the Inebriate Woman*** (1971), a tragi-comic piece in which Patricia Hayes played a down-and-out.

C.A.T.S. Eyes

Action-Adventure | TVS for ITV | episode duration 50 mins | broadcast 12 Apr 1985–6 Jun 1987

Regular Cast

Rosalyn Landor · *Pru Standfast*
Jill Gascoigne · *Maggie Forbes*
Leslie Ash · *Fred Smith*
Nigel Beaumont · *Don Warrington*
Tracy-Louise Ward · *Tessa Robinson*

Creator Terence Feely **Producers** Rex Firkin (executive), Frank Cox, Dickie Bamber, Raymond Menmuir **Writers** Terence Feely, Jeremy Burnham, Don Houghton, Ben Steed, Francis Megahy, Barry Appleton, Andy de la Tour, Reg Ford, Ray Jenkins, Jenny McDade, Gerry O'Hara, Anthony Skene, Paul Wheeler, Martin Worth **Theme Music** John Kongos produced the up-tempo dynamic first season theme, Barbara Thompson provided the saxophone-led, sultrier version for the second season onwards.

Some people have accused *C.A.T.S. Eyes* of being no more than a cheap, lower-budget British interpretation of international mega-hit ***Charlie's Angels***. And they'd be right. Despite this fact, *C.A.T.S. Eyes* is a true guilty pleasure, and unfortunately the last of a breed of light-hearted action/adventure series that had been a staple of the ITV schedules since the days of ***The Adventures of Robin Hood*** and ***Ivanhoe*** in the 1950s. By combining the glamorous talents of ice-maiden Rosalyn Landor and gorgeous tomboy Lesley Ash (long before her ***Men Behaving Badly*** days) with the presence of much-loved Jill Gascoigne (recreating her character from ***The Gentle Touch***), ITV managed to create a series that appealed to men, women and (of course) teenage boys.

The Eyes Enquiry Agency is the cover story for a group of Home Office special investigators working with the moniker 'Covert Activities, Thames Section' (C.A.T.S., geddit?). Leader of the group is posh Oxbridge graduate Pru Standfast, who, together with ex-copper Maggie Forbes and computer whiz Fred (short for Frederica) Smith, solve international spy conspiracies and foil the villainous activities of smugglers, terrorists and general do-badders. Their main ministry contact is the ever-so-posh Nigel Beaumont, who would end up joining the women in their crime-fighting capers every now and again.

The Eyes Enquiry Agency lost their leader after the first series, when actress Rosalyn Landor moved to the USA to take guest roles in such programmes as ***Star Trek: The Next Generation*** and as a voice artist for animated hits like *The Incredibles* (2004). Jill Gascoine's Maggie Forbes took over the running of the agency and a new operative joined the team, posh society girl Tessa Robinson. Made by TVS, the series used its home base of the Medway towns to great effect during location filming on and around the Thames.

Catweazle

Children's Fantasy Comedy | LWT for ITV | episode duration 25 mins | broadcast 15 Feb 1970–4 Apr 1971

Cast

Geoffrey Bayldon · *Catweazle*
Robin Davies · *Carrot*
Neil McCarthy · *Sam Woodyard*
Charles 'Bud' Tingwell · *Mr Bennet*
Gary Warren · *Cedric Collingford*
Moray Watson · *Lord Collingford*
Elspet Gray · *Lady Collingford*
Peter Butterworth · *Groom*
Gwen Nelson · *Mrs Gowdie*

Creator/Writer Richard Carpenter **Producers** Joy Whitby (executive), Quentin Lawrence, Carl Mannin **Theme Music** 'Busy Boy' by Ted Dicks

The 1960s saw ***Adam Adamant*** displaced from his own time into ours, a prototype Austin Powers reacting to the strangeness of the modern world. In 1970, a time traveller would lack the sophistication and status of Adamant, while the age gap between him and his 20th-century friends would be greater. Catweazle was a peasant from the Middle Ages and a dabbler in sorcery. When the Norman soldiers came for him, he panicked and surprised himself by performing an escape spell that worked, although not how he'd planned: he found himself shot into the 20th century. There, he befriended a farmer's son called Carrot, who helped him evade the grown-ups and eventually find his way back to his own time. In the second series, the old fool managed to do the trick again and this time he found help from Cedric, the son of Lord and Lady Collingford. Luckily, Catweazle had one friend who understood everything he'd been through – his pet toad, Touchwood.

The comedy elements in the programme came mainly from Catweazle's reaction to commonplace modern inventions like light bulbs (powered through 'electrickery') and telephones ('telling bones'), with broad but endearing slapstick elements akin to those in ***Worzel Gummidge***, which *Catweazle* star Geoffrey Bayldon would later appear in as the more dignified Crowman.

Catweazle came from the pen of Richard Carpenter, who also wrote for ***Look and Read*** (notably 'The King's Dragon') and would continue to explore his fascination for sorcery and life in the time of the Norman occupation in ***Robin of Sherwood***.

CD:UK

See SM:TV LIVE

Celebrity Big Brother

See BIG BROTHER, *pages* 90–7

Celebrity Squares

Quiz Show | ATV/Reg Grundy for ITV | episode duration 30 mins | broadcast 1975–1979, 1993–1995

Cast
Bob Monkhouse · *Host*
Kenny Everett · *Voice-over*

Creator Ian Messiter **Producers** Paul Stewart-Laing, Glyn Edwards, Peter Harris, Gill Stribling-Wright, Danny Greenstone

Another Bob Monkhouse-hosted show that scores high in the immortality stakes, mostly because the audience wondered how on earth the celebrities billeted in the top row of the 6m (18ft) high noughts and crosses board got there without mortally injuring themselves.

Two contestants were charged with firing questions at the nine celebrities arranged across the board, and then had to decide if the celebrities were giving the right answer or not. If the contestant guessed correctly, they were awarded with an X or an O, earning various rewards for a row of three. Monkhouse presided over everything like a showbiz god, always ready with a quip to move things along while ably assisted by wacky voiceovers from Kenny Everett.

The main attraction of *Celebrity Squares* (which was cribbed from America's *Hollywood Squares*) was to see just how far down the barrel the producers could scrape for the celebrity guests. Regulars included Willie Rushton (who always sat in the centre box), Diana Dors, Alfred Marks and Beryl Reid, but it was always a thrill to see Hinge and Bracket squeezed into the same box.

The original series ended in 1979, but returned to ITV for a short-lived run in 1993. The quality of the guests remained joyfully and consistently mediocre.

Century Falls

Children's Drama | BBC One | episode duration 25 mins | broadcast 17 Feb–24 Mar 1993

Principal Cast
Catherine Sanderson · *Tess Hunter*
Simon Fenton · *Ben Naismith*
Emma Jane Lavin · *Carey Naismith*
Heather Baskerville · *Mrs Hunter*
Bernard Kay · *Richard Naismith*
Mary Wimbush · *Esme Harkness*
Georgine Anderson · *May Harkness*
Eileen Way · *Alice Harkness*
Tatiana Strauss · *Julia*

Creator/Writer Russell T. Davies **Producer** Richard Callanan
Theme Music David Ferguson

After his earlier sci-fi serial ***Dark Season*** had been so well received, Russell T. Davies followed it up with a second six-part children's drama that easily surpassed it. Whereas *Dark Season* had been a loving tribute to ***Doctor Who***, with an evil villain trying to take over the world via a supercomputer, with *Century Falls* Davies produced his own sinister tale of myth and superstition, a ***Children of the Stones*** or even ***Quatermass and the Pit*** for the 1990s.

Fat, lonely teenager Tess Hunter moves with her mother to the remote village of Century Falls, a village that harbours a terrifying secret. No children have been born in the village since 17 July 1953, a day on which a terrible catastrophe befell the residents. But if that is the case, where have Tess's new friends, young twins Ben and Carey Naismith, come from? And, perhaps even more worryingly, why does the fact that Tess's mother is pregnant fill the villagers with fear?

Century Falls was a very different and challenging type of children's drama, with no typical 'lead' character for young viewers at home to empathise with. Tess is simply too shy and repressed to provide audience identification to many viewers, and the twins Ben and Carey turn out to have motives and agendas of their own. In the end, the hero of the piece turns out to be someone quite unexpected – one of the elderly residents of the village. With psychic powers, flashbacks to mass deaths and spirits possessing unborn children, *Century Falls* was dark, disturbing and a million miles away from the typical kiddie fare you'd expect to find at five o'clock on a Wednesday afternoon.

Chalk

Comedy | Pola Jones Productions for BBC One | episode duration 30 mins | broadcast 20 Feb–22 Oct 1997

Regular Cast

David Bamber · *Eric Slatt*
Nicola Walker · *Suzy Travis*
Martin Ball · *Dan McGill*
John Wells · *Richard Nixon*
Geraldine Fitzgerald · *Janet Slatt*
Amanda Boxer · *Amanda Trippley*
John Grillo · *Mr Carkdale*
Andrew Livingston · *Mr Humboldt*
Duncan Preston · *J. F. Kennedy*
Damien Matthews · *Jason Cockfoster*

Creator/Writer Steven Moffat **Producers** Andre Ptaszynski, Steven Moffat, Kevin Lygo **Theme Music** Howard Goodall

Far better than its disastrous reputation suggests, *Chalk* is a sitcom with a distinctly acquired taste. Discarding any semblance of reality, *Chalk* deposits viewers into a school that's part zoo, part bacchanalian nightmare, part product of a warped mind. That mind belongs to Galfast High School's deputy head, Eric Slatt – neurotic and anal-retentive to degrees that would make Gordon Brittas look like the epitome of laid-back cool. Slatt's determination to control both staff and pupils is largely a result of the so-hands-off-he's-absent policy of headmaster Richard Nixon. Having to cope with the frenzied behaviour of Eric is his ever-suffering wife Janet, who, for her sins, is also the school's secretary. Additional oddball characters include profanity-spouting English teacher Mr Carkdale and slovenly PE teacher Mr Humboldt.

Coming into this world of insanity is new teacher Suzy Travis (a marvellous performance from Nicola Walker, who went on to track down terrorists in ***Spooks***), desperate to be the best teacher she can but constantly frustrated by both the school and Slatt's hyper behaviour. She thinks she's got a friend in fellow young teacher Dan, but sadly he's far more interested in copping off with her than developing children's minds.

On its first transmission, critics decided this was trying to be '***Fawlty Towers*** in a school' (it wasn't) and decided to make *Chalk* their latest target for abuse (the series became a reviewer by-word for 'worst TV comedy ever' for about six months). Its second and final season was much better received – perhaps simply because the critics had finally got used to this show's twisted and misanthropic style or possibly because they'd found something new to hate. Whatever, *Chalk* is in serious need of re-evaluation.

It's ironic that despite no intentional attempt to ape Basil Fawlty, the casting of the lead character proved the idea that Fawlty worked because John Cleese was already popular, whereas David Bamber's talent as a character actor has ensured that he remains largely unknown to the general public. Eric Slatt was such a well-formed unpleasant character that it really needed a likeable leading man in the part to help the audience overcome Slatt's short-fallings, or at least find some level of empathy. Still, the scripts compare well to Steven Moffat's earlier sitcom, ***Joking Apart***, and offer the kind of titter/trauma balancing act that made his children's drama ***Press Gang*** so popular. Thankfully, Moffat managed to put the pain of *Chalk* behind him to give us ***Coupling***, a sitcom that was similarly cursed with being erroneously compared to another show (in this case, ***Friends***) but fortunately this time it was meant as a compliment.

Champion the Wonder Horse

Children's Adventure | Flying A Productions for CBS (shown on BBC One) | episode duration 25 mins | broadcast 30 Sep 1955–3 Feb 1956

Regular Cast

Barry Curtis · *Ricky North*
Jim Bannon · *Uncle Sandy North*
Rebel · *Himself*
Champion · *Himself*
Francis McDonald · *Will Calhoun*
Ewing Mitchell · *Sheriff Powers*

Creator Gene Autry **Producers** Armand Schaefer (executive), Gene Autry, Louis Gray, Eric Jenson **Writers** Oliver Drake, Paul Franklin, Orville H. Hampton, Eric Freiwald, Paul Gangelin **Theme Music** Norman Luboff; lyrics by Marilyn Bergman. Though the theme tune was recorded by Frankie Laine, one of the biggest stars of the 1950s, the version used on the programme was sung by its composer, Norman Luboff. A truly memorable piece, perfect for waking up the neighbours when you're staggering back from the pub: 'Like a mighty cannonball he seems to fly' – apparently.

In the American West of the 1880s, a wild stallion befriends a 12-year-old boy and his German shepherd dog Rebel. With a nose for trouble, Ricky relies on his animal friends to keep him out of it, and – with such regular problems as horse rustlin', daring mountainside rescues and race relations with the local 'Red Indians' – trouble is one thing Ricky is always guaranteed.

The exploits of Champion the Wonder Horse and his owner Ricky became a regular TV fixture of summer holidays from the 1950s until well into the 1980s. Shown in the US under the name *The Adventures of Champion*, this was ostensibly a spin-off from the many movies of screen cowboy Gene Autry, whose horse Champion was (although the one seen in the TV version was actually the second of four Champions to appear in Autry productions). The series ran to 26 episodes but only 19 of them were broadcast in the original run after the series was pulled from the CBS Network mid-season in favour of the instantly memorable (!) *My Friend Flicka*.

The Champions

Action-Adventure | ITC Productions for ITV | episode duration 50 mins | broadcast 25 Sep 1968–30 Apr 1969

Regular Cast
Stuart Damon · *Craig Stirling*
Alexandra Bastedo · *Sharron Macready*
William Gaunt · *Richard Barret*
Anthony Nicholls · *Tremayne*
David Bauer · *Opening Voice-over*

Creator Monty Berman, Dennis Spooner **Producer** Monty Berman **Writers** Dennis Spooner, Donald James, Philip Broadley, Tony Williamson, Brian Clemens, Gerald Kelsey, Ralph Smart, Terry Nation, Ian Stuart Black, John Kelsey **Theme Music** Tony Hatch

While on a mission to recover evidence of biological weapons in China, agents of Nemesis Craig Stirling, Richard Barret and Sharon Macready are critically wounded in a plane crash. Only the intervention of a forgotten race of spiritual people in Tibet saves their lives – and gives them superhuman powers too, including increased strength and telepathy. Realising how useful their powers are, they decide to keep their new abilities a secret and continue to work as a team, the 'Champions of law, order and justice'.

In development at the same time as ***Randall and Hopkirk (Deceased)***, *The Champions* ended up with a more straightforward approach to the fantastical change that the three leads experience. As a result, it ended up a little dry and stuffy compared to the exploits of Jeff Randall and his ghostly chum. Still, the series sits well with other ITV adventure shows of the time, and did no harm to the careers of its stars. Twenty-year-old Alexandra Bastedo had previously tasted fame as the face of Shell Oil abroad, and became known as one of the 'It' girls of the late 1960s (and later joined the list of stars to make appearances on ***Absolutely Fabulous***), while in the 1980s William Gaunt starred in the cosy BBC sitcom ***No Place Like Home***.

Chancer

Drama | Central for ITV | episode duration 50 mins | broadcast 6 Mar 1990–28 May 1991

Principal Cast
Clive Owen · *Stephen Crane/Derek Love*
Leslie Phillips · *James Xavier Blake*
Benjamin Whitrow · *Robert Douglas*
Lynsey Baxter · *Victoria Douglas*
Caroline Langrishe · *Penny Nichols*
Matthew Marsh · *Gavin Nichols*
Sean Pertwee · *Jamie Douglas*
Susannah Harker · *Joanna Franklyn*
Peter Vaughan · *Thomas Franklyn*
Simon Shepherd · *Piers Garfield Ward*
Karen Archer · *Vanessa*
Tom Bell · *Derek's Father*
Cathryn Bradshaw · *Sonya Morris*
Trevor Byfield · *Dudley*
Stephen Tompkinson · *Markus Warton*
Melanie Kilburn · *Angela*
Jennie Linden · *Olivia*
Cliff Parisi · *'Lunchbox'*
Ralph Riach · *Stebbings*
Tom Tudgay · *Joseph Franklyn*
Louise Lombard · *Anna*

Producers Ted Childs (executive), Sarah D. Wilson **Writers** Guy Andrews, Simon Burke, Tony Grounds **Theme Music** Jan Hammer, unsuccessfully repeating his ***Miami Vice*** tricks, which now seem to date the show horrifically

Financier Stephen Crane knows exactly who he is – smug, reckless and a bit of a bastard. He doesn't have a friend that he wouldn't use for his own means. So when his old mate Gavin Nichols calls out of the blue to ask for his help, Stephen's not sure Gavin's got the right man. Gavin has married into a family of car manufacturers, headed by the idealistic Robert Douglas, whose small production line of hand-built vintage cars is under threat of collapse after a fire at the workshop. Now Gavin wants Stephen to find the means of financing Douglas Motors' rise from the ashes. Stephen manages to save the day, but only after embezzling big cheese Jimmy Blake and putting his own girlfriend Joanna at risk of arrest for insider dealing.

Douglas Motors is far from safe yet; there's the small matter of Robert Douglas's long-lost son returning out of the blue after absconding from the Foreign Legion; then Jimmy Blake wants his money back; and Joanna just happens to be the daughter of the city's most ruthless businessman – so why is he offering Stephen a job?

And the biggest problem of all, which none of them suspects, is that Stephen Crane doesn't even exist. But Derek Love does, and he's terrified of anyone finding out who he really is . . .

An inventive romantic drama, *Chancer* is full of twists, revelations and triple-bluffs. Just as you feel you have a handle on the on-going crises of Douglas Motors, another plot emerges that will take the story off in another direction. Clive Owen is captivating as the charming Stephen/Derek, though it's Leslie Phillips as the roguish Jimmy Blake that keeps us watching. A second series followed Derek ('Dex') on his release from prison after being arrested for a fraud he committed in his teens. Jimmy Blake is on the scene again as the owner of a casino, which naturally ties in with one of Dex's scams to finance the restoration of a stately home.

Changing Rooms

Lifestyle | Bazal for BBC Two/One | episode duration 30 mins | broadcast 4 Sep 1996–22 Nov 2004, 28 Dec 2004

Cast
Carol Smillie, Andy Kane, Laurence Llewelyn-Bowen, Linda Barker, Anna Ryder Richardson, Graham Wynne, Oliver Heath, Michael Jewitt, Laura McCree, Gordon Whistance, Rowena Johnson · *Presenters*

Producers Various, including Linda Clifford (executive), Anna Hill, Pauline Doidge, Suzy Carter, Caspar Peacock, Mary Ramsay, Victoria Richardson, Susannah Walker, Corinne Sturmer, Joanne Haddock, Rachel Palin **Theme Music** Jim Parker

The DIY and lifestyle trend that threatened to swallow British television whole by 2004 began with a modest show on BBC Two. *Changing Rooms* took neighbours, friends or relatives and split them into two teams with the challenge of creating a makeover for a room in each other's houses. Each team had experts on hand to help with design ideas and practical tips that viewers at home might like to try, including how to create stencils for decorative painting on walls, how to run up a new set of curtains and how to create everything else through large sheets of MDF (medium density fibreboard).

Hosted initially by the eternally sunny 'Smiley smiley' Carol Smillie, the series had its successes and its disasters, with some participants overawed by the transformations and others reduced to tears as they discover just how little their friends/relatives knew about their own personal tastes. Some of the experts have become household names, including carpenter 'Handy' Andy Kane, Anna Ryder Richardson and Linda Barker. When Carol Smillie left in 2002, flamboyant interior designer Laurence Llewellyn-Bowen stepped in as the show's presenter.

Its legacy was far-reaching: as well as exporting the format overseas, there have been numerous copycat DIY shows, plus ***Ground Force***, which took the concept into people's gardens, and *Home Front*, in which Laurence Llewelyn-Bowen and Diarmuid Gavin would challenge each other to design a room and a garden for one property.

With the Beeb changing trends away from lifestyle programming, *Changing Rooms* was brought to an end after 15 series in 2004. Its final regular edition in 2004 preceded a Christmas special in which the team took on the Cornish village town of Boscastle, which had been decimated by extreme flash floods the previous summer.

Charlie Brown

Animation | Lee Mendelson/Bill Melendez/Charles M. Schulz Creative Associates/United Feature Syndicate for CBS (shown on BBC One) | episode duration 25–60 mins | broadcast 9 Dec 1965–present (USA)

Regular Voice Cast
Various, including:
Peter Robbins · *Charlie Brown*
Bill Melendez · *Snoopy, Woodstock*
Tracy Stratfor, Pamelyn Ferdin · *Lucy Van Pelt*
Christopher Shea, Glenn Gilger · *Linus Van Pelt*
Kathy Steinberg · *Sally Brown*
Chris Doran, Andy Pforsich · *Schroeder*
Karen Mendelson, Sally Dryer · *'Peppermint' Patty*
Geoffrey Ornstein, Christopher DeFaria · *Pig-Pen*

Creator/Writer Charles M. Schulz, based on his daily comic strip *Peanuts* **Producers** Lee Mendelson, Bill Melendez **Theme Music** Vince Guaraldi, whose 'Linus and Lucy' was used throughout the series to accompany more than just the Van Pelt kids – most notably in scenes where child protégé Schroeder would play the piano while the other kids danced in that curious way where their heads would lift up and their arms would wiggle at their sides.

The story of a group of philosophical primary-age kids from Birchwood School first appeared as a daily comic strip in newspapers on 2 October 1950. The star of the piece, Charlie Brown, was a child with an exceptionally round head and browbeaten demeanour, though his trademark zig-zag T-shirt didn't appear for some months. He was accompanied by his freakish beagle Snoopy, who insisted on walking around on two legs, his nemesis, the confident Lucy Van Pelt, and eventually his baby sister Sally and Lucy's baby brother Linus, the sensitive, blanket-hugging little boy who nevertheless manages to nail every situation with assessments that have frightening perspicacity.

The first TV special, *A Charlie Brown Christmas*, inspired over 50 *Peanuts* TV shows, including a Saturday morning serial (USA airdates: 17 Sep 1983–12 Oct 1985). It began with producer Lee Mendelson, who in 1963 made a documentary about *Peanuts*' creator, Charles Schulz, that had included short animated sequences created by Bill Melendez. An approach from a representative of the Coca-Cola company led to the corporation sponsoring the first TV special, a production that was surprisingly controversial. On Schultz's instruction, the special contained a strong Christian message, with Linus quoting the Bible, while he and Mendelson had decided not only to eschew the customary laughter track but to use the voices of real children to create the characters (the kids had to be coached to read the dialogue phonetically, often line by line). Oh, and it had a modern jazz soundtrack, courtesy of jazz pianist Vince Guaraldi. Despite such concerns, the special attracted the attention of over half the available viewing population in America, reaching No. 2 in the ratings (pipped by ***Bonanza***). The following year, it won an Emmy for 'Outstanding Children's Program'.

Charlie Brown seasonal specials soon became a regular fixture, including a memorable Thanksgiving episode where Linus reveals his fervent belief in 'the Great Pumpkin' and 'It's the Easter Beagle, Charlie Brown', in which Snoopy dances with Easter bunnies. In later editions, we get to see more of the *Peanuts* universe, with the little league baseball matches that inevitably lead to disaster for Charlie Brown and his team; the familiar scene where Lucy holds out the football for Charlie to kick, only to snatch it away every time; the kite-eating tree; his exchanges with tomboy Peppermint Patty, who calls him 'Chuck', and her friend Marcie, who addresses him as 'Charles' (and therefore become the only characters, aside from Charlie's own sister, who don't call him 'Charlie Brown'); Charlie's teacher, whose voice is that of a muted trumpet, delivering messages to the class in a 'wahwuwuwahwahwah' tone; and of course, whenever things went wrong, Charlie Brown would always say 'Good grief!'

The final *Peanuts* strip was syndicated on 3 January 2000. Just a month later, the 77-year-old Charles Schulz died from colon cancer. On 27 May that year, nearly 100 other cartoonists added *Peanuts*-related material to their own strips in tribute to Schultz, whose *Peanuts* characters were celebrating their 50th anniversary.

Trivia

Why 'Peanuts'? In the USA, small children would often be referred to as 'little peanuts'. It has nothing to do with Linus and Lucy having vaguely peanut-shaped heads.

Charlie's Angels

Adventure/Crime Drama | Spelling/Goldberg Productions for ABC (shown on ITV) | episode duration 50 mins | broadcast 21 Mar 1976, 22 Sep 1976–24 Jun 1981 (USA)

Regular Cast

Kate Jackson · *Sabrina Duncan*
Farrah Fawcett-Majors · *Jill Munroe*
Jaclyn Smith · *Kelly Garrett*
David Doyle · *John Bosley*
John Forsythe · *Charles Townsend (voice only)*
Cheryl Ladd · *Kris Munroe*
Shelley Hack · *Tiffany Welles*
Tanya Roberts · *Julie Rogers*

Creators Ivan Goff, Ben Roberts **Producers** Leonard Goldberg, Aaron Spelling (executive), Shelley Hull (associate), Elaine Rich (co-producer), Ronald Austin, James D. Buchanan, Rick Husky, Robert Janes, Edward J. Lakso, David Levinson, Barney Rosenzweig **Writers** Various, including Ronald Austin, John D. F. Black, James D. Buchanan, Richard Carr, Robert George, Edward J. Lasko, Laurie Lasko, Brian McKay, B. W. Sandefur, Lee Sheldon **Theme Music** Jack Elliott and Allyn Ferguson composed one of the most iconic pieces of 1970s music for the titles.

In 1974, Aaron Spelling – the media mogul behind such hits as *The Mod Squad* and ***Starsky and Hutch*** – came up with a concept for a new TV series. Following in the footsteps of Angie Dickinson's *Police Woman*, Spelling's idea was to create a series starring three glamorous detectives – the proposed title being 'The Alley Cats'. After a year of pitching the series to different networks, a 90-minute pilot movie was made in 1975. It was a ratings smash, and inevitably a series followed soon after.

Initially, this new series was conceived as a star vehicle for actress Kate Jackson, who had appeared in Goldberg and Spelling's series *The Rookies* (never shown in the UK). Joining her as Charlie's other two angels was Southern belle actress Jaclyn Smith and, most famously, wife of the Six Million Dollar Man, Farrah Fawcett-Majors. In the series, the three women worked at the Charles Townsend Investigations, having been head-hunted from their existing 'boring' jobs working for the police force. Sabrina was the 'clever' Angel, Jill the 'athletic' and Kelly the 'tough' one. Strangely though, the Angels never get to meet their boss, Charlie – instead, they receive their latest mission from him via his office manager Bosley, or when need be, direct from Charlie via a speakerphone on a desk. For many years, the identity of the mystery voice behind Charlie wasn't widely circulated, but when actor John Forsythe began starring as Blake Carrington in ***Dynasty***, the conundrum was soon solved.

Charlie's Angels became an almost overnight sensation in the USA – all of the three leading actresses were transformed into international superstars. However, most famous by far was Farrah, a woman whose hair launched a million copycat cuts right around the globe. With her husband receiving a far higher salary for his leading role as the Bionic Man, Farrah decided to quit *Charlie's Angels* after the first season, in the hope of capitalising on her massive fame. But she'd forgotten about the little matter of the contract that she'd signed, and eventually came to an agreement with producers that liberated her from that contract in return for several guest appearances in the second and third seasons of the show. Farrah's replacement was Cheryl Ladd, who portrayed Jill Monroe's younger sister Kris. This line-up of Angels – Sabrina, Kelly and Kris – became even more popular than that of the first season, and the programme's ratings soared even higher. When Kate Jackson finally got fed up with all of the back-combing and running around in high heels, she was replaced in quick succession first by Shelley Hack and then by future Bond girl Tanya Roberts (who starred opposite Roger Moore in *A View to a Kill*, 1985).

All good things come to an end, and after six seasons Charles Townsend Investigations closed for business. Nearly 20 years later, though, the Angels came out of retirement for two big-budget Hollywood films, starring

Cameron Diaz, Lucy Liu and Drew Barrymore (*Charlie's Angels* in 2000 and *Charlie's Angels: Full Throttle* in 2003, the latter featuring a cameo appearance by Jaclyn Smith as the heavenly Kelly Garrett) – empty-headed, all-style-no-substance, *massively* entertaining action movies that were perfect re-imaginings of their source material.

Cheers

Sitcom | Charles/Burrows/Charles for Paramount (shown on Channel 4) | episode duration 25 mins, plus 3 × 60-90-min specials | broadcast 30 Sep 1982–20 May 1993 (USA)

Regular Cast

Ted Danson · *Sam Malone*
Shelley Long · *Diane Chambers*
Kirstie Alley · *Rebecca Howe*
Rhea Perlman · *Carla Tortelli-LeBec*
John Ratzenberger · *Cliff Clavin*
George Wendt · *Norm Peterson*
Nicholas Colasanto · *Ernie 'Coach' Pantusso*
Woody Harrelson · *Woody Boyd*
Kelsey Grammar · *Dr Frasier Crane*
Bebe Neuwirth · *Dr Lilith Sternin-Crane*
Harry Anderson · *Harry 'The Hat' Gittes*
Dan Hedaya · *Nick Tortelli*
Jean Kasem · *Loretta Tortelli*
Timothy Williams · *Anthony Tortelli*
Tom Skerritt · *Evan Drake*
Jay Thomas · *Eddie LeBec*
Roger Rees · *Robin Colcord*
Jackie Swanson · *Kelly Gaines*
Keene Curtis · *John Allen Hill*
Alan Koss · *Alan*
Jack Knight · *Jack*
Steve Giannelli · *Steve*
Tim Cunningham · *Tim*
Al Rosen · *Al*
Larry Harpel · *Larry*
Paul Willson · *Paul*

Creators Glen Charles, James Burrows, Les Charles **Producers** Various, including Glen Charles, Les Charles, James Burrows, Phoef Sutton, Dan O'Shannon, Tom Anderson, Cheri Steinkellner, Bill Steinkellner (executive), Peter Casey, David Lee (supervising), Ken Estin, Heide Perlman, Sam Simon, David Angell, Mary Fukuto **Writers** Various, including Glen Charles, Les Charles, Tom Reeder, Ken Levine, David Isaacs, David Lloyd, Heide Perlman, David Angell, Peter Casey, David Lee, Cheri Steinkellner, Bill Steinkellner, Phoef Sutton, Sue Herring, Brian Pollack, Mert Rich, Dan O'Shannon, Tom Anderson, Dan Staley, Rob Long, Kathy Ann Stumpe **Theme Music** 'Where Everybody Knows Your Name' by Judy Hart-Angelo. Gary Portnoy sang this rather lovely little title song, which was an ode to every great pub you've ever been to.

With 270 episodes, *Cheers* joins the upper echelons of TV comedy in terms of sheer volume alone: 150 million viewers (surpassing even the vast 125 million who tuned in to the final episode of ***M*A*S*H****) in the USA watched the last edition of *Cheers* – but even that wasn't the end of the story, with spin-off series ***Frasier*** equalling *Cheers*' tally of 11 seasons. Not bad at all for a programme with the simplest of formats – a Boston bar, its staff and the regular patrons who propped up that bar.

Former Boston Red Sox baseball pitcher Sam Malone owns and manages Cheers, a friendly neighbourhood bar (we'd call it a pub in the UK!) where, as the title song says, 'everybody knows your name'. Sam is an incorrigible flirt with the ladies, relying on his former (somewhat fleeting) fame as one of his opening gambits. At the start of the series, Sam's staff consisted of his old friend and former baseball coach Ernie (always known as 'Coach' though), a man with a somewhat oblique hold on reality, logic and clarity of thought; Carla, a diminutive, hot-blooded Italian with a fierce tongue, a spiky temperament and a huge brood to care for; and snobby intellectual Diane (who joins the Cheers staff in the first episode). Regular customers at the bar included nerdy postal worker Cliff and beer-monster Norm, with psychiatrist Dr Frasier Crane joining the gang two years in as Diane's fiancé.

For the first four seasons, the on-off relationship between Sam and Diane formed the core of the programme, with both of them confused by the attraction to types of people they'd normally completely avoid. Sam and Diane's relationship finally reached a crisis point and they split (with actress Shelley Long leaving to embark on a movie career). Sam sold the bar and bought a boat to travel around the world in order to forget about Diane. However, the boat sank and he returned to the bar to discover Rebecca Howe, now in place as the manager. With Sam reduced to the role of barman, the dynamic of the series was changed completely, centring on Sam's inability to deal with a woman boss. Other cast changes affected the series too – following the death of actor Nicholas Colasanto, Coach was written out of the programme and future Hollywood superstar Woody Harrelson arrived as the equally intellectually challenged barman Woody (must have taken them a long time to think up that name . . .). Shortly after, prickly, humour-free Dr Lilith Sternin started frequenting the bar, eventually marrying Frasier and bearing a son, Frederick.

Created by the team behind earlier hit sitcom ***Taxi***, *Cheers* was consistently funny throughout its lengthy run. Whereas some sitcoms would focus on moments of poignancy or (God forbid) saccharine, slushy sentimentality, *Cheers* just relied on strong scripts and quality direction (series co-creator James Burrows directed 237 of the 270 episodes). The ensemble cast of performers was among the very finest ever assembled for television, perfectly complementing the high-class, behind-the-scenes team. Because it was transmitted on Channel 4 in the UK (normally on Friday nights at 10.00 p.m., establishing the network's long-standing Friday night comedy strand), audiences never really matched those for the big, mainstream sitcoms on BBC One or ITV. Having said that, the people who watched *Cheers* knew that what they were getting was the real deal – the equal of anything produced on this side of the Atlantic.

Chef!

Sitcom | Crucial Films for BBC One | episode duration 30 mins | broadcast 28 Jan 1993–30 Dec 1996

Cast

Lenny Henry · *Gareth Blackstock*
Caroline Lee-Johnson · *Janice Blackstock*
Roger Griffiths · *Everton Stonehead*
Gary Bakewell · *Donald*
Elizabeth Bennett · *Lola*
Dave Hill · *Cyril Bryson*
Lorelei King · *Savanna Concord*
Pui Fan Lee · *Debra*
Hilary Lyon · *Alice*
Tim Matthews · *Crispin*
Ian McNeice, Jeff Nuttall · *Gustave LaRoche*

Creator Lenny Henry **Producers** Polly McDonald (executive), Charlie Hanson, Beverly Randall **Writers** Peter Tilbury, Geoff Dean **Theme Music** Jakko M. Jakszyk wrote the theme song *Serious Profession*, which was performed by Omar.

In the television present, as schedules become littered with gastronomic fare such as *Hell's Kitchen* fuelling the ever upward rise of TV celebrity chefs, one can't help but feel that Lenny Henry and Peter Tilbury were a good ten years early with this comedy about an egomaniac chef, and that it would do much better in 2005.

Henry, who devised the series, gives a great performance as Gareth Blackstock, ruling the kitchen at the rural Le Chateau Anglais with a rod of iron, while hiding behind a deceptively delicate sense of self. Gareth's efforts to strive for food perfection are hindered by his useless kitchen staff and, of course, the customers. Blackstock regularly lambastes his ignorant clientele like Basil Fawlty in chef's whites, much to the chagrin of his long-suffering wife, Janice.

It's a wonder that Lenny Henry insists on persevering with seriously off-target sketch shows when he can be this good. The early scripts by actor Peter Tilbury (who also created ***Shelley*** and wrote episodes of ***Birds of a Feather***) are particularly biting, but the third series, which came a couple of years later, tweaked the format and lost its way. The series was BAFTA nominated in 1994.

Chigley

Animation | Gordon Murray Puppets for BBC One | episode duration 15 minutes | broadcast 6 Oct–29 Dec 1969

Voice Cast

Brian Cant

Creator/Producer Gordon Murray **Writers** Gordon Murray, Alison Prince **Theme Music** The music to the 6 o'clock dance, courtesy of the Dutch Organ, came from Freddie Phillips.

For commentary, see THE TRUMPTONSHIRE TRILOGY, *pages 776–9*

Child's Play

Quiz Show | LWT for ITV | episode duration 30 mins | broadcast 1984–1988

Cast

Michael Aspel · *Host*

Producers Keith Stewart, Richard Hearsay

Child's Play is a supposedly hysterical celebrity quiz show in which guests have to decipher the correct word or phrase from video clips of children describing that word. The poor mites clearly barely understand what is being asked of them and the humour comes from the pulled faces and odd sounds the little ones make in their efforts to be understood. If they uttered the word, a comedy cartoon 'Ooops!' bubble was plastered over their mouths by video trickery.

Based on a short-lived American show of the same name, *Child's Play* came from LWT, which over the years provided plenty of disposable light entertainment fodder, and this is no exception. Michael Aspel lends as much gravitas to the proceedings as is possible, given the material.

Children of the Stones

Children's Science Fiction/Horror | HTV West for ITV | episode duration 25 mins | broadcast 10 Jan–21 Feb 1977

Cast

Iain Cuthbertson · *Rafael Hendrick*
Gareth Thomas · *Adam Brake*
Freddie Jones · *Dai*
Veronica Strong · *Margaret*
Peter Demin · *Matthew 'Matt' Brake*
Katherine Levy · *Sandra*
Ruth Denning · *Mrs Crabtree*
June Barrie · *Miss Clegg*
Ian Donnolly · *Bob*
Darren Hatch · *Kevin*
Gary Lock · *Jimmo*
Peggy Ann Wood · *Mrs Warner*
Richard Matthews · *Dr Lyle*
John Woodnutt · *Link*

Producers Patrick Dromgoole (executive), Peter Graham Scott **Writers** Jeremy Burnham, Trevor Ray **Theme Music** Sidney Sager, featuring the Ambrosia Singers

A cross between a sexless *Wicker Man* (1973) and a horror-lite ***Quatermass*** but for a younger audience, *Children of the Stones* is far more sophisticated and mature than its timeslot might suggest.

Widower scientist Adam Brake and his son Matthew arrive in the isolated West Country village of Milbury to study its stone circle and settle into the local community. Soon, Adam and Matthew begin to realise that there's a connection between the stone circle, the villagers and the local Squire Hendrick – a retired astronomer famed for his discovery some years before of a black hole. The locals are possessed with an uncomfortable level of happiness, a side effect of which is that the village children all seem at ease with solving astronomically complex mathematical equations, far beyond the ability of even scientist's son Matthew. Adam's scientific approach to his studies of the stone circle is challenged by his own son's apparent psychic awareness and paranormal links to those around him. As more of the village's 'outsiders' become converted to the 'happy' ways of Milbury, Adam and Matthew (aided by the new local historian Margaret, her daughter Sandra and a local disturbed down-and-out, Dai), examine maps, ley-line charts, ancient artefacts and an eerie painting, desperately hoping to find a solution to the mystery before time runs out for them all.

Filmed largely on location in the Wiltshire village of Avebury (which boasts its own genuine stone circle), *Children of the Stones* has lost little of its power to unnerve. From the discordant choral music sung by the brainwashed villagers through to a wholly impressive cast (in particular Freddie Jones as Dai) and the devastating finale, watching *Children of the Stones* is a truly unsettling experience.

Almost 30 years after its broadcast, this is a drama that remains original, which is all the more surprising considering its reliance on the traditional iconography of horror movies: a deconsecrated church, ley lines, a telepathic child with a link to the future (or is it the past?), a painting that portrays the village struck down by an unimaginable evil, the sinister local squire and his village of brainwashed 'happy' people, and sophisticated computers deciphering a link to a supernova. Even the villagers themselves are distinctly odd – only ever a sole parent with one same-gender child: father and son, mother and daughter.

The cyclical nature of the story – in which our heroes finally escape the village only for events to begin all over again – references another telefantasy classic, ***The Prisoner***, with the chorus of 'Happy day' mimicking the 'Be seeing you . . .' of that other famous village.

Children's Ward

Children's Drama | Granada for ITV | episode duration 25 mins | broadcast 15 Mar 1989–4 May 2000

Principal Cast

Carol Harvey · *Dr Charlotte Woods*
Ian McCulloch · *Dr McKeown*
Janette Beverley · *Sister Diane Meadows/Gallagher*
Tim Stanley · *Nurse Gary Miller*
Jenny Luckraft · *Keely Johnson*
Rita May · *Mags*
Alan Rothwell · *Dr Davies*
Tim Vincent · *Billy Ryan*
Leyla Nejad · *Dawn Khatir*
Ken Parry · *Jack Crossley*
Tom Higgins · *Dr Kieran Gallagher*
Judy Holt · *Sister Sandra Mitchell*
Dean Gatiss · *Mathew McCann*
Paul Lally · *Dr Strickland*
Mark Hamer · *Spida*
Mark Dixon · *Cal Spicer*
Chris Bisson · *'JJ'*
Nicola Stephenson · *Amanda*
Natalie Wiblin · *Helen Jordan*
Emily Aston · *Sally Jordan*
Martin Corrigan · *Colin Jordan*
Sarah Cooper · *Bryony Shaeffer*
Catherine Grimes · *Rowena Easson*
Will Mellor · *Ben Rowlingson*
Chloe Newsome · *Thea Bartlett*
Matthew Marsh · *Dr Brian Stoker*
Steven Arnold · *Joe Lloyd*
Patrick Connolly · *Swifty*
Jane Danson · *Paula*
David Elliot · *Dr Adam Sullivan*
Phillip King · *Charge Nurse Nick Williams*
Chris Cooke · *Chas*
Andrea Young · *Trish*
Paul Fox · *Tim O'Halloran*
Sharon Muircroft · *Fiona*
Gregg Baines · *Greg Casson*
Anthony Lewis · *Scott Morris*
Brigit Forsyth · *Sylvia Dickinson*
Trevor Cooper · *Big Bob*
Victoria Finney · *Julie Barrow*
Tina O'Brien · *Claire*
Kelly Greenwood · *Geri Stevens*
Ralf Little · *Robbie*
Vicky Binns · *Tash*
John Cattermole · *Davey Pearson*
Jonathan Taylor · *Si*

Creators Paul Abbott and Kay Mellor **Producers** Nick Wilson, David Liddiment (executive), Rod Natkiel, Gareth Morgan, Russell T. Davies **Writers** Paul Abbott, Kay Mellor, John Chambers, Martin Riley, Garry Lyons, Russell T. Davies, Sally Wainwright, Jan McVerry, Julian Preston, Catherine Hayes, Paul Cornell, Tom Eliott, Martin Jameson, Lee Pressman, Tony Basgallop, Joe Turner, Bill Taylor, Peter Kerry, Patrea Smallacombe, Karin Young, Chris Thompson, Julie Wilkinson, Matt Jones **Theme Music** Matthew Strachan

Granada's multi-award-winning drama set in a children's hospital ward came with an impressive pedigree. It was created by two of ***Coronation Street***'s top writers, both of whom later went on to greater success with their own series (Paul Abbott with ***State of Play*** and ***Shameless***, Kay Mellor with ***Band of Gold*** and *Fat Friends*). It also managed to tackle many of the issues the 'grown-up' shows addressed, including terminal illness, bereavement, abuse, drugs and bullying.

With a high turnover of characters that one would expect in any hospital-based drama, Granada slowly worked their way through hundreds of juvenile actors and actresses during the run, with many of them going on to more prominent roles in other shows. Steven Arnold, Alan Halsall, Tina O'Brien, Chris Bisson and Jane Danson were just some of the youngsters who went on to become lead performers on *Coronation Street*, while others include Anna Friel and Nicola Stephenson (***Brookside***), Ralf Little (***The Royle Family***, ***Two Pints of Lager and a Packet of Crisps***) and Will Mellor (***Hollyoaks, Casualty, Two Pints of Lager***).

The series title was reduced to *The Ward* for its eighth series, though for its 12th and final year it reverted to *Children's Ward*.

Chocky

Children's Science Fiction | Thames for ITV | episode duration 25 mins | broadcast 9 Jan 1984–16 Oct 1985

Principal Cast

James Hazeldine · *David Gore*
Carol Drinkwater · *Mary Gore*
Andrew Ellams · *Matthew Gore*
Glynis Brooks · *Voice of Chocky*
Penny Brownjohn · *Phyl*
Zoë Hart · *Polly Gore*
Colin McCormack · *Alan*
Paul Russell · *Paul Barclay*
Devin Stanfield · *Colin*
Jeremy Bulloch · *Landis*
Annabel Worrell · *Albertine Meyer*
Prentis Hancock · *Arnold Meyer*
Ed Bishop · *Dr Deacon*
Michael Crompton · *Luke*
Angela Galbraith · *Aunt Cissie*
Joan Blackham · *Mrs/Major Gibson*
Roy Boyd · *Professor Fraycott*
Freddie Brooks · *Mike*
Kristine Howarth · *Professor Wade*
Illona Linthwaite · *Dr Liddle*
Norma Ronald · *Voice of Chocky's parent*
Katrina Wilsher · *Su Lin*
Richard Wordsworth · *Professor Ferris*

Producers Pamela Lonsdale, Brian Walcroft (executive), Vic Hughes, Richard Bates **Writer** Anthony Read, from the novel by John Wyndham **Theme Music** John Hyde

Matthew Gore has always been a bright child, but one day something changes within him. His adoptive parents notice how much more inquisitive he has become about all sorts of things. He suddenly begins to excel at school, particularly in science and art, but he's also become easily distracted as if he's listening to something . . . or someone.

Intelligent science fiction dramas for children are still incredibly rare; only a handful have been made in the last 40 years. More common is the type of programme that has committed SF fans foaming at the mouth in frustration (***Captain Zep***, *Galloping Galaxies!* and any other series where the setting of a story in space is taken as an excuse for the performers to overact and the designers to cover everything in tinfoil). But Anthony Read's adaptation remains faithful to the tone of the novel by John Wyndham (also the author of *The Day of the Triffids*), retaining quite a sinister aspect to proceedings. We're not sure until the end that Chocky is a benign force, when we discover the reason for 'her' presence on Earth is to find intelligent life. Unfortunately, by making contact with Matthew, Chocky appears to have placed his life in danger as government scientists want to use him to access her energy source.

Though that was the point at which Wyndham's original novel ends, Thames negotiated with his estate to create two sequels, *Chocky's Children* and *Chocky's Challenge*, in which we meet other children who have conversed with Chocky and learn that their activities have attracted the attention of the military, represented by the sinister Major Gibson. Not quite as solid as the first series, let down by some of the younger cast members, the sequels were still head and shoulders above most other kiddie drama series at the time, crediting their youthful audience with enough brains not to need a gunge sequence or 'cute' anthropomorphic animal sidekick.

Chorlton and the Wheelies

Animation | Cosgrove Hall for ITV | episode duration 10 mins plus 30-min special | broadcast Sep 1976–Jun 1979

Voice Cast

Joe Lynch

Creators/Producers Brian Cosgrove and Mark Hall **Writers** Brian Trueman, Joe Kemp **Theme Music** Joe Griffiths – 'Jump in, we'll take you for a spin, and show you round the Wheelie World'

Wheelie World is a place where all the people have wheels instead of legs. On the outskirts of the town, high on a hilltop, is Spout Hall, a building in the shape of a kettle. That's where Fenella the Witch lives. With the help of her telescope, Reilly, a spellbook called Clapp Trapp Von

Spill-da-Beans and her tiny minions, the spikeys and the mushroom-shaped toadies, she keeps the people of Wheelie World miserable and under her thrall. One day, an egg appears in the centre of the town – an egg containing a happiness dragon who the Wheelies named Chorlton. Such was the infectious nature of Chorlton's happiness, Fenella's power over the Wheelies was broken. Now Fenella waits for opportunities to regain control of Wheelie World, while Chorlton hopes to show the 'little old lady' the ways of happiness.

Chorlton's Wheelie friends include Zoomer, who wears a flying cap, Jenny, a pink Wheelie with a ponytail, Good King Otto and Queen Doris and their pompous Minister. There's also Fenella's son, Clifford, who is so tall we only ever see his legs. Fortunately, he didn't inherit his mother's vile disposition.

The first production to be released under the name of Cosgrove Hall made great use of Joe Lynch's talent for accents, with Fenella shrieking in Welsh, Reilly the telescope in Irish mumbles, Clap Trapp in German and good ole Chorlton (named after the Greater Manchester home of Cosgrove Hall) in a thick Lancashire accent. *Chorlton and the Wheelies* ran for three series of 39 episodes, plus a 30-minute special. 'Right gradely!'

The Chronicles of Narnia

Children's Fantasy | BBC/WonderWorks for BBC One | episode duration 25 mins | broadcast 13 Nov 1988–23 Dec 1990

Principal Cast

Jonathan R. Scott · *Edmund Pevensie*
Sophie Wilcox · *Lucy Pevensie*
Richard Dempsey · *Peter Pevensie*
Sophie Cook · *Susan Pevensie*
Michael Aldridge · *The Professor*
Barbara Kellerman · *The White Witch, Green Lady*
Ronald Pickup · *Voice of Aslan*
Jeffrey S. Perry · *Mr Tumnus*
Kerry Shale · *Mr Beaver*
Lesley Nicol · *Mrs Beaver*
Big Mick · *Little Man, Trumpkin*
Maureen Morris · *Mrs Macready*
David Thwaites · *Eustace Clarence Scrubb*
Jean Marc Perret, Samuel West, Geoffrey Russell · *Prince/King Caspian*
Warwick Davis · *Reepicheep, Glimfeather*
John Hallam, Roy Boyd · *Captain/Lord Drinian*
Robert Lang · *King Miraz*
Angela Barlow · *Queen Prunaprismia*
Guy Fithen · *Rhince*
Neale McGrath · *Rynelf*
Henry Woolf · *Dr Cornelius*
Julie Peters · *Trufflehunter*
Camilla Power · *Jill Pole*
Tom Baker · *Puddleglum*
Richard Henders · *Prince Rilian*
Christopher Birch · *Old Giant*
Nick Brimble · *Giant Porter*
Patsy Byrne · *Giant Nanny*
June Ellis · *Giant Cook*
Melanie Gibson · *Giant Chambermaid*
Lesley Nicol · *Giant Queen*
Stephen Reynolds · *Giant King*
Jack Purvis · *Golg*

Producers Dale Bell, Jay Rayvid, Colin Shindler (executive), Paul Stone, Ellen Freyer **Writer** Alan Seymour, from *The Lion, the Witch and the Wardrobe, Prince Caspian, The Voyage of the Dawn Treader* and *The Silver Chair*, by C. S. Lewis **Theme Music** Geoffrey Burgon

One of the great British classics of the 20th century, *The Chronicles of Narnia* was C. S. Lewis's Christian parable that proved more accessible to younger readers than the Middle Earth sagas of his good friend J. R. R. Tolkien. *The Lion, The Witch and the Wardrobe* first came to television in a ten-part ATV serial for ITV in which Bernard Kay played Aslan and Elizabeth Wallace (***Compact***) the White Witch in a script by Trevor Preston. There, all of the animals were realised through actors wearing half-masks, like a Greek play or pantomime. In 1979, Bill Melendez, the man behind ***Charlie Brown***, collaborated with ***Sesame Street***'s Children's Television Workshop to bring an animated version of the tale to TV. But it was the BBC's 1989 version that came the closest to the magic of the original novel. The production shared many of the same techniques as ***The Box of Delights***, with the many strange and fearsome creatures realised through a combination of animation and the traditional men in suits.

Bypassing Lewis's prequel, *The Magician's Nephew*, the story beings with *The Lion, The Witch and the Wardrobe*, in which four children are evacuated from London and arrive at the country estate of an old professor. While playing hide-and-seek with her sister Susan and brothers Peter and Edmund, Lucy Pevensie enters a wardrobe and is startled to discover it acts as a portal into another world. Eventually, her siblings follow her in and the children discover a land that's forever winter but never Christmas, a land populated by fawns, centaurs, talking animals and an evil White Witch who has usurped the true ruler of Narnia, Aslan the Lion.

The adaptation was enough of a success to justify a second series, this time condensing two more books – *Prince Caspian* and *The Voyage of the Dawn Treader* – into a six-part serial. In *Prince Caspian*, the Pevensie children return to Narnia to discover that though a year has passed in their time, it's a generation further on in Narnia. The land is in the midst of civil war, with the heir to the throne, Prince Caspian, fleeing for his life from his evil uncle, King Miraz. The following summer, Lucy and Edmund are forced to spend time with their spiteful cousin Eustace only for all three children to be drawn into a picture of a Narnian ship – the *Dawn Treader*. Aboard the ship, Eustace struggles to make sense of things while Edmund and Lucy are reunited with Caspian, now a young king on a voyage to find lost Narnian lords. A final series, *The Silver Chair*, paired Eustace off with a girl at his school, Jill Pole, and a marsh-dwelling and thoroughly miserable frog-like creature called Puddleglum in a quest to rescue another heir to the Narnian throne from the thrall of a wicked queen of the underworld.

Sadly, *The Silver Chair* brought the short series to a close without adapting the remaining books (*The Horse and His Boy* and *The Last Battle*). However, in 2003, *The Magician's Nephew* was eventually serialised as a storytelling series for deaf children, signed by Jean St Clair and narrated by Jane Lapotaire. A major Hollywood motion picture adaptation of *The Lion, The Witch And The Wardrobe* (starring Tilda Swinton as the White Witch) reached cinemas in 2005, bringing the tales of Narnia to a whole new generation of adults and children alike.

Chucklevision

Children's Comedy | BBC One | episode duration 20 mins | broadcast 26 Sep 1987–present

Regular Cast
Paul Elliott · *Paul Chuckle*
Barry Elliott · *Barry Chuckle*

Creators Paul Elliott, Barry Elliott **Producers** Chris Bellinger, Anne Gilchrist (executive), Martin Hughes, Ken Robertson, Dominic MacDonald **Writers** Various, including the Chuckle Brothers, Russell T. Davies, John Sayle, Martin Hughes, Terry Randall, Nick McIvor, Philip Hazelby, Ramsay Gilderdale, Rory Clark, Robert Taylor, Ian Billings, Richard Preddy, Gary Howe, Dominic MacDonald, Jo Boyle, Isabelle Amyes, Peter Symonds, Gail Renard, Marie Findlay, Emma Millions, George Poles, Simon Littlefield **Theme Music** Dave Cooke

Paul and Barry Chuckle – known collectively as the Chuckle Brothers – are two children's comedy performers who deserve an award for perseverance, if nothing else. They first burst onto TV screens in 1985 in a short-lived show aimed at toddlers called *Chucklehounds*, in which they dressed up in giant fluffy dog costumes and got up to the usual assortment of short-attention-span mischief. Then, in 1987, a TV legend was born – *Chucklevision* arrived. Each 20-minute episode relies upon the brothers' old-school slapstick comedy for laughs, and it has to be said that they must be doing something right. Still enormously popular with their chosen audience of 7–10-year-olds (and university students, naturally), *Chucklevision* continues in production nearly 20 years after it was first broadcast. At the time of writing, the brothers had notched up an astonishing 234 episodes over the course of 16 seasons, with no sign on the horizon of ever calling it a day. Not ones to be typecast as mere comedy performers, in 1996 the Chuckle Brothers also tried their hand at hosting a children's game show called *To Me, To You* (one of their catchphrases – normally invoked in the middle of a slapstick routine whilst passing a heavy object back and forth between themselves).

Citizen Smith

Sitcom | BBC One | episode duration 30 mins | broadcast 12 Apr 1977, 3 Nov 1977–31 Dec 1980

Regular Cast
Robert Lindsay · *Walter 'Wolfie' Smith*
Cheryl Hall · *Shirley Johnson*
Mike Grady · *Ken Mills*
Anthony Millan · *Tucker*
John Sweeney · *Speed*
Peter Vaughan, Artro Morris, Tony Steedman · *Dad/Charles Johnson*
Hilda Braid · *Mum/Mrs Johnson*
Stephen Greif · *Harry Fenning*
Anna Nygh · *Desirée*
David Garfield · *Ronnie Lynch*
Susie Baker · *Mandy Lynch*

Creator/Writer John Sullivan **Producers** Peter Whitmore, Dennis Main Wilson, Ray Butt **Theme Music** Socialist anthem 'The Red Flag', performed in full heckle mode by Robert Lindsay

BBC scenery shifter John Sullivan was busy working on other people's comedy programmes – shows he considered on the whole to be distinctly unamusing – when he decided to put his money where his mouth was and submit a script of his own. After a few comments and alterations, a pilot episode for Sullivan's first series, *Citizen Smith*, was eventually transmitted in 1977 under the *Comedy Special* label, leading to a full series later the same year.

Wolfie Smith is the leader of the Tooting Popular Front, a revolutionary Marxist organisation dedicated to dismantling the capitalist straightjacket that holds the population in its decadent grip. Despite Wolfie's stated aim to bring about revolution on the streets of south London, his very limited support means that his goals are forever way beyond his reach. The other members of the TPF include best friend and wimpy vegetarian Buddhist Ken, hen-pecked husband Tucker and unpredictably violent thug Speed, who spends as much time in jail as he does out and about trying to overthrow the system. Away from the TPF, however, Wolfie's life continues to be rather mundane and ordinary. His girlfriend Shirley's dad is a blunt-speaking northerner with no time for Wolfie's politics or behaviour, whereas her mum is a slightly bewildered lady who insists on calling him 'Foxy'. Meanwhile, Wolfie does whatever he can to avoid having to get a job, believing that work of that sort would do nothing to help in his fight to liberate the proletariat. Occasionally, his path crosses those of local gangland villains Harry Fenning and Ronnie Lynch, which normally spells trouble for Wolfie and his friends.

Not only was *Citizen Smith* the first hit for writer John Sullivan, it was also the first lead role for actor Robert

Lindsay, who'd made an impression as part of the ensemble in ITV's national service sitcom ***Get Some In!*** He would later achieve further sitcom success in *Nightingales* and ***My Family***, as well as portraying more serious roles in shows as diverse as ***GBH*** and ***Hornblower***. Peter Vaughan, who played Shirley's dad in the first two seasons of *Citizen Smith*, is perhaps best known as the sinister 'Genial' Harry Grout in ***Porridge***. Appearing as Shirley's mum was actress Hilda Braid, who took on the role of another doddery lady as Nana Moon in ***EastEnders***. For writer John Sullivan, the end of *Citizen Smith* marked the beginning of further sitcom success, for less than a year after Wolfie Smith bellowed, 'Power to the People!' for the final time, a certain Del Boy Trotter made his first appearance on BBC One . . .

Civilisation

Documentary | BBC Two | episode duration 50 mins | broadcast 23 Feb–18 May 1969

Cast/Writer Sir Kenneth Clark **Producers** Michael Gill, Peter Montagnon

Sir Kenneth Clark's personal journey through the history of mankind took us from the fall of the Roman Empire right up to the 20th century. Clark eschewed clever graphics and special effects in favour of a simple story well told. His quest took him the scenic route through the evolution of civilisation, examining art and architecture through the ages. The series was rightly recognised as a landmark in British broadcasting and a major coup for BBC Two. It also spawned a successful book.

Clangers

Children's Science Fiction | Smallfilms for BBC One | episode duration 10 mins | broadcast 16 Nov 1969–10 Oct 1974

Cast

Oliver Postgate · *Narrator and Clanger Voices*
Stephen Sylvester · *Additional Clanger Voices*

Creator/Producers Oliver Postgate and Peter Firmin
Writer/Director Oliver Postgate **Theme Music** Vernon Elliott

The most easily imitated of all Oliver Postgate's creations, the Clangers reflected our fascination with all things spacey in the late-1960s. The Clangers – Major, Mother, Small and Tiny Clanger, plus an extended family of Granny, uncles and aunts – were a family of pink, long-eared rodents who lived underneath clanging bin-lids that covered the craters on a small blue planetoid not far from Earth. They communicated through a series of sounds produced by a Swannee whistle and seemed to exist on a diet of green soup, glow-honey and blue-string pudding. They shared their home with the Soup Dragon, a benign lizard, the orange froglets and a rather cantankerous creature called the Iron Chicken.

Most of their charming adventures involved exploring the oddness of their environment, such as harvesting the musical trees, whose notes are used to power the Clangers' short-trip spaceship, traversing the soup wells or conversing with Skymoos, inhabitants of a nearby planet, who came to rid the Clanger world of a rather persistent weed.

An early Clanger made an appearance in the two-dimensional animated series ***The Saga of Noggin the Nog***, but for their own show, they became three-dimensional thanks to metal armatures, knitted woollen skins and pipe-cleaners for fingers. The sets and models were constructed by Peter Firmin, with help from his wife Joan, who created the dresses for the female Clangers. This charming programme was clearly a major contributor to popular culture; a clip appeared in an episode of ***Doctor Who*** where the Doctor's archenemy, the Master, feigned belief that they were real aliens, while pop group The Soup Dragons had a top five hit with 'I'm Free' in 1990. The show has been dubbed into a number of European languages, where viewers have believed the cute little creatures to be speaking fluent Swedish, German or whatever. Clever, eh?

The final episode, 'Vote for Froglet!', was broadcast on election night, 10 October 1974, almost a year after the transmission of the final regular episode. The only one of the run not to be subsequently repeated, it saw Small Clanger join forces with a froglet to canvass support for the planetoid's own elections.

The Clifton House Mystery

Children's Drama | HTV for ITV | episode duration 25 mins | broadcast 8 Oct–12 Nov 1978

Cast

Sebastian Breaks · *Timothy Clare*
Ingrid Hafner · *Sheila Clare*
Peter Sallis · *Milton Guest*
Derek Graham · *Officer*
Elizabeth Havelock · *The Lady*
Amanda Kirby · *Jenny*
Joshua Le Touzel · *Steven*
Michelle Martin · *Emily*
Robert Morgan · *Ben*
Peter Sallis · *Milton Guest*
Margery Withers · *Mrs Betterton*

Writers Henry Moore and Daniel Parson **Producers** Patrick Dromgoole (executive), Leonard White **Theme Music** Sidney Sager

HTV's annual kiddie-fantasy slot had already mined straight sci-fi (***Sky***, 1975), time travel (*The Georgian House*, 1976) and the mystical (***Children of the Stones***, 1977). For the fourth excursion into the unknown, genre maestro Patrick Dromgoole turned his hand to out-and-out horror. Of course, the series was acted with the usual mechanical apathy (adults) and clumsy enthusiasm (children), the sets were over-lit and the budget low, but as a script, *The Clifton House Mystery* is cut from the cloth of nightmares, taking many of its cues from more X-rated fare, at times even pre-empting scenes from *The Amityville Horror* (1979). As the Clare family – predictably nuclear, with RP accents and unpleasant hair – move into an old house in Bristol, they quickly discover that they are sharing the property with a couple of restless revenants. Dusty skeletons are found in sealed rooms, wild-eyed, disembodied faces leer from the furniture, and, most shockingly of all, a dinner party is interrupted by blood dripping from the ceiling. In a scenario only remotely reminiscent of *The Exorcist* (1973), Peter Sallis is summoned to exorcise the unruly phantoms.

Overall, though, this a competent and enjoyable thriller with some moments of genuine atmosphere, although Sidney Sager's haunting music-box melody will haunt you longer than any of the visuals. Sadly, the series tends not to make it into the beery reminiscences of nostalgic thirtysomethings, although in recent years it has achieved some trophy status on the cult video collectors' circuit.

Clive James/Floyd/Tarrant on TV

Comedy | ITV | episode duration 30 mins | broadcast 1987–present

Cast

Clive James, Keith Floyd, Chris Tarrant · *Host*

A now long-running format that was originally hosted by Clive James in a late Sunday evening slot, exhausting reams and reams of footage showing the cultural differences in advertising and broadcasting across the world. *On TV* is genuinely funny and many of the clips will have you laughing out loud or looking on in open-mouthed amazement. The series is probably best remembered as showcasing the bonkers Japanese game show *Endurance*, where contestants were put through the most excruciating agony week in, week out.

Clive James was succeeded by celebrity chef Keith Floyd, who seemed an odd choice of host without a glass of something in his hand, but Chris Tarrant made the format his own when he took over the chair from Floyd. This series eventually led to Tarrant's TV rehabilitation after the shock of the flop *OTT*, and eventually put him in the right place and the right time to host ***Who Wants to be a Millionaire?***

Clocking Off

Drama Anthology | Red Productions for BBC One | episode duration 30 mins | broadcast 23 Jan 2000–6 Apr 2003

Regular Cast

Philip Glenister · *James 'Mack' Mackintosh*
Lesley Sharp · *Trudy Graham*
Sarah Lancashire · *Yvonne Kalakowski*
Siobhan Finnerman · *Julie O'Neill*
Christine Tremarco · *Katherine Mackintosh*
Jason Merrells · *Martin Leach*
Diane Parish · *Sylvia Robinson*
Ricky Tomlinson · *Ronnie Anderson*

Creator Paul Abbott **Producers** Gareth Neame, Tessa Ross, Nicola Shindler (executive), Des Hughes, Alison Law (associate), Juliet Charlesworth, Ann Harrison-Baxter **Writers** Paul Abbott, Daniel Brockelhurst, John Fay, Bill Gallagher, Richard Zajdlic **Theme Music** Murray Gold

The staff-members of Mackintosh Textiles all have a tale to tell, because when they clock off, their lives don't end. This brilliant series, devised by the always excellent dramatist Paul Abbott, showcases the private lives of the many workers in rotation from week to week. Although there is an ensemble cast, one character is placed in the spotlight in each episode, with most of the cast getting their shot in the spotlight at some point, from factory boss James Mackintosh, his PA Trudy to factory worker Yvonne Kalakowski. The guest cast reads like a Who's Who of top British drama talent, with turns from Abbott stalwarts Christopher Eccleston, John Simm and David Morrissey, with upcoming actresses like the (since) Oscar nominated Sophie Okonedo putting in appearances.

Clocking Off was rightly feted by critics and audiences for challenging the usual narrative form of British drama and for combining intelligent writing with superb performances. The series garnered many award nominations and wins, including a Best Drama Series BAFTA in 2001.

The Cloning of Joanna May

Drama | Granada for ITV | episode duration 90 mins | broadcast 26 Jan–2 Feb 1992

Cast

Patricia Hodge · *Joanna May*
Brian Cox · *Carl May*
Emma Hardy · *Jane Jarvis*
Helen Adie · *Alice Morthampton*
Laura Eddy · *Gina Herriot*
Billie Whitelaw · *Mavis*
Jean Boht · *Mrs Love*

Producers Sally Head (executive), Gub Neal **Writers** Ted Whitehead, from the novel by Fay Weldon **Theme Music** Rachel Portman

Joanna and Carl May were once very much in love, but were forced to divorce when Joanna had a casual love affair. Carl is a very wealthy nuclear energy magnate and remains obsessed with Joanna to the extent that he creates three clones of her. He sits back and watches as the clones grow to maturity, and eventually gathers them together to inform the sub-Joannas that he will pick one of them as his bride. The reaction is not quite what he's expecting, but that's nothing to what Joanna has to say when she drops by for a visit.

Adapted from the novel by Fay Weldon, *The Cloning of Joanna May* is, like ***The Life and Loves of a She-Devil*** before it (also directed by Phillip Saville), an effective parable on love, obsession and fidelity with a nice line in unobtrusive sci-fi thrills.

The Clothes Show

Lifestyle | BBC One | episode duration 30 mins | broadcast 13 Oct 1986–13 Apr 1998

Cast

Jeff Banks, Brenda Emmanus, Caryn Franklin, Andy McNair, Selina Scott, Margherita Taylor, Tim Vincent · *Presenters*

Producers Roger Casstles (editor) Colette Foster, Karen Hughes **Theme Music** 'In the Night' by The Pet Shop Boys

Before *What Not to Wear*, this was a popular venture for the BBC. The Birmingham-based Pebble Mill arm of the Corporation launched *The Clothes Show* as a daytime programme with an evening repeat, before it took up a decade-long residence on Sunday afternoons. Fashion designer Jeff Banks had apparently lobbied for a show of this nature for years, and he finally got his wish, presenting the show for much of its run, alongside Selina Scott, and, towards the end of its run, ***Blue Peter*** presenter Tim Vincent joined the team.

BBC Magazines launched an accompanying magazine, while *The Clothes Show Live* took place at London's Olympia. Throughout the year, amidst the usual fashion tips and style news, various national competitions would be held. Presenter Andy McNair, who arrived in 2000 for the show's last hurrah, would go on to star as Dan Hunter in teen Channel 4 soap ***Hollyoaks***.

Cluedo

Game Show | Action Time /Granada in association with Waddingtons Games for ITV | episode duration 30–45 mins | broadcast 1990–1993

Cast

James Bellino, Chris Tarrant, Richard Madeley · *Hosts*
Stephanie Beacham, Rula Lenska, Susan George, Joanna Lumley, Kate O'Mara · *Mrs Peacock*
June Whitfield, Mollie Sugden, Pam Ferris, Liz Smith, Joan Sims · *Mrs White*
Robin Ellis, Michael Jayston, Lewis Collins, Leslie Grantham, David Robb · *Colonel Mustard*
Tracy-Louise Ward, Koo Stark, Lysette Anthony, Jerry Hall, Toyah Willcox · *Miss Scarlet*
Robin Nedwell, Richard Wilson, Christopher Biggins, Nicholas Parsons, Derek Nimmo · *Reverend Green*
Kristoffer Tabori, David McCallum, Tom Baker, John Bird, Ian Lavender · *Professor Plum*

Creator Stephen Leahy, inspired by the board game thought up by Anthony Pratt in 1944 **Producers** Dianne Nelmes (executive) Mark Gorton, Stephen Leahy, Brian Park, Kieran Roberts, Oscar Whitbread **Theme Music** Richard G. Mitchell, Kevin Malpass

Based around the ever-popular board game of the same name, *Cluedo* brought the familiar characters from the game to life in a series of live action murder vignettes that contestants in the studio would watch. They then had the opportunity to cross-examine the characters in real time and ultimately solve the murder and win. Amusingly, the host would always ask the murderer to stay behind for questioning, although they were clearly acquitted, as we'd see them back at work the following week.

Devised by Action Time head Steven Leahy, the show used the characters from the board game – Mrs Peacock, Mrs White, Colonel Mustard, Miss Scarlet, Reverend Green and Professor Plum (although the cast would be changed every series) – and the fictional location was Arlington Grange (in actual fact, Tatton Park in Cheshire) as opposed to Tudor Close.

Chris Tarrant, who hosted season two, has since confessed to hating the show, as it took too long to make. He was replaced in the final two seasons by ***This Morning*** host Richard Madeley. A Christmas special was broadcast in 1990, again using a different cast. ***Doctor Who*** fans might like to note the name of Russell T. Davies having penned an episode.

The Colbys

Soap | Aaron Spelling Productions for ABC (shown on BBC One) | episode duration 50 mins | broadcast 20 Nov 1985–26 Mar 1987 (USA)

Regular Cast

Charlton Heston · *Jason Colby*
Barbara Stanwyck · *Constance Colby Patterson*
Stephanie Beacham · *Sable Colby*
Katherine Ross · *Frankie Colby*
John James · *Jeff Colby*
Emma Samms · *Fallon Carrington Colby*
Maxwell Caulfield · *Miles Colby*
Tracy Scoggins · *Monica Colby*
Claire Yarlett · *Bliss Colby*
Ken Howard · *Garrett Boydston*
Ricardo Montalban · *Zach Powers*

Creators Eileen and Robert Pollock, Esther Shapiro **Producers** Richard and Esther Shapiro, Aaron Spelling, E. Duke Vincent, Douglas S. Cramer (executive), Dennis Hammer, Paul Huson, Christopher Morgan, William Bast **Writers** Various, including Rick Edelstein, Frank Furino, Paul Huson, Mary Ann Kasica,

Charles Pratt Jr, Don Roos, Michael Scheff, Doris Silverton, E. Jeffrey Smith, Dennis Turner **Theme Music** Bill Conti

Created as a sister show to the already hugely successful ***Dynasty*** (in fact, for the first four episodes, the programme was actually called *Dynasty II: The Colbys*), few people could have predicted that *The Colbys* would prove to be even more outrageously over-the-top than its parent show. In order to try and guarantee an audience for the new series, two of the most popular characters from Dynasty – Jeff and Fallon Colby – were moved from *Dynasty*'s home town of Denver to the sunnier climes of Los Angeles, where Jeff attempted to get to know the rest of his family better while simultaneously winning back the love of his wife, Fallon (who had developed amnesia and fallen in love with Jeff's cousin, bad-boy Miles).

Patriarch of this new 'dynasty' was hyper-rich businessman Jason Colby, Jeff's uncle. Much like Blake Carrington, Jason was rather humourless and authoritarian in his dealings with his family, which often alienated them and provided the source of a lot of the show's dramatic tension. Jason was married to glamorous vixen Sable, a woman determined to do whatever she could to hang on to her husband and his riches. Unfortunately for Sable, Jason was actually deeply in love with her sister Frankie (who also happened to be Jeff's mother!), a love triangle that lasted the duration of the series. Adding extra fun and games to proceedings were the antics of Jason and Sable's three children, Miles, Monica and Bliss. Rounding off the family was Jason's older sister Connie, a no-nonsense elderly lady who delivered home truths to her wayward brood whenever the opportunity arose.

One of the great strengths of *The Colbys* was in the casting of several major Hollywood legends: Charlton Heston, Barbara Stanwyck and Katherine Ross were all already well known to viewers. By adding a smattering of glamorous younger cast members of both sexes, the already familiar charms of two *Dynasty* veterans, and of course the inestimable glamour of Stephanie Beacham (out-Joaning Joan Collins as the show's resident British bitch), *The Colbys* whipped up a soufflé-light confection of typically tawdry soap storylines.

Despite what appeared to be a winning formula, audience figures never seemed to reach the dizzy heights that the networks expected. *The Colbys* was an extremely expensive show to make, even after the departure at the end of the first series of Barbara Stanwyck (who later claimed that the series was 'the biggest pile of garbage that I ever did'). So it came as little surprise that the series was cancelled at the end of its second year, after just 49 episodes. Unfortunately, this meant that many of the plot threads left dangling in the cliffhanger finale were never resolved. The most famous one – in which Fallon Carrington is abducted by a UFO – was discussed in *Dynasty* the following season, when Fallon failed to convince anyone except her brother Steven that she'd been for a quick tour around the galaxy in a spaceship.

When *The Colbys* was quickly put to sleep, several characters moved over to *Dynasty*, including Fallon, Jeff, Sable and Monica. Cast members from *The Colbys* are still doing the rounds today – Maxwell Caulfield played dashing-yet-doomed doctor Jim Brodie in ***Casualty***, Tracy Scoggins was the captain of ***Babylon 5*** in its final season, while Stephanie Beacham is locked up with her other co-stars in ***Bad Girls***.

Cold Feet

Comedy Drama | Granada for ITV | episode duration 50 mins | broadcast 30 Mar 1997, 15 Nov 1998–16 Mar 2003

Regular Cast

James Nesbitt · *Adam Williams*
Helen Baxendale · *Rachel Bradley*
John Thomson · *Pete Gifford*
Robert Bathurst · *David Marsden*
Hermione Norris · *Karen Marsden*
Fay Ripley · *Jenny Gifford*
Jacey Sallés · *Ramona Ramirez*
Kimberley Joseph · *Jo Ellison*
Rosie Cavaliero · *Amy*
Ben Miles · *Robert*
Yasmin Bannerman · *Jessica*
Richard Armitage · *Lee*
Steve Edge · *Sean*
Laurie Jenkins · *Baby Adam*
Daniel O'Brien, Liam O'Brien · *Baby Josh*
Sean Pertwee · *Mark Cubitt*
Lorelei King · *Natalie*
Victoria Smurfit · *Jane Fitzpatrick*
Samantha Spiro · *Ruth*
Doreen Keogh · *Audrey Gifford*
Lucy Robinson · *Robyn Duff*

Creator Mike Bullen **Producers** Mike Bullen, Andy Harries, Robert C. Thompson (executive), David Meddick (associate), Emma Benson, Spencer Campbell, Christine Langan **Writers** Mike Bullen, David Nicholls **Theme Music** Mark Russell

A warm, clever and touching series that focused on the lives of three couples living in Manchester, *Cold Feet* was one of ITV's greatest drama successes of recent years, regularly gaining audiences in excess of 10 million viewers. When *Cold Feet* first began, some critics compared it to the American comedy series ***Friends***, primarily because it starred three professional men and women talking about their love lives and relationships. However, *Cold Feet* was much more of a drama than a comedy, revealing all of the pain and agony of being in love, as well as delivering the more palatable laughs and fun. In keeping with this, comedic performers like ***The Fast Show***'s John Thompson and Robert Bathurst from ***Joking Apart*** were mixed with 'straight' actors such as Helen Baxendale, Fay Ripley and James Nesbitt – who, thanks to a few carefully shot nude scenes (including one where his character woos Rachel by appearing at her garden gate with a rose between his buttocks), became a bit of a sex symbol.

Chirpy Irishman Adam meets and falls in love with advertising executive Rachel. Although he's wary of settling down, eventually they declare their undying love for each other. Pete and Jenny Gifford are trying for a baby, hoping that a child will help to paper over the cracks that have begun to appear in their marriage. And David and Karen Marsden are beginning to realise that external pressures can strain even the strongest of relationships. As the series goes on, Pete and Jenny do split up, enabling actress Fay Ripley to leave the show. Another of the programme's stars had a brief flirtation with transatlantic fame when Helen Baxendale joined the cast of *Friends* as Ross's new English fiancée, Emily.

Over the course of he four series, audiences became incredibly involved with the ongoing storylines, investing a great deal of emotional time and effort in the show, in much the same way that viewers do with the best soap operas. So when tragic events struck the series, the impact was almost unbearable. In the penultimate episode Rachel was killed in a freak – and distressingly sudden – road accident. After her funeral, Adam scattered her ashes in the beautiful setting of Portmeirion, North Wales. A nation mourned, vastly increasing the profits of Kleenex tissues overnight.

Equally loved by critics and public alike, the pilot episode of *Cold Feet* won acclaim at the Montreux Festival, thereby guaranteeing that ITV would commission the show for a full series. The show picked up the 1999 and 2000 British Comedy Award for best series, neatly proving that it wasn't just about tears and tragedy by any means.

Cold Warrior

See BLOOD MONEY

Colditz

Drama | BBC/Universal for BBC One | episode duration 50 mins | broadcast 19 Oct 1972–1 Apr 1974

Regular Cast

Jack Hedley · *Lieutenant Colonel John Preston*
Edward Hardwicke · *Captain Pat Grant*
Robert Wagner · *Flight Lieutenant/Major Phil Carrington*
David McCallum · *Flight Lieutenant Simon Carter*
Bernard Hepton · *The Kommandant*
Christopher Neame · *Lieutenant Dick Player*
Paul Chapman · *Captain George Brent*
Hans Meyer · *Hauptman Franz Ulmann*
Richard Heffer · *Captain Tim Downing*
Peter Penry-Jones · *Pilot Officer Peter Muir*
Anthony Valentine · *Major Horst Mohn*
Jeremy Kemp · *Squadron Leader Tony Shaw*
Dan O'Herlihy · *Lieutenant Colonel Max Dodd*
Nicholas McArdle · *Captain Richard Walters*
Al Mancini · *Captain Harry Nugent*
Malcolm Stoddard · *Captain Christopher Mawson*

Creators Brian Degas and Gerard Glaister, based on *Colditz* by P. R. Reid, and Ivan Foxwell's film *The Colditz Story* (1955) **Producer** Gerard Glaister **Writers** Brian Degas, Ian Kennedy Martin, Arden Winch, N. J. Crisp, John Kruse, Marc Brandel, John Brason, Bryan Forbes, Thom Keyes, David Ambrose, Ken Hughes, Ivan Moffat, Robert Muller **Theme Music** 'The Colditz March' by Robert Farnon

During World War Two, it was the duty of every captured British officer to escape from German imprisonment or die trying. For the habitual escapee, the Germans had one particular stronghold near Leipzig that was renowned for its lack of escape possibilities – Castle Colditz. It's here that the BBC's most famous wartime drama was set.

In the first episode, wartime newsreel footage was used to set the scene, footage that dissolved seamlessly into the drama to add to the air of realism. Some facts were omitted to aid popular myths, however. Though life was grim at Colditz, producer Gerard Glaister realised that the five square meals a day and the senior officers' adherence to the British social structure might not convey the misery quite as effectively or clearly as was hoped. Yet Glaister's writers managed to produce stories that were suitably grim without being relentlessly depressing, although one scene in which a prisoner claws the stone cobbles as his mind breaks still haunts viewers who watched it.

The series took its time to even reach the infamous castle: the first three episodes were set in other camps until certain key characters found themselves moved to Colditz. Initially, these included Captain Grant (a pre-***Sherlock Holmes*** Edward Hardwicke), Flight Lieutenant Carter (a post-***Man from U.N.C.L.E.***, pre-***Sapphire and Steel*** David McCallum) and American Air Force officer Carrington (Robert Wagner, in his last major role before ***Hart to Hart***). What made the series such a stand-out production was the refusal to paint the Germans as mere mindless automatons or stereotypical sadists. For this drama, the propaganda was put to one side to show real human beings on opposite sides of the conflict – including the stern Kommandant (Bernard Hepton), who battles against internal politics and external interference by the SS.

Gerard Glaister would return to stories of World War Two with his next production, ***Secret Army***, which managed to surpass even the standards set by *Colditz* thanks to continuity behind the scenes: directors Viktors Ritelis and Terence Dudley, writers John Brason and N. J. Crisp and actors Bernard Hepton and Christopher Neame all worked on both series.

Columbo

Crime Drama | Universal for NBC (shown on ITV/BBC One) | episode duration 90 mins | broadcast 20 Feb 1968, 1 Mar 1971, 15 Sep 1971–13 May 1978, 6 Feb 1989–30 Jan 2003 (USA)

Regular Cast

Peter Falk · *Lieutenant Philip Columbo*

Creators Richard Levinson and William Link **Producers** Roland Kibbee, Dean Hargrove, Richard Alan Simmons (executive), Edward K. Dodds, Everett Chambers **Writers** Various, including Richard Levinson, William Link, Dean Hargrove, Steven Bochco, Jackson Gillis, Larry Cohen, Peter S. Fischer, William Driskill, Howard Berk, Peter S. Feibleman, William Read Woodfield, Jeffrey Bloom, Peter Falk **Theme Music** *Columbo* did not have its own theme tune initially; it shared a Henry Mancini-composed theme with the other shows broadcast in the USA as part of the *Sunday Mystery Movie* series. For UK broadcast, this music was retained as the theme tune for *Columbo*.

While many great TV heroes come from literature, occasionally the medium generates one of its own. Along with Sherlock Holmes, Sexton Blake, Poirot and Miss Marple, we submit for your approval one Lieutenant Columbo of the Los Angeles Police Department's Homicide division. Although his creators were inspired by Porfiry Petrovich, a character in Dostoyevski's *Crime and Punishment*, he's a true original. Determined, dishevelled and disarming, it's a foolish villain who underestimates his ability to find the culprit. The trick with *Columbo* is that unlike most other super-sleuth stories, we, the audience, know who the murderer is from the very start - we saw them do it, in painstaking detail.

The fun comes from watching the villain's façade crumble as Columbo pieces the crime together bit by bit while appearing to be the most absent-minded buffoon ever allowed out in a raincoat and shabby brown suit. Working near Hollywood, Columbo is always called to the homes of the rich and famous, and just the sight of such a man pulling up to their driveway in his similarly ramshackle 1959 Peugeot convertible is enough to make these snobbish, vain people desperate to get rid of him - never mind the fact that he's there to tie them to the horrible and convoluted murder we witnessed in the first act. Often he'll get the suspect talking by pointing to an object in their home, an ornament or a clock. 'Y'know, my wife would love something like that,' he begins. 'Now, forgive me for asking, but how much would one of those set you back?' When the reply comes in figures of six digits, Columbo looks embarrassed and changes the subject - which is usually the point at which the off-guard suspect lets a vital piece of information slip, and when they know they've done so, begin to scramble for a new alibi. But by then, we know he's just treading water until the moment, 80 minutes in, when he delivers that inevitable line: 'By the way, sir, just one more thing. I think you did it.' They're doomed!

It's such a marvellous creation and Peter Falk can take much of the credit for the character's popularity. Polite, modest yet confident in his own abilities, he skilfully plays two parts simultaneously: the idiot who has no chance of solving the crime (i.e. the man the villains see at first); and the experienced crime-catcher who knows that his softly-softly approach will always come up trumps. It's strange to discover that Falk was neither the first person to play the part, nor the first choice when it was developed for a series. Bert Freed played the detective in 'Enough Rope', an episode of *The Chevy Mystery Show*, broadcast on 31 July 1960. Writers Richard Levinson and William Link then incorporated the character into a play, where he was played by Thomas Mitchell in one of his last stage roles before his death in 1962; Mitchell had played Scarlet O'Hara's father in *Gone with the Wind* (1939). When Levinson and Link decided to develop the part for a television series, their first choices were Bing Crosby and Lee J. Cobb, but Crosby turned down the offer, preferring to spend his time playing golf, while Cobb proved similarly unavailable. Peter Falk stepped in for the first TV movie, *Prescription: Murder*, and made the part his own.

When the second TV movie led to the commission of a full series, *Columbo* was initially placed on rotation with *McCloud* and *McMillan and Wife* as part of NBC's *Sunday Mystery Movie* slot before gaining its own billing in the schedules. It also kick-started the careers of several people who would become big names in entertainment, including writer and ***Hill Street Blues*** creator Steven Bochco and a young director by the name of Steven Spielberg. But it's the celebrity villains that are the show's biggest boast, with the likes of Ray Milland, William Shatner, Robert Vaughn and Patrick McGoohan lining up for an uneven battle of wits. Though the series came to an end in 1979 after just 45 episodes, repeat runs kept *Columbo* on air almost constantly until Peter Falk agreed to resurrect the character in 1989 for another run of 24 TV movies spanning 14 years. Surprisingly, there were not only enough murders to keep him working but enough people stupid enough not to know that you can't escape the world's greatest TV detective.

Trivia

The first TV movie in the series marked the first and only time that Columbo's Christian name, Philip, was revealed, though when later asked about the character's first name, Peter Falk claimed it was 'Lieutenant'.

Come Dancing

Entertainment | BBC One | episode duration various | broadcast 29 Sep 1950–11 Sep 1995, 19 May 2004–present

Cast

Michael Aspel, Judith Chalmers, Peter Dimmock, Noel Edmonds, Rosemarie Ford, Keith Fordyce, MacDonald Hobley, David Jacobs, Brian Johnston, Mary Malcolm, Peter Marshall, Don Moss, Pete Murray, Sylvia Peters, Angela Rippon, Peter West, Terry Wogan, Bruce Forsythe, Natasha Kaplinsky · *Presenters*

Creator Eric Morley **Producers** Simon Betts, Barrie Edgar, Ray Lakeland, Philip Lewis

Not so much a TV programme, more an institution, *Come Dancing* has been around in one form or another since 1949, with a reappearance in the Noughties as a re-tooled celebrity show, *Strictly Come Dancing*, along with the Graham Norton-hosted *Strictly Dance Fever*.

Not many shows do what they say on the tin, but *Come Dancing* is as close as you get. Under the auspices of many presenters over the years, leading dance couples would compete in regional 'dance-offs', progressing on to that all-important final. It was never cutting edge and *Come Dancing* attempted to embrace new musical styles, but, like ***One Man and His Dog***, became a programme with a shrinking audience, however fondly regarded it was, and the show was cancelled in the mid-1990s. Many presenters came and went over the years, but the most notable were Michael Aspel, Judith Chalmers, David Jacobs, Terry Wogan (obviously), Angela Rippon and Rosemarie Ford.

In 2004, the BBC returned to the format under the title *Strictly Come Dancing*, hosted by Bruce Forsyth, reviving it with the country's obsession for celebrities away from their natural habitat. Certainly the sight of the likes of Julian Clary and gardening guru Diarmuid Gavin throwing themselves around the dance floor has proved to be a huge ratings smash, regularly beating ITV's ratings juggernaut *The X Factor* (see ***Popstars***). Newsreader Natasha Kaplinsky won the first year of the contest, with ***EastEnders*** actress Jill Halfpenny winning the second outing.

Comic Relief

Telethon | BBC One | Duration 90–485 mins | broadcast 5 Feb 1986–present

Principal Cast

Griff Rhys Jones, Lenny Henry, Jonathan Ross, Dawn French, Jennifer Saunders, Stephen Fry, Hugh Laurie, Rowan Atkinson, Hugh Grant, Joanna Lumley, Billy Connolly · *Presenters*

Theme Music While there's no common musical theme for the events, each *Comic Relief* night has its own connected song. Inspired by Band Aid, the first *Comic Relief* single was a 1986 cover of 'Living Doll', performed by its original singer Cliff Richard alongside Hank Marvin and the cast of ***The Young Ones*** (that's the anarchic sitcom, not Cliff's movie). The following Christmas, Mel (Smith) and Kim (Wilde) covered Brenda Lee's 'Rockin' Around the Christmas Tree'.

The other *Comic Relief* singles to date are:

* 1989: 'Help!', by Bananarama and La Na Nee Nee Noo Noo (French and Saunders with Kathy Burke), which got to No. 3
* 1991: 'The Stonk', by Hale and Pace and the Stonkers (which included Brian May and Roger Taylor of Queen, and Dave Gilmour of Pink Floyd), another No. 1
* 1992: '(I Want To Be) Elected' by *Mr Bean* (Rowan Atkinson) and Smear Campaign, featuring Bruce Dickinson
* 1993: 'Stick It Out' by Right Said Fred and friends
* 1994: 'Absolutely Fabulous', a dance track from Pet Shop Boys, featuring samples of Jennifer Saunders and Joanna Lumley from ***Absolutely Fabulous***
* 1995: 'Love can Build a Bridge' by Cher, Chrissie Hynde, Neneh Cherry with Eric Clapton – another No. 1
* 1997: The Spice Girls offered up the profits from their double A-sided No. 1 'Mama'/'Who Do You Think You Are?'
* 1999: Boyzone covered Billy Ocean's 'When the Going Gets Tough' and got to No. 1, although on the programme itself Ronan Keating was called away to the birth of his first child, so fellow band member Mikey Graham took his place on lead vocals
* 2000: 'Uptown Girl', an unsurprising cover of the Billy Joel classic, taken to No. 1 by Boyzone's stablemates Westlife
* 2003: ***Pop Idol*** (see ***Popstars***) runner up Gareth Gates performed 'Spirit in the Sky' with the cast of ***The Kumars*** (incidentally the third time the song had been at the top spot since it was first performed by Norman Greenbaum in 1970)
* 2005: While McFly's double A-side 'All About You/You've Got a Friend' was the official 2005 campaign song, a video prepared by Peter Kay miming to Tony Christie's 'Is This the Way to Amarillo?' stole the show. The song was released as a single three days later and remained at No. 1 for eight weeks.

The impact of ***Live Aid*** can never be underestimated. Writing in the 21st anniversary about the event, we can look back and see that it not only drew the world's attention to the plight of Ethiopia and other African countries but also opened the eyes and ears of the public to expect telethons and charity records in the wake of tragedies and disasters. The BBC had been hosting the *Children in Need* appeals on television for the previous five years, but *Live Aid* also took the work of events like the Amnesty International benefits *The Secret Policeman's Balls* and raised them to another level.

Comic Relief was launched on Christmas Day 1985, just five months after *Live Aid*, with a broadcast from a refugee camp in Sudan as part of Noel Edmonds' then-customary Christmas morning broadcasts. A few months later, the first of three *Comic Relief* concerts held in London started the ball rolling on what has become a now biennial, live extravaganza of fund-raising hilarity that rivals the success of *Children in Need*. The first live telethon was broadcast in 1988, hosted by Lenny Henry and Griff Rhys Jones and raising around £15 million for charities in Africa and the UK. Thanks to the distinctive nasal garments sold in aid of the appeals, the day of the broadcast has since become known as Red Nose Day.

Comedians and performers galore have given their time to the event, with many travelling abroad to make films highlighting the plight of the people that the charity raises money for. Largely coordinated by writer/director Richard Curtis, the evening involves live performances and classic comedy clips bid for by the public, with the profits from calls and pledges all adding to the final total at the end of the night.

The evening has also provided the opportunity for some one-off specials of comedy favourites, such as ***Blackadder*** ('The Cavalier Years'), ***The New Statesman***, ***Butterflies*** and ***Men Behaving Badly***, among others. In 1999, ***Coupling*** writer Steven Moffat penned '***Doctor Who*** and the Curse of Fatal Death', starring Rowan Atkinson as the Time Lord in a spoof that also featured Julia Sawalha and Jonathan Pryce, with cameos from Hugh Grant, Jim Broadbent, Richard E. Grant and Joanna Lumley as different incarnations of the Doctor. In 2005, the boys from ***Little Britain*** released a DVD of specially recorded sketches that included cameo appearances by Robbie Williams, Elton John and 'George Michaels'.

Websites

While *Comic Relief* is a hugely entertaining night, it also has a serious ongoing mission. Take a look at the official website, www.comicrelief.com, and Richard Curtis's banner project, Make Poverty History – www.makepovertyhistory.org – which brings together the efforts of numerous other organisations, including Band Aid.

The Comic Strip Presents

Comedy | Michael White/Comic Strip/Filmworks for Channel 4/BBC Two | episode duration 30–35 mins, plus 25–65-min specials | broadcast 2 Nov 1982–27 May 1993, 12 Apr 1998, 4 Jan 2000

Regular Cast

Adrian Edmondson, Peter Richardson, Dawn French, Jennifer Saunders, Daniel Peacock, Robbie Coltrane, Ronald Allen, Ron Tarr, Nigel Planer, Keith Allen, Serena Evans, Nosher Powell, Alan Pellay, Neil Cunningham, Rowland Rivron, Christopher Malcolm · *Various Characters*

Creator Peter Richardson **Producers** Various, including Lolli Kimpton, Nira Park, Elaine Taylor, Michael White, Andrew St John, Michael Hall, Victoria Poushkine-Relf, Sarah Radcliffe, Chris Brown, Simon Wright, Peter Richardson **Writers** Peter Richardson, Pete Richens, Adrian Edmondson, Dawn French, Rik Mayall, Jennifer Saunders, Keith Allen, Roland Rivron, Daniel Peacock, Alexei Sayle, Pauline Melville, David Stafford, Doug Lucie, Nigel Planer, Paul Bartel, Barry Dennen, Robbie Coltrane, Morag Fullarton

Along with ***Countdown*** and ***Brookside***, *The Comic Strip Presents* formed part of the first night of Channel 4. 'Five Go Mad in Dorset' was a savage critique of Enid Blyton's *Famous Five* books and of post-war Britain, depicting Julian, Dick and the 'mere girls' as racist, snobbish prigs who report a station porter to the police because he 'looks foreign' and discover to their horror that their beloved Uncle Quentin is 'a screaming homosexual' – thereby adding homophobia, as well as racism, as a target for the programme's satire.

The series came from the Comic Strip, Michael White's Soho-based comedy nightclub. The club gave rise to the alternative comedy movement (often dismissively referred to by the 'Old Guard' as 'alternative to comedy') that strove to avoid the racism, sexism and religious mockery inherent in 'traditional' comedy. The performers who got their big breaks there included four-fifths of ***The Young Ones***, the two halves of ***French and Saunders*** and one entire Alexei Sayle. But *The Comic Strip Presents* was the creation of Peter Richardson, a writer-performer who blustered his way through the commissioning process at Channel 4 and only revealed his plans to the other comics after he'd secured the deal to produce the new station's first home-grown comedy series.

Each episode began with a quaint, 'seaside' introductory jingle accompanying an animated bomb (the words 'Wish you were here' scrawled on the side) plummeting down onto a map of rural England and heralding another unmissable slice of satire. Unmissable because everyone would talk about it the next working/school day, even if it was just to say, 'It wasn't as good as *Five Go Mad*', or to endlessly quote from it. There were plenty of misses alongside hits during its on-off 37-episode run – 'The Yob' and 'Oxford' in particular – but we come to praise Richardson et al., not to bury them. Whether or not anyone ever really remembered the precise doings of the Famous Five, the phrase 'lashings of ginger beer' has now become inextricably linked with the odious little toffs. For some British viewers, the mockumentary 'Bad News' resonates much more than *This is Spinal Tap* (1983) ever did, while the criminally neglected 'Mr Jolly Lives Next Door' (directed by Stephen Frears) offers a delightful amalgam of comedy generations with Peter Cook playing an assassin hired to bump off Nicholas Parsons.

A few projects that were *Comic Strip* in approach weren't actually part of the official canon: *The Bullshitters* mocked macho action series ***The Professionals*** by playing it out as a homoerotic thriller (and decimating *The Professionals'* public standing as a result); the film *The Pope Must Die* (1991) starred Robbie Coltrane and was written by Richardson and his co-scribe Pete Richens but, like *The Glam Metal Detectives* (a disjointed seven-part series produced by Richardson), was made independently from the *Comic Strip*.

By 1998, when Channel 4 celebrated *The Comic Strip Presents* among its *First on Four* strand, the once-anarchic, alternative brand of comedian had become the establishment, hosting telethons and enjoying golden handcuff deals with the BBC. Like the Pythons, the *Carry On* team and the Goons before them, they've given way to the new generation of comedians – ***Little Britain***'s David Walliams and Matt Lucas, ***The League of Gentlemen*** and the multi-cast repertoire of Leigh Francis in ***Bo' Selecta!*** – who set out to push those boundaries even further.

Compact

Soap | BBC TV | episode duration 25 mins | broadcast 2 Jan 1962–30 Jul 1965

Regular Cast

Jean Harvey · *Joanne Minster*
Ronald Allen · *Ian Harmon*
Betty Cooper · *Alison Gray/Morley*
Marcia Ashton · *Lily Todd/Kipling*
Newton Blick · *Sir Charles Harmon*
Pauline Letts · *Marion Layne*
Justine Lord · *Kay Livingstone/Babbage*
Donald Morley · *Arnold Babbage*
Nicholas Selby · *Jimmy Saunders*
Sonia Graham · *Beryl Doyle*
Monica Evans · *Sally Henderson/Harmon*
Anna Castaldini · *Ruth Munday*
Leo Maguire · *Alec Gordon*
Sonia Graham · *Maggie Clifford/Brent*
Bridget McConnel · *Lynn Bolton*
Moray Watson · *Richard Lowe*
Tony Wright · *Paul Constantine*
Richard Clarke · *Harold Apthorpe*
Gareth Davies · *Mark*
Penny Morrell · *Kathy Sherwood*
June Murphy · *Maureen*
Scott Finch · *Tim Gray*
Donald Hewlett · *Tom Brent*
Dawn Beret · *Lois James/McClusky*
Clinton Greyn · *Mike McClusky*
Jemma Hyde · *Beth Francis*
Frances Bennett · *Gussie Brown/Beatty*
Vicky Harrington · *Sylvia Grant*
Dilys Watling · *Gillian Nesbitt*
Karen Stephanie Beaumont, Louise Dunn · *Iris Alcott/Miller*
Ann Morrish · *Clancey*
Margot Christiensen · *Shirley Hawkins*
Edwaard Evans · *Ken Hawkins*
Brenda Kaye · *Lorna Willis-Ede*
Mandy Miller · *Copper*
Keith Buckley · *Bryan Merchant*
David Langton · *Marmot James*
Shane Rimmer · *Russell Corrigan*
Patricia Haines · *Vivien*
Carmen Silvera · *Camilla Hope*
Bill Kerr · *Ben*
Sonia Dresdel · *Mrs Beatty*
Bernard Kaye · *Dennis Farrow*
David Swift · *Theo Clay*
Horace James · *Jeff Armandez*
Polly Adams · *Julia Preston*

Creators Hazel Adair and Peter Ling **Producers** Alan Bromly, Douglas Allen, Morris Barry, Bernard Hepton, Joan Craft, Harold Clayton, William Sterling **Writers** Hazel Adair, Peter Ling, Ted Dicks, David Whitaker, Sheila Ward

Though they weren't known as such at the time, ***The Appleyards, The Grove Family*** and to some extent *Starr and Company* were early examples of British soap operas. But it was *Compact* that first consciously set itself up as a soap. The twice-weekly serial, often broadcast live, revolved around the staff on a women's magazine – *Compact*. Sir Charles Harmon was the money man but all the decisions fell on the shoulders of the magazine's editor, Joanne Minster.

Storylines were as much governed by the characters' interaction with each other as the articles in the magazine; in the second episode, 'Agony Aunt' Alison Gray discovers her daughter Rosemary has run away again. Fortunately, disaster is averted when Rosemary confesses that she wants to be a writer and she's introduced to Ted Willis, the man who created ***Dixon of Dock Green***. An early continuing story was a competition to find the ideal husband, which culminated in a final involving omelette cooking and baby feeding. Racy stuff!

Away from Enterprise House, the home of *Compact*, the staff fell in and out of love, conducted affairs and harboured the most dreadful of secrets – all in a rather chaste and charming way: this was the BBC, remember! Episodes would often end on a shocking cliffhanger. There was also plenty of boardroom banter, with the dashing Ian Harmon brought in from America by the owner to improve the magazine's sales, while the accountant, Mr Babbage, pours over the figures. Eventually, *Compact* amalgamates with its rival, *Lady Fair*, to save money.

After three years and 373 episodes, the BBC decided to close *Compact* for good. Its last episode was appropriately entitled 'Journey's End'. Its place was eventually taken by a new series, *United!*, about the management board of a football team. *Compact*'s creators, Hazel Adair and Peter Ling, left the series for an invitation by Lew Grade to produce a drama serial for ITV. Set in the Midlands it would run five times a week. ***Crossroads*** would become infamous within the world of soap opera – and not necessarily for all the right reasons.

Connie

Soap/Drama | Central for ITV | episode duration 50 mins | broadcast 26 May–25 Aug 1985

Regular Cast

Stephanie Beacham · *Connie*
Brenda Bruce · *Madam Bea*
Paul Rogers · *'Hot Pants' Hector*
Richard Morant · *Jamieson*
Pam Ferris · *Nesta*
George Costigan · *Arnie*
Claire Parker · *Babs*
Peter Straker · *Dev*
Georgia Allen · *Lisa*
Roy Lee · *Leroy*

Karen Meagher · *Marie*
Kate Dorning · *Annie*

Creator/Writer Ron Hutchinson **Producer** Nicholas Palmer **Theme Music** Written by legendary playwright Willy Russell, 'The Show' was performed by Rebecca Storm. It reached No. 22 in the charts in July 1985, and featured the immortal lyrics 'I'm getting dressed up, to win some affection/To get messed up, to win just a mention/So . . . I'm putting on the show. . .'

Set in the oh-so-glamorous world of the Midlands fashion industry, *Connie* was one of the few attempts made by British TV in the mid-1980s to emulate the success of the American mega-soaps like ***Dallas*** and ***Dynasty***. Stephanie Beacham (previously seen on British television as emaciated prison-camp internee Rose in ***Tenko***) starred as Connie, a woman determined to make her own way in the fashion industry. Some years prior to the start of the series, Connie had fled the UK after being diddled out of her rightful share in the family fashion business. After having spent several years living the good life in the Mediterranean, she flies back to Britain, determined to use either fair means or foul to claw her way back to power. Chief enemy is future ***Darling Buds of May*** star Pam Ferris as Connie's deeply unlikeable sister, the ferocious-looking Nesta, who had been instrumental in her downfall years before.

Never truly able to rival the glamour of the American soaps, *Connie* instead relied upon plotlines crammed full of power play, gambits and back-stabbing of almost epic proportions. Lasting for just one season and 13 episodes, *Connie* boasted a fantastic cast of quality character actors. Although the show wasn't renewed, the success of Stephanie Beacham's portrayal as the determined yet bitchy heroine directly led to her being cast in – ironically enough – American mega-soap ***The Colbys***.

The Coronation of Elizabeth II

Live Broadcast | BBC TV | duration c.7 hours | broadcast 2 Jun 1953

Cast

Sylvia Peters, Max Robertson, Michael Henderson, Mary Hill · *Presenters*
Berkeley Smith, Chester Wilmot, Richard Dimbleby · *Commentators*

Producer Peter Dimmock

We've tried to steer clear of televised events in this book. Generally, sporting fixtures will take place anyway, and news tends not to be about just one broadcaster reporting it. But the coronation of Queen Elizabeth II was a national event *because* of the presence of the BBC TV cameras. It was broadcast to 2.5 million homes – the first time television had achieved higher ratings than radio.

The British Cabinet and church authorities had initially refused permission for Westminster Abbey to be invaded by cameras, fearing the bright lights would dazzle the 26-year-old Elizabeth, but pressure from the press convinced them to relent. The man representing the BBC on the day was 32-year-old Peter Dimmock, a former RAF pilot who had joined BBC TV in time to cover the 1948 Olympics. Dimmock would be in overall control of 15 cameras on the procession route, which would cover 29 bands, 13,000 troops and 27 carriages in addition to the young Queen herself. Dimmock directed the five cameras inside Westminster Abbey itself. There was a very good reason for this: Buckingham Palace's representative, the Duke of Norfolk, Earl Marshal of England, had forbidden the BBC from using any close-ups – partly in deference to Royal protocol (which had no clear instructions on the business of television) but also because of concerns in some quarters that the television cameras would give the people at home a better view of proceedings than the invited dignitaries inside the Abbey. But Dimmock recognised just how important that close-up would be, for those people at home and for the future of television. He was determined to ignore the palace and give the viewers what they wanted.

The morning began with an introduction from Sylvia Peters and views of the Victoria Memorial in central London. Soon after, the eager viewers got their first glimpse of Elizabeth's gold carriage. Max Robertson, Michael Henderson and Mary Hill were positioned along the route to describe the procession and capture a sense of the excitement of the people lining the streets to cheer their Queen. Additional commentary came from Berkeley Smith and Chester Wilmot until, finally, Elizabeth's coach reached Westminster Abbey.

Positioned in a specially constructed control room, Peter Dimmock began to select the shots of the inside of the Abbey while Richard Dimbleby took over the commentary, identifying the invited guests for the benefit of the viewers and explaining the importance of each stage of the ceremony. Finally, with the investiture complete, the Queen proceeded down the aisle of the Abbey and, with one camera discreetly placed above the Abbey door, Dimmock was able to get that all-important close-up shot. Significantly, if anyone at the Palace noticed, nothing was said.

The seven-mile procession round Hyde Park and back to Buckingham Palace took two hours to complete. An unexpected star of the day emerged in the considerable form of Queen Salote of Tonga, who, despite the heavy rain, insisted on travelling with the canopy of her carriage down so that she could wave to the crowds. As a consequence, she immediately endeared herself to the British public, most of whom would be unable to point to her country on a map. With the tail end of the procession reaching Buckingham Palace, the cameras gave viewers a final view of the now empty Westminster Abbey.

The cooperation of the RAF enabled film canisters to be flown to Canada. Thanks to the different time zones, the coronation was broadcast to over 2 million Canadians at the same hour of day there as it had taken place in the UK.

The coronation marked a change in the British public's relationship with the monarchy in more ways than one. Certainly it had united the country, which, if nothing else, made for an impressive first day for a new monarch. However, there was a darker side. Shortly before the big day, journalists became aware of persistent rumours surrounding Elizabeth's sister Margaret and her relationship with Group Captain Peter Townsend. The press chose not to report this out of respect for the incumbent Queen, but just days after the coronation the story finally broke.

Thanks to Peter Dimmock's cool-headed direction, the coronation of Queen Elizabeth II remains one of the greatest moments in television history. Elizabeth's children and grandchildren are now perfectly aware of the power of TV, as are we. It's highly likely that, with digital TV and other technological developments yet to come, any future coronation will be an entirely different affair. For starters, the viewers will be much more in control of what they see. It'll be a far cry from the moment in 1953 when Britain made those unsteady steps towards becoming a TV nation.

Trivia

The Queen's coronation dress was designed by Norman Hartnell, who incorporated diamonds, pearls and amethysts to take advantage of the lights needed for the TV cameras.

Coronation Street

See pages 196–202

The Corridor People

Crime Drama | Granada for ITV | episode duration 50 mins | broadcast 26 Aug–16 Sep 1966

Principal Cast

Gary Cockrell · *Phil Scotty*
Alan Curtis · *Inspector Blood*
William Maxwell · *Sergeant Hound*
John Sharp · *Kronk*
Elizabeth Shepherd · *Syrie Van Epp*
Donald Webster · *Weedy*
Windsor Davies · *Sullavan*
William Trigger · *Nonesuch*
June Watson · *Miss Dunner*
Tim Barrett · *Chris Vaughan*
Clive Morton · *Sir Wilfred Templar*
Kevin Brennan · *Whitebait*
Ingrid Hafner · *Abigail Whitebait*
Aubrey Morris · *Robag*
Betty McDowall · *Beryl Kempstead*
Ivor Salter · *Blinky*
John Woodnutt · *Colonel Lemming*
Nina Baden-Semper · *Pearl*
Barbara Couper · *Queen Helen*
Roger Hammond · *Ferdinand*

Creator/Writer Edward Boyd **Producer** Richard Everitt **Theme Music** Derek Hilton's jazz theme accompanies crude animated graphics – black-and-white blocks and lines, similar to Saul Bass's titles for films like *North by Northwest* (1959) and *Psycho* (1960), with a very 'Sixties' logo, similar to that of a pop music show.

Intelligence agency Department K, headed by the portly Kronk, handle matters of national security for the British government. Kronk is on the trail of the supremely wealthy Persian siren Syrie Van Epp, who somehow manages to stay one step ahead of the game through means most foul. Aiding Kronk in his investigations are Blood and Hound, a pair of bumbling policemen, and an American Humphrey Bogart-obsessed detective called Scrotty, who once had Van Epp as a client – until he ended up dead . . .

Before transmission, Granada displayed a fair bit of misplaced confidence in this series, even promoting it on the front of the northwest editions of the *TVTimes* (*TVTimes* editions for other regions that week favoured Jane Asher), but today *The Corridor People* is fondly remembered solely by fans of telefantasy and by the performers themselves. At times impenetrable, it's very difficult to label, lurching from a kidnap plot to sub-***Avengers*** stories involving resurrecting the dead and a suffocating perfume. Even self-proclaimed *Corridor People* enthusiasts find it difficult to describe coherently.

Actor John Sharp, who played Kronk, was also one of a long line of Number 2s in ***The Prisoner***, while the criminal mastermind Syrie Van Epp was brought to life by the elegant Elizabeth Shepherd, who came to the series via *The Avengers* where she'd won the role of John Steed's partner Emma Peel until producers dropped her in favour of Diana Rigg after already filming two episodes. This connection inspires many to compare the show with the early videotaped *Avengers* seasons.

The Corridor People lasted for just four episodes – the title of each instalment begins 'Victim as . . .', with just the suffix revealing a tenuous clue to the content ('. . . Birdwatcher', '. . . Whitebait', '. . . Red' and '. . . Black'). For its time, it was beautifully directed and edited (certain scenes were framed through rectangles and squares more reminiscent of the multi-frame techniques used in ***24*** and ***Trial and Retribution***), but it does appear almost wilfully obscure and perverse, viewers soon getting the feeling that it might even be possible to watch the four episodes in any order without any effect on the meaning at all. Still, we're glad that there was once a time when a TV company would take such a risk on a show as challenging as this – and give it a prime slot on a Friday night (9.40 p.m.!) – so for that, we salute you, Granada. You complete lunatics.

Trivia

The final episode, 'Victim as Black', was recorded just two days before it was broadcast, which possibly explains a

Continued on page 203

Coronation Street

Julie Goodyear as Bet Lynch (later Bet Gilroy).

There probably never was a street like *Coronation Street* – not really. But that's never stood in the way of it becoming the most-watched street on British TV, nor has it prevented it from being seen across the world. Ever since it first appeared on television in 1960, the residents have opened their doors to millions of viewers, giving them a unique insight into modern life through good times and bad. Births, marriages, deaths, this street has seen them all – and more. Not bad for a show that was initially given just 16 weeks to prove itself.

In 1960, 23-year-old writer Tony Warren was working unhappily on adaptations of *Biggles* for Granada Television. He longed to be writing about characters from a world he could recognise as his own: a working-class world; a northern world. Warren had previously submitted an idea for a comedy to the BBC, which he redeveloped as a drama called 'Florizel Street' (until someone pointed out that 'Florizel' sounded too much like a detergent). His idea was simply to peak through the net curtains and letterboxes of a northern backstreet and follow the goings on of a community of ordinary people. Renamed *Coronation Street*, it was initially commissioned for just 16 episodes, and not every ITV region took it up from the start (it wouldn't be fully networked until May 1961).

Corrie, as it's affectionately known, appeared during a time of great social change. The final effects of World War Two were wearing off, with rationing replaced by greater spending power. There was the concept of the 'teenager' to content with, an idea that even five years earlier simply hadn't existed. Working-class men were gaining university educations only to come back home feeling dissatisfied with having to do the jobs their fathers and grandfathers had done. Against this, they had the backdrop of the traditional northern

Soap
Granada Television for ITV
Episode Duration: 25 mins
Broadcast: 9 Dec 1960–present

Regular Cast
Betty Alberge · *Florrie Lindley*
Violet Carson · *Ena Sharples*
Lynne Carol · *Martha Longhurst*
Margot Bryant · *Minnie Caldwell*
Frank Pemberton · *Frank Barlow*
Noel Dyson · *Ida Barlow*
William Roache · *Ken Barlow*
Alan Rothwell · *David Barlow*
Patricia Phoenix · *Elsie Tanner/Howard*
Philip Lowrie · *Dennis Tanner*
Anne Cunningham · *Linda Tanner/Cheveski*
Doris Speed · *Annie Walker*
Arthur Leslie · *Jack Walker*
Daphne Oxenford · *Esther Hayes*
Ivan Beavis · *Harry Hewitt*
Christine Hargreaves · *Christine Hardman/Appleby*
Joan Heath · *May Hardman*
Jennifer Moss · *Lucille Hewitt*
Doreen Keogh · *Concepta Riley/Hewitt*
Arthur Lowe · *Leonard Swindley*
Ernst Walder · *Ivan Cheveski*
Jack Howarth · *Albert Tatlock*
Eileen Derbyshire · *Emily Nugent/Bishop/Swain*
Peter Adamson · *Len Fairclough*
Joan Francis · *Dot Greenhalgh*
Derek Benfield · *Walter Greenhalgh*
Kenneth Farrington · *Billy Walker*
Bryan Mosley · *Alf Roberts*
Anne Reid · *Valerie Tatlock/Barlow*
Kenneth Cope · *Jed Stone*
Peter Noone · *Stanley Fairclough*
Graham Haberfield · *Jerry Booth*
Reginald Marsh · *Dave Smith*
Jack Watson · *Petty Officer Bill Gregory*
Susan Jameson · *Myra Dickenson/Booth*
Jean Alexander · *Hilda Ogden*
Bernard Youens · *Stan Ogden*
Jonathan Collins, Don Hawkins · *Trevor Ogden*
Sandra Gough · *Irma Ogden/Barlow*
Barbara Knox · *Rita Littlewood/Fairclough/Sullivan*
Wendy Jane Walker, Suzy Patterson, Joanna Foster · *Susan Barlow/Baldwin*
Linus Roache, Christopher Dormerr, Joseph McKenna, David Lonsdale, Chris Gascoine · *Peter Barlow*
Julie Goodyear · *Bet Lynch/Gilroy*
Neville Buswell · *Ray Langton*
Stephen Hancock · *Ernest Bishop*
Paul Maxwell · *Steve Tanner*
Betty Driver · *Betty Turpin/Williams*

working class; people who'd had to survive the war knew all too well how hard life could be and how embittered it could make a person; people who knew that sometimes you just had to make do with what you have. The working-class voice was still very much a rarity in TV terms, with the possible exception of that of the Londoner. Certainly few northern accents were heard in anything other than comedies. *Coronation Street* would change that.

Tony Warren had a talent for characters. The inhabitants of his fictional street were drawn from real people he'd known in Salford and were all skilfully designed to appeal to a wide section of the audience. There was social-climbing publican Annie Walker and her put-upon husband, Jack; Elsie Tanner, who was tough as nails but still glamorous enough to turn men's heads despite being the mother of a rebellious teenage son and wayward married daughter; puritanical pug-faced 'battle-axe' Ena Sharples, who, with Minnie Caldwell and Martha Longhurst, would become gossiping mainstays of the snug in the Rover's Return; timid shopkeeper Florrie Lindlay; miserable pensioner Albert Tatlock; plus the Barlows, Frank and Ida and their sons, the teenage David and his idealistic university graduate brother, Ken. The most important 'character' was the street itself, re-created inside Granada's Manchester studios at first, with a railway viaduct and a corner shop at one end and the Mission and the Rover's at the other. And running all along the street were small cobbles, a lasting reminder of the old roads of Lancashire.

The first episode of *Coronation Street* went out on Friday, 9 December 1960. It was performed and broadcast live, like most television drama of the time, which added to its naturalistic approach. Perhaps predictably, the reception from the snooty press was generally unfavourable. Ken Irwin, writing in the *Daily Mirror*, claimed the show was 'doomed'. Still, some were optimistic – the critic in the *Guardian* even went to far as to suggest the show might run 'for ever'. One of them was right at least . . .

Over the coming months, new characters were introduced, such as mild-mannered businessman Leonard Swindley, an aggressive builder by the name of Len Fairclough and the shy Emily Newgent. Like Ken Barlow, Emily is still with the show all these years later. At first Leonard Swindley's business partner, she was at one time engaged to him, though she eventually called the wedding off. She married Ernest Bishop in 1970 – he was later shot dead during a robbery in Baldwin's factory – and in 1980 she married Arnold Swain, only to discover that he was both violent and a bigamist (the marriage was annulled). In recent years, egged on by her nephew Spider, she has become an environmental campaigner and was central to one of the biggest stories post-2000, left for dead by Richard Hillman, the *Street*'s own multiple murderer.

The *Street* had its first death just six episodes in. May Hardman, mother of Christine, had only recently returned to No. 13 after a serious nervous breakdown. She suffered a heart attack on New Year's Eve 1960 and tried in vain to attract the attention of her neighbours. Almost a year later, Ida Barlow was knocked down by a

William Moore · *Cyril Turpin*
Judith Barker · *Janet Reid/Barlow*
Bill Kenright, Geoffrey Leesley · *Gordon Clegg*
John Sharp · *Les Clegg*
Irene Sutcliffe · *Maggie Clegg/Cooke*
Mollie Sugden · *Nellie Harvey*
Lynne Perrie · *Ivy Tilsley/Brennan*
Thelma Barlow · *Mavis Riley/Wilton*
Anne Kirkbride · *Deirdre Hunt/Langton/Barlow/Rachid*
Roy Barraclough · *Alec Gilroy*
Geoffrey Hughes · *Eddie Yeats*
Helen Worth · *Gail Potter/Tilsley/Platt/Hillman*
Elizabeth Dawn · *Vera Duckworth*
Patricia Cutts, Maggie Jones · *Blanche Hunt*
Fred Feast · *Fred Gee*
Madge Hindle · *Renee Bradshaw/Roberts*
Johnny Briggs · *Mike Baldwin*
Peter Baldwin · *Derek Wilton*
Cheryl Murray · *Suzie Birchall*
Christabel Finch, Holly Chamarette, Dawn Acton, Kate Ford · *Tracy Langton/Barlow/Preston/Cropper*
Christopher Quinten · *Brian Tilsley*
Sue Nicholls · *Audrey Potter/Roberts*
William Tarmey · *Jack Duckworth*
Peter Dudley · *Bert Tilsley*
George Waring · *Arnold Swain*
Amanda Barrie · *Alma Sedgewick/Baldwin/Halliwell*
Warren Jackson/Adam Rickitt · *Nicky Tilsey/Nick Platt*
Meg Johnson · *Eunice Nuttall/Gee*
Tracie Bennett · *Sharon Gaskell*
Christopher Coll · *Victor Pendlebury*
Jill Summers · *Phyllis Pearce*
Veronica Doran · *Marion Willis/Yeats*
Jill Kerman · *Maggie Dunlop/Redman*
Kevin Kennedy · *Norman 'Curly' Watts*
Michael Le Vell · *Kevin Webster*
Peter Armitage · *Bill Webster*
Sue Devaney · *Debbie Webster*
Bill Waddington · *Percy Sugden*
Nigel Pivaro · *Terry Duckworth*
Sean Wilson · *Martin Platt*
Judy Gridley · *Elaine Prior/Webster*
Sally Ann Matthews · *Jenny Bradley*
Jane Hazlegrove · *Sue Clayton*
Johnny Leeze · *Harry Clayton*
Caroline O'Neill · *Andrea Clayton*
Sue Jenkins · *Gloria Todd*
Sally Whittaker · *Sally Seddon/Webster*
Mark Eden · *Alan Bradley*
Leah King, Lynsay King, Tina O'Brien · *Sarah Louise Tilsley/Platt*
Geoffrey Hinsliff · *Don Brennan*
Beverley Callard · *Liz McDonald*
Charles Lawson · *Jim McDonald*

bus – one of the rare occasions the character was seen outside her own living room. But life continued: Ida's son Ken married Valerie Tatlock, daughter of his elderly next-door neighbour Albert; Minnie Caldwell took in a lodger, the scheming but lovable Jed Stone (Liverpool actor Kenneth Cope, who'd later find fame as one half of the supernatural detective duo in ***Randall and Hopkirk (Deceased)***); Len and Elsie prowled around each other in a lustful, but ultimately ill-matched relationship; and on one occasion, the entire population of the street were forced to spend the night in the local Mission Hall after the discovery of a burst gas pipe – strong stuff, all. But in 1964, Fate dealt the inhabitants of the street a hand that would have long-reaching effects on the show.

When the role of producer was handed over to the young, enthusiastic Tim Aspinall, he was determined to shake up the cosiness of the *Street* a little. He'd already decided to write out a number of 'unwanted' characters, although largely on the strength of a bet, when – to the horror of both his production team and, later, the cast – he announced that Martha Longhurst, the much-loved gossip and friend of Ena and Minnie, would suffer a fatal heart attack in the snug of the Rover's Return. Recording the scenes, actor Peter Adamson postponed delivering the line 'She's dead' as long as he could in the hope of a reprieve, but none came. When the episode was eventually broadcast, the shocked viewers sat and watched Martha clutch her chest and collapse, unseen by the rest of the Rover's regulars, who were celebrating Frank Barlow's £5000 Premium Bond win. The end credits rolled in silence.

Though Tim Aspinall's reign as producer lasted only a few months, the effects of his decisions persisted much longer. Fans of the show reacted as if the actress herself had died. Many went into mourning for the character, flowers were sent to Granada on behalf of Martha, and it's a reaction that's continued to happen, be it for births, marriages or deaths. Actress Violet Carson threatened to resign in protest but was talked round by Granada supremo Cecil Bernstein. Years later, Bernstein confessed to Carson that he regretted letting Martha's demise go ahead and, with typical bluntness, Carson is reported to have replied: 'It's a bit late for that!'

The production team therefore received first-hand experience of the love the nation had for their show. It's no surprise that all the dramatic exits of popular soap-opera characters ever since stem from this one decision. It's certainly true to say that many an incoming producer has realised that the best way to put their own stamp on a show is to copy Aspinall and cull as many characters in one go as possible. But Aspinall's legacy was not all doom and gloom. As Martha Longhurst was on her way out, a middle-aged married couple were moving in. Destined to forever 'bring down the tone' of the street, busybody Hilda and her useless, work-shy husband Stan would become *Corrie*'s most adored couple. While Stan tried to find more and more excuses why 'supping' at the bar of the Rover's was better than working for a living, Hilda worked hard taking whatever cleaning work she could – and all the better if it put her in a position to hear or pass on gossip.

Coronation Street's most popular characters have usually been of the more earthy variety, more fitting for comedy storylines than high drama. The Ogdens' best friend, Eddie Yates, who turned up one day announcing that he was a former friend of Jed Stone from 'inside', was an ex-criminal dustbin man with a heart of gold but not much else. Shopkeeper Reg Holdsworth had pretensions of grandeur, with his lopsided toupee and comedy glasses, yet we all knew deep down he was just a randy old man. Reg left just as Fred Elliot was introduced, the foghorn-throated proprietor of a string of butcher shops and other small businesses across the area. Though Fred has often been the source of comedy, the character is also a surprisingly deep one, emotional, well meaning but bitter at the cards he's been dealt. In 1996, he was joined by his nephew, Ashley Peacock, who, it was later revealed, was actually his natural son. The booming Fred and the squeaky-voiced Ashley have created yet another enduring *Corrie* double act, equally adept at comedy or the utter depths of tragedy, and they've had their share of both. When Vera Duckworth's husband Jack was introduced in the late 1970s, the couple replaced the Ogdens as the 'lower class' element of the street, horrifying residents by keeping pigeons and having their house fitted with stone cladding (thus devaluing the property considerably). By the mid-1980s, the Duckworths had replaced the Ogdens as the favourite 'common' characters, so the Claytons were introduced, but, proving unpopular with viewers, they were hurriedly ditched after just six months, to be replaced by the McDonalds. Father, ex-army man Jim, mum Liz who, for a time, managed her own pub, and twin sons Andy and Steve, mirroring the *Street*'s first brothers, David and Ken Barlow. Jim's violent temper and alcoholism (a disappointingly clichéd representation of an Irishman, it has to be said) drew many complaints after one episode in which Jim punched Liz and then left her abandoned, sobbing, in a car park. The McDonalds unsurprisingly split up, though they also got back together and split up again. Liz ran off with Jim's friend, Jim ended up in prison and Andy washed his hands of his family, heading off to travel the world, leaving Steve as the sole permanent McDonald resident of the street. Liz has subsequently returned after years managing various pubs across the Northwest . . . and Jim has been known to make the odd jail break too. The position of most hated family in the street is currently occupied by Les Battersby and his brood of misfits. Originally it was Les, his second wife Janice and their daughters (from previous relationships) Leanne and Toyah. As with all ghastly families, they've softened over the years, with Toyah becoming a hard-working and highly moral student and Janice divorcing Les to become an independent and very popular woman. Luckily, Les has been preserved as the *Street*'s example of Neanderthal man, currently shacked up with Cilla Brown and numerous other strays.

In the 1960s, the sight of a pregnant woman being beamed into people's homes might not have been an appealing one, but by the late 1970s, Ray and Deirdre Langton had been blessed with a daughter, Tracy. Tracy was abducted, became the product of a

Simon Gregson · *Steve McDonald*
Nicholas Cochrane · *Andy McDonald*
Ken Morley · *Reg Holdsworth*
Thomas Ormson, Jack P. Shepherd · *David Platt*
Sarah Lancashire · *Raquel Wolstenhulme/Watts*
Philip Middlemiss · *Des Barnes*
Amelia Bullmore · *Steph Barnes*
Tommy Boyle · *Phil Jennings*
Deborah McAndrew · *Angie Freeman*
Shirin Taylor · *Jackie Ingram/Baldwin*
Chloe Newsome · *Vicky Arden/McDonald*
Denise Black · *Denise Osbourne*
Chris Cook, Paul Fox · *Mark Redman*
Catherine Cusack · *Carmel Finnan*
Angela Griffin · *Fiona Middleton*
Caroline Milmoe · *Lisa Horton/Duckworth*
Sherrie Hewson · *Maureen Naylor/Holdsworth/Elliott*
Al Nedjari · *Samir Rachid*
Ellie Haddington · *Josie Clarke*
Malcolm Terris · *Eric Firman*
Eva Pope · *Tanya Pooley*
Malcolm Hebden · *Norris Cole*
John Savident · *Fred Elliott*
Elizabeth Bradley · *Maud Grimes*
Tracy Brabin · *Tricia Armstrong*
David Neilson · *Roy Cropper*
Ian Mercer · *Gary Mallett*
Gaynor Faye · *Judy Mallett*
Tracy Shaw · *Maxine Heavey/Peacock*
Lee Warburton · *Tony Horrocks*
Steven Arnold · *Ashley Peacock*
Eve Steele · *Anne Malone*
Tina Hobley · *Samantha Failsworth*
Glenn Hugill · *Alan McKenna*
Vicky Entwistle · *Janice Battersby*
Bruce Jones · *Les Battersby*
Jane Danson · *Leanne Battersby/Tilsley*
Georgia Taylor · *Toyah Battersby*
Owen Aaronovitch · *Jon Lindsay*
Joanne Frogatt · *Zoe Tattersall*
Denise Welch · *Natalie Horrocks/Barnes*
Martin Hancock · *Geoffrey 'Spider' Nugent*
Matthew Marsden · *Chris Collins*
Julie Hesmondhalgh · *Hayley Patterson/Cropper*
Margi Clarke · *Jackie Dobbs*
Alan Halsall · *Tyrone Dobbs*
Stephen Billington · *Greg Kelly*
Jacqueline Chadwick/Pirie · *Linda Sykes/Baldwin*
Naomi Radcliffe · *Alison Wakefield/Webster*
Lee Boardman · *Jez Quigley*
Chris Bisson · *Vikram Desai*
Saeed Jaffrey · *Ravi Desai*
Rebecca Sarker · *Nita Desai*
John Bowe · *Duggie Ferguson*
Richard Standing · *Danny Hargreaves*

Angela Lonsdale · *WPC/Sergeant/Inspector Emma Taylor*
Melanie Kilburn · *Evelyn Sykes*
Nikki Sanderson · *Candice Stowe*
Dean Ashton · *Aidan Critchley*
Jimmi Harkishin · *Dev Alahan*
Sue Cleaver · *Eileen Grimshaw*
Bruno Langley · *Todd Grimshaw*
Ryan Thomas · *Jason Grimshaw*
Jonathan Wrather · *Joe Carter*
Samia Ghadie · *Maria Sutherland*
Suranne Jones · *Karen Phillips/McDonald*
Andrew Whyment · *Kirk Sutherland*
Charles Dale · *Dennis Stringer*
Brian Capron · *Richard Hillman*
Shobna Gulati · *Sunita Parekh*
Jennie McAlpine · *Fiz Brown*
Sally Lindsay · *Shelley Unwin/Barlow*
Thomas Craig · *Tommy Nelson/Harris*
Kathryn Hunt · *Angela Nelson/Harris*
Lucy-Jo Hudson · *Katy Nelson/Harris*
Richard Fleeshman · *Craig Nelson/Harris*
Katy Carmichael · *Lucy Richards/Barlow*
Keith Duffy · *Ciaran McCarthy*
Stephen Beckett · *Dr Matt Ramsden*
Iain Rogerson · *Harry Flagg*
Roy Hudd · *Archie Shuttleworth*
Julia Haworth · *Claire Casey/Peacock*
Pauline Fleming · *Penny King*
Wendi Peters · *Cilla Brown*
Sam Aston · *Chesney Brown*
Bill Ward · *Charlie Stubbs*
Susie Blake · *Bev Unwin*
Antony Cotton · *Sean Tully*
Bradley Walsh · *Danny Baldwin*
Debra Stephenson · *Frankie Baldwin*
Rupert Hill · *Jamie Baldwin*
Danny Young · *Warren Baldwin*
Jenny Platt · *Violet Wilson*

broken home, and was adopted by Ken Barlow when he married Deirdre. As a wayward teenager, Tracy nearly died after a drugs overdose in a nightclub – only to be saved by an organ donation made available by the death of her mother's third husband, Moroccan toyboy Samir. Her parents breathed a sigh of relief when she eventually settled down and married, only for her to return with the marriage in tatters in 2002. Any hope that marriage might have mellowed her has quickly been dispelled – she's become quite the most malicious soap bitch to be seen in years (pretending to seduce Roy Cropper, getting him to marry her and pay for the birth of her illegitimate baby only to reveal it was actually the product of a one-night stand with Steve McDonald, which in turn led to her working to split up Steve and his wife to provide a father for her daughter – and so on). Other 'Soap Children' have been used as pawns in custody battles, but for little else (most of them being sent upstairs to listen to tapes until they're old enough to generate storylines – usually five years does the trick). But increasingly, enough child actors have been produced in the Northwest to keep *Corrie* busy, with the 13-year-old Sarah-Louise Platt giving birth, Rosie Webster inspiring her mother Sally to become a 'pushy mum', forcing her into stage school, and young Sam Aston providing an award-winning turn as Chesney Brown, the neglected but oh-so-cute son of Les Battersby's monstrous lover Cilla.

And, over 40 years on, William Roach is still with the programme, albeit older and a little more cynical. *The Guinness Book of Records* lists him as the longest-serving actor in the world to be associated with one show. Though Ken is often criticised for being 'boring', critics have failed to recognise the complex nature of a character whose education, which once inspired him, became a cause for frustration as he went from local journalist to schoolteacher, never able to find a job that really taxed his intellect. Ken found himself right at the heart of the *Street*'s most famous love triangle when he learned of wife Deirdre's affair with factory owner Mike Baldwin. Though Deirdre tried to end the affair with Mike, Ken threw her out. Such was the nation's interest in the outcome of this that when Ken and Deirdre finally got back together, the news was flashed on a display at Old Trafford to a stadium of cheering Manchester United fans (the writers tried the same trick some years later, when Ken became involved with Wendy Crozier – and it took a lot longer for he and Deirdre to get over that little blip). Ken and Mike's paths have crossed on many occasions since, and we hope these now pensionable men will have the strength to be scrapping until their dying days.

The Rover's Return has provided the perfect location for revelations, heartbreak, raucous laughter and punch-ups. When Annie Walker finally relinquished the licence in 1983, the pub was briefly managed by her son Billy, but it eventually fell into the well-manicured hands of barmaid Bet Lynch, and then, when she married in 1987, jointly with Alec Gilroy. After she and Alec split up, and brewery Newton and Ridley had put the pub on the market, Bet found herself unable to raise the necessary cash to buy the place that had been her home since 1970. Bet left the street with her head held high but her heart sunk low. In stepped Jack and Vera Duckworth, who seriously underestimated the work that goes into running a busy pub like the Rover's. Widowed businesswoman Natalie Barnes took over for a while until, traumatised by the murder of her second husband, Des Barnes, she too sold up to a consortium of local businessmen, builder Duggie Ferguson, factory owner Mike Baldwin and butcher Fred Elliot. After a round of bargaining and double-dealing, Fred became the sole owner, expanding his business empire still further.

As an openly gay man at a time when such things were still very much taboo, Tony Warren had constant battles with other writers dismissing ideas, dialogue and entire scenes as 'too poofy'. Yet *Coronation Street* has managed to hold on to a certain level of campery over the years because of the characters Warren created at the beginning. Elsie Tanner, thanks in part to the vampishness of Pat Phoenix, was the TV equivalent of Katharine Hepburn, hard as nails but rarely seen without the trademark bouffant hairdo of flame-red locks piled high on her head like an Ascot hat. It became the archetype that all wounded women eventually grew into. Elsie's immediate successor in the role was Bet Lynch, the former good-time girl who evolved into the kind of working-class woman often seen in the North. The hair grew bigger, the jewellery more vulgar until she began to look every inch the panto dame, brash, lippy and sporting make-up like it was war paint.

Thus the *Street* managed to remain defiantly camp, even after other soaps pretended that the only way forward was gritty realism. In the mid-1990s, one producer made the error of forcing the show down the competitive route of tackling one big issue a month; she didn't last. *Corrie* never works when it's issue-led (in fact no TV drama ever does). During the big issue-chasing of the 1990s, the introduction of a lesbian character was briefly considered until one of the more experienced writers pointed out that the *Street* already had its own lesbian couple – Percy Sugden and Emily Bishop!

Yes, *Corrie* has 'done' issues and got away with it. But the introduction of Hayley Patterson, a transsexual, wouldn't have worked had she not also been a strong character. Likewise, the *Street* has never gone in for casting Black characters to make an issue of colour (although we're forced to confess that this argument falls apart when we consider the number of Asian characters linked to the corner shops in the show). The successful integration of homosexuality into the *Street* combined honesty with stealth. As viewers joined young Todd Grimshaw on his journey of discovery with a pin-up male nurse, Sean Tully (played by the incomparable Antony Cotton) crept in and effortlessly assimilated himself into Mike Baldwin's underworld knicker factory. The move came 20 years behind ***EastEnders*** and ***Brookside*** but *Corrie* has never really been about keeping up with the times – or the Fowlers.

While other soaps have rushed to court younger viewers (and indeed *Corrie* itself has been guilty of this on occasion), January 2003 heralded the beginning of a string of storylines that focused on the

Creator Tony Warren

Producers Stuart Latham, Derek Granger, H. V. Kershaw, Margaret Morris, Tim Aspinall, Howard Baker, Peter Eckersley, Jack Rosenthal, Michael Cox, Richard Everitt, Richard Doubleday, John Finch, June Howson, Brian Armstrong, Eric Prytherch, Leslie Duxbury, Susi Hush, Bill Podmore, Pauline Shaw, Mervyn Watson, John G. Temple, David Liddiment, Carolyn Reynolds, Tony Wood, Sue Pritchard, Brian Park, David Hanson, Jane Macnaught, Kieran Roberts.

Writers Various, including Tony Warren, H. V. Kershaw, John Finch, Jack Rosenthal, Adele Rose, Vince Powell, Peter Eckersley, Tony Williamson, John Pennington, Jim Allen, Geoffrey Lancashire, Leslie Duxbury, Ron McDonnell, Malcolm Lynch, Susan Pleat, James Bryant, Peter Tonkinson, Julian Roach, Brian Finch, Tony Perrin, Leo Knowles (aka Bernard Aspen), Barry Hill, Kay McManus, John Stevenson, Paula Milne, Peter Whalley, Bob Mason, Kay Mellor, Stephen Mallatratt, Paul Abbott, Stephen Lowe, Ken Blakeson, Phil Woods, Tom Eliott, Patrea Smallacombe, Frank Cottrell Boyce, Sally Wainwright, Mark Wadlow, Peter Mills, Jan McVerry, Catherine Hayes, Phil Ford, Maureen Chadwick, Martin Allen, David Lane, Susan Wilkins, Joe Turner, Stephen Bennett, Julie Gearey, Jo O'Keefe, Daran Little, Jayne Hollinson

Theme Music Eric Spear

TRIVIA

An early star turn in *Coronation Street* was Leonard Swindley, played by Arthur Lowe, who in 1967 took the character off in his own spin-off series, a sitcom called *Turn Out the Lights*.

older characters – culminating in the heinous activities of twisted property developer and financial adviser Richard Hillman. It was a complete coincidence that teen soap ***Hollyoaks*** just happened to be running a storyline about a multiple murderer at the same time. But whereas that programme was about teen characters having teen crises, the *Street*'s plot was much more credible. Richard wasn't a loony drafted in to make headlines; he was a genuinely desperate man whose situation grew worse and worse as events spiralled out of control. First he accidentally killed his money-grabbing wife, then his treacherous business partner Duggie Ferguson fell from the top floor of one of their building sites and Richard let him die. There was a near miss with Audrey Roberts, who suddenly realised that Richard had been trying to poison her, and finally came the savage attack on Maxine Peacock, who stumbled on Richard after he'd whacked Emily Bishop across the head with a crowbar. Emily recovered to learn that Maxine had been brutally murdered. In a painful twist, Richard was called upon to deliver a reading at Maxine's funeral, leading to a marvellous tease where for a moment it appeared that Richard was about to confess all to the congregation . . .

Births, marriages, deaths, this street has seen them all – and more. Not bad for a show that was initially given just 16 weeks to prove itself.

The effect of Hillman on the *Street* is still being felt. His story has reinvigorated the parts of the senior cast members, giving them all major storylines for the first time in years. Audrey went from silly, interfering mother-in-law to lead role, giving Sue Nicholls the chance to show off acting abilities that have rarely been called upon. The shattering effect of Maxine's tragic death on poor husband Ashley Peacock was equally dramatic. But *Corrie* doesn't want us to be glum for too long. When Richard finally confessed his doings to wife Gail, the writers couldn't resist giving us a small chuckle with Gail describing her husband as 'Norman Bates with a briefcase'. It felt natural, it didn't harm the drama and it reminded us once again why *Coronation Street* is still the nation's favourite.

It might be on more regularly now than it was in the past (currently four times a week, including two full half-hour episodes on Mondays), but despite many changes, it remains intrinsically the same. In a way, this is how *Coronation Street* has been able to achieve a timeless quality, recognisably contemporary yet belonging to a world of its own. While other soaps tackle modern issues head on, *Coronation Street* has always been at its best sticking to what it knows best – good characters.

cryptic comment about TV critics having a 'licence to knock', considering how badly the series had gone down . . .

The Cosby Show

Comedy | Carsey-Werner Company for NBC/Channel 4 | episode duration 25 mins | broadcast 20 Sep 1984–30 Apr 1992 (USA)

Regular Cast

Bill Cosby · *Dr Cliff Huxtable*
Phylicia Rashad · *Clair Huxtable*
Lisa Bonet · *Denise Huxtable Kendall*
Sabrina Le Beauf · *Sondra Huxtable Tibideaux*
Geoffrey Owens · *Elvin Tibideaux*
Malcolm-Jamal Warner · *Theo Huxtable*
Tempestt Bledsoe · *Vanessa Huxtable*
Keshia Knight Pulliam · *Rudi Huxtable*
Joseph C. Phillips · *Lieutenant Martin Kendall*
Allen Payne · *Lance Rodman*
Raven-Symoné · *Olivia Kendall*
Erika Alexander · *Pam Tucker*

Creators Michael Leeson, Ed Weinberger and William Cosby Jr (aka Bill Cosby) **Producers** Marcy Carsey, Tom Werner, Caryn Sneider, Bill Cosby **Writers** Various, including Chris Auer, Walter Allen Bennett Jr, Susan Fales, Carmen Finestra, Gordon Gartrelle, Winifred Hervey, Bernie Kukoff, Janet Leahy, John Markus, Earl Pomerantz, Elliott Shoenman, Matt Williams **Theme Music** Over the years, there were a number of different tunes and songs that opened *The Cosby Show*, including one performed in human-instrument style by Bobby McFerrin. Most, though, were variations on the same tune, written by Stu Gardner and Bill Cosby himself.

When *The Cosby Show* was launched on American TV in 1984, few casual observers would have given the programme much chance of success. At that time, it was believed that the sitcom was a dying genre, with few other successful comedies still on the air. Worse still, *The Cosby Show* was a programme about an entirely black family – an inevitable ratings disaster, surely? But just as Bill Cosby had broken down barriers in *I Spy* (in which he was the first ever black co-star of a prime-time American TV series), so *The Cosby Show*, Bill's own labour of love, would rewrite the rule books, eventually running for over 200 episodes and becoming one of the most lucrative sitcoms in US history.

Cliff and Clair Huxtable are two very successful middle-class parents (he's an obstetrician, she's a lawyer), living in a beautiful terraced house in New York City. They have five marvellous children, too – Sondra, Denise, Theo, Vanessa and Rudi. Together the family face the normal kind of problems that most families face – marriage difficulties, wayward kids, moral dilemmas – but together, the Huxtables manage to overcome them all. During the course of the series, the two eldest daughters go off to college (in fact, the exploits of Denise Huxtable at Hillman College were the basis of spin-off series, *A Different World*, which ran for six seasons from 1987 – albeit only two of them with Denise in!), and then both get married.

A warm, witty and charming sitcom, *The Cosby Show* was revolutionary in its portrayal of black people on TV, but could never said to be truly challenging or innovative with its comedy, which remained resolutely 'nice' and predictable throughout its eight-year run. Four years after the series ended, Bill Cosby returned to TV screens in the US in a show called simply *Cosby*, which was in fact a remake of Britain's own ***One Foot in the Grave***, running for four seasons.

Count Dracula

Horror Drama | BBC One | duration 151 mins | broadcast 22 Dec 1977

Cast

Louis Jourdan · *Count Dracula*
Frank Finlay · *Professor Van Helsing*
Susan Penhaligon · *Lucy Westenra*
Judi Bowker · *Mina Westenra*
Jack Shepherd · *Renfield*
Mark Burns · *Dr John Seward*
Bosco Hogan · *Jonathan Harker*
Richard Barnes · *Quincey P. Holmwood*
Ann Queensberry · *Mrs Westenra*
George Raistrick · *Bowles*
George Malpas · *Swales*
Michael MacOwan · *Mr Hawkins*
Susie Hickford, Belinda Meuldijk, Sue Vanner · *Brides of Dracula*

Producer Morris Barry **Writer** Gerald Savory, from the novel by Bram Stoker **Theme Music** Kenyon Emrys-Roberts

Although there have been many dozens of movie adaptations of Bram Stoker's classic Gothic horror novel, television has rarely ventured into the realm of the un-dead. The BBC two-parter from 1977 is a notable exception, featuring a stellar cast, incredibly high production values and an eerie and unsettling atmosphere that's more art-house than any Hammer horror film.

Louis Jourdan stars as the eponymous Count, a centuries-old vampire who's planning to relocate from his home in Transylvania to Victorian England. Jourdan's performance is both charismatic and considerably more erotically charged than previous interpretations of the role. Having a ball as vampire slayer Van Helsing is the ever-reliable Frank Finlay, and both Judi Bowker and Susan Penhaligon deliver the customary heaving cleavages of Dracula's victims with great aplomb. The whole production reeks of class and style, with the art department, in particular, going berserk and replacing the standard 'wafting smoke' of vampire films with what looks like a cocaine trail of drug-induced psychedelia. In fact, the only thing that might be slightly off-putting to modern audiences is a very occasional dated visual effect – but look past that and revel in one of the BBC's greatest ever period dramas . . . albeit one with a touch more bite than usual.

Count Duckula

Animation | Cosgrove Hall/Thames for ITV | episode duration 25 mins | broadcast 6 Sep 1988–16 Feb 1993

Regular Voice Cast
David Jason · *Count Duckula*
Jack May · *Igor*
Brian Trueman · *Nanny*
Barry Clayton · *Narrator*
Jimmy Hibbert · *Von Goosewing*
Ruby Wax · *Assorted Voices*

Creators Mike Harding, Brian Trueman **Producers** Brian Cosgrove, Mark Hall, Chris Randall, John Hambley **Writers** Brian Trueman, Jimmy Hibbert, John Broadhead, Joyce McAleer, Chris Randall, John Sayle, Peter Richard Reeves **Theme Music** Mike Harding wrote the catchy theme, with vocals provided by Doreen Edwards.

A spin-off from legendary cartoon series ***Danger Mouse***, *Count Duckula* provided an almost equally marvellous series of chuckles and chills for children of all ages. In the heart of Transylvania lives Count Duckula, the latest reincarnation in a long line of vicious vampire ducks who have terrorised the locality for centuries. However, Duckula is not like most vampires: thanks to the bungling of well-meaning but dim servant Nanny during the revivification process (she used tomato ketchup rather than blood), Duckula is now a vegetarian vampire – much to the dismay of sinister servant Igor, who longs for the olden days when previous counts had been vicious bloodsuckers. Although Duckula just wants to lead a quiet life, Igor keeps doing his best to turn his young master to the dark side, while Nanny wanders round in a perpetual state of bewilderment, normally messing things up for everyone with her utter stupidity and complete clumsiness.

With voices supplied by comedy superstar David Jason and veteran actor Jack May (the voice of Nelson Gabriel in *The Archers* and star of TV shows such as ***Adam Adamant Lives!***), *Count Duckula* could be relied upon to provide superior-quality entertainment for the whole family. Like its parent series, *Count Duckula* was also sold to several countries around the world, including the Nickelodeon Network in the USA.

Website
www.chf.co.uk – the official Cosgrove Hall site

The Count of Monte Cristo (1956)

Drama | ITC for ITV | episode duration 25 mins | broadcast 5 Mar–7 Dec 1956

Principal Cast
George Dolenz · *Edmond Dantes*
Nick Cravat · *Jacopo*
Robert Cawdron · *Rico*
Faith Dormergue · *Princess Anne*

Producers Leon Fromkess (executive), Sidney Marshall, Dennis Vance **Writers** Various, from the novel by Alexandre Dumas **Theme Music** Emil Newman

For commentary, see THE COUNT OF MONTE CRISTO (1964)

The Count of Monte Cristo (1964)

Drama | BBC One | episode duration 25 mins | broadcast 4 Oct–20 Dec 1964

Principal Cast
Alan Badel · *Edmond Dantes, The Count of Monte Cristo*
Natasha Parry · *Mercedes*
Anthony Newlands · *Morrel*
Michael Bilton · *Cocles*
Morris Perry · *Danglars*
Bob Raymond · *Penelon*
Philip Madoc · *Fernand*
Michael Robbins · *Caderousse*
Michael Gough · *DeVillefort*
Rosalie Crutchley · *Madame Danglars*
Anna Palk · *Valentine*
Valerie Sarruf · *Haydee*

Producer Campbell Logan **Writer** Anthony Steven, from the novel by Alexandre Dumas **Theme Music** Roberto Gerhard

Edmond Dantes is falsely imprisoned in Chateau d'If. There he learns of a fortune in treasure secreted on the island of Monte Cristo and subsequently escapes, finding the treasure and setting himself as a nobleman. From here, he becomes a dashing benefactor, helping those in need with some finely placed swashbuckling.

The first British TV adaptation of Alexandre Dumas's classic novel of dual identities and adventure was a UK/US co-production, starring George Dolenz (father of ***Monkees*** star Mickey) as Dantes. The first 12 episodes were filmed in California at the Hal Roach Studio, with the remaining 27 shot on the backlot at Borehamwood in the UK. The normally moustachioed Dolenz went clean-shaven for his heroic role as Dantes. A later production from the BBC was made on a lower budget but stuck closer to the source novel.

Countdown

Quiz Show | Yorkshire Television/Granada Yorkshire for Channel 4 | episode duration 25–40 mins | broadcast 2 Nov 1982–present

Regular Cast

Richard Whiteley · *Presenter*

Carol Vorderman, Beverly Isherwood, Kathy Hytner, Dr Lynda Barrett, Karen Loughlin, Lucy Summers · *Co-presenters*

Keith Barron, Gyles Brandreth, Barry Cryer, Richard Digance, Geoffrey Durham, Philip Franks, Jan Harvey, David Jacobs, Martin Jarvis, Denis Norden, Tom O'Connor, Eve Pollard, Nigel Rees, Tim Rice, Ned Sherrin, Richard Stilgoe, Bill Tidy, Rick Wakeman, Kenneth Williams, Simon Williams · *'Dictionary Corner' Guests (appearing most frequently)*

Catherine Clark, Suzie Dent, Damian Eadie, Mark Nyman, Richard Samson, Julia Swannel, Della Thompson, Freda Thornton · *Lexicographers (appearing most frequently)*

Creator Armand Jammot **Theme Music** Alan Hawkshaw

A perennially popular brain-teasing programme, ideal for putting your feet up to, *Countdown* was the very first show broadcast on Channel 4's launch night. Based on a much less exciting French show (*Des Chiffres et des lettres*), the format of *Countdown* has changed little since it began as a regional programme broadcast only in the ITV Yorkshire area. After a short run as *Calendar Countdown* (*Calendar* being the name of Yorkshire's local TV news programme), the show became the cornerstone of Channel 4's early evening /afternoon schedule.

In each episode, two contestants take part in a number of rounds testing two key skills: the ability to make the longest word possible out of a randomly chosen series of nine letters; and arithmetic, by using six randomly selected numbers and standard arithmetic functions (add, subtract, divide and multiply) in order to reach another randomly chosen number. Finally, the last round presents the contestants with a nine-letter anagram, the 'Countdown Conundrum' – first person to buzz in with the unjumbled word wins extra points. Alongside genial presenter Richard Whiteley is maths expert Carol Vorderman, a woman who's now become more famous for appearing in glossy magazines and adverts for credit companies than for *Countdown* itself. However, when *Countdown* started, Carol was only wheeled on to check the working-out by the contestants in the maths rounds; there were other glamorous assistants to do the challenging job of selecting the vowels and consonants on behalf of the contestants. It took several years (and several other glamorous presenters) before Carol assumed all of the co-presenter functions and the legendary double-act between her and Richard was consolidated.

In the very first edition, contestants Jeff Andrews and Michael Goldman (who won!) battled to create the longest words, which were checked by celebrity farmer and Everest double-glazing salesman Ted Moult, the first guest in 'Dictionary Corner'. Over the years, many hundreds of celebrities have tried their hand at coming up with a longer word than the contestants. However, we don't think that we'll be shattering too many illusions if we let on that quite often the celebrities are secretly fed a few nice long words (courtesy of a hidden earpiece) to show off with. Also on hand to help out the celebrities is an expert (usually associated with the *Oxford Dictionary* itself), whose job it is to ensure that the occasionally baffling words suggested by the contestants are in fact real and not some figment of the imagination.

The programme jumped in length (including adverts) from 30 to 45 minutes in 2001. When in 2003 it was moved to 3.15 p.m. on Channel 4, there was a national uproar, with questions even being asked in Parliament about the possible negative impact such a move would have on the nation's literacy and numeracy. Channel 4 refused to budge, however, and a whole nation's afternoon schedules were rejigged, much to the chagrin of many people who were perfectly happy putting their feet up with a cup of tea at 4.30 p.m. to listen to Richard Whiteley's appalling puns. At the time of writing (Spring 2005), Channel 4 is screening the 53rd series – a feat made manageable by the fact that up to three series are often squeezed into any one calendar year. Sadly, it was the last for Whiteley, who died following surgery after a short illness.

As reassuring as a chocolate digestive, *Countdown* will hopefully continue into the future and deserves its place in any hall of fame for TV quiz shows.

Trivia

Carol deals out from piles of 73 vowels (15 As, 20 Es, 14 Is, 14 Os and 10 Us, fact fans!) and 82 consonants. The random number generator device actually has a nickname, CECIL – which stands for *Countdown* Electronic Computer In Leeds (which probably sounded more sophisticated and futuristic in 1982, when the programme started, than it does today).

Website

www.thecountdownpage.com/index.htm

Countryfile

Factual | BBC One | episode duration 30–60 mins | broadcast 24 Jul 1988–present

Regular Cast

John Craven, Chris Baines, Ben Fogle, Adam Henson, Bob Langley, Miriam O'Reilly, Michaela Strachan · *Presenters*

Producers Teresa Bogan, Sarah Elgin **Theme Music** Spike MacLaren

As much an essential part of the Sunday morning hangover experience as the ***Hollyoaks*** and *Archers* omnibus, *Countryfile* has a soothing quality that has the ability to gently wash over you, even if you probably don't have a clue what they're talking about.

John Craven, still with the ability to remind us of a golden age of TV gone by, presides over this rural affairs magazine programme (alongside one-time ***Castaway*** Ben Fogle and former *The Really Wild Show* presenter Michaela Strachan) with avuncular style. Features typically include coverage of wildlife, rural transport, farming issues, video diaries and a detailed weather report on the week ahead. An annual photography competition is well subscribed, with amateur snappers itching to show off their often-stunning views of the countryside. In fact, a calendar produced each year from the best of the competition entries sells many hundreds of thousands of copies in aid of the BBC's *Children in Need* appeal.

Website
www.bbc.co.uk/nature/environment/programmes/countryfile/

Coupling

Sitcom | Hartswood Films for BBC Two | episode duration 30 mins | broadcast 12 May 2000–14 Jun 2004

Regular Cast
Jack Davenport · *Steve Taylor*
Sarah Alexander · *Susan Walker*
Richard Coyle · *Jeff Murdock*
Kate Isitt · *Sally Harper*
Gina Bellman · *Jane Christie*
Ben Miles · *Patrick Maitland*
Richard Mylan · *Oliver Morris*
Mariella Frostrup · *Herself*

Creator/Writer Steven Moffat **Producers** Beryl Vertue, Geoffrey Perkins, Sophie Clarke-Jervoise (executive), Sue Vertue **Theme Music** 'Perhaps, Perhaps, Perhaps' was originally a hit for Doris Day – this version was covered by Mari Wilson, '50s retro singer who'd had a No. 8 hit in the UK charts in 1982 with 'Just What I Always Wanted'.

When *Coupling* first hit TV screens, some TV critics predictably categorised it as 'The British ***Friends***', largely because of the line-up of six attractive twenty-something lead actors, three men and three women. But scratch beneath the superficial similarities and *Coupling* is a very different programme from *Friends* – just as funny as the American show, but aimed at a much more mature audience, with humour and situations that would never get past the US network's censors.

Coupling is all about the life and loves of six friends, and the twists and turns that their relationships undergo. Steve breaks up with his slightly potty girlfriend Jane, despite her protestations that she simply won't let him leave her. Steve's mate Jeff soon introduces him to a girl he works with, the lively and bubby Susan – who has just broken up with über-confident womaniser Patrick. The moment that Patrick is free, Susan's friend Sally decides to seduce him – thus the basic web of tangled emotions and love-lives is set up, with permutations on the relationships forming much of the narrative throughout the rest of the series.

Writer Steven Moffat, who had enjoyed earlier success with ***Press Gang*** and ***Joking Apart***, created characters and scripts that felt as if they'd come from real-life events – complete with moments of wince-inducing embarrassment, social *faux pas* and gags that often took a whole episode to build up to a devastating punchline. One of Moffat's great strengths came in the innovative way he structured his scripts, using a variety of interesting techniques and tricks to keep the series fresh and interesting. One episode used split-screen to show two different perspectives on the break-up between Steve and Susan, another was told in a non-linear format, with the end of the storyline revealed well before the events that led up to it. Moffat used his own relationship with wife Sue Vertue (also the show's producer) as the initial starting block for *Coupling*, basing the relationship between Steve and Susan on certain incidents from their own history (embellished for comic purposes, we hope!).

Coupling was a huge hit for BBC Two, gaining a devoted audience eager to discover what was going to happen next in the turbulent love lives of their favourite characters. Even the departure of perhaps the most popular character – Welsh joker Jeff – at the start of the fourth season didn't dim enthusiasm for the series, with replacement Oliver doing a great job of fitting swiftly into the well-established quintet. The series was a big success in the USA, too, becoming very popular on the BBC America cable channel. American network NBC believed that *Coupling* might have been a potential replacement series for their show *Friends* and created their own version, which was launched in September 2003. Unfortunately, most critics compared the new Americanised version less favourably than the British original and the series was dropped after transmission of just a handful of episodes.

Cracker

Crime Drama | Granada for ITV | episode duration 50 mins | broadcast 11 Oct 1993–28 Oct 1996, 2005

Regular Cast
Robbie Coltrane · *Dr Eddie 'Fitz' Fitzgerald*
Geraldine Somerville · *DS Jane 'Panhandle' Penhaligon*
Barbara Flynn · *Judith Fitzgerald*
Lorcan Cranitch · *DS Jimmy Beck*
Christopher Eccleston · *DCI David Bilborough*
Ricky Tomlinson · *DCI Charlie Wise*
Kieran O'Brien · *Mark Fitzgerald*
Colin Tierney · *DC Bobby Harriman*
Kieran O'Brien · *Mark Fitzgerald*
Tess Thomson · *Katie Fitzgerald*
Amelia Bullmore, Isobel Middleton · *Catriona Bilborough*
Ian Mercer · *DS George Giggs*
Wilbert Johnson · *DC Skelton*
Robert Cavanah · *DC Alan Temple*

Creator Jimmy McGovern **Producers** Gub Neal, Hilary Bevan Jones **Writers** Jimmy McGovern, Paul Abbott

Better known at the time for comedic roles in *Tutti Frutti* and ***The Comic Strip Presents***, Robbie Coltrane proved himself a consummate serious actor as Fitz, the star of Jimmy McGovern's psychological police drama *Cracker* (Robert Lindsay had been the producers' first choice but turned the part down). Cynical psychology lecturer Fitz – overweight, alcoholic, chain-smoking and a habitual gambler – is a mess. His wife has left him, his son and daughter loathe him and he hasn't spoken to his mother or brother in years. He's rude to the point of being obnoxious and arrogant with it (when a taxi driver asks him not to smoke, complaining about passive smoking, Fitz points out that he's getting the smoke for free – which prompts the driver to kick him out of the cab). But when his mind is on the job, he is a master at assessing the criminal mind. He sees patterns that escape the police officers he often works with, which they resent completely.

Fitz was initially hired as a profiler at the Anson Road police station in Greater Manchester. It was evident to most that his involvement was more of a PR exercise than anything else, and while the real killer wasn't caught, Fitz did prove the innocence of their only suspect – not a popular result for the CID team. Initially, Fitz's point of contact in the Manchester police force was DI Bilborough, an ambitious but popular high-flyer. Frustrated by complaints from the surly Penhaligon, Bilborough assigns her to be Fitz's minder, in effect killing both the 'bird' and the burden with one stone. None of them expects the pair to develop a strong partnership – in more ways than one.

Also on the team is Jimmy Beck – sexist, racist, homophobic and lazy, his attitudes seem old-fashioned and outdated in a modern police force. He resents Fitz's smart intellectualising of criminals – to Beck, they're all perverts and low-lifes who should be strung up from the nearest tree. He also resents Penhaligon's presence, feeling that police work is no job for a woman. Beck's frustrations manage to obstruct more than one case, and eventually he becomes a criminal himself when he rapes Penhaligon, an act of brutality that serves to haunt him.

Cases tended to be spread across two or three episodes and tackled numerous issues in an uncompromising manner. The programme's highlight is widely recognised as 'To Be A Somebody'. Series creator Jimmy McGovern had tried and failed to introduce a story about the Hillsborough football disaster into ***Brookside***. In *Cracker*, he shows us Alby (a subtle but terrifying creation from Robert Carlyle), a disaffected man who blames the disaster for the distance that has grown between himself and his father. But it is his father's death that acts as the catalyst for him becoming a murderer, picking targets that he blames for the alienation of white, working-class males: an Asian shopkeeper, a tabloid journalist and a policeman. That policeman is DI Bilborough, who stabbed by Alby in a lengthy, harrowing scene, delivers 'the testament of a dying man' on his police radio as he lies bleeding to death in the street. Bilborough's death affects everyone, most of all Jimmy Beck, who had interviewed Alby in relation to the previous murders but had discounted him as a suspect. Unable to cope with the double guilt of Bilborough's death and Penhaligon's rape, Jimmy arrests a suspect for a series of brutal murders, takes him to the top of a Manchester hotel and makes a full confession to Penhaligon before jumping from the roof – taking the murder suspect with him.

Jimmy McGovern left *Cracker* behind in 1995 to work on his dramatisation of the events of ***Hillsborough***, while the series ended in 1996 with a one-off special set in Hong Kong. 'White Ghost' paired Fitz with Bilborough's replacement, the jolly Scouser DCI Wise, to investigate the killing of a businessman. It's been many long years since then, but at the time of writing, a new *Cracker* is being prepared, once more written by Jimmy McGovern.

Website

www.crackertv.co.uk – a fan site maintained by Sarah K.

Crackerjack

See pages 208–10

Crimewatch UK

Factual | BBC One | episode duration 50–60 mins | broadcast 7 Jun 1984–present

Cast

Nick Ross, Sue Cook, Jill Dando, Fiona Bruce · *Presenters*

Producers Peter Chafer, Nikki Cheetham, Gerry McClelland, Liz Mills, Seetha Kumar, Owen Gay, Karen Benveniste, Sally Dixon, Kate Thomson **Theme Music** 'Rescue Helicopter' by John Cameron

Originally scheduled to run for only four editions, *Crimewatch UK* was inspired by the German series *Aktenzeichen XY Ungelost*, which roughly translates as *File XY Unsolved*. Over the course of 20 years, the series has become a comforting guardian in assisting the police in bringing a range of serious crimes to wider public attention. The BBC's continued commitment to the series has clearly been worthwhile, with over 400 arrests made as a result of information provided by viewers phoning in. Although the reconstructions of crimes and interviews with investigating officers form the backbone of each edition, there are also regular features on effective crime prevention and a look at particularly tasty items of loot that have been recovered in the 'Treasure Trove' section.

The reassuring form of Nick Ross has been with the series since the word go, and he was joined by Sue Cook for the first 11 years. Jill Dando then took over until her tragic murder in 1999. For the last five years, newsreader Fiona Bruce has been standing faithfully beside Mr Ross, who always signs off the programme with the regular as clockwork, 'Don't have nightmares.'

Crackerjack

'... CRAC - KER - JACK!'

From 1955 until the mid-1980s, *Crackerjack* ('CRA-CKER-JACK!') was one of those shows that defined your generation. If you were 'old' you remembered when Michael Aspel presented it. It you were really old, you remembered Eamonn Andrews for something other than ***This is your Life***. While for anyone who was 25 plus in 2005, you'd remember Stu Francis boasting about his grape-crushing prowess while Ian Tough threatened to beat up his wife Jeanette, who was dressed up as a schoolboy, as part of their act, the Krankies. The presenters came and went but amazingly the games tended to stay the same.

Children's Television's first great variety show was fronted by former boxer and TV presenter Eamonn Andrews, a star at the age of 33 and the host of popular panel game ***What's My Line?*** The cool Irishman displayed few of the traits we might associate with children's TV presenters today. While various other performers came in to do the clowning around in the pre-filmed and live sketches (including future *Carry On* star Jack Douglas, Ronnie Corbett and Leslie Crowther), Andrews appeared unfazed by, even uninvolved in, the madness around him. He mimed along to the songs at the end of the show, explained each of the games to the children with passionless calm and never allowed the volume of his voice to rise above that of a vicar's at a christening. No wonder then that the children of the 1950s sat attentively in polite regard for the proceedings while Eamonn got on with the serious task of providing the linking material between the guests (a singer, an

Children's Variety/Game Show
BBC TV/BBC One
Episode Duration: 45–55 mins
Broadcast: 14 Sep 1955–21 Dec 1984

Regular Cast
Eamonn Andrews, Leslie Crowther, Michael Aspel, Ed Stewart, Stu Francis · *Hosts*
Jack Douglas, Joe Baker, Eddie Mendoza, Michael Derbyshire, Ronnie Corbett, Eddie Leslie, Teddy Johnson, Pearl Carr, Raymond Rollett, Vivienne Martin, Peter Glaze, Pip Hinton, Jillian Comber, Harold Taylor, Valerie Walsh, Christine Holmes, Rod Mclennan, Frances Barlow, Little and Large, Elaine Page, Stuart Sherwin, Heather Barbour, Jacqueline Clarke, Don Maclean, Jan Hunt, William Wallace (Ali Bongo), Bernie Clifton, Val Mitchell, Jan Michelle, Keith Harris, Ian and Jeanette Tough ('The Krankies), Sally Ann Triplett, Leigh Miles, Julie Dorne Brown, Geoffrey Durham (The Great Soprendo), Basil Brush, Sarah Hollamby, Ling Tai · *Co-presenters*

Creator Johnny Downes

Producers Johnny Downes, Peter Whitmore, Brian S. Jones, Robin Nash, Michael Hurll, Brian Whitehouse, Brian Penders, Paul Ciani

Theme Music There were various theme tunes throughout *Crackerjack*'s 29-year run, including various compositions from Bert Hayes and his orchestra. The final theme was written and performed by Chas and Dave ('Come on, are you ready? Come on, let's hear you shout/It's Crackerjack!').

acrobatics troupe or the resident 'nitwits' performing their latest sketch). It could simply have been the nature of live TV itself, and it was a far cry from the shrieking, messy cacophony that the show would be by the end, yet Andrews seemed to genuinely enjoy it. When the time came for him to leave for pastures new after ten years (he'd been moonlighting as host of *This is your Life* for eight of them), Eamonn appeared to be genuinely touched by the cast's gift of an inscribed silver salver ('To Eamonn with affection, from *Crackerjack*').

Leslie Crowther graduated from stooge to star as he stepped into Andrews' shoes as the show's host, and with his manic, gung-ho approach the show became more a showcase for vaudeville and pop acts and less reliant on the dull games for the kids. Not that this affected the general atmosphere of perfectly choreographed mayhem. When HM the Queen paid a visit to the studios, she confessed to Crowther that she often watched the show with her eldest two, Charles and Anne.

Peter Glaze had been the principal straight man in the comedy segments since the late 1950s, and with Crowther moving centre-stage, the search for a new comic performer was on. Don Maclean came first, with his permanent toothy grin and lanky frame making him a perfect stand-in for Crowther (and kids are so fickle – they don't care who it is getting the custard pie in the mush). When Crowther followed Andrews over to ITV, the role of host went to Michael Aspel, a return to the more pedestrian, sensible approach to children's telly, even if he did have a horrific line in curtain-style flowery shirts.

In the early days, the show had bounced around the schedules but by the 1970s it was able to affirm its slot in the introduction to each edition: 'It's Friday,' someone would shout, 'it's five to five and it's *Crackerjack*!' Eamonn Andrews' legacy was evident in *Crackerjack*'s most famous game – Double or Drop. Devised by Andrews back in the 1950s, the game was revived in the 1970s with only the nature of the prizes themselves marking the passage of time. The contestants would have to answer general knowledge questions, with right answers rewarded with a prize and wrong ones with a cabbage. If the kids dropped their prizes, they were disqualified (it's a harsh world out there). Never mind; there was always the consolation of a branded *Crackerjack* pencil just for taking part.

These games, always designed so they could be played at home with household objects, were regular fixtures well into the 1970s, when host Ed 'Stewpot' Stewart was battling against Peter Glaze and his latest sidekick, Bernie Clifton (who wowed kids with his hilarious ostrich-riding act). As time and trends passed, the special guests reflected the gentler side of the popular entertainment of the time. The show could attract such mega-stars as the Wombles or Little Jimmy Osmond as well as regular visits from magician Ali Bongo.

In the 1980s, though, the show suffered a noticeable shift. Stu Francis was introducing the acts by this point, a man whose faux-camp presentation style included such intentionally lame boasts as 'Ooh, I could rip a tissue', 'I could jump over a doll's house' and 'I could crush a grape'. Peter Glaze disappeared just as Francis arrived, his and Bernie Clifton's places taken by husband-and-wife team the Krankies, who honed their angry man/cheeky schoolboy act in front of a generous audience of cub scouts, girl guides and assorted school parties. The easy-to-copy party games were ditched in favour of manic question-and-answer sessions that inevitably resulted in someone being gunged (smothered in a thick gooey mess that would have left *The Exorcist*'s Linda Blair feeling queasy).

With Leslie Crowther's manic, gung-ho approach, the show became more a showcase for vaudeville and pop acts and less reliant on the dull games for the kids.

The kids might well have been an easily pleased crowd but the grown-ups in charge were not. As Michael Grade began looking for cuts that could be made to finance BBC One's new daytime schedule, *Crackerjack* joined *Pop Quiz* and ***Doctor Who*** in the list of casualties. While *Doctor Who*'s fans campaigned for a brief reprieve, the lack of similar loyalty for Stu Francis and the gunk tank meant *Crackerjack* was brought to an end just a couple of months past its 29th birthday.

Variety as a whole is a dying genre. Talent spots like ***New Faces*** and ***Opportunity Knocks*** have been usurped by ***Pop Idol*** and ***Stars in their Eyes***, while Saturday morning TV serve up the sketches and games at a faster pace. But it's hard for any Brit over 30 to watch *Dick and Dom in Da Bungalow* or even *Ministry of Mayhem* (while waiting for the latest adventures of ***Captain Scarlet***, naturally) without thinking of them as heavily inspired by the same tomfoolery that Peter Glaze and Leslie Crowther got up to 50 years before.

Crossroads

See pages 212–15

Crown Court

Drama | Granada | episode duration 25 mins | broadcast 18 Oct 1972–29 Mar 1984

Regular Cast
Various, including:
John Alkin · *Barry Deeley*
John Barron · *Justice Mitchioner*
Joseph Berry · *Usher*
Bernard Brown · *Andrew Logan QC*
Richard Colson · *Clerk of the Court*
Bernard Gallagher · *Johnathan Fry QC*
Michael Gover · *Peter Carson QC*
Terrence Hardiman · *Stephen Hardesty QC*
Derek Hockridge · *Clerk of the Court*
Edward Jewesbury · *Judge Bragg*
Charles Keating · *James Eliot QC*
William Mervyn · *Justice Cambell*
Dorothy Vernon · *Helen Tate*
Richard Warner · *Honourable Justice Waddington*
Peter Wheeler · *Court Reporter, Narrator*
Richard Wilson · *Jeremy Parsons QC*

Producers Jonathan Powell, Dennis Woolf **Writers** Various, including James Follett, Jeremy Sandford, John Foster, John Godber, Roger Parkes, Alun Richards, Ben Steed **Theme Music** 'Distant Hills' by Haseley and Preno

In 1972, ITV set about building its daytime schedule: Yorkshire TV presented their new rural soap opera ***Emmerdale Farm***; Border gave us the cosy game show ***Mr and Mrs***; and Granada came up with a drama set in the courts of a fictional town called Fulchester. Each week, three episodes (Wednesday, Thursday, Friday) would slowly present an entire case, from black and white photographs submitted as evidence (over which Court Reporter Peter Wheeler would lay out the facts), through to the verdict being given in the third episode.

Hundreds of familiar faces appeared as the accused or as vital witnesses, including Michael Elphick, Juliet Stevenson, Connie Booth, Fulton Mackay, Brenda Fricker, Mark McManus, John Le Mesurier and T. P. McKenna. Only the court staff and occasional police representatives provided any continuity through the weeks. All manner of cases were heard in the court, although rarely the dull ones: arson, kidnapping, burglary, robbery, rape and, of course, the odd juicy murder were the staple diet in this particular courtroom. What made this particular drama so innovative was that the jury were composed of members of the public and their verdict was unscripted, coming as a genuine response to the facts of the case.

In 1998, Granada attempted a revival of sorts with *The Verdict*, in which Richard Madeley presented the case and the audience at home got to decide the outcome. In 2004, Mersey Television, the company behind ***Brookside*** and ***Hollyoaks***, launched their first daytime soap – *The Courtroom* – which shared similarities with *Crown Court* except each case was wrapped up in one episode.

The Crystal Maze

Game Show | Chatsworth for Channel 4 | episode duration 50 mins | broadcast 1990–1995

Regular Cast
Richard O'Brien, Edward Tudor-Pole · *Presenter*
Sandra Caron · *Mumsie/Auntie Sabrina*

Creators Jacques Antoine, Adam Howarth, Simon Taylor, Bob Thorne, Lloyd Bettell-Higgins, David Bodycombe **Producers** Malcolm Heyworth, David G. Croft **Theme Music** 'Forcefield' by Zach Laurence

The Crystal Maze was a game show that worked harder than any other before it to be truly unique. A big-budget bastard offspring of ***The Adventure Game*** and those puzzle books people buy for long journeys, this weekly series was a huge hit for Channel 4, coming from the same production company that had been behind the similarly successful ***Treasure Hunt***. During each episode, six ordinary members of the public (typically marketing executives or local government officers in their twenties and thirties) would be guided around four themed 'zones' by genial host Richard O'Brien, the man behind legendary cult musical *The Rocky Horror Show*. In each of the four zones – Medieval, Future, Aztec and Industrial (which was substituted in later seasons with 'Ocean') – contestants would have the opportunity to play a series of games in order to try and win a time crystal. Each crystal counted as five seconds of time for completing the final game at the end of the programme, the 'Crystal Dome'.

The great joy in watching *The Crystal Maze* came from a smug sense of superiority in watching contestants floundering in games they had no possible chance of winning. Each game was situated inside an individual 'cell' with a lockable door, and had a set time limit – if the contestant failed to solve the puzzle or complete the task within the time limit, they failed to win that particular time crystal. If, in addition, the contestant didn't manage to get back out of the cell before time ran out, they would be 'locked in'. The only way to free a trapped contestant would be to buy their freedom by sacrificing one of their hard-earned crystals. Games were divided into four different categories: physical, skill, mental and mystery. These games would inevitably involve such things as mazes, giant puzzles, shooting tests and mental agility challenges. Some games were created with an extra challenge: if the contestant made more than the allowed number of errors of judgement (such as putting a foot on the floor when

Continued on page 216

Crossroads

Noele Gordon (left), Queen of the Crossroads Motel.

The story of *Crossroads* began in the 1950s, when actress Noele Gordon was a familiar face to viewers in the Midlands thanks to her daily chat show, *Lunchbox*. When she hosted one edition of the programme from a location in Nottingham, thousands of fans turned up to catch a glimpse of her, a show of loyalty that caught the imagination of Lew Grade, then head of ATV (the ITV franchise-holder for the Midlands region). He approached *Lunchbox*'s producer Reg Watson to see if something could be done to tap into this adoration, only to have Watson pitch the idea for a daytime soap, like the ones that filled the schedules in America, but made five times a week. Grade decided to mull the idea over. In the meantime, the BBC began screening the glamorous ***Compact***, a soap opera about a women's weekly magazine. Lew Grade approached the show's creators, Peter Ling and Hazel Adair, to work on a series he was about to launch, but the writers instead offered to create an entirely new serial drama for ATV to be made from Birmingham.

Called 'The Midland Road', their series would revolve around Noele Gordon as Meg Richardson, a widow who decides to convert her country house into a motel with the help of her daughter Jane and son Sandy. Meg also had a sister, Kitty Jarvis, not as well off as Meg but living in the same village, just down the road from the motel. This relationship immediately established the split between the successful and glamorous types whom they hoped would appeal to viewers in the home counties, and the working-class folk who might attract viewers in the Midlands and the North. Though Gordon's starring role meant that her beloved *Lunchbox* would have to close after 3000 shows, the thrill of making live TV every working day appealed to her increasingly.

With a quick name change to *Crossroads*, the series hit TV screens in the autumn of 1964, the first words being 'Crossroads Motel, can I help?' – spoken by 18-year-old Jane Rossington as Meg's daughter Jill. The first six weeks were only shown on ATV in the Midlands, though other regional stations followed. The only exception was Granada, which already had its own soap, ***Coronation Street***, and which held out until it picked up the story in 1971. By the late 1960s, *Crossroads* had moved from its daytime slot to early evenings, 6.00 or 6.30 p.m., which was more or less where it would remain until the 1980s.

Made as if it were live (i.e. any mistakes or fluffs were kept in), the ambitious task of producing enough episodes to fill the working week left its mark on the gloss and sheen; throughout its run, even after the episode count was reduced and production values were on a par with any other prime-time soap, *Crossroads* was considered to be cheap and shoddy, with characters going missing at a moment's notice, never to return, and plots that stretched credulity to the limit. Yet for all its faults, *Crossroads*' fans were loyal to the end. They felt a genuine connection to the on-off romance of Jill and the charmer Adam Chance; to dim-witted Benny (poor Paul Henry, who suffered more than anyone from typecasting after the show) and the object of his affection, 'Miss Diane'; and most of all to the queen of soap, Meg. The collective memory of wobbly sets is something that the makers never tried to defend. Made on a shoestring budget in the early days, the sets were theatrical flats, like the ones used in theatres, which made them portable and easy to erect and strike, but also not very stable. When the permanent sets were built, the memories of those early days proved too strong to shift.

The fast turnover of scripts began to take its toll, and in 1968 newspapers reported the shock resignation of the show's leading lady, though in the end an increase in salary and a reduction of her working hours eventually managed persuade Noele Gordon to stay. Head of production at ATV Bill Ward had tried to axe the programme in 1966 but had been prevented from doing so by Lew Grade. The axe once again hovered above the show in 1968 when Thames took over ATV 's franchise and dropped *Crossroads* from its London schedules. This time, one of the people pushing for it to continue was the prime minister himself, Harold Wilson, whose wife was a fan. The only concession allowed was that *Crossroads* would drop to four days a week to help production become less shoddy (a decade later it would be reduced to three, for the same reasons, which was still more episodes per week than any other soap at the time).

Reg Watson left the production team in 1974 to return to his native Australia (there, he'd create numerous other shows, including ***Prisoner: Cell Block H*** and ***Neighbours***). His replacement, Jack Barton, had been a director on the show since the beginning. His only real change was to introduce stories with more social awareness to them, playing to the serious storylines that the soap had occasionally included since it began. It was then that the show began to hit ratings peaks of 20 million. Sadly, just four years later, Sir Lew Grade retired, the show's champion throughout its early days. With Grade no longer able to protect the show, it was once again vulnerable to attack. The demise of *Crossroads* was steady and unjustified. Charles Denton, head of programmes at ATV, tried to bring the show to an end. Though he was overruled, like his predecessors, he did succeed in one small victory – the axing of Noele Gordon after 17 years. Meg was believed to have been killed in a fire that gutted the motel before a later episode revealed in

Soap Opera
ATV/Central for ITV
Episode Duration: 25 mins
Broadcast: 2 Nov 1964–4 Apr 1988, 5 Mar 2001–30 May 2003

Regular Cast
Noele Gordon · *Meg Richardson/Mortimer*
Jane Rossington · *Jill Richardson/Harvey/Chance*
Roger Tonge · *Sandy Richardson*
Beryl Johnstone · *Kitty Jarvis*
Sally Adcock · *Jane Smith*
Arnold Ridley · *Reverend Guy Atkins*
Deke Arlen · *Benny Wilmott*
Peggy Aitchison · *Vi Blundell*
Vincent Ball · *Kevin McArthur*
Peter Brookes · *Vince Parker*
Alan Gifford · *Lloyd Munroe*
Jimmy Hanley · *Jimmy Gudgeon*
Mollie Maureen · *Granny Fraser*
Anthony Morton · *Chef Carlos Raphael*
Sue Nicholls · *Marilyn Gates*
Wendy Padbury · *Stevie Harris*
Ann George · *Amy Turtle*
Susan Hanson · *Diane Lawton/Parker/Hunter*
Elisabeth Croft · *Edith Tatum*
Sheila Keith · *Mrs Cornet*
Joy Andrews · *Tish Hope*
Jack Haig · *Archie Gibbs*
Lew Luton · *Geoffrey Steele*
Rosalie Ashley · *Jane Templeton*
Gillian Betts · *Josephina Rafael*
Diane Grayson · *Penny Richardson*
David Lawton · *Bernard Booth*
Tony Norton · *Carlos Rafael*
Jo Richardson · *Mrs Whitton*
Ronald Allen · *David Hunter*
Diane Keen · *Sandra Gould*
Stan Stennett · *Harry Silver, Sid Hooper*
Edward Clayton · *Stan Harvey*
Sonia Fox · *Sheila Harvey/Mollison*
Chris Sullivan · *Jim Davis*
Zeph Gladstone · *Vera Downend*
Derek Farr · *Timothy Hunter*
David Valla · *Bill Warren*
Stephanie De Sykes · *Holly Brown*
Angus Lennie · *Shughie McFee*
Gretchen Franklin · *Myrtle Cavendish*
Stephen Hoye · *Chris Hunter*
Paul Henry · *Benny Hawkins*
Sue Lloyd · *Barbara Brady/Hunter*
Johnny Briggs · *Clifford Leyton*
Fiona Curzon · *Faye Mansfield*
Jack Woolgar · *Sam 'Carney' Carne*
Janet Hargreaves · *Rosemary Hunter*
Justine Lord · *Angela Kelly*
Peter Hill · *Arthur Brownlow*
Jean Rogers · *Julie Shepherd*
Pamela Vezey · *Kath Brownlow/Fellowes*

June Bolton · *Lia Hua*
Jeremy Sinden · *Anthony Mortimer*
Nell Curran · *Maureen Flynn*
Tony Adams · *Adam Chance*
Kathy Staff · *Doris Luke*
Merdelle Jordine · *Trina MacDonald*
Elaine Paige · *Caroline Winthrop*
Carl Andrews · *Joe MacDonald*
Lesley Daine · *Josie Welch*
Theresa Watson · *Linda Welch*
Kate Robbins · *Kate Loring*
Sandor Elès · *Paul Ross*
Dorothy Brown · *Lorraine Baker*
Charmain Eyre · *Mavis Hooper*
Denis Gilmore · *Terry Lawton*
Francesca Gonshaw · *Lisa Walters*
Jo Anne Good · *Carole Sands*
Anthony Woodruff · *Percy Dobson*
Ian Liston · *Ron Brownlow*
Reginald Marsh · *Reg Lamont*
Martyn Whitby · *Ashley Lamont*
Jean Kent · *Jennifer Lamont*
Frances White · *Kate Hamilton*
Margaret Nolan · *Denise Paget*
Nina Weill · *Nina Paget*
Paul Ashe · *Larry Wilcox*
Annette Andre · *Sarah Alexander*
Gabrielle Blunt · *Penelope Farrar*
Ann Castle · *Angela Reece*
Beth Ellis · *Helen Walker*
Arthur Howard · *Cecil Beecher Blount*
Mary Lincoln · *Joanna Freeman*
Gina Maher · *Patsy Harris*
Ken Parry · *'Dolly' Dolman*
Andrew Rattenbury · *Gary Corbett*
Angela Webb · *Iris Scott*
Dorota Zienska · *Anna Radek*
Arthur White · *John Latchford*
Gerald Sim · *Philip Reece*
Gabrielle Drake · *Nicola Freeman*
Philip Goodhew · *Daniel Freeman*
Dee Hepburn · *Anne Marie Wade*
Elsie Kelly · *Mrs Tardebigge*
Shona Lindsay · *Sara Briggs*
Norman Bowler · *Sam Benson*
Patrick Jordan · *Mr Darby*
Steven Pinder · *Roy Lambert*
Rachel Davies · *Elaine Winters*
Colette Barker · *Tracey Hobbs*
Kate Binchy · *Gloria Tilling*
Jim Dunk · *Gary Bristow*
Claire Faulconbridge · *Miranda Pollard*
John Line · *Stephen Fellowes*
Martin Smith · *Mickey Doyle*
Bernard Kay · *Harry Maguire*
Mary Kenton · *Edna Tilling*
Michael McNally · *Pete Maguire*
Jill Meers · *Maggie Bristow*
David Moran · *Kevin Banks*
Harry Nurmi · *Barry Hart*
Wendy Seely · *Sheila Maguire*

flashback that she'd survived – shortly before she, and Noele Gordon, sailed off on the *QE2* after more than 3000 melodramatic episodes.

With the arrival of William Smethurst (the man who'd ruled radio soap *The Archers* with a rod of iron), Hazel Adair and Peter Ling were felt to be surplus to requirements – Smethurst reckoned he could do their job himself. Finally, the soap that everyone loved to snigger at was given a refit and renamed *Crossroads: King's Oak* in a move to include more of the villagers – the idea being to make it a Midlands version of *Emmerdale*. But when the axe finally fell after 4510 episodes, it wasn't because the ratings were down or that the money had run out. *Crossroads* came off the air simpy because Andy Allen, head of drama at Central, decided he didn't like it.

With the closure of the motel on 4 April 1988, and Jill Chance delivering the final line, the gloves came off. What had once been a friendly joke that *Crossroads* wasn't perhaps the best-made show on TV became a simple statement of fact: the programme was rubbish and everyone knew it. Damning, but widely believed to be true by everyone except the viewers who'd loved it through thick and thin.

The decision to resurrect *Crossroads* in 2001 was not perhaps the most widely anticipated revival. Designed to spearhead ITV's new-look daytime schedule, it was an uneasy mix of the old and the new. No longer a motel, but a four-star hotel, Crossroads had a new manager, played by ex-***Casualty*** star Jane Gurnett. It's the common misconception in the soap genre that details more than six months old don't matter – a dangerous underestimation of viewers' memories. Familiar faces like Jill and Adam returned, but the continuity was slightly off (for instance, Jill has apparently reverted to her first married name without any real explanation) as if no-one thought it would matter or that anyone would ever notice. The ultimate betrayal was when the producers announced that they'd be killing Jill off, not for any other reason than because they could.

The series was put on hold for 18 months to give the production team a chance to rethink their approach. What emerged was possibly the most crass and offensive approach to soap ever. The logic went something like this (and please excuse the ***Little Britain***-type tone of voice): the gays are the style leaders in Britain – what the gays love one minute becomes the thing that mainstream culture loves next. The gays love soaps, so let's make *Crossroads* something the gays like. What do the gays like? Why, superficial characters, celebrity guest appearances for no reason whatsoever, lots of pink and gold paint, and fluff and . . . as we said, quite offensively crass.

There were some elements that were easier to accept, such as the addition of Sherrie Hewson, late of *Coronation Street*, and the lovely Jane Asher as the new hotel owner, a cold, calculating bitch called Angel. But when the *final* final end came, the only tears rolling down anyone's cheeks were of laughter: the entire year's-worth of episodes were revealed to have been the fantasies of a sad, deluded Angel, working on a checkout in a supermarket. For sheer brazen cheek, we wish the show had been more like that from the start.

Nigel Williams · *Douglas Brady*
David Sterne · *Brian Hobbs*
Shirin Taylor · *Sue Kirk*
Rosemary Smith · *Pat Reddington*
Terence Rigby · *Tommy 'Bomber' Lancaster*
Al Ashton · *Ray Grice*
Caroline Evans · *Fiona Harding*
Meryl Hampton · *Margaret Grice*
Kathryn Hurlbutt · *Debbie Lancaster*
Karen Murden · *Beverley Grice*
Ashok Kumar · *Ranjit Singh Rupal*
Simon Lowe · *Jason Grice*
Glynn Pritchard · *Paul*
Graham Seed · *Charlie Mycroft*
Margaret Stallard · *Mrs Babbitt*
Tara Shaw · *Tara James*
Alison Dowling · *Lisa Lancaster*
Christopher Duffy · *Jamie Maddingham*
Trevor Harrison · *Terry Butterworth*
Jeremy Nicholas · *John Maddingham*
Sean Blowers · *Tony Morris*
Nikki Brooks · *Rosie Harding*
Sophie Cook · *Sarah Jane Harvey*
Frances Cuka · *Mary Lancaster*
Valerie Holliman · *Eve Maddingham*
David Lodge · *The Walrus*
Breffni McKenna · *Dave Gould*
Terry Molloy · *Stan Harvey*
Jane Gurnett · *Kate Russell*
Sherrie Hewson · *Virginia Raven*
Roger Sloman · *Rocky Wesson*
Rebecca Hazlewood · *Beena Shah*
Cindy Marshall-Day · *Tracey Booth*
Di Sherlock · *Oona Stocks*
Jim Dunk · *Dave Stocks*
Colin Wells · *Jake Booth*
Gilly Gilchrist · *Billy Taylor*
Neil McCaul · *Patrick Russell*
Marc Jordan · *Des White*
Joanne Farrell · *Sarah-Jane Harvey, Louise Dixon*
Anne Charleston · *Betty Waddell*
Jane Asher · *Angel Samson/Angela*
Stuart Milligan · *Max Samson*
Luke Roberts · *Ryan Samson*
Graham McGrath · *Jimmy Samson*
Clare Wilkie · *Cleopatra Samson*
Shauna Shim · *'Phil'omena Wise*
Jessica Fox · *Belle Wise*
Freema Agyeman · *Lola Wise*
Ben Porter · *Vince Vaccaro*
Richard Burke · *Joe Lacey*
Matthew Maude · *Scott Booth*
Jim Dunk · *Dave Stocks*
Di Sherlock · *Oona Stocks*
Rebecca Hazlewood · *Beena Shah*
Cindy Marshall-Day · *Tracey Booth*
Lucy Pargeter · *Helen Raven*
John Bowler · *Ethan Black*

Creators Hazel Adair and Peter Ling (with Reg Watson)

Producers Reg Watson, Jack Barton, Philip Bowman, William Smethurst, Pieter Rogers, Eric Fawcett, Michele Buck

Writers Various, including Hazel Adair, Peter Ling, Keith Mills, Michaela Crees, Terrance Dicks, Malcolm Hulke, Paul Erickson, Don Houghton, David Whitaker, Gerald Kelsey, Bill Lyons, Paula Milne, Jon Rollason, Matthew Robinson, Andy Bernhardt, Gurpreet Bhatti, Tracy Brabin, Colin Brake, Robyn Charteris, Candy Denman, Helen Eatock, William Gallagher, Nandita Ghose, Tanika Gupta, Clive King, Pippa McCarthy, Paul Mousley, Lee Pressman, Paul Rose, Kevin Scouler, Arnie Smith, Keith Temple, Rick Waghorn, Alison Watt, Katharine Way

Theme Music A classic example of 'cheesy listening' music, Tony Hatch's theme began as a simple electric guitar and clarinet piece. An alternative clarinet-based version was played in a minor key for episodes with really sad endings. Paul McCartney covered it on Wings' *Venus and Mars* album, a version that was used on the show from 26 June 1975 until 1984. When the series changed its name to *Crossroads: King's Oak*, the familiar intro music was ditched completely for a combination of 'Greensleeves' and the theme from ***Emmerdale***. For the final revival of the show, the theme music was reduced to a soulless camp-fest on a harp.

TRIVIA

In 1990, producer William Smethurst would return to the same studios to make BSB's ill-fated sci-fi soap *Jupiter Moon*, an ambitious attempt to make a *Neighbours*-style, youth-centric soap opera set on board a European space station in orbit around Jupiter in the year 2050. Perhaps better than it had any right to be, *Jupiter Moon* sadly fell prey to the takeover of BSB by Sky, and was cancelled just as it was hitting its stride.)

WEBSITES

Crossroads has a surprisingly strong on-line presence, with websites focusing on either the classic series or either of the two revivals (and it is at least encouraging to learn that even that final series has its fans). Best place to start is the website of the official fan club: www.crossroads appreciation society.co.uk

that wasn't permitted, or making the wrong decision in a mental test), they would be automatically locked in, thereby requiring them to be 'bought out' of their confinement.

After about ten minutes in each zone, presenter O'Brien would lead the contestants through the twisted passages of the maze into the next themed area. Once the fourth zone had been completed, the remaining contestants would be led to the centre of the Crystal Maze, to the Crystal Dome. Inside the dome, the contestants were allotted five seconds for each of the time crystals they had won in order to gather as many gold paper tokens as they possibly could. Any silver tokens collected would be deducted from their gold total. An added inconvenience to their attempts to collect the paper tokens was the giant fans that would be switched on for the duration of the final game. If the total after deductions was more than 100, the contestants won an action-adventure holiday of their choice, such as white-water rafting, parachuting or stock car racing. In the first few series, a score between 50 and 100 resulted in the contestants winning a secondary, less expensive prize of a similar nature.

The Crystal Maze benefited in its first four seasons from a highly charismatic 'performance' by presenter Richard O'Brien. In particular, his bizarre ad-libs and asides to the camera about the mishaps befalling the inept contestants were a joy to behold. One especially entertaining element of the series concerned Richard's fictitious family life. Apparently, he lived in Medieval Zone with his Mumsie, who would pop up in most episodes to quiz the contestants in return for a time crystal. For the final two years, Richard O'Brien (having apparently decided to emigrate to California with Mumsie and her New Age biker boyfriend, Ralph) was replaced by ex-Tenpole Tudor lead singer Edward Tudor-Pole. Ed's style was very different from Richard's, and for most people he sadly was a bit of a pale imitation.

The maze itself was constructed inside one of the few studios in Britain big enough to encompass its vast sets, at Shepperton Studios. When the series was recommissioned for further episodes, Shepperton was unfortunately already booked, and the maze had to be relocated to an abandoned aircraft hanger in North Weald. Four Christmas children's specials, featuring younger contestants tackling the challenges of the maze, were also broadcast.

Trivia

The Crystal Maze was voted the second greatest TV game show of all time by readers of website www.ukgameshows.com. First place went to the rarely seen and barely remembered *The Mole* on Channel 5, which just shows how unrepresentative internet polls can be.

The Crystal Maze was based on a similar French game show called *Fort Boyard*, which had just been launched. *Boyard* co-creator Jacques Antoine – the man behind Chatsworth's other big hit, *Treasure Hunt* – came to the UK to develop this new spin on the same format. In 1998, Channel 5 (and subsequently satellite station Challenge TV) produced their own versions of *Fort Boyard*, filming in the very same French marine fort used by the original Gallic series.

Various locations around the UK boasted their very own *Crystal Maze* attractions, courtesy of Cyberdrome, which combined basic physical challenges with computer-simulated versions of some of the puzzles that had appeared in the TV show. In addition, a version of the game for home computers was developed by Sherston Software.

CSI: Crime Scene Investigation

Crime Drama | Jerry Bruckheimer Television/Alliance Atlantis for CBS (shown on Channel 5) | episode duration 50 mins | broadcast 6 Oct 2000–present (USA)

Regular Cast

William Petersen · *Gil Grissom*
Marg Helgenberger · *Catherine Willows*
Gary Dourdan · *Warwick Brown*
George Eads · *Nick Stokes*
Jorja Fox · *Sara Sidle*
Paul Guilfoyle · *Captain Jim Brass*
Eric Smanda · *Greg Sanders*
Robert David Hall · *Dr Al Robbins*

Creator Anthony E. Zuiker **Producers** Jerry Bruckheimer, Anthony E. Zuiker, Ann Donahue, Carol Mendelsohn (executive) William L. Petersen, Cynthia Chvatal (co-executive) Josh Berman, Danny Cannon, Andrew Lipsitz **Writers** Anthony E. Zuiker, Josh Berman, Danny Cannon, Carol Mendelsohn, Naren Shankar, Eli Talbert, Quentin Tarantino **Theme Music** 'Who Are You?' performed by Pete Townshend and The Who

Against the glitzy and seedy backdrop of a city that never sleeps, the forensic scientists of the Las Vegas Crime Lab apply brain and technological smarts to solving a ceaseless parade of grisly and often gruesome crimes. Headed by modern-day Sherlock Holmes Gil Grissom, the team – single mother and ex-stripper Catherine Willows, sometimes reformed gambler Warwick Brown, pretty boy Nick Stokes and the caustic Sara Sidle – apply their individual skills to the job in hand. Working alongside (and sometimes against) the police, in the form of the dour Captain Jim Brass, the crimes on offer range from the sublime (doppelgänger serial-killer judges), the ridiculous (scuba divers found dead in the middle of the Nevada Desert) to the wonderfully deranged (bodies coming alive on the slab), all supplemented by stylishly visceral post mortem sequences.

The very model of a modern television series, *CSI: Crime Scene Investigation* grew from small beginnings to a ratings-busting powerhouse of a franchise, single-handedly reviving the fortunes of the struggling CBS network (and on its transmission in the UK, that of Channel 5), and the career of William Petersen, whose star had briefly shone as FBI agent Will Graham in the first Hannibal Lecter movie, *Manhunter* (1986). Schlock

Hollywood action movie producer Jerry Bruckheimer brought this surprisingly intelligent series to TV screens after Disney passed it up, and Brit movie director Danny Cannon (*Judge Dredd*, 1995) was hired to shape much of the look and directorial style. Its insane pace, sharp scripting, well-drawn ensemble and pop video visuals have brought enough success to spawn two spin-offs, the sun-drenched *CSI: Miami* (headed by once-disgraced ***NYPD Blue*** actor David Caruso) and *CSI: New York* (top-billed by movie actor Gary Sinise). Most weeks on the US Neilson chart are dominated by the various incarnations of the show, and in 2005, with the likes of Quentin Tarantino attracted to write and direct, the *CSI* star shows no signs of dimming. Furthermore, with the launch of spin-off series *CSI: NY* and *CSI: Miami*, the programme seems to be becoming as much of a franchise as ***Star Trek*** once was. We look forward to watching '*CSI: Scunthorpe*' or '*CSI:* ***Trumpton***' sometime soon.

Cybill

Sitcom | Carsey Werner/Chuck Lorre/Jay Daniel/River Siren Productions for CBS (shown on Channel 4) | episode duration 30 mins | broadcast 2 Jan 1995–13 Jul 1998

Cast

Cybill Shepherd · *Cybill Sheridan*
Christine Baranski · *Maryann Thorpe*
Dedee Pfeiffer · *Rachel Blanders*
Alicia Witt · *Zoey Woodbine*
Alan Rosenberg · *Ira Woodbine*
Tom Wopat · *Jeff Robbins*

Creator Chuck Lorre **Producers** Tom Werner, Marcy Carsey, Cybill Shepherd, Alan Ball, Chuck Lorre, Jay Daniel (executive) **Writers** Various, including Chuck Lorre, Elaine Aronson, Howard M. Gould, Linda Wallem, Mike Langworthy, Lee Aronsohn, Alan Ball, Maria A. Brown, James L. Freedman, Erin A. Bishop, Susan Nirah Jaffee, Michael Poryes, Joey Murphy, John Pardee, Mark Hudis **Theme Music** Bobby Martin, Jim Latham

It's a trial being a middle-aged actress in the harsh climate of Hollywood, and feeling the pinch is the harassed Cybill Sheridan, formerly a successful performer, but now relegated to bit parts and commercials. Her life is made more complicated by those around her – daughters Zoey (redheaded feisty teenager) and Rachel (married with child), two ex-husbands who just won't go away and Cybill's hard drinking, hard loving best pal, Maryann. Living on a crumbling hillside overlooking LA, Cybill takes on the challenges of life after 40, and while life may have its ups and downs, it's certainly never all down hill.

The nearest America ever got to its own ***Absolutely Fabulous***, Cybill was a well-scripted sitcom that cast the always-likeable Cybill Shepherd in a role that has more than its fair share of asides to her career off screen. Since ***Moonlighting*** and an early movie career, the former model's career had by her own admission been on the slide, and this provided her with something of an outlet. The hits of the series, however, were Christine Baranski's gin-soaked turn as Maryann, always out for revenge on her ex, 'Dr Dick' (Cybill and Maryann are arrested for his murder in the final episode), and Alicia Witt as youngest daughter Zoey.

Although the series lasted just four seasons, both Cybill Shepherd and Christine Baranski would be nominated several times for Golden Globes and Emmys, with wins for both in 1995 and 1996.

Dad

Sitcom | BBC One | episode duration 30 mins | broadcast 25 Sep 1997–19 Dec 2000

Cast

George Cole · *Brian Hook*
Kevin McNally · *Alan Hook*
Julia Hills · *Beryl Hook*
Toby Ross-Bryant · *Vincent Hook*

Producers Andrew Marshall (executive), Marcus Mortimer **Writer** Andrew Marshall **Theme Music** Julian Stewart Lindsay

A gently amusing generation gap comedy that casts Kevin McNally as Alan, stuck in the middle between his cheerfully old-fashioned and set in his ways father, Brian, and 18-year-old son, Vincent. Alan and Brian have had time apart, and the middle Hook finds it difficult adapting, especially when he finds himself adopting some of his father's irritating habits. This doesn't sit well when he tries to be a hip, understanding father to Vincent.

Andrew Marshall seems destined to be a cut-price alternative to his former writing partner, David Renwick. Where Renwick has the all-conquering hits ***One Foot in the Grave*** and ***Jonathan Creek*** to his name, Marshall has the lesser hit ***2 Point 4 Children*** and the laughably lame *Strange* on his cv. *Dad* seemed to slip under the radar, which is a shame as it is much subtler than any of his other work. George Cole is endearingly loveable as Brian, and Kevin McNally is always watchable (and notable recently for his role in the Disney movie, *Pirates of the Caribbean*, 2002). A Christmas special, broadcast six months after the end of season two, rounded off the series.

Dad's Army

See pages 220–4

Daktari

Adventure Drama | Ivan Tors Films Inc./MGM Television for CBS (shown on BBC One) | episode duration 60 mins | broadcast 11 Jan 1966–15 Jan 1969 (USA)

Cast

Marshall Thompson · *Dr Marsh Tracy*
Cheryl Miller · *Paula Tracy*
Hari Rhodes · *Mike*
Hedley Mattingly · *District Officer Hedley*
Ross Hagen · *Bart Jason*
Erin Moran · *Jenny Jones*
Yale Summers · *Jack Dane*

Creators/Writers Ivan Tors and Art Arthur **Producers** Ivan Tors (executive), Harry Redmond Jr (associate), Leonard Kaufman **Theme Music** Al Mack

Replacing *Rawhide* in the CBS television schedules, *Daktari* (translates as 'Doctor') starred Marshall Thompson as a vet working from an animal reserve in the heart of Africa alongside his daughter, Paula, and assisted by various conservationists and natives. The series was spun off from the theatrically released pilot, *Clarence the Cross-Eyed Lion* (1965), and it is arguably the animals that are the real attractions, with Clarence and the cheeky chimp Judy garnering much attention. Stories frequently revolved around the team fending off poachers, finding injured animals in the jungle and tackling heavy conservation issues.

Producer Ivan Tors had a track record of working on TV series involving animals, having been producer on theatrical and TV versions of ***Flipper***, and would also turn his attention from cross-eyed lions to bears in 1967's *Gentle Ben*. Tors was experienced in all matters wildlife-related, and was also credited with supplying diving equipment and frogmen for the James Bond film *Thunderball* (1965). The series was filmed quite convincingly on the wildlife park that Tors owned in Los Angeles, and child star Erin Moran, who joined the cast for the final year, would later star as Joanie in ***Happy Days***.

Dallas

See pages 225–9

Dalziel and Pascoe

Detective | BBC One | episode duration 120 mins | broadcast 16 Mar 1996–present

Cast

Warren Clarke · *DS Andy Dalziel*
Colin Buchanan · *DS/DI Peter Pascoe*
Susannah Corbett · *Ellie Soper/Pascoe*
David Royle · *DS Edgar Wield*
Navin Chowdhry · *Cadet Sanjay Singh*
Peter Halliday · *Edward Soper*
Sylvie Kay · *Mary Soper*
Fred Pearson · *Dr Vickery*
Malcolm Tierney · *Deputy Chief Constable Raymond*
Jo-Anne Stockham · *WDC Shirley Novello*
Pippa Haywood · *ACC Rebecca Fenning*

Creator Reginald Hill, from his novels **Producers** Mal Young (executive), Warren Clarke (consulting), Michael Darbon (associate) Ann Tricklebank, Emma Hayter, Eric Abraham, Chris Parr, Paddy Higson, Andrew Rowley **Writers** Reginald Hill, Alan Plater, Malcolm Bradbury, Stan Hey, Robin Chapman, Bill Gallagher, Tony McHale, Elizabeth-Anne Wheal **Theme Music** Daemion Barry, Mark Thomas, Colin Towns, Rick Wentworth

The first outing for Reginald Hill's duo of mismatched northern detectives came in 1994 when comedians ***Hale and Pace*** attempted to go straight in a Yorkshire TV adaptation of the Hill novel *A Pinch of Snuff*. It was a fairly disastrous attempt, and Hill reportedly despised it so much that he became reluctant to sanction any further adaptations. Thankfully the BBC persuaded him otherwise, and *Dalziel and Pascoe* became a popular backbone to the schedules.

Warren Clarke is the perfect Andy Dalziel (pronounced Dee-Ell), big, brash, obnoxious but strangely likeable. Colin Buchanan provides the foil in the more empathic and sensitive Peter Pascoe. Each feature length episode sees the duo investigating crimes in and around the fictional town of Wetherton, with the bleakness of industrial Yorkshire providing much of the backdrop.

The early episodes chose to faithfully adapt the Hill novels, but as the source material was soon exhausted, original stories were required, adopting a less whimsical tone to its nearest rival, ***A Touch of Frost***. The series has been able to attract a high pedigree of writer, with Malcolm Bradbury, Stan Hey and Alan Plater all contributing scripts over the years.

Danger Man

Action-Adventure | ITC/ATV for ITV | episode duration 25/50 mins | broadcast 11 Sep 1960–12 Jan 1968

Principal Cast
Patrick McGoohan · *John Drake*

Creator Ralph Smart **Producers** Ian Stuart Black, Aida Young (associate), Ralph Smart **Writers** Various, including Brian Clemens, Ralph Smart, Ian Stuart Black, Jo Eisinger, John Roddick, Michael Pertwee, Donald Jonson, Wilfred Greatorex, David Stone, Philip Broadley **Theme Music** Edwin T. Astley

John Drake is an agent for a secret branch of NATO (and later MI9), working alone and across the globe. His brief is to prevent any interference with vital treaties between governments. That means no distractions, no messy solutions, no guns and definitely *no* girls.

The series that made Patrick McGoohan a household name was eclipsed by the one it inspired him to create, ***The Prisoner***. That inspiration came from the first episode of *Danger Man*, which was filmed in Portmeirion, the setting for the later series; and after four years, it also provided the catalyst for McGoohan's feeling trapped in a job he felt he couldn't resign from.

It's a shame *Danger Man* has been usurped somewhat as McGoohan's best-known work. It was intelligent (for an action series) and had strong traditional values (Drake's refusal to carry a gun or philander with women came at McGoohan's request). It also ran for 84 episodes – considerably longer than *The Prisoner*. But more than that, it was ahead of its time. With both the Profumo scandal and Kim Philby's defection to the USSR breaking in between its first and second series, British viewers had at least one spy they could count on to keep his eyes on the job.

Danger Mouse

Animation | Cosgrove Hall /Thames for ITV | episode duration 5–20 mins | broadcast 28 Sep 1981–19 Mar 1992

Regular Voice Cast
David Jason · *Danger Mouse, Colonel K, Nero, The Narrator – Isambard Sinclair*
Terry Scott · *Ernest Penfold*
Brian Trueman · *Nasaccio Mafiosa Cornetto/Stiletto*
Edward Kelsey · *Colonel K, Baron Silas Greenback, Professor Squawkencluck*

Creator Mike Harding, Brian Trueman **Producers** John Hambley (executive), Brian Cosgrove, Mark Hall **Writers** Brian Trueman, Angus Allen, Keith Scobie **Theme Music** Mike Harding

Every generation has its own TV superhero. Children of the 1960s thrilled to ***The Avengers***; kids in the 1970s got all worked up about ***The Six Million Dollar Man***; while in the 1980s there was nobody braver, stronger, tougher and more dashing than a small white mouse with an eyepatch.

Danger Mouse lived in a swanky hi-tech bachelor pad hidden inside a bright red letterbox in London's Baker Street (or 'Mayfair', as the announcer would have it). Whenever incidents of national security required specialist help, DM received a message on his living room video-phone from his boss, Colonel K. Upon receiving the briefing, DM and his faithful (if rather blundering and frightened) sidekick Penfold headed off in the superhero's flying yellow car to thwart the schemes of whatever dastardly villain was causing chaos. The Professor Moriarty to DM 's Sherlock Holmes is Baron Silas Greenback, a sinister toad with plans for world domination and a seemingly perpetual sore throat. Baron Greenback's sidekicks were Italian gangster crow Stiletto and a giant white hairy caterpillar called Nero. Whatever the threat to national or international security, Danger Mouse could always be relied upon to right wrongs and defeat the villain, whether that threat came from Baron Greenback, Professor Squawkencluck or the horrifically evil vegetarian vampire duck, Count Duckula (who proved so popular that he received his own highly successful spin-off series).

A rather cheeky send-up of everything from Patrick McGoohan's ***Danger Man*** through to the *Bond* films and the Republic serials of the 1930s (such as *Flash Gordon*), *Danger Mouse* represented another huge success from Britain's animation geniuses Cosgrove Hall productions (the people behind classic children's shows such as ***Chorlton and the Wheelies***, *Cockleshell Bay* and *The Wind in the Willows*). Running for nearly 150 episodes over ten seasons, *Danger Mouse* was so highly regarded and successful that the programme was sold to 31 countries

Continued on page 230

Captain Mainwaring (Arthur Lowe) and the U-Boat Commander (Philip Madoc).

Dad's Army

On 14 May 1940, Secretary of State for War Anthony Eden announces the formation of the Local Defence Volunteers, an organisation that enables men aged between 17 and 75 to enlist as voluntary defenders of our great nation against invasion from German paratroopers. Two months later, directed by Prime Minister Winston Churchill, the oversubscribed and under-resourced LDV becomes known as the 'Home Guard'. In the small town of Walmington-on-Sea, on the south coast of England, a Home Guard platoon is formed under the control of local bank manager George Mainwaring. His recruits – including his deputy manager at the bank, an elderly butcher, a black-marketeer and a very 'stupid boy' – may lack vitality, but they more than make up for this with their enthusiasm, determination and patriotism.

Created by Jimmy Perry initially as a vehicle for himself to star in, *Dad's Army* is far more important from a historical point of view than it ever receives credit for. If it weren't for Perry, we might never have even heard of a long-forgotten element of British life during World War Two. As a teenager, Perry had actually served in the Local Defence Volunteers. After the war, Perry became a writer and actor, learning his crafts in weekly rep before moving into television. But Perry soon realised that if he wanted a starring part he'd have to write one for himself. While scouting around for ideas for a script, he remembered his time in the LDV and began researching the history of the Home Guard, but was dismayed to find that aside from a few pamphlets, there existed a pitiful amount of documentation on the subject – the efforts of the Home Guard had, in effect, been forgotten. This made him determined to forge ahead with his idea. Inspired by the Will Hay movie *Oh, Mr Porter* (1937), Perry structured his first script (which at that point was called 'The Fighting Tigers') around three characters – a pompous, middle-aged man, an old man and a boy.

It was while acting in the BBC sitcom *Beggar My Neighbour* that Perry met the producer David Croft and eventually plucked up the courage to show him his script. It was a meeting that led to the formation of one of TV comedy's most inventive and productive partnerships. With the support of the BBC's head of comedy Michael Mills and head of light entertainment Tom Sloan, the series – by now called *Dad's Army* at Sloan's suggestion – was given the go-ahead, with Perry as writer and Croft as producer and co-writer.

Arthur Lowe had always been Jimmy Perry's choice for Mainwaring, though David Croft had originally favoured Thorley Walters or Jon Pertwee. It was Michael Mills who suggested John Le Mesurier for Wilson, noting, 'He suffers so well.' The part of elderly butcher and war veteran Jack Jones was offered to Clive Dunn, who although only 48 at the time had made a name for himself playing old duffers. Again, things could have been so different: original first choice for Jonesie was Jack Haig (whom many will remember as the spectacle-raising Leclerc in Perry and Croft's other wartime sitcom ***'Allo, 'Allo***), while in reserve was a 28-year-old David Jason (think of him as Blanco in ***Porridge*** to imagine that!).

At just 22, Ian Lavender was the baby of the bunch, almost 50 years younger than Arnold Ridley (a noted playwright whose work included *The Ghost Train*), who played the sleepy Godfrey with the dicky bladder. Although young Pike was effectively Perry as a young man, the writer had created the part of Walker, the black-marketeer, for himself to play. As the principal roles began to be cast, Perry was advised that there was a conflict of interests; even if the team was able to give equal weight to each player in the ensemble, some might feel the writer was giving himself the best lines. Somewhat reluctantly, Perry stepped aside and James Beck was duly cast in the role that would make him a household name.

Just a few months younger than Arnold Ridley, John Lawrie had been a classical actor, a regular at the Old Vic and Stratford, a contemporary of Gielgud and had twice collaborated with Alfred Hitchcock. For him, the material was forever sub-standard, perhaps because he was always more than a little put out that his morbid Scottish sailor-turned-philatelist-turned-undertaker received greater critical acclaim than his Hamlet.

With such an unimpressive bunch of rather weak men, it wouldn't have been appropriate to have them face the genuine enemy (and in fact only a very few episodes contained any Germans at all). Therefore the nemesis of the platoon became the air raid warden Hodges, with his aggressive booming voice and dislike for Mainwaring and his 'toy solders'. For this contemptible character, the producer chose Bill Pertwee, an actor with a reputation for being one of the most likeable and pleasant men in the business. Croft knew that Pertwee would be able to soothe any friction that might arise among such a large cast – and also knew that the stalwart Pertwee would be less likely to complain during all those scenes in which someone had to end up falling into a freezing cold river that inevitably became part of the stories as the years passed by.

The vast majority of British comedy is performed against a backdrop of class awareness and never more so than on the field of battle. In the case of *Dad's Army*, that 'battlefield' would be near the aforesaid freezing cold river somewhere on the outskirts of

Sitcom
BBC One
Episode Duration: 25 mins
Broadcast: 31 Jul 1968–12 Nov 1977

Regular Cast
Arthur Lowe · *Captain George Mainwaring*
John Le Mesurier · *Sergeant Arthur Wilson*
Clive Dunn · *Lance Corporal Jack Jones*
John Laurie · *Private James Frazer*
Arnold Ridley · *Private Charles Godfrey*
Ian Lavender · *Private Frank Pike*
James Beck · *Private Joe Walker*
Bill Pertwee · *ARP Warden Willy Hodges*
Frank Williams · *Reverend Timothy Farthing/The Vicar*
Edward Sinclair · *Mr Yateman/The Verger*
Janet Davies · *Mavis Pike*
Harold Bennett · *Mr Blewitt*
Pamela Cundell · *Mrs Fox*
Caroline Dowdeswell · *Janet King*
Olive Mercer · *Mrs Yeatman*
Queenie Watts · *Mrs Peters*
Robert Raglan · *Colonel Pritchard*
John Ringham · *Captain Bailey*
Talfryn Thomas · *Private Cheeseman*
Colin Bean · *Private Sponge*
Eric Longworth · *Mr Gordon – Town Clerk*
E. V. H. Emmett · *Newsreel Commentator*

Creators/Writers Jimmy Perry and David Croft

Producer David Croft

Theme Music While music from the 1940s was used in the episodes themselves, the theme song – 'Who do you think you are kidding, Mr Hitler?' – was written especially for the series by Jimmy Perry (lyrics) and Derek Taverner (music). Its authentic sound was created by the Band of the Coldstream Guards and the vocal talents of Bud Flanagan (one half of hugely popular wartime entertainers Flanagan and Allen). Sadly, the song would be Flanagan's last; he died, aged 72, just a few months after it was recorded.

TRIVIA

We must address a matter of pronunciation. While pretty well everyone knows that the name of Arthur Lowe's character is pronounced 'Mannering' there are still some people who will insist on pronouncing 'Mesurier' as if it were actual French ('Mezooriay'). The man himself always said it to rhyme with 'treasurer'.

Walmington-on-Sea, while the class awareness centred on Sergeant Wilson, who had it, and Captain Mainwaring, who didn't – or at least felt insecure about the extent to which Wilson was aware of class. Huw Weldon, head of television when the series was first broadcast, had expressed his surprise when he discovered that Arthur Lowe would be playing the bumbling captain and John Le Mesurier the well-spoken subordinate; he'd assumed the casting would be the other way round and regarded this as a clever twist on the part of the two writers. When Wilson points out the class reversal to Mainwaring, the captain replies: 'There's no chip on my shoulder, Wilson. I'll tell you what there is on my shoulder – three pips, and don't you forget it.' Mainwaring's pomposity is punctured by his never-seen wife, Elizabeth. The only hint we ever get of her comes when Mainwaring is trying to get to sleep in the bottom level of a bunk bed while eyeing an intimidatingly rounded dip in the underside of the top bunk. Aside from that heavy curve, Elizabeth exists solely in the timid facial expressions of Arthur Lowe during Mainwaring's calls home.

Wilson's primary characteristic is laziness. Despite his public school background and aristocratic pretensions, all he wants is an easy life. Unfazed by Mainwaring's insecurities, he's happy to be only second in command; even then it was a position of seniority he took only at Mainwaring's insistence. His relationship with Mrs Pike is hinted at through innuendo rather than openly confirmed, as is the suggestion that he is the biological father of Pike. Limp, mollycoddled 17-year-old Frank is too young to be in the regular army but signed up to join the Home Guard despite his mother's concerns that he might catch a cold, or worse – croup. He's not quite the 'stupid boy' Mainwaring has labelled him, however. In one exchange, Pike asks 'Uncle' Arthur why he's always at his house last thing at night and first thing in the morning yet he never hears him leave or arrive. As Wilson tries to avade embarrassing questions by claiming that he comes and goes very quietly, Pike mutters: 'You never do anything else quietly.'

Clive Dunn had been a prisoner of war during World War Two, but Corporal Jones first saw active service in 1884 in the Sudan, fighting the 'fuzzy wuzzies'. Despite his advancing years, Jonesie remains a popular figure in Walmington-on-Sea, admired by Mainwaring (possibly because he's the only member of the platoon to ever show him respect), and when it looks as if he'll be removed from the Home Guard because he's too old (in 'The Showing Up of Corporal Jones'), the rest of the gang help out to ensure that Jones is seen to complete an assault course in record time (thanks to a little assistance and subterfuge on the part of the men). First in line to volunteer, forever at hand to make ridiculous suggestions and always one beat out of step on parade, Corporal Jones became the series' most adored character, and many of his sayings evolved into catchphrases that are indelibly linked to the show: 'Permission to speak, Sir'; 'The cold steel – they don't like it up 'em' (to which we can only add: who does?); and of course the oft-bellowed 'Don't panic!' a phrase later appropriated by ***The Hitchhiker's Guide to the Galaxy***.

There are far too many brilliant episodes to list here, but each season has its own outright classics, many of which gave Arthur Lowe the chance to shine among the bunch of scene stealers that made up the rest of the cast. The very first episode, 'The Man and the Hour', begins with a flash forward to the 'present day', where Mainwaring is addressing the 'I'm Backing Britain' campaign, explaining how he's been backing Britain since 1940, while the episode ends with the captain summing up the feelings of a nation: 'Come on, Adolf – we're ready for you!' 'Mum's Army' replayed *Brief Encounter* (1945) with an ill-fated love affair between George Mainwaring and Mrs Gray (Carmen Silvera), while the 1975 Christmas special, 'My Brother and I', gave Arthur Lowe the chance to play an alternative Mainwaring in the form of the captain's louche brother, Barry. In the most famous episode of all, 'A Deadly Attachment', the platoon captured the crew of a German U-boat. Affronted by the arrogance of the British, the U-boat commander (Philip Madoc) decides to keep a list of the names of all who dare to challenge Germany and after Pike sings a song that begins 'Whistle while you work/Hitler is a twerp', the commander demands to know the boy's name too. Mainwaring's foolish response has become the stuff of legend: almost as soon as the episode ended, 'Don't tell him, Pike!' had joined the series' long list of wonderful catchphrases.

With so many elderly actors and with the real war only lasting six years, the show couldn't have gone on for ever, but it did its best, amassing nine series in all. That the first one to die happened to be the second youngest in the cast, James Beck, was a loss that affected the rest of the cast terribly. Missing from all but some brief location footage in the last two episodes of series six, Private Walker's last lines come in the series finale, 'The Recruit'. Mainwaring makes his way down the line inspecting the troops as usual, but where Walker should be there's just a gap and a scrap of paper, a letter from Walker explaining that he's popped up to London to do a deal with a 'geezer [for] a pony' and thanking the captain for letting him off. After much agonising, Croft and Perry decided that they wanted to keep the front row of the parade even, so drafted in a character from a previous episode, the buck-toothed Welshman Mr Cheeseman, a war correspondent (as signified by the initials on his armband – 'WC'). Though no reflection on Talfryn Thomas, Cheeseman was not deemed a success and for the final two series, Private Sponge (one of the regular supporting artists) was promoted to the front line to make up the numbers.

Though the team continued to produce the programme after Beck's death, it was inevitable that the series would have to come to an end eventually. John Le Mesurier had been very ill for that final year (his face looks distressingly gaunt throughout the series), while Arthur Lowe had begun to suffer from bouts of narcolepsy that were affecting his performance. Carrying on without James Beck had been hard for everyone and they all agreed they didn't wish to go through that again. The ninth series therefore became their last, while they were all still able to show up and say their lines. 'Never Too Old' brought the series to a close with old Jack Jones finally making an

TRIVIA

Dad's Army was also a hit on radio from 1973 to 1977, with actor Graham Stark (and later Larry Martyn) standing in for James Beck. A feature film was released through Columbia Pictures in 1971, revising and condensing the events of the first series, and a successful stage show toured the country in 1975–6.

A little-known sequel was broadcast by Radio 4 in the early 1980s. Written by Michael Knowles and Harold Snoad, *It Sticks Out Half a Mile* was due to star Arthur Lowe again as Mainwaring, who decides to buy Walmington-on-Sea's pier and turn it into a major tourist attraction. Returning to Swallow Bank, where he was once manager, he's surprised to find Wilson now in charge there. Sadly, after a pilot episode was recorded, Arthur Lowe died suddenly. Encouraged by Lowe's widow, Joan Cooper, the producers remounted the series with John Le Mesurier joined by Ian Lavender as Frank Pike and with the entrepreneurial Mainwaring replaced by Bill Pertwee as former ARP Warden Hodges. Aired from 13 November 1983 to 9 October 1984, the series ran for 13 episodes, though it's never been repeated in full. The central concept was later recycled by Knowles and Snoad for television, first in 1985 as *Walking the Planks*, a 30-minute one-off for the BBC starring Michael Elphick as Ron Archer (effectively the role played by Bill Pertwee in the radio series) and Richard Wilson as the bank manager, Talbot. In 1987, a seven-part series called *High and Dry* was made by Yorkshire Television for ITV, with Bernard Cribbins as Archer and Richard Wilson once again playing Talbot.

TRIVIA
The BBC's 2004 poll for Best British Sitcom placed *Dad's Army* fourth, despite a valiant defence from comedian Phil Jupitus. Its position below ***The Vicar of Dibley, Blackadder*** and ***Only Fools and Horses*** might well be due to the fact that World War Two is now more a moment in history than an event in the living memory of most of its audience. But *Dad's Army* was also the oldest sitcom in the Top Ten and the highest ranking out of any comedy produced during the 1970s. Its longevity and the fact that its repeats continue to attract healthy ratings nearly 30 years after its last episode show just how adored the series still is. For us, *Only Fools* may have won the battle, but without a doubt it is *Dad's Army* that won the war.

WEBSITE
www.dadsarmy.cwc.net/ – site of the official *Dad's Army* Appreciation Society.

honest woman of his lady friend Mrs Fox ('Does she love me for myself . . . or does she love me for my meat?' asks the nervous butcher) only for their wedding night to be interrupted by the threat of invasion. The final scene, in which the ageing actors turn to face the camera to toast 'Britain's Home Guard', is so poignant it can reduce a grown man to tears. Other series might have timed their curtain call to coincide with the end of the war, but as this episode draws to a close, the war is still raging. Nevertheless, despite the power of their enemy (so wittily observed in those opening titles of the swastika arrowheads cornering quivering Union flags on the southern tip of a map of England), these old men know that they're playing their part to help win it. And they did, you know.

What pervades the series is a sense of accuracy that makes it much easier to believe that these characters actually existed. In the first series, the voice-over on the newsreels was provided by E. V. H. Emmett, who'd fulfilled that function for real during the war. The attention to detail matched that of any high-budget period drama: Mainwaring's spectacles were a genuine artefact from the 1940s, the many rows of tins and boxes of food were designed to match real products from the time, and the costume designers even made sure that Mainwaring's uniform was made of a better-quality material than the others to show his higher status in the community. The first series poked fun at the men's ramshackle equipment and uniforms but even that was a pretty accurate reflection of the truth. The Local Defence Volunteer groups across the country were so over-subscribed that in the first weeks the official uniform consisted solely of an armband bearing the initials 'LDV', while the lengths some battalions went to in order to obtain weapons leave the *Dad's Army* gang's assault on Jonesie's father's war museum ('Museum Piece') look almost tame by comparison.

Nostalgia is the stuff of many a television programme, but in the case of *Dad's Army* it's its greatest asset; moreover, as Victoria Wood has noted, by being already set in the past a programme will never date like a contemporary situation comedy does. When *Dad's Army* first appeared, the war had ended over 20 years ago and recollection of the daily hardships of the time, such as rationing, would have already faded to a large degree in the memories of those viewers who had lived through them. The series was filmed in the town of Thetford, and it's said that the arrival of the cast each year seemed to guarantee long, hot summers. Even this, the great British obsession with the weather, seemed affected by the warmth of these brave old men, another element that helped make the series the stuff of rose-tinted memories. The Home Guard may well have been at war with a deadly enemy, but summers were long and everyone knew they had a part to play and everyone's contribution was valued, even if they were incompetent (or merely incontinent).

Nostalgia is the stuff of many a television programme, but in the case of *Dad's Army* it's its greatest asset

No, you're not dreaming – it's Bobby Ewing in the shower.

Dallas

On Sunday 2 April 1978, the CBS Network in the USA aired the first episode of a series that was to change the face of television across the globe. Initially, they didn't have much faith in their new show. It was one of a number of programmes that had been created as possible long-running series; they commissioned only five episodes, intending to give the go-ahead for more if the show took off. Following the broadcast of that first 'mini series', CBS recommissioned a whole season for the following autumn, realising they had a potential hit on their hands.

When *Dallas* began, it was originally planned to be the story of a young woman from a middle-class background and her marriage into a hugely wealthy family. In fact, the series was created to be a star vehicle for actress Linda Evans, whom producers felt would be ideal as naïve Pamela. However, Evans turned down the part, thinking that it wasn't really for her (a decision she soon regretted, but which she made sure didn't happen again when a very similar role in ***Dynasty*** was offered to her!), and young actress Victoria Principal (who'd had a minor role in disaster flick *Earthquake*, 1974, among others) took on the pivotal role of Pamela, the woman responsible for bringing two warring families together. Viewers quickly discover that there is a history of bad blood between Pamela's family, the Barneses, and the wealthy Ewings. Way back in the 1930s, Pam's father Digger Barnes felt that his old friend Jock Ewing had diddled him out of the oil reserves, money and land that were rightfully his. Not only that, Jock also stole the beautiful Miss Ellie away from him. For 40 years, that hatred and mistrust between the Barnes and Ewing families had been simmering away, with Jock now in charge of the hugely successful Ewing Oil company and Digger an alcoholic and practically penniless. When Jock Ewing's youngest son, Bobby, fell in love with Digger's daughter Pam, the lovebirds decided to marry in secret, largely because they knew that both families wouldn't be in the slightest bit happy about what they'd done.

And so began the first short season of *Dallas*. Predictably enough, having a Barnes in the family caused no end of heartache for the

Soap
Lorimar for CBS (shown on BBC One/ITV)
Episode Duration: 50 mins
Broadcast: 2 Apr 1978–3 May 1991 (USA)

Regular Cast
Barbara Bel Geddes, Donna Reed · *'Miss Ellie' Ewing/Farlow*
Jim Davis · *John Ross 'Jock' Ewing Sr*
Patrick Duffy · *Bobby Ewing*
Linda Gray · *Sue Ellen Ewing*
Larry Hagman · *John Ross 'JR' Ewing Jr*
Steve Kanaly · *Ray Krebbs*
Ken Kercheval · *Cliff Barnes*
Victoria Principal · *Pamela Ewing*
Charlene Tilton · *Lucy Ewing/Cooper*
Susan Howard · *Donna Krebbs*
Howard Keel · *Clayton Farlow*
Priscilla Presley · *Jenna Wade*
Dack Rambo · *Jack Ewing*
Sheree J. Wilson · *April Stevens*
George Kennedy · *Carter McKay*
Cathy Podewell · *Cally Harper/Ewing*
Kimberly Foster · *Michelle Beaumont/Barnes*
Sasha Mitchell · *James Richard Beaumont*
Lesley-Anne Down · *Stephanie Rogers*
Barbara Stock · *Liz Adams*
John Beck · *Mark Graison*
Barbara Carrera · *Angelica Nero*
Mary Crosby · *Kristin Shepard*
Omri Katz · *John Ross Ewing*
Joshua Harris · *Christopher Ewing*
David Wayne, Keenan Wynn · *Willard 'Digger' Barnes*
Audrey Landers · *Afton Cooper*
Jared Martin · *'Lusty Dusty' Farlow*
Morgan Brittany · *Katherine Wentworth*
Christopher Atkins · *Peter Richards*
Steve Forrest · *Ben Stivers, Wes Parmalee*
Deborah Rennard · *Sly Lovegren*
Deborah Tranelli · *Phyllis*
Deborah Shelton · *Mandy Winger*
Andrew Stevens · *Casey Denault*
Jack Scalia · *Nicholas Pearce, Joey Lombardi*

Creator David Jacobs

Producers Leonard Katzman, Philip Capice, David Paulsen, James H. Brown, Peter Dunne, Joel J. Feigenbaum, Cliff Fenneman, Arthur Bernard Lewis, Lee Rich, Larry Hagman

Writers Various

Theme Music Jerrold Immel

Ewings – and one member of the clan in particular found Pam's presence too much to bear. Jock's eldest son, and heir to the Ewing fortune was JR, a man to whom lying, cheating, stealing, backstabbing and manipulating came as easily as breathing, eating or sleeping. Cast as JR was Larry Hagman (after future ***Falcon Crest*** star Robert Foxworth declined the part), revelling in a rare opportunity for him to play the villain. Audiences used to seeing Hagman as a light comedy actor in shows like ***I Dream of Jeannie*** watched, enraptured, as JR pulled off yet another underhand trick or attempted to destroy a rival's life or career. The person on the receiving end of much of JR's plotting was Digger Barnes's son Cliff – the pair of them would lock horns throughout the entire series. Indeed, Larry Hagman and Ken Kercheval (Cliff) would become the only actors to appear right the way through the 13-year run. Completing the Ewing clan were veteran actor Jim Davis as patriarch Jock, Hollywood legend and one-time Hitchcock collaborator Barbara Bel Geddes as the saintly and forever-suffering Miss Ellie, former *Man from Atlantis* star Patrick Duffy, Steve Kanaly as cowboy Ray Krebbs (who turns out to be Jock's illegitimate son) and the vertically challenged actress Charlene Tilton as cousin Lucy (nicknamed 'the poison dwarf' by *Dallas* fan and radio DJ Terry Wogan).

The character that the audience had the most sympathy with was JR's put-upon wife Sue Ellen, a woman for whom life's whisky bottles were perpetually more than half empty. When JR cruelly points out her failings – 'Sue Ellen, you're a drunk, a tramp and an unfit mother!' – we can't help but agree with him while simultaneously shouting back at the TV that all of poor Sue Ellen's problems are a direct result of JR's appalling behaviour towards her. JR and Sue Ellen's marriage was a tumultuous one, a textbook example of a couple that couldn't live with *or* without each other either. For every affair JR had, Sue Ellen would do her best to try to match him, with both 'Lusty Dusty' Farlow and toyboy Peter Richards (played by a post-*Blue Lagoon* (1980) Christopher Atkins) bedding the former Miss Texas, much to JR's fury. As their marriage fell apart and a custody battle for their son John Ross loomed, JR tried to get rid of his wife once and for all and had her committed to a lunatic asylum. Life was certainly never dull at the Ewing family home of Southfork Ranch . . .

Over the course of the first few years, *Dallas*'s format began to alter. Even when recommissioned for a full-length season on the back of the mini series, it still bore the pretence of being a 'serious drama', with episodes largely consisting of stand-alone plotlines rather than ongoing stories. However, by the third season viewing figures had rocketed and the decision was taken to further 'soapify' the programme by allowing plots to develop over a long period of time. Along with its own spin-off series, ***Knots Landing*** (detailing the life of another Ewing brother, Gary, in suburban California), *Dallas* was usually regarded by viewers and critics as the most serious and realistic of the batch of 1980s prime-time American soap operas – although we realise the very nature of the genre means this is a little like saying being shot with a Colt .45 is the classiest way of having two slugs pumped into one's chest.

Speaking of which, *Dallas* was more than happy when flirting with high camp and melodrama: the most famous storyline in soap opera history – Who Shot JR? – came about when producers were suddenly told by the network that they had been granted an additional few episodes for that season. With no storylines prepared, it was decided to go ahead with a classic whodunit that would both conclude that series and open up the next one. Practically every single character was given a motive for the attempted murder, and in order to maintain the secret of the attacker's identity for as long as possible, every member of the cast (with the exception of Charlene Tilton) was filmed pulling the trigger.

For several months, it appeared as though that might be the end of Larry Hagman and JR. Contract negotiations between Hagman and the producers had broken down, and they were already talking about having JR's ambulance crash on the way to hospital, resulting in him having to undergo plastic surgery (and thus enabling the producers to recast the part). While on a promotional tour of the UK, Hagman appeared on ***Wogan*** to publicise the forthcoming shooting episode. When Hagman revealed live on air that he might not be returning to the series, the public uproar was immense and immediate. Newspapers and magazines across the globe were dumbfounded by the producers' hesitancy to sign their leading star back up again, and loudly proclaimed that *Dallas* simply wouldn't be *Dallas* without JR. Shortly after, Hagman was back on board with an increased salary and more input into the storylines and production as a whole – an outcome more favourable than Hagman had probably ever imagined. In the end, the episode in which the attacker's identity was revealed gained astronomical viewing figures, with sealed film canisters being shipped under armed guard to broadcasters such as the BBC to ensure no 'leaks' took place prior to transmission. All around the world, people donned 'I Shot JR' T-shirts, and bookmakers raked in the money from punters eager to wager on the identity of the culprit, who in the end turned out to be Kristen, Sue Ellen's sister and JR's spurned lover, motivated by revenge in its most classic guise. Hell hath no fury . . .

When Hagman revealed live on air that he might not be returning to the series, the public uproar was immense and immediate.

While Hagman successfully clung to the part of a lifetime, not everyone's fortunes on *Dallas* were so good. Producers were taking a tougher line, with the sudden recasting or departure of regular characters. The first was Jock Ewing, written out in an aeroplane crash in South America following the sudden death of actor Jim Davis. When Barbara Bel Geddes fell ill, Donna Reed (famed for *It's a Wonderful Life*, 1946) was brought in to fill Miss Ellie's comfy shoes. But the recasting just didn't seem to work. As soon as Geddes was well enough to return, Reed's contract was abruptly terminated (tragically Donna Reed died shortly afterwards). However, none of these come close to the revolving door that was Bobby Ewing's departure from and shock return to Southfork.

Patrick Duffy had become concerned about being typecast as Bobby and asked to be permanently written out of *Dallas*. In an end-of-series cliffhanger, Bobby was mown down by Katherine Wentworth while trying to save Pam's life. Millions of viewers sobbed into their hankies as Bobby died in hospital. However, nowhere near as many of them returned the following year to watch a Bobby-less *Dallas*. Producers began to panic at the falling ratings and asked Hagman to try to persuade Duffy to make a return to the programme. In conditions of the utmost secrecy, Hagman managed to convince his friend to come back, but aside from those two individuals and a few very senior production staff, nobody in the rest of the cast or crew had any clue about Duffy's return. Producer Leonard Katzman flew from the usual studios in Los Angeles to New York to film Patrick Duffy in a shower for a 'soap commercial'. Meanwhile, Victoria Principal recorded a scene in which her character Pam conducts an innocuous conversation with her new boyfriend, Mark Graison, who is having a shower. However, the episode as transmitted combined these two pieces of footage, providing a shock reversal that left Victoria Principal as uproariously baffled as the rest of the viewing audience. It's reported that Principal was so shocked that she instantly telephoned Duffy and started screaming with excitement down the line at him.

For *Dallas* aficionados, the 'lost season' of Pam's dream provides them with endless hours of amusement trying to work out at exactly which point the true events stopped and the dream events began.

Of course, the resurrection of Bobby Ewing presented producers with a challenge: exactly how were they going to rationalise such a plainly daft decision without losing the respect of viewers? In the end, they went for perhaps the simplest yet most outrageous concept, that Pam had in fact dreamt the entire previous season. For *Dallas* aficionados, the 'lost season' of Pam's dream provides them with endless hours of amusement trying to work out at exactly which point the true events stopped and the dream events began. And how could actors and characters introduced to the series during Pam's dreams now be walking around in the 'awake' world? Perhaps it's best not to think about it too much and just revel in the rare moment of apology from a TV network combined with audacity demonstrated by the *Dallas* production team in acknowledging that they had made a mistake in letting Patrick Duffy go, and then doing whatever they had to do in order to bring him back. By simply brushing over the matter and getting on with telling gripping stories, *Dallas* achieved what ***EastEnders*** spectacularly failed to do in resurrecting Den Watts: not losing the faith of their viewers.

In fact, viewers stayed remarkably loyal to *Dallas*, ensuring it had a place among the top-rated shows for many years. However, by the end of the 1980s the programme had begun to show its age. Many of the former regular cast members had left to pursue other projects, and the replacement characters (such as JR's young hillbilly bride Cally Harper and illegitimate son James Beaumont) simply lacked the charisma and depth of those that had departed. *Dallas* came to a close in May 1991 after a staggering 356 episodes, having outstayed its welcome by perhaps just one series. In the last episode, JR faces a crisis of self-belief. He has lost everyone and everything that he values and he considers taking his own life. Suddenly, he is visited by an otherworldly figure who offers to show him how the lives of his family and friends would have turned out had he never existed. What could easily have turned out to be 'It's a Wonderfully Lucrative Life' is saved by the fact that *Dallas* was the 'soap that dared to dream'. Naturally enough, there is a final twist in the tale as we discover that the strange figure guiding JR (played with sinister glee by *Cabaret* (1972) star Joel Grey) turns out to be a demon rather than an angel. Hearing a shot ring out in JR's room, Bobby rushes through the door and stops in his tracks, with a look of horror on his face . . .

You simply can't keep a good bastard down (particularly in ratings-driven TV) and the Stetson-wearing man we love to hate returned to our screens along with the rest of his family in two TV movies – *JR Returns* (1996) and *War of the Ewings* (1998). Unfortunately, neither of these telemovies successfully recaptured the feel of *Dallas* the series. Little better was a spin-off movie screened during the show's original run. *Dallas: The Early Years* (1986) flashed back to the events of the feud between Jock and Digger and filled in a lot of the background story. However, if you were a regular viewer, little of what was shown in the prequel movie came as any surprise.

By the dawn of the 1990s, *Dallas* simply didn't fit into the TV schedules. The avaricious culture of the 1980s had made way for a much less money-focused and selfish attitude. Greed wasn't good any more, and as such the exploits of the mega-wealthy no longer seemed something to aspire to for many viewers, merely crude. *Dallas* charted the acquisitive forces of the 1980s from their roots in the late 1970s through to their last gasps in the dawn of the 1990s. *Dallas* was also a soap opera that revelled in displays of overt wealth and (almost uniquely for a soap) a programme that eschewed a traditional female-centric series of family and relationship issues for the more macho arena of the boardroom. In JR, the Eighties had its ultimate icon – a self-made man not ashamed to trample over anyone to get his own way and satiate his basest desires. And although JR Ewing-like activity seems to have diminished since the yuppie years, we're delighted that a TV show like *Dallas* allowed us to watch and observe such behaviour at a safe distance. With rumours perpetually circulating about a possible cinema film of *Dallas* (complete with all-new cast), it's intriguing to think about whether the series will make the transition to the 21st century intact. Provided the central character remains JR – Stetson, sneer, amorality and all – we're sure it will be highly entertaining!

WEBSITE

www.ultimatedallas.com is one of the very best fan sites anywhere on the internet, providing regular interviews with cast members, message boards for people to chat on, as well as photos and facts and figures from long-forgotten storylines. Highly, highly recommended.

and eventually appeared on the Nickelodeon Network in the USA from 1984 (with one slight change: so as not to offend American sensibilities, the Italian accent for Greenback's henchman Stiletto was swapped for a Cockney one). One of the primary reasons for the success of *Danger Mouse* was in the top-notch voice cast that Cosgrove Hall hired. It took American movie animators many years to realise the benefits of employing 'big name' actors to work in their films, but with such vocal talent as David Jason (*Danger Mouse* and ***Only Fools and Horses*** both starting in the same month) and Terry Scott (still enjoying prime-time success in ***Terry and June***) bringing life to the show's two heroes, success must surely have been even more certain.

The series survived/thrived on some excruciating puns that never failed to raise a giggle (our absolute favourite involved a trip to the moon where DM pointed out the crater of Copernicus, causing Penfold to titter, 'Hee hee – "Copper knickers"!'). Some of the biggest laughs in the programme came from the deadpan narration by David Jason, a mock-serious introduction to each episode that at first appeared to present the programme as gritty action series, then rapidly descended into a display of muddled-up words, hyperbole about Danger Mouse's and Penfold's skills as superheroes, and general exasperation that his lot in life wasn't as good as it could be. Many episodes ended with the Narrator sighing with frustration at the events he's just witnessed; some reminded viewers to return next episode to see how our heroes might escape the cliffhanging ending; others mocked the convention of having a narrator on a TV show at all. However they played out, the brief voice-overs by David Jason topping and tailing each episode were an undoubted highlight.

Beginning with serialised adventures (a five-minute episode shown every day of the week) and then moving on to longer stories, *Danger Mouse* maintained its quality right to the very end of its life. A true British classic.

Website

www.chf.co.uk – the official Cosgrove Hall site

Danger UXB

Drama | Euston Films/Thames for ITV | episode duration 50 mins | broadcast 8 Jan–2 Apr 1979

Regular Cast

Anthony Andrews · *Brian Ash*
Maurice Roëves · *Sergeant James*
Gordon Kane · *Sapper Mulley*
George Innes · *Sapper/Lieutenant Corporal Wilkins*
Ken Kitson · *Corporal Horrocks*
Robert Pugh · *Sapper Powell*
Peter Cartwright · *Major Luckhurst*
Kenneth Cranham · *Sapper/Lieutenant Corporal Salt*
Robert Longden · *Sapper Copping*
Deborah Watling · *'Naughty' Norma Baker*
Marjie Lawrence · *Mrs Baker*
Jeremy Sinden · *Lieutenant Rodgers*
Norman Chappell · *Corporal Mould*
Osmund Bullock · *Lieutenant /Captain Pringle*
Royston Tickner · *Lieutenant /Captain Leckie*
Kenneth Farrington · *Captain/Major Francis*
David Shaughnessy · *Lieutenant Carter Brown*
Judy Geeson · *Susan*
Iain Cuthbertson · *Doctor Gillespie*
David Auker · *Sapper Baines*
John Bowler · *Sapper Scott*

Creators John Hawkesworth and John Whitney **Producers** John Hawkesworth, Christopher Neame, Johnny Goodman **Writers** John Hawkesworth, Jeremy Paul, Don Shaw, Paul Wheeler, Kenneth Clark, from the novels by Major A. B. Hartley, MBE, RE **Theme Music** Simon Park

One of TV drama's great maestros, John Hawkesworth, moved on from his work on Edwardian period shows such as ***Upstairs, Downstairs*** and ***The Duchess of Duke Street*** to tackle the astonishing real-life story of the teams of dedicated workers sent to defuse German bombs during World War Two. These unexploded bombs (or UXBs) often landed in sensitive areas, such as in the middle of a residential street, next to a school, or even in a church crypt very close to a tube line. Worse still for the teams working in these Explosive Ordnance Disposal units was the fact that German scientists did everything they could to make their bombs tamper-proof – one false move while attempting to defuse it, and the poor unfortunate officer would be no more.

Following a tragic accident very much along the lines detailed above, Lieuteant Brian Ash is seconded to work in an EOD unit. With a bare minimum of training, he is let loose on bomb after bomb, with only the loyal support of Sergeant James and his team of Sappers. Unsurprisingly for a series about unexploded bombs, *Danger UXB* manages to crank up the tension – the sequences where Ash or one of his colleagues perform their delicate work on Adolf's devices are enough to bring viewers out in a cold sweat. Attention to historical detail is quite remarkable, with not even a glimpse of a 1970s haircut to be seen. Shot entirely on colour film (something Euston Films always tried to do, in contrast with the half-film, half-videotape productions that were still common at the time), *Danger UXB* still looks quite sumptuous, and apart from an occasionally slow-moving episode, it's still a rollicking good series. Aside from the manly heroics of the EOD unit, there's the usual round of people falling in and out of love, notably the sweet romance between one of the soldiers and 'Naughty' Norma, a young woman (played by former child star and ***Doctor Who*** girl Deborah Watling) who gets a thrill out of bedding men while the bombs rain down.

The series concluded with a bitter and self-pitying Ash, wounded in the line of duty, facing promotion that would effectively invalid him out of active service, while Norma's wedding to a member of Ash's team inevitably takes place during a German bombing raid.

Daniel Deronda

Drama | WGBH/BBC for BBC One | episode duration 70 mins | broadcast 24 Nov–8 Dec 2002

Cast
Hugh Dancy · *Daniel Deronda*
Romola Garai · *Gwendolen Harleth*
Hugh Bonneville · *Henleigh Grandcourt*
Jodhi May · *Mirah Lapidoth*
Edward Fox · *Hugo Mallinger*
Amanda Root · *Mrs Davilow*
David Bamber · *Lush*
Greta Scacchi · *Lydia Glasher*
Barbara Hershey · *Contessa Maria Alcharisi*
Celia Imrie · *Mrs Meyrick*
Jamie Bamber · *Hans Meyrick*

Producers Rebecca Eaton, Kate Harwood, Laura Mackie (executive), Louis Marks, Lee Morris **Writer** Andrew Davies, from the novel by George Eliot **Theme Music** Rob Lane

Young Daniel Deronda meets the feisty Gwendolen at the roulette table, where an obvious spark ignites between them, but neither is able to act on their feelings. The honourable Daniel hails from an uncertain background and is involved with the beautiful 'Jewess' Mirah. Gwendolen is unable to inherit her father's estate as she is a woman and becomes bride to the conniving Grandcourt, who subjects her to torment and manipulation. When Gwendolen turns to Daniel for help, he must come to terms with his own past and separate his feelings for the two women in his life.

Daniel Deronda is a typically lavish costume drama from the BBC, which generally does this kind of thing with its eyes closed. The pedigree is good, with the consummate Andrew Davies providing the script, although it lacks the genuine greatness of his previous work on ***Pride and Prejudice***. A previous adaptation of the George Eliot novel was attempted by the BBC in 1970, starring Robert Hardy as Grandcourt.

Dark Season

Children's Drama | BBC One | episode duration 25 mins | broadcast 14 Nov–19 Dec 1991

Principal Cast
Victoria Lambert · *Marcie Hatter*
Kate Winslet · *Reet*
Ben Chandler · *Thomas*
Brigit Forsyth · *Miss Maitland*
Jacqueline Pearce · *Miss Pendragon*
Grant Parsons · *Mr Eldritch*
Cyril Shaps · *Mr Polzinski*
Samantha Cahill · *Olivia*
Rosalie Crutchley · *Mrs Polzinski*
Tim Barker · *Dr Osley*
Roger Milner · *Headmaster*
Martina Berne · *Inga*
Stephen Tedre · *Luke*
Marsha Fitzalan · *Voice of Behemoth*

Creator/Writer Russell T. Davies **Producer** Richard Callanan **Theme Music** David Ferguson

Marcie Hatter becomes very suspicious when a strange blond man called Mr Eldritch spearheads a delivery of free Abyss Computers for everyone at her school – she reasons that corporations simply aren't that generous. Marcie's right to be suspicious, because the computers seem to have mind-altering abilities. Together with her friends Thomas and Reet, Marcie soon uncovers a plan by Eldritch to enslave the world by linking all the planet's computers together, every single one of them working to his will. Although the young friends thwart Eldritch's plan, they soon notice an elegant woman with a group of blond followers digging up their school's playing field. Could this have a connection to Eldritch's attempt to take over the world? And who – or what – is Behemoth?

The first TV drama script from a young writer called Russell T. Davies came about because he despaired of the poor quality of drama being served up for children – either adaptations of 'worthy' children's classics, or patronising stories with old-fashioned moral messages. Having begun his TV career as a researcher and then assistant producer for ***Why Don't You?***, Davies felt that he knew what children would enjoy – and he served up a fantastical science fiction adventure grounded in everyday reality. What set *Dark Season* apart from most similar dramas was a dynamic script packed full of sharp and witty dialogue, and a trio of lead juvenile characters that didn't pander to stereotypes. Featuring a very early starring role for *Titanic* (1997) star Kate Winslet, *Dark Season* also boasted a fabulous guest-starring appearance from ***Blake's 7***'s cocktail dress-wearing villainess Servalan, actress Jacqueline Pearce. Russell T. Davies would return to family friendly science fiction when he masterminded the 2005 revival of ***Doctor Who***.

The Dark Side of the Sun

Drama | BBC/Gryphon Productions for BBC One | episode duration 50 mins | broadcast 13 Sep–19 Oct 1983

Principal Cast
Peter Egan · *Raoul Lavalliere*
Patrick Mower · *Don Tierney*
Emily Richard · *Anne Tierney*
Betty Arvaniti · *Ismini Christoyannis*
Michael Sheard · *Colonel Von Reitz*
Godfrey James · *Harry Brennan*
Trevor Baxter · *Dr Phillimore*
Christopher Scoular · *David Bascombe*
Dimitri Andreas · *Andreas Seferis*

Brian Attree · *Simon*
Victor Baring · *Voice*
Max Barrat · *Max*
Willy Bowman · *Niedermann*
Michael Chesdon · *Major Lambrinos*
Ray Marioni · *Manzini*
Morris Perry · *Wilhelm Ruiter*
Steve Plytas · *Nikolaidis*
Peter Whitaker · *Sir Joseph Marcus*

Creator/Writer Michael J. Bird **Producer** Vere Lorrimer **Theme Music** Stavros Xarhakos

Having based his thrillers ***The Lotus Eaters, Who Pays the Ferryman?*** and ***The Aphrodite Inheritance*** in a Greek setting, in 1983 Michael J. Bird plunged further into Greek mythology and the legend of the Knights Templar, barely disguising the supernatural elements of *The Dark Side of the Sun*, which this time was set on Rhodes. Peter Egan (***Ever Decreasing Circles***) got the chance to play against type as the villainous Raoul Lavalliere, a man with the chameleon-like ability to impersonate other people, which he uses to bed the widow of photographer Don Tierney and convince her that her husband had returned to her.

Surreal at times, deeply creepy at others, *The Dark Side of the Sun* was an inventive way of revisiting familiar territory, but after four series set in Greek locations, the public seemed to tire of all that Mediterranean sun and sea. His follow-up, ***Maelstrom***, would be set in Norway.

Website
An authorised tribute site to Michael J. Bird can be found at birdland2.netfirms.com.

The Darling Buds of May

Comedy Drama | Excelsior/Yorkshire Television for ITV | episode duration 100 mins | broadcast 7 Apr 1991–4 Apr 1993

Regular Cast
David Jason · *Sidney Charles/Pop Larkin*
Pam Ferris · *Ma Larkin*
Philip Franks · *Cedric 'Charley' Charlton*
Catherine Zeta-Jones · *Mariette Larkin*
Julie Davis, Abigail Rokison · *Primrose Larkin*
Christina Giles · *Petunia Larkin*
Katherine Giles · *Zinnia Larkin*
Stephanie Ralph · *Victoria Larkin*
Ian Tucker · *Monty Larkin*
Moray Watson · *The Brigadier*
Rachel Bell · *Edith Pilchester*
Kika Mirylees · *Angela Snow*
Steven Brand · *Tom Sargent*
Tyler Butterworth · *Reverend John Candy*
Ross Marriott · *Baby Oscar Larkin*
Martyn Read · *Sergeant Wilson*
Michael Jayston · *Ernest Bristow*
Carol MacReady · *Mrs Daws*

Producers Richard Bates, Vernon Lawrence (executive), Robert Banks Stewart, Simon Lewis, Peter Norris **Writers** Bob Larbey, Robert Banks Stewart, Paul Wheeler, Stephen Bill, from the Larkin novels of H. E. Bates **Theme Music** Pip Burley composed a theme tune to the series that's so uplifting and melodic that it can instantly take even the hardest-hearted of viewers back to the long hot summers of their youth.

This was a beautifully languid and gorgeously filmed series of nostalgic family stories, based upon the five Larkin novels by H. E. Bates. In the rolling Kent countryside of the 1950s, Pa and Ma Larkin live what can only be described as an idyllic existence. The sun always shines, the farm they live on is verdant and bountiful, and they have a large family of kids who all adore them and each other. Nothing looks as though it could ever shatter this paradise, until one day a man from the Inland Revenue arrives on the farm to discuss Pa Larkin's somewhat 'innovative' efforts at paying tax. To cause further complications, Pa and Ma announce that they've never actually got married – their distaste for rules, regulations and formal procedures encompassing their marital status too. Pa manages to persuade young Cedric Charlton from the Inland Revenue to stay for lunch. Before he knows what's happening, Cedric's fallen in love with the Larkins' eldest daughter, Mariette, and very soon they are married.

Another vehicle to show off the chameleon talents of David Jason, *The Darling Buds of May* was absolutely 'perfick' (sorry) Sunday night entertainment – safe, charming and with nothing to offend even the most uptight of viewers. Pam Ferris's buxom Ma Larkin was always seen with a frying pan in hand, a marvellous antidote to the stick-thin leading ladies seen in most TV programmes. Philip Franks – subsequently a stalwart of ***Countdown***'s dictionary corner – had just the right touch of naïvety and wide-eyed innocence to convince as Charley the tax inspector. And of course, the programme brought Catherine Zeta-Jones, a young actress from the Welsh valleys, straight onto the front of the tabloids and eventually to the glamour of a Hollywood career and an A-list marriage to actor Michael Douglas.

The term 'Capra-esque' has never befitted a series more than this, in some ways a rustic, spring-filled colour version of Frank Capra's *You Can't Take It With You* (1938), complete with a dotty but lovable family and a setting that puts visitors so at ease that they find it hard to leave. Co-produced by H. E. Bates's son Richard, *The Darling Buds of May* utilised top-notch writing talent such as ***The Good Life***'s Bob Larbey and ***Bergerac***'s Robert Banks Stewart. The gorgeous village of Pluckley in Kent (and Buss Farm therein) provided the locations for the series. Ironically, for such a sunny and good-hearted programme, Pluckley is listed in *The Guinness Book of Records* as being the most haunted village in the whole of England – presumably the ghosts of all of those killed by overindulgence in Ma Larkin's scrumptious food . . .

Das Boot

Drama | Bavaria Film/Radiant Film GmbH/Süddeutscher Rundfunk/Westdeutscher Rundfunk production (shown on BBC Two) | episode duration 50 mins | broadcast 17 Sep 1981 (Germany)

Principal Cast

Jürgen Prochnow · *Der Alte/Kapitän Leutenant Heinrich Lehmann-Willenbrock*
Herbert Grönemeyer · *Leutnant Werner*
Klaus Wennemann · *Leitender Ingenieur*
Hubertus Bengsch · *Erster Wachoffizier*
Martin Semmelrogge · *Zweiter Wachoffizier*
Bernd Tauber · *Obersteuermann*
Erwin Leder · *Johann, Das Gespenst*
Martin May · *Ullmann*
Heinz Hoenig · *Hinrich*

Producers Günter Rohrbach **Writer** Wolfgang Petersen, from the novel by Lothar G. Buchheim **Theme Music** Klaus Doldinger

In World War Two, duty aboard on one of the many U-boats was considered something of a glamour job in the German Navy. *Das Boot* disavows its audience of that notion in this brutal, claustrophobic mini series that later saw life as a theatrical release, also in 1981, with a Director's Cut version having 60 minutes of the original mini series stitched back in for a 1997 release.

The series follows the lives of a U-boat crew as they undertake a tour of duty under Kapitän Lehmann-Willenbrock, a commander who has the respect of his men, but is portrayed as a flawed human being who makes mistakes. The action takes place mostly aboard the submarine and is seen through the eyes of war correspondent Leutnant Werner, who observes these young men transform from enthusiastic individuals to haggard, pale figures of their former selves.

Wolfgang Petersen brings a mix of claustrophobia interspersed with action, a style that would propel him on to directing Hollywood fare such as *Air Force One* (1997) and *In the Line of Fire* (1993). Petersen kept his cast indoors throughout much of the filming of *Das Boot* to accentuate the washe- out complexion of the submariners. As no Type VII-C U-boats existed, much of the $15 million budget was spent on constructing a sea-worthy replica, a task undertaken by the original builders of the boats. The theatrical release of *Das Boot* was nominated in several Academy Award categories, including Best Director for Petersen, but it failed to win any gongs.

David Copperfield

Drama | WGBH/BBC for BBC One | episode duration 90 mins | broadcast Christmas 1999

Principal Cast

Ciaran McMenamin · *David Copperfield*
Daniel Radcliffe · *Young David Copperfield*
Emilia Fox · *Clara Copperfield*
Pauline Quirke · *Peggotty*
Maggie Smith · *Betsey Trotwood*
John Normington · *Dr Chillip*
Trevor Eve · *Murdstone*
Michael Elphick · *Barkis*
James Thornton · *Ham Peggotty*
Alun Armstrong · *Daniel Peggotty*
Patsy Byrne · *Mrs Gummidge*
Laura Harling · *Little Emily*
Zoë Wanamaker · *Miss Murdstone*
Jacqueline Tong · *Lady in Coach*
Karl Johnson · *Tungay*
Ian McKellen · *Creakle*
Bob Hoskins · *Micawber*
Imelda Staunton · *Mrs Micawber*
Nicholas Lyndhurst · *Uriah Heep*
Thelma Barlow · *Mrs Heep*

Producers Jane Tranter, Rebecca Eaton (executive), Katrine Dudley (associate), Kate Harwood **Writer** Adrian Hodges, from the novel by Charles Dickens **Theme Music** Rob Lane

Daniel Radcliffe, a couple of years away from *Harry Potter* superstardom, takes the role of the young David Copperfield in this highly regarded, star packed period drama, brought to life by much the same team as ***Daniel Deronda***, although Adrian Hodges handled the adaptation. John Sullivan was originally the driving force behind the BBC's plan to adapt the story, but the project fell through and the ***Only Fools and Horses*** scribe took the project to ITV, called it *Micawber* and drafted in David Jason as the eponymous lead. The BBC adaptation, however, retained the services of Nicholas Lyndhurst as a fabulously creepy Uriah Heep.

The story is impeccable, but the draw here is the amazing cast, from Pauline Quirke as Peggoty and Bob Hoskins as Micawber, to Trevor Eve as Murdstone, but even the walk-ons have pedigree, with quick turns from stars such as Paul Whitehouse. This was not the first attempt the BBC made at bringing *David Copperfield* to the TV screens. Other productions have cropped up in 1956, starring Robert Hardy, 1966 (also featuring Ian McKellen), 1974 and 1986. On previous form, the 1999 version is unlikely to be the last . . .

Dawson's Creek

Drama | Columbia TriStar for the WB Network (shown on Channel 4) | episode duration 45 mins | broadcast 20 Jan 1998–14 May 2003 (USA)

Regular Cast

James Van Der Beek · *Dawson Leery*
Katie Holmes · *'Joey' Potter*

Michelle Williams · *Jen Lindley*
Joshua Jackson · *Pacey Witter*
Mary Beth Peil · *Evelyn 'Grams' Ryan*
Kerr Smith · *Jack McPhee*
Mary-Margaret Humes · *Gail Leery*
John Wesley Shipp · *Mitch Leery*

Creator Kevin Williamson **Producers** Kevin Williamson, Paul Stupin, Greg Prange, Tom Kapinos (executive) **Writer** Various, including Kevin Williamson, Jon Harmon Feldman, Mike White, Dana Baratta, Greg Berlanti, Darin Goldberg, Shelly Meals, Jeffrey Stepakoff, Gina Fattore, Tom Kapinos, Maggie Friedman, Jonathan Kasdan, Rina Mimoun, Anna Fricke **Theme Music** For airings in the UK, season one's theme song was 'Run Like Mad', performed by Jann Arden. From season two onwards it was the more familiar 'I Don't Want to Wait' by Paula Cole.

Dawson's Creek 'defined a network', according to the mouthpiece of the fledgling Warner Brothers Television Network (the WB for short), and there was certainly something about this coming of age teen drama that struck a chord with a desirable youthful audience.

Four friends come together in the picturesque setting of Capeside, Massachusetts: they are movie-obsessed Dawson Leery, the shy Joey Potter, macho Pacey Witter and the feisty Jen Lindley. Together they go through high school, learning about life, forging loyalties that lasted beyond the fallouts that happened from time to time. Throughout the course of six seasons, the youngsters grow into young adulthood, entering college and gradually losing the last vestiges of innocence. At the heart of the series was the ongoing love triangle between Dawson, Pacey and Joey that seemed to take on different permutations season by season. A nation, as they say, was hooked.

Dawson's Creek was created by Kevin Williamson, the creative mind behind the *Scream* movies, and the series fizzed with the same snappy dialogue that was occasionally far too knowing for its own good (teenagers just aren't *that* wise). The series made several landmarks, chiefly the first male gay kiss seen on US prime-time television.

All four main cast members have become stars in their own right, graduating quickly to movies, although the star that has shone most brightly is that of Katie Holmes, with roles in blockbuster movies such as *Batman Begins* (2005) – not to mention a relationship with Tom Cruise – confirming her A-list status.

The Day of the Triffids

Science Fiction | BBC/ABC and RCTV for BBC One | episode duration 25 mins | broadcast 10 Sep–15 Oct 1981

Principal Cast

John Duttine · *Bill Masen*
Emma Relph · *Jo Payton*
Maurice Colbourne · *Jack Coker*
Jonathan Newth · *Dr Soames*
Cleo Sylvestre · *Nurse Barbara*
Stephen Yardley · *John*
Claire Ballard · *Alice*
Andrew Paul · *Gang Member*
Albie Woodington · *Gang Leader*
Max Faulkner · *Jo's Attacker*
Morris Barry, Elizabeth Chambers · *Car Attackers*
John Benfield · *Ted*
Gordon Case · *Dying Man*
Desmond Cullum-Jones · *Tom*
Beryl Nesbitt · *Tom's Wife*
David Swift · *Michael Beadley*
Denis De Marne · *Major Anderson*
Caroline Fabbri · *Tina*
Susie Fenwick · *Blind Girl*
Eva Griffiths · *Girl*
Ian Halliburton · *Grant*
John Hollis · *Alf*
Andrea Miller · *Dr Vorless*
Perlita Neilson · *Miss Durrant*
Emily Dean, Lorna Charles · *Susan*
Christopher Owen · *Vicar*
Edmund Pegge · *Walter*
Christina Schofield · *Shirley*
Desmond Adams · *Dennis Brent*
Jenny Lipman · *Mary Brent*
Gary Olsen · *Torrence*

Producer David Maloney **Writer** Douglas Livingstone, from the novel by John Wyndham **Theme Music** Christopher Gunning

The triffids were a novelty once: giant, orchid-like plants that could walk, found on a distant island. But then they were discovered to produce oil and became another commodity for mankind to farm, like fowl or cattle. It was soon apparent that the plants were equipped with defences – a sting that springs from the bell-shaped 'mouth' at the top of their stalks – but with care, these were easily docked. What humans hadn't bargained for was the possibility that the plants possessed intelligence. When a spectacular shower of meteorites left anyone who witnessed it blind, the triffids broke free of their pens and headed to the cities, picking off their sightless victims one by one, waiting for their bodies to decompose sufficiently for them to devour.

A trio of early 1980s' BBC dramas left their marks on those who saw them, ***The Nightmare Man***, ***The Mad Death*** and *The Day of the Triffids*. Each of them contained sequences that left young viewers quaking behind cushions and checking behind their bedroom doors at night. From its sickly-green opening titles and foreboding choral theme music, *The Day of the Triffids* set the tone just right. Of all our senses, sudden loss of sight is the one that leaves the individual most at risk, from attack, from a clumsy fall or from simply eating the wrong thing, and it's this primal fear that the production plays on.

The Day of the Triffids faithfully adapted (with only minor tweaks and a shift in time period to near-present day) John

Wyndham's horticultural horror story of deadly daffodils that leap to the top of the food chain after society breaks down. Producer David Maloney was only able to realise Douglas Livingstone's script thanks to a co-production deal with Australian broadcaster ABC and American cable network RCTV. Though the series was shown in six 25-minute slots on BBC One, abroad it was re-edited into three 50-minute episodes (the format it's been more recently repeated in on UK Gold). John Duttine, fresh from ***To Serve Them All My Days***, starred as Bill Masen, a triffid farmer who spent the meteor shower in hospital after a near miss from a triffid sting left him temporarily blinded.

While the triffids themselves were a triumph for the Beeb's designer Steve Drewett, the credit should be shared with the sound department who were responsible for the 'pop-pop-pop' noises that Bill at least believes is the sound of the plants talking to each other. Often we hear the popping before we see the triffid, making for a truly creepy experience courtesy of director Ken Hannam.

Some of the series' most upsetting moments don't involve the triffids at all: images of the newly blind looting shops for food but instead opening boxes of washing powder; football louts terrorising the streets and thugs bullying the sighted into becoming their unwilling guides; the sound of a woman breaking down in tears while playing her guitar. It's the utter panic that sets the day after the meteor shower and the chilling silences that follow that frighten us the most. When Bill Masen's doctor deliberately leaps to his death in the second episode, it's difficult to judge him, especially when we see what humanity faces in the days and weeks ahead when the bodies of the dead begin to spread disease and the survivors become even more desperate to retain what little hold on life they have.

Like ***Survivors***, the similarly post-apocalyptic drama from Terry Nation, *The Day of the Triffids* spells out just how useless we are as individuals at self-sufficiency. Such a disaster would divide people – not along class lines, but along those sighted people who wish to help the less fortunate and those who'd wish to dominate them. A common theme in science fiction, we see the rapid establishment of martial law in some areas, local dictatorships in others, all with their eyes towards controlling the stricken and removing such luxuries as freedom of choice. In their vision of the future, men and women will have the primary role of procreation merely to replace the lost humans.

Though the series occasionally veers towards slowdown, usually in the scenes spent establishing the relationship between Bill and Jo, these brief moments are only ever the eye of the storm. For the most part, *The Day of the Triffids* remains both the best science fiction drama produced by the BBC in the last 30 years and (to date at least) the most successful translation of a John Wyndham novel to the screen.

The Day Today

Comedy | Talkback Productions for BBC Two | episode duration 30 mins | broadcast 19 Jan–23 Feb 1994

Regular Cast
Chris Morris, Steve Coogan, Doon Mackichan, Patrick Marber, Rebecca Front, David Schneider

Creators Chris Morris, Armando Iannucci **Producer** Armando Iannucci **Writers** Chris Morris, Armando Iannucci, Peter Baynham, Andrew Glover, Steven Wells, David Quantick, Graham Linehan, Arthur Mathews, Steve Coogan, Doon Mackichan, Patrick Marber, Rebecca Front, David Schneider **Theme Music** Jonathan Whitehead and Chris Morris, a superb parody of theme tunes that never quite know when to end

In a fast paced, multi-media international news bundling envioromode, only one equation matters: Fact × Importance = News. Comprehending the importance of the highest quality, fastest paced news delivery machinery, *The Day Today* accurately represented the high standards of professionalism, empathy and downright ball-breaking brilliance of TV journalism.

In reality, *The Day Today* was a spot-on parody of the excesses, conventions and utter cliché-ridden stupidity of many news broadcasts. For far too long, the public service nature of news programmes had absolved them from the piercing gaze of the satirists' eye – thankfully in 1994 Armando Iannucci and Chris Morris decided to eviscerate pompous, bloated newsreaders' egos in a TV series that took no prisoners, be they sports reporters, weather forecasters, reconstructions of 'real' events or hidden camera footage.

The Day Today was to all intents and purposes a TV version of Morris and Iannucci's earlier Radio 4 series *On The Hour*, in which the kind of dreary current affairs programming often found on earnest radio stations was parodied. The move from radio to TV enabled the team to revel in many of the excesses that were uniquely visual, including the insanely over-the-top graphics and blue-screen work that was beginning to creep into the ever more competitive TV news productions, the thought being that just telling the news to viewers simply wasn't exciting or interesting enough to hold their attention any more.

Chris Morris fronted *The Day Today* as the chief newsreader of this fictitious news programme, a posturing and vain man who's far more concerned with his own ego and public profile than in any of the words that get spewed from his babbling mouth. He regularly berates his rubbish political reporter Peter O'Hanraha'hanrahan (Patrick Marber), flirts outrageously with glamorous yet incomprehensible business reporter Collaterlie Sisters (Doon Mackichan), is baffled by bearded 'environmation' (environmental information) expert Rosie May (Rebecca Front) and, of course, deals with the undoubted

incompetence of chief sports correspondent Alan Partridge, played by Steve Coogan. So popular was the character of the inept Partridge that he soon graduated to his own spin-off series, ***Knowing Me, Knowing You***.

Although *The Day Today* lasted for just six episodes, its impact on both genres of comedy and news broadcasting is long-lasting. *The Day Today* – and its Channel 4 successor, ***Brass Eye*** – provided the first major TV exposure for a whole new set of comics who would move on to other, equally successful, projects (such as Doon Mackichan in Channel 4 sketch series ***Smack the Pony***). On the other hand, news programmes seem not to have taken on board any of the cautionary warnings contained within *The Day Today* – ten years on, many of the jokes about dim yet attractive presenters, over-the-top computer graphics, too literal montages and all-style-no-substance broadcasting seem to not just have come true, but to have exceeded any of the worst predictions thrown up by the satirists.

Dead Ringers

Comedy | BBC Two | episode duration 30 mins | broadcast 15 Mar 2002–present

Regular Cast

Jon Culshaw, Jan Ravens, Mark Perry, Kevin Connelly, Phil Cornwell

Producers Jon Plowman (executive), Bill Dare **Writers** Nev Fountain, Tom Jamieson, Jon Holmes, Laurence Howarth, Jon Culshaw, Simon Blackwell, Richard Ward, Jan Ravens, Mark Perry **Theme Music** John Whitehall

The *Dead Ringers* team of impressionists had been an award-winning troupe of comics on BBC Radio 4, with three full seasons of programmes having been broadcast on the wireless before the idea was put forward to switch the show to television. Everybody knew that the talented impressionists would have no trouble replicating the voices of their famous victims, but would they be any good attempting to look like them too? Furthermore, with *Alistair McGowan's Big Impression* still pulling in the viewers on BBC One, was there really room for two impressionist shows on TV at the same time?

Of course, viewers needn't have worried – the *Dead Ringers* team managed to create a programme with a very different feel to any previous impression show, affectionately mocking current political figures (in much the same way that ***Spitting Image*** had done in the 1980s) while simultaneously tapping into a country-wide well of nostalgia by faultlessly resurrecting Tom Baker's Doctor Who (perhaps the programme's signature character, brought to life by *Who* fan Jon Culshaw). Each member of the team got a good chance to show off their own individual skills of mimicry, with Jan Ravens proving particularly good, tackling all of the female roles single-handedly. With a team of quality writers providing an endless stream of gags, the *Dead Ringers* crew have brought impressionism right up to date and revitalised the genre. It's as if Mike Yarwood was just a bad dream.

Dear John

Sitcom | BBC One | episode duration 30 mins, plus 1 × 50-min Christmas special | broadcast 17 Feb 1986–21 Dec 1987

Regular Cast

Ralph Bates · *John Lacey*
Peter Blake · *Kirk St Moritz*
Peter Denyer · *Ralph Dring*
Rachel Bell · *Louise*
Belinda Lang · *Kate*
Jean Challis · *Mrs Arnott*
Lucinda Curtis · *Sylvia*
Kevin Lloyd · *Ricky Fortune*
Wendy Allnutt · *Wendy Lacey*
Irène Prador · *Mrs Lomenski*
William Bates · *Toby Lacey*

Creator/Writer John Sullivan **Producer** Ray Butt **Theme Music** John Sullivan, sung by Joan Baxter

The pain and misery of the recently divorced provided material for another comedy classic from the pen of John Sullivan, creator of ***Citizen Smith***, ***Just Good Friends*** and ***Only Fools and Horses***. Schoolteacher John Lacey finds himself single after his wife Wendy reveals she's having an affair with his best friend. Or rather, her solicitor informs him of this at the same time as serving him with divorce papers. With the divorce settlement falling firmly in Wendy's favour, she keeps the family home and custody of their young son while John is forced to rent a bedsit next door to a Polish immigrant who is convinced John is a 'crazy person'. Frustrated with being excluded by his married friends, who mask their thoughtlessness with assumptions of John's innate happiness over his newfound bachelorhood, John enrols with a '1-2-1 Club' for the divorced and separated . . .

Star of the series Ralph Bates came to prominence in some of Hammer Studios' more lurid feature films of the early 1970s, including *The Horror of Frankenstein* and *Lust for a Vampire*. For non-horror fans he was known for his leading role as George Warleggan in the BBC's romantic drama ***Poldark***; he was not known for comedy. Peter Blake was a singer-songwriter who had made minor appearances in a few of Euston Films' gritty dramas for Thames, though he'd also played a supporting role in Maureen Lipman's ***Agony***. But of the entire cast of *Dear John*, only Peter Denyer could be described as an experienced sitcom performer, not that anyone could recognise the woolly-haired pupil he'd once played in ***Please Sir*** or the gay neighbour from *Agony*. But then, assembling a cast from different strands and spinning gold from them is what we'd expect from sitcom king John Sullivan.

Each of the characters manages, over time, to pull our heartstrings and encourage us to empathise without ever coming across as too pathetic. Group leader Louise, renowned for her 'okay yah' vernacular and intense fascination in other people's 'sexual problems', is certainly not a cause for pity. When her ex-husband (who she'd divorced because of his S&M interests) feigned a split personality, Louise sued them both for alimony. Kate may be prickly and defensive but she's also the sanest member of the group. Divorced three times due to self-confessed frigidity on her part, she sees John as a kindred spirit. Mrs Arnatt, who sits at the back and rarely speaks, can often be relied upon to chip in with the most shocking revelation just as the group is about to retire to the nearest pub; many's the time Louise has decided to extend a session after one of Mrs Arnatt's sexual confessions.

Everyone spots Kirk St Moritz as a fake as soon as he explodes into the room. More 'Friday Evening Headache' than *Saturday Night Fever*, he's painfully tactless and rude to everyone he meets. He's also a particularly blatant pathological liar. He claims to work in espionage, though only Ralph believes him (Kate tells a newcomer to the group that his life story was novelised under the title 'Tinker, Tailor, Soldier, Dickhead') and few of them suspect that he's joined the group for any reason other than to seduce some desperate divorcee – though he's hindered at every turn by his 1970s' togs and his insistence on calling all women 'chicks'. There's another side to Kirk, though, the real side that only John sees: Eric Morris has been horrifically bullied by his sadistic mother all his life. His boring nylon-clad wardrobe of hand-me-downs and the tedious drudgery of his situation inspired him to create Kirk as a façade, a brash, over-confident superstar instead of a wet, big-eared drip.

The only person who is taken in by Kirk's tall (and long, though never deep) stories is poor, trusting Ralph Dring. Ralph is a deeply boring man (like Peter Cook's E. L. Wisty only without the sparkling wit), which is a shame considering how he finds everything so fascinating. His Polish bride left him when the ink on the all-important marriage certificate was still wet. A rather innocent man, he was offended by the suggestion that the lovely Blomlika had wed him purely to evade deportation. When he loses his job, Ralph spends his redundancy on a mobile disco. Sadly, it's not the success he hoped for: his only record is 'Green Door' by Shakin' Stevens.

A second series introduced Sylvia, a gentle soul with a ghastly laugh, and Ricky Fortune, a minor support player in the 1960s' music scene desperately trying to rekindle the flame of success. John claims to be his biggest fan, though in truth the only person who remembers Ricky is Mrs Arnatt. Despite a momentary possible fling with Kate (the pair were too drunk to remember if anything actually happened) and the chance of a reconciliation with his wife, the series ended with John staying in for the evening to keep his elderly neighbour Mrs Lomenski company. No matter how hard he tried, John was just too nice.

The series' title was inspired by the 'Dear John' letters that soldiers receive when their girlfriends dump them, and by the close of the second series and a successful Christmas special John Lacey and his chums had a sizeable audience hanging on their every perfectly timed word. Sadly, that was it for *Dear John*. Ralph Bates was diagnosed with pancreatic cancer and died in 1991 aged just 50, survived by his second wife, actress Virginia Wetherall, their son William (who had played John Lacey's son Toby in the series) and daughter Daisy.

As the second series was in production, John Sullivan successfully sold the format to Paramount in the United States. Starring Judd Hirsch from ***Taxi***, it soon ate up Sullivan's 14 original scripts – *Dear John USA* (as it was known over here) racked up 90 episodes, though the final eight were not transmitted due to the fourth run being prematurely cut short mid-season.

From the cast of the English original, Rachel Bell made a small appearance as a psychotic gun-wielding psychotic in three episodes of ***Doctor Who*** before joining the cast of ***Grange Hill*** as teacher Mrs Holmes; Peter Blake starred alongside Anita Dobson in the critically mauled *Split Ends* and Belinda Lang acquired a family thanks to another hugely popular sitcom, ***2 Point 4 Children***.

The Demon Headmaster

Children's Drama | BBC One | episode duration 25 mins | broadcast 15 Jan 1996–1999

Principal Cast

Terrence Hardiman · *The Demon Headmaster*
Tessa Peake-Jones · *Mrs Hunter*
Frances Amey · *Dinah Glass/Hunter*
Gunner Cauthery · *Lloyd Hunter*
Thomas Szekeres · *Harvey Hunter*
Danny John-Jules · *Eddy Hair*

Producers Richard Langridge (executive), Roger Singleton-Turner, Richard Callanan **Writer** Helen Cresswell, adapted from the novel by Gillian Cross

The Hunter brothers and their foster sister Dinah are convinced that their headmaster is not quite what he seems – and they're right! He's actually an evil genius who is hypnotising his pupils to prevent them going home and spilling the beans to their parents about his plans for world domination. The three youngsters form SPLAT – Society for the Protection of our Lives Against Them – and defeat the headmaster's plans, but he would return to make lives difficult for Lloyd, Harvey and Dinah twice more.

Great fun and a popular vehicle for the BBC's children's output, with ***Secret Army***'s Terrence Hardiman providing a suitably terrifying presence to scare the willies of the show's young fans. The series was nominated for a BAFTA Children's award in 1996.

Dempsey and Makepeace

Crime Drama | Golden Eagle Films/LWT for ITV | episode duration 50 mins | broadcast 11 Jan 1985–1 Nov 1986

Regular Cast
Michael Brandon · *Lieutenant James Dempsey*
Glynis Barber · *DS/Lady Harriet Makepeace*
Ray Smith · *Chief Superintendant Gordon Spikings*
Tony Osoba · *DS Chas Jarvis*

Creator Tony Wharmby **Producers** Nick Elliott (executive), Tony Wharmby, Ranald Graham **Writers** Ranald Graham, Jesse Carr-Martindale, Dave Humphries, Jonathan Hales, Murray Smith, Roger Marshall, Paul Wheeler, Jeffrey Caine, David Wilks, John Field **Theme Music** Alan Parker

After he uncovers corruption in his own precinct, hard-nosed New York Detective James Dempsey is transferred to the UK, joining Scotland Yard's covert department SI-10. There he's partnered with the haughty Harriet Makepeace, a toff with a Cambridge degree and a no-nonsense attitude. Together, they fight crime, he with his fists, she with her contacts, while their Liverpudlian Chief Super, Spikings, and mild-mannered colleague Chas Jarvis lend a hand and try to stay out of the firing line.

Dempsey and Makepeace benefited from a move towards action-adventure police dramas in the 1980s. With its mid-Atlantic approach, but filmed in the UK with all the country's overcast weather conditions to contend with, it was often preposterously posey and ludicrously lacking in realism, but the promise of fast action and the hint of sexual tension between the leads kept viewers tuning in for a regular dose of will-they-won't-they (they did, in real life at least, when Brandon and Barber married in 1989 – at the time of writing, they are still together, a true celebrity marriage success story). Tony Osoba played Jarvis, having previously starred in the sitcom ***Porridge*** in the 1970s.

The set-up was parodied in a 1987 BBC comedy drama from ***Last of the Summer Wine*** writer Roy Clarke called *Pulaski*, in which an American actor playing a cop on TV finds himself drawn into real-life investigations. David Andrews and Caroline Langrishe starred in the eight episodes.

Department S/Jason King

Action-Adventure | ITC for ITV | episode duration 50 mins | broadcast 9 Mar 1969–24 Mar 1970 (*Department S*), 15 Sep 1971–28 Apr 1972 (*Jason King*)

Regular Cast
Peter Wyngarde · *Jason King*
Joel Fabiani · *Stewart Sullivan*
Rosemary Nicols · *Annabelle Hurst*
Dennis Alaba Peters · *Sir Curtis Seretse*
Anne Sharp · *Nicola Harvester*
Dennis Price · *Sir Brian*
Ronald Lacey · *Ryland*

Creators Monty Berman and Dennis Spooner **Producer** Monty Berman **Writers** Gerald Kelsey, Philip Broadley, Terry Nation, Donald James, Tony Williamson, Leslie Darbon, Harry H. Junkin, Robert Banks Stewart, Dennis Spooner **Theme Music** Edwin T. Astley

If a case proves too baffling for Interpol, when regular detective work isn't enough, they turn to Department S, a secret division specialising in the mysterious. Headed by Sir Curtis Seretse, the team includes Former FBI agent Stewart Sullivan, the methodical Annabelle Hurst and flamboyant Jason King, who combines investigations with a lucrative career as a spy novelist (his Mark Caine books have sold over 60 million copies in 18 languages!). King lives the playboy lifestyle, always with a different girl on each arm and rarely treating the investigations with the respect they deserve. To him, crime fighting is a diverting hobby.

Another of ITC's extravagant adventure series, *Department S* ran for 28 episodes and made a star of actor Peter Wyngarde to such an extent that for the show's second series of 26 episodes – retitled *Jason King* – his character was the only element retained. King was very much a model for the later *Austin Powers* films (1997–2002), both in outrageously loud clothes and his insatiable sexual appetite. Wyngarde himself became a huge international sex symbol, being mobbed so badly upon his arrival in Australia that he had to be rescued from a crowd of screaming fans by the local police.

Deputy Dawg

Animation | Terrytoons for CBS (shown on BBC One) | episode duration 7 mins | broadcast 5 Sep 1959–1972 (USA)

Voice Cast
Dayton Allen · *Deputy Dawg*
Lionel G. Wilson · *Various Characters*

Creator Larz Bourne **Producer** Bill Weiss **Writers** Larz Bourne, Ralph Bakshi, Al Bertino, T. Hee, Carl Howard, Chris Jenkins, Dick Kinney, Jack Mercer **Theme Music** Phillip A. Schieb

Deputy Dawg attempts to keep a chicken shed free of varmints such as Musky the muskrat, Vince the nearly blind mole and Ty Coon the raccoon. He reports to the sheriff, the only human character in the show, who frequently lambastes the poor hound for getting things wrong. Deputy Dawg probably introduced children to the concept of swearing, throwing around 'Dagnabit's like they were going out of fashion.

Ralph Bakshi, who served as a director and writer on this long running US cartoon would go on to bigger things, with animated versions of *The Lord of the Rings* (1978) and the

Kim Basinger vehicle *Cool World* (1992) among his Hollywood credits.

Derren Brown

Documentary | Objective Productions for Channel 4 | episode duration 30–60 mins | broadcast 27 Dec 2000

Producers Andrew O'Connor, Derren Brown (executive), David Britland, Andy Nyman (consultants), Anthony Owen, Debbie Young **Theme Music** Steve Beresford

From the buffoonery of Tommy Cooper and Ali Bongo to the pompous, ego-driven stunts of Davids Copperfield and Blaine, TV has always loved magicians. It's a medium that allows us to get near enough to the performer to see where his hands go without getting too close for comfort. Derren Brown is not a traditional magician. For a start, he's perfectly up-front and honest in stating that there is no such thing as magic – it's all misdirection, suggestion and showmanship. But even when we're repeatedly told that he possesses no paranormal ability at all, we're not convinced – he's just too good at what he does.

Brown got his big break thanks to fellow TV magician Andrew O'Connor who executive-produced the first of his TV specials, *Mind Control*. Unlike his Channel 4 stable-mate David Blaine, whose persona relies upon a creepy, almost autistic sullenness, Brown is neatly dressed, charming, polite and slightly nervous, which gives us the impression that things can go wrong, and that no-one's as surprised as Derren himself when the act succeeds.

The typical trick might be a simple case of 'mind reading' – guessing a card, predicting a drawing that a participant has done. Once we've become used to Brown's style, we might pick up on the subtle suggestions he slips into his preamble, but it's the reactions of the participants – and Derren's reactions to them – that make the moment.

The specials led to a series, *Trick of the Mind*, with its signature motif of passers-by answering a ringing payphone and then falling asleep within seconds of picking up the receiver. Other tricks include making taxi drivers or London Underground passengers forget their destinations, pre-preparing a response in Braille that a blind participant will give, or creating a voodoo doll that apparently controls the actions of an unbeliever. Terrifying!

But it's the big stunt shows that have brought him the most attention. In 2003, *Derren Brown Plays Russian Roulette*, saw Derren invite members of the public to load a gun for him. Some 12,000 volunteers were whittled down to just one, a man Derren hoped would be the most likely to accept one hypnotic suggestion from him to place one bullet in a specific chamber of the gun in a time-delayed live broadcast. Viewers who had been paying attention breathed a sigh of relief when the volunteer placed the bullet in chamber number one – something Derren had been leading up to right from the beginning of the show. But even with the confidence in his abilities as a hypnotist and showman, the final event was blood chilling.

Russian Roulette was followed in 2004 by *Séance*, in which students were invited to join Derren in an experiment – in this case the test was whether Derren could use psychological tricks to convince sceptics of the presence of contact from the spirit world. Again, it paid to pay attention as the act relied upon a well-thought-out parlour game and a spooky setting; Derren claimed the séance was being held in the same location as where a death cult committed mass suicide in the 1970s – a complete fiction on his part, but it provided an initial fear that helped to carry the participants into hysteria (the final shot of the show reveals that one of the supposed suicide victims of the cult is, in fact, an actress waiting in the wings to greet the unsuspecting participants). Remarkably, Channel 4 received over 700 complaints about the séance, compared to just 20 for the prospect of Brown blowing his brains out on live TV.

In January 2005, Brown gave us *Messiah*, a deliberately provocative title for a look into the commercial aspect of faith in America. Derren posed as five different individuals looking for recommendations from five leading figures in the worlds of psychic phenomena, evangelist conversion, alien abductees, New Age crystals and finally spiritual mediums. Less sensational than his previous specials, it still provided an insight into how opinion leaders can themselves be influenced by a self-confessed charlatan. Throughout the show, Brown stressed that he had no desire to undermine individual faith, but merely to reveal the methods by which some people choose to exploit that belief for monetary gain.

A second series of *Trick of the Mind* in 2005 concluded with a special live performance, *The Gathering*. Now one of Channel 4's biggest stars, Brown's self-effacing approach will always win over David Blaine's ego-driven nonsense (sitting in a Perspex box for a month and a half – we ask you!). Britain's greatest wit, Stephen Fry, who was one of Brown's guests on *Trick of the Mind*, commented that he wanted to 'burn him at the stake and watch his witch's heart bubble'. If Fry is impressed, that's good enough for us.

Desmond's

Sitcom | Humphrey Barclay Productions for Channel 4 | episode duration 25 mins, plus 50-min special | broadcast 5 Jan 1989–19 Dec 1994

Regular Cast

Norman Beaton · *Desmond Ambrose*
Carmen Munroe · *Shirley Ambrose*
Geff Francis · *Michael Ambrose*
Kim Walker · *Gloria Ambrose*
Justin E. Pickett · *Sean Ambrose*
Ram John Holder · *Porkpie Grant*
Gyearbour Asante · *Matthew*

Robbie Gee · *Lee*
Lisa Geoghan · *Louise*
Dominic Keating · *Tony*
Matilda Thorpe · *Mandy Ambrose*
Count Prince Miller · *Vince*
Dean Gatiss · *Ricky*

Creator Trix Worrell **Producers** Humphrey Barclay, Al Mitchell (executive), Charlie Hanson, Paulette Randall **Writers** Various, including Trix Worrell, Annie Bruce, Carol Williams, Paul McKenzie, Laurence Gouldbourne, Joan Hooley, Alrick Riley **Theme Music** Written by John Collins with lyrics by Trix Worrell, the title song was performed by Norman Beaton.

When series creator Trix Worrell was thinking up ideas for a new sitcom, he thought back to his youth in Peckham, south London. He remembered how barbershops were pivotal hubs for the Afro-Caribbean community, places where people dropped in for a chat, hung out with their friends and caught up on gossip, rather than just somewhere to get a short back and sides. Thus *Desmond's* was born, a sitcom set in a Peckham barbershop.

Desmond Ambrose is a grumpy old goat, whose bad-tempered outbursts annoy his wife Shirley and three grown-up children, Gloria, Sean and Michael. Immigrants from the Caribbean, Desmond and Shirley arrived in the UK in 1959 and set themselves up in business in south London. Despite the grouchy nature of its owner, Desmond's barbershop is always busy, filled with a combination of passing trade and regular hangers-on. Seemingly permanently in the shop is Porkpie (who gets his nickname from the hat he always wears), one of Desmond's mates from back in Guyana, along with Desmond's other friend Matthew.

A classy, well-written sitcom very much in the American mould (multiple writers, rounds of applause for the regular cast when they made their first appearance in each episode), Desmond's brought together two highly respected black actors (Norman Beaton and Carmen Munroe), gave screen time for a new generation of black performers, and also saw an early sighting of future ***Enterprise*** crewmate Dominic Keating as one of Desmond's barbers. Producers and cast had already decided to call it a day after the sixth series, when six days prior to transmission of the final episode, Norman Beaton died at the age of 60 while on a trip back to his birthplace of Guyana. Although *Desmond's* came to an end at that point, a spin-off series based on the antics of regular customer Porkpie was launched on Channel 4, running from 13 November 1995 to 26 September 1996. *Porkpie* showed what happened to the slightly past-it eponymous hero after he suddenly won £10 million on the lottery.

Desperate Housewives

Comedy Drama | Cherry Television/Touchstone for ABC (shown on Channel 4) | episode duration 45 mins | broadcast 3 Oct 2004–present (USA)

Regular Cast
Teri Hatcher · *Susan Mayer*
Felicity Huffman · *Lynette Scavo*
Marcia Cross · *Bree Van De Kamp*
Eva Longoria · *Gabrielle Solis*
Nicolette Sheridan · *Edie Britt*
Steven Culp · *Rex Van De Kamp*
Ricardo Antonio Chavira · *Carlos Solis*
Mark Moses · *Paul Young*
Andrea Bowen · *Julie Mayer*
Jesse Metcalfe · *John Rowland*
Cody Kasch · *Zach Young*
Brenda Strong · *Mary Alice Young*
James Denton · *Mike Delfino*
Doug Savant · *Tom Scavo*
Shawn Pyfrom · *Andrew Van De Kamp*
Shane Kinsman · *Porter Scavo*
Brent Kinsman · *Preston Scavo*
Zane Huett · *Parker Scavo*
Lupe Ontiveros · *Mama Juanita Solis*

Creator Marc Cherry **Producers** Marc Cherry, Michael Edelstein, Charles Pratt Jr, Tom Spezialy, Kevin Murphy (executive), Oliver Goldstick, Joey Murphy, John Pardee, (consulting), Stephanie Hagen (associate), Alexandra Cunningham, Patty Lin, Larry Shaw, George W. Perkins, Tracey Stern, David Schulner, Charles Skouras III **Writers** Marc Cherry, Oliver Goldstick, Tom Spezialy, Alexandra Cunningham, Tracey Stern, John Pardee, Joey Murphy, Kevin Murphy, Jenna Bans, Patty Lin, David Schulner, Chris Black, Kevin Etten, Joshua Senter **Theme Music** Danny Elfman

When suburban housewife Mary Alice Young suddenly takes her own life, the shockwaves reverberate around the close-knit community of Wisteria Lane in which she lived. At first glance, her neighbours can think of absolutely no reason for Mary Alice to have committed suicide. Then as time passes, clues and secrets about Mary Alice's life begin to surface, much to the amazement and curiosity of her friends. Of course, her friends have their own problems to deal with. Single parent Susan Mayer is so busy with her job and looking after her daughter Julie that she's suddenly realised that there's no man in her life. Working mum Lynette Scavo is run ragged trying to raise a large family, whereas Bree Van De Kamp is apparently so immaculately perfect as a mother and wife that nobody suspects the deep unhappiness lurking beneath her anally-retentive exterior. And then there's young trophy bride Gabrielle Solis, wealthy beyond her wildest dreams but so bored and restless with her loveless marriage that she begins an affair with her gardener.

An instant ratings smash-hit in the USA, *Desperate Housewives* filled the gap for an intelligent, edgy female-focused drama series left by the demise of the late, lamented ***Sex and the City***. Although it wasn't anywhere near as wilfully shocking or provocative as the antics of the Manhattan foursome, *Desperate Housewives* has nevertheless proven to be hugely entertaining, with a fine combination of humour, drama and shocking plot twists to keep us all gripped.

The Detectives

Sitcom | BBC One | episode duration 30 mins | broadcast 27 Jan 1993–28 Dec 1997

Principal Cast
Jasper Carrott · *DC Bob Lewis*
Robert Powell · *DC Dave Briggs*
George Sewell · *DS Frank Cottam*

Producers Nic Phillips (executive), Ed Bye **Writers** Steve Knight, Mike Whitehill **Theme Music** Keith Strachan, Matthew Strachan

The Detectives was a spin-off of a popular strand in the Jasper Carrott vehicle *Canned Carrott*, allowing the hapless detectives of Lewis and Briggs their own 30-minute slot. The pair are fairly useless, but despite this drawback they manage to get results on a variety of cases, often going undercover with hilarious consequences.

Robert Powell and Jasper Carrott actually make an endearing duo in this decent, if obvious, comedy series. Serious actor Powell has since given Carrott the credit for teaching him about comedy. It's not the sort of series where you'd expect to find intertextuality, but two episodes feature characters from other BBC shows – a story set on Jersey features John Nettles as ***Bergerac***; another episode takes the lads undercover as musicians at *The Paradise Club*. Writers Steve Knight and Mike Whitehill were long-time scribes for Jasper Carrott, although Whitehill's greatest contribution to television was in co-devising ***Who Wants to be a Millionaire?***

The Dick Emery Show

Comedy | BBC TV/BBC One | episode duration 25–50 mins | broadcast 13 Jul 1963–7 Feb 1981

Regular Cast
Dick Emery · *Various Characters*

Producers David Croft, James Gilbert, John Street, Dennis Main Wilson, Ernest Maxin, Colin Chapman, Harold Snoad **Writers** Various, including Dick Emery, David Cumming, John Warren, John Singer, Steven Singer, Mel Brooks, Mel Tolkin, David Nobbs, Peter Tinniswood, Maurice Wiltshire, Peter Robinson, Eric Davidson, Garry Chambers, Barry Cryer, Dick Clement, John Esmonde, Bob Larbey, Marty Feldman, Talbot Rothwell **Theme Music** Alan Roper

One of the longest-running and most successful sketch shows in history, *The Dick Emery Show* is surprisingly almost forgotten nowadays. That's a terrible shame, for although Emery's comedy does seem rather more a product of its time than comparable shows like ***Morecambe and Wise*** or ***The Two Ronnies***, it's still truly funny and a perfect representation of what people liked to laugh at throughout the 1960s and 1970s, as well as remaining Harry Enfield's biggest influence.

Richard Emery was born in 1915 in London to music-hall performers Callan and Emery. His early career included work as part of the *Gang Show* on radio before joining several 1950s TV comedy shows such as *Round the Bend*, ***Two's Company*** and even the legendary ***The Army Game***, in which he appeared for a year as Chubby Catchpole. In 1963, the BBC gave him his very own sketch series, which, amazingly, remained on air for 18 years. With an array of top-notch writers providing material for his shows (including several big-name American scribes such as Mel Brooks, *Carry On* maestro Talbot Rothwell, Marty Feldman, ***Likely Lads*** co-author Dick Clement and ***The Good Life***'s Esmonde and Larbey), the jokes came thick and fast.

Emery's most memorable characters returned week after week to appear in yet more outrageous incidents. Chief among them were dark-haired man-eater Hettie, a vicar with a set of gnashers big enough to crack open beer bottles, ancient, wheezing old geezer Lampwick, flagrantly camp Clarence ('Oooh, hello, honky tonk!'), a nearly tough skin-head, Bovver Boy, and of course the irrepressible blonde Mandy, forever being accosted in the street by a vox-pop reporter and being asked for her opinion, only to misinterpret his comments as being salacious and then wallop him in the stomach saying, 'Oooh, you are awful – but I like you!' before clattering away in her high heels. So popular was Mandy that her catchphrase became the title of a 1972 feature film showcasing the whole range of Emery's characters.

Following the last of his sketch shows, an elderly Emery starred in two seasons of a comedy detective/thriller series called *Emery Presents*. He played Jewish detective agency boss Bernie Weinstock, investigating two specific cases, 'Legacy of Murder' (broadcast 16 Feb–23 Mar 1981) and 'Jack of Diamonds' (3 Jun–15 Jul 1982), which was transmitted six months after Emery's death on 13 January 1983.

Dick Spanner

Animation | Anderson Burr for Channel 4 | episode duration 6 mins | broadcast 3 May–27 Sep 1987

Regular Voice Cast
Shane Rimmer · *Dick Spanner*

Creator Terry Adlam **Producers** Gerry Anderson and Christopher Burr **Writer** Harry Bolt (actually Tony Barwick under a pseudonym, a habit he'd acquired during the production of ***Terrahawks***) **Theme Music** Christopher Burr

When broadcaster and journalist Janet Street Porter came to Channel 4, one of her first big, brave acts was to create a current affairs strand aimed at 16-24-year-olds called ***Network 7***, which went out on Sunday early afternoons. Using handheld cameras to move around the presenters and with the screen littered with fast-scrolling information and trivia, it probably wasn't the best concept for a presentation aimed at people who'd be nursing hangovers from the night before. One regular element of the show managed to eclipse the rest. This contained no social commentary or current affairs content, just insanely daft puns and very craftily lame visual gags. *Dick Spanner* starred a metallic private detective from a dimension not far from our own, with long-time Anderson collaborator Shane Rimmer narrating the stories in the Raymond Chandler style. Many of the best jokes weren't scripted but added to the sets by director and creator Terry Adlam in the form of signs in the background or visual puns (when Dick says he was caught red-handed, we just know he's going to show us his fingers to prove it).

Two connected stories of eleven six-minute episodes each made up the series, 'The Case of the Human Cannon Ball' and 'The Case of the Maltese Parrot'. The stories were later re-edited and shown late at night on Channel 4 as four 24-minute episodes.

Dick Turpin

Action-Adventure | LWT for ITV | episode duration 30 mins | broadcast 6 Jan 1979-6 Mar 1982

Principal Cast

Richard O'Sullivan · *Dick Turpin*
Michael Deeks · *Swiftnick*
Christopher Benjamin · *Sir John Glutton*
David Daker · *Captain Nathan Spiker*

Creator Richard Carpenter **Producers** Sidney Cole, Paul Knight **Writers** Richard Carpenter, Charles Crichton, John Kane, Paul Wheeler **Theme Music** Denis King

Dick Turpin is an action-adventure series from the always-reliable stable of Richard Carpenter (***The Ghosts of Motley Hall, Catweazle***) that does what his later ***Robin of Sherwood*** would repeat by turning a violent criminal into a folk hero for children.

After returning from a tour of duty on Flanders, Dick Turpin is cheated out of a hefty inheritance and so, penniless, takes to the road as a highwayman, ably accompanied by young sidekick Swiftnick. This Turpin doesn't seem as motivated by stealing hard cash as his historical reputation suggests, and he turns benefactor, helping out people where he finds them in strife. His adventures usually bring him into conflict with the blustering Sir John Glutton and his military commander, the ruthless Spiker.

By 1979, this type of gung-ho, Saturday tea time adventure series was a dying breed, with only Knight and Carpenter's mid-eighties *Sherwood* series keeping the home fires burning on ITV. Richard O'Sullivan, known for sitcom roles up to this point, brought a heroic edge to the role of Turpin, and there was always lots of horseplay, swashbuckling and firing of flintlocks. The fun of the series, though, was in the villainous partnership of Glutton and Spiker, and in wondering just how many times Dick and Swiftnick could be captured and escape episode after episode.

The Dick Van Dyke Show

Sitcom | Calvada Productions for CBS (shown on BBC) | episode duration 25 mins | broadcast 19 Jul, 3 Oct 1960-25 May 1966, 11 May 2004 (USA)

Regular Cast

Dick Van Dyke · *Rob Petrie*
Mary Tyler Moore · *Laura Petrie*
Morey Amsterdam · *Maurice B. 'Buddy' Sorrell*
Rose Marie · *Sally Rogers*
Larry Mathews · *Richie Rosebud Petrie*
Carl Reiner · *Alan Brady*
Richard Deacon · *Mel Cooley*
Jerry Paris · *Jerry Helper*
Ann Morgan Guilbert · *Millie Helper*

Creator Carl Reiner **Producers** Sheldon Leonard, Danny Thomas (executive), Ronald Jacobs (associate), Sam Denoff, Bill Persky, Carl Reiner **Writers** Carl Reiner, David Adler, John Whedon, Sheldon Keller, Howard Merrill, Bill Idelson, Bill Persky, Sam Denoff, Garry Marshall, Jerry Belson, Dale McRaven, Carl Kleinschmitt **Theme Music** Earle H. Hagen

Rob Petrie works as an unappreciated scriptwriter on *The Alan Brady Show*, a top-rated sitcom with an obnoxious star. Luckily he has the support of his wife, Laura, and occasional good cheer from his neighbours in New Rochelle, Jerry and Millie.

The Dick Van Dyke Show might have suffered from a few hangovers from the 1950s – a perfectly normal married couple were seen to sleep in separate single beds at the behest of the network – but in other ways it was hugely progressive. Rob Petrie was shown at work (as opposed to just returning from 'the office', like most TV dads) and stories were equally balanced between his work and home life. Laura Petrie was a domestic goddess, the perfect wife, but she was also intelligent and never written merely to be 'the little woman' (and her decision to wear trousers instead of skirts was another thing that worried the network). They were a couple who knew their roles, but were pretty much an equal, loving partnership (many viewers were convinced that Van Dyke and Tyler Moore were a real married couple). They were also blessed with a cute kid, Richie, who unconsciously revealed his parents' wit when he complained about being teased at school because of his middle name, 'Rosebud'. Despite what his parents told him, it *wasn't* an acronym of all his uncles' names – Robert Oscar Sam Edward Benjamin Ulysses David.

The archetypal American sitcom, *The Dick Van Dyke Show* forms an important branch on the TV comedy family tree. It began life as a pilot called *Head of the Family*, written by and starring Carl Reiner, but TV executives felt it was 'too Jewish' and 'too New York'. Reworking his script as a vehicle for Broadway actor Dick Van Dyke, Reiner offered viewers a fresh, youthful series with attractive, quick-witted leads. In addition to Van Dyke, the series gave us Mary Tyler Moore as his wife, Laura. Having spent years in commercials and bit parts, Tyler Moore relished the chance of a starring role and displayed a canny knack for comedy. Her reward was ***The Mary Tyler Moore Show***, which became one of the most successful sitcoms ever, made Tyler Moore a TV megastar and led to the creation of her own production company, MTM, responsible for ***Rhoda, Hill Street Blues*** and ***St Elsewhere***, among many others.

Having starred in two of the most successful film musicals of the 1960s – *Mary Poppins* (1964) (in which he created a vocal style that's since become synonymous with similarly atrocious 'cockernee' accents) and *Chitty Chitty Bang Bang* (1968) – Dick Van Dyke returned to television in 1971 with *The New Dick Van Dyke Show*, in which he played a chat-show host. In the 1990s, he gave us another successful TV character, police consultant Dr Mark Sloan of *Diagnosis Murder*.

Trivia

Though we caught glimpses of it during *The Dick Van Dyke Show*, the fictional sitcom that Rob Petrie wrote for, *The Alan Brady Show*, finally reached TV screens in 2003 in the form of a short-lived, three-dimensional, computer-animated sitcom. Carl Reiner re-created the voice of Alan Brady.

Diff'rent Strokes

Sitcom | Embassy Television/Norman Lear/Tandem Productions for NBC/ABC (shown on ITV) | episode duration 25 mins | broadcast 3 Nov 1978–Mar 1986 (USA)

Regular Cast

Conrad Bain · *Philip Drummond*
Gary Coleman · *Arnold Jackson*
Todd Bridges · *Willis Jackson*
Dana Plato · *Kimberly Drummond*
Charlotte Rae · *Edna Garrett*
Nedra Volz · *Adelaide Brubaker*
Mary Jo Catlett · *Pearl Gallagher*
Danny Cooksey · *Sam McKinney*
Dixie Carter, Mary Ann Mobley · *Maggie McKinney*
Rosalind Chao · *Miss Chung*
Dody Goodman · *Aunt Sophia*
Jason Hervey · *Charlie*
Janet Jackson · *Charlene DuPrey*
Steven Mond · *Robbie Jason*
Shavar Ross · *Dudley Ramsey*
Nikki Swasey · *Lisa Hayes*
Le Tari · *Ted Ramsey*

Creators Jeff Harris and Bernie Kukoff **Producers** Bob Brunner, Budd Grossman, Ken Hecht, Blake Hunter, Howard Leeds (executive), John Maxwell Anderson, Barbara Cramer, Roxie Wenk Evans (associate), Al Aidekman, Martin Cohan, Richard Gurman, Herbert Kenwith, Ben Starr **Writers** Ben Starr, Alan Rosen, Fred Rubin, Albert E. Lewin, Sandy Veith, Howard Leeds, Martin Cohan, Ed Jurist, Dawn Aldredge, Scott Rubenstein, Calvin Kelly, Glenn Padnick, Bruce Taylor, A. Dudley Johnson Jr, Howard Meyers, Bob Brunner, Ken Hecht, Robert Jayson, Blake Hunter **Theme Music** Alan Thicke, Gloria Loring and Al Burton, who reminded us that 'It takes Diff'rent Strokes to move the world'

Had *Diff'rent Strokes* been made in the UK, it probably would have been just another class-conscious comedy. While class played a part in the series, it was inherent in the set-up that brothers Willis and Arnold weren't felt to be different because of their social standing but because of their colour. After his terminally ill housekeeper asks him to take on her boys after her death, millionaire Philip Drummond decides to offer Willis and Arnold a home. The boys are displanted from the familiar surroundings of Harlem into his lavish pad, along with new housekeeper Mrs Garrett and Mr Drummond's 13-year-old daughter Kimberley.

The series tackled many social issues, including drink-driving, teenage sex and drug abuse (featuring a visit from Nancy Reagan during her 'Just Say No' campaign). But it's remembered chiefly for the diminutive genius of Gary Coleman, whose perfect comic timing and expressively cute face stole many a scene (often just by repeating his catchphrase: 'What you talking 'bout, Willis?').

As the older juvenile leads matured, it grew more and more obvious that Gary Coleman never would (a liver complaint and a transplant at the age of five had left him permanently the height and build of a child). So Arnold was given a younger brother to interact with, in the form of the carrot-haired son of Mr D's new wife. But after eight seasons and 189 episodes, *Strokes* just wasn't different enough and the series was dropped by its network. The child actors who'd starred in the series found it difficult to adjust to their lives away from their fictional millionaire mansion. Gary Coleman struggled to find roles significantly different from Arnold and later sued his parents and agent for mismanagement of his earnings. Dana Plato died of a suspected suicidal drug overdose in 1999; Todd Bridges also had his own battles with drugs, though thankfully he overcame his problems.

dinnerladies

Sitcom | Good Fun/Pozzitive Productions for BBC One | episode duration 30 mins | broadcast 12 Nov 1998–27 Jan 2000

Regular Cast

Victoria Wood · *Brenda*
Thelma Barlow · *Dolly*
Anne Reid · *Jean*
Andrew Dunn · *Tony*
Celia Imrie · *Philippa*
Duncan Preston · *Stan*
Maxine Peake · *Twinkle*
Shobna Gulati · *Anita*
Julie Walters · *Petula*

Creator/Writer Victoria Wood **Producers** Geoff Posner, Victoria Wood **Theme Music** 'Day by Day' was composed by Victoria Wood, and originally ran as an instrumental track. As events in the final season took a decidedly melancholy turn, Wood provided poignant lyrics that played out over appropriate credits at the end of each episode.

The 1990s saw a downturn in the number of on-screen appearances by 1980s TV icon Victoria Wood, who by that stage was making an enormous name for herself performing as a stand-up comedienne in front of vast audiences. *Victoria Wood's All Day Breakfast*, a one-off, semi-sequel to ***Victoria Wood: As Seen on TV***, was shown on Christmas Day 1992; two years later, a one-woman special, *Live in Your Own Home*, was transmitted. Her other major work was a *Screen One* comedy drama entitled 'Pat and Margaret' (broadcast on 11 September 1994), which once again reunited Wood with her long-time collaborators Julie Walters, Duncan Preston and Celia Imrie. 'Pat and Margaret' focused much more on the melancholic aspects of life than anything Wood had previously created for television, revealing a genius for conveying the bittersweet nature of life with deftness and assurance, plus an unerring eye for detail.

When Victoria Wood announced that her next project would be a sitcom, viewers were naturally expecting a full-blown return to the rip-roaring comedy of *As Seen on TV*. However, Wood took those preconceptions and turned them on their head. Yes, *dinnerladies* was absolutely hilarious, but lying scant millimetres below the surface of the comedy was a strand of sadness and disappointment, a peculiar form of humour that has its roots in the lives of northern working-class women, one that had paid rich ratings dividends for many years via the comedic characters and storylines of ***Coronation Street***. The setting for *dinnerladies* was a factory canteen on the outskirts of Manchester, where the lives and loves of the women who prepare the dinners (or 'lunches', as southerners would call them) for the factory workers formed the core of the series. Leader of the women is Bren, good-natured, warm-hearted and eager to crack a joke with everyone; Dolly and Jean are the 'senior' members of staff, constantly bitching at each other; dumb Anita and slovenly, foul-mouthed Twinkle are the younger team-members. Managing them all is ever-suffering Tony, a man who puts up with all of their 'women's talk' with an air of patient understanding and who engages in light-hearted flirting with the women more out of the understanding that that's what is expected of him rather than because he has wandering hands and eyes. Also working in the factory are dour, by-the-rulebook handyman Stan, and fish-out-of-water human resources officer Philippa, who manages to put people's noses out of joint simply by being from the South. A regular visitor to the canteen kitchen is Bren's elderly mother Petula, a fantasist who claims to enjoy sexual encounters with Hollywood celebrities and live the glamorous life of an international superstar. In reality, she's actually a smelly old lady with a wind problem whose appearances in the canteen tend to embarrass her very understanding daughter. However, there's never quite enough evidence to dismiss her fanciful claims entirely. . .

When *dinnerladies* first began, critics weren't as kind to it as perhaps the show deserved, finding its broad northern comedy difficult to get to grips with. Audiences on the other hand adored it, and a second, longer series was rapidly commissioned. Even before the second run of episodes was broadcast, however, Wood announced that this season would be the last time she would ever attempt to write a traditional sitcom, the process having exhausted her utterly. If anything, these episodes moved even further away from the traditional sitcom format, delving much deeper into the realm of tragedy, sadness and soap-style drama (it's telling that most of the cast, including Anne Reid and Thelma Barlow, had already been regulars in *Coronation Street* – newcomer Shobna Gulati would later join the permanent *Corrie* cast). When in the final episode Petula died in hospital, viewers didn't know whether to laugh, cry or do both at the same time. With Bren and Tony preparing to make a new life for themselves, the time felt right to draw the story to a close. Although it ran for just 16 episodes, *dinnerladies* managed to quickly grab itself a place among the all-time sitcom greats.

Disappearing World

Documentary | Granada for ITV | episode duration 60 mins | broadcast 1970–93

Producer Brian Moser

Disappearing World provided a long-running series of in-depth films that showed, from the perspective of the peoples of remote corners of the world, how the modern age was intruding on and destroying their lives. Each film had no narrator, allowing the images to tell the story, with occasional subtitles providing the necessary translations.

Brian Moser was the man behind the concept, having previously served a stint as producer on Granada TVs seminal current affairs magazine programme, *World in Action*.

The District Nurse

Drama/Soap | BBC One | episode duration 30–50 mins | broadcast 10 Jan 1984–24 May 1987

Regular Cast
Nerys Hughes · *Nurse Megan Roberts*
John Ogwen · *David Price*
Deborah Manship · *Nesta Mogg*
Margaret John · *Gwen Harris*
Nathalie Price · *Nora*
Rio Fanning · *Dr O'Casey*
Ian Saynor · *Dylan Roderick*
Ifan Huw Dafydd · *Reverend Geraint Rhys*
Ernest Evans · *Will Hopkin*
Elen Roger Jones · *Sarah Hopkin*
Elizabeth Morgan · *Mrs Prosser-Davies*
Beth Morris · *Evalina Williams*
Gareth Potter · *Bryn Morris*
Philip Raymond · *Hugh Morris*
Philip Hurdwood · *Dr Charles Barclay*
Freddie Jones · *Dr Emlyn Isaacs*
Bethan Jones · *Lily Thomas*
Janet Aethwy · *Ruth Jones*
Nicholas Jones · *Dr James Isaacs*

Creators Julia Smith, Tony Holland **Producers** Julia Smith, Tony Holland (executive), Brian Spiby, Peter Edwards **Writers** Various, including Tony Holland, Julia Smith, William Ingram, Peter King, Frank Vickery, Juliet Ace, Gwenlyn Parry, Michael Robartes, Jane Hollowood, Harry Duffin, Rob Gittins **Theme Music** David Mindel composed the lovely twinkly, harp-based theme tune.

In the small Welsh mining town of Pencwm, new district nurse Megan Roberts encounters resistance to her new-fangled ways. The local medics are tired and uninterested in helping people who can't pay for their services, and the poor themselves are more used to getting help from local herbalist Nesta Mogg. Despite these barriers, Megan still ploughs on, riding up and down the valleys on her bicycle, determined to help people out – whether they want to be helped or not.

Created by ***EastEnders*** supremo Julia Smith to fill the twice-weekly early evening slot occupied by shows like ***Angels*** and ***Triangle***, *The District Nurse* was a well-crafted if slow-moving drama series that combined two of British TV's great obsessions – medical dramas with nostalgic trips down memory lane. Nerys Hughes seemed born to play this role of a bossy, slightly dowdy nurse – a much greater acting challenge for her than the ditzy comedy roles (such as in ***The Liver Birds***) she'd been known for up to that date, and one that she rose to with aplomb. With quality support from John Ogwen as the kind-hearted mine worker David, *The District Nurse* seemed to run its natural course when *EastEnders* arrived as a permanent fixture in the schedules in February 1985. So it came as quite a surprise when Megan Roberts returned to TV two years later, this time in the mid-Wales seaside town of Glanmore and working alongside Freddie Jones as Dr Emlyn Isaacs.

Dixon of Dock Green

See pages 246–8

The 'Doctor' . . . Series

See pages 249–51

Dr Finlay's Casebook

Drama | BBC TV/BBC One | episode duration 45–50 mins | broadcast 16 Aug 1962–3 Jan 1971

Principal Cast
Bill Simpson · *Dr Alan Finlay*
Andrew Cruickshank · *Dr Angus Cameron*
Barbara Mullen · *Janet*
Eric Woodburn · *Dr Snoddie*
Tracy Reed · *Barbara Davidson*
James Copeland · *Hooky Buchanan*
Effie Morrison · *Mistress Niven*
Geraldine Newman · *Mary*
Fulton Mackay · *Jamie*
Anthony Valentine · *Bruce Cameron*
John Humphrey · *Dr Maddock*
Wilfred Pickles · *Mr Finlay*
Duncan Macrae · *Cogger*

Creator A. J. Cronin **Producers** Campbell Logan, Andrew Osborn, Gerard Glaister, Douglas Allen, Royston Morley, John Henderson **Writers** Various, including Donald Bull, John Lucarotti, Harry Green, Dick Sharples, Elaine Morgan, Jan Read, Vincent Tilsley, John Pennington, Pat Dunlop, Anthony Steven, Robert Holmes, N. J. Crisp, from the stories of A. J. Cronin **Theme Music** 'March' from *Little Suite* by Trevor Duncan

One of the BBC's longest-running and most popular medical dramas began very modestly, as a six-episode run of stories adapted from A. J. Cronin's *The Adventures of a Black Bag*. Viewers took the stories of Dr Finlay, Dr Cameron and their housekeeper Janet to their hearts, and soon those six episodes became the first of a staggering 191 episodes, spread over nine years.

The year is 1928, and young junior doctor Alan Finlay arrives in the small Scottish town of Tannochbrae to join the established Arden House practice belonging to crusty Dr Angus Cameron. Throughout the series, Finlay's radical ideas and methods for treating the sick were shown to

Continued on page 252

Dixon of Dock Green

Jack Warner as George Dixon

If someone uses the name 'Dixon of Dock Green' nowadays, odds on they're referring to someone out of touch with modern living. The cosiness and old-fashioned approach of television's most famous copper represent both a nostalgia for a time when you could leave your front door open and not worry about someone breaking in, and a feeling that a man in a police uniform was someone you could trust.

Audiences first saw George Dixon in the 1949 film *The Blue Lamp*, brought to life by well-known variety actor Jack Warner. Warner's cheery attitude made for the perfect community bobby on his beat. A constable at Paddington Green police station, George Dixon has 20 years' service behind him and just six months to go before retirement. He's a married man, though their only son, Bert, was killed during the war, so when George is asked to 'puppy-walk' a

Crime Drama

BBC TV/BBC One
Episode Duration: 30/45 mins
Broadcast: 9 Jul 1955–1 May 1976

Regular Cast
Jack Warner · *PC/Sergeant George Dixon*
Peter Byrne · *PC/DC/DS/DI Andy Crawford*
Billie Whitelaw, Jeanette Hutchinson, Anna Dawson · *Mary Dixon/Crawford*
Arthur Rigby · *Sergeant Flint*
Dorothy Casey · *Nancy Murphy*
Neil Wilson · *PC 'Tubb' Barrell*
Moira Mannion · *WP Sergeant Grace Millard*
Robert Cawdron · *Inspector/DI Cherry*
David Lyn · *PC Jenkins*
Anthony Parker · *PC Bob Penney*
Graham Ashley · *PC/DC Tommy Hughes*
Geoffrey Adams · *PC/DC 'Laudie' Lauderdale*
David Webster · *Cadet/PC Jamie MacPherson*
Hilda Fenemore · *Jennie Wren*
Jocelyn Rhodes · *WPC Kay Shaw*
Michael Nightingale · *DC Jack Cotton*
Nicholas Donnelly · *PC/Sergeant Johnny Wills*
Max Latimer · *PC 'Tiny' Bush*
Ruth Lodge · *WP Sergeant 'Scotty' Scott*
Anne Ridler · *WP Sergeant Chris Freeman*
Christopher Gilmore · *PC Clyde*
Janet Moss · *WPC 'Barney' Barnes*
John Hughes · *PC John Jones*
Jan Miller · *WPC Alex Johns*

young policeman on his first day he adopts a paternal aspect, showing him the kind of local knowledge only experience can bring. His fellow officers look up to him and his superiors can depend on him. He's the model officer. All of which makes his sudden death in the middle of the picture, shot by a panicked thief (a young Dirk Bogarde) all the more shocking.

Dixon's co-creator, Ted Willis, found it difficult to let go of the character and wrote him into a stage play before finally grooming him for television as the star of his own series, a replacement for the popular ***Fabian of the Yard***. Dock Green stood in for Paddington, while Dixon became a widower and proud father of a daughter, Mary, in her 20s (initially played by Billie Whitelaw). Willis had done his research to ensure the show was an accurate representation of community policing. But he'd also remembered that viewers like their heroes with a bit of heart. The first episode took its lead from the opening act of the movie, with Dixon once again taking under his wing a new recruit – Andy Crawford, who would become a part of the family in more ways than one when he married Mary Dixon at the end of the show's second year.

Each episode, which in early series bore the subtitle 'Some Stories of a London Policeman', began and ended with George standing underneath the lamp outside the station. George's cheery 'Evenin' all' became as much a part of the British language as 'You're nicked' would be a decade or more later. He spoke directly to camera, anecdotally sharing his memories of policework and family life. He spoke to viewers as old, trusted friends, valued members of his community; at the show's peak, 16 million people visited Dock Green every Saturday night. At the end of a series, George was even known to let his viewers know that he was 'going on holiday for a few weeks' so that they wouldn't worry about not seeing him around. Talk about being in touch with your audience.

Like almost all TV at the time, Dixon was broadcast live in the early days, which is one reason why so few of the original run of episodes remain in the archives (just five from the first seven years, in fact). It means that early TV appearances by the likes of Sean Connery, David Hemmings, Michael Caine and Nigel Hawthorne are probably lost forever. There are, nevertheless, still some treats to be found in the extant episodes, mainly from the second season. In 'The Rotten Apple', a well-known gentleman thief is arrested for resuming his career of crime, only for George to discover that the real thief is one of his own officers (played by Paul Eddington), trying to pay off mounting gambling debts. George's reaction to the bent officer's suggestion that he's on the payroll of a local bookie is one of the few times Dixon is seen to lose his temper. 'The Roaring Boy' echoed

George's cheery 'Evenin' all' became as much a part of the British language as 'You're nicked' would be a decade or more later.

Paul Elliott · *Cadet Michael Bonnet*
Peter Thornton · *PC Burton*
Geoffrey Kenion · *PC Roberts*
Robert Arnold · *PC/DC Swain*
Zeph Gladstone · *WPC Liz Harris*
Anne Carroll · *WPC Shirley Palmer*
Duncan Lamont · *Sergeant Bob Cooper*
Ronald Bridges · *PC Ted Bryant*
Jean Dallas · *WPC Betty Williams*
Joe Dunlop · *DC Pearson*
Andrew Bradford · *PC Brian Turner*
Pamela Buchner · *WDC Ann Foster*
Jenny Logan · *WPC Sally Reed*
Michael Osborne · *PC David Newton*
Kenneth Watson · *DI Scott*
Derek Anders · *DC Webb*
Gregory de Polnay · *DS Mike Brewer*
Stephen Marsh · *PC Harry Dunne*
Richard Heffer · *DS Alan Bruton*
Ben Howard · *DC Len Clayton*

Creator Ted Willis

Producers Douglas Moodie, G. B. Lupino, Ronald Marsh, Robin Nash, Philip Barker, Eric Fawcett, Joe Waters

Writers Various, including Paul Ableman, Cyril Abraham, Bill Bassett, Derek Benfield, Bill Craig, N. J. Crisp, Pat Dunlop, David Ellis, David Fisher, Tom Greene, Luanshya Greer, P. J. Hammond, Robert Holmes, Derek Ingrey, Ivor Jay, Gerald Kelsey, Neil Kingsley, Peter Ling, Geoffrey Matthews, Eric Paice, Ludovic Peters, Roy Russell, Dick Sharples, Robert Storey, Jack Trevor Story, Arthur Swinson, Richard Waring, Mike Watts, John Wiles, Tony Williamson, Ted Willis, Michael Winder

Theme Music Originally 'Maybe It's Because I'm a Londoner', a traditional musical hall tune by Hubert Gregg and whistled by Jack Warner. However, the theme most usually identified with the series is 'An Ordinary Copper' by Jeff Darnell.

certain scenes in *The Blue Lamp*, with George staring down the barrel of a gun once again, courtesy of an AWOL soldier (Kenneth Cope). 'Father-in-Law' gives us a chance to see George in a social environment, the marriage of his daughter to Andy Crawford (now a detective in Dock Green CID). Despite a token concession to the drama with the matter of a stolen wallet, it's really just an opportunity for Jack Warner to return to his variety roots and give us all a good singsong.

In 1960, viewers were introduced to Newtown, the setting for ***Z Cars***. With its earthy Northern characters and more modern approach to policing, it left poor Dixon looking a little tame in comparison. Dixon's writers tried to compete, but the fact of the matter was the viewers liked the show because of its homely feel, not in spite of it. George was promoted to Sergeant in 1965, which meant his little introductory homilies could be performed from behind a counter inside the station. Episodes began to be pre-recorded instead of going out live, and in 1969 the show switched to colour, but little else changed. In fact, the more the writers tried to make the show more contemporary, the more obvious it was that it could never be anything of the sort.

Jack Warner was already 60 when the show began, but he was closer to 80 when the show came to an end in 1976 after 429 episodes (the series' record for longest-running police drama series was only beaten in 2003, when ***The Bill*** celebrated its 21st birthday). Strong competition from hard-knock shows like ***Special Branch*** and ***The Sweeney***, plus Warner's own ill health, eventually took their toll, and George Dixon told his final anecdote in a bitter-sweet episode called 'Reunion'. When Jack Warner died five years later, his coffin was carried by officers from Paddington Green station, just as they must have done for the original George Dixon in 1949.

In 1988, BBC Two screened a one-off play called *The Black and Blue Lamp* as part of their *Screenplay* season, a satirical look at how attitudes had changed to policing. Set initially in the hours after George Dixon's fatal shooting at the end of *The Blue Lamp*, his captured killer and a young constable suddenly find themselves transported forward 30 years into an episode of a Sweeney-like action series in which Kenneth Cranham plays a hard-nosed ball-breaking crooked cop.

The 'Doctor'... Series

Clockwise from top: Simon Cuff, George Layton, Robin Nedwell, Barry Evans, Geoffrey Davies and Jonathan Lynn.

In 1954, a movie adaptation of Richard Gordon's best-selling novel *Doctor in the House* was released, with Dirk Bogarde starring as the trainee doctor finding his feet at St Swithin's Hospital. A series of movies ensued, with Bogarde and legendary 'bounder' Leslie Phillips, along with Michael Craig (who later starred in soap opera ***Triangle*** for the BBC), and while not exactly challenging the *Carry On* films for variety, it proved hugely successful throughout the 1950s and 1960s. Eventually the films prompted the creation of a TV series based on the same source material, but updated to take into account the changing face of British society as the Sixties swung into the Seventies. With scripts written by an astonishing array of writing talent (*Pythons* Chapman and Cleese, *Goodies* Garden and Oddie, and comedy stalwart Barry Cryer among others), *Doctor in the House* soon became an enormous success for ITV.

Barry Evans initially starred as medical student Mike Upton, an earnest young man determined to become a good doctor, yet often led astray by his birds-and-booze obsessed friends Duncan Waring, Phil Collier and Dick Stuart-Clark. Their nemesis was stern Professor Loftus, a character cast straight from the same mould as James Robertson-Justice's immortal Sir Lancelot Spratt from the films. Like the films, successive series looked at another aspect of the medical profession, so after two seasons and 26 episodes, the student medics finally qualified as 'proper doctors' and their story progressed in the follow-on series, *Doctor at Large*.

Sitcom
LWT for ITV/7 Network Australia, BBC One
Episode Duration: 25–30 mins
Broadcast: 12 Jul 1969–3 Jul 1970 (*Doctor in the House*), 28 Feb–12 Sep 1971 (*Doctor at Large*), 9 Apr 1972–29 Dec 1973 (*Doctor in Charge*), 21 Apr–16 June 1974 (*Doctor at Sea*), 27 Apr 1975–10 Apr 1977 (*Doctor on the Go*), 5 Feb 1979–10 May 1980 (*Doctor Down Under* - Aus.), 28 Feb–4 Apr 1991 (*Doctor at the Top*)

Regular Cast
Barry Evans · *Mike Upton*
Robin Nedwell · *Duncan Waring*
George Layton · *Paul Collier*
Geoffrey Davies · *Dick Stuart-Clark*
Ernest Clark · *Professor Geoffrey Loftus, Captain Norman Loftus*
Richard O'Sullivan · *Dr Lawrence Bingham*
Simon Cuff · *Dave Briddock*
Ralph Michael · *The Dean*
Martin Shaw · *Huw Evans*
Yutte Stensgaard · *Helga*
Kirsten Lindholm · *Ingrid*
Jonathan Lynn · *Danny Hooley*
Arthur Lowe · *Dr Maxwell*
Madeline Smith · *Sue Maxwell*
Brian Oulton · *Dr Griffin*
Joy Stewart · *Sister Fowles*
Joan Benham · *Lady Elizabeth Loftus*
Helen Fraser · *Dr Mary Parsons/Bingham*
Sammie Winmill · *Nurse Sandra Crumpton*
Elizabeth Counsell · *Nurse Joyce Winton*

Having successfully qualified as a doctor, Mike Upton ventures forth into the big wide world in the hope of getting a permanent position somewhere. At first abandoning the sitcom's initial 'sit' of St Swithin's Hospital, Mike attempts to get work at a GP's practice before eventually ending back with his friends Paul and Dick at the hospital he graduated from. Following the vaguely saucy stereotype inherent in most 'doctors and nurses' comedies of this era, *Doctor at Large*, like its immediate predecessor, is notable for the quality writers it attracted. One of John Cleese's episodes is particularly worthy of note, being set in a seaside boarding house complete with obstreperous hotelier – the genesis of ***Fawlty Towers***. Having played a supporting role in *Doctor in the House*, Jonathan Lynn went behind the camera to deliver a script for the show – he would later go on to write ***Yes, Minister***. Now under the banner of *Doctor in Charge*, one long series of 29 episodes (six made in black and white owing to an industrial dispute) saw the last appearance of lead character Barry Evans, before the programme made its bow in late 1973.

With Dr Mike having fallen in love and moved to a different hospital, the dynamic of the *Doctor* . . . series changed radically. Returning medic Duncan Waring joined forces with Collier and Stuart-Clark to create a terrible trio of lady-killer medics. Forty-four episodes across two seasons were produced, three of which heralded the beginning of a long career in television for a young Liverpudlian script-writer called Phil Redmond – who would, of course, go on to create ***Grange Hill***, ***Brookside*** and ***Hollyoaks***.

The following year saw the series being renamed *Doctor at Sea* – when Dick Stuart-Clark is fired from St Swithin's Hospital, he and his friend Duncan Waring take new positions as medics aboard the HMS *Begonia*. To their horror, they discover that the captain is the identical twin of their old adversary Professor Loftus (a handy way of keeping series regular Ernest Clark employed in this new setting!). A single series of 13 episodes was produced.

Back on dry land again, Duncan and Dick once more indulge in their regular nurse-chasing activities at St Swithin's Hospital for a further two seasons and 26 episodes of *Doctor on the Go*. One episode was co-written by ***Monty Python*** star Graham Chapman and a young writer called Douglas Adams, who would achieve huge success the following year with the radio broadcast of *The Hitch-Hiker's Guide to the Galaxy*. In the final episode, Duncan's playboy years come to an end as he marries pretty colleague Kate Wright. And as Duncan's bachelor life came to an end, so did the *Doctor* . . . series of programmes on LWT. It was the end of an era – or so people thought, until the 7 Network in Australia decided to revive the series with *Doctor Down Under*.

One of John Cleese's episodes is particularly worthy of note, being set in a boarding house complete with obstreperous hotelier – the genesis of *Fawlty Towers*.

Following a successful stage tour of *Doctor in the House* in Australia and New Zealand in 1974, it seemed inevitable that the *Doctor* . . . series would be an ideal candidate to follow in the footsteps of ***Are You Being Served?*** and ***Love Thy Neighbour*** by producing its very own special episodes for an Australian audience. Robin Nedwell and Geoffrey Davies duly hopped on a plane and headed 'down under' to record a single season of 13 episodes, reprising the roles they had last played on TV two years before. Also travelling to Australia was producer William G Stewart, a TV producer responsible for a number of comedies at the time but who would later become a household name when presenting long-running quiz show *Fifteen to One*. Sadly, the scripts lacked the sparkle of previous versions. The show wasn't a great hit either in Australia or back in the UK when it was transmitted on an easily avoided Sunday afternoon slot in 1981.

For a few years in the early 1990s, the BBC began to revive, Frankenstein-like, sitcoms that had perished years previously, and so the *Doctor* . . . series joined the ranks of ***The Liver Birds***, ***Are You Being Served?*** and ***Agony*** in a short-lived resurrection. *Doctor at the Top* brought us up-to-date with what had been happening to the staff of St Swithin's Hospital in the years since we last witnessed their antics. Former ladies' man Duncan Waring had become father to five daughters while holding down a job as resident paediatrician at St Swithin's, and astonishingly (not!), both of his former friends Paul Collier and Dick Stuart-Clark found themselves as permanent staff members there too. Of course, this being the 1990s, it was impossible for veteran scriptwriters Oddie and Layton to resort to the skirt-chasing antics of old. Sadly, this seemed to restrict the opportunities for humour and the revival flatlined after just seven episodes. Despite being one of the longest-running sitcoms to be listed within these pages, the TV series has rarely been repeated, largely thanks to the original films still being available to fill daytime gaps in the schedule.

John Grieve · *Purser*
Bob Todd · *Cyril*
John Drake · *Chief Officer*
Desmond Stokes · *Radio Officer*
Jacquie-Ann Carr · *Kate Wright*
John Kane · *Dr Andrew Mackenzie*
Andrew Knox · *Dr James Gascoigne*
Alison King · *Nurse Reynolds*
Gerald Cross · *Sir Edmund Steele*
Derek Deadman · *Porter*
Frank Wilson · *Norman Beaumont*
John Derum · *Dr Maurice Griffin*
Joan Bruce · *Sister Cummings*
Jennifer Mellet · *Linda*
Ken Wayne · *Professor Wilkinson*
Georgina Melville · *Geraldine Waring*
Jill Benedict · *Emma Stuart-Clark*
Chloë Annett · *Rebecca Stuart-Clark*
Roger Sloman · *Dr Lionel Snell*

Creator Richard Gordon (pen-name for Gordon Ostlere)

Producers Humphrey Barclay, William G. Stewart, Susan Belbin

Writers Graham Chapman, John Cleese, Graeme Garden, Bill Oddie, Barry Cryer, Bernard McKenna, David Sherlock, Oliver Fry (aka George Layton), Jonathan Lynn, Andy Baker, Geoff Rowley, David Yallop, Phil Redmond, David Askey, Gail Renard, Richard Laing, Chris Beetles, Rob Buckman, Selwyn Roberts, Steve Thorn, Paul Wolfson, Bernie Sharp, Jon Watkins, Douglas Adams

Theme Music Alan Tew

contrast wildly with Cameron's much more traditional approach, and although they rarely seriously fell out with each other, each doctor learned a great deal from the other's techniques, knowledge and experience. The other main character to appear throughout the programme's run was Arden House's loyal housekeeper, Janet – a down-to-earth, gentle, elderly lady who was always on hand to calm troubled waters and prepare a good cup of tea.

Just as ***All Creatures Great and Small*** and ***Heartbeat*** garnered good ratings by evoking a warm, rosy nostalgia for simpler, nicer times gone by, so *Dr Finlay's Casebook* provided the viewers of the 1960s with a gentle way to relax and think back to a rural golden age. That's not to say that the programme's storylines were bland or wishy-washy – indeed, some episodes dealt with issues as sensitive as illegal abortions and incest. In fact, *Dr Finlay's Casebook* was so well received that Scottish TV decided to bring the show back to a whole new generation of viewers (naming it simply *Dr Finlay*), this time starring David Rintoul as Dr Finlay, Ian Bannen as Dr Cameron and ***One Foot in the Grave***'s Annette Crosbie as Janet.

Doctor in the House

See THE 'DOCTOR' . . . SERIES, *pages* 249–51

Dr Kildare

Drama | Arena Productions/MGM for NBC (shown on BBC One) | episode duration 60/30 mins | broadcast 28 Sep 1961–5 Apr 1966 (USA)

Principal Cast

Richard Chamberlain · *Dr James Kildare*
Raymond Massey · *Dr Leonard Gillespie*
Eddie Ryder · *Dr Simon Agurski*
Jud Taylor · *Dr Thomas Gerson*
Joan Patrick · *Susan Deigh*
Lee Kurty · *Nurse Zoe Lawton*
Steven Bell · *Dr Quint Lowry*
Jean Innes · *Nurse Fain*

Creator Max Brand **Producers** Norman Felton (executive), Douglas Benton, Calvin Clements Jr, Herbert Hirshchman, David Victor **Writers** Various, including Theodore Apstein, William Bast, Douglas Benton, Jerry de Bono, Gene Roddenberry **Theme Music** 'Three Stars Will Shine Tonight' by Jerry Goldsmith. Richard Chamberlain released a lyrical version of the tune.

Although *Dr Kildare* made a star out of Richard Chamberlain, he was not the first actor to take on the mantle of the idealistic young intern at the Blair General Hospital. Lew Ayres made the role famous in a series of films between 1938 and 1942, starting with *Young Dr Kildare* (1938), also featuring Lionel Barrymore in the role of Dr Gillespie.

The same format as the films was adopted for the TV series, with Chamberlain perfectly cast as the fresh-faced Kildare, arriving to a new job at the hospital, specialising in internal medicine under the mentorship of Raymond Massey's Dr Gillespie. From there it was all standard fare that managed to portray a fairly accurate account of working in a hospital during the 1960s. Much like ***ER*** today, there was discussion of medical ethics, career pressures and the effect of illness on patients and their families. With Kildare promoted to resident by the third season, the show evolved as it went, with the focus shifting away from the doctors and on to the many patients. For the fifth and final season in 1965–6, *Dr Kildare* was transformed into a twice weekly, half hour serial.

Richard Chamberlain has regularly confessed to finding the role of Dr Kildare difficult to shake off, but he will forever be remembered for this well-regarded ratings winner.

Dr Quinn, Medicine Woman

Drama | Sullivan Company for CBS (shown on ITV) | episode duration 60 mins | broadcast 1 Jan 1993–16 May 1998 (USA)

Principal Cast

Jane Seymour · *Dr Michaela 'Mike' Quinn*
Joe Lando · *Byron Sully*
Chad Allen · *Matthew Cooper*
Erika Floress, Jessica Bowman · *Colleen Cooper*
Shawn Toovey · *Brian Cooper*

Creator Beth Sullivan **Producer** Beth Sullivan, Carl Bunder, Phillip Gerson, Chris Abbott, Jane Seymour (executive)

It is 1860 and Dr Michaela 'Mike' Quinn leaves the pratice she worked at with her father after his death and heads to the remote wilderness town of Colorado Springs. As a female surgeon in a man's world, Mike has had it tough already and she take to this new challenge with gusto, eventually winning over the initially distrustful townsfolk. Shortly after her arrival in the village, she takes on the responsibility of bringing up three orphaned children after their mother dies and, of course, there is the handsome and mysterious Byron Sully to provide assistance when needed. By the end of the series, Mike and Sully marry and have a child of their own.

Dr Quinn, Medicine Woman ended in 1998, but the dedicated fanbase of the frontier adventures of Dr Mike has been such that two TV movies have been produced since, the last being broadcast in 2001. As always, there is a strong campaign for further exploits. Despite Jane Seymour's lengthy career, Dr Quinn remains her most recognised role, and the actress won a Golden Globe for Best Actress in 1996, along with a later Emmy nomination.

Doctor Who

See pages 254–60

Dodger, Bonzo and the Rest

Drama | Thames for ITV | episode duration 25 mins | broadcast 18 Feb 1985–24 Mar 1986, 22 Dec 1986

Regular Cast
Lee Ross · *Dodger*
Sophy McCallum, Jodie Gordon · *Bonzo*
Mark Fletcher · *Ronnie*
Lyndon Hayes · *Brian*
Richard Holgate · *Delmont*
Stephen Sweeney · *Gerry*
Caroline Jay · *Teacher*
Jenny Jay · *Elaine*
Mark McKenzie · *Mickey*
Zeph Ponos · *Nikos*
Jennie Goossens · *Steph*
Leesa Williams · *Liza*

Creator Geoffrey Case **Producer** Brian Walcroft (executive), Sheila Kinany **Writers** Geoffrey Case, Johnny Byrne **Theme Music** 'Our House' by Madness

A spin-off from an episode of ***Dramarama***, *Dodger, Bonzo and the Rest* followed brother and sister Dodger and Bonzo, inhabitants of a children's home. In among the typical light-hearted scrapes we might expect from a children's drama, there were serious elements, such as coping with a thief in the house or looking at the greater likelihood of white children being fostered over non-white children, and how siblings often face the threat of being split up.

Series writer Geoffrey Case had previously written a six-part series for Children's ITV (in the *Watch It!* segment that preceded CITV) called *Nobody's Hero*, which had also looked at the life of a child in care. Lee Ross went on to star in the first three series of ITV's hit children's drama ***Press Gang***.

Don't Forget Your Toothbrush

Game Show | Ginger Productions for Channel 4 | episode duration 60 mins | broadcast 12 Feb 1994–(date unknown)

Regular Cast
Chris Evans · *Presenter*
Rachel Tatton-Brown, Jadine Doran · *Hostess*
Jools Holland · *Band Leader*

Creator Chris Evans **Producers** Jon Harvey, Will Macdonald, Rachel Tatton-Brown **Theme Music** David Arnold

Though Saturday nights are currently dominated by Ant and Dec, and for most of the 1980s it was the kingdom of Noel Edmonds, it was Chris Evans who really rocked the format in the mid-1990s. Riding high after his departure from ***The Big Breakfast***, Evans brought us *Don't Forget Your Toothbrush*, a live game show where every member of the audience had to arrive with their passport, a suitcase and either permission from their boss to have a week off work or enough attitude not to care if they get sacked. For everyone was in with a chance of playing for the big prize – a holiday that they would fly off to at the end of the show.

Excitable, seemingly random and inventive, the show would pit a celebrity in a quiz about their own life against one of their fans. It would invite the viewers at home to flash their houselights on and off. Somewhere around the country was a camera watching a secret area, and if one of the houses flashed their lights on cue, the inhabitants would end up playing a game where they'd have to find objects around the house and throw them out of their windows. Fine if it's a treasured teddy bear; not so fine if it's the family TV set. The games were often risqué, but rarely beyond seaside postcard levels.

In the final, two contestants would compete for the grand prize – a holiday in Barbados or Mauritius, perhaps – while the 'loser' would have to make do with somewhere less glamorous like Clacton or Skegness. Inevitably, this drew complaints from tourist boards across the country, unhappy that their holiday destination was being written off as a booby prize, but in comparison to a tropical get-away, could they honestly think of themselves as anything else? Famously, one edition saw the entire audience packed off to EuroDisney.

The format became only the first of Evans's successful exports. On winning the 1995 Golden Rose of Montreux award, he was able to sell the formula to over 20 countries around the world – though probably not the Seychelles or Mauritius, which would have been odd. After two series, Evans went out on a high by handing over his very own Ferrari to the winner. Next for him was pop/rock chat show ***TFI Friday***, which continued to break new ground for entertainment – and fall foul of the ITC thanks to potty-mouthed guests. We might remember his audacious purchase of Virgin Radio, or his dismissal from the station after he called in sick for his morning show only to be caught on a drinking binge that afternoon by a tabloid photographer, or even the string of guest presenters on *TFI* when Chris became noticeable by his absence. But we also shouldn't forget that if you have a creative person who bores easily, they're never going to want to do the same thing for too long, which can only be of benefit to the viewers. While *TFI Friday* clearly went off the boil almost as soon as Evans himself grew tired of it, *Don't Forget Your Toothbrush* was a prime example of the man at his absolute best. Inventive, witty and crowd-pleasing to the *n*th degree.

Doctor Who

Tom Baker as the fourth Doctor, Louise Jameson as Leela and their trusty robotic dog, K-9.

Why a programme about a man travelling through time and space in a London Metropolitan Police box should have captured the British public's admiration and affection is anyone's guess. But for over 20 consecutive years, *Doctor Who* managed to do just that. Surviving changes in cast and colossal advances in technology that remained outside the show's budget, it managed to endear itself to millions and (prior to the 2005 revival), still had an active, dedicated and vocal fanbase more than a decade after it was a regular part of the schedules.

Doctor Who remains the show that people love above all others. Sure, more people may like ***EastEnders***, but not so many people *love* it in the way viewers seem to love *Doctor Who*. It has a magical quality that defies explanation or genre classification. It's not really science fiction in its purest sense (certainly, some hardcore SF fans feel uncomfortable with it being lumped in with the works of Brian Aldiss, Arthur C. Clarke or Philip K. Dick); it's not really action-adventure in the same way that, say, ***Robin Hood*** or ***Star Trek*** were; and it's supposed initial educational remit was gradually ditched in favour of what the viewers really wanted – monsters, and lots of them.

One rather pithy description of *Doctor Who* described it as a 'sci-fi panto', which isn't quite as cruel or dismissive as that might sound. The show's greatest successes came when it played with and worked against familiar conventions. Furthermore, while, for the most part, it had production values that might have shamed 'serious' period dramas made at the same time, its over-ambition just added to its charm.

Doctor Who came about because the bosses at the Beeb had identified a gap in the early-evening Saturday schedules between the sports round-up and news at 5.00 p.m. and the music show ***Juke Box Jury***. Though the history books often credit TV mogul Sydney Newman (***A for Andromeda***, ***The Avengers***) as the show's sole creator, this is a bit of an oversimplification, somewhat akin to discussing the dawn of the Beatles and only focusing on John Lennon, ignoring the contributions of McCartney, Harrison, Epstein, Martin and Pete Best. (Similarly, despite what *Trivial Pursuit* might have you believe, the show wasn't created by Terry Nation either. To extend The Beatles metaphor further, Nation was *Doctor Who*'s McCartney – he made it popular, but it wasn't exclusively his.)

The creation of *Doctor Who* is also down to a number of other key BBC personnel. In 1962, Donald Wilson, then the BBC's Head of Drama Serials, commissioned a report from Alice Frick and Donald Bull of the BBC Survey Group as to the viability of a science fiction-based TV series and then helped to apply the survey's findings to Newman's desire for a family-friendly sci-fi show. While Bull's involvement in the project gradually diminished, it was Frick who first suggested time travel as a possible concept for the series, noting that the show could become 'the ***Z Cars*** of science fiction'. Cecil Edwin 'Bunny' Webber of the BBC Script Department helped develop the central characters from 'Lola, Cliff and Biddy' into 'Barbara, Ian and Susan' as well as shaping the 'bible' used in the early years. Verity Lambert (later producer of ***Widows***, ***Minder*** and many more) produced the first few series and, along with the first script editor, David Whitaker, shaped the programme's direction in defying Sydney Newman's instruction to avoid 'bug-eyed monsters'; and Anthony Coburn, who wrote the first episode, was responsible for the Doctor's time machine appearing as the familiar police box.

The programme began with the kidnapping of two London school teachers who, concerned about one of their pupils (a peculiar girl called Susan), followed her home to a junkyard. There, they discovered a Police Box and a crotchety old man who refused to help them search for the girl. When they heard Susan's voice coming from inside the police box, they assumed she was being held captive and barged their way inside – only to discover the box was, in fact, a time and space machine infinitely bigger on the inside than the outside (or 'dimensionally transcendental', as it's often been described). The old man explains that he is the Doctor, Susan's grandfather, and that they are actually aliens from 'another time, another world'. Worried that the teachers will warn the authorities about his 'ship', the Doctor sets his time machine going and before you can say 'bigger on the inside than the outside', they've travelled

Science Fiction
BBC One
Episode Duration: 25 mins/ 45–50 mins
Broadcast: 23 Nov 1963–6 Dec 1989, 28 May 1996, 26 Mar 2005–present

Regular Cast
William Hartnell, Patrick Troughton, Jon Pertwee, Tom Baker, Peter Davison, Colin Baker, Sylvester McCoy, Paul McGann, Christopher Eccleston, David Tennant · *Doctor Who*
Carole Ann Ford · *Susan Foreman*
William Russell · *Ian Chesterton*
Jacqueline Hill · *Barbara Wright*
David Graham, Peter Hawkins, Roy Skelton, Michael Wisher, Royce Mills, Nick Briggs · *Dalek Voices*
Maureen O'Brien · *Vicki*
Peter Purves · *Steven Taylor*
Adrienne Hill · *Katarina*
Jackie Lane · *Dodo Chaplet*
Anneke Wills · *Polly*
Michael Craze · *Ben Jackson*
Frazer Hines · *Jamie McCrimmon*
Deborah Watling · *Victoria Waterfield*
Nicholas Courtney · *Colonel/Brigadier Lethbridge Stewart*
Wendy Padbury · *Zoe Heriot*
John Levene · *Corporal/Sergeant/RSM Benton*
Caroline John · *Liz Shaw*
Katy Manning · *Jo Grant*
Richard Franklin · *Captain Mike Yates*
Roger Delgado, Anthony Ainley · *The Master*
Elisabeth Sladen · *Sarah Jane Smith*
Ian Marter · *Harry Sullivan*
Louise Jameson · *Leela*
John Leeson, David Brierley · *Voice of K-9*
Mary Tamm, Lalla Ward · *Romana*
Matthew Waterhouse · *Adric*
Sarah Sutton · *Nyssa*
Janet Fielding · *Tegan Jovanka*
Mark Strickson · *Vislor Turlough*
Nicola Bryant · *Peri Brown*
Bonnie Langford · *Melanie*
Sophie Aldred · *Ace*
Daphne Ashbrook · *Grace Holloway*
Billie Piper · *Rose Tyler*
Camile Coduri · *Jackie Tyler*
Noel Clarke · *Mickey Smith*
John Barrowman · *Jack Harkness*

Creators Sydney Newman (et al.)

Producers Verity Lambert, Mervyn Pinfield (associate), John Wiles, Innes Lloyd, Peter Bryant, Derrick Sherwin, Barry Letts, Philip Hinchcliffe, Graham Williams, John Nathan-Turner, Philip Segal, Peter Ware, Russell T. Davies, Phil Collinson

Writers Various, including Anthony Coburn, Terry Nation, David Whitaker, John Lucarotti, Dennis Spooner, Donald Cotton, Gerry Davis, Kit Pedler, Ian Stuart Black, Malcolm Hulke, Mervyn Haisman, Henry Lincoln, Terrence Dicks, Peter Ling, Robert Holmes, Don Houghton, Bob Baker, Dave Martin, Robert Sloman, Robert Banks Stewart, Chris Boucher, Douglas Adams, David Fisher, Steve Gallagher, Johnny Byrne, Christopher H. Bidmead, Christopher Bailey, Eric Saward, Peter Grimwade, Philip Martin, Ian Briggs, Ben Aaronovitch, Rona Munro, Russell T. Davies, Steven Moffat, Paul Cornell, Mark Gatiss, Rob Shearman

Theme Music Ron Grainer and the Radiophonics Workshop. Though the theme has been tweaked, stretched and misshapen by many over the years, none can compete with the original arrangement by Delia Derbyshire, which involved taking samples of plucked guitar strings and electronic whines and splicing them together note by note. The result was a truly unearthly piece of music that terrified viewers for 17 years until it was ungraciously retired in favour of a more modern sound that now seems much more dated. The 2005 revival saw Murray Gold reinterpreting Derbyshire's original arrangement to great effect, combining a modern reworking with many of her familiar elements from the 1963 original.

backwards in time to Palaeolithic Earth and are helping cavemen to rediscover the lost secret of fire.

In these early serials, the remit was to be as educational as possible, with the Doctor and his reluctant chums popping around the royal courts of history; Kublai Khan, Nero and Richard the Lionheart were to be seen more often than bug-eyed monsters. But inevitably it was the arrival of the sci-fi mainstay of horrible monsters – and specifically the infamous Daleks in the second story – that grabbed the ratings. Soon, historical adventures began to look odd among the exploits of the giant ant-like Zarbi, the hideous Rills and the chilling part-man, part-machine Cybermen (like a corruption of the old Steven Wright joke, early versions of these fellas had metal arms but real hands).

It wasn't just the history plays that were looking tired and past their best. By 1966, lead actor William Hartnell had seen all of his co-stars leave the series and was slowly finding it harder and harder to remember his lines (later discovered to be the onset of arteriosclerosis). For any 'normal' show, that would be the end of it, but, recognising that the show's format was infinitely forgiving (and, more importantly, very popular with viewers), the decision was taken to 'regenerate' the Doctor and cast another actor in Hartnell's place. The lucky man was character actor Patrick Troughton, who, having first considered playing the role as a sea captain or (gasp) blacked up, eventually settled on the guise of a space tramp, like an intergalactic Charlie Chaplin. The stories of the Troughton era played with a successful formula of alien invaders holding a base (space station, gas refinery, monastery in the Himalayas, London Underground . . .) under siege. It worked for a while and introduced a menagerie of popular monsters, such as the robotic Yeti, Martian reptiles the Ice Warriors and the giggling killer Quarks. It also managed to rejuvenate the Cybermen from the campy, cloth-faced metaphors that Hartnell had encountered into metallic, silver-suited armies – the scarier they were, the more the kids adored them.

By 1969, however, the joke was wearing a bit thin, with every corner of the galaxy held under siege at least twice already. Having successfully replaced the lead actor once, producers decided to press that recast button again and came up with comedy actor Jon Pertwee, who took on the persona of a pompous dandy with a penchant for gadgets. Troughton was last seen in 'The War Games' having finally been captured by his own people – revealed as the Time Lords – who he went on the run from all those years ago. Tried and convicted of interfering in the affairs of other races, the Doctor finds himself with a new face exiled to Earth – a budgetary decision, allowing the production team to stick to more realistic (cheaper) settings. During this time, the Doctor was allied with the paramilitary organisation UNIT, headed by Brigadier Lethbridge Stewart (a character that had been road-tested to great success during the Troughton years) and his companions were generally the token female on the UNIT staff roster: first Dr Liz Shaw, a scientist far too independent, witty and clever to be anyone's companion; and then Jo Grant, a dizzy '70s chick with a penchant for screaming, stumbling into trouble and getting captured – the perfect model for Doctor Who assistants. Pertwee's most notable villain was the Master, a suave, charming renegade Time Lord played to perfection by Roger Delgado as the Professor Moriarty to Pertwee's Sherlock Holmes.

For the show's 10th birthday, a celebratory tale was concocted that would involve the first three Doctors ganging up against the megalomaniac Omega. It was a brave move in some ways as it could have exposed Pertwee's weaknesses in the presence of his predecessors and reminded viewers of how good 'it used to be'. Fortunately, viewers are a fickle bunch and Pertwee's position was never stronger.

Many people currently in their late thirties or early forties will talk fondly of Jon Pertwee, while other members of the public might boast of remembering 'the first one'. For most, however, Tom Baker was the definitive portrayal, with his disarming grin, mad glaring eyes, unruly curly hair and shabby clothes (including that all-important 20-feet-long scarf). Subsequent Doctors (most often Colin Baker) would struggle to escape the trappings of their predecessor. Tom Baker became possessed by his role in a way few other actors ever are.

Baker was accompanied initially by Sarah Jane Smith (a journalist who had accompanied Pertwee in his final year) and the burly UNIT medical officer Lieutenant Harry Sullivan. Harry was ditched after just one year, leaving Sarah alone to take on the insane renegade Time Lord Morbius (or, more accurately, what was left of him – his addled brain), the Egyptian God Sutekh and the vegetable parasite the Krynoid before being unceremoniously dumped back on Earth by a distressed Doctor, having received a summons to return home to his home planet once again. While Sarah Jane remains among the most popular companions for fans, for the general public it is the savage Leela who is best remembered, and it's no surprise why. Having taken the perhaps cynical decision to start trying to grab the interest of the dads, the producers created a leggy, stunningly attractive savage called Leela. Tanned and loin-clothed, this 'something for the dads' policy certainly helped bolster the ratings. If Tom Baker felt pushed aside by the glamour, the situation can't have improved when he was also saddled with a gimmicky side-kick for the kids to adore too – a pompous robotic dog called K-9.

Tom Baker's was the definitive portrayal, with his disarming grin, mad, glaring eyes and shabby clothes (including that all-important 20-foot-long scarf). Tom Baker became possessed by his role in a way few other actors ever are.

After Leela came another Time Lord – or rather Lady. Romanadvoratrelundar (or 'Romana' for short) was loaned to the Doctor from the Time Lord Academy in his quest to find the Key to Time and defeat the Black Guardian. By the time the Black Guardian was defeated, Romana had decided to stay. Original Romana, Mary Tamm, presented the producer with a brand new problem when she revealed between seasons that she was pregnant. Aware that having a 'glowing' beautiful assistant might raise all the wrong type of questions in young minds, Romana's Time Lord heritage was exploited and a new model arrived in season 17 to see the fourth Doctor through to almost the end of his run.

With Baker having almost indelibly stamped his persona on the role for seven years, casting his replacement was a difficult task. Attempting to go for as many opposites as possible in one man (the idea of a female Doctor having been rumoured and then dismissed just to fluff up the tabloids for a while), the producer cast 29-year-old Peter Davison as a more human, fallible Doctor to see the series into the 1980s. Davison inherited three companions from Tom Baker's final season: the delicate Nyssa of Traken, who had seen her stepmother, her father and finally her entire planet destroyed by the evil Master (regenerated in the form of Anthony Ainley – Delgado having been tragically killed in a car crash back in 1973); the headstrong 'mouth on legs', Australian air stewardess Tegan Jovanka; and Adric, a less likeable intergalactic version of the Artful Dodger. With the TARDIS a little crowded, the decision was taken to kill one of the companions – and millions of viewers were left reeling when Adricfailed to survive the surprise return of the Cybermen in 'Earthshock'.

The year 1983 saw the show celebrate its 20th anniversary with an entire season of retrospective stories that featured the return of old villains such as Omega, the Black Guardian and the Master again. November that year brought an anniversary special – the imaginatively titled 'The Five Doctors' in which the late William Hartnell was played by a not-very-look-alike and old companions and enemies were mixed together to battle the Doctor's old headmaster on his home planet Gallifrey (no, really!). This introspection seemed to stay with the programme long after its 20th birthday party and by the time Colin Baker took over the TARDIS controls in 1985, the show was rooted in its past and struggling to escape. As a consequence, the show was cancelled.

Or at least, that's how the fans would have it. In truth, it was somewhat different. The fact that the different ITV companies rarely aired the same show across all the regions at the same time had always worked in *Doctor Who*'s favour. The first time it faced networked opposition, with 1980's ***Buck Rogers in the 25th Century***, viewers deserted it in droves in favour of the glossy American sci-fi show. For Davison's seasons, *Doctor Who* was moved to a mid-week slot as part of a strong BBC One line-up that included glossy US soaps ***Dallas*** and ***Dynasty***. In essence, *Doctor Who* was being used to test out the timeslot eventually handed over to

EastEnders in 1985. When *Doctor Who* was moved back to its old Saturday slot for Colin Baker's first series, it faced strong competition once again from a networked action-adventure series – this time, the moronic ***A-Team***, a show with a budget for explosions per episode that would have kept the good Doctor in polystyrene and bubble-wrap for *decades*. *Doctor Who*'s ratings begin to drop. With a directive to save money across the board to pay for daytime TV, BBC One boss Michael Grade simply cancelled those shows that were in prime slots and under-performing, including long-running family favourites ***Ask the Family***, *Pop Quiz* and ***Crackerjack***.

Grade's binning of *Crackerjack* proves that it doesn't matter how much the public likes you, when you're down on your luck, you need your fans to *love* you to save you from cancellation. And so the Krankies and Stu Francis were resigned to the scrap heap and *Doctor Who* continued for three more years in the form of comedic performance artist Sylvester McCoy.

At this point, recognising that *Doctor Who* was going to get five million viewers (give or take) no matter when it was scheduled, the BBC bosses did something that was actually quite canny from their point of view, but will forever be associated by fans with the death of the series – they moved it to a timeslot directly opposite ***Coronation Street***. The move was a comparative success and did exactly what it was meant to do – claw back a couple of million viewers from ITV. Before *Doctor Who*, the best ratings a show had achieved in that time slot on BBC One were in the region of 3 million – *Doctor Who* almost doubled that. But by this time, few people wanted to work on a show that was clearly being used as a ratings tool rather than for its own merits and eventually, in 1989, the show was put on hold for what seemed like forever. Ask a 'fan', though, and you'll be told the show was killed by the casting of Bonnie Langford as an assistant.

Not that *Doctor Who* was actually killed off, mind. There have been a number of 'revivals' over the years, including two charity spoofs: one, a three-dimensional special called 'Dimensions in Time', placed multiple Doctors and companions battling the Rani (Kate O'Mara, in her third appearance) on the set of *EastEnders* to raise funds for *Children in Need*; another, 1989's 'The Curse of Fatal Death', was an affectionate story in aid of ***Comic Relief*** that saw Rowan Atkinson, Richard E. Grant, Jim Broadbent, Hugh Grant and Joanna Lumley as a Doctor running out of regenerations as he pits his wits against the manic Master (Jonathan Pryce in an uncanny recreation of Delgado's original) and the dreaded Daleks.

The first new series managed to capture the excitement, comedy and level of fear that everyone involved remembered from when they were children.

But the one genuine attempt to resurrect the legend was a 1996 TV movie called simply *Doctor Who*, an Anglo-American co-production starring Paul McGann intended as a pilot for a proposed new series. Despite massive ratings for the showing on BBC One (the highest for any drama series pilot that year), the lack of success across the Atlantic, where it was screened opposite the last ever episode of the hugely popular sitcom ***Roseanne***, meant that a full series was not commissioned and that consequently Paul McGann became the George Lazenby of Doctor Whos.

While *Doctor Who* has been off our screens, he has flourished in other media. Over 400 original novels have been published since 1991 (a Guinness World Record for most novels based on one character); full-cast audio dramas with Doctors five, six, seven and eight have taken the Doctor into previously unimagined realms; the official *Doctor Who Magazine* is still going strong, 26 years after it first hit the shelves; and BBCi brought us a new Doctor in the form of an animated webcast series starring Richard E. Grant as an all-new Doctor.

What the fans were really waiting for, though, was a return to primetime TV – a vindication of their ardour, persevering despite a lack of interest from BBC executives. In the autumn of 2003, their prayers were answered when it was announced that the show would finally be returning in 2005 under the wing of top TV writer Russell T. Davies (***Dark Season***, *Revelations*, ***Queer as Folk***), a lifelong fan of the show.

With Christopher Eccleston taking on the part of the Doctor in 13 brand new adventures, it was finally time to close the door on the past and look expectantly to the future – which was, after all, where *Doctor Who* came from in the first place. The first new series managed to capture the excitement, comedy and level of fear that everyone involved remembered from when they were children, with adventures taking place underneath the London Eye, on far-flung space stations awaiting the media-friendly destruction of Earth in the far future . . . and Cardiff. The Daleks returned in new, chunkier livery and with a step-by-step rebuttal of each and every criticism that had been levelled at the creatures since 1963 (who would have thought a sink plunger could do that to a human face!?), and for those that missed them do it in the original series, the producers made sure everyone knew they could also fly.

The Daleks returned in new, chunkier livery and with a step-by-step rebuttal of every criticism that had been levelled at the creatures since 1963.

With press interest and viewer appreciation at an all-time high, the news that Eccleston was on board for just one series came as a shock to many. But with his replacement announced as ***Casanova*** star David Tennant (a lifelong fan of the series), a Christmas special and at least two more seasons in the pipeline, for the time being, at least, *Doctor Who*'s future once more looks secure.

Don't Wait Up

Sitcom | BBC One | episode duration 30 mins | broadcast 25 Oct 1983–25 Mar 1990

Principal Cast
Tony Britton · *Dr Toby Latimer*
Nigel Havers · *Dr Tom Latimer*
Dinah Sheridan · *Angela Latimer*
Jane How · *Helen Latimer*
Richard Heffer/Simon Williams · *Dr Charles Cartwright*
Susan Skipper · *Madeleine*

Writer George Layton **Producer** Harold Snoad

Nigel Havers and Tony Britton are the doctors Latimer – Tom and Toby. Toby is the pompous private doctor whose marriage to Tom's mother, Angela, has broken down. Similarly, Tom (the idealist NHS GP) has just lost his surgery in the divorce settlement from his ruthless ex-wife Helen. Father and son are forced to share a flat together, setting the scene for much clashing of character over politics, career, morals and ethics, alongside more traditionally slapstick moments. Throughout the series, Tom attempts to reconcile his parents, while pursuing his father's receptionist, Madeleine. Thankfully, the series finishes with Toby and Angela back together, and the by then married Tom and Madeleine having their first child.

George Layton, better known as an actor in ***Doctor in the House***, among others, had just gone through his own divorce when he penned this generation gap comedy, leading to some very dry, even raw dialogue on the subject. Tony Britton and Dinah Sheridan are perfectly cast and a likeable Nigel Havers finds his feet quickly in uncharted sitcom territory.

Doogie Howser, MD

Drama | Steven Bocho Productions/20th Century Fox Television for ABC (shown on BBC One) | episode duration 25 mins | broadcast 19 Sep 1989–21 Jul 1993 (USA)

Regular Cast
Neil Patrick Harris · *Doogie Howser*
James B. Sikking · *Dr David Howser*
Max Casella · *Vinnie Delpino*
Belinda Montgomery · *Katherine Howser*
Kathryn Layng · *Nurse Curly Spaulding*
Lisa Dean Ryan · *Wanda Plenn*
Lawrence Pressman · *Doctor Canfield*
Mitchell Anderson · *Dr Jack McGuire*

Creators Steven Bochco and David E. Kelley **Producers** Steven Bochco, Stephen Cragg (executive), Mark Horowitz, Phil Kellard, Rick Wallace **Writer** Various, including Steven Bochco, David E. Kelley, Todd Fischer, David Greenwalt, Phil Kellard, David Pitlik, Michael Swerdlick **Theme Music** Mike Post

Doogie Howser is a boy genius. He breezed through high school in weeks and graduated college with a top class medical degree by the time he was 14 years old. Doogie followed in his father's footsteps into the world of medicine, and the series revolves around his work at Los Angeles' Eastman Medical Center. Doogie has a bit of a hard time – his adult colleagues are not exactly happy about this 16 year-old upstart coming into their world, while other teenagers think he's a bit weird. Mixing comedy with drama, the series has Doogie trying to make his way through a world where he tries to be a normal kid, while getting on with his difficult professional life. Thankfully on hand are wise parents, a best buddy, and the local hottie.

Doogie Howser, MD was an odd, if popular, mix of styles, adopting a vogue that was quite new at the time and was quickly labelled a 'dramedy'. It has less schmaltz than a lot of US drama of the period thanks to the economies in writing from Steven Bochco and David E. Kelley, both of who made their names in some of the best TV drama around. Neil Patrick Harris, who went on to a highly successful career in films, TV and theatre (including a cameo as himself in ***The Simpsons***), reportedly drew his inspiration from watching episodes of *Marcus Welby, MD*, starring Robert Young. When Harris learnt that Young was suffering from ill health, he would visit the actor with tapes of *Doogie Howser* in an attempt to cheer him up.

The series enjoyed a briefly popular run on BBC One in a prime-time slot, but was eventually shunted to Sunday nights at 11 p.m.

Doomwatch

Science Fiction | BBC One | episode duration 50 mins | broadcast 9 Feb 1970–10 Jul 1972

Regular Cast
John Paul · *Dr Spencer Quist*
Simon Oates · *Dr John Ridge*
Robert Powell · *Toby Wren*
Joby Blanshard · *Colin Bradley*
Wendy Hall · *Pat Hunisett*
Jean Trend · *Dr Fay Chantry*
John Nolan · *Geoff Hardcastle*
Vivien Sherrard · *Barbara Mason*
John Barron · *The Minister*
Vivien Sherrard · *Barbara Mason*
Elizabeth Weaver · *Dr Anne Tarrant*
John Bown · *Commander Neil Stafford*

Creators Gerry Davis and Kit Pedler **Producer** Terence Dudley **Writers** N. J. Crisp, Gerry Davis, Terence Dudley, Brian Hayles, Robert Holmes, Elwyn Jones, Louis Marks, Roger Parkes, Kit Pedler, Don Shaw, Dennis Spooner, Martin Worth **Theme Music** Max Harris created an ominous, percussion-driven theme tune that seemed to spell out the two syllables of the programme's title: 'Doom-Watch! Doom-Watch!'

Doomwatch co-creators Gerry Davis and Kit Pedler graduated from their work on family-friendly science fiction programme ***Doctor Who*** (where they created the famous monsters the Cybermen, humans that had swapped their body parts for cybernetic replacements) to a programme that relished in giving its viewers cautionary tales about the dangers of unchecked scientific progress. *Doomwatch* wasn't just the title of the programme, it was the name of a government-sponsored organisation (the Department for the Observation and Measurement of Science) whose job it was to investigate science-related disasters and prevent potential problems from occurring.

Leader of *Doomwatch* was stubborn, argumentative Dr Spencer Quist, a man who never shied from a verbal confrontation with politicians, the armed forces or the heads of powerful multi-national corporations. Quist's two right-hand men were dapper ladies' man John Ridge and shy, bookish yet brilliant Toby Wren. Over the course of the first series, *Doomwatch* investigated such threats as a plastic-eating virus (that caused jet liners to fall out of the sky), intelligent carnivorous rats, and even a nuclear device that had washed up on the support legs of a seaside pier. Never afraid to shock and surprise its audience, the first season ended with heroic Toby Wren being killed outright in a (non-nuclear) explosion while trying to defuse the bomb on the pier. Quist appeared as shocked as the viewers at home, and took several episodes of the subsequent series to recover from his sense of guilt at the death of his subordinate. Later on, accusations of sexism were addressed (if only to a degree) with the introduction of some regular female members of the team, Dr Fay Chantry and Dr Anne Tarrant – although neither part was ever truly written as a powerful, independent female role model.

Doomwatch lasted for three seasons and 37 episodes until creators Pedler and Davies eventually became disillusioned with an increase in the mundane and unremarkable elements that had begun to creep into the series and the show was canned. However, one final episode of *Doomwatch* caused such controversy that nervous TV executives decided never to broadcast it. In 'Sex and Violence' the Doomwatch team investigate a very unusual threat to society – permissiveness and its impact on human behaviour. There were fine performances from the guest cast (including a young June Brown as a 'clean-up TV' campaigner, years before she played a similar role in ***EastEnders*** as morality junkie Dot Cotton) and an intriguing, intelligent discussion of the debate – which was a public obsession at the time because of Mary Whitehouse and her National Viewers' and Listeners' Campaign – but the theme of this particular instalment was not why the episode was banned. It was pulled from the schedules because it featured the investigators watching footage of a real-life execution in Africa, footage that we viewers would have seen too. It made a very valid point that observing real violence on screen has a different effect on viewers than watching make-believe violence. Nevertheless, the episode was felt to be just too strong to broadcast and it remains unseen to this day.

Doomwatch was a challenging and intelligent slice of science fiction that raised questions in the mind of viewers who were more used to sci-fi that presented an optimistic view of the future or bug-eyed monsters trying to conquer the earth. By making the audience think about the consequences of unregulated commercial exploitation of the planet and its resources, *Doomwatch* was in fact one of the first examples of environmentally conscious television. A spin-off film starring Ian Bannen was released in 1972, and Five produced a pilot film for a potential new series (broadcast on 16 December 1999) with former ***Shoestring*** star Trevor Eve in the lead role. Sadly this amounted to nothing, despite the far greater public awareness towards the potential perils of technology going wrong during the year of the Millennium Bug scare. Indeed, it took another six years for a 'Doomwatch' revival to reach TV screens: in 2005, ITV announced a new science fiction programme called *Eleventh Hour*, written by horror novelist Stephen Gallagher and starring ex-Captain Picard Patrick Stewart. Based around a government department investigating problems connected with technology, it all seemed a tad familiar. . .

Double Deckers

See HERE COME THE DOUBLE DECKERS

Double Your Money

Quiz Show | Associated Rediffusion for ITV | episode duration 30 mins | broadcast 26 Sep 1955–1968

Cast

Hughie Green · *Host*

Monica Rose, Amanda Barrie · *Hostesses*

Creator John Beard **Theme Music** Alex Leader

A quiz show that does what it says on the tin, and one that was a popular feature of the early ITV schedules until Associated Rediffusion lost its franchise in 1968. The legendary Hughie Green asked members of the public questions for money, allowing them to double up their £1 winning on the first question by answering more questions correctly up to a maximum £32. The contestant could then go on to the Treasure Trail, leading them all the way to cash prize of £1000.

The series was based on the popular US game show *The $64,000 Question* (a UK version of which ran concurrently with *Double Your Money* from 1956–1956, and again with Bob Monkhouse in 1990). Hughie Green was a highly jocular host, accompanied by a bevy of hostesses, the mainstay being Monica Rose, but an early appearance can be seen by *Carry On* and ***Coronation Street*** star Amanda

Barrie. Rose would accompany Green in another spin on the format, *The Sky's the Limit* in the early 1970s. Rose sadly committed suicide some years after the end of the show.

Dragnet

Crime Drama | Mark VII Ltd for NBC (shown on ITV) | episode duration 60 mins | broadcast 16 Dec 1951–23 Aug 1959 (USA)

Regular Cast
Jack Webb · *Sergeant Joe Friday*
Barton Yarborough · *Sergeant Ben Romero*
Barney Phillips · *Sergeant Ed Jacobs*
Herbert Ellis, Ben Alexander · *Officer Frank Smith*
Harry Morgan · *Officer Bill Gannon*
George Fennerman, Hal Gibney · *Announcer*

Creator/Writer/Producer Jack Webb **Theme Music** Miklos Rosa

One of the original and arguably best TV cop shows of the time, *Dragnet* centred in the investigations of Sergeant Joe Friday, played by the creator, producer and sometimes director of the series, Jack Webb. Following the format of the original radio series, which also starred Webb, each episode would open with the same voiceover from Friday: 'This is the city, Los Angeles, California. I work here, I carry a badge.' Friday is supported by various police officers, and the investigations had a sheen of realism with many of them being taken from the files of the LAPD. Regular narration by Friday as the episode progressed added a certain documentary element.

The series ended in 1959, but would be resurrected in 1967 under the imaginative title *Dragnet 1967*. This time Friday (once more played by Webb) would be partnered by ***M*A*S*H****'s Harry Morgan as Officer Bill Gannon. This was the first time a previously cancelled show was successfully resurrected. Further revivals would not fair so well. Aside from the vaguely amusing spoof, *Dragnet* (1987) starring Dan Aykroyd, Tom Hanks and Harry Morgan (reprising his role as Gannon), a generally forgotten TV revival without Friday (Jack Webb died in 1982) came and went in 1989. Most recently, Ed O'Neill – better known as Al Bundy in ***Married, With Children*** – took on the mantle of Joe Friday for a 2003 version of the series, ***LA Dragnet***. Again it was short lived.

Dragnet left an important legacy to television – without it, the crime/police genre may have developed in a different direction altogether. It also provided a great TV detective in the form of Joe Friday, who regularly chewed out the immortal words: 'My name is Friday. I'm a cop.'

Dramarama

Anthology | ITV | episode duration 25 mins | broadcast 18 Apr 1983–21 Aug 1989

Producers Pamela Lonsdale (executive), Charles Warren, Vic Hughes, Alistair Clarke, John Dale, Geoff Husson, Peter Miller
Writers Various, including Maggie Wadey, Paula Milne, Trevor Preston, David Hopkins, R. Chetwynd-Hayes, Richard Handford, Jane Hollowood, Leon Garfield, Alan Garner, Adele Rose, Alan England, Gerry Huxham, Nigel Baldwin, Geoffrey Case, George Markstein, David Blake, Alan Banham, Peter Grimwade, Adele Rose, Kay Mellor, Robin Driscoll, Alex Norton, Bill Oddie, Brian Trueman, Gary Hopkins, Anthony Horowitz

Dramarama began where ITV's horror-for-kids anthology *Shadows* (see ***Ace of Wands***) had ended, with a series of seven thematically connected, stand-alone ghost stories. The first series, subtitled 'Spooky', was produced by the Thames region, with highlights including Alan Garner's 'The Keeper' and Paula Milne's 'The Exorcism of Amy' – an exorcism in *Children's Hour* being just one brave element that today's kids are denied.

The series continued after 'Spooky' with repeats of selected episodes from an earlier children's anthology, *Theatre Box*, including 'Marmalade Atkins in Space' and 'School for Clowns'. Ironically, it's a *Theatre Box* story that's now remembered as one of *Dramarama*'s scariest episodes. 'Death Angel', written by actor Brian Glover and partly inspired by his own experiences as a wrestler, contained a terrifying brawler whose face was hidden behind a mask – for very good reasons.

Dramarama soon became the name of the timeslot rather than a specific production, as *Watch with Mother* had been for the BBC. It became a collaborative project for the ITV regions with TVS, Central and Tyne Tees producing episodes, and Granada and other regions pitching in later.

Each series mixed up a variety of styles and forms, from broad farce and comedy to suspense and straight drama, though it was the scarier episodes that are best remembered. Trevor Preston made a return to children's TV with 'Mr Stabs', a sequel to an episode of his early 1970s series *Ace of Wands* starring David Jason as Stabs. 'The Comeuppance of Captain Katt' also had telefantasy connections, starring Alfred Marks as the grumpy star of a clapped-out science fiction TV show. Written and directed by Peter Grimwade, the episode acted as a thinly veiled criticism of the production team behind ***Doctor Who***, on which Grimwade had recently brought to an end many years as a contributor.

Most admirable of all though were the stories involving social issues: 'Because I Say So' was one of a few to look at the subject of bullying; in the award-winning 'Look at Me', a deaf boy tries to find help for his dog after it's knocked down by a car and is befriended by a passing cyclist; 'A Couple of Charlies', about a boy who's being abused at home, was made alongside advice from the NSPCC; and 'Dodger, Bonzo and the Rest' by Geoffrey Case featured a brother and sister living in a children's home; it led to its own series.

Driving School

Reality TV | BBC One | episode duration 30 mins | broadcast 1997

Cast

Quentin Willson · *Narrator*

Maureen Rees · *Herself*

Producer Mark Fielder

An early example of the modern obsession for docusoaps and reality TV, *Driving School* followed seven pupils from a Bristol driving school as they battled against the odds to get that all important licence. There was much hilarity was to be had for the pupils' atrocious driving skills and the trials of their patient but long-suffering partners in attempting to teach them how to get from A to B.

One pupil shone above the rest: Maureen Rees, a cleaner who had already failed a total of seven driving tests. From her performance on screen, the thought of her taking to the roads filled motorists with horror. Maureen became an overnight star, one of the very first reality TV celebrities. She has made appearances on many chat shows and magazine programmes, and even recorded a novelty cover version of the Madness hit 'Driving In My Car'.

In 2003, a celebrity version of *Driving School* was broadcast to coincide with ***Comic Relief***, featuring the driving mishaps of Simon Day, Natalie Cassidy, Gareth Gates, Jade Goody, Paul O'Grady and Nadia Sawalha.

Drop the Dead Donkey

Sitcom | Hat Trick Productions for Channel 4 | episode duration 25 mins | broadcast 9 Aug 1990–9 Dec 1998

Regular Cast

Jeff Rawle · *George Dent*

Neil Pearson · *Dave Charnley*

Stephen Tompkinson · *Damien Day*

Robert Duncan · *Gus Hedges*

David Swift · *Henry Davenport*

Victoria Wicks · *Sally Smedley*

Susannah Doyle · *Joy Merrywether*

Ingrid Lacey · *Helen Cooper*

Haydn Gwynne · *Alex Pates*

Sara Stewart · *Jenny*

Louisa Millwood-Haigh · *Deborah Dent*

Creator Andy Hamilton and Guy Jenkin **Producers** Denise O'Donoghue (executive), Andy Hamilton, Guy Jenkin **Writers** Andy Hamilton, Guy Jenkin, Malcolm Williamson **Theme Music** Matthew Scott

The offices of Globelink News were the setting for this cutting-edge sitcom from Channel 4, a programme ostensibly about the journalists and broadcasters working on a TV news programme, but also about the events occurring in the real world, too. The unique way in which *Drop the Dead Donkey* was made enabled the programme to deliver knockout up-to-the-minute satirical punches – unlike most other TV comedy shows, *Drop the Dead Donkey* was recorded on the day prior to transmission, with the main scripts deliberately leaving one or two lines blank to enable the writers to insert topical jokes about politicians or world events into the middle of the storyline. Each episode was then edited on the afternoon of transmission, with cast members recording a voiceover for the end credits (an idea 'borrowed' from the children's series about a newspaper office, ***Press Gang***) that often included some even more up-to-the-minute jokes.

However, *Drop the Dead Donkey* wasn't a success simply because of its radical production technique – it was a darned funny sitcom too, featuring pitch-perfect performances from a large ensemble cast. George Dent runs the Globelink newsroom, but it's clear to most people that George's hypochondria, dithering and general ineffectualness mean that he's more of a hindrance than a help. Thankfully he has a no-nonsense deputy in the shape of Alex Pates (later replaced by Helen Cooper) who helps to keep the newsroom functioning. George's two main reporters are confident ladies' man and gambling addict Dave Charnley, and the unscrupulous and ambitious field reporter Damien Day (a man not averse to carrying around a teddy bear with him so that he can place it into the middle of a pile of rubble or the aftermath of a car crash, simply to give his report more poignancy). The two Globelink newsreaders are old-school wig-wearing alcoholic Henry Davenport and vacuous glamour girl Sally Smedley, a woman with an unfortunate predilection for rough sex with truckers and workmen. Of course, neither Sally nor Henry can stand each other, and often resort to back-stabbing and other unprofessional attempts to sabotage each others' careers. The final member of the team is secretary Joy Merryweather, a foul-tempered, cynical and deeply unpleasant young woman who never even attempts to conceal the contempt in which she holds the rest of the staff.

The owner of Globelink News is the international media magnate Sir Royston Merchant (a kind of Murdoch/Maxwell-type figure) whose orders are delivered to the newsroom floor courtesy of his fawning, obsequious yes-man Gus Hedges. Hedges isn't a journalist or reporter, more a buzzword-spouting yuppie cliché who hasn't the faintest idea how to motivate or manage a team of creatives. Much of the comedy in *Drop the Dead Donkey* came from Hedges' gloriously inept attempts to 'rally the troops' or introduce another new bit of management-speak into the lives of the uninterested reporters.

Drop the Dead Donkey was a huge hit on Channel 4, running for six seasons over nine years, and winning the BAFTA for Best TV Comedy Series in 1994. It proved to be a rich launching pad for future TV acting talent, most notably Neil Pearson (who went on to a variety of heart-throb roles in shows such as ***Between the Lines***) and Stephen

Tompkinson, portraying the English priest who moved to the town of ***Ballykissangel***. The final season saw the Globelink team facing redundancy as Sir Royston sold off the channel, with Gus finally meeting his beloved employer only to discover that Sir Royston had absolutely no idea who Gus was – a devastating blow to this most loyal of corporate flunkies.

Writers Andy Hamilton and Guy Jenkin's original title for the series was going to be 'Dead Belgians Don't Count' – neatly summarising the kind of prioritisation process that goes on behind-the-scenes of real-life TV news stations when they're trying to decide which stories deserve to be featured and which don't. Instead, they opted for a title that confused many people – why is there a dead donkey, and who's doing the dropping? In fact, the name refers to the kind of filler item that's often used as the last item on a TV news programme (normally introduced with the words, 'And finally . . .'), about a brave child, an unusual animal or a celebrity in crisis. If the rest of the broadcast overruns, the production team are easily able to 'drop' that item from the programme – hence, 'Drop the Dead Donkey'.

The Duchess of Duke Street

Drama | BBC One | episode duration 50 mins | broadcast 4 Sep 1976–24 Dec 1977

Regular Cast

Gemma Jones · *Louisa Leyton/Trotter*
Christopher Cazenove · *Charlie Tyrrell/Lord Haslemere*
Victoria Plucknett · *Mary Phillips*
John Welsh · *Merriman*
John Cater · *Starr*
Richard Vernon · *Major Toby Smith-Barton*
Donald Burton · *Augustus Trotter*
June Brown · *Mrs Violet Leyton*
John Rapley · *Mr Ernest Leyton*
Joanna David · *Lady Margaret Haslemere*
Mary Healey · *Mrs Cochran*
Sammy Winmill · *Ethel*
Holly de Jong · *Violet*
Lalla Ward · *Lottie*

Creator/Producer John Hawkesworth **Writers** Various, including John Hawkesworth, Julia Jones, Jeremy Paul, Jack Rosenthal **Theme Tune** Alexander Faris

By the time viewers experienced the unique charms of Louisa Trotter, owner of London's exclusive Bentinck Hotel, they'd been spoiled by a number of high-quality period dramas for almost a decade. Funnily enough, most of them were thanks to the work of one man – John Hawkesworth – who'd already given us ***Upstairs, Downstairs*** and ***The Forsyte Saga***.

What made *Duchess* so special was that Mrs Trotter was spiteful, vindictive, stubborn, bigoted, opinionated and quite the rudest person ever to mix in royal circles. But we forgave such 'small' faults because by the time they became a major part of her character most of us had already fallen utterly in love with her.

Charting her dream to become 'the best cook in England', we followed Louisa's exploits from lowly kitchen assistant to mistress of the Prince of Wales and then on to the privileged but fraught position as proprietor of the Bentinck. There, lords and gentlemen could be assured of two things – the excellence of the menu and the discretion of the staff. Said staff included a decrepit head waiter called Merriman (a miserable chap whose name was a cruel irony), porter Mr Starr and his dog, Fred, head parlour maid Mary and cook Mrs Cochrane, as well as Louisa's one permanent resident, Major Smith-Barton, who lived in the hotel for free in return for vetting the guests.

At the heart of the show was a bitter-sweet romance with the heir to a lordship who Louisa was lucky enough to know as 'Charlie'. Charming, roguish yet thoroughly decent, his and Louisa's paths were destined to entwine on more than one occasion. The result of this passionate affair was their love child, Lotty, who was initially palmed off onto a childless couple on Charlie's father's estate, before she would move to the Bentinck as a teen and make her mark on London society.

Though the show ran for just two seasons, it is still fondly remembered by many. It was all the more enchanting because of its basis in truth – a loose adaptation of the memoirs of real-life society hostess Rosa Lewis.

The Dukes of Hazzard

Action-Adventure | Lou Step/Piggy Productions/Warner Bros for CBS | episode duration 50 mins | broadcast 26 Jan 1979–8 Feb 1985, 25 Apr 1997, 19 May 2000

Principal Cast

Tom Wopat · *Luke Duke*
John Schneider · *Bo Duke*
Catherine Bach · *Daisy Duke*
Denver Pyle · *Uncle Jesse Duke*
James Best · *Sheriff Rosco P. Coltrane*
Sorrell Booke · *Jefferson Davis 'Boss' Hogg*
Sonny Shroyer · *Deputy Enos Strate*
Ben Jones · *Cooter Davenport*
Rick Hurst · *Deputy Cletus Hogg*
Byron Cherry · *Coy Duke*
Christopher Mayer · *Vance Duke*
Waylon Jennings · *Voice of the Balladeer*
Jeff Altman · *Hughie Hogg*
Don Pedro Colley · *Sheriff Ed Little*
Peggy Rea · *Lulu Coltrane Hogg*
Dick Sargent · *Sheriff Grady Byrd*
Nedra Volz · *Miz Emma Tisdale*

Creator Gy Waldron **Producers** Philip Mandelker, Paul R. Picard (executive), Wesley J. McAfee, Albert J. Salzer, Gilles de Turenne, Skip Ward, Ron Grow (associate), Gy Waldron, Joseph Gantman, Rod Amateau, Hy Averback, Robert Jacks, Bill Kelley, Ralph Riskin,
Continued on page 269

Dynasty

Krystle (Linda Evans), Claudia (Pamela Bellwood), Sammy-Jo (Heather Locklear), Fallon (Pamela Sue Martin), Alexis (Joan Collins) and Blake Carrington (John Forsythe).

Following the huge worldwide success of CBS's ***Dallas***, the other American networks began putting together treatments for their own glamorous mega-soaps. ABC formulated a series that perhaps summed up the excesses of the 1980s better than any other programme – *Dynasty*. Husband-and-wife writer/producer team Richard and Esther Shapiro created a saga about the massively wealthy Carrington family of Denver, Colorado, in a blatant attempt to out-glitz the Ewings of Dallas. Head of the clan was silver-haired oil magnate Blake Carrington, played by former movie star (and voice of 'Charlie' in ***Charlie's Angels***) John Forsythe. Joining the cast as Blake's new trophy wife Krystle was the actress originally earmarked for the role of Pam Ewing in *Dallas*, Linda Evans. The first series of *Dynasty* was a moderate success for ABC, but hardly set the ratings alight. The final episode – detailing Blake's trial for the murder of his son Steven's gay lover – ended on a cliffhanger when Blake's ex-wife, shrouded in a veil that masked her face, strode into the courtroom as a witness for the prosecution. Rumours quickly flew about who was going to play Blake's ex-wife, with Sophia Loren being an early contender for the part.

Of course, when the producers finally got round to casting the scheming, manipulative Alexis Morell Carrington Colby Dexter Rowan (she did seem to get through husbands rather quickly), they pulled off a masterstroke by hiring British Seventies sex siren Joan Collins. Suddenly, the dynamic of the series altered, and the legendary board- and bedroom antics of Blake, Krystle and Alexis hooked millions of viewers. As Alexis and Blake wrestled for control of Denver-Carrington Oil, the antics of their family became increasingly bonkers too. Blake's long-lost son Adam tried to murder arch-rival and all-round do-gooder Jeff Colby by redecorating his office with toxic paint; Krystle was kidnapped and replaced by an identical double; and son Steven got so badly burned in an exploding oil rig that when he returned to the series he was played by an entirely different actor – the first of several 'head changes' of the regular cast. Of course, whenever the producers feared that the storylines were beginning to flag, all they had to do was write in a catfight between Alexis and Krystle. The most notable of these regular hair-pulling squabbles was probably the one in the lily pond of the Carrington mansion, which quickly reduced the glamorous Joan Collins and Linda Evans to two bedraggled mud-caked urchins.

Whether it was just for the shock value or in a genuine effort to push the boundaries of what was acceptable on network television, *Dynasty* was able to claim two 'firsts' for the world of prime-time soap operas: the first gay character (Steven Carrington – although his sexuality fluctuated according to the demands of the plotlines) and the first major black regular (Diahann Carroll as Blake's half-sister Dominique).

For *Dynasty*, no storyline was too outrageous, and no frock too over-the-top. As the acting got bigger, so did the shoulder pads: the budget for Nolan Miller's costumes often exceeded $10,000 per episode. Members of the American elite even made guest appearances in the series, including former President Gerald Ford, Betty Ford and Henry Kissinger playing themselves. By the end of the 1984–5 season, *Dynasty* had become a ratings juggernaut, boasting over 250 million viewers in 70 countries and topping the ratings in the USA. To capitalise on the show's success, the ABC Network decided to create a spin-off series set in Los Angeles: *Dynasty II: The Colbys*. And to crown their most successful year yet, the producers came up with their most outrageous storyline, a plot that would come to rival 'Who Shot JR?' . . .

Blake and Alexis's daughter Amanda had fallen in love with handsome Prince Michael of Moldavia (played by ***Robin of Sherwood*** himself, Michael Praed) and the whole Carrington family decamped to Europe for a spectacular royal wedding. But of course, this being a soap opera, no wedding can ever go without a hitch. In most soap weddings, the worst thing that can happen is the bride jilting the groom at the altar or perhaps the organist not showing up. This being *Dynasty*, things were a touch more extreme: a group of machine gun-toting rebels determined to overthrow the government of Moldavia burst into the church and opened fire

Soap
Aaron Spelling Productions for ABC (shown on BBC One)
Episode Duration: 50 mins
Broadcast: 12 Jan 1981–11 May 1989

Regular Cast

John Forsythe · *Blake Carrington*
Linda Evans · *Krystle Carrington*
Pamela Sue Martin, Emma Samms · *Fallon Carrington/Colby*
Al Corley, Jack Coleman · *Steven Carrington*
Pamela Bellwood · *Claudia Blaisdel/Carrington*
John James · *Jeff Colby*
Joan Collins · *Alexis Morrell/Carrington/Colby/Dexter/Rowan*
Heather Locklear · *Sammy-Jo Reece/Carrington/Fallmont*
Gordon Thomson · *Adam Carrington*
Michael Nader · *Farnsworth 'Dex' Dexter*
Diahann Carroll · *Dominique Carrington/Deveraux*
Catherine Oxenberg, Karen Cellini · *Amanda Carrington*
Michael Praed · *Prince Michael of Moldavia*
Maxwell Caulfield · *Miles Colby*
Christopher Cazenove · *Ben Carrington*
Kate O'Mara · *Cassandra 'Caress' Morrell*
Stephanie Beacham · *Sabella 'Sable' Scott/Colby*
Tracy Scoggins · *Monica Colby*
Wayne Northrop · *Michael Culhane*
Bo Hopkins · *Matthew Blaisdel*
Katy Kurtzman · *Lindsay Blaisdel*
Lee Bergere · *Joseph Aynders*
James Farentino · *Dr Nick Toscanni*
Lloyd Bochner · *Cecil Colby*
Geoffrey Scott · *Mark Jennings*
Kathleen Beller · *Kirby Aynders/Colby*
Helmut Berger · *Peter De Vilbis*
Ken Howard · *Garrett Boydston*
Ted McGinley · *Clay Fallmont*
Terri Garber · *Leslie Carrington*
Leann Hunley · *Dana Waring/Carrington*
James Healy · *Sean Aynders Rowan*
Billy Dee Williams · *Brady Lloyd*
Ali MacGraw · *Lady Ashley Mitchell*
Rock Hudson · *Daniel Reece*
George Hamilton · *Joel Abrigore*

Creators Richard and Esther Shapiro

Producers Aaron Spelling, Richard and Esther Shapiro, Nancy E. Barr, Douglas C. Cramer, Edward DeBlasio, Edward Ledding, John B. Moranville, Philip L. Parslow, David Paulsen, Elaine Rich, E. Duke Vincent

Writers Various, including Daniel King Benton, Edward DeBlasio, Loraine Despres, Norman Katkov, Chester Krumholz, Eileen Pollock, Robert Pollock, Mann Rubin, Esther Shapiro, Richard Shapiro, Elizabeth Wilson, Richard Wilson

Theme Music Bill Conti

on the congregation. The final shot of the season saw the whole main cast sprawled on the floor of the church, covered in blood. Unfortunately, the resolution of the cliffhanger was somewhat less than satisfactory – only two people lost their lives, Ali McGraw's pointless photographer Ashley Mitchell and poor Steven's latest boyfriend.

A steady stream of guest stars queued up to appear in *Dynasty*, ranging from perma-tanned George Hamilton to *Star Wars* alumnus Billy Dee Williams. Following in the footsteps of Joan Collins, other British actresses were soon recruited to up the 'bitchy glamour' stakes, including Kate O'Mara (as Alexis's sister Caress) and Stephanie Beacham. Perhaps the most notorious guest appearance came from Hollywood legend Rock Hudson. Perpetually known as a suave, romantic leading man, Hudson's gaunt appearance shocked many viewers. Shortly after his episodes were broadcast, Hudson announced that he was suffering from AIDS – the first famous person to publicly admit to having the disease. Scare stories ran in the press alleging that Linda Evans, who had shared several lingering on-screen kisses with Hudson, was terrified that she might have been exposed to the disease (a revealing insight into the lack of information available about HIV/AIDS in 1985). Tragically, Rock Hudson died only three months after announcing his illness.

When *Dynasty* finally came to an end in 1989, it marked the end of an era for excess in the TV schedules. As the values of the 'me, me, me' '80s were being replaced by the more 'caring, sharing' '90s, *Dynasty*'s evocation of a world of glamour, greed and all-round selfishness just didn't match the audience's expectations. After eight seasons of excess and a spin-off series, the programme went out on another epic multiple cliffhanger – Fallon buried with Nazi treasure in a collapsed tunnel under the Carrington mansion, Blake being shot by a policeman, and Alexis and Dex plunging off a balcony to their possible doom. Just another ordinary day for the Carringtons of Denver, then.

When the producers finally got round to casting the scheming, manipulative Alexis Morell Carrington Colby Dexter Rowan, they pulled off a masterstroke by hiring British Seventies sex siren Joan Collins.

Myles Wilder **Writers** Various, including Gy Waldron, Bruce Howard, William Raynor, Fred Freiberger, Si Rose, Martin Roth, Myles Wilder, Jim Rogers, Len Kaufman **Theme Music** 'The Dukes of Hazzard (Good Ol' Boys)', written and sung by Waylon Jennings, who also sang the narrative ballads throughout each episode

Beginning in 1977, Burt Reynolds' *Smokey and the Bandit* films spawned a trend for high-speed Hick-flicks involving red-faced sheriffs and miles of dusty roads. That was the formula that kept the Duke family on TV screens for six years from 1979.

At first, the bane of Sherrif Rosco's life is cousins Luke and Bo Duke, whose hooch-brewing antics paled in comparison to the dodgy schemes Rosco himself was up to – thanks to the domineering influence of corrupt politician 'Boss' Hogg. With Boss Hogg and Sherrif Rosco on their tale at every turn, Bo and Luke had their work cut out just trying to stay one step ahead. Occasionally they'd recruit help from their Uncle Jesse and cousin Daisy (she had legs that went all the way up, and cut-off jeans short enough for you to know it). But as with almost every action series of the time, it wasn't about characters – it was the car. In this case, the car was The General Lee, a 1969 Dodge Charger adorned with Confederate regalia and boasting an offensively loud horn that played bars of 'Dixie' as its victory cry.

After pay disputes led to a brief departure for Tom Topat and John Schneider, Bo and Luke's places in the General Lee were filled by Coy and Vance, two more distant cousins of the Duke family. Luckily the dispute was sorted out quick enough for the original Duke boys to make a return.

Even after the show came to an end, *The Dukes of Hazzard* enjoyed a healthy repeat run in syndication and in 1997 and 2000 it spawned revival TV movies. In 2005, the Dukes made their first appearance on the big screen, with Seann William Scott as Bo, Johnny Knoxville as Luke and Jessica Simpson as Daisy in even more 'nothing-left-to-the-imagination' shorts than her predecessor. The all-important part of Boss Hogg was taken by . . . Burt Reynolds, the star of the movie that inspired *The Dukes of Hazzard* in the first place. Isn't that just perfect?

Duty Free

Sitcom | Yorkshire for ITV | episode duration 25 mins, plus 50-min special | broadcast 13 Feb 1984–25 Dec 1986

Regular Cast

Keith Barron · *David Pearce*
Gwen Taylor · *Amy Pearce*
Joanna Van Gyseghem · *Linda Cochran*
Neil Stacy · *Robert Cochran*
Carlos Douglas · *Waiter*

Creators/Writers Eric Chappell, Jean Warr **Producer** Vernon Lawrence **Theme Music** Peter Knight's theme was a pastiche of every bit of tourist-friendly Spanish flamenco music ever to blight a package holiday to the Costas, complete with guitar and castanets.

When Yorkshire couple David and Amy Pearce book a holiday to the Spanish Costa del Sol with his redundancy money, they never expected their first trip abroad to be quite as eventful as it turned out. David hopes for a bit of excitement from his foreign jaunt, but little did he know that he'd meet the woman of his dreams, the posh and glamorous Linda. As the holiday progresses, David and Linda begin a surreptitious affair behind the backs of their respective partners. Although Amy is highly suspicious of David's behaviour, Linda's ex-army husband Robert is less aware of the strange mid-afternoon naps she suddenly needs to have. Indeed, the only person who has noticed David and Linda's infidelity is the ever-suffering and blind-eye turning hotel waiter.

An amazingly popular sitcom, *Duty Free* was recorded almost entirely within the Yorkshire TV studios, with only a one-off special warranting location filming in Spain. Each season ran for seven episodes, reflecting one day of each week of their holiday – hence at the end of the second season, the fortnight's holiday in Spain came to an end and the couples returned home to Blighty. A Christmas special, in which David and Linda once again tried to shake off their spouses for a bit of extra-marital shenanigans, was followed by a third season that represented yet another week in the sun for the four 'holidaymaters'.

With such a limited premise, it's not really surprising that *Duty Free*'s shelf-life was as perishable as an opened bottle of sun-tan lotion. Having said that, occasional twists to the formula (such as one episode featuring Judith Chalmers 'filming' a report on the hotel for ***Wish You Were Here?***) kept the jokes bubbling along. Thankfully, the quality of the writing (from ***Rising Damp***'s Eric Chappell) and acting were largely superior to standard sitcom fare, with particular kudos going to the ever-reliable Gwen Taylor in her standard role as a brassy stroppy Northern woman.

Dynasty

See pages 266–8

EastEnders

See pages 272–6

Edge of Darkness

Drama | BBC One | episode duration 50 mins | broadcast 4 Nov–9 Dec 1985

Principal Cast

Bob Peck · *Ronald Craven*
Joe Don Baker · *Darius Jedburgh*
Jack Watson · *James Godbolt*
Imogen Staley, Joanne Whalley · *Emma Craven*
Charles Kay · *Guy Pendleton*
Ian McNeice · *Henry Harcourt*
Sean Caffrey · *McCroon*
Tim McInnerny · *Terry Shields*
Kenneth Nelson · *Jerry Grogan*
Hugh Fraser · *Robert Bennett*
John Woodvine · *Chief Superintendant Ross*
David Fleeshman · *Jones*
Randal Herley · *Elliott*
Bill Stewart · *DI Dingle*
Paul Humpoletz · *Detective Chief Superintendent Elham*
Anthony Douse · *Carlisle*
Joel Cutrara · *Colonel Mike Merryweather*
Jay Roberts · *Shadow*
Zoë Wanamaker · *Clementine 'Clemmy'*
Allan Cuthbertson · *Bernard Chilwell*
Sarah Martin · *Polly Pelham*
Paul Williamson · *Harold Bewes*
Trevor Bowen · *Childs*
Rowland Davies · *Maberley*
Struan Rodger · *Mac*
Roy Heather · *Lowe*
Jerry Harte · *Kurt Wagner*
David Jackson · *Colonel Taffy Lawson*
Tony Mathews · *Toby Berwick*
Jo Ross · *Miriam Berwick*
Ann Scott-Jones · *Jemima*
Mac McDonald · *Colonel Robert Kelly*

Creator/Writer Troy Kennedy Martin **Producer** Michael Wearing **Theme Music** Eric Clapton, Michael Kamen

When his daughter Emma is gunned down outside their home, police detective Ronald Craven believes he was the killer's intended target and assumes there must be a connection with the IRA. Trying to make sense of Emma's death, Craven meets some of her friends and learns that she had been part of an environmental pressure group called Gaia. This 'green' group had recently mounted a raid on a supposedly abandoned mine to find evidence that it was being used as a dumping ground for nuclear waste. In addition, there are the interests of the British government to consider – whatever they may be – as represented by a ferret-faced, cocksure man called Pendleton. And then there's Darius Jedburgh, an American operative who's investigation into Craven's blind stumbling across certain secrets leads him to join with Craven in a search for the truth – which isn't the story so many people seem desperate to put across . . .

Edge of Darkness is rightly considered a high point of British television drama (as the series completed its run on BBC Two, the schedule was being cleared on BBC One for a full repeat). It arrived with the cover of the *Radio Times* depicting Bob Peck in profile and gun in hand, spot-lit against a brick wall, and Joanne Whalley lurking in the shadows holding a bouquet of black flowers. It was a striking image, and a clever one too, as many of the clues to events in the series were there in that one photo.

Part murder mystery, part political thriller, with a heavy dose of environmental angst, terrorism and even a hint of incest, the series is densely layered and packed with symbolism. There is even a huge sub-plot involving descendants of the Knights Templar coming together, unaware that their actions are bringing the planet closer to its own destruction. Intervening are present-day representatives of an even older civilisation, including Craven, who takes his daughter's place as a saboteur of the nuclear age. Thanks to a (probably very prudent) decision by director Martin Campbell to focus on the more literal story, much of this background story only became clear in interviews with writer Troy Kennedy Martin years after the event.

The biggest change to the story was its resolution, which – had Campbell and Bob Peck not insisted on another rewrite – would have given us Peck, as Craven, turning into a tree. Instead we get an irradiated Craven crying out his dead daughter's name on a mountainside while the camera focuses on the small patches of black flowers (as depicted on that *Radio Times* cover). A much more subtle suggestion of the same idea that was meant by the scripted tree transformation (that the planet somehow finds a way to sustain life), the last-minute change prevented an original if baffling conclusion from spoiling an otherwise thought-provoking and accessible thriller.

Website

A superb online resource can be found at: www.fabulousbakers.tripod.com/edge/.

Edna, the Inebriate Woman

Drama | BBC One | episode duration 90 mins | broadcast 21 Oct 1971

Principal Cast

Patricia Hayes · *Edna*
Barbara Jefford · *Josie*
Pat Nye · *Irene*
June Watson · *Attendant at The Spike*

Denis Carey · *Doctor at The Spike*
Jerry Verno · *Old Man*
Rex Rashley · *Old Man*
Walter Sparrow · *Proprietor of Common Lodging House*
Amelia Bayntun · *Jessie*
Douglas Ditta · *Social Security Clerk*
Chris Gannon, Talfryn Thomas, Charles Farrell · *Tramps*

Producer Irene Shubik **Writer** Jeremy Sandford

Not quite as powerful as writer Jeremy Sandford's earlier, seminal ***Cathy Come Home***, *Edna, the Inebriate Woman* is no less compelling, charting the world's indifference to the homeless and destitute through the experiences of the tragic-comic Edna.

After a spell in prison, Edna develops schizophrenia and ends up wandering the streets with a 'cloudy' mind, bouncing from one hostel to another and finding many doors closed thanks the her abusive behaviour. She eventually finds some stability at the Jesus Saves refuge, but that comes under threat of closure from local residents. Will Edna ever find the respite and help she so desperately needs?

Edna, the Inebriate Woman was broadcast as a *Play for Today*, but started life as *The Lodging House*, one part of a trilogy that Jeremy Sandford started working in 1968 under the heading *In the Time of Cathy*. By the time 1971 came around, the idea for *The Lodging House* was considerably expanded, with the doss house location becoming just one backdrop among many for the aimless meanderings of Edna.

Sandford claimed that the backbone of his research for writing the film came from two separate stints living as a tramp, allowing him to open up to and absorb the experiences of the homeless. For the role of Edna, Sandford and director Ted Kotcheff (who went on to direct *First Blood* (1982)) felt they needed an actress with comedy experience to give the fairly difficult character an air of sympathy with the audience, and they found Patricia Hayes working as a regular on ***The Benny Hill Show***. The production team arranged for Hayes to be released to film *Edna*, and the brave casting choice clearly paid off, with Hayes winning a BAFTA for Best Actress in 1972.

Edward and Mrs Simpson

Drama | Thames for ITV | episode duration 50 mins | broadcast 6 Nov–18 Dec 1978

Principal Cast
Edward Fox · *King Edward VIII*
Cynthia Harris · *Wallis Simpson*
Peggy Ashcroft · *Queen Mary*
Maurice Denham · *Archbishop of Canterbury*
Marius Goring · *King George V*
Nigel Hawthorne · *Walter Monkton*
Cherie Lunghi · *Lady Thelma Furness*
Kika Markham · *Freda Dudley Ward*
Jessie Matthews · *Aunt Bessie Merryman*
Andrew Ray · *Duke of York*
John Shrapnel · *Major Alexander Hardinge*
David Waller · *Stanley Baldwin*

Producers Brenda Ennis (associate), Andrew Brown
Writer Simon Raven, from the biography by Frances Donaldson
Theme Music 'I Danced With a Man, Who Danced With a Girl, Who Danced with the Prince of Wales', a cheekily appropriate ditty from Ron Grainer.

Edward and Mrs Simpson was a multi-BAFTA-winning drama that charted the love affair between Prince Edward (later King Edward VIII) and divorcée Wallis Simpson and the king's subsequent abdication. Edward meets and falls in love with Wallace Simpson and shortly afterwards his father, King George V, dies. Edward is forced to fight politicians and the church for his right to take the throne and marry Simpson. On the one side, he has Prime Minister Stanley Baldwin and the Archbishop of Canterbury challenging him, while allies include the might of Winston Churchill.

The real-life Wallace Simpson was reportedly unhappy with the depiction of her life in this series – based on the biography by Frances Donaldson – and possibly rightly so. The drama does not present her in a particularly good light, and the Duchess of Windsor, as she was named after the abdication, successfully managed to have the series banned in France, where she was living. Highly acclaimed, *Edward and Mrs Simpson* was an international success, winning BAFTAs for Best Drama Serial, Best Costume Design and Best Actor for Edward Fox in 1978, alongside numerous other nominations. The series won an International Emmy in 1980 after it was broadcast in America.

El CID

Comedy Drama | Granada for ITV | episode duration 50 mins | broadcast 7 Feb 1990–2

Regular Cast
Alfred Molina · *Bernard Blake*
John Bird · *Douglas Bromley*
Simón Andreu · *Delgado*
Viviane Vives · *Mercedes*
Niven Boyd · *Graham*
Donald Churchill · *Metcalf*
Kenneth Cranham · *Gus Mercer*
Tony Haygarth · *Frank*
María Isbert · *Señora Sanchez*
Amanda Redman · *Rosie Bromley*
Robert Reynolds · *Stevie Blake*

Creators/Writer Chris Kelly, Iain Roy **Producer** Mathew Bird
Theme Music Georgie Fame

Down-at-heel police clerk Douglas Bromley discovers he is about to be relocated to Surrey, which he's not best

Continued on page 277

EastEnders

The original Fowler and Beale families: Mark (David Scarboro), Michelle (Susan Tully), Arthur (Bill Treacher), Pauline (Wendy Richard), Kathy (Gillian Taylforth), Pete (Peter Dean), Ian (Adam Woodyatt) and, seated, matriarch Lou (Anna Wing).

While the BBC arguably kickstarted the genre in the UK, ITV seemed to have the better success rate with its soaps – and king of the lot was ***Coronation Street***. To some extent, there was a certain amount of sniffiness about soaps at the Beeb, with a fair few believing it to be a low-grade form of entertainment. However, the arrival of ***Brookside*** in late 1982 showed the potential for the twice-weekly drama; it wasn't just gossip over the garden wall and melodramatic silliness (at least, not in the beginning), it was often tackling hard-hitting issues usually reserved for 'serious' drama.

It became clear to all that the Beeb needed to overcome their snobbery and tackle the soap issue head on. A number of existing popular shows were used to test the schedules, with ***Angels***, ***Triangle***, ***The District Nurse*** and even ***Doctor Who*** dotted about the midweek line-up to see which nights performed best. Meanwhile, formidable producer Julia Smith, along with her *Angels* script editor Tony Holland, retreated to a Spanish villa to bash out the format for the proposed show. Avoiding direct comparisons to existing soaps set in the north and midlands of England, it made sense to set their stories in a London location, and the East End was chosen. Combining the charm and family-centred appeal of *Coronation Street* with *Brookside*'s gritty issue-led agenda, this new soap opera would form the backbone to the BBC One weekday schedules every Tuesday and Thursday at 7.00 p.m. Several different names for the new soap were tried out and abandoned (the most popular alternative being the fictional postcode in which the programme was going to be set, E20) before *EastEnders* finally lurched onto the nation's TV screens in February 1985, like a sulky, petulant teenager with a particularly vicious hangover.

Soap
BBC One
Episode Duration: 30 mins
Broadcast: 19 Feb 1985–present

Regular Cast
Wendy Richard · *Pauline Fowler*
Bill Treacher · *Arthur Fowler*
David Scarboro, Todd Carty · *Mark Fowler*
Susan Tully · *Michelle Fowler*
Jon Peyton Price, James Alexandrou · *Martin Fowler*
Samantha Crown, Samantha Leigh, Scarlett Johnson · *Vicki Fowler*
Lucy Benjamin · *Lisa Shaw/Fowler*
Anna Wing · *Lou Beale*
Peter Dean · *Pete Beale*
Gillian Taylforth · *Kathy Beale/Mitchell*
Adam Woodyatt · *Ian Beale*
Pam St Clement · *Pat Harris/Beale/Wicks/Butcher/Evans*
Michelle Collins · *Cindy Williams/Beale*
Tamzin Outhwaite · *Melanie Healey/Beale/Owen*
Hannah Waterman · *Laura Dunn/Beale*
Leslie Grantham · *Den Watts*
Anita Dobson · *Angie Watts*
Letitia Dean · *Sharon Watts/Mitchell*
Nigel Harmon · *Dennis Rickman*
June Brown · *Dot Cotton/Branning*
Christopher Hancock · *Charlie Cotton*
John Altman · *Nick Cotton*
Nejdet Salih · *Ali Osman*
Sandy Ratcliff · *Sue Osman*
Gretchen Franklin · *Ethel Skinner*
Tom Watt · *George 'Lofty' Holloway*
Leonard Fenton · *Dr Harold Legg*
Linda Davidson · *Mary Smith*
Oscar James · *Tony Carpenter*
Paul J. Medford · *Kelvin Carpenter*
Delanie Forbes · *Cassie Carpenter*
Sally Sagoe · *Hannah Carpenter*
Ross Davidson · *Andy O'Brien*
Shirley Cheriton · *Debbie Wilkins*
Nick Berry · *Simon Wicks*
Michael French · *David Wicks*
Paul Nicholls · *Joe Wicks*
Jacqueline Leonard · *Lorraine Wicks*
Michael Cashman · *Colin Russell*
Michael Melia · *Eddie Royle*
Mike Reid · *Frank Butcher*
Edna Doré · *Mo Butcher*
Sophie Lawrence · *Diane Butcher*
Sid Owen · *Ricky Butcher*
Rebecca Michael, Alexia Demetriou, Charlie Brooks · *Janine Butcher*
Jo Warne, Barbara Windsor · *Peggy Mitchell*
Ross Kemp · *Grant Mitchell*
Steve McFadden · *Phil Mitchell*

At least two things were on the fledgeling show's side. First, *Coronation Street* had clearly become complacent. Consequently, it was perceived as being out of touch with real life and far too twee for a modern audience. Second, someone had the bright idea of providing an omnibus edition on Sundays. The message was clear: you won't want to miss an episode.

Set in the fictional London suburb of Walford (situated more or less where you'd find Bromley-by-Bow on a London tube map), *EastEnders* initially focused on the lives and loves of a small number of families living and working around Albert Square, the Queen Victoria pub and the Bridge Street Market. The heart of the show was found in two linked families, the Fowlers and the Beales. Pauline Fowler shared a small terraced house with her unemployed husband Arthur, teenage children Mark and Michelle, and battleaxe mother, Lou Beale. Living in a block of flats behind the square were Pauline's twin brother Pete, Kathy, his second wife, and their son Ian. But slowly the focus of attention shifted to the married couple who ran the pub, the Queen Vic. By *EastEnders*' first birthday, the stars were undoubtedly Den and Angie Watts, whose tempestuous love-hate relationship had audiences hooked.

Before the show had even begun, broadcaster Terry Wogan had mocked its predictability in killing off a central character in the first episode (Rex Cox, who was found unconscious in his flat by Den Watts, Arthur Fowler and Ali Osman). But few could have been prepared for just how unrelentingly grim it all was. Few shows would have had the sheer nerve to begin with the news that a middle-aged woman was pregnant by accident and view this as anything other than a happy occasion. Not for *EastEnders*, as newly-expectant parents Pauline and Arthur had to face the wrath of Lou, disgusted at her daughter's irresponsibility. The baby was duly born nine months later and named Martin (20 years, two recasts, a prison sentence and a marriage later, Martin is still causing his mother headaches).

While Wendy Richard (Pauline) and Susan Tully (Michelle) were familiar faces to the audience (Richard from playing Miss Brahms in ***Are You Being Served?***, Tully from her memorable run on ***Grange Hill***), the majority of the cast were relatively inexperienced. This brought a freshness and realism to many of the performances, but it also meant that the cast was generally unprepared for the kind of instant fame such a show brought. Leslie Grantham ('Dirty' Den) found his past exposed when a tabloid newspaper revealed he'd served a prison sentence for manslaughter, while the love lives of the cast served to increase the show's profile further. For one cast member, however, the pressure became too much. Young David Scarboro, who played Mark Fowler, began to suffer from bouts of depression and left the show. He eventually took his own life in 1988. In 1989, Mark returned in the form of another former *Grange Hill* alumnus, Tucker Jenkins himself, Todd Carty.

Arriving just a few months into the series were the Bible-bashing, chain-smoking legend that is Dot Cotton, and the blonde battleaxe 'Fat' Pat Harris-Beale-Wicks-Butcher-Evans (she's been married many times!). Over the years, Pat's many and varied relationships

Danniella Westbrook, Kim Medcalf · *Sam Mitchell/Butcher*
Casey Anne Rothery, Melissa Suffield · *Lucy Beale*
Joseph Shade, James Martin · *Peter Beale*
Perry Fenwick · *Billy Mitchell*
Jack Ryder · *Jamie Mitchell*
Jill Halfpenny · *Kate Tyler/Mitchell*
Tommy Eytle · *Jules Tavernier*
Leroy Golding · *Celestine Tavernier*
Jacqui Gordon-Lawrence · *Etta Tavernier*
Steven Woodcock · *Clyde Tavernier*
Michelle Gayle · *Hattie Tavernier*
Nicola Stapleton · *Mandy Salter*
Sean Maguire · *Aidan Brosnan*
Ian Reddington · *Richard 'Tricky Dicky' Cole*
Paul Bradley · *Nigel Bates*
Nicola Duffett · *Debbie Tyler/Bates*
Gemma Bissix · *Clare Tyler*
Deepak Verma · *Sanjay Kapoor*
Shobu Kapoor · *Gita Kapoor*
Lindsey Coulson · *Carol Jackson*
Howard Anthony · *Alan Jackson*
Patsy Palmer · *Bianca Jackson/Butcher*
Natalie Cassidy · *Sonia Jackson/Fowler*
Dean Gaffney · *Robbie Jackson*
Mona Hammond · *Blossom Jackson*
John Bardon · *Jim Branning*
Craig Fairbrass · *Dan Sullivan*
Gavin Richards · *Terry Raymond*
Martine McCutcheon · *Tiffany Raymond/Mitchell*
Andrew Lynford · *Simon Raymond*
Carol Harrison · *Louise Raymond/Simmonds*
Roberta Taylor · *Irene Hills/Raymond*
Mark Homer · *Tony Hills*
Daniela Denby-Ashe · *Sarah Hills*
Brian Croucher · *Ted Hills*
Tony Caunter · *Roy Evans*
Shaun Williamson · *Barry Evans*
Lucy Speed · *Natalie Price/Evans*
Russell Floyd · *Michael Rose*
Joe Absalom · *Matthew Rose*
Louise Jameson · *Rosa di Marco*
Michael Greco · *Beppe di Marco*
Marc Bannerman · *Gianni di Marco*
Leila Birch · *Teresa di Marco*
Carly Hillman · *Nicky di Marco*
Martin Kemp · *Steve Owen*
Laila Morse · *Maureen 'Big Mo' Harris*
Derek Martin · *Charlie Slater*
Elaine Lordan · *Lynne Slater/Hobbs*
Jessie Wallace · *Kat Slater/Moon*
Kacey Ainsworth · *Maureen 'Little Mo' Morgan/Mitchell*
Michelle Ryan · *Zoe Slater*
Ricky Groves · *Garry Hobbs*
Alex Ferns · *Trevor Morgan*
Corrine Skinner Carter · *Audrey Trueman*
Nicholas R. Bailey · *Dr Anthony Trueman*

ensured that she could be relied on to have some direct link to almost every single character in the show – either through marriages, employment or accommodation. As the only original cast member not to have taken any lengthy time away from Albert Square, the mighty Adam 'Ian Beale' Woodyatt takes the long-service crown from his fellow cast members. It's a credit to Woodyatt that such a loathsome, selfish and weasley character as Ian should remain so popular with audiences as they rejoice in seeing him built up and knocked down with Jobian regularity.

In addition to the regular twice-weekly episodes, there have also been several spin-offs (or 'soap bubbles'), with varying degrees of success. 1988's 'Civvy Street' stepped back to the Walford of World War Two to look at the lives of Lou Beale, her husband Albert (played by ***2 Point 4 Children***'s Gary Olsen), and her friend Ethel; the heartbreaking 'Dot's Story' came in 2003 and saw Dot Branning revisit the old woman she'd lived with as an evacuee during the war; and a 1960s-set edition explained the long-standing bad blood between Pat and Big Mo Harris. Other bubbles helped to extend the on-going stories by catching up with departed characters like Ricky and Bianca or even the irredeemable Nick Cotton. The show has also become famous for its occasional two-handers, episodes where we get a more in-depth look at a pair of characters, usually as they reach a turning point in their lives, such as Den and Angie's blazing rows; Michelle confessing the identity of her daughter's father to her best friend Sharon (the father being Sharon's dad, Den); Dot and Ethel reminiscing, or the aftermath of Kat Slater's revelation that her youngest sister is actually her daughter, the result of a coerced sexual relationship with her abusive uncle Harry.

Throughout the 1980s and '90s, *EastEnders* seemed to be an unstoppable juggernaut. Moved back to 7.30 p.m. from its original timeslot of 7.00 p.m. (allegedly to counter complaints about the sordid nature of the programme, but more likely to capitalise on the show's success and build the ratings still further), it managed to pull in a record-breaking 30 million viewers for the double Christmas episode where Arthur suffered a nervous breakdown and trashed the family's Christmas tree while Den stunned Angie by giving her a present to remember – divorce papers. *EastEnders* then expanded into a third weekly episode from 1994 before gaining a fourth episode in 2001.

The trick of bringing in a large family has been pulled regularly with variable results. The Jacksons were a mixed-race family headed by Carol, whose four children had four different fathers. Even when Carol left the Square after entering the witness protection programme (!), her children remained with their grandfather, Jim Branning. Flame-haired harpy Bianca narrowly avoided an incestuous relationship when it was revealed that David Wicks, Pat's eldest son who Bianca had been flirting with, was actually her biological father. Luckless Robbie emerged as a strong comedy character who was also occasionally capable of generating pathos, but, unquestionably, the surprise star of the family was Sonia, who evolved from trumpet-playing moppet to the show's leading young dramatic actress. Her shock pregnancy to Martin Fowler, doomed relationship with Jamie Mitchell and later about-turn and marriage to Martin has given viewers some of *EastEnders*' most heart-rending moments in the last few years.

The Mitchells arrived in 1991 with Phil and Grant, two skinhead mechanics who fancied themselves as ladies' men, taking over the garage in 'The Arches'. Soon, their younger sister, Sam, and their mother, Peggy, moved to the Square and, in 1998, Phil's godson Jamie Mitchell popped up to escape from his violent uncle, Billy. Inheriting some of the gangland storylines that had been attached to Den Watts, Phil and Grant have both had spells in prison, slept with the same women and both had unsuccessful custody battles for their children. When Grant left in 1999, Phil seemed to take on many of his character traits, while Billy took on the mantle of the more sympathetic face of Mitchelldom. Peggy also evolved – not least thanks to the recasting of the part in the shape of former *Carry On* films star Barbara Windsor. Installed as owner of the Queen Vic, her formidable cry of 'Wossgoinon? Gerroutta my pub!' was heard right across the Square.

Another great success was the decision to allow the Slaters (matriarch 'Big' Mo' Harris, son-in-law Charlie Slater and his daughters Kat, Lynne, 'Little' Mo and Zoe) to arrive in a blaze of glory, but then bed in for a year in advance of their first major story. This gave viewers the chance to overcome their initial dislike of the intentionally brash characters. Recognising their immense popularity, however, the writers became too reliant on the Slater girls to carry storylines, resulting once again in a shift away from the older characters and too much in favour of the new kids on the block. Tabloid rumours of cast dissent over a belief in the 'Not a Slater, See ya Later' policy coincided with a culling of a number of characters who were felt to be past their best.

One area in which *EastEnders* has drawn justified criticism is in its representation of ethnic minorities. Few, if any, of the non-white characters seem to be particularly well drawn or integrated into Walford life – tokenism that is hardly an accurate reflection of the real vibrant multi-cultural East End of London. This is a shame, because at its best, *EastEnders*' commitment to other issues can't really be beaten. Mark Fowler's HIV status was more than just sensationalism as it fought to break down barriers and prejudice, and also show the many options open to people who've discovered they

Throughout the 1980s and '90s, *EastEnders* seemed to be an unstoppable juggernaut. It managed to pull in a record-breaking 30 million viewers for the double Christmas episode where Arthur suffered a nervous breakdown and Den stunned Angie by giving her a present to remember – divorce papers.

Gary Beadle · *Paul Trueman*
Rudolph Walker · *Patrick Trueman*
Angela Winter · *Yolande Duke/Trueman*
Shane Richie · *Alfie Moon*
Christopher Parker · *Spencer Moon*
Hilda Braid · *Victoria 'Nana' Moon*
Michael Higgs · *Andy Hunter*
Ian Lavender · *Derek Harkinson*
Joel Beckett · *Jake Moon*
Jake Maskall · *Danny Moon*
Billy Murray · *Jonny Allen*
Joe Swash · *Mickey Miller*
Gerry Cowper · *Rosie Miller*
David Spinx · *Keith Miller*
Charlie G. Hawkins · *Darren Miller*
Shana Swash · *Demi Miller*
Laurie Brett · *Jane Collins*
Tracy-Ann Oberman · *Chrissie Watts*

Producers Julia Smith, Tony Holland, Christopher Ballantyne, Richard Bramall, Jane Fallon, Jane Harris, Corinne Hollingworth, Matthew Robinson, John Yorke, Louise Berridge, Kathleen Hutchison

Writers Various, including Colin Brake, Tony Jordan, Tony Holland, Simon Ashdown, Tony Basgallop, Nazrin Choudhury, Andrew Collins, Robin Mukherjee, Colin Wyatt

Theme Music Simon May

have contracted the disease without necessarily being promiscuous or gay. Teenage pregnancy has reared its head on a number of occasions (most recently with a girl of 13) and, early on, the show looked at the trauma that Sudden Infant Death Syndrome (or 'cot death') leaves behind. Unsurprisingly, we've also seen incidents and after-effects of rape, alcoholism, drugs, infidelity and an increasingly ludicrous number of headline-grabbing murders (usually with a 'Whodunnit?' element attached that often results in the slightly less exciting response of 'Who cares?'). The treatment of domestic violence shows how the drama has matured. While the site of Pauline smacking Arthur over the head with a frying pan was almost played for laughs, the on-going story of Little Mo's abuse at the hands of her sadistic estranged husband Trevor culminated in her being charged with attempted murder after she hit him across the head repeatedly with an iron. Though the episode in question drew criticism for the level of violence being shown pre-watershed, it was also lavished with praise by concerned support groups who know that this kind of incident sadly represents a daily reality for many of the show's viewers.

Despite winning the top gong in the Soap awards almost every year, many have recognised that *EastEnders* is no longer the guaranteed Corrie-beater it once was. The year 2004 marked a very difficult time for the soap: at more than one point it attracted the lowest recorded ratings in its history (6.2 million – although this doesn't take into account its omnibus or digital channel repeats); the head of the new Ferreira family had to be swiftly written out after actor Dalip Tahil learned his work visa had expired (the rest of the family followed in 2005); the departure of three of the four Slater girls (one permanent, two for maternity leave) necessitated rewrites for months of scripts; and the audacious resurrection of Den Watts from the dead was hampered by tabloid reports of Leslie Grantham's internet sexploits with a fan.

So long as the producers remember that *EastEnders* should be more about families than gangsters, the show's future should be assured.

Late 2004 saw the introduction of the Miller family in much the same way we've seen before – upsetting their neighbours, being brash and aggressive towards anyone who has cause to remonstrate with them – in fact, pretty much the same as the Jacksons and the Slaters had done when they arrived. It remains to be seen how well or otherwise the public takes to them, but so long as the producers remember that *EastEnders* should always be more about families than gangsters, the show's future should be assured.

pleased about and decides to retire to Marbella aboard his yacht, the appropriately named *El CID* He manages to persuade his long-time colleague Bernard to accompany him, and together they set sail with the intention of opening a bar. Things don't quite go to plan, and the bar literally goes up in smoke, the retired coppers ending up in a feud with local crime boss Gus Mercer and his henchman, Graham. Help is on hand from local restaurateur Frank and detectives Delgado and Mercedes, whom Bromley and Blake form an alliance with. The third season saw the departure of Blake (Alfred Molina clearly destined for big things in Hollywood), to be replaced with Amanda Redman as Blake's long-lost daughter, Rosie.

Punning the name of the 1961 Charlton Heston epic *El Cid*, *El CID* was a gently amusing comedy drama from TV presenter Chris Kelly, who also created the action series, *Saracen*, but one can't help but feel that the title was dreamt up long before the mechanics of the series were worked out. Although highly enjoyable, *El CID* is probably more remembered for bringing future well-known names to a wider audience. John Bird would become inseparable from his work alongside satirists Rory Bremner and John Fortune, while Alfred Molina has risen to stardom in films such as *Spider-Man 2* (2004). Amanda Redman has since become a high-profile TV star in the UK on both ITV and BBC with drama hits ***At Home with the Braithwaites*** and *Old Tricks*.

Eldorado

Soap | Cinema Verity for BBC One | episode duration 30 mins | broadcast 6 Jul 1992–9 Jul 1993

Principal Cast

Jesse Birdsall · *Marcus Tandy*
Sandra Sandri · *Pilar Moreno*
Patricia Brake · *Gwen Lockhead*
Campbell Morrison · *Drew Lockhead*
Julie Fernandez · *Nessa Lockhead*
Josh Nathan · *Blair Lockhead*
Polly Perkins · *Trish Valentine*
Leslee Udwin · *Joy Slater*
Hilary Crane · *Rosemary Webb*
William Lucas · *Stanley Webb*
Roland Curram · *Freddie Martin*
Faith Kent · *Olive King*
Patch Connolly · *Snowy White*
Roger Walker · *Bunny Charlson*
Kathy Pitkin · *Fizz Charlson*
Tessa Wojtczak · *Natalie Jackson*
Ben Murphy · *Terry Flynn*
Darren Newton · *Gavin Hindle*
Jon Morrey · *Allan Hindle*
Buki Armstrong · *Gerry Peters-Smith*
Ravi Aujla · *Jaskaran Singh*
Amerjit Deu · *Ranjit Singh*
Marchell Betak, Clare Wilkie · *Trine Svendsen*
Iker Ibáñez · *Javier 'Paco' Fernandez*
Jorge Cano · *Pablo Fernandez*
Stella Maris · *Rosario Fernandez*
Franco Rey · *Roberto Fernandez*
María Sánchez · *Maria Fernandez*
María Vega · *Abuela Fernandez*
Bo Corre · *Ingrid Olsson*
Daniel Lombart · *Philippe Leduc*
Framboise Gommendy · *Isabelle Leduc*
Mikael Philippe · *Arnaud Leduc*
Kai Maurer · *Dieter Shultz*
Kim Romer · *Per Svendsen*
Nanna Møller · *Lene Svendsen*

Creators Julia Smith and Tony Holland **Producers** Verity Lambert, John Dark, (executive) James Todesco (associate), Julia Smith, Corinne Hollingworth, Matthew Kuipers, David Shanks **Writers** Various, including Tony Holland, Maureen Chadwick, Alison Davis, Lilie Ferrari, Gilly Fraser, Jane Galletly, Valerie Georgeson, Rob Gittins, Andrew Holden, Jane Hollowood, Gary Hopkins, Gerry Huxham, Tony Jordan, Dean Lemmon, Bill Lyons, Rosemary Mason, Glen McCoy, Tony McHale, John Pennington **Theme Music** Simon May and Simon Lockyer

While ITV's ***Albion Market*** also failed to find a loyal audience, it manages to escape scorn partly because it was such a low-key series created predominantly to capture some of ***EastEnders***' glory. But the BBC's *Eldorado* was ripped apart by the press before it had even begun and continues to be used as a euphemism for bad TV ideas. The corporation had attempted to copy ***Brookside***'s idea of building an entire complex that would house its sets and provide an attractive filming location, the mountains of Coin, Spain, doubling for the fictional Los Barcos. *EastEnders*' creators Julia Smith and Tony Holland mapped out the series' characters and plots: there was ex-pat family the Lockhead, whose daughter Nessa was wheelchair-bound; middle-aged couple Rosemary and Stanley Webb; lively, earthy part-time singer Trish Valentine in the 'tart-with-a-heart' mould; a fair mix of European families to spice things up a little; and the dastardly bad-boy Marcus Tandy.

The series was plagued from the start by poor acoustics, something that had also affected *Brookside*, but with so many strong foreign accents and at times whole conversations conducted in German, Spanish or Danish, it proved a frustrating element to a show that was already struggling to find its target audience (who, frankly, were already living the ex-pat life rather than staying at home to watch it on telly). Many of the cast-members were savaged by the tabloids for being inexperienced actors (notably poor Josh Nathan as Blair and Kathy Pitkin, who played teen bride Fizz), but despite cast reshuffles and assurances that it was getting better, honest, viewers just weren't interested. Having genuinely tried all they could to recoup their losses, BBC One Controller Alan Yentob decided to accept defeat and brought *Eldorado* to an end almost a year to the day that it had begun, with Marcus Tandy and his on-off girlfriend Pilar sailing away into the sunset.

Elizabeth R

Drama | BBC Two | episode duration 90 mins | broadcast 17 Feb–24 Mar 1971

Principal Cast
Glenda Jackson · *Queen Elizabeth I*
Ronald Hines · *William Cecil, Lord Burghley*
Robert Hardy · *Robert Dudley, Earl of Leicester*
Hamilton Dyce · *Sir Amyas Paulet*
Peter Egan · *Earl of Southampton*
Robin Ellis · *Robert Devereaux, Earl of Essex*
David Garfield · *Father Ballard*
Robert Garrett · *Sir Thomas Wyatt*
David Hargreaves · *Bolingbroke*
Bernard Hepton · *Archbishop Cranmer*
Bernard Holley · *Gifford*
Julian Holloway · *Ambassador de Noailles*
Bernard Horsfall · *Sir Christopher Hatton*
Peter Jeffrey · *King Phillip II of Spain*
Jason Kemp · *Edward VI*
Stanley Lebor · *Sir Robert Tyrwhitt*
Stephen Murray · *Sir Francis Walsingham*
John Nettleton · *Sir Francis Bacon*
Clifford Rose · *Egerton*
Leonard Sachs · *Count de Feria*
Nicholas Selby · *Sir Walter Raleigh*
John Shrapnel · *Earl of Sussex*
Anthony Ainley · *Sir Henry Sidney*
David Strong · *Duke of Norfolk*
John Woodvine · *Sir Francis Drake*
Michael Culver · *John Tregannon*
Vivian Pickles · *Mary of Scotland*
Margaretta Scott · *Catherine de Medici*
Daphne Slater · *Mary I*
Judith South · *Lady Essex*
Angela Thorne · *Lettice Knollys*
Rosalie Crutchley · *Catherine Parr*
Sarah Frampton · *Lady Jane Grey*

Producers Christopher Sarson (executive), Roderick Graham
Writers John Hale, Rosemary Anne Sisson, Julian Mitchell, Hugh Whitemore, John Prebble, Ian Rodgers **Theme Music** 'The Leaves Be Green' by David Munrow

For commentary, see THE SIX WIVES OF HENRY VIII

Ellen

Sitcom | Black-Marlens Company/Touchstone Television for ABC (shown on Channel 4) | episode duration 30 mins | broadcast 29 Mar 1994–22 Jul 1998 (USA)

Regular Cast
Ellen DeGeneres · *Ellen Morgan*
Joely Fisher · *Paige Clark*
Arye Gross · *Adam Green*
Jeremy Piven · *Spence Kovak*
David Anthony Higgins · *Joe Farrell*
Clea Lewis · *Audrey Penney*
Maggie Wheeler · *Anita*
Holly Fulger · *Holly*

Creators/Writers Neal Marlens, Carol Black, David Rosenthal
Producers Warren Bell, Mark Driscoll, Lawrence Broch, Neal Marlens, Carol Black (executive), Ellen DeGeneres
Theme Music Sharleen Spiteri, John McElhone (theme music), W. G. 'Snuffy' Walden (music)

Originally titled *These Friends of Mine* during the broadcast of season one in America, *Ellen* quickly became more than just another ensemble spin on the ***Friends*** format by pushing star Ellen DeGeneres firmly to the front. As the quirky manager/owner of an independent bookstore called Buy The Book, Ellen goes through her days making wry observations on the bizarreness of life and what it has to throw at her. Her best friends make the process easier – bubbly redhead Paige, flatmate photographer Adam and, later, her gung-ho but insecure cousin Spence, who moves in after Adam takes his leave. Playing like a hybrid between *Friends* and ***Seinfeld***, Ellen is most famous for the double episode in which Ellen comes as out as gay, the first time in US TV history that a lead character and actress had been openly out. DeGeneres became an icon overnight.

Although popular for a time, *Ellen* surprisingly lasted only five seasons – in the fickle world of American network television, that amounts to a respectable run. Throughout the show's years on air, Ellen DeGeneres was nominated for Best Actress on four occasions, but came away with nothing (although she would share an award for writing at the 1997 ceremony). As has become de rigueur in American sitcoms, *Ellen* attracted some heavyweight cameo stars, with appearances by Carrie Fisher, Jay Leno, the Bee Gees, Laura Dern and Emma Thompson all walking through Ellen's door, the latter also bagging herself an Outstanding Guest Actress Emmy for her troubles.

Ellen DeGeneres made a return to network sitcoms in 2001 with *The Ellen Show*. Viewer response was so negative that the show was cancelled after just 12 episodes, with the final six unaired episodes eventually seeing the light of day on the UK's Paramount Comedy Channel. At the time of writing, she's now moved into the arena of chat shows, with a hugely popular and successful series called simply *Ellen: The Ellen DeGeneres Show*.

Emergency Ward 10

Soap | ATV for ITV | episode duration 30 mins | broadcast 19 Feb 1957–27 Jun 1967

Regular Cast
Charles 'Bud' Tingwell · *Dr Alan Dawson*
Desmond Carrington · *Dr Chris Anderson*

Frederick Bartman · *Dr Simon Forrester*
John Carson · *Dr Donald Latimer*
Richard Thorp · *Dr John Rennie*
Jill Browne · *Nurse/Sister Carole Young*
Tom Adams · *Mr Guy Marshall*
John Alderton · *Dr Richard Moon*
Gene Anderson · *Sister Joy Shelley*
John Arnatt · *Dr Fitzgerald*
Sydney Arnold · *Richard Sainsbury*
Jean Aubrey · *Nurse Julie Mayne*
Ray Barrett · *Dr Don Nolan*
John Barrie · *RSO Miller*
John Barron · *Harold de la Roux*
Michael Baxter · *Dr Alex Grant*
Richard Bidlake · *Dr Ted Bryan*
Caroline Blakiston · *Lena Hyde*
John Brooking · *Mr Stephen Brooks*
Anne Brooks · *Staff Nurse Jill Craig*
David Butler · *Dr Nick Williams*
Paula Byrne · *Dr Frances Whitney*
Kathleen Byron · *Margaret de la Roux*
John Carlisle · *Mr Lester Large*
Richard Carpenter · *Mr Victor*
Erik Chitty · *Ignatius Small*
Barbara Clegg · *Nurse Jo Buckley/Anderson*
Noel Coleman · *Dr Richmond*
Ian Colin · *Rupert Marsden*
Anthony Collin · *Mr Unwin*
Geoffrey Colville · *Dr Mike Beckett*
John Crocker · *George Rudd*
Ian Cullen · *Mr Kent*
Paul Darrow · *Mr Verity*
Carol Davies · *Sally Bowen*
Zuleema Dene · *Sister Wright*
Jane Downs · *Audrey Blake/Dawson*
Pamela Duncan · *Sister Doughty*
Colette Dunne · *Staff Nurse Lyle*
Sheila Fearn · *Elizabeth Benskin*
Hilda Fenemore · *Mrs Sainsbury*
Albert Finney · *Tom Fletcher*
Anne Firbank · *Miss Nesbitt*
Sonia Fox · *Staff Nurse Amy Williams*
Rosemary Frankau · *Helen Booth*
Joan Frank · *Tania Trimble*
David Garth · *Mr Dorsey*
Norah Gorsen · *Nurse Ann Guthridge*
Noel Hood · *Mrs Anderson*
Joan Hooley · *Dr Louise Mahler*
Basil Hoskins · *Dr Reginald Lane-Russell*
Peter Howell · *Dr Peter Harrison*
Cecily Hullett · *Sister Crawford*
Douglas Ives · *Potter*
Langton Jones · *Dr Green*
Desmond Jordan · *Dr Bob Coughlin*
Elizabeth Kentish · *Sister Cowley*
Karen Kessey · *Dinny Jackson*
Katherine Kessey · *Penny Jackson*
David King · *Mr Bailey*
Robert Lang · *Dr Griffiths*
Janet Lees-Price · *Nurse Jones*
Pik Sen Lim · *Nurse Kwe Kim-Yen/Kwei*
John Line · *Andrew Shaw*
Anne Lloyd · *Staff Nurse/Sister Jane Beattie*
Robert MacLeod · *Dr Matthews*
Kerry Marsh · *Nurse O'Keefe*
Joan Matheson · *Sister Rhys*
Michael McKevitt · *Dr James Gordon*
Monica McLeod · *Sister Walker*
Therese McMurray · *Nurse Parkin*
Rosemary Miller · *Nurse Pat Roberts*
Tricia Money · *Nurse Michaela Large/Davies*
Elizabeth Murray · *Jean Twillow*
Jonathan Newth · *Mr Booth*
Brian Nissen · *Dr Derek Bailey*
Shaun O'Riordan · *Jake O'Dowd*
Glyn Owen · *Dr Patrick O'Meara*
John Paul · *RSO Hughes*
Salmaan Peer · *Dr Murad*
David Pinner · *Mr Bacon*
Chips Rafferty · *Mick Doyle*
Jane Rossington · *Nurse Kate Ford*
Geoffrey Russell · *Mr Barrett*
Iris Russell · *Nurse/Sister/Matron Mary Stevenson*
Ann Sears · *Staff Nurse Jane Morley*
Honor Shepherd · *Elizabeth Fairfax*
Dorothy Smith · *Sister MacNab*
Stella Tanner · *Sister Ransome*
Grant Taylor · *Jim Singleton*
Shirley Thieman · *Staff Nurse Craigie*
Hilary Tindall · *Amanda Brown*
Jean Trend · *Nurse Ann Webb*
Julie Webb · *Mrs Brooks*
Peter Welch · *Gunner Clarke*
John Welsh · *Professor Jenkins*
John White · *Mr Giles Farmer*
William Wilde · *Dr Brook*
Victor Winding · *Dr Fairfax*
Edward Woodward · *Reverend Posset*
Jennifer Wright · *Dr Linda Stanley*
Pauline Yates · *Estelle Waterman*
Felicity Young · *Nurse Gregg*

Creator Tessa Diamond **Producers** Antony Kearey, Rex Firkin, Hugh Rennie, John Cooper, Cecil Petty, Jacqueline Douglas, Pieter Rogers **Writers** Various, including Tessa Diamond, Rachel Grieves, Hazel Adair, Michael Ashe, Margot Bennett **Theme Music** 'Silks and Satins' by Peter Yorke

Aside from the police force, there's nothing more likely to form the background to a TV series than the medical profession. Hospitals are perfect for television as you have unexpected drama, crises and human emotion on tap 24 hours a day. No-one can predict where the next patient will come from, or even if they will survive their ordeal. And of course, the uniforms are generally quite sexy. Why else would 'Doctors and Nurses' be such an important rite of

passage for young children? And why else would the *Carry On* team have set four of their farces in hospitals?

Britain's first twice-weekly serial took advantage of our love for other people's health in the form of *Emergency Ward 10*, delving into the ins and outs of Ward 10 of the fictional Oxbridge General Hospital. In those gentler times, few of the patients ever suffered anything particularly serious, and indeed there were limits on how many deaths per year the series was allowed (a limit that had even been reduced in the 1960s from five to just two; on average, ***Casualty*** as that many per episode).

The show proved a wonderful stepping stone for many of Britain's best-loved TV faces. Joanna Lumley, Pauline Collins, John Alderton, Albert Finney and Ian Hendry all started out in the *Ward*. Richard Thorp, who since 1982 has starred in ***Emmerdale*** played Dr John Rennie in both this and a short-lived spin-off, *Call Oxbridge 2000*, which was aired in 1961. That show eventually led to another series in 1963, *24-Hour Call*. *Emergency Ward 10* also received the big-screen treatment in 1959 with *Life in Emergency Ward 10*.

In 1967, head of ATV Lew Grade decided to axe the series just a few months after its tenth anniversary, although he later claimed that it was one of the worst decisions he'd ever made. This might explain the arrival on 19 October 1972 of *General Hospital*, which might as well have been called *Emergency Ward 11*. That series also enjoyed a particularly good run, lasting until 26 January 1979. By that time, the BBC's ***Angels*** had taken off, and from then on the BBC pretty much dominated the genre, with *Angels* leading to *Casualty* and then *Holby City*. Such is the TV medic's family tree.

Emmerdale

See pages 282–5

Emu

See ROD HULL AND EMU

Enemy at the Door

Drama | LWT for ITV | episode duration 50 mins | broadcast 21 Jan 1978–29 Mar 1980

Regular Cast

Alfred Burke · *Major-Doktor Dieter Richter*
Bernard Horsfall · *Doctor Philip Martel*
Simon Cadell · *Hauptmann Reineke*
John Malcolm · *Oberleutnant Otto Kluge*
Simon Lack · *Major Ernst Freidel*
Richard Heffer · *Peter Porteous*
Emily Richard · *Clare Martel*
Antonia Pemberton · *Olive Martel*
Helen Shingler · *Helen Porteous*
Peter Williams · *The Vicar*
Richard Borthwick · *Major Kirk*
Pauline Menear · *Ruth – Martel's Maid*
Anthony Head · *Clive Martel*
Richard Hurndall · *John Ambrose*
David Waller · *Generalmajor Müller*
Patrick Godfrey · *Doctor John Forbes*
David Ryall · *Captain Tom Foster-Smythe*

Creator Michael Chapman **Producers** Tony Wharmby (executive), Michael Chapman, Jonathan Alwyn **Writers** Michael Chapman, N. J. Crisp, James Doran, Kenneth Clark, Robert Barr, John Kershaw, John Brason, James Andrew Hall **Theme Music** Wilfred Josephs

While the BBC's ***Secret Army*** showed the effects of German occupation on the people of Belgium, ITV had a go at reminding the viewers just how close Germany got to invading Britain as well, with the story of life on the German-occupied isle of Guernsey. It's a historical event many remain unaware of: when France fell to the German forces, the British government took the decision to strengthen defences on the mainland and leave the Channel Islanders to their own devices. On 30 June 1940, when the series starts, the inhabitants of Guernsey await the arrival of German troops while wealthy landowner Peter Porteous plans to flee the island and join the Allies. Unfortunately, the attempt leaves him wounded and trapped on Guernsey with the Germans.

Unlike *Secret Army*, the story is not about evasion lines and underground resistance, but simple survival. It's also about maintaining a balance, with Doctor Martell trying to prevent any kind of action that might lead to reprisals and German officer Major-Doktor Richter turning a blind eye every now and then to reduce the need for the Guernsey residents to rebel. However, not all of the Germans have such a tolerant attitude; Hauptmann Reineke certainly disagrees with Richter's methods (a chilling performance by Simon Cadell a few years before he starred in ***Hi-De-Hi!***).

Although never achieving the brilliance of *Secret Army*, *Enemy at the Door*'s best episodes come pretty close, mainly thanks to scripts by John Brason and N. J. Crisp, who both worked on the BBC serial. *Enemy at the Door* still managed to attract a fair few guest stars, including Michael Sheard (Mr Bronson from ***Grange Hill*** and Hitler in an episode of ***The Tomorrow People***), Joss Ackland, Alun Armstrong and Martin Jarvis, and early TV appearances for John Nettles (***Bergerac***), Pam St Clement (***EastEnders***) and Anthony Head (***Buffy the Vampire Slayer*** and ***Little Britain***).

Secret Army may have been overshadowed by ***'Allo, 'Allo*** but *Enemy at the Door* seems to have been obliterated from the minds of almost everyone. So much so that almost no-one referred to it when Granada unveiled their very similar series *Island at War* in 2004.

An Englishman Abroad

Drama | BBC One | duration 65 mins | broadcast 29 Nov 1983

Cast
Alan Bates · *Guy Burgess*
Coral Browne · *Herself*
Charles Gray · *Claudius*
Harold Innocent · *Rosencrantz*
Vernon Dobtcheff · *Guildenstern*
Czeslaw Grocholski · *General*
Matthew Sim · *Boy*
Mark Wing-Davey · *Hamlet*
Faina Zinova · *Hotel Receptionist*
Douglas Reith · *Toby*
Peter Chelsom · *Giles*
Judy Gridley · *Tessa*
Bibs Ekkel · *Scarf Man*
Alexei Jawdokimov · *Tolya*
Molly Veness · *Mrs. Burgess*

Creator/Writer Alan Bennett **Producer** Innes Lloyd **Theme Music** George Fenton

It's 1958, and British actress Coral Browne is touring the Soviet Union in a production of *Hamlet*. There she bumps into a fellow Englishman – and is surprised to discover that he is the defected spy Guy Burgess. Browne is even more surprised when Burgess asks to meet her in his State-provided apartment. Browne goes along, curious to discover what this spy could possibly want with her. In fact, all Burgess wants Browne to do is to run an errand for him – when she returns to England, he wants her to visit his old tailor and arrange to have a new suit made for him. After reminiscing for a while with the former spy, Browne leaves for the theatre. On her return to England, Browne follows Burgess's request and, despite the reluctance of the tailor to make a suit for a spy, ships the items to the USSR, where Burgess is a grateful recipient of a small piece of the 'old country'.

Based on a genuine incident, *An Englishman Abroad* gained an added air of realism and poignancy by the appearance of actress Coral Browne as herself (albeit playing a version of herself 25 years younger). It came as quite a surprise to many people to see a drama about one of the loathed 'Cambridge Spies' of the 1950s portrayed in a relatively sympathetic fashion. Although it's clear from the screenplay that Burgess believed in what he was doing, it's also clear that abandoning all of his friends, family and cultural connections has left him a gloomy, depressed individual. *An Englishman Abroad* was, quite simply, a masterpiece of subtle and restrained comedy/drama from the pen of the immortal Alan Bennett. Critics were lavish in their praise – *An Englishman Abroad* won BAFTAS for Best Actor (Alan Bates), Actress (Coral Browne), Film Sound, Costume Design and Best Single Drama for director John Schlesinger.

Enid Blyton's Famous Five

Children's Drama | Southern TV/Portman Productions for ITV | episode duration 25 mins | broadcast 3 Jul 1978–8 Aug 1979

Cast
Marcus Harris · *Julian*
Gary Russell · *Dick*
Michele Gallagher · *George*
Jennifer Thanisch · *Anne*
'Toddy Woodgate' · *Timmy the Dog*
Michael Heinz · *Uncle Quentin*
Sue Best · *Aunt Fanny*
Frederick von Thun · *Rogers*

Producers James Gatwood (executive), Don Leaver, Sidney Hayers **Writers** Richard Carpenter, Gail Renard, Richard Sparks, Gloria Tors **Theme Music** 'We are the Famous Five' by Rob Andrews, sung by the Italia Conti School Choir – not the cast

Perennial adventure favourites by a writer who falls in and out of grace change with the decades. Although the books were set in the 1930s–1950s, in 1977 it was clearly thought that wasn't sufficiently long ago to be charmingly 'period', so shirts and slacks were replaced by T-shirts and trainers. The heart of the actual stories, however, remained unchanged. Each adventure saw the three siblings Julian, Dick and George, their tomboy cousin Anne and her dog deal with smugglers, less-than-jolly gypsies, crooked businessmen and dodgy 'European' villains, re-creating as faithfully as possible 18 of Blyton's 21 books. Two of the stories not dramatised, *Five on a Treasure Island* and *Five Have a Mystery to Solve*, were caught up in a rights wrangle (the Children's Film Foundation owned them), while the other missing story, *Five Have Plenty of Fun*, was dropped simply because the producers believed it was too similar to every other story in the canon.

Filmed entirely in and around the New Forest, the series made good use of its locations, occupying Exbury House for an ever-changing series of interiors rather than head off to Southern's studios. At the time it was made, the first series was the most expensive children's programme produced by the ITV network (it was a co-production with Germany), and although a third series was discussed, the Enid Blyton Foundation refused permission for new 'non-canon' adventures to be written. Ironically, less than a year later, they allowed a series of contemporary new novels to be written, but to date these remain untranslated to film.

In 1996, the series was remade by Zenith and Tyne Tees for ITV, this time with a more faithful period setting. With such distractions as PlayStation and computers to compete with, this revival wasn't quite as big a hit with the younger generation as the 1970s version had been.

Emmerdale

Matriarch of the Yorkshire Dales, Annie Sugden (Sheila Mercier).

The very nature of soap opera as the most melodramatic form of TV drama has meant that they've tended to revolve around two core elements: family and business. The BBC's first soap, ***The Grove Family***, gave us the former, while ***Compact*** and ***The Troubleshooters*** provided variations on the latter, but the very best of the genre have managed to combine the two. We might recall Ewing Oil in ***Dallas*** and the battle for power within the Ewing family, or perhaps ***EastEnders***, where the Beales/Fowlers have their market stall and shops, while ownership of the Queen Vic has bounced in and out of the hands of various members of the Watts and Mitchell clans. Similarly back in 1972, it was the day-to-day infighting of the Sugdens that fuelled *Emmerdale Farm*. The Sugdens were the central family in an old farming community in the fictitious Yorkshire village of Beckindale. In the first episode, the family members attended the funeral of old Jacob Sugden. Jacob's decision to leave the farm to his prodigal son Jack, who had left the family home nine years earlier to find his fortune in London, leaves the family reeling. Jack returns to a frosty reception from his brother Joe, who had assumed the farm would fall to him.

The first episode also featured the introduction of the Wilks family, the wealthy Henry and his daughter Marion, whose appearance on horseback in the opening scene prompted the first line of dialogue – Peggy Skilbeck asking, 'Who's she?' Henry Wilks in particular would emerge as a popular character, particularly after his purchase of local pub The Woolpack in partnership with the mutton-chopped Amos Brierley. Amos and Mr Wilks were the show's central double-act for nearly 20 years until Arthur Pentelow's death in 1991 brought Henry Wilks's reign in Beckindale to an end.

Aside from the brutal rape and murder by Jim Latimer of Sharon Crossthwaite (played by Louise Jameson) in the first year, events in Beckindale in the 1970s could rarely be described as action-packed. But slowly the soap began to pick up speed – albeit at a much slower pace than its rivals. Its rather pedestrian attitude to drama has in fact been one of the series' biggest attractions over the years. Its fans enjoyed brief moments of titillation as characters started up relationships with people they shouldn't and others brokered deals that shifted the balance of power in the local community. The fact that *Emmerdale* (as it became known in 1989) has been shifted around the TV schedules like the last pea on the plate doesn't seem to have done it much harm either. In its early years, *Emmerdale Farm*'s status in ITV's priorities never seemed to even rival that of the much-maligned ***Crossroads***, with its daytime transmission slot meaning it never attracted much of a following beyond housewives and students. In 1981, a whole slew of episodes were recorded but never shown because of an ITV strike. Astonishingly, when the strike ended, the network simply picked up where they would have been, rather than using the episodes already in the can – these six episodes remain untransmitted to this day. Furthermore, regional variations meant that the show was not shown at the same time across the country until the late 1980s. But eventually *Emmerdale* emerged as one of the top three British soaps and that's partly down to the intervention of Phil Redmond.

Redmond had already proven himself as both a dramatist and producer when he created the BBC's school drama ***Grange Hill*** in 1978, and again with Channel 4's soap ***Brookside*** in 1982. When *Emmerdale*'s ratings (and more importantly, its advertising revenue) began to dip dramatically, Redmond was drafted in to see if the ailing soap could be saved. His solution was kill-or-cure: the programme had to change in tone dramatically. Out went the cosy farming storylines; in came glamour and spectacle. To herald this shift in tone, Redmond unleashed what is still to this day the most spectacular and controversial storyline ever to be seen in a British soap. Aping the real-life devastation suffered in the Scottish town of Lockerbie, Redmond devised a story where a plane crashed in Beckendale on the evening of 30 December 1993. Some characters were killed outright by the falling plant; others were killed by flotsam from the burning plane (Archie Brooks is burnt alive after being caught in a shower of fuel while inspecting his burning sheep). Eric Pollard murders his wife Elizabeth, then makes use of the crash to mask the foul deed (his crime remaining undiscovered to this day). The disaster also gave the producers the chance to change the name of the village from Beckindale to Emmerdale, realising that the names might cause confusion to all the morbid, rubbernecking new viewers they were attracting. The feeling regarding Beckendale was that the show used to be about a specific farm called Emmerdale Farm. Now the show was about the village, but the village is called Beckendale, which is confusing. Hence why they renamed the village Emmerdale, so they could have stories of a wider setting. In short, Redmond found a way to rid the series of its dead wood while setting up a single story that would have repercussions for all the characters in many different ways.

Though never to quite the same degree, *Emmerdale* has used similar stunts since then to provide exits for characters: a bus crash in 2000; a horrific storm in 2004. But it has also managed to regenerate itself thanks to one other 'natural' disaster that struck

Soap
Yorkshire Television for ITV
Episode Duration: 25 minutes
Broadcast: 16 Oct 1972–9 Nov 1989 (as *Emmerdale Farm*), 14 Nov 1989–present (as *Emmerdale*)

Regular Cast
Various, including:
Sheila Mercier · *Annie Sugden*
Frazer Hines · *Joe Sugden*
Andrew Burt, Clive Hornby · *Jack Sugden*
Toke Townley · *Sam Pearson*
Jo Kendall · *Peggy Skilbeck*
Frederick Pyne · *Matt Skilbeck*
Ronald Magill · *Amos Brearly*
Arthur Pentelow · *Mr Henry Wilks*
Gail Harrison, Debbie Blythe · *Marion Wilks*
Alan Tucker · *Alec Saunders*
Louise Jameson · *Sharon Crossthwaite*
Miles Reithermann, Dennis Blanch · *Jim Latimer*
Stan Richards · *Seth Armstrong*
Jean Rogers · *Dolly Skilbeck*
Hugh Manning · *Reverend Donald Hinton*
Ian Sharrock · *Jackie Merrick*
Lynn Dalby, Helen Weir · *Pat Merrick/Sugden*
Jane Hutcheson · *Sandie Merrick*
Julian Garlick · *Fred Armstrong*
Lennox Greeve · *Jimmy Armstrong*
Catherine Terris · *Susan Armstrong*
Ursula Camm · *Meg Armstrong*
Neil McCarthy · *Enoch Tolly*
Margaret Stallard · *Grace Tolly*
Alison Ambler · *Hannah Tolly*
Jenny Tomasin · *Naomi Tolly*
Carl Rigg · *Richard Anstey*
Sara Roache · *Jenny Anstey*
Sarah Atkinson · *Janet Anstey*
James Ottaway · *Fred Anstey*
Richard Thorp · *Alan Turner*
Tony Pitts · *Archie Brooks*
Sally Knyvette · *Kate Hughes/Sugden*
Diana Davies · *Caroline Bates*
Malandra Burrows · *Kathy Bates/Merrick/Tate/Glover*
Cy Chadwick · *Nick Bates*
Christopher Chittell · *Eric Pollard*
Glenda McKay · *Rachel Hughes*
Craig McKay · *Mark Hughes*
Madeleine Howard, Alyson Spiro · *Sarah Sugden*
Fionnuala Ellwood · *Lynn Whiteley*
Richard Franklin · *Dennis Rigg*
Christopher Smith, Karl Davies · *Robert Sugden*
Claire King · *Kim Tate*
Norman Bowler · *Frank Tate*
Peter Amory · *Chris Tate*

Leah Bracknell · *Zoe Tate*
Kate Dove · *Elizabeth Pollard*
Matthew Vaughan · *Michael Feldman*
Naomi Lewis · *Elsa Feldman*
Bernard Archard · *Leonard Kempinski*
Rachel Davies · *Shirley Foster*
Deena Payne · *Viv Windsor/Hope*
Adele Silva · *Kelly Windsor*
Toby Cockerell, Ben Freeman · *Scott Windsor*
Alun Lewis · *Vic Windsor*
Sophie Jeffrey, Verity Rushworth · *Donna Windsor*
Rachel Tolboys · *Alice Bates*

in 1994 – the arrival of the Dingle family. Lazy, uncouth and initially very, very unpopular, the Dingles' domination of the series started with a few characters at a time. But within just a couple of years they owned it utterly. As family members have departed, new ones have arrived (such as Cain and Chastity) and though the Sugdens are still around in the form of Jack and his kids, they're no longer the guaranteed focus of events.

One thing that the new-look *Emmerdale* has proven to be especially good at is creating top-notch 'bitches', characters whose motivations rarely stray beyond sheer self-interest and who are consequently guaranteed more than their fair share of the best dialogue. Longest serving and undoubtedly the most popular of these madams of mayhem was Kim Tate, wife of local landowner Frank and stepmother to wheelchair-bound bounder Chris (paraplegic after the injuries he sustained in the plane disaster) and lesbian vet Zoe. Kim's wickedness knew no bounds – she was never happier than when she was breaking up somebody's marriage or driving a metaphorical knife into their back. When in 1997 the producers decided that Kim's character had run its course, she was killed off when a body was discovered in her car at the bottom of a quarry. Some two months later – in one of the biggest shock storylines ever – the Bitch came back from beyond the grave (the earlier body had, in fact, been of somebody else entirely, dressed up in Kim's clothes). Frank Tate was so stunned by the resurrection of his wife that he promptly collapsed and died from a heart attack – Kim waiting and watching just long enough to ensure that he really was dead (by holding her make-up compact mirror to see if he was still breathing, before applying a fresh coat of powder on herself). Kim's eventual departure in January 1999 in a helicopter was the sort of ending all fans secretly adore – outrageous, over-the-top, entirely appropriate for the character and thankfully open enough to allow her to return one day. Since Kim's departure, both Charity Dingle and, more recently, Sadie King have done a splendid job at keeping the vitriol levels topped up.

One thing that the new-look *Emmerdale* has proven to be especially good at is creating top-notch 'bitches'.

It's officially Britain's second-longest-running TV soap but still few would have predicted its win at the 2001 BAFTAs in the 'Best Soap' category, traditionally a two-horse race between ***Coronation Street*** and *EastEnders*. Even host Angus Deayton had described the rural soap as an 'also-ran' in his introduction to the nominations. Deayton had clearly not been paying attention, as for many of its loyal fans it had been a strong contender for much of the previous decade. In 2004, a combination of smart scheduling and bad luck on the part of *EastEnders* saw *Emmerdale* trounce its BBC rival in the ratings for the first time. While we have no doubt whatsoever that the Walford lot will return to prominence, for the moment ITV is once again out of top, with *Corrie* and *Emmerdale* broadcast almost every night of the week.

Noah Huntley · *Luke McAllister*
Camilla Power · *Jessica McAllister*
Brendan Price · *Dr Bernard McAllister*
Amanda Wenban · *Angharad McAllister*
Stuart Wade · *Biff Fowler*
Samantha Hurst · *Dolores Sharp*
Paula Tilbrook · *Betty Eagleton*
Johnny Leeze · *Ned Glover*
Nicky Evans · *Roy Glover*
Roberta Kerr · *Jan Glover*
Tonchina Jeronimo · *Linda Glover/Fowler*
Ian Kelsey · *Dave Glover*
Niven Boyd · *Reg Dawson*
Paul Loughran · *Butch Dingle*
Steve Halliwell · *Zak Dingle*
Jacqueline Pirie · *Tina Dingle*
Sandra Gough, Maggie Tagney · *Nellie Dingle*
Billy Hartman · *Terry Woods*
Michelle Holmes · *Britt Woods*
James Hooton · *Sam Dingle*
Lisa Riley · *Mandy Dingle*
Tony Barton · *Des Burtenshaw*
Bobby Knutt · *Albert Dingle*
Paul Opacic · *Steve Marchant*
Kelvin Fletcher · *Andy Hopwood/Sugden*
Jane Cox · *Lisa Clegg/Dingle*
Mark Charnock · *Marlon Dingle*
John Middleton · *Reverend Ashley Thomas*
Dominic Brunt · *Paddy Kirk*
Sally Walsh · *Lyn Hutchinson*
Claudia Malkovitch · *Dee de la Cruz/Pollard*
Paul Fox · *Will Cairns*
Edward Peel · *Tony Cairns*
Sarah Neville · *Becky Cairns*
Rebecca Loudonsack · *Emma Cairns*
Sarah Graham · *Charlie Cairns*
Anna Brecon · *Lady Tara Oakwell*
Rupam Maxwell · *Lord Alex Oakwell*
David Crellin · *Billy Hopwood*
Sheree Murphy · *Tricia Stokes/Dingle*
Samantha Giles · *Bernice Blackstock/Thomas*
Stephen McGann · *Sean Reynolds*
Freya Coupland · *Angie Reynolds*
Kate McGregor · *Emily Wylie/Dingle/Kirk*
Mark Powley · *Liam Hammond*
Vicky Binns · *Ollie Reynolds*
Anthony Lewis · *Mark Reynolds*
Elizabeth Estensen · *Diane Blackstock*
Gary Turner · *Carlos Diaz*
James Carlton · *Jason Kirk*
Kevin Pallister · *Graham Clark*
Emma Atkins · *Charity Dingle/Tate*
Jeff Hordley · *Cain Dingle*
Janice McKenzie · *Gloria Weaver/Pollard*
Shirley Stelfox · *Edna Birch*
Antony Audenshaw · *Bob Hope*
Patrick Mower · *Rodney Blackstock*
Amy Nuttall · *Chloe Atkinson*
Nicola Wheeler · *Nicola Blackstock*
Peter Martin · *Len Reynolds*
Emily Symons · *Louise Appleton*
Cleveland Campbell · *Danny Daggert*
Danielle Henry · *Latisha Daggert*
Nathan Gladwell · *Syd Woolfe*
Lorraine Chase · *Steph Stokes*
Andy Devine · *Shadrach Dingle*
Lucy Pargeter · *Chastity Dingle*
Sammy Winward · *Katie Addyman/Sugden*
Charlotte Bellamy · *Laurel Potts*
Richard Moore · *Jarvis Skelton*
Charley Webb · *Debbie Jones*
Julia Mallam · *Dawn Hope/Woods*
Carolyn Pickles · *Shelly Williams*
Meg Johnson · *Pearl Ladderbanks*
Luke Tittensor · *Daz Eden*
Dale Meeks · *Simon Meredith*
Charlie Hardwick · *Val Lambert*
Tom Lister · *Carl King*
Nick Miles · *Jimmy King*
Kenneth Farrington · *Tom King*
Matt Healy · *Matthew King*
Patsy Kensit · *Sadie King*
Paul Shane · *Solomon Dingle*
Sherrie Hewson · *Lesley Meredith*
Charlie Kemp · *Max King*

Creator Kevin Laffan

Producers Various, including Nicholas Prosser, Mervyn Watson, Keiran Roberts, Keith Richardson, Stuart Doughty, Timothy J. Fee, Steve Frost, Richard Handford, John Michael Phillips, Lisa Williams

Writers Various, including Phil Collinson, Shirley Cooklin, Matthew Cooper, Helen Eatock, Tom Eliott, Chris Farrer, Rob Gittins, Helen Greaves, James Hall, Peter Hammond, Ginnie Hole, Mark Illis, Martin Jameson, Freda Kelsall, Peter Kerry, Andrew Kirk, Rupert Laight, David Lane, Rebecca Levene, Bill Lyons, Barbara Machin, Pippa McCarthy, Glen McCoy, Colin McKeown, David Millard, Hugh Miller, Lance Parkin, Jyoti Patel, Alison Pennells, Robert Perry, Mickey Poppins, Gareth Roberts, Dave Simpson, Patrea Smallacombe, Greg Snow, Chris Thompson, Andrew S. Walsh, Matthew Westwood, Lindsay Williams, Simon Winstone, Barry Woodward, Karin Young

Theme Music Tony Hatch

Enterprise

Science Fiction | Paramount Televison/Rick Berman Productions (shown on Channel 4) | episode duration 45 mins | broadcast 26 Sep 2001–13 May 2005 (USA)

Regular Cast
Scott Bakula · *Captain Jonathan Archer*
Jolene Blalock · *Commander T'Pol*
Connor Trinneer · *Commander Charles 'Trip' Tucker III*
Dominic Keating · *Lieutenant Malcolm Reed*
Anthony Montgomery · *Ensign Travis Mayweather*
Linda Park · *Ensign Hoshi Sato*
John Billingsley · *Dr Phlox*
Gary Graham · *Ambassador Soval*
Vaughan Armstrong · *Admiral Maxwell Forrest*

Creators Gene Roddenberry, Rick Berman, Brannon Braga **Producers** Various, including Rick Berman, Brannon Braga, Manny Coto (executive), Peter Lauritson, Merri D. Howard **Writers** Various, including Rick Berman, Brannon Braga, Fred Dekker, Andre Bormanis, Phyllis Strong, Mike Sussman, Chris Black, Manny Coto **Theme Music** Russell Watson, who decided that it would be a good idea to perform it as a ***Stars in their Eyes*** auditionee in the style of Rod Stewart (Rod Stewart actually performed the song first). Ghastly – one of the most truly awful and inappropriate TV themes ever.

In the 22nd century, a hundred years before Captain Kirk would ever 'boldly go' anywhere, humanity began taking its first faltering steps out into the Universe. With only very basic equipment and vehicles, untried and untested transporter technology and no real allies out in space (except for the Vulcans, and they're decidedly sniffy about humanity as it happens), it falls to the crew of the *Starship Enterprise*, registration number NX-01, to seek out new life and new civilisations. Headed by genial yet determined Captain Jonathan Archer, the crew consists of a Texan engineer called Trip, a British security chief called Malcolm, an alien doctor and a Vulcan 'adviser' who seems to spend most of her time trying to prevent them from going anywhere.

It was a very good idea by the ***Star Trek*** producers to have a spin-off series that was set in the future, but at an earlier point in time than the adventures of Kirk, Picard, Sisko or Janeway. By divesting the *Enterprise* heroes of most of the really advanced technology that we'd been used to seeing on the various *Star Trek* series, it made the threats these pioneers faced seem a heck of a lot more dangerous. However, *Enterprise* just didn't seem to catch on with viewers – either casual channel surfers or more dedicated sci-fi viewers. Even a change of name from the original '*Enterprise*' to '*Star Trek: Enterprise*' didn't manage to attract in many new viewers. Fans also became disillusioned with storylines that just seemed rather mundane and unoriginal, with only the arrival of new producer/writer Manny Coto in the third season getting Trekkers excited again. Typically though, the damage had been done and *Star Trek: Enterprise* came to an end after its fourth season, ironically after a run of its best ever episodes. Perhaps audiences were just 'Trekked Out' after 18 consecutive years of new *Star Trek* episodes being aired since the arrival of ***Star Trek: The Next Generation*** back in autumn 1987. Many people have speculated that a break from the airwaves might just be what the *Star Trek* franchise needs to revitalise itself.

The Equalizer

Crime Drama | Universal for CBS (shown on ITV) | episode duration 50 mins | broadcast 18 Sep 1985–24 Aug 1989

Regular Cast
Edward Woodward · *Robert McCall*
Robert Lansing · *Control*
Steven Williams · *Lieutenant Burnett*
Ron O'Neal · *Lieutenant Isadore Smalls*
William Zabka · *Scott McCall*
Keith Szarabajka · *Mickey Kostmayer*
Chad Redding · *Sergeant Alice Shepard*
Maureen Anderman · *Pete O'Phelan*
Eddie Jones · *Lieutenant Brannigan*
Richard Jordan · *Harley Gage*

Creator Michael Sloan **Producers** Stuart Cohen, James Duff McAdams, Heywood Gould, Coleman Luck, Ed Waters, Michael Sloan (executive), Bernadette Joyce, Dan Lieberstein (associate), Alan Barnette, Gail Morgan Hickman, Maurice Hurley, Alan Metzger, Joel Surnow **Writers** Various, including Michael Sloan, Grenville Case, Loraine Despres, Kevin Droney, Carleton Eastlake, Heywood Gould, Gail Morgan Hickman, Maurice Hurley, David Jackson, Coleman Luck, Donna Powers, Wayne Powers, Marc Rubin, Scott Shepherd, Michael Sloan, Joel Surnow, Tom Towler, Jim Trombetta, Jacqueline Zambrano **Theme Music** Stuart Copeland

Robert McCall is a retired expert in the art of espionage who now helps those people who were victims of crime but have been let down by the legal system. Based in New York, he can be traced by his advert in the classifieds: 'Got a problem? Odds against you? Call the Equalizer.' Though retired from the governmental security services, McCall can still request a little favour or three from his former boss, 'Control', and rely on the help of some of his other old colleagues.

The Equalizer could almost be a continuation of Woodward's previous big TV role, ***Callan***, were it not for *Callan*'s superior scripts and *The Equalizer*'s inflated budget. In some ways, Callan and McCall were different sides of the same coin – both were polite and neatly attired, both were deeply troubled by their time in security agencies. But McCall had clearly been through therapy and emerged with a desire to put his skills to some use that benefit ordinary people.

Though quite successful in the USA (during the series' run in the US, Woodward won a Golden Globe and was nominated for an Emmy), *The Equalizer* was little more than a schedule filler in the UK, its episodes symptomatic of the formulaic nature of many action-based US dramas at the time. But it still managed to acquire a strong following and Woodward's character even won a Channel 4 poll to find TV's toughest hard man.

Trivia

In 1987, legendary actor Robert Mitchum made a guest appearance in a two-part story as Richard Dyson, a man brought in by McCall's son to discover the whereabouts of the missing McCall. In reality, this was to bridge a gap while Edward Woodward recovered from a heart attack.

ER

Drama | Constant c/John Wells/Amblin Entertainment/ Warner Bros for NBC (shown on Channel 4) | episode duration 50 mins, plus 90-min pilot | broadcast 19 Sep 1994–present

Regular Cast

Noah Wyle · *Dr John Carter*
George Clooney · *Dr Douglas Ross*
Anthony Edwards · *Dr Mark Greene*
Eriq La Salle · *Dr Peter Benton*
Sherry Stringfield · *Dr Susan Lewis*
Julianna Margulies · *Head Nurse Carol Hathaway*
Laura Innes · *Dr Kerry Weaver*
Gloria Reuben · *Jeanie Boulet*
Alex Kingston · *Dr Elizabeth Corday*
Paul McCrane · *Dr Robert Romano*
Maria Bello · *Dr Anna Del Amico*
Kellie Martin · *Lucy Knight*
Goran Visnjic · *Dr Luka Kovac*
Michael Michele · *Dr Cleo Finch*
Erik Palladino · *Dr Dave Malucci*
Maura Tierney · *Dr Abby Lockhart*
Ming Na · *Dr Jing Mei 'Deb' Chen*
Sharif Atkins · *Dr Michael Gallant*
Mekhi Phifer · *Dr Gregory Pratt*
Parminder Nagra · *Dr Neela Rasgotra*
Linda Cardellini · *Nurse Samantha Taggart*
Shane West · *Dr Ray Barnett*

Creator Michael Crichton **Producers** Various, including Lydia Woodward, Mimi Leder, Robert Nathan, Meredith Stiehm, John Wells, Neal Baer, Christopher Chulack, Michael Crichton, Carol Flint, Walon Green, Dee Johnson, R. Scott Gemmill, Jack Orman (executive) **Writers** Various, including Michael Crichton, John Wells, Lydia Woodward, Paul Manning, Robert Nathan, Lance Gentile, Neal Baer, Carol Flint, Joe Sachs, Samantha Howard Corbin, Jack Orman, David Mills, Linda Gase, R. Scott Gemmill, Dee Johnson, David Zabel, Julie Hébert **Theme Music** James Newton Howard

The names Michael Crichton and Steven Spielberg almost certainly conjure up impressive action films about dinosaurs more vividly than a Chicago-based emergency ward. Produced by Spielberg's Amblin Entertainment, *ER* ('Emergency Room' – the American terminology for a casualty or accident and emergency department) was created from Michael Crichton's own experiences as a medical student, delving into the green-smocked world of County General Hospital, a 'Level One Trauma Center', and the lives of its personnel. An ensemble show, the stories in the first season revolved around a few core characters, including: idealistic doctor Mark Greene; paediatric doctor Doug Ross, a romantic-at-heart ladies' man who maintained an off-on relationship with nurse Carol Hathaway; the ambitious Dr Benton; and medical student John Carter in his first year of residency. Dr Carter rose through the ranks to become the centre's attending physician after ten years at the hospital.

In the States, it's become one of the prime examples of the 'water-cooler' show, with viewers discussing each instalment at work (in the UK, it's got a strong and loyal minority following on Channel 4 and its digital channel E4). The appeal isn't just the endurance test of watching all the gory operations, but the human story of the doctors, often expected to perform miracles in dire situations while their own lives lurch from disaster to disaster. In the first series, Carol Hathaway returns to work after a suicide attempt and soon after finds herself counselling a woman who's been raped; Dr Benton tries to juggle a high-pressure position with a demanding sick mother; while Dr Greene struggles to maintain a work-life balance with his wife, who lives in Milwaukee, and in later seasons has to deal with his own terminal illness; children are brought in after swallowing drugs; there are regular clashes with the families of deceased or near-death patients over organ donation; and grieving family members often throw their anger at losing a loved one into malpractice law-suits. It's not a job anyone does for the money or the sociable hours, but for vocational reasons – and it comes as a surprise to some to discover their vocation just isn't as strong as they'd thought.

Throughout the show, odd episodes have been handed over to deal with major events – a viral outbreak, a helicopter crash – while others have been notable for what was going on behind the cameras. Quentin Tarantino directed an episode, for instance, while in tribute to the pressures of early daytime TV, one instalment was broadcast live (a trick later copied by British shows like ***Coronation Street*** and ***The Bill***). Some would argue that later seasons dwelt too much on gimmicks, but they're forgetting that *ER* has always produced challenging, multi-stranded stories when they might have been expected to stick to a formula, in the manner of ***Hill Street Blues*** and ***St Elsewhere*** – with only three plot strands at any one time. Thankfully the most recent episodes of *ER* seem to show signs of a return to the character-led storytelling of the programme's first few years.

The departure of major cast members is a traumatic time for any TV series, and indeed with *ER* having made George Clooney a star, many fans thought the final appearance of Dr Ross (to enable Clooney to concentrate on his film career) would lead to the end of the show. But the programme – like a real emergency ward – carries on, with new arrivals appearing each year (one of the most enduring is Goran Visnjic as Dr Luka Kovac, a Croatian who's already had more than his fair share of tragedy). The series has amassed 21 Emmy awards over the years and over 112 nominations Indeed, *ER* continues to be a ratings success 11 years after it first appeared.

Eurotrash

Comedy | Rapido TV for Channel 4 | episode duration 25–40 mins | broadcast 24 Sep 1993–present

Regular Cast

Antoine de Caunes, Jean-Paul Gaultier · *Presenters*
Maria McErlane · *Narrator*
Kate Robbins · *Voice-overs*
Eddy Wally, Mr Penguin, The Romeo Cleaners, Lolo Ferrari, Eva and Adele – The Eggheads, Victoria Silvstedt, Sister Bendy, Melinda Messenger

Producers Various, including Kurt Seywald **Theme Music** A marvellous slice of Sixties French pop, 'St Tropez' was released by legendary movie star Brigitte Bardot and instantly wafts you away to a sunny Mediterranean café, glass of wine in hand, watching the world go by.

A naughty late-night Channel 4 series that combines mild nudity with funny voiceovers and puppet giraffes, *Eurotrash* takes the British obsession with nudge-nudge-wink-wink sex and combines it with another of our favourite pastimes – laughing at those wacky Europeans and their strange ways. A natural spin-off from the earlier pre-watershed BBC Two show *Rapido*, Eurotrash is hosted by Gallic charmer Antoine de Caunes (also the host of *Rapido*) accompanied for the first six seasons by his fellow Frenchman, fashion designer Jean-Paul Gaultier.

Each week viewers are presented with a selection of short films showcasing the weird, the wacky, the perverse, or the just plain bonkers. Whether it's the two skinny German men who like to clean peoples' houses in the nude (the Romeo Cleaners), aging Dutch pop star Eddy Wally's attempt to get to grips with gangster rap, or a feature on adults who like to dress up as babies, no topic is too obscure or too taste-free to be covered on *Eurotrash*. Another regular feature of the programme is 'Sit on Me', in which host de Caunes invited a glamorous model to sit on his lap. Although 'Sit on Me' is incredibly chaste and nothing untoward ever happens, the saucy subtext is never far from most viewers' minds. The unsung stars of *Eurotrash* are the two principal voiceover performers. Maria McErlane's prim and proper narration of the clips is an inspired combination of wide-eyed innocence and near-the-knuckle innuendo. Kate Robbins then provides handy 'translations' of the foreign languages being spoken in the film clips, usually adding hilariously inappropriate British regional accents, making the antics of our European neighbours even funnier still.

The programme's biggest star discovery (in every way) was porn star Lolo Ferrari (real name Eve Valois), who'd had many surgical procedures to enhance the size of her breasts – she was reputed to have achieved a 71in chest measurement. As a regular guest presenter of *Eurotrash*, Lolo starred in an ongoing series of features called 'Look at Lolo', in which she would be seen engaging in everyday activities such as blowing up a li-lo or playing with a ball with two scantily clad male companions. Sadly, Lolo died at her home on the French Riviera in Mar 2000, aged just 30 – the cause of her death remains contentious to this day.

Sixteen seasons of continental muckiness have so far been transmitted. Although politicians may still struggle to convince British voters of the benefits of closer European integration, it seems as though many British TV viewers can never get enough naked Germans or middle-aged Italian housewife porn stars.

Eurovision Song Contest

See pages 290–3

Ever Decreasing Circles

Sitcom | BBC One | episode duration 30 mins plus 80-min special | broadcast 29 Jan 1984–6 Dec 1987, 24 Dec 1989

Regular Cast

Richard Briers · *Martin Bryce*
Penelope Wilton · *Ann Bryce*
Peter Egan · *Paul Ryman*
Stanley Lebor · *Howard Hughes*
Geraldine Newman · *Hilda Hughes*

Creator/Writers John Esmonde, Bob Larbey **Producers** Sydney Lotterby, Harold Snoad **Theme Music** Piano Prelude No. 15 from Op. 34 by Dmitri Shostakovitch

Martin Bryce is a man who likes systems, routines, order, procedures and to be in charge of things. He's on a hundred different organisational committees, and likes to think of himself as the pillar of the community. His wife Ann just about tolerates his spreadsheets, timetables, forms and unrelenting need to ensure that the handset of the phone in the hallway is always put the correct way round. With oddball neighbours Howard and Hilda willing footsoldiers in Martin's campaigns to categorise and organise the world, life was almost perfect for Martin – until one day, Paul Ryman moves in next door and, in one fell swoop, undermines almost everything that Martin stands for.

Paul isn't malicious, nasty or even chaotic – he's simply insightful, creative and able to get to the crux of the community's problems in a tenth of the time Martin can. His natural charm, ability and charisma make him a born leader – a fact that rankles Martin to the core. Worse still, Ann, Howard and Hilda listen to what Paul has to say. This, in turn, increased Martin's inherent paranoia, jealousy and bitterness, driving Ann to the brink of unfaithfulness with (of course) her charming, sophisticated and distinctly single new neighbour.

Having already hit sitcom gold with ***The Good Life***, *Ever Decreasing Circles* once again reunited actor Richard Briers with the scripts of John Esmonde and Bob Larbey. Although Tom Good had been a generally likeable character with a few flaws and weaknesses, Briers had always felt him to be a patronising and annoying man. Martin Bryce was to all intents and purposes an example of where Tom might have ended up, a hideous creature with little or no redeeming features. Viewers gasped in horror as Martin committed yet another social faux pas, embarrassing himself, his ever-suffering wife Ann or his loyal friends Howard and Hilda (who were usually seen wearing matching garishly-coloured woolly pullovers), all in a vain attempt to prove he was better, funnier or cleverer than his nemesis Paul. Many people hoped that Ann (flawlessly portrayed by the ever-marvellous Penelope Wilton) would ditch her hopeless hubby and run off with the charming Paul – this being sitcom, of course, her patience and fortitude in the face of unbearable odds meant that she stayed with her loathsome hubby throughout all 27 episodes. Equally, it's testament to the acting skills of Richard Briers, who was able to rescue a few shreds of decorum and sympathy from such an unsympathetic and undignified character, bringing believability to a character and relationship that might have looked completely unrealistic in the hands of a less able or experienced performer.

Every Second Counts

Quiz Show | Talbot Television/Group W for BBC One | episode duration 30–35 mins | broadcast 8 Feb 1986–29 Oct 1993

Regular Cast

Paul Daniels · *Host*

Producers David Taylor, Stanley Appel **Theme Music** Ronnie Hazlehurst

This long-running midweek 'comedy quiz show' from BBC One helped magician Paul Daniels to stretch his wings from his usual role of family-friendly conjuror. Each week, three married couples would compete against each other, answering true-or-false questions posed by Daniels. Couples took it in turns to answer, with partners seated in a kind of 'front seat-back seat of a car'-type arrangement. After several rounds of questions, the couple would swap places for the remainder of the quiz. Instead of winning points or money, in the early rounds of the quiz the couples were aiming to bank as many seconds as possible – the couple with the most seconds on the clock would go through to the final round, with the amount of time they had accumulated earlier in the show hopefully enough for them to win a big prize. Sadly, the losing couples went away with just a time-based souvenir – an allegedly 'lovely' clock. Lucky winners won up to two prizes – a lower value one for getting four correct answers in a row ('easy peasy'), or something like an exotic foreign holiday for getting seven answers in a row correct (tricky, and only possible if they'd banked lots of seconds earlier in the game).

Eurovision Song Contest

The 1981 winners, Bucks Fizz – Cheryl Baker, Bobby G, Jay Aston and Mike Nolan.

Television has been blamed for many of society's ills. Does increased exposure to on-screen violence create an equally violent young viewer? Has the arrival of swearing on the small screen stunted the linguistic capabilities of an entire generation? And can a pop contest cause more harm than good to international relations?

For the uninitiated, the *Eurovision Song Contest* is an annual contest put together by the European Broadcasting Union and specifically created to be broadcast on Europe-wide television (unlike, for example, European sporting events that would exist without the presence of cameras). Inspired by the popular San Remo Festival, the idea behind the contest is simple. A major broadcaster in each country arranges the selection of one song each year that is then put forward into the competition itself (normally held on a Saturday in May). Each song is performed live, with the order of performance decided by the drawing of lots. After all of the contestants have finished singing, a brief interval is held, during which viewers are treated to some kind of dance or musical celebration of the host country. Also during the interval, votes for the best song are collated from each country. Originally, countries assembled a representative panel of judges to decide whom to give their votes to. In recent years, thanks to advances in technology, a phone vote is usually conducted in most competitor countries. One by one, in the same order in which they performed, countries report their voting results back to the competition venue. As the contest is a pan-Europen and multi-lingual one, results are always announced in the two official Eurovision languages, English and French (and occasionally in the host nation's tongue, too). The act with the most votes receives 12 points ('douze points'); the next receives

Music
BBC TV/BBC One
Duration: 120–180 mins
Broadcast: 3 Mar 1957–present (UK)

Cast

Katie Boyle, Moira Shearer, Angela Rippon, Jan Leeming, Ulrika Jonsson, Terry Wogan · *Presenters of UK contests*
Terry Wogan, Michael Aspel, John Dunn, Pete Murray, Rolf Harris, Dave Lee Travis, David Jacobs · *Commentators*

Contest Winners

Lys Assia, Switzerland – 'Refrain' (1956)
Corry Brokken, Netherlands – 'Net Als Toen' (1957)
André Claveau, France – 'Dors Mon Amour' (1958)
Teddy Scholten, Netherlands – 'Een Beetje' (1959)
Jacqueline Boyer, France – 'Tom Pillibi' (1960)
Jean-Claude Pascal, Luxembourg – 'Nous Les Amoureux' (1961)
Isabelle Aubret, France – 'Un Premier Amour' (1962)
Grethe and Jorgen Ingmann, Denmark – 'Dansevise' (1963)
Gigliola Cinquetti, Italy – 'No Ho L'Eta' (1964)
France Gall, Luxembourg – 'Poupée de Cire, Poupée de Son' (1965)
Udo Jurgens, Austria – 'Merci Chérie' (1966)
Sandie Shaw, United Kingdom – 'Puppet on a String' (1967)
Massiel, Spain – 'La La La' (1968)
Salome, Spain – 'Vivo Cantando'/Lennie Kuhr, Netherlands – 'De Troubadour'; Frida Boccara, France – 'Un Jour, Un Enfant/Lulu, United Kingdom – 'Boom Bang-a-Bang' (1969)
Dana, Ireland – 'All Kinds of Everything' (1970)
Severine, Monaco – 'Un Banc, Un Arbre, Une Rue' (1971)
Vicky Leandros, Luxembourg – 'Après Toi' (1972)
Anne-Marie David, Luxembourg – 'Tu Te Reconnaîtras' (1973)
Abba, Sweden – 'Waterloo' (1974)
Teach-Inn, Netherlands – 'Ding Dinge Dong' (1975)
Brotherhood of Man, United Kingdom – 'Save Your Kisses for Me' (1976)
Marie Myriam, France – 'L'Oiseau et l'Enfant' (1977)
Yizhar Cohen and Alphabeta, Israel – 'A Ba Ni Bi' (1978)
Milk and Honey, Israel – 'Hallelujah' (1979)

10 points; then 8, 7, 6, etc. right down to 1 point. As there are many more countries competing than points to be given out, the lowest-scoring competitor nations can often remain on 'nul point' right the way through to the end of the competition. Naturally enough, no country can vote for itself. At the end of the results, the competitor with the highest score receives a trophy, returns to the stage to perform their winning song again, and goes on to become a staple of the gay pub circuit for all eternity. The country of the winning act then has to host the following year's contest – a great (albeit expensive) honour.

Indeed, the honour of hosting Eurovision is so great that some competing countries take the whole process of trying to win the contest terribly seriously. Others (such as Italy), perhaps fed up with never really making much of an impact on the competition, no longer even bother to take part. However, with the expansion of eligible nations throughout the 1990s (owing to the collapse of the Communist Bloc and the break-up of Yugoslavia into a number of separate states), a single night eventually proved to be too small to accommodate all of the countries that wished to take part. For a short while, countries that finished at the bottom of the results table were 'relegated' to a second division of countries who would have to battle to gain the privilege of being 'promoted' back to the main competition the following year. Realising that this system was perhaps a little unfair, since 2004 a 'semi-final' has taken place on the Thursday prior to the contest in order to whittle down the 39 competing countries to a more manageable 24 taking part in the final. Some countries have a permanent place in the final (rather akin to the permanent members of the UN Security Council) owing to the amount of money they contribute to the upkeep of the European Broadcasting Union: specifically Germany, France, Spain and (thankfully, considering the disastrous performance by Jemini in 2003) the UK. In fact, it is membership of the European Broadcasting Union that qualifies a country to take part in Eurovision, not simply geographically residing within Europe. For instance, many countries in North Africa and the Middle East are theoretically able to take part; Israel has in fact won the contest on three separate occasions (most recently thanks to transsexual Dana International). At present, there is no restriction on the language in which each country can perform their song. Many choose to sing in English because of the perceived benefit it will bring to their final score. However, in the major European countries this is often frowned upon as totally unpatriotic and simply not the done thing.

The very first contest – held on 24 May 1956 in Lugano, Switzerland – was a rather smaller affair than the grand multi-hour (and now multi-day) epic we've come to know and endure nowadays. Just seven countries – Netherlands, Switzerland, Belgium, Germany, France, Luxembourg and Italy – took part, with each country submitting two songs to make up the time. Voting was kept a completely secret matter, with the winner decided by a panel made up of two judges from each of the participating countries. In the end, the first winner of the Eurovision Song Contest was

Johnny Logan, Ireland – 'What's Another Year?' (1980)
Bucks Fizz, United Kingdom – 'Making Your Mind Up' (1981)
Nicole, Germany – 'Ein Bisschen Frieden' (1982)
Corinne Hermes, Luxembourg – 'Si La Vie Est Cadeau' (1983)
Herreys, Sweden – 'Diggi Loo-Diggi Ley' (1984)
Bobbysocks, Norway – 'La Det Swinge' (1985)
Sandra Kim, Belgium – 'J'Aime La Vie' (1986)
Johnny Logan, Ireland – 'Hold Me Now' (1987)
Celine Dion, Switzerland – 'Ne Partez Pas Sans Moi' (1988)
Riva, Yugoslavia – 'Rock Me' (1989)
Toto Cotugno, Italy – 'Insieme: 1992' (1990)
Carola, Sweden – 'Fångad Av En Stormvind' (1991)
Linda Martin, Ireland – 'Why Me?' (1992)
Niamh Kavanagh, Ireland – 'In Your Eyes' (1993)
Paul Harrington and Charlie McGettigan, Ireland – 'Rock 'n' Roll Kids' (1994)
Secret Garden, Norway – 'Nocturne' (1995)
Eimear Quinn, Ireland – 'The Voice' (1996)
Katrina and the Waves, United Kingdom – 'Love Shine a Light' (1997)
Dana International, Israel – 'Diva' (1998)
Charlotte Nilsson, Sweden – 'Take Me To Your Heaven' (1999)
Olsen Brothers, Denmark – 'Fly on the Wings of Love' (2000)
Tanel Padar, Dave Benton and 2XL, Estonia – 'Everybody' (2001)
Marie N, Latvia – 'I Wanna' (2002)
Sertab Erener, Turkey – 'Everyway That I Can' (2003)
Ruslana, Ukraine – 'Wild Dances' (2004)
Helena Paparizou, Greece – 'My Number One' (2005)

Theme Music The title music for each broadcast changes every year. However, the Eurovision fanfare that plays before the start of the contest – 'Te Deum' – was written by Marc Antoine Charpentier.

Switzerland's Lys Assia, who won with a tragedy-infused ballad called 'Refrain', which she sang in French. It wasn't until the following year's contest that the United Kingdom joined in the fun. Sadly our first entry (Patricia Bredin singing 'All') didn't set the continent alight and came seventh out of the ten entrants. Stung by such a low placing, we Brits decided to have a year off from all that European malarky and crawled back to Blighty to lick our collective wounds until 1959's contest.

Upon our return, chirpy singing partners Pearl Carr and Teddy Johnson did the UK proud, warbling out their memorable ditty 'Sing Little Birdie'. Although they held the lead at one point during the edge-of-the-seat voting, they were eventually pipped to the post, finishing in a respectable second place. In fact, the UK has finished second in the Eurovision Song Contest an amazing 15 times. Here are the other UK runners-up, a catalogue of pop talent that contains some surprising names: Bryan Johnson – 'Looking High, High, High' (1960); the Allisons – 'Are You Sure?' (1961); Matt Monro – 'I Love the Little Things' (1964); Kathy Kirby – 'I Belong' (1965); Cliff Richard – 'Congratulations' (1968); Mary Hopkin – 'Knock Knock, Who's There?' (1970); the New Seekers – 'Beg, Steal or Borrow' (1972); the Shadows – 'Let Me Be the One' (1975); Lynsey de Paul and Mike Moran – 'Rock Bottom' (1977); Scott Fitzgerald – 'Go' (1988); Live Report – 'Why Do I Always Get It Wrong?' (1989); Michael Ball – 'One Step Out Of Time' (1992); Sonia – 'Better the Devil You Know' (1993); and Imaani – 'Where Are You?' (1998). And it's not just British acts that failed to win Eurovision; other internationally famous performers didn't quite make the grade with the voters either, such as Baccara (seventh in 1978 for Spain with 'Parlez-vous Français?'), Julio Iglesias (fourth in 1970 for Spain with 'Gwendolyne'), Olivia Newton-John (fourth in 1974 for the UK – despite being Australian – with 'Long Live Love') and even Nana Mouskouri (eighth in 1963 for Luxembourg with 'A Force de Prier'). Another strange feature of Eurovision is that it's not the nationality of the performer that's the important factor – it's the nationality of the songwriter that has to match the country making the entry. This explains how Canadian Celine Dion managed to win for Switzerland (by just one point) in 1988, and how American Katrina Leskanitch and Australian Gina G both represented the UK in the late 1990s.

It's the performing of the songs that forms the core of the Eurovision Song Contest, but for many people it's the arrival of the voting that brings the most entertaining part of the whole evening. It's always more than a little bit soul-destroying to sit through two hours of songs being performed in languages you don't understand by people whose artistic ability is at best questionable. However, everybody can comprehend the cut and thrust of the voting, much of which is normally tainted with at least a whiff of partiality. No matter how much viewers would like to believe that it's always the quality of the song that determines which country receives the most points, only the most trusting, naïve and innocent of viewers could ever truly believe that the reason Cyprus and Greece give each other 'douze points' virtually every year is because they honestly believe each other's song is the best. Furthermore, the arrival of new voting blocs – the Baltic and the Adriatic nations – has created another batch of countries that seem perfectly happy to vote for their neighbours first, then for their favourite songs. Of course, there is some merit in the view that countries in close proximity to each other might have very similar musical taste, but even so . . . Dodgy voting practices among many juries have led to long-standing Eurovision commentators questioning if there isn't something that should be done about it.

The Eurovision Song Contest is a poisoned chalice – designed to promote international harmony among the diverse nations and populations of this great continent, but sadly in fact responsible for more blatant xenophobia, favouritism and regional nepotism than any major conflict. Furthermore, it takes a very brave artist to decide to enter either the main competition itself or the Song for Europe/Making Your Mind Up preliminary competition. With an established track record as a recording artist no guarantee of success, entering the Eurovision does seem akin to taking part in an especially vicious bout of Russian roulette – only one performed live in front of 600 million viewers. Aside from the legendary ABBA, very few Eurovision winners have had a great deal of long-term international success. When asked if he'd ever enter the competition again, star of West End musicals Michael Ball commented, 'I'd rather stick rusty pins in my eyes.' Go on, Michael – tell us what you really think.

The Eurovision Song Contest is a poisoned chalice – designed to promote international harmony among diverse nations, it is sadly in fact responsible for more blatant xenophobia, favouritism and regional nepotism than any major conflict.

WEBSITES

www.eurovision.tv is the official website of the Eurovision Song Contest, containing facts, figures and sound and video clips of each year's new contestants. There's also a very useful section on prior contests and more behind-the-scenes information about how each event is staged than is probably at all healthy to know.

Fabian of the Yard

Crime Drama | Trinity Productions (Charles Wick/Telefilm Enterprises) for BBC TV | episode duration 25 mins | broadcast 13 Nov 1954–26 Mar 1956

Regular Cast
Bruce Seton · *DI Robert Fabian*
Robert Fabian · *Himself*
Robert Raglan · *DS Wyatt, Detective Sims*
Betty Cooper, Kenneth Cope, Michael Craig, Elspet Gray, Reginald Hearne, Ursula Howells, Jean Ireland, Maurice Kaufmann, Betty McDowall, Charles Mortimer, Cicely Paget-Bowman, Nicolas Tannar · *Various Characters*

Creator Anthony Beauchamp **Producers** John Larkin, Anthony Beauchamp **Theme Music** Eric Spear; Tommy Reilly on harmonica

The first successful BBC police drama series, *Fabian of the Yard* was based on the real-life cases documented and solved by 'the man the press call England's Greatest Detective', DI Robert Fabian. In each episode, Fabian (played by Bruce Seton) would calmly tell the audience the nature of the crime that was about to be shown to them, before explaining precisely why criminals will never get away with their bounder-like behaviour. 'In the nation's war on crime, Scotland Yard is the brain of Great Britain's man-hunting machine,' proudly exclaims the title sequence. 'Routine, detail, science and tenacity are the weapons used by squads of highly trained men,' it goes on to exclaim (ironically over a picture of a female lab technician). The rest of the title sequence is very much in the style of *The Blue Lamp* (1949) and other police films of the time, complete with a stirring theme tune by Eric Spear – the man who would go on to create ***Coronation Street***'s instantly memorable theme music six years later.

Amazingly for a programme made 50 years ago, production values on *Fabian of the Yard* are infinitely glossier and more modern than later programmes like ***Dixon of Dock Green*** or ***Z Cars***. This is because it was recorded on film, often on location, which enabled producers to edit each story into a relatively fast-paced episode. Additionally, having the entire episode pre-recorded meant that schedulers were able to transmit and then repeat episodes with much more flexibility than practically any other programme being made at the time (indeed, some episodes were edited together and released as cinema films, *Fabian of the Yard* (1954) and *Handcuffs, London* (1955)). Although most of the 30 episodes dealt with relatively mundane exploits, more sensational subjects were covered, including terrorism (in 'Bombs of Piccadilly', never screened in the UK) and an acid-bath serial killer (in 'The Executioner'). Once each episode had drawn to a close, the real Inspector Fabian would appear on screen and address the audience. Not only did this reassure viewers that our noble boys in blue were always one step ahead of the villains, but it also reassured actors right across the UK that their jobs would always be safe – Fabian might very well have been an astounding detective, but he was utterly lousy when it came to speaking in front of a camera.

Many familiar faces appeared in *Fabian of the Yard*, playing either criminals, victims or other assorted characters. These included classic British actors such as Michael Craig, Elspet Gray and future star of ***Randall and Hopkirk (Deceased)*** Kenneth Cope. Unlike in modern drama, these actors and actresses often played several different roles over the course of the series, rather as a repertory theatre group might play multiple parts throughout a season of plays. Another unusual fact about the series was that it was also sold to a number of different territories abroad – some countries screening it as *Fabian of Scotland Yard*, others (such as the CBS network in the USA) renaming it *Patrol Car*, in tribute to Fabian's huge black Humber Hawk squad car. *Fabian of the Yard* is a charming example of vintage crime-fighting; it's a true delight that at least nine of these vintage capsules of British social history have survived the archive purges of the 1960s and 1970s.

Face the Music

Quiz Show | BBC Two | episode duration 30–35 mins | broadcast 3 Aug 1967–16 Dec 1984

Regular Cast
Joseph Cooper · *Host*
Richard Baker, Robin Ray, Joyce Grenfell · *Panellists*

Producers Walter Todds, Peter Butler **Theme Music** 'Clog Dance' from Frederick Ashton's ballet *La Fille Mal Gardée*.

A popular if slightly intellectual (well, it was on BBC Two) quiz show that consisted of host Joseph Cooper sitting at a silent piano, beating out sections of tunes on the dead keys. Regular panellists included Richard Baker, Robin Ray and Joyce Grenfell attempting to guess the tune based on the thump of the keys. *Name that Tune* for the thinking man meets ***Never Mind The Buzzcocks***.

Falcon Crest

Soap | Lorimar Television for CBS (shown on ITV) | episode duration 60 mins | broadcast 4 Dec 1981–17 May 1990

Regular Cast
Jane Wyman · *Angela Channing*
David Selby · *Richard Channin*
Lorenzo Lamas · *Lance Cumson*
Susan Sullivan · *Maggie Gioberti*
Robert Foxworth · *Chase Gioberti*
Ana Alicia · *Melissa Agretti*
William R. Moses · *Cole Gioberti*
Margaret Ladd · *Emma Channing*

Abby Dalton · *Julia Cumson*
Chao Li Chi · *Chao-Li*
Jamie Rose, Dana Sparks · *Vicki Gioberti*
Simon MacCorkindale · *Greg Reardon*
Sarah Douglas · *Pamela Lynch*
Paul Freeman · *Gustav Riebmann*
Ken Olin · *Father Christopher*
Cesar Romero · *Peter Stavros*
Ursula Andress · *Madam Malec*
Anne Archer · *Cassandra Wilder*
Jane Badler · *Meredith Braxton*
Morgan Fairchild · *Jordan Roberts*
Mel Ferrer · *Phillip Erikson*
Celeste Holm · *Anna Rossini*
Gina Lollobrigida · *Francesca Gioberti*
Kim Novak · *Kit Marlowe*
John Saxon · *Tony Cumson*
Rod Taylor · *Frank Agretti*
Roy Thinnes · *Nick Hogan*
Lana Turner · *Jacqueline Perrault*

Creator Earl Hamner Jr **Producers** Earl Hamner Jr, Michael Filerman, Jeff Freilich, Joanne Brough, Malcolm R. Harding, Barry Steinberg, John F. Perry, Philip L. Parslow, Rod Peterson, Claire Whitaker **Writers** Various, including Stephen Black, Robert Cochran, Cynthia Darnell, David Ehrman, Jeff Freilich, James Fritzhand, Richard Gollance, Earl Hamner Jr, Scott Hamner, Suzanne Herrera, Kathleen Hite, Diana Kopald Marcus, Howard Lakin, Ann Marcus, Robert L. McCullough, Alan Moskowitz, Dick Nelson, Cyrus Nowrasteh, Katharyn Powers, William Schmidt, Lisa Seidman, Barry Steinberg, Henry Stern, Greg Strangis, Joel Surnow, Ernie Wallengren **Theme Music** Bill Conti

Apparently just another one of those mega-soaps to jump onto the bandwagon set rolling by the success of ***Dallas*** and ***Dynasty***, *Falcon Crest* very quickly established itself as one of the most consistently entertaining programmes in TV history. Set in the lush vineyards of Tuscany Valley, Northern California (actually filmed in Spring Mountain Winery, Napa Valley), *Falcon Crest* tells the story of the eponymous vineyard, owned by the ever-scheming Angela Channing (a marvellous performance by Hollywood legend and former Mrs Ronald Reagan, Jane Wyman). In the first episode, Angela's nephew Chase inherits a large stretch of land adjoining Falcon Crest from her late brother. Incensed at being deprived of the land that she imagined to be rightfully hers, Angela sets out to win back the land by hook or by crook – and so began nine seasons of bitching, backstabbing and general ruthlessness.

Falcon Crest was generally less concerned with the glitz and glamour than its oil-rich rival soaps *Dynasty* and *Dallas*: more often than not, storylines would often come back to matters of family, the influence of the Catholic church and general power-broking. Add in the Italian-American heritage of its central family, and perhaps the best analogy to describe the series is '*The Godfather* with grapes'.

Where *Falcon Crest* scored above its more famous rivals was in its casting. Almost every recurring guest role was filled by some famous legend from Hollywood history – often to the disgust of leading lady Wyman. In fact, it is rumoured that the scenes featuring both Wyman and Lana Turner had to be recorded in split-screen, as the actresses had grown to hate each other so much that they refused to be in the same room together. When Kim Novak (best known for her role in Alfred Hitchcock's classic thriller *Vertigo*, 1958) appeared in the series, the producers gave her almost exactly the same role to play as she'd done for Hitchcock back in 1958 – that of a woman involved in a plot to fake a death and appear as somebody else. As an extra bit of trivia, Novak's character name in *Falcon Crest* was Kit Marlowe – Novak's original choice for her screen name.

As the series progressed, plotlines veered from the appearance of a Nazi-funded business cartel intent on taking control of the winery to the lengthy tussles between Angela and her nephew Richard (who actually turned out to be her son), owner of the local newspaper. Cliffhangers too became more and more outlandish, with particularly memorable season finales including a plane crash with most of the regular cast on board, and an earthquake rupturing the vats in the winery and drowning several characters in a flood of Cabernet Sauvignon. In fact, looking back at the series, it may come as little surprise to discover the reason for some of the intricate and downright Machiavellian plotting – one of the writers for *Falcon Crest* was a young Joel Surnow, the mastermind behind real-time thriller series ***24***.

The Fall and Rise of Reginald Perrin

Sitcom | BBC One | episode duration 30 mins | broadcast 8 Sep 1976–24 Jan 1979, 22 Sep–31 Oct 1996

Regular Cast

Leonard Rossiter · *Reginald Iolanthe Perrin/Martin Wellbourne*
Pauline Yates · *Elizabeth Perrin*
John Barron · *CJ*
Sue Nicholls · *Joan Greengross/Webster*
John Horsley · *'Doc' Morrisey*
Trevor Adams · *Tony Webster*
Bruce Bould · *David Harris-Jones*
Theresa Watson · *Prue Harris-Jones*
Geoffrey Palmer · *Jimmy Anderson*
Tim Preece/Leslie Schofield · *Tom Patterson*
Sally-Jane Spencer · *Linda Patterson*
David Warwick · *Mark Perrin*
Glynn Edwards · *Mr Pelham*
Joan Blackham · *Miss Erith*
Derry Power · *Seamus Finnegan*
Joseph Brady · *McBlane*
Jacki Piper · *Esther Pidgeon*
Patricia Hodge · *Geraldine Hackstraw*
Michael Fenton-Stevens · *Hank*
David Ryall · *Welton Ormsby*
James Bannon · *Morton Radstock*

Creator/Writer David Nobbs **Producers** Gareth Gwenlan, John Howard Davies **Theme Music** Ronnie Hazlehurst

In the summer of 1974, Labour MP John Stonehouse faked his own death on Miami Beach, leaving a pile of clothes on the beach and his friends and family in no doubt that he had drowned at sea. The following year, writer David Nobbs released a comic novel called *The Death of Reginald Perrin* – he'd actually been working on it for several years, so the timing seemed more than just perfect for a TV adaptation of the work, in which a man on the verge of a nervous breakdown fakes his own death in order to gain some control back over his life.

Nobbs' original choice to play Reggie was Ronnie Barker, having already written several sketches for him to perform in ***The Two Ronnies*** – however, the casting of Leonard Rossiter as the funny yet fragile Reggie was the element that turned this sitcom from being merely great into a true classic, Rossiter's performance bringing extra layers of subtlety and nuance to an already sophisticated script that revelled in delving into the darker corners of middle-aged, middle-class existence. Desk-bound sales executive Reginald Perrin works at Sunshine Desserts, where his life is harassed by his baffling boss CJ ('I didn't get where I am today by . . .') and his loathsome colleagues Tony and David. Even his loyal secretary Joan causes him trouble, always being just a bit too flirty and forward for Reggie's comfort. At home, things are not much better. Despite having a loyal and supportive wife in Elizabeth, other family members drive him potty – in particular his barmy brother-in-law Jimmy, who has views and opinions that would make the Gestapo blush.

Eventually, things just get too much for Reggie and he decides to fake his own death, curious to see what his own funeral might be like. Donning the new identity of Martin Wellbourne, Reggie speaks to his new 'widow' Elizabeth and falls back in love with her – she, in turn, falls for 'Martin', only revealing later that she'd been aware of his true identity. Later seasons saw Reggie establishing his own business selling useless items in a shop he names 'Grot', which naturally enough becomes a massive international success. Reggie even gives jobs to his former colleagues at Sunshine Desserts when that business goes under – however, his slow transformation into a CJ-alike (even beginning to adopt his catchphrase) brings a completely new set of stresses to his life, leading to yet another faked suicide attempt at the end of the second series (this time in conjunction with Elizabeth and CJ). A third and final series brought Reggie back for yet more mayhem, this time launching a hippy-style commune aimed exclusively at people just like him – disenfranchised, middle-aged, middle-class people fed up with their lot in life.

Almost 20 years after Reggie's last TV adventure, David Nobbs brought his story up to date with *The Legacy of Reggie Perrin*, a seven-part series once again shown on BBC One. With actor Leonard Rossiter having died in 1984, the story now focused on Reggie's friends and family and the impact he had on their lives. In order to gain a share of the £1m he left to them, they are charged with undertaking an act of extreme stupidity – if lawyer Geraldine Hackstraw judges their act to be ludicrous enough, they will gain a portion of the cash. Unfortunately, despite reuniting virtually every single original cast member, this new series failed to gain either the audience or critical success of *The Fall and Rise of Reginald Perrin* and it lasted for just one season.

The Fall Guy

Action-Adventure | Glen A. Larson / 20th Century Fox for ABC (shown on ITV) | episode duration 50 mins | broadcast 4 Nov 1981–2 May 1986 (USA)

Regular Cast

Lee Majors · *Colt Seavers*
Douglas Barr · *Howie Munson*
Heather Thomas · *Jody Banks*
Jo Ann Pflug · *Samantha 'Big' Jack*
Markie Post · *Terri Shannon*
Nedra Volz · *Pearl Sperling*

Creator Glen A. Larson **Producers** Glen A. Larson, Bruce E. Kalish, Mark Evans, Sam Egan, David Garber, Andrew Schneider, Lou Shaw (executive), Larry Brody (supervising), Harry Thomason, Paul Mason, Lee Majors **Writers** Glen A. Larson, Nick Thiel, Mark Jones, Lou Shaw, Larry Brody, Burton Armus, Harry Thomason, Deborah Davis, Ron Friedman, Andrew Schneider, Bruce E. Kalish, David Garber, Sam Egan **Theme Music** 'The Unknown Stuntman', written by Glen A. Larson, David Sommerville and Gail Jensen, was performed by series star Lee Majors himself. This lovely little ditty namechecked a wide range of glamorous leading ladies from the late 1970s, including Farrah Fawcett-Majors (Lee's then-wife), Sally Field, Bo Derek, Cheryl Tiegs and Raquel Welch – as well as action heroes Robert Redford and Clint Eastwood.

In *The Fall Guy*, former ***Six Million Dollar Man*** Lee Majors paid tribute to the behind-the-scenes heroes of the action/adventure genre who had made the action sequences in his previous series so realistic – the stunt men. Majors played Colt Seavers, a moderately successful movie stunt man who supplements his income during quiet times by tracking down criminals who have gone on the run – bail jumpers, fugitives, that kind of thing – and bringing them back to face the law. In his bounty hunting, Colt is helped by beautiful stunt woman Jody and his cousin Howie; together they use the skills and talents of the movie stunt man to apprehend evildoers and bring them to justice.

Five seasons of adventure were served up by Lee Majors until the Unknown Stunt Man hung up his cowboy hat for good. An undemanding and typically gung-ho series from Glen A. Larson (the genius behind popular successes like *Quincy*, ***Battlestar Galactica, Knight Rider***, *Cover Up* and ***Magnum, P.I.***, *The Fall Guy* provided ideal entertainment for teenage boys everywhere who wished they too could be an action star in the movies.

Fame

Musical Drama | MGM Television for NBC (shown on BBC One) | episode duration 50 mins | broadcast 7 Jan 1982–18 May 1987 (USA)

Regular Cast

Debbie Allen · *Lydia Grant*
Erica Gimpel · *Coco Hernandez*
Carlo Imperato · *Danny Armatullo*
Lee Curreri · *Bruno Martelli*
Valerie Landsburg · *Doris Schwartz*
Gene Anthony Ray · *Leroy Johnson*
P. R. Paul · *Montgomery MacNeil*
Carol Mayo Jenkins · *Elizabeth Sherwood*
Albert Hague · *Professor Benjamin Shorofsky*
Lori Singer · *Julie Miller*
Michael Thoma · *Mr Crandall*
Carmine Caridi · *Angelo Martelli*
Morgan Stevens · *David Reardon*
Ann Nelson · *Mrs Gertrude Berg*
Cynthia Gibb · *Holly Laird*
Billy Hufsey · *Christopher Donlon*
Ken Swofford · *Quentin Morloch*
Jesse Borrego · *Jesse Valesquez*
Janet Jackson · *Cleo Hewitt*

Creator Christopher Gore **Producers** William Blinn, Donald Reiker, Patricia Jones, Harry Longstreet, Renee Longstreet (executive), Parke Perine, Frank Merwald (associate), Stan Rogow, Christopher N. Seiter, Mel Swope, Ken Ehrlich, Michael McGreevey, Claylene Jones, Ira Steven Behr **Writers** Various, including Christopher Gore, Christopher Beaumont, Ira Steven Behr, Ken Ehrlich, Lee Curreri **Theme Music** 'Fame' by Michael Gore, with lyrics by Dean Pitchford, was performed for the TV series by Erica Gimpel, not, as many people believe, by Irene Cara (who, of course, played the same role and sang the same tune in the original movie, *Fame*).

At New York's High School for the Performing Arts, students take lessons in dance, singing and music alongside their regular academic studies. For the students, life is a constant rollercoaster of hopes and dreams, many of which are dashed by the harsh realities of life in the entertainment business. The teachers constantly strive to keep their charges motivated – a particular struggle for the teachers of the traditional school subjects.

A direct spin-off from Alan Parker's smash-hit 1980 film of the same name, many of the cast and crew involved in the movie transferred over to the TV show, including Debbie Allen, Lee Curreri, Albert Hague and Gene Anthony Ray. Several other characters were recast, such as Coco, Doris, English teacher Mrs Sherwood and school secretary Mrs Berg. Viewers all around the world avidly followed the antics of the 'Kids from *Fame*' (as they came to be known); furthermore, the release of two albums (*The Kids from Fame* and *The Kids from Fame Again*), featuring songs that had been performed in the series, helped to reinforce the multi-media domination of *Fame* during 1982 and 1983. Two singles reached the UK top ten – 'Hi-Fidelity' in August 1982 (at No. 5), and 'Starmaker' in October of the same year (at No. 3). The release of the tear-jerking 'Starmaker' takes on an added poignancy owing to a sad real-life story connected with the filming. In the series, the kids and cast sing 'Starmaker' to say farewell to their teacher Mr Crandall, who is retiring. However, what most of them didn't know is that actor Michael Thoma was seriously ill at the time – he died shortly after the episode was transmitted.

Over the course of six seasons and 136 episodes, practically every possible plotline was mined in relation to the life of performing arts students. In the early years of the series, awards came thick and fast, with Debbie Allen winning Best Actress (Comedy/Musical) at the 1983 Golden Globes, and the series itself winning the Best TV Show (Comedy/Musical) at the Golden Globes in both 1983 and 1984. Gradually, as with most television shows, several cast members drifted away to be replaced by new blood. A notable addition to the cast in 1984–5 was Janet Jackson, younger sister of the 'King of Pop' – luckily, she didn't appear to suffer any 'wardrobe malfunctions' during her time on the show. A sequel series, *Fame LA*, was launched in 1997 and lasted for one season of 22 episodes.

Website
www.fameforever.com

The Family

Documentary | BBC One | episode duration 30 mins | broadcast 3 Apr–26 Jun 1974

Cast
The Wilkins Family

Producer Paul Watson **Theme Music** Stanley Myers

Inspired by an American series made for PBS in 1973 entitled *An American Family*, and arguably Britain's very first docusoap long before the term existed, *The Family* was producer Paul Watson's 12-part chronicle of the turbulent lives of Reading's Wilkins family. Mother Margaret was a terrifying creature who brow-beat the rest of the family with little or no success. Bus driver husband Terry would frequently arrive home from work to find the house erupting into all-out war as Margaret gave it out to kids Gary, Christopher, Marion and Heather. Supporting cast came in the form of Gary's wife Karen (along with young baby), Marion's live-in boyfriend and Heather's teenage beau.

The Family provided a viewing spectacle and no mistake, with the family put through the wringer for their coarse behaviour, lewd language and some of the frank

discussions caught by Watson's camera crew who followed the Wilkins for three months. There were questions raised in the House of Commons about issues surrounding invasion of privacy and, predictably, Mary Whitehouse had a great deal to say on the subject of *The Family*.

One year after the series aired, the marriage of Margaret and Terry ended after 26 years, but a repeat for the series in the 1980s allowed the indomitable figure to air her views once again on ***Wogan***. As a seminal piece of documentary making, modern television owes a lot to *The Family* (or it needs to take the blame, depending on your viewpoint). Watson tried a similar format in the mid-1990s in the far sunnier Australian-based *Sylvania Waters* with similarly explosive results.

Family Affairs

Soap | Fremantle/Thames for Five | episode duration 25 mins | broadcast 30 Mar 1997–present

Recurring Cast
Various, including:
David Easter · *Pete Callan*
Miles Petit · *Roy Farmer*
Tina Hall · *Claire Toomey Callan*
Annie Miles · *Maria Simons Starr*
Kay Adshead · *Barbara Fletcher*
Ian Ashpitel · *Chris Hart*
Fleur Bennett · *Belinda Rhodes*
Cordelia Bugeja · *Melanie Hart/Farmer*
Michael Cole · *Jamie Hart*
Liz Crowther · *Annie Hart*
Ian Cullen · *Angus Hart*
Sandra Huggett · *Holly Hart*
Barbara Young · *Sadie Hargreaves Lloyd*
Nicola Duffett · *Cat Matthews/Webb/MacKenzie*
Leah Coombes · *Chloe Costello*
Kazia Pelka · *Chrissy Costello*
Gary Webster · *Gary Costello*
Kate Williams · *Myra Costello*
Gareth Hale · *Doug MacKenzie*
Gabrielle Glaister · *Trish Wallace*

Producers Mal Young, Brian Park, Corinne Hollingworth, Paul Marquess (executive), David Harvey, Alison Davis, Jane Harris, Vivien Adam, Mike Hudson, Johann Knobel, Kirstie MacDonald, Dominic Treadwell-Collins **Writers** Various, including Mark Cairns, Helen Childs, Rupert Laight, Rebecca Levene, Paul Mousley, Jake Riddell, David Robertson, Andrew Taft, Paula Webb, Kate Wood, Stephen Wyatt **Theme Music** Rick Turk

It's pretty much accepted now that every channel needs at least one soap opera. Although *Family Affairs* has been the flagship production of Britain's fifth channel since its launch, it's generally felt to be an also-ran in the battle of the soaps (especially now that ***Emmerdale*** has become a major BAFTA-award-winning player). The series has its own regulars based on the standard soap archetypes of other established leaders in the genre (soap tart, soap villain, soap families, etc.), and indeed its cast has consisted primarily of refugees from other series – notably ***Brookside***, ***The Bill*** and ***EastEnders***.

What mainly makes *Family Affairs* stand out is that it successfully managed to relocate the show's setting (from the fictional Midlands town of Charnham to the fictional London borough of Charnham) and write out almost the entire cast in one go – for which incoming producer Brian Park (formerly the 'axeman' producer of ***Coronation Street***) took the blame/credit. Unforgivably, the series has since attempted the same trick again with a huge chunk of the cast replaced in 2003. Still, despite the fact that it won't win any awards for originality, *Family Affairs* enjoys a loyal (if rather small) and devoted audience.

Trivia
From 29 Oct 1949–18 Feb 1950, the comedy series *Family Affair(s)* was broadcast live from Alexandra Palace. It bears no relation to the modern soap of the same name, aside from the fact that its own loyal fans will also be disappointed by how we've decided to represent it in this book.

A Family at War

Drama | Granada for ITV | episode duration 50 mins | broadcast 14 Apr 1970–16 Feb 1972

Regular Cast
Colin Douglas · *Edwin Ashton*
Shelagh Fraser · *Jean Ashton*
Coral Atkins · *Sheila Ashton*
Colin Campbell · *David Ashton*
David Dixon · *Robert Ashton*
Keith Drinkel · *Philip Ashton*
Barbara Flynn · *Freda Ashton*
Ian Thompson · *John Porter*
Patrick Troughton · *Harry Porter*
Ian Bowen · *John Porter*
Margery Mason · *Celia Porter*
Lesley Nunnerley · *Margaret Ashton/Porter*
Richard Beckinsale · *Grey*
Adrienne Corri · *Grace Gould*
Trevor Bowen · *Tony Briggs*
John McKelvey · *Sefton Briggs*
David Bradley · *Alfred*
James Bree · *Mr Brehaut*
Prunella Ransome · *Dominique Brehaut*
Mark Jones · *Michael Armstrong*
Bryan Marshall · *Stashek*
Maurice Roëves · *Sergeant Hazard*
Ray Smith · *Sergeant Connor*
Amelia Taylor · *Peggy Drake*
Mark Dignam · *Dennis Pringle*
Mark Edwards · *Owen Thomas*
Tenniel Evans · *Norton*
Mel Martin · *Barbara*

John Nettles · *Ian McKenzie*

Creator John Finch **Producers** James Brabazon, Michael Cox, Richard Doubleday **Writers** John Finch, John Wiles, Jack Ronder, Jonathan Powell, Alexander Baron, John Brabazon, John Ellison, Stan Barstow, David Weir, H. V. Kershaw, Geoffrey Lancashire, John Foster, Robert Furnival, Elaine Morgan, Philip Purser, Susan Pleat, Roy Russell, Leslie Sands, John Stevenson **Theme Music** Vaughan Williams

This seminal, highly expensive (at the time) Granada serial charted the fortunes of a Liverpool family, the middleclass Ashtons, from the brink of war in 1938 right through to 1945. The family is varied, from father Edwin (forced to work in the family printworks and under the thrall of brother-in-law Sefton), and matriarch Jean, to eldest son David. Coral Atkins played Sheila, David's wife, and became the best known face from the series, which itself became incredibly popular very quickly. The depiction of wartime on home soil was often stark and accurate, if not a little soapy in execution. Relationships strengthen and fall apart, faces come and go as the men leave for war, all wrapped up in a never ending conveyor belt of angst and problems for the Ashtons. The series' evocative opening title sequence depicted a sandcastle being destroyed by the encroaching tide.

A Family at War's main writer John Finch was well versed in the social realism of the industrial north, having cut his teeth as a writer on ***Coronation Street*** between 1961 and 1970, when he took up his pen for this well-remembered series. Alongside already well known names such as Colin Douglas, Tenniel Evans and Patrick Troughton, early appearances from future names John Nettles and Barbara Flynn can be seen. In 2000, Granada produced *Seeing Red*, being an adaptation of Coral Atkins's biography. Starring Sarah Lancashire as Atkins, it charts her trials in opening a care home for children while still making *Family at War*.

Family Fortunes

Quiz Show | ATV/Central/Carlton for ITV | episode duration 25 mins | broadcast 1978–2002

Regular Cast

Bob Monkhouse, Max Bygraves, Les Dennis, Andy Collins · *Presenters*

Producers Various, including William G. Stewart, Dennis Liddington, Andrew Wightman, Tony Wolfe, Graham C. Williams

As famous for some of the stupid answers given by the contestants and the ridiculous fake 'computer' Mr Babbage, *Family Fortunes* was a mainstay of Sunday evening viewing for much of the 1980s, before being shunted into a daytime slot in 2002.

One hundred members of Joe Public are polled with various questions, usually amounting to nothing more difficult than 'Name something blue' or 'Name something that has arms'. Back in the studio, two families compete to come up with the most popular answer and whoever guesses the highest placed answer wins the opportunity to play and guess the remaining hidden answers on the board. If they guess incorrectly three times (signalled by a pop culturally invasive farting sound), the opposing family has the opportunity to steal the money on the board. Round two (after the break, naturally) sees the stakes raised in the self-explanatory 'Double Money' round, with the winning family going on to the tense against the clock round and play for 'Big Money'!

Based on the US game show *Family Feud* (which sounds immeasurably more exciting), ATV wisely selected the demigod figure of Bob Monkhouse to host *Family Fortunes*. So why, three years later, they dropped the ball and replaced Monkhouse with Max Bygraves is anyone's guess. After two years off the air, *Family Fortunes* returned with comedian Les Dennis at the helm who remained until the show transferred to the daytime schedules with the little known Andy Collins, after which it was quietly dropped.

Trivia

Producer William G. Stewart (who was also instrumental in ***The Price is Right*** and presenter of Channel 4's *Fifteen to One*) was reportedly unhappy that only 10,000 families applied to come on the show.

Website

An entire book could be devoted to some of the hysterical answers given on *Family Fortunes* over the years, but you can find a list at: www.ukgameshows.com/index.php/Family_Fortunes_Cockups. We're not sure how many of these are actually genuine, but they still make for some rib-tickling reading.

The Famous Five

See ENID BLYTON'S FAMOUS FIVE

The Far Pavilions

Drama | Geoff Reeve/Goldcrest Films/HBO for Channel 4 | episode duration 105 mins | broadcast 3 Jan–5 Jan 1984

Principal Cast

Ben Cross · *Ashton 'Ash' Pelham-Martyn*
Amy Irving · *Princess Anjuli*
Christopher Lee · *Kaka-ji Rao*
Benedict Taylor · *Wally*
Rossano Brazzi · *Rana of Bhithor*
Saeed Jaffrey · *Biju Ram*
Robert Hardy · *Commandant*
Sneh Gupta · *Shushila*
Omar Sharif · *Koda Dad*
John Gielgud · *Major Sir Louis Cavagnari*
Jennifer Kendal · *Mrs Viccary*
Felicity Dean · *Belinda Harlowe*

Peter Arne · *General*
Michael Cochrane · *Crimpley*
Rupert Everett · *George Garforth*
John Forbes-Robertson · *Squadron Commander*
Clive Francis · *Kelly*
William Gaunt · *Commissioner*
Art Malik · *Zarin*

Producers John Peverall (executive), Geoffrey Reeve **Writer** Julian Bond, from the novel by M. M. Kaye **Theme Music** Carl Davis

A contemporary of ***The Jewel in the Crown*** (both catching a ride on the popular vogue for India generated by the success of Richard Attenborough's *Gandhi*, 1982), *The Far Pavilions* cost a whopping £8 million to make. The series stars Ben Cross as Ash Pellam-Martyn, an officer in the Corps of Guards and serving in India at the time of brewing troubles in India's plight to free itself from English rule. His ancestry makes his life difficult, being of Anglo-Indian descent, and the presence of former childhood friend, Princess Anjuli, does not help matters.

Full of love and political intrigue, *The Far Pavilions* is a beautifully shot piece of television, featuring plenty of stunning Indian backdrops with some tense battle sequences adding to a rich cooking pot. The three-part serial unfortunately lost out to *The Jewel in the Crown* at that year's BAFTAS, the rival serial sweeping the boards. Ben Cross's co-star, Amy Irving, who played Princess Anjuli, was previously married to Steven Spielberg, and has recently played the recurring role of Emily Sloane in the US spy series *Alias*. Sadly, *The Far Pavilions* would mark the final screen role of actor Peter Arne, who was tragically murdered in 1984 after attending a costume fitting for a forthcoming ***Doctor Who*** story. The story of *The Far Pavilions* refuses to go away, however, with a West End musical based on the same story premiering in Spring 2005.

The Fast Show

See pages 302–3

Father Ted

See pages 304–5

Father, Dear Father

Sitcom | Thames Television for ITV | episode duration 30 mins | broadcast 5 Nov 1968–6 Feb 1973

Regular Cast
Patrick Cargill · *Patrick Glover*
Ann Holloway · *Karen Glover*
Natasha Pyne · *Anna Glover*
Noel Dyson · *Nanny*
Ursula Howells · *Barbara*
Joyce Carey · *Patrick's Mother*

Producer William G. Stewart **Writer** Brian Cooke, Johnnie Mortimer

Patrick Glover is a writer of James Bond-esque adventure novels, but his life in Surrey is far from suave and sophisticated as he is left to bring up two feisty daughters after his wife runs off with his best friend. To help with the trials of bringing up Karen and Anna, Patrick hires Nanny, whose approach to any domestic problem (i.e. every episode) is to go and make a nice cup of tea. Male companionship for the harassed father comes from his sleepy St Bernard, H. G. Wells. By the time season six came round, Anna had found love and married, but her husband moved into the family pile, adding to Patrick's woes rather easing them.

Before turning his hand to game shows, William G. Stewart was a ratings winning sitcom producer, but before he 'carried on' with Sid James in ***Bless this House***, he helmed the highly successful domestic shenanigans of *Father, Dear Father*. Patrick Cargill, already a well-known name from films and television (including an appearance as Number Two in ***The Prisoner***) became a prime-time star thanks to this series, and for a time you couldn't move for the Glovers. Cargill, Ann Holloway and Natasha Pyne appeared in character on a 1970 edition of *The Golden Shot*, and the three also popped up in *The Edward Woodward Hour* in August 1971 where they met Woodward's secret agent character, ***Callan***. Not to be outdone, Cargill's own hour-long entertainment special, *Patrick, Dear Patrick*, broadcast in January 1972, featured segments set in the Glover's sprawling Surrey residence. As was the vogue in the 1970s, a big screen version of the series followed in 1972.

Father, Dear Father ended after six seasons in 1973, but that was not the end for Patrick and Nanny. Cargill and Noel Dyson travelled down under to star in the imaginatively titled *Father, Dear Father in Australia*, with Patrick taking responsibility for his equally feisty Antipodean nieces. Predictably, it didn't last long.

Patrick Cargill sadly died in 1996, the victim of a hit and run accident.

Fawlty Towers

See pages 306–9

Film...

Factual | BBC One | episode duration 30 mins | broadcast Nov 1971–present

Cast
Jacky Gillott, Barry Norman, Joan Bakewell, Frederic Raphael, Tina Brown, Maria Aitken, Russell Harty, Iain Johnstone, Miles Kington, Philip Oakes, Michael Parkinson, Glyn Worsnip, Jonathan Ross · *Presenters*

Theme Music 'I Wish I Knew How It Felt To Be Free' by Billy Taylor

Back in 1971, who could possibly have imagined that a regional film review programme, initially hosted by Jacky Gillott and broadcast solely in the southeast of England, would still be going nearly 35 years later? Yet the simplicity of the format for *Film '71* was the key to its success and longevity. By reviewing the latest cinema releases, showing clips and trailers and interviewing the stars of the silver screen, the programme remains continually relevant and a must-see for any movie buff. In 1972, three presenters (Barry Norman, Joan Bakewell and Frederic Raphael) took it in turns to host the now networked programme, until one of those three eventually took solo responsibility.

That host was, of course, Barry Norman, who will be perennially linked to this programme, acting as the knowledgeable presenter right through to 1999 (albeit with a brief break in 1982, during which time other stand-in hosts took over). In 1999, Norman accepted an offer from Sky to become their film critic, and so the omnipresent Jonathan Ross inherited the role of presenter. Ross brought a new perspective to the programme's reviews – for example, whereas a fantasy or horror film would rarely receive more than a perfunctory nod from Norman (and westerns remained his favourite genre long after the public tired of them), Ross revelled in his geek-chic adoration of cult movies of all kinds, an appreciation he'd already revealed on Channel 4's *The Incredibly Strange Film Show*, where he championed Mexican wrestling movies, Hong Kong action films, and the king of Spanish cinema, Pedro Almodovar, long before anyone else knew who he was.

Filthy, Rich and Catflap

Sitcom | BBC Two | episode duration 30 mins | broadcast 7 Jan–11 Feb 1987

Regular Cast
Adrian Edmondson · *Eddie Catflap*
Rik Mayall · *Richie Rich*
Nigel Planer · *Ralph Filthy*

Creator/Writer Ben Elton, with additional material from Rik Mayall **Producer** Paul Jackson **Theme Music** Peter Brewis

Sandwiched in between ***The Young Ones*** and ***Bottom***, and abandoned after just six episodes, *Filty, Rich and Catflap* never really got the chance to catch on like its stable-mates in the Edmondson–Mayall hit list. The shouting, violence and smut increased, but sadly the laughs didn't follow suit as we watched the exploits of permanently out-of-work actor Richie Rich, his lodger-cum-bodyguard Eddie Catflap and Rich's manager Ralph Filthy (allegedly based on a real Soho theatrical agent). Increasing numbers of murdered milkman, paternity cases, extortion and scandal seemed to haunt Richie Rich – and that was just the first episode. With its knowing asides to camera and references to TV legends such as Jimmy Tarbuck ('Tarby!'), Bruce Forsythe ('Brucey!') and the rest of the celebrity golf set, it felt like it was supposed to be an assault on the nature of celebrity, but missed most of its targets. There were some subtle links to *The Young Ones*, with Michael Redfern reviving his vicious policeman character for three appearances (one as a prison officer) and Andy de la Tour popped in to play a club owner. But really this was just a rehearsal for *Bottom*. Oo-err!

The Final Cut

Drama | BBC One | episode duration 60 mins | broadcast 12 Nov–26 Nov 1995

Principal Cast
Ian Richardson · *Francis Urquhart*
Diane Fletcher · *Elizabeth Urquhart*
Glyn Grain · *Rayner*
David Henry · *General Gough*
Erika Hoffman · *Princess*
Isla Blair · *Claire Carlsen*
Nickolas Grace · *Geoffrey Booza Pitt*
Paul Freeman · *Tom Makepeace*
David Ryall · *Sir Bruce Bullerby*
Yolanda Vazquez · *Maria Passolides*
Leon Lissek · *Evanghelos Passolides*
Julian Fellowes · *Sir Henry Ponsonby*
Nicholas Blane · *Dicky Withers*
Duggie Brown · *Joe Badger*
Joseph Long · *President Nicolaou*
Cherith Mellor · *Hilary Makepeace*
Boyd Clack · *Hywell Harris*
Julian Fellowes · *Sir Henry Ponsonby*
Michael Wardle · *Hugh Pugh*
Ian Mercer · *Graham Glass*
John Rowe · *Sir Clive Watling*
Susannah Harker · *Mattie Storin*

For commentary, see HOUSE OF CARDS

Fingerbobs

Pre-School Puppetry | Q3 London for BBC One | episode duration 10 mins | broadcast 14 Feb–3 May 1972

Cast
Rick Jones · *Yoffy*
Continued on page 310

The Fast Show

Charlie Higson (Ralph) and Paul Whitehouse (Ted).

Whether it was simply reacting to the idea of the shortened attention span or partly contributing to it we'll probably never know, but *The Fast Show* boasted more sketches per episode than any comedy show to that date. On average, no sketch lasted longer than a minute, which led to a staggering number of characters popping onto our screens. It was also responsible for an impressive amount of catchphrases that wormed their way slowly into the British language.

Having met at university, Charlie Higson and Paul Whitehouse had become friends with Harry Enfield during the glory days of ***Saturday Live*** on Channel 4. Enfield rescued them from jobs as decorators to become his chief writers for characters like Stavros and Loadsamoney. When Enfield moved to the BBC, Whitehouse became his foil for double acts like Smashy and Nicey, Lee and Lance and The Old Gits. Higson and Whitehouse also wrote for rising star Vic Reeves, an experience that inspired them to create a show where the sketches came at lightning speed without a pause for breath.

The Fast Show relied heavily on one essential element of comedy – repetition. Part of the charm of traditional sitcoms like ***Dad's Army*** was seeing how the familiar catchphrase would make it into each episode. For *The Fast Show*, entire characters would revolve around variations around a single phrase: 'Does my bum look big in this?', 'Ooh! Suits you, sir!', 'Today I have mostly been eating . . .', 'Oh bugger' or 'Where's me washboard?' Ron Manager was a football TV pundit stuck in the past with his memories of schoolyard football. Whether it was a Premiership match or the World Cup final, discussion would inevitably sway towards 'Jumpers for goalposts – an enduring image.' In an increasingly cynical age, one adorable creation of Whitehouse's was a bobble-hat-wearing Mancunian enthusiast who delivered monologues in a free-flowing stream of consciousness. Though his location changed every three seconds (from market stall to beach to housing estate), the monologue continued unbroken as he explained why such subjects as mums, gravity and Jesus are 'brilliant'. Another Whitehouse creation, Rowley Birkin, was a QC whose warm fireside anecdotes would ramble incoherently towards the final admission that he had been 'vahry, vahry drunk.' Occasionally, the programme would be interrupted by interference from the Continent and we'd be treated to a brief snatch of the vaguely Mediterranean 'Channel 9' in which the only words we'd be able to pick out were 'Scorchio!', 'Boutros Boutros Ghali' and 'Chris Waddle'. The most ingenious use of the art of repetition came with 'The Pissed family', in which entire sketches consisted of one-liners like 'Dad's home!' and 'I'm not pissed, y'know' from a family so intoxicated that they had the memory capacity of a goldfish.

Such repetition also had hidden bonuses, for the slightest deviation from the formula could delight. An inspired example of thiscame with one of Rowley's stories where his usual glee about a fond memory was replaced by a rather sombre tone. As before, much of the story is lost in his mumbling, but this time it's not through excitement that his words are muffled but through grief. We can decipher only that it involves a lost love. When he tells us that, bereft, he got 'very, very drunk', the audience is silent. It's an unexpected and painful surprise that we can care so much about a character we've previously dismissed as an old drunken buffoon – and that the effect was achieved in less than 60 seconds.

With such a rate of progression, not all of the characters were hits and certainly the majority of Simon Day's creations seemed to miss the mark, including the hugely irritating 'Competitive Dad', who plays cricket with his sons but refuses to allow them any concessions for being just children; pub bore Billy Bleach, the despot of the quiz machine who's not as smart as he thinks; or tough-guy TV detective Monkfish. Despite the brevity of each of their scenes, these characters somehow managed to outstay their welcome.

The best-loved of all had to be Ted and Ralph. At first it appeared to be a comment about the chasm between the classes, with the Lord of the Manor attempting and failing to make anything other than stilted conversation with his groundsman, Ted. But Higson and Whitehouse eventually revealed in an interview that there was a deeper subtext to the characters, that Ralph was, in fact, madly in love with Ted and used any excuse to be near him.

The Fast Show came to an end with three specials under the banner of 'the last ever', which featured a guest appearance by a huge fan – Johnny Depp. But that wasn't quite the end as a live stage show followed which, like the series itself, became a best seller on home video. Ted and Ralph appeared in their own one-off TV special in 1998 in which Ralph was forced to find a wife or face disinheritance. Swiss Tony, who had a talent for being able to compare anything to 'making love to a beautiful woman', also bagged his own show in 2003, first broadcast on BBC Three, while the same year saw Simon Day's Billy Bleach star in *Grass*, in which fantasist Bleach finds himself living in Norfolk on the witness protection programme. The show also made a star of John Thompson, who joined another ensemble cast for one of ITV's biggest hits of recent years, ***Cold Feet***.

Comedy
BBC Two
Episode Duration: 30 mins
Broadcast: 27 Sep 1994–28 Dec 2000

Regular Cast
Paul Whitehouse, Charlie Higson, John Thomson, Arabella Weir, Caroline Ahearne/Hook, Simon Day, Mark Williams, Maria McErlane, Robin Driscoll, Rhys Thomas, Paul Shearer, Eryl Maynard, Colin McFarlane, Donna Ewin, Louise Brill, Rosie Fellner · *Various roles*
Jeff Harding · *Ed Winchester*

Creators Charlie Higson, Paul Whitehouse

Producers Charlie Higson, Geoffrey Perkins, Paul Whitehouse

Writers Caroline Aherne, Jane Bussmann, Craig Cash, Dave Cummings, Simon Day, Dave Gorman, Charlie Higson, Gary Howe, Graham Linehan, Arthur Mathews, Lise Mayer, Bob Mortimer, Henry Normal, Richard Preddy, Rhys Thomas, John Thomson, Arabella Weir, Paul Whitehouse, Mark Williams

Theme Music Opening music by Philip Pope. End theme a reworking of Engelbert Humperdinck's classic 'Please Release Me'

TRIVIA

On its screenings in America, *The Fast Show* was renamed *Brilliant*, which was nice.

Father Ted

Ardal O'Hanlon (Father Dougal), Dermot Morgan (Father Ted) and Frank Kelly (Father Jack).

Father Ted is a huge crossover hit of a sitcom – a series dangerous and surreal enough to be a favourite among students and trendy Londoners, yet simultaneously warm and nostalgic enough to appeal to middle-aged mums and dads. Despite its potentially controversial source material, *Father Ted* was equally beloved by Catholic viewers, who found its gentle ribbing of their religion just about disrespectful enough to laugh at rather than get angry about – unlike BBC Three cartoon series *Popetown*, which was canned in late 2004 without ever receiving a screening owing to fears it would offend Catholics.

Father Ted is a simple story about three simple Irish country priests, their simple housekeeper and the simple folk whose lives they mess up by being, well, rather simple. Father Ted Crilly finds himself in charge of the parish on the remote, desolate Craggy Island. Although he's largely well meaning, Ted is at heart a rather lazy and opportunistic man, who would love the chance to work in a more glamorous region of the world. His main woes come from two priests who share the presbytery with him, dumped there because nobody in their right mind would want them to look after any proper people. Ted's eager right-hand man is youthful Father Dougal McGuire, endowed with so little sense he doesn't have two brain cells to rub together. Dougal lacks any of the basic skills required to be an effective priest – memory, communication skills, even a belief in God – but Ted struggles on with his attempts to train him up in the arcane ways of the Catholic church and in more worldly matters such as the concept of electricity. At the other end of the age spectrum is Father Jack Hackett, a potty-mouthed drunken letch who spends as much time as he possibly can asleep in his chair or hollering obscenities at anyone within hearing distance ('Drink!' 'Feck!' 'Girls!' 'Arse!' being his favourite exclamations). Tending to the three priests' every need is their housekeeper, the ever-loyal Mrs Doyle. Mrs Doyle is never happier than when she's cooking or cleaning, and her particular obsession is making sure that everyone in the Craggy Island presbytery has a good hot cup of tea – whether they want one or not.

Sitcom
Hat Trick Productions
for Channel 4
Episode Duration: 25 mins
Broadcast: 21 Apr 1995–1 May 1998

Channel 4 owes *Father Ted*'s huge success to some lovingly surreal and affectionate scripts from Graham Linehan and Arthur Mathews, and a core cast of four performers who realised that they were on to a real winner. Ardal O'Hanlon's permanently befuddled yet wide-eyed and enthusiastic Dougal was perhaps the most popular character with viewers; when *Father Ted* came to an end, O'Hanlon would recycle many of the same character traits in BBC One's superhero sitcom *My Hero*. Pauline McLynn, who is much younger and more attractive in real life than she appears as Mrs Doyle, made the most of what could have been a pretty thankless part. In particular, her repeated catchphrases ('Go on, go on, go on . . .' and 'You will, you will, you will . . .') entered mainstream public consciousness – so much so that Mrs Doyle was even utilised by the Inland Revenue in a campaign encouraging people to send in their tax returns. Poor Frank Kelly had very little to do as Father Jack, but what he did proved to be utterly hysterical. Jack's bouts of extreme violence (usually when someone tried to take his whisky away from him) and foul-mouthed outbursts were often the most eagerly anticipated moments of the whole programme. To see him out of the vomit and drool-encrusted black suit and wild flyaway hair as a sweet-faced, cheery crooner in the final episode was a wonder, though our favourite Father Jack scene remains the one in which he's sitting in the play pen at the department store surrounded by infants shrieking 'Feck!' and 'Arse!'

A sign of a great comedy success is the amount of artistes queuing up to make a guest appearance. Actor Richard Wilson took great joy in re-enacting his most famous on-screen persona as a grumpy old git when Ted (urged on by Father Dougal, which is surely not a clever idea) decides to creep up behind the actor and bellow his *One Foot in the Grave* catchphrase 'I don't believe it!' down his ear – with predictably violent results. Meanwhile Dervla Kirwan and Stephen Tompkinson re-created their ***Ballykissangel*** roles in a deliciously subversive cameo. A fair few young Irish comedians showed up along the way, including Tommy Tiernan as a depressive priest and Graham Norton, who made several appearances as the insanely chirpy priest Father Noel Furlong.

Holding the entire show together, though, was Dermot Morgan, an actor initially unfamiliar to many British viewers, despite having had a long and successful career in comedy in Ireland. Ted's exasperation with everything and everyone around him was always a joy to behold – be it Dougal's latest act of stupidity or the bizarre behaviour exhibited by the potty parishioners he had to deal with. Tragically, just days before the first episode of the third series was due to be screened, Dermot Morgan died suddenly from a heart attack at just 45 years of age. Understandably, the final eight episodes were viewed by most people with more than a hint of melancholy, for although they were (and still are) blisteringly funny, no one could forget about the tragic event overshadowing the series. With just 25 episodes made, *Father Ted* joined the ranks of that select group of programmes with not a single duff instalment to its name.

Regular Cast
Dermot Morgan · *Father Ted Crilly*
Ardal O'Hanlon · *Father Dougal McGuire*
Frank Kelly · *Father Jack Hackett*
Pauline McLynn · *Mrs Doyle*
Jim Norton · *Bishop Len Brennan*
Graham Norton · *Father Noel Furlong*
Patrick Drury · *John O'Leary*
Rynagh O'Grady · *Mary O'Leary*
Maurice O'Donaghue · *Father Dick Byrne*
Tony Guilfoyle · *Father Larry Duff*
Don Wycherley · *Father Cyril MacDuff*
John Ridgeway · *Father Ken Dillon*

Creators/Writers Graham Linehan, Arthur Mathews

Producers Geoffrey Perkins, Lissa Evans, Mary Bell

Theme Music Pop group the Divine Comedy created such a lovely, lolloping melody that they later added lyrics to it, called it 'Songs of Love', and released it on their album *Casanova*.

TRIVIA

Father Ted was as big a hit with critics as it was with audiences, winning the BAFTA award for Best Comedy in 1996 and 1999, as well as the Silver Rose of Montreux in 1999. Dermot Morgan won a posthumous bafta for Best Comedy Performance in 1999, something that surely he deserved to receive before his untimely death.

Fawlty Towers

Basil tries (and fails – again) to explain things to Manuel.

Jaws slackened, eyes rolled and minds clouded in confusion when the BBC's 2004 poll to find Britain's Best Sitcom placed *Fawlty Towers* at No. 5. Without wishing to take anything away from the shows placed fourth and higher, *Fawlty Towers* is widely agreed to be the genuine article, and only a fool, an alien or (it seems) the Great British Public would argue with that. But we all conveniently forget that it wasn't always so highly regarded.

While John Cleese and his fellow *Monty Pythonistas* were staying in Torquay, they encountered a hotelier, one Donald Sinclair of the Gleneagles Hotel, who proceeded to instruct Terry Gilliam on how to use cutlery, allegedly threw Eric Idle's suitcase over a cliff after hearing his ticking alarm clock and fearing it was a bomb, and generally being rude and obnoxious to all. The Pythons soon tired of this maltreatment and moved to another hotel. All except John Cleese, who called his wife, actress Connie Booth, and invited her to join him in a spot of people watching.

Initially, Cleese was thinking he could channel the man's misanthropy into a sketch for the ***Monty Python*** show. As the idea grew he incorporated a similar character to the hotelier into a script for the ITV sitcom *Doctor at Large* (see ***Doctor in the House***) – 'No Ill Feelings' (broadcast 30 May 1971) – but still the idea that he could make a series out of the man remained. Eventually, Cleese decided to leave the *Monty Python* team to collaborate with Connie Booth on what evolved into *Fawlty Towers*, the examination of a man on the verge of a nervous breakdown.

Cleese had of course been part of a septet of perceived smugness and intellectual superiority for five years as part of the *Monty Python's*

Sitcom
BBC Two
Episode Duration: 30–35 mins
Broadcast: 19 Sep 1975–25 Oct 1979

Regular Cast
John Cleese · *Basil Fawlty*
Prunella Scales · *Sybil Fawlty*
Andrew Sachs · *Manuel*
Connie Booth · *Polly Shearman*
Ballard Berkeley · *Major Gowen*
Gilly Flower · *Miss Abitha Tibbs*
Renée Roberts · *Miss Ursula Gatsby*
Brian Hall · *Terry – The Chef*

Creators/Writers John Cleese and Connie Booth

Producers John Howard Davies, Douglas Argent

Theme Music Dennis Wilson

Flying Circus gang of Cambridge graduates. Out on his own for the first time, it was an opportunity for critics to give him the mauling he richly deserved (it's perhaps for this reason that Eric Idle's *Rutland Weekend Television* and Terry Jones and Michael Palin's ***Ripping Yarns*** also failed to gain the kind of acclaim they would not receive until years after the event). Then there's the matter of Connie Booth, who with Carol Cleveland had been one of the token 'real women' in *Python* (i.e. not the ones played by Terry Jones in a pair of big baggy knickers), but as far as the public and critics were concerned certainly didn't have a track record for writing. So was her credit on *Fawlty Towers* a result of nepotism or was she the real reason for the single greatest success in Cleese's writing career? Even after the first few episodes had gone out, the ratings did not reflect the talent – just over 3 million viewers does not a hit make.

Fawlty Towers is initially difficult to like, let alone adore. It's an almost hero-less situation: only Polly, the maid, has any truly redeeming features at all – an invaluable member of staff whose quick thinking and loyalty to the job save the establishment from ruination on a weekly basis. Basil Fawlty himself is not a sympathetic character, riddled as he is with middle-class insecurities and deep-rooted snobbishness that make him fawn and creep to those he feels are of a higher social standing (as we see, he's the perfect victim for a conman posing as a lord), yet thinks nothing of being unspeakably rude to his other guests and the staff.

It's nearly possible to picture Basil and his young bride Sybil blissfully happy once, even though we suspect her family felt she married beneath her (and indeed if we substitute Cleese for Richard Briers, we can see how this might have been thanks to Prunella Scales's 1963 sitcom ***The Marriage Lines***). At some point they believed that investing in a hotel might make a tidy nest egg, never thinking it would be the millstone around their necks that ensured they could never afford to part but never bear living or working together either. Basil is simply not built to be servile to the majority of people who'd be looking to stay at his hotel, while Sybil, marginally more adept at basic customer service, is still more interested in golf than serving up gourmet cuisine. She has got to the stage in this marriage where she automatically assumes that Basil is up to something and never gives him the benefit of the doubt. That Basil usually *is* up to something merely turns this into a rather vicious circle. Sybil channels her dissatisfaction into retail therapy, her social group and well-aimed jibes in Basil's direction; Basil foists his frustration upon the guests, who then turn to Sybil to complain. Still, at least they love each other enough to have pet names for each other: Sybil is Basil's 'little piranha fish'; he is her 'ageing, Brilliantine, stick-insect'.

Spanish waiter Manuel is adored, because there's nothing the British like more than to laugh at than stupid foreigners. With old colonial Basil there, we get the opportunity to revel in our xenophobia, reinforcing the idea that the world would be a much better place if everyone spoke English. Unlike Basil, Manuel is so servile, so beautifully loyal, like a well-behaved puppy that keeps returning to the master who kicks it. Too willing to please for his own good, Manuel is the only person in the whole hotel who is doing his ideal job. But it's typical of Basil to hire someone because of their enthusiasm, rather than for their ability to communicate (it often amazed Andrew Sachs that he could ever be mistaken for a real Spaniard; the most ironic thing of all is that Manuel's grasp of Spanish is only slightly better than his English). No, Basil hired Manuel because he was cheap – just as he hired O'Reilly the builder to refit the hotel because of his own false sense of economy.

The world of *Fawlty Towers* is determined not by Newton's or Einstein's Laws but Sod's – something perfectly illustrated in the series' most famous episode, 'Gourmet Night'. All Basil wants is some social standing, but typically, to try to achieve this, he arranges a gourmet night without any evidence that his cook (or perhaps most importantly himself) is up to the job. Fawlty is an ambitious man. The world is his Brutus, conspiring to stab him in the back at every opportunity. His chef gets steaming drunk and can no longer do his job. Basil drives to a restaurant to collect some special replacement food (entirely the wrong dish, as it turns out – with excruciatingly comic results), only for his car to break down. Significantly, it's an Austin Estate 1300 – possibly the most tragically ridiculous car that a man of John Cleese's height and build could ever squeeze into. At the absolute end of his patience, Basil decides that what his car needs right now is not a mechanic, but a damn good thrashing. But Mother Nature hasn't finished with him yet. For the twig that Fawlty grasps as a weapon gives his vehicle a punishment as weak and ineffectual as Fawlty himself. Et tu, Austin?

One other great Basil moment comes with the arrival of German tourists to the hotel. World War Two was of course the biggest cultural event of the 20th century, shaping everything in the British psyche (hence the famous football chant: 'Two World Wars and One World Cup – doo-dah, doo-dah . . .'). A concussed Basil finds himself arguing with a family of German residents and refuses to admit that he was the one who started the row. When the German father denies doing any such thing, Basil says, 'Yes you did, you invaded Poland.' As the scene progresses towards car-crash levels of unwatchability, Basil stage-whispers, 'Don't mention the war. I mentioned it once, but I think I got away with it all right.' It's said just once, yet it became one of the nearest things this sitcom ever had to a catchphrase.

Sybil might be every bit of a match for Basil, but there's one woman in his world who manages to get the better of him on every level: the hard-of-hearing and short-of-temper Mrs Richards. At first, it doesn't appear to be a fair fight at all. Mrs Richards's hearing aid provides Fawlty with an advantage from the beginning, as does her ridiculous complaints about the view from her window that prompt Basil to enquire: 'Might I ask what you expected to see out of a Torquay hotel bedroom window? Sydney Opera House, perhaps? The hanging gardens of Babylon? Herds of wildebeest sweeping majestically . . . ?!' She is the perfect nemesis for Fawlty, though, a

TRIVIA

One of the great joys of *Fawlty Towers* was to see what rearrangement of the letters would appear on the roadside sign to the hotel. As only revealed in the second episode of series two, this is down to a young boy who mischievously rearranges the words into new and exciting combinations. For the record, these are the variations shown in the episodes they're seen in: 'Warty Towels' ('Gourmet Night'), 'Watery Fowls' ('The Psychiatrist'), 'Flay Otters' ('Waldorf Salad'), 'Fatty Owls' ('The Kipper and the Corpse'), 'Farty Towers' ('Basil the Rat') and the outrageously vulgar 'Flowery Twats' ('The Anniversary').

woman so spiteful that quite by chance – and very unjustly – she ends up the victor in this battle of witlessness; just as it looks as though for once Basil will come out on top, the Major's ill-timed interjection causes Fawlty to lose both his grip on her very expensive vase and his winnings from an illicit bet on the horses.

Each script for *Fawlty Towers* was intricately crafted, more than double the average length for comedy. Having wrung what they thought to be every last possibility out of the characters in just six episodes, Cleese and Booth were reluctant to attempt any more. After such a disappointing beginning, the series slowly found its audience and by the series' end both the viewers and the BBC wanted more. The second series took four years to write and reach the screen, and while Cleese and Booth's divorce almost certainly contributed to that delay, it was also simply that it took that long to construct another six episodes of perfection. But for many viewers it remains a show that cannot be watched for pleasure. There's very little that's televisual about it; it's a work of structural genius, though, more like a live Pinter play squished down from one and a half hours on stage to a glorious 35 minutes of TV Schadenfreude, much the same as Ricky Gervais's ***The Office*** would become 25 years later.

Fawlty Towers is a work of structural genius: a glorious 35 minutes of TV Schadenfreude, much the same as Ricky Gervais's _The Office_ would become 25 years later.

Due to BBC industrial action, a sketch Cleese had recorded for the new BBC Two sitcom ***Not the Nine O'Clock News*** (in which he refuses to make any more *Fawlty Towers* and suggests the BBC do a 'tacky revue' instead) was actually broadcast before Fawlty's final episode, 'Basil the Rat'. After just 12 episodes, *Fawlty Towers* had finally managed to eclipse John Cleese's former role as a Python in the minds of the British viewers. The same can't be said for viewers Stateside, thanks to the *Monty Python* films and a live gig at the Hollywood Bowl, although this is more a blessing in disguise. There have been two attempts to adapt *Fawlty Towers* for an American audience: one didn't get past the pilot stage; the other, *Amanda's*, was created as a starring vehicle for Bea Arthur, years before she became a Golden Girl, in which (astonishingly) Basil's role was completely removed.

The British Academy of Film and Television awarded *Fawlty Towers* the BAFTA for Best Comedy Series for both series (1976 and 1980), while Cleese won the Best Light Entertainment Performer award. In 2000, the British Film Institute selected the series for the accolade of Best-Ever Comedy Series, and we're pretty certain its low placing in that BBC poll of 2004 was more to do with the perceived inevitability of its win than a downturn in popularity. It might not be Britain's favourite, but there's little doubt as to its being Britain's best.

Creator/Producer Michael Cole **Writers** Joanne and Michael Cole **Theme Music** Michael Jessett

Inventive paper fun came to *Watch with Mother* in 1972 courtesy of Yoffy, a bearded mime artist played by Canadian actor and ***Play School*** presenter Rick Jones. As the theme song went, 'Yoffy lifts a finger and a mouse is there/Puts his hands together and a seagull takes the air'. The mouse was Fingermouse, a grey paper cone popped on the end of a grey glove and adorned with paper ears and a curly tail, while the seagull was Gulliver, a pair of white, outstretched gloved hands forming his wings with a customised ping-pong ball forming the head. There were also schools of Scampi (purple gloves with fronted red heads popped on each finger) and the steady Flash, the Tortoise.

Rerun in rotation throughout the 1970s, the format returned in September 1985 as *Fingermouse*, in which Yoffy's place was taken by Iain Lauchlan, also from *Play School*.

Fireball XL5

Children's Science Fiction | AP/ITC/ATV for ITV | episode duration 25 mins | broadcast 28 Oct 1962–27 Oct 1963

Regular Voice Cast
Paul Maxwell · *Colonel Steve Zodiac*
Sylvia Anderson · *Dr Venus*
David Graham · *Professor Matthew Matic, Lieutenant 90*
John Bluthel · *Commander Wilbur Zero*
Gerry Anderson · *Robert the Robot*

Creator Gerry and Sylvia Anderson **Producers** Gerry and Sylvia Anderson, Reg Hill (associate) **Writers** Gerry and Sylvia Anderson, Alan Fennell, Anthony Marriott, Dennis Spooner **Theme Music** Barry Gray, sung by Don Spencer

Fireball XL5 is one of the flagship spacecraft of the World Space Patrol. She's piloted by top-notch astronaut Colonel Steve Zodiac, a blond, square-jawed pin-up kind of guy, and he's accompanied on his missions by space medicine doctor, Venus, Professor Matthew Matic and a translucent robot nicknamed Robert. They also have a pet, an ape-like alien Lazoon that they name Zoonie. Among the villains they tackled were the Green Men from Planet 46 and Mr and Mrs Space Spy.

Taking the go-anywhere approach of ***Supercar*** into outer space, Gerry Anderson's second main 'Supermarionation' series was his first to be set around a global security organisation, complete with uniforms, insignia, ranks and, of course, hardware – and lots of it. *XL5* was a curious mix of *Supercar* and ***Stingray***, with old-style overly-caricatured puppets in hugely impressive sets. Made in a pre-Apollo era, the sight of a space rocket being catapulted up a ramp and into space might not entertain any little ones used to the effects of *Star Wars* (1977–2005), but the sheer ambition of the show is its charm. Thanks to the addition of jetpacks and jetmobiles (flying space bikes), Anderson finally overcame his biggest problem with the whole marionette thing – getting them to walk without looking, well, like puppets! The show was a huge success, both for AP and ITC, the only Anderson series to be fully networked across the USA. But after 39 episodes, Anderson was keen to move onto a new project. *Stingray* was just around the corner.

Fireman Sam

Animation | Bumper Films/Siriol Productions for S4C/BBC One | episode duration 10 mins | broadcast 17 Nov 1987–present

Voice Cast
John Alderton, John Sparkes · *Narrator and Character Voices*

Creators Rob Lee, from an idea by firemen Dave Gingell and Dave Jones **Producers** Ian Frampton, John Walker, Simon Quinn **Writer** Nia Ceidiog, from the stories by Rob Lee **Theme Music** Sung by Maldwyn Pope, with lyrics by Robin Lyons and music by Ben Heneghan

In the same animated style of ***Postman Pat*** comes another cheerful hero, *Fireman Sam*. First shown on Welsh channel S4C, Sam came to the BBC's *Watch with Mother* slot (even though no-one called it that any more) for his first national broadcast. Sam hails from the town of Pontypandy in Wales where he works with Sam, Elvis and Station Officer Steele, driving the fire engine Jupiter. Sometimes, in serious cases, help comes from nearby Newtown with Penny Thomas and her rescue vehicle Venus. Other Pontypandy residents include bus driver Trevor Evans, Bella Lasagne, an Italian restaurateur, naughty skateboarder Norman Price and his mum Dilys, and Sam's niece Sarah and nephew James.

A regular fixture in the kiddies' timeslot for nearly 20 years, a whole new series of *Fireman Sam* episodes began in 2004, with former *Absolutely*/***Naked Video*** star John Sparkes stepping into the narration booth previously occupied by John Alderton.

First of the Summer Wine

See LAST OF THE SUMMER WINE

Fist of Fun

Comedy | BBC Two | episode duration 30 mins | broadcast 11 Apr 1995–22 Mar 1996

Regular Cast
Stewart Lee, Richard Herring, Peter Baynham, Kevin Eldon, Mel Giedroyc, Sally Phillips, Alistair McGowan, Rebecca Front, Bill Cashmore

Producer Sarah Smith **Writer** Stewart Lee, Richard Herring **Theme Music** Chris Morris, Jonathan Whitehead

Fist of Fun saw youthful comedy duo Stewart Lee and Richard Herring bringing a combination of their live act and Radio 4/Radio 1 shows to TV in typically minimal, post-modernist style. The pair debuted on Radio 4 with *Lionel Nimrod's Inexplicable World* in 1992, before moving to Radio 1 for *Lee and Herring's Fist of Fun* in 1993, followed by the eponymous *Lee and Herring* in 1994.

Graduating from duties on the radio precursor to ***The Day Today***, *On the Hour*, Lee and Herring's comedy shared much in common with contemporaries such as Reeves and Mortimer and Newman and Baddiel. *Fist of Fun* was presented from a minimal set, supposedly in a BBC basement, and featured the comics' observations on a range of mundane issues and appearances by off-the-wall comics. Peter Baynham regularly guested as the lonely Twiglet chef, Welsh Peter. The second series of the show was slicker when the pair were given the honour of broadcasting from a proper studio, with new features like the 'News for Ians'.

After *Fist of Fun*, Lee and Herring came back in 1998 with the imaginatively titled *This Morning with Richard not Judy* in a bizarrely placed Sunday lunchtime slot. The aesthetics were a skit on ITV's ***This Morning***, from the opening graphics to the studio set, but that's where it ended, a simple device on which to hang the wacky, if sometimes patchy, comedy of Lee and Herring. The most memorable element of the show was Paul Putner (later of ***Little Britain***) as a sentient talking citrus fruit, the Curious Orange. A condensed repeat of the Sunday show was usually broadcast in a Friday evening slot.

Following a live tour of *This Morning with Richard not Judy*, Lee and Herring have contributed as writers to the Al Murray vehicle, *Time Gentlemen Please*, while Lee has also garnered great acclaim for writing the controversial stage show *Jerry Springer the Opera*.

The Flintstones

Animation | Hanna-Barbera for ABC (shown on ITV) | episode duration 25 mins | broadcast 30 Sep 1960–1 Apr 1966 (USA)

Voice Cast
Alan Reed · *Fred Flintstone*
Jean Vander Pyl · *Wilma Flintstone, Pebbles Flintstone*
Mel Blanc, Daws Butler · *Barney Rubble, Dino*
Bea Benaderet, Gerry Johnson · *Betty Rubble*
Don Messick · *Bamm-Bamm Rubble*
John Stephenson · *Mr George Slate*
Verna Felton · *Pearl Slaghoople – Wilma's Mother*

Creators William Hanna and Joseph Barbera (with Dan Gordon and Ed Benedict) **Producers** William Hanna and Joseph Barbera **Writers** Ray Allen Saffian, Joseph Barbera, Tony Benedict, Walter Black, Barry Blitzer, Harvey Bullock, Alan Dinehart, Herb Finn, Warren Foster, Ralph Goodman, Joanna Lee, Mike Maltese, Larry Markes, George O'Hanlon, Arthur Phillips, Jack Raymond, Dalton Sandifer, Sydney Zelinka **Theme Music** Everybody knows the title song with its catchy 'Meet the Flintstones' hook and its garbled lyrics: 'Let's ride with the family down the street/through the courtesy of Fred's two feet' (boy, do those fellas love their awkward scansion!). But that wasn't always the theme. Originally, Fred drove home from work to the tune of an instrumental piece called 'Rise and Shine' and then sat down to watch himself on TV (to provide the all-important sponsorship sequences), while the end sequence involved Fred covering the birdcage before failing to put the sabre-toothed cat out. 'Meet the Flintstones' was introduced for the show's third series with a brand new title sequence showing Fred sliding down the tail of a dinosaur to leave work before picking up his wife and neighbours to take them all to the movies. The end sequence showed them all leave the drive-in and head for a fast food drive-through that delivers a set of ribs that are so big they tip the car over (the last shot, as before, being Fred banging on his own front door after the cat has put him out). The end music changed for the later episodes to include a song from Bam-Bam and Pebbles called 'Open Up Your Heart and Let the Sunshine In'. For syndication and overseas repeats, the familiar 'Meet the Flinstones' sequence was edited onto the beginning of all the episodes. It was also aped wonderfully for the first live-action feature film. The original sequences were believed to be lost for ever until they turned up in the mid-1990s. The Cartoon Network restored ten of the early episodes with their 'proper' titles just in time for the show's 35th anniversary.

The Honeymooners is not a particularly well-remembered programme in the UK, but the 1950s sitcom, which starred Jackie Gleason as loudmouth mailman Ralph Kramden, was a huge hit in the States. So when Hanna-Barbera came to make their first prime-time animated sitcom, they lifted *The Honeymooners*' Ralph, his wife Alice and his neighbours Ed and Trixie Norton and transformed them into the pre-hysterical Fred and Wilma Flintstone (after previous names 'Flagstone' and 'Gladstone' were rejected) and their friends Barney and Betty Rubble.

Much of the comedy came from blurring the lines between history and modern times. All houses in Bedrock have waste disposal units and vacuum cleaners, but only thanks to the inventive use of all manner of prehistoric wildlife (a record player's needle is the sharp beak of a very much alive bird, for instance). Fred is the proud owner of a stone-wheeled car too, which is powered by propulsion from Fred's feet (and anyone sitting in the front passenger seat). There's the family dog, a licky purple dinosaur called Dino, and in time Fred and Wilma are blessed with an adorable toddler called Pebbles, while Barney and Betty adopt a foundling, whose fondness for banging a wooden club on the ground earns him the name Bamm-Bamm.

One of Hanna-Barbera's most enduring series, *The Flintstones* held the record for the longest-running prime-time animated series until 9 February 1997, when ***The Simpsons*** overtook them (and cheekily included a few references to their predecessors in the commemorative

episode – No. 167). Fred, Barney and their families have since appeared in stacks of revival series, specials and Hanna-Barbera team-ups, including the feature film *A Man Called Flintstone* (1966), *Scooby's All-Star Laff-A-Lympics* (a 1977 reworking of the ***Wacky Races*** idea, with loads of characters competing against each other), *The Flintstones Meet Rockula and Frankenstone* (1979) and *The New Fred and Barney Show* (1979). The next generation of youngsters even got a look in with the 1971 series *The Pebbles and Bamm-Bamm Show*. In 1994 came the release of a pretty decent, live-action feature film starring John Goodman and Rick Moranis delivering note-perfect impressions of Fred and Barney. A less satisfying 'prequel', *The Flintstones in Viva Rock Vegas* (2000), saw British actor Mark Addy (fresh from *The Full Monty*, 1997) take on Fred with a completely miscast Stephen Baldwin as Barney.

Cable/satellite channel the Cartoon Network has become the regular home for Fred Flintstone, though they've taken the strange decision to air the majority of episodes without their original laughter track. Which isn't funny.

Trivia

Fred's catchphrase 'Yabba-Dabba-Doo' came from Alan Reed, the voice of Fred (the script had ready simply 'yahoo').

Website

One of the absolute best *Flintstones* sites around is John Paul Murphy's superb resource www.topthat.net/webrock/. As well as offering a comprehensive background to the show, this also answers many of the questions that have vexed us over the years, such as how come we see a cat in the title sequence that never seems to appear in the show itself?

The Flipside of Dominick Hide

Science Fiction | BBC Two | episode duration 85 mins | broadcast 9 Dec 1980, 14 Dec 1982

Cast

Peter Firth · *Dominick*
Caroline Langrishe · *Jane*
Pippa Guard · *Ava*
Patrick Magee · *Caleb Line*
Trevor Ray · *Alaric*
Sylvia Coleridge · *Great Aunt Mavis*
Jean Trend · *Helda*
Timothy Davies · *Jim*
Denis Lawson · *Felic*
Bernadette Shortt · *Midge*
Tony Melody · *Harry*
Bill Gavin · *Brian*
David Griffin · *Carl*
Karl Howman · *Geoffrey*
Jenny Donnison · *Carole*
Jean Trend · *Helda*
Ron Berglas · *Pyrus Bonnington*
Michael Gough · *Professor Burrows*
Antonia Pemberton · *Mrs Burrows*
Gillian Raine · *Magistrate*
Godfrey James · *Police Sergeant*
Geoffrey Leesley · *Police Constable*
Mary Jo Randle · *Pilar*
Peter Cann · *Home Help*
Steve Alder · *Duncan*
Ysanne Churchman · *Voice of SOO the Computer*

Creator Alan Gibson **Producer** Chris Cherry **Writers** Jeremy Paul and Alan Gibson **Theme Tune** 'You'd Better Believe it Babe' by Rick Jones and David Pierce, performed by Meal Ticket

The post-holocaust London of 2130 is much like that of our own. People live in apartments and go to work on public transport. There are some differences though: relationships are arranged according to compatibility by computer; nudity is not a cause for concern because sex is no longer used for titillation and procreation is a rather antiseptic affair; and the realities of time travel – or going to the 'flipside' – are commonplace. Dominick Hide is married to Ava and works in Pinner as a correlator (or 'corro'), whose job it is to research the mundane data of the past that was lost during the holocaust. Sent on a mission to 1980 to study London bus routes, he decides to break off and meet his great great grandfather. Instead, he embarks upon a relationship with a woman called Jane, which leaves Jane pregnant and Dominick his own great great great grandfather . . .

A charming dip into science fiction, *The Flipside of Dominick Hide* starred former ***Double Deckers*** cast member Peter Firth – fresh from lead roles in the films *Equus* (1977) and *Tess* (Roman Polanski, 1979) – as the naïve but endearing Dominick. Such was the success of this *Play for Today* that a follow-up was commissioned – *Another Flip for Dominick* – broadcast two years later following a repeat of the original instalment. The sequel saw Dominick banned from flips after his transgressions in 1980. But when one of his students goes missing after a trip to 1982, Dominick is despatched to rescue him. Reunited with Jane and his son, Dominick must choose whether to stay in 1980 and risk changing the timelines or return to 2132 to his wife and son there.

Not repeated since the 1982 transmission, this pair of plays have become something of a legend among cult TV enthusiasts. Fortunately, they're worth their attention as they managed to take a time travel cliché and create something wholly original out of it. As a consequence, the plays were lauded by critics and viewers alike (both received nominations for British Science Fiction Awards).

Flipper

Childrens' Drama | Ivan Tors/MGM for NBC (shown on ITV) | episode duration 30 mins | broadcast 19 Sep 1964–15 Apr 1967 (USA)

Regular Cast
Brian Kelly · *Porter Ricks*
Luke Halpin · *Sandy Ricks*
Tommy Norden · *Bud Ricks*
Andy Devine · *Hap Gorman*
Ulla Stromstedt · *Ulla Norstrand*

Creator Ivan Tors **Producers** Ivan Tors (executive), Harry Redmond Jr (associate) **Writers** Ivan Tors, Art Arthur (Ricou Browning), James Buxbaum, Alan Caillou, Jess Carneol, Jack Cowden, Peter L. Dixon, Sylvia Drake **Theme Music** Henry Vars

'They call him Flipper, Flipper, faster than lightning', warbled the theme tune to this Ivan Tors produced Florida-based children's adventure series, not dissimilar to other Tors fare like ***Daktari*** and *Gentle Ben*. Brian Kelly is Porter Ricks, responsible for the animals (and humans) in Coral Key Wildlife Park. Porter, however, is forced to play second fiddle to his two precocious sons – Sandy (15) and Bud (10), but it's their smug dolphin pet, Flipper, who is the star of the show. The series, as is traditional with this genre, revolved around Flipper finding trouble, swimming off to tell the kids in a series of hoots and clicks, kids head off to sort trouble out, get into danger, dad comes to the rescue – and for three seasons. Porter is assisted in his work by Norwegian biochemist Ulla, who also happened to be rather attractive.

Flipper was spun off from the Ivan Tors' feature film of the same name, starring Chuck Connors as Porter Ricks, although Bud Halpin still played Sandy. The TV cast was allowed to take to the cinemas in the big screen sequel, *Flipper's New Adventure* (aka *Flipper and the Pirates*) (1964). A second slice of *Flipper* adventures was made in 1995, lasting for five years under the title *The New Adventures of Flipper*, while a further big screen adventure for the adventurous dolphin was made in 1996. *Flipper* starred Paul Hogan as Porter Ricks and Elijah Wood as Sandy, with a cameo from original star Luke Halpin as a fisherman.

The original Flipper was called Mitzi, but the pampered dolphin had a stunt double called Mr Gipper to handle all the difficult tail walking sequences. Mitzi died of a heart attack in 1972.

Flower Pot Men

See pages 314–15

The Flumps

Animation | David Yates Productions for BBC One | episode duration 15 mins | broadcast 14 Feb–3 May 1977

Voice Cast
Gay Soper · *Narrator, Singer*

Creator/Writer Julie Holder **Producer** David Yates **Theme Music** Paul Reade, performed by George Chisholm

A family of fluff balls living somewhere in Northern England became the next generation of *Watch with Mother* stars, stepping into the domestic roles of ***The Woodentops*** 20 years earlier.

Mother Flump was a great cook, Father built things in his shed and Grandfather Flump kept everyone entertained with tunes from his big brass flumpet – when he wasn't snoozing, that was. The kids were Perkin, Posie and the littlest member of the family, Poodle, whose confusions and childish questions were just the kind of things little kids say.

If you were a Flump, it wasn't unknown for bad moods to be accompanied by small black clouds floating above your head; if you were a little Flump, you might even have experienced a distressing night when you thought the moon was trapped in a bucket of water (until someone was kind enough to explain it was only the moon's reflection); and if you were a girl Flump, you might decide to keep all of your secrets in a safe place – just don't put it under your hat as it might blow away.

Gay Soper provided all the voices and the odd song too. Only 13 episodes were made, but they ran in rotation for ages, and ***Blue Peter*** even showed kids how to make models of the entire family using pipe cleaners, plasticine and balls of wool.

The Flying Doctors

Drama | Crawford Productions for 9 Network (shown on BBC One) | episode duration 45 mins | broadcast 15 May 1986–13 Aug 1991 (Aus.)

Regular Cast
Andrew McFarlane · *Dr Tom Callaghan*
Robert Grubb · *Dr Geoff Standish*
Liz Burch · *Dr Chris Randall*
Lenore Smith · *Kate Wellings/Standish*
Lewis Fitz-Gerald · *David 'Gibbo' Gibson*
Peter O'Brien · *Sam Patterson*
Bruce Barry · *George Baxter*
Max Cullen · *Hurtle Morrison*
Mark Little · *Ron Miller*
Pat Evison · *Violet Carnegie*
Maurie Fields · *Vic Buckley*
Val Jellay · *Nancy Buckley*
Terry Gill · *Sergeant Jack Carruthers*
George Kapiniaris · *D. J. Lonniadis*
Vikki Blanche · *Paula Patterson*
Sarah Chadwick · *Dr Rowie Lang*
Brett Climo · *Dr David Ratcliffe*
Alex Papps · *Nick Cardaci*
Louise Siversen · *Debbie O'Brien*
Gerard Kennedy · *Luke Mitchell*
Nikki Coghill · *Jackie Crane*
Beverley Dunn · *Claire Bryant*
Continued on page 316

Flower Pot Men

Bill and Ben. (Or is it Ben and Bill? It's hard to tell if they're not talking ...)

At the back of a small house, down the bottom of the garden, lies a shed in which the gardener leaves all his equipment. But he doesn't know that at the front of the shed, inside two flower pots, live Bill and Ben, twin scamps who love to make play with the gardener's tools. Their neighbour, a sunflower called Weed, keeps lookout for them in case the gardener returns, and sometimes their friend Slowcoach the tortoise calls in.

Those two tiny, mischievous string puppets, seemingly made of flowerpots, kept children captivated for years before colour TV turned up and ruined it all. They were the original bad boys of *Children's Hour*, with their inarticulate language (officially known as 'Oddle Poddle') that every expert who offered an opinion claimed would corrupt young viewers and stunt their capacity for language. Said experts were, of course, talking out of their flobblelobs. Kids knew that Bill was the high-pitched one and Ben the deeper one, and they always understood exactly what the Flower Pot Men were saying, just like other generations would understand the Clangers, Pob, the Teletubbies and foul-mouthed Kenny McCormack on ***South Park***. And only one of those could ever be accused of truly being a bad influence.

The genius of the *Flower Pot Men* was that it was the first television show ever that talked up to its audience. They knew that the 'flobbles' would entertain the kids and also be easy to imitate, which of course helped with parent–child bonding. And as the songs didn't have any words to speak of, the child could join in with the fun just by gurgling along to the music (yes, the children who benefited

Pre-School Puppetry/Animation
Westerham Arts Ltd for BBC TV
Episode Duration: 15 mins
Broadcast: 12 Dec 1952–27 Oct 1954, Jan–29 Mar 2001

Voice Cast
Peter Hawkins · *Bill, Ben, Weed*
Gladys Whitred, Julia Williams · *Narrators*
John Thomson · *Bill, 2002*
Jimmy Hibbert · *Ben, 2002*

Creator Hilda Brabban

Producer Freda Lingstrom

Writer Freda Lingstrom, based on Hilda Brabban's stories

Theme Tune Maria Bird, a simple song possibly based around the first three notes of 'This Old Man': 'Bill and Ben, Flower Pot Men/Bill and Ben/Bill and Ben, Flower Pot Men.'

from this truly wondrous experience would be the same ones who complained about the damage that the Teletubbies were doing to their grandchildren).

The naughty Bill and Ben themselves were based on the brothers of writer Hilda Brabban (while her sister inspired the gentle Weed who lived in a nearby pot). The characters had already appeared in stories read on the BBC's *Listen with Mother* radio series, and were later adapted for BBC TV's *For the Very Young* strand, placed alongside other shows like ***Andy Pandy***. Although all 26 episodes had been shown by the time *Watch with Mother* was introduced in the autumn of 1953, repeats of *Flower Pot Men* continued to feature in the timeslot until the 1970s, by which time few black-and-white programmes were still being aired outside of *Open University* broadcasts.

In 2001, Cosgrove Hall animation studios unveiled a brand new series of Bill and Ben adventures, though this time, thanks to stop motion, there were no strings attached. Voiced by John Thomson and Jimmy Hibbert, *Bill and Ben* saw the introduction of new characters like Whoops the worm and Whimsey the spider. The series was accompanied by a bit of a merchandising boom in the form of talking plush toys and even a single ('Floppadance').

The particular genius of the *Flower Pot Men* was that it was the first television show ever that talked up to its audience.

Producers Hector Crawford, Ian Bradley (executive), Stanley Walsh, Oscar Whitbread, Jan Marnell, Barbara Burleigh **Theme Music** Garry McDonald, Laurie Stone

In 1984, a six-part mini series took us across some of the most remote parts of Australia, following the travels and traumas of a young and enthusiastic doctor called Tom Callaghan, who leaves the city behind to join up with the Royal Flying Doctors Service (RFDS). Tom's arrival in the remote Cooper's Crossing was not met with universal eagerness from the residents of the area, many of whom believing him to be too young, too naïve and too 'City' for their liking. But his determination and skills as a medic soon won most of them over. Thankfully the mini series wasn't the last we saw of Callaghan and the residents of Cooper's Crossing, with the series returning as an ongoing soap opera from 1986.

Australian soaps have inevitably garnered a reputation for being a bit tacky and low budget, but despite heavy doses of melodrama this series was much closer to the early films of Peter Weir than a soap. Episodes usually involved a minor problem affecting the residents of Cooper's Crossing, interwoven with a guest performer's disaster/injury/embarrassing snake-bite incident. A desperate radio call would be the sign for the RFDS to fly out to the stricken victim, with time always being the crew's biggest obstacle.

Medical dramas tend to have a fast turnover of characters due to the generally distressing storylines and the high stress levels under which the characters exist. Never more so than with *The Flying Doctors* who also had to contend with the forces of nature and the overwhelming distances that separate the communities they cared for. One of the most naturally deadly countries on the planet, the Australian Outback also offers the courageous traveller some unique vistas and natural wonders that *The Flying Doctors* was only too ready to exploit. Filming took place in Victoria's Minyip (doubling for the town of Cooper's Crossing) and Nulla Station, New South Wales and the Mundi Mundi plains, all providing those important stretches of empty outback.

Over 30 years earlier, Richard Denning starred as Dr Greg Graham in *The Flying Doctor*, a series that ran for a year (13 Sep 1959–4 Jun 1960). Half of that series was filmed in Elstree Studios London, the rest on location in Australia.

Website

www.crawfords.com.au/libary/drama/flyingdocs.shtml

Follyfoot

Drama | Yorkshire for ITV | episode duration 25 mins | broadcast 28 Jun 1971–16 Sep 1973

Principal Cast

Gillian Blake · *Dora*
Arthur English · *Slugger*
Paul Guess · *Lewis Hammond*
Steve Hodson · *Steve*
Desmond Llewelyn · *The Colonel/Uncle Geoffrey*
Christian Rodska · *Ron Striker*

Producers Tony Essex (executive), Audley Southcott **Writers** Francis Stevens, Audley Southcott, Jennifer Stewart, from the books *Follyfoot* and *Cobbler's Dream* by Monica Dickens **Theme Music** 'The Lightning Tree', written by Steven Francis, performed by the Settlers – 'Grow, grow, the lightning tree/Never give in too easily' – which is one of the very best TV theme tunes ever; far more memorable than the programme it was attached to

With her parents emigrating to Brazil to work at the High Commission, Dora comes to stay with her uncle Geoffrey, who lives in a huge dusty mansion. It doesn't take long for adventure to find her when she is a sole witness of a botched horse-rustling attempt. She befriends a stable boy called Steve and begins to visit the nearby Follyfoot Farm on her uncle's estate, home to maltreated or injured horses. There, her uncle shows her a tree that has been dead ever since it was struck by lightning many years ago – the Lightning Tree.

Often misremembered as a quaint little series for girls in the vein of ***The Adventures of Black Beauty***, *Follyfoot* began with a horrific attack on the horses by rustlers that led to the animals needing to be shot to put them out of their misery. Right from the beginning, the programme never shied away from the brutal realities of life in the country, nor did it avoid showing us the cruelty that people can inflict on animals or each other. The death of Uncle Geoffrey leaves Dora with the dilemma of taking on full responsibility for the horse sanctuary and management of her uncle's estate or rejoining her family on their return from Brazil.

Food and Drink

Factual | Bazal Productions for BBC Two | episode duration 30 mins | broadcast 6 Jul 1982–5 Mar 2002

Regular Cast

Simon Bates, Gillian Miles, Jonathan Choat, Henry Kelly, Susan Grossman, Chris Kelly, Michael Barry, Jilly Goolden, Oz Clarke, Anthony Worrall-Thompson, Emma Crowhurst · *Presenters*

Producers Peter Bazalgette, Gloria Wood (executive), Henry Murray, Elaine Bancroft

Cookery and home economics had been a part of British television from its inception. But while cook after chef after ***Why Don't You?*** child encouraged us to get in the kitchen and have a go, *Food and Drink* was the first programme to invite us to think about what we consume and take notice of things like branding as well as the psychological tricks supermarkets were beginning to employ in order to get us to buy their premium brands.

It seemed pretentious to some, but then wine tasters and gourmands are prone to over-enthusing because of their passion for the subjects. What the series did offer was at least an attempt to bring this world within the reach of the average viewer, pointing out how supermarkets were making inroads in stocking more adventurous products, offering more than just Chardonnay and Cheddar.

It didn't completely abandon the traditional approach to foodie TV, with at least a couple of recipes a week, but for most it's remembered by the sights of Jilly Goulden and Oz Clarke encouraging the public to ditch the Leibrfraumilch with an effusive eulogy to a Pinot Noir.

The year 2002 saw *Food and Drink* replaced by a more interactive approach. *Full on Food* had a studio audience and a rather graphic but honest depiction of the food process (the sight of a carcass in its title sequence drew a fair few complaints). Elsewhere, the Beeb has stripped weekend mornings with *Saturday Kitchen*, a compilation of clips and recipes from other cookery programmes, framed with live links presented by Antony Worrall Thompson.

Footballers' Wives

Soap/Drama | Shed/Carlton for ITV | episode duration 45–75 mins | broadcast 8 Jan 2002–present

Regular Cast

Zoe Lucker · *Tanya Turner/Laslett*
Gillian Taylforth · *Jackie Pascoe*
Alison Newman · *Hazel Bailey*
John Forgeham · *Frank Laslett*
Susie Amy · *Chardonnay Lane/Pascoe*
Gary Lucy · *Kyle Pascoe*
Cristian Solimeno · *Jason Turner*
Chad Shepherd · *Ron Bateman*
Lee-Anne Baker · *Lara Bateman*
Daniel Schutzmann · *Salvatore Biagi*
Philip Bretherton · *Stefan Hauser*
Jessica Brooks · *Freddie Hauser*
Julie Legrand · *Nurse Janette Dunkley*
Laila Rouass · *Amber Gates*
Ben Price · *Conrad Gates*
Caroline Chikezie · *Elaine Hardy*
Jamie Davis · *Harley Lawson*
Sarah Barrand · *Shannon Donnelly/Lawson*
Jesse Birdsall · *Roger Webb*
Ben Richards · *Bruno Milligan*
Helen Latham · *Lucy Milligan*
Marcel McCalla · *Noah Alexander*
Peter Ash · *Darius Fry*
Elaine Glover · *Katie Jones*
Tom Swire · *Seb Webb*

Creators Maureen Chadwick, Ann McManus **Producers** Brian Park (executive), Liz Lake, Sean O'Connor, Claire Phillips, Cameron Roach **Writers** Various, including Maureen Chadwick, Ann McManus, Guy Picot, Helen Childs, Phil Ford, Jaden Clark, Liz Lake, Harriet Warner **Theme Music** Colin Winston-Fletcher

The players at Earls Park Football Club are among the best in the country – talented, young, attractive, and paid an absolute fortune. So it's not surprising that they attract a certain type of woman: the money-grabbing, gold-digging, image-conscious fashion victim with fewer brain cells than pairs of shoes. However, these women usually get cast aside sooner or later, as the ambitious football players keep scouting around for the next conquest. It takes a very special kind of woman to be more than just a happy memory – to become a footballer's wife, in other words.

One of the true guilty pleasures of modern television, it comes as no great surprise to most people to learn that *Footballers' Wives* was created by the same team that had earlier made life inside a women's prison into top-quality entertainment with ***Bad Girls***.

The concept behind *Footballers' Wives* is the true star of the programme rather than any one character, as players and their partners have come and gone (some in rather unpleasant ways – Chardonnay due to anorexia, Jason plummeting off a roof, Frank of a heart attack mid-coitus). However, there's one woman who stands head and shoulders ahead of the rest of the pack – cocaine-snorting, manipulative, baby-swapping goddess Tanya Turner, possibly the most loathsome (yet completely adored) bitch to be seen on television since the heady days of ***Dynasty***'s Alexis. It remains to be seen if *Footballers Wives* will be able to carry on without Tanya's shiny talons clutching their way to the top.

The Forsyte Saga

Drama | BBC Two | episode duration 50 mins | broadcast 7 Jan–1 Jul 1967

Principal Cast

Eric Porter · *Soames Forsyte*
Nyree Dawn Porter · *Irene Heron*
Kenneth More · *Jolyon 'Jo' Forsyte*
Susan Hampshire · *Fleur Mont*
John Welsh · *Uncle James Forsyte*
Joseph O'Conor · *Old Jolyon Forsyte*
Margaret Tyzack · *Winifred Dartie*
Terence Alexander · *Monty Dartie*
John Barcroft · *George Forsyte*
June Barry · *June Forsyte*
John Baskcomb · *Uncle Timothy Forsyte*
John Bennett · *Phillip Bosinney*
A. J. Brown · *Uncle Roger Forsyte*
Jonathan Burn · *Val Dartie*
Fay Compton · *Aunt Ann Forsyte*
Ursula Howells · *Frances Forsyte*
Lana Morris · *Helene Hilmer/Forsyte*
Suzanne Neve · *Holly Forsyte/Dartie*
Nora Nicholson · *Aunt Juley Forsyte*
Dalia Penn · *Annette Lamotte/Forsyte*
Kynaston Reeves · *Uncle Nicholas Forsyte*

Fanny Rowe · *Emily Forsyte*
Nora Swinburne · *Aunt Hester Forsyte*
George Woodbridge · *Uncle Swithin Forsyte*
Michael York · *Jolyon 'Jolly' Forsyte*
Richard Armour · *Jack Cardigan*
Christopher Benjamin · *Prosper Profond*
Caroline Blakiston · *Marjorie Ferrar*
Anne De Vigier · *Imogen Cardigan*
Karin Fernald · *Anne Wilmot*
Hal Hamilton · *Francis Wilmot*
Martin Jarvis · *Jolyon 'Jon' Forsyte*
Sarah Harter · *Francie Forsyte*
Cyril Luckham · *Sir Lawrence Mont*
Nicholas Pennell · *Michael Mont*

Producer Donald Wilson **Writers** Lennox Phillips, Donald Wilson, from the novels by John Galsworthy **Theme Music** 'Halcyon Days' from *The Three Elizabeths Suite* by Eric Coates

With the arrival of BBC Two in 1964, channel controller Michael Peacock commissioned a hugely ambitious, 26-part adaptation of John Galsworthy's *The Forsyte Saga*. Such is the slow-moving nature of TV production, by the time the Forsytes reached the screen, Peacock had been moved onto BBC One and his replacement, David Attenborough, received all the credit. But the serial was really the work of Donald Wilson, who had nagged the Beeb to negotiate for the rights (the tale having previously been made by MGM into a 1949 film, *That Forsyte Woman*, which starred Errol Flynn and Greer Garson). Wilson convinced Michael Peacock to have faith that the viewing public would appreciate a costume drama that would blow their drama budget for the year (at a cost of £250,000, it was the corporation's most expensive drama production to date) and run for six months.

Wilson's sense of conviction was rewarded by six million viewers (two-thirds of the available audience for the channel), while over 18 million tuned in for a BBC One repeat the following year. The show was a major hit when exported to America and became the first BBC serial to be bought by stations in the Soviet Union. Thanks to *The Forsyte Saga*, the BBC acquired both a reputation and a taste for exquisitely made costume dramas and literary adaptations of the works of Tolstoy, George Eliot and Anthony Trollope.

The Forsyte Saga concerns the lives and interconnected relationships of two cousins, Jo and Soames Forsyte. Jo abandons his wife for his mistress (pregnant with his child) to the shame of his large, extended family. The successful but grim lawyer Soames finds himself a trophy wife in Irene, but his neglect of her leads to Irene seeking solace in the arms of another. Soames's response is to rape Irene – a shocking scene that had viewers as appalled as they were captivated by such melodrama. Irene divorces Soames and marries Jo; Soames finds himself a new wife and the offspring from these pairings form the backbone to the second, much less involving, half of the serial.

In 2002, Granada Television felt enough time had passed for another attempt at adapting Galsworthy's novels. Their *Forsyte Saga*, produced across two series, starred Damian Lewis as Soames, Rupert Graves as Jolyon and ***Our Friends in the North***'s Gina McKee as Irene.

Trivia

The Forsytes also inspired the name of a 1969 comedy series, *The Fossett Saga*, starring Jimmy Edwards and Sam Kydd, and written by Dave Freeman. Edwards played a Victorian novelist whose attempts to make his fortune by ridiculous means are always quashed by his servant, played by Sam Kydd.

Four Feather Falls

Children's Puppet Drama | AP Films/Granada for ITV | episode duration 13 mins | broadcast 25 Feb–27 Oct 1960

Regular Cast

Nicholas Parsons · *Tex Tucker, Dan Morse*
Denise Bryer · *Ma Jones, Little Jake*
Kenneth Connor · *Rocky, Dusty, Pedro, Marvin Jackson, Doc Haggerty, Slim Jim, Chief Kallamakooya*
David Graham · *Grandpa Twink, Fernando, Big Ben, Red Scalp*

Creators Gerry Anderson and Barry Gray **Producer** Gerry Anderson **Writers** Mary Cathcart Borer, Phil Wrestler, Jill Allgood **Theme Music** Barry Gray, sung by Michael Holliday

Gerry Anderson's first independent production was this quirky fantasy western starring Tex Tucker. En route to take up the post of sheriff at Four Feather Falls with his trusty horse, Rocky, and dog, Dusty, Tucker meets a little lost Indian boy. When he returns the boy to his father, a powerful Indian chief, he is rewarded with four magic feathers that enable his animal companions to talk and his pistolsto operate automatically in times of danger.

The marionettes for *Four Feather Falls* were the first incarnation of the 'Supermarionation' puppets that would become Anderson's trademark, featuring lip-synch courtesy of solenoids fitted inside the puppets' heads that responded to the electrical impulses of the recorded character voices. The episodes still hadn't reached the level of sophistication of later Supermarionation productions, but they were getting there.

Fox

Drama | Euston Films/Thames for ITV | episode duration 50 mins | broadcast 10 Mar–2 Jun 1980

Regular Cast

Peter Vaughan · *Billy Fox*
Elizabeth Spriggs · *Connie Fox*
Bernard Hill · *Vin Fox*
Derrick O'Connor · *Ray Fox*
Larry Lamb · *Joey Fox*
Eamon Boland · *Phil Fox*

Ray Winstone · *Kenny Fox*
Rosemary Martin · *Renie Fox*
Margaret Nolan · *Sheila Fox*
Yvette Dotrice · *Anne Pegram*
Cindy O'Callaghan · *Nan*
Richard Weinbaum · *Andy Fox*
Shaun Curry · *George Macey*
Sidney Livingstone · *Frank Macey*
Patricia Quinn · *Liz*
Maggie Steed · *Bette*
Karl Howman · *Griff*
Trudie Goodwin · *Carol*
Bill Nighy · *Colin Street*
Helen Gelzer · *Madeline*
Dave Arlen · *Clem*
Mary Peach · *Peg*
Robert Urquhart · *Jerry*
David Calder · *DI Davin*

Creator Trevor Preston **Producers** Graham Benson, Verity Lambert (executive) **Writer** Trevor Preston **Theme Music** George Fenton

Billy Fox was once a major player in the south London underworld. Tough as nails, yet well regarded by the community, he was affectionately known as 'King Billy', a last reminder of the honour of old-school villainy. In the run-up to his 70th birthday, we meet Billy's family: sons from his first marriage, Vin, Ray and Joey, and his younger sons from second wife, Connie – Phil and Kenny.

A well-regarded drama from Euston Films, *Fox* presented a romanticised image of South London that still managed a bit of grit along the way. It boasted a powerful cast, including an impressive early role for Ray Winstone as a boxer left bereft and disillusioned when an opponent dies from injuries sustained during their fight. Peter Vaughan plays the softer side of 'Grouty' from ***Porridge*** as a larger-than-life old man who idolises his family – especially his deaf grandson, Andy – and whose death leaves his large family without the focus he had always provided.

Fun can be had looking out for future TV stars like Christopher Ryan (***The Young Ones***), or Trudie Goodwin and Mark Wingett, who would become the longest-serving members of ***The Bill***'s Sun Hill station. The one slightly odd element is the use of original – and not particularly subtle – songs (sung by Peter Blake) to bridge the narrative in some scenes.

Foyle's War

Drama | Greenlit/Paddock Productions for ITV | episode duration 100 mins | broadcast 27 Oct 2002–14 Nov 2004

Regular Cast
Michael Kitchen · *DCS Foyle*
Anthony Howell · *Sergeant Paul Milner*
Honeysuckle Weeks · *Samantha Stewart*
Julian Ovenden · *Andrew Foyle*
Geoffrey Freshwater · *Sergeant Eric Rivers*
Mali Harries · *Jane Milner*

Creator Anthony Horowitz **Producers** Jill Green, Jim Reeve (executive), Michael Kitchen (consulting), Claudine Sturdy, Averil Brennan, Simon Passmore, Keith Thompson **Writers** Anthony Horowitz, Rob Heyland, Michael Russell, Matthew Hall **Theme Music** Jim Parker

Neatly combining two popular genres – nostalgic rural dramas and detective thrillers – *Foyle's War* brought Michael Kitchen (***To Play the King***) to prime-time TV as '***Inspector Morse*** with a ration book'. Though the series is set in the middle of World War Two, it avoided the popular myth of everyone working together, bolstered with Dunkirk Spirit and a drive to beat the Bosch.

DCS Christopher Foyle is embittered after he learns that his age precludes him from joining his colleagues who have already signed up to fight the Nazis. Nevertheless, he realises his particular talents as a catcher of criminals can still be of some use; despite the threat of invasion, serious crime did not end in 1939. With many of the younger police officers away, Foyle is left with a young female driver (he himself cannot drive). Samantha Stewart is a quiet, intelligent young lady, daughter of a clergyman and seconded from the Women's Royal Army Corps. She accompanies Foyle on his investigations and becomes one of his few trusted colleagues; his second in command, Paul Milner, has been invalided out of the army after losing part of a leg, but disappoints Foyle when he is revealed to be a member of a Nazi-supporting social club. Local police officers are responsible for savagely beating German refugees while young women take part in sabotage and murderous spouses use the horrific bombings to conceal their crimes.

Series creator Anthony Horowitz had previously written for a variety of genres, contributing to ***Robin of Sherwood***, ***Boon***, ***Murder Most Horrid*** and ***Midsomer Murders*** before *Foyle's War* came to mind. We try not to mention that he also gave us the Saturday night dud *Crime Traveller*.

Fraggle Rock

Muppetry | Jim Henson Television/TVS for HBO/ITV | episode duration 25 mins | broadcast 10 Jan 1983–30 Mar 1987 (USA)

Cast
Jerry Nelson · *Gobo Fraggle, Marjorie the Trash Heap, Pa Gorg, Architect*
Steve Whitmire · *Wembley Fraggle, Sprocket the Dog*
Dave Goelz · *Boober Fraggle, Philo, Uncle 'Travelling' Matt Fraggle, Wrench*
Kathryn Mullen · *Mokey Fraggle, Cotterpin Doozer*
Karen Prell · *Red Fraggle*
Richard Hunt · *Junior Gorg, Gunge, Turbo, Wizard*
Cheryl Wagner · *Ma Gorg*

Jim Henson · *Cantus the Minstrel, Convincing John*
Fulton Mackay · *Captain*
John Gordon Sinclair · *John*
Simon O'Brien · *Simon*

Creator Jim Henson **Producers** Jim Henson (executive), Martin Baker (associate), John Dimon, Jerry Juhl, Duncan Kenworthy, Lawrence S. Mirkin **Writers** Jerry Juhl, Jocelyn Stevenson, David Young, Carol Bolt, David Brandes, B. P. Nichol, Sugith Varughese, Laura Phillips, Susan Juhl, Bob Sandler **Theme Music** Phil Balsam, lyrics by Dennis Lee

For commentary, see THE MUPPETS, *PAGES 501–6*

Frankie Howerd

Comedy | BBC One | episode duration 30 mins | broadcast 22 Feb–29 Mar 1966

Regular Cast
Frankie Howerd, Arthur Mullard, Hugh Paddick, Sheila Steafel, John Le Mesurier, June Whitfield · *Various Characters*

Producers Bill Lyon-Shaw, Ernest Maxin, George Inns, Kenneth Carter, Duncan Wood **Writers** Various, including Eric Sykes, Spike Milligan, Johnny Speight, Ray Galton, Alan Simpson

Like many of his contemporaries, Yorkshire native Francis Alick Howard got his first taste for showbiz while in the army, where he participated in troop shows and concert parties. Post-WWII, he joined a number of different variety troops (working alongside such people as Eric Sykes and Hattie Jacques) and changed his surname to Howerd before becoming a regular performer on radio in the early 1950s. His first television show, 1952's *The Howerd Crowd*, allowed him to develop the camp 'ooh's, 'aaah's and over-familiarity with his audience that would become his trademark. Despite being one of Britain's most legendary comedians, he failed to achieve a consistent run of hits on television with his willingness to experiment with new styles, writers and routines leading to as many misses as hits in the early days.

Despite this, lack of consistency, Howerd's act was bolstered by support from such writers as Eric Sykes, Johnny Speight and Galton and Simpson. By the late 1950s his popularity was on the decline (in particular, a disastrous 1959 sitcom called *Frankly Howerd* did little to endear him to the public), to the extent that Galton and Simpson were turned down when they suggested to TV bosses that they should write a sitcom for Howerd. Instead, they were given the chance to write a series of comedy pilots in the *Comedy Playhouse* strand (which gave birth to ***Steptoe and Son***), only one of which ('Have you Read this Notice?') starred poor Frankie.

In 1963, Howerd resuscitated his career by making a guest appearance on ***That Was the Week that Was*** – suddenly, he was cool again, and as a consequence Galton and Simpson were finally allowed to write that long-awaited sitcom for him, *The Frankie Howerd Show*. This series featured a 'sit-down' comic routine as Howerd introduced the setting for each episode, which then led into a sitcom-style expanded sketch for the rest of the show, often featuring some top-notch co-stars. From then on, Howerd enjoyed a full decade's worth of prime-time TV work (as well as guest appearances in several of the *Carry On* films), culminating in the classic sitcom ***Up Pompeii*** and its sequel/spin-off *Whoops Baghdad*.

Frankie Howerd successfully weathered the arrival of Alternative Comedy in the 1980s (Howerd had been alternative for his entire career!) and by the early 1990s his career was enjoying something of a renaissance, with a new series of stand-up shows on ITV (*Frankie's On . . .*) attracting good critical comments and the adoration of a new generation of fans. Sadly with Frankie's death the titters came to an end on 19 Aapril 1992, with *Frankie's On . . .* only half-completed.

Frasier

Sitcom | Grub Street Productions for Paramount (shown on Channel 4) | episode duration 25 mins | broadcast 16 Sep 1993–13 May 2004

Regular Cast
Kelsey Grammer · *Dr Frasier Winslow Crane*
David Hyde Pierce · *Dr Niles Crane*
John Mahoney · *Martin Crane*
Jane Leeves · *Daphne Moon/Crane*
Peri Gilpin · *Roz Doyle*
Dan Butler · *'Bulldog' Briscoe*
Edward Hibbert · *Gil Chesterton*
Patrick Kerr · *Noel Shempsky*
Harriet Sansom-Harris · *Bebe Glazer*
Tom McGowan · *Kenny Daly*
Millicent Martin · *Gertrude Moon*
Anthony Lapaglia · *Simon Moon*
Saul Rubinek · *Donny Douglas*
Bebe Neuwirth · *Dr Lilith Sternin-Crane*
Mercedes Ruehl · *Kate Costas*
Luke Tarsitano, Trevor Ironhorn · *Frederick Gaylord Crane*
Griffin Dunne · *Bob*
Ashley Thomas · *Alice May Doyle*
Jane Adams · *Dr Mel Karnofsky*
Marsha Mason · *Sherry Dempsey*
Virginia Madsen · *Cassandra Stone*
Moose · *Eddie*

Creators David Angell, Peter Casey, David Lee **Producers** David Angell, Peter Casey, David Lee, Christopher Lloyd, Kelsey Grammer, Rob Hanning, Sam Johnson, Joe Keenan, Lori Kirkland, Jay Kogen, Steven Levitan, Jon Sherman, Eric Zicklin, Vic Rauseo, Mark Reisman, Chris Marcil, Linda Morris, Dan O'Shannon (executive) **Writers** Various, including David Angell, Peter Casey, David Lee, Sy Dukane, Denise Moss, Anne Flett-Giordano, Chuck Ranberg, Christopher Lloyd, David Lloyd, Ken Levine, David Isaacs, Linda Morris, Vic Rauseo, Joe Keenan, Rob Greenberg,

Suzanne Martin, Jeffrey Richman, Jay Kogen, Rob Hanning, Lori Kirkland, Sam Johnson, Chris Marcil, Bob Daily, Dan O'Shannon, Jon Sherman, Peter Casey, Saladin K. Patterson, Eric Zicklin, Heide Perlman **Theme Music** Bruce Miller wrote the jazz-based theme ('Tossed Salad and Scrambled Eggs'), with the dulcet tones of series star Kelsey Grammar providing the vocal backing over the end credits.

When long running Boston-based sitcom **Cheers** came to an end, producers created two spin-off programmes. One featured bad-tempered barmaid Carla Tortelli and her huge Italian-American family (*The Tortellis*, not shown in the UK) – the other was an intellectual exercise in wit, sophistication and pretension centred around perhaps the least likeable of all of the regular characters. Few people could have expected *Frasier* to be a success – even fewer could honestly have predicted that the show would last as long as its parent series, would regularly come away from award shows with trophies, and would remain one of the last bastions of intelligent comedy programming on American network television.

Following a messy divorce from his uptight wife Lilith, psychiatrist Frasier Crane moves from Boston back home to Seattle to begin a new career as a phone-in host on KACL Radio. His arrival home coincides with the retirement of his policeman father Marty, invalided out of the force following a gunshot wound to his leg. Frasier's equally prissy brother Niles is extremely reluctant to have their traditionally macho father living with him and his hypochondriac wife Marls, so after a considerable amount of arm-twisting, Frasier agrees to have Marty move in with him. Marty brings along his live-in carer, Mancunian Daphne Moon, and his seemingly preternaturally aware terrier Eddie – a dog that manages to creep Frasier out at least once per episode. Despite an initial clash of personalities between Frasier and his father, household harmony is largely established, although Marty's vile green recliner chair spoils Frasier's otherwise immaculately-furnished designer apartment. Meanwhile at work, Frasier is beginning to make a name for himself as a local radio personality, thanks largely to his ever-suffering man-hungry producer Roz.

Relying upon word-play, badinage and culture-clashes for its comedy rather than slapstick or innuendo (unlike most other shows), highlights of *Frasier* included the occasional returns of his ex-wife Lilith and son Frederick and the odd appearances by his former *Cheers* drinking buddies – indeed, every single regular member of the *Cheers* cast appeared in *Frasier* with the exception of Kirstie Alley's Rebecca. The growing love of Niles for Daphne (a love unspoken for seven years!) was a prevailing feature of early seasons – when they eventually did become a couple, the embarrassed and awkward nature of their relationship was a sheer joy to behold. Less pleasurable were appearances by Australian actor Anthony Lapaglia as Daphne's brother Simon, boasting the worst 'English' accent (London? Manchester? Cornwall?) committed to screen since Dick Van Dyke's mockney disaster in *Mary Poppins* (1964).

With an outstanding ensemble cast of performers, *Frasier* was an outstanding sitcom that matched the giddy heights of quality established by its parent show *Cheers*. Witty, charming and consistently well written, it's hardly surprising that it enjoyed such longevity. Indeed, having played Dr Frasier Crane for the last eight seasons of *Cheers* as well as the ten years of the spin-off, Kelsey Grammer equalled the record of 20 years playing the same character on TV established by James Arness, who played Marshall MacDillon on *Gunsmoke* from 1955 to 1975.

Fred Basset

Animation | BBC One | episode duration 5 mins | broadcast 25 Apr–20 May 1977

Voice Cast

Lionel Jeffries, Victor Spinnetti, Ann Beach

Creator Alex Graham **Producers** Bill Melendez (executive), Graeme Spurway **Writers** Nick Spargo, Hitce Hitchins

Fred Basset made his debut as a comic strip character in the *Daily Mail* on 8 July 1963. The rather basic animation of the TV version might not evoke the greater sophistication (or even budget) of Disney or Warner Bros, but it owed its existence to a man who had worked for both, Bill Melendez, who had already brought Charlie Brown and Snoopy to life.

Voiced by British film legend Lionel Jeffries, Fred was a curious but likeable dog. He frequently gave his owners cause to be angry, leaving chewed up slippers around the house or digging up the garden to deposit and then reclaim bones. He barked at cats (even though he was terrified of them) but his ultimate fear was a ferocious dog that lived around the corner. His friends Fifi the poodle and Jock the Terrier were no help either.

With its melancholy music and wry observations, *Fred Basset* was a perfect bridge between the weekday children's programming and the evening news. Melendez productions made just 20 episodes at breakneck speed before taking on another newspaper strip, the *Mirror*'s *Perishers*.

French and Saunders

Comedy | BBC Two/BBC One/Saunders and French Production for BBC One | episode duration 30–50 mins | broadcast 9 Mar 1987–present

Regular Cast

Dawn French, Jennifer Saunders, Rowland Rivron, Simon Brint, Liza Tarbuck

Creators Dawn French, Jennifer Saunders **Producers** Jon Plowman (executive), Geoff Posner, Janice Thomas, Emma Cornish, Jo Sargent, Anil Gupta, Jon Rolph **Writers** Dawn French, Jennifer Saunders, Adrian Edmondson, Sue Perkins, Mel Giedroyc

Theme Music Simon Brint composed the theme tune that became synonymous with French and Saunders' first seasons. Since then they have occasionally used other stock pieces of music as their themes.

The reigning queens of British TV comedy, Dawn French and Jennifer Saunders began their television careers as members of the cutting-edge radical comedy troupe The Comic Strip. Some 20 years later, they are the epitome of the comedy establishment, criticised by some for being traditional, safe and stuck in their ways. If nothing else, those criticisms go to prove that French and Saunders have now enjoyed success for such a long time that they've become legitimate targets for the next generation of comedians to attack.

French and Saunders came to the BBC in 1987, having cut their teeth on Channel 4 (***The Comic Strip Presents***) and ITV (***Girls on Top***). Their new show was a sketch series along similar lines to ***The Two Ronnies***, albeit from a distinctly feminine perspective. There were few recurring characters (unlike the sketch shows of, say, Dick Emery or Kenny Everett), Dawn and Jennifer preferring instead to run with one-off jokes, parodies or songs. However, some characters and set-ups were reused, the most famous of which were two grotesquely fat men (played in giant foam rubber outfits by French and Saunders themselves) who made horrifically inappropriate and politically incorrect comments at any passing female. A later spin on the joke involved two 'stuff and nonsense' upper-class country housewives, again corpulently padded, who brushed off horrifically violent accidents with guns, knives and large blades as nothing more than nicks or scratches. Most episodes would also feature a sketch set in Dawn and Jennifer's sparsely-decorated living room, inevitably featuring Dawn doing something to annoy or irritate a bored and listless Jennifer (who inexplicably wore a comedy turban-like hat throughout).

For the first four seasons (all of which were screened on BBC Two), French and Saunders also boasted the talents of musical duo Raw Sex, the hilariously un-sexy Rowland Rivron and Simon Brint. This enabled the programme to include parodies of current and classic pop stars, including a particularly effective send-up of ABBA's video for their song 'Knowing Me, Knowing You'. For many viewers the highlight of most episodes were the immaculately presented recreations of classic feature films. No genre of film was safe from French and Saunders' satirical treatment, with movies as diverse as Ingmar Bergman's *The Seventh Seal*, science fiction classic *Aliens* and legendary horror movie *The Exorcist* being lampooned. Few people who saw Dawn and Jennifer recreating the Joan Crawford/Bette Davis picture *Whatever Happened to Baby Jane?* will ever be able to forget it – similarly, the spot-on send-up of *The Silence of the Lambs* means that it's nigh on impossible to watch the original movie without picturing Dawn French standing in the underground glass-walled cell making vile slurping noises.

Dawn and Jennifer are always careful not to merely churn out a new batch of episodes ever year, with lengthy gaps of up to three years inbetween their TV appearances. Indeed, their output consisted solely of one-off specials (normally at Christmas or Easter) from 1996 to 2004, at which point they returned with a whole new season of episodes, this time linked with an overarching theme, in which Dawn and Jennifer tried and failed repeatedly to write sketches for their new BBC series, irritating their increasingly frustrated producer Liza Tarbuck.

French and Saunders' careers blossomed when they were not appearing together in their BBC sketch show, with Dawn scoring major hits with homicide-themed comedy show ***Murder Most Horrid*** and ecclesiastical comedy ***The Vicar of Dibley***, and Jennifer becoming an international megastar courtesy of ***Absolutely Fabulous***. However, a sitcom set just prior to the French Revolution that reunited the two performers, *Let Them Eat Cake*, fared less well in the ratings and lasted just one series.

The Fresh Prince of Bel-Air

Sitcom | Stuffed Dog/Quincy Jones – David Salzman for NBC (shown on BBC Two) | episode duration 25 mins | broadcast 10 Sep 1990–10 May 1996

Regular Cast
Will Smith · *Himself*
James Avery · *Philip Banks*
Janet Hubert-Whitten, Daphne Maxwell Reid · *Vivian Banks*
Alfonso Ribeiro · *Carlton Banks*
Karyn Parsons · *Hilary Banks*
Tatyana M Ali · *Ashley Banks*
Joseph Marcell · *Geoffrey*
Ross Bagley · *Nicky Banks*
Nia Long · *Lisa*
Tyra Banks · *Jackie Ames*
Jeffrey A. Townes · *Jazz/DJ Jazzy Jeff*

Creators Jeff Pollack, Benny Medina (format), Andy and Susan Borowitz **Producers** Various, including Quincy Jones, Winifred Hervey Stallworth, Gary H. Miller, David Steven Simon, Kevin Wendle, Josh Goldstein, Cheryl Gard, Will Smith (executive), Samm-Art Williams, Deborah Oppenheimer, Joanne Curley Kerner, Werner Walian, David Pitlik **Writers** Various, including Susan Borowitz, Shannon Gaughan, Cheryl Gard, Bennie R. Richburg Jr, Sandy Frank, Lisa Rosenthal, Samm-Art Williams, Gary H. Miller, Eddie Gorodetsky, David Zuckerman, Barry Gurstein, David Pitlik, Maiya Williams, Joel Madison, Jeff Pollack **Theme Music** Will Smith and QJIII (Quincy Jones III)

One of the world's biggest movie stars is Will Smith, having been nominated for an Oscar for his portrayal of Muhammad Ali as well as single-handedly saving the world in summer blockbusters like *Men In Black* (1977) and *Independence Day* (1996). He's also been able to sustain a career as a non-threatening rap artist, garnering a string of No. 1s on both sides of the Atlantic. It was in the guise of a non-threatening rap artist that Smith first attracted the attention of TV producers, who cast in as *The Fresh Prince of Bel-Air*.

The Fresh Prince developed many of the themes present in the 1970s' racial class comedy ***Diff'rent Strokes***, with Smith playing a borderline hoodlum from Philadelphia sent to live with his wealthy Bel-Air resident relatives. Initially co-starring Smith's musical partner DJ Jazzy Jeff Townes, the show was as schmaltzy as any other American family-friendly sitcom, but saved by its recognition of urban fashion and culture. In the UK, it was first aired as part of BBC Two's *Def II* strand. Unfortunately, excessive repeats (primarily because of the loss of ***The Simpsons*** to Channel 4) meant that BBC Two controllers decided to schedule another American comedy in the same timeslot, have blunted its bite somewhat.

Friday Night Live

See SATURDAY LIVE

Friday Night with Jonathan Ross

Chat Show | Callender/Channel X for Channel 4/Open Mike for BBC One | episode duration 45–60 mins | broadcast 1987–1988 (*The Last Resort*), 2 Nov 2001–present (*Friday Night*)

Regular Cast
Jonathan Ross · *Host*
Andy Davies · *Co-host*
Rowland Rivron · *Dr Martin Scrote*
Stephen de Martin, Ian Parkin, David Roper, David Wickenden · *Four Poofs and a Piano*

Producers Colin Callender, Katie Lander (*The Last Resort*); Addison Cresswell (executive), Deborah Cox, Andrew Beint, Suzi Aplin, Ruth Wallace (*Friday Night*) **Writers** Various, including Jonathan Ross, Shaun Pye, Jim Pullin, Fraser Steele, Jez Stevenson

Inspired by the more irreverent, less fawning approach of American chat show *Late Night with David Letterman*, TV researcher-turned-presenter Jonathan Ross represented the epitome of the 1980s, with sharp suits, an immovably hairsprayed quiff and a passion for all forms of entertainment (without any seeming discernment) combined with a brutally honest willingness to admit that everything on the show was a bit of a sham. Ross's effortless presentation style and mock vanity/ego allowed him to get away with a lot more than most other interviewers would ever attempt, resulting in a number of hugely important A-list celebrities queuing up to appear on his shows over the years.

For *The Last Resort*, Ross was accompanied by Rowland Rivron as Dr Martin Scrote, the 'court jester' of the programme and the butt of many of Ross's jokes. Ross also fronted *Saturday Zoo*, *The Incredibly Strange Film Show* and *Mondo Rosso*, the latter programmes allowing him to indulge in his passion for world cult cinema. With Ross's move to the BBC to take over from Barry Norman as the presenter of the ***Film . . .*** series, he soon returned to his familiar stomping ground of the chat show with *Friday Night with Jonathan Ross*. Over the years, Ross has also become the regular host of the British Comedy Awards and one of the anchormen for the bi-annual ***Comic Relief*** telethons.

Friends

See pages 324–6

The Fugitive

Thriller | Quinn Martin for ABC (shown on ITV) | episode duration 45 mins | broadcast 17 Sep 1963–29 Aug 1967 (USA)

Regular Cast
David Janssen · *Dr Richard Kimble*
Barry Morse · *Lieutenant Philip Gerard*
Bill Raisch · *Fred Johnson – the One-Armed Man*
J. D. Cannon · *Lloyd Chandler*
Richard Anderson · *Leonard Taft*
Jacqueline Scott · *Donna Taft*
William Conrad · *Narrator*

Creator Roy Huggins **Producers** Quinn Martin (executive), Wilton Schiller **Writers** Various, including Arthur Weiss, George Eckstein, Harry Kronman, Sheldon Stark, Philip Saltzman, William Link, Richard Levinson, Dan Ullman, William D. Gordon, Jack Turley, Don Brinkley, John Kneubuhl, Barry Oringer **Theme Music** Peter Rugolo

Wrongly accused of murdering his wife, Dr David Kimble is arrested and charged with her murder. Circumstantial evidence leads a jury to find him guilty and he's despatched by train to be executed. But on the road to prison, Kimble takes advantage of a disruption and flees the scene, for Kimble knows that the one-armed man who did kill his wife is still roaming free and is determined to track him down to prove his own innocence – even if he has to cover every inch of America to find him.

The Fugitive had viewers gripped for four years as Kimble's journey kept him one step behind the one-armed man, while doggedly pursued by Lieutenant Gerard), the officer in charge of him at the time of the train crash. Taking in almost the entire USA, plus Canada and Mexico, the series kept moving from location to location and introducing random characters to keep things interesting. Thankfully, viewer loyalty was rewarded when at the end of the final series, Kimble finds the one-armed man and Gerard shoots him – now convinced of Kimble's innocence.

Continued on page 327

Friends

From L–R: Chandler, Rachel, Ross, Monica, Joey and Phoebe.

The fan mindset is a curious thing. Typified as 'geeky' by the wearing of T-shirts, collecting of merchandising and regurgitating of quotes ad nauseam, it's the kind of behaviour that have led some studies to conclude that your average fanatic can often be a borderline case for Asperger's syndrome or even autism. Fans are able to make near-*Rainman* connections, to approach cast lists like an Underground map that makes the links to long-forgotten TV and film projects as fast as the Internet Movie Database. The stereotype – in the main, the comic book or science fiction fan – is a bespectacled, anorak-wearing, social inadequate whose closest relationships have been fostered over the internet.

There are of course elements of this that we identify with – the list-building and obsession for detail being just two – but what makes this particular stereotype so uncomfortable is that the exact same patterns of behaviour are thought of as normal when applied elsewhere, notably with regard to sport, where a memory for detail is seen as an advantage. Sport is of course a social activity to be enjoyed in crowds. Not so the art of watching TV. *Friends* figures large in the cultural make-up of the close of the 20th century as the first American sitcom to be a crossover for the fanishly minded. It was a series that not only appealed to the kind of person with fan sensibilities but also catered for them with merchandising and TV specials, almost to the same degree as the release of a new ***Star Trek*** might do. For a vast proportion of its audience, this would be the first time where being able to quote back a line of dialogue ('Did I say that out loud?') or identify a cultural reference would give them credibility around the water-cooler that they'd never previously enjoyed. It also meant their Friday nights in front of the box became a social thing, with each episode deconstructed and analysed just as last Saturday's game would be.

Part of the explanation for this was, of course, canny marketing on the part of Warner Bros in the USA and Channel 4 in the UK. The range of merchandising was extensive, from oversized coffee mugs and 'A Quote a Day' desk calendars to Smelly Cat T-shirts and soundtrack albums containing middle-of-the-road bands like Hootie and the Blowfish and REM (performing their least-whiny track, 'It's a Free World, Baby'), all of which was also unlikely to stick out as 'culty' if seen on your desk at the office or in your bag. But the canniness also harked right back to the moment when the creators of the show came up with the idea of six reasonably attractive late twenty-somethings living in apartments they could never afford across the hall from each other.

In the first episode, Monica Geller is telling her former room mate Phoebe Buffay and her neighbours Joey and Chandler about her forthcoming date. In walks Monica's older brother Ross, depressed after his wife finally moved out to be with her girlfriend after a gradual realisation that she's a lesbian. Just as Ross says that he wishes he was still married, in rushes a woman in a bridal gown (prompting Chandler to wish for a million dollars). The bride is Monica's best friend from high school who for some reason had elected not to invite her to her wedding to Barry, an orthodontist. At her wedding reception, Rachel realised she didn't love Barry and bolted. Only once she was in the rain and out on her own did she realise that the only person she knew in the city was Monica. Ross is amazed that Rachel has joined their group; back in high school he'd nurtured a secret crush on her. Joey decides to give Ross some advice about the ways of love, while Chandler says that he wishes he were a lesbian.

This is how Monica ended up acquiring a new room mate and how we discovered the facets of each character. Economical, concise and instantly involving, that first episode showed us how Ross frets and worries about everything for so long that the moment almost always passes him by; how Phoebe is a spiritual being with a deeply tragic past that never seems to drag her down; how Joey, an out-of-work actor, has never had success on stage or screen, but has also never had to face the idea of rejection from a woman; how impulsive and spoilt Rachel is, and how she's forced to take a job as a waitress not only to be able to afford her rent but to discover how to survive without her daddy's credit cards; how detail-fixated and unlucky in love Monica is; and how at the end of every scene Chandler will deliver a perfect punchline. That's the series in a nutshell.

The romance between Ross and Rachel became the series' first big over arching story, with Rachel discovering Ross's feelings for her at the end of series one and realising she feels the same way, only for Ross to return from a trip to Japan with a girlfriend. The will-they won't-they continued until eventually the pair got together, but a year later, after Rachel leaves waitressing for a career in the fashion industry, she and Ross split up. The possibility that they were 'on a break' becomes a bone of contention for the rest of the series as Ross has a drunken one-night stand and Rachel decides she can't forgive him. Thus their dynamic changes from coy lovers to fierce bitchy rivals for that all-important last word. It's an interesting switch as it has the unfortunate effect of turning Ross from a lovable geek into a distressingly childish and aggressive

Sitcom
Bright/Kauffman/Crane/Warner Bros for NBC (shown on Channel 4)
Episode Duration: 25 mins
Broadcast: 22 Sep 1994–6 May 2004 (USA)

Regular Cast

Jennifer Aniston · *Rachel Green*
Courteney Cox Arquette · *Monica Geller/Bing*
Lisa Kudrow · *Phoebe Buffay-Hannigan/Ursula Buffay*
Matt LeBlanc · *Joey Tribbiani*
Matthew Perry · *Chandler Bing*
David Schwimmer · *Ross Geller*
James Michael Tyler · *Gunther*
Anita Barone, Jane Sibbett · *Carol Willick-Bunch*
Jessica Hecht · *Susan Bunch-Willick*
June Gable · *Estelle Leonard*
Mitchell Whitfield · *Barry Farber*
Cosimo Fusco · *Paolo*
Larry Hankin · *Mr Heckles*
Hank Azaria · *David*
Morgan Fairchild · *Nora Tyler Bing*
Maggie Wheeler · *Janice Litman*
Lauren Tom · *Julie*
Michael G. Hagerty · *Mr Treeger the Caretaker*
Marlo Thomas · *Sandra Green*
Ron Leibman · *Dr Leonard Green*
Tom Selleck · *Dr Richard Burke*
Giovanni Ribisi · *Frank Buffay Jr*
Debra Jo Rupp · *Alice Knight/Buffay*
Charles Thomas Allen, John Christopher Allen, Cole Mitchell Sprouse · *Ben Geller*
Steven Eckholdt · *Mark Robinson*
Jon Favreau · *Pete Becker*
Christine Taylor · *Bonnie*
Teri Garr · *Phoebe Abbott Sr*
Paget Brewster · *Kathy*
Tate Donovan · *Joshua Bergen*
Helen Baxendale · *Emily Waltham-Geller*
Michael Rapaport · *Gary*
Elle Macpherson · *Janine Lecroix*
Reese Witherspoon · *Jill Green*
Alexandra Holden · *Elizabeth Stevens*
Bruce Willis · *Paul Stevens*
Eddie Cahill · *Tag Jones*
Kathleen Turner · *Charles Bing*
Paul Rudd · *Mike Hanigan*
Dermot Mulroney · *Gavin Mitchell*
Aisha Tyler · *Charlie Wheeler*
Anna Faris · *Erica*

Creators Marta Kauffman and David Crane

Producers Kevin Bright, David Crane, Marta Kauffman, Sherry Bilsing, Michael Borkow, Brian Buckner, Adam Chase, Ted Cohen, Michael Curtis, Shana Goldberg-Meehan, Sebastian Jones, Alexa Junge, Seth Kurland, Greg Malins, Ellen Plummer, Andrew Reich, Scott Silveri, Todd Stevens (executive)

Writers Various, including Marta Kauffman, David Crane, Jeffrey Astrof, Mike Sikowitz, Alexa Junge, Adam Chase, Ira Ungerleider, Doty Abrams, Michael Curtis, Greg Malins, Michael Borkow, Sebastian Jones, Wil Calhoun, Scott Silveri, Seth Kurland, Shana Goldberg-Meehan, Andrew Reich, Ted Cohen, Sherry Bilsing, Ellen Plummer, Brian Buckner, Dana Klein Borkow, Mark J. Kunerth, Robert Carlock

Theme Music 'I'll Be There For You', which was a No. 3 hit in the UK singles chart for the Rembrandts in 1995.

TRIVIA

Although there are no on-screen episode titles, it's widely known that the ones used by the production team follow a formula, each beginning with 'The One with . . .' or 'The One Where . . .' and alluding sometimes cryptically to some element of the story. Examples include: 'The One with the Sonogram at the End', 'The One After the Superbowl' (which had nothing to do with the content of the episode and everything to do with its scheduling on the NBC network), 'The One with Five Steaks and an Eggplant', 'The One Where Ross and Rachel . . . You Know' and 'The One with the Princess Leia Fantasy'. Two of the 230-odd episode titles only just conform – 'The One Hundredth' and 'The Last One'.

brat. Conversely, it opened the writers' eyes up to the fact that Jennifer Aniston, as Rachel, could deliver a killer punchline just as well as Matthew Perry's Chandler.

Chandler and Monica were paired off at the end of the show's two-episode trip to London (or 'London, BABY!' as Joey kept on telling everyone), a trip that was ostensibly to see Ross marry his British girlfriend Emily (Helen Baxendale) after a whirlwind romance. Though Ross does eventually marry Emily, it's not before accidentally saying Rachel's name at the altar by mistake. The marriage is doomed before it's even begun while Chandler and Monica decide to keep their own relationship secret for the time being. While Chandler and Monica are of course perfect for each other (the episode where they propose to each other being the most blub-tastic emotional half-hour of *Friends* ever), the decision to pair them off meant that they inherited the responsibility for the ongoing relationship plots at the expense of much of the comedy. And that didn't manage to bring a close to the ongoing saga of Ross and Rachel either. After a drunken night in Vegas, they discover that they're married and, shortly later, that Rachel is pregnant. In due time, the gang of six becomes seven, with the arrival of baby Emma.

As the popularity of the show soared, its cast became megastars, which inevitably led to those rumours that one or all of them had resigned over pay deals. They all became the richest people in American sitcomland, appearing on the cover of thousands of magazines and starring in films of variable quality. The women fared better than the men, with Lisa Kudrow excelling as a waspish wife in *The Opposite of Sex* (1998), Courtney Cox starring in the three *Scream* films (1996/1997/2000) and Jennifer Aniston in a run of romantic comedies like *The Object of My Affection* (1998) and *Bruce Almighty* (2003). Matthew Perry made a few forgettable lightweight comedies before he struck gold with *The Whole Nine Yards* (2000) opposite Bruce Willis (who also made a guest appearance in Friends around the same time). David Schwimmer also did his time with romantic comedies before striking out to do serious stage work and bagging a few straight roles in films like the adaptation of Stephen King's *Apt Pupil* (1998) and the World War Two TV series ***Band of Brothers***. Matt LeBlanc's hit ratio was not so strong, the sci-fi remake *Lost in Space* (1998) being the only film of note. Perhaps this was a deciding fact for choosing LeBlanc's character for the spin-off series that would follow on from *Friends*; a solid, dependable performer, he was less likely than the others to be distracted by other projects.

By series end, after ten hugely successful seasons, everything was geared towards one thing – leaving Joey excluded from the gang enough to make him move to LA for the start of that spin-off show, called simply *Joey*. So Phoebe marries her long-time boyfriend Mike (Paul Rudd), Chandler and Monica decide to move into a bigger house with their new babies, acquired through surrogacy, and in the final act Ross and Rachel get together again. In the last episode, the gang decide to have one last coffee at their regular haunt, Central Perk, before heading their separate ways. In the UK, the episode pulled in 9 million viewers for Channel 4, who had more reasons than most for lamenting its passing (in a Channel 4 poll, the *Friends'* finale was voted No. 1 in the 100 Best TV Moments of 2004). Of course, not everyone warmed to the show's ten-year reign as America's top sitcom. Some felt it was too saccharine-sweet or at worst smug, and yes, occasionally it was guilty of both, but it was also supremely witty. It perpetuated an idea that things will work out fine in the end, and that you're never alone when you've got friends.

A 1993 big-budget movie version of *The Fugitive* starred Harrison Ford as Kimble and Tommy Lee Jones as his pursuer, Marshal Samuel Gerard. The film led to a spin-off for Tommy Lee Jones, *US Marshals* (1998). A TV remake followed in 2000, with Timothy Daly as the man on the run.

Full Circle

See AROUND THE WORLD IN 80 DAYS

The Further Adventures of Oliver Twist

Comedy Drama | ATV for ITV | episode duration 25 mins | broadcast 2 Mar–1 Jun 1980

Principal Cast

Daniel Murray · *Oliver Twist*
John Fowler · *Artful Dodger*
David Swift · *Fagin*
Bryan Coleman · *Mr Brownlow*
Harold Innocent · *Mr Bumble*
Geoffrey Larder · *Monks*
Leonard Preston · *Noah Claypole*
Pauline Quirke · *Charlotte*
Gary Shail · *Ned Fingers*
Derek Smith · *Mr Grimwig*

Producers Ian Fordyce, David Reid **Writer** David Butler, based on characters created by Charles Dickens **Theme Music** Syd Amos

For commentary, see OLIVER TWIST (1999)

Game for a Laugh

Entertainment | LWT for ITV | episode duration 50 mins | broadcast 26 Sep 1981–5

Regular Cast
Jeremy Beadle, Henry Kelly, Matthew Kelly, Sarah Kennedy, Rustie Lee, Martin Daniels, Lee Peck, Debbie Rix · *Hosts*

Producers Alan Boyd (executive), Keith Stewart, Phil Bishop, Brian Wesley, Bob Merrilees

The idea of playing pranks on the public was spearheaded by ***Candid Camera***, an American show shipped over to the UK in the 1960s. In 1981, the format was given a twist by a show that professed to be 'Watching You, Watching Us – Watching Us, Watching You'. *Game for a Laugh* was hosted by four presenters (rather excessive, we feel!) who sat on stools and laughed uproariously while introducing clips of the public being duped by stunts being filmed on hidden cameras. They also played surprises on their studio audience – a trait of Saturday night TV to this very day.

Sarah Kennedy is now a Radio 2 DJ, Henry Kelly enjoyed a lengthy spell presenting daytime quiz show *Going for Gold*, while Matthew Kelly dabbled with sitcoms such as *Holding the Fort* and *Relative Strangers* before stepping into Leslie Crowther's shoes on ***Stars in their Eyes***. Jeremy Beadle continued terrorising innocent members of the public with *Beadle's About* – another show that relied on hidden cameras and practical jokes. Strangely unpopular with viewers, Beadle is nevertheless a hyper-intelligent and (by all accounts) highly likeable chap – something you'd never guess from the choices he's made in his TV career. A second generation of *Game for a Laugh* hosts arrived in the form of Brummie TV cook Rustie Lee (a woman with one of the loudest and most infectious laughs ever heard on telly), magician's son Martin Daniels, Debbie Rix (daughter of farce king Brian Rix) and Lee Peck.

Game On

Sitcom | Hat Trick Productions for BBC Two | episode duration 30 mins | broadcast 27 Feb 1995–6 Feb 1998

Principal Cast
Ben Chaplin, Neil Stuke · *Matthew Malone*
Samantha Janus · *Mandy Wilkins*
Matthew Cottle · *Martin Henderson*
Tracy Keating · *Clare Monohan*
Crispin Bonham-Carter · *Archie*
Mark Powley · *Jason*

Creators/Writers Andrew Davies, Bernadette Davis **Producers** Geoffrey Perkins, Sioned William **Theme Music** 'Where I Find My Heaven' by the Gigolo Aunts, which reached No. 29 in May 1995

When Matthew Malone's parents are killed in a horrific car accident, the loss leaves him emotionally scarred, agoraphobic and filthy stinking rich – result! He shares his flat with Martin, a 'ginger sad bastard' who's been his friend (and emotional punch bag) since they were children, and is now his semi-willing slave. Matthew rents out the last bedroom in his apartment to hard-working attractive blonde temp Mandy, for no other reason than he wants to get into her knickers – and isn't she furious when one day she comes home from work early and finds him wearing a pair of them.

Unable to leave his flat, Matthew spends most of his long, boring days recreating scenes from his favourite movies, or polishing his surfboard (not a euphemism). When Martin gets himself a girlfriend (the shag-obsessed Irish nurse Clare), Matthew befriends Mandy's caring friend Jason, who helps him overcome his agoraphobia. Matthew's overjoyed to have a friend who can 'go birding' with him – however he's sadly blind to the fact that not only is Jason gay, he's also completely besotted with him.

Game On pushed the boundaries in terms of taste and decency by being the crudest sitcom to date – however, it didn't really advance the genre in the way that Andrew Davies's previous success ***A Very Peculiar Practice*** had done. Played in the first series by Ben Chaplin (who quit the show to make a career for himself in Hollywood), Matthew was re-imagined for seasons two and three by Neil Stuke, successfully making him much more thetic and as a consequence much funnier. Samantha Janus put the memory of her disastrous ***Eurovision Song Contest*** performance behind her, showcasing her not inconsiderable talents as a comic actress. Sadly her next choice of sitcom, *Babes in the Wood* (opposite Denise Van Outen and Karl Howman), was a ghastly disaster of a show.

Gardeners' World

Factual | BBC Two | episode duration 15–60 mins | broadcast 19 Feb 1969–present

Cast
Percy Thrower, Peter Seabrook, Geoff Hamilton, Alan Titchmarsh, Monty Don, Arthur Billit, Geoffrey Smith, Clay Jones, Diarmuid Gavin, Chris Baines, Chris Beardshaw, Rachel de Thame, Pippa Greenwood, Sarah Raven, Gay Search, Joe Swift, Ali Ward · *Presenters*

Producers Various, including Owen Gay, Tony Laryea, Nick Patten (executive), Andy Vernon, Sarah Moors, Colette Foster, Richard Simkin, Louise Hampden **Theme Music** The lovely languid theme tune to *Gardeners' World* is called 'Morning Light' and was written by Nick Webb and Greg Carmichael. Rik Carter remixed the version currently in use on the show.

Amazingly, programmes featuring plants, gardens and flowers have been a fixture on the TV schedules ever since the first week of regular TV transmissions in the UK, way back in 1936 (a fascinating programme about prize-winning chrysanthemums, apparently). The BBC's studios at Alexandra Palace boasted lots of nearby gardens in which programmes could be recorded. From 1956, a monthly programme aimed at the more hands-on gardener began transmission – *Gardening Club* was hosted by genial Percy Thrower and was a popular, long-running success story.

However, it was the arrival of colour television that really transformed gardening programming, enabling viewers at home to marvel at the rich colours and shades available to use in British gardens. *Gardeners' World* became a regular series from 1969 and has remained on screens ever since (and yes, the use – or otherwise – of an apostrophe in the programme's title has varied many times over the years!). Percy Thrower became the first lead presenter, and looked set to remain so, until in 1976 he made a commercial for Garden Plus fertiliser. This contravened BBC regulations that state that none of their presenters can be seen to promote any individual products – as a result, Thrower was quickly replaced by Peter Seabrook, who presented the show throughout most of the 1980s. One of the best-loved presenters was Geoff Hamilton, the host for six years from 1990 until his untimely death. In later years, Alan Titchmarsh and Monty Don have been the primary presenters, with a wide range of talented and passionate gardeners providing enthusiastic support.

With the huge boom in lifestyle programming on all channels in the 1990s, many other gardening programmes began to spring up across the schedules. Most have been fly-by-night visitors, occupying the schedules for a year or two at most. However *Gardeners' World* remains a pivotal part of the BBC Two schedules to this day, normally shown on a Friday evening so as to capture an audience ready to get their hands dirty over the weekend. An annual Gardener of the Year competition and a hugely popular *Gardeners' World* magazine have helped to reinforce the brand still further – for as long as the British like to potter around in their gardens, there will always be a place in the TV schedules for *Gardeners' World*.

GBH

Drama | Channel 4 | episode duration 50 mins | broadcast 6 Jun–18 Jul 1991

Principal Cast

Robert Lindsay, Stephen Hall · *Michael Murray*
Lindsay Duncan · *Barbara Douglas/Critchley*
Julie Walters · *Mrs Murray*
Michael Palin · *Jim Nelson*
David Ross · *Mr Weller*
Jake Abrahams · *Black Waiter*
Jean Anderson · *Dr Goldup*
Michael Angelis · *Martin Niarchos*
Peter Armitage · *Mr Burns*
Judith Barker · *Margie*
Peter-Hugo Daly · *Bubbles*
Paul Daneman · *Mervyn Sloan*
Jane Danson · *Eileen Critchley*
Colin Douglas · *Frank Twist*
Hayley Fairclough · *Jessica Nelson*
Dearbhla Molloy · *Laura Nelson*
Edward Mallon · *Mark Nelson*
Anna Friel · *Susan Nelson*
William Franklyn · *Distinguished Gent*
William Gaunt · *J. B. Hunnigdon*
Tom Georgeson · *Lou Barnes*
Kulvinder Ghir · *Ravi*
Alan Igbon · *Teddy*
Daniel Massey · *Grosvenor*
Jimmy Mulville · *Philip*
Clifford Rose · *Judge Critchley*
Andrew Schofield · *Peter Grenville*
Gareth Tudor Price · *Richard Grenville*
Philip Whitchurch · *Franky Murray*
Noreen Kershaw · *Maureen Murray*
Niall Toibin · *Michael Murray Snr*

Creator/Writer Alan Bleasdale **Producers** Verity Lambert (executive), David E. Jones, Alan Bleasdale **Theme Music** Elvis Costello, Richard Harvey

At the beginning of the 1980s, Alan Bleasdale offered us his ***Boys from the Blackstuff*** – a story of unemployment set in Bleasdale's home town of Liverpool. In 1991, without stating the exact location of the setting, Bleasdale summed up the attitudes of Liverpool's Militant political movement of the mid-1980s in his tragi-comic GBH.

Michael Murray is an ambitious man and head of the city's Labour council. But power corrupts and having beaten most of his political adversaries, Murray begins to get his revenge on those from his past. His targets include the schoolteacher who tried to put him 'with the loonies' and whom Murray has transferred to a school for children with learning difficulties. Head of that school is Jim Nelson (Michael Palin), who breaks a strike during a city-wide day of action to protect the children in his care who are terrified of the near-riotous picketers. When Murray tries to turn Nelson's mistake to his advantage, he unwittingly sets in motion a chain of events that brings about his own downfall.

In Bleasdale's critique of the rise in the 1980s of opportunist local politicians like Derek Hatton, he still leaves almost enough room for us to feel sorry for his central character. Murray's mother loathes him (a sturdy performance from the always great Julie Walters) and the pressures of his job cause him to develop a debilitating stammer and a nervous twitch that makes his arm flash upwards in a parody of Lindsay's earlier political creation, 'power to the people' Wolfie in ***Citizen Smith***. Cruellest of all is the onset of his nervous breakdown, which begins to manifest itself during a ***Doctor Who*** convention being staged at the hotel where he's staying (complete with

Daleks mocking his attempts to sleep with the mysterious Barbara with taunts of 'Fornicate! Fornicate!').

While Robert Lindsay shines as Murray, it's Michael Palin, as the bullied, sensitive teacher Jim Nelson, who truly excels, proving what we've often suspected, that he was by far the most versatile of the Pythons.

Gemini Man

Science Fiction | Universal for NBC (shown on BBC One) | episode duration 50 mins | broadcast 10 May–28 Oct 1976

Principal Cast
Ben Murphy · *Sam Casey*
William Sylvester · *Leonard Driscoll*
Katherine Crawford · *Dr Abby Lawrence*

Producers Harve Bennett (executive), Leslie Stevens **Writers** Leslie Stevens, Frank Telford, Robert F. O'Neill, James D. Parriott, Steven E. De Souza, loosely inspired by the novel by H. G. Wells **Theme Music** Lee Holdridge and Mark Snow

For commentary, see THE INVISIBLE MAN

The Generation Game

Game Show | BBC One | episode duration 45 mins | broadcast 2 Oct 1971–3 Jan 1982, 7 Sep 1990–13 Apr 2002

Cast
Bruce Forsyth, Anthea Redfern, Roy Castle, Larry Grayson, Isla St Clair, Rosemary Ford, Jim Davidson, Sally Meen, Melanie Stace, Francine Lewis, Lea Kristensen · *Presenters*

Producers James Moir, Robin Nash, Alan Boyd, Marcus Plantin, David Taylor, Guy Freeman, Jonathan Beazley, Sue Andrew, Jonathan Glazier, Ben Kellett **Theme Music** It enjoyed a number of themes through the years, but the one everyone remembers was sung by Bruce Forsyth himself: 'Life is the name of the game,/And I wanna play the game with you/Life can be terribly tame,/If you don't play the game with two.'

Taking the 'My dad's better than your dad' idea to the limit, *The Generation Game* pitted two couples, each comprising of family members of different generations – dad and daughter, aunt and nephew, grandparent and grandchild. Shown a series of challenges by visiting experts – a potter's wheel, an auctioneer – and acting in a farce with bits of the script plastered all over the set, the contestants simply have to copy whatever they're shown, and the pair awarded the highest marks goes on to the final while another pair of couples go through the same ordeals. The winning pairs from each game go to a head-to-head and the winners of that round get to choose which of them will face the conveyer belt – a parade of prizes that always included luggage and a cuddly toy – which they then have to remember (with the help of the studio audience) in order to win the lot.

Simple, eh?

The idea came from a Dutch show called *Een Van De Aacht*, but became a vehicle for the talents of the king of variety, Bruce Forstyth. Accompanied by the toothsome Anthea Redfern (who became Brucie's wife), Brucie created a string of catchphrases during his tenure, including 'Good game, good game!', 'Give us a twirl' and 'Didn't they do well?', Bruce left the series with the Christmas 1977 edition. After a short run of compilations of the series' best bits, Bruce's replacement came in the form of the unique Larry Grayson, joined by Isla St Clair, who ruled Saturday nights until 1982.

At its peak, *The Generation Game* drew in over 23 million viewers (making it the highest-rated game show in British TV history). With the nostalgia trend in full swing by 1990, *The Generation Game* was resurrected with Brucie once more in the driving seat. A couple of episodes saw possible replacements standing in for the great man, Roy Castle and Jim Davidson. For some reason, Davidson became the prime choice when Forsythe once again tired of the show, and went on to host the show for seven years (one more than Bruce Forsythe's original run). Since 2002, the BBC has been experimenting with possible hosts to continue the series (two pilots are rumoured to have been recorded with Paul O'Grady, aka Lily Savage). We're sure it'll be back in some form or other in the future, but at the time of writing it's the waiting game at play.

The Gentle Touch

Crime Drama | LWT for ITV | episode duration 50 mins | broadcast 11 Apr 1980–24 Nov 1984

Regular Cast
Jill Gascoigne · *DI Maggie Forbes*
William Marlowe · *DCI Bill Russell*
Brian Gwaspari · *DI Bob Croft*
Paul Moriarty · *DS Jake Barrett*
Kevin O'Shea · *DS Peter Philips*
Nigel Rathbone · *Steve Forbes*
Derek Thompson · *DS Jimmy Fenton*

Creator Brian Finch **Producer** Kim Mills, Jack Williams, Michael Verney-Elliott **Writers** Various, including Tony Wharmby, Geoff McQueen, P. J. Hammond, John Reardon, Christopher Hodson **Theme Music** Roger Webb

Inspired by the hit American series *Police Woman*, starring Angie Dickinson, *The Gentle Touch* was a true milestone in television programming, presenting viewers with their own first ever British policewoman in a lead role in a TV series (the BBC's ***Juliet Bravo*** reached screens just five months later). Jill Gascoigne played DI Maggie Forbes, a career policewoman who moves to work in CID. With her policeman husband Ray shot and killed in the line of duty in the first episode of the series, Maggie faces a dual challenge – to raise her son Steve single-handedly, and to challenge the traditional chauvinistic attitudes of the Metropolitan Police Force. Based at the Seven Dials Police Station in the heart of Soho, Maggie tackles a wide range of investigations, including (in one particularly memorable moment) dealing with a hand-grenade attack on her life that brought the fourth season to a close on a white-knuckle cliffhanger ending. Maggie's regular sparring partner was her boss, DCI Russell, a fair-minded if rather unapproachable officer from the old school of policing.

Jill Gascoigne's sensitive and intelligent portrayal of Maggie Forbes won the hearts of many viewers, not just the women who normally turned off police dramas, but also male viewers who enjoyed watching a heroine who was gutsy, glamorous and a heck of a lot more realistic than the jiggling catwalk models of ***Charlie's Angels***. *The Gentle Touch* came to an end after 56 episodes over five seasons – but that wasn't the end of Maggie Forbes. The following year, Jill Gascoigne joined the cast of a new, more action-oriented drama series called ***C.A.T.S. Eyes***, a programme that ironically was lambasted by critics for trying to be a British version of *Charlie's Angels*.

George and Mildred

Sitcom | Thames for ITV | episode duration 25 mins | broadcast 6 Sep 1976–25 Dec 1979

Regular Cast

Yootha Joyce · *Mildred Roper*
Brian Murphy · *George Roper*
Norman Eshley · *Jeffrey Fourmile*
Sheila Fearn · *Ann Fourmile*
Nicholas Bond-Owen · *Tristram Fourmile*
Roy Kinnear · *Jerry*
Reginald Marsh · *Humphrey*
Avril Elgar · *Ethel*
Gretchen Franklin · *Mum*

Creators/Writers Johnnie Mortimer and Brian Cooke **Producer** Peter Frazer-Jones **Theme Music** Johnny Hawkesworth composed the theme tune for the first two seasons, after which Roger Webb provided the new bouncy melody.

When the council issues a compulsory purchase order for their ***Man About the House*** Earls Court home, George and Mildred Roper decide to move onwards and upwards to suburbia – specifically to 46 Peacock Crescent, Hampton Wick. Mildred is delighted to be living in a nice middle-class environment where all of her dreams of social climbing can come true. George is steadfast in his determination to remain resolutely slovenly and working class, much to Mildred's shame and embarrassment. Their next-door neighbours are arch-snob Jeffrey Fourmile, his much nicer wife, Ann, and their adorable moppet/brat, Tristram. Other characters showing up every now and again included Mildred's rich-bitch sister, Ethel, and her dotty mum, played by future ***EastEnders*** actor Gretchen Franklin; George's work-shy mate, Jeffrey (the irrepressible Roy Kinnear); and sitcom stalwart Reginald Marsh (see also ***The Good Life*** and ***Terry and June***) in a traditional pompous role as Humphrey.

George and Mildred was regularly watched by 20 million viewers, a figure almost unimaginable today. Looking back at the programme, it's remarkable just how well the episodes have stood the test of time – undoubtedly due to the writing talents of the hugely prolific Mortimer and Cooke. Like most other sitcoms in the 1970s, *George and Mildred* was rewarded with a spin-off feature film in 1980 (not the best of its ilk, unfortunately) and plans were proceeding apace for a sixth TV season when series star Yootha Joyce tragically died on 24 August 1980, aged just 53. Her untimely death robbed an adoring public of one of its great comic performers; although Brian Murphy delivers his lines with finesse and aplomb, Joyce steals every single scene that she's in.

Get Some In!

Sitcom | Thames for ITV | episode duration 25 mins | broadcast 16 Oct 1975–18 May 1978

Regular Cast

Tony Selby · *Corporal Marsh*
David Janson · *Ken Richardson*
Robert Linsday, Karl Howman · *Jakey Smith*
Brian Pettifer · *Bruce Leckie*
Gerard Ryder · *Matthew Lilley*
Lori Wells · *Alice Marsh*
John D Collins · *Squadron Leader Baker*
Madge Hindle · *Min*
Jenny Cryst · *Corporal Wendy Williams*

Creators/Writers John Esmonde, Bob Larbey **Producers** Michael Mills, Robert Reed **Theme Music** Alan Braden produced a theme tune that combined a military-ish melody with lyrics that summed the show up: 'It's time for National Service lads, so Get Some In!'

In 1955, another intake of nervous young National Service-men are inducted into RAF Skelton. Much to their shock, they are faced with a monster of a commanding officer, the hectoring and bullying Corporal Marsh. Marsh despises pretty much all of the young men assigned to him, using every kind of insult under the sun to belittle them. Marsh dislikes Ken Richardson because he's a polite, middle-class grammar school boy; he loathes Scot Bruce Leckie; he has nothing good to say about wimpy vicar's son Matthew Lilley; and he particularly hates Teddy Boy Jakey Smith. Thankfully for the new recruits, Marsh isn't blessed with the sharpest of intellects, so one way or another the boys are able to run rings around their belligerent Commanding Officer. Later seasons saw the recruits training as nursing assistants and even working in an RAF hospital.

In the spirit of that other great ITV army sitcom ***The Army Game***, *Get Some In!* gave Robert Lindsay his first taste of fame before he took on ***Citizen Smith***, and later

Karl Howman, who went on to play Jacko in ***Brush Strokes***. Perhaps because National Service was ancient history by the mid-1970s, it didn't quite hit the meteoric heights of Esmonde and Larbey's greatest work, ***The Good Life***, but it's also been criminally left in the cold these last three decades.

A Ghost Story for Christmas

Anthology | BBC Two | episode duration 35–55 mins | broadcast 24 Dec 1971–25 Dec 1978

Principal Cast
Clive Swift · *Dr Black*
Robert Hardy · *Archdeacon Haynes*
Peter Vaughan · *Mr Paxton*
Joseph O'Connor · *Mr Abney*
Simon Gipps-Kent · *Stephen*
Paul Lavers · *Lord Peter Dattering*
Michael Bryant · *Reverend Justin Somerton*
Edward Petherbridge · *Sir Richard Fell*
Lalla Ward · *Lady Augusta*
Barbara Ewing · *Anne Mothersole*
Denholm Elliott · *The Signalman*
Kate Binchy · *Katherine*
Peter Bowles · *Peter*
John Stride · *Paul*

Producers Lawrence Gordon Clark, Rosemary Hill **Writers** Lawrence Gordon Clark, Robin Chapman, John Bowen, David Rudkin, Andrew Davies, from novels by M. R. James and Charles Dickens, with original scripts from Clive Exton, John Bowen

No Christmas is complete without a ghost story, and with the tinsel in one hand and a coffin lid in the other, the BBC tingled the nation's spines with a series of fondly remembered plays throughout most of the 1970s under variations of the above title (*A Christmas Ghost Story, An English Ghost Story . . .*). Dr Jonathan Miller had created the template in 1968 with an adaptation of *Whistle and I'll Come to You, my Lad* by M. R. James (Miller's version sported the slightly briefer name *Whistle and I'll Come to You*). Billed as a tale of 'solitude and terror', the beautifully shot production was a note-perfect exercise in atmospheric filmmaking – from eerie opening shots of a deserted beach, to Michael Hordern's uncomprehending horror as he comes face to face with the forces of the supernatural. The film was never less than hauntingly effective, although aficionados of M. R. James still complain that Miller added psychological undertones to the story that were simply not present in the original, even going as far to suggest that the ghost may simply be a fantasy brought on by overwork, anxiety or even sexual impotence.

Three years later, Lawrence Gordon Clark of the BBC's General Features Department followed up Miller's film with his own adaptation of another James story, *The Stalls of Barchester*, which was the first to be broadcast under the infamous *A Ghost Story for Christmas* banner. A tale of sinister black cats, cursed timbers and vengeful spirits, the film failed to re-create either the general eerie ambience or the crescendos of terror evoked by Miller's original, but for the festive thrill seeker, the best was yet to come. Clarke looked again to the stories of M. R. James and in 1972 produced a film that rivalled Miller's vision, both in its outstanding cinematography and its sheer power to chill the blood. *A Warning to the Curious* saw a return to the bleak, open beaches of *Whistle and I'll Come to You*, and from the moment that a superbly harried Peter Vaughan invokes the ire of a vengeful, remorseless spirit, the viewer barely dares breathe out until the curse has worked to its unnatural conclusion.

Christmas Night 1973 was greeted with *Lost Hearts*, another classic that ensured that the image of two eviscerated children, swaying in ghastly unison to ethereal hurdy-gurdy music, would be etched into memories well past Boxing Day – even decades later. Indeed, it wouldn't be until Hideo Nakata's *Ringu* (1998) that the device of simply painting a child a different colour would prove so devastatingly effective.

The Treasure of Abbott Thomas (1974) continued the run of successful scares, although the following year's *The Ash Tree* was a disappointing affair. David Rudkin's script drifting off into psychosexual ruminations while the production's dénouement relied on an abundance of latex spiders that in recent times have raised more giggles in art house cinemas than hairs on the back of the neck. Despite the pleas of cult TV enthusiasts, it is not without reason that this play remains the only one of the 'classic' productions not to have been repeated since the early 1980s.

The following year saw the first changes to the series format with the decision to adapt a non-M. R. James story – namely Charles Dickens' *The Signalman*. Denholm Elliott is on top form as the haunted railwayman facing a fate as inexorable as the trains he regulates, his performance effortlessly stealing what is essentially a two-hand play. Although the film lacks the aura of sheer malevolence that pervades the earlier productions, its horrifying conclusion is no less effective for it.

The final two entries in the canon are more forgettable affairs, altogether abandoning the classic ghost stories with their period trappings in favour of two new plays with modern-day settings. The first, *Stigma* (1977), offers an updated version of the 'unleashed curse' format as workmen remove an ancient stone to reveal a skeleton, ritually slain. As Kate Binchy starts to bleed with the same wounds, the emphasis is again on subtext and metaphor rather than chills and thrills, and digging further beneath both stone and skeleton, it doesn't take a *Late Review* panellist to unearth themes of female sexuality, menstruation and the sacred feminine.

The show's final outing was the lamentable *The Ice House* in 1979. The only production not to be directed by Lawrence Gordon Clark – and it shows – it all but ignored traditional notions of scaring the audience in favour of a weak and wilfully perplexing fantasy-cum-mystery. What is the secret of the mysterious health spa? What horror lurks in the eponymous ice house? Are siblings Clovis and Jessica really engaged in the sexual relationship they seemed keen to imply? Or are they really spirit projections of a strange nocturnal flower? Questions abounded, but sadly the only one worth answering was 'Is there anything better on ITV?' and this entry proved to be the death knell for the series.

Ironically, the following year, something better *was* on ITV, as the newly defected Lawrence Gordon Clark directed a version of M. R. James' *Casting the Runes* for Yorkshire Television. Although sturdy and entirely respectable, the production failed to recapture the atmosphere of the BBC originals, due in no small part to being shot largely on videotape rather than film, and with the script again updating events to a modern setting. The age of the classic TV ghost story, it seemed, was dead, although examples of the series have been periodically exhumed on both terrestrial and satellite channels, held up as exemplars of the genre.

Ghostwatch

Telefantasy | BBC One | episode duration 90 mins | broadcast 31 Oct 1992

Cast
Michael Parkinson, Sarah Greene, Mike Smith, Craig Charles · *Themselves*
Brid Brennan · *Pamela Early*
Michelle Wesson · *Suzanne Early*
Cherise Wesson · *Kim Early*
Gillian Bevan · *Dr Lin Pascoe*

Producer Ruth Baumgarten **Writer** Stephen Volk **Theme Music** Philip Appleby

Ghostwatch still lingers in the minds of the people who saw it on its one and only screening on Halloween 1992. Its reputation has extended through word of mouth, from those who enjoyed it as a bit of spooky hokum to those who prefer not to talk about it. They're the ones who thought it was all real and are still harbouring a grudge, bless them.

To be fair though, despite the show being promoted as a drama on the front cover of the *Radio Times*, those that believed it to be a documentary possibly didn't read the accompanying article inside. They might not have understood why it was being shown in BBC One's drama slot *Screen One* and, if so, they almost certainly missed the 'written by' credit at the start. The presence of a trusted broadcaster like Michael Parkinson can't have helped either; it was he, after all, who told them it was all live, an investigation into a suspected haunting incident at the home of the Early family. Mike Smith took viewers' calls (on 01 811 8181, significantly the same familiar number used on Saturday morning kids' TV), while his wife, Sarah Greene, was on site with comedian Craig Charles in 'haunted' Foxhill Drive. Charles exchanged witty banter with the assembled crowds in the street and Greene conducted sensitive interviews inside the house with the distressed mother and daughters.

Gradually, as the programme went on, the light-hearted nature of the programme turned more sinister. Just as it began to look like it had all been the work of one of the daughters, the spectral presence of the ghost, 'Pipes', began to make blink-and-you'll-miss-it appearances in the house. When the programme reached its terrifying climax, Greene appeared to have been trapped with the poltergeist under the stairs of the haunted house, and 'something' began to affect the cameras and lights of the TV studio, leaving a bewildered Michael Parkinson wandering a chaotic studio while Mike Smith tried in vain to get some kind of reassurance that his wife was still alive. . .

When the drama came to a close, having peaked at 11 million viewers, the BBC switchboards were flooded with calls, and few of them were happy. Some were convinced that the programme had been real, desperate to know if the presenters were still alive. Some were simply furious that the BBC had been so complicit in an attempt to con them into believing in the occult. The tabloids were quick off the mark to report the public outrage at the irresponsible BBC, with one *Sun* headline screeching 'Viewers blast BBC's "sick" ghost hoax'. Five days after the broadcast, another tabloid told of a teenage boy who'd committed suicide because of *Ghostwatch* (strangely though, the coroner made no mention of this in the eventual inquest), and one woman tried to gain compensation from the programme makers for her husband's soiled trousers.

It was, of course, not live, but a work heavily influenced by the writing of Nigel Kneale, who had terrified audiences in the 1950s with ***Quatermass*** and whose own play ***The Stone Tape*** had played with the idea of recording ghosts in the 1970s. Writer Stephen Volk had originally pitched the idea as a six-part drama in which the final episode was set in a live studio environment, but when his producer began to get cold feet over the idea of six hours worth of science fiction (a genre the Corporation remained resolutely against for decades), it was reformatted as a one-off play. Thanks in part to the controversy that surrounded it after its original broadcast, the BBC has made little mention of it ever since. Thanks to the BFI, though, it eventually resurfaced on DVD and has lost none of its bite as a drama, though it's unlikely to convince anyone else that it's real any more.

Gimme Gimme Gimme

Comedy | Tiger Aspect Productions/Hartswood Films for BBC Two/One | episode duration 30 mins | broadcast 8 Jan 1999–14 Dec 2001

Regular Cast
Kathy Burke · *Linda La Hughes*
James Dreyfus · *Tom Farrell*

Rosalind Knight · *Beryl Merit*
Brian Bovell · *Jez*
Beth Goddard · *Suze*
Simon Shepherd · *Himself*
Elaine Lordan · *Sugar Walls*
Doña Croll · *Norma*

Creator/Writer Jonathan Harvey **Producers** Sue Vertue, Jon Plowman, Mark Chapman, Peter Bennett-Jones (executive), Matthew Francis **Writer** Jonathan Harvey **Theme Music** Bjorn Ulvaeus and Benny Anderson of ABBA are the men behind the original song 'Gimme! Gimme! Gimme! (A Man After Midnight)', which was murdered, karaoke-style, by the show's stars Kathy Burke and James Dreyfus.

Drop-dead gorgeous Linda La Hughes lives in her glamorous apartment in north London with her gay actor flatmate Tom Farrell. Men's jaws hit the floor whenever she walks past - she spends all of her time trying to fend off the studs who throw themselves at her (all the ones who aren't obviously just a bunch of homos). Her downstairs neighbour - despite being married to a very plain woman - clearly has the hots for her too. Her famous sister, Sugar Walls, is a TV and glamour actress who isn't anywhere near as good-looking as Lynda, but who still pops over for a visit every now and again.

It must be said, of course, that Lynda happens to have the most deluded perspective on life ever. In reality, Lynda is neither the sharpest knife in the drawer, nor the most attractive of women - she thinks she's a supermodel, but in fact she looks more like Olive from ***On the Buses***. Her flatmate Tom is a vain, preening, lazy and totally untalented 'actor' whose main claim to fame was one line of dialogue with 'Dame Patsy Palmer' on ***EastEnders***. In short, they make ideal flatmates for each other. They're both so unrelentingly horrid that it's for the best that they've each found someone equally unpleasant to shout and scream their insults at. Completely oblivious to the vile behaviour of Tom and Lynda is their landlady Beryl, who lives in the flat above. An ageing prostitute, Beryl's comings and goings are often even more surreal and disturbing than Tom and Lynda's. In the downstairs flat are picture-perfect couple Jez and Suze - Tom and Lynda both fancy the pants off Jez and loathe Suze in equal measure.

The adventures of the hilariously vile flatmates included such memorable moments as an escaped murderer with a scar fetish (Phil Daniels) shacking up with Lynda (and eventually showing more of an interest in Tom); Tom's romance with the actor from a discount sofa warehouse TV commercial; a tragically lonely Millennium Eve which left the two of them passed out on the settee as their party guests deserted them; and the sudden arrival of Tom's all-time favourite TV heart-throb, ***Peak Practice***'s 'Sir' Simon Shepherd. The series ended with the mismatched pair finally throwing caution to the wind and having a farewell shag before Tom left London to work on his fantasy acting job on ***Crossroads***.

Written by Jonathan Harvey - famous for gay teen romance movie *Beautiful Thing* (1996) and more recently a writer for ***Coronation Street*** - *Gimme Gimme Gimme* was a vile, unpleasant and yet extremely funny sitcom that was definitely an acquired taste for many viewers. Both Kathy Burke and James Dreyfus turned in performances of over-the-top grotesqueness that took the breath away, with Burke in particular stealing every single scene that she was in. After two seasons on BBC Two, *Gimme Gimme Gimme* became so popular that it was transferred to BBC One for its final run of six episodes.

Girls on Top

Sitcom | Witzend Productions/Central for ITV | episode duration 25 mins | broadcast 23 Oct 1985-11 Dec 1986

Regular Cast
Dawn French · *Amanda Ripley*
Jennifer Saunders · *Jennifer Marsh*
Ruby Wax · *Shelley Dupont*
Tracey Ullman · *Candice Valentine*
Joan Greenwood · *Lady Carlton*

Creators/Writers Ruby Wax, Dawn French, Jennifer Saunders **Producers** Allan McKeown (executive), Paul Jackson **Theme Music** Squeeze's Glenn Tilbrook and Chris Difford composed the theme tune to the series, which was sung by the main members of the cast.

Described at the time as a female version of ***The Young Ones***, *Girls on Top* was a frantic, frenetic comedy series that boasted an all-female lead cast, female writers and a higher than average gag count. The Girls were four flatmates renting top-floor rooms in Kensington from their aristocratic yet distinctly odd landlady, romantic novelist Lady Carlton. Candice Valentine was a dizzy blonde pathological liar who used her good looks, charm and light-fingered tendencies to get what she wanted out of life. Shelley Dupont was an abrasively loud-mouthed, pushy and generally obnoxious American, surviving in the UK thanks to her wealthy daddy rather than any ability in her chosen career of acting. Amanda Ripley was a placard-waving feminist, environmentalist and anti-nuclear campaigner, dismissive of all men but secretly longing for the right chap to sweep her off her feet. Finally, Jennifer Marsh was one of Amanda's childhood friends, a dim creature without two brain cells to rub together.

Whereas *The Young Ones* revelled in anarchic, stream of consciousness plotting, *Girls on Top* featured much more traditional linear plots, with much of the comedy coming from another round of bitching, back-stabbing and general unpleasantness between all four of the women. The quality of the writing and performances was plain for all to see - ***French and Saunders*** launched their own BBC series just six months after the end of *Girls on Top*; Ruby Wax featured in her own unique series of chat shows/ interviews as well as script-editing ***Absolutely Fabulous***;

and Tracey Ullman was so successful that she upped sticks and left the UK after the first season in order to launch her own series (the same show that introduced ***The Simpsons*** to the world) – Candice getting bumped off thanks to a hereditary medical complaint (or was she murdered by her flatmates? We never found out . . .).

Guest stars flocked to take part in the series, with Robbie Coltrane, Hugh Laurie, Harry Enfield and even ***Soap***'s Katherine Helmond dropping in. Sensibly, the antics of the *Girls on Top* came to an end after just 13 episodes, with everyone involved realising that they had probably mined all of the comedy they could out of these bizarre characters.

Give Us a Clue

Panel Game | Thames for ITV/Grundy for BBC | episode duration 25 mins | broadcast 1979–1991 (ITV), 10 Nov–19 Dec 1997 (BBC)

Cast
Michael Aspel, Michael Parkinson, Tim Clark · *Host*
Lionel Blair, Una Stubbs, Liza Goddard, Christopher Blake, Julie Peasgood · *Team Captains*

Producers Various, including Juliet Grimm, David Clark, Robert Reed, Keith Beckett, Danny Greenstone **Theme Music** For the first few seasons, the theme to *Give Us a Clue* was 'Chicken Man' by Alan Hawkshaw – exactly the same piece of stock music as was being used over on BBC One as the ***Grange Hill*** theme tune. Realising how odd this was, a second, bland and totally forgettable melody was introduced for Michael Aspel's last episodes in the host's chair. When Parky took over, a third theme was launched that incorporated the names of the host and team captains in a ghastly (yet oddly unforgettable) vocal: 'Give us a Clue! With Michael Par-kin-son . . . Liza Goddard . . . and Lionel Blair!'

It's not often that the name of a specific product, service or item replaces its real name and becomes the noun associated with it – for instance, everybody knows what you're talking about if you say you've got the Hoover out. Similarly, whenever families get together to play parlour games (ghastly name!) with each other, odds are somebody will suggest a round of '*Give us a Clue*' rather than charades. In this TV version of the classic family favourite, a team of four men would compete against four women to see which sex was better at using a bizarre series of signs and mimes to convey the title of a famous book, film, play or TV show to their colleagues.

For the first few years, a member of the public joined three celebrities on each team, but producers soon realised that nobody at home cared less if Betty Smith from Nottingham was any good at miming if something was a book (put palms of hands together then open them like the pages of a book), a play (use index fingers to draw imaginary theatre curtains opening), a TV show (use index fingers to draw a box) or a film (look through a 'lens' formed with one fist whilst 'cranking a handle' near the opposite ear with the other hand). So *Give us a Clue* rapidly became a straight fight between four celebrity 'girls' and four celebrity 'boys', with two points to be won on each round if the correct title was guessed by the teammates of the person playing within 60 seconds, one point if they got it within two minutes. There were no actual prizes for the winning team, simply the satisfaction of knowing you'd proven that yours was the superior gender.

Titles to be mimed varied in difficulty from an easy one like '*Jaws II*' through to something really tricky (or riddled with innuendo) like 'My Ding-A-Ling'. The two resident team captains usually got the most difficult titles to mime, with Lionel Blair in particular being given songs or books with 20 or 30 word-titles to mime on more than one occasion. Following the departure of original captain of the ladies Una Stubbs, Liza Goddard took over for the remainder of the show's original run. *Give us a Clue* eventually came to an end on ITV in 1991, but (as is so often the case) it's impossible to keep a good format down for long, and the programme was briefly resurrected for the BBC daytime schedules in 1997 with team captains Christopher Blake and Julie Peasgood being posed questions by Tim Clark.

Gladiators

Game Show | LWT for ITV | episode duration 50 mins | broadcast Oct 1992–1 Jan 2000

Regular Cast
Ulrika Jonsson, John Fashanu, Jeremy Guscott · *Hosts*
John Anderson · *Referee*
John Sachs · *Commentator*
Michael Van Wijk · *Wolf*
Michael Willson · *Cobra*
Mike Lewis · *Saracen*
Kim Betts · *Lightning*
Michael Ahearne · *Warrior*
Helen Haddison · *Panther*
Diane Youdale · *Jet*
Nikki Diamond · *Scorpio*
Jefferson King · *Shadow*
Sandy Young · *Phoenix*
Alex Georgijev · *Hawk*
Kimbra Standish · *Flame*
James Crossley · *Hunter*
Mark Griffin · *Trojan*
Bernadette Hunt · *Falcon*
Judy Simpson Cook · *Nightshade*
Mike Harvey · *Bullet*
Kate Staples · *Zodiac*
Suzanne Cox · *Vogue*
Sharron Davies · *Amazon*
Carlton Headley · *Raider*
Eunice Huthart · *Blaze*
Mark Smith · *Rhino*
Tina Andrews · *Laser*
Warren Furman · *Ace*

Jennifer Stoute · *Rebel*
Jaine Omorogbe · *Rio*
Tami Marie Baker · *Fox*
Radosav Nekic · *Kahn*
Lize Van Der Walt · *Gold*
Alison Paton · *Siren*
Pauline Richards · *Rocket*
Darren Crawford · *Diesel*
John Seru · *Vulcan*

Producers John Kaye Cooper (executive), Nigel Lythgoe, Ken Warwick

Unashamedly American-styled, glitzy, glamorous, more than a little bit camp, *Gladiators* was a highly popular fixture in the ITV Saturday night schedules for nearly a decade. Recorded in Birmingham's vast National Indoor Arena, *Gladiators* combined the same kind of games and challenges seen in ***It's a Knockout*** with the razzmatazz, high production values and heroes and villains you'd normally associate with WWF Wrestling. Presented by former weathergirl Ulrika Jonsson and ex-footballer John Fashanu (replaced in later seasons by Jeremy Guscott), *Gladiators* was a competition that stretched the competitors' sinews, muscles and Lycra outfits to the limit.

Each week, two male and two female contenders would battle against each other and the resident team of muscle-bound Gladiators (each given a suitably silly name such as 'Flame', 'Hawk' or, most memorably, 'Wolf' – the most senior of the 'Glads' by quite a few years, and the show's boo-hiss panto villain). In a series of challenges with equally silly names (like 'Atlaspheres', 'SkyTrak' and 'Hang Tough'), contenders would score points by knocking the Gladiators off an elevated platform, by climbing up a wall quickly, or simply by hanging on to a gigantic swinging pendulum suspended 10m (30ft) in the air for 60 seconds. All the time, the Gladiators would do their best to return the favour by holding the contenders back, chucking them off the top of a padded pyramid, or (in many peoples' favourite round, 'Duel') clobbering them with a padded giant cotton wool bud called a pugil stick. After a number of rounds, the contenders would compete against each other in the Eliminator, an assault course containing scramble nets, death slides, rope climbs and a fiendishly painful conveyor belt travelling very quickly in the wrong direction. The number of points that the contenders had earned throughout the early rounds would determine how much of a head start the leader would get in the Eliminator – the first person to complete the course would win the contest, to return in the semi-finals and then possibly the finals. The most famous winner of *Gladiators* was Liverpudlian Eunice Huthart, whose determination and bubbly personality won her a temporary place on the Gladiators' team the following year (as 'Blaze').

Although *Gladiators* was based on the already-established *American Gladiators* (which was screened late-night in some ITV regions), the UK version was, surprisingly, an altogether bigger-budget affair. With the popularity of the programme spreading around the globe, a series of *International Gladiators* programmes were produced, with a selection of the Gladiators and the best contenders from a number of countries all travelling to the glamorous celebrity-studded mecca of Birmingham.

In 2005, ITV1 unveiled *Celebrity Wrestling*, in which D-list celebs battled it out in rounds tenuously related to wrestling and more than a little inspired by *Gladiators*. An embarrassing flop, it was soon relegated to Sunday mornings where hopefully everyone would forget about it.

Going Live!

Children's Magazine | BBC One | episode duration 180 mins | broadcast 26 Sep 1987–17 Apr 1993

Regular Cast

Phillip Schofield, Sarah Greene · *Hosts*
Paul Smith · *Gordon the Gopher*
Trevor Neal and Simon Hickson, Nick Ball and James Hickish · *Comedy Performers*
Phillip Hodson · *Agony Uncle*
Annabel Giles · *Fashion Expert*
Emma Forbes · *Cookery Expert*
Mark Chase · *Reporter*

Producers Chris Bellinger, Cathy Gilbey **Theme Music** Peter Gosling

Saturday morning kids' television matured in 1987 when the framing devices of shops and superstores were binned in favour of an honest embracing of the joys of live TV. Host Phillip Schofield had presented weekday children's TV from a small booth affectionately known as the 'Broom Cupboard' as well as doing the TV reviews for ***Saturday SuperStore*** in its final year. He was joined by another popular children's TV personality, Gordon the Gopher, a very basic glove puppet that squeaked, yet became one of the show's greatest assets as he was able to comment on the guests in ways the human adults couldn't (yawning in the background, quivering with fear as a little dog tried to take a chunk out of his nose). *SuperStore* refugee and former ***Blue Peter*** presenter Sarah Greene played 'big sister' to the family unit, and for most of its run they were accompanied by comedy duo Trevor and Simon, the 'naughty little brothers' whose daft characters, like the Singing Corner ('swing your pants' while singing Donovan's 'Jennifer Juniper') or the terrifying Moon Monkey, whose crazy, and possibly drug-fuelled, rave motions would only be comprehensible to the older teens, while younger kids and their parents just thought he was a freak in a body stocking. Trevor and Simon won the hearts of millions and became regulars on the student circuit for years afterwards (when they took a year off from the show, Nick Ball and James Hickish sadly failed to achieve the same kind of success).

Though the structure of the programme was similar to that of both of its BBC predecessors – cartoons, pop music and interviews – there were subtle changes that made *Going Live!* the perfect magazine programme for a Saturday morning. The live phone-ins were retained from *SuperStore*, though now with a new number thanks to BT's reshuffle of the regional numbers ('081-811 8181' we sang each week). The addition of kids in the studio meant that the presenters could always cut to a primed question if things went a bit awry, though that didn't help poor Sarah Greene when a teenager called Elliot Fletcher called in to ask pop family Five Star 'Why are you so f**king crap?' It's a clip now played again and again on TV compilations, but we do wish they'd let the clip play on just a little more; the horrified voice of the next caller saying 'I heard that!' is heartbreaking. Young Master Fletcher started a trend for telephonic abuse, however, as a short while later Simon Roberts phoned in to tell Matt Bianco that they were 'a bunch of wankers'.

It wasn't all unbridled profanity, though. There were some really strong educational sections that didn't feel like an extra morning of school: Emma Forbes stepped in to do the cookery slots pioneered on ***Multi-Coloured Swap Shop*** by Delia Smith (though the segments were more memorable for those times when Schofield ballsed things up); Philip Hodson returned from *SuperStore* to comment on viewers' problems in a section called 'Growing Pains', which never shied away from the genuine worries of the kids, from eating disorders to bullying and child abuse; and 'All About Me' was a forerunner of the video diary – even though some kids chose that bit to go and get a second helping of Coco Pops, it was still a major step forward for children's programming. Which is more than can be said for *Double Dare* and *Run the Risk*, messy, gunge-fuelled game shows fronted by Peter Simon that were just ***TISWAS***-meets-*Cheggers Plays Pop* on a larger scale.

Going Straight

Comedy | BBC Two | episode duration 30 mins | broadcast 24 Feb–7 April 1978

Regular Cast
Ronnie Barker · *Norman Stanley Fletcher*
Richard Beckinsale · *Lennie Godber*
Patricia Brake · *Ingrid Fletcher*
Nicholas Lyndhurst · *Raymond Fletcher*
Rowena Cooper · *Shirley Chapman*
David Swift · *Mr McQween*

Creators/Writers Dick Clement and Ian La Frenais **Producer/Director** Sydney Lotterby **Theme Music** Tony Macauley, Dick Clement, sung by Ronnie Barker

Though Ronnie Barker had decided to bring ***Porridge*** to a close before audiences tired of it, there was still enough enthusiasm for his character that a spin-off series was proposed that would show Fletcher newly released from prison and trying to become rehabilitated. The first episode of *Going Straight* was almost a replay of the original pilot, with Fletch once again on a train journey with Mr Mackay, though this time their shared journey is just a coincidence. While this introduction to Fletch's new life serves as an effective cushioner, replaying for the last time his verbal sparring with the stern prison officer, from then on it's clearly a different series. Fletch's beloved wife Isobel has ran off with another man, leaving him to support his gormless son Raymond and daughter Ingrid (once again played by Patricia Brake). It's almost home from home, though, as his old cell-mate Lennie (Richard Beckinsale), now working as a long-distance lorry driver, spends most of his time at Fletch's house after starting a relationship with Ingrid. Meanwhile, Fletcher's parole officer, Mrs Chapman, despairs of his flippancy and inability to find work, though she eventually places him in a position as a night porter.

Despite temptations from all sides, Fletch just about manages to remain on the straight and narrow, and in the final episode of the series acts as both best man and father of the bride when his daughter Ingrid marries Lennie.

Lasting just six episodes and gaining very respectable ratings, *Going Straight* was, nevertheless, a pale reflection of the show that spawned it and a second series was not forthcoming. Rather confusingly, the next time audiences saw Fletcher, he was back behind bars for *Porridge the Movie* (1979), which was set some time before he and Lennie were released.

The Golden Girls

Sitcom | Witt-Thomas-Harris for NBC (shown on Channel 4) | episode duration 25 mins | broadcast 14 Sep 1985–9 May 1992 (USA)

Regular Cast
Bea Arthur · *Dorothy Zbornak*
Rue McClanahan · *Blanche Devereaux*
Betty White · *Rose Nylund*
Estelle Getty · *Sophia Petrillo*
Herbert Edelman · *Stan Zbornak*
Harold Gould · *Miles Webber*
Bill Dana · *Uncle Angelo*
Richard Mulligan · *Dr Harry Weston*

Creator Susan Harris **Producers** Paul Junger Witt, Tony Thomas, Susan Harris, Marc Sotkin (executive), Kathy Speer, Terry Grossman, Marsha Posner Williams, Paul Bogart, Winifred Hervey, Mort Nathan, Barry Fanaro, Jeffrey Ferro, Fredric Weiss, Eric Cohen, Martin Weiss, Robert Bruce, Terry Hughes, Tom Whedon, Philip Jayson Lasker, Gail Parent, Tracy Gamble, Richard Vaczy, Don Seigel, Jerry Perzigian, Nine Feinberg, Jamie Wooten, Marc Cherry, Mitchell Hurwitz **Writers** Various, including Susan Harris, Winifred Hervey, Barry Fanaro, Mort Nathan, Kathy Speer, Christopher Lloyd, Robert Bruce, Terry Grossman, Tracy Gamble, Richard Vaczy, Martin Weiss, Gail Parent, Mitchell Hurwitz, Tom Whedon, Jamie Wooten, Marc Sotkin, Don Siegel, Jerry Perzigian **Theme Music** 'Thank You for Being a Friend', music by George Aliceson Tipton, lyrics by Andrew Gold, performed by Cynthia Fee

'Picture the scene – Channel 4, 1986 . . .' A freshly launched TV network buys a new comedy series from the USA, little realising that it was going to become one of its most popular shows. Who would have thought that a programme about four little old ladies with a cheesecake habit would have lasted for 180 episodes? The answer is anybody who spotted that *The Golden Girls* was in fact a female twist on the already successful ***Last of the Summer Wine*** format, transposed to the USA and blessed with the writing talent of ***Soap*** supremo Susan Harris. In short, it was a programme that simply couldn't fail.

Miami Beach, Florida – the American equivalent of Eastbourne, a seaside resort somewhat cruelly labelled 'God's waiting room' because of the high proportion of senior citizen residents who move there to retire to a warmer climate. The four core characters in the series are all women of a 'certain age' – gruff divorcee Dorothy, her octogenarian mother Sophia, randy Southern belle Blanche and not-quite-all-there Rose. Throughout the series, viewers watched in delight as these women faced the challenges of growing older together with good grace, good humour and more than their fair share of cheesecake.

Bea Arthur and Rue McClanahan had worked together previously in Arthur's sitcom *Maude*, which had been a huge success in the early 1970s for the CBS network (although strangely it didn't make much of an impression in the UK). Although Arthur reprised her somewhat world-weary performance from *Maude*, McClanahan switched from playing a slightly dim character in that show to a man eater. Ironically, Betty White had been famous in the States for portraying a man-hungry vamp on ***The Mary Tyler Moore Show***, so portraying the ditzy Rose was a big career shift for her too. Only Estelle Getty was a relative unknown. She was in fact two months younger than Bea Arthur, who played her daughter, relying upon a charming performance and some top-notch make-up to 'age her up'.

The Golden Girls refused to consign older women to a metaphorical shelf; the women in this series were always on the lookout for romance – indeed, Blanche was often shown juggling the affections of more than one 'gentleman caller' at the same time. Perhaps the relationship with the most humour and greatest poignancy was the one between Dorothy and her mother Sophia. With Sophia unable to moderate anything she says (owing to a stroke), Dorothy constantly had to fight to maintain her sense of humour and simultaneously indulge her mother's little eccentricities or regular rambling stories about her past (which inevitably began with, 'Picture the scene – Sicily, 1923 . . .' or some such place/date).

After seven hugely successful seasons, Bea Arthur decided that enough was enough and chose not to renew her contract. However, the network was reluctant to lose such a popular series from their schedules and created a spin-off entitled *The Golden Palace*. When Dorothy moves to Atlanta to be with her new husband, Lucas, the remaining three 'girls' decide to sell their house and invest their money in a run-down Miami Beach hotel called the Golden Palace. Helping them run the place are manager Roland (Don Cheadle) and chef Chuy (Cheech Marin). Sadly, the magic didn't survive the relocation from domestic to work-based comedy, and the show was canned after just 24 episodes. A much more successful spin-off (in the USA at least) was *Empty Nest*, which featured former *Soap* star Richard Mulligan as recent widower Dr Harry Weston. Lasting an amazing seven series, *Empty Nest* saw the arrival of one of the *Golden Girls* into its cast when *The Golden Palace* shut its doors, with Estelle Getty reprising her role as Sophia. Although both *The Golden Palace* and *Empty Nest* received screenings on Channel 4, neither grabbed the attention of audiences in the way their parent series had done.

Back in 1983, Bea Arthur had starred in a particularly ill-thought-out and short-lived remake of ***Fawlty Towers*** called *Amanda's*. As if to enact revenge, ten years later ITV served up *Brighton Belles*, Carlton TV's attempt to re-create the *Golden Girls* magic with a British cast. Despite casting Sheila Hancock, Wendy Craig, Sheila Gish and Jean Boht, the series failed to make best use of the talent available and was written off before it had even begun, possibly because the viewers and critics knew they were being fed second-hand ideas and very probably because the original characters were a very hard act to follow.

The Good Life

See pages 340–2

The Good Old Days

Variety | BBC One | episode duration 45–60 mins | broadcast 20 Jul 1953–31 Dec 1983

Cast

Don Gemmell, Leonard Sachs · *Master of Ceremonies*
Plus many hundreds of guests

Producer Barney Coleman **Theme Music** Not a theme as such, but each show would feature the signature ditty, 'The Old Bull and Bush'.

Awash with nostalgia for the songs your grandmother used to sing, *The Good Old Days* re-created the glory of music-hall variety each week, with performers and audience members alike dressing up in Victorian garb and stepping back a century. Celebs of the day would take on the roles of the stars of yesteryear, as singers, dancers, comedians and all manner of other good, clean acts. Don Gemmell was the show's first master of ceremonies, introducing the acts, but it's Leonard Sachs that everyone remembers, each relished word of his sesquipedalian speeches and indulgent introductions would be greeted by whoops of appreciation from the audience.

Each edition was recorded in the City Varieties in Leeds, one of the last standing music halls in the country, while the Players' Theatre Company and BBC Northern Dance Orchestra performed some of the bigger numbers. *The Good Old Days* ran for an astonishing 30 years until the curtain finally came down on its performances for one last time.

The Goodies

See pages 343–5

Goodness Gracious Me

Comedy | BBC Two | episode duration 30 mins, plus specials | broadcast 12 Jan 1998–19 Feb 2001

Principal Cast
Meera Syal, Sanjeev Bhaskar, Kulvinder Ghir, Nina Wadia, Dave Lamb

Producers Jon Plowman (executive), Anil Gupta **Writers** Various, including Meera Syal, Sanjeev Bhaskar, Kulvinder Ghir, Nina Wadia, Dave Lamb, Richard Pinto, Anil Gupta, Sharat Sardana **Theme Music** Herbert Kretzmer and Dave Lee composed the original song 'Goodness Gracious Me' (which got to No. 4 in the charts in November 1960, performed by Peter Sellars and Sophia Loren) – this version was arranged by Sanjeev Bhaskar and Nitin Sawhney.

It's very easy to over-use the adjective 'groundbreaking' when describing innovations in television programme-making, but *Goodness Gracious Me* was a true groundbreaker – the first comedy series written by, for and examining the culture of, second generation Asians living in Britain today. The team (who had scored a big hit with *Goodness Gracious Me* on radio when unconvinced TV execs passed on the idea first time round) set out their stall quite clearly with the programme's title and theme music. 'Goodness Gracious Me' has been a stock catchphrase (spoken in a dodgy Asian/Welsh accent) used by generations of people whenever a politically incorrect stereotype of British Asians is required. In fact, it was legendary comic Peter Sellars, 'blacked-up' and putting on that very same accent on the original song 'Goodness Gracious Me', that started the whole thing off – so when this team of young comics replaced Sellars' dodgy pseudo-Asian delivery with a gruff Northern voice, their hijacking and reclamation of that original joke was complete.

For much of the time, *Goodness Gracious Me* was a competent but never spectacular sketch show, with many good characters and scenarios, but only a few that were real classics. Some of their best sketches included the Kapoor family (pronounced Cooper, of course – shades of Hyacinth Bucket), determined to out-English the most English of English people; a father who's convinced that every innovation and great person in history came from India; and, of course, the justly famous 'Going for an English' sketch. Perhaps the reason why this one sketch (in which a group of drunken Asians finish off their boozy night out by going for an English, determined to sample the blandest items on the menu) became so popular is because it provided laughs for viewers whether they'd been a customer in an Indian restaurant, worked in one, or never even sampled the delights of a Chicken tikka masala.

Goodness Gracious Me was making a real impact on audiences by the end of its third season, so much so that the whole team went on a nationwide sell-out theatre tour. Critics loved the programme too, with a decent smattering of awards going the team's way over the course of the series. It therefore came as quite a surprise when *Goodness Gracious Me* ground to a rather sudden halt in 2001, with Bhaskar and Syal jumping ship to create their even more successful follow-on series ***The Kumars at No. 42***.

Goodnight Sweetheart

Comedy | Alomo Productions for BBC One | episode duration 30 mins | broadcast 18 Nov 1993–28 Jun 1999

Regular Cast
Nicholas Lyndhurst · *Gary Sparrow*
Victor McGuire · *Ron Wheatcroft*
Michelle Holmes, Emma Amos · *Yvonne Sparrow*
Dervla Kirwan, Elizabeth Carling · *Phoebe Bamford*
Christopher Ettridge · *PC Reg Deadman*
David Ryall · *Eric Bamford*
Yvonne D'Alpra · *Mrs Bloss*
David Benson · *Noel Coward*

Creators Laurence Marks, Maurice Gran **Producers** John Bartlett, Nic Phillips, Allan McKeown, Claire Hinson **Writers** Laurence Marks and Maurice Gran, Gary Lawson, John Phelps, Sam Lawrence, Geoff Rowley, Paul Makin, Paul Alexander, Simon Braithwaite **Theme Music** Ray Noble, Jimmy Campbell, Reg Connelly and Rudy Vallee – a World War Two standard that inspired the title of the series

'It's a love story between a guy of 30 and a woman of 80 who might be dead . . .' Thus said series co-creator Maurice Gran about *Goodnight Sweetheart*. A hugely popular and oddly heart-warming series from the team behind such hits as ***Shine on Harvey Moon***, ***The New Statesman*** and ***Birds of a Feather***, it was a sitcom unlike any other. For a start, not many other comedy series portray an adulterer and bigamist in a sympathetic fashion, and, furthermore, few prime-time comedy series boasted a concept that could have come straight out of an episode of ***Doctor Who***.

Amiable TV repairman Gary Sparrow discovers one day that a nearly hidden alleyway – Duckett's Passage – is, in fact, a time portal that links present-day London with the Blitz-ravaged streets of 1940. Exploring the past, he meets chirpy barmaid Phoebe and falls in love with her. Trouble is, Gary is already married, to the prickly and ever so slightly disappointed Yvonne. Realising that his time-travelling exploits will allow him to have the best of both

Continued on page 346

The Good Life

Richard Briers and Felicity Kendal as Tom and Barbara Good.

On his 40th birthday, Tom Good walks out on his middle-ranking career in the marketing department of JJM Plastics to completely change his life. With the support of his loving wife, Barbara, Tom quits the rat race entirely and attempts to live an entirely self-sufficient lifestyle. Tom and Barbara dig up the large garden behind their suburban house and use the land to plant crops and raise a variety of farmyard animals – much to the dismay of their friends and next-door neighbours Jerry and Margo Leadbetter. Although Jerry and Margo support the Goods in their ambitions, the everyday practicalities of self-sufficiency grate against their desperately middle-class aspirations and lifestyle.

It came as no surprise at all when ***The Young Ones*** royally ripped into *The Good Life* for being 'so bloody nice'. The definitive 1970s sitcom, it stood for all the values and concerns of that decade that the more aggressive and self-obsessed anarchists were reacting to and rebelling against. Life in the UK of the early 1970s was more unstable and unsettling than it had been for decades: oil shortages, power cuts, strikes and a mandatory three-day working week all took their toll on peoples' quality of life. As a direct result, many ordinary families began to think about what they could do to provide for themselves, should things get even worse, and the Goods are perhaps an extreme example of that. Needless to say, the concept of self-sufficiency was clearly on many people's minds in 1975, with the post-apocalyptic science fiction series ***Survivors*** (covering similar themes in a much more 'serious' way) starting to be broadcast just 12 days after the first episode of *The Good Life*.

Although it did tap into many of the concerns facing audiences of the 1970s, *The Good Life* was more than just a product of its time – it was perhaps the most consistently funny sitcom that the BBC has ever produced. Although Esmonde and Larbey's scripts were exceptional, the programme's massive ratings and longevity are undoubtedly down to the accomplished, career-defining

Sitcom
BBC One
Episode Duration: 30 mins
Broadcast: 4 Apr 1975–10 Jun 1978

Regular Cast
Richard Briers · *Tom Good*
Felicity Kendal · *Barbara Good*
Penelope Keith · *Margo Leadbetter*
Paul Eddington · *Jerry Leadbetter*
Reginald Marsh · *'Sir'/ Andrew*
Moyra Fraser · *Felicity – Andrew's Wife*

Producer John Howard Davies

Creators/Writers John Esmonde and Bob Larbey

Theme Music Burt Rhodes

performances by the four leads. Richard Briers had already been a massive star in programmes such as ***The Marriage Lines***, but it was his charismatic and totally believable portrayal of the ever-so-slightly annoying Tom that he will forever be associated. Similarly, Briers' on-screen wife, Barbara, provided a career-making role for luminous actress Felicity Kendall, a woman whose rear view became, for a time, even more famous than the person it was attached to. Tom and Barbara's relationship was so utterly real and grounded in the everyday little details that it went beyond realism into the realm of fantasy wish-fulfilment. Indeed, to many people even today, Tom and Barbara Good remain the absolute epitome of the ideal married couple.

On the surface, Margo and Jerry seemed to have a much less affectionate relationship, but that initial impression couldn't have been further from the truth. Yes, Margo does bully her husband to an unbearable degree, but the reality is that Jerry craves Margo's attention and simply couldn't function without her, either on a personal or, especially, on a professional level. Margo's talents and abilities at supporting Jerry and keeping them both in the lifestyle to which they have become accustomed is one of her great strengths. Her biggest weakness is, of course, her innate snobbery and the sense of disappointment and personal betrayal she feels as the result of the changes Tom and Barbara have made to their lives. By throwing aside everything that she values and turning their backs on her capitalistic lifestyle, Margo believes that the Goods are actually cocking a snook at her and Jerry. Thankfully, though, Margo soon comes to terms wlth the changes to her Surbiton neighbourhood and relations mostly return to normal.

The Good Life was more than just a product of its time – it was perhaps the most consistently funny sitcom that the BBC has ever produced.

Paul Eddington's performance as Jerry is a masterstroke of sublime understatement, proving without question that he was one of the greatest 'straight men' ever seen in British sitcoms. However, everyone remembers the louder, more obviously 'funny' partner in a comedy double-act, and in Margo, Penelope Keith provided one of the greatest comedy performances ever recorded in a British TV studio. Margo was initially written as more of a supporting character, but when the writers and producer noticed just how magnificent Keith's performance was, subsequent episodes boosted her role, thereby creating a television legend. Forever battling against Miss Mountshaft for the lead role in the musical society's latest production, or doing her best to butter up the very well-connected Mrs Doomes-Patterson, Margo's middle-class aspirations are a joy to behold. Unsurprisingly, Keith won a BAFTA in 1977 for Best Light Entertainment Performance and Best Funny Lady in the ***Multi-Coloured Swap Shop*** awards. With hindsight, it's almost impossible to imagine how Margo might have turned out had Hannah Gordon won the role (as was originally mooted).

Most people who have ever watched *The Good Life* will undoubtedly have their favourite episode, but particularly noteworthy ones include 'Backs to the Wall' (in which Margo, dressed from head to toe in bright yellow waterproofs, helps out in the garden when Tom damages his back), the utterly hilarious 'Silly, But It's Fun' (in which all four neighbours get very tiddly during their Christmas party) and the heartbreaking 'Anniversary' (when the Goods' house is vandalised). The show boasted a very important fan when it was revealed that it was the Queen's favourite TV programme – in fact, a special final episode was recorded in 1978 with HM sitting in the audience in Television Centre. *The Good Life* became extremely popular in the USA too, where it was transmitted on the PBS network for many years. The title was changed for USA broadcasts to *The Good Neighbors* in order to avoid confusion with an earlier, short-lived sitcom on NBC with the same title, starring Larry Hagman and Donna Mills.

The Young Ones did have a point, however. *The Good Life* was 'bloody nice'. But it was also pragmatic enough to accept that Tom and Barbara had a very hard life too. On one occasion a heavy storm devastates their crops and leaves them facing a very lean winter; on another, Margo forces Tom to sell his pigs to an abattoir and then, when she realises her error, Tom has to buy look-alikes to spare his neighbour from the fact that the originals are now bacon. We tend to forget, also, that as a consequence of tackling someone for stealing his valuable crops, Tom ends up with a criminal record and serves time for contempt of court. And who would ever have expected Margo to berate Jerry for ignoring her sexual advances with a line like 'That's the last time I play the whore for you!'

Funnier, saucier and much more accomplished than practically every single other sitcom made during the 1970s, *The Good Life* richly deserves every accolade that it has received.

Funnier, saucier and much more accomplished than practically every single other sitcom made during the 1970s, *The Good Life* richly deserves every accolade that it has received (including reaching the top ten in the 2004 Britain's Best Sitcom survey). Creators John Esmonde and Bob Larbey did the sensible thing and quit after just 30 episodes while the show was ahead (finishing with that special Royal Command Performance for the Queen and Prince Philip). Although fewer people may nowadays be actively considering a self-sufficient lifestyle, there will always be a place in most people's hearts for Tom, Barbara, Jerry and Margo – oh, and Geraldine the goat.

The Goodies

Bill Oddie, Graeme Garden and Tim Brooke-Taylor.

Often regarded as little more than a juvenile take on ***Monty Python's Flying Circus***, few programmes have been as harshly judged as *The Goodies*. Not a sitcom, not a sketch show, not simply a series of pastiches of films (though *Jaws* (1975), *Saturday Night Fever* (1977) and *Close Encounters of the Third Kind* (1977), all got the Goodies treatment), *The Goodies* is both more than and (sadly) less than the sum of its parts. When it was good, it was head-achingly funny – when it was bad, it was just painful.

The Goodies had its genesis in a show called *Broaden Your Mind*, a kind of pre-*Python* sketch show starring Tim Brooke-Taylor, Graeme Garden, Graham Chapman, Terry Jones, Michael Palin, Nick McArdle, Jo Kendall and Roland MacLeod. Running for two series from October 1968 to December 1969, a guest star on the show was a certain Bill Oddie. Soon Oddie had teamed up with Brooke-Taylor and Garden and a long-lasting comedy team was formed.

The basic format of the series (stretching over nine seasons and 74 episodes) was that the Goodies were men for hire, ready, willing and able to do 'anything, anytime' for a paying client. Tim was the slightly effete Tory-supporting patriot, Bill the anarchy-loving socialist prone to taking visionary trips thanks to his special sherbert, and Graeme was the archetypal mad inventor whose schemes and plans were often the cause of the gang's (mis)adventures. Many of the episodes featured their custom-made three-seater vehicle – the trandem.

Many fans will tell you that the early episodes were the best of the bunch, but it's unlikely you'd agree as, in all fairness, very few of those early seasons matched the brilliance that the team were later capable of. An exception was the award-winning and genuinely marvellous 'Kitten Kong' (which snagged the Silver Rose of Montreux award in 1972), in which a tiny white fluffy kitten called Twinkle grows to epic size (courtesy of another of Graeme's mad schemes) and goes on a destructive rampage through London – knocking the dome off the top of St Paul's, demolishing the Post Office Tower and squashing Michael Aspel. Equally memorable moments from early episodes include a send-up of telly sci-fi in 'Invasion of the Moon

Comedy
BBC Two/ITV
Episode Duration: 30 mins
Broadcast: 8 Nov 1970–13 Feb 1982

Regular Cast
Tim Brooke-Taylor, Graeme Garden, Bill Oddie

Creators Tim Brooke-Taylor, Graeme Garden, Bill Oddie

Producers John Howard Davies, Jim Franklin, Bob Spiers

Writers Graeme Garden, Bill Oddie (with Tim Brooke-Taylor)

Theme Music The first theme ('Take a little good advice . . .') came from the collaboration of Bill Oddie and Michael Gibbs, though it's Bill Oddie's solo-penned theme ('Goody goody yum yum') that most people remember.

Creatures' and the epic Christmas panto special 'The Goodies and the Beanstalk'. But despite an uneven hit rate, *The Goodies* themselves were enormously popular. They made guest appearances on other shows and they even had several UK chart hits ('The Funky Gibbon' reached number 4 in March 1975, 'Black Pudding Bertha' number 19 in June of the same year).

It wasn't until the boys launched their fifth series on the UK public in early 1975 that the classic episodes began to come thick and fast: 'Kung Fu Kapers' saw the boys learning the ancient Lancashire martial art of Ecky Thump, utilising black puddings to clobber people around the head; in 'Bunfight at the OK Tea Rooms', the trio duel with squeezy tomato ketchup bottles over the valuable resources of a Cornish clotted cream mine; and 'The End' presented just the three regulars trapped in their office, endlessly waiting for their next client to arrive. The most iconic episode of this era was 'The Goodies Rule O.K.', in which our heroes have to defeat an attempt by an assortment of children's TV characters to take over the country. Appearances by Sooty, the Wombles and Bill and Ben were hilarious in themselves, but surely everybody who ever saw this episode will never be able to forget the sight of a gigantic Dougal from ***The Magic Roundabout*** chasing the Goodies through an ornamental maze.

The enthusiasm and sheer verve that *The Goodies* displayed in ridiculing any target in sight (though never with any hint of cruelty) often managed to carry the audience through any under-par instalments. Everything from the advertising industry to the Cod War was lampooned, even such venerable institutions as the Scouts, the Salvation Army, Tony Blackburn and the TV series *Black Beauty* weren't safe from having the mickey taken lock, stock and barrel. Like a well-directed banana-skin joke, the house style of *The Goodies* was to signpost the jokes a mile off, tell you they're coming, and then stand back and watch as the jokes are delivered with every possible ounce of gusto that they can manage. Depending on the episode, this approach either leaves viewers gasping with laughter, or sighing at the predictability of it all. Thankfully, on most occasions, the gags worked marvellously. The perfect example of this approach comes in an episode called 'The Goodies and Politics', in which Tim has (for a very convoluted series of reasons!) adopted a persona called 'Timita', a combination of Margaret Thatcher and Evita. Filming her Party Political Broadcast, Timita was shown visiting two sobbing girls working at a supermarket checkout, who are concerned that the public won't vote for her, simply because Timita is a woman. Breaking into a song instantly recognisable to anyone who's ever seen the musical *Evita*, Timita trills, 'Don't cry for me, Marge and Tina. . . .' Just sublime.

An unexpected gap of three years between seasons seven and eight led the Goodies to question just how committed the BBC were to their programme. Despite the fact that the show was still being transmitted at 9.00 p.m. on BBC Two, many people considered *The Goodies* to be little more than fodder for hyperactive children. Still, putting aside their qualms about their working environment, Tim,

Graeme and Bill managed to produce possibly their finest series yet, touching on topics as varied as ***It's a Knockout*** (with Graeme providing an uncanny impression of Eddie Waring); the Common Market with its butter mountains, wine lakes and fears of nuclear conflict; the Olympics, *Watership Down* (1978) and World War Two.

One episode of this series, 'Saturday Night Grease', attracted a formal complaint from Mary Whitehouse's National Viewers and Listeners' Association. She protested that a scene featuring Tim trying to squeeze into a pair of impossibly tight trousers – while only clad in a pair of underpants bearing a carrot motif – was bordering on the obscene. Of course, the three Goodies saw this complaint from Mrs Whitehouse as the ultimate vindication of their work and were delighted. If Mary Whitehouse had seen beyond the rude pants, she would have enjoyed a marvellously topical parody of both *Grease* (1978) and *Saturday Night Fever*. Tim, smitten with the lovely 'Livvy' Newton-John, tries to model himself on her on-screen beau John Travolta. When he's asked if he's seen Travolta in *Saturday Night Fever*, Tim exclaims that of course he hasn't – the film has an X certificate and he might be frightened watching it . . . a perfect example of tapping into the zeitgeist and simultaneously undermining the icons of 'cool' by just being terribly fluffy and British.

Finally tiring of the struggles they were having with BBC management, the three Goodies jumped ship to an eager ITV. Unfortunately, the Goodies' style of humour just didn't seem to fit in a commercial environment and their unique brand of anarchic humour came to a halt after just one more season, with notorious axeman Michael Grade terminating their three-year contract. Thankfully, less than a year later, the trio were reunited when they provided the voices to cartoon series ***Bananaman*** – Graeme playing the eponymous hero who gains his super powers Popeye-style after eating a banana; Tim playing Bananaman's weedy alter-ego Eric; and Bill playing the wisecracking sidekick Crow. Garden and Brooke-Taylor have since become regular panellists on the Radio 4 comedy 'I'm Sorry, I Haven't a Clue', while Oddie changed tracks to become the BBC's ornithology and wildlife expert, fronting shows such as *Birding with Bill Oddie* and *Britain Goes Wild*.

The Goodies has rarely been repeated or seen again for the past 20 years. People have speculated upon the reasons for this, but one factor that has to be taken into account is the reputation the programme has for displaying some of the worst excesses of '70s attitudes. In particular, several episodes contain instances of racist phrases and jokes that would be completely unacceptable to audiences today. Having said that, the one episode that is regularly identified as being particularly unacceptable to modern audiences ('South Africa') is, in fact, clearly a blatant attack on apartheid and racism. Yes, it does contain words that modern viewers would wince at, but its heart is very much in the right place. It's a real shame that preconceived notions about the programme have apparently denied modern audiences the enjoyment of a show that contains some of the finest moments of TV comedy ever seen.

worlds, Gary spends his time flitting back and forward between the past and the present, only ever confiding in his best friend Ron about the precise nature of what's going on. At the end of the series, the portal inexplicably collapses on VE Day, leaving Gary trapped in his life with Phoebe and their son Michael and poor Ron to explain to Yvonne exactly what's happened.

Goodnight, Mr Tom

Drama | Carlton for ITV | duration 110 mins | broadcast 25 Oct 1998

Cast

John Thaw · *Tom Oakley*
Nick Robinson · *William Beech*
Annabelle Apsion · *Mrs Beech*
Thomas Orange · *Zacharias Wrench*
William Armstrong · *Dr Stelton*
Geoffrey Beevers · *Vicar*
Mossie Smith · *Mrs Fletcher*
Peter England · *Michael Fletcher*
Ivan Berry · *George Fletcher*
Harry Capehorn · *Edward Fletcher*
Merelina Kendall · *Mrs Holland*
Marlene Sidaway · *Mrs Webster*
John Cater · *Dr Little*
Denyse Alexander · *Mrs Little*
Avril Elgar · *Mrs Ford*
Michael Cronin · *Matthew Parfitt*
Pauline Turner · *Annie Hartridge*
Thomas Russell · *David Hartridge*
Stephanie Perry · *Ginnie Thatcher*
Tanya Perry · *Carrie Thatcher*
Geoffrey Hutchings · *Ralph Briggs*
Mary Healey · *Gladys Rigby*
Charles Kay · *Mr Greenway*

Producers Ted Childs, Lewis Rudd, Ray Frift (executive), Chris Burt **Writer** Brian Finch, from the novel by Michele Margorian **Theme Music** Carl Davies

William Beech is a quiet, anxious and lonely boy from a poor background, who is evacuated during World War Two to the lovely village of Little Weirwood, along with a set of equally deprived London kids. They are allocated to various families in the village, with the exception of William, whom nobody wants. He finds himself nevertheless allocated to Tom Oakley who, as well as being cantankerous, doesn't see why at his age he should be lumbered with one of the 'London lot'.

Although gruff and unsentimental, Tom slowly takes to William and teaches him to read, as well as treating lightly William's occasional bed-wetting, so that slowly they become friends. Just when William has come to love Tom and to appreciate his gentle and beautiful surroundings, his mother demands his return. The comparison with the countryside William has become used to and wartime London is stark and for William frightening, for his mother (Annabelle Apsion) has become a fearsome figure, viewing the world outside of her basement tenement as 'filth'.

One of John Thaw's last great roles sees him in sentimental form as the old widower Tom, who grows so attached to the boy that he becomes alarmed when he does not hear from him and so sets out for London, where he comes face to face with the horror that has now become William's world.

This television adaptation of Michelle Magorian's award-winning novel (which picked up 13.8 million viewers on first transmission) deals realistically with the themes of loneliness, loss and redemption, as Tom and William come to terms with their own demons, eventually returning to the certainties and calm of an idyllic village life.

Gormenghast

Fantasy Drama | WGBH Boston/BBC Two | episode duration 60 mins | broadcast 17 Jan–7 Feb 2000

Principal Cast

Jonathan Rhys-Meyers · *Steerpike*
Celia Imrie · *Lady Gertrude*
Ian Richardson · *Lord Groan*
Neve McIntosh · *Lady Fuchsia*
Christopher Lee · *Flay*
Richard Griffiths · *Swelter*
Cameron Powrie, Andrew Robertson · *Titus Groan*
John Sessions · *Dr Prunesquallor*
Fiona Shaw · *Irma Prunesquallor*
June Brown · *Nannie Slagg*
Zoë Wanamaker · *Clarice Groan*
Lynsey Baxter · *Cora Groan*
Stephen Fry · *Professor Bellgrove*
Warren Mitchell · *Barquentine*
Spike Milligan · *Death*
James Dreyfus · *Professor Fluke*
Gregor Fisher · *Fly*
Eric Sykes · *Mollocks*
Windsor Davies · *Rottcodd*
Steve Pemberton · *Professor Mule*
Olga Sosnovska · *Keda*
Martin Clunes · *Professor Flower*
Phil Cornwell · *Professor Shred*

Producer Estelle Daniel **Writer** Malcolm McKay, from *Titus Groan* and *Gormenghast* by Mervyn Peake **Theme Music** Richard Rodney Bennett

It's a tricky business trying to make TV or movie adaptations of epic sprawling fantasy novels – Frank Herbert's *Dune* series has been attempted (rather badly) on a couple of occasions, and it took until the advent of realistic CGI for Tolkien's *Lord of the Rings* books to be more than a fantasy on a producer's storyboard. Mervyn Peake's *Gormenghast* novels are equally challenging to realise, with their vast collection of grotesque characters and an enormous city-sized castle for a setting. BBC Two's first big drama for a new millennium was therefore perhaps an odd choice, but thankfully everyone concerned just about managed to achieve their lofty goals.

Gormenghast is the story of a young kitchen servant called Steerpike, a devious and resourceful chap who manages (through a combination of plotting, skulduggery and sheer villainy) to scramble his way up the social order inside Gormenghast Castle. En route, Steerpike encounters all kinds of strange people, most of them suffering from a variety of personality defects at best, the advanced stages of madness at worst. Shown in four episodes, *Gormenghast* wasn't an easy programme to either watch or enjoy, with many people getting quickly lost in the overwhelming deluge of characters, plots and settings. Perhaps best enjoyed by people who had already familiarised themselves with Peake's novels, *Gormenghast* can only really be judged as a partial success, notable mostly for proving categorically that the BBC was still able to produce drama that didn't involve vets, doctors or policemen. Oh, and *Gormenghast* reminded people of one other thing – that actress June Brown is even better at playing other roles than she is at portraying everyone's favourite chain-smoking Bible basher Dot Cotton/Branning in ***EastEnders*** (for further evidence, see also ***The Duchess of Duke Street***).

The Governor

Drama | La Plante Productions/Yorkshire TV for ITV | episode duration 45 mins | broadcast 14 May 1995–18 Jun 1996

Regular Cast
Janet McTeer · *Helen Hewitt*
Derek Martin · *Gary Marshall*
Ron Donachie · *Russell Morgan*
Dave Nichols · *'Jumbo' Jackson*
Eamonn Walker · *Snoopy Oswald*
Sophie Okonedo · *Moira Lavitt*
Jeremy Sheffield · *Dr Thomas*
Mal Whyte · *John Bunny*
Martin Herdman · *Damon O'Keefe*
David Barrass · *Tom Doughen*
John Flanagan · *Brian Langham*
Steven Hartley · *Billy Howel*
Christine Moore · *Mavis O'Connell*
James Malahide · *Paul Kynman*
Eric Allan · *Governor Lyons*
Terry O'Neill · *Victor 'Tarzan' Braithwaite*
Jake Abrahams · *Brian Samora*
Charlotte Cornwell · *Annette Bullock*
Craig Charles · *Eugene Buffy*
Idris Elba · *Officer Chiswick*
Pat Laffan · *Governor Syons*
John Ringham · *Judge Simms*
Philip Elsmore · *Mr Winchwood*
Gillian McCutcheon · *Mrs Winchwood*
Alec Linstead · *Norman Sewell*
Anthony Brophy · *Winchwood*

Creator/Writer Lynda La Plante **Producers** Steve Lanning (executive), Lynda La Plante **Theme Music** Joe Campbell, Paul Hart

Renowned TV scriptwriter Lynda La Plante has returned to the theme of a woman making her way in a traditionally all-male environment in many of her TV dramas (***Prime Suspect*** and ***Widows***). In *The Governor*, La Plante dumped her lead character Helen Hewitt into the heart of perhaps the toughest of all-male environments – a high-security men's prison. Helen becomes the first-ever female governor of Barfield, and is given the task upon arrival of trying to rebuild trust between inmates and staff following a disastrous riot. Although Helen is quite modern-minded and progressive in her views on rehabilitation and prison reform, she's no lily-livered liberal pushover – towering over most of the inmates and fiercely determined, she's more than capable of looking after herself. Well, with *most* of the men . . . this is a high-security prison for violent murderers and rapists, after all. Helen faces just as many challenges from her own staff, died-in-the-wool traditionalists who resent her presence and are happy to undermine her new regime at any opportunity.

The Governor ran for two seasons, and although not up with the very finest of La Plante's work, it was nevertheless powerful, thoughtful and challenging drama. The series was notable for giving a major role to an actor called Derek Martin, who for many years had carved a career out for himself as a stuntman or background artist. Today, he's best known as the head of the Slater family in ***EastEnders***. Even braver casting came in the form of ***Red Dwarf*** star Craig Charles, who took a role as an inmate not long after being imprisoned himself on an unproven allegation of rape.

Grace and Favour

See ARE YOUR BEING SERVED?

Grandstand

Sports | BBC TV/BBC One | episode duration c.60–420 mins (average 300 mins) | broadcast 11 Oct 1958–present

Regular Cast
Peter Dimmock, David Coleman, Frank Bough, Des Lynam, Steve Rider, Bob Wilson, Helen Rollason, Sue Barker, David Icke, John Inverdale, Hazel Irvine · *Presenters*

Producers Various, including Dave Gordon, Carl Hicks, Peter Allden, Paul Armstrong, Michael Cole (editors), Ken Burton, Martin Hopkins, Jonny Bramley, Helen Kuttner, Paul Davies, Sharon Lence **Theme Music** Specially composed for the show, the *Grandstand* theme tune was written by Keith Mansfield.

Grandstand is the world's longest-running live sports programme and has been a fixture of Saturday afternoons

on the BBC for almost 50 years. The format has barely changed since the first edition – a studio-bound presenter links live coverage from a number of different BBC outside broadcast units scattered across the UK. Everything from horse racing through to rugby league, test cricket matches, boxing and rugby (both league and union) have been covered over the years, with national events such as the Grand National from Liverpool's Aintree racecourse and the University Boat Race on the Thames uniting the whole country around their televisions.

The most iconic element of *Grandstand* has always been its coverage of football, from the pre-match pontificating of Football Focus (initially Football Preview) through to regular updates throughout the afternoon of goals as they're scored and the eventual Final Score roundup at around 4.45 p.m. For 20 years, ITV produced a rival show, *World of Sport* (1965–85, hosted by Eamonn Andrews and Dickie Davies), which covered many of the sports that the BBC didn't traditionally handle, such as darts, wrestling, snooker and motor sports, such as motorbike racing. Just as *Grandstand* had Football Focus, so *World of Sport* had *On the Ball* (hosted by Brian Moore and Jimmy Hill, later spun off to a standalone programme after *World of Sport*'s demise) and later *Saint and Greavsie*, presented by the eponymous Ian St John and Jimmy Greaves.

Grange Hill

See pages 350–5

Ground Force

Factual/Lifestyle | Bazal/Endemol for BBC Two/One | episode duration 30 mins, plus specials | broadcast 19 Sep 1997–Jul 2005

Regular Cast

Alan Titchmarsh, Charlie Dimmock, Tommy Walsh, Kirsty King, Will Shanahan · *Presenters*

Producers David Bernath (executive – America episodes), Carol Haslam, John Thornicroft, Michael Robins **Theme Music** Jim Parker composed the theme, which was performed (along with much of the incidental music for the show) by one of the world's most famous brass bands, the Black Dyke Mills Band.

Gardening programmes have been a staple of the TV schedules since time immemorial, but until the late 1990s, they'd always been fairly staid affairs, littered with long incomprehensible Latin plant names and lugubrious presentation. When ***Changing Rooms*** single-handedly revitalised one of the country's favourite pastimes (DIY), it was inevitable that a programme that showed people how to transform their gardens from derelict wasteland to a lush tropical paradise in just two days would soon appear. In order to provide some much-needed continuity with the established roster of gardening shows, Alan Titchmarsh was roped in as chief designer and presenter for *Ground Force*. Joining him were hard-working geezer Tommy Walsh and flame-haired bra-free tomboy Charlie Dimmock, who was always pottering around with her water features. Her complete lack of awareness about her own ample charms only added to the number of viewers tuning in to admire this most unlikely of sex symbols.

The format of *Ground Force* was fairly simple – a relative or friend of that week's selected 'victim' would ensure that they were away for the weekend, giving the team two clear days to work on transforming the garden. This being Britain, the weather would rarely cooperate, leaving the team struggling to achieve their aims while being ankle-deep in mud and shivering from gale force winds and horizontal rain. As the victim of the make-over returned to their home, the team would hide in the garden and then surprise the gob-smacked home-owner who, by this stage, would usually be in tears of admiration and joy over their new pergola and decking. *Ground Force* rapidly gained an enthusiastic following and as a consequence switched to BBC One in 1998.

Many special editions of the programme were staged, the first of which saw the team heading to South Africa to makeover Nelson Mandela's own garden. On 25 August 2002, another special episode was transmitted, detailing the team's work on a small patch of derelict land in New York – less than a year after the 9/11 attacks, this proved to be an emotional edition, and forged the way for 13 *Ground Force America* specials (made as a co-production with BBC America) in which the team weaved their magic on the back yards of our colonial cousins. Another special edition featured the construction in her home town of Weston Super-Mare of a tribute garden to the murdered TV presenter Jill Dando – many of her friends and family lent a hand, including Sir Cliff Richard.

Recognising the domination of the TV schedules by lifestyle/makeover programming, two special editions broadcast in 2000 saw the regular presenters of *Changing Rooms* swap places with their *Ground Force* colleagues in the highly amusing *When Changing Rooms met Ground Force* – needless to say, just because you happen to be good at stencilling, it doesn't necessarily follow that you'll be adept at handling a garden spade.

The public support for *Ground Force* was so strong that the series managed to survive the departure of Alan Titchmarsh in 2003, promoting Charlie and Tommy to co-hosts and introducing new 'workies' in the form of Kirsty King and Will Shanahan. However, with other members of the founding team announcing their decision to quit after the 2005 season, BBC bosses took the wise decision to call it a day for *Ground Force*.

The Grove Family

Serial Drama | BBC TV | episode duration 15–20 mins | broadcast 2 Apr 1954–28 Jun 1967

Regular Cast
Edward Evans · *Mr Bob Grove*
Ruth Dunning · *Mrs Gladys Grove*
Nancy Roberts · *Gran*
Peter Bryant · *Jack*
Sheila Sweet, Carole Mowlam · *Pat*
Christopher Beeny · *Lennie*
Margaret Downs · *Daphne*

Creator/Producer John Warrington **Writers** Roland and Michael Pertwee **Theme Music** Eric Spear

Although children's drama ***The Appleyards*** began transmission a year earlier, *The Grove Family* is generally recognised as the first British soap opera. Named after the BBC's Lime Grove Studios, the series invited viewers into the home of a lower middle-class family from Hendon, North London. Father ran his own small construction company while mother looked after their four children and her elderly mother, whose comically grumpy persona turned her into one of TV's first great characters.

Broadcast live at 7.30 p.m. on Fridays, only two episodes survive in the archives, though they are thought to be representative of the series as a whole. With performances that would be at home in Harry Enfield's newsreel sketches, the oh-so-jolly attitudes to life hardly bear comparison to the soaps of today (the 'dramatic' storylines in the extant episodes involved a shady door-to-door salesman and a family outing that results in a cheery call to the lifeguard). Still, it was watched by 9 million people and led to a spin-off film, *It's a Great Day* (1955). When father-and-son writing team Roland and Michael Pertwee requested a holiday after 147 episodes, the Beeb decided to retire the Groves permanently.

In 1965, Edward Evans later joined ***Coronation Street*** as Lionel Petty. Child actor Christopher Beeny would star in both ***Upstairs, Downstairs*** and *In Loving Memory* and eldest son Peter Bryant moved behind the camera to produce ***Doctor Who***, which would later star Roland Pertwee's other son, Jon. A one-off 1991 re-creation to mark the anniversary of Lime Grove Studios starred Sue Johnston, Leslie Grantham, Anna Wing and Nick Berry.

The Growing Pains of Adrian Mole

See THE SECRET DIARY OF ADRIAN MOLE, AGED 13¾

The Growing Pains of PC Penrose/Rosie

Comedy Drama | BBC One | episode duration 30 mins | broadcast 2 Sep–17 Oct 1975, 5 Jan 1977–30 Oct 1981

Regular Cast
Paul Greenwood · *PC Michael Penrose*
Bryan Pringle · *Sergeant Flagg*
Christopher Burgess · *Inspector Fox*
Catherine Chase · *WPC Dean*
Alan Foss · *PC Toombs*
David Pinner · *PC Buttress*
Tony Haygarth · *PC Wilmot*
Frankie Jordan · *Gillian Chislehurst*
Lorraine Peters · *Aunt Ida*
Allan Surtees · *Uncle Norman*
Avril Elgar, Patricia Kneale · *Millie Penrose*
Paul Luty · *Chief Inspector Dunwoody*
Penny Leatherbarrow · *WPC Brenda Whatmough*
Don McKillop · *Bill Chislehurst*
Maggie Jones · *Glenda Chislehurst*
Robert Gillespie, John Cater · *Merv*

Creator/Writer Roy Clarke **Producers** Douglas Argent, Bernard Thompson **Theme Music** Sung by Paul Greenwood

Another gentle Northern comedy from the pen of the prolific Roy Clarke (***Last of the Summer Wine, Open All Hours, Keeping Up Appearances***), *The Growing Pains of PC Penrose* introduced viewers to the character of young, naïve policeman Michael Penrose – nicknamed 'Rosie' because of his surname. Having left his home seaside town of Ravensby, Rosie gets a job at Slagcaster Police Station, where his life is made difficult by the gruff, bullying Sergeant Flagg – an old-fashioned copper determined to mould the next generation of Bobbies in his own image.

From the second season onwards, the programme was renamed simply *Rosie*, and showed his urgent return home to Ravensby to look after his 'seriously ill mother'. He soon discovers that his mum Millie is far from poorly – she just missed having him around to mother and manipulate. Her sister Ida, who lives in the Penrose family home along with her husband Norman, shares Millie's dismay at her beloved son's choice of profession. Norman and Rosie are often forced to gang together in a bit of male solidarity to fight back against the nagging might of the combined women in their lives. The other main characters in the series included Rosie's on-off girlfriend Gillian (who was far more desperate to get him down the aisle than he was), his best mate at work PC Wilmot, and Merv, his regular 'snout' into the decidedly lightweight Ravensby underworld. Eventually, Rosie manages to free himself from his suffocating mother's apron strings and moves into a flat-share with his mate Wilmot.

Far more of a wry examination of domineering Northern women and weak-willed, frustrated Northern men (see Nora Batty, Hyacinth Bucket, etc.) than a comedy about the police force, *Rosie* ran for 34 episodes over five seasons.

Grange Hill

Michael Sheard as the fearsome Mr Bronson.

In that most influential sitcom of the 1980s ***The Young Ones***, Ben Elton played a schoolboy in a sketch that drew the audience's attention to the fact that *Grange Hill* kids are the only ones in Britain who don't say the f-word. It's a fair point and a sound comeback for all of those parents who have complained about the supposedly bad language and the overall tone of the BBC's long-running school drama series. The problem for those parents is that it's also the only school in TV Land to use words like 'menstruation', 'heroin', 'pregnancy', 'homosexuality' and, er, 'arse' (admittedly that last one was only written down). It was the first show to admit that school days are not the best days of one's life, that underage sex happens (often) and that while some teachers were much better than the kids would ever admit, a few of them really are bastards – as are some of the children.

Comedy writer Phil Redmond had approached producers at ATV back in 1975 with an idea concerning a comprehensive school, but to no avail. Luckily, BBC producer Anna Home was much more accommodating and placed Redmond's series in the children's midweek schedule. *Grange Hill* began in 1978, following a new intake of pupils beginning their first term, almost every one of them instantly at odds with the BBC's traditional E. Nesbit-informed view of childhood. Trisha Yates is a sullen, lank-haired girl who seems uninspired by all around her, in contrast to Judy, a posh kid who's frightened of everything. Benny Green is an Afro-Caribbean lad from the nearby housing estate whose only interest is football. Justin, like Judy, is well spoken and middle class, but not at all happy about being lumped in with common kids. And then there is Tucker Jenkins, cheeky, not that academically minded but quick witted and charming when he wants to be. Tucker's mates, Benny, plus Alan and Tommy, follow him everywhere, which usually means running for their lives being chased by gangs from one of their rival schools, Brookdale.

Every school needs their bullies and for the first-years at Grange Hill that position was filled by Michael Doyle. We knew he was bad because of his tendency to call Benny Green a 'golly', although when Trisha Yates tried to be supportive to Benny she almost blew it by consoling him that he couldn't help being 'a nig nog'. That Benny pointed out that she couldn't help being a 'honky' showed both a great restraint on his part and the level of influence programmes like ***Love Thy Neighbour*** had already had on children of such an impressionable age. Still, racism was the first major issue to be tackled by *Grange Hill*, and not for the last time either.

In contrast to the stereotypical masters of *Whack-O!* and ***Billy Bunter***, the teachers were human too, and miraculously the kids sometimes acknowledged this. Head of Year One was nice Mr Mitchell, a cheery and good-humoured man who showed his disapproval of Tucker's mischief but rarely blew his top or raised his voice for more than a few seconds. As the kids moved up the years they got to meet more of the staff (as you do). In their second year the children encountered PE teacher Mr Baxter, nicknamed 'Bullet'. Balding with an impressively bushy beard, Baxter belonged to that breed of teacher who commanded respect but wasn't afraid to occasionally demand it too. All manner of mischief would instantly cease the second the cry went out: 'Bullet – leg it!' Although he was stern and gruff, the kids respected Baxter and never more so than when he discovered that fellow teacher Mr Hicks was a sadistic and violent bully. Witnessing a physical assault by Hicks on a pupil, Baxter punches the man and sneers, 'Slipped on the wet floor, did you?' before ushering the boys to safety.

Though there had been other head teachers in the first three years of the series, none of them left an impression as deeply ingrained as Mrs Bridget McClusky, who arrived in 1981 and quickly showed the children who was in charge. Her reign lasted until 1991 when she decided to take up a post helping foreign teachers. By this time, McClusky had become a popular figure around the school, although the sad faces at her departure were as much to do with regret at her leaving as the prospect of deputy head Mr Hargreaves taking her place.

Season eight saw the arrival of a man synonymous with the series, pompous disciplinarian language teacher Mr Bronson. A humourless, unforgiving man whom Grange Hill inherited after its merger with another comprehensive, Rodney Bennett, Bronson might have seemed like an ogre to the pupils had it not been for his vanity, or more accurately his toupee. Actor Michael Sheard has

Children's Drama
BBC/Mersey TV for BBC One
Episode Duration: 30 mins
Broadcast: 8 Feb 1978–present

Regular Cast
Todd Carty · *Peter 'Tucker' Jenkins*
Terry Sue Patt · *Benny Green*
James Jebbia, Paul McCarthy · *Tommy Watson*
George Armstrong · *Alan Hargreaves/ Humphries*
Michelle Herbert · *Trisha Yates*
Robert Craig-Morgan · *Justin Bennett*
Abigail Brown/Arundel · *Judy Preston*
Vincent Hall · *Michael Doyle*
Michael Percival · *Mr Tony Mitchell*
Denys Hawthorne · *Mr Starling*
Graham Ashley · *Mr Garfield*
Hilary Crane · *Mrs Jenkins*
Lucinda Duckett · *Ann Wilson*
Lindy Brill · *Cathy Hargreaves*
Mark Farmer · *Gary Hargreaves*
Linda Slater · *Susi McMahon*
Paul Miller · *Simon Shaw*
Mark Eadie/Chapman · *Andrew Stanton*
Sarah Sugarman · *Jessica Samuels*
Vivian Mann · *Antoni Karamanopolis*
Lesley Woods · *Madelin Tanner*
Michael Cronin · *Mr Geoff 'Bullet' Baxter*
James Wynn · *Mr Graham 'Sooty' Sutcliffe*
Sean Arnold · *Mr Llewelyn*
Brenda Cavendish · *Mrs Schubert*
Sheila Chandra · *Sudhamani Patel*
Ruth Davies · *Penny Lewis*
Jill Dixon · *Miss Pauline Clark*
Robert Hartley · *Mr Keating*
Peter Moran · *Douglas 'Pogo' Patterson*
Mark Baxter · *Duane Orpington*
Brian Capron · *Mr Stuart 'Hoppy' Hopwood*
Lucinda Gane · *Miss Terri Mooney*
Graham Ashley · *Mr Garfield*
Neville Barber · *Mr John Curtis*
Joanne Boakes · *Anita Unsworth*
Carey Born · *Karen Stanton*
Cheryl Branker · *Miss Susan Peterson*
Alex Kingston · *Jill Harcourt*
Rene Alperstein · *Pamela Cartwright*
Paula Ann Bland · *Claire Scott*
Susan Tully · *Suzanne Ross*
Mark Burdis · *Christopher 'Stewpot' Stewart*
David Lynch · *'Booga' Benson*
Gwyneth Powell · *Mrs Bridget McClusky*
Allyson Rees · *Miss Jenny Lexington*
Timothy Bateson · *Mr Thomson the Caretaker*
Paul Jerrico · *Mr Hicks*
Dulice Liecier · *Precious Matthews*
Nicholas Pandolfi · *Matthew Cartwright*
Jennifer Piercey · *Mrs Scott*
Mark Savage · *Gripper Stebson*

WEBSITE

www.grangehill.com – the official site that serves to support the current episodes. There is a separate section that looks at *Grange Hill*'s history and includes a superb Friends Reunited-style section where old characters give updates on their lives. All except Tucker, that is, who hasn't contributed anything; according to his mate Alan Humphries, Tucker thinks it's all 'a bit sad'.

since lapped up the adoration of fans by making numerous public appearances at cult TV events where he's been known to show off his party piece – miming along to Alice Cooper's 'School's Out'.

Any long-running drama has to be able to bring in new characters to keep the series fresh. The beauty of *Grange Hill* is that its cast reboots are built into the format, with no child ever outstaying his or her welcome. Though the faces change, many of the archetypes remain the same. In 1980, the series included its first entrepreneur, the modern equivalent of the scheming and skiving Billy Bunter of old: Pogo Patterson. One of Pogo's funniest attempts at skiving was when, having heard girls use the same excuse, he asked to be let off games because of 'the time of the month'. Pogo's successor was Gonch Gardener just as Tucker and Trisha were followed by Stewpot and Suzanne, Zammo and Annette, Tegs and Chrissy.

Michael Doyle and the sneering Madelin Tanner might have held the distinction of being Grange Hill's first school bullies, but it was Gripper Stebson who transformed the role from hobby to profession, extorting 50p pieces from other kids, pushing heads down toilets, beating up 'bun heads' and almost instigating the school's first race war until Bullet Baxter was finally able to put an end to his career and expel him. After Gripper, Imelda Davies and Mauler McCaul seemed no more than troubled attention seekers.

The series has never been afraid to court controversy by taking a mature approach to serious life issues. Any lesson on the danger of dares came with the death of Antoni Karamanopolis, who fell from the top of a shopping precinct. Another dare saw the demise of the loathsome Jeremy Irvine after a stunt at the swimming baths misfired. Some pupils have experienced the consequences of shoplifting, truancy, smoking and consumption of alcohol. But *Grange Hill*'s turning point came with the decision to face the rise of serious drug abuse among teenagers. The production team selected Zammo as their addict because he was so popular and was in the best position to illustrate how destructive drugs can be. His descent into the life of a junkie was so gradual that his sulky mood swings and secretive behaviour could have been hormonal rather than narcotic. The truth was finally revealed when Roland Browning found Zammo slumped in the back room of a penny arcade after a fix of heroin. Even after revealing Zammo's addiction the story wasn't over. First he was seen to deceive his mother, his best friend Kevin and his girlfriend Jackie before he was finally arrested and forced to undergo counselling. The production team worked with ***Newsround*** and campaign group Drugwatch on *It's Not Just Zammo*, a discussion programme highlighting the dangers of drug and solvent abuse, while a pop single called 'Just Say No' combined flat vocals and a rather naff arrangement to make the same point. As a result of the single, the

Grange Hill has never been afraid to court controversy by taking a mature approach to serious life issues.

cast also travelled to Washington DC to meet anti-drug campaigner Nancy Reagan.

Aside from drug abuse, there were other 'issues' that *Grange Hill* took a while to tackle. We're not taking too much of a risk when we boldly state that by the mid-1980s there couldn't have been a single mixed-sex school in Britain that hadn't experienced teen pregnancy in some form or another. *Grange Hill*'s tardiness in dramatising serious issues possibly delayed it tackling this thorny subject, but it finally came to the fore with Tegs and Chrissy. The series explored the options as best it could within the confines of the timeslot and Chrissy eventually gave birth to a healthy baby boy. She later broke up a potentially lethal gang war between boys from Grange Hill and new rivals St Joseph's by standing between both groups and pointing out that this wasn't the sort of world she wanted her baby to grow up in. Poignant stuff.

Since then, each series has had a shopping list of issues to get through. Though the issue of homosexuality was hinted at in an early season with one victim of Gripper Stebson's verbal abuse realising he wasn't 'normal' after he 'looked it up in the encyclopedia', *Grange Hill* tackled the subject head on with the arrival of Mr Brisley, who was seen entering a gay bar and later forced to justify his position as a teacher. We've also experienced by proxy Asperger's syndrome, AIDS, homelessness, disability and date rape, each time drawing complaints and congratulations in almost equal measure from TV audiences.

Just as *Grange Hill* creator Phil Redmond was preparing for his other great success, ***Brookside***, to be axed, his production company was on the verge of taking on *Grange Hill* as an independent production. Production relocated from the BBC's Elstree studios, *Grange Hill*'s home since 1985, to Mersey TV's headquarters in Childwall, Liverpool. Fears that the series would ditch its issue-led plots in favour of the skiving and childish mischief of its early years proved to be unfounded. Since reverting back to Redmond's control, *Grange Hill* has looked at domestic violence, obesity, stalking, suicide and racism, while the classrooms have become hi-tech with the arrival of electronic blackboards and computers courtesy of new headmistress Mrs Bassinger.

Grange Hill had always been part drama, part soap. In the mid-1980s the series was the top-rated drama among teens, with audience figures regularly achieving the levels that most adult dramas would kill for nowadays. But then ***EastEnders*** and ***Neighbours*** arrived and eventually began to target the same audience. As a consequence, *Grange Hill* lost out a little as the younger teens began watching the exploits of Scott and Charlene or Ricky and Bianca, all dealing with grown-up issues that made those shows a more aspirational experience than watching kids of their own age trying to rescue donkeys. With competition from prime-time TV and from the multiple channels that have sprouted up over the last ten years, *Grange Hill*'s position is no longer as unique as it once was, but it still holds a valued place as a gateway for older children into quality drama.

Lee Sparke · *Gordon 'Jonah' Jones*
Jenny Twigge · *Mrs Maguire*
Alison Bettles · *Fay Lucas*
Fraser Cains · *Mr Bill 'Scruffy' McGuffy*
Nadia Chambers · *Annette Firman*
Lisa East · *Christine Everson*
Julian Griffiths · *Denny Rees*
Terry Kinsella · *Jimmy Flynn*
Lee Macdonald · *Samuel 'Zammo' Maguire*
Erkan Mustafa · *Roland Browning*
Mike Savage · *Mr Browning*
Kaka Singh · *Randir Singh*
Julie-Ann Steel · *Diane Cooney*
Lisa York · *Julie Marchant*
Joanne Eversdon-Bell · *Sarah Wilks*
Freddie Brooks · *Arthur Knowles*
Simon Heywood · *Mr Nick Smart*
Tony MacPherson · *Derek 'Woody' Woods*
Vincent Matthews · *Jeremy Irvine*
Keith Meade · *Terry Mitchell*
Mark Monero · *Steven Defley*
Simone Nylander · *Janet St Clair*
Anita Savage · *Mandy Firth*
Melissa Wilkes · *Jackie Wright*
Joanne Boakes · *Anita Unsworth*
Mmoloki Chrystie · *Kevin Baylon*
Gary Hailes · *Nigel Flavin*
Gary Love · *Jimmy McLaren*
David Rippey · *Gluxo Remington*
Michael Sheard · *Mr Maurice Bronson*
Bradley Sheppard · *Paul 'Hollo' Holloway*
Steven West · *Vince Savage*
John Alford · *Robbie Wright*
Tony Armatrading · *Mr Peter McCartney*
Amma Asante · *Cheryl Webb*
John Drummond · *Trevor Cleaver*
Karen Ford · *Miss Ginny Booth*
Caroline Gruber · *Miss Gillie Washington*
John Holmes · *Luke 'Gonch' Gardner*
Simone Hyams · *Caroline 'Cally' Donnington*
Joann Kenny · *Jane Bishop*
Tina Mahon · *Ronnie Birtles*
Tim Polley · *Steven 'Banksie' Banks*
Ricky Simmonds · *Anthony 'Ant' Jones*
David Straun · *Mr Peter King*
Fleur Taylor · *Imelda Davis*
Vincent Brimble · *Mr Martin Glover*
Ruth Carraway · *Helen Kelly*
George Wilson/Christopher · *Eric 'Ziggy' Greaves*
George A. Cooper · *Mr Eric Griffiths*
Lucinda Curtis · *Mrs Liz Reagan*
Alison Etienne · *Sharon Burton*
Jeffery Kissoon · *Mr Chris Kennedy*
Jonathan Lambeth · *Danny Kendall*
Karen Lewis · *Mrs Roz Partridge*
Samantha Lewis · *Georgina Hayes*
Alison McLaughlin · *Louise Webb*
Fiona Lee-Frasere · *Laura Reagan*
Sara McGlasson · *Julia Glover*

Simon Vaughan · *Freddy Mainwaring*
Aran Bell · *Mr Phil Scott*
Darren Cudjoe · *Clarke Trent*
Nicholas Donnelly · *Mr Craig McKenzie*
Joshua Fenton · *Francis 'Mauler' McCaul*
Michelle Gayle · *Fiona Wilson*
Sonya Kearns · *Chrissy Mainwaring*
Ian Lee Congden · *Ted Fisk*
Sean Maguire · *Terence 'Tegs' Ratcliffe*
Stuart Organ · *Mr Peter Robson*
Paul Adams · *Matthew Pearson*
Imran Pishori · *Rajesh Patel*
Lynne Radford · *Susie Young*
Rachel Victoria Roberts · *Justine Dean*
Julie Buckfield · *Natalie Stevens*
Lee Cornes · *Mr Geoff Hankin*
David Crane · *Barry Timpkin*
Alice Dawnay · *Alice Rowe*
Jamie Lehane · *'Jacko' Morgan*
Otis Munyangiri · *Kevin 'Locko' Lockery*
Kevin O'Shea · *Mr 'Mad' Max Hargreaves*
John Pickard · *Neil Timpson*
Natalie Poyser · *Becky Stevens*
Anna Quayle · *Mrs Kate Monroe*
Ian Rushmere · *Brian Shaw*
Margo Selby · *Julie Corrigan*
Sundeep Suri · *Akik Rashim*
Veena Tulsiani · *Aichaa Rashim*
René Zagger · *Mike Bentley*
Desmond Askew · *Richard*
Luisa Bradshaw-White · *Maria Watts*
Karen Ford · *Miss Ginny Booth*
Nina Fry · *Robyn Stone*
Kelly George · *Ray Haynes*
Rebekah Joy Gilgan · *Fran Williams*
Denzil Kilvington · *Kenny Haynes*
Clare Buckfield · *Natasha Stevens*
Alan Cave · *Dennis 'Techno' Morris*
Danny Cunningham · *Liam Brady*
Mark De Couteau · *Stuart*
Jamie Golding · *Graham 'Grimbo' Pike*
Jenny Howe · *Mrs Angela Keele*
Melanie Joseph · *Lauren Phillips*
Joseph Kpobie · *Mick Daniels*
Christopher McGown · *Frank Buttrey*
Adam Ray · *Mr Tom Brisley*
Zander Ward · *Andy 'Spanner' Walker*
Flip Webster · *Mrs Marjorie Mason*
Paul Bigley · *Dave Greenman*
Belinda Crane · *Lucy Mitchell*
Steven Hammett · *Dudley Wesker*
Darren Kempson · *Gabriel Woods*
Natalie Tapper · *Jodie Abadeyo*
Kevin Bishop · *Sam Spalding*
Aidan David · *James 'Arnie' Arnold*
Rochelle Gadd · *Delia 'Dill' Lodge*
Jamie Groves · *Josh Davis*
Lisa Hammond · *Denny*

Abigail Hart · *Paula Webster*
Peter Leeper · *Mr Malcolm Parrott*
Jenny Long · *Anna Wright*
Francesca Martinez · *Rachel Burns*
Karen O'Brien · *Mrs Siobhan Maguire*
Amy Phillips · *Jessica Arnold*
David Quilter · *Jim Arnold*
Colin Ridgewell · *Colin Brown*
Amy Simcock-Phillips · *Jessica Arnold*
Daryl Webster · *Caroline Arnold*
Ayesha Antoine · *Poppy Silver*
Kate Bell · *Kelly Bradshaw*
Tim Bentinck · *Fred Mitchell*
Sally Geoghegan · *Miss Jayne Carver*
Laura Hammett · *SarahJane Webster*
Stephen Humby · *Mark Jenkins*
Martino Lazzeri · *Joe Williams*
Simon Long · *Rick Underwood*
Madelaine Newton · *Pamela Jenkins*
Nicholas Pinnock · *Jerome Cairns*
George Stark · *Kevin Jenkins*
Thomas Carey · *Alec Jones*
David Case · *Russell Joseph*
Stephen Earle · *Paul Longworth*
Julie Foulds · *Esther Longworth*
Peter Morton · *Wayne Sutcliffe*
Sam Powell · *Robert Buckley*
Nitzan Sharron · *Gerald Benn*
Sian Welsh · *Laurie Watson*
Fiona Wade · *Joanna Day*
Rachel Bell · *Mrs Margaret Holmes*
Oliver Elmidoro · *Tom Smith*
Ben Freeman · *Chris Longworth*
Leona Kadir · *Janet Hunt*
Diana Magness · *Evelyn Wright*
Jonathon Marchant-Heatley · *Sam 'Cracker' Bacon*
Maggie Mason · *Gemma Lyons*
Marcel McCalla · *Nathan Charles*
Charlotte McDonagh · *Lisa West*
Sally Morton · *Tracy Long*
Tracey Murphy · *Claire Sullivan*
Laura Sadler · *Judi Jeffreys*
Robert Stuart · *Matt Singleton*
Ashley Walters · *Andy Phillips*
Lorraine Woodley · *Carlene Joseph*
Sam Bardens · *Adam Hawkins*
Francesco Bruno · *Franco Savi*
John Hudson · *Ian Hudson*
Michael Obiora · *Max Abassi*
Iain Robertson · *Sean Pearce*
Jade Williams · *Zoe Stringer*
Jenny Galloway · *Harriet Davenport*
Rhydian Jai-Persad · *Saheed Hussain*
Daniel Lee · *Ben Miller*
Jalpa Patel · *Anika Modi*
Arnold Oceng · *Calvin Braithwaite*
Emma Pierson · *Becky Radcliffe*

Lindsey Ray · *Amy Davenport*
Taylor Scipio · *Kamal Hussain*
Adam Sopp · *Darren Clarke*
Colin White · *Spencer Hargreaves*
Don McCorkindale · *Mr Forbes*
Renee Montemayor · *Briony Jones*
David Schaal · *Tom Hargreaves*
Joanne Howarth · *Sue Hargreaves*
Lucas Lindo · *Abel Benson*
Judith Wright · *Miss Emily Fraser*
Emma Waters · *Katy Fraser*
Naomi Osei-Mensah · *Clare Chaplin*
Simon Pearsall · *Don West*
Jon Newman · *Kieran 'Ozzie' Osborne*
La Charne Jolly · *Amelia Nkebe*
Shane Leonidas · *Josh Irving*
Phillip Lester · *Waiter*
Amanda Fahy · *Shannon Parkes*
Matthew Buckley · *Martin Miller*
Michael Brogan · *Alan Clarke*
Kacey Barnfield · *Maddie Gilkes*
Max Brown · *Danny Hartson*
Phillip Lester · *Walter*
Sophie Shad · *Shona West*
Cindy Shelley · *Ros Meyer*
Jessica Staveley-Taylor · *Leah Stewart*
Emma Wills · *Vikki Meedes*
Chris Perry-Metcalf · *Patrick Togger*
Tom Graham · *Nick Edwards*
Nikki Grosse · *Miss Dyson*
Nicholas Tizzard · *Mr Stephen Deverill*
Sara Stockbridge · *Suzie Gilkes*
Reggie Yates · *Carl Fenton*
Thomas Hudson · *Barry 'Baz' Wainwright*
Reece Noi · *Taylor Mitchell*
Simon O'Brien · *Wally Scott*
Celyn Jones · *Mr Steve Green*
Sarah Lawrence · *Mel Adams*
Valerie Lilley · *Mrs Knuckle*
Jonathan Dixon · *Matthew 'Mooey' Humphries*
Lauren Bunney · *Annie Wainwright*
Ben Friswell · *Jeremy Bishop*
Jacqui Boatswain · *Mrs Bassinger*
Josh Abdelfatah · *Michael Tranter*
Edward Baker-Duly · *Mr Chris Malachay*
Kirsten Cassidy · *Tanya Young*
Daniella Fray · *Emma Bolton*
Celyn Jones · *Mr Steve Green*
Valerie Lilley · *Mrs Knuckle*
James Wignall · *Max Humphries*
Terri Dwyer · *Miss Adams*

Creator Phil Redmond

Producers Anna Home, Richard Callanan, Phil Redmond (executive), Colin Cant, Susi Hush, Kenny McBain, Ben Rea, Ronald Smedley, David Leonard, Albert Barber, Christine Secombe, Josephine Ward, Steven Andrew, Diana Kyle, Jo Hallows, Lee Hardman

Writers Phil Redmond, Margaret Simpson, Alan Janes, Sandy Welch, Jane Hollowood, Barry Purchese, David Angus, Paula Milne, Frances Galleymore, John Godber, Rosemary Mason, Sarah Daniels, Chris Ellis, John Smith, Kay Trainor, Kevin Hood, Alison Fisher, Diane Whitley, Ol Parker, Judith Johnson, Leigh Jackson, Tanika Gupta, Tim O'Mara, Jeff Povey, Annie Wood, Philip Gerard, Philip Gladwin, Michael Butt, Eanna O'Lochlainn, Judy Forshaw, Lin Coghlan, Paul Smith, Suzie Smith, Si Spencer, Lisselle Kayla, Rachel Dawson, Helen Eatock, Tara Byrne, Bridget Colgan, Mark Hiser, Carolyn Sally Jones

Theme Tune Somehow surviving its use as the theme for the panel-game show ***Give us a Clue***, the original *Grange Hill* theme, 'Chicken Man' by Alan Hawkshaw, remains definitive, accompanying the comic book-style opening graphics that showed kids missing the bus and being startled by the appearance of a sausage in mid-air. The theme remained basically the same (a slight re-arrangement aside) until 1990, when some idiot decided to 'modernise' the theme tune and turn it into a generic electro-mess that managed to date the series rather than update it. Peter Moss's theme has now been with the series longer than Alan Hawkshaw's, but it's Hawkshaw's that we all still remember, especially the final notes on that electric guitar: wadam wah waoow . . .

H. G. Wells' Invisible Man

Science Fiction | Official Films/ATV for ITV | episode duration 30 mins | broadcast 13 Jun–19 Dec 1959

Regular Cast
Tim Turner · *Voice of Dr Peter Brady*
Johnny Scripps · *The Invisible Man*
Lisa Daniely · *Diane Brady*
Deborah Watling · *Sally Brady*

Creator/Producer Ralph Smart, from the novel by H. G. Wells **Writers** Michael Connor, Michael Cramoy, Ralph Smart, Stanley Mann, Leslie Arliss, Lindsay Galloway, Philip Levene, Lenore Coffee, Ian Stuart Black, Doreen Montgomery, Brenda Blackmore, Michael Pertwee, Brian Clemens **Theme Music:** Sydney John Kay

For commentary, see THE INVISIBLE MAN (1984)

Hamish Macbeth

Comedy Drama | Skyline Films/Zenith for BBC One | episode duration 50 mins | broadcast 26 Mar 1995–4 May 1997

Regular Cast
Robert Carlyle · *Hamish Macbeth*
Ralph Riach · *TV John McIver*
Jimmy Yuill, Billy Riddoch · *Lachie McCrae Snr*
Stuart Davids · *Lachie McCrae Jr*
Valerie Gogan · *Alex MacLaine*
Shirley Henderson · *Isobel Sutherland*
Brian Pettifer · *Rory Campbell*
Stuart McGugan · *Barney*
Anne Lacey · *Esme Murray*
Duncan Duff · *Doc Brown*
Campbell Morrison · *Harry Balfour*
Brian Alexander · *Jubel*
David Ashton · *Major Roddy Maclean*
Mona Bruce · *Edie*
Morag Hood · *Delores Balfour*
Anne Kristen · *Miss Meikeljohn*
Barbara Rafferty · *Agnes*
James Young · *Tusker Gray*
Iain McColl · *Neil the Bus*
Zippy · *Wee Jock*
Fraoch, Dexter · *Wee Jock Two*

Producers Scott Meak, Trevor Davies, Andrea Calderwood (executive), Deirdre Keir **Writers** Dominic Minghella, Daniel Boyle, from the novels by M. C. Beaton **Theme Music** John Lunn

Hamish Macbeth is a small-town policeman pounding the beat in the tiny village of Lochdubh (pronounced 'Lock-doo') in the Scottish Highlands. Because the town is so far away from any other kind of authority, Hamish's style of policing is far more laid-back than a traditional copper's. He's happy to turn a blind eye to lock-ins in pubs, poaching or other petty offences of that kind, dedicated instead to tracking down real criminals. In fact, Hamish's attitude is so laissez-faire that he's even known to smoke the odd joint every now and again. With the help of his right-hand man, 'second sight'-blessed TV John (so called because he owned the first set in the village), Hamish tries to keep the peace while studiously avoiding any attempts at gaining a promotion – keenly aware that an advance in his career might take him away from his idyllic home. Hamish's best friend is his beloved West Highland terrier Wee Jock – it's a terrible trauma for Hamish when Wee Jock is run over and killed, with only the arrival of Wee Jock Two helping to ease his grief.

Hamish Macbeth was a much more satisfying type of gentle Sunday night series than the overly inoffensive blandness of shows like ***Heartbeat*** and *Born and Bred*. Largely filmed on location in the Scottish town of Plockton, *Hamish Macbeth* was also the first major starring role for Robert Carlyle, who would go on to international fame in movies as diverse as *Trainspotting* (1995) and Bond flick *The World Is Not Enough* (1999). Just prior to being cast in *Hamish Macbeth*, Carlyle made an impressive guest appearance as psychotic football supperter Alby in the memorable ***Cracker*** story 'To be a Somebody'.

Hammer House of Horror/Mystery and Suspense

Anthology | Cinema Arts International/Hammer Film Productions/ITC for ITV | episode duration 50/90 mins | broadcast 13 Sep–6 Dec 1980

Principal Cast
Patricia Quinn · *Lucinda Jessop*
Jon Finch · *David Winter*
Prunella Gee · *Mary Winter*
Denholm Elliott · *Norman Shenley*
Norman Beaton · *Mr Ngenko*
Barbara Kellerman · *Laurie Morton*
Nicholas Ball · *William Peters*
Rachel Davies · *Emma Peters*
Brian Croucher · *George Evans*
Leigh Lawson · *Graham*
Angela Bruce · *Sarah*
Marius Goring · *Heinz*
Michael Culver · *Mark*
Peter Cushing · *Martin Brueck*
Brian Cox · *Chuck Spillers*
Elaine Donnelly · *Annie Spillers*
Diana Dors · *Mrs Ardoy*
Christopher Cazenove · *Tom*
Anthony Valentine · *Inspector Clifford*
Siân Phillips · *Mrs Henska*
Suzanne Danielle · *Natalie*
Rosalyn Landor · *Alison*
Ray Lonnen · *Michael Roberts*
Paul Darrow · *Simon Andrews*

Simon MacCorkindale · *Harry*
Gareth Thomas · *Richard*
Philip Latham · *Hargreaves*
Jenny Laird · *Mrs Roberts*
Emrys James · *Dr Harris*
Georgina Hale · *Stella*

Producers Brian Lawrence, David Reid, Roy Skeggs **Writers** Anthony Read, Jeremy Burnham, Gerald Savory, David Lloyd, Bernie Cooper, Francis Megahy, Francis Essex, Murray Smith, David Fisher, John Elder (pseudonym for Hammer producer Anthony Hinds), Don Shaw **Theme Music** Roger Webb

The world-famous Hammer studio had, at one point, been Britain's leading film production company, with successful horror franchises built around stories of vampires, monsters and reanimated corpses, all with the trademarked fierce red blood. Hammer had also sporadically dabbled with television, first in the 1950s with a pilot for a series called *Tales of Frankenstein* that never got past its first episode, then in 1968 with an anthology series called ***Journey to the Unknown***.

A series entitled *The Hammer House of Horror, Mystery and Suspense* had previously been mooted back in 1973 as one of a number of attempts to save the fortunes of the company which, by that time, was struggling to re-create the successes of the previous two decades After Hammer's managing director Michael Carreras was ousted from the company in 1979, remaining members of the board Roy Skeggs and Brian Lawrence licensed the Hammer brand and created the *Hammer House of Horror* TV series. Taking their lead from anthology series like ***Tales of the Unexpected*** and ***Armchair Thriller***, each of the 13 50-minute instalments would, like *Journey to the Unknown*, play on situations of tension, violence and ultimately an ironic twist. Hammer regular Peter Cushing showed up for one episode, 'The Silent Scream', concerning an ex-con (Brian Cox) ensnaring a sadistic pet-shop owner in his own trap. Unfortunately, the rather tame stories were unable to compete with either the restrictions on TV broadcasts or the more visceral cinema franchises like *Halloween* (1978–2002, 8 films) or *Friday the 13th* (1980–2003, 11 films).

The TV series was, however, sufficiently successful for Skeggs and Lawrence to eventually buy Hammer outright from its creditors. Though a second series of *Hammer House of Horror* failed to materialise, Skeggs managed to set up a new series – *Hammer House of Mystery and Suspense* – with Fox, Hammer's partners for *Journey into the Unknown. Hammer House of Mystery and Suspense* unfortunately suffered the same fate as the company's previous series – low ratings in the USA and transmitted only sporadically by ITV's different television networks. As before, *Hammer House of Mystery and Suspense* ran for just one series of 13 90-minute episodes.

One final Hammer related TV show arrived in 1990, *The World of Hammer*, a documentary series exploring the themes of Hammer's film library and narrated by ex-Hammer star Oliver Reed. Although handsomely put together, the series pre-empted the nostalgia boom of the end of the decade and was relegated to schedule-filler status mid-week on BBC One.

Hancock's Half Hour

Sitcom | BBC TV, ATV/ABC for ITV | episode duration 25–30 mins | broadcast 6 Jul 1956–6 May 1960 (Hancock's Half Hour, BBC), 26 May–30 Jun 1961 (Hancock, BBC), 3 Jan–28 Mar 1963, 16 Jun–18 Jul 1967 (Hancock, ITV)

Regular Cast
Tony Hancock, Sidney James, June Whitfield, Joe Ritchie

Producers Duncan Wood, Graeme Muir, Bernard Delfont, Tony Hancock, Mark Stuart **Writers** Ray Galton, Alan Simpson (BBC), Godfrey Harrison, Richard Harris, Dennis Spooner, Terry Nation, Ray Whyberd, John Muir, Eric Green (ITV) **Theme Music** Wally Stott, Derek Scott

For many people, Tony Hancock is simply the greatest TV comic of all time. Rewatching his BBC programmes, it's very hard to disagree with this interpretation, with many of the episodes of the single series of *Hancock* shown in 1961 standing the test of time as the equal of anything shown before or since – 'The Bowmans' (a send-up of radio's *The Archers*), 'The Radio Ham', 'The Bedsitter' and the oft-quoted 'The Blood Donor' being among the finest half-hours of comedy ever committed to videotape.

Tony Hancock was born in Birmingham in 1924, but grew up in the seaside town of Bournemouth where he first grew fascinated by the variety acts passing through the town throughout the summer season. During the war, he joined the RAF Gang Show and gained a great deal of experience at performing comedy on stage. After the war, he was soon spotted by the BBC and made his first TV appearance on a talent show called *New to You* in 1948. Work on a number of sketch shows on both radio and TV led to his first starring work on BBC Radio's Light Programme, when in 1954 he broadcast the first of 104 editions of *Hancock's Half-Hour* to an enraptured audience listening at home. Hancock's first starring TV series was 12 episodes of *The Tony Hancock Show*, a sketch series for Associated Rediffusion featuring appearances by stars such as Hattie Jacques, Clive Dunn, Dick Emery, June Whitfield and the sublime Kenneth Williams. It was, however, his seven seasons on the BBC that turned Tony Hancock from a lugubrious radio personality into one of the first TV superstars.

In the move to television there were casualties, the most notable being Kenneth Williams (something Williams himself only found out about third-hand). Sharing Hancock's limelight for most of TV run of *Hancock's Half Hour* was co-star Sid James, acting as the 'straight man' and foil for Hancock's jokes several years prior to his first appearance in the *Carry On* movies. Together with top-notch scripts courtesy of writers Ray Galton and

Alan Simpson, Hancock and James's performances created a new benchmark for TV comedy. Each episode was a completely different story, and although Hancock played the same character each week, his job, aims in life and the challenges facing him changed with every individual episode. Some things remained the same though – Hancock would always be put-upon, unlucky and generally downbeat in life, with his best-laid plans (whatever they were) usually coming to naught, and he'd always return to his home on 23 Railway Cuttings, East Cheam, Surrey.

For Hancock's final year at the BBC he decided that he would rather appear as a solo star, and so Sid James was let go and the show was retitled just *Hancock* (running times were cut to 25 minutes too). These six episodes are rightly regarded as the high-spot of his career – unfortunately, when Hancock returned to TV screens with further shows on ATV and ABC, things just weren't the same. Not only had Hancock now also disposed of the services of his long-term scriptwriters Galton and Simpson, he had also unfortunately started to rely upon alcohol to a near-disastrous extent. His final run of episodes on ITV were based around a single concept, of Hancock as the manager of a variety theatre – the idea being that if the rest of the scripts or Hancock's performance itself failed to live up to expectations, other acts and performers could be wheeled on to take up the slack. With no new work in the UK on the cards, Hancock travelled to Australia to record *The Tony Hancock Show* for the 7 Network. While he was there, he tragically took his own life on 25 June 1968 – he was just 44 years old. It was an unbearably sad conclusion to the life of one of the greatest comedy talents ever seen on British TV.

The Hanged Man

Crime Drama | Yorkshire Television for ITV | episode duration 50 mins | broadcast 15 Feb–5 Apr 1975

Principal Cast

Colin Blakely · *Lew Burnett*
Michael Williams · *Alan Crowe*
Gary Watson · *John Quentin*
John Rees · *Brian Nelson*
Angela Browne · *Elizabeth Hayden*
Brian Croucher · *Sammy Grey*
William Lucas · *George Pilgrim*
Frank Wylie · *David Larson*
Julian Glover · *Joe Denver*
Jenny Hanley · *Druscilla*
Peter Halliday · *Jean-Claud de Salle*
John Bay · *Sam Lambert*
William Russell · *Peter Kroger*
Michael Coles · *Hans Ericksen*
Gareth Hunt · *Eddie Malone*
Jack Watson · *Douglas McKinnon*
Bill Mitchell · *Harry Friedman*
Alan MacNaughtan · *Charles Galbraith*
Beth Morris · *Sue Harrington*
Gareth Hunt · *Eddie Malone*
Ray Smith · *Milojek*
James Maxwell · *Frengel*
Tony Jay · *Laszlo*
Gordon Reid · *Willie O'Keefe*
Frederick Jaeger · *Hans Dieter*
Naomi Chance · *Jane Cowley*
Al Mancini · *Joe Shapiro*
Jan Francis · *Captain Jane Ashley*
James Grout · *Sam McGuire*
Laurence Payne · *Prendergast*
Richard Shaw · *Joe Hennessy*
John F. Landry · *Turtle*
Richard Bebb · *Sir Charles Hammond*
Colin George · *George Seagram*
Ann Morrish · *Margaret Burnett*
Jane Seymour · *Laura Burnett*

Creator/Writer Edmund Ward **Producers** Peter Willes (executive), Edmund Ward, Marc Miller **Theme Music** Written by Alan Tew and performed by Bullet, this is a macho jazz funk fusion of heavy bass, frenetic drumming and a rather whiney synthesiser sound that should be familiar to any fans of ***The Two Ronnies*** (see below).

Lew Burnett is a self-made man, owner of a hugely successful construction corporation that grew from a one-man business. But success also breeds resentment and Burnett's enemies are numerous. After his wife is killed in a plane crash and a third attempt is made on his life, Burnett realises the only chance he has of staying alive is to play dead. By maintaining the deception he hopes to be able to find out who wants to kill him and why. Assisted by Alan Crowe, an old friend and former mercenary, Burnett stages a wages snatch to fund his mission, travelling around the world to trace nine potential suspects who might be behind his 'death'.

A little-remembered 1970s' thriller that ran for just eight episodes on consecutive Saturday nights, each episode was named after a Tarot card relating to one of the suspects Burnett was tracking down – Wheel of Fortune, Tower of Destruction, Knave of Coins, etc. Burnett himself was the Hanged Man, a symbol for a person undergoing a massive change. Like all the best crime thrillers of the 1970s, there was violence aplenty, with Burnett caught in brutal fight sequences every week.

The final episode led to the shock revelation of who wanted Burnett dead, but it also introduced a shady thief called Turtle who later won himself his own series, ***Turtle's Progress***. But *The Hanged Man*'s real place in TV history is due to its theme tune later being used by *The Two Ronnies* for their detective spoof 'Stop! You're Killing Me . . .' featuring the bumbling Charley Farley and his sidekick Piggy Malone.

The Hanged Man's creator, Edmund Ward, had previously written for *The Power Game* and ***Man in a Suitcase***, and later scripted episodes of ***The Professionals*** and ***Bergerac*** as well as providing the screenplay for *A Prayer for the Dying* (1987).

Happy Days

Sitcom | Paramount/Henderson/Miller-Milkis-Boyett Productions for ABC (shown on ITV) | episode duration 25 mins | broadcast 15 Jan 1974–24 Sep 1984, 3 Mar 1992, 3 Feb 2005

Regular Cast
Ron Howard · *Richie Cunningham*
Henry Winkler · *Arthur 'Fonzie' Fonzarelli*
Tom Bosley · *Howard Cunningham*
Marion Ross · *Marion Cunningham*
Erin Moran · *Joanie Cunningham*
Anson Williams · *Warren 'Potsie' Weber*
Donny Most · *Ralph Malph*
Gavan O'Herlihy, Randolph Roberts · *Chuck Cunningham*
Pat Morita · *Matsuo 'Arnold' Takahashi*
Al Molinaro · *Alfred Delvecchio*
Scott Baio · *Charles 'Chachi' Arcola*
Lynda Goodfriend · *Lori Beth Allen Cunningham*
Cathy Silvers · *Jenny Piccalo*
Ted McGinley · *Roger Phillips*
Crystal Bernard · *K. C. Cunningham*
Linda Purl · *Ashley Pfister*
Heather O'Rourke · *Heather Pfister*
Billy Warlock · *Leopold 'Flip' Phillips*
Beatrice Colen · *Marsha Simms*
Suzi Quatro · *Leather Tuscadero*
Denis Mandel · *Eugene Belvin*
Scott Mitchell Bernstein · *Melvin Belvin*
Ed Peck · *Officer Kirk*

Creator Garry Marshall **Producers** Garry Marshall, Edward K. Milkis, Thomas L. Miller (executive), William Bickley, Bob Birnbaum, Bob Brunner, Ronny Hallin, Michael Warren (associate), Lowell Ganz, Walter Kempley, Gary Menteer, Jerry Paris, Nick Abdo, Mark Rothman, Ed Scharlach **Writers** Various, including Rob Reiner, Phil Mishkin, Garry Marshall, Dick Bensfield, Perry Grant, William Bickley, Bob Brunner, Mark Rothman, Lowell Ganz, Frank Buxton, Steve Zacharias, David Ketchum, Arthur Silver, Bob Howard, Barry Rubinowitz, Joe Glauberg, Michael Warren, Brian Levant, Fred Fox Jr, Walter Kempley, Beverly Bloomberg, Paula A. Roth **Theme Music** For the first two seasons, the theme was a cover version of 'Rock Around the Clock', though for later broadcasts the Bill Hailey original was used. However, it's the song by Jerry McClain and Truett Pratt ('Sunday, Monday, Happy Days . . .') that we usually associate with the series.

The decent time for nostalgia to gestate is around 15 years. At the moment, in the middle of the 2000s, we're seeing a revival of all things early 1990s – Bez from the Happy Mondays winning *Celebrity Big Brother 2005* being a prime example. In the summer of 1973 it was time to look back at the mid-1950s when George Lucas, yet to convince anyone that there was merit in an idea he had called *Star Wars*, released a film called *American Graffiti*. Lucas's film, about teenagers and their cars, was a huge smash in the States and featured a young actor by the name of Ronny Howard in a lead role. Though the success of *American Graffiti* obviously led to the decision to make the TV series *Happy Days*, *Happy Days* itself actually pre-dated the movie by a couple of years.

The first incarnation of the show came in the form of a pilot written and produced by Garry Marshall (former writer for Dick Van Dyke and Lucille Ball). 'New Family in Town' introduced the Cunninghams, an All-American family that included Ronny Howard as the son, Marion Ross as the mother and Harold Gould as the father. ABC passed on the pilot, instead using it as an episode in their anthology series *Love American Style*. When *American Graffiti* exploded into cinemas, ABC execs realised their mistake and commissioned Marshall to turn his pilot into a series. The series retained many of the pilot's cas tmembers, although Tom Bosley took Gould's place as Mr Cunningham (Gould got the chance to play Dad to Valerie Harper and Julie Kavner in another sitcom, ***Rhoda***).

The Cunninghams were too perfect to be true. Dad ran a local hardware store (Dads should always be good with tools), and Mrs Cunningham was forever in the kitchen. They had four children: eldest boy Chuck was about to go off to college (he disappeared after the second series never to be seen or mentioned ever again), middle child Richie and only daughter Joanie. Richie and his friends, ginger joker Ralph Malph and self-assured Potsie, usually hung out at Arnold's drive-in restaurant (owned by Japanese chef Arnold Takahashi and later by hang-drawn Italian Al Delvecchio) trying to pick up girls and act as cool as the Fonz, the coolest High-school dropout in Milwaukee.

Considering its position in TV history, and its impact on American culture during the 70s, *Happy Days* was not a success to start with, *Time* magazine mauled it and viewers weren't that keen either. But gradually it found its audience and convinced people that 'Sit on it!' was a pretty cool thing to say.

Tom Bosley and Ron Howard still got top billing, but as the series progressed it became obvious that the true star of the show was the Fonz, a character who had barely appeared in the pilot and was originally scripted with an astonishingly limited vocabulary ('Heyyyy', pretty much) and an almost paranormal hold over any woman he desired. The image of the short, dark Italian-American in biking leathers was at odds with Garry Marshall's original vision of a tall, blond, cardigan-wearing surfer dude, but at the auditions Henry Winkler struck Marshall as being so at odds with the character-as-written that he decided to change it all to fit Winkler. Having gradually eclipsed the other characters over two years, by the third series the writers had moved Fonzie into the spare room above the Cunningham's apartment to ensure they could maximise the potential for the character's involvement in other stories. 'Fonzie Moves In' also coincided with a change in the production. For the third season onwards, *Happy Days* would be 'filmed before a live studio audience', as would be

obvious by the maniacal cheering whenever any of the characters walked through the door.

Garry Marshall had never been afraid to fiddle with the series to get the effect he wanted and to road test other ideas. In a 1975 episode, he cast sister Penny Marshall alongside Cindy Williams as Fonzie's girlfriends Laverne DeFazio and Shirley Feeney. The pair impressed the network enough to allow Marshall to shape a sitcom around their characters and so *Laverne and Shirley* was born. It was the first of several spin-offs from *Happy Days*: in 1977, Howard Cunningham's cousin Nancy Blansky (Nancy Walker, who later played Ida Morgernstern, the interfering mother in *Rhoda*) popped in to celebrate his and Marion's wedding anniversary and returned to Las Vegans to star in *Blansky's Beauties*, a short-lived sitcom that also featured appearances by Pat Morita as Arnold – the same character he'd played in early episodes of *Happy Days*. A year later, a dream episode introduced Mork, a fast-talking and massively confused alien played by the energised Robin Williams. Again, Williams was given his own show, ***Mork & Mindy***, in which Mork tries to understand life on Earth while reporting back to his unseen boss on the planet Ork.

As Richie's gang grew up and moved on, younger characters were brought in to take their place. Fonzie's cousin, the hugely popular Chachi stepped into the mix in the fifth series in 1977 and promptly became Joanie's on-off love interest for the duration of the series. Inevitably, the story was plucked out of *Happy Days* and into yet another spin-off – *Joanie Loves Chachie*, which ran from 1982 for two seasons. Fonzie and his friends were even treated to cartoon versions, with three different *Laverne and Shirley* series (including the Bilko-esque *Laverne and Shirley in the Army*), plus *Fonz and the Happy Days Gang* and *Mork and Mindy* segments in the *Mork and Mindy/Laverne and Shirley/Fonz Hour*, all of which make *Happy Days* a contender for the title of 'Most Reproductive Sitcom'.

But not all of Marshall's experiments were successful. One episode in the fifth series took Fonzie and the gang to Hollywood, where the Fonz was being screen tested to become the next James Dean. A climactic scene in which Fonzie performs a spectacular motorcycle leap over a caged shark has become infamous for all the wrong reasons. Among television enthusiasts, the phrase 'Jump the Shark' is now used to refer to the moment when a TV show loses its way to the point where its origins are unrecognisable. The website jumptheshark.com even categorises shows that 'jump the shark' for specific reasons, including 'death of the star', 'child characters reaching puberty', 'major cast changes' and 'Ted McGinley joins'. McGinley became a *Happy Days* regular from 1980 to fill the gap left by Ron Howard's abrupt departure between seasons to take on a directing job.

In its final years, *Happy Days* had definitely lost its way. The 1950s' elements were phased out as 1970s' fashions and hairstyles took over, and the Fonz went from cool chick-magnet to high-school teacher (as a mechanic tutor) and surrogate father to a young orphan called Danny. Still, after 11 seasons, no-one was complaining. Gearing towards the perfect happy ending, Richie and Joanie returned to the family home in preparation for the final, 256th, episode in which Joanie finally married Chachi.

The *Happy Days* gang got together in 1992 for a 90-minute 'Reunion Special'. In May 1995, rock band Weezer intercut clips from *Happy Days* seemlessly into an ingenious video for their song 'Buddy Holly' (which peaked at number 12 in the British singles charts). In 1999, Henry Winkler acted as creative consultant on *Happy Days – The Musical*, and another reunion – this time to celebrate the show's 30th anniversary – brought cast members back together again in 2005. Anyone who still thinks nostalgia ain't what it used to be can, frankly, sit on it.

Trivia

Happy Days creator Garry Marshall directed the feature films *Beaches* (1988) and *Pretty Woman* (1990), among many others. His sister, Penny Marshall (Laverne), is now also one of Hollywood's leading directors; her films include *Jumpin' Jack Flash* (1986), *Big* (1988), *Awakenings* (1990) and *A League of Their Own* (1992). Ron Howard left the series to become a director. One of his first films, *Night Shift* (1982) starred Henry Winkler, while his later pictures include *Splash*, (1984) *Cocoon* (1985), *Parenthood* (1989) and *Apollo 13* (1995). In 2001 he won the Academy Award for Best Director for *A Beautiful Mind* and executive produced the hugely successful TV thriller **24**.

Happy Ever After

See TERRY AND JUNE

Harry Enfield

SEE PAGES 362–5

Harry Hill

Comedy | Channel 4 | episode duration 25 mins | broadcast 30 May 1997–24 Apr 2000

Regular Cast

Harry Hill · *Himself*
Barrie Gosney · *Himself/Ken Ford*
Al Murray · *Alan Hill*
Matt Bradstock · *Little Alan Hill*
Evie Garratt · *Nana Hill/various*
Steve Bowditch · *various*
Burt Kwouk · *Himself*

Creator/Writer Harry Hill **Producers** Richard Allen-Turner, Jon Thoday (executive), Charlie Hanson

Kent native Matthew Hall was born in October 1964 and began life training to be a doctor. Thankfully, he soon realised that his calling in life wasn't to set people's broken bones, it was to tickle their funny bones instead. Adopting the stage name Harry Hill, he established himself quickly by winning the Perrier Award for best new comedian at the 1992 Edinburgh Festival. Hill's first TV show was a series of six 15-minute black-and-white comedy films, broadcast on BBC Two (19 Sept–24 Oct 1994) under the banner *Harry Hill's Fruit Fancies*. With a successful career on Radio 4 already well under way, it was only a matter of time before Hill's real breakthrough series – the self-titled *Harry Hill* – arrived: on Channel 4 in May 1997.

For the uninitiated, Harry Hill's brand of comedy can come across as utterly incomprehensible. It takes a while to realise that the whole point of his humour is to veer wildly from one surreal moment to another – from a discussion with Ken Ford, the man from the *Joy of Sex* books through to the appearance of blue plastic glove-puppet Stouffer the Cat. And as for the obsession with badgers – what's that all about then? Regular guests on the show included Burt Kwouk (the camp commandant from ***Tenko*** and Inspector Clouseau's implacable opponent Cato, playing himself), Al (the Pub Landlord) Murray as Harry's older brother Alan and a number of people in badger outfits (playing, among others, Tasmin Archer Badger, Gareth Southgate Badger and Windsor Davies Badger). To Harry, nothing was too odd or strange to obsess about – indeed, the weirder the obsession, the funnier it was. Even scenarios that seemed to have no relevance to the rest of the programme were relevant, with Hill carefully setting up punchlines some 20 minutes before he delivered them.

After three seasons and two Christmas specials of fun on Channel 4, Hill jumped ship to the mainstream waters of ITV (what are the chances of that happening, eh?) where he began hosting *Harry Hill's* TV Burp, an offbeat and often hilariously funny look at the best (and worst) programmes screened over the past seven days. One of Hill's favourite gags is to get look-alikes of celebs or actors into the studio and get them to (mock) fight with each other to 'see who's best' – sparring partners have included 'soap stars', 'sportsmen' and 'politicians', among many others. Aside from *TV Burp* (which at time of writing is still in production), Hill has also enjoyed a single run of *The All-New Harry Hill Show* (ITV, 9 Feb–6 Mar 2003), a variation/development on his original Channel 4 sketch show, and now provides the voiceovers for ***You've Been Framed!***, where he's single-handedly revitalised a programme on the verge of cancellation. Although Hill's comedy is very much an acquired taste, he's become one of the true leading lights of ITV's comedy portfolio in the 21st century, getting a prestigious ***An Audience With . . .*** special in 2004.

Harry's Game

Drama | Yorkshire for ITV | episode duration 50 mins | broadcast 25–27 Oct 1982

Regular Cast

Ray Lonnen · *Captain Harry Brown*
Geoffrey Russell · *Home Secretary*
Nicholas Day · *Bannen*
Geoffrey Chater · *Colonel George Frost*
Derek Thompson · *Billy Downes*
Charles Lawson · *Seamus Duffryn*
Rita Howard · *Mrs Duffryn*
Sean Caffrey · *Inspector Howard Rennie*
Denys Hawthorne · *Minister of Defence*
Benjamin Whitrow · *Davidson*
Carole Nimmons · *Mrs Rennie*
Linda Robson · *Theresa McCorrigan*
Gary Waldhorn · *Commissioner of Police*
Geoffrey Leesley · *Asst.istant Commissioner*
Robert Morris · *The Right Honourable Henry Danby MP*

Producers David Cunliffe (executive), Keith Richardson **Writers** Gerald Seymour, from his own novel **Theme Music** Clannad produced the beautifully haunting theme to *Harry's Game* – an early example of the kind of music they would later provide for ***Robin of Sherwood***. It reached No. 5 in November 1982.

When a cabinet minister is gunned down on the streets of London by an IRA assassin, the public outcry is so intense that the government is forced to take unusual steps to deal with the problem. With the assassin's trail long gone cold, Captain Harry Brown is sent undercover to Northern Ireland in the hope of infiltrating the Republican terrorist groups that operate in Belfast. With no time to establish an in-depth cover story (or even to perfect his accent), Harry is dropped in the deep end, isolated from any back-up or support, in a place where one slip of the tongue could prove fatal. Can Harry track down the assassin before he himself becomes the latest victim of 'the troubles'?

This nail-biting three-part thriller was penned by former ITN journalist Gerald Seymour, an adaptation of his own best-selling novel. Screened over three consecutive nights, viewers barely had time to draw their breath before being plunged into the next dramatic instalment. Featuring an early TV dramatic role for ***Casualty*** stalwart Derek Thompson as the assassin, and an even rarer dramatic performance by Linda 'Birds of a Feather' Robson, *Harry's Game* was an outstanding thriller that left a lingering impression on the minds of everyone who saw it.

Hart to Hart

Detective/Romance | RONA II/Columbia Pictures/Aaron Spelling Productions for ABC (shown on ITV) | episode duration

Continued on page 366

Harry Enfield

Harry Enfield and Kathy Burke as teenagers Kevin and Perry.

The British like nothing better than a good comedy catchphrase to quote back at each other. It's like membership of a secret club or society – you're only in with the in-crowd if you know the correct phrase or saying. From Miriam Karlin's 'Everybody out!' in ***The Rag Trade*** through to Matt Lucas's 'I wan' tha' one!' in ***Little Britain***, building a comedy series around catchphrases has often been a easy way of getting big laughs. However, it takes something very special for catchphrases to enter the public psyche and to live on long after the original source has finished broadcasting. Based upon the sheer volume of instantly recognisable characters he created and the longevity of their catchphrases and tics, Harry Enfield must therefore be someone very special indeed.

Harry Enfield was born in Sussex in 1961 and graduated from York University with a politics degree. He got a taste for performing while at university and even performed at the Edinburgh Fringe Festival. Enfield's first big break came when he got a job providing many of the voices for the latex unlovelies of ***Spitting Image***. He soon graduated to stand-up comedy, appearing on Channel 4's seminal youth programmes ***The Tube*** and ***Saturday Live***. Enfield realised he had a special talent for playing characters – his two early successes being wide-eyed and innocent Greek kebab-shop owner Stavros and the loathsome yuppie plasterer Loadsamoney, who scrored a top five hit in the UK singles charts in 1988 with 'Loadsamoney (Doin' up the House)'. However, one thing that Enfield quickly became well known for was dumping characters that he'd become bored with: Loadsamoney was killed off in a hit-and-run accident during the middle of a telethon, reportedly because Enfield was shocked to find out that some yuppies had actually adopted the 'Loadsamoney' persona more as a hero figure than the deeply ironic, despicable monster he'd been intended to be (he was equally ruthless with another character, the flat-capped know-it-all whose catchphrase was 'It's only meeee'). In 1989, Enfield created a new character for a one-off Channel 4 mockumentary, *Norbert Smith: A Life*, hosted by Melvyn Bragg and telling the story of a legendary British film icon. Here, Enfield and Channel 4 parted company; the following year, the BBC offered him a contract to develop a full sketch show for them – the result was *Harry Enfield's Television Programme*.

Throughout this series, Enfield assembled a cornucopia of iconic characters that would become TV legends, every one of them completely believable and so well drawn that viewers eagerly awaited their appearances in subsequent episodes. Wayne and Waynetta Slob (and their children Frogmella and Spudulika – 'It's exotic!') were prototype chavs, characters so repellent and disgusting that even Albert Steptoe might turn his nose up at spending time with them (in one episode, Waynetta bemoans the fact that she doesn't have a 'brown baby . . . like all the other mothers on the estate'). Tim Nice-But-Dim was a gentle attack on the kind of chinless wonder seen hanging around Chelsea courtesy of Daddy's money, and Tory Boy was a much more blatant attack on the government of the day and expressive of Enfield's inability to understand how any young people could possibly support them. At the opposite end of the age spectrum were the vile Old Gits, Alf and Fred, two vindictive old men who took great pleasure in popping kids' balloons, stealing babies' sweets, scanning the newspaper obituaries to gloat ('You're dead; I'm not!') and generally being totally reprehensible. There was also a series of Pathé News-style films starring Mr Cholmondley-Warner (pronounced 'Chumley'), the moral of which was usually 'Women, know your place!'

Enfield assembled a cornucopia of iconic characters that became TV legends, every one of them completely believable.

Almost single-handedly, Enfield completed the job Carla Lane had begun with her sitcom ***Bread*** in creating an unshiftable stereotype for the people of Merseyside. Aggressive, bevvy-sinking LFC supporters, 'the Scousers' were permanently one sniff away from a brawl ('Ey! Ey! Ey! You staaaartin'?!'), though war is always averted thanks to a last-minute instruction to 'Caaaalm down'. The permed, moustached trio consisted of Enfield himself and genuine

Comedy
Hat Trick Productions/ Tiger Aspect Productions/Pozzitive Productions for BBC Two (*Harry Enfield's Television Programme*)/ BBC One (*Harry Enfield and Chums*)
Episode Duration: 30 mins
Broadcast: 8 Nov 1990–24 Dec 1992 (*Harry Enfield's Television Programme*), 4 Nov 1994–24 Dec 1997 (*Harry Enfield and Chums*)

Regular Cast
Harry Enfield, Paul Whitehouse, Kathy Burke, Gary Bleasdale, Joe McGann, Mark Moraghan, Jon Glover, Charlie Higson, Duncan Preston, Stephen Moore, Louisa Rix, Carla Mendonça

Creator Harry Enfield

Producers Denise O'Donoghue, Peter Bennett-Jones, Maureen McMunn (executive), Mary Bell, Geoffrey Perkins, Geoff Posner, Harry Thompson, Sophie Clarke-Jervoise

Writers Various, including Harry Enfield, Paul Whitehouse, Charlie Higson, Geoffrey Perkins, Ian Hislop, Nick Newman, Graham Linehan, Arthur Mathews, Richard Preddy, Gary Howe, David Cummings, Harry Thompson

Theme Music Simon Brint and Kate St John (*Harry Enfield's Television Programme*), Kate St John (*Harry Enfield and Chums*)

Liverpudlians Gary Bleasdale from ***Boys from the Blackstuff*** and Joe McGann, star of ***The Upper Hand*** and one quarter of the prolific McGann brothers (McGann's role was later taken by fellow Scouser Mark Moraghan shortly before he joined the casts of ***Brookside*** and ***Holby City***). Unlike Carla Lane's creations, these Scousers were taken to Liverpool's heart, recognised as an affectionate (if repetitive) parody rather than a potentially defamatory character study. Indeed, one Scousers sketch featured a guest appearance by Paul Usher, the man who arguably inspired the characters in the first place when he played loveable rogue Barry Grant in *Brookside*.

Two of Enfield's most popular and enduring characters (brought back time and again, sometimes even to host Channel 4 'Top 100', countdown-style programmes) were Smashey and Nicey, veteran DJs very loosely styled on the likes of Radio 1 veterans Alan Freeman and Tony Blackburn. With their theme tune – in fact, only tune – 'Ain't Seen Nothing Yet' by Bachman Turner Overdrive, the duo waffled over the airwaves on all manner of banalities. At the heart of the success of *Harry Enfield's Television Programme* was the input of two key collaborators – series co-writer and old-time friend of Enfield, the irrepressibly talented Paul Whitehouse (who would go on to front a sketch show of his own, ***The Fast Show***), and character actress and comedian Kathy Burke. The three performers handled the vast majority of the show's character requirements between them, with Whitehouse becoming Mike Smash, Fred Git and many others and Burke playing Waynetta Slob.

One returning character was Kevin – formerly just the annoying younger brother, now the antichrist-like Kevin the Teenager, Enfield's most astutely observed creation.

Harry Enfield's Television Programme came to an end following a Christmas Eve special in 1992, after which the programme switched channels (to BBC One) and changed its title to *Harry Enfield and Chums* – perhaps reflecting the increased role played in the proceedings by Burke and Whitehouse. Many of the old favourites from the *Television Programme* returned, but lots of new characters were introduced too. We met the aggressive Self-Righteous Brothers Frank and George, who would predict precisely how angry they would get should a celebrity ever do them a highly unlikely injustice ('Oi! Vorderman – NO!'); the Lovely Wobbly Randy Old Ladies, who kept springing traps on unsuspecting youths before jumping on them ('Young MAN!'); toddler Harry, who loved 'accidentally' inflicting pain on his younger sister Lulu just to get his mother's attention; the Understanding Dad who desperately didn't want to say or do the wrong thing in the presence of his gay son and new boyfriend; and the pair of wealthy Brummies who took great delight in explaining that they 'are considerably richer than yow!' Paul Whitehouse played Julio Geordio (a foretaste of the Channel 9 'Scorchio' joke in *The Fast Show*), a Spanish football player now living in Newcastle, who over the course of the series assimilates Geordie lingo into his own. In the second series of *Harry Enfield and Chums*, they introduced one new character per episode, characters that wouldn't be brought back in later episodes but which would have three or four different gags in that one half-hour. An example of this was Paul Whitehouse's nosy neighbour Michael Paine, a very accurate impersonation of Cockney movie-star Mr Caine.

A returning (yet different) character for *Harry Enfield and Chums* was Kevin – formerly just the annoying younger brother, now the antichrist-like Kevin the Teenager, Enfield's most astutely observed creation. His best friend Perry was played utterly convincingly by Kathy Burke and named after Burke's friend and future ***EastEnders*** star Perry Fenwick (aka Billy Mitchell), but at least Perry was quite sweet really. Kevin's antics represented one of the first times that the true nature of loathsome, hormone-raddled truculent teenagers was ever parodied in a comedy series. Louisa Rix played Kevin's ever-suffering mum and both Duncan Preston and latterly Stephen Moore portrayed his dad. Kevin and Perry were such overwhelmingly popular characters that they were given their own TV special (a compilation of old and new sketches) before heading off to the big screen for the feature film *Kevin and Perry Go Large* (2000), in which the boys travel to Ibiza for a week of hedonistic partying that of course goes horribly wrong.

Harry Enfield and Christmas Chums brought the series to an end on Christmas Eve 1997. Whitehouse had moved on to write and star in *The Fast Show*, and Burke revelled in another grotesque comic character when she starred in ***Gimme Gimme Gimme***. Enfield returned to his original TV home of political satire with a one-off special called *Norman Ormal: A Very Political Turtle* (broadcast on 1 November 1998), a stinging attack on a typical old-school Tory MP. Not content to merely throw brickbats at one political party, Enfield then delivered a very competent impression of Tony Blair in a series of short Sunday evening ITV shows called *Sermon from St Albion's*. Tempted over to Sky One for a new attempt at a sketch series – *Harry Enfield's Brand Spanking New Show* – the moment was lost by the decision to release the series on home video ahead of its first TV airing. Sadly, it wasn't a patch on his previous work, relying on cheap, bodily fluid-based humour and swearing for its few laughs. After just one series for Sky, Enfield jumped back to the BBC for a traditional sitcom called *Celeb*, in which he played ageing rock guitarist Gary Bloke. Although better than his dismal Sky One series, *Celeb* was not a great hit and wasn't recommissioned for a second run. Thankfully, viewers will always have Enfield's sublimely superb BBC sketch shows to watch and watch again. Perhaps Enfield might listen to one of his own characters the next time he decides to switch to Sky One – 'You don't want to do that! You want to stick with the BBC!'

50 mins | broadcast 25 Aug 1979, 29 Sep 1979–4 May 1984, 5 Nov 1993–25 Aug 1996 (USA)

Regular Cast
Robert Wagner · *Jonathan Hart*
Stefanie Powers · *Jennifer Hart*
Lionel Stander · *Max*
Richard B. Shull · *Lieutenant Gillis*

Creator Sidney Sheldon **Producers** Aaron Spelling, Leonard Goldberg (executive), Mart Crowley, David Levinson **Writers** Various, including Donald Ross, David Solomon, Edward Martino, Allyn Freeman, Bill LaMond, Jo LaMond, Mary Ann Kasica, Michael Scheff, Lawrence Hertzog, Don Roos **Theme Music** Mark Snow

With their grizzled driver Max and their shaggy dog Freeway, the Harts have it all. He's a self-made millionaire, she a famous journalist with gravity-defying hair. Together they indulge in capers and solve crimes, activities that keep their romance sparkling. Makes ya sick, doesn't it? Throughout it all, Max takes care of them – 'Which ain't easy, cause when they met, it was murder!'

I Dream of Jeannie creator Sidney Sheldon came up with the idea of a married pair of amateur sleuths back in the 1960s, originally calling it *Double Twist*. By the time Robert Wagner was available for another high-profile TV series, it had become *Hart to Hart*. Though the pilot episode was apparently written with Wagner's real-life wife Natalie Wood in mind, the part of Mrs Hart went to Stephanie Powers; Wagner and Powers later hooked up in real life.

Lightweight and reminiscent of the *Thin Man* movie capers that had starred Myrna Loy and William Powell (and the TV spin-off starring Peter Lawford and Phyllis Kirk), *Hart to Hart* ran for five years until a combination of increasingly poor scripts, dissatisfaction among the stars and a change of management at ABC conspired to bring the show to a timely close. Later reunion movies kept the Harts beating though.

Have I Got News For You?

Panel Game | Hat Trick for BBC Two/One | episode duration 30 mins | broadcast 28 Sep 1990–present

Regular Cast
Angus Deayton · *Host*
Ian Hislop, Paul Merton · *Team Captains*

Producers Denise O'Donoghue, Jimmy Mulville, Mary Bell, Richard Wilson (executive), John Ryan, Paul McGettigan, Margaret Johonnett, Darren Smith, Rachael Webb, Andrew Morgan (associate), Harry Thompson, Colin Swash, Giles Pilbrow, Nick Martin, Steve Doherty, Rebecca Papworth **Theme Music** Big George

Effectively a TV version of Radio 4's *The News Quiz*, without ever officially acknowledging it, *Have I Got News For You?* has been the BBC's primary alternative political commentator for over 15 years. The show is pre-recorded to allow the BBC legal team to review the content for possible libel; despite what people might believe, saying 'allegedly' after a comment isn't enough. Editor of *Private Eye* Ian Hislop and noted improvisational comedian Paul Merton are the regular captains, each accompanied by a politician, comedian or media commentator to make up the rest of the team. Often the guests will be people who've been in the news themselves, though that doesn't stop them from being the butt of jokes, sometimes from their own team captain (famously, when Roy Hattersley failed to show up for one show, he was replaced by a tub of lard).

Rounds have previously consisted of: team members coming up with a caption for a photograph of a public figure; a headline with certain words obscured, which the contestants have to either work out what it says or come up with a funny alternative; Odd One Out – four people, three of whom are connected, one of whom isn't; and general rounds based on discerning the news story behind the headlines of the week.

An uncompromising show like *Have I Got News For You?* can afford to take no prisoners, even when the host of the show is exposed for sexual improprieties in the tabloids. After Angus Deayton's sex life became headline news in October 2002, his aloofness became more than a little inappropriate for the show. The quiz programme has enjoyed guest hosts ever since, including Bruce Forsyth (who turned the show into a collection of witty parodies of some of his own series), Jeremy Clarkson, ***Frasier*** star Jane Leeves, former BBC director general Greg Dyke, Anne Robinson, *Spectator* editor and foot-in-mouth politician Boris Johnson and comedy performer Alexander Armstrong. The format has also been rolled out to cover other types of quiz show, including sport (***They Think It's All Over***), pop music (***Never Mind The Buzzcocks***) and television (*It's Only TV, But I Like It*).

Hawaii Five-O

Drama | Leonard Freeman Productions for CBS (shown on ITV) | episode duration 50 mins | broadcast 20 Sep 1968–5 Apr 1980

Regular Cast
Jack Lord · *Detective Steve McGarrett*
James MacArthur · *Detective Danny Williams*
Zulu · *Detective Kono Kalakaua*
Al Harrington · *Detective Ben Kokua*
Kam Fong · *Detective Chin Ho Kelly*
William Smith · *James 'Kimo' Carew*
Sharon Farrell · *Lori Wilson*
Herman Wedemeyer · *Edward D. 'Duke' Lukela*
Moe Keale · *Truck Kealoha*

Creator Leonard Freeman **Producers** Various, including Leonard Freeman, Philip Leacock, Douglas Greene **Writers** Various, including Leonard Freeman, Herman Groves, Jerome Coopersmith, Mel Goldberg, John D. F. Black, Robert C. Dennis,

Jerry Ludwig, Meyer Dolinsky, Anthony Lawrence, Ken Pettus, Eric Bercovici, E. Arthur Kean, Stephen Kandel, Alvin Sapinsley, Bill Stratton, Frank Telford, Norman Lessing, Glen Olson, Rod Baker, Walter Black, Tim Maschler, Bud Freeman, Orville H. Hampton, Anne Collins, Robert Janes, Seeleg Lester **Theme Music** Morton Stevens wrote arguably the most famous theme tune of them all – even if people don't know what it is, as soon as the drum-beats begin they assume the surfing position and begin to air-surf.

As Detective Steve McGarrett cried 'Book 'em, Danno' in almost every episode of *Hawaii Five-O*, we were rarely ever thinking about the crime that 'villain of the week' had committed – it was all about Hawaii itself: the wide, sandy beaches, the sunshine and the beauties on the seafront. Hubbada-hubbada.

Jack Lord starred as McGarrett, having previously played second fiddle to James Bond as Felix Leitner in *Dr No* (1962) but here heading up an elite crime-busting team. Every week it was another bunch of Chinese gangsters or Floridian drug barons, predating both ***Magnum*** and ***Miami Vice*** in location and style respectively. His second in command, Detective 'Danno' Williams caused a major stir when actor James MacArthur tired of the series and was promptly killed off in 1979. From then on, the series was merely treading water until it finally sunk. Still, at 270 episodes, *Hawaii Five-O* ranked as the longest-running cop show in American TV history.

Hazell

Drama | Thames for ITV | episode duration 50 mins | broadcast 16 Jan 1978–30 Jan 1980

Regular Cast
Nicholas Ball · *James Hazell*
Roddy McMillan · *'Choc' Minty*
Desmond McNamara · *Cousin Tel*
James Faulkner · *Gordon Gregory*
Celia Gregory · *Vinne Rae*
Barbara Young · *Dot Wilmington*
Maggie Riley · *Maureen*

Creators Terry Venables and Gordon Williams (as P. B. Yuill) **Producers** June Roberts, Tim Aspinall, Juliet Grimm **Writers** Various, including Terry Venables, Brian Glover, Gordon Williams, Richard Harris, Tony Hoare, Trevor Preston, Murray Smith, Marek Kanievska, Leon Griffiths, Willis Hall, P. J. Hammond, Jim Hawkins, Stan Hey, from the novels of 'P. B. Yuill' **Theme Music** Andy Mackay

Divorced, discharged from the police force due to a dodgy ankle and still only 33, James Hazell sets up a private investigations company with his cousin Tel. Generally surviving on his cockney charm, his powers of persuasion don't help him when he's faced with obstruction from a Scottish CID officer known as 'Choc' Minty.

An engaging series which spoofed the detective genre with Nicholas Ball's knowing narration, *Hazell* came from the minds of footballer Terry Venables and Gordon Williams, who had together written the source novels under the pen-name P. B. Yuill. Another surprising name associated with this series (as a writer) is that of bald-headed Yorkshire actor and ex-wrestler Brian Glover, perhaps best known for his voice-overs for Tetley tea bags and his starring role opposite Peter Davison in *Campion*.

Heartbeat

Drama | Yorkshire for ITV | episode duration 45 mins | broadcast 10 Apr 1992–present

Regular Cast
Nick Berry · *PC/Sergeant Nick Rowan*
Derek Fowlds · *Sergeant Oscar Blaketon*
William Simons · *PC Alf Ventress*
Mark Jordon · *PC Phil Bellamy*
Tricia Penrose · *Gina Ward*
Niamh Cusack · *Dr Kate Rowan*
Bill Maynard · *Claude Jeremiah Greengrass*
Frank Middlemass · *Dr Alex Ferrenby*
Juliette Gruber · *Jo Weston/Rowan*
David Lonsdale · *David Stockwell*
Kazia Pelka · *Maggie Bolton*
Bernard Gallagher · *Graham Weston*
Wanda Ventham · *Fiona Weston*
Stuart Golland · *George Ward*
Anne Stallybrass · *Eileen Reynolds*
Peter Benson · *Bernie Scripps*
Jason Durr · *PC/DC Mike Bradley*
Fiona Dolman · *Jackie Bradley*
Rupert Vansittart · *Lord Charles Ashfordly*
Dominic Rickhards · *Steve Adams*
Philip Franks · *Sergeant Raymond Craddock*
Geoffrey Hughes · *Vernon Scripps*
Duncan Bell · *Sergeant Dennis Iain Merton*
Sarah Tansey · *Jenny Latimer/Merton*
James Carlton · *PC Steve Crane*
Vanessa Hehir · *Rosie Cartwright*
Jonathan Kerrigan · *PC Rob Walker*
Gwen Taylor · *Peg*
Sophie Ward · *Dr Helen Trent*
John Duttine · *Sergeant George Miller*

Creator Johnny Byrne devised the format of the series from the original *Constable* novels by Nicholas Rhea, using the characters and settings rather than adapting many of the storylines **Producers** Keith Richardson (executive), Pat Brown (associate), Stuart Doughty, Steve Lanning, Martyn Auty, Archie Tait, Carol Wilks, Gerry Mill **Writers** Various, including Johnny Byrne, Peter N. Walker (the real name of Nicholas Rhea), Peter Gibbs, Brian Finch, Adele Rose, John Stevenson, Eric Deacon, Jane Hollowood, John Flanagan, Andrew McCulloch, Bill Lyons, Jane McNulty, Rob Heyland **Theme Music** The Buddy Holly classic 'Heartbeat' (which reached No. 30 in both January 1959 and

April 1960) was covered by series star Nick Berry; oddly, the theme's stayed the same despite his character having departed the show many years back. Berry released the title tune as a single – it reached No. 2 in the charts in June 1992.

Writer Johnny Byrne had long been successful in his work on other nostalgic drama series – like ***All Creatures Great and Small, One by One*** and, erm, ***Doctor Who*** – when he decided to take the basic concept of the *Constable* novels by Nicholas Rhea and create them into the perfect heart-warming TV show for Sunday night viewing – it's been a ratings juggernaut and a staple of the ITV weekend schedules for almost 15 years. In the first episode, London-based copper Nick Rowan decides to up sticks to the countryside with his doctor wife Kate, fed up of the hassle and stress of being a bobby on the beat in the heaving metropolis. They move to Kate's original stomping ground of the North Yorkshire moors, where Nick gets a job working at Ashfordly police station. His colleagues are his grumpy boss Sergeant Blaketon, world-weary Alf Ventress and enthusiastic young Phil Bellamy. Kate joins the local surgery of her old friend Alex Ferrenby, eventually taking over the duties of the practice when he's killed in a train crash. Most of Nick's duties tend to involve the latest hare-brained scheme or act of mischief caused by local elderly troublemaker Claude Greengrass, a man with his fingers in many pies and an eye always open for something that's fallen off the back of a lorry. When Nick's not on duty, the welcoming environment of the local pub, the Aidensfield Arms (with pretty young Scouser Gina as the barmaid), provides a welcome home from home.

Heartbeat is different from other nostalgia-driven TV shows in that its 1960s setting provides one of the main reasons for people turning in. Instead of just using specially composed incidental music, the producers of *Heartbeat* also rely upon contemporary pop songs of the 1960s, liberally sprinkling them throughout the action. Indeed, some songs match the events that occur in the programme so well that they have been used several times in different episodes. The first episode of *Heartbeat* was set in 1964 – consequently, if one year on screen is supposed to represent one year in real life, events in *Heartbeat* would now revolve around the dawn of disco and the arrival of punk rock. However, Aidensfield remains trapped in a sort of 'Bradford Triangle' – a mysterious area of Yorkshire where people disappear into a time-warp that's forever the 1960s.

Heartbeat was built around the swoonsome charms of former ***EastEnders*** star Nick Berry. When he announced his departure from the show, many people felt that the programme would inevitably be consigned to the scrap heap. However, TV executives hate to get rid of programmes that are raking in the advertising revenue and consequently they introduced a new young copper to be the heart-throb of *Heartbeat*. Jason Durr lasted for seven years as PC Mike Bradley (one more than Berry), before being replaced by the ill-fated PC Steve Crane (who fell from a bridge to his death) and the hopefully less accident-prone PC Rob Walker. Other characters came and went, too. When Sergeant Blaketon retired due to ill-health, he soon took over the running of the Aidensfield Arms from the late-lamented landlord, George Ward. Similarly, when running around the countryside with his dog on a string became too much for Greengrass, other lovable rogues were introduced – notably ne'er-do-wells Bernie and Vernon Scripps.

Largely filmed on location in the towns of Goathland and Otley as well as on the North Yorkshire moors themselves, *Heartbeat* looks sumptuous and provides family-friendly entertainment that's neither offensive nor particularly challenging. Realising that viewers can't get enough of this kind of thing, Yorkshire Television decided to do what ***Casualty*** had successfully achieved with ***Holby City***, and create a spin-off series that operated as a sister show to *Heartbeat*. Hence, in 2003 *The Royal* opened for duty, a programme about the comings and goings in a hospital in the nearby seaside town of Elsinby. Characters from *Heartbeat* regularly cross over into episodes of *The Royal* and vice versa; similarly, as soon as a season of *The Royal* has finished broadcasting on Sunday nights, it's usually replaced by a new run of episodes of *Heartbeat*, and so on ad infinitum...

Hector's House

Puppetry | Europe 1-Telecompagnie (shown on BBC One) | episode duration 5 mins | broadcast 9 Sep 1968–8 Jan 1970

Voice Cast
Paul Bacon · *Hector*
Denise Bryer · *Zsa Zsa, Kiki*

Creators/Writers Régine Artarit, Georges Croses **Producer** Peggy Miller **Theme Music** Francis Lai

Inspired by the success of ***The Magic Roundabout***, the BBC bought in another French series in the late 1960s to be shown just before the main evening *News*. *La Maison de Toutou* was the tale of a dog called Toutou who lives with a cat called Zouzou. Their next-door neighbour is a frog called Kiki who befriends them, accompanies them on days out and helps Zouzou calm down Toutou's bad moods. For British audiences, Peggy Miller hired British voice artists to dub over the French ones and renamed the dog and cat Hector and Zsa Zsa – thus the title of the show became *Hector's House*. Hector acquired a catchphrase of sorts; acknowledging his mood *du moment*, he'd grumble, 'I'm a great big [insert adjective] old Hector.'

In 2003, a series of adverts for the Royal Bank of Scotland re-created the world of Hector and his chums, with Hector's house now sporting a satellite dish.

He-Man and the Masters of the Universe

Animation | Mattel/Filmation (shown on ITV) | episode duration 25 mins | broadcast 5 Sep 1983–present (USA)

Voice Cast
John Erwin · *Prince Adam/He-Man*
Alan Oppenheimer · *Cringer, Man-at-Arms, Skeletor*
Linda Gary · *Teela, Evil-Lyn, Queen Marlena, Sorceress*
Lou Scheimer · *King Randor, Whiplash*
Melendy Britt · *She-Ra/Princess Adora*

Producers Norm Prescott, Patricia Ryan, Lou Scheimer **Writers** Various, including Robby London, Paul Dini, Brynne Chandler Reaves, Larry DiTillio, Ron Schultz, Richard Pardee, Sam Schultz, Janis Diamond, Douglas Booth, David Wise, Misty Taggart, Jeffry O'Hare, Rowby Goren, Antoni Zalewski, Robert Lamb, J. Michael Straczynski, D. C. Fontana **Theme Music** 'I Have the Power' by Shuki Levy, Haim Saban and Erika Scheimer. In his role as He-Man, John Erwin added some spoken vocals to the title sequence.

Though it became an utter cash cow in the end, when *Star Wars* first hit cinemas in 1977 there were no McDonalds Happy Meal tie-ins or collectable action-figure ranges. No one expected it to do any business at all so the mania that followed caught almost everyone by surprise. Everyone except George Lucas, who'd prudently made sure he retained his film's merchandising rights – which helped fund five sequels.

By the mid-1980s, entertainment lawyers and executives knew that the quickest way to make some dosh was to ensure that the retailing of the toys would not only coincide with a film's release but that they were an essential element of the creative process. It wasn't enough to ask designers to make the characters appealing to eight-year-olds; now they had to appeal to eight-year-olds as a toy – and as part of a collection.

He-Man and the Masters of the Universe was a big deal for Mattel, a boy's toy to rival (and at times eclipse) Barbie. Launched in 1981, the range revolved around a prince with a secret identity – He-Man – and a group of friends who had sworn to protect Eternia from evil, personified by Skeletor, Evil-Lyn and all manner of other rather literal-sounding characters. Whenever Castle Greyskull came under threat, Prince Adam would hold his magic sword aloft and cry 'By the power of Greyskull', an incantation that would turn him into the rippling, muscular form of He-Man. His sister Princess Adora also maintained an alter-ego, the heroic She-Ra, Princess of Power, who soon got her own spin-off series. Each episode would conclude with Adam's man at arms – called Man-at-Arms – talking directly to the viewers at home, underlining the heavy-handed moral of the story.

Masters of the Universe spawned a live-action film in 1987, starring Dolph Lundgren as He-Man and Frank Langella as Skeletor. The series has been revived numerous times since, most recently for a 2002 series by Mike Young Productions. Another live-action film version is in production for a planned 2006 release.

Henry's Cat

Animation | Bob Godfrey Films for BBC One | episode duration 5–15 mins | broadcast 12 Sep 1983–30 Dec 1992

Voice Cast
Bob Godfrey · *Narrator*

Creator/Writer Stan Hayward **Producer** Bob Godfrey **Theme Music** The original series carried a theme tune by Peter Shade, while later series had music by Jonathan P. Hodge.

Lazy, greedy and bright yellow, Henry's Cat has no name of his own (Henry himself is never seen; this is a world where animals rule). Despite the encouragement of his friend Chris Rabbit, he never seems to accomplish anything, even though he has loads of ideas. Henry's Cat has a nasal, moaning voice and the features of his face spell out the word 'Miow' vertically.

The original animation – by the cartoon god Bob Godfrey – mirrored that of the 1970s classic ***Roobarb***, with the excitable felt-tipped colouring that was easy for kids to copy. As the series evolved, the animation became more sophisticated and Henry's Cat's adventures with Chris more and more glamorous. Thankfully, none of these changes affected the characterisations that made the series so appealing in the first place.

Website
Brand new stories can be found at www.henryscat.com.

The Herbs

Animation | FimFair for BBC One | episode duration 13 mins | broadcast 1968

Cast
Gordon Rollings · *Narrator*

Creator/Writer Michael Bond **Producer/Animator** Ivor Wood

Behind the huge wall that surrounds the garden of Sir Basil and Lady Rosemary lies the 'Herbidacious' domain of the Herbs. This is where you can find a dragon called Tarragon, an owl called Sage and, lest we forget, a rather gentle green lion called Parsley. Bayleaf the gardener and Constable Knapweed try to keep order, while the rather unpleasant Bella Donna the Witch masquerades as a nice old lady while trying to get the other Herbs to do her bidding. Boo!

For a generation who grew up with *Watch with Mother*, *The Herbs* and its successor, ***The Adventures of Parsley***, represent everything that was perfect about the children's programming of the 1960s and '70s: simple stories well told, with a short song or two, and clearly defined characters. *The Herbs* also benefited from being one of the first BBC Children's programmes to be made on colour film stock (even though most viewers didn't know this until their parents finally got a colour TV in the mid-1970s when the series was still regularly repeated).

The Herbs were created by Michael Bond and brought to life by animator Ivor Wood, who had worked together on ***The Magic Roundabout*** and who later gave us ***The Wombles*** and ***Paddington***. Like many other shows of the time, the characters have found new fans within

successive generations thanks to selected episodes being released on home video and DVD compilations. We suspect the mums and dads watch them more often than their *Pokemon*-addicted kids though.

Here Come the Double Deckers

Musical Comedy | 20th Century Fox for ABC (shown on BBC One) | episode duration 25 mins | broadcast 1 Jan–30 Apr 1971

Principal Cast
Peter Firth · *Scooper*
Brinsley Forde · *Spring*
Gillian Bailey · *Billie*
Michael Audreson · *Brains*
Douglas Simmonds · *Doughnut*
Bruce Clark · *Sticks*
Debbie Russ · *Tiger*
Melvyn Hayes · *Albert*

Creators Harry Booth and Roy Simpson **Producers** David Gerber (executive), Roy Simpson **Writers** Harry Booth, Glyn Jones, Peter Miller, Melvyn Hayes, Michael Watson, Jan Butlin, John Tulley **Theme Music** A wonderfully uplifting anthem by Harry Booth, Melvyn Hayes and Johnny Anthey: 'Fun and laughter is what we're after/On our double double double decker bus'. Vocals were performed by the Double Deckers themselves.

What fun we had in the 1970s – especially if we were members of the Double Deckers gang, a group of kids whose HQ is a disused doubled-decker London bus. The only adult supervision they had came from road-sweeper Albert, who's a big kid at heart himself (played by Melvyn Hayes, who had been a member of a similar but slightly older gang when he starred alongside Cliff Richard in the film *Summer Holiday*, 1963). The kids are high-spirited but rarely wilfully naughty (although when Doughnut was mistreated by shop assistants at the toy shop and bakery, he took advantage of Brains's invisibility pudding to get his revenge). Scooper was nominally the leader of the gang, but it was usually Brains's experiments that acted as the catalyst for their adventures, such as when he built a robot that went on to cause mayhem. Whatever scrapes they find themselves in, the gang made time for a good ol' sing-sing every now and then, which gave the series a definite whiff of ***The Monkees***.

Peter Firth carried on acting after the series ended, starring in films such as *Equus* (1977) and *The Hunt for Red October* (1990) and TV shows, including a *Play for Today*, ***The Flipside of Dominick Hide***, and, more recently, the spy drama ***Spooks***. Brinsley Forde was a member of Britain's most successful reggae band, Aswad, whose hits included 'Don't Turn Around' and 'Shine'.

Website
www.thedoubledeckers.com is a lovely site with clippings from magazines, messages from the original cast and bags of info.

Here's Lucy

Sitcom | Universal/Lucille Ball Productions for CBS (shown on BBC One) | episode duration 25 mins | broadcast 23 Sep 1968–2 Sep 1974 (USA)

Regular Cast
Lucille Ball · *Lucy Carter*
Gale Gordon · *Harrison Carter*
Lucie Arnaz · *Kim Carter*
Desi Arnaz Jr · *Craig Carter*
Mary Jane Croft · *Mary Jane Lewis*

Creator Lucille Ball **Producers** Cleo Smith, Gary Morton **Writers** Various **Theme Music** Wilbur Hatch

For commentary, see I LOVE LUCY

Hetty Wainthropp Investigates

Crime Drama | BBC One | episode duration 50 mins, plus 75-min specials | broadcast 3 Jan 1996–4 Sep 1998

Regular Cast
Patricia Routledge · *Hetty Wainthropp*
Derek Benfield · *Robert Wainthropp*
Dominic Monaghan · *Geoffrey Shawcross*
Suzanne Maddock · *Janet Frazer*
John Graham-Davies · *DCI Adams*
Frank Mills · *Frank Wainthropp*
Wanda Ventham · *Margaret Balshaw*

Creators John Bowen, David Cook **Producers** Michael Wearing, Rebecca Eaton, Jo Wright, Mal Young (executive), Mike Hudson, Ian Hopkins (associate), Carol Parks **Writers** John Bowen, David Cook, Philip Martin, Jeremy Paul, Brian Finch, Peter Gibbs **Theme Music** Nigel Hess

Hetty Wainthropp is a 60-ish housewife living in a small Lancashire town. Happily married to Robert, but bored and short of money, Hetty sets herself up as a private investigator, roping in her husband and a 17-year-old reformed former shoplifter called Geoffrey to help her. Although she doesn't look or act like a typical detective, Hetty's innate curiosity and busybody nature make her particularly effective when it comes to solving crimes. Plain spoken and quietly determined, Hetty Wainthropp always gets her man.

A wonderful change of pace and character for Patricia Routledge (who faced typecasting for ever more thanks to her marvellous creation of Hyacinth Bucket in ***Keeping Up Appearances***), *Hetty Wainthropp Investigates* was based upon the 1986 novel *Missing Persons* by David Cook. Cook worked alongside other writers to come up with a whole new range of investigations for Hetty's television adventures. A charming yet completely unchallenging detective series, *Hetty Wainthropp Investigates* is now perhaps best remembered for being the launching pad for a young actor called Dominic Monaghan, who would achieve Hollywood superstardom as Merry, one of the Hobbits in the *Lord of the Rings* trilogy of movies.

Hi-De-Hi!

Sitcom | BBC One | episode duration 30-60 mins | broadcast 1 Jan 1980-30 Jan 1988

Regular Cast
Simon Cadell · *Jeffrey Fairbrother*
Paul Shane · *Ted Bovis*
Ruth Madoc · *Gladys Pugh*
Spike Dixon · *Jeffrey Holland*
Peggy Ollerenshaw · *Su Pollard*
Felix Bowness · *Fred Quilly*
Diane Holland · *Yvonne Stuart-Hargreaves*
Barry Howard · *Barry Stuart-Hargreaves*
Leslie Dwyer · *Mr Partridge*
David Griffin · *Squadron Leader Clive Dempster*
Ben Aris · *Julian Dalrymple-Sykes*
Nikki Kelly · *Sylvia*
Rikki Howard · *Betty*
Penny Irving · *Mary*
Chris Andrews, the Webb Twins · *Yellowcoat Boys*
Kenneth Connor · *Uncle Sammy*

Creators/Writers Jimmy Perry and David Croft **Producers** David Croft, John Kilby, Mike Stephens **Theme Music** 'Holiday Rock', written by Jimmy Perry and performed by Paul Shane

In the Britain of the late 1950s, the prospect of a package holiday to Benidorm was still about ten years away from being an affordable option for most families. The traditional seaside holiday resort was thus still the choice for many people, but increasingly it was the new-fangled holiday camps, originally started by entrepreneur Billy Butlin, that attracted families with their offer of cheap, cheerful entertainment all in one place. It was in this environment that writers Jimmy Perry and David Croft chose to set their next sitcom. Perry had been a Butlin's 'Redcoat' (the name given to the camp staff owing to their brightly coloured uniforms) and Croft had worked as one the entertainment team producing shows for holiday-makers. As they had with ***Dad's Army***, Perry and Croft chose a historic setting for their comedy series, proving that nothing sells like nostalgia when it comes to getting laughs.

It is 1959 and the staff of Maplin's Holiday Camp return to work for the summer season after the long winter break. They discover to their surprise that the new camp manager is ex-academic Jeffrey Fairbrother, a well-meaning but charisma-free bloke with no experience whatsoever of leading a team of entertainers. Jeffrey's right-hand woman is Gladys Pugh, a lusty lady from Wales and Chief Yellowcoat (all Maplin's staff are required to wear the corporate yellow blazers) who instantly finds herself smitten with Jeffrey's polite behaviour and educated ways. Initially hostile and dismissive of Jeffrey's attempts to run the holiday camp is bluff northern comic Ted Bovis, a traditional comedian training up hapless young protégé Spike Dixon with a bewildering variety of rules each of which is dubbed 'the first rule of comedy', just like the last one was. Upper-crust ballroom dancers Barry and Yvonne Stuart-Hargreaves, surly jockey Fred Quilly, and alcoholic, child-hating Punch and Judy man Mr Partridge complete the line-up of principal entertainment staff. The final member of the Maplin's team is junior chalet maid Peggy, perpetually effervescent and yearning to get the chance to give up cleaning duties and join the ranks of the Yellowcoats.

The comedy in *Hi-De-Hi!* revolved around the day-to-day interaction between the Maplin's staff and occasionally the holiday-makers who stayed there. In particular, the well-observed snatches of 1950s life, and the completely differing attitudes as to what constituted entertainment then compared with the 1980s made *Hi-De-Hi!* a joy to behold. Of particular note was Ruth Madoc as permanently frustrated Gladys Pugh. Her ever-so-cheery greeting over the camp's public address system (complete with three-note glockenspiel melody) would invariably include an update about what she'd just had for lunch in the camp canteen ('I had a steak and kidney pie followed by a spotted dick with custard – yum yum. My compliments to our cordon bleu chef . . .'), followed by a rundown of the day's main activities: 'This afternoon we've got our Knobby Knees Competition at 2 o'clock by our Olympic-sized swimming pool, and don't forget the "Get-to-Know-You Dance" in the Hawaiian Ballroom tonight at eight.' You don't get that kind of glamour on a fortnight in Ibiza, now do you?

After four seasons, star Simon Cadell (writer/producer David Croft's son-in-law, incidentally) chose to move on to pastures new and a replacement Chief Entertainments Officer, the slightly smarmy Clive Dempster, was drafted in. Although David Griffin did a good job, the show just didn't feel quite the same without shy, ineffectual Jeffrey in charge of the camp. Eventually the gates of Maplin's Holiday Camp closed after eight years on screen, with Peggy finally freeing herself from the iron rule of cleaning manager Miss Cathcart and donning the yellow coat she'd always longed for. *Hi-De-Hi!* was another quality sitcom from the Perry/Croft stable (which as well as *Dad's Army* included ***It Ain't Half Hot Mum*** and ***You Rang, M'Lord?***) that enjoyed creditable audiences throughout its run of 58 episodes.

The High Chaparral

Action-Adventure | Xanadu Productions for NBC (shown on BBC One) | episode duration 50 mins | broadcast 10 Sep 1967-12 Mar 1971 (USA)

Regular Cast
Leif Erickson · *John Cannon*
Cameron Mitchell · *Buck Cannon*

Mark Slade · *Billy Blue Cannon*
Henry Darrow · *Manolito Montoya*
Linda Cristal · *Victoria Montoya Cannon*
Don Collier · *Sam Butler*
Bob Hoy · *Joe Butler*
Roberto Contreras · *Pedro Carr*
Ted Markland · *Reno*
Jerry Summers · *Ira Bean*
Frank Silvera · *Don Sebastian Montoya*
Rudolfo Acosta · *Vaquero*
Anthony Caruso · *El Lobo*
Rudy Ramos · *Wind*
Gilbert Roland · *Don Domingo Montoya*

Creator David Dortort **Producers** David Dortort (executive), Buck Houghton, William F. Claxton, James Schmerer **Writers** Various, including David Dotort, Walter Black, Don Balluck, Michael Fessier, Tim Kelly, William F. Leicester, Ken Pettus, Jack Sowards, D. C. Fontana **Theme Music** David Rose, Harry Sukman

In the Arizona of the 1870s, the Cannon family own The High Chaparral cattle ranch. Patriarch of the family is 50-year-old John Cannon, determined to build himself an empire while simultaneously co-existing with the Apaches and Mexicans who live nearby. The rest of the family include his younger brother Buck, a dead-eye shot and a mean bar-room brawler, his 20-year-old son Billy Blue and his new Mexican wife Victoria Montoya. The final member of the family is Victoria's brother Manolito, who originally came to supervise the marriage of convenience between Victoria and John, but who stayed when the marriage turned into a true love-match. Together, the family face a wide variety of challenges, including rustlers, drought and raids from assorted renegade Mexicans and Apaches.

Created and produced by the man behind ***Bonanza***, David Dotort, *The High Chaparral* set a new benchmark for realism in TV westerns, with the heat and dirt of life in the Arizona desert clearly coming across to viewers – primarily because it was shot on a real-life western set, Old Tucson (which had been created for the 1939 movie *Arizona*). It also marked a shift in the way in which Native Americans were shown on screen. From *The High Chaparral* onwards, 'Indians' would no longer be simplistically depicted as the bad guys. Instead, the portrayal of good and bad in both the 'Indians' and the 'cowboys' would make westerns a much more sophisticated genre.

The High Life

Sitcom | BBC Two | episode duration 30 mins | broadcast 9 Jan 1994, 6 Jan–10 Feb 1995

Regular Cast
Alan Cumming · *Sebastian Flight*
Forbes Masson · *Steve McCracken*
Siobhan Redmond · *Shona Spurtle*
Patrick Ryecart · *Captain Duff*

Creators/Writers Alan Cumming, Forbes Masson **Producers** Tony Dow **Theme Music** 'The High Life' was composed and sung by Alan Cumming and Forbes Masson, arranged by Graham Jarvis: 'Here's how to get that adrenaline flowing, just step aboard a Boeing, going high. . .'

On board Air Scotia, airline trolly dollies Sebastian and Steve do whatever they can to make their lives a little more comfortable. They're not averse to siphoning off the miniature bottles of vodka and replacing the liquid with water, and they're perfectly bitchy behind the backs of sweaty or unpleasant passengers. Although they're both as camp as a row of tents, Steve nevertheless has an eye for the ladies and often makes a fool of himself with unwanted approaches towards the female Air Scotia staff and (even worse) the passengers. One woman that simultaneously attracts and repels Steve is 'Hitler in tights', their senior in-flight supervisor Shona Spurtle – a woman with a nasty turn of phrase and an even nastier attitude to lazy, good-for-nothing stewards. Their regular pilot is the frankly bonkers Captain Duff, a man with the slightest possible grip on reality and zero sense of direction.

A true cult classic in every sense of the word, *The High Life* was adored by the few people who watched it and either ignored or forgotten by everybody else. Written by and starring long-time friends Forbes Masson and Alan Cumming, it was a frantic, surreal and exceptionally odd viewing experience, with moments of complete comedy genius interspersed among the thick Scottish vernacular and accents (one *Batman* pastiche, in which sound effects are superimposed as words on the screen, includes the onomatopoeic word 'Fud!' which is horrifically crude in Scotland but unknown further south than Hadrian's Wall). With storylines veering from a hostage crisis (instigated by a pro-Scottish Independence terrorist) through to the theft of a secret recipe for a Scottish confectionary delicacy called Tablet, there was a distinctly Caledonian taste to the programme: even legendary Scottish actress Molly Weir (best known to Sassenach viewers of a certain age as Hazel the McWitch from ***Rentaghost***) was tempted out of retirement to take part. The funniest moment of the show involved Steve and Sebastian's attempt to compose a Scottish entry for the ***Eurovision Song Contest*** – their masterpiece, 'Pif Paf Pof' ('I want to have it off, have it off 'til I cough') neatly summarised everything that's ludicrous, camp and completely entertaining in this programme. Sadly, only one series (plus an earlier pilot episode) of *The High Life* was produced – more may well have followed if Alan Cumming hadn't suddenly become the toast of Hollywood, making a name for himself in such films as *Goldeneye* (1995), *Emma* (1986), *Eyes Wide Shut* (1999) and the *X-Men* sequel *X2* (2003).

Highway

Religious/Factual | Various Regions/Anglia/Tyne-Tees for ITV | episode duration 25 mins | broadcast 1983–93

Regular Cast
Harry Secombe · *Host*

Creator Reverend Maxwell Deas **Producers** Bill Ward (executive), David Hammond-Williams, Roy Norton, Malcolm Alsopp

For many years, the 'God Slot' was a regular fixture on Sunday early evenings on ITV, with the much loved *Stars on Sunday* running for ten years between 1969 and 1979, a celebrity-led rival to the BBC's more traditional ***Songs of Praise***. In the 1980s, ITV handed the job of co-ordinating its religious programming to just one of its regional companies, Tyne Tees Television, under the auspices of their head of religious programming, Reverend Maxwell Deas. One of Deas' first ideas was to bring back a Sunday evening religious programme that would have significant entertainment content – the end result was *Highway*, a weekly collection of hymns, interviews and music, all hosted by much-loved national treasure (and former Goon) Harry Secombe.

Broadcast at 7 p.m. every Sunday, *Highway* travelled around the country visiting a different location each week – and, appropriately, ITV regions would take it in turns to produce each edition. In each programme, Harry would invite his guests to sing their favourite religious songs, to talk about their particular faiths, or even just to show him around their part of the UK. On one occasion, the programme arrived at a small Scottish school, where a young teacher had come up with the idea for a drama series based around a student newspaper. *Highway*'s executive producer Bill Ward liked the idea so much that he decided to take this young teacher's scripts to Central Television – the teacher was called Steven Moffat, and ***Press Gang*** would be his first TV hit, with ***Joking Apart*** and ***Coupling*** following on afterwards.

Highway's death warrant was signed in 1992 when Margaret Thatcher liberated ITV from its long-standing obligation to feature religious programming in its early Sunday evening schedule. *Highway* was quickly shunted to an afternoon slot for its final run in 1993 before being dropped by the network – the older demographic watching *Highway* simply wasn't attractive enough to a ratings-hungry network. The same year, Harry began hosting *Sunday Morning with Secombe*, another religious programme that could survive more happily away from competitive prime-time slots. Unfortunately, Harry Secombe's health began to deteriorate from 1997, and in 1999 he retired from television presenting. He passed away the following year, on 11 April 2000.

Hill Street Blues

Crime Drama | MTM Enterprises for NBC (shown on Channel 4) | episode duration 50 mins | broadcast 15 Jan 1981–12 May 1987 (USA)

Regular Cast
Daniel J. Travanti · *Captain Frank Furillo*
Taurean Blacque · *Detective Neal Washington*
Barbara Bosson · *Fay Furillo*
René Enríquez · *Lieutenant Ray Calletano*
Charles Haid · *Officer Andy Renko*
Veronica Hamel · *Joyce Davenport*
Ed Marinaro · *Officer Joe Coffey*
Kiel Martin · *Officer J. D. LaRue*
James B. Sikking · *Lieutenant Howard Hunter*
Joe Spano · *Sergeant/Detective Henry Goldblume*
Betty Thomas · *Officer/ Sergeant Lucy Bates*
Bruce Weitz · *Sergeant Mick Belker*
Michael Conrad · *Sergeant Phil Esterhaus*
Robert Prosky · *Sergeant Stan Jablonski*
Barbara Babcock · *Grace Gardner*
Robert Clohessy · *Officer Patrick Flaherty*
Lindsay Crouse · *Kate McBride*
Jon Cypher · *Chief Fletcher Daniels*
Dennis Franz · *Detective Sal Benedetto, Lieutenant Norman Buntz*
Megan Gallagher · *Officer Tina Russo*
Robert Hirschfeld · *Officer Leo Schnitz*
Peter Jurasik · *Sid the Snitch*
Mimi Kuzyk · *Detective Patsy Mayo*
Vincent Lucchesi · *Captain Jerry Fuchs*
Gary Miller · *EAT Officer Jack Ballantine*
Lynne Moody · *Martha Nichols*
Ken Olin · *Detective Harry Garibaldi*
Trinidad Silva · *Jesus Martinez*
Lisa Sutton · *Officer Robin Tataglia*
Jeffrey Tambor · *Judge Alan Wachtel*
Jennifer Tilly · *Gina Srignoli*
Michael Warren · *Officer Bobby Hill*
George Wyner · *Assistant District Attorney Irwin Bernstein*
Pat Corley · *Chief Coroner Wally Nydorf*
Larry D. Mann · *Judge Lee Oberman*
Tony Perez · *Officer Mike Perez*

Creators Steven Bochco, Michael Kozoll **Producers** Various, including Steven Bochco, Michael Kozoll, Jeffrey Lewis (executive), Anthony Yerkovich, Gregory Hoblit, Scott Brazil (supervising), David Anspaugh, David Latt, Ellen S. Pressman, James C. Hart (associate), Christian Williams, Jeffrey Lewis, Michael Vittes, Sascha Schneider, Walon Green **Writers** Various, including Steven Bochco, Michael Kozoll, Anthony Yerkovich, Gregory Hoblit, Jeffrey Lewis, Michael Wagner, David Milch, Mark Frost, Karen Hall, Roger Director, Elia Katz, Jacob Epstein, Walon Green, Robert Ward, Dick Wolf, David Mamet **Theme Music** Mike Post composed the beautifully understated and slightly melancholic theme, a piece of music completely at odds with (and therefore complementing magnificently) the frenzied pace of the programme itself.

The importance of *Hill Street Blues* on modern TV drama simply cannot be underestimated. It single-handedly rewrote the rulebook on how drama should be staged on television, shifting from a carefully controlled and neat, multi-camera formula to a much more realistic,

chaotic style, thanks to the use of handheld cameras that followed the characters rather than waiting for them to step into position. In one fell swoop, television drama was dragged kicking and screaming into the 1980s, sweeping aside all of the conventions of established TV production and making everything screened before it seem more than a little bit slow, stagy and artificial.

Hill Street precinct is a police station in the heart of a major city on America's East Coast (never actually named in the show itself, although location filming was done in Chicago). It's located in the roughest part of town and deals with the absolute lowest of the low – drug addicts, prostitutes, pimps, armed robbers, et cetera – on a daily basis. In charge of a motley assortment of cops is noble Captain Frank Furillo, a determined and dedicated man whose commitment to the job is an inspiration to his world-weary team. Furillo's right-hand man is the charming and genial Sergeant Esterhaus, who leads the early-morning roll-call, assigning specific officers to duties, briefing the team on the latest news, and then of course warning: 'Let's be careful out there . . .' Other memorable team members included SWAT team leader Howard Hunter, undercover specialist (and perpetual tramp-a-like) Mick Belker, easy-going officer partners Lucy Bates and Joe Coffey, and the two principal cops, Bobby Hill and Andy Renko. Hill and Renko's relationship was often strained, largely due to the latter's latent racism and the fact that he'd been assigned to work with Hill, a black man, as his partner. Furillo's private life formed a major element to the storylines too – his ex-wife Fay was always on the scene, casting a shadow over his new relationship with glamorous defence attorney Joyce Davenport. As with most other long-running shows, characters came and left according to the needs of the stories and as actors chose to quit. The most poignant departure was that of Sergeant Esterhaus, when actor Michael Conrad died suddenly in the middle of filming. Esterhaus's replacement was the less affable Sergeant Stan Jablonski.

The appeal of *Hill Street Blues* lay in the multi-layered storylines and innovative camera work. As we have stated, it was the first series to extensively use handheld cameras, huge numbers of extras and a rowdy background hubbub with characters talking over each other. All of these tricks created an air of immediacy and realism more normally associated with news reports and documentaries. Furthermore, *Hill Street Blues* broke the rule normally associated with police TV series – the villains weren't always brought to justice at the end of each episode. Solutions to investigations were sometimes impenetrable, sometimes unforthcoming. In each individual episode, viewers would follow multiple storylines, many of them stretching across several weeks. To audiences more familiar with police shows like ***The Sweeney*** or ***Starsky and Hutch***, in which storylines were neatly wrapped up within the space of the hour-long episode, it came as both a shock and a breath of fresh air. Although *Hill Street Blues* never attracted a vast audience either in the US or the UK (where it was screened as one of Channel 4's first acquisitions), its critical acclaim was immense, and its influence on programme making of every genre is felt to this day. Indeed, the creators of ***The Bill*** specifically adopted *Hill Street Blues* as the template for their programme. A product of Mary Tyler Moore's highly successful production company, each episode of *Hill Street Blues* ended with the MTM logo – a kitten mewing in a pastiche of the old MGM roaring lion – subtly adapted to feature the kitty wearing a policeman's cap. Other MTM shows would ape this, with ***St Elsewhere*** boasting a kitten in a surgeon's mask and *Newhart* endowing the kitten with Bob Newhart's own deadpan delivery of the word 'miaow'.

Hillsborough

Drama | Granada for ITV | duration 100 mins | broadcast 5 Dec 1996

Cast

Christopher Eccleston · *Trevor Hicks*
Ricky Tomlinson · *John Glover*
Annabelle Apsion · *Jenni Hicks*
Rachel Davies · *Theresa Glover*
Mark Womack · *Eddie Spearritt*
Tracey Wilkinson · *Jan Spearritt*
Scot Williams · *Joe Glover*
Maurice Roëves · *Chief Superintendant David Duckenfield*
Ian McDiarmid · *Dr Popper*
Stephen Walters · *Ian Glover*
Kevin Knapman · *Adam Spearritt*
Sarah Graham · *Sarah Hicks*

Producers Gub Neal (executive), Nicola Shindler **Writer** Jimmy McGovern **Theme Music** Robert Lane

On the morning of 15 April 1989, members of the Hicks, Glover and Spearritt families left their homes on Merseyside to travel to Hillsborough football stadium in Sheffield where an FA Cup semi-final football match was due to take place between Nottingham Forest and their beloved Liverpool FC. However, something went wrong that day, and as kick-off time approached, huge numbers of Liverpool fans were still outside the stadium waiting to gain admission. A gate was opened to allow large numbers of fans rapid access – as a result of this surge, the people who were already at the front of the stands were crushed against security fences. Before anybody realised what was happening, 96 people were dead.

Hillsborough was a dramatised account of the events of that terrible day, written by Liverpudlian playwright Jimmy McGovern. McGovern began his career on Scouse soap ***Brookside***, only quitting the series when his suggestions to cover the Hillsborough tragedy in the show's plotlines fell on deaf ears. McGovern's next major hit was in gritty detective drama ***Cracker*** – in perhaps the most memorable storyline, Robert Carlyle played a young man traumatised both by Hillsborough and by the press's reporting of the event. Still eager to feature the individual stories of the families bereaved in the tragedy, McGovern then wrote *Hillsborough*, a one-off drama that delved into what many of the families of the victims felt was an official cover-up into incompetent crowd management by the police force on that day. An astoundingly powerful play (winning the 1997 Best Single Drama BAFTA), not least because of uniformly believable performances from a top-notch ensemble cast, *Hillsborough* was written in the hope that it would force a full public enquiry into the events of 15 April 1989. Unfortunately, although this aim never came to pass, few people who watched this drama could have failed to be convinced of the need for some genuine closure for the families involved.

Himalaya

See AROUND THE WORLD IN 80 DAYS

The History Man

Drama | BBC One | episode duration 60 mins | broadcast 4 Jan–25 Jan 1981

Regular Cast

Antony Sher · *Howard Kirk*
Geraldine James · *Barbara Kirk*
Isla Blair · *Flor Beniform*
Michael Hordern · *Professor Marvin*
Maggie Steed · *Myra Beamish*
Paul Brooke · *Henry Beamish*
Jonathan Bruton · *Martin Kirk*
Charlotte Enderby · *Celia Kirk*
Milo Sperber · *Dr Zachery*
Bill Buffery · *Peter Madden*
Peter-Hugo Daly · *George Carmody*
Miriam Margolyes · *Melissa Tordoroff*
Zienia Merton · *Miss Ho*
Laura Davenport · *Annie Callendar*
Jack Elliott · *Leon*
Jane Galloway · *Chloe*
Judy Liebert · *Jane McIntosh*
Graham Padden · *John McIntosh*
Arthur Lugo · *Hashmi Sadeck*
Henry Moxon · *Dr Petworth*
Lloyd Peters · *Michael Bernard*
Elizabeth Proud · *Moira Millikin*
Veronica Quilligan · *Felicity Phee*
Chloe Salaman · *Anne Petty*
Jane Slaughter · *Joanna*
Julia Swift · *Beck Pott*
Juliet Waley · *Marjorie*

Producer Michael Wearing **Writer** Christopher Hampton, from the novel by Malcolm Bradbury **Theme Music** George Fenton

A four-part adaptation of Sir Malcolm Bradbury's novel, *The History Man* is set at the fictional Watermouth University and centres on the life of lecturer Howard Kirk and his wife Barbara. Howard is a radical sociologist, who likes nothing better than trying to encourage his colleagues and students to challenge the established way of doing things. Howard and Barbara enjoy what's euphemistically known as a 'modern marriage', and their views on politics and sexuality cause upheaval and conflict within the academic community at the university.

Noted at the time for its controversial content and both frequent and (relatively) graphic sex scenes, in hindsight perhaps the most shocking thing about *The History Man* is Antony Sher's gigantic Afro hairdo and handlebar moustache. For many years, Professor Laurie Taylor of York University was believed to have been the inspiration for Howard Kirk. However, Taylor confirmed after Bradbury's death that he had never met the author before the book was written. The series was partly filmed on location at Lancaster University, for that bleak Sixties 'new university' concrete look.

A History of Britain by Simon Schama

Documentary | BBC Two | episode duration 60 mins | broadcast 30 Sep 2000–18 Jun 2002

Regular Cast

Simon Schama · *Presenter*
Timothy West, James Bolam, David Threlfall, Bill Paterson, Samuel West, Lindsay Duncan, Michael Kitchen, Matthew Rhys, Emilia Fox, Christian Rodska, Jane Lapotaire, Ray Lonnen, Richard Griffiths, Jonathan Price, Juliet Stevenson, Prunella Scales, Charles Dance · *Voice-overs*

Creator/Writer Simon Schama **Producers** Martin Davidson (executive), Mike Ibeji (associate), Janet Lee, Claire Beavan, Ian Bremner, Martina Hall, Liz Hartford, Tim Kirby, Paul Tilzey, Jamie Muir, Helen Nixon, Ben Ledden **Theme Music** John Harle

One of the great achievements in documentary making in the past ten years, *A History of Britain by Simon Schama* revealed, in an easily understood fashion, the ongoing saga behind the development of the peoples, leaders and countries of the British Isles. Beginning just prior to the Norman invasion of 1066, *A History of Britain* travelled in chronological order, using narration, re-enactments and dramatisations of key events in British history. Throughout all 16 episodes (with dynamic titles like 'Dynasty', 'Britannia Incorporated', 'King Death' and 'The Wrong Empire'), Simon Schama's calm, involving narration helped to make even the trickiest period in history accessible to couch potatoes with little or no knowledge of the events or people involved.

Simon Schama had already made a name for himself as a talented interpreter of history, having published

successful works on the French Revolution and Dutch history in the 1970s and 1980s. He taught modern history at Brasenose College, Oxford, before spending 13 years teaching at Harvard. Schama's easy style of presentation and delivery was backed up by a starry cast of voice-over performers, many of them re-creating the words of some of the most important people in history. *A History of Britain* re-established the kind of epic documentary series that many people felt had disappeared from TV schedules for ever, and for that reason alone it deserved all of the awards and plaudits that rained down upon it.

The Hitch Hiker's Guide to the Galaxy

Comedy | BBC Two | episode duration 35 mins | broadcast 5 Jan–9 Feb 1981

Cast
Peter Jones · *Voice of The Book*
Simon Jones · *Arthur Dent*
David Dixon · *Ford Prefect*
Joe Melia · *Mr Prosser*
Martin Benson · *Vogon Captain*
Michael Cule · *Vogon Guard*
Sandra Dickinson · *Trisha 'Trillian' McMillan*
Mark Wing-Davey · *Zaphod Beeblebrox*
David Learner · *Marvin*
Stephen Moore · *voice of Marvin*
David Tate · *voice of Eddie*
Richard Vernon · *Slartibartfast*
Valentine Dyall · *voice of Deep Thought*
David Leland · *Majikthise*
Charles McKeown · *Vroomfondel*
Antony Carrick · *Lunkwill*
Timothy Davies · *Fook*
Matt Zimmerman · *Shooty*
Marc Smith · *Bang Bang*
Jack May · *Head Waiter at the Restaurant at the End of the Universe*
Colin Jeavons · *Max Quordlepleen*
Peter Davison · *Dish of the Day*
Colin Bennett · *Zarquon*
Aubrey Morris · *Captain of the Golgafrincham 'B' Ark*
Matthew Scurfield · *Number One*
David Neville · *Number Two*
Geoffrey Beevers · *Number Three*
Beth Porter · *Marketing Girl*
Jon Glover · *Management Consultant*

Creator/Writer Douglas Adams **Producers** Alan J. W. Bell, John Lloyd **Theme Music** 'Journey of the Sorcerer' by Bernie Leadon of the Eagles, arranged by Paddy Kingsland

When Arthur Dent wakes up to the sound of a demolition squad of bulldozers amassing on his front lawn, he has no idea that by the end of the day he'll have discovered his best friend is an alien and not, as he'd always believed, from Guildford, see his planet destroyed by a fleet of Vogons spaceships, be thrown out of an airlock into deep space, bump into a girl he once spectacularly failed to get off with, on the bridge of an impossible spaceship, discover that the beings most pissed off about the earth's destruction are the white mice who footed the bill for it to be built in the first place, and learn that the number 42 is slightly more connected to life's great mysteries than anyone had ever suspected. Oh, and struggle to find anywhere in the universe that can provide him with a decent cup of tea.

Straddling the comic generations between the ***Monty Python*** set and the anarchic ***Comic Strip*** bunch, Douglas Adams' *The Hitch Hiker's Guide to the Galaxy* provides a tightly packed story which sustains a rather precarious internal logic that simultaneously succeeds in making absolute sense largely due to the conviction with which it's delivered. His much-imitated and frequently recycled science fiction comedy was first produced as a radio series the likes of which had never been heard before – a jumbled mix of ***Doctor Who***, Isaac Asimov, the Beatles' *Sergeant Pepper's Lonely Heart's Club Band*, Pink Floyd's *Dark Side of the Moon* and far too many books on existentialism and quantum physics. Prior to its translation to the TV screen, it had been novelised and adapted for stage. Each form added to and remixed the original story until many hard-core fans now find it difficult to remember which version included what specific elements.

Though a few of the original radio players re-created their roles for television (Simon Jones, Mark Wing-Davey and Stephen Moore among them), producer Alan J. W. Bell battled with Adams to recast as many parts as possible, figuring that a note-by-note retread would be pointless. It was a decision that gave us the superb David Dixon (replacing Geoffrey McGivern) as the mercurial and very *Doctor Who*-ish Ford Prefect, but sadly also delivered the shrill Sandra Dickinson as Trillian. One of the more surprising elements of continuity came in the form of David Learner – who had previously played the body of Marvin in a stage production – reprising his dialogue-free role.

Douglas Adams' dexterity with language was combined with a rational atheist approach to the creation of the universe, which makes his popularity in America all the more inexplicable. God is proven not to exist purely because of the presence of a small parasitic fish that, when placed in the ear of any being, can instantly translate any language (a nifty sidestep of the issue of why all aliens in science fiction speak perfect English), while another faith system is revealed to be based upon the theory that the universe was the product of a giant goat suffering a sneezing fit. Such accounts and anecdotes are delivered by the voice of the book, as provided by Peter Jones. A necessary narrative device for radio, the voice of the book survived for this adaptation and is now thought to be such an essential ingredient that much nail biting ensued as fans awaited the casting of the 2005 feature film (with Peter Jones having died in 2000, the part eventually went to Stephen Fry, a self-confessed *Hitch Hiker* fan). Jones's voice was accompanied by groundbreaking 'computer' graphics that were actually one of the series' biggest cons – not one pixel of CGI was used; instead, traditional cell animation was used to create the colourful line drawings that illustrate the *Guide*, although some of the subtlest jokes were hidden in these animated sequences.

Not everything from the radio series made it through to TV land, though ideas such as an alien that changed its shape every few seconds would have severely tested an already over-stretched budget. Adams had tweaked the story considerably for the novelisations that covered the first radio series (*The Hitch Hiker's Guide to the Galaxy* and *The Restaurant at the End of the Universe*), and one of the TV show's defining moments actually came from the stage play – 'the Dish of the Day'. Adams' logic of creating an animal that actually wants to be eaten can't really be faulted, although that doesn't stop Arthur from turning white at the thought of it and ordering a green salad instead. That the mooing space pig itself is played by Sandra Dickinson's then husband Peter Davison, shortly before he stepped into the role of *Doctor Who*, makes it all the more surreal.

As with the first radio series, the TV show ends with Arthur and Ford separated from their space chums and trapped on a prehistoric earth with a bunch of alien marketing consultants, hair designers, lifestyle documentarians and other members of the useless third of the Golgafrinchan race, a bunch of knuckleheads so deeply involved in the whole process of point-missing that their only concern in the development of the wheel is what colour it should be. As Arthur and Ford stroll off, realising that their very presence on the planet will lead to the extinction of the cavemen, we hear 'What a Wonderful World' by Louis Armstrong and realise that two million years for the lifespan of a planet is really no time at all.

With Adams' notorious inability to deliver scripts on time (his oft-quoted excuse being because he loved the sound deadlines make as they whiz past his head), a second series was never really on the cards. But the success of the TV series (winning three BAFTAS) almost managed to overshadow the radio series that spawned it. Not that this means much. Even fans keep harping on about how the TV show (and now the film) differs from the book. Pah!

Website
See the real-life *Hitch Hiker's Guide to the Galaxy* at work at www.bbc.co.uk/h2g2.

Holby City

Drama | BBC One | episode duration 50 mins | broadcast 12 Jan 1999–present

Regular Cast
George Irving · *Anton Meyer*
Michael French · *Nick Jordan*
Phyllis Logan · *Muriel McKendrick*
Jan Pearson · *Kath Shaughnessy/Fox*
Lisa Faulkner · *Victoria Merrick*
Dawn McDaniel · *Kirstie Collins*
Sarah Preston · *Karen Newburn*
Angela Griffin · *Jasmine Hopkins*
Nicola Stephenson · *Julie Fitzjohn/Bradford*
Ian Curtis · *Ray Sykes*
Julie Saunders · *Ellie Sharpe*
Jeremy Edwards · *Danny Shaughnessy*
Thusita Jayasundera · *'Tash' Bandara*
Jeremy Sheffield · *Alex Adams*
Peter De Jersey · *Steve Waring*
Laura Sadler · *Sandy Harper*
Siobhan Redmond · *Janice Taylor*
Tina Hobley · *Chrissie Williams/Davis*
Hugh Quarshie · *Ric Griffin*
Dominic Jephcott · *Alistair Taylor*
Paul Shane · *Stan Ashleigh*
Mark Moraghan · *Owen Davis*
Ian Aspinall · *Mubbs Hussein*
Luisa Bradshaw-White · *Lisa Fox*
Verona Joseph · *Jess Griffin*
David Paisley · *Ben Saunders*
Denis Lawson · *Tom Campbell-Gore*
Rocky Marshall · *Ed Keating*
Sharon Maughan · *Tricia Williams*
Kim Vithana · *Rosie Sattar*
Art Malik · *Zubin Khan*
Amanda Mealing · *Connie Beauchamp*

Creators Jeremy Brock, Paul Unwin **Producers** Geraint Morris, Foz Allan, Sophie Anwar, Tim Bradley, Pippa Brill, Jeremy Brock, Diana Brookes, Edwina Craze, David Crean, Michael Ferguson, Fiona Francombe, Lowri Glain, Richard Handford, Sally Haynes, Corinne Hollingworth, Tim Holloway, Sue Howells, Alexei de Keyser, Chris Le Grys, Steve Lightfoot, Laura Mackie, Peter Norris, Alex Perrin, Bronagh Taggart, Paul Unwin, Mervyn Watson, Rachel Wright, Jonathan Young, Mal Young **Writers** Many dozens, including Jeremy Brock, Paul Unwin, Simon Ashdown, David Ashton, Tony Basgallop, Peter Bowker, Joe Broughton, Paul Cornell, Wally K. Daly, Clive Dawson, Julie Dixon, Greg Evans, Lisa Evans, Lilie Ferrari, Emma Frost, Rob Gittins, Steve Griffiths, Billy Hamon, Jim Hill, Jackie Holborough, Andrew Holden, Ginnie Hole, Chris Jury, David Lane, Chris Lang, Steve Lightfoot, Barbara Machin, Paul Marx, Lise Mayer, Stephen McAteer, Tony McHale, Stuart Morris, Simon Moss, Robin Mukherjee, Rona Munro, Chris Murray, Jim O'Hanlon, Christopher Penfold, Ashley Pharoah, Margaret Phelan, Jeff Povey, Barry Purchese, Nick Saltrese, Robert Scott-Fraser, Manjit Singh, Sam Snape, Julian Spilsbury, Keith Temple, Richard Vincent, Don Webb, Sam Wheats, Julie White, Patrick Wilde, Susan Wilkins, James Wood, Colin Wyatt, Stephen Wyatt **Theme Music** Ken Freeman provided the *Holby City* theme, based upon the electronic pulsing of an ECG machine.

For commentary, see CASUALTY, *pages 168–72*

Hollyoaks

Soap | Mersey TV for Channel 4 | episode duration 25 mins, plus specials | broadcast 23 Oct 1995–present

Principal Cast

Jeremy Edwards · *Kurt Benson*
Lisa Williamson · *Dawn Cunningham*
Paul Leyshon · *Ollie Benson*
Kerrie Taylor · *Lucy Benson*
James Quinn · *Kirk Benson*
Martine Brown · *Juliet Benson*
Terri Dwyer · *Ruth Osborne*
Adam Booth, Ashley Taylor Dawson · *Darren Osborne*
Natalie Casey · *Carol Groves*
Julie Buckfield · *Julie Matthews*
Yasmin Bannerman · *Maddie Parker*
Bernard Latham · *Gordon Cunningham*
Liz Stooke · *Angela Cunningham*
Laura Crossley, Stephanie Waring · *Cindy Cunningham*
Ben Sheriff, Matt Littler · *Max Cunningham*
Nick Pickard · *Tony Hutchinson*
Will Mellor · *James 'Jambo' Bolton*
Stephanie Schonfield · *Janice Bolton*
Brett O'Brien · *Louise Taylor*
Shebah Ronay · *Natasha Anderson*
Alvin Stardust · *Greg Anderson*
Robert Weatherby · *Kevin Daniels*
Darren Jeffries · *Sam 'OB' O'Brien*
Dannielle Brent · *Gina Patrick*
Paul Danan · *Sol Patrick*
Lynda Rooke · *Jill Patrick/Osborne*
Natasha Symms · *Kate Patrick*
James McKenna · *Jack Osborne*
Warren Derosa · *Rob Hawthorn*
Kathryn George · *Helen Richardson/Cunningham*
Sarah Jayne Dunn · *Mandy Richardson/Hutchinson*
Ben Hull · *Lewis Richardson*
Davinia Taylor · *Jude Cunningham*
Daniel Pape · *Sean Tate*
James W. Redmond · *Rory 'Finn' Finnigan*
Kelly Greenwood · *Zara Morgan*
David Brown · *Adam Morgan*
Ross Davidson · *Andy Morgan*
Elizabeth O'Grady · *Beth Morgan*
Eve White · *Sue Morgan*
Tim Downie · *Sam Smallwood*
Wendy Glenn · *Nikki Sullivan*
Lisa Kay · *Anna Green*
Martino Lazzeri · *Alex Bell*
Gary Lucy · *Luke Morgan*
David McAllister · *Dennis Richardson*
Lorna Pegler · *Emily Taylor*
Joanna Taylor · *Geri Hudson Cunliffe*
Sarah Vandenbergh · *Kerry*
Zander Ward · *Paul Millington*
Marcus Patric · *Ben Davies*
Carley Stenson · *Steph Dean*
Mikyla Dodd · *Chloe Bruce*
Kristian Ealey · *Matt Musgrove*
Elize Du Toit · *Izzy Cornwell Davies*
Fiona Mollison · *Victoria Hutchinson*
Helen Noble · *Abby Davies*
Colin Parry · *Mark Gibbs*
Julie Peasgood · *Jacqui Hudson*

Creator Phil Redmond **Producers** Various, including Phil Redmond (executive), David Crean, Jo Hallows, Liza Mellody, Sean O'Connor **Writers** Various, including Maurice Bessman, Roy Boulter, Anna Clements, Judith Clucas, Nicky Cowan, Simon Crowther, Elizabeth Delaney, Matthew Evans, Darren Fairhurst, Chris Gill, Lucy Gough, Mark P. Holloway, Neil Jones, Andy Lynch, Anna McHugh, Lisa O'Donnell, Louise Osborn, Chris Parker, Ian Pike, Allan Swift, Mariam Vossough **Theme Music** Gordon Higgins and Steve Wright

The baby sibling of ***Brookside***, *Hollyoaks* was developed to take advantage of the younger audiences who had become soap addicts with the arrival of ***Neighbours*** and ***Home and Away***. While all of the major soaps had tried to reduce the average age of their casts to attract younger viewers, *Hollyoaks* was the first British soap to aim itself directly at that market. But with *Brookside* – already fairly youth-focused – already dominating Channel 4's schedules, many argued there really wasn't room or need for another soap on a minority channel. Phil Redmond disagreed and Mersey TV's second soap hit the air in October 1995.

It was a tale of middle-class teens in a quiet suburb outside Chester: the Bensons – Kurt, a keen mechanic and biker, his brother Ollie and sister Lucy; Kurt's friends Jambo, a lively joker, and serious-minded Tony; the Cunninghams, Dawn, Jude and Cindy; and their friends, who included Ruth, Maddie, Natasha, Julie and mad Carol. Initially, audiences were decidedly lukewarm to the setting and the cast, but luckily Channel 4 stuck with it and rewarded the show with a second weekly episode and a weekend omnibus. The series experimented with stripping special episodes across an entire week, as *Brookside* had done and, in 2003, the soap went permanently five nights a week.

As he'd done with *Brookside* and ***Grange Hill***, Redmond set about bringing together a cast comprising of experienced child actors and complete novices to bring a sense of realism. The difference with *Hollyoaks* though was that this cast was trying to compete with the glamour of their Australian rivals, and so the actors chosen would be much more traditionally attractive than realism would usually allow. This move prompted criticisms of the series' shallowness and characters with quirks that were too contrived (Jambo – played by Will Mellor – only ever entered his friend's houses through their windows, for example). But the series proved to be an excellent place for young actors to start or advance their careers: Will Mellor and Natalie Cassidy ended up playing a couple in the BBC sitcom ***Two Pints of Lager and a Packet of Crisps***;

Jeremy Edwards and James Redmond both headed off to Holby for the BBC's two medical soaps; in 2005, original cast member Yasmin Bannerman made a high-profile guest appearance in the revival of ***Doctor Who*** as a tree-person; and *Hollyoaks* is currently the only major soap to hold regular open auditions ('Hollyoaks on the Pull').

Hollyoaks has managed to replenish its stocks of youthful and nubile babes and hunks on a regular basis (and successfully marketed them in calendars). When it looked as if the series was haemorrhaging its most popular characters, producers created a spin-off series, *Hollyoaks: Moving On* (a title describing both the characters and the series), which aired in 2001 to bridge the gap. Despite the glitz and glamour that Chester has to offer, *Hollyoaks* remains proudest of its attempts to tackle serious issues – often through late-night specials and in ways few other soaps would have dared attempt. A commendable examination of the effects of rape upon a male victim catapulted future ***Footballers' Wives*** star Gary Lucy into the big league, while other stories have looked at credit car fraud, domestic abuse, suicide and serial murder (unfortunately at the same time that ***Coronation Street*** was running the Richard Hillman saga, which stole all of *Hollyoaks*' glory on that topic).

That Channel 4 decided to retain *Hollyoaks* in favour of *Brookside*, we can see how much has changed in television in just ten years as social realism was replaced with celebrity. Ironically, at the time of writing, *Coronation Street* remains Britain's biggest soap, having boosted its ratings and credibility of its storylines by once again giving ample numbers of storylines to its most senior cast members.

Trivia
In 2000, actor Kristian Ealey moved to *Hollyoaks* from *Brookside*, surprisingly playing the same character, Matt Musgrove. Though set in Chester, *Hollyoaks* was recorded in the same Liverpool location as *Brookside*. The Childwall complex that housed the *Brookside* shopping parade and sports centre was often divided by diagonal splits in décor – viewed from one angle it was *Brookside*, viewed from the other it was *Hollyoaks*.

Website
The official site contains information not only on the characters but advice on how to enter the TV industry in all manner of roles: www.hollyoaks.com.

Holocaust

Drama | Titus Productions for NBC (shown on BBC One) | episode duration 90–135 mins | broadcast 16–19 Apr 1978 (USA)

Regular Cast
Meryl Streep · *Inga Helms Weiss*
Joseph Bottoms · *Rudi Weiss*
Fritz Weaver · *Dr Josef Weiss*
Rosemary Harris · *Berta Palitz Weiss*
Sam Wanamaker · *Moses Weiss*
James Woods · *Karl Weiss*
Blanche Backer · *Anna Weiss*
Michael Moriarty · *Erik Dorf*
Deborah Norton · *Marta Dorf*
Robert Stephens · *Uncle Kurt Dorf*
Lee Montague · *Uncle Sasha*
Marius Goring · *Heinrich Palitz*
Tovah Feldshuh · *Helena Slomova*
Tony Haygarth · *Heinz Muller*
George Rose · *Lowy*
Tom Bell · *Adolf Eichmann*
Ian Holm · *Heinrich Himmler*
David Daker · *Rudolf Hoess*
David Warner · *Reinhard Heydrich*
Sean Arnold · *Hoefle*
Edward Hardwicke · *Biberstein*
Nigel Hawthorne · *Oldendorf*
T.P. McKenna · *Colonel Blobel*

Producers Herbert Brodkin (executive), Pia Arnold (associate), Robert 'Buzz' Berger **Writer** Gerald Green **Theme Music** Morton Gould

Charting the progress of the darkest moment in modern history through the lives of two very different German families, *Holocaust* was a hugely ambitious and largely successful mini series. The Weiss family are upstanding, professional German citizens, including father Josef (a doctor), mother Berta (an accomplished pianist), and their children Rudi, Karl and Anna. They also happen to be Jewish. Lawyer Erik Dorf is another professional German – only he happens to be unemployed, married to an ambitious wife Marta and with a young family to support. As the series begins in 1935, hostility in Germany towards Jewish people begins to grow. Soon Dorf finds a new job with the SS, one where he feels like he's truly contributing towards Germany's future. As the years of Nazi rule turn into the years of war in Europe, the 'Final Solution' is slowly implemented, and one by one the Weiss family meet horrific fates in the concentration camps.

Holocaust attracted some criticism at the time of broadcast from some Jewish groups about its alleged trivialisation of such an important subject – in particular, some of the dialogue and historical accuracy was called into question. However, for most people *Holocaust* provided them with their first real insight into the true horror and inhumanity of this most atrocious of periods in history. With a star-studded cast featuring Hollywood A-listers and the cream of British acting talent (as the Nazis, predictably enough), *Holocaust* followed in the footsteps of the previous year's ***Roots*** in opening the eyes of huge audiences around the globe to periods in history that must never, ever happen again.

Home and Away

Soap | Seven Network (shown on ITV/Five) | episode duration 25 mins | broadcast 16 Jan 1988–present (Aus.)

Principal Cast
Roger Oakley · *Tom Fletcher*
Vanessa Downing, Debra Lawrance · *Pippa Fletcher/Ross*
Ray Meagher · *Alf Stewart*
Kate Ritchie · *Sally Fletcher*
Dennis Coard · *Michael Ross*
Alex Papps · *Frank Morgan*
Nicolle Dickson · *Bobby Simpson/Morgan/Marshall*
Ross Newton · *Greg Marshall*
Justine Clarke · *Roo Stewart*
Sharyn Hodgson · *Carly Morris/Lucini*
Adam Willits · *Steven Matheson*
Helena Bozich · *Lynn Davenport*
Judy Nunn · *Ailsa Stewart*
Dannii Minogue · *Emma Jackson*
Lyn Collingwood · *Colleen Smart*
Julian McMahon · *Ben Lucini*
Tina Thomsen · *Finlay Roberts*
Jacquy Phillips, Lynne McGranger · *Irene Roberts*
Fiona Spence · *Celia Stewart*
Norman Coburn · *Donald Fisher*
Dieter Brummer · *Shane Parrish*
Melissa George · *Angel Brooks/Parrish*
Emily Symons · *Marilyn Chambers/Fisher*
Greg Benson · *Matt Wilson*
Mat Stevenson · *Adam Cameron*
Craig Thompson · *Martin Dibble*
Peter Vroom · *Lance Smart*
Frank Lloyd · *Neville McPhee*
Sheila Kennelly · *Floss McPhee*
Cornelia Frances · *Morag Stewart/Bellingham*
Craig McLachlan · *Grant Mitchell*
Alistair McDougall · *Ryan Lee*
Guy Pearce · *David Croft*
Rebekah Elmaloglou · *Sophie Simpson*
Les Hill · *Blake Dean*
Belinda Jarrett · *Karen Dean*
Nic Testoni · *Travis Nash*
Christopher Egan · *Nick Smith*
Isla Fisher · *Shannon Reed*
Daniel Amalm · *Jack Wilson*
Tina Thomsen · *Finlay Roberts*
Matt Doran · *Damian Roberts*
Tempany Deckert · *Selina Cook/Roberts*
Lisa Lackey · *Roxy Miller*
Tristan Bancks · *Tug O'Neale*
Kristy Wright · *Chloe Richards/Fraser*
Ben Unwin · *Jesse McGregor*
Ryan Clark · *Sam Marshall*
Kylie Watson · *Shauna Bradley*
Beau Brady · *Noah Lawson*
Rebecca Cartwright · *Hayley Smith/Lawson*
Danny Raco · *Alex Poulos*
Ada Nicodemou · *Leah Poulos/Patterson*
Ryan Kwanten · *Vinnie Patterson*
Kimberley Cooper · *Gypsy Nash/Smith*
Sam Atwell · *Kane Phillips*
Christie Hayes · *Kirsty Sutherland/Phillips*
Kate Garven · *Jade Sutherland*
Mitch Firth · *Seb Miller*
Tammin Sursok · *Dani Sutherland*
Kip Gamblin · *Scott Hunter*
Paula Forrest · *Shelley Sutherland*
Michael Beckley · *Rhys Sutherland*
Sebastian Elmaloglou · *Max Sutherland*
Martin Dingle-Wall, Joel McIlroy · *Flynn Saunders*
Clarissa House · *Beth Hunter*
Jason Smith · *Robbie Hunter*
Tobi Atkins · *Henry Hunter*
Indiana Evans · *Matilda Hunter*
Laurie Foell · *Josie Russell*
Isabel Lucas · *Tasha Andrews*
Tim Campbell · *Dan Baker*
Chris Hemsworth · *Kim Hyde*
Ivar Kants · *Principal Barry Hyde*

Creator Alan Bateman **Producers** Many, including Alan Bateman, Victor Glynn, John Holmes, Julie McGauran, Des Monaghan, Russell Webb **Writers** Many hundreds **Theme Music** 'Home and Away' was written by Mike Perjanik and has been performed by a number of different male and female vocalists over the years, with a new arrangement of the tune seemingly being launched every 18 months or so.

The Australian Seven Network was the original home of mega-soap ***Neighbours***, but when the programme was launched to somewhat middling ratings, they cancelled it after less than a year. A rival channel, Ten Network, then took in the homeless residents of Ramsay Street and ratings went through the roof. After this, bosses at Seven decided that they needed their own teen-centric soap opera, and gambled with a series format that challenged the cosy and safe nature of goings-on in Erinsborough.

Home and Away began with married couple Tom and Pippa Fletcher. When Tom loses his job, the Fletchers decide to change their lives by selling up their home in Sydney and relocating to a large house complete with caravan park in the picturesque coastal resort of Summer Bay. Having more room enables Tom and Pippa to expand their family of foster children and soon they have a brood of kids around them – bookish Steven, rebellious wild-child Bobby, shy and retiring Lynn, self-confident and slightly bitchy Carly, and baby of the brood Sally. Other residents of Summer Bay when the programme first started were Floss and Neville McPhee, an elderly couple living in one of the Fletchers' caravans; local shop owner Alf Stewart, his ex-con wife Ailsa and busybody sister Celia; stuffy headmaster of Summer Bay High Donald 'flat-head' Fisher; and local wide-boys Frank, Lance and Martin.

The basic format of *Home and Away* provided many more opportunities for conflict and trauma than the happy families of *Neighbours*. With Pippa and Tom regularly getting new children to foster, most of whom came with their own baggage and personal problems, a wide variety of different storylines became possible. Other families soon decided to take waifs and strays in – Alf and Ailsa provided a home to several of them, as did recovering alcoholic Irene Roberts, mother to two of Pippa's temporary charges, Fin and Damian. Sadly, earth mother Pippa never had much luck in her life – first husband Tom died of a heart attack and second husband Michael drowned in a flash flood during a tropical storm. Summer Bay seemed particularly vulnerable to all manner of floods, earthquakes, storms, shark attacks and bush fires. The beach and surf-friendly lifestyle might look idyllic, but Mother Nature was always ready to deliver another crippling blow to the town (usually when a boost to the ratings was required). Eventually, the parade of traumas and natural disasters caused too much strain and Pippa decided to flee to somewhere (anywhere!) safer. A new family moved into the Summer Bay Caravan Park house, the Sutherlands – this being soap, they naturally inherited the bad luck that had blighted Pippa and her kids.

Throughout the show's lengthy run (4000 episodes produced by the middle of 2005), the basic format has changed little, focusing much more on the lives and loves of the town's resident youngsters with only an occasional storyline for the older members of the cast. With the departure of teacher Donald Fisher in 2003, only two characters from the first episode remain: grumpy yet good-hearted Alf Fisher (who looks after the café following the sudden death of his wife Ailsa) and Sally Fletcher, who is now a very happy young woman working as a teacher in the school she once attended. Having been a major success for ITV from 11 February 1989 (who showed it in a pre-*News* timeslot, much as *Neighbours* was broadcast on BBC One), it came as a great shock when in 2001 the programme moved to Five, following a bidding war. Although it attracts decent enough ratings for Five, the channel's smaller share of the available audience means that *Home and Away* no longer connects with the British public the way it once did. Which is rather ironic, considering that back home in Australia it regularly trounces *Neighbours* in the ratings.

Hong Kong Phooey

Animation | Hanna Barbera for ABC (shown on BBC One) | episode duration 20 mins | broadcast 7 Sept–21 Dec 1974

Principal Voice Cast

Scatman Crothers · *Penrod 'Penry' Pooch/Hong Kong Phooey*
Kathy Gori · *Rosemary*
Don Messick · *Spot, Narrator*
Joe E. Ross · *Sergeant Flint*

Producers Joseph Barbera, William Hanna (executive), Iwao Takamoto **Writers** Larz Bourne, Fred Fox Jr, Seaman Jacobs, Len Janson, Jack Mendelsohn, Chuck Menville **Theme Music** Joseph Barbera, William Hanna and Hoyt Curtin

Thanks to Bruce Lee, martial arts were huge in the 1970s. How fortuitous then that Hanna Barbera once again had their fingers on the pulse when they gave us a superhero and martial artist in one.

Hong Kong Phooey is a hero with two secrets. His identity remains a mystery: is he Sarge of the local police station? Or Rosemary the telephone operator? Or could it possibly be Penry the mild-mannered janitor (clue: could be!)? The second, rather startling secret remains hidden from Penry himself: though Hong Kong Phooey takes the credit for capturing all the villains, the real hero is a striped cat called Spot. As Hong Kong prepares a special attack for the criminal ('The Lychee Nut Thousand Stop', maybe? He'd better look that up in his *Hong Kong Book of Kung Fu*), Spot whacks the villain over the head with a bin lid – case closed.

That a cat should have the opposable digits necessary to pick up a bin lid in the first place shouldn't be cause for concern; anthropomorphic domestic pets didn't worry the person who hired Penry as a janitor – unless they thought that exploiting a talking dog was a neat idea. The real neat idea, though, was the Phooeymobile, an all-purpose super-vehicle fitted with a snazzy pagoda that turns into a helicopter, a jet – even a pogo-stick. Hong Kong Phooey was definitely our number one super guy, a 'fanriffic!' cartoon with more than enough wit and humour to keep big kids as well as little kids entertained. Phooey's voice came courtesy of legendary jazz singer, dancer and actor Scatman Crothers, who'd achieved significant fame in films such as *Hello Dolly* (1969), *Lady Sings the Blues* (1972), and as a voice artist for Disney's *The Aristocats* (1970).

Horizon

Documentary | BBC Two | episode duration 50 mins | broadcast 2 May 1964–present

BBC Two's flagship science and technology programme began as a monthly round-up show a few weeks after the channel's launch day. It went bi-weekly a year later and by 1968 it was a weekly series. By 2004 it had celebrated 40 years with the BBC and is now supported by a website and occasional TV specials. Though *Horizon*'s remit is pretty broad in itself, its scientific approach has been used to examine archaeological subjects like the lost civilisations of Peru, as well as advances in medicine, social trends like the Atkins diet and GM foods, scientific applications to solve murders, as well as reconstructions of natural disasters and tragedies like the shocking collapse of the World Trade Center after the attack in September 2001. Its prestige has always attracted the top actors and presenters to narrate its films. The first presenter was TV scientist Michael Burke, while more recent programmes have been narrated by the likes of Martin Shaw, Sinéad Cusack, Juliet Stevenson, Lindsay Duncan, Bernard Hill, Bill Paterson and Neil Pearson.

Website

www.bbc.co.uk/horizon

Hornblower

Action-Adventure | Meridian/Granada/LWT/United/A&E for ITV | episode duration 90 mins | broadcast 7 Oct 1998–6 Jan 2003

Regular Cast
Ioan Gruffudd · *Horatio Hornblower*
Robert Lindsay · *Captain Sir Edward Pellew*
Paul McGann · *Lieutenant Bush*
Dorian Healy · *Midshipman Jack Simpson*
Jamie Bamber · *Midshipman Archie Kennedy*
Michael Byrne · *Captain Keene*
Robert Bathurst · *Lieutenant Eccleston*
Duncan Bell · *Midshipman Clayton*
Paul Copley · *Matthews*
Sean Gilder · *Styles*
Simon Sherlock · *Oldroyd*
Chris Barnes · *Finch*
Colin MacLachlan · *Master Bowles*
Roger May · *Lieutenant Chadd*
Vincent Grass · *Captain Forget*
Richard Lumsden · *Midshipman Hether*
Denis Lawson · *Captain 'Dreadnought' Foster*
Ian McNeice · *Tapling*
Cherie Lunghi · *Duchess of Wharfedale*
Christopher Fulford · *Hunter*
Ronald Pickup · *Don Massaredo*
John Woodvine · *Sir Hew Dalrymple*
Antony Sher · *Colonel Moncoutant*
Samuel West · *Major Edrington*
Peter Vaughan · *Admiral Lord Hood*
David Warner · *Captain James Sawyer*
Nicholas Jones · *Lieutenant Buckland*
Philip Glenister · *Gunner Hobbs*
David Rintoul · *Dr Clive*
Terence Corrigan · *Midshipman Wellard*
Gilly Gilchrist · *Seaman Randall*
Paul Brightwell · *Marine Sergeant Whiting*
Lorcan Cranitch · *Wolfe*
Tony Haygarth · *Master Prowse*
Julia Sawalha · *Maria Mason*
Barbara Flynn · *Mrs Mason*

Producers Delia Fine, Vernon Lawrence (executive), Pavel Douvidzon, Stepan Pojenian (associate), Emilio Nunez (supervising), Andrew Benson, Peter Richardson, Michele Buck, Liz Bunton **Writers** Russell Lewis, Mike Cullen, Patrick Harbison, Chris Ould, T. R. Bowen, Ben Rostul, Stephen Churchett, from the novels by C. S. Forester **Theme Music** John Keane

Based upon C. S. Forester's novel *Mr Midshipman Hornblower* (the first chronologically in Hornblower's life, but not the first one published – that was 1937's *The Happy Return*), the first episode of the TV series followed the exploits of the 1- year-old fresh-faced recruit to the HMS *Justinian*, at a period of time where Britain's supremacy of the sea would lead it into conflict with a variety of other maritime nations. From his first faltering steps on board a ship in 1794, the ongoing movie-length adaptations of Forester's other novels showed the seaman gain experience and climb up the ranks to the position of lieutenant.

Lavishly filmed, *Hornblower* used a combination of real-life ships (the *Julia* and the *Grand Turk*) and dry-dock sets to portray the hardship and excitement of life at sea. Rising star Ioan Gruffudd (who finally won his first feature film starring role in 2005's *The Fantastic Four*) was ably supported by a combination of fresh young talent and weather-beaten veteran performers, including a memorable performance by David Warner (who'd spent much of the 1990s underneath prosthetic make-up as a variety of aliens in the ***Star Trek*** movies and TV series) as the tyrannical Captain Sawyer in the episode 'Mutiny'. In the end, it wasn't a lack of interest on the part of audiences that brought Hornblower's adventures to an end – it was a combination of the escalating costs of production and the ever-increasing lack of availability for the show's main cast. Fingers crossed ITV will be able to get both the cast and the money back together again in the not-too-distant future.

Hot Metal

Comedy | ITV | episode duration 25 mins | broadcast 16 Feb 1986–17 Apr 1988

Regular Cast
Robert Hardy · *Russell Spam, Twiggy Rathbone*
Geoffrey Palmer · *Harold Stringer*
Richard Wilson · *Dicky Lipton*
Richard Kane · *Greg Kettle*
John Gordon Sinclair · *Bill Tytla*
Caroline Milmoe · *Maggie Troon*
Don Henderson · *Voice of 'Sore Throat'*

Creators/Writers Andrew Marshall and David Renwick
Producer Humphrey Barclay **Theme Music** Alan Price

This bizarre and sometimes surreal exposé of the world of the tabloid newspaper, shown in the Sunday night ***Spitting Image*** timeslot, came from the writers behind ***2 Point 4 Children, One Foot in the Grave*** and ***Jonathan Creek***.

Robert Hardy (in his first major comic role, and taking time out from sticking his hand up a cow's bum in ***All Creatures Great and Small***) starred as demented press baron Twiggy Rathbone, the new owner of boring broadsheet the *Daily Crucible*. Rathbone appoints gutter hack Russell Spam (also played by Hardy) as the new editor, leaving former boss Harold Stringer (a marvellously exasperated Geoffrey Palmer) aghast at his paper's declining standards and rocketing circulation in its reincarnation as a tabloid. Following a mysterious 'accident' between seasons, Richard Wilson replaced Geoffrey Palmer as the perpetually frustrated new managing editor Dicky Lipton.

Both seasons had a distinct overarching storyline. In the first series, the *Crucible*'s enthusiastic young reporter Bill Tytla manages to link together a sinister government informant (nicknamed 'Sore Throat') with a murder perpetrated by the prime minister's wife and the assassination of a man mistakenly believed to be Nikita Kruschev. By the second series, Maggie Troon is left on her own to uncover the links between the mass murder of a judge and his family and the appearance of a space yeti in the Home Counties. Also featured were shorter storylines about such insane concepts as the war between the *Crucible* and the other tabloids over an abused donkey in South America, and the invention of a new three-diminsional technology for Page 3, known as 'Wobblevision'.

Hotel

Drama | Aaron Spelling Productions for ABC (shown on ITV) | episode duration 50 mins | broadcast 21 Aug 1982, 21 Sep 1983–1985 May 1988

Principal Cast
James Brolin · *Peter McDermott*
Anne Baxter · *Victoria Cabot*
Connie Sellecca · *Christine Francis*
Shea Farrell · *Mark Danning*
Nathan Cook · *Billy Griffin*
Michael Spound · *Dave Kendall*
Heidi Bohay · *Megan Kendall*
Shari Belafonte-Harper · *Julie Gillette*
Michael Yama · *Kei*
Harry George Phillips · *Harry*
Efrem Zimbalist Jr · *Charles Cabot*
Michelle Phillips · *Elizabeth Bradshaw Cabot*
Valerie Landsburg · *Cheryl Dolan*
Susan Walters · *Ryan Thomas*
Ty Miller · *Eric Lloyd*

Creator Arthur Haley **Producers** Aaron Spelling, Douglas S. Cramer (executive), Stephen K. Rose (associate), Henry Colman, Geoffrey Fischer, James Fritzhand, Dennis Hammer, Bill La Mond, Jo La Mond, Andrew Laskos, Duane Poole, Tom Swale, E. Duke Vincent, Joseph B. Wallenstein **Writers** Various, including John Furia, Barry Oringer, Jo La Mond, Bill La Mond, Andrew Laskos, James Fritzhand, Geoffrey Fischer, Michael Marks, Mitch Paradise, Duane Poole, Tom Swale **Theme Music** Henry Mancini

Arthur Hailey's successful potboiler of a novel *Hotel* detailed the lives and loves of the owners and staff of a major hotel in New Orleans and was turned into a feature film (starring Rod Taylor and Merle Oberon) in 1967. Not a major hit, the appeal of the novel as an ideal basis for an ongoing TV series caught the eye of American mega-producer Aaron Spelling, the man responsible for shows as diverse as ***Starsky and Hutch***, ***Charlie's Angels*** and ***Dynasty***. A pilot telemovie was produced in early 1983, starring Hollywood legend Bette Davis as the hotel's owner Laura Trent – unfortunately, Davis suffered a stroke shortly afterwards and wasn't able to take part in the full series. Instead, ownership of the San Francisco-based St Gregory Hotel transferred to Laura Trent's sister-in-law Victoria Cabot, played by another great from Hollywood's golden age, Anne Baxter – a casting decision that's painfully ironic to anyone who's ever seen the movie *All About Eve* (1950), which starred both Davies and Baxter.

In each episode of *Hotel*, a new batch of guests would check in to the St Gregory, bringing with them an assortment of their own problems, issues, romances and secrets. Their paths cross with many members of the staff, including hotel manager Peter McDermott and his assistant Christine, head of security Billy Griffin and public relations officer Mark Danning. *Hotel* was a moderate success on American TV, running for five glamorous five-star years of unchallenging entertainment.

House of Cards

Drama | BBC One | episode duration 60 mins | broadcast 18 Nov–9 Dec 1990

Principal Cast
Ian Richardson · *Francis Urquhart*
Susannah Harker · *Mattie Storin*
Miles Anderson · *Roger O'Neill*
David Lyon · *Prime Minister Henry Collingridge*
Malcolm Tierney · *Patrick Woolton*
Nicholas Selby · *Lord Billsborough*
Alphonsia Emmanuel · *Penny Guy*
James Villiers · *Charles Collingridge*
Kenny Ireland · *Ben Landless*
Diane Fletcher · *Elizabeth Urquhart*
Isabelle Amyes · *Anne Collingridge*
William Chubb · *John Krajewski*
John Hartley · *Greville Preston*
Kenneth Gilbert · *Harold Earle*
Damien Thomas · *Michael Samuels*
Colin Jeavons · *Tim Stamper*
John Arnatt · *Sir Jasper Grainger*
Richard Braine · *Kevin Spence*
Justine Glenton · *PR Girl*
Vivienne Ritchie · *Stephanie Woolton*
Tommy Boyle · *Stephen Kendrick*
Eric Allan · *Adrian Shepherd*
Robin Wentworth · *Sir Humphrey Newlands*
Christopher Owen · *McKenzie*

Creator Michael Dobbs **Producers** Michael Wearing (executive), Ken Riddington **Writer** Andrew Davies, from the novels by Michael Dobbs **Theme Music** Jim Parker

The series that placed the phrase 'You might well think that; I couldn't possibly comment' into popular usage, the *House of Cards* trilogy and its star, the insidious Francis 'FU' Urquart, delighted audiences with his delicious wickedness and Machiavellian plotting straight out of Tudor history.

He also made the audience complicit in his schemes through barbed asides to camera, which helped viewers to like the old monster all the more, even if even we weren't completely trusted with the whole truth.

When Urquart is passed over for promotion in the Prime Minister's new cabinet, he puts to use the information he's collected while Chief Whip (the office that ensures party members toe the line with government policy and suppress all scandal until the time is right) to disgrace, discredit and politically dismember all opposition to his route to the top. Urquart's conspiracy takes in a washed-up political journalist with a drug habit, the Prime Minister's alcoholic brother and finally the Prime Minister himself before he begins to pick off his opponents for the premiership one by one.

Aiding him at first is the naïve journalist Mattie Storrin, who falls under Urquart's spell and eventually becomes his lover (thanks to the implicit consent of Urquart's wife, who we learn is the Lady Macbeth of proceedings, quietly urging him forward at every step). But when others conspire to inform Mattie of her mentor's duplicity she realises her error. When Mattie confronts him about his deceit, Urquart pushes her from the top of the House of Commons and then constructs her death as the suicide of a crazed obsessive (diverting from the source novel, in which it's Urquart who plunges to his death – an event conveniently rewritten for Michael Dobbs' follow-up).

In the first sequel, ***To Play the King***, the newly appointed Prime Minister Urquart finds himself poles apart from the King (a performance from Michael Kitchen that drew criticism for appearing to mock Prince Charles), whose liberal views and misplaced idealism make him a hindrance to Urquart and his government. There's also trouble closer to home as the new Chief Whip, Stamper, reveals that he too has ambition and tries to play FU at his own game. Stamper and his incriminating evidence are easily removed, but Francis has to play a longer game with the King, one in which ore or the other will have to resign. That there's another series of this does rather spoil the outcome though (God save the King!). In the last series, ***The Final Cut***, Francis Urquart has removed most of his political enemies and even outlived Margaret Thatcher ('that bloody woman'). Intent on making his mark on history, Francis chooses to push forward the Cyprus Peace Treaty, having spent time in there as a young man while in the army. But here, Urquart's past catches up with him as a vengeful woman and a patient one both hold him in their sights . . .

We've always liked nothing better than cheering on a good villain and Francis Urquart never disappoints. Even his eventual demise has that exquisite satisfaction that comes with the downfall of any overly ambitious character, from Macbeth to the Wicked Witch of the West. It's a part Ian Richardson clearly relishes, and for good reason – it's not many actors who can play a part only to find themselves endlessly quoted by the very people they were mocking in their performance.

Trivia
Producer Ken Riddington had a long heritage of quality BBC dramas to his credit, including ***To Serve Them All My Days, Tenko*** and ***A Very Peculiar Practice***.

The House of Eliott

Drama | BBC/Arts & Entertainment Network for BBC One | episode duration 50 mins | broadcast 31 Aug 1991–6 Mar 1994

Regular Cast
Stella Gonet · *Beatrice Eliott*
Louise Lombard · *Evangeline 'Evie' Eliott*
Barbara Jefford · *Lady Lydia Eliott*
Aden Gillett · *Jack Maddox*
Francesca Folan · *Penelope Maddox*
Peter Birch · *Arthur Eliott*
Cathy Murphy · *Tilly Watkins*
Jill Melford · *Lady Haycock*
Robert Daws · *Piggy Garstone*
Jeremy Brudenell · *Sebastian Pearce*
Kelly Hunter · *Daphne Haycock*
David De Keyser · *Sir Desmond Gillespie*
Judy Flynn · *Madge Howell*
Diana Rayworth · *Betty Butcher*
Victoria Alcock · *Agnes Clarke*
Burt Kwouk · *Peter Lo Ching*
Maggie Ollerenshaw · *Florence Ranby*
Michael Culver · *Ralph Saroyan*
Richard Lintern · *Daniel Page*
Elizabeth Garvie · *Lady Elizabeth Montford*
Rupert Frazer · *Lord Alexander Montford*

Creators Eileen Atkins and Jean Marsh **Producers** Jeremy Gwilt, Ken Riddington **Writers** Jill Hyem, Peter Buckman, Deborah Cook, Alan Seymour, Michael Robson **Theme Music** Though it sounded very much of the period, the theme tune was especially written for the series by Jim Parker.

The creative forces behind such programmes as ***Upstairs, Downstairs, A Very Peculiar Practice*** and ***Tenko*** united to work on a programme that became one of the BBC's flagship drama series of the early 1990s. The first of the three seasons alone cost more than £6 million to produce, an astonishing amount of money for the time. And of course, ***French and Saunders*** mercilessly lampooned the show in a hilarious send-up that left even fans of the series referring to it as *The House of Idiot*.

It's the early 1920s, and sisters Beatrice and Evie Eliott live in a large house with their stick-in-the-mud bully of a father. When he dies suddenly, the sisters learn to their horror that not only was he conducting an illicit affair, but that he was a gambler with significant debts. With no means of supporting themselves, Beatrice starts work for (and eventually marries) louche photographer Jack Maddox, while Evie decides to work with Jack's sister Penelope to try to help the homeless and poverty-stricken. Soon, the girls' skills as fashion designers are discovered, and after producing some one-off commissions for private clients, the House of Eliott is soon launched.

Over the course of 34 episodes, viewers followed the exploits of Beatrice and Evie in their attempts to launch a successful business in the female-unfriendly environment of the 1920s. Of course, this being a family-friendly drama series, a lot of the storylines revolve around the Eliott sisters developing relationships, and how they interact with the women who end up working for them on the factory floor. The second series takes a much darker turn, and follows Evie's exploits as she does her very best to throw off the shackles of 1920s society and live the life she wants. She embarks on a reckless affair with Lord Alexander Montford, a romance that threatens to bring humiliation on both herself and her sister, as well as bring down the House of Eliott itself. By the third series, reconciliation appears to be on the cards for former love birds Beatrice and Jack – but will the simmering rivalries that are brewing between the two sisters put a halt to everybody's happiness?

With the streets of Bristol doing a marvellous job of standing in for the London of the roaring Twenties, *The House of Eliott* managed to look remarkably sumptuous and glossy, despite being entirely made on videotape rather than more expensive-looking film. Managing to attract more than ten million viewers throughout its life, *The House of Eliott* was also a major success for the BBC in terms of overseas sales. Although not quite managing to achieve the same level of success as their previous series *Upstairs, Downstairs*, creators Jean Marsh and Eileen Atkins have every reason to be proud of the success of *The House of Eliott*, one of the last great original period drama series made by the BBC.

How Green Was My Valley

Drama | BBC Two | episode duration 50 mins | broadcast 29 Dec 1975–2 Feb 1976

Regular Cast
Stanley Baker · *Gwilym Morgan*
Siân Phillips · *Beth Morgan*
Norman Comer · *Ifor Morgan*
Nerys Hughes · *Bronwen Morgan*
Sue Jones-Davies · *Angharad Morgan*
Keith Drinkel · *Ianto Morgan*
Rhys Powys, Dominic Guard · *Huw Morgan*
Gareth Thomas · *Reverend Mr Gruffyd*
Jeremy Clyde · *Iestyn Evans*
Sheila Ruskin · *Blodwen Evans*
Aubrey Richards · *Mr Elias*
Clifford Rose · *Mr Jones*

Producers Robert Kline (executive), Martin Lisemore **Writer** Elaine Morgan, from the novel by Richard Llewellyn

To many people, Richard Llewellyn's *How Green Was My Valley* (first published in 1939) is the definitive novel about life in the valleys of South Wales in the 'olden days' – a story of hardship, mining, families, oppression and the perpetual hope of escape to a better life. The novel was made into an Oscar-winning film (directed by John Ford and starring Donald Crisp, Roddy McDowall and Maureen O'Hara) in 1941, but for those who saw it in 1975, there's no question that the six-part TV version is an even better adaptation.

Centring on the trials and tribulations of the Morgan family, *How Green Was My Valley* told the story of stern father Gwilym, loving mother Beth and their children, focusing largely on the growth towards maturity of youngest son Huw. With a cast list that read like a *Who's Who* of Welsh acting talent (including Siân Phillips from ***I, Claudius***, Nerys Hughes of ***Liver Birds*** fame and even ***Blake's 7*** star Gareth Thomas), *How Green Was My Valley* was a perfect slice of historical drama, containing all of the elements necessary for a rattling good family story, including unrequited love (Huw for his sister-in-law Bronwyn), tragedy (when Gwilym is killed in an accident in the mine) and romance (Huw's sister Angharad falling for the local minister).

How!

Children's Factual | Southern/TVS/Meridian/Scottish for ITV | episode duration 20–25 mins | broadcast 1966–1981 (*How!*) 1990–present

Regular Cast
Fred Dineage, Jack Hargreaves, Bunty James, Jon Miller, Jill Graham, Marian Davies, Carol Vorderman, Gareth 'Gaz Top' Jones, Siân Lloyd, Gail Porter, Gail McKenna · *Presenters*

Producers Angus Wright (*How!*), Tim Edmunds, Jonathan Sanderson, Adrian Edwards (*How 2*)

Ever wondered why the sky is blue? Want to know the science behind rockets? Need to understand why soap bubbles form themselves into spheres? The answers to these, and many other questions like them, formed the basis of a long-running ITV series for children called *How!* – presented by a panel of grown-ups who always seemed to be a darn sight better at explaining scientific concepts than your teachers at school were. Beginning way back in the 1960s, *How!* combined basic scientific concepts with a chirpy, enthusiastic presentation style, which meant that even the most tricky of ideas suddenly became interesting. The first group of four presenters included genial older gent Jack Hargreaves (also known for his lunchtime rural travelogue *Out of Town*), bubbly Bunty James, gadget-obsessed Jon Miller and young bespectacled Fred Dineage. After Bunty left the show, she was replaced by Jill Graham and then Marian Davies. *How!* came to an end in 1981 with a shake-up of the ITV franchise holders, disappearing from the airwaves for almost a decade.

When *How 2* was launched in 1990, the concept behind the show remained the same, as did returning presenter Fred Dineage. As the most mature member of the new team, Dineage assumed Jack Hargreaves' old role as the more laid-back presenter, as source of wisdom that the other younger hosts would turn to for explanations. Dineage was initially joined by well-established children's presenter Gareth Jones and brainbox ***Countdown*** number wizard Carol Vorderman, with others including weathergirl Siân Lloyd and lads' mag favourite Gail Porter taking over the duties as the years went by.

Howards' Way

Soap | BBC One | episode duration 50 mins | broadcast 5 Sep 1985–29 Nov 1990

Regular Cast

Maurice Colbourne · *Tom Howard*
Jan Harvey · *Jan Howard*
Stephen Yardley · *Ken Masters*
Glyn Owen · *Jack Rolfe*
Tony Anholt · *Charles Frere*
Nigel Davenport · *Sir Edward Frere*
Tracey Childs · *Lynne Howard*
Edward Highmore · *Leo Howard*
Susan Gilmore · *Avril Rolfe*
Ivor Danvers · *Gerald Urquhart*
Willoughby Gray · *Sir John Stevens*
Cindy Shelley · *Abby Urquhart*
Dulcie Gray · *Kate Harvey*
Patricia Shakesby · *Polly Urquhart*
Kate O'Mara · *Laura Wilde*
Lana Morris · *Vanessa Andenberg-Rolfe*

Creators Gerard Glaister and Allan Prior **Producers** Gerard Glaister, Tony Rowe, Sean Birton **Writers** Various, including Allan Prior, Harry Duffin, Raymond Thompson, Douglas Watkinson **Theme Music** 'Always There' by Simon May and Leslie Osbourne. Marti Webb recorded a vocal version of the theme (which was used on later seasons); it reached No. 13 in the charts in September 1986.

With a new generation of American prime-time soap operas filling the TV schedules in the early 1980s, it was surely only a matter of time before British TV – and especially the BBC – decided to have a go at making their own glamorous suds-fest. The hugely popular – yet critically derided – result was *Howards' Way*, the story of everyday shipbuilding and fashion industry folk in the south of England. Telling the story of the entire Howard family (note the positioning of the apostrophe in the title!), the series begins when noted aeroplane designer Tom Howard is made redundant. Always keen to work in an area where his true passion lies – namely shipbuilding – Tom invests his redundancy pay and most of his savings into the rundown local 'Mermaid' boatyard. Working alongside heavy drinker Jack Rolfe, Tom Howard soon re-establishes the Mermaid as one of the leading shipyards in the town of Tarrant (a fictional locale roughly doubling for Southampton).

However, also based in Tarrant is Relton Marine, a prosperous and dynamic boat-building company run by Ken Masters, and multi-national Frere Holdings – neither of which is keen to see a new company treading on 'their' patch. Big business isn't the only of Tom's concerns. Having initially been quite happy as a housewife, Jan soon decides she wants a career of her own and sets herself up as a fashion designer with her own boutique. Inevitably, the antics of their two children Leo and Lynne also cause Tom and Jan sleepless nights, as do the machinations of Charles Frere and Ken Masters.

Howards' Way did a pretty decent job of portraying the south coast as a wealthy and glamorous location to rival the south of France, but to be brutally honest, the series never had anywhere near enough of a budget to rival ***Dallas*** or ***Dynasty*** in the glamour stakes. Where it made up for that was in more than competent acting and writing, and an experienced series producer in the form of Gerard Glaister (the man behind riveting wartime dramas like ***Colditz*** and ***Secret Army***). One of Glaister's earlier successes had been boardroom drama series ***The Brothers***, which dramatised the behind-the-scenes antics of a family running a haulage company. *Howards' Way* was very much based on this format, only updated and moved upmarket to satisfy the tastes of the wannabe-affluent 1980s audience.

With four successful seasons under their belts, it was decided to tie up all of the loose ends for *Howards' Way* and finish the series off. However, a bumper crop of overseas sales and increased viewing figures led to the show being brought back for a fifth season, with post-*Dynasty* Kate O'Mara being brought into the show to add an even greater infusion of glitz (astonishing, really, that O'Mara decided to join the cast of a BBC water-based soap opera after the disaster that was ***Triangle***!). Extra location filming in Malta added still further gloss to the series and all seemed well. Tragically though, just as the fifth season was being wrapped up, series star Maurice Colbourne suddenly died from a heart attack. Producer Gerard Glaister was left with a near-impossible task of rewriting and reworking the storylines, which eventually explained that Tom Howard had drowned during a storm at sea. A sixth and final series was given the go-ahead in order to tie the storylines up and provide a fitting end to the series, but, unsurprisingly, neither the production staff nor the performers seemed to have any stomach for it following the death of their colleague. Undoubtedly one of the best shows of its type, *Howards' Way* was unfairly panned by critics at the time, and is more than due for a reappraisal – even if that reappraisal comes with tongue firmly planted in cheek.

I Dream of Jeannie

Sitcom | Screen Gems Television/Sidney Sheldon Productions for NBC (shown on ITV) | episode duration 25 mins | broadcast 18 Sep 1965–26 May 1970 (USA)

Principal Cast
Barbara Eden · *Jeannie*
Larry Hagman · *Captain/Major Tony Nelson*
Bill Daily · *Captain/Major Roger Healey*
Hayden Rorke · *Colonel Alfred E. Bellows*
Emmaline Henry · *Amanda Bellows*
Vinton Hayworth · *General Winfield Schaeffer*
Barton MacLane · *General Martin Peterson*

Creator Sidney Sheldon **Producers** Sidney Sheldon, (executive), Sheldon Schrager, Joseph Goodson, Herb Wallerstein (associate), Claudio Guzmán **Writers** Sidney Sheldon, Tom Waldman, Frank Waldman, William Davenport, Arnold Horwitt, Harry Essex, Jerry Seelen, Irma Kalish, Ausin Kalish, Arthur Alsberg, Bob Fisher, James Allardice, Tom Adair, Charles Tannen, Martin Ragaway, Allan Devon, Peggy Chantler Dick, Douglas M. Dick, Robert Marcus, James Henerson, Dennis Whitcomb, Ron Friedman, Christopher Golato, Mark Rowane, Bruce Howard, Searle Kramer **Theme Music** Buddy Kaye and Hugo Montenegro here gave us the joint most unshiftably catchy theme song in existence (a tie with ***Bewitched***). Once it enters your brain it will never leave.

The space race was of paramount importance in 1960s America; with the assassination of the man who'd promised Americans that they'd be first to have a man on the moon, it became even more important to make JFK's dreams come true. As astronauts replaced cowboys as every little boy's dream occupation, the spacemen, in people's minds, went from being invaders to pioneers. Working in space was no longer a science fantasy starring *Flash Gordon*'s Buster Crabbe: spacemen were everyday folk doing an extraordinary job.

That a sitcom could be shaped around an astronaut would have seemed highly improbable in 1960, but one of the big hits of the mid-to-late 1960s was exactly that. In fact, the astronaut in question, Tony Nelson, was an average guy – it was his girlfriend who was odd, a genie that he released from a bottle after bailing out of his test rocket over a desert island. The comedy came from the trouble that 2,000-year-old genie had in understanding modern terminology. Of course, the great joy of *I Dream of Jeannie* was the warm relationship between Barbara Eden's genie-out-of-water and Larry Hagman's bewildered spaceman – a role a million miles away from his conniving and scheming persona in ***Dallas***.

A huge success in the 1960s, *I Dream of Jeannie* enjoyed many years of repeat cycles and syndication for new generations to enjoy. In 1985, a TV movie was screened in the States called *I Dream of Jeannie: 15 Years Later* with Wayne Rogers standing in for Larry Hagman (by then a huge star, again thanks to *Dallas*). A 1991 TV movie, *I Still Dream of Jeannie*, starred Barbara Eden once more; in the final act, Jeannie gets herself a new master, played by Larry Hagman's old *Dallas* nemesis, Ken Kercheval. A big-screen version is, at the time of writing, scheduled to hit cinemas in 2006.

I Love Lucy

Sitcom | Desilu Productions/CBS (shown on ITV) | episode duration 25 mins (*I Love Lucy*), 50 mins (*The Lucille Ball Show*) | broadcast 15 Oct 1951–6 May 1957 (*I Love Lucy*), 6 Nov 1957–1 Apr 1960 (*The Lucille Ball Show*) (USA)

Regular Cast
Lucille Ball · *Lucy Ricardo*
Desi Arnaz · *Ricky Ricardo*
William Frawley · *Fred Mertz*
Vivian Vance · *Ethel Mertz*
Richard Keith · *Little Ricky*
Frank Nelson · *Ralph Ramsey*
Mary Jane Croft · *Betty Ramsey*

Creators Jess Oppenheimer, Madelyn Pugh, Bob Carroll Jr **Producers** Jess Oppenheimer, Desi Arnaz, Bert Granet **Writers** Jess Oppenheimer, Madelyn Pugh, Bob Carroll Jr, Bob Schiller, Bob Weiskopf **Theme Music** Eliot Daniel

I Love Lucy isn't just the most famous early sitcom: to all intents and purposes it created the entire genre, in the process making series star Lucille Ball an astonishingly wealthy woman, one of the first international TV superstars, and a major player in TV production herself.

I Love Lucy portrayed the misadventures of feisty redheaded housewife Lucy Ricardo, a woman prone to complications, misunderstandings, accidents and just about every kind of slapstick disaster imaginable. Lucy is married to her Cuban bandleader husband Ricky (portrayed by Lucille Ball's real-life Cuban bandleader husband Desi Arnaz) and is constantly enthralled by the brief glimpses and exposure she gets to the glamorous life of celebrity that her husband enjoys. Next door live old-fashioned couple Ethel and Fred Mertz, whose paths regularly cross those of Lucy and her husband.

When pitching the idea for their sitcom to the CBS network, Lucille Ball and Desi Arnaz suggested an innovative and revolutionary method of production. Rather than broadcasting the episodes live, as virtually all sitcoms had been prior to this point, they decided to invest a fairly significant amount of money to ensure that each episode would be recorded onto high quality film. This move ensured that *I Love Lucy* would be an easily saleable commodity for syndication markets, guaranteeing the programme's longevity. In fact, *I Love Lucy* has been shown consistently on American TV every single year since for more than half a century, its 180 episodes providing an easy way for channel controllers to fill their schedules with a minimum of effort. The money that Lucille Ball and Desi Arnaz recouped from *I Love Lucy* helped them to establish their own production company Desliu, the firm behind some of the most popular TV shows of all time, including ***The Twilight Zone*** and the original ***Star Trek***.

After *I Love Lucy* came to a conclusion, an occasional series of 13 hour-long episodes of *The Lucille Ball Show* was broadcast over the course of three years, reuniting the principal cast in episodes set in different locations around the globe. Soon after the end of *The Lucille Ball Show*, the two stars of the show divorced. Although Desi Arnaz remained as a producer of her next big series, from this point on Lucille Ball was very much the solo star of her sitcoms. ***The Lucy Show*** saw the lead character as a widow, a much more acceptable state of affairs to early 1960s audiences than a divorcee. Lucy Carmichael is a hard-working widow trying to bring up her two kids Chris and Jimmy as best she can. She flatshares with her friend Vivian, who's also a widow, and works for the First National Bank where her scatty behaviour gets up the nose of her bosses Mr Barnsdahl and Theodore Mooney. Of the 156 episodes that were produced, 126 of them were made in colour.

Lucille Ball's final major TV series was called ***Here's Lucy***, with few scant changes made to the overall format from the previous *The Lucy Show*. Lucy Carter is an over-efficient yet very forgetful woman who works as a secretary for her brother in law Harrison Otis Carter. At home, she cares for her two kids Craig and Kim, and often gets visits from her confidante Mary Jane. Yet again cast from the well-established mould already established in Lucille Ball's earlier shows, *Here's Lucy* ran for an amazing 144 episodes, and featured guest appearances from Hollywood royalty including Johnny Carson, Liberace, Shelley Winters and even Elizabeth Taylor and Richard Burton. Lucille Ball eventually retired from performing from the mid-1970s, only rarely venturing back in front of the camera. She eventually died from heart surgery complications in 1989 at the age of 77, the passing of a true TV legend.

I, Claudius

Drama | BBC/London Film Productions for BBC Two | episode duration 100/50 mins | broadcast 20 Sep–6 Dec 1976

Principal Cast

Ashley Knight, Derek Jacobi · *Claudius*
Siân Phillips · *Livia*
Brian Blessed · *Augustus*
George Baker · *Tiberius*
Ian Ogilvy · *Drusus*
Angela Morant · *Octavia*
Sheila Ruskin · *Vipsania*
Frances White · *Julia*
John Paul · *Marcus Agrippa*
Amanda Kirby, Margaret Tyzack · *Antonia*
Christopher Guard · *Marcellus*
Kevin Stoney · *Thrasyllus*
Kevin McNally · *Castor*
Katharine Levy, Patricia Quinn · *Livilla*
Simon MacCorkindale · *Lucius*
Earl Rhodes · *Gaius*
Russell Lewis · *Lucius*
Alister Kerr, John Castle · *Postumus*
Fiona Walker · *Agrippina*
Douglas Melbourne · *Gemellus*
Karin Foley · *Helen*
Robert Morgan, John Hurt · *Caligula*
Beth Morris · *Drusilla*
Freda Dowie · *Caesonia/The Sybil*
Barbara Young · *Agrippinilla*
Gary Locke, David Robb · *Germanicus*
Michael Clements, James Faulkner · *Herod Agrippa*
Patrick Stewart · *Sejanus*
Kate Lansbury · *Apicata*
Jo Rowbottom · *Calpurnia*
Stratford Johns · *Piso*
John Rhys-Davies · *Macro*
Sheila White · *Messalina*
Bernard Hill · *Gratus*
Geoffrey Hinsliff · *Rufrius*
Bernard Hepton · *Pallas*
John Cater · *Narcissus*
Norman Eshley · *Marcus*
Barbara Young · *Agrippinilla*
Christopher Biggins · *Nero*
Graham Seed · *Britannicus*

Producer Martin Lisemore **Writer** Jack Pulman, from the novels *I Claudius* and *Claudius the God* by Robert Graves
Theme Music Wilfred Josephs's theme is wonderfully evocative, bold, brassy and snaking, just like the adder that slithers across the mosaic in the opening title sequence – a concept blatantly parodied for ***Blackadder II***.

In the last years of his life, Emperor Claudius begins to compile the history of his family – the true history, not the one his family would necessarily wish to be known. Many secrets and treacheries would be revealed, many follies and misguided loyalties – even his own. It begins with the reign of Augustus, a benign but trusting man who has no idea that his second wife, Livia, has conspired to poison her way to his side and continues to remove all obstacles to her son Tiberius becoming Augustus's heir. Livia's treachery includes arranging the murder of her own son and all bar one of his children; the sole survivor is Claudius, teemed to be too much of an idiot to be a threat to anyone.

Livia's grandson Caligula is identified as a perverted monster as a child; he's repeatedly pulled from the beds of his sisters or chastised for his callous attitude. But he finds himself in line to succeed Tiberius after exposing (with Claudius' help) a plot to kill him. Certain that his destiny is to be Emperor, Caligula assists Tiberius's death and so begins a reign of terror where servants, senators and anyone in sight can be given a death sentence on the whims of the insane Caligula. He proclaims himself a living god and insists on being referred to as Zeus; his sister is similarly exalted and takes the mantle of Hera.

Eventually, with the assassination of Caligula, there is no-one left but Claudius to take command of the Empire, and it comes as some surprise for the senators to learn that the fool is much wiser than they'd believed – even if he completely fails to notice that his wife cuckolds him repeatedly (while Claudius is away conquering England, she competes in public against the most notorious prostitute in Sicily to see who can wear out the most men in a day). Still, even after he's poisoned by his wife to leave the role of Emperor open to her fat son Nero, Claudius gets the last laugh, as one copy of his family history lied buried, protected by a prophecy that claims his words will finally be read, 1900 years later . . .

With *I, Claudius*, while some might have been shocked by the amount of bare flesh and depravity put on show for the sake of entertainment, they couldn't deny they'd also learned a lot about the lives of the emperors. Director Herbert Wise makes the best use of some of the most impressive sets ever seen in BBC Television Centre, keeping the camera moving to avoid the proscenium arch approach of so much television of the time. Derek Jacobi gives an astounding performance, playing Caligula from late teens to old age, limping and with a debilitating stammer that seems to ease only in times of anger. But it's Siân Phillips as Livia who steals every scene she's in. The coiled viper in the bosom of the Roman Empire, she relishes every last drop of hatred in her body. Though John Hurt almost matches her as the spoilt, decadent and thoroughly wicked Caligula, the series does dip slightly after Livia's passing, her stand-out moment being a soliloquy over the corpse of her husband (lying still, eyes glazed, throughout – a staggering achievement on the part of Brian Blessed).

First broadcast in the 40th anniversary of BBC Television, *I, Claudius* was one of the most expensive drama productions the Corporation had attempted. It had the superficial approach of the BBC Shakespeare adaptations, but with its tales of infidelity, political manoeuvring and murder it could also be classed as a particularly innovative soap opera. It's certainly yet another contender from the BBC for greatest TV drama serial of all time.

I'm a Celebrity . . . Get Me Out of Here!

Game Show | Granada for ITV | episode duration 50 mins | broadcast 25 Aug 2002–present

Regular Cast

Anthony McPartlin, Declan Donnelly · *Hosts*
Tony Blackburn, Phil Tufnell, Kerry McFadden, Joe Pasquale · *Winners*
Tara Palmer-Tomkinson, Nigel Benn, Rhona Cameron, Darren Day, Uri Geller, Christine Hamilton, Nell McAndrew · *Series 1 Contestants*
Linda Barker, Chris Bisson, John Fashanu, Catalina Guirado, Siân Lloyd, Wayne Sleep, Toyah Willcox, Antony Worrall Thompson, Danniella Westbrook · *Series 2 Contestants*
Peter Andre, Alex Best, Jennie Bond, Charles Ronald George Nall-Cain (aka Lord Charlie Brockett), Jordan/Katie Price, John Lydon, Diane Modahl, Mike Read, Neil Ruddock · *Series 3 Contestants*
Paul Burrell, Janet Street-Porter, Sophie Anderton, Fran Cosgrave, Antonio 'Huggy Bear' Fargas, Sheila Ferguson, Brian Harvey, Nancy Sorrell, Vic Reeves, Natalie Appleton · *Series 4 Contestants*

Producers Alexander Gardener, Nigel Hall, John Saade, Natalka Znak (executive), Christopher Lore, Claire Zolkwer
Theme Music Grant Buckerfield

Pampered poseurs, past-it players and famous faces just looking for a new challenge are thrown into a jungle having been warned about all the poisonous and deadly creatures that might greet them in the camp. Living off basic rations, the celebs must perform 'bushtucker trials' for their food – which involve the kind of stunts that ensure you wouldn't want to eat anyway – swimming with crocodiles, milling around hard-pecking ostriches, being submerged in a hole in the ground with rising water and scurrying rats, standing underneath containers of horrific creepy crawlies that are then dropped on their heads and . . . the horror of eating fat, squirming witchetty grubs and prairie oysters (kangaroo testicles to you and me).

In their first week in the camp, the contestants are subjected to the trials by the whim of public votes back in the UK. In the second, it becomes a popularity contest as the viewers vote to keep their favourites in (and the celeb with the least number of votes is released early for a long, hot bath). It's ostensibly all for charity, but it's also to debase the contestants as much as possible – something presenters Ant and Dec never try to hide as they laugh along with the rest of us at the lengths the players will go to in order to be crowned King (or Queen) of the Jungle.

As with *Celebrity Big Brother* (see ***Big Brother***) part of the fun is seeing the celebs tired and with their guards down, which is when they start to irritate each other until the fireworks begin to fly. In the third series, having calculated that the more time he spent in the jungle, the more exposure he'd get to plug his ailing pop career, Peter Andre left the jungle with a girlfriend (fellow contestant and 'glamour model' Jordan) and a single, the baffling 'Insania'. Punk god John Lydon kept us all entertained by 'keeping it real' and treating his fellow contestants with the contempt they deserved before deciding to leave partway through the second week, confident that he would have won the show (he would have, if the bookies were to be believed), leaving timid Atomic Kitten singer Kerry McFadden to emerge as a surprise but much-deserved winner. A second 2004 series gave squeaky-voiced comedian Joe Pasquale the crown, although former royal butler Paul Burrell emerged the moral victor, having entered as public enemy number one for his perceived betrayal of the memory of Diana but leaving teary-eyed as a genuine people's hero, mainly for confronting so many personal phobias – including eating those kangaroo testicles – and being rather charming and likeable throughout the experience.

I'm a Celebrity is admittedly an endurance test as much for the viewers as the participants, with echoes of ***The Word***'s 'Hopefuls' segment in the way it puts people through stomach-churning ordeals in the name of entertainment. But for ITV it's currently a bit of a ratings saver as one of their few non-soap shows to be able to pull in the viewers. It's also been a successful export for the channel, with versions produced and shot in the same camp for American and German TV.

I'm Alan Partridge

Sitcom | BBC Two | episode duration 30 mins | broadcast 3 Nov–8 Dec 1997, 11 Nov–16 Dec 2002

Regular Cast

Steve Coogan · *Alan Partridge*
Felicity Montagu · *Lynn*
Simon Greenall · *Michael*
Phil Cornwell · *Dave Clifton*
Barbara Durkin · *Susan*
Sally Phillips · *Sophie*
Amelia Bullmore · *Sonja*

Creators Peter Baynham, Armando Iannucci, Steve Coogan **Producer** Armando Iannucci **Writers** Peter Baynham, Armando Iannucci, Steve Coogan **Theme Music** John Whitehall

Having been fired from his prime-time BBC chat show *Knowing Me, Knowing You . . .*, renowned and beloved broadcaster Alan Partridge has sunk into a bit of a career lull. Now reduced to working the (very) early morning shift on Radio Norwich (presenting *Up With the Partridge*), Alan has been kicked out of the family home by his wife Carol and is living semi-permanently in one of those cheap motels often found by the side of trunk roads. The motel staff treat him either with the utmost respect or the utmost contempt, with Alan completely unable to understand the thick Geordie accent of Michael, the motel handyman, who happens to be a fan. Despite all of these disappointments, Alan always has one person to rely upon, his trusty middle-aged PA Lynn. Naturally enough, he treats her like dirt, belittling and humiliating her in public in order to satiate his still rampant ego.

Through Alan, Steve Coogan's parody of clueless DJs is faultless: in one episode ('To Kill a Mocking Partridge'), he claims to understand the meaning of U2's 'Sunday Bloody Sunday' because he too finds Sundays frustrating, while his exploitation of his 'number one fan', Jed (played by ***Emmerdale Farm***'s Ian Sharrock), backfires when he discovers that Jed is an obsessive 'mentalist' who's papered his living room wall with pictures of him – and David Copperfield from ***Three of a Kind***.

A marvellous development of the long-established character of rubbish reporter Alan Partridge, it was an inspired idea to plonk Alan in the middle of a sitcom and investigate just how warped and pathetic an individual he was. The answer, naturally enough, was that he was even more vile that we might ever have imagined – especially in the second season (made five years later) in which Alan reveals he's suffered from a nervous breakdown and is now living in a caravan waiting for his new house to be built. Despite the marvellous character study from Steve Coogan, *I'm Alan Partridge* makes for deeply uncomfortable viewing, however, with many moments of cushion-hugging agony to be endured in every episode as Alan blunders around either making a fool of himself or a fool out of the people who associate with him. On 24 March 2003, a one-off special was broadcast on BBC Two, entitled 'Anglian Lives – Alan Partridge', a mock regional TV interview with the man himself. In between the two seasons of *I'm Alan Partridge*, Steve Coogan ventured down an altogether more sinister comedy path in his affectionate tribute to Hammer Horror films in the miss-and-hit *Dr Terrible's House of Horrible*, with Coogan portraying storyteller Dr Terrible and the leading man in each story.

In Sickness And In Health

Sitcom | BBC One | episode duration 30 mins | broadcast 1 Sep 1985–3 Apr 1992

Regular Cast

Warren Mitchell · *Alf Garnett*
Dandy Nichols · *Else Garnett*
Carmel McSharry · *Mrs Hollingberry*
Arthur English · *Arthur*
Eamonn Walker · *Winston*
Ken Campbell · *Fred Johnson*
Eileen Kennally, Tricia Kelly · *Mrs Johnson*
Una Stubbs · *Rita*
James Ellis · *Michael*
Harry Fowler · *Harry*
Patricia Hayes · *Min Reed*
Vas Blackwood · *Pele*
Hugh Lloyd · *Wally Carey*
Pat Coombs · *Mrs Carey*

Creator/Writer Johnny Speight **Producers** Roger Race, Richard Boden **Theme Music** 'In Sickness And In Health' was written and performed by the archetypal Cockney duo Chas and Dave (aka Chas Hodges and Dave Peacock) in a 'knees-up' style, complete with honky-tonk piano and lyrics explaining Alf's new circumstances. In the first season, they focused on the fact that Alf was now Else's carer: 'Now after all these years I've started pushing you about'; following Dandy Nichols' death, the lyrics were changed to reflect Alf's loss.

For commentary, see TILL DEATH US TO PART

Inch High, Private Eye

Animation | Hanna Barbera for NBC (shown on BBC One) | episode duration 25 mins | broadcast 8 Sep–1 Dec 1973 (USA)

Voice Cast
Lennie Weinrib, Alan Oppenheimer · *Inch High*
John Stephenson · *Mr Finkerton*
Jean Vander Pyl · *Mrs Finkerton*
Kathy Gori · *Laurie*
Bob Lutell · *Gator*
Don Messick · *Braveheart*

Creators William Hanna, Joseph Barbera **Producers** Joseph Barbera, William Hanna (executive), Art Scott (associate), Iwao Takamoto **Theme Music** Hoyt S. Curtin

A short-lived but much-loved Hanna Barbera cartoon, *Inch High, Private Eye* detailed the exploits of a diminutive private investigator and his detective friends. Inch High works for the Finkerton Detective Agency, and has to constantly reassure his dubious boss Mr Finkerton that he's (ahem) big enough to handle the cases he's given. Thankfully, Inch High has a gang to help him – his normal-sized blond niece Laurie, slow-on-the-uptake Gator and a loveable old St Bernard dog called Braveheart. Together the four crime-fighters go in search of their prey in the Hushmobile, a gadget-heavy, cherry-red vehicle.

Another innovative animation from William Hanna and Joseph Barbera – the geniuses behind such worldwide hit cartoons as ***Yogi Bear, The Flintstones, Wacky Races, Scooby-Doo, Where Are You?, Hong Kong Phooey*** and ***Captain Caveman*** – *Inch High, Private Eye* was not one of their greatest commercial successes, lasting for just 13 episodes. However, both the outfit worn by Inch High and the cartoon's obsession with hidden gadgets would later be reborn in another animated series, *Inspector Gadget*.

The Incredible Hulk

Action-Adventure | Marvel/Universal for CBS (shown on ITV) | episode duration 90/50 mins | broadcast 4 Nov 1977–12 May 1982, 22 May 1988, 7 May 1989, 18 Feb 1990 (USA)

Recurring Cast
Bill Bixby · *Dr David Banner*
Lou Ferrigno · *The Incredible Hulk*
Jack Colvin · *Jack McGee*

Creator Kenneth Johnson, based on the characters created by Stan Lee and Jack Kirby **Producers** Kenneth Johnson (executive), Alan Cassidy (associate), Chuck Bowman, Nicholas Corea, Jill Sherman, James D. Parriott, Robert Bennett Steinhauer, Jeff Freilich, Karen Harris, James G. Hirsch **Writers** Various, including Kenneth Johnson, Karen Harris, Jill Sherman, Nicholas Corea, Andrew Schneider, Allan Cole, Reuben Leder **Theme Music** Joe Harnell

As in sport, comic book fans' favourite heroes tend to come from the same team. Until the 1990s, it was generally a choice between DC's heavily patriotic *Superman* and the *Justice League of America* or Marvel's teen angst metaphors in *Spider-Man* and *The X Men*. Sadly, in TV land, DC wiped the floor with its friendly rival. We only need to look at the programmes themselves to see why. For while DC managed to capture the spirit of their comic book worlds, Marvel's outlandish and imaginative concepts didn't sit easily with the largely formulaic production line of American television in the Sixties, Seventies and Eighties.

The *Incredible Hulk* comics were not a huge success when they first launched in 1962. Lasting just six issues before being cancelled, the Hulk became a supporting character who took most of the 1960s to find his audience. In the 1970s, Marvel attempted to exploit their properties by making deals to transfer their characters to television. Doctor Strange, Captain America and Spider-Man would all appear in TV movies in time, but the biggest success was *The Incredible Hulk*. CBS gave the show to Kenneth Johnson, who had helped make ***The Six Million Dollar Man*** and ***The Bionic Woman*** top-rated programmes.

The part of David Banner was given to Bill Bixby, an actor and director known to American viewers for his starring role as *The Magician*, but the problem was who they could get to play the monstrous Hulk. First choice Richard Kiel ('Jaws' from the *James Bond* films) was thought to lack the bulk the character needed and world-class body builder Arnold Schwarzenneger lacked the stature. But Schwarzenneger's co-star in a 1977 body building documentary (*Pumping Iron*), Lou Ferrigno, caught the eye of the producers. At 6ft 5in and with an impressively muscular frame, he more than matched the expectations of the Hulk's physique.

Johnson succeeded in making *The Incredible Hulk* a ratings winner for sure, but he achieved so by jettisoning almost everything from the comic books except the presence of a green man in torn clothing: 'Robert Bruce Banner' became David Banner ('Bruce' was thought to be too gay and too stuck in the manner of other alliterative superhero characters like Peter Parker and Lois Lane); his unpredictable, uncontrollable, monosyllabic alter ego was reduced to an anger-induced growling mute. Furthermore, his legion of typically inventive super-villains were replaced by small-town bullies and an investigative journalist called McGee whose pursuit of David in search of a scoop turned the series from a comic book adaptation into a remake of popular 1950s' series ***The Fugitive***. This last point, however, is what actually made the series so successful. Viewers had no need to understand a backstory or character motivation when the show's premise was summarised in the opening titles each week: 'Don't make me angry, Mr McGee – you wouldn't like me when I'm angry.'

As well as the 80-plus episodes of the series, Bill Bixby and Lou Ferrigno starred in three feature-length reunion movies between 1988 and 1990. Two of them (*The Incredible Hulk Returns* and *The Trial of the Incredible Hulk*) guest-starred other characters from the Marvel world for the first time – Norse god Thor and blind lawyer Daredevil. A fourth movie was planned but Bill Bixby's illness and eventual death from prostate cancer brought the series to

an end. Ang Lee's 2003 movie version, starring Eric Bana, stuck much closer to the story of the original comic books but its CGI Hulk failed to impress viewers who missed Lou Ferrigno's green-thatched giant.

Website
www.incrediblehulktvseries.com/

Inigo Pipkins

See PIPKINS

The Inspector Alleyn Mysteries

Detective | BBC One | episode duration 100 mins | broadcast 2 Dec 1990, 18 Apr 1993–29 Aug 1994

Principal Cast
Patrick Malahide · *Chief Inspector Roderick Alleyn*
William Simons · *Inspector Fox*
Belinda Lang · *Agatha Troy*

Producer George Gallaccio **Writers** T. R. Bowen, Barbara Machin, Kevin Laffan, Hugh Leonard, Alfred Shaughnessy, Ken Jones, Cyril Williams, based on the stories of Ngaio Marsh **Theme Music** Anne Dudley

Roderick Alleyn is a man born with a silver spoon in his mouth and a cut-glass accent. Educated at Oxford (where he graduated with an outstanding Double First), Alleyn grew to notice and resent the lack of law, honesty and good manners prevalent in the world and made it his life's work to do something about it. Joining Scotland Yard, Alleyn soon progresses to the rank of Chief Inspector, becoming a particularly effective enemy of lawbreakers and blaggards everywhere. Alleyn is supported in his investigations by the ever-loyal Inspector Fox, a rather crumpled-faced man from a more lowly background, but just as dedicated as Alleyn to bringing criminals to justice. Throughout his adventures, Alleyn gently romances aristocratic artist Agatha Troy, a woman with a keen mind and opinions that she's never afraid to voice.

The first time that Inspector Alleyn appeared on television was back in the 1960s anthology series *Detective*, when he was portrayed by both Geoffrey Keen and Michael Allinson. A pilot episode for a new interpretation of Alleyn's stories was broadcast in 1990, with ***Upstairs, Downstairs***' Simon Williams appearing opposite William Simons (***Heartbeat***) and Belinda Lang (***2 Point 4 Children***). When the BBC eventually decided to commit to a full season of adventures, Patrick Malahide – already well known to viewers for playing cynical and bumbling Sergeant Chisholm in ***Minder*** as well as baring his bum in ***The Singing Detective*** – took over the part. Although Ngaio Marsh's novels happily portrayed Alleyn's life over a long career (from the 1930s to 1980), the TV adaptations were all set in the years just after the end of World War Two. In total, eight mysteries were transmitted – one season of five stories, followed by three one-off episodes.

The Inspector Lynley Mysteries

Detective | BBC One | episode duration 90–100 mins | broadcast 12 Mar 2001–present

Principal Cast
Nathaniel Parker · *Inspector Thomas Lynley*
Sharon Small · *DS Barbara Havers*

Producers Jane Tranter, Sally Haynes, Rebecca Eaton, Pippa Harris (executive), Julia Stannard, Yvonne Isimeme Ibazebo (associate), Ruth Baumgarten **Writers** Lizzie Mickery, Simon Block, Valerie Windsor, Kate Wood, Anne Marie di Mambro, Simon Booker, Julian Simpson, Mark Greig, Peter Jukes, from the novels by Elizabeth George **Theme Music** Robert Lockhart

The adventures of yet another aristocratic detective, *The Inspector Lynley Mysteries* are at least different from *Campion* or ***Inspector Alleyn*** in so far as they're based in the present day, and that rather than relying upon or enjoying his aristocratic heritage, Thomas Lynley actively wishes he could rid himself of it. Bored of being a titled nobleman (the Eighth Earl of Asherton), Lynley decides to give something back to society and joins the police force. Naturally enough, the modern Met isn't the easiest of places for a gent with blue blood to survive within. However, Lynley's dogged determination and quick mind ensure that he solves his cases quickly and gains the begrudging respect of his colleagues. Lynley's partner in crime solving is down-at-heel DS Barbara Havers, a bedraggled looking young woman brought up on a council estate in west London. Havers and Lynley are chalk and cheese – he's self-confident and sophisticated; she's gauche and clumsy. Together, however, they make an outstanding pair of gumshoes.

Based upon the detective novels by American author Elizabeth George, *The Inspector Lynley Mysteries* is a perfectly harmless, by-the-book detective series that manages to fill a gap in the weekday schedules without shocking or offending viewers. However, this also means that it's not going to be remembered as anything innovative, challenging or particularly memorable either. The decidedly non-starry casting also adds an air of averageness to proceedings, with Nathaniel Parker and Sharon Small delivering accomplished and unshowy performances that are a million miles away from the celebrity-led stunt casting that seems to dominate the genre.

Inspector Morse

Crime Drama | Zenith/Central/Carlton for ITV | episode duration 120 mins | broadcast 6 Jan 1987–15 Nov 2000

Regular Cast
John Thaw · *Chief Inspector Morse*
Kevin Whately · *Detective Sergeant Lewis*
James Grout · *Chief Superintendent Strange*
Peter Woodthorpe · *Max*
Amanda Hillwood · *Dr Grayling Russell*
Clare Holman · *Dr Laura Hobson*
James Grout · *Chief Superintendent Strange*

Producers Ted Childs, Rebecca Eaton, John Thaw (executive), Ray Frift, Laurie Greenwood (associate), Kenny McBain, Chris Burt, David Lascelles, Deirdre Keir **Writers** Anthony Minghella, Julian Mitchell, Thomas Ellice, Charles Wood, Michael Wilcox, Peter Buckman, Alma Cullen, Jeremy Burnham, Daniel Boyle, Geoffrey Case, Peter Nichols, John Brown, Russell Lewis, Malcolm Bradbury, Stephen Churchett, from the books and stories by Colin Dexter **Theme Music** Barrington Pheloung famously created the theme around the Morse code for the word 'Morse'.

Adored the world over for its romanticised view of Oxford, Colin Dexter's laconic copper might not seem like a natural successor to ***The Sweeney***, but in reuniting *Sweeney* producer Ted Childs with John Thaw, paired this time with Kevin Whately as Sergeant Lewis, it could almost have been called 'What Regan Did Next'. Thaw's return to police drama after over a decade certainly invited comparisons with his former role as TV's toughest detective. They might share the same face but Regan and Morse are poles apart: Regan was bullish, violent and likely to punch first and ask questions later, in an interview room; Morse is squeamish (not the most helpful attribute for a homicide detective), but thoughtful, intelligent, a lover of opera and favouring crosswords than cross words. But, like Regan, there was a blunt honesty about Morse: he liked real ale, for starters, and was often impatient with Lewis's inability to make the vital connections to solve the case.

The series took advantage of its Oxford setting and its two-hour running time to take viewers via the scenic route to the killer's identity. The decision to make each episode feature-length – an idea that some suspected might test the patience of the viewers – actually allowed the audience to settle in and relax with the characters while being drawn in by the subtlest of dramatic events.

Inspector Morse managed to remain consistently captivating thanks to the guiding hand of his creator. Most of the episodes were based on Dexter's books, and when those ran out original scripts were inspired by storylines suggested by Dexter (the writer also made cameo appearances, Hitchcock-style, in every episode). His final case came with 'The Remorseful Day', adapting Dexter's final novel in which Morse dies. But the show's popularity has ensured the character lives on in welcome repeats on ITV1, 2 and 3, while its influence on television can be seen in other rural detective series such as ***A Touch of Frost*** and ***Midsomer Murders***. At the time of writing, a spin-off series focusing on DS Lewis is in production.

Trivia
John Thaw won Best Actor BAFTAs for Morse in 1990 and 1993 (with nominations in 1991 and 1992). After a great deal was made over his character's reluctance to reveal his first name, it was eventually made public in 'Death is Now My Neighbour', one of a number of specials made after the official end of the series (it's 'Endeavour', by the way).

Website
www.inspectormorse.co.uk/

Inspector Wexford

See THE RUTH RENDELL MYSTERIES

Interceptor

Game Show | Chatsworth TV for Channel 4 | episode duration 50 mins | broadcast 19 Jul 1989–1 Jan 1990

Regular Cast
Annabel Croft · *Presenter*
Sean O'Kane · *The Interceptor*
Michael Malric-Smith · *Mikey the Helicopter Pilot*

Creators Jacques Antoine and Malcolm B. Heyworth
Producer Malcolm B. Heyworth **Theme Music** Zach Laurence

Two contestants are dropped by helicopter in the middle of the British countryside, at which point they have to navigate their way to finding each other using maps, compasses and an audio link with presenter Annabel Croft. The only thing standing in their way to a prize of £1000 is the villainous Interceptor, who will use his wrist-mounted laser to 'shoot' their backpacks thereby locking the prize money away. Created by the same team responsible for ***Treasure Hunt***, *Interceptor* was a variation on the same theme – only this time involving a high-tech game of 'tick' or 'cowboys and Indians'. For more information on *Interceptor*, see ***Treasure Hunt***.

Website
www.interceptors-lair.com

Interludes

Documentary | BBC TV | episode duration up to 11 mins | broadcast 7 Feb 1952 to well into the 1960s

Back in the day when television was a much more frightening experience for those that made it, the vast majority of broadcasts were live. As we've noted elsewhere, TV was still very much the new kid on the block as far as entertainment was concerned, coming a distant fourth in terms of importance behind theatre, radio and cinema. As a consequence, it was as ephemeral as a stage performance, one run and that was it. No home video release, no repeat on a digital channel – if the BBC wanted to repeat something, they had to get the actors and technical crew to do it live all over again. Naturally, shows that had been rehearsed as, say, 60 minutes long, wouldn't always be that exact on the night. Nerves might make all the actors deliver their lines fractionally faster, just as they might during a stage production, or a line might be fumbled and the rest of the cast might need to contract the scene to hide the mistake. And then there was the simple matter of the interval (like stage productions, these live plays would occasionally need a break to move the cast to another part of the studio or to arrange the set in some way). Whatever the cause, there was on occasion a gap that would need to be filled somehow, and by 1952 that 'somehow' took the form of the 'interlude'.

Made predominantly by the BBC Film Unit, interludes were short films designed to be soothing on the eyes and unlikely to upstage the next programme. Though some of the films lasted up to ten minutes, often only a portion of the film would actually be shown, depending on the gap it was filling in the schedule. One of the first such films was 'Vespers', a nine-minute piece showing the rituals of the Feast of Holy Guardian Angels (so presumably filmed on 2 October 1951) at the Monastery of St Benedict in Ealing. Throughout the next decade many other films would pop up unexpectedly as schedule fillers or to cover a breakdown in transmission in a more attractive, pleasing way than a mere testcard. Viewers were taken to the River Ouse in Buckinghamshire, to the Kaieteur Falls of British Guiana, to a sandy shore in Jamaica, to watch the waves crashing at Portland Bill or Regent Park Zoo's angel fish darting around their tank. Many of the films were of a pastoral nature, showing aspects of daily life that for most viewers might as well have been from a century ago: farmers ploughing fields in Essex; the slowly turning sails of Pakenham Mill, Bury St Edmonds; a woman making a tapestry; a spinning wheel whirring away. The most famous of these, though, was 'The Potter's Wheel', in which the potter's hands were seen scoring grooves in the clay to help the pot take shape. Action-packed they were not, but there was something strangely hypnotic about the slow, steady movement of plough horses making their way across a field, a bonfire crackling away or Snowy the kitten going ape with a ball of wool.

In addition to these interludes were a number of slightly more ambitious short films that, while not captioned as interludes, fulfilled the same function of bridging the gap between the 'proper' programmes. 'London to Brighton in Four Minutes' used what David Lloyd James, the narrator, called 'trick photography' to make the Brighton Belle soar down the Victoria-to-Brighton line at an average of 756 miles per hour. Unfortunately, there were limitations to the technology then, and not all of the journey was actually filmed; the bits missed when the camera was being reloaded were bridged by cutting away to shots of the train driver. Similar films were later made covering journeys from Paddington to Birmingham and from Kings Cross to Peterborough.

One of the last interludes, from the mid-1960s, could have come from an edition of ***The Twilight Zone***, featuring dolls and toys apparently coming alive while unattended by their child masters. This particular film is remembered by ***Doctor Who*** fans for its inclusion of a 'Tricky Action' Dalek toy among the dolls and teddy bears.

Into the Labyrinth

Children's Drama | HTV West for ITV | episode duration 25 mins | broadcast 13 May 1981–8 Sep 1982

Regular Cast
Ron Moody · *Rothgo*
Pamela Salem · *Belor*
Lisa Turner · *Helen*
Simon Henderson · *Terry*
Simon Beal · *Phil*
Jeremy Arnold · *Theseus*
Chris Harris · *Lazlo*
Howard Goorney · *Bran*

Creators Bob Baker and Peter Graham Scott **Producers** Patrick Dromgoole (executive), Peter Graham Scott **Writers** Bob Baker, Andrew Payne, Ray Jenkins, Anthony Read, Christopher Priest, John Lucarotti, Ivan Benbrook, Robert Holmes, Martin Worth, Jane McClarkey, Gary Hopkins, Moris Farhi, Dave Martin **Theme Music** Sidney Sager

Another subterranean fantasy series from HTV in the same vein as ***King of the Castle***, *Into the Labyrinth* took teenagers Helen, Terry and Phil down into a network of caves where they find Rothgo, a kindly sorcerer, whose mission it is to prevent the evil witch Belor from obtaining a powerful artefact called the Nidus. While the Nidus is lost, Belor is prevented from using it for evil purposes, but its absence means that Rothgo grows ever weaker. If he can get to the relic before Belor, he'll be able to regain his powers and rid the Labyrinth of her menace. The teens then find themselves on an ongoing quest to locate the Nidus in different time periods within the labyrinth, every one of them a potential trap with Belor lurking in disguise. They manage to defeat Belor each time, but not before she was able to cast the all-important Nidus back through the labyrinth and out of Rothgo's reach by reciting the words: 'I deny you the Nidus!'

Legendary musical star Ron Moody (Fagin in *Oliver!*) left the show after two series, but his role as pursuer of Belor was taken by Chris Harris as Lazlo, now in search of the Scarabeus. The role of the glamorous witch Belor was played by Pamela Salem, who's perhaps best known as Miss Moneypenny in Sean Connery's return Bond movie

Never Say Never Again (1983). In 2005 she made a guest appearance in ***The West Wing*** as the new British Prime Minister Maureen Graty.

The Invaders

Science Fiction | Quinn Martin for ABC (shown on BBC Two) | episode duration | broadcast 10 Jan 1967–26 Mar 1968, 12–19 Nov 1995 (USA)

Regular Cast
Roy Thinnes · *David Vincent*
Kent Smith · *Edgar Scoville*
Hank Simms · *Narrator*

Creator Larry Cohen **Producers** Quinn Martin (executive), David W. Rintels, Anthony Spinner (associate), Alan A. Arme **Writers** Various, including Franklin Barton, John W. Bloch, Don Brinkley, Robert E. Collins, Meyer Dolinsky, George Eckstein, Laurence Heath, Norman Klenman, John Kneubuhl, Barry Oringer, David W. Rintels, Robert Sabaroff, Robert Sherman, Jerry Sohl, Dan Ullman, Anthony Wilson **Theme Music** Dominic Frontiere

The 'better dead than red' paranoia of the 1950s spawned a multitude of allegorical science fiction movies, including *Invaders from Mars* (1953) and *Invasion of the Body Snatchers* (1955). The idea of invaders that look like everyone else but are really subversive aliens was a metaphor that ran deep into American culture at the time, not just in science fiction but across the board, from sitcoms to melodrama. It also led to a revival of the 'innocent man on the run' thrillers that had been a mainstay of the films of Alfred Hitchcock since the 1920s.

In 1967, Larry Cohen revisited the fear and mistrust of the previous decade with *The Invaders*, in which David Vincent is the only man who knows of the existence of aliens who have taken human form. When killed, their bodies disintegrate into nothing, meaning evidence is hard to come by. As the very people he's trying to warn turn against him, Vincent becomes obsessed with proving the existence of extraterrestrial life already here on Earth.

Eventually, Vincent finds a group who believe his stories and join him in the fight for truth, but the series came to an end after two years and 43 episodes, without concluding the adventure. In 1995, a two-part mini series saw Scott Bakula (***Quantum Leap, Enterprise***) take up the baton in the quest for evidence. Original series star Roy Thinnes returned to the search for aliens as Jeremiah Smith in ***The X Files***, although that time he actually *was* the alien.

The Invisible Man (1959)

For credits, see H. G. WELLS' INVISIBLE MAN; *for commentary see* THE INVISIBLE MAN (1984)

The Invisible Man (1975)

Science Fiction | Silverton Productions/Universal for NBC (shown on BBC One) | episode duration 50 mins | broadcast 6 May–8 Sep 1975–19 Jan 1976

Regular Cast
David McCallum · *Dr Daniel Westin*
Melinda Fee · *Dr Kate Westin*
Craig Stevens · *Walter Carson*

Creators Harve Bennett and Steven Bochco, inspired by the novel by H. G. Wells **Producers** Harve Bennett, Steven Bochco, Robert F. O'Neill, Leslie Stevens **Writers** Steven Bochco, James D. Parriott, Seeleg Lester, Rick Blaine, Leslie Stevens, Philip DeGuere Jr, Brian Rehak **Theme Music** Henry Mancini

For commentary, see THE INVISIBLE MAN (1984)

The Invisible Man (1984)

Science Fiction | BBC One | episode duration 25 mins | broadcast 4 Sep–9 Oct 1984

Principal Cast
Jonathan Adams · *Teddy Henfrey*
Donald Bisset · *Professor Hobbeman*
Ruby Buchanan · *Miss Hood*
Deddie Davies · *Margaret Bunting*
Pip Donaghy · *Griffin*
Helen Gold · *Rose*
David Gwillim · *Dr Kemp*
Roy Holder · *Sandy Wadgers*
Gerald James · *Dr Edward Cuss*
Lila Kaye · *Jenny Hall*
Merelina Kendall · *Lucy*
Esmond Knight · *Blind Man*
Jimmy Mac · *Old Silas*
Alan Mason · *Charlie Wicksteed*
Frank Middlemass · *Thomas Marvel*
John Patrick · *Officer Hinton*
Ron Pember · *George Hall*
John Quarmby · *Constable Charlie Jaffers*
Ivor Salter · *Barman*
Cyril Shaps · *Landlord*
Michael Sheard · *Reverend Edward Bunting*
Frederick Treves · *Colonel Adye*
Anna Wing · *Mrs Sarah Roberts*

Producers Ros Wolfes (associate), Barry Letts **Writer** James Andrew Hall, from the novel by H. G. Wells **Theme Music** Stephen Deutsch

H. G. Wells' science fiction novel has inspired numerous film and TV adaptations, though for some reason few of them have ever been faithful to the source. This results in a few curiosities released under the same title but with wildly differing approaches. We begin with an action-adventure series from the same stable as the 1950s' adventures of ***Ivanhoe*** and ***The Adventures of Robin Hood***.

Here, brilliant scientist Dr Peter Brady is an expert in the field of optical density and regularly conducts experiments into light reflection and refraction. One day, an experiment goes horribly wrong and Peter's body is left permanently invisible – the only evidence of his presence is seen when he wears clothing, smokes a cigarette or moves objects like chairs and opens doors. Peter's invisibility comes as a shock to his sister Diane and niece Sally, who both do their best to give him some kind of corporeal form by covering him in bandages and sunglasses when it's required. At first, the presence of an invisible man is viewed by the government with hostility and fear – soon, though, they realise just how valuable Peter's new ability could be, and in a short space of time he's being used for security work, spying on foreign governments, drug smugglers and gangsters alike. All the while, Peter eagerly searches for an elusive cure for his invisibility . . .

For its time, this reworking of *The Invisible Man* was a highly accomplished series with cutting-edge special effects (courtesy of backstage boffin Jack Whitehead) and storylines based on contemporary issues and concerns. Producer Ralph Smart (who had worked on *The Adventures of William Tell* and who would later create ***Danger Man*** for Patrick McGoohan) opted to keep an air of mystery about the identity of the lead actor, never crediting him on-screen. Young Sally Brady was played by actress Deborah Watling, who would go on to star opposite Patrick Troughton's ***Doctor Who*** as assistant Victoria Waterfield.

Our next brilliant scientist was Dr Daniel Westin, hero of a 1975 American series capitalising on the popularity of ***Man from U.N.C.L.E.*** star David McCallum. Westin has discovered the secret of invisibility and is immensely proud of that discovery – until he realises that the government wants to get their hands on his invention and use it to give an invincible advantage to their military forces. Appalled at the misuse of his research, Westin memorises his techniques, destroys all physical evidence of his research and then turns himself invisible, determined that he won't be tracked down and forced into handing his secrets over. Unfortunately, Westin doesn't have a reversal process, so he's forced into making a realistic flesh-coloured facemask and flesh-coloured gloves in order to gain some semblance of a life. He also takes his wife Kate and goes to work for the Californian-based KLAE Corporation, every now and again performing invisible undercover operations for KLAE boss Walter Carlson.

The series was even further removed from H. G. Wells' original material than before, instead being a more up-to-date twist on the 1958 British TV series. Unfortunately, it wasn't a huge success and the programme was quickly dropped. Producer Harve Bennett was reluctant to give up the concept of invisibility and all of the special effects techniques that they had developed, so the same year a rejigging and renaming of the format saw the launch of ***The Gemini Man***. Starring Ben Murphy as secret agent Sam Casey, the twist in *The Gemini Man* was that Casey was able (following an exposure to undersea radiation) to turn himself invisible for short bursts of time – however, if he stayed invisible for more than 15 minutes a day, he would die. Sadly, audiences liked this idea even less than David McCallum's series and it was quickly dropped.

The most recent *The Invisible Man* to date was made in 1984 and was as close to a faithful adaptation of H. G. Wells' original novel as we've so far seen on screen. It's quite refreshing to see the story told in its original Victorian setting, complete with flickering gas lamps and sinister laboratories – in fact, it's not far removed from the similar tale of *Dr Jekyll and Mr Hyde*. This being a BBC studio-based drama, you'd expect the special effects to be somewhat less than special, but for the time they hold up remarkably well. Unfortunately, by sticking to the source material, on this occasion the Invisible Man in question (Griffin, played by Pip Donaghy) isn't a hero or even particularly sympathetic. As the invisibility begins to effect Griffin's mind, he turns from well-meaning if rather dull scientist into psychotic killer, making the final few episodes of this adaptation much more exiting than the first.

The Irish RM

Drama | Rediffusion Films/Ulster/RTE/Little Bird for Channel 4 | episode duration 50 mins | broadcast 6 Jan 1983–7 Jul 1985

Principal Cast

Peter Bowles · *Major Sinclair Yeates*
Bryan Murray · *Flurry Knox*
Doran Godwin · *Philippa Butler/Yeates*
Lise-Ann McLaughlin · *Sally Knox*
Beryl Reid · *Mrs Knox*

Producer Adrian Hughes **Writer** Rosemary Anne Sisson, from the novel *Some Experiences of an Irish R. M.* by Somerville and Ross (aka Edith Somerville and Violet Florence Martin) **Theme Music** Nick Bicât

At the end of the 19th century, when Britain still ruled the world and 'a third of the globe was pink', British staff were often sent to parts of the Empire to maintain law, order and instil proper values into the restless natives. One such man is Major Sinclair Yeates, sent to the rural west coast of Ireland to become a Resident Magistrate (RM). Yeates hopes that his job will be a peaceful and tranquil one, but soon he's neck-deep in local squabbles and concerns that shatter those dreams of a quiet life. Although Yeates is far from stupid, his rather deadpan manner and closed mind make him an easy target for scams and confidence tricks from the locals – most of who seem to have been regularly kissing the Blarney Stone. Particularly mischievous when it came to dealing with Yeates is his landlord Flurry Knox, a man with a twinkle in his eye and a formidable mother on hand to dispense wit and wisdom.

Fresh from his ratings-smashing success in ***To the Manor Born***, Peter Bowles took a step back from his recent work in sitcoms and signed up for this amiable drama series, co-produced on behalf of Channel 4 and Irish broadcasters Ulster TV and RTE. Its potentially controversial plotline (British rule over Ireland at the end of the 19th century) was quite a brave step for any broadcaster to put onto screens, considering that the mid-1980s saw a marked increase in IRA activity on both sides of the Irish Sea. However *The Irish RM* made its political points in such a quaint, charming and quietly amusing way that few people in Ireland or the UK were offended by its content. This series also marked the first major TV appearance for Bryan Murray, who'd go on to much greater success in programmes as diverse as comedy show ***Bread*** and gritty soap ***Brookside*** (in which, as violent wife-beater Trevor Jordache, Murray's character was stabbed to death and buried underneath a patio).

It Ain't Half Hot Mum

Sitcom | BBC One | episode duration 30 mins | broadcast 3 Jan 1974–3 Sep 1981

Regular Cast

Windsor Davies · *Sergeant Major Williams*
Melvyn Hayes · *Bombadier 'Gloria' Beaumont*
Donald Hewlett · *Colonel Reynolds*
Michael Knowles · *Captain Ashwood*
Michael Bates · *Rangi Ram*
George Layton · *Bombadier Solly Solomons*
Don Estelle · *Gunner 'Lofty' Sugden*
John Clegg · *Gunner Graham*
Christopher Mitchell · *Gunner Perkins*
Mike Kinsey · *Gunner Evans*
Kenneth MacDonald · *Gunner Clark*
Stuart McGugan · *Gunner Mackintosh*
Dino Shafeek · *Char-Wallah Muhammed*
Babar Bhatti · *Punka-Wallah Rumzan*
Andy Ho · *Ah Syn*

Creators/Writers Jimmy Perry, David Croft **Producers** David Croft, Graeme Muir **Theme Music** 'Meet the Gang', composed by Jimmy Perry and Derek Taverner and sung by the boys of the concert party

Looking for another hit comedy series to go alongside their mega-success ***Dad's Army***, Jimmy Perry and David Croft turned to another neglected period of the Second World War to come up with the basis of *It Ain't Half Hot Mum*. Most people think that the British Army was largely confined to Europe – however, many campaigns took place in the steaming jungles of Asia and the Indian sub-continent, and just like army units based closer to home, the troops needed supplies, back-up facilities and, of course, entertainment. Concert Parties were set-up among the soldiers to put on songs, shows and all-round entertainment for their fellow troops – *It Ain't Half Hot Mum* showed the behind-the-scenes shenanigans that went into the formation of such performances.

Sergeant Major Williams leads the Royal Artillery Concert Party stationed in Deolali, India – resolutely old-school bullying officer, Williams hates the fact that he's been put in charge of 'a bunch of pooftahs' rather than a group of 'real men'. Most of his bile is aimed at effeminate Gloria Beaumont, the one of the party normally happiest to stick on a frock and sing a show-tune, although 'La-de-dah' Gunner Graham (the posh one who plays the piano) and the vertically challenged Lofty Sugden also receive their fair share of Williams' bellowing. In fact, about the only one of the troup that Williams really likes is 'lovely boy' Perkins – and that's undoubtedly due to the suspicion on Williams' part that Perkins might be his own illegitimate son. Meanwhile, officers Reynolds and Ashwood do whatever they can to avoid getting their hands dirty, preferring to stay out of the way of any actual work and simply sit back and take the credit later on. Looking on with a wry air of amusement at the silly goings-on are a cross-section of the locals, namely staunchly patriotic Indian servant Rangi Ram and two less anglophilic Wallahs Rumzan and Muhammed.

It Ain't Half Hot Mum, although undeniably popular and successful when first broadcast, is nowhere near as well remembered or loved today as its contemporaries like *Dad's Army* or ***Are You Being Served?*** This has to be down to its somewhat politically incorrect comedy – not only is homophobia rampant in the scripts, but you've also got a British actor, Michael Bates, 'blacked-up' to play Indian Rangi Ram (although Bates was born in India and was a fluent speaker of Hindustani, it's still no real excuse, is it?). Although this humour was considered perfectly acceptable at the time when the series was being made, it does make the programme much more difficult to repeat for modern audiences. It's a shame that there are such objectionable elements inherent in the scripts, as leaving these elements aside, *It Ain't Half Hot Mum* is just as funny and enjoyable as Perry and Croft's other comedies. When the time came to wind up the programme, viewers followed the soldiers as the war drew to a close and they returned home to be 'demobbed'. The final episode (featuring a blink-and-you'll-miss-him cameo appearance from future chat-show host Jonathan Ross as another demobbed soldier) saw Sergeant Major Williams facing an uncertain future with nowhere to go and nothing to look forward to on Civvy Street – until his 'lovely boy' Perkins offers to put him up until he gets himself sorted. Aw!

Trivia

Windsor Davies and Don Estelle scored a 1975 No. 1 hit with 'Whispering Grass', an in-character pastiche of the 1940 Ink Spots song, written by Fred and Doris Fisher.

It'll Be Alright On The Night

Comedy | LWT for ITV | episode duration 40–50 mins | broadcast 1977–present

Regular Cast

Dennis Norden · *Presenter*

Producers Paul Smith, Paul Lewis, Sean Miller, Simon Withington **Writer** Dennis Norden

It's hard to believe that this perennial favourite of the schedules has been running for almost 30 years, but *It'll Be Alright On The Night* did indeed first hit TV screens in 1977. At the time of its first broadcast, it was an absolute revelation to TV viewers, containing, as it did, clips of actors, newsreaders, reporters, presenters and sports stars all stumbling over their words, being attacked by random animals, losing items of clothing, crashing into the scenery and generally making fools of themselves. For most people, this was the very first time that they'd had seen footage of celebrities not being 100% perfect, and it created an appetite for witnessing the human frailties of our top stars that remains unabated to this day. Thankfully, genial host Dennis Norden (who also wrote his own scripts) was always on hand to point out any mitigating circumstances in the displays of stupidity he presented to viewers.

Every two years or so, Norden has hosted another edition of *It'll Be Alright On The Night* (we're up to number 17 at time of writing), with clips being gladly donated by TV production companies right across the globe. One notable exception was the BBC, who maintained an air of detachment over this kind of thing until 1991, when *Auntie's Bloomers* took to the airwaves, hosted by Terry Wogan – later replaced by *Outtake TV* (presented by Paul O'Grady and then Anne Robinson). Even digital channel BBC Three got in on the game with *Three's Outtakes*, consisting almost entirely of expletives from the mouths of the ***Little Britain*** and ***Two Pints of Lager and a Packet of Crisps*** performers. It seems as though the public's appetite for cock-ups remains as insatiable as ever.

It's a Knockout

Game Show | BBC One/Ronin TV for Channel 5 | episode duration 50–60 mins | broadcast 28 May 1967–29 Oct 1982, 15 Jun 1987 (*It's a Royal Knockout*), 1999–2001

Cast

David Vine, Stuart Hall, Vince Hill, Keith Chegwin, Lucy Alexander · *Hosts*

McDonald Hobley, Katie Boyle, Eddie Waring, Brian Cant, Su Pollard, Frank Bruno, Nell McAndrew · *Co-hosts, Score-keepers*

Creator Inspired by the French game show *Intervilles* by Guy Lux, Charles De Gaulle (no, really!) initiated the *Jeux Sans Frontières* that led to Britain's *It's a Knockout* **Producers** Barney Colehan, Cecil Korer, Geoff Wilson **Theme Music** 'Bean Bag' by Herb Alpert

One of the most bonkers game-show ideas ever, the concept behind *It's a Knockout* was to pit British towns against each other to see who was best at traversing a moving platform while being splashed with water, or navigating along an obstacle course while dressed in a ten-feet-tall giant's costume. The winning team from the national competition would then represent the UK in the international *Jeux Sans Frontières*, taking on European teams in similar games.

David Vine was the show's first host, accompanied by McDonald Hobley and later Katie Boyle, but it was the arrival of manic cackler Stuart Hall in 1972 that the show found its real star. Hall's laugh became the most famous in TV history as he collapsed in uncontrollable fits at the spectacle of grown-ups falling over. His joy was completely infectious and made the show immeasurably more enjoyable. Stuart Hall's co-host was sports commentator Eddie Waring, whose northern drawl made him an ideal target for impressionists like Mike Yarwood. The original series ended in 1982 with a Christmas special hosted by Vince Hill and Brian Cant.

In 1987, HRH Prince Edward came up with the idea of orchestrating a one-off *It's a Royal Knockout* in aid of various charities. Princess Anne, Prince Edward and the Duke and Duchess of York were team captains while celebrities of the day did the hard work. Prince Edward was disappointed by the apathy of the press on the day.

Channel 5 resurrected the format for two series in 1999–2001 with Keith Chegwin as host and boxer Frank Bruno as referee. Model and ***I'm a Celebrity . . . Get Me Out of Here*** contestant Nell McAndrew kept score.

Ivanhoe (1958–9)

Action-Adventure | Sydney Box Television Presentation for ITV | episode duration 25 mins | broadcast 5 Jan 1958–4 Jan 1959

Principal Cast

Roger Moore · *Ivanhoe*
Robert Brown · *Gurth*
John Pike · *Bart*
Andrew Keir · *Prince John*
Bruce Seton · *King Richard the Lionheart*

Producer Peter Rogers (executive), Bernard Coote
Writers Various, including Geoffrey Orme, Bill Strutton, Joel Carpenter, Saul Levitt, Thomas Law, Richard Fiedler, Larry Forrester, Shirl Hendryx, Felix Van Lieu, Aubrey Feiest, Anthony Verney, M. L. Davenport, George Baxt, Sheldon Stark, Lawrence Hazard, from the novel by Sir Walter Scott
Theme Music Albert Elms

For commentary, see IVANHOE (1997)

Ivanhoe (1970)

Action-Adventure | BBC One | episode duration 25 mins | broadcast 4 Jan–8 Mar 1970

Principal Cast

Eric Flynn · *Ivanhoe*
Anthony Bate · *Sir Brian de Bois Guilbert*

Bernard Horsfall · *Black Knight*
Vivian Brooks · *Rebecca*
Clare Jenkins · *Rowena*
Tim Preece · *Prince John*
Clive Graham · *Locksley*

Producers Campbell Logan, John McRae **Writer** Alexander Baron, from the novel by Sir Walter Scott

For commentary, see IVANHOE (1997)

Ivanhoe (1997)

Action-Adventure | BBC/A&E (shown on BBC One) | episode duration 50 mins | broadcast 12 Jan–16 Feb 1997

Principal Cast
Steven Waddington · *Wilfred of Ivanhoe*
Victoria Smurfit · *Rowena*
James Cosmo · *Cedric of Rotherwood*
Ciaran Hinds · *Sir Brian de Bois-Guilbert*
Ralph Brown · *Prince John*
Rory Edwards · *King Richard*
Siân Phillips · *Queen Eleanor*
Ronald Pickup · *Waldemar Fitzurse*
David Horovitch · *Isaac of York*
Susan Lynch · *Rebecca*
Chris Walker · *Aethelstane*
Trevor Cooper · *Gurth*
Jimmy Chisholm · *Wamba*
Nick Brimble · *Sir Reginald Front de Boeuf*
Valentine Pelka · *Sir Maurice de Bracy*
Aden Gillett · *Robin of Locksley*
David J. Nicholls · *Little John*
Christopher Lee · *Lucas de Beaumanoir*

Producer Jeremy Gwilt **Writer** Deborah Cook, from the novel by Sir Walter Scott **Theme Music** Allyn Ferguson

Towards the end of the 12th century, England is caught up in turbulent times. With Richard the Lionheart off fighting the Crusades in the Holy Land, his brother Prince John has assumed control of the country and is ruling with a rod of iron. Ivanhoe returns home from fighting alongside King Richard and is appalled at the corruption and abuses of power being demonstrated by wicked Prince John. Ivanhoe frees Gurth and Bart, two lowly serfs who were about to be executed, and they become his squires as he sets about trying to right wrongs and undermine John's tyranny.

Ivanhoe was the first major success for a young actor called Roger Moore. Throughout the 1960s he would become internationally famous for playing another upstanding hero on television, ***The Saint***. Of course, by 1973 he had assumed the mantle of 007 in the James Bond film series – yet another role as a noble hero bringing wicked villains down to earth. Remarkably, executive producer Peter Rogers was working on another project at exactly the same time as he was supervising *Ivanhoe* – it was a low-budget feature film called *Carry On Sergeant*, the first of the long-running series of comedy films.

The next adaptation of the Ivanhoe legend was broadcast on BBC One in the first weeks of 1970, and starred Eric Flynn as the daring hero. A much more accurate ten-part adaptation of Sir Walter Scott's original novel, this was a grimmer and more realistic portrayal of 12th-century England, with none of the tongue-in-cheek light-hearted derring-do portrayed in Roger Moore's version. No, this was dark, gritty and totally camp-free, and as such it came as quite a revelation to audiences. Ivanhoe returns to England to redeem his name, reclaim his inheritance and win back the hand of his beloved Rowena, who is now betrothed to Saxon prince Aethelstane.

A third approach to the legend reached TV screens in 1997, and once more the realism was cranked up still further. Ivanhoe returns from the Crusades in disguise, largely because his reputation has been left in tatters, thanks to false accusations of disloyalty to King Richard that have been made against him. Again in this version Ivanhoe has to fight to win back his love Rowena – however, this time he also falls in love with young Jewish girl Rebecca. Ivanhoe then does battle with the wicked Sir Brian de Bois-Guilbert as well as facing the wrath of the Knights Templars, and (in an expansion of the original text) meets another fictional hero, Robin of Locksley, and his best mate Little John. With a staggering cast of acting heavyweights (such as Christopher Lee as the leader of the Knights Templars and ***I, Claudius***'s Siân Philiips as the most fearsome English queen in history, Eleanor of Aquitaine), this six-part adaptation was certainly the most lavish version yet seen on TV.

Ivor the Engine

See pages 400–2

Ivor the Engine

Jones the Steam poses with his trusty engine Ivor.

When it comes to level of importance on television, children's programmes tend to be pretty near the bottom of the pile for the corporations and networks that commission them. So long as they're deemed not to offend and don't encourage the little'uns to start marauding around the house with loaded weapons or kitchen knives, generally no one gives two hoots. Certainly, the vast majority of children's TV productions that we all grew up with were made with the absolute minimum of expense. Perversely, that makes us a hell of a lot luckier than the children of today.

That phrase 'the children of today' is one that programme maker Oliver Postgate takes issue with. In an article published on his website in May 2003 ('Does Children's Television Matter?'), he asserts that 'apart from a few in-built instincts, they [children] are blank pages happily waiting to be written on'. Small children have no preconceptions, no ideas of what good storytelling is. As long as it keeps them entertained, they don't really care if it consists of shadow puppets or computer graphics. A prejudice about programme format is not something they're born with; it's something they learn – or more accurately, something they are taught, often by the kind of TV executive who's actually a bit embarrassed to be working in children's programmes and so wants to impose grown-up production values on an audience that doesn't need them.

How do we know this? It's easy: just sit a three-year-old in front of a television set and show them any one of the TV shows that Oliver Postgate created with his creative partner Peter Firmin. The child won't care that the programmes were created using crudely animated cardboard cutouts or homemade stop-motion puppets. Such things don't matter to the fresh imaginations of young children. All they'll know is the storyteller has a comforting reassurance to his voice and that the characters are every bit as real as the people around him. Put simply, Postgate and Firmin, under the banner of 'Smallfilms', knew how to spin a yarn.

Oliver Postgate's first animated work was *Alexander the Mouse* (1958), which was performed live as part of Small Time, ITV's

Animation
Smallfilms for Associated Rediffusion/ITV (black and white)/BBC TV (colour)
Episode Duration: 5/10 mins
Broadcast: Dec 1958–3 Feb 1964, 26 Jan 1976–13 Dec 1979

Cast
Oliver Postgate · *Narrator, Character Voices*

Creators/Producers Oliver Postgate and Peter Firmin

Writer Oliver Postgate

Theme Music Vernon Elliott, played by the Vernon Elliott Ensemble

equivalent of the BBC's *Watch with Mother* timeslot. The problems that ensued led him to invest in a 16mm film camera to produce his next series, *The Journey of Master Ho*, a six-part animated series for deaf children in which a small Chinese boy and his buffalo explored the world of the famous Willow Pattern. *Ivor the Engine* followed in 1958 and became Postgate's first major collaboration with illustrator Peter Firmin. While at drama school in the late 1940s, Postgate had met a former railwayman who told him of the effort that went into warming up the steam engine every morning. This memory inspired the tale of Ivor, the steam engine that pulls the carriages along the tracks of the Merioneth and Llantisilly Rail Traction Company Limited, a local service covering 'the top left-hand corner of Wales'. 'The Locomotive of the Merioneth and Llantisilly Rail Traction Company Limited' struck the driver, Edwin Jones (aka 'Jones the Steam'), as a pretty long name for an engine to endure, so he called him 'Ivor' and the name stuck.

Oliver Postgate narrated the stories, voicing the characters and providing the distinctive sound of Ivor as he puffed along the tracks – 'Pssch-ti-kuff . . . Pssch-ti-kuff . . .' Peter Firmin supplied the illustrations on pieces of card that could be manipulated to create basic poses. What's evident from these drawings is just how much love and attention was being poured into the show from the beginning. Ivor isn't just a block on wheels; he's intricately designed with fancy scrolling and what looks to us like a clear idea of the workings of a real engine. Though the people of Llantisilly are caricatures, they're imbued with just enough personality to make them real in the imagination (confession: in our innocent childhood minds, Jones the Steam and Lofty from ***It Ain't Half Hot Mum*** were one and the same!).

The first series of six black-and-white episodes was shown over Christmas 1958 on Associated Rediffusion, the ITV franchise-holder for the London region. The series told how Jones the Steam discovered that Ivor (the most human of steam engines) was unhappy with just being a locomotive. What Ivor really wanted to do (he later learned) was sing. Thanks to a train doctor, Ivor was eventually fitted with a new set of musical pipes that enabled him to join the local choral society as their bass accompaniment. This first series was repeated in 1962 immediately prior to the beginning of a new series, in which Jones discovers a dragon's egg and hatches it inside Ivor's furnace. The dragon who emerges, Idris, becomes a recurring character along with a few other local residents: Dai Station, the station master whose concern over timetables often overshadows any recognition that Ivor and Jones provide a good service for the community; the wealthy but batty Mrs Porty and her donkey, Bluebell; Mr Hughes who works at the gasworks at Grumbly Town; the elephant, Alice, who turns up at the gasworks one day and is cared for until her owner, Bani Moukerjee of Banger's Circus, comes to fetch her; and a hermit called Meredith Dinwiddy.

Thirty-two monochrome masterpieces of Ivor's adventures were made for ITV up to 1963, at which point the series began repeat runs that lasted until the end of the decade. While Ivor had been chuffing

WEBSITES

Oliver Postgate's own website can be found at www.oliverpostgate.co.uk, while the official Smallfilms Treasury, maintained by Nigel Baker, resides at www.smallfilms.co.uk.

away, Smallfilms had also produced a series of Norse adventures for the BBC, ***The Saga of Noggin the Nog***, which first appeared on our screens in autumn 1959, and *The Pingwings*, a series of 32 short episodes about a group of penguin-like animals who lived in a barn. This latter series marked Smallfilms' first break away from two-dimensional animation into three-dimensional models. Oliver Postgate then starred as himself in 1962 for a live series of 26 episodes called *The Dogwatch*, where he played a lighthouse keeper whose puppet dog Fred was voiced by Ivan Owen (Peter Firmin and Ivan Owen later created another TV legend in the form of ***Basil Brush***). In 1964, Smallfilms brought us the Pogles of ***Pogles' Wood***, followed in 1968 by the first appearance of those lunar rodents the ***Clangers***. From 1973, Smallfilms were occupied by the comings and goings in a bric-a-brac shop run by a girl called Emily, aided by a large, saggy, stuffed cat called ***Bagpuss***.

Smallfilms' output was prolific considering how long stop-motion animation takes, but more than that – it was immensely popular, a little matter recognised by BBC head of children's programmes Monica Simms when she approached the company to remake their classic *Ivor the Engine* episodes in colour for the celebrated pre-*News* slot on weekday evenings that had been kept warm by ***The Magic Roundabout***, ***The Wombles*** and ***Paddington***. Postgate and Firmin then successfully negotiated to buy the rights to their old black-and-white episodes from Associated Rediffusion (who had lost their ITV franchise when they were amalgamated into Thames in the 1968 ITV reshuffle). All of the original episodes were remade, recycling Peter Firmin's designs, plus a few new ones were added to the mix to create a batch of two seasons, each made up of 20 episodes. What's more, none of the target audience ever knew that they weren't watching a series that hadn't been made specifically for them, and the episodes were repeated virtually until the series' 30th anniversary. See what we mean about children recognising good storytelling?

Smallfilms continued with *The Doll's House*, an adaptation of the books by Rumer Godden, and *Pinny's House*, written and illustrated by Firmin in the two-dimensional style of *Ivor the Engine*. But by this time fashions were changing and 'modern' executives eventually convinced themselves that Ivor and his Smallfilms stable-mates weren't what 'the children of today' actually wanted. In 1987, it was decided that Ivor had run his course.

The rise in digital entertainment has been of some benefit to Ivor's fans. In 2004, the Welsh regional service for BBC Two commissioned a series of trailers to promote the extra channels now available via digital telly. Written and voiced by Oliver Postgate, the films featured Ivor the Engine, Jones the Steam and other examples of Peter Firmin's artwork, now animated on computer but looking just as wonderfully jerky as the series always had been. In 2005, the complete episodes in colour were released on DVD. Oliver Postgate and Peter Firmin now give talks on the birth of children's TV animation to adults who still remember the joy of being a child when Smallfilms ruled their world.

Jackanory

Children's Anthology | BBC One/Two | episode duration 15 mins | broadcast 13 Dec 1965–24 Mar 1996, 24–27 Dec 2001

Cast
Over 400 storytellers presented Jackanory, including Lee Montague, Bernard Cribbins, Kenneth Williams, Rodney Bewes, Judi Dench, Clement Freud, Jane Asher, Arthur Lowe, HRH Prince Charles, Susan Hampshire, Spike Milligan, Peter Sellers, Gareth Thomas, Bernard Holley, Willie Rushton, Tom Baker, Tony Robinson, Terry Jones, Annette Badland, Alexei Sayle, Rik Mayall, Alan Bennett

Creators Joy Whitby, Anna Home, Joanne Symons, Molly Cox **Producers** Various, including Joy Whitby, David Coulter, Anna Home, Christine Seacombe, Roger Singleton-Turner

A subtle educational programme disguised as story time, *Jackanory* was improving standards of literacy among children long before J. K. Rowling came along. It took its name from a nursery rhyme that went: 'I'll tell you a story about Jack-a-Nory/And now my story's begun/I'll tell you another 'bout Jack and his brother/And now my story is done' (the word 'Jackanory' possibly coming from rhyming slang for 'story'). Each week, a famous actor, actress or personality would read a story, carefully abridged to be able to be split across five 15-minute segments stripped from Monday to Friday. The first story presented in this way was *Cap of Rushes*, read by Lee Montague. Bernard Cribbins became the most prolific of readers, with 111 appearances, often narrating Joan Aitken's stories about Arabel and her pet crow Mortimer (*Nevermore!*), which were illustrated by Quentin Blake. Kenneth Williams came a distant second at 69 shows, many of which involved the great detective Agaton Sax. A couple of the stories were later adapted for live-action serials, such as *Lizzie Dripping and the Witch* and ***Jonny Briggs***. Prince Charles had a bash at it too, reading his own story, *The Old Man of Lochnagar*, while a substantial cast assembled for the show's 3000th edition to perform *The Hobbit*, with Bernard Cribbins as Bilbo Baggins.

Despite attempts to keep the stories up to date with presenters like Alexei Sayle and Rik Mayall popping in (whose manic delivery of Roald Dahl's *George's Marvellous Medicine* caused outrage among concerned parents), *Jackanory* was looking decidedly slow by the mid-1980s. The final regular edition starred Alan Bennett, reading *Winnie the Pooh*. In 2005, the BBC announced their long-overdue intention to revive *Jackanory*.

Jamie and the Magic Torch

Animation | Cosgrove Hall/Thames for ITV | episode duration 15 mins | broadcast 3 Apr 1978–21 Jan 1980

Voice Cast
Brian Trueman

Creators/Producers Brian Cosgrove and Mark Hall **Writer** Brian Trueman **Theme Music** 'Down the helter skelter, faster and faster/Towards Cuckoo Land', written and sung by Joe Griffiths. Listen to the beginning: the piano soundtrack tinkles a melody that progresses in a way that is not dissimilar to the incredibly long 'Layla' by Eric Clapton.

In the annals of children's entertainment, there is *no other* cartoon series with a better, more engrossing and uplifting opening title sequence than the one that introduced all 39 episodes of *Jamie and the Magic Torch*. Beginning with a spooky journey through the deserted night-time streets of a northern suburb, the picture focuses in on a typical house, and the bedroom of a small boy. The boy's mum tucks him up in bed and with a loving 'Sleep well, Jamie' shuts the door. With that, all hell breaks loose – a frantic electric guitar starts thrashing, Jamie throws back the covers of his bed and fishes underneath it for his magical torch. He switches the torch on, points it at the floor, and all of a sudden a magic hole appears there. Along with his faithful dog Wordsworth, Jamie then drops through the hole and slides down a psychedelic helter-skelter into Cuckoo Land.

Once in Cuckoo Land, Jamie and Wordsworth would regularly meet a selection of weird, wonderful and downright strange characters, from number-obsessed Mr Boo, motorised unicycling policeman Officer Gotcha and giant-footed, florid-voiced rabbit Bulli Bundy. Even Wordsworth is no longer an ordinary dog – in Cuckoo Land, he speaks with a laid-back west-country drawl and is often keen to point out to Jamie just how odd everything they encounter appears to be.

Wordsworth was absolutely correct – things in *Jamie and the Magic Torch* really *were* genuinely weird. Every generation of TV viewers have a programme that, in hindsight, appears as though it might have been dreamt up while under the influence of certain illegal substances. Indeed, most third-rate comedians appearing on 'I Love the 1970s'-type programmes can usually be guaranteed to lapse into the standard refrain of 'Ooh, the writers must have been on drugs'. What such people tend to forget, however, is that programmes like *Jamie and the Magic Torch* and ***The Magic Roundabout*** before it were popular simply because they tapped into two critical elements – situations and characters that encouraged kids to use their imagination, and writers who were able to think back to the way in which children dream.

A live-action remake was announced in 2002, with producers on the scout for a young actor to play Jamie. However, as with many similar projects, nothing has so far come of this live-action version of Jamie's adventures.

Website
www.chf.co.uk – the official Cosgrove Hall site.

Jane Austen's Emma

Drama | Meridian for ITV | duration 100 mins | broadcast 1996

Principal Cast
Kate Beckinsale · *Emma Woodhouse*
Mark Strong · *Mr Knightley*
Samantha Morton · *Harriet Smith*
Bernard Hepton · *Mr Woodhouse*
Prunella Scales · *Miss Bates*
Dominic Rowan · *Mr Elton*
Lucy Robinson · *Mrs Elton*
Raymond Coulthard · *Frank Churchill*
Samantha Bond · *Mrs Weston*
James Hazeldine · *Mr Weston*
Olivia Williams · *Jane Fairfax*

Producer Sue Birtwistle **Writer** Andrew Davies, from the novel by Jane Austen

Emma Woodhouse is 21, 'handsome, clever and rich' and lives in a small country village with her hypochondriac father. The mistress of the house from quite a young age, Emma is used to being the centre of attention in the local community, and likes nothing better than to match-make relationships between her friends and neighbours. Unfortunately, Emma is atrociously bad at picking suitable matches, often causing much heartache for the people whose lives she meddles with. Emma encourages her best friend Harriet Smith to believe that local vicar Mr Elton might be interested in her – but Harriet is distraught when she discovers that Mr Elton carries a torch for the much more eligible Emma. With a community far too polite to point out her failings and inappropriate behaviour, it's down to old family friend Mr Knightley to tell Emma some home truths about her spoiled and arrogant behaviour. But could Mr Knightley be the knight in shining armour that Emma's been looking for all along?

Having had a major hit with ***Pride and Prejudice*** on the BBC the previous year, producer Sue Birtwistle and screenplay writer Andrew Davies turned their attentions to another one of Jane Austen's novels, the equally marvellous *Emma*. A one-off feature length adaptation of the story, this version does tend to rattle through the events of Austen's novel quite quickly, ditching much of the fine word play and characterisation that the longer screen-time of *Pride and Prejudice* had managed to maintain. However, Kate Beckinsale (daughter of ***Porridge*** star Richard Beckinsale and ***Ace of Wands/Casualty*** actress Judy Loe) made an appealing Emma, making enough of a mark for herself as an actress that she was soon appearing in blockbuster Hollywood movies like *Pearl Harbor* (2002) and *Van Helsing* (2004). Jane's best friend Harriet was played by Samantha Morton, who would also forge a movie career for herself in arthouse flick *Sweet and Lowdown* (1999) and Steven Spielberg's sci-fi action flick *Minority Report* (2003).

Two previous attempts at bringing this story to the small screen had been attempted by the BBC. The first was in 1960, starring Diana Fairfax as Emma and Paul Daneman as Mr Knightley; the second was shown on BBC Two in 1972 and featured Doran Goodwin as Emma with John Carson as Knightley. With such a talented cast and another quality screenplay from Andrew Davies, *Jane Austen's Emma* provided a highly enjoyable way of passing a couple of hours, and proved an accessible version of the story to people who might never have picked up the original text.

Jane Eyre (1954)

Drama | BBC TV | episode duration 30 mins | broadcast 24 Feb–30 Mar 1954

Principal Cast
Daphne Slater · *Jane Eyre*
Stanley Baker · *Mr Rochester*

Producer Campbell Logan **Writer** Constance Cox, from the novel by Charlotte Brontë

For commentary, see JANE EYRE (1997)

Jane Eyre (1963)

Drama | BBC One | episode duration 30 mins | broadcast 7 Apr–12 May 1963

Principal Cast
Ann Bell · *Jane Eyre*
Richard Leech · *Mr Rochester*

Producer Douglas Allen **Writer** Constance Cox, from the novel by Charlotte Brontë

For commentary, see JANE EYRE (1997)

Jane Eyre (1973)

Drama | BBC One | episode duration 30 mins | broadcast 27 Sep–25 Oct 1973

Principal Cast
Sorcha Cusack · *Jane Eyre*
Michael Jayston · *Mr Rochester*

Producer John McRae **Writer** Robin Chapman, from the novel by Charlotte Brontë

For commentary, see JANE EYRE (1997)

Jane Eyre (1983)

Drama | BBC One | episode duration 30 mins | broadcast 9 Oct–18 Dec 1983

Principal Cast
Zelah Clarke · *Jane Eyre*
Timothy Dalton · *Mr Rochester*

Producer Barry Letts **Writer** Alexander Baron, from the novel by Charlotte Brontë

For commentary, see JANE EYRE (1997)

Jane Eyre (1997)

Drama | LWT/A&E for ITV | duration 100 mins | broadcast 9 Mar 1997

Principal Cast
Samantha Morton · *Jane Eyre*
Ciaran Hinds · *Mr Rochester*
Gemma Jones · *Mrs Fairfax*
Richard Hawley · *Mr Richard Mason*
Emily Joyce · *Miss Temple*
Deborah Findlay · *Mrs Reed*
Timia Berthome · *Adele*
Rupert Penry-Jones · *St John Rivers*
Elizabeth Garvie · *Diana Rivers*
Gemma Eglinton · *Helen Burns*
Abigail Cruttenden · *Blanche Ingram*
Val McLane · *Grace Poole*

Producer Sally Head, Delia Fine (executive), Greg Brenman **Writer** Kay Mellor, from the novel by Charlotte Brontë

Jane Eyre is a hard-working young woman who becomes the governess of Thornfield Hall, in charge of young Adele Varens, the ward of elusive Mr Rochester. When Rochester returns home, an attraction between himself and Jane soon builds, and in time he asks her to become his wife. Jane is slightly perturbed when wedding plans take on an almost indecent air of haste – the reason becomes clear when, on their wedding day, she's appalled to discover from a Mr Richard Mason that Rochester is already married to Mason's sister Bertha, a raving lunatic who's confined to a locked room inside Thornfield Hall. Jane flees Thornfield and is taken in by a kindly clergyman, St John Rivers. She's about to accompany Rivers and his wife to India when a subconscious voice tells her she should return to Thornfield – there she discovers her former love Rochester, blinded and living in the wrecked shell of the house. Rochester had sustained the injuries in an unsuccessful attempt to rescue his wife from the fire that she, in her madness, had started. Now free to follow their hearts, Jane and Rochester are married.

As befitting its status as one of the most popular novels ever written in the English language, *Jane Eyre* has been adapted for television on many occasions over the years – the 1963 version starred a pre-***Tenko*** Ann Bell as Jane, and surely Timothy Dalton's 1983 appearance as Rochester must have stood him in good stead for portraying the suave spy James Bond in the late Eighties. The 1997 version was adapted by talented screenwriter Kay Mellor, the woman behind ***Band of Gold*** and *Fat Friends*, and starred future Hollywood actress Samantha Morton as the vulnerable young governess.

Jason King

See DEPARTMENT S

Jeeves and Wooster

Comedy Drama | Picture Partnership for Granada (shown on ITV) | episode duration 50 mins | broadcast 22 Apr 1990–20 Jun 1993

Regular Cast
Stephen Fry · *Jeeves*
Hugh Laurie · *Bertie Wooster*
Robert Daws · *Tuppy Glossop*
Mary Wimbush, Elizabeth Spriggs · *Aunt Agatha*
Brenda Bruce, Vivian Pickles, Patricia Lawrence, Jean Heywood · *Aunt Dahlia*
John Turner · *Roderick Spode*
Francesca Folan, Diana Blackburn, Elizabeth Morton · *Madeline Bassett*
Adam Blackwood, Martin Clunes · *Barmy Fotheringay-Phipps*
Richard Dixon · *Oofy Prosser*
Richard Garnett, Richard Braine · *Gussie Fink-Nottle*
John Woodnutt · *Sir Watkyn Bassett*
Michael Ripper · *Drones Porter*

Creator/Writer Clive Exton, from the stories by P. G. Wodehouse **Producers** Sally Head (executive), Brian Eastman, Al Burgess, Ron Purdie **Theme Music** Anne Dudley produced a marvellously appropriate Twenties-style melody.

Although the BBC had already adapted P. G. Wodehouse's *Jeeves and Wooster* stories into a TV series in the late 1960s (*The World of Wooster*, starring Dennis Price as Jeeves and Ian Carmichael as Bertie Wooster), it is ITV's sumptuous production of the early 1990s that is justifiably remembered as the definitive interpretation of Wodehouse's work. However, when members of the Wodehouse Society learned of the casting of alternative comedians Stephen Fry and Hugh Laurie (then best known for their BBC sketch series ***A Bit of Fry and Laurie***), they were up in arms. Their fears, although understandable at the time, simply couldn't have been more ill placed, with Laurie creating a charmingly daffy Bertie Wooster and Fry managing to convey a million words with the slightest raise of an eyebrow as Jeeves.

In the London of the Roaring Twenties, the chaps and chapesses of high society were still living it up to the nines. Bertie Wooster is one of the in-crowd, a wealthy young gentleman well connected to all of the most fashionable events and people. An altogether decent chap, Bertie is none the less not one of life's intellectuals – in fact, he's thick as two short planks. Considerable embarrassment is only avoided thanks to the timely intervention of Bertie's butler, the ever-suffering Jeeves, who manages to extricate his master from a continual stream of self-inflicted crises. Also causing Bertie much grief are his terrifyingly bossy aunts Dahlia and Agatha, two elderly women who won't stand for any stuff and nonsense from anybody – least of all silly young Bertie.

With sumptuous-looking location filming (including several episodes being set in New York City) and a stellar cast, *Jeeves and Wooster* was that rarity among ITV drama series – a programme that both looked good and didn't pander to the lowest common denominator. Four short seasons (23 episodes in total) were made.

The Jetsons

Sitcom | Hanna Barbera for ABC (shown on ITV) | episode duration 25 mins | broadcast 23 Sep 1962–3 Mar 1963, 1 Sep 1984–9 Nov 1987

Voice Cast
George O'Hanlon · *George Jetson*
Penny Singleton · *Jane Jetson*
Janet Waldo · *Judy Jetson*
Daws Butler · *Elroy Jetson, Henry Orbit, W. C. Cogswell*
Mel Blanc · *Cosmo S. Spacely*
Jean Vander Pyl · *Rosie the Robot, Mrs Starla Spacely*
Don Messick · *Astro*

Creators Joseph Barbera, William Hanna **Producers** Joseph Barbera, William Hanna (executive), Jeff Hall, Alex Lovy (associate), Bob Hathcock **Writers** Larry Markes, Harvey Bullock, R. S. Allen, Barry E. Blitzer, Tony Benedict, Walter Black, Warren Foster, Joanna Lee, Dalton Sandifer **Theme Music** Joseph Barbera, William Hanna and Hoyt Curtin

With ***The Flintstones*** proving an unprecedented success in a prime-time slot, Hanna Barbera flipped the concept to bring viewers another animated sitcom, this time set in the future. But while the gadgets and technology were more advanced, the show's gender roles were stuck in the 1950s. While George flew to and from work every day in his very chic flying car, his wife Jane stayed at home with her kids, Elroy and Judy, dog Astro and robot maid Rosie. Less boorish than Fred, George Jetson was a squeaky-clean Dick Van Dyke type, always trying to engage his family in his latest interest while working hard to get his permanently aggravated boss off his back.

Running originally for just one series of 24 episodes, *The Jetsons* returned for a revival series in the 1980s, culminating in the canon-colliding 'The Jetsons meet the Flintstones'. An animated feature film was released in cinemas in 1990, with former pop starlet Tiffany playing Judy Jetson, despite having already hired Janet Waldo to re-create her character.

Jeux Sans Frontières

See IT'S A KNOCKOUT

The Jewel in the Crown

Drama | Granada for ITV | episode duration 1 x 120-minute episode, 13 x 60-min episodes | broadcast 9 Jan–3 Apr 1984

Regular Cast
Tim Pigott-Smith · *Ronald Merrick*
Peggy Ashcroft · *Barbie Batchelor*
Derrick Branche · *Ahmed Kasim*
Geraldine James · *Sarah Layton*
Art Malik · *Hari Kumar*
Wendy Morgan · *Susan Layton/ Bingham/Merric*
Judy Parfitt · *Mildred Layton*
Eric Porter · *Dimitri Bronowsky*
Charles Dance · *Guy Perron*
Susan Wooldridge · *Daphne Manners*
Rachel Kempson · *Lady Manners*
Sarah Neville · *Sister Prior*
Om Puri · *Mr De Souza*
Zohra Sehgal · *Lili Chatterjee*
Marne Maitland · *Pandit Baba*
Kamini Kaushal · *Aunt Shalini*
Janet Henfrey· *Edwina Crane*
Rosemary Leach · *Aunt Fenny*
Fabia Drake · *Mabel Layton*
Nicholas Farrell · *Teddy Bingham*
David Allister · *Travers*
Geoffrey Beevers · *Captain Coley*
Anita Bhardwag · *Shinaz*
James Bree · *Colonel Grace*
Antony Brown · *Arthur Peplow*
Ishaq Bux · *Aziz*
Jeremy Child · *Robin White*
Rowena Cooper · *Connie White*
Anna Cropper · *Nicky Paynton*
John Emmanuel· *Khansamar*
Matyelok Gibbs · *Sister Ludmila*
Carol Gillies · *Clarissa Peplow*
Rennee Goddard · *Dr Anna Klaus*
Sheila Grant· *Clara*
Kumal Grewal · *Aziz*
Saeed Jaffrey · *The Nawab of Mirat*
Warren Clarke · *'Sophie' Dixon*
Robert James · *Colonel Beames*
Dominic Jephcott · *Reggie*
Siddharth Kak · *Rajendra Singh*
Karan Kapoor · *Colin Lindsey*
Rashid Karapiet · *Judge Menen*
Roly Lamas · *Ramaswami*
David Leland · *Purvis*
Jamila Massey · *The Maharani*
Zia Mohyeddin · *Mohammad Ali Mak' Kasim*

Albert Moses · *Suleiman*
Salmaan Peer · *Sayed Kasim*
Frederick Treves · *Colonel John Layton*
Bhasker Patel · *Gay Muslim Boy*

Producers Denis Forman (executive), Milly Preece (associate), Christopher Morahan **Writer** Ken Taylor, from *The Raj Quartet* by Paul Scott **Theme Music** George Fenton

The BBC tends to be regarded as the home of literary adaptations – and, indeed, in the United States it is often assumed to be responsible for all quality British productions thanks to the BBC America channel, which provides a home for UK output regardless of the originating channel. But along with ***Brideshead Revisited***, *The Jewel in the Crown* is considered to be the best of independent TV production of the 1980s.

The source novels, *The Raj Quartet*, were written by Paul Scott between 1966 and 1975, at a time of great social change in the UK, with levels of immigration from former British colonies rising like never before and with some quarters questioning the wisdom in allowing the dissolution of the Empire. By the time the novels reached the screen, Britain was once again facing social unrest – the riots of the early 1980s, rising unemployment and a war for an area of 'British' soil that few people were even aware of prior to its invasion by Argentine forces. Furthermore, by 1984 a mounting problem between British industry and the government led to the year-long miners' strike. In entertainment, though, we saw a shift back to the days of the Empire. An earlier adaptation of a Paul Scott story, *Staying On*, starring Trevor Howard and Celia Johnson, had appeared on ITV in 1982. *The Jewel in the Crown* was followed by ***The Far Pavilions***, and in cinemas by *A Passage to India* (1984). Suddenly, Indian culture – or at least the British understanding of it – seemed to be a popular subject for re-examination.

What makes *The Jewel in the Crown* so remarkable now is its willingness to let its audience be the judge. Although our eyes and ears are those of the British ex-pats still protecting the ideals of the Empire at the end of World War Two, we also gain insight into the troubles of the people of India, the political and cultural split between Muslim and Hindi and their resentment towards their outgoing British masters. Hari Kumar tells English nurse Daphne Manners how he feels disassociated – raised in an English public school, yet unable to fit in with either the English community in India or with his own family's people due to his inability to speak Urdu. But the Muslims also feel cut off, believing that their representatives will only support the Hindu people. Such frustrations inevitably lead to violence. But while we feel revulsion at the sight of the massacre of Muslims aboard a train, it's difficult to feel any sympathy for the British witnesses, one of whom condemns the 'savages' responsible but in a way that suggests her scorn extends beyond the perpetrators to include anyone native to the continent.

Running through the series is the ownership of a painting, 'The Jewel in the Crown', which depicts Queen Victoria on her throne being worshipped by the Indian people and presented with a large gem. The picture is allegorical, of course – such a scene never took place in real life – but its message is that India was the 'jewel' in the British Empire, and where it once represented optimism and hope, now it stood only for missed opportunity and lost potential. At one point, the painting passes into the hands of Ronald Merrick, a middle-class man who feels inferior about his grammar-school education among so many Oxbridge graduates. Like Hari Kumar, Merrick doesn't really fit in with the people around him. Sardonic, emotionally lacking and with a semi-permanent sneer on his lips, he is difficult to like from the beginning. We meet him first as the District Superintendent of the local police where he reveals a cold attraction to Daphne Manners and a distain for her friendship with Hari Kumar. The brutal rape of Daphne becomes a catalyst for events that continue to haunt Merrick. Hari is arrested for her rape and brutally tortured by Merrick, despite Daphne's insistence that Hari is innocent. When Daphne informs the authorities that she will undermine Merrick's case, should it come to trial, Hari is instead held in connection with acts of terrorism and imprisoned.

By episode four, Hari remains in prison unaware that Daphne has died in childbirth (a child she believed to be his). The story shifts to the extended family of Susan and Sarah Layton and for a while it seems Kumar and 'the Manners girl' will be forgotten. Ronald Merrick is now a high-flyer in the army, stationed with Teddy Bingham, the fiancé of Susan Manners. But certain sections will not let Merrick forget his part in the wrongful imprisonment without trial of six men, including Kumar, who, though innocent of any seditious acts, is now being used as a pawn by political agitator Pandit Baba. When Teddy is caught in an attack on his jeep, Merrick tries to save his life, believing that the attack was meant for himself. Teddy is killed and Merrick is left disfigured and loses his left arm. Strangely, though Merrick now looks like the monster we've always believed him to be, we gain an insight into his psyche that makes him almost sympathetic, as we eventually learn that his self-loathing is in part motivated by a deeply suppressed homosexuality, which emerges only through masochism; his torture of Kumar was, presumably linked on some level to a sexual connotation to him in Merrick's mind.

Though the issue of Kumar's imprisonment is eventually resolved, it happens off-screen. He doesn't appear again until the very end, and even then, like Godot, he fails to show up for the final act. What we are left with is a frustratingly uneven drama that offers few easy answers. But with such a talented cast and exotic settings, it's no surprise that the production was so highly acclaimed. Though it only pulled in an average of 8 million viewers, this was still an achievement for an ITV drama that could be described as more worthy than populist. But it was the critical response that secured its reputation, winning five

BAFTAS (including Best Actor for Tim Pigott-Smith and Best Actress for Peggy Ashcroft) and nominations for a further eight. It also won Best Mini Series at the Golden Globes and Best Limited Drama at the Emmys. Since then, *The Jewel in the Crown* has been repeatedly cited as a representative of a bygone age, where values and standards were met and surpassed repeatedly. Not the British Empire, but a time when a British TV company could spend four years making a drama and rightly justify a £5 million expenditure just by pointing to the screen.

Jim'll Fix It

Children's Entertainment | BBC One | episode duration 35 mins | broadcast 31 May 1975–24 Jul 1994, 2 Jan 1995

Cast

Jimmy Savile · *Presenter*

Producer Roger Ordish **Theme Music** *Jim'll Fix It* boasted theme tunes by Dave Mindel, the same man who wrote the themes to the chat show *Harty* and the drama *The District Nurse*. The first theme to *Jim'll Fix It* was performed by Dazzle and went a bit like this: 'If you have a vision you want to achieve/Then we know a man who's so eager to please/Jim'll fix it and we know that he can/Jim'll fix it 'cos he's that kind of man.' In 1982, a new opening theme came from Dave Mindel and producer Roger Ordish, performed by a band called Good Looks and featuring lyrics that promised: 'If you'd even like to fly a plane/You can even learn to drive a train/All you have to do is leave it up to Jim . . .'. The end theme, however, is the one everyone remembers. Also performed by Good Looks (with a later remixed version by Musical Youth), it reminded us that 'Your letter was only the start of it/One letter and now you're a part of it . . .' A final tweak of the theme from Dave came with the 1988 series.

There was never anything cuddly about Jimmy Savile, and he certainly never displayed much of a love for kids, but he was every kid's hero back in the Seventies and Eighties. A DJ and dead ringer for the first ***Doctor Who***, throughout the 1960s he had the coolest job on the planet as regular presenter on the BBC's flagship music programme ***Top of the Pops***. But in 1975, thanks to a call for submissions via the magazine programme *Nationwide*, Jimmy went from pop picker to dream maker in a Saturday teatime series for kids that would unite fans with their idols and life-long ambitions fulfilled.

People wrote to Jimmy Savile asking for him to fix it for them to perform alongside *Top of the Pops*' dance troupe Pan's People, swim with a dolphin, drive a steam train or design their own Christmas wrapping paper. Some of the 'fix it's would take place in the studio, some in filmed segments at the end of which the fixee would receive their ultimate prize – the shiny metal 'Jim fixed it for me' medallion that hung from a red ribbon. Anyone could ask Jim to fix it for them, and over 350,000 people a year sent in letters. Some wanted to blow up a chimney or drive James Bond's car, one young lad got to appear in his very own *Doctor Who* Adventure, 'A Fix With Sontarans' alongside Colin Baker, and a troop of cub scouts famously rode the Revolution rollercoaster at Blackpool Pleasure Beach while trying (and failing) to eat their packed lunches – drinks and crumbs went everywhere. Actor Peter Cushing even wrote in, to ask for a rose to be named after his beloved late wife Helen – one of the most heartbreaking, poignant and utterly magical moments ever seen on television.

By 1989, kids were still writing in to meet their pop idols, though by the last show, it was Worlds Apart rather than Showaddywaddy that the girls were screaming for. But the late 1980s saw a change in viewing patterns where Saturday night was no longer pulling in the viewers, and Jimmy Savile, his badges and his magic chair were not invited back. Now, the only place you can get a 'Jim fixed it for me' badge is on Ebay.

Joe 90

Children's Science Fiction | Century 21 Television/ITC for ITV | episode duration 25 mins | broadcast 29 Sep 1968–20 Apr 1969

Regular Voice Cast

Len Jones · *Joe McClaine*
Rupert Davies · *Professor Ian 'Mac' McClaine*
Keith Alexander · *Sam Loover*
David Healy · *Shane Weston*
Sylvia Anderson · *Mrs Ada Harris*
Gary Files, Martin King, Jeremy Wilkin, Shane Rimmer · *Other Voices*

Producers Reg Hill (executive), David Lane **Writers** Gerry and Sylvia Anderson, Tony Barwick, Shane Rimmer, David Lane, Donald James, Keith Wilson, Pat Dunlop, John Lucarotti **Theme Music** Barry Gray

Professor 'Mac' McClaine invents a machine called BIG RAT – Brain Impulse Galvanoscope Record And Transfer – which is capable of recording a person's brain patterns and transferring their entire sum of knowledge into another person's mind via special glasses. To show how safe it is, he tests the machine on his adopted son, nine-year-old Joe. But when Mac's best friend Sam Loover informs his bosses at WIN – the World Intelligence Network – they beg Mac to let them use BIG RAT and recruit young Joe as their latest very special agent.

Hanging from the coat-tails of ***Captain Scarlet and the Mysterons***, *Joe 90* was a major disappointment to Anderson's legions of fans. No cool uniforms or futuristic settings, just a smart-arsed kid and his dad. Children tend to be quite aspirational, which is probably why the idea of a 4ft 3in hero younger than most of the audience didn't quite appeal as much as *Scarlet* or ***Thunderbirds***. This is an immense shame as *Joe 90* is possibly Anderson's most slick Supermarionation production with some of the best direction in any of his series. The first episode alone sports a photomontage scene that is more emotionally fraught than anything that had gone before, and there are some beautifully subtle touches, such as the way the characters' postures are less stiff-backed than usual; we see them lounge around, fiddle absent-mindedly with glasses and display quite human body language – a major leap forward from the days of ***Fireball XL5***.

Anderson tried two further Supermarionation productions after *Joe 90: The Secret Service* combined live action with puppets and cast Stanley Unwin (inventor of the gibberish language Unwinese) as a priest who also moonlighted as a spy; and *The Investigator*, which didn't go beyond pilot stage. *Joe 90* marked the end of Anderson's original puppet empire, a genre he wouldn't return to until ***Terrahawks***, 15 years later.

Trivia

There are two explanations as to why Joe McClaine was dubbed 'Joe 90': one is that the WIN organisation already had 89 field agents, so he became their 90th; the other is that the BIG RAT project was assigned the codename 'Project 90', and Joe was the very special agent assigned to it.

John Craven's Newsround

See NEWSROUND

Joking Apart

Sitcom | Pola Jones for BBC Two | episode duration 30 mins | broadcast 15 Jan 1991, 7 Jan 1993–7 Feb 1995

Regular Cast

Robert Bathurst · *Mark Taylor*
Fiona Gillies · *Becky Johnson/Taylor*
Tracie Bennett · *Tracy Glazebrook*
Paul Raffield · *Robert Glazebrook*
Paul-Mark Elliott · *Trevor*

Creator Steven Moffat **Producer** Andre Ptaszynski **Writer** Steven Moffat **Theme Music** 'Fool If You Think It's Over', written by Chris Rea, performed by Kenny Craddock

It's an unusual set-up for a sitcom when the entire series is performed in flashback. *Joking Apart* is the story of the disintegration of the marriage of Mark and Becky Taylor, young newlyweds who at first appear to be ideally suited. Becky is initially attracted to Mark's sense of humour – as a stand-up comedian, Mark always has a quick one-liner or smart-alec remark ready. This charm quickly turns to resignation, frustration and then loathing from Becky, who eventually walks out on the marriage, sick of being the 'straight man' in their relationship.

We, the audience, discover all of these facts bit by bit, as Mark uses elements of his failed relationship as part of his stand-up act. We then follow Mark's increasingly embarrassing and amusing attempts to wrest his ex-wife's affections back, despite her now going out with dull but safe estate agent Trevor. Adding extra levels of farce and stupidity to proceedings are Becky's dim yet well-meaning neighbours Tracy and Robert, who are determined to do whatever they can to protect Becky and thwart Mark's attempts at reconciliation.

Although not strictly autobiographical, writer Steven Moffat used certain elements from the break-up of his first marriage as source material for this, his first prime-time TV series. Moffat had honed his comedy skills on children's comedy-drama ***Press Gang*** and would go on to write ***Chalk***, ***Coupling*** and episodes of Dawn French's ***Murder Most Horrid***. Series star Robert Bathurst would find much greater fame in the ensemble cast of ITV1 hit ***Cold Feet***, and Tracie Bennett would return to the programme that initially made her a star, as Rita's foster daughter Sharon Gaskell in ***Coronation Street***.

Unfathomable scheduling by BBC Two, which left the second series on the shelf for more than a year after it was recorded, meant that any momentum built up by the first series was lost. A fan-led campaign and the support of star Robert Bathurst to see the programme released on DVD attracted media attention in early 2005.

Jonathan Creek

Crime Drama | BBC One | episode duration 50 mins, plus 50–120-min specials | broadcast 10 May 1997–present

Regular Cast

Alan Davies · *Jonathan Creek*
Caroline Quentin · *Maddy Magellan*
Julia Sawalha · *Carla Borrego*
Anthony Head, Stuart Milligan · *Adam Klaus*
Adrian Edmondson · *Brendan Baxter*

Creator/Writer David Renwick **Producers** David Renwick (executive), Susan Belbin, Verity Lambert, Jonathan Paul Llewellyn, Matthew Hamilton **Theme Music** 'Danse Macabre' by Camille Saint Saëns

Jonathan Creek is the name of the behind-the-scenes assistant to odious stage magician Adam Klaus. Responsible for inventing many of the illusions and tricks that his better-known colleague takes the credit for, Jonathan spends much of his time in his windmill home, constructing new props and gadgets for Klaus's stage show. Jonathan's ability at thinking laterally around seemingly-impossible problems attracts the attention of self-serving journalist Maddy Magellan, who soon taps into Jonathan's unique brain to assist her in her investigations, emotionally blackmailing or manipulating him into getting involved. Over the course of time, Maddy and Jonathan grew closer and closer, with the ever-present possibility of a relationship between them looming over their investigations.

Jonathan Creek was created and written by ***One Foot in the Grave***'s David Renwick, and it's clear that this detective series played upon Renwick's strengths for convoluted, twisted yet utterly believable plots – strengths that had been obvious throughout Victor Meldrew's bizarre adventures. Viewers thrilled at being faced with storylines and plots that were intellectually challenging rather than tediously predictable, as most other detective shows tended to be. *Jonathan Creek* was equally popular with critics, winning both the BAFTA and National Television Awards for Best Drama Series in 1998. More likely to be seen as one-off specials rather than as long-running seasons, the programme handled the departure of series co-star Caroline Quentin very well (Maddy having left the UK on an international book tour), drafting in ***Absolutely Fabulous*** and ***Press Gang*** star Julia Sawalha as Jonathan's new partner, theatrical agent Carla Borrego, from 2001 onwards.

Trivia

If you fancy wandering around Jonathan's windmill, it's located in the town of Shipley, West Sussex, and is open to the public.

Jonny Briggs

Children's Drama | BBC One | episode duration 15 mins | broadcast 11 Nov 1985–20 Jan 1987

Principal Cast

Richard Holian · *Jonny*
Jane Lowe · *Mam*
Leslie Schofield · *Dad*
Sue Devaney · *Rita*
Jeremy Austin · *Humphrey*
Tommy Robinson · *Albert*
Debbie Norris · *Mavis*
Georgina Lane · *Pam*
Karen Meagher · *Miss Broom*
Adele Parry · *Jinny*
Rachel Powell · *Josie*
John Forbes-Robinson · *Mr Badger*

Creator Joan Eadington **Producer** Angela Beeching **Writer** Valerie Georgeson

A drama series aimed at younger school children, *Jonny Briggs* was to all intents and purposes a kind of 'My First Soap Opera', detailing the ins and outs of family life in twice weekly episodes. Jonny is the youngest child of the Briggs family who live in a Yorkshire town not too far from Leeds. Jonny's eldest brother Humphrey is the intellectual of the family, Albert is the ne'er do well who's always trying to find new ways of making money, and sister Rita is a fashion victim who's in the middle of hormonally charged temper tantrums. Thankfully, there's always his beloved and reliable dog Razzle, who never does anything that confuses or upsets our young hero. At school, Jonny is picked on by vindictive twins Jinny and Josie and, as a result of their pranks, he's often shouted at by teacher Miss Broom or (worse still) the headmaster Mr Badger.

Joan Eadington's *Jonny Briggs* stories had been a fixture on ***Jackanory*** for many years (read by actor Bernard Holley) when it was decided to turn them into a live action BBC One drama. With relatively few sets needing to be built (Jonny's house and classroom, mainly), it's interesting to see a programme that's clearly written very accurately from the perspective of the horizons of a young child. For although there might be a few weird and wacky excursions into Jonny's imagination (courtesy of a haunted cupboard), this series remained firmly fixed in the everyday problems that most young kids go through – the queue for the bathroom first thing in the morning, looking after the school rabbit, that kind of thing. Thirty-three episodes of *Jonny Briggs* were produced, broadcast across two seasons.

Judge John Deed

Drama | One-Eyed Dog Productions/BBC Worldwide for BBC One | episode duration 90 mins | broadcast 9 Jan 2001–present

Regular Cast

Martin Shaw · *Judge John Deed*
Jenny Seagrove · *Jo Mills QC*
Louisa Clein · *Charlie Deed*
Caroline Langrishe · *'George' Channing QC*
Barbara Thorn · *Rita Cooper*
Dave Norman · *Stephen Ashurst*
Christopher Cazenove · *Row Colemore*
Donald Sinden · *Sir Joseph Channing*
Jemma Redgrave · *Lady Francesca Rochester*
Simon Chandler · *Sir Ian Rochester*
Trevor Bowen · *Sir Michael Nivan*

Creator/Writer/Producer Gordon F. Newman **Theme Music** Debbie Wiseman

A former barrister who was renowned for his fearsome reputation in court and determined attempts to seek real justice for his clients, John Deed accepts promotion to the bench, becoming a judge with an even more formidable attitude. For Deed, it's not simply good enough for the letter of the law to be upheld – it's far more important that Justice (with a capital J) is *seen* to be served. As a result of his innovative interpretation of the letter of the law, Deed comes into conflict with the barristers he deals with in court, and sometimes faces the wrath of the Lord Chancellor himself. When he's not in court, Deed has to deal with his ex-wife George Channing (who's also a QC and is more than capable of handling Deed's sharp mind) and his student daughter Charlie. A resolutely single man, Deed's charm, mature good looks and powerful intellect enable him to bed a succession of attractive young women – a trait that can border on professional misconduct at times.

Judge John Deed is a rarity in modern television making, in so far as one individual (Gordon F. Newman) has been solely responsible for the creation, writing and production of every episode of the programme so far transmitted, a phenomenal feat considering the complexity involved in getting a television programme to our screens. *Judge John Deed* saw the return to our screens of Martin Shaw, still perhaps best known for his early role in ***The Professionals*** (a fact that apparently pains him greatly!), but more recently seen in Anglia's police drama for ITV *The Chief*. Complex and perhaps a touch soapier than many legal dramas, *Judge John Deed* has so far enjoyed a lengthy and successful run on BBC One.

Juke Box Jury

Music | BBC One/Two | episode duration 30 mins | broadcast 1 Jun 1959–27 Dec 1967, 16 Jun–18 Aug 1979, 19 Mar 1989, 24 Sep 1989–25 Nov 1990

Cast

David Jacobs, Noel Edmonds, Jools Holland · *Hosts*

Creator Peter Potter **Producers** Stewart Morris, Harry Carlisle, Neville Wortman, Barney Colehan, Barry Langford, Terry Henebery, Colin Charman, Roger Ordish, Philip Chilvers, Graham K. Smith **Theme Music** The first series was accompanied by 'Juke Box Fury' by Ozzie Warlock and the Wizards, but the theme most people remember was the appropriate 'Hit and Miss' by John Barry, a virtual, 'with-it' mash-up of 'What Do You Want?' by Adam Faith and a Shadows song.

Juke Box Jury – the name says it all – invited celebrities to listen to the latest crop of pop songs prior to their release and decide whether, in their opinion, the composition would be a hit or a miss. David Jacobs was the host who got to ring a bell if the jury liked the song or a klaxon if they didn't. In the event of a hung jury, members of the audience would cast the deciding vote. There'd be the occasional surprise for the jury, though, as the artist(s) responsible for one of the tracks under discussion would be lurking behind the scenes ready to be unveiled once their masterwork had been praised or (much more satisfying) ripped apart.

The show was a major part of the Saturday TV line-up, bridging the football results and early evening family entertainment. Regular jurors included Pete Murray, Alma Cogan, Katie Boyle, Gary Miller and a pre-***Magpie*** Susan Stranks. One special edition in 1963 had the four jury places filled by the Beatles, in which the boys professed to being fans of Elvis but not his songs, while John Lennon tipped 'I Could Write a Book' by the Chance 'the bestest gear' (sadly, despite John's recommendation, it failed to gain a place in the charts). The experiment was repeated the following year with the Rolling Stones (the only time the panel was five instead of four) and again with the Seekers.

Noel Edmonds resurrected the format in 1979; on the 30 June edition, Sex Pistol and iconoclast Johnny Rotten tried to perform an 'Emperor's New Clothes' by dismissing everything as boring, rowing with fellow juror Alan Freeman, to the visible discomfort of Joan Collins and Elaine Paige, and storming off at the end. A 1989 reunion special starring Jacobs and Pete Murray preceded another revival later that year, with Jools Holland as the chairman. This version illustrated the changes in attitudes, with the rather formal, polite critiques of the 1960s replaced with more savage group bitching sessions.

Juliet Bravo

Drama | BBC One | episode duration 50 mins | broadcast 30 Aug 1980–21 Dec 1985

Regular Cast

Stephanie Turner · *Inspector Jean Darblay*
Anna Carteret · *Inspector Kate Longton*
David Ellison · *Sergeant Joseph Beck*
Noel Collins · *Sergeant George Parrish*
C. J. Allen · *PC Brian Kelleher*
Edward Peel · *DCI Mark Perrin*
Tony Caunter · *DCI Jim Logan*
Mark Drewry · *PC Roland Bentley*
David Hargreaves · *Tom Darblay*
Martyn Hesford · *PC Ian Shelton*
Gerard Kelly · *PC David Gallagher*
James Grout · *DS Albert Hallam*
David Gillies · *PC Peter Sims*
Mark Botham · *PC Danny Sparks*
Sebastian Abineri · *DS Dick Maltby*

Creator Ian Kennedy Martin **Producers** Terence Williams, Colin Shindler, Jonathan Alwyn, Geraint Morris **Writers** Ewart Alexander, Chris Boucher, Tony Charles, Kenneth Clark, Wally K. Daly, Keith Dewhurst, James Doran, Colin Haydn Evans, Brian Finch, John Foster, John Fraser, Valerie Georgeson, Robert Holmes, William Humble, Ray Jenkins, Julia Jones, Henry Livings, Bill Lyons, Ian Kennedy Martin, Simon Masters, Nick McCarty, Paula Milne, Steven Morgan, Tony Parker, Susan Pleat, Allan Prior, Douglas Watkinson, Don Webb **Theme Music** Derek Goom

In the small fictional northern town of Hartley, the local police force gets a shock when their new Inspector arrives and turns out to be a woman. Jean Darblay faced the problems of many professional women – having to combine family life with a challenging career. After three years of fighting crime (everything from the kidnapping of babies through to robbery, arson and even paedophilia), Darblay was replaced by the even more dynamic Inspector Kate Longton. A career copper, Longton was keen to get promotion and move on in her career, but regularly clashed with DCI Perrin about her future in the force. The show ended on a surprisingly downbeat note with the shock death of PC Danny Sparks in a house fire, an incident that prompted Kate to change her mind about leaving the force.

Created by Ian Kennedy Martin as both a replacement for the long-running ***Z Cars*** and the BBC's response to ITV's ***The Gentle Touch***, *Juliet Bravo* was a huge success, raking in ratings for BBC One of up to 17 million viewers. Its bite might well have been overshadowed by grittier shows such as Lynda La Plante's ***Widows***, while its homespun philosophies have been taken up by the even cosier nostalgia of ***Heartbeat***, but for a generation of viewers, there's still a level of reassurance from that familiar title sequence with the rotating police badge and the soaring strings of Derek Goom's theme tune.

Junior Showtime

Entertainment | Yorkshire TV for ITV | episode duration 25 mins | broadcast 1969–1974

Regular Cast
Bobbie Bennett · *Presenter, 'Mr Interlocutor'*
The Showtime Minstrels · *Resident Performers*
Glyn Poole, Joe Longthorne, Mark Curry, Bonnie Langford, Marjorie Philips, Ken Dodd, Joe Brown, Billy Dainty, Peter Simon, Pauline Quirke · *Guest Presenters*

Producer Jess Yates

When people look back on television from the 'olden days', they often have a nostalgic glow about the programmes they enjoyed as children. Sadly, that glow can often be little more than the memory cheating – the harsh reality of the fact is that many old programmes were, to put it bluntly, a bit rubbish. One of the programmes least likely to ever be resurrected on DVD for nostalgia's sake is *Junior Showtime*. Perhaps best described as ITV's cross between ***The Good Old Days***, ***The Black and White Minstrel Show*** and your local church hall's junior talent show, *Junior Showtime* was presented by hyper-enthusiastic Bobbie Bennett, and gave a first TV break to a number of top-notch celebrities, including ***Emmerdale***'s Malandra Burrows (then going by her real name of Malandra Newman), Joe Longthorne, ***The Generation Game***'s Rosemarie Ford, ***Blue Peter***'s Mark Curry, and even burly ***Coronation Street*** actor Charles Dale. Created and produced by Jess Yates (father of Paula Yates – although it later transpired that her biological father was actually been ***Opportunity Knocks***' presenter Hughie Greene), each week viewers were treated to an array of youngsters, all fresh out of singing or music lessons, ready to perform a routine for the viewers at home. Whether it was playing the accordion or doing an impression of Frank Spencer in ***Some Mothers Do 'Ave 'Em***, *Junior Showtime* had them all.

Other regular performers on *Junior Showtime* included a pre-***Just William*** Bonnie Langford, the Poole Family (who had become famous on producer Jess Yates' other programme, the religious-based *Stars on Sunday*) and the Showtime Minstrels, a less accomplished (yet still blacked-up) version of the artistes performing on *The Black and White Minstrel Show* over on BBC One. In between such highlights, current chart acts like Herman's Hermits would come on to play their latest single, hopefully keeping the viewers at home at least as enthralled as they had been by the latest seven-year-old juggler who'd appeared before them.

Just Good Friends

Sitcom | BBC One | episode duration 30 mins | broadcast 22 Sep 1983–25 Dec 1986

Regular Cast
Paul Nicholas · *Vince Pinner*
Jan Francis · *Penny Warrender*
Sylvia Kay · *Daphne Warrender*
John Ringham · *Norman Warrender*
Ann Lynn · *Rita Pinner*
Shaun Curry · *Les Pinner*
Adam French · *Clifford Pinner*

Creator/Writer John Sullivan **Producer** Ray Butt **Theme Music** Paul Nicholas sang the syrupy yet annoyingly memorable theme song, which was written by series creator/writer John Sullivan. Legendary BBC band leader Ronnie Hazlehurst arranged the music.

He might be more famous nowadays for creating the exploits of Peckham's finest dodgy dealer Del Boy Trotter, but by the early 1980s writer John Sullivan's biggest success had been the exploits of revolutionary Wolfie in ***Citizen Smith***. His next hit was a sitcom based upon a classic will-they, won't-they relationship between star-crossed lovers Vince Pinner and Penny Warrender. *Just Good Friends* proved so popular that its final episode was broadcast on Christmas Day 1986, wedged in between two legendary episodes of ***EastEnders*** (Den's 'Merry Christmas, Ange!' and Arthur Fowler's breakdown), attracting an audience of almost 21 million viewers.

Young sweethearts Penny and Vince first met at a Rolling Stones concert in Hyde Park during the long hot summer of 1976. They fell in love and, like lots of young people, decided to get married. However, Vince got cold feet and jilted poor Penny at the altar. Five years later, Penny accidentally bumps into her former fiancé and, much to the surprise of them both, they find themselves falling in love once again. Penny's snobby middle-class mother is appalled that the common wide-boy who broke her daughter's heart is back on the scene and does nothing to hide her feelings about it. On the other hand, Vince's common-as-muck parents are delighted that their son has a chance to put right the mistake he made when he left posh Penny heartbroken in the church.

Over the course of two series, the ebb and flow of the relationship between Penny and Vince captivated viewers. Realising that there was only limited mileage in keeping the audience guessing whether these two characters were truly destined to be together, John Sullivan decided to call it a day with a Christmas special in 1984, in which Penny chooses to break off their relationship and flits over to Paris. Two long years passed before a final third season was transmitted, with Penny finally returning to Blighty for a tear-soaked reunion and triumphant marriage in the above-mentioned mega-rating Christmas episode.

Although Sullivan's scripts are sharp, witty and the characterisation excellent, it's undoubtedly the performances from leads Jan Francis (more used to appearing in straight dramas like ***Secret Army***) and Paul Nicholas that made this series such a success.

Just William (1977)

Comedy Drama | LWT for ITV | episode duration 25 mins, plus 50-min special | broadcast 6 Feb 1977–22 Jan 1978

Regular Cast
Adrian Dannatt · *William Brown*
Tim Rose · *Douglas*
Colin McFarlane · *Henry*
Michael McVey · *Ginger*
Bonnie Langford · *Violet Elizabeth Bott*
Diana Fairfax · *Mrs Brown*
Hugh Cross · *Mr Brown*
Stacy Dorning · *Ethel Brown*
Diana Dors · *Mrs Bott*

Producers Stella Richman (executive), John Davies **Writer** Keith Dewhurst, from the novels by Richmal Crompton

For commentary, see JUST WILLIAM (1994)

Just William (1994)

Comedy Drama | Talisman Films for BBC One | episode duration 25 mins | broadcast 13 Nov 1994–17 Dec 1995

Regular Cast
Oliver Rokison · *William Brown*
David Horovitch · *Mr Brown*
Polly Adams · *Mrs Brown*
Naomi Allisstone · *Ellen the Maid*
Tiffany Griffiths · *Violet Elizabeth*
Olivia Hallinan · *Susie Chambers*
Jonathan Hirst · *Ginger*
Benjamin Pullen · *Robert Brown*

Producers Anna Home, Alan Shallcross (executive), Alan Wright **Writer** Allan Baker, from the novels by Richmal Crompton

Richmal Crompton's stories of naughty schoolboy William Brown were first published in women's magazine *Home* in 1917. Throughout her productive career, Crompton wrote 38 *William* books, as well as screenplays for several films and radio adaptations. William made his first appearance on TV in 1946 in a one-off play entitled *Just William at the Zoo* (in which he was portrayed by John Clark); two later one-off plays were broadcast in 1947 and 1951. In 1962, writer C. E.Webber (who the following year would be instrumental in the creation of ***Doctor Who***) adapted Crompton's work for two seasons of adventures. The first series featured future ***Sweeney*** and ***Minder*** star Dennis Waterman as the naughty schoolboy, while in the second he had been replaced by Denis Gilmore. Even though these adaptations were popular, it is the mid-1970s version of the tale that is the one that's best remembered by the general public.

Eleven-year-old William Brown is the leader of his gang of friends, nicknamed the Outlaws. William, Ginger, Henry and Douglas get up to all sorts of mischief, both at school and at home – much to the dismay of their parents. However, William's biggest enemy isn't one of his teachers, it's the red-headed lisping spoilt girl Violet Elizabeth Bott, who threatens to 'thcweam and thcweam and thcweam until I'm thick!' if William doesn't let her get involved in his adventures, or if he gets into anything too naughty. Two seasons of William's adventures were made by LWT, totalling 26 episodes, and although many people enjoyed watching the exploits of the eponymous hero, it was Bonnie Langford's occasional supporting role as Violet Elizabeth that was the greatest legacy of the show – poor Bonnie became forever typecast as a nauseatingly precocious flame-haired monster, an albatross that she's unfortunately been unable to shake off ever since, despite proving her ability as a versatile stage and screen performer.

In 1994, the BBC commissioned another adaptation of the *William* stories from Talisman Films. Broadcast in two seasons between 1994 and 1995, this version of *Just William* unfortunately didn't capture the public's imagination like previous adaptations, despite being arguably the most faithful of the lot.

Kavanagh QC

Crime Drama | Carlton for ITV | episode duration 70 mins | broadcast 3 Jan 1995–29 Mar 1999, 25 Apr 2001

Regular Cast
John Thaw · *James Kavanagh QC*
Lisa Harrow · *Lizzie Kavanagh*
Anna Chancellor · *Julia Piper-Robinson*
Oliver Ford Davies · *Peter Foxcott QC*
Nicholas Jones · *Jeremy Aldermarten QC*
Daisy Bates · *Kate Kavanagh*
Tom Brodie · *Matt Kavanagh*
John Carlisle · *Judge Trafford*
Sam Cox · *Dr Derek Buxton*
Carol Harrison · *Susan Hutton*
Cliff Parisi · *Tom Buckley*
Jenny Jules · *Alex Wilson*
Geraldine James · *Eleanor Harker QC*
Valerie Redmond · *Emma Taylor*

Creators Chris Kelly, Susan Rogers, Ted Childs **Producers** Ted Childs (executive), Ray Frift, Lars MacFarlane, Rupert Ryle-Hodges, Neville C Thompson, Liz Watkins (associate), Chris Kelly **Writers** Various, including Nigel Kneale, Andy de la Tour, Malcolm Bradbury, Edward Canfor-Dumas, Stephen Churchett, Matthew Hall, Russell Lewis, Peter Moffat, Douglas Watkinson, Charles Wood **Theme Music** John E. Keane

James Kavanagh is one of the UK's top Queen's Counsels, a working class liberal Mancunian who believes in the basic integrity of the legal system. A dedicated barrister, Kavanagh loves to defend underdogs from unfair prosecutions and is relentless in getting justice for his clients in court. However, at home, Kavanagh is much less confident – he often finds himself juggling the normal ups and downs of family life with stressful cases, with the family sometimes having to accept that they're not always his first priority. Perhaps that's the reason why his wife Lizzie has begun an affair . . .

In many ways, *Kavanagh QC* is a deliberately humour-free version of the earlier smash hit TV legal series ***Rumpole of the Bailey***, featuring a determined and dedicated barrister fighting for the rights of those unfairly accused of crimes. Providing a welcome respite for John Thaw from all that mucking around on location in Oxford hunting for corpses and murderers, Kavanagh was a man at the other end of the legal process from ***Inspector Morse***, and somebody with a much more traditional background and attitude to life than the secretive bachelor Chief Inspector. Co-created by former TV presenter Chris Kelly (you know, him from ***Wish You Were Here?***, *Clapperboard* and ***Food and Drink***), 29 episodes of *Kavanagh QC* were made in total, with a bold decision taken en route to kill off James's wife Lizzie. Kavanagh drew to a close to enable John Thaw to return to play Morse for one last time (the plan being to kill him off). The final episode of *Kavanagh QC* left the distinct possibility of further storylines, with Kavanagh's promotion to becoming a judge looking like a distinct possibility – sadly this was not to be, with John Thaw's untimely death in February 2002 leaving fans worldwide in mourning.

Keep it in the Family

Sitcom | Thames for ITV | episode duration 25 mins | broadcast 7 Jan 1980–19 Oct 1983

Principal Cast
Robert Gillespie · *Dudley Rush*
Pauline Yates · *Muriel Rush*
Glyn Houston · *Duncan Thomas*
Stacy Dorning · *Susan Rush*
Jenny Quayle, Sabina Franklin · *Jacqui Rush*

Creator Brian Cooke **Producers** Mark Stuart, Robert Reed **Writers** Brian Cooke, Dave Freeman, Greg Freeman, David Barry, Peter Learmouth, Alex Shearer

'Barney: The Adventures of a Bionic Superdog' is a popular newspaper cartoon strip, whose artist/author Dudley Rush is the dad of a typical family. He and wife Muriel live in the upstairs half of their house on Highgate Avenue, Highgate, North London, Dudley working from home on creating the latest adventure for his cartoon superhero. Dudley also worries a great deal about his two gorgeous daughters Susan and Jacqui, so (being a typically overprotective and conservative parent) he decides it would be a good idea to move the two of them into the downstairs flat so he can keep an eye on them. However, to Dudley's horror, the only thing that he observes are more and more boyfriends coming and going out of his daughters' apartment.

Another ITV generation gap sitcom (very much along the same lines as the earlier hit ***Bless this House***), *Keep it in the Family* is perhaps as well remembered for the unusual profession of its lead character as much as for its jokes. Normally driven to distraction by his lusty daughters' reckless behaviour, Dudley often has conversations with the glove puppet he uses to make his drawings of Barney more realistic. Later in the series, his understanding-yet-worried newspaper editor Duncan even moves into Dudley's house to keep him company (neatly coinciding with Pauline Yates' absence from some episodes). A generally harmless and relatively amusing show, *Keep it in the Family* lasted for 31 episodes over five seasons. An American adaptation of the show, *Too Close For Comfort*, fared better with 151 episodes reaching US TV screens.

Keeping Up Appearances

Sitcom | BBC One | episode duration 30 mins, plus 50–60 min specials | broadcast 29 Oct 1990–25 Dec 1995

Regular Cast
Patricia Routledge · *Hyacinth Bucket*
Clive Swift · *Richard Bucket*
Judy Cornwell · *Daisy*
Geoffrey Hughes · *Onslow*
Josephine Tewson · *Elizabeth Warren*
David Griffin · *Emmet Hawkesworth*
Shirley Stelfox, Mary Millar · *Rose*
Jeremy Gittins · *Michael – the Vicar*
Marion Barron · *Vicar's Wife*
David Janson · *Postman*
George Webb · *Daddy*

Creator/Writer Roy Clarke **Producer** Harold Snoad **Theme Music** Nick Ingram produced the suitably pompous and regal-sounding theme tune

For Hyacinth Bucket ('It's "boo-*kay*",' she insists), life is a never-ending battle to maintain certain standards. Everything must be just-so: from the correct way of keeping her house and lawn neat and tidy, to the correct people to be seen in public with, to the correct way of dealing with minions like postmen. Heaven forbid anyone whose behaviour fails to meet Hyacinth's exacting standards – and woe betide anyone who mispronounces her surname.

In creating Hyacinth Bucket, writer Roy Clarke and star Patricia Routledge creating one of comedy's great monsters, a woman with an astonishing lack of self-awareness and a booming voice to strike fear into the hearts of ordinary mortals. The primary focus of Hyacinth's disapproval is her doormat of a husband, Richard. Initially able to just about tolerate his wife's domineering attitude, his retirement means he's subjected to Hyacinth's demands and bullying 24 hours a day, much to his dismay. Equally keen to steer clear of Hyacinth are her next door neighbours, brother and sister Emmet and Elizabeth – however, Elizabeth rarely manages to set a foot outside her front door without being 'invited' in for coffee, which she normally ends up spilling all over Hyacinth's floor because of her shredded nerves. Hyacinth can't even turn to her sisters for support – Daisy is married to vile working class slob Onslow and has adopted many of his habits, and Rose is no better than she ought to be, with a long chain of gentleman callers discarded by the wayside. A further sister, Violet – 'the one with the country house and room for a pony' – is nowhere to be seen, and even her beloved, sensitive son Sheridan (away studying at University) normally only ever calls his mummy to beg for some money. And, worst of all, Hyacinth's Daddy is a sandwich short of a picnic and prone to running off at the slightest opportunity, despite Onslow and Daisy's best attempt to keep him under control. This necessitates Hyacinth having to go round to their slum of a house and putting everything right – as per usual.

With *Keeping Up Appearances*, writer Roy Clarke created yet another long-running sitcom hit, following his earlier success with ***Open All Hours*** and perfectly complementing his ongoing saga of geriatric misbehaviour ***Last of the Summer Wine***. Much of the success of the programme came down to the British obsession with class, snobbery and puncturing the egos of those who consider themselves to be better than everybody else. However, this doesn't automatically explain why *Keeping Up Appearances* became a relatively major hit in the USA, where it was shown on the PBS network. Perhaps the British aren't entirely unique in their obsession at laughing at the pompous. . .

Keith Floyd on TV

See CLIVE JAMES ON TV

Kenny Everett

Comedy | Thames for ITV/BBC One | episode duration 25–60 mins | broadcast 3 Jul 1978–21 May 1981 (ITV), 24 Dec 1981–18 Jan 1988 (BBC)

Regular Cast
Kenny Everett, Anna Dawson, Cleo Rocos, Lionel Blair, Billy Connolly, Terry Wogan, Barry Cryer, Joanna Lumley, Sheila Steafel, Hot Gossip (choreographed by Arlene Philips), Teresa Codling, Carol Kenyon, Jane Newman, Kate Rabette, Paula Sommers, Lesley Ann Wootten

Producers David Mallet, Royston Mayoh, Bill Wilson, John Bishop, Paul Ciani **Writers** Kenny Everett, Barry Cryer, Ray Cameron, John Langdon, Brian Levenson, Andrew Marshall, Paul Minett, David Renwick **Theme Music** During his time with ITV, Kenny didn't use 'theme music' as such, more a collection of *a capella* ditties recited over Terry Gilliam-esque animation sequence. There were a number of different theme tunes for Kenny's BBC shows, including one co-written by Mike Moran (which was reworked into the hit single 'Snot Rap' – No. 9 in March 1983) and 'We are Electro People', written by Kenny Young and performed by Fox.

Maurice Cole was born on Christmas Day 1944 in Liverpool – as Kenny Everett, he became one of the country's best-loved entertainers. Everett was one of the founding fathers of the radio revolution, making a name for himself on Pirate Radio London before 'jumping ship' to the newly formed BBC Radio 1 as one of its first DJs. His radio career was dogged with incident, getting fired for making jokes about politicians' wives (which today is practically part of the job description) on the one hand, and championing an unlikely B-side from rock group Queen that nobody else wanted to play – a song called 'Bohemian Rhapsody'. His early ventures onto TV were similarly mixed, with a short-lived sketch show for Granada called *Nice Time* (co-starring ***Candid Camera***'s Jonathan Routh and future feminist icon Germaine Greer) lasting for just two seasons in selected ITV regions (11 Aug 1968–8 Jun 1969 – the producer was future BBC Director General John Birt). He then made three

consecutive six-part sketch shows for Thames TV, *The Kenny Everett Explosion* (10 Jul–11 Sep 1970), *Making Whoopee* (18 Sep–24 Oct 1970) and *Ev* (31 Oct 1970–2 Jan 1971), none of which really made much of an impression on viewers.

Everett is best remembered for two very similar programmes of dynamic sketch-based innovative comedy – *The Kenny Everett Video Show* (which was shown on ITV) and the subsequent *The Kenny Everett Television Show* (for the BBC). With many of the same characters and writers, it was really only a change of network and a very slight toning down of the material that distinguished these two shows from each other – that and the commercial breaks, obviously. Everett presented viewers with an array of different characters and jokes each week, but very soon some became staples of his programmes – 1950s' style biker Sid Snot, French ladykiller Marcel Wave, 'glamour actress' Cupid Stunt (the lady whose films normally involved all of her clothes falling off at an inopportune moment – despite the fact that it was 'all done in the best *possible* taste'!), and perhaps most memorably the animated adventures of futuristic space pilot Captain Kremmen and his busty assistant Carla. Produced by ***Jamie and the Magic Torch*** animators Cosgrove Hall, The Adventures of Captain Kremmen were so popular that a feature film (*Kremmen – The Movie*) was released in 1980. The final year of the ITV show (renamed *The Kenny Everett Video Cassette*) saw the animated adventures of the Captain realised in real-life form, with Anna Dawson taking the role of Carla. Pop artists would appear to plug their latest record and appear in a few sketches, and saucy dance troupe Hot Gossip would gyrate their 'naughty bits' much to the delight of teenage boys and their dads. However, when ITV scheduled this final run of episodes directly opposite ratings juggernaut ***Top of the Pops***, Everett tired of working for Thames and switched channels to the BBC.

A whole new range of characters greeted Everett's arrival at 'Auntie Beeb', including gob-spitting punk Gizzard Puke, General Norm Bomb-the-Bastards ('Round 'em all up, put 'em in a field and *bomb the bastards*!'), Verity Treacle, the delicate lady presenter of religious song show *Up Your End* who sat with legs so far akimbo they were at right angles, and the lethally clumsy DIY programme presenter Reg Prescott, the only man able to mark out the right place to cut a piece of his wood with his own blood. Many of his ITV characters returned too, including the furiously angry Colonel Muriel Clean, the stockings-and-suspenders-wearing leader of the Campaign For Nice Things On TV ('You've all got a knob there – use it!'), and the huge-handed preacher Brother Lee Love. Celebrity guests became regular foils for Everett's humour, with dancer Lionel Blair chained up in a dungeon being whipped by busty hostess Cleo Rocos; Billy Connolly dressing up as a prim old lady in a kind of tribute to Hinge and Bracket, and even Spider-Man making occasional appearances – most memorably in a sketch where he discovered the downside of getting out of his spandex suit when bursting to go to the toilet.

When the sketch series came to an end, Everett returned to his former love of radio, where he presented a show on London's Capital Gold. He also tried his arm at presenting the BBC One game show *Gibberish*. Sadly, Kenny Everett died in 1995, a tragically early end to one of the most innovative and talented comedians ever to have polluted early evening TV screens with his 'naughty bits'.

Kessler

Drama | BBC/BRT Belgium (shown on BBC One) | episode duration 50 mins | broadcast 13 Nov–18 Dec 1981

Regular Cast

Clifford Rose · *Ludwig Kessler/Manfred Dorf*
Alan Dobie · *Richard Bauer*
Nitza Saul · *Mical Rak*
Ralph Michael · *Ruckert*
Alison Glennie · *Ingrid Dorf*
Nicholas Young · *Franz*
Guy Rolfe · *Yqueras*
Oscar Quitak · *Josef Mengele*
Richard Addison · *Heinrich Himmler*
John Moreno · *Garriga*
Jerome Willis · *Hugo Van Eyck*
Robert Morris · *Leider*
Harold Innocent · *Deakin*
Jeremy Wilkin · *Gidney*
Ishia Bennison · *Ruth*
Bernard Hepton · *Albert Foiret*
Angela Richards · *Monique Durnford*
Juliet Hammond-Hill · *Natalie Chantrens*

Creators Gerard Glaister and John Brason **Producer** Gerard Glaister **Writer** John Brason **Theme Music** A slightly more militaristic version of Robert Farnon's 'Wall of Fear', which had already been used on ***Secret Army***

A spin-off/sequel series to the hugely successful *Secret Army*, *Kessler* was set 35 years after the end of the World War Two, when most people across Europe have managed to put the horrors of Nazi occupation behind them. But there are some who dedicate their lives to tracking down the few senior Nazis who managed to escape justice. One such man is Ludwig Kessler, former leader of the SS in occupied Belgium and the man personally responsible for a number of outrages and atrocities across the Low Countries. Investigator Richard Bauer teams up with Israeli Mical Rak as they put together a case against successful German industrialist Manfred Dorf. Albert, Monique and Natalie, former members of the Lifeline organisation during the war, confirm that Dorf is indeed the hated Kessler, but both Bauer and Rak discover to their cost that bringing a Nazi officer to justice is fraught with danger...

Although *Kessler* is undoubtedly an extremely well-made programme, it does lack emotional connection to the two main Nazi-hunters, thereby losing a lot of the power of its

parent series, *Secret Army*. In fact, *Kessler* is a reworking of the never-transmitted final episode of *Secret Army* – entitled 'What Did You Do in the War, Daddy?' – which also detailed Kessler's post-war attempts to hide from the authorities. By the end of the six episodes, Kessler and his Nazi colleagues have fled to South America, where Bauer and Rak discover that infamous characters such as Mengele and Himmler are still very much alive and well. Can our two heroes finally bring Kessler and his loathsome kind to justice?

Kilroy

Chat Show | BBC One | episode duration 45–60 mins | broadcast 12 Oct 1987–8 Jan 2004

Cast

Robert Kilroy-Silk · *Presenter*

Producers Various, including David Wickham

Former Labour MP Robert Kilroy-Silk branched out from his political beginnings in 1986 when he became the host of a BBC daytime chat show called *Day to Day* (24 Nov 1986–15 May 1987 on BBC One). This programme followed the format of a dozen other American 'Talk Shows', inviting a handful of guests into a TV studio where they would discuss their own problems, issues or viewpoints on a particular subject. The audience would then chip in with their own views and opinions, with Kilroy-Silk acting as mediator, moderator and ringmaster for some of the more confrontational debates.

Within a year, *Day to Day* had quickly been renamed to take into account the presenter's increasing fame (and also following the format established by American talk shows like *Donohue* and *Geraldo*, simply using the host's name as programme title) and *Kilroy* first hit screens on 12 October 1987, with the first topic centring on the tricky subject of harassment in all its forms. For over 15 years, Kilroy-Silk hosted five programmes each week for most of the calendar year (only breaking for the summer and Christmas). Everything seemed to be going swimmingly for Kilroy-Silk, especially as (by the late 1990s) he now ran his own production company that made the show for the BBC. Then, one day in early 2004, it all came crashing to a sudden and spectacular halt when *Kilroy* was pulled from the schedules. Kilroy-Silk had written a personal opinion article in a Sunday newspaper that was deemed to be offensive to Muslims. Although BBC editorial policy states that its employees are entitled to voice their own opinions, it's equally clear that presenters, newsreaders and 'impartial' bastians of the airwaves are not permitted to write about or voice their own personal political views in public. With his programme suddenly whipped from the air, Kilroy-Silk switched back to his original career path of politics, this time no longer campaigning for the Labour party but instead for the minority UK Independence party before spearheading his own party Veritas. At the 2005 General Election, Kilroy-Silk didn't manage to get himself elected, but just about managed to hold onto his deposit. As a side note, the final broadcast episode of *Kilroy* on BBC One was entitled 'I've Taken Revenge'.

King of the Castle

Children's Fantasy | HTV West for ITV | episode duration 25 mins | broadcast 8 May–19 Jun 1977

Principal Cast

Philip DaCosta · *Roland Wright*
Angela Richards · *June Wright, Lady*
Sean Lynch · *Ron Wright, Lord*
Milton Johns · *Hawker, Ergon*
Fulton Mackay · *Dr Spurgeon, Hawkspur*
Talfryn Thomas · *Vine, Vein*
Majelia Dennehy · *Della, Delta*
Edward Dentith · *Sergeant Tarr, Governor*
Jamie Foreman · *Ripper, Warrior*
Derek Smith · *Voss, Voysey*
Kevin Hudson · *Alf, Alfie*
Georgina Kean · *Betty, Beattie*
Paul Nicholson · *PC Briggs, Guard*
Patrick Durkin · *1st Engineer, Chef*
David Trevena · *2nd Engineer, Sous Chef*

Creators/Writers Bob Baker and Dave Martin **Producers** Patrick Dromgoole (executive), Leonard White **Theme Music** Sidney Sager

Roland Wright is finding it hard to adapt to his new life. His father has only recently remarried and he's still not sure if he likes his stepmother. He attends a private choir school but finds himself on the receiving end of frequent and fearsome outbursts from the headmaster Dr Spurgeon and choirmaster Hawker. Worst of all, his family has moved to a tower block held in the grip of a gang of teenage thugs who take time out from fighting among themselves to torment Roland. But when Roland is pushed into a faulty lift carriage by the thugs, the carriage hurtles to the bottom of the lift shaft, crashing with a thud and knocking Roland unconscious. He awakes to find himself deep within forgotten catacombs beneath the tower block, a fantasy realm where the inhabitants look strangely familiar . . .

King of the Castle really is an odd one. What starts as a quite perturbing story of bullying soon becomes something else entirely as events take a more metaphorical turn. Scenes set in the subterranean world were shot on videotape, distinguishing them from those scenes filmed up on the surface, where engineers battle to rescue Roland from the lift shaft. Each of the people Roland knows in real life are mirrored in a contorted form down below: a gatekeeper called Vein looks identical to the tower block's caretaker Mr Vine (the unforgettable Talfryn Thomas); his headmaster and teacher are transformed into mad scientist Hawkspur and his hideous monster Ergon; leader of the bullies, Ripper, is represented by a sword-wielding warrior; and his father and stepmother appear as Lord of the Tower and a witch, respectively.

The realism of the first episode soon gives way to a dreamlike story that combines ***Into the Labyrynth*** with *The Wizard of Oz*, and whether or not the events are actually taking place all depends on whether you believe Dorothy Gale really did met Munchkins and battled a witch or just got a bang on the head during a storm.

Although created to be shown mid-week in a traditional children's ITV timeslot, *King of the Castle* was held back by the channel schedulers and instead screened in a Sunday teatime drama slot. Although just seven episodes long, its point was as difficult to fathom as many of the more convoluted episodes of ***The Prisoner***. That's possibly why it's still held in such high esteem by hardcore TV enthusiasts, among whom it's achieved legendary status. No-one seems to be 100 per cent sure if it all still exists in broadcast quality, with at least a couple of episodes being rumoured to have disappeared over the years (though VHS copies are known to exist in the hands of private collectors).

King Rollo

Animation | King Rollo/Children's Entertainment for BBC One | episode duration 5 mins | broadcast 1 Oct–31 Dec 1980

Voice Cast
Ray Brooks · *Narrator*

Creator/Writer David McKee **Producer** Clive Juster **Theme Music** Duncan Lamont

Another example of a children's series that everyone thinks ran for much longer than it did, *King Rollo* was a crudely animated yet enchanting series about life in a castle. Kindly King Rollo lives in the castle with his wife Queen Gwen and an assortment of other characters, such as a magician (clad in typical Merlinesque robes and hat) and the ever-busy cook. Ray Brooks – the same chap who narrated ***Mr Benn*** and who would later star in '80s gambling drama *Big Deal* – provided the languid narration for these gentle adventures.

Only one note of concern really creeps in for older viewers. The castle's resident cat is called Hamlet – for those familiar with Shakespeare's play, it's difficult not to get nervous about the possible dreadful fates that might befall the King and Queen with a mischief-minded Hamlet in the castle . . .

Knight Rider

Action-Adventure | Glen A. Larson Productions/Universal for NBS (shown on ITV) | episode duration 50 mins | broadcast 24 Sep 1982–4 Apr 1986, 19 May 1991 (USA)

Regular Cast
David Hasselhoff · *Michael Knight*
Edward Mulhare · *Devon Miles*
William Daniels · *Voice of KITT*
Patricia McPherson · *Bonnie Barstow*
Rebecca Holden · *April Curtis*
Peter Parros · RC3 *(Reginald Cornelius III)*

Creator Glen A. Larson **Producers** Glen A. Larson, Robert Foster (executive), Bruce Golin, Ron Martinez (associate), Robert Ewing, Tom Greene, Gino Grimaldi, Robert A. Cinader, Hannah Louise Shearer, Steven E. de Souza, Stephen Downing, Rob Gilmer, Joel Rogosin, Burton Armus, Gerald Sanford, Calvin Clements Jr, Gregory S. Dinallo, Bruce Lansbury **Writers** Various, including Glen A. Larson, William Schmidt, Robert Foster, Janis Hendler, Tom Greene, Robert Gilmer, Richard C. Okie, Gerald Sanford, Burton Armus, Gregory S. Dinallo **Theme Music** Stu Phillips and Glen A. Larson's synthesiser theme has since become one of the most mobile popular ringtones in the UK. Rap artist Busta Rhymes scored a No. 2 hit in the UK singles charts with 'Fire It Up', which featured a sample of the theme.

During a police stakeout, a young detective is ambushed and left for dead. When he wakes up after the attack, he learns that his has been given a new face and a new identity – Michael Knight. It's all the work of one Wilton Knight (Richard Basehart), a dying billionaire in search of an heir and standard-bearer for his secret project. Wilton Knight believes that he can put his wealth to good use in fighting crime, but with time so short he needs someone to provide the muscle. Michael is equipped with a state-of-the-art, high-security car – Knight Industries Two Thousand, or KITT for short – which can hit speeds of over 300 mph and has been programmed with a rather snooty personality (yep, the car can talk). Guided by Devon Miles, the man who inherits the responsibilities for the Knight Foundation after Wilton Knight's death, Michael now becomes a hero of the roads – the Knight Rider.

Catapulting David Hasselhoff to stardom, *Knight Rider* was your typical 1980s action-adventure series. ***Airwolf*** had its helicopter, ***Street Hawk*** its motorbike and ***Magnum, P.I.*** its bright red Ferrari. KITT, Michael Knight's sleek black phallic symbol of choice, was a customised Pontiac Trans-Am with a red LED strip on the front that make it look like it had just had a collision with a Cylon from ***Battlestar Galactica***. A natural successor to Chitty Chitty Bang Bang as the smuggest smart car on the road, KITT was fitted with auto-pilot, ski mode (driving on two wheels), turbo power and as many other features as the writers needed each week. KITT could also remain in communication with Michael via a rather swanky wristwatch.

It was also symptomatic of mid-1980s formulaic shows in that, the car aside, there was nothing truly unique about it. The token female was a cipher, a mechanic with no other function apart from looking pretty and waiting around for Michael to flirt in a purely platonic, non-threatening way. Yet it was a hugely popular show.

Just goes to show how seductive a sexy-looking car can be . . .

David Hasselhoff returned to the driving seat in 1991 for *Knight Rider 2000*, a reunion movie for television. Another TV movie, *Knight Rider 2010*, this time without Hasselhoff, was broadcast in the US on 13 February 1994 (going straight to video in the UK), and was followed by *Team Knight Rider*, which ran for a series of 22 episodes (9 October 1997–23 May 1998). In this version of the show, KITT was joined by KAT and other vehicles.

Website

knightrideronline.com looks like a car showroom, just as it should.

Knots Landing

Soap | Lorimar/Roundlay/MF for CBS (shown on BBC One) | episode duration 45 mins | broadcast 1979–1993 (USA)

Principal Cast

Ted Shackleford · *Gary Ewing*
Joan Van Ark · *Valene Ewing/Gibson/Waleska*
Douglas Sheehan · *Ben Gibson*
Sam Behrens · *Danny Waleska*
Michele Lee · *Karen Fairgate/MacKenzie*
Don Murray · *Sid Fairgate*
Kevin Dobson · *Mack MacKenzie*
John Pleshette · *Richard Avery*
Constance McCashin · *Laura Avery/Sumner*
William Devane · *Gregory Sumner*
Kim Lankford · *Ginger Ward*
James Houghton · *Kenny Ward*
Claudia Lonow · *Diana Fairgate*
Pat Petersen · *Michael Fairgate*
Steve Shaw · *Eric Fairgate*
Donna Mills · *Abby Cunningham/Ewing/Sumner*
Bobby Jacoby, Brian Austin Green · *Brian Cunningham*
Tonya Crowe · *Olivia Cunningham/Dyer*
Julie Harris · *Lilimae Clements*
Lisa Hartman · *Ciji Dunne, Cathy Geary/Rush*
Alec Baldwin · *Joshua Rush*
Ava Gardner · *Ruth Galveston*
Nicolette Sheridan · *Paige Matheson*
Michelle Phillips · *Anne Winston/Matheson*
Red Buttons · *Al Baker*
Kristy Swanson · *Jody Campbell*
Melinda Culea · *Paula Vertosick*

Creator David Jacobs **Producers** David Jacobs, Lee Rich, Michael Filerman (executive) **Writers** Various, including David Jacobs, John Pleshette, Bernard Lechowick and many others **Theme Music** Jerrold Immel

A spin-off soap opera from mega-soap ***Dallas***, *Knots Landing* actually managed to stay on screen for just as long as its parent show, an amazing 13 years. The series centred on a small residential cul-de-sac in the town of Knots Landing, California. As the show began, viewers saw the arrival in Knots Landing of Gary Ewing – alcoholic younger brother of J. R. and Bobby from *Dallas* – and his ever-suffering wife Valene. Their new neighbours included car dealer Sid Fairgate, his wife Karen and their three teenage kids; double-dealing slimy lawyer Richard Avery and his estate agent wife Laura; and a younger couple Kenny and Ginger Ward. Over time, other characters arrived in the cul-de-sac, including Sid's sister (and arch bitch) Abby Cunningham and mob-connected senator Greg Sumner.

With storylines much more based in reality than any of the other prime-time early '80s soap operas, *Knots Landing* held a mirror up to the American middle classes, who thoroughly enjoyed watching a twisted reflection of their own lives. Viewers in the UK were less enthusiastic though, with *Knots Landing* only surviving for a few years in a prime-time slot before being bumped to weekday afternoons for the rest of its run. More than any other US soap, watching *Knots Landing* felt more akin to watching a British soap such as ***Brookside*** (the weather and standard of living were a darn sight better for the Americans, though) – a group of families clustered together on one street, all of them working for a living, and facing the kind of issues that many people could identify with.

Knowing Me, Knowing You . . . With Alan Partridge

Comedy | Talkback Productions for BBC Two | episode duration 30 mins, plus 40-min special | broadcast 16 Sep–21 Oct 1994, 29 Dec 1995

Regular Cast

Steve Coogan · *Alan Partridge*
Steve Brown · *Glenn Ponder*
Rebecca Front, Patrick Marber, Doon Mackichan · *Various Characters*

Producers Peter Fincham (executive), Armando Iannucci **Writers** Steve Coogan, Armando Iannucci, Patrick Marber, Rebecca Front, Steve Brown, Doon Mackichan **Theme Music** Bjorn Ulvaeus and Benny Andersson of ABBA composed the original song 'Knowing Me, Knowing You' (a sad song about the break-up of a long-term relationship), which got to No. 1 in the UK charts in February 1977. Of course, Steve Coogan (as Partridge) would interject a boisterous 'A-HA!' into the middle of these poignant lyrics, completely undermining the whole point of the song.

With ***The Day Today*** having successfully been translated into a TV hit from the earlier radio series *On the Hour*, it seemed only logical to do the same thing with *On the Hour*'s spin-off series *Knowing Me, Knowing You*. One of the most popular of the ensemble of characters created by Armando Iannucci and Chris Morris for *On the Hour* was inept sports reporter Alan Partridge, a man incapable of grasping the basics of journalism, common sense or even

communication skills. So it seemed only right and proper, in a decade that had already begun to celebrate mediocrity, that such a monumental waste of skin would be given his own TV series, a show in which he could be insensitive and patronising towards an entirely new group of people.

Knowing Me, Knowing You . . . With Alan Partridge was a mock chat show, hosted by the eponymous multi-talented broadcaster Mr Partridge. Each week, Partridge would exchange some forced and unfunny (and therefore to us viewers, hilarious) banter with his resident band leader Glenn Ponder, a man who never seemed able to keep the name of his group the same for more than a week at a time. Partridge would then welcome a number of guests onto his show, usually consisting of 'celebrities' or experts in some field or another. Unfortunately, Alan wasn't one of the world's great listeners or communicators, failing to understand anything but the most basic of discussion topics. He was also unable to disguise how he really felt about his guests – if he liked them, he fawned and flirted; if he disliked them, they might leave the stage in tears. Eventually, Alan's incompetence led to his own downfall when he assaults the BBC's programme commissioner with a 'dead foul'. With the BBC now determined never to allow Alan back on television, he headed off into the wilderness years, as shown in follow-up series *I'm Alan Partridge*.

Knowing Me, Knowing You . . . With Alan Partridge was undoubtedly very funny, with a central performance from Steve Coogan that's the equal of any of the great sitcom characters. However for some people, the endless parade of embarrassment contained in a single episode of the series made it too uncomfortable to watch for pleasure, a criticism levelled at the next great 'squirmedy', Ricky Gervais's ***The Office***.

Kojak

Detective | Universal for CBS (shown on BBC One) | episode duration 50 mins | broadcast 24 Oct 1973–18 Mar 1978 (USA)

Regular Cast

Telly Savalas · *Lieutenant Theo Kojak*
Dan Frazer · *Captain Frank McNeil*
Kevin Dobson · *Lieutenant Bobby Crocker*
George Savalas · *Detective Stavros*
Mark Russell · *Detective Saperstein*
Vince Conti · *Detective Rizzo*
Borah Silver · *Detective Prince*

Creator Abby Mann **Producers** Matthew Rapf (executive), James McAdams, Jack Laird, Chester Krumholz **Writers** Various, including Matthew Rapf, James McAdams, Jack Laird, Chester Krumolz, Donald P Bellisario, Robert Earll, Jerrold Freedman, Mort Fine, Harriet Margulies, Joseph Polizzi, Ross Teel **Theme Music** Billy Goldberg

A very different of police detective, Theo Kojak stood out from the rest of the pack of television sleuths for a number of reasons. First of all, he was a natty dresser, never showing up to the scene of a homicide unless he was immaculately turned out in suit, tie, snazzy-looking waistcoat and often an elegant-looking trilby. Second, he had a fondness for sucking on lollipops – perhaps a Freudian sublimation of his own shiny bald pate? And finally, not many cops working out of New York City's Manhattan South Precinct were in the habit of addressing people as 'Pussycat' or asking complete strangers, 'Who loves ya, baby?'

Another reason for *Kojak* standing out from the rest of the crowd of TV detectives was an immaculate performance by Hollywood bad guy Telly Savalas, star of movies like *The Dirty Dozen* (1967) and Bond flick *On Her Majesty's Secret Service* (1969), in which he played über-villain Blofeld. Having already 'made it' as a film star, Savalas simply oozed charisma and style, lighting up the entire television screen with his widescreen-sized personality. Savalas had quality back-up, too, with Kevin Dobson (future star of ***Knots Landing***) playing Kojak's partner Bobby Crocker and Savalas's real-life younger brother George showing up as the rotund laid-back Detective Stavros (no, not Harry Enfield, or the guy who invented the Daleks). Kojak was a policeman who really cared about his job, someone who felt he was on a personal crusade to clean up the streets – occasionally, Kojak didn't object to breaking rules if it meant justice could truly be served. *Kojak* attracted much praise from police forces worldwide, who admired the realism of the show – although much of that realism was undoubtedly down to a higher than normal proportion of location filming on the streets of Manhattan. Savalas took the opportunity of starring in *Kojak* to re-use some of the skills he'd developed in the early part of his career working as a director for ABC News, getting behind the camera and directing several episodes of the series himself. Although the series came to an end in 1978, *Kojak* returned to TV screens in the USA in 1989 in several TV movies (not screened in the UK), in which the detective had been promoted all the way up to Inspector.

The Krypton Factor

Game Show | Granada for ITV | episode duration 25 mins | broadcast 1977–95

Cast

Gordon Burns, Penny Smith · *Hosts*

Creator Jeremy Fox **Producers** Jeremy Fox, Stephen Leahy, David Jenkins, Geoff Moore, Patricia Pearson, Rod Natkiel, Kieran Roberts, Caroline Gosling, Wayne Garvey **Theme Music** In the mid-1980s, the theme came from pop experimentalists The Art of Noise.

Taking its name from that of Superman's home planet, *The Krypton Factor* was dubbed 'the toughest quiz on TV'. In a succession of rounds testing observation, mental

agility, intelligence, general knowledge, coordination and physical endurance, it certainly looked like anyone who could do well in the challenges was worthy of the title 'Superperson'.

For observation, the contestants would watch a film or near-identical pair of films and answer questions on slight differences or continuity errors. The general knowledge round framed the contestants in profile, side by side and in semi-darkness, with a spotlight on the person giving the answer. Mazes or in later series a computer flight simulation would test response times, while the most feared of the studio-bound rounds was a three-dimensional jigsaw puzzle that the players would have to construct (viewers at home would be shrieking, 'It's that one, you fool!'). But the greatest test of all was the army assault course, with start times for each contestant staggered according to age and sex.

Granada news reporter Gordon Burns hosted the show for almost its entire run, but GM:TV newsreader Penny Smith stepped in for the final series, which junked most of the older ideas to create a curious mismatch of ***The Crystal Maze*** and something not quite as good as either show. Ross King also presented a junior version of the show, *Young Krypton*, in 1988.

The Kumars at No. 42

Sitcom/Chat Show | Hat Trick Productions for BBC Two/One | episode duration 30 mins | broadcast 12 Nov 2001–present

Principal Cast
Sanjeev Bhaskar · *Sanjeev Kumar*
Meera Syal · *Shushila Kumar*
Indira Joshi · *Madhuri Kumar*
Vincent Ebrahim · *Ashwin Kumar*

Producers Denise O'Donoghue, Jimmy Mulville (executive), Richard Pinto, Sharat Sardana, Lissa Evans **Writers** Sharat Sardana, Richard Pinto, Sanjeev Bhaskar **Theme Music** Morgan Pochin

An innovative combination of scripted sitcom, improvised performance and traditional chat show, *The Kumars at No. 42* was brought to screens by several of the team behind the barrier-busting sketch show ***Goodness Gracious Me***. The concept behind the show was rather unique – in an effort to prove how successful they are, the Kumar family of Wembley decide not to build a conservatory or some other boring extension onto the back of their house. Instead, they choose to flatten their back garden and build an entire state-of-the-art television studio, solely in order to enable them to welcome celebrity guests into their house and onto their own chat show. Sanjeev is the ambitious wannabe chat-show host, perpetually embarrassed by his charming yet often inappropriately behaved parents, Ashwin and Madhuri. However, the star of the show is really Sanjeev's granny, Sushila, a randy old lady who likes to flirt with the handsome male celebrities who visit the Kumars' house (look out for her awe at meeting Michael 'Parky' Parkinson).

One of the best things about *The Kumars at No. 42* is the way in which the celebrity 'chat show' guests throw themselves into the fiction of the piece, willingly taking part in the scripted segments of the programme (playing themselves, of course) as they arrive and leave the Kumars' home. Because the guests are already relaxed and playing along with the spirit of the programme, the interview section frequently manages to get better and more in-depth answers out of the guests than more traditional chat shows.

Trivia
The number of the Kumars' house was chosen by Sanjeev Bhaskar because he's a big fan of Douglas Adams's book, radio and TV series ***The Hitch Hiker's Guide to the Galaxy***, in which the number 42 is revealed to have universally important significance.

KYTV

Sitcom/Comedy | BBC Two | episode duration 30 mins | broadcast 12 May 1989, 3 May 1990–22 Oct 1993

Principal Cast
Helen Atkinson Wood · *Anna Daptor*
Angus Deayton · *Mike Channel*
Geoffrey Perkins · *Mike Flex*
Michael Fenton-Stevens · *Martin Brown*
Philip Pope · *Various Characters*

Producer Jamie Rix **Writers** Angus Deayton, Geoffrey Perkins **Theme Music** Philip Pope

KYTV (not to be confused with SkyTV, *obviously* – the KY stands for the channel's owner, media magnate Sir Kenneth Yellowhammer) is a low-budget satellite television channel that's just about a step above incompetent and a long way below mediocre. Each week, viewers are treated to KYTV's latest programming, introduced by the network's three main anchors Mike Channel, Mike Flex and Anna Daptor (with occasional interruptions from bumbling reporter Martin Brown). For regular viewers, KYTV's programming does seem to be somewhat fluid – one week the network seems to focus on travel programmes, another week it's reformatted as a religious channel or a *Crimewatch*-style police reconstruction network. Whatever that week's particular focus, some things remained the same – no-budget production values, dodgy camera work and increasingly desperate presenters just about managing to hold everything together.

KYTV was brought to TV screens by the same team who'd had an earlier hit on Radio 4 with their send-up of local radio stations, *Radio Active*. The change in target for their satire came naturally enough, with the recent launch of low-budget satellite TV channels coming at just the right time. Writers and performers Angus Deayton and Geoffrey

Perkins tapped into everybody's fears that the launch of new channels would lead to a slap-dash approach and an overall reduction in quality television – and looking back with the benefit of hindsight, they weren't far off. In the wildest dreams of *KYTV*, nobody could ever have expected that programmes like *Celebrity Wrestling* and *Celebrity Love Island* would find their way onto prime-time Saturday night TV, could they? Beginning with a one-off pilot transmitted as part of the *Comic Asides* anthology of possible new shows, *KYTV* ended up running for three seasons. Perhaps the most memorable episode was a hilarious send-up of po-faced period costume dramas, a behind-the-scenes special of 'The Making of *David Chizzlenut*'.

LA Law

Drama | 20th Century Fox for NBC | episode duration 45 mins | broadcast 15 Sep 1986–19 May 1994, 12 May 2002 (USA)

Principal Cast
Harry Hamlin · *Michael Kuzak*
Susan Dey · *Grace Van Owen*
Michele Greene · *Abby Perkins*
Jimmy Smits · *Victor Sifuentes*
Susan Ruttan · *Roxanne Melman/Meyer*
Larry Drake · *Benny Stulwicz*
Blair Underwood · *Jonathan Rollins*
Sheila Kelley · *Gwen Taylor*
Amanda Donohoe · *Cara Jean 'CJ' Lamb*
John Spencer · *Tommy Mullaney*
Cecil Hoffmann · *Zoey Clemmons*
Michael Cumpsty · *Frank Kittredge*
Conchata Ferrell · *Susan Bloom*
A. Martinez · *Daniel Morales*
Lisa Zane · *Melina Paros*
Alan Rosenberg · *Eli Levinson*
Debi Mazar · *Denise Ianello*
Alexandra Powers · *Jane Halliday*

Creators Steven Bochco, Terry Louise Fisher **Producers** Steven Bochco, William M. Finkelstein, Gregory Hoblit, David E. Kelley, John Masius, John Tinker, Mark Tinker, Rick Wallace (executive) **Writers** Various, including Steven Bochco, Terry Louise Fisher, Jacob Epstein, David E. Kelley, William M. Finkelstein, Michele Gallery, Judith Parker, Patricia Green, Carol Flint, Alan Brennert, Paul Manning, Anne Kenney, Julie Martin, John Tinker, Roger Lowenstein, Peter Schneider, Paul Haggis **Theme Music** Written by Mike Post, performed by David Sanborn

A hugely popular American drama set in the legal firm of McKenzie, Brackman, Cheney, Kuzack (and later Becker), *LA Law* was also a hit for ITV in the UK, where it held on to a mid-week slot for many years (although ITV dropped the series before the end, the later episodes were picked up by satellite channel Sky One). The series was co-created by Steve Bochco – whose ***Hill Street Blues*** had been a major influence on 1980s TV – and Terry Louise Fletcher, herself a former deputy district attorney, who had worked on ***Cagney and Lacey***. *LA Law* drew from both shows, combining the 'day job' of legal cases that touched upon a variety of issues (prejudice, unfair dismissal, sexism) while juggling the private lives of the staff. One of the show's lead writers, David E. Kelley, later created legal romantic comedy ***Ally McBeal***.

The Lakes

Drama | Company Television for BBC One | episode duration 60–80 mins | broadcast 14 Sep 1997–14 Mar 1999

Principal Cast
John Simm · *Danny Kavanagh*
Emma Cunniffe · *Emma Quinlan*
Paul Copley · *Peter Quinlan*
Mary Jo Randle · *Bernie Quinlan*
James Thornton · *Pete Quinlan*
Jessica Perry · *Annie Quinlan*
Robert Pugh · *Father Matthew*
Charles Dale · *Chef*
Kevin Doyle · *John Parr*
Clare Holman · *Simone Parr*
Matt Bardock · *Albie*
Zienia Merton · *Anna Guest*
Elizabeth Berrington · *Ruth*
Debbie Chazen · *Delilah*
Kaye Wragg · *Lucy Archer*
Elizabeth Bennett · *Mrs Archer*
Nicholas Day · *Mr Archer*
Amanda Mealing · *JoJo*
Robin Laing · *Joey*
Bob Mason · *Sergeant Eddie Slater*
Danny McGrath · *Father Steve*
Ryan Pope · *Robert*
Elizabeth Rider · *Sheila Thwaite*
Jenna Scruton · *Paula Thwaite*
David Westhead · *Arthur Thwaite*
Sally Rogers · *Juliet Bray*
Samantha Seager · *Julie*
Barbara Wilshere · *Dr Sarah Kilbride*
Lee Oakes · *Tharmy*
Andy Devine · *Bus Driver*

Creator Jimmy McGovern **Producers** George Faber, Lynn Horsford, Charles Pattinson, Suzan Harrison (executive), Melanie Howard (associate), Matthew Bird **Writers** Jimmy McGovern, William Gaminara, Joe Ainsworth, Julie Rutherford **Theme Music** Simon Boswell, Nina Humphreys

Filmed in the splendour of Patterdale and Glenridding in the Lake District, Jimmy McGovern's potboiler centred around Danny Kavanagh, a young man with a destructive gambling habit that wrecks the lives of everyone round him. Escaping from his native Liverpool he steals money to fund a journey to the Lake District. There he initially falls in with a gang of youths and indulges himself in a cycle of promiscuity and routine work in another hotel. But when a relationship with the quiet, intelligent Emma results in Emma falling pregnant, Danny is forced to try for a life of normality and security, providing a home for Emma and the baby back in Liverpool. Predictably, his gambling addiction soon sends Emma back home to her parents and results in Danny serving a brief jail sentence.

It's when Danny returns to the Lakes that we discover all is not as serene and peaceful as we might have suspected. Emma's mother is having an affair with a priest while a local schoolteacher learns that his wife is sleeping with Chef, a bullish thug who works in the nearby hotel. And when Danny takes a job looking after boats on the lakeside, he's witness to a horrific accident when a group of girls are drowned. Many of the locals blame Danny, but that's just the beginning of a hellish journey for him and the other residents of the village as they try to put their lives back together after such a dreadful tragedy. Then there's a hit-and-run attack on Chef, which sends him into a bout of predatory promiscuity in an attempt to infuriate the culprit of the attack to reveal himself; a murder and a particularly gruesome revenge pact among the women of the village . . .

No stranger to controversy, with ***Brookside, Cracker*** and ***Hillsborough*** under his belt, McGovern's story attracted complaints for the graphic sex and, in the second series, a brutal gang rape. The character of Chef was voted one of TV's 'biggest bastards' in a Channel 4 poll.

Trivia

Second series writer William Gaminara is also an actor; among other roles, he played Dr Richard Locke in radio soap *The Archers* and Duffy's husband Andrew Bower in ***Casualty***.

Land of the Giants

Science Fiction | Irwin Allen Productions/20th Century Fox TV for ABC (shown on ITV) | episode duration 50 mins | broadcast 22 Sep 1968–22 Mar 1970 (USA)

Regular Cast

Gary Conway · *Captain Steve Burton*
Don Matheson · *Mark Wilson*
Stefan Arngrim · *Barry Lockridge*
Don Marshall · *Dan Erickson*
Deanna Lund · *Valerie Scott*
Heather Young · *Betty Hamilton*
Kurt Kasznar · *Alexander Fitzhugh*

Creator Irwin Allen **Producers** Jerry Briskin (associate), Irwin Allen **Writers** Various, including Irwin Allen, Sidney Marshall, Bob Mitchell, Esther Mitchell, Richard Shapiro, William L. Stewart, Daniel B. Ullman **Theme Music** Composed by the legendary movie music maestro John Williams, the man who brought us the themes for *Star Wars* (1977) and *ET* (1982), among others.

It's the year 1983, and the crew and passengers of the commercial spaceship *Spindrift* are on a sub-orbital flight from New York City to London. However, they crash-land and are shocked to discover that everyone and everything have grown to a massive size – or have *they* shrunk? Soon they discover that this planet isn't in fact Earth, and that they have flown through a space warp to a far-off distant world. The totalitarian authorities of this alien planet soon become aware of their presence and begin to hunt the crew down. Can they escape back to the *Spindrift*, make the repairs and escape from this brutal land of giants?

Another glossy adventure series from the mind of Irwin Allen (creator of *The Time Tunnel*, ***Voyage to the Bottom of the Sea*** and ***Lost in Space***), *Land of the Giants* was perhaps the most serious and 'grown-up' of his shows, with a genuine air of dread and peril present in many of the episodes. As with most TV sci-fi of the period, it's perhaps best not to dwell too much on any of the scientific inaccuracies or the fact that the crew, stranded for years, seems never to run out of hairspray and mascara or to dirty their limited supply of multi-coloured jumpsuits. Less than two years after the final adventure of Captain Burton and the others (which saw them still stranded on the giants' world), Irwin Allen branched out from his fantasy TV shows into the disaster movie genre, producing two of the most famous films of all time in quick succession – *The Poseidon Adventure* (1972) and *The Towering Inferno* (1974).

The Larry Sanders Show

Sitcom | Brillstein-Grey Entertainment for HBO (shown on BBC Two) | episode duration 30 mins, plus 2 × 60-min specials | broadcast 15 Aug 1992–31 May 1998 (USA)

Principal Cast

Garry Shandling · *Larry Sanders*
Rip Torn · *Artie*
Jeffrey Tambor · *Hank Kingsley*
Wallace Langham · *Phil*
Penny Johnson · *Beverly*
Janeane Garofalo · *Paula*
Linda Doucet · *Darlene*
Megan Gallagher · *Jeannie Sanders*
Jeremy Piven · *Jerry*
Kathryn Harrold · *Francine*
Scott Thompson · *Brian*
Mary Lynn Rajskub · *Marylou*

Guest Stars

Various, including David Duchovny, Roseanne, David Letterman, Sally Field, Jim Carrey, William Shatner, Elvis Costello

Creators Garry Shandling, Dennis B. Klein **Producers** Garry Shandling, Brad Grey (executive) John Ziffren **Writers** Various, including Garry Shandling, Maya Forbes, Judd Apatow, John Riggi, Jon Vitti, Keli Cahoon, Molly Newman, Fred Barron, Chris Thompson **Theme Music** Frank Fitzpatrick

Garry Shandling had already enjoyed some major sitcom success with *It's Garry Shandling's Show* several years before *The Larry Sanders Show* catapulted him into the big-time. The earlier show had at first glimpse been a fairly ordinary sitcom, with Garry playing himself and actors portraying other members of his family. However, all of them were aware that they were in a sitcom, and would often discuss how implausible the plotlines were, or whether there were enough jokes in a particular week's episode – an effective destruction of the 'fourth wall' not dissimilar to ***Moonlighting***. Like the earlier sitcom, *The Larry Sanders Show* was also shown on American cable TV, thereby allowing the use of far more colourful language and enabling Shandling to co-create a series that was much less juvenile than most television sitcoms.

Larry Sanders is the host of a US late night chat show (the sort of show hosted by people like Jay Leno and David Letterman). He gets some top-notch guests onto his sofa, and in front of the camera he's the consummate professional. However, we also get to see what happens behind the scenes, where Sanders is a different person altogether – whiny, insecure, petulant and a 'high-maintenance' individual for his poor embattled assistants and production staff. The only person who refuses to put up with Sanders' attention-seeking and introspection is the show's producer Artie, a dedicated man who's used to Sanders' little hissy fits and who manages to use a number of underhand techniques into getting his own way most of the time. Artie's complete opposite was Sanders' on-screen right-hand man Hank, another deeply insecure individual who hopes to maintain his position on air through endless sucking-up to Sanders.

Using a novel technique of switching between videotaped material for the 'on-air' chat show segments and film for the behind-the-scenes sequences, *The Larry Sanders Show* once again showcased Garry Shandling's attempts to stretch the sitcom format. Blessed with a veritable galaxy of celebrities (playing both Sanders' production staff and the guests arriving to appear on the show – many of whom were far nastier than their public facing persona might suggest), this was a truly hilarious sitcom, especially if you've ever stopped to ponder if the smiles you see night after night from your favourite TV presenters might ever be just a tiny bit fake.

Lassie

Children's Adventure | Lassie Television/Wrather Corporation for CBS (shown on ITV) | episode duration 25 mins | broadcast 1954–1974 (USA)

Principal Cast

Tommy Rettig · *Jeff Miller*
Jan Clayton · *Ellen Miller*
George Cleveland · *Gramps Miller*
Jon Provost · *Timmy Martin*
Cloris Leachman, June Lockhart · *Ruth Martin*
Jon Shepodd, Hugh Reilly · *Paul Martin*
Andy Clyde · *Cully Wilson*
Robert Bray · *Ranger Corey Stuart*
Jed Allan · *Ranger Scott Turner*
Jack De Mave · *Ranger Bob Erickson*
Ron Hayes · *Garth Holden*
Skip Burton · *Ron Holden*
Joshua Albee · *Mike Holden*
Larry Wilcox · *Dale Mitchell*
Larry Pennell · *Keith Holden*

Creator Eric Knight **Producer** Jack Wrather, Robert Maxwell (executive), Bonita Granville-Wrather, William Beaudine Jr, Rudy E. Abel, Sherman A. Harris, Robert 'Bob' Golden **Writers** Various, including Eric Scott, John McGreevey **Theme Music** William Lava

Based upon the much-adored 1943 movie *Lassie Come Home* (starring a youthful Elizabeth Taylor and Roddy McDowall), the TV version of *Lassie* ran for almost 25 years, providing families all over the world with a safe, family entertainment that proved once and for all that dogs are indeed man's best friend. As unfortunately young humans age very quickly and are fairly easy to tell apart from one another, a number of different masters looked after Lassie over the years (and yet, not one of them noticed when replacement dogs were shipped in to play the perpetually-youthful Lassie – worse still, most of them were males).

Lassie's first owner was young Jeff Miller, who lived with his widowed mother and doddery old grandfather on a farm. When the Millers moved to the city, they cruelly abandoned their beloved pet and left her to be taken in by adopted orphan little Timmy Martin. As the years passed, still more owners proved to be heartless swines who'd forgotten the old adage that 'a dog is for life, not just for a few seasons of a children's TV drama'. New owners included elderly gent Cully Wilson, and rangers Corey Stuart, Scott Turner and Bob Erickson. Tired of constantly being abandoned by people she loved, Lassie decided to make it on her own, and spent several years wandering the roads of the USA on her own – wise move, girl. Finally she decides to give another bunch of humans a chance, and finishes the programme living with a family called the Holdens. No matter who she was living with, Lassie managed to use her supernatural intelligence and barking abilities to save youngsters trapped down wells, to warn people about fires and to rescue thousands of other stupid humans who, without Lassie's intervention, would have gone to meet their maker. The world's probably better off without 'em, we reckon.

Last of the Summer Wine

Sitcom | BBC One | episode duration 30 mins | broadcast 4 Jan 1973, 12 Nov 1973–present

Regular Cast

Peter Sallis · *Norman Clegg*
Bill Owen · *William 'Compo' Simonite*
Michael Bates · *Cyril Blamire*
Brian Wilde · *Walter 'Foggy' Dewhurst*
Michael Aldridge · *Seymour Utterthwaite*
Frank Thornton · *Herbert 'Truly' Truelove*
Kathy Staff · *Nora Batty*
Joe Gladwin · *Wally Batty*
Jane Freeman · *Ivy*
John Comer · *Sid*
Blake Butler · *Mr Wainwright*
Rosemary Martin · *Mrs Partridge*
Philip Jackson · *Gordon*
Gordon Wharmby · *Wesley Pegden*
Jonathan Linsley · *'Crusher' Milburn*
Jean Fergusson · *Marina*
Robert Fyfe · *Howard*

Danny O'Dea · *Eli Duckett*
Juliette Kaplan · *Pearl*
Thora Hird · *Auntie Edie Pegden*
Mike Grady · *Barry*
Jean Alexander · *Auntie Wainwright*
Sarah Thomas · *Glenda*
Stephen Lewis · *Smiler*
Keith Clifford · *Billy Hardcastle*
Tom Owen · *Tom Simonite*
Burt Kwouk · *Entwistle*
Brian Murphy · *Alvin Smedley*
Julie T. Wallace · *Mrs Avery*
Josephine Tewson · *Miss Davenport*
Dora Bryan · *Roz*

Creator/Writer Roy Clarke **Producer** Alan J. W. Bell
Theme Music Ronnie Hazlehurst

Last of the Summer Wine isn't just a record-breaker in the UK; it's the world's longest-running sitcom (although, of course, lengthy seasons of 20-plus episodes every year mean that many American shows – such as ***The Simpsons*** and ***The Beverly Hillbillies*** – have produced more individual programmes). At the time of writing, *Last of the Summer Wine* was enjoying its 25th season on air, having produced more than 230 episodes since its pilot in the *Comedy Playhouse* series was screened in January 1973, and despite doom-sayers predicting its demise for the past 20 years at least, it seems as though it's not about to leave our screens any time soon.

As a comedy series, *Last of the Summer Wine* is the antithesis of every 'alternative' and 'challenging' comedy show that's come and gone in its wake over the past 30 years. Resolutely family friendly and gentle in its humour, it neatly separates the distinctly unimpressed critics from its adoring audience; indeed, as time passes, its nostalgic focus seems simultaneously less relevant and more attractive than ever. Filmed in and around the Yorkshire Pennines village of Holmfirth, the programme takes great delight in showing off the glorious northern countryside, providing an ideal backdrop to its typically northern brand of comedy. The humour in *Last of the Summer Wine* is very similar to that of ***Coronation Street*** (set in Manchester, barely 20 miles from Holmfirth) – strong, brassy women look disapprovingly on the spineless antics of their ineffectual men, all of whom would much rather be left alone to play with their latest invention or to spy on the object of their affections. For the first 21 seasons (until the sad death of actor Bill Owen), chief trouble-maker among the boys was tramp-like Compo, a man obsessed beyond reason by the wrinkled stockings of broom-wielding battleaxe Nora Batty. Always there to back Compo up was reluctant hellraiser Clegg, someone who'd much sooner keep out of trouble, thank you very much. Their first colleague in mischief was former army sergeant Cyril Blamire. When actor Michael Bates was forced to leave after just two seasons owing to ill-health, Blamire was replaced by another ex-army man, Foggy (played by ***Porridge*** star Brian Wilde), thereby creating the line-up that most people remember. In 1988–9 viewers were treated to a glimpse of how their favourite characters met, way back in the 1930s. *First of the Summer Wine* started life as a one-off special (3 January 1988) followed by two six-part seasons (4 September 1988–8 October 1989). All of the familiar characters were featured, with younger actors portraying them in their first flush of youth (David Fenwick as Clegg, Paul Wyett as Compo, Richard Lumsden as Foggy, Paul McLain as Seymour and Helen Patrick as Nora). In a moment of sheer inspiration, Peter Sallis turned up playing Clegg's father ('Mind the gate'/'He always says, "Mind the gate"!').

With such a senior cast, it's not surprising that many have joined and left the programme as the years have passed. There are a few characters that have stayed with the show more or less since day one – namely Clegg, Nora Batty and Ivy. Another stalwart of the show is the series writer, Roy Clarke (the man behind other sitcoms like ***Open All Hours*** and ***Keeping Up Appearances***), who has single-handedly penned every one of the episodes. *Last of the Summer Wine* is a vintage institution that is precisely to the taste of a significant section of the viewing audience – long may it continue.

The Late Late Breakfast Show

Entertainment | BBC One | episode duration 45 mins | broadcast 4 Sep 1982–8 Nov 1986

Principal Cast
Noel Edmonds, Mike Smith · *Presenters*

Producer Michael Hurll **Theme Music** Composed by Spandau Ballet's Gary Kemp

Having been responsible for a whole new generation of Saturday morning children's programmes with *Swap Shop*, Noel Edmonds turned his attention to the competitive Saturday night variety show in autumn 1982 with the launch of *The Late Late Breakfast Show*. The show's title didn't reveal much about the programme's content – it was merely reflecting the imminent launch of Breakfast TV (which arrived on 17 January 1983 with the first broadcast of BBC's *Breakfast Time*). Each week, Noel would introduce a variety of regular features including game show elements, hidden camera stunts ('The Hit Squad'), out-takes of celebrities messing things up on BBC TV programmes ('The Golden Egg Awards' – see the breakfast theme there?) and the ever-popular 'Give it a Whirl'.

On 'Give it a Whirl', a member of the public would be selected to take part in an over-the-top stunt on the following show. In the interim, they would receive coaching and rehearsal from professionals in order to ensure their safety. For more than four years, the results of the Whirly Wheel (which decided which stunt the willing volunteers would face) were the most successful part of the programme. Tragically, during the rehearsals for a bungee jump-based stunt, daredevil volunteer Michael Lush was killed. An immediate investigation was launched within the BBC to find out how things could have gone so drastically wrong, and *The Late Late Breakfast Show* was pulled from the schedules. Subsequently, Health and Safety procedures within the Corporation were appropriately tightened up, hopefully ensuring that no similar accidents could ever happen again. Noel Edmonds returned to Saturday evening TV in 1988 with the moderately successful *Noel's Saturday Roadshow*, a precursor to his crowning achievement ***Noel's House Party***.

The League of Gentlemen

See pages 428–31

The Lenny Henry Show

Comedy/Sitcom | BBC One | episode duration 30 mins, plus specials | broadcast 4 Sep 1984–24 Dec 1987, 27 Oct 1987–3 Nov 1988 (sitcom), 1 Apr–6 May 1995, 5 Sep–10 Oct 1998 (*Lenny Goes to Town*), 30 Dec 2000–2 May 2003 (*Lenny Henry in Pieces*), 6 May–24 Jun 2005

Regular Cast
Lenny Henry, Mark Gatiss, Steve Pemberton, Omid Djalili, Tony Gardner, Tracy-Ann Oberman, Roger Griffiths, Gina Yashere, Sheridan Smith · *Various Characters*
Lenny Henry · *Delbert Wilkins*
Vas Blackwood · *Winston*
Ellen Thomas · *Rose*
Gina McKee · *Julie*
Naim Kahn · *Wazim*
Michael Mears · *Alex*

Producers Various, including Geoff Posner, Kevin Lygo, Polly McDonald, Geoff Atkinson, Jonathan Beazley, Jon Rowlands, Lucy Robinson, Alex Jackson-Long **Writers** Various, including Lenny Henry, Kim Fuller, James Hendrie, Tony Sarchet, Andrea Solomons, Ian Brown, David Hansen, Paul Owen, Geoff Atkinson, James Bibby, Bob Sinfield, Garry Chambers, Moray Hunter, Jack Docherty, Stan Hey and Andrew Nickolds (sitcom season)

Lenworth Henry was born in 1958 in the Birmingham suburb of Dudley, and following his appearance on talent show *New Faces* in 1975, he's hardly ever been off our television screens. Lenny honed his comedy skills on Saturday morning kids' show ***TISWAS*** before joining Tracey Ullman and David Copperfield on BBC One sketch show ***Three of a Kind***. Realising that they had a true family-friendly talent on their hands, BBC bosses soon gave Lenny his own series, which combined the same kind of sketch-based comedy that had been such a hit in *Three of a Kind* with Lenny's own stand-up routines. Some of Lenny's characters became instant favourites with the public: Theophilus P. Wildebeeste, a kind of black Tom Jones singing sex-god; Minister for Reggae Fred Dread; PC Ganga; and, of course, the 'crucial' Brixton-based DJ Delbert Wilkins.

Delbert Wilkins was so popular that the 1987 and 1988 seasons of *The Lenny Henry Show* changed format, ditching the sketches and instead running as a traditional scripted sitcom based around the antics of Wilkins and his friends at Pirate Radio Brixton. One-off sketch shows were a regular feature of the Christmas and New Year schedules throughout the late 1980s and 1990s, and Lenny successfully tried another sitcom when he played short-tempered cook Gareth Blackstock in ***Chef!*** The late 1990s and 2000s saw Lenny return to sketch shows once again, with *Lenny Goes to Town* boasting support from up-and-coming comics Mark Gatiss and Steve Pemberton (***The League of Gentlemen***) and *Lenny Henry in Pieces*, featuring future landlady of the Queen Vic Tracy-Ann Oberman.

Whatever the format of his comedy, Lenny Henry has been part and parcel of the TV comedy establishment for more than 20 years. Never one to forget that there's always a place for mainstream comedy in the heart of the schedules, Lenny Henry has successfully adjusted his style and output over time, tapping into current vogues, interests and fashions and parodying current pop stars, films and TV programmes (the spot-on Michael Jackson send-ups of 'Thriller' and 'Bad', for example). It's a shame that Lenny recently announced his intention to retire from making any more seasons of sketch shows, but we feel sure that he won't be away from our television screens for long.

The Life and Loves of a She-Devil

Drama/Telefantasy | BBC Two | episode duration 60 mins | broadcast 8–29 Oct 1986

Regular Cast
Julie T. Wallace · *Ruth Beaswell*
Dennis Waterman · *Bobbo Beaswell*
Patricia Hodge · *Mary Fisher*
Miriam Margolyes · *Nurse Hopkins*
Paul Herzberg · *Garcia*
Liz Smith · *Mrs Fisher*
Tom Baker · *Father Ferguson*
Bernard Hepton · *Judge Bissop*
Stephen Greif · *Dr Ghengis*
Malcolm Terris · *Geoffrey Tupton*
Kim Thomson · *Elsie Flowers*
Noel Dyson · *Brenda*
Pippa Guard · *Lady Bissop*

Producer Sally Head **Writer** Ted Whitehead, from the novel by Fay Weldon **Theme Music** Richard Thompson and Peter Filleul; Christine Collister performed the melancholy vocals.

To the casual observer, Ruth has it all – a nice house, two children, and a successful husband, Bobbo, who's possibly

Continued on page 432

The League of Gentlemen

Steve Pemberton (Tubbs) and Reece Shearsmith (Edward).

'Welcome to Royston Vasey', beams a sign on the road to Royston Vasey. 'You'll never leave.' What might be a confident advertising slogan for a holiday resort in Florida or the Caribbean becomes a thinly veiled threat on this barren moorland. For nearby is the Local Shop, a black-slated shack where a weary traveller might stop to admire the 'precious things', count up to twelvety different items for sale and maybe enquire about purchasing 'I can I can't' before being warned off by the proprietor, Edward, and his wife/sister, the pig-faced Tubbs. For this is a local shop, for local people, and they'll have no trouble here . . .

Jeremy Dyson, Mark Gatiss, Steve Pemberton and Reece Shearsmith met at college and eventually got together to work on a stage show. So the legend goes, they took the show to the Edinburgh Festival and picked up the Perrier award that also catapulted Frank Skinner and Steve Coogan into the big time. In 1997, they adapted their show for Radio 4 as the six-part *On the Town* (the town being Spent, a prototype Royston Vasey with many of the same characters and incidents), which won the team a Sony award. They then reworked the radio show for television, won a Royal Television award, a BAFTA and the Golden Rose of Montreux, at which point they realised that they'd better write some new material pretty quick.

Almost uniquely among comedy writers, *The League of Gentlemen* (as they are collectively known) don't cite ***Monty Python*** as their biggest influence. For them, the comedy comes from such exquisite, British-made horror films as *Don't Look Now* (1973) and the bloodier output of Hammer Film Studios. The first episode features a

Comedy
BBC Two
Episode Duration: 30 mins
Broadcast: 11 Jan 1999–31 Oct 2002 (to date)

Recurring Cast
Mark Gatiss · *Dr Matthew Chinnery, Val Denton, Mickey Michaels, Hilary Briss, Les McQueen, Brian Morgan, Phil Proctor, Iris Krell and Other Characters*
Steve Pemberton · *Tubbs Tattsyrup, Pauline Campbell-Jones, Herr Wolf Lipp, Harvey Denton, Charlie Hull, Tish Guppy, Mike Harris, Voice of Barbara Dixon, Dave Parkes, Maurice Evans, Reenie Calver, Ally Welles and Other Characters*
Reece Shearsmith · *Edward Tattsyrup, Papa Lazarou, Ross Gaines, Stella Hull, Benjamin Denton, Vinnie Wythenshaw, Geoff Tipps, Ollie Plimsolls, Dean Tavalouris, Reverend Bernice Woodall, Pamela Doove, Judee Levinson, Sam Chignell, Henry Portrait and Other Characters*
Roy 'Chubby' Brown · *Mayor Larry Vaughan*
Frances Cox · *Annie Raines*
Helen Lambert · *Eunice Evans*
Don Estelle · *Little Don*
Megan De Wolf · *Chloe Denton*
Rosy De Wolf · *Radclyffe Denton*
Jeremy Dyson · *Various Characters*

Creators/Writers Jeremy Dyson, Mark Gatiss, Steve Pemberton, Reece Shearsmith

Producers Jon Plowman (executive), Jemma Rodgers (associate), Sarah Smith

Theme Music Joby Talbot

performance by Mark Gatiss that lifts Edward Woodward's Scottish policeman from *The Wicker Man* (1973) and plonks him in the middle of the insidious Local Shop (a later episode sees two construction workers tied to a post as Tubbs strips naked and performs her own version of Britt Ekland's *Wicker Man* dance number while suckling a pig – euw!). The laughter tracks that accompanied early episodes might wrong-foot the innocent, but these are not comedies in the traditional sense, unless, like ***The Addams Family***, you find merriment in suffering, torture and humiliation. Fortunately, we do.

Taking its name from a 1959 Jack Hawkins crime caper, *The League of Gentlemen* combines sketches featuring multiple characters in the spirit of ***The Fast Show***, with Gatiss, Shearsmith and Pemberton populating the entire town. Driving Royston Vasey's only cab is Barbara of Babs' Cabs. Gravel-voiced, hairy-armed Barbara is in the final stages of gender realignment, sparing no-one's blushes in detailing every last snip and tuck of her operations. At the job centre we find Pauline, the tyrannical leader of a 'restart' group that has less to do with helping the unemployed find work and everything to do with keeping them on the dole so Pauline can keep her job. While smart-arse Ross spends his time undermining her lectures on pens ('Everything I know about people I learned from pens. If they don't work, you shake 'em. If they still don't work, you chuck 'em away, bin them!'), the buck-toothed, bemulleted 'Mickeyluv' pines to be a fireman but stays at the restart centre out of love for Pauline. The Dentons have their own special ways of living, as their nephew Benjamin discovers when he comes to stay. Uncle Harvey is a collector of prize toads, while in the bathroom Aunty Val maintains a complicated system of towels for each body part (and, thanks to an unsettling naked body-suit sported by Mark Gatiss for 'Nude Monday', we also learn Val has a pubic bush like Davy Crockett's hat). Benjamin spends two years trying to escape the Denton household, until he finally uses Harvey's collection to entrap him in a huge glass case (setting us up for quite the most exquisite pun in history as Harvey laments: 'Hoist by my own pet toad . . .').

The essence of much of the interaction between characters is conflict. Charlie and Stella Hull are one of those married couples who feel trapped, terrified to live apart yet unable to live together without expressing their utter hatred of each other. Geoff, Mike and Brian have been friends since childhood and now work at a local plastics factory. Geoff has aspirations as a stand-up comic, but he's simply rubbish at telling jokes. He's also a psychotic nutcase who's been known to pull a gun on his friends just so he can force someone else to tell the 'Death by Mau Mau' joke to him one more time. Then there's the foul-mouthed vicar, the Reverend Bernice, whose antipathy for her flock hides a dark secret from her childhood, linked

These are not comedies in the traditional sense, unless, like *The Addams Family*, you find merriment in suffering, torture and humiliation. Fortunately, we do.

WEBSITE

www.lofg.com houses an on-line community as well as all the background material to the show that you might want, although at the time of writing it looked like they needed to update their links section as almost every one of them was out of date.

to a black-faced monster who kidnapped her mother. A creature in search of a man called Dave and a woman to be his next wife, it was the genuinely terrifying circus performer Papa Lazarou . . .

The League (can we really call them the Gentlemen?) clearly have two goals here: to prove that there's no such place as 'too far' and to destroy their idols. Worst culprit (or greatest iconoclast) of them all is Mark Gatiss – the tall one – who most frequently targets the career high points of actor Peter Davison, former ***Doctor Who*** star and TV vet in ***All Creatures Great and Small***. Gatiss's hapless-but-deadly vet Mr Chinnery is responsible for the deaths of many an animal in the most distressing conditions – burned to a crisp on an open fire or pylon-mounted electric cable, or simply decimated from within thanks to some explosive gases. (Gatiss also wrote *League*-esque sketches for a BBC Two *Doctor Who* night in 1999 in which he and ***Little Britain***'s David Walliams kidnap a terrified Peter Davison and threaten to kiss him). As tributes go it's right up there with Mark Chapman and John Lennon, really.

In the second series, the Gents introduce a story arc – the mystery of the nosebleeds that begin to strike the inhabitants of the town at a frightening rate. Mayor of Royston Vasey Roy 'Chubby' Brown (whose real name lent the town its name) is called upon to give an interview to the local TV news but warned he mustn't swear – something he almost manages to pull off. Meanwhile, as attention focuses on the strange disappearances surrounding the Local Shop, the real cause of the outbreak is revealed to be 'special meat' served up by local butcher Hilary Briss, the product – it's heavily suggested – of a sexual relationship he's conducting with a cow.

The series even flirts with the subject of paedophilia in the form of Herr Lipp, the choir master from Duisberg, Germany, who takes a shine to one of the boys in his care. However, hidden among the other grotesques, Herr Lipp is one of the least offensive of the lot, a tragically closeted man pursuing an unrequited love affair with a schoolboy over the age of 16. We'd almost feel sorry for him if he didn't end up burying the target of his misplaced affections under the flowerbeds of the boy's home.

Despite their hideously deformed faces and murderous ways, the most adored of the original characters remain Edward and Tubbs, inbred proprietors of that 'local shop for local people'.

Despite their hideously deformed faces and murderous ways, the most adored (if that's the right word) of the original characters remain Edward and Tubbs, inbred proprietors of that 'local shop for local people' on a remote stretch of moorland road some distance from Royston Vasey. That the multiple-murdering, pig-suckling, snub-nosed parents of a hideous man-beast should endear themselves to their audience isn't all that surprising – Tubbs's subservient innocence and Edward's fear of outsiders have a charm all of their own. They've been killed off twice – once after an angry mob torched the Local Shop and again after an altercation with the front end of a high-speed train. But you can't keep a great comedy duo down for long. The stage show that toured the country offered one alternative existence for the pair – as angels pouring scorn on the perverted audiences in the stalls, while the spin-off feature film, *The League of Gentlemen's Apocalypse* (2005), gave us a far more terrifying alternative.

The BBC's tradition of serving up ghost stories for Christmas by the likes of M. R. James was not forgotten by the League for their own Christmas special, which aped the old Amicus anthology films of the late 1960s and early 1970s, such as *Dr Terror's House of Horror* (1965) and *Tales from the Crypt* (1972). Here we discover the truth behind Dr Chinnery's misfortunes with animals and learn of the existence of a secret society of women that empowers them with dark forces. The third – and to date final – series was an inventive experiment with narrative, with different plot strands unravelling around the journey of a lost plastic bag. Each week, extra details, told from different perspectives, were added to a scene that closed every episode until eventually we got to see the final picture: how a plastic bag from the charity shop obscured the vision of the driver of a van entering the town at high speed, causing him to swerve to avoid hitting Pauline and instead crashing into a wall and burying the recently murdered wife of a B&B proprietor along with Lawrence Llewellyn-Bowen.

Paedophiles, transsexuals, murderers, bestiophiles, travellers and the unemployed – all subjects guaranteed to get Middle England hot under the collar. While *Little Britain* managed to find its way onto BBC One thanks to some judicious pruning, there's virtually no chance that *The League of Gentlemen* will make such a leap due to the nature of their material. And quite right too. Though that didn't stop the League heading instead for their local cinema (yes, that word 'local' again) for their 2005 feature film, in which the characters of Royston Vasey broke into our own world to run amok. With the film completed (and in fact by the time this book's published almost certainly out on DVD), the four Gentlemen will be free to look at other projects, which might even include a return to Royston Vasey. We can only hope.

a bit 'out of her league'. Despite reservations, Ruth's life is mostly happy – that is, until one day Bobbo embarks on an affair with glamorous romantic novelist Mary Fisher. At first, Ruth is humiliated and traumatised by her husband's infidelity. However, she soon decides that the only way to survive is to get her own back, both on Bobbo and on the detested Mary Fisher. So begins Ruth's transformation into the She-Devil – a woman prepared to do literally anything to gain the revenge she so desperately wants.

Adapted from the best-selling novel by Fay Weldon, *The Life and Loves of a She-Devil* was a four-part journey into the deep dark recesses of the psyche of a woman who has been betrayed – and everybody knows that hell hath no fury like a woman scorned . . . Twenty-five-year-old Julie T. Wallace created a memorably sympathetic monster in the form of lumpy, warty Ruth, a woman so desperate to love and be loved that she resorts to the ultimate in make-overs – a ***Nip/Tuck*** so extreme that she literally becomes her hated nemesis, Mary Fisher. Alternately hilarious and deeply unsettling, Ted Whitehead's script gave all three leads some marvellous lines and scenes to play with – and hardly anyone who saw the series will ever be able to get the image of Tom Baker's bum frantically copulating with Ruth out of their minds!

Unfortunately, when Hollywood decided to have a go at interpreting Weldon's novel in 1989, they opted to turn the story into a much broader slapstick farce. Despite being directed by *Desperately Seeking Susan*'s Susan Seidelman and starring Meryl Streep, Ed Begley Jr and Roseanne Barr in the three lead roles, *She-Devil* was truly disappointing.

Life on Earth

Documentary | BBC/Warner Bros/Reiner Moritz for BBC Two | episode duration 55–60 mins | broadcast 16 Jan 1979–10 Apr 1979

Creator/Writer/Presenter David Attenborough **Producers** Christopher Parsons, John Sparks, Richard Brock, Michael Salisbury **Theme Music** Composed by Edward Williams and conducted by Marcus Dods

Although David Attenborough was already an experienced television presenter (of programmes like *Zoo Quest* as far back as the mid-1950s), by the mid-1970s he had become much better known as a television executive, having been one of the first controllers of BBC Two. However, Attenborough had become tired of a desk-bound job and jumped at the chance to become involved in an epic natural history series in the mould of previous BBC Two successes like ***Civilisation*** and ***The Ascent of Man***. *Life on Earth* was to be an undertaking on an entirely more massive scale than anything that had ever been attempted by the BBC's Natural History Unit in Bristol. Attenborough's unique ability, of making what can be quite difficult concepts understandable to an audience of novice naturalists, was the show's unique selling point. In 13 beautifully crafted episodes, the programme revealed how life had evolved on this planet from small, single-celled organisms through to the ascent of man. One slight flaw in this chronological approach is that the first few episodes, fascinating though they are, contain almost no footage of any exciting animals – focusing instead on mosses, fungi and other assorted plant life.

It took 19 cameramen three years to film *Life on Earth*, with material being shot in more than 30 countries around the globe. At the time, this was the most intensive and expensive filming ever undertaken for a wildlife series. This investment of money – and most importantly time – enabled the series to show the full life cycle of species that had never before been captured on film. It also rewrote scientific theories on several species – for instance, prior to *Life on Earth*, it was believed that mother crocodiles had no maternal instinct whatsoever and that often they would eat their own young. It was the film crews of *Life on Earth* who observed, by contrast, the tender way in which mother crocodiles pick their young up in their mouth before taking them down to the river to swim.

Life on Earth also provided one of the first-ever recordings on film of the cooperative nature of lionesses stalking their prey. This was a TV event that took the filming of natural history to a completely new level of realism – it didn't shy away from showing the cruelty of nature but instead demonstrated to fascinated audiences the truth about the sometimes harsh reality of an animal's need for survival. The renowned sequence of Attenborough getting up close and personal with a family of mountain gorillas in Rwanda was another landmark in television, and was put together with the assistance of gorilla expert Diane Fossey (whose tragic story would later be told in the 1988 film *Gorillas in the Mist*, with Sigourney Weaver playing the part Fossey). The original intention was not for David to get quite as close to the animals as he did – the depth of interaction on screen came as a surprise to everyone concerned. Nowadays such close interaction is banned, for fear of human diseases being passed to the gorilla population (and vice versa). Astonishingly, the film (and the crew) nearly didn't reach home because Rwandan authorities thought that an anti-government propaganda film was being made and arrested the entire production team. It was only quick thinking on the part of the cameraman that prevented a disaster – he quickly switched the exposed film of the gorillas for a reel of unexposed film, a reel that was then confiscated, never to be seen again.

The importance of *Life on Earth* cannot be underestimated. On its first screening on BBC Two, it caused an absolute sensation among critics and viewers alike, and rapidly became a major hit around the world. Ironically, despite some significant investment from an American backer, the programme was not screened in the United States for several years. US backers were concerned that David Attenborough's accent would be off-putting for American viewers and suggested replacing him with specially filmed inserts recorded by a major Hollywood star such as Robert Redford. Quite apart from the massive extra cost such an undertaking would have entailed, Attenborough rightfully stuck to his guns and pointed out a clause in the original contract that gave him final approval over any foreign transmissions. As a consequence, the 'Americanised' version was binned and *Life on Earth* remained unscreened in the USA for several years until it eventually appeared on the PBS network. It was, of course, a huge hit, as it had been everywhere else, and it's now estimated that *Life on Earth* has been seen and loved by more than half a billion people around the globe.

The Likely Lads

See pages 434–6

Linda Green

Comedy | Red for BBC One | episode duration 30 mins | broadcast 30 Oct 2001–17 Dec 2002

Regular Cast
Liza Tarbuck · *Linda Green*
Claire Rushbrook · *Michelle Fenton*
Jimmy McKenzie · *Sean Gallagher*
Darren Alexander · *Daniel Ryan*
Rachel Davies · *Iris Green*
Dave Hill · *Frank Green*
Jessica Harris · *Katy Green*
Bruno Langley · *Fizz Green*
John Donnelly · *Ricky Pinder*
Christopher Eccleston · *Tom Sherry/Neil Sherry*
Jimmy Tarbuck · *Uncle Vic*

Creator Paul Abbott **Producers** Jane Tranter, Paul Abbott (executive), Nicola Shindler, Matthew Bird, Phil Collinson **Writers** Paul Abbott, Russell T. Davies, Daniel Brocklehurst, Catherine Johnson, Chris McHallern, Tom Higgins, Chris Bucknall **Theme Music** Guy Pratt

Linda Green is an attractive, upbeat and slightly overweight 30-something woman living in the north of England. By day, she works in a car showroom, selling finance packages to people who want to own a new vehicle; by night, she's a singer in the local 'working men's' club. Although Linda's happy living on her own, she's still on the lookout for a man to spend some time with. Her best friend Michelle is happily settled with Darren, so Linda often worries about being left on the shelf. Having said that, she's never short of male company – when she's in between boyfriends and needs a quick jump, there's always Jimmy the mechanic who works down the showroom.

Over two seasons, *Linda Green* explores the ups and downs of life for a sassy single woman at the start of the 21st century. While Bridget Jones is still very much the fantasy of a 'normal' woman winging her way in a media career, Linda Green hasn't got time for any of that crap. Although she's an independent woman, she survives thanks to a strong and close network of friends and a nearby family who are there to back her up whenever she encounters a problem, such as when she's burgled, or when she's trying to tell which identical twin she's having sex with.

From the talented and prolific Paul Abbott (who worked on shows as diverse as ***Coronation Street, Cracker, Clocking Off*** and *Touching Evil*), *Linda Green* is a hilarious and occasionally poignant examination of modern-day life. The first series was a huge and popular success on BBC One, but the second suffered from awkward scheduling and significantly lower viewing figures. With *Linda Green* prematurely cancelled after just 20 episodes, Paul Abbott changed channels and created another series about working-class life in the North, the much more blatant and outrageous ***Shameless*** for Channel 4.

The Lion, the Witch and the Wardrobe

See THE CHRONICLES OF NARNIA

Lipstick on Your Collar

Drama | Whistling Gypsy for Channel 4 | episode duration 45 mins | broadcast 21 Feb–28 Mar 1993

Principal Cast
Ewan McGregor · *Private Mick Hopper*
Giles Thomas · *Private Francis Francis*
Louise Germaine · *Sylvia Berry*
Peter Jeffrey · *Colonel Bernwood*
Clive Francis · *Major Hedges*
Douglas Henshall · *Corporal Pete Berry*
Nicholas Farrell · *Major Church*
Nicholas Jones · *Major Carter*
Kim Huffman · *Lisa Trekker*
Roy Hudd · *Harold Atterbow*
Maggie Steed · *Aunt Vickie*
Bernard Hill · *Uncle Fred*
Shane Rimmer · *Lieutenant Colonel Trekker*
Carrie Leigh · *Dream Girl*
Frederick Treves · *Brigadier Sanders*

Producers Dennis Potter (executive), Michael Brent (associate), Alison Barnett, Rosemarie Whitman **Writer** Dennis Potter **Theme Music** 'Lipstick on Your Collar' by George Goehring

Having already achieved the two most accessible hits of his career with musical dramas ***Pennies from Heaven*** and ***The Singing Detective***, Dennis Potter returned to this unique genre with *Lipstick on Your Collar*, another series that mixed a traditional narrative with song-and-dance routines. Set in the 1950s, the series focuses on the lives of young adults trying to discover what their roles in life

Continued on page 437

The Likely Lads

James Bolam (Terry) and Rodney Bewes (Bob).

Comedy programmes, by their very nature, normally revolve around some kind of conflict between their core characters – the antagonistic relationship between Albert and Harold Steptoe; Alf Garnett's disgust at his 'lazy Scouse git' of a son-in-law; even the class war between the Goods and the Leadbetters. It's rare, therefore, to come across a sitcom that has at its heart a strong friendship; and even less common for that friendship to be between two men. When Dick Clement and Ian La Frenais created *The Likely Lads* in the mid-1960s, they tapped into the vibrancy of the northern, working-class, youth culture being spearheaded by the Beatles. Although *The Likely Lads* was transmitted on the fledgling BBC Two (a channel that most TV sets of the time were unable to receive) and was on screen for just 18 months, it instantly became a zeitgeist-surfing classic, a programme with public and critical appeal and an influence that lasted longer than anyone might have expected.

Terry Collier and Bob Ferris are lifelong friends, brought up and still living in Newcastle. The boys work in an electrical factory and, like most 21-year-olds, are obsessed with the usual things – football, beer and girls. Terry is proud of his working-class roots and is always ready with a smart-alec remark when dealing with figures in authority. Deeply cynical about most things in life, Terry enjoys nothing more than getting involved in some kind of hare-brained scheme, trying to pull a fast one or run rings around people less canny than him. Bob, on the other hand, is more timid and less reluctant to get involved in Terry's mischief-making – perpetually torn between a desire to be live the high life and a concern about upsetting anybody or letting Terry down.

At the heart of the success of *The Likely Lads* were the witty and dynamic scripts by Clement and La Frenais, their first collaboration together. So successful were these scripts that a lengthy writing partnership soon developed, with programmes as diverse as ***Porridge***, ***Auf Wiedersehen, Pet*** and ***Lovejoy*** springing from the imaginations of these prolific authors. Relative newcomers Rodney Bewes and James Bolam – both 'proper' actors rather than veterans of the comedy circuit – grabbed hold of the opportunity provided in Clement and La Frenais's scripts and created a pair of characters that were totally believable, coincidentally supplying the newly launched BBC Two with one of its first big hits.

After three seasons, it seemed as though Bob and Terry's adventures were naturally drawing to a close. In the 20th and final episode, Bob makes a bold decision and decides to join the army in order to see the world. With the prospect of losing his best friend for several years, Terry goes to the recruiting office and signs up too. However, to Terry's horror, he finds out too late that Bob has been rejected because of his flat feet – Bob will be staying at home, but Terry has signed his life away to the army with no best mate to keep him company.

Six years later, the boys came back to TV – this time on BBC One, thanks to a successful repeat run of the original series on that channel – in *Whatever Happened to the Likely Lads?*, again written by Clement and La Frenais. Terry returns from the army and goes back home to Newcastle, where he discovers that all the former certainties in life no longer hold true. Just as the enthusiasm and vibrancy of the 1960s degenerated into the uncertainty and disillusionment of the 1970s, so this new run of programmes reflected the harsh realities facing young men as they're forced to grow up. Terry is shocked to discover that Bob now hankers after a life of domestic bliss with his fiancée Thelma, his boss's daughter. Thelma's steadying influence over Bob means that Terry's attempts to lead him off the straight and narrow are less successful. In turn, Bob realises that Terry's tall tales and determined attempts to remain young, free and single are self-destructive and not to be aspired to. Indeed, it's Bob's dilemma – whether to spend more time with his middle-class, aspirational (yet dull) fiancée or his good-for-nothing, retrogressive best friend – that forms the heart of the comedy in *Whatever Happened to the Likely Lads?* Although the original series had been extremely popular, the follow-up proved to be an enormous hit, cementing the reputation of actors and writers alike as the leading exponents in their genre.

Despite Terry's efforts to waylay Bob, Thelma managed to get her man up the aisle at the end of the first season. But, like a bad smell on a landing, Terry refuses to go away – much to Thelma's dismay. Indeed, Terry's continual interference in their relationship eventually leads them to split up for a short while, Thelma moving back home to her mother's house. Despite this brief hiccup, Bob and Thelma's marriage is able to

The Likely Lads instantly became a zeitgeist-surfing classic, a programme with public and critical appeal.

Sitcom
BBC Two/One
Episode Duration: 25–30 mins
Broadcast: 16 Dec 1964–23 Jul 1966 (*The Likely Lads*), 9 Jan 1973–24 Dec 1974 (*Whatever Happened to the Likely Lads?*)

Regular Cast

James Bolam · *Terry Collier*
Rodney Bewes · *Bob Ferris*
Sheila Fearn · *Audrey Collier*
Irene Richmond · *Mrs Ferris*
Olive Milbourne · *Mrs Collier*
Alex McDonald · *Mr Collier*
Brigit Forsyth · *Thelma Chambers/Ferris*
Joan Hickson, Noël Dyson · *Mrs Chambers*
Bill Owen · *George Chambers*
Anita Carey · *Susan Chambers*
Tony Haygarth · *Les*
Elizabeth Lax · *Terry's Secretary*

Creators/Writers Dick Clement and Ian La Frenais

Producers Dick Clement, James Gilbert, Bernard Thompson

Theme Music For the original series, Ronnie Hazlehurst produced a somewhat generic theme tune. The sequel was an altogether different matter: 'Oh, what happened to you, whatever happened to me?/What became of the people we used to be?' sang Mike Hugg, formerly of pop group Manfred Mann. The lyrics of the tune 'Whatever Happened to You?' were written by Ian La Frenais.

survive the depredations of a dodgy best friend, and when the series finally came to a close after 27 episodes it appeared as though Bob was finally shaking free of Terry's relentless laddism.

Like most sitcoms of the early 1970s, *Whatever Happened to the Likely Lads?* was honoured with a movie adaptation, released in 1976 and starring the three main cast members once again reunited in a crumbling and decaying Newcastle. For its type, it's one of the very best, thanks to a Clement and La Frenais script and a surprising guest appearance by ***Coronation Street***'s Mike Baldwin (a very young-looking Johnny Briggs) as a milkman. And that was the last we saw of Terry Collier and Bob Ferris – that is, until 2002, when a bizarre experiment by ITV brought the boys back for one last shout. Current ITV golden boys (and, of course, native northeast lads) Anthony McPartlin and Declan Donnelly – better known of course as Ant and Dec – took on the parts for a one-off special called *A Tribute to the Likely Lads*. 'No Hiding Place' – an episode, possibly the best known, from *Whatever Happened to the Likely Lads?* – was remade and updated from its original 1973 setting to 2002. It featured Terry (Ant) and Bob (Dec) desperately trying to avoid hearing the result of an England football match, having accepted a bet that they can go a whole day without finding out the score. Donnelly and McPartlin were perfectly adequate in their new roles, but audiences couldn't help feeling as though there simply wasn't much point in remaking a series that had been so iconic. Having said that, it didn't seem to put off Rodney Bewes, who made a tiny cameo appearance as a one-legged newspaper seller.

***Whatever Happened to the Likely Lads?* cemented the reputation of the actors and writers alike as the leading exponents in their genre.**

should be. Private Mick Hopper does his National Service working as a translator for the War Office. Bored and unstimulated in his day job, by night Gary lives life to the full, playing the drums in a rock and roll band. Throughout the six episodes, we follow Gary's romance with the beautiful Lisa (daughter of a senior officer) whilst his best friend Francis flirts with danger as he falls in love with a married woman.

Eagerly awaited at the time, *Lipstick on your Collar* didn't thrill critics as much as they'd hoped. Having said that, it was nevertheless an entertaining series, with the musical routines definitely contributing to the authentic historical feel of the programme. *Lipstick on your Collar* is also notable for providing an early opportunity for a young Scottish actor called Ewan McGregor to shine in a leading role. Two years later, he was cast in the movie *Trainspotting* – the rest, as they say, is history.

Little Britain

See pages 438–40

Little House on the Prairie

Drama | Ed Friendly Productions for NBC (shown on BBC One and ITV) | episode duration 45 mins | broadcast 11 Sep 1974–21 Mar 1983, 12 Dec 1983, 6 Feb 1984, 17 Dec 1984 (USA)

Regular Cast
Melissa Sue Anderson · *Mary Ingalls/Kendall*
Melissa Gilbert · *Laura Ingalls/Wilder*
Sidney Greenbush · *Carrie Ingalls*
Karen Grassle · *Caroline Ingalls*
Lindsay Greenbush, Michael Landon · *Charles Ingalls*
Brenda Turnbaugh, Wendi Turnbaugh · *Grace Ingalls*
Matthew Laborteaux · *Albert Quinn Ingalls*
Jonathan Gilbert · *Willie Oleson*
Alison Arngrim · *Nellie Oleson*
Allison Balson · *Nancy Oleson*
Richard Bull · *Nels Oleson*
Katherine MacGregor · *Harriet Oleson*
Bonnie Bartlett · *Grace Snider Edwards*
Jason Bateman · *James Cooper*
Missy Francis · *Cassandra Cooper*
Linwood Boomer · *Adam Kendall*
Dean Butler · *Almanzo Wilder*
Shannen Doherty · *Jenny Wilder*
Woody Eney, Nicholas Pryor · *Royal Wilder*
Aileen Fitzpatrick · *Millie Wilder*
Lucy Lee Flippin · *Eliza Jane Wilder*
Ruth Foster · *Melinda Foster*
Victor French · *Isaiah Edwards*
Dabbs Greer · *Reverend Alden*
Kevin Hagen · *Dr Hiram Baker*
Patrick Laborteaux · *Andy Garvey*
Merlin Olsen · *Jonathan Garvey*
Hersha Parady · *Alice Garvey*
Ketty Lester · *Hester-Sue Terhune*
Steve Tracy · *Percival Dalton*

Producers Michael Landon (executive), Ed Friendly, Kent McCray, Marvin Coil, Gary L. Wohlleben (associate), John Hawkins, Winston Miller, B. W. Sandefur, William F. Claxton **Writers** Various, including Blanche Hanalis, Gerry Day, Harold Swanton, Michael Landon, Arthur Heinemann, John Hawkins, Carole Raschella, Michael Raschella, John T. Dugan, Don Balluck, Chris Abbott, from the novels by Laua Ingalls Wilder **Theme Music** David Rose

Leaving the thrills and action of ***Bonanza*** behind, serial frontiersman Michael Landon starred in a ***Waltons***-alike drama series based on the autobiographical novels of Laura Ingalls Wilder and set in Minnesota and later Dakota. Landon came to the series after an invitation to direct and star in the pilot movie came from Ed Friendly, a TV executive who had become fascinated by the novels and wanted to bring them to the screen.

The Ingalls family have none of the traditional problems with 'Injuns' and cattle thieves that haunt almost every other western. This was a simple example of the Protestant work ethic, a story of a family existing with nature and generally getting along with their neighbours as told from the point of view of the Ingalls' middle child, Laura. The drama came from commonplace incidents, silly accidents, trivial fallings-out and the odd tragedy. Eldest daughter Mary discovers she's going blind and begins attending blind school to learn how to cope with her disability. There, she meets Adam Kendall and eventually the couple fall in love and marry. Laura also marries and has a baby girl – Rose. Having been the series' narrator throughout its run, for the final series (when Michael Landon had left the production entirely) Laura became the central character as stories revolved more around her own family, with both her father and elder sister having moved away.

Trivia
The opening sequence where Sidney Greenbush (as little Carrie) falls over while running down the side of a hill was actually an out-take that Michael Landon felt was so charming he decided to keep it in.

Live Aid

Live Broadcast | BBC One/Two | duration c.16 hours | broadcast 13 July 1985

Cast
Coldstream Guards, Status Quo, Style Council, Boomtown Rats, Adam Ant, INXS, Ultravox, Loudness, Spandau Ballet, Bernard Watson, Joan Baez, Elvis Costello, The Hooters, Opus, Nik Kershaw, Four Tops, B. B. King (video from The Hague), Billy Ocean, Ozzy Osbourne and Black Sabbath, Sade, Run DMC, Yu Rock Mission, Sting, Rick Springfield, Phil Collins, REO

Continued on page 441

Little Britain

David Walliams and Matt Lucas as Lou and Andy.

Little Britain is a poignant, often painful, documentary series that first aired on the opening night of BBC Three. Brutal and uncompromising but always truthful, it was a wholly accurate depiction of life across the classes in Britain today. The fly-on-the-wall series masqueraded as a comedy sketch show until viewers began to recognise something within each of the short vignettes – themselves. The successful pilot episode eventually led to a series that was so honest and uncompromising that – oh, wait, have we used uncompromising? Ah. Er . . .

Let's start again, shall we? From ***Steptoe*** to ***Monty Python*** and beyond to ***Spitting Image*** and ***The League of Gentlemen***, the very best comedies have never shied away from issues that some would prefer never to raise their ugly heads in polite society. With that heritage behind it, *Little Britain* succeeded in being truly offensive to as many people as possible in its short half-hour slot – and, like the freak shows of Victorian carnivals, its audience love nothing more than to groan in disgust and recoil in horror. Graphic descriptions of hardcore homosexual practices, obese naked old ladies with hyperactive libidos, vomiting Women's Guild members and casual racism are just a few of the guilty seams that the series mines, making its ever-growing audience complicit in the creation of each and every foul aberration.

Matt Lucas and David Walliams were rightly praised for their genius; media darlings who could be guaranteed to turn up at every single awards ceremony or opening night and dare the assembled stuffed shirts to have a bit of fun. Like many great successes, their overnight rise to fame took a fair few years to achieve. Matt Lucas began his TV career as 'George Dawes', the 'glamorous assistant' on Reeves and Mortimore's potty game show ***Shooting Stars*** – a gig he won after sending in a letter to the duo claiming he could do better. Dressed in a baby romper and grinning like a loon, 'George Dawes' simply kept score during the game but somehow he managed to upstage the lot of them. Occasionally, baby George would be replaced by his mother, the diet-obsessed Marjorie. More on her later.

A spin-off from *Shooting Stars* was a one-off comedy special starring Ulrika Jonsson called *It's Ulrika!*, in which some of the characters were played by David Walliams. Walliams, who also co-created the Channel 4 mock pop-documentary *Boyz Unlimited* (shown in 1999), slowly began to pop up in other comedy roles, including a hilariously rubbish alien and an obsessive kidnapper in a series of sketches written by *The League of Gentlemen*'s Mark Gatiss for a BBC Two ***Doctor Who***-themed night. But the first major collaboration for Walliams and Lucas was UK Play's *Rock Profiles*, a razor-sharp satire of the legends of the pop and rock industry, first shown on the cable channel in 1999. Just one glimpse of the mercilessly funny way in which *Rock Profiles* demolishes icons like Tom Jones, Shirley Bassey ('She doesn't have the range!') and The Bee Gees gave only a hint of what was to follow.

Based upon the traditional sketch show format, *Little Britain* combined the high-camp of Dick Emery with the speed of ***The Fast Show*** and the savagery of their friends *The League of Gentlemen*. Like The League, Walliams and Lucas's show debuted on Radio 4 with a fair few characters surviving the transition to telly. The most important character of all, though, was one not played by the show's creators but by one of their all-time heroes. Former Time Lord Tom Baker has evolved into one of this country's great eccentrics, with his meandering anecdotes about his amazing paranormal effect on the bosoms of pensioners and how he was once (or maybe thrice) mistaken for (former Liberal politician) Shirley Williams. As narrator for the series, Baker sets the tone with his aristocratic, sometimes pompous, voice delivering quite the most magnificent stream of nonsense ever heard by anyone ('If you disagree, you must be a woman, a mental or a gay', being one of many).

Every viewer of *Little Britain* has their own favourite character, but the test of any multi-character show like this is which ones are being imitated in playgrounds and offices the next morning. *Little Britain* can boast at least two who make the grade on that score. Teenage delinquent Vicki Pollard, resident of Darkly Noone, is the walking, talking personification of the term 'chav'. Her breathless delivery of excuses, always beginning with the hesitant, 'Yeah, but no, but yeah, but . . .' and outraged indignation at being accused of something she so obviously *has* done have replaced the tongue-twister as Britain's modern example of vocal dexterity.

A duo that began as a fictional exploration of the last years in the life of Andy Warhol, as cared for by rock star Lou Reed, soon evolved into something much funnier (no doubt due to the realisation that one of those two could still sue). Lou Todd is the lisping day-care worker responsible for looking after wheelchair-bound monosyllabic lump Andy Pipkin. While Lou tries to guide Andy through life's difficult decisions, like which book to get out of the library or whether to have a flake in his ice cream, Andy merely mumbles, 'Ah want tha' one', regardless of what 'that one' actually is. Lou checks with him that this decision is indeed what he wants, and reminds him of previous occasions when he's expressed opinions to the contrary, to which Andy grunts, 'Yeah, ah know.' Only when Lou

Comedy
BBC Three/Two/One
Episode Duration: 30 mins
Broadcast: 9 Feb 2003, 16 Sep 2003–present

Regular Cast

Matt Lucas · *Vicki Pollard, Marjorie Dawes, Dafydd, Bubbles deVere, Dame Sally Markham, Andy Pipkin and Various Characters*
David Walliams · *Emily Howard, Des Kaye, Ray McCooney, PM's aide Sebastian, Harvey Pincher, Lou Todd and Various Characters*
Tom Baker · *Narrator*
Anthony Head · *Michael the Prime Minister*
Paul Putner · *Various Roles*
Steve Furst · *Various Roles*
Charubala Chokshi · *Meera*
Joann Condon · *Fat Pat*
Evie Garratt · *Gran*
Ruth Jones · *Myfanwy*
Stephen Aintree · *Fat Fighters Taxi Driver*
Sterling Gallacher · *Prime Minister's Wife/Voice of Margaret*
Siobhan Hayes · *Julie*
Tony Tang · *Chinese Waiter*
David Soul · *Himself*
Les McKeown · *Himself*
Ewan Macintosh · *Himself*
Ted Robbins · *Reporter/Restaurant Customer*
Barbara Keogh · *Marjorie Dawes' Mum*
Sophie Raworth · *Herself*
Jennie Bond · *Herself*
Peter Serafinowicz · *Interviewer*
Mark Gatiss · *Theatrical Agent*
Helen Coker · *Samantha*
Veronica Roberts · *School Secretary*
Mollie Sugden · *Herself*
David Foxxe · *Vicar*
Vanessa Feltz · *Herself*
Nigel Havers · *Leader of the Opposition*
Geraldine James · *Mrs Pincher*
Habib Nasib Nadar · *Gregory Merchant*
Ruth Madoc · *Mrs Thomas*
Paul Darrow · *Conservative MP*
Pik-Sen Lim · *Simone*
Hywel Simons · *Gay Vicar*
Vincent Marzello · *US President*
Jamie Theakston · *Andrew Wiltshire*
Jon Culshaw · *Andrew Lloyd Webber*
Gavin Esler · *Himself*

Creators/Writers Matt Lucas and David Walliams

Producers Jon Plowman, Geoff Posner, Myfanwy Moore, Andrew Wiltshire

Feem Toon David Arnold

TRIVIA
Realising that some of the jokes that were just about acceptable on BBC Three would be completely inappropriate on BBC One, Lucas and Walliams recorded slight variations on some scenes – notably some of the more risqué comments by Dafydd's fellow gays about their specific lifestyle choices.

has done as instructed and wheeled Andy some distance away do we hear him change his mind: 'Don' like it.' What slowly becomes obvious about Andy (to get a little sociological for a second) is that he's both a victim of, and highly exploitative of, a society that sees disability as a complete removal of any ability to make one's own choices. Lou is insufferably patronising, so Andy continues the façade of being confined to his wheelchair just until Lou is distracted, at which point Andy will shin up a tree, leap off a diving board, run into the sea or simply get off his fat arse and fetch the TV remote control for himself. Lazy beyond belief, Andy is more cunning than he'll ever be given credit for – and we love him for it.

Lucas's creation Marjorie Dawes also makes regular appearances, now acting as the monstrous leader of a local branch of 'Fat Fighters' and taking gleeful joy in humiliating her members and suggesting they're so fat the only thing they can risk eating is dust. Other characters include Sebastian, predatory homosexual and insanely jealous assistant to the Prime Minister (a wonderfully baffled performance from ***Buffy the Vampire Slayer*** star Anthony Head); rubbish transvestite Emily Howard; Dafydd Thomas, the self-proclaimed 'only gay' in the Welsh village of Llandewi Breffi; Dennis Waterman (yes, the actor from ***Minder***), who is depicted as a micro-midget living in a giant's world while rejecting any part his agent gets him that doesn't allow him to write the 'feem toon, sing the feem toon'; Bubbles deVere, the obese health farm resident with the unfortunate habit of disrobing at every opportunity (performed with such glee by Matt Lucas in a prosthetic suit so horrific it deserved its own 18 certificate); and two prim and proper 'women's guild' ladies, one of whom has a habit of projectile vomiting whenever she eats anything cooked by any form of minority group.

Boasting a range of guest appearances by celebrities playing either themselves or grotesques connected with the core series characters, *Little Britain* keeps itself fresh and constantly pushing back the boundaries of what is and isn't acceptable in TV comedy. BBC Three's first big success soon found its way onto BBC Two, a fairly safe location for 'alternative' and challenging comedy programmes. However, BBC One controller Lorraine Heggesey soon realised the extent of this potential break-out hit and arranged for the second and subsequent seasons to be re-broadcast on the BBC's primary channel, where it soon attracted massive viewing figures and critical acclaim. Not everyone was pleased with *Little Britain*, however – the Women's Institute reacted angrily to suggestions that their members might be racist or homophobic, and as a result of their complaints, subsequent repeats of the 'women's institute ladies' sketches saw all offending logos blurred out.

Despite such concerns, *Little Britain* is now one of the biggest stars in the comedy firmament. In February 2005, a special DVD was released by the *Little Britain* team in aid of ***Comic Relief***. Featuring an appearance by pop star Robbie Williams as another 'rubbish transvestite', the DVD sold 110,000 copies in just four days. The British public, delighted that they finally had something decidedly politically incorrect to enjoy, seem to be lapping it up in spades.

Speedwagon, Howard Jones, Autograph, Bryan Ferry, Dave Gilmour, Paul Young, Alison Moyet, Bryan Adams, U2, Beach Boys, Dire Straits, Sting, George Thorogood and the Destroyers, Bo Diddley, Albert Collins, Queen, Simple Minds, David Bowie, Thomas Dolby, Pretenders, Who, Santana, Pat Metheny, Ashford & Simpson, Teddy Pendergrass, Elton John, Kiki Dee, Wham!, Madonna, Paul McCartney, Tom Petty and the Heartbreakers, Crosby Stills & Nash, Kenny Loggins, Cars, Neil Young, Power Station, Thompson Twins, Eric Clapton, Phil Collins, Robert Plant, Jimmy Page, John Paul Jones, Duran Duran, Patti LaBelle, Hall & Oates, Eddie Kendricks, David Ruffin, Mick Jagger, Tina Turner, Bob Dylan, Keith Richards, Ron Wood, Lionel Richie · *Music Acts*
Jack Nicholson, Maryilyn McCoo, Mel Smith, Griff Rhys Jones, Billy Connolly, Bette Bidler, John Hurt, Chevy Chase, Jeff Bridges · *Compères*
Richard Skinner, Janice Long, Andy Kershaw, David Hepworth, Paul Gambaccini, Tommy Vance, Steve Blacknell, Mike Smith, Mark Ellen · *UK Presenters*

Creator Bob Geldof **Producers** Various, including Mike Appleton (UK), Mike Mitchell (USA)

The recording in late 2004 of Band Aid 20's version of 'Do They Know It's Christmas?' brought home two very unsettling facts. The pop stars of today weren't even born when the original song was released (some of them had never even heard of Bob Geldof before being invited to take part in the 20th-anniversary project). More importantly, though, many of us had assumed that the mass starvation of the people of Africa had been consigned to history. We'd seen the success stories of the survivors and footage of the verdant plains, hadn't we? Band Aid had been No. 1 in the UK charts twice already (in 1984 and 1989) and in 12 other countries. And for those of us old enough to remember, the televised Live Aid concert was the most important live broadcast ever.

Before 1985, the collective noun for a bigger-than-normal live rock concert was a 'Woodstock'. The famous 1969 event wasn't shown on TV. Most people who claim to have been there are either lying or were too busy enjoying the atmosphere to remember who actually played there; in fact, the only recorded evidence that it ever took place was a small movie directed by an up-and-coming film director called Martin Scorsese. We'd imagine pretty much every music festival since has been called 'the next Woodstock' at some point. But there was only one *Live Aid*. And never again will there be an event that brings the world together in such a gloriously ramshackle way, with satellite links conking out, feedback drowning out the acts and cameras unable to cope with the sheer volume of noise being generated around the globe.

This was a musical event that was so big, so ridiculously ambitious that when Bob Geldof approached Tyne Tees TV (where his then-wife Paula Yates presented pop show ***The Tube***) to ask them produce it, they instantly baulked at the idea and pointed him in the direction of the BBC, the only broadcaster that had even half the equipment needed for such an event (the Beeb didn't quite have everything Geldof would need, but frankly he wouldn't have wanted to wait 20 years for instant satellite link-ups, internet feeds and Nicam stereo . . . although he did happen to have Concorde at his disposal). BBC One head man Michael Grade (who, many forget, had given Band Aid an enormous boost by adjusting the schedules for a broadcast of the 'Do They Know It's Christmas?' video in a slot of its own the previous December) did something staggering – he negotiated for 16 hours of programming to be dropped across BBC One and Two in order for *Live Aid* to be shown uninterrupted and uncut.

It all began with DJ Richard Skinner announcing: 'It's 12 noon in London, 7 a.m. in Philadelphia and around the world it's time for *Live Aid*.' Prince Charles and Princess Diana took their seats next to Bob Geldof and Paula Yates, which in itself shows us just how long ago this all was (a decade later, both of these marriages would be over, and subsequently both wives died in horrifically tragic circumstances). After the national anthem, one of the biggest touring bands of the time, Status Quo, strolled onto the stage, gave a cheeky 'hallo' and went straight into 'Rockin' All Over the World'. They'd never played to such an audience – but then, no-one else had either. At the end of the event, Ultravox's Midge Ure, co-writer with Geldof of the song that had inspired the concert, overheard the Quo's Francis Rossi jokily asking Rick Parfitt why they'd been singing 'Feed the Welsh'. And so, they were off, with the Quo stepping aside for The Style Council, then Geldof's band The Boomtown Rats came on, followed by Adam Ant, Ultravox, Spandau Ballet, Elvis Costello . . . a line-up that today seems ridiculously unorchestrated, such were the clash of styles, but which was timed almost to the second – any band that dared over-run on their set had already been warned that the stage would revolve and cut them off regardless.

In the UK it was the TV event of the year, perhaps of the whole decade. The exact line-up still wasn't clear when the show started, and though newspapers had speculated that The Beatles were going to re-form, with Julian Lennon standing in for his late father (it didn't happen), Led Zeppelin *did* get back together (with Phil Collins in place of the late John Bonham), while Mel Smith and Griff Rhys Jones claimed to have split up their comedy partnership the previous week just so they too could re-form for the day. Bruce Springsteen and Prince were also no-shows, but Mick Jagger dueted with Tina Turner! The front cover of the *Radio Times* that week prepared us for an event dubbed 'the Global Jukebox'. It was the main news item on the day itself, and the day after it was the lead story on the front cover of every single newspaper; even the *New Musical Express*, which up until this point had been decidedly sniffy about the whole affair, reluctantly offered up its cover to one of David Bowie's photos of starving children.

This wasn't just a concert. Its place in this book marks a huge turning point in the whole notion of the telethon. The sheer scale of the event makes it even more baffling – in a time where reports can be logged from war zones using video-phones and mobiles, it's sometimes difficult to imagine just how difficult it was to obtain a link-up to Philadelphia that worked even some of the time. Another live-by-satellite broadcast, from Moscow, marked the first uncensored broadcast from the Soviet Union ever, for the sheer love of music and a need to take part in a global effort to save lives. In Australia, INXS led Men at Work, Midnight Oil and a line-up of other artists we'd not really heard of; Austria's Band Aid sang their own song, 'Why?'; bands from Japan appeared by satellite; and in the good old USA, MTV broadcast a highlights show lasting just an hour, in which hoary old rock fans chanted 'Who's on next?' during the performance of a young woman who was known only for a couple of disco hits and a so-so movie. That would be Madonna, by the way. It has to be said that the line-up from Philadelphia probably didn't mean much to the crowds and audience in the UK. Jack Nicholson, Chevy Chase, Bette Midler and Jeff Bridges introduced acts like Rick Springfield (who pre-recorded a video for the day), REO Speedwagon and Bryan Adams, a Canadian whose biggest UK hits were still some six years away.

There were some who participated out of sheer ego, for sure, but for every Adam Ant promoting his latest single, there was a Bono, a Bowie and some Beach Boys. In fact, one of the show's biggest dangers was that it was just too bloody good to turn away from to make the all-important call and donate money. This provoked the most famous utterance of an expletive since Kenneth Tynan first used the f-word on a televised debate in 1965. Frustrated that people just weren't pledging fast enough, Bob Geldof made an impassioned plea for people to 'give us the money'. David Hepworth, the anchorman for that part of the day, made an effort to recite the many ways people could donate, beginning with the address they could write to. 'Fuck the address,' snapped Bob impatiently, painfully aware that the phone numbers were much more important. He was tired, he was emotional and, for those viewers perceptive enough not to get upset by an ill-chosen word, he was a hero.

Out of so many performances, two tend to receive the most praise. Queen were of course experienced in the art of stadium performances, but Freddie Mercury pranced around the stage with the confidence of a man who knows the world is watching him. Getting the audience to perform singing warm-ups with him was inspired, showing just how much in control of them he was. But that's what Freddie did every show. The band's skill was condensing their stage act into a perfect, 20-minute summary, seguing from classic to classic. You only have to watch the sea of arms clapping along to 'Radio Gaga' – how many bands get to have their own clapping sequence that the entire audience knows?

But the other act that took people by surprise was U2. With a lesser band, the antics it performed – clambering around the stage to dance with audience members or urging a cameraman to stand centre-stage to record the audience – could have been a disaster. Indeed, so the legend goes, Bono was distraught that his decision to go down into the crowd had led to the need to drop one of their songs, believing that such self-indulgence had ruined their set. Nothing could be further from the truth, however. If anything, Bono's warmth and eagerness to connect with the crowd caused U2's profile to rocket higher after *Live Aid* than that of any other act that performed alongside them.

Band Aid and *Live Aid* started out as an emotional response on Bob Geldof's part to Michael Buerke's heartbreaking news report on the famine in Ethiopia. Only later did it become clear that the problems were much, much greater than anyone had begun to imagine. What the people of Africa needed wasn't just grain and powdered milk. They needed an ally in the West to help them get rid of mounting debts. For every pound that went into Ethiopia and the Sudan in the form of aid, ten times as much had to come out of the regions to pay off loans to Western banks. *Live Aid*'s real legacy was in getting high-profile, articulate people like Geldof and Bono to challenge the world's governments to cancel the debt. At the time of writing, it now looks as if the UK's prime minister, Tony Blair, will be pushing to do just that – in time for *Live Aid*'s 20th anniversary.

Live and Kicking

Magazine | BBC One | episode duration 180 mins | broadcast 2 Oct 1993–15 Sep 2001

Regular Cast

Emma Forbes, Andi Peters, John Barrowman, Zoë Ball, Jamie Theakston, Emma Ledden, Steve Wilson, Katy Hill, Sarah Cawood, Ortis Deley, Trey Farley, Heather Suttie · *Presenters*
Mitch Johnson · *Voice-over Continuity Announcer*
Paul Brophy · *Ratz*
Trev Neal, Simon Hickson · *Trevor and Simon*
Don Austen, John Eccleston, Rebecca Nagan · *Sage, Onion and Shamrock – The Leprechauns*
Peter Simon, Shane Ritchie · *Run the Risk Compères*
Barry Killerby · *Mr Blobby*
Ben Ward, Gerard Foster, Richard Webb · *Men in Trousers*
Louise McClachy, Jai Simeone · *SuperGirly*

Producers Chris Bellingham, Angela Sharp, Annette Williams, Simon Parsons (editors) **Theme Music** David Arnold, who re-orchestrated the classic James Bond theme tune for the Pierce Brosnan movies.

Live and Kicking retained the format of previous Saturday morning magazine show ***Going Live!*** but with Emma Forbes brought out of the kitchen to be the co-host with Andi Peters (like Phillip Schofield, a graduate of the weekday Children's BBC continuity announcer 'broom cupboard'). For the first series, Scottish-American stage actor John Barrowman chipped in, but Saturday morning kids TV really wasn't his thing and he soon leapt back to Broadway (and eventually to join the crew of the TARDIS in the revived ***Doctor Who***). Aside from the new set and opening titles, Trevor and Simon still did their comedy sketches, for a while at least, and the role of cheeky puppet was divided between two 'Oirish' ginger leprechauns, Sage and Onion (eventually joined by girl leprechaun Shamrock). Guests popped in for live phone-ins to plug their latest record, and pop videos were sprinkled throughout the show.

The big difference between *Going Live!* and *Live and Kicking*, though, was that the latter was not a vehicle for its presenters, as became evident when Peters and Forbes decided to leave at the end of the third year in a highly emotional show of surprises and tears all round. Rather than come up with a new show, the Beeb decided to make *Live and Kicking* a brand, and brought in Zoë Ball and Jamie Theakston. Whether or not this is how they actually felt, there was something about the slightly cooler personas of Ball and Theakston that suggested they felt kids' TV was a bit beneath them – which we actually loved because it meant they were never patronising and always spoke to the kids like equals. The show was filled out by ***Juke Box Jury***-styled 'Hit, Miss or Maybe', 'Star Driving Test', cartoons like *Eek the Cat, Spider-Man, The Addams Family* and, of course, ***Rugrats***, which became a major feature of the show, while live-action comedy came from American imports *Kenan and Kell* and *Sweet Valley High*.

The problem with having presenters who can be easily slotted into place, however, was that the departure of Ball and Theakston left the programme without any feeling of continuity – presenters simply came and went (the show even found a home for Mr Blobby, the inflatable pink, yellow-spotted buffoon created for ***Noel's House Party***). The series became the BBC's longest-running Saturday morning kids show – racking up eight long years – and even managed to add in a Friday afternoon support show and a digital-only mid-week edited repeat. But this longevity was as much to do with a lack of a suitable opponent on ITV as anything else; the independent station went from *Motormouth*, through *Ghost Train, What's Up Doc?* and *Gimme 5* before they finally struck gold with ***SM:TV Live***, which starred Ant and Dec. It was this final show that managed to regularly trounce the Beeb in the ratings for the first time in over a decade. Despite a slight trendification of the name (to *L&K*), the BBC's Saturday morning champion was finally vanquished, to be replaced (from 22 September 2001) by *The Saturday Show*, alternating with *Dick and Don in Da Bungalow*.

The Liver Birds

Sitcom | BBC One | episode duration 30–40 mins | broadcast 14 Apr, 25 Jul 1969–5 Jan 1979, 6 May–24 Jun 1996

Principal Cast

Nerys Hughes · *Sandra Hutchinson*
Polly James · *Beryl Hennessey*
Elisabeth Estensen · *Carol Boswell*
Pauline Collins · *Dawn*
Mollie Sugden · *Mrs Hutchinson*
Ivan Beavis, John McKelvey, William Moore · *Mr Hutchinson*
Sheila Fay, Carmel McSharry · *Mrs Hennessey*
Cyril Shaps · *Mr Hennessey*
Eileen Kennally, Carmel McSharry · *Mrs Boswell*
Ray Dunbobbin · *Mr Boswell*
Michael Angelis · *Lucien Boswell/Hennessey*
John Nettles · *Paul*
Jonathan Lynn · *Robert*
Tom Chadbon · *Derek*

Creators Carla Lane and Myra Taylor **Producers** Sydney Lotterby, Douglas Argent, Roger Race, Philip Kampff **Writers** Carla Lane, Myra Taylor, Lew Schwartz, Jack Seddon, David Pursall **Theme Music** The Scaffold, the Liverpool group (including poet Roger McGough and Paul McCartney's brother Mike) behind the No. 1 hit 'Lily the Pink' and famous anthem 'Thank U Very Much', composed the theme tune 'On a Hillside Stands a Lady'. It was deliberately sung in such a thick Scouse accent that many of the words slide into each other becoming nigh on impenetrable. The whistling intro is instantly memorable bringing back memories of watching a faded 1970s film of the Mersey Ferries and the Mersey Tunnel entrances.

A much-loved slice of life from post-Beatles Merseyside, *The Liver Birds* told the story of two young women sharing a flat on Huskisson Street, not far from Liverpool's Anglican Cathedral. At the start of the series, the flatmates were Dawn and Beryl – however, Dawn soon moved out and Sandra took her place. The two girls had to deal with the normal problems of any young singleton – boys, money, work, parental pressure, etc. Despite all of their worries, their natural chirpy nature and optimistic outlook on life helped them to get by. They also had to deal with the changing nature of what it meant to be a young woman in the 1970s – after the sexual revolution of the late Sixties, just what kind of behaviour was expected of them? Could they – or should they – behave like they were supposed to act as young, liberated women? Or was it just easier to follow the old rules and regulations that their parents wished of them?

Perhaps more than anything else, *The Liver Birds* is an outstanding documentary record of the concerns facing young single women in a world where the old rulebook of finding a husband, settling down and having kids as soon as possible had been ripped up and thrown away. Creators Carla Lane and Myra Taylor used many of their own experiences as the basis for the plotlines and characters in the series. After working together on the first few seasons (and with the support of veteran scriptwriter Lew Schwartz), Taylor soon departed the series and left Carla Lane to write the vast majority of the subsequent episodes. The format of the series remained the same though – slightly snobby Sandra (Nerys Hughes) would always be slightly embarrassed by her more vulgar flatmate, whether that was brash Beryl (Polly James) or, for the final half of the show's run, gobby Carol (Elizabeth Estensen, children's show star ***T-Bag*** and ***Emmerdale***'s Bernice). The girls would often have to put up with visits by their parents (leading to the standard sitcom generation gap misunderstandings), with Mollie Sugden especially good as Sandra's monstrous mother. Affairs of the heart played heavy on their minds, with future ***Bergerac*** star John Nettles becoming a long-term love interest for Beryl. Perhaps the best-remembered of all of the supporting characters was Carol's rabbit-obsessed brother Lucien, played by ***Boys from the Blackstuff***'s Michael Angelis.

The Liver Birds came to an end in 1979 with Sandra getting married and settling down, drawing to a close the free-living days of the single Scouse girls. Seventeen years later, Carla Lane brought back two of her *Liver Birds* to BBC One, reuniting Beryl and Sandra as middle-aged women rather than the chirpy youngsters they used to be. It was a joy to see such talented performers as Nerys Hughes and Polly James revisiting their old characters, both of them now having to deal with the reality of failed relationships and downscaled ambitions for life. In a bizarre continuity cock-up, Beryl suddenly inherited Carol's mother and brother Lucien – a switch that angered many viewers and proved to programme makers that viewers have much longer memories than they're often given credit for. Sadly, the new run of *The Liver Birds* wasn't a great success, with audiences finding it difficult to warm to the melancholy women who used to be such lively and vibrant young 'birds'.

Trivia

The real-life Liver Birds are two gigantic carved seabirds – shags, to be accurate – that reside on top of the famous Liver Buildings on the Mersey waterfront.

The Living Planet

Documentary | BBC/Time-Life for BBC One | episode duration 55 mins | broadcast 19 Jan–10 Apr 1984

Cast

David Attenborough · *Presenter*

Producers Richard Brock (executive), Ned Kelly, Andrew Neal, Adrian Warren **Writer** David Attenborough

Life on Earth had proven to television executives that David Attenborough's unique style of natural history documentary making was hugely popular with viewers in dozens of different countries. *The Living Planet* was Attenborough's follow-up series, this time focusing on Earth's present-day life forms and showing in intimate detail how these plants, animals and other organisms had adjusted and evolved over time to better suit their habitats.

Produced by the respected BBC Natural History Unit in Bristol, *The Living Planet* was filmed on location in deserts, rainforests, tundra and oceans right across the world. Once again, David Attenborough's seemingly effortless style of presentation managed to make a fascinating subject even more interesting. Six years later, *The Trials of Life* concentrated on the fauna of Earth, whereas in 1995 *The Private Life of Plants* showed that you don't have to have a central nervous system to be a good subject for a TV programme. Later series from David Attenborough and his team included *The Life of Mammals*, *The Life of Birds* and *Life in the Freezer*, all of which maintained *The Living Planet*'s extraordinarily high benchmark of quality.

Logan's Run

Science Fiction | MGM Television for CBS (shown on ITV) | episode duration 50 mins | broadcast 16 Sep 1977–30 Jan 1978 (USA)

Regular Cast

Gregory Harrison · *Logan*
Heather Menzies · *Jessica*
Donald Moffat · *Rem*
Randy Powell · *Francis*

Creators William F. Nolan, George Clayton Johnson (original novel) **Producers** Ben Roberts, Ivan Goff **Writers** Leonard Katzman, D. C. Fontana, Harlan Ellison, John Meredyth Lucas, William F. Nolan, Shimon Wincelberg, Katharyn Powers **Theme Music** Jerry Goldsmith's original movie score was re-used for the TV series

Based upon the 1976 feature film starring Michael York, Jenny Agutter, Leo McKern and Farrah Fawcett (which in itself was based upon the novel by William F. Nolan and George Clayton Johnson), the TV series of *Logan's Run* followed pretty much the same basic premise.

In the far future of the 23rd century, mankind is still recovering from the trauma of a nuclear holocaust. The few survivors have huddled together inside protective domed cities, to shelter from the radioactive fallout in the outside world. Inside the City of Domes, humanity has managed to rebuild itself an excellent quality of life – people are young, happy, healthy and carefree. However, the ever-present worry about overcrowding inside a strictly limited space has led to the creation of one overriding law – at the age of 30, everyone must submit themselves to 'Carousel', a ritual wherin they are killed and reborn in the next generation. To ensure that everyone obeys the rule of taking part in Carousel, an armed group of citizens called the Sandmen has been created. Two such Sandmen are best friends Logan and Francis and everything in their lives seems fine, until one day Logan comes to the realisation that Carousel is simply a fancy public execution, and decides to go on the run from his own people, out into the wilderness, in search of a mythical place called Sanctuary, where people can live to a ripe old age. Logan is joined in his hunt for Sanctuary by another 'runner', Jessica, and eventually by a friendly robot called Rem. Unfortunately, his old friend Francis is sent to hunt Logan down and terminate him.

Much better quality than many movie spin-off sci-fi shows, *Logan's Run* sadly lasted for just 14 episodes before being cancelled, despite boasting scripts written by established science fiction bigwigs like author Harlan

Ellison and ***Star Trek***'s D. C. Fontana. Even Leonard Katzman, the chap who produced ***Dallas***, contributed a script. Another name of note behind the camera was one of the show's directors, an actor called Nicholas Colasanto, who would find fame as the slow-witted barman Coach in ***Cheers***.

Lois and Clark: The New Adventures of Superman

Action-Adventure/Romance | December 3rd Productions/Warner Bros for ABC (shown on BBC One) | episode duration 45 mins | broadcast 12 Sep 1993–14 Jun 1997 (USA)

Principal Cast

Dean Cain · *Clark Kent/Kal-El/Superman*
Teri Hatcher · *Lois Lane*
Lane Smith · *Perry White*
Michael Landes, Justin Whalin · *Jimmy Olsen*
Tracy Scoggins · *Catherine 'Cat' Grant*
Eddie Jones · *Jonathan Kent*
K. Callan · *Martha Kent*
John Shea · *Lex Luthor*

Creators Inspired by characters created by Joe Shuster and Jerry Siegel **Producers** Various, including Brad Buckner, Jim Crocker, David Jacobs, Brad Kern, Deborah Joy LeVine, Eugenie Ross-Leming, Robert Singer, Randall Zisk (exectuive) **Writers** Various, including Deborah Joy LeVine, Daniel Levine, Tony Blake, Paul Jackson, John McNamara, Grant Rosenberg, Dean Cain, Chris Ruppenthal, Eugenie Ross-Leming, Brad Buckner, Brad Kern, Teri Hatcher, Tim Minear **Theme Music** Jay Gruska's title music was designed to sound as much like Jerry Goldsmith's score for the *Superman* movies as possible.

For commentary, see ADVENTURES OF SUPERMAN

London's Burning

Drama | LWT for ITV | episode duration 90/50 mins | broadcast 7 Dec 1986, 20 Feb 1988–25 Aug 2002

Regular Cast

Katharine Rogers · *Josie Ingham*
James Hazeldine · *Mike 'Bayleaf' Wilson*
Glen Murphy · *George Green*
Richard Walsh · *Bert 'Sicknote' Quigley*
Gerard Horan · *Leslie 'Charisma' Appleby*
Mark Arden · *Roland 'Vaseline' Cartwright*
Sean Blowers · *John Hallam*
Ross Boatman · *Kevin Medhurst*
Treva Etienne · *Tony Sanders*
Shirley Greenwood · *Maggie*
Amanda Dickinson · *Jean Quigley*
Kim Clifford · *Sandra Hallam*
Valerie Holliman · *Claire*
Rupert Baker · *Malcolm Cross*
James Marcus · *Sidney Tate*
Vanessa Pett · *Kelly Green*
Demetri Jagger · *Micky*
Samantha Beckinsale · *Kate Stevens*
Craig Fairbrass · *Gary 'Technique' Pagnall*
Stephen North · *Colin Parrish*
Andrew Kazamia · *Nick Georgiadis*
John Alford · *Billy Ray*
Michael Garner · *Geoffrey 'Poison' Pearce*
Sara Powell · *Sally Reid*
Brad Clayton · *Chris 'Skippy' Newman*
Zoe Heyes · *Carole Webb*
Clive Wood · *Jack Morgan*
Minna Aaltonen · *Marianne*
Stephen Houghton · *Gregg Blake*
Jim Alexander · *Joe Walker*
Helen Anderson · *Fiona Hoddle Pearce*
Melanie Barker · *Lisa Hammond*
Sharon Gavin · *Jacqui Parker*
Brad Gorton · *Dan Barratt*
Jonathan Guy Lewis · *Chris Hammond*
Daniel Maiden-Wood · *Stephen Morgan*
Ben Onwukwe · *Stuart 'Recall' McKenzie*
Heather Peace · *Sally 'Gracie' Fields*
Sian Radinger · *Linda Morgan*
Joanne Adams · *Andie Green*
Connor Byrne · *Rob 'Hyper' Sharpe*
Fuman Dar · *Ronnie 'Hi-Ho' Silva*
Sharon Duce · *Elaine Reeve*
Heather-Jay Jones · *Zoe*
Edward Peel · *John Coleman*
Terry Alderton · *Charlie Mead*

Creator Jack Rosenthal **Producers** Linda Agran, Nick Elliot, Sarah Wilson (executive), Paul Knight, Gerry Poulson, David Shanks, Angus Towler, David Newcombe **Writers** Various, including Tony Hoare, Anita Bronson, Gerry Mill, David Humpfries, Roger Marshall, Simon J. Sharkey, Neil McKay, Richard Zjajdlic, Len Collin, Jeff Dodds, Doug Briggs, Colin Steven, Jonathan Guy Lewis, Joe Turner, Ed McCardie **Theme Music** The original music was composed by Simon Brint and Roddy Matthews. Later seasons used a completely new composition, though neither theme was particularly distinctive, consisting of generic 'supermarket music' rather than a memorable melody.

Inspired by the TV movie by Jack Rosenthal, *London's Burning* followed the Blue Watch crew of London Blackwall fire station through their daily lives, in and out of uniform. Almost all of the characters carried a nickname, whether they wanted one or not. 'Vaseline' was sex-mad, Bert Quigley became 'Sicknote' as he had the worst attendance record on the crew, 'Bayleaf' was the station's cook and Les Appleby was the most boring man in the world – what else, but 'Charisma'. But the station had to adapt to new ways with the arival of firefighter Josie Ingham, their first woman officer.

At one time, one of ITV's highest-rated dramas (drawing in a peak of almost 19 million viewers in December 1991),

London's Burning succeeded in combining well-drawn characters and comic moments with genuinely life-threatening incidents in which we'd never be sure if our heroes would come out unscathed or even alive (the second series ended with popular character Vaseline drowning during a rescue operation, leaving behind a pregnant widow). Many of the stories came from real life (or at least popular fire brigade mythology), with one early episode seeing the crew called out to rescue a cat only for the engine to back over the poor moggie, resulting in the station's cat being handed over to the grief-stricken owner as a replacement (though the cat's name was hastily changed from 'Brown Balls' to 'Brambles' to save causing further offence).

As we might expect, the series continued thanks to a regular turnover of new characters. Vaseline's place on the crew as chief Lothario was taken by bodybuilder and part-time male stripper 'Technique' (***Prime Suspect***'s Craig Fairbrass, who later played Dan Sullivan in ***EastEnders***), while Josie left to be replaced as token firewoman by Kate Stevens (Samantha Beckinsale). By 2000, only one of the original stars remained – Glen Murphy, who played George.

Though *London's Burning* was always a show of spectacle, major stunts tended to be spaced out within seasons. But towards the end, each episode revolved around a huge set piece, leaving little room for character development or the human elements that had made it so popular. From its heights in the 1990s, by 2002 ratings had slumped to under 5 million and Blue Watch were decommissioned.

The Lone Ranger

Western | Apex/Wrather for CBS (shown on BBC TV) | episode duration 25 mins | broadcast 15 Sep 1949–12 Sep 1957

Regular Cast
Clayton Moore, John Hart · *John Reid/The Lone Ranger*
Jay Silverheels · *Tonto*
Chuck Courtney · *Dan Reid*
Ralph Littlefield · *Jim Blaine*

Creators George W Trendle, Fran Striker, James Jewell
Producers George W. Trendle, Jack Wrather (executive), Sherman A. Harris, Jack Chertok, Paul Landers, Harry Poppe **Writers** Various, including Fran Striker, Dan Beattie, Ralph Goll, Charles Larson, Joe Richardson, Tom Seller, George B Seitz, Ed Earl Ropp, Curtis Kenyon, Walker A. Tompkins **Theme Music** Rossini's *William Tell Overture* became forever associated with galloping horses and masked cowboys rather than with crossbows and apples on heads. . .

Probably the most famous Western TV series ever made, *The Lone Ranger* ran for 221 episodes. The character of *The Lone Ranger* was created for a radio programme in 1933 on a small local station in Detroit. So popular were *The Lone Ranger*'s adventures that the radio episodes were played right across the USA and eventually spawned two Saturday morning cinema serials by Republic Pictures (the people who gave us Buster Crabbe as *Flash Gordon*).

The first TV episode revealed the history behind the mysterious Lone Ranger. John Reid becomes the sole survivor of a group of six Texas Rangers ambushed by a group of dastardly outlaws. Reid's life is saved by a friendly Indian named Tonto, amazingly somebody whose life Reid had himself saved years previously. When Tonto says 'You lone ranger now', Reid takes this description as a career opportunity and sets off on his horse Silver to right wrongs and bring the villains who killed his buddies to justice. Keen to preserve his identity, Reid always wears a mask to cover his face. This leads to the perpetual cry from those he's saved and those he's caught: 'Who was that masked man?'

Aimed squarely at a family/juvenile audience, *The Lone Ranger* was immensely popular with parents too, because there was never any bad language, no displays of overt violence or aggression on the part of the Ranger, and a ruling from the producers that our hero would never shoot to kill. Clayton Moore, a former male model, portrayed the rugged hero for most of the programme's run, but for the two seasons during which he was locked in financial and contract negotiations with producers, John Hart (a much less satisfactory stand-in) took over. Jay Silverheels, who played Tonto, was, in fact, the son of a Mohawk Chief from Canada, so despite the (now) politically incorrect terminology of referring to him as an 'Indian', at least Tonto wasn't played by a white or Hispanic actor.

The Long Firm

Crime Drama | BBC Two | episode duration 60 mins | broadcast 7–28 Jul 2004

Principal Cast
Mark Strong · *Harry Starks*
Derek Jacobi · *Lord Teddy Thursby*
Judy Parfitt · *Lady Ruth Thursby*
George Costigan · *DI George Mooney*
Lena Headey · *Ruby Ryder*
Joe Absolom · *Tommy*
Shaun Dingwall · *Lenny*
Israel Aduramo · *John Ogungbe*
Geoff Bell · *Jock McClusky*
Robert Boulter · *Craig*
Neil Conrich · *Manny Gould*
Charles Barker · *Compère*
Tracie Bennett · *Judy Garland*
Tim Flavin · *Johnnie Ray*
Diana Brooks · *Harry's Mum*
Sidney Kean · *Harry's Dad*
Phil Daniels · *Jimmy*
Bryan Dick · *Beardsley*
Samuel Gough · *Hippy*
Anna Hope · *Samantha the Dolly Bird*

Katherine Ingle · *Jimmy's Tart*
Derek Jacobi · *Lord Teddy Thursby*
Billy Keating · *Freddie Bird*
Gregor Truter · *Joe Meek*

Creator Jake Arnott **Producers** David Bernath, Laura Mackie, Hilary Salmon (executive), Liza Marshall **Writer** Joe Penhall, from Jake Arnott's novel **Theme Music** Rob Lane

Jake Arnott's brutal novel about the underbelly of London's Soho in the 1960s came to the small screen losing little of its shocking details – notably a torture scene in which a white-hot poker is forced down a man's throat, which drew as many complaints as one would expect and probably hope for. Retaining the narrative device of the book, each episode told the story of a character somehow linked to Harry Starks, a West End gangster and proprietor of The Stardust club in the heart of Soho.

We first meet Harry through Teddy Thursby, member of the House of Lords whose promising career is now very much in decline. Though married, he occasionally indulges in sex with pretty young boys, often procured for him by Starks (who, unlike Teddy, is very open about his homosexuality). When Teddy encourages Harry to invest in a property development venture in Africa that quickly collapses, the gangster drags him across the world to sort out the matter, only to be confronted by post-colonial insolence and frustration.

Next is Ruby Ryder, a graduate of the Rank Charm School and actress in the Diana Dors mould who accepts a job running the entertainments at Harry's club after her useless housebreaking husband is arrested and sent to jail. But the temptation to start an affair with Harry's 'boy', Tommy, leads to a tragic conclusion. A feature of the novel included here is the merging of fiction and history as Harry and his friends socialise with Judy Garland (a stunning portrayal by Tracie Bennett, unrecognisable from her days as Rita's adopted daughter in ***Coronation Street***). Here we learn that Harry's a huge 'Judy' fan, suffering from that classic affection for tragic torch singers, so to see her at the end of her career, drunken and desperate for affection is a hard thing for Harry to witness.

Best of the four episodes was also the one that was the most altered from the source, where the pill-popping drunkard was Jack 'The Hat' McVitie, one of the real-life victims of the Krays. Here, he emerged as the more likeable but nonetheless tragic figure Jimmy, played by Phil Daniels. At the end of the episode, Jimmy is killed by a young wannabe gangster while Harry is arrested and imprisoned. The final episode, told from the perspective of a failed sociology lecturer called Lenny, sees Harry's audacious jail break and escape to Spain in search of the man he believes caused his arrest – retired DI Mooney, formerly of the 'Dirty Squad' of the Metropolitan police, who had once controlled the porn trade through Soho.

Very classy, capturing the seduction and glamour of the 1960s' gangster scene without shying away from the brutality behind it, *The Long Firm* was critically acclaimed on first broadcast (which, like many BBC dramas now, premiered on digital channel BBC Four), particularly thanks to Mark Strong, who excelled as Harry Stark just as he'd done back in 1996 in ***Our Friends in the North***. Hailed as one of the best TV productions of 2004, it left us hoping that the BBC get round to adapting Arnott's further novels, *He Kills Coppers* and *Truecrime*.

Look and Read

See pages 448–51

Look Around You

Comedy | Talkback/Talkback Thames for BBC Two | episode duration 10/30 mins | broadcast 10 Oct 2002–present

Regular Cast
Nigel Lambert · *Narrator*
Peter Serafinowicz · *Scientist/Peter Packard*
Robert Popper · *Scientist/Jack Morgan*
Olivia Colman · *Pam Bachelor*
Josie D'Arby · *Pealy Maghti*

Creators/Writers Robert Popper, Peter Serafinowicz **Producers** Peter Fincham (executive), Robert Popper, Peter Serafinowicz **Theme Music** A loving tribute to the electronic bleeps and whines of the BBC Radiophonic Workshop's 'futuristic' music, the *Look Around You* theme was composed by Gelg.

Tapping into people's nostalgic memories of their own childhood proved to be a rich source of comic material for the team behind *Look Around You*, creators, producers, writers and performers Robert Popper and Peter Serafinowicz. The first season of the show was a painfully accurate pastiche of schools' science programming in the late 1970s. In order to make the show as accurate a send-up as possible, spot-on fashions, haircuts and attitudes were re-created in painstaking detail, as was an uncannily old-fashioned title sequence and incidental music. Another lovely detail was recording the programme on faded film stock, giving the whole show a 'feel' of genuine age. Each of the eight episodes lasted just ten minutes, covering a specific science-related topic (such as germs, music, water, calcium and the brain) 'in depth'. At regular intervals during the programme, the on-screen scientists would conduct an assortment of experiments with test tubes, Bunsen burners and Van der Graaf generators in order to prove their hypotheses – viewers were then advised to 'write that down in your copybook' by the portentous narrator.

The second season, made over two years later, decided to turn its attentions to another vintage science programme, the late (and very much lamented) ***Tomorrow's World***. Again spoofing the fashions, technological advances and broadcasting styles of the early

Continued on page 452

Look and Read

Cosmo and Wordy read 'The Boy From Space'.

The problem with programmes for schools and colleges is that we tend to forget that they carried on long after our own school year stopped watching them. So it was with some surprise that we learned *Look and Read* is still (at the time of writing at least) a fixture of BBC educational broadcasting. Another thing about schools programmes is that, like sex, you're vaguely aware that it must have taken place before you came along – largely because there are books about other people's experiences available for you to read – but you're really only interested in your own experience. So, throughout this entry, you may find yourself skipping past 'Joe and the Sheep Rustlers' to get to 'Cloud Burst' or 'Sky Hunter', if that was 'your' year. Don't worry; it's quite understandable and a perfectly normal thing to do.

Unlike other BBC factual productions, programmes for schools were not aimed at the self-motivated but at the plodders, those children who found lessons difficult or struggled to keep up with the rest of the class (or, as BBC documentation said at the time, 'backward' children'). Programmes tended to use a variety of obvious devices like repetition, music and animation – what shows such as ***Sesame Street*** had relied on for pre-schoolers.

Look and Read was developed by ex-teacher and BBC producer Claire Chovil. Having been responsible for radio broadcasts in *Children's Hour*, one of Chovil's first TV productions was a couple of test pieces shown within the 'Merry-Go-Round' slot, an overall title for a variety of broadcasts for seven-to-nines on science history and society. The educational content for the shows was developed by Dr Joyce M. Morris, co-founder of the United Kingdom Reading Association. Both 'Fishing for Fivers' and 'Tom, Pat and Friday' helped establish the format for what became *Look and Read*. They were simple dramas showing children, probably a year or two older than the target audience, observing crimes and helping the police to catch the perpetrators. Each episode was shown in two halves, with the educational content, such as animations of word construction, slipped into the middle. 'Tom, Pat and Friday' also came with a pamphlet for teachers to help them relate the stories to their lessons.

The first series to go out under the *Look and Read* banner was 'Bob and Carol Look for Treasure'. Like its 'Merry-Go-Round' predecessors, it told the story of children spoiling the criminal's plans by solving clues and piecing together information. Still considered an experimental broadcast, it was largely deemed a success, although one reviewer, in the educational journal *Visual Education*, noted that children had difficulty reading the on-screen text when it was presented black on white (this was remedied in subsequent programmes, with all text appearing in white on a black background).

Still, a success it was, so after a few years of repeats for 'Bob and Carol' a second series was prepared. For 'Len and the River Mob', the educational segments were introduced by one of the characters, Len, played by George Layton. Len works on the river docks and his adventures begin when he stumbles across a gang of thieves smuggling toys recently stolen from a local toy shop. There are a couple of points to note here. First, bringing the character out of the story to speak directly to the children was a clever device, as was tying his disappearance in one episode into the studio action – his part as narrator being taken by Angela Crow as Mrs Green, to preserve an air of mystery. Secondly, one of the young actors in the story was Christopher Chittell, who'd starred alongside Sidney Poitier and Lulu in the film *To Sir With Love* (1966) and would go on to play the villainous Eric Pollard in ***Emmerdale***.

One of the best-remembered stories was 'The Boy from Space', a science fiction adventure involving a young space boy called Peep-Peep and the children who help him evade capture by the terrifying Thin Spaceman. Considering that in 1970 it would have only ever been planned to be shown in black and white at this point, the production team took the surprising decision to shoot the story segments on colour film, directed by former Radiophonic Workshop alumnus Maddalena Fagandini (under the guise of 'Ray Cathode', Fagandini was responsible for the Workshop's experimental single 'Time Beats'). At one point it was mooted that the segments might be collated into a feature film, although nothing ever came of this. Still, using colour film turned out to be a fortuitous decision as it allowed the story to be recycled in 1980 with the addition of new framing sequences involving Wordy, and fresh educational segments.

The success of *Look and Read* inspired Claire Chovil to create a similar show for younger children. *Words and Pictures*, which began in 1970, again used the device of stories and animated sections, and had its own non-human host, like Wordy (see below) – an animated cartoon character called Charlie who appeared to be animated 'live' as he was superimposed into the action within the studio.

The last of the original format editions was 'Joe and the Sheep Rustlers', which was also the first to be made entirely in colour. As before, the in-between teaching segments were presented by the main character, Joe himself. But, as from the next story, 'Cloud

Education
BBC Two
Episode Duration: 25 mins
Broadcast: 9 Jan 1967–present

Regular Cast
Charles Collingwood · *Mr Watchword/Wordy*
Katie Hebb · *Wordy Puppeteer*
Colin Marsh, Sean Barrett · *Narrator*
Jane Carr, Derek Griffiths, Gerald Down, Dave Royal, Julie Stevens, Jeremy Birchall, Donald Greig, Miriam Stockley, Tony Wharmby, Michael Dore, Robert Fardell · *Singers*

Story Casts
'Bob and Carol Look for Treasure'
Tom Gibbs · *Presenter*
Jean Anderson · *Miss Brown*
Veronica Purnell · *Carol*
Stephen Leigh · *Bob*
Robert Bridges · *The Fat Man*
Peter Hempson · *Mike*
Carl Gonzales · *Dan*

'Len and the River Mob'
Harvey Hall · *Narrator*
George Layton · *Len Tanner*
Philip Brack · *Bill*
Denise Powell · *Pat*
Christopher Chittell · *Micky*
Kenneth Colley · *Mr Moon*
Paul Sarony · *Dave*
Kenneth Gardnier · *Roy*
Angela Crow · *Mrs Green*

'The Boy from Space'
Sylvestra Le Touzel · *Helen*
Loftus Burton · *Tom*
Stephen Garlick · *Dan*
Colin Mayes · *Peep-Peep*
John Woodnutt · *The Thin Spaceman*
Anthony Woodruff · *Mr Bunting*

'Joe and the Sheep Rustlers'
Struan Rodger · *Joe Norland*
Martine Howard · *Jill Sharp*
Ken Jones · *Mr West*
Paul Humpoletz · *Ted Beasley*
Michael Grady · *Denis Beasley*
David Sadgrove · *Mike Burns*
Rita Howard · *Mrs Sharp*
Powell Jones · *Pat*
Ray Dunbobbin · *Mr Burns*

'Cloud Burst'
Tina Heath · *Jenny Barber*
Anne Ridler · *Mrs Green/Number Three*
Miles Anderson · *Dick Turner*
Nigel Rathbone · *Tim Barber*

Renu Setna · *Ram, Ravi Pandit*
Michael Sheard · *Number Two*
Kenneth Watson · *Mr Barber*
Bill Gavin · *Sir Robert Blain*

'The King's Dragon'
Kenneth Watson · *Jack Dunbar*
Frankie Jordan · *Ann Mills*
Sean Flanigan · *Billy West*
Reg Lye · *Stan West*
John Quayle · *Mr Carter*
Anne Pichon · *Miss Wood*
Peter Settelen · *Clive Manning*
Charles Lloyd Pack · *Mr Day*

'Sky Hunter'
Nigel Anthony · *Narrator*
Geoffrey Bayldon · *Mr Charles Trim*
Luke Batchelor · *Butch*
Isobil Nisbet · *'Cat' Mary MacBride*
Emma Jean Richards · *Sharon Blake*
Mike Savage · *Bert Badger*
Jayne Tottman · *Jackie Blake*
Donald Waugh · *Trevor*
Lennox Greaves · *Tom Roberts, The Birdman*
Michael Maynard · *Dave*

'The Boy from Space' (1980)
Phil Cheney · *Cosmo*
with rest of cast same as 1970 edition

'Dark Towers'
Denise Coffey · *Presenter, Jenny Jackson*
Christopher Biggins · *Mr Benger*
Harry Jones · *Mr Bunce*
David Collings · *Lord Dark, The Friendly Ghost*
Juliet Hammond Hill · *Miss Hawk*
Peter Mayhew · *The Tall Knight*
Gary Russell · *Lord Edward Dark*
Juliet Waley · *Tracy Brown*

'Fair Ground!'
Wayne Laryea · *Presenter, Martin Salisbury*
Judy Cornwell · *Jean Watson*
Percy Herbert · *Bert Thurston*
Bruce Montague · *Mr Turnbull*
Elizabeth Morgan · *Mrs Leach*
Iain Ormsby-Knox · *Sidney*
Lynne Pearson · *Rachel Thurston*
Paul Russell · *Ozzie Watson*
George Sweeney · *Steve*
Kenneth Waller · *Mr Grant*

'Badger Girl'
Gary Watson · *Narrator*
Margo Gunn · *Jane Miles*
John Hollis · *Mr Barker*
Ashiek Madhvani · *Kiran Singh*
James Marston · *Mr Deal*

Burst', the educational sections would change completely, thanks to the introduction of a limbless, orange fellow with a head covered in typewriter keys. This was Mr Watchword – or 'Wordy' – who became the only constant element of the show from now on until 1992. For 'Cloud Burst', and the next story, 'The King's Dragon', Wordy was accompanied by writer Richard Carpenter, who helped explain how he came to write the story as well as providing the linking sections previously supplied by the characters in the story. Carpenter later admitted that his first *Look and Read* script was the most difficult writing assignment of his career as it took him some time to adjust to limiting his vocabulary to just 100 or so words.

'Cloud Burst' also saw the introduction of the singers who would help illustrate particular points in grammar, such as 'Magic E' or adding 'ly' to create adverbs. Derek Griffiths would become the musical voice of *Look and Read* for many subsequent series, and he was joined by Jane Carr, who as a child had appeared as Mary Macgregor in the film version of *The Prime of Miss Jean Brodie* (1969).

One other story that is fondly remembered is 'Sky Hunter', concerning a group of children and their involvement in a ring of bird thieves attempting to trade in peregrine falcons. Accounting for a significant rise in memberships for the RSPB, 'Sky Hunter' was recycled, like 'The Boy from Space' had been, in 1992, presented by the now grown-up child stars of the original.

From 1993 onwards, the format of *Look and Read* might well be unrecognisable to children of the 1970s. But while new stories continue to be told, many of the originals have been reshown on the BBC digital channel CBBC, a chance for us all to reminisce with Wordy and that all-important 'Magic E'.

June Marlow · *Mrs Rudge*
Julia Millbank · *Debbie West*
Nick Orchard · *Mick Rudge*
Kieron O'Shea · *Norman Bolt*
William Squire · *Sam North, The Badgerman*

'Geordie Racer'
Michael Heath · *Narrator*
Leon Armstrong · *Spuggy Hilton*
Lien Lu · *Janie Chung*
Lesley Casey · *Cath Hilton*
Brian Hogg · *Victor*
Madelaine Newton · *Bev Hilton*
Fred Pearson · *Baz Bailey*
Kevin Whately · *Ray Hilton*
Peter Rowell · *Mickey Stone*

'Through the Dragon's Eye'
Sean Barrett · *Voice of Gorwen*
David Collings · *Charn*
Charles Collingwood · *Voice of Rodey*
Simon Fenton · *Scott Bates*
Marlaine Gordon · *Amanda Jackson*
Michael Heath · *Morris*
Katie Hebb · *Rodey's Puppeteer*
Timothy Lyn · *Boris*
Carolyn Pickles · *Doris*
Nicola Stewart · *Jenny*

'Earth Warp'
David Cooper · *Martin Rowlands*
Rachna Kapur · *Amina Patel*
Ellie Beavan · *Jenny Steel*
Helen Martin · *Ollie*
Caroline Holdaway · *Mrs Rowlands*
Mark Benton · *Chef*
Dean Harris · *Mr Belcher*
Anthony Milner · *Joe Lowin*
Joanna Wake · *Miss Enid Grant*
Rhoda Lewis · *Mrs MacDonald*
Michael Garner · *Mr Steel*

'Spywatch'
Raymond Pickard · *Norman Starkey*
Russell Tovey · *Dennis Sealey*
Sophie Ward · *Polly Hobbs*
Josie McCabe · *Mary Parker*

Rosemary Leach · *Aunty Amy*
Lesley Joseph · *Miss Millington*
Guy Henry · *Phillip Grainger*
Norman Bird · *Cyril Jenkins*
Joseph Alessi · *Luigi Balzoni*
Abigail Thaw · *Vivienne Belling*
Terence Maynard · *Mike Johnson*
Rab Christie · *Private Wilson*
Pauline Delaney · *Mrs Calver*
Victoria Hasted · *Ethel Higson*
Carol Harvey · *Mrs Starkey*
Reinhard Michaels · *The German Pilot*
Colin Starkey · *Dr Simpson*
Vincent Pickering · *Harrison*
Keith Barron · *adult Starkey*
Josephine D'Arby · *Miss Lee*
Roger Kitter · *CD Rom*

'Captain Crimson'
Ben Brooks · *Thomas Rickard*
Helen Ryan · *Whizz*
Paul Bigley · *Jeff Rickard*
Lucy Wood · *Amy*
Beverley Hills · *Gina Clough*
Felix Dexter · *Captain Crimson*

'The Legend of the Lost Keys'
Andrew Sachs · *George Gardener*
Jonathan Kitchens · *Mark Astor*
Abigail Ansell · *Lisa Astor*
Sabra Williams · *Erica Turner*
Richard Morant · *Sir Derek Janus*
David Gant · *Professor Humphrey Waters*
Tatiana Strauss · *Dr Burns*
Nicole Arumugan · *Ariana*
Sonia Graham · *Anna*
Sita Ramamurphy · *The Taker*
Stafford Gordon · *The Catcher*

'Zzaap and the Word Master'
Neil Morrissey · *Voice of Zzaap*
Jamie Gill · *Frances*
Amanda Riley · *Josie*
Kieran Hardcastle · *Peter*
Stephen Mapes · *Victor Virus*
Deborah Steele · *Miss Wordsworth*
Tom Mullion · *Simon*
Michael Windsor · *Rock Face, Skinless, Grendel*
Lawrie McNichol · *The Carved Heads*
Roy Barraclough · *Sir Clifford Clank*
Miriam Acharki · *Scheherezade*
Paul Sharma · *The Green Man*
James Bryce · *Lord Hamish*
Sarah Patterson · *The Snow Queen*
Nick Ball · *The Scarecrow*
Philip Bird · *The Word Master*

'Shadow Play'
Angellica Bell · *Presenter*
Jack Bannon · *Ben*
Naomi Miller · *Emma*
Patrick Robinson · *Cal*
Sophie Aldred · *Roz*
Anabel Barnston · *Hester Moreton*
Timothy Bentinck · *Uncle Augustus*
Laura Davenport · *Aunt Sophie*
Janine Duvitski · *Katie*
Faye Jackson · *The Girl in Blue*
Cameron Crighton · *Nathan*
Francis Magee · *Mr Bob Trimby*
Patience Tomlinson · *Mrs Alice Trimby*
Adam Donnelly · *George Moreton*
Ben · *Meg the Dog*
Doreen Mantle · *Queen Victoria*
Paul Bigley · *Dogsbody*

Creator Claire Chovil

Producers Claire Chovil, Andrée Molyneux, Sue Weeks, Roger Tonge, Susan Paton, Ronald Smedley, Nicholas Whines, Cas Lester, Karen Johnson, Sarah Miller

Writers Joy Thwaytes, Roy Brown, Leonard Kingston, Richard Carpenter, Andrew Davies, Christopher Russell, Christine Russell, David Angus, Derek Farmer, Jim Eldridge, Berlie Doherty, Carolyn Sally Jones

Theme Music Each series had its own theme, usually created by members of the BBC Radiophonic Workshop, including Paddy Kingsland, Roger Limb and Peter Howell. Some of these also featured vocals by Derek Griffiths, including the theme for the second version of 'The Boy from Space'. Later editions had music by Elly Brewer, Debbie Wiseman and Gregor Philip.

1980s, these longer, half-hour episodes were hosted by four 'presenters' (Peter, Jack, Pam and Pealy) and featured regular interviews with new inventors. Each week, three competitors would arrive in the studio to compete for the prestigious 'Inventor of the Year' competition – memorably, these included a treatment for the debilitating condition 'cobbles', a 'psilence' spray to cut out extraneous noise by temporary sealing up the user's ear and a hilariously rubbish Japanese plastic surgery robot called Medi-Bot (that called out 'ME-DI-BOT!' at regular intervals).

Wonderfully daft, both series of *Look Around You* were hilarious, clever and warm in equal measure. The final episode featured a guest appearance from a youthful Prince Charles (referred to throughout the series as 'HRH Sir Prince Charles') in a staggeringly well-edited piece that combined archive footage with the 'live' reactions of the presenters.

Lost in Space

Science Fiction | Irwin Allen Productions/20th Century Fox TV for CBS (shown on ITV) | episode duration 50 mins | broadcast 15 Sep 1965–6 Mar 1968

Regular Cast

Guy Williams · *Professor John Robinson*
June Lockhart · *Maureen Robinson*
Mark Goddard · *Major Don West*
Marta Kristen · *Judy Robinson*
Bill Mumy · *Will Robinson*
Angela Cartwright · *Penny Robinson*
Jonathan Harris · *Dr Zachary Smith*
Bob May · *Robot Voice*
Dick Tufeld · *Robot Operator*

Creator Irwin Allen **Producers** Irwin Allen, Jerry Briskin **Writers** Various, including Irwin Allen, William Welch, Carey Wilber, Jackson Gillis, Herman Groves, Norman Lessing, Barney Slater, Shimon Wincelberg **Theme Music** John Williams, here credited as 'Johnny Williams' – the future, multi-Oscar-winning composer of classic motion picture scores – composed two different themes. The first (for the first season) was quite stern and dramatic, the second (for subsequent series) was much more memorable in a groovy Sixties kind of way.

In the far future of 1997, the world is suffering from extreme overpopulation. Determined to find other planets that might be able to support life, a programme of research trips begins to identify future homes for humanity. Professor John Robinson, his wife Maureen and their children Penny, Judy and Will are selected to board the Jupiter II spacecraft, under the careful control of Major Don West. However, sneaky Dr Zachary Smith – an agent for an enemy power – sabotages the ship's robot and accidentally gets trapped on board during take-off. The combination of his sabotage and his extra weight sends the Jupiter II hurtling off into the uncharted depths of space. The family then has to struggle against alien menaces and Dr Smith's skulduggery in order to find their way home.

Created by ***Voyage to the Bottom of the Sea***'s Irwin Allen (he'd later create ***Land of the Giants***, among others), *Lost in Space* began in black and white as a fairly serious attempt at a science fiction 'Space Family Robinson' but soon ended up as a comedy double-act between the cowardly Dr Smith and the eternally chirpy and optimistic young Will Robinson. With the demented robot trundling around the place, shouting 'Danger! Will Robinson, Danger!' you could pretty much guarantee that any attempts at creating a credible science fiction universe had gone to pot. Having said that, *Lost in Space* is enormously entertaining TV, provided you have the right temperament to find gigantic talking carrots amusing (the cast certainly did – several of them can be seen on screen laughing at the whole thing). Generally speaking, if you like your science fiction serious, you'll prefer the early black and white episodes. If you like nothing better than laughing along with a ***Batman***-style camp classic, go for the later episodes in their lurid Technicolor. Indeed, *Lost in Space* has something to appeal to everyone, which must be one of the principal reasons that a feature film version of the series was released in 1998, starring John Hurt as John Robinson, ***Friends***' Matt LeBlanc as Major West and Gary Oldman as the evil Dr Smith. Boo hiss!

The Lost Prince

Drama | Talkback/WGBH Boston for BBC One | episode duration 90 mins | broadcast 19–26 Jan 2003

Cast

Gina McKee · *Lalla*
Tom Hollander · *King George V*
Miranda Richardson · *Queen Mary*
Daniel Williams, Matthew Thomas · *'Johnnie'*
Brock Everitt-Elwick, Rollo Weeks · *Prince George*
Bill Nighy · *Stamfordham*
Bibi Andersson · *Queen Alexandra*
Ron Cook · *Lloyd George*
Frank Finlay · *Asquith*
David Westhead · *Fred*
John Sessions · *Mr Hansell*
Michael Gambon · *King Edward VII*
David Barrass · *Kaiser Wilhelm*
Vanessa Ackerman · *Olga*
Holly Boyd · *Tatiana*
Suzanne Burden · *Lady Warrender*
Dominic Colenso · *David*
Jonathan Coy · *Dr Hetherington*
James Crooke · *Henry*
Graham Crowden · *Callender*
Ingeborga Dapkunaite · *Tsarina Alexandra*
Algina Lipskyte · *Anastasia*
Ivan Marevich · *Tsar Nicholas*
Sam Page · *Alexei*
Nicholas Palliser · *Knutsford*

Nastya Razduhova · *Maria*
John Rowe · *Dr Longhurst*
Neil Stacy · *The General*

Producers David Thompson, Rebecca Eaton, Peter Fincham, Joanna Beresford (executive), John Chapman **Writer** Stephen Poliakoff **Music** Adrian Johnston

At the turn of the 20th century, one vast inter-connected family controlled much of Europe, with the British Royal family at its centre. But though the eldest son of George V would ascend to the throne, history has forgotten George's other son, John, a child who was epileptic and who would nowadays be described as autistic. But his governess, Lalla, never gave up on 'Johnnie', even after the family had him sent to a remote cottage out of sight. As Johnnie's family prepared for war against Uncle Wilhelm and his cousins the Romanovs were murdered during the October Revolution, his governess Lalla dedicates her life to ensuring that he is not forgotten, that he is regarded by his family – and specifically his mother – as a true prince.

Another masterpiece from writer-director Stephen Poliakoff, and, like ***Shooting the Past*** and *Relative Strangers*, a story about lost connections in history, *The Lost Prince* draws from numerous sources, including the writings of royal courtier Stamfordham, which provide amazing insight into, for example, Lloyd George's decision not to allow the Tsar of Russia asylum in Britain and the consequences of that decision. By focusing on the forgotten member of the family, Poliakoff provides us with a contrast between the boy's often tactless but endearing naïvety and the controlling, obsessive actions of his parents, forced to abandon their family name in the interests of patriotism and become the Windsor family that we all know today.

The Lotus Eaters

Drama | BBC One | episode duration 50 mins | broadcast 23 Apr 1972–12 Aug 1973

Principal Cast
Ian Hendry · *Erik Sheppard*
Wanda Ventham · *Anne Sheppard*
James Kerry · *Donald Culley*
Maurice Denham · *Nestor Turton*
Thorley Walters · *Major Edward Wooley*
Sylvia Coleridge · *Miriam Wooley*
Stefan Gryff · *Captain Krasakis*
Timothy Carlton · *Gerard Mace*
Carol Cleveland · *Leigh Mervish*
Karan David · *Katerina*
Julia Goodman · *Kirsten McLuhan*
Karl Held · *Philip Mervish*
John Horsley · *Sir Hugh Russell*
Ronald Howard · *Dr Dartington*
Godfrey James · *Nicholson*
Paul Maxwell · *Sam Webber*
Calliope Petrohilos · *Ariadne Mazonaki*

Creator Michael J. Bird **Producers** Michael Glynn (associate), Anthony Read **Writers** Michael J. Bird, David Fisher, David Weir **Theme Music** 'Ta Trena Pou Fyghan', a track from the album *Hellespontus* by Stavros Xarhakos

After a successful career writing for series like *Brett*, *Paul Temple* and ***Danger Man***, Michael J. Bird's memorable first series as creator started off as the apparently mundane story of two ex-pats living in Greece, running a bar, and getting caught up in the lives and loves of their neighbours. However, as the story progressed over its nine episodes, a series of black-and-white flashbacks suggested that both Erik and Anne Sheppard have far darker backgrounds and reasons for being in the bar than they tell even each other. Are they both sleeper agents, sent to oversee, maybe assassinate, someone – or even one another?

A truly ground-breaking thriller, making the most of the overseas location and using monochrome to denote flashbacks at a time when British TV was still adjusting to colour (and therefore quite ready to think of the past in terms of black and white). A second, six-part season sadly became more of a run-around adventure series, lacking the element of mystery and intrigue that had made the first so distinctive.

Michael J. Bird continued the Mediterranean thriller theme with ***Who Pays the Ferryman?***, ***The Aphrodite Inheritance*** and ***The Dark Side of the Sun***, as well as scripting episodes of the BBC's wartime drama ***Secret Army***.

Website
An authorised tribute site to Michael J. Bird can be found at birdland2.netfirms.com.

Lou Grant

Drama | MTM for NBC (shown on Channel 4) | episode duration 45 mins | broadcast 20 Sep 1977–13 Sep 1982 (USA)

Regular Cast
Edward Asner · *Lou Grant*
Robert Walden · *Joe Rossi*
Linda Kelsey · *Billie Newman McCovey*
Mason Adams · *Charlie Hume*
Jack Bannon · *Art Donovan*
Daryl Anderson · *Dennis 'Animal' Price*
Nancy Marchand · *Margaret Jones Pynchon*
Thomas Carter · *Chris*
Allen Williams · *Adam Wilson*
Cliff Potts · *Ted McCovey*
Richard B. Shull · *Jack Towne*
Barbara Jane Edelman · *Linda*

Creators James L. Brooks, Allan Burns, Gene Reynolds **Producers** James L. Brooks, Allan Burns, Gene Reynolds (executive), Seth Freeman, Gary David Goldberg **Writers** Various

Theme Music Lance Rubin, Patrick Williams

Fired from his job as head of television news at WJM-TV in Minneapolis, Lou Grant moves to Los Angeles to become city editor for the *Los Angeles Tribune*. There he finds himself in conflict with his editor in chief, Charlie Hume, and with the paper's proprietor, the highly opinionated Mrs Jones Pynchon. But Grant knows that his reporters can be a force for good in Los Angeles, uncovering corruption and drawing attention to the plight of people who too often fall through the cracks.

Lou Grant was a direct spin-off from ***The Mary Tyler Moore Show***, which also spawned ***Rhoda*** and was itself a spin-off of sorts from ***The Dick Van Dyke Show***. Taking the grumpy news editor Grant from a sitcom and placing him into a drama was a courageous move, MTM's first on-going drama series (the company later gave us ***Hill Street Blues*** and ***St Elsewhere***, among others). An outspoken activist, Ed Asner's campaigning and political views are often cited as one reason why *Lou Grant* was dropped by NBC. However, Asner continues to be one of America's most respected actors. His sparring partner Margaret Jones Pynchon was played by Nancy Marchand, who later became Tony Soprano's poisonous mother Livia in HBO's hit mobster drama ***The Sopranos***.

The Love Boat

Comedy Drama | Douglas S. Cramer for ABC (shown on ITV) | episode duration 45 mins | broadcast 17 Sep 1976, 21 Jan, 24 Sep 1977–5 Sep 1986 (USA)

Regular Cast

Gavin MacLeod · *Captain Merrill Stubing, Marshall Stubing, Milo Stubing*
Bernie Kopell · *Doctor Adam Bricker*
Fred Grandy · *Yeoman-Purser Burl 'Gopher' Smith*
Ted Lange · *Isaac Washington*
Lauren Tewes · *Julie McCoy*
Jill Whelan · *Vicki Stubing*
Ted McGinley · *Ashley Covington Evans*
Pat Klous · *Judy McCoy*

Creator Jeraldine Saunders **Producers** Aaron Spelling, Douglas S. Cramer (executive), Hudson Hickman (associate), Henry Colman, Gordon Farr, Lynne Farr, Allen Brown, Alan Rafkin, Paul Stanley, Ben Joelson, Art Baer, Harvey Bullock, William A. Porter, Dennis Hammer, William Bickley, Duane Poole, Tom Swale, Michael Warren **Writers** Various, including Dawn Aldredge, Marion C. Freeman, Carl Kleinschmitt, Michael Norell, Art Baer, Ben Joelson, Richard Albrecht, Ann Gibbs, Casey Keller, Joel Kimmel, Howard Albrecht, Sol Weinstein, Lee Aronsohn, Tom Dunsmuir, Lan O'Kun, Ray Jessel **Theme Music** Written by Charles Fox and Paul Williams, the theme song was performed by Jack Jones for most of the series' run, and by Dionne Warwick for its final regular season: 'Soon we'll be making another run/The Love Boat promises something for everyone.'

Pretty much '*Fantasy Island* on a cruise liner', each episode began with the passengers as they embarked on the *Pacific Princess*, introduced each of the sub-plots for the week by chatting to various members of the crew, resolved their problems at some point, and by the end everyone had left with blissful smiles on their faces. Part of the fun was in trying to remember where you'd seen each of the passengers before (consisting of celebrities of the time and of yesteryear; they changed every episode). The show was almost an anthology series in some ways, in that the regular cast were present only to facilitate exposition and resolve the various issues of the guest characters.

A TV movie, *The Love Boat: A Valentine Voyage*, was broadcast in 1990, while a revival TV series, *The Love Boat: The Next Wave* aired in 1998 and starred Robert Urich as Captain Jim Kennedy.

Website

Jeraldine Saunders, creator of *The Love Boat*, has her own website: www.loveboatlady.com.

Love Thy Neighbour

Comedy | Thames for ITV | episode duration 25 mins | broadcast 13 Apr 1972–22 Jan 1976

Regular Cast

Jack Smethurst · *Eddie Booth*
Rudolph Walker · *Bill Reynolds*
Kate Williams · *Joan Booth*
Nina Baden-Semper · *Barbie Reynolds*
Tommy Godfrey · *Arthur*
Keith Marsh · *Jacko Jackson*
Ken Parry · *Cyril*
Paul Luty · *Nobby Garside*

Creators Vince Powell, Harry Driver **Producers** Stuart Allen, Ronnie Baxter, Anthony Parker, William G. Stewart **Writers** Vince Powell, Harry Driver, Brian Cooke, Johnnie Mortimer, George Evans, Sid Colin, Lawrie Wyman **Theme Music** 'Roger Webb', sung by Stuart Gillies

Left-wing trade unionist and ardent chauvinist Eddie Booth lives in what passes for domestic harmony with his long-suffering wife Joan. But when new neighbours – Bill and Barbie Reynolds – move in next door, Eddie can't decide whether he's more appalled by the prospect of living next door to black immigrants or that the new neighbours are Tories.

Actors always love playing the antagonist as it gives them opportunities to express sides of human behaviour that the heroic roles rarely offer. We can't fault any of the actors in *Love Thy Neighbour* for playing to the strengths of the scripts rather than shying away from them. It's not at all surprising to see Jack Smethurst being comfortable with casually using words like 'nignog' in every episode because it's not him, it's Eddie. Likewise, Rudolph Walker's chance to retaliate to a racist in ways that Afro-Caribbeans simply couldn't in the 1970s, frees his performance tremendously and ensures that, theoretically, he's representing his character's stubbornness and refusal to be beaten, not the suffering of his race.

Though it was written with the idea of examining racial conflict within the confines of a comedy, *Love Thy Neighbour*'s attempt at race relations would inevitably end up uneven, despite the fact that the Reynolds family always ended up with another minor victory, with even Eddie's wife Joan on their side. The point of the conflict wasn't that Eddie was racist per se – we never saw Barbie sobbing because of the abuse she and her husband suffered. They disliked Eddie because he was boorish, lazy and generally obnoxious and his racism was just one example of the many ways these traits manifested themselves. But while the wives winced and looked apologetically at each other throughout Eddie's and Bill's sparring matches, we only have to listen to the studio audience's hearty and enthusiastic laughter following every use of the word 'Sambo' to know that any potential message inherent in the script had been lost. As far as they were concerned, the comedy – and therefore the power – of the series was always on Eddie's side.

We pride ourselves on being a much more sophisticated audience today. When ***The League of Gentlemen*** or the ***Little Britain*** guys black up, the comedy comes from their confidence that we *know* it's racist; it's funny because it's wrong. With *Love Thy Neighbour*'s audience, we're not convinced that for them the comedy isn't in witnessing a Trotskyite trying to get one over on the 'Wog' next door. While plenty of sitcoms from this period are enjoying positive re-evaluation, it's highly unlikely *Love Thy Neighbour* will be one of them simply because too many of the punch lines rely on words that we're not comfortable hearing any more.

Trivia

Love Thy Neighbour spawned a short-lived American remake, a feature film version and, in 1980, a seven-part sequel – *Love Thy Neighbour in Australia* – with Jack Smethurst re-creating the charms of Eddie Booth Down Under.

Rudolph Walker now plays Patrick Trueman in ***EastEnders***, while Kate Williams currently appears in ***Family Affairs***.

Lovejoy

Comedy Drama | Witzend/McShane Productions for BBC One | episode duration 50 mins, plus 2 × 90-min specials | broadcast 10 Jan 1986–27 Dec 1993

Regular Cast

Ian McShane · *Lovejoy*
Dudley Sutton · *Tinker Dill*
Phyllis Logan · *Lady Jane Felsham*
Chris Jury · *Eric Catchpole*
Malcolm Tierney · *Charlie Gimbert*
Cassie Stuart · *Amanda Gimbert*
Caroline Langrishe · *Charlotte Cavendish*
Diane Parish · *Beth Taylor*

Creator Ian La Frenais, from the novels by Jonathan Gash **Producers** Tony Charles, Allan McKeown (executive), Robert Banks Stewart, Emma Hayter, Jo Wright, Paul Richmond, Colin Shindler, Richard Everitt **Writers** Various, including Ian La Frenais, Terry Hodgkinson, Francis Megahy, Dick Clement, Douglas Watkinson, Roger Marshall, Steve Coombes, Dave Robinson, Jeremy Paul, Geoff McQueen, Tony Marchant, John Milne, Andy de la Tour, Eric Deacon, John Goldsmith, Paul Alexander **Theme Music** Denis King

Dodgy dealings in East Anglia within the antiques market make for an unusual spin on both the 'lovable rogue' series and the investigation-based drama. Despite the casual appearance (white T-shirt, jeans and leather jacket), Lovejoy is a little classier than your usual wheeler-dealer and he has some equally classy support from a local Lady, Jane Felsham, and later Charlotte Cavendish, head of an auction house. He's clumsily assisted by his apprentice Eric, the well-meaning Tinker and, when Eric leaves, the young but level-headed Beth. As much as Lovejoy has an eye for a bargain, his business rival Charlie Gimbert knows how to pull a few fast ones to ensure that the bargains are all in his favour.

Ian La Frenais developed the series for television, creating the interesting narrative trick of having Lovejoy speak directly to the audience. After its first successful season, the series went off the air for five years while the production team negotiated to deviate from Jonathan Gash's stories and create their own (the hiatus was explained away in the story as being due to Lovejoy serving a prison sentence after being set up by person or persons unknown).

The Lucy Show

Sitcom | Desilu for CBS (shown on both BBC One and ITV) | episode duration 25 mins | broadcast 1 Oct 1962–16 Sep 1968 (USA)

Regular Cast

Lucille Ball · *Lucy Carmichael*
Vivian Vance · *Vivian Bagley*
Gale Gordon · *Theodore J. Mooney*
Candy Moore · *Chris Carmichael*
Jimmy Garrett · *Jerry Carmichael*
Ralph Hart · *Sherman Bagley*
Dick Martin · *Harry Connors*
Mary Jane Croft · *Mary Jane Lewis*
Charles Lane · *Mr Barnsdahl*

Creator Lucille Ball **Producers** Lucille Ball, Desi Arnaz, Gary Morton **Writers** Various **Theme Music** Wilbur Hatch, William Julian Davidson

For commentary, see I LOVE LUCY

The Mad Death

Drama | BBC One | episode duration 50 mins | broadcast 16–30 Jul 1983

Cast
Richard Heffer · *Michael Hilli*
Barbara Kellerman · *Anne Maitland*
Richard Morant · *Johnny Dairy*
Brenda Bruce · *Mrs Stonecroft*
Debbi Blythe · *Jane Stoddard*
Paul Brooke · *Bob Nicol*
Ed Bishop · *Tom Siegler*
Valerie Holliman · *Norma Siegler*
Tom Watson · *Andrew Dowie*
Jimmy Logan · *Bill Stanton*
Jack McKenzie · *Fergus*
Léon Sinden · *James Galbraith*

Creator Nigel Slater **Producer** Bob McIntosh **Writer** Sean Hignett **Theme Music** Philip Sawyer

It begins when a cat infected with rabies is smuggled by her owner from France into Scotland. When the cat is knocked over by a car, its body is eaten by a fox, which is later found lying dazed on a roadside, where it's adopted by an American businessman. Then the man falls ill and dies of what doctors suspect to be rabies. Michael Hilliard is tasked with containing the outbreak, but even he cannot be certain just how far the disease has already spread.

First shown in 1983, *The Mad Death* remains one of the single most unsettling dramas produced in the UK. Playing on public paranoia over Britain's integration with Europe, its three episodes looked at what might happen in the event of a rabies epidemic on our shores. The stand-out moment comes in the second episode where an infected dog runs amok in a shopping centre, although the feral fox at the beginning and the culling in the finale provide a few effective scares. Brenda Bruce excels as a fanatical collector of stray dogs. The only downside is a pretty uninvolving love triangle that never seems to amount to much.

Maelstrom

Drama | BBC/Gryphon Productions for BBC One | episode duration 50 mins | broadcast 5 Feb–12 Mar 1985

Principal Cast
Tusse Silberg · *Catherine Durell*
David Beames · *Anders Bjørnson*
Susan Gilmore · *Anna Marie Jordahl*
Christopher Scoular · *Lars Nilsen*
Edita Brychta · *Ingrid Nilsen*
Ann Todd · *Astrid Linderman*
John Abineri · *Olav Tunheim*
Trevor Baxter · *Dr Albrigtsen*
Thane Bettany · *Mr Tovan*
Marisa Campbell · *Freya*
Paul Darrow · *Oliver Bridewell*
Thomasine Heiner · *Fru Tovan*
Lorna Lewis · *Liv Albrigtsen*
Alan MacNaughtan · *Professor Solberg*
John Rowe · *Stoddard*
Peter Tuddenham · *Bjarne Langva*
Shelagh Wilcocks · *Gerda*

Creator/Writer Michael J. Bird **Producer** Vere Lorrimer **Theme Music** Johnny Pearson

For Michael J. Bird's final BBC series, 1985's *Maelstrom*, he turned to the icy winds and grey skies of Norway as Tusse Silbery tried to solve the mystery of her vanished sister. Although not as well received as his earlier efforts (such as ***The Lotus Eaters, Who Pays The Ferryman?*** and ***The Dark Side of the Sun***), *Maelstrom* did provide us with one of television's most alarming images when actress Susan Gilmore (later to find fame in ***Howards' Way***) was found by Silberg surrounded by hundreds of disfigured dolls.

The nature of TV drama was changing in favour of more populist soaps (***EastEnders*** began transmission the night of *Maelstrom*'s third episode). Having been responsible for many psychological thrillers in the 1970s, Michael J. Bird parted company with the BBC after this series to work with Yorkshire Television for the very down-to-earth *The Winning Streak*, a poor-man's ***Dallas*** about the Savage family's dealings in the motor industry that lacked any of the exciting locales or mysteries of his earlier works. However, 1988's *West of Paradise*, a thriller set in the Seychelles and again created for YTV, was notable for reuniting director David Cunliffe and producer Michael Glynn, who'd both worked on *The Lotus Eaters* back in 1972. His final TV work was providing a dramatisation of Andrea Davidson's novel *Out of the Shadows*, which starred Charles Dance as a Scotland Yard detective investigating art theft in Athens. Bird died in May 2001.

Website
An authorised tribute site to Michael J. Bird can be found at birdland2.netfirms.com.

The Magic Roundabout

See pages 458–9

Magnum, P.I.

Action-Adventure | Belisarius/Glen A. Larson/Universal for CBS (shown on ITV) | episode duration 50–120 mins | broadcast 11 Dec 1980–1 May 1988

Principal Cast
Tom Selleck · *Thomas Magnum*
John Hillerman · *Jonathan Quayle Higgins III*
Roger E. Mosley · *Theodore 'TC' Calvin*

Larry Manetti · *Orville 'Rick' Wright*
Orson Welles · *Voice of Robin Masters*

Creators Donald P. Bellisario, Glen A. Larson **Producers** Donald P. Bellisario, Glen A. Larson, Chas. Floyd Johnson, Tom Selleck (executive), Gilbert M. Shilton, Rick Weaver, David Bellisario, John David, Walton Dornisch, Mark R. Schilz (associate), Tom Greene, J. Rickley Dumm, Douglas Green, Andrew Schneider, Joel Rogosin, Reuben Leder, Nick Thiel, Chris Abbott-Fish, Jay Huguely, Jill Sherman Donner, Jeri Taylor, Stephen A. Miller **Writers** Various, including Donald P. Bellisario, Glen A. Larson, Babs Greyhosky, Frank Lupo, Allan Cole, Chris Bunch, Craig Buck, Ken Pettus, Rogers Turrentine, Robert Hamilton, T. J. Miles **Theme Music** The first series had horrible music by Ian Freebairn-Smith that felt like it had been composed for another show entirely, but the more familiar theme came from Pete Carpenter and king of the American TV theme Mike Post.

Combining Raymond Chandler mysteries with a backdrop of sun and surf, *Magnum, P.I.* stepped in where ***Hawaii Five-O*** had left off (and, indeed, used many of the sets of its predecessor). Played by the charismatic Tom Selleck, Thomas Magnum was a Vietnam vet and private eye who accepted a position as a house sitter for eccentric millionaire author Robin Masters (played in voice-over only by Orson Welles no less!). With Mr Masters away all the time, the task of running the house fell to his snotty English butler, Higgins, who openly displays his dislike for Magnum's casual manner, Hawaiian shirts, misuse of his master's red Ferrari and general ability to attract trouble. Magnum was often helped in his investigations by old war buddies TC (who ran a helicopter hire company) and Rick (real name Orville) who was the proprietor of a Casablanca-style bar.

The series ran for eight seasons and made a star of Tom Selleck, who had missed out on playing Indiana Jones for Steven Spielberg because he was tied to the show. But he got his chance at cinema roles eventually, starring in *Three Men and a Baby* (1987) and its sequel, among many other films. He was also a semi-regular in the sitcom ***Friends***, playing Monica's 'older man' boyfriend Richard.

Magpie

Children's Magazine | Thames for ITV | episode duration 25–40 mins | broadcast 30 Jul 1968–6 Jun 1980

Cast
Pete Brady, Tony Bastable, Susan Stranks, Douglas Rae, Mick Robertson, Jenny Hanley, Tommy Boyd · *Presenters*

Creator Susan Turner **Producers** Lewis Rudd (executive), Sue Turner, Tony Bastable, David Hodgson, Randal Beattie, Tim Jones, Leslie Burgess **Theme Music** The Murgatroid Band (actually members of The Spencer Davis Group), providing yet another groovy ITV theme tune: 'One for sorrow, Two for joy/Three for a girl and Four for a boy/Five for silver, Six for Gold/Seven for a story never to be told.'

When ITV decided to muscle in on ***Blue Peter***'s weekday magazine programme for children, they were at least honest enough to give their version a name that acknowledged a degree of theft. *Magpie* was one of a number of new programmes shown on Thames' first day of transmission. To begin with, it was a once-weekly 40-minute affair, though within six months it switched to two 25-minute editions, like its BBC rival – though never on the same days.

They had three presenters, a lady and two chaps, they showed kids how to recycle household crap into play items and even raised money for charity. The difference though was in the attitudes. *Blue Peter* was respectable, middle-class and with the full weight of those traditional BBC values on its shoulders. *Magpie* had Susan Stranks (and later Jenny Hanley) running around in a T-shirt without the support of a bra. It also had Mick Robertson, who looked like a footballer and (we suspected) had the home phone numbers for the Bay City Rollers and Marc Bolan. They also had badges on *Magpie* and not just one – there were loads to collect, one of each of the magpies listed in the song, awarded for different endeavours, like swimming or being really brave while in hospital. The only unsexy thing about the show really was their magpie mascot, a particularly lardy bird called Murgatroyd, about as aerodynamic as a cushion.

Magpie was plainly on an even smaller budget than even the very low-tech *Blue Peter*, but they didn't seem to care. While the BBC visual effects department cobbled together a flashing totaliser for their appeals, *Magpie* just stuck a line of tape around the walls of Studio 3 Teddington Lock, Middlesex, and when they ran out of walls they carried on down the corridors outside until they ended up in Thames TV's reception.

Accused of aiming to be 'all things to everyone' by Thames head of children's programmes, John Hambley, *Magpie* came to an end in 1980. Susan Stranks went on to present the potty pre-school show *Paper Play* alongside woollen spiders Itsy and Bitsy and plenty of Copydex glue, while late-comer Tommy Boyd headed Saturday Morning show *The Wide Awake Club* for TV AM before becoming an in-vision continuity announcer on Children's ITV in the late Eighties.

Maid Marian and Her Merry Men

Children's Comedy | BBC One | episode duration 25 mins | broadcast 16 Nov 1989–11 Apr 1995

Regular Cast
Tony Robinson · *The Sheriff*
Kate Lonergan · *Marian*
Wayne Morris · *Robin*
Forbes Collins · *King John*
Danny John-Jules · *Barrington*
Howard Lew Lewis · *Rabies*
Mike Edmonds · *Little Ron*
Continued on page 460

The Magic Roundabout

It's clearly not 'time for bed' yet in the magic garden …

If we were to tell you that this beloved show started out as the story of how an old man procured young children for his magical fairground ride, courtesy of a Jack-in-the-box that entrapped the kiddies by turning into a balloon, you'd probably think we'd been watching a Stephen King mini series or a Chris Morris comedy by mistake. But *The Magic Roundabout* was the product of a more innocent time, where such events would not be thought of as worrying by anyone, when a hippy rabbit could speak of peace and love without being thought of as a stoner, and where a dog with a love for sugar cubes would be suspected of neither diabetes nor drug addiction. Sorry to spoil the fun, but *The Magic Roundabout* wasn't 'trippy'. It really was as simple as it looked. Like ***Captain Pugwash***, *The Magic Roundabout*'s reputation has been much maligned over the years.

Serge Danot's original animated TV show, *Le Manège enchanté*, introduced French children to Père Pivoine, the owner of an abandoned carousel. A strange springy creature called Zebulon offered to help Pivoine fix the roundabout, restore its magic and find children to ride the carousel horses; eventually a little girl called Margotte came to visit. In the enchanted world of the carousel, Margotte met a laid-back rabbit called Flappy, a snail called Amboise, a cow called Azalée and a nosey dog called Pollux, who followed Margotte into the Magic Garden.

A huge success in France, the show caught the eye of the head of family programmes at the BBC, Doreen Stephens, who decided to buy the rights for British viewing. Responsibility for making the French production suitable for English-speaking viewers fell to ***Play School*** producer Joy Whitby, who in turn passed it to Eric Thompson, an actor and performer already familiar to *Play School* viewers as a presenter. Thompson was initially hired to provide the narration, but he was so unimpressed by the simplistic translations provided for him that he asked to be allowed to rewrite the scripts himself. Having viewed each episode without its soundtrack, he came back with what were completely original stories inspired by the action and that had little relation to the original scripts. Thompson even reinterpreted the characters and changed their names. Père Pivoine emerged as Mr Rusty, Margotte became Florence, Zebulon was renamed Zebedee, and although he remained responsible for bringing Florence to and from the Magic Garden as in the original programme, he also acquired a catchphrase that became synonymous with the show – 'Time for bed' (again, let us stress, these were innocent times; the characters were simply sleepy). The snail was renamed Brian, the cow Ermintrude and the hairy dog was crowned Dougal. Thompson also ensured that there were elements that the grown-ups would enjoy, references to contemporary culture – such as pop groups or politicians of the day – that were above the heads of your average five-year-old. Few children would recognise that Thompson voiced Dougal to sound very like Tony Hancock, while changing Flappy the rabbit's name to Dylan was a nod to American folk singer Bob Dylan. *Le Manège enchanté*'s theme tune, a rather jaunty organ track with an adult male and young child singing, was also ditched in favour of the more pacey instrumental organ piece we know and love.

British viewers had never seen anything like it. While the BBC had hoped people would like their reworking of Danot's concept, they had no idea its success would become quite so massive. Scheduled in the five minutes before the 6 o'clock *News*, *The Magic Roundabout* began pulling in as many as 8 million viewers, nearly double that for any other show ostensibly just for children. When the Beeb shifted the show back an hour to join the rest of their children's programming, the howls of protest from adults across the country made them quickly reconsider their decision.

The feature film *Pollux et le chat bleu* (1970) was also adapted by Thompson for UK audiences. Watching *Dougal and the Blue Cat* was the first time many fans were able to experience the Magic Garden in its full-colour glory. It co-starred Fenella Fielding as the Blue Queen and introduced Buxton, the Derbyshire-accented cat.

Though Serge Danot ceased production of *Le Manège enchanté* in 1971, there was sufficient a backlog of episodes for Eric Thompson to continue until 1977. The ongoing story of the original batch of 39 episodes had long been dropped in favour of self-contained stories that could be shown in any order and so, theoretically, the series could exist on reruns for ever. However, a couple of Thompson's episodes were rejected by the BBC – and not for the drug-related reasons some might expect. One saw Dougal hiding in a fridge, another involved fireworks – definitely not activities the BBC wanted to be seen encouraging children to copy. One additional *Roundabout*-related programme of note was a Christmas special of ***The Goodies*** – 'Goodies Rule OK' – which saw Graeme, Bill and Tim terrorised by giant versions of Zebedee and Dougal.

Eric Thompson died in 1982, but in 1990 Nigel Planer took on the mantle of providing stories and narration for episodes bought by Channel 4 that, for some reason, Thompson hadn't taken on. Broadcast on 2 January 1992, Planer's stories were impressively close to those we all grew up with, and for a new generation of children – and parents – Dougal and his friends were born again.

Animation
Danot Films/BBC One
Episode Duration: 15 mins
Broadcast: 18 Oct 1965–12 Feb 1994

Cast
Eric Thompson, Nigel Planer · *Narrator*

Creator/Producer Serge Danot

Writers Eric Thompson, Nigel Planer

Theme Music Alain Legrand

TRIVIA

The children seen riding the Magic Roundabout with Florence are called Basil, Paul and Rosalie.

In 2005, a computer-generated movie combined Thompson's characters with the multi-voice cast of the French originals as Tom Baker, Ray Winstone and Bill Nighy joined Ian McKellen (Zebedee), Robbie Williams (Dougal) and Kylie Minogue (Florence) in an all-new adventure. It wasn't *The Magic Roundabout* we knew and loved, but then again, that's probably what the French said back in 1965 . . .

Mark Billingham · *Gary*
David Lloyd · *Graeme*
Hilary Mason · *Gladys*
Robin Chandler · *Snooker*
Ramsay Gilderdale · *Guy of Gisborne*

Creator/Writer Tony Robinson **Producer** Richard Callanan **Theme Music** Nicholas Russell-Pavier, David Chilton

It comes to something when after years of seeing the same old lies trotted out in endless feature films and serious adult drama series, the truth about the Robin Hood legend has to be uncovered in a children's comedy. But that's exactly what happened in *Maid Marian and Her Merry Men*, in which we found out the cold hard truth about the so-called 'hero' Robin, who, in fact, turned out to be a rather effete tailor from London, and not from Loxley after all. It was, of course, Maid Marian who led the group of outlaws in Sherwood Forest, her guts and determination more than making up for their general lack of brains and bravery. Marian's troops included cool black rapper Barrington, the extremely dim Rabies and Ron, who in reality was very little indeed. Of course, Marian's nemesis was the sneaky, sly and totally underhand Sheriff of Nottingham, who together with his bumbling guards Gary and Graeme, never quite manages to capture the outlaws.

Written by and starring ***Blackadder***'s very own Baldrick, *Maid Marian and Her Merry Men* was an outstanding piece of children's television, with scripts and performances witty enough for it to have easily held its own as a 'proper' prime-time comedy series. There were 28 episodes of stupendously silly comedy, with episode titles giving a clue as to the neat way in which the scripts combined the Robin Hood legend with modern references: 'Much the Minimart Manager's Son', 'The Miracle of St Charlene', etc. Robinson enjoyed sterling support from his cast, including ***Red Dwarf***'s Danny John-Jules as the coolest Merry Man in history and Kate Lonergan as a charmingly eager Maid Marian.

Maigret (1960)

Crime Drama | BBC TV | episode duration 75/50 mins | broadcast 6 Dec 1959, 31 Oct 1960–24 Dec 1963, 9 May 1969

Regular Cast

Basil Sydney, Rupert Davies · *Inspector Maigret*
Neville Jason · *Inspector LaPointe*
Victor Lucas · *Torrence*
Helen Shingler · *Madame Maigret*
Ewen Solon · *Sergeant Lucas*

Producer Andrew Osborn **Writers** Giles Cooper, Margot Bennett, Vincent Tilsley, John Elliot, Donald Bull, from the stories by Georges Simenon **Theme Music** Ron Grainer's Maigret theme perfectly captured the flavour of old Paris, with the sound of an accordion playing in the title sequence as Maigret's face is dramatically illuminated by a struck match as he lights his pipe.

for commentary, see MAIGRET (1992)

Maigret (1992)

Crime Drama | Granada for ITV | episode duration 50 mins | broadcast 9 Feb 1992–18 Apr 1993

Cast

Michael Gambon · *Inspector Jules Maigret*
Ciaran Madden, Barbara Flynn · *Madame Maigret*
Geoffrey Hutchings · *Sergeant Lucas*
Jack Galloway · *Inspector Janvier*
James Larkin · *Inspector LaPointe*

Producer Jonathan Alwyn **Writers** Robin Chapman, William Humble, Douglas Livingstone, Alan Plater, from the stories by Georges Simenon **Theme Music** Nigel Hess

Georges Simenon's Commissioner Maigret is matched only by Sherlock Holmes in terms of international fame. In 1959, the BBC adapted Simenon's 1954 novel *Maigret and the Lost Life* as part of their *Saturday Night Theatre* series. Basil Sydney played the detective alongside Patrick Troughton, Henry Oscar, Mary Merrall and Andre Van Gyseghem. Produced by Campbell Logan with a script from Giles Cooper, it was deemed enough of a success to pursue to the idea of adapting further novels as part of a series. Basil Sydney proved unavailable due to ill-health, so for the series the lead role was taken by Rupert Davies. The great Charles Laughton had played Maigret in a 1950 film, *The Man on the Eiffel Tower*, and many French actors had attempted to play the part in films from the 1930s onwards as well as in a long-running French TV show that began in 1965. But, in Simenon's own words, Rupert Davies was 'the perfect Maigret'. In contrast to the violent, action-packed detectives shown in American imports, his Maigret was a cool, methodical and insightful chap, often choosing to interview his witnesses in the privacy of their own homes where he could get a feel for who they are, rather than in his own office. He was accompanied in his investigations by the more impetuous Sergeant Lucas, played by Geoffrey Hutchings.

When the BBC brought Maigret's investigations to an end in 1963, they softened the blow by commissioning *Detective*, a series of one-off plays about other great sleuths. The stories were adapted by Maigret's chief writer Giles Cooper and hosted by Rupert Davies. That series led to the BBC's 1965 series of ***Sherlock Holmes*** adaptations. Davies's final association with the part that made him a household name came in 1969 for a 90-minute TV play, *Maigret at Bay*. For nearly 20 years, Maigret became a star of radio in a series of sporadic productions from Radio 4. In 1976–7 and 1984, Maurice Denham played the part, with Michael Gough playing the narrator (as Georges Simenon). Bernard Hepton (***Secret Army***) and Barry Foster (***Van der Valk***) both separately starred in *Maigret* radio productions, and from 2002 Nicolas Le Provost became the great detective in an on-going run of adaptations.

In 1988, Richard Harris starred in a TV movie from Columbia Tri-Star and shown in the UK on ITV (9 Feb 1988). Four years later, Michael Gambon became the character's fourth and to date last TV incarnation in two lavish series filmed in Budapest (a much closer match to old Paris than Paris itself).

Malcolm in the Middle

Sitcom | Satin City/Regency for Fox (shown on Sky One/BBC Two) | episode duration 25 mins | broadcast 9 Jan 2000–present (USA)

Principal Cast
Frankie Muniz · *Malcolm*
Jane Kaczmarek · *Lois/Mom*
Bryan Cranston · *Hal/Dad*
Christopher Kennedy Masterson · *Francis*
Justin Berfield · *Reese*
Erik Per Sullivan · *Dewey*
Craig Lamar Taylor · *Stevie*
Emy Coligado · *Piama*

Creator Linwood Boomer **Producers** Linwood Boomer, David Richardson, Alan J. Higgins (executive), Gordon Wolf **Writers** Various, including Linwood Boomer, Alan J. Higgins, Michael Glouberman, Andrew Orenstein, Dan Kopelman, Alex Reid, Michael Borkow, Bob Stevens, Maggie Bandur, Pang-Ni Landrum, Ian Busch **Theme Music** They Might Be Giants (famous for 'Birdhouse in your Soul') recorded the theme tune, 'Boss of Me'. It reached No. 21 in Jan 2001.

Most children aspire to do better in their schoolwork and exams – for Malcolm, the reverse is true. He's a true child genius with an IQ of 165. As a result, much to his dismay, Malcolm has been put into a class full of nerds and swots. In fact, Malcolm's only real friend at school is wheelchair-bound Stevie, whose sharp brain and verbal dexterity shine out past his physical limitations. Things aren't much better at home either – with eldest son Francis away at military school, Malcolm is now the middle child, younger than his thuggish brother Reese, older than the dreamy, away-with-the-fairies Dewey. His parents Lois and Hal aren't much help either, with dad never much interested in anything that goes on at home and mum ruling the roost single-handedly.

Malcolm in the Middle is a wonderfully quirky, often downright surreal sitcom that takes a skew-wiff glance at a fairly average kind of family. At the heart of the show is a remarkable performance by young actor Frankie Muniz, a performer who's as precociously talented as the character he portrays. Equally marvellous is Jane Kaczmarek at Malcolm's domineering mother Lois, a role that could easily have proved one-dimensional and unsympathetic in the hands of a lesser actor.

Man About the House

Sitcom | Thames for ITV | episode duration 25 mins | broadcast 15 Aug 1973–7 Apr 1976

Regular Cast
Richard O'Sullivan · *Robin Tripp*
Paula Wilcox · *Chrissy Plummer*
Sally Thomsett · *Jo*
Yootha Joyce · *Mildred Roper*
Brian Murphy · *George Roper*

Creator/Writer Johnnie Mortimer, Brian Cooke **Producer** Peter Frazer-Jones **Theme Music** We challenge anybody to listen to the chirpy, upbeat theme to *Man About the House* without grinning from ear to ear. This definitive piece of 1970s feel-good music was written by Alan Hawkesworth, and underscored two equally fantastic title sequences (one showing Robin on his broken-down motorbike and Chrissy losing a shoe on the bus, the other featuring the three flatmates messing about on a boat).

When their female flatmate moves out of their three-bed apartment at 6 Myddleton Terrace, Earls Court, Chrissy and Jo throw a leaving party to wish her well. The next morning they ponder over how to find a new flatmate, but soon their prayers are answered in an unconventional way. They discover a man asleep in their bath, a remnant from the previous night's party. He is catering student Robin Tripp, and soon the girls agree to let Robin move in – on the strict understanding that there's to be no funny business. Chrissy and Jo's only problem then is trying to convince their landlords, the Ropers (who live in the ground-floor flat below them), that having a man about the house is going to be a good idea . . .

Man About the House is a true gem of 1970s comedy. Because it was shown on the rerun-phobic ITV network, it hasn't been seen by modern audiences anywhere near as many times as similar 1970s fare from the BBC, such as ***The Good Life*** or ***Porridge*** – and that's a crying shame. To modern viewers there will be a few wince-inducing moments of political incorrectness (such as when Chrissy explains to Robin how she persuaded George Roper into allowing a single man to share with two girls – 'I told 'im you were a puff!'), but there's never any maliciousness behind the humour as there is in ***Love Thy Neighbour*** or ***Mind Your Language***, for example. *Man About the House* was so popular with viewers that Thames managed to squeeze six seasons out of the show in less than three years.

Performances from the regular cast are top-notch, with particular praise due to Paula Wilcox as Chrissy. She shruggs off Robin's ham-fisted attempts at seduction so effortlessly that it is a joy to see precisely how she'll pop his balloon of over-confidence on the next occasion he tries to flirt with her. Writers Cooke and Mortimer knew that they had assembled the perfect ensemble of characters, and so when ideas for *Man About the House* began to diminish,

they span three of the five regulars off into two distinct series – the Ropers (who had begun the show very much as supporting characters and rapidly become the most popular) moved to suburbia in ***George and Mildred*** and Robin graduated from catering college and opened up his own restaurant in ***Robin's Nest***. In common with most sitcoms of the period, *Man About the House* enjoyed a cinema adaptation. Made in 1974 by the ailing Hammer organisation, it's one of the best of its kind, boasting guest appearances from legendary comic stars like Arthur Lowe and Spike Milligan as well as the two protagonists of *Love Thy Neighbour*, Jack Smethurst and Rudolph Walker. *Man About the House* became an even bigger success in the USA, where the show was renamed *Three's Company* and ran for seven years. Like its parent show, *Three's Company* also span off two sequel shows – *The Ropers* (their version of *George and Mildred*) and *Three's a Crowd* (an adaptation of *Robin's Nest*).

A Man Called Ironside

Detective | Harbour Productions/Universal for NBC (shown on BBC One) | episode duration 50 mins, plus specials | broadcast 28 Mar 1967–16 Jan 1975, 4 May 1993 (USA)

Regular Cast
Raymond Burr · *Chief Robert Ironside*
Don Galloway · *DS Ed Brown*
Barbara Anderson · *Detective Eve Whitfield*
Don Mitchell · *Mark Sanger*
Elizabeth Baur · *Detective Fran Belding*
Gene Lyons · *Commissioner Dennis Randall*
Johnny Seven · *Lieutenant Carl Reese*
Joan Pringle · *Diana Sanger*

Creator Collier Young **Producers** Collier Young, Cy Chermak, Joel Rogosin, Frank Price (executive), Albert Aley, Douglas Benton, Norman Jolley, Paul Mason, Winston Miller, Lou Morheim, Jerry McAdams **Writers** Various, including Collier Young, Don Mankiewicz, Albert Aley, Francine Carroll, Cy Chermak, Lou Morheim **Theme Music** Monty Paich, Oliver Nelson

A police drama with an unusual concept, *A Man Called Ironside* (simply called *Ironside* when broadcast in its home territory of the USA) provided a meaty follow-up role for ***Perry Mason*** star Raymond Burr. San Francisco-based Chief of Detectives Robert Ironside has been a scourge in the side of criminals for a quarter of a century, when one day he's shot through the spine and paralysed from the waist downwards. Ironside confounds his colleagues when he asks Commissioner Randall that he be allowed to stay on the payroll in a consultative capacity. Unable to play the same kind of active role in investigations as he'd previously enjoyed, Ironside relies upon his colleagues Ed Brown and Eve Whitfield (later Detective Fran Belding) to do the legwork. He also takes on former hoodlum Mark Sanger as his personal assistant/driver/bodyguard.

Raymond Burr's portrayal of the wheelchair-bound detective was so utterly convincing that many viewers honestly believed that the actor had suffered some kind of spinal injury – thankfully his return to the role of *Perry Mason* in a revival of his old hit in the mid-1980s put paid to that misconceived idea. A rather traditional police drama, each episode would see the criminals caught and good triumph over evil, with no loose plot strands or ongoing storylines left dangling to confuse viewers.

The Man from U.N.C.L.E.

Action-Adventure | Arena Productions/MGM for NBC | episode duration 50 mins | broadcast 22 Sep 1964–15 Jan 1968

Regular Cast
Robert Vaughn · *Napoleon Solo*
David McCallum · *Illya Kuryakin*
Leo G. Carroll · *Alexander Waverly*
Barbara Moore · *Lisa Rogers*

Creators Norman Felton (with Ian Fleming and Sam Rolfe) **Producers** Norman Felton (executive), Joseph Calvelli, George Lehr, Irv Pearlberg (associate), Boris Ingster, Mort Abrahams, Sam Rolfe, Robert Foshko, David Victor, Anthony Spinner **Writers** Various, including Sam Rolfe, Harold Jack Bloom, Alan Cailou, Alvin Sapinsley, Dick Nelson, Peter Allan Fields, Robert Hill, Mark Weingart, Henry Slesar, Harlan Ellison, Joseph C. Cavella, Robert E. Thompson, Jack Turley **Theme Music** Jerry Goldsmith

Spies were big business in the 1960s, and not just on the big screen. The Profumo affair and Kim Philby's defection to Russia mirrored the public's fascination for more glamorous fictional spies like James Bond. On TV, viewers were captivated by the activities of the United Network Command for Law Enforcement and their agents, the suave Napoleon Solo and his cool Russian colleague Illya Kuryakin. Every agency needs its opposite, and while James Bond faced SMERSH in the films (and SMERSH in the books), Napoleon Solo was forced to endure THRUSH. Sorry, that acronym was never explained in the series.

The Man from U.N.C.L.E. came from producer Norman Felton's desire to make a TV show like Alfred Hitchcock's 1959 thriller *North by Northwest*, in which Cary Grant had played an innocent man on the run for a murder he didn't commit and fleeing a group of gangsters who have mistaken him for a spy. Felton turned to James Bond author Ian Fleming, who gave him the name of the lead character, Napoleon Solo (a name that Fleming had used in his novel *Goldfinger*). But with Fleming tied to the Bond movies, his involvement was cut short. Felton instead turned to writer Sam Rolfe, who came up with the idea of U.N.C.L.E. – an international organisation dedicated to preserving peace that wasn't tied to one government. He also suggested that the innocent man from *North by Northwest* might be a good role for the guest star of the week to take on, so that each episode would see their heroes working alongside a fresh face.

Though Robert Vaughn was the show's star, it was David McCallum who received the most attention from the fans – something the producers exploited by organising tours and public appearances. Extending the show's appeal further was spin-off series, *The Girl From U.N.C.L.E.* (13 Sep 1966–29 Aug 1967, 29 episodes). It starred Stefanie Powers as April Dancer, with Leo G. Carroll reprising the role of *U.N.C.L.E.* boss Alexander Waverly.

With sillier affairs like ***Get Smart*** and ***Batman*** influencing the direction of the show, viewers began to lose interest; few of them stuck around to notice the return to serious thriller action for the show's fourth and final year. Inevitably, the men from U.N.C.L.E. returned for a reunion movie in the 1980s – snappily titled *The Return of the Man from U.N.C.L.E.* – though it remains a one-off largely thanks to a lack of interest on the part of its original stars.

Man in a Suitcase

Detective | ITC/ATV for ITV | episode duration 50 mins | broadcast 27 Sep 1967–17 Apr 1968

Regular Cast
Richard Bradford · *McGill*

Creators Dennis Spooner, Richard Harris **Producer** Sidney Cole
Writers Various, including Wilfred Greatorex, Roger Parkes, Kevin Laffan, Bernie Cooper, Francis Megahy, Jan Read, Vincent Tilsley
Theme Music Ron Grainer composed the jaunty, dynamic theme that was so good Chris Evans nicked it for the theme tune to ***TFI Friday*** in the late 1990s.

McGill (known to his few friends as Mac) was a successful officer in the CIA until one day he was framed for the crime of failing to stop an American scientist from defecting to the Soviet Union. As this offence was so serious, McGill was fired from the Agency and travelled to Europe – partly to make a living for himself as a private investigator, partly to work out exactly who it was that set him up and clear his name. Living out of just one suitcase (containing little more than a gun and a few spare pairs of undies), McGill travels across Europe, happily working for anyone who will cough up his fee of $500 a day (plus expenses, naturally).

Yet another one of those seemingly endless ITC action-adventure series from the late 1960s (see also ***The Prisoner, Randall and Hopkirk (Deceased)*** and ***The Champions***), *Man in a Suitcase* was rather more serious and po-faced than many of its stablemates. Sharing much in common (in terms of plot and locales, anyway) with Roger Moore's ***The Saint***, *Man in a Suitcase* ditched the camp and sophisticated lead character and settled on a cynical, sneery performance from Richard Bradford that was clearly inspired by Marlon Brando's oeuvre. With a cigarette permanently in hand, McGill's exploits were gritty and quite realistic – so much so that in several episodes there was no happy ending, with our hero getting a good beating or seeing his friends or employers meet unpleasant demises. Blessed with fine direction, scripts and a distinctive and charismatic central performance, *Man in a Suitcase* is one of the most underrated shows of the 1960s.

Marion and Geoff

Sitcom | Baby Cow Productions for BBC Two | episode duration 10–30 mins | broadcast 26 Sep 2000–5 Mar 2003, 3 Sep 2001

Regular Cast
Rob Brydon · *Keith Barratt*
Tracy-Ann Oberman · *Marion Barratt*
Steve Coogan · *Geoff*
Mary Healey · *Edie*
Tim Wylton · *Neville*
Mark Benton · *Euros*

Producers Steve Coogan, Henry Normal (executive), Hugo Blick
Writers Hugo Blick, Rob Brydon

Taxi driver Keith Barratt is a cheerful chappy, the kind of bloke who's able to see the positive side of almost any disaster that befalls him. And to be perfectly honest, that's quite a lot of disaster – his wife Marion has walked out, taking their two children Rhys and Alun with her, and moved in with her work colleague Geoff. However Keith doesn't take this news personally – instead he tries his best to understand the reasons why Marion left him and to make friends with her new boyfriend. Even when Marion turns his kids against him, Keith manages to rationalise their vile behaviour, hoping that they'll get over it soon and putting their unpleasantness down to the trauma of being part of a broken home. As time goes by, however, it becomes clear that Keith's positivity may simply be just his way of coping with the bleakness in his life.

Marion and Geoff began life as a series of ten ten-minute solo monologues, all starring Welsh actor Rob Brydon as the unfortunate Keith. It crept onto the TV schedules with hardly any fanfare, but the taut scripts and beautifully underplayed performance soon grabbed a keen audience of fans. A second series expanded the episodes to 30 minutes, but still maintained the dramatic monologue format, showing Keith in his new role as chauffeur to a loathsome wealthy American family. In between the two seasons, viewers were treated to the one-off special episode 'A Small Summer Party', which filled in a lot of the back-story. With a full cast of actors playing the roles of Marion, Geoff, their friends and neighbours, this cringe-making episode showed – through the conceit of 'home video camera footage' – the final disintegration of Keith and Marion's relationship while they were throwing a party at their home. Taking comedy way beyond the realm of 'dark' and 'uncomfortable' viewing, *Marion and Geoff* was often so painful to watch that it stopped being funny. Thankfully, the top-quality scripts from Rob Brydon and Hugo Blick always managed to raise more than a few smiles in between the psychological hand-wringing.

(The) Marriage Lines

Sitcom | BBC One | episode duration 25–30 mins | broadcast 16 Aug 1963–3 Jun 1966

Regular Cast

Richard Briers · *George Starling*
Prunella Scales · *Kate Starling*
Edward de Souza · *Miles*
Ronald Hines · *Peter*
Christine Finn · *Norah*
Dorothy Black · *Kate's Mother*
Diana King · *George's Mother*
Geoffrey Sumner · *George's Father*

Creator/Writer Richard Waring **Producers** Graeme Muir, Robin Nash

The Marriage Lines (which dropped the definite article after the first season) was subtitled 'A Quizzical Look at the Early Days of Married Life'. The first episode begins with newlyweds George and Kate Starling arriving back home after their honeymoon, only to discover that George has lost the key to his flat. A series of entirely predictable farcical encounters then take place, with the happy couple being mistaken for burglars, having no change to ring their friends to help them out, then being dragged into a party being held by their next-door neighbours. A typical plotline for an archetypal 'safe' sitcom that spent much of its time dwelling on such lofty matters as George's desire to spend more time down the pub with his single mates, and Kate's growing irritation with being stuck at home.

Written by Waring with the youthful Richard Briers specifically in mind (they had previously worked together in 1962 on the short-lived legal sitcom *Brothers in Law*), *Marriage Lines* is very much a product of its times – a family-friendly sitcom that never pushed back any boundaries, but which was enjoyed by many millions of viewers. Indeed, the programme was so popular that new short sketches featuring the Starlings were included in the *Christmas Night with the Stars* specials in 1963 and 1964.

Kate and George survived money worries, jealousy and all of those other minor irritants that get in the way of a harmonious relationship, until the newlyweds were blessed with a daughter Helen in the third season. Writer Richard Waring (who would go on to write for such programmes as ***Robin's Nest*** and ***...And Mother Makes Three***) had planned to finish the series at the end of the fourth season, and sent the family abroad when George got a job in Lagos. However, a recommission for a fifth season saw the Starlings return to the UK for a final run of seven episodes, culminating in the birth of a second child.

Married . . . with Children

Comedy | Embassy Television for Fox (shown on ITV) | episode duration 25 mins | broadcast 5 Apr 1987–9 Jun 1997 (USA)

Regular Cast

Ed O'Neill · *Al Bundy*
Katey Sagal · *Peggy Wanker Bundy*
Christina Applegate · *Kelly Bundy*
David Faustino · *Bud Bundy*
Amanda Bearse · *Marcy Rhoades D'Arcy*
David Garrison · *Steve Rhoades*
Ted McGinley · *Jefferson D'Arcy*

Creators Ron Leavitt, Michael G. Moye **Producers** Barbara Blachut Cramer, Harriette Regan, Kevin Curran; Ellen L. Fogle, Kim Weiskopf, Ralph R. Farquhar (supervising), Katherine Green, Kim Weiskopf, Michael G. Moye, Pamela Eells, Richard Gurman, Ron Leavitt (executive) **Writers** Many dozens, including Ron Leavitt, Michael G. Moye, Amanda Bearse **Theme Music** 'Love and Marriage' by Sammy Cahn and Jimmy Van Heusen, performed by Frank Sinatra

When a programme is put into development with the working title 'Not the Cosbys', you do tend to get the general gist of the type of show that *Married . . . with Children* was created to satirise. For 11 seasons and an astonishing 260 episodes, *Married. . . with Children* outraged conservative viewers with its constant references to bodily functions, sex and slovenly behaviour and its determined effort to undermine American family values.

Al Bundy (named after the famous serial killer Ted?) is a man who has constantly been disappointed with life. After a brief moment of local fame in his youth, when he played American Football, nothing seems to have gone right for him, now reduced to working as a ladies' shoe salesman. His wife Peg is a randy white-trash chain-smoker with zero skills in the kitchen and no desire to either get a job or keep her house in order; daughter Kelly is a brain-dead slut with a new boyfriend in town every few days; and son Bud is controlled by his hormones so much that he never manages to snag a girlfriend no matter how hard he tries. Even the family dog Buck rejected the standard all-American work ethic.

Next-door neighbours Marcie and Steve were the complete antithesis of the Bundys, high-achieving career-minded newlyweds with everything to look forward to. That optimism lasted until the fourth series when Steve (David Garrison) left the show, to be replaced as Marcie's doormat by eternal series new-boy Ted McGinley.

Initially scheduled as a late-night filler programme for ITV regions to broadcast as they saw fit, *Married. . . with Children* became so successful that a British adaptation, *Married for Life*, was commissioned. Russ Abbott was cast in the role of shoe salesman Ted Butler, and future Oscar nominee Hugh Bonneville appeared as next-door neighbour Steve Hollingsworth. Like so many British

adaptations of US successes, *Married for Life* was quickly dropped after just seven episodes.

Extremely vulgar and exceptionally funny, *Married . . . with Children* managed to shatter many of the boundaries associated with tired and clichéd American sitcoms. Without *Married. . . . with Children*, the sitcom genre would have stayed safe and predictable. Thankfully, we were blessed with over a decade's worth of vile innuendo and politically incorrect behaviour, some of which fortunately flew straight over the heads of most American viewers. In particular, Peggy's maiden name (as shown in the credits above) certainly didn't raise as many eyebrows in the USA as it did here . . .

Martin Chuzzlewit

Drama | BBC One | episode duration 55 mins | broadcast 7 Nov–12 Dec 1994

Principal Cast
Ben Walden · *Young Martin*
Paul Scofield · *Old Martin Chuzzlewit, Anthony Chuzzlewit*
Pauline Turner · *Mary Graham*
Pete Postlethwaite · *Tigg Montague*
Tom Wilkinson · *Seth Pecksniff*
Julia Sawalha · *Mercy Pecksniff*
Roger Ashton-Griffiths · *George Chuzzlewit*
Emma Chambers · *Charity Pecksniff*
Keith Allen · *Jonas Chuzzlewit*
Lynda Bellingham · *Mrs Lupin*
Steve Nicolson · *Mark Tapley*
Cyril Shaps · *Mr Fips*
Joan Sims · *Betsy Prig*
Elizabeth Spriggs · *Mrs Gamp*
Graham Stark · *Nadgett*
Maggie Steed · *Mrs Todgers*
Julian Fellowes · *Dr Jobling*
Peter-Hugo Daly · *Chevy Slyme*
Jenny Tomasin · *Maidservant*
John Mills · *Mr Chuffey*
Philip Franks · *Tom Pinch*
Sam Kelly · *Mr Mould*
Joanna Kirkland · *Georgina Jones*
Janet Lees-Price · *Mrs Jones*

Producers Michael Wearing, Rebecca Eaton (executive), Chris Parr **Writer** David Lodge, from the novel by Charles Dickens **Theme Music** Geoffrey Burgon

Where there's a will there's a way, goes the old saying. Due to the machinations of his seemingly many 'close relatives', Old Mr Chuzzlewit has come across them all. There are nephews and nieces, cousins and second cousins, and cousins so far removed they are off the family tree altogether. They each think they are perfectly entitled to his money. These relatives, however tenuous their kinship, sit outside Old Mr Chuzzlewit's room, day after day, waiting for him to die.

Mr Chuzzlewit's grandson, Young Martin, has been disinherited. The old man becomes aware that Young Martin is in love with his companion, Mary. As a consequence of this relationship, Mary's only benefit from the elder's will is to receive an annuity. By this action the older Mr Chuzzlewit intends to thwart any plans his grandson may have to gain a pecuniary advantage via his love for Mary. While Young Martin seeks his own salvation and fortune in America, the malevolent relatives and their supporters work their duplicitous schemes for their own ends to not only outwit each other but also bring about the death of the old man and thereby gaining access to his vast fortune.

Though the BBC attempted their first adaptation of this Dickens classic in the form of a 13-part serial in 1964, their 1994 production is greatly enhanced by the sheer talent brought together – a cast any director would die for. Paul Schofield is superb playing the twin parts of Old Martin and his brother Anthony. Although no physical difference can be detected between them, the subtle variations of his speech immediately determines which is the good Chuzzlewit and which the bad. Philip Franks as Mr Tom Pinch is so believable that he is at once pitiable yet lovable, while the inspirational casting of Elizabeth Spriggs and Joan Sims as the nurses, hideously dirty, drunk and in constant competition for their charges, brings some much needed broad comedy into a richly layered tale.

Mary, Mungo and Midge

Animation | BBC Two | episode duration 15 mins | broadcast 7 Oct–30 Dec 1969

Voice Cast
Richard Baker · *Narrator*
Isabel Ryan · *Mary*

Creator/Writer Daphne Jones **Producer** John Ryan **Theme Music** Johnny Pearson

Mary, her dog Mungo and her pet mouse Midge live in the top apartment in a block of flats with Mary's parents. Mungo can be a grumpy old thing, so Midge often tries to soothe him by playing music on the flute (although he only knows one tune – 'Three Blind Mice').

Not every family lived in a house in the 1960s – some would be watching TV from one of the many hundreds of new tower blocks that were springing up around the country. It might be an obvious thing to say now, but very few TV shows for kids reflected this, with the tradition of 2.4 kids living in a semi-detached still very much the norm in TV land. That Mary's family lived in a nine-storey block of flats was an attempt to address this.

The 13-part series was quite a step away from John Ryan's previous projects, ***Captain Pugwash*** and *Sir Prancelot*, though it still consisted of the same sliding sections of card that was Ryan's 'house style'.

The Mary Tyler Moore Show

Sitcom | MTM for CBS (shown on BBC One) | episode duration 25 mins | broadcast 19 Sep 1970–19 Mar 1977

Regular Cast

Mary Tyler Moore · *Mary Richards*
Edward Asner · *Lou Grant*
Gavin MacLeod · *Murray Slaughter*
Valerie Harper · *Rhoda Morgenstern*
Ted Knight · *Ted Baxter*
Cloris Leachman · *Phyllis Lindstrom*
Lisa Gerritsen · *Bess Lindstrom*
John Amos · *Gordy Howard*
Nancy Walker · *Ida Morgenstern*
Joyce Bulifant · *Marie Slaughter*
Georgia Engel · *Georgette Franklin Baxter*
Betty White · *Sue Ann Nivens*

Creators James L. Brooks and Allan Burns **Producers** James L. Brooks, Allan Burns (executive), Budd Cherry, Michael Zinberg (associate), David Davis, Ed Weinberger, Stan Daniels **Writers** Various, including James L. Brooks, Allan Burns, Treva Silverman, Steve Pritzker, David Davis, Lorenzo Music, Martin Cohan, Susan Silver, Dick Clair, Jenna McMahon, Ed Weinberger, Elias Davis, David Pollock, Stan Daniels, David Lloyd, Bob Ellison, Les Charles, Glen Charles **Theme Music** 'Love Is All Around' by Sonny Curtis

When Mary Richards comes to Minneapolis after the break-up of a relationship, she applies for a job as a secretary in the newsroom at local TV station WJM-TV, only to be hired as an assistant producer by the irascible news editor Lou Grant. There, she quickly befriends the witty but unappreciated head writer Murray while steering clear of the brainless egomaniac anchorman Ted Baxter. Mary also finds herself a new home, courtesy of snobbish landlady Phyllis Lindstrom, only for a young New Yorker called Rhoda to claim that Mary's apartment is actually hers. Luckily, she and Mary soon become fast friends.

The Mary Tyler Moore Show functions not only a piece of well-crafted television but as a nexus point in American entertainment. With Tyler Moore stepping out from ***The Dick Van Dyke Show*** to form her own production company, she assembled a group of individuals who between them became the most influential team in American television: it spawned three spin-offs, sitcoms ***Rhoda*** and *Phyllis*, and hard-hitting drama ***Lou Grant***; Betty White went off to head *The Betty White Show* before joining ***The Golden Girls***; producer James L. Brooks brought us ***Taxi***, *The Tracey Ullman Show* and ***The Simpsons***; and Glen and Les Charles (who wrote an episode in the final season) went on to create ***Cheers*** and ***Frasier***.

The series came to an end after seven years with the staff of WJM-TV all given their notices and singing 'It's a Long, Long Way to Tipperary'. A 2000 TV movie called *Mary and Rhoda* reunited both the characters Mary Richards and Rhoda Morgenstern and the actresses, Mary Tyler Moore and Valerie Harper. Meanwhile, as well as the spin-offs listed above, Mary Tyler Moore's MTM went on to produce such hits as WKRP in Cincinnati, Newhart, Remington Steele, ***Hill Street Blues, St Elsewhere*** and *The Trials of Rosie O'Neill*.

If you're ever playing 'Six Degrees of Separation', odds are the link you're looking for is Mary Tyler Moore.

The Mary Whitehouse Experience

Comedy | Spitting Image Productions for BBC Two | episode duration 30 mins | broadcast 3 Oct 1990–6 Apr 1992

Principal Cast

Rob Newman, David Baddiel, Steve Punt, Hugh Dennis

Producer Marcus Mortimer **Creator/Writers** Rob Newman, David Baddiel, Steve Punt, Hugh Dennis **Theme Music** Simon Brint, Steve Brown

BBC Radio has proven to be a fertile breeding ground for successful comedy series over the years, with everything from ***The Day Today*** to ***Little Britain*** having started off life on the wireless. Another such example was *The Mary Whitehouse Experience*, an achingly cool sketch show that was, for about two years, one of the most overly quoted productions in the country. On Radio 1, the show had starred, among others, Mark Thomas and Jo Brand. On its transfer to BBC Two, however, Thomas and Brand were out and the show effectively became two double acts: student heartthrob Rob Newman and cynical David Baddiel, alongside writers and impressionists Steve Punt and Hugh Dennis – the programme felt like a breath of fresh air, the first of a new generation of comedians that had come along to brush aside the now-established 'alternative' comedians of the early 1980s. Sketches were fast-paced and breathless, and the performers often played up to the 'undergraduate' humour their critics accused them of. Indeed, naming a programme 'The Mary Whitehouse Experience' was a sure-fire way of raising the show's profile, with infamous clean-up TV campaigner Mary Whitehouse (and her supporters) guaranteed to tune in and complain about any programme that blatantly went out of its way to be controversial.

The series was a curious mash-up of styles, from ***Not the Nine O'Clock News*** to ***Harry Enfield's Television Programme***). Observational sketches and stand-up routines were combined with very few characters who would return week after week. Newman and Baddiel created the 'History Today' slot, in which two doddery old lecturers debated historical theories in depth only to descend to playground put-downs ('that's you, that is'); a bunch of aliens newly arrived on earth had the habit of pointing at objects and shouting their names out – 'Tree!', 'Car!', 'LickleBabyJesus!'; and the disgusting Mr Strange (Hugh Dennis), an anorak-clad freak with a fetish for drinking sour milk ('Milky milky!'). The only downside of

this approach is that with few particularly memorable or recognisable characters, there's little nostalgic warmth felt towards such a series – more a general sense that it must have been a good programme at the time.

Punt and Dennis still to this day occasionally collaborate together, while Newman and Baddiel went on to create *Newman and Baddiel in Pieces*, taking the popular 'History Today' segment from Mary Whitehouse with them. After a successful live tour, Rob Newman and David Baddiel parted company and Baddiel hooked up with his then-flatmate Frank Skinner to create *Fantasy Football League* and *Baddiel and Skinner Unplanned*, an improvised chat show.

M*A*S*H*

Comedy/Drama | 20th Century Fox for CBS (shown on BBC Two) | episode duration 25 mins | broadcast 17 Sep 1972–28 Feb 1983 (USA)

Cast

Alan Alda · *Captain Benjamin Franklin 'Hawkeye' Pierce*
Wayne Rogers · *Captain 'Trapper' John McIntyre*
Mike Farrell · *Captain B. J. Hunnicutt*
Loretta Swit · *Major Margaret 'Hotlips' Houlihan*
McLean Stevenson · *Colonel Henry Blake*
Harry Morgan · *Colonel Sherman T. Potter*
Larry Linville · *Major Frank Burns*
Gary Burghoff · *Corporal Walter 'Radar' O'Reilly*
David Ogden Stiers · *Major Charles Emerson Winchester III*
Jamie Farr · *Corporal/Sergeant Max Klinger*
William Christopher · *Captain Father Francis Mulcahey*

Creator Larry Gelbart, from the film *M*A*S*H** (1970), based on the book *M*A*S*H** by Richard Hooker (being the pen name of Dr Richard Hornberger) **Producers** Larry Gelbart, Gene Reynolds, Burt Metcalfe (executive), John Rappaprt, Thad Mumford **Writers** Various, including Larry Gelbart, Robert Klane, Laurence Marks, Alan Alda, Sid Dorfman, Linda Bloodworth, Jim Fritzell, Everett Greenbaum, Simon Muntner, Burt Prelutsky, Jay Folb, Gene Reynolds, Ken Levine, David Isaacs, Ronny Graham, Larry Balmagia, Dennis Koenig, Thad Mumford, Dan Wilcox, John Rappaport, Mike Farrell, David Pollock, Elias Davis, Karen L. Hall **Theme Music** Written by Mike Altman (son of Robert, who directed the movie) and Johnny Mandel, 'Theme from M*A*S*H* (Suicide is Painless)', performed by The MASH, reached No. 1 in the UK singles chart in May 1980, more than a decade after it was written. The Manic Street Preachers covered it in 1992, which reached No. 7, shortly before their lead singer went missing, presumed dead.

The Korean War ran from 25 June 1950 to 27 Jul 1953. The staff of the 4077 Mobile Army Surgical Hospital were on duty for nearly four times that long. The men and women of the 4077th M*A*S*H* (Mobile Army Surgical Hospital) unit battle to save the lives of the wounded servicemen choppered in from the front line, often working in a basic operating theatre for more than 24 hours straight. These brave souls survive the tedium of long days and nights through a mix of practical jokes, well mixed martinis and the occasional round of golf over a minefield. Hawkeye Pierce and Trapper John McIntyre are two brilliant surgeons who were drafted into the US army as captains and want to be sent home more than anything, regularly challenging the chain of command to see how far they can push. They are masters of the wisecrack, and their tent, fondly nicknamed 'The Swamp' is a focal point of their escapades. Colonel Henry Blake is their bumbling CO, backed up by the protocol obsessed Major Frank Burns and chief nurse, Major Margaret 'Hotlips' Houlihan. Keeping the whole unit from falling apart is the youthful Corporal O'Reilly, otherwise known as Radar.

*M*A*S*H** was based on the film of the same name, directed by Robert Altman, who has since claimed that his movie saved 20th Century Fox thanks to the subsequent success of the TV series. Larry Gelbart, who was tasked with writing the pilot, had the problem of how to adapt a film that was essentially about blood and sex into a palatable form for a prime-time TV audience. He wrote the pilot episode in two days while in London working for Marty Feldman, and he would stay with the series for four years.

The only cast member from the movie who took up regular residence in the 4077th when it started filming on the 20th Century Fox ranch in California was Gary Burghoff, who reprised the role of Radar. The rest of the cast were essentially upcoming but reasonably unknown actors. In the lead role of Hawkeye, Alan Alda would become a star the world over, and in the 11 years the series was on air, would win Emmy awards for acting, writing and directing, a unique achievement in the history of US broadcasting.

After three seasons, both Wayne Rogers and McLean Stevenson departed the 4077th, making way for two new characters – Mike Farrell as Captain B. J. Hunnicut, a new partner in crime for Hawkeye, and the regular army CO, Colonel Sherman Potter, played by US TV veteran Harry Morgan. Weathering the storm of the cast change, *M*A*S*H** continued, seemingly unstoppable. Frank Burns eventually left the unit in a straight jacket, replaced by the impeccably snobbish Major Charles Winchester. Radar would also return home, replaced in the clerks' office by Corporal Klinger, a semi-regular character who frequently wore a dress in an attempt to be declared insane and be sent home. It never worked. Taking care of the spiritual side of the unit's well-being (and more often than not, administer last rites to the young men who die in battle), was Father Francis Mulcahey.

With its place now firmly earned in broadcasting history (running for 11 years – seven more than the Korean War itself), it's hard to believe that *M*A*S*H** very nearly didn't make it past a first season. Languishing at the bottom of the US TV ratings, a timely intervention by the wife of CBS president who asked her husband to move her favourite show to a better time slot ensured this series, part sitcom, part wartime drama, would enter the TV hall of fame.

*M*A*S*H** started life as a sitcom, complete with

canned laughter, but as time went on, themes of a more hard-hitting nature came to the fore, although the laugh track remained, much to Gelbart's frustration. In the UK, the BBC transmitted the vast bulk of the series without the laugh track, requesting that Fox provide it with a canned laughter-free version.

The final episode of *M*A*S*H**, 'Goodbye, Farewell, Amen', was afforded a two-and-a-half-hour feature-length slot, and was a national event. More than 50 million homes tuned in for this TV movie, a record that went unchallenged for many years. Although the *M*A*S*H** family decided to quit while they were ahead in the ratings and quality stakes, the record audiences who had tuned in for the final episode convinced network CBS that they certainly had a need for the audience pulling power, and so *After M*A*S*H** was premiered soon after the 4077th bugged out for the last time. Harry Morgan, William Christopher and Jamie Farr were convinced to reprise their *M*A*S*H** roles, with the series following their characters' lives working in a civilian hospital Stateside. However, something didn't quite gel, and the show was cancelled after just two seasons.

*M*A*S*H** ended in 1984, the show's legacy as an icon of broadcasting was ensured in an exhibit in the Smithsonian Museum when the set of the Swamp was donated to the establishment. Reruns in syndication and on cable seem to have been scheduled for the next 50 years, and with the series finding new audiences all the time, the enjoyment of this rare example of TV brilliance is clearly far from painless.

Masterchef

Game Show | Union Pictures Productions for BBC One/Two | episode duration 30 mins, plus specials | broadcast 2 Jul 1990–3 Jul 2001, 22 Feb 2005–present (*Masterchef Goes Large*)

Regular Cast

Loyd Grossman, Gary Rhodes, John Torode, Greg Wallace · *Presenters*

Creator Franc Roddam **Producers** Richard Kalms, Bradley Adams (executive), Glynis Robertson (associate), Richard Bryan, Karen Ross **Theme Music** Richard G. Mitchell

An intriguing combination of game show, recipe programme and reality TV, *Masterchef* ran for more than ten years throughout the 1990s until a recent reinvention of the format brought it back to our screens with an increased emphasis on the reality section of the format.

Hosted by ***Through the Keyhole***'s curiously Midlantic-accented Loyd Grossman, each week *Masterchef* invites three contestants from one region of the UK into a TV studio fitted out with three colour-coded kitchens. Armed with just £10-worth of ingredients, the contestants have two and a half hours to prepare a three-course meal – starter, main course and dessert – under the glare of the studio lights and with cameras following their every move. Throughout the programme, Grossman and his special guests (normally a celebrity and a renowned chef) would chat to the contestants about their menu, ask them about the provenance of their ingredients, and generally have a bit of a natter to put them at their ease. Then, with time up, the tastings would begin, with Grossman and his guests emitting a series of oohs, aahs and sighs of appreciation. They would then retire to a separate room to 'cogitate, ruminate and digest' on whose overall menu was the best. The winner of each particular round would be invited to return to take part in semi-finals and then a grand final.

After having enjoyed reasonable success on BBC One for more than a decade, *Masterchef* moved over to BBC Two in 2001 and gained a new host in the form of TV chef Gary Rhodes. However, these changes didn't go down well with many viewers and the show was dropped after just one season. In 2005, the format was revived with *Masterchef Goes Large*, in which chefs Greg Wallace and John Torode supervised a large group of chef wannabes, putting them through a variety of different challenges in the hope of discovering the next great restaurant cook. The revived programme became a surprise hit for BBC Two, and further programmes are currently being planned.

Mastermind

Quiz Show | BBC One/Two | episode duration 30 mins | broadcast 11 Sep 1972–1 Sep 1997, 7 Jul 2003–present

Cast

Magnus Magnusson, John Humphrys · *Interrogators*

Creator Bill Wright **Producers** Bill Wright, Mary Craig, Roger Mackay, Peter Massey, David Mitchell, Penelope Cowell Doe, Pam Cavannagh, Naomi Dennison, Sally Evans **Theme Music** The utterly terrifying 'Approaching Menace' by Neil Richardson

Appearing on TV can be a petrifying experience at the best of times. The fear is doubled for a quiz show, where one wrong answer could mean humiliation back at work or in the pub. The ultimate test of nerve for over 30 years has been *Mastermind*, in which four contenders at a time are placed in a black leather chair to answer questions in the most intimidating of circumstances. The kind of mind that decided on that piece of music and that spot-lit black chair really understood the panic that can be experienced while being interrogated – the mind in question being that of former RAF gunner Bill Wright, who came up with the idea of the show from the standard answers to 'name, rank, number' that preceded interrogation from the Germans during World War Two. For the less life-threatening but no less petrifying *Mastermind*, those questions became: 'Name? Occupation? Chosen specialist subject?'

It was the first 'interrogator', Magnus Magnusson, who coined so many of the phrases we associate not just with *Mastermind* but quiz shows in general, such as saying 'pass' instead of 'dunno', or the firm statement 'I've

started, so I'll finish' when the buzzer signals the end of the round (sometimes followed by the reassuring '. . . and you may answer'). Each edition was recorded in a university or church hall somewhere in the UK (although the revived 2003 version of the programme was somewhat disappointingly recorded from a standard BBC Manchester studio). The first round contains two minutes of questions on the contestant's 'specialist subject', a notion that provided a clever sketch for ***The Two Ronnies*** ('answering the question before last') and a withering put-down for John Cleese as Basil Fawlty ('Specialist subject: the bleeding obvious. . . .'). The second half of the show, in which the contender with the lowest number of points so far goes first, is a two-minute general knowledge round. At the end, the person with the most correct answers is the winner; in the event of a tie, the number of passes each contender made is taken into account.

The very first question asked on the series, which was recorded at Liverpool University, was as follows: 'Picasso's *Guernica* was a protest about the bombing by Spanish planes of a village. What was the year when the event took place which inspired this painting?' Despite the fact that they were German – not Spanish – planes, print-maker Alan Whitehead got it right (1936). As an in-joke, that same question was the very last to be asked by Magnus Magnusson when the series came to an end in 1997.

The series was thought to be too highbrow for prime-time TV on its inception and so was relegated to a late-night slot. Fortunately a scheduling reshuffle placed it at a more family-friendly time, transforming it into the most highly regarded of British quiz shows. When the series was finally brought to an end in 1997, Magnus Magnusson got to choose the location, St Magnus's Cathedral in Orkney, and at the end of the contest he was presented with that demonic black chair.

Huw Evans was the first to step into Magnus's seat, presenting a *Mastermind International* competition between 1979 and 1983. When the regular TV series came to an end, it reappeared on Radio 4, fronted by Peter Snow for three years before Clive Anderson became the interrogator for a brief revival on the cable and satellite channel Discovery in 2001. Finally, after a 30th-anniversary special, the series returned as a regular fixture to BBC One and Two with John Humphrys asking the questions. Humphrys drew criticism for his rather more informal approach, interviewing contenders in between rounds. The question-setters too came under fire after it was revealed that contenders could now set specialist subjects on slightly more 'lowbrow' subjects such as television programmes (heaven forbid they should have *any* value) and pop acts. Humphrys is also the host of *Junior Mastermind* and even hosted the 2005 ***Doctor Who*** *Mastermind* special.

Trivia

The first ever Mastermind was 1972 champion Nancy Wilkinson, whose specialist subject in the final was 'The History of Music 1550–1900'. Kevin Ashman set the record for highest-ever score in 1995 when he racked up 41 points. Fred Housego became the most famous winner in 1980; a London cabbie, Housego later became a TV presenter. In 2004, Shaun Wallace became the 27th Mastermind champion – and the very first black winner. For the final, Shaun's specialist subject was 'FA Cup Finals since 1970'. Arfor Wyn Hughes became famous for scoring the lowest ever on his specialist subject, but the record for the lowest score is held by Gill Perry, who specialised in the TV series ***Babylon 5*** and scored just eight points overall during her appearance in 2004.

Masters of the Universe

See HE-MAN AND THE MASTERS OF THE UNIVERSE

Match of the Day

Sport | BBC Two/One | episode duration 45–120 mins | broadcast 22 Aug 1964–19 May 2001, 14 Aug 2004–present

Cast

Kenneth Wolstenholme, David Coleman, Jimmy Hill, Bob Wilson, Desmond Lynam, Gary Lineker, Ray Stubbs, Adrian Chiles · *Presenters*
Wally Barnes, John Motson, Barry Davies, Idwall Robling, Tony Gubba, Alan Parry, Gerald Sinstadt, Clive Tyldesley, John Champion · *Commentators*
Terry Venables, Alan Hansen, Trevor Brooking, Mark Lawrenson · *regular pundits*

Producers Various, including Niall Slone, Paul Armstrong (series editors), Phil Bigwood, Ian Finch, Paul McNamara **Theme Music** Barry Stoller, perfectly capturing the jollity of 1960s football matches. While it might sound a little old-fashioned now, it's become so closely linked with the game it really doesn't matter.

'Welcome to *Match of the Day*, the first of a weekly series coming to you every Saturday on BBC Two. As you can hear we're in Beatleville for this Liverpool versus Arsenal match.' So spoke Kenneth Wolstenholme introducing the first edition of a programme that became a national institution. Roger Hunt scores the first *Match of the Day* goal, though as Liverpool's all-time league-match goal-scorer with 245 to his name, it's not that surprising. The final score? Liverpool beat Arsenal 3–2 and went on to win the league title. Shown on BBC Two (broadcasting on 625-line format, allowing for clearer picture), only 20,000 viewers tuned in – less than half those who saw the game live from Liverpool's home ground Anfield. But the BBC persevered. Some clubs tried to bring the show down fearing it would affect ticket sales, but it returned in 1965 – admittedly two months after the season had begun, with conditions attached. It could only be broadcast after 10 p.m., and then only for 45 minutes.

On 20 August 1966, bolstered by England's win in the

World Cup (where Kenneth Wolstenholme had uttered the immortal words, 'They think it's all over'), *Match of the Day* moved to BBC One, where it remained for 35 years. In 1969, improvements in technology allowed the previously pre-recorded show to be broadcast live for the first time, while 1971 saw the arrival of the video-disc, a method of recording that allowed for slow-motion replays - which proved its worth almost straight away as it showed a West Bromwich Albion goal against Leeds to be offside.

Changes in the commentary box brought Jimmy Hill over from ITV and when he left after a record 15 years, his chair was taken by 'housewives' favourite' Des Lynam. Disaster struck in 2001 when ITV and Sky Sports outbid the BBC for the rights to screen league matches. On 19 May that year, *Match of the Day* came to an end. . . but not for long. On 14 August 2004, *Match of the Day* returned, accompanied by an extended commentary programme, MOTD2, which was screened on BBC Two, almost 40 years to the day that the channel that had first brought us the series.

Max Headroom

Comedy/Music (UK) Science Fiction (USA) | Lorimar/Chrysalis/Lakeside (shown on Channel 4) | episode duration 50 mins | broadcast 4 Apr 1985-5 May 1988

Regular Cast

Matt Frewer · *Max Headroom/Edison Carter*
Amanda Pays · *Theora Jones*
George Coe · *Ben Cheviot*
Chris Young · *Bryce Lynch*
William Morgan Sheppard · *Blank Reg*
Jeffrey Tambor · *Murray*
Concetta Tomei · *Blank Dominique*
Sharon Barr · *Lauren*
Hank Garrett · *Gene Ashwell*
Lee Wilkof · *Edwards*

Creators Peter Wagg, George Stone, Rocky Morton, Annabel Jankel **Producers UK**: Terry Ellis (executive), Peter Wagg, Chris Griffin **US**: Philip DeGuere, Peter Wagg (executive), Andrew Adelson (supervising), Steve Roberts, Brian E. Frankish **Writers UK**: Tim John, David Hansen **US**: Various, including Philip DeGuere, Howard Brookner, Martin Pasko, Steve Roberts, Dennis Rolfe, Joe Gannon, Adrian Hein, Rebecca Parr **Theme Music** Michael Hoenig

The character of Max Headroom is a pretty unique beast with a convoluted genesis and a number of different programme formats featuring the plastic-headed presenter. Max Headroom was first born in a Channel 4 1985 science fiction movie entitled *Max Headroom: 20 Minutes into the Future*. In this drama, set sometime in the not-too-distant future, an American TV reporter called Edison Carter (actor Matt Frewer) is involved in a motorcycle crash that leaves him on the verge of death. In order to stabilise his condition, Edison's personality and memories are downloaded into a computer, which, with the help of a whizz-kid named Bryce, promptly creates an artificial reality version of the poor chap. This computerised creation - nicknamed Max Headroom after the sign that was the final thing Edison saw before his crash - is a loud-mouthed, fast-talking arrogant creature and, of course, a ratings bonanza for Edison's TV network.

Although the pilot movie of *Max Headroom* was a critical success, it didn't really take off as a drama series - at least not initially. Realising that the character of Max had a huge amount of potential as a real-life TV presenter, Channel 4 execs gave him his own series the same year, *The Max Headroom Show*. Max would welcome viewers in his own inimitable style before introducing the latest pop videos - most of them blessed with a sarcastic comment of quip from the electronic host. Viewers were genuinely confused as to whether the digitised images of Max were entirely computer generated or whether (as was, in fact, the case) they were simply images of an actor pumped through a box of electronic gizmos.

With Max a huge cult star thanks to his own TV show, American executives suddenly became interested in him. In 1987, they created a full ongoing science fiction drama series about Max Headroom, re-using many of the cast from the original Channel 4 movie and slightly reworking the plot of the film for the pilot episode. Fourteen episodes were made in total, featuring some outstandingly good science fiction storylines and an impressive visual look on what was (for an American show) a fairly limited budget. Whether in a drama or presenting the latest Dire Straits video, Matt Frewer's inspired gurning and grinning as the 'perfect TV host' was a sublime treat.

Trivia

In 1986, Max released a record with The Art of Noise, 'Paranoimnia', which peaked at No. 12.

May to December

Sitcom | Cinema Verity for BBC One | episode duration 30 mins, plus 55-min special | broadcast 2 Apr 1989-27 May 1994

Principal Cast

Anton Rodgers · *Alec Callender*
Eve Matheson, Lesley Dunlop · *Zoe Angell*
Frances White · *Miss Flood/Mrs Tipple*
Paul Venables · *Jamie Callender*
Rebecca Lacey · *Hilary*
Clive Francis · *Miles Henty*
Ashley Jensen · *Rosie MacConnachy*
Carolyn Pickles · *Simone*
Kate Williams · *Dot Burgess*
Ronnie Stevens · *Mr Burgess*
Chrissie Cotterill · *Debbie Burgess*

Creator Paul A Mendelson **Producers** Verity Lambert (executive), Sydney Lotterby, Sharon Bloom **Writers** Paul A. Mendelson, Geoff Deane, Paul Minett, Brian Levenson **Theme Music** 'September Song' by Kurt Weill and Maxwell Anderson

Love blossoms between 26-year-old PE teacher Zoe Angell and her 53-year-old solicitor Alec Callender when she visits Semple, Callender and Henty to finalise plans for her divorce. Despite the big age gap between them, the two sweethearts fall further and further in love, eventually marrying and having a baby daughter Fleur. Luckily for them both, their respective families get on well with their new other halves. Alec's son Jamie (who works in his dad's law firm too) finds he has much in common with Zoe, and despite their initial surprise that such a lively young woman could ever be happy with an old stick-in-the-mud like Alec, Zoe's mum and dad soon become good friends with him. Thankfully, there's more than just a sexual attraction between the mis-matched couple – they share a fondness for detective stories (Alec in particular is obsessed by ***Perry Mason***) and old Hollywood musicals. In fact, the only people who are a bit put out by the relationship (and only a bit, mind you) are the girls working in Alec's office, prim and proper Miss Flood and nosy gossipmonger Hilary.

May to December was never what you'd describe as a hilarious comedy – belly laughs were rarely thick on the ground. It did, nevertheless, provide some nice pleasant chuckles throughout its 39 episodes. Executive produced by television legend Verity Lambert (the woman behind such hits as ***Doctor Who, Minder*** and ***Widows***), Lambert followed *May to December* with the ill-fated soap ***Eldorado***.

The Mayor of Casterbridge

Drama | BBC One | episode duration 50 mins | broadcast 22 Jan–5 Mar 1978

Cast

Alan Bates · *Michael Henchard*
Janet Maw · *Elizabeth Jane Henchard*
Jack Galloway · *Donald Farfrae*
Anne Stallybrass · *Susan*
Anna Massey · *Lucetta Templeman*
Avis Bunnage · *Mrs Goodenough*
Peter Bourke · *Abel Whittle*
Ronald Lacey · *Jopp*
Richard Owens · *Newson*
Jeffrey Holland · *Carter*
Freddie Jones · *Fall*
Alan Rowe · *Mr Joyce*

Producer Jonathan Powell **Writer** Dennis Potter, from the novel by Thomas Hardy **Theme Music** Carl Davies

The BBC's consumption of literary greats reached Thomas Hardy's tragic *Mayor of Casterbridge* in 1978. A faithful adaptation, from the usually iconoclastic Dennis Potter follows Michael Henchard from his drunken disgrace in selling his wife for five guineas to his rise to respectability as the Mayor of Casterbridge. Potter uses the framing device of the return of the maltreated wife, Susan, and her daughter, to stall the inevitable tragic revelation and reversal of fortune for the bullying Henchard. Alan Bates made for a sympathetic lead, gracing the character of Henchard with both the stature and shame that the character carries, while Janet Maw is the innocent whose very existence causes the downfall of the surrogate father she loves dearly.

A TV movie from Pearsons for ITV was broadcast on 17 August 2003, starring Ciarán Hinds as Michael Henchard with Juliet Aubrey as Susan Henchard, Jodhi May as Elizabeth Jane and James Purefoy as Donald Farfrae.

Men Behaving Badly

Sitcom | Hartswood Films /Thames for ITV/BBC One | episode duration 30 mins, plus specials | broadcast 18 Feb–13 Oct 1992 (ITV), 1 Jul 1994–28 Dec 1998 (BBC)

Regular Cast

Martin Clunes · *Gary*
Neil Morrissey · *Tony*
Harry Enfield · *Dermot*
Caroline Quentin · *Dorothy*
Leslie Ash · *Deborah*
John Thompson · *Ken*
Dave Atkins · *Les*
Ian Lindsay · *George*
Valerie Minifie · *Anthea*

Creator/Writer Simon Nye **Producer** Beryl Vertue **Theme Music** Alan Lisk

Although most people remember *Men Behaving Badly* as one of the BBC's great sitcom successes of the 1990s, it actually started life over on ITV. For two seasons, ITV viewers enjoyed the foul-mannered antics of Martin Clunes as Gary and Harry Enfield as Dermot, two flatmates revelling in their bachelorhood and mounting a determined stand against the phenomenon of the caring, sharing, supportive 'new man'. Gary and Dermot aren't interested in having a deep and meaningful relationship with the woman of their choice – all they care about is getting tanked up on lager and dreaming about shagging Kylie Minogue.

Although *Men Behaving Badly* was well received by critics, it wasn't initially a big ratings success, so the ITV network decided not to commission a third season. Production company Hartswood then made a very bold move and offered the series to the BBC, who eagerly snapped it up (a rare example of a British TV programme swapping networks mid-run). The switch of channels also meant a change in transmission time, from a pre-watershed 8.30 p.m. slot on ITV to a post Nine O'Clock *News* broadcast on the BBC. This enabled scripts to be ruder, cruder and full of more realistically laddish language. Another change with the move to the BBC was the departure of Harry Enfield's Dermot (who decided to go travelling around the world) and the arrival of former ***Boon***

star Neil Morrissey as Gary's new flatmate Tony. The combination of sharper scripts and Morrissey's easy-going charm helped to turn *Men Behaving Badly* from a minor success into a fully fledged triumph, with ratings soaring and the programme becoming a true cultural icon that neatly encapsulated the growing culture of 'laddism' in the mid-1990s. With fine support from Leslie Ash and Caroline Quentin as the pair's ever-suffering girlfriends, *Men Behaving Badly* deserves its reputation as one of the finest sitcoms of recent years.

The Men from Shiloh

See THE VIRGINIAN

Metal Mickey

Comedy | LWT/ITV | episode duration 30 mins | broadcast 6 Sep 1980–15 Jan 1983

Regular Cast
Michael Stainton · *Father*
Georgina Melville · *Mother*
Irene Handl · *Granny*
Askley Knight · *Ken*
Lucinda Bateson · *Haley*
Lola Young · *Janey*
Gary Shail · *Steve*
Metal Mickey · *Himself*

Creator John Edward, Michael Dolenz **Producer** Michael Dolenz **Writer** Colin Bostock-Smith **Theme Music** Phil Coulter

Riding the crest of the *Star Wars* wave, Metal Mickey began life with a novelty record called 'Lollipop' in 1978. He was also a guest-for-hire on *Saturday Banana*, ***TISWAS***, ***The Generation Game*** and ***That's Life*** before someone had the idea of giving him his own Saturday evening sit-com. That 'someone' being Micky Dolenz, late of ***The Monkees***.

Sit-com Mickey was the invention of child protégé Ken, youngest child of the Wilberforce family. With dad, mum, a dotty Gran (a scene-stealing Irene Handl) and various siblings, Ken and Mickey would find themselves in incredible scrapes of the type guaranteed to keep pre-teens entertained for 30 minutes; many an episode, whether involving robot hiccups or visiting space aliens, would be resolved thanks to 'Mickey Magic'.

Metal Mickey had his own comic strip in the weekly *Look-in* magazine. His face adorned lunch-boxes and annuals, and his favourite sweets – Atomic Thunderbusters – were available in the form of extra-fizzy bonbons (and, thankfully, not pink detergent tablets as depicted in the show). His catchphrases, 'Boogie boogie' and 'Give us a kiss' – delivered in the same voice as the Cylons from ***Battlestar Galactica*** – helped him become part of Britain's cultural landscape, lending his name to any number of mechanical devices (and even an unconnected song by pop group Suede).

At the time of writing, a pilot for a new TV show is said to be in production, written by his real-life inventor, John Edward.

Miami Vice

Crime Drama | The Michael Mann Co for NBC (Shown on BBC One) | episode duration 50 mins | broadcast 16 Sep 1984–28 Jun 1989 (USA)

Regular Cast
Don Johnson · *Detective James 'Sonny' Crockett*
Philip Michael Thomas · *Detective Ricardo Tubbs*
Edward James Olmos · *Lieutenant Martin Castillo*
Saundra Santiago · *Detective Gina Navarro Calabrese*
Olivia Brown · *Detective Trudy Joplin*
Michael Talbott · *Detective Stan Switek*
Martin Ferrero · *Izzy Moreno*
John Diehl · *Detective Larry Zito*
Sheena Easton · *Caitlin Davies*
Charlie Barnett · *Neville 'Noogie' Lamont*
Belinda Montgomery · *Caroline Crockett*
Gregory Sierra · *Lou Rodriguez*
Pam Grier · *Valerie Gordon*

Creator Anthony Yerkovich **Producers** Michael Mann, Anthony Yerkovich, George Geiger, Dick Wolf, Robert Ward (executive), Michael Attanasio, Richard Brams, Michael A. Cherubino, Dennis Cooper, George E. Crosby, Michael Duggan, John Nicolella, Liam O'Brien, Michael Piller, Mel Swope **Writers** Various, including Anthony Yerkovich, Joel Surnow, Maurice Hurley, Chuck Adamson, Daniel Pyne, Dennis Cooper, Marvin Kupfer, Dick Wolf, David Jackson, Michael Duggan, John Schulian, Peter McCabe, Peter Lance, Scott Shepherd, Ken Solarz **Theme Music** Jan Hammer's electro-rock 'Miami Vice Theme' reached No. 5 in the UK charts in 1985. Two years later, 'Crockett's Theme', an instrumental piece that figured heavily in the series, peaked at No. 2 in the charts.

As the rock video became a powerful force in America, NBC exec Brandon Tartijoff gave instructions to writer Anthony Yerkovich to develop a two-word idea of his: 'MTV Cops'. What Yerkovich came up with was a show that defined the fashions and styles of the 1980s and influenced a hundred copycats on TV and film.

Undercover Miami detective Sonny Crockett is partnered with a New York cop (Ricardo Tubbs) with a grudge – a drugs baron hiding out in Florida murdered his brother. What starts as a fractious, uncomfortable working relationship soon becomes a friendship based on trust and respect. Women may come and go, but the pair stay together through thick and thin.

What helped the series evade the stench of generic writing and cliché was its sense of style and quality direction (thanks to directors like Abel Ferrara, former ***Starsky and Hutch*** star Paul Michael Glaser, Dick Miller

and executive producer Michael Mann). Each shot would be matched for colour to evoke a mood – soft white suits for bright outdoor scenes or pastel shades that would have gotten any schoolboy a severe beating. Of course, anyone who tried to emulate the T-shirt-and-Armani look back then must be looking back at his photos in shame, but at the time it was the ultimate in decadent cool.

The series lived up to its initial promise of 'MTV Cops' by using contemporary rock and pop songs for its soundtrack and even inviting genuine music stars to make cameos and guest appearances, including Little Richard, James Brown and Phil Collins (who was surprised to see the word 'wanker' given to his character to use, as the writers hadn't realised it was more than just a 'London expression'). Sheena Easton was a regular guest, her character marrying Sonny Crockett before being brutally murdered after the writers realised that a wife would get in the way of the central 'buddy' relationship.

At the time of writing, renowned movie director Michael Mann (responsible for such hits as *The Last of the Mohicans* (1992), *Heat* (1995), *Ali* (2001) and 2004's Oscar-nominated *Collateral*) is returning to his roots with a *Miami Vice* feature film, starring Colin Farrell as Crockett and Jamie Foxx as Tubbs for a projected 2006 release.

Michael Palin's Hemingway Adventure

See AROUND THE WORLD IN 80 DAYS

Middlemarch

Drama | BBC/WGBH Boston for BBC Two | episode duration 50–90 mins | broadcast 12 Jan–16 Feb 1994

Principal Cast

Juliet Aubrey · *Dorothea Brooke*
Patrick Malahide · *Reverend Edward Casaubon*
Douglas Hodge · *Dr Tertius Lydgate*
Trevyn McDowell · *Rosamond Vincy*
Robert Hardy · *Arthur Brooke*
Rufus Sewell · *Will Ladislaw*
Peter Jeffrey · *Bulstrode*
Caroline Harker · *Celia Brooke*
Clive Russell · *Caleb Garth*
Jonathan Firth · *Fred Vincy*
Rachel Power · *Mary Garth*
Pam Ferris · *Mrs Dollop*
Michael Hordern · *Peter Featherstone*
Roger Milner · *Pratt*
Stephen Moore · *Mayor Vincy*
John Savident · *Raffles*
Jeremy Sinden · *Captain Lydgate*
Elizabeth Spriggs · *Mrs Cadwallader*
Jacqueline Tong · *Mrs Vincy*
Judi Dench · *Voice of George Eliot*

Producer Louis Marks **Writer** Andrew Davies, from the novel by George Eliot **Theme Music** Stanley Myers

Dorothea Brooke lives with her staid Uncle Arthur, her uncle's mother-in-law and her younger sister Celia. None of Dorothea's immediate relatives want or feel the need for change, even though Uncle Arthur likes to give the impression he is in touch with all the new ideas. Dorothea sacrifices love for what she perceives could be a more useful and worthy life by marrying her cousin, Edward Casaubon, and helping him with his great work – his 'Key to all Mythologies'. Sadly, Edwin wants nothing more than to be left alone, preferring the life of the perpetual student, studying for its own sake, publishing nothing, sharing his discoveries with no one.

Dr Lydgate is as frustrated as Dorothea. His inner weakness, his extravagant wife and the 'stick in the mud' attitudes of those around him thwart his plans for the local hospital, his work on a possible eradication of certain diseases and his ambition to work for the good of all. Even Will Ladislaw, who loves Dorothea, has to stand by as she throws her life away on a dull academic who doesn't appreciate his wife nor want her genuine help.

Middlemarch is a town waiting for change. The railways are being constructed; people like Dorothea, Dr Lydgate and others are welcome to new ideas but feel that they can put these ideas into practice if only they can persuade those in positions of influence to open their limited minds . . .

Andrew Davies's adaptation supplants BBC Two's previous, rather stagey 1968 effort with a glorious £6 million production, which opened the doors for serials based on other literary works – most notably ***Pride and Prejudice***.

Midsomer Murders

Detective | Bentley Productions/Hallmark/A&E for ITV | episode duration 105 mins | broadcast 23 Mar 1997–present

Regular Cast

John Nettles · *DCI Tom Barnaby*
Daniel Casey · *DS Gavin Troy*
John Hopkins · *DS Dan Scott*
Jane Wymark · *Joyce Barnaby*
Laura Howard · *Cully Barnaby*
Barry Jackson · *Dr Bullard*

Producers Delia Fine, Kris Slava (executive), Pat Greenland, Veronica Castillo, Patricia Greenland (associate), Brian True-May, Betty Willingale, Peter Cregeen, Ian Strachan **Writers** Various, including Anthony Horowitz, P. J. Hammond, Alan Plater, Andrew Payne, David Hoskins, Douglas Livingstone, Douglas Watkinson, Christopher Russell, from the novels by Caroline Graham **Theme Music** Jim Parker used a wonderfully 'space-age' instrument called a theremin (the high-pitched whine used on the soundtracks to those 1950s sci-fi movies and several tracks by New Age electro-rockers Goldfrapp) to create the creepy theme tune.

Ever since ***Inspector Morse*** introduced British audiences to the two-hour long detective series format, ITV has searched for other programmes that would ideally fit this lengthier timeslot and which could attract the same kind of huge audiences that had enjoyed Morse's Oxford-based sleuthing. In 1997, ITV launched a series of detective dramas based on Caroline Graham's *Midsomer Murders* novels, perhaps hoping that they'd have a success on their hands. Little did the ITV commissioners realise what a hit *Midsomer Murders* would be – at the time of writing, the programme has screened 41 separate mysteries and has been sold to over 100 countries around the world.

In the fictional county of Midsomer, things are pretty much idyllic. People live in beautiful old mansion houses or on picturesque farms. You can usually stop and enjoy the locals playing a game of cricket on the village green. There's no litter in the quaint lanes, no graffiti or vandalism on the bus stops, and the weather is sunny much more often than anywhere else in the country. Yet Midsomer houses a terrible secret – its homicide rate would give South-Central Los Angeles a run for its money. Thankfully, DCI Barnaby and his colleague Troy (later Scott) are on hand to track down the culprits responsible for the fiendish murders and bring them to justice.

Midsomer Murders thankfully never takes itself or its subject matter too seriously – any long-running TV show about murder in one small part of the world inevitably becomes less and less realistic as time goes by. Thankfully the *Midsomer Murders* producers have always been aware of this fact and have largely brushed over the implausibility of such a high death count in a rural English county (110 murders and counting, plus eight suicides and eight accidental deaths – roughly double the recorded murder rate for the whole of the Thames Valley region in the same period of time), instead concentrating on creating murder mysteries with intricate plots and a first-rate cast of guest suspects each week. Filmed largely on location in Buckinghamshire and Gloucestershire, in 2005 producers faced a major shock when Rover car manufacturers went out of business, leaving DCI Barnaby with a defunct vehicle to cruise the country lanes. Producers responded by announcing that in future, Barnaby will be seen driving a Jaguar X-type instead.

Minder

Comedy Drama | Euston Films/Thames for ITV | episode duration 50 mins | broadcast 29 Oct 1979–10 Mar 1994

Regular Cast

George Cole · *Arthur Daley*
Dennis Waterman · *Terry McCann*
Gary Webster · *Ray Daley*
Glynn Edwards · *Dave Harris*
Patrick Malahide · *Detective Sergeant Albert 'Charlie' Chisholm*
Michael Povey · *DC/DS 'Taff' Jones*
Michael Troughton · *DC Mellish*
Peter Childs · *Detective Sergeant Ronald 'Kenny' Rycott*
Emma Cunningham · *Gloria*
Nicholas Day · *Detective Sergeant Morley*
George Layton · *Des*
Mark Farmer · *Justin James*
Diana Malin · *Debbie Mitchell*

Creator Leon Griffiths **Producers** Verity Lambert, Johnny Goodman, John Hambley (executive), Ian Toynton, Simon Channing-Williams, Laura Julian (associate), Lloyd Shirley, George Taylor **Writers** Leon Griffiths, Paul Wheeler, Murray Smith, Bernie Cooper, Francis Megahy, Tony Hoare, Andrew Payne, Willis Hall, Jeremy Burnham, Stanley Price, Dave Humphries, George Day, Trevor Preston, Geoffrey Case, Barry Purchese, Alan Janes, David Yallop, Alistair Beaton, Anita Bronson, Kevin McNally **Theme Music** 'I Could be so Good for You', written by Dennis Waterman and Gerard Kenny, sung by Waterman on the end titles with an instrumental arrangement opening the show. For some reason, the twisted minds behind ***Little Britain*** have decided, on the basis of this song, that Dennis Waterman now insists on singing the 'feem toon' to everything he appears in. No real grounds for this, but still funny.

When you've got as many fingers in as many dodgy pies, and know as many unsavoury characters as Arthur Daley does, you're going to rely on having a bit of backup. For Arthur, that backup is Terry McCann, boxer and ex-con, who accepts Daley's offer of a few readies in return for being at the businessman's beck and call. Driver, courier, bodyguard and general dogsbody, there's more to being Arthur Daley's minder than Terry ever realised.

What became known as *Minder* was originally written as a film, before Leon Griffiths decided to pitch it as a TV show. Production company Euston Films saw the series as a starring vehicle for Dennis Waterman, who'd just completed four years opposite John Thaw in ***The Sweeney***. As Thaw had done for him, Waterman pushed for his *Minder* co-star, George Cole, to be his equal on the show; ironically, by well before the end of the series, Cole would be the star.

Like ***Only Fools and Horses***, *Minder* was not an instant success. In fact it was sheer good fortune for the series that it was allowed to run for three seasons before it eventually caught on. And again like *Only Fools*, once the audience took to it, it became its network's biggest hit. Arthur Daley was transformed into a cultural leader for a while, along with his malapropisms ('the world's your lobster'), Mockney rhyming slang and the never-seen ''er indoors'. The stream of guest stars, usually as villain of the week, helped keep proceedings light and interesting for the viewers.

Taking a leaf out of John Thaw's book, Dennis Waterman decided not to return for an eighth series, preferring to jump in 1989 while the programme was still at its peak. So, out went Terry McCann and in came Ray Daley, Arthur's nephew with yuppie pretensions. *Minder* continued for another three series before George Cole finally decided to hang up Arthur Daley's camel coat for the last time. The

actor's next big TV project was *Root into Europe* – based on William Donaldson's satirical collection of letters ostensibly by the fictional Henry Root. More miss than hit, it would still have been good to have seen a little more.

Mind Your Language

Sitcom | LWT/Tri Films for ITV | episode duration 25 mins | broadcast 30 Dec 1977–15 Dec 1979, 4 Jan–12 Apr 1986

Principal Cast
Barry Evans · *Jeremy Brown*
Zara Nutley · *Miss Courtney*
Dino Shafeek · *Ali Nadim*
Albert Moses · *Ranjeet Singh*
Françoise Pascal · *Danielle Favre*
Jacki Harding · *Anna Schmidt*
George Camiller · *Giovanni Capello*
Ricardo Montez · *Juan Cervantes*
Pik-Sen Lim · *Chung Su-Lee*
Kevork Halikyan · *Maximillian Papandrious*
Robert Lee · *Taro Nagazumi*
Jamila Massey · *Jamila Ranjha*
Gabor Vernon · *Zoltan Szabo*
Anna Bergman · *Ingrid Svenson*
Iris Sadler · *Gladys*
Tommy Godfrey · *Sid*

Producer Stuart Allen **Writer** Vince Powell **Theme Music** Max Harris

Another show from the prolific pen of ***Love Thy Neighbour*** author Vince Powell, this sitcom had a rather unusual topic for its 'sit' – an adult education class for people for whom English was not their first language. Teacher Jeremy Brown is a kind-hearted, well-meaning chap who goes out of his way to help his students with their work, despite their habit of playing practical jokes on him and getting him into trouble with the school's stern headmistress Miss Courtney. Jeremy's class consists of people from a wide variety of different cultures, including Japan, Sweden, Spain, India, Pakistan, Greece, Italy, France and Germany, and the vast majority of the humour in the programme came from linguistic misunderstandings and the students' inability to grasp the subtleties of the English language.

Whether or not *Mind Your Language* could actually be described as racist is a matter of personal opinion – certainly its humour relied upon the most broadly drawn of national stereotyping (dour, humourless German, sexy French woman, libido-driven Italian, etc.), the kind of jokes that nowadays would be seen as distinctly inappropriate. The series came to an end in 1979 after 29 episodes – however, some six years later, series star Albert Moses was instrumental in staging a revival of the programme with many of the same cast and scripts once again provided by Vince Powell. For this new series, 13 episodes were made, but (perhaps owing to increasing concerns about politically incorrect humour) it failed to get a full ITV network screening, only popping up in the HTV, Ulster, Central and Granada regions.

Miss Marple

Crime Drama | BBC One | episode duration 50–110 mins | broadcast 26 Dec 1984–27 Dec 1992

Regular Cast
Joan Hickson · *Miss Jane Marple*
David Horovitch · *DI Slack*
Ian Brimble · *DS Lake*
Gwen Watford · *Dolly Bantry*

Producers Guy Slater, George Gallaccio **Writers** Alan Plater, David Giles, Julia Jones, T. R. Bowen, Jill Hyem, Ken Taylor, from the stories by Agatha Christie **Theme Music** Ken Howard

Miss Jane Marple, resident of the sleepy village of St Mary Mead, is every murderer's nightmare. With a knack for solving mysteries, her keen mind is always able to make connections and piece together clues that seem to escape the professional constabulary.

Some fans of Agatha Christie are often tempted to consider Miss Marple to be her alter-ego, though Christie purists would suggest Ariadne Oliver, co-sleuth to Poirot, is more Agatha's own 'Mary Sue extrusion'. On 30 December 1956, the pride of Lancashire, Gracie Fields, played the part on US TV for a Goodyear Television Playhouse adaptation of *A Murder is Announced*. While many other actresses have attempted the role since, notably Margaret Rutherford in a series of movie adaptations in the 1960s, and Angela Lansbury in the 1980 TV movie adaptation of *The Mirror Crack'd*, the most widely-known interpretation came with the BBC's series starring Joan Hickson.

Back in the mid-1960s, Agatha Christie reportedly told Hickson that she'd make a perfect Marple. Twenty years on, Agatha Christie had become popular once again thanks to two TV movies from LWT/ITV (*Why didn't they ask Evans?* and *The Seven Dials Mystery*) and the subsequent *Partners in Crime* series. Cashing in on the zeitgeist, the Beeb decided to make their own version of Marple, choosing to make it on film instead of videotape, and spending a lot of money on locations, guest stars and some seriously good adaptations. Everything seemed perfect. The only drawback really was that, two decades on from when the writer had mooted her, Hickson was simply too old, too immobile to really portray the fact that Jane Marple is a nosey old busybody that not too many people actually like. By playing her as everyone's favourite grandmother, Hickson scored with the viewers but didn't really serve the stories. As the BBC reached the end of their canon, it was noticeable that the frail Hickson was getting less and less to do with each outing. The actress, undoubtedly one of Britain's finest, died in 1998, just a few years after the broadcast of her last *Miss Marple*, 'The Mirror Crack'd from Side to Side'.

Move forward another couple of decades and, flushed with the success of their David Suchet-led ***Poirot*** mysteries, LWT took up the gauntlet and produced four Marple TV movies, *The Body in the Library, Murder at the Vicarage, 4.50 from Paddington* and *A Murder is Announced*. The casting of Geraldine McEwan as the amateur detective raised a few eyebrows – again, a tad too old for the role, but actually approaching it with a dynamism and wicked glint in the eye lacking from the BBC version. McEwan's Marple leaves no doubt that she can be a nasty piece of work when she needs to be and is all the better for it. Just as ITV proved with the Jeremy Brett ***Adventures of Sherlock Holmes***, and indeed some of the latter Suchet *Poirots*, your lead character doesn't have to be the nicest person to nevertheless carry the show, and McEwan certainly relishes that. Let down by some less-than-faithful adaptations, with an over-emphasis on sex and violence, plus a determination to overburden the films with more famous faces than the story can support, the 21st-century *Marple* almost sinks under the weight of its own expectations, but without a doubt, it is Geraldine McEwan who saves it from doing so. We look forward to more with eager anticipation.

Mission: Impossible

Action-Adventure | Desilu/Paramount for CBS (shown on ITV) | episode duration 50 mins | broadcast 17 Sep 1966–30 Mar 1973 (USA)

Regular Cast

Steven Hill · *Daniel Briggs*
Peter Graves · *Jim Phelps*
Barbara Bain · *Cinnamon Carter*
Martin Landau · *Rollin Hand*
Greg Morris · *Barney Collier*
Peter Lupus · *Willy Armitage*
Leonard Nimoy · *Paris*
Sam Elliott · *Doug*
Lesley Ann Warren · *Dana Lambert*
Lynda Day George · *Lisa Casey*
Barbara Anderson · *Mimi Davis*

Creator Bruce Geller **Producers** Bruce Geller (executive), Robert F. O'Neill, John W. Rogers, Robert H. Justman, Barry Crane (associate), Allan Balter, Barry Crane, Joseph Gantman, Bruce Geller, Laurence Heath, Stanley Kallis, Bruce Lansbury, Robert E. Thompson, William Read Woodfield **Writers** Various, including Ed Adamson, Allan Balter, Howard Browne, Jackson Gillis, Laurence Heath, James L. Henderson, Stephen Kandel, Norman Katkov, Harold Livingston, Ken Pettus, Paul Playdon, Samuel Roeca, William Read Woodfield **Theme Music** Lalo Schiffrin's theme has become a TV icon – it's even been used memorably as a backing track for a wildlife film about squirrels tackling a complex 'assault course' (which was then adapted into a lager commercial). It's also one of the more bearable popular mobile phone rings.

What does the Government of any country do when it has to engage in activities that are at best highly improper and at worst highly illegal? Well, if you're the US Government, you could always send in the CIA-like agents of your super-secret agency 'Impossible Missions'. Just contact the team's chief (Daniel Briggs, or later, Jim Phelps) and he'll get you a bunch of highly trained operatives to resolve any embarrassing situation. Need top-secret plans stolen? Want to overthrow a Communist regime? Planning to assassinate a drug baron? Well, Impossible Missions are your people. Just don't forget that any message left for them will self-destruct in five seconds.

A hugely popular long-running action/adventure series, *Mission: Impossible* tapped into Cold War paranoia and a love of spies, gadgets and secret missions that had exploded since the arrival of the James Bond movies. Real-life husband and wife actors Martin Landau and Barbara Bain (as Rollin Hand and Cinnamon Carter) supplied the brains and the beauty of the team, with Barney Collier providing the gadgets and Willy Armitage the brawn. When Landau and Bain departed the series after three years, they were replaced by ***Star Trek***'s Leonard Nimoy and a variety of other leading ladies. So beloved by audiences was *Mission: Impossible* that it became one of a raft of vintage TV series to receive the motion picture makeover treatment, with Tom Cruise starring in two movies (in 1996 and 2000).

Mr and Mrs

Quiz Show | HTV/Border for ITV/UK Living/LWT for ITV | episode duration 25 mins | broadcast 1964–26 Mar 1999

Principal Cast

Alan Taylor, Norman Vaughan, Derek Batey, Nino Feretto, Julian Clary · *Presenters*
Lynda Thomas, Helen McArthur, Sue Cuff, Sara Long, Katrina Buchanan, Stacey Young · *Hostesses*

Creator Roy Ward Dixon **Producers** Various, including Derek Clark, Derek Batey, William Cartner

One of the best-remembered quiz shows from the Sixties right through to the Eighties, *Mr and Mrs* began life as a regional programme broadcast from the HTV region and presented by Alan Taylor. However, it was the nationwide screenings, hosted by Norman Vaughan and (most famously) Derek Batey that ensured *Mr and Mrs* a place in the quiz show hall of fame.

The concept of *Mr and Mrs* was simplicity itself. A married couple would be presented with three multiple-choice questions, each of them answering them in turn. While the husband was answering the questions, his wife would be placed into a soundproof booth so that she couldn't overhear his answers. A typical question might be something like: 'What does your wife prefer to drink last thing at night – a cup of tea, a cup of warm milk, or something else?' The husband would then give his answer, and if it matched his wife's responses, they would win some cash. After the wife had given her responses to the three questions her husband had initially answered (to much hilarity at any incorrect answers, of course!), it was the husband's turn to be stuck in the soundproof booth and the wife's turn to predict what her hubby's answers might be. If the couple got all six questions right (his three and her three) then they won the jackpot prize – if they didn't, the jackpot would increase until a couple finally managed to prove how well they knew each other by getting a clean sweep.

Aimed primarily at a more mature age range of contestants and viewers, it was always fun to compare how well the newlyweds did against those who'd celebrated their Golden Wedding Anniversaries, *Mr and Mrs* was supremely unchallenging and unthreatening entertainment, with the hosts gently teasing any partner who got (what their spouse thought to be) easy questions wrong. The original run of episodes came to an end in 1988 with ITV realising that the format was perhaps a little bit tired. Satellite channel UK Living briefly revived the show with mulletted kids TV presenter Nino Feretto hosting before a camp makeover saw Julian Clary hosting the show for LWT. Universally despised by critics and viewers alike, Julian's version of *Mr and Mrs* was pulled from the airwaves after just two episodes – perhaps people just weren't ready for a post-modern send-up of a programme that was the epitome of old-fashioned TV light entertainment.

Mr Bean

Comedy | Tiger/Tiger Aspect Productions for Thames/Central for ITV | episode duration 25 mins | broadcast 1 Jan 1990–31 Oct 1995

Principal Cast
Rowan Atkinson · *Mr Bean*
Matilda Ziegler · *Irma*

Creator Rowan Atkinson **Producers** John Howard Davies, Peter Bennett-Jones, Sue Vertue, Richard Wilmore **Writers** Richard Curtis, Rowan Atkinson, Ben Elton, Robin Driscoll **Theme Music** Howard Goodall

With the benefit of hindsight, it's easy to forget just how much of a culture shock it was for viewers to see Rowan Atkinson starring as Mr Bean – after all, he had spent most of the 1980s plotting and scheming his way through the intricate plots of ***Blackadder***. To place Atkinson in an almost dialogue-free comedy series in which he portrayed a simple-minded gormless nerd of the highest order was a radical move. However, to anyone familiar with his earlier work on the sketch show ***Not the Nine O'Clock News***, Atkinson's physical comedy skills and rubber-faced gurning were already well known.

Mr Bean is a strange individual, with an outlook on life that's distinctly naïve and child-like, but also with an insatiable curiosity and a habit for getting caught up in all manner of stupid situations – these varied from something as innocent as trying to stop himself from sneezing while in church, through to the challenge of cooking an enormous turkey for Christmas lunch with his long-suffering girlfriend Irma. In total, just 13 half-hour episodes of Mr Bean were broadcast, averaging two or three a year. A feature film of Bean's exploits – *Bean: The Ultimate Disaster Movie* – became a worldwide box-office smash in 1997, laying claim to being the most successful British TV comedy spin-off film ever. In 2002, an animated version of Mr Bean's adventures hit ITV screens, with Atkinson providing the necessary brief vocals.

Mr Benn

See pages 478–9

Mr Majeika

Children's Sitcom | TVS for ITV | episode duration 25 mins, plus 50-min special | broadcast 13 Mar 1988–14 Feb 1990

Principal Cast
Stanley Baxter · *Mr Majeika*
Claire Sawyer · *Melanie Brace-Girdle*
Andrew Read · *Thomas Grey*
Roland MacLeod · *Headmaster*
Simeon Pearl · *Hamish Bigmore*
Fidelis Morgan · *Mrs Bunty Brace-Girdle*
Eve Ferret · *Mrs Pam Bigmore*
Miriam Margolyes · *Wilhelmina Worlock*
Pat Coombs · *Miss Flavia Jelley*
Sonia Graham · *Miss Lammastide*
Sanjiv Madan · *Prince*
Adele Silva · *Mrs Fenella Fudd*
Christopher Mitchell · *Ron Bigmore*
Robin Driscoll · *Sergeant Sevenoaks*
Richard Murdoch · *Voice of The Worshipful Wizard of Walpurgis*

Creator Humphrey Carpenter **Producers** J. Nigel Pickard (executive), Roger Cheveley, John Price **Writer** Jenny McDade, from the novels by Humphrey Carpenter **Theme Music:** Paul Hart

Thomas Grey and Melanie Brace-Girdle get a big surprise one day when their new teacher at St Barty's School turns out to be a real-life wizard. His name is Mr Majeika, and he's been exiled to the UK (or, as he calls it, Britland) from his home of Walpurgis for failing his O-level Sorcery exam on no less than 17 occasions. Majeika is under strict instructions not to use any magic while he's living in Britland, but despite his decidedly dodgy skills, he just can't resist using the odd spell every now and again – usually to thwart the behaviour of Hamish Bigmore, the world's most horrible schoolboy.

Based on the three *Mr Majeika* novels by Humphrey Carpenter, the TV version was brought to screens by Jenny McDade, the producer behind the earlier hit ***Supergran***.

Continued on page 480

Mr Benn

Mr Benn goes shopping for a clown suit. Do you think he'll find one?

Children's TV has all the best theme tunes, and it's heartbreaking to hear so many of them mangled by conversion to mobile phone ringtones. Such is the fate of Mr Benn, whose 13-part adventure has been on near-constant rerun since he first graced our screens in 1971. Bored city-worker Mr Benn of 52 Festive Road, London, visits a costume shop in search of ideas for a fancy dress party, only to encounter a fez-sporting shopkeeper who appears 'as if by magic'. The shopkeeper invites Mr Benn to try on a costume and while in the fitting room Mr Benn discovers a magical doorway into a world where the costume suddenly becomes rather handy.

Mr Benn represented those pre-Thatcherite values of individuality and escapism that 1970s viewers were later to enjoy with ***The Good Life*** and ***The Fall and Rise of Reginald Perrin***; office workers trapped in the machine who desperately want an outlet for their creativity. In Mr Benn's case it was dressing up and playing at being a cowboy, a knight, a zookeeper or a pirate. Such innocent times.

After each adventure, he'd return the costume to the shopkeeper, who never asked for a hire fee and always allowed Mr Benn to take something as a memento, whether it be an Indian feather or a cowboy's sheriff badge. Then, as Mr Benn enjoyed a leisurely stroll back home, he'd invariably see the children of his road playing, perhaps unconsciously mirroring his latest adventures by 'peeow'ing each other in a game of cowboys and Indians.

Gently political in its encouragement of children to consider other cultures and points of view, it was nevertheless a typically cosy series, made all the more comfy by the warm tones of narrator Ray Brooks and the wonderfully simplistic designs of creator David McKee. Though rumours of a film version circulate every now and then (most recently with John Hannah cast as the eponymous hero), it's unlikely to ever eclipse McKee's original vision of a man in a pin-striped suit who has the ability to change his clothes simply by removing his hat. Bless him.

Mr Benn represented those pre-Thatcherite values of individuality and escapism: office workers trapped in the machine who desperately want an outlet for their creativity.

Animation
Zephyr Film Productions for BBC One
Episode Duration: 15 mins
Broadcast: 25 Feb 1971–31 Mar 1972

Cast
Ray Brooks · *Narrator*

Creator/Writer David McKee

Theme Music Don Warren

Note Mr Benn's complete adventures were: The Red Knight, The Big Game Hunter, The Clown, Mr Benn goes Ballooning, The Wizard, The Spaceman, The Cook, The Caveman, The Zookeeper, The Frogman, The Cowboy, The Magic Carpet, The Pirate.

TRIVIA

Mr Benn's Festive Road address is believed to have been inspired by David McKee's old home in Festing Road, Putney.

Mr Majeika also saw a welcome return to the small screen of Stanley Baxter, the Scottish comic who had propped up the TV schedules throughout the Sixties and Seventies with his own variety and sketch shows on both BBC and ITV. In total, 20 episodes were made of *Mr Majeika*, the final run of which saw a new character Prince replace Thomas as one of Majeika's best friends.

Mr Men

Animation | Flicks Films for BBC One | episode duration 10 mins | broadcast 31 Dec 1974–2 Sep 1976, 14 Feb 1983–2 May 1984

Voice Cast
Arthur Lowe, John Alderton, Pauline Collins

Creator/Writer Roger Hargreaves **Producers** Terry Ward, Trevor Bond **Theme Music** Tony Hyams, Joe Campbell

The BBC's reputation for faithful literary adaptations was sorely tested when it decided to adapt a series of books that had been originally written for a notoriously critical audience. Thankfully, the series was a word-for-word translation from page to screen with the characters accurately realised, even down to their distinctive footwear.

Flicks Films' *Mr Men* series began with an advert for spam written by Roger Hargreaves and voiced by ***Dad's Army*** star Arthur Lowe. Hargreaves had just published his first *Mr Men* books, a range of six, one per character, and managed to persuade the Flicks crew to record Arthur Lowe reading one of them – *Mr Bump*. The recording was then used to pitch for a series for the BBC, which they delivered in two batches of 13 (featuring the stories of two characters per episode) between 1974 and 1976.

With Hargreaves proving prolific, and with a new *Little Miss* range also on shelves across the world, a second series, *The Mr Men and Little Misses*, was commissioned in the early 1980s. Arthur Lowe had died in 1982, so husband-and-wife team John Alderton and Pauline Collins each narrated one story (one Mr Man, one Little Miss) in each edition.

Many children have taken their first literary steps thanks to Hargreaves' characters. Each of them is created using primary colours and a reliance on geometric or other simple shapes that children can copy. The stories are often moralistic but never too preachy, with some stories concluding with characters ironically losing the trait that gave them their names in the first place; certainly, we can assume Mr Nosey no longer peers around corners after the threat of having his nose sawn off, and that Mr Greedy is now fully sated after being force fed by a giant. Luckily, Mr Tickle (the very first Mr Man) is still at large to cause mayhem and mirth.

Trivia
Mr Sneeze is the only Mr Man who doesn't have arms – perhaps this is the reason why his nose is so red.

Website
www.mrmen.com carries a full list of Mr Men and Little Miss characters as well as a brilliant 'Make your Own Mr Man' game.

Mrs Merton Show

Chat Show/Sitcom | Granada for BBC Two/One | episode duration 30 mins | broadcast 10 Feb 1995–2 Apr 1998, 22 Feb–29 Mar 1999

Principal Cast
Caroline Aherne · *Mrs Merton*
Craig Cash · *Malcolm Merton*

Producers Various, including Andy Harries, Clive Tulloh (executive), Peter Kessler, Mark Gorton, Spencer Campbell, Philippa Robinson **Writers** Caroline Aherne, Craig Cash, Dave Gorman, Henry Normal **Theme Music** 'Hooky and the Boys' (aka Peter Hook from New Order) provided Mrs Merton's chat show with its first theme music and were the resident house band for the first few seasons. After Aherne and Hook's split, the Patrick Trio became the house band.

A bizarre hybrid between scripted comedy, celebrity chat show and the kind of 'heated debates' shown on morning discussion programmes like ***Kilroy***, *The Mrs Merton Show* was consistently entertaining – largely down to the inspired performance by talented young comedian Caroline Aherne as the wicked pensioner Mrs Merton.

In each episode, Mrs Merton would welcome a number of celebrity guests onto her show and would interrogate them about their life and career. Unfortunately, Mrs Merton was a bit of a mischief-maker, and managed to get away with asking gasp-inducing questions that sailed across the line of what was acceptable and unacceptable (one particularly memorable comment, to magician's wife Debbie McGee – 'So Debbie, what first attracted you to millionaire magician Paul Daniels?'). Egging her on were a crowd of genuine pensioners (many of them known personally to Caroline Aherne prior to the series) and most of them were attendees every week. Mrs Merton herself wasn't above letting certain guests know how she felt about them – in particular, poor Michael Parkinson ('Ooooh, Parky, Parky, Parky,' she sighed) was left in no doubt about his attractiveness to a woman of a certain age like Mrs Merton. Thirty episodes of the show were screened in total, including a short run of three programmes recorded in Las Vegas with American celebrity guests.

A six-part spin-off sitcom followed from 27 February 1999, in which we were introduced to the family life of Mrs Merton, her dopey son Malcolm (who'd made the occasional appearance on the chat show) and their neighbour Arthur Capstick (played with great élan by former ***George and Mildred*** star Brian Murphy). Set in the Manchester suburb of Heaton Norris, we discover that there is a Mr Merton – however, he's bedridden and never makes an appearance in the show. A poignant and often

painfully funny series (in the awkward and uncomfortable sense), *Mrs Merton and Malcolm* managed to focus on the minutiae of Northern life in beautiful detail – a trait that the show's writers used to great effect in their next project, the beloved and justly adored ***The Royle Family***.

Mogul

See THE TROUBLESHOOTERS

Monarch of the Glen

Drama | Ecosse Films for BBC One | episode duration 50–60 mins | broadcast 27 Feb 2000–present

Regular Cast
Alastair Mackenzie · *Archie MacDonald*
Dawn Steele · *Alexandra 'Lexie' MacDonald*
Susan Hampshire · *Molly MacDonald*
Richard Briers · *Hector MacDonald*
Lloyd Owen · *Paul Bowman-MacDonald*
Hamish Clark · *Duncan McKay*
Alexander Morton · *Golly Mackenzie*
Julian Fellowes · *Lord Angus Kilwillie*
Jason O'Mara · *Fergal Maclure*
Angus Lennie · *Badger*
Tom Baker · *Donald MacDonald*
Lorraine Pilkington · *Katrina Finlay*
Martin Compston · *Ewan Brodie*
Rae Hendrie · *Jess Mackenzie*
Paul Freeman · *Andrew Booth*
Simone Lahbib · *Isobel Anderson*
Kirsty Mitchell · *Iona*

Creators Michael Chaplin **Producers** Douglas Rae, Victoria Evans, Barbara McKissack, Gaynor Holmes (executive), Michael Chaplin (associate), Graeme MacArthur, Ian D. Tootle, Jennifer Booth, Rob Bullock, Stephen Garwood, Jeremy Gwilt, Paddy Higson, Nick Pitt **Writers** Various, including Michael Chaplin, Niall Leonard, Patrick Wilde, Stuart Hepburn, Mark Holloway, John Martin Johnson, James Mavor, Harriet O'Carroll, Rob Fraser, Leslie Stewart, Colin Wyatt, Jeremy Front, Andrew Taft, Andrew Rattenbury, Dan Sefton, from the 'Highland' novels by Compton MacKenzie **Theme Music** Simon Brint

Another one of the seemingly endless stream of 'warm', 'cosy' and 'heartwarming' dramas that TV executives seem to feel are the only form of entertainment that people want to watch on Sunday evenings, *Monarch of the Glen* at least set itself apart from rival shows like ***Heartbeat***, *Where the Heart Is* and *Born and Bred* by being set in the highlands of Scotland rather than the north of England.

In the first episode we meet Archie MacDonald, who's established a good career for himself in London as a restaurateur. Archie suddenly finds himself called back to Scotland to assume the role of Laird of Glenbogle (a tax dodge on the part of his father). Not only does Archie have to adjust to life as a Laird, he's also charged with getting the 40,000-acre estate financially back on its feet. Luckily, Archie has his eccentric father Hector and lovely mother Molly to keep him grounded as he struggles with his new title and responsibilities as well as a new romance with housekeeper Lexie. As the years go by and Archie decides to leave Glenbogle, he hands responsibility for the estate over to his half-brother Paul Bowman. After Hector dies in a tragic accident, the estate reels from the arrival of his even more eccentric brother Donald and from the news that Glenbogle's finances are far from secure . . .

Thankfully, although *Monarch of the Glen* delivers its fare share of heartbreak, doomed romances and family struggles, it does manage to avoid too many of the cloying excesses or simplistic moral messages that pollute many similar programmes. And, of course, the astonishingly beautiful scenery (Ardverikie Estate in the Scottish Highlands, on the shores of Lake Laggan, stands in for the fictional Glenbogle Estate) and attractive young lead cast members go a long way towards making up for any occasional deficiencies in the plotting. *Monarch* has also developed a huge international fan following (fans of the show call themselves 'Boglies', by the way), having been screened in 44 countries to date. Sadly for all Boglies out there, the BBC has announced that the forthcoming seventh season is likely to be the last.

The Monkees

Music/Comedy | Screen Gems Television/Raybert Productions for NBC (shown on BBC One) | episode duration 25 mins | broadcast 12 Sep 1966–6 Nov 1968, 14 Apr 1969

Principal Cast
Davy Jones, Mickey Dolenz, Michael Nesmith, Peter Tork

Creators Bert Schneider and Bob Rafelson **Producers** Bert Schneider, Bob Rafelson (executive), Gerald Shepard, Ward Sylvester, Michael Burns (associate) **Writers** Various, including Robert Schlitt, Peter Meyerson, Treva Silverman, David Panich, Dave Evans, Gerald Gardner, Dee Caruso, Robert Rafelson, Jack Winter, Coslough Johnson, Neil Burstyn **Theme Music** Tommy Boyce and Bobby Hart wrote the 'Theme from *The Monkees*' (often mistitled 'Hey Hey, We're the Monkees') as they did for most of the band's early songs. Only Micky Dolenz contributed to the song, though, singing the lead vocals, all the other parts being taken by the songwriters themselves and an ensemble of session musicians. 'For Pete's Sake', a song written by Peter Tork with Joseph Richards, was used as the end theme for some repeat screenings.

Manufactured to ride the wave of Beatlemania and the success of Rick Lester's films *A Hard Day's Night* (1964) and *Help* (1965), *The Monkees* was never meant to be the story of a real-life band. Columbia Records, who were supplying the musical talent for the series, pushed an English singer they had under contract, former ***Coronation Street*** actor

Davy Jones, onto the producers. The rest of the band were cast from 400 hopefuls, more on their personalities than any musical ability – and indeed their original contracts forbade them from having any influence on the songs aside from providing vocals. That aside, they were still one of the best-loved bands of the 1960s – not surprising considering some of their most memorable songs (or at least, the best-known ones not penned by Tommy Boyce and Bobby Hart) were written by the likes of Neil Diamond, Carole King and Harry Nilsson.

Each episode followed a familiar structure, with three songs interspersed around a loosely chaotic plot usually involving a pretty girl in peril and the boys evading their landlord. The idea of the series being solely about a fictional act was swiftly abandoned when the producers realised the quality of the songs they were sitting on; they rushed them into production and began racking up the chart hits, beginning with 'Last Train to Clarkesville' and 'I'm a Believer' (Mickey Dolenz has been quoted as saying that at the time the band's first songs entered the US Billboard singles charts, he didn't even know what 'Billboard' was). While the individual performers had been happy playacting as musicians, when it became known that they didn't play their instruments on the records the backlash began. This was especially embarrassing for Michael Nesmith and Peter Tork, the two genuine musicians in the band.

The band came to an acrimonious end after its members (not unreasonably) requested to have more input into the songwriting and performing, only for the producers to release Davy Jones's version of 'Valleri' (produced using session musicians, just like the early hits) without consulting the other three. A bafflingly psychedelic movie co-written by Dennis Hopper and Jack Nicholson (*Head*, 1968) and an unsuccessful TV special brought their reign to a close. Their legacy, though, was massive, and not just for inspiring Hanna Barbera's similarly crazy band ***The Banana Splits***. While Mickey Dolenz became the TV producer behind such hits as ***Metal Mickey***, Mike Nesmith gained recognition as a genuine music star. He also came up with a little idea that was slow to take off but became moderately popular – MTV.

Monkey

Action-Adventure | Kokusai Hoei for NTV (shown on BBC Two) | episode duration 25 mins | broadcast 16 Nov 1979–3 Apr 1981

Regular Cast

Masaaki Sakai · *Sun Wu-Kong/Monkey*
Toshiyuki Nishida, Tonpei Hidari · *Zhu Ba-Jie/Pigsy*
Shirô Kishibe · *Sha Wu-Jing/Sandy*
Masako Natsume Xuanzang Sanzang · *Tripitaka*
Shunji Fujimura · *Yu-Lung*
Mieko Takamine · *Buddha*
David Collings · *Voice of Monkey*
Peter Woodthorpe · *Voice of Pigsy*
Gareth Armstrong · *Voice of Sandy*
Miriam Margolyes · *Voice of Tripitaka*
Andrew Sachs · *Voice of Yu-Lung*
Cecile Chevreau · *Voice of Buddha*
Frank Duncan · *Narrator*
Peter Marinker · *Additional Voices*

Creator The series was based on the tales of Ch'eng-En Wu, a 16th-century storyteller, who had adapted the 7th-century legends of Tripitaka **Producers** Teisho Arikawa, Tsuneo Hayakawa, Yoji Katori, Ken Kumagaya, Kazuo Morikawa, Tadahiro Nagatomi, Muneo Yamada **Writer** David Weir, adapting translations of the Japanese scripts **Theme Music** 'Birth of the Odyssey'/'Monkey Magic' by the band Godiego, sung in English by Yukihide Takekawa (the theme was never recorded in Japanese)

'In the worlds before Monkey,' the opening titles told us, 'primal chaos reigned.' Then elemental forces brought an egg from a rock, from which hatched a stone monkey who was 'irrepressible!' An English-language version of the Japanese series *Saiyûki*, *Monkey* was based on the tale of a 7th-century Buddhist priest Tripitaka, who travelled across continents in search of enlightenment. In the imaginative TV series, Tripitaka was played by a woman and accompanied by a group of animals in human form – Sandy, the thoughtful, timid fish, Pigsy the greedy, impetuous swine; even her horse, Yu-Lung, eventually takes human shape. But central to the quest was the personal journey of Monkey, a being who needed to be taught a lesson. Monkey's strength comes from a gold band on his head, which, when he gets out of line, can be shrunk by a chant from Tripitaka to cause him a severe headache. As a consequence, Monkey tends to behave himself when Tripitaka is around. Monkey can summon clouds to bear him across distances, and the Princess of the Western Ocean gives him a wishing staff that can be used to fight with or grown to any size, from matchstick to pole-vault.

Inventive and energetic, *Monkey* was scripted by David Weir (he'd scripted the British version of *The Water Margin* too), improvising liberally around the Japanese translation to include jokes that would only work in English. Weir had no knowledge of Japanese – but then, neither did any of the British actors cast to play the parts. Monkey himself was voiced by David Collings, who played Silver in ***Sapphire and Steel***, while Miriam Margolyes provided the voice for the androgynous Tripitaka.

Monkey Dust

Adult Animation | Talkback Productions for BBC Two/Three | episode duration 30 mins | broadcast 9 Feb 2003–date

Regular Voice Cast

Morwenna Banks, Frances Barber, Brian Bowles, Saraj Chaudhry, Rebecca Front, Simon Greenall, Tom Hillenbrand, Nick Holder, Sharon Horgan, Simon Lipson, Enn Reitel, Kate Robbins · *Various characters*

David Baddiel, Stuart Maconie · *Voices, Themselves*

Creator Harry Thompson and Shaun Pye **Producers** Harry Thompson, David Z. Obadiah, Claire Jennings **Writers** Harry Thompson, Shaun Pye, Chris Sussman, Sharon Horgan, Peter Baynham, Marcus Berkmann, Dan Hine, Conor Lennon, Chris Sussman **Theme Music** 'That's Not Really Funny' by The Eels

The adjective 'dark' is often attributed to modern comedy series, particularly for programmes where the jokes are in such poor taste that viewers can feel pangs of guilt for laughing out loud. Forget ***Little Britain*** – forget ***The League of Gentlemen***. Even forget *Nighty Night* – the 'darkest' comedy made for TV so far is the twisted and warped animated sketch show *Monkey Dust*. Originally made for the youth-oriented channel BBC Three, *Monkey Dust* soon received a terrestrial airing on BBC Two when it rapidly developed a vociferous cult following.

Monkey Dust features a variety of regular characters, some of which are seen each episode, some of which disappear for weeks at a time before making a comeback. The first series introduced viewers to a divorced father, constantly seen awaiting rare visits from his son Timmy. The dad's hopes for a wonderful weekend with his son are always crushed when Timmy reveals something about his mum's new boyfriend, and, regular as clockwork, the father takes his own life – just prior to the audience overhearing Timmy telling his now-dead dad that he was only kidding. Other characters include the two young Muslim boys from Dudley in the West Midlands being prepared for a suicidal jihad by a demonic-eyed mullah, only to be interrupted from their plans by the arrival of their mum with promises of a lovely tea consisting of oven chips and Findus Crispy Pancakes. Perhaps the best loved of all *Monkey Dust* characters is Ivan Dobsky, a poor man with the mental age of a young boy who was falsely imprisoned in the 1970s for 'The Meat Safe Murders'. Ivan is released from prison when 'Two nice men called D 'n' A' proved he couldn't have been the killer. 'I only said I done it so they'd sew me hands back on,' explains Ivan. Accompanied only by his trusty orange space-hopper Mr Hoppy, Ivan tries unsuccessfully to adapt to life in the 2000s, only to end up committing a horrible crime in order to get put back into his home, a prison cell.

Add in characters such as 'first-time cottager', the Paedo-Finder General, a laboratory experimentation rabbit called Noodles with the healing abilities of a Warner Bros cartoon character and even semi-regular appearances by England coach Sven-Göran Eriksson, and you've got a unique, challenging and extremely guilty treat.

The Monocled Mutineer

Drama | BBC One | episode duration 75–90 mins | broadcast 31 Aug–21 Sep 1986

Cast

Tony Williams, Paul McGann · *Percy Topliss*
Cherie Lunghi · *Dorothy*
Timothy West · *Brigadier Thompson*
Penelope Wilton · *Lady Angela Forbes*
Philip McGough · *Woodhall*
Matthew Marsh · *Charles Strange*
Jane Wood · *Annie Webster*
Dave Hill · *Frank Webster*
Malcolm Terris · *Johnson*
Bert Parnaby · *Todd*
Antony Brown · *Judge*
Anthony Benson · *Salvation Army Captain*
Ian Mercer · *Wheelchair-Bound Soldier*
Dorian Healy · *Cockney*
Billy Fellows · *Geordie*
Ian Hart · *Scouse*
Robert Putt · *RAMC Sergeant*
Nick Reding · *Cruikshank*
Rowena Cooper · *Mrs Cruikshank*
Ron Donachie · *Strachan*
Anthony Calf · *Guiness*
Jonathan McKenna · *Corporal Reeve*
P. H. Moriarty · *Wall Eye*
Jerome Flynn · *Franny*
Julian Ronnie · *Carrothead*
Patrick Doyle · *Gilzean*
David Allister · *General Asser*
Robert Reynolds · *Captain Davies*
Geoff Morrell · *Aussie Gas Mask*
Louis Mellis · *Scots Gas Mask*
Philip Martin Bell · *Turner*
Aran Bell · *Fallows*
Jim Carter · *Spencer*
Ted Richards · *PC Fulton*
Anthony Carrick · *Decourcy Parry*
Peter Hutchinson · *Norman*
Richard Ireson · *Inspector Ritchie*
David Miller · *Spruce*
Terry Cundall · *Bertram*
Frank Duncan · *Reverend Law*

Producer Richard Broke **Writer** Alan Bleasdale, from the book by William Allison and John Flynn **Theme Music** George Fenton

The subject of Alan Bleasdale's 1986 drama was a deserter, a thief, an impostor, a mutineer and, very possibly, a murderer. The British establishment would also have had us believe that he didn't exist, or at the very least, that events he was said to have took part in or even instigated never actually happened.

Catapulting actor Paul McGann to fame, *The Monocled Mutineer* told the story of Percy Topliss, a charming con-man who escapes the drudgery and danger of the Nottinghamshire miles for the trenches of World War One. At first, he manages to live from one dodge to the next, but after witnessing the execution for cowardice of a captain whose only crime was fear, Topliss decides to steal the dead officer's uniform and live in his place for a while. He visits the man's mother and convinces her that her son

was a hero – an act of kindness that proves profitable. He soon realises that an officer's uniform can open many doors to him. Eventually he is arrested for desertion and sent to the infamous retraining 'bullring' at Etaples where the soldiers are subjected to brutal and inhuman acts of cruelty by their superior officers, including Brigadier Thompson (Timothy West).

Topliss's intelligence and quick wits help to gain the trust of the men around him, and when the soldiers eventually mutiny for better conditions, Topliss emerges as their reluctant leader. By the time the mutineers have won their cause, Topliss escapes and begins a new life back in England with a widow called Dorothy. He might well have succeeded in evading capture had he not decided to re-enlist in the army in 1920 when, recognised by one of his fellow former mutineers, he becomes embroiled in a petrol-siphoning scam. A problem with one of his buyers results in a cab driver's murder and when another soldier identifies Percy as the culprit, Topliss is declared guilty in absentia. He is eventually found in the Lake District by local policemen and shot.

The Monocled Mutineer opened BBC One's autumn season in 1986 with Paul McGann gracing the front cover of the *Radio Times* (billed as 'The most wanted man in Britain'). Despite popular acclaim, the drama was attacked by both the Government and ex-soldiers for the scene in which a young officer is shot by his own side for refusing to lead his man to almost certain death (despite the fact that similar events were described by, among others, musician Victor Sylvester). However, despite popular myth to the contrary, *The Monocled Mutineer* was repeated on BBC One in August 1988, and remains McGann's most celebrated performance.

Monty Python's Flying Circus

See pages 486–9

Moonlighting

Comedy/Drama | Picturemaker Productions for CBS (shown on BBC Two) | episode duration 45 mins | broadcast 3 Mar 1985–14 May 1989

Regular Cast

Cybill Shepherd · *Maddie Hayes*
Bruce Willis · *David Addison*
Alice Beasley · *Miss Agnes Dipesto*
Curtis Armstrong · *Bert Viola*
Eva Marie Saint · *Virginia Hayes*
Robert Webber · *Alex Hayes*
Jack Blessing · *MacGillicuddy*
Mark Harmon · *Sam Crawford*
Charles Rocket · *Richard Addison*
Paul Sorvino · *David Addison Sr*
Virginia Madsen · *Lorraine Anne Charnock*

Creator Glenn Gordon Caron **Producers** Glenn Gordon Caron, Jay Daniel, Charles H. Eglee, Barbara Hall, Karen Hall, Artie Mandelberg, Philip Carr Neel, Ron Osborn, Jeff Reno, Christopher T. Welch **Writers** Glenn Gordon Caron, Eric Blakeney, Ron Clark, Frank Dandridge, Roger Director, Charles H. Eglee, Kerry Ehrin, Debra Frank, Joe Gannon, Dale Gelineau, Scott Spencer Gordon, Barbara Hall, Karen Hall, Jim Kramer, Jeremy Lew, Merrill Markoe, Ali Matheson, Gene Miller, Pauline Miller, Ron Osborn, Michael Petryni, Jeff Reno, Chris Ruppenthal, Carl Sautter, William Shakespeare, Bruce Franklin Singer, Jerry Stahl **Theme Music** The sweeping, sophisticated theme to *Moonlighting* was written by Alf Clausen, Lee Holdridge and Richard Lewis Warren, and was beautifully performed by silky-voiced Al Jarreau. It reached No. 8 in the UK singles charts in March 1987.

Former high fashion model Maddie Hayes receives a shock when her business partner embezzles all of her money. She's appalled to discover that her only remaining assets are her house and the City of Angels Detective Agency, which she had only bought as a tax loss. Initially intent on selling the business off, she visits the agency and meets the charming, handsome and wise cracking manager, David Addison. Realising that David is lazy, lecherous, irresponsible and (thankfully) a rather effective detective, she renames the company the Blue Moon Detective Agency (after a brand of shampoo she used to advertise) and becomes David's hands-on boss. Of course, this leads to fireworks between the two headstrong bosses, of both the managerial and romantic variety.

Perhaps more than anything else, *Moonlighting* is remembered today as the TV show that launched the career of a then-unknown actor called Bruce Willis. He was the last person to be interviewed for the part of smart-alec David Addison – viewing early episodes of *Moonlighting* today, it's not difficult to see why producers fell instantly in love with his charisma, charm and wit, because we as an audience did exactly the same thing. So, in the fiction of the programme, did stuck-up, self-important Maddie Hayes, much against her better judgement. Indeed, *Moonlighting* became one of the best representations of the 'will-they-won't-they' relationship ever seen on screen, crossed with the kind of verbal dexterity normally associated with the screwball comedies of 1930s and '40s cinema. For three seasons, viewers watched enraptured, hoping against hope that these two people (who were clearly destined to be together) would finally get over their issues with each other and just do it!

Unfortunately, from the moment that Maddie and David became a couple, the precise element that made *Moonlighting* such a wonderfully funny and witty programme disappeared. Rather than enjoying yet another venom-filled flirty argument (which usually involved much slamming of doors and the intervention of receptionist Miss Dipesto to resolve things), viewers were shocked to realise that *Moonlighting* had become just another soap opera, with relationship and baby problems dominating much of the narrative and excluding the very jokes that people had tuned into *Moonlighting* for.

Another unique feature of *Moonlighting* was in the way that it broke through the 'fourth wall' of the studio sets, allowing the characters to directly address the audience. In one episode, for example, David and Maddie learn how to 'get funky' with the Temptations in the pre-credits sequence; in a Christmas episode they walk off the set entirely into the CBS studio and share festive cheer with the behind-the-scenes crew that worked on the show. Other episodes played with the narrative format – one was filmed entirely in black and white, another was a parody of Shakespeare's *The Taming of the Shrew*, with all dialogue written in iambic pentameter. *Moonlighting* was an innovative joy, a programme that challenged the format of what a TV drama series could be – without *Moonlighting*, there could never have been an ***Ally McBeal***, a ***Sex and the City***, or even a ***Desperate Housewives***.

The Morecambe and Wise Show

See pages 490–2

Mork & Mindy

Sitcom | Henderson/Miller-Milkis/Paramount for ABC (shown on ITV) | episode duration 25 mins | broadcast 14 Sep 1978–27 May 1982

Regular Cast
Robin Williams · *Mork*
Pam Dawber · *Mindy McConnell*
Conrad Janis · *Fred 'Fredzo' McConnell*
Elizabeth Kerr · *Cora Hudson*
Ralph James · *Voice of Orson*
Jeffrey Jacquet · *Eugene*
Robert Donner · *Exidor*
Morgan Fairchild · *Susan Taylor*
Gina Hecht · *Jean Da Vinci*
Jay Thomas · *Remo Da Vinci*
Tom Poston · *Franklin Delano Bickley*
Jim Staahl · *Nelson Flavor*
Shelley Fabares · *Cathy McConnell*
Jonathan Winters · *Mearth*
Foster Brooks · *Miles Sternhagen*
Crissy Wilzak · *Glenda Faye 'Crissy' Comstock*

Creators Joe Glauberg, Garry Marshall, Dale McRaven
Producers Anthony W. Marshall, Garry Marshall, James O'Keefe (executive), Elizabeth Kerr Hudson, Bruce Johnson, Crissy Wilzak Comstock, Dale McRaven **Writers** Various, including Dale McRaven, Lloyd Turner, April Kelly, Gordon Mitchell, Tom Tenowich, Bruce Johnson, Ed Scharlach **Theme Music** Perry Botkin Jr

Hailing from the planet Ork, Mork visits Boulder, Colorado in the American Midwest to investigate human culture and report back his findings to his Orkan boss Orson. Luckily he quickly finds a friend in human girl Mindy, who generously allows him to become her room mate at 1619 Pine Street – much to the concern of her father. Mork might look human, but there are constant reminders of his origins. He peppers his language with words and phrases from his home planet, such as the exclamation 'Shazbot' and the all-purpose pleasantry 'Nanoo Nanoo'. He also drinks through his finger, sleeps upside down in a wardrobe, offers a handshake by interlocking hands held in a position like Mr Spock's Vulcan salute from ***Star Trek***. But Mork wants so much to be able to pass for human, which is why Mindy tries so hard to protect his secret from the outside world.

Loveable Mork's first TV appearance was as a guest character in an episode of ***Happy Days*** after Garry Marshall's son suggested he put an alien into the show. The episode was effectively a test for the character to see how audiences took to comedian Robin Williams, whose brand of manic humour had been wowing audiences at the Comedy Store. Mork's naïvety allowed him to say things that most humans would never dare, but it also gave him a fresh approach to life on Earth that the writers exploited to make him a tool for social commentary, although this rarely went any deeper than 'Sometimes it's okay to lie.'

The show was a major hit, at one point occupying a top three place in the US ratings. But then there were cast changes for later seasons and the show began to be used as a pawn in the ratings battle to the extent that the viewing figures plummeted. There were changes to Mork and Mindy's relationship too, as they moved on from being platonic friends to become a married couple. Mindy accompanied Mork for a honeymoon on Ork and on their return to Earth, Mork announced that he was going to have a baby. He laid an egg that later hatched to reveal Mearth – an infant with the body of a middle-aged man (comic legend Jonathan Winters).

Though the series officially ended in summer 1982, it continued in the autumn of the same year as an animated series, starring the voices of the live-action cast. Robin Williams moved towards feature films, having already starred in *Popeye* (1980) and *The World According to Garp* (1982). *Moscow on the Hudson* (1984), *Good Morning, Vietnam* (1987), *Dead Poets Society* (1989) and *Awakenings* (1990) defined his screen persona as alternating manic/mawkish. In 1997 he won a Best Supporting Actor Academy Award for underplaying his role in the critically acclaimed *Good Will Hunting*.

Mother Love

Drama | BBC Two | episode duration 60 mins | broadcast 29 Oct–19 Nov 1989

Regular Cast
Diana Rigg · *Helena Vesey*
David McCallum · *Alex Vesey*
James Wilby · *Kit Vesey*
Continued on page 493

Monty Python's Flying Circus

Cleese, Gilliam, Jones (in a frock – again), Chapman, Palin and Idle.

For much of the early part of the 20th century, popular comedy was the realm of the working class. End-of-the-pier shows, working men's clubs and army concert parties were the training ground for entertainers. But in the 1960s, the intelligentsia reclaimed ground; the Cambridge Footlights with the *Beyond the Fringe* group (Jonathan Miller, Alan Bennett, Peter Cook and Dudley Moore) and David Frost over at ***That Was the Week That Was***. Their successors at the Cambridge Footlights' 1963 tour (headed by Humphrey Berkley), Graham Chapman, John Cleese and Eric Idle, followed them to television, while Terry Jones and Michael Palin came from Oxford University at around the same time. This generation of performers and writers took inspiration from both the intellectual savagery of the iconoclastic Peter Cook and the banal anarchy of the Goons, Peter Sellers, Michael Bentine, Harry Secombe and of course Spike Milligan.

For TV viewers in the 1960s, David Frost's *That Was the Week That Was* (or 'TW3') was the last word in topical political satire. It was also the way into television for the future Pythons – Cleese appearing in numerous sketches alongside Ronnie Barker and Ronnie Corbett (notably the class-conscious sketch where the working-class Corbett 'knows my place'). In 1967, Cleese and Chapman joined forces to create *At Last, the 1948 Show* (the title being a side-swipe at the BBC's bureaucracy that ensures it takes for ever to get anything done), which co-starred Marty Feldman, Tim Brooke-Taylor and Eric Idle. The following year, the children's comedy series *Do Not Adjust Your Set* combined sketches from Eric Idle, Michael Palin and Terry Jones and mind-boggling animated sequences from American filmmaker/designer Terry Gilliam. The series also featured appearances by the Bonzo Dog Doo Dah Band, whose members included Vivian Stanshall and Neil Innes.

After Jones and Palin created *The Complete and Utter History of Britain* in 1969, BBC producer Barry Took decided to bring together an ensemble of talent to see what they could create. The result was a commission to produce 13 shows that would exploit the strengths of

Comedy
BBC Two
Episode Duration: 30 mins
Broadcast: 5 Oct 1969–5 Dec 1974

Regular Cast
Graham Chapman, John Cleese, Terry Gilliam, Eric Idle, Terry Jones, Michael Palin, Connie Booth, Carol Cleveland, Ian Davidson, Neil Innes, the Fred Tomlinson Singers

Creators
Barry Took, Graham Chapman, John Cleese, Terry Gilliam, Eric Idle, Terry Jones, Michael Palin

Producers
John Howard Davies, Ian MacNaughton

Writers Graham Chapman, John Cleese, Terry Gilliam, Eric Idle, Terry Jones, Michael Palin, Neil Innes, Douglas Adams, Connie Booth

Theme Music 'Liberty Bell March' by John Philip Sousa

each of the writing teams. John Cleese and Graham Chapman would continue to write together, as would Terry Jones and Michael Palin; Eric Idle would work alone and in collaboration with the others, while Terry Gilliam would go off and single-handedly create the animated sequences for which the programme became famous. After numerous suggestions for a title for the series (which included 'Owl Stretching Time', 'Arthur Megapode's Cheap Show', 'Vaseline Review', 'Ethel the Frog' and 'Gwen Dibley's Flying Circus' – many of which would return as episode titles for the series), the name *Monty Python's Flying Circus* was chosen. For years afterwards, ill-prepared journalists would ask which of them was actually 'Monty'. Pah!

The first episode was transmitted at 11.00 p.m. on Sunday 5 October 1969. With such an unhelpful and decisively odd title, viewers who tuned in that night had very little concept of what to expect – neither, as it happens, did the studio audience. The first proper sketch features John Cleese, dressed as Mozart, introducing some of the greatest deaths in history. The stony silence of the studio audience is testament to the radical nature of the comedy. It took that audience – both at home and in the studio – the best part of the first season to 'get' this new form of 'jokeless comedy', which abandoned the traditional linear structure: introduction, set-up, then punchline. The *Python* team would often wander haphazardly into the middle of a situation, loiter around its edges for just as long as they could be bothered, before heading off to whichever comic situation grabbed their attention next.

If the Pythons ever succumbed to something as boring as a catchphase, 'And now for something completely different', first heard in the second episode, was it. Also the title of the Pythons' first film (a compilation of re-created classic sketches made in 1971), 'something different' was a promise that the team pretty much kept throughout the 45 episodes they amassed over four series. As far as the team were concerned, it wasn't necessary to deliver a punchline to order if the concept of simply leaving it halfway through and moving on to the next one would be funnier. Extensive pre-filmed sequences made the whole series seem much more cinematic and expensive than perhaps it was. The introduction for each of the first season's episodes must have been a huge culture shock to viewers; building the suspense as a figure appeared on the horizon, making his way towards the camera to reveal an exhausted, dishevelled man clothed in rags and with long, matted hair and beard, stumbling along the way until finally he collapsed and rasped the word 'It's . . .' before the title sequence completed his sentence with the name of the show (his work done, the shaggy man would turn and make his way back into the sea or over a barren landscape as the end titles rolled). Baffling beyond belief, it became one of the only motifs that the series repeated.

Comedy high points included any occasion on which the team dressed up in women's clothes. For some bizarre reason, the sight of a group of less-than-pretty men making no effort whatsoever to disguise the fact that they're just a bunch of blokes in frocks is

TRIVIA
The giant squashing foot from the opening titles was a detail taken from Agnolo di Cosimo's painting *Venus, Cupid, Folly and Time* (1545).

WEBSITE
The Pythons' on-line presence can be found at www.pythonline.com.

instantly and utterly hilarious. Added to the fact that the shrieking, piercing, high-pitched caterwaul of a 'woman's voice' that was always used sounds more like a hedgehog being dragged backwards through a mincing machine, and you've got pure comedy gold. In particular, Terry Jones was born to play a loud, working-class woman, with a face (framed in curlers and headscarf) twisted to resemble the proverbial bulldog chewing a wasp. Nevertheless, all of the Pythons took their turn under the headscarf (one of these grotesque parodies was identified as a 'Mrs Niggerbaiter', a name so intent upon shocking that it's hard to imagine that particular sketch finding an American audience open-minded enough to accept it for what it was, though we can only assume that it did). For those vignettes where a real woman was absolutely necessary, Carol Cleveland or Connie Booth would oblige: only very rarely did either of them have anything to do but look beautiful and dim.

There are simply far too many memorable sketches, scenarios and characters to adequately list. Aside from the ubiquitous parrot sketch and the nearly as famous 'Lumberjack Song' ('I put on women's clothing, and hang around in bars'), some of our favourites include: John Cleese's dislocative Minister of Funny Walks; Chapman's army officer who interrupted sketches because they were 'getting a bit silly'; the surprise appearance of the Spanish Inquisition (which of course, nobody expects); the horrifically sadistic gameshow 'Blackmail' (which now seems positively tame compared to the reality TV humiliations that people actually volunteer to take part in); and the knotted-hankie-wearing Gumbies ('My brain hurts!'). Even the very first episode has some classic moments. We meet Ernest Scribbler, writer of 'the funniest joke in the world', who causes mass carnage because of his lethally funny quip. The discovery of this joke leads to the creation of the Geneva Convention on Joke Warfare and the destruction of German forces across the whole of Europe, in an utterly sublime sequence that's just as funny today as it ever was. Another hilariously inappropriate joke is the marvellous mouse organ – unfortunately not a mechanical mouse organ, like in ***Bagpuss***, but one that's powered by real mice and a mallet-wielding Terry Jones . . .

Without question, though, it's Terry Gilliam's completely bizarre animation that has stood the test of time better than the rest of the sketches. Gilliam's source material tended to incorporate photographs and images of people throughout history as well as classical works of art. By cutting them out, animating them and putting them into contemporary settings, Gilliam provided both neat segues between other jokes and exceptionally funny sequences in their own right. The nightmare giant Siamese cat walking around on its hind legs; the flasher being eaten by a pram; and the savage group of man-eating cars all etch themselves on the memory thanks to Gilliam's work, a combination of Dali-esque landscapes mixed with the imagery of Flemish artist Pieter Bruegel, all animated in the style of ***Captain Pugwash***.

Critical and public acclaim grew to an almost exponential degree. Europe beckoned too – the boys won the Silver Rose of Montreux and were shipped off to Germany to record a special edition of the series – *Monty Python's Fliegender Zirkus* – which combined lengthy mockery of historical documentaries with re-creations of some of the better-known sketches from the series (the German version of the 'Lumberjack Song' in particular is amusing for British viewers as it changes the line 'Just like my dear mama' to 'Just like my Uncle Walter' to aid the rhyme).

As comedians like Steve Martin and Richard Pryor took comedy from the clubs into stadiums, the Pythons were waiting in the wings to storm America and join what many were calling 'the new rock 'n' roll'. *Monty Python – Live at Hollywood Bowl* elevated that wretched dead parrot to the level of a rock anthem, a 'Smoke on the Water' or 'Layla' for pub bores to repeat ad nauseam. For which we can only say: thanks, *Monty*. Thanks so much!

Tired of the slog of writing new material, the Pythons not so much disbanded as drifted apart. John Cleese went off to create ***Fawlty Towers*** with Connie Booth, and although he contributed sketches for the fourth series (which was retitled simply *Monty Python*), he chose not to appear (instead, former Bonzo Dog Doo Dah Band member Neil Innes joined the team). Michael Palin and Terry Jones went on to make ***Ripping Yarns***, a quirky series in the style of the kind of *Boy's Own* adventure stories that the pair had enjoyed as children. Eric Idle took Neil Innes with him to make *Rutland Weekend Television*, from which grew Beatles mickey-take the Rutles, and Terry Gilliam and Terry Jones collaborated on *Jabberwocky* (1977), a comic horror feature film inspired by the beast of Lewis Carroll's nonsense poem. As the later Python films showed, it wasn't that the individuals didn't want to work together; rather they were simply too busy doing other things. They were also keen to take part in the Amnesty International fundraising concert *The Secret Policeman's Ball* (and subsequent shows), which saw many a classic Python sketch replayed for a new generation (one such 'ball' marked the last occasion on which Cleese and Palin performed the parrot sketch, in which Cleese declared the parrot to be dead, Palin agreed and the matter was sorted out amicably – possibly the first time that sketch had been funny since its initial performance a decade and a half before).

Michael Palin has nominated ***The Day Today/Brass Eye*** mastermind Chris Morris as the true inheritor of the 'Pythonesque' tag – a man totally unafraid to push back the boundaries of comedy; just as the Pythons had done 30 years earlier. Our problem is that the adjective 'Pythonesque' is abused and misapplied almost as often as that other hyperbolic descriptor 'Hitchcockian'. Too few critics ever stop to question what they mean when they use the term, to the point where it's evolved into a generic word for anything that isn't a traditional sitcom or purely linear narrative. Only the *Monty Python* films could ever be truly described as Pythonesque – vaguely similar to the rhythms and themes of that influential TV series, yet simultaneously something completely different.

The Morecambe and Wise Show

Ernie Wise and Eric Morecambe.

The undisputed kings of television comedy, Morecambe and Wise are so beloved and well regarded even today that their position in the television firmament is undoubtedly forever assured. Ernest Wiseman and John Eric Bartholomew were both born in the north of England in the mid-1920s, Ernie in Leeds and Eric in the Lancashire seaside resort he would adopt as his stage name. The two boys first met as children when working together for theatre impresario Jack Hylton, joining the touring talent show *Youth Takes a Bow*. Over the next 30 years, their paths would cross on several occasions; each time, Eric's mother Sadie would try to encourage them to become a double-act. Finally, in 1951, Morecambe and Wise made their TV debut on the BBC's *Parade of Youth* talent show, an appearance that led to a long-lasting comedy partnership.

The duo having appeared on programmes as diverse as *Running Wild, The Winifred Atwell Show, Double Six* and ***Sunday Night at the London Palladium***, the first edition of *The Morecambe and Wise Show* was broadcast (live from the Wood Green Empire in North London) on ITV at 8.00 p.m. on Thursday 12 October 1961. Instantly, network chiefs felt that they were on to a hit, with Eric and Ernie's combination of stand-up comedy and sketches proving to be a winner with audiences. Very soon, the formula for the next 20 years was established – Eric was the quick-witted gag-master, Ernie the butt of Eric's jokes. The boys stayed with ATV for six seasons and 67 episodes of their show, but after producing their final run of ten episodes in colour (thanks to American investment, with the specific intention that they would be sold overseas – they went down particularly well in Canada), Eric and Ernie were unwilling to revert to their former monochromatic ways and decided to up sticks to the only UK channel then broadcasting in colour – BBC Two.

Comedy
ATV for ITV/BBC Two/One/Thames for ITV
Episode Duration: 30-60 mins
Broadcast: 12 Oct 1961-31 Mar 1968 (ATV), 2 Sep 1968-25 Dec 1977 (BBC), 18 Oct 1978-26 Dec 1983 (Thames)

Regular Cast
Eric Morecambe, Ernie Wise

Producers Colin Clews (ATV), John Ammonds, Ernest Maxin (BBC), Keith Beckett, John Ammonds, Mark Stuart (Thames)

Writers Eric Morecambe, Ernie Wise, Sid Green, Dick Hills, Eddie Braben, Mike Craig, Lawrie Kinsley, Barry Cryer, John Junkin, Ron McDonnell

Theme Music 'Bring Me Sunshine' was normally performed by the boys as they skipped away from the camera on their BBC shows – words were written by Sylvia Dee, music by Arthur Kent. However, other lesser-known tunes were used for their ITV series, including one called 'The Two of Us' and 'Positive Thinking' by ***Neighbours*** theme maestro Tony Hatch. When Eric and Ernie returned once again to ITV, a special version of the 'Salute to Thames' theme (originally written by Johnny Hawkesworth) was premiered, matching the words 'Here they are, it's Morecambe and Wise!' to the famous Thames logo and melody.

This marked the beginning of a nine-year run of programmes that forever linked Morecambe and Wise with the BBC in the minds of the general public. These BBC episodes are the ones that everybody remembers – a top-notch example of how to do sketch-based comedy programmes. However, things didn't always go smoothly for the new giants of British TV comedy. Shortly after the transmission of the first BBC Two season, Eric Morecambe suffered a major heart attack. For several months there were real fears that Morecambe and Wise would be no more, with Eric's ability to recover sufficiently to return to the rigours of TV production remaining in doubt. Thankfully, he was eventually able to return to work, although unfortunately the break in production between the first and second BBC seasons had resulted in regular scriptwriters Sid Green and Dick Hills signing up to write exclusively for new shows on ATV. Drafted in to write the sketches for Morecambe and Wise's second BBC series was a former gag writer for Ken Dodd, Eddie Braben. Braben's arrival was the missing element that escalated the show from merely excellent into genuine brilliance. The writer had a knack of being able to produce material that played to the strengths of both performers – in particular, he established the dynamic wordplay between the two comics that at times came to resemble a Bjorn Borg v. Jimmy Connors tennis rally.

With ratings for Morecambe and Wise's comedy going through the roof, it came as no surprise that BBC bosses were delighted to make the duo the centrepiece of their schedules. Following the success of their second BBC series, a special was broadcast on BBC One on Christmas Day 1969 – the first time that these two comics appeared in the slot for which they will forever be associated. Not only were Morecambe and Wise popular with critics and network bosses, they were also the number one draw for celebrities from the worlds of film, theatre, TV, music and even newsreading. The duo regularly welcomed an array of quality guests on to their show, allof whom were delighted to have the mickey gently taken out of them. Many guests showed up to take part in the weekly plays 'wot Ernie wrote', a parade through history normally featuring Ernie in the leading role. Everybody who was anybody in the 1970s queued up to appear in Ernie's plays – from Shirley Bassey to Vincent Price, Vanessa Redgrave to Elton John, Cliff Richard to Laurence Olivier, and even to ***Sweeney*** stars John Thaw and Dennis Waterman (which led in turn to a reciprocal appearance by Eric and Ernie on the gritty cop show).

Possibly one of the most shocking celebrity moments came when an episode was apparently interrupted by a newsflash from the BBC Newsroom. The fragrant Angela Rippon appeared behind what seemed to be a standard desk, reading the headlines – until suddenly the desk hatched open to permit the previously staid and entirely respectable Angela to show off her spectacular legs while performing a song-and-dance routine with the boys to 'Let's Face the Music and Dance'. It was, quite simply, a revelation – something that had never been seen before on British television. In one fell swoop, the long-established wall between 'serious' journalism and celebrity was demolished by a pair of very long pins. It's highly likely that, had any other performers made such a request of the BBC Newsroom, they would have been laughed out of the building. But Eric and Ernie had such a hold on the hearts of a nation that the rules that normally prevented a serving newsreader performing on a light entertainment show were understandably allowed to be bent for once. As a consequence of this, the following year saw all of the male BBC newsreaders and weather presenters guested on the show in sailor suits in a gigantic song and dance routine.

After nine years, Morecambe and Wise's Christmas specials had become an integral part of festive TV broadcasts. Indeed, the 1977 special clocked up an astonishing 28 million viewers. So it came as a huge shock that their highest-rated programme became the last thing they ever did for the BBC. The following year, the pair switched channels to Thames TV, the ITV franchise holder that had inherited the ATV region in the late 1960s.

Unfortunately for Thames, the one thing that they had forgotten about in their big-league poaching was Morecambe and Wise's master scriptwriter, Eddie Braben. Braben was still contracted to work for the BBC and was therefore unable to immediately make the switch along with his former colleagues. Despite employing seasoned and highly talented scriptwriters such as Barry Cryer and John Junkin, things just didn't seem right on ITV. Even when Braben was able to finally join them there, the magic just didn't materialise. Four full-length series and seven specials were screened on ITV, but even the Christmas specials seemed no longer to be sacrosanct: horror of horrors, ITV shifted them away from their traditional Christmas Day slot and stuck them at any point over the festive season, each time with diminishing viewers and fading critical support. It seems especially cruel that Eric and Ernie's unique comedy talents were taken away from viewers at a time when their popularity was at a low ebb; unfortunately, however, the Boxing Day show of 1983 proved to be their final TV special together. Some five months later, Eric Morecambe died of a heart attack while leaving a charity concert in Gloucestershire, at the tragically young age of 58.

Although they had actually recorded a rare 'straight' piece together prior to Eric's death (*Night Train to Murder*, which received a posthumous screening in January 1985), it is for a series of comedy vignettes and catchphrases that Eric Morecambe and Ernie Wise will forever be remembered. They left behind memories of a perfect comedy double-act that raise a melancholy smile even now. We recall constant references to Ernie's 'short, fat, hairy legs'; Eric miming the 'invisible coin into a brown paper bag' gag or putting his glasses on askew; the repetition of tea, Ern?/tea urn; the unashamed cheapness of it all, with guests complaining of their low fees and Peter Cushing making repeated appearances and claiming he still hadn't been paid for the last one; the sight of two grown men in their pyjamas sharing a double bed; the duo preparing breakfast to the tune of 'The Stripper'; their immaculate pastiche of 'Singing in the Rain'; and oh so many more. Forgiving them their early disappointing feature films, Morecambe and Wise's TV work never failed to raise a smile. We miss them today as much as ever.

TRIVIA

Two celebrities do stand out from the rest of the crowd for subjecting themselves to embarrassment and humiliation above and beyond the call of duty. Celebrated concert pianist and conductor André Previn (or 'Andrew Preview', as Eric called him) took it neatly on the chin when Eric insisted that, contrary to Previn's criticism, he was playing all of the right notes in his piano piece (Grieg's Piano Concerto) – just 'not necessarily in the right order'. TV legend Des O'Connor was the perpetual butt of Eric's jokes: poor Des's singing ability (or lack of it) became a running gag that lasted for many years. Des didn't let this prevent him making several guest appearances on the show, however.

Isla Blair · *Ruth*
Fiona Gillies · *Angela*
James Grout · *George Batt*
Holly Aird · *Emily*
Jonathan Burn · *Chief Inspector Strachan*
Louisa Janes · *Helena*
Liliana Komorowska · *Danuta*
Grant Parsons · *Leo*
Trevor Cooper · *Sergeant Bear*

Producer Ken Riddington **Writer** Andrew Davies, from the novel by Domini Taylor (real name Laura Black) **Theme Music** Patrick Gowers

Renowned screenwriter Andrew Davies, fresh from his success on ***A Very Peculiar Practice***, adapted Domini Taylor's novel into this gripping and powerful four-part drama. Beginning as a standard family drama series, *Mother Love* centred on the overbearing and suffocating relationship between Helena Vesey and her beloved son Kit. Although Kit is a successful lawyer, he still lives at home with his mother and finds himself tied to her proverbial apron strings. When Kit falls in love with art gallery worker Angela, Helena's passion for her child twists into a dangerous obsession that will tolerate no interlopers.

Mother Love was a *tour de force* for Diana Rigg, who played Helena with an air of vengeful malice and controlled menace that was a million miles away from her most famous TV role as ***Avenger*** Emma Peel. Former ***Man from U.N.C.L.E.*** David McCallum also delivered a quality performance as Helena's estranged husband Alex. Boasting a grade A script and a star-studded cast of past and future acting talent, *Mother Love* is a perfect example of the kind of drama series that really captures the imagination of the viewing public. The series rightfully won two BAFTA awards in 1990 – Best Actress to Diana Rigg, and Best Drama Series/Serial.

Muffin the Mule

See pages 494–6

Mulberry

Sitcom | BBC One | episode duration 30 mins | broadcast 24 Feb 1992–20 May 1993

Regular Cast

Karl Howman · *Mulberry*
Geraldine McEwan · *Miss Rose Farnaby*
John Bennett · *The Stranger*
Tony Selby · *Bert Finch*
Mary Healey, Lill Roughley · *Alice Finch*
Caroline Blakiston · *Adele*
Sylvia Syms · *Springtime*

Creators/Writers John Esmonde and Bob Larbey **Producers** John B. Hobbs, Clive Grainger **Theme Music** Chris Adoni and Chris Nicolaides composed the melancholy theme tune, with series star Karl Howman providing the vocals.

Miss Farnaby is an elderly, crotchety recluse who lives in her large isolated house with only lifelong servants Bert and Alice Finch for company. Despite having been friends with them for many years, Miss Farnaby now resents having the Finches around, believing that they only stay working with her so that they can inherit some money when she dies. Bert and Alice meanwhile are so fed up with the old lady's constant bad attitude that they're prepared to walk out on her, disgusted that such an old friend could ever treat them so badly. They're just about to place an advert for a replacement housekeeper/gardener/odd job man in the local newsagent's window when a strange young man arrives at Miss Farnaby's front door. His name is Mulberry, and very soon, with his natural charm and cheek, he's become an irreplaceable part of the household, mending bridges between Miss Farnaby and the Finches, and breathing new life into the twilight years of a woman who doesn't expect to have many of them left.

However, all is not what it seems. Over the course of the first series of six episodes, we see Mulberry leave the house and talk to a mysterious, black-clad stranger, who keeps urging Mulberry to hurry up and 'get on with it'. It transpires that this stranger is none other than Death himself, and that Mulberry is his son – a trainee Grim Reaper-in-waiting. Mulberry's first 'job' is to escort Miss Farnaby from this world to the next, but to his father's disgust, Mulberry begs to be allowed some time with Miss Farnaby, to help her experience joy and happiness and just live a little before she has to move on. With his father reluctant to agree, Mulberry asks his mother, Springtime, to intercede on his behalf, and eventually he gets a (literal) stay of execution for Miss Farnaby.

A charming, subtle and at times deeply moving sitcom, *Mulberry* came from the pens of ***The Good Life***'s John Esmonde and Bob Larbey, who had previously made Karl Howman a star with ***Brush Strokes***. The unusual supernatural theme provides a deeply poignant backdrop to the gentle comedy. Although the characters of the Finches seem as though they belong in a broader, more traditional sitcom, the performances of Howman and McEwan as the supernatural manservant and the crabby spinster are, quite simply, an utter joy. Moderately popular at the time, *Mulberry* sadly lasted for just 13 episodes. A third season was planned, which would have revealed the final fates of Miss Farnaby, the Finches and Mulberry himself, but unfortunately a change of BBC management (rather than poor viewing figures) meant this was not to be. One of the great 'forgotten' sitcoms, *Mulberry* richly deserves to be re-evaluated and rediscovered by a new generation of viewers.

Muffin the Mule

Annette Mills and Muffin say hello.

Muffin was already a television veteran of more than a decade by the time he became a household name. His first appearance took place in November 1934 during an experimental broadcast of a performance by husband and wife team Jan Bussell and Ann Hogarth and their 'Hogarth Puppets'. Built by Fred Tickner, famous for his Punch and Judy puppets, the mule appeared in a sequence set at a circus. He had been designed to have a deliberately comical look, with an enlarged head and rather stiff legs. After this brief taste of fame, the still nameless puppet was placed into storage.

In 1946, actress Annette Mills (elder sister of actor John Mills) was the host of *For the Children*, a musical programme for the very young shown at 5 o'clock. After stumbling on the notion that the top of her piano resembled a stage, she approached Bussell and Hogarth to see if they had any puppets that might suit the kind of songs Mills was writing and performing. There, in their store cupboards, she found two that took her fancy: a clown, which she named Crumpet, and a bandy-legged mule, who became known as Muffin. The puppets were operated by Ann Hogarth, who stood on one side of the piano concealed behind a partition. Mills and Hogarth realised the potential in Muffin and so he eventually won his own series.

Pre-School Puppetry
Parthian/Maverick Entertainment for BBC TV
Episode Duration: 15 mins
Broadcast: 20 Oct 1946–1955

Regular Cast
Annette Mills · *Presenter*
Muffin · *Himself*

Creators Ann Hogarth, Annette Mills

Producer Andrew Miller Jones

Writers Ann Hogarth, Annette Mills

Theme Music Written and performed by Annette Mills, who sang the infamous line 'We want Muffin, Muffin the Mule!'

Early episodes, as was common to all television at the time, were broadcast live from Alexandra Palace, although eventually some programmes were recorded to enable them to be reshown at a later date. Each edition involved Annette Mills singing a few songs while Muffin danced along as best he could. Some of the songs would be inspired by a basic story, such as Muffin preparing for a holiday in France (complete with a French beret and stripy top), while another involved making a wish (he wished that it would rain carrots, which of course Annette Mills mocked until, with perfect comic timing, a bunch of carrots plummeted down onto poor Muffin's head). The show also gave Ann Hogarth the chance to resurrect some of her other puppets were too, each of whom had their own theme tune, like Muffin. There was a 'penguin so important' called Mr Peregrine Esquire, Louise the Lamb ('Wearing buttercup and daisy/Just a trifle crazy!'), Sally the dancing Sea-lion ('She can use her flippers/Just like dancing slippers'), plus a couple of characters that almost certainly wouldn't be invited back for any reunions – Big Chief Carrot Top ('Waller waller waller woo') and Wally the Gog, who was a minstrel golliwog.

Muffin's BBC career was brought to an abrupt end in 1951 when Annette Mills died. Ann Hogarth later took Muffin to ITV and then to the States. Aside from compilation shows, that was it for the excitable mule until 2004, when the BBC announced the commissioning of a new animated series from Maverick Entertainment along the same lines as their revivals of ***Andy Pandy*** and the ***Flower Pot Men***. Gone are the cheesy songs and very upper-class accents, as Muffin now lives on a farm with other animals and has adventures far away from the top of a piano. The new show is scheduled to appear on our screens just in time for Muffin's 6th anniversary, in 2006.

Other puppets almost certainly wouldn't be invited back for any reunions – Big Chief Carrot Top and Wally the Gog.

Multi-Coloured Swap Shop

See pages 498–500

The Munsters

Sitcom | Kayro-Vue Productions for CBS/The Arthur Company for MCA (shown on ITV) | episode duration 25 mins | broadcast 24 Sep 1964–12 May 1966, 9 Oct 1988–24 May 1991 (USA)

Regular Cast

Fred Gwynne, John Schuck, Edward Herrmann, Sam McMurray · *Herman Munster*

Yvonne De Carlo, Lee Meriwether, Veronica Hamel, Ann Magnuson · *Lily Munster*

Al Lewis, Howard Morton, Robert Morse, Sandy Baron · *'Grandpa' Dracula*

Beverley Owen, Pat Priest, Hilary Van Dyke, Christine Taylor, Elaine Hendrix · *Marilyn Munster*

Butch Patrick, Jason Marsden, Mathew Botuchis, Bug Hall · *Eddie Wolfgang Munster*

Creators Joe Connelly and Bob Mosher **Producers** Joe Connelly, Bob Mosher (*The Munsters*), Lloyd J. Schwartz, Arthur Annecharico, Dustin Nelson (*The Munsters Today*) **Writers** Various, including Joe Connelly, Bob Mosher, Norm Liebmann, Ed Haas, James Allardice, Tom Adair, Dick Conway, Richard Baer, Douglas Tibbles **Theme Music** Jack Marshall

It's unfortunate that *The Munsters'* television debut coincided with that of ***The Addams Family***. Both are fine examples of creative producers thinking outside of the box to develop something original, and both involve engaging and likeable characters in bizarre situations. *The Addams Family* often comes out on top simply because of its subtlety, in contrast to the broader comedic strokes of Herman Munster and his brood.

Created from the people who made *Leave it to Beaver* (a top-rated show in the States), *The Munsters* was shaped around the talents of Al Lewis and Fred Gwynne, stars of the hit comedy *Car 54, Where Are You?* It began 'unlife' in 1963 as a 16-minute pilot shot in colour on the set of Hitchcock's *Psycho* (1960). The biggest difference between the pilot and the series (aside from the series being made in black and white) was Herman's wife, who in the pilot was called Phoebe and played by Joan Marshall. Happy Derman (yes, that's a real name!) played a rather feral Eddie, though the character's wolfish tendencies would be toned down when Butch Patrick played him in the series.

The programme relied on audience recognition of Universal Studios' horror films of the 1930s, 40s and 50s. Herman sported a flat-top head, sunken face and looming physique that undermined the memorable image of Karloff's 1930s Frankenstein with his thin-lipped but expansive grin; while Lily's raven mane with its lock of white hair evoked both Elsa Lanchester's Bride of Frankenstein and Vampira, a character that used to present the horror flicks on American television. Their son, Eddie, was a diminutive Lon Chaney from *The Wolf Man* (1941), while Grandpa was the family's very own vampire, related in some way to Count Dracula and modelled on the versions played by Bela Lugosi (1931) and John Carradine (*House of Dracula*, 1945). The misfit in the family in more ways than one is the Munsters' niece Marilyn, an attractive blonde, like Ms Monroe, whose conventional good looks pass for disappointing plainness in the eyes of her relatives. A running gag in the series involved Marilyn being escorted home by a date only for him to flee in terror at the sight of Herman, who naturally assumed that it was Marilyn and not himself from whom the young man was running away.

Like the Addams' spooky abode, 1313 Mockingbird Lane was filled with all manner of ghoulish artefacts, cobweb-strewn torture equipment and funereal decor (appropriate considering Herman's job as a grave digger at the local funeral parlour). Likewise, the foundations of the buildings must have been equally strong, especially in the Munster household, where Herman's hefty frame caused the destruction of walls and doorways galore. But one thing the Munsters had over their ghoulish neighbours on the other network was the family car, a converted stretch hearse with a gothic canopy that matched that of the family home. The Munster Koach and Grandpa's 'Dragula' car were made by George Barris, the 'Kustom Car King' who also gave us the classic Batmobile for the ***Batman*** TV series.

Unhappy at living so far away from her New York home, Beverley Owen abandoned Marilyn after just 14 episodes, necessitating the swift casting of Pat Priest in her place. After just 70 episodes in two series, *The Munsters* was dropped by executives, uncomfortable with the kind of nonconformist values the show was espousing. Ironically, *The Addams Family* was dropped at the same time for similarly daft reasons. Reruns and an animated series (*The Mini-Munsters*) helped keep the show alive until 1981 when a reunion movie, *The Munsters' Revenge* (1981), gave viewers their first sight of the cast in lurid colour. The format was revived in 1988 as *The Munsters Today*. Though starring a completely new cast (including John Schuck as Herman and Lee Meriwether as Lily), the characters were intended to be the very same that we'd seen in the 1960s, the premise being that one of Grandpa's experiments had placed them all in suspended animation for 22 years. Surprisingly (no, scratch that–*inexplicably*), this series ran for three years and just managed to beat the original series' count with 72 episodes, although it has to be said that being recorded on videotape made it look cheap compared to the classy black and white film episodes. Two TV movies followed – *Here Come the Munsters* (1995) and *The Munsters' Scary Little Christmas* (1996) – with the characters recast again each time. At the time of writing, a feature film version penned by Marlon and Keenen Ivory Wayans is in production. We're genuinely surprised it's taken this long, considering the glut of other TV characters to have

been given the big-screen treatment, including *The Addams Family* (1991 and 1993), *Car 54, Where Are You?* (1994) and the ill-advised *Sgt Bilko* (1996).

Trivia

The opening titles for the first series were a witty parody of *The Donna Reed Show* (a popular sitcom that ran in the USA from 1955 until 1966), with Lily shown waving her family off with their packed lunches. James Allardice wrote for both shows.

Muppet Babies

Animation | Jim Henson Productions/Marvel Productions for CBS (shown on BBC One) | episode duration 25 mins | broadcast 15 Sep 1984–29 Dec 1990 (USA)

Voice Cast

Frank Welker · *Kermit, Beaker, Skeeter*
Greg Berg · *Fozzie, Scooter*
Laurie O'Brien · *Piggy*
Howie Mandel · *Animal, Bunsen, Skeeter*
Katie Leigh · *Rowlf*
Barbara Billingsley · *Nanny*
Russi Taylor · *Gonzo, Robin*
Dave Coulier · *Uncle Waldorf*

Creator Jim Henson **Producer** Roy Allen Smith **Writer** Jeffrey Scott **Theme Music** Hank Saroyan: 'Muppet Babies, we make our dreams come true!/Muppet Babies, we'll do the same for you!'

For commentary, see THE MUPPETS, pages 501–6

The Muppet Show

Comedy/Muppetry | ATV/ITC for ITV | episode duration 25 mins | broadcast 24 Oct 1976–15 Mar 1981 (UK)

Regular Voice Cast

Jim Henson · *Kermit the Frog, Rowlf, Link Hogthrob, Swedish Chef, Dr Teeth, Muppet Newsman, Waldorf*
Frank Oz · *Animal, Fozzie Bear, Miss Piggy, Sam the Eagle*
Jerry Nelson · *Camilla, Sergeant Floyd Pepper, Robin the Frog, Crazy Harry, Uncle Deadly, Dr Julius Strangepork, Pops, J. P. Grosse, Thog, Lew Zealand, Fleet Scribbler, Announcer*
Richard Hunt · *Beaker, Miss Piggy, Janice, Wayne, Scooter, Statler, Sweetums*
Dave Goelz · *The Great Gonzo, Dr Bunsen Honeydew, Zoot, Muppy, Beauregard, Timmy Monster*
Louise Gold · *Annie Sue Pig*
John Lovelady · *Crazy Harry, Nigel*
Eren Ozker · *Janice, Wanda, Hilda*
Steve Whitmire · *Foo-Foo, Rizzo the Rat, Lips*
Kathryn Mullen · *Gaffer the Backstage Cat, Various Voices*
Betsy Baytos · *Betsy Bird, Various Voices*
Brian Muehl, Karen Prell · *Various Voices*

Creator Jim Henson **Producers** Jim Henson, David Lazer (executive) **Writers** Joseph A. Bailey, Jack Burns, Jim Henson, Don Hinkley, Jerry Juhl, Chris Langham, Marc London, David Odell, James Thurman **Theme Music** 'It's time to play the music, it's time to light the lights, it's time to raise the curtain on the *Muppet Show* tonight . . .' by Jim Henson and Sam Pottle

For commentary, see THE MUPPETS, pages 501–6

The Muppets

See pages 501–6

Muppets Tonight!

Comedy/Muppetry | Jim Henson Productions for ABC (shown on BBC One) | episode duration 25 mins | broadcast 8 Mar 1996–17 Nov 1997 (USA)

Voice Cast

Frank Oz · *Miss Piggy, Fozzie Bear, Sam the Eagle, Lion, Animal*
Steve Whitmire · *Kermit the Frog, Rizzo the Rat, Beaker, Andy Pig, Captain Pighead, Mr Poodlepants*
Brian Henson · *Seymore, Sal Manilla, Dr Phil Van Neuter, Nigel*
Jerry Nelson · *Lew Zealand, Statler, Announcer*
Dave Goelz · *The Great Gonzo, Dr Bunsen Honeydew, Beauregard, Waldorf, Randy Pig, Bill the Bubble Guy*
Allan Trautman · *Various Voices*
Bill Barretta · *Bobo, Johnny Fiama, Pepe the Prawn, Rowlf the Dog, Zippity-Zap, Big Mean Carl, David Hoggselhoff*
Leslie Carrara · *Spamela Hamderson*
Kevin Clash · *Clifford, Mulch*

Creator Jim/Brian Henson **Producers** Patric Verrone, Brian Henson (executive) **Writers** Jennifer Barrow, Dick Blasucci, Paul Flaherty, Darin Henry, Bernie Keating, Jim Lewis, Dan McGrath, Kirk R. Thatcher, Patric Verrone **Theme Music** Though the series' music, by Eric Colvin and Philip Giffin, continued the old ***Muppet Show*** traditions, the programme's theme wasn't particularly memorable, being a generic, glitzy intro that sounded just like everything else from that time.

For commentary, see THE MUPPETS, pages 501–6

Murder Most Horrid

Comedy/Anthology | Talkback Productions for BBC Two | episode duration 30 mins | broadcast 14 Nov 1991–2 Apr 1999

Regular Cast

Dawn French · *Various Roles*

Producers Peter Fincham, Jon Plowman (executive), Sophie Clarke-Jervoise **Writers** Ian Hislop, Nick Newman, Paul Smith, Terry Kyan, James Hendrie, Graham Alborough, Jez Alborough, Ian Brown, Steven Moffat, Chris England, Jon Canter, Mark Burton,

Continued on page 507

Multi-Coloured Swap Shop

Cheggers, Maggie, John and Noel.

It's hard to imagine it now, but prior to the autumn of 1976, Saturday mornings on television were not the exclusive domain of the ankle-biters and rugrats. Although the TV schedules often boasted a few cartoons or repeats of ***Thunderbirds*** and ***Joe 90***, there wasn't a coherent, overall policy to permanently dedicate those hours to children's programming. In fact, you were just as likely to stumble across an instalment of *Farmhouse Kitchen* or *Asian Magazine* as an episode of ***Scooby-Doo***. There had been a couple of previous attempts to provide some kind of linking continuity around a child-centric Saturday morning line-up in the late 1960s and early 1970s (the all-but forgotten *Zokko* and *Outa-Space!*), but it wasn't until 1976 that the BBC decided to tackle the problem properly.

Trying to come up with a workable format for a lengthy live-broadcast show, the new programme's producer Rosemary Gill met with ***Blue Peter***'s head honcho Biddy Baxter and head of children's programmes Edward Barnes. They had already approached Radio 1 DJ Noel Edmonds to front the show, having been very impressed by the cool and collected way he handled the live phone-ins during 1975's teenage problem show *Z-Shed*. Gill suggested that a running theme for the programme might be based around the fact that kids loved swapping things – a truism that the manufacturers of Pokémon used to their financial advantage in the mid-1990s. Thus *Multi-Coloured Swap Shop* was born, the first full-length, live, Saturday morning children's programme to be shown across the whole of the UK. In fact, *Swap Shop* wasn't actually the first Saturday morning show – another programme beat it to air by a couple of years. However, this other programme was only shown in the ATV (Midlands) region for its first four or five years of life; it gradually spread across the other regions until it was eventually networked in 1980/1 as ITV's response to the success of *Swap Shop*. Its name? ***TISWAS*** ...

The very first edition of *Swap Shop* was transmitted on 2 October 1976 and featured a line-up of guests that set the scene for the next 20-odd years of Saturday morning children's telly on the BBC. The

Children's Entertainment
BBC One
Episode Duration: 175 mins
Broadcast: 2 Oct 1976–27 Mar 1982

Regular Cast Noel Edmonds, Keith Chegwin, John Craven, Maggie Philbin, Posh Paws, Eric, Igor, Lamb · *Presenters*

Creator Rosemary Gill

Producers Rosemary Gill (editor), Crispin Evans, Chris Bellinger, Angela Sharp

Theme Music Mike Batt's theme ran for the first five seasons ('Swap Shop! Doo-do, do-do-do-do-do-do-do-do-do dooooo . . . !'), until a new, revamped one – courtesy of B. A. Robertson ('Hello . . . hello . . . hello . . .') and performed by Brown Sauce (see below) – arrived in autumn 1981.

star of ***Doctor Who*** and his sidekick Sarah Jane (Tom Baker and Elisabeth Sladen) turned up to promote the first episode of 'The Hand of Fear', transmitted later that same afternoon at 6.10 p.m.; glam-pop group Flintlock (seemingly everywhere and really only ever famous for being on kids' TV shows) played their one hit, 'Dawn'; and young actor Kevin Moreton (who'd played the lead in Geordie drama *Sam*) turned up to let viewers know about the new ghost-story series he was appearing in, ITV's *Nobody's House*. Over the rest of the series, guests as wide-ranging as Patrick Moore, Tavares, the **Liver Birds**, Queen, Pussycat, ABBA, Percy Thrower and Suzi Quatro showed up – a veritable *Who's Who* of 1970s light entertainment performers. All of them would inevitably face a grilling from young viewers over the phone (calling in on 01 811 8055) before offering up a 'Prize Swap', such as a signed copy of their latest album.

Aside from the celebrity guests, each edition would revolve around a number of key elements. Noel would read out letters that had been sent in by viewers, and would share some banter with Posh Paws, the bright purple tyrannosaurus that sat on his desk. It took many viewers quite some time to realise that 'Posh Paws' was very nearly the name of the programme spelled backwards rather than a comment on his sartorial state. A half-hour cartoon would break up proceedings (usually a Hanna-Barbera or Filmation production like ***Tarzan*** or *Valley of the Dinosaurs*) before the competition results were read out (often thanks to the 'helping hand' of Igor (a stagehand wearing a big hairy 'horror' glove). ***Newsround*** presenter John Craven might then introduce a feature based loosely around an item that had been topical in the news that week; glamorous 'roving reporter' Maggie Philbin (who joined from the third season onwards) would have young male viewers glued to the screen; and insanely chirpy Scouser Keith 'Cheggers' Chegwin would inevitably end up standing outside in the pouring rain in a desolate windswept car park somewhere in the Midlands, surrounded by hundreds of kids waving broken Action Men and Etch-a-Sketches in the air. Cheggers' 'Swaparama' became one of the most popular elements in the programme, giving children in 'the provinces' the chance to both appear on telly and get rid of that useless birthday present they'd just received from Auntie Betty.

The core of the whole programme was the 'Swap Board', a 'Top Ten' list of items that viewers wanted to get rid of in exchange for something more desirable. The camera would slowly pan up the board, revealing each number in turn, along the lines of 'Damian, Preston. Has: Mastermind Game. Wants: Scalextric'. Very often the people wanting to make a swap were highly optimistic of their chances, offering to exchange a low-value item like a Slinky or a *Girl's World* for the ultimate in 1970s cool, a Raleigh Chopper bike. For those viewers who simply wanted to throw away a bit of old tat, the board might read: 'Peter, Hounslow. Has: Six Million Dollar Man figure. Wants: Anything.' If any of the viewers at home wanted to swap their property for the item advertised on the show, they then wrote in to the programme ('BBC TV, Wood Lane, London W12 8QT') and an army of unfortunate BBC researchers would match the postcard sent in by the swappers to those of the swapees.

Each year, *Swap Shop* would organise the Star Awards, voted for by the kids. The awards were presented on or around Easter Sunday each year and consisted of typical categories like 'Favourite Man on TV' and 'Best Pop Act'. These awards weren't Oscars, though, they were Erics, named after the mysterious BBC wage-slave whose job it was to raise and lower the large plastic spheres that contained all of the correct postcards sent in as the answers to competitions. During the ceremony there would even be a musical act in the interval (shades of the **Eurovision Song Contest**), usually consisting of Cheggers and Maggie singing a nauseating ballad at each other. However, one year chart-troubling Caledonian crooner B. A. Robertson decided to pen the interval song – 'I Just Wanna Be a Winner', which was performed by Noel, Maggie and Cheggers (collectively known as 'Brown Sauce'). Once again highlighting the woeful taste of the British public when it comes to novelty records, this song proved so popular that it was released as a single – eventually hitting No. 15 in December 1981.

Swap Shop drew to a close after six highly successful years on the air, primarily because host Noel Edmonds had decided he wanted to have a crack at the Saturday evening family entertainment audience with ***The Late, Late Breakfast Show***. Although the last 'proper' episode went out on 27 March 1982, it was followed by the annual Star Awards, two specials replaying many of the musical guests seen on the programme over the years, and then finally two '*Swap Shop* on the Road' specials – following pop stars 10CC and Adam Ant – shown in August 1982. In the end, some 146 episodes of *Swap Shop* were screened on BBC One, establishing an entirely new genre of programming and essentially banishing 'adult' programmes from the two main channels at any time before noon on Saturdays. *Swap Shop* lived on in its follow-up programme, ***Saturday Superstore*** – a show that wasn't so much an evolved version, more a photocopy of the format with just the main presenters swapped over.

At heart, *Multi-Coloured Swap Shop* was always a much more sedate, refined and (dare we say) middle-class programme than its main ITV rival *TISWAS*. Whereas *TISWAS* prided itself on the copious quantities of slime and water hurled around the studio, *Swap Shop* was far more likely to feature a young viewer who had just won a scholarship to the Northern Music School for being precociously talented at playing the flute. And perhaps that's the reason for its success – by providing a programme that educated as well as entertained, *Swap Shop* enabled parents to feel much happier leaving their young 'uns in front of the antics of Noel and Cheggers than they would have been letting their offspring witness the subversive behaviour taking place under Chris Tarrant's gaze. It's rather ironic, therefore, that as soon as Noel graduated to prime-time 'adult' programming, the first thing he introduced was a gunge tank. Perhaps this goes to show that as far as adults are concerned, there's no point in being grown up if you can't be childish sometimes . . .

TRIVIA

Looking at the guests who made an appearance in the final year of the programme, it's amusing to see just how much tastes had changed, while simultaneously remaining curiously the same: they included Toyah, the Carpenters, Ken Dodd, new *Doctor Who* star Peter Davison, Barry Manilow, Stu Francis and 'interesting' Steve Davis, the snooker player.

WEBSITES

The fan site www.come.to/swapshop features information on *Swap Shop*, such as which episodes have survived in the BBC archives. TV Cream's 'Saturday, Saturday' page – www.tv.cream.org/lookin/saturdaymorning – has a fantastic chronological history of the genre; while the astounding Satkids site www.paulmorris.co.uk/satkids/index2.htm – has a chart showing precisely which programme was on air in which year. Quite brilliant.

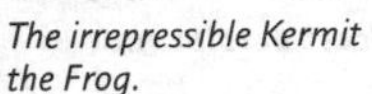

The Muppets

The irrepressible Kermit the Frog.

In 1954, a college student called Jim Henson began making appearances on a local TV station in Washington, accompanied by homemade hand puppets – or 'muppets' as he would have it – including a character called Pierre the French Rat. The following year, Henson's first TV show, *Sam and Friends*, featured a wide-eyed dog puppet called Rolf and a lizard puppet called Kermit. In an amazing quirk of Darwinism, Kermit would evolve into a frog and become one of the world's best-loved TV performers, star of umpteen movies, recipient of the 2208th star on the Hollywood Walk of Fame, and even model for a campaign for Calvin Klein. His mentor Jim Henson wouldn't do too badly out of the arrangement either.

Henson and his Muppets grew in popularity in Washington and eventually across America (thanks to regular appearances on *The Ed Sullivan Show*), but it was with an educational programme that Henson's creations would become internationally famous. ***Sesame Street*** first appeared on National Educational Television and its successor, PBS, courtesy of the publicly funded Children's Television Workshop. People who work in the television industry often rebuff the idea that television ever influences anyone, but the makers of *Sesame Street* acknowledged that this was a misconception that could be put to some good.

Even at an early age, a toddler will have been exposed to many hours of advertising and might even be able to sing along to TV jingles and theme songs. Each hour-long episode of *Sesame Street* would be structured like an hour of grown-up's TV, with ad breaks at regular intervals, except the 'products' the show would be advertising were the alphabet, numbers and word usage. Each episode would be sponsored by a letter and a number ('*Sesame Street* was brought to you today by the letters E and H and by the number 4'), and the sketches, soap-style plots and other elements would be interrupted by eye-catching sequences promoting the day's sponsored letters and number with catchy songs that veered in style from the nursery to the jazz halls of Harlem (one particularly memorable one accompanied a bouncy funk song counting from one to 12 while a

See* FRAGGLE ROCK, MUPPET BABIES, THE MUPPET SHOW, MUPPETS TONIGHT! *and* SESAME STREET *for broadcast details and individual credits

silver ball-bearing made its way across an intergalactic pin-ball machine straight out of the Beatles' *Yellow Submarine*, 1968). The characters would also illustrate examples of words like 'cooperation', the importance of understanding signs like 'Exit', 'Stop', 'Open' and 'Close', and, for the large proportion of Latin-American viewers, some of the sequences would be repeated in Spanish ('*Abierto . . . cerrado*!'). And, like proper adverts, some of the segments would be endorsed by celebrities, from sports stars like Michael Jordon to A-list film stars like Whoopi Goldberg and Mel Gibson.

The street itself was a set, but for its viewers it was real – a small, multi-cultural community where blacks, whites, Latinos and Muppets lived in harmony. Mr Hooper owned a shop on the street and the residents eventually included couples, Luis and Maria and Gordon and Susan, plus single man Bob and 'odd couple' room mates Bert (the po-faced bore) and Ernie (the playful one with the spitty laugh and love for a rubber ducky). The first Muppet to make an appearance on *Sesame Street* was Big Bird, a seven-foot-tall yellow bird with a long, broad beak and huge orange feet. Big Bird nests in an alley that runs off the back of the street, near to where the trash cans are kept. It's also where another character from that first series lives, Oscar, a grouch – a species of rude, grumpy beings who delight in misery and self-pity. First seen sporting orange fur, he appeared for the show's second year with the matted green fur he's had ever since.

As well as a change of coat for Oscar, year two introduced a few other characters, who became firm favourites with the children. Gangly blue monster Grover replaced Fuzzy Face as an excitable and curious creature who would star in comedy sketches. Grover eventually paired up with magician the Amazing Mumford to frustrate his every move. Then there was Count von Count, a benign vampire who loved to count in a thick, Transylvanian accent, often to the accompaniment of a thunderclap and gentle but slightly unhinged laughter ('Four – four wonderful bats' (KA-BOOM!) 'Ah ha ha haa'). And old faithful Kermit became a reporter for 'Muppet News', investigating such earth-shattering events as Bo Peep's lost sheep and the frustrations of an ambitious songwriter suffering from creative block ('I'll never get it! Never! Never!' and then his head would hit the piano keys – do not try this at home).

The series was socially aware from the beginning, as its multi-racial cast shows. In the mid-1970s, the viewers were introduced to Linda, who was deaf but could lip-read (though she was no use to Oscar when his TV broke and he wanted to watch 'Grouch News' – not because Muppets don't have lips (don't be silly) but because the newsreader's massive beard obscured his. Soon, Big Bird found himself a friend, a woolly mammoth called Mr Snuffleupagus. The intention with 'Snuffy' was to share in the magic of invisible friends that children sometimes invent, and so each time Big Bird went to introduce the *Sesame Street* residents to his friend, Snuffy would have wandered off, leaving Luis, Maria and the rest convinced that Big Bird was just making things up. Kids loved Snuffy, with his shaggy pelt, long eyelashes and deep, slow voice. Sadly, children's safety groups were worried that showing a 'child' (i.e. Big Bird) being frustrated by adults refusing to believe him might make victims of child abuse unwilling to report their attackers. Snuffleupagus was swiftly integrated into the *Sesame Street* community.

While we British viewers stuck with the same show that America got, in other countries the Muppets were restyled and even re-voiced to suit the local population (*Sesamstrasse* in Germany, *Ulitsa Sezam* in Russia, *Zhima Jie* in China). This has also meant that issues that might not be thought of as appropriate for an American pre-school child might well be a daily reality elsewhere in the world: since 1998, both the Israeli and Palestinian territories have been offered essentially the same show, *Rechov Sumsum Shara'a Simsim*, designed as a beacon of hope for racial harmony; while in 2002, an HIV-positive character was introduced to the South African version of the show, *Takalani Sesame*.

In 1979, a small, red-furred baby Muppet called Elmo was introduced. Designed to appeal to the very young, Elmo was so ruthlessly cute that he could have staged a bloodless coup in any country of his choosing. He has inspired vibrating 'Tickle-Me-Elmo' toys and become the firm favourite for any child who grew up with the series, to the extent that he's now pretty much the star of the show.

The success of *Sesame Street* encouraged Jim Henson to develop a vehicle for his creations that could be watched by the whole family rather than just the kiddie audience. In the mid-1970s, Henson pitched the idea for a comedy-variety show to all of the major US TV networks – all of whom thought it was a lousy idea that would never be a hit. Henson then took the concept to Lew Grade at ATV in the UK. Grade, who had long been an entrepreneur ready to take risks on an innovative idea, stumped up the cash – the Muppets had a new home. A couple of pilot specials (including one entitled 'The Muppet Show: Sex and Violence') preceded the full series, but when *The Muppet Show* finally hit the airwaves in 1976, it was like a breath of fresh air. It simultaneously revitalised and sent up the old variety show format, a genre that was practically on its last legs as a TV staple on both sides of the Atlantic. Kermit – who had done such a good job playing a news reporter on *Sesame Street* – was now producer and backstage guru behind the Muppets' weekly show. With the programme staged inside a beautifully ornate theatre, TV viewers were privileged to see the acts just as the theatre audience (including two rude hecklers, Waldorf and Stadtler) saw them: everything from Fozzie Bear's comedy stand-up routine (rarely any good) and the Great Gonzo's death-defying stunts and magic (which looked very painful) through to Miss Piggy's glossy production numbers (which rewrote the rulebook on camp) – woe betide anyone who messed things up for Piggy, for they would soon see the back of her hand in a brutal karate-chop ('hi-yaa!').

Other regular performers in the show included: Dr Teeth and his Electric Mayhem Band (Zoot, Floyd, Janice and Animal on drums); Muppet Lab's scientist Dr Bunsen Honeydew and his terrified assistant Beaker; Delia Smith-wannabe the Swedish Chef; and the amazingly patriotic and humourless Sam Eagle. Each week, if we were lucky, we would be treated to a new episode of ongoing drama

'Veterinarian's Hospital', Rowlf would give us a tune on the piano, and we might even share a few jokes with the competition ballroom dancers. Songs were an important part of the show too, with Kermit's nephew Robin performing 'Halfway Down the Stairs' (a No. 7 hit in 1977) and a group of strange creatures singing the unforgettable 'Mah Na Mah Nah' (which hit No. 8 in the same year for its original artist Piero Umiliani).

However, we viewers at home were also treated to the behind-the-scenes goings-on within the Muppet Theatre; the intrigues, power struggles and downright stupidity that went into producing each week's show. Thankfully, Kermit was able to rely upon his chirpy assistant Scooter to make sure that each of the celebrity special guests were ready for their curtain call: Scooter's chirpy knock on their dressing room door was often the first thing we viewers saw each week. And what a line-up of guest stars!

Willing volunteers in the Muppet madness included Peter Ustinov, Twiggy, Vincent Price, Ethel Merman, Steve Martin, George Burns, Elton John (memorably performing 'Crocodile Rock' with a whole crowd of singing toothy terrors), Peter Sellars, Liberace, Raquel Welch, Spike Milligan, Cheryl Ladd, Sylvester Stallone, Liza Minelli, Diana Ross, Gene Kelly, Loretta Swit, Glenda Jackson, Roger Moore, and John Denver in a Christmas special. Even Mark Hamill, R2D2 and C3Po from *Star Wars* (1977) showed up to appear in the latest instalment of 'Pigs in Space', opposite hunky captain Link Hogthrob, boffin Dr Julius Strangepork and glamorous first mate Miss Piggy. On one occasion, special guest Richard Pryor was unable to make it to the recording, so scriptwriter Chris Langham suddenly found himself in front of the camera, the Muppets (in a moment of life imitating art) being so desperate to get a replacement guest on stage, even if he was a nobody. Chris Langham has since gone on to appear in (and write) several BBC sitcoms, such as *Kiss Me Kate* and, more recently, *Help!* with Paul Whitehouse.

It comes as a big surprise to many people to discover that the entire series of *The Muppet Show* was actually recorded at ATV's studios in London. It was testament to the popularity and success of the series that such a galaxy of international stars were willing to fly all the way to the UK to record a half-hour comedy series with a bunch of puppets (luckily, many other shows were willing to make it worth their while – many a Muppet guest would end up doing the circuits on chat shows like ***Parkinson***). It wasn't just guest stars that were impressed by the Muppets, though – ratings on both sides of the Atlantic were simply astronomical, pretty much from the very first episode. Critics loved the programme too – it collected a whole bevy of awards including the Golden Rose of Montreux (1977), a Peabody Award (1979), the Emmy Award for Best Comedy (1978) and the BAFTA (1977) for Best Light Entertainment Show. With the programme still at the height of its popularity, it span off into the first of a series of feature films with *The Muppet Movie* (1979), in which the gang leave the Muppet Theatre behind and head off to Hollywood to make their fortune. Amazingly, with the Muppets practically everywhere in popular culture (only surpassed, perhaps, by the *Star Wars* phenomenon), Jim Henson took the very bold step of deciding to finish the programme while it was still 'at the top', shutting the doors of the Muppet Theatre in 1980 after 120 uproariously funny episodes.

That wasn't the end for the endearing fuzzy characters, however. Two more motion pictures followed in fairly quick succession, *The Great Muppet Caper* (1981) and *The Muppets Take Manhattan* (1984). Establishing a specific studio in London called the Jim Henson Creature Shop, Henson and his team lent their talents to the *Star Wars* films (creating retired Jedi master Yoda and the Max Rebo band for Jabba the Hutt's palace in *Return of the Jedi* (1983) – an ensemble that was effectively a reworking of Dr Teeth's band from *The Muppet Show*) and then began producing their own films such as *The Dark Crystal* (1982) and *Labyrinth* (1986), and the TV series ***The Storyteller***.

Their next TV project was a bit of a departure – a new series featuring Muppet-like characters, but with a completely new set of friends to discover. ***Fraggle Rock*** featured a race of creatures that lived (in the UK version at least) in the rock underneath a lighthouse. Gobo, Mokey, Wembley, Boober and Red tried to avoid the giant, monstrous Gorgs and help out the tiny builders the Doozers. Gobo's Uncle 'Travelling' Matt (whose name was an in-joke: a travelling matte is a trick used in film-making to block out small parts of the screen, like those blurs they put across people's faces in documentaries) would send back messages to the rest of the Fraggles from his travels in 'outer space' – i.e. our world. An interesting feature of *Fraggle Rock* was that every country that showed it had a different setting 'upstairs': in the USA, a mad inventor called Doc (played by Gerry Parkes) lived with his Muppet dog Sprocket. In Germany, he was a chef, and in the UK he was a retired captain and was played by ex-***Porridge*** star Fulton MacKay. Following Fulton's death, later series saw *Gregory's Girl* (1981) leading man John Gordon Sinclair and lastly ***Brookside*** player Simon O'Brien looking after Sprocket.

Unwilling to let his immortal main Muppet characters lie dormant, Henson then launched in 1984 an animated version in collaboration with Marvel Comics, *Muppet Babies*. Although most of the regular characters were present, the much younger-sounding voices were provided by new performers (Frank Welker as Kermit, Laurie O'Brien as Piggy and Greg Berg as Fozzie and Scooter, for example). Lasting for eight seasons and more than 100 episodes, *Muppet Babies* was even more surreal and left-field than its parent programme, with clips from movies often intercut with the animation to represent the wild flights of imagination the little ones were undertaking. Needless to say, the sight of such adorable characters crawling around in nappies was almost too cute to bear.

Dinosaurs (a spin on ***The Simpsons*** but featuring a human-sized, animatronic dinosaur family complete with the cutest, most violent baby in TV history) was about to go before the cameras when suddenly, on 16 May 1990, Jim Henson died from bacterial pneumonia at the cruelly young age of 54. His last Muppet work was to provide voices for an inspired theme park attraction – Muppet-

Vision 3-D – for the Disney-MGM Studios park in the Walt Disney World Resort in Orlando, Florida. Jim's son Brian soon took over both the running of his father's creative business and the responsibility of providing vocal duties for the world's most famous frog, Kermit (although that onerous task was eventually passed on to Steve Whitmire). Two further feature films followed, *The Muppet Christmas Carol* (1992) and *Muppet Treasure Island* (1996), before the unthinkable/obvious was suggested – why not bring them back to television?

So in 1996, ***Muppets Tonight!*** launched itself upon a public with high expectations. Although it introduced some fantastic new regular characters into the fold of Muppet regulars (including Pepe the Prawn, Seymore the Elephant and mafia boss Johnny Fioma), many viewers felt alienated by the sudden switch from a variety theatre to a TV studio. Still worse was the sidelining of many of the original Muppet characters – Kermit was no longer the host, having been supplanted by wisecracking smooth presenter Clifford. Despite this, guests lined up once again to appear, with Leonard Nimoy, Mickey Dolenz, John Goodman and Whoopi Goldberg (among many others) taking their turn in the Muppet spotlight. The Artist Formerly (and subsequently) known as Prince guest starred in one hilarious episode in which the Muppets pretty much took the piss out of the diminutive pop legend by failing to understand how he'd moved on with his styles and music (causing one Muppet to complain that he'd spend ages ripping the buttocks out of his leather trousers just for the occasion). Prince not only took it all in good spirits but actually showed a side to himself rarely seen, singing a song wearing a hideous 'Christmas jumper'. Rather irritatingly, though, we Brits never got to see this – the second series never aired here.

Unfortunately *Muppets Tonight!* didn't take off in the ratings and it was cancelled in the US after just 22 episodes. Although the original line-up of Muppets reunited for yet another cinema film in 1999 (*Muppets from Space*, in which the gang join together to discover where exactly Gonzo comes from), it looked as though that might be the end for Henson's most famous creations. The company's other projects, meanwhile, were going from strength to strength, with programmes as diverse as *Bear in the Big Blue House*, *The Hoobs* and the sci-fi series *Farscape* benefiting from the Creature Shop's expertise. In 2004, after many years of backroom negotiations and power struggles, the Walt Disney Corporation finally negotiated the rights to own and exploit the back catalogue of Muppet characters. How this development pans out is anybody's guess – Disney has never struck us as the kind of self-deprecating organisation Henson Productions has always been – but it's unlikely that an organisation as driven as Disney would allow one of their assets to remain 'resting' for very long. One possible hint might come from the news of a new Muppet TV movie due to be screened in 2005 – *The Muppets' Wizard of Oz*. Quite frankly, we can't wait.

John O'Farrell, Anthony Horowitz, Nick Vivian, Jonathan Harvey **Theme Music** Simon Brint

A little bit of black comedy is always a delicious addition to the TV schedules, particularly when it's performed with as much flair, panache and downright mischief as the anthology series *Murder Most Horrid*. Designed to showcase the skills of Dawn French at the same time as her 'comedy partner' Jennifer Saunders was busy developing ***Absolutely Fabulous***, *Murder Most Horrid* was an anthology series of wickedly funny, comic murder-based stories, set in a wide variety of different locations and with an outstanding guest cast. Each week Dawn played a different role, whether that be a bumbling policewoman promoted to investigate a murder, an ambitious and amoral cookery writer or even the presenter of a children's TV show who's lethally jealous of her younger male co-presenter.

One of the great strengths of *Murder Most Horrid* was the way in which it used a variety of different, well-established writers to pen the episodes. Alongside a number of talented but lesser-known writers, scripts were provided by famous scribes such as ***Midsomer Murders***' Anthony Horowitz, ***Coupling***'s Steven Moffat, ***Gimme Gimme Gimme***'s Jonathan Harvey and even ***Have I Got News For You*** panellist Ian Hislop. Four seasons of *Murder Most Horrid* were made in all, spaced out fairly evenly throughout the 1990s. Perhaps the best episode of them all, 'Overkill', guest starred ***LA Law***'s Amanda Donohoe as an assassin trying to take out a top businessman. When she stumbles across a suicidal Brummie social worker called Tina (Dawn French), the assassin realises that a woman trying to end her life might be just the most reliable (and disposable) remote control killing machine ever devised. Unfortunately, Tina's general incompetence leaves a trail of butchered office staff behind her, and a lethal plan that inevitably finds even more unsuspecting victims.

Murder, She Wrote

Detective | Universal TV for CBS (shown on ITV) | episode duration 45 mins, plus specials | broadcast 30 Sep 1984–19 May 1996, 2 Nov 1997, 18 May 2000, 2 May 2001, 9 May 2003 (USA)

Regular Cast

Angela Lansbury · *Jessica Fletcher*
Tom Bosley · *Sheriff Amos Tupper*
William Windom · *Dr Seth Hazlett*
Ron Masak · *Sheriff Mort Metzger*
Michael Horton · *Grady Fletcher*
Richard Paul · *Mayor Sam Booth*
Keith Michel · *Dennis Stanton*
Ken Swofford · *Lieutenant Perry Catalano*
Alan Oppenheimer · *Dr Raymond Auerbach*
Julie Adams · *Eve Simpson*

Creators Peter S. Fischer, Richard Levinson, William Link **Producers** Various, including Peter S. Fischer, Richard Levinson, Angela Lansbury (executive), Douglas Benton, Todd London, Robert Van Scoyk **Writers** Various, including Bruce Lansbury, J. Michael Straczynski, Tom Sawyer, Lawrence G. DiTillio, William Bigelow **Theme Music** Bruce Babcock, Richard Markowitz, Lance Rubin

Veteran murder mystery novelist Jessica Fletcher must be the unluckiest person in the world. Although she lives in the pretty New England fishing village of Cabot Cove, a suspiciously large number of her friends and relatives become murder victims. Furthermore, whenever Jessica travels away from her hometown, she's often plunged into yet another homicide investigation. Luckily Jessica's reputation as a renowned detective of criminals means that she's only rarely a suspect for the crimes she stumbles into. Sometimes with (but usually without) the help of the police, Jessica manages to deduce who the villain of the piece is, just in time for the boys in blue to arrive and cart the evil-doers off to jail.

A rather blatant tribute/rip-off of Agatha Christie's ***Miss Marple***, *Murder, She Wrote* provided a charming and undemanding role for former movie star Angela Lansbury. Lansbury portrayed Jessica as everyone's favourite auntie, a younger and livelier old lady than Joan Hickson's Miss Marple (which launched the same year). Although there were a few other semi-regular characters in the show (such as Cabot Cove's Mayor and Sheriffs Amos and Metzger), nobody tuned in to *Murder, She Wrote* to watch any of the other characters. This was Jessica Fletcher/Angela Lansbury's show, and in over 260 different episodes, she provided viewers with a mildly diverting hour's worth of harmless homicide-based entertainment.

My Family

Sitcom | DLT Entertainment/Rude Boy Productions for BBC One | episode duration 30 mins, plus 50-min special | broadcast 19 Sep 2000–18 Jun 2004, 24 Dec 2004

Regular Cast

Robert Lindsay · *Ben Harper*
Zoë Wanamaker · *Susan Harper*
Kris Marshall · *Nick Harper*
Daniela Denby-Ashe · *Janey Harper*
Gabriel Thomson · *Michael Harper*
Siobhan Hayes · *Abi Harper*
Daisy Donovan · *Brigitte*

Creator Fred Barron **Producer** Fred Barron, Donald Taffner Jr, Geoffrey Perkins, Sophie Clarke-Jervoise (executive), John Bartlett **Writers** Various, including Fred Barron, Andrea Solomons, Ian Brown, James Hendrie, Jim Armodida, Steve Armogida **Theme Music** Graham Jarvis

Ben Harper is a bad-tempered dentist, married to the sharp-tongued and piercingly intelligent Susan. Between them they have three children – elder son Nick (who's a dim-witted layabout and dreamer), daughter Janey (petulant typical teenager) and youngest son Michael (sharp as one of his dad's dental drills). Together they face the normal kind of problems that many households have to go through, most of them brought about or exacerbated by Ben's fiery temperament.

An old-fashioned genre of sitcom (the everyday happenings affecting an ordinary family) written in a non-traditional fashion (by a committee of writers as opposed to a single author or partnership, as is traditional with UK sitcoms), *My Family* showed conclusively that there's still place in TV schedules for a comedy series that isn't daring, radical, innovative or filled with bad language. Created by an American sitcom writer called Fred Barron (who'd worked on programmes like *Caroline in the City*), *My Family*'s committee-authored scripts were often tailored on the day of recording, adding extra jokes and scenes to the production – something that had almost never happened before in the production of a British comedy series.

Although many critics viewed *My Family* as little more than an updated version of ***No Place Like Home*** for the Noughties, it's true that the superior performances by Robert Lindsay and Zoë Wanamaker lifted the programme beyond its rather predictable premise. *My Family* also created its own star – Kris Marshall as lovable layabout Nick landed a role in the major feature film *Love, Actually* (2003) as a direct result of his appearance in the programme. With his career blossoming, Marshall departed as a regular cast-member, only making occasional visits back to the show.

Robert Lindsay has indicated that the 2004 series (which concluded with a Christmas special) would be his last, something that was confirmed by Zoë Wanamaker in 2005. But as we know, good sitcoms have a habit of returning when we least expect them.

My Two Dads

Sitcom | Michael Jacobs Productions/Columbia/Tristar for NBC (shown on Channel 4) | episode duration 25 mins | broadcast 20 Sep 1987–30 Apr 1990 (USA)

Principal Cast

Paul Reiser · *Michael Taylor*
Greg Evigan · *Joey Harris*
Staci Keanan · *Nicole Bradford*
Florence Stanley · *Judge Margaret Wilbur*
Dick Butkus · *Ed Klawicki*
Chad Allen · *Zach Nichols*
Vonni Ribisi · *Cory Kupkus*
Amy Hathaway · *Shelby Haskell*

Creators Michael Jacobs, Danielle Alexandra **Producer** David Steven Simon, Roger Garrett, Mark Brull **Writers** Various, including Chuck Lorre, Tom Moore, Bill Streib, Richard Vaczy, Bryan Winter **Theme Music** Michael Jacobs and Lenny Macaluso

When 13-year-old Nicole Bradford's mother dies, her final act is to get in touch with the two men she'd had an affair with years ago – the two potential natural fathers for her beloved Nicole. Up-tight and conservative financial adviser Michael and laid-back artist Joey are both shocked to discover that they might be dads, but they're even more shocked when the genetic tests prove inconclusive. Eventually, formidable old Judge Wilbur makes an even more shocking pronouncement – both men will share joint guardianship of young Nicole. Fortuitously, Judge Wilbur owns the building in which all three members of this new family live, so she's able to keep an eye on Nicole and her two dads. As the years go by, Michael and Joey's very differing parenting styles are tested as Nicole matures into a young woman with typically active hormones . . .

With most sitcoms, there's at least one element that makes it stand out from the rest of the pack, ensuring its longevity in the annals of television history. Unfortunately, *My Two Dads* had little that made it stand out from many other bland, formulaic shows that never darkened our shores. Up until this point, Channel 4's record in selecting only the very best American comedy series for transmission was fairly faultless – after all, they had brought us ***Cheers*** and ***The Golden Girls***, comedies that provided something that was a little bit different from the norm. The best thing that can be said about *My Two Dads* is that for people who enjoyed gentle, family-centred sitcoms with a traditional 'family values' moral supplied to neatly wrap things up, this programme provided a perfectly acceptable form of entertainment.

My Wife Next Door

Sitcom | BBC One | episode duration 30 mins | broadcast 19 Sep–12 Dec 1972

Regular Cast

John Alderton · *George Bassett*
Hannah Gordon · *Suzy Bassett*
Tim Barrett · *Henry*
Diana King · *Suzy's Mother*
Mollie Sugden · *George's Mother*
Paddy Frost · *Liz*

Creators Brian Clemens, Richard Waring **Producer** Graeme Muir **Writer** Richard Waring **Theme Music** Ronnie Hazlehurst

For its time, the concept behind *My Wife Next Door* was verging on the controversial – a couple in the throes of a messy divorce both quit their city-based lifestyles and buy a house in the country. To their shock, they discover that they've purchased adjacent cottages and realise that far

from it being the end of their story, their tempestuous relationship is set to continue. George, who never truly wanted the divorce, takes the opportunity to try and woo back Suzy, who (against her better judgement) often looks as though she's on the verge of falling for him again before George puts his foot in it, she comes to her senses and realises that they're better off apart. Chuck in regular appearances from both meddling mothers and you've got a very traditional 'will-they, won't they?' sitcom with a twist – will they or won't they get back together again?

Just one season of *My Wife Next Door* was made, 13 episodes in total. Co-created by ***The Avengers*** and ***The Professionals*** veteran writer Brian Clemens, *My Wife Next Door* was a moderate hit on its first transmission, largely due to a pair of outstanding performances from stars Hannah Gordon and John Alderton. The series was repeated in full in early 1980, when it attracted astronomical viewing figures that belied its fairly humble beginnings.

My Wonderful Life

Sitcom | Granada for ITV | episode duration 25 mins | broadcast 25 Feb 1996, 1 May 1997–18 Jul 1999

Regular Cast

Emma Wray · *Donna*
Philip Glenister · *Phil*
Gary Webster · *Lawrie*
Elizabeth Berrington · *Marina*
Tony Robinson · *Alan*
Hannah McVeigh, Amanda Riley · *Rhiannon*
Elizabeth Earl, Vicky Connett · *Shirley*
Hamish Clark · *Roger*
Oliver Furness · *Simon*
Nicola Stephenson · *Gail*
Marcel McCalla · *Ben*
Aingeal Grehan, Joan Kempson · *Briedah*
Race Davies · *Lydia*
Clare Perkins · *Bridget*
Charlie Hunnam · *Wes*
Ben Miles · *Brian*
Suzanne Jones · *Linda*

Creator Simon Nye **Producer** Andy Harries, Justin Judd (executive), Brian Park, Mark Redhead, Sophie Clarke-Jervoise, Spencer Campbell **Writers** Simon Nye, Amanda Swift, Paul Dornan **Theme Music:** 'I Am, I Feel' by Alisha's Attic, which reached No. 14 in the charts in August 1996

It's always nice when a one-off programme is so well received by viewers that it spawns an ongoing series. An hour-long comedy drama called *True Love* was the first post-***Watching*** project for actress Emma Wray, who'd made quite an impression on viewers as the gobby Scouser with the heart of gold Brenda. In *True Love* and its follow-on series *My Wonderful Life*, Wray played young mum Donna, a nurse who's bringing her two daughters up on her own after finally mustering the courage to throw her useless husband Phil out on his ear. Luckily Donna has two suitors at work vying for her attention – boring nerdy (yet reliable) doctor Roger and lively, fun (and untrustworthy) ambulance driver Lawrie.

Walking a fine line between comedy and drama, *My Wonderful Life* eschewed the traditional laughter track in favour of allowing viewers to laugh and cry at the material. Storylines evolved over multiple episodes, giving the quality cast (including ***Minder***'s Gary Webster and ***Blackadder***'s Tony Robinson) the chance to shine. Created by ***Men Behaving Badly*** writer Simon Nye, *My Wonderful Life* ran for 23 episodes and provided a very welcome change from cutesy sitcoms in which every episode provided a resolution to the 'storyline of the week'.

The Naked Civil Servant

Drama | Thames for ITV | episode duration 90 mins | broadcast 17 Dec 1975

Principal Cast
John Hurt · *Quentin Crisp*
Liz Gebhardt · *Art Student*
Patricia Hodge · *Ballet Teacher*
Stanley Lebor · *Mr Pole*
Katherine Schofield · *Mrs Pole*
Colin Higgins · *Thumbnails*
John Rhys-Davies · *Barndoor*
Stephen Johnstone · *Young Quentin*
Antonia Pemberton · *Mrs Longhurst*
Lloyd Lamble · *Mr Crisp*
Joan Ryan · *Mrs Crisp*
Frank Forsyth · *Family Doctor*
Shane Briant · *Norma*
Ron Pember · *Black Cat Proprieter*
Roger Lloyd-Pack · *Liz*

Producers Verity Lambert (executive), Barry Hanson
Writer Philip Mackie, from the autobiography by Quentin Crisp
Theme Music Carl Davis

The memoirs of the self-proclaimed 'stately homo of England' were brought to the screen in this film from director Jack Gold. Crisp wore make-up and open-toed sandals, coloured his hair and paraded along streets as an openly gay man 20 years before homosexuality was legalised (in the winter of 1965). The self-deprecating, withering wit of Crisp was ably served by John Hurt's decadent, deceptively languid delivery, which acted as a prelude to his scene-stealing turn as Caligula in ***I, Claudius***. Hurt picked up a BAFTA for Best Actor the following year while in 2000 the film came fourth in a British Film Institute poll for the 100 Greatest British Television Programmes.

Naked Video

Comedy | BBC Two | episode duration 30 mins | broadcast 12 May 1986–18 Nov 1991

Regular Cast
Gregor Fisher, Helen Lederer, John Sparkes, Tony Roper, Elaine C. Smith, Andy Gray, Jonathan Watson, Ron Bain, Kate Donnelly, Louise Beattie

Producers Colin Gilbert, Philip Differ **Writers** The cast
Theme Music David McNiven

When the shock success of ***Not the Nine O'Clock News*** revitalised the format of the sketch show, BBC Two spent much of the 1980s trying to find a suitable replacement team to capture the public's imagination in much the same way as Rowan, Pamela, Mel and Griff had done. BBC Scotland in particular seemed to provide many of these programmes, some of them more successful than others. The best remembered of them included *A Kick Up the Eighties* (BBC Two, 21 Sep 1981–24 Jan 1984, featuring Tracey Ullman, Robbie Coltrane and Miriam Margolyes) and *Laugh??? I Nearly Paid My Licence Fee* (BBC Two, 29 Oct–3 Dec 1984 with Louise Gold, John Sessions and Robbie Coltrane). At more or less the same time, a Radio Scotland series called *Naked Radio* was making a rather large impact north of the border. After a successful stint at the Edinburgh Fringe Festival, the team transferred their show to BBC Two and *Naked Video* was born.

Thirty episodes of *Naked Video* were broadcast over five seasons, consisting of solid and occasionally inspired comedy. Gregor Fisher scored two remarkable hit characters in the form of ***Rab C. Nesbitt*** (who got his own BBC Two show) and The Baldy Man, a chap with the most pathetic comb-over in the world, who had a moderately successful spin on ITV (Yorkshire for ITV, 13 episodes, 13 Apr 1995–17 Dec 1997), largely as a result of a commercial he made for Hamlet cigars. Alongside established Scots from the *Naked Radio* days, such as Andy Gray, Ron Bain and Elaine C. Smith, *Naked Video* tried to woo the Sassenach vote by roping in posh English comedienne Helen Lederer (often performing a monologue from a yuppie wine bar) and comic John Sparkes, whose turn as an ineffectual Welsh poet called Siadwell (pronounced Shadwell) was perhaps the most popular character in the show.

Neighbours

See pages 512–15

Never Mind The Buzzcocks

Quiz show | Talkback for BBC Two | episode duration 30 mins | broadcast 19 Nov 1996–present

Cast
Mark Lamarr · *Host*
Phill Jupitus, Sean Hughes, Bill Bailey · *Team Captains*
Appleston · *Recurring Line-up Guest*

Producers Peter Fincham (executive), Simon Bullivant, Bill Matthews (associate), Steve Doherty, Jim Pullen, Harry Thompson, Richard Wilson

Taking its lead from ***Have I Got News For You?*** and ***They Think It's All Over***, *Never Mind The Buzzcocks* is the panel game for the cooler TV addict. Former ***The Word*** presenter and ***Shooting Stars*** panellist Mark Lamarr is quizmaster for two teams, both captained by comedians. In the early days, Phill Jupitus took on Sean Hughes, whose lethargic approach usually led to a humiliating defeat for his team. Since his departure in 2002, 'part-troll' Bill Bailey has led his guests to victory on many occasions. Guests tend to come from a mix of old-school music legends, new fresh-faced teeny-bop band-members and up-and-coming comedians glad to get a little exposure.

The first round is usually be a chance to guess the connections between pop acts, decipher lyrics or determine the pop-related news story behind Lamarr's cryptic clues. Next it's beat-the-intro in which two competitors from one team have to perform the musical lead-in to a song *a capella* for the delight and often bafflement of their remaining teammate. It might sound easy to perform 'The Final Countdown' or 'Day Tripper', but you just try making any recent R 'n' B track sound distinctive. Next it's the identity parade, where a poor, forgotten pop performer (a drummer, a bassist, the vocalist of a 1990s' dance act) is placed alongside four other possibles and asked to stand there while the panellists hurl abuse at them. A baffling figure known only as 'Appleston', a stern-faced black man who never blinked, often appeared in this section, regardless of whether he was an appropriate look-alike or not (for instance, if the other four in the line-up were all white women).

Finally, the quick-fire round – in which the teams have to supply the next line to a series of lyrics – decides which of the teams will be declared the winner. Not that even that is straightforward, for Mark Lamarr has been known to allow personal prejudice to creep in to ensure a team he's chosen to dislike doesn't win. Meanwhile, we all laugh as the teenybopper completely fails to recognise the lyrics from his or her own record.

It's not really a genuine test of popular musical knowledge – it's much more important to get a laugh than a point. But musicians young and old, and a never-ending stream of comedians keep stepping forward for the humiliation and the kudos. Meanwhile, we keep watching for the wealth of archive music clips – there aren't many other places you get to see rare performances of Lieutenant Pigeon and Chicory Tip, y'know.

Never the Twain

Sitcom | Thames for ITV | episode duration 25 mins | broadcast 7 Sep 1981–9 Oct 1991

Regular Cast

Donald Sinden · *Simon Peel*
Windsor Davies · *Oliver Smallbridge*
Julia Watson, Tacy Kneale · *Lyn Smallbridge/Peel*
Robin Kermode, Christopher Morris · *David Peel*
Derek Deadman · *Ringo*
Teddy Turner · *Banks*
Marla Charles · *Mrs Sadler*
Honor Blackman · *Veronica Barton*
Żara Nutley · *Aunt Eleanor*

Creator Johnnie Mortimer **Producers** Peter Frazer-Jones, Anthony Parker **Writers** Johnnie Mortimer, Vince Powell, John Kane, Dick Hills, Brian Platt, Peter Tilbury

In the 1960s, a much-quoted sketch on *The Frost Report* presented John Cleese, Ronnie Barker and Ronnie Corbett as representatives of the Upper, Middle and Working Classes: Cleese looked down on the other two; Barker looked up to Cleese but down on Corbett; Corbett knew his place. In the 1980s, that sketch was drawn out into a bewilderingly long-lasting sitcom in which Donald Sinden (as the snooty Simon Peel) sparred with the grubby upwardly-mobile yet fiercely working class Windsor Davies (Oliver Smallbridge), while their gopher Derek Deadman knew his place.

Created as a starring vehicle for Sinden and Windsor, *Never the Twain* was never challenging, but it did provide us with ten years'-worth of barbed comments. In the first series, the pair were exasperated when their respective children decided to get married while in the last they were arguing over who was the better grandparent. It rarely required any stretch of talent for either star, with Davies repeating the moustache-twitching boor he'd played in ***It Ain't Half Hot, Mum*** and Sinden over-annunciating every syllable to ensure he maintained the (very much unofficial) title of biggest ham in British comedy. Between them, they gave us 11 seasons of mid-week laughs.

The New Avengers

Fantasy/Action-Adventure | Avengers (Film & TV) Enterprises/IDTV (France)/Nielsen-Ferns (Canada) for ITV | episode duration 50 mins | broadcast 17 Oct 1976–17 Dec 1977

Regular Cast

Patrick Macnee · *John Steed*
Gareth Hunt · *Mike Gambit*
Joanna Lumley · *Purdey*

Creators Sydney Newman, Leonard White, Brian Clemens **Producers** Albert Fennell, Brian Clemens, Ron Fry **Writers** Brian Clemens, Dennis Spooner, John Goldsmith, Terence Feely **Theme Music** Laurie Johnson, playing with his own theme for the original series, creates something that combines military bands with funky 1970s porno music. We're sure there's an untapped fetish market there somewhere.

While making a champagne commercial for French television in 1975, Patrick Macnee shocked the producer by telling him that he hadn't made any new episodes of ***The Avengers*** since 1969. *The Avengers*, which had enjoyed huge success on French TV as *Chapeau melon et bottes de cuir* (Bowler Hat and Leather Boots), was still being repeated. Seeing an opportunity, the producer contacted former *Avengers* executive Brian Clemens and suggested a co-production deal. With a new financial backer, the scene was set for the return of one of the most successful programmes of the 1960s: *The New Avengers* was here.

Macnee returned, this time accompanied by two partners, ostensibly because he was considered too old to

Continued on page 516

Neighbours

Jason Donovan (Scott Robinson) and Kylie Minogue (Charlene Mitchell) becoming good friends ...

In the middle-class Melbourne suburb of Erinsborough, life on cul-de-sac Ramsay Street is pretty much like life everywhere else. Kids fall in and out of love with each other, parents have financial and marital problems, and there's always something happening next door that's good for a gossip. But no matter how bad things get, you can always be sure of two things – that sunny skies are never far away, and that good neighbours can always become good friends.

In 1985, the Australian production company Grundy Television began work on a cosy, domesticated soap opera that would go on to be an astonishing international success. Indeed, it would prove to be far more popular abroad than it was in its home country. Many Australian soaps had previously been targeted at a more adult audience – either the violence and drug-dealing of ***Prisoner: Cell Block H***, or the historically based ***The Sullivans***. From the outset, *Neighbours* was designed to appeal to a broad cross-section of the public, from adults to children, and had a timeslot and appropriate storylines to match. However, things didn't go as Grundy had planned. Australian audiences on the Seven Network just weren't tuning in, and after a brief six months on air, Seven pulled the plug on the fledgling programme and dismantled their Ramsay Street sets. *Neighbours* had been cancelled.

But that wasn't the end. In an almost unprecedented move, Grundy Productions pitched their programme to a different channel, and to their relief the rival Ten Network decided to buy the show from them. There were conditions, however – *Neighbours* was now to be aimed even more obviously at a teenage/young adult demographic. As a result of this shift, many of the show's cast were unceremoniously dumped. Several characters were simply written out; others were recast with younger and more obviously attractive actors. Sets that had been rather dingy yet realistic representations of a typical Australian suburb suddenly became more brightly lit and rather more lavishly decorated (in fact, the first episode of the new run showed several of the surviving characters redecorating their house – primarily because the original sets had already been trashed!). Slowly but surely, *Neighbours* was on its way to becoming an international phenomenon.

Neighbours arrived in the UK courtesy of a newly expanded BBC One. Until 1986, large sections of daytime television were often just turned over to the Testcard, the thought being that it simply wasn't worth spending lots of money filling the schedules with programmes that few people would be around to tune in to. New BBC One controller Michael Grade was tasked with filling the whole daytime schedule with programmes that were both cheap and plentiful. With the success of ***EastEnders*** still ringing in his ears, Grade decided that *Neighbours* would be an ideal programme to purchase, and scheduled it to run twice a day, once at about 10.00 a.m., once after the lunchtime *News* at 1.30 p.m. Over several months, *Neighbours* built up a small but dedicated following. But when the UK started broadcasting the new-look Ten Network episodes, something very strange began to happen. Children and teenagers alike were suddenly asking if they could have a TV set up in their school classrooms at lunchtime so that they could watch *Neighbours*. Those whose afternoon lessons began before 1.30 p.m. were starting to take 'sickies' so that they could be at home to catch up with the goings-on down under. When Michael Grade's daughters alerted him to this phenomenon, he made a change in scheduling that in one fell swoop demolished a long-held British TV tradition (the cartoon just prior to the 6 o'clock *News*) and created an all-new one. By moving the repeat of *Neighbours* from early morning to 5.35 p.m, Grade created the ideal timeslot for this new demographic of soap addicts, cleverly managing at the same time to drag in parents who were waiting for the *News*.

From 1987, for about five solid years, *Neighbours* wasn't just another imported TV show – it was a genuine broadcasting and cultural rule-breaker. Viewing figures regularly topped 12 million and both the fictional events of the soap and the real-life antics of the cast filled page after page of the tabloid press. It was, of course, the wedding (in episode 523) between the show's two young romantic leads that became the show's first major event. The romance between tomboy mechanic Charlene Mitchell (Kylie Minogue) and budding journalist Scott Robinson (Jason Donovan) held viewers rapt for months. The ceremony itself attracted an unprecedented 17 million viewers, making international celebrities out of fresh-faced Kylie and Jason. Other favourite characters in the early years of *Neighbours* included busybody neighbour Mrs Mangel, swan in ugly duck's clothing 'plain Jane super-brain', tragedy-magnet Des Clarke and his former stripper wife Daphne (her deathbed croak of 'I love you, Clarkie!' was a real tearjerker), and even chirpy golden retriever

Soap
Grundy Productions for Seven Network/Ten Network Australia (shown on BBC One)
Episode Duration: 25 mins
Broadcast: 18 Mar 1985 (Aus)/ 27 Oct 1986-present (UK)

Regular Cast

Jade Amenta · *Melissa Jarrett*
Ben Anderson · *Tim Collins*
Andy Anderson · *Mick Scully*
Janet Andrewartha · *Lyn Scully*
Michelle Ang · *Lori Lee*
Jeremy Angerson · *Josh Anderson*
Felice Arena · *Marco Alessi*
Lisa Armytage, Shaunna O'Grady · *Beverly Marshall/Robinson*
Lesley Baker · *Angie Rebecchi*
Elspeth Ballantyne · *Cathy Alessi*
Natalie Bassingthwaighte · *Izzy Hoyland*
Francis Bell · *Max Ramsay*
Melissa Bell, Sasha Close, Kylie Flinker · *Lucy Robinson*
Andrew Bibby · *Lance Hails/Wilkinson*
Andrew Blackman · *Mike Healy*
Dasha Blahova · *Maria Ramsay*
Rachel Blakely · *Gaby Willis*
Gayle Blakeney · *Christina Alessi/Robinson*
Gillian Blakeney · *Caroline Alessi*
Vikki Blanche, Julie Mullins · *Julie Robinson/Martin*
Brett Blewitt · *Brett Stark*
Carla Bonner · *Steph Scully/Hoyland*
Ernie Bourne · *Rob Lewis*
Peta Brady, Amelia Frid · *Cody Willis*
Jay Bunyan · *Jack Scully*
Joy Chambers · *Rosemary Daniels*
Nicola Charles · *Sarah Beaumont/Hannay*
Anne Charleston · *Madge Ramsay/Mitchell/Bishop*
David Clencie · *Danny Ramsay*
Shane Connor · *Joe Scully*
Fiona Corke · *Gail Lewis/Robinson*
Brett Cousins · *Ben Atkins*
Lucinda Cowden · *Melanie Pearson*
Lochie Daddo · *Stephen Gottlieb*
Alan Dale · *Jim Robinson*
Kimberley Davies · *Annalise Hartman*
Myra De Groot · *Eileen Clarke*
Maggie Dence · *Dorothy Burke*
Stefan Dennis · *Paul Robinson*
Terence Donovan · *Doug Willis*
Jason Donovan, Darius Perkins · *Scott Robinson*
Anthony Engelman · *Stonefish Rebecchi*
Dan Falzon · *Rick Alessi*
Gary Files · *Tom Ramsay*
Alan Fletcher · *Karl Kennedy*

Bouncer the Soap Dog (who was such a popular character the producers even wrote in a staggeringly inept dream sequence for him – a decision that backfired utterly; the dog may have had his fans, but nobody wanted to see inside his mind!).

In Britain at least, *Neighbours* is a soap where continuity simply isn't all that important – viewers begin watching it in their early teens and then quit as soon as they get their first proper job. Young romantic leads Scott and Charlene were soon replaced by Annalise and Mark; the Ramsay, Robinson and Mitchell clans were eventually phased out and replaced by the Willis, Martin, Hancock, Scully and Kennedy families. In short, although the archetypes of family grouping and relationships stay the same, every few years pretty much the whole cast can renew itself with little worry about alienating viewers. There are now no characters left in *Neighbours* who were in the series when it first began – the longest-serving cast members include Ian Smith (former scriptwriter and producer on other Aussie soaps such as *Prisoner: Cell Block H*) as blustering, bumbling Harold Bishop, and Tom Oliver as former car salesman Lou Carpenter. The programme's 20th anniversary saw the return of an original cast member to the series after an absence of over ten years – Stefan Dennis made a surprise comeback as amoral businessman Paul Robinson, returning to Erinsborough (a near-anagram of 'Neighbours', by the way!) just in time to see his former business-place, the Lassiter's Hotel complex, burn to the ground.

As a teen-focused import, *Neighbours* has always been considered to be somewhat less 'credible' than its prime-time, British-made, fellow soap operas. However, its storylines and performances can often be relied upon to be at least the equal of those in ***EastEnders*** or ***Hollyoaks***. Indeed, without the huge success of *Neighbours*, there is no way in which a soap like *Hollyoaks* would ever have been commissioned in the UK. Another major impact that *Neighbours* had on British TV was the way in which other programmes suddenly realised the ratings bonanza that could be enjoyed by the introduction of additional attractive young characters. On the other hand, other children's drama programmes that had traditionally enjoyed healthy ratings really felt the pinch after the arrival of *Neighbours*. For instance, ***Grange Hill*** had normally been watched by children and teenagers who saw their own lives reflected in the programme. But why bother to watch the drab, boring lives of London schoolchildren when the sexy and sunny Antipodean storylines of *Neighbours* were much more attractive to viewers? As a result, viewing figures for the CBBC series dropped markedly from their mid-1980s peak and have never really recovered to this day.

Slick, entertaining and seemingly almost effortless in the way in which it pumps out over two hours of drama every week (approximately 4800 episodes have been recorded at the time of writing), *Neighbours* has itself seen viewing figures drop significantly from its heyday in the Scott and Charlene years. In fact, back in Australia the programme suffered from such low ratings that for a time the only reason production continued was because of its profitability in overseas sales. Still regularly screened in dozens of countries around the globe, *Neighbours* underwent something of a critical renaissance throughout 2004 and 2005. With the 20th-anniversary celebrations taking place at the end of 2005, many former cast members were approached to make a return visit to Ramsay Street. Perhaps that's the lasting appeal of *Neighbours* – unlike practically every other soap opera street or square (complete with their horrifically high death counts!), Erinsborough seems to be an almost idyllic place to live – the 'perfect blend' of 'good neighbours', sunshine and light-hearted cares. It's a great place to go back to once in a while.

Rachel Friend · *Bronwyn Davies*
Ben Geurens · *Toby Mangel*
Caroline Gillmer · *Cheryl Stark*
Nathan Godkin · *Pinhead Pinders*
Delta Goodrem · *Nina Tucker*
Vivean Gray · *Mrs Nell Mangel*
Richard Grieve · *Sam Kratz*
Anne Haddy · *Helen Daniels*
Kevin Harrington · *David Bishop*
Linda Hartley · *Kerry Bishop/Mangel*
Patrick Harvey · *Connor O'Neill*
Virginia Hey · *Beth Travers*
Raelee Hill · *Ren Gottlieb*
Richard Huggett · *Glen Donnelly*
Stephen Hunt · *Matt Hancock*
Natalie Imbruglia · *Beth Brennan/Willis*
Irene Inescort · *Aunt Edie Chubb*
Sally Jensen · *Katie Landers*
Annie Jones · *Jane Harris*
Sue Jones · *Pam Willis*
Paul Keane · *Des Clarke*
Amber Kilpatrick · *Tiffany 'Lochy' McLachlan*
Maxine Klibingaitis · *Terry Inglis/Robinson*
Mark Little · *Joe Mangel*
Stephen Lovatt · *Max Hoyland*
Todd MacDonald · *Darren Stark*
Daniel MacPherson · *Joel Samuels*
Lawrence Mah · *Mr Udugawa*
Kyal Marsh · *Boyd Hoyland*
Blair McDonough · *Stuart Parker*
Stephanie McIntosh · *Sky Bishop*
Craig McLachlan · *Henry Mitchell/Ramsay*
Benjamin McNair · *Mal Kennedy*
Scott Michaelson · *Brad Willis*
Maggie Millar · *Rosie Hoyland*
Kylie Minogue · *Charlene Mitchell/Robinson*
Ryan Moloney · *Toadfish Rebecchi*
Ben Nicholas · *Scott 'Stingray' Timmins*
Richard Norton · *Ryan McLachlan*
Peter O'Brien · *Shane Ramsay*
Isabella Oldham · *Emily Hancock*
Tom Oliver · *Lou Carpenter*
Nicholas Opolski · *Evan Hancock*
Moya O'Sullivan · *Marlene Kratz*
Geoff Paine · *Dr Clive Gibbons*
Dan Paris · *Drew Kirk*
Ashley Paske · *Matt Williams/Robinson*
Guy Pearce · *Mike Young*
Mark Raffety · *Darcy Tyler*
Ian Rawlings · *Philip Martin*
Marnie Reece-Wilmore · *Debbie Martin*
Rebecca Ritters · *Hannah Martin*
Simone Robertson · *Pheobe Bright/Gottlieb*
Marcella Russo · *Liljana 'Lil' Bishop*
Lara Sacher · *Serena Bishop*
Bruce Samazan · *Mark Gottlieb*
Brooke Satchwell · *Anne Wilkinson*
Kristian Schmid · *Todd Landers*
Anne Scott-Pendlebury · *Hilary Robinson*
Marisa Siketa · *Summer Hoyland*
Elaine Smith · *Daphne Lawrence/Clarke*
Ian Smith · *Harold Bishop*
George Spartels · *Benito Alessi*
Jesse Spencer · *Billy Kennedy*
Mark Stevens · *Nick Page*
Kym Valentine · *Libby Kennedy*
Sarah Vandenbergh · *Lauren Carpenter*
Marisa Warrington · *Sindi Watts*
Madeleine West · *Dee Bliss*
Ian Williams · *Adam Willis*
Jackie Woodburne · *Susan Kennedy*

Creator Reg Watson

Producers Many dozens, including Don Battye, Ian Bradley, Philip East, John Holmes, Jan Russ, Marie Trevor

Writers Many hundreds, including Don Battye, Ysabelle Dean, Coral Drouyn, Ray Kolle, Lyn Ogilvy, Michael O'Rourke, Betty Quin, Ian Smith, Reg Watson

Theme Music Tony Hatch and Jackie Trent were the dynamic duo behind the most sing-a-long theme tune for a soap opera ever committed to videotape.

handle much of the 'rough stuff' himself. The new male lead was Gareth Hunt as former navy man Mike Gambit, handy with his fists and a sucker for a pretty lady. Perpetual source of Gambit's desires was Purdey, the first leading role for up-and-coming actress Joanna Lumley. An ex-ballerina, Purdey's lethal high leg kicks and talent with motor vehicles became almost as famous as her 'Purdey bob' haircut – the only serious challenger to 'the Farrah' as the most copied female hairdo of the 1970s.

The style of *The New Avengers* was somewhat different from that of the final years of the original show. Rather than fantastical situations and over-the-top characters, *The New Avengers* battled much more contemporary foes. No longer were spies simply from 'foreign governments' – now they were definitely Soviets. Fight scenes no longer pulled any punches (pun intended), preferring the gritty style of ***The Sweeney*** to the old-fashioned balletic charm of the original run. In the process, a lot of the humour of the series seemed to fall by the wayside, relying on the endless single-entendre flirting between Purdey and Gambit rather than on wit or on the outrageous plotting of the villain of the week. The emphasis in many episodes is most definitely sex rather than romance. We might (just) have believed that Steed's relationships with Emma or Tara were chaste, and of course, being a 'modern' man, Gambit's obsession with chasing skirt (and particularly Purdey) is indicative of the time *The New Avengers* was created in. However, Steed's transformation from the perfect gentleman to randy old man – with a brand new filly gracing his stable each week – just seems rather crass. Furthermore, the cliché counter does tend to work overtime registering the number of times that either an agent and/or one of Steed's friends bursts into his house, mortally wounded, before revealing a crucial plot point just prior to expiring. Far too many of the episodes revolve around Steed's old address book rather than his files.

Having said that, there is still a great deal to enjoy in *The New Avengers*. In 'The Eagle's Nest', a group of Nazis-disguised-as-monks on a remote Scottish island attempt to resurrect a freeze-dried Hitler, and in 'Gnaws' a giant rat hunts down its prey from the sewers. In the first run of episodes, the producers made every attempt to get the audience to feel as if this was the same show they'd loved back in the 1960s: 'Sleeper' is a virtual remake of 'The Morning After', with some marvellous high comedy when Purdey, clad only in a pair of blue silk pyjamas, has to hide from an armed gang by pretending to be a shop window mannequin. Her cover is eventually blown when her pyjama bottoms slip off, distracting the gunmen just long enough for her to kick them into unconsciousness; 'Last of the Cybernauts . . .?' sees the welcome return of the mechanical murderers that made two appearances in the original series, now led by a chilling villain who wears plastic masks depicting an assortment of fixed emotions to hide the hideously disfigured face beneath. 'To Catch a Rat' is a splendid hark-back to the very first season of *The Avengers* with original co-star Ian Hendry playing an agent who's been missing for 17 years (at the episode's conclusion, Macnee and Hendry are reunited, with Macnee uttering the touching line, 'Welcome back'). But then just in case anyone was becoming a little cosy, they did the unthinkable. In 'Dead Men Are Dangerous' Steed's former best friend (and defecting traitor) Mark Crayford returns to England to take his final revenge, by systematically destroying everything Steed holds dear – including (gasp!) his beloved racing green Bentley. For long-term fans it makes for a painful viewing as we share in Steed's anguish at seeing everything he cares about being attacked. Any one of the above could be a contender for best *New Avengers* episode, and it's largely a matter of personal taste whether the series was at its peak when paying tribute to its heritage or rebelling against it.

The first series of 13 episodes were a moderate success, and a second run was quickly commissioned. Some French money was again forthcoming, this time with the proviso that several episodes should be shot on location in France. However, the French money wasn't sufficient to complete the whole 13 episodes and money had to be found from elsewhere. This resulted in the final four being recorded in and around Toronto and broadcast as *The New Avengers in Canada*. Sadly, with a few notable exceptions such as the first part of 'K is for Kill' and the so-silly-it's-fun 'Emily', these foreign excursions weren't up to the standard of the rest of the series.

The New Avengers remains a highly enjoyable series, especially if you are able to watch the programme through nostalgia-tinted spectacles. However, despite the handful of aforementioned episodes that may be compared with the best *The Avengers* produced, and considering it sprung the luminous Joanna Lumley upon the viewing public, it doesn't stand up as well as its illustrious predecessor, or not as much as we'd hoped, particularly in its second season. With the benefit of hindsight, it seems as though the next project worked upon by Brian Clemens gives a clearer indication of the direction he perhaps wished to work in. In *The New Avengers* episode 'Obsession', two young actors appeared together in several action sequences. Their names were Martin Shaw and Lewis Collins, who would of course go on to star in Clemens' next project, ***The Professionals***.

The New Statesman

Sitcom | Yorkshire/Alomo Productions for ITV/BBC One | episode duration 25 mins, plus special | broadcast 13 Sep 1987–26 Dec 1992, 30 Dec 1994

Principal Cast

Rik Mayall · *Alan B'Stard*
Michael Troughton · *Piers Fletcher-Dervish*
Marsha Fitzalan · *Sarah B'Stard*
John Nettleton · *Sir Stephen Baxter*
Terence Alexander · *Sir Greville McDonald*
Nick Stringer · *Bob Crippen*

Steve Nallon · *Mrs Thatcher*
Charles Gray · *Roland Gidleigh-Park*
Rowena Cooper · *Norman Bormann*
Vivien Heilbron · *Beatrice Protheroe*
Berwick Kaler · *Geoff Dicquead*

Creators/Writers Laurence Marks, Maurice Gran
Producers David Reynolds, Michael Pilsworth (executive), Tony Charles, Andrew Benson, Bernard McKenna, Claire Hinson
Theme Music Alan Hawkshaw

Television villains are a tricky thing to get right – many fail to be villainous enough, with writers often giving their creations annoying streaks of morality or occasional glimpses of compassion to make them more 'realistic'. What nonsense! Most viewers want to enjoy watching a villain so dastardly, so malicious, so irredeemably bad that they come to actively look forward to his or her next act of wickedness. Throughout the history of television, no long-running character has ever been quite as malignant, as self-obsessed, as downright evil as Alan Beresford B'Stard, Conservative MP for Haltemprice, North Yorkshire. B'Stard was, to put it bluntly, a bastard of the highest order.

B'Stard was created by writers Laurence Marks and Maurice Gran, the duo responsible for earlier hits *Holding the Fort* and ***Shine on Harvey Moon***. B'Stard held views and beliefs that were so right wing that Hitler himself might have thought them a tad extreme – he was involved with the Keep Britain Nuclear campaign and the Friends of South Africa, and in his spare time was a director of a missile manufacturing company. Perpetually hanging onto B'Stard's every word (and as a consequence, the recipient of many of his violent outbursts) was fellow Tory MP Piers Fletcher-Dervish, a wimpy lapdog who seemed to masochistically revel in the abuse that B'Stard heaped upon him. Less subservient was his wife Sarah – they'd never truly been in love with each other, the marriage being one of convenience for both of them (him marrying her for status, she marrying him for money-making and power-grabbing opportunities). Throughout the programme's 28 episodes, B'Stard lied, cheated, slept around, sabotaged his political rivals and made so many enemies that it came as no great surprise that at one point an assassination was attempted on him. The last ever episode of *The New Statesman* was a one-off special entitled 'A B'Stard Exposed', which was screened on BBC One in 1994.

Newsround

News | BBC One | episode duration 10 mins | broadcast 14 Apr 1972–present

Regular Cast
John Craven, Lucy Mathen, Roger Finn, Helen Rollason, Paul McDowell, Juliet Morris, Krishnan Guru-Murthy, Julie Etchingham, Chris Rogers, Kate Sanderson, Lizo Mzimba, Matthew Price, Becky Jago · *Presenters*

Theme music Though it's changed over the years, the first decade's worth opened with a short sample from 'Johnny One-Note' by Ted Heath and His Music. The distinctive twanging ruler end-theme is the last six notes of a piece called 'New Worlds' by John Baker of the BBC's Radiophonic Workshop.

Beginning with just two short bulletins a week on a six-week trial, *John Craven's Newsround* was an attempt to educate children to the importance of news – traditionally a major turn-off for younger viewers. It's tackled world issues like war, AIDS, disasters and topics that might cause worry for children, but always in a responsible and carefully-worded way so as to inform without ever being sensationalist or patronising.

Since 1987, the slot has been called simply *Newsround* (Craven left the series in 1989). It currently runs five days a week, airing just before 5.30 p.m.

The Nightmare Man

Science Fiction/Thriller | BBC One | episode duration 30 mins | broadcast 1–22 May 1981

Regular Cast
James Warwick · *Michael Gaffikin*
Celia Imrie · *Fiona Patterson*
Maurice Roëves · *Inspector Inskip*
Tom Watson · *Dr Goudry*
Jonathan Newth · *Colonel Howard*
James Cosmo · *Sergeant Carch*
Fraser Wilson · *PC Williamson*
Tony Sibbald · *Dr Symonds*
Elaine Wells · *Mrs Mackay*
Jon Croft · *McGrath*
Ronald Forfar · *Campbell*
Jeff Stewart · *Drummond*
Robert Vowles · *Lieutenant Carey*
Pat Gorman · *The Killer*

Creator David Wiltshire **Producer** Ron Craddock **Writer** Robert Holmes, from the novel *Child of the Vodyanoi* by David Wiltshire
Theme Music Robert Stewart

Another great example of how the BBC got around producing science fiction in the early 1980s by pitching it as something else entirely (see also ***The Day of the Triffids*** and ***The Mad Death***), *The Nightmare Man* paired director Douglas Camfield and writer Robert Holmes together for a story that was part murder mystery, part horror tale and part . . . something else.

It begins with an almost *Wicker Man*-like Scottish island, remote and cut off from the mainland by a sudden fog. The community's dentist, Michael Gaffikin, stumbles across the badly mutilated body of a local woman, the result of a frenzied attack by a mad man. A second body is found – a visiting ornithologist whose camera managed to snap a

few stills of the masked attacker, and soon the entire island is in a state of panic.

Made on videotape, the four-part serial has the air of a soap opera, until we witness our first murder at the end of the first episode. With both the director and writer veterans of ***Doctor Who***, they relished the opportunity to ramp up the gore for an older audience. The feeling of there being 'something out there' has ensured that while this is by no means a well-remembered production, those that saw it at the time at least recall that it was terrifying, even if the story's resolution might have some feeling a little cheated.

Nineteen Eighty-Four

See pages 520–1

1990

Drama | BBC Two | episode duration 50 mins | broadcast 18 Sep 1977–10 Apr 1978

Regular Cast
Edward Woodward · *Jim Kyle*
Robert Lang · *Herbert Skardon*
Barbara Kellerman · *Delly Lomas*
George Murcell · *'Tiny' Greaves*
Clifton Jones · *Henry Tasker*
John Savident · *Home Secretary Dan Mellor*
Michael Napier Brown · *Jack Nichols*
Paul Hardwick · *'Faceless'/Mawdsley*
Honor Shepherd · *Marly*
Tony Doyle · *Dave Brett*
Donald Gee · *Dr Vickers*
Mathias Kilroy · *Tommy Pearce*
Lisa Harrow · *Lynn Blake*
Stanley Lebor · *'Digger' Radford*
David McKail · *Inspector Macrae*
Yvonne Mitchell · *Kate Smith*
Clive Swift · *Tony Doran*

Creator Wilfred Greatorex **Producer** Prudence Fitzgerald **Writers** Wilfred Greatorex, Edmund Ward, Arden Winch, Jim Hawkins **Theme Music** John Cameron provides a curious theme tune that could easily have come from ***Tomorrow's World***, with a rather tinny high-pitched synth providing the main theme.

An unsuccessful military coup a few years back has left Britain in the grip of a terrifying totalitarian state. All citizens have been issued with identity cards and ration books, every telephone call is monitored, houses and clothes are fitted with bugs and, in a reversal of the concerns from the 1970s, the biggest issue of the day is *emigration*, with over 26,000 professionals waiting in vain for the results of their application for exit visas. While governments around the world condemn the UK for restricting free movement across boundaries, in direct contradiction of the European agreement, the British government justifies its stance to prevent the loss of more doctors, engineers, academics and other essential professionals to overseas where they can earn much more money and live in relative freedom. Many try to escape, those who survive being recaptured face the Adult Rehabilitation Centres run by the Public Control Department (PCD).

Jim Kyle is the chief reporter for one of the biggest independent newspapers still permitted to publish by the government. Highly critical of the Home Secretary and the PCD, the paper is often willing to report the government's successes in capturing escaping citizens and closing down emigration lines. Secretly though, Kyle is running his own emigration line, helped by 'Faceless', his very own 'Deep Throat' informer from within the civil service. But as his scoops begin to anticipate government announcements, head of the PCD Herbert Skardon realises that Kyle must be implicated in the emigration business personally and vows to bring him down.

Bucking the system from within as he did in ***Callan***, Edward Woodward starred as journalist/people smuggler Jim Kyle. Enjoying the guilty pleasure of evading the bugs and prying eyes of the PCD's surveillance operatives, Kyle also liked to flirt with the PCD's deputy controller, the attractive Delly Lomas, an ambitious woman with plans to depose her boss, the fiery Herbert Skardon. When her Machiavellian schemes failed, Kyle found himself within the radar of Government minister Lynn Blake.

Running for just two series of eight episodes each, *1990* was a clever update of the threats of George Orwell's *1984*, though sadly the series has languished in the BBC archives since transmission with, at the time of writing, no sign of a home video release on the horizon.

Nip/Tuck

Drama | Shephard/Robin/Stu Segal Productions for Warner Bros (shown on Channel 4) | episode duration 45 mins | broadcast 22 Jul 2003–present (USA)

Regular Cast
Julian McMahon · *Christian Troy*
Dylan Walsh · *Sean McNamara*
Joely Richardson · *Julia McNamara*
John Hensley · *Matt McNamara*
Valerie Cruz · *Grace Santiago*
Roma Maffia · *Liz Cruz*
Vanessa Redgrave · *Dr Erica Noughton*
Linda Klein · *Nurse Linda*
Kelsey Batelaan · *Annie McNamara*
Jessalyn Gilsig · *Gina Russo*
Famke Janssen · *Ava Moore*
Kelly Carlson · *Kimber Henry*

Creator Ryan Murphy **Producers** Ryan Murphy, Michael M. Robin, Greer Shephard (executive), Hoot Maynard, Bonnie Weis (associate), Michael Weiss, Patrick McKee **Writers** Ryan

Murphy, Lyn Greene, Jennifer Salt, Hank Chilton, Brad Falchuk, Sean Jablonski, Richard Levine **Theme Music** 'The Engine Room' by The Perfect Lie

Christian Troy and Sean McNamara are two friends who run a plastic surgery partnership in Miami, Florida. Sean is a family man with a beautiful wife and teenage son, who appreciates that there's a lot to be said for a happy domestic life. Unfortunately, he doesn't have anything approaching a happy family life, with his wife Julie needy, selfish and insecure and his son Matt on the verge of outright hatred towards him. Christian, meanwhile, is a voracious slut, sleeping his way round as many women as he can possibly manage and determined to maintain his carefree bachelor status for as long as possible. As a consequence, Christian is keen to maintain his sexual attractiveness, and therefore isn't averse to undergoing a few minor surgical procedures to keep him looking good – after all, as he says to Sean, his face is his professional calling card.

A slick, glamorous and often horrifically gory drama series, *Nip/Tuck* is a perfect demonstration of the concerns facing a lot of people in the early 21st century. When one of the surgeons asks their patient, 'What don't you like about yourself?', it's difficult for anybody at home not to imagine what it would be like to have the money to be able to sculpt the perfect version of themselves. Naturally enough, this being a 'realistic' drama, the surgery sequences are often almost impossible to watch without squirming – the prosthetics and special effects involved are stomach-churningly authentic. Although it's lovely to see British actress Joely Richardson starring in a US drama series, it does still come as a bit of a shock for many British viewers to see former ***Home and Away*** star (and former Mr Dannii Minogue) Julian McMahon starring as the amoral Christian, especially as he's spent many years cultivating a TV career in the States on a number of shows that haven't really made it over here.

No Place Like Home

Sitcom | BBC One | episode duration 30 mins | broadcast 13 Dec 1983–22 Dec 1987

Principal Cast
William Gaunt · *Arthur Crabtree*
Patricia Garwood · *Beryl Crabtree*
Stephen Watson · *Paul Crabtree*
Martin Clunes, Andrew Charleson · *Nigel Crabtree*
Dee Sadler · *Tracy Crabtree*
Daniel Hill · *Raymond Codd*
Beverley Adams · *Lorraine Codd*
Marcia Warren, Ann Penfold · *Vera Botting*
Michael Sharvell-Martin · *Trevor Botting*

Creator/Writer John Watkins **Producer** Robin Nash **Theme Music** A faltering, inaccurately played solo piano interpretation of the classic folk song 'There's no Place Like Home' (which was based originally on the poem by John Howard Payne).

A staple of weekday early evenings on BBC One throughout the mid-1980s, *No Place Like Home* told the story of middle-aged, middle-class couple Arthur and Beryl Crabtree. Having raised four children, Arthur eagerly looks forward to finally getting his house back to himself and enjoying some quality time with his wife in peace. However, his kids have other ideas – whenever they have problems with their relationships or cashflow, they all pile back to the family home, much to Arthur's dismay. Eldest daughter Lorraine has married a man who drives Arthur up the wall – Raymond is overly familiar with him, insisting on calling him 'Dad' and treating Arthur's house like his own. In fact, the only time that Arthur gets to himself is when he retreats to his garden shed with his next door neighbour Trevor to have a glass or three of sherry. Trevor likes these quiet moments too, for his eccentric wife Vera is an animal fanatic and keeps a veritable menagerie of beasts in their suburban semi.

Another amiable if unspectacular comedy series, *No Place Like Home* falls very much into the same type of show as ***Terry and June*** and ***My Family***, programmes that the whole family can enjoy with little chance of anybody getting offended by the material. Holding the whole thing together was renowned actor William Gaunt, somebody who'd been a bit of a heartthrob in his earlier career starring in glossy action-adventure series ***The Champions***. It also gave Martin Clunes his first TV comedy experience, something he was able to capitalise upon years later in the much nearer-the-knuckle ***Men Behaving Badly***.

No – Honestly

Sitcom | LWT for ITV | episode duration 25 mins | broadcast 4 Oct 1974–5 Jan 1975

Principal Cast
Pauline Collins · *Clara Burrell/Danby*
John Alderton · *Charles Danby*

Creator Charlotte Bingham **Producer** Humphrey Barclay **Writers** Charlotte Bingham, Terence Brady **Theme Music** Lynsey de Paul wrote the title song, 'No – Honestly', which reached No. 7 in the charts in November 1974

Charles Danby (known as 'CD' to his friends) meets Clara Burrell, a young woman of noble birth, at a party in Hampstead. Despite being an out-of-work actor with few prospects, the two of them get married and enjoy a long and happy life together. Each episode of the series begins with Clara and CD talking directly to the audience at home, discussing a particular event in their past round about the time when they first met and got married. Then, in flashback, we find out the truth about the incident.

Starring real-life husband and wife team Pauline Collins and John Alderton (who'd become huge stars thanks to their starring role in ***Upstairs, Downstairs*** – later, they'd get their own *UpDown* spin-off series called *Thomas and*

Continued on page 522

Nineteen Eighty-Four

The public face of Big Brother.

Here is a society where certain thoughts are classed as crimes and where language is shaped into 'Newspeak' to be as economical and uncomplicated as possible. Television rules the population; it cannot be switched off and its function is to watch, not to be watched. The symbol of authority is Big Brother, a man who is never seen, although his face adorns posters everywhere, accompanied by slogans like 'Ignorance is Strength', 'War is Peace' and 'Big Brother is watching you'. Britain, now known as 'Airstrip One', is part of Oceania, one of three power blocs that control the world. Thought itself is a crime here, as decreed by the Thoughtpolice, while sex is an activity reserved purely for the purpose of procreation. At the heart of London lies a huge pyramid, the Ministry of Truth, where Newspeak is developed and where Winston Smith works as part of the system, rewriting history so that it always matches the current policies rather than the original facts. Winston tries to be a good citizen, attending 'Hate' rallies and joining in with the crowd as they shout abuse at the Party's enemy, Emmanuel Goldstein, and express their love for Big Brother. But then Julia enters his life and he discovers to his combined joy and horror that he has fallen in love with her. When the couple are betrayed and arrested, Winston is taken to Room 101, a place of torture that houses his worst nightmare ...

Science Fiction
BBC TV
Episode Duration: 120 mins
Broadcast: 12, 16 Dec 1954

Nineteen Eighty-Four had been published just six years before the BBC acquired the rights for a TV adaptation. The success of ***The Quatermass Experiment*** prompted the BBC to invite producer/director Rudolph Cartier and writer Nigel Kneale to tackle the adaptation of George Orwell's novel, which the opening narration calls 'one man's alarmed vision of the future'. Cartier hired John Hotchkis to compose and conduct the music, which was played in live from an adjoining studio. Several pre-filmed sequences were shot, at Alexandra Palace and on a site of demolished houses where, six years later, the BBC's Television Centre would be built. The inserted film footage had the advantage of giving the performers time to move between sets.

The play was performed live twice, first on Sunday 12 December 1954, and then again the following Thursday, this being telerecorded for posterity (the only way that a live show could be recorded back then was to point a film camera at a TV monitor, but the process was expensive so not every production got the treatment). By the time of its repeat, the play had hit the front pages of the British press, with headlines like 'Tortures on TV start biggest protest storm' (referring to the scene in which Peter Cushing, as Smith, had his head encased in a glass helmet with rats fed into it from a tube), 'Wife dies as she watches' and 'No! No! No! No! TV won't drop "1984"'. Questions were asked in Parliament and sack-loads of complaints flooded in from viewers furious that the BBC could broadcast something so grim and sadistic – until, that is, the Queen was quoted as having enjoyed the play immensely. Suddenly the BBC's *Nineteen Eighty-Four* was hailed as an outstanding piece of work and its reputation was assured.

The Beeb had another go at adapting the novel in 1965, as part of the *Theatre 625* series. With a new script, again by Nigel Kneale, David Buck and Jane Merrow played the doomed lovers. Ironically, while the telerecording of the 1954 production survives in the archives, the more recent production does not.

Principal Cast
Richard Williams · *Narrator*
Peter Cushing · *Winston Smith*
André Morell · *O'Brien*
Yvonne Mitchell · *Julia Dixon*
Donald Pleasance · *Syme*
Arnold Diamond · *Emmanuel Goldstein*
Campbell Gray · *Parsons*
Hilda Fenemore · *Mrs Parsons*
Pamela Grant · *Parsons Girl*
Keith Davis · *Parsons Boy*
Janet Barrow · *Woman Supervisor*
Norman Osborne · *First Youth*
Tony Lyons · *Second Youth*
Malcolm Knight · *Third Youth*
John Baker · *First Man*
Victor Platt · *Second Man*
Van Boolen · *Barman*
Wilfrid Brambell · *Old Man, Thin Prisoner*
Leonard Sachs · *Mr Charrington*
Roy Oxley · *Big Brother*

Producer Rudolph Cartier

Writer Nigel Kneale, from the novel by George Orwell

Theme Music Composed and conducted by John Hotchkis

Sarah), *No – Honestly* was adapted from her own semi-autobiographical novel by Charlotte Bingham and *her* real-life husband Terence Brady. The show ran for 13 episodes, after which Bingham and Brady created a sequel programme of sorts, ***Yes – Honestly***. In truth, only the title of the programme and the behind-the-scenes talent remained the same, with the characters and storylines completely different to the Collins/Alderton season. Ditching the flashback format, *Yes – Honestly* simply portrayed the relationship between Lily Pond (her parents should have been reported to the NSPCC, giving her a name like that!) and Matthew Browne, (Liza Goddard and Donal Donnelly) watching them as they fell in love and got married. Two seasons of *Yes – Honestly* of 13 episodes each were made.

Noel's House Party

Entertainment | BBC One | episode duration c. 60 mins | broadcast 23 Nov 1991–20 Mar 1999

Regular Cast

Noel Edmonds · *Presenter*
Mr Blobby · *Himself/Barry Killerby*
Graham Cole, Andrew Paul · *Visiting Policeman*
Tony Blackburn · *Butler*
Pat Coombs · *Pru the Organist*
Shane Richie · *Sebastian*
Bernard Cribbins · *Himself*

Creator Noel Edmonds **Producers** Michael Leggo (executive), Jonathan Beazley, Guy Freeman, John McHugh, Philip Kampff **Writers** Various, including Andy Parsons, Henry Naylor **Theme Music** James Simpson

Born out of the wreckage of the not-especially good *Noel Edmonds Saturday Roadshow*, and the much earlier ***The Late Late Breakfast Show***, *Noel's House Party* rapidly became perhaps the definitive Saturday teatime entertainment programme, regularly attracting audiences in excess of 14 million. The *House Party* differed from previous Saturday shows in so far as it was broadcast completely live – thereby making the programme just a little bit more exciting because neither the audience at home nor host Noel Edmonds ever knew precisely what was going to happen. Each episode consisted of a bewildering array of stunts, games and sketches, all hosted from within the 'Grand House' (i.e. studio set) of the fictional town of Crinkley Bottom. House guests included a variety of different celebrities, many of them playing themselves or slight variations on their familiar TV characters – for instance, Noel would often be interrupted in the middle of the party by two policemen calling at the house, played by ***The Bill***'s PCs Quinnan and Stamp.

Favourite segments included the Gotcha Oscars (later renamed simply the Gotchas after the American Academy of Motion Picture Arts and Sciences objected to the blatant send-up of their own beloved icon), pre-filmed sequences in which a celebrity would be 'set-up' via hidden cameras – particularly funny examples included ***Blue Peter*** presenter Yvette Fielding trapped in a room with a rotary-action paint sprayer and former ***Doctor Who*** Jon Pertwee attending a shambolic local radio phone-in. Many of the Gotchas were set up with the help of a fake children's TV character called Mr Blobby, a gigantic pink creature prone to messing things up, falling over and generally being obnoxious. When Mr Blobby's cover as a stooge for Noel had been blown, he became a regular guest within the studio-bound segments of the show and simultaneously a huge star himself. Indeed, as a result of *Noel's House Party*, Blobby became a recording star, grabbing the Christmas 1993 No. 1 slot with his eponymous hit single.

Viewers at home had a chance to win some money courtesy of a sports star, a sealed box and a wind machine in 'Grab a Grand' (suspiciously similar to the final round of Channel 4's ***The Crystal Maze***), and studio-bound celebrities shuddered in fear of the results of a public vote in 'The Gunge Tank'. A far more charming sequence saw children filmed by hidden cameras conversing with talking books, plants and toys in 'My Little Friend', and in the most memorable and eagerly-awaited segment of the programme, Noel would activate 'NTV' – a hidden camera secreted into somebody's living room, the victim then becoming part of the live broadcast, much to their shock and amazement. On certain occasions, the star of 'NTV' would be a celebrity, with people like Dale Winton, Garry Bushell and Chris Evans being set up (and apparently Chris wasn't even watching *Noel's House Party* – he was tuned to ***Baywatch*** instead . . .).

One of the great strengths of *Noel's House Party* was the way in which it refused to trot exactly the same features out year after year – new games and guests were essential to maintain the show's freshness. Indeed, towards the end of the run Noel Edmonds himself realised that the programme was relying too much on its old standards and insisted that two episodes of the show not be transmitted until he could revamp the show properly. In the end, despite a much-improved final season, audiences simply grew tired of gunge andMr Blobby and the show was dropped from BBC One Saturday night schedules. Ironically, ITV scored their biggest Saturday night hits in years when Ant and Dec hosted a remarkably similar show with their own ***Saturday Night Takeaway***.

Noggin the Nog

See THE SAGA OF NOGGIN THE NOG

Northern Exposure

Comedy/Drama | Universal TV for CBS (shown on Channel 4) | episode duration 45 mins | broadcast 12 Jul 1990–26 Jul 1995 (USA)

Regular Cast
Rob Morrow · *Dr Joel Fleischman*
Barry Corbin · *Maurice J. Minnifield*
Janine Turner · *Maggie O'Connell*
John Cullum · *Holling Gustaf Vincoeur*
Darren E. Burrows · *Ed Chigliak*
John Corbett · *Chris Stevens*
Cynthia Geary · *Shelly Marie Tambo Vincoeur*
Elaine Miles · *Marilyn Whirlwind*
Peg Phillips · *Ruth-Anne Miller*
Richard Cummings Jr · *Bernard Stevens*
William J. White · *Dave, the cook*
Doug Ballard · *Ron Bantz*
Anthony Edwards · *Mike Monroe*
Graham Greene · *Leonard Quinhagak*
James L. Dunn · *Hayden Keyes*
Paul Provenza · *Dr Phil Capra*
Teri Polo · *Michelle Schowdoski Capra*
Earl Quewezance · *Eugene*
Adam Arkin · *Adam*

Creators Joshua Brand, John Falsey **Producers** Various, including Joshua Brand, John Falsey, Henry Bromell, David Chase, Diane Frolov, Robin Green, Jeff Melvoin, Andrew Schneider, Michael Vittes **Writers** Various, including Joshua Brand, John Falsey, Mitchell Burgess, Diane Frolov, Robin Green, Jeff Melvoin, Andrew Schneider, Jerry Stahl **Theme Music** David Schwartz

Young medical graduate Joel Fleischman arrives in the remote Alaskan town of Cicely to set himself up in practice, largely as the result of not having read the small print on a contract he'd signed (a salutary warning to us all!). For a New Yorker like Joel, life in Cicely moves at nothing more than a snail's pace. Add in the local weirdoes and eccentrics that seem to make up the vast majority of the population (not to mention the moose that spends much of its time wandering up and down Cicely's main street) and Joel soon realises that life in the far north is going to be a very strange experience indeed.

Touted by some people as the natural successor to ***Twin Peaks*** (remote US setting, bizarre characters, etc.), *Northern Exposure* was, in fact, a much gentler and funnier show, one that revelled in its developing characters rather than an ongoing plotline. Many people enjoyed *Northern Exposure* for the love-hate, will-they-won't-they relationship between Joel and Maggie – others enjoyed it for the background characters and the heartwarming representation of a small-town community that mostly gets on with each other pretty well. The town of Roslyn, Washington State, was used to represent the fictional Alaskan town of Cicely, and few people who weren't from those particular states probably noticed. *Northern Exposure* lasted for six seasons, although most fans think it probably should have ended a year earlier with the departure of Rob Morrow as Joel (the final year saw Dr Capra take over Joel's surgery – what a Wonderful Life, eh?).

Not In Front of the Children

Sitcom | BBC One | episode duration 30 mins | broadcast 26 May 1967, 25 Aug 1967–9 Jan 1970

Principal Cast
Wendy Craig · *Jennifer Corner*
Paul Daneman, Ronald Hines · *Henry Corner*
Roberta Tovey, Verina Greenlaw · *Trudi Corner*
Hugo Keith-Johnston · *Robin Corner*
Jill Riddick · *Amanda Corner*

Creator/Writer Richard Waring **Producer** Graeme Muir

Jennifer and Henry Corner have a typical kind of family life – they've got three lovely children and live in a very average sort of house in a run-of-the-mill suburban street. Trying to cope with three demanding children and an occasionally unsympathetic husband drives Jennifer up the wall – but some of the problems in the household can be blamed on her own scatterbrained behaviour.

Not In Front of the Children started life as a pilot episode in the *Comedy Playhouse* strand entitled 'House in a Tree'. Although it was very popular with viewers at the time, many critics felt that *Not In Front of the Children* was simply too tame, too twee and too darned nice to provide much in the way of comedy. In total, 38 episodes were made, with the last of four seasons being made in colour. By the time of the final episodes, people could have been forgiven for assuming that the format had reached the end of its natural life: however, viewers tuning in to ***And Mother Makes Three*** on ITV the following year may well have detected some pretty large similarities. This was largely down to the defection to ITV of writer Richard Waring and series star Wendy Craig, who would play a very similar character to Jennifer Corner in her new show.

Not Only . . . But Also

Comedy | BBC Two / ABC (shown on BBC One)| episode duration 30–50 mins | broadcast 9 Jan 1965–26 Dec 1966, 18 Feb–13 May 1970, 18–25 Jun 1971

Cast
Dudley Moore, Peter Cook · *Various Characters*

Producers Joe McGrath, Dick Clement, John Street, James Gilbert **Writers** Various, including Peter Cook, Dudley Moore, Robert Fuest, Dick Clement, Joe McGrath, John Law, Jonathan Abbot, Robert Sale **Theme Music** Pete and Dud released their famous closing titles song, 'Goodbye-ee', which peaked at No. 18 in the charts in June 1965.

When people are asked to name the greatest TV comedy double-acts, Peter Cook and Dudley Moore are often right at the top of the list – and it's *Not Only . . . But Also* that launched the genius of these two comics onto the viewing public. Initially established to showcase the talents of

Beyond the Fringe comedian/musician Dudley Moore (Not Only . . .), comedy partner Peter Cook (. . . But Also) rapidly assumed equal, if not greater, acclaim. Perhaps the best-remembered segments of each programme featured 'Pete' and 'Dud' as two working class men clad in macs and flat caps, sitting in a pub and putting the world to rights. The sketch that most people recall was the very first one they performed, in which Pete recalls how he was subjected to the unwanted sexual attentions of 'Greta bleedin' Garbo'. Although these 'Dagenham dialogue' sketches were largely scripted, viewers were enthralled by the obvious ad-libs that often left the performers (usually Moore!) gasping with laughter in the middle of the sketch. In fact, in retrospect, we're now more aware of how barbed their off-screen relationship was, to the point that it's perhaps fair to describe Cook and Moore as not so much a comedy partnership – more a comedy duel to the death, using their fearsome brains and barbed wit as weapons.

Other regular features of the later shows included a slot in which guest comics showed off their spontaneous rhyming skills, 'Poets Cornered'. If they failed, they got dunked into a tank of gunge – who says that Chris Tarrant and the ***TISWAS*** team started that kind of thing off? Moore would also perform new songs at the piano or with a jazz backing band, and a wide range of celebrities would show up to get involved in the surreal madness (a good indicator of how popular and cool the duo were at the time is shown in the fact that John Lennon turned up twice on the series). Two seasons were made in black and white, and a further run four years later in colour. Two extra episodes – 'Peter Cook and Dudley Moore in Australia' – were recorded for ABC in Australia and then shown on BBC One. Both Cook and Moore would go on to international fame in feature films, but tragically both men died far too early, robbing us all of their comic talents. Unfortunately, many of the original episodes of *Not Only . . . But Also* were wiped from the BBC Archives in the 1970s – thankfully, we at least have some examples of the wit and wisdom of Pete and Dud.

Not the Nine O'Clock News

Comedy | BBC Two | episode duration 30 mins | broadcast 16 Oct 1979–12 Mar 1982

Principal Cast

Rowan Atkinson, Pamela Stephenson, Griff Rhys Jones, Mel Smith, Chris Langham · *Various Roles*

Producers Sean Hardie, John Lloyd **Writers** Various, including Guy Jenkin, Andy Hamilton, Richard Curtis, Howard Goodall, Colin Bostock-Smith, Andrew Marshall, David Renwick, Rowan Atkinson, Mel Smith, Griff Rhys Jones, Nigel Planer, Peter Richardson, John Lloyd, Philip Pope, Paul Smith, Peter Brewis, Laurie Rowley, Douglas Adams **Music** Peter Brewis, Howard Goodall, Philip Pope, Nic Rowley

An especially fine satirical sketch show, *Not the Nine O'Clock News* was broadcast on BBC Two directly opposite BBC One's *Nine O'Clock News*, using its timeslot as a unique selling point by providing a literal 'alternative comedy' to the programming on the main channel. There hadn't been an up-to-the-minute sketch show on TV for many years, so the arrival of *Not the Nine O'Clock News* felt like a breath of fresh air – particularly as the performers involved were all virtual television unknowns.

The first season of the show starred Rowan Atkinson, Chris Langham, Pamela Stevenson and Mel Smith, and together they poked fun at politicians and current affairs (with Stevenson particularly memorable when doing impressions of female newsreaders), performed send-ups of pop songs and performed traditional slapstick comedy routines. An occasional support artist in the first season, Griff Rhys Jones was promoted to a full-time member of the team when Chris Langham departed before the second series began. In total, 27 episodes were produced, with a wide variety of genuinely funny sketches scattered throughout the run. Two of the best remembered include 'Nice Video – Shame About the Song', a parody of the New Romantic pop music movement and the promotional videos that looked as though they took longer to record than the music; and 'Gerald the Talking Gorilla', a strong contender for the title of the funniest sketch of all time.

When the series came to an end, all of its performers went on to enjoy successful careers: Mel and Griff moving on to their own long-running sketch show ***Alas Smith And Jones***, Pamela flirting with Hollywood fame before settling down with Billy Connolly and becoming a celebrated author, and Rowan writing and starring in a sitcom of his own called ***The Black Adder*** . . .

Number 73

Magazine | TVS for ITV | episode duration 95 mins | broadcast 2 Jan 1982–27 Mar 1988

Regular Cast

Sandi Toksvig · *Ethel Davies*
Nick Staverson · *Harry Stern*
Andrea Arnold · *Dawn Lodge*
Neil Buchanan · *Himself*
Kim Goody · *Herself*
Jeannie Crowther · *Hazel Edwards*
Richard Addison · *Martin Edwards*
Patrick Doyle · *Percy Simmons, Alec Simmons*
Tony Aitken · *Fred the Postman*
Nick Wilton · *Tony Deal*
Michael Maynard · *Frederick Crossfield*
Tony Hippolyte · *Eazi Target*
David Taylor · *Vet*
Kate Copstick · *Maisie McConachie*
Andrew O'Connor · *Himself*
Chris Sievey · *Frank Sidebottom*
Julian Callaghan · *Jules*
Nadia De Lemeny · *Herself*
Nicholas Barnes · *Geoffrey Edwards*

Hamilton Dent · *Richard Waites*
Jo Connor · *Herself*
Chris Donat · *James Squire*
Bill Stewart · *J. C. Birch*
Robert Denenham · *Rob the Builder*
Tessa Morton · *Phillipa*
David Rubin · *Himself*

Creator John Dale **Producers** Various, including Richard Leyland, Janie Grace (executive), John Dale, Tim Edmunds **Theme Music** Peter Gosling wrote the theme for the little-seen first series, but it's Ray Shulman's theme that we all remember: 'Hey you, get ready get on your feet/Get into gear and hit the street...'

While over on BBC One they were pretending to be running a TV studio-shaped shop, on ITV's TVS region they built a soap-styled magazine show around an entire house, complete with living room and kitchen areas, and with neighbours popping in and out all the time. The idea was that elderly landlady Ethel (Sandi Toksvig) runs an open house – anyone can come and stay so long as they have a lively personality and are prepare to join in all the fun. Ethel's lodgers took the place of presenters and everything was styled to be able to be re-created in the homes of the kids – especially 'The most daring, dazzling, death-defyingly dull, devastatingly dangerous, delectable, delicatessenable, divinely decadent Sandwich Quiz!' in which trivia questions were rewarded with slices of bread with numerous fillings. Ethel's second-in-command was Dawn, a roller-skating free spirit who later brought in her friend Neil who was a great artist. If Ethel couldn't do the Sandwich Quiz, Neil would step in with his own version – 'Salt and vinegar, green mushy peas, scallops and chips all covered in grease, a big fat sausage, the curry's the biz, frying tonight – the Chip Butty Quiz!' Ahem!

Number 73 began life as TVS's attempt to distance itself from ***TISWAS***. A short local-only run in 1982 eventually led to TVS winning the chance to go national (aided by *Tiswas*'s disappearance and the fact that none of the subsequent replacements being much cop). With the move to a fully-networked broadcast, Sandi Toksvig was allowed to lose the old lady make-up and play her own age, and eventually the format settled down into a comfortable alternative to Mike Reid's ***Saturday SuperStore*** on the other side. The soap elements continued, nevertheless, with threats to bulldoze the house or sell it off, issues that often involved Ethel being nice to her bank manager boyfriend. The series also moved location, from Southampton to Maidstone, resulting in a change for the postal address (with the legendary postcode 'ME15 6RS' – or 'Me Fifteen, Six Rs').

With Ethel emigrating to Australia unexpectedly in the show's sixth year (Toksvig left the series), her nephew Harry was promoted to head of the house, which is where most of us lost interest, despite the addition of papier mâché-headed nasal Northern comic Frank Sidebottom. The show got a regular Sunday edition too, but an attempt to zjush things up a little by relocating to a Wild West theme park called '7t3' didn't cut it and the show was brought to an end to make way for *Motormouth*, which also starred Neil Buchanan and Andrea Arnold, this time out of character (and roller boots in Arnold's case) and simply presenting a standard ITV Saturday morning kids' show.

Nuts in May

Comedy Drama | BBC One | episode duration 85 mins | broadcast 13 Jan 1976

Principal Cast

Alison Steadman · *Candice Marie Pratt*
Roger Sloman · *Keith Pratt*
Anthony O'Donnell · *Ray*
Stephen Bill · *Finger*
Sheila Kelley · *Honky*
Richenda Carey · *Miss Beale*
Eric Allan · *Quarryman*

Producer David Rose **Writer** Mike Leigh

Keith and Candice Marie are two London-based trendy liberal vegetarians who decide to get back to nature by going on a camping holiday in rural Dorset. Unfortunately, their ambitions and expectations completely dwarf their abilities, with the holiday proving to be far from the relaxing break they hoped for. Quite aside from their own relationship problems, Candice Marie and Keith quickly manage to annoy the locals and other people staying on the campsite with their attitudes, their behaviour and most importantly with Candice Marie's ghastly guitar playing. Their peace is disturbed too, first by Ray with his radio, and then by the arrival of Brummie bikers Finger and Honky. When the newcomers decide to light a campfire – strictly against the rules of the site – the tension and stress that's been building up in Keith finally snaps and he challenges Finger to a duel with sticks.

Mike Leigh is unquestionably one of Britain's great playwrights and directors – *Nuts in May* was the first exposure most of us got to his genius. As he does with most of his work, Leigh sketched out the basic storyline of *Nuts in May* and then allowed his cast to improvise their way through the events, creating dialogue and characters that were painfully acute in their realism. It's impossible to single out either Roger Sloman (as the neurotic uptight bully Keith) or Alison Steadman (as the meek, lisping Candice Marie), who was at that point married to Mike Leigh – both of them are simply outstanding, creating a comedic double-act that has you alternately gasping with horror and screaming with laughter at their social *faux pas*. Leigh's next TV project was his equally well-received dissection of the middle-class social gathering, ***Abigail's Party***.

NYPD Blue

Drama | Steven Bochco Productions/20th Century Fox for ABC (shown on Channel 4) | episode duration 45 mins | broadcast 21 Sep 1993–1 Mar 2005 (USA)

Regular Cast

Dennis Franz · *Detective Andy Sipowicz*
James McDaniel · *Lieutenant Arthur Fancy*
Nicholas Turturro · *Detective James Martinez*
Sharon Lawrence · *Assistant District Attorney Sylvia Costas*
David Caruso · *Detective John Kelly*
Sherry Stringfield · *Laura Michaels Kelly*
Amy Brenneman · *Officer Janice Licalsi*
Jimmy Smits · *Detective Bobby Simone*
Justine Miceli · *Detective Adrianne Lesniak*
Gail O'Grady · *Donna Abandando*
Gordon Clapp · *Detective Greg Medavoy*
Kim Delaney · *Detective Diane Russell*
Andrea Thompson · *Detective Jill Kirkendall*
Rick Schroder · *Detective Danny Sorenson*
Bill Brochtrup · *John Irvin*
Henry Simmons · *Detective Baldwin Jones*
Mark-Paul Gosselaar · *Detective John Clark Jr*
Jacqueline Obradors · *Detective Rita Orti*
Currie Graham · *Lieutenant Thomas Bale*
Bonnie Somerville · *Detective Laura Murphy*
Esai Morales · *Lieutenant Tony Rodriguez*
Charlotte Ross · *Detective Connie McDowell*
Garcelle Beauvais-Nilon · *ADA Valerie Heywood*
John F. O'Donohue · *Sergeant Eddie Gibson*

Creators Steven Bochco and David Milch **Producers** Various, including Steven Bochco, David Milch, Bill Clark, Walon Green, Charles H. Eglee, William M. Finkelstein, Gregory Hoblit, Matt Olmstead, Michael M. Robin, Mark Tinker, Nicholas Wootton, Robert J. Doherty, Bonnie Mark (executive) **Writer** Various, including David Milch, Ted Mann, Burton Armus, Gardner Stern, Leonard Gardner, Theresa Rebeck, David Mills, Nicholas Wootton, Meredith Stiehm, Jody Worth, Matt Olmstead, Buzz Bissinger, Jonathan Lisco, Keith Eisner, Tom Szentgyorgyi, Greg Plageman, William M. Finkelstein **Theme Music** Mike Post

Picking up pretty much where Steven Bochco's ***Hill Street Blues*** left off, *NYPD Blue* offered up challenging, gritty drama. The series managed to be a hit without bowing to the right-wing Christian campaigners who were baying for its removal from American screens before it had even aired, largely because of the promise of a little bare flesh (and to be fair, while there were indeed a few nude scenes in the first series, they were just as likely to be of a male form as a female one – the show was striking out for equality if nothing else).

What made the show such a success was its refusal to paint its characters as either squeaky-clean or completely corrupt: Sipowicz was a wise-cracking, likeable guy who just happened to have dubious views on the race of some of his arrestees. As Detective John Kelly, David Caruso came across as brash but charismatic (though Caruso's over-estimating of his public appeal led to his early departure from the show for a disappointing film career and a humble return to serial TV a decade later as the lead in one of the CSI spin-offs); and notable later additions included Jimmy Smits (whose character is suspended from the force and then exonerated only to die of a heart attack that took everyone by surprise) and former child star Rick Schroder as Andy Sipowicz's final partner and surrogate son. Often the case in hand was secondary to the personal lives of the characters, which occasionally left the series open to accusations of becoming a soap opera, but anyone familiar with Bochco's other creations would recall just how important he appeared to value character over plot.

Dennis Franz and David Caruso had both made appearances in *Hill Street Blues* while Jimmy Smits, who arrived after Caruso's controversial departure for the series, had previously starred in Bochco's ***LA Law***.

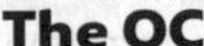

The OC

Drama | Hypnotic/College Hill Pictures/Wonderland/Warner Bros for Fox (shown on Channel 4) | episode duration 45 mins | broadcast 5 Aug 2003–present (USA)

Regular Cast

Adam Brody · *Seth Cohen*
Benjamin McKenzie · *Ryan Atwood*
Peter Gallagher · *Sandy Cohen*
Kelly Rowan · *Kirsten Cohen*
Mischa Barton · *Marissa Cooper*
Chris Carmack · *Luke Ward*
Melinda Clarke · *Julie Cooper-Nichol*
Rachel Bilson · *Summer Roberts*
Alan Dale · *Caleb Nichol*
Tate Donovan · *Jimmy Cooper*
Travis Van Winkle · *Kyle*
Samaire Armstrong · *Anna Stern*
Amanda Righetti · *Hailey Nichol*
Michael Cassidy · *Zach Stevens*
Olivia Wilde · *Alex Kelly*
Shannon Lucio · *Lindsay Gardner*

Creator Josh Schwartz **Producers** Josh Schwartz, McG, Bob DeLaurentis, Dave Bartis, Doug Liman, Melissa Rosenberg, Allan Heinberg, Stephanie Savage (executive), Ian Toynton (supervising), Mike Kelley (consulting), Ben Kunde, Judith Blume (associate), Loucas George, John Stephens, Drew Z. Greenberg **Writers** Various, including Josh Schwartz, Jane Espenson, Drew Z. Greenberg, Allan Heinberg, J. J. Philbin, Stephanie Savage **Theme Music** 'California' by Phantom Planet, a typical piece of American soft 'college rock'. It was written by band members Alex Greenwald and Jason Schwartzman, and it became a moderate hit when it was released into the UK charts in Spring 2005.

When troubled teenager Ryan Atwood is thrown out of his own home, he well and truly lands on his feet when he's invited by his wealthy lawyer Sandy Cohen to come and live with him and his family. Ryan moves into the Cohens' palatial house in Newport Beach, Orange County (the 'OC' of the title), California, and soon makes friends with Sandy's son Seth, who's the same age as him. The pair become the best of friends and spend their time worrying about girls, grades and the usual kind of things that trouble teenagers. However, all is not entirely hunky-dory – Sandy's wife Kirsten is aware of Ryan's past as a young hoodlum and loathes the idea of having a criminal living under their roof. Meanwhile, Ryan falls in love with Marissa Cooper, a beautiful and rich young girl living nearby. Marissa doesn't return the affection though – she has her own hidden feelings that she keeps close to her chest. Marissa's best friend Summer fancies Ryan, though – but completely fails to notice that Seth is madly in love with *her*.

Another well-produced if rather soulless teen drama series from the same kind of mould as ***Dawson's Creek*** and ***Beverly Hills 90210***, *The OC* benefits from its glamorous location, glamorous stars and so-hip-it-hurts scripting (many of the scriptwriters cut their teeth on the much smarter ***Buffy the Vampire Slayer***) and direction. But for British and Australian audiences of a certain age, it still comes as a huge shock to see ***Neighbours***' Jim Robinson (Alan Dale) acting with a faultless American accent.

The Odd Couple

Sitcom | Paramount for ABC (shown on ITV) | episode duration 25 mins | broadcast 24 Sep 1970–4 Jul 1975 (USA)

Principal Cast

Jack Klugman · *Oscar Madison*
Tony Randall · *Felix Unger*
Al Molinaro · *Murray Greshner*
Larry Gelman · *Vinnie*
Garry Walberg · *Speed*
Archie Hahn · *Roger*
Ryan McDonald · *Roy*
Joan Hotchkis · *Dr Nancy Cunningham*
Janis Hansen · *Gloria Unger*
Brett Somers · *Blanche Madison*
Penny Marshall · *Myrna Turner*
Elinor Donahue · *Miriam Welby*
Monica Evans · *Cecily Pigeon*
Carol Shelly · *Gwendolyn Pigeon*

Creator Neil Simon **Producers** Sheldon Keller, Garry Marshall (executive), Jerry Belson, Tony Marshall **Writer** Various, including Harvey Miller, Carl Gottleib, Ruth Brooks Flippen, Garry Marshall **Theme Music** Sammy Cahn and Neil Hefti's original movie theme was re-used for this television series.

When Felix Unger's wife kicks him out of their family home, he's left with a dilemma – where should he go? Luckily Felix's old childhood friend Oscar Madison has just been divorced from his wife too, so the two bachelors decide that the best thing to do is to share an apartment together. However, this apparently good idea rapidly falls to pieces when the two of them discover that they have diametrically opposing views and opinions about how to live – uptight, anal-retentive and skinny Felix is a neatness freak, demanding that everything should be perfectly clean and tidy at all times. On the other hand, Oscar is so laid back and lazy about the whole 'keeping things clean' thing that he can barely aspire to slovenliness.

Based upon the hit 1968 Neil Simon movie of the same name (starring Jack Lemmon and Walter Matthau), *The Odd Couple* was quite unusual for most traditional sitcoms in so far as it featured no one lead character, no smarter half of the partnership, no-one whom the audience identified with more than the other. Instead, the comedy came out of the equally matched conflicts between these two extremely intelligent men: Felix (Tony Randall) a professional photographer, Oscar (future ***Quincy*** star Jack Klugman) a sports reporter for the *New York*

Herald. Regular visitors to the mismatched flatmates' world included their poker pals Murray the cop, soft-hearted Vinnie, gambler Speed and Roy (later Roger), as well as a number of different on-off girlfriends, who included Dr Nancy and the charming flighty English Pigeon sisters. After 114 episodes, Felix was eventually reunited with his estranged wife Gloria and moved back in with her, splitting up this most mismatched of couples forever. However, we in Britain have never seen this final episode, with both ITV (on the original screening) and BBC One (on a late Eighties repeat run) failing to get far enough into the run of episodes to reveal the programme's eventual outcome. We Brits have never had the privilege of seeing two twists on the format either – *The New Odd Couple* (which featured two black performers, Ron Glass and Desmond Wilson, in much the same show) and *The Oddball Couple*, a short-lived cartoon series starring a neat cat called Spiffy and a dirty dog called Fleabag.

The Office

Sitcom | BBC Two/One | episode duration 30 mins, plus 2 × 45-min specials | broadcast 9 Jul 2001–4 Nov 2002, 26–27 Dec 2003

Regular Cast

Ricky Gervais · *David Brent*
Mackenzie Crook · *Gareth Keenan*
Martin Freeman · *Tim*
Lucy Davis · *Dawn*
Stirling Gallagher · *Jennifer Taylor-Clark*
Ralph Ineson · *Chris Finch*
Joel Beckett · *Lee*
Ewen MacIntosh · *Keith*
Robin Hooper · *Malcolm*
Oliver Chris · *Ricky Howard*
Sally Bretton · *Donna*
Patrick Baladi · *Neil Godwin*
Stacey Roca · *Rachel*

Creators/Writers Ricky Gervais, Stephen Merchant **Producers** Jon Plowman, Anil Gupta (executive), Ash Atalla **Theme Music** An instrumental version of 'Handbags and Gladrags', written by Mike d'Abo and arranged by Big George Webley. Originally released by Chris 'Out of Time' Farlow (reaching No. 33 in 1967), it was famously covered by Rod Stewart (never released as a single in the UK) and Stereophonics (reaching No. 4 in December 2001).

For the staff at the Slough branch of leading paper merchants Wernham Hogg, life suddenly gets much more interesting when a fly-on-the-wall documentary series begins filming the everyday goings-on in their office. The main target for their cameras is office manager David Brent, the extremely popular life and soul of the party whom everybody looks up to and admires.

Or at least, that's what *he* thinks. But the camera picks up the truth about David Brent all too clearly – that his staff sees him as little more than a complete and utter joke. Utterly self-obsessed and completely disinterested in the lives of his team (except in how they reflect on him, naturally) as Brent is, the only person who has any time for him is his junior office manager Gareth, an obsequious crawler who butters Brent up in the hope of advancing his own career. Gareth's nemesis is sales rep Tim, always ready with a bit of backchat or a sarcastic retort to Gareth's latest bit of officiousness. Tim is madly in love with shy receptionist Dawn, who unfortunately is already going out with a loathsome boyfriend called Lee, much to Tim's chagrin. Brent reports up to Wernham Hogg regional manager Jennifer Taylor-Clark, who only normally drops by to the Slough office in order to deliver some piece of bad news, such as the merger with the Swindon office announced at the end of the first series. With a nearly permanent threat of redundancy hanging over the workers, morale and motivation is never very high; and it tends to slip even lower whenever Brent attempts to raise people's spirits with a dirty joke, an ill-timed comment or (God forbid) doing a dance for them in the middle of the office.

The success of *The Office* took most commentators by surprise – a small sitcom on BBC Two with no big-name stars would seem an unlikely hit. However, after just one series, word of mouth had turned the show into a real success story. This has to be largely down to the acutely accurate portrayal of the tedium and mundaneity prevalent in most offices across the UK – the petty point-scoring, the unrequited love for a colleague, the realisation of being stuck in a dead-end role. Viewers empathised with the plight of Tim and Dawn, and everybody watching at home recognised at least an element of Brentian behaviour in their own bosses at work. However, for many people *The Office* was simply too uncomfortable to sit through. It elevated the comedy of embarrassment to an entirely new plane, making viewers squirm in horror at Brent's latest *faux pas*. For a significant proportion of the audience, there just wasn't any pleasure to be obtained from such agonising viewing, perhaps explaining why although it was a massive critical success (winning practically every comedy award going), *The Office* never achieved similarly huge ratings. Having said that, sales of the programme on DVD were so healthy that they actually broke records, with the season one becoming the biggest-selling non-movie DVD in UK sales history.

Having completed two seasons, star and co-writer Ricky Gervais decided not to accept the BBC's offer of another run of *The Office*, instead opting for two extended Christmas special episodes over the 2003 festive season, shown over on BBC One. These formed a kind of catch-up for the 'fly-on-the-wall' crew, who had decided to interview Brent, Tim and the rest to see how their lives had changed following the broadcast of the documentary. Another inspired concept for a comedy series, this final look at the lives of the Wernham Hogg staff had TV viewers cheering for joy as Tim and Dawn finally got together and Brent capitalised on his temporary fame in still more horrifically embarrassing ways. Gervais created a true TV monster in David Brent – we're very glad that he exists, if only to help give all office workers a perfect example of an incompetent manager to compare their own demon boss against.

Oh Brother!

Sitcom | BBC One | episode duration 30 mins | broadcast 13 Sep 1968–27 Feb 1970/12 Sep–24 Oct 1973

Regular Cast
Derek Nimmo · *Brother Dominic*
Felix Aylmer · *Father Anselm*
Colin Gordon · *Master of Novices*
Derek Francis · *Father Matthew*
Laurence Naismith · *Father Harris*
Pearl Hackney · *Mrs Carr*
David Kelly · *Walter*

Creators/Writers David Climie, Austin Steele **Producers** Duncan Wood, Johnny Downes, Harold Snoad **Theme Music** Mike Sammes

While Derek Nimmo was still appearing as the Reverend Mervyn Noote in ***All Gas and Gaiters***, he simultaneously moonlighted as another calamitous cleric in another BBC One religious comedy series, *Oh Brother!* However, on this occasion, the setting wasn't a public-facing religious establishment like a cathedral – it was the sheltered, secluded environs of Mountacres Priory. Nimmo starred as bumbling novice monk Brother Dominic – a man with his heart in the right place, but his common sense well and truly missing. Incredibly accident prone, Brother Dominic is prone to overhearing conversations and getting the wrong end of the stick, with occasionally hilarious consequences – the Prior, Father Anselm, is fairly understanding when it comes to Dominic's latest misadventure. However, Father Matthew finds Dominic's stupidity and clumsiness distinctly wearying and longs to see Mountacres Priory returned to a haven of peace and Godliness.

After 19 episodes of monk-eying about, Brother Dominic left our TV screens for three years – upon his return, he'd received a promotion (astonishingly!) and was now Father Dominic, thereby warranting a name change for the series too. Little else about the show had changed though – Dominic was still distinctly incompetent, causing a never-ending parade of disasters for his boss Father Harris. Just seven episodes of *Oh Father!* were made. Never the most cutting-edge or challenging comedy series that the BBC has ever made, *Oh Brother!* and *Oh Father!* now seem positively antediluvian, with only the most determinedly old-fashioned of modern viewers able to find much within to entertain.

The Old Grey Whistle Test

Music | BBC Two | episode duration 30–90 mins | broadcast 21 Sep 1971–3 Jun 1983, 23 Dec 1984 31 Dec 1987

Cast
Ian Whitcomb, Richard Williams, Bob Harris, Anne Nightingale, Mark Ellen, Richard Skinner, Andy Kershaw, Ro Newton · *Hosts*

Producer Michael Appleton **Theme Music** Each edition would open with an animated figure composed of stars kicking (hence the sequence's unofficial name, the 'Starkicker'). The distinctive harmonica tune, 'Stone Fox Chase', was written by Charlie McCoy and Kenny Buttrey of Area Code 615, a supergroup of Nashville session players who'd performed on Bob Dylan's 1969 *Nashville Skyline* album. In 2003, the tune was sampled by Deep South rapper Bubba Sparxx on 'Johnny Mathis'.

While ***Top of the Pops*** has traditionally (with only brief exceptions) stuck to the singles charts, the point of *The Old Grey Whistle Test* was to provide exposure to bands yet to chart or to artists whose primary income came from albums and live performances. Programmes featured one or two artists playing live; Bob Marley and the Wailers played their first British TV performance on the show, as did The Stone Roses towards the end of the programme's run (famously blowing the BBC's fuses with their amps, causing singer Ian Brown to call the Beeb's technicians 'amateurs'). There was also a leaning towards prog-rock acts like Yes, or artists known for having a serious approach to music, like David Bowie. An ephemeral pop act likely to hit number one was unlikely to be a feature of the show.

Considered the home for serious music on BBC Television, it was to *The Old Grey Whistle Test* team, and not *Top of the Pops*, that the Beeb turned to for its presentation of the mammoth ***Live Aid*** concert in 1985. *The Old Grey Whistle Test* had been presented initially by Richard Williams, former assistant editor of *Melody Maker*, but it's co-founder of *Time Out* Bob Harris that's most closely associated with the show. Famous for a quiet, intense delivery that earned him the nickname 'Whispering' Bob Harris, it was a style he developed because he was aware that his voice was echoing around the undressed studio.

The 'Old Greys' of the title were the elderly cleaners and doormen who worked in the buildings of record companies in the 1920s; the test being that a good song would have the 'Old Greys' whistling the tune after only a couple of plays. For its 1984 series, the show's title was shortened to *Whistle Test* in an attempt to remove some of the dusty connotations the show had acquired, having weathered both punk and the new romantic movements without being too bothered by either. The format of *The Old Grey Whistle Test* survives to this day, with *Later with Jools Holland* providing a similar showcase for 'serious' music.

Oliver Twist (1962)

Drama | BBC TV | episode duration 30 mins | broadcast 7 Jan–1 Apr 1962

Principal Cast
Bruce Prochnik · *Oliver Twist*
Max Adrian · *Fagin*

Peter Vaughan · *Bill Sikes*
Melvyn Hayes · *The Artful Dodger*
Carmel McSharry · *Nancy*
Willoughby Goddard · *Mr Bumble*
Donald Eccles · *Mr Sowerberry*
Barbara Hicks · *Mrs Sowerberry*
John Breslin · *Harry Maylie*
Gay Cameron · *Rose Maylie*
John Carson · *Monks*
George Curzon · *Mr Brownlow*
Aimée Delamain · *Old Sally*
Alec Foster · *Carter*
Priscilla Morgan · *Charlotte*
Alan Rothwell · *Charley Bates*
Peggy Thorpe-Bates · *Widow Corney*

Producer Eric Tayler **Writer** Constance Cox, from the novel by Charles Dickens **Theme Music** Ron Grainer

For commentary, see OLIVER TWIST (1999)

Oliver Twist (1985)

Drama | BBC One | episode duration 30 mins | broadcast 13 Oct–29 Dec 1985

Principal Cast
Ben Rodska, Scott Funnell · *Oliver Twist*
Eric Porter · *Fagin*
Michael Attwell · *Bill Sikes*
David Garlick · *The Artful Dodger*
Amanda Harris · *Nancy*
Dominic Jephcott · *Harry Maylie*
Lysette Anthony · *Agnes Fleming/Rose Maylie*
Pip Donaghy · *Monks*
Frank Middlemass · *Mr Brownlow*
Raymond Witch · *Mr Sowerberry*
Elizabeth Proud · *Mrs Sowerberry*
Terry Molloy · *Brittles*
Charles Pemberton · *Warden*
Julian Firth · *Noah Claypole*
Alan Bennion · *Magistrate*
Dicken Ashworth · *Sergeant*
Hilda Braid · *Mrs Bedwin*
June Brown · *Mrs Mann*
Edward Burnham · *Mr Grimwig*
Janet Henfrey · *Martha*
Miriam Margolyes · *Mrs Corney, Mrs Bumble*

Producer Terrance Dicks **Writer** Alexander Baron, from the novel by Charles Dicken **Theme Music** Dudley Simpson

For commentary, see OLIVER TWIST (1999)

Oliver Twist (1999)

Drama | HTV/Diplomat Films/United Productions/WGBH Boston for ITV | episode duration 90 mins | broadcast 21 Nov–5 Dec 1999

Principal Cast
Sam Smith · *Oliver Twist*
Robert Lindsay · *Fagin*
Andy Serkis · *Bill Sikes*
Alex Crowley · *Artful Dodger*
Emily Woof · *Nancy*
David Ross · *Mr Bumble*
Julie Walters · *Mrs Mann/Bumble*
Roger Lloyd-Pack · *Mr Sowerberry*
Ger Ryan · *Mrs Sowerberry*
Marc Warren · *Monks/Edward Leeford*
Tim Dutton · *Edwin Leeford*
Lindsay Duncan · *Elizabeth Leeford*
Michael Kitchen · *Mr Brownlow*
Annette Crosbie · *Mrs Bedwin*
Keira Knightley · *Rose Fleming*
Sophia Myles · *Agnes Fleming*
Liz Smith · *Sally*
Sam Kelly · *Giles*
Alun Armstrong · *Mr Fleming*
Annette Badland · *Chertsey Cook*
David Ryall · *Mr Fang*
Hugh Lloyd · *elderly vicar*

Producers Alan Bleasdale, Michele Buck, Rebecca Eaton (executive), Keith Thompson **Writer** Alan Bleasdale, from the novel by Charles Dickens **Theme Music** Paul Pritchard, and Elvis Costello

Two cinematic versions of Charles Dickens's most famous novel have dominated the public perception of the tale: David Lean's 1948 film, which starred Robert Newton as Bill Sikes and Alec Guinness as Fagin; and Lional Bart's musical, filmed by Carol Reed in 1968 with Ron Moody as Fagin, Oliver Reed as Sikes, Jack Wild as the Artful Dodger and Mark Lester as the angelic Oliver. There have, however, been a number of TV adaptations through the years – as well as a sequel of sorts.

With so many adaptations, the story is familiar: a young orphan boy escapes the life of the workhouse and the cruelty of a family of funeral directors only to fall in with a gang of juvenile offenders led by the seedy Fagin. Fagin's associates include a teen rogue known as the Artful Dodger, a kind-hearted prostitute called Nancy and her violent partner, Bill Sikes, a murderous thug. Trained in the art of pickpocketing, Oliver proves to be too good-hearted to be adept at crime and finds himself in front of a judge only for a distant relative of his mother's to step forward and adopt him. Then Bill Sikes comes looking for him. . .

Despite the singing and dancing of Bart's musical version, *Oliver Twist* is not a happy tale and almost every adaptation has worked hard to get Dickens' social commentary across in different ways. The 1962 version was criticised for its violence, notably in Sikes' brutal murder of Nancy, while for the 1999 adaptation, Alan Bleasdale chose to pull out some of the back-story from the end of the book and construct a new prologue that took up much of the first episode of his four-part script. Bleasdale's scripts also show how the circumstances of Oliver's parents led to him being handed over to the workhouse. In this version, Robert Lindsay chooses to avoid the heavy Jewish stereotype suggested by Dickens' novel (and invariably played up in almost every other depiction of the character), making him much less fun than usual, but infinitely more credible as a rather sleazy individual whose exploitation of children and general criminal activities leave him a broken man in jail. Also of note is Bill Sikes, played by Andy Serkis, who two years later would have audiences gripped by his characterisation – via computer-generated graphics – of Gollum/Smeagol in the epic film version of Tolkien's *The Lord of the Rings* trilogy.

A curious oddity among these adaptations is *The Further Adventures of Oliver Twist*. Made in 1980, it came out of discussions between a group of writers about how they'd create sequels to well-known stories. Remembering his disappointment at how grim the BBC's 1962 production of *Oliver Twist* had been, writer David Butler came up with an idea to continue Oliver Twist's 'adventures' in a setting that would be suitable for a younger audience. In this 13-part ATV production for ITV, Oliver's half-brother, Monks, conspires to get his hands on Oliver's fortune, with the help of Noah Claypole and old Mr Bumble from the workhouse, who he manipulates into a position at Oliver's school. The Artful Dodger makes an appearance too, as does the duplicitous Fagin, played by David Swift.

On the Buses

Sitcom | LWT for ITV | episode duration 25 mins | broadcast 28 Feb 1969–6 May 1973

Principal Cast

Reg Varney · *Stan Butler*
Michael Robbins · *Arthur*
Anna Karen · *Olive*
Stephen Lewis · *Inspector 'Blakey' Blake*
Cicely Courtneidge, Doris Hare · *Mrs Butler*
Bob Grant · *Jack Harper*
Pat Ashton · *Doreen*

Creator Ronald Wolfe, Ronald Chesney **Producer** Stuart Allen, Derek Goodwin, Bryan Izzard **Writers** Ronald Wolfe, Ronald Chesney, Bob Grant, Stephen Lewis, George Layton, Jonathan Lynn, Garry Chambers, Wally Malston, Myles Rudge **Theme Music** 'Happy Harry' by Tony Russell.

On the Buses ran for 74 episodes across seven seasons, spawned no less than three spin-off feature films (*On the Buses* in 1971, *Mutiny on the Buses* in 1972 and *Holiday on the Buses* in 1973), a follow-on series for Blakey called *Don't Drink the Water*, and enough well drawn characters and dialogue to ensure its longevity. In short, *On the Buses* was one of the most successful sitcoms that ITV ever enjoyed.

Stan Butler is a bus driver (the Number 11 route, usually) operating out of Luxton and District Traction Company bus depot. He and his conductor mate Jack Harper spend most of their time working on the buses chasing after the sexy young ticket collectors and trying to run rings around the sour-faced authoritarian Inspector Blake – Blakey knows that Stan and Jack try to get the better of him, but most of the time he can't prove anything, leading him to exclaim 'I 'ate you, Butler!' on a regular basis. Home life is tricky for Stan too – he still lives with his bingo-obsessed mum, his aesthetically challenged sister Olive and her work-shy husband Arthur. A typical episode would see some kind of minor challenge (for instance, Olive deciding to become a ticket collector and joining Stan on the Number 11), which would be neatly wrapped up within 25 minutes courtesy of a few politically incorrect double entendres ('Going all the way. . .?'), a crack about Olive's lack of good looks and a threat from Butler.

On the Buses was a formulaic sitcom-by-numbers that happened to be staggeringly popular with the viewing public. Written by the same duo as the earlier BBC hit show ***The Rag Trade***, it didn't stretch the formula of the sitcom in any way, didn't try out anything novel or innovative, but it simply did the job of making its viewers laugh a hell of a lot.

On the Move

Education | BBC One | episode duration 10 mins | broadcast 12 Oct 1975–3 Oct 1976

Cast

Polly James · *Presenter*
Bob Hoskins · *Alf*
Donald Gee · *Bert*
Martin Shaw, Gay Hamilton, Peter Jones, Patricia Hayes, Rosemary Leach, Norman Rossington, Nigel Stock, M. P. Jackson, Bella Pocock · *Various Characters*

Producer David Hargreaves **Writer** Barry Took **Theme Music** Written by Hawkshaw/Tempest and sung by The Dooleys

This educational programme was designed to improve adult literacy and remove the shame from taking evening classes. Bob Hoskins and Donald Gee played removal men whose encounters with different clients provoked discussions about certain words and phrases that are common causes of embarrassment. Fifty episodes were made.

One by One

Drama | BBC One | episode duration 50 mins | broadcast 29 Jan 1984–2 May 1987

Regular Cast

Rob Heyland · *Donald Turner*
James Ellis · *Paddy Reilly*

Sonia Graham · *Ethel Ledbetter*
Liz Smith · *Gran Turner*
Jack Hedley · *Peter Raymond*
Heather James · *Maggie Raymond*
Rosie Kerslake · *Jenny Blount*
Peter Jeffrey · *Maurice Webb*
Garfield Morgan · *Howard Rundle*
Peter Gilmore · *Ben Bishop*
Clifford Rose · *Challon*
Catherine Schell · *Lady Anne Pendle*
Andrew Robertson · *Jock Drummond*

Creator Anthony Read **Producer** Bill Sellars **Writers** Various, including Johnny Byrne, Freda Kelsall, Terry Hodgkinson **Theme Music** Michael Omer

One by One consisted of three seasons of stories based upon the real-life incidents that happened to internationally renowned 'Zoo Vet' David Taylor (note the slight change in name of the lead character, David to Donald). In this respect, *One by One* was an obvious follow-on series to the already hugely popular James Herriot saga ***All Creatures Great and Small***, which was experiencing an eight-year gap in production at the time.

As the series (set in the late 1950s) begins, newly qualified vet Donald Taylor arrives home in Rochdale to take up his job at the veterinary practice run by the grumpy Maurice Webb. To his astonishment, this includes a small local zoo, and instead of just treating cats and dogs he soon finds himself working on the rather more exotic residents of the zoo. The second season moved the action on a few years to the 1960s and saw Donald setting up his own practice in response to the opening up of the new Manford Safari Park, owned by Ben Bishop. By the third and final season, action had moved on to the early 1970s, by which point Donald had become a globetrotting expert in exotic animal care. Always by Donald's side was ever-suffering Irish keeper Paddy Reilly, portrayed with great gusto and conviction by former ***Z Cars*** actor James Ellis.

Hugely popular with the public at the time, *One by One* seems to have become almost a forgotten series nowadays, which is a terrible shame. Rather more graphic in its depiction of animal surgery than the gentler *All Creatures Great and Small*, the series never shied away from the reality of the problems facing Donald in handling exotic animals when little or no documented knowledge existed on how to treat such patients. Adding to the realism was the fact that Dudley Zoo and Knowsley Safari Park allowed filming on their premises throughout the show's run.

One Foot in the Grave

See pages 534–6

One Man and his Dog

Game Show | BBC Two | episode duration 25 mins | broadcast 17 Feb 1976–present

Cast
Phil Drabble, Robin Page, Ben Fogle, Shauna Lowry, Clarissa Dickson Wright · *Presenters*
Eric Halsall, Ray Ollerenshaw, Gus Dermody · *Commentators*

Creator Philip S. Gilbert **Producers** Philip S. Gilbert, Ian Smith, Joy Corbett, Daniel Brittain-Catlin

There's a power to old countryside ways that will always draw an audience of some form or other. It runs through dramas like ***Dr Finlay, All Creatures Great and Small, Heartbeat*** and ***Emmerdale***, through comedies such as ***Last of the Summer Wine*** and to some extent ***The Good Life*** – and, of course, many of us would like to think it runs through us. We feel energised, refreshed by the Great Outdoors, which is why, even if few of us would ever watch a show like *One Man and his Dog*, we're glad that it exists.

It takes its name from a song about a man mowing a meadow, in itself an unlikely concept for a TV show (although it was, funnily enough, the subject of one of many ***Interludes*** broadcast by the BBC in the 1950s and early '60s). This is, of course, about sheepdog trials, where farmers show off their training and control of Man's Best Friend over a series of set courses. A series of tinnitus-inducing whistles and the odd 'come by' were all it took to herd a flock of sheep from one pen to another. Never the most heart racing of pastimes, but as the movie *Babe* (1995) showed (in which the herding was done by a rather identity-befuddled pig), it has a lot of simple charm. That was, after all, what had attracted series creator and first producer Philip Gilbert to it in the first place.

Though its audience was small, there were howls of outrage when the series was dropped in the late 1990s. With fears of foot-and-mouth disease sending countryside tourism to frighteningly low levels, it was clear to many that *One Man and his Dog* was a confident ambassador for country ways, and so the programme has continued to the present day, albeit as occasional specials rather than ongoing regular series. The programme itself has also evolved, from solitary farmers and their collies to a team-based game. Evidently, there was more than one man and his dog eager to have a go.

The Onedin Line

Drama | BBC One | episode duration 50 mins | broadcast 15 Oct 1971–26 Oct 1980

Regular Cast
Peter Gilmore · *James Onedin*
Anne Stallybrass · *Anne Webster/Onedin*

James Hayter · *Captain Webster*
Timothy Slender, Christopher Douglas · *Samuel Onedin*
Howard Lang · *Captain Baines*
Victoria Thomas, Laura Hartong · *Charlotte Onedin*
Mary Webster · *Sarah Onedin*
James Garbutt, Brian Rawlinson · *Robert Onedin*
Jessica Benton · *Elizabeth Onedin/Frazer/Lady Fogarty*
Michael Billington, Tom Adams · *Daniel Fogarty*
Philip Bond · *Albert Frazer*
Edward Chapman · *Mr Callon*
John Phillips · *Jack Frazer*
Pamela Salem, Jane Seymour · *Emma Callon/Fogarty*
Caroline Harris · *Caroline Maudslay*
Robert James · *Rowland Biddulph*
Kate Nelligan · *Leonora Biddulph*
Jill Gascoigne · *Letty Gaunt/Onedin*
John Rapley · *Mr Dunwoody*
Ken Hutchison · *Matt Harvey*
Marc Harrison · *William Frazer*
Warren Clarke · *Josiah Beaumont*
Maurice Colbourne · *Charles Marston*
Michael Walker · *Seth Burgess*
John Wentworth · *Mr Dawkins*
Keith Jayne · *Tom Arnold*
Roberta Iger · *Margarita Juarez/Onedin*
Frederick Jaeger · *Max Van Der Rheede*

Creator Cyril Abraham **Producers** Geraint Morris, Peter Graham Scott **Writers** Cyril Abraham, Ian Kennedy Martin, John Lucarotti, Mervyn Haisman, Roger Parkes, Martin Worth, Nick McCarthy, Simon Masters, Alun Richards, Barry Thomas, Douglas Watkinson **Theme Music** Aram Khachaturyan's classic 'Adagio' from *Spartacus and Phrygia* was used as the theme to *The Onedin Line*, perhaps the best ever match of a classical track to a TV show. It's impossible to listen to that piece of music now without instantly being able to smell the brine and the salt air!

Another great example of the kind of quality drama coming from BBCtv in the 1970s, *The Onedin Line* was the story of an ambitious Victorian seaman called James Onedin and the ups and downs of his business. James begins his empire by purchasing a ship called the *Charlotte Rose* from its former owner Captain Webster, for the sum of just £25. However, as part of the deal, James agrees to marry Webster's headstrong daughter Anne, an arrangement that eventually suited both parties. Tragically, Anne later died in childbirth but James remarried twice – first to Letty Gaunt (played by ***The Gentle Touch***'s Jill Gascoigne) and then, as the series drew to a close, to Spanish widow Margarita Juarez.

The stories of *The Onedin Line* revolved around a combination of bitter business wrangling, exciting adventures and incidents at sea, and, of course, standard drama fare such as weddings, deaths and illnesses. Extra authenticity was added to the proceedings by a great deal of the programme being filmed on board a real ship, the *Soren Larsen* (which is still in use today as a passenger vessel sailing around the South Pacific). Doubling up for the old-fashioned sea port of Liverpool were a number of different locations, including Dartmouth and Milford Haven. At the very heart of the series, though, was a powerhouse performance by Peter Gilmore as the determined, gruff James Onedin – a massive departure from his earlier career, in which he'd normally played in comic films such as *The Great St Trinian's Train Robbery* (1966) and ten of the best *Carry On* movies.

Only Fools and Horses

See pages 537–9

Only When I Laugh

Sitcom | Yorkshire TV for ITV | episode duration 25 mins | broadcast 29 Oct 1979–16 Dec 1982

Principal Cast
James Bolam · *Roy Figgis*
Christopher Strauli · *Norman Binns*
Peter Bowles · *Archie Glover*
Richard Wilson · *Dr Gordon Thorpe*
Derrick Branche · *Gupte*

Creator/Writer Eric Chappell **Producer** Vernon Lawrence **Theme Music** 'I'm H-A-P-P-Y. . . I know I am, I'm sure I am, I'm H-A-P-P-Y. . .' half-heartedly sung by James Bolam

A fondly remembered sitcom that seemed like a cross between 'Carry on NHS' and the world-weariness of ***Hancock, Only When I Laugh*** was written by ***Rising Damp*** author Eric Chappell – he'd later go on to pen the package holiday adultery comedy ***Duty Free***. With a remarkably small regular cast and a single setting, it's quite impressive that Chappell managed to keep the storylines as fresh and funny as he did throughout the 29 episodes.

Only When I Laugh starred former ***Likely Lad*** James Bolam as Figgis, one of three semi-permanent residents in an NHS hospital ward. Figgis actually enjoys the rest he's getting while in hospital from his regular job as a lorry driver, and takes great pleasure in winding up his 'bedmates' Binns (a pampered mummy's boy) and Glover (snotty, upper class and used to being waited on hand and foot). Together and separately, the three men cause no end of wearisome troubles for the easily confused porter Gupte and the crabby medic Dr Thorpe.

Not quite up to the extremely high standards of either Chappell or Bolam's earlier comedy work, *Only When I Laugh* undoubtedly benefited from the simultaneous mega-success of series star Peter Bowles in BBC One's ***To the Manor Born*** (an unusual example of a top sitcom actor starring in two hit shows for rival networks at the same time). It also provided the first major outing for Richard Wilson, ten years before the advent of Victor Meldrew.

One Foot in the Grave

Another typical day for Victor Meldrew.

It's a common complaint from many people that modern society has become ever more obsessed with the cult of youth. Programmes are refashioned and reformatted so that they appeal to the ever more important youth market. People who are old enough and people who are old enough to know better now spend thousands of pounds on facelifts, Botox injections and beauty treatments in order to hold back the inevitable march of time. Ironically, flying in the face of all this is the cold hard fact that the average age of the UK's population is climbing ever higher. People are living longer and are just as active and lively in their retirement years as they were prior to getting a bus pass. It's this dichotomy between the pigeonhole that society wants to put older people into and their increasing reluctance at being forced into it that formed the core of *One Foot in the Grave*.

On his 60th birthday, security guard/receptionist Victor Meldrew is made redundant from his job welcoming visitors to the headquarters of Watson-Mycroft Ltd. Appalled that he's now on the scrapheap five years before retirement age, Victor is even more aghast to discover that his replacement isn't even another human being – it's nothing more than a small electronic box that will be able to do everything that Victor had previously done, but at a fraction of the cost. Burdened with additional leisure time he'd never asked for, Victor is at a loss to know what to do with himself. With his wife Margaret still working part time in a flower shop, he's left home alone with little to do except rant and rail against the injustices he believes that society has dealt him. From the perpetual crisp packets that find themselves blown into his front garden, to the rudeness, inefficiency and general ineptitude of staff in the service sector, nothing is small enough or minor enough to slip underneath Victor's radar. He is an unwilling consumer vigilante, a man with sufficient time on his hands and a similarly sufficient lack of embarrassment to be able to say the things that we, as viewers, never have the guts and quickness of thought to vocalise.

Although many of the bizarre events that overtake Victor seem to be outrageously cruel acts of God (a spiteful and vengeful God with a

Sitcom
BBC One
Episode Duration: 30–90 mins
Broadcast: 4 Jan 1990–20 Nov 2000

Principal Cast
Richard Wilson · *Victor Meldrew*
Annette Crosbie · *Margaret Meldrew*
Doreen Mantle · *Mrs Jean Warboys*
Owen Brenman · *Nick Swainey*
Angus Deayton · *Patrick Trench*
Janine Duvitski · *Pippa Trench*
Tim Brooke-Taylor · *Derek McVitie*
Marian McLoughlin · *Betty McVitie*
Gordon Peters · *Ronnie*
Jean Challis, Barbara Ashcroft · *Mildred*

Writer/Creator David Renwick

Producers Susan Belbin, Jonathan P. Llewellyn, Esta Charkham

Theme Music Written and performed by ***Monty Python***'s Eric Idle, the theme tune for *One Foot in the Grave* sums up the whole concept behind the series: 'I'm a wrinkly, crinkly, set in my ways / It's true that my body has seen better days / But give me 'alf a chance and I can still misbehave . . .'

distinctly wicked sense of humour) – his house burning down while he's on holiday, a stray street lamp plummeting (still illuminated) through his bedroom window, for example – Victor himself has to take a significant amount of blame for the other surreal things that happen to him. Because of his short temper, he unfortunately rubs people up the wrong way. In retribution for his outbursts, people go to extraordinary lengths to get him back. In the world of *One Foot in the Grave*, we understand Victor's anger and share his utter frustration at the insane lengths to which they go. Victor might be many things – stubborn, foolish, irritable, impulsive – but downright mean is not one of them. That's why semi-regular characters Mrs Warboys and Nick Swainey have a great deal of time and affection for Victor, putting his outbursts down to just examples of 'typical' behaviour rather than a reason never to set foot in his house again. In short, that's why viewers will always empathise with Victor and Margaret Meldrew – at heart, they're simply decent people dealt a very bad hand by life.

The core of *One Foot in the Grave* was the perfectly drawn relationship between Victor and his ever-suffering wife, Margaret. For the first few seasons, viewers scratched their head about why such a reasonable and even-tempered woman would bother to stay with such a ranting monster of a husband. However, when Margaret is offered the chance of an affair with a handsome, charming, attentive man called Ben, she declines, telling him that although Victor is at times the most annoying and frustrating person she knows, she loves him and appreciates how kind and sensitive he is – only somebody who really cares about life and about people would get as worked up about things as Victor does. Annette Crosbie's considerable acting skills are allowed full rein in the show – it's always much more difficult to be the foil to a larger-than-life character. However, Crosbie succeeds in making Margaret a completely believable and well-rounded character, someone prepared to grit her teeth and sigh – or occasionally roar back – at the latest embarrassment or humiliation brought upon the Meldrew family name because of Victor's current hobbyhorse. Similarly, the character of Victor Meldrew could have risked being a much less likeable figure in the hands of a lesser actor. TV veteran Richard Wilson (who had appeared in shows as diverse as ***Crown Court***, ***The Sweeney*** and ***Only When I Laugh***) invests Victor with a nobility and sense of morality that shines out from underneath his perpetual scowl and flat cap. When Victor phones up the garage to find out if his car has been fixed, his opening words betray far more than just the colour and make of his vehicle: 'Victor Meldrew – the Crimson Avenger.'

Writer David Renwick had cut his teeth working with Andrew Marshall (***2 Point 4 Children***, *Strange*) on ITV sitcoms such as ***Hot Metal*** and ***Whoops Apocalypse*** and providing sketches for ***The Kenny Everett Television Show*** and ***Not the Nine O'Clock News***. In common with his early work, *One Foot in the Grave* is at times almost labyrinthine in its plotting, with throwaway lines of dialogue or easily missed actions by minor supporting characters becoming crucial to the episode's (normally) hilarious denouement. Renwick would further develop his skill for complex and thought-provoking plotting when he created and wrote murder-mystery series ***Jonathan Creek***. In *One Foot in the Grave*, Renwick played with the standard sitcom format in several episodes by using a much-reduced cast or single set. For example, 'The Beast in the Cage' is set entirely within Victor's car, stuck in one of those interminable motorway traffic jams. 'Timeless Time' is set solely within Victor and Margaret's bedroom during one sleepless night. In the episode we're treated to lots of Victor's typical rants and moans, but also we discover a sad secret of the Meldrews – that they once had a son, Stuart, who has died. Up until this point, viewers had never even questioned that the Meldrews were childless. Discovering that they had lost a child adds another layer to the reality of these characters, going some small way to explain Victor's boiling anger at the inherent unfairness of life. The format was stretched to its absolute limit when in 'The Trial' only Richard Wilson appears, performing a 30-minute monologue that is utterly compelling to watch.

Although the quality of the characterisation and acting is impeccable, it's the surreal and downright bizarre situations that Victor finds himself in that provide the fondest memories. Only in a programme as weird as this could Victor's new next-door neighbour Pippa (the sublime Janine Duvitski) truly believe that he'd take his ventriloquist's dummy to have a wee in their downstairs bathroom. There are dead cats discovered frozen stiff in the Meldrews' freezer, though, and wigs being pulled out of the middle of a loaf of bread – events that conspire to shock you with a guilty belly laugh at an inappropriate moment. Small animals always seemed to have a short life expectancy: a tortoise is accidentally burnt in a garden bonfire (the tortoise's replacement is then accidentally buried alive); Victor mistakes a decaying hedgehog for a slipper in the dark – it's surprising that the RSPCA didn't complain to the BBC. And what they made of the bizarre monkey-attracting pheromones that Victor gave off is anybody's guess . . . Add the ongoing feud between Victor and his equally stubborn (yet much less sympathetic) next-door neighbour Patrick (a fine performance from gameshow host and satirist Angus Deayton), and it's hardly surprising that *One Foot in the Grave* became such a huge hit.

The show proved that a mass-market sitcom could do a number of things at once – deliver huge, gasping-for-air belly laughs; bring tears of sadness and poignancy to the eyes; and make viewers question the current state of society. By challenging the automatic assumption made prevalent by the cult of youth that old equals useless, *One Foot . . .* made a clear point that the end of a traditional working life needn't mean the end of your usefulness to society. When, in the last ever episode, Victor was knocked down and killed in a hit-and-run accident (by everyone's favourite *Watercolour Challenge* host Hannah Gordon, incidentally), it seemed the perfect conclusion to the series that had made us sob at regular intervals throughout its run.

TRIVIA

Four months after the show finished, there was a final slice of Victor thanks to a short sketch broadcast as part of that year's ***Comic Relief***. In a knowing tribute to the movie *The Sixth Sense* (1999), we discover that Victor is ranting and raging as normal, but that Margaret can't hear him. He is in fact a ghost, and even passing over won't stop him from airing his views. Anyone who'd followed Victor's misadventures over the 42 episodes of *One Foot in the Grave* should have known that no grave would ever shut Victor Meldrew up for long. 'I don't believe it'? Well, we do.

Only Fools and Horses

Rodney, Del-Boy and Uncle Albert.

When *Only Fools and Horses* won the BBC's public vote for Best Sitcom, it did seem just a little inevitable. After all, a caricature of Del Boy appeared on the winning trophy. Whether or not it actually deserved the title is another matter – ***Fawlty Towers***' position as the most structurally perfect collection of scripts ever recorded is almost universally acknowledged. But certainly, John Sullivan's brainchild beats all other applicants as most *popular* comedy, hands down. It's certainly come a long way since its first run of episodes, which pulled in just 7 million viewers – almost half as many as most other BBC One sitcoms could attract at the time. Indeed, were it not for the persistence of Sullivan and his producer, Ray Butt – and the conveniently timed repeat run – *Only Fools and Horses* might have been consigned to the scrap heap long ago.

In casting the show, Ray Butt had no problems finding Grandad and he knew who he wanted for Rodney (he'd seen the 19-year-old Lyndhurst on Carla Lane's ***Butterflies***). But the central part of Del proved harder to fill. Roger Lloyd Pack auditioned, as did Jim Broadbent (both would play other characters in the series) until Butt caught a repeat of ***Open All Hours*** and cast David Jason. John Sullivan was not impressed, believing Jason wouldn't be able to convince as the tough guy he envisaged Del-Boy to be. Thankfully, Jason's East End roots soon put the writer's mind at rest.

One reason why *Only Fools* works is its rooting in classic comedy situations. Its debt to ***Steptoe and Son*** is clear, both shows dealing with the dashed dreams of family members clinging to each other in fear of being left to run the family business alone. Here, it's two brothers, Derek 'Del-Boy' Trotter, a quick-talking wheeler-dealer market trader, lumbered with his younger brother Rodney. Though 'Rodders' left school with qualifications (two O-levels, neither of

Sitcom
BBC One
Episode Duration: 30/50 mins, plus specials 60-85-min specials
Broadcast: 8 Sep 1981-29 Dec 1996, Christmas 2001-3

Regular Cast
David Jason · *Derek 'Del-Boy' Trotter*
Nicholas Lyndhurst · *Rodney Trotter*
Lennard Pearce · *Grandad*
Buster Merryfield · *Uncle Albert Trotter*
Roger Lloyd-Pack · *Trigger*
John Challis · *Aubrey 'Boycie' Boyce*
Sue Holderness · *Marlene Boyce*
Patrick Murray · *Mickey Pearce*
Paul Barber · *Denzil*
Kenneth MacDonald · *Mike Fisher*
Jim Broadbent · *DCI Roy 'The Slag' Slater*
Tessa Peake-Jones · *Raquel Turner/Rachel Slater*
Gwyneth Strong · *Cassandra Parry/Trotter*
Denis Lill · *Alan Parry*
Wanda Ventham · *Pamela Parry*
Roy Heather · *Sid Robertson*
Grant Stevens, Patrick McManus, Roger Liddement, Jamie Smith, Douglas Hodge · *Damien Derek Trotter*

Creator/Writer John Sullivan

Producers Ray Butt, Bernard Thompson, Gareth Gwenlan

Theme Music For the first series, Ronnie Hazlehurst provided the theme. This was soon dropped in favour of 'Only Fools and Horses' and the end theme 'Hooky Street', written and sung by John Sullivan.

them in anything useful), a suspended sentence for possession of cannabis has been a mill-stone around his neck ever since and Rodney has always felt trapped by Trotters Independent Traders, wondering how his life might have been without that early stupid mistake. Likewise, though Del was popular with the ladies, he always felt duty-bound to make sure that his younger brother was cared for, which inevitably meant that Del remained single well into adulthood. This sacrifice, along with the many 'last words' that Del claims their mother uttered on her deathbed, have helped Del-Boy keep Rodney in his place – by his side. Despite the heavy burden of his responsibilities, Del remains an eternal optimist, with 'more bounce than Zebedee', convinced with every passing year that by the next one they'll all be millionaires.

Selling their dodgy gear from the back of a three-wheeled yellow Robin Reliant, they live in Nelson Mandela Heights, a tower block in darkest Peckham. There's always the suspicion that the items littering their flat are at best 'hooky' and at worst stolen goods. But while they might cut corners on the legitimacy of their wares, we can't help but be impressed by how hard working and determined they are. Despite his pretensions, the cod-French and the ridiculous cocktails, we know that Del is no slacker, always working, always thinking ahead to his next great plan. Rodney, meanwhile, might long to break out and become his own boss – or at least work for someone he's not related to – but his loyalty to Del is unflinching. When we first meet them, they share the flat with their Grandad, a vague, simple man who was always willing but not altogether able to help out where he could. Lennard Pearce's sudden death during the making of series four necessitated a speedy rewrite of the scripts. Grandad's funeral was filmed just a week after the cast had done the real thing for Pearce. His role as bumbling older relative was filled by Buster Merryfield as Grandad's brother Uncle Albert, who wasted no time in boring his nephews with tales of his time in the navy during the war.

Sullivan's Peckham is populated by a cast of brilliantly-realised characters, whether it's the intellectually lacking Trigger, who insists on calling Rodney 'Dave' for reasons no-one can fathom, the oily Boycie and his wife Marlene (whose reputation precedes her as the good time had by all), Mike the barman at the Nag's Head or luckless entrepreneurs Denzil and Mickey. And, of course, there's the villainous Slater, a bent copper and sadistic bully who Del-Boy knew from school. This is a world where Del-Boy is king only because almost everyone else around him is dafter than he is. It's a perfect comedy situation made all the more believable because many of the situations come from real life.

By that fourth season, *Only Fools* had managed to more than double its ratings. Proof that the BBC recognised its success came when the sixth season's episodes were all increased to 50 minutes, giving John Sullivan more time to explore his creations and let them mature just a little. Rodney begins dating Cassandra, and the close of the season sees them married. With Rodney finally out of his hands, Del is free to continue his relationship with Raquel, an actress and former stripper he'd been dating on and off for a while.

There had been concerns that the addition of women into a predominantly male cast might have shifted the balance towards a more traditional domestic sitcom. Thankfully, the women added an extra dimension to the equation as voices of sanity for the Trotter brothers and were pivotal in turning the show from a sitcom into something much deeper.

Among many classic moments we can highlight, one of the funniest must be the scene where Del and Rodney stand at the top of ladders holding a tarpaulin waiting for Grandad to unscrew an expensive chandelier, only to realise too late that Grandad has been working on the wrong one when they see it crashing to the floor (Lyndhurst recounts how, during filming of the scene Ray Butt put enormous pressure on his shoulders telling him that if he laughed during the once-only take he'd be sacked and the show would be finished for good). And possibly the single most replayed clip saw Del-Boy leaning on a bar only to fall straight through the bar-hatch that someone had lifted up seconds before.

It's not always belly laughs, though. Sullivan has an amazing skill for pathos. The realisation that Del-Boy has suffered a savage beating the night before Rodney's wedding and the final shot where he's left standing alone at the reception apparently had the live audience in stunned silence, broken only by the tag scene at the end of the episode where Rodney returns home from his honeymoon having forgotten that he no longer lives there. The birth of Del and Raquel's son Damien combined superb one-liners with heavy sentimentality that was absolutely note perfect. Bravest of all was the decision to show Rodney's despair after Cassandra suffers a miscarriage. It's not a suitable subject for comedy, and at no point did Sullivan play it as such. By then, he trusted that the audience cared enough about the Trotters to forgive them for being too grief-stricken to play it for laughs and, as a result, it allowed Nicholas Lyndhurst to show us why he's more than just a brilliant comic actor.

When *Only Fools* came to an end in 1986 with the Trotters' discovery that an old watch they'd had for years was worth over £6 million, it was the perfect way to finish. The Trotter boys were finally millionaires, just as Del had often promised they would be. Their efforts were rewarded with a whopping 24 million people tuning in to see them off. That should have been it, but eventually John Sullivan bowed to pressure from the public and the nation's press by resurrecting the Trotters in three specials, to be shown at Christmas in 2001, 2002 and 2003. With such an enormous amount of expectation, the first special was not well received, despite strong ratings. Set just four months after the finale, it saw the Trotters penniless again after a stock market crash. Having already said goodbye to the Trotters once before, we're not altogether convinced that this really is the end. Though it has to be said, we're also concerned that the show's current fate, as schedule filler in continual repeat cycles, may dull its brilliance. Although we may have seen the last of the Trotters, Ray Sullivan's spikn-off comedy *The Green, Green Grass* (featuring the adventures of Boycie, Marlene and their teenage son) was due to reach TV screens in Autumn 2005.

Open all Hours

See pages 542–3

Operation Good Guys

Sitcom | Fugitive Group for BBC Two | episode duration 30 mins | broadcast 29 Dec 1997–31 Aug 2000

Regular Cast
David Gillespie · *DI Jim Beach*
Ray Burdis · *DS Raymond Ash*
Dominic Anciano · *Sergeant Dominic De Sade*
Perry Benson · *Bones*
Mark Burdis · *Mark Kemp*
John Beckett · *Strings*
William Scully · *Bill Zeebub*
Gary Beadle · *Gary Barwick*
Kim Taylforth · *Boo-Boo Finch*
Roy Smiles · *Roy Leyton*
Hugo Blick · *Smiler McCarthy, Hugo Crippin, Narrator*

Creators Dominic Anciano, Ray Burdis **Producers** Geoffrey Perkins, Jim Beach (executive), Dominic Anciano, Ray Burdis, Hugo Blick **Writers** Dominic Anciano, Ray Burdis, Hugo Blick **Theme Music** John Beckett

DI Jim Beach has a lot to contend with – not only is he in charge of a brand new crack police outfit nicknamed 'Operation Good Guys', but the team he hand-picked himself has turned out to be more than a little bit useless. And then there's the matter of the fly-on-the-wall documentary crew that he invited to follow every stage of 'Operation Good Guys', who are on hand to record every single failure and cock-up that befalls him and his team.

Pre-dating Ricky Gervais's great 'spoof documentary' comedy series ***The Office*** by some four years, *Operation Good Guys* was a rather unique experiment in the writing and production of a sitcom. Created by and starring Dominic Anciano and Ray Burdis, the basic outline of each episode was prepared prior to recording, but the dialogue and performances were largely improvised by the cast, in much the same way as acclaimed film director Mike Leigh had done with (among other things) ***Nuts in May*** way back in 1976. Although this kind of off-the-cuff comedy often worked very well, there were also more than a few occasions on which the 'cobbled together as it went along' reality of the programme came through to the surface. Having said that, *Operation Good Guys* was an interesting and unusual experiment – and it's not often nowadays that television allows people to be as creative as this.

Opportunity Knocks

Entertainment | Associated Rediffusion/ATV/Thames for ITV/BBC One | episode duration 45–60 mins | broadcast 1956–1978 (ITV), 21 Mar 1987–2 Jun 1990 (BBC)

Regular Cast
Hughie Green, Bob Monkhouse, Les Dawson · *Hosts*

Producers Various, including Peter Dulay, Milo Lewis, Royston Mayoh, Robert Fleming, Keith Beckett, Stewart Morris **Theme Music** Although the original ITV series didn't boast a successful theme, the BBC revival was blessed with 'Star' by Elton John's former collaborator Kiki Dee, which had reached No. 13 in February 1981.

The great-granddaddy of all TV talent shows, *Opportunity Knocks* began life as a BBC radio series in the early 1950s, created and presented by popular all-round entertainer Hughie Green (who many people mistakenly believe was Canadian – in fact, he was born in the UK but brought up for much of his childhood in Canada). When the BBC decided not to continue with the show, Green took the format over to TV station Associated Rediffusion and the rest, as they say, is history. In each edition of *Opportunity Knocks*, a number of acts (six, most weeks) would compete against each other to win the approval of the studio audience and the viewers at home. Before they had their few minutes of fame, their 'advocate' (a friend or a family member, usually) would have a chat with Hughie to explain a bit more about the contestant, their life, their background, and why they deserve the public's affection. Then the performer would do their 'turn' – singing, dancing, stand-up comedy, impressionism, whatever. As each act finished, the volume of the studio audience's thunderous applause would be measured by the patented 'clapometer' – at the end of each programme, the act with the highest score on the clapometer would be announced as the studio audience's favourite act. However, it was entirely down to the number of letters and postcards received each week supporting an individual contestant that decided whether or not they'd be invited back the following week to perform again – Hughie's entreaty for the folks at home to write in was always preceded by the famous comment, 'It's "make your mind up" time!'

With an original run of more than 20 years, it's not in the slightest bit surprising that *Opportunity Knocks* was responsible for launching the careers of a catalogue of famous faces, including Mary Hopkin, Les Dawson, Bonnie Langford, Lena Zavaroni, Peters and Lee, Bobby Crush, Freddie Starr, Frank Carson, and Little and Large. The programme came to an end in 1978, despite continuing to receive massive viewing figures – a curious decision indeed, and one that defies explanation even to this day. When the BBC decided to revive *Opportunity Knocks* in 1987, legal wrangles took place when the question of Hughie Green's copyright over the format was disputed. In the end, although Hughie had no direct involvement in the production of the new epsiodes (now hosted by Bob Monkhouse and latterly Les Dawson), he did receive an on-screen credit as 'programme adviser'. The new BBC series ran for four years but never achieved either the massive ratings or grabbed the imagination of the public in the same way as the original run.

During the 1970s, another talent show made significant waves on ITV, *New Faces* (produced by ATV and broadcast between 1973 and 1978). Instead of relying upon the vagaries of the British public, *New Faces* also included a panel of 'expert critics' who'd criticise or praise the contestants as they saw fit, hoping to influence the outcome of the public's vote. Hosted by Derek Hobson, some of the more famous winners of *New Faces* included Victoria Wood, Jim Davidson, Lenny Henry and Marti Caine, who would return as hostess of *New Faces* when it was revived for a short run in the mid-1980s.

It's not an exaggeration to say that without *Opportunity Knocks*, the current vogue for Saturday night 'interactive' entertainment programmes would almost certainly never have happened. Phoning a premium-rate phone line and texting in may have replaced the quaint old method of sending a postcard to register your vote, but the principal is exactly the same. Without *Opportunity Knocks*, there'd be no ***X Factor***, no ***Fame Academy***, no ***Popstars***. And, as Hughie Green might have said, we mean that most sincerely, folks.

The Oprah Winfrey Show

Talk Show | Harpo Productions (shown on Channel 4) | episode duration 45 mins | broadcast 8 Sep 1986–present

Cast

Oprah Winfrey · *Host*
Dr Phillip McGraw · *Medical Expert*

Producers Dianne Atkinson Hudson (executive), Oprah Winfrey (supervising), Melissa Geiger, Amie Baker (associate), David Boul, Alice McGee, Dana Newton, Ellen Rakieten (senior), Mollie Allen, Kandi Amelon, Amy Craig, Angie Kraus, Katy Murphy Davis, Laura Grant Sillars, Jill Van Lokeren

It's said that, should she ever stand for office, Oprah Winfrey could become America's first non-white and first female president – and probably with a landslide. This is not based solely on ratings, (though they certainly support the theory), but on the level of trust the American people have for the reigning queen of talk shows.

While some of the subjects of her shows might have been similar to her salacious rivals like Rikki Lake or Jerry Springer, the tone of Oprah's Chicago-based programmes has been very different. Indeed, after years of delving into her guests' private lives for the shock of exposing an affair or addiction, Oprah decided to lead by example and focus on more life-affirming stories and self-help features. Meanwhile other shows continue to feature mulleted trailer trash brawling for the crowd's entertainment – just one more reason why our vote goes to Oprah every time.

We've followed her weight losses and gains, her fashion disasters and snippets about her long-term relationship with Stedman Graham. She's brought us 'The Blue Eyes vs Brown Eyes Experiment', a study in racism that reveals to the audience evidence that brown-eyed people are more intelligent to see how people's behaviour begins to change, only to reverse their opinions by then claiming the opposite. Oprah challenged the people of Forsyth County, Georgia – which has been white-only for 40 years – to justify their stance and even explain why they believe there's a difference between a black person and a 'nigger'. It was a show that clearly disturbed Oprah, but she continued anyway. In a follow-up show she revealed that campaigns to integrate the county continue, and that the population is now only 92% white. She's created a nationwide 'book group' where her audience joins her in recommending books to the viewers, from literature heavyweights like *Anna Karenina* to *What Not to Wear* by our own Trinny and Susannah. Authors have also visited the studio to discuss their work. And one spectacular 2004 edition involved a lottery with the audience that led to everyone in the studio leaving with a brand new car (Oprah leading them out of the studio to see the vehicles for themselves while chanting, '*You* got a car. . . *you* got a car!').

It's deeply significant that Oprah regularly tops lists like '100 most powerful people in TV' or 'Pop culture icons of the 20th century', making her not just the most successful African-American or even the most successful woman but the most successful individual overall.

Trivia

Oprah has occasionally acted, most notably in Steven Spielberg's adaptation of Alice Walker's *The Color Purple* (1985). Her company name, Harpo, is 'Oprah' backwards.

Oranges are Not the Only Fruit

Drama | BBC Two | episode duration 55 mins | broadcast 10–24 Jan 1990

Principal Cast

Emily Aston, Charlotte Coleman · *Jess*
Geraldine McEwan · *Mother*
Kenneth Cranham · *Pastor Finch*
Mark Aspinall · *Ian*
Sharon Bower · *Mrs Vole*
Cathryn Bradshaw · *Melanie*
Freda Dowie · *Mrs Green*
Pam Ferris · *Mrs Arkwright*
Peter Gordon · *William*
Richard Henders · *Graham*
Barbara Hicks · *Cissy*
Celia Imrie · *Miss Jewsbury*
Elizabeth Spriggs · *May*
David Thewlis · *Doctor*

Continued on page 544

Open All Hours

Granville (David Jason) and Arkwright (Ronnie Barker)

Roy Clarke, the man behind the 'gentle' comedies ***Last of the Summer Wine***, ***Rosie*** and (later) ***Keeping Up Appearances***, created this sitcom way back in 1973 as an episode of the anthology series *Seven of One* designed to showcase comedian Ronnie Barker's talents. Although 'Prisoner and Escort' was immediately rushed into production as ***Porridge***, it would take three years before the exploits of miserly shopkeeper Arkwright would be graced with a full series. In fact, although *Open all Hours* eventually ran for 26 episodes and four seasons, there was a huge gap of five years between the first and second seasons.

Set in a typical small northern town, *Open All Hours* tells the story of Arkwright, owner of his own corner shop and grumpy mentor to his daydreaming nephew/delivery boy Granville. Arkwright spends much of his time fantasising about one of two things: prising cash out of the hands of his customers, and the buxom delights of his paramour Nurse Gladys Emmanuel. Forever just out of reach of Arkwright's grasp, Nurse Gladys seemed to genuinely like her admirer, but she never succumbed to her moustachioed Romeo's charms. Poor Granville longs to free himself from the shackles of life working for his uncle, but never seems to be able to muster the energy or the determination to cut his apron strings. Granville has his own object of affection, the nameless milk lady, who often seems to be on the verge of showering her erotic charms on the poor young lad, but never quite manages to divert her attention away from her semi-skimmed and gold top.

In many respects, *Open All Hours* follows a similar format to the ***Steptoe and Son*** model – two male characters trapped together, with the older man ensuring the youngster never breaks out to make a life of his own. Unlike *Steptoe*, though, *Open All Hours* is bathed in an air of cosy familiarity and Northern warmth.

Although there's sometimes pathos in Arkwright and Granville's situation, the humour is never as cruel or hurtful as in Albert and Harold's relationship. This warmth also helps the show to avoid any accusations of political incorrectness: although Arkwright's stammer is often the cause of humour in the programme, it never feels as if jokes are made *at* Arkwright and his physical condition.

By creating a sitcom around one member of the 'Nation of shopkeepers', Roy Clarke tapped into a common social memory that's as deeply ingrained in British society today as it ever has been. Up and down the land, there could hardly have been anyone who didn't feel a twinge of empathy for the voracious appetite of Arkwright's lethal cash register, which would slam shut with a brutality that threatened to remove at least two or three of Arkwright's fingers each episode. For anyone who's felt hard done by through the extra pence added to the price of goods in local 'convenience' stores, these weekly tussles were a particular highlight of the programme.

Of course, more than anything else, *Open All Hours* cemented Ronnie Barker's reputation as the greatest comedy actor the UK has ever produced. In the mid-1970s, Barker was simultaneously appearing in three classic shows – *Open All Hours*, *Porridge* and, of course, ***The Two Ronnies***. Whereas Fletcher is perhaps the better loved by the British public, we feel it would be remiss of us not to sing the p-p-praises of Britain's favourite shopkeeper, Arkwright.

By creating a sitcom around one member of the 'Nation of shopkeepers', Roy Clarke tapped into a social memory that's as deeply ingrained in British society today as it ever has been.

Sitcom
BBC One
Episode Duration: 30 mins
Broadcast: 25 Mar 1973, 20 Feb–26 Mar 1976, 1 Mar 1981–6 Oct 1985

Regular Cast
Ronnie Barker · *Arkwright*
David Jason · *Granville*
Sheila Brennan, Lynda Baron · *Nurse Gladys Emmanuel*
Kathy Staff · *Mrs Blewitt*
Stephanie Cole · *Mrs Featherstone*
Barbara Flynn · *The Milk Woman*
Maggie Ollerenshaw · *Wavy Mavis*

Producer Sydney Lotterby

Writer Roy Clarke

Theme Music A mournful trumpet solo from Max Harris

TRIVIA

The exterior sequences for *Open all Hours* were recorded in Balby, Doncaster, south Yorkshire. At the time of filming, Arkwright's corner shop was a hairdressing salon called 'Helen's Beautique', located at 15 Lister Avenue. BBC set dressers simply added signs and external props to transform the salon into a general store.

In 1981, US TV network ABC attempted a vague remake of the show with *Open all Night*, set in a 24-hour convenience store in Los Angeles. Starring George Dzundza, the programme lasted for just a few months before being cancelled.

Producer Phillippa Giles **Writer** Jeanette Winterson, from her own novel **Theme Music** Rachel Portman

Adopted by an evangelist couple as a young child, flame-haired Jess has known nothing but obedience and the Bible for as long as she can remember. Evenings by the wireless listening for prayers to Africa and quick quizzes on the Bible have left her with a world view out of step with those of other children. As a teenager, she meets and befriends Melanie only to experience a sexual awakening that, when discovered, sends a wave of shock and revulsion through her closed community. But Jess's mother knows what must be done and so Jess is brought to the Pastor to seek redemption.

Jeanette Winterson adapted her own critically acclaimed novel as a three-part serial for BBC Two. Its depiction of the 'cult' of religion and of a lesbian affair between teenage girls predictably attracted complaints, but it also brought plaudits for BBC Two in the form of three BAFTA awards, including Best Actress for Geraldine McEwan, as Jess's adoptive mother.

The teen Jess was a standout role for Charlotte Coleman, who'd previously starred in ***Worzel Gummidge*** and as another wayward teen, *Marmalade Atkins*. Coleman went on to movie fame in *Four Weddings and a Funeral* (1994), but tragically died of a severe asthma attack in 2001 at the age of just 33 years. Young Jess was played by Emily Aston, who appears to come from a family of talented and adorable moppets: her younger brother Sam is currently breaking hearts and scooping awards as Chesney Brown in ***Coronation Street***.

The Osbournes

Documentary/Comedy | JOKS/Big Head Productions for MTV (shown on MTV/Channel 4) | episode duration 25 mins | broadcast 5 Mar 2002–21 Mar 2005

Regular Cast

Ozzy Osbourne, Sharon Osbourne, Kelly Osbourne, Jack Osbourne · *Themselves*

Producers Various, including Sharon Osbourne, Lois Clark Curren, Jonathan Taylor, Jeff Stilson, Greg Johnston (executive), Jordan Doran (associate), Marcus Fox (co-ordinating), Melanie Graham (supervising), Rod Aissa, Shari Brooks, Francis Gasparini, Charles Kramer, Claudine Magre, Ann Meek, Dan Murphy, Brad Spotto **Theme Music** 'Crazy Train', written and performed by Ozzy Osbourne, Randy Rhoads and Bob Daisley (aka Ozzy Osbourne's Blizzard of Ozz). This tune was Ozzy's first solo single after leaving Black Sabbath, and peaked at No. 49 in September 1980.

Reality TV shows are ten-a-penny – with the advent of multi-channel television, they're the easiest and cheapest way to come up with original programming. However, this also means that the vast majority of reality shows are little more than an attempt to convert a nameless functionary from a regional airport or some other loathsome individual into a 'wacky' or 'crazy' real-life celebrity. Thankfully, with *The Osbournes*, MTV already knew that the subjects of their programme were going to be a little off the wall – in truth, they probably had no idea what they were letting themselves in for. Ever since John Michael Osbourne (from Aston in the West Midlands) had his first hit with band Black Sabbath, he's enjoyed massive success as one of the world's most famous heavy metal artists. When the suggestion came that TV cameras should be allowed into Ozzy's home, the opportunity was simply too good to pass up. Not only did *The Osbournes* revitalise his career, it also garnered new careers as presenters for son Jack and wife Sharon, as well as a rock career of her own for daughter Kelly.

Each episode of *The Osbournes* follows some of the everyday goings-on in the life of a super-wealthy heavy metal rock and roll band family with vast mansions in Beverly Hills and London. From the minutiae of aeroplane delays on their way to the latest gig through to the really important stuff like the unsanitary toilet habits of Sharon's massive collection of pets, viewers shared practically every intimate moment of this bizarre family's life. Some critics of the series railed against the show and the Osbournes themselves, claiming that their bad language and unconventional behaviour (such as throwing joints of meat and logs over their fence at noisy neighbours) were promoting poor values to impressionable young viewers. These critics missed a crucial point though – that throughout the whole programme, despite all of their trials and troubles (Ozzy's near-fatal quad-bike crash, Kelly's and Jack's drug and alcohol-related issues), the Osbournes were a hugely supportive and mutually respectful family. Yes, they may have spent hour upon hour shouting and screaming at each other, but underneath it all you always knew that this family was a family that really cared for each other.

If nothing else, *The Osbournes* revitalised Ozzy's chart career too – prior to the series, the last time he troubled the UK singles charts was with the No. 4 Was Not Was single 'Shake Your Head', in which both Ozzy and actress Kim Basinger weren't credited for their guest vocals. Following the series, Ozzy and Kelly Osbourne reached No. 1 in December 2003 with 'Changes', a cover of an old Black Sabbath track. With Sharon now a regular judge on music talent show ***The X Factor***, it seems as though taking part in a reality TV series was a very good move for this quirky family.

Our Friends in the North

Drama | BBC Two | episode duration 60 mins | broadcast 15 Jan–11 Mar 1996

Recurring Cast

Christopher Eccleston · *Nicky Hutchinson*
Daniel Craig · *George 'Geordie' Peacock*

Gina McKee · *Mary Soulsby/Cox/Hutchinson*
Mark Strong · *Terry 'Tosker' Cox*
David Bradley · *Eddie Wells*
Peter Vaughan · *Felix Hutchinson*
Freda Dowie · *Florrie Hutchinson*
Alun Armstrong · *Austin Donohue*
Margery Bone · *Barbara Cox*
Matthew Baron, Adam Pearson, Nick Figgis, Daniel Casey · *Anthony Cox*
Tracey Wilkinson · *Elaine Craig/Cox*
Malcolm McDowell · *Benny Barratt*
Tony Haygarth · *Deputy Chief Constable Roy Johnson*
Trevor Cooper · *DCS Dennis Cockburn*
Frank Couchman · *Patrick Soulsby*
Val McLane · *Rita Cox*
Terence Rigby · *Berger*
Julian Fellowes · *Claud Seabrook MP*
William Hoyland · *Commander Arthur Fieldson*
Peter Jeffrey · *Commissioner Sir Colin Blamire*
Larry Lamb · *Alan Roe*
Louise Salter · *Julia Allen*
Nicholas Selby · *Commissioner Sir Edward Jones*
Daniel Webb · *DS/DI Ron Conrad*
Granville Saxton · *Commissioner Michael Jellicoe*
David Schofield · *DS/DI/DCS John Salway*
Chris Walker · *DCI Paul Boyd*
Saskia Wickham · *Claudia Seabrook MP*
Craig Conway, Alan Gilchrist · *Christopher Collins*

Creator/Writer Peter Flannery **Producers** Michael Wearing (executive), Melanie Howard (associate), Charles Pattinson **Theme Music** Colin Towns

It is 1964 and idealist student Nicky Hutchinson returns home to Newcastle after travelling America's Deep South to witness the race riots. His extreme left-wing views catch the eye of local entrepreneur and politician Austin Donohue who offers him a job as his personal assistant. Against the advice of his father (a disillusioned Jarrow Crusader) and his father's friend MP Eddie Wells, Nicky accepts. But Nicky's obsession with the class struggle makes him blind to the feelings of those around him, including his girlfriend Mary, who ends up dating and eventually marrying would-be pub singer 'Tosker' Cox. Meanwhile, Nicky's friend Geordie Peacock goes on the run after a fight with his violent and abusive father. His travels take him to London where he falls under the wing of Soho gangster and pornography baron Benny Barratt. As the years go by, the personal fortunes of Nicky, Mary, Tosker and Geordie change, sometimes for the worse, sometimes for better as they witness changes to the country's political and social make-up and live through turbulent, often harrowing times.

Peter Flannery took 20 years to bring his stage play to the screen, by which time he – and his characters – had aged (his play had ended with the rise to power of Margaret Thatcher's Conservative government in 1979). Flannery's story came to television thanks to BBC producer Michael Wearing, who'd brought viewers ***Boys from the Blackstuff*** in the early 1980s and who championed the series for over 13 years. It finally hit the screen in 1996, a searing social commentary spanning 30 years where each episode was set in the year of an election from 1964 until 1987, with a final instalment in 1995 as an end to the Conservatives' 18-year rule was in sight.

The drama examined the scandals surrounding poor housing, police corruption and the rise of dirty politics, with the music of the times liberally interspersed through each episode. The irony is that while political activist Nicky, his jaded father and the smart Mary discuss some of the bigger issues of the times, it's the more politically naïve characters Tosker and Geordie who unconsciously illustrate the points. Tosker carries the working-class dream of being a star with him, and blames Mary for holding him back, which in some ways is borne out in the encouragement and support he receives from his second wife, Elaine. Thanks to her, Tosker becomes a successful businessman (though after Black Wednesday wipes out their savings, it's Tosker's suggestion that they reinvest in pubs and karaoke machines that gets them back on their feet). Geordie meanwhile sinks lower and lower until he becomes a down-and-out, a victim of the lack of care in the community. In the final frame, as Nicky and Mary attempt some kind of reconciliation, it's Geordie that we follow as he hits the road once more, with Oasis's 'Don't Look Back in Anger' playing over the final credits.

With a cast of 160 speaking parks and over 3000 extras, many of whom played protesters and police officers during scenes recreating the violent miners strike of 1984, *Our Friends in the North* was the last great epic of British television. It was also a springboard to a successful career for all of its young leads – Christopher Eccleston in dramas like ***Hillsborough, The Second Coming*** and ***Doctor Who***; Daniel Craig into movies like *Lara Croft: Tomb Raider* (2001), *The Mother* (2003) and *Layer Cake* (2004); Gina McKee has starred in movies like *Notting Hill* (1999) and TV epics like ***The Lost Prince*** and the remake of ***The Forsyte Saga***; and Mark Strong has starred in TV shows as diverse as ***Prime Suspect*** and ***The Long Firm***.

Out

Crime Drama | Euston Films/Thames for ITV | episode duration 50 mins | broadcast 24 Jul–28 Aug 1975

Principal Cast
Tom Bell · *Frank Ross*
Lynn Farleigh · *Anne Ross*
Pamela Fairbrother · *Eve Ross*
Norman Rodway · *DI Bryce*
Robert Walker · *Rimmer*
Katherine Schofield · *Cimmie*
John Junkin · *Ralph Veneker*
Brian Croucher · *Chris Cottle*
Andrew Paul · *Paul Ross*
Brian Cox · *McGrath*

Katherine Schofield · *Crimmie Vincent*
Frank Mills · *Vic Lee*
Oscar James · *Bernie Machen*
Peter Blake · *Pretty Billy Binns*
Bryan Marshall · *Hallam*
Colin McCormack · *Keith*
Maurice O'Connell · *Eddy Archer*
Derrick O'Connor · *John Pavey*
Dawn Perllman · *Linda*
Tania Rogers · *Alison*

Creator/Writer Trevor Preston **Producers** Johnny Goodman (executive), Barry Hanson **Theme Music** George Fenton

Having scripted episodes of ***Callan, The Sweeney*** and ***Hazell*** as well as created his own telefantasy series ***Ace of Wands***, Trevor Preston returned to south London for this six-part thriller. Tom Bell starred as Frank Ross, recently released from prison after eight years. His wife has suffered a severe nervous breakdown and is on constant suicide watch in a mental hospital; his son Paul, taken in by friends when Frank was arrested, is turning into a yob, drinking heavily and spending time with his girlfriend; and his best friend Chris is struggling to keep his car business afloat. But all Frank wants to do is find out who it was that grassed him up after his gang did their last big job.

Each episode was given ironic titles like 'It Must Be The Suit' (referring to the fact that Frank Ross looks like he's only just been released from prison) and the final episode, 'I Wouldn't Take Your Hand If I Was Drowning'. Naturalistic writing from Preston and a solid ensemble cast (including a young Andrew Paul, who later starred as PC Quinnan in ***The Bill***) helped make another hit for Euston Films. Sadly, although the series pointed towards a cliffhanger, with the identity of the traitor revealed and Frank Ross vowing to catch him, a second series never materialised. Trevor Preston and director Jim Goddard instead collaborated again on another series (shown in 1980) about a south London family linked to the criminal underworld–***Fox***.

Out of the Unknown

Anthology | BBC Two | episode duration 50/90 mins | broadcast 4 Oct 1965–30 Jun 1971

Principal Cast

Hannah Gordon, Geoffrey Palmer, Sylvia Coleridge, Judy Parfitt, Patsy Rowlands, Milo O'Shea, Eric Thompson, Burt Kwouk, Warren Mitchell, Fulton Mackay, Peter Bowles, John Abineri, Sam Kydd, David Langton, Michele Dotrice, Caroline Blakiston, Nigel Stock, Deborah Watling, Anton Rodgers, Ed Begley, Marius Goring, Wendy Craig, Donald Morley, Ian Ogilvy, George Cole, Bryan Mosley, Ed Bishop, Keith Barron, Arnold Ridley, Molly Weir, Chloe Ashcroft, Lynda Marchal, Bernard Hepton, Kevin Stoney, Glynn Edwards, Francis Matthews, Peter Barkworth, Peter Jeffrey, Lesley-Ann Down, Arthur Pentelow, Pamela Salem, Anthony Ainley, Patrick Troughton, Brian Wilde, Freddie Jones, Tessa Wyatt · *Various Characters*

Creator Sydney Newman **Producers** Irene Shubik, Alan Bromly **Writers** Stanley Miller, Philip Broadley, David Campton, Jeremy Paul, Paul Erickson, Mike Watts, Meade Roberts, Terry Nation, Bruce Stewart, Leon Griffiths, Stanley Miller, Troy Kennedy Martin, Kenneth Cavander, Clive Donner, Hugh Whitemore, J. B. Priestley, Hugh Leonard, Robert Gould, Julian Bond, William Trevor, Robert Muller, Jack Pulman, Jeremy Paul, Allan Prior, Donald Bull, Owen Holder, Brian Hayles, Michael Ashe, Clive Exton, David Climie, John Wiles, Michael J. Bird, John Tully, Edward Boyd, Moris Rahi, Martin Worth, Nigel Kneale, David T. Chantler, from novels by: Alan Nourse, Angus Hall, C. M. Kornbluth, Clifford D. Simak, Colin Kapp, E. M. Forster, Frederik Pohl, Henry Kuttner, Isaac Asimov, J. G. Ballard, John Brunner, John Rankine, John Wyndham, Kate Wilhelm, Larry Eisenberg, Mordecai Roshwald, Peter Phillips, Ray Bradbury, Robert Sheckley, Rog Phillips, William Tenn **Theme Music** Norman Kay's theme ran for seasons one to three, while an except from a stock track–'Lunar Lanscape' by R. Roger–was used for season four.

For four years, the Canadian Sydney Newman had cast a long shadow over British television, at times even threatening to dim the lights of Broadcasting House itself. As the drama supervisor at ABC, Newman was behind the reinvigoration of *Armchair Theatre*, the creation of ***The Avengers*** and the sci-fi hits ***Pathfinders*** and ***Out of this World***, among many others. Auntie responded by poaching him from commercial TV (reportedly luring him with a paycut of £3000), and Newman would, over the following years, strive to create rivals for all four of these series. *Armchair Theatre* begat *The Wednesday Play, The Avengers* would clash swordsticks with ***Adam Adamant Lives!***, the concept of *Pathfinders* wasn't light years away from ***Doctor Who***, but only but it was the advent of BBC Two–and the concomitant increase in BBC broadcasting hours–that would see a reprise of the sci-fi anthology format of *Out of this World*.

When Newman defected to the BBC, he had taken with him one Irene Shubik–the other driving force behind *Out of this World*–and installed her as producer of the new series, which, with scant regard for the decades of confusion which would follow, would be titled *Out of the Unknown* (Hammer films would later compound this problem even further with their *Journey to the Unknown*).

Like its forerunner, *Out of the Unknown* relied on a mixture of adaptations of sci-fi stories by established authors such as Asimov, Bradbury and Pohl, a selection of lesser-known names (Larry Eisenberg submitted his two stories on spec after seeing an advert placed by Shubik in an American science fiction magazine) and the final slots were filled with a smattering of original screenplays from TV writers (although by the fourth series, the balance shifted and all of the plays would be new).

After a poor start (the opening instalment was deemed 'excruciatingly slow' by *The Times*), the show rapidly found its feet and the opening episode of the second season is, simply put, one of the greatest triumphs of genre television. *The Machine Stops* was a story by E. M. Forster, telling of a future dystopia where human relationships have broken down due to an over-reliance on machines. Adapted by Kenneth Cavander and Clive Donner, the script has an epic, filmic feel, with superb dialogue that actually embraces the period staginess of the original and allows it to glisten with a rare poetry. Philip Saville's direction rises to the occasion, both visually and technically, and the production is nothing if not *lavish* – a fully working monorail installed in a TV studio would be a rare sight in any age. The moving production ends with the final moments of mankind, memorably conveyed in starkly personal terms. Yvonne Mitchell sits among the heaps of dying flesh in an unending corridor, cradling her dying son – and discovering, far too late, the true nature of human love.

Also worthy of recognition is the *The Prophet* – an adaptation of Isaac Asimov's *Reason*, which told of the universe's first robotic rebellion. Unable to accept the absurd possibility that a being as inferior as a man could have created them, the robots, led by a mechanical Tenniel Evans, form a new religion based upon the worship of their one true lord, a piece of inanimate machinery that provides their power. It was their robotic hymn of praise that is now better known to electronic music enthusiasts as 'Ziwzih Ziwzih OO-OO-OO', a peerless classic by the BBC Radiophonic Workshop's in-house genius Delia Derbyshire.

After a long break, the series returned – now in colour – for a third series in 1969 under the stewardship of Alan Bromly, who took the show away from traditional sci-fi paraphernalia and towards more psychological or supernatural thrillers. The show faded away from the public consciousness after a fourth and final series in 1971; the science fiction anthology genre was rarely examined by British television again.

Out of this World

Anthology | ABC for ITV | episode duration 50 mins | broadcast 30 Jun–22 Sep 1962

Cast

Boris Karloff · *Host*

Nigel Stock, Maxine Audley, Clifford Evans, Peter Wyngarde, Jane Asher, John Carson, Patrick Allen, Glyn Owen, William Gaunt, Julian Glover, Aubrey Morris, Jacqueline Hill, Reginald Marsh, Milo O'Shea, David Hemmings, Maurice Denham, Ronald Radd, Gerald Harper, Bernard Horsfall, Rosemary Miller, Gary Raymond, Michael Golden, Dinsdale Landen, Paul Eddington, Philip Madoc, Charles Gray, Geraldine McEwan, Jill Curzon · *Various Characters*

Creator Irene Shubik **Producer** Leonard White **Writers** Leon Griffiths, Leo Lehman, Clive Exton, Terry Nation, Julian Bond, Bruce Stewart, Richard Waring, Denis Butler **Theme Music** Eric Siday

This little-remembered ITV series was a milestone of sorts, being the first science fiction anthology show on British television. In many ways it was a logical extension of *Armchair Theatre*, which, since its inception, had embraced the kitchen sink theatrical revolution, turning its back on the traditional 'well-made play' to reflect the present day lives of the working man and woman. It is no surprise therefore that this idea-hungry medium should also give us glimpses of the future.

One week before the series began, a prestigious *Armchair Theatre* slot was given over to a production of John Wyndham's *Dumb Martian*, by way of introduction to the show's sci-fi sibling – easing the passage from kitchen sink to 'the oxygenated roses of Hyper Base Seven', from angry young man to little lost robot, in one easy step.

Running in a Saturday night slot throughout the summer of 1962, the show was created by Irene Shubik, the chief story editor of ABC Television, while production duties were handled by Leonard White, who came fresh from producing the earliest episodes of ***The Avengers***. A 75-year-old Boris Karloff was installed as series host, topping and tailing each edition with a suave, if somewhat bemused, assurance. Episodes would include adaptations of stories by sci-fi luminaries such as Isaac Asimov, Philip K. Dick and Clifford Simak in addition to other lesser-known writers.

The series featured early contributions from several talents who would later rise to prominence in the field – most notable being Shubik herself, who would go on to produce ***Out of the Unknown*** and *The Mind Beyond* (as well as ***Edna, the Inebriate Woman*** and ***Rumpole of the Bailey***); while on the scripting side was Terry Nation, who just one year later would create a race of robotic pepperpots for a new BBC show called ***Doctor Who***. Nation also provided a brand new story of his own for the series, *Botany Bay*, in which a student of psychiatry discovers that the patients of an institution are possessed by aliens.

Sadly, only one programme from the series survives in the archives, Asimov's wonderful 'Little Lost Robot', which provides a tantalising glimpse of what, for its time, were the high production values and slick direction of a popular mainstream show. It's interesting to compare the rather clunky but immensely tense atmosphere of this, with its very functional robots, to the Will Smith-starring blockbuster *I, Robot* (2004), reliant on clever computer-generated imaging to create emotional responses and menace. No doubt, most would understandably prefer the movie, but for ambition alone, this one programme makes us wish more episodes of *Out of this World* still existed.

The Outer Limits

Anthology | Villa Di Stefano/Daystar/United Artists for ABC (shown on ITV/BBC Two) | episode duration 50 mins | broadcast 16 Sep 1963–16 Jan 1965, 26 Mar 1995–18 Jan 2002

Regular Cast

Vic Perrin, Kevin Conway · *Introduction Control Voice*

Creator Leslie Stevens **Producers** Leslie Stevens (executive), Leon Chooluck, John Erman, Seeleg Lester, Louis Morheim (associate), Joseph Stefano, Ben Brady **Writers** Various, including Leslie Stevens, Joseph Stefano, Lou Morheim, Harlan Ellison,

Seeleg Lester, Charles Beaumont, Milton Krims, Jerry Sohl, Jonathan Glassner, Brad Wright, Alan Brennert, Grant Rosenberg, Steven Barnes, Chris Dickie, James Crocker, Sam Egan, Naren Shankar, Scott Peters, Mark Stern, A. L. Katz **Theme Music** Not as distinctive as the music for ***The Twilight Zone***, the music accompanying the first season was written by Dominic Frontiere and by Harry Lubin for the second.

The only real challenger to *The Twilight Zone*'s hold on the spooky sci-fi anthology genre in the 1960s, *The Outer Limits* is often cited as the anthology series of preference for the serious science fiction buff. Taking advantage of the still-primitive TV sets that were prone to technical problems, each episode began with sine-wave interference before the announcer would explain: 'We control the vertical. We control the horizontal.' From that point, *The Outer Limits* confidently took audiences to worlds that *The Twilight Zone* would never consider visiting, with the quirky, psychological themes of Rod Serling usurped by grotesque monsters-of-the-week and tales with moralistic endings.

The series evolved from Leslie Stevens' script 'Please Stand By', which became the first episode, 'The Galaxy Being'. Stevens then handed over control to Joseph Stephano, a writer who'd given audiences the shock of their lives with *Psycho*, made as a feature film by Alfred Hitchcock in 1960.

Episodes that stand out include 'The Zanti Misfits', featuring a race of human-faced insect criminals from another world, and 'Demon with a Glass Hand', in which a man from the future evades aliens by travelling back to present-day Earth. Once there, he discovers he's in fact an android sent back in time with the last survivors of humanity encoded inside a wire in his chest.

Prior to the second series, Joseph Stefano left the production, unhappy with interference from network executives and erratic scheduling. His replacement, Ben Brady, pushed the show towards more rational explanations than the pure science fiction stories of the first series. As a consequence, the audiences dwindled and *The Outer Limits* was cancelled mid-season.

The programme had managed to notch up just 49 episodes, but thanks to syndication it soon found a wider audience. In the UK, a late-night repeat run on BBC Two combined episodes from both series to create a patchy but captivating show. With the rise in nostalgia at the end of the 20th century, *The Outer Limits* was selected for revival in 1995. Unlike its predecessor, the new production ran for seven complete series and 154 episodes, with Kevin Conway now providing the 'Control Voice'.

Paddington

Animation | FilmFair for BBC One | episode duration 5 mins, plus 3 × 25-min specials | broadcast 5 Jan 1976–14 Nov 1980, 15 Mar 1983, 3 Jan 1986, 26 Dec 1987

Cast

Michael Hordern · *Narrator, Character Voices*

Creator/Writer Michael Bond **Producers** Graham Clutterbuck (executive), Barrie Edwards **Theme Music** 'Size Ten Shuffle' by the Boyfriends

It's highly unlikely that any unsuspecting person could be asked to make a sentence including the words 'marmalade' and 'Peru' without them using the name 'Paddington' at some point. Paddington was the small brown bear who arrived by train from Darkest Peru with a little 'Please look after this bear' tag hanging from around his neck. Adopted by the Brown family, he soon settled in at their home, 32 Windsor Gardens, made himself at home and started to get to know the neighbours, including the irascible Mr Curry, and nice Mr Gruber who runs the nearby antique shop. Naturally inquisitive, his curiosity would often lead him into all sorts of mischief, though his usual defence against anyone telling him off was to issue one of his hard stares. A well-brought-up and polite bear, Paddington simply couldn't do with anyone making a scene and was never happier than when enjoying his favourite treat, marmalade sandwiches.

Paddington is of course famous thanks to both Ivor Wood's hugely popular stop-motion animation series from the mid-1970s onwards, and the slightly generic cell-animated, Canadian-made show that young 'uns saw towards the end of the 1990s. But his stardom pre-dates even Ivor Wood's version, of course, his adventures having first appeared in print in 1958.

The adorable bear started out as a toy bought by Michael Bond as a last-minute Christmas present for his wife Brenda. Named Paddington after the London station, the bear inspired Bond to write a series of short stories without ever thinking they'd be seen by anyone else. But gradually the stories began to take shape and Bond showed them to his agent. The result was a book, *A Bear Called Paddington*, published on 13 October 1958 by William Collins & Sons (the company that evolved into the publishers of the book you're currently reading). In the book, Paddington appeared in black and white sketches by Peggy Fortnum. (See, all the best things started out in black and white!) Paddington slowly began to draw a very loyal following and eventually inspired Michael Bond to conjure up a further 17 books. In 1964, the bear from Peru was sufficiently famous to appear in a specially written story for that year's ***Blue Peter*** annual, and by the mid-1960s, the tales were proving lucrative enough for Bond to quit his day job as a BBC cameraman and dedicate his time to writing, including reworking his original Paddington stories for a series of books aimed at younger children. In 1975, Paddington was brought to life by FilmFair and Ivor Wood, who had worked on ***The Magic Roundabout*** in the 1960s and would also help to animate ***The Wombles*** and Michael Bond's other creations, ***The Herbs*** and Parsley the Lion.

Slotted in the old *Magic Roundabout* slot right before the evening *News*, *Paddington* was an instant success. Paddington himself became something of a trendsetter, with his blue dufflecoat and wide-brimmed, black hat. Michael Hordern's gravel-voiced narration ran through all 56 episodes, plus three half-hour specials, 'Paddington's Birthday Bonanza', 'Paddington Goes to School' and the sublime 'Paddington Goes to the Movies', in which Paddington acts out Gene Kelly's dance routine from *Singing in the Rain* (1952). The series was visually quite innovative, with Paddington realised in all his three-dimensional fuzziness but all the other characters created in the form of free-standing two-dimensional cut-outs, highlighting the 'him' and 'us' aspect of the show.

Paddington returned to our screens in 1989, courtesy of Hanna Barbera, and again in 1997 in a brand new, fully animated cartoon series from Canadian company Cinar. Unlike the earlier FilmFair series, all the characters were given their own voices rather than performed by one narrator (including Jon Glover as Mr Brown). Although many of the episodes were based on original stories from the books, new storylines were also introduced which took Paddington and his friend Mr Gruber to different countries and places throughout the world.

The Pallisers

Drama | BBC One | episode duration 50 mins | broadcast 19 Jan–2 Nov 1974

Cast

Susan Hampshire · *Lady Glencora MacCluskie/Palliser*
Philip Latham · *Plantagenet Palliser*
Barbara Murray · *Madame Max Goesler*
Donal McCann · *Phineas Finn*
Roland Culver · *The Duke of Omnium*
Moray Watson · *Barrington Erle*
Roger Livesey · *The Duke of St Bungay*
Donald Pickering · *Dolly Longstaffe*
Bryan Pringle · *Mr Monk*
Doris Rogers · *Lady Hartletop*
Fabia Drake · *Countess of Midlothian*
Sonia Dresdel · *Marchioness of Auld Reekie*
Barry Justice · *Burgo Fitzgerald*
Gary Watson · *George Vavasor*
Caroline Mortimer · *Alice Vavasor*
Karin MacCarthy · *Kate Vavasor*
John Glyn-Jones · *John Vavasor*
Bernard Brown · *John Grey*
Anna Massey · *Lady Laura Standish*
Lockwood West · *Lord Brentford*

Mel Martin · *Violet Effingham*
Ellen Pollock · *Lady Baldock*
Derek Godfrey · *Robert Kennedy*
John Hallam · *Lord Chiltern*
Maire Ni Ghrainne · *Mary Flood*
Derek Jacobi · *Lord Fawn*
Brenda Cowling · *Mrs Bunce*
Hayden Jones · *Mr Bunce*
Robin Bailey · *Mr Gresham*
Edward Burnham · *Mr Turnbull*
Neil Stacy · *Laurence Fitzgibbon*
Norman Shelley · *Mr Mildmay*
Rosalind Knight · *Aspasia Fitzgibbon*
Clifford Rose · *Quintus Slide*
Sarah Badel · *Lizzie Eustace*
Anthony Ainley · *Reverend Emilius*
Martin Jarvis · *Frank Greystock*
Peter Sallis · *Mr Bonteen*
June Whitfield · *Mrs Bonteen*
Penelope Keith · *Mrs Hittaway*
Jo Kendall · *Adelaide Palliser*
Jeremy Clyde · *Gerard Maule*
Sheila Fay · *Mrs Meager*
John Phillips · *Sir Gregory Grogram*
Michael Spice · *Inspector Staple*
Peter Vaughan · *Mr Chaffanbrass*
Carleton Hobbs · *Lord Chief Justice*
Brian Coburn · *Peter Praska*
Stuart Wilson · *Ferdinand Lopez*
David Ryall · *Sextus Parker*
Sheila Ruskin · *Emily Wharton*
Gareth Forwood · *Everett Wharton*
Brewster Mason · *Abel Wharton*
Basil Dignam · *Sir Orlando Drought*
Anthony Andrews · *Lord Silverbridge Palliser*
Anna Carteret · *Lady Mabel Grex*
Jeremy Irons · *Frank Tregear*
Kate Nicholls · *Lady Mary Palliser*
Michael Cochrane · *Gerald Palliser*
Angus MacKay · *Mills Happerton*
John Ringham · *Major Tifto*
Jerry Stovin · *Mr Boncassen*
Eileen Erskine · *Mrs Boncassen*
Lynne Frederick · *Isabel Boncassen*
Josie Kidd · *Miss Cassewary*

Producer Martin Lisemore **Writer** Simon Raven from the novels by Anthony Trollope **Theme Music** Herbert Chappell

For generations, the Pallisers have been at the very heart of the Liberal Party. Head of the family, the Duke of Omnium, finds himself without an heir, though most believe that his middle-aged nephew, Plantagenet Palliser, will inherit the title. The Duke decrees that the rather staid Plantagenet should be wed, and selects the flighty Lady Glencora as his bride-to-be, despite her very visible displays of love for the wastrel Burgo Fitzgerald. But the Duke has spoken, so wed they shall be . . .

A 26-part adaptation of Anthony Trollope's much-loved six-volume saga, *The Pallisers* takes us through Plantagenet's rather cold courtship of Glencora, showing how he wins her compliance, her trust and eventually her love, though the process turns her into a ruthlessly ambitious society hostess. The best episodes concern the tribulations of poor Phineas Finn, a principled, determined Irish politician whose luck deserts him at almost every step, usually thanks to the hounding of Quintus Slide, the sickeningly malicious editor of *The People's Voice* (an astounding character study by Clifford Rose that manages to avoid descending into caricature). Thankfully, his loyalty to and support from Plantagenet is unflinching, which often leads to his salvation. A disappointingly undiverting story involving an heiress's appropriation of the Eustace Diamonds leaves us hungry for the later installments, which take us through Plantagenet's time as Prime Minister of a coalition government, Finn's trial for murder and Plantagenet's eldest son Silverbridge's first steps in the political arena – as a Tory!

Complex political manoeuvring and social etiquette drive the plot, but it's the wide range of characters that is both the production's greatest asset and its biggest stumbling block as it can take a while to get used to so many characters and their relationships to each other. So it can't have helped viewers when the series was disrupted by a BBC strike just before the end. A repeat run of five episodes helped bridge the gap and allow the production team to complete work on the final episodes before the series eventually came to a belated close.

Often unjustly ignored in favour of ***The Forsyte Saga***, the series is a fine example of the BBC at the height of its creative powers, producing the kind of period costume drama that it has always excelled at.

Panorama

Factual/Current Affairs | BBC TV/ BBC One | episode duration 30–60 mins | broadcast 11 Nov 1953–present

Regular Cast

Various, including Patrick Murphy, Max Robertson, Richard Dimbleby, James Mossman, Robin Day, Alistair Burnet, David Dimbleby, Charles Wheeler, Fred Emery, Robert Kee, Christopher Chataway, John Freeman, Malcolm Muggeridge, Pat Murphy · *Presenters*

Michael Barratt, Tom Mangold, Jane Corbin, Sarah Barclay, Martin Bashir, John Ware, Vivian White · *Reporters*

Creator Grace Wyndham Goldie **Producers** Various, including Dennis Bardens, Michael Barsley, Rex Moorfoot, Michael Peacock, Paul Fox, Jeremy Isaacs, Brian Wenham, Frank Smith, Roger Bolton, Mark Thompson, Glenwyn Benson (editors), David Webster, Charles Wheeler, Alasdair Milne, David Harrison, Nick Hudson, Lorraine Heggessey, Andrew Miller-Jones, Andrew Martin **Theme Music** There have been three different theme tunes to *Panorama* over the years. First of all, 'Pelléas et Mélisande' by Sibelius (which only lasted a few months), then through until 1969 was a piece called 'Openings and Endings' by Robert Farnon. The tune that we all know today, which has been the title music for *Panorama* for more than 35 years now, is by Francis Lai and is called 'Aujourd'hui C'est Toi'.

The world's longest-running current affairs programme, *Panorama* has been investigating corrupt politicians, unearthing dodgy business practices and highlighting the latest bit of information in the public's best interests for well over 50 years. It began life as a fortnightly programme billed as a 'reflection of the contemporary scene' before developing less than two years later into the hard-hitting flagship of BBC television's news and documentary department. Subjects covered in *Panorama* investigations have ranged from the activities of trade unions and the police force through to uncovering the effects of dangerous prescription medications and, of course, the economic influences that impact on the everyday lives of the British public. Other less conventional – but no less memorable – *Panorama* reports have included Martin Bashir's infamous interview with Diana, Princess of Wales (in which she confirmed that there were 'three people' in her marriage to Prince Charles – a reference to the future Duchess of Cornwall) and the much-loved 1957 April Fool's joke about the bumper spaghetti harvest in Switzerland.

Parkinson

Chat Show | BBC One/Granada for ITV | episode duration 50 mins | broadcast 19 Jun 1971–3 Apr 1982, 9 Jan 1998–present

Cast List
Michael Parkinson · *Host*

Theme Music Laurie Holloway

Parkinson is widely regarded as the king of British chat-show hosts – only Terry Wogan comes close to challenging him, and then largely because of his ubiquity in the 1980s. Parkinson's television career began with Granada on shows like *World in Action* before he switched to the BBC. His chat show began in 1971 with an interview with comic actor Terry-Thomas. The show quickly gained a reputation for the quality of his guests, who included (on more than one occasion) boxer Muhammad Ali, Kenneth Williams, Peter Cook and Billy Connolly. ***Rod Hull and Emu*** famously mauled Parky, who was less than amused.
The series ran to 361 editions over 11 years, with nearly 1000 guests.

Parkinson was poached in 1983 to be one of the first presenters of TV AM, alongside his wife, Mary. Aside from his lead role in the spoof drama ***Ghostwatch*** and a guest appearance on ***The Mrs Merton Show***, he rarely appeared on the BBC until a run of repeats of some of his best interviews led to a return to the BBC's Saturday night schedule (his first guests for this new series were Michael Palin and Sir Elton John). The series maintained its high calibre of guest; one special edition was dedicated to George Michael, who performed some of his new material and talked candidly about his arrest in LA for indecent exposure. Not all the interviews went well, however, for Parky's blunt style was not appreciated by Hollywood actress Meg Ryan, who became reticent and uncooperative as the interview progressed.

In April 2004, Michael Parkinson left the BBC after a dispute over his timeslot and took his chat-show format to ITV. The need to break for adverts took time to get used to, but it also meant that he could get world-class guests like Tom Cruise and Samuel L. Jackson. At the time of writing, Parkinson continues to be the reigning champion of the chat show.

Partners in Crime

See AGATHA CHRISTIE'S PARTNERS IN CRIME

The Partridge Family

Sitcom | Screen Gems for ABC (shown on BBC One and ITV) | episode duration 25 mins | broadcast 25 Sep 1970–31 Aug 1974 (USA)

Principal Cast
Shirley Jones · *Shirley Partridge*
David Cassidy · *Keith Partridge*
Susan Dey · *Laurie Partridge*
Danny Bonaduce · *Danny Partridge*
Jeremy Gelbwaks, Brian Foster · *Christopher Partridge*
Suzanne Crough · *Tracy Partridge*
Dave Madden · *Reuben Kinkaid*

Creator Bernard Slade **Producers** Various, including Bob Claver (executive), Paul Junger Witt **Writer** Various, including Bernard Slade, Susan Harris, William Bickley, Ron Friedman, Gordon Mitchell, Dick Bensfield **Theme Music** Wes Farrell and Danny Janssen wrote the theme tune. During the first season, one set of lyrics ('When We're Singing') and a slightly different rearrangement of the tune was used, however, from the second season onwards the unforgettable 'Come On, Get Happy' lyrics and arrangement were used.

Widow Shirley Partridge has been left to raise her children Keith, Laurie, Danny, Christopher and Tracy on her own in the Californian town of San Pueblo. Shirley is rather surprised when eldest son Keith forms the family into a rudimentary pop group (him on vocals, Laurie on keyboards, Danny on guitar, Christopher on drums and young Tracy shaking a tambourine) – she's even more surprised when their first record ('I Think I Love You') becomes an overnight success. Soon, the singing Partridge Family is making a name for itself on the road, travelling in a brightly painted bus to gigs arranged by manager Reuben

Kinkaid. Shirley finds herself sharing the lead vocal limelight with Keith, a strange state of affairs that she, as a middle-aged woman, certainly hadn't expected.

Just like ***The Monkees*** in the 1960s, *The Partridge Family* was specifically set up as a comedy series with the potential for a simultaneous music career. The first single released in the fiction of the show also made it big in the real-life American charts, with 'I Think I Love You' hitting the No. 1 spot. Undoubtedly the appeal of both the programme and the music was down to the clean-cut, teen-friendly appeal of lead singer David Cassidy, one of the 1970s' true heart-throbs. *The Partridge Family* were almost as successful here in the UK, with 'Breaking Up Is Hard to Do' reaching No. 3 in July 1972 and follow-ups 'Looking Thru' the Eyes of Love' and 'Walking in the Rain' both reaching the Top Ten in 1973. Soon Cassidy had no need to release singles as part of *The Partridge Family*, forging a career for himself in the music charts as a solo artist and grabbing two UK No. 1s ('How Can I Be Sure?', September 1972 and 'Daydreamer/The Puppy Song' in October 1973).

After the first dozen or so programmes were screened on the BBC, the rest of *The Partridge Family*'s 96 episodes were shown on ITV, mostly at lunchtimes on Saturdays - surely not an attempt to encourage viewers to dash down to their nearest record shop afterwards and spend their pocket money on a Partridge Family record? Although David Cassidy's television career didn't last very long, his on-screen sister Susan Dey starred in 1980s'drama ***LA Law***, and series producer Paul Junger Witt went on to have a hand in the development of some of the most iconic American comedy series of all time, including ***Soap, Benson*** and ***The Golden Girls***.

Pathfinders

Children's Science Fiction | ABC for ITV | episode duration 25 mins | broadcast 11 Sep 1960–23 Apr 1961

Regular Cast

Peter Williams · *Professor Wedgwood*
Harold Goldblatt · *Dr O'Connell*
Gerald Flood · *Conway Henderson*
Gillian Ferguson · *Valerie Wedgwood*
Irene Sutcliffe · *Jean Cary*
Stewart Guidotti · *Geoffrey Wedgwood*
Richard Dean · *Jimmy Wedgwood*
Pamela Barney · *Professor Meadows*
Hugh Evans · *Ian Murray*
Astor Sklair · *John Field*
Michael Guest · *Michael Kennedy*
George Coulouris · *Harcourt Brown*
Gerald Flood · *Conway Henderson*
Hester Cameron · *Margaret Henderson*
Graydon Gould · *Captain Wilson*
Bob Bryan · *The Venusian*
Brigid Skemp · *Venusian child*

Producer Sydney Newman **Writers** Malcolm Hulke, Eric Paice

In the early 1960s, ABC's head of drama had a visionary moment of inspiration - he saw a gap in the schedules and knew at once the show that would fill it. He pictured a weekly science fiction serial aimed at bridging the gap between family viewing and grown-up telly, that would take young and old alike on a mysterious yet enthralling trip through space. In its initial incarnation, the show was called *Target Luna* (also 1960) and told of little Jimmy Wedgwood who, having got lost in his father's personal rocket launch station, ends up, a mere two cliffhangers later, in orbit around the moon with only a pet hamster for company. The remaining episodes were then spent ensuring that Jimmy - and 'Hamlet' - returned safely to Earth. The series, which capitalised on the recent Sputnik mission and the birth of the space race, along with a child's desire to see him- or herself centre-stage, was a big success and a sequel was rapidly commissioned.

Pathfinders in Space saw Jimmy and his entire family regenerate into a new cast. The all-new family, along with Gerald Flood's dashing newspaper reporter, venture to the moon and, in a couple of rather nice twists, discover not only relics of an ancient civilisation, but also 'a calcified figure and a spaceship in the caverns', that is proof of 'a previous landing sometime in the distant past.' What is pleasantly surprising is that the story is propelled by an ancient mystery that borders on profound philosophical issues rather than an imminent threat from what Sydney Newman is reported to have dismissed as 'bug-eyed monsters'.

Pathfinders to Mars swiftly followed and saw the heroic Gerald Flood promoted to a more central role. Also added to the mix was George Coulouris's scheming Harcourt Brown, who, we are swiftly made aware, is never to be trusted when you're a million miles away from home. Brown contrives a landing on Mars where, this time, our heroes *are* attacked by alien life (albeit a fast-growing lichen). *Pathfinders to Venus* rounded off the trilogy (the series now proudly boasting a credit for special effects), and saw the Wedgwoods landing on that titular planet. Finally, the show caved in to genre expectations and the cast are assaulted by a fine variety of alien attackers from all rungs of the evolutionary ladder, from carnivorous plants, to pterodactyls, and even Mars' own 'Cro-Magnon' ape-men.

Although not massively remembered outside of fan circles, *Pathfinders* is an undeniably worthwhile series, if only as a fascinating statement of intent from Sydney Newman. Defecting to the BBC, he followed the same formula with the addition of time travel, which resulted in *Pathfinders*' natural successor - the indestructible ***Doctor Who***.

The Paul Hogan Show

Comedy | JP Productions/7 Network/9 Network (shown on Channel 4) | episode duration 50 mins | broadcast 11 May 1973–21 Sep 1982 (Aus)

Principal Cast
Paul Hogan, Delvene Delaney, John Cornell, Marguerite Frewin, Andrew Harwood, Marion Edward, Roger Stephen, Sue McIntosh · *Various Characters*

Producers Peter Faiman, John Cornell **Writer** Paul Hogan

Paul Hogan entered Australia's version of talent show *New Faces* as a joke, creating what he felt would be the all-time worst act ever. To his surprise, the voting public recognised a spark of genius in his performance and brought him back week after week. Eventually, he began to make occasional specials involving sketches and character studies that appealed directly to the Australian audience. Hogan's ignorant alter ego 'Hoges' was a boor, togged up in Aussie football gear and with a best friend called Strop, whose stupidity was the only thing that made an-answer-for-everything Hoges look smart. Smartened up a little, Hoges formed the basis of Hogan's fish-out-of-water frontman for Fosters in a series of adverts for the Australian lager (at the ballet, he's heard to shout 'Strewth – there's a bloke down there with no strides on!').

When screened in the UK and the States, Paul Hogan's 50-minute episodes were trimmed of their more Oz-specific jokes to create 25-minute versions. The first cut-down episode was shown here on 2 November 1982 – Channel 4's first day of transmission, giving viewers a taste of the Vegemite-fuelled madness to come. His 'overnight' rise to fame in America after only a decade of award-winning work is, of course, legendary, playing on the stereotypes about and ignorance towards Australians as the star of *Crocodile Dundee* (1986).

Peak Practice

Drama | Central/Carlton for ITV | episode duration 45 mins | broadcast 10 May 1993–30 Jan 2002

Regular Cast
Kevin Whately · *Dr Jack Kerruish*
Amanda Burton · *Dr Beth Glover/Kerruish*
Simon Shepherd · *Dr Will Preston*
Gary Mavers · *Dr Andrew Attwood*
Saskia Wickham · *Dr Erica Matthews*
Adrian Lukis · *Dr David Shearer*
Haydn Gwynne · *Dr Joanna Graham*
Joseph Millson · *Dr Sam Morgan*
Gray O'Brien · *Dr Tom Deneley*
Maggie O'Neill · *Dr Alex Redman*
Jamie Bamber · *Dr Matt Kendal*
Sylvia Syms · *Isabel de Gines*
Shaun Prendergast · *Trevor Sharp*
Jacqueline Leonard · *Sarah Preston*
Veronica Roberts · *Laura Elliott*
Shelagh McLeod · *Kate Preston*
Yolanda Vazquez, Fiona Gillies · *Clare Shearer*
Sarah Parish · *Dawn Rudge*
Anne Reid · *Rira Barrat*
John Bowler · *Mike Pullen*
Melanie Kilburn · *Liz*
Eva Pope · *Claire Brightwell*
Jamie Bamber · *Dr Matt Kendall*
Victor McGuire · *Shaun Carter*

Creator Lucy Gannon **Producers** Ted Childs, Sharon Bloom (executive), Charles Hubbard, Nicholas Brown (associate), Michele Buck, Richard Handford, Damien Timmer, Tony Virgo **Writers** Various, including Lucy Gannon, Andy de la Tour, Jeff Dodds, Andrea Earl, Rio Fanning, John Flanagan, Stewart Harcourt, Ginnie Hole, Maria Jones, Andrew McCulloch, Stuart Morris, Anita J. Pandolfo, Laura Phillips, Andrew Rattenbury, Patrea Smallacombe, James Stevenson, Patrick Wilde, Colin Wyatt **Theme Music** John Altman

When *Peak Practice* first arrived on TV screens, viewers might well have expected to see yet another cosy rural series about a charming group of friendly doctors working in their country practice. However, *Peak Practice* was decidedly different, right from the start. Created by former nurse Lucy Gannon (who was also behind ITV's other smash-hit series ***Soldier, Soldier***), *Peak Practice* built up a hugely devoted following from fans right across the globe, captivated by storylines and characters that seemed just a little bit more realistic and believable than your average TV medical drama.

As the series began, viewers were introduced to Dr Jack Kerruish (a role written for star Kevin Whately, incidentally), an idealistic medic working in a remote African hospital. Forced to return to the UK, Jack soon ends up working at The Beeches surgery in the Peak District village of Cardale, alongside doctors Beth Glover and Will Preston. At first the relationship between Jack and Beth is strained, but soon they fall in love and marry. As the years go by, the medical staff at The Beeches come and go (Jack and Beth heading off to Africa at the end of the third season), but the beautiful countryside and above-average storylines remained the same. With the majority of the show's leads a good ten years older than the youthful, shiny-faced cast of ***Casualty*** (for example), *Peak Practice* just *felt* more real than other TV medical dramas. Many viewers were furious when ITV decided not to continue with *Peak Practice*, especially as the final episode ended on a literal cliffhanger with psychotic nurse Claire Brightwell dragging nice Dr Alex with her as she plunged into a very deep quarry. What galled fans still further was that ITV replaced their beloved show with an almost identikit series called *Sweet Medicine* (starring Patricia Hodge and Jason Merrells, 4 Sep–2 Nov 2003), also set in a medical practice in Derbyshire, which spectacularly failed to ignite the passions in quite the same way.

Pebble Mill at One

Magazine | BBC One | episode duration 45 mins | broadcast 2 Oct 1972–23 May 1986, 14 Oct 1991–29 Mar 1996

Regular Cast
Bob Langley, Marian Foster, Donny McLeod, Bob Hall, David

Freeman, Jan Leeming, Marjorie Lofthouse, Chris Baines, Magnus Magnusson, Sarah Greene, David Seymour, Ross King, Alan Titchmarsh, Judi Spiers, Ross Kelly, Josephine Buchan, Paul Coia · *Presenters*

Creator Phil Sidey

Though a later incarnation saw a studio-based daytime chat show of a similar name, the original *Pebble Mill at One* production was famously broadcast from the foyer of the BBC's Pebble Mill studios in Birmingham. The building itself had been opened on 10 November 1971 by HRH Princess Anne.

It was producer Phil Sidey who came up with the idea of hosting the show from the foyer after being unimpressed with the look of the studio available to him. It was what's known in the business as a 'good plan' for it allowed viewers a glimpse of the Pebble Mill garden, designed by regular contributor Peter Seabrook and gave the locals a little excitement when the likes of Sophia Loren or Cliff Richard came to visit. Cookery slots, antiques, pop music and behind-the-scenes features were interspersed with the celebrity interviews, while the rather casual approach led to a feeling of familiarity between the presenters, the guests and the audience, sitting on the sidelines but all still very much an essential part of the atmosphere.

Though *Pebble Mill at One* came to a close in 1986 to make way for the all-new daytime schedule (including Australian import ***Neighbours***), it was resurrected briefly from 1991 as *Pebble Mill*, with Alan Titchmarsh, Judy Spiers and Ross King presenting. This second version lacked the essential making-it-up-as-we-go-along charm of those 1970s and 80s editions. In 2004, the BBC moved out of its long-term Midlands home of Pebble Mill and into a new specially-designed studio and office facility in Birmingham City Centre.

Perfect Scoundrels

Comedy Drama | TVS for ITV | episode duration 50 mins | broadcast 22 Apr 1990–May 1992

Regular Cast
Peter Bowles · *Guy Buchanan*
Bryan Murray · *Harry Cassidy*
Ian Bartholomew, Stephen Tate · *Inky*
Zoot Money · *Ted*
Arkie Whiteley · *Fleur*
Eric Mason · *Willie*
Kyle Gordon · *Young Buchanan*

Creator Ray Connelly, based on an idea by Peter Bowles and Bryan Murray **Producer** Graham Benson **Writers** Ray Connolly, Russell Lewis **Theme Music** Nigel Hess

Inspired by their happy working relationship on ***The Irish RM***, Peter Bowles and Bryan Murray worked with writer Ray Connelly to develop a return vehicle for the pair. *Perfect Scoundrels* reunites the lovable rogues as conmen who meet at the funeral of a mutual associate and decide to enter into an uneasy partnership to avenge their friend's death. Though they eventually discover they've been duped by the dead man (who is anything but dead), they realise the strength in numbers and become modern-day Robin Hoods who steal from their rivals and occasionally each other. While Irishman Harry Cassidy lacked the subtle sophistication of Guy Buchanan, he could still charm his way out of most situations.

Perfect Strangers

Drama | Talkback for BBC One | episode duration 60–90 mins | broadcast 10–24 May 2001

Cast
Michael Gambon · *Raymond*
Lindsay Duncan · *Alice*
Matthew MacFadyen, Daniel Williams · *Daniel*
Claire Skinner, Courtney Bolden · *Rebecca*
Toby Stephens, Mitchell Finlay · *Charles*
Jill Baker · *Esther*
Timothy Spall · *Irving*
Anton Lesser · *Stephen*
Paul Alexander · *Uncle Bill*
Michael Culkin · *Sidney*
Kelly Hunter · *Poppy*
Kathleen Byron, Emma Sackville · *Edith*
Muriel Pavlow, Rebecca Tarry · *Violet*
Sheila Burrell, Miranda Raison · *Grace*
Peter Howell · *Ernest*
Tony Maudsley · *Peter*
Camilla Power · *Martina*
Marianne Borgo · *Nazik*
J. J. Feild, Ben Heffer · *Richard*
Jay Simon · *Raymond's Father*

Producer John Chapman **Writer** Stephen Poliakoff **Theme Music** Adrian Johnson

According to one character in Stephen Poliakoff's three-part play, every family has at least three great stories. For Daniel, who has never known his father's relations, a huge reunion of the Symon family is the beginning of a journey through the past, the beginning of new friendships and relationships and the unearthing of a dreadful secret.

Though Daniel (Matthew MacFadyen, shortly before he began work on ***Spooks***) is our guide through the labyrinthine family tree, he's by far the least interesting of the family, which includes a boorish property developer called Irving, the family genealogist Stephen, and a co-dependent brother and sister, Rebecca and Charles, whose fraught relationship with their Aunt Alice is the catalyst that draws Daniel into the heart of the family. While the reunion awakens Daniel's curiosity in a family he's never known, it's a second function at a country house that provides some of the answers. It's there that he discovers the reason for his father's distance from the rest of the family as well as an unexpected link to his own grandfather. As with Poliakoff's ***Shooting the Past***, *Perfect Strangers* captures the magic of photography to tell its tales, with much of the story revolving around two pictures in particular, one of Daniel's father and uncle standing by a pair of stone beasts, and another of a boy dressed as a little prince.

The Perishers

Animation | FilmFair/Bill Melendez for BBC One | episode duration 5 mins | broadcast 21 Mar–4 May 1979

Voice Cast

Leonard Rossiter, Sheila Steafel, Peter Hawkins, Judy Bennett

Creator/Writer Maurice Dodd, based on his comic strip **Producers** Graham Clutterbuck (executive), Graeme Spurway **Theme Music** Trevor Evan Jones; if you're in the right mood this might recall sections of the Beatles' 'Obla-Di Obla-Da'

The *Daily Mirror*'s popular strip cartoon came to the golden 'before the early-evening news' slot courtesy of Bill Melendez, who'd been responsible for animating ***Charlie Brown*** in the States. Retaining the original designs from Dennis Collins's drawings and Maurice Dodd's witty scripts, the estuary-accented Perishers were forever dropping their 'g's and 'h's, or getting words wrong. They comprise Wellington, a bombastic boy; Maisie, a bullying spoilt brat; the vacuous buggie-obsessed Marlon ('Vroom-vroom'); baby Grumbling, who is the voice of reason in the group; and Boot, an exasperated Old English sheep dog with the voice of Leonard Rossiter.

Perry Mason

Crime Drama | Paisano Productions for CBS (shown on BBC One) | episode duration 50 mins, plus specials | broadcast 21 Sep 1957–22 May 1966, 1 Dec 1985–10 Apr 1993 (USA)

Principal Cast

Raymond Burr · *Perry Mason*
Barbara Hale · *Della Street*
William Hopper · *Paul Drake*
William Talman · *District Attorney Hamilton Burger*
Ray Collins · *Lieutenant Arthur Tragg*
Karl Held · *David Gideon*
Wesley Lau · *Lieutenant Anderson*
Richard Anderson · *Lieutenant Steve Drumm*
Lee Miller · *Sergeant Brice*
Dan Tobin · *Terence Clay*
William Katt · *Paul Drake Jr*
William R Moses · *Ken Malansky*
David Ogden Stiers · *Michael Reston*

Producers Various, including Gail Patrick Johnson, Arthur Marks (executive), Ben Brady, Art Seid, Sam White, Herbert Hirschman **Writers** Various, including Erle Stanley Gardner, Stanley Niss, Gene Wang, Samuel Newman, Robert C. Dennis, Jackson Gillis, Stirling Silliphant, from the novels by Eric Stanley Gardner **Theme Music** Composed by movie composer Bernard Hermann, the genius responsible for many of Alfred Hitchcock's most memorable movie scores such as *North by Northwest* (1959) and *Psycho* (1960).

Simply judged by the sheer volume of episodes produced, *Perry Mason* is one of the most successful detective shows in television history, with 271 episodes being recorded over nine years. Quite apart from that rather impressive statistic, the programme is perhaps best remembered for launching the career of actor Raymond Burr, someone who'd spent much of his early career appearing as villains in the movies (playing the killer in Hitchcock's *Rear Window* (1954) for instance). Burr took his big break seriously, spending time in Los Angeles courtrooms studying the way in which the performance and personality of attorneys could swing the outcome of a case. The series was based upon the series of novels written by lawyer/author Eric Stanley Gardner, the first (*The Case of the Velvet Claws*) appearing in 1933.

Perry Mason is a dedicated and determined Los Angeles defence attorney, who (with the unstinting help of his secretary Della Street) works alongside private detective Paul Drake to uncover evidence that will prove the innocence of his clients. In most of the cases Mason is given, it seems as though his client's guilt is pretty much cut-and-dried, with the evidence supplied by police detective Arthur Tragg making life easy for his courtroom opponent, prosecution attorney Hamilton Burger. However, Mason's scalpel-sharp legal mind, probing questioning and lateral thinking ability help him to punch holes in the prosecution's case, and his innocent clients inevitably avoid a horrific miscarriage of justice at best, a death sentence at worst.

Although the series came to a conclusion in 1966 (Burr moving on to play another lead role in a legal/police show, ***Ironside***), that wasn't the last we heard of Perry Mason. In 1985 a reunion movie *Perry Mason Returns* reunited Burr and Barbara Hale; a number of further feature-length investigations followed, with Hale's actor son William Katt taking over as the fictional son of Paul Drake.

Peter Kay's Phoenix Nights

Sitcom | Ovation/Goodnight Vienna for Channel 4 | episode duration 25 mins | broadcast 14 Jan 2001–12 Sep 2002

Regular Cast

Peter Kay · *Brian Potter, Max*
Dave Spikey · *Jerry St Clair*
Neil Fitzmaurice · *Ray Von*
Patrick McGuinness · *Paddy*
Steve Edge · *Alan*
Toby Foster · *Les*

Janice Connolly · *Holy Mary*
Bea Kelley · *Marion*
Archie Kelly · *Kenny*
Justin Moorhouse · *Young Kenny*
Ted Robbins · *Den Perry*

Creator Peter Kay **Producers** Phil McIntyre (executive), Mark Herbert, John Rushton **Writers** Peter Kay, Neil Fitzmaurice, Dave Spikey **Theme Music** James McColl

This blisteringly funny comedy series sprang from the fertile mind of Bolton-born stand-up comedian Peter Kay, a semi-familiar face on TV since his first big break on the barely lamented BBC Two lunchtime youth-focused comedy show *The Sunday Show*. In 1999, Channel 4 gave Kay a chance to shine in a pilot episode called 'The Services', a mock behind-the-scenes documentary on the life and loves of staff working at a motorway service station. The episode was so successful that the following year a full six-part season showcasing Kay's comic characters was launched, *That Peter Kay Thing*. Each of the six episodes dealt with a different character living in and around Bolton, from an aggressive ice cream van man, a slightly effete yet highly competitive bingo caller, through to a talent-free singer-songwriter who achieves chart success. However, there was one episode of *That Peter Kay Thing* that really leant itself to further examination: 'In The Club'. The story of wheelchair-bound working men's club manager Brian Potter and his motley collection of staff, regulars and hangers-on was so popular that in 2001 Potter returned to Channel 4 screens in the first episode of his very own series, *Peter Kay's Phoenix Nights*.

The Phoenix Club in Bolton has suffered from a number of unfortunate incidents in its life, having been burned down on more than one occasion (hence the name). Never one to let a minor problem like an incinerated property knock him back, belligerent boss Brian Potter marshals his troops and sets the Phoenix back up in business, hosting regular comedy nights, cabaret and search for a star competitions in his club. Brian's right-hand man and compère is the ever-suffering Jerry St Clair, a man who always wanted to be a top-notch singer, but who has ended up stuck working for the wheelchair-bound bully Potter. Other members of the team include musicians Les and Alan ('Les Alanos'), religion-obsessed barmaid Holy Mary, and the two bumbling doormen Max and Paddy.

Phoenix Nights was one of Channel 4's true break-out hits, a comedy series from the same mould of northern working-class humour as ***Coronation Street*** or ***dinnerladies***, only this time with a distinctly male spin on the laughs. Indeed, Kay's comedy was so in tune with the Corrie sensibility that one of his best friends, actress Sally Lindsay, was cast as new Rovers Return barmaid Shelley Unwin shortly after appearing in *Phoenix Nights*. In return, Kay then made a cameo appearance in *Coronation Street* as a socially inept drayman trying to woo the hand of 'Sunshine Shelley'. After just 12 episodes of witnessing Brian Potter's struggles against rival club boss Den Perry (a fabulous performance by Ted Robbins), the doors of the Phoenix Club closed in order to make room for a spin-off show featuring the two boneheaded bouncers of the Phoenix, *Max And Paddy's Road to Nowhere* (broadcast on Channel 4 in 2005), in which Kay revived his role as Max (in fact, many viewers when watching *Phoenix Nights* were unaware that Peter Kay played both Brian Potter and Max the doorman – a tribute to Kay's abilities). Thankfully, despite the end of *Phoenix Nights*, Brian Potter made a few reappearances in the middle of *Max And Paddy's Road to Nowhere* to cause his normal brand of mayhem to the unfortunate pair. Later still, Brian Potter, Max and Paddy all featured in the pop video produced to support the 2005 Comic Relief single, a re-release of Tony Christie's hit 'Is this the way to Amarillo?', which topped the charts in the UK for an amazing eight weeks.

The Peter Principle

Sitcom | Hat Trick Productions for BBC One | episode duration 30 mins | broadcast 4 Sep 1995, 2 Jun–7 Jul 1997, 3 Feb–6 Mar 2000

Principal Cast
Jim Broadbent · *Peter Duffley*
Lesley Sharp, Claire Skinner · *Susan Harvey*
Linda Bassett, Janette Legge · *Iris*
David Schneider · *Bradley Wilson*
David Gant, Stephen Moore · *Geoffrey Parkes*
Stuart McQuarrie, Daniel Flynn · *David Edwards*
Zoe Heyes, Tracy Keating · *Brenda*
Beverley Callard · *Barbara*
Helena McCarthy · *Mrs Parkes*
Clive Russell · *Kevin Mott*
Michael J Shannon · *Milton Macrae*
Wendy Nottingham · *Evelyn Walker*

Producers Denise O'Donoghue (executive), Dan Patterson **Writer** Dan Patterson, Mark Burton, John O'Farrell **Theme Music** Mark Russell

The 'Peter Principle' is a phrase used to describe a common trait that's familiar to many office workers – when an individual is promoted to their precise level of incompetence. In this sitcom, the 'Peter' in question is bank manager Peter Duffley, a pompous, idiotic, self-obsessed man who simply hasn't got a clue about how to do his job properly. The rest of the staff at the Aldbridge Branch of the County & Provincial Bank have cottoned on to Peter's cluelessness and take one of two tacks – either to use his failings to further their own careers, or to support him in the hope that he'll promote *them* one day. Chief among them is Peter's assistant manager Susan Harvey, who knows full well that she's far more competent than he'll ever be – half of the time she rails against his stupidity, the rest of the time she covers up his mistakes (especially when regional manager David Edwards visits the branch).

The Peter Principle showcased the comic talents of Jim

Broadbent, a man perhaps now better known for his critically lauded performances in serious movie dramas like *Topsy Turvy* (1999), *Moulin Rouge!* (2001) and especially his Oscar-nominated turn opposite Judi Dench in *Iris* (2001). An outstanding pilot episode of *The Peter Principle* shown in 1995 led to a full series two years later – however, by this point, almost all of the supporting cast were unavailable and had to be replaced. Unfortunately, although some decent laughs were to be had, the 12 follow-on episodes never quite lived up to the promise of the pilot.

Peyton Place

Soap Opera | 20th Century Fox for ABC (shown on ITV) | episode duration 25 mins | broadcast 15 Sep 1964–2 Jun 1969 (USA)

Regular Cast

Dorothy Malone, Lola Albright · *Constance MacKenzie/Carson*
Mia Farrow · *Allison MacKenzie*
Ed Nelson · *Dr Michael Rossi*
Warner Anderson · *Matthew Swain*
Paul Langton · *Leslie Harrington*
Ryan O'Neal · *Rodney Harrington*
Christopher Connelly · *Norman Harrington*
Barbara Parkins · *Betty Anderson/Harrington/Cord/Harrington*
Kasey Rogers · *Julie Anderson*
Henry Beckman · *George Anderson*
Kent Smith · *Dr Robert Morton*
Patricia Breslin · *Laura Brooks*
Mary Anderson · *Catherine Harrington*
Frank Ferguson · *Eli Carson*
Tim O'Connor · *Elliot Carson*
Dayna Ceder · *Sharon Purcell*
Whit Bissell · *Calvin Hanley*
Richard Evans · *Paul Hanley*
Patrick Whyte · *Theodore Dowell*
Gregory Morton · *Mr Wainwright*
Erin O'Brien Moore · *Nurse Choate*
Patricia Morrow · *Rita Jacks/Harrington*
Mickey Dolenz · *Kitch Brunner*
Edith Atwater · *Grace Morton*
Mariette Hartley · *Dr Claire Morton*
Evelyn Scott · *Ada Jacks*
James Douglas · *Steven Cord*
Ruth Warrick · *Hannah Cord*
Leslie Nielson · *Dr Vincent Markham, Kenneth Markham*
Don Quine · *Joe Chernack*
William Smithers · *David Schuster*
Gail Kobe · *Doris Schuster*
Kimberly Beck · *Kim Schuster*
Lee Grant · *Stella Chernack*
Bruce Gordon · *Gus Chernack*
David Canary · *Dr Russ Gehring*
John Kerr · *John Fowler*
Joan Blackman · *Marion Fowler*
George Macready, Wilfred HydeWhite · *Martin Peyton*
Susan Oliver · *Ann Howard*
Stephen Oliver · *Lee Weber*
Lana Wood · *Sandy Weber*
Gary Haynes · *Chris Weber*
Leigh TaylorYoung · *Rachel Welles*
John Kellogg · *Jack Chandler*
Gena Rowlands · *Adrienne Van Leyden*
Dan Duryea · *Eddie Jacks*
Elizabeth Tippy Walker · *Carolyn Russell*
Barbara Rush · *Marsha Russell*
Joe Maross · *Fred Russell*
Bob Hogan · *Reverend Tom Winter*
Diana Hyland · *Susan Winter*
Percy Rodriguez · *Dr Harry Miles*
Ruby Dee · *Alma Miles*
Glynn Turman · *Lew Miles*
Joyce Jillson · *Jill Smith*
Michael Christian · *Joe Rossi*

Creators Grace Metalious, Paul Monash and Irna Phillips **Producers** Various, including Paul Monash (executive) **Writers** Various, including Don Balluck, Franklin Barton, Gene Boland, Steven W. Carabatsos, Dick Carr, Gerry Day, Richard DeRoy, Lee Erwin, Mathilda Ferro, Theodore Ferro, Harold Gast, Michael Gleason, James P. Griffith, Kenneth Hartman, Wharton Jones, Nina Laemmle, Rita Lakin, Ann Marcus, Malcolm Marmorstein, Grace Metalious, Paul Monash, Irna Phillips, Del Reisman, Laurence Richards, Sonya Roberts, Miriam Rosamond, Mark Saha, Peggy Shaw, Robert J. Shaw, Lionel E. Siegel, Carol Sobieski, Jessica Stephans, Glynn Turman, Sam Washington, John Wilder, Jerry Ziegman **Theme Music** 'The Wonderful Season of Love' (also known as 'Allison's Theme'), with lyrics by Paul Francis Webster, music by Franz Waxman. For *Return to Peyton Place*, Webster and Waxman wrote 'For Those Who Are Young'.

Though it had been a best-selling novel (by Grace Metalious) and a feature film, when people talk about *Peyton Place* they're almost certainly referring to the soap opera that held TV audiences in its grip in the mid-1960s. One of the first soaps to break into prime time – shown on the ABC network in the USA and ITV in the UK – its heady mix of sexual intrigue, deception and betrayal cast the mould from which evolved many other melodramas, including ***Dallas, Dynasty*** and ***Twin Peaks***. Though initially it drew flak from critics for being morally dubious, viewers loved it – it topped the ratings in America a month after it launched.

Most soaps revolve around families, and *Peyton Place* was no exception. The filthy-rich Harringtons were the descendents of the Peyton family, the founders of the town. Martin Peyton (played by George Macready) was the head of the family and the wealthy owner of a large part of the town. Much of his involvement in the show came from the many power struggles in and out of the boardroom as he challenged opposition from other businessmen. Peyton's extended family included his grandson, Rodney Harrington (played by Ryan O'Neal in one of his first major TV roles). Rodney found himself in a love triangle, having been entrapped into an engagement by the scheming Betty Anderson, while secretly in love with Allison

MacKenzie (Mia Farrow), illegitimate-but-virtuous daughter of Constance MacKenzie (former 1950s film star Dorothy Malone). Though Rodney married Betty believing she was pregnant with his child, when he found out that she had miscarried long before their wedding, he abandoned her and ran away with Allison . . . and the melodrama continued for five years.

Popular cast members came and went. Mia Farrow's high-profile departure from the show (having abandoned her husband André Previn for Frank Sinatra) unsettled audiences, though her character's off-screen adventures was alluded to for many years to come (one storyline saw the arrival of a woman carrying what was claimed to be Allison's child – the story's proximity to the release of Farrow's 1968 film *Rosemary's Baby* was unlikely to be a coincidence). However, plenty of other actors, old and young, were keen to play a part in proceedings, including Patricia Morrow, Gena Rowlands, Leslie Nielsen, Wilfrid Hyde White and John Kerr.

In its final years, though, changes in front and behind the cameras led to a drop-off in viewers. Too few of the original stars had stuck with the show, the schedule was changed and the show was reshaped in an attempt to capture the attentions of the lucrative youth market. When this failed, the show was given its eviction notice. After 514 episodes and the trial of Mike Rossi for murder, *Peyton Place* was closed down.

There have been a number of revival attempts and TV movies in subsequent years – including one that reunited many of the original cast members and finally solved the mystery of what had happened to Mia Farrow's character all those years before. But what was once shocking and fresh seemed pretty twee and way too cosy for audiences who have grown up with HBO, JR Ewing and Laura Palmer.

The Phil Silvers Show

Sitcom | CBS (shown on BBC) | episode duration 25 mins | broadcast 20 Sep 1955–19 Jun 1959 (USA)

Regular Cast

Phil Silvers · *Sergeant Ernie Bilko*
Harvey Lembeck · *Corporal Rocco Barbella*
Allan Melvin · *Corporal Steve Henshaw*
Paul Ford · *Corporal John T. Hall*
Hope Sansbury · *Nell Hall*
Maurice Gosfield · *Private Duane Doberman*
Herbie Faye · *Private Sam Fender*
Billy Sands · *Private Dino Paparelli*
Mickey Freeman · *Private Fielding Zimmerman*
Terry Carter · *Private Sugarman*
Karl Lucas · *Private 'Stash' Kadowski*
Joe E Ross · *Sergeant Rupert Ritzik*
Beatrice Pons · *Emma Ritzik*
Jimmy Little · *Sergeant Francis Grover*
Elisabeth Fraser · *Sergeant Joan Hogan*
Harry Clark · *Sergeant Stanley Sowici*
Ned Glass · *Sergeant Andrew Pendleton*
Nick Saunders · *Captain Barker*
John Gibson · *Chaplain*

Creator Nat Hiken **Producers** Nat Hiken, Edward J. Montagne **Writers** Various, including Nat Hiken, Terry Ryan, Arnie Rosen, Leonard Stern, Coleman Jacoby, Billy Friedberg, Tony Webster, Phil Sharp, Sydney Zelinka, A. J. Russell, Neil Simon

The motor pool at Fort Baxter, Kansas might be under the command of one Colonel Hall, but it's wholly controlled by Ernie Bilko. The men jump to his every command and can be mobilised in seconds to complete any task required of them. Their motivation is not loyalty to the American army, nor to discipline or respect for their commanding officer. They jump because Bilko ensures they have the easiest life any soldier ever experienced. Scams, schemes, gambles and games ensure that Bilko always comes out on top – although they all know that it requires everyone to play their part, even the smelly, dopey Doberman. Plans might not bring them the riches they desire – the ultimate prize often has a habit of going to a more deserving cause to due Bilko's sentimental side – but so long as the scam itself isn't exposed, Bilko will always win on points.

Phil Silvers' motormouth con-artist team leader has become the archetype for hundreds of characters in films and sitcoms for 50 years now. *The Phil Silvers Show* began as *You'll Never Get Rich* but is popularly known as 'Sergeant Bilko' after Silvers' dominating character in the series. With some of the top comedy writers in the business providing the laughs, the show bagged three Emmy awards in consecutive years and, thanks to its intricate plotting, remains one of the most highly respected TV comedy works among industry figures. Bilko later inspired the brilliant Hanna Barbera series ***Top Cat***, while an ill-advised 1996 film version starred Steve Martin and was directed by ***Yes, Minister*** co-creator Jonathan Lynn.

The Phoenix and the Carpet

Children's Drama | BBC One | episode duration 25 mins | broadcast 29 Dec 1976–16 Feb 1977

Cast

Gary Russell · *Cyril*
Tamsin Neville · *Anthea*
Max Harris · *Robert*
Jane Forster · *Jane*
Richard Warner · *Voice of the Phoenix*
Joe Barton · *Phoenix Puppeteer*
Daphne Neville · *Mother*
Edward Brooks · *Father*
V. M. Hartman · *'The Lamb'*

Producers Anna Home (executive), Dorothea Brooking **Writer** John Tulley, from the novel by E. Nesbit **Theme Music** A passage from *The Firebird* by Igor Stravinsky

The first BBC production of Edith Nesbit's classic Victorian adventure series was based on the second of three books about this particular family of children (the others being *The Five Children and It* and the to-date untelevised *The Story of the Amulet*). A mix of location filming, Ealing studios interiors and videotaping at Pebble Mill combined to make this adaptation one of the best of the Seventies series overseen by the prestigious Brooking. The five children (the fifth is the baby, referred to as 'The Lamb' and played by a set of twins, Victoria and Michelle Lambert) discover the legendary phoenix egg within a second-hand rug. The egg hatches and the phoenix explains that the carpet is a magic one that can fly them anywhere – although they discover in an early jaunt to a French castle that they only have three wishes per day. Further exploits involving a Caribbean island (populated by blacked-up white actors no less), burglars, a cow and hundreds of Persian cats (well, a handful and lots of polystyrene replicants) followed. The cat storyline provoked strong criticisms from Mary Whitehouse as the kids were seen dumping the unwanted moggies on people's doorsteps, and the entire sequence was edited from the Sunday repeat later in 1977. Whitehouse also reared her head over the climax to episode one in the aforementioned French castle as she felt that the children of the 1970s were too delicate to be scared by apparent ghosts at 5.15 on a Wednesday afternoon.

Looking back on the series, it might appear unsophisticated and clunky in places, but it certainly compares well to pretty much every other TV production of the time, with Clive Doig's inventive direction handling the rather creatively realised phoenix rather well, while the psychedelic kaleidoscope patterns that accompanied the flights of the magic carpet were captivating.

The story was remade in the 1990s, shortly after a successful new version of *Five Children and It* and a wholly original sequel, *The Return of the Psammead*. While the carpet flew more realistically, the phoenix itself was disappointing, trying too hard to depict a realistic bird rather than having fun with a fantasy one as the 1970s version did.

Pingu

Animation | Trickfilmstudio/Hit Entertainment (shown on BBC One) | episode duration 5 mins | broadcast 1986–present

Voice Cast
Carlo Bonomi, Marcello Magni, David Sant
Creator/Producer Otmar Gutmann

Pingu is a naughty little penguin with a bright red beak and over a billion fans worldwide. He lives on the South Polar ice cap with his mum, his dad (a postman), baby sister Pinga and friends Pingo and Robby the baby seal. In this wonderful Plasticine world, igloo houses have fire-stoves and electricity (yet they never melt) while Pingu is surprisingly versatile for a penguin, often seen skating, fishing (fish is both food and currency at the South Pole), using a telephone and skiing. Such versatility runs in the family; his chick-in-arms sister can play the trumpet even though she's only recently hatched from an egg and still has her baby plumage, while his dad does the ironing and smokes a pipe (like all dads should).

Pingu is yet another astoundingly imaginative show that causes concern for some parents with its open acceptance that kids find toilet habits hilarious – a realisation exploited in one episode (known by some as 'Little Accidents') in which baby Pinga wets herself (complete with a huge, yellow Plasticine puddle) and Pingu is seen relieving himself rather dramatically. But any show that has its own language (Pinguish), which can be understood by children all over the world, has got to be a force for good. More recent episodes have been criticised by purists for losing some of the rough-and-ready charm of the originals, but even these are head and shoulders about the competition. *Pingu* – a modern masterpiece.

Pink Windmill Show

See ROD HULL AND EMU

Pinky and Perky

Puppetry | BBC TV/Thames for ITV | episode duration 25–30 mins | broadcast 20 Oct 1957–1968 (BBC), 1969–1972 (ITV)

Cast
Charles Young · *Singing Voice of Pinky*
Michael John · *Singing Voice of Perky*
John Slater, Roger Moffat, Jimmy Thompson, Bryan Burdon, Fred Emney · *Human Stooges*

Creators Jan and Vlasta Dalibor **Producers** Stan Parkinson, Trevor Hill **Writers** Various, including Don Nicholl, Robert Gray, Margaret Potter **Theme Music** 'We Belong Together' by Norman Newell and Alyn Ainsworth

Two of the biggest stars of the 1950s and 60s were a pair of puppet pigs called Pinky and Perky (to tell them apart, Perky always wore a hat or beret). 'Discovered' by Czech refugees Jan and Vlasta Dalibor, the pigs were basic marionettes that could do little but bob in time to music. But what made them popular was their talent for singing the hits of the day in their imitable high-pitched voices, achieved by hiring baritones to sing the songs slowly so they could be sped up to the proper tempo and sound like they'd been at the helium.

They first appeared as part of the Dalibors' puppet act on *It's up to You*, a BBC North programme produced by Barney Coleham (who later gave us ***It's a Knockout***). On Colehan's suggestion, the pigs were moved to centre-stage and soon took over the act. For their 1960s BBC series, they became the managers of PPC TV, a broadcasting corporation housed underneath the BBC's Television Centre responsible for

'Channel 2X'. The piglet twins would be joined by all manner of other anthropomorphic animal puppets: feathered friends Belinda Bird, Caraway Crow, Debbie Duckling, Dick and Dock the singing sparrows, Gertie Goose and, by the mid-1960s, mop-topped crows The Beakles; loads of mice, including Midge, the Whiskerley Sisters (the Beverley Sisters, basically); Basil Bloodhound, D'Arcy Dog and the sexy Vera Vixen; Morton Frog, who sang baritone, played sax and even dressed up as a doctor on occasion; George Hare and Horace Hare (a Ken Dodd-alike); Bertie the baby elephant; Ambrose Cat, Gusty Goat, Conchita Cow; in fact, over 50 different characters made appearances over the years.

Pinky and Perky were also seen having adventures in filmed inserts, driving around in their mini car or on river boats. Often these film sequences would dictate the theme for the series, with titles like *Pinky and Perky's American Journey* and *Pinky and Perky's Island* (other series titles were *Pinky and Perky's Pop Parade* and *Pinky and Perky Times*).

The pigs even went transatlantic, appearing on *The Lucy Show* and *The Ed Sullivan Show*. It's possible that the attention went to their heads as in 1966 they went head to head with Prime Minister Harold Wilson in a sketch called 'You Too Can Be a Prime Minister'. The BBC panicked, not wanting to risk political content in an election year, but all that happened was their stooge Jimmy Thompson stood for election only to be bombarded by cabbages.

Pinky and Perky left the BBC in 1968. The following year they made their debut 'on the other side' thanks to a deal with Thames, the ITV region for the southeast. Their show ended in 1972, though the basic format for the show was revived in 1989 for the bizarre *Dooby Duck's Disco Bus* (5 Jan–30 Mar 1989), which once again had marionette animals performing contemporary pop hits.

Pipkins

Children's Puppetry | ATV Television for ITV | episode duration 15/30 mins | broadcast 1 Jan 1973–29 Dec 1981

Regular Voice Cast

George Woodbridge · *Inigo Pipkin*
Wayne Laryea · *Johnny*
Nigel Plaskitt · *Hartley Hare, Tortoise, Narrator*
Lorain Bertorelli, Heather Tobias, Anne Rutter, Diana Eden · *Pig*
Lorain Bertorelli, Heather Tobias, Elizabeth Lindsay · *Topov, Octavia*
Jumoke Debayo · *Bertha*
Sue Nicholls · *Mrs Muddle*
Anne Rutter · *Sophie the Cat*
Jonathan Kydd · *Tom*
Paddy O'Hagan · *Peter Potter*
Royce Mills · *Fred Pipkin*
Charles McKeown · *Charlie, the Dustman*
Preston Lockwood · *The Old Gentleman*
Billy Hamon · *The Genie*
Heather Tobias · *The Bag Lady*
Janet Dale · *Granny*

Creator/Producer Michael Jeans **Writers** Susan Pleat, David Cregan, Billy Hamon, Denis Bond, Gail Renard, Steve James, Johnny and Sandy Byrne, Michael Jeans, Vicky Ireland **Theme Music** The original theme songs were by Frank Weston and Ron Roker, and sung by Jackie Lee. A later theme, in which the puppets are name-checked while Hartley tries to maintain his prominence over the others, featured interjections from Nigel Plaskett, voicing Hartley.

Pipkins came about thanks to a request from the Independent Broadcasting Authority for UK-produced alternatives to the hugely popular ***Sesame Street***. Four different programmes emerged from around the ITV regions, which would be stripped across weekday lunchtimes: Mondays and Fridays came from Thames in the form of ***Rainbow***; Tuesdays saw ATV's offering, *Inigo Pipkins*; on Wednesdays it was over to Yorkshire for the adventures of *Mr Trimble*; and on Thursdays it was Granada's turn with *Hickory House*, which introduced former ***Corrie*** star Alan Rothwell to Humphrey Cushion and Dusty Mop (yes, a cushion and a mop). Each of them took a little from *Sesame Street*, lively puppets, cheery songs and a little education mixed in with the entertainment. While *Rainbow*'s double shift helped it become one of the best-remembered children's shows of all time, for our money *Inigo Pipkins* was by far the superior show.

Created by producer/director Michael Jeans and writer Susan Pleat, it told of an elderly puppet maker Inigo Pipkins (played by George Woodbridge) and his assistant Johnny. Pipkin's puppets assisted him in his altruistic enterprise 'The Help People'. Tragically, Woodbridge died just a few weeks into recording the show's second series. Rather than recast the role, the production team did something unthinkably brave – they told their young viewers the truth that Mr Pipkin had died. An almost surreal experience, the puppets, led by Hartley Hare, spent an episode learning about what 'dead' means and slowly coming to terms with the matter, as indeed the children watching were doing. From then on, the show became simply *Pipkins*.

There were other puppets apart from Hartley: Pig, who spoke with a thick West Midlands accent and spent many episodes knocking up imaginative labour-saving – often food-related – devices; Topov the monkey; the monotonous Tortoise who sat on top of the till or lurked under the workbench; and the beautiful ostrich Octavia. But it was Hartley we watched out for. Rude, bullying, spiteful, acquisitive and utterly selfish, he was everything we were never allowed to be. His catchphrase, if you will, was a petulant 'Meh!', expressing his deep dissatisfaction every time things didn't go his way. Nevertheless, each episode would offer a glimmer of hope that Hartley might have learned an important lesson, even if he was reluctant to admit it.

A regular feature of each programme was the point when Johnny would say 'It's time . . .' and, evoking the intro to Pink Floyd's 'Time', a series of clocks would tick away frantically while alarms would chime and Speaking Clock pips would sound. Once the noise had stopped, Johnny would continue: '. . . for the story'.

After 313 episodes, *Pipkins* became a victim of ATV's hand-over to Central Television. With the matter-of-factness we'd come to expect, Hartley told viewers that the series had come to an end and that in its place would be 'a new programme with new people'. That programme turned out to be *Let's Pretend*, in which an enthusiastic gang of grown-ups made up a play. Like *Pipkins*, it was created by Michael Jeans. But without scruffy old Hartley Hare and his friends, it could never compete.

Planet of the Apes

Drama | 20th Century Fox for CBS (shown on ITV) | episode duration 50 mins | broadcast 13 Sep–20 Dec 1974

Cast

Roddy McDowell · *Galen*
Mark Lenard · *General Urko*
Ron Harper · *Virdon*
James Naughton · *Burke*
Booth Coleman · *Dr Zaius*

Creator Based on concepts created by Pierre Boulle in his novel *La Planète des singes* **Producers** Herb Hirschman (executive), Stan Hough **Writers** Art Wallace, Edward J. Lakso, Robert W. Lenski, Robert Hamner, Barry Oringer, Anthony Lawrence, Ken Spears, Joe Ruby, David P. Lewis, Richard Collins, Walter Black, Howard Dimsdale, Shimon Wincelberg, Arthur Browne Jr **Theme Music** Lalo Schifrin

Hard to believe, but in the old days TV shows span off from successful movie franchises, and not the other way round. *Planet of the Apes* is possibly the weirdest and most unexpected of these – bearing in mind that unlike ***Logan's Run***, *Alien Nation* or even ***Buffy the Vampire Slayer***, the *Apes* films were over and done with by 1974. But it was a TV showing of the first film that encouraged America's classrooms to 'Go Ape' and it was not too surprising that it was considered a cheaper way to cash-in on this via the little box rather than the big screen routes the franchise had all but exhausted.

Essentially ignoring the ongoing story of the movies without actually contradicting them, the series mirrored the first two films – human astronauts thrown through time find themselves in the future where apes rule the planet. Here, befriended by the chimp Galen (played by movie monkey actor Roddy McDowell), they are constantly on the run from Urko, the gorilla soldier who wants them slaughtered before they can spread sedition through the human slaves. Perhaps, ironically, coming closer in spirit to Boulle's novel than the films, the longer the series ran meant more character development could be squeezed into the storylines – most memorably in the episode 'The Trap' where Urko learns how apes were treated in Virdon and Burke's day.

Despite a successful merchandising plan, the series bombed in America (it was vastly more popular in Europe) and was cancelled after only 14 episodes were shown. Boulle himself might have been happier to see the short-lived DePatie-Freleng cartoon series that came afterwards, *Return to the Planet of the Apes*, which actually featured the apes living in modern cities, driving cars, etc., just as they do in his original book, *Monkey Planet*.

Play Away

Children's Entertainment | BBC Two | episode duration 30 mins | broadcast 20 Nov 1971–11 Feb 1984

Regular Cast

Brian Cant, Toni Arthur, Floella Benjamin, Derek Griffiths, Carol Chell, Jeremy Irons, Nerys Hughes, Fred Harris, Tony Robinson, Julie Stevens, Matthew Devitt, Linda Williams, Alex Norton, Delia Morgan, Janine Sharp, Pam Ellis, Heather Williams · *Presenters*
Jonathan Cohen · *Pianist*
Spike Heatley, Alan Rushton, Henry McKenzie, Martyn David, Dill Katz, Dave Roach, David Rose, Paul Robinson, Paul Boita, Paul Carmichael, John Hayman · *House Musicians*

Producers Cynthia Felgate, Ann Reay **Theme Music** 'It really doesn't matter if it's raining or it's fine, just as long as you've got time, to p-l-a-y, play away-ay, play-away ah play play-ah-way-way, ah-play away play away . . . Play Away!' – this unforgettable theme was composed by Lionel Morton and was arranged by the show's resident pianist and band leader Jonathan Cohen.

Whereas ***Play School*** was shown on weekdays and, like a real-life school, focused on gentle bits and pieces of educational value, come the weekend it was time to play – and so *Play Away* was born, a programme containing many of the same basic elements as *Play School*, but this time focusing on simply having fun. Broadcast on Saturday afternoons, *Play Away*'s lynchpin was the irrepressible entertainer Brian Cant, a man seemingly able to make even the most inconsequential of everyday objects into the basis of a song, dance or series of groan-inducing gags.

Each week, Brian would be joined by three other presenters who'd join in with the fun – one of the regulars in the mid-1970s was future Oscar-winning actor Jeremy Irons. Depending on when it was that you might have tuned into *Play Away*, you might have caught Floella Benjamin, Toni Arthur, Derek Griffiths or future Baldrick Tony Robinson performing for a youthful audience. Charming and innocent, *Play Away* seems today like the product of an entirely different time – it's rather sad that there's nothing really like it currently being made for kids today, because children of all ages like nothing better than a few jokes and a sing-song.

Play School

See pages 562–3

Hamble, Jemima, Big Ted, Little Ted and Humpty on top of a collection of Play School *props.*

Play School

For generations of children, *Play School* was the entry point to TV addiction. Introduced by a jaunty theme tune and a two-dimensional illustration of a house with a door and windows, its power, like that of ***Sesame Street***, lay in repetition and structure. Each episode was based around themed days – 'useful box day', 'dressing-up day', 'pets day' – while an ornate clock taught kids how to identify the big hand from the little hand and learn how to tell the time (said clock is rumoured to have been the catalyst for a series of BBC strikes in the 1970s as electricians and prop men argued over whose job it was to switch the damned thing on). It also holds an unplanned position in TV history: after a power cut wiped out BBC Two's official opening night, *Play School* became the first scheduled broadcast on the new channel the next morning.

The format for the series remained the same for 24 years. A pair of presenters would work through the week, with artistes appearing on rotation throughout the series' run. One of the longest-serving *Play School*ers was Brian Cant, while other regulars included Eric Thompson (voice of ***The Magic Roundabout***) and his wife Phyllida Law, Derek Griffiths, Floella Benjamin, the effervescent Johnny Ball and the manic Fred Harris. A shocking amount of the male presenters had beards or moustaches (just count how many presenters on children's TV nowadays are even capable of displaying facial hair). But it was the toys that were the real stars. Unlike *Sesame Street*'s talking furry characters, *Play School*'s approach was more honest and straightforward – toys were just toys and they only came to life within the realms of imagination (and a helpful hand to prop them up): Big Ted, the egg-shaped Humpty and rag doll Jemima, eventually joined by Little Ted and Hamble, quite the most ugly plastic monstrosity outside of the 'Finger Frights' collection (she was ditched in 1986 in favour of Afro-Caribbean doll Polly). Dapple the rocking horse occasionally put in an appearance, and like ***Blue Peter*** the show usually had a pet or three for the young ones to look forward to seeing, including Henry and Henrietta the mice, rabbits Peter, Benjamin, Pippa, Buffy and Becky, a Cockatoo called K'too, and a pair of goldfish named Bit and Bot.

Aside from the clock, the most exciting element each day would come when one of the presenters would invite the viewers to look through one of the *Play School* windows. Contrary to the opening sequences, there were just three – the round window, the square window and the arched window. The simple act of guessing which one they'd pick was enough to energise the most placid of viewers as children up and down the country would bellow 'ROUND!' or 'SQUARE!' only to suffer a minor disappointment as the camera zoomed in on the arched frame, the image blurred and from somewhere off screen a harp would begin to play by way of an introduction to the day's short film.

The decision to axe *Play School* in 1988 led to complaints to the *Radio Times*, and looking at its replacement, *Playbus* (later renamed *Play Days*), it's not hard to see why the complaints were so vehement, the replacement show being almost entirely derivative of its predecessor except for an attempt to include a greater regional variation in the voices of the children. If it ain't broke, don't fix it, that's what we say.

But it was the toys that were the real stars: Big Ted, the egg-shaped Humpty and rag doll Jemima, eventually joined by Little Ted and Hamble, quite the most ugly plastic monstrosity outside of the 'Finger Frights' collection.

Pre-School
BBC Two/One
Episode Duration: 20–25 mins
Broadcast: 21 Apr 1964–28 Aug 1988

Cast
Virginia Stride, Gordon Rollings, Marian Diamond, Brian Cant, Carole Ward, Rick Jones, Phyllida Law, Eric Thompson, Valerie Pitts, Terence Howard, Miranda Connell, Paul Danquah, Carol Chell, Jennifer Naden, Colin Jeavons, Ann Morrish, John White, Julie Stevens, Wally Whyton, Marla Landi, Johnny Ball, Carmen Munroe, Lionel Morton, Mela White, Gordon Clyde, Diane Dorgan, Kerry Jewel, Derek Griffiths, Johnny Silvo, Chloe Ashcroft, Don Spencer, Stuart McGugan, John Golder, Jon Glover, Karen Platt, Samantha Wyse, Floella Benjamin, Sarah Long, Carol Leader, Bruce Allan, Delia Morgan, Chris Tranchell, Sheelagh Gilbey, Fred Harris, Christopher Bramwell, Elizabeth Millbank, Iain Lauchlan, Patrick Abernethy, Fraser Wilson, Ben Thomas, Rosalind Wilson, Simon Davies, Stuart Bradley, Brian Jameson, Liz Watts, Wayne Jackman, Jane Hardy, Kate Copstick, Mike Amatt, Lloyd Johnston, John Agard, Nick Mercer, Robert Kitson, Lesley Woods, Janet Palmer, Nigel Makin, Robin Kingsland · *Presenters*
William Blezard, Richard Brown, Jonathan Cohen, Philip Colman, Rudi Van Dyk, Graham Evans, Roger Fiske, Reg Flowers, Martin Frith, Martin Goldstein, Alan Grahame, Patrick Harvey, Harry Hayward, Peter Howland, Don Lawson, David Moses, Bill Nickson, Michael Omer, Peter Pettinger, Paul Reade, Winifred Taylor · *Musicians*

Creator Joy Whitby
Producers Cynthia Felgate, Anne Gobey, Judy Whitfield, Barbara Roddam, Christine Hewitt (executive), Joy Whitby, Michael Grafton-Robinson, Peter Ridsdale Scott, Ann Reay, Peter Wiltshire, Sue Peto, Penny Lloyd, Greg Childs, John Lane

Theme Music Paul Reade's four-note theme gave us the description of the play school: 'A House . . . with a door/Windows . . . one, two, three, four.' The next line – 'Ready to play? What's the day?' – later evolved into 'Ready to knock? Turn the lock!'

Playhouse: The Mind Beyond

Anthology | BBC Two | episode duration 50 mins | broadcast 29 Sep–3 Nov 1976

Principal Cast
Donald Pleasance, John Bluthal, Janet Street-Porter, Charles Keating, Jeremy Kemp, Anthony Bate, Geraldine Cowper, Clifford Rose, Anna Massey, William Lucas, Michael Bryant, Megs Jenkins, Peter Sallis, George Coulouris, T. P. McKenna, John Wells, Richard Pascoe, Judy Parfitt, Willie Jonah, Cyril Cusack, Geoffrey Bayldon

Producer Irene Shubik **Writers** David Halliwell, Brian Hayles, William Trevor, Bruce Stewart, Malcolm Christopher, Evan Jones **Theme Music** Joseph Horovitz

Irene Shubik had begun her career as a producer with two seasons of the genre classic ***Out of the Unknown***. Following successful stints on the more mainstream waters of *The Wednesday Play* and *Play for Today* (which included the unforgettable ***Edna, the Inebriate Woman***), Shubik returned to the fantasy anthology with *The Mind Beyond*, a series that was showcased as part of the *Playhouse* strand. Gone was the sci-fi hardware and tinfoil spacewear of old (Gerry Anderson was one of the very few still bothering), this new show searched out mysteries closer to home, with six plays linked by the common theme of ESP.

Quite appropriately for a series that set out to explore hidden areas of the mind, *The Mind Beyond*, like many shows of the period, requires the viewer to do some of the work. This is never TV that washes over the audience – it is often oblique or tantalising open-ended, but without ever being impenetrable. The opening play, *Meriel, the Ghost Girl*, is close to masterful – a definitive statement on the slippery, contradictory nature of 'psychic phenomena', the conflicting accounts of the people who witness and record them and the hopelessness of trying to reconcile them into a useful 'truth'. It opens with the ever-faultless Donald Pleasance witnessing and commentating on a séance that utterly convinces him of its authenticity. Fifteen minutes later, a surprise 'second act' begins, shot in black and white in a clear film-noir pastiche (although with poor quality BBC film stock and inadequate lighting, 'film gris' might be more appropriate). Stock American John Bluthal arrives as a Marlowe-esque private eye, who, having researched the case minutely, now denounces the earlier account as deliberate and wilful fraud by a tired man at the end of his life. Not so, says a third researcher, whose startling arrival is only further enhanced when it becomes clear that we are being harangued by a youthful Janet Street-Porter. Again, she has researched the case, uncovered further witnesses and proven that Meriel was the genuine article. Next, we meet the woman who claims that as a child 'played' Meriel during the séance. Then a psychologist who, in a wry commentary on the predilections of armchair Freudians, boils the whole case down to the original researcher's sexual frustration (which borders virtually on the paedophilic according to this reading).

The Daedalus Equations covers similar ground, which is a shame, as it's not as effective – genuine mathematical equations from a deceased scientist are being delivered from the spirit world to a psychic. But she is a demonstrable fraud who, just to complicate matters, is in it just for the money. And yet the equations continue to come. . .

The Love of a Good Woman is the only entry in the canon to border on the dull side, while *Stones* is the closest to a traditional ghost story. All the paraphernalia is present and correct – ancient curses, stone circles and indecipherable inscriptions. Throw in a great cameo by John Wells and you've onto a winner, but it's *The Man with the Power* that really stands out – alongside *Meriel*, it's worth the price of admission on its own. This is an audacious tale of the second coming of (a black) Christ who spends 30 days in the wilderness of a dingy flat while being tempted by Satan – whose evil tricks vary from homosexuality to some cheap visual effects.

Also worthy of a mention are the two editions of *Playhouse* that preceded the series – *Mrs Acland's Ghosts* is sturdy enough, but it's the adaptation of du Maurier's *The Breakthrough* that wins top honours. Bleak and haunting, the production drips with atmosphere from start to finish, as a research team on a lonely island probe the mysteries of life after death – and succeed in capturing the soul of a dying man. This edition contains some stunning filmic iconography, in particular shots of a girl with learning difficulties (possibly affected by the death of her twin) pushing a rackety pram along a deserted beach. The moment where she piles stones on top of the dolly within until its face is completely submerged is undeniably shocking.

The Pogles

Animation | Smallfilms for BBC One | episode duration 10 mins | broadcast 7 Apr 1966–4 Jan 1968

Regular Voice Cast
Oliver Postgate · *Narrator, Amos Pogle*
Olwen Griffiths · *Edna Pogle, Pippin*
Steve Woodman · *Plant, Tog*

Creators/Producers Oliver Postgate and Peter Firmin **Writer** Oliver Postgate **Theme Music** Vernon Elliott

The Pogles (not to be confused with the dentally challenged Irish folk band The Pogues) were tiny woodland folk who lived in an old tree stump deep within Pogles' Wood. When a fairy-child is left on their doorstep, Amos and Edna Pogle adopt him as their own and call him Pippin. Other inhabitants of the wood include the Pipecleaner family, who live in a slide-top pencil box, and the rather odd looking woodland sprite Tog, who looks like a tailless squirrel/rabbit hybrid and who speaks in a manner not unlike Bill and Ben. Occasionally the Pogles explore the woods and discover the wonders of nature, and sometimes their neighbour, the Magic Plant, tells them all a story.

From the wonderfully creative minds of Oliver Postgate and Peter Firmin, the men responsible for ***Clangers***, ***Ivor the Engine*** and ***Bagpuss***, this gorgeous stop-motion series ran for six episodes, telling the story of an evil shape-shifting witch who spent her time trying to steal the Pogles' magical crown. Deemed too scary for the *Watch with Mother* slot it had been commissioned for, *The Pogles* was instead shown within the children's cinema series *Clapperboard*. A second series, *Pogles' Wood*, finally made it to *Watch with Mother* and ran for a further 26 episodes.

Points of View

Feedback | BBC One | episode duration 5–25 mins | broadcast 2 Oct 1961–24 Aug 1971, 31 Aug 1979–present

Principal Cast
Robert Robinson, Sarah War, Gaynor Morgan-Rees, Cathy McGowan, Kenneth Robinson, Barry Took, Anne Robinson, Carol Vorderman, Eamonn Holmes, Terry Wogan · *Presenters*

Theme Music There have been many themes, but one particularly charming one was inspired by a line from The Beatles 'When I'm 64', in which Paul McCartney sang, 'Send me a postcard, drop me a line/Stating point of view'.

Viewers' letters and phone calls on the content of BBC programmes became the focus for the first edition of *Points of View*, hosted by Robert Robinson. It became famous for outpourings of scorn and moans from people who would insist on asking 'Why, oh why, oh why . . .?' or insisting that, though they were not prudes, they were utterly disgusted by such-and-such a programme. *Junior Points of View* was shown from 1963 to 1970, though some editions were clearly steered by letters from parents on behalf of their little ones. Barry Took resurrected the series in 1979 (although the series was only shown in the southeast region until 1980), with a ten-minute format that sat just before the *Nine O'Clock News*. Eventually the theatrical actors who read out the letters were phased out in favour of the letter being voiced by its author.

Though it's by far the most enduring of the feedback shows, *Points of View* is not the only one to have graced our screens. With the arrival of Channel 4 came *Right to Reply*, where viewers were given the same resources as the TV companies to help them make their own short videos illustrating their points. The viewers were then invited into the studio to meet the people who had upset them (with hilarious results . . . not really). In 1985, BBC One's weekday daytime schedule included a live discussion programme called *Open Air*. Hosted by, among others, Bob Wellings, Patti Caldwell and Eamonn Holmes, the show invited viewers to put their complaints direct to the programme makers and channel controllers – in fact, just as *Points of View* had done in the 1960s. A similar arena-style show, *Biteback*, invited the viewers of the 1990s to have a go, with host Phillip Schofield trying to diffuse the mood of the mobs.

In recent years, with the prominence of the Beeb's website forums providing an arena for 'disgusted of Tunbridge Wells', *Points of View* has been relegated to a Sunday late-afternoon slot, with the ever-genial Terry Wogan introducing the letters.

Poldark

Drama | BBC One | episode duration 50 mins | broadcast 5 Oct 1975–4 Dec 1977, 3 Oct 1996

Regular Cast
Robin Ellis · *Ross Poldark*
Angharad Rees · *Demelza Poldark*
Jill Townsend · *Elizabeth Chynoweth/Poldark/Warleggan*
Nicholas Selby · *Nicholas Warleggan*
Frank Middlemass · *Charles Poldark*
Clive Francis · *Francis Poldark*
David Garfield · *Jacka Hoblyn*
Norma Streader · *Verity Poldark*
Paul Curran · *Jud Paynter*
John Blythe · *Constable Vage*
Mary Wimbush · *Prudie Paynter*
Tilly Tremayne · *Ellen*
Eric Dodson · *Reverend Johns*
Cynthia Grenville · *Constance Bodrugan*
John Baskcomb · *Nathaniel 'Nat' Pearce*
Ruth Trouncer · *Mrs Chynoweth*
Jonathan Newth · *Captain Blamey*
Forbes Collins · *Zacky Martin*
Stuart Doughty · *Jim Carter*
Gillian Bailey · *Jinny Martin*
Richard Morant · *Dr Dwight Enys*
Ralph Bates · *George Warleggan*
Martin Fisk · *Mark Daniel*
Sheila White · *Keren Daniel*
Barry Jackson · *Charlie Kempthorne*
Judy Geeson · *Caroline Penvenen*
Christopher Benjamin · *Sir Hugh Bodrugan*
Donald Douglas · *Captain Malcolm McNeil*
Ralph Nossek · *Harris Pascoe*
Clifford Parrish · *Sir John Trevaunance*
Don Henderson · *Tom Carne*
Philip Madoc · *Sir Henry Bull*
Peter Miles · *Manners*
John Ringham · *Henshawe*

Producer Morris Barry **Writers** Jack Pulman, Jack Russell, Paul Wheeler, Peter Draper, from the novels by Winston Graham
Theme Music Kenyon Emrys-Roberts

A hugely popular early evening drama series based upon the four novels by Winston Graham, *Poldark* captured the imaginations of a whole generation of viewers, entranced by the beautiful Cornish settings for the series and the epic romance portrayed in the show. The series began with

Captain Ross Poldark returning home to Cornwall after having fought in the American War of Independence. Eager to win back the attentions of his true love Elizabeth Chynoweth, Ross is shocked to discover that Elizabeth is now in love with his cousin Francis. Ross then decides to restore his father's ruined estate Nampara, and goes on to cause much shock and consternation in the local community by marrying a lowly miner's daughter called Demelza. Soon Ross finds himself locked in a power struggle with the cruel and ambitious George Warleggan, a conflict that will have major implications for both of them...

With a powerful, romantic backdrop that could have come straight out of Daphne Du Maurier's *Jamaica Inn*, *Poldark* was screened in 22 countries around the globe and inspired many people to read the original source novels. The first season of 16 episodes used up all of the plotlines of Winston Graham's books, so when the time came to commission a second season, the BBC worked closely with Graham to devise the ongoing storylines for his characters – sensibly, Graham then worked these storylines into two new novels. Despite a large and vocal fan following (and Graham publishing still more novels in the *Poldark* series – 12 in total), the saga drew to an end after just two series.

Fans were delighted when it was announced that ITV was to broadcast a TV movie based on Graham's eighth *Poldark* novel, *The Stranger from the Sea*. Despite the presence of an impressive cast – John Bowe, Mel Martin and Ioan Gruffudd – the finished product most definitely did not live up to their expectations and is viewed by most *Poldark* fans as an abject mistake.

Website

www.poldark.org.uk/index.html gives details of the *Poldark* TV series and Winston Graham's novels (including his other work, such as *Marnie*, which was filmed by Alfred Hitchcock in 1964).

Pole to Pole

See AROUND THE WORLD IN 80 DAYS

Police Squad!

Comedy | Zucker/Zucker/Abrahams/Paramount for ABC (shown on ITV) | episode duration 25 mins | broadcast 4 Mar–8 Jul 1982 (USA)

Principal Cast

Leslie Nielsen · *Detective Frank Drebin*
Alan North · *Captain Ed Hocken*
Rex Hamilton · *Abraham Lincoln*
Ed Williams · *Ted Olson, Scientist*
William Duell · *Johnny the Snitch*
Peter Lupus · *Norberg*

Creators Jerry Zucker, David Zucker, Jim Abrahams **Producers** Jim Abrahams, David Zucker, Jerry Zucker (executive), Rich Correlli, Deborah Hwang (associate), Robert K. Weiss **Writers** Jim Abrahams, David Zucker, Jerry Zucker, Deborah Hwang, Robert Wuhl, Robert K. Weiss, Tino Insana, David Misch, Pat Proft, Nancy Steen, Neil Thompson **Theme Music** Ira Newborn

Though ***Monty Python***'s John Cleese has often asserted that the three rules of comedy are 'No puns, no puns and no puns', it often depends on how the rules are broken. Creators of the *Airplane* films Jim Abrahams and Jerry and David Zucker have been responsible for some of the side-splittingest pun-abusage of all time.

In *Police Squad!*, Detective Frank Drebin of the Los Angeles Police Department is our hero and narrator, delivering deadpan, Chandleresque voiceovers dripping with irony and contradiction. Each episode featured a real celebrity guest star, though their only contribution was to be brutally murdered before the end of the opening title sequence (Lorne Greene is stabbed and then thrown out of a moving car; William Shatner escapes a shoot-out only to drink a glass of poisoned wine; Florence Henderson from ***The Brady Bunch*** is riddled with bullets). The episode titles never matched what appeared on screen – it might say 'A Substantial Gift' but the narrator claims it's 'The Broken Promise'. And, of course, as the cast took their places for the freeze-frame ending, the frame wouldn't freeze – they'd all just stand in position, leaving their criminal to escape or their pot of coffee to keep on pouring – and all without the burden of a laughter track. Priceless.

Shockingly, *Police Squad!* bombed on its first appearance and ran to just six episodes, but under the banner of *Naked Gun* it later spawned a hugely successful run of films all based on the same premise – there's no such thing as too silly.

Pop Idol

Reality TV/Talent Show | 19 TV and Pearson Television | episode duration 50 mins, plus shorter 'results' show | broadcast 5 Oct 2001–present

Principal Cast

Anthony McPartlin, Declan Donnelly · Pop Idol *Presenters*
Simon Cowell, Pete Waterman, Nicki Chapman, Neil Fox · Pop Idol *Judges*
Will Young · Pop Idol *Winner, 2002*
Michelle McManus · Pop Idol *Winner, 2004*

Creator Simon Fuller **Producers** Various, including Simon Fuller, Nigel Lythgoe, Richard Holloway (executive) **Theme Music** Cathy Dennis

For commentary, see POPSTARS

Popstars

Documentary/Reality TV/Talent Show | ITV | episode duration 25–50 mins | broadcast 10 Jan 2001–present

Principal Cast
Paul Adams, Nicki Chapman, Nigel Lythgoe · Popstars *Judges*
Danny Foster, Myleene Klass, Kym Marsh, Suzanne Shaw, Noel Sullivan, · Popstars *Winners as Hear'Say*
Davina McCall · Popstars: The Rivals *Presenter*
Pete Waterman, Geri Halliwell, Louis Walsh · Popstars: The Rivals *Judges*
Nadine Coyle, Sarah Harding, Nicola Roberts, Cheryl Tweedy, Kimberley Walsh · Popstars: The Rivals *Winners as Girls Aloud*

Producers Various, including Nigel Lythgoe, Jennifer Heftler, Des Monaghan, Scott A. Stone, David G. Stanley, Lisa Page (executive)
Theme Music David Foster

It began as an Australian show that led to the creation of girlband True Bliss. When *Popstars* came to ITV, the decision was out of our hands as the judges had already chosen their winners and the judges' decision was final. The search for five talented young singers resulted in the formation of Hear'say (a name chosen by the final members of the group: Danny, Kim, Mylene, Noel, Suzanne) and a string of hits – including 'Pure and Simple' – before internal group politics, Kim's departure, a rather suspect audition for a replacement and an under-performing fourth single brought the dream to an end. The five finalists who didn't make it later formed Liberty X and continue to be one of the UK's biggest pop acts. Liberty X's success sent a clear message to the judges of *Popstars*: at the end of the day, it's the public who gets to decide. For ITV's next big talent contest, that's exactly what happened.

Pop Idol was the show that set the format for every talent show since. From thousands of hopefuls, shortlists are created, with the winners of each round (voted for by the public) entering the finals. None of the contestants are prisoners: every one of them is a number. For the final, those numbers are even more important as each week the hopeful with the least number of votes is ejected until finally we have a winner. Throughout the selection process and the live finals, our hosts are Ant and Dec, former child stars whose partnership has made them TV's top light entertainment hosts.

Will Young became the first *Pop Idol* winner, beating Gareth Gates thanks to a distinctive singing style (something most of the contenders lack) and a decent performance of Jose Feliciano's cover of The Doors' 'Light my Fire'. Will, like Hear'Say, scored a No. 1 with the song given to him to perform by the judges – he's since had great success with self-penned hits like 'Leave Right Now' and 'Your Game'.

It wasn't until Young's victory was announced as 'the winner of *Pop Idol* 2002' that ITV's scheduling strategy became clear – these shows had become ratings gold and would be returning to screens for years to come. *Popstars* returned soon after *Pop Idol* finished, but with a difference – '*The Rivals*' would create two acts, a boyband and a girlband, but with Boyzone/Westlife manager Louis Walsh mentoring the girls and pop legend Pete Waterman guiding the boys. Arbitrating between the two was former Spice Girl Geri Halliwell. Girls Aloud won, leaving One True Voice (the 'male vocal harmony group') dumped within months.

In 2004, *Pop Idol* judge Simon Cowell came up with a spin on the format that would silence the show's critics. ***The X Factor*** had no upper age limit and acts could be groups as well as soloists (though the focus was still on singing rather than playing an instrument, and definitely not open to rappers). Louis Walsh returned alongside Sharon Osbourne, who quickly became the real star of the show as she combined the warmth and passion that the other two lacked with a surprisingly vicious streak.

And so the machine continues, very much in the traditions of older talent shows like ***Opportunity Knocks*** and *New Faces* but with a more cynical edge. Now the viewers know they're in control. As Pete Waterman noted on the *Pop Idol* final that elevated Michelle McManus, few of these shows are solely about finding talent; now, it's as much an examination of voting patterns.

Porridge

See pages 568–70

Porterhouse Blue

Comedy Drama| Channel 4 | episode duration 50 mins | broadcast 3–24 Jun 1987

Regular Cast
David Jason · *Skullion*
Ian Richardson · *Sir Godber Evans*
John Sessions · *Lionel Zipser*
Charles Gray · *Sir Cathcart D'Eath*
Griff Rhys Jones · *Cornelius Carrington*
Paul Rogers · *Dean*
John Woodnutt · *Senior Tutor*
Harold Innocent · *Bursar*
Paula Jacobs · *Mrs Biggs*
Barbara Jefford · *Lady Mary Evans*
Ian Wallace · *Praelector*
Willoughby Goddard · *Professor Siblington*
Lockwood West · *Chaplain*
Bob Goody · *Walter*
John Rogan · *Chef*
Roy Evans · *Arthur*

Producer Brian Eastman **Writer** Malcolm Bradbury, from the novel by Tom Sharpe **Theme Music** '*Dives in Omnia*' ('There's Money in Everything') by Rick Lloyd, performed *a capella* by the Flying Pickets

Continued on page 571

Porridge

Mr Mackay points out a few rules to Fletch and Godber.

Ronnie Barker was already a familiar face to British TV audiences by the time *Porridge* came to our screens. A regular on shows like *The Frost Report* (a satirical news show fronted by David Frost) and, with comedy partner Ronnie Corbett, one half of ***The Two Ronnies***, Barker displayed a knack for accents and unparalleled comic timing. As part of the deal in poaching Barker from LWT (a division of the ITV network), the BBC lined up a number of projects for him, which included *Seven of One*, a series of seven stand-alone half-hour plays created with the hope of finding a new long-running sitcom for him to star in. In among the selected batch was ***Open All Hours***, a script by Roy Clarke (creator of ***Last of the Summer Wine***) about a stuttering shopkeeper that would eventually be taken up for series in 1976, and two from writing duo Dick Clement and Ian La Frenais – 'I'll Fly You for a Quid', about a family of gamblers, and 'Prisoner and Escort'. Although Barker's personal favourite was 'I'll Fly You for a Quid', Clement and La Frenais's prison idea particularly lent itself to an ongoing story and so became the first to be developed into a series.

Broadcast seventh in the run, on 1 April 1973, 'Prisoner and Escort' saw Barker as Norman Stanley Fletcher, a convicted criminal travelling to Cumbria with his escorts, two prison wardens called Mackay and Barrowclough. Whereas Barrowclough is a gentle, forgiving man who believes that prison's aim is rehabilitation, for Mackay it's purely about punishment. Well-known character actors Brian Wilde and Fulton Mackay were cast as the wardens.

Clement and La Frenais considered 'Stir' and 'Inside' as a title for the show before settling on *Porridge* – slang for a stretch in prison (so called because of the porridge-like gruel that used to be served up in prison kitchens). Coincidentally, Ronnie Barker had also come up with the same name, which convinced all concerned that it was the right way to go. Worried that they might not be able to find the comedy in a prison stretch without trivialising crime or depressing the audience, the writers consulted Jonathan Marshall, author of *How to Survive in the Nick*, who described to them the language of the prisoners themselves – terms such as 'screw' for a warden, or 'snout'

Comedy
BBC Two
Episode Duration: 30 mins
Broadcast: 1 Apr 1973, 5 Sep 1974–25 Mar 1977

Regular Cast
Ronnie Barker · *Norman Stanley 'Fletch' Fletcher*
Richard Beckinsale · *Lennie Godber*
Fulton Mackay · *Mr Mackay*
Brian Wilde · *Mr Barrowclough*
Michael Barrington · *Governor Venables*
Sam Kelly · *'Bunny' Warren*
Peter Vaughan · *'Genial' Harry Grout*
Ken Jones · *'Horrible' Ives*
Christopher Biggins · *'Lukewarm' Lewis*
David Jason · *'Blanco' Webb*
Patricia Brake · *Ingrid Fletcher*
Ronald Lacey · *Harris*
Maurice Denham · *Judge Rawley*
Tony Osoba · *McLaren*
Brian Glover · *Heslop*
Ray Dunbobbin · *Evans*
Eric Dodson · *Banyard*

Creators/Writers Dick Clement and Ian La Frenais

Producer Sydney Lotterby

Theme Music While the opening sequence of each episode featured a voice-over re-creating the judge sentencing Fletcher to five years, Max Harris provided the tune that ran over the end credits.

for tobacco – and the routine of prison life: how prisoners tend to keep themselves going by looking for the 'little victories' each day, like obtaining extra helpings of food, managing to get an easy job for their prison tasks or just winning at cards. These 'little victories' would ultimately become the driving force behind the show.

The pilot had been a three-hander character study, but the series would have to become more of an ensemble. Pivotal to the expanded cast was the part of a first-time inmate called Lennie Godber. Having two old-timers as the main characters might make any explanations seem fake or forced, so Clement and La Frenais decided to create a character who needed to have things explained to him. It would fall to Fletch to show Lennie how to survive in prison and how to get the most of his time there; how to score those 'little victories'. One of the best examples of this comes in the episode 'A Night In', where Fletch and Lennie talk after 'lights out'. Fletch's experience comes to the fore as he tries to cheer the spirits of his depressed young cellmate. For Lennie, Ronnie Barker had suggested Paul Henry – familiar to TV viewers as Benny from the soap opera ***Crossroads*** yet not yet typecast as he would become – but producer and director of the series, Sydney Lotterby, suggested the actor Richard Beckinsale, who had starred in the romantic comedy ***The Lovers***. Beckinsale was a popular choice, bringing an honesty and believability to a difficult role.

The expanded cast also included Sam Kelly (who would later appear in the World War Two-based comedy ***'Allo, 'Allo***) as the illiterate Warren, Christopher Biggins as the gay cook, 'Lukewarm' (so named because by the time he served up the evening meal it would be near-cold), and Peter Vaughan as Harry Grout. Though he actually appears in just three episodes, Grouty's menace and influence runs throughout the series, representing the ever-present threat that prisoners faced from each other. Mr Venables might have been the governor, but it was the Godfather-like Harry Grout that ruled Slade Prison. A vicious, intimidating man, he had his own cell and a network of informers who kept him in touch with everything going on inside. An illegal card game could not progress until Grouty had given his permission and stated his cut of the prize money.

An ironic twist of fate brought a new face to Slade Prison in the third series with the episode 'Poetic Justice'. Rawley (played superbly by the veteran actor Maurice Denham) is an elderly man, but to Fletcher he is much more than that; he is the judge who sent Fletch to prison in the first place. Sentenced to three years after being found guilty of corruption, Rawley was later released after his appeal was accepted. The news comes as no surprise to Fletch, especially considering Rawley and the governor are old friends.

One of the cleverest and most surprising stories came in series two with 'Happy Release', which saw the 63-year-old convict 'Blanco' (played under heavy make-up by a very youthful David Jason) released from prison after gaining a pardon for a crime he always maintained he didn't commit – the murder of his wife. Blanco had always claimed that it was his wife's lover who had murdered her and finally, after 16 years, the authorities believed him and granted him his freedom. Before he departs, Blanco tells Fletcher that it was true that he hadn't killed his wife, though – he reveals in confidence to a stunned Fletch – he did kill her lover.

In the BBC's 2004 survey to find Britain's best sitcom, *Porridge* came in at a respectable No. 7. Many would argue that it deserved to be much higher. While its debt to shows like ***Steptoe and Son*** are clear, *Porridge* was still a groundbreaker in its own right, focusing on a type of largely working-class character who is generally not thought to be suitable for comic relief, unless played as a horrific Jewish stereotype in a performance of *Oliver*. *Porridge* never seeks to disguise that these men are habitual criminals, but neither does it set out to dehumanise them either. It could never depict in gory detail the true horrors of a shared cell with a shared toilet, the outbreaks of violence, bad language and the genuine terror that many experience once they're the other side of those huge iron gates. But it comes close, with Lennie Godber's rite of passage steered by Fletch, with the terrified reactions of the inmates towards Grouty that convey a threat that never needs to be enacted. Few TV programmes get to add a new swearword to the language, but *Porridge* gave us two, 'nurk' (as in 'charmless nurk') and 'naff' (as in 'naff off'). That last one was even heard coming from the lips of Princess Anne, y'know. (The trick of creating a new swearword was emulated by the creators of ***Red Dwarf*** with the word 'smeg' 15 years later.) As for the inconvenience of sharing an 8 × 12 with another man for three years, how many other sitcoms could claim to be the first to make masturbation the subject of an entire episode without once even alluding to it? Why else do you think Fletch was so eager to be left alone in the season two finale, 'No Peace for the Wicked'?

After 20 episodes of the series (including two Christmas specials), Ronnie Barker decided to move on. In the final episode Lennie is released, leaving Fletch to serve out the rest of his sentence with a new cellmate. Lennie has one final bombshell for Fletch, however – he's now dating Fletch's daughter, Ingrid!

Fletch did get the chance to ride again in both a six-part sequel – ***Going Straight*** – as well as a feature film, which finished filming shortly before the untimely death of Richard Beckinsale at just 31. Then in 2003, the mockumentary series *Life Beyond the Box* had as its subject Norman Stanley Fletcher. Re-creating Fletcher's early life (with Gareth Farr delivering an eerily accurate portrayal as Fletch), the programme also caught up with many of his old inmates, including Bunny Warren, now working as a sign writer for 'Bowlton Sity Kownsil', McLaren a successful businessmen and Ives running a charity scam raising money for 'blind doggies'. Patricia Brake once again played Fletcher's daughter Ingrid, still married to Lennie (though he remains unseen), and as a lovely final surprise, Ronnie Barker himself appeared as Fletch, living out his retirement in Muswell Hill in luxury, thanks (it's heavily implied) to the spoils of a bank robbery bequeathed to him by Harry Grout before his death. As we left Fletch for probably the final time, he sang us out at a local karaoke pub with 'You Belong to Me', the 1953 Jo Stafford tune that he often hummed while in Slade Prison.

TRIVIA

As often happens with successful British shows, Clement and La Frenais were able to sell the format of *Porridge* to America in the form of *On the Rocks*, a 22-part sitcom for the ABC network. What was unusual about this particular show, though, was that after they had adapted the initial run of episodes, Clement and La Frenais were forced to write new ones for the American series, which – as they were working on both shows almost simultaneously – they then rewrote for the British version.

WEBSITE

www.porridge.org.uk

The bawdy comic novels of Tom Sharpe had already enjoyed almost two decades of popular appeal before BBC One launched an adaptation of ***Blott on the Landscape*** onto an unwitting public. Although *Blott* had undoubtedly been a success, Channel 4 took the opportunity of adapting one of Sharpe's most celebrated novels, *Porterhouse Blue*. Hiring the same production and writing team that had worked on the earlier *Blott*, Channel 4 was able to splash out a bit more money on the series, creating a far glossier and more polished four-part adaptation.

At Porterhouse College, Cambridge, tradition permeates every single fibre of the students, staff and building itself. Steadfastly rejecting any form of modernisation, the college prides itself on its poor academic reputation, success on the sports field and – most importantly – the quality of the 'gentlemen' it produces. However, Porterhouse is shaken to its very foundations when its elderly vice-chancellor dies from a stroke (a 'Porterhouse Blue') without naming his successor. Following ancient rules, the Prime Minister has to make the appointment – and to the utter horror of all of the elderly college staff, the new vice-chancellor is named as former Porterhouse man Sir Godber Evans. Sir Godber is a socially aware reformer who is disgusted by the excess, crudity and stubbornness on display in the college. On his first day, he promises to scrap the legendary 'Feasts' (including swans and a roast boar!), improve the academic standards within college and – most controversial of all – make Porterhouse co-educational. Although the staff are shocked, it's college porter Skullion who is most outraged by Sir Godber's reforms, and he vows to do everything he can to prevent his beloved Porterhouse from changing.

In one of his first 'serious' roles (albeit one heavily laced with dark, dark comedy), David Jason excels as the tradition-worshipping Skullion, a man whose depths of plotting and double-dealing know no bounds. Without this performance he'd have almost certainly never stood a chance to star in a leading role like the grumpy detective in ***A Touch of Frost***, and considering ***Only Fools and Horses*** was at its peak at the time, it's a minor miracle the BBC let him out on such a long lead. The ever-marvellous Ian Richardson's portrayal of Sir Godber is lower key than his legendary Tory chief whip Francis Urquhart in the ***House of Cards*** trilogy, but only just. *Porterhouse Blue* is a much more assured and all-round successful adaptation than *Blott on the Landscape*, and moments such as the ill-fated Zipser's lustful fantasies about his matronly cleaner, and the hilariously perverse way in which he meets his maker (courtesy of hundreds of gas-filled condoms) linger long in the memory.

Portland Bill

Animation | FilmFair/ Central for ITV | episode duration 10 mins | broadcast 1983–6

Voice Cast

Norman Rossington · *Narrator, Character Voices*

Creator John Grace **Producers** Graham Clutterbuck (executive), John Grace, Barrie Edwards **Writers** John Grace, Ian Sachs **Theme Music** Mik Parsons, John Grace

Here's a novelty: a TV show where all the characters are named after locations listed in the UK Shipping Forecast. Portland Bill is a lighthouse keeper on Guillemot Rock, the perfect remote location for a bagpipe-player like himself. Bill shares the lighthouse with Cromarty, a rather clumsy amateur inventor and fan of retro fashions, and young Ross, who likes to spend time fishing as it indulges his habit of daydreaming. Fourth member of the team is Dogger, Bill's dog.

Other characters include residents of McGuillycuddy, a village on the mainland. It's there that we meet Finisterre the crofter, Ronaldsway the lighthouse inspector, Edward Stones, owner of the village shop (the grandly named Edward Stones Emporium) and part-time policeman, postman and many other roles (he keeps the different hats for each job on the front of his bike), and villagers Mrs Lundy and Grandma Tiree.

Portland Bill offered an enchanting world in the style of ***Postman Pat***, brought to us by FilmFair using 'stop motion' animation. The series was the work of John Grace, research fellow in animation studies at Loughborough University School of Art and Design. Each episode contained two short stories bridged by nautically themed songs written by Mik Parsons and John Grace. Two series were made, each lasting 13 episodes.

Postman Pat

Animation | Woodland Animations for BBC One | episode duration 15 mins | broadcast 16 Sep 1981–14 Oct 2004

Cast

Ken Barrie · *Narrator, Voice Characters*

Creator/Writer John Cunliffe **Producer** Ivor Wood **Theme Music** Written by Bryan Daly, sung by Ken Barrie

Postman Pat is another classic show that brought a new generation of fans to discover Ivor Wood's stop-motion talents. This time the hero was a friendly postman called Pat Clifton who drove around the Lake District village of Greendale with his black-and-white cat, Jess. Each episode would introduce us to the residents of the village, including Granny Dryden, Mrs Goggins the postmistress, the Reverend Timms and Tim and Katie, twins. Pat's daily routine would sometimes be disturbed by sheep blocking the road, or wind blowing his letters away.

The original *Postman Pat* series ran for just 13 episodes, but popular demand has seen him return in specials and later series thanks to Cosgrove Hall, the team behind ***Chortlon and the Wheelies*** and ***Danger Mouse***.

p

Pot Black

Sport/Game Show | BBC Two | duration various | broadcast 23 Jul 1969–17 Apr 1986

Cast

Ted Lowe · *Commentator*
Keith Macklin, Alan Weeks, David Icke, David Vine, Eamonn Holmes · *Hosts*

Pot Black Champions Ray Reardon (1969), John Spencer (1970), John Spencer (1971), Eddie Charlton (1972), Eddie Charlton (1973), Graham Miles (1974), Graham Miles (1975), John Spencer (1976), Perrie Mans (1977), Doug Mountjoy (1978), Ray Reardon (1979), Eddie Charlton (1980), Cliff Thorburn (1981), Steve Davis (1982), Steve Davis (1983), Terry Griffiths (1984), Doug Mountjoy (1985), Jimmy White (1986), Steve Davis (1991)

Creator Philip Lewis **Producers** Philip Lewis, Reg Perrin, David Kenning, John G. Smith **Theme Music** 'The Black and White Rag' by George Botsford, performed by Winifred Atwell

Pot Black emerged out of a number of limitations and two conflicting remits for BBC Two. At its inception, the channel was to make the most of the new 625-line picture format in anticipation of colour transmissions, and take every advantage to broadcast in colour. However, it also had to ensure that its programmes could be watched by those viewers who had already invested money in the expensive new black-and-white, 625-line TV sets.

Most of the major sporting fixtures were already evenly divided between BBC One and ITV, but broadcast in black and white. With colour cameras still some way off from being widespread, any programme intended for colour broadcast would have to make best use of the limited cameras available. The suggestion came from the BBC's Sports department that with the arrival of colour, the corporation could finally begin showing snooker, a sport that had always caused problems with its reliance on being able to identify the colour of each ball in play (leading to the probably apocryphal story of whispering commentator Ted Lowe saying, 'And for those of you watching in black and white, the pink is next to the green'), plus three cameras at different positions (one either side of the table, one looking down onto it) could capture all of the action. The format for the series would be a sporting event unique to BBC Two – handily avoiding a bidding war – in which world-class snooker players would compete in a single-frame knock-out tournament that could run for weeks, pre-recorded and edited as necessary. An immediate success, it further established BBC Two as an innovator while capturing an audience that might not have been drawn to the highbrow documentaries or period melodrama of ***The Forsyte Saga***.

Soon, snooker was everywhere, becoming one of the biggest causes of complaint as programmes later in the schedule would be delayed or cancelled while Cliff Thorburn took forever to work his way round a frame. With access to 'proper' world-class tournaments, *Pot Black* had outlived its quirky usefulness and came to an end after the 1986 tournament. *Junior Pot Black* ran from 1981 to 1985, while the game was revived in 1991 as *Pot Black Timeframe*, hosted by Eamonn Holmes.

Press Gang

See pages 574–6

The Price is Right

Game Show | Central/Talbot/Yorkshire for ITV | episode duration 25 mins | broadcast 1984–1988, 1989 *The Price is Right*, 1995–2001 (*Bruce's Price is Right*)

Cast

Leslie Crowther, Bob Warman, Bruce Forsyth · *Hosts*
Simon Prebble, Peter Dickson · *Voice-overs*
Marie Elise, Jacqueline Bucknell, Julia Roberts, Cindy Day, Gillian de Terville, Judy Bailey, Denise Kelly, Kimberley Cowell, Emma Noble, Emma Steadman, Lea Kristensen, Brian Tattersall, Simon Peat · *Models*

Creators Mark Goodson, Bill Todman, Bob Stewart **Producers** William G. Stewart, Howard Huntridge

The consumer's dream game show, *The Price is Right* came from America, where it had been a hit since 23 November 1956. Cockney entertainer Joe Brown hosted a pilot for the British series, but über-slick Leslie Crowther got the presenting gig for the actual show and brought with him the closest thing to an American game-show host that Britain had ever seen. Some criticised the show for glamorising greed, but this was the 1980s and everyone was at it.

Four members of the audience would be invited to 'Come on down' to take part in an auction for items on display. Players could freeze their bids or continue to outbid each other until the end of the round when the player closest to the actual price of the item – without overbidding – would be taking home the prize. The final winner would be the one who amassed the biggest hoard of booty over the course of the show. The game show had other elements to it though, with mini-games loosely based on seaside carnival activities like mini-golf or slot machines, where players who'd won the most money began the game with more playing discs with which to activate the game.

After a brief spell on Sky, the series returned to ITV in 1995 now hosted by the king of the game show Bruce Forsythe – *Bruce's Price is Right*.

Pride and Prejudice

Drama | BBC/A&E for BBC One | episode duration 55 mins | broadcast 24 Sep–29 Oct 1995

Principal Cast
Colin Firth · *Mr Fitzwilliam Darcy*
Jennifer Ehle · *Miss Elizabeth Bennet*
Alison Steadman · *Mrs Bennet*
Susannah Harker · *Miss Jane Bennet*
Julia Sawalha · *Lydia Bennet*
Benjamin Whitrow · *Mr Bennet*
Crispin Bonham-Carter · *Mr Charles Bingley*
Anna Chancellor · *Miss Caroline Bingley*
Barbara Leigh-Hunt · *Lady Catherine de Bourgh*
Adrian Lukis · *Mr George Wickham*
David Bamber · *Mr Collins*
Christopher Benjamin · *Sir William Lucas*
Joanna David · *Mrs Gardiner*
Emilia Fox · *Georgiana Darcy*
Rupert Vansittart · *Mr Hurst*

Producers Michael Wearing (executive), Julie Scott (associate), Sue Birtwistle **Writers** Andrew Davies, from the novel by Jane Austen **Theme music** Carl Davis

Pride and Prejudice is probably the UK's most beloved novel, having come second in the BBC's 2003 *The Big Read* competition (pipped to the post by *The Lord of the Rings*, then enjoying a huge boost in popularity courtesy of the movie adaptations making huge waves in cinemas). It's therefore not really surprising to discover that the story has been made into a television series on no less than five separate occasions. The first version was a 55-minute-long play broadcast on 22 May 1938, just two years after the start of BBC Television, with Curigwen Lewis playing Elizabeth Bennet and Andrew Osborn as Mr Darcy. Eager Jane Austen fans had to wait until well after World War Two for the first serialised adaptation, with a six-part series starring Daphne Slater and future Hammer Horror star Peter Cushing beginning transmission on 2 February 1952. Another six-part adaptation began broadcasting on 10 September 1967, this time featuring Celia Bannerman and Lewis Fiander as the couple destined to be together. A fourth version hit screens on 13 January 1980, this time as a feature-length adaptation starring David Rintoul as Darcy and Elizabeth Garvie as Elizabeth Bennet. However, this wasn't at all well received by critics, and Jane Austen's comedy of manners remained off television screens for a further 15 years.

But the production of *Pride and Prejudice* that was created in 1995 can honestly lay claim to being the most popular, successful and critically acclaimed costume drama in BBC history, collecting a very large handful of international awards and being screened in countries as far apart as Australia, the Netherlands and the USA. Viewers thrilled to the sumptuously filmed goings-on of the Bennet family, empathising with the determined Elizabeth and amused by the behaviour of her parents. It was, however, one particular scene (not featured in the original book) that etched itself into the minds of many viewers – a soaking-wet Mr Darcy rising from the lake. Colin Firth became an overnight heartthrob to a whole country of women of a certain age, even prompting the *Radio Times* to produce a special Darcy poster that viewers could send off for. In fact, so great was the impact of Colin Firth as Mr Darcy that author Helen Fielding based a character in her book *Bridget Jones's Diary* on him – it was a moment of sheer casting bliss when Colin Firth won the role of Darcy in the 2001 movie version of *Bridget Jones*.

Prime Suspect

See pages 577–80

Prince Caspian

See THE CHRONICLES OF NARNIA

The Prisoner

See pages 581–4

Prisoner: Cell Block H

See pages 585–8

The Professionals

See pages 589–91

'P' is continued on page 592

Press Gang

Dexter Fletcher (Spike) and Julia Sawalha (Lynda).

Matt Kerr is a hotshot newspaper man with big ideas for a local paper. He comes up with the idea of the *Junior Gazette* – 'a voice for today's youth' – and recruits pupils from Norbridge to run it. With the help of English teacher Mr Sullivan, he manages to get the cream of the crop – the determined and ruthless Lynda Day, and her moral guides Kenny Phillips and Sarah Jackson. However, Sullivan also wants to use the paper to give some of his more troublesome kids something to focus on – namely Frazz Davies, Danny McColl and an American known as Spike, whose troubled family life has led to him achieving little academic success on either side of the Atlantic.

In 1984, the religious programme ***Highway***, which starred former Goon Harry Secombe, came to a high school in Paisley to film the school choir. During filming, headmaster Bill Moffat showed *Highway*'s executive producer Bill Ward an environmental studies module he'd created based around a school newspaper. Ward decided to show the module – called 'The Norbridge Files' – to Sandra Hastie, an American producer on the verge of jacking it all in and moving back home. Moffat's idea gathered dust and in the meantime his son, Steven, who was also a teacher, began working towards a career as a scriptwriter. When Hastie eventually decided to produce a series based upon Moffat's idea, it was Steven, not Bill, who was contracted to write the scripts. For that, we can all be thankful, as 'The Norbridge Files' evolved into a masterpiece of children's drama – *Press Gang*. Every review of *Press Gang* comes to the same conclusion: in its first two years, the programme managed to prove that it was the best children's drama series we're ever likely to see; in its final three years, it managed to shake off the 'children's' qualifier to be regarded as a very good drama series in its own right. This is one trend we're not looking to buck: *Press Gang* remains unbeaten in its field.

Moffat's influences were more Steve Bochco than E. Nesbit, which is unusual for someone targeting a younger audience. The central love-hate relationship of Spike and Lynda aped ***Moonlighting***'s David and Maddie, resting on a long game of who'd

Children's Drama
Central/Richmond Films & Television for ITV
Episode Duration: 25 mins
Broadcast: 16 Jan 1989–21 May 1993

Regular Cast
Julia Sawalha · *Lynda Day*
Dexter Fletcher · *Spike Thomson*
Paul Reynolds · *Colin Mathews*
Kelda Holmes · *Sarah Jackson*
Lee Ross · *Kenny Phillips*
Lucy Benjamin · *Julie Craig*
Mmoloki Chrystie · *Fraser 'Frazz' Davies*
Joanna Dukes · *Toni 'Tiddler' Tildesley*
Clive Wood · *Matt Kerr*
Nick Stringer · *Mr Sullivan*
Gabrielle Anwar · *Sam Black*
Angela Bruce · *Chrissie Stuart*
David Collings · *Mr Winters*
Andy Crowe · *Billy Homer*
Charlie Creed-Miles · *Danny McColl*
Claire Hearnden · *Laura*
Rosie Marcel · *Sophie*
Sadie Frost · *Jenny Eliot*
Aisling Flitton · *Dublin Girl/Kelly*
Penelope Nice · *Mrs Day*
Claire Forlani · *Judy Wellman*
Christien Anholt · *Donald Cooper*
Hugh Quarshie · *Inspector Hibbert*

Creator Steven Moffat, from an idea by Bill Moffat

Producers Sandra C. Hastie, Bill Ward

Writer Steven Moffat

Theme Music Peter Davis, John Mealing, John G. Perry

get the last word (inevitably Lynda). Moffat's characters reported the real world, but thankfully they didn't live there. These were teenagers who spoke with the self-confidence and wit that no real teen is ever capable of, and as a consequence managed to capture that aspirational desire every young person that age has.

Where *Press Gang* really scored over its stable-mates was in the unpatronising and uncompromising approach it took towards different issues. In the first series, Lynda stands up to a bully who tries to blackmail his way onto the paper's writing team, but when he shoots himself right after hearing Lynda's harsh comments, the repercussions hit hard. A story about the dangers of glue sniffing turns into an attack on the shopkeepers who sell solvents rather than the kids who use them. A child abuse story avoids the traps of sensationalism by having office clown Colin as the one person who identifies a younger child's subconscious cries for help (an impactful approach that won the show a BAFTA). The gun lobby came under the spotlight in 'The Last Word', a two-part story from series three that sees the shocking death of a member of the *Junior Gazette* team at the hands of a clown-masked gunman. And after putting it off for four years, the show took on the subject of drugs in its final episode with a daringly unsympathetic view: when a member of their own team dies of a heroin overdose, Spike argues that they should do a feature for the paper, but Lynda convincingly argues that not only do people do things because they're dangerous but that those kinds of people are losers they can do without. Though Lynda's hard-nosed approach softens in the end, the point is still made more effectively than any number of 'Just Say No' slogans.

The series was not without its lighter moments, even if the wit grew darker as the show matured. Early examples of out-and-out comedy include Colin returning from his little sister's birthday party trapped in a bunny rabbit costume scant minutes before an important meeting with an advertiser (Colin's solution, to announce himself as a bunny-gram falls flat when he learns he's barged into the middle of the advertiser's own funeral); an episode in series four light-heartedly targets children's TV itself, specifically Saturday morning shows that treat the viewer as a 'backward three-year-old with the attention span of a goldfish'; and in the final year, Colin arrives for a date with deputy editor Julie and manages to accidentally kill her dove, goldfish and (apparently) her cat within the space of ten seconds.

Aside from Moffat's scripting, *Press Gang*'s greatest strength lay in its amazingly strong cast. Dexter Fletcher had been a familiar face since playing Baby Face in *Bugsy Malone* (1976), while Lee Ross had led the cast of ***Dodger, Bonzo and the Rest*** (as well as starring in a toothpaste commercial with a catchy re-arrangement of 'Baggy Trousers' by Madness) and Mmoloki Chrystie had recently graduated from ***Grange Hill***. The rest of the leads, though, were largely newcomers, although for many of them this marked the beginning of solid careers. Dexter Fletcher bagged a part in one of the UK's coolest films of the 1990s, *Lock, Stock and Two Smoking Barrels* (1998), and Lee Ross (who left the show after its third year) worked with Mike Leigh on *Secrets & Lies* (1996) and in the first ***Trial and Retribution***. Charlie Creed-Miles starred alongside Ray Winstone as Kathy Burke's drug-dealing brother in *Nil by Mouth* (1997); Gabrielle Anwar left the UK for Hollywood (and almost straight away landed a prominent role in *Scent of a Woman* (1992) as Al Pacino's dance partner); Lucy Benjamin eventually joined the cast of ***EastEnders*** and found herself at the centre of the 'Who Shot Phil Mitchell' storyline; and Paul Reynolds has managed to maintain his reputation for scene stealing in shows like *Maisie Raine* and the films *Let Him Have It* (1991), and *Croupier* (1998). Even guest star Sadie Frost swapped newspapers for vampires in *Bram Stoker's Dracula* (1992).

But it's Julia Sawalha who's really hit the big time. Thanks to the part of put-upon Saffy in ***Absolutely Fabulous***, she's worked with Kenneth Branagh (*In the Bleak Midwinter*, 1995) and Mel Gibson (as the voice of his romantic interest in *Chicken Run*, 2000) and starred in a major adaptation of ***Pride and Prejudice*** (as Lydia Bennet). It's telling that Julia won the Royal Television Society Award for Best Actress in 1993 for her work on *Press Gang*, beating every other performance in 'adult' drama. Like everything else about this 'children's' series, the acting from the lead performer put that of most prime-time programmes to shame.

These were teenagers who spoke with the self-confidence and wit that no real teen is ever capable of, and as a consequence managed to capture that aspirational desire every young person that age has.

Press Gang ended on a cliffhanger. With their offices burned down, it's not clear whether the *Junior Gazette* could have been remounted anyway, but following a change in management at Children's ITV, *Press Gang* was decommissioned in any case. Steve Moffat scripted a 90-minute film that would have placed Spike and Lynda in a TV studio instead of a newsroom but to date the script remains unproduced. Moffat went on to create the hilarious black comedy ***Joking Apart***, the critically underrated ***Chalk*** and the thirty-something comedy ***Coupling*** before joining the writing team on the resurrected ***Doctor Who*** series in 2005. Richmond Films produced the children's dramas *The Lodge*, focusing on the residents of a children's home, and *Wavelength*, a series created by writer (and *Press Gang* fan) Paul Cornell that revolved around a community radio station.

Prime Suspect

Helen Mirren as Jane Tennison.

High-ranking police officer Jane Tennison feels she's being continually passed over for major cases in favour of her male colleagues. So when DCI John Shefford dies of a heart attack while investigating the brutal murder of a prostitute, Tennison demands (with indecent haste) to be given the case. She faces resistance from Shefford's team, led by DI Bill Otley, especially when she realises that the evidence against Shefford's prime suspect, George Marlow, is not as tight as Shefford had thought. With time running out, Tennison is forced to release Marlow and begin the investigation again from square one. But when another body is found bearing identical marks of torture as the first, Tennison realises their murderer might be a serial killer.

Lynda La Plante's next series after ***Widows*** was a long time coming. Written almost on the spur of the moment, *Prime Suspect* catapulted La Plante into the big league as one of Britain's premier writers. It also tapped into an obsession with serial killers kick-started by Jodie Foster's Oscar-winning turn in *Silence of the Lambs* (1990), released the previous year. La Plante, dependable as ever, took a less sensationalist, no-nonsense approach in which the drama's appeal lay in the details, the elements of police procedure we rarely see. We followed every step of the way from the scene of

Drama
Granada Television for ITV
Episode Duration: 50-120/100 mins
Broadcast: 7 Apr 1991-9 Nov 2003 (to date)

Regular Cast
Helen Mirren · *DCI/DCS Jane Tennison*
Tom Bell · *DS Bill Otley*
John Benfield · *DCS Mike Kernan*
John Bowe, Tim Woodward · *George Marlow*
Zoë Wanamaker · *Moyra Henson*
Bryan Pringle · *Felix Norman*
Tom Wilkinson · *Peter Rawlins*
John Forgeham · *DCI John Shefford*
Gary Whelan · *DS Terry Amson*
Jack Ellis · *DI Tony Muddyman*
Craig Fairbrass · *DI Frank Burkin*
Ian Fitzgibbon · *DC Jones*
Mossie Smith · *WPC Maureen Havers*
Philip Wright · *DC Lillie*
Andrew Tiernan · *DC Rosper*
Richard Hawley · *DC Haskons*
Mark Spalding · *DC Oakhill*
Tom Bowles · *DC Avison*
Dave Bond · *DS Eastel*
Seamus O'Neill · *DC Caplan*
Marcus Romer · *DI Caldicott*
Wilfred Harrison, Frank Finlay · *Arnold Tennison*
Noel Dyson · *Mrs Tennison*
Colin Salmon · *DS Robert Oswalde*
Lloyd McGuire · *Sergeant Calder*
Stephen Boxer · *DCI Thorndike*
Claire Benedict · *Esme Allen*
George Harris · *Vernon Allen*
Fraser James · *Tony Allen*
Ashley James · *Cleo Allen*
Junior Laniyan · *David Allen*
Jenny Jules · *Sarah Allen*
Josephine Melville · *Esta*
Tom Watson · *David Harvey*
June Watson · *Eileen Reynolds*
Matt Bardock · *Jason Reynolds*
David Ryall · *Oscar Bream*
Peter Capaldi · *Vera Reynolds*
Greg Saunders · *Colin 'Connie' Jenkins*
David Thewlis · *James Jackson*
Danny Dyer · *Martin Fletcher*
Richard Rees · *Mike Chow*
Terrence Hardiman · *Commander Chiswick*
Mark Strong · *Inspector/Detective Chief Superintendant Larry Hall*
Karen Tomlin · *WPC Norma Hastings*
Struan Rodger · *Superintendent Halliday*
Terence Harvey · *John Kennington*
Lewis Jones · *Judge Syers*
Ciarán Hinds · *Edward Parker-Jones*
Gilbert Wynne · *Frampton*

the crime, through discussions with pathology in the neon strip-lit morgue, to meeting the parents of the victims and eventually honing down the evidence until one suspect remains. Told in three two-hour episodes, the mini-series format allowed La Plante to go much deeper into the mechanics of crime solving than the traditional hour-long episode ever could.

It's not just details of police work that hooked viewers but a cast of highly believable characters. The snide Otley, whose dependence on the Old Boys' network is undermined by Tennison's very presence on the case, nevertheless possesses a commendable side, such as the loyalty he shows towards his late Guv'nor, a loyalty that leads to him being removed from the case. Burly Frank Burkin, pride of the station after winning a charity boxing match, is revealed to be a racist who (it's heavily implied) consorts with prostitutes. Even Jane's own superiors and colleagues, including DCI Thorndike, conspire to restrict her investigations into a suspected murderer. But it's her dogged determination to do a thorough job that finally wins her team onto her side. Shefford might have been a copper of the old school, but they know that Tennison will get results without snatching all the glory for herself.

With *Prime Suspect*, Lynda La Plante can take the credit for once again providing strong parts for women, just as *Widows* had done several years before, such as Moyra (played by Zoë Wanamaker), the loyal and feisty common-law wife of George Marlow. But from the beginning it's been about Helen Mirren, a highly respected stage and screen actress who finally got the public recognition she deserved for playing the uncompromising and at times unlikeable Jane Tennison. It made her a star in the eyes of audiences who tend not to go to the theatre or watch the kind of films she'd previously made, and helped raise her profile in the USA (Mirren has gone on record to state that her Oscar nomination for *The Madness of King George* in 1995 was thanks in no small part to *Prime Suspect*).

La Plante created the storyline and Alan Cubitt wrote the script for *Prime Suspect 2*, in which Jane and her team face the prospect of another multiple murderer and too many suspects. The discovery of a decomposed body beneath a patio and another in nearby woodlands opens up long-forgotten missing-persons cases and ignites tensions between the police and a London-based Afro-Caribbean community. The murder investigation is handed to Jane Tennison's team, but her life is made more complicated when DS Oswalde, a young black officer that she's recently had an affair with, is transferred to the team. Ambitious but conscious of the racism inherent in the force, Oswalde's insensitivity in arresting Tony Allen (a member of the Afro-Caribbean community and the claustrophobic and troubled brother of one of the murder victims) indirectly results in Allen's suicide while in police custody. David Harvey, a tenant in the property where the body was found, is traced; during questioning by Tennison, the elderly Harvey confesses on his deathbed to the murder, but his testimony doesn't add up. It's only when Tennison commissions a bust of one of the murdered girls that her mother steps forward and reveals that her daughter sang in a reggae band, a connection that leads the investigation to the nephew of the man who confessed and a former neighbour of the Allen family.

Lynda La Plante wrote the script for a third mini series – a different type of story this time, but arguably the best of the original batch. Here, Tennison moves to Soho's vice squad and begins an investigation into the death of rentboy Colin 'Connie' Jenkins after a fire in the flat of a transsexual drag queen called Vera Reynolds (sensitively portrayed by Peter Capaldi). Attention immediately focuses on James Jackson, an unsavoury character suspected of procuring under-aged boys as prostitutes. He is connected in some way to Edward Parker-Jones, manager of a boys' club not far from Vera Reynolds's flat. Digging further, Jane discovers that Parker-Jones has a history of complaints of child abuse against him spanning decades, but thanks to the intervention of a high-ranking police officer none of them has ever come to trial. As the investigation becomes more and more hampered by Parker-Jones's connections to other high-ranking police officers, Jane is frustrated at every turn. Unable to bring him to justice, she takes the decision to show her case file on him to a tabloid journalist . . .

Lynda La Plante's involvement with Jane Tennison ended with *Prime Suspect 3*, but Granada and, more importantly, Helen Mirren, were willing to continue. The next series departed from the standard 'series' format to present three self-contained stories: one about a rehabilitated paedophile whose past is exposed to his new family after a child is reported missing; the second concerning a close-knit community harbouring a murderer; and the third a rather pointless sequel to the first series that should have been reconsidered when it was discovered that John Bowe would be unable to play George Marlow (though in the event Tim Woodward made a fine job of it).

Prime Suspect 5 returned to the original, two-hour, single-plot format, but by this point the only reason to keep watching was for Helen Mirren. Her hard-as-nails portrayal of Tennison is mesmerising. Tennison is tactless and often ruthlessly ambitious. She's a chain smoker and possibly a bit of a drinker, eager to beat the men at their own game and as a result can often be as sexist and belittling to the women officers in her team as the blokes. We've seen her ruin her father's birthday because it clashed with her appearance on a crime appeals programme (think ***Crimewatch***), as good as reduce at least one of her partners to the role of house husband and another to a 'token' bit on the side. To survive in a man's world, she has to not only be as good as the men but better. The problem with this is the tendency in later series to make her less of a woman – an abortion and continually unsuccessful love life smack almost of punishing her for abandoning her femininity in favour of success.

With *Prime Suspect*, Lynda La Plante can take the credit for once again providing strong parts for women, just as she had done with *Widows* several years before.

Pearce Quigley · *Red*
Andrew Woodall · *DI Brian Dalton*
Mark Drewry · *DI Ray Hebdon*
Richard Cadman · *Alan Thorpe*
Steven Crossley · *Mark Lewis*
Christopher Fairbank · *Chief Inspector David Lyall*
Beatie Edney · *Susan Covington*
Robert Glenister · *Chris Hughes*
Lesley Sharp · *Anne Sutherland*
Tracy Keating · *Carolyn Norwood*
David Phelan · *DC Pride*
Tony Rohr · *DS McColl*
Mark Bazeley · *DC Aplin*
Chris Brailsford · *DC Westbrook*
Caroline Selby · *Alison Sutherland*
Candice Paul · *Gayle Sutherland*
Adrian Lukis · *John Warwick*
Fergus O'Donnell · *DC Hawker*
Stuart Wilson · *Dr Patrick Schofield*
Stephen Tindall · *DCI White*
Patrick Cremin · *DI Andrews*
Sam Cox · *DCI Birnam*
James Laurenson · *Paul Endicott*
Helene Kvale · *Lynne Endicott*
Jill Baker · *Maria Henry*
Kelly Reilly · *Polly Henry*
Gareth Forwood · *Denis Carradine*
Anthony Bate · *James Greenlees*
Phillida Sewell · *Olive Carradine*
Jonathan Copestake · *Micky Thomas*
Julie Rice · *Sheila Bower*
Sam Rumbelow · *PC Wilson*
Ralph Arliss · *DCI Raymond*
Sophie Stanton · *DS Cromwell*
Thomas Craig · *DS Booth*
Cristopher John Hale · *DC Bakari*
Nick Patrick · *Hamish Endicott*

Ian Flintoff · *Superintendent Mallory*
Alan Perrin · *Derek Palmer*
Michael Stainton · *George*
Penelope Beaumont · *Elizabeth Bramwell*
Christopher Fulford · *DCI Tom Mitchell*
John McArdle · *DCS Ballinger*
Julia Lane · *DI Devanny*
David O'Hara · *DS Jerry Rankine*
John Brobbey · *DC Henry Adeliyeka*
Steven Mackintosh · *The Street*
Ray Emmet Brown · *Michael Johns*
Joseph Jacobs · *Campbell Lafferty*
Marsha Thomason · *Janice Lafferty*
Vanessa Knox-Mawer · *Louise Ballinger*
Oleg Menshikov · *Milan Lukic*
Ben Miles · *DCI Simon Finch*
Robert Pugh · *DS Alun Simms*
Clare Holman · *Elizabeth Lukic*
Liam Cunningham · *Robert West*
Velibor Topic · *Zigic*
Barnaby Kay · *DC Michael Phillips*
Tanya Moodie · *DC Lorna Greaves*
Phoebe Nicholls · *Shaw*
Rad Lazar · *Kasim*
Serge Soric · *Dr Mulagu*
Ingeborga Dapkunaite · *Jasmina*
Sam Hazeldine · *DC David Butcher*
Eileen Battye · *Carsen*
Nadia Cameron-Blakey · *Sarah Ford*

Creator Lynda La Plante

Producers Sally Head, Rebecca Eaton, Gub Neal, Andy Harries (executive), Lynda La Plante, Nicola Shindler (associate), Don Leaver, Paul Marcus, Lynn Horsford, David Boulter

Writers Lynda La Plante, Allan Cubitt, Paul Billing, Eric Deacon, Guy Hibbert, Guy Andrews, Peter Berry

Theme Music Stephen Warbeck, Robert Lane

At the same time, we can't help but admire her. When investigating possible connections to the Della Mornay case, Jane's respect for a group of prostitutes helps her obtain valuable leads. At the morgue, she manages to retain her lunch, while Jonesey is not so lucky. And when she's saddled with Otley once again, her former antipathy is replaced by respect as she witnesses the compassion he shows towards the street kids who sell their bodies, in particular a young teenager called Billy, whose death from an AIDS-related illness leaves Otley shaken. In short, we like Jane as much because of her faults as in spite of them.

The overall effect of the post-La Plante series was that they'd actually done more damage than good. When *Prime Suspect 6* was announced, expectations were not exactly high, though within the first few moments it became obvious that finally we were once more getting the kind of script that Helen Mirren – and we – deserved. Easily on a par with the first three serials, *Prime Suspect 6* delved into the world of Britain's East European refugees, an underclass of terrified and abused people. Seven years after we last saw Jane, we find her nearing the end of her career. The dawning of retirement gives her a new edge as she becomes fearless in her determination to find the killer of a Bosnian refugee. The grimmest *Prime Suspect* so far, it's also the most far-reaching one, with Jane travelling to Bosnia with an old friend (Robert West, played by Liam Cunningham) before setting her targets – against the instructions of her superior officers and representatives of the Home Office – on an optician whom Jane believes is a former war criminal who'd been granted immunity for informing on other suspects after the Bosnian massacres.

The announcement in spring 2005 of a final *Prime Suspect* serial (provisionally scheduled for screening sometime in 2006) came as somewhat of a surprise, but hopefully it will maintain the high standards of its immediate predecessor and give Jane Tennison a suitable send-off.

The Prisoner

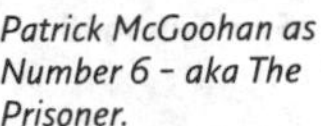

Patrick McGoohan as Number 6 – aka The Prisoner.

Accepted wisdom will have you convinced that *The Prisoner* is the most impenetrable 'text' ever performed and that it's as impossible to explain as *Waiting for Godot*, the Schleswig-Holstein question or the American electoral college system. It's not quite as esoteric as some would claim – though it was often too self-indulgent for its own good – but it at least had lofty intentions in its aim to get its audience thinking.

The Prisoner was the brainchild of Irish-American actor Patrick McGoohan, in collaboration with David Tomblin and George Markstein. By the late 1960s, McGoohan was one of British TV's top actors, thanks to his lead role in the ITC action series ***Danger Man***. But McGoohan had grown increasingly frustrated by the series, despite a hefty amount of influence on its direction (he'd managed to persuade the writers not to give him any scripts where he was asked to tote a gun or seduce loose women), but evidently this wasn't enough.

The exact starting point for *The Prisoner* is difficult to pin down, with the accounts of those concerned differing significantly. Portmeirion had been used as a location in *Danger Man*, and McGoohan had appeared in a one-off teleplay called *The Prisoner* in 1963 (where he'd played the part of the interrogator rather than the prisoner). At some point, McGoohan began discussing his theories

Science Fiction
ITC/Everyman Films Ltd for ITV
Episode Duration: 50 mins
Broadcast: 29 Sep 1967–1 Feb 1968

Regular Cast
Patrick McGoohan · *The Prisoner*
Angelo Muscat · *The Butler*
Peter Swanwick · *The Supervisor*

Guest Cast
Guy Doleman, George Baker, Leo McKern, Colin Gordon, Eric Portman, Anton Rodgers, Georgina Cookson, Mary Morris, Peter Wyngarde, Rachel Herbert, Derren Nesbitt, Andre Van Gysegham, John Sharpe, Clifford Evans, David Bauer, Kenneth Griffith · *Number 2*
Alexis Kanner · *The Kid – Number 48*
Robert Rietty · *Voice of 'New Number 2' in Titles*
Fenella Fielding · *Voice of Village Public Address System*
Christopher Benjamin · *Potter*
Virginia Maskell · *The Woman – Number 9*
Paul Eddington · *Cobb*
Nadia Gray · *Nadia Rakowski*
Richard Wattis · *Fotheringay*
Kevin Stoney · *Colonel J.*
Katherine Kath · *Engadine*
Sheila Allen · *Number 14*
Peter Bowles · *'A'*
Jane Merrow · *Alison – Number 24*
John Castle · *Number 12*
Peter Howell · *The Professor*
Donald Sinden · *The Colonel*
Annette André · *Watchmaker's Daughter*
Mark Eden · *Number 100*
Wanda Ventham · *Computer Attendant*
Nigel Stock · *The Colonel*
Hugo Schuster · *Seltzman*
Justine Lord · *Sonia*

Creator Patrick McGoohan (with David Tomblin and George Markstein)

Producers David Tomblin, Patrick McGoohan (executive producer)

Writers George Markstein, David Tomblin, Vincent Tilsley, Anthony Skene, Paddy Fitz (pseudonym for Patrick McGoohan), Terence Feely, Lewis Greifer (writing as Joshua Adam), Gerald Kelsey, Roger Woddis, Michael Cramoy, Roger Parkes, Ian L. Rakoff

Theme Music 'The Age of Elegance' by Ron Grainer

about individuality and personal identity with both Tomblin and Markstein, who were both working on *Danger Man* (Tomblin as assistant director, Markstein as script consultant) and that Tomblin and McGoohan eventually formed Everyman Films Ltd to develop programme ideas. The pair brought in Markstein, who had worked in espionage during the war. Although Markstein has since claimed that he thought up the idea of *The Prisoner* himself while commuting back from Shepperton one evening, most accounts at least agree that it was he who told McGoohan about real-life villages in remote areas of Scotland where former agents had been sent during the war. This almost certainly provided the spark for McGoohan's eventual idea. He and Tomblin then drafted the series format with a view to selling the idea to ITC, *Danger Man*'s distributors. McGoohan approached Lew Grade, head of ITC, with a pitch. Grade is said to have put the document to one side and instead asked the actor to tell him what the show was all about. McGoohan's conviction persuaded Grade to greenlight the show.

Aware perhaps that his creation's strength lies in the questions it raises, not the answers it might offer, McGoohan has stuck to his guns in never stating what exactly it was all about – despite many invitations to do just that from foolhardy journalists and ardent fans alike. The basic idea was retold in the opening title sequence for almost every episode. A man resigns dramatically from a top government position. Returning home in his custom-made sports car, he enters his apartment and begins to pack a suitcase. Suddenly, the room begins to fill with suffocating gas and the man passes out. When he awakes, he does so in an exact replica of his home, but he is no longer in London – he's been taken to a remote community called the Village, where no-one has a name, just a number and where (it's suggested) even the establishment is a prisoner. Presiding over the Village is a succession of people called 'Number 2', whose sole task is to crack their latest resident – and find out why he resigned . . .

Number 2's methods varied from allowing him – The Prisoner, or Number 6 – to think he can escape only for him to return to the Village again, encouraging the other villagers to shun him for being 'unmutual', feeding him hallucinogenic drugs and employing every psychological trick they can think of (one marvellous episode sees the current Number 2, in utter desperation, inviting Number 6 to tell some children a bedtime story in the hope that he might slip up and tell them anything of use).

Much has been made of the fact that the name of McGoohan's character was never revealed (he asserted week after week that he was 'not a number' but to the viewers, and to the villagers, he was – 'Number 6'). Though Grade almost certainly intended it to be so – and despite the production sharing some of the same cast members and liberally using old publicity stills of McGoohan – *The Prisoner* is not a direct continuation of *Danger Man*, nor is the main character called 'John Drake' (although even this is a matter of debate: Markstein says he is; McGoohan insists he isn't). Some believe that the sanest interpretation is that Number 6's name must be Patrick McGoohan. After all, he and his character share the same time and date of birth: 4.31 a.m., 19 March 1928. But as with most of the questions raised in its 17 episodes, there is no one definitive answer.

ITC was astoundingly prolific in the 1960s, churning out action series after action series, but very few of them left their mark like *The Prisoner*. This is undoubtedly due to McGoohan's bloody-mindedness in not giving away any answers. But it's also because the show itself was so iconic, boasting indelible images like the huge, almost shapeless white guardian of the Village – 'Rover' – that prevents anyone from escaping. Then there's the penny-farthing symbol that adorns everyone's number badges (an emblem that McGoohan claimed was symbolic of 'inverse progress'). And there's the ultra-stylish fashions with blazers that sport white piping and T-shirts that suggest a nautical flavour – like a world of GAP adverts 30 years too early. And we shouldn't forget McGoohan's car, the green and yellow Lotus 7 that's seen in the title sequence and in selected episodes, which was provided for the show by Graham Nearn of Caterham Cars, who at that time manufactured the Lotus 7 kit (McGoohan chose the model in preference to the Lotus Elan he'd initially considered). Plus there were mini-moke taxis, lava lamps, umbrellas, 'human chess' games, crazy phones, sexy interior décor, big circular chairs that look like carved-up ping-pong balls, a game called Kosho involving two trampolines, a small pool of water and lots of padding . . . and a rather sinister butler who lurks inside Number 2's Green Dome. But the most iconic element of all was the Village itself. The sprawling layout and Italianate architecture convinced many viewers that the entire series had been filmed abroad. Only in the opening titles of the final episode was it revealed to be Portmeirion, a small village-hotel in North Wales created by the late Sir Clough Williams-Ellis. The location has naturally become a Mecca for the show's legions of fans, who meet there each year for 'PortmeiriCon', the official convention.

Aware perhaps that his creation's strength lies in the questions it raises, not the answers it might offer, McGoohan has stuck to his guns in never stating what exactly it was all about.

The final element of the show was the identity of the person behind the Village – Number 1. It was a question asked every week – 'Who is Number 1?' – and many of the cast members had their own ideas, from the Butler to the telex machine in Number 2's chamber. It turned out to be a bit of a Maguffin, yet another question that would not be satisfactorily answered by the end. After a finale in which a callow youth and a former Number 2 are held up as examples of feckless rebellion, Number 6 decides to take matters into his own hands and helps his fellow prisoners to stage a coup. Entering the lair of Number 1, our hero unmasks him to reveal first a chattering ape and then Number 6's own face leering back at him.

TRIVIA

While the first and last episodes of *The Prisoner* are easy to pin down, from then on things get a little confusing. Few of the different ITV regions stuck to a specific order and fans have continued to debate the 'true' order ever since. Here, we simply offer our own recommended viewing order.

Arrival; Dance of the Dead; Checkmate; Free for All; The Chimes of Big Ben; Living in Harmony; Many Happy Returns; The Schizoid Man; The General; A, B and C; It's your Funeral; The Girl who was Death; Do not Forsake Me; A Change of Mind; Hammer into Anvil; Once Upon a Time; Fall Out.

Number 6, the former Number 2, the youth and the creepy butler finally escape from the Village as 'Number 1' flees in a space rocket (!). In the final seconds, Number 6 collects his sports car, parked outside his old apartment. As he drives off along the same route that appeared in the opening titles for the series, the Butler enters Number 6's home – the door to which has acquired a disconcerting hum, just like the doors in the Village.

Does this mean that The Prisoner had been holding himself captive, victim of some kind of mental breakdown? Does the humming door at the end suggest that society at large is the Village and that we will all remain prisoners? Whatever, the lack of a clear resolution left viewers feeling cheated and McGoohan had to flee the country to avoid the public's wrath. But they forgave him eventually and when Channel 4 selected *The Prisoner* to be repeated in 1983–4, the fan club 'Six of One' received record applications for membership.

Ah yes, the fans. In *Monty Python's Life of Brian* (1979), the ersatz Messiah tells an attentive crowd, 'You are all individuals,' to which the crowd reply in unison, 'We are all individuals' – apart from one gent at the back who indignantly points out, 'I'm not!' With its ingrained values of personal freedom and the right to individuality, it might strike an outsider as painfully ironic that *Prisoner* enthusiasts celebrate McGoohan's vision by dressing alike and voluntarily wearing their numbers with pride. But then they do so entirely of their own volition – and freedom of choice is, of course, vital for a sense of individuality. By re-creating the human chess games, writing huge articles, maintaining websites and taking over Portmeirion every now and again, they've managed to keep *The Prisoner* alive for 40 years. Not bad going for a show that had such a small batch of episodes in the first place.

Prisoner: Cell Block H

Officer Joan Ferguson – aka 'The Freak' (played by Maggie Kirkpatrick).

A genuine cult phenomenon, *Prisoner* is a series that had no right to become a huge mainstream hit in the UK, but succeed it did. *Prisoner* (the 'Cell Block H' suffix was added to the programme's title for international transmission so as to avoid confusion with Patrick McGoohan's fantasy series ***The Prisoner***) was originally purchased by a handful of ITV regions in 1987. With the arrival of 24-hour TV, the ITV network was looking for ways to fill its late-night schedule, and the opportunity to capitalise on the ***Neighbours***-inspired boom in popularity for Australian programming was too good to miss. The problem was that each region showed it at different times and on different days of the week (some showed it on two or more nights) meaning that it was impossible for the press to cover the series, as each different ITV region would be at a different point in the storylines. Consequently, every viewer tended to discover it by accident or word of mouth and the ITV regions weren't really aware of how popular the show had become until the point when they stopped showing it for a short while – when the letters of complaint would arrive. What appeared to be at first glance a cheesy, low-budget drama would have night owls across the UK hooked by a parade of grotesque and outrageous storylines and characters.

By the time the theme tune was released as a single in April 1989 (reaching number 3 in the UK charts), *Prisoner* fever was everywhere. The actors from the series were flown over from Australia by the Prisoner Fan Club, getting mobbed by crowds of housewives and students (the core audience for *Prisoner*) when making personal appearances at shopping centres and nightclubs. At one point, it was estimated that in excess of ten million viewers were tuning in for their late-night melodrama each week (but with no collated data for non-networked programmes, it's hard to verify this claim).

The series came from writer-producer Reg Watson, who had also created *The Young Doctors*. Australian viewers had already been treated to a British drama called ***Within These Walls***, which had looked at life in a women's prison from the point of view of the prison staff. Watson felt that it would have been more interesting to

Soap
Grundy for Channel 10
(shown on ITV)
Episode Duration: 50 mins
Broadcast: 27 Feb 1979–16 Dec 1986 (Aus)

Regular Cast

Elspeth Ballantyne · *Officer Meg Jackson/Morris*
Patsy King · *Governor Erica Davidson*
Val Lehman · *Bea Smith*
Sheila Florance · *Lizzie Birdsworth*
Collette Mann · *Doreen Anderson/Burns*
Fiona Spence · *Officer Vera 'Vinegar Tits' Bennett*
Peita Toppano · *Karen Travers*
Barry Quin · *Greg Miller*
Kerry Armstrong · *Lynn Warner*
Carol Burns · *Franky Doyle*
Mary Ward · *Mum Brooks*
Amanda Muggleton · *Chrissie Latham*
Joy Westmore · *Officer Joyce Barry*
Jude Kuring · *Noeline Bourke*
Gerard Maguire · *Officer Jim 'Fletch the Letch' Fletcher*
Judith McGrath · *Officer Colleen 'Po Face' Powell*
Reylene Pearce · *Phyllis Hunt*
Ian Smith · *Ted Douglas*
Margot Knight · *Sharon Gilmour, Terri Malone*
Betty Bobbitt · *Judy Bryant*
Jane Clifton · *Margo Gaffney*
Jentah Sobott · *Mouse*
Caroline Gillmer · *Helen Smart*
Belinda Davey · *Hazel Kent*
Anthony Hawkins · *Bob Morris*
Anne Phelan · *Myra Desmond*
Alan Hopgood · *Wally Wallace*
Maggie Millar · *Marie Winter*
Olivia Hamnett · *Kate Peterson*
Louise Le Nay · *Sandy Edwards*
Wayne Jarratt · *Officer Steve Fawkner*
Maggie Kirkpatrick · *Officer Joan 'The Freak' Ferguson*
Lisa Crittenden · *Maxine Daniels*
Carole Skinner · *Nola McKenzie*
Gerda Nicolson · *Governor Ann Reynolds*
Judy McBurney · *Pixie Mason*
Tina Bursill · *Sonia Stevens*
Babs McMillan · *Cass Parker*
Maxine Klibingaitis · *Bobbie Mitchell*
Andy Anderson · *Officer Rick Manning*
Janet Andrewartha · *Reb Keane*
Lois Collinder · *Alice 'Lurch' Jenkins*
Louise Siversen · *Lou Kelly*
Nigel Bradshaw · *Officer Dennis 'The Yorkshire Pud' Cruickshank*
Genevieve Lemon · *Marlene 'Rabbit' Warren*

tell the stories of the inmates too and so set about developing a series where the prisoners would be as integral to the story as the warders. He and his production team visited a number of women's prisons and spoke to real prisoners about their lives and crimes. The result was *Prisoner*, set in the fictional Wentworth Detention Centre for Women, located in a suburb of Melbourne. The series began with the case of schoolteacher Karen Travers, found guilty of murder and sent to Wentworth. Few of the characters she met there were what could be described as glamorous: stern yet fair 'top dog' Bea Smith, locked up for murdering her adulterous husband; outrageous old lag Lizzie (sent down for poisoning a whole bunch of sheep shearers) and her best friend drippy Doreen; and the borderline psychotic lesbian Franky Doyle. The first 20 or so episodes of *Prisoner* were, in fact, created as a serious stand-alone drama series, with no plan for this to become a year-round soap opera. When the cast were approached to renew their contracts for an ongoing series, one of the few performers to turn the offer down was theatre actress Carol Burns, who had made an astonishing impact as Franky. Producers opted to give her a memorable exit, gunned down by police while on the run with her on-off girlfriend Doreen.

One of the key achievements of *Prisoner* was in its realistic portrayal of lesbian relationships. One of the first programmes ever to handle this sensitive subject in any depth, certainly on British screens, *Prisoner*'s lesbian characters were three-dimensional: some were likeable despite their crimes, some were downright nasty. Following the death of Franky, the next major gay character was American earth mother Judy Bryant, who would stay with the series for more than four years. Judy deliberately committed a crime to get put inside to be with her girlfriend Sharon – unfortunately for her, Sharon was soon murdered by psychotic warder Jock Stewart, leaving Judy to suffer both her loss and a lengthy prison stretch alone.

On the other side of the bars was prim and proper governor Erica Davidson, a woman whose bouffant hair and twin-set seemed modelled upon Googie Withers, who played liberal governor Faye Boswell in *Within these Walls*. Working alongside her was the perpetually nice 'Saint' Meg Jackson, the only character to last the entire run of the series. Meg would always give the prisoners the benefit of the doubt – even when one of them stabbed her first husband to death in the middle of a riot with a pair of scissors – which inevitably brought her into conflict with the sour-faced disciplinarian Vera Bennett. Effectively the first villain of the series, Vera was a woman always happier sending a prisoner to solitary confinement ('the pound') than worrying about rehabilitation. Her callous approach led Franky Doyle to name her 'Vinegar Tits' – speculating that she was so sour-faced that it was impossible to imagine her ever nursing a child. It was this kind of shockingly cruel humour that became one of the series' most unexpectedly attractive qualities.

After the first 20 episodes, *Prisoner* began to evolve. After all, it wasn't a documentary series and its first responsibility was to entertain. It retained a sense of social responsibility and tackled many difficult issues, including the extremes of severe pre-menstrual depression, drug abuse and child murder. But it also gave us some staggering plotlines that weren't exactly restricted by realism. The amount of over-the-top incidents that befell Wentworth Detention Centre provided such blissful moments of pure melodrama: an escape attempt through long-forgotten secret tunnels hidden under the prison, which took place during a pantomime staged by the women for the local kiddies; an unhinged warder who started to bump off the women one by one; a particularly selective poisonous snake working its way through the prison, and even an outbreak of Lassa fever. In fact, there was very little that *didn't* happen to the inmates. Even the potentially fun week-and-a-half when the prison officers went out on strike was ruined by the arrival of lunatic Bev the Butcher, a woman so terrifyingly unhinged that she murdered one of the temporary social worker staff with a knitting needle and sliced open Bobbie Mitchell's already damaged palms with a razor blade prior to killing herself via an embolism just to find out what it felt like.

The single worst thing to strike the inmates – and the best addition to the show by miles – was the arrival in episode 287 of a new warder. Her name was Joan Ferguson, better known as the Freak. Ferguson would become synonymous with the series. The Freak was a violent, towering lesbian with a penchant for black leather gloves who'd often conduct late-night body searches on the younger, prettier women. She made the lives of the inmates a living hell and the series infinitely more watchable. As with all great villains, though, the nastier the Freak behaved, the more audiences loved it. Secretly, viewers loved to have a character to boo and hiss at. The occasional glimpses into Miss Ferguson's lonely private life just made her character infinitely more believable. Just as Joan began to show a softer side – either when meeting a new girlfriend, or on the bizarre occasion when she fostered a young boy called Shane – some cruel twist of fate would wrench her happiness away from her and she'd take out her frustration on the inmates.

For more than a hundred episodes, titanic struggle raged between Bea Smith and the Freak, creating some of the most entertaining episodes Australian soap opera had ever seen. However, when actress Val Lehman decided to quit the series (having won just about every TV award available to her), Bea finally lost the war when Ferguson managed to persuade the governor to get Bea transferred to Barnhurst Prison and out of the series for good. If nothing else, this marvellously staged punch-up proved that the misconception about *Prisoner*'s wobbly cardboard sets was wrong, seeing the brute force with which actors Lehman and Kirkpatrick threw each other against the set walls without even the slightest scenic tremble.

With more and more of the original characters departing, *Prisoner* began to lose its way with few of the replacements having anywhere near the charisma of Bea, Lizzie and Doreen. However, there were a few notable exceptions, including the new governor Ann Reynolds (portrayed by Gerda Nicolson with less hair lacquer and infinitely more depth than her predecessor) and Myra Desmond, former leader of the Prison Reform Group who found herself on the wrong side of the law. Myra's reign as top dog was brought to an abrupt end by the

Victoria Nicolls · *Officer Heather Rogers*
Maggie Dence · *Bev 'The Butcher' Baker*
Robert Summers · *Shane Munroe*
Dorothy Cutts · *Officer Pat Slattery*
Peter Bensley · *Matt Delaney*
Les Dayman · *Geoff Macrae*
Trevor Kent · *Frank Burke*
Pepe Trevor · *Lexie Patterson*
Lois Ramsay · *Ettie Parslow*
Ernie Bourne · *Mervin Pringle*
Kirsty Child · *'Weeping' Willie Beacham*
Billie Hammerberg · *May Collins*
Jackie Woodburne · *Julie 'Chook' Egbert*
Debra Lawrence · *Daphne Graham*
Sonja Tallis · *Nora Flynn*
James Condon · *James Dwyer*
Lynda Stoner · *Eve Wilder*
Glenda Linscott · *Rita 'The Beater' Connors*
Julia Blake · *Nancy McCormack*
Sean Scully · *Dan Moulton*
Kate Hood · *Kath Maxwell*
Paula Duncan · *Lorelei Wilkinson*
Michael Winchester · *Marty Jackson*
Rosanne Hull-Brown · *Merle Jones*
Philip Hyde · *Rodney Adams*
Desiree Smith · *Delia Stout*
Taya Stratton · *'Spider' Simpson*
Terrie Waddell · *Lisa Mullins*
Ray Meagher · *Geoff Butler, Kurt Renner, Ernest Craven*
Shane Connor · *Bongo Connors*

Creator Reg Watson

Producers Reg Watson, Ian Bradley, Philip East, Sue Masters, John McRae, Marie Trevor, Lex Van Os

Writers Various, including Ian Bradley, Michael Brindley, Marcus Cole, Ian Coughlan, Coral Drouyn, Andrew Kennedy, Ray Kolle, Bevan Lee, Margaret McClusky, Gail Meillon, Chris Milne, John Mortimore, Betty Quin, Barbara Ramsay, Fay Rousseaux, Sheila Sibley, James Simmonds, Patrea Smallacombe, Ian Smith, Alister Webb, Bryon Williams, John Wood, Dave Worthington

Theme Music 'On The Inside' by Allan Caswell, sung by Lynne Hamilton

single most outrageously magnificent plotline ever to feature in *Prisoner*, the infamous three episode-long 'Ballinger Siege'.

Ruth Ballinger, the wife of a gangland boss, had been thrown into Wentworth prior to her trial. Her husband, eager to ensure that Ruth never got the opportunity to testify against him in the witness box, arranged for a gang of armed mercenaries to break *into* the prison and spring his wife. However, the attempt went wrong when the Freak raised the alarm and armed police surrounded Wentworth. Inside, the mercenaries decided to up the stakes by shooting one of the inmates each hour until their demands were met. One by one, various extras were executed, until finally top dog Myra faced the horror of having to decide which one of her friends would be the next victim. Myra chose the noble option and goaded the lead gunman into shooting her instead. This shocking turn of events, which happened ten minutes into an episode rather than at the cliffhanger, left Myra without the back of her head and the women without a leader. Finally, Ballinger and her mercenaries got their comeuppance as they tried to make their escape at a nearby airport, with hostage the Freak turning the tables and stopping Ruth at gunpoint.

Thankfully, the final year of *Prisoner* heralded the introduction of a new leader for the women, a tough six-foot-tall biker called Rita Connors. Rita's arrival finally brought the Freak another worthy rival. Explosive, energetic and full of hilarious anecdotes, Rita was an immediate hit with the women and more importantly the viewers. She could handle herself – as her regular tussles with Ferguson proved – and, despite being a criminal, her strong code of honour earned her the respect of the Governor and Meg.

The final episodes played an absolute blinder in the form of the double-whammy revelation that Rita had been struck down with leukaemia and that a disillusioned Ferguson was planning to leave the prison service. The news that both women would no longer need to spar led to a jaw-dropping alliance where Rita offered to share with the Freak half of the money she had stashed away from a bank raid. After Rita's sudden death, Ferguson thought she had nothing to lose and collected the cash from Rita's hiding place only to be arrested. In a beautiful combination of irony and bad planning on the part of the prison board, the Freak was sent to Wentworth for a single night before being shipped to another prison. The inmates, of course, already knew and taunted the woman who'd help make their lives a misery for so long. But the final pay-off came when Ferguson realised too late that Rita's death and the stashed loot had been part of an elaborate set-up to entrap her. Rita hadn't actually died – and both Ann Reynolds and Meg Morris, the nice prison officers who had long attempted to get rid of her, were in on the deception too.

As the cell walls of Wentworth Detention Centre were being torn down, Reg Watson's next project was being constructed – the interiors of the suburban homes of Ramsay Street were erected in the same studios. Had it not been for the success of ***Neighbours*** on British TV, it's highly unlikely that *Prisoner: Cell Block H* would ever have been screened over here. And that *would* have been criminal.

TRIVIA

In 1989, two years after the show came to an end, Elspeth Balantyne, Patsy King and Glenda Linscott came to Britain to star in the first *Prisoner* stage play, an adaptation of the first six episodes of the series. The part of Franky Doyle was taken by British actress Joanna Monro, formerly of ***Angels*** and ***That's Life!***, while Brenda Longman stood in as Bea Smith – a far cry from her previous major role as the voice of Sooty's girlfriend Soo. A year later, the production was revived for a 13-week tour of the UK, this time starring Fiona Spence and Jane Clifton.

By the time some of the ITV regions had completed the run of original episodes, the play had been reworked as a crowd-pleasing musical shaped around the unique comedy talents of drag queen Lily Savage. Savage found herself flung into Wentworth for the suspected murder of her sister Vera while on holiday. While she awaited the authorities to discover that Vera had simply been washed away while looking for crabs, Lily took on the Freak, re-created with relish and cheese by Maggie Kirkpatrick.

Prisoner was one of the few Australian soaps to have been successfully exported to the USA. There it attracted the attention of one celebrity fan – Sammy Davis Jr – who approached producers regarding a possible guest role, though ultimately his schedule prevented this from happening.

In 1997, ten years after it had hit British shores, Channel 5 gave *Prisoner* its first fully networked transmission in the UK.

The Professionals

Lewis Collins and Martin Shaw as The Professionals.

George Cowley is the head of CI5, an elite division of the British Security Services nicknamed 'the Professionals'. Though they appear to cover similar territory to MI5 – terrorism, serious crimes against the public – their remit allows them to achieve results by any means necessary. Cowley's two top men are Bodie and Doyle. They have different approaches to their work – Doyle favours a softly-softly method, Bodie is more brash and cock-sure of himself – but together, they get results.

Criticised at the time for its violence and bad language, *The Professionals* no longer offends in quite the same way. Now, we're more likely to be concerned by its attitude to women as tarts and victims, which revisionists will claim was true to life or always done with tongue firmly in cheek.

Bodie, Doyle and Cowley came to our screens after Brian Clemens and Albert Fennell realised they wouldn't be able to pull together a third run of ***The New Avengers***, which had been in production for two years thanks to investment from France and Canada. With that investment withdrawn, the adventures of Steed, Purdey and Gambit were coming to their natural end, but at the same time Clemens and Fennel were invited to pitch for a new action-adventure series that would set out to rival Euston Films' ***The Sweeney***. Their idea – the adventures of two members of an elite anti-terrorist squad – was given the working title 'The A Squad' (which sounds like something George Peppard might have starred in), though thankfully this was changed early on to 'The Professionals'.

On the producers' shortlist were Jon Finch – who apparently accepted and then rejected the part of Doyle in quick succession –

Crime Drama/Action-Adventure
Avengers Mark 1/lwt for ITV
Episode Duration: 50 mins
Broadcast: 30 Dec 1977–6 Feb 1983, 19 Sep–19 Dec 1999

Regular Cast
Lewis Collins · *William Andrew Philip Bodie*
Martin Shaw · *Raymond Doyle*
Gordon Jackson · *George Cowley*
Steve Alder · *Murphy*
Bridget Brice · *Betty - Cowley's Secretary*

Creator Brian Clemens

Producers Brian Clemens, Albert Fennell (executive), Sidney Hayers, Raymond Menmuir

Writers Anthony Read, Brian Clemens, James McAteer, Dennis Spooner, Gerry O'Hara, Edmund Ward, Don Houghton, Ranald Graham, Stephen Lister, John Goldsmith, Philip Loraine, Christopher Wicking, Ted Childs, Michael Feeney Callan, Douglas Watkinson, John Kruse, Roger Marshall, Tony Barwick, David Humphries

Theme Music Laurie Johnson. Johnson's theme is one of the classic signature tunes of the 1970s, brassy, strident and with the right level of sleazy porn funk. Remixed by Blue Boy in 1997, it reached No. 37 in the UK singles chart.

and Clive Revill, whom Brian Clemens wanted for Cowley. With Revill about to leave the UK for America, Gordon Jackson accepted the part, excited by the chance to break away from the potential typecasting facing him after five years of playing Hudson the butler in ***Upstairs, Downstairs***. There was still an air of Hudsonian authority about Cowley, but little of his sentimentality. Cowley was the original old soldier, intolerant of disrespect or frivolity in his subordinates and hampered by a gammy leg (a bullet wound from his own days of more active service that is eventually forgotten in the later series), but still capable of bringing down a villain or too if necessary.

With Doyle's boots now filled by Martin Shaw (who had appeared in an episode of *The New Avengers*), the important role of Bodie, his partner in crime fighting, was given to rising actor Anthony Andrews, who had appeared in *Upstairs, Downstairs* in its final year and would go on to star in ***Danger UXB*** and ***Brideshead Revisited***. But after viewing the rushes for the first few episodes, the producers realised that the two younger leads lacked the sense of friction they'd been working towards: as old friends, Andrews and Shaw simply got on too well. Andrews was quickly dropped. In his place came Lewis Collins, who had appeared in the same *New Avengers* episode as Shaw. Played by Collins, Bodie was smug, abrasive, witty and often a little callous. Smartly dressed in a blazer or casual suit and with his close-cropped police-standard hair only just beginning to grow out, he was exactly the right character to provide contrast to the more thoughtful, compassionate one-time art student Doyle, with his bubble perm and clad in faded denim.

Right from the beginning, Martin Shaw identified the scripts as being formulaic and not really what he'd hoped for, but he was contracted for four years and unable to escape (he later tried and failed to block video releases of the episodes, believing it would be best all round if the tapes were left in the archives and quietly forgotten about). While it delivered on the action front, with fight sequences that looked savage and brutal, and car chases that always seemed inches away from the camera, the downfall of the series was its posturing as something grittier and more mature than it actually was. It played directly to that part of the audience that thinks all blacks are foreign, all foreigners can't be trusted and all women should look like Pamela Stephenson. One particularly infamous episode, 'Klansman', was omitted from the series. Dealing with a British branch of the Ku Klux Klan, it revealed that Bodie was actually a racist with no sympathy for 'Spades'. When he ends up in hospital after being stabbed by a black gang member, the fact that he's cared for by a black doctor and – more significantly – an attractive black nurse cures him of his prejudice. We know this because at the close of the episode the black nurse takes the place of the usual blonde on Bodie's arm as he sets off with her on a date. Having avoided any representation of black characters in the original *New Avengers* show, this was quite a brave move for Clemens and Fennel. The problem is that its position as rather cack-handed tokenism is all too obvious when viewed alongside the vast majority of other episodes.

The Professionals is a guilty pleasure for many, a series that is so wrong in so many ways, yet still manages to deliver competent action sequences, attractive leads and an exciting premise, even if that premise is often botched through ridiculous machismo and a tendency to ignore characterisation for action. Many female *Professionals* fans (and a fair few male ones) enjoyed the series for what it suggested as much as what it showed. Doyle's almost flirty interaction with Bodie, for instance, fuelled fantasies and inspired page after page of homoerotic fiction.

The series' critical reputation had always been poor, but viewers remained loyal – for a while at least. Unfortunately, the flirtatious banter between the two leads was so wide open to misinterpretation that when Channel 4 broadcast a parody by members of ***The Comic Strip Presents*** team, 1984's 'The Bullshitters', all it took was the sight of Keith Allen and Peter Richardson running around back streets in their underpants and *The Professionals* became unbroadcastable. The reputation of many a TV production has been damaged by a well-aimed comedy lampoon, and *The Comic Strip Presents* was responsible for a fair few. But *The Professionals* was savaged beyond repair. Allan and Richardson made those guilty fantasies real with possibly the most graphic televisual depiction of homosexual behaviour performed by heterosexual men until 1999's ***Queer as Folk***. The result was a few people became a little confused as to how gay *The Professionals* actually was. Not very, as it happens, but, as with those unfounded rumours surrounding Captain Pugwash and his friends, why let the facts stand in the way of a good story?

With erratic scheduling and the odd strike or two, *The Professionals* died a rather drawn-out death, with episodes made for one season but clumped together to pad out the next. With the four-year-long handcuffs released, Martin Shaw bolted after production of the episodes that would make up the show's fifth and final series, eventually starring in ITV's *The Chief* and the BBC One legal drama ***Judge John Deed***. Lewis Collins meanwhile starred in the film *Who Dares Wins* (1982) as a cocky SAS officer, and as well as undertaking numerous stage roles, he popped up as 'guest-star-for-hire' in TV series such as ***Robin of Sherwood*** and ***The Bill***. He also played Colonel Mustard in the third series of ITV's game show ***Cluedo***.

Towards the end of the 1990s, in a move to break away from the reputation of being a channel that only broadcast imports, Sky One began commissioning original British-produced dramas. A beneficiary of this was David Wickes Television, a production company who successfully negotiated with Avengers Mark 1 and Laurie Johnson to resurrect *The Professionals* with an all-new cast. *CI5: The New Professionals* featured former ***Callan*** star Edward Woodward as head of CI5 Harry Malone, now running three operatives: Sam Curtis (played by Colin Wells), Chris Keel (Kal Weber) and – blimey! – a female by the name of Tina Backus (Lexa Doig). Sexual equality had finally struck CI5. Sadly, despite input from the series' creator Brian Clemens and some pretty decent performances, the series didn't last beyond its first run of 13 episodes.

TRIVIA

The opening titles for the first series depicted Cowley timing Bodie and Doyle on an assault course. Later series sported a more fast-cut sequence beginning with a car smashing through a window and consisting of various shots of the men in action. This was subsequently used in place of the original titles on repeats and home video releases. The downside of the use of this pacier opener is the loss of Cowley's voice-over, which explained the premise of the show: 'Anarchy, acts of terror, crimes against the public. To combat it I've got special men – experts from the army, the police, from every service – these are the professionals.'

The Protectors

Detective | Group Three/ITC for ITV | episode duration 25 mins | broadcast 7 Jul 1972–1 Feb 1974

Regular Cast
Robert Vaughn · *Harry Rule*
Nyree Dawn Porter · *Contessa Caroline di Contini*
Tony Anholt · *Paul Buchet*
Anthony Chinn · *Chino*
Yasuko Nagazami · *Suki*

Creator Lew Grade **Producers** Gerry Anderson, Reg Hill **Writers** Various, including Dennis Spooner, Robert Banks Stewart, Terry Nation, Brian Clemens, Sylvia Anderson, Shane Rimmer, David Butler, Terence Feely, John Goldsmith, Donald James, Ralph Smart, Lew Davidson **Theme Music** Mitch Murray and Peter Callender wrote the magnificent end title music, 'Avenues and Alleyways', which was belted out with gusto by Tony 'Amarillo' Christie. Released as a single, it peaked at No. 37 in March 1973.

Led by ultra-cool American Harry Rule, the Protectors are a team of international freelance crime-fighters, available for hire by private individuals, corporations or even governments – whoever can afford to pay their fees. Based in a mock-Tudor mansion in London, Harry coordinates his two main colleagues – glamorous widow the Contessa di Contini (who lives in her late husband's villa in Rome) and young Parisian playboy Paul Buchet. Together, the Protectors travel around the globe, freeing kidnap victims, capturing escaped Nazi war criminals, recovering stolen valuables and generally making the world a better place. When needed, they're also able to call upon the services of a world-wide network of extra Protectors based in their own cities – and in the first episodes, they were also assisted by karate expert Chino (the Contessa's chauffeur) and judo expert Suki (Harry's glamorous au pair).

The Protectors was created and filmed with the explicit intention of selling the series to as many different countries as possible – this being so, the programme spared no expense in jetting off to film the episodes in a variety of European locations (Madrid, Venice, Salzburg and Copenhagen) rather than using studios and back projection, as was common practice with many other programmes at the time. Furthermore, casting the worldwide superstar Robert Vaughn (from ***The Man from U.N.C.L.E.***) in the lead role further ensured the series' marketability. Produced under duress by puppet series maestro Gerry Anderson after Lew Grade cancelled the second series of ***UFO***, *The Protectors* was rollicking good entertainment, with the very best of British TV writers and directors queuing up to work on the show. In total, 52 episodes of *The Protectors* were produced, several of them shot entirely on location abroad.

Public Information Films

Animation/Live Action | duration <5 mins | broadcast c.1945–present

Messages from the government telling us how to behave might sound a little 'Big Brother', but for over 60 years now the Central Office of Information has commissioned short films to pass on guides for common sense instruction, new road signs or child safety warnings. Early examples were shown in cinemas on such subjects as how to use kitchen scraps to feed your chickens during rationing (no worries about salmonella then) or promoting civic pride in a city that's been devastated by the Blitz. When BBC television returned in 1945, such films would pop up at the ends of daily programming at lunchtime and late evening, or with the arrival of commercial TV, in gaps during advertising slots that were donated at the discretion of the broadcaster.

A fair few of the films were designed to get the messages across as plainly and concisely as possible but some were genuinely terrifying: a live-action film of a woman trying to clean windows on a wobbly chair only for her hand to go through the glass (a campaign for blood donors); in 'Lonely Water', a spectral hooded figure (voiced by Donald Pleasance) warning of the dangers of playing near the riverside; and the little boy running barefoot on the sand whose foot freeze-frames mere inches away from the pointed shards of a broken bottle.

Road safety films often used the same techniques as adverts to get their messages across. After all, if a celebrity can get you to buy a Mars Bar or drink a particular brand of beer, why can't they get you to pay attention when crossing the road? Ken Dodd played all the characters in one film from 1963 that explained how to use a pelicon crossing (that's 'Pedestrian Light Controlled', hence the weird spelling), while the same idea was used for the 'flashing green man' in a pair of films starring the cast of ***Dad's Army*** ('Don't panic!'). Jon Pertwee starred in a staggering road safety campaign that involved a convoluted mnemonic: First, find a **S**afe place to cross, then stop. Stand on the **P**avement, **L**ook all round for traffic, and **I**f traffic is coming, let it pass. When there is **N**o traffic near, walk straight across the road. **K**eep looking and listening for traffic while you cross. Apparently, that spells 'SPLINK', though if you had to remember all that in a crisis it would probably spell 'Accident and Emergency'. The film also included a very young Dexter Fletcher and Todd Carty, both of whom managed to avoid traffic accidents long enough to have acting careers as adults (Fletcher in ***Press Gang*** and the film *Lock, Stock and Two Smoking Barrels* (1998), Carty in ***Grange Hill***, ***EastEnders*** and ***The Bill***).

Pertwee wasn't the only celebrity to be called upon for road safety advice. In a series of films called 'Children's heroes', Les Gray of Mud, Alvin Stardust and boxer Joe

Bugner stopped children from running out into the roads. They were never our idea of children's heroes; Alvin Stardust was naff even then, while we weren't cheering Joe Bugner when he fought Muhammad Ali – at least they got it right when they hired Kevin Keegan.

Road safety got a lot easier when the Green Cross Code man arrived in 1975, played by bodybuilder Dave Prowse. As would later happen in *Star Wars*, where he played Darth Vader, Prowse's West Country burr was over-dubbed for some of the Green Cross films, though at least we all knew to Stop, Look and Listen for ourselves because we knew that the Green Cross Man 'won't be there when you cross the road'.

The most popular films were the animated kind, used to illustrate all manner of problems, from painting over polystyrene tiles with gloss paint to being rude on the roads. Many of these animated classics were voiced by Peter Hawkins, famous for creating the voice of Bill and Ben, Captain Pugwash and the original Daleks in ***Doctor Who***. Stars of a small number of these were Joe and Petunia, a skinny man and his lumpen wife, were voiced by Hawkins and Wendy Craig (and in the last of the series, Brigit Forsyth). The couple would be seen lounging by the seaside and observing danger flags, having a picnic on a cliff and spotting a man in a 'sailing Dinjee' in need of a coastguard or littering a farmer's fields and making him do 'a country dance' with fury. The hazardous couple eventually met a sticky end in a horrific car-crash due to worn tyres.

Most famous of all of these – and indeed the cartoons that lent their name to a home video collection of Public Information Films – is the 'Charley Says' series. Kenny Everett voiced Charley, an orange-striped cat whose 'Mrraowrorow' noises were interpreted by his young owner as warnings against playing with matches, going off without telling mummy or avoiding strangers' invitations 'to see some puppies'. The films also inspired the first hit single for 'twisted firestarters' The Prodigy, whose 'Charly' got to No. 3 in 1991.

With the arrival of 24-hour television, a lot of the more obvious Public Information Films have been relegated to very late at night (just before BBC One hands over to News 24), or immediately before Breakfast TV begins in the morning. But films fulfilling the same function still occasionally make it into primetime and now Public Information Films aren't limited to low-budget animations. A transport for London road safety campaign called 'Don't die before you've lived' featured a young pop star showing off her home, or a man starring in a trailer for a blockbuster movie, which in both cases were cut short by the star of the film being knocked over as a teenager. Another technically impressive and harrowing film simply shows in slow motion a car ploughing into a teenager with the message for drivers to 'kill your speed'.

Quantum Leap

Science Fiction | Belisarius Productions/Universal for NBC (shown on BBC Two) | episode duration 45 mins | broadcast 26 Mar 1989–5 May 1993

Regular Cast

Scott Bakula · *Dr Sam Beckett*
Dean Stockwell · *Al Calavicci*
Deborah Pratt · *Narrator, Voice of Ziggy*

Creator Donald P. Bellisario **Producers** Donald P. Bellisario, Chas Floyd Johnson, Deborah Pratt, Michael Zinberg (executive), David Bellisario (associate), Robin Bernheim, Paul Brown, Scott Ejercito, Jimmy Giritlian, Jeff Gourson, John Hill, Chris Ruppenthal, Scott Shepherd, Tommy Thompson, Harker Wade, Robert Wolterstorff **Writers** Various, including Donald P. Bellisario, Deborah Pratt, Paul Brown III, Scott Shepherd, Chris Ruppenthal, Tommy Thompson, Beverly Bridges, Richard C. Okie, Robin Jill Bernheim **Theme Music** Mike Post

A ***Twilight Zone*** combined with *The Littlest Hobo* and ***The Incredible Hulk***, *Quantum Leap* placed scientist Sam Beckett inside a quantum accelerator just in time for him to leap through time into the body of an experimental pilot. So begins a journey through the latter half of the 20th century with Sam righting wrongs and putting people's lives back on course – aided by his colleague Al, who appears to him in the form of an intangible hologram who is connected by a handheld device to a computer called Ziggy. Unlike practically every other time-travelling adventure series, Sam's purpose in life was explicitly to change history. Though there were some episodes that were set in such a way as he merely had to ensure established history happened as planned, generally his job was to correct mistakes that individuals had made, whether that was in the form of a black man conceding to the prejudices of a small town, a baseball player in need of a decent hit, a boxer standing up to gangsters who want him to take a dive or a woman fending off unwanted sexual approaches from her boss. Oh yes, Sam can leap into anyone, male, female, black or white.

Some episodes where played for laughs – young boys in certain episodes revealed themselves to be Buddy Holly or Stephen King – but generally this was a show with a strong moral centre and a willingness to make a difference, even if many of the outcomes were a bit schmaltzy. After five years of leaping – including leaps into Sam's own background where he helped out himself as a child, into the body of his own grandfather and one episode where it was Al who did the leaping – the final episode revealed that Sam is destined to continue leaping, sent by a higher power. (God? Time? Fate? You choose.)

Quatermass

Science Fiction | Euston Films for ITV | episode duration 60 mins | broadcast 24 Oct–14 Nov 1979

Principal Cast

John Mills · *Professor Bernard Quatermass*
Simon MacCorkindale · *Joe Kapp*
Barbara Kellerman · *Clare Kapp*
Brewster Mason · *Gurov*
Margaret Tyzack · *Annie Morgan*
Ralph Arliss · *Kickalong*
Paul Rosebury · *Caraway*
Jane Bertish · *Bee*
Rebecca Saire · *Hettie Carlson*
Annabelle Lanyon · *Isabel*
Toyah Willcox · *Sal*
Bruce Purchase · *Tommy Roach*
David Yip · *Frank Chen*
Brenda Fricker · *Alison Thorpe*
Tony Sibbald · *Chuck Marshall*
Neil Stacy · *Toby Gough*
Larry Noble · *Jack*
Gretchen Franklin · *Edna*
Clare Ruane · *Jane*
Kathleen St John · *Winnie*
Beatrice Shaw · *Susie*
James Ottaway · *Arthur*
David Ashford · *David Hatherley*
Donald Eccles · *Chisholm*
Joy Harrington · *TV Producer*
Rita Webb · *Charm Seller*
Kevin Stoney · *Prime Minister*

Creator/Writer Nigel Kneale **Producers** Johnny Goodman, Verity Lambert (executive), Norton Knatchbull (associate), Ted Childs **Theme Music** Nic Rowley, Marc Wilkinson

For commentary, see THE QUATERMASS SERIES, *pages* 596–601

Quatermass II

Science Fiction | BBC TV | episode duration 30 mins | broadcast 22 Oct–26 Nov 1955

Cast

John Robinson · *Professor Bernard Quatermass*
Monica Grey · *Paula Quatermass*
Hugh Griffith · *Dr Leo Pugh*
John Stone · *Captain John Dillon*
Brian Hayes · *Sergeant Grice*
Eric Lugg · *Fred Large*
Hilda Barry · *Mrs Large*
Herbert Lomas · *Robert*
Richard Cuthbert · *Landlord*

Peter Carver · *Australian Commentator, Inspector Clifford*
Derek Aylward · *Ward*
Rupert Davies · *Vincent Broadhead*
Austin Trevor · *Fowler*
John Miller · *Stenning*
Wilfrid Brambell · *Tramp*
Michael Brennan · *Dawson*
Sheila Martin · *Child*
Ilona Ference · *Mother*
Sydney Bromley · *Father*
Melvyn Hayes · *Frankie*
Philip Levene · *Supervisor*
Roger Delgado · *Conrad*
Michael Golden · *Paddy*
John Rae · *McLeod*
Elsie Arnold · *Mrs McLeod*
Ian Wilson · *Ernie*
Cyril Shaps · *Control Assistant*

Creator/Writer Nigel Kneale **Producer** Rudolph Cartier **Theme Music** As with ***The Quatermass Experiment***, the opening music, played once again over sinister burning letters forming the serial title, is a segment from 'Mars' from *The Planets* by Gustav Holst, with 'Inhumanity', a piece of stock music by Trevor Duncan, closing each episode.

For commentary, see THE QUATERMASS SERIES, *pages* 596–601

Quatermass and the Pit

Science Fiction | BBC TV | episode duration 30 mins | broadcast 22 Dec 1958–26 Jan 1959

Cast
André Morell · *Professor Bernard Quatermass*
Cec Linder · *Dr Matthew Roney*
Anthony Bushell · *Colonel Breen*
John Stratton · *Captain Potter*
Alexander Moyes · *Narrator*
Brian Worth · *James Fullalove*
Christine Finn · *Barbara Judd*
Arthur Hewlett · *Baines*
Michael Bird · *Armitage*
Janet Burnell · *Interviewer*
Robert Perceval · *The Minister*
Nan Braunton · *Miss Dobson*
Ian Ainsley · *Police Inspector*
Michael Ripper · *Sergeant*
Harold Goodwin · *Corporal Gibson*
John Walker · *Private West*
Victor Platt · *PC Ellis*
Hilda Barry · *Mrs Chilcot*
Howell Davies · *Mr Chilcot*

Creator/Writer Nigel Kneale

Producer Rudolph Cartier

Theme Music 'Mutations', a piece of stock music by Trevor Duncan

For commentary, see THE QUATERMASS SERIES, *pages* 596–60

The Quatermass Experiment

Science Fiction | BBC TV | episode duration 30 mins | broadcast 18 Jul–22 Aug 1953

Cast
Reginald Tate · *Professor Bernard Quatermass*
Isabel Dean · *Judith Carroon*
Duncan Lamont · *Victor Carroon*
Hugh Kelly · *John Paterson*
Moray Watson · *Peter Marsh*
W. Thorp Deverreux · *Blaker*
Van Boolen · *Len Matthews*
Iris Ballard · *Mrs Matthews*
Katie Johnson · *Miss Wilde*
Paul Whitsun-Jones · *James Fullalove*
John Glen · *Dr Gordon Briscoe*
Ian Colin · *Chief Inspector Lomax*
Frank Hawkins · *DS Best*
Christopher Rhodes · *Dr Ludwig Reichenheim*
Peter Bathurst · *Charles Greene*
Enid Lindsay · *Louisa Greene*
Wilfrid Brambell · *A Drunk*
John Kidd · *Sir Vernon Dodd*
Tony Van Bridge · *TV Producer*
Neal Arden · *TV Commentator*

Creator/Writer Nigel Kneale **Producer** Rudolph Cartier **Theme Music** The distinctive opening titles for the serial were formed by smouldering powder clouded in smoke, accompanied by a segment from 'Mars' from *The Planets* by Gustav Holst. 'Inhumanity', a piece of stock music by Trevor Duncan, closed each episode.

For commentary, see THE QUATERMASS SERIES, *pages* 596–601

The Quatermass series

See pages 596–601

Queer as Folk

See pages 602–4

The Quatermass series

André Morell (centre) as the third Quatermass.

The Quatermass Experiment came to our screens by accident when a gap appeared in the BBC television schedules. Waiting in the wings was Nigel Kneale, a young staff writer who was becoming increasingly frustrated by, as he later put it, 'radio men content to make radio plays with pictures'. Kneale's opinion was shared by a director who was fighting to make productions that were more cinematic and less static. The problem was technology. Lumbered with 20-year-old cameras and the traditions of live TV, the resources to perform more than the most basic of edits on film just didn't exist. Television as a medium was yet to reach a point where it was thought to be of any value at all, let alone culturally significant. The coronation of Elizabeth II had led to a dramatic increase in the potential audience, but there remained very little for that audience to enjoy after the event. The very ethos in the BBC of the time leaned more towards informative, worthy adaptations of Greek tragedies and Victorian novels. Science fiction was not considered to be of any merit whatsoever. It was a minor miracle that Kneale's 'serial in six parts' reached the screen at all.

The first of three *Quatermass* serials to be made by the BBC (a fourth being made by Euston Films for ITV in 1978), *The Quatermass Experiment* introduced us to the British Rocket Group, a research team headed by Professor Bernard Quatermass. To a 21st-century mind, the idea of the UK being a world leader in rocket science, ahead of America and Russia, might seem ludicrous. But in the wake of the Festival of Britain, good old imperial patriotism had never been stronger, so *of course* Quatermass's rocket was ahead of the game. But before the backslapping got too hearty, Kneale added another element – Cold War paranoia – and in this, the series pre-dates Don Siegal's *Invasion of the Body Snatchers* (1955) by two years.

See **QUATERMASS, QUATERMASS II, QUATERMASS AND THE PIT** *and* **THE QUATERMASS EXPERIMENT** *for broadcast details and individual credits*

When Quatermass's manned space rocket, the Q1, crash-lands after successfully becoming the first such craft to leave the earth's atmosphere, the first concern is for the three astronauts trapped inside it. But when the rocket's door is opened, only one of the crew – Victor Carroon – emerges, the other two having disappeared. For Quatermass, this is the beginning of a nightmare, as the astronaut begins to transform into a monstrous, shapeless killer. What's left of Carroon is eventually tracked to Westminster Abbey where Quatermass talks him – now a writhing blob of vegetable matter – into committing suicide.

Like almost all TV drama at that time, *The Quatermass Experiment* was performed and broadcast live, aside from a very few pre-filmed inserts to set up scenes of London. The scripts for the final episodes were still being written when the first episode went on air; only Nigel Kneale and producer/director Rudolph Cartier knew how it would end. Over 20 years before *Star Wars*, it all looked rather low-tech; one important scene is staged with characters listening to it on the radio, while the final appearance of the alien was created by Kneale himself donning a pair of tendril-covered rubber gloves and waggling them menacingly through a photographic blow-up of the Abbey. But as far as television went, nothing like this had ever been seen before.

To a 21st-century mind, the idea of the UK being a world leader in rocket science might seem ludicrous. But in the wake of the Festival of Britain, good old imperial patriotism had never been stronger, so *of course* Quatermass's rocket was ahead of the game.

Nigel Kneale has often rebuffed the idea that he was the progenitor of British science fiction, preferring to think of himself merely as a dramatist who used science fiction elements to tell his stories. The technological limitations of course shaped how the finished production would look, but Kneale's economical approach meant that the story came through the characters rather than through special effects.

Kneale's scripts were adapted for the big screen two years later, in 1955, as *The Quatermass Xperiment* (neatly capitalising on the brand new 'X' certificate films aimed at adult audiences). Starring American actor Brian Donlevy, who appeared to be making up his dialogue as he went along, the film marked the beginning of a long association with horror for a British company called Hammer Film Productions.

Following the huge success of *The Quatermass Experiment*, a sequel, *Quatermass II*, was made two years later, forming part of BBC television's assault on rival network ITV, which had finally begun broadcasting just a month before. This time round, Nigel Kneale's scripts were less hokum 'monster-on-the-run' and more a sociological horror story, looking at the damaging effects industrial new towns were having on older communities, voicing concerns over pollution and warning against the corruption of government by big business. Of course this was all played out against a backdrop of alien invasion and possession. This wasn't a heavy-handed didactic onslaught; Kneale wasn't that daft.

This time Quatermass finds himself swept up in events almost by accident, guilt-ridden and facing the end of his career after one of his prototype rockets under test in Australia misfires and causes a nuclear explosion that kills thousands. As the news reaches the horrified scientist, his daughter's fiancé John Dillon is investigating reports of a meteor that has landed in nearby farmland. Soon, Quatermass is drawn into investigating an industrial complex that has seemingly been built overnight, dominated by a series of domes and protected by guards that appear to have been brainwashed. When Dillon joins their number, the professor tries in vain to convince the locals of the menace growing on their doorstep. Returning to his research laboratory, Quatermass is shocked to discover that Dillon and his possessed troops have surrounded the building. Running out of options, Quatermass realises his only chance of success might lie with his disgraced rocket project . . .

The death of Reginald Tate just weeks before *Quatermass II* was filmed led to the lead role being recast. That John Robinson had come to the production late was not hard to spot as he stumbles over his lines through most of the serial. But the fact that he wasn't word perfect just added to the feeling of authenticity. Besides, in the early days of live TV, no-one was word perfect.

If *The Quatermass Experiment* had ruffled a few feathers, that was nothing compared to the effect *Quatermass II* would have. Having already terrified the nation back in 1953, and created outrage and indignation with ***Nineteen Eighty-Four*** the following year, this serial set out to maintain the horror levels right from the first episode when, investigating strange meteors, Quatermass notices an alien spore growing from the side of Dillon's face (an effect that relies entirely on John Robinson's ability to convey concern as, due to the series being broadcast live, there was no chance to actually put anything on actor John Stone's face until the recap at the start of the next episode). When the complaints began to pour in, two things became apparent: the BBC would have to broadcast a warning before some of the later episodes; and Kneale and Cartier had another hit on their hands.

If *The Quatermass Experiment* had ruffled a few feathers, that was nothing compared to the effect *Quatermass II* would have.

Some viewers would have seen the kind of American horror films that studios like Universal had released in the UK, so the sight of a grown adult being scared witless was not a new one. But there's quite a difference between showing that kind of image in a cinema and beaming it into someone's living room. *Quatermass II* was chock-full of moments to chill the blood: the conclusion to episode three has Quatermass's colleague Ward emerging from one of the huge containers covered in a steaming black substance and smearing it like oil along a wall before collapsing; at the end of episode four, Quatermass finally sees what is inside the factory domes – a pulsating alien parasite, its tendrils thrashing into the smoky air; and the moment where a journalist called Conrad (a mesmerising performance from future ***Doctor Who*** villain Roger Delgado) realises he's been infected with the alien spores and phones in a news story to his editor knowing it will be his last.

As with its predecessor, *Quatermass II* was given the Hammer treatment in 1957 with another big-screen adaptation starring the truly dire Brian Donlevy. The following year, Nigel Kneale wrote his last *Quatermass* serial for the BBC – *Quatermass and the Pit.*

In this third serial, digging at a construction site in the East End of London is halted after the discovery of a skull. What begins as a murder investigation soon spirals out of control after a large metallic object is also unearthed from deep within the ground. The authorities move nearby residents from their homes, fearful that the object is an unexploded bomb left over from the Blitz, but after Quatermass investigates further, he concludes that the object is alien. The object is cut open and the dried remains of an alien race are revealed. But then the noises begin, and the visions of an alien world in the throes of destruction. Is this a recording of the past, or a warning about the future?

Having spent much of the 1950s scaring the nation witless, Kneale and Cartier collaborated to create their most impressive – certainly their scariest – *Quatermass* to date. The story combined the no-nonsense scientific approach that Quatermass was known for with a hint of olde worlde mythology. The presence of the strange, locust-like creatures found within the craft re-awakens atavistic memories in the minds of some people, images of the aliens tearing each other apart in an apocalyptic end to life on Mars. Through this, Kneale manages to provide a science fiction-based rational explanation for a belief in demons: the excavation work takes place in Hobbs Lane – formerly 'Hobs Lane' ('Hob', or 'Hobgoblin', being an old name for the Devil). Using this theory he's able to deduce that the spark of life that caused the evolution of humanity, coupled with human urge to wage war on itself, may have come from Mars.

The concept might appear far-fetched, and in retrospect the production (broadcast live with a few pre-filmed sequences inserted, as before) would appear crude and simplistic by today's flashy standards, but at the time it was riveting. André Morell, replacing John Robinson in the title role, delivered what many fans consider to be the definitive portrayal, a reserved Englishness that nevertheless had a sense of urgency about it.

Like its predecessors, *Quatermass and the Pit* received the big-screen treatment, courtesy of Hammer Films. The 1967 adaptation, directed by Roy Ward Baker, was made in lurid colour, with Hammer regular Andrew Keir as the professor, James Donald as Dr Roney, Barbara Shelley as Quatermass's assistant Barbara Judd and Julian Glover as the stubborn Colonel Breen. Faster paced and with some impressive set pieces (notably the climax in which the demon is destroyed by a courageous act of self-sacrifice), it's the most accessible of all *Quatermass* productions; its shorter running time and links to the grand Hammer company at its peak have ensured that more people have seen this version of *Quatermass* than any other (it was released in the USA under the title *Five Million Years to Earth*).

With the success of Hammer Films' adaptations of Kneale's *Quatermass* teleplays, what became the final *Quatermass* serial began in 1973 as an original *Quatermass* film for Hammer. When that fell through, Kneale took it to the BBC under the auspices of BBC Head of Drama Ronnie Marsh and producer Joe Waters, but there too the project faltered, mainly due to lack of budget. Eventually, the script went to Euston Films, the drama production subsidiary of ITV regional franchise-holder Thames. The decision was taken to assemble two versions, one a four-part TV production, the other a 100-minute film for overseas distribution. Shot on 35mm film on location, and starring British film legend John Mills as the eponymous professor, it was by far and away the most lavish of the TV versions of *Quatermass*.

In this version, Quatermass has retired and turned his back on society, living for many years in a remote area of Scotland. Called upon as a guest for a London-based TV programme to offer a commentary on a joint Soviet–American space station project, he unleashes a scathing attack on both superpowers. When the space station is mysteriously destroyed by unknown forces, Quatermass finds himself targeted as a scapegoat. Meanwhile, a group calling themselves the Planet People have assembled at the Ringstone Round stone circle to welcome a new world thanks to amazing powers they believe they've gained from an immensely potent spiritual force. Instead, a blinding light obliterates them. Quatermass soon realises that rather than granting the Planet People power, this alien force is harvesting them. Around the world, street gangs and Planet People alike are gathering together. Quatermass, aided by a radio-astronomer called Kapp, fears that the only way to prevent the complete destruction of the human race is to deliver himself as the ultimate sacrifice . . .

Kneale had often used *Quatermass* to comment on the society of the time but here his story becomes much more overtly critical. Through the professor's eyes we see the gang warfare in the inner cities, the police force are now 'contract police' and a wave of anarchy is bubbling under the surface with graffiti calling for the death of 'HM the King' (in this near future, Prince Charles has ascended to the throne). The world's disaffected youth rises up in protest against the establishment, but even here Kneale offers a science fictional explanation for what we'd usually attribute to hormones: that this alien influence is causing them to react with violence and surges of emotion that make them ripe for the picking. Their social alienation is replaced by a physical one, their bodies literally 'made alien' and harvested.

There's also a brief jab at spirituality in all its forms: the faith of the Planet People is contrasted with that of Kapp and his family, practising Jews, but both faiths ultimately fail to save any of the believers. Even Quatermass's own faith in science, specifically a belief that a bomb will bring an end to the alien menace, is an uneasy one as he knows the exact same technology has caused so many of the world's problems – and possibly led to the planet being exposed to the alien attack in the first place.

Though *Quatermass* hasn't endured in the same way as its successor *Doctor Who*, it has been a reassuring presence in entertainment now for over 50 years, with subsequent generations still eager to prolong its memory. In 1996, a five-part BBC Radio 4 series, *The Quatermass Memoirs*, merged interviews with Nigel Kneale and dramatic audio re-creations of classic scenes. Movie Quatermass Andrew Keir played the professor once again, trying to live out his retirement peacefully while a persistent biographer forces him to relive his past. The programme placed the *Quatermass* series within a historical perspective, drawing lines from the atomic tests, espionage defections and race riots of the 1950s with the fantastical events of Quatermass's own life.

Though *Quatermass* hasn't endured in the same way as its successor *Doctor Who*, it has been a reassuring presence now for over 50 years, with subsequent generations still eager to prolong its memory.

An unusual approach greeted audiences in the summer of 1997 when *Quatermass and the Pit* was adapted into a theatrical production. Staged in a quarry on the outskirts of Nottingham by Creation Productions, the play starred David Longford as Quatermass with Daniel Hogarth as Dr Roney, whose final confrontation of the aliens was achieved through the combination of an impressive light show and an industrial digger.

Finally (so far at least), 2005 saw a BBC Four season called 'TV on Trial' in which the television of the past and present was attacked and defended by a critic and an advocate of each decade from the 1950s. With much of the material from the 1950s no longer available (only the first two episodes of *The Quatermass Experiment* exist in the archives, for instance, preserved on a 16mm film telerecording – achieved by literally pointing a camera at a TV monitor and hoping for the best), the centrepiece of the season was a new adaptation of *The Quatermass Experiment*, broadcast live on Saturday 2 April 2005. Boasting an impressive cast of established and up-and-coming performers – Jason Flemyng as Professor Quatermass, with ***League of Gentlemen*** star Mark Gatiss as Paterson, Indira Varma as Judith Carroon, David Tennant as Briscoe, Andy Tiernan as Victor Carroon and Adrian Dunbar as Detective Lomax – it was an ambitious, fitting tribute that also showed there's life in the old professor yet.

Queer as Folk

Manchester's Canal Street, the 'Gay Village'.

This is the one about the one-night stand that wouldn't go away: Nathan Maloney, a schoolboy (not yet 16) who goes out on Manchester's gay scene for the first time and ends up having sex with Stuart Alan Jones (King of Canal Street and doesn't he know it), who rarely shags the same bloke twice. It's also about Stuart's best friend, Vince, a ***Doctor Who*** fan and habitual liar who's just too nice to tell the truth. It's about Vince's mum, Hazel, who's out on the scene almost as much as he is. It's about Alexander – well, he'd like to think it is. His parents treat him as if he's invisible, though it's impossible to miss someone as screamingly gay as him. It's about Janice Maloney, Nathan's worried mother, just wanting to be allowed into his life but scared that her husband's homophobia might drive their son away for good. It's about a baby and a pair of lesbians – but only just. And it's definitely not about issues. Who's got time for issues while the clubs are open?

Coronation Street took over 40 years to develop its first regular gay character, surprising considering its creator was himself gay and all manner of over-rouged hot-tempered lasses in the series' history have inspired copy-cat drag acts in seaside towns and back-street revue clubs across the country. The soap genre is exceedingly camp, yet all too often the soaps shy away from having homosexuality on at tea time in case this puts viewers off their fish fingers. And of course, when the gays finally do come out of the closet, they're forced to carry the weight of 'their people' on their shoulders because you can't be gay and happy in soap land. This is what Russell T. Davies was reacting against when he created *Queer as Folk*.

Queer as Folk refused to ask for anything as dreary as to be accepted as an equal – there were no aims to grasp the 'Good As You' slogan as a campaign banner. For the characters, the gay lifestyle is better than a conformist straight life. Vince's mum certainly thinks so, with her gay son, gay lodger and love for the clubs. But this attitude, embodied by the vain, selfish and ruthless Stuart Alan Jones, was never meant to stand for every single gay man in the UK; representation of all gay men was never the series' agenda any more than *Coronation Street* represents every facet of life in Manchester. Yet some of the strongest criticisms came from the gay community itself, concerned that the drama reinforced the stereotypes of predatory, promiscuous men targeting schoolboys (which apart from anything else ignores the fact that here it's the schoolboy doing most of the chasing).

The decision not to shy away from the process of gay sex by including the most explicit man-on-man scene ever shown on British TV halfway through the first episode drew condemnation from almost every facet of the fourth estate, as might be expected (and indeed was probably one of the reasons that scene was there in the first place). Of course there was more than a little hypocrisy in the fact that the same critics who roared against the sight of two men getting hot and sweaty had no such complaints when two women did the same in *Tipping the Velvet*. What did disappoint was beer manufacturers Becks pulling their sponsorship after the first episode was aired. It was an action that left Russell T. Davies perplexed. After all, Becks were more than happy to stock the gay bars of Manchester and the rest of the UK, so it couldn't have been motivated by corporate homophobia, could it?

The series also drew complaints from *Doctor Who* fans: in the first episode, while Stuart and Nathan are indulging in a sex scene that wouldn't have raised an eyebrow if it had been between a straight couple on BBC Two, Vince, identified early on as a major fan of *Doctor Who*, is watching the cliffhanger to part one of 'Pyramids of Mars' in which a black-masked alien 'bring[s] Sutekh's gift of death to all humanity'; in the penultimate episode Stuart buys Vince a remote-controlled version of Doctor Who's robot dog K-9; in the finale, Vince dumps his boyfriend for thinking that his inability to name all the actors to have played the Time Lord doesn't matter, while Stuart names them in order, dismissing Paul McGann as 'he doesn't count'. While the inclusion of K-9 drew a complaint from one 'Whoover', who felt it inappropriate to include a children's favourite in such a show, some fans were simply concerned about the acknowledgement of the disproportionate amount of gay male viewers that *Doctor Who* attracted (as in *Time Out* magazine's euphemism 'traditional *Doctor Who* fan' suggests).

But for every gay man who felt that they weren't represented by the series, thousands more felt that they were. While sexuality was a significant part of the make-up of these characters, it was more important that they resonated as real, believable people, which they did. In a follow-up mini series (which incidentally featured the first bad-taste joke on British TV about the death of Princess Diana,

Drama
Red Productions for Channel 4
Episode Duration: 50 mins
Broadcast: 23 Feb 1999–22 Feb 2000

Principal Cast
Aidan Gillen · *Stuart Alan Jones*
Craig Kelly · *Vince Tyler*
Charlie Hunnam · *Nathan Maloney*
Denise Black · *Hazel Tyler*
Antony Cotton · *Alexander Perry*
Andy Devine · *Bernard Thomas*
Peter O'Brien · *Cameron Roberts*
Esther Hall · *Romey Sullivan*
Saira Todd · *Lisa Levene*
Jason Merrells · *Phil Delaney*
Caroline O'Neill · *Janice Maloney*
Paul Copley · *Roy Maloney*
Jonathon Natynczyk · *Dazz Collinson*
Ben Maguire · *Christian Hobbs*
Caroline Pegg · *Rosalie Cotter*
Ger Ryan · *Margaret Jones*
Ian McElhinney · *Clive Jones*
Maria Doyle Kennedy · *Marie Jones Threepwood*
Andrew Mawdsley · *Thomas Jones*
Stuart Mawdsley · *Ben Jones*
John Brobbey · *Lance Amponah*
Alison Burrows · *Sandra Docherty*
Adam Zane · *Dane McAteer*
Juley McCann · *Siobhan Potter*
Sarah Jones · *Suzie Smith*
Susan Cookson · *Marcie Finch*
Andrew Lancel · *Harvey Black*
Michael Culkin · *Martin Brooks*
Jack Deam · *Gareth Critchly*
Kate Fitzgerald · *Mrs Delaney/Phil's Mum*
Lee Warburton · *Striking Man*
Clinton Kenyon · *Mickey Smith*
Susan Cookson · *Marcie Finch*
Pearce Quigley · *Graham Beck*
Judy Holt · *Claire Fletcher*
Naomi Radcliffe · *Judith Collins*
James Lauren · *Adrian Collins*
Alan Rothwell · *Dudley Jackson*
Ben Maguire · *Christian Hobbs*

Creator/Writer Russell T. Davies

Producers Russell T. Davies, Nicola Shindler

Theme Music Murray Gold taps into the Mardi Gras carnival themes of San Francisco Gay Pride marches and combines them with the Manchester club sound.

courtesy of Alexander) Stuart avoids blackmail by his young nephew by finally coming out to his parents. He and Vince decide to escape Manchester to explore America, leaving Nathan to rule Canal Street. In a coda to the story, Stuart and Vince give an ignorant homophobe the *Thelma and Louise* treatment.

Sadly, that was that for the show. A proposed spin-off series, provisionally entitled 'Misfits', was in advanced stages of development when it was unexpectedly dropped by Channel 4, as was another drama Davies was developing for the channel, ***The Second Coming***, which subsequently materialised on ITV. Davies ditched *Misfits* completely and instead created a new drama, *Bob and Rose*, for ITV.

Russell T. Davies's series attracted its very own fans, one of whom, film director Joel Schumacher, was so impressed by its wit and bravery that he bought the rights and made his own version. In *Queer as Folk* USA, broadcast on cable channel Showtime, the action has relocated from Manchester to Pittsburgh, names of the main parts are changed and the Vince character is a comic-book fan instead of a Whovian, but the main plot strands are there for the first few series (a comparatively runaway success, the American version has racked up over 70 episodes and, at the time of writing, four series). Back in the UK, Antony Cotton (Alexander) emerged as TV's greatest new find, wrote and starred in his own short-lived sitcom, the acidic *Having It Off*, before being cast as one of *Coronation Street*'s first regular gay characters, Sean Tully (just being pipped to the post by confused teen Todd Grimshaw). Meanwhile, having upset all those *Doctor Who* fans, Russell T. Davies made amends by bringing their favourite show back to Saturday nights in a 2005 high-budget series starring Christopher Eccleston as the Doctor. Quite right too.

***Queer as Folk* refused to ask for anything as dreary as to be accepted as an equal – for the characters, the gay lifestyle is better than a conformist straight life.**

A Question of Sport

Panel Game | BBC One | episode duration 30 mins | broadcast 5 Jan 1970–present

Regular Cast

David Vine, David Coleman, Sue Barker · *Presenters*
Henry Cooper, Cliff Morgan, Freddie Trueman, Brendan Foster, Gareth Edwards, Emlyn Hughes, Bill Beaumont, Willie Carson, Ian Botham, John Parrott, Ally McCoist, Frankie Dettori, Matt Dawson · *Team Captains*

Producers Nick Hunter, Hazel Lewthwaite, Mike Adley, Carl Doran, Phil Wye, Caroline Roberts, Ade Rawcliffe, Gareth Edwards
Theme Music The original theme tune was called 'Tio Pepe', and the current arrangement is by Vitamin.

A perpetually popular panel game, *A Question of Sport* has been on our TV screens for 35 years and shows absolutely no sign of running out of steam. The programme's format has stayed pretty much the same since the first show – two regular team captains (both champions in the field of sports) are joined each week by two pairs of sports stars to answer sporting questions in a number of different rounds. In the first series, presenter David Vine posed the puzzlers and Henry Cooper and Cliff Morgan were the team captains. As the years have passed, only three people have sat in the presenter's chair, with David Coleman lasting the longest and helming the show during the high-rating glory years of the mid-1980s. Team captains have come and gone too, but the cheeky, chirpy charm of Emlyn Hughes and latterly Ally McCoist attracted a wide range of viewers who might normally switch off from any TV show that was remotely sport-related.

Favourite rounds have included 'What Happens Next?', in which a clip of sporting action is stopped just before something bizarre or unpredictable occurs, and 'Mystery Guest', where another sports star is filmed in disguise or in extreme close up (sometimes in a parody of a pop music performance or classic film clip). With constant slight variations on the standard games, *A Question of Sport* keeps itself refreshed and relevant for each new generation of viewers. For the show's 200th edition (broadcast 5 Feb 1987), HRH Princess Anne was a panellist.

Rab C Nesbitt

Sitcom | BBC Two | episode duration 30 mins, plus specials | broadcast 31 Dec 1989, 27 Sep 1990–18 Jun 1999

Principal Cast

Gregor Fisher · *Rab C Nesbitt*
Elaine C. Smith · *Mary Nesbitt*
Andrew Fairlie · *Gash Nesbitt*
Tony Roper · *Jamesie Cotter*
Barbara Rafferty · *Ella Cotter*
Eric Cullen · *Burney Nesbitt*
David McKay · *Screech Nesbitt*
Brian Pettifer · *Andra*
Iain McColl · *Dodie*
John Kazek · *Norrie*
Charlie Sim · *Dougie*

Creator/Writer Ian Pattison **Producer** Colin Gilbert

Gregor Fisher's foul-mouthed and largely incomprehensible alcoholic Glaswegian first appeared in the long-running Scottish sketch show ***Naked Video***, in which he would often be seen staggering along the road, drunkenly berating the camera for some unfathomable reason or another. Amazingly, a character that at first sight appeared to be so limited in its comedy potential managed to spin off into a very long-running, successful and surprisingly emotional sitcom.

Rab C Nesbitt lives in a fairly permanent drunken haze, normally clad in a string vest and with a bandaged head (either as a result of a fight or a booze-induced tumble). His ever-suffering wife Mary just about puts up with Rab's dodgy deals, skiving, sexism and regular arrests by the police. Rab is led astray by his drinking partner Jamesie, who spends as much time in the pub as Rab, largely to keep out of the way of his nagging wife Ella. Rab and Mary's children, Gash and Burney, seem to be heading in the same direction as their father, with a punch-up or an arrest never very far away. With such a bleak premise, it's down to Ian Pattison's quality scripts to turn these characters (who could quite easily have fallen out of a hard-hitting gritty domestic drama) into believable and (almost) lovable comic creations. However, sadness and tragedy did sometimes creep into the Nesbitt's lives, such as the moment when Rab discovered he was suffering from cancer. By and large, Rab C Nesbitt was a triumphant comic creation, running for a very healthy 52 episodes across eight seasons.

Rab C Nesbitt was significant for one other reason: exploiting the North-South divide by slipping in obscenities that are never heard south of the Border. It caused one of the biggest uptakes in use of Ceefax subtitles to enable English viewers to get more of the jokes.

The Rag Trade

Sitcom | BBC TV/LWT for ITV | episode duration 25–30 mins | broadcast 6 Oct 1961–30 Mar 1963 (BBC), 11 Sep 1977–20 Oct 1978 (ITV)

Principal Cast

Miriam Karlin · *Paddy*
Peter Jones · *Harold Fenner*
Reg Varney · *Reg*
Sheila Hancock · *Carole*
Esma Cannon · *Little Lil*
Wanda Ventham · *Shirley*
Barbara Windsor · *Judy*
Irene Handl · *Reg's Mum*
Claire Davenport · *Myrtle*
Amanda Reiss · *Janet*
Stella Tanner · *Olive*
Patricia Denys · *Betty*
Carmel Cryan · *Gloria*
Sheena Marshe · *Sandra*
Christopher Beeny · *Tony*
Anna Karen · *Olive*
Diane Langton · *Kathy*
Deddie Davies · *Mabel*
Gillian Taylforth · *Lyn*
Lucita Lijertwood · *Jo-Jo*
Rowena Cooper, Joy Stewart · *Sylvia Fenner*

Creators/Writers Ronald Wolfe, Ronald Chesney **Producers** Dennis Main Wilson, Bryan Izzard **Theme Music** The original theme tune was written by Gordon Franks. For the '70s revival, Eurovision entrant Lynsey de Paul wrote and performed 'The Rag Trade Rag'.

A top-quality sitcom from the same team behind the later ***On the Buses***, *The Rag Trade* detailed the conflicts between Harold Fenner, manager of small clothes manufacturers Fenner Fashions, and the women who work for him in his factory. Chief spokesman and union rep for the women was the dynamic, no-nonsense Paddy, a woman always ready with her whistle and perpetual cry of 'Everybody Out!' should Fenner ever break any employment laws. Reg was the factory foreman, sorting out problems with the equipment and always ready with a bit of banter for the ladies. The factory workers were a real cross-section – glamorous, busty younger women and doddery older ladies worked side-by-side (or more accurately, skived side-by-side).

It wasn't just *The Rag Trade*'s scripts that were good – the quality of the cast was pretty outstanding too. Future stage and screen actress (and Mrs John Thaw) Sheila Hancock played the lippy Carole in the show's first two seasons, and a pre-*Carry On* Barbara Windsor strutted her stuff too. When the third BBC season seemed to lack a bit of the sparkle and dynamism of the first two, the decision was taken to shut the doors of Fenner Fashions – writers

Chesney and Wolfe moved off to create *On the Buses* (which starred *The Rag Trade*'s Reg Varney) and that seemed to be that. It came as a pretty big surprise when the programme was revived, 14 years after its last transmission, and on ITV rather than on its original home of the BBC. Paddy and Fenner resumed their battles (Miriam Karlin and Peter Jones were the only two returning cast members) for another 22 episodes that were almost on a par with the 36 BBC originals. Working in the factory this time were Christopher Beeny (straight from working for the Bellamy Household in ***Upstairs, Downstairs***), future ***EastEnder*** Gillian Taylforth, and (playing almost exactly the same character as she'd done in *On the Buses*) Anna Karen as bespectacled Olive.

Rag, Tag and Bobtail

Pre-School Puppetry | Westerham Arts Ltd for BBC TV | episode duration 15 mins broadcast 10 Sep 1953–c.1954

Voice Cast
Charles E. Stidwell, David Enders, James Urquhart · *Narrators*

Creator/Writer Louise Cochrane **Producers** Freda Lingstrom and David Boisseau

When *Watch with Mother* finally arrived in 1953, children's programming had been in evidence for over a decade, with ***Muffin the Mule, Andy Pandy*** and the ***Flower Pot Men*** holding the fort. But there had never been a deliberate effort to schedule programmes to suit that time of day when mum takes a break from the housework to spend some 'quality time' with the little 'un. *Andy Pandy* had been created as an experiment, which was deemed successful, and thanks largely to the efforts of Freda Lingstrom, September 1953 saw the new *Watch with Mother* timeslot bring a little order to the schedule: *Andy Pandy* and his chums appeared on Tuesdays; Wednesdays remained the domain of Bill and Ben, and Thursdays became the home of a trio called *Rag, Tag and Bobtail*. (In later years, the strand would be expanded to fill out the weekdays, with shows such as *Picture Book* and ***The Woodentops*** appearing on Mondays and Fridays.)

Rag, Tag and Bobtail lived out in the countryside. Rag was a slow-talking hedgehog, Tag was a mouse and Bobtail was a rabbit whose padded rear could give Jennifer Lopez a run for her money.

Unlike the other string-puppet *Watch with Mother* treats, Rag, Tag and Bobtail were brought to life through the magic of hand puppetry by Sam and Elizabeth Williams, very much in the traditions of Punch and Judy only with less domestic abuse. The settings were the burrowed-out tree hollows and logs that the characters called home, with each episode featuring an aspect of country life, such as using a hazel twig to divine a source of water. In almost constant rotation until 1965, very few of the original episodes have survived, which perhaps explains why these particular characters are not as well remembered as their contemporaries.

Trivia
Oddly, the term 'rag, tag and bobtail' originates from the 17th century as a derogatory term for peasants, though we think it's unlikely we'll ever see a modern equivalent; 'Pikey, Chav and Dole-scum' doesn't have the same ring to it.

The Railway Children (1951)

Children's Drama | BBC TV | episode duration 30/60 mins | broadcast 6 Feb–27 Mar 10–31 Jul 1951

Principal Cast
Jean Anderson · *Mother*
Marian Chapman · *Roberta*
Ysanne Churchman · *Ruth*
Michael Croudson · *Peter*
David Duncan · *Station Master*
Carole Lorimer · *Phyllis*
John Stuart · *Father*

Producer/Writer Dorothea Brooking, from the novel by E. Nesbit **Theme Music** *Symphonic Dances* by Grieg

For commentary, see THE RAILWAY CHILDREN (2000)

The Railway Children (1957)

Children's Drama | BBC TV | episode duration 30/60 mins | broadcast 3 Mar–21 Apr 1957

Principal Cast
Jean Anderson · *Mother*
Anneke Wills · *Roberta*
Cavan Kendall · *Peter*
Sandra Michaels · *Phyllis*
Donald Morley · *Station Master*
Richard Peters · *Jim*
John Richmond · *Father*
Norman Shelley · *Old Gentleman*
Richard Warner · *Perks*

Producer/Writer Dorothea Brooking, from the novel by E. Nesbit **Theme Music** *Symphonic Dances* by Grieg

For commentary, see THE RAILWAY CHILDREN (2000)E.

The Railway Children (1968)

Chiildren's Drama | BBC One | episode duration 25 mins | broadcast 21 May–23 Jun 1968

Principal Cast
Ann Castle · *Mother*
Jenny Agutter · *Roberta Waterbury*

Neil McDermott · *Peter Waterbury*
Gillian Bailey · *Phyllis Waterbury*
Gordon Gostelow · *Perks*
Brian Hayes · *Station Master*
Mary Healey · *Ruth*
Joseph O'Conor · *Old Gentleman*
John Ringham · *Dr Forrest*
Frederick Treves · *Father*
Christopher Witty · *Jim*

Producer Campbell Logan **Writer** Denis Constanduros, from the novel by E. Nesbit **Theme Music** *Symphonic Dances* by Grieg

For commentary, see THE RAILWAY CHILDREN (2000)

The Railway Children (2000)

Children's Drama | Carlton for ITV | episode duration 30 mins | broadcast 23 Apr 2000

Cast
Jenny Agutter · *Mother*
Jemima Rooper · *Bobbie*
Jack Blumenau · *Peter*
Clare Thomas · *Phyllis*
Michael Kitchen · *Father*
Valerie Minifie · *Cook*
Melanie Clark Pullen · *Ruth*
Georgie Glen · *Aunt Emma*
Gregor Fisher · *Perks*
Amanda Walker · *Mrs Ransome*
Clive Russell · *Station Master*
Richard Attenborough · *Old Gentleman*
David Bamber · *Dr Forrest*

Producers Jonathan Powell (executive), Freya Pinsent (associate), Charles Elton **Writer** Simon Nye, from the novel by E. Nesbit **Theme Music** Simon Lacey

At the turn of the century, siblings Roberta ('Bobbie'), Peter and Phyllis are surprised and a little upset to learn that they are to leave their city home and move to the country while their father is away. Their mother looks distressed and soon Bobbie discovers that their father has been arrested and is awaiting trial for spying, a detail she decides not to burden her younger brother and sister with. While Mother works hard to sell stories to magazines, the children begin to explore their new surroundings and their attentions turn to the local railway station and grumpy old Perks, who is soon begrudgingly won over by the love and affection the children show him. Every day, they sit by the side of the railway to wave to an elderly gentleman – and he waves back.

The classic tale by Edith Nesbit was adapted for a live drama serial in 1951, remounted for another, shorter version the same year and remade in 1957. The 1968 adaptation combined studio-recorded scenes with location filming – something the earlier live productions could never have done. This version also marked the first time Jenny Agutter would be associated with the story. Two years later, she'd re-create the role of Bobby for Lionel Jeffries' lavish film version. Most recently, a TV movie from ITV starred Agutter once more – this time as Mother.

Trivia
Storytelling series ***Jackanory*** also offered up an abridged reading of the tale from 5 to 9 October 1981, read by Jane Asher.

Rainbow

See pages 610–11

Randall and Hopkirk (Deceased) (1969–70)

Action-Adventure | ITC for ITV | episode duration 50 mins | broadcast 21 Sep 1969–13 Mar 1970

Regular Cast
Mike Pratt · *Jeff Randall*
Kenneth Cope · *Marty Hopkirk*
Annette André · *Jeannie Hopkirk*
Ivor Dean · *Inspector Large*
Judith Arthy · *Jenny*
Michael Griffiths · *Inspector Nelson*

Creator Dennis Spooner **Producer** Monty Berman **Writers** Ralph Smart, Mike Pratt, Ian Wilson, Donald James, Tony Williamson, Gerald Kelsey **Theme Music** Edwin T. Astley; a quirky harpsicord piece

For commentary, see RANDALL AND HOPKIRK (DECEASED), *pages* 612–5

Randall and Hopkirk (Deceased) (2000–01)

Comedy Drama | Working Title for BBC One | episode duration 50 mins | broadcast 18 Mar 2000–10 Nov 2001

Regular Cast
Vic Reeves · *Jeff Randall*
Bob Mortimer · *Marty Hopkirk*
Emila Fox · *Jeannie Hurst*
Tom Baker · *Wyvern*
Charlie Higson · *Various Characters*

Producers Simon Wright (executive), Analisa Barreto (associate), Charlie Higson **Writers** Charlie Higson, Paul Whitehouse, Gareth Roberts, Kate Wood, Mark Gatiss, Jeremy Dyson, based on the characters created by Dennis Spooner **Theme Music** Unlike the deliciously quirky original, David Arnold's theme for the remake is tediously generic.

For commentary, see RANDALL AND HOPKIRK (DECEASED), *pages* 612–5

Record Breakers

Children's Entertainment | BBC One | episode duration 25–30 mins | broadcast 15 Nov 1972–21 Dec 2001

Regular Cast

Roy Castle, Norris McWhirter, Ross McWhirter, Fiona Kennedy, Cheryl Baker, Julian Farino, Ron Reagan Jr, Kriss Akabusi, Dan Roland, Mark Curry, Linford Christie, Kate Sanderson, Fearne Cotton, Shovell, Jez Edwards · *Presenters*

Producers Alan Russell, Eric Rowan, Michael Forte, Greg Childs, Sally Fraser, Jeremy Daldry **Theme Music** The version of the theme that everybody remembers was called 'Dedication' and was performed by the programme's legendary presenter Roy Castle – he'd even whip out his trumpet to round things off. This original version (with the Geoff Sanders Quartet backing Roy up) was released on several compilation albums.

Few subjects fascinate children more than world records – most ankle-biters are endlessly intrigued by information about the tallest, fastest, longest, smallest, highest, widest, and most *things* in the world, like, *ever*. The first printed edition of the *Guinness Book of Records* was released to an eagerly awaiting public in August 1955. The book's two editors, twin brothers Norris and Ross McWhirter, became co-hosts and 'record experts' when the BBC launched a series for children that was essentially a televised version of their book. *The Record Breakers* (it maintained a 'the' in the title until 22 December 1982) was first screened in 1972 and became a popular and long-running series, primarily down to the sheer enthusiasm and charisma of its long-term presenter, all-round entertainer and good egg Roy Castle.

Roy would keep things ticking along in the studio, and the McWhirters would be on hand to verify if any records had been broken. There would also be a segment in which children in the studio audience could pose questions to the brothers, to try and test their encyclopaedic knowledge of world records. Roy himself broke several world records while presenting the programme, including one in the very first edition for playing the same tune on the most number of musical instruments within four minutes (he managed 43 in his astounding one-man band!) as well famously breaking the record for the fastest tap-dancing. Each year between 1974 and 1982, *Christmas All-Star Record Breakers* would give TV presenters and pop stars the chance to do a few song and dance routines in between another couple of record-breaking attempts. The 1977 special featured the legendary mass tap-dance in the circular courtyard in the middle of BBC Television Centre, breaking yet another world record at the same time.

However, *Record Breakers* wasn't always blessed with good memories and happy times. On 27 November 1975, Ross McWhiter – who had been an outspoken critic of the IRA – was assassinated outside his north London home in front of his wife and children. His brother Norris continued to present *Record Breakers* throughout the 1970s and '80s, with the 'Norris on the Spot' feature one of the most popular segments until he quit the show in 1994. Roy Castle sadly passed away from lung cancer in 1994, despite never having smoked himself – he blamed his illness on passive smoking, after years of performing in smoky clubs.

It might have been expected for the programme to come to an end with the loss of both of its long-running presenters, but the format was so strong that *Record Breakers* ran for a further seven successful years – including two seasons during which it was renamed *Linford's Record Breakers* (16 Oct 1998–8 Dec 2000), after new host, Olympic medal-winning sprinter Linford Christie.

Red Dwarf

See pages 616–19

Rentaghost

Children's Comedy | BBC One | episode duration 25/40 mins | broadcast 6 Jan 1976–6 Nov 1984

Regular Cast

Michael Staniforth · *Timothy Claypole*
Edward Brayshaw · *Harold Meaker*
Ann Emery · *Ethel Meaker*
Anthony Jackson · *Fred Mumford*
Michael Darbyshire · *Hubert Davenport*
Molly Weir · *Hazel the McWitch*
Sue Nicholls · *Nadia Popov*
Christopher Biggins · *Adam Painting*
Hal Dyer · *Rose Perkins*
Jeffrey Segal · *Arthur Perkins*
Betty Alberge · *Mrs Mumford*
John Dawson · *Mr Mumford*
Lynda Marchal (aka Lynda La Plante) · *Tamara Novek*
William Perrie, John Asquith · *Dobbin*
Jana Sheldon · *Catastrophe Kate*
Kenneth Connor · *Whatsisname Smith*
Aimi MacDonald · *Suzi Starlight*
Vincent White · *Bernie St John*
Patsy Smart · *Aunt Mable*

Creator/Writer Bob Block **Producers** Jeremy Swan, Paul Ciani **Theme Music** ***Play Away***'s Jonathan Cohen wrote the melody and actor Michael Staniforth performed the vocals to this most distinctive of kids' TV themes: 'If your mansion house needs haunting, just call Rentaghost/We've got spooks and ghouls and freaks and fools, at Rentaghost!'

This long-running children's sitcom was based around the most unusual of premises – an agency of ghosts for hire.

Continued on page 620

Rainbow

Roger, Rod, Jane, Geoffrey and Bungle, with Zippy and George (centre).

Rainbow formed part of a package of lunchtime children's programming from around the bigger ITV regions. In its first series, it shared the timeslot with *Larry the Lamb* and *Happy House*, but from its second run it appeared on Mondays and Fridays, with ***Pipkins***, *Mr Trimble* and *Hickory House* filling the same slot from Tuesday to Thursday.

The show was presented by David Cook and a bear called Bungle, played by John Leeson, an actor who would later voice the robot dog K-9 in ***Doctor Who***. The duo were joined by puppets – bright yellow Sunshine, the purple Moony, and the oval-headed Zippy, so called because he had a zip for a mouth, so that anyone could shut him up if he bragged about how clever he was. In the second year, Zippy introduced his friend George, a shy, pink hippo, and Bungle got a make-over – his head became less like a scabby terrier's and more like a friendly teddy-bear's, while his fur became an attractive rusty brown. Some younger viewers were distraught that they'd brought in a new Bungle, though they soon got over their trauma.

When David Cook left the show after the second series, a young actor called Geoffrey Hayes was cast as Bungle's new best friend. Hayes, who had previously spent three years on the BBC' s ***Z Cars***, completed the 'classic' *Rainbow* line-up and stayed with the show until 1992. Sunshine and Moony, meanwhile, were sent to the same farm that all animal puppets go to when they're no longer appearing on TV. Either that or they were simply disappointed that it was producer Pamela Lonsdale and not they who accepted the BAFTA from Princess Anne for Best Children's Series in 1975. You know how petulant puppets can be.

As well as celebrity guests, who'd come to read the puppets a story, and animated short films (including regular visits to Robin and Rosie of *Cockleshell Bay*), the regular team included singers and musicians. Early episodes starred three of the members of Telltale, the band who also sang the theme tune. In time, though, the musical segments were taken over by Jane Tucker, Rod Burton and Matthew Corbett. When Corbett left to join his father on ***The Sooty***

Show, Roger Walker took his place and the team became known simply as Rod, Jane and Roger. For the final decade, Freddy Marks joined Rod and Jane for songs and musical sketches, and from 1981 the trio divided their time between *Rainbow* and *The Rod, Jane and Freddy Show*.

For a children's programme, there was, it has to be said, rather a lot of cross-dressing. Bungle needed no encouragement to don a frock and blonde plaits, but then he also wore pyjamas to bed after spending all day naked (sorry, but we had to mention that). It was George who worried us most, however, as he seemed to be ashamed of his little habit. He'd go to the pretence of claiming he'd decided to go to the country, only for a rather George-like 'Georgina' to step through the doors moments later. Hmmm . . .

As a result of Thames losing the ITV franchise in 1992, *Rainbow* was given a rather fatal shake-up. The entire cast found themselves surplus to requirements. With the remaining characters now working in a toy shop (shades of *Pipkins* there), *Rainbow* returned in 1994 with the puppets remade and recast with younger voices – including Bungle, who lost the use of his legs and joined Zippy and George behind the counter – and a female puppet was brought in: Cleo, a floppy-eared blue rabbit. In 1996, it was renamed *Rainbow Days* and became more of a sketch-based comedy for the very easily impressed.

Away from the TV studios, Geoffrey Hayes and Roy Skelton continued their relationship with *Rainbow* by creating a stage act designed to appeal to students. Though written for a much more adult audience, most of the truly risqué material was delivered by Zippy, who we'd always suspected was a bit of a potty-mouth on the sly. More family-friendly tours have continued to run ever since, with original puppeteer Ronnie Le Drew still lending a hand, while Zippy and George have become celebrity DJs at venues up and down the country.

Children's Entertainment
ITV
Episode Duration: 20 mins
Broadcast: 16 Oct 1972–22 May 1995

Regular Cast
David Cook, Geoffrey Hayes · *Presenters*
John Leeson, Stanley Bates, Malcolm Lord, Richard Robinson, Paul Cullinan · *Bungle*
Peter Hawkins, Roy Skelton, Ronnie Le Drew · *Zippy*
Roy Skelton, Craig Crane · *George*
Jane Tucker, Rod Burton, Matthew Corbett, Roger Walker, Freddy Marks · *Musicians*
Gillie Robic · *Cleo*
Hugh Frazer, Hugh Portnow, Tim Thomas, Julian Littman, Karl Johnson, Charmian Dore · *Themselves*

Creator Pamela Lonsdale

Producers Pamela Lonsdale, Ruth Boswell, Vic Hughes, Charles Warren, Lesley Burgess, Shelia Kinany

Writers Various, including John Kershaw and the cast

Theme Music Written and performed by Hugh Frazer, Hugh Portnow and Tim Thomas of the band Telltale, the theme was accompanied by an animated title sequence created by Brian Cosgrove and Mark Hall.

TRIVIA

Like many broadcasters in the 1970s and early 1980s, Thames TV used to compile a selection of the juicier out-takes from their shows to screen to staff at Christmas parties. Occasionally the casts and crews of the shows would also write special sketches never to be seen by the general public, and *Rainbow* was no exception. The sketch in question involved small musical instruments called 'twangers' which, Geoffrey suggested, children could play on their own, or they could play with a friend's twanger. Meanwhile, Zippy ate a banana and counted its skins (yes, there were four of them). A tape of the sketch eventually passed into the public domain and can usually be found after a good search on the internet, but it should be stressed that, despite misleading assertions in other books, this was not an actual episode of the show, nor was it ever intended to be seen by anyone but Thames staff members.

Incidentally, such Christmas tapes were gradually phased out after an embarrassing incident for the BBC over one tape containing clips of Princess Anne making off-colour remarks. The tape fell into the hands of a tabloid journalist and the usual cries of misuse of licence fee money ensued. Some of the clips that had been compiled for these presentations materialised some years later – as segments on *Auntie's Bloomers*.

Oh, and if you're wondering what Zippy is, according to the man himself he's a 'unique'. No, not a tortoise . . .

Randall and Hopkirk (Deceased)

Kenneth Cope (Marty Hopkirk), Annette André (Jeannie Hopkirk) and Mike Pratt (Jeff Randall)

Thanks to production companies like ITC, the 1960s and early 1970s were awash with detectives, crime fighters and action heroes, each with their own unique selling points (USP): 'he's a loner – with a suitcase'; 'he's a playboy/porn star-alike who works as a spy'; 'he's a playboy Bond-alike whose initials are the same as the abbreviation for "Saint" '; 'he wears a bowler hat, she wears kinky boots – together they battle killer robots and career-obsessed maniacs'; 'there's three of them and they all have special powers'; and of course 'he's not a number – he's a free man!'

In autumn 1969, a series began with a USP that certainly distanced it from its contemporaries: 'two detectives – one of them is dead'. *Randall and Hopkirk (Deceased)* came from the mind of Dennis Spooner, a writer whose previous work included ***Doctor Who***, ***The Avengers*** and *The Baron*, and whose collaborations with producer Monty Berman led to the creation of ***The Champions*** and ***Department S***. Spooner came up with the idea of Martin Hopkirk, a bumbling detective who ends up dead as a result of his own clumsiness and who decides to make amends for holding back the success of his business partner, Steve Randall, by helping him from beyond the grave without his knowledge. With the help of Berman and Australian writer-producer Ralph Smart, Spooner changed the storyline slightly: 'Steve' became 'Jeff'; instead of having Martin help Jeff invisibly, the concept of the 'buddy' partnership was retained, with Jeff being the only one who can see and hear his late partner; Marty isn't killed by carelessness but deliberately, through mistaken identity; and Marty also leaves behind an attractive young widow – Jeannie. Finally, the reason why Marty doesn't go wherever it is the newly departed go to is explained when he fails to return to his grave before dawn. This mishap traps him on earth for 100 years with only Jeff (and the odd psychic) for company.

Randall and Hopkirk (Deceased) never managed to scale the heights of TV stardom like *The Avengers*, but in ITC's stable it was one of the few to leave a substantial mark on its audience. In fact, all of its negatives were actually what made it so much fun. It never quite

See **RANDALL AND HOPKIRK (DECEASED) (1969–70)** *and* **(2000–01)** *for broadcast details and individual credits*

knew whether it was a detective series with a supernatural gimmick or a paranormal adventure series rooted in the real world. Was it a light-hearted action-adventure series or a fully fledged comedy drama? Although for the purposes of this book we favour the former, the latter is equally valid as it dealt with very serious issues like death and grieving but it was also genuinely funny.

The two male leads were unusual choices. Mike Pratt had been a singer-songwriter for Tommy Steele (he was responsible for Steele's 'Little White Bull', among many others). He wasn't the traditionally handsome kind of actor that usually played the action hero, but somehow his ordinariness made him both more appealing and strangely more credible as a single jack-the-lad Lothario who manages to get the girl to his apartment but rarely anything more. Kenneth Cope had moved from serious dramatic acing (having played a gun-toting psychotic teenager in an episode of ***Dixon of Dock Green***) to playing lovable rogue Jed Stone in ***Coronation Street*** – the only person in living memory to have asked Ena Sharpes to 'give us a kiss'. Though he gave a successful audition for the part of Marty, the producers later told him that he'd been their choice all along anyway. By casting such average, normal men for the starring roles, their friendship seemed all the more credible, and helped to ground some of the more fantastic elements of the series. Rounding off the regulars was Annette André as Marty's widow Jeannie. André, a stunningly attractive blonde, had narrowly missed out on the lead role in *The Champions* that eventually went to Alexandra Bastedo.

There were some concerns over the somewhat flippant approach to death in the series (notably in America, where the show was syndicated under the name *My Partner the Ghost*), but it is the fact that so many scenes were played for laughs that makes this one of our favourite programmes from that era. While the first episode was suitably grief-stricken over the loss of Marty, without descending into morbid self-pity, the second, 'A Disturbing Case', sees Jeff undergo psychotherapy (on the suggestion of Jeannie's sister, Jennifer) to erase this 'delusion' of Marty's ghost. In a state of deep hypnosis, Jeff is completely under the spell of a corrupt doctor using his abilities to make people rob themselves, and it's only thanks to Marty's ability to mimic the doctor's vaguely European accent ('Go through ze door . . .' BANG! 'No, open ze door!') that he is able to guide Jeff towards solving the case.

The central premise might require us to believe in ghosts, but the series never claims that the vast majority of money-making psychics are anything other than charlatans. 'All Work And No Pay' involves a company that scour the obituary columns to find victims for their complicated poltergeist-faking trickery. 'That's How Murder Snowballs' sees Jeff investigating a suspected murder after a mind reader is shot dead by his assistant (a very young David Jason) right in the middle of their stage act in front of a full house of witnesses. Using Marty to help him cheat, Jeff replaces the mind reader to allow himself to go undercover and expose the real murderer. And while 'The House on Haunted Hill' exposes yet another criminal plot on the part of a gang who employ the most basic ***Scooby-Doo***

TRIVIA

As the ghostly Marty in the original series, Kenneth Cope wore an immaculate white suit, which kept the wardrobe women on edge in case it picked up a single patch of dirt. Cope remembers how he was leapt upon at the end of takes to protect the jacket from getting damaged. Cope also wore a wig for the role; unfortunately, for the first three episodes the wig was fitted backwards, which explains his slight change of haircut from the fourth episode onwards.

techniques to keep people away from their hideout, a good honest Irish drunkard is shown to be able to see Marty while under the influence. Cheats seldom prosper but at least the pure of heart and clouded of mind might see something a little unusual.

One other celebrated episode, 'The Ghost Who Saved the Bank at Monte Carlo', concerns an aunt of Marty's who claims to have a new system for winning at the casino. An inventive script by Tony Williamson is dominated somewhat - for TV buffs at least - by the presence of Brian Blessed, fresh from ***Z Cars***, and Roger Delgado and Nicholas Courtney, both of whom were about to join the regular cast of *Doctor Who*.

Sadly, like the majority of ITC productions, the series wasn't shown at the same time, or even the same day, across the ITV network, meaning it was difficult for the TV Times and other listings magazines to coordinate any kind of accurate coverage for the series. After just 29 episodes, things came to a close with Marty still popping up in his white suit to help Jeff and nothing properly resolved. It meant that there was never really an end to the series, but it also resulted in fans never having to say goodbye. Aside from a few repeats in the 1970s, *Randall and Hopkirk (Deceased)* might have lain forgotten on some dusty archive shelf had it not been for some ITV regions deciding to schedule a repeat run in the daytime during the late 1980s, and BBC Two doing the same a decade later as part of their midweek Cult TV slot. It's possibly this final run - incidentally the first time the series enjoyed a fully networked transmission - that rekindled distant memories in the minds of two comedy performers at the top of their game, resulting in a remake that hit the screens in spring 2000 . . .

Vic Reeves and his comedy partner Bob Mortimer have never been famed for their acting prowess. To some, they're comedy gods walking a fine tightrope between the gleefully absurd and the genuinely mentally disturbed. Vic Reeves made his first TV appearances as house fool for Jonathan Ross's Channel 4 show *The Last Resort* before exploding onto screens with *Vic Reeves' Big Night Out. Bang! It's Reeves and Mortimer* and two BBC series of *The Smell of Reeves and Mortimer* followed, each of which peddled a kind of comedy that left some clutching their sides in agony and others genuinely baffled as to how it could be construed as funny. The very definition of Hit and Miss, their material was uniformly consistent, but that didn't necessarily mean the viewers interpreted it in the same way.

Their decision to star in a reworking of *Randall and Hopkirk (Deceased)* was, however, completely inconsistent with what had gone before. Would they be tempted to play the parts as they'd done with Marvin Gaye and Otis Redding, as high-pitched falsetto marionettes trapped inside a wardrobe? Maybe the detectives' office would be relocated to Novelty Island where Jeff could dress up as a wannabe entertainer with a string of desperately unlikely acts? These kinds of question and many other ('Will they sing the theme tune themselves?') hampered the first run of the series. The duo had a long way to go to overcome the prejudices of the audience even before they addressed the prejudices of the original series' patient but frustrated fans.

The casting for the show was the first surprise. Surely Bob would be the cheeky ghost and Vic the surviving partner, Jeff? Nope – not in this version. Vic would don the white suit and be assisted by the ghostly guru Wyvern, played by Tom Baker, a former Doctor Who and great British eccentric, well used to delivering streams of drivel in the name of fantasy dialogue. Bob, meanwhile, would instead play the serious, unlucky straight man to Marty's antics. Updating the series slightly, Marty would not be married, but portraying his independent, kick-boxing fiancée was Emilia Fox, while supporting characters would be cast from a combination of respected British actors (Charles Dance, Steven Berkoff, Hywel Bennett, Freddie Jones) and performers from the current crop of comedy such as the cast of ***The Fast Show*** (Paul Whitehouse, Arabella Weir and *Randall and Hopkirk* producer/writer Charlie Higson), ***The League of Gentlemen***'s Mark Gatiss and Steve Pemberton, Hugh Laurie, Martin Clunes, Simon Pegg and Jessica Stevenson from ***Spaced***, plus David Walliams and Matt Lucas (soon to take British comedy by storm with their ***Little Britain*** but for the moment content to play supporting parts in other people's shows – Matt Lucas was a regular performer on Vic and Bob's comedy panel game ***Shooting Stars***). Guy Pratt – son of the late Mike Pratt – even showed up in one episode.

As for the episodes themselves, the first series played with some of the original stories quite neatly: the first episode had a false start when a near shot-for-shot remake of Marty's original death serves as a tease before he's killed off moments later in a much more sadistic manner. The second episode, 'Mental Apparition Disorder', owed a lot to the original series' 'A Disturbing Case', concerning a crooked doctor running a scam from the safety of a mental institution, while 'A Blast from the Past' swapped the ghostly Chicago mobster from 'Murder Ain't What It Used To Be!' for a deceased London hood with a vendetta against Marty, whose late policeman father caused the villain's death in the first place.

The second series was a much more confident affair, thanks in part to a decision on the part of some of the writers to attempt to ape another 1960s series in its entirety: the best episodes, 'Pain Killers' among them, were pure *Avengers* and all the better for it. By the close of the season finale, 'Two Can Play at that Game', *Randall and Hopkirk (Deceased)* had finally exorcised the ghost of the original series and gained respectable ratings. Sadly there was a feeling in certain quarters that it had achieved what it had set out to do, but not to the extent that it would be worth carrying on for a third run. It's a shame, as there was plenty of life left in the format, but at least the show left the audience wanting more than outstaying its welcome.

Kryten, Cat, Lister and Rimmer, with Holly on a screen (rear).

Red Dwarf

Red Dwarf is a minor miracle. Despite being a BBC Two sitcom, it managed to bag a special effects budget that, per episode, was bigger than any BBC Two sci-fi drama ever (it visually outclassed the ***Doctor Who*** of the 1980s at every turn, despite using the same effects team – going to prove that the BBC could do decent effects when they had sufficient cash). It tackled stories that, minus the laughter track, wouldn't look out of place in the more po-faced ***Star Trek***, and it resulted in BBC Two's most lucrative sitcom ever with the type of hardcore audience unseen since the stadium-playing days of ***Monty Python***.

When the crew of the Jupiter Mining Corporation's ship *Red Dwarf* is wiped out by a massive radiation leak, the only survivor is Dave Lister, the lowest-ranking bum in space, who had been locked in suspended animation as a punishment for smuggling a pregnant cat on board. When he is finally defrosted by the ship's sentient computer, Holly, Dave learns that Holly took the decision to pilot *Red Dwarf* out of harm's way until the radiation died down, which is how the ship is now three million years in the future and billions of miles away from home. To keep Dave sane while he comes to terms with this, Holly activates a hologram of one of the crew and makes his selection from the person Dave exchanged the most words with. Unfortunately, that person just happens to be Arnold Rimmer, his ex-room mate and the biggest 'smeg-head' in the universe. As a hologram, Rimmer can't touch anything, but that doesn't stop him from making Dave's life hell. Just as he thinks that things can't get any stranger, Dave Lister discovers that they are not alone on *Red Dwarf*. Deep in the hold lurks a life form that's the last survivor of a race that evolved over millions of years from the kittens of his pet cat . . .

Science Fiction Comedy
Grant Naylor Productions for BBC Two
Episode Duration: 30 mins
Broadcast: 15 Feb 1988–7 Apr 1999

Recurring Cast
Chris Barrie · *Arnold Judas Rimmer*
Craig Charles · *David Lister*
Danny John-Jules · *Cat*
David Ross, Robert Llewellyn · *Kryten*
Norman Lovett, Hattie Hayridge · *Holly*
Clare Grogan, Chloë Annett · *Kristine Kochanski*
Tony Hawks · *Various Characters*
Mac McDonald · *Captain Frank Hollister*
Mark Williams · *Peterson*
Paul Bradley · *Chen*
David Gillespie · *Selby*
John Lenahan, David Ross · *Voice of Talkie Toaster*
Graham McTavish · *Warden Ackerman*
Jake Wood · *Kill Crazy*
Kalli Greenwood · *Mrs Rimmer*
Simon Gaffney · *Young Rimmer*

When they began developing the idea that became *Red Dwarf*, Rob Grant and Doug Naylor were jobbing writers-for-hire for comedians like Little and Large and Jasper Carrott. They were also sketch writers for ***Spitting Image*** – they'd been responsible for *Spitting Image*'s No. 1 single 'The Chicken Song' and had indulged in sci-fi comedy before with 'Dave Hollins: Space Cadet', a regular character from their radio show *Son of Cliché*. But science fiction was not a popular genre at the BBC in the 1980s and when they tried to pitch a science fiction-based sitcom they found it to be a hard sell: everyone who read the script rejected it.

Thanks to a quirk of BBC budgeting, money had been allocated for a second series of *Happy Families*, a self-contained, six-part sitcom from the creative team behind ***The Comic Strip Presents***. There had never been any plans for a second series; *Happy Families* 2 had merely been a means of ensuring BBC North had some money put aside for a new project. That year, with no other contenders materialising, the lucky recipient turned out to be *Red Dwarf*.

Grant and Naylor had suggested to producer Paul Jackson hiring serious actors rather than comics, with Alan Rickman and Alfred Molina as early choices. Fortunately, the final casting didn't quite match such lofty aspirations. Craig Charles was known only as a satirical Scouse poet who was once a regular fixture on ***Wogan*** and ***Saturday Live***, yet he now found himself playing the lead role in a sitcom. Still in his mid-twenties, Charles's natural cheekiness allowed the comedy to be much more bawdy than might have been appropriate with an older actor. Norman Lovett, a stand-up comic, became the disembodied face of Holly, the ship's computer. The part of the Cat was filled by Danny John-Jules, a dancer who'd decided to audition for the part as a zoot-suited Little Richard, squeals and all. For Rimmer, they chose Chris Barrie, an impressionist who'd been one of the lead performers on *Spitting Image* (and, like Grant and Naylor, could lay claim to a No. 1 record, having provided the voice of Ronald Reagan on the 12-inch single of Frankie Goes to Hollywood's 'Two Tribes'). This may have been some way short of the cast of serious actors that had been planned, but somehow it was a perfect mix.

To ensure late viewers were able to keep up with the concept, the first two series began with a 'story so far' courtesy of Holly, which invariably finished with a one-liner, such as a reference to an asteroid that looks like Felicity Kendal's bottom. Similarly 'anachronistic' references occur throughout the series, with jokes about footballer Peter Beardsley, the Osmonds and ***The Flintstones*** mixed in with futuristic personalities like sports hero Jim Bexley Speed and Sabrina Mulholland J-Jones, richest beauty on Earth (played by Koo Stark). When the crew encounter a plant of warring celebrity waxworks, it's 20th-century figures we see, Hitler, Einstein, Elvis and Mother Teresa.

Episodes of the first two seasons that stand out include 'Confidence and Paranoia', in which a hyper-evolved dose of space flu results in the physical manifestations of aspects of Lister's personality (played by Lee Cornes and Craig Ferguson); 'Me^2', where

TRIVIA

For the recordings, the studio audience were treated to warm-up routines from, among others, Eddie Izzard and Alistair McGowan.

Rimmer finds out just how much of a pain in the arse he is after moving in with his identical holographic twin; an episode where Holly is replaced by an extreme disciplinarian called 'Queeg'; and of course 'Kryten', which opened the second series and introduced the Norman Bates of deep space, a mechanical butler who's been labouring away unaware that his mistresses have been dead for centuries.

Red Dwarf and *Red Dwarf II* established the characters but in retrospect were not representative of the bulk of episodes, too closely resembling ***The Odd Couple*** in space. It was with the third season that *Red Dwarf* found the format for the rest of the series. A move from BBC North's Manchester studios to London led to Holly actor Norman Lovett deciding to quit, reluctant to commute from his home in Edinburgh. His part was taken by Hattie Hayridge, who had played Holly's female alter ego in 'Parallel Universe', the final episode of series two. With *Red Dwarf III* came an increased special effects budget, a shift in tone towards plots involving scampering across brave new worlds (thanks to space exploration vehicle Starbug) and the reintroduction of Kryten as a permanent member of the team. The android allowed the writers to provide Lister with a subordinate; helpful, considering that in the beginning at least Rimmer was intangible and so unable to touch anything, while the Cat simply wasn't interested in helping anyone. The addition of Kryten was also useful in creating conflict between Rimmer and Lister, the former only too happy to have a willing slave on hand, the latter desperate to help Kryten break his programming and rebel. But with an encyclopedic knowledge and an ability to interact more than a head on a screen ever could, Kryten also led to a reduction in the appearance and eventual phasing out of Holly.

Few comedies could be a western on one occasion and a Jane Austen farce or film noir pastiche the next, while simultaneously juggling shape-shifting aliens or monsters genetically bred from mutant curry.

With the characters now firmly established, there came a more experimental approach. Few comedies could be a western on one occasion (as in the Emmy-award-winning 'Gunmen of the Apocalypse') and a Jane Austen farce or film noir pastiche the next, while simultaneously juggling shape-shifting aliens or monsters genetically bred from mutant curry. But *Red Dwarf* managed it week after week. The cast were even given opportunities to stretch themselves by playing alternative versions of their characters. Chris Barrie became the suave space hero Ace Rimmer, Danny John-Jules created the buck-toothed, nylon-clad über-geek Duane Dibley and Robert Llewellyn gave us Kryten's grumpy Yorkshireman in the form of 'Spare Head Three'.

The science fiction grapevine being what it is, TV producers in the States approached Doug Grant and Rob Naylor with an offer to develop an American version. Two pilots were recorded, with only

Robert Llewellyn's Kryten retained from the original cast. Ultimately (and thankfully), nothing came of the pilots, possibly because the American producers failed to grasp the essence of what had made the original series so funny.

Problems during the production of *Red Dwarf VI* led to Rob Grant deciding to end his writing partnership with Doug Naylor to allow him to try new ideas (which have included *The 10%ers*, *Dark Ages* and *The Strangerers*). Grant's departure meant that, for the first time, outsiders were invited to write for the show, with mixed results. Chris Barrie also requested a reduced role for the seventh series, though he returned full time for series eight. A final departure was . . . the studio audience. With more and more of the scenes reliant on special effects, the live studio audience had become more of a hindrance than an asset, so from *Red Dwarf VII*, the production team were able to take a more cinematic approach, both in terms of story structure and editing. The biggest change though was the reintroduction of Kochanski, a female officer aboard *Red Dwarf* who had been the object of Lister's desires. Introduced thanks to a parallel universe where it was she rather than Lister thrown into stasis, she elects to join the 'Boys from the *Dwarf*' on their adventures. The character had been played by former Altered Images singer Claire ('CP') Grogan in the first episode and in subsequent flashbacks, but for her return she was played by Chloë Annett. Despite the many changes, series seven marked an all-time high for the team with ratings of over 8 million.

By *Red Dwarf VIII*, the cast were already gearing up for a mooted feature film, though as of 2005, there is little sign of it hitting cinema screens in the near future. Until the movie shifts into production or is abandoned, it looks as if we won't be seeing the Dwarfers for some time yet. We look forward to that last sentence becoming the first obsolete line in this book.

Creators Rob Grant and Doug Naylor

Producers Paul Jackson, Rob Grant, Doug Naylor (executive), Gilly Archer, Candida Julian-Jones, Julian Scott, Ann Zahl (associate), Hilary Bevan Jones, Ed Bye, Justin Judd

Writers Rob Grant, Doug Naylor, Paul Alexander, Kim Fuller, Robert Llewellyn, James Hendrie

Theme Music There have been a few different themes for *Red Dwarf*, all of them composed by Howard Goodall. The opening theme for the first two series, with the shot of a space-suited man painting the outside of *Red Dwarf* and the slow pan along one side of the ship, was a deliberate parody of *2001: A Space Odyssey*'s use of Richard Strauss's *Also Sprach Zarathustra*. The end theme song ('It's cold outside – there's no kind of atmosphere . . .') was Howard Goodall's tribute to Phil Spector and the Wall of Sound, sung by Jenna Russell in the style of Ronnie Spector. From the third series onwards the opening titles (a generic montage of clips from the show) were accompanied by a jazzed-up version of the end theme with an intentionally self-indulgent electric guitar riff replacing the vocals. Goodall has also recorded alternative title music for specific episodes, including one in the style of Rimmer's favourite Hammond organ player, Reggie Wilson, and one sung by Elvis impersonator Clayton Mark.

Fred Mumford comes back to Earth from the spirit world and decides to set up a business hiring himself out to needy clients. He's joined in his new business by two fellow ghosts, Edwardian gent Hubert Davenport and medieval jester Timothy Claypole. They initially set up shop in a property owned by Harold Meaker, who eventually becomes the owner of Rentaghost itself.

Other ghosts soon join the agency, including cowgirl Catastrophe Kate, Hazel the McWitch, and two highly allergic cousins, Tamara Novek and Nadia Popov, both of whom have the unfortunate habit of sneezing and disappearing whenever they go near flowers. To add to the mayhem, a ghostly pantomime horse called Dobbin regularly puts his nosebag into things – much to the dismay of Harold and Ethel Meaker, their non-ghost-aware neighbours the Perkinses (who think Harold and Ethel are barking mad) and friendly department store owner Adam Painting.

Much good-natured slapstick comedy and groan-inducing puns filled every episode of *Rentaghost*, one of the most beloved children's programmes of the 1970s and 1980s. In total, 58 episodes of the show were made over nine seasons, including a couple of slightly longer Christmas panto specials. Perhaps best remembered now for the enthusiastic performances put in by future ***Prime Suspect*** writer Lynda La Plante (under her stage name Lynda Marchal) and ***Coronation Street***'s Audrey Roberts (Sue Nicholls), there's no arguing that *Rentaghost* is simplistic, extremely juvenile fun. But where's the harm in that, eh? And haven't you always wanted to hire a ghost to terrify somebody *you* didn't like? Thought so.

When the doors of the *Rentaghost* office shut for the last time, series writer Bob Block and producer Jeremy Swan went on to create a very similar type of programme in *Galloping Galaxies!*, a children's panto comedy series set in outer space with Kenneth Williams providing the voice for ship's computer SID. It ran from 1 October 1985 to 18 December 1986 and was, if it's possible to imagine, even more juvenile and silly than *Rentaghost*.

Website

www.welcome.to/rentaghost

Return of The Saint

Adventure | ITC for ITV | episode duration 50 mins | broadcast 1978–1979

Principal Cast

Ian Ogilvy · *Simon Templar, 'The Saint'*

Creator Leslie Charteris **Producer** Robert S. Baker (executive), Anthony Spinner **Writers** Ray Austin, Roy Ward Baker, Tom Clegg, Kevin Connor, Charles Crichton, Cyril Frankel, Peter Medak, Leslie Norman, Peter Sasdy, Jeremy Summers, Sam Wanamaker **Theme Music** Brian Dee and Irving Martin

For commentary, see THE SAINT

Rhoda

Sitcom | MTM for CBS (shown on BBC Two) | episode duration 25 mins | broadcast 9 Sep 1974–9 Dec 1978

Regular Cast

Valerie Harper · *Rhoda Morgenstern/Gerard*
Julie Kavner · *Brenda Morgenstern*
Lorenzo Music · *Voice of Carlton the Doorman*
David Groh · *Joe Gerard*
Nancy Walker · *Ida Morgenstern*
Harold Gould · *Martin Morgenstern*
Barbara Sharma · *Myra Morgenstein*
Ron Silver · *Gary Levy*
Anne Meara · *Sally Gallagher*
Ray Buktenica · *Benny Goodwin*
Rafael Campos · *Amon Diaz Jr*
Michael Delano · *Johnny Venture*
Kenneth McMillan · *Jack Doyle*
Nancy Lane · *Tina Molinari*

Creators James L. Brooks and Allan Burns **Producers** James L. Brooks, Allan Burns (executive), Budd Cherry (associate), David Davis, Lorenzo Music, Charlotte Brown, Don Reo, Allan Katz **Writers** Various, including Pat Nardo, James L. Brooks, Allan Burns, Lorenzo Music, Charlotte Brown, Gloria Banta, Coleman Mitchell, Geoffrey Neigher, Allan Katz, Don Reo, David Lloyd, Deborah Leschin **Theme Music** Billy Goldenberg

This spin-off from the monolithic ***Mary Tyler Moore Show*** saw Rhoda Morgenstern pop back to New York for two weeks from her home in Minneapolis only to end up staying. Her mother sets her up on a date with Joe, who owns a construction company, and the couple quickly fall in love, get married and move into an apartment in the same building as Rhoda's sister, dumpy, luckless Brenda. Rhoda sets up her own window-dressing company with a friend with a similar surname (the business is called 'Morgenstern & Morgenstein'). All the while, her mother lurks in her life, waiting for opportunities to interfere.

A text-book example of great sitcom writing, *Rhoda* featured some astounding scene-stealers, including Nancy Walker as Rhoda and Brenda's mom, and producer/writer Lorenzo Music as the voice of Carlton, the hesitant doorman in Rhoda's apartment (in 1980, the character starred in his own animated special, *Carlton, Your Doorman*, while Music later voiced another popular character, *Garfield*, in the hugely successful animated series). Both Valerie Harper and Julie Kavner won Emmy awards for their performances in the show, while Harper won a Golden Globe (as did the show). Viewers loved the plodding romance of Rhoda and Joe, and were disappointed by the decision for them to divorce, but the producers wanted to have a show about an independent woman to prove it could be done. Sadly, it failed, with ratings tailing off almost straight away. Rhoda was brought to an end with some of its later episodes still to be aired.

Valerie Harper returned to sitcom with *Valerie*, and a 2000 TV movie called *Mary and Rhoda* reunited both the characters Mary Richards and Rhoda Morgenstern and the actresses, Mary Tyler-Moore and Valerie Harper. Julie Kavner has worked with Woody Allen on numerous films, including *Hannah and Her Sisters* (1986) and *Radio Days* (1987). However, Kavner is best known for voicing the queen of American domestic comedy, Marge Simpson.

Website
Catch up with Valerie at valerieharper.com.

Richard and Judy

See THIS MORNING

Ripping Yarns

Comedy | BBC Two | episode duration 30 mins | broadcast 7 Jan 1976, 27 Sep 1977–24 Oct 1979

Principal Cast
Michael Palin · *Tomkinson, Eric Olthwaite, Major Phipps, Charles/Hugo Chiddingfold, Captain Walter Snetterton, Sir Kevin Orr, Uncle Jack, Gerald Whinfrey, Gordon Ottershaw, Roger Bartlesham*
Terry Jones · *Mr Ellis*
Ian Ogilvy · *School Bully*
Barbara New · *Vera Olthwaite*
John Barrett · *Mr Olthwaite*
Anita Carey · *Irene Olthwaite*
Roy Kinnear · *Herr Vogel*
Frank Middlemass · *Sir Clive Chiddingford*
Denholm Elliott · *Mr Gregory*
Don Henderson · *RSM Urdoch*
Aubrey Morris · *Grosvenor*
Maria Aitken · *Mrs Otway*
Jack May · *General Chapman*
Gerald Sim · *Lord Raglan*
Gwen Taylor · *Mrs Ottershaw*
Bill Fraser · *Arthur Foggen*
Richard Vernon · *Lord Bartlesham*
Joan Sanderson · *Lady Bartlesham*
John Le Mesurier · *Colonel Runciman*
Jan Francis · *Miranda*

Creators Terry Hughes, Michael Palin, Terry Jones **Producers** Terry Hughes, Alan J. W. Bell, Sydney Lotterby **Writers** Michael Palin, Terry Jones

Michael Palin and Terry Jones's first post-***Python*** success story was a gleeful tribute to the type of *Boy's Own* storybook adventures that had proliferated in the UK during the 19th and early 20th centuries – the kind of story that promised its readers that joining the army would be a 'jolly good wheeze', and that Johnny Foreigner would never amount to much if he were confronted with a good old-fashioned English stiff upper lip. In much the same way that ***The Comic Strip*** would parody the antics of the Famous Five in the early 1980s, each *Ripping Yarns* adventure lampooned the air of wide-eyed naivety present in those original stories, poking gentle fun at the attitudes of a time long since vanished. Each episode of *Ripping Yarns* told a standalone story and, unlike virtually every other comedy series, the entire show was all recorded on top quality colour film, bringing a distinctly expensive feel to the series.

Michael Palin starred in every episode of the series, portraying a wide range of different characters from one week to the next. The most fondly remembered episodes of *Ripping Yarns* include the pilot, 'Tomkinson's Schooldays' (a hilarious send-up of public schools), and 'The Testing of Eric Olthwaite', in which Palin played the world's most boring man. Other adventures included an Agatha Christie tribute, 'Murder at Moorstones Manor', a derring-do tale of wartime heroism ('Escape from Stalag Luft 112b') and 'Golden Gordon', in which a football fan fights to save his favourite team from being closed down. In total, just nine episodes of *Ripping Yarns* were made, but they are of such high quality, made with oodles of love and respect for the stories they were parodying, that they have stood the test of time a great deal better than many comedy shows from the 1970s.

Rising Damp

Sitcom | Yorkshire for ITV | episode duration 25 mins | broadcast 2 Sep, 13 Dec 1974–9 May 1978

Principal Cast
Leonard Rossiter · *Rupert Rigsby*
Frances de la Tour · *Miss Ruth Jones*
Richard Beckinsale · *Alan Moore*
Don Warrington · *Philip Smith*
Gay Rose · *Brenda*
Derek Newark · *Spooner*

Creator/Writer Eric Chappell **Producers** Ian MacNaughton, Ronnie Baxter, Vernon Lawrence, Len Lurcuck **Theme Music** Dennis Wilson

Regarded by many people as the finest sitcom ever to have been transmitted on ITV, *Rising Damp* is a perfect example of a comedy series benefiting from a tiny regular cast, outstandingly good performances and scripts all written by the same author right the way through the show's run. *Rising Damp* began as a stage play called 'The Banana Box' in which a vile landlord called Rooksby caused trouble for his tenants. Originally starring Old Man ***Steptoe***, Wilfrid Brambell, the play was recast with Leonard Rossiter in the lead, opposite actors Don Warrington, Frances de la

Tour and Manfred Mann singer Paul Jones. The play grabbed the attention of Yorkshire TV commissioners, who decided to ask the play's author Eric Chappell to rework the material into a sitcom pilot – the rest, as they say, is history.

Rigsby is the landlord of a rather dilapidated house sub-divided into bedsits, located in a seaside resort somewhere in the North of England. A repressed, unhappy man, Rigsby spends much of his time skulking outside the doors of his tenants' rooms, hoping in vain to catch them doing something rude or, better still, hoping to catch Miss Jones in a state of undress. University administrator Miss Jones is completely immune to Rigsby's 'charms', partly because of her obsession with Philip, a well-spoken man who claims to be the son of an African chief and isn't afraid to use the prejudice of others to his advantage. The other regular tenant in Rigsby's hovel is medical student Alan, a long-haired lad whose attempts to lead an active sex life are normally frustrated by Rigsby's snooping/barging in. Episodes revolved around Rigsby either mishearing or misunderstanding something, inevitably leading to a tirade of sexist, racist or homophobic whining from the loathsome landlord. However, all of Rigsby's aspirations and plotting usually came to nothing – especially as far as getting to grips with Miss Jones was concerned.

A total masterpiece, *Rising Damp* was elevated to legendary status by exemplary performances by the four main leads. Although he ostensibly had the least to do, Richard Beckinsale's understated portrayal of Alan was simply brilliant, a slightly more upmarket version of Lenny Godber from ***Porridge***, though equally as likeable. Similarly, both Don Warrington and Frances de la Tour were able to make both of their characters shine – characters that *might* have seemed like stereotypes had they been performed by less capable artists. But, of course, *Rising Damp* was Leonard Rossiter's show, the man shamelessly stealing every scene whether clutching his flea-bitten moggy Vienna or standing hands on hips, moth-eaten cardigan half unbuttoned, stammering with furious indignation about the latest indignity the world had heaped on him. It's not surprising that *Rising Damp* is considered the pinnacle of ITV comedy – what is perhaps very surprising is the fact that in the 2003 Britain's Best Sitcom survey it only managed to reach No. 27 in the charts: 26 sitcoms funnier than *Rising Damp*? Surely not. . .

Roald Dahl's Tales of the Unexpected

See TALES OF THE UNEXPECTED

Robin of Sherwood

See pages 624–6

Robin's Nest

Sitcom | Thames for ITV | episode duration 25 mins | broadcast 11 Jan 1977–31 Mar 1981

Regular Cast

Richard O'Sullivan · *Robin Tripp*
Tessa Wyatt · *Vicky Nicholls/Tripp*
Tony Britton · *James Nicholls*
David Kelly · *Albert Riddle*
Honor Blackman, Barbara Murray · *Marion Nicholls*

Creators Johnnie Mortimer and Brian Cooke **Producer** Peter Frazer-Jones **Writers** Johnnie Mortimer, Brian Cooke, George Layton, Bernard McKenna, Adele Rose, David Norton, Roger Taylor, Terence Brady, Charlotte Bingham, Dave Freeman, John Watkins, Terence Feely, Ken Hoare, Willis Hall, Richard Waring, Gail Renard **Theme Music** Arranged by Brian Bennett, the rather melancholic synthesised theme music for *Robin's Nest* was written by series star Richard O'Sullivan.

Johnnie Mortimer and Brian Cooke, the writers behind the hugely successful sitcom ***Man about the House***, from the early 1970s, had already spun one series off from that original show, the even more popular ***George and Mildred***. With the Ropers now living in middle-class bliss, Mortimer and Cooke returned to the ostensible star of *Man about the House*, young chef Robin Tripp, and wrote a new show based around him. Whereas Robin had never been successful in love in *Man about the House* (Chrissie and Jo being immune to his charms), in *Robin's Nest* he has settled down and is living with his girlfriend, air hostess Vicky. Keen to make a living from his culinary skills, Robin decides to go into business with Vicky and open up a bistro of their own – Robin's Nest. However, they don't have sufficient money to fund the enterprise on their own and turn to Vicky's stern and stuffy father, James, for the extra cash. James is less than delighted that his daughter is 'living in sin' with a long-haired hippy layabout, having hoped for someone with far better breeding for his daughter. Having a share in the business enables James to keep a close eye on their relationship, however, and to ensure that Robin isn't letting his little girl down in any way.

Joining the team at the Fulham bistro is Albert Riddle, their one-armed Irish washer-up (actor David Kelly doing a fine job of keeping his perfectly healthy left arm hidden during filming), in a stereotypical portrayal of a thick Irishman with the gift of the gab.

As the series progresses, Robin and Vicky's relationship goes through the standard ups and downs, until eventually they get married at the end of the second season.

(Mortimer and Cooke had to get special permission from the Independent Broadcasting Authority in order to be allowed to show an unmarried couple living together in a sitcom. This was the very first British comedy series to feature such a relationship in an otherwise 'regular' setting.) By the fifth series, the Tripps had been blessed with twin children.

Unfortunately, *Robin's Nest* never seemed to gel quite as well as either *Man about the House* or *George and Mildred*, in particular after Mortimer and Cooke stopped being sole writers and merely undertook script-editing duties from the third series onwards. Having said that, the show survived for 48 episodes over six seasons and spawned an American adaptation, *Three's a Crowd* (which was, of course a spin-off of the American *Man about the House*, *Three's Company*).

Robot Wars

Game Show | Mentorn for BBC Two/Five | episode duration 30–45 mins | broadcast 1998–2003

Cast

Jeremy Clarkson, Philippa Forrester, Craig Charles, Jayne Middlemiss, Julia Reed · *Presenters*
Jonathan Pearce · *Commentator*

Producers Stephen Carsey, Joe Shaw

Homemade mechanical battle-robots enter the arena to face a succession of opponents (including some lethal house robots with names like Sergeant Bash and Sir Killalot) in deadly mazes and traps. The losers face being dismantled or terminally damaged while the winner has the dubious honour of surviving to battle another day.

What might have been simply a kids' show became a real niche for itself with construction enthusiasts customising plans available on the internet to create their own machines. While we might have experienced a little malicious thrill as their tin terror is ripped apart by a robot called Matilda, it could be quite harrowing to see months of work dismembered in seconds.

Top Gear's Jeremy Clarkson presided over the first series, but from the second it was Craig Charles's Scouse charms whooping and cheering through the carnage. Sadly, a move from BBC Two to Five left the series in pieces.

Rock Follies

Drama | Thames for ITV | episode duration 25 mins | broadcast 24 Feb 1976–6 Dec 1977

Regular Cast

Charlotte Cornwell · *Anna Ward*
Rula Lenska · *Nancy 'Q' Cunard de Longchamps*
Julie Covington · *Devonia 'Dee' Rhodes*
Denis Lawson · *Ken Church*
Emlyn Price · *Derek Huggin*
Derek Thompson · *Harry Moon*
Angela Bruce · *Gloria*
Beth Porter · *Kitty Schreiber*
Sue Jones-Davies · *Rox*
Stephen Moore · *Jack*
Billy Murray · *Spike*
Tim Curry · *Stevie Streeter*

Creator/Writer Howard Schuman **Producers** Verity Lambert (executive), Andrew Brown **Theme Music** Composed by Andy Mackay, lyrics by Howard Schuman

Long before Girls Aloud and even Bananarama, a group of friends from different backgrounds form a pop trio called the 'Little Ladies' and head off to find fame and fortune – only to encounter manipulation, disappointment and sleazy industry types who are more interested in sex than music. The drama is interspersed by musical numbers, some of which, in the style of Dennis Potter's ***Pennies from Heaven*** (which came two years later) are fantasies. For the second season (*Rock Follies of '77*); the Little Ladies are joined by Rox and go on the road with superstar Steve Streeter, but jealousies and bad feeling among the band itself causes things to implode.

Within the story, the four-piece record a single, 'OK?', which flops. Ironically in real life, Cornwell, Lenska, Covington and Jones-Davies got the song to No. 10 in the charts in 1977 – one of many songs written by Roxy Music's Andy Mackay. Between seasons Julie Covington had a number one with 'Don't Cry for Me, Argentina', a song from Andrew Lloyd-Webber's musical *Evita*.

Website

www.therockfollies.co.uk

The Rockford Files

Drama | Universal/Public Arts/Cherokee for NBC (shown on BBC One) | episode duration 50 mins | broadcast 27 Mar 1974, 13 Sep 1974–10 Jan 1980, 27 Nov 1994–20 April 1999 (USA)

Regular Cast

James Garner · *Jim Rockford*
Noah Beery Jr · *Joseph 'Rocky' Rockford*
Stuart Margolin · *Evelyn 'Angel' Martin*
Joe Santos · *Detective Dennis Becker*
Gretchen Corbett · *Beth Davenport*
Tom Atkins · *Lieutenant Alex Diehl*
James Luisi · *Lieutenant Doug Chapman*
Luis Delgado · *Officer Billings*
Dennis Dugan · *Richie Brockleman*
Bo Hopkins · *John 'Coop' Cooper*
Joe Santos · *Detective Dennis Becker*
Pat Finley · *Peggy Becker*
Al Stevenson · *'LJ'*

Continued on page 627

Robin of Sherwood

The men of Sherwood Forest provide backup for Robin (Michael Praed).

Almost universally admired by viewers as the definitive interpretation of the legend (just as Joan Hickson's ***Miss Marple*** and Jeremy Brett's ***Sherlock Holmes*** are similarly lauded), HTV's *Robin of Sherwood* wipes the floor with every other version – and that includes Hollywood movies like Kevin Costner's *Robin Hood: Prince of Thieves* (1991), even though the film liberally 'borrowed' many elements that had been specifically created for the television show.

Michael Praed originally starred as Robin of Loxley, one of the few survivors of a Norman massacre that wiped out his home village. Along with miller's son Much, Robin attempted to strike back at the corrupt regime of Robert de Rainault, the sheriff of nearby Nottingham and his less-than-bright right-hand man, Guy of Gisburne. Robin was guided in his acts of terrorism/freedom-fighting by a mysterious figure called Herne the Hunter, pagan god of the forests and possessor of mystical powers. Nicknamed 'Herne's Son', Robin dedicated his life to fighting back against the Norman oppressors.

Soon, Robin's band of followers (never once referred to by the twee term 'merry men') expanded. John Little, possessed by evil sorcerer Simon de Belleme, was freed when Robin killed his master. John joined the gang of rebels, simultaneously adopting the nickname 'Little John' as an ironic comment about his great height. Will Scatlock, burning with an intense hatred for the Normans following the rape and murder of his wife, became 'Will Scarlet' – not because he wore red, but because of the furious temper he had and his liability to burst into frenzied bouts of prolonged violence against the occupying Norman forces. Marion, daughter of Sir Richard of Leaford, soon found herself falling in love with Robin, abandoning her life of privilege and wealth to join the rebels, bringing with her faithful family friend Friar Tuck. The final member of the team was Saracen warrior Nasir, who rarely spoke a word but whose skill as a swordsman was unsurpassed. When writer Richard Carpenter introduced a Saracen for the very first time into the Robin Hood

Fantasy/Action-Adventure
Goldcrest/HTV for ITV
Episode Duration: 60 mins
Broadcast: 28 Apr 1984–28 Jun 1986

Regular Cast
Michael Praed · *Robin of Loxley*
Jason Connery · *Robert of Huntingdon*
Nickolas Grace · *Robert de Rainault – the Sheriff of Nottingham*
Judi Trott · *Lady Marion*
Clive Mantle · *Little John*
Peter Llewellyn Williams · *Much*
Robert Addie · *Sir Guy of Gisburne*
Ray Winstone · *Will Scarlet*
Phil Rose · *Friar Tuck*
John Abineri · *Herne the Hunter*
Mark Ryan · *Nasir*
Philip Jackson · *Abbot Hugo de Rainault*
Jeremy Bulloch · *Edward of Wickham*
Claire Toeman · *Meg of Wickham*
Stuart Linden · *The Old Prisoner*
Philip Davis · *Prince John*
Anthony Valentine · *Simon de Belleme*
Robbie Bulloch · *Matthew of Wickham*
George Baker · *Sir Richard of Leaford*
Richard O'Brien · *Gulnar*

Creator Richard Carpenter

Producers Patrick Dromgoole (executive), Paul Knight, Esta Charkham

Writers Richard Carpenter, Anthony Horowitz, John Flanagan, Andrew McCulloch

Theme Music 'The Hooded Man' by Clannad

legend, he undoubtedly never realised that Hollywood star Morgan Freeman would soon be providing some ethnic diversity to Kevin Costner's film version, due to members of the film's production team not realising that the character had been an invention of Carpenter's and not present in the original legend.

Robin of Sherwood's success can be attributed to a number of different factors. First and foremost, the acting by the entire regular cast was head and shoulders ahead of that of any previous dramatisation of the legend. Clive Mantle, who played Little John, went on to star as sympathetic consultant Mike Barrett in ***Casualty*** for many years. Michael Praed quit *Robin of Sherwood* after the second series to join the cast of ***Dynasty*** in the USA before embarking on a highly successful career in theatre. Nickolas Grace joined Robin straight from a powerhouse turn in ***Brideshead Revisited*** and has remained a familiar face in high-profile comedy and drama series. And, of course, Ray Winstone's career, which had seemed to grind to a halt after his juvenile breakthrough role in *Scum*, was given a much-needed boost by his portrayal of the permanently angry Will Scarlet, before he became the most highly sought after British actor of his generation.

Another reason for the programme's success was its clever combination of brutal realism and otherworldly fantasy. This interpretation of the Robin Hood legend presented the outlaws living in a dirty, cold environment in Sherwood – no immaculate Lincoln green tights here. For Robin and his supporters, the threat of starvation or being turned in by hostile villagers was just as great as the chance of being caught and executed by the sheriff. The inclusion of fantastical elements such as magic and sorcery would never have worked if the rest of the programme had presented an unconvincing portrayal of medieval life.

For two series, audiences were hooked as the outlaws took on the sheriff, witches and the Knights Templar, and even came across Richard the Lionheart. In 'The Swords of Weyland', a hugely memorable two-part adventure in the second series, Robin and his men leave Sherwood to defend a distant village from attack by the 'Hounds of Lucifer', horse-riding servants of Morgwyn, prioress of Ravenscar. Lapping up the opportunity to play a Satan-worshipping nun, Rula Lenska created a memorable study in evil as a woman determined to use the seven magic swords of Weyland to summon up the Devil. This story attracted much criticism from Mary Whitehouse's much-vilified National Viewers and Listeners Association, angry that a portrayal of satanic worship was being broadcast at Saturday teatime.

One of the great worries in any programme like *Robin of Sherwood*, in which our heroes defeat the same villain, is that the threat of that villain is undermined by the constant defeats they suffer. In the case of the Sheriff of Nottingham, however, a unique behind-the-scenes chain of circumstances would ensure Nickolas Grace's place in the TV villain hall of fame.

Michael Praed's decision to quit the programme in order to get work in the USA left producers with both a problem and an

TRIVIA

One of the greatest strengths of *Robin of Sherwood* was undoubtedly the hauntingly beautiful soundtrack provided by Irish folk group Clannad. Their traditional ethereal melodies, matched with modern (for the 1980s) synthesisers, provided a unique atmosphere to the series. However, the group could provide only a limited amount of music for the first two series, which unfortunately resulted in a great deal of repetition – the piece of music used during the battle sequences becoming especially repetitive. It was a joy when Clannad were able to record new tracks for the third series.

opportunity – how could they write out their star yet still keep the programme going? The answer came from the Robin Hood legend itself, which told of two separate men who might have been the people's hero. Neatly combining both versions of the story, 'The Greatest Enemy' saw the sheriff finally cornering Robin on the top of a rocky outcrop. As dozens of Norman crossbowmen released their quarrels arrows into Robin's body, the sheriff gasped in delight that he had finally won.

The audience watched in shock as the outlaws, captured by Guy of Gisburne, realised that their leader was dead. Just as all hope began to evaporate, a man wearing a hood freed them and led them back to Sherwood. It transpired that this mysterious figure was a disaffected young nobleman called Robert of Huntingdon. Disgusted at the way in which his fellow Normans abused their power, Robert found himself driven to assume the mantle of 'The Hooded Man' and carry on the work of Herne the Hunter – as well as eventually taking the place of the first Robin in Marion's heart.

The new leading man was Jason Connery, son of Bond legend Sean. Although many fans of the series felt Connery's performance to be not of the same standard as Praed's, there is in reality little to separate the two, and in fact episodes in the third series turned out to be on average much stronger than many of those seen earlier. Plotlines were much more evenly shared amongst the ensemble rather than focusing solely on a single lead actor. Joining the series as a new recurring villain was *Rocky Horror* and ***Crystal Maze*** maestro Richard O'Brien as flesh-creeping soothsayer and magician Gulnar. Adding an element of 'soap' to the story was the revelation that Robert and Guy of Gisburne were in fact half-brothers.

Admired by many viewers as the definitive interpretation of the legend, *Robin of Sherwood* wipes the floor with every other version.

Robin of Sherwood came to a premature conclusion, unfortunately, when Marion – stricken with grief when she thought she had lost a second love in quick succession – consigned herself to a convent. Judi Trott, who played Marion, decided not to return to the programme should a fourth series be commissioned. In the event, the collapse of Goldcrest (the production company behind such movie hits as *Chariots of Fire*, 1981) meant that neither HTV nor American network Showtime (which had bought the series for screening Stateside) were able to finance a fourth season on their own. Series creator Richard Carpenter (the man behind other such mystical medieval hits as ***Catweazle***) is on record as saying that, had he known the series was going to come to an end, he would have written a much happier ending for Marion and her second Robin.

For a generation of viewers, *Robin of Sherwood* was the definitive adaptation of the legend, Richard Greene's televised ***Adventures of Robin Hood*** from the mid-1950s relegated to distant parental memory. Kevin Costner's version doesn't get a look in, frankly.

Creators Roy Huggins and Stephen J. Cannell **Producers** Meta Rosenberg (executive), William F. Phillips, John David, J. Rickley Dumm (associate), Stephen J. Cannell, Jo Swerling Jr, Juanita Bartlett, David Chase, Chas Floyd Johnson **Writers** Stephen J. Cannell, Juanita Bartlett, Robert Hamner, Jo Swerling Jr, Gloryette Clark, Edward J. Lakso, Howard Berk, Rudolph Borchert, Zekial Marko, Charles Sailor, Eric Kalder, Don Carlos Dunaway, Gordon Dawson, Walter Dallenbach, Donald L. Gold, Lester William Berke, David Chase, David C. Taylor, James S. Crocker, William R. Stratton, Rogers Turrentine, Shel Willens **Theme Music** Mike Post

So the saying goes, 'Set a thief to catch a thief.' That was the premise of *The Rockford Files*, in which James Garner played an ex-convict who became a private detective. The twist was that the man had been the victim of a miscarriage of justice, wrongfully convicted and released after seeing through five years of his sentence before new evidence proved his innocence. The experience inspired Jim Rockford to become a private detective and help others who find themselves in need of a little help.

It's a way of life unlikely to make Jim rich. Living in a caravan on a beach, his only luxury is an answerphone. Every episode would begin with his answerphone message ('This is Jim Rockford, at the tone leave your name and message and I'll get back to you'), followed by someone leaving a message that would invariably be unrelated to the episode itself. Jim's father, retired truck driver Rocky, occasionally helped out, though more often than not it was just to needle him about getting a proper job. Other colleagues include his ex-girlfriend Beth Davenport, now an attorney (which proves useful when needing to be bailed out of jail) and later 'Coop' Cooper, a former attorney who now offers himself as a legal researcher. Where Jim succeeds where others fail is with his contacts from the wrong side of the tracks; his time inside left him with many associates on the wrong side of the law – notably 'Angel', a little pleader who often provides him with a few choice morsels of info.

In what turned out to be the final series of *The Rockford Files*, Jim Rockford encountered the suave, smug Lance White, an altogether more successful detective. Played by Tom Selleck, the character later inspired the series ***Magnum, P.I.***, which also starred Selleck.

The Rockford Files came to an abrupt end in 1980, but in yet another revival wave, eight TV movies ran on US television between 1994 and 1999, again starring Garner, whose profile had been boosted somewhat by starring opposite Mel Gibson in the movie remake of Garner's old TV western *Maverick* (1994).

Rockliffe's Babies

Crime Drama | BBC One | episode duration 50 mins | broadcast 9 Jan 1987–18 Mar 1988 (*Rockliffe's Babies*), 2 Nov–14 Dec 1988 (*Rockliffe's Folly*)

Regular Cast

Ian Hogg · *DS Alan Rockliffe*
Bill Champion · *PC David Adams*
John Blakely · *PC Keith Chitty*
Brett Fancy · *PC Steve Hood*
Joe McGann · *PC Gerry O'Dowd*
Martyn Ellis · *PC Paul Georgiu*
Susanna Shelling · *WPC Karen Walsh*
Alphonsia Emmanuel · *WPC Janice Hargreaves*
Edward Wilson · *DI Charlie Flight*
Malcolm Terris · *DS Munro*
Brian Croucher · *Chief Superintendent Barry Wyatt*
James Aubrey · *DI Derek Hoskins*
Ian Brimble · *Inspector Leslie Yaxley*
Aaron Harris · *DC Paul Whitmore*
Carole Nimmons · *DS Rachel Osborne*
Craig Nightingale · *PC Guy Overton*
Elizabeth Morton · *WPC Hester Goswell*
John Hartley · *PC Alfred Duggan*

Creator Richard O'Keefe **Producer** Leonard Lewis **Writer** Don Webb **Theme Music** Joe Campbell and Paul Hart composed the theme for *Rockcliffe's Babies*, featuring children from the Corona Stage School singing a playground chant, while Richard Harvey provided a more stately theme for *Folly*, with Chris Hirons on violin.

'The Young Arm of the Law – they're green but they're keen.' So proclaimed the *Radio Times* announcing the arrival of a new urban cop show to rival ***The Bill***. The series followed seven rookies fresh out of the training academy, placed under the watchful eye of the grumpy Detective Rockliffe. Though Rockliffe has years of experience he's often more fallible than his trainees, which funnily enough earns him the young 'uns' respect. Ian Hogg aside, the principal cast were as new to television as their characters were to police work; following in the footsteps of his younger brothers Paul and Mark (with youngest McGann – Stephen – a few years away from joining them all), Joe McGann went on to star in ***The Upper Hand***, while Alphonsia Emmanuel's work includes political thriller ***House of Cards*** and the movie *Peter's Friends* (1992).

After two series of *Rockliffe's Babies*, Ian Hogg took *Rockliffe* to new pastures in a spin-off series, *Rockliffe's Folly*, set in the quieter but no less dramatic Wessex countryside.

Rod Hull and Emu

Children's Entertainment | BBC One/Central for ITV | episode duration 25 mins | broadcast 18 Nov 1975–27 Jan 1980 (BBC), 1982–1988 (ITV)

Cast

Rod Hull, Emu, Billy Dainty, Barbara New · *Various Characters*
Carol Lee Scott · *Grotbags*

Creator Rod Hull **Producer** Peter Ridsdale-Scott

Rod Hull was the human counterpart in this immortal double-act that is difficult to categorise as they cropped up everywhere, in many TV shows over the years, a showbiz sensation that eventually came to a tragic end in 1999. Rod Hull's act was simple, using the Emu puppet (which was allegedly found in a props cupboard while Hull was working for Australia's Channel 9 in the mid-1960s) to cause havoc and mayhem wherever he went. Returning to England in 1971, it was on the 1972 *Royal Variety Performance* that the comedian and his cheeky puppet would gain early notoriety after attacking host Dickie Henderson and the Queen Mother's posy of flowers!

To children of the 1970s, Rod Hull and Emu are best known for *Emu's Broadcasting Company* that saw the pair running a pirate TV station, assisted by Billy Dainty as their harassed technician and Barbara New as the tealady. EBC1 took over the BBC's broadcast for 25 minutes of madcap fun, sketches and all round hilarity that had shades of ***Python*** and ***The Goodies*** about it.

The series was produced by Peter Ridsdale-Scott (who later found ***Red Dwarf*** for the BBC), and featured the well-remembered skit 'Dr Emu' (Rod and Emu in full Tom Baker outfits, battling the evil Deadly Dustbins – something the ***Doctor Who*** revival remembered in 2005, where one character was attacked by a wheelie-bin), as well as spoof weather forecasts and 'Yesterday's World'. In what would prove to be a painfully ironic twist, the final episode of EBC included a scene in which Rod and Emu scaled the outside of the BBC's Broadcasting House because they needed to fix an aerial.

After EBC1 shut up shop, Rod and Emu jumped to ITV for *Emu's Pink Windmill Show*, which begat *Emu's World*, neither of which being a patch on previous hilarity. The format evolved over its years on air, with a live version featuring phone-ins, but always with the same mix of horribly phoney stage school kids and regular appearances from olive-skinned witch Grotbags and various henchmen (including Robot Redford – geddit? – and the scaly yet terribly camp Croc). Rod and Emu's days at ITV are better known for the cringeful catchphrase 'There's somebody at the door!' Grotbags and her minions later got their own eponymously named series, allowing Carol Lee Scott to terrorise more 'brats'.

Rod and Emu's finest hour, a moment that burned the act across the consciousness of popular culture was a 1977 appearance on the BBC's flagship chat show, ***Parkinson***. Hull (and Emu) famously wrestled the unflappable host off his chair, leading to Michael's Parkinson's fear of the bird ever since, although he did appear on *Emu's Broadcasting Company* shortly afterwards.

Sadly, the success of Emu was not to continue into the 1990s, with interest in an increasingly hackneyed light entertainment act waning. Despite lucrative merchandise deals for glove puppets, games and comics, Rod Hull was declared bankrupt in 1994. The performer was killed in 1999 after falling from the roof of his Sussex cottage while trying to fix a TV aerial.

Roobarb

Animation | BBC One | episode duration 5 mins | broadcast 21 Oct 1974–16 May 1975

Cast

Richard Briers · *Narrator*

Creator Grange Calveley **Producer** Bob Godfrey
Theme Music Johnny Hawksworth

Roobarb is a lucky beast – a children's TV show that shows no signs of dating. With a theme tune that's too enthusiastically energetic to ever be annoying and a crazy, uneven wobbliness about its animation, the additional casting of cuddly Richard Briers as the narrator kicks it right into the zone known as 'TV perfection'.

Originally created for publication as a children's book, *Roobarb* was the creation of writer-illustrator Grange Calveley, whose own border collie inspired the eponymous moss-green dog of the series. Having been unable to find an interested publisher, Calveley instead took his idea to the BBC where it was eventually picked up by head of Children's Television Monica Simms. Calveley was introduced to animation director Bob Godfrey (who with Calveley also gave us *Noah and Nelly Aboard the Skylark* and ***Henry's Cat***) and, with the help of animators Anne Jolliffe and Terry Moesker, the team created 30 five-minute giddy episodes.

The adventures revolved around Roobarb's latest hair-brained scheme – hatched up in his shed – such as building himself a spike (a beak) so that he too can go searching for rubber bands (or worms) just like birds do, or going in search of the source of the river and somehow discovering its sauce instead. The result was twofold: invariably it left a shamefaced Roobarb fleeing from the mocking laughter of the birds in the trees, egged on by his nemesis, Custard, the sneering pink cat from next door. It also left a generation of adults with the Pavlovian need to simulate the fusion of guitar, harmonica and electric organ whenever his name is mentioned. Just don't try to correct anyone who insists the show was called 'Roobarb and Custard' though. They won't be told.

Roobarb returned in 2003 in *Roobarb and Custard Too* on Five with an enlarged cast of characters, including computer whizz Mouse.

Trivia

Grange Calveley neglected to tell his own next-door neighbour that he'd inadvertently inspired the voice of Custard. Luckily, the neighbour thought it was based on a man who lived further down the road.

The *Roobarb* theme tune managed to get into the UK singles charts in 1991, courtesy of Shaft. It peaked at No. 7.

Room 101

Entertainment | Hat Trick Productions for BBC Two | episode duration 30 mins | broadcast 4 Jul 1994–present

Regular Cast

Nick Hancock, Paul Merton · *Presenters*

Producers Denise O'Donoghue, Jimmy Mulville, Dan Patterson (executive), Lissa Evans, Toby Stevens, Richard Wilson, Victoria Payne **Writers** Various, including Sarah Parkinson, Ged Parsons, Pete Sinclair, Dan Gaster, Mark Burton, John O'Farrell, John Irwin, Rob Colley

In George Orwell's prophetic novel *Nineteen Eighty-four*, poor unwitting rebel Winston Smith is captured by the minions of all-seeing, all-powerful ***Big Brother***. Inside ***Room 101***, he is tortured by all of the worst imaginings from the darkest pits of his mind.

Quite aside from inspiring reality TV programmes, dramatic TV adaptations and any number of sinister telly adverts, the book has also been responsible for one of the funniest entertainment shows of recent years, named after that room of horrors from the novel. In *Room 101*, the programme's host (Nick Hancock initially, Paul Merton from July 1999 onwards) invites one celebrity guest per week to propose a number of different personal bugbears, irritations or phobias. After a few choice clips pertaining to the selection have been screened, the host then shares a bit of banter with the guest, trying to decide if the selection is awful enough to warrant being consigned to Room 101 for all eternity. Over the years, subjects put forward have included: London buses (proposed by Michael Gambon), the *Children In Need* telethon (Ricky Gervais), hard-boiled eggs (Boris Johnson), champagne (Fay Ripley), 'pedal-bin hair' (Lorraine Kelly) and – infamously – the Welsh (an unrepentant Anne Robinson).

The programme's very first guest was veteran comic Bob Monkhouse, and the first person Paul Merton got to interrogate was outgoing presenter Nick Hancock. With a never-ending stream of celebrities and an even greater list of potential pet peeves (we British like nothing better than to have a good moan about things, don't we?), it seems as though the concept of *Room 101* still has a great deal of mileage left in it.

Roots

Drama | David L. Wolper Productions/Warner Bros for ABC (shown on BBC One) | episode duration 60–120 mins | broadcast 23–30 Jan 1977

Cast

Maya Angelou · *Nyo Boto*
Thalmus Rasulala · *Omoro – Kunta's Father*
Cicely Tyson · *Binta – Kunta's Mother*
LeVar Burton, John Amos · *Kunta Kinte/Toby Reynolds*
Edward Asner · *Captain Thomas Davies*
Ralph Waite · *Slater*
Louis Gossett Jr · *Fiddler*
Robert Reed · *Dr William Reynolds*
Lorne Greene · *John Reynolds*
Lynda Day George · *Mrs Reynolds*
Sandy Duncan · *Missy Anne Reynolds*
Vic Morrow · *Ames*
Paul Shenar · *John Carrington*
Madge Sinclair · *Bell*
Gary Collins · *Grill*
Lee de Broux · *Trumbull*
Tanya Boyd · *Genelva*
Beverly Todd · *Fanta*
Thayer David · *Harlan*
Lawrence Hilton-Jacobs · *Noah*
John Schuck · *Ordell*
Leslie Uggams · *Kizzy*
Roxie Roker · *Melissa*
Elma Jackson · *Mama Ada*
Carolyn Jones · *Mrs Moore*
Scatman Crothers · *Mingo*
George Hamilton · *Stephen Bennett*
Ian McShane · *Sir Eric Russell*
Lillian Randolph · *Sister Sara*
Richard Roundtree · *Sam Bennett*
Ben Vereen · *'Chicken' George Moore*
Lloyd Bridges · *Evan Brent*
Georg Stanford Brown · *Tom Harvey*
Brad Davis · *Ol' George Johnson*
Doug McClure · *Jemmy Brent*
Lynne Moody · *Irene Harvey*
Lane Binkley · *Martha Johnson*
Richard McKenzie · *Sam Harvey*
Austin Stoker · *Virgil*
Sally Kemp · *Lila Harvey*
Burl Ives · *Senator Arthur Johnson*
John Quade · *Sheriff Biggs*
Charles Cyphers · *Drake*
Todd Bridges · *Bud*

Creator Alex Haley **Producers** David L. Wolper (executive), Stan Margulies **Writers** William Blinn, M. Charles Cohen, Ernest Kinoy, James Lee, from the novel by Alex Haley **Theme Music** Quincy Jones

In 1767, son of a Gambian chief, Kunta Kinte, is kidnapped by slave traders and brought to America. Sold into slavery, he is forced by torture to take a new name, Toby Reynolds (the surname coming from his master). When Kunta rebels and tries to escape, his 'master' orders than one of his feet must be removed. The threat of worse reprisals, coupled with his love for Bell, a fellow slave, compels him to remain a slave until his death. He and Bell leave behind a daughter, Kizzy, who is sold to a neighbouring landowner who makes her his concubine. When Kizzy falls pregnant, her son George becomes a favoured slave of the master (who is all too aware that he is the boy's father) and soon his skill as a trainer of fighting birds earns him the nickname 'Chicken George'. George raises his own family, but after his prize chicken loses a fight, his master sells him to a visiting Englishman and he is separated from them and sent off to England. Though the Civil War eventually results in the freedom of all slaves, George's sons learn just how crafty the white men can be at maintaining their servitude. But George's return as a freed man offers his family hope at last of finally being free themselves. . .

One of the highest-rated dramas in American TV history, *Roots* brought the story of slavery into the limelight. The cast alone was impressive, featuring some noted liberals in the roles of racist slave owners and oppressors (Ed Asner, Ralph Waite from ***The Waltons***, Todd Bridges) as well as the largest African-American cast ever assembled for television, including many who would become major stars over the following years (notably LeVar Burton, the young Kunte Kinte, who would join the cast of ***Star Trek: The Next Generation***). The mini series also led to a rise in traditional African baby names and an increased awareness and respect for black history. Accusations of plagiarism dogged Alex Haley for years after his book's success, as did allegations that the purportedly true story was actually a work of fiction heavily inspired by the work of a white writer. But even as a work of fiction it was a powerful and more convincingly honest depiction of slavery than had been seen before. A six-part follow-up mini series, *Roots: The Next Generation*, continued the tale right up to the present day, with James Earl Jones playing the author.

Roseanne

Sitcom | Carsey-Werner/Wind Dancer for ABC (shown on Channel 4) | episode duration 25 mins | broadcast 18 Oct 1988–20 May 1997

Regular Cast

Roseanne Barr/Arnold · *Roseanne Conner*
John Goodman · *Dan Conner*
Laurie Metcalf · *Jackie Harris*
Sara Gilbert · *Darlene Conner/Healy*
Lecy Goranson, Sarah Chalke · *Becky Conner-Healy*
Sal Barone, Michael Fishman · *David Jacob 'DJ' Conner*
Tom Arnold · *Arnie Thomas*
Ned Beatty · *Ed Conner*
Sandra Bernhard · *Nancy Bartlett*
Bonnie Sheridan · *Bonnie Watkins*
George Clooney · *Booker Brooks*
Johnny Galecki · *David Healy*
Martin Mull · *Leon Carp*
Michael O'Keefe · *Fred*
Estelle Parsons · *Beverly Harris*
Ron Perkins · *Pete*
Glenn Quinn · *Mark Healy*
Cole Roberts · *Jerry Garcia Conner*
Natalie West · *Crystal Anderson-Conner*
James Pickens Jr · *Chuck Mitchell*
Adilah Barnes · *Anne-Marie Mitchell*
John McConnell · *Bob*
Shelley Winters · *Nana Mary*
Fred Willard · *Scott*

Creators Matt Williams, Roseanne **Producers** Roseanne, Tom Arnold, Eric Gilliland, Marcy Carsey, Jay Daniel, Jeff Harris, Bruce Helford, Stacie Lipp, Chuck Lorre, Bob Myer, Daniel Palladino, Nancy Steen, Allan Stephan, Rob Ulin, Tom Werner, Matt Williams Matt Williams **Writers** Matt Williams, Roseanne Barr/Arnold/Thomas, Bill Pentland, David McFadzean, Grace McKeaney, Laurie Gelman, Danny Jacobson, Joss Whedon, Tom Arnold, Norma Safford Vela, Bob Myer, Chuck Lorre, Brad Isaacs, Jennifer Heath, Amy Sherman-Palladino, Joel Madison, Don Foster, Maxine Lapiduss, Sid Youngers, David Forbes, Eric Gilliland, Mike Gandolfi, Rob Ulin, Betsy Borns, David Raether, Lois Bromfield, Miriam Trogdon, Kevin Abbott, Michael Borkow, Pat Bullard, Stevie Ray Fromstein, Lawrence Broch, Leif Sandaas, Drew Ogier, Allan Stephan, Carrie Fisher **Theme Music** Dan Foliart and Howard Pearl, with additional laughter by Roseanne. For the final season, the theme was accompanied by lyrics by John Popper of Blues Traveler.

Based on the character comedian Roseanne Barr had shaped around herself for her stand-up act, it's confusing to see one-time head writer Matt Williams's name on the credits as creator. But someone judged in favour of Williams and who are we to argue? Regardless of who was responsible, *Roseanne* stands in US TV history as a uniquely important series. It starred a woman few would describe as traditionally attractive and whose voice is shrill and aggressive, while her husband, kids, friends and extended family were cast to be average people. In a time when silicone ruled the airwaves, this was a naturally funny show.

The stories were often decisively controversial, involving homosexuality (the series featured American prime-time TV's first ever lesbian kiss), infidelity, spousal abuse, overt critiques of big corporate business, in-bred racism (which Roseanne and her husband Dan are horrified to realise has manifested itself in their young son, DJ) and an honest approach to the situations many families find themselves when living on the breadline. Roseanne herself was uncompromising on and off-screen, clashing publicly with Matt Williams and other production personnel and allowing her private and fictional lives to blur: in an episode from the final series she alludes to her very public divorces and marriages when she jokes that she's going to 'dump Dan for some pig, then dump him for some really buff guy'.

Roseanne remained central to the series, but she wasn't afraid to let her co-stars share the limelight. The series catapulted John Goodman into the big league, many episodes allowed Sara Gilbert the last word or the lion's share of the jokes and Laurie Metcalf was often given very dramatic sub-plots. But there was only one character for whom Roseanne ever deferred to: her antipathy for her own mother led her to identify more with the previous generation, represented by her hilarious silver rebel grandmother, played by two-time Oscar-winner Shelley Winters. Whenever she made a guest appearance, Roseanne would willingly step back and let her steal the show.

Although it was one of the most realistic sitcoms ever, it also played loose with the idea that it was a fictional TV show. In the 100th episode, Roseanne's sister Jackie is shown polishing an Emmy that the actress had won a short time before. When actress Lecy Goranson decided to leave the series, her replacement Sarah Chalke was introduced in an episode where the family watched a rerun of ***Bewitched*** and debated the merits of recasting (Becky number two claims to prefer the second Darin, to the shock of all). In later series, the two Becky actresses alternated, leading to the title sequence for series seven to show the two actresses morphing from one to the other (and a witty aside when the second Becky returns for a one-off appearance when the family are about to leave for Disneyland and Roseanne says to her, 'I'll bet you're glad you're here THIS week!').

With the conflicts behind the scenes well known, many kept expecting each successive series to be the last. Indeed, Roseanne herself had planned to call it quits with the eighth year, only to be tempted back for a ninth and definitely final time. For the last series, the Conners became multi-millionaires after winning a $100 million on the state lottery. With John Goodman unable to appear in the whole season because of filming commitments elsewhere, Dan was written out and the whole series became a succession of wish-fulfilment stories and high-concept stunts (one episode featured Jennifer Saunders and Joanna Lumley in character as Edina and Patsy from ***Absolutely Fabulous*** – Roseanne had recently purchased the American remake rights). For such a consistently funny and rewarding show, the final series was a major disappointment for the viewers – until the last episode aired. An hour-long special, it revealed that the whole final season had been a fantasy ever since Dan had survived a heart attack the previous year. Dan had *not* survived and Roseanne had decided to help her grieving by writing a fictionalised version of her life in the study that we saw Dan build for her in the basement years earlier. In a voice-over, she reveals that in constructing the fictional life, she'd swapped Becky's and Darlene's partners, and that her friend Nancy wasn't gay, but her sister Jackie was. Such a brave and unexpected revelation marked the first time since *The Wizard of Oz* in 1939 where a dream ending wasn't a cop-out. It also meant that *Roseanne* could remain in the running for the title of greatest American sitcom ever.

Rosie

See THE GROWING PAINS OF PC PENROSE

The Roy Rogers Show

Action-Adventure | Frontier/Roy Rogers Productions for CBS (shown on ITV) | episode duration 25 mins | broadcast 30 Dec 1951–23 Jun 1957 (USA)

Principal Cast
Roy Rogers, Dale Evans, Pat Grady · *Themselves*
Reed Howes, Harry Harvey Sr · *Sheriff Tom Blodgett*

Creator Roy Rogers **Producers** Roy Rogers, Jack Lacey, Bob Henry, Leslie H. Martinson **Writers** Various, including Milton Raison, Dwight Cummins, William Lively, Ray Wilson, Al Demond **Theme Music** Roy Rogers and Dale Evans duetted on the show's theme song, 'Happy Trails To You', which was composed by the lovely Dale herself.

The Roy Rogers Show is perhaps the one television programme that encapsulates the 1950s just as neatly as ***The Avengers*** tells you all you need to know about the Sixties and ***Dynasty*** is virtually a textbook analysis of the concerns and interests of the Eighties. Real-life singing 'king of the cowboys' Roy Rogers lives on the Double R Bar Ranch in Paradise Valley near Mineral City, along with his wife Dale Evans, her horse Buttermilk, man's best friend Bullet and dopey 'pardner' Pat Grady. Last, but not least, Roy was never far from his faithful steed Trigger, a horse that got him out of all kinds of trouble. In each one of the 100 episodes, Roy would saddle up Trigger and sort out whatever problem stumbled across his path – cattle rustlers, missing children, that kind of thing. Thankfully, by the end of each edition everything would once again be right with the world, just in time for Roy and Dale to join in a chorus of 'Happy Trails to You'.

If this sounds almost unbearably sickly to modern audiences, it's largely because the wholesome values and aims of *The Roy Rogers Show* were clearly identified when the programme was being devised. Aimed squarely at a junior audience, Roy Rogers was a cowboy in the loosest sense – i.e., he rode a horse and wore a hat. With the programme being set in contemporary 1950s America, traditional values of politeness, respect for your elders and the safe handling of firearms were drilled into a nation of eager young viewers, plonked in front of the television by parents who knew that their little 'uns wouldn't be exposed to anything offensive. Of course, there's always a place for quality family friendly entertainment, but surely most sane people must draw the line at the idea of a 1950s' singing cowboy, perched on top of his horse Trigger, putting the wrongs of the world to rights? Where was he when McCarthy was leading his witch-hunts? On a happy trail, presumably. On a side note, Rogers was elected to the Country Music Hall of Fame on two separate occasions – once as a solo artist, and once as a member of the Sons of the Pioneers vocal group (who also popped up regularly in the TV show).

The Royle Family

Sitcom | BBC Two/One | episode duration 30 mins | broadcast 14 Sep 1998–25 Dec 2000

Regular Cast

Caroline Aherne · *Denise Royle/Best*
Ricky Tomlinson · *Jim Royle*
Sue Johnston · *Barbara Royle*
Ralf Little · *Antony Royle*
Craig Cash · *Dave Best*
Jessica Stevenson · *Cheryl Carroll*
Liz Smith · *Norma 'Nana' Speakman*
Geoffrey Hughes · *Twiggy*
Doreen Keogh · *Mary Carroll*
Peter Martin · *Joe Carroll*
Andrew Whyment · *Darren Sinclair-Jones*
Sheridan Smith · *Emma Kavanagh*

Creator Caroline Aherne **Producers** Caroline Aherne, Craig Cash, Henry Normal (associate), Andy Harries (executive), Glenn Wilhide, Kenton Allen **Writers** Caroline Aherne, Craig Cash, Henry Normal, Carmel Morgan, Ricky Tomlinson **Theme Music** 'Half the World Away' by Oasis

Another comedy great to have emerged from the stand-up circuit in the 1990s, Caroline Aherne possessed a laid-back gossipy delivery that disguised the amount of observation and hard work that had gone into her routines. Though her most famous creation, the quick-witted pensioner ***Mrs Merton***, had hosted her own chat-show from 1995 to 1998, and had even starred in a sitcom alongside screen son Malcolm (played by Craig Cash), behind her glasses and blue-rinsed wig she was barely recognisable as the same woman who had played the chatty till-girl in ***The Fast Show***.

The Royle Family was Aherne's attempt to tear up the rulebook for situation comedy. The family members rarely left the comfort of their chairs (dad Jim in his armchair, mum Barbara, daughter Denise and her fiancé/husband Dave on the couch), all eyes fixed on the telly. Occasionally, their son Antony would be despatched to the kitchen to 'make a brew' or to fetch some ciggies from the local shop, and the house had an open door to the next door neighbours, Denise's best friend Cheryl (in early read throughs, this part was played by Kathy Burke), plagued by her inability to lose weight, and her parents, chatty Mary and the taciturn Joe. Even when Jim's friend Twiggy arrives, usually with a bag full of 'knock-off' casual wear, little really happens beyond the day-to-day repetition of conversations. Every character has their catchphrases, but they're disguised as everyday phrases like 'Had your tea, Dave?' or Jim's oft-quoted 'My arse!'

It's the observation that makes *The Royle Family* such a gem; naturalistic responses to mundane situations captured perfectly. Were it not for the presence of former ***Brookside*** stars Ricky Tomlinson and Sue Johnson, re-creating the fondly remembered Grants in another form, you'd be forgiven for thinking you'd stumbled across a docusoap – except docusoaps never feel as real as this. We followed Denise and Dave's romance, from its last-minute stumbling blocks after Denise thought Dave was flirting with Beverley Macca during one of his DJ nights, through to the preparations for the wedding. We witnessed the announcement of Denise's pregnancy (which gave her the perfect excuse to be even more lazy than before – and take advantage of the opportunity to 'drink for two') and cried buckets along with Jim as his heavily pregnant daughter waited for an ambulance on the floor of the Royle bathroom on Christmas Day. We've giggled at Nana's inability to understand the meaning of vegetarianism ('Can she have some wafer-thin ham, Barbara? Oh, that's a shame . . .') and shared the family's bafflement as Antony and his friend Darren re-create a dubious scene from *The Fast Show*. We love the Royle family because they're like our own families – petty, argumentative, trivial and as loving as every family should be.

The tragedy of *The Royle Family*'s success is the attention it brought on its creator. Press intrusion on her relationship problems, drunken nights out and rumoured suicidal tendencies led to Aherne fleeing the UK for Australia. There, she wrote and produced *Dossa and Joe*, a sitcom, before returning to the UK in 2002. Most of *The Royle Family* cast have managed to remain in the spotlight with various projects. Ralf Little and Sheridan Smith were reunited in the bawdy sitcom ***Two Pints of Lager and a Packet of Crisps***; Jessica Stevenson joined Simon Pegg in ***Spaced*** and in 2005 won her own BBC One show *According to Bex*. Andrew Whyment became one of ***Coronation Street***'s great comic assets and Craig Cash went on to create *Early Doors*. But as Ricky Tomlinson noted in his autobiography, they all still hope to return to the Royle couch one day – and we hope to be there when that day comes.

Rugrats

Animation | Klasky-Csupo for Nickelodeon (shown on BBC One) | episode duration 25 mins | broadcast 11 Aug 1991–present (USA)

Voice Cast

E. G. Daily · *Tommy Pickles*
Christine Cavanaugh, Nancy Cartwright · *Chuckie Finster Jr*
Cheryl Chase · *Angelica Pickles*
Kath Soucie · *Phil DeVille, Lil DeVille, Betty DeVille*
Cree Summer · *Susie Carmichael*
Dionne Quan · *Kimi Wantabe-Finster*
Jack Riley · *Stu Pickles*
Melanie Chartoff · *Didi Kerpacketer-Pickles*
Michael Bell · *Drew Pickles, Chaz Finster, Sr, Boris Kerpacketer*
Philip Proctor · *Howie DeVille*
Tress MacNeille · *Charlotte Pickles*
David Doyle, Joe Alaskey · *Louis Kalhern 'Grandpa' Pickles*
Tara Charendoff · *Dylan Prescott 'Dil' Pickles, Timmy McNulty*

Creators Gabor Csupo and Arlene Klasky **Producers** Gabor Csupo, Arlene Klasky, Eryk Casemiro (executive), Cella Nichols Duffy, Jim Duffy, Paul DeMeyer, Paul Germain, Mark Risley, Margot Pipkin, Lorraine Gallacher, David T. Blum, Kate Boutilier, Geraldine Clarke, Richard Gitelson, Pernelle Hayes, Arlene Klasky, Susan Ward **Writers** Various, including Paul Germain, Craig Bartlett, Steve Viksen, Joe Ansolabehere, Peter Gaffney, Douglas Petrie, Jonathan Greenberg, Michael Ferris, Rachel Lipman, Vinny Montello, Steve Ochs, David Maples **Theme Music** Mark Mothersbaugh

One of the original hits for the US Nickelodeon channel, *Rugrats* came to the UK via the BBC One Saturday morning children's TV show ***Live and Kicking***, where it fast became one of the most-watched segments. The episodes revolve around a group of babies and toddlers (the 'rug rats' of the title), with Tommy Pickles as the nominal head of the gang. While still a baby in nappies, Tommy's no-nonsense approach is often essential to control the likes of Chuckie, his best friend, who's scared by everything around him – not surprising when you're only a couple of feet tall in a grown-up world. Other members of the gang, Phil and Lil DeVille, are twins, while Tommy's dog Spike often gets involved. Of course, grown-ups often don't understand the subtle differences between babies and toddlers, which is why they leave the infants in the care of Angelica, a spoilt monster who bullies the gang into obeying her will, though she almost always gets her comeuppance.

The Rugrats Movie was released in 1998, with a sequel, *Rugrats in Paris*, following in 2000 and *Rugrats Go Wild* in 2003. *Rugrats* passed ***The Flintstones***' old benchmark of 165 episodes on 30 November 2002, though it still has a long way to go to top ***The Simpson***'s record-breaking 380-and-counting. The toddlers have also been seen a few years older in the States, in the spin-off series *All Grown Up*, while September 2005 saw two of the older children star in *Angelica and Susie's School Daze*.

Rumpole of the Bailey

Drama | BBC One Thames for ITV | episode duration | broadcast 16 Dec 1975, 3 Apr 1978–3 Dec 1992

Regular Cast

Leo McKern · *Horace Rumpole*
Peter Blythe · *Samuel 'Soapy Sam' Ballard, QC*
Julian Curry · *Claude Erskine-Brown*
Patricia Hodge · *Phyllida 'Portia' Trant/Erskine-Brown*
Peggy Thorpe-Bates, Marion Mathie · *Hilda Rumpole*
Peter Bowles · *Guthrie Featherstone*
Bill Fraser · *Judge Roger 'The Mad Bull' Bullingham*
Richard Murdoch · *Uncle Tom*
Joanna Van Gyseghem · *Marigold Featherstone*
Peter Whitaker · *Jack Pommeroy*
David Yelland · *Nick Rumpole*
Moray Watson · *George Frobisher*
Maureen Derbyshire · *Diana*
Maurice Denham · *Mr Justice Gwent-Evans*
Samantha Bond, Abigail McKern · *Liz Probert*
Camille Coduri · *Dot Clapton*
Rowena Cooper · *Matron Margerite 'Matey' Ballard*
Robin Bailey · *Judge 'Gravestone' Graves*
Jonathan Coy · *Henry the Clerk*
Denys Graham · *Percy Hoskins*
James Grout · *Mr Justice Ollie Oliphant*
Rosalyn Landor · *Fiona Allways*
Denis Lill · *Mr Bernard*

Creator/Writer John Mortimer **Producers** Lloyd Shirley, Brian Walcroft (executive), David Ball, Juliet Grimm (associate), Irene Shubik, Jacqueline Davis **Theme Music** Joseph Horowitz

Middle-aged barrister Horace Rumpole isn't your average kind of dull grey legal man. He's bizarre, eccentric and has the amusing habit of thinking up nicknames for practically everybody he meets in his professional life working at London's Old Bailey. Interestingly, Rumpole refuses to prosecute any cases, always preferring to be a defence counsel – he turns his razor sharp legal mind onto a wide variety of different cases, sometimes even finding to his shock that he's managed to get guilty people off scot-free. However, there's nothing that Rumpole likes better than taking an innocent underdog client (usually bewildered and overawed by being in a courtroom) and winning the case on their behalf through a combination of crafty legal manoeuvrings and verbal dexterity. Unfortunately, at home, Rumpole is far from being the confident master of all he surveys, living under the thumb of his wife Hilda – 'She who must be obeyed.'

Rumpole of the Bailey began life as a one-off *Play for Today* on BBC One, broadcast in December 1975. Written by real-life barrister John Mortimer, the dialogue and situations, although occasionally somewhat fantastical, never felt fake or contrived. When the BBC decided not to commission a whole series of Rumpole, Mortimer took the show to Thames, who eagerly snapped up the idea. In total, some seven seasons of legal skulduggery took place between 1978 and 1992 with some large gaps explained away by having Rumpole retire to Florida for a few years. Throughout the whole run of *Rumpole of the Bailey*, a towering comic performance by Leo McKern helped to make this series compulsively watchable

The Ruth Rendell Mysteries

Drama/Anthology | Blue Heaven Productions/TVS for ITV | episode duration 50–100 mins | broadcast 2 Aug 1987–11 Oct 2000

Regular Cast

George Baker · *DCI Reg Wexford*
Christopher Ravenscroft · *DI Mike Burden*
Louie Ramsay · *Dora Wexford*
Ann Penfold · *Jean Burden*
Diane Keen · *Jennie Ireland /Burden*

Producers Christine Benson, Colin Rogers, Graham Benson (executive), George Baker, Graeme MacArthur, Fiona B. McTavish (associate) Neil Zeiger, Phillippa Giles, Jacky Stoller **Writers** Barbara Rennie, Michael Baker, Julian Bond, Jacqueline Holborough, Sandy Welch, Trevor Preston, George Baker, Guy Meredith, John Harvey, Geoffrey Case, Piers Haggard, Ken Blakeson, Alex Ferguson, Peter Ransley, Ted Whitehead, P. J. Hammond, Douglas Livingstone, Clive Exton, J. E. M. Brooks, Paula Milne, Geoffrey Cox, Roger Marshall, Matthew Jacobs, John Brown, Robert Smith, Peter Berry, Guy Hibbert, Rosemary Anne Sisson, Alan Plater, Christopher Russell, based on the stories by Ruth Rendell **Theme Music** 'Kissing the Gunner's Daughter' by Brian Bennett, formerly of pop group The Shadows

With the success of ***Inspector Morse*** came a glut of laconic rural detectives concerning themselves with the murderous pursuits of the upper classes. Ruth Rendell's Inspector Wexford arrived seven months after *Morse* with a videotaped serial adaptation of 'Wolf to the Slaughter'. Noticing the success of *Morse*, subsequent series would be made on film.

George Baker admits in his autobiography that he'd never read any Ruth Rendell prior to being offered the part of Wexford, but was immediately struck by the intelligence and stature of the character as well as the way each case challenged his principals and personal philosophies. Stories not only dealt with the obligatory murder but political and social matters, such as Alan Plater's adaptation of 'Simisola', which looks at racial tensions in a community where few black people live, or 'Road Rage' in which a group of militant environmentalists use Wexford's wife as a bargaining tool.

Adapting all of Rendell's *Wexford* novels, the series also featured original stories using the same characters (some written by its star, Baker, having become a devotee of the character). Over 20 non-*Wexford* stories were also adapted, justifying the series' generic, author-centric title that was used for the majority of the episodes.

Sabrina, the Teenage Witch

Children's Sitcom | Finishing the Hat/Hartbreak Films for ABC/WB (shown on ITV) | episode duration 25 mins | broadcast 27 Sep 1996–present (USA)

Regular Cast
Melissa Joan Hart · *Sabrina Spellman*
Caroline Rhea · *Hilda Spellman*
Beth Broderick · *Zelda Spellman*
Nick Bakay · *Voice of Salem the Cat*
Nate Richart · *Harvey Kinkle*
Michelle Baudoin · *Jenny Kelly*
Jenna Leigh Green · *Libby Chessler*
Emily Hart · *Amanda Spellman*
Lindsay Slone · *Valerie Birkhead*
Paul Feig · *Mr Eugene Pool*
Martin Mull · *Willard Kraft*
Alimi Ballard · *The Quizmaster*
Robby Benson · *Edward Spellman*
Elisa Donovan · *Morgan*
Soleil Moon Frye · *Roxie King*
Trevor Lissauer · *Miles Goodman*
David Lascher · *Josh*

Creator Nell Scovell **Producers** Nell Scovell, Bruce Ferber, Paula Hart, Miriam Trogdon, David Babcock (executive), Kenneth R. Koch, Gary Halvorson, Frank Conniff, Melissa Joan Hart **Writers** Various, including Nell Scovell, Laurie Gelman, Adam England, Jon Vandergriff, Jon Sherman, Miriam Trogdon, Bruce Ferber **Theme Music** Danny Lux and Paul Taylor composed the typical sub-rock title theme.

Sabrina Spellman is just like any other teenage girl – she gets exasperated with school, boyfriends and her family. But unlike most teenagers, Sabrina has an astonishing secret: on her 16th birthday she finds out that she's a witch, like most of the women in her family. Sent to live with her witch aunts Hilda and Zelda, Sabrina learns how to use her powers sensibly, often being reminded about what to do by her familiar, a black cat called Salem (the home, of course, of the famous witch trials).

During the first few years, Sabrina attended Westbridge High School with her best friend Jenny and fell in chaste love with heart-throb Harvey. Unusually for an American TV series (which tend to like the status quo being kept in all of their programmes), Sabrina was seen to grow up over the course of the programmes. Soon she moved on to college, where her room mates were Roxie, Morgan and Miles. Love was in the air for Sabrina too – after Harvey, Josh became the object of her affections.

An easy-going sitcom that wasn't a hundred miles away from the successful *Tabitha* (itself a spin-off from legendary ***Bewitched***) of the 1970s, Sabrina is actually quite an old character, having originally appeared in the *Archie* comics in the 1960s. When that comic book was transformed into a Saturday morning series, *The Archie Comedy Hour*, Sabrina joined the gang in an animation of her own, eventually getting her own animated series (running from 1970 to 1974). Two decades later, Sabrina was brought to (real) life with a pilot movie broadcast on 7 April 1996, starring 20-year-old Melissa Joan Hart, fresh from the long-running *Clarissa Explains It All*. Realising they had a hit on their hands, the ABC network rushed to sign Hart up for an ongoing series based around the exploits of Sabrina and her family. Indeed, so successful was the live action show that Sabrina returned to her original animated 'roots' when a spin-off, *Sabrina – The Animated Series*, hit TV screens in September 1999. Determined to ensure a good deal for her young daughter, Hart's mother Paula became an executive producer for the series, with young Melissa Joan eventually graduating to become a producer herself.

The Saga of Noggin the Nog

Animation | Smallfilms for BBC TV/BBC One | episode duration 10–15 mins | broadcast 11 Sep 1959–26 Sep 1965, 26 Aug 1970–30 Mar 1973, 19–28 Apr 1982

Voice Cast
Oliver Postgate

Creators/Producers/Writers Oliver Postgate and Peter Firmin
Theme Music Vernon Elliott

In 1952, while studying at art college, Peter Firmin became obsessed by the Isle of Lewis chess pieces on display in the British Museum. He began to whittle away at an idea, a story about the adventures of a benign Viking. Thus Noggin the Nog was born, an inhabitant of the cold North Lands, where dragons fly and winters are long. When Firmin established a creative partnership with Oliver Postgate in the late 1950s (forming Smallfilms in the process), he revealed his Noggin stories and Postgate became a fellow 'Nogmaniac'. Postgate reworked the stories into scripts and the pair gained the interest of the BBC children's department, who commissioned them to make *The Saga of Noggin the Nog* into a series.

The animation was identical to that in Smallfilms' ***Ivor the Engine***, with characters created on sections of adjustable card brought to life with stop-motion animation. In the first stories, Noggin, son of Knut, King of the Nogs, and Queen Grunhilda, went in search of an Eskimo bride called Nooka, made friends with an ice dragon called Grolliffe and faced his uncle, the evil Nogbad the Bad.

Thirty episodes were made in black and white. With the advent of colour, Firmin and Postgate remade the episodes in 15-minute instalments, with 'new' episodes appearing, until the spring of 1982. Noggin the Nog also appeared in a series of storybooks, one of which, *Noggin and the Moon Mouse*, marks the first appearance of a race of pink space rodents who would become famous in the 1970s when they got their own TV series. The 'moon mouse' was of course one of the ***Clangers***!

Sahara

See AROUND THE WORLD IN 80 DAYS

The Saint

Action-Adventure | New World/Bamore/ITC/ATV for ITV | episode duration 50 mins | broadcast 1962–1969

Principal Cast

Roger Moore · *Simon Templar – 'The Saint'*

Creators Robert S. Baker, Monty Norman, inspired by the novels by Leslie Charteris **Producers** Robert S. Baker, Monty Norman **Writers** Various, including Terry Nation, Ian Stuart Black, Robert Holmes, Richard Harris, Gerald Kelsey, Harry W. Junkin, John Knise, Norman Borisof, Julian Bond, Michael Cramoy, John Gilling, Lewis Davidson, Dick Sharples, Donald James, Leigh Vance **Theme Music** Edwin Astley

Simon Templar (ST = Saint) is a wealthy adventurer who loves a fight. He travels around the globe, always on the lookout for some criminal or villain to battle, or preferably some damsel in distress to rescue. He answers to no higher authority, not working specifically for any organisation or government, and because he's a man of means, he asks for no reward for his efforts. Driving around in his sexy yellow Volvo P1800 (the same make of car driven years later by Steve McQueen in the movie *Bullitt*), registration plate ST 1, Simon Templar fights smugglers, murderers, spies, thieves and kidnappers alike (usually literally, with a lengthy fight sequence at least once every episode), only stopping to drop off his calling card – a stick figure with a halo.

Leslie Charteris created the character of Simon Templar in 1928, and had seen the Saint blossom into a popular character in both cinema films (starring George Sanders) and on the radio. The original casting idea for the TV version of *The Saint* was suave David Niven, Leslie Charteris's preferred choice. However a TV version didn't progress until Lord Lew Grade showed an interest in the property, originally planning to use ***Danger Man*** star Patrick McGoohan (who turned it down, uncomfortable with playing a hero who was both a womaniser and happy to resolve problems with a gun). Eventually the role went to ***Ivanhoe*** star Roger Moore, whose own natural debonair charm and occasional raising of the eyebrow ensured that the adventures of Simon Templar, exciting though they were, never took themselves too seriously. It was this approach that made him the likely successor for James Bond when the post became available in the 1970s.

The character of *The Saint* had been away from TV screens for nearly a decade when ITC decided to revive Simon Templar for a whole new generation of viewers. Just as before, Simon Templar travelled around the globe from exotic locale to exotic locale, hobnobbing with the international jet set, romancing the most glamorous of women, and fighting the wicked plans of villains wherever he finds them.

With a much higher budget than the 1960s series, *Return of The Saint* actually went to glamorous locations rather than recreating them within a studio. With a far more up-tempo jazzy theme tune and a Roger Moore lookalike in the form of Ian Ogilvy, it's difficult to understand why *Return of The Saint* was utterly panned by critics – perhaps the viewers of the 1970s were more interested in the gritty realism of shows like ***The Sweeney*** rather than in the escapist fantasy of Simon Templar's adventures.

Exec producer Robert Baker was still trying to resurrect *The Saint* well into the 1990s. An unsuccessful 1987 pilot movie called *The Saint in Manhattan* starred Australian actor Andrew Clarke as Simon Templar. When the series finally materialised in 1989, the lead role was taken by Simon Dutton. Consisting of six 90-minute movies, the series was not recommissioned. The Saint's final screen appearance to date was in a 1997 feature film, directed by Philip Noyce and starring Val Kilmer.

St Elsewhere

Drama | MTM for NBC (shown on Channel 4) | episode duration 50 mins | broadcast 26 Oct 1982–25 May 1988

Principal Cast

Norman Lloyd · *Dr Daniel Auschlander*
Howie Mandel · *Dr Wayne Fiscus*
Denzel Washington · *Dr Philip Chandler*
William Daniels · *Dr Mark Craig*
Eric Laneuville · *Luther Hawkins*
Sagan Lewis · *Dr Jacqueline Wade*
Bonnie Bartlett · *Ellen Craig*
Ed Begley Jr · *Dr Victor Ehrlich*
Ed Flanders · *Dr Donald Westphall*
Ellen Bry · *Nurse Shirley Daniels*
Terence Knox · *Dr Peter White*
G. W. Bailey · *Dr Hugh Beale*
David Birney · *Dr Ben Samuels*
Stephen Furst · *Dr Elliot Axelrod*
Mark Harmon · *Dr Robert 'Bobby' Caldwell*
Bruce Greenwood · *Dr Seth Griffin*
Ronny Cox · *Dr John Gideon*
Cynthia Sikes · *Dr Annie Cavanero*
Kim Miyori · *Dr Wendy Armstrong*
Nancy Stafford · *Joan Halloran*
David Morse · *Dr Jack 'Boomer' Morrison*
France Nuyen · *Dr Paulette Kiem*
Cindy Pickett · *Dr Carol Novino*
Christina Pickles · *Nurse Helen Rosenthal*
Kavi Raz · *Dr V. J. Kochar*
Jennifer Savidge · *Nurse Lucy Papandrao*

Creators Joshua Brand and John Falsey **Producers** Joshua Brand, Channing Gibson, Bruce Paltrow, Abby Singer, John Tinker,

Mark Tinker **Writers** Various, including Joshua Brand, John Falsey, Tom Fontana, John Masius, Joel Surnow, Mark Tinker, Steve Lawson, John Tinker, Steve Bello, Channing Gibson, Charles H. Eglee, Eric Overmyer **Theme Music** Dave Grusin

St Eligius Hospital in south Boston is known to one and all as 'St Elsewhere', such is the feeling of abandonment there. But each member of staff is determined to do their job, no matter what the problem.

St Elsewhere had a troubled existence from the start. With disappointing ratings it was cancelled by the network after its first season only for NBC to change their mind again. The production team were certain they'd be canned after their fifth year so deliberately created an incredibly down-beat ending to the season involving the hospital being sold off and the regular characters' plotlines abruptly brought to a less-than life affirming close. Miraculously, NBC brought the show back for one more year, much of which was spent trying to work around the various problems caused by the previous season finale.

Such a reckless attitude might suggest a lack of care but nothing could be further from the truth. *St Elsewhere* wore its heart on its sleeve and, like its stable-mate ***Hill Street Blues***, continually pushed the boundaries both in production and dramatic terms. It was the first US series to deal with the subject of AIDS and the first prime-time drama to have a central character contract the disease (Dr Bobby Caldwell, played by sometime heart-throb Mark Harmon). It was also the first series to portray a man as a victim of rape.

Playing to its audience of Generation Xers, *St Elsewhere* is a nexus point for crossovers: Dr Westphall announces his resignation in a certain Bostonian bar where the barflies include Norm and Cliff and the waitress is called Carla (and all three characters were played by the ***Cheers*** regulars); Dr Roxanne Turner hopped over to *Homicide: Life on the Streets*, a show that featured a crossover to ***The X Files***, which featured a crossover to ***The Simpsons*** – as did *Cheers*. To cap it all, St Eligius was bought in its final year by Weigert Medical Corporation, the same company that supplies the medical centre in Oswald Maximum Security Penitentiary – the prison in HBO's *Oz* – and there are also tenuous one-liner links to ***M*A*S*H****, *Wings*, *Newhart* and other shows.

If the suggestion that *St Elsewhere*, *M*A*S*H**, *Homicide*, *Cheers* and *The X Files* all share the same universe as *The Simpsons* strikes you as being a little too much, prepare yourself for a shock. The final episode of *St Elsewhere* reveals that the entire series has been concocted within the imagination of Tommy, an autistic boy who owns a snowglobe that contains a model of St Elsewhere. What a way to finish – and take half of the rest of television with you!

Trivia
The little cat that featured in the MTM logo at the end of each episode was seen wearing a surgeon's green smock and cap. The cat's name, by the way, was Mimsie, who, for the final episode was shown hooked up to a life-support before flat-lining (the real Mimsie died the same year as the show was cancelled). Nice, eh?

Sale of the Century

Quiz Show | Anglia for ITV/Sky One/Challenge TV | episode duration 25 mins | broadcast 1971–1984 (ITV)

Regular Cast
Nicholas Parsons, Peter Marshall, Keith Chegwin · *Hosts*
John Benson · *Announcer*
Jennifer Cresswell, 'Canasta', Carole Ashby, Me Me Lai · *Hostesses*

Creator Al Howard **Producers** John Jacobs (executive), Peter Joy, Bill Perry **Theme Music** 'Joyful Pete' by Peter Fenn

Another quiz show with its roots in the USA, the UK version of *Sale of the Century* was proud of the fact that it came 'Live . . . from Norwich' and unashamedly boasted that it was 'The quiz of the week!' Converting points into prize money to be spent on a range of household items at knockdown prices, *Sale of the Century* made Nicholas Parsons one of the biggest names in game shows, though sadly this also put an end to his career as an actor, aside from guest roles in ***The Comic Strip Presents*** and ***Doctor Who***.

A BBC strike in 1978 led to viewers watching one *Sale of the Century* edition to the tune of just over 21 million, making it the highest-rated ITV game show ever. The format has been exported around the world, with particular success in Australia, while in the UK it's been resurrected on satellite/cable channels Sky One (with Peter Marshall as host) and Challenge TV, where former ***Multi-Coloured Swap Shop*** presenter Keith Chegwin posed the questions.

Salem's Lot

Horror | Warner Bros Television for CBS (shown on BBC One) | episode duration 90 mins | broadcast 17–24 Nov 1979 (USA)

Regular Cast
David Soul · *Ben Mears*
James Mason · *Richard K. Straker*
Ed Flanders · *Dr William 'Bill' Norton*
Lance Kerwin · *Mark Petrie*
Bonnie Bedelia · *Susan Norton*
Bonnie Bartlett · *Ann Norton*
Joshua Bryant · *Ted Petrie*
Barbara Babcock · *June Petrie*
James Gallery · *Father Donald Callahan*
Brad Savage · *Danny Glick*
Ronnie Scribner · *Ralphie Glick*
Clarissa Kaye · *Majorie Glick*
Ned Wilson · *Henry Glick*
Julie Cobb · *Bonnie Sawyer*
George Dzundza · *Cully Sawyer*

Fred Willard · *Larry Crockett*
Kenneth McMillan · *Constable Parkins Gillespie*
Lew Ayres · *Jason Berk*
Geoffrey Lewis · *Mike Ryerson*
Elisha Cook · *Weasel Phillips*
Barney McFadden · *Ned Tebbets*
Marie Windsor · *Eva Miller*
Robert Lussier · *Deputy Constable Nolly Gardner*
Reggie Nalder · *Mr Kurt Barlow*

Producers Stirling Silliphant (executive), Anna Cottle, Richard Kobritz **Writer** Paul Monash, from the novel by Stephen King **Theme Music** Harry Sukman, a rather apt surname for the composer of music in a film about vampires.

An entire generation of children were left petrified beyond the ability to sleep after watching this adaptation of Stephen King's classic horror novel. Directed by Tobe '*The Texas Chain Saw Massacre*' Hooper, no programme before or since has been quite as successful in its stated intention of scaring the wits out of anybody watching.

Struggling novelist Ben Mears returns to his childhood home town of 'Jerusalem's Lot' in New England in the hope that it might inspire his work. Unfortunately, the town has become decidedly more sinister since he was last there – in particular, Mr Barlow, the new owner of the old and derelict Marsten House (long rumoured to be haunted by *something*) seems notable by his absence. His business associate Mr Straker seems pleasant enough at first – but what secret is he hiding? And why has Straker arranged for a gigantic crate full of soil from Europe to be shipped to this quiet town? Soon, the residents of Salem's Lot start to die, one by one. The only problem is they don't stay buried for very long. . .

Shown initially in two 90-minute episodes, *Salem's Lot* begins slowly, held back by a strangely underwhelming performance from ***Starsky and Hutch*** star David Soul. However, as soon as the supernatural evil begins to take hold, the atmosphere and tension never let up for one second. It's not until the end of the first episode that most people's suspicions – that Mr Barlow is, in fact, an ancient, powerful vampire out to bleed the town dry – are horribly confirmed when a young boy rises out of his coffin and sinks his fangs into the poor unfortunate grave-digger. For anyone who's ever watched *Salem's Lot*, there are several sequences that will remain imprinted on the mind forever. One is Mr Barlow himself, a blue-tinged decaying Nosferatu-esque skull complete with two gigantic fangs where the incisor teeth should be – portrayed to perfection (albeit silently) by former Hitchcock collaborator Reggie Nalder. The other is the image of one of the vampirised Gluck boys, hovering outside his friend's bedroom window, red eyes glowing, scratching with his long, sharp fingernails on the glass and asking to be let in.

Salem's Lot was also released in cinemas as a cut-down, two-hour version. Unfortunately, that edit cut out a great deal of the important tension-building scenes and left in all of the dull stuff from the first episode – so if you're hoping to scare yourself again by revisiting this programme on video or DVD, try to ensure that you track down the full three-hour version or you may be terribly disappointed. In 2004, the American cable channel TNT staged another two-part adaptation of *Salem's Lot*, this time starring Rob Lowe as Ben Mears, Donald Sutherland as the creepy Mr Straker, and Rutger Hauer as the ancient vampire.

Sapphire and Steel

Science Fiction | ATV for ITV | episode duration 25 mins | broadcast 10 Jul, 1979–31 Aug 1982

Regular Cast

Joanna Lumley · *Sapphire*
David McCallum · *Steel*
David Collings · *Silver*

Creator P. J. Hammond **Producers** David Reid (executive), Shaun O'Riordan **Writers** P. J. Hammond, Don Houghton, Anthony Read **Theme Music** Cyril Ornadel composed a deeply creepy theme tune that bombastically blared out from beneath the surreal title sequence.

Writer P. J. Hammond had contributed to everything from ***Ace of Wands*** to ***Z Cars*** by the time he pitched a children's drama serial to Thames about two agents fighting a war against an invisible enemy. The agents were 'Elements', beings that appear human but have properties connected to gold, lead, copper, jet, diamond, radium, silver . . . and, of course, sapphire and steel (don't fret that not all of these are genuine elements; it's really not important). Thames passed the series to ATV, who realised the show probably wasn't meant for kids and instead pushed for a teatime slot.

Sapphire and Steel is essentially a programme about two Time Agents who are dispatched by a mysterious higher power to correct mistakes in time and to prevent either time itself or evil entities from 'breaking through' into the real world. Beautiful blue-clothed Sapphire was the heart of the duo of time-travelling investigators; she'd be the one who'd inevitably be sent to calm down the terrified humans while Steel tackled the problem, finding it too difficult to hide his concern about the severity of the situation. Sapphire also had the ability to turn time back, briefly, which came in handy when trying to find Time's point of entry. And while the setting changed each time – an apartment block, an abandoned railway station, a petrol station – the threat was always the same: time trying to break through to now, wanting to exist beyond its own limitations. It chooses to do this in various ways, such as hiding inside nursery rhymes, re-animating soldiers who were killed after the armistice was called on World War One or by passing through photographs. Whatever, it must be prevented from succeeding – which is where the elements come in.

Occasionally, the threat will be too great for just Sapphire and Steel and other elements will be despatched, such as Lead, which takes the form of a tall, muscular man, or Silver, a technician with the ability to control pretty much any bit of manufactured machinery or technology. Special effects were, if anything, rather unambitious, but the series' strength was its performances. Almost all of the atmosphere and terror was created by the actors, with only the subtlest of superimposed shadows or lights used to convey the ever-present abstract threat of time.

With ATV absorbed into Central Television, and both Lumley and McCallum increasingly difficult to get hold of, *Sapphire and Steel* came to a jolting end, left trapped by time and looking through a window in space. But the series left us with so many other iconic images, not least the Magritte-like man with no face, and was as much a series of chilling ghost stories as science fiction.

P. J. Hammond later contributed to ***The Bill*** in the 1980s and '90s – his episodes were typified by quirky and often disturbed characters and staggering twists in the tale. His retirement from writing has left British television without one of its most innovative talents.

Trivia

For many years, the portentous voice speaking out over the opening title sequence was believed to be that of *Poirot* actor David Suchet. However, in recent interviews he has stated that he has no memory of recording such a voice-over – we might have to chalk this one down to yet another baffling *Sapphire and Steel* mystery.

Saturday Live

Entertainment | LWT for Channel 4 | episode duration 50–70 mins | broadcast 12 Jan 1985–11 Apr 1987 (*Saturday Live*), 19 Feb–29 Apr 1988 (*Friday Night Live*)

Regular Cast

Ben Elton · *Host*
Adrian Edmondson, Rik Mayall · *The Dangerous Brothers*
Mark Arden, Stephen Frost · *The Oblivion Boys*
Stephen Fry, Hugh Laurie, Harry Enfield, Jack Docherty, Moray Hunter, Josie Lawrence

Producers Marcus Plantin (executive), Paul Jackson, Geoff Posner, Geoffrey Perkins **Writers** Various, including Ben Elton, Mark Arden, Stephen Frost, Geoff Atkinson, Pete McCarthy, Rebecca Stevens, Adrian Edmondson, Rik Mayall, Stephen Fry, Hugh Laurie, Guy Jenkin, Ricky Greene, Paul Whitehouse, Harry Enfield, Josie Lawrence, Jack Docherty, Moray Hunter, Charlie Higson

There are some programmes that have a cultural impact much greater than their ratings might suggest. Though less than 2 million people actually bothered to tune in, *Saturday Live* (and its successor *Friday Night Live*) was responsible for bringing to our screens a staggering amount of comedy talent. Since the creation of the Comic Strip in the late 1970s, stand-up comedy had become a huge industry. Having already given us ***The Young Ones*** (notably featuring Rik Mayall and Adrian Edmondson, with appearances from Mark Arden, Steve Frost and Ben Elton), producer Paul Jackson cherry-picked his way through London's many comedy clubs and brought the very best of them to Channel 4 viewers each week.

Regular performers on *Saturday Live* read like a *Who's Who of TV Comedy*. Edmondson and Mayall developed their 'Dangerous Brothers' act, which later evolved into ***Bottom***; Fry and Laurie brought an air of intellectual silliness to proceedings, while motormouth leftie Ben Elton became the show's permanent host from its second series. *Saturday Live*'s politics were quite obvious, with Elton's use of the nickname 'Thatch' for Prime Minister Mrs Thatcher neatly combining over-familiarity with an equal dose of contempt. Harry Enfield was Elton's co-performer on the vast majority of shows, with his comic creations Stavros the Greek kebab shop owner and boorish plasterer Loadsamoney offering a different social commentary to Elton's more in-your-face rapid fire delivery.

Other performers taking their first unsteady steps on television included Julian Clary (then appearing in his punk-drag persona of The Joan Collins Fan Club, accompanied by Fanny the Wonder Dog) and The Sea Monster – a curiously sing-song-voiced feminist creation of former psychiatric nurse Jo Brand. The series also brought in the cream of American comedy performers (or at least all of those who weren't booked to appear on America's own long-running *Saturday Night Live*) such as Emo Phillips, as well as representatives from the previous generation of rabble-rousers such as Spike Milligan, Frankie Howerd and Peter Cook. The programme also continued the long-established variety/entertainment show mix of combining comedians with performances from top music acts.

From 1988, the programme shifted days to Fridays for its final season. There were few other obvious changes, with Elton and Enfield remaining with the show to its conclusion. In 1996, LWT resurrected the format for an eight-part series once again called *Saturday Live* (only this time on ITV) (1 Jun–20 Jul 1996). Like its predecessors, the new *Saturday Live* was also transmitted live and featured Lee Hurst as the compère.

The Saturday Night Armistice

Comedy | BBC Two | episode duration 30–35 mins | broadcast 24 Jun–5 Aug, 22 Dec 1995 (*The Saturday Night Armistice*), 14 Jun 1996–13 Feb 1998 (*The Friday Night Armistice*)

Regular Cast

Armando Iannucci, David Schneider, Peter Baynham

Producer Sarah Smith **Writers** Armando Iannucci, Peter Baynham, David Schneider, Jane Bussmann, Kevin Cecil, Graham Linehan, Arthur Mathews, David Quantick, Andy Riley **Theme Music** Jonathan Whitehead, Jonny Moore

Radio 4's *On the Hour* fed Nineties comedy in much the same way as ***That Was The Week That Was*** had done three decades earlier. Two of its writers, Stewart Lee and Richard Herring, went on to create and star in ***Fist of Fun*** and Sunday lunchtime comedy show *This Morning With Richard Not Judy*. In addition, *On the Hour* spawned two massively influential comedy monsters – Steve Coogan's Alan Partridge and Chris Morris' double-barrelled assault on the media, ***The Day Today*** and ***Brass Eye***. *The Saturday Night Armistice* was a vehicle for three figures who'd also been key players in many of *On the Hour*'s illegitimate, slightly deformed offspring: sharp-suited, pock-marked smug Scot/Italian Armando Iannucci; rubber-faced, not-Rowan Atkinson David Schneider; and the other one, Peter Baynham.

The Saturday Night Armistice took a faux, improvised three-handed discussion format, dissecting the week's news and its key participants. Driving the comedy was a combination of apathy, sneering and extreme cynicism, with a high level of topicality (the show was recorded a day before broadcast) making the barbs and jibes hit home even harder. One of the programme's regular features was 'Hunt the Old Woman', a member of the public planted in the audience or in the background of other programmes. There were regular attacks on the then-Leader of the Opposition Tony Blair, a more viable target for comedy than the actual Prime Minister John Major. The programme also used carefully re-edited clips from genuine news interviews to mildly comic effect. Shifting days of transmission didn't alter much about the programme. In truth, each of the show's performers was vastly superior to the material they were given to deliver – or at least we'd like to think so.

Saturday SuperStore

Magazine | BBC One | episode duration 180 mins | broadcast 2 Oct 1982–18 Apr 1987

Regular Cast

Mike Read, Sarah Greene, Keith Chegwin, John Craven, David Icke, Vicky Licorish, Philip Hodson, Peter Simon, Phillip Schofield

Producers Rosemary Gill, Chris Bellinger (editors), Christopher Tandy, Nick Wilson, Cathy Gilbey, Richard Simkin **Theme Music** 'Down at the Superstore', written by B. A. Robertson, performed by The Assistants (B. A. Robertson, Cheryl Baker, Dave Edmunds, Junior Giscombe and Suzi Quatro). The same theme was re-arranged by Steve Levine for its fourth series.

With Noel Edmonds leaving ***Multi-Coloured Swap Shop*** in 1982 for the giddy heights of grown-up, prime-time telly, the golden BBC One Saturday morning slot was left wide open. In came Mike Read with *Saturday SuperStore*, a high-concept show in which Read was general manager of the store, Keith Chegwin was the delivery boy (i.e. he went on location as he'd done for *Swap Shop*), Sarah Greene was in charge of 'Customer Services' and most of the interviews took place in the coffee shop or the staff room. But the concept didn't really hide the fact that there's little difference between a 'Shop' and a 'Store', especially if the sets have almost the same layout, the phone-ins use the same number (altogether now, '01 – if you're outside London – 811 8055'), and the shows have a similar structure of interviews with celebs interspersed with cartoons and pop music. Oh, and they both had news items presented by John Craven (bolstered by sports roundups from David Icke, before he became famous for believing that the royal family were aliens).

There were, however, some innovations. There was the 'Saturday SuperStore Search for a SuperStar', which 'discovered' at least three acts from the northwest who went on to enjoy some success. One was Juvenile Jazz, an accomplished trad-jazz band consisting of teenagers, another was a young lad called Shaun Duggan, who wrote and performed a skit of the Famous Five with some friends. Shaun later appeared in a 1987 edition of ***The South Bank Show*** as a fan of the band the Smiths and wrote a play called William, based on the song 'William It Was Really Nothing', which led to him being interviewed by his idol, Morrissey, on Channel 4's ***The Tube***. From there, he's become a professional writer, scripting for ***Brookside*** and, from 2003, ***EastEnders***. Biggest success of all in our minds though was Claire Usher, who performed 'It's 'Orrible Being in Love (When You're Eight and a Half)' and later scored a No. 13 hit with the song in the UK Singles charts. But we digress . . .

Edmonds had Posh Paws, Read had a small clunky robot called 'Sieve-head' who whirred around his desk. Better, though, was the Crow, a Liverpudlian bird puppet who popped up from the back of the sofa or through bits of the set to interject with punchlines and general heckling.

Saturday SuperStore also scored a few coups with guests – including the leaders of the three main political parties. Margaret Thatcher claimed that she liked the honesty of children's questions, though she did appear more than a little flustered by the directness of one of them: 'If the bomb goes off, where will you be?' Another impressive guest was HRH Prince Edward, who had come to present the award to the 'Search for a SuperStar' winner and agreed to answer some questions.

Scarlet and Black

Drama | BBC One | episode duration 80 mins | broadcast 31 Oct–14 Nov 1993

Principal Cast

Ewan McGregor · *Julien Sorel*
Alice Krige · *Madame de Renal*
Stratford Johns · *Abbé Pirard*
T. P. McKenna · *Marquis de la Mole*
Rachel Weisz · *Mathilde de la Mole*

Christopher Fulford · *Napoleon*
Martin Jarvis · *Monsieur de Renal*
Georges Corraface · *Comte Altamira*
Jo Ross · *Marquise de la Mole*
Michael Attwell · *Monsieur Valenod*
Peter Benson · *Monsieur de Moirod*
Sarah Berger · *Madame Derville*
Crispin Bonham-Carter · *Comte de Croisenois*
Lisa Coleman · *Elisa*
Joe Duttine · *François*
Ian McNeice · *Prosecutor*
Jeremy Young · *Duke of Wellington*

Producer Rosalind Wolfes **Writer** Stephen Lowe, from Stendhal's novel *Le Rouge et le Noir*

In the France of the 1830s, young son of a carpenter Julien Sorel realises that unless he does something soon with his life, he will forever be trapped in the provinces, with no power or influence over others. With an air of confident ruthlessness, Julien decides that the best way to achieve his aims is not to join the army (the 'Scarlet') but instead to enter the church (the 'Black'). Through a combination of perseverance, duplicity and love, Julien manages to climb the social ladder all the way to Paris, hiding behind a façade of piety that belonging to the Church gives him. However, the truth about Julien's behaviour and the shameless methods he uses to climb to the top are destined to come spilling out – after having climbed such a high and precarious 'ladder' all the way to the top, there's only one way that Julien can go . . .

One of the most sumptuous and beautiful mini series ever filmed for British television, *Scarlet and Black* benefits from truly cinematic direction, photography, costumes and sets. The cast list's not too shabby either, with a healthy combination of veteran British actors (Stratford Johns, Martin Jarvis, T. P. McKenna) working well alongside two young performers Rachel Weisz and Ewan McGregor – both of whom would spiringboard off the back of *Scarlet and Black* into long-running movie careers in Hollywood. A particularly notable performance comes from Alice Krige (better known to ***Star Trek*** fans as the Borg Queen) as Madame de Renal, with the chemistry between her and Ewan McGregor's characters crackling with sexual tension.

The Scarlet Pimpernel

Drama | ABC Australia/A&E/BBC for BBC One | episode duration 90 mins | broadcast 24 Jan 1999–1 Nov 2000

Principal Cast
Richard E. Grant · *Sir Percy Blakeney/The Scarlet Pimpernel*
Elizabeth McGovern · *Lady Marguerite Blakeney*
Martin Shaw · *Chauvelin*
Anthony Green · *Sir Andrew Ffoulkes*
Ronan Vibert · *Robespierre*
Christopher Fairbank · *Fumier*
Gerard Murphy · *Planchet*
Ron Donachie · *Mazzarini*
Beth Goddard · *Suzanne De Tourney*
Milton Johns · *Fisher*
Jonathan Coy · *The Prince of Wales*
Emilia Fox · *Minette*
Jamie Bamber · *Lord Tony Dewhurst*
Dominic Mafham · *James Danby*
Pascal Langdale · *Armand St Just*
Gillian Cally · *Countess de Martignac*
Nicholas Gecks · *Auguste Didier*
Matthew Graville · *J. M. W. Turner*
Anton Lesser · *Antoine Picard*
John McEnery · *Sir William Wetherby*
Harry Meacher · *Count de Martignac*
Daniel Webb · *Libersac*
Simon Williams · *Henry Cavendish*

Producers Johan Eliasch, Delia Fine, Morgan Mason, Hannah Rothschild, Tony Virgo (executive), Kevan Van Thompson, Julian Murphy **Writer** Richard Carpenter, from the novels by Baroness Emmuska Orczy **Theme Music** Michal Pavlícek

Baroness Orczy's stories of the noble English lord Sir Percy Blakeney risking life and limb by travelling to Revolutionary France in order to rescue his fellow aristocrats from a sudden messy death on the guillotine have been filmed on many occasions. First, Leslie Howard and Merle Oberon starred in a 1934 movie adaptation, followed in 1950 by Powell and Pressberger's classic *The Elusive Pimpernel* (with David Niven effortlessly portraying Sir Percy). An early TV version of the story from the ever-reliable ITC production company starred Marius Goring, and ran for 30 episodes on ITV (24 Feb 1955–22 Jun 1956). Yet another interpretation came in 1982, with a one-off TV movie made for US TV starring Anthony Andrews, Jane Seymour and Ian McKellen as Sir Percy, his wife Marguerite and the villainous Chauvelin. Even the *Carry On* crowd had a go, with *Don't Lose Your Head* (1966) mercilessly lampooning the story, featuring Sid James as Sir Rodney Effing ('Two effs'), aka The Black Fingernail.

For many people, the recent adaptation starring Richard E. Grant as Sir Percy is one of the best. It's by no means the most accurate adaptation of the source material, but the sheer verve, enthusiasm and excitement contained in the production is breathless. Grant makes a charismatic and believable Scarlet Pimpernel, a hero who's more like an 18th-century James Bond than an effete 'aristo' lauding it over the proletariat villains. Packed full of excellent cameo appearances and lushly filmed in Prague in order to get a better representation of what the 'Reign of Terror' Paris might have looked like, it's a shame that only six feature-length episodes were made.

Scooby-Doo

Animation | Hanna-Barbera for CBS (shown on BBC One) | episode duration 25–50 mins | broadcast 13 Sep 1969–31 Oct 1970, 9 Sep 1972–present

Regular Cast

Don Messick, Frank Welker · *Scoobert 'Scooby'-Doo*
Casey Kasem · *Norville 'Shaggy' Rogers*
Stefianna Christopherson, Heather North, Grey DeLisle, Kellie Martin · *Daphne Blake*
Nichole Jaffe, Patricia Stevens, Christina Lange, Mindy Cohn · *Velma Dace Dinkley*
Frank Welker, Carl Stevens · *Fred Jones, Dynomutt*
Daws Butler · *Scooby-Dum*
Julie McWhirter · *Scooby-Dee*
Lennie Weinrib · *Scrappy-Doo/Yabba-Doo*
Mel Blanc · *Speed Buggy*

Creators Joe Ruby, Ken Spears **Producers** Joseph Barbera, William Hanna, Alex Lovy, Lewis Marshall **Writers** Various, including Joe Ruby, Ken Spears, Larz Bourne, Jameson Brewer, Tom Dagenais, Ruth Brooks Flippen, Fred Freiberger, Willie Gilbert, Heywood Kling, Bill Lutz, Larry Markes, Norman Maurer, Jack Mendelsohn, Sidney Morse, Ray Parker, Gene Thompson, Paul West, Harry Winkler **Theme Music** Though each successive incarnation of Scooby-Doo has sported its own theme, the classic *Scooby Dooby Doo, Where Are You?* theme came from David Mook and Ben Raleigh. This was not the original theme for the show though; musical director Ted Nichols composed an instrumental piece that is still present on some copies of the first series of episodes – the Mook/Raleigh was recorded just days before the show aired. David Mook himself sang the first vocal theme, while Dan Janssen sang the version used on the second series.

Zoinks! It's the most famous TV dog of all time, the Great Dane whose name came from the misheard lyrics of 'Strangers in the Night', as sung by Frank Sinatra. *Scooby-Doo, Where Are You?* started out as a new animated comedy for Saturday mornings with the name 'W-Who's S-S-Scared?' The answer to that question soon came – the network executives, who felt that production designs by Joe Ruby and Ken Spears were simply too nightmarish for children. The horror was toned down and the gang's dog was given centre stage. Who could possibly be scared with a big lummocking dog to protect you?

Scooby was the mascot of Mystery Inc., a gang of high-school students who make it their mission to solve crimes – the spookier the better. Leader of the pack is Fred Jones, a tall, blonde, good-looking lad with a fondness for cravats (hmmm – we know it's the end of Swinging Sixties, but even so . . .). Daphne Blake is all legs and red hair. Sensible and confident, she doesn't actually do much, but she's pretty, so she gets away with it. Velma (not 'Thelma', note) Dinkley is the brains of the bunch and the one who usually pieces together the clues to reveal it was the gardener/property developer/janitor all along. Smart she may be, but she's also blind as a bat without her glasses. Norville Rogers is better known by the apposite epithet 'Shaggy', a description of his hair and goatee beard, not his social life. He's a committed vegetarian – most of the time – and best friends with Scooby, 'Ol' buddy, ol' pal'.

The gang love poking their noses into other people's business – very much in the traditions of ***The Famous Five***, only minus the ginger beer and with the addition of a dog that talks, pops on fancy dress costumes and wolfs down scooby snacks like they're going out of fashion. Every time they went anywhere they'd be dragged into another investigation – the phantom at the local fair, a mummy at a museum – and it would be left to Scooby and Shaggy to . . . well, to put no fine a point on it, let themselves be used as bait to lure the villains into the open so they could be caught and unmasked.

Scooby-Doo, Where Are You? came to an end in 1970, but the characters and format had proven popular, so they were back two years later with *The New Scooby Doo Movies*, hour-long episodes in which the gang would team up with animated version of stars like Sonny and Cher, Laurel and Hardy, the Three Stooges or the Harlem Globetrotters. One fine crossover took place in a 1973 episode called 'Weird Winds of Winona' in which Speed Buggy's gang are amazed by Mystery Inc.'s talking dog – until Scooby's chums remind them that they have a talking car. Priceless.

The idea of teaming up with other Hanna Barbera characters – which had been such a winner for ***Wacky Races*** – was repeated with a series of spin-offs in which Scooby Doo's gang (which included Scooby-Dum, Shaggy, Speed Buggy and Dynomutt) took on teams led by Yogi Bear and Dastardly Dalton, with his dog Mumbly (fans of *Wacky Races* will ask – who were they trying to kid with those two?). But after *Scooby's All-Star Laff-A-Lympics*, *Scooby's All Stars* and even *Scooby's Laff-A-Lympics*, fate struck as the golden Mystery Inc. line-up was ruined forever by the arrival of . . . *that* puppy!

Son of Scooby's sister Ruby, young Scrappy was designed to appeal to younger viewers (because, like, Scooby was *so* the wrong demographic – or something). Scrappy was eager, pugnacious and damn-well annoying (his catch-phrase was: 'Tadadadah dadah – puppy power!'). Some might ask if he was so unpopular why did he stick around for six more seasons? Well, it just shows how great the original characters were to withstand such an onslaught of tweeness and survive. Scrappy arrived in a crate in 'The Scarab Lives!', the first episode of *The Scooby and Scrappy-Doo Show*, which premiered on ABC on 22 Sep 1979. Some Scooby fans still wear black armbands on 22 September each year.

Scooby has continued to reinvent himself across 14 different series, numerous animated films and even two big-screen, live-action movies (one of which featured Scrappy-Doo in a role that pleasured audiences for the first time in his long career – though this book won't spoil exactly how). In 1998, the first of a new series of those full-length animated features was released straight to video. *Scooby-Doo on Zombie Island* was notable for three things: first, it went right back to the original format of *Scooby-Doo, Where Are You?* and dispensed with the puppy; second, it took a very post-modern approach, with familiar clichés exploited and common questions answered almost before the bore in the audience can point them out; and third – and most importantly – the zombies the gang face . . . are real! No rubber masks, no 'It was Mr Smith, the plumber!' These are real, terrifying monsters that will have kids reaching for cushions to hide behind while the grown-up fans just think, 'Bloody Nora!'

Screen Test

Children's Quiz Show | BBC One | episode duration 20–25 mins | broadcast 23 Nov 1970–20 Dec 1984

Regular Cast
Michael Rodd, Brian Trueman, Mark Curry · *Presenters*

Producers David Brown, John Buttery, Tony Harrison
Theme Music 'Marching There And Back' by Syd Dale

One of the great children's TV programmes from the pre-CBBC era, *Screen Test* lasted for 14 years. Hosted initially by Michael Rodd (at roughly the same time as he was telling grown-ups about the latest scientific innovations on ***Tomorrow's World***), *Screen Test* was a quiz show based around simple observation questions. Rodd would show the kids in the studio a clip from a movie (or if they were very lucky, a TV programme) before asking them such tricky teasers as 'What was the girl holding in her hand?', 'How many cakes were on the table', or 'What colour was the car?' (the type of question that always annoyed anybody at home who didn't have a colour set yet). The first contestant to buzz in got the points – the winner was the child with the highest score at the end of the programme.

Halfway through each edition, there would be a short break from the questions for the latest entry in the 'Young Film-maker of the Year Competition', which was basically an excuse for kids from rich families to bully Mummy and Daddy into buying them a cine-camera so that they could film a bit of basic animation using cardboard cut-outs, or worse still, a drama featuring their friends, family and pets. One of the winners of this competition did make it as a professional animator – Jan Pinkava, a young boy born in Czechoslovakia, went from the giddy heights of *Screen Test* to working on a couple of little-known feature films called *A Bug's Life* (1998) and *Toy Story 2* (1999), at least partially making up for all of the rest of the rubbish that was shown in between the good clips.

Some of the movies regularly used as clips for the main part of the programme were the latest offerings from the Children's Film Foundation. These family-friendly features packed out Saturday morning cinemas in the 1970s and early 80s, and usually involved a group of kids (on one occasion a preciously young Keith Chegwin) discovering a group of villains up to no good and implausibly bringing them to justice. Typical titles included *Danger on Dartmoor*, *A Hitch In Time*, *Calamity the Cow* (starring Phil Collins), *The Boy who Turned Yellow* and *Hunted in Holland*. Many of these films were shown regularly on TV on summer weekend mornings or as fillers in the schedules, but if you were a fan you could always guarantee at least one clip per week from a CFF production on *Screen Test*.

For most children watching, the thing that kept them glued to the box was the hope that there might be a clip from a forthcoming Disney movie, a James Bond film, or better still the latest *Star Wars* or Indiana Jones flick. When Michael Rodd left for pastures new, he was replaced in the host's chair by Brian Trueman (producer/voice artist responsible for numerous Cosgrove Hall children's cartoons such as ***Chorlton and the Wheelies***, ***Jamie and the Magic Torch*** and ***Danger Mouse***). For the final episodes, ***Blue Peter***'s Mark Curry took the helm, with the very last edition pitting the 1984 winners against a team from ***Grange Hill***.

Scully

Comedy Drama | Granada Television for Channel 4 | episode duration 30 mins, plus 1 × 55-min episode | broadcast 14 May–25 Jun 1984

Regular Cast
Andrew Schofield · *Franny Scully*
Ray Kingsley · *'Mooey' Morgan*
Mark McGann · *'Mad Dog'*
Cathy Tyson · *Joanna*
Richard Burke · *'Snooty Dog'*
Jean Boht · *Gran*
Val Lilley · *Mum*
David Ross · *Steve*
Gary Bleasdale · *Bignall*
Judith Barker · *Mrs Heath*
Tom Georgeson · *'Isaiah'*
Gilly Coman · *Marie Morgan*
Peter Christian · *Tony*
Tony Haygarth · *'Dracula'*
Jimmy Gallagher · *Arthur Scully*
Elvis Costello · *Henry Scully*
Paula Jacobs · *Florrie*
Angie Catherall · *Rita*
Kenny Dalglish, Bruce Grobbelaar, Bob Paisley, Ian St John · *Themselves*

Creator/Writer Alan Bleasdale **Producer** Steve Morrison
Theme Music 'Turning the Town Red' by Elvis Costello, who also appears in the series as Scully's model railway-obsessed brother. The opening title music fades out to the sound of the supporters of Liverpool's football ground, Anfield, chanting Scully's name.

Everywhere you go in Liverpool you'll see his name. Scully is a legend in his own lunchtime. On the verge of leaving school with no qualifications or prospects, he expects little from life and is determined to give nothing in return.

Accompanied by his friends, the Dog brothers and the painfully backward 'Mooey' Morgan, Scully's only goal is to avoid having anything to do with 'Dracula', the school caretaker, or sadistic policeman 'Isaiah' (so called because one eye's higher than the other). He dreams of playing for Liverpool and sometimes imagines that Kenny Dalglish is his personal guardian angel, but his only chance of ever getting a trial for the world's greatest football team is if he does a favour for a teacher and appears in the school play. No chance!

The Walter Mitty-esque Scully had already appeared in two novels and a BBC *Play for Today, Scully's New Year's Eve*, when creator Alan Bleasdale adapted him for television. Returning from the BBC production was Andrew Schofield who, while clearly too old to still be at school, made a captivating and witty lead for what evolves into quite a bleak comedy overall. Joanna, the object of Scully's affection, was played by a young Cathy Tyson, while Gilly Coman (who went on to play Aveline in ***Bread***) is the scene-stealing Marie Morgan. There are also cameo appearances by several members of the Liverpool football squad of the time – predominantly Kenny Dalglish – who are mainly figments of Scully's imagination.

Sean's Show

Comedy | Channel X for Channel 4 | episode duration 25 mins | broadcast 15 Apr 1992–29 Dec 1993

Regular Cast

Sean Hughes · *Himself*
Victor McGuire · *Tony Benetti*
Michael Troughton · *Barry Bullsit*
Jeff Shankley · *Barry from the Shop*
Eileen Way · *Mrs Pebbles*
John Barrard · *Mr Pebbles*
Colin McFarlane · *Announcer*
Jo Powell/Brian Poyser · *Bosnian Lodgers*
Philip McGough · *Bobby Workman*
Owen O'Neill · *Voice of Elvis the Spider*

Creator Sean Hughes **Producers** Mike Bolland (executive), Katie Lander **Writers** Sean Hughes, Nick Whitby **Theme Music** Steve Lironi, Tony De Meur; performed during the title sequence by Sean Hughes while sitting in the bath.

Some shows like to occasionally break down that invisible wall between the audience at home and the cast; Sean Hughes' sitcom *Sean's Show* simply forgot that wall could ever have existed. An extension of Hughes' stand-up comedy routines (with a spotlight descending on him at various moments each week), the stories appeared rambling and chaotic at first until subsequent episodes revealed a twisted kind of logic.

Abandoned by his one true love, Susan, Sean spends each instalment lurching from the depths of depression to mere self-pity. His pained emotional state isn't helped by his neighbours, an elderly couple called Mr and Mrs Pebbles, Barry from the local pub, always thinking of the next theme night to bring the punters in, and the other Barry, from the Corner Shop, where Sean buys his coleslaw in bulk. In the first series, burglars break into Sean's flat, but decide to take pity on him, leaving friendly messages on his answerphone and furnishing his sparse apartment each week with loads of new stuff (until the final episode of the first series when they take it all back and return it to the original owner, sports announcer Elton Welsby).

Characters frequently stroll around the gaps between sets that are visible to the studio audience rather than through the doors, as theatrical rules would demand. Everyone appears perfectly aware that their characters exist solely within and at the control of the script; the first episode involves the mysterious arrival of a script by dead writer Samuel Beckett, while the last is ruined when the plot is carelessly revealed in advance by Sean's best friend Tony (played by Victor McGuire from ***Bread*** and appearing later in ***Goodnight Sweetheart***), necessitating some quick thinking on Sean's part that involves his parents phoning to reveal that he was adopted, leading Sean to suspect that his natural mother might be Robert Smith from The Cure.

In the second series, Sean relocates to a Chelsea apartment that he shares with a dog and a pair of Bosnian refugee lodgers. Bea Arthur from ***The Golden Girls*** pops in to give him advice on how to maintain a long-running sitcom and Sean discovers that Elvis has been reincarnated as a spider.

Sean Hughes left the realm of sitcom behind after just 14 episodes. He later became a team captain on music panel game ***Never Mind The Buzzcocks***.

The Second Coming

Drama/Fantasy | Red Production for ITV | episode duration 75 mins | Broadcast 9–10 Feb 2003

Regular Cast

Christopher Eccleston · *Stephen Baxter*
Lesley Sharp · *Judith Roach*
Mark Benton · *Johnny Tyler*
William Travis · *Dave Morris*
Annabelle Apsion · *Fiona Morris*
Ahsen Bhatti · *Peter Gupta*
Peter Armitage · *Frank Baxter*
Peter Wight · *Chief Superintendent Len Chadwick*
John Henson · *Clive Saxon*
Judith Barker · *Eileen Saxon*
Rory Kinnear · *Father James Dillane*
Tim Woodward · *Chief Constable Richard Tanner*
Angel Coulby · *PC Louise Fraser*
Kenny Doughty · *PC Simon Lincoln*
Denise Black · *Rachel Craig*

Creator/Writer Russell T. Davies **Producers** Nicola Shindler, Russell T. Davies (executive), Ann Harrison-Baxter **Theme Music** Murray Gold

Steve Baxter works in a video shop in Manchester. He's got a perfectly ordinary life – he enjoys a drink with his mates in the pub, he loves his football and he's got a chequered love-life. Then, one day, Steve disappears – his friends have no idea where he's gone. Forty days later, Steve reappears. He tells his friends that he's been walking on Saddleworth Moor, and that he is in fact the Son of God. At first, his friends think he's had some kind of breakdown. But Steve isn't mad – he really is the Second Coming. Slowly, people begin to believe Steve's story. As authorities in the Vatican reel from the sudden death of the Pope, they too begin to realise that Stephen could very well herald the arrival of Judgement Day. Doubt falls away when Steve's miracle takes place: in the middle of the night, he calls thousands of people to Manchester City's Maine Road stadium, where a shaft of daylight descends from the heavens and turns night into day. Having got the world's attention, Stephen makes a proclamation: mankind has become corrupt, self-serving and arrogant beyond measure. If humanity isn't able to produce a Third Testament in five days, Judgement Day itself will come and the world will end. However, with the arrival of God in human form on Earth, the Devil can't be far behind. Can humanity find the Third Testament in time, or is this truly the end of the world?

The Second Coming was one of the most challenging, controversial and downright brilliant pieces of drama made for TV in the past ten years. Astonishingly, it was produced by ITV, a network not renowned for straying too far from the cosy familiarity of dramas like ***Heartbeat*** or *Where the Heart Is*. Perhaps the pedigree of the production staff involved might have given the game away. Russell T. Davies, Nicola Shindler and Ann Harrison-Baxter had been responsible for some of the most critically acclaimed dramas in recent years, such as *Bob and Rose*, ***Clocking Off*** and of course boundary-trampling gay drama ***Queer as Folk***. In *The Second Coming*, Davies challenged viewers to hypothesise what they would do if, all of a sudden, any doubt about the existence of God was suddenly whisked away. How would you react? How would the press report it? How would the world change? The very ordinary nature of Stephen Baxter's life helps to drive home to viewers the parallels with the story of Christ – in fact, even the most famous joke about Christ's crucifixion ('I can see your house from up here!') is referenced in a script that subtly parallels the Gospel stories – such as an infertile father, a best friend called Peter, a 'last supper', and an ultimately treacherous follower called Judith (Judas).

Undoubtedly, it is the two powerhouse performances from Eccleston and Sharp that breathe life into Davies' astounding script. The drama originally being written with the intention that it would be shown on more controversy-friendly Channel 4, it's nothing short of a miracle that ITV decided to pick it up when nervous Channel 4 executives passed on it. Of the two episodes, it's the first that works best – the palpable air of tension and utter awe that is created by filming the unfilmable is more akin to that of a thriller than a serious drama. Ironically, the second and final episode, in which mankind faces the real possibility of the end of everything, is perhaps a little anti-climactic. However, the final realisation by Judith that humanity has to fend for itself and say 'Thanks, but we don't need you any more' to God is a bold, innovative and extremely powerful thing to portray. Of course, with the benefit of hindsight, Eccleston's performance in *The Second Coming* can be seen as an audition piece for his next major TV role, another super-powered being sent to save humanity – ***Doctor Who***, again working with Russell T. Davies.

Secret Army

See pages 646–9

The Secret Diary of Adrian Mole, Aged 13¾

Sitcom | Thames Production for ITV | episode duration 30 mins, plus 1 × 60-min special | broadcast 16 Sep 1985–9 Feb 1987

Regular Cast

Gian Sammarco · *Adrian Mole*
Julie Walters, Lulu · *Pauline Mole*
Stephen Moore · *George Mole*
Beryl Reid · *Grandma Mole*
Lindsey Stagg · *Pandora Braithwaite*
Bill Fraser · *Bert Baxter*
Doris Hare · *Queenie Baxter*
Steven Mackintosh · *Nigel*
Paul Greenwood · *Mr Lucas*
Su Elliott · *Doreen Slater*
Freddie Jones · *Mr Scruton*
Robin Herford · *Ivan Braithwaite*
Louise Jameson · *Tania Braithwaite*

Creator/Writer Sue Townsend, from her novel **Producers** Peter Sasdy, Lloyd Shirley **Theme Music** 'Profoundly in Love with Pandora', performed by Ian Dury, reached No. 45 in the UK singles charts in October 1985.

One of the defining novels of the 1980s became a hugely successful TV series when author Sue Townsend adapted her own book into an ITV series, *The Secret Diary of Adrian Mole, Aged 13¾*. Adrian Mole is a young wannabe-intellectual who spends his spare time writing rubbish pseudo-intellectual poetry, fantasising about his classmate Pandora Braithwaite, coping with the slow break-up of his parents' marriage, and visiting his curmudgeonly old friend Bert Baxter. All of his exploits are scribbled down in his private diary, which charmingly and sensitively charts the growing pains of a teenage boy in 1980s Britain, angry and frustrated by the Conservative government and frustrated by his ability to never get his girl. Adrian's story juxtaposes moments of high comedy with ones of extreme pathos –

Continued on page 650

Secret Army

Jan Francis as Lisa Colbert – codename: Yvette.

The single greatest popular drama series ever produced by the BBC – and we'll fight anyone who dares disagree – *Secret Army* is today one of its least-remembered gems. And the reason for this? A certain bawdy sitcom set in wartime Europe about the owner of a café and his wacky adventures with the Germans . . .

Gerard Glaister, the creator of such programmes as ***The Brothers*** and ***Colditz***, used his own experiences as an RAF pilot during World War Two as the basis for *Secret Army*. During the war, many Allied pilots were shot down over occupied Europe by German aeroplanes and gun batteries. The survivors, urgently needed back in Britain, were often helped to escape from Nazi-occupied territory by ordinary members of the public, people who risked their lives working on so-called 'evasion lines'. These chains of people harboured airmen and helped them to escape either north into neutral Scandinavia or south into Spain, where the airmen would be met by British agents and escorted back to Blighty. For workers in these evasion lines, there was no salvation from the rules of the Geneva Convention – anyone suspected of assisting British airmen to escape faced summary torture and execution by the Gestapo. In reality, it's estimated that over 3000 airmen were returned back to the UK. Glaister himself was helped back along an evasion line while (unbelievably) dressed as a little old lady – a storyline that was re-used as an episode of the second series of *Secret Army*.

Secret Army tells the story of a fictional Belgian evasion line called 'Lifeline'. Created by the young and determined Lisa Colbert (played by Jan Francis, later to achieve massive fame in ***Just Good Friends***), Lifeline's headquarters is Albert Foiret's Café Candide, located in a back street close to the Grand Place in Brussels city centre. Working alongside Albert in the smoky and slightly seedy café (and for Lifeline too) are his mistress Monique and barmaid Natalie. Unfortunately for Albert and Monique, his invalid wife Andrée lives in a depressed and bedridden state above the café, and has begun to suspect that something might be happening between her husband and Monique.

Drama
BBC One
Episode Duration: 50 mins
Broadcast: 7 Sep 1977–15 Dec 1979

Regular Cast
Bernard Hepton · *Albert Foiret*
Jan Francis · *Lisa 'Yvette' Colbert*
Angela Richards · *Monique Duchamps*
Juliet Hammond-Hill · *Natalie Chantrens*
Clifford Rose · *Sturmbahnführer Ludwig Kessler*
Michael Culver · *Luftwaffe Major Erwin Brandt*
Ron Pember · *Alain Muny*
Valentine Dyall · *Dr Pascal Kelderman*
Hazel McBride · *Madeleine Duclos*
Terrence Hardiman · *Major Hans Dietrich Reinhardt*
Christopher Neame · *Flight Lieutenant John Curtis*
James Bree · *Gaston Colbert*
Maria Charles · *Louise Colbert*
Timothy Morand · *Jacques Bol*
Eileen Page · *Andrée Foiret*
Robin Langford · *Rennert*
Stephen Yardley · *Max Brocard*
Nigel Williams · *François*
John D. Collins · *Inspector Paul Delon*
Paul Shelley · *Major Nick Bradley*
Robin Langford · *Rennert*
Gunnar Möller · *Hans Van Broecken*
Marianne Stone · *Lena Van Broecken*
Ralph Bates · *Paul Vercors*
Hillary Minster · *Müller*
Neil Danish · *Wullner*
Morris Perry · *Maître Guissard*
Stephen Chase · *Captain Durnford*

Creators Gerard Glaister, Wilfred Greatorex

Producer Gerard Glaister

Writers John Brason, N. J. Crisp, Gerard Glaister, Willis Hall, Arden Winch, James Andrew Hall, Robert Barr, Simon Masters, Michael Chapman, David Crane, Lloyd Humphries, Allan Prior, Eric Paice, Michael J. Bird

Theme Music Re-arrangement of 'Wall of Fear' by Robert Farnon

Meanwhile, Lisa works as a nurse in Dr Kelderman's surgery, the elderly medic (played by Valentine Dyall, the bloodcurdling voice behind the 1950s radio series *The Man in Black*) using his skills to patch up injured airmen before they try to make their escape. Lisa's uncle Gaston helps with the production of forged travel documents so that the airmen can pass through German checkpoints. Hence, although a hazardous operation, Lifeline seems to be operating quite successfully – until, that is, SS officer Ludwig Kessler arrives in Brussels to assist the local Luftwaffe officer Erwin Brandt in terminating the evasion lines. Brandt operates by the book and is largely honourable. Kessler, on the other hand, is despicable, underhand and quite ruthless when it comes to tracking down the leaders of Lifeline and stopping them – in fact, Brandt feels that Kessler gets just a little bit too much pleasure out of his work.

Throughout the series, Lifeline has several successes in getting airmen down the evasion line (the route metaphorically shown in Alan Jeapes and Michael Sanders' memorable title sequence). However, they also suffer some terrible losses, with beloved regular members of the team falling prey to the Nazis – and in one horrible incident, being killed during an Allied bombing raid. Lisa, travelling with some airmen to the docks at St Nazaire, falls victim to a bomb dropped by the very people she had worked to save. The irony of her meaningless death is not lost on her surviving colleagues in Lifeline.

Lisa's tragic death comes at a time of major success for Lifeline. Following some very positive reports from British officer John Curtis (who had been sent to Brussels to help with the organisation of the evasion line), Albert receives a huge supply of money from London in order to upgrade his café. The new headquarters for Lifeline is to be the swanky and upmarket Restaurant Candide, this time located slap-bang in the heart of Brussels and designed specifically to cater for the dining needs of the local senior German officers. After all, where better to overhear the plans of the Gestapo and Luftwaffe? And where better to hide than right under their noses? This high-risk policy seems to pay off, as both Kessler and Brandt become regular customers of Albert at his new restaurant.

As the series (and the war) progresses, the threats to the safety of Lifeline grow ever more deadly. The Communist resistance movement infiltrates the organisation, hoping to usurp new leader Albert and replace him with somebody who would be sympathetic to their post-war political ambitions. Perhaps still in shock over the deaths of both his wife Andrée and colleague Lisa, Albert fails to spot anything suspicious about Lifeline's new forger, Max Brocard, only discovering the treachery when Natalie's boyfriend François falls prey to the Nazis. Determined to protect both the organisation and the stability of his profitable business, Albert resorts to the unthinkable and betrays the location of Max and many of his Communist colleagues to the Nazis, who machine gun the nest of Communist resistance fighters with their usual efficiency.

One of the great strengths of *Secret Army* was that (unlike virtually every other dramatic representation of World War Two) viewers were encouraged almost to empathise with the actions of the German officers. The vile Kessler remained as brutal and despicable as ever in his working activities, but over time viewers saw him fall in love with disillusioned local woman Madeleine Duclos. Kessler's wooing of Madeleine was tender, gentle and sensitively handled, providing the audience with an understanding of how so many women found themselves falling in love with men whose activities would go down in infamy. We still regarded Kessler as a monster, though, no matter how he behaved in private, precisely because, unlike Madeleine, we knew what he got up to in his day job. Brandt was always a much easier character to empathise with. He believed in the German cause, like Kessler, but he didn't relish it quite so much. His concerns with Lifeline were simply a matter of war, rather than being personal. It was for this reason that we shared in Brandt's pain when his wife and children were killed in a bombing raid on Berlin. Still further, it came as a terrible shock when Brandt, mistakenly linked to a failed assassination attempt on Hitler, took his own life rather than face disgrace.

As the second season concludes, Lifeline rejoices to hear that the Allies have finally landed on the beaches of Normandy. However, if they thought that the rapid advance of friendly troops would make their lives easier, they are to be sadly mistaken. The raging battle lines in northern Europe quickly cut off the long-established evasion line, meaning that there is simply nowhere for Lifeline to take the British airmen to. As a result, life becomes even more dangerous for Albert and his team – where on earth are they to hide all of the British airmen?

The single greatest popular drama series ever produced by the BBC – and we'll fight anyone who dares disagree – *Secret Army* is today one of its least-remembered gems.

Just when things seem that they can't get any worse for Albert, he is arrested by Belgian police on a trumped-up charge: the murder of his late wife Andrée. Left to manage Lifeline on her own, Monique faces yet more challenges to the security of the organisation, not least an outbreak of bubonic plague among the airmen in one of their safe houses. Following the suicide of Brandt, his replacement, Reinhardt, quickly becomes a potential threat as he studies Brandt's notes and discovers just how close he had been to working out the identities of the Lifeline leaders. Reinhardt's mission, joining the dots between Brandt's files, turns the third and final season into a ticking clock: we know that he will catch up with Albert eventually; we just don't know when . . .

In the final episodes of the series, the Allies encircle Brussels and the tension reaches almost unbearable levels. Albert is released from prison just as the Communist resistance makes its final move to seize control of the Candide and take revenge for the death of Max Brocard. Viewers lurch from one horror to another, as the Communists attempt to lynch Albert, and as the Belgian civilians line Monique up with other collaborator women for a head shaving. And of course, the viewers wait with bated breath to see if Kessler will escape back to Germany with Madeleine, or if he will finally get his come-uppance.

The final recorded episode of *Secret Army*, 'What Did You Do in the War, Daddy?', is set 25 years after the liberation of Brussels and reveals what happened to the characters who survived. However, this episode has never been transmitted, omitted from repeat screenings and home video releases. Several contradictory theories have been put forward by members of the production team to account for this. Producer Gerard Glaister points to the BBC strike that had dogged the final season, which resulted in the production values, specifically the old age make-up on the lead characters, not being up to the standard of the rest of the series. Meanwhile, script editor John Brason believed it was due to the lack of balance in the anti-Communist diatribe by one of the programme's regular characters, which could have been viewed as undervaluing the suffering of the countries and people who had fought and died during the war. By claiming that humanity had 'learned nothing' from the war and that the Communists around the world have been more successful mass killers than the Germans, it does somewhat undermine everything that the characters and the viewers had been through during the past 39 episodes. The episode was subsequently remade in part as the first episode of the 1981 six-part spin-off series ***Kessler***, which looked at Kessler's attempts to pose as a respectable businessman while simultaneously working towards the formation of a new Nazi army.

At the core of *Secret Army* are two astounding performances, by Bernard Hepton and Angela Richards. Albert is such an iconic character that his look, personality and behaviour were copied almost exactly for the core character in the 1980s sitcom ***'Allo, 'Allo***. The songs that Monique performs at the Candide – so mercilessly lampooned by *'Allo, 'Allo*'s Madame Edith – are amazing re-creations of the kinds of ballads made popular during the war. These songs were in fact co-written by Angela Richards along with Ken Moule and Leslie Osbourne. Several of them were later released on a tie-in album, *Songs from the Candide*, which went on to be a moderate success.

Whereas at first *Secret Army* appears to be the story of Albert, by the end of the final series it suddenly becomes clear that the programme has actually been Monique's story all along. Monique goes through the biggest journey of self-discovery of all of the characters – from put-upon mistress afraid to admit her love, to a self-confident woman single-handedly running a resistance organisation and leading the Nazis a merry dance. Monique initially sees herself ending her days with Albert, but it's only when it's nearly too late that she finally realises her love for Albert is simply not enough and makes a surprising decision that many viewers found baffling and enthralling in equal measure.

Heartbreaking, riveting, educational and utterly convincing, *Secret Army* is our favourite BBC drama series and deserves to be seen by everyone who enjoys quality television programming. Unmissable.

revelling in the launch of Channel 4 (a network aimed at 'minorities and intellectuals' like him), then reeling from the discovery that both his parents were having affairs, Mum with the oily Mr Lucas, Dad with 'stick insect' Doreen Slater.

Of course, we see the truth behind Adrian's pretensions; a prig of the highest order, his observations are deeply ironic as he continually misses the point and misinterprets his role in society, like George and Weedon Grossmith's Mr Pooter from *Diary of a Nobody*, an equally deluded diarist who overrates his own importance.

The Growing Pains of Adrian Mole, encompassing the events of Sue Townsend's sequel novel, reached screens in January 1987. Adrian is still 'profoundly in love with Pandora' and still obsessed by the volume of Norwegian wood exports (a wall chart he uses to measure the ever-changing size of his manhood) and the latest single by pop star Toyah. Only one major cast change took place in between seasons – Julie Walters was replaced as Adrian's mum by former pop singer Lulu.

Charming, totally evocative of its period and one of those true rareties – a sitcom recorded on film without an intrusive laugh-track – *The Secret Diary of Adrian Mole, Aged 13¾* did for teenage boys what Bridget Jones would do for singleton women 20 years later. However, Adrian's story didn't finish during his teenage years. Author Sue Townsend continued to write additional Adrian Mole novels, one of which – 1999's ***Adrian Mole: The Cappuccino Years*** – was turned into a BBC series.

Seinfeld

Sitcom | West-Shapiro Productions/Castle Rock for NBC (shown on BBC Two) | episode duration 25 mins | broadcast 5 Jul 1989, 31 May 1990–14 May 1998 (USA)

Principal Cast

Jerry Seinfeld · *Himself*
Julia Louis-Dreyfus · *Elaine Benes*
Jason Alexander · *George Costanza*
Michael Richards · *Cosmo Kramer*
Phil Bruns, Barney Martin · *Morty Seinfeld*
Wayne Knight · *Newman*
Liz Sheridan · *Helen Seinfeld*
Jerry Stiller · *Frank Costanza*
Estelle Harris · *Estelle Costanza*
Len Lesser · *Uncle Leo*

Creators Larry David, Jerry Seinfeld **Producers** Larry David, George Shapiro, Howard West, Andrew Scheinman, Jerry Seinfeld (executive), Andy Ackerman, Suzy Mamann Greenberg, Tim Kaiser
Writers Various, including Jerry Seinfeld, Larry David, Larry Charles, Peter Mehlman, Alec Berg, Jeff Schaffer, Tom Gammill, Max Pross, Gregg Kavet, Andy Robin
Theme Music Jonathan Wolff

In the heart of Manhattan lives stand-up comedian Jerry Seinfeld. In between his performances, he hangs out with his three closest friends – cynical, nervous worrier George, ex-girlfriend Elaine, and eternally cheerful lanky neighbour Kramer. Sometimes they spend time ruminating over life's great mysteries in Monk's Deli, other times they just pass the time in Jerry's apartment.

It comes as quite a surprise to many Americans to discover that the most successful comedy series of recent years in their homeland is, at best, little more than a cult hit in the UK, while other less successful sitcoms in America have become big hits over here. It's equally difficult for us in Britain to appreciate just how huge *Seinfeld* was in the USA – a ratings juggernaut that dominated the schedules for eight years and 169 episodes. People who enjoy *Seinfeld* become rabid in their appreciation, turning into passionate advocates for the show and keenly trying to get the unconverted masses into watching the series. Unfortunately, *Seinfeld*'s unique style of comedy (relying upon character moments and observational humour about the mundanity of life rather than on plots or events), famously described by one critic as a 'show about nothing', didn't appeal to a wide cross-section of UK audiences with ratings never anything to write home about. It seems that for viewers in this country, *Seinfeld* was a programme you either loved passionately or simply weren't moved by.

Sergeant Bilko

See THE PHIL SILVERS SHOW

Sesame Street

Pre-School/Muppetry | Children's Television Workshop, Sesame Workshop, Jim Henson Productions for NET, PBS (shown on ITV, Channel 4, Five) | episode duration 60 mins | broadcast 10 Nov 1969–present (USA)

Regular 'Human' Cast

Will Lee · *Mr Harold Hooper*
Bob McGrath · *Bob*
Loretta Long · *Susan Robinson*
Emilio Delgado · *Luis Rodriguez*
Linda Bove · *Linda*
Northern Calloway · *David*
Roscoe Orman · *Gordon Robinson*
Sonia Manzano · *Maria Figeuroa Rodriguez*
Alaina Reed Hall · *Olivia*
Clarice Taylor · *Harriet*
Miles Orman · *Miles*
Desiree Casado · *Gabriella*
Alan Muraoka · *Alan*
Tarah Schaeffer · *Tarah*
Paul Benedict · *The Number-Painter*
Stockard Channing · *Number Painter's Victim*

Muppet Voice Cast
Carroll Spinney · *Big Bird, Oscar the Grouch*
Jim Henson, Steve Whitmire · *Kermit the Frog, Ernie*
Jim Henson · *Guy Smiley*
Frank Oz · *Grover, Bert, Cookie Monster*
Jerry Nelson · *Count von Count, Sherlock Hemlock, The Amazing Mumford, The Announcer, Fred the Wonder Horse, Two-Headed Monster*
Richard Hunt · *Don Music, Sonny Friendly, Sully, Two-Headed Monster*
David Rudman · *Baby Bear, Sonny Friendly, Two-Headed Monster*
Martin P. Robinson · *Aloysius 'Snuffy' Snuffleupagus, Telly Monster*
Kevin Clash · *Elmo*

Creators Jim Henson, Joan Ganz Cooney **Producers** Various, including Joan Ganz Cooney, Jon Stone, Dulcy Singer, Eva Saks, David D. Connell, Al Hyslop **Writers** Many hundreds of people have written for *Sesame Street* over the years, but here we'd like to raise a glass to the late Jeff Moss, who died on 25 September 1998, aged just 56. Jeff won 15 Emmys and four Grammys for his work on the show, and was responsible for creating both Cookie Monster and Oscar the Grouch, among many others. If this isn't enough to raise a smile in thanks, he also wrote Ernie's song, 'Rubber Duckie'. **Theme Music** '(Can You Tell Me How to Get to) Sesame Street', music by Joe Raposo, lyrics by Bruce Hart and Jon Stone. Dance band Smart E's scored their only UK singles chart hit in 1992 with 'Sesame's Treat', a rave-fuelled reworking of the classic *Sesame Street* theme, which peaked at No. 2. Two! (cue thunderclap, 'Ha ha ha ha. . .')

For commentary, see THE MUPPETS, *pages* 501–6

Seven Up!

See pages 652–5

Sex and the City

See pages 656–9

Sexton Blake

Crime Drama | Associated-Rediffusion and Thames for ITV | episode duration 25 mins | broadcast 25 Sep 1967–13 Jan 1971

Regular Cast
Laurence Payne · *Sexton Blake*
Roger Foss · *Edward 'Tinker' Bell*
Dorothea Phillips · *Mrs Bardell*
Ernest Clark · *Inspector Cutts*
Meredith Edwards · *Inspector 'Taff' Evans*
Eric Lander · *Inspector Cardish*
Charles Morgan · *Inspector Davis*
Leonard Sachs · *Inspector Van Steen*

Creator Harry Blyth **Producer** Ronald Marriott **Writers** Peter Ling, Ivor Jay, David Edwards, Max Oberon, Roy Russell **Theme Music** Frank Chacksfield

Sexton Blake is one of a handful of fictional characters to have enjoyed massively long-lasting success. Unjustly, nicknamed the 'Poor Man's Sherlock Holmes', Blake's adventures often lacked the intellectual or artistic values of Conan Doyle's creation, but more than made up for that with exciting adventure, derring-do and more than a touch of good old-fashioned British stiff-upper-lip. To date, over 4000 different Sexton Blake adventures, written by more than 200 authors, have seen print since his debut in 1893 (in *The Halfpenny Marvel* story paper), so it's hardly surprising that both movies and television would seek to tap into such a rich vein of source material. Feature films of Blake's adventures included many silent movies (including *The Jewel Thieves run to Earth by Sexton Blake* in 1910, *Sexton Blake vs Baron Kettler* in 1912, and *The Mystery of the SS Olympic* in 1919) and two 1930s' features starring George Curzon as Blake, *Sexton Blake and the Mademoiselle* and *Sexton Blake and the Bearded Doctor* (both 1935).

When television turned its gaze towards Blake, it did so first in 1967 with a long-running ITV series, starring actor Laurence Payne. Fifty-nine episodes of adventures were made, with the show proving so popular that when Thames Television took over the London ITV franchise from Associated-Rediffusion they decided to keep making episodes of *Sexton Blake* – one of the very few shows to survive the switch-over in management companies. Adventures were bold, daring and exciting – so much so, that on one occasion, an accident during the filming of a sword fight left Payne blinded in one eye. Seven years after the end of the ITV series, the BBC brought *Sexton Blake* back with a brand new adventure (not based on one of the original stories, as the original TV series had been) called ***Sexton Blake and the Demon God***. Sadly, most Blake aficionados have little time for this particular script, which seemed to mock the great detective rather than celebrate him – neither did viewers at the time, and the show was never brought back for a further run of episodes. The BBC version survives intact in the archives, whereas the much-loved ITV version has been all but destroyed.

Website
www.sextonblake.co.uk is an exhaustive resource of the detective's adventures and is highly recommended for anybody who enjoys a bit of old-fashioned pulp fiction.

Sexton Blake and the Demon God

Adventure | BBC One | episode duration 25 mins | broadcast 10 Sep–15 Oct 1978

Principal Cast
Jeremy Clyde · *Sexton Blake*
Philip Davis · *Edward 'Tinker' Bell*
Barbara Loft · *Mrs Bardell*
Continued on page 660

Seven Up!

The original Seven Up! *children in 1964.*

ITV's *World in Action* ran for 35 years, starting in January 1963. It was the channel's prime current affairs programme and spearheaded a dynamic movement of investigative journalism into such subjects as the Troubles in Northern Ireland, protests against the Vietnam War and the rise of drug use in Britain (one famous edition orchestrated a debate on the subject between Mick Jagger – only recently convicted of drug possession – a Jesuit priest, an Anglican bishop and a former home secretary).

World in Action's first editor was an Australian called Tim Hewat. A conversation in a London pub with Canadian filmmaker Paul Almond veered onto the subject of the prejudice inherent in the British class system. Hewat went on to recite the much-quoted Jesuit boast 'Give me a child until he is seven and I will give you the man', which inspired the pair to develop a documentary series that would begin with seven-year-olds and follow them through life to get a glimpse of 'the shop-steward and the executive in the year 2000'. Head of Granada Television Sidney Bernstein green-lit the project and gave it the name 'Seven Up' (a title neither Hewat nor Almond was keen on). Joined by researchers Michael Apted and Gordon McDougall, the team began looking for children who could represent not only the different classes in England but a good mix of the English regions.

Documentary
Granada for ITV/Granada Television for BBC One
Episode Duration: 40/60 mins
Broadcast: 5 May 1964–22 Jul 1998, 13 Apr 2000–present

Regular Cast
Douglas Keay, Derek Cooper, Wilfrid Thomas · *Narrators*
Michael Apted · *Interviewer*
Bruce Balden, Jackie Bassett, Lynn Johnson, Susan Sullivan, Symon Basterfield, Andrew Brackfield, John Brisby, Suzanne Dewey, Charles Furneaux, Nicholas Hitchon, Neil Hughes, Peter Davies, Paul Kligerman, Tony Walker · *The 'Children'*

Creator Tim Hewat

Producers Derek Granger, Steve Morrison, Rod Caird, Ruth Pitt, Stephen Lambert (executive), Tim Hewat, Michael Apted, Margaret Bottomley, Claire Lewis

Using hand held cameras, Almond's cameramen were able to get down to the height of the children as they were interviewed. These were, after all, views of the world as they saw it, so it was important to meet them on their level rather than looking down on them.

Fourteen children were selected for interview and every seven years Michael Apted has caught up with them to see what changes they've gone through and what obstacles they've encountered. While the first three editions (*Seven Up!*, *7 Plus Seven!* and *21 Up!*) looked at the children's education and first experiences in the workforce, later shows (*28 Up!*, *35 Up!*, *42 Up!* and *7 Up: 2000!*) have included contributions from their wives or husbands while detailing their experiences on becoming mums or dads and with the loss of their own parents. Some recognise that they've done better in life than their parents, one or two of them have simply repeated the cycles they were part of, being sent to the same schools their parents and grandparents went to (and to which they are continuing to send their own children).

Symon was the only black child involved in the study, and as such has often been asked questions about his understanding of racial issues, his responses offering greater insight into the subject than those of the other children (whose early responses range from Suzy's comment that she doesn't know any 'coloured' people and doesn't want to, to Neil's glorious explanation of how he doesn't like the word 'coloured' because it makes him think they'll be green).

Both the artistic Symon and the shy Paul were children of single-parent families and at the beginning were being raised in a children's home. When Apted met Paul again at 14, he was reunited with his father and living in Australia, where he's remained ever since. His story might be used to exemplify the limited horizons of expectation in many children of his background, sweetly asking as a seven-year-old, 'What's university?' Yet Nick, a farmer's son from Yorkshire, ends up as a published author and lecturer at the University of Wisconsin and, partly thanks to his appearance in the show, Tony manages a sideline in acting for shows like ***EastEnders*** and ***The Bill*** (usually as a cabbie). It is their upper-class contemporaries who were most able to identify their futures with frightening prescience. John, Andrew and Charles, attending an exclusive Kensington prep school, seem to have their whole lives mapped out for them at seven; only Charles deviates at all from 'the plan', going from the predicted Charterhouse and Marlborough schools to Durham University (rather than Oxbridge) and on to work at Channel 4, rather than the legal firm his parents were probably hoping for.

Jackie, Lynn and Susan have always been interviewed as a trio, despite Jackie's move to Scotland prior to the *35 Up!* edition. All three of them married young, though only Lynn remains married to her first husband, and Jackie and Lynn have both faced life-threatening illness, events that have made them appreciate all the more their families and lives.

The star of the series, if indeed it's fair to say there is one, is Tony, whom we met as a cheeky East End kid with one aspiration – to be a

TRIVIA

The full names of the children were only revealed for the first time in the credits to *21 Up!*, when all of the participants had come of age.

jockey. By 14 he was working in stables and by 21 he had achieved his ambition, but with a sense of realism that already had him formulating a back-up plan of working as a cabbie; by 28, he had indeed become a taxi driver and was married with two children. At the age of 42, Tony is one of a few of the children who has lost both his parents. The experience has affected him deeply, as we see, for the first time in 35 years, tears welling up in his eyes. He and his wife are very frank about the difficulties their marriage has undergone, partly because of Tony's own infidelities. However, we get a sense that the regular visits from Michael Apted act as a form of therapy for the couple, a chance to assess how far they've come and how many of life's challenges they've beaten together.

From a Liverpool suburb came Neil and Peter. Though Peter would eventually disappear from the series after the age of 14, Neil would contribute to each successive edition and provide many of the biggest jolts of the series as we witness the steady deterioration of his circumstances. At seven, he's bright, cheery and very comfortable with the cameras, articulate and imaginative. By 14, we see that he is much more serious, experiencing the pressures of being in the top stream at his local comprehensive. In *21 Up!* he's living in a squat in London, by 35 he's in a caravan in a remote area of the Scottish Highlands, having spent time living rough. He's painfully thin, tense and uncomfortable with society and the world around him, yet there is still some sense of the fierce intelligence that we saw when he was just seven. It's of some comfort to those who've followed the story over a number of editions that we learn that by 42 he's become an elected Liberal Democrat councillor in the London borough of Hackney. Though he readily admits that he's never had a paid job and has spent his entire adult life living on benefits, his council work shows that he's willing and able to give something back to his community in other ways. The biggest surprise of all comes with the discovery that, thanks to the *35 Up!* edition, Neil has struck up an unlikely friendship with Bruce, the would-be missionary, who allowed Neil to lodge at his London home. Neil delivered a reading at Bruce's wedding and has remained in touch. Of all the children, it's Neil who we wait to hear from most, and who we suspect most disproves the theory that the seven-year-old will show you the man he'll become – no-one could have ever predicted the man that Neil is. At the age of 42, he tells Michael that he's finally begun to look to the future as, for the first time in many years, he thinks he actually has one.

Using hand held cameras, Almond's cameramen were able to get down to the height of the children as they were interviewed.

All of the children have treated the shows as a mixed blessing. While Andrew states that he would never wish such a burden on his own children and John describes each edition as a 'pill of poison', Jackie notes how she would never have recorded her life in such detail if it weren't for the programme, while Paul admits to being slightly excited when the time comes for another meeting with Michael Apted, and Tony laughs that it's the only time when the celebrities recognise him in the cab rather than the other way round. It's Sue's comment that we would like to think about, though, that the 'children' are all linked now, like family who only meet every seven years. With at least nine of the original 14 still contributing, it's clear that there are enough of them still willing, should Michael wish to speak to them again. We certainly hope he does.

In the conclusion to the first programme, viewers were invited to join the children again on Granada Television in the year 2000. When the 'children' returned for a catch-up with Michael Apted in 1998, *World in Action* itself was no more, but Apted was determined to continue the stories and so took the concept to the BBC. As a consequence, it was the BBC who picked up the baton when Apted wanted to begin interviewing a new cycle of children in the year 2000. The new batch of 19 subjects, while still representing the differences across the classes, also included children from Scotland, Northern Ireland and Wales as well as England, a wider mix of ethnicity, more children from single-parent families as well as children growing up with disabilities. Apted hopes to meet them all again in 2007.

Of all the children, it's Neil who we suspect most disproves the theory that the seven-year-old will show you the man he'll become – no-one could have predicted the man that Neil is.

The *Seven Up!* series has inspired a number of similar projects. Michael Apted himself oversaw versions of the show involving children from the Soviet Union (1990), the United States (1991) and South Africa (1992). In 2000, Professor Robert Winston began a more in-depth study, to chronicle the development of 25 babies and their families (the initial recruitment of the families was one of the last projects in the sadly defunct ***Tomorrow's World***). More scientific than the sociological approach of *Seven Up!*, the open-ended *Child of Our Time* continues to be updated each year, looking at such subjects as the growth of personality, how the babies begin to display recognition of gender roles, the 'terrible twos' and social interaction with other children.

Sex and the City

Samantha, Carrie, Charlotte and Miranda raise a glass to NYC.

As the 20th century became the 21st, the United States of America seemed more polarised than ever before. The rise of the religious right wing resulted in campaigns against sex education in schools and in protests against abortion clinics, evolution, homosexuality and the perceived general decline in morality. At the same time, television viewers were lapping up the comedic exploits of four female friends in New York who would all much rather be sitting in a bar chatting about their latest boyfriends' deficiencies in the oral sex department than in a Bible study class. This juxtaposition of a society that's simultaneously getting *less* tolerant and yet *more* tolerant of sexual 'freedom' provided both a backdrop to and the rationale for the success of *Sex and the City*, the archetypal 'girls' night in' television programme.

Thirty-something journalist Carrie Bradshaw lives in the heart of Manhattan and gets just about as much out of life as is physically possible. Single and happy with that fact (most of the time), Carrie makes a living writing a column for the *New York Star* newspaper about how she sees contemporary life, and in particular, how women of her age deal with the important issues in life – namely sex,

Comedy
Sex and the City **Production for HBO (shown on Channel 4)**
Episode Duration: 30 mins
Broadcast: 6 Jun 1998–22 Feb 2004 (USA)

Regular Cast
Sarah Jessica Parker · *Carrie Bradshaw*
Kim Cattrall · *Samantha Jones*
Kristin Davis · *Charlotte York*
Cynthia Nixon · *Miranda Hobbes*
Chris Noth · *Mr Big/'John'*
Willie Garson · *Stanford Blatch*
David Eigenberg · *Steve Brady*
Ben Weber · *Skipper Johnston*
Bridget Moynahan · *Natasha*
John Slattery · *Bill Kelley*
John Corbett · *Aidan Shaw*
Kyle MacLachlan · *Trey MacDougal*
Frances Sternhagen · *Bunny MacDougal*
Evan Handler · *Harry Goldenblatt*
Sarah Michelle Gellar · *Debbie*
Craig Bierko · *Ray King*
Sonia Braga · *Maria Diega Reas*
James Remar · *Richard Wright*
Amy Sedaris · *Courtney Masterson*
Blair Underwood · *Dr Robert Leeds*
James Remar · *Richard Wright*
Lynn Cohen · *Magda*
Ron Livingston · *Jack Berger*
Jason Lewis · *Smith Jerrod*
Mikhail Baryshnikov · *Aleksandr Petrovsky*

Creator Darren Star, from the book by Candace Bushnell

Producers Darren Star, Michael Patrick King, Barry Jossen, Sarah Jessica Parker (executive), Jenny Bicks, John Melfi, Cindy Chupack, Allen Heinberg (supervising), Judith Stevens, Jane Raab, Candace Bushnell, Mark McGann, Amy B. Harris, Antonia Ellis, Grace Naughton

Writers Candace Bushnell, Darren Star, Michael Patrick King, Nicole Avril, Jessica Bendiger, Jenny Bicks, Cindy Chipack, Michael Green, Becky Hartman-Edwards, Allan Heinberg, Jenji Kohan, Terri Minsky, Julie Rottenberg, Aury Wallington, Elisa Kuritsky

Theme Music A Latin-flavoured track by Douglas J. Cuomo

relationships and men. Sometimes using the experiences of her friends and acquaintances to form the basis of her weekly article, Carrie poses important questions like: Are men pre-programmed to cheat? Can men and women ever just be friends? Why do people automatically assume that if you're a single woman in your thirties, you must therefore be a lesbian? Most of the money that Carrie earns goes on eating and drinking out on the town with her three best friends, and on her *other* best friends – expensive designer shoes. In between shopping and writing, Carrie often finds time for love, dating a steady stream of men but normally finding them wanting. Reluctant to go for second best (sounds like a Madonna lyric . . .), Carrie would much sooner spend time with her pals than with a man who isn't quite right – after all, your best friends never let you down and will always be there for you. And that goes for Manolo Blahniks and Jimmy Choos, too.

Carrie's three friends have exciting lives too. Miranda Hobbes is a flame-haired, highly successful corporate lawyer who's never afraid to say what she thinks in her working life, but who spectacularly fails to express what she really means when it comes to relationships. Initially coming across as cynical and sarcastic, Miranda is actually a bit of an idealist who has had her fingers burned so many times that she's now just a bit sceptical about men in general. Although Miranda attracts her fair share of eligible bachelors, it's not until she meets bar manager Steve Brady that she finds someone who would be just perfect for her. Miranda being Miranda can therefore not see this, and the couple spend several years skirting around each other, even having a baby together, before finally realising that they really should settle down.

Beautiful brunette Charlotte York works in an art gallery and is, by some significant measure, the most reserved and sexually inexperienced of the four friends. On many occasions during their lunches and dinners together, Charlotte is left red-faced and flustered by her friends' frank admissions of what they've been up to. Charlotte tends to attract clean-cut, 'preppy' types of men and dreams of nothing more than a fantasy fairytale wedding with a handsome, wealthy man. At first, her engagement and marriage to successful doctor Trey MacDougal seems perfect – he's good-looking, charming and comes from a well-connected and monied family. However, after many months of trying to make the marriage work and dealing with interference from Trey's overly protective mother, Bunny, Charlotte realises that sometimes the fantasy just doesn't live up to expectations. Against all the odds, Charlotte eventually discovers true love – with short, balding and tubby Harry Goldenblatt. To her own amazement, Charlotte realises that in the end it's only love that really counts for anything. She even becomes Jewish so that she can marry Harry 'properly'. In the final season, their quest to start a family together is utterly heartbreaking, with the joyous news that they are to be allowed to adopt a child coming in the last episode of the series.

Without doubt, the most iconic and memorable of all of the *Sex and the City* girlfriends is outrageous PR Agent Samantha Jones, a woman with the sexual appetite of a hundred rabbits and the self-confidence to bed practically any man she wants. Samantha's bedroom gymnastics provide *Sex and the City* with some of its funniest moments – both in the literal portrayal of her outrageous exploits, but more often in the matter-of-fact way in which she casually drops into conversation her latest sexual peccadillo. For Samantha, nothing is off-limits; she's the ultimate hedonist who's willing to try things at least once that most people don't even know the name of. With a string of beaus all around New York, it came as a huge shock to both her and her friends when she even tried being a lesbian for a while. In the end, it wasn't that she was still straight that spelled the end for her fling with Mexican artist Maria, it was the fact that Samantha just didn't 'do relationships' and had been kidding herself to even try. But even Samantha Jones eventually grew up, and much to her surprise she eventually realised that a relationship was indeed what she'd been missing all her life. Happily shacked up with a beautiful male model, Samantha faces her biggest challenge when she's diagnosed with breast cancer, which thankfully she manages to beat.

Despite the fascinating three supporting characters, *Sex and the City* is undoubtedly Carrie Bradshaw's story. Her narration of the episodes allows us to get into Carrie's mind and discover what she really feels about situations, and we groan and cheer with her as the mistakes and successes in her life and loves are revealed. Carrie's most famous infatuation is with a mysterious high-flyer whom she nicknames 'Mr Big'. Despite the fact that neither of them seem either inclined or willing to commit to a monogamous relationship, Big and Carrie always end up circling around each other, even when they are in other relationships. Indeed, Carrie's long-term affair with furniture-maker Aidan seemed as though it was going to be the real thing – he was so obviously the person most suited to being with her that it was so frustrating when their relationship eventually came to naught. In fact, the only man who was more suitable to be Carrie's boyfriend was her gay friend Stanford Blatch, but even in liberal-minded New York that kind of relationship was never going to be a real possibility.

Despite the fascinating three supporting characters, *Sex and the City* is undoubtedly Carrie Bradshaw's story and we groan and cheer with her as the mistakes and successes in her life and loves are revealed.

For six seasons, *Sex and the City* attracted rave reviews and huge ratings for the American cable network HBO. As HBO is a subscription channel, it is not governed by the strict sex and strong-language restrictions that the main four networks (ABC, CBS, NBC and Fox) have to deal with. This meant that viewers of *Sex and the City* were treated to both male and female nudity and the regular use of extremely strong swearwords. Without being able to use both, and in a realistic way, *Sex and the City* simply wouldn't have worked: it was the sheer frankness and honesty of the programme that made it hit home with viewers all over the planet. Emmy Award voters loved it too: it won Best Comedy series in 2001 and picked up nominations in 1999, 2000, 2003 and 2004. After having received nominations for Lead Actress in a Comedy Series every year, Sarah Jessica Parker eventually picked up the award for the final 2004 season. Although Kim Cattrall (who, incidentally, was born in Liverpool and is therefore a Scouser by birth) was nominated most years in the Best Supporting Actress category, she never collected that particular Emmy; Cynthia Nixon was the only one of the three co-stars who received that honour, also for the final season.

Actor/producer Sarah Jessica Parker made the bold decision to end *Sex and the City* while it was still both hugely popular and critically on top of the game. In the final storyline Carrie had to decide whether or not to move to Paris to be with her new artist boyfriend (ballet star Mikhail Baryshnikov delivering a highly unsympathetic performance). Fans waited with baited breath to see if Carrie really would say goodbye to her friends and her home. Although it was the most obvious and 'traditional' conclusion to use, the shock appearance of Big, who flew to Paris to win back Carrie's heart, seemed to be about the best way to bring things to a conclusion. In the process, we finally learned Big's first name (John) and watched as Carrie realised what her one true love really was: not Big, not Aidan, not her friends – but New York City itself. NYC was always lovingly portrayed in *Sex and the City*, filmed to show off its beauty no matter what the weather. The idealised portrayal of the Big Apple was never more clearly evident than after the horrifying attacks of 11 September 2001. *Sex and the City* never directly mentioned the atrocity, but discreetly removed a shot of the Twin Towers from its opening title sequence from episode 61 onwards.

Like the city that spawned it, *Sex and the City* was challenging, beautiful, scary, unpleasant, superficial and intensely complex all at the same time. Its portrayal of women as unashamedly sexual beings was long overdue – something that perhaps only Joanna Lumley's Patsy in ***Absolutely Fabulous*** had previously managed. Witty, intelligent and often almost unbearably poignant, it's hardly surprising that *Sex and the City* became must-see TV for its fans. It's reputation as one of the best comedies of recent years is richly deserved. We wait to see if its heir apparent, ***Desperate Housewives***, will be able to match *Sex and the City*'s longevity and downright fabulousness.

Derek Francis · *Hubba Pasha*
Natasha Parry · *Cassandra*
Linal Haft · *Maremma Bey*
Jacquey Chappell · *Zigiana*

Producer Barry Letts **Writer** Simon Raven **Theme Music** Anthony Isaac

For commentary, see SEXTON BLAKE

Shameless

Comedy Drama | Company Pictures for Channel 4 | episode duration 50 mins | broadcast 13 Jan 2004–present

Principal Cast
David Threlfall · *Frank Gallagher*
Maggie O'Neill · *Sheila Jackson*
Anne-Marie Duff · *Fiona Gallagher*
James McAvoy · *Steve*
Jody Latham · *Philip 'Lip' Gallagher*
Gerard Kearns · *Ian Gallagher*
Rebecca Ryan · *Debbie*
Elliot Tittensor · *Carl*
Joseph Furnace · *Liam Gallagher*
Chris Bisson · *Kash*
Kelli Hollis · *Yvonne*
Maxine Peake · *Veronica Fisher*
Dean Lennox Kelly · *Kev*
Marjorie Yates · *Carol*
Jack Deam · *Marty*
Rebecca Atkinson · *Karen Jackson*
Anthony Flanagan · *Tony*
Rebecca Ryan · *Debbie Gallagher*
Marjorie Yates · *Carol*
Alice Barry · *Lillian*
Chris Coghill · *Craig*
Lindsey Dawson · *Jez*
Samantha Siddall · *Mandy*
Warren Donnelly · *Stan*

Creator Paul Abbott **Producers** Emma Burge, Matt Jones **Writers** Paul Abbott, Danny Brocklehurst, Carmel Morgan, Phil Nodding, Amanda Coe, John Griffin **Theme Music** Murray Gold (and Johnny Marr 2004 Christmas special)

Once upon a time, before the mighty hunters Paul Abbott and Russell T. Davies destroyed its native habitats, the genus of 'comedy drama' was overpopulated and undernourished, encompassing, as it did, the most anodyne – yet most widely feared – of all the atrocities created in the name of family viewing. From ***Heartbeat*** to *Harbour Lights*, every fond, Frankensteinian fusion was cloyingly scented and saccharine seasoned, and sure to leave the senses – and frequently the memory – untroubled by the experience. So when *Shameless* burst onto TV screens in early 2004, it hit home with all the iconoclastic vigour of a brick through ***Hamish Macbeth***'s windshield and literally redefined popular television drama.

With a large ensemble cast (mostly youthful, often unfamiliar, always superb) and a set of razor-sharp scripts, *Shameless* celebrates the lives of the Gallagher family who live on the fringes of poverty – and frequently the law – on Manchester's rundown Chatsworth estate. Mum has vanished and father Frank is a pint-guzzling, pill-popping Madchester throwback with a fear of gainful employment who spends his time (and his giros) down the local pub, leaving eldest daughter Fiona to look after the rest of the family.

Abbot makes no bones about the autobiographical origins of the show – his own parents both deserted the family home when he was a child, leaving his 16-year-old sister to assume maternal duties. These stories are character-driven and marked by a rare range and variety – from the lethal consequences of Steve's entanglement with a drug cartel (drama as stark and gritty as Channel 4 could ever wish for), to the broad farce that ensues when the debt-bound Frank pretends to be dead (complete with mourners paying their respects to the open coffin). The horrors of a missing child turn out to be a highlight of the first series as it materialises that the angelic younger daughter Debbie kidnapped the child to save him from his rotten parents. Debbie learns the vital tricks to lying as a result of coaching from her family, who concoct an elaborate plan to return the child and leave Debbie hailed a hero. Viewers are taken on a jump-cut joyride that veers from sitcom to tragedy, pathos to farce, ***The Waltons*** to kitchen sink, all without pausing for breath.

If anyone *has* successfully encapsulated *Shameless*, it might well be the judges at the Royal Television Society Awards, who called the show 'exciting, intelligent, mucky, poignant, raw, amusing, involving and always entertaining', before underlining their praise with a hat-trick of awards – for Best Drama Series, Best Writer and, for Paul Abbott, the judges' award for Outstanding Contribution to TV Drama.

For its second series, Channel 4 chose to create a billboard advertising campaign that some say mirrored Da Vinci's *Last Supper*. Bad taste? For a show that actually celebrates the power of family, friendship and surviving by your wits, that'd be a matter for you to decide. We loved it.

She's Out

Crime Drama | Cinema Verity/La Plante Productions/Carlton for ITV | episode duration 50 mins | broadcast 6 Mar–10 Apr 1995

Principal Cast
Ann Mitchell · *Dolly Rawlins*
Linda Marlowe · *Ester Freeman*
Maureen Sweeney · *Gloria Radford*
Anna Patrick · *Julia Lawson*
Zoe Heyes · *Connie Stephens*
Indra Ové · *Angela Dunn*

Maggie McCarthy · *Kathleen O'Reilly*
Adrian Rawlins · *DS Mike Withey*
Hugh Quarshie · *DCI Ron Craigh*
Kate Williams · *Audrey Withey*
Buffy Davis · *Norma Walker*
Anthony Allen · *Mr Crow*
Terence Beesley · *Jim Douglas*
Milo Bell · *Brian Mills*
Eve Bland · *Heather Dunn*
Charlie Caine · *Lennie Black*
Philip Croskin · *Raymond Dewey*
Jim Dunk · *George Fuller*
Sophie Heyman · *Susan Withey*
Huggy Leaver · *Eddie Radford*
Richard Lintern · *John Maynard*
Roger Martin · *DS Lenton*
Douglas McFerran · *DS John Palmer*
Sharon McKevitt · *WPC Marilyn*
Ian Minney · *PC Ian Pointer*
Jon Morrison · *Ashley Brent*
Jeff Nuttall · *Tommy Malin*
Nicholas Palliser · *Steven Rooney*
Antony Webb · *Jimmy Donaldson*

Creator/Writer Lynda La Plante **Producers** Lynda La Plante, Verity Lambert, David Shanks, Ray Singer **Theme Music** The intro music was by Michael Storey, while the end theme, 'Widow's Tears', was written by Richard La Plante and sung by Lorraine Crosby.

The second series of ***Widows*** had concluded with Dolly arrested for the murder of Harry, although a caption card tells us the charge is later reduced to manslaughter after Dolly helps the police with their enquiries into the security van raid. We're told she's been sentenced to prison for five years. The location of the diamonds remains a secret – Dolly handed them over to Bella before setting off to kill Harry. While Lynda La Plante was busy creating Jane Tennison for ITV's crime thriller ***Prime Suspect***, fans of *Widows* began to write to her, pointing out that Dolly should have been released long ago and they wanted to know what happened next.

Dolly was finally released for the appropriately named sequel *She's Out*, in which a collection of her former inmates ask her to invest in a run-down old mansion. Dolly decides to turn it into a children's home, but for that she'll need money. Luckily, the property is conveniently situated near a railway track that just happens to carry a mail wagon several times a week.

The plot unravels, with the man investigating Dolly revealed to be the (previously unseen) brother of Shirley from *Widows*, and with Shirley's mum determined to get revenge against the woman she still blames for her daughter's death (another sterling performance from ***Love Thy Neighbour*** star Kate Williams). But it's the interplay between the women behind the raid that once again provides the real gems. Liverpudlian beauty Connie lures men with all the seductive fragility of Marilyn Monroe, while the brash Gloria manages to put her foot in it with every step. Vying for position as top dog among the women is Ester Freeman, a former madam whom Dolly wisely mistrusts from the start, for Ester plans to con her out of the loot she suspects Dolly still has from her previous raids.

The death of Dolly at the end of the series – shot by an increasingly paranoid Ester, believing Dolly is about to sell her out to the police – left many viewers feeling cheated as she had been a strong character with whom they had empathised from the beginning. There's little the public admires more than honour among thieves – Dolly's demise signalled the end of that way of life.

Shelley

Sitcom | Thames for ITV | episode duration 25 mins | broadcast 12 Jul 1979–12 Jan 1984 (*Shelley*), 11 Oct 1988–1 Sep 1992 (*The Return of Shelley*)

Principal Cast
Hywel Bennett · *James Shelley*
Belinda Sinclair · *Fran Smith/Shelley*
Josephine Tewson · *Edna Hawkins*
Frederick Jaeger · *Gordon Smith*
Sylvia Kay · *Isobel Shelley*
Warren Clarke · *Paul Kay*
Garfield Morgan · *Desmond*
Caroline Langrishe · *Carol*
Andrew Castell · *Graham*
James Grout · *George*
David Ryall · *Ted Bishop*

Creator Peter Tilbury **Producer** Anthony Parker
Writers Peter Tilbury, Andy Hamilton, Guy Jenkin, Barry Pilton, Bernard McKenna, Colin Bostock-Smith, David Firth
Theme Music Ron Grainer

Twenty-eight-year-old James Shelley is fed up with the unfairness of life – despite being an educated man (a geography graduate), he's quite happy living on social security, believing that people who work for a living are mugs. Shelley shares a flat with his girlfriend Fran, who eventually becomes Mrs Shelley soon after they have a daughter, Emma. Shelley's work-shy attitude doesn't endear him to their landlady Mrs Hawkins, nor to Fran's father Gordon. Eventually his inability to hold down any kind of job for any length of time leads a desperate Fran to kick him out, Shelley deciding to take the opportunity to move to America and see if he can make a new life for himself there.

Shelley was created by Peter Tilbury, based upon a period of time in which he found himself living on the dole. Hywel Bennett's central performance was a magnificent Hancock-style portrayal of a man convinced that the whole world is mad and that he's the only one who can see that life's too short to worry about working and earning money. Such an attitude might have spelt disaster as far as the viewing public were concerned, but courtesy of careful scripting and a charming central performance, the public took Shelley to their hearts. In fact, *Shelley* was so popular that four years after the series left the airwaves it came back for another four seasons in *The Return of Shelley* – this time, the main focus for the eternal moaner's rants was the new capitalistic money-focused society that had cropped up in his lengthy absence from the UK.

Sherlock Holmes

See pages 664–7

Sherlock Holmes (1968)

Crime Drama | BBC TV | episode duration 50 mins | broadcast 18 May 1964, 20 Feb 1965–8 May 1965, 9 Sep–12 Dec 1968

Regular Cast

Douglas Wilmer, Peter Cushing · *Sherlock Holmes*
Nigel Stock · *Dr Watson*
Peter Madden · *Inspector Lestrade*

Producers David Goddard, William Sterling (and Donald Tosh) **Writers** Giles Cooper, Nicholas Palmer, Clifford Witting, Jan Read, Vincent Tilsley, Anthony Read, Jennifer Stuart, Hugh Leonard, Michael and Mollie Hardwick, Bruce Stewart, John Gould, Harry Moore, Alexander Baron, Richard Harris, Donald Tosh, Stanley Miller, from the stories by Sir Arthur Conan Doyle **Theme Music** Max Harris provided music for the first series, while the second used stock music that bore the distinction of being one of the very few *Sherlock Holmes* adaptations with a theme tune that wasn't played on a violin.

For commentary, see SHERLOCK HOLMES , *pages* 664–7

The Shield

Crime Drama | 20th Century Fox/Sony Pictures/The Barn Productions for FX Network (shown on Five) | episode duration 50 mins | broadcast 12 Mar 2002–present

Regular Cast

Michael Chiklis · *Detective Vic Mackey*
Jay Karnes · *Detective Holland 'Dutch' Wagenbach*
CCH Pounder · *Detective Claudette Wyms*
Benito Martinez · *Captain David Aceveda*
Catherine Dent · *Officer Danny Sofer*
Walton Goggins · *Detective Shane Vendrell*
Michael Jace · *Officer Julien Lowe*
Kenneth Johnson · *Detective Curtis 'Lemonhead' Lemansky*
Cathy Cahlin Ryan · *Corrine Mackey*
Autumn Chiklis · *Cassidy Mackey*
Joel Rosenthal · *Matthew Mackey*
Aasha Davis · *Lucy*
Matt Gerald · *Tommy Hisk*
Elijah Kelley · *Jaymon*
John Diehl · *Assistant Chief Ben Gilroy*
Brian J. White · *Detective Tavon Garris*
Nicki Micheaux · *Detective Trish George*
David Rees Snell · *Detective Ronnie Gardocki*
Glenn Close · *Captain Monica Rawling*

Creator Shawn Ryan **Producers** Shawn Ryan, Kevin Arkadie, Scott Brazil, Scott Brazil, Charles H. Eglee, Reed Steiner (executive), Ryan D. Adams, Craig Yahata (associate), James Manos Jr, Paul Marks, Glen Mazzara, Scott Rosenbaum, Michael Chiklis, Kevin G. Cremin, Adam Fierro, Kurt Sutter, Dean White, Elizabeth Craft, Sarah Fain **Writers** Shawn Ryan, Glen Mazzara, Kevin Arkadie, Kurt Sutter, Scott Rosenbaum, Reed Steiner, Kim Clements, Charles H. Eglee, Adam E. Fierro, Diego Gutierrez, Elizabeth Craft Sarah Fain, Lia Langworthy, Jennifer R. Richmond **Theme Music** 'Just Another Day ' by Vivian Romero

The Shield has its roots in a fly-on-the-wall documentary series called *Cops*, in which lightweight, handheld cameras followed police officers around during their shifts. Here, in a drama series that's shot in a very similar way, we follow the officers of Farmington District Police Station, Los Angeles – both at work and at home. Commanding officer David Aceveda rose through the ranks to his position by passing all the tests, but he's also aware that his promotion is partly political; it looks good to have a Hispanic on the team. Aceveda is ambitious but his strong moral code leaves him in a dilemma, as his most successful officer just happens to be corrupt. Vic Mackey, head of an elite group known as the Strike Team, is known to accept bribes and run drug pushers on the streets of LA. For Vic, it's all part of a bigger picture as he knows they can never remove all the pushers, so it makes sense to know he can control the ones he does permit to work. Vic also has a strong moral code; it's just that his isn't quite as restricted as Acevada's, and he doesn't have any qualms about profiting from his successes. Vic runs his team like a high-school football squad and expects his men to be treated similarly, even if that means the occasional practical joke or intimidating quiet word with other officers or detectives who don't fall in with his way of doing things.

With a battle for control for the station between Aceveda and Mackey, it falls to Detective Claudette Wyms to provide balance; she accepts that Vic gets results even if she doesn't condone his methods. Often though, her main responsibility is preventing her partner, the would-be psychological profiler Detective Dutch Wagenbach from allowing his smart mouth and by-the-book attitude to get his ass whooped by Mackey.

This is a world where drugs, murder, prostitution and violence are a daily occurrence, and the show never shies away from showing that. It's also brave enough to allow its audience to make up their own minds. While we might hate Mackey's cocky, bullish attitude, we also see his sensitivity with a drug addict prostitute trying to make enough money to feed her child, his loyalty to his crew and the love he has for his wife and children, especially his son, recently diagnosed as autistic (although later he finds himself separated from the family when his wife leaves him and files for divorce). We may also support Aceveda's loathing for Mackey's ways, but we have a grudging appreciation for the way he uses violence on a remorseless paedophile to get a confession. It refuses to guide our loyalties or depict any character in such bland turns as good or bad, which is why in the UK it's become (along with ***CSI***) one of Five's few really addictive shows.

Shine on Harvey Moon

Comedy Drama | Witzend Productions for Central/Meridian for ITV | episode duration 25–50 mins | broadcast 8 Jan 1982–23 Aug 1985, 23 Apr–28 May 1995

Principal Cast

Kenneth Cranham, Nicky Henson · *Harvey Moon*
Elizabeth Spriggs · *Nan*
Maggie Steed · *Rita Moon*
Lee Whitlock · *Stanley Moon*
Linda Robson · *Maggie Moon*
Nigel Planer · *Lou Lewis*
Pauline Quirke · *Veronica*
Fiona Victory · *Harriet Wright*
Linal Haft · *Monty Fish*
Dudley Sutton · *Connie Rosenthal*
Christopher Benjamin · *Mr Hartley*
Suzanne Bertish · *Freida Gottleib*
Leonard Fenton · *Erich Gottleib*
Clive Merrison · *Dick Elliot*
Mark Kingston · *Leo Brandon*
Gwen Nelson · *Mrs Brandon*
Michele Winstanley · *Janice*
Glen Murphy · *Alfie*
Tenniel Evans · *Geoff Barratt*
Lee Ross · *Roy*
Marlon Bailey · *Avis*
Colin Salmon · *Noah Hawksley*

Creators Laurence Marks, Maurice Gran **Producers** Allan McKeown, Tony Charles **Writers** Laurence Marks, Maurice Gran, Alan Clews, Francis Megahy, Barry Lamato, Gary Lawson, John Phelps, Dick Clement, Ian La Frenais **Theme Music** A reworking of the 1903 song 'Shine on Harvest Moon' by Nora Bayes and Jack Norworth

The Harvest Moon is a term used in agriculture to describe the full moon nearest to the autumn equinox of 23 September – traditionally the time of the year when farmers are out and about collecting in their crops. Harvey Moon, on the other hand, was a former professional footballer who, during World War Two, had served in India as a stores clerk with the RAF. At the end of the war, Harvey returns home to Hackney only to discover that his life has been ripped apart by the war. Not only has his home been demolished in the Blitz, but his family have mistakenly assumed that he's dead – as a consequence, his wife Rita has spent much of the war entertaining a variety of different men, and his young daughter Maggie has started dating his old mate Lou. But despite all of these trials and struggles, Harvey has his dear old mum to rely upon as he attempts to rebuild his life.

Shine on Harvey Moon was the first real breakthrough hit for writers Laurence Marks and Maurice Gran, two hugely talented scribes who would go on to create and write programmes as diverse as ***The New Statesman, Birds of a Feather*** and ***Goodnight Sweetheart***. *Shine on Harvey Moon* began in the traditional half-hour sitcom format, but soon expanded into the more traditional hour long drama slot – an indication of the fine balancing job the authors did in creating a show that was simultaneously very very funny and at times almost heartbreaking. After four seasons, the storyline had brought Harvey to 1948, by which time he had more or less rebuilt his life by winning back Rita and becoming a Labour councillor.

Ten years later, ITV revived the series for a final run of six half-hour episodes. Most of the cast returned (with the exception of Kenneth Cranham as Harvey, necessitating Nicky Henson's swift casting) to update viewers on how life in the early 1950s was treating the Moon family. Nostalgic yet never sentimental or cynical, *Shine on Harvey Moon* was a real treat for viewers, with quality scripts and casting making this show a cut above the standard crop of TV drama.

Shoestring

Crime Drama | BBC One | episode duration 50 mins | broadcast 30 Sep 1979–21 Dec 1980

Principal Cast

Trevor Eve · *Eddie Shoestring*
Michael Medwin · *Don Satchley*
Doran Godwin · *Erica Bayliss*
Liz Crowther · *Sonia*

Creator Robert Banks Stewart **Producer** Robert Banks Stewart **Writers** Various, including Robert Banks Stewart, Bob Baker, Philip Martin, Chris Boucher, John Kruse, Peter King, William Hood, Terence Feely, Dave Humphries, Robert Bennett, Peter Miller, Bill Craig **Theme Music** George Fenton wrote a theme tune that began with a brief radio station-style jingle before moving into a more traditional TV theme melody.

After suffering a nervous breakdown, computer programmer Eddie Shoestring decides to ditch his former high-pressure yet repetitive career and take up a new role, one that would help solve other peoples' problems. Eddie sets himself up as a private detective and enjoys moderate success, until one of his early investigations takes him to the Radio West station. Impressed by Eddie's abilities, and keen to get some more local interest into the schedules, station manager Don Satchley offers Eddie a regular job as the host of a phone-in programme. Instead of taking requests for the latest pop singles, Eddie becomes Radio

Continued on page 668

Sherlock Holmes

Jeremy Brett at Holmes, with David Burke as Watson in the Granada TV *series.*

Sir Arthur Conan Doyle's most famous creation first appeared in the novel *A Study in Scarlet* in 1887, but it's mainly the short stories, published by *Strand Magazine* between 1891 and 1927, that have been the inspiration for the TV appearances of Sherlock Holmes. The first British TV version was broadcast live on 29 July 1951 as part of the For the Children slot that pre-dated *Watch with Mother*. Set solely within Holmes's study, the adaptation of 'The Adventure of the Mazarin Stone' starred Andrew Osborn as Holmes and Philip King as Watson. Not thought to be important enough to record for posterity, it nevertheless convinced the BBC to attempt something a little more ambitious for adults. Six months later, Alan Wheatley took up the role in *Mr Sherlock Holmes*, a six-part series that adapted 'The Empty House', 'A Scandal in Bohemia', 'The Dying Detective', 'The Reigate Squires', 'The Red-Headed League' and 'The Second Stain'. As with 'The Adventure of the Mazarin Stone', these live broadcasts were not retained by the BBC.

Holmes's next appearance on TV came thanks to a number of factors coming together at just the right time. In 1963, BBC producer Vere Lorrimer and Tom Sloan, head of light entertainment, looked into the rights situation of Conan Doyle's works. Pleased to discover they were available, Sloan put a proposal to the head of drama, the

See **THE ADVENTURES OF SHERLOCK HOLMES** *and* **SHERLOCK HOLMES (1968)** *for broadcast details and individual credits*

legendary Sydney Newman, only to find Newman was already ahead of him. The long-running detective serial ***Maigret*** was coming to an end and Newman had already commissioned a new anthology series, *Detective*, to showcase certain classic characters with the intention of rewarding the most popular ones with a full TV show – and Holmes was already on that list. When the series went out, on 18 May 1964, 'Sherlock Holmes and the Speckled Band' came eighth in the run, adapted by Giles Cooper, who'd adapted and edited the scripts for *Maigret*. Four days after its first broadcast, Douglas Wilmer's *Sherlock Holmes* was confirmed for a full 12-part series.

Wilmer developed the character more for the series, making his performance less the charming socialite and more aggressive. The changes did not suit many of the critics, who felt him to be an unsuitable man for the job. The Sherlock Holmes Society, however, had no such qualms and gave their wholehearted support to the series in the letters page of the *Radio Times*. Sadly, the BBC board of governors were not impressed, by Wilmer or by the production as a whole.

By 1966, the BBC's head of drama was former actor Andrew Osborn, who by a staggering coincidence had portrayed the first BBC TV Holmes back in 1951. With a repeat run of Wilmer's *Holmes* attracting good ratings, Osborn was keen to repeat the magic for a second series, but with Wilmer filming in Hong Kong a new Holmes would need to be cast. After John Neville and Eric Porter declined offers to play the great detective, the lead role in the remount of the series (now called *Sir Arthur Conan Doyle's Sherlock Holmes* to stress its authenticity), went to Peter Cushing, who'd played the role of Holmes in the Hammer film *The Hound of the Baskervilles* (1959). The new series, consisting of 16 episodes (including a two-part adaptation of *The Hound of the Baskervilles*), would be the first dramatisation to be made for TV in colour. Concerns over a rapidly escalating budget meant that much of the series would end up being made in studio on videotape, as opposed to the film that most of the directors had been hoping for. Cost-cutting across the board also led to a few stylistic touches such as narrating some scenes by use of static illustrations, akin to those seen in the original publication of the stories in *Strand Magazine*. These scenes might have looked cheap had they not been so well executed.

With some episodes scripted by Michael and Mollie Hardwick, favoured writers of the Conan Doyle estate and the people behind the popular radio adaptations of the late 1950s and early 1960s, the series was warmly received by viewers, with ratings peaking at 15.5 million. Sadly, behind-the-scenes disputes ensured that Cushing's episodes would bring the series to an end. A shame, as it was a part Cushing clearly relished, even if the producers had taken a rather safe approach, playing on the hearty hero aspect of the character and politely ignoring his darker moods and habitual drug taking.

This wasn't the end of the BBC's association with the character, though. In December 1974, the Beeb broadcast a one-off original drama by Kingsley Amis called *Dr Watson and the Darkwater Hall Mystery*. Edward Fox played Watson, drawn into an investigation of the secrets of the wealthy Fairfax family and their dealings with a poacher called 'Black Paul' after Holmes has decided to take a holiday. In 1982, Tom Baker left behind ***Doctor Who***'s TARDIS and long scarf to don the deerstalker for yet another adaptation of *The Hound of the Baskervilles*. The serial ran over four successive Sundays from 3 October, slotting neatly into the BBC's classic serial teatime schedule. Baker might well have been the definitive Time Lord, but even he felt his Holmes to have been a failure, possibly because the story itself writes Holmes out for much of the third quarter. Luckily for fans of Conan Doyle, the truly definitive portrayal was only a couple of years away. Granada Television was about to launch their own version and beat the Beeb at their own game with *The Adventures of Sherlock Holmes*.

Sherlock Holmes came to Granada and the ITV network thanks to John Hawkesworth, a man who had already given British television ***Upstairs, Downstairs***, ***Danger UXB*** and ***The Duchess of Duke Street***. Such a pedigree would ensure that this particular incarnation of *Holmes* would come to be recognised as the greatest. In Jeremy Brett, Holmes gained the depth that had been missing from almost every other interpretation; he also gained the ritual use of cocaine that had been quietly forgotten about since the literary version quit the habit in 1904 (with 'The Missing Three-Quarter'). What also marked this adaptation out for special praise was that the character of Watson, played initially by David Burke, was allowed some intellect – he was, after all, a doctor – whereas almost every screen interpretation of the character had been guided by Nigel Bruce (opposite Basil Rathbone in the 1930s feature films), who played him as a bumbling buffoon.

The plan had been to begin the series in 1981 with an adaptation of *The Sign of Four*, but logistical problems delayed the series. When it finally aired in 1984 under the banner of *The Adventures of Sherlock Holmes*, it was 'A Scandal in Bohemia' that was first out of the gate. Awesome sets, including a full-scale replica of Baker Street built at Granada Studios, Manchester, and an amazing attention to detail drew viewers back in time to the turn of the century (19th to 20th, that is). Fans rejoiced as the producers made a point of being faithful to the spirit of the originals, ensuring Holmes smoked the right kind of pipe and never wore that damned deerstalker except when in the countryside. Such care and attention also enabled the writers to take the odd diversion from the texts, notably with 'The Adventure of Charles Augustus Milverton', which became 'The Master Blackmailer', as the original tale had run to just six pages. Moriarty also appeared in double the amount of tales that Doyle had written for him (i.e. two), inserted into 'The Red-Headed League' as a means of reinforcing the importance of the rivalry between the two characters whose first meeting in the original stories was also their last. After a massively successful couple of series, *The Adventures of Sherlock Holmes* came to an end with 'The Final Problem' and that fateful battle at the top of the Reichenbach Falls.

The death in 1985 of Jeremy Brett's wife, American producer Joan Wilson, left the actor deeply grief-stricken. He ploughed his way into work for a third series for Granada (*The Return of Sherlock Holmes*) but the strain proved too great for him: the following year, he suffered what he later described as a 'nervous breakdown' but which was diagnosed as a bipolar disorder that he'd had most of his life yet had simply dismissed as being part of the 'actor temperament'.

Sherlock Holmes returned but David Burke did not, the actor having chosen to join the Royal Shakespeare Company. In his place came former ***Colditz*** star Edward Hardwicke, who captured Watson's intelligence but also made him a warmer character. With the addition of Hardwicke, viewers were treated to the sight of a genuinely deep friendship and equal partnership between Holmes and Watson, as opposed to the traditional approach of having Watson merely as Holmes's immediate audience.

In total, the Granada TV series ran to 45 episodes, which included five feature-length editions – 'The Sign of Four', an obligatory 'Hound of the Baskervilles', 'The Master Blackmailer', 'The Last Vampyre' and 'The Eligible Bachelor'. Having initially felt miscast as the moody Holmes, Brett grew to love him. Indeed, he often commented that he'd become him; it was Brett's suggestion, for instance, that Holmes should quit his drug habit, as shown by the symbolic burial of his syringe in the opening episode of the second series of *The Return* . . . ('The Devil's Foot'). In 1988, he and Edward Hardwicke starred in Jeremy Paul's play *The Secret of Sherlock Holmes*, a character piece erroneously billed as a thriller, which ran in London's West End for 200-odd performances. Their final appearance together on screen came with *The Memoirs of Sherlock Holmes*. One episode had to be rewritten due to Brett's ill health, with Holmes's much smarter but lazy brother Mycroft (Charles Gray) taking the central role. Brett died on 12 September the following year of heart failure, caused by the drugs he was taking to combat the bipolar disorder combined with years of heavy smoking.

In Jeremy Brett, Holmes gained the depth that had been missing from almost every other interpretation

Such was Brett's mastery of the part that few would have dared to undertake the more difficult role of stepping into his shoes so soon after his passing. When the BBC decided to remake *The Hound of the Baskervilles* again for broadcast in 2002, there could have been few who felt that the adaptation was overdue. With Richard Roxburgh as Holmes and Ian Hart as quite the youngest TV Watson yet, the best that could be said of Allan Cubitt's script was that it was adequate. The BBC's next visit to Baker Street, this time with Rupert Everett in the lead role, was an original tale, *The Case of the Silk Stocking*, again by Alan Cubitt. At the time of writing, we're told that ITV has decided to build another interpretation around the redoubtable Stephen Fry, with Hugh Laurie as Watson, though this time we suspect they won't be so much competing with Brett as making play with the original stories. As a recent repeat run on BBC Two and release on DVD has shown, there's no sign of Brett's version ever dating.

West's 'Private Ear', listening to people's problems and then investigating them. Because all of the listeners were normally pretty ordinary, the crimes and problems that Eddie investigated were fairly mundane at first sight. However, some of them would become much more convoluted than they first appeared, with some storylines venturing into the pitch-black world of a serial rapist, lethal children's toys and even driving Eddie close to a second breakdown.

Created by Robert Banks Stewart (who had enjoyed earlier writing success on programmes as diverse as ***Doctor Who*** and ***Callan***), *Shoestring* was a very popular series with viewers, who for once enjoyed watching a detective series that wasn't all about car chases, gun running or drug smuggling. A major factor in the success of *Shoestring* was star Trevor Eve's charismatic and charming portrayal of the down-at-heel gumshoe, his first major television role (but by no means his last). With viewing figures very high, it came as a big surprise to everyone involved behind-the-scenes when Trevor Eve opted not to make any more episodes of *Shoestring* after just two short seasons. With several storylines and scripts more or less completed, Robert Banks Stewart made the sensible decision not to abandon them, but to switch their location from Bristol to Jersey, and to create a new detective to investigate the crimes. Thus ***Bergerac*** was born . . .

Shogun

Drama | Paramount/Toho/Asahi National Broadcasting/Jardine Matheson for NBC (shown on BBC One) | episode duration 100 mins | broadcast 15 Sep–c. 6 Oct 1980 (USA)

Regular Cast

Richard Chamberlain · *Pilot-Major John Blackthorne/Anjin-san*
Toshirô Mifune · *Toranaga*
Yôko Shimada · *Lady Toda Buntaro-Mariko*
Frankie Sakai · *Yabu*
Alan Badel · *Father Dell'Aqua*
Damien Thomas · *Father Alvito*
John Rhys-Davies · *Vasco Rodrigues*
Vladek Sheybal · *Captain Ferriera*
Yuki Meguro · *Omi*
Hideo Takamatsu · *Lord Buntaro*
Nobuo Kaneko · *Ishido*
Hiromi Senno · *Fujiko*
Michael Hordern · *Friar Domingo*
George Innes · *Vinck*
Leon Lissek · *Father Sebastio*
Edward Peel · *Pieterzoon*
Eric Richard · *Maetsukker*
Steve Ubels · *Roper*
Stewart MacKenzie · *Croocq*
Neil McCarthy · *Spillbergen*
William Morgan Sheppard · *Specz*
Mika Kitagawa · *Kiku*
Seiji Miyaguchi · *Muraji*
Orson Welles · *Narrator*

Producers James Clavell (executive), Eric Bercovici, Ben Chapman, Kerry Feltham **Writer** Eric Bercovici, from the novel by James Clavell **Theme Music** Maurice Jarre

One of the best-loved and most critically acclaimed of the rash of mini series that swept into production in the late 1970s and early 1980s, *Shogun* was based on the popular novel by author James Clavell, originally published in 1975. Clavell had already made a name for himself as a screenwriter for such films as *The Great Escape* (1960) and *To Sir, With Love* (1967), but the overwhelmingly enthusiastic reception to his greatest novel *Shogun* made it a natural candidate for conversion into a movie or a TV series. Opting for the latter choice, Clavell chose to stay closely involved with practically every element of the mini-series' production, resulting in an adaptation that remained remarkably true to his original novel.

Based in part on a true story (that of Elizabethan seaman Will Adams), *Shogun* was the tale of an English sailor called John Blackthorne. When he and his vessel are shipwrecked off the shore of Japan, Blackthorne and his crew are captured by the noble Samurai warriors of local nobleman Toranaga. Barely escaping summary execution for failing to obey simple matters of courtesy such as bowing in the presence of another, Blackthorne struggles to understand both the language of Japan and the intricacies of their feudal culture. Eventually he begins an affair with his married translator Mariko, risking both of their lives in the process. As the years go by, Blackthorne adopts the new name Anjin-san, as he trains to become the first Western Samurai warrior.

Running for 12 hours in total, *Shogun* is definitely longer and more in-depth than your average mini series. Filmed entirely on location in Japan, the series gained international kudos thanks to the casting of renowned Japanese actor Toshirõ Mifune as Toranaga (star of Kurosawa's legendary 1954 movie *The Seven Samurai*), dozens of his countrymen in the other leading roles and a whole host of British acting talent as the unfortunate shipwreck victims and the sinister Portuguese Jesuit missionaries. But, of course, the star of *Shogun* was ***Dr Kildare*** himself, Richard Chamberlain, proving once and for all a gravitas in his performance that belied his earlier reputation as little more than a pretty-boy actor.

Shooting Stars

Game Show | BBC/Channel X for BBC Two/Choice | episode duration 30 mins | broadcast 26 Dec 1993, 22 Sep 1995–Dec 1997, 13 Jan–22 Dec 2002

Regular Cast

Vic Reeves, Bob Mortimer · *Hosts*
Ulrika Jonsson, Mark Lamarr, Will Self · *Team Captains*
Johnny Vegas · *Regular Panellist*
Matt Lucas · *George Dawes/Marjorie Dawes*

Rhys Thomas · *Voice of Donald Cox, the Sweaty Fox*
Steven Burge · *Naughty Boy on a Rope*

Creators Vic Reeves (Jim Moir) and Bob Mortimer
Producers John Whiston, Jon Plowman, Alan Marke (executive), Charlie Higson (associate), Franny Moyle, David Housham, Lisa Clark **Writers** Vic Reeves, Bob Mortimer, Matt Lucas, Shane Allen, Rhys Thomas **Theme Music** Peter Baikie

Almost certainly the single most bizarre and surreal comedy game show ever broadcast on television, *Shooting Stars* is a beautiful fusion of traditional quiz show, celebrity panel show and surreal comedy sketches. Beginning as a short pilot episode as part of Vic Reeves and Bob Mortimer's 1993 Christmas special *At Home with Vic and Bob, Shooting Stars* soon established itself as unmissable student-friendly comedy, and was the birthplace of one of ***Little Britain***'s favourite characters Marjorie Dawes.

The format for *Shooting Stars* was simple. Genial hosts Vic and Bob would ask questions to two teams of three celebrities, some real questions, some made up or with ridiculously obscure answers – the fun of the programme was watching which celebrity guests 'got' the joke and played along, and which ones became increasingly frustrated at their inability to ever get a question right (as if *that* was the main aim of the programme!). Rounds included questions brought in by 'The Dove from Above' and 'Donald Cox, the Sweaty Fox'; having to guess which song Vic was singing 'In the Club style'; short sketches acted out by the regulars, and a battery of true or false questions. Certain elements felt like hangovers from the hosts' previous shows, such as Vic's inability to tell jokes (accompanied by rolling tumbleweeds and a church bell tolling mournfully) or the use of made-up words to signify success ('Iranu') or failure ('Uvavu').

Team captains Ulrika ('-ka-ka-ka-ka') Jonsson and 'Fifties throwback' Mark Lamarr (later Will Self) threw themselves gamely into the madness and tried to drag their often bewildered teammates along too. For the 2002 series, Ulrika was joined by permanently drunk Johnny Vegas, whose empty pint glasses amassed during the show. Keeping (arbitrary) score throughout proceedings was giant baby George Dawes (Matt Lucas), who'd often bang out a beat on his drum kit before announcing in his plummiest accent which team was in the lead. On a few occasions, when George wasn't able to make it along, his distinctly odd mother Marjorie Dawes would keep the scores, showing the same level of tact and sympathy as she would do in years to come with her *Little Britain* Fat Fighters group. The final winner's bonus round – often for the princely sum of five or six quid – was a large-scale stunt game guaranteed to embarrass and possibly physically scar the celebrity concerned. The guest could be suspended on a harness and swung across the studio, spun around inside a makeshift washing machine or forced to wear some kind of oversized animal costume. The effect was the same each time and it was rarely important if they won or not.

Shooting Stars was very much an acquired taste – if you'd never come across Vic and Bob before, then it might have seemed fairly impenetrable. If you were already a fan from their earlier shows, then *Shooting Stars* undoubtedly seemed perfectly *normal*.

Shooting the Past

Drama | Talkback for BBC One | episode duration 50–70 mins | broadcast 10–24 Jan 1999

Cast

Lindsay Duncan · *Marilyn Truman*
Timothy Spall · *Oswald Bates*
Liam Cunningham · *Christopher Anderson*
Billie Whitelaw · *Veronica*
Emilia Fox · *Spig*
Arj Barker · *Garnett*
Blake Ritson · *Nick*
Andy Serkis · *Styeman*

Producers Simon Curtis, Peter Fincham (executive), John Chapman **Writer** Stephen Poliakoff **Theme Music** Adrian Johnston

In a large 18th-century house outside central London lies the Fallon Photo Library and Collection: ten million photographs from the 19th and 20th centuries, assembled from countless sources. On a day in December, the staff of the library awaits Mr Anderson, a representative of their new owner, an American business corporation. When he arrives, Mr Anderson is surprised to see the library in operation as he faxed instructions for it to be closed down and boxed out before he got there. Thanks to an apparent breakdown in communication that might be due to an act of rebellion on the part of the library's curator, Oswald Bates, head of staff Marilyn Truman is shocked to learn that the building is to be gutted for development, that the small valuable part of the photo collection is to be sold off and the remaining pictures (the vast bulk of the ten million items) destroyed.

Oswald suggests that they 'lose' each of the valuable pieces by shifting them through the rest of the collection, but Marilyn refuses to descend to blackmail. Instead, with the assistance of Oswald's encyclopaedic knowledge, she shows Mr Anderson a story illustrated by pictures from all over the collection, a story of a little Jewish girl whose father was an amateur photographer, who was fostered by a rich German family to protect her from the Nazis, who then appears in pictures of Berlin on the day of a Nazi rally, in a picture of Jews being sent to a concentration camp and then, finally, in a photo of the Old Kent Road in London in the 1980s, an old woman raging. It's not much, but it at least buys Marilyn a week to find a buyer for parts of the election, to ensure their survival. But then Oswald decides to do something really stupid that threatens the futures of them all . . .

Stephen Poliakoff's skill as a storyteller is brought to the fore in this sentimental but never mawkish tale of histories, of the story of the 20th century and its importance to today. Timothy Spall pulls just short of playing Oswald as a buffoon while the frosty Marilyn (Lindsay Duncan) bewitches the American (Irish actor Liam Cunningham, underplaying to enormous effect) with further stories that soon take on a personal significance for the businessman. In a time where dramas tend to be cutting scenes faster and faster, it's all the more enthralling to be offered a tale that insists that we pay attention to a series of static images, images that produce an overwhelming emotional response.

The Silver Chair

see THE CHRONICLES OF NARNIA

Simon in the Land of Chalk Drawings

Animation | FilmFair for BBC One | episode duration 5 mins | broadcast 1977–8

Voice Cast

Bernard Cribbins · *Narrator*

Creator Edward MacLachlan **Producer** Ivor Wood **Writer** Glyn Frewler **Theme Music** Mike Batt

Six-year-old Simon is surprised to discover that everything he draws on the blackboard in his playroom comes to life in a land of chalk drawings, a place he can only get to by climbing up a ladder and over a fence that lie on his way to school. Simon is introduced to the Land of Chalk Drawings by Henry, a boy Simon once drew. But Simon's excitement is cut short when he is shown the hospital wing full of all the chalk people he never got round to finishing off. Soon Simon is paying regular visits to the land to see what other calamities he's caused by not thinking through the consequences of his drawings. The boy should probably be kept away from chalk for good, if you ask us.

Adapted from the stories by Edward MacLachlan, *Simon in the Land of Chalk Drawings* was an odd one for FilmFair to produce, cell animated instead of the usual stop-motion puppetry of other shows like ***The Herbs*** and ***Paddington***. However, it would have been difficult to create the feel of a two-dimensional world had Simon been a three-dimensional model. If his best friend was a chalk-based stick boy, it's possible that Simon was not a popular child at school – especially if he was as chummy with his real teacher as he was with the one in the Land of Chalk Drawings (in one episode he draws an alarm clock to wake the children up in time for school . . . bet that made him popular with the chalk kids). Two series of 12 episodes each were made, with adventures such as a trip to the moon, a football match where Simon draws himself extra players, an encounter with a dinosaur and a sudden outbreak of chalk measles.

The Simpsons

See pages 672–7

The Singing Detective

Drama | BBC Two | episode duration 50 mins | broadcast 16 Nov–21 Dec 1986

Principal Cast

Lyndon Davies, Michael Gambon · *Philip E. Marlow*
Patrick Malahide · *Mark Finney/Raymond/Mark Binney*
Joanne Whalley · *Nurse Mills*
David Ryall · *Mr Hall*
Gerard Horan · *Reginald Dimps*
Ron Cook, George Rossi · *Mysterious Men*
Leslie French · *Mr Tomkey/Noddy*
Geff Francis · *Hospital Porter*
Sharon D. Clarke · *Night Nurse*
Janet Suzman · *Nicola*
Alison Steadman · *Mrs Marlow/Lili*
Bill Paterson · *Dr Gibbon*
Jim Carter · *Mr Marlow*
Janet Henfrey · *Schoolteacher/Scarecrow*
Imelda Staunton · *Nurse White*
Kate McKenzie · *Sonia*
Charon Bourke · *Amanda*
Charles Simon · *George Adams*
Mary MacLeod · *Nurse Malone*
William Speakman · *Mark Binney*
Wally Thomas · *Grandad Baxter*
Trevor Cooper · *Cloth Cap/Barman*
Niven Boyd, David Thewlis · *Soldiers*
Simon Chandler · *Dr Finlay*

Creator/Writer Dennis Potter **Producers** Kennith Todd and John Harris **Theme Music** Stanley Myers

Philip Marlow is a writer of detective pulp fiction – but no, he's not *that* Philip Marlow. Trapped in a hospital bed with a debilitating skin disease (psoriatic arthropathy) that's left his entire body covered in scabs and flaking skin, his medication keeps him in a semi-permanent state of delirium and fantasy. Characters and situations from his novels merge with memories of childhood in the Forest of Dean that have left him emotionally as well as physically scarred. His hallucinations recall his mother's infidelities as well as his fantasies as a crooner with a jazz orchestra.

The Singing Detective is thought by many to be not just Potter's greatest work, but the greatest television drama ever. It's also one of his least accessible works, part autobiography, part 'greatest hits' with elements taken from his 1973 novel *Hide and Seek*, his highly acclaimed drama ***Pennies from Heaven*** and from his own life (Potter suffered from the same disease, and experienced the same discomforts that plague Marlow) as well as casual references to other influences. For example, in the Sherpa Tensing ward of the hospital is a '***Doctor Finlay***', while Philip Marlow at one point states that he would have been a better writer if his mother had called him Christopher). It also provided a controversial high-point to his career, for while critics fell over themselves to praise the series and claim to understand its meta- and intertexual narrative first time, it shocked some viewers with its graphic (for the time) sex scenes, notably one in which Patrick Malahide's buttocks are seen. The outrage voiced by Mary Whitehouse and others perhaps influenced the judges at BAFTA who nominated *The Singing Detective* but gave the Best Drama award to Fay Weldon's ***Life and Loves of a She-Devil***. It would eventually be transferred to the big screen in 2003, after a lengthy time in development hell, starring Robert Downey Jr. Despite strong performances all round, the film was predictably mauled by critics.

Fans of Potter would enjoy a third music/memory drama in ***Lipstick on your Collar***, set within the sexual awakening of the 1950s, while controversy was courted once more in *Blackeyes*, based on Potter's novel and marking his debut as a director. Dennis Potter died in 1994 of pancreatic cancer. A fierce champion of British television drama, he pulled off one last significant coup by getting the BBC and Channel 4 to collaborate on the production of his final two works: *Karaoke* delved into the mind of writer Daniel Feeld (Albert Finney), whose illness causes his fictional work and real life to blur; its sequel, *Cold Lazarus*, was shown on Channel 4, a science fiction tale about an Earth of the future where Daniel Feeld's head has been removed from cryogenic freezing to enable scientists to tap into his memories of 20th-century Earth. But even as a disembodied head, Feeld proved uncooperative.

The Singing, Ringing Tree

Children's Fantasy | DEFA Studio für Spielfilme (shown on BBC One) | duration 73 mins | broadcast 15 Dec 1957 (East Germany)

Regular Cast

Christel Bodenstein · *Arrogant Princess*
Eckart Dux · *Handsome Prince*
Richard Krüger · *Wicked Dwarf*
Günther Polensen · *Guard Captain*
Friedrich Teitge · *Gärtner*
Dorothea Thiesing · *Nurse*
Charles H. Vogt · *Aged King*
Antony Bilbow · *Narrator*

Writers Francesco Stefani, Anne Geelhaar, a reworking of the story 'Snow White and Rose Red' by the Brothers Grimm
Theme Music Heinz-Friedel Heddenhausen

When a snooty, self-absorbed Princess rejects the advances of a handsome Prince, she sets in motion a train of events that will affect them both. Rejecting the Prince's offer of pearls, the Princess instead demands that he bring her a magical singing, ringing tree to show his devotion. The Prince searches for such a tree for a long time, and eventually he discovers one. Unfortunately for the Prince, the tree is growing in a land owned by an evil dwarf. The Dwarf tells the Prince that he can take the tree and give it to the Princess – but if, when he hands it over, the Princess still doesn't love him, there will be a terrible price to pay. Sure enough, the Princess doesn't have any true love for the Prince in her heart, and the Dwarf's magical curse on the magical tree turns him into a bear and makes her ugly . . .

In the spirit of other Brothers Grimm fairy tales, *The Singing, Ringing Tree* is a heck of a lot darker than most parents might imagine. Transmitted in Britain as a three-part serial, *The Singing Ringing Tree* first hit our screens on 19 November 1964, as part of the *Tales from Europe* strand of re-dubbed programmes. Unable to afford to get the whole programme re-dubbed with separate voice-overs replacing each of the actors, a single clipped RP (received pronunciation) narrator told the story, with the original German voices often coming through. Along with similar European kids' fare like *Heidi* and ***Belle and Sebastian***, *The Singing, Ringing Tree* was repeated several times throughout the 1960s and 70s, its unique art-house production style (with sets looking like a real-life version of the backdrops on ***The Magic Roundabout***) and incredibly sinister atmosphere terrifying several generations of children.

Six Feet Under

Drama | Actual Size/Greenblatt-Janollari for HBO (shown on Channel 4) | episode duration 60–65 mins | broadcast 3 Jun 2001–21 Aug 2005 (USA)

Regular Cast

Peter Krause · *Nate Fisher*
Michael C. Hall · *David Fisher*
Rachel Griffiths · *Brenda Chenowith*
Frances Conroy · *Ruth Fisher*
Lauren Ambrose · *Claire Fisher*
Freddy Rodriguez · *Rico Diaz*
Mathew St Patrick · *Keith Charles*
Richard Jenkins · *Nathaniel Fisher Snr*
Jeremy Sisto · *Billy Chenowith*
Ed Begley, Jr · *Hiram*
Justina Machado · *Vanessa Diaz*
Dina Waters · *Tracy Montrose Blair*
Joanna Cassidy · *Margaret Chenowith*
Robert Foxworth · *Bernard Chenowith*
Lili Taylor · *Lisa Kimmel/Fisher*
James Cromwell · *George Sibley*
Kathy Bates · *Bettina*
Ayre Gross · *Frank Muehler*
Veronica Cartwright · *Peg Kimmel*
Justin Theroux · *Joe*
Michelle Trachtenberg · *Celeste*
Patricia Clarkson · *Aunt Sarah*
Mena Suvari · *Edie*
Continued on page 678

The Simpsons

Clockwise, from top: Marge, Homer, baby Maggie, Bart and Lisa – the Simpson family.

Though a few rare Brits experienced the joys of satellite TV in the mid-1980s (many of whom were ***Doctor Who*** fans wanting to watch their reruns of Tom Baker's best years on Superchannel), it was with Sky television that most got their first dose of space-age TV entertainment. The movie, sports and music packages were hugely attractive but the television drama and comedy output was less so. With virtually no UK-originated programming on Sky's main channel, it was wall-to-wall imports, the majority of which seemed to come from America's Fox network (also owned by media magnate Rupert Murdoch).

Cable and satellite television, almost by definition, offers a much more niche experience than its terrestrial counterpart; in 2005 science fiction, drama, comedy, music, sport, documentaries and children's programmes could all be found on their own genre-defined channels via digital cable. With most channels delivering at least six hours of programming a day, and with many filling the whole 24, there's simply too much of it to keep track of. It's for this reason that we've made the rule in this book to restrict our attentions to TV shows that reached their audience on BBCs One and Two, ITV (1), Channel 4 and the occasional non-Nazi-related show on Five.

Naturally every rule has its exceptions; ours is *The Simpsons*. Sure, it's had long runs on BBC Two and later Channel 4, but its home really is Sky One. Not that we really have to justify the inclusion of

Comedy
Gracie Films for Fox (shown on Sky One/BBC One/Two/Channel 4)
Episode Duration: 25 mins
Broadcast: 17 Dec 1989, 14 Jan 1990–present

Regular Voice Cast
Various, including:
Dan Castellaneta · *Homer Simpson, Grampa Abe Simpson, Barney Gumble, Krusty the Klown, Groundskeeper Willie, Mayor Quimby*
Julie Kavner · *Marge Simpson, assorted Members of the Bouvier Family*
Nancy Cartwright · *Bart Simpson, Nelson Muntz, Todd Flanders, Ralph Wiggum* Yeardley Smith · *Lisa Simpson*
Hank Azaria · *Moe Szyslak, Chief Wiggum, Apu Nahasapeemapetilon, Comic Book Guy, Professor Frink*
Harry Shearer · *Mr Montgomery Burns, Waylon Smithers, Ned Flanders, Kent Brockman, Reverend Lovejoy, Principal Skinner, Dr Hibbert*
Marcia Wallace · *Edna Krabappel*
Pamela Hayden · *Milhouse Van Houten*
Phil Hartman · *Lionel Hutz, Troy McClure*
Maggie Roswell, Marcia Mitzman Gaven · *Maude Flanders, Helen Lovejoy*
Joe Mantegna · *Fat Tony*
Kelsey Grammer · *'Sideshow Bob' Underdunk Terwilliger*
Jon Lovitz, Karl Wiedergott, Jo Ann Harris · *Various Characters*

the single most culturally relevant – and, annoyingly, misunderstood – TV show of the last 20 years. We can understand why Channel 4 wanted to get their hands on *The Simpsons*, and to show off about it as much as possible. But allowing *The Simpsons* to win a poll of the Top 100 Children's Programmes poll wasn't even remotely accurate and suggests that whoever compiled the list has missed the point somewhat. Still, the show was once part of Saturday morning telly on BBC One so they're not exactly alone in this view.

Matt Groening created *The Simpsons* mere minutes prior to a meeting with producer James L. Brooks about adapting Groening's comic strip 'Life is Hell' (a philosophical world that starred a bitter, one-eared rabbit) into a series of animated sketches for *The Tracey Ullman Show*. Realising that such a move would almost certainly mean he'd lose the rights to the characters he'd spent years making a success, when the meeting began Groening instead pitched an entirely different setting, a dysfunctional family with names plucked from his own relatives. 'Life is Hell' continued as a newspaper-syndicated strip and *The Simpsons* emerged as quite the best thing about *The Tracey Ullman Show*. This is more of a compliment than might be evident as Ullman herself was superb and her ensemble cast, many of whom ended up voicing characters on *The Simpsons*, included Harry Shearer (one-time member of spoof rock band Spinal Tap) and Julie Kavner, who had co-starred in a hugely popular sitcom in the 1970s (***Rhoda***) and since worked with Woody Allen on one of his all-time funniest films, *Radio Days* (1987).

These early vignettes took up just four minutes per show, but it soon became apparent that many viewers were tuning in for them rather than Ullman's brilliant characterisations (for some reason, the animated sequences had been excised when they were broadcast on BBC Two).

For the channel airing the show in the States, this was the beginning of a change of fortunes. In 1989, Fox had been broadcasting for just two years but was still not available in every region of the USA. For its competitors, it was little more than a minority channel without a hit to its name. It certainly wasn't in a position to take any risks, yet it gave Matt Groening and James L. Brooks half a season (12 episodes) to prove themselves – and it did so without wresting creative control from Brooks's team.

The first episode, 'Simpsons Roasting on an Open Fire', aired on 17 December 1989. The money Marge has been saving for Christmas is instead going on the removal of Bart's tattoo. Luckily, Bart has enough faith in the festive messages in other TV shows to convince his father to bet on a dog race; the dog fails to win but Homer adopts him and thus the family has something to celebrate. And with their highest-rated Sunday broadcast ever, so did Fox.

When the series began, all eyes were on Bart – 'under-achiever and proud of it' as the millions of T-shirts proclaimed. It took the writers – and us – two years to realise the show's real star was Homer. Ten years before the arrival of ***The Sopranos***' James Gandolfini, Homer gave balding, over-weight, middle-aged men some hope of being sex symbols and the unlikeliest of life coaches. A slave to his

Creators Characters by Matt Groening, series developed by Groening with James L. Brooks and Sam Simon

Producers *The Simpsons* has an astounding amount of people attached to the job title of producer (including animation producers on top of your normal execs, associates and supervisors). So the following come in under the 'executive' group: James L. Brooks, Matt Groening, David X. Cohen, Gabor Csupo, Al Jean, George Meyer, David Mirkin, Bill Oakley, Mike Reiss, Mike Scully, Sam Simon, Josh Weinstein

Writers Various, including Matt Groening, Jon Vitti, Jay Kogen, Wallace Wolodarsky, Al Jean, Mike Reiss, John Swartzwelder, George Meyer, Sam Simon, Jeff Martin, Bill Oakley, Josh Weinstein, Mike Scully, David X. Cohen, Dan Greaney, Ian Maxtone-Graham, Matt Selman, Tim Long, John Frink, Don Payne

Theme Music Danny Elfman

id, Homer is the only man whose own brain uses reverse psychology on him; who needs to phone directory enquiries for the 911 emergency number; who thinks that the best way to wipe away a crying child's tears is with a hairdryer. The pull of instant gratification drives this man from blunder to disaster with hilarious 'Mmmmm's and 'D'OH!'s along the way.

Homer has individually been responsible for more life-threatening incidents than any other inhabitant of Springfield, possibly the world. But for some reason he manages to escape retribution. No one story illustrates this more effectively than 'Homer's Enemy', a season eight episode in which a celebrated hero, Frank Grimes, finds himself at the Springfield Nuclear Plant in Sector 7G alongside Homer Simpson, a crass, rude, painfully stupid man – our hero. Appalled by Homer's lack of basic safety knowledge, insensed by his apparent success in life (his large home contains photos of him with president Gerald Ford and other celebrities, while Grimes is forced to take an extra job just to be able to afford an apartment crammed in between two bowling alleys) and finally exasperated by Homer's popularity, Grimes mocks Homer openly, aping his actions until an encounter with some dangerous electric cables brings his tragic life to an end. Even at Grimes's funeral, Homer's behaviour is reprehensible, with him falling asleep and asking Marge to 'change the channel' during the Reverend Lovejoy's sermon. An episode that polarises fans (if the extremes of A+s and Fs in online polls are anything to go by at least), it's fitting that the show reserves its most savage of critiques for its most popular character. Why should he get off scot-free when so many other celebrities are routinely maltreated by the show?

Ah yes, the celebrity voices. Ever since crooner Tony Bennett made a cough-and-you'll-miss-him appearance in season two's 'Dancin' Homer', the famous and would-be-famous have been queuing up to pay a visit to Springfield. Some have appeared as themselves – including rock group Cypress Hill, ex-Beatles Paul McCartney, Ringo Starr and George Harrison, Hollywood megastar Mel Gibson, Mr Spock himself (Leonard Nimoy), the cast of ***Cheers*** and even British Prime Minister Tony Blair (apparently because he wanted to do at least one thing his kids would be proud of).

Blair in particular was being rather canny in accepting the invitation to voice himself – an honour no other world leader has so far accepted – and at least one American president has been denied. When President Bush Snr spoke in 1992 of his desire to make families 'a lot more like the Waltons and a lot less like the Simpsons', the *Simpsons'* creative team swiftly put together a short scene in just three days to be tagged onto the beginning of a rerun of 'Stark Raving Dad'. The scene showed the family watching Bush delivering that speech on TV (curiously not 'Simpsonified' either) one of the very rare times in the show's history that real video footage is used. On hearing the unfavourable comparison to the Waltons, Bart exclaimed: 'Hey, we're just like ***The Waltons***. We're praying for an end to the Depression too!'

Celebrities don't just sign up to see themselves given the yellow *Simpson* make-over, though. Many of them are content to take whatever roles are available. Danny DeVito played Homer's half-brother Herb, Glenn Close his activist mother; playwright Harvey Fierstein was Homer's ultra-efficient secretary Karl, Kathleen Turner was Stacy Lovell (creator of the Malibu Barbie dolls so adored by Lisa) and Kirk Douglas played Chester J. Lampwick, creator of the Itchy and Scratchy cartoons. Elizabeth Taylor provided Maggie with her first word ('Daddy') and Michael Jackson voiced a huge white man who thought he was Jackson and lived in a mental institution (Jackson also reputedly wrote Bart Simpson's hit single 'Do the Bartman').

Best of the lot, though, is Kelsey Grammer, cast in series one as the voice of Krusty the Klown's sidekick, 'Sideshow Bob' Terwilliger, sent to jail for robbing the Kwik-E-Mart thanks to evidence uncovered by Bart (in 'Krusty Gets Busted'). Parolled two years later, largely thanks to his new relationship with Bart's spinster aunt Selma, Sideshow Bob begins years of revenge plots that always result in him returning to jail. His plot to take control of Springfield fails when Lisa exposes the corruption behind his election (he included votes from dead people); his protests at innocence even extend to hiring a lawyer to explain that his tattoo, 'Die Bart, Die', actually means 'The Bart, the' in German. In the hugely entertaining 'Cape Feare', the *Simpsons* writers parody the 1991 Martin Scorsese/Robert De Niro film of (almost) the same name, replacing De Niro's vengeful Max Cady with a buffed and tatooed Sideshow Bob, a masterful Bernard Hermann-esque musical score and a joke involving Sideshow Bob being hit repeatedly in the face by a load of rakes that have been left lying around, causing him to mutter something that sounds like 'Urroghruh'. Grammer has returned as Sideshow Bob four further times, once accompanied by his ***Frasier*** co-star David Hyde Pierce, who played Bob's even more evil brother, Cecil.

Ten years before the arrival of *The Sopranos*' James Gandolfini, Homer gave balding, over-weight, middle-aged men some hope of being sex symbols and the unlikeliest of life coaches.

The *Cape Fear* connection here underlines just how culturally literate the producers expect fans to be. Every fan can list their own favourite obscure references and there are hundreds that probably go unnoticed. 'Homer 3D', a segment of one of the now annual Treehouse of Horror episodes, mimicked an episode of ***The Twilight Zone*** in explaining how Homer had somehow slipped into a parallel world of 'three dimensions' (created through computer graphics animation). The sequence with Homer exploring the three-dimensional world included a shot of a temple accompanied by a piece of music that might have been familiar to fans of the computer game Myst but almost certainly passed everyone else by. But then there are the more obvious ones where we slowly realise just what is being aped. The makers are clearly fans of Hitchcock, as shown by their loving re-creation of a jacket-tearing scene from *Saboteur* (1942; Millhouse's shirt in 'Three Men and a Comic Book') the finale

WEBSITES
The official site-thesimpsons.com – is pretty decent, with all of the basic info you'd want. One of the best fan sites is '*The Simpsons* Archive' (www.snpp.com), which combines a brain-aching amount of trivia with simple navigation.

from *The Birds* (1963; Homer removing Maggie from a crèche in 'A Streetcar Named Marge', itself a pastiche of the Tennessee Williams play), James Stewart in *Rear Window* (1954; Bart in 'Bart of Darkness') and a re-creation of the shower scene from *Psycho* (1960) involving Maggie, Homer, a mallet and a tin of red paint ('Itchy and Scratchy and Marge').

Bart and Homer hog the limelight, but they're not the only stars. In Japan, where the values embodied in *The Simpsons* jar with those of the country as a whole, the series was not a success until it was repositioned to make Bart's sister Lisa the star. In the Tracy Ullman shows, Lisa had been merely Bart's little sister, but by the first season of their own programme she had somehow become a child genius, possibly the most intelligent citizen of Springfield and the moral centre of the show. She likes Malibu Stacy dolls, ponies and cartoons like any other kid of her age, but she just happens to be ever so slightly brilliant. A vegetarian Zen Buddhist, saxophonist and political activist, she avoids being a preachy, judgemental pain because she's still only eight years old and knows it.

Marge Simpson's might seem like the most thankless existence of all. Homer keeps his expectations of life deliberately low to avoid disappointment, Lisa is never more content than when campaigning against something and Bart has a near limitless capacity to keep himself entertained with chaos and comic books. Even Maggie has her dummy, but what does Marge have except cooking, cleaning and looking after her family? Aside from her neighbours, the creepily peppy Flanders family, she appears to be the only person in Springfield who sees Sunday Church rituals as something to look forward to (yes, including the Reverend Lovejoy). In fact, she embodies everything the American housewife should be and in doing so undermines those values in quite the most understated but persuasive act of subversion delivered by the series. As viewers we see how much effort Marge puts into her domestic chores every day, including three different breakfasts and packed lunches. When Lisa decides to become a vegetarian, Marge supports her without too much concern for the extra load it'll place on her own shoulders come teatime. The clue to Marge's raison d'être comes in an exchange with Lisa about not giving up on people: 'When I first met your father he was loud, crude and piggish, but now he's a whole new person,' claims Marge. 'But Mom . . .' Lisa tries to interrupt. 'He's a whole new person,' Marge repeats firmly. Does this mean she survives the repetitive, unappreciated life as matriarch of the Simpson brood through sheer self-delusion or just that giving has its own reward? *The Simpsons* rarely preaches. It's unlikely to mean anything beyond Marge being some kind of supermom. But it

Marge embodies everything the American housewife should be and in doing so undermines those values in quite the most understated but persuasive act of subversion.

does (or at least should) make us re-assess our relationships with our own stay-at-home parents.

Owner of the Springfield Nuclear Plant (and the funnel-web spider at the heart of the community) is of course corrupt old monster Mr Burns, a man with conscience and emotion in inverse proportion to his years upon years of decrepitude. Burns is a cold-hearted brute, a man with desires for nothing but money and power (to the extent that he was perfectly prepared to blot out the sun over Springfield just so people would need to buy more electricity from his power station). The only person with desires for him is his ever-so-gay personal assistant Waylon Smithers (another member of the Malibu Stacy collectors' club), a man so transfixed with love for his boss that he simply fails to register much of the evil work Burns does. Thankfully, Burns's attempts at achieving world domination are usually thwarted either by his ageing body or the incompetence of the people he surrounds himself with – which quite often ends up being his single laziest employee, Homer Simpson of Sector 7G.

As the years have passed, the ensemble cast of characters has grown too. Apu, the only Asian character on prime-time TV when *The Simpsons* first arrived on American screens, has evolved from shopkeeper stereotype to major supporting player. Barney Gumble, Homer's bar-fly friend, can always be relied on for a well-timed belch. School bully Nelson Muntz lives for those Schadenfreude moments when he can deliver his cold, mocking 'Ha, ha!' laugh. Seymore Skinner is Springfield Elementary's principal, yet this veteran of the Vietnam War is driven more by rules and regulations than any desires to educate the masses. Lisa's teacher, Edna Krabappel, is no better, running from her classes to the nearest bar. Chief Wiggum represents Law and Order in Springfield – rather badly. The only order he considers is the one in which he eats his donuts. His son Ralph goes to Springfield Elementary, in Lisa's class but not her league. Ralph is lovably dim, the child most likely to be rebuked for eating glue. He's the prince of the priceless non sequitur – 'My cat's breath smells of catfood' and 'I bent my Wookie' being just two. We could go on.

One might not consider the figure 167 to represent a particularly special milestone, but it does for *The Simpsons*. Episode 167 marked the point at which the show had surpassed the record number of instalments previously set by ***The Flintstones***, prime-time TV's first animated family. The production team celebrated with one of their legendary couch sequences that open each episode by having the Simpson family rush in as normal only to find their places taken by Fred, Wilma and Pebbles Flintstone. That was back in season eight. At the time of writing, *The Simpsons* is about to begin its 18th series.

Creator Alan Ball **Producers** Alan Ball, Robert Greenblatt, David Janollari, Alan Poul, Christian Williams, Bruce Eric Kaplan (executive), Rick Cleveland, Scott Buck, Laurence Andries (supervising), Christian Taylor, Jill Soloway, Lori Jo Nemhauser **Writers** Various, including Alan Ball, Christian Williams, Bruce Eric Kaplan, Laurence Andries **Theme Music** Thomas Newman, who also composed the unforgettable music for Alan Ball's film *American Beauty*, created this haunting yet quirky title music.

When *Six Feet Under* was first screened, critics didn't know quite how to classify it: was it the blackest of comedy series, or a damned funny drama? Of course, the answer is both – *Six Feet Under* combines incredibly strong family-focused adult drama with a distinctly sick and twisted sense of humour. Perhaps that's to be expected when the setting for the series is a small funeral parlour business. Indeed, every episode would begin with somebody's death – sometimes through sad or tragic circumstances, but often in a hilariously warped and messy fashion (chopped up in a giant bread mixing machine, crashing a motorbike dressed as Santa Claus while waving at a group of excited young children, electrocuted in the bath when a cat knocked a set of heated hair rollers into the tub, etc., etc.).

In the first episode, the scattered members of the Fisher family are heading home to celebrate Christmas together when patriarch Nathaniel is killed in a road accident. Against his better judgement, eldest son Nate agrees to abandon his carefree life in Seattle and move back to the family home in Pasadena, California to help keep the family funeral parlour business above water. Nate's brother David is initially unhappy at the idea of sharing the business with his sibling – he had, after all, stayed at home and invested a lot of time and effort in preparing to take over from his father in due course. Their sister Claire is deeply affected by her father's death, going off the rails and falling in love with a rather dodgy character. And Nathaniel's widow Ruth reels from her loss, trying to find a new role and purpose in life while simultaneously attempting to break out from her own self-imposed control freak behaviour. One problem that the whole Fisher family suffers from is an inability to open up and talk about their problems or share their secrets – chief of which is David's sexuality, a taboo subject that he simply can't bring himself to talk about with his mother and siblings.

The other principal characters in *Six Feet Under* included the Fishers' embalmer/mortician Rico Diaz, a kind-hearted yet very traditional young Hispanic man; Keith Charles, David's on-off policeman boyfriend; and Nate's girlfriend Brenda Chenowith – a hyper-intelligent woman who appears at first sight to be cool, calm and totally collected, but who is actually deeply messed up courtesy of her mentally ill brother and oddball psychiatrist parents.

Six Feet Under was created by Alan Ball, scriptwriter of 1999's Best Picture Oscar-winning movie *American Beauty*. Having enjoyed such a success as a movie screenplay writer, it came as a shock to most observers when Ball didn't just create *Six Feet Under*, he remained with it throughout its run, writing and directing many of the episodes himself. The programme boasts a uniformly excellent cast, with extra-special praise owing to the three female leads, Frances Conroy, Lauren Ambrose and Australian actress Rachel Griffiths (star of *Muriel's Wedding*, among many other films) who all put in outstanding performances of depth, subtlety and real emotion. With the programme being broadcast by subscription channel HBO, *Six Feet Under* was able to break taboos on all manner of subjects that simply wouldn't be allowed anywhere near one of the main US TV networks. Challenging, innovative and consistently outstanding, *Six Feet Under* is perfect evidence that the best TV drama in the world is currently being produced in the USA.

The Six Million Dollar Man

Action-Adventure | Harve Bennett/Silverton/Universal for ABC (shown on ITV) | episode duration 50 mins | broadcast 7 Mar 1973–6 Mar 1978, 17 May 1987, 30 Apr 1988, 29 Nov 1994

Regular Cast

Lee Majors · *Colonel Steve Austin*
Richard Anderson · *Oscar Goldman*
Jennifer Darling · *Peggy Callahan*
Martin E. Brooks, Alan Oppenheimer · *Dr Rudy Wells*
Lindsay Wagner · *Jaime Sommers*

Creator Kenneth Johnson and Harve Bennett, from Martin Caidin's novel *Cyborg* **Producers** Allan Balter, Harve Bennett, Lionel E. Siegel (executive), Rod Holcomb, Arthur E. McLaird, Arnold F. Turner (associate), Donald R. Boyle, Joe L. Cramer, Fred Freiberger, Kenneth Johnson, Richard H. Landau, Lionel E. Siegel, Sam Strangis **Writers** Larry Brody, Richard Carr, Robert C. Dennis, Steven E. de Souza, Peter Allan Fields, D. C. Fontana, Fred Freiberger, Mark Frost, Kenneth Johnson, Stephen Kandel, Edward J. Lakso, Richard H. Landau, John Meredyth Lucas, Del Reisman, Mann Rubin, Sy Salkowitz, Wilton Schiller, James Schmerer, Elroy Schwartz, Lionel E. Siegel, Michael I. Wagner **Theme Music** The theme music for the first three seasons came from Oliver Nelson, while J. J. Johnson provided music for seasons four and five. The opening sequence also provided a handy summary of the backstory with Oscar Goldman speaking over shots of the operation and Steve's training: 'We can rebuild him. We have the technology. We can make him better than he was. Better . . . stronger . . . faster.' Sadly not cheaper though.There are a number of fun one-off themes too. The third TV movie featured a song written by Glen A. Larson and sung by Dusty Springfield ('And he's my man . . . Six Million Dollar Man'). The two 'Bionic Woman' episodes of series two featured two songs, 'Got to Get Loose' and 'Sweet Jaime', written by Lionel E. Siegel and Oliver Nelson and sung by Lee Majors. The 1987 TV movie *Return of the Six Million Dollar Man and the Bionic Woman* featured a cover version of The Pointer Sisters' 1982 song 'Automatic', with lyrics so apt they could almost have been written especially for the film.

The test flight of a new aircraft results in tragedy when it crashes and leaves its pilot, NASA astronaut Steve Austin, critically injured. Then Oliver Spenser, head of the Office of Scientific Operations (OSO), steps forward with an offer to fund groundbreaking operations on Austin involving the latest in bionic technology. When Austin wakes up he discovers that his right arm and both legs have been replaced by machinery, and that his left eye now contains a telephoto lens. The bionic additions give him a top running speed of 66 mph, he can leap up to 30ft, lift up to half a ton unassisted and his eye can zoom in across 200yd. After a long and painful period of recovery, Austin comes to terms with his new superhuman abilities (accompanied in the series by a metallic juddering sound that was mimicked by every child in every playground in the world) and accepts a post as an agent with the OSO's sister organisation, the Office of Scientific Intelligence, working with Oscar Goldman.

In 1972, author Martin Caidin hawked his recently published novel *Cyborg* around every network in America trying to pitch it as a TV series until ABC decided to adapt it into a TV movie. A second and third movie acted as a prelude to the long-awaited TV series, but, by this time, the format for the show bore little resemblance in tone or structure to the source novel. With a strong, tough-looking heroic figure like Lee Majors in the role, the Bionic Man (as he was often known) became every young boy's hero – to the extent that parents became concerned by a spate of incidents involving children jumping off garden sheds and buildings trying to ape his bionic leaps. For the most part, episodes involved routinely generic crime investigations, the only difference being how Steve Austin battled the villains (with a fight in slow motion or by gripping the rear fender of their vehicle to stop them from escaping).

For the show's second series, the producers decided to soften Steve's personality a little by giving him a girlfriend, Tennis pro Jaime Sommers, who ends up becoming the first bionic woman after a parachute jump goes tragically wrong. With the characters due to be married, Jaime suffered a relapse as her body rejected the implants and she died on the operating table. Such was the public reaction to Jaime, the third series began with a two-part story 'The Return of the Bionic Woman', in which Jaime's death was explained away and the character returned. Later that same season, a third appearance by Jaime acted as a crossover for her own show, *The Bionic Woman*, which was about to start its own three year run. With this, Steve Austin and Jaime Sommers became American TV's golden couple, while in real life, Lee Majors shared the celebrity limelight with Farrah Fawcett, his then wife and star of equally huge series ***Charlie's Angels***.

Later *Six Million Dollar Man* episodes began to exploit the realms of science fiction more and more as the series lurched from basic detective series to a proto-***X Files*** with Steve Austin chasing down aliens and even Bigfoot (played by ***The Addams Family***'s Ted Cassidy, no less). By this time, the show had clearly been repositioned for younger viewers as characters from the series began to appear on toy shelves: the Six Million Dollar Man figure wore a red NASA track suit and boasted a clunky 'bionic' function where a button in his back slowly lifted light objects while a lens in his eye (viewed through a hole in the back of his head) made objects appear far away (he also had a layer of rubber skin on his forearm that could be rolled back to reveal removable circuitry within clear plastic blocks); the Jaime doll was much more attractive, despite the circuitry panels on her legs and the same rubber skin on her arm; and other dolls in the range included Oscar, who had his own, er, briefcase, and the villains Maskatron (a robot with switchable face-plates that allowed him to impersonate Steve and Oscar or pose as another human), Fembot (a female version of Maskatron) and Bigfoot.

The series was eventually brought to an end after five series and 101 episodes. TV movie sequels appeared in the late 1980s and early '90s, originally as a means to kickstart a new generation of bionic heroes starring Steve Austin's son Michael (Tom Schanley). After the first film failed to attract high enough ratings, subsequent TV movies, bringing together the Six Million Dollar Man and Bionic Woman, were mainly for nostaligic purposes. In the final film, *Bionic Ever After?*, Steve and Jaime are wed at last.

The Six Wives of Henry VIII

Drama | BBC Two | episode duration 90 mins | broadcast 1 Jan–5 Feb 1970

Principal Cast

Keith Michell · *Henry VIII*
Annette Crosbie · *Catherine of Aragon*
Dorothy Tutin · *Anne Boleyn*
Patrick Troughton · *The Duke of Norfolk*
John Woodnutt · *Henry VII*
Martin Ratcliffe · *Prince Arthur*
John Baskcomb · *Cardinal Woolsey*
Verina Greenlaw · *Princess Mary*
Anne Stallybrass · *Jane Seymour*
Sheila Burrell · *Lady Rochford*
Michael Osborne · *Mark Smeaton*
Jonathan Newth · *Viscount Rochford*
Hilary Mason · *Lady Boleyn*
Wolfe Morris · *Thomas Cromwell*
Bernard Hepton · *Archbishop Cranmer*
Daniel Moynihan · *Edward Seymour*
Gillian Bailey · *Dorothy Seymour*
Dorothy Black · *Lady Margaret Seymour*
John Ronane · *Thomas Seymour*
Howard Land · *Sir John Seymour*
William Abney · *Sir Francis Bryan*
Louis Haslar · *Sir Nicholas Carew*
Jo Kendall · *Anne Stanhope*
Elvi Hale · *Anne of Cleves*
Mollie Sugden · *Lotte*
Angela Pleasance · *Catherine Howard*

Julia Cornelius · *Anne Carey*
Catherine Lacey · *The Dowager Duchess of Norfolk*
Howard Goorney · *Will Somers*
Ralph Bates · *Thomas Culpeper*
Rosalie Crutchley · *Catherine Parr*
Patrick Godfrey · *Sir Thomas Wriothesley*
Alison Frazer · *Mary*
Karen Ford · *Lady Lane*

Creator Maurice Cowan **Producers** Ronald Travers, Mark Shivas, Roderick Graham **Writers** Beverley Cross, Nick McCarty, Jean Morris, John Prebble, Rosemary Anne Sisson, Ian Thorne **Theme Music** David Munrow

Something Americans love about Britain is its sense of history, which explains why, when screened on Masterpiece Theatre in the USA, both *The Six Wives of Henry VIII* and ***Elizabeth R*** were deluged by praise and Emmys in abundance. Here in the UK, they were similarly well-received, making stars of Keith Michell as Henry and Glenda Jackson as Elizabeth, and drawing record ratings to BBC Two (still regarded by many as a minority channel) with the promise of sexual impropriety, political misdirection and an insight into the most infamous of English monarchs that was simply too great to miss.

Henry VIII's reign is often summarised by the schoolroom rhyme about the fate of each of his wives: 'Divorced, beheaded, died/Divorced, beheaded, survived.' In *Six Wives*, Henry's life was similarly divided, each episode written by a different writer who focused on the period of time that covered each of the six marriages. We begin with the last years in the reign of Henry's father Henry VII, where young Prince Henry is burdened by his father's political manoeuvring to appease Spain by providing him with a wife, Catherine of Aragon (his own brother's widow). Their marriage is initially happy but even though Catherine bears him a child, Mary, she is not the son Henry demands as his heir. His divorce from Catherine overlaps with his secret wedding to Anne Boleyn, but after she too gives birth to a daughter, we witness Henry's despotic, violent and spiteful moods as he allows himself to be convinced that Anne Boleyn is an adulteress. And so on, through death, disappointment and despair to create a picture of a highly complex man who's neither god nor demon. Critics reserved special praise for Keith Michell's portrayal of Henry, a handsome and confident performance that eclipsed the bloated, monstrous image popularised by Charles Laughton in the film *The Private Life of Henry VIII* (1933).

A year later, *Elizabeth R* offered us a sequel of sorts as we follow the life of Henry's second daughter, a woman who witnessed her mother's execution and the deaths of two of her step-mothers and lived in fear for her life while her half-sister was on the throne. Elizabeth eventually became Queen only to find challenges to her right to ascend to the throne from both Scotland and from Thomas Cranmer, a former adviser to her father. Glenda Jackson threw herself into the part, to the extent of shaving her hair back to the crown and enduring lengthy make-up sessions to portray the older Queen, caked in white pancake to hide the her smallpox scars.

The two productions might be considered a little too theatrical and stagey for modern viewers, yet both productions are still held in high regard today; certainly the 1998 film *Elizabeth*, starring Cate Blanchett, and ITV's (admittedly very impressive) 2004 revisionist mini series *Henry VIII* starring Ray Winstone, were both compared unfavourably to the 1970s versions. This is even more impressive when you consider that Keith Michell blotted his copybook by releasing a novelty record – 'Captain Beaky' in 1980. But when you've given the definitive portrayal of the most famous English king in history, people will forgive you everything.

Skippy the Bush Kangaroo

Children's Adventure | Norfolk International/Fauna for 7 Network Australia (shown on ITV) | episode duration 25 mins | broadcast 1966–1968 (Aus)

Regular Cast
Ed Devereaux · *Matt Hammond*
Garry Pankhurst · *Sonny Hammond*
Ken James · *Mark Hammond*
Tony Bonner · *Jerry King*
Liza Goddard · *Clarissa 'Clancy' Merrick*
Frank Thring · *Dr Alexander Stark*
Elke Neidhart · *Dr Steiner*
John Warwick · *Sir Adrian Gillespie*

Creators John McCallum, Lee Robinson, Dennis Hill **Producers** John McCallum, Bob Austin (executive), Dennis Hill, Lee Robinson, Joy Cavill **Writers** Various, including Ross Napier, Ed Devereaux, Ted Roberts, Joy Cavill **Theme Music** Eric Jupp

Widower Matt Hammond lives with his two sons, younger Sonny and teenager Mark in the Waratah National Park, New South Wales, where he's the head ranger. Together with his chopper-flying colleague Jerry King, Matt's in charge of looking after all of the wildlife within the park, rescuing them from danger, and, of course, keeping his family out of trouble. One day Matt comes across an injured kangaroo and brings her home to recuperate. Sonny bonds with the 'roo, names her 'Skippy' and the two become inseparable. Skippy's smarter than your average marsupial, though, and she often manages to communicate surprisingly complex messages to the various members of the Hammond family or their young English friend Clancy Merrick – more often than not alerting the adults if somebody happens to be trapped down a well somewhere. That's by no means Skippy's only skill – she's equally adept at undoing locks, tying knots, posting letters, scaring off poisonous snakes and even (believe it or not) playing the piano when the mood takes her.

Another children's adventure series with a friendly fauna theme (very much along the lines of similar programmes like ***Lassie, Daktari, Flipper*** and *Gentle Ben*), *Skippy* – the suffix *The Bush Kangaroo* was only added for overseas sales – is perhaps the most successful television show in Australian history, having been screened in just as many countries as ***Neighbours*** but also having been a major success in the USA. One of the main reasons for this success is because the whole programme was made on colour film, something that might have seemed an extravagance to the Aussie production company (considering that Australia never got colour television until 1975), but which ensured its marketability and longevity overseas. *Skippy* is best remembered in the UK for two things – for providing an early acting role for Liza '***Give us a Clue***' Goddard, well before her starring roles in ***The Brothers*** and ***Bergerac***, and for the utterly preternaturally implausible skills that *Skippy* exhibited. Still, such freakish behaviour didn't seem to matter much when we were watching the programme as kids – it's the kind of strangeness that only adults really notice.

Skorpion

See BLOOD MONEY

Sky

Children's Drama | HTV for ITV | episode duration 25 mins | broadcast 7 Apr–19 May 1975

Cast
Mark Harrison · *Sky*
Stuart Lock · *Arby*
Cherrald Butterfield · *Jane*
Robert Eddison · *Goodchild*
Jack Watson · *Major Briggs*
Richard Speight · *Roy*

Creators Bob Baker, Dave Martin **Producers** Patrick Dromgoole (executive), Leonard White **Theme Music** Eric Wetherell

When Arby and Jane Vennor find Sky naked in the same woods where local landowner Major Briggs is running a pheasant shoot, they think hiding him might get complicated. That's nothing once they realise that Sky isn't exactly human – he's a force of nature given human form, only the local nature of 1970s Somerset doesn't want him there.

One of the most intelligent kids TV shows – but then coming out of Patrick Dromgoole's HTV stable, what do we expect – *Sky* was never going to be fluffy brain candy. A show that demanded its young audience think about what was going on and follow a complicated plot was rare enough; a show that presented characters with decidedly uncompromising shades of grey was unheard of. No whiter-than-white good guys, Arby is a bit of a troublemaker with a criminal record, Sky is an amoral user of people with (occasionally) terrifying blank eyes, while Roy Briggs is a coward. Throw into the mix an incorrigible drunk in the hospital who can commune with spirits and, in Goodchild, a creation you are meant to see as a force for evil but is, in fact, far more on the side of the angels, and it's easy to see why Sky only ever got one network showing. This is a shame as it was one of the better children's fantasy show of its time. But then, would children of the 21st century really sit through seven episodes in which the titular hero is trying not to be killed by tree branches and leaves?

Even at the end, when Arby realises that Sky has to be removed from the area before nature is permanently wrecked by his presence (he acts like a virus to it), we get an extended jaunt into the future (via an explanation for Stonehenge) and a brand new set of supporting characters worshipping a nuclear bomb, the radiation from which has destroyed much of the local area (an ending possibly inspired by the film *Beneath the Planet of the Apes*). Sky ends on a slightly downbeat note that nevertheless kept a generation of kids hooked for seven weeks and, hopefully, made them question a few things that were taken for granted back then.

The Sky at Night

Factual | BBC TV/BBC One | episode duration 30 mins | broadcast 24 Apr 1957–present

Regular Cast
Patrick Moore · *Presenter*

Producers Paul Johnstone, Patricia Owtram, Patricia Wood, Pieter Morpurgo, Ian Russell, Jane Fletcher **Theme Music** 'At the Castle Gate', from *Pelléas et Mélisande* by Sibelius

In the mid-1950s, the 'space age' as we now know it hadn't yet come to pass. No artificial satellites circled the earth, no spacecraft had been sent up into orbit – and the idea of a man walking on the moon was little short of a science fiction pipedream. Into this rocket-free environment came a television programme that helped people to explore the stars from the comfort of their own gardens, a programme that's still in production nearly 50 years later – astonishingly, with the same presenter handing out advice in his typically eccentric and accessible fashion. Sir Patrick Moore is, quite simply, a national institution of the highest order, and *The Sky at Night* is a broadcasting phenomenon. Although both ***Panorama*** and *What the Papers Say* pre-date it, *The Sky at Night* has both continuity and a place in the hearts of the British people that make it the grand-daddy of all TV shows. Throughout its history, thousands of amateur stargazers have turned to Patrick Moore for advice about what astronomical events will be occurring over the next month. Moore, along with regular guests and advisers, tells viewers on which part of the sky to train their telescopes, and covers all of the important developments taking place in astronautics.

Moore and *The Sky at Night* have covered every single major event in astronomy, from the launch of Sputnik (just a few months after the start of the series) through to the moon landing in July 1969, and even more recently to the UK's total eclipse of the sun in 1999. The influence of this programme on at least three generations of astronomers cannot be underestimated – and even if you've never picked up a telescope in your life, virtually everyone in the UK knows precisely who Patrick Moore is. And that's no mean feat.

SM:TV Live

Magazine | Blaze/Dec and Ant Productions/Zenith for ITV | episode duration 120 mins | broadcast 29 Aug 1998–27 Dec 2003 (*SMTV Live*), 29 Aug 1998–present (*CD:UK*)

Regular Cast
Cat Deeley, Anthony McPartlin, Declan Donnelly, Tess Daly, James W. Redmond, Jonathan Wilkes, Claire Richards, Brian Dowling, Ian 'H' Watkins, Des Clarke, Stephen Mulhern, Shavaughn Ruakere · *Presenters*

Producers Conor MacAnally (executive), David Staite

After years of repetitive shows like *Ghost Train, What's Up Doc?* and *Gimme 5*, ITV finally got a children's Saturday morning TV show to beat the BBC in the ratings. The long reign of the Beeb, from ***Multi-Coloured Swap Shop*** to ***Live and Kicking*** had seen off all the competition. But the combination of Ant McPartlin and Declan Donnelly (formerly of ***Byker Grove*** and their own *Ant and Dec Show*) with the ever-lovely Cat Deeley in two shows broadcast side by side was a stroke of genius.

Ant and Dec brought to ITV the irreverence and naughtiness that had been the cause of many a furrowed brow while presenting their own innuendo-laden show at the BBC. Together with Cat they performed in ongoing sketches, such as their hilariously formulaic ***Friends*** mickey-take, 'Chums', less-than-flattering flashbacks to their childhood (when Cat had buck-teeth and the nickname 'Cat the Dog'), a phone-in quiz called 'Wonky Donkey' where a cryptic posed puppet would apparently reveal the name of a rhyming object (such as 'plucky Ducky'), which the kids never seemed to get, and an utterly brilliant game show called 'Challenge Ant' where contestants could ask Ant a series of questions to win videogames. But if Ant won, he'd taunt them (with the help of the audience) to an enthusiastic chorus of 'You're thick – and you know you are', to the tune of The Village People's/Pet Shop Boys' 'Go West'. It was savage, it was cruel – and audiences flocked to tune in.

The show also played a part in the evil cult known as Pokemon, with the presenters embracing utterly its satanic brainwashing techniques while simultaneously mocking it for being so utterly rubbish. Then, miraculously, the team would step into a studio next door and host CD:UK, a chart rundown and pop performance show that showed ***Top of the Pops*** how it should be done (to the extent that the BBC eventually created their own Saturday version of *TOTP*).

When Ant and Dec left the show for grown-up TV (hosting ***Pop Idol, I'm a Celebrity . . . Get Me Out of Here*** and their own innovative game show/variety hybrid ***Ant and Dec's Saturday Night Takeaway***), Cat was given a new set of playmates, including the less-than-sparkling former ***Hollyoaks*** actor James Redmond (great actor, crap presenter). When Cat also left (though continuing to present the *CD:UK* slot), one of a number of presenters drafted in to keep the show afloat was ***Big Brother*** winner Brian Dowling, whose slightly clueless approach was his most endearing quality. Playing on the cheeky qualities that won him the public vote on *BB*, Dowling was also a bit of a TV first as the first out gay presenter on children's TV, something that, rather wonderfully, no-one seemed to be in any way bothered by.

With ratings plummeting towards the end, the series decided to play on its heritage and became *SMTV* Gold for a few months of classic clips. The final *SMTV* show reunited the original presenters for one last edition of 'Chums'. At the time of writing, *CD:UK* continues to dominate Saturday mornings alongside *The Ministry of Mayhem*, which is the closest that ITV has so far got to reviving ***TISWAS*** for a new generation of kids.

Smack the Pony

Comedy | Talkback Productions for Channel 4 | episode duration 25 mins | broadcast 19 Mar 1999–3 Jan 2003

Regular Cast
Fiona Allen, Sally Phillips, Doon Mackichan, Sarah Alexander, Darren Boyd

Producers Peter Fincham (executive), Vicki Pile **Writers** Various, including Doon Mackichan, Sally Phillips, Fiona Allen, Vicki Pile, Kevin Eldon, Mark Love, Richard Vranch, Darren Boyd**Theme Music** 'In the Middle of Nowhere', sung by Jackie Clune, was originally a hit for a true feminist icon Dusty Springfield.

Although female comics have often been seen in sketch shows, it's normally been either as part of a mixed-sex ensemble or simply as a foil for the jokes of the male writers/performers. With *Smack the Pony*, sketch comedy truly came of age, providing an innovative outlet for the comic stylings of Fiona Allen, Sally Phillips and Doon Mackichan. The *Pony* regulars didn't appear to be interested in using their comedy as a feminist tract, belittling men or treating them as the butt of their humour – rather, they took a typically British tack and turned the comedy against the average modern woman, the life she lives, the relationships she messes up and the neuroses that fill her every waking hour. The programme's most memorable recurring sketch featured the regulars recording messages for a video-dating agency – every possible quirk of female behaviour was put on display, from paranoia through nymphomania to utter male co-dependency, each one getting progressively funnier and funnier.

As time went by, two supporting performers (***Coupling*** star Sarah Alexander and Darren Boyd, fulfilling much the same role as Carol Clevelend had done in ***Monty Python***, looking pretty and setting up the jokes) added a great deal of extra energy and pizzazz to the show. *Smack the Pony* boasted a far higher ratio of laughs to gags than most sketch shows, with the scripts (most written by the cast or by other female writers) playing to the performers' strengths at slapstick and physical comedy as well as satirical barbs against the general rubbishness of modern women's lives. Three seasons and two festive specials of *Smack the Pony* have so far been broadcast – with other women performers such as Catherine Tate coming along with their own comedy sketch shows, it proves that there's still definitely a place in the schedules for more from this talented bunch of performers.

A Small Problem

Comedy | BBC Two | episode duration 30 mins | broadcast 26 Jan–2 Mar 1987

Principal Cast
Christopher Ryan · *Howard Massingham*
Mike Elles · *Roy Pink*
Dickie Arnold · *Fred Harris*
Christine Ozanne · *Lily Harris*
Cory Pullman · *Jenny*
David Simeon · *George Pink*
Joan Blackham · *Heather Pink*
Big Mick · *Sid*
Tetsu Nishino · *Mr Motokura*
Sayo Inaba · *Mrs Motokura*

Producer/Director David Askey **Writers** Tony Millan, Mike Walling **Theme Music** Mo Foster, Mike Walling, Tony Millan

Dwarf-hating Roy Pink is distressed to discover that he's been reclassified a 'Small' after a European directive for metric-only measurements leaves him one centimetre short of the new 155cm benchmark for 'normal' height. Rehoused in a squalid tower block in a Small ghetto, Roy meets other residents, including officious Fred and his wife Lily, belligerent Douglas Bader-obsessed Sid, right-on Jenny, and Howard, leader of terrorist group the Small Liberation Front, who all struggle to cope with the increasingly restrictive establishment intent on keeping down the 'Smalls'.

Satirising prejudice by focusing on sizeism, *A Small Problem* was condemned at the time by people distressed by the use of offensive terms like 'midget', thereby showing that they'd missed the point. The writers had been regulars in long-running sitcoms (Millan in ***Citizen Smith***, Walling in ***Brush Strokes***), so the brevity of this series was a disappointment for some. In truth, though, the comedy was rather gentle and the social satire rather naïve; the biggest belly-laughs came from fictional news reports showing cruelty to old ladies and the implied expectation that the audience would be shocked by depictions of the police as power-abusing thugs. Coming three years after the same point had been made by ***The Young Ones*** (which had also starred Ryan), the impact of that last point was somewhat diminished.

Smallville: Superman – The Early Years

Science Fiction | Warner Bros/Smallville Films/Tollin/Robbins Productions for the WB Network (shown on Channel 4) | episode duration 45 mins | broadcast 16 Oct 2001–present (USA)

Principal Cast
Tom Welling · *Clark Kent*
Kristin Kreuk · *Lana Lang*
Michael Rosenbaum · *Lex Luthor*
Allison Mack · *Chloe Sullivan*
Eric Johnson · *Whitney Fordman*
Sam Jones III · *Pete Ross*
John Glover · *Lionel Luthor*
Jensen Ackles · *Jason Teague*
Annette O'Toole · *Martha Kent*
John Schneider · *Jonathan Kent*

Creators Alfred Gough and Miles Millar, inspired by characters created by Joe Shuster and Jerry Siegel **Producers** Various, including Alfred Gough, Miles Millar, Greg Beeman, Kenneth Biller, Joe Davola, Ken Horton, Brian Robbins, Alex Taub, Mike Tollin, Ken Horton, Mark Verheiden, Michael W. Watkins (executive) **Writers** Alfred Gough, Miles Millar, Mark Verheiden, Michael Green, Philip Levens, Todd Slavkin, Darren Swimmer, Jeph Loeb, Brian Peterson, Holly Harold, Kelly Souders, Steven S. DeKnight, Luke Schelhaas **Theme Music** 'Save Me' by Remy Zero

For commentary, see ADVENTURES OF SUPERMAN

Smiley's People

see TINKER, TAILOR, SOLDIER, SPY

Smith and Jones

See ALAS SMITH AND JONES

The Snowman

Animation | TVC/Murakami-Wolf Productions for Channel 4 | duration 25 mins | broadcast 25 Dec 1982

Cast
Peter Auty · *Singer*
David Bowie · *Host*

Creator/Writer Raymond Briggs **Producers** John Coates, Iain Harvey **Theme Music** Howard Blake

One of the all-time bleakest Christmas films is also one of the most loved. When a small boy builds a snowman one Christmas Eve, the snowman comes alive and takes him flying through the air with other snowmen to meet Father Christmas. But when the boy wakes up on Christmas morning, the Snowman has melted away. Based on Raymond Briggs' own illustrations from his book, *The Snowman* takes on extra significance thanks to an introduction by, of all people, the Thin White Duke himself, David Bowie, who as good as suggests he was the little boy. Aled Jones got to No. 5 in the UK charts with the song 'Walking in the Air', and has been associated with the film ever since. Despite this, it was not Jones who sang on *The Snowman* but Peter Auty.

So Graham Norton

Chat Show | So Television/United for Channel 4/Comedy Central for BBC Three | episode duration 25–50 mins | broadcast 3 Jul 1998–1 Mar 2002 (*So Graham Norton*), 6 May 2002–12 Dec 2003 (*V Graham Norton*), 30 Jan–2 Apr 2004 (*NY Graham Norton*), 24 Jun–16 Sep 2004 (*The Graham Norton Effect*)

Regular Cast

Graham Norton · *Presenter*
Betty Hoskins · *Betty*
Miles O'Keeffe · *Himself*

Producers Jon Magnusson, Graham Stuart **Writers** Various, including Graham Norton, David Quantick, Jon Magnusson, Jane Bussmann **Theme Music** 'History Repeating' by The Propellerheads Featuring Miss Shirley Bassey (a No. 7 hit in October 1997) was the theme tune to *So Graham Norton*. For *V Graham Norton*, it was replaced by a Turkish-type tune reminiscent of 'Kiss Kiss' by Holly Valance, but not enough for them to need a payout on it.

When Graham Norton first popped up on our TV screens as a hyper-happy priest in Channel 4 comedy ***Father Ted***, few people could have anticipated just how much of a star he'd become. For six solid years, Graham became *the* face of a whole TV network, shoring up Channel 4's schedules with a combination of quirky Irish charm and downright filth.

Graham's first chat show, *So Graham Norton*, was transmitted late on Friday nights. Each edition would begin with Graham doing a bit of stand-up material for the studio audience, normally including extremely topical jokes about celebrity gossip that had recently been in the papers, or referring to storylines from trendy television programmes – an early precursor to the type of entertainment that seems to dominate schedules in this *Heat* magazine era of broadcasting. Graham would then run into his studio audience and play a game with them, ordering 'Everybody up!' onto their feet. People had to 'stay standing' if they had a particularly embarrassing secret in their past. Astonishingly, people seemed perfectly at ease with talking about horrific scatological incidents or sexual misfortunes on national television – testament, perhaps to Graham's cheeky yet non-threatening persona.

Then Graham would invite on his special guests – normally two, one each side of the commercial break. The very first edition set the tone for the kind of guests who would frequent the show – American celebrity rich wife Ivana Trump, and beloved British sitcom goddess/serious thespian Kathy '***Gimme Gimme Gimme***' Burke. Graham would often delight in finding a website or somebody somewhere in the world who had an oddball connection to his special guests. One particularly memorable moment featured Graham telephoning (via the adorably cute 'Doggyphone' – a stuffed toy dog with a phone in its belly) a gentleman with a fetish for actresses who wore long-sleeved gloves in their starring roles. When the man discovered to his joy that Graham's guest was former ***Dynasty*** actress Joan Collins, he was in a state of utter joy. When Joan started describing over the phone the different gloves she used to wear on *Dynasty*, audible sounds of the gentleman's 'excitement' could be heard – much to the shrieking delight of the studio audience.

A regular guest on the programme was a lovely old lady called Betty, who had, in fact, been one of the canteen ladies when Graham was a student. Betty would be sent out to interview movie stars arriving for their red carpet premieres in Leicester Square, and would often turn up in a wig or silly costume as the punchline to a comedy sketch or audience-related game show. Another of Graham's regular collaborators/victims was muscular actor Miles O'Keeffe, the star of the 1981 Bo Derek 'classic' *Tarzan the Ape Man*, who played along quite marvellously as the object of Graham's adolescent lust now brought back in a camp celebration of his long and varied 'career'. After one guest appearance on the show, Graham proceeded to phone him up each week on the most tenuous of pretexts.

In total, five seasons of weekly shows were broadcast before Channel 4 experimented with the format and decided to 'strip' Graham's programmes five nights a week at 10 p.m. The show renamed itself *V Graham Norton* (V = Roman numeral for five), but the format remained much the same, even if the shorter half-hour timeslot and increased number of editions meant only one celeb guest for each programme. Although the programme was still entertaining, there was a definite feeling that Graham was risking over-exposure. Even a trip to New York for three months' worth of episodes didn't manage to rid the feeling that we'd seen much of what was going on before. Graham then announced two shock moves – a season of programmes (*The Graham Norton Effect*) recorded for the Comedy Central network in the USA (an attempt to crack the American market already aware of his work thanks to screenings of his earlier shows on BBC America); and even more shocking, the decision to quit the smut-friendly environs of late night Channel 4 for the family viewing heartland of Saturday night BBC One. Although Graham took a while to settle in to his role as host of *Strictly Dance Fever*, its rather sincere tone doesn't really fit well with Graham's mocking persona. It's hard to shake off the feeling that his own personal style is perhaps better suited for a channel and timeslot where he can revel in single entendres to the hilt.

Soap

Sitcom | Witt-Thomas-Harris for ABC (shown on ITV) | episode duration 25–50 mins | broadcast 13 Sep 1977–20 Apr 1981 (USA)

Regular Cast

Katherine Helmond · *Jessica Tate*
Robert Mandan · *Chester Tate*
Cathryn Damon · *Mary Campbell*
Robert Mulligan · *Burt Campbell*
Robert Guillaume · *Benson*
Jennifer Salt · *Eunice Tate*
Dana Canova · *Corrine Tate*
Jimmy Baio · *Billy Tate*
Arthur Peterson · *The Major*
Ted Wass · *Danny Dallas*
Billy Crystal · *Jodie Dallas*
Jay Johnson · *Chuck and Bob Campbell*
Roscoe Lee Browne · *Saunders*
Donnelly Rhodes · *Dutch*
John Byner · *Detective Donahue*
Rebecca Balding · *Carol David*
Dinah Manoff · *Elaine Lefkowitz*
Sal Viscuso · *Father Tim*
Gregory Sierra · *El Puerco*

Creator Susan Harris **Producers** Paul Junger Witt, Tony Thomas, Susan Harris **Writers** Susan Harris, Stu Silver, Dick Clair, Jenna McMahon, Barry Vigon, Danny Jacobson, Jordan Crittenden, Tony Lang **Theme Music** George Aliceson Tipton

Outrageous, controversy-provoking and barrier breaking in so many different ways, *Soap* was a sitcom that started off as a simple parody of ghastly American daytime soap operas that seem to go on and on without a single decent storyline or performance between them. Created by Susan Harris (who went on to equally massive success with ***The Golden Girls***), *Soap* attracted literally hundreds of thousands of complaints from 'concerned viewers' in America before the first episode had ever been screened – presumably they had been appalled by advance publicity that promised a comedy show filled to the brim with adultery, promiscuity, mob killings, homosexuals and smart-ass black servants. Little did they know, but *Soap* took all of these typical 'soapy' issues and kept twisting them until they popped, creating a programme that reinforced every soap opera viewer's hidden beliefs that what they'd been glued to for years was, in all truth, more than a little bit rubbish.

This is essentially the story of two sisters and their families. Jessica Tate is a dizzy, naïve woman married to hugely wealthy philanderer Chester. Together they have three children – flirty and loose-moraled daughters Eunice and Corrine and younger son Billy. Jessica's shell-shocked and insane old father (who still believes he's fighting World War Two) lives with them, and the Tates are looked after by their surly butler Benson, who never even attempts to conceal his utter contempt for Chester and the two girls. On the poor side of town lives Jessica's sister Mary, a widow who's recently got married to nervous and jumpy Burt Campbell. Mary's two sons live with them, mobster Danny and gay Jodie: Burt is appalled by both of these facts, primarily because he's never met anyone gay before, but also because Danny has worked out that Burt was the person who accidentally killed his father. Burt's son Chuck also moves into the house with them all, bringing along with him his permanent companion, a ventriloquist's dummy called Bob (who gets to say all of the rude and offensive things that Chuck would never dream of vocalising himself).

With such an over-the-top array of characters, the storylines themselves had to be equally extravagant. Sure enough, they were: Burt was abducted by aliens and replaced by an extraterrestrial replica – when Mary fell pregnant, she didn't know if Burt or an alien was the father of her child; Billy was brainwashed by an obscure religious cult; Corrine's baby was possessed by the Devil and took to flying around its bedroom before Jessica accidentally managed to exorcise the evil spirit; and Jodie managed to father a child despite being resolutely gay (the first regular gay character ever seen on prime-time American television). Part of the reason for the success and strength of the characters was the astounding performances delivered by the core cast, with Katherine Helmond's Jessica one of the greatest sitcom characters of all time and Billy Crystal making an entire film career for himself out of the part of confused gay Jodie. The other most memorable performer was Robert Guillaume, who played the Tates' first butler, Benson. So beloved by audiences was Benson that he was given his own spin-off series – shockingly titled ***Benson*** – that actually ran for longer than its parent show.

Soap finally came to an end after 92 half hours of jaw-dropping incidents and hilarity when producers realised that they'd poked just about as much fun at the conventions of the soap opera as they could manage without diluting the show through repetition. We wish that some genuine soap operas could have been as brave and called it a day rather than lingering on well beyond their 'best before' date.

Soldier, Soldier

Drama | Central for ITV | episode duration 50 mins | broadcast 10 Jun 1991–1997

Regular Cast
Holly Aird · *Corporal/Sergeant Nancy Thorpe/Garvey*
Jerome Flynn · *Lance Corporal/Corporal/Acting Sergeant Paddy Garvey*
Robson Green · *Fusilier/Lance Corporal Dave Tucker*
Gary Love · *Corporal/Sergeant Tony Wilton*
Rosie Rowell · *Donna Tucker*
Annabelle Apsion · *Joy Wilton*
Miles Anderson · *Lieutenant Colonel Dan Fortune*
Richard Hampton · *Reverend Simon Armstrong*
Sean Baker · *CSM Chick Henwood*
Susan Franklyn · *Juliet Grant*
Robert Glenister · *Colour Sergeant Ian Anderson*
David Haig · *Major Tom Cadman*
Cathryn Harrison · *Laura Cadman*
Melanie Kilburn · *Carol Anderson*
Samantha Morton · *Clare Anderson*
Gareth Parrington · *James Anderson*
Peter Wingfield · *Lieutenant Nick Pasco*
Lesley Vickerage · *Lieutenant/Captain Kate Butler/Voce*
Mo Sesay · *Fusilier Michael 'Midnight' Rawlings*
Mark Aiken · *Captain Andrew Beamish*
Simon Donald · *Major Bob Cochrane*
Angus Macfadyen · *Lieutenant Alex Pereira*
Lesley Manville · *Rachel Elliot/Fortune*
Denise Welch · *Marsha Stubbs*
Rob Spendlove · *CSM/RSM/Lieutenant Michael Stubbs*
Dorian Healy · *Captain/Major Kieran Voce*
William Ash · *Jack Stubbs*
Rakie Ayola · *Bernie Roberts*
Suzanne Burden · *Sandra Radley*
Robert Gwilym · *Lieutenant Colonel Nick Hammond*
Akim Mogaji · *Fusilier Luke Roberts*
Tara Simpson · *Sarah Stubbs*
Adrian Rawlins · *Major Tim Radley*
Ben Nealon · *Lieutenant/Captain Jeremy Forsythe*
Angela Clarke · *Colette Daly*
David Groves · *Fusilier Joe Farrell*
Debra Beaumont · *Sergeant Sally Hawkins*
John Bowe · *Lieutenant Colonel Ian Jennings*
Paterson Joseph · *Fusilier Eddie Nelson*
John McGlynn · *Major James McCudden*
Colin Salmon · *Colour Sergeant Dennis Ryan*
Tracy Whitwell · *Kelly Deeley*
Gabrielle Reidy · *Isabelle Jennings*
Danny Cunningham · *Fusilier Andy Butcher*
Shaun Dingwall · *Lance Corporal Steve Evans*
Duncan Bell · *Lieutenant Colonel Paul Philips*
Richard Dillane · *Sergeant Brad Connor*
Sophie Dix · *Captain Sadie Williams*
Dougray Scott · *Major Rory Taylor*
Fiona Bell · *Angela McCleod*
Ian Curtis · *Corporal Mark Hobbs*
Jonathan Guy Lewis · *Sergeant Chris McCleod*
Kate O'Malley · *Private Stacey Grey/Butcher*
Philip Bowen · *Lieutenant Colonel Mike Eastwood*
Kate Ashfield · *Cate Hobbs*
James Callis · *Major Tim Forrester*
Biddy Hodson · *2nd Lieutenant Samantha Sheridan*
Laura Howard · *Deborah Osbourne/Briggs*
Simon Sherlock · *Fusilier Mel Briggs*
Alison Skilbeck · *Dr Sarah Eastwood*

Creator Lucy Gannon **Producers** Ted Childs (executive), Chris Kelly, Christopher Neame, Ann Tricklebank **Writers** Lucy Gannon, Peter Barwood, Ann Brown, Jack Chaney, Ted Childs, James Clare, Len Collin, Bernadette Davis, Bill Gallagher, Rob Gittins, Billy Hamon, Patrick Harbinson, Mark Holloway, Jane Hollowood, Michael Jenner, Julian Jones, Chris Lang, Garry Lyons, Roy MacGregor, Jesse Carr Martindale, Nicholas Martin, Richard McBrien, Jo O'Keefe, Chris Ould, Shaun Prendergast, James Quirk, Robert Smith, Sam Snape, Simon Andrew Stirling, Heidi Thomas **Theme Music** Jim Parker

Well regarded by the public and the professionals alike, *Soldier, Soldier* followed the fictional King's Fusiliers (and after amalgamations with another regiment, the King's Own Fusiliers) on their various tours of duty around the world – Hong Kong, New Zealand, Germany, Cyprus and Australia. For the first five series, the story revolved around mischievous best friends Paddy and Tucker – Robson Green (***Casualty***) and Jerome Flynn (***Between the Lines, London's Burnin***), with Paddy's girlfriend/wife Nancy, a military policewoman, often struggling to keep him on the straight and narrow while Tucker's wife Donna humiliates him with her loose morals. They were good blokes who women could idolise and men could imagine enjoying a pint with. But among the horse-play and shenanigans was a serious tale to be told. With the British army facing major reshuffles in real life, the series examined the effect of these changes on the men who'd often assumed they were in a job for life, or at least assumed, before the end of the Cold War, that the British Army had a clearly defined place on the world stage. Lives are lost and friendships betrayed along the way.

An episode that required Paddy and Tucker to sing 'Unchained Melody' at a wedding reception led to demands for their recording to be released as a single. Though Flynn and Green were reluctant, the persuasive powers of pop guru Simon Cowell eventually compelled them to record the song in May 1995; it got to No. 1, the first of three chart-toppers for the duo. At its peak, the series attracted over 16 million viewers.

Some Mothers Do 'Ave 'Em

Sitcom | BBC One | episode duration 30–50 mins | broadcast 15 Feb 1973–25 Dec 1978

Regular Cast
Michael Crawford · *Frank Spencer*
Michele Dotrice · *Betty Spencer*

Creator/Writer Raymond Allen **Producers** Michael Mills, Sydney Lotterby **Theme Music** Another masterpiece from 70s sound superstar Ronnie Hazlehurst

Frank Spencer is, by and large, a rather happy man. After all, he's got a lovely wife in Betty, and as time goes by he gets a gorgeous little daughter Jessica to complete his family. Unfortunately, life isn't very kind to him: if things can possibly go wrong, then they will. If any kind of implausible disaster is going to impact on any specific individual, then fate will definitely single Frank out to receive the full impact of any unpleasantness. Despite being seemingly cursed by bad luck, Frank manages to maintain a positive outlook, happy to count his blessings and look on the bright side. Betty, meanwhile, is supportive of her husband, fretting and worrying about the rotten hand of cards that life has dealt them both, but still deeply in love with Frank in spite of his quirks, idiosyncrasies and generally wimpy and effete behaviour.

Frank Spencer is a TV character whose longevity and fame have way surpassed the programme that spawned him. Most people are shocked to discover that there were only ever three seasons and three specials of *Some Mothers Do 'Ave 'Em* broadcast, totally just 22 episodes. It's down to the amazingly distinctive performance by Michael Crawford that even today, nearly 30 years since the last sighting of Frank Spencer on TV, impressionists up and down the country can still be guaranteed a laugh simply by putting a raincoat and a beret on and simpering 'Ooooh, Betty – the cat's done a whoopsie on the carpet!' Crawford's astonishing physical comedy came straight from the school of black and white cinema slapstick – no stunt was too outrageous or dangerous for Crawford to attempt himself. In fact, many of the most famous and memorable moments in the whole of *Some Mothers Do 'Ave 'Em* seemed to involve Crawford dangling off the outside of a moving train, precariously balanced on top of a car on the edge of a cliff, or careering underneath a lorry on a pair of roller-skates. Neither before nor after *Some Mothers Do 'Ave 'Em* has slapstick comedy been performed better on television – undoubtedly one of the reasons for its frequent and very welcome repeat runs.

Songs of Praise

Music | BBC One | episode duration 35 mins | broadcast 1 Oct 1961–present

Regular Cast
Alan Titchmarsh, Geoffrey Wheeler, Toyah Willcox, Kevin Woodford, Sally Magnusson, Diane-Louise Jordan, Huw Edwards, Jonathan Edwards, Eamonn Holmes, Aled Jones, Penelope Keith, Anne Kirkbride, Pam Rhodes · *Presenters*

Creators Stuart Hood, Donald Baverstock, John Morgan
Producers Various, including Norman Ivison, Maurice Maguire, R. Medwyn Hughes, Diane Reid

British television's longest-running 'God slot' came about due to a number of converging factors and various BBC heads realising what a nice idea it would be to have a weekly series that filmed hymns being sung in various churches and cathedrals around the country. Mocked by many (including ***The Vicar of Dibley***) for its shots of pews full to bursting point with people wanting to get on the telly, it nevertheless provides comfort to those concerned by statistics that claim fewer people than ever are attending church of any kind. The series has also offered viewers the chance to choose some of their favourite hymns in special compilation shows such as *Songs of Praise Choice* and, from 1984, *Praise Be*, in which Thora Hird spoke to the viewers like dearly loved old friends. The music might not be to everyone's tastes, but when a show tries so hard to be uplifting in times of strife, you've got to be really hard-hearted not to be slightly moved.

The Sooty Show

See pages 688–9

The Sopranos

See pages 690–3

Sorry!

Sitcom | BBC One | episode duration 30 mins | broadcast 12 Mar 1981–10 Oct 1988

Principal Cast
Ronnie Corbett · *Timothy Lumsden*
Barbara Lott · *Phyllis Lumsden*
William Moore · *Sidney Lumsden*
Marguerite Hardiman · *Muriel*
Roy Holder · *Frank*
Wendy Allnutt · *Jennifer*
Bridget Brice · *Pippa*

Creator/Writers Ian Davidson, Peter Vincent **Producer** David Askey **Theme Music** Gaynor Colbourn and Hugh Wisdom

Timothy Lumsden is a shy, easily embarrassed man who finds it very difficult to speak to members of the opposite sex. This is unfortunate, because at heart he's bright, sensitive and good company to be around. The reason for Timothy's bumbling nature around women is because of one factor – his domineering, monstrous, control freak of a mother, Phyllis. Timothy still lives at home with his parents, unlike his sister Muriel, who's managed to get away from the overbearing oppressive Phyllis. Timothy's father Sidney is no use either, a proverbial doormat who's regularly trampled over by Phyllis's nannying, controlling ways. Every time that it looks as though Timothy might find some kind of happiness, Phyllis uses emotional blackmail, bullying and manipulative techniques to get Timothy to come running back to her apron strings.

Continued on page 694

The Sooty Show

Sweep the dog and Sooty the bear.

There are many contenders for 'Best TV Bear': Paddington, the marmalade-craving Peruvian; Rupert, inhabitant of Nutwood; Gentle Ben, who miraculously was never put to sleep for mauling a child . . . but with nearly 50 series, the most enduring of the lot is a small yellow hand-puppet bear with black ears called Sooty. Electrical engineer and part-time conjurer Harry Corbett (nephew of legendary fish-and-chips king Harry Ramsden) bought him in 1948 for 7s 6d from a shop on Blackpool Pier. He named him 'Teddy' and soon added him to his stage act, which at the time was limited to appearances at shows in the Yorkshire region near his home in Guiseley. It was Corbett's wife, Marjory, who christened the bear Sooty after Corbett had given him little black ears using soot from the fireplace. Starting out as a guest on the show, Sooty soon became a permanent part of Corbett's act as he cannily realised the bear was getting bigger laughs than he was getting on his own. Sooty gained his own miniature conjuring table and took over as the magician, with Corbett 'relegated' to the role of assistant. All the while, the bear remained silent to audiences, only ever whispering his instructions to Harry.

All of this had been a sideline for Harry, who was still working as an electrical engineer by day. But in 1952 he went full time into show business and after an appearance on the variety show *Talent Night* he bagged a regular guest slot for himself and Sooty on the TV show *Saturday Special*, which starred Peter Butterworth. The duo made appearances on other programmes at the time, including *Whirligig* and *Sugar and Spice*, but finally, in 1955 they won their own BBC TV show, thanks to Frieda Lingstrom, the matriarch behind *Watch with Mother*. *The Sooty Show* was set in Sooty's own magic shop, where Corbett would come to visit and inevitably leave soaked by Sooty's water pistol or beaten by collapsing props. Each show would end with a deflated Corbett saying 'Bye bye everybody. Bye bye.' Sooty founded his own Magic Circle, a fan club where kids could learn basic magic tricks (Corbett later handed over the club to the National Children's Homes organisation as a lucrative fundraiser).

Children's Puppetry
BBC TV/Thames and Granada for ITV
Episode Duration: 20–25 mins
Broadcast: 16 Jan 1955–present

Regular Cast
Harry Corbett, Matthew Corbett, Richard Cadell, Liana Bridges · *Presenters*
Marjorie Corbett, Connire Creighton, Brenda Longman · *Voice of Soo*
Eva Gray · *Portia du Pont*

Creator Harry Corbett

Writers Harry Corbett, Matthew Corbett, Peter Corey

By 1957, Sooty had been joined by Sweep, a squeaky-voiced spaniel who, in Corbett's words, was 'as thick as a brick'. Sweep was fond of the xylophone, which was odd for a dog, and bones, which was not. In 1964, Sooty gained a girlfriend, a panda called Soo, though being children themselves the romance was chaste, especially with Soo being so disapproving of everything the boy puppets did. Soon, Corbett had a whole menagerie on his hands with characters like Butch, a gruff bulldog who terrified Sweep, Kipper the cat and a snake called Ramsbottom who sported a strong Yorkshire accent.

When Paul Fox became controller of BBC One, he cleared out many 'old favourites' that he felt were past their best. So 1967 saw *The Sooty Show* cancelled. Harry Corbett took the decision hard – he and his wife considered Sooty to be part of the family. Corbett's love for the bear might have gone to extremes (keeping him in a box with air-holes, for example), but his tenderness and conviction that Sooty was real helped children believe it too. Luckily, the bear was offered a new home on ITV, thanks to a deal with Thames which eventually saw him in colour on telly for the first time (in fact, some viewers wouldn't have been aware that Sooty was yellow, especially if they bought the annuals, which depicted him in black and white on the covers).

When Harry suffered a heart attack on Christmas Eve 1975, it could well have been the end for Sooty and his friends. Eventually, his youngest son Matthew (an actor and performer on ***Rainbow***) took on the role of Sooty's stooge, though it was not without a struggle as Harry Corbett's family had to force him to accept he was simply too old now for the rigours of TV production. A compromise was reached where Harry was allowed to be Sooty's carer for the roadshows while Matthew remained his TV companion. In 1976, the same year that Matthew bought the rights to Sooty from his father for £35,000, Harry was presented with an OBE by the Queen, along with a miniature version for Sooty himself.

Matthew's approach to the series was much more manic and physical than his father's. A Frank Spencer for kids, the gentle splashes of a water pistol and soft flumps of custard pies were not enough for him; regularly seen hanging from the rear of a moving vehicle or thrown into the nearest lake, the younger Corbett became as much a part of the tomfoolery as the puppets, which was probably what helped him win over the audience. For two generations of children, it was Matthew who was the Sooty man.

Harry Corbett died on 17 August 1989, aged 71. His legacy as a children's entertainer is that since his first appearance on TV in 1952, Sooty has been in almost constant demand. When Thames lost their franchise in 1992 and were forced to drop the series, Granada stepped in and produced *Sooty & Co*, and the sale of the series in 1996 to Japanese-owned merchant bank Guinness Mahon for more than £1.4 million led to an animated series (*Sooty's Amazing Adventures*). From 2000, Sooty moved into the hotel industry with *Sooty Heights*. Though it ensured Sooty's continuation, the series brought one chapter of the saga to a close as Matthew Corbett handed over the reins to another performer, Richard Cadell. Corbett's final episode on the series was called 'Bye Bye, Everybody, Bye Bye'.

The Sopranos

The extended family of Tony Soprano (pictured, bottom right).

There's something seductive about the lifestyle of a gangster that has kept novelists, biographers and of course filmmakers in business since the year dot. Gangsters do what they want, have their own code of practice and an uncompromising approach to the resolution of conflict, and their appetite for food and sex is as admirable as it's repugnant. Two of the greatest films of the 1970s, Francis Ford Coppola's *The Godfather* parts I and II (1971 and 1974), depicted the upper echelons of the criminal underworld, on the cusp of transition from first-generation Sicilian emigrants to second-generation Italian-Americans.

In the world of the fictional gangster, the Corleone family was like royalty, consorting with politicians, heads of state, even the Pope. In Martin Scorsese's *Goodfellas* (1990), however, the stars are the foot soldiers, lower-ranking families who look after their districts like barons of old. It tells the the real-life story of Henry Hill, a former gangster who lived the mod lifestyle to the full before gang in-fighting led him to submit himself and his family to the witness protection programme. What made *Goodfellas* the definitive study of the life of a gangster was the attention to detail, the ritual of food and the inclusion of the immediate family in the picture, elements that, *The Godfather* aside, tended to be forgotten.

When *The Sopranos* first aired in January 1999, it was understandably regarded by many as 'Goodfellas – the Series'. The same middle-ranking mobsters, the same appetite for sex, violence, food and drugs, and many shared cast members: Lorraine Bracco (Dr Melfi) was Oscar-nominated for her role as Henry Hill's wife, Karen; Michael Imperioli, who plays Christopher Moltisanti, was Spider, the waiter killed on a whim by Joe Pesci's character; Tony Sirico (Paulie) and Vincent Pastore ('Pussy') also appeared (and continuing the Martin Scorsese connection, David Proval starred in Scorsese's film *Mean Streets*, 1973). There's also the shared sense of a family within a family. For the Italian-American mobster, the term 'family' means more than a husband's wife and children. Tony Soprano grew up in a closed community where everyone he associates with is family, including the hoods and career criminals who form his gang. Those gang members also show how the idea of being a gangster has been blurred by their depiction in the movies. Paulie is an old-school gangster who dresses the part with wing-collar shirts and immaculate suits. Silvio does impressions of Al Pacino and believes that *The Godfather* parts I and II and *Goodfellas* are the best films ever made (they don't rate *The Godfather Part III* (1990), though – and who does?). Christopher Moltisanti is Tony's cousin, a young turk in the business. Though eager to climb the ladder to become Tony's successor (no-one, least of all Tony, thinks that his son AJ would ever make the grade), Christopher also harbours ambitions of becoming a screenwriter. His hopes of becoming the next Tarantino are dashed, however; instead, he ends up a junkie with a serious drug habit and a destructive attitude towards his long-suffering girlfriend Adriana (whose dog he accidentally kills when he falls asleep on it in a drug-fuelled haze one night) and to everyone in general. No wonder that the FBI decide to target Adriana as an informer . . .

Creator David Chase's own experience in therapy led him to wonder how a mobster might respond to the process, and how it might inform him of the motivations for the relationships around him. While the timing of the series was unfortunate – Robert De Niro was appearing in cinemas with *Analyse This*, a comedy based around the same concept – it didn't diminish the impact of *The Sopranos* one bit. While De Niro was mugging for laughs, Tony Soprano was dealing with the one part of life that can often be the most complicated for a gangster – the family that you *don't* choose.

Tony Soprano lives in a world with a strict moral code – you do what you have to do to make your money, but never betray your friends and always remember that every gangster belongs to two families, one tied by blood, one by associations generations long. Tony grew up in this world. His father and uncle (Uncle Junior) had risen through the ranks to run one of the top families in New York and no-one ever questioned that Tony would inherit the family business when his uncle became too old. Living within this very close community gave him a strong sense of who he was, or at least who he should be, and a self-assurance that the answers to life's questions were almost always physical ones: if you want a woman, you have her; if you're hungry, eat; if someone crosses you, beat 'em up; if they cross you again, whack 'em. The idea that the psychological could have an effect upon the physical simply never occurred to anyone. But when Tony begins to suffer blackouts and a physical cause can't be found, his doctor refers him to a psychiatrist, Dr Jennifer Melfi.

The series begins with Tony's first reluctant visit to Melfi's office. It's clear from the outset that Tony is keeping things from her, such as his job (he claims unconvincingly to be in 'waste management') and the fact that his mother, Livia, is a soulless monster with no joy in her life and no intentions of allowing anyone else to have any (a notion that is borne out when Tony learns that she, his own mother, conspired to have him killed). The root of the problem appears to be

Drama
Brad Grey Television/Chase Films for HBO (shown on Channel 4)
Episode Duration: 60 mins
Broadcast: 10 Jan 1999–present

Recurring Cast
James Gandolfini · *Tony Soprano*
Edie Falco · *Carmela Soprano*
Michael Imperioli · *Christopher Moltisanti*
Lorraine Bracco · *Dr Jennifer Melfi*
Drea de Matteo · *Adriana La Cerva*
Dominic Chianese · *Corrado 'Junior' Soprano*
Steven Van Zandt · *Silvio Dante*
Tony Sirico · *Paulie 'Walnuts' Gualtieri*
Jamie-Lynn Sigler/DiScala · *Meadow Soprano*
Robert Iler · *Anthony 'AJ' Soprano Jr*
Nancy Marchand · *Livia Soprano*
Jerry Adler · *Herman 'Hesh' Rabkin*
John Ventimiglia · *Artie Bucco*
Kathrine Narducci · *Charmaine Bucco*
Vincent Pastore · *Salvatore 'Big Pussy' Bonpensiero*
Michael Santoro, Paul Schulze · *Father Phil Intintola*
Michael Rispoli · *Jackie Aprile*
Al Sapienza · *Mikey Palmice*
Oksana Babiy · *Irina*
Joe Badalucco · *Jimmy Altieri*
Vincent Curatola · *Johnny 'Sack' Sacramoni*
Frank Santorelli · *Georgie*
Frank Pando · *Agent Grasso*
Matt Servitto · *Agent Harris*
Richard Portnow · *Attorney Melvoin*
Lillo Brancato Jr · *Matt Bevilaqua*
Chris Tardio · *Sean Gismonte*
Steve Schirripa · *Bobby 'Bacala' Baccalieri*
Peter Bogdanovich · *Dr Elliot Kupferberg*
David Proval · *Richie Aprile*
Sharon Angela · *Rosalie Aprile*
Aida Turturro · *Janice Soprano*
Federico Castelluccio · *Furio Giunta*
Saundra Santiago · *Jean Cusamano*
Joseph R. Gannascoli · *Vito Spatafore*
Dan Grimaldi · *Patsy Parisi*
Toni Kalem · *Angie Bonpensiero*
Maureen Van Zandt · *Gabriella Dante*
Denise Borino · *Ginny Sack*
George Loros · *Raymond Curto*
Richard Maldone · *Albert Barese*
Max Casella · *Benny Fazio*
Patrick Tully · *Noah Tannenbaum*
Jason Cerbone · *Jackie Aprile Jr*
Joe Pantoliano · *Ralph Cifaretto*
Annabella Sciorra · *Gloria Trillo*
Carl Capotorto · *Little Paulie Germani*
Lola Glaudini · *Agent Deborah Ciccerone*
Robert Funaro · *Eugene Pontecorvo*
Steve Buscemi · *Tony Blundetto*

TRIVIA

Steven Van Zandt, who plays Silvio, the Pacino-impersonating mobster, was a musician before becoming an actor. In the 1970s and 1980s, he was known as 'Little Steven', guitarist with Bruce Springsteen and the E-Street Band.

When Nancy Marchand died shortly before series three, the producers decided to re-create her with computer graphics for one episode shortly before Livia Soprano was to die. The scene skilfully combined existing footage of the actress in character with clever editing to let Livia interact with her usual dismissiveness: 'I wish the Lord would take me now . . .' The very next scene, Livia, dear. The very next scene . . .

a family of ducks that had recently been living in the Soprano family swimming pool but have now flown away. Tony's daughter Meadow is on the verge of leaving for university and his son is a listless academic plodder with no skills, but Tony either won't or can't see the connection between his own family and the ducks. Nevertheless, he makes his second appointment and so begins a love-hate relationship with Melfi.

Carmela Soprano has the perfect life, a beautiful house, two great kids and a husband who spoils her rotten. But the suppressed awareness of where the money has come from to pay for her luxuries – and the knowledge that each of Tony's presents in some way alleviates his own guilt for cheating on her time and time again – leaves her feeling emotionally empty. It's not that Carmela necessarily judges Tony for his chosen career – she knew about that before she married him, and as her actions in obtaining a reference for Meadow's university application show, she's not averse to using her husband's reputation to get what she wants. But with the kids grown up and Tony spending less and less time at home, she longs to feel appreciated. A brief affair with a local priest leaves her feeling used after she discovers she's not the only bored housewife he favours, while a mutual attraction between her and one of Tony's men, the taciturn Furio, ends with the latter returning to Sicily rather than give in to their desires. Realising that Tony will never remain faithful for long, and concerned for the family's future, Carmela decides to push him towards providing an investment for her future . . .

As some of Tony's flashbacks reveal, it's not easy being a Soprano kid. When Tony was young he saw his dad viciously beating another man after following him one day. That's how he learned what his father really did for a living. Tony's children are of the MTV generation; everything they know about life comes from the media. A news report first alerts Meadow to her father's other life. Though he initially lies about it when she asks him straight out if he's a gangster, he's impressed that his daughter is mature enough to ask him outright, just as Meadow admits that some of her friends had realised what his job was and think it's kind of cool (he could after all be a lawyer or something boring like that). In contrast, the youngest Soprano child, AJ, has no direction or sense of purpose. When he shows some skill on the football pitch, he discovers with horror that his father's blackouts are hereditary.

Unlike most American dramas, which tend to churn out episode after formulaic episode, *The Sopranos* dishes out half-seasons of well-served, high-quality fare.

In contrast to the stereotype for American TV shows, *The Sopranos* is often quite ponderous, taking its time and allowing scenes to last. (One scene in the first series shows Tony taking his prescribed medication for the first time. As they begin to take effect and his mind turns numb, he sits in his shower blankly as we hear 'White

Rabbit' by Jefferson Airplane played all the way through.) Occasionally, events step outside the ultra-realism of the ongoing story to show us Tony's fantasies and nightmares. This might be a dream where he's having energetic sex with the wife of a Sicilian Godfather while dressed as a Roman soldier, or, at the close of the second season, when a bout of food poisoning causes him to hallucinate conversations with Pussy, his former friend whom Tony killed after realising he'd been speaking to the FBI in return for his own freedom.

Unlike most American dramas, which tend to churn out episode after formulaic episode, *The Sopranos* dishes out half-seasons of well-served, high-quality fare. It has been one of HBO's biggest successes in recent years (and one of the leading champions of American drama that challenge the notion that British television is the best in the world), yet surprisingly, for a show about characters prone to excess, David Chase has always made sure to leave us wanting more. With season five ending with Tony and Carmela on the wrong side of marital breakdown and the Feds and rival gangs closing in on him, the long wait for season six was almost too much to bear . . .

Robert Loggia · *Michele 'Feech' La Manna*
Frank Vincent · *Phil Leotardo*
Ray Abruzzo · *Little Carmine Lupertazzi*

Producers David Chase, Brad Grey, Robin Green, Mitchell Burgess, Ilene S. Landress, Terence Winter, Henry J. Bronchtein (executive), Matthew Weiner, Martin Bruestle, Gianna Smart, Scott Hornbacher

Writers David Chase, Mark Saraceni, Jason Cahill, James Manos Jr, Frank Renzulli, Mitchell Burgess, Robin Green, Joe Bosso, Terence Winter, Todd A. Kessler, Michael Imperioli, Lawrence Konner, Salvatore J. Stabile, David Flebotte, Matthew Weiner, Michael Caleo, Toni Kalem

Theme Music 'Woke Up This Morning', performed by Alabama 3 (despite the name, the band hail from Brixton, south London)

Although Ronnie Barker had enjoyed several sitcom successes during his tenure on ***The Two Ronnies*** (such as ***Porridge*** and ***Open All Hours***), it took until 1981 for his comedy partner to achieve a similar hit. *Sorry!* was at times a painful comedy to sit through, with viewers aghast that a grown man would ever enable himself to be treated so badly by his own mother. Ronnie Corbett had shown his acting ability time and time again throughout *The Two Ronnies*, and *Sorry!* finally gave him the opportunity to shine on his own. It even gave the country a short-lived new catchphrase – 'Language, Timothy!' – which was bellowed by his mother and father whenever he dared to utter the slightest of expletives. Forty-two episodes were made, until finally Timothy mustered the courage to stand up to his mother, finally making a life for himself with girlfriend Pippa.

The South Bank Show

Documentary | LWT for ITV | episode duration 50–90 mins | broadcast 14 Jan 1978–present

Cast

Various, including Melvyn Bragg, Richard Hoggart, Germaine Greer, Tina Brown, Paul Gambaccini, David Liddiment

Theme Music 'Variations', Andrew Lloyd Webber's reworking of Paganini's 24th Caprice, originally performed by Andrew's brother Julian. The opening titles sequences have incorporated many iconic images, but they always conclude with the spark of electricity between two fingers – inspired by Leonardo Da Vinci's ceiling in the Sistine Chapel.

In the 16th and 17th centuries, London's South Bank was thought to be the disreputable part of the city – the perfect place to build theatres when such a practice was outlawed within the city walls. Now, we might think of it as the home of the National Film Theatre, the Royal Festival Hall and an IMAX cinema. For nearly 40 years it's also been the name of ITV's fourth-longest-running programme, after ***Coronation Street***, ***Emmerdale*** and the *News*.

Arriving in 1978 with a programme about Paul McCartney, Germaine Greer and Gerald Scarfe, *The South Bank Show* replaced ITV's previous arts slot, *Aquarius*. Though Melvyn Bragg is most closely associated with the series he's by no means the only person to have fronted it. Having previously hosted the BBC's *Lively Arts* series, Bragg moved to ITV and stayed there, presenting a show with one of the widest remits in broadcasting. Everything is art, so therefore everything is a fair subject for discussion, whether that be the work of David Hockney, a stage production about a serial killer, a rock band or a soap opera. Subjects have included Ken Dodd, Harold Pinter, Billy Connolly, Francis Ford Coppola, ***Coronation Street***, Talking Heads, Akira Kurosawa, Elvis Costello, Catherine Cookson, Francis Bacon, the Darkness, the TV work of Jimmy McGovern, Kay Mellor, Alan Bleasdale and Paul Abbott, ***The Sopranos***, Steve Coogan and Craig David, to name but a very few.

South Park

Adult Animation | Baniff for Comedy Central (shown on Channel 4) | episode duration 25 mins | broadcast 13 Aug 1997–present (USA)

Voice Cast

Trey Parker · *Stan Marsh, Eric Cartman, Mr Herbert Garrison, Mr Mackey, Philip Niles Argyle, Satan, Tom the News Reporter, Timmy, Randy Marsh, Grandpa Marvin Marsh, Miss Diane Choksondik, Officer Barbrady, Big Gay Al, Jimmy Swanson, God, Additional Voices*

Matt Stone · *Kyle Broslofski, Kenny McCormick, Jimbo Kearn, Terrance Henry Stoot, Pip Pirrup, Token Williams, Leopold 'Butters' Stotch, Tweek, Gerald Broslofski, Saddam Hussein, Stuart McCormick, Jesus Christ, Priest Maxi, Additional Voices*

Shannen Cassidy, Mona Marshall, Eliza Schneider · *Principal Victoria, Liane Cartman, Sharon Marsh, Sheila Broslofski, Mrs McCormick, Nurse Gollum, Wendy Testaberger, Mrs Crabtree, Additional Voices*

Isaac Hayes · *Jerome 'Chef' McElroy*

Creators Trey Parker and Matt Stone **Producers** Anne Garefino, Brian Graden, Deborah Liebling, Trey Parker, Matt Stone (executive), Jennifer Howell, David Niles White, Frank C. Agnone II **Writers** Various, including Trey Parker, Matt Stone, David Goodman, Nancy Pimental **Theme Music** Sung by Les Claypool from the band Primus, accompanied by Matt and Trey as members of the cast

Every day, millions of email boxes around the world ping with excitement because someone's decided to send a joke round to their friends. Sometimes it's a piece of brilliant viral marketing, such as the infamous John West Salmon advert with a man wrestling with a grizzly bear for its fish; sometimes it might be a clip of something so gross you hope they haven't sent it to your mother. Very rarely does the content of those emails lead to a multi-million-dollar TV franchise that sets out to offend pretty well everyone.

In 1991, film students at the University of Colorado Matt Stone and Trey Parker created a crude animated short film in which a little boy made of geometric pieces of coloured paper constructs a monstrous snowman that ends up being decapitated by the halo of the baby Jesus. The film began doing the rounds and by 1995 had reached the desks of executives at Fox who, flushed with the success of ***The Simpsons***, commissioned Trey and Matt to create an animated Christmas card for them. 'The Spirit of Christmas', made in the same style as their first film, featured Jesus and Santa coming to an understanding about the meaning of Christmas. It was then that the internet took control as the video began surging through the information superhighway like hormones through a teenager. But in the event it was Comedy Central and not Fox who commissioned the boys to make their first series, which, thanks to advances in technology, was deliberately animated to look as if it had been made out of coloured paper.

The episodes revolve around a group of young boys, Stan Marsh, Kyle Broflovski, Kenny McCormick and Eric Cartman. Kenny's dialogue is mumbled throughout as he wears the hood of his coat over his mouth – and good job too because everything he says would give the censors panic attacks (example: the opening title music has him mumbling either 'I like girls with big fat titties; I like girls with big vaginas' or 'I have got a ten-inch penis; use your mouth to help me clean it' – no, we're not joking). Kenny comes from a poor family and, in the early series, each episode would build to the point when Kenny is killed – horrifically, often with rats rushing in to eat his eyeballs. While this prompts Stan to cry: 'Oh my God, they killed Kenny!' and Kenny to follow with 'You bastards!' the incident is almost always forgotten by the next episode as Kenny is revived and the status quo returns to normal. We might feel sorry for Kenny and trying to decipher his Tourette's syndrome-peppered speech makes for fun late-night viewing, but it's Eric Cartman who's the show's real star. Cartman is fat, greedy, thoroughly spoilt and guilty of every kind of 'ism' you can think of. He's part of a heritage of comic characters that hark back to Archie Bunker for American viewers and Alf Garnet for us Brits. He's funny because he's so very wrong, although the sight of him briefly transformed into a Thai prostitute ('Love you long-time five dollar') has left its scars.

There are many similarities to *The Simpsons* – although its animation and humour are both much cruder – and it's a debt that Parker and Stone acknowledge regularly (one entire episode sees adorable semi-regular character Butters plotting to take over South Park only to be told with mounting frustration that his every idea has already been done by *The Simpsons*). The biggest connection between both shows is that know where they sit politically, and the biggest difference is that *South Park*'s team rarely pull their punches. The name 'Barbra Streisand' is reduced to the worst swearword in Cartman's profanisauros; Ben Affleck is revealed to have been the missing son of a couple who have 'asses' for faces; heiress Paris Hilton is forced to crawl head first to freedom via a sex-slave's anal canal; Bill Clinton is revealed to have slept with Cartman's mom – along with every other man in South Park; and in 'The Passion of the Jew', Mel Gibson's *The Passion of the Christ* (2004) is slated by Stan ('That wasn't a movie. That was a snuff film!'). Those celebs that the team take to aren't treated that much better: while the real Robert Smith of the Cure gets to battle the Mecha-Streisand, George Clooney's contribution to the series was in creating the woofs and growls for a gay dog.

Almost no topic is taboo, which means that the funniest episodes each year are the ones where they go another step beyond too far. Yet it's not all just for the sake of shock value; these episodes have a strong moral point to make, even if it's just 'don't accept what they tell you at face value'. One episode discusses the issue of stem-cell research by having *South Park*'s two disabled kids, Timmy and Jimmy, challenge Christopher Reeve's claims that stem-cell research should benefit people like him when he's not been disabled all his life (and therefore not 'pure' in his disability like they themselves are). It's a very contentious issue and even the *South Park* regulars (and by proxy the writers) instantly distance themselves from the debate, as if it were questionable to have brought it up in the first place. Possibly the most extreme example of pushing an issue to its limits comes in the fourth series, in which Cartman abandons his friends to seek out more mature company only to find himself the poster boy for NAMBLA – the (terrifyingly real) North American Man/Boy Love Association. Before the protests begin, though, the programme is quite clear which side of the fence it sits on regarding this issue. Stan tells a NAMBLA representative: 'I know the Founding Fathers fought for equality and all, but with all due respect, f— you!'

In 1999 came the *South Park* movie *Bigger, Longer and Uncut*. We don't think we're exaggerating when we say it's one of the greatest films made in our lifetimes, exposing the crassness and hypocrisy of governments and religious organisations who want to stamp out bad language while sponsoring wars. It's a point made by an attack on Canadian entertainers Terrence and Phillip who inadvertently instigate a war between Canada and the USA because of the effect their film has on Cartman's 'fragile little mind'. That the film is an intricate pastiche of the dreary musical version of *Les Misérables* diminishes its power not one jot.

Trivia

Chef, who serves food to the children at South Park elementary school, is voiced by Isaac Hayes, the man who sang 'The Theme from Shaft' in 1971 ('You're damn right!'). As Chef, Hayes also voiced 'Chocolate Salty Balls (PS I Love You)', an innuendo-riddled No. 1 single, in December 1998.

Space: 1999

Science Fiction | Group Three/ITC/RAI for ITV | episode duration 50 mins | broadcast 4 Sep 1975–12 Nov 1977

Regular Cast

Martin Landau · *Commander John Koenig*
Barbara Bain · *Dr Helena Russell*
Barry Morse · *Professor Victor Bergman*
Tony Anholt · *Tony Verdeschi*
Nick Tate · *Captain Alan Carter*
Prentis Hancock · *Controller Paul Morrow*
Zienia Merton · *Sandra Benes*
Catherine Schell · *Maya*
Clifton Jones · *David Kano*
John Hug · *Bill Fraser*
Anton Phillips · *Dr Bob Mathias*
Suzanne Roquette · *Tanya Alexandria*
Yasuko Nagazumi · *Yasko*
Barbara Kelly · *Voice of Moonbase Alpha Computer*

Creators Gerry and Sylvia Anderson **Producers** Sylvia Anderson, Fred Freiberger **Writers** George Bellak, Christopher Penfold, Art Wallace, Johnny Byrne, David Weir, Edward di Lorenzo, Anthony Terpiloff, Elizabeth Barrows, Jesse Lasky Jr, Pat Silver, Bob Kellett, Donald James, Tony Barwick, Keith Miles, Thom Keyes, Charles Woodgrove, Lew Schwartz, Jack Ronder, Terence Feely, John Goldsmith, Terrance Dicks, Pip and Jane Baker, Michael Winder **Theme Music** Season one's theme was by Barry Gray, while Derek Wadsworth wrote the replacement theme for series two.

By 1999, mankind has colonised the moon in the form of Moonbase Alpha, a massive base drilled deep into the moon's crust and capable – with regular supplies – of supporting over 300 lives. But on 13 September 1999, an explosion in a nuclear waste dump on the far side of the moon triggers a massive chain reaction that catapults it and its inhabitants out of Earth's orbit and into deep space. Hopelessly lost, Commander John Koenig and his staff must face the probability that they will never see Earth again, and instead begin the search for a new home.

It was during a meeting with TV mogul Lew Grade that Gerry Anderson, having just heard that his proposed second series of *UFO* had been cancelled, learned that he'd be spending the next couple of years working on a similar science fiction-based drama for Grade with a much bigger budget. Anderson had been responsible for a significant number of hit TV shows, mainly for children, and the despite blip in confidence caused by *UFO*'s lukewarm reception in the States, Grade knew he could rely on Anderson to deliver. With the head of ITC, Abe Mandell, insisting that the show had to be set somewhere other than Earth, Anderson revised his plans for *UFO* 2 (which he'd envisaged as featuring SHADO's moonbase to a greater extent anyway). Instead, the series would be set *entirely* on the moon, separated from Earth and roaming the outer reaches of known space.

Aware that the series, eventually named *Space: 1999*, would require support from American networks to achieve the funding it needed, Anderson began considering American stars for the leads. One such was Robert Culp, famous for his starring role in *I Spy* opposite Bill Cosby. But after just one meeting, it became clear that Culp was looking for greater creative involvement than just saying the lines and avoiding the furniture – indeed, he had dropped unsubtle hints that he would like to both write and direct the series. Anderson turned down that offer and instead approached well-known American actor Martin Landau to play the head of Moonbase Alpha, John Koenig. He was able to offer Landau's wife, Barbara Bain, the part of Dr Helena Russell (the pair were already familiar to TV audiences through their roles in the American series ***Mission: Impossible***). Though the couple would cost Anderson a hefty chunk of his budget, it was a worthwhile expense.

The rest of the regular cast echoed the international flavour that Anderson had worked towards with *UFO*, with Australian Nick Tate as Alan Carter and Zienia Merton as the Euro-Asian Sandra Benes, while the second season would see the addition of Tony Anholt (fresh from Anderson's ***The Protectors***) as Italian Tony Verdeschi and Yasuko Nagazumi as Yasko.

For the majority of Anderson's shows, the spacecraft, miniature sets and special effects had been the work of a team led by Derek Meddings. By the mid-1970s, Meddings was fully immersed in doing a similar job for the James Bond movies, so the task fell to Meddings' alumni Brian Johnson, who had worked on ***Thunderbirds*** and *UFO* as well as Stanley Kubrick's *2001: A Space Odyssey* (1968). From the nuclear explosion that kick-started the series to numerous lunar surface and deep-space shots, the model work on *Space: 1999* was nothing short of brilliant, with Johnson's cinematic approach perfectly matching the traditional Anderson feel for action sequences. At the heart of the show were the Eagles – lean, vaguely rectangular spacecraft with four chunky landing pads and an arrowhead cockpit. In the 1970s, these were reproduced as die-cast models by Dinky – one of the most sought-after toys of the decade.

The first series had been a success, but the American offices of ITC wanted a number of changes to make the show fit their market better. With Anderson and his wife having separated during the production of the first series, former ***Star Trek*** producer Fred Freiberger was brought in as producer. It was a decision that has since divided many fans. Those who loved the austere, serious first season of the show often feel it ruined the concept completely. Others love the way Freiberger somehow managed to thaw out Bain's performance (which she had chosen to deliberately underplay, but which gave her rather a wooden appearance in comparison with some of the characters rather more overplayed by guest actors) and lighten the mood so that the Alpha crew look like they'd settled into their surroundings. While he had every respect for Barry Morse, Freiberger disliked his character, Professor Bergman, an old man with an electronic heart. With Morse's agent haggling for more money, Professor Bergman was quickly forgotten and a new character introduced – the shape-changing Maya, played by the beautiful Catherine Schell in less-than-flattering make-up.

The title sequence of the first series originally featured a curious mix of iconic poses by the main cast and a series of *Thunderbirds*-style, fast-paced clips to summarise the episode. Sadly this too was ditched for the Freiberger season, in favour of a more stable series of space shots and computer banks intercut with shots of the cast in posed action sequences (Koenig firing a laser gun, Maya's eyes reflecting some of the exciting beasts she could turn into, Helena Russell looking vacant . . .).

An episode that really encapsulates the Freiberger approach is 'Brian the Brain', in which a sentient computer holds the moon to ransom in order to obtain fuel that will keep it 'alive' for ever. Despite the computer being voiced by Bernard Cribbins as (initially) a cute, mid-Atlantic robot of the kind you'd see on a kids' show, the episode is otherwise a lot of fun.

One of the most expensive ongoing series ever produced in the UK at that time, *Space: 1999* was ultimately too much of an investment to continue beyond a second series and was soon relegated to the position of Sunday afternoon schedule filler. But it had proven to be a timely show, drawing British children to the excitement of science fiction just in time for George Lucas's *Star Wars*, which hit cinema screens during *Space: 1999*'s second series.

Spaced

Sitcom | LWT/Paramount UK for Channel 4 | episode duration 25 mins | broadcast 24 Sep 1999–13 Apr 2001

Regular Cast
Simon Pegg · *Tim Bisley*
Jessica Stevenson · *Daisy Steiner*
Mark Heap · *Brian Topp*
Julia Deakin · *Marsha Klein*
Katy Carmichael · *Twist Morgan*
Nick Frost · *Mike Watt*
Peter Serafinowicz · *Duane Benzie*
Bill Bailey · *Bilbo*
Michael Smiley · *Tyres O'Flaherty*
Anne Wilson Jones · *Sarah*

Creators/Writers Jessica Stevenson, Simon Pegg **Producers** Humphrey Barclay, Tony Orsten, Lisa Clark executive), Gareth Edwards, Nira Park **Theme Music** Guy Pratt

When wannabe comic-book artist Tim is dumped by his long-term girlfriend Sarah, he's forced to find somewhere new to live. Similarly, writer Daisy wants to move out of her bedsit into somewhere nicer now that her boyfriend Richard has gone away to become a mature student. The two meet in a café while scouring through the accommodation listings in a newspaper, and they soon become good friends. Eventually they spot an advert for what seems to be an ideal two-bedroom flat, at 23 Meteor Street, Tufnell Park, north London. However, as the advert states that the landlady will only rent her flat out to a professional couple, Daisy and Tim decide to pretend to be an item in order to convince fearsome and rather odd Marsha to let the flat to them. Soon they move into Marsha's house and get to know both her (chain-smoker, heavy drinker, weird) and her other tenant Brian (artist, shy, creepy). Regular visitors to Tim and Daisy's flat included their best friends Twist (dizzy) and Mike (weapons-obsessed).

An outstanding comedy series with a huge cult following, *Spaced* felt like the first in an entirely new breed of sitcom. It wasn't the 'sit' that set it apart – dozens of comedies had already been screened that centred around mismatched housemates. No, it was the direction that set *Spaced* apart, more akin as it was to a fast-paced pop video than a traditional half hour comedy series. Dream sequences, montage, jump cuts and dozens of other innovative techniques added depth and texture to scripts that were already dripping with references to pop culture that were shared by viewers and the writers/stars Stevenson and Pegg. When Tim was revealed to be in shock as a result of having been traumatised by the awfulness of *Star Wars: The Phantom Menace* (1999), it was a gag that everyone of a certain age could empathise with. Indeed, the joke was even more subversive, considering that the loathsome character Duane Benzie (the man who Tim's girlfriend Sarah dumped him for) was played by Peter Serafinowicz, the man who provided the voice for Darth Maul in *The Phantom Menace*.

Sadly, only two seasons of *Spaced* have so far been produced, with many of the programme's key players branching out into successes of their own, such as Bill Bailey into ***Black Books*** and Peter Serafinowicz into ***Look Around You***. However, Simon Pegg's career has really hit the big time, having starred in the 'rom-zom-com' *Shaun of the Dead* (2004), a massive transatlantic hit horror movie, alongside fellow *Spaced* star (and real-life best mate) Nick Frost.

Spender

Drama | BBC One | episode duration 50 mins | broadcast 8 Jan 1991–29 Dec 1993

Regular Cast
Jimmy Nail · *DS Freddie Spender*
Berwick Kaler · *DS Dan Boyd*
Sammy Johnson · *Kenneth Norman 'Stick' Oakley*
Denise Welch · *Frances Spender*
Paul Greenwood · *Superintendent Yelland*
Peter Guinness · *DCS Gillespie*
Tony McAnaney · *Keith Moreland*
Siv Borg · *Astrid Moreland*
Dawn Winlow · *Laura Spender*
Lynn Harrison · *Kate Spender*
Amanda Redman · *Bobby Montgomery*
Christopher Fairbank · *Joe Phelan/John Ives*
Mickey Hutton · *'Spud' Tate*
David Telfer · *Det. Sergeant Colin Driver*
Maurice Roëves · *Mal Balmer*
Timothy Spall · *Robert Cunningham*
Kris Watson · *Vincent Hackett*
David Whitaker · *DS Terry Knowles*

Creator/Writers Ian La Frenais and Jimmy Nail **Producers** Steve Lanning, Martin McKeand, Paul Raphael **Theme Music** Tony McAnaney

When his partner is injured during a high-risk undercover operation in London, police officer Freddie Spender is relocated back home to Newcastle for his own safety. On one hand, at least that means he's not in immediate danger any more – well, not from criminals anyway. On the other hand, it means he's got the chance to catch up with his ex-wife Frances and his daughters Laura and Kate, at which point he really *could* be in serious trouble. Soon the 'one-off' assignment in Newcastle turns into a permanent relocation – can Spender really settle back into live up north? Thankfully, although Spender's been working with the Met for several years, he still has quite a few contacts on the streets, notably ex-bank robber Stick.

Following his major success as Oz in ***Auf Wiedersehen, Pet***, Jimmy Nail's next small-screen success was in a programme he was personally responsible for co-creating and writing (alongside *Auf Wiedersehen*'s Ian La Frenais), *Spender*. The programme was quite a departure from the kind of detective series that was prevalent on BBC One at the time – set in the murky and dangerous world of the undercover policeman, it was much grittier than most of the same kind of output. The show also benefited greatly from its distinct regional identity, with the Newcastle location and accents setting the programme apart from pretty much everything else on the television. Spender drew to a close after three seasons and a Christmas special – Jimmy Nail's next project would be the country music-influenced show *Crocodile Shoes*, which he once again was responsible for creating and writing.

Spitting Image

Comedy | Spitting Image/Central Production for ITV | episode duration 25–40 mins | broadcast 26 Feb 1984–18 Feb 1996

Principal Voice Cast
Chris Barrie, Rory Bremner, Steve Coogan, Hugh Dennis, Harry Enfield, Jon Glover, Alistair McGowan, Jessica Martin, Steve Nallon, Jan Ravens, Enn Reitel, Kate Robbins, John Sessions

Creators Peter Fluck and Roger Law, with Martin Lambie-Nairn
Producers John Lloyd, Jon Blair, Tony Hendra, Geoffrey Perkins, David Tyler, Bill Dare, Giles Pilbrow **Writers** Various, including Ian Hislop, Richard Curtis, Rob Grant, Doug Naylor, Nick Newman, Geoff Atkinson, Moray Hunter, Jack Docherty, Guy Jenkin, Tony Sarchent, Steve Punt, Alistair McGowan, John Coleman, Andrea Solomons, Laurie Rowley **Theme Music** Philip Pope

The most successful satire show of all time, *Spitting Image* ran for an amazing 141 episodes over 12 years, an amazing feat for a programme that was much more expensive and time-consuming to produce than traditional satire or impression-based programmes. Each week, caricaturists Roger Law and Peter Fluck would produce savagely unflattering puppet parodies of politicians, celebrities and royalty, and the country's leading impressionists would provide uncannily accurate voices to bring life to these foul creations. Scripts were written at the last minute, and several sequences would not be filmed until the last possible moment before transmission in order to incorporate topical gags about the stories in the news.

No individual was above being lampooned – including the Royal Family, who only a few years earlier had felt the love of the nation during the Queen's Silver Jubilee and the marriage of Charles to Diana. The last 'sacred cow' to be sacrificed on the rubber altar was the beloved Queen Mother, a move that caused outrage among the tabloid press, especially from the *Sun*, which had been trying for months to get a photo of the 'secret' puppet of the Queen Mum that *Spitting Image* had made. In fact, no such puppet had been created at all – eventually one *was* constructed (complete with Beryl Reid soundalike voice) simply to shut the *Sun* up. For the more ambitious or fame seeking, having a puppet of themselves appear on *Spitting Image* was a sign of 'having made it' – it's unlikely that many politicians working for the Thatcher government of the 1980s would have been anywhere near as well-known as they were without the tender ministrations of the *Spitting Image* team.

Speaking of the Iron Lady, her portrayal on *Spitting Image* was initially intended to mock her overly masculine style of leadership – however, many viewers saw this as confirmation of her strength and ability, leading the *Spitting Image* scriptwriters to gradually convert Mrs Thatcher into a manic, psychotic monster with mad, flashing red eyes. When John Major eventually succeeded Thatcher as Prime Minister, *Spitting Image*'s interpretation of a grey man only interested in peas undoubtedly coloured many people's perception of their new PM. Other politicians' careers were seemingly damaged by the series too – any perception that the partnership between the two leaders of the SDP/Liberal alliance was an equal one were quashed by *Spitting Image* portraying Liberal leader David Steel as a tiny, whining sycophant desperately trying to impress the much larger, suave David Owen of the SDP. The Labour Party's inadequacies weren't ignored either, with Michael Foot and later Neil Kinnock portrayed as bumbling dolts without any of the skills necessary to run the country.

Spitting Image didn't just make careers for politicians – it also launched impressionists and comedy performers like Harry Enfield, Chris Barrie (***Red Dwarf***), Jan Ravens (***Dead Ringers***) and Alistair McGowan. Special editions of *Spitting Image* centred on individual characters, such as US President Ronald Reagan (often portrayed as searching for his missing brain) and the fearsome Mrs T (Steve Nallon's uncanny impression becoming more famous than Thatcher's own voice). In the spirit of ***That Was The Week That Was***, most episodes would finish with a satirical musical number – some were so successful that they were blessed with a single release. The No. 1 hit 'The Chicken Song' (a parody of those ghastly summer sing-a-long hits like 'Agadoo') featured an anti-apartheid ditty called 'I've Never Met a Nice South African' on the B-side (charted in May 1986), and a special festive single called 'Santa Claus is on the Dole' reached No. 22 in December of the same year. One song wasn't played for laughs though – 'Every Bomb You Make', a deadly serious spin on the words of The Police's 'Every Breath You Take', once again satirising Mrs Thatcher's government, performed by Sting himself.

In the end, the loss of many of the big political personalities and the arrival of other satire- and impression-based shows meant that *Spitting Image* was simply no longer essential viewing, and it came to an end a year before Tony Blair's New Labour came to power. It would have been very interesting to see how the latex unlovelies of *Spitting Image* would have handled a whole new set of politicians and celebrities to lampoon.

Spooks

See pages 700–3

Star Cops

Science Fiction | BBC Two | episode duration 50 mins | broadcast 6 Jul–31 Aug 1987

Regular Cast
David Calder · *Nathan Spring, Voice of 'Box'*
Erick Ray Evans · *David Theroux*
Linda Newton · *Pal Kenzy*
Trevor Cooper · *Colin Devis*
Jonathan Adams · *Alexander Krivenko*
Sayo Inaba · *Anna Shoun*

Creator Chris Boucher **Producer** Evgeny Gridneff **Writers** Chris Boucher, Philip Martin, John Collee **Theme Music** 'It Won't Be Easy', composed and sung by Justin Hayward, formerly of The Moody Blues, a middle-of-the-road track which feels completely out of touch with the futuristic setting.

'Space Cops to Zap Dull Dr Who' declared one newspaper in 1986 ahead of *Star Cops'* transmission. It wasn't just the name of the show the article got wrong, sadly, as *Star Cops* turned out to be much more pedestrian than ***Doctor Who*** had been in even its most troubled times. The problem was that *Star Cops* was never intended to be a rival to the BBC's longest-running drama series, it was closer to a traditional police drama in structure, determined to avoid the clichés of monsters and ray guns.

Commander Nathan Spring is reluctant to take on a position with the International Space Police Force until his superiors make it difficult for him to refuse the offer. Nathan was bequeathed a talking digital assistant called 'Box' by his late father, an interesting device that pre-dates the PDAs and mobile phones we almost take for granted at the beginning of the 21st century but was still akin to ***Blake's 7***'s Orac back in 1987.

Spring soon becomes aware that anything he forgets to take with him into space could kill him, anything he did bring could kill him and anything that fails to work could kill him. One of the series' great strengths was this realisation of how claustrophobic and unsettling space living could be. Another was its range of characters, most of whom appeared more than mere sci-fi ciphers. Spring's second in command, David Theroux, was a smart-mouthed American with a love for film quotes, while other officers included Colin Devis, a rather tactless former copper with an impressive track record for failed marriages (though his chat-up line, 'I'm cuddly' does have its merits), and Pal Kenzy, a hot-headed Australian woman who as good as blackmails her way onto Spring's team and almost lives to regret it. Sadly, two other regular characters introduced during the short nine-week run were less credible – a humourless Russian called Alexander Krivenko and Anna Shoun, a Japanese Buddhist-cum-racial stereotype.

Star Cops took a logical approach to the kind of cases faced by Spring and his team. Unlike ***Star Trek***, with its warp drive and ability to get anywhere it needs to in the space of an hour, real thought was given to how current technology might progress within just 50 years and how this might affect society. For instance, an exploration vehicle in space suffers a power failure, rescue teams have to calculate whether they could reach the ship before its life support systems fail; this means that a crew could be declared legally dead while still alive, and if sabotage is suspected, the crew members could even assist in compiling evidence against their own technical murderer.

Designed as a ten-part series, one episode had to be dropped due to a BBC strike. Sadly, ratings for the series were pitifully and undeservedly low – supporting former BBC One controller Michael Grade's belief that science fiction simply wasn't popular in the UK at the time. Perhaps its heritage as the latest show in the tradition of ***Bergerac*** and ***Shoestring*** would have been a better strategy than to pitch it as a replacement for *Doctor Who*. It might not have been the action-packed thriller that the tabloids had been expecting, but it offered an intelligent and thought-provoking response to the sci-fi genre while also adding something to the great tradition of crime mysteries. Ratings aside, a second series would definitely have been welcome.

Website
www.geocities.com/thestarcopssite/

Star Trek

See pages 704–8

Star Trek: Deep Space Nine

Science Fiction | Paramount Television (shown on Sky One/BBC Two) | episode duration 45 mins | broadcast 3 Jan 1993–2 Jun 1999 (USA)

Regular Cast
Avery Brooks · *Commander Benjamin Sisko*
Nana Visitor · *Major Kira Nerys*
Rene Auberjonois · *Constable Odo*
Armin Shimerman · *Ferengi Quark*
Colm Meaney · *Chief Miles O'Brien*
Alexander Siddig (aka Siddig El Fadil) · *Dr Julian Bashir*
Cirroc Lofton · *Jake Sisko*
Continued on page 709

Spooks

Peter Firth as MI5 boss Harry Pearce.

MI5 – a world of secrets, intrigue and treachery; a world where you can go anywhere, be whoever you want to be and hopefully save your country from its enemies in the process. But as well as the excitement and danger of working under cover, there's also the routine, the office politics and the general air of insecurity and paranoia that comes with any day job. To us, they're spies, living in the underworld of the British establishment. Among themselves, they're known simply as 'spooks'.

Spooks arrived with appropriate stealth thanks to a cool campaign of trailers depicting schoolchildren discussing what their family members do for a living. One boy reluctantly confesses that his brother is a computer programmer. Boring, huh? Except we then see what his brother really does – covert operations for MI5 With the tagline 'MI5, not 9 to 5', *Spooks* had arrived to usurp Le Carré, sack ***The Professionals*** and give 007 his carriage clock. It was sexy, slick, dangerous . . . and broadcast about six months after ***24***.

It's a shame that *24* was first out of the gate (although both shows went into production at about the same time) as it meant some people decided to dismiss *Spooks* as a copy-cat (in fact if we're looking for a comparison, *The Professionals* is actually nearer the

Drama
Kudos for BBC One
Episode Duration: 50 mins
Broadcast: 13 May 2002–present

Regular Cast
Matthew MacFadyen · *Tom Quinn*
Keeley Hawes · *Zoe Reynolds*
David Oyelowo · *Danny Hunter*
Peter Firth · *Harry Pearce*
Jenny Agutter · *Tessa Phillips*
Esther Hall · *Ellie Simm*
Heather Cave · *Maisie Simm*
Hugh Simon · *Malcolm Wynn-Jones*
Graeme Mearns · *Jed Kelley*
Shauna Macdonald · *Sam Buxton*
Nicola Walker · *Ruth Evershed*
Megan Dodds · *Christine Dale*
Hugh Laurie · *Jools Siviter*
Natasha Little · *Dr Vicki Westbrook*
Lisa Faulkner · *Helen Flynn*
Rory MacGregor · *Colin Wells*
Rupert Penry-Jones · *Adam Carter*
Olga Sosnovska · *Fiona Carter*
Richard Harrington · *Will North*
Tim McInnerny · *Oliver Mace*
Anna Chancellor · *Juliet Shaw*

Creator David Wolstencroft

Producers Jane Featherstone, Stephen Garrett, Gareth Neame, Simon Crawford Collins, Julie Scott (executive), Alison Barnett, Andrew Woodhead

Writers David Wolstencroft, Simon Mirren, Howard Brenton, Steve Bailie, Mathew Graham, Ben Richards, Rupert Walters, Raymond Khoury

Theme Music Jennie Muskett

mark – they even use the same building as their base of operations, the Masonic Temple in Covent Garden). *24* and *Spooks* both use a split screen to deliver information at breakneck speed. The sheer volume of information imparted during one hour-long episode is such that it's easy to get lost in the drama and miss vital information. But while fans of each show love to deride each other, there's actually very little in common between the two programmes, other than a slight superficial resemblance and an involvement in the lives of the security services of the UK and America. *24* plays a long game and relies upon its real-time gimmick. *Spooks* tells multiple stories and can afford to dip into bigger issues without always having to link them into the story arc for the season.

Spooks came initially from production company Kudos, whose chief exec, Stephen Garrett, had looked at the way television tended to focus on the same 'precincts' for ideas – principally police stations and hospitals. Looking for a 'precinct' that was untapped, or at least a concept that hadn't been done to death on television in the last decade or so, Garrett realised that espionage hadn't really been explored much on television in the last 20 years – certainly not since the BBC's adaptations of Le Carré's ***Tinker, Tailor, Soldier, Spy*** and *Smiley's People* in the early 1980s. The more he thought about it, the more a modern approach to the security services appealed to him. Of particular interest was the idea of looking at people who lie professionally, something that other shows naturally didn't do. Unlike, say, a policeman or a medic, a spy cannot share anecdotes about their day job with loved ones. Their life in effect becomes a series of lies. After commissioning some initial research into the world of spies in general and MI5 in particular, Stephen approached David Wolstencroft to see if it was an idea he thought he could develop into a series. Entirely coincidentally, David had been developing a similar idea with a view to perhaps selling it as a feature film but in a way that departed from the usual James Bond/glamorous type and instead featured ordinary people who just happened to be spies.

For the first series that's exactly what *Spooks* was about, as Tom Quinn balanced his work life with his secret identity, Matthew Archer, a character who just happens to be heavily involved with a restaurateur called Ellie who has a young daughter, Maisie. The challenge for Tom therefore was to maintain a sense of having a normal life while simultaneously being a spy. When he's eventually forced to reveal his true identity, Ellie slowly accepts the idea until an IRA splinter group plant a bomb in their home: Tom's work thus puts the lives of his girlfriend and her daughter at risk.

Spooks remains one of the few intelligent, challenging dramas still in production that puts good storytelling over vanity stunt casting and easy choices.

That final episode of the first series, where Tom is locked out of his high-security home with Ellie and Maisie trapped inside, waiting

TRIVIA

When creator David Wolstencroft submitted the first script to the producers, he replaced his name on the front page with 'anonymous', simply as a joke to play with the idea of the characters' anonymity within the world he was creating. But the production team liked the idea so much they negotiated for the episodes to be shown without credits on their first BBC One screenings (the compromise was that they'd appear on the official website and on DVD releases). Since its third series, the preview screenings on BBC Three have in fact had credits at the end, but the BBC One screenings continue to drop them.

for the bomb to go off, left viewers on a horrifically cruel cliffhanger. When the second series began, it teased the audience further by showing the bomb exploding only to reveal that it had in fact gone off in a completely different location. That's been a trademark of the series throughout, mixing sleight of hand and trickery with genuine shocks. One of the most controversial scenes came as early as the second episode, where a young and eager trainee spook (played by Lisa Faulkner, at that stage possibly the best-known member of the cast) was killed by a sadistic racist by being shoved head-first into a deep-fat fryer and then shot in the head. Although the action was actually not shown on screen, even the suggestion that a character (especially one billed as one of the main stars) could be killed off so callously left many viewers shocked beyond what they felt to be an acceptable level of violence on TV. It also raised questions for TV producers. In an age where magazines like *Heat*, *What's on TV* and even the *Radio Times* are able to pre-warn viewers about every shock and surprise in our favourite soaps, how can a television producer maintain suspense in a programme?

What this one episode also did was send a clear signal to its audience that this was a show where no one is safe, something that's become more and more clear as the seasons have progressed. Though the first series was focused mainly on Tom Quinn, from the second series onwards it became much more of an ensemble. After the shock departure of senior officer Tessa Phillips the previous year (caught running 'phantom' agents and pocketing the money herself), head of the section, the stoical but calculating Harry Pearce was forced to take an even more hands-on approach. Tom's fellow operatives, Danny and Zoe, were pushed to the fore, the department gained a new junior in the form of Sam and a genius collator, Ruth (the subtly astounding Nicola Walker, who'd been one of the best things about the sitcom ***Chalk*** a few years before). The back-room boys, bookish Malcolm and geeky Colin, also became essential parts of the team. By more than doubling the regular cast, it encouraged us to develop emotional attachments to more characters, all of whom could then be potential 'victims' for every episode.

Tom's departure in series three caused outrage among fans of the series who for weeks after kept expecting Matthew MacFadyen to pop back and surprise them all.

The highlight of the second series involved a security lock-down within the Grid (the main operations room for Harry's section). Initially everyone treats it all with excitement, believing it to be a drill, but as the situation worsens and tempers become frayed, the team begins to panic and take it seriously. Even though this came right in the middle of the series and we hoped that it would all be revealed to be a drill (as indeed it is), that doesn't stop it from being a nail-gnawingly tense 50 minutes. It also sows the seeds for Tom's departure from the show as we the audience (but not the other characters) see his anger at being tested unnecessarily. It kick-starts a slow-burning storyline that sees him commence an unvetted relationship with the department's CIA representative, Christine Dale, become increasingly frustrated with Harry's direction of the department, find himself embroiled in a conspiracy that leaves everyone believing he's an assassin, before ultimately being dismissed from the service after trying to wreck a delicate operation involving a government scientist.

Tom's departure in series three caused outrage among fans of the series who for weeks after kept expecting Matthew MacFadyen to pop back and surprise them all. But that was not the kind of surprise that series three was about to offer. In fact MacFadyen's exit was just the beginning of a year of major changes for *Spooks* as each of the three original young leads chose to call it a day. Bridging the gaps were suave new arrival Adam Carter, seconded from MI6 and then retained as Tom's replacement at Harry's request. To stir things up a little, Adam brought in his wife Fiona, also a spook for MI6. Having married spies as the lead characters provided an interesting new angle – highlighted in an episode where Fiona is forced to play Mata Hari with a corrupt businessman. This just left the writers facing the problem of writing out two more existing characters: Zoe and Danny. Even here, though, they succeeded in throwing us all a few red herrings.

With press reports of the cast exodus removing some of the surprise, Zoe was given a new boyfriend and a marriage proposal that set up her departure for a new life over a number of episodes. But then from nowhere we learn that she's on trial for incitement to murder after a suspect she'd been trailing accuses her of goading him into committing murder. The shock verdict of the jury, that Zoe is indeed guilty, isn't the end, though, as Harry manages to pull a few strings that see her offered a new life in South America. When her fiancé threatens to expose the deceit, Danny gives him information to enable him to find Zoe, so that at least they can be together. Danny's departure is not so happy, however: taken hostage with Fiona in the final episode of the series, he taunts their captor and draws his attention from Fiona to give her a better chance of survival. Sadly, it also results in Danny getting a bullet in the head. For once, *Spooks* decided not to tease us with another cliffhanger. Danny is dead and that's that.

One of BBC One's real success stories of the early 21st century, *Spooks* does, however, show just how much television has changed. With ratings rarely above 9 million viewers, it will never compete with the success of earlier shows like ***The Sweeney*** or *The Professionals* simply because, with a greater choice of channels and way too many other leisure activities nowadays (DVDs, games consoles, the internet), the days of 20 million for a drama are long gone. But *Spooks* remains one of the few intelligent, challenging dramas still in production that puts good storytelling over vanity stunt casting and easy choices. For that, it can be counted as one of our absolute favourite modern TV shows.

Star Trek

William Shatner as James T. Kirk, captain of the USS Enterprise.

Out of all of the programmes listed in this book, *Star Trek* is the purest example of a show surviving against all odds; of a TV series whose cultural importance and impact belies its brief original lifespan. Many people are astounded to discover that *Star Trek* ran for just 79 episodes and three seasons, largely because those episodes seemed to be repeated on the BBC at least once a year for decades. Indeed, it's the ability of *Star Trek* to stand up to multiple repeat screenings that granted it telly immortality, and its sudden switch from just television series to feature film and then to multiple spin-off shows that made it a cultural icon.

Star Trek was created by scriptwriter Gene Roddenberry, who had spent a significant part of his career working on TV westerns like *Have Gun Will Travel*. Westerns were still dominating the American prime-time schedules in the mid-1960s, so Roddenberry's concept was pitched to network executives as a '*Wagon Train* to the stars', a programme that would mix those all-American values of exploration and adventure with a more unusual science fiction element, something which he hoped would prove popular as the US space programme neared its goal of placing a man on the moon. Although home-grown TV science fiction was proving to be extremely popular in the UK (valiantly represented by ***Doctor Who***, following on from the event-TV spectacle of ***Quatermass*** in the 1950s), it had never been an especially successful genre in the USA for anything other than the kiddie slot – only Rod Serling's bizarre tales of the strange and unexpected in ***The Twilight Zone*** had made much of an impact on the public consciousness. So when *Star Trek* was finally launched in 1966, broadcasters were taking quite a risk.

Star Trek was set in the 23rd century, charting the voyages of the Starship USS *Enterprise* (registration number NCC 1701). In this vision of the future, Earth is part of the United Federation of Planets, who have formed an organisation to promote mutual defence (a bit like the UN) while simultaneously exploring the galaxy to 'seek out new life and new civilisations' and 'boldly go where no man has gone before' (a mission statement that if nothing else gave grammar tutors a practical example of the split infinitive, even if it didn't explain why the linguistic transgression was such a big deal in the first place). Key to the success of these ideals is Starfleet, a multi-cultural organisation that maintains ships such as the *Enterprise* to perform both exploratory and defensive functions on behalf of the entire Federation. Captain of the *Enterprise* is all-American Iowan native James T. Kirk, a man who flies by the seat of his pants and who lives on his instincts. A real one for the ladies – whatever their skin colour or number of extra eyes – Kirk tends to have a 'shoot first, ask questions later' style of leadership. Moderating Kirk's impulsive streak is First Officer Mr Spock, half human, half Vulcan and a man dedicated to living his life logically; calmly and sensibly collating as much information as possible before making any decisions. Kirk and Spock often lock horns about the best way of achieving their goals. However, despite their occasionally stormy relationship, they are the best of friends. Completing the trio of leading characters is crusty old ship's doctor Leonard 'Bones' McCoy, a man who never suffers fools (either human or half Vulcan) gladly.

The other chief officers of the *Enterprise* include Chief Navigator Mr Sulu, eager young Russian officer Mr Chekov (introduced in the second season of the programme following wry comments from the Soviet Space Agency), and dour Scottish Chief Engineer Mr 'Scotty' Scott (a name that must have taken them *ages* to come up with . . .). Perhaps reflecting the nature of society in the late 1960s, female role models among the crew were largely restricted to more 'supporting' parts – Bones's glamorous right-hand woman, Nurse Chappell (played by Roddenberry's real-life wife Majel Barrett), Kirk's occasional personal assistant Janice Rand (written out fairly early on in the show's run) and of course Chief Communications Officer Uhura. The mere presence of Uhura (a black woman) on the bridge of the *Enterprise* caused major consternation among many of the local television stations in the Southern States, aghast at such a blatant example of multi-culturalism hitting their screens. They were even more offended when, in the third series, Kirk and Uhura shared

Science Fiction
Norway-Paramount-Desilu for NBC (shown on BBC One)
Episode Duration:, 45 mins
Broadcast: 8 Sep 1966–3 Jun 1969 (USA)

Regular Cast
William Shatner · *Captain James Tiberius Kirk*
Leonard Nimoy · *Mr Spock*
DeForest Kelley · *Dr Leonard 'Bones' McCoy*
George Takei · *Mr Sulu*
Nichelle Nichols · *Lieutenant Uhura*
James Doohan · *Engineer Montgomery 'Scotty' Scott*
Walter Koenig · *Ensign Pavel Chekov*
Majel Barrett · *Nurse Christine Chapel*
Grace Lee Whitney · *Yeoman Janice Rand*

Creator Gene Roddenberry

Producers Various, including Gene Roddenberry, Gene L. Coon, John Meredyth Lucas, Fred Freiberger

Writers Various, including Gene Roddenberry, George Clayton Johnson, D.C. Fontana, Gene L. Coon, Sam Peebles, Richard Matheson, Robert Bloch, Adrien Spies, Shari Lewis, Jerry Sohl, Harlan Ellison, Theodore Sturgeon, Don Mankiewicz, Gilbert Ralston, John Meredyth Lucas, Max Ehrlich, Margaret Armen, Chet Richards, Judy Burns, Shimon Wincelberg, Stephen Kandel

Theme Music Alexander Courage was responsible for creating a TV music icon with the *Star Trek* theme. Instantly recognisable, the tune is none the less more than a little bit camp, with a demented soprano vocalist wailing at the top of her voice as the orchestra gleefully belts out the melody.

a passionate kiss; one of the first inter-racial smooches ever seen on American TV. For many years, this episode ('Plato's Stepchildren') was omitted from screenings in certain areas of the USA.

One of the great strengths of *Star Trek* as a series was its ability to address current Sixties concerns. Thanks to its science fiction setting, the metaphors were shrouded, thereby either going completely under the radar or simply making them more acceptable to sensitive network bosses. This meant that producer/creator Gene Roddenberry was able to surreptitiously engineer episodes of prime-time drama about racism ('Balance of Terror'), the Vietnam War ('A Private Little War') and corrupt totalitarian regimes ('Patterns of Fear') without either alienating his core audience or the notoriously conservative network and advertisers. The two most regular adversaries for the *Enterprise* crew were the cold and calculating Romulans (an offshoot from the Vulcan species) and the aggressive, warrior-like Klingon empire. Although *Star Trek*'s production values were unsurprisingly light-years ahead of those seen on contemporary science fiction shows in the UK, the imagination shown in the various alien species rarely matched that seen in either anthology programmes like ***The Outer Limits*** or even Irwin Allen camp-fest ***Lost in Space***: the majority of alien races in *Star Trek* consisted of humans in silver foil clothes with either green skin or a pair of giant caterpillars for eyebrows.

Star Trek is the purest example of a show surviving against all odds; a TV series whose cultural importance and impact belies its brief original lifespan.

Although most people automatically associate Captain Kirk with the Starship *Enterprise*, he was in fact not the first man to sit in the 'big chair' on the bridge. In a pilot episode entitled 'The Cage', actor Jeffrey Hunter portrayed the very first captain of the *Enterprise*, Christopher Pike. Gene Roddenberry wanted this crew to be far more representative of a future that prided itself on equality and opportunity for all, so Captain Pike's first officer was in fact a woman (a first acting appearance in *Star Trek* for Roddenberry's future wife, Majel Barrett). Although there were elements of 'The Cage' that NBC liked, they chose to ditch former movie star Hunter in favour of Canadian actor William Shatner. Furthermore, the network felt that audiences would never accept a woman in a position of such authority and ordered Roddenberry to write out the female Number One. Finally, they expressed grave concerns about an alien character that had appeared in the pilot – with his cold, emotionless demeanour and pointed ears, certain NBC executives seriously believed that they would face criticism for portraying a Satan-like character in one of their series. Thankfully, although Roddenberry lost his fight to keep a woman as second-in-command, he managed to retain Spock in *Star Trek*, thereby assuring his place as one of the most famous aliens ever to be created.

Despite the network's concerns, *Star Trek* finally made it to the screen in 1966 (with segments of 'The Cage' finally being re-used as flashbacks in the two-part story 'The Menagerie', in which Kirk meets Pike). Although it proved to be popular with some viewers, *Star Trek* was never a huge success in the ratings. After two years, NBC decided to pull the plug. Fans of the show were outraged at this decision and launched a letter-writing campaign to get a reprieve for their favourite programme. The network was so taken aback by the support the programme received (particularly from younger, more affluent men, regarded as the ideal target audience for potential advertisers wishing to buy slots within the show) that *Star Trek* returned for a third and final run of episodes in 1968–9. Unfortunately, the producer that they installed to oversee this new series, Fred Freiberger, never seemed to grasp the real essence of what made *Star Trek* different from other TV sci-fi programmes. Previously, writers such as award-winning science fiction novelist Harlan Ellison had contributed to the show, with challenging stories like 'City on the Edge of Forever' – guest starring Joan Collins as one of Kirk's doomed loves. Under Freiberger's auspices, alien races stole Spock's brain (leaving neither a scar nor a hair out of place) and operated his body by remote control; hippies sat in otherworldly gardens and sang of peace and love; and viewers unsurprisingly switched off in droves, embarrassed at how juvenile everything had become. NBC once again cancelled the programme, and this time no amount of letter writing from devoted Trekkies could save the show.

However, this wasn't the end. With a decent number of episodes in the can, *Star Trek* soon found itself being rescreened on local stations around the USA and across the world in an almost endless loop. Along with shows like ***Batman*** and ***The Addams Family***, *Star Trek* became much more successful in syndication than it had ever been while being shown on the main US network. As the years went by, *Star Trek* catchphrases soon became part of society's vernacular: 'Warp factor six', 'Phasers on stun', 'He's dead, Jim!' and of course 'Beam me up, Scotty' (although that precise phrase was *never* actually uttered in any episode of *Star Trek*!) became iconic phrases. In 1973, capitalising upon this increased interest, came *Star Trek: The Animated Series*. Screened in a Saturday morning children's slot, this new show ran for 17 episodes and featured scripts written by many of the best of the original series' scribes. The majority of the cast returned to give voices to their animated on-screen counterparts, and the cartoon medium enabled the show to feature an otherworldly array of regular characters that would have proved either uneconomic or unconvincing to produce before the advent of computer graphics in the late 1990s.

With *Star Trek* still failing to fall out of fashion, Gene Roddenberry (who had not had a major success with any of his post-*Trek* projects) decided that the late 1970s would be a good time to bring his baby back to television. Plans were fairly far advanced for a new series – *Star Trek II* – to come back to network television for the 1977–8 season, when all of a sudden, a certain feature film set 'a long time ago, in a galaxy far, far away . . .' hit cinema screens in

1977. With *Star Wars* raking in stellar-sized wads of cash for 20th Century Fox, Paramount chose to rework the plans for *Star Trek II* into a feature film, and in 1979 *Star Trek: The Motion Picture* appeared in cinemas. Although this film was disliked by most viewers and critics for its ponderous and self-important attitude (a marked contrast to the action-adventure fun of *Star Wars*), the box office returns were so good that Paramount agreed to make a sequel: *Star Trek II: The Wrath of Khan* (1982). This film featured Ricardo Montalban reprising his role as the genetically enhanced human Khan from the original series episode 'Space Seed' and was an enormous success with critics, Trekkies and members of the public alike, held enthralled by a genuinely great sci-fi adventure movie. Two more sequels followed in 1984 and 1986 (*The Search for Spock* and *The Voyage Home*), at which point some wise guy within Paramount's television division suddenly had an inspired thought. Wouldn't this movie series make a great television programme . . .?

At the heart of *Star Trek*'s success is its astonishingly positive view of the future of humanity.

At the heart of *Star Trek*'s enduring success is its astonishingly positive view of the future of humanity. In a time when East and West were poised on the verge of destroying each other with their batteries of nuclear missiles, Roddenberry created a future in which not only were Russians happy to work alongside Americans and Japanese, but also beings from different planets were perfectly delighted to subscribe to the typically American Protestant work ethic and conquer the rest of the universe 'peacefully' together. As pop group the Firm so eloquently put it in their 1987 chart-topping hit 'Star Trekkin', Kirk and his crew's philosophy could be neatly summed up as 'We come in peace – shoot to kill'. As we move into the 21st century (only two centuries to go until we'll all be able to use transporters, tricorders and warp drive!), *Star Trek*'s appeal may now be starting to wane. Although (with the recent cancellation of prequel series *Star Trek: Enterprise*) there's now currently no new Star Trek series in production (for the first time since ***Star Trek: The Next Generation*** debuted in 1987, through the other spin-offs ***Star Trek: Deep Space Nine*** and ***Star Trek: Voyager***), Trekkers around the world – the politically correct term of address that many fans of the series prefer to the better-known 'Trekkie' – will undoubtedly keep the spirit of Gene Roddenberry's original series alive until humanity's voyages into deep space become a reality. Indeed, perhaps the greatest legacy of *Star Trek* was the naming of one of NASA's space shuttles after Captain Kirk's interstellar craft. How many other TV shows can boast something as historically important as that?

Terry Farrell · *Lieutenant Jadzia Dax*
Michael Dorn · *Lieutenant Commander Worf*
Nicole deBoer · *Lieutenant Ezri Dax*
Felecia M. Bell · *Jennifer Sisko*
Camille Saviola · *Kai Opaka*
Marc Alaimo · *Gul Dukat*
Rosalind Chao · *Keiko O'Brien*
Max Grodenchik · *Rom*
Aron Eisenberg · *Nog*
Andrew Robinson · *Garak*
Majel Barrett · *Lwaxana Troi*
Louise Fletcher · *Kai Winn*
Philip Anglim · *Vedek Bareil*
Salome Jens · *Female Shapeshifter*
Robert O'Reilly · *Gowron*
Chase Masterson · *Leeta*
Penny Johnson Jerald · *Kasidy Yates*
Robert Foxworth · *Admiral Leyton*
Hana Hatae · *Molly O'Brien*
Jeffrey Combs · *Weyoun*
Jeffrey Combs · *Brunt*
Ken Marshall · *Lieutenant Commander Michael Eddington*
Barry Jenner · *Admiral Ross*
Mark Allen Shepherd · *Morn*
James Darren · *Vic Fontane*
Garman Hertzler · *Martok*
Casey Biggs · *Damar*
William Sadler · *Sloan*

Creators Rick Berman and Michael Piller, based on ***Star Trek***, created by Gene Roddenberry **Producers** Rick Berman, Michael Piller, Ira Steven Behr, Ronald D. Moore (executive), Hans Beimler, James Crocker, René Echevarria, Peter Lauritson, David Livingston (supervising), Robert Della Santina, J. P. Farrell, Peter Allan Fields, Steve Oster, Terri Potts, Robert Hewitt Wolfe **Writers** Various, including Michael Piller, Rick Berman, Ira Steven Behr, Robert Hewitt Wolfe, Peter Allan Fields, David Livingston, Evan Carlos Somers, Joe Menosky, Jim Trombetta, Jeri Taylor, Mark Gehred-O'Connell, James Crocker, Hans Beimler, Ronald D. Moore, René Echevarria, Michael Taylor, Jane Espenson, Bradley Thompson, David Weddle, Majel Barrett, Mike Vejar **Theme Music** Dennis McCarthy

Midway through the run of ***Star Trek: The Next Generation***, executives at Paramount TV realised that they sitting on a potential sci-fi goldmine. *Star Trek* movies (featuring the cast of the original TV series) were still enjoying remarkable success at the box office, and the ratings and revenue brought in by *The Next Generation* had surpassed everyone's expectations. So why settle for just one TV show when you could have two? *Star Trek: Deep Space Nine* was therefore put into production, with a unique selling point. Rather than providing a rival series to *The Next Generation*, it would act as a companion piece, occasionally with characters from one series crossing over into the other. In order to achieve this, *Deep Space Nine* had to be set in the same time period as *The Next Generation* – in fact, storylines would switch back and forward between the two programmes in much the same way that ***The Colbys*** and ***Dynasty*** had done in the mid-1980s. However, one thing was blatantly obvious from the outset: unlike *The Next Generation, Deep Space Nine* was dark, nasty and completely different from any version of *Star Trek* seen either before or since.

Towards the edge of Federation-friendly space, the planet Bajor had been under the occupation of the Cardassians, a brutal lizard-like race of warmongers. After many years of sabotage and rebellion, the humanoid Bajorans finally won their freedom when the Cardassian forces withdrew from their planet. At the same time, the Cardassians abandoned the space station (called Terek Nor) they had built nearby. The newly liberated Bajorans called for help from the Federation, and soon Starfleet arrived and began the process of converting the derelict station into a useful intergalactic staging post – Deep Space Nine was born.

As the series begins, a new commander arrives on board DS9. His name is Ben Sisko, a single parent following the death of his wife Jennifer during the Borg attack on Earth (as seen in *Star Trek: The Next Generation*). Sisko's job is simple: to maintain the peace on board DS9, to win over the trust of the Bajoran people – many of whom see the arrival of Starfleet as simply swapping one occupying force with another – and to represent Federation interests in that remote part of the galaxy. Sisko's job gets more complex when a wormhole is discovered near to DS9 – a kind of intergalactic secret passage providing high-speed access to another distant quadrant of the galaxy. For not only does Sisko have concern himself about the various existing races trying to lay claim to the wormhole, he also has to worry about what might come back through it. . .

Sisko is assisted by a rag-tag collection of crew members, including several fellow Starfleet officers (Dr Julian Bashir, symbiotic life form Jadzia Dax and *Enterprise* veteran Miles O'Brien), a former leader in the Bajoran resistance (Kira Nerys) and an alien shapeshifter called Odo, acting as the head of on-board security. Odo in particular has regular run-ins with the Ferengi Quark, who manages the station's rough bar. Throughout the series, threats to the security of the station arise from the Cardassians, fundamentalist Bajorans, the Klingons, and eventually from a mysterious and extremely powerful group of aliens called the Dominion, who travel down the wormhole determined to conquer everything in their path.

Deep Space Nine was, as a direct result of its location and background history, much less of a story about travel and exploration, and much more of a programme about politics, subterfuge and good old-fashioned intrigue. Far more than they had to with any previous incarnation of *Star Trek*, viewers of *Deep Space Nine* needed to keep up to date with the latest shenanigans in the assorted intergalactic power games. Whose side were the Klingons on this week? Who were the other strange shapeshifting aliens – and if they turned out to be evil, did that mean Odo was evil too? Some ongoing storylines eventually took many years to be resolved, resulting in a programme that felt much more like a cohesive story than a series of episodic events. However, this also had an impact on viewing figures – newcomers to the series found it increasingly difficult to get up to speed with what was happening. In order to counteract this problem, producers decided to transfer an extremely popular character from *The Next Generation* over to *Deep Space Nine*. So at the start of the fourth series, with the TV adventures of the *Enterprise* now at an end, Klingon warrior Worf came on board Starfleet's most dangerous space station, bringing his customary scowls, an increased fanbase and even more convoluted plotlines. Worf even fell in love and married Jadzia Dax – until she was shot and killed (and then partially reincarnated in the form of Ezri Dax – this is sci-fi, after all!).

Although *Deep Space Nine* never achieved the audience figures of *The Next Generation*, critically it was just as popular. The casting of black actor Avery Brooks as the station's commanding officer was certainly a move worthy of praise (particularly when you consider the reluctance of many stations in certain parts of America to cast non-white performers in leading roles), it's a little unfortunate that Ben Sisko is among the least interesting of all of the characters in the series. Despite this, among many *Star Trek* fans, *DS9* is held up as an ideal example of how to make a long-running science fiction series, with plotting and character development for once taking precedence over mindless action sequences.

Star Trek: Enterprise

See pages 712–14

Star Trek: The Next Generation

SEE PAGES 00–00

Star Trek: Voyager

Science Fiction | Paramount Television for UPN (shown on Sky One and BBC Two) | episode duration 45 mins | broadcast 15 Jan 1995–23 May 2001 (USA)

Regular Cast

Kate Mulgrew · *Captain Kathryn Janeway*
Robert Beltran · *Commander Chakotay*
Tim Russ · *Lieutenant Commander Tuvok*
Robert Duncan McNeill · *Tom Paris*
Robert Picardo · *The Doctor*
Roxann Biggs-Dawson · *B'Elanna Torres*
Garrett Wang · *Ensign Harry Kim*
Ethan Phillips · *Neelix*
Jennifer Lien · *Kes*
Jeri Ryan · *Seven of Nine*
Scarlett Pomers · *Naomi Wildman*
Martha Hackett · *Seska*
Manu Intiraymi · *Icheb*
Alexander Enberg · *Ensign Vorik*
Nancy Hower · *Ensign Samantha Wildman*
Dwight Schultz · *Lieutenant Reg Barclay*
Carolyn Seymour · *Mrs Templeton*
John de Lancie · *Q*
Brad Dourif · *Suder*
Raphael Sbarge · *Michael Jonas*
Ed Begley Jr · *Henry Starling*
John Rhys-Davies · *Leonardo Da Vinci*
Richard Herd · *Admiral Paris*
Susanna Thompson/Alice Krige · *Borg Queen*
Marina Sirtis · *Deanna Troi*

Creators Rick Berman, Michael Piller and Jeri Ryan, based on ***Star Trek***, created by Gene Roddenberry **Producers** Rick Berman, Michael Piller, Jeri Taylor, Brannon Braga, Kenneth Biller, Ronald D. Moore (executive), Merri D. Howard, James Kahn, Peter Lauritson, David Livingston, Joe Menosky (supervising), Robin Burger, J. P. Farrell, Wendy Neuss, Dawn Velazquez, Stephen Welke, Brad Yacobian **Writers** Various, including Michael Piller, Jeri Taylor, Rick Berman, Brannon Braga, Kenneth Biller, Joe Menosky, Ron Wilkerson, Jimmy Diggs, Lisa Klink, Andrew Shepard Price, Mark Gaberman, Mike Sussman, Andre Bormanis, Alexander Singer, Harry Doc Kloor, Bryan Fuller, Nick Sagan, Michael Taylor, Robert J. Doherty, Ronald D Moore, Robin Burger, Raf Green, Robert Picardo, James Kahn, Phyllis Strong, Robert Doherty **Theme Music** Jerry Goldsmith

In this, the fourth interpretation of the *Star Trek* series, the crew of the Starship *Voyager* find themselves in uncharted territory when they, and a ship of anti-Federation rebels they have been pursuing, are flung across to the other side of the galaxy. With fatalities high among both crews, the Maquis rebels and the Starfleet officers are forced to combine forces under the command of no-nonsense Katherine Hepburn-alike Captain Kathryn Janeway. Second in command is Chakotay, leader of the Maquis, who manages to strike up a mutually respectful relationship with Janeway after some initial friction. Other members of the newly combined *Voyager* crew include Vulcan security chief Tuvok, the young and enthusiastic Tom Paris and Harry Kim, and half Klingon engineer B'Elanna Torres. With the ship's doctor dead, an emergency medical hologram is activated to act as temporary chief medical officer. Completing the crew are two aliens from this remote part of the galaxy – Talaxian chef and 'morale officer' Neelix, and his Ocampan girlfriend Kes. Janeway and her crew set off for home in *Voyager*, realising that they have been catapulted so far away from home that even if they travel at maximum speed, it will take them at least 70 years to get back to Earth. . .

Set in the same time period as ***Star Trek: The Next Generation*** and ***Star Trek: Deep Space Nine***, *Star Trek: Voyager* made a concerted effort to provide a programme that was both familiar to viewers and yet simultaneously didn't tread the same ground. By relocating the action to a different part of the galaxy, producers effectively cut away a huge amount of the continuity-based baggage that was perceived to be *Deep Space Nine*'s weakness. In *Voyager*, there would be *Next Generation*-style exploration and adventure, but there would be no reliance upon the heritage of *Star Trek* to provide storylines – these really would be places that no-one had gone before.

That was the theory at least. Sadly, the format failed to grab either the love or the loyalty of critics or viewers. Many felt that the new characters were simply not interesting enough (in fact, some argued that Janeway was the only member of the crew who actually possessed a personality); others believed that abandoning all links with the past had essentially robbed the series of its *Star Trek*-iness. Gradually, as the programme went on, more and more 'kisses to the past' were introduced – each of which seemed more and more like a desperate attempt to win back viewers.

The ultimate sign of this was the introduction into *Star Trek: Voyager* of one of the biggest villains from *The Next Generation*, the machine-like Borg. Half of the audience were enthralled at the prospect; the other half sighed at what seemed to be a blatant ratings-grabbing move. However, it was a move that paid off in one respect: the introduction of a new regular character, Seven of Nine. Played by the pneumatically blessed Jeri Ryan, Seven of Nine is a woman freed from a lifetime of being controlled by the Borg, who slowly begins to discover what it was like to be human thanks to the intervention of Captain Janeway and her love of figure-hugging Lycra catsuits. Ryan's introduction was quite clearly an attempt to attract an adolescent male audience, and to that end it succeeded. However, what came as a very nice bonus was the subtlety and depth with which Seven of Nine's story was told. The show's writers finally found a character they could get their teeth into, and the programme clearly benefited from her presence.

Eventually, in the sixth season, *Voyager* finally made contact with Earth (thanks to the efforts of former *Enterprise* crewman Reg Barclay, played with geeky finesse by former ***A-Team*** star Dwight Schultz) and efforts were redoubled to hasten their mission to return to familiar territory. After 172 episodes, Janeway and her crew managed to get home at last, thanks to a convoluted trick they played on the evil Borg. As viewers, we were just as exhausted and at our wits' end as the crew were by the time the series finished. Undoubtedly the least satisfying of all of the incarnations of *Star Trek*, *Star Trek: Voyager* was none the less a slickly produced and fairly entertaining series. What it wasn't, unfortunately, was shocking, innovative or particularly memorable, Jeri Ryan's figure-hugging costume aside. Thus, the attempt to really push the boundaries ended up taking us not only where plenty of people had gone before but to places that weren't really worth going to anyway.

Stargate SG-1

Science Fiction | Double Secret Productions/Gekko Film Corp/Kawoosh! Productions/MGM Television for Showtime/Sci-Fi Channel (Shown on Channel 4) | episode duration 45 mins | broadcast 27 Jul 1997–present

Regular Cast
Richard Dean Anderson · *Colonel Jack O'Neill*
Amanda Tapping · *Lieutenant Colonel Samantha Carter*
Christopher Judge · *Teal'c*
Michael Shanks · *Dr Daniel Jackson*
Don S. Davis · *Major General George S. Hammond*
Corin Nemec · *Jonas Quinn*
Ben Browder · *Lieutenant Colonel Cameron Mitchell*
Gary Jones · *Sergeant Walter Harriman*
Teryl Rothery · *Dr Janet Fraiser*

Creator Dean Devlin, developed for TV by Jonathan Glassner and Brad Wright **Producers** Brad Wright, Jonathan Glassner, Michael Greenberg, Richard Dean Anderson (executive), Joseph Mallozzi, N. John Smith, Paul Mullie, Ron French **Writers** Various, including Brad Wright, Jonathan Glassner, Katharyn Powers, Robert C. Cooper, Joseph Mallozzi, Paul Mullie, Damian Kindler **Theme Music** Joel Goldsmith, utilising elements from David Arnold's original movie theme.

A spin-off series from the 1994 sci-fi feature film *Stargate* (starring Kurt Russell as Colonel O'Neill and James Spader as Daniel Jackson), *Stargate SG-1* is the story of an elite group of soldiers and scientists who utilise the alien portal of the show's title to explore the universe from their underground base. With the American Government only too well aware of both the potential and threat caused by having a fully active alien doorway operating on US soil, Stargate Command has been set up to both protect the Earth from any forces that might try to come through the gate, and to travel to any of the myriad of other stargates located across the universe. The SG-1 team (led by Colonel O'Neill and consisting of scientist Daniel Jackson, Lieutenant Samantha Carter and an alien called Teal'c) travel through the stargate and discover the ominous threat to humanity posed by the sinister architects of the stargates, the Egyptian-like Goa'uld.

A quality science fiction epic with superficial similarities to ***Star Trek*** (gang of military bods dashing around the galaxy fighting aliens) that's actually quite a novel spin on the genre, *Stargate SG-1* has beaten all the odds to (at the time of writing) equal ***The X Files***' record as the longest-running TV science fiction series, lasting for nine seasons and counting. This is especially surprising considering the fact that it's bounced around a number of different networks in the USA, normally a sure-fire way of getting a show cancelled. *Stargate SG-1* has also spawned a spin-off series, *Stargate: Atlantis* (which has yet to reach terrestrial screens in the UK).

Star Trek: The Next Generation

Patrick Stewart as Jean-Luc Picard, captain of the Enterprise.

Although the original series of ***Star Trek*** had never been a huge success in the ratings, subsequent years of repeats had turned the programme into a genuine cultural phenomenon. In the late 1970s, executives at Paramount Television toyed with the idea of bringing *Star Trek* back, with the aim of riding on the back of the science fiction boom brought about by *Star Wars* (1977). Scripts were written and most of Kirk's original crew agreed to reprise their roles. In the end, the TV series never came to pass – instead, the *Enterprise* went boldly into a series of extremely popular cinematic adventures, beginning with *Star Trek: The Motion Picture* (1979). When the fourth in the series – *Star Trek IV: The Voyage Home* (1986) – became the most successful of the run in both critical and financial terms, the previously shelved idea of a new *Star Trek* TV series was dusted off. However, Paramount realised that it would be impossible to make a new programme with the original cast: first, their movie-star salaries would make an ongoing TV show prohibitively expensive; second, tying the original crew up in a TV series would prevent any future lucrative movies being made. Furthermore, the prospect of a younger, sexier (and therefore inevitably cheaper!) cast must have been the final factor that convinced the studio that *Star Trek* could (ahem) live long and prosper without Spock, Bones and the others.

So in autumn 1987, viewers were introduced to a whole new crew of space explorers. Set nearly a century *after* the voyages of the original crew, *Star Trek: The Next Generation* told the continuing story of humanity's exploration of the galaxy and the alien races and cultures encountered on the way. Captain of the *Enterprise D* (a much bigger and more advanced model than Kirk's ship) is Frenchman Jean-Luc Picard, a diplomat and true leader and a particular expert in 'first contact' situations with new civilisations.

Science Fiction
Paramount Television (shown on BBC Two/Sky One)
Episode Duration:, 45 mins
Broadcast: 26 Sep 1987–21 May 1994

Regular Cast
Patrick Stewart · *Captain Jean-Luc Picard*
Jonathan Frakes · *Commander Will Riker*
Brent Spiner · *Lieutenant Commander Data*
LeVar Burton · *Lieutenant Commander Geordi La Forge*
Michael Dorn · *Lieutenant Worf*
Gates McFadden · *Dr Beverly Crusher*
Marina Sirtis · *Counsellor Deanna Troi*
Wil Wheaton · *Wesley Crusher*
Denise Crosby · *Lieutenant Tasha Yar/Sela*
Michelle Forbes · *Ensign Ro Laren*
Diana Muldaur · *Dr Kate Pulaski*
Colm Meaney · *Chief Miles O'Brien*
John de Lancie · *Q*
Whoopi Goldberg · *Guinan*
Rosalind Chao · *Keiko O'Brien*
Dwight Schultz · *Lieutenant Reg Barclay*
Majel Barrett · *Lwaxana Troi*
Carel Struycken · *Mr Homn*
Suzie Plakson · *Dr Selar/K'Ehleyr*
Andreas Katsulas · *Commander Tomalak*
Tony Todd · *Kurn*
Patrick Massett · *Duras*
Robert O'Reilly · *Gowron*
Natalia Nogulich · *Admiral Nechayev*
Jennifer Hetrick · *Vash*
Eric Menyuk · *The Traveller*
Susan Gibney · *Dr Leah Brahms*
Barbara March · *Lursa*
Gwynyth Walsh · *B'Etor*
Mark Lenard · *Sarek*
Brian Bonsall · *Alexander Rozhenko*
Georgia Brown · *Helena Rozhenko*
Jonathan Del Arco · *Hugh*
Daniel Davis · *Professor Moriarty*
Ashley Judd · *Ensign Robin Lefler*

Creator Gene Roddenberry

Producers Various, including Gene Roddenberry, Maurice Hurley, Michael I. Wagner, Rick Berman, Michael Piller, Jeri Taylor (executive), Robert H. Justman, Frank Abatemarco, David Livingston (supervising), D. C. Fontana, Burton Armus, Ira Steven Behr, Peter Lauritson, John Mason, Robert McCulloch, Ronald D. Moore, Lee Sheldon

Writers Various, including Gene Roddenberry, D. C. Fontana, Herbert Wright, Tracy Torme, Robert Lewin, Maurice Hurley,

Picard's 'Number One' is Will Riker, normally assigned to lead the 'away teams' that beam down to planets, and a man with a definite hint of the Kirks about him (at least at the start of the series). Also manning the bridge of the *Enterprise* is ship's counsellor Deanna Troi, half-human half-empathic Betazoid who is completely invaluable to Picard when he's involved in sensitive negotiations; blind navigator Geordi La Forge (who 'sees' courtesy of a high-tech 'VISOR'), security chief Tasha Yar and hyper-advanced android Data. The changing shape of the future is reflected in the fact that many families are also on board the *Enterprise*. Having realised that long missions in the depths of space away from their loved ones could have an adverse affect on any crew member, Starfleet took the decision to allow families of their personnel on board – for example, Wesley Crusher, teenage son of ship's doctor Beverly. Another shock to viewers familiar with the politics of the original series of *Star Trek* is the fact that by this stage in future history, the good guys of the Federation have signed a peace treaty with their former mortal enemies, the Klingon Empire. Finding it hard to reconcile his genetic heritage with his new role as a Starfleet officer, Lieutenant Worf quickly became one of the most popular characters among fans of the series.

Quite sensibly, series producers decided that not only would the look and feel of the show be updated to reflect advances in real-life technology (for instance, the hand held communicator devices were replaced by badges worn on the chest that switched on when touched), but the themes and topics touched on in the plotlines would also reflect the world of the late 1980s. Just as the original series of *Star Trek* had addressed contemporary concerns such as the Cold War and racism, *The Next Generation* tackled such weighty issues as drug addiction, the arms race and the environmental impact of new technological developments. An initial attempt to confront concerns about the dangers of rampant capitalism was created in the shape of the new big villains, the Ferengi – a race of money-obsessed, treacherous and self-obsessed aliens with huge ears and tiny morals. Unfortunately, neither viewers nor production staff liked the Ferengi and they were quickly sidelined into comic relief baddies. The archetypal Next Generation enemy was introduced half-way through the second season – the robotic, relentless Borg. Travelling across the universe inside gigantic cube-shaped ships, the Borg exist solely to assimilate other species into their own hive mentality. The *Enterprise* crew faced the Borg on several occasions, barely escaping with their lives and never totally defeating this remorseless menace.

Star Trek: The Next Generation continued to be an enormous success for its producers – so much so, that it quickly superseded the three seasons that the original series had enjoyed. One of the new series' key strengths was in the way it focused on the lives of every single one of the regular crew, often featuring plotlines that would refer back to episodes shown several years before. Perhaps the biggest of these ongoing stories was Worf's discovery of a vast conspiracy within the Klingon Empire, a conspiracy that initially

Hannah Louise Shearer, Hans Beimler, Joseph Stefano, Melinda M. Snodgrass, Michael Piller, Ronald D. Moore, Ira Steven Behr, René Echevarria, Rick Berman, Jeri Taylor, Joe Menosky, Brannon Braga, Peter Allan Fields, Naren Shankar, Ron Wilkerson

Theme Music Jerry Goldsmith (re-using the theme he'd written for *Star Trek: The Motion Picture* in 1979)

TRIVIA

An amazing addition to the cast from the second season onwards was Oscar-nominated actress Whoopi Goldberg. Goldberg had been a lifelong fan of *Star Trek* – largely because of its positive portrayal of a multi-cultural society in the future where black women (such as Uhura) had a part to play that wasn't subservient. Goldberg asked her friend LeVar Burton (Geordi) if he could speak to someone on her behalf about creating a part for her in the show – producers didn't believe him until Goldberg wrote to them herself begging to join the cast. As a consequence, Goldberg became the mysterious Guinan, an ancient alien being for some reason working as bartender and hostess of the *Enterprise*'s Ten Forward lounge, where crew members would come to share their worries, concerns (or in the case of Troi, simply enjoy a chocolate sundae). More than just a gimmick, Guinan was rarely pivotal to the plot, but her use as a catalyst to uncover and highlight character development in the regulars was something that helped distinguish this series from its predecessor.

caused him and his family to be made outcasts, and eventually led to his involvement in the uncovering of the duplicitous schemes orchestrated by Duras and his sisters Lursa and B'Etor. Even 'lesser' characters were often allowed their moments to shine: Chief O'Brien began as little more than a background role for Irish actor Colm Meaney (the dad in the marvellous 1991 musical comedy *The Commitments*) – by the fourth series, he had found a wife, had a child and eventually became one of the lead characters in spin-off series ***Star Trek: Deep Space Nine***.

As the series progressed, some characters fell by the wayside. In the first season episode 'Skin of Evil', security chief Tasha Yar was suddenly killed off by a malevolent oil slick called Armus. This drastic turn of events made the universe of the Next Generation a great deal more dangerous and unpredictable than Kirk's journeys had been – from now on, there would be no guarantee that each episode would finish with all of the problems sorted out and the crew sharing a happy joke with each other. For the second series, Beverly Crusher was replaced as ship's doctor by the crusty Dr Pulaski, a woman never backwards about coming forwards with her opinions on anything. Unfortunately, her character didn't sit comfortably alongside her much more 'PC' comrades and Beverly soon found her way back into sickbay.

Producers at Paramount were so content with the success of *Star Trek: The Next Generation* that they decided to launch a spin-off series that would run alongside their existing show. *Star Trek: Deep Space Nine* used alien races (the Cardassians and Bajorans) and events (the Borg attack on Earth shown in two-part episode 'The Best of Both Worlds') from *The Next Generation* as the basis for their new show, set on board a space station locked in a delicate political situation.

With contract negotiations approaching for the *Next Generation* crew, a decision was taken that the seventh season would be the last, with any further adventures for the crew taking place on the cinema screen – a rather sweet circular turn of events for a TV show that only came about because of the success of cinematic movies based on the original *Star Trek* series. After 176 episodes – nearly 100 more than Kirk and his crew managed – *Star Trek: The Next Generation* came to a conclusion with a double episode called 'All Good Things', which not only referred back to the very first episode but also suggested how events in the future might pan out – Picard and Dr Crusher getting married and later divorced, for instance.

In hindsight, *The Next Generation* has to be looked upon as a huge success. By completely re-inventing and re-imagining an old TV series for a new audience in a new decade, producers managed to launch a franchise that managed to run for 18 years (only coming to a halt with the end of ***Star Trek: Enterprise*** in 2005). They also managed to make a version of *Star Trek* that wasn't just for 'Trekkies' (that much-despised word that fans avoid in favour of 'Trekkers') – by combining the traditional sci-fi elements with soapier plotlines, (much) better acting and cutting edge (for the time!) special effects, producers breathed much-needed life into not just *Star Trek*, but into the whole genre of science fiction on TV.

Stars in their Eyes

Entertainment | Granada for ITV | episode duration 45 mins | broadcast 1990–present

Cast
Leslie Crowther, Russ Abbott, Matthew Kelly, Davina McCall, Cat Deeley · *Hosts*

Producers Various, including Nigel Hall, Jane Macnaught (executive)

Combining the rising love for karaoke with the talents of Granada's make-up artists, *Stars in their Eyes* began as an event competition but is now a standard variety jewel in ITV's crown: members of the public audition to be the best sound-alikes for all genres of singers, from the latest chart-toppers to the stars of the 1950s. Many winning entrants have earned the right to have 'as seen on *Stars in their Eyes*' on the promotional material for their performances on cruise ships and in nightclubs across the country. Sometimes, the finalists on each series are sent gifts by the people they're taking off, while occasionally we're confronted with a person who's managed to win the finals performing as artists who would struggle to get on TV themselves – a situation exemplified by 2000 winner Ian Moor, who portrayed Chris De Burgh.

Chris Tarrant presented the original pilot show, but it was Leslie Crowther who was the show's host for its first few years. After Crowther was involved in a car accident in 1992, his place was taken by Matthew Kelly, while Kelly was eventually replaced by ***SMTV*** presenter Cat Deeley. Occasional celebrity editions have brought an added note of occasion to the show, although coming from Granada its reliance on the stars of ***Coronation Street*** and ***Emmerdale*** has been noted. One spectacular celebrity turn was ***Z Cars*** legend Brian Blessed as Pavarotti, while a low-point was possibly ***The Fast Show***'s Simon Day as an indescribably poor Boy George.

Starsky and Hutch

Crime Drama | Spelling-Goldberg Productions/Columbia for ABC (shown on BBC One) | episode duration 50 mins | broadcast 30 Apr 1975, 10 Sep 1975–15 May 1979 (USA)

Principal Cast
David Soul · *Detective Ken 'Hutch' Hutchinson*
Paul Michael Glaser · *Detective Dave Starsky*
Bernie Hamilton · *Captain Harold Dobey*
Antonio Fargas · *Huggy Bear*

Creator William Blinn **Producers** Aaron Spelling, Leonard Goldberg (executive), Michael Hiatt, Shelley Hull (associate), Adrian Samish, Joseph T. Naar **Writers** Various, including William Blinn, Fred Freiberger, Michael Mann, Edward J. Lakso, Robert I. Holt, Michael Fisher, James Schmerer, Ron Friedman, Ben Masselink, Robert Earll, Don Patterson, Tim Maschler, Rick Edelstein, Robert Swanson, Robert Dellinger **Theme Music** While Lalo Schifrin and Mark Snow provided versions of the theme for seasons two and four, it's Tom Scott's 'Gotcha' that's playing on everyone's mobiles. The James Taylor Quartet recorded a superb version of the tune for their 1988 album *Wait a Minute* (it's the version you get on almost every cool Acid Jazz or TV themes CD).

Butch Cassidy and the Sundance Kid redefined the buddy movie in the late 1960s, re-creating two of the most famous outlaw anti-heroes the Wild West ever saw. Ironically, it was on the other side of the law that its influence was most visible, with cop stories on the big and small screen revolving around pairs: Cagney and Lacey; Riggs and Murtaugh in *Lethal Weapon*; Turner and Hooch . . .

On TV, the ultimate police partnership was Ken Hutchinson and David Starsky, even though they were designed to be total opposites. Starsky was a dark, wiry-haired, cocky, happy-go-lucky fella fond of junk food, while Hutch was more fair, thoughtful and into healthy living. When they're not beating up drugs barons and exposing organised crime rackets they're chatting about their latest girlfriends or getting it in the neck from their grumpy boss. With heavy overtones of *The French Connection* (1971), their cases often involved high-speed car chases and lots of undercover work, for which they cultivated a number of very shady contacts.

The characters of Starsky and 'Hutch' Hutchinson came about after TV producer Leonard Goldman read about two New York policemen – David Greenberg and Robert Hantz – who drew attention for their high arrest rates and strong friendship. Goldman suggested to writer William Blinn that the concept of best friends working the same beat might make a good TV show. Blinn set about creating the characters and came up with an idea called 'Nightwork', which would have seen the cops working after dusk to catch the criminals. As night-shoots are so expensive the idea was adjusted to be set mainly during the day. David Soul was always in line for Hutch, but the casting process took forever to find their Starsky until Paul Michael Glaser wowed the producers by playing a tough, gritty audition scene in a light-hearted manner – the opposite of everyone else who auditioned. Glaser and Soul hung out before filming began to get to know each other and became friends both on and off screen.

The series was also notable for having prominent roles for African-American actors: Bernie Hamilton played the guys' brusque boss, Captain Dobey, who created the archetype that's appeared in every cop drama ever since; and Antonio Fargas, whose streetwise, jive-talking Huggy Bear stole every scene he was in. Such was the strength of Fargas's performance that when he participated in ITV's celebrity endurance show ***I'm a Celebrity . . . Get Me Out of Here*** he was known by his character's name rather than his own.

For many fans, though, the car was the star – that distinctive cherry-red 1976 limited edition Ford Gran Torino with the white 'tick' stripe running down its length. One of TV's sexiest vehicles, it wasn't perhaps the subtlest of cars to give undercover cops to drive around in, but it looked the business screeching round corners and displacing litter with such style.

Dealing with criticisms of the violence and adult themes (prostitution, drug use, spousal abuse), the producers decided to soften the show's hard edge – a move that left the show devoid of the elements that made people watch it in the first place. While Paul Michael Glaser tried (and failed) to bail ahead of the end of his five-year contract, viewers were bailing in droves. Fortunately for Glaser, the network decided to give the show an early retirement after the fourth year.

Defining much of the kitsch quality of the 1970s, with their tight denim jeans and baggy woollen pullovers, Starsky and Hutch's reappearance on the big screen in 2002 was more parody than tribute, with stars Ben Stiller and Owen Wilson playing up the laughs.

Trivia

Back in the 1970s, David Soul scored five top 20 hits in the UK singles charts, including two No. 1s ('Don't Give Up on Us' and 'Silver Lady'). Both of the show's leads moved behind the camera to directors – Soul on TV shows such as *China Beach* and ***Miami Vice***, Glaser on the film *The Running Man* (1987) and various other TV shows (including Steven Spielberg's ***Amazing Stories***). David Soul has also continued acting; in 2004 he began a long stage run as the (non-singing) lead in the controversial *Jerry Springer: The Opera*.

State of Play

Drama | Endor for BBC One | episode duration 45 mins | broadcast 18 May 2003–present

Principal Cast

David Morrissey · *Stephen Collins*
John Simm · *Cal McCaffrey*
Kelly Macdonald · *Della Smith*
Polly Walker · *Anne Collins*
Bill Nighy · *Cameron Foster*
Amelia Bullmore · *Helen Preger*
Michael Feast · *Andrew Wilson*
Deborah Findlay · *Greer Thornton*
Philip Glenister · *DCI Bell*
James Laurenson · *George Fergus*
Johann Myers · *Sonny Stagg*
Michael Pennington · *Richard Sieglar*
Geraldine James · *Yvonne Shaps*

Creator/Writer Paul Abbott **Producers** Paul Abbott, Laura Mackie, Gareth Neame (executive), Hilary Bevan Jones
Theme Music Nick Hooper

Paul Abbott graduated from the soap opera stories of ***Clocking Off*** for one of 2003's stand-out dramas, a political thriller intertwined with scandal, conspiracies and the corruption of the political process by big business. Beginning with two seemingly unconnected deaths – a murdered teenager and a researcher working for and conducting an affair with MP Stephen Collins – the six-part serial takes us into the unscrupulous world of tabloid journalism as Cal McCaffrey, Collins' former campaign manager and now writer for the *Herald*, is asked to investigate whether the two deaths are connected. Exactly what the connection is remains a secret until near the end, but it results in the near-disgrace of Collins, whose wife is also sleeping with Cal, and an ever-widening range of targets for an assassin.

The series scored a BAFTA award for Best Drama Serial and a Best Actor award for the always-great Bill Nighy as newspaperman Cameron Foster (Nighy had previously played a low-end tabloid journalist in the ITV drama ***Fox***). A second series is in production at the time of writing, expected to be aired sometime in 2005.

Stella Street

Comedy | Tiger Aspect/Stella Street Productions for BBC Two | episode duration 10–15 mins, plus specials | broadcast 22 Dec 1997–11 Dec 2001, 21 Mar 2004

Cast

John Sessions · *Various Characters, Keith Richards, Roger Moore, Marlon Brando, Al Pacino*
Phil Cornwell · *Various Characters, Mick Jagger, Michael Caine, Jack Nicholson, David Bowie*
Ronnie Ancona · *Various Characters, Madonna, Jerry Hall, Victoria Beckham, Penélope Cruz*

Producers Charles Brand, Andrew Zein (executive), Ben Swaffer
Writers John Sessions, Phil Cornwell, Peter Richardson
Theme Music Gary DeMichele

In the late 1990s, BBC Two had a temporary vogue for comedies that only ran to ten or 15 minutes, a significant departure from the sitcom standard 30 minutes. Alongside the marvellous ***Marion and Geoff***, *Stella Street* attracted quite a lot of positive press and a small but dedicated viewership. Written by and starring impressionists John Sessions and Phil Cornwell, Stella Street turned the usual conventions of an impressionist show on its head – rather than simply having a series of different impressions in different sketches one after another, *Stella Street* was instead a sitcom populated entirely by Sessions and Cornwell's impressions of famous people (Cornwell relying on many of the voices he'd used when providing vocals for Gilbert, the nasally-dribbling alien puppet star of Saturday morning kids' TV show *Get Fresh*). In this small suburban street, Mick Jagger and Keith Richards are the owners of the corner shop and movie legends like Jack Nicholson, Marlon Brando and Roger Moore are all neighbours.

More than simply a showcase for the stars' admittedly impressive abilities at looking and sounding like the stars they were 'taking off', *Stella Street* also worked simply because of the ludicrous idea of these international megastars living in a perfectly ordinary suburban street – the concept of them all having to pop down to the corner shop for a pint of milk and a loaf of bread, only to have to put up with a steaming drunk Keith Richards and a 'lippy' Mick Jagger was simply inspired. The only down side of a sitcom/sketch show/comedy series written by and starring just two people is that if you're not a particular fan of those individuals, there's not a great deal on offer for you. Perhaps realising that (or just a little bit wary of playing yet more female characters), Sessions and Cornwell roped in female impressionist Ronnie Ancona for an impressive final 80-minute-long special, screened in March 2004.

Steptoe and Son

See pages 718–21

Stig of the Dump (1981)

Children's Drama | Thames Television | episode duration 25–30 mins | broadcast 38 Sep–28 Oct 1981

Principal Cast
Keith Jayne · *Stig*
Grant Ashley Warnock · *Barney*
Kenneth Gilbert · *Chief*
Nigel Patterson · *Tribesman*
Janine Tidman · *Lou*
Bay White · *Gran*

Producers Pamela Lonsdale (executive), Sheila Kinany
Writer Maggie Wadey, from the novel by Clive King
Theme Music Paul Lewis

For commentary, see STIG OF THE DUMP (2002)

Stig of the Dump (2002)

Children's Drama | Childsplay Ltd for BBC One | episode duration 25–30 mins | broadcast 3 Jan–17 Feb 2002

Principal Cast
Thomas Sangster · *Barney*
Robert Tannion · *Stig*
Nick Ryan · *Voice of Stig*
Geoffrey Palmer · *Robert Tollworth*
Phyllida Law · *Marjorie Tollworth*
Perdita Weeks · *Lou*
Saskia Wickham · *Caroline*
Andrew Schofield · *Billy Snarget, Craig*

Producers Elaine Sperber (executive), Peter Tabern **Writer** Peter Tabern, from the novel by Clive King **Theme Music** Debbie Wiseman

The classic children's story by Clive King has twice been adapted into a TV series. Young Barney and his sister Lou are on holiday, staying with their gran. One day Barney discovers a shambling figure living in a nearby quarry. For years, people living in the area had dumped their rubbish into the quarry, little knowing that somebody had made their junk his own home. Barney befriends the primitive, caveman-like figure Stig, and soon they become the best of friends, Barney helping him to make a window for his cave out of jam jars and to get a running water supply. Just as Stig learns about the conveniences of modern living, so Barney learns what it's like to be free from worries about parents, school and other mundane matters like that.

The original adaptation of *Stig of the Dump* featured former ***Onedin Line*** actor Keith Jane as the rubbish-dwelling primitive, with little more than the odd smudge of dirty make-up and a vocabulary consisting of grunts to indicate his un-evolved status. Twenty years later, and the full joys of animatronics and costly prosthetics made the new-look Stig much more like the Neanderthal the story implied he must be. Both versions of the story were charming children's drama series, perfectly suited to the eras in which they were broadcast. There was an additional TV outing for Stig when, in 1986, actor Christopher Guard read an adaptation of the story on ***Jackanory***.

Stingray

Children's Puppet Drama | AP Films/ITC for ITV | episode duration 25 mins | broadcast 4 Oct 1964–2 Jun 1965

Regular Voice Cast
Don Mason · *Captain Troy Tempest*
Robert Easton · *Lieutenant George 'Phones' Sheridan, Surface Agent X Two Zero*
Lois Maxwell · *Lieutenant Atlanta Shore*
Ray Barrett · *Commander Sam Shore, Titan*
David Graham · *Oink*

Creators Gerry and Sylvia Anderson **Producers** Gerry Anderson, Reg Hill (associate producer) **Writers** Gerry and Sylvia Anderson, Alan Fennell, Dennis Spooner **Theme Music** Composed, arranged and conducted by Barry Gray. End theme, 'Aqua Marina', also by Barry Gray, was sung by Gary Miller, a British artist who sang in an American style and who had hits in the late 1950s and early 1960s, including 'Robin Hood' and 'The Garden of Eden'.

It's 2064 and the world's oceans are protected by an organisation called WASP – the World Aquanaut Security Patrol – which is based at Marineville on the west coast of America. It's an impressive complex that, during a security alert, can be lowered completely underground courtesy of massive hydraulic jacks. Head of operations at Marineville is Commander Shore, a grumpy old warhorse who, though crippled, can glide about his office in a state-of-the-art hoverchair. He's ably assisted by his daughter, Atlanta, who

Continued on page 722

Steptoe and Son

Harold Steptoe is tormented by his dad Albert (he's the one on the right . . .).

Ray Galton and Alan Simpson had supplied Tony Hancock with scripts for five years before the idea of a comedy set in a junkyard occurred to them. When their pitch for a new series for Frankie Howerd was rejected (on the basis that, it was then felt, Howerd had no future in television) BBC Head of Light Entertainment Tom Sloan made Galton and Simpson a remarkable offer, the chance to write ten new one-off comedies with any setting and their choice of cast. Sloan's idea, which he called *Comedy Playhouse*, effectively placed the writers above the title, where names like Howerd or Hancock usually went.

Though Galton and Simpson accepted the offer as a means of escaping the treadmill of scripting another long-running sitcom, for Tom Sloan each of the episodes was being viewed as a potential pilot. There were some strong contenders in the mix – actor Graham Stark was convinced that the one he starred in opposite Alfred Marks, 'The Status Symbol' had 'series' written all over it. But after the fourth play, 'The Offer', was broadcast it became the obvious choice for further development. 'The Offer' starred Wilfrid Brambell, who was just 49 at the time but had been playing old men for much of the previous decade, with bit-parts in both ***Quatermass II***and ***Nineteen Eighty-Four***. Harry H. Corbett, meanwhile, was an up-and-coming stage actor earning a reputation as the 'British Brando'. A graduate of the Joan Littlewood Theatre Workshop Company, he added the 'H' to distance himself from Harry Corbett, Sooty's creator.

Though 'The Offer' was about two rag-and-bone men, the story was more about two people trapped together through circumstances rather than a genuine insight into the junk trade. The motivations for the Steptoe men barely changed from this first pilot until their final appearance in 1974: approaching middle age, Harold longs to escape the drudgery of totting and enjoy a life of decadence but he feels his father always holds him back; Albert accepts his lot in life but is frightened of being abandoned by his only son. What makes the show is the constant wrestling for power between the two. Harold puts his father down at every opportunity for being ignorant while clearly being little better (in 'The Economist' he mocks the old man for not knowing what the Acropolis is, but by way of explanation refers to 'the four horsemen of the Acropolis'). Admittedly, Albert makes it easy for him by dressing in second-hand moth-eaten rags, eating pickled onions in the bath and having only the most casual of relationships with the notion of hygiene, personal or otherwise.

Albert resents his son's obsession with bettering himself, expressing the opinion that 'books lead to Communism' and that things were better when the working man knew his place. This reverse snobbery might appear like just another trick to stop the son from leaving but it's much deeper than that. Albert knows that Harold is a dreamer, that if he were to indulge his son's fantasies, they'd starve (as we see when Harold invests £40 in 4000 sets of false teeth, which Albert correctly predicts he'll never sell), or worse, Harold would suffer ridicule from the hoi polloi he so desperately wants to ingratiate himself with. Instead, Albert belittles Harold to keep him from getting carried away with his fantasies, or if he feels he's losing the battle, he feigns a heart attack (Brambell always claimed that while the attacks were clearly psychosomatic or even faked, for the old man they were real; his fear of being alone would induce a panic that convinced him his time was running out).

Harold is his own worst enemy, but he's right to blame his father for holding him back, and in the first series episode, 'The Bird', we see just how malicious Albert can be. Harold's date for the evening hasn't shown up and, feigning sympathy, his father convinces him that she's only agreed to the date out of pity. Eventually, the date arrives as if nothing has happened to be greeted by a distraught Harold telling her to sling her hook. With Harold sloping off to bed alone, we see the old man turn the hands of an old grandfather clock back an hour: the girlfriend had been on time all along.

One other recurring subject for discussion was the annual holiday, which invariably involved Harold's attempts to go abroad alone while his father, claiming he vowed never to return to mainland Europe after his time in the trenches in World War One, pushes for their regular trip to Bognor, with its boarding houses and petting zoo. For Harold, the foreign holidays are merely another facet of his desire to mix with the likes of Brigitte Bardot and Frank Sinatra; he never really stands a chance of escaping Bognor, but it's important for him to keep up the pretence because making his father beg is the only way he knows to get him to show affection. References abound to Harold's childhood when, he claims, Albert used to beat him and maltreat him. When we see the well-built younger man shouting at his stick-insect father it's hard to imagine which is the more physically intimidating in Harold's mind; these emotional scars run deep.

This war of domestic politics plays the audience like a finely tuned violin, making us swing from shock at the old man's persistent cruelty to the recognition of certain harsh realities of life that the son is blind to, from supporting Harold's ambition to agreeing with his dad that he should stick to what he knows in fear of exposing his lack of other talents. Gradually we realise that Harold's threats to leave home and Albert's frequent heart attacks are merely ammunition in

Sitcom
BBC TV/BBC One
Episode Duration: 30 mins
Broadcast: 5 Jan 1962, 14 Jun 1962–26 Dec 1974

Regular Cast
Wilfrid Brambell · *Albert Edward Ladysmith Steptoe*
Harry H. Corbett · *Harold Albert Kitchener Steptoe*

Creators/Writers Ray Galton and Alan Simpson

Producers Duncan Wood, John Howard Davies, David Croft, Graeme Muir, Douglas Argent

Theme Music 'Old Ned' by Ron Grainer

this never ending war. Both know the other's tricks of old but are incapable of crossing that line because they know deep down they depend upon each other utterly.

Within two years, *Steptoe and Son* had established itself as a major success. Such was the series' popularity that Prime Minister Harold Wilson expressed serious concerns that it was scheduled to be broadcast at 8.00 p.m. on the day of the 1964 General Election, the belief being that *Steptoe and Son* attracted the same audience as the Labour Party hoped to, which might prevent the voters from showing up at the polls (the episode was slipped an hour to 9.00 p.m. that evening, though whether that was down to governmental influence or because the news of the day made that the first available slot is at least debatable).

Brambell's success in the Beatles' film *A Hard Day's Night* (1964) raised his profile overseas, including America, and when he was offered a leading part in a Broadway musical *Kelly*, he accepted it. With Brambell possibly out of the UK, Galton and Simpson were confronted by a dilemma: should they kill off the show or just the old man. For a time, the writers considered the latter, with the introduction of a new character, Harold's illegitimate son. Fortunately for the series (but unfortunately for Brambell), *Kelly*'s long Broadway run never materialised – it closed after just one night. Brambell returned to the UK and almost immediately commenced work on a fourth series of *Steptoe*. With the writers and the stars eager to be seen capable of doing something other than *Steptoe*, the gates of the junkyard at Mews Cottage, Oil Drum Lane, Shepherd's Bush, closed seemingly for the last time. The scripts were re-cycled and adapted for radio, with Corbett and Brambell recreating their roles, but by then audience familiarity with the characters meant that scenes that had initially left viewers floored with the pathos of it all sent the live radio audiences into gales of laughter. *Steptoe and Son* was no longer poignant now that even the most utterly tragic scenes were guaranteed laughs.

Despite the absence of new episodes for the remainder of the 1960s, *Steptoe and Son* enjoyed regular repeats. But the arrival of colour TV inspired a downturn in the successes of black-and-white shows. With the increased licence fee, viewers resented being offered programming in black and white – particularly repeats. Hence Galton, Simpson, Brambell and Corbett were persuaded back for a colour series. The fact that the return of *Steptoe and Son* was designed to be a big-hitter for the BBC as part of the new all-colour schedules (promoted on the front cover of the *Radio Times*) is strange considering that the only real change was from dirty greys to equally dirty browns. In fact, colour was never *Steptoe and Son*'s selling point (though making any major show in black and white would have been unthinkable by 1970). Once again, its strength was found in its scripts and performances.

Just as it had done from the beginning, the series continued to push the boundaries of what was and wasn't acceptable for a BBC sitcom. The first colour episodes 'treated' viewers to the sight of Albert shovelling up horse manure, sniffing his fingers appreciatively

TRIVIA

In 1963, Galton and Simpson were called to write a special *Steptoe and Son* script for a Royal Variety Performance. The sketch revealed that Old Man Steptoe had just returned from a call to a big house at the end of the Mall and accepted a load of 'junk' from a little boy (presumably Prince Charles) in exchange for a windmill on a stick. The performance was overshadowed slightly by another group of working-class heroes, The Beatles (John Lennon famously inviting the members of the Royal box to 'rattle yer jewellery'), and while a recording of Brambell and Corbett performing the sketch didn't prevent The Beatles' 'I Wanna Hold Your Hand' reaching No. 1, its own position in the singles charts – climbing to No. 25 – was impressive for a comedy disc.

and eating a sandwich in one gut-wrenching move. A later episode shows him using a recently drained beer bottle as a rolling pin and using a pair of false teeth to serrate the edges of his pie crust.

A highlight from this colour period was 'The Desperate Hours'. Late at night, two criminals, recently escaped from prison, invade the Steptoe house. The older of the two (played by J. G. Devlin, who had been second choice for the part of Albert Steptoe had Brambell refused the role) is struggling to keep pace with the younger (Leonard Rossiter) and begs to use the Steptoe's abode for shelter. Often regarded as one of the all-time great episodes, 'The Desperate Hours' plays upon the similarities between the two pairs of men; one old and weak, one relatively young and resentful of being lumbered with someone who he knows is holding him back. It's a situation played surprisingly straight; even when Harold and Albert deliver characteristically brilliant comic lines, Devlin and Rossiter always react with irritation, never stepping outside of their dramatic function to mug to the audience (indeed Rossiter is particularly threatening at some points, leaving us to feel genuine concern for the outcome). The realisation that the criminals were richer in prison than the two junk men are, supposedly free, leads them to return to jail, leaving both Steptoes feeling sorry for their new comrades, and themselves. 'I'm glad they stayed together,' sighs Albert, prompting Harold to growl, 'Yeah, I expect you are . . . .'

Two moderately successful feature films followed in 1972 and '73. Having already produced two unsuccessful pilots for the USA, an American version finally arrived on 14 January 1972. *Sanford and Son* took the brave step of recasting the roles as African-Americans. Starring Redd Foxx as Fred Sanford and Demond Wilson as his son Lamont, *Sanford and Son* ran until 1977 and spawned three separate spin-offs, *Sanford Arms* (1977) in which Fred took over a bar, *Grady* (1975), starring one of the regular characters, Grady Wilson (played by Whitman Mayo), and a 1980 revival called simply *Sanford*. As for the originals, well it's well known that by the end of the series Corbett and Brambell were barely talking, having grown to loathe each other, a feeling worsened by a disastrous tour of Australia together. Their final appearance together was for a 1980 TV commercial for Kenco coffee, performed in character and scripted by Galton and Simpson.

It's no exaggeration that ***The Likely Lads***, Alf Garnet, the Trotters of Peckham, even 'the Boys from the *Dwarf*' owe their very existence to two grotty rag-and-bone men from Shepherds Bush, yet it's a debt that's no longer acknowledged by the British public if the BBC's 2004 Best Sitcom is anything to go by. Perhaps the problem with *Steptoe and Son* is that it was first in a long line of sitcoms that relied upon fractious but loving relationships that involve debates about class, sex, work and feeling trapped by the people who love us most. It could also be that stories about rag-and-bone men seem too much like ancient history for a generation who consider themselves poor if they haven't got the right brand of trainers and think of television as a right rather than a privilege. For the rest of us, it's the most important sitcom ever made. Fact.

we soon discover is besotted with WASP's greatest pilot, Troy Tempest. Troy and his best buddy Phones make up the crew of the super-powered submarine Stingray, the pride of WASP and the fastest thing on or under water. After an encounter with Titan, the despotic leader of the Undersea World and his hideous soldiers, the Aquaphibians, Stingray is placed on constant alert against attack from their new aquatic enemies. Luckily, not all of the oceanic inhabitants are set on destruction, as the beautiful Marina of Pacifica proves . . .

Of all the programmes we've looked at for this book, there is none with a title sequence as thrilling as *Stingray*. From its opening undersea explosion and Commander Shore's promise that 'Anything can happen in the next half hour!' to the sight of a mechanical fish and Stingray itself performing a salmon-leap out of the water and back down again, all to the accompaniment of Barry Gray's energetic theme music, bongo drums, a dynamic brass-and-strings section and the male vocals chanting 'Sting-raaaaay – STINGRAY!'. . . there's barely chance to catch your breath before the main episode begins.

Like all of his early Supermarionation series, Gerry Anderson's *Stingray* is primarily for kids, but this is the first series where the sophistication of the production really warrants the grown-ups' attention too. Thanks to ITC head Lew Grade's confidence in Anderson's team, *Stingray* was afforded a bigger-than-average budget for a children's show. It was the first British TV show of any kind to be made wholly in colour (mainly for the American market; ITV wouldn't convert to colour broadcasts for another four years), and the model effects were of largely the same quality as one might expect to see in a feature film – courtesy of miniature set designer Derek Meddings, who later worked on the James Bond and Superman movies. Thanks to the use of a slimline fish tank placed in front of the camera, the dry sets that Stingray passed through on strings looked as if they were filmed in the very depths of the sea.

The puppets retained the caricatured aspects of ***Fireball XL5*** and ***Supercar***, but for the first time Anderson's designers used glass eyes to give a greater sense of realism, and each character had a range of different heads, which allowed for varied facial expressions. This was also the first time the puppets began to look strangely familiar, thanks to a casual remark by Anderson that he envisaged the main hero, Troy Tempest, as a 'James Garner' type. So Tempest was created in Garner's image, while the undersea temptress Marina, who the Stingray crew rescue in the first episode, was Anderson's idea of a perfect woman – she had the face of Brigitte Bardot, but she was completely mute! Unusually, only Atlanta Shore appears to have been modelled on the person who voiced her, Miss Moneypenny herself, Lois Maxwell.

The villains of the series were also modelled after famous actors. Titan, the despot ruler of the undersea world, was supposedly based on Laurence Olivier (though we can't see it ourselves), while his minion on the surface, Agent X Two Zero was modelled on Claude Rains, but voiced to sound like a snivelling Peter Lorre. X Two Zero lives on a remote island in an old abandoned house where the paintings and furniture exist solely to act as camouflage for X Two Zero's sophisticated computers and other equipment that allows him to communicate directly with Titan. Most memorable of all though were those fearsome Aquaphibians, sulky-faced fish people whose language sounds suspiciously similar to someone running their finger across their lips and saying 'flubblubble' (thereby making then easy to imitate in the playground). In the 1980s, impressionist and facial contortionist Phil Cool made a career out of recreating Aquaphibians for comic effect.

The show ran for 39 episodes. While it's clearly intended for young children (underlined by the addition of Oink the Seal to the crew in later episodes), *Stingray* is much less po-faced than ***Thunderbirds*** and its episodes are mercifully shorter, leading to tighter plotting and an engaging simplicity. Some of its stories are decidedly less aimed at realism than those of Anderson's later series; in the first episode, Titan places Troy on trial for his life in an ordeal that consists of a staring contest with the bloated fish God Teufel (no, really!), while in 'Tom Thumb Tempest' we see Troy shrunk to, well, puppet size, in one of Anderson's most annoying recurring plot devices, the dream sequence. But with the eternal love triangle between Atlanta, Troy and Marina (poor Phones just didn't get a look in), consistently strong visual effects and model work, and the excitement that comes each week with another pair of representatives of the undersea civilisations (funny how they always travel in twos), *Stingray* remains one of the most popular shows of Gerry Anderson's long career, and it's not hard to see why.

Trivia

While Thunderbirds had 'FAB', the Stingray crew got there first with the slightly less catchy 'PWOR' – Proceed With Orders Received. Most male viewers would have used the callsign for a more gutteral word to describe Marina.

Though it's never mentioned in the TV show, the mystery of Marina's inability to talk was solved on 'Marina Speaks', one of a series of flexidisc records released by TV 21 comic in the 1960s. Marina decides to write Atlanta a letter explaining how the cruel Titan cursed all of Marina's people so that if any of them ever uttered one word they would all die.

The Stone Tape

Science Fiction | BBC One | episode duration 90 mins | broadcast 25 Dec 1972

Cast

Michael Bryant · *Peter Brock*
Jane Asher · *Jill Greeley*
Iain Cuthbertson · *Roy Collinson*
Michael Bates · *Eddie Holmes*
Reginald Marsh · *Crawshaw*

Tom Chadbon · *Hargrave*
John Forgehan · *Maudsley*
James Cosmo · *Cliff Dow*
Philip Trewinnard · *Stewart Jessop*
Neil Wilson · *Sergeant Paterson*
Hilda Fenemore · *Bar Helper*
Peggy Marshall · *Bar Lady*
Michael Graham Cox · *Alan*
Christopher Banks · *Vicar*

Creator/Writer Nigel Kneale **Producer** Innes Lloyd **Theme Music** A discordant collection of white noise and ambient electronic organ created by Desmond Briscoe, head of the BBC Radiophonic Workshop

Sponsored by Ryan Electric Products to develop an entirely new recording medium, experimental scientist Peter Brock and his team take over an old mansion as their base. Exploring the building, computer programmer Jill Greeley finds a storeroom that was once part of the original house the mansion was built on top of. There she experiences a vision of a maid falling to her death. The apparition leaves Jill shaken, but Peter becomes obsessed by it, changing the focus of the team's research towards re-creating the vision. As he and Jill investigate further, Peter becomes convinced that the new recording medium they were hired to find could well be literally under their noses. However, not all of the team can see the images and remain unconvinced by, or at least sceptical of, Peter's theory that the rocks in the building's foundations might have 'recorded' images from centuries before.

The revelation that the site has twice played host to an exorcism and that the hauntings extend further back in history than the Victorian servant girl's attire would suggest, leaves Jill on the verge of hysteria as she continues to be the focal point of both the visitations and Peter's experiments. Even after the tape that has been made of the recordings is accidentally wiped, Jill is terrified that she might lose her mind before the project is over . . .

Almost certainly inspired by Charles Dickens' *A Christmas Carol*, Christmas plays about the supernatural became quite a tradition for the Beeb in the 1970s, with adaptations of M. R. James's short stories a regular festive fixture in a series appropriately named ***A Ghost Story for Christmas***. *The Stone Tape*, however, was a wholly original story not shown as part of that particular anthology series but as a stand-alone play.

Written by Nigel Kneale, who had electrified audiences with ***Nineteen Eighty-Four*** and the ***Quatermass*** series, the play relies almost entirely on the performances of the cast, in particular Jane Asher as Jill, who slowly discovers that she may have latent psychic abilities, and the somewhat bombastic Michael Bryant as Peter, striving for a rational explanation of events even if none can be found. Peter Sasdy's direction makes full use of lighting and camera angles to convey the menace within the mansion walls, with only very basic video techniques and clever editing providing the special effects. In some ways a forerunner of BBC One's ***Ghostwatch***, *The Stone Tape* avoided the overly sensationalist approach and as a consequence has enjoyed a reputation greater than its two TV airings would usually demand. Thanks to a DVD release from the British Film Institute in 2001, new audiences can experience a terrifyingly effective chiller.

The Storyteller

Anthology | Henson Associates/TVS for NBC/Channel 4 | episode duration 25 mins | broadcast 15 May–10 July 1988, 1–22 Dec 1991

Regular Cast
John Hurt, Michael Gambon · *The Storyteller*
Brian Henson · *Voice of the Dog*

Creators Jim Henson, Anthony Minghella **Producers** Jim Henson (executive), Martin G. Baker (associate), Duncan Kenworthy, Mark Shivas **Writers** Anthony Minghella, Nigel Williams **Theme Music** Rachel Portman

When people used stories to tell their past, explain their present and foretell their future, the best place by the fireside would be kept for the Storyteller, a wizened old man whose constant companion was a rather shaggy dog.

A superbly creative series, *The Storyteller* brought the talents of Jim Henson's Creature Shop to the small screen. Each episode told a familiar story in an unfamiliar way, weaving different versions of the tale together, much as the brothers Grimm had done. 'Sapsorrow' was a version of 'Cinderella', but this time the girl is also a hideous hairy hag whose transformation into the Prince's true love involves more than just a pair of glass slippers. 'Three Ravens' plays with the wicked stepmother idea, a witch who turns the King's three sons into ravens, a curse that can only be lifted if the King's daughter remains mute for over three years. Every story begins with the Storyteller himself, telling the tale in the style of ***Jackanory***. The difference here is that his dog can talk and isn't afraid of interrupting to correct the odd detail.

The series attracted superb guest casts, from Bob Peck as a soldier who manages to catch Death itself and Miranda Richardson as a wicked stepmother, to Dawn French and Jennifer Saunders as the ugly sisters of Sapsorrow. But the real stars were of course the creatures, which included demons, a griffin, a hedgehog riding a cockerel and a hideous troll.

When *The Storyteller* was finally revealed to American TV executives, they were baffled as to what to do with it. The stories were too scary to be shown alongside other children's programming, but each episode was a fairy tale, which they felt would be wrong for grown-ups. This lukewarm reaction, coupled with the time and money the production consumed, meant that only nine episodes were made of the original series. A second brief series, *The Storyteller: Greek Myths*, cast Michael Gambon as a storyteller wandering the labyrinth of Knossos, accompanied by the dog who, as before, passed comment on the stories. Just four episodes were made this time, 'Perseus and the Gorgon', 'Theseus and the Minotaur', 'Daedalus and Icarus' and 'Orpheus and Eurydice'.

Street Hawk

Action-Adventure | Universal for ABC (shown on ITV) | episode duration 45 mins | broadcast 4 Jan–16 May 1985 (USA)

Regular Cast
Rex Smith · *Jesse Mach*
Joe Regalbuto · *Norman Tuttle*
Richard Venture · *Captain Leo Altobelli*
Jayne Modean, Jeannie Wilson · *Rachel Adams*
Raymond Singer · *Bernie*

Creators Robert Wolterstorff and Paul M. Belous **Producers** Various, including Bruce Lansbury, Burton Armus, Karen Harris, Stephen Cragg **Writers** Various, including Nicholas Corea, Bruce Cervi, Hannah Louise Shearer, Deborah Davis, Burton Armus **Theme Music** Tangerine Dream, legendary German techno group, composed the synth-heavy theme. The band – consisting of Christopher Franke (who later wrote incidental music for ***Babylon 5***), Edgar Froese and Johannes Schmölling – actually put together a suite of nearly three hours' incidental music, much of which was used during action sequences in the episodes.

Motorcycle cop Jesse Mach is injured and his partner is killed in the line of duty. While he's recuperating, Mach is assigned to a desk job in the police PR department, a job he's less than happy with. Mach is eventually approached by a government engineer called Norman Tuttle and offered a place on the team working on a top-secret prototype called Street Hawk, a super-advanced motorbike designed specifically for tackling urban crime. Jesse signs up for the project, and once he's used to handling the 300 mph+ vehicle, decides to get revenge on the criminals who killed his partner.

One of the better efforts from the 'super-vehicle action series' boom of the mid-1980s (see also ***Airwolf*** and ***Knight Rider***), *Street Hawk* unfortunately never really caught on with the public, lasting for only 13 episodes. Having said that, it's really not at all bad, with a decent concept behind the show and charming performances from the two leads – especially Regalbuto, who went on to achieve major success in *Murphy Brown*. Guest stars in the first episode included future ***Star Trek: Voyager*** star Robert Beltran as Jesse Mach's ill-fated partner and Christopher Lloyd (of *Back to the Future*) playing very much against type as a villainous gang leader. The motorbike upgraded and modified to create Street Hawk was a Honda CR250 (although the less expensive C125 model was used for stunt work, just in case things went wrong).

The Streets of San Francisco

Crime Drama | Quinn Martin for ABC (shown on ITV) | episode duration 50 mins | broadcast 16 Sep 1972–23 Jun 1977, 27 Jan 1992 (USA)

Regular Cast
Karl Malden · *Detective Lieutenant Mike Stone*
Michael Douglas · *Inspector Steve Keller*
Darleen Carr · *Jeannie Stone*
Richard Hatch · *Inspector Dan Robbins*
Reuben Collins · *Inspector Tanner*
Fred Sadoff · *Dr Lenny Murchison*
Lee Harris · *Lieutenant Lessing*
Vic Tayback · *Officer Haseejian*
Art Passarella · *Sergeant Sekulovich*

Creator Carolyn Weston (the original pilot movie was based on her novel *Poor, Poor Ophelia*) **Producers** Quinn Martin (executive), Russell Stoneman, Cliff Gould, John Wilder, William Robert Yates **Writers** Various, including Rod Baker, Walter Black, Larry Brody, Gene L. Coon, Paul Robert Coyle, Theodore J. Flicker, Cliff Gould, Shirl Hendryx, Edward Hume, Rick Husky, Charles McDaniel, Eugene Price, Del Reisman, Michael Russnow, James Schmerer, Hal Sitowitz, Guerdon Trueblood, John Wilder **Theme Music** Pat Williams

Another great 1970s American cop show as much remembered for its theme music as its action, *The Streets of San Francisco* cast a young Michael Douglas as 28-year-old graduate cop Steve Keller and Karl Malden as the veteran Mike Stone. Stone's tried and tested police methods often clashed with Keller's enthusiastic modern approach but they somehow came through in the end. The characters were first seen in a TV movie, which was followed by the series. Looking back at the show, it's fun to notice Academy Award-winner Malden guiding Douglas through what was effectively a supporting part; at that point, Douglas was still only the son of a movie star rather than a leading man in his own right. During the third season, Douglas told the producers he would not return for a fourth as he was about to produce the film adaptation of *One Flew Over the Cuckoo's Nest* (1975), a production that would bag Douglas the first of two Oscars (the second would be for his performance in *Wall Street*, 1987). The series was popular with viewers and critics alike: Douglas was nominated for Emmy Awards for each of his three years on the show, while Malden was nominated for the 1976 and 1977 seasons and the show itself received a nod for its third year.

With Douglas's character written out to become a teacher, the final season introduced another rookie, Richard Hatch as Dan Robbins. Fans generally point to this casting as the reason why the show didn't return for a fifth year, which is a shame as the storytelling was just as sharp as it had always been, with a greater focus on the cases themselves (input from Mike Stone's college-student daughter having been gradually reduced). Though *The Streets of San Francisco* ended in 1977 (with final episodes reaching British shores in 1980), both Mike Stone and Dan Robbins returned for a reunion movie – *Back to the Streets of San Francisco* – in 1992. At the time of writing, rumours persist that a feature film remake is on the cards, with fans hoping to see the return of Michael Douglas, this time as the experienced detective taking on a new recruit.

Strictly Come Dancing

See COME DANCING

Strictly Dance Fever

See COME DANCING

Strike it Lucky

Game Show | Thames/Central for ITV | episode duration 25 mins | broadcast 1986–1999

Cast
Michael Barrymore · *Host*

Producer Maurice Leonard

Three couples would compete for prizes and money, with one half of each couple standing to one side to answer questions while the other half acted as a playing piece on a board-game, traversing the arched set to strike the screens that would reveal what (if anything) they'd won. Occasionally a 'hot spot' would appear on the screens to wipe out all of the prizes that one couple had won in that round. The way to avoid these would be to halt progression and bank all of the prizes, but there was always the temptation to race as far as possible to get the end of the row and bag a change for a bigger prize.

The end game featured a bank of 30 screens containing ten questions, ten arrows and ten hot spots. The winning couple would choose whether to risk being stopped after two hotspots, three hotspots or four. Choosing four would give them a better chance of winning but a lower prize, while two hotspots raised both their chances of going bust and getting a top prize. They had to work their way across the board, stopping for questions, advancing with arrows and praying they'd avoid the right amount of hotspots.

In 1996, the show changed production companies and its name became *Strike it Rich*, with an increased jackpot of £10,000.

Host Michael Barrymore had a talent for putting people at ease; acting in mock exasperation at some of the things the contestants came out with but always with a genuine, infectious affection. Even after his troubled private life became public and he began to go a bit off the rails, Barrymore remained adored by the public. He made light entertainment look easy, which is a skill in itself.

The Sullivans

Soap | Crawford Productions for 9 Network (shown on ITV) | episode duration 30 mins | broadcast 15 Nov 1976–Mar 1983 (Aus)

Principal Cast
Paul Cronin · *Dave Sullivan*
Lorraine Bayly · *Grace Sullivan*
Andrew McFarlane · *John Sullivan*
Steven Tandy · *Tom Sullivan*
Richard Morgan · *Terry Sullivan*
Susan Hannaford · *Kitty Sullivan/McGovern*
Vivean Gray · *Mrs Ida Jessup/Pike*
Norman Yemm · *Norm Baker*
Vikki Hammond · *Maggie Baker*
Jamie Higgins · *Geoff Sullivan*
Michael Caton · *Harry Sullivan*
Maggie Dence · *Rose Sullivan*
Genevieve Picot · *Caroline Sullivan*
Megan Williams · *Alice Watkins/Sullivan*
Andy Anderson · *Jim Sullivan*
Penny Downie · *Patty Spencer Sullivan*
Dinah Shearing · *Mary Sullivan*
Fiona Paul · *Maureen Sullivan*
David Clencie · *Steve Sullivan*
Graham Harvey · *Robbie McGovern*
John Walton · *Michael Watkins*
Myra de Groot · *Laura Watkins*
Wallas Eaton · *Arthur Pike*
Ilona Rodgers · *Kate Meredith*
Lisa Crittenden · *Sally Meredith*

Creator Jack Blair, Ian Jones **Producers** Henry Crawford, John Barringham, Hector Crawford, Ian Jones, Ian Crawford, Jock Blair **Writers** Various, including Lynn Bayonas, Ray Kolle, Tony Morphett, Charlie Strachan **Theme Music** Geoff Harvey

One of the perennial staples of the ITV weekday lunchtime schedules throughout the 1980s, *The Sullivans* told the story of a suburban middle class family in Melbourne, Australia throughout World War Two. Head of the family was stern patriarch Dave Sullivan, World War One veteran perpetually grimacing for the family photograph in the opening title sequence. Along with his wife Grace, Dave shepherded his family through the trials and tribulations of the war. Eldest sons John and Tom soon enlist for the army, along with Dave and his best friend Norm. Soon, the standard soap plotlines are interwoven with the dramas and threats of the conflict, and eventually several of the regular cast meet tragic fates. In particular, when Lorraine Bayly decided to leave the series, an especially sad fate lay in store for Grace. Having travelled all the way to London to be with her injured son, the ever-loving mother of the Sullivans was killed in a German bombing raid.

The Sullivans is notable for seeing early acting appearances by performers who would go on to much bigger and better things; both Mel Gibson and Kylie Minogue appeared in this long-running and highly satisfying slice of Aussie soap.

Sunday Night at the London Palladium

Variety | ATV for ITV | episode duration 50 mins | broadcast 25 Sep 1955–1967, 1973–1974, 2000

Principal Cast

Tommy Trinder, Bob Monkhouse, Bruce Forsyth, Dickie Henderson, Robert Morley, Don Arroll, Des O'Connor, Norman Vaughan, Jimmy Tarbuck, Jim Dale · *Hosts*
Eric Rogers, Cyril Ornadel, Jack Parnell · *Music Directors*
The Tiller Girls · *Resident Dancers*

Creator Val Parnell **Producers** Val Parnell (executive), Brian Tesler **Theme Music** 'Startime' composed by Eric Rogers, the original music director for the show

For more than a decade, there was one television programme that week in, week out could be relied upon to deliver the absolute best in variety entertainment – *Val Parnell's Sunday Night at the London Palladium*. Created and produced by long-time variety theatre and television producer Val(entine) Parnell, this hour-long live programme held audiences enthralled. Each episode would be introduced by the programme's regular host (beginning with Tommy Trinder in 1955) and would feature a number of performers such as comedians, ventriloquists, acrobats and musicians.

Towards the end of the first 'act', there would also be the regular game show, entitled 'Beat the Clock'. Based on an American game show of the same name, it involved taking married couples out of the theatre audience and inviting them to take part in a number of silly/strange/bizarre games, such as copying an expert dance troupe, or trying to assemble a complicated puzzle. If they managed to do it within the specified time, they could win a jackpot prize of anything up to £1800 – a huge amount of money for the time. One of *Sunday Night at the London Palladium*'s most accomplished presenters was showbiz legend Bruce Forsyth – years later, he would revive the basic concept of 'Beat the Clock' (with more than a few modifications and enhancements) with the launch of ***The Generation Game***.

With the start of the second act, several more acts would be given their seven or eight minutes of fame. Then, finally, the top-of-the-bill performer would arrive – people as diverse as Frank Ifield, Tony Hancock, Gracie Fields or even The Beatles. When the series drew to a close in 1967, many people felt that it was the end of an era for Variety on television screens. Despite two attempts to resurrect the show in 1973 and 2000, the format never really seemed to grab the attention of the viewing public. In fact, only LWT's *Live From Her Majesty's* (1982–8), presented by ex-*Palladium* host Jimmy Tarbuck, had any kind of longevity. Unfortunately, even that success is now best remembered for the tragic death of veteran comic magician Tommy Cooper live on stage on 15 April 1984. Nowadays, only the annual *Royal Variety Performance* can really give us an idea of what these old-school shows were really like.

Superboy

Action-Adventure | Alexander Salkind/Cantharaus Productions NV/Lowry Productions (shown on ITV) | broadcast 8 Oct 1988–17 May 1992 (USA)

Principal Cast

John Haymes Newton, Gerard Christopher · *Superboy/Clark Kent*
Stacy Haiduk · *Lana Lang*
Scott Wells, Sherman Howard · *Lex Luthor*
Jim Calvert · *T. J. White*
George Chakiris · *Dr Peterson*
Peter J. Fernandez · *Matt Ritter*
R. Emmett Fitzsimmons · *Trucker*
Salome Jens · *Martha Kent*
Stuart Whitman · *Jonathan Kent*
George Lazenby · *Jor-El*
Robert Levine · *C. Dennis Jackson*
Michael Manno · *Leo*
Ilan Mitchell-Smith · *Andy McAllister*
Tracy Roberts · *Darla*

Creators Inspired by characters created by Joe Shuster and Jerry Siegel **Producer** Julia Pistor **Writers** Various, including Fred Freiberger, Toby Martin, Michael Carlin, Andrew Helfer, Cary Bates, Ilya Salkind, Mark Jones, Michael Maurer, Stan Berkowitz, Paul Stubenrauch, Gerard Christopher, J. M. DeMatteis **Theme Music** Kevin Kiner

For commentary, see ADVENTURES OF SUPERMAN

Supercar

Children's Science Fiction | AP Films/ATV/ITC for ITV | episode duration 25 mins | broadcast 28 Jan 1961–29 Apr 1962

Regular Voice Cast

Graydon Gould · *Mike Mercury*
Sylvia Thamm · *Jimmy Gibson*
George Murcell, Cyril Shaps · *Professor Rudolph Popkiss, Masterspy*
David Graham · *Mitch, Dr Horatio Beaker, Emil Zarin*

Creators Gerry Anderson, Reg Hill **Producer** Gerry Anderson **Writers** Hugh and Martin Woodhouse, Gerry and Sylvia Anderson **Theme Music** Barry Gray, sung by Mike Sammes

Gerry Anderson's connection with puppets had begun with his collaborations with producer Roberta Leigh on

The Adventures of Twizzle and ***Torchy the Battery Boy***. Anderson's own AP Films also created their own puppet adventures, the fantasy western series ***Four Feather Falls***, but it was with the company's first journey into science fiction, in the form of *Supercar*, that the Anderson legend really began. It kick-started Anderson's long association with Lew Grade's ITC, and in its second series, it introduced the concept of 'Supermarionation', a term used to describe Anderson's sophisticated lip-synched puppets.

The Supercar of the title is a rocket-powered car that can drive at high speeds of 1500 miles an hour or more; it can fly through the air; and it can dive to the deepest ocean. Housed in a secret laboratory in the Nevada desert, it was the creation of Professor Popkiss and his assistant, the stammering Dr Beaker (an early creation of David Graham, who would create many of Andersons' most famous characters, including Brains and Parker in ***Thunderbirds***). Its pilot/driver was Mike Mercury, who, in turn, was helped by Jimmy Gibson, an annoying ten-year-old with a talking pet monkey called Mitch. Each episode, the team would take on their main adversary, the villainous Masterspy, who would usually despatch a couple of his henchmen in the on-going quest to steal the Supercar.

Voice artist Sylvia Thamm would become known by her married name, Sylvia Anderson. The show also boasted the talents of puppeteer Christine Glanville, model master Derek Meddings and composer Barry Gray, all of whom would become staple ingredients for future Anderson productions.

Superman

See ADVENTURES OF SUPERMAN

Surgical Spirit

Sitcom | Humphrey Barclay Productions/Granada for ITV | episode duration 25 mins | broadcast 14 Apr 1989–7 Jul 1995

Principal Cast
Nichola McAuliffe · *Sheila Sabatini*
Duncan Preston · *Jonathan Haslam*
Marji Campi · *Joyce Watson*
Emlyn Price · *Neil Copeland*
David Conville · *George Hope-Wynne*
Suzette Llewellyn · *Sister Cheryl Patching*
Beresford Le Roy · *Michael Sampson*
Simon Harrison · *Giles Peake*
Lyndham Gregory · *Simon Field*
Andrew Groves · *Daniel Sabatini*

Creator Peter Learmouth **Producers** David Liddiment, Al Mitchell, Andy Harries, Antony Wood (executive), Humphrey Barclay **Writers** Peter Learmouth, Graeme Garden, Raymond Dixon, Annie Bruce, Annie Wood, Paul McKenzie **Theme Music** David Cullen

The most feared thing at Gillies Hospital isn't an old-fashioned battleaxe of a matron or even the canteen food – it's tyrannical senior surgeon Sheila Sabatini, a woman with a tongue sharper than any scalpel. Unwilling to suffer fools gladly (or otherwise), Sheila barks orders at her colleagues, patients or anyone who happens to get in her way. Despite her fearsome nature, Sheila does have some friends, including the hospital surgical administrator Joyce and the kindly anaesthetist Jonathan (with whom she slowly develops a relationship). Other members of the team are less to her liking – in particular the crusty old misogynistic consultant George Hope-Wynne, and any vulnerable junior staff who make mistakes in her operating theatre.

A well above-average ITV sitcom, *Surgical Spirit* had a well-deserved lengthy run of 50 episodes, spread across six seasons. Without a doubt, *Surgical Spirit*'s success has to be attributed to Nichola McAuliffe's dynamic performance as Sheila Sabatini – eyes glaring, shoulder-pads braced and hair scraped back into the severest of hairdos. It's not common for sitcoms to boast a lead female character who's as powerful, self-confident and shameless as Sheila, and viewers revelled in the chance to enjoy seeing a woman ranting and raving just as magnificently as any man could.

Survivors

Science Fiction/Drama | BBC One | episode duration 50 mins | broadcast 16 Apr 1975–8 Jun 1977

Regular Cast
Carolyn Seymour · *Abby Grant*
Lucy Fleming · *Jenny Richards*
Ian McCulloch · *Greg Preston*
Denis Lill · *Charles Vaughan*
Chris Tranchell · *Paul Pitman*
Talfryn Thomas · *Tom Price*
Terry Scully, Hugh Walters · *Vic Thatcher*
Hana Maria Pravda · *Emma Cohen*
John Abineri · *Hubert Marks*
Celia Gregory · *Ruth Anderson*
Michael Gover · *Arthur Russell*
Eileen Helsby · *Charmian Wentworth*
Lorna Lewis · *Pet Simpson*
Anna Pitt · *Agnes Carlsson*
Gordon Salkilld · *Jack Christensen*
John Hallet · *Barney*
Julie Neubert · *Wendy*
Stephen Dudley · *John*
Tanya Ronder, Angie Stevens · *Lizzie*
Peter Bowles · *David Grant*
Richard Heffer · *Jimmy Garland*
Peter Duncan · *Dave*

Creator Terry Nation **Producer** Terence Dudley **Writers** Terry Nation, Terence Dudley, Ian McCulloch, M. K. Jeeves,

Roger Parkes, Jack Ronder, Martin Worth, Don Shaw, Roger Marshall **Theme Music** Anthony Isaac

Somewhere in the Far East, a scientist is working with a flask of a new deadly virus. His hand slips and the flask falls to the floor, releasing its lethal contents. The virus spreads quickly across the globe, and within a few weeks, 99.9 per cent of the earth's population is dead. The few people who survive The Death are forced to band together in order to carry on living. Some resort to scavenging tinned food and other remnants of 20th-century society, others decide to revert to an agrarian existence. For upper middle-class housewife Abby Grant, the death of her husband David is just the start of her saga. Soon she finds herself allied with young former secretary Jenny Richards and ex-engineer Greg Preston in a desperate battle just to survive. For Abby, her personal quest to try and find whether her missing son Peter was dead or alive became a personal obsession.

Survivors was created by writer Terry Nation, a man who started off writing comedy for Hancock before going on to create the Daleks in ***Doctor Who*** and script editing the final year of ***The Avengers***. Later he would create another group of sci-fi heroes in ***Blake's 7***, but for *Survivors* he based his fantasy fiction on a very realistic premise. The basic concept of an apocalypse decimating humanity had been a sci-fi staple for years, encompassing books, films and TV shows as diverse as ***The Day of the Triffids***, Steven King's *The Stand*, ***Threads*** and even ***Nineteen Eighty-Four***. However, in *Survivors*, Terry Nation chose to focus on the long-term impact on very ordinary middle-class people whose entire world had suddenly come to an end. In the first season, viewers' sympathies mostly lay with poor Abby Grant, a woman discovering to her own surprise the resources and leadership ability that had lain dormant within her. Abby vocalises the concerns that everyone watching the programme must have felt: if society collapsed tomorrow, would you have the skills to make a simple knife from scratch? Could you melt the iron required? Could you dig the ore from the rocks? No, of course you couldn't – and viewers shared in the increasing realisation of the survivors that they would have to learn some very basic skills just to get through the first winter.

As the series progressed, new people joined Abby and Greg's community – self-serving repulsive Welsh tramp Tom Price, bitter wheelchair-bound Vic Thatcher, happy-go-lucky Paul Pitman and cheerful children John and Lizzie. In perhaps the most heartbreaking and memorable episode, mentally sub-normal labourer Barney was suspected of raping and murdering a member of their community. Faced with a terrible choice of banishing him into a wilderness of a slow lingering death from starvation, Abby and the other members of her commune chose to put Barney to death – only to discover to their horror that it was Tom Price who was the killer. Abby and Greg faced a number of challenges and successes – for every tanker of petrol they located, crops and livestock would be deliberately destroyed by a jealous bunch of rival survivors. At the end of the first series, despite having been responsible for founding a vaguely successful self-sufficient community, Abby left the programme to continue her quest for her missing son.

At the start of the second season, a fire rages through our heroes' community and kills many of the characters we had come to know and love. The lucky ones join forces with Charles Vaughan's commune many miles away and carry on the fight to rebuild their lives. When one of their number falls ill, a desperate mission to find necessary drugs takes our heroes into the heart of disease-and rat-ridden London, a journey that in itself costs the life of one of the long-running characters. Even the nominal leads of the series weren't safe – indeed, by the third series poor Greg falls prey to disease but nonetheless manages to posthumously establish a new government structure for Britain. In the 38th and final episode of the series, the survivors manage to restore electricity thanks to a hydroelectric power station: it's a rare note of unabashed hope and positivity for a series that prided itself on its melancholic view of humanity. With recent airborne viruses like SARS making the news, *Survivors* is perhaps even more relevant and scary today than it was back in the 1970s.

The Sweeney

See pages 730–2

Sykes

Sitcom | BBC TV/BBC One | episode duration 25–30 mins | broadcast 29 Jan 1960–16 Nov 1965 (*Sykes and a . . .*), 14 Sep 1972–16 Nov 1979 (*Sykes*)

Principal Cast
Eric Sykes · *Himself*
Hattie Jacques · *Hat Sykes*
Deryck Guyler · *PC Wilfred 'Corky' Turnbull*
Richard Wattis · *Charles Brown*

Creator Eric Sykes **Producers** Dennis Main Wilson, Sydney Lotterby, Philip Barker, Roger Race **Writers** Eric Sykes, Johnny Speight, John Antrobus, Spike Milligan **Theme Music** Ken E. Jones

Eric Sykes was born in 1923 in Oldham, near Manchester. Although he wrote material for many other performers (including Frankie Howerd, Peter Sellers and even Lenny the Lion and Terry Hall), he's best remembered for two long-running runs of a sitcom that paired him with *Carry On* actress Hattie Jacques. The first run of 59 episodes was titled *Sykes and a . . .*, the final word changing each week according to the nature of the plot. The set-up of the series was rather basic: brother and sister Eric and Hattie Sykes share a house together at 24 Sebastapol Terrace, East Acton.

Both Eric and Hat are single, and they spend a lot of their time simply dealing with life's minor irritating challenges, such as trapping a mouse that's on the loose in the house, or perhaps trying to deflect the attentions of an unsuitable romantic admirer. A regular visitor to their house is neighbourhood policeman Wilfred Turnbull, whom they nickname Corky, and occasionally they have to deal with their snobbish next-door neighbour Mr Brown.

The first season of *Sykes and a . . .* was written by future ***Till Death Us Do Part*** scribe Johnny Speight, and Spike Milligan contributed a couple of scripts to the second season. However, from the start of the third season in January 1961, every single episode of Sykes was written by Eric Sykes himself – a tremendous feat of consistent work. After nine seasons, *Sykes and a . . .* came to an end with Hattie Jacques busy as one of the stalwarts of the *Carry On* film series. A seven-year gap followed, after which Hattie, Eric and Deryck returned for an additional seven seasons of fun on BBC One. This time, the programme was simply called *Sykes* and was made in glorious colour. Many of the new run of episodes were adaptations of the earlier black-and-white ones, but others were brand new stories, too. Perhaps the only significant change to the series was the bizarre change in location of Eric and Hat's house, from number 24 to number 28 Sebastapol Terrace, but the style of comedy and the gentle friendly nature of the relationship between Eric and Hattie were a nostalgic throwback to a much simpler age. *Sykes* came to a conclusion after 68 colour episodes when series co-star Hattie Jacques died of a heart attack at the age of 58 – a tragic loss of a talented lady. Thankfully, Eric Sykes's career continues right to the time of writing, having starred in a number of guest roles in comedy series and in the feature film *The Others* (2001) opposite Nicole Kidman.

The Sweeney

A badly bruised Carter (Dennis Waterman) and Regan (John Thaw).

The Sweeney emerged out of the embers of Euston Films' first production, *Special Branch*, a cop show that was curiously popular with viewers while being loathed by the people who made it. Many members of the production team resented that the real work of special branch – such as undercover activities in Northern Ireland – was deemed to be unsuitable for their show, leaving it curiously out of touch with reality. One of the writers on *Special Branch*, Ian Kennedy Martin, was invited to pitch an idea for a replacement series and came up with something called 'The Outcasts', about an old-school detective in the Flying Squad struggling to come to terms with the changing face of the force and the reorganisation of Scotland Yard. Belligerent to his superiors and contemptuous of criminals, the man – and the first episode – would be called 'Regan' (an anagram of 'anger'), and Ian Kennedy Martin already had in mind who should play him: John Thaw.

The opening episode, 'Regan', was screened as part of Thames's *Armchair Cinema* anthology series, a spin-off from the long-running *Armchair Theatre*. Although it was designed to work as a stand-alone play, it wasn't a pilot in the traditional sense; with a series already assured before production on 'Regan' had finished, *The Sweeney* was not reliant on it being a success. Ian Kennedy Martin had assumed that he would retain some degree of creative control over the series, but after clashes with the producer that led to the original director, Douglas Camfield, being replaced, Kennedy Martin negotiated a release that allowed the TV show to continue without him while retaining the rights to develop his characters for feature films.

The series was planned as a more dramatic, action-packed and representative police drama than the BBC's ***Z Cars*** had become, just as *Z Cars* had been created (by Kennedy Martin's older brother, Troy) as a reaction to the staid comfort of ***Dixon of Dock Green***. Regardless of such intentions, though, the series began just as *Z Cars* had done, with the death of a copper. Regan's guilt over his own possible negligence is what motivates him to find and arrest young DS Cowley's killers. Regan brings in George Carter, a detective sergeant who left the Squad to work in Divisional due to pressure from his wife, but hopes that a return to the Squad will help his chances of promotion. Right from the word go, 'Regan' sets up the character of the series we'd all grow to love. Regan's first words are: 'Get your trousers on – you're nicked', a phrase that would become a favourite recurring feature throughout the series.

Each episode by and large stuck to a formula. In the first act – often before the main titles – a crime would be committed and Regan and his men would be despatched to solve it. In the second act, the pieces would come together and the final act would see them tracking down the criminals. The trick was that the 'Mr Big' of the criminal underclass sometimes got away – there were rarely any easy resolutions in this series. *The Sweeney* drew complaints from people upset by the depiction of a police force as violent, foul-mouthed (though never anything stronger than the odd 'bastard' and 'slag') and often as loose with the law as the criminals; Regan would frequently be seen to ignore the need for a warrant if he felt it would speed up a successful pinch, and in the first episode he threatens to get a suspect's sentence increased by alleging that he attacked a police officer. While senior officers condemned it for besmirching the reputation of the good honest copper, the Metropolitan Police's foot soldiers loved it as much as the great British public because they recognised it to be true. The sense of realism that drove each episode was partly thanks to two advisers to the series who had experience of the real Flying Squad, one a retired senior officer who received an on-screen credit, another still active in the police force, who chose to remain anonymous.

Though Ian Kennedy Martin was no longer willing to work on the show after his experience of the pilot, help came from a number of writers familiar from other shows of the time, including Allan Prior and Robert Banks Stewart. Ian Kennedy Martin's brother Troy wrote a fair few of the best episodes, as did Trevor Preston, a London-born writer with a flair for creating local colour (responsible for the children's fantasy series ***Ace of Wands***, he also wrote for ***Callan*** and *Special Branch* and later created ***Out*** and ***Fox***). One of Preston's best scripts, 'Abduction', concluded the first series. Regan hears that his daughter has been kidnapped to prevent him from following up on a lead from one of his informers. While trying to look after his emotionally fraught ex-wife, Regan is shown to be both driven by his job and so invaluable to the police force that he never seems to get time off even when he needs it. We also see for the first time just how much he values Carter; unwilling to confide in the officer investigating the kidnapping, Regan turns to Carter as the only man he can trust not to prevent him from solving the case himself. When the man behind the kidnapping is finally apprehended, it's Carter who pulls Regan away from beating him to a pulp and risking his job in the process.

Though John Thaw was nominally the star, he felt that Dennis Waterman was worthy of sharing the limelight and pushed to have

Crime Drama
Euston Films/Thames for ITV
Episode Duration: 50 mins
Broadcast: 4 Jun 1974, 2 Jan 1975–28 Dec 1978

Regular Cast
John Thaw · *DI John Albert 'Jack' Regan*
Dennis Waterman · *DS George Hamilton Carter*
Garfield Morgan · *Chief Inspector Frank Haskins*
John Alkin · *DS Tom Daniels*
John Flanagan · *DS Matt Mathews*
Morris Perry · *Detective Chief Superintendent Maynon*
Martin Read · *DC Jimmy Thorpe*
Benjamin Whitrow · *DCI Braithwaite*
Jennifer Thanisch · *Susie Regan*
Stephanie Turner · *Alison Carter*

Creator Ian Kennedy Martin

Producers Lloyd Shirley, George Taylor (executive), Ted Childs

Writers Ian Kennedy Martin, Trevor Preston, Troy Kennedy Martin, Ranald Graham, Tudor Gates, Martin Hall, Allan Prior, Robert Banks Stewart, Murray Smith, Roger Marshall, Ray Jenkins, Andrew Wilson, Tony Hoare, Peter Hill, Richard Harris, P. J. Hammond, Robert Wales, Ted Childs, Donald Churchill

Theme Music 'Regan', the pilot episode, had a theme called 'The Loner' by Mark Duval (not to be confused with the piece of the same name that was used on the first series of ***Budgie***), but the series itself sported a theme by Harry South. It remains one of the best known of all 1970s cops theme tunes, partly because it was possible to sing the show's title along with the music: 'The Sweeney . . . The Sweeney, Da dada da dah dah dadah dah . . .'

the latter's character beefed up a little. Carter had largely been a supporting role for the first series with little to do except stand at Regan's side. The fifth episode of the second season, 'Hit and Run', marked the beginning of the change in prominence for Carter and included Dennis Waterman's best ever performance, enacting Carter's grief over the sudden death of his wife, deliberately run over to ensure her silence (Alison Carter was played by Stephanie Turner, who would return to TV police work when she took on the title role in ***Juliet Bravo***). It also gives John Thaw the chance to stretch himself a little while also sitting back to let Waterman take centre stage. Although a harrowing episode, it also gave Regan and Carter an opportunity to build upon their relationship after hours, including the kind of late-night drinking sessions that Carter couldn't have taken part in as a married man.

By the third season, the writers were comfortable enough to experiment. Although *The Sweeney* had always mixed hard-hitting stories with more light-hearted ones (notably the third episode of the first series, 'Thin Ice', in which Alfred Marks played a doggie-obsessed gangster whose flight to southern France is hampered when he learns that Regan has sent his beloved pooch to the pound), by now more humour was being injected into each episode week by week. When John Thaw told Dennis Waterman about his plans to leave *The Sweeney* after the fourth season, Waterman agreed to jump ship too, figuring it'd be better to go out on a high. That fourth series became a celebration of the previous three years, even going so far as to have Morecambe and Wise star as themselves in one episode (returning a favour – or perhaps getting revenge – after Thaw and Waterman appeared as guest stars in an episode of ***The Morecambe and Wise Show***). Though the humour levels increased, the character of Regan became much more morose and irritable, foreshadowing the final episode where, arrested but later acquitted of corruption, he finally turns his back on the job and leaves.

Two feature films followed – *Sweeney!* (1977), which earned John Thaw an Evening Standard British Film award for Best Actor, and *Sweeney 2* (1978). Though costing only a little more than a couple of episodes of the TV show to produce, the violence level alone lifted the films into an altogether different bracket. After the second film, *The Sweeney* itself came to an impressive end, having had a consistent run of 53 episodes. For many, it remains one of the best police TV dramas ever produced.

John Thaw's biggest hits in later life were both crime related – ***Inspector Morse*** and ***Kavanagh QC*** – and he himself was widely recognised as one of British TV's true greats (for which reason we tend not to discuss one almighty blip – the critically mauled ***A Year in Provence***). His death in 2002 due to cancer represented a tremendous loss, as the viewing public showed. Dennis Waterman meanwhile went on from *The Sweeney* to star in ***Minder*** and ***The Life and Loves of a She-Devil***, before being bafflingly sent up in ***Little Britain***.

Tabitha

Sitcom | Columbia Pictures for ABC (shown on BBC One) | episode duration 25 mins | broadcast 24 Apr 1976, 7 May 1977, 10 Sep 1977–14 Jan 1978 (USA)

Regular Cast
Lisa Hartman · *Tabitha Stephens*
Robert Urich · *Paul Thurston*
David Ankrum · *Adam Stephens*
Karen Morrow · *Aunt Minerva*
Mel Stewart · *Marvin Decker*
Bernard Fox · *Dr Bombay*

Creator Jerry Mayer **Producers** Jerry Mayer (executive), George Yanok **Writers** Jerry Mayer, George Yanok, Bernie Kahn, Martin Donovan, Robert Stambler, Roland Wolpert

Young Tabitha Stephens finds her life working for a Los Angeles radio station quite taxing. Fortunately, she comes from a long line of magical witches . . .

For commentary, see BEWITCHED

Taggart

Crime Drama | STV for ITV | episode duration 50–100 mins | broadcast 6 Sep 1983–present

Regular Cast
Mark McManus · *DCI Jim Taggart*
James MacPherson · *DS/DI/DCI Michael Jardine*
Iain Anders · *Superintendent Jack McVitie*
Neil Duncan · *DS Peter Livingstone*
Blythe Duff · *DC/DS Jackie Reid*
Harriet Buchan · *Jean Taggart*
Robert Robertson · *Dr Stephen Andrews*
Colin McCredie · *DC Stuart Fraser*
John Michie · *DI Robbie Ross*
Alex Norton · *DCI Matthew Burke*
Tom Watson · *Superintendent Murray*

Creator Glenn Chandler **Producers** Robert Love, Philip Hinchcliffe, Eric Coulter, Murray Ferguson, Graeme Gordon **Writers** Glenn Chandler, Stuart Hepburn, John Milne, Barry Appleton, Russell Lewis, Richard Maher, Robert Smith, Phil Ford, Julian Spilsbury, Steve Griffiths, Danny McCahon, Mark Greig, Steve Griffiths, Nick Doughty, Peter Mills, Brian McGill, John Brown, Anne Marie Di Mambro, Michael Jenner, Julie White, Julie Dixon, Chris Dolan, James McIntyre **Theme Music** 'No Mean City' by Mike Moran. For many years, the titles also featured a vocal accompaniment, performed by husky-voiced singer Maggie Bell.

When, in 1983, a young woman called Eileen Ballantyne is found strangled and washed up on the banks of Glasgow's River Kelvin, enthusiastic university-educated DS Peter Livingstone is partnered with craggy, seen-it-all-before DCI Jim Taggart. Some 22 years later, the programme that bears Taggart's name is still running on ITV, making it the longest-running police drama still in production on UK television. With episodes commissioned until at least the end of 2006, it seems as though nothing is likely to call a halt to yet another series of gruesome 'murrrdurrrs' in the foreseeable future.

There were in fact two original stars of the series: Mark McManus as the dour, humour-free Taggart, and the grey and rainy streets of the city of Glasgow itself. Rarely for an ITV drama series, *Taggart* was not just set north of the border, it was also based firmly within the kind of gritty urban environment that had long been synonymous with English cities, abandoning the stereotypical view of Scotland as the home of heather, whisky and terribly nice rural communities. Location and leading man complemented each other perfectly to create a drama series that stood out from the rest. For one thing, *Taggart* could make viewers wince in shock and disgust far more often than any other series – the murders portrayed were normally screened with a maximum of panache, inventiveness and (more often than not) a great deal of blood and gore. In particular, scripts written by series creator Glenn Chandler could always be relied upon to be innovative, horrific and a real brain-teaser for audiences.

Taggart's first on-screen partner was yuppie Peter Livingstone, a career copper whose ambitions were in stark contrast to Taggart's dedicated cynicism. Livingstone's replacement (and the longest-running character in the series to date) was blond teetotal Christian Mike Jardine, a detective with a much cheerier, brighter attitude towards his work that slowly changed into a slightly less brusque version of Taggart's own viewpoint as the series progressed.

Starting life in 1983 as a one-off pilot movie entitled *Killer*, *Taggart* rapidly became a key weapon in ITV's ratings battle. For several years in the 1990s, *Taggart* was a fixture on or around ITV's Hogmanay, with the episode transmitted on 1 January 1992 ('Violent Delights') gaining an astonishing 18.3 million viewers. The series has been sold around the globe to more than 50 countries, and as a consequence makes more money for Scottish TV than it costs to produce. However, *Taggart* faced its toughest challenge in 1994 when star of the series Mark McManus sadly passed away. Perhaps not surprisingly, considering the huge success they had on their hands, Scottish Television and the ITV decided not to end the series, but opted to continue the exploits of Mike Jardine and his team of detectives, Jackie Reid and Stuart Fraser. More controversially, though, the series continued with the name 'Taggart' despite the fact that neither Jim nor his wheelchair-bound wife Jean were in the series. In fact, *Taggart* has now survived as a programme longer without its eponymous hero than with him. As the series enters its third decade, the core group of crime-solvers includes sour-faced Taggart-alike DCI Burke, ladies' man DI Ross, and long-term foot soldiers Reid and Fraser. We're glad to say the producers of *Taggart* have yet to resort to outrageous and over-the-top storylines like their colleagues working on ***The Bill***. If *Taggart* continues to make intelligent, surprising and genuinely realistic police drama, there's no reason why it won't still be around in another 20 years.

Website

www.taggart-fanclub.co.uk

Take Hart

Entertainment | BBC One | episode duration 25 mins | broadcast 15 Feb 1977–30 Dec 1983, 14 Sep 1984–17 Nov 1993

Cast

Tony Hart · *Host*
Colin Bennett · *The Caretaker*
Margot Wilson, Joanna Kirk, Gabrielle Bradshaw, Liza Brown, Alison Millar · *Artists*
Amanda Swift · *Elvira Muckett*

Producers Patrick Dowling, Christopher Pilkington

Tony Hart had been a regular illustrator for BBC children's programmes since the 1950s (he designed the ***Blue Peter*** ship and contributed designs for title sequences including one for ***Billy Bunter***), and in 1977 was known for being the gentle-voiced, neck-scarf-wearing artist on ***Vision On***. With *Take Hart*, Tony finally got his own series, although a lot of the arty features from *Vision On* were retained, such as the gallery of paintings sent in by viewers, accompanied by the soporific 'Cavatina' by John Williams – otherwise known as 'Theme from *The Deer Hunter*'. As before, they couldn't return pictures, but there was a vaguely unspecific prize for all those they showed.

As is now the norm for 'do it yourself' art shows (such as ITV's *Art Attack* with Neil Buchanan), Tony would create collages using bits of wood and leaves, or paint masks using a simple design and while the overall effect would be fairly impressive it was never outside of the capabilities of most BBC-watching children. Of course, it was all terribly middle class, but that never stopped children of all backgrounds being encouraged to take an interest in art.

Tony wasn't totally alone, though, as his features would be regularly interrupted by the hugely irritating Mr Bennett, the caretaker of Tony's studio. Guaranteed to be the one to put his foot in a tin of paint only to inspire Tony to create a mural of footprints, Mr Bennett was possibly present to keep the very young entertained but for most of us he just got in the way of proceedings. Another provider of constant interruptions was much more welcome, Aardman Animations' diminutive terracotta plasticine man Morph, whose 'bah bah bah' dialogue was perfectly understandable to Tony and us kids but seemed to leave our parents baffled. Morph and his alabaster chum Chas would scrap, bicker and end up rolling around Tony's worktop, sending ink and paintbrushes everywhere. Another regular participant was a rather basic dinosaur called Auggie, created by Avril Johnson. Captivating though he was, he wasn't Morph.

Morph and Chas eventually got their own TV series, shown in the coveted pre-News slot kept warm by ***The Magic Roundabout*** and ***Willo the Wisp***. *The Amazing Adventures of Morph* (13 Oct 1980–18 May 1981) introduced other characters that would be relatively easy for kids to make at home, including Folly, a lady made of tin foil, and a scrubbing brush that thought it was a dog.

In 1984, *Take Hart* evolved into *Hartbeat*. Morph and Mr Bennett came too, but now Tony's rather desirable art studio was shared with a rotating group of female artists who joined him to explain various alternative approaches to art, be it sculpting, brass rubbings, cave paintings or chalk carvings on hillsides.

Website

Yes! Tony has his own website, which rejoices at: www.tonyhart.co.uk/.

Tales of the City

Drama | American Playhouse/KQED San Francisco/Les Productions La Fête/Propaganda Films/Showtime/Working Title/Les Productions Bleu Blanc Rouge for Channel 4 | episode duration 50 mins | broadcast 10 Jan 1994–7 May 2001

Principal Cast

Olympia Dukakis · *Mrs Anna Madrigal*
Donald Moffat · *Edgar Warfield Halcyon*
Chloe Webb, Nina Siemaszko, · *Mona Ramsey*
Laura Linney · *Mary Ann Singleton*
Marcus D'Amico, Paul Hopkins · *Michael 'Mouse' Tolliver*
Bill Campbell · *Dr Jon Philip Fielding*
Thomas Gibson · *Beauchamp Talbot Day*
Paul Gross, Whip Hubley · *Brian Hawkins*
Barbara Garrick · *Deirdre Denise 'DeDe' Ligon Halcyon Day*
Nina Foch, Diana Leblanc · *Frances 'Frannie' Alicia Ligon Halcyon*
Edie Adams · *Ruby Miller*
Robert Downey Sr · *Edgar's Doctor*
Meagen Fay · *Binky Gruen*
Lou Liberatore · *Chuck*
Country Joe McDonald · *Joaquin*
Mary Kay Place · *Prudence Susan 'Prue' Giroux*
Parker Posey · *Connie Bradshaw*
Kevin Sessums · *Peter Prescott Cipriani*
McLean Stevenson · *Roger 'Booter' Manigault*
Syd Straw · *Laurel*
David Brisbin · *Lemon Candles*
Hank Stratton · *Robert*
Lou Cutell · *Herb Siegel*
Carolyn Lowery · *Hillary*
Phillip Moon · *Lionel Wong*
Amy Ryder · *Frieda*
Stanley DeSantis · *Norman Neal Williams*
Cynda Williams, Françoise Robertson · *Dorothea/Dorothy Wilson*
Paul Dooley · *Herb Tolliver*

Belita Moreno · *Alice Tolliver*
John Fleck · *Vincent*
Amanda Fuller · *Lexy*
Michael Jeter · *Carson Callas*
Paul Bartel · *Charles Hillary Lord*
Lance Loud · *William Deveraux Hill III*
Bob Mackie · *Richard Evan Hampton*
Ian McKellen · *Archibald Anson Gidde*
Stephanie Faracy · *Candi Moretti*
Meadow Sisto · *Cheryl Moretti*
Rod Steiger · *Bookstore Owner*
Don Novello · *Father Sarducci*
Howard Platt · *Leroy Wilson*
Colin Ferguson · *Burke Christopher Andrew*
Domini Blythe · *Helena Parrish*
Thomas Gibson · *Beauchamp Talbot Day*
Swoosie Kurtz · *Betty Borg Ramsey*
Sonia Dubé · *Lady Eleven*
Michel Perron · *Bruno Koski*
Brigid Tierney · *'Douchebag' Heidi*
Jackie Burroughs · *Mother Mucca*
Heath Lamberts · *Arnold Littlefield*
Sharman Sturgess · *Melba Littlefield*
Janine Theriault · *Bobbi*
Sonia Benezra · *Charlene*
Edward Asner · *Jack Lederer*
Janet Wright · *Vita Keating*
Sheila McCarthy · *Mildred*
Gwen Tolbart · *Nurse Thelma*

Creator Armistead Maupin **Producers** Tim Bevan, Luc Châtelain, Suzanne Girard, Richard Kramer, Matt Loze, Armistead Maupin, Alan Poul, Sigurjon Sighvatsson (executive), Debra Kouri, Rebecca Yates (associate), Antony Root, José Lacelle, Kevin Tierney **Writers** Richard Kramer, Nicholas Wright, James Lecesne and Armistead Maupin, from the novels by Armistead Maupin **Theme Music** John E. Keane and Richard Grégoire

Anna Madrigal runs a boarding house at 28 Barbary Lane, situated in a fashionable part of San Francisco. Her residents accept her Bohemian ways, her free spirit and her supplies of marijuana, which she grows lovingly in plant pots around the house. The house is home to waifs and strays in search of something, and Anna sees it her mission to provide them with a safe house until they find whatever they're looking for.

Her latest waif is Mary Ann Singleton, an innocent from the Midwest who initially finds the sexuality of the city and its residents intimidating. She's befriended by Mona Ramsey, a devil-may-care habitual drug-user who proudly talks her way out of her copywriter job by verbally abusing a client. She comes in tow with Michael 'Mouse' Tolliver, a cheerful gay serial monogamist and her best friend. Then there's Brian, a handsome straight guy who knows the odds of picking up women are stacked in his favour in the gay capital of the world. But not everyone is happy to tolerate this enclave of free spirits and not everyone is as open and honest as they'd like to be. Particularly Anna Madrigal herself, whose past is littered with revelations waiting to burst out...

Tales of the City began as a newspaper column in the *San Francisco Chronicle* but blossomed when Armistead Maupin adapted them into six, million-seller novels. Channel 4's initial six-part co-production captured both Maupin's picaresque multi-threaded plots and the carefree pre-AIDS spirit of the 1970s. Maupin himself suggested Olympia Dukakis for the part of Anna Madrigal (an anagram of 'A man and a boy', which hints at only one of the secrets in her past), while other big-name stars included Ian McKellen as society queen Archibald Anson Gidde, Rod Steiger as a bookstore owner and Karen Black as herself. Littered with homages to Alfred Hitchcock's *Vertigo*, which was also set in San Francisco, the series acted as a tribute to one of the world's most beautiful cities as well as offering gay viewers a serial that spoke to them in ways the later ***Queer as Folk*** arguably didn't.

A sequel, *More Tales of the City*, came four years later, with cast changes and more twists and turns (one involving the arrival of Mother Mucca, a former brothel-owner with shocking links to a number of major characters). A third series, *Further Tales from the City*, sadly wasn't shown on terrestrial TV in the UK, while three other *Tales of the City* novels, *Babycakes*, *Significant Others*, and *Sure of You*, have yet to be adapted for television.

Tales of the Riverbank

Pre-School | Riverbank Productions for BBC TV/ITV | episode duration 15–25 mins | broadcast 3 Jul 1960–1964

Regular Cast

Johnny Morris · *Narrator, Character Voices*

Creators Dave Ellison and Paul Sutherland **Writers** Dave Ellison, Paul Sutherland, Roy Billings **Producers** Dave Ellison, Paul Sutherland, Roy Billings, Peggy Miller

Made in Canada, *Tales of the Riverbank* took the woodland settings of *Wind in the Willows* and placed real rodents into specially constructed sets. Hammy the hamster was the star, with back-up from his friends Roderick the mouse and GP the guinea pig, all interacting (through clever editing) with other animals. Hammy was a curious animal, always exploring, whether it be in a barge, a diving bell, a car or – most exciting of all – his bi-plane. Narrator Johnny Morris created the characters' voices as he'd done with ***Animal Magic***.

Beginning in 1960 in a 5 p.m. slot, *Tales of the Riverbank* moved into *Watch with Mother* from 1963 and stayed there until the early 1970s. New colour episodes were bought in by ITV who stripped them into their own lunchtime children's programmes for the next decade. A hilarious 1990 series *The Adventures of Dynamo Duck* used the same principals, placing a ducking (voiced by ***The Simpsons***' Dan Castellaneta) in mortal peril week after week.

Tales of the Unexpected

Anthology | Anglia for ITV | episode duration 25 mins | broadcast 24 Mar 1979–13 May 1988

Regular Cast

Roald Dahl, John Houseman · *Presenters*

Creator Roald Dahl **Producers** John Fleming Ball, John Woolf (executive), John Rosenberg, David Deutsch, Norman Lloyd, Louis Pitzele, Bert Salzman, John Woolf, Graham Williams **Writers** Various, including Ronald Harwood, Robin Chapman, Denis Cannan, Johnny Byrne, John Rosenberg, Julian Bond, Chaim Bermant, Bert Salzman, David Scott Milton, Ross Thomas, Jeremy Paul, Alan Seymour, Peter Ransley, Paul Ableman, Gerald Savory, from stories by Roald Dahl, Robert Bloch, John Collier, Stanley Ellin, Henry Slesar, Jack Ritchie, Ruth Rendell, W. Somerset Maugham **Theme Music** Ron Grainer's theme music is guaranteed to make drunk people perform the most hypnotically unpleasant 'sexy' dancing you've ever witnessed. Best leave it to the original, Karen Standley, whose silhouette graced the opening titles for the series, accompanied by shots of tarot cards, demons and flames.

While ***The Twilight Zone*** is undoubtedly the most famous anthology series worldwide, the UK's own series of twists and chills, *Tales of the Unexpected*, has a similar ability to place a person in a particular frame of mind whenever they hear the theme song (as the above description shows). Created by Norwich-based Anglia Television, the series initially consisted of adaptations of stories by Roald Dahl (some of which had already been adapted for the ***Alfred Hitchcock Presents*** series), with the man himself providing introductions. Unlike Rod Serling's 'Ain't life tough?' introductions for *The Twilight Zone*, Dahl's were more judgemental, with strong moral lessons to be learned that could usually be boiled down to: 'Bad things happen to bad people.' As fewer of the episodes began to depend on input from Dahl, he was eventually replaced as presenter by John Houseman.

Episodes tended to be divided between those with big American guest stars (Joseph Cotten, Eli Wallach, Telly Savalas, Janet Leigh, David Cassidy, Sharon Gless and Don Johnson, among others) and those sporting the best of British talent (Joan Collins, Michael Hordern, Robert Morley, Pauline Collins, John Mills, Ralph Bates, Derek Jacobi, Charles Dance), making it a truly transatlantic show. Among 112 episodes a few stand out: 'Lamb to the Slaughter' saw Susan George kill her abusive husband with a leg of lamb that she then cooked to hide the evidence from police inspector Brian Blessed (this particular twist was later used by Spanish filmmaker Pedro Almodóvar for his 1984 film *What Have I Done to Deserve This?*); vegetarians got a fright with 'The Sound Machine', in which a scientist accidentally discovers that plants scream when they die; in 'Skin', Derek Jacobi played a tattoo artist offered a life-changing sum of money for a work of art created by a friend, a piece inked onto the tattooist's own back and therefore a little difficult to just hand over while still alive (this particularly gruesome story won the 1980 Edgar Allan Poe Award for Best Television Episode); Peter Cushing starred in 'The Vorpal Blade' as an old man remembering an incident from his school days when he was an expert dueller (the twist being that the old man is now interred within a prison for Nazi war criminals); and probably the most well-known episode, 'Royal Jelly', in which a bee-keeper (played by Timothy West) feeds royal jelly to his baby daughter with devastating side-effects for both of them.

As audiences grew used to the rhythm and inevitable outcomes of some of the later episodes, the series was unfairly dubbed 'Tales of the Bleeding Obvious', and we're pretty certain that by the end of its run a fair few viewers switched off after the dance number at the start.

Talking Heads

Anthology | BBC Two | episode duration 40 mins | broadcast 19 Apr 1988–11 Nov 1998

Cast

Alan Bennett, Patricia Routledge, Maggie Smith, Stephanie Cole, Julie Walters, Thora Hird, Eileen Atkins, David Haig, Penelope Wilton

Creator/Writer Alan Bennett **Producers** Innes Lloyd, Mark Shivas **Theme Music** George Fenton

Alan Bennett's series of monologues display much of his dry wit and ear for naturalistic dialogue, characters who punctuate anecdotes with 'he said . . . she said' and little of consequence in between. The characters are unexceptional folk, people whose lives are at a standstill or in a crisis where their screams of frustration never leave their lips. In the first play, *A Chip in the Sugar*, Bennett himself plays a middle-aged man recovering from a nervous breakdown and facing the prospect of his elderly mother finding love again, a man who seems destined to note 'I didn't say anything' after each carefully noted sleight against him. Patricia Routledge's *Lady of Letters* acted as a more credible companion to the floral Hyacynth Bucket of ***Keeping Up Appearances***, a serial complainer whose letters bring trouble to her own front door.

While some of the plays were whimsical but bittersweet, others were decidedly darker. David Haig's park keeper in *Playing Sandwiches* begins as hugely sympathetic, chattering through his soliloquy as other characters have done. Only as we near the end of the tale do we realise that he is a paedophile; the final scene, revealing him severely beaten in prison leaves us feeling raw and scared at the place Bennett has led us, but immensely impressed at his skill as a dramatist. Most memorable of all were two plays starring Thora Hird: *A Cream Cracker under the Settee* cast her as an elderly lady ranting against her home help while lying immobile on her living room floor after a fall; and in

Waiting for the Telegram she was a 99-year-old looking forward to receiving her telegram from the Queen to mark her centenary while remembering a correspondence from the previous monarch.

Tarrant on TV

See CLIVE JAMES ON TV

Tarzan

Action-Adventure | Banner Productions for NBC (shown on ITV) | episode duration 45 mins | broadcast 8 Sep 1966–5 Apr 1968

Regular Cast
Ron Ely · *Tarzan*
Manuel Padilla Jr · *Jai*

Creator Inspired by the character created by Edgar Rice Burroughs **Producer** Steve Shagan **Writers** George F. Slavin, Don Brinkley, Oliver Crawford, S. J. Loy, Robert Sabaroff, John Considine, Tim Considine, Lee Erwin, Jack H. Robinson, Sam Rocca, Alan Crosland, Jim Leighton, Robert L. Goodwin, Sid Saltzman, Carey Wilber, Jackson Gillis, William Driskill, Don Mullaly **Theme Music** For the first season, Quinn Amper and Fred Strittmatter composed a piece arranged by Walter W. Greene, with closing music by Sydney Lee. The second season's music was by Nelson Riddle.

Edgar Rice Burroughs' 1912 novel about the English Lord Greystoke's metamorphosis into the jungle warrior Tarzan had first reached cinema screens in 1918, with Stellan Windrow playing the lead in a silent movie, *Tarzan of the Apes*. Since then over 20 different actors have portrayed the character, with Olympic swimmer Johnny Weissmuller being the most famous (with 12 films alongside co-star Maureen O'Sullivan as Jane), followed by Gordon Scott, the 1950s Tarzan, who made six *Tarzan* films. By the 1960s, James Bond had become a major movie success and so the Tarzan of the movies evolved into a more articulate, civilised man who wore sharp suits in the city and only donned the loin cloth when in the jungle. Mike Henry had been an American football player for the Pittsburgh Steelers and the Los Angeles Rams before he became the 15th actor to play at being Lord of the Jungle. He starred in three films, made back-to-back between 1965 and '66: *Tarzan and the Valley of Gold*, *Tarzan and the Great River* and *Tarzan and the Jungle Boy*. When the decision was made to bring the character to television, Henry was first choice for the role, but by the time the films began to be released, Henry was locked in a dispute with the movie's producers after being mauled by a chimpanzee. Henry passed on returning to the jungle, so the part instead went to Ron Ely.

Ely's Tarzan retained Henry's quiet, articulate approach as a rather placid Tarzan – until he was called upon to wrestle with alligators or fend off poachers, at which point he leapt into action. Ely also inherited a young actor from Henry's final film, Manuel Padilla Jr, who played the jungle boy Jai (though how a Mexican child star came to be living in the jungle was never really explained). The series expanded upon many of the themes of the original novels, with Tarzan acting as a go-between for the white colonists and the native animals and people, invariably showing the Westerners that they're either unsuited to a life in Africa or teaching them a lesson about how to survive in such an inhospitable environment.

Rising budgets and falling ratings were blamed for the show's inevitable cancellation, but for many, Ron Ely was their very first Tarzan. Younger viewers, though, might recall an animated series that ran from 1976 until 1982. It was made by Filmation – the company responsible for many animated superhero shows, including ***Batman***, ***Superman***, *The Space Sentinels* and animated *Star Trek*, and with rather simplistic animation was a fairly formulaic affair. It had the same music samples used repeatedly throughout the show and with certain scenes repeated almost every episode (the elephant stampede, Tarzan swinging through the vines), but it ran for years in BBC One's children's week-day children's slot. This TV Tarzan was voiced by Robert Ridgely, but with his dark hair and chiselled jaw, his look was very much that of Sixties' movie Tarzan, Mike Henry.

Taxi

Sitcom | John Charles Walters Productions/Paramount for ABC and NBC (shown on BBC One) | episode duration 25 mins | broadcast 12 Sep 1978–15 Jun 1983 (USA)

Principal Cast
Judd Hirsch · *Alan Rieger*
Marilu Henner · *Elaine O'Connor Nardo*
Tony Danza · *Tony Banta*
Danny DeVito · *Louie De Palma*
Andy Kaufman · *Latka Gravas*
Jeff Conaway · *Bobby Wheeler*
Christopher Lloyd · *'Reverend' Jim Ignatowski*
Randall Carver · *John Burns*
Carol Kane · *Simka Dahblitz Gravas*

Creators Ed Weinberger, James L. Brooks, Stan Daniels, David Davis **Producers** Ed Weinberger, James L Brooks, Stan Daniels, David Davis (executive), Ken Estin, Howard Gewirtz, Ian Praiser, Sam Simon, Richard Sakai **Writers** Various, including Glen Charles, Les Charles, Barry Kemp, Ken Estin, Sam Simon, David Lloyd, Ian Praiser, Howard Gewirtz, Earl Pomerantz **Theme music** 'Angela' by Bob James is a wonderfully sad and wistful melody that seems perfectly at home with the Manhattan setting for the programme.

New York's Sunshine Cab Company is home to a motley assortment of drivers – failed actor Bobby Wheeler, rubbish boxer Tony Banta, single mother Elaine Nardo, spaced out ex-hippie the Reverend Jim, and all-round nice guy Alex Rieger. They're dispatched on jobs by foul-tempered, short

in stature Louie, a walking personification of the Napoleon complex who takes out his own petty insecurities on his staff. The final member of the team was the Sunshine Cab Company's resident mechanic, oddball immigrant with a loose grip on the English language Latka Gravas.

Ostensibly Judd Hursch's show, he was effectively eclipsed by a large ensemble cast of truly great performers, notably Danny DeVito, Christopher Lloyd and the ever-scene-stealing Andy Kaufman, whose behind-the-scenes antics were the subject of a 1999 biopic, *Man on the Moon*, starring Jim Carrey.

After five series, *Taxi* closed its doors – twice. The official final episode, 'A Grand Gesture' was an upbeat finale that the production team had prepared in case the series was canned. However, the actual final episode, 'Simka's Monthlies' was broadcast the following month, making 114 episodes in all. Producer James L. Brooks had an even bigger hit lurking in the wings – their next television show was a certain comedy set in a bar in Boston. . .

T-Bag

Children's Comedy | ITV | episode duration 25 mins | broadcast 1985–92

Regular Cast

Elizabeth Estensen · *Tallulah Bag*
Georgina Hale · *Tabitha Bag*
John Hasler · *T-Shirt 'Thomas'*
Jennie Stallwood · *Debbie*
Diana Barrand · *Holly-Anna Jones*
Kellie Bright · *Sallie Simpkins*
Natalie Wood · *Polly-Zena*
Evelyn Sweeney · *Penny Hunt*
Bea Julakasiun · *Tow-Ling Shirt*

Creators/Writers Lee Pressman, Grant Cathro

A series of individual children's programmes featuring the adventures of evil witch T-Bag, her faithful young 'T-Caddy' T-Shirt, and an assortment of brave youngsters who challenge her. Titles of the individual stories (each of which ran for ten episodes) were: 'Wonders in Letterland', 'T-Bag Strikes Again', 'T-Bag Bounces Back', 'Turn on to T-Bag', 'T-Bag and the Revenge of the T-Set', 'T-Bag and the Pearls of Wisdom', 'T-Bag and the Rings of Olympus', 'T-Bag and the Sunstones of Montezuma' and 'Take Off With T-Bag'. Four Christmas specials were also shown: 'T-Bag's Christmas Cracker', 'T-Bag's Christmas Carol', 'T-Bag's Christmas Ding-Dong' and 'T-Bag's Christmas Turkey'.

Elizabeth Estensen (previously famous for appearing in the final seasons of ***The Liver Birds***, now better known for ***Emmerdale***) played the panto-villainous Tallulah (usually known as 'T') Bag for the first five seasons, after which she was replaced by Georgina Hale, who played her on-screen sister, Tabitha. In total, writer/creators Lee Pressman and Grant Cathro wrote a staggering 94 episodes over seven years and ten seasons.

Website
www.angelfire.com/rings/tbag/index.html

Teachers

Drama | Tiger Aspect for Channel 4 | episode duration 45 mins | broadcast 21 Mar 2001–21 Dec 2004

Regular Cast

Andrew Lincoln · *Simon Casey*
Adrian Bower · *Brian Steadman*
Navin Chowdhry · *Kurt McKenna*
Raquel Cassidy · *Susan Gately*
Nina Sosanya · *Jenny Page*
James Corden · *Jeremy*
Tamzin Malleson · *Penny Neville*
Shaun Evans · *John Paul Keating*
James Lance · *Matt Harvey*
Vicky Hall · *Lindsay Pearce*
Daon Broni · *Damien Wallace*
Mathew Horne · *Ben Birkett*
Lee Williams · *Ewan Doherty*
Gillian Bevan · *Clare Hunter*
Ursula Holden Gill · *Carol*
Lloyd McGuire · *Bob Porter*
Ellen Thomas · *Liz Webb*
Bob Mason · *Steven*
Zoe Telford · *Maggie*

Creator Tim Loane **Producers** Greg Brennan, Jane Fallon (executive), Liz Lewin (associate), Tim Bradley, Matthew Patnick, Dean Sipling, Rhonda Smith **Writers** Tim Loane, Andrew Rattenbury, Julie Rutterford, Richard Stoneman, Charlie Martin, Ed Roe, Tony Basgallop, Jack Lothian, Linton Chiswick **Theme Music** 'The Boy with the Arab Strap' by Belle and Sebastian

We never think as children that the teachers might be as bored of history, maths and literature as we are, but Channel 4's four-season drama comedy looked at the education system from the point of view of a group of late twenty/early thirty-somethings who, through various life choices, end up teaching at Summerdown School in Bristol. Simon hates school, hates his job, hates Jeremy the class swot, gets on well with some of the girls, cadges cigarettes from some of the boys and spends the rest of the time avoiding year head Jenny, who wants his reports on the pupils in his charge. His friend Kurt shares his dual obsession with loathing Jenny but finding her rear view utterly captivating. The pair can often be found in the early hours of the morning with their fellow teachers drunk and in search of a kebab shop.

With the success of both the show and its cast, the fourth and final year of *Teachers* is greeted with an amalgamation of schools that sees a near-complete cast change (the few remaining characters from the previous year had been killed off, off-screen, in an unexplained accident). Now, the pupils and staff have to confront inter-school rivalries and the continuing apathy for their own subjects ('I just teach this bollocks', moans atheist religious teacher Ben). Unsurprisingly, viewers and interest rapidly declined and school was out for summer permanently.

Teddy Edward

Pre-School | BBC One | episode duration 5 mins | broadcast 5 Jan–30 Mar 1973

Regular Cast

Richard Baker · *Narrator*

Creators/Writers Patrick and Mollie Matthews **Producer** Howard Kennett **Theme Music** 'Glad Gadabout' by Johnny Scott

It's possibly the rite of passage that is *going to school* that turns a child's mind towards cynicism and violence. Pre-school viewers are nowhere near as critical or discerning a their school-attending elder siblings. It's this vital flaw in the child's psychology that allowed many a TV producer to get away with the kind of shows that anyone over the age of seven might possibly scoff at. More fool them.

Shown alongside *Ring-a-Ding* in the famed *Watch with Mother* slot, *Teddy Edward* was gloriously basic. Each episode consisted of a series of photographs depicting Teddy and his friends (including Jasmine the Rabbit and Snowy Toes the Panda) standing next to a country gate or in a field. Newsreader Richard Baker supplied the narration, simple stories about picnics and children's games like 'Hide and Seek', while the episodes were framed by a glorious theme tune played on recorder and flute (with electric bass guitar as backing) that still manages to bring back memories of long, hot summers and drives through country lanes.

Teletubbies

Pre-School | Ragdoll Productions for BBC One | episode duration 25 mins | broadcast 31 Mar 1997–5 Jan 2001

Cast

Dave Thompson, Mark Heenehan, Simon Shelton · *Tinky-Winky*

John Simmit · *Dipsy*

Nikky Smedley · *Laa-Laa*

Pui Fan Lee · *Po*

Rolf Saxon · *Narrator*

Tim Whitnall · *Narrator, Periscope Voice*

Toyah Willcox, Eric Sykes, Penelope Keith, Toni Barry, Sandra Dickinson, Alex Pascall, John Schwab, Rudolph Walker · *Additional Voices*

Jessica Smith · *Sun Baby*

Creators/Writers Anne Wood and Andy Davenport **Producers** Anne Wood, Andy Davenport, Sue James **Theme Music** 'Teletubbies Say "Eh-Oh"!' by Andrew McCrorie-Shand and Andy Davenport, which was also a Christmas No. 1 single in 1997

What became one of the most controversial and pervasive educational programmes ever made was developed from an idea by Ragdoll Productions' Andy Davenport. Andy thought up a sitcom for young children involving spacemen at the bottom of the garden, reasoning that there was something wonderfully ironic about spacesuits being developed from the very latest technology that simultaneously made the wearer look like a nappy-wearing toddler taking their first steps. From here came the Teletubbies – four alien babies in romper-suits fitted with television screens in the chests and aerials on the heads.

Tinky Winky was purple, the biggest of the gang, and his antenna was triangular. His decision to carry a handbag caused certain conservative Christian groups in the USA, led by Jerry Falwell, to out him as homosexual (though we find any attempt to ascribe sexual behaviour to children much more a cause for concern than a handbag – shame on you Mr Falwell). Green-adorned Dipsy was Afro-Caribbean with a straight antenna and loved big hats and dancing. Laa-Laa was a bright yellow girl Teletubby with a curly antenna who, when not playing with her ball, would sometimes count in Welsh. Finally, little Po, in fetching red and with a circular antenna, liked to play on her scooter and sometimes counted in Cantonese.

In Teletubby land, everyone is their friend, including the automated hoover, Noo-Noo, who helps keep the Tubby Dome clean and tidy from Tubbytoast crumbs and blobs of Tubby custard ('Tubby Tusted!'). Giant rabbits lollop around the landscape surrounding the Tubby Dome – and it's said that many of them were caught doing . . . what rabbits do in the backgrounds to some shots, necessitating a retake or five (though a rumour we've heard claiming that the cameras got their revenge in a rather messy way as they navigated the set cannot and probably should not be substantiated).

As with many other pre-school programmes, the key to *Teletubbies* was repetition. They'd watch a video of children engaged in some playtime activity only to cry 'again, again!' at the end, while each episode followed the basic structure of introducing each of the Teletubbies at the beginning and saying goodbye at the end, only for one of them to pop up again and say 'Boo!' – a moment that matched ***Play School***'s 'Which window shall we look through today?' trick in wondering which Teletubby it might be this time. Some parents complained about the baby-talk language that the Teletubbies spoke in, forgetting that Bill and Ben seemed to get away with exactly the same thing 40 years before (an earlier Ragdoll production, Channel 4's *Pob*, was similarly dogged by complaints about baby talk).

Teletubbies was brought to an end only after it was realised that enough episodes had been made for almost every day of the year. It's successfully been exported across the world (it's called *Teletapit* in Finland, *Telepuziki* in Russia) and has been awarded BAFTAS and Emmys. It's also been embraced, like ***The Magic Roundabout***, by students for its supposed 'trippy' elements, like the sparkling

windmill, gurgling baby face in the sun and ***Prisoner***-esque public address systems. 'Time for Tubby Bye-Bye.'

Telly Addicts

Quiz Show | BBC One | episode duration 30 mins | broadcast 3 Sep 1985–1998

Regular Cast
Noel Edmonds · *Host*
Charles Collingwood · *Scorer*

Producers John King, Richard L. Lewis, Helen Lott, Juliet May
Theme Music Richard Lewis

Making up another vital part of 1980s mid-week entertainment was the family oriented quiz show where a mix of generations was a distinct advantage. Noel Edmonds came out of the safety of Saturdays and dazzled us all with a wardrobe of ghastly jumpers to match the oh-so-eighties set crammed full of telly-related imagery. Two teams of four, often families, would answer questions of telly through the ages. As you can imagine, this was the perfect show for us.

Noel would introduce each round with his fake remote control. For the first few years the format was a knockout tournament, but after the Paynes beat all-comers with their truly impressive general TV knowledge, the rules were changed just to get rid of them. Rounds included: themes from one show played over the titles of another and 'On the Spot', where one member of the team answered questions on a specialist subject, general knowledge or questions set by the opposition (the round changed format through the years). The prop round would offer three items, with the highest points awarded if the team guessed the TV show it came from with the first object. This was followed by 'Guess the Year', where a group of clips would be shown, and the final round was a quick-fire round where each team would get one minute between them to answer 12 questions (three each)–with no guarantee that the questions would even reach the final person before time ran out. This round was often the one that flipped the overall result of the show.

From 1994 to 1996, Charles Collingwood looked after the scores, dressed in a 1940s suit and speaking in his best Alexandra Palace accent. Collingwood had previously earned his place in TV history by playing Wordy, the floating torso from ***Look and Read***.

The Tenant of Wildfell Hall

Drama | BBC/CBC/WGBH Boston for BBC One | episode duration 45 mins | broadcast 17 Nov–1 Dec 1996

Principal Cast
Tara Fitzgerald · *Helen Graham*
Toby Stephens · *Gilbert Markham*
Rupert Graves · *Arthur Huntingdon*
James Purefoy · *Mr Lawrence*
Cathy Murphy · *Mrs Myers*
Pam Ferris · *Mrs Markham*
Kenneth Cranham · *Reverend Millward*
Sean Gallagher · *Hargrave*
Jonathan Cake · *Hattersley*
Janet Dale · *Mrs Wilson*
Miranda Pleasence · *Eliza Millward*
Karen Westwood · *Jane Wilson*
Paloma Baeza · *Rose Markham*
Joe Absolom · *Fergus Markham*
Linda Marlowe · *Helen's Aunt*
Aran Bell · *Richard Wilson*

Producers Rebecca Eaton, Kevin Loader (executive), Joanna Newbery (associate), Suzan Harrison **Writers** David Nokes and Janet Barron, from the novel by Anne Brontë **Theme Music** Richard G. Mitchell

The Tenant of Wildfell Hall is a morality tale, and could be described as the triumph of love over experience. It was criticised when it was published in 1848 for its shocking portrayal of the lives of married women. At that time, whatever a woman owned before marriage became the sole property of her husband. When Helen Graham and her son become the tenants of Wildfell Hall, Helen's forthright opinions and radical views cause her to stand out from the quiet, staid and settled community of Yorkshire farming folk. She becomes drawn to the young farmer Gilbert Markham, and he to her, but there is a mystery surrounding Mrs Graham and her little boy. She seems determined to maintain her privacy and will not let the child out of her sight, an attitude that gives great offence to the community who consider her behaviour towards the child as possessive and unhealthy. But naturally the secrets and insecurities surrounding Helen slowly emerge when a stranger appears whose presence leaves Helen terrified for herself and her son . . .

The BBC's first adaptation of a lesser-known Bronte novel came in 1968, with BBC Two trying to capitalise on their success with ***The Forsyte Saga***. Then, Janet Munro starred as Helen Graham, with William Gaunt as Mr Lawrence, Bryan Marshall as Gilbert Markham and Corin Redgrave as Arthur Huntingdon. The 1996 production followed renewed interest in period dramas thanks to Mr Darcy's breeches in ***Pride and Prejudice***. *The Tenant of Wildfell Hall* might have disappointed those looking for more of the same effusive jollity of Austen's work, but it faithfully captured the menace and loneliness that pursued Helen Graham throughout the tale.

Tenko

See pages 742–6

Terrahawks

Children's Puppetry | Anderson Burr/LWT for ITV | episode duration 25 mins | broadcast 8 Oct 1983–12 Jul 1986

Regular Voice Cast

Jeremy Hitchen · *Dr 'Tiger' Ninestein, Lieutenant Hiro, Colonel Johnson, Sram, Moid, Lord Tempo, Chick King, It-Star (aka Birlgoy, Goybirl)*
Anne Ridler · *Kate Kestrel, Cy-Star, It-Star (aka Birlgoy, Goybirl)*
Denise Bryer · *Mary Falconer, Zelda*
Windsor Davies · *Sergeant Major Zero*
Ben Stevens · *Hawkeye, Space Sergeant 101, Yung-Star, HUDSON, Dix-Huit, Stew Dapples, Five-Five*

Creator Gerry Anderson **Producers** Gerry Anderson, Christopher Burr, Bob Bell **Writers** Gerry Anderson, Tony Barwick (under a series of pseudonyms, all ending in '-stein'), Trevor Lansdown **Theme Music** Richard Harvey

In the year 2020, alien androids from the planet Guk attack and destroy NASA's base on Mars and seize the planet for themselves. Leader of the androids is the witch-faced Zelda, assisted by her ever-growing family (including Yung-Star and Cy-Star) and a menagerie of hideous monsters.

On Earth, Doctor 'Tiger' Ninestein sets up a crack team of pilots – the Terrahawks – as Earth's last defence from attack. The Terrahawks are Captain Kate Kestrel, Lieutenant Hiro and Lieutenant Hawkeye, plus spherical robots the Zeroids, led by Sergeant Major Zero.

Gerry Anderson's return to puppets was a controversial one. Having successfully broken away from kiddie-fodder with ***UFO***, ***The Protectors*** and ***Space: 1999***, Anderson's fortunes had dipped by the end of the 1970s. Changes at ITC, the parent company that had supported Anderson's career since the late 1950s, had resulted in him being without a sponsor for the first time in more than 20 years. A co-production with Japanese producer Banjiro Uemara ultimately came to nothing, although Uemara later developed an animated anime-style series called *Techno-Voyager* (though it was cheekily renamed *Thunderbirds 2086* when screened in the UK and America), which Anderson had nothing to do with.

Eventually, Anderson was able to set up Anderson-Burr with Christopher Burr and in 1983 he unveiled a brand new puppet series. *Terrahawks* was vastly different to his earlier string-animated Supermarionation productions; these puppets were hand-operated, similar to muppets, but with rubber faces and radio-controlled eyes. Though the model work was well up to Anderson's usual standard, including the various aircraft (Battlehawk, Terrahawk, Hawkwing, shuttle craft Treehawk and Spacehawk) and Ninestein's futuristic Rolls-Royce called HUDSON, many of his long-term fans despised the new series, feeling it to be puerile compared to his earlier successes. But then, this wasn't made for them but for a younger generation of newcomers to the Anderson world who loved the combination of cinematic battle sequences and excruciating puns. There was also the bizarre casting of Windsor Davies, effectively recreating his character of the shouty Sergeant Major from ***It Ain't Half Hot, Mum***. We're not quite sure what the kids thought of this character but the parents must have been baffled.

The series was a step in another direction in other ways too, most notably for the development of an increasing number of villains who were much more entertaining than the main heroes. Zelda's second in command is her son Yung-Star, a gurgling brat whose voice was much imitated in playgrounds (and, it has to be said, by quite a few adults who'd recognised just how much fun the series was). As Zelda built most of her android relatives, the family tree did get a little confusing at times, especially when her sister, Cy-Star, gave birth (!) to a bi-gendered creature called Goybirl or Birlgoy, depending on which gender was the most dominant at any time (though officially the baby was called 'It-Star'). Zelda's army also included a 'villain of the week' who was created or hired to do her bidding in the continued war against Earth: Sram, the scaly-faced monster with a roar that could collapse buildings; Moid, the master of disguise; and our favourite, Yuri, who is described by Zelda's spawn as the ugliest monster of them all, but is in reality an all-too-cute teddy-bear with disruptive psychic powers.

Terrahawks was slow to take off, possibly due to the resistance of the old guard towards both the new form of puppetry (dubbed 'Supermacromation') and the much heavier comedic aspect of the show, but more likely because the generation of kids watching the show simply didn't know that a Gerry Anderson production was something to look forward to. But at its peak, the series was attracting nine million viewers – more than many peak-time grown-up shows could achieve. The *Terrahawks* puppets even became TV presenters, hosting a month of Children's ITV programmes in specially filmed sequences in October 1984. There were three series, racking up an impressive 39 episodes; the last Anderson puppet series to reach that many episodes was ***Stingray***, back in 1965.

Terry and June

Sitcom | BBC One | episode duration 30 mins | broadcast 7 May 1974–20 Dec 1978 (*Happy Ever After*), 24 Oct 1979–31 Aug 1987 (*Terry and June*)

Regular Cast

Terry Scott · *Terry Fletcher/Medford*
June Whitfield · *June Fletcher/Medford*
Beryl Cooke · *Aunt Lucy*
Lena Clemo, Pippa Page · *Susan Fletcher*
Caroline Whitaker · *Debbie Fletcher*
Terence Alexander, Tim Barrett, John Quayle · *Malcolm*
Rosemary Frankau · *Beattie*
Reginald Marsh · *Sir Dennis Hodge*

Continued on page 747

Dr Bea (standing), Marion, Blanche and Joss dread the calling of another Tenko.

The harrowing story of women suffering under the cruel regime of their Japanese captors, *Tenko* (the Japanese word for 'roll call') has lost little of its power in the 20 years since it was originally transmitted. *Tenko* was created by Lavinia Warner, who began researching the facts of female prisoners of war while working on editions of ***This is your Life*** and *Omnibus*. Aware that there had already been numerous accounts of the harsh regime faced by male prisoners of war in films such as *The Bridge on the River Kwai* (1957), Warner realised that there was a whole other story still to be told – that of the women interred for years in conditions of squalor and deprivation. *Tenko* would redress the balance somewhat, with a particular focus on how formerly privileged women managed to survive such an ordeal.

The series begins in December 1941 among the Western colonials living in the tropical paradise of Singapore. We meet Marion Jefferson, a bored wife of an army officer who spends her days longing for something worthwhile to do and hoping for a greater purpose in life than just to 'make up the numbers at dinner'. Marion's plans to return to London are put in jeopardy by the news that the Japanese army is advancing quickly towards Singapore. Along with hundreds of other women, married couples, children and the elderly, Marion is packed onto a cargo ship heading for Australia. But when a Japanese torpedo strikes the ship in the middle of the night, Marion and the other passengers are forced to swim for their lives. By the next morning, they've washed up on the shore of a nearby island, but not everyone has made it. Marion has little time to mourn the loss of her best friend Vicky (two episodes in, the first instance in *Tenko* of the unexpected killing off of a popular character – there would be many more to come), when suddenly the terrified survivors are surrounded by a passing patrol of Japanese soldiers. The women are brutally separated from the few male evacuees who survived the shipwreck and marched off through the jungle to a prisoner-of-war camp.

Arriving at their new home, the women are shocked to discover that it is little more than a few huts in the middle of the jungle surrounded by a fence. Sanitation is non-existent and the sleeping arrangements so basic that disease is soon rife among the women. Much against her better judgement, Marion agrees to be the elected leader of the British women, with the formidable nun Sister Ulrica leading the Dutch-speaking internees. Dr Beatrice Mason (Stephanie Cole, in a dry-run for her withering performance as curmudgeonly Diana in ***Waiting for God***) starts to assemble what passes for a sickbay, where she is helped by two of her former nurses, Nelly and Kate. A constant theme in the series is the lack of medical supplies such as quinine, a life-saving treatment for the malaria carried by tropical mosquitoes.

Although it might be expected that a programme with a largely all-female cast could be read as a feminist treatise, this is not the case with *Tenko*. Very often, the women are at each other's throats, plotting and manipulating the situation to do whatever they can to survive. In particular, class issues still caused divisions, with upper-crust racist Sylvia initially refusing to mix with people she considered to be 'beneath' her, such as mixed-race linguist Christina or former good-time-girl Blanche. Sylvia's stubborn refusal to acknowledge the Japanese in any kind of position of authority gets her, and by association all the women, into serious trouble and it takes her a long time to learn which fights are worth picking, and which she should let go. In contrast, the similarly upper-class Joss (who arrives in the second series) takes great pleasure in subtly taking the mickey out of the Japanese and any fellow prisoners who have ideas above their station, such as the nauseating Dutch woman Mrs Van Meyer (nicknamed 'Metro-Goldwyn' Meyer by the British women for her diva-like attitude), who takes every opportunity she can to brag about how wonderful her life used to be, and how awful it is for her to have to suffer the privations of camp life.

The character who goes through the biggest changes in the series is undoubtedly Dorothy, who begins the series witnessing her husband being shot dead by the Japanese. A short time into her stay in the camp, her daughter Violet dies from a combination of disease and malnutrition, sending the grieving Dorothy into a depression she only barely climbs out of. In the face of overwhelming odds, Dorothy finds resourcefulness deep within her that, in her previous pampered life, she would never have imagined she possessed. Dorothy risks accusations of collaboration from her fellow prisoners when she associates with friendly guard Shinya and offers him English lessons and, later, sexual favours in exchange for food. When Dorothy falls pregnant and has to seek an abortion from one of the local native

Drama
BBC/Australian Broadcasting Company, BBC One
Episode Duration: 50 mins
Broadcast: 26 Oct 1981–16 Dec 1984

Regular Cast
Ann Bell · *Marion Jefferson*
Stephanie Cole · *Dr Beatrice Mason*
Stephanie Beacham · *Rose Millar*
Louise Jameson · *Blanche Simmons*
Patricia Lawrence · *Sister Ulrica*
Veronica Roberts · *Dorothy Bennett*
Emily Bolton · *Christina Campbell*
Elizabeth Chambers · *Mrs Dominica Van Meyer*
Claire Oberman · *Kate Norris*
Burt Kwouk · *Captain/Major Yamauchi*
Jean Anderson · *Lady Jocelyn 'Joss' Holbrook*
Joanna Hole · *Sally Markham*
Jeananne Crowley · *Nellie Keene*
Renée Asherson · *Sylvia Ashburton*
Rosemary Martin · *Verna Johnson*
Josephine Welcome · *Miss Hasan*
Carolle Rousseau · *Dr Natalie Trier*
Cindy Shelley · *Alice Courtenay*
Elizabeth Mickery · *Maggie Thorpe*
Philippa Urquhart · *Lillian Cartland*
Nicolas Corry · *Bobby Cartland*
Kerry Tovey · *Suzy*
Ann Queensberry · *Judith Bowen*
Karin Foley · *Debbie Bowen*
Anna Lindup · *Daisy Robertson*
Wendy Williams · *Vicky Armstrong*
Ivor Danvers · *Jack Armstrong*
Daniel Hill · *Tom Redburn*
Edmund Pegge · *Bernard Webster*
Eiji Kusuhara · *Lieutenant Sato*
Takashi Kawahara · *Shinya*
Takahiro Oba · *Kasaki*
Sabu Kimura · *Lieutenant Nakamura*
Jonathan Newth · *Clifford Jefferson*
Damien Thomas · *Jake Haulter*
Preston Lockwood · *Stephen Wentworth*
Elspet Gray · *Phyllis Bristow*
Bernard Gallagher · *Mr Courtney*

Creator Lavinia Warner

Producers Vere Lorrimer, Ken Riddington

Writers Lavinia Warner, Jill Hyem, Anne Valery, Paul Wheeler

Theme Music James Harpham

women, her sheer determination and will to survive means that even in this most terrible of circumstances, you always know that Dorothy will pull through. Other women are less fortunate, however – young bubbly 'jolly hockey sticks' Sally is crushed by the death of her child and takes her own life during an inspection of the camp, an act that brings extensive retributions onto the rest of the women.

Throughout the first series of *Tenko*, the women struggle to make their lives in the camp as tolerable as possible, but a lack of food and basic medical supplies leads them into acts of rebellion that regularly see them being punished by sadistic guard Sato and camp commandant Captain Yamauchi. Burt Kwouk (perhaps best known for playing Cato in the *Pink Panther* films) does a sterling job of portraying the dignified Yamauchi, a Japanese officer who it's possible to respect if not exactly like. It is, of course, slightly ironic that Kwouk – famously of Chinese descent – was cast as a Japanese officer, considering that *Tenko* made an especially hard effort to portray the political situation in South-East Asia during World War Two with sensitivity and accuracy. In a similar way to earlier BBC World War Two dramas, such as ***Colditz*** and ***Secret Army***, *Tenko* makes a concerted effort never to simply portray 'us' as the good guys and 'them' as the villains – life was much more complex than that. By avoiding broad brush-strokes in its portraits of both the Japanese and the prisoners, *Tenko* gains an air of realism and sophistication that most war films would dearly love to possess.

At the start of the second series of *Tenko*, the women are relocated to a different camp where they meet some surprising new challenges. Having grown used to their own systems and routines in their impoverished environment, it comes as some surprise to be moved to a comparatively luxurious, well-run facility. In charge of this camp is Lieutenant Nakamura, who speaks no English. His interpreter, Miss Hasan, is a truly vile woman with a ferocious temper and expensive tastes. Working closely with Miss Hasan is leader of the prisoners, Verna Johnson, who at first appears friendly and welcoming, but who very quickly reveals her true colours as self-centred and manipulative. As the internees adjust to their lives in the new camp, they learn that luxury has a price – both financial and in terms of their own self-respect. Beatrice, who has started to lose her eyesight, finds herself being browbeaten by the camp's own snotty medic Dr Trier; Marion discovers that being an unrecognised leader means her voice is no longer heard; and Sister Ulrica is sworn to a vow of silence by a visiting priest for being complicit in Sally's burial (it being a sin for anyone who commits suicide to have a Christian funeral), a vow she only breaks in an attempt to prevent Dorothy's abortion.

The discovery by the women that there is a men's prison camp nearby is the main storyline for the last half of the second season. When posh society girl Rose discovers that her boyfriend Bernard is alive and well and living in a camp nearby, she risks all to spend one night with him. The lovers share a blissful reunion but, unknown to them, somebody has informed the Japanese. Inside the camp, the women watch in horror as a patrol is sent out into the jungle –

shortly afterwards, two shots ring out. Bernard is killed at the scene, but Rose is brought back into the camp, shot through the back and paralysed from the waist down.

Stephanie Beacham's performance as the dying Rose is undoubtedly the greatest of her TV career. An actress famed for her glamorous roles in programmes such as ***Dynasty*** and ***Connie***, it must have been a fantastic opportunity to portray a woman dying in possibly the least dignified way imaginable, and Beacham rises to it admirably. Rose's agony is matched by Beatrice's, when she realises that she must compromise her long-held belief in the sanctity of human life in order to ease her friend's suffering. Marion later realises, much to her disgust, that it was her friend Lilian who informed on Rose to get extra food for her young son Bobby. Although Marion does the decent thing and asks for Lilian and Bobby to be moved to another camp, she cannot forgive: Lilian has gone too far, and cannot be excused for her actions, even if they were done to protect her child.

The second season ended with a shocking double blow for the women. First, the women discover that Verna Johnson, on the orders of Miss Hasan, has been hoarding Red Cross parcels and selling the contents back to them at extortionate prices. The quinine that could have saved so many lives has been in the camp all along. Marion's abilities as leader of the women are stretched to breaking point when she only barely manages to stop Blanche and Dorothy from lynching Verna right then and there. Marion promises to confront Yamauchi with the evidence of Miss Hasan's corruption, but she never gets the chance. The next day, an Allied aeroplane attempts to bomb Yamauchi's headquarters – tragically, it misses and the bomb hits the camp. Miss Hasan and several of the women are killed, and just as the survivors manage to liberate their Red Cross parcels, a furious Yamauchi arrives and threatens to shoot every single one of the women then and there. 'You are a defeated race!' he bellows. 'Not for long,' replies Marion defiantly.

Sadly, Marion was wrong in that assessment. Two years have passed by the time the third season started. The women have yet again been relocated to another prison, and several of their number (including Blanche and Verna) have died in the intervening years from disease and malnutrition. When actress Louise Jameson fell pregnant in between seasons, it was reluctantly decided to kill off her character Blanche. In one of the few obvious flaws in the whole of *Tenko*, all of the dialogue and situations that would clearly have been Blanche's ended up going to a new character. Although this is no criticism of a fine performance by Elizabeth Mickery, it's easy to imagine her copies of the scripts with 'Blanche' crossed out and 'Maggie' hastily scrawled in.

In the final days of the war, it appears as though time is rapidly running out for the women. Christina sees a document in Yamauchi's office ordering all prisoners to be massacred prior to any retreat. The women arm themselves with rocks and sticks as they assemble for what will be their final tenko. In an almost unbearably tense scene, the guards line up opposite the women and raise their

TRIVIA

Although all of the prison camp sequences were recorded in a specially constructed set in a Dorset sand quarry, *Tenko* received an added boost of realism thanks to extensive location filming each season in Singapore and the Far East.

The third season was nominated for Best Drama Series in the BAFTA awards of 1985.

weapons, at which point Yamauchi announces that the Japanese have surrendered and the war is over. Marion goes to Yamauchi's office and formally accepts his surrender, gratefully accepting the protection of the guards until the camp can be liberated by the Allied forces. This marvellous reversal of fortune proves to the audience that their support for Marion throughout the series was entirely justified. In victory, she is a magnanimous leader, calmly making the right decisions to ensure the safety of her friends until they can finally be liberated. With the war over, the women are repatriated back to Singapore where, to their amazement, they are billeted in the luxury of Raffles Hotel.

Although this final series lacks the tense drama of the first two years, it does contain a beautifully realised portrayal of the culture shock facing prisoners of war as they try to re-adapt to life back in the 'real' world. Young Alice, who had gone through puberty while in the camps, is at first mistaken for a boy by one of her rescuers. As she struggles to come to terms with her freedom and her womanhood, she has to learn from her friends about the trials of courting. Marion, who had always been something of a reluctant leader, finds it impossible to settle back into the role of a subservient military wife and, as a consequence, the reunion with her husband Clifford is filled with melancholy and a dawning realisation that their marriage is over. As *Tenko* draws to a close, Beatrice stays in Singapore to run a clinic providing healthcare for the native population. Dorothy, Alice, Maggie and Marion return to Britain, and Sister Ulrica visits Major Yamauchi, who is on death row waiting to be executed for war crimes.

The series ends with the women making promises to keep in touch. We're lucky enough to be party to their reunion, shown a year later, but set five years on. The movie-length *Tenko Reunion* (1985) returns to Singapore where a slightly strained party at the home of Dominica Van Meyer becomes entwined in an attack by an armed Communist insurgence. Once more, the former internees face death, only this time they discover that their friend Christina is the leader of the band of Communists. Though they all feel betrayal by their own friend, she reveals her own sense of betrayal, an outcast from East and West, the two cultures she was simultaneously part of and abandoned by.

Despite such a consistently grim situation, *Tenko* provided a fine combination of humour, pathos and drama that gave a unique insight into a historical event few people might otherwise have known about. By focusing on the impact that war can have on the gender that normally has little to do with front-line conflict, *Tenko* also gave a group of top-notch actors the chance to raise their game to the highest of levels. Louise Jameson (Blanche) has stated that *Tenko* was her favourite ever TV role. 'The *Tenko* cast had such a hard-core sisterhood, which still exists,' she said. 'There's six of us who meet up regularly and chat on the phone once a week.' Watching the episodes today, it's easy to see why.

John Warner · *Reverend Austin Doyle*
Allan Cuthbertson · *Tarquin*
Joanna Henderson · *Miss Fennell*
Patsy Smart · *Nora Dingle*

Creators John Chapman, Eric Merriman, Christopher Bond, John Kane (*Happy Ever After*), John Kane (*Terry and June*) **Producers** Peter Whitmore, Ray Butt, Robin Nash, John B. Hobbs **Writers** John Chapman, Eric Merriman, Christopher Bond, John Kane, Jon Watkins, Terry Ravenscroft, Dave Freeman, Greg Freeman, Colin Bostock-Smith, David Grigson **Theme Music** John Shakespeare (astonishingly, not Ronnie Hazlehurst for once) created a theme tune that's so redolent of mid-week early evenings that it sets off nervous tics about getting homework finished in a generation of people across the UK.

On 7 May 1974, an episode of the *Comedy Playhouse* series of pilot shows brought together two comic actors into a partnership that would become synonymous with middle-class, middle-of-the-road sitcoms. In the process, they would become two of the most beloved performers in the country, simultaneously ensuring that the names 'Terry' and 'June' would join a list of names inextricably linked in much the same way as Laurel and Hardy, Morecambe and Wise, and Bill and Ben.

Although Scott and Whitfield had actually worked together before on the 1960s sketch show *Scott On*, it was with the sitcom *Happy Ever After* that they honed their comedic double-act into an exercise in patience, stupidity and lots of 'Cor, June'. In *Happy Ever After*, Scott and Whitfield play Terry and June Fletcher, a happily married couple living in suburbia. With daughters Susan and Debbie having flown the coop, Terry and June now spend their time looking after elderly Aunt Lucy and her irritating talking mynah bird, Gunga Din. Things stayed much the same throughout 42 episodes, with Terry acting like a great big spoiled kid (much as he had done earlier in adverts for Curly Wurly chocolate bars) and June exasperatedly raising her eyes to heaven at her on-screen husband's utter idiocy.

Eventually, chief scriptwriter John Chapman grew tired of thinking up new storylines for the series and asked the BBC to call it a day on *Happy Ever After*. However, the BBC was unhappy about cancelling such a successful programme and decided to carry on making the show anyway. Without Chapman's input as co-creator of the original series, it was decided to simply rename the show and make a few minor tweaks to it in order to avoid any potentially nasty legal wrangles. Thus, just ten months after *Happy Ever After* came to an end, *Terry and June* burst onto BBC One in an all-new show that felt remarkably similar. In the new show, the Fletchers had become the extremely similar Medfords, again living in middle-class suburban bliss. No longer tied down by visiting daughters or an elderly auntie, they were instead visited on a regular basis by snotty next-door neighbours Malcolm and Beattie and Terry's belligerent boss, Sir Dennis (a performance by Reginald Marsh that's almost identical to his earlier turn as 'Sir' in ***The Good Life***). Indeed, Sir Dennis dropping in on the Medfords at unexpected and inopportune moments provided much of the programme's comedy.

Regular viewers of *Terry and June* might have found plotlines and situations becoming familiar and repetitious. However, one part of the programme was rarely the same each week: would it be Terry's sun-lounger or June's that collapsed during the opening titles? Or instead might it be the parasol that fell down on top of them both? Such adrenalin-pumping antics were enough to keep viewers of a nervous disposition gripped each week.

Neither *Happy Ever After* nor *Terry and June* were particularly welcomed by critics at the time, feeling old-fashioned even when new episodes were still in production (possibly because certain situations from their earlier shows seemed alarmingly similar to those being served up in the 1980s). This archetypal, 'safe', middle-class sitcom inspired the format for outrageous comedian Julian Clary's own inimitable take on the format, *Terry and Julian* (shown on Channel 4, in six episodes in 1992). For younger viewers, Terry Scott became known as the voice of Danger Mouse's friend Penfold and for the series of adverts for Curly Wurly. Meanwhile, June Whitfield has enjoyed worship from a whole new generation of fans thanks to ***Absolutely Fabulous***, something we always knew she was.

TFI Friday

Entertainment | Ginger Productions for Channel 4 | episode duration 45 mins | broadcast 9 Feb 1996–22 Dec 2000

Regular Cast

Chris Evans, Will Macdonald, Danny Baker, Holly Samos, Andrew Carey · *Andrew the Barman*
Steve Vermont · *Ugly Bloke*
Catalina Guirado · *Model Rejected by Ugly Bloke*
Johnny Boy Revell and His Wheels of Steel, Cedric
Ronald Fraser · *The Lord of Love*

Creator Chris Evans **Producers** Chris Evans (executive), Will Macdonald, David Granger, Suzi Aplin **Writers** Chris Evans, Danny Baker **Theme Music** Ron Grainer's original theme tune for **Man in a Suitcase** was re-used for *TFI Friday*.

For about three years, *TFI Friday* was simply unmissable, headline-making television. Part chat show, part music show, part variety special, *TFI* (which stood for 'Thank Four It's Friday') was broadcast live at 6 p.m. on Channel 4 and tapped into the very essence of the Britpop movement. Each week the guests would consist of the coolest of indie bands, the most cutting edge of comedians and the biggest of celebrities – and the ringmaster leading this parade of fun and seemingly effortless confidence was former ***Big Breakfast*** presenter Chris Evans.

Chris's relaxed style of presentation was ideal for a show that seemed to revel in its spontaneity. Surrounding himself with a team of talented staff (both in front of and behind the camera), Chris introduced regular features that included 'Freak or Unique' (a rather unusual talent show

segment), 'Fat Lookalikes' and 'Ugly Bloke' (each new Ugly Bloke would rebuff glamorous model Catalina's advances with the phrase 'I'm sorry love, you're just not my type!'). Chris's main on-screen sparring partner was show producer Will Macdonald, and his off-screen sparring partner (and eventually wife) became popstar Billie Piper after they met on the show. More controversy was courted when Happy Mondays' frontman Shaun Ryder used exceptionally strong language live (on two separate occasions!) during the show's run. As a direct result, the programme was forced to be pre-recorded, a move that seemed to lessen the adrenaline rush and took the edge off the series. Of course, all good things come to an end, and by 2000 it was clear that Chris Evans had become bored with hosting *TFI*. In fact, he didn't even bother to present the final seven episodes, with special guest hosts including the Spice Girls and Elton John being drafted in. Evans' next big project for TV after the demise of *TFI Friday* was an innovative game show called ***Don't Forget Your Toothbrush***, which offered members of the studio audience the chance to jet directly off on holiday if they won the big prize. Like so much of what Chris Evans does, it had a certain touch of ginger gold about it.

That Was The Week That Was

Comedy | BBC TV | episode duration 50 mins, plus 20-/100-/150-min specials | broadcast 24 Nov 1962–28 Dec 1963

Cast

David Frost, Millicent Martin, Bernard Levin, Lance Percival, Kenneth Cope, David Kernan, Roy Kinnear, Willie Rushton, Timothy Birdsall, Al Mancini, Robert Lang, Cleo Laine

Creator Ned Sherrin **Producers** Alasdair Milne (executive), Ned Sherrin **Writers** Various, including David Frost, Keith Waterhouse, Willis Hall, Gerald Kaufman, David Nathan, Dennis Potter, David Nobbs, Peter Tinniswood, Jack Rosenthal, Dave Lee, Caryl Brahms, Bill Oddie, Richard Ingrams, Brian Glanville, John Cleese, Robert Gillespie, Bernard Levin, Ned Sherrin, William Rushton, Kenneth Tynan, Granville Barker, Richard Rodney Bennett, John Betjeman, John Bird, Timothy Birdsall, Malcolm Bradbury, Graham Chapman, David Climie, Peter Cook, Kenneth Cope, David Cumming, Roald Dahl, Johnny Dankworth, Barry Fantoni, William Franklyn, Michael Frayn, Al Mancini, John Mortimer, Frank Muir, Denis Norden, Alan Plater, Peter Schaffer, Johnny Speight, Eric Sykes, John Wells **Theme Music** Ron Grainer, sung by Millicent Martin with different topical lyrics set to the same tune

In 1962, BBC Director General Hugh Carleton Greene tasked Ned Sherrin with the responsibility of shaking up the BBC's news coverage with an aggressive, no-holds barred attack on public figures. Produced within the News and Current Affaris department rather than Light Entertainment, *That Was The Week That Was* satirised politicians, religious leaders and anyone else who dared place themselves in a position of responsibility. Sherrin assembled one of the most important creative forces in British entertainment, fronted by 23-year-old David Frost and including singer Millicent Martin and writers Bernard Levin and Lance Percival. After a pilot that nearly frightened off Sherrin's bosses, *That Was The Week That Was* finally went to air – live – in November 1962.

The show mixed song-and-dance routines, often written by Percival, with straight-to-camera monologues, comic sketches and rants from Bernard Levin (one surly playwright broke into the studio during one live show to physically attack Levin, while being incredibly polite about it). In both content and style, *TW3* (as it became known) was unlike any programme the BBC had ever made. Exposing the trappings of TV production by allowing cameras and lighting gantries into shot, or having the performers read from their scripts, gave it a more off-the-cuff, immediate feeling that complemented the bang up-to-date edge to the show. In the early days of television, it wasn't unknown for programmes to over- or under-run, but by the early 1960s, programmes were expected to be disciplined enough to finish bang on time. This was something *TW3* rarely managed to do, mainly because – as the last item in the Saturday night schedule – the only thing it would be affecting was the National Anthem, played at closedown. To bring the show in on its allotted end-time, the Beeb decided to schedule repeats of the popular thriller serial ***The Third Man*** – until David Frost began reading out detailed synopses of the episode in advance. *The Third Man* was rapidly dropped from Saturday nights to allow *TW3* to continue as before.

While most British viewers were enjoying ***The Black and White Minstrels***, *TW3* attempted to parody the show in an attack on the racial disturbances in America's Deep South, although its joke was missed by most. Its most famous edition, however, saw it drop all of its regular items for an unrepresentatively reverent show the night after the assassination of President John F. Kennedy. Including a tribute sung by Millicent Martin, the soundtrack to the programme was later released in the USA as a long-playing record – *The British Broadcasting Corporation's Tribute to John Fitzgerald Kennedy*.

Prime Minister Harold Macmillan brushed off criticisms, allegedly because he believed it was better to be criticised than ignored. Harold Wilson was also said to have defended the show against Postmaster General Reginald Bevins' campaign to have it dropped. But in 1964, it was felt that it would be inappropriate to broadcast such a deliberately iconoclastic programme during an election year. After its final episode (brought to a close by Frost's final words: 'That was *That Was The Week That Was*, that was'), the series was quietly pushed to one side and forgotten about. David Frost successfully exported the format to the USA (where it was broadcast by the same name), fronting some editions as he'd done in the UK, running from January 1964 to May 1965. Next came *The Frost Report*, another satirical current affairs show that saw Ronnies Barker and Corbett brought together for the first time and gave John Cleese his first major TV exposure.

That's Life!

Factual | BBC One | episode duration 40 mins | broadcast 26 May 1973–19 Jun 1994

Regular Cast

Esther Rantzen, Cyril Fletcher, George Layton, Glyn Worsnip, Kieran Prendiville, Victoria Wood, Paul Heiney, Chris Serle, Gavin Campbell, Bill Buckley, Adrian Mills, Doc Cox, Joanna Monro, Mollie Sugden, Maev Alexander, Simon Fanshawe, Michael Groth, Grant Baynham, Kevin Devine, Howard Leader · *Presenters*

Producers Peter Chafer (executive), John Lloyd, John Morrell, Esther Rantzen **Theme music** Tony Kinsey composed the legendary *That's Life!* theme tune, complete with blaring brass instruments. It's a great piece of music that instantly grabs the viewer's attention.

That's Life was created as a follow-on series to BBC One's successful consumer-focused show *Braden's Week*. Respected journalist Bernard Braden had hosted the series (13 Sep 1968–29 Apr 1972), until he was sacked by the BBC for appearing in a TV commercial on ITV (see also Percy Thrower on ***Gardeners' World*** and Hugh Scully on ***Antiques Roadshow***). Esther Rantzen was one of the reporters on *Braden's Week*, and it seemed a natural fit for her to take over as presenter of the new show *That's Life!*

For 21 years, Esther and her compatriots at *That's Life!* presented viewers with a live Sunday night TV show that informed, educated and entertained – warning them about newly discovered health risks and worries, telling them about companies who were guilty of dodgy dealings or bad service, and warming their hearts with stories of 'talking' animals, cute children and amusingly shaped root vegetables. Esther was normally backed up by two desk-bound co-presenters, who would 'dramatise' the letters and discussions between a disgruntled viewer and British Telecom, Tesco or whoever was the subject of their investigations that particular week. Esther would also be able to call upon Cyril Fletcher (later, Doc Cox and Mollie Sugden) to read out viewers' letters and 'odd odes' for a little bit of light relief inbetween the more serious stories. For a short while, comedienne Victoria Wood was even on hand to chip in with a humorous song about a topical subject. The 'Jobsworth' Awards were also given out to public officials who took the letter of the law above and beyond the call of duty, and Esther would regularly go out onto the streets of London to get the public's opinion about a new delicacy or fashion/fad (memorably leading to Esther's arrest on one occasion for 'blocking the pavement').

That's Life!'s achievement weren't just transitory though. As a result of the programme featuring the story of young Ben Hardwick, who was dying because there were no suitable livers available to be transplanted into him, organ donations shot up. Sadly, the benefits came too late to help Ben, who tragically died of his condition. In order to raise still more funds and awareness of the problem, West End singer Marti Webb released a cover version of Michael Jackson's 'Ben', which reached No. 5 in the charts in June 1985. But *That's Life!*'s greatest legacy was the establishment of children's charity Childline, which provides an invaluable service to abused and lonely children to this day.

They Think it's all Over

Panel Game | Talkback for BBC One | episode duration 30 mins | broadcast 14 Sep 1995–present

Regular Cast

Nick Hancock · *Host*

David Gower, Gary Lineker, David Seaman, Phil Tufnell · *Team Captains*

Lee Hurst, Rory McGrath, Jonathan Ross, Phill Jupitus, Jo Brand · *Regular Team Members*

Creators Bill Matthews and Simon Bullivant **Producers** Various, including Peter Fincham (executive), Harry Thompson, Jim Pullin

Reworking the irreverent format of ***Have I Got News For You?*** for sporting matters, *They Think it's all Over* was originally developed for radio before finally reaching our screens in 1995. The game combines professionals with comedians. It also unashamedly pinches from ***A Question of Sport***, the BBC's other jocular sport quiz, although, as with ***Never Mind The Buzzcocks***, it's more about being funny than winning. Rounds include a rapid-fire name game where one team member has to describe a sportsperson without using their name and the others have to guess who it is; 'Feel the Sportsperson' involves two team members groping a sport-related person or group of people while blindfolded – often with objects from the sport included in the portmanteau (a surf board, a javelin . . .); and a few 'What Happened Next?' type affairs. The show, of course, takes its name from the infamous utterance of ***Match of the Day*** presenter Kenneth Wolstenholme at the end of the 1966 World Cup.

The Thin Blue Line

Sitcom | Tiger Aspect Productions for BBC One | episode duration 30 mins | broadcast 13 Nov 1995–23 Dec 1996

Regular Cast

Rowan Atkinson · *Inspector Raymond Fowler*
Serena Evans · *Sergeant Patricia Dawkins*
James Dreyfus · *PC Kevin Goody*
Mina Anwar · *WPC Maggie Habib*
Rudolph Walker · *PC Gladstone*
David Haig · *DI Derek Grim*
Kevin Allen · *DC Kray*
Mark Addy · *DC Boyle*
Lucy Robinson · *Mayoress Wickham*

Producers Geoffrey Perkins, Ben Elton **Writer** Ben Elton **Theme Music** Howard Goodall

Inspector Fowler would like to believe that he runs Gasforth Police Station with a rod of iron – sadly, it's more like a rod of slightly damp cardboard, with Fowler's ineffectual nature and frankly rather rubbish leadership style causing no end of problems both for him and his team. His subordinates included the astonishingly camp PC Goody (who is, in fact, in love with go-getting WPC Habib), laid-back West Indian copper PC Gladstone, and the sour-faced and ambitious (yet utterly incompetent) DI Grim and his plain-clothes detective colleagues. Longest suffering of all of his staff is Desk Sergeant Dawkins, an earnest and romantic woman who's been Fowler's girlfriend for ten years. Despite Fowler being rather inept on the romance front, Dawkins keeps hoping against hope that underneath his stern, geeky exterior there lays a heart just waiting to be kick-started into life.

When ***Blackadder***'s star and writer Rowan Atkinson and Ben Elton announced their new comedy series would be set in a police station, most viewers probably expected a stinging satire on the modern police force, or at the very least a show jam-packed with banter of the highest order. Instead, Elton's scripts harked back to the Seventies, the golden era of sitcoms (and television in general). Instead of jokes about bodily fluids or backstabbing, the comedy in *The Thin Blue Line* was gentle, character-based and remarkably traditional in its style and delivery. Perhaps because of this deviation from what people were anticipating, *The Thin Blue Line* never really grabbed the attention of the viewing public. The show's greatest success was in reviving the career of former ***Love Thy Neighbour*** star Rudolph Walker (who'd quickly be snapped up by ***EastEnders*** as Patrick Trueman) and launching the career of James Dreyfuss, whose double-takes and adept physical comedy would be given an even bigger opportunity to shine in ***Gimme Gimme Gimme***.

Third Rock from the Sun

Sitcom | Carsey-Werner for NBC (shown on BBC Two) | episode duration 25 mins, plus specials | broadcast 9 Jan 1996–22 May 2001 (USA)

Principal Cast

John Lithgow · *Dick Solomon*
Jane Curtin · *Dr Mary Albright*
Kristen Johnston · *Sally Solomon*
French Stewart · *Harry Solomon*
Joseph Gordon-Levitt · *Tommy Solomon*
Simbi Khali · *Nina Campbell*
Shay Astar · *August*
Wayne Knight · *Officer Don*
Ian Lithgow · *Leon*
Danielle Nicolet · *Caryn*
Chris Hogan · *Pitman*
David DeLuise · *Bug*
William Shatner · *Big Giant Head*

Creators Bonnie Turner, Terry Turner **Producers** Various, including Bonnie Turner, Terry Turner, Marcy Carsey, Tom Werner, Caryn Mandabach (executive), Patrick Kienlen, Christine Zander, Bob Kushell **Writers** Various, including Bonnie Turner, Terry Turner, Christine Zander, Mike Schiff, Bill Martin, Andrew Orenstein **Theme Music** Ben Vaughn, Jeff Sudakin

The Solomons are a group of aliens who have come to Earth on a field trip. Their high commander assumes the identity of Dick, the head of a family, who discovers that he has formed an emotional attachment to an Earth human called Mary and decides to postpone the return home indefinitely. The news does not sit well with the team, the First Lieutenent (who's taken the form of an Amazonian woman called 'Sally'), the most senior crew member, 'Tommy', who has ironically appeared on Earth in the form of a randy teenager, and 'Harry', who was apparently part of the team because they 'had an extra seat'. Harry doesn't seem to understand either the most basic of human activities or the need for the crew to maintain their pretence at being human to avoid being Area 51'd.

While some would have us believe aliens are slimy, deadly and in possession of more than their fair share of teeth, others have speculated that all our extra-terrestrial friends want is to make us laugh. From Mork the Orkan to the dog-faced ***ALF***, the sitcom genre has long realised the potential for comic situations coming from the simple fact that aliens won't always be 100 per cent up on human culture before they try to integrate into our world. *Third Rock* tapped into the same 'illegal alien' vein that had fuelled ***Mork & Mindy***, but with a much more pop-cultural awareness; ***Star Trek***'s William Shatner guest starred in a few episodes as the team's glorious leader, the Big Giant Head.

thirtysomething

Drama | Bedford Falls Productions/MGM Television for ABC (shown on Channel 4) | episode duration 50 mins | broadcast 29 Sep 1987–28 May 1991 (USA)

Regular Cast

Ken Olin · *Michael Steadman*
Mel Harris · *Hope Murdoch Steadman*
Timothy Busfield · *Elliot Weston*
Patricia Wettig · *Nancy Krigger Weston*
Luke Rossi · *Ethan Weston*
Melanie Mayron · *Melissa Steadman*
Polly Draper · *Ellyn Warren*
Peter Horton · *Professor Gary Shepherd*
David Clennon · *Miles Drentell*
Erich Anderson · *Billy Sidel*
Terry Kinney · *Steve Woodman*
Richard Gilliland · *Jeffrey Milgrom*
Patricia Kalember · *Susannah Hart Shepherd*

Andra Millian · *Angel Wasserma*
Corey Parker · *Lee Owens*

Creators Marshall Herskovitz and Edward Zwick **Producers** Edward Zwick (executive), Jeanne Byrd (associate), Paul Haggis, Joseph Dougherty, Marshall Herskovitz, Winnie Holzman, Richard Kramer, Lindsley Parsons III, Ellen S. Pressman, Scott Winant **Writers** Various, including Marshall Herskovitz, Edward Zwick, Richard Kramer, Liberty Godshall, Susan Shilliday, Joseph Dougherty, Ann Lewis Hamilton, Winnie Holzman, William H. Macy **Theme Music** W. G. Snuffy Walden

With most TV executives aiming their output at a young, 16–24 demographic, *thirtysomething* acknowledged the presence of an age group who are just as likely to be influenced by advertising but might actually also have the money to buy the products too. By the age of 30, most people have either paired off, are in the process of building their lives up again after their first serious split or else are still playing at being 21.

Here, Philadelphians Hope and Michael are married and getting to grips with that period in their lives where the honeymoon is over and they begin to face the harder task of sharing their lives together. In contrast, Michael's best friend Gary is happy to continue playing the field and doesn't think there's much wrong in being a professor who has his pick of his students. Gary's colleague and agency business partner Elliot was always the joker in the pack, but with two kids and a wife who gets on his nerves at times, *he's* beginning to suspect that maybe getting married wasn't such a great idea. The series followed Michael and Hope learning to cope with their first child and, on Hope's part, about having to choose between a career and motherhood. Hugely sentimental and hopeful, *thirtysomething* became the number one show for women during its original run, an archetypal 'watercooler' show as office pals talked about not just the events of each episode but their emotional responses towards them.

This is your Life

Chat Show | BBC/Thames for ITV/BBC One | episode duration 25–30 mins | broadcast 29 Jul 1955–c. 1989, 2 Nov 1994–8 Aug 2003

Cast

Ralph Edwards, Eamonn Andrews, Michael Aspel · *Hosts*

Creator Ralph Edwards **Producers** Various, including T. Leslie Jackson, Vere Lorrimer, Robert Trell, Malcolm Morris, David Croft, Sue Green, John Graham, Jack Crawshaw **Theme Music** 'Gala Performance' by Laurie Johnson

This is your Life was originally created for radio before appearing on American television for the first time on 2 October 1952. When the BBC brought the format to the UK, the first guest scheduled for the red book treatment had been football manager Stanley Matthews but after the surprise was scuppered by the *Daily Sketch*, a little quick thinking resulted in the show's host Eamonn Andrews being the surprise first guest – creator of the American show Ralph Edwards was flown over to do the honours. Andrews proceeded to host the show for more than 30 years, nine of which were on the BBC, then, after a five-year hiatus, the series was picked up by new ITV franchise-holder Thames, where it remained until Thames lost their franchise in 1994. After the death of Eamonn Andrews in 1987, Michael Aspel took on responsibilities for handing over the red book, bridging the point where *This is your Life* returned to the BBC (Aspel had himself been the subject of an edition in 1980).

Each episode would begin with a surprise 'sting', with the subject taken by surprise as the host stepped forward to say those blood-chilling words, 'This . . . is your life.' Once the shock had numbed, they'd be taken to the studio where the audience would be waiting. The guest would be led in from the rear of the auditorium, through the audience and down towards the stage (although this changed in later editions, perhaps because of an increasing awareness that celebs and members of the public in close proximity aren't a very good combination). Sat stage right, guests would first arrive as a mystery voice introducing an anecdote before stepping through the sliding double doors at the back of the stage to the (hopeful) surprise and delight of the edition's subject – though it was often clear from their facial expressions that they often had no idea who the person was. The subject's family members would then take their place in the tiered seating behind the subject, while friends and colleagues sat opposite. The final guest was always one designed to jerk a tear or two – a long-lost relative, the subject's grandchildren or some other figure who had great sentimental attachment. At the end of the show, the guest would be treated to a party with their family and friends, at which point they'd finally learn the relevance of certain codewords they'd probably heard over and over again in snatched phone calls for the previous few weeks.

Evergreen entertainer Des O'Connor was the first guest of the Thames version of the show, while Andrew Lloyd-Webber was the subject when it returned to the BBC. The final guest to date was former boy soprano and host of ***Songs of Praise*** Aled Jones. Jones was stunned at being chosen for the honour at just 32 years old, though he wasn't the youngest recipient of the Red Book: Bonnie Langford was caught in 1986 when she was just 21, and the youngest ever subject was the model Twiggy, who was just 19 at the time.

Not everyone has been willing to be subjected to an enforced trip down memory lane; Richard Gordon, who wrote the *Doctor in the House* novels, was just one 'victim' who declined to participate initially, though he did eventually appear in a later edition. Former ***Goodie*** Bill Oddie also refused, though was likewise turned around for a 2002 edition. Only one person has refused outright, footballer Danny Blanchflower. The series eventually took to pre-recording shows to avoid embarrassment and in later years to allow producers to edit out some of the choicer reactions (legend has it that ***Coronation Street***'s Jill Summers (Phyllis) was mid-way through a particularly inappropriate choice anecdote about one of her fellow cast-members at the point when Michael Aspel reached her to hand over the big red book).

Though *This is your Life* came to an end when Aspel decided to leave the series, then-channel controller Lorraine Heggessey expressed the opinion that it's more *au revoir* than goodbye.

This Life

Drama | World Productions for BBC Two | episode duration 45 mins | broadcast 18 Mar 1996–7 Aug 1997

Regular Cast

Jack Davenport · *Miles Stewart*
Amita Dhiri · *Milly Nassim*
Andrew Lincoln · *Edgar 'Egg' Cook*
Daniela Nardini · *Anna Forbes*
Jason Hughes · *Warren Jones*
Ramon Tikaram · *Ferdy*
Luisa Bradshaw-White · *Kira*
Steve John Shepherd · *Jo*
David Mallinson · *O'Donnell*
Geoffrey Bateman · *Hooperman*
Cyril Nri · *Graham*
Sacha Craise · *Kelly*
Gillian McCutcheon · *Therapist*
Natasha Little · *Rachel*

Creator Amy Jenkins **Producers** Tony Garnett (executive), Edwina Craze (associate), Jane Fallon **Writers** Amy Jenkins, Joe Ahearne, Matthew Graham, Amelia Bullmore, William Gaminara, Annie Caulfield, Jimmy Gardner, Eirene Houston, Mark Davies Markham, Ian Iqbal Rashid, Patrick Wilde, Richard Zajdlic **Theme Music** Written by Mark Anderson and Cliff Freeborn and performed by The Way Out

Five young London lawyers share a big house together in South London – Miles fancies Anna, Anna fancies Miles but is too busy to admit it, Egg and Milly are all loved up and Warren's so far back in the closet he could be in Narnia. Together they face the trials of living life as a twentysomething in the Nineties.

When *This Life* first appeared on TV screens, it was like a breath of fresh air, portraying a type of people and their lifestyles that had never been seen on screen before. For the lawyers of *This Life*, being young wasn't about rebelling or dropping out – it was about achieving as much as possible, working and partying hard and enjoying life to the absolute limits. The series did attract criticism for its portrayal of casual sex and drug taking, but many more viewers were put off by the swaying, dizzying in-your-face direction that dropped them slap-bang into the heart of the action like never so before.

Critically acclaimed, *This Life* was nominated for the Best Drama Series BAFTA in both 1997 and 1998, and stand-out star Daniela Nardini won the Best Actress BAFTA for her work in the second season. Just two seasons were made, and fans were left gasping for more by a final episode that saw former housemate Warren reunited with his friends just as repressed, up-tight Milly finally blew her top and lashed out at loathsome Rachel in perhaps the most satisfying right-hook in television history.

This Morning

Magazine | Granada for ITV | episode duration 90 mins | broadcast 1988–present

Cast

Various, including Richard Madeley, Judy Finnigan, Vanessa Feltz, Caron Keating, John Leslie, Fern Britton, Twiggy, Matthew Wright, Phillip Schofield, Coleen Nolan, Lorraine Kelly, Gloria Hunniford · *Hosts*
Fred Talbot · *Weatherman*
Dr Chris Steele · *Health Expert*
Denise Robertson · *Agony Aunt*
Susan Brookes, Phil Vickery, Simon Rimmer, Charles Metcalfe, Chef Gino D'Acampo · *Food and Drink*
Rosemary Conley, Joanna Hall · *Diet and Ftness*
Ross Kelly, Richard Orford, Anthea Turner, Philippa Forrester, Alison Hammond, Ingrid Tarrant · *Segment Presenters*
Jaci Stephen, Sharon Marshall, Beverley Turner, Ian Hyland, Paul Ross · *Entertainment, TV Critics*
Raj Persaud, Anjula Mutanda · *Psychologists*
Eric Knowles · *Antiques*

In Alan Bleasdale's masterpiece ***Boys from the Blackstuff***, we get to see Liverpool's Albert Dock as it was at the beginning of the 1980s, with silted, oily water and soot-smeared walls. Just a few years later, a conversion programme saw the old warehouses turned into luxury apartments, boutiques, a museum dedicated to the Beatles and studio space for Granada Television. It was from here that their flagship daytime show *This Morning* was broadcast in its first ten years. Each weekday morning from 10.30 until noon, husband-and-wife partnership Richard Madeley and Judy Finnigan hosted a mix of lifestyle features and celebrity chat. Dr Chris Steel answered medical queries, Denise Robertson tackled 'agony aunt' material, Susan Brookes was the resident cook and weatherman Fred Talbot leapt his way across a relief map floating in the dock. Fred's map drew crowds daily to watch him jump over to Northern Ireland and back. He never fell into the water, though the segment was occasionally interrupted by a streaker, braving the jellyfish infested water to stage a cheeky map invasion.

Realising that the programme was missing out on some of the bigger international guests by being at the 'wrong' end of the country, Richard and Judy took *This Morning* to

London before hopping over to Channel 4 for a more specialised late afternoon chat show called *Richard and Judy* (which was what most people had called *This Morning* anyway). Their old programme continued with Fern Britton and John Leslie (later Phillip Schofield) as the hosts.

This Morning with Richard not Judy

Comedy | BBC Two | episode duration 45 mins | broadcast 15 Feb 1998–13 Jun 1999

Regular Cast
Stewart Lee, Richard Herring, Kevin Eldon, Paul Putner, Trevor Lock, Richard Thomas, Nathalie Brandon, Jo Unwin, Roger Mann, Emma Kennedy, Gordon Parnis, Mark Gatiss

Producers Jon Plowman (executive), Charlie Hanson, Carlton Dixon **Writers** Stewart Lee, Richard Herring **Theme Music** Richard Thomas

For commentary, see FIST OF FUN

Thomas the Tank Engine and Friends

Animation | Clearwater/Britt Allcroft/Central/HIT Entertainment for ITV | episode duration 5–25 mins | broadcast 9 Sep 1984–present

Cast
Ringo Starr, Michael Angelis · *Narrators*

Producers Various, including Jocelyn Stephenson, Peter Ure (executive), Britt Allcroft, Robert D. Cardona, David Mitton, Phil Fehrle **Writers** Various, including Reverend W. Awdry, Christopher Awdry, Britt Allcroft, David Mitton, from the books by Reverend W. Awdry **Theme Music** Junior Campbell

A perennial favourite even before he came to TV screens, generations have grown up with the Reverend Awdry's stories about Thomas, a blue steam engine and his many locomotive friends who keep to the racks and sidings of the railway network on the fictional island of Sodor. Awdry's anthropomorphised trains first appeared in 1942 with the illustrated book *Three Railway Engines*, a tale of a green engine called Henry, a blue one called Edward and a very big one called Gordon. The adventures were inspired by stories Awdry told to his young son Christopher (as an adult, Christopher took over from his father to write some of the books himself).

The Sodor railway is owned by Sir Topham Hatt, aka the Fat Controller, so-called because he's a portly chap who wears a top hat and runs everything. Other trains include Skarloey, one of the oldest trains, Percy, a small engine, James the Red Engine, Montague 'Duck', the Great Western Engine, Donald and Douglas the Scottish Twin Engines, and Duncan, an ambitious and bossy boiler.

The TV show arrived in 1984, realised by intricate model railways and with animation created through clever editing and a variety of facial expressions for the trains themselves. Former Beatle Ringo Starr voiced the first batch, though his fellow Liverpudlian Michael Angelis (***The Liver Birds, Boys from the Blackstuff***) took over in 1991. Internationally, each country has their own narrator, with George Carlin, Alec Baldwin and Michael Brandon each taking a turn in the USA (hence Baldwin's appearance in the 2000 film *Thomas and the Magic Railroad).* Each 'episode' lasts just five minutes, but they tend to be shown in blocks of four or five at a time. Surprisingly, not all of the stories even feature Thomas, with so many other trains and vehicles to include on a regular basis.

The Thorn Birds

Drama | Warner Bros for ABC (shown on BBC One) | episode duration 120 mins | broadcast 27 Mar–30 Mar 1983 (USA)

Principal Cast
Richard Chamberlain · *Ralph de Bricassart*
Sydney Penny, Rachel Ward · *Meggie Cleary*
Barbara Stanwyck · *Mary Carson*
Christopher Plummer · *Archbishop Vittorio Contini-Verchese*
Jean Simmons · *Fiona 'Fee' Cleary*
Richard Kiley · *Paddy Cleary*
Ken Howard · *Rainer Hartheim*
Piper Laurie · *Anne Mueller*
Earl Holliman · *Luddie Mueller*
Mare Winningham · *Justine O'Neill*
Bryan Brown · *Luke O'Neill*
Philip Anglim · *Dane O'Neill*
John Friedrich · *Frank Cleary*
Stephen Burns · *Jack Cleary*
Brett Cullen · *Bob Cleary*
Dwier Brown · *Stuart Cleary*
Allyn Ann McLerie · *Mrs Smith*
Richard Venture · *Harry Gough*
Stephanie Faracy · *Judy*
Barry Corbin · *Pete*
Antoinette Bower · *Sarah MacQueen*
John de Lancie · *Alastair MacQueen*

Producers Edward Lewis, David L. Wolper (executive), Irving Paul Lazar (associate), Stan Margulies, Lee Stanley **Writer** Carmen Culver, from the novel by Colleen McCullough **Theme Music** 'Anywhere the Heart Goes' by Henry Mancini

Colleen McCulloch's familiar themes of forbidden love and redemption come to the fore in the relationship between a proud, ambitious Catholic priest, Ralph de Bricassart, and Meggie, the daughter of an Irish-Australian farmer. Meggie's family harbour a secret – that her elder brother Frank was the product of an affair her mother had before marrying their father. Bryan Brown played the man Meggie married after being rejected by Father Ralph, a hardworking sheep-farmer who neglects Meggie and works her like a slave. Barbara Stanwyck shone as Meggie's grandmother, the wealthy Mary Carson and owner of the Drogheda estate, who takes in Meggie's family for little reason other than to attract Father Ralph's attention (she too has feelings for him).

A four-part American mini series, showing *The Thorn Birds* was a big deal for the BBC. It took pride of place on the front cover of the *Radio Times*, headlined as 'The Piety and the Passion', and was scheduled opposite ITV's ***The Jewel in the Crown***. Richard Chamberlain had already experienced the life of a heart-throb when he'd starred in the American hospital drama ***Dr Kildare***. He'd return to the role of Ralph for a 1996 sequel, *The Thorn Birds: The Missing Years*.

Threads

Drama | BBC/9 Network/Western-World Television for BBC One | episode duration 115 mins | broadcast 23 Sep 1984

Principal Cast

Karen Meagher · *Ruth Beckett*
Reece Dinsdale · *Jimmy Kemp*
David Brierley · *Mr Kemp*
Rita May · *Mrs Kemp*
Nicholas Lane · *Michael Kemp*
Jane Hazlegrove · *Alison Kemp*
Henry Moxon · *Mr Beckett*
June Broughton · *Mrs Beckett*
Sylvia Stoker · *Granny Beckett*
Harry Beety · *Clive Sutton*
Ruth Holden · *Marjorie Sutton*
Ashley Barker · *Bob*
Michael O'Hagan · *Chief Superintendent Hirst*
Phil Rose · *Medical Officer*
Steve Halliwell · *Information Officer*
Brian Grellis · *Accomodation Officer*
Peter Faulkner · *Transport Officer*
Anthony Collin · *Food Officer*
Michael Ely · *Scientific Advisor*
Sharon Baylis · *Manpower Officer*
David Stutt · *Works Oficer*
Phil Askham · *Mr Stothard*
Anna Seymour · *Mrs Stothard*
Fiona Rook · *Carol Stothard*
Maggie Ford · *Peace Speaker*
Mike Kay · *Trade Unionist*
Richard Albrecht · *Officer at Food Depot*
Ted Beyer · *Policeman*
Dean Williamson · *Policeman*
Joe Holmes · *Mr Langley*
Andy Fenn-Rodgers · *Patrol Officer*
Graham Hill · *Soldier*
Nigel Collins · *Soldier*
Victoria O'Keefe · *Jane*
Lee Daley · *Spike*
Marcus Lund · *Gaz*
Lesley Judd · *Newscaster*
Colin Ward-Lewis · *Newscaster*
Paul Vaughan · *Narrator*

Producers Graham Massey, John Purdie (executive), Peter Wolfes (associate), Mick Jackson **Writer** Barry Hines

In 1965, the BBC produced a horrifying drama documentary about the probable effects of a limited nuclear attack on a British city. Thought to be too violent and lingering on human suffering, *The War Game* was eventually refused a slot in the TV schedules. Instead it was given a limited cinema release, winning both a BAFTA and an Oscar for best documentary (despite being fiction!). The film eventually received its first TV broadcast 20 years later, as part of a season examining the still-widespread fear of a nuclear attack on Britain from the Soviet Union. In a year where pop band Frankie Goes to Hollywood sat at No. 1 with 'Two Tribes' and the Central Office of Information prepared the 'Protect and Survive' leaflets about how a household door or a blanket could save us all from nuclear fallout, the BBC once again attempted a fictional look at the effects of a nuclear attack on a British city, this time Sheffield.

Threads followed the weeks leading up to the attack through the lives of two connected families, the Becketts and the Kemps. After the bomb hits the city centre, we learn that Ruth Beckett survives but her boyfriend Jimmy is missing, feared killed. Ruth ventures out of her home to witness the devastation, the breakdown of society and the scale of loss around her. Scenes of women clutching dead babies, dismembered limbs in rubble and the cadavers of dead animals littering the streets eventually give way to the story of Ruth's daughter, and finally to the harrowing birth of the daughter's malformed child. *Threads* still haunts those who saw it at the time and viewers who've since caught it on home video. Though the Cold War has ostensibly ended, we now face threats from elsewhere in the world that make this no less effective a warning.

Three of a Kind

Comedy | BBC One | episode duration 30 mins, plus special | broadcast 1 Jul 1981–8 Oct 1983

Principal Cast

David Copperfield, Lenny Henry, Tracey Ullman · *Various Characters*

Producer Paul Jackson **Writers** Various, including Kim Fuller, Rob Grant, Doug Naylor, Ian Hislop, Nick Revell, Gareth Hale, Norman Pace, Mike Radford, Bob Sinfield, David McKellar, Tony Sarchet, David Copperfield, Lenny Henry

At the same point in time when ***The Young Ones*** and ***Not the Nine O'Clock News*** were forging a new wave of 'alternative' comedy on BBC Two, the mainstream channel

BBC One was showcasing the talents of three young comedians in a much more traditional sketch show. *Three of a Kind* gave breaks to relative unknowns Tracey Ullman and David Copperfield (real name Stanley Barlow) and matched them with the established star of ***TISWAS***, Lenny Henry. Foregoing any political or satirical elements, *Three of a Kind* relied instead upon good old-fashioned jokes, parodies and even brief segments of stand-up at the start of each programme. Sketches were kept to an absolute minimum length, with on-screen text-based gags from 'Gagfax' (courtesy of the BBC's own teletext service Ceefax) used to bridge the gaps between sketches.

David Copperfield created one of the most enduring characters for the series, Medallion Man, a hairy-chested wine-bar letch dressed in *Saturday Night Fever*-style white suit and loads of bling, but sadly didn't maintain much of a TV presence after *Three of a Kind* came to a close (after many years off the screen Copperfield participated in a 2004 Channel 4 reality TV show called *Kings of Comedy*). Lenny Henry went on to star in his own stand-up series ***The Lenny Henry Show*** and through his work on *Comic Relief* has become one of the leaders of the British comedy establishment. Henry is also responsible for raising the profile of black performers in the UK, possibly inspired by his own rather degrading stint as house comic on ***The Black and White Minstrel Show***. Tracey Ullman appeared in ITV sitcom ***Girls on Top*** for a year before heading off to make her own multi-award-winning show for American TV (a show that also gave ***The Simpsons*** its first television airing).

The comedy might have been up to date, but the format itself wasn't new. In 1967, the BBC put together three rising stars for a musical comedy sketch show called *Three of a Kind*, starring Mike Yarwood, Lulu and Ray Fell. Two of them went on to greater success, one of them didn't. It seems on each occasion three of a kind was more three's a crowd.

3-2-1

Game Show | Yorkshire Television for ITV | episode duration 50 mins | broadcast 1978–1987

Regular Cast

Ted Rogers · *Host*
Dusty Bin · *Booby Prize*
Chris Emmett, Dougie Brown, Debbie Arnold · *In-house Comedians*
Anthony Schaeffer · *Announcer*
John Benson · *Announcer*
Gail Playfair, Patsy Ann Scott, Tula, Mireille Allonville · *The Gentle Secs*
Alison Temple-Savage, Libby Roberts, Fiona Curzon, Karan David, Lynda Lee Lewis, Caroline Munro · *Hostesses*

Creator Chicho Ibáñez-Serrador, who came up with the original Spanish format *Un Dos Tres* **Producers** Alan Tarrant (executive), John Bartlett (associate), Derek Burrell-Davis, Mike Goddard, Ian Bolt, Terry Henebery, Graham Wetherell **Theme Music** The brash, bold and bouncy theme tune to *3-2-1* was composed by Johnny Pearson.

One of the best-remembered and highest-rated game shows of the 1980s was a fixture in ITV's Saturday night schedules for almost a decade. *3-2-1* – 'It's a quiz! It's a game! It's fortune and fame!' proclaimed the opening titles – was hosted by genial comic Ted Rogers, and consisted of three separate sections. The first was a general knowledge quiz, the second some kind of elimination party game, then the third the fiendishly tricky word puzzles that accompanied a variety of sketches, songs and variety turns. Three couples began the show competing against each other – after each round, one couple would be eliminated . . . three being whittled down to two and then one (hence the title). Throughout the programme, Ted would be assisted by an array of glamorous hostesses. In early years, the hostesses were nicknamed 'The Gentle Secs' and took to wearing large spectacles (albeit with no lenses in them) to show that they were secretaries (bet it took them hours to come up with that one!). One of the show's final hostesses was the former Lamb's Navy Rum girl (and James Bond/Hammer Horror film star) Caroline Munro.

Like any self-respecting Saturday night show should, *3-2-1* featured performances by stars old and new, pop groups, comedians, impressionists and ventriloquists, among others. Indeed, the programme even had its own gang of three in-house comedians (Chris, Debbie and Dougie) to help out. However, what most people recall about *3-2-1* was the impenetrably complex clues of the final round. The last remaining couple had to select their prize via a completely unsolvable riddle – clues that seemed to suggest that the prize might be a wonderful new car ('It's made of metal and sits on your drive') would inevitably turn out to be the booby prize, Dusty Bin (which, if the contestants won him, meant that they went home with nothing more than a brand new shiny dustbin). Other typical prizes of the era might include 'his and hers' matching fur coats, a silver canteen of cutlery, or perhaps even a luxury holiday to Spain. Throughout all the madness, Ted Rogers would skilfully keep everything ticking over, welcoming and sending off viewers with his trademark *3-2-1* spinning finger salute, which we recommend that you practice long and hard before attempting in front of anyone, lest you end up insulting any passers-by.

Three Up, Two Down

Sitcom | BBC One | episode duration 30 mins | broadcast 15 Apr 1985–18 Jun 1989

Regular Cast

Angela Thorne · *Daphne Trenchard*
Michael Elphick · *Sam Tyler*
Lysette Anthony · *Angie Tyler*
Ray Burdis · *Nick Tyler*

Neil Stacy · *Major Giles Bradshaw*
John Grillo · *Wilf*
Vicki Woolfe · *Rhonda*

Producers David Askey, John B. Hobbs **Writer** Richard Ommanney **Theme Music** Ronnie Hazlehurst

Happily married couple Angie and Nick Tyler come from the opposite ends of the social spectrum – she from a posh country family, he from a family of East End ne'er-do-wells. When they have a baby, Angie and Nick realise that they need two things – a bit of extra income, and some extra pairs of hands about the place to help look after their little bundle of joy. Cue their parents – snobby Daphne and common Sam, both of whom are happy to look after their grandchild. Soon (after a convoluted chain of financial and other circumstances) Sam and Daphne find themselves moving into Angie and Nick's basement flat, despite their obvious 'Odd Couple' status. However, opposites do attract, and over time Sam and Daphne discover a slow-burning mutual attraction.

A perfectly adequate little sitcom, *Three Up, Two Down* combined two of the genres great clichés (the generation gap and class warfare) to create an enduring and very popular series. Angela Thorne was a revelation as the uptight Daphne, a mile away from her much softer and nicer portrayal of Marjory in ***To the Manor Born***, and much closer in demeanour and spirit to the then Prime Minister Maggie Thatcher. Ever-reliable Michael Elphick (a year away from his own ITV comedy/drama ***Boon***) provided a neat contrast to Thorne's histrionics, and the young leads Ray '*Scum*' Burdis and Lysette Anthony (best known for her role in the 1983 fantasy movie *Krull*) gave attractive supporting performances. There was even a semi-permanent role for ***Duty Free***'s Neil Stacy as (yet another) chinless wonder military man, this time intent on wooing Daphne. In total, 25 episodes were produced, with the final one seeing Daphne and Sam united (as we'd all secretly hoped they would be).

Through the Keyhole

Panel Game | ITV/BBC One | episode duration 25–30 mins | broadcast 1983–present

Regular Cast

Sir David Frost · *Host*
Loyd Grossman, Catherine Gee · *House Snoops*

Here's a weird one: a show hosted by a man who made Richard Nixon apologise to the American people, who interviewed a former head of the Hitler Youth and who was thought to be such a threat to the British government that his first TV success was taken off in the 1964 election year and not brought back. In *Through the Keyhole*, Sir David Frost hosts a panel game show that involves a peculiar mid-Atlantic-accented being strolling around the homes of minor celebrities. And yet, because we're a nation of curtain-twitching voyeurs, we loved it! The show was a reworking of the 'Homes of the Rich and Famous' features that fill mags like *Hello*, only with a vague game attached in which three celebrities try to 'guess whose house this is' (not much of a catchphrase, admittedly, but it's done okay for Sir David these last 20-odd years). We always suspected each of the celebs had been primed as they'd make meteoric leaps to identify the mystery guest based on the most spurious of evidence – or perhaps intimate knowledge of their own friend's interior decor. We didn't mind that they might have cheated; it just made the show even cuddlier while we had a good laugh at the expense of whichever guest thought horse brasses and pine walls was classy.

The series spent a short while on Sky before returning to terrestrial television as part of BBC One's daytime schedule, this time with lovely posh lady Catherine Gee doing the snooping round celebrities' houses.

Thunderbirds

See pages 758–60

Till Death Us Do Part

Sitcom | BBC One/ATV for ITV | episode duration 25–40 mins | broadcast 22 Jul 1965, 6 Jun 1966–16 Feb 1968, 12 Sep 1972–17 Dec 1975 (BBC), 22 May–3 Jul 1981 (ATV)

Regular Cast

Warren Mitchell · *Alf Garnett*
Dandy Nichols · *Else Garnett*
Una Stubbs · *Rita Garnett*
Anthony Booth · *Mike*
Spike Milligan · *Paki-Paddy*
Alfie Bass · *Bert Reed*
Patricia Hayes · *Min Reed*
Joan Sims · *Gran*
Hugh Lloyd · *Wally Carey*
Pat Coombs · *Mrs Carey*
John Fowler · *Michael Jr*

Creator/Writer Johnny Speight **Producers** Dennis Main Wilson, William G. Stewart **Theme Music** Dennis Wilson composed the theme (no, not the show's producer Dennis Main Wilson), the same chap who wrote the theme tune to *Rising Damp* and *Fawlty Towers*, among other shows.

With ***Steptoe and Son*** already doing a fine job of shattering TV viewers' preconceptions about precisely what the sitcom was able to do and say, many people were left reeling by the arrival of loud-mouthed boorish Alf Garnett, the walking, talking personification of stubborn-minded, right wing, working class bigotry.

To Alf Garnett, life is a constant stream of disappointments and injustices to be shouted down and railed against. He despises the laziness and liberalism of 'Yer common workin' man', instead placing his trust and belief in ''Er Majesty', the better educated and the better connected. Alf's wife Elsie (nicknamed Else) is not so much a doormat, more a carefully placed drawing pin on the floor – somebody's who's barely seen or acknowledged until she delivers the sharpest of points into the conversation. Else might not be especially knowledgeable or clever, but she knows exactly what to say at exactly the right moment to burst Alf's insufferable smugness and self-righteousness.

Similarly upset by Alf's ranting is his daughter Rita and her new husband Mike. Rita tries to be a part of the Swinging Sixties' revolution taking place all around her in London, but her lowly upbringing means she's not a part of the Carnaby Street scene she'd love to be involved in. Mike's eternal shame is that he's unable to afford to buy a house for him and Rita to live in – instead, they have to share with Alf and Else, which leads to an endless onslaught of arguments between the two men. Mike is politically the complete opposite of Alf, a 'randy Scouse git' Socialist who believes in the dismantling of the monarchy. However Mike and Alf share many things in common – notably a stubbornness and complete refusal to acknowledge that they could ever be wrong about anything. Often Alf would end up in his local pub, putting the world to rights with his mates and moaning about yet another group in society who are 'responsible' for everything that's going wrong.

Till Death Us Do Part certainly wasn't everybody's cup of tea. For a start, the brutal honesty and naturalism of the scripts were like a proverbial slap in the face to anybody who was more used to polite sitcoms about husbands and wives having a tiff about whose responsibility it was to leave the milk bottles out. *Till Death Us Do Part* was raw, real and included words and terminology that made most dockers wince with embarrassment. Indeed, many of the racist words and phrases employed by Alf makes *Till Death Us Do Part* a very difficult series to repeat nowadays, despite the fact that writer/creator Johnny Speight's had in fact created Alf as a satirical attack on racism rather than as a poster-boy for undesirable elements in society. However, the use of a blacked-up Spike Milligan to play a half Irish half Pakistani character (called Paki-Paddy, of all things) seems pretty indefensible to modern audiences. However, ignoring the uncomfortable elements, *Till Death Us Do Part* is still today an amazingly confident and accomplished comedy, with four strongly defined characters brought to life by a quartet of quality performers.

With Dandy Nichols opting to quit the show after the sixth season owing to ill-health (Else was sent to Australia to care for a sick relative), the time seemed right to draw the series gradually to a close after 54 episodes. For five years, Alf and his ill-informed rantings vanished from TV screens, until he made a surprise switch to ITV in time for a Christmas stand-up special (*The Thoughts of Chairman Alf at Christmas*, shown on Boxing Day 1980) and a single season of further adventures, this time just called *Till Death*... In the ITV series, Alf and Else had retired to live in Eastbourne, playing hosts to the odd visit by their daughter Rita and punky grandson Michael Jr and learning to deal with the trials of retirement.

Another five-year gap followed, after which Alf returned to his natural home of the BBC for a long-running sequel series called ***In Sickness and in Health***. Back in his natural home of London, Alf is now responsible for looking after his frail, wheelchair-bound wife Else. To his horror, the council sends them a care assistant – a camp black man called Winston, who quickly gets the measure of Alf's old-fashioned attitudes and deliberately plays upon them in order to wind him up as much as possible. Alf has to learn to live without his 'silly moo' of a wife when Else dies (Dandy Nichols passed away after the first season), sending Alf into even deeper rants and rages against the unfairness of life. He soon had another woman making his life hell, though, his new bolshy landlady Mrs Hollingberry – they even for a while contemplated marriage to each other, but decided better of it after one too many arguments. Although *In Sickness and in Health* could never match the atavistic energy and sheer shock of its parent show, it was nevertheless a very funny and thought-provoking comedy that provided an ideal counterpoint to the Conservative government of the time – Alf could never get over the fact that his beloved Tory Party was now being led by (gasp!) a woman who was (shock, horror!) the daughter of a shopkeeper rather than somebody 'proper' or posh.

Trivia

The pilot episode for *Till Death Us Do Part* saw the whole Garnett clan called Ramsay, in honour of the England football manager Alf (whose greatest hour came in 1966 during the transmission of the first full season when England won the World Cup). With Ramsay not deemed an entirely appropriate name, Alf, Else and Rita became the Garnetts, named after a street in Wapping by the same name. In the pilot, Else was played by future ***EastEnder*** Gretchen Franklin.

Timeslip

Children's Science Fiction | ATV for ITV | episode duration 25 mins | broadcast 28 Sep 1970–22 Mar 1971

Regular Cast

Spencer Banks · *Simon Randall*
Cheryl Burfield · *Liz Skinner*
Denis Quilley · *Commander Charles Traynor*
Derek Benfield · *Frank Skinner*
Iris Russell · *Jean Skinner*
Mary Preston · *Beth Skinner*
John Barron · *Deveraux*
David Graham · *2957*
Ian Fairbairn · *Doctor Frazer/Alpha 4*
Merdelle Jordine · *Vera*

Continued on page 761

Thunderbirds

Thunderbird 2 *blasts into action.*

In the year 2065, on the Pacific island of Moyla, lies an impressive luxury villa, home to retired millionaire astronaut Jeff Tracy and his five sons, Scott, Virgil, Gordon, John and Alan. The island is fitted with everything one might expect on a millionaire's private island: palm trees, swimming pool, secret rocket launching bay . . . for Jeff Tracy is also the head of a secret organisation called International Rescue. If disaster strikes, Jeff and his boys get ready for action with their call sign – 'F-A-B'. Every super team needs their super villain and International Rescue's was The Hood, a vaguely oriental criminal mastermind who was able to control his half-brother Kyrano. Fortunately for him, the Tracy family employs Kyrano as a chef and butler, while Kyrano's daughter Tin-Tin helped Brains in his laboratory. Though Kyrano's loyalty to Jeff Tracy is unquestionable, The Hood still manages to exploit their tenuous blood-ties to the full.

Anyone claiming that today's children have no attention span would be hard pressed to explain why *Thunderbirds* is still adored. Fifty minutes of puppetry doesn't sound quite as exciting as the latest instalment of Harry Potter but for three generations of kids it's been their entry point for the action-adventure genre. From the very beginning of each episode, with its ominous '5 . . . 4 . . . 3 . . . 2 . . . 1' and short précis of the story (a hook that would be repeated in ***Space: 1999***), *Thunderbirds* continues the traditions of ***Stingray*** in making sure it grabs the audience by the throat immediately and refuses to let go. As might be suggested by the strident theme tune from Barry Gray (destined to be murdered by school bands ever since), this is Gerry Anderson's most confident production.

In search of a replacement for the enormously successful *Stingray*, Anderson read of a rescue operation on a mine in Germany.

Children's Puppet Adventure
ITV
Episode Duration: 50 mins
Broadcast: 30 Sep 1965–25 Dec 1966

Principal Voice Cast
Peter Dyneley · *Jeff Tracy*
Shane Rimmer · *Scott Tracy*
David Holliday · *Virgil Tracy*
Matt Zimmerman · *Alan Tracy*
David Graham · *Gordon Tracy, Brains, Aloysius Parker, Kyrano*
Ray Barrett · *John Tracy, The Hood*
Sylvia Anderson · *Lady Penelope Creighton-Ward*
Christine Finn · *Tin-Tin, Grandma*
Brian Cobby · *Intro Sequence Voice-over*

Creators Gerry and Sylvia Anderson

Producer Gerry Anderson

Writers Gerry and Sylvia Anderson, Alan Fennell, Dennis Spooner, Alan Pattillo, Donald Robertson, Martin Crump, Tony Barwick

Theme Music Barry Gray

He began to develop an idea initially called 'International Rescue', with the popular western series ***Bonanza*** providing the inspiration for the Tracy family (the Tracy boys were named after American astronauts Scott Carpenter, Virgil Grissom, Alan Shepard, Gordon Cooper and John Glenn). On viewing rushes for the first episodes, studio head Lew Grade was so impressed that he decided to double the length of each episode and increase the budget accordingly. This meant Anderson's team had to go back and reshoot extra material for the eight episodes they'd already completed as well as rethink the ones still in production. Because of that unexpected increase to the running time, some of the earlier episodes were severely padded. If a scene involved cutting tools, the camera would linger far longer than was comfortable; the launch of every craft from Tracy Island was shown in full. But strangely this just added to the suspense. Had later episodes skimped on the footage of Tracy Island's palm trees splaying and the swimming pool sliding back to let Thunderbird 1 emerge from the underground base, we would have felt sorely cheated.

Having already conquered impossible speeds, the frontiers of space and the depths of the ocean in his previous shows, Anderson chose to combine them all here. Courtesy of stuttering boffin Brains, International Rescue had no shortage of impressive hardware at its disposal. Pride of the squadron was Thunderbird 1, a rocket-powered aircraft piloted by Virgil. Jeff's eldest son Scott (he was the looker of the clan) was in the hotseat for Thunderbird 2. The favourite among fans, it was a huge green air freighter that also housed the Mole (a drilling machine), Firefly (a state-of-the-art fire-fighting vehicle) and a few hover-scooters – another of Anderson's methods of avoiding shots of the puppets walking. The youngest son Alan was usually found at the controls of Thunderbird 3, a red space rocket, the biggest craft at International Rescue's disposal. Thunderbird 4, a small yellow submarine operated by Gordon, was usually transported inside Thunderbird 2, while Thunderbird 5 was International Rescue's communication centre out in space, manned alternately by Alan and John. For some reason, Anderson took a dislike to the puppet created to play John Tracy, hence why he ended up on his own aboard Thunderbird 5 for most of the time.

International Rescue's British secret agent, Lady Penelope Creighton-Ward, and her butler-cum-chauffeur (and former jailbird) Aloysius Parker, were the best characters in the Anderson collection. Like the Tracy family, Lady Penelope had her own hi-tech mode of transport – FAB 1, a high-speed pink Rolls-Royce. While the Tracy boys were the undoubted stars of the show, these two British characters managed to steal every episode they appeared in, and Parker's adenoidal delivery of the line 'Yus, m'lady' (courtesy of David Graham, who also voiced Brains), became synonymous with the show. Penelope herself was modelled on co-creator Sylvia Anderson – though the puppet maker Mary Turner didn't tell her this at the time.

As with *Stingray*, the model work was uniformly impressive, with up to 120 individual effects per episode courtesy, once again, of

TRIVIA

In 1990, 'Thunderbirds are Go', a novelty record by 'FAB featuring MC Parker', reached number 5 in the UK singles charts. It used samples of the *Thunderbirds* theme tune and David Graham's Parker saying 'N-n-not so loud' against a generic dance beat, while the video gave us the joyous vision of Parker dressed for a rave in white baseball cap and chunky medallion.

Derek Meddings. Pre-dating the disaster movie trend of the 1970s, each set piece was a warning against the hubris of any architect; if a construction is the tallest, spans the furthest, reaches the deepest or just happens to be the newest, you can bet it'll be in peril within the first ten minutes, especially if a family of tourists just happens to be visiting.

Sadly, Grade's insistence on the extended episode length proved to be the show's downfall as a 50-minute puppet show proved to be a harder sell overseas than even Grade could overcome. After 36 episodes and two superior feature films (one of which included an appearance by Supermarionation versions of pop group The Shadows), the Thunderbirds were put back on the shelf. Many of them were later sold off in auctions for headline-grabbing sums of money. A Japanese animated series *Thunderbirds 2086* was released in 1986. Despite retaining elements such as the 'International Rescue Organization', it had nothing to do with Anderson productions and was a rather disappointingly cheap-looking affair.

Thanks to the way the ITV network operated back then, *Thunderbirds* was shown at different times across the regions. So, it wasn't until BBC Two repeated the series in full in 1993 that it was shown at the same time across the British Isles. Such was the public interest in this blast from the past that model Tracy Island sets became the desirable item for Christmas, and when ***Blue Peter*** tried to help out by showing kids how to make their own, the *BP* offices were swamped with requests for a fact sheet. The BBC were forced to release a home video, *How to Make Tracy Island*, which became a best seller. The entire series, and its spin-off movies, *Thunderbirds are Go* (1967) and *Thunderbird Six* (1968), have now found a new audience on DVD, along with most of Anderson's other shows. However, the least said about the 2004 live-action movie the better.

Had later episodes skimped on the footage of Tracy Island's palm trees splaying and the swimming pool sliding back to let Thunderbird 1 emerge from the underground base, we would have felt sorely cheated.

Creators James Boswell and Ruth Boswell **Producer** John Cooper **Writers** Ruth Boswell, James Boswell, Bruce Stewart, Victor Pemberton **Theme Music** Edouard Michael composed the stirring, dramatic theme tune

A fondly remembered children's science fiction series, *Timeslip* was a cut above the juvenile storytelling that blights most attempts to portray sci-fi for a younger audience. On holiday with her parents, Liz Skinner and her friend Simon Randall become intrigued by a nearby abandoned wartime weapons base. Breaking into the complex, the pair find themselves back in 1940 when the base was still fully active. They soon meet a younger version of Liz's dad and discover he was mixed up in a top-secret project to dismantle an experimental laser before it could be stolen by the Germans. Later, the pair travel into the future of 1990 where, at an Antarctic base called the Ice Box, sinister tests were being carried out to increase humanity's life-span. And lurking behind the scenes of all of these locations is Commander Traynor – is he really what he seems to be, or is he also able to travel in time?

Handling 'grown-up' issues as diverse as the fears of cloning, global warming, medical experimentation and their ethical consequences, *Timeslip* was no light-hearted romp. Consisting of four self-contained stories ('The Wrong End of Time', 'The Time of the Ice Box', 'The Year of the Burn Up' and 'The Day of the Clone'), *Timeslip* benefited from decent performances by its young leads Spencer Banks and Cheryl Burfield, and a knockout performance by acting heavyweight Dennis Quilley as the kids' friend/foe Traynor. Two years after the end of *Timeslip*, producer Ruth Boswell brought another kids' sci-fi show to ITV, the rather more traditionally hokum-filled ***The Tomorrow People***.

Tinker, Tailor, Soldier, Spy

Drama | BBC Two | episode duration 50 mins | broadcast 10 Sep–22 Oct 1979 (*Tinker, Tailor, Soldier, Spy*), 20 Aug–25 Oct 1982 (*Smiley's People*)

Principal Cast

Alec Guinness · *George Smiley*
Michael Jayston, Michael Byrne · *Peter Guillam*
Anthony Bate · *Oliver Lacon*
Bernard Hepton · *Toby Esterhase*
Ian Richardson · *Bill Haydon*
Ian Bannen · *Jim Prideaux*
Hywel Bennett · *Ricki Tarr*
Michael Aldridge · *Percy Alleline*
Terence Rigby · *Roy Bland*
Alexander Knox · *Control*
George Sewell · *Mendel*
Beryl Reid · *Connie Sachs*
Joss Ackland · *Jerry Westerby*
Siân Phillips · *Ann Smiley*
Nigel Stock · *Roddy Martindale*
Patrick Stewart · *Karla*
John Standing · *Sam Collins*
Thorley Walters · *Tufty Thessinger*
Eileen Atkins · *Madame Ostrakova*
Barry Foster · *Saul Enderby*
Michael Lonsdale · *Anton Grigoriov*
Bill Paterson · *Lauder Strickland*
Mario Adorf · *Claus Kretschmar*
Curd Jürgens · *The General*
Vladek Sheybal · *Otto Leipzig*
Rosalie Crutchley · *Mother Felicity*
Michael Gough · *Mikhel*
Maureen Lipman · *Stella Craven*
Dudley Sutton · *Oleg Kirov*

Producer Jonathan Powell **Writers** Arthur Hopcraft, from John Le Carré's novel *Tinker, Tailor*; John Hopkins, from John Le Carré's novel *Smiley's People* **Theme Music** 'Nunc Dimittis' by Geoffrey Burgon, performed by chorister Paul Phoenix. The music for *Smiley's People* was composed by Patrick Gowers.

When George Smiley was head of Personnel in 'The Circus', offices of British Intelligence, his superior, 'Control', began to suspect the presence of a mole in the department. When it was discovered that Control was being manipulated by a Soviet agent, he and Smiley were forcibly retired. But when an agent thought to have been lost to the 'other side' comes out of the cold to confirm the existence of a mole, George Smiley is recalled to flush out the mole. George's wife is conducting an affair, and he feels unfairly disgraced by the way he was released from the service, but reluctantly he proceeds with his investigation into the prime suspects – all of whom have been given code names – 'Tinker', 'Tailor', 'Soldier'. . .

George Smiley had already had one outing in the 1965 feature film *The Spy Who Came in from the Cold*, where he'd been played by Rupert Davies. Here, though, Alec Guinness sparkles as the methodical Smiley, carefully piecing together the evidence, conducting face-to-face conversations with some of his oldest rivals to get to the truth. Guinness reprised his role in *Smiley's People* (the Hong Kong setting of the next novel in John Le Carré's saga, *The Honourable Schoolboy*, made it prohibitive for the BBC to film), where Smiley was called upon to settle the affairs of an old friend while Soviet assassins try to ensure he doesn't expose a particularly nasty secret.

John Le Carré's work lacks the whizz-bang approach of modern shows like ***Spooks***, but it's all the richer for it. These kind of spies are working to a long game, where plans take years to ferment to the extent where most of the main players here are old men and women; one of the reasons why *Tinker, Tailor, Soldier, Spy* and *Smiley's People* were so highly regarded was that it gave a number of experienced senior actors and actresses riveting roles to play.

For most, Guinness was the definitive George Smiley, but after his death, Denholm Elliott made a decent job of the role in a 1994 TV movie, *A Murder of Quality*, made by Thames and Portobello Productions for ITV.

TISWAS

Children's Entertainment | ATV for ITV | episode duration 120 mins | broadcast 5 Jan 1974–3 Apr 1982

Cast

Chris Tarrant, John Asher, Trevor East, Peter Tomlinson, Sally James, Lenny Henry, John Gorman, Sylvester McCoy, Bob Carolgees, Joan Palmer, Den 'Den Bong' Hegarty, Fogwell Flax, Clive 'Wizard Webb' Webb, David 'Shades' Rappaport, Gordon Astley, Jim Davidson

Producers Mike Smith (executive), Chris Tarrant, Peter Harris
Theme Music 'Saturday is *TISWAS* Day' by Tom Bright

The BBC's stranglehold on Saturday morning might leave us thinking they invented it. But if you grew up within the catchment of ITV's ATV region, you'll know better. For five years, *TISWAS* kept kids in Birmingham, Nottingham, Coventry and the rest of the Midlands gripped with the sheer power of adrenalin, long before the rest of the country learned the phrase 'This Is Saturday, Watch And Smile'.

As more and more of the ITV regions began to drop their own programmes in favour of ATV's output, *TISWAS* became a serious challenger to ***Multi-Coloured Swap Shop***, which had started transmission in 1976. Chris Tarrant rejoiced with the freedom that live TV afforded him. 'This is what they want!' he cried as he chucked a bucket of water across an audience of ten-year-olds, and he was right – they loved it. So did the dads, but for entirely different reasons, undoubtedly related to the tight T-shirts worn by Sally James. And when Lenny Henry joined the series, he embraced the mania and near-the-knuckle humour wholeheartedly, impersonating naturalist David Bellamy ('gwapple me gwapenuts') and newsreader 'Trevor McDoughnut', creating characters like Algernon Winston Spenser Castleray Razzmatazz – a dreadlocked, Rastafarian, reggae-performing newsreader ('Ooooooooooohhh Kaaaaaaaaaay'), and contributing to the unashamedly Birmingham-centric attitude of the show. And so they should have – they'd have never been allowed to get away with such behaviour had they been broadcasting from London.

Feeling restricted by the things he could and couldn't do on children's television, Chris Tarrant left the series in 1981 to set up *OTT* – officially 'Over The Top' but it could just as easily have been 'Old-Timers' *TISWAS*'. Taking most of the male *TISWAS* cast with him, Tarrant's *OTT* featured strippers doing routines on pool tables and grown men performing a naked balloon dance with a diminishing number of balloons. Too much for Middle England, it lasted one series, thereby consigning Tarrant to the TV wilderness for more than a decade until he began hosting global telly review *Tarrant on TV* (see ***Clive James on TV***) in the mid-1990s and later the smash game show ***Who Wants to be a Millionaire?*** – both of which cast Tarrant as a rather less frantic figure, in his sober suit and calm aura.

Back at ATV, Sally James struggled on with new presenters, but eventually even she grew tired of it all. Her departure came scant months after ATV was taken over by Central. Other regions began to produce their own Saturday morning entertainment – Southern came up with ***Number 73***, for instance – and *TISWAS* began to look like it had outstayed its welcome. When the autumn TV season began in 1982, the show was nowhere to be seen. But the ground rules for making cheap Saturday morning TV had been set. You could have live phone-ins with the risk of your guest being called a 'wanker' or worse by a naughty teenager, or you could employ someone to make lots of gunge and custard pies for you. At the time of writing, Saturdays are dominated by *Dick and Dom in Da Bungalow* on BBC One and *The Ministry of Mayhem* on ITV. Both shows favour mild innuendo, general mischief and copious amounts of water and gunk over educational items and chatty phone-ins. Twenty-five years after *Swap Shop* and *TISWAS* left our screens, it's now obvious which of them was the real victor in the battle for the hearts of our nation's children.

Trivia

The identity of the Phantom Flan Flinger has been a source of confusion ever since his first masked and caped appearance to push a custard pie into the face of a startled celebrity. In 2004, comedian Jim Davidson shed some light – and further confusion – on the mystery. While some sources maintain that the original Flan Flinger was Helen Piddock, a *TISWAS* writer, Davidson claims that title for himself, with the role then being handed to Davidson's then girlfriend, Jane Beaumont. What we do know is that at least one of the Flan Flingers was a driver and part-time cabaret performer called Benny Mills, while 'Flanderella', the Phantom's wife, was played by Oliver Spencer.

As the Four Bucketeers, the cast members released 'The Bucket of Water Song' in 1980, reaching No. 26 in the UK singles chart.

Website

www.tiswasonline.com

To Play the King

Drama | BBC One | episode duration 60 mins | broadcast 21 Nov–12 Dec 1993

Principal Cast

Ian Richardson · *Francis Urquhart*
Michael Kitchen · *The King*
Kitty Aldridge · *Sarah Harding*
Colin Jeavons · *Tim Stamper*
Diane Fletcher · *Elizabeth Urquhart*
Erika Hoffman · *The Lady*
Tom Beasley · *Young Prince*
Leonard Preston · *John Stroud*
Rowena King · *Chloe Carmichael*
Nicholas Farrell · *David Mycroft*

Michael Howarth · *Dick Caule*
Merelina Kendall · *Hilda Cordwainer*
Barry Linehan · *Henry Hotson*
Nick Brimble · *Corder*
Bernice Stegers · *Princess Charlotte*
Frederick Treves · *Lord Quillington*
Joanna Archer-Nicholls · *Young Girl*
David Ryall · *Sir Bruce Bullerby*
Pip Torrens · *Andrew Harding*
Jack Fortune · *Ken Charterhouse*
Don Warrington · *Graham Gaunt*
John Bird · *Bryan Brynford-Jones*
George Raistrick · *Gropeham*
Kenneth Gilbert · *Harold Earle*
Christopher Owen · *McKenzie*
Elizabeth Chambers · *Baroness Craske*
Susannah Harker · *Mattie Storin*

For commentary, see HOUSE OF CARDS

To Serve Them All My Days

Drama | BBC Two | episode duration 50 mins | broadcast 11 Oct 1980–16 Jan 1981

Regular Cast
John Duttine · *David Powlett-Jones*
Frank Middlemass · *Algy Herries*
Alan MacNaughtan · *Howarth*
Neil Stacy · *Carter*
David King · *Barnaby*
Charles Kay · *Alcock*
Belinda Lang · *Beth Marwood/Powlett-Jones*
Kim Braden · *Julia Darbyshire*
Susan Jameson · *Christine Forster/Powlett-Jones*
Peter Arne · *Dr Farrington*
Phillip Joseph · *Emrys Powlett-Jones*
Patricia Lawrence · *Ellie Herries*
Cyril Luckham · *Sir Rufus Creighton*
Simon Gipps-Kent · *Boyer*

Producer Ken Riddington **Writer** Andrew Davies, from the novel by R. F. Delderfield **Theme Music** Kenyon Emrys-Roberts

Invalided out of the army during the World War One and suffering quite badly from shell-shock, David Powlett-Jones is sent to be interviewed for a job at Bamfylde, a large public school in Devon. He has little faith in his own abilities as a teacher, and is very aware of his own working-class upbringing and strong Welsh valley accent. However, headmaster Algy Herries takes him on – partly because he desperately needs new staff, and partly because he's willing to take a gamble on the young man.

After a shaky start, Powlett-Jones ('PJ') soon manages to get into the swing of being a teacher. Unfortunately, his progressive attitudes lead him into conflict with some of the other masters at Bamfylde, most notably Carter, head of the school's army training corps – a man whose bad cartilage has meant that he's sent many boys off to fight, having never seen active service himself, much to PJ's disgust. As the years pass by, PJ falls in love and marries the effervescent Beth before tragedy strikes the couple and their children. Years later, when Herries retires as headmaster, PJ is persuaded to stand against Carter as a candidate for Herries's replacement, but the well-known animosity between the two men leads to the governors selecting an outsider. The new headmaster, Alcock, is a softly spoken tyrant loathed by staff and pupils alike. PJ finds himself having to stand up to Alcock's bullying ways, resulting in a showdown that only one of them can win. But the outcome surprises them all. . .

In part a reworking of James Hilton's *Goodbye, Mr Chips*, *To Serve Them All My Days* is sentimental without being too sickly-sweet. A number of key events contribute to this, such as the loss of Powlett-Jones's first wife early on, which comes as a great shock, while the face-off between Alcock and PJ provides us with a particularly chilling resolution. A fallible hero, Powlett-Jones is frequently his own worst enemy, being moody, impetuous and often unable to bite his tongue at times when tact would be more productive than honesty. But it's his understanding of the boys, his modesty and his ardent conviction in the value of an institution like Bamfylde, despite his left-wing politics, that makes him such an engaging and likeable character. The series made a name for John Duttine, who went on to star in ***The Day of the Triffids***, while the cast of pupils included Nicholas Lyndhurst, whose later credits include ***Butterflies*** and ***Only Fools and Horses***, and Matthew Waterhouse, known to ***Doctor Who*** fans as Adric.

To the Manor Born

Sitcom | BBC One | episode duration 30 mins | broadcast 30 Sep 1979–29 Nov 1981

Regular Cast
Penelope Keith · *Audrey fforbes-Hamilton*
Peter Bowles · *Richard DeVere*
Angela Thorne · *Marjory Frobisher*
Daphne Heard · *Mrs Polouvicka*
John Rudling · *Brabinger*
Michael Bilton · *Ned*
Gerald Sim · *Rector*
Daphne Oxenford · *Mrs Patterson*

Creator Peter Spence **Producer** Gareth Gwenlan **Writers** Peter Spence, Christopher Bond **Theme Music** Ronnie Hazlehurst composed a grand, sweeping melody that's more than a little similar to the title music for ***Yes, Minister***.

When Martin fforbes-Hamilton dies, he leaves his stately home and estate to his widow Audrey. Unfortunately, Martin didn't have much money. Unable to pay inheritance taxes and death duties, Audrey fforbes-Hamilton is forced

to sell her beloved home and move into the tiny lodge at the end of the drive, taking only her butler Brabinger with her. The new owner of Grantleigh Manor is supermarket magnate Richard DeVere, owner of Cavendish Foods. To Audrey's shock, she discovers that DeVere isn't his real name – he's half Polish half Czech, from an immigrant family who fled Europe in 1939. DeVere's mother, Mrs Polouvicka (or 'Mrs Poo', as Audrey calls her), constantly bullies her son into taking more of an interest in the local community. Audrey, meanwhile, spends time with her best friend Marjory and, as time passes, finds herself becoming increasingly drawn to Richard . . .

Designed as a vehicle to showcase the talents of ***The Good Life***'s Penelope Keith, *To the Manor Born* was a wittily written and charming sitcom based on class-conflict issues. In a clever reversal of the situation she faced as Margo, Keith here finds herself playing a character who is forced to come to terms with a definite diminution in her social status. Audrey is a true member of the aristocracy rather than a grasping middle-class social climber (like Margo), and amazingly the series paints her as an underdog rather than one of the privileged set – and there's nothing that the British public likes better than siding with an underdog. Shown on Sunday evenings, *To the Manor Born* hit a nerve with viewers and attracted audiences so enormous that one in three of the UK population were regularly tuning in. The series peaked with its final episode, in which Audrey and Richard were finally married. Safe, unchallenging and very, very funny, it's not surprising that it was such a success.

Tom Jones (aka 'The History of Tom Jones, a Foundling')

Drama | BBC/A&E for BBC One | episode duration 95 mins | broadcast 9 Nov–7 Dec 1997

Principal Cast

Max Beesley · *Tom Jones*
Samantha Morton · *Sophia Western*
James D'Arcy · *Blifil*
Benjamin Whitrow · *Squire Allworthy*
Frances de la Tour · *Aunt Western*
Brian Blessed · *Squire Western*
John Sessions · *Henry Fielding*
Paul Barber · *Adderley*
Kathy Burke · *Honour*
Peter Capaldi · *Lord Fellamar*
Camille Coduri · *Jenny Jones*
Lindsay Duncan · *Lady Bellaston*
Julian Firth · *Northerton*
Christopher Fulford · *Mr Square*
Tim Healy · *Mr Nightingale Snr*
Brian Hibbard · *George Seagrim*
Celia Imrie · *Mrs Miller*
Sara Kestelman · *Mrs Wilkins*
Caleb Lloyd · *Young Blifil*
Roger Lloyd-Pack · *Anderson*
Norman Lovett · *Mr Follett*
Amy Marston · *Susan*
Sylvester McCoy · *Mr Dowling*
Stuart Neal · *Young Tom*
Richard O'Callaghan · *Mr Fitzpatrick*
Con O'Neill · *Captain Blifil*
Tessa Peake-Jones · *Bridget Allworthy*
Alexei Sayle · *Puppeteer*
Neil Dudgeon · *Puppeteer's Assistant*
Rachel Scorgie · *Mollie Seagrim*
Ruth Sheen · *Mrs Harris*
Mossie Smith · *Goody Seagrim*
June Whitfield · *Mrs Whitefield*

Producer Michael Wearing, Delia Fine (executive), Nigel Taylor (associate), Suzan Harrison **Writer** Simon Burke, from the novel by Henry Fielding **Theme Music** Jim Parker

Tom Jones is a foundling – found in Squire Allworthy's bed in fact. The Squire decides to bring him up as his own and to educate him. The boy, who was 'born to be hanged', scandalises the surrounding neighbourhood by whoring, fighting, drinking and generally having a good time. Tom, though, is something of an oddity, for while engaged in all of his 'wicked' activities, he is nevertheless an honest boy. In spite of his bed hopping, Tom genuinely loves Sophia Western, the daughter of another county squire. Sophia is above Tom in social standing, but Tom has an honest and faithful heart and will help his friends out of any difficulty, even if it means trouble for himself. . .

Perhaps because of the 1963 film starring Albert Finney, television had left Henry Fielding's novel alone, prior to this romping BBC production. Max Beesley approaches the part of a lifetime with gusto, while Fielding's theme of hypocrisy in the upper classes (a central notion that also runs through both adaptations of the diaries of ***Casanova***) never gets in the way of the fun and frolics that inspire the hypocrisy in the first place.

The Tomorrow People

Science Fiction | Thames for ITV | episode duration 25 mins | broadcast 30 Apr 1973–19 Feb 1979, 18 Nov 1992–8 Mar 1995

Regular Cast

Nicholas Young · *John*
Elizabeth Adare · *Elizabeth M'Bondo*
Sammie Winmill · *Carol*
Stephen Salmon · *Kenny*
Peter Vaughan-Clarke · *Stephen Jameson*
Dean Lawrence · *Tyso*
Michael Holoway · *Mike Bell*
Misako Koba · *Hsui Tai*
Nigel Rhodes · *Andrew Forbes*
Philip Gilbert · *voice of TIM/Timus*
Michael Standing · *Ginge Harding*

Derek Crewe · *Lefty*
Francis de Wolff, Roger Bizley · *Jedikiah*
Richard Speight · *Peter*
Christopher Chittell · *Chris Harding*
Brian Stanion · *Professor Cawston*
Ann Curthoys · *Patricia Conway*
Denise Cook · *Evergreen Boswell*
Joanna Tope · *Mrs Boswell*
Dominic Allen · *Bruce Forbes*
Kristian Schmid · *Adam Newman*
Kristen Ariza · *Lisa Davies*
Stephen Pollard · *Kevin Wilson*
Christian Tessier · *Marmaduke 'Megabyte' Damon*
Naomie Harris · *Ami Jackson*
Jeff Harding · *General Bill Damon*
Sally Sagoe · *Mrs Hasana M'Bundo Jackson*
Alexandra Milman · *Jade Weston*

Creator Roger Price **Producers** Roger Price, Ruth Boswell, Vic Hughes, Grant Cathro, Alan Horrox, Lee Pressman **Writers** Roger Price, Brian Finch **Theme Music** A superbly creepy piece by Dudley Simpson that only *just* escapes being structurally similar to the ***Doctor Who*** theme tune

David Bowie's 1971 album *Hunky Dory* features the song 'Oh! You Pretty Things' in which we hear the lyrlc 'You gotta make way for the Homo Superior'. Two years later, Thames unveiled a new science fiction series for kids. Created by Roger Price as a replacement for ***Ace of Wands***, it announced the dawn of the next stage in human development that begins showing itself in teenagers on the verge of 'breaking out' as 'Tomorrow People'. These evolved superhumans – the 'Homo Superior' of Bowie's song – have innate skills they can draw upon, such as teleportation and telepathy, but these abilities must be trained, honed and perfected or else the potential Tomorrow Person might hurt themselves or suffer mental anguish as they struggle to make sense of the sensations rushing through them. This is why the Galactic Federation has sent them TIM – a dryly voiced computer hidden inside a secret base deep within a disused London underground station – to find the first generation of Tomorrow People, group them together and show them the way.

As a metaphor for puberty, it wasn't all that subtle, and indeed in retrospect some viewers have read the metaphor as being more about dawning homosexuality (though of course that kind of reading can be imposed on practically any children's programme – witness Batman's relationship with Robin, or the urban myths surrounding Captain Pugwash and his cabin boy). There were Tomorrow People of different stages of development, which made the show appealing to different age ranges. The older ones, like stern John, affectionate Carol and socially conscious schoolteacher Elizabeth, would often have to hold back the younger, impetuous ones (initially Stephen, later young traveller Tyso, musician Mike and Scottish lad Andrew) while they thought through the problems of each week's alien invasion or extraterrestrial manifestation. In a move towards full integration, there were also non-Tomorrow People in the gang, who more often than not found themselves getting into trouble and having to wait for their talented friends to rescue them (one of these, Chris Harding, was played by Christopher Chittell, who would grow up to play devious Eric Pollard in ***Emmerdale***).

Some of the best-known adventures involved the shape-changing robot Jedikiah. There were also the tribal badges that divided the nations youth ('The Blue and the Green'); an astoundingly camp adventure called 'A Man for Emily' in which Peter Davison and Sandra Dickinson appeared in space swimwear that we're not sure was appropriate for the timeslot; and Hitler – yes, even the head of the Nazi party put in appearance courtesy of Michael Sheard (Mr Bronson from ***Grange Hill***). Hitler was revealed to be a shape-changing alien from the planet Vashir called Neebor, and not the Austrian despot we'd all thought he was.

The series made stars of its young actors; the pages of *Look-In* magazine were filled with *Tomorrow People* comic strips and features, and Mike Holloway and his band Flintlock also featured in two light entertainment programmes developed for kids by Roger Price (**You Must Be Joking!** and *Pauline's Quirks*, both of which starred future **Birds of a Feather** Pauline Quirke and Linda Robson).

The series came to an end in 1979 after eight series of variable quality, punk becoming a greater influence on youth than the hippyish values of the early Seventies. In 1991 *The Tomorrow People* enjoyed something of a revival. Starring ***Neighbours***' Kristian Schmid, it was a much more internationally flavoured group of Homo Superior, and the show boasted both impressive special effects and a strong cast list (guest villains included Jean Marsh and Christopher Lee). A further re-invention of the show came in 2001, this time in a series of feature-length audio dramas from Big Finish, the company behind a successful and ever-growing collection of *Doctor Who* audio plays. Combining various members of the original cast with new characters, they've now produced more hours of drama than the original series. But it's that flared-trousered, wing-collared, paisley-shirted 1970s series that everyone remembers. Whenever people have mocked the production values of *Doctor Who*, fans of *The Tomorrow People* have tended to remain rather quiet on the matter, knowing all too well that it managed to look much cheaper and descend much more rapidly into childishness than the adventures of the good Doctor. Yet the imaginative stories and aspirationally selected cast left its mark none the less on children of the 1970s who wished they too could grow up to be Homo Superior.

Website
Catch up with the new adventures of *The Tomorrow People* courtesy of Big Finish: www.bigfinish.com/tpeople.

Tomorrow's World

Documentary/News | BBC One | episode duration 30 mins | broadcast 7 Jul 1965–29 May 2002, 3 Jul 2002–16 Jul 2003

Cast
Raymond Baxter, Derek Cooper, James Burke, William Woollard, Judith Hann, Michael Rodd, Kieran Prendiville, Peter McCann, Howard Stableford, Su Ingle, Kate Bellingham, Anna Ford, Maggie Philbin, Shahnaz Pakravan, John Diamond, Vivienne Parry, Carmen Pryce, Carol Vorderman, Philippa Forrester, Craig Doyle, Anya Sitaram, Jez Nelson, Peter Snow, Sophie Raworth, Lindsey Fallow, Nick Baker, Danielle Meagher, Roger Black, Adam Hart Davis, Kate Humble, Gareth Jones, Katie Knapman · *Presenters*

Producers Various, including Michael Blakstad, Martin Mortimore, Amanda Murray, Saul Nassé **Theme Music** The first theme tune came from Marius Constant, but the rather jazzy version that ran from the end of the 1960s through to 1981 came from Johnny Dankworth's Big Band. An electro-pop theme for the early 1980s came from Richard Denton and Martin Cook (and can be found on pop mixer Richard X's superb *Back to Mine* compilation). Paul Hart composed the sophisticated trumpet-led theme of the late-1980s and early '90s while The Divine Comedy's 'In Pursuit of Happiness' became the final *Tomorrow's World* signature tune.

The BBC's flagship popular science programme ran for over three decades, looking at the current state of technology and putting new inventions to the test. The series was broadcast live at first with pre-recorded editions introduced by the 1980s to reduce the embarrassment of experiments completely failing to impress.

In the late 1990s, *Tomorrow's World* became a BBC brand for all things experimental, with a BBC website that also incorporated cult TV. But by the early 2000s it was felt that the TV show that brought us the CD, the cashpoint machine and the mobile phone had finally been overtaken. The technology of tomorrow was already here. The series continued for a time as *Tomorrow's World Roadshow* before finally coming to a close in 2003. The website closed at about the same time.

Trivia
Tomorrow's World was the primary target of retro parody ***Look Around You*** for its 2004 series.

Top Cat

Animation | Hanna-Barbera for ABC (shown on BBC One) | episode duration 25 mins | broadcast 27 Sep 1961–2 May 1962 (USA)

Voice Cast
Arnold Stang · *Top Cat*
Maurice Gosfield · *Benny the Ball*
Marvin Kaplan · *Choo Choo*
Leo DeLyon · *Spook, The Brain*
John Stephenson · *Fancy-Fancy*
Allen Jenkins · *Officer Dibble*

Creators/Producers William Hanna and Joseph Barbera **Writer** Kin Platt **Theme Music** Joseph Barbera, William Hanna and Evelyn Timmens, responsible for one of the most annoying mondegreens (or misheard phrases) of all time. For the record, the lyric was 'Close friends get to call him TC/Pro-vi-ding it's with dignity'.

Top Cat is the craftiest alley cat on the block. Always up to some scheme or other, he's aided – or more often hindered – by his gang: the Brain (a deeply ironic moniker, considering how the orange moggy begins every sentence with 'Dur . . .'); Benny the Ball, so called because he's fat and round (and blue!); lothario Fancy-Fancy (always on the verge of a female feline conquest just as Top Cat summons the gang with a clash of bin-lids that echo round the district); Spook, who's a cool, hip cat; and Choo Choo – the pink one in the white polo-necked sweater. Hot on their tails is Officer Dibble, always watching out for evidence of gambling, scamming or – worst of all – misuse of the police telephone that's conveniently situated right by the trash can that Top Cat calls home. The gang spends countless hours evading Dibble's truncheon, but secretly they're rather fond of him. They'd far sooner have him patrolling the neighbourhood than any other copper.

In the 1960s, Hanna-Barbera began shifting the focus of their output from simply targeting kids to making shows that the whole family could enjoy. Like ***The Flintstones*** before it, *Top Cat* was shown in America on prime-time TV (Wednesdays 8.30 p.m.), and just as Fred and his gang aped ***The Honeymooners***, *Top Cat* drew upon another popular live-action sitcom, ***The Phil Silvers Show***, with Top Cat stepping in for the fast-talking Bilko and Benny for Bilko's greasy sidekick Dwane Doberman (Maurice Gosfield, who'd played Doberman, provided the voice for Benny), all combined with some of the cool gangster trappings of Frank Sinatra's Rat Pack. The final twist of making the lead character a cat who lives in a rubbish bin shows just how the genius of Hanna-Barbera made the company and its cartoon figures so successful.

Over in the UK, the programme found itself renamed *Boss Cat* to avoid inadvertently advertising a well-known brand of cat food (hence that jump in the opening sequence where the show's title should have appeared). The show's 30 episodes remained in almost constant rotation for over 40 years, although they're now more likely to be found on dedicated kiddie cable and satellite channels.

Top Gear

Magazine | BBC Two | episode duration 30 mins | broadcast 1978–2001, 2002–present

Regular Cast
Angela Rippon, Barrie Gill, Noel Edmonds, William Woollard, Sue Baker, Jeremy Clarkson, Quentin Willson, Tiff Needell, Chris

Goffey, Tony Mason, Janet Trewin, Michelle Newman, Steve Berry, Andy Willman, James May, Kate Humble, Jason Barlow, Vicki Butler-Henderson, Julia Bradbury, Jason Dawe, Steve Lee, Andy Wilman, Adrian Simpson, Richard Hammond · *Presenters/Reporters*

Producers Various, including Dennis Adams, Gary Hunter (executive), Gary Broadhurst, Julie Clive, Richard Pearson, Ken Pollock, Derek Smith, John Wilcox **Theme Music** The main theme is an arrangement of 'Jessica', written by Dickie Betts and originally performed by the Allman Brothers Band. For many years, Elton John's 'Out of the Blue' was used for the end titles.

Top Gear began as a rather stiff-fronted news magazine looking at the latest developments in the motor trade. With its Reithian values pinned high, and with Angela Rippon as an unlikely presenter, it was more about road safety than the petrol-head laddism it later became renowned for. This change in tone came in the 1990s with the arrival of the smooth Quentin Willson and the bellicose Jeremy Clarkson, who refused to play to the sales brochure scripts and allowed his own personal opinions and prejudices to colour his reports. He also introduced a style of car reviewing that had never been seen before; long, meandering metaphors that instantly captured an emotional response rather than a dry, factual rundown on the car's stats. It spoke directly to the original *Loaded* generation, some of whom were buying their first cars, others looking aspirationally to the kind of vehicles that made Clarkson and co foam at the mouth. While the series still contains features on innovation and car safety, its main purpose is to road test new models and allow its presenters (which currently includes racing driver Tiff Needell) the chance to live out their fantasies on test tracks. A recent addition to the series is 'Celebrity Laps', in which well-known faces are timed driving around a course. Ubiquitous comedian Jimmy Carr achieved the highest time, followed by ***X Factor***'s Simon Cowell and snooker player Ronnie O'Sullivan.

The series inspired copycat production such as ITV's *Pulling Power* and Channel 4's *Driven*. After Jeremy Clarkson decided to try his had at other TV formats and *Top Gear*'s ratings dipped, the BBC ditched the show after 23 years. Channel Five stepped in, gathered the presenters together and created *5th Gear*. Realising their mistake, the BBC quickly resurrected *Top Gear* in 2002, now with a more 'Zoo TV' format in the form on a studio audience. Clarkson was instrumental in the show's return and has continued to juggle *Top Gear* with other projects, such as evangelising the achievements of Isambard Kingdom Brunel for the BBC's *Great Britons* series.

Website
www.bbc.co.uk/topgear/

Top of the Pops

See pages 768–70

Torchy the Battery Boy

Pre-School Puppets | AP/Associated British-Pathe/Pelham Films/Associated Rediffusion for ITV | episode duration 13 mins | broadcast 23 Feb 1960–14 Feb 1961

Regular Cast
Olwen Griffiths · *Torchy*
Kenneth Connor · *Mr Bumbledrop, King Dithers, Gillygolly*
Jill Raymond · *Narrator, Flopsy, Bossy Boots*
Patricia Somerset · *Other Characters*

Creator/Producer/Writer/Theme Music Roberta Leigh

Gerry Anderson's second and last children's marionette series for Roberta Leigh was, like ***The Adventures of Twizzle***, pretty crude when compared with what Anderson's own company would later produce. This time, the star was a toy called Torchy who was built in order to rescue other toys that had been blown away on a kite to Topsy Turvy Land, a place where cream buns grow on trees and animals can talk. The voice cast included Kenneth Connor, who was already a film star courtesy of the *Carry On* series, but who would return to voice characters for Anderson's own series, ***Four Feather Falls***.

After 26 episodes, Roberta Leigh was keen to make a second series of *Torchy* but Anderson and his team had decided to go it alone (and in fact had already begun production in secret for *Four Feather Falls*). Leigh instead hired Vivian Milroy to direct another 26 instalments.

A Touch of Frost

Crime Drama | Excelsior/Yorkshire Television for ITV | episode duration 105 mins | broadcast 6 Dec 1992–present

Regular Cast
David Jason · *DI William George 'Jack' Frost*
Bruce Alexander · *Superintendent Norman Mullett*
James McKenna · *Sergeant Don Brady*
Arthur White · *PC Ernest 'Ernie' Trigg*
David Gooderson · *Derek Simpkins*
Lindy Whiteford · *Shirley Fisher*
Neil Phillips · *DCI Jim Allen*
Matt Bardock · *DC/DS Clive Barnard*
Bill Stewart · *Sandy Longford*
Christopher Rickwood · *PC Keith Stringer*
Nigel Harrison · *DCI Jim Peters*
Susannah Doyle · *DS Liz Maud*
Paul Jesson · *DS Dorridge*
Ian Driver · *PC Ken Jordan*
Tricia Thorns · *Miss Grey*
Robert Glenister · *DS Terry Reid*

Producers Richard Bates, Philip Burley, Martyn Auty, Vernon Lawrence, David Reynolds, David Jason (executive), Peter Lover

Continued on page 771

Top of the Pops

Dave Lee Travis discovers a Jimmy Saville-shaped growth under his arm.

Leaving aside television itself, it's arguable that the most influential and successful art form of the late 20th century was the pop music single. From the publication of the very first UK singles chart on 12 November 1952 (Al Martino's 'Here in My Heart' grabbing the first prestigious No. 1 spot), children, adults and especially teenagers have eagerly absorbed the output from the latest artists, each listener having a soundtrack to their life that instantly identifies them as a rocker, an indie kid, a punk, a skater girl or a disco queen. One programme has done more to bring those soundtracks to the British public than anything else, an institution that has been as much a part of our culture as the music it plays. But when it started, nobody could ever have predicted that such an insignificant programme would become a television legend.

When the BBC launched *Top of the Pops* in 1964, it was originally commissioned for just six episodes. The first edition went out at 6.35 p.m. on New Year's Day 1964, and was presented by Radio 1 DJ genial Jimmy Savile. The format of that first programme was remarkably similar to the show that's still being made today, with groups riding high in the pop chart performing their latest hits.

Top of the Pops' greatest strength as a programme format is that, by its very nature, it accurately reflects the musical genres and songs that are the most popular at a point in time. The rise of Beatlemania and Merseybeat carried the show through the mid-1960s; Motown and the psychedelic music of the hippy movement closed the decade. In the 1970s, glam rock eventually gave way to punk and disco, before the New Wave and the New Romantics saw in the 1980s. Dance music and the Stock Aitken Waterman 'hit factory' bridged the transition into the 1990s, by which point Britpop was riding high in the charts. Throughout all of these changing fads and musical movements, *Top of the Pops* has persisted, providing an opportunity for both new and established performers to reach a new, wider audience.

For three years from its outset in 1964, *Top of the Pops* was broadcast live from Manchester. Eventually, though, the sheer logistical problems of trying to get the world's top recording artists

Music
BBC One/Two
Episode Duration: 25–60 mins
Broadcast: 1 Jan 1964–present

Cast
Jimmy Savile, Pete Murray, David Jacobs, Alan Freeman, John Peel, Tony Blackburn, Stuart Henry, Kenny Everett, Simon Dee, Noel Edmonds, Ed Stewart, Dave Lee Travis, Emperor Rosko, David Hamilton, Kid Jensen, Peter Powell, Paul Burnett, Mike Read, Simon Bates, Steve Wright, Richard Skinner, Tommy Vance, Andy Peebles, Gary Davies, Janice Long, Mike Smith, Pat Sharp, Bruno Brookes, Dixie Peach, Simon Mayo, Nicky Campbell, Andy Crane, Mark Goodier, Caron Keating, Anthea Turner, Liz Kershaw, Phillip Schofield, Andi Peters, Jakki Brambles, Simon Parkin, Jenny Powell, Sybil Ruscoe, Tony Dortie, Mark Franklin, Femi Oke, Adrian Rose, Claudia Simon, Lisa I'Anson, Claire Sturgess, Bear Van Beers, Sarah Cawood, Zoe Ball, Jayne Middlemiss, Mark Lamarr, Jo Whiley, Jamie Theakston, Gail Porter/Hipgrave, Kate Thornton, Richard Blackwood, Sara Cox, Scott Mills, Dermot O'Leary, Josie D'Arby, Vernon Kaye, Lisa Snowdon, Liz Bonnin, Richard Bacon, Tim Kash, Fearne Cotton, Reggie Yates · *Presenters*

Producers Chris Cowey, Andi Peters (executive), Johnnie Stewart, Colin Charmey, Stanley Dorfman, Mel Cornish, Robin Nash, Brian Whitehouse, David G. Hillier, Stanley Appel, Michael Hurll, Paul Ciani, Ric Blaxill, Sally Wood

Theme Music The theme that greeted viewers in 1964, written by Johnnie Stewart and Harry Rabinowitz, was more influenced by jazz than genuine pop. In 1972, the definitive *TOTP* theme came in the form of a cover of Led Zeppelin's 'Whole Lotta Love' performed by CCS (Collective Conciousness Society). Phil Lynott's 'Yellow Pearl' came in 1981 and since then new versions have come from Paul Hardcastle, Tony Gibber and Vince Clarke. Another reworking of 'Whole Lotta Love' ran for the early 2000s until Andi Peters decided to change the theme back to Vince Clarke's version again.

to travel 200 miles away from the centre of the musical world became too much to deal with. So in 1967, *Top of the Pops* relocated to London, a mere Rolling Stones' throw away from Carnaby Street and the groovetastic excesses of the Swinging Sixties. With the move south, new presenters were drafted in from their regular DJ-ing gigs on Radio 1, including such groovy names as Simon Dee (for about 12 months, the coolest man in the country) and wild-child Kenny Everett.

With the programme still being broadcast live, the perennial problem of what to do if an artist wasn't available to perform on the show was solved by the introduction of a *Top of the Pops* dance troupe, a collection of attractive ladies who would perform their own innovative routines while the record in question was played. The first troupe was called the Go-Jos, but it was the arrival in 1968 of choreographer Flick Colby's dancers, Pan's People (performing to Tommy James and the Shondells' 'Mony Mony'), that really grabbed the attention of the public – and particularly the dads who were watching. Named after the pipe-playing Greek god, Pan's People consisted of Babs Lord, Ruth Pearson, Dee Dee Wilde, Louise Clarke and Andi Rutherford. Flick Colby (an original member of the gang, who dropped out because of the pressures of both dancing and putting together the routines) would often only have a short amount of time to choreograph an exciting series of moves for the dancers, a sad fact of life that unfortunately led to some routines looking more like a send-up of the song than was ever intended. Andi was replaced by Cherry Gillespie in 1972, and Sue Menhenick came in for Louise when she left to get married in 1974. Pan's People carried on performing on *Top of the Pops* until April 1976, when the girls finally decided to call it a day. Their short-lived replacements were mixed-sex group Ruby Flipper (Cherry, Floyd, Lulu, Gavin, Sue, Philip and Patti), but soon producers realised that many viewers missed seeing an all-girl dance group and introduced Legs and Co. – Lulu Cartwright, Patti Hammond and Sue Menhenick, who had all been in Ruby Flipper, were joined by Gill Clark, Pauline Peters and Rosie Hetherington – in November 1976. Legs and Co. supplied dance routines (still choreographed by Flick Colby) until 1981, by which point the pop video had more or less removed the need for 'fill-in' dancers. A big, mixed-sex dance troupe called Zoo then provided any required backing dancers for the groups performing in the studio.

Throughout the 1970s and 1980s, *Top of the Pops* attracted huge audiences, a true entertainment programme for the whole family. If there was one major criticism that could be levelled at the show it's that it was much less likely to feature controversial or innovative music than rival, 'cooler' shows such as ITV's 1980s *Pops*-alike *The Roxy* and Channel 4's influential ***The Tube***. Some musicians and labels even went as far as to say that *Top of the Pops* was deliberately suppressing acts that didn't seem to fit in with a cosy, family-friendly broadcast slot. Indeed, for many years, simply appearing on *Top of the Pops* would virtually guarantee that a particular act's record would leapfrog up the charts the following Sunday – record companies would lobby the *Top of the Pops* production team just to

TRIVIA

Acts on the first show on New Year's Day 1964 included the Rolling Stones (with 'I Wanna Be Your Man'), Dusty Springfield ('I Only Want To Be With You'), the Dave Clark Five ('Glad All Over') and the Swinging Blue Jeans ('The Hippy Hippy Shake'). Several groups were unable to make it to the studio, a converted church in Manchester, in which that first edition was recorded, so pre-filmed sequences were shown for Cliff Richard and The Shadows, Freddie and the Dreamers, and the No. 1 act that week – The Beatles (who else?) with 'I Wanna Hold Your Hand'.

make sure that their acts could get a vital three minutes of airtime on the show.

However, by the early 1990s, things were beginning to change with the record-buying public. In 1991, Canadian rocker Bryan Adams stayed at No. 1 for a record-breaking 16 weeks with his dreary ballad 'Everything I Do, I Do It For You'; the following year, Shakespear's Sister racked up eight weeks with 'Stay'; and Whitney Houston lasted ten weeks at the top with 'I Will Always Love You'. By the time Wet Wet Wet's 'Love Is All Around' had sat at the top of the singles charts for a week shy of four months in 1994, record executives had realised that the charts were in serious danger of stagnating. Their response was a bold one – rather than allowing radio stations to play forthcoming tracks just a week or two before their release, they instead started to promote new singles weeks and weeks ahead of time, in order to generate advance 'buzz' about releases and thereby reinvigorate the charts. *Top of the Pops* reacted to this new phenomenon, and for the first time permitted artists to appear on the programme before their singles had even been released – changing the very nature of the programme in one fell swoop. Although this was an entirely understandable move on the part of *Top of the Pops* producers, it did remove a great deal of the freshness and innovation from the programme. Subsequently, acts rarely climbed up the charts; instead, the first week's sales were normally the greatest that the act would ever achieve, with a new single seemingly entering chart at No. 1 practically every single week.

With the ever-increasing spread of information via multi-media outlets, by the dawn of the 2000s *Top of the Pops* was suddenly looking irrelevant. With the new chart announced each Sunday evening on Radio 1, every newspaper, website and radio station had already got the news about the new No. 1 into public circulation by Monday morning. In the fast-paced world of instant gratification, having to wait almost a week to see on television which record was 'Top of the Pops' seemed positively geriatric – almost like sending a message by carrier pigeon in an age of emails. When *Top of the Pops* was shifted from its long-term Thursday-night slot at 7.00 p.m. to the infamous 'death' slot opposite ***Coronation Street*** on Friday nights, it looked as though the show's days were numbered. In a multi-channel environment with 24-hour pop videos instantly available on demand, surely an old-fashioned format like *Top of the Pops* would simply just shrivel up and die? Well amazingly, it didn't. Ratings plunged to a fraction of what they were in the show's heyday, but the public's affection for the programme gave it a stubborn hold on life that seems nigh impossible to shake off. Indeed, the news in late 2004 that *Top of the Pops* would abandon its traditional BBC One home and move to BBC Two sometime in 2005 seemed to be an innovative response to the problem of what to do with it. In the less ratings-driven environment of BBC Two, we hope that *Top of the Pops* will be able to find a format that once again excites and enthuses a mass audience of music lovers. After all, a world without the Christmas Day edition of *Top of the Pops* scarcely bears thinking about.

(associate), Don Leaver, Simon Lewis, Lars MacFarlane **Writers** Various, including Christopher Russell, Richard Harris, Malcolm Bradbury, Russell Gascoigne, Sian Orrells, Michael Russell, Robert Smith, from the novels by R. D. Wingfield **Theme Music** The echoing, plaintive theme for the series is by Barbara Thompson and John Hiseman.

In the fictional town of Denton, the police force seems to encounter the same kind of everyday scumbag that most major conurbations face. However, most towns aren't blessed by the piercing intellect of Detective Inspector Frost, a small, crumpled looking man who nonetheless possesses a brain that can usually find its way round the trickiest or most convoluted of crimes. Unfortunately, Frost doesn't seem to have much of a life outside of the police force, with his terminally ill wife dying in the very first episode. Perhaps as a result of this, Frost believes passionately in his police work, despite coming across to many of his more formal superiors as rather slapdash and disorganised. Indeed, Frost tests the patience of Superintendent Mullet in virtually every episode.

For TV viewers back in 1992, the concept of casting Britain's biggest sitcom star as the lead in a serious drama series was quite a radical one. Audiences familiar with David Jason's work in everything from ***Porridge*** to ***Open All Hours*** might very well have taken against one of their favourite performers switching genres. However, Jason's natural skill and charisma shone through, and *Frost* has been a staple of the ITV schedules for more than ten years, with one-off specials and short seasons being recorded whenever Jason has enough spare time. Unlike the other big detective successes of the early '90s such as ***Cracker*** or ***Prime Suspect***, *A Touch of Frost* never set out to venture too far away from the cosiness you'd expect from most TV police shows, a factor that's gone a long way in ensuring its longevity.

Traffik

Drama | Carnival/Picture Partnership for Channel 4 | episode duration 50 mins | broadcast 22 Jun–17 Jul 1989

Principal Cast
Bill Paterson · *Jack Lithgow*
Lindsay Duncan · *Helen Rosshalde*
Jamal Shah · *Fazal*
Talat Hussain · *Tariq Butt*
Fritz Müller-Scherz · *Ulli*
Vincenzo Benestante · *Domenquez*

Creator/Writer Simon Moore **Producers** Christabel Albery, Brian Eastman **Theme Music** Tim Souster

The most intricate examination of the drug routes so far, *Traffik* looked at the whole issue of drugs from three perspectives: the farmer dependent on selling the drugs to feed his starving family; the trafficker, whose arrest prompts his wife to take his place and continue the business; and the politician whose campaign to close down the drug routes contrasts with his private life, battling to keep his own daughter's addictions at bay. The story moves in a triangle from London to northeast Pakistan via Germany. The series rarely allows sentimentality to get in the way or influence our sympathies, as all three main characters are caught in situations not of their own making and trying to find the solutions.

The story was retold by director Steven Soderberg in *Traffic* (2000), starring Michael Douglas and Catherine Zeta-Jones, while a mini series spun from the movie aired in the USA during Jan 2004.

Treasure Hunt

Game Show | Chatsworth Television Productions for Channel 4/BBC Two | episode duration 50 mins | broadcast 28 Dec 1982–18 May 1989, 10 Dec 2002–2 Aug 2003

Regular Cast
Kenneth Kendall, Dermot Murnaghan · *Presenter*
Anneka Rice, Annabel Croft, Suzi Perry · *Sky-runners*
Anne Meo, Annette 'Netty' Lynton, Wincey Willis · *Adjudicators*
Graham Berry · *Cameraman*
Frank Meyburgh · *Sound Recordist*
Keith Thompson · *Helicopter Pilot*

Creator Anne Meo **Producers** Malcolm Heyworth, Peter Holmans, Hester Davies **Theme Music** Zach Laurence (Channel 4), Francis Haines (BBC Two)

Channel 4's first prime-time game show was also one of its longest-running and most successful. Based upon a French game show by prolific TV format maestro Jacques Antoines (see also ***The Crystal Maze*** and *Fort Boyard*), *Treasure Hunt* was the first UK prime-time action/adventure quiz show – a genre that had previously been the reserve of children's programmes like ***The Adventure Game*** and *On Safari*.

The concept behind *Treasure Hunt* was simple: a kind of 'cryptic crossword' meets ***Wish You Were Here?*** if you like. Two contestants based in a London studio had 45 minutes to guide a 'sky-runner' in a helicopter around a pre-determined course somewhere in the UK (or if they were particularly lucky, in one of the series' occasional sojourns abroad). The course was broken down into five distinct stages, with the location of the next clue hidden within a deliberately obtuse word puzzle. Resources available to help the befuddled contestants included a large library of reference books, maps and tourist guides to the area concerned. Also on hand was series presenter (and former newsreader), the perpetually unflappable Kenneth Kendall. Occasionally, Kendall's leaps of deduction seemed so utterly inspired that it did make you question whether or not he'd been primed beforehand with the solutions to the riddles or the locations of where the next clue was hidden.

The studio-bound contestants were utterly reliant on their mobile arms and legs (the Sky-runner) to do the difficult job of tracking down the final location of the next clue. Often this would involve her having to climb up or down something, swim or row across a river, abseil down a cliff-face, or even, on one occasion, grab the clue (usually written on a piece of pink card) from the top of a fairground log-flume ride. The first and best remembered of the sky-runners was Anneka Rice, whose bottom became one of the best-known in the entire country thanks to cameraman Graham's habit of focusing on her rear view as she dashed to the next clue location. Although viewers at home were able to see what the sky-runner was doing, the only live link back to the studio was via audio – therefore, the contestants often had an agonising wait, leaving them to ask, 'Have you found it yet?' periodically until the triumphant shriek of, 'I've found it – stop the clock!' from Anneka.

Slight variations in the format included the introduction of an in-studio adjudicator to keep an eye on the ticking clock. Contestants had 45 minutes to get from the starting point to the location of the final 'treasure' – if they succeeded, they would win the grand total of £1000. If they only managed to complete four stages, the prize money was halved to £500 – on the rare occasion of only three stages being completed, the prize money was just £300. One of the adjudicators happened to be former TV:AM weather girl Wincey Willis, who developed a wonderful repartee with 'Annie' and Kenneth. After seven seasons of out-of-breath derring-do, Anneka Rice left *Treasure Hunt* to host her own BBC One series *Challenge Anneka*. Her replacement was former British tennis star Annabel Croft, who (if it was possible) managed to cause even more stress among the contestants than her predecessor by simply either not listening to their directions or being too keen to stop and talk to the members of the public who would inevitably gather at the first sighting of the familiar *Treasure Hunt* helicopter (one particular task required her to find a clue near a Minster, which prompted the rather dazed question 'What's a Minster?' from poor Annabel).

Eventually the series drew to a close in 1989, with production company Chatsworth creating a variation on the same theme the following year with ***Interceptor***. In this remarkably samey programme, it was presenter Annabel Croft who stayed stationery as the two contestants, dumped into the middle of the countryside, attempted to find their way to each other while dodging the malevolent black-clad Interceptor (Sean O'Kane). Although everyone involved in the show threw themselves into it with gusto, the format produced an uninvolving programme that not surprisingly lasted just one season.

You can't keep a good format down, though. In 2002, BBC Two revived *Treasure Hunt* with a new sky-runner (Suzi Perry), a new presenter (newsreader Dermot Murnaghan) and similar challenges and clues as before. However, the BBC never seemed to promote this revival to any great extent, sometimes showing five episodes in one week in a tea-time slot, sometimes dropping the programme with no notice in order to screen sporting events. Frustratingly, the series was soon consigned to history once more. One of the main criticisms of this re-launch was the choice of location for the 'hunts' themselves. The first run of five episodes was all filmed in and around one county, Kent – the second all shot abroad. Fans argued that the great joy in watching the original series of *Treasure Hunt* was to wallow in the glories of the British countryside and to identify stately homes, national parks and funfairs to go on visits to yourself (many of which had benefited from increased admissions thanks to a visit from Anneka and her crew), something that sadly the revived programme failed to offer.

Trial and Retribution

Crime Drama | La Plante Productions for ITV | episode duration 80–100 mins | broadcast 19 Oct 1997–present

Regular Cast

David Hayman · *DS/Detective Chief Superintendent Mike Walker*
Victoria Smurfit · *DCI Roison Connor*
Kate Buffery · *DI Pat North*
Dorian Lough · *DS David Satchell*
Inday Ba · *DC Lisa West*
Sarah Ozeke · *DC Lisa West*
George Asprey · *DC Jack Hutchins*
Sandra James Young · *DC Vivien Watkins*
Michael Simkins · *Police Chief Superintendent Bradley*
David Kennedy · *PC Phelps*
Daniel Ryan · *PC Brown*

Creator/Writer Lynda La Plante **Producers** Lynda La Plante, Steve Lanning, Keith Richardson, Steve Christian, Lorraine Goodman, Peter Richardson, Liz Thorburn

Lynda La Plante's level of research is legendary, spending years obsessing over the specific details of procedure to ensure her details are unfaultable. It ran through ***Prime Suspect*** but with *Trial and Retribution* her obsession to detail rises to degrees of near-fetishism as a split-screen technique is employed to allow us to see the story unfolding from various viewpoints or locations simultaneously. The realism extends to a batch of regular characters that we warm to out of familiarity rather than because they're genuinely likeable. Mike Walker in particular ferrets around with a face like thunder playing up to the genuine pretensions of real-life coppers who are informed as much by the tough guys on TV as the training schools.

We first join Walker as he heads a murder investigation after a small child is abducted, abused and left to die on a building site inside a concrete pipe. The residents have their own prime suspect, a drunkard with an unreliable memory whose flat seems to be open to all the children on the housing estate, but it's up to Walker and the team that he inherits from a resentful DI Pat North to prove that he committed the murder through solid forensic evidence.

Each two-part series begins with the realisation that a crime has been committed, the police being called and the investigations commencing. Mistakes are made – in the first story, a young PC falsifies evidence motivated by trauma caused by finding the girl's body too late to save her, while in the second case the guilty man walks free only for his own wife to frame him for her own murder/suicide. But what could become a formulaic series is elevated by La Plante's knowledge of the huge variety of possible cases, which, in turn, affect the way the concluding trial (or retrial) unravels.

Website
Lynda La Plante's production company can be found at www.laplanteproductions.com.

Triangle

Soap | BBC One | episode duration 25 mins | broadcast 5 Jan 1981–28 Jun 1983

Regular Cast
Michael Craig · *Captain John Anderson*
Larry Lamb · *Matt Taylor*
Kate O'Mara · *Katherine Laker*
Nigel Stock · *Wally James*
Paul Jerrico · *Charles Woodhouse*
Jonathan Owen · *Peter Nuttall*
Douglas Sheldon · *Arthur Parker*
George Baker · *David West*
Diana Coupland · *Marion Terson*
Sandra Dickinson · *Penny Warrender*
Peter Arne · *Kevin Warrender*
Penelope Horner · *Sarah Hallam*
Sandra Payne · *Christine Harris*

Creator Bill Sellars **Producer** Bill Sellars **Writers** Michael Armstrong, Colin Davis, Robert Del Valle, Luanshya Greer, David Hopkins, Sue Lake, Dawn Lowe-Watson, Jack Mott, Bill Sellars, Ben Steed, Leslie Elizabeth Thomas **Theme Music** Johnny Pearson

Legendary among TV viewers and executives alike, *Triangle* is a programme that's sometimes been labelled as one of the very worst ever made – a criticism that's far more unkind than the show truly deserves. Having said that, the high concept of the series was fundamentally flawed – trying to create a glamorous soap about the staff and passengers on board a North Sea ferry travelling in a triangular route between the three ports of Felixstowe, Gothenburg and Amsterdam is hardly going to match the wealth and sunshine of ***Dallas***.

One of the first programmes to be entirely recorded on location and on videotape as opposed to film, *Triangle* suffered from the inherent weaknesses of its setting: namely that the North Sea is a cold grey expanse of featureless water. The drama between the actors had to be filmed inside small, dark cabins for much of the time, and many of the cast and crew suffered from roaring seasickness. One of the most memorable moments of *Triangle* (and the one often selected by TV researchers to represent the series) was in its opening minutes, where poor benighted Kate O'Mara tried to convince a boggling public that sunbathing topless on the deck of a freezing cold North Sea ferry was a) a bright idea, and b) not likely to give her frostbite. However, enough viewers kept tuning in to ensure that the show got recommissioned for three seasons of high-seas intrigue and boardroom shenanigans.

Trigger-Happy TV

Comedy | Absolutely/First Television for Channel 4 | episode duration 25 mins | broadcast 2000–2001

Cast
Dom Joly, Sam Cadman, Travis Draft, Lindsey Ellis, Jessica Makinson, Jerry Minor · *Various Characters*

Producers Dom Joly, Sam Cadman, Michael Dugan **Theme Music** 'Connection' by Elastica – or at least a decent soundalike

Decisively apolitical, *Trigger-Happy TV* riffs off ***Candid Camera*** and other hidden camera shows to undermine the famous and baffle the elderly purely to celebrate the power of silliness. In a variety of guises, Dom Joly chats casually to pensioners while dressed as a cub scout, poses as a tourist guide to deliver bogus information about local landmarks, dresses as a giant squirrel or a dog to frolic in the park. Two men in fat suits walk towards each other down a corridor or in opposite segments of a revolving door, trapping anyone unfortunate enough to be caught in-between. Most pervasively he mocks the Nokia default ringtone with a gigantic mobile phone and a very loud voice: 'HELLO? . . . I'M IN BELGIUM . . . IT'S RUBBISH!' Such was Joly's hatchet job on that particular tune ('Diddle doodoo, diddle doodoo, diddle doodoodoo') that we can now be sure anyone who still has the Nokia ringtone on their phone should be avoided at all costs. To make up for this, the series also sported an ultra-cool soundtrack, with the likes of Stereophonics, Faithless and Massive Attack accompanying each example of comedy terrorism.

The Tripods

Science Fiction | BBC/Seven Network Australia for BBC One | episode duration 25 mins | broadcast 15 Sep 1984–23 Nov 1985

Principal Cast
John Shackley · *Will Parker*
Jim Baker · *Henry Parker*
Ceri Seel · *Jean-Paul 'Beanpole' Deliet*
Robin Hayter · *Fritz Eger*
Roderick Horn · *Ozymandias*
Lucinda Curtis · *Mrs Parker*
Peter Dolphin · *Mr Parker*

Michael Gilmour · *Jack*
Robin Langford · *Duc de Sarlat*
Charlotte Long, Cindy Shelley · *Eloise de Ricordeau*
Pamela Salem · *Countess de Ricordeau*
Jeremy Young · *Count de Ricordeau*
Cecilia Boorman · *Kirsty Vichot*
Imogen Boorman · *Fiona Vichot*
Nicola Boorman · *Lucy Vichot*
Maria Evans · *Shelagh Vichot*
Stephen Marlowe · *Monsieur Vichot*
Clare Nimmo · *Helen Vichot*
Anni Lee Taylor · *Madame Vichot*
Barbara Wilshere · *Jeannie Vichot*
Victor Baring · *Mayor*
Richard Wordsworth · *Julius*
Richard Beale · *Ulf*
Vass Anderson, Ian Brimble, Ian Cinderby · *Black Guards*
Mark Nicholls · *Gabriel*
John Woodvine · *Voice of Will's Master, West 468*
Julian Battersby · *Pierre*
James Coyle · *Borman*
Geraldine Griffiths · *Nurse*
Edward Highmore · *Boll*
Alfred Hoffman · *Speyer*
Bernard Holley · *Voice of the Power Master*
Christopher Guard · *Cognosc*
Alex Leppard · *Dorfen*
Garfield Morgan · *Slave Master*

Producer Richard Bates **Writers** Alick Rowe, Christopher Penfold, from John Christopher's novels *The White Mountains* and *The City of Gold and Lead* **Theme Music** Ken Freeman's electronic theme was evocative of Holst's 'Mars' from *The Planets*, with bombastic opening music replaced by a more languid, romantic piece for the closing titles. Definitely one of the best synth-based themes of the 1980s.

John Christopher's apocalyptic science fiction tale bears some comparison to H. G. Wells' *The War of the Worlds*: giant three-legged machines from another world attempt to take over the planet Earth. The difference is, in Christopher's version, they've already won before the story begins. For the BBC adaptation, the differences become greater still; the BBC Special Effects department succeeded where Hollywood had failed in creating three-legged machines to stalk the countryside – the 1953 film version cheated by having the invaders fly.

It's 2089 and the Tripods have been masters of the planet Earth for many years with the once great cities now reduced to rubble. Technology has been retarded to the level of the pre-industrial age with little manufactured items available that aren't made by a blacksmith or carpenter. Every adult over the age of 16 is fitted with a cap – a thin piece of gold mesh embedded into the scalp to prevent sedition and uprising. For Will Parker and his cousin Henry, Capping Day is not far off and the prospect of becoming another puppet of the Tripods fills them with dread. But then a vagrant called Ozymandias tells them of a community of Free Men who live in The White Mountains where the Tripods can never reach.

On their travels across the English Channel towards France, Will and Henry pretend to be young travellers wanting to see the world before their Capping. They make a new friend in France, Jean-Paul, a lanky young inventor who quickly earns himself the nickname 'Beanpole'. But their journey is not all fun and adventure. They must evade the Tripods' agents, the Black Guards, and stay away from populated areas in case they are handed over to the metallic masters. But then, en route to the White Mountains, they are taken in by a kind Count and Countess, and Will falls in love with their daughter Eloise, only to watch in horror as she is handed over as an offering to the Tripods and taken to their legendary City of Gold . . .

Producer Richard Bates had been trying to bring the *Tripods* trilogy to the screen ever since the first book was released in 1967. Sadly, the series failed to draw in audiences from the very beginning, despite a striking *Radio Times* front cover and a Saturday evening slot. By the mid-1980s, ITV ruled Saturday nights – even ***Doctor Who*** had struggled in its old traditional slot. Also, the promise of the mechanical monsters was not fulfilled, with far too many episodes tied up with repetitive captures and escapes (including a completely superfluous sub-plot at a vineyard not present in the source novel) and not enough of the aliens themselves.

The second series, adapting John Christopher's *The City of Gold and Lead*, was much more satisfying, as Will and his friends are sent by the Free Men to infiltrate the Tripod's huge domed city by competing in Olympic-styled games. Only Will and his rival, the cold German Fritz, succeed and soon they are within the dome, an impressive covered citadel with tall pyramids pulsing with light. There they meet the beings within the Tripods, hulking three-legged creatures called the Masters who use the humans as slaves and who plan to pollute the planet with air that only they can breathe and turn it into their second home.

Frustratingly, while the ongoing story and special effects were a vast improvement on the first series, the second suffered from almost as much padding. With ratings still nowhere near high enough for a show so expensive, *The Tripods* was cancelled, leaving the downbeat ending of the series unresolved and the final part of the trilogy, *The Pool of Fire*, untold.

The Troubleshooters

Drama | BBC One | episode duration 50 mins | broadcast 7 Jul 1965–29 Sep 1965 (*Mogul*), 30 Apr 1966–3 Jan 1972 (*The Troubleshooters*)

Regular Cast
Ray Barrett · *Peter Thornton*
Geoffrey Keen · *Brian Stead*
Philip Latham · *Willy Izzard*
John Carson · *James Langley*

Philippa Gail · *Jane Webb*
Wanda Ventham · *Moira Hart*
Robert Hardy · *Alec Stewart*
Deborah Stanford · *Roz Stewart*
Ronald Hines · *Derek Prentice*
Barry Foster · *Robert Driscoll*
Virginia Wetherell · *Julie Serres*
Isobel Black · *Eileen O'Rourke*
David Barron · *Mike Szabo*
Edward de Souza · *Charles Grandmercy*
Jayne Sofiano · *Dr Ginny Vickers*

Creator John Elliot **Producers** Peter Graham Scott, Anthony Read, David E Rose, Michael Glynn **Writers** John Elliot, Mike Watts, Kenneth Ware, James Mitchell, John Lucarotti, Kenneth Salter, David Weir, Vincent Tilsley, Anthony Read, Ian Kennedy Martin, Bryan Cooper, George Byatt, Lee Dunne, Ray Jenkins, John Gould, Eve Martell, Roy Russell, Ray Jenkins, Hugh Forbes, Roy Clarke, Michael Winder, Ludovic Peters, David Fisher, Joe Lorigan **Theme Music** Tom Springfield

The original oil industry drama series, ***Mogul*** revealed the everyday ins-and-outs of the executives of Mogul Oil, years before JR Ewing ever donned a ten-gallon hat. As the series began, viewers watched Brian Stead, deputy managing director of Mogul, as he struggled to maintain his firm's commercial advantage in a cut throat marketplace. Aiding Stead were Mogul's company secretary Willy Izzard, Robert Driscoll (PR) and personnel manager Derek Prentice. Together they faced such problems as North Sea oil rig disasters, industrial espionage and negotiating deals with Middle Eastern governments.

Although the first series of *Mogul* was a moderate success (gaining particular praise from oil industry insiders for its realism), some changes were made before it returned the following year. Most notable was the change in title to *The Troubleshooters*, reflecting a shift in focus with the cast, too. Although boardroom shenanigans were still a part of the series, the focus would now be on Mogul Oil's two main field operatives, Peter Thornton and Alec Stewart. Plotlines uncannily seemed to predict major events in the news, with incidents in *The Troubleshooters* taking place either immediately before or after similar events happening in the real world.

Lasting for seven years, the exploits of Mogul Oil and its employees are fondly remembered to this day, not least because of its high-quality scripting from such luminaries as John Elliot (***A For Andromeda***) and Ian Kennedy Martin (***The Sweeney***, ***Juliet Bravo***).

Trumpton

Animation | Gordon Murray Puppets for BBC One | episode duration 15 mins | broadcast 3 Jan–28 Mar 1967

Voice Cast
Brian Cant

Creator/Producer Gordon Murray **Writers** Gordon Murray, Alison Prince **Theme Music** 'The Chimes of the Trumpton Clock', written by Freddie Phillips and narrated by Brian Cant, introduces us to the clock at the top of the Trumpton Town Hall, which tells the time for Trumpton, 'steadily, sensibly, never too quickly, never too slowly'. Cue the two brass characters who emerge from tiny doors on the clock, one holding a bell, the other a small hammer. Together they create the nine chimes for the clock before shuffling back inside.

For commentary, see THE TRUMPTONSHIRE TRILOGY, *pages* 776–9

The Tube

Music Magazine | Tyne Tees for Channel 4 | episode duration 60 mins | broadcast 1982–7

Cast
Jools Holland, Paula Yates, Muriel Gray, Gary James, Leslie Ash, Felix Howard · *Presenters*

Creators Malcolm Gerrie and Andrea Wonfor **Producers** Andrea Wonfor, Malcolm Gerrie, Paul Corley, John Gwyn, Jill Sinclair

Broadcast live on Friday evenings, *The Tube* held two proud fingers up to ***Top of the Pops*** and carved a confidently chaotic sway through 1980s' television. Former pianist with Squeeze, Jools Holland and the permanently flirtatious Paula Yates set the irreverent tone, frequently admonished for swearing (most notably Holland, who used the dreaded f-word during a trail being shown live on ITV) and treading the line between enthusiasm and cool apathy.

Unlike *Top of the Pops*, *The Tube* didn't just reflect the high-flyers and the usual suspects from the chart. Within its remit was a desire to contribute to music, to shape the industry, not just reflect it. It's biggest success came with Liverpool band Frankie Goes to Hollywood, who made their first TV appearance in a specially shot video for their song 'Relax'. Pop producer Trevor Horn saw the edition and quickly snapped up the boys; they went on to have three consecutive No. 1 singles and a No. 1 album. Other acts receiving their big break on the show included Wet Wet Wet, the Housemartins and, in her first UK TV appearance, Madonna, who performed 'Holiday' (thought to be little more than a novelty dance act at the time, her record company refused to pay her travel expenses from an appearance in London, so Tyne Tees offered to pay for her tickets in exchange for the broadcast rights to the performance – a very canny move there).

Established acts also saw the show as something worthy of their attention, although Paul McCartney showed himself to be an especially patient man when he was interviewed by Felix Howard, a barely teenage boy who'd

Continued on page 780

The Trumptonshire Trilogy

The people of Trumpton look to the skies .

Gordon Murray's association with children's television harks back to the early days of *Watch with Mother* as a puppeteer on shows like ***The Woodentops*** and his own creation *Rubovian Legends*. But by 1964, Murray had grown tired of the back-biting and internal politics of the BBC Children's Department and decided to strike out as an independent producer, taking husband-and-wife design team Andrew and Margaret Brownfoot and animators Bob Bura and John Hardwick with him. Providing the music and sound effects was another *Rubovia* graduate, Freddie Phillips, while Brian Cant, a familiar face to viewers of ***Play School***, narrated the stories. Murray set up shop in a converted house in Crouch End in London, an inauspicious location for the beginning of a legendary series, a new generation of programmes for the *Watch with Mother* slot made with stop motion animation – and in colour . . .

As this was his first independent production, cost-conscious Murray was willing to make *Camberwick Green* on 16mm black-and-white film, but Bura and Hardwick convinced him to also use colour film stock, mindful of the imminent introduction of colour TV. So the black-and-white camera was set up next to the colour one and each of them were in operation almost simultaneously. It's lucky they did, as otherwise the series might not have enjoyed the long repeat life it subsequently did. As soon as BBC One was ready to move over to complete colour broadcasting, Gordon Murray's shows were able to simply switch to their colour versions and those viewers yet to acquire a colour TV would barely notice the difference.

Camberwick Green is a small village in the county of Trumptonshire. The green itself sports park benches around a tree in the middle of an arc of shops including the post office (run by

See **CAMBERWICK GREEN, CHIGLEY** *and* **TRUMPTON** *for broadcast details and individual credits*

Mrs Dingle and her puppy, Packet), Mickey Murphy's bakery (which also provides a home for Mrs Murphy and their children, Paddy and Mary) and Mr Carraway's fishmongers with its striped awning. Dr Mopp has his surgery there, PC McGarry (number 452) patrols the streets, Thomas Tripp delivers the milk, Peter Hazel delivers everyone's letters, and news of a different sort comes from local gossip Mrs Honeyman, wife of an unseen chemist and with a young baby in her arms.

Mr Crockett's garage can be found not far from the green (you'll often see car salesman Mr Dagenham's sports car parked up there) while on the outskirts of the village lie Jonathan Bell's farm and Pippin Fort, home to Captain Snort, his soldiers – Privates Armitage, Featherby, Higgins, Hopwood, Lumley and Meek (plus an unnamed bugler) – and their 'humpety bumpety army truck'.

The most popular character was the owner of Colley's Mill, Mr Miller, known affectionately as 'Windy'. Windy's a placid man with a fondness for home-brew cider and a trust of the old country ways. like wetting his finger to test for wind. Every week we'd tune in to see if that would be the episode where Windy got whacked by one of the windmill's sails, but somehow he always managed to dart between the gaps.

The star of each episode of *Camberwick Green* would appear via the trap door at the top of that music box in the title sequence. Each of the characters was constructed with a ping-pong ball for its head with eyes painted on and a nose added. The models did not have mouths, however, thereby voiding the additional problem of lip-synch. *Camberwick Green* was a picturesque slice of life, a soap opera for tots – of a more sophisticated and intricate form than the very basic storylines of *The Woodentops*. It featured a curious mix of 18th- and early 20th-century styles. Women all wore long, floor-length dresses and shawls, while Captain Snort's soldiers could easily have been called into battle on the moors of Culloden and not looked out of place (although the boys of Pippin Fort were never actually called upon to face an enemy of any kind during the series' run). Dr Mopp drove a car that might have been either vintage or contemporaneous with whichever time period the stories were set in: it's been suggested that while the stories did in fact take place in the modern world, the people of *Camberwick Green*, and later *Trumpton*, seemed to inhabit an era frozen in time, with all the charm and eternal happiness that can only exist in the realm of nostalgia – or children's telly.

Every week we'd tune in to see if that would be the episode where Windy got whacked by one of the windmill's sails, but somehow he always managed to dart between the gaps.

With the simple stories and catchy, folk-styled music, *Camberwick Green* was deemed successful enough for a second series. For this, Murray's team would head over to Camberwick Green's nearest neighbour – Trumpton.

WEBSITE
The impressively detailed Trumptonshire website – www.t-web.co.uk/trumpgo.htm – has interviews, episode guides and pictures from all of Gordon Murray's productions.

Trumpton is a town in the heart of Trumptonshire. At its centre is the Town Hall where His Worship the Mayor oversees the many municipal services that keep the town running, as detailed in one of the songs performed by Brian Cant: 'Fire brigade, library, road repairs, postage stamps, rubbish bins, swimming baths, broken window panes/Park gates, waterworks, painting all the street lamps, dust cart, youth club, church bazaar, drains'. The Mayor is assisted by Mr Troop, the town clerk, and driven to all manner of civic functions by his chauffeur, Philby, who knows his place and never speaks.

The Town Hall faces onto the Market Square with a statue of Queen Victoria in the centre and shops all around. On the far corner is Miss Lovelace's hat shop, the owner being a haughty woman identifiable by her constant companions, three unruly Pekinese dogs, Mitzy, Daphne and Lulu; there's Mr Platt the clock maker and watch repairer, who'll tell you that 'Clocks are like people/Clocks are like you and me/Each has its own personality'; Mr Munnings, who runs the print works and produces posters for the daily concerts in Trumpton park – posters that are placed around the town by the bill sticker, Nick Fisher; Mr Clamp the greengrocer who gets daily deliveries of fresh fruit and veg; and Police Constable Potter, who, along with Mrs Cobbett the flower-seller (who specialises in roses and violets), is always first one in the Square every morning. There are a number of tradesmen and handymen who visit Trumpton too: Mr Crockett from the Camberwick Road; Mr Antonio the ice cream man; Mr Robinson the window cleaner; Raggy Dan the rag and bone man; painter and decorator Walter Harkin; Mr Wilkins the plumber; and telephone engineers Mr Wantage and his assistant Fred.

In Trumpton Park we find the bandstand, duck pond and the tool shed belonging to Mr Craddock the park keeper. There was at one point a greenhouse – until an unfortunately positioned chimney demolition destroyed it. Elsewhere in the town we find the home of Mrs Cobbet. Her next-door neighbours are the Mintons – Dora, husband Chippy, who's a carpenter, and son Nibbs. The Mintons' cottage also houses Chippy's workshop. On the outskirts of the town is the fire station with its bright red engine and shiny fireman's pole. Chief fire officer Captain Flack and his men (twins Pugh and Pugh, old man Barney McGrew, Cuthbert, Dibble and Grubb) never actually put out a fire, but as the owners of the only crane platform in the town they're called out daily to help with fixing crowns onto statues or looking for lost people across the treetops in the park. They also double up as the town's featured act at the bandstand each day.

It should be noted here that while we find the complete lack of fires for the fire brigade to put out rather charming, this narrative device came from a much more practical concern of being unable to animate water or flames with any degree of success. Sheer serendipity, as the inferno-free brigade and the rollcall of its crew remain the most memorable aspect of any Gordon Murray production.

Chigley was effectively the lap of honour for the residents of Trumptonshire. Characters from *Camberwick Green* and *Trumpton* would pop up at the beginning of each episode and Brian Cant would ask them if he could follow them. They'd nod their agreement and soon we'd all be off to Chigley. Often the character that took us there would only be involved at the very beginning before introducing us to a Chigleyite, such as Mr Creswell, the efficiency-crazed proprietor of Creswell's Chigley Biscuit Factory (a rather cheeky CCB for the BBC); Harry Farthing and his androgynous daughter Winnie at the pottery; or Mr Swallow, driver of the impressive crane at Treddles' Wharf, where cargo brought in by train could be transferred to lorry or barge. The train, Bessie, belonged to the potty Lord Belborough of Winkstead Hall, faithfully assisted by his butler, Brackett. Though Brian Cant's script would invariably read, 'Brackett rushed to find Lord Belborough', the butler would never do anything so undignified as rush; his was a plodding, reliable, steady existence where rushing simply wouldn't do.

Each working day (and therefore each episode) would end with the factory whistle signalling 6 o'clock and the start of the evening's entertainment. As Lord Belborough's Dutch organ (not as rude as it sounds) hooted out a waltz-time tune, the factory workers would dance with what looked like a pair of Romany women, complete with the floor-length dresses and head-scarves that were all the rage in Trumptonshire.

As with *Camberwick Green* and *Trumpton*, Gordon Murray and his team made just 13 episodes of the series that gave us the classic song 'Time Goes by When You're the Driver of a Train', so mercilessly parodied by satirical northern punk band Half Man Half Biscuit on their 1986 'Trumpton Riots' single. After 39 *Trumpton*-based stories, Gordon Murray felt he'd said all he could about the region. His next project would take him right back to the beginning of his career, to the fairytale kingdom of *Rubovia* . . .

Sadly, as all of the Trumptonshire puppets were made of perishable materials like foam rubber, few of them survived past the 1980s. One of the Pippin Fort soldiers was given to a friend of Gordon Murray's daughter, while the rest were thrown onto a bonfire by their creator. When Murray let this slip during an interview, newspapers were outraged that another part of their childhood was gone for ever, but Murray himself wasn't sentimental about the little fellas. Besides, they were fairly easy to remake, as indeed they were for a 1988 advert for Hovis bread. A decade later, they joined the casts of the ***Flower Pot Men***, ***Postman Pat*** and ***The Magic Roundabout*** for the BBC's 'Future Generations' promotions for the licence fee (which also made a star of Scott Chisolm, the chubby-cheeked young actor who was shown strolling through scenes from the childhood TV favourites of his parents). Since then, of course, the DVD boom has struck and the retro TV market has soared. Playing its part is a DVD collection of the entire *Trumptonshire* trilogy, currently available in a three-box set.

appeared in Madonna's video for 'Open Your Heart' but struggled to remember his questions or display any prior knowledge of Macca's career.

Turtle's Progress

Comedy Drama | ATV for ITV | episode duration 50 mins | broadcast 23 Apr 1979–11 Jul 1980

Regular Cast

John Landry · *Turtle*
Michael Attwell · *Edward Winston 'Razor Eddie' Malone*
Ruby Head · *Aunt Ethel Wagstaff*
Tony London · *George Wagstaff*
James Grout, David Swift · *Superintendent Rafferty*
Paul Shelley · *Alex Corton*

Creator/Writer Edmund Ward **Producers** David Reid (executive), Nicholas Palmer, Joan Brown **Theme Music** Written and sung by Alan Price, the theme was released as a single by Kenny Ball and his Jazzmen. Price reworked the tune into 'Mr Sunbeam', a track on his 1980 album *Rising Sun*.

Despatched to steal a van by Turtle, Razor Eddie makes a huge mistake when he steals a van that was used to steal safe deposit boxes worth over £1 million. While the criminal underworld, the police and the original owners close in, Turtle and Eddie begin to work their way through each of the boxes to uncover rackets, extortion, even espionage. But can they get rid of the boxes before someone gets rid of them?

A spin-off from the equally forgotten 1975 crime series ***The Hanged Man***, *Turtle's Progress* continued the story of the unlikely partnership between a balding low-level crook with middle-aged spread and a hulking heavy with a distracting facial scar from the days when the word 'hooligan' meant something. The duo were well known down at their local pub, the Robin Hood, where Eddie would often stockpile on pasties, six at a time.

Sadly, this series has been overshadowed by ***Minder***, which first appeared just a few months after *Turtle's Progress* aired, running for ten series compared to *Turtle*'s two. It's a shame as the dialogue here came thick and fast – very sharp, quick-fire banter, thick with East-End criminal lingo and a cast almost the equal of *Minder*'s, especially Ruby Head as Aunt Ethel, barmaid at the Hood and adept at avoiding awkward questions from dodgy customers and associates, even the tax-man.

Tweenies

Pre-School | Tell-Tale for BBC One | episode duration 20 mins | broadcast 6 Sep 1999–present

Cast

Colleen Daley · *Voice of Fizz*
Justin Fletcher · *Voices of Jake and Doodles*
Bob Golding · *Voices of Max and Milo*
Sally Preisig, Emma Weaver · *Voice of Bella*
Sinead Rushe · *Voice of Judy*
Jenny Hutchinson · *Fizz*
C. H. Beck · *Milo*
Simon Grover · *Max, Judy*
Tamsin Heatley · *Bella*
Alan Riley · *Doodles*
Samantha Dodd · *Jake*

Creator Iain Lauchlan **Producers** Clare Elstow, Judy Whitfield (executive), Iain Lauchlan, Will Brenton, Kay Benbow, Robin Carr **Writers** Iain Lauchlan, Will Brenton, Simon Grover, Philip Hawthorn, Wayne Jackman, Gillian Juckes, Alan Macdonald, Jan Page, Alan Riley

Aimed at slightly older pre-school children than ***The Teletubbies***, *Tweenies* are egg-faced, brightly coloured children who come to a playroom run by Max and Judy. Bella is the tallest and oldest, but also the bossiest, Milo is the most imaginative, Fizz is a child of nature and Jake is the youngest and often needs help with his pronunciation. Max and Judy's red and yellow dog Doodles often plays along while the children use the playroom clock to decide what to do next (is it going to be song time, news time, story time or telly time?). As in the real world, but pretty unique for TV, these children don't always get along; there are squabbles, rivalries, teasing and falling in and out of friends, though such disputes are always sorted out in the end.

24

See pages 782–3

The Twilight Zone

See pages 784–8

Twin Peaks

See pages 789–91

Two Pints of Lager and a Packet of Crisps

Sitcom | BBC Two/Choice/Three | episode duration 30 mins | broadcast 26 Feb 2001–present

Regular Cast

Natalie Casey · *Donna Henshaw*
Will Mellor · *Gaz Wilkinson*
Ralf Little · *Jonny Keogh*
Sheridan Smith · *Janet Smith/Keogh*
Kathryn Drysdale · *Louise Brooks*

Beverley Callard · *Flo Henshaw*
Jonathon Dutton · *David Fish*
Alison Mac · *Kate*
Lee Oakes · *Munch*

Creator/Writer Susan Nickson **Producers** Geoffrey Perkins, Sophie Clarke-Jervoise, Michael Jacob (executive), Jez Nightingale, Stephen McCrum **Theme Music** Simon Brint, Christian Henson

Life in Runcorn can be more than a little bit dull if you're a young person with sex, booze and biscuits on your mind. Layabout Jonny does his best to laze around as much as possible and is resolved to live a life of indolence, until one day his friend Gaz takes him out on the town and he throws up over a girl in a pub. That girl turns out to be Janet, and after such a romantic introduction, the two soon find themselves dating. Against her better judgement, Janet's friend Donna ends up shagging arrogant and laddish Gaz, eventually moving in with him. Completing the regular line-up is Janet and Donna's oddball friend Louise, a girl with a decidedly warped perspective on the world. Throw in Donna's slutty mother Flo, Louise's Australian boyfriend David, Gaz's knuckle-dragging brother Munch and you've got a recipe for comedy that's not just politically incorrect but downright wrong. Fantastic!

Having begun life on BBC Two (the traditional home for comedy series on the BBC since it was launched in the 1960s), *Two Pints* was moved from its second series onwards to the more youth-oriented BBC Choice (which was rebranded as BBC Three shortly after). Virtually slaughtered by critics during its first season, the programme soon found its niche on BBC Three, rapidly earning a repeat run back on the terrestrial channel it had moved from. It's perfectly understandable why *Two Pints* alienates so many people, however. When it comes to comedy, most people in Britain are still unused to watching women swearing and find it quite distasteful. *Two Pints* positively revels in its crudity, giving an equal measure of the most unpleasant lines of dialogue to its female leads. A working-class sitcom in the great tradition, *Two Pints* makes no concessions to any audience members who may take offence at humour of the gynaecological or scatological kind. In so doing, writer Susan Nickson created a show that out-'grossed' practically every other programme in TV history. What other sitcom would ever have described how one of its characters burned off his excess pounds through months of dedicated masturbation (or as he put it, 'Gaz-turbation')?

The programme stretched the sitcom format in other ways, too. A flashback episode presented in the form of a musical showed 'How Janet Met Jonny', featuring lurid songs such as 'Can I Get a Blow Job?' and was craftily timed to take advantage of Will Mellor's recent victory in the first *Comic Relief Does Fame Academy*. The final episode of the fourth season ended on a cliffhanger, with Johnny having been shot by police due to a mistaken identity. Encouraged to take interactivity to a level normally reserved for talent contests like ***Pop Idol***, viewers were asked to vote to say whether Jonny should live or die. Thankfully for actor Ralph Little (***The Royle Family***), most people said they wanted more of the lovable layabout, and he consequently survived the shooting. However, producers weren't averse to toying with their viewers – season five began with a funeral, and for a while we believed Jonny to be dead. It was quickly revealed that it was Donna's mum Flo who had died, primarily as a direct result of actress Beverly Callard returning full time to ***Coronation Street***, where she played another character to whom the words 'mutton' and 'lamb' were familiar friends. This fifth season was supposed to be the last, but extremely high ratings led to a rapid decision by BBC Three to commission a sixth series for 2006.

2 Point 4 Children

Comedy | BBC One | episode duration 30 mins | broadcast 3 Sep 1991–30 Dec 1999

Regular Cast
Belinda Lang · *Bill Porter*
Gary Olsen · *Ben Porter*
Julia Hills · *Rona*
Clare Woodgate, Clare Buckfield · *Jenny Porter*
John Pickard · *David Porter*
Kim Benson · *Christine*
Alex Kew · *Declan*
Leonard O'Malley · *Gerry*
Ray Polhill · *The Biker/Angelo Shepherd*
Patricia Brake, Sandra Dickinson · *Tina*
Barbara Lott · *Auntie Pearl*
Roger Lloyd Pack · *Jake 'The Klingon' Klinger*
Liz Smith · *Bette, Aunt Belle*

Creator Andrew Marshall **Producers** Andrew Marshall, Richard Boden, Rosemary McGowan, Marcus Mortimer **Writers** Andrew Marshall, Paul Smith, Paul Alexander, Simon Braithwaite **Theme Music** Howard Goodall

Initially touted in the press as a British version of ***Roseanne***, *2 Point 4 Children* does bear a passing resemblance to that highly successful American series, in so far as it follows the life and adventures of a slightly dysfunctional family in a middle-class neighbourhood. Aside from that – and a vague similarity in appearance between Gary Olsen and *Roseanne*'s John Goodman – there's little to support that initial interpretation. If anything, *2 Point 4 Children* is more of a bed-fellow to Britain's own ***One Foot in the Grave*** (which was written by Andrew Marshall's former writing partner David Renwick), in that both shows depict ordinary families dealing with day-to-day events just a few degrees off-centre from our own normality.

Bill (short for Wilhemlina) and Ben (surely a deliberate reference to the ***Flower Pot Men***) Porter are a typical early-1990s married couple dealing with a typical set of issues. Bill works in a baker's shop with best friend man-mad Rona, and Ben runs his own business repairing

Kiefer Sutherland as Jack Bauer.

24

In the 1930s and '40s, children of all ages would be thrilled by adventure serials starring Buster Crabbe and Crash Corrigan. In *Flash Gordon*, ***Buck Rogers*** and many others, each episode would end with our hero trapped facing certain death from all sides and time running out. Jump forward to January 2002 and British viewers were about to see a drama series that had been sending viewers wild Stateside. *24* starred former teen badboy Kiefer Sutherland as Jack Bauer, the head of a counter-terrorism organisation called CTU, the events of one frantic day unfolded in real time, an hour an episode (although this included time for commercial breaks – its BBC transmissions were closer to 45 minutes). Events also took place simultaneously, or overlapped, so occasionally the screen would divide up to give us a catch-up on what was happening with other characters. None of this was what made this show special though. It was that it had been transmitted at all. After all, the first instalment concluded with a terrorist planting a bomb aboard an aeroplane and escaping just seconds before it exploded. That's not an easy sell for an audience still shell-shocked by the destruction of the World Trade Center just two months before.

Initially commissioned for just 13 of the 24 episodes that would make up the series, it's ever so slightly obvious in the first series that the producers were winging it a little, notably where Jack's wife Teri lost her memory (always a bad sign in drama) and the point where we – but not the characters – discover that Nina Myers, Jack's former lover and second-in-command at CTU, is actually a traitor operating under the codename 'Yelena'. But it's jaw-dropping moments like that that have helped *24* make the crossover from macho thriller into something much more arch and intelligent. Almost anything can happen within the next 60 minutes – and it usually does.

Each series represents a day in the life of Jack Bauer, so 'day one' is the story of how Jack saved a Presidential candidate but lost his wife; day two was the fight to prevent the detonation of a nuclear bomb in LA; day three, a race to contain a lethal virus. After three years, viewers became too familiar with the characters and locations, hence an almost complete recast, aside from Jack himself, heralded the fourth season.

David Palmer, like Bartlet in ***The West Wing***, represents the fantasy of a commander-in-chief who appears to have integrity, intelligence and a reputation for being incorruptible (qualities many would like to see more evident in the real world). That Palmer is also an African-American just extends that fantasy, at least while the Democrats struggle to get a white candidate elected.

24 benefited hugely in the UK from the digital TV revolution. BBC Choice broadcast a live 'post mortem' on the night of the final episode's transmission, with studio guests and an audience of fans (24 of them) debating the finale and the series as a whole. Choice became BBC Three by the time series two came around, and *24 Post Mortem* became *Pure 24*, a weekly, half-hour chat show broadcast live after each week's episode.

Having become the biggest 'watercooler' show on TV, it was a shame that a bidding war led to the third and subsequent seasons premiering on Sky One rather than BBC Two. With the audience now divided between satellite, home video and the hope that later series might eventually surface on terrestrial, *24* went from the most-discussed drama of 2002 to a near-guaranteed conversation-stopper in fear of spoiling the surprises ahead.

Drama
Imagine Entertainment for Fox Television (shown on BBC Two/Sky One)
Episode Duration: 45–60 mins
Broadcast: 6 Nov 2001–present (USA)

Regular Cast
Kiefer Sutherland · *Jack Bauer*
Leslie Hope · *Teri Bauer*
Elisha Cuthbert · *Kimberly Bauer*
Sarah Clarke · *Nina Myers*
Dennis Haysbert · *Senator/President David Palmer*
Carlos Bernard · *Tony Almeida*
Xander Berkeley · *George Mason*
Penny Johnson · *Jerald Sherry Palmer*
Karina Arroyave · *Jamey Farrell*
Richard Burgi · *'Alan York'/Kevin Carroll*
Mia Kirshner · *Mandy*
Rudolf Martin · *Martin Belkin, Jonathan*
Megalyn Echikunwoke · *Nicole Palmer*
Michael Massee · *Ira Gaines*
Glenn Morshower · *Aaron Pierce*
Vicellous Shannon · *Keith Palmer*
Eric Balfour · *Milo Pressman*
Jude Ciccolella · *Mike Novick*
Zeljko Ivanek · *Andre Drazen*
Misha Collins · *Alexis Drazen*
Paul Schulze · *Ryan Chappelle*
Dennis Hopper · *Victor Drazen*
Lou Diamond Phillips · *Mark DeSalvo*
Reiko Aylesworth · *Michelle Dessler*
Sarah Wynter · *Kate Warner*
James Badge Dale · *Chase Edmunds*
Jim Abele · *Ralph Burton*
Anthony Azizi · *Mamud Rasheed Faheen*
Billy Burke · *Gary Matheson*
Timothy Carhart · *Eric Rayburn*
Michelle Forbes · *Lynne Kresge*
Sara Gilbert · *Paula Schaeffer*
Laura Harris · *Marie Warner*
Skye McCole Bartusiak · *Megan Matheson*
Tracy Middendorf · *Carla Matheson*
Phillip Rhys · *Reza Naiyeer*
John Terry · *Bob Warner*
Harris Yulin · *Roger Stanton*
Francesco Quinn · *Syed Ali*
Daniel Dae Kim · *Agent Tom Baker*
Alan Dale · *Vice President Jim Prescott*
Lucinda Jenney · *Helen Singer*
Vincent Laresca · *Hector Salazar*
Zachary Quinto · *Adam Kaufman*
Mary Lynn Rajskub · *Chloe O'Brian*
Riley Smith · *Kyle Singer*
D. B. Woodside · *Wayne Palmer*
Joaquim de Almeida · *Ramon Salazar*
Geoffrey Pierson · *Senator/President John Keeler*
Andrea Thompson · *Dr Nicole Duncan*
Greg Ellis · *Michael Amador*
Julian Rodriguez · *Sergio*
Albert Hall · *Alan Milliken*
Jamie McShane · *Gerry Whitehorn*
Gina Torres · *Julia Milliken*
Lothaire Bluteau · *Marcus Alvers*
Michael Cavanaugh · *Joseph O'Laughlin*
Paul Blackthorne · *Stephen Saunders*
Alexandra Lydon · *Jane Saunders*
Anil Kumar · *Kalil Hasan*
William Devane · *James Heller*
Alberta Watson · *Erin Driscoll*

Creators Robert Cochran, Joel Surnow

Producers Various, including Ron Howard, Brian Grazer, Robert Cochran, Remi Aubuchon, Howard Gordon, Stephen Hopkins, Tony Krantz, Evan Katz, Joel Surnow, Kiefer Sutherland (executive), Bob Johnston, Chris Cheramie (associate), Michael Chernuchin, Gil Grant, Stephen Kronish (consulting), Jon Cassar, Robert P. Cohen, Paul Gadd, Robin Chamberlain, Michael Loceff, Andrea Newman, Cyrus Yavneh, Danielle Weinstock, Tim Iacofano, Michael Klick, Norman S. Powell

Writers Various, including Robert Cochran, Joel Surnow, Michael Loceff, Howard Gordon, Andrea Newman, Virgil Williams, Lawrence Hertzog, Michael Chernuchin, Maurice Hurley, Gil Grant, Elizabeth Cosin, Evan Katz, Duppy Demetrius, Stephen Kronish, Peter M. Lenkov

Theme Music Sean Callery

The Twilight Zone

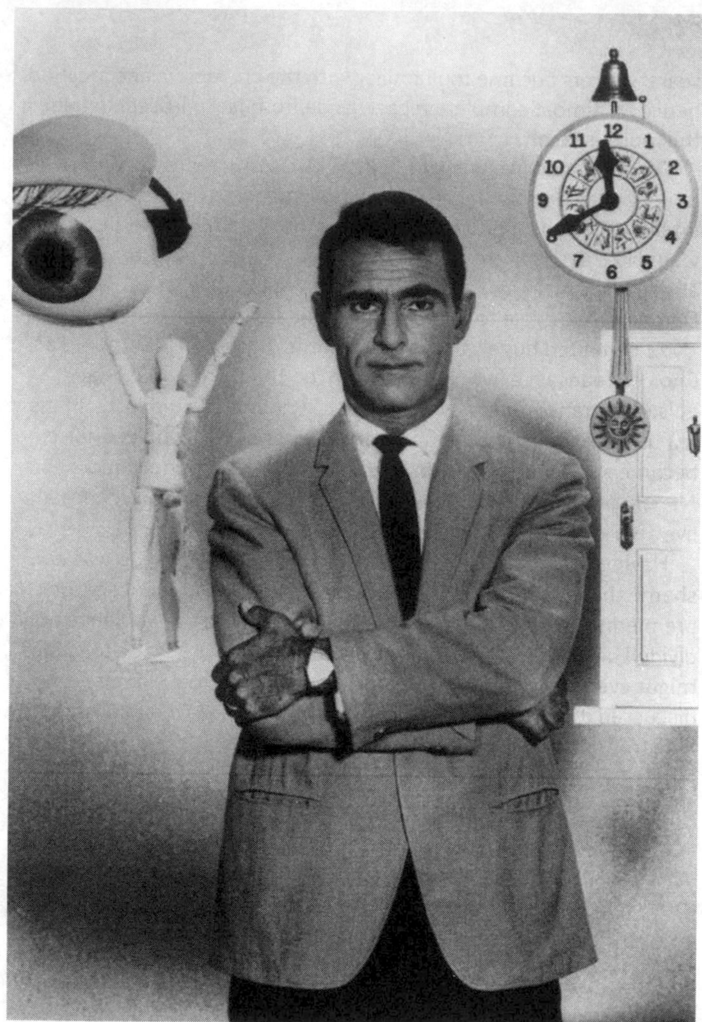

Rod Serling, accompanied by props from the title sequence of The Twilight Zone.

Witness Rod Serling, a husband, a father, a workaholic, 35 years old and with a track record in success. Short, unassuming with a featherweight boxer's physique and a heaving smoking habit. Rod Serling, whose power comes not from force, but from words. Words that can transport people across light years to meet aliens on another planet, or to the other side of the wall to spy on neighbours embroiled in a bitter fight that results only in losers. Rod Serling, gatekeeper to The Twilight Zone.

Such ominous introductions brought viewers together from across the globe in their admiration for one of the 20th century's greatest storytellers and creator of *The Twilight Zone*. One of the single most enduring TV shows of all time, *The Twilight Zone* had no regular cast except its narrator, no standing sets, no continuity of any kind. What it did have was the courage to treat its audience with intelligence and the skill to rarely disappoint them. And of the 156 episodes of the original series, 92 of them came from Serling.

A jobbing writer, Serling achieved early success with the teleplay *Patterns*, which had been broadcast live on two occasions before

Anthology
Cayuga Productions for CBS Television (shown on BBC Two)
Episode Duration: 25/50 mins
Broadcast: 2 Oct 1959–19 Jun 1964, 27 Sep 1985–15 Apr 1989, 18 Sep 2002–present

Regular Cast
Rod Serling · *Host (original series)*
Charles Aidman, Robin Ward · *Narrators (1985–1989 series)*
Forest Whitaker · *Host (2002 series)*

Creator Rod Serling

Producers Rod Serling (executive), William Self, Buck Houghton, Herbert Hirschman, Bert Granet, William Froug

Writers Various, including Rod Serling, Charles Beaumont, Richard Matheson, George Clayton Johnson, Montgomery Pittman, Earl Hamner Jr, Ray Bradbury, Jerry Sohl

Theme Music Everyone knows the theme tune to *The Twilight Zone* – it's hummed or whistled every time something strange happens in our lives. But Marius Constant's theme – plucked, undulating electric guitar strings, discordant brass and bongo drums – replaced the music used to introduce most of the first season's episodes, an ethereal tune written by much-sought-after film composer and regular Hitchcock collaborator Bernard Herrmann. A major element of the feel of the series was the title sequence that accompanied the music. In the beginning, the sequence consisted of a painting of an alien horizon puckered by ancient stone slabs, but from the second season it began to feature more surreal elements such as a swirling, hypnotic pattern, a doorway, a doll's eye opening like a flower, shattering glass, a ticking clock and an artist's mannequin.

being made into a film. But though Serling's writing was critically acclaimed and seemed to be popular with viewers, it wasn't so popular with the corporations that sponsored many of the productions. One of his scripts had the word 'America' changed to 'United States' and 'Lucky' switched for 'Fortunate' as the tobacco-producing sponsors were afraid viewers would be subconsciously encouraged to think of rival brands of cigarettes. Another had originally been a searing critique on a true case where the murderers of a young black boy were found not guilty by an all-white jury, but with changes to the script that included (but were not limited to) the removal of the words 'Coca-Cola' and 'lynch' because the sponsors felt they carried connotations that were too Southern, the end result was as anodyne as Serling's original had been courageous.

After another script had been butchered to the point where its political stance had been lost amid made-up motivations and legal terminology that bore no resemblance to reality, Serling realised that American TV at that time just wasn't the place for reality-based dramas and that he'd be better served if his stories were set in the realms of science fiction.

With science fiction still thought of as a dirty word, many had viewed Serling's move towards the genre as a career-ending act of folly. Certainly, when he first offered the series to CBS, in the form of a play called 'The Time Element', they paid him off and shelved the script with no intention to produce it. But then producer Bert Granet haggled with CBS to buy the script and subsequently produced it as part of the *Desilu Playhouse* series (an anthology vehicle for Lucille Ball and her husband Desi Arnaz). The story told of a man who describes to his psychiatrist a recurring dream where he tries to warn the people of Honolulu about the attack on Pearl Harbor. When the psychiatrist visits a nearby bar some time later, he sees a picture of the man on the wall and learns that he died in the Pearl Harbor attacks in 1941. Such an eerie open-ended conclusion proved unsatisfactory for the sponsors, who insisted that the play should have a proper ending. Though a compromise was reached by having Desi Arnaz himself step in at the end to offer viewers his own explanation (that the psychiatrist had been to the bar some time before, noticed the photo and subsequently had a dream about it), one critic reportedly responded with 'GO HOME, DESI!' He wasn't alone – critics across the country loved 'The Time Element' for its quirkiness and CBS soon realised their mistake in not producing the play themselves. Promptly they commissioned Serling to write a pilot script for his idea, which he called *The Twilight Zone*, an umbrella title for stories of imagination and from another dimension.

Each episode would involve an ironic twist at some point, usually the end. But what marked *The Twilight Zone* from its competitors was that many of the outcomes were not the standard morality play that audiences had come to predict. In Serling's universe, bad things happen to people, with many an episode closing with a worryingly cruel resolution. 'Time Enough at Last', from the first season, introduces us to Henry Bemis, a near-sighted bank teller whose bullying wife bans him from pursuing his only true love – reading books. Hiding inside the bank vault to sneak in a few chapters of a book during his lunchtime, Bemis is protected from a massive explosion that devastates the city above, killing everyone. As Bemis explores the ruins, he comes across the city library and realises that no-one is left to stop him reading every book every written – but then his glasses fall from his face and shatter. Left almost blind without them, he sobs, 'It's not fair,' to which we can only say, 'Amen.' Another Serling classic sees James Corry, a convicted murderer, exiled to a distant asteroid. Every three months a supply ship lands to bring him the essentials, but its captain, convinced of Corry's innocence, often brings him little items to keep him sane, and one such gift comes in the form of an android (played by a young Jean Marsh), almost completely human in appearance and capable of displaying emotion. Inevitably, Corry falls in love with the android and when the captain returns unexpectedly with news of an official pardon, his joy is short-lived when he's told that due to weight restrictions, the android must stay behind . . .

The idea of having Serling himself top and tail the shows with narration came at a late stage in the development of the series. Westbrook Van Voorhis had been hired for the pilot episode because of his narration for newsreel documentaries and series like *The March of Time*, but his approach was felt to be too pompous. Orson Welles was put forward as a possible name, but when reality struck with the realisation that they'd never be able to afford his fee, Rod Serling stepped in. Rod's delivery was a mass of contradictions. For the first series, he narrated through a voice-over, his slow and articulate delivery purring with seductive ease. However, when the decision was taken to bring him in vision, viewers saw for the first time how he spoke through almost clenched teeth and with a body language that suggested tension and discomfort. The truth is, Serling was filled with terror each time he was called on to stand before the camera. The directors began employing numerous tricks to help him relax, including letting him smoke during the presentation and even catching him off-guard with rehearsals that were anything but. As the production team learned how to work around Serling's nerves, they began to experiment with ways to introduce him: after the first scene, for example, the camera would pan to one side to reveal him standing just out of sight of the characters, or, in one notable episode, 'Nervous Man in a Four Dollar Room', standing at right angles to the room, feet fixed to the wall (a shot achieved by shooting Serling against a back-projection of the room shot from above).

Though Serling wrote around 80 per cent of the episodes, a couple of other writers racked up a fair share of the remainder, among them Richard Matheson. Matheson's 'Little Girl Lost' was inspired by an incident with his own daughter where he couldn't find her one night because she'd fallen between her bed and the wall. *The Twilight Zone* version played upon every parent's fear of being separated from their child, except in this instance the cause is a gateway into another dimension (the episode, which inspired the film *Poltergeist* (1982), was famously parodied by ***The Simpsons*** in a sequence where a scientist explains how Homer has left his normal two-dimensional world and stepped into a theoretical 'third' dimension).

By 1963, *The Twilight Zone* faced a challenge from ***The Outer Limits***, a similarly sci-fi-orientated anthology series put together by Joseph Stefano, author of *Psycho* (1960). Boasting a whole hour of mystery and suspense, but with a greater reliance on aliens and monsters, the newcomer was perceived by studio execs as a serious threat to Serling. For its fourth series then, *The Twilight Zone* mimicked its competitor in switching to an hour-long format (it also lost the '*the*' from its title). The experiment was not a success and for the show's final year it reverted back to the half-hour format. With Serling's original producer long gone, and with a widely held suspicion that the switch to hour-long episodes had damaged the show irreparably, few people were surprised when the fifth season became its last. Still, after five years it was nevertheless capable of conjuring up some all-time greats, the most famous of which is undoubtedly 'Nightmare at 20,000 Feet' in which a passenger on a plane (played by a pre-***Star Trek*** William Shatner) spends a terrifying flight catching glimpses of a hideously woolly gremlin ripping off sections of the wing.

Domestic violence is the subtext of 'What's in the Box?', in which a TV repairman (played by Sterling Holloway, the voice of Disney's Winnie the Pooh) decides to teach an abusive husband a harsh lesson. The conclusion to the play is actually revealed just before the mid-point ad break, courtesy of the couple's prophetic TV set. This serves to make the second half a sadistic tease as we're led to hope for a happy resolution, or at least a hugely ironic alternative, only for the spooky TV set's tragic prediction to come true as the wife accidentally falls backwards through the apartment window to her death. Having already seen the TV's vision of the husband sentenced to death in the electric chair, we don't need to be shown any more.

Although the series continued to pull in ratings, the network was constantly looking for ways to keep the budget down almost as hard as Serling and his team were dedicated to spending it as creatively as possible. Six episodes of the second series had been made on videotape instead of film to bring down costs and things were no better by the show's final year. With such concerns on his mind, producer William Froug decided to save money by buying the rights to a French film called *An Occurrence at Owl Creek Bridge*, about a Confederate soldier about to be hanged, who miraculously escapes only to discover his flight has been one last fantasy before his execution. Almost entirely silent, apart (conveniently enough) from a few lines of an English ballad, the film was trimmed down and given the customary introduction from Serling. The original French version went on to win the Academy Award for Best Short Film.

The anthology format wasn't created for *The Twilight Zone* (indeed, ***Alfred Hitchcock Presents*** pre-dates it by four years – and even that wasn't the first), and though Rod Serling's creation remains by far the best known, a few honorary mentions should go to a couple of forgotten examples of the genre that were produced in the UK around the same time: ITV's ***Out of this World*** had as its presenter Boris Karloff, an inspired choice. The BBC responded with ***Out of the Unknown***, which ran for four seasons on BBC Two between 1965 and 1971.

By *Twilight Zone*'s close, Serling was a bona fide celebrity. While trying to pitch new ideas to different TV stations, he accepted the job of hosting *Liar's Club*, a TV panel game in which two contestants had to work out which of four celebrities was telling the truth in offering their explanation for the purpose of an unusual object. Though his later anthology series, *Rod Serling's Night Gallery*, was inspired by an original movie of his and still bore his name, he found he had little control over the way the show evolved. He grew increasingly frustrated as his own scripts were rejected by producers in favour of material he felt was too like everything else out there. But tied by a contractual obligation, he continued to host *Night Gallery* until its cancellation in 1972. Serling died in June 1975 after complications during a coronary by-pass operation.

Steven Spielberg got his first TV break directing a segment for the original *Night Gallery* movie. By 1981 he was the biggest name in Hollywood thanks to a series of hit movies including *Close Encounters of the Third Kind* (1977) and *ET: The Extra-Terrestrial* (1982). Thanks largely to his efforts, science fiction was no longer the dirty word it had been when Serling first pitched *The Twilight Zone*. He'd longed to make something in the same vein as Serling's show, and in 1983 Spielberg collaborated with John Landis, Joe Dante and George Miller on *The Twilight Zone – The Movie*. The film consisted of four different stories, three of which were adaptations of original *Twilight Zone* episodes – 'Kick the Can', 'It's a Good Life' and 'Nightmare at 20,000 Feet' (with John Lithgow stepping into William Shatner's shoes as the petrified aeroplane passenger). Possibly as a result of this, the mid-1980s saw a revival in the anthology series, facing competition from *Alfred Hitchcock Presents* – new scripts framed by 'colorised' introductions from Hitch's original episodes – as well as from Steven Spielberg's own ***Amazing Stories***, a rather blatant attempt to do '*Twilight Zone*-lite'. Only *Alfred Hitchcock Presents* would go past two series, and *The Twilight Zone*'s second run was only commissioned to bump up its episode count in order to make it more suitable for syndication.

Fortunately, trends come around again and again. *The Outer Limits* re-appeared in 1995, followed by yet another *Twilight Zone* revival in 2000, which suggests there's life in the anthology series yet. As with many of the American shows we feature in this book, *The Twilight Zone*'s place in history might well have been assured anyway, but it was certainly confirmed thanks to repeat runs and syndication in the US. Despite newer episodes to tease and tantalise us with, Rod Serling's originals continue to pop up as late-night schedule fillers on BBC Two and satellite/cable channels while an impressive series of digitally re-mastered DVD box-sets are currently available in the USA.

TRIVIA

Theme park freaks can experience a real-life version of *The Twilight Zone* in the Disney-MGM Theme Park, part of Walt Disney World Resort in Orlando, Florida. This attraction – The Twilight Zone Tower of Terror – takes you on a ride up a haunted lift shaft into the upper reaches of an 'abandoned hotel' before plunging back down to earth faster than gravity. The pre-ride introduction is provided by a holographic representation of Rod Serling, and you're guaranteed to have your heart in your mouth for the duration of the ride ... along with your intestines, too.

Twin Peaks

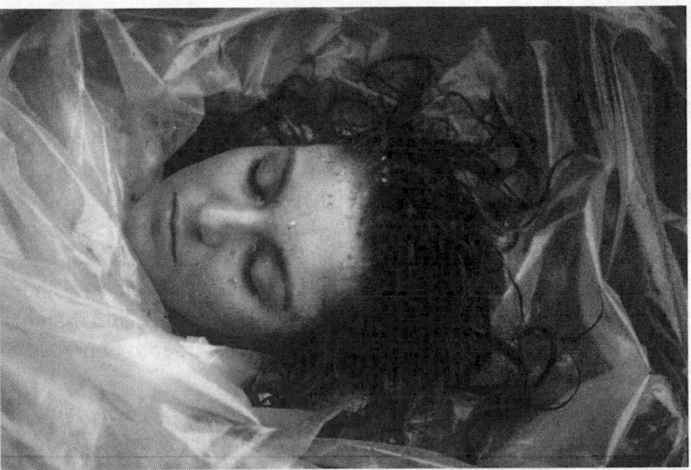

Laura Palmer (Sheryl Lee) – wrapped in plastic

In the small logging town of Twin Peaks (population 51,201 – located in the Pacific North West of the USA), life seems idyllic. There's little crime, the residents keep themselves to themselves, and the scenery is breathtaking – until one day, the town's beautiful prom queen is found murdered and wrapped in plastic. Thus began one of the great television cult successes, a soap opera masquerading as a drama series, with the added extra spice of horror and fantasy elements thrown in. In the early 1990s, millions of people around the globe were enraptured by the mystery of just who killed Laura Palmer . . .

The central character in *Twin Peaks* was quirky FBI Special Agent Dale Cooper, a man whose oddball perspective on life both captivated and confused the local law enforcement officers. As Cooper's investigations gather pace, the façade of happiness and normality presented by the town of Twin Peaks seems to crumble away. Soon it becomes clear that Laura wasn't the golden girl she was supposed to be – in fact, she had posed for pornographic magazines and had a cocaine habit. Cooper's search for possible suspects in Laura's murder turned up dozens of people with a motive for silencing her: violent drug dealer Leo Johnson, her lover James Hurley, her boyfriend Bobby Briggs, her infatuated psychiatrist Dr Jacoby, local hotel owner Ben Horne, even the town's medic Dr Hayward. But gradually Cooper began to focus his investigations on two individuals – a travelling shoe salesman with one arm called Mike Gerard, and a mysterious lank-haired, denim-clad demonic figure known only as 'BOB'.

When *Twin Peaks* first burst onto our TV screens, it was billed as a strange murder mystery from noted movie director David Lynch, the warped genius behind such films as *Eraserhead* (1977) and *The Elephant Man* (1980). *Twin Peaks* appeared to follow a similar narrative path to Lynch's most recent movie *Blue Velvet* (1986), which also portrayed the slimy underbelly of the small town American Dream. However, *Twin Peaks* was always supposed to be much more than just a murder mystery. In fact, Lynch (and co-creator Mark

Soap/Horror/Drama
Lynch/Frost Productions for ABC (shown on BBC Two)
Episode Duration: 50 mins
Broadcast: 8 Apr 1990–10 Jun 1991 (USA)

Regular Cast

Kyle MacLachlan · *FBI Special Agent Dale Cooper*
Michael Ontkean · *Sheriff Harry S. Truman*
Mädchen Amick · *Shelly Johnson*
Dana Ashbrook · *Bobby Briggs*
Richard Beymer · *Ben Horne*
Lara Flynn Boyle · *Donna Hayward*
Ray Wise · *Leland Palmer*
Sherilyn Fenn · *Audrey Horne*
Warren Frost · *Dr William Hayward*
Peggy Lipton · *Norma Jennings*
James Marshall · *James Hurley*
Everett McGill · *'Big Ed' Hurley*
Jack Nance · *Pete Martell*
Kimmy Robertson · *Lucy Moran*
Joan Chen · *Josie Packard*
Piper Laurie · *Catherine Packard Martell*
Grace Zabriskie · *Sarah Palmer*
Eric DaRe · *Leo Johnson*
Harry Goaz · *Deputy Andy Brennan*
Michael Horse · *Deputy Tommy 'Hawk' Hill*
Sheryl Lee · *Laura Palmer/Madeleine Ferguson*
Russ Tamblyn · *Dr Lawrence Jacoby*
Gary Hershberger · *Mike Nelson*
Don S. Davis · *Major Briggs*
Mary Jo Deschanel · *Eileen Hayward*
David Patrick Kelly · *Jerry Horne*
Wendy Robie · *Nadine Hurley*
Chris Mulkey · *Hank Jennings*
Ian Buchanan · *Richard 'Dick' Tremayne*
Catherine E. Coulson · *Margaret Lanterman, The Log Lady*
Miguel Ferrer · *FBI Agent Albert Rosenfield*
David Lynch · *FBI Regional Bureau Chief Gordon Cole*
Charlotte Stewart · *Betty Briggs*
Michael J. Anderson · *Mike, 'The Man from Another Place'*
Frank Silva · *BOB*
Victoria Catlin · *Blackie O'Reilly*
Heather Graham · *Annie Blackburn*
Al Strobel · *Mike Gerard, The One-Armed Man*
John Boylan · *Mayor Dwayne Milford*
Dan O'Herlihy · *Andrew Packard*
Robyn Lively · *Lana Budding Milford*
Walter Olkewicz · *Jacques Renault*
Michael Parks · *Jean Renault*
David Duchovny · *Agent Dennis/Denise Bryson*
James Booth · *Ernie Niles*
Kenneth Welsh · *Windom Earle*

Frost) originally intended that Laura Palmer's murderer would never be found, the plan being for the discovery of her body to merely be the catalyst to the rest of the series' plotlines. However, both the media and the general public instantly latched onto the concept of the murder mystery (a much 'safer' genre to the public than the twisted fantasy-tinged soap opera that surrounded the murder plot), with theories being swapped left, right and centre by eager fans. Viewers would tune in religiously to watch each new episode, ready with their 'damn fine' cups of coffee and slices of cherry pie (as consumed with eager glee by Cooper in Twin Peaks' Double R Diner). Fans would swap theories as to the identity of the killer, and many would record and re-watch the episodes later in order to hopefully find any clues left by Lynch and Frost.

As the first season of eight episodes drew to a close, it seemed that Dale Cooper was beginning to close in on the identity of Laura's killer. The crime scene had been located and additional clues had been gleaned from the strange 'Log Lady'. However, a multiple-cliffhanger ending to the season left Cooper at the receiving end of three bullets, Catherine Martell seemingly burned to death in her sawmill, Laura's father Leland suffocating one of the main suspects, and glamorous Audrey Horne trapped in her father's brothel having to fend off paternal amorous advances.

When the second full-length season of *Twin Peaks* began, viewers were caught in an impossible situation – many wanted to see the resolution of the main mystery, but equally didn't want to lose the most gripping part of the programme. Producers faced a similar dilemma – would the programme survive once the primary storyline had been resolved? Eight episodes into the second series, the true killer of Laura Palmer was revealed, in the most unpleasant and horrifying sequence ever recorded for a TV drama. Laura's cousin Maddy, who had been staying with Leland and Sarah Palmer to help them come to terms with their horrible bereavement, had been having terrifying dreams of a man with long straggly hair, clad in denim. One day, Maddy discovers who (and what) this mysterious figure is – her uncle, Leland. Suddenly realising that it was, in fact, Leland who raped and murdered his own daughter, Maddy tries to flee, but isn't quick enough. In brutal slow motion, Leland beats up his niece, all of the time his visage flicking back-and-forwards between his normal face and that of the killer, BOB. Shortly, there is a second corpse from the Palmer household, and it's only Maddy's disappearance that finally leads Cooper to the murderer.

In prison, Cooper realises the true horror of what happened to Leland – he's been possessed by an evil spirit called BOB, an entity based in a mysterious multi-dimensional space called the Black Lodge. BOB then takes his final possession of Leland and forces him to commit suicide. BOB's spirit escapes back to the Black Lodge, and Leland dies in Cooper's arms, truly horrified at the evil he has been forced to commit and – finally – being welcomed into the afterlife by his daughter.

With the mystery of Laura's death now solved, Cooper remains in Twin Peaks, to answer charges that he acted illegally in his

Creators Mark Frost, David Lynch

Producers Mark Frost, David Lynch (executive), David J. Latt, Robert Engels, Gregg Fienberg, Harley Peyton, Robert D. Simon

Writers Mark Frost, David Lynch, Harley Peyton, Robert Engels, Jerry Stahl, Barry Pullman, Scott Frost, Tricia Brock

Theme Music 'Falling' by Angelo Badalamenti

investigations into Laura's death. Sadly, in the next eight to ten episodes, events seem to stall somewhat. Just as the producers feared, audiences seemed less interested in the other ongoing plotlines than they had been in the murder of Laura Palmer, and viewers drifted away as the programme itself began to appear rudderless. Some critics had viewed the first series of *Twin Peaks* as an exercise in artisitic masturbation – weirdness for weirdness' sake, with few characters or storylines ever evolving into a coherent whole. The promise that 'the next episode will explain it all' never seemed to materialise and, as the second series drew to a close (with Lynch seemingly away working on other projects), many people began to accuse *Twin Peaks* of suffering from 'Emperor's New Clothes' syndrome, and dismissed it as a load of old cobblers.

In hindsight, there is some merit in these claims – particularly when it comes to that second season. Some storylines that had been introduced to maintain viewers' interest were so dull and unmemorable that it's hardly surprising that ratings plummeted. Furthermore, the lack of any real clarity to the exposition provided in the few interesting episodes left even the brightest of viewers scratching their heads. Did Leland know he'd murdered his own daughter? Was BOB real? Could characters really dream about the future? And just what significance did the backwards-talking dancing dwarf have to *anything*?

Having said that, there is much to enjoy and relish with *Twin Peaks*. When the storylines began to gather pace towards the end of the second (and final) season, the programme once again became unmissable viewing. Cooper's investigation into the supernatural occurrences around the town leads him to the Black Lodge and a meeting with the spirits of Laura, Leland and BOB. As the series ends, Cooper returns to the real world – but his soul has been left there, and BOB has hitched a lift back to Twin Peaks . . .

Twin Peaks' real legacy was enormous. First it broke the mould of 'precinct-based' prime-time drama series on US television, paving the way for the equally radical (but far more successful) ***The X Files*** shortly afterwards (note an early TV appearance in *Twin Peaks* by *The X Files'* David Duchovny, playing a transvestite). Second, it actively encouraged what we now call 'water-cooler TV' – for a few months back in 1990/1, *Twin Peaks*, its catchphrases and characters were pop culture icons. Everybody had to have their own theory as to who Laura Palmer's killer was. Personally, we thought it was Donna's father; he was just far too nice to be innocent! Finally, it proved that it was possible to have intelligent programming on American network television – even though at times *Twin Peaks* took things just a little bit too far.

TRIVIA

One of the most memorable elements of *Twin Peaks'* success is the haunting theme music, a melancholic orchestral piece that seems to sum up the programme's tragedy and beauty in one perfect piece of music. Composer Angelo Badalamenti had worked with David Lynch previously on *Blue Velvet*. In several sequences in the programme, a female singer performing heart-rending ballads was required. Unable to track down anyone suitable, Lynch's secretary Julee Cruise offered to step in and perform herself, thereby getting herself a recording career in the process. Cruise's vocals – deliberately performed with an air of 'heroin chic' about them – are particularly memorable in tracks such as 'Rockin Back Inside My Heart' and 'Into the Night', tunes performed in the series at especially dramatic moments.

***Twin Peaks*' real legacy was enormous: for a few months back in 1990/1, its catchphrases and characters were pop culture icons.**

The Two Ronnies

Ronnies Corbett (left) and Barker (right).

For more than 15 years, the annual series of songs, sketches and occasional satire from *The Two Ronnies* was an eagerly awaited treat, the kind of apparently effortless light entertainment that was a staple of the schedules in the 1970s and 1980s. It's not an exaggeration to say that aside from ***Morecambe and Wise***, Messrs Corbett and Barker are just about the most popular double-act ever seen on British television, a reputation that's entirely justified, as a recent season of repeats on the BBC has demonstrated to viewers both old and new.

Edinburgh native Ronnie Corbett (the shorter one) began his TV career on editions of ***Crackerjack*** in the late 1950s. He had worked alongside comics like Jimmy Tarbuck and Dickie Henderson before joining David Frost on his seminal 1960s satire *The Frost Report*. There, he first worked alongside Bedford-born Ronnie Barker (the taller one), who had enjoyed early TV success opposite Michael Bentine and Jimmy Edwards before joining David Frost's comedy troupe. *The Frost Report* ran for two years from 1966 to 1967 and was also the show that featured the famous 'I am upper class – I look down on him. He is middle class . . .'/'I know my place!' sketch, in which Ronnie Barker and Ronnie Corbett were joined by future Python John Cleese. When the comedy-focused *Frost Report* changed channels (to ITV) and mutated into a more serious chat show called *Frost on Sunday*, there was still space within the format for occasional comedy interludes, which were still performed by Barker and Corbett. Spotting the potential of the double-act, BBC bosses lured the duo back to the corporation for their own series.

The two Ronnies were unlike most other comedy double-acts, in so far as there was never simply one straight man and one funny man – both Corbett and Barker were equally funny and would take it in turns to provide either the punchlines or the feeds. Each show would open up with the two presenters seated behind a newsreader-style desk. They would go on to inform viewers what was coming up

Comedy
BBC One/Two
Episode Duration: 45–50 mins
Broadcast: 10 Apr 1971–25 Dec 1987, 16 Jul 1999, 18 Mar–22 Apr 2005

Regular Cast
Ronnie Barker, Ronnie Corbett

Producers James Gilbert, Beatrice Ballard (executive), Sam Donnelly, Terry Hughes, Michael Hurll, Paul Jackson, Ben Kellett, Marcus Mortimer, Marcus Plantin, Brian Penders, Peter Whitmore, Bill Wilson

Writers Various, including Gerald Wiley (Ronnie Barker), Michael Palin, Terry Jones, John Cleese, Graham Chapman, Eric Idle, Tim Brooke-Taylor, Ian Davidson, Peter Vincent, Spike Mullins, David Nobbs, Barry Cryer, David Renwick, Dick Vosburgh, David McKellar, Garry Chambers, Spike Milligan

Theme Music If one man could be said to be responsible for the sound of the BBC in the 1970s, it was Ronnie Hazlehurst, the genius behind this title tune and dozens of others.

'in a packed programme' (a list of fake items and guests) followed by a few brief 'news headlines' – again, quips or wordplays based around the traditional format of a news report. Then, it was straight into the main body of the programme, a collection of sketches and monologues that fizzed with top-notch comedy writing, provided from a wide pool of authors. Sketches often took place in the middle-class environments like cocktail parties or restaurants, neatly reflecting the status quo of the TV establishment and the aspirational aims of the viewers throughout the 1970s. Many sketches revolved around a bewildering variety of wordplay, confused conversations and even muddled quizzes in a game show. From the famous 'four candles'/'fork handles' sketch through to the similarly well-known send-up of ***Mastermind*** (where Ronnie Corbett's specialist subject is 'answering the question before last'), *The Two Ronnies* delighted to play with the conventions of language and consistently challenged and stretched its audience.

With punters still chortling, a musical interlude then followed. Regular guests tended to be female solo performers who either had already or were imminently due to appear in West End musicals – two of the most frequent and beloved performers were Elaine Paige and Barbara Dickson. Another regular feature of the show was an ongoing story, which would feature episodically across every instalment of a specific series. The most famous of these included the exploits of blundering detectives Charlie Farley and Piggy Malone in 'Stop – You're Killing Me!'; a sci-fi adventure set in a gender-swap future in which men wear frocks and women wear the trousers ('The Worm that Turned', starring Diana Dors as the brutally glamorous chief of police) and the Spike Milligan-authored Hammer Horror pastiche 'The Phantom Raspberry Blower of Old London Town'. These stories often ended in cliffhangers that would encourage viewers to tune in again the next week – would the Ronnies manage to shed their dresses in 'The Worm that Turned' or would yet another member of the aristocracy have been traumatised into insensibility by a especially vulgar raspberry?

Both Barker and Corbett were patently aware that although they had a hugely successful series as a comedy partnership, it would be prudent to be seen to be capable of solo comedy as well. To this end, every episode of *The Two Ronnies* featured sketches that allowed both men to blossom on their own. Ronnie Barker took the opportunity of portraying a series of outrageous characters, often a spokesman for a particular organisation or perhaps a political party. On the other hand, Corbett entertained viewers with his weekly 'shaggy dog story'. Sitting in a comfy chair, directly facing the audience, Corbett would take several minutes to tell a very brief joke, wandering all around the subject and often getting a few digs in about their alcoholic producer. For many viewers, Corbett's rambling jokes would either be the highlight of the programme or the moment to pop out and put the kettle on.

The final main sketch of each edition of *The Two Ronnies* was a large-scale musical number, often featuring Corbett and Barket taking alternate lines in a musical duet. One particularly amusing

TRIVIA

One person watching as a child who wouldn't have missed Corbett's monologues must surely have been ***Bo Selecta!*** maestro Leigh Francis – spot the similarities between Corbett and the latter's diminutive 'chat show host' the Bear; although we're pretty sure that Francis came up with the concept of the Bear's 'tail' popping out, rather than copying it from Ronnie C . . .

number had them participating in a ***Come Dancing***-style contest, with Corbett dressed in a frilly frock that made him look as if he'd fallen from the top of a Christmas tree. And then the two hosts would announce some more late-breaking 'news stories' before signing off with the unforgettable 'It's goodnight from me . . .' from Corbett, followed by '. . . and it's goodnight from him' by Barker.

Both performers were wise (and lucky) enough to star in other programmes at the same time that *The Two Ronnies* was being produced, largely due to a special deal made with BBC bosses that provided them with other avenues for their talents. Barker struck gold first, thanks to a series of comedy show pilots called *Six of One*. Two long-running shows came directly from this one brief run – 'Prisoner and Escort' was quickly fast-tracked into legendary prison sitcom ***Porridge***, and ***Open All Hours*** followed shortly after. Corbett was less lucky with his first few attempts at a sitcom – neither *Now Look Here . . .* nor *The Prince of Denmark* were a success. Finally in 1981, Corbett had a major hit on his hands, playing put-upon mummy's boy Timothy Lumsden in ***Sorry!***

By Christmas Day 1987, *The Two Ronnies* had clocked up 94 episodes across 12 full seasons and a number of highly successful specials. Then, seemingly without warning, Ronnie Barker decided that he'd had enough of life in the public gaze and announced his retirement from TV. Perhaps it wasn't very surprising – by that time, Barker was approaching his 60th birthday and wanted to spend more time with his wife and family. He opened up a small antiques shop and disappeared from our TV screens, only being tempted back to the world of acting for a straight role playing Churchill's butler in the 2002 drama *The Gathering Storm* (opposite Albert Finney). Gradually, Barker made more and more public appearances (including accepting a lifetime achievement award from BAFTA) until in early 2005 he and Corbett were reunited on BBC One for *The Two Ronnies Sketchbook*, a compilation show of the best clips from their old programmes topped and tailed by newly recorded footage. *The Two Ronnies Sketchbook* gathered highly satisfactory ratings and as a consequence a whole new generation of fans for their witty, heart-warming and memorable style of comedy.

***The Two Ronnies* delighted to play with the conventions of language and consistently challenged and stretched its audience.**

people's central heating, employing assistant Gerry (and later stroppy Christine). Daughter Jenny is a typical whining, complaining teenager, whereas younger son David is mostly too busy playing computer games or watching telly to care about his mum and dad's problems. Although Bill and Ben are deeply in love, an early crisis in the marriage comes when Bill meets a mysterious leather-clad biker. They meet several more times, with Bill beginning to fantasise about what might happen between them, until one day she hears the news that a biker matching his description has been killed in a traffic accident. Although Bill is initially upset, she soon realises that she could never have been unfaithful to her husband and is grateful that she enjoyed the brief possibility of a flirtatious affair.

One of the great things about *2 Point 4 Children* was the portrayal of realistic family relationships. At one point, characters would be shouting and screaming at each other – shortly afterwards, without any tedious saccharine apology or 'message of the week', the family would be seen functioning once again, just like real people do. In sharp contrast to this reality was the series' propensity to disappear into flights of bizarre fantasy at the drop of a hat. During Christmas episodes there would often be a song-and-dance number, and any episode featuring Ben's central heating rival, Jake the Klingon, would inevitably end up with a tribute to classic fantasy series – most memorably in an impressive pastiche of ***The Prisoner***, recorded, like Patrick McGoohan's classic sci-fi series, in Portmeirion, North Wales.

The addition of members of the extended family always added an extra frisson to episodes, including Ben's nauseatingly prissy sister Tina, Bill's mother Bette and Auntie Belle (both portrayed by incomparable character actress Liz Smith) and Windsor Davies as Ben's vulpine long-lost uncle. When daughter Jenny left home to go to university, Bill and Ben fostered charming young moppet Declan, and the series seemed set to continue into the new millennium.

Bill, Ben and their children helped to encourage the BBC's latest adult literacy series at one point – a testament to their popularity (regularly attracting audiences in excess of 12 million), and went out on a high with a Millennium special at the end of 1999. Sadly, towards the end of the series Gary Olsen was diagnosed with terminal cancer. He emigrated to Australia with his family for the last months of his life and finally died in September 2000.

Trivia

Clare Buckfield and John Pickard both have twin siblings who are also actors. Clare's sister Julie and John's brother Nick both starred in ***Hollyoaks***, and all four of them appeared in ***Grange Hill***.

Clare Woodgate effectively disappeared from acting after she auditioned unsuccessfully for a part in Mike Newell's 1995 film *An Awfully Big Adventure*. Woodgate was such a fan of the Beryl Bainbridge novel the film was based on that she reinvented herself as 16-year-old Liverpool actress Georgina Cates, re-auditioned and got the part. She only confessed to her deception well into the film's production (and indeed some of her fellow cast-members had no idea until shortly before the film's premiere). Though she dropped the Liverpudlian persona, she retained the name Georgina Cates for subsequent parts.

The Two Ronnies

See pages 792–4

UFO

Science Fiction | Century 21 Television/ITC for ITV | episode duration 50 mins | broadcast 16 Sep 1970–1 Apr 1971 (The transmission of UFO was inconsistent across the ITV regions, with many of them holding back the final episode for up to two years or more. Only Anglia showed the complete run in one go, and even then they slipped the last episode, 'The Long Sleep', to a late-night slot.)

Regular Cast

Ed Bishop · *Commander Ed Straker*
George Sewell · *Colonel Alec Freeman*
Michael Billington · *Colonel Paul Foster*
Peter Gordeno · *Captain Peter Carlin*
Gabrielle Drake · *Lieutenant Gay Ellis*
Wanda Ventham · *Colonel Virginia Lake*
Antonia Ellis · *Lieutenant Joan Harrington*
Keith Alexander · *Lieutenant Keith Ford*
Dolores Mantez · *Lieutenant Nina Barry*
Gary Myers · *Lieutenant /Captain Lew Waterman*
Grant Taylor · *General James Henderson*
Vladek Sheybal · *Dr Doug Jackson*
Norma Ronald · *Miss Ealand*
Harry Baird · *Lieutenant Mark Bradley*
Jon Kelley · *Lieutenant John Masters*
Jeremy Wilkin · *Lieutenant Gordon Maxwell*
Ayshea Brough · *Lieutenant Ayshea Johnson*
Georgina Moon · *Lieutenant Sylvia Howell*
Mel Oxley · *Voice of Space Intruder Detector*

Creators Gerry and Sylvia Anderson, Reg Hill **Producers** Gerry Anderson (executive), Reg Hill **Writers** Gerry and Sylvia Anderson, Tony Barwick, Ian Scott Stewart, Ruric Powell, Alan Pattillo, Alan Fennell, Donald James, David Lane, Bob Bell, David Tomblin, Dennis Spooner, Terence Feely **Theme Music** One of Barry Gray's funkiest compositions

Ed Straker is the head of Harlington-Straker, a film studio based in England. Harlington-Straker is also a cover for a military organisation called SHADO (Supreme Headquarters Alien Defence Organisation), which must remain hidden from public knowledge to prevent mass panic. Responsible for maintaining Earth's security against alien attack, SHADO has operatives beneath the sea in the submarine Skydiver, tank-like Mobiles that track down landed UFOs, an early warning surveillance satellite orbiting the Earth and a base on the moon that houses Interceptors, which can take out UFOs with nose-mounted missiles. But just as SHADO is a mission of survival, so too are the frequent raids by UFOs. The aliens are a dying race; they come to Earth to harvest humans for their internal organs.

Gerry Anderson left Supermarionation behind with his first live action series. Inspired in part by the feature film *Doppelganger* (1969), which his team had made the previous year, Anderson's *UFO* was set in the near future and, like ***Captain Scarlet***, took a much more serious approach than his earlier shows. In fact, the series was thought to be too adult, dealing in quite grim topics (in addition to the matter of organ theft, some episodes dealt with drug use and sex). As a consequence, *UFO* was relegated to a late-night slot in many ITV regions, with a couple of episodes effectively banned from repeat runs.

One of the most notable elements of *UFO* was the style and fashions. Female operatives working on the moon were kitted out in silver mini-skirts and purple wigs, while the collarless jackets, wing-hatch cars and portable phones add an attractive quirkiness to the production. With Anderson's Century 21 studios completely taken up by Derek Meddings and his crew, the model effects for *UFO* were the most impressive yet. Meddings' experiences on *Stingray* ensured that the Skydiver sequences were top notch, while the increased space available to his team meant that the models could be made at a larger scale than before, making them that little bit more convincing. Though the Interceptors are perhaps a little impractical, with their one-shot-and-your-out missiles fired from their nose cone, their potential for space battle is somewhat limited. But the UFOs themselves are simply gorgeous, shimmering, rotating craft accompanied by an undulating high-pitched whine.

As ever with Anderson productions, *UFO* had an energetic and instantly captivating title sequence, lots of fast cuts between shots of autopsies on green-skinned aliens, SHADO personnel in a variety of vehicles and a gratuitous ass shot of one of the SHADO ladies walking across a room. It sets the tone perfectly, as it hints at the great number of story options that the series will go on to explore: you have disaster stories set on board a submarine ('Sub-Smash') or on the moon ('Flight Path'); there's the possibility for chase sequences, with UFOs and interceptors playing cat and mouse ('Conflict'); SHADO's ethnically diverse staff would suggest an examination of racism in the military at some point ('Computer Affair'); and there are opportunities for human interest too.

It's in this last area that *UFO* really excels. Two episodes in particular give us insight into the difficulties that Ed Straker is forced to face when his work and his private life collide. In the flashback episode 'Confetti Check A-OK', we learn how Straker's marriage split up because security measures prevented Straker from telling his wife why he's been out all night. And one of the fan favourites, 'A Question of Priorities', sees Straker forced to choose between using a SHADO mobile to get life-saving medicine to his dying son or diverting the mobile to help capture one of the aliens. The devastating outcome has repercussions felt in a few later episodes.

Production on the series had to be halted due to the closure of MGM's Borehamwood Studios, at the time the largest studios in Britain. By the time new accommodation could be found at Pinewood, George Sewell had been called to his next project. His replacement came in the slightly sexier form of Wanda Ventham, re-creating Virginia Lake, a character first seen early on in the series. Many of the episodes made in the second production block are among the fan favourites, though they also have a tendency towards surrealism and plain weirdness that doesn't always sit comfortably alongside the generally gritty approach of the earlier batch.

While Anderson began planning a second series of *UFO*, with more focus on the moonbase personnel, he was told that the series had not performed well in the USA and as a consequence the series was to come to an end after just 26 episodes. Lew Grade instead ordered Anderson to take on a project for him, a detective series called ***The Protectors*** that would act as a vehicle for ***Man from U.N.C.L.E.*** star Robert Vaughn and Nyree Dawn Porter, who had been one of the principal leads in the BBC's ***The Forsyte Saga***. Anderson brought in Tony Anholt to play the third central character and proceeded to produce two successful series, despite loathing Robert Vaughn and not having that much interest in the concept. Thankfully, though, it wasn't too long before he and his team were back on familiar ground, as the ideas for series two of *UFO* evolved into a different programme entirely – ***Space: 1999***.

Ultraviolet

Drama/Horror | Channel 4 | episode duration 45 mins | broadcast 15 Sep–20 Oct 1998

Regular Cast

Jack Davenport · *DS Michael Colefield*
Susannah Harker · *Dr Angie Marsh*
Idris Elba · *Vaughan Rice*
Philip Quast · *Father Pearse Harman*
Corin Redgrave · *Dr Paul Hoyle*
Colette Brown · *Kirsty Maine*
Stephen Moyer · *Jack Beresford*
Fiona Dolman · *Frances Pembroke*
Thomas Lockyer · *Jacob Keanault*

Creator/Writer Joe Ahearne **Producers** Bill Shapter, Sophie Balhetchet **Theme Music** Sue Hewitt provided a gorgeously understated tonal piece.

Police Sergeant Michael Colefield is due to be best man for his friend Stephen until the latter goes missing on the night before the wedding, to the understandable distress of fiancée Kirsty (who also happens to be Michael's ex). Stephen's disappearance seems to be linked to a bizarre killing that's been captured on CCTV – a murder where the victim can be clearly seen, but the perpetrator is invisible. Slowly, the truth begins to dawn on Michael . . . that his friend has become a creature of the night. Michael is inducted into a secret government organisation, supported for centuries by the Vatican, determined to keep the 'leeches' under control. Leading the organisation is Father Pearse, backed up by a doctor and an ex-army man. Soon Michael is embroiled in a desperate attempt to discover what the enemy are up to, and why the established relationship of parasite and host may soon be under threat . . .

An astonishingly intelligent and sophisticated interpretation of the traditional vampire story, *Ultraviolet* never once talks down to its audience nor panders to the old-fashioned 'cloak and fangs' camp. In fact, the word 'vampire' is never once mentioned throughout the series – the bloodsuckers are normally referred to as a 'Code 5' ('V' of course being the Roman numeral for 5). With this programme writer/director Joe Ahearne created a modern horror parable ('horrable'?) in which vampires utilise the trappings of today's society to advance their cause, such as research into blood substitutes. As the series progresses, the human heroes realise to their horror that the vampires are finally beginning to work together in order to control threats to their food supply from things such as HIV/AIDS and global warming. Rising to the high quality of the scripts, the entire cast deliver top-notch performances, with guest star Corin Redgrave especially memorable as a sinister, imprisoned, Hannibal Lecter-style vampire. *Ultraviolet* stands as one of those rare instances where the audience was left eager for more – only six episodes were produced. It's a terrible shame that bosses at Channel 4 never saw fit to recommission such an innovative and intelligent programme for a second series. Rumours of an expanded American remake remain unfounded to date.

University Challenge

Quiz Show | Granada for ITV/BBC Two | episode duration 25–30 mins | broadcast 21 Sep 1962–1987, 1994–present

Cast

Bamber Gascoigne, Jeremy Paxman · *Quizmasters*
Jim Pope, Roger Tilling · *Announcer*

Creator Don Reid **Producers** Barrie Heads, Douglas Terry, Patricia Owtram, Peter Mullings, Kieran Roberts
Theme Music 'College Boy' by Derek New

Inspired by the American show *College Bowl*, created by Don Reid in 1959, *University Challenge* figured large in TV quiz show land for decades, challenged only by ***Mastermind*** for the title of television's most cerebral quiz. Two teams from different universities faced each other (despite how they were framed, they were not situated one above the other; that effect was achieved with split-screen). The fun for the viewer would always be to see an Oxbridge team thrashed by a group from a 'lower establishment'.

Each round begins with a 'Starter for Ten' points. The fastest person on the buzzer with a correct answer (and no conferring) wins control of the round for his or her team (an incorrect answer will incur a penalty of five minus points, meaning it's possible to finish with a negative score). The round then continues with three linked questions for five points each. Then the host returns to another Starter for Ten, and so on until a loud gong signals the end. Each challenge forms part of a series-long tournament.

The series took an enforced break between 1987 and 1995, and when it returned, Bamber Gascoigne had regenerated into Jeremy Paxman. Paxman's no-nonsense, belligerent approach was criticised at first, but his baiting of the elite rapidly became one of the main reasons to tune in ('Oh, *do* come on!'). The year 1999 saw the first series champions to come from the Open University.

University College, Oxford's 1987 team hold the record for highest score with 520 points, while the 1972 series saw the lowest ever score, with Sussex amassing just 10 points. According to statistics, you're most likely to be on a high-scoring team if you attend Trinity College, Cambridge, Durham University or the Open University.

Trivia
University Challenge was famously parodied by ***The Young Ones***, complete with an actual two-tier set to allow Vyvian (of Scumbag College) the opportunity to kick down into the lower tier while Neil frets about peeing on the head of Lord Snot (Footlights College, Oxbridge).

Website
www.blanchflower.org/uc/

The Untouchables

Crime Drama | Desilu/Langford for ABC (shown on ITV) | episode duration 50 mins | broadcast 20–27 Apr 1959, 15 Oct 1959–21 May 1963, 10 Nov 1991, 11 Jan 1993–22 May 1994

Regular Cast
Robert Stack · *Eliot Ness*
Paul Picerni · *Agent Lee Hobson*
Nicholas Georgiade · *Agent Enrico Rossi*
Abel Fernández · *Agent William Youngfellow*
Bruce Gordon · *Frank Nitti*
Steve London · *Agent Jack Rossman*
Frank Wilcox · *Beecher Asbury*
Jerry Paris · *Agent Martin Flaherty*
Chuck Hicks · *LaMarr Kane*
Anthony George · *Agent Cam Allison*
Jason Wingreen · *Captain Dorsett*
Robert Bice · *Captain Jim Hale Johnson*
Grant Richards · *Frankie Resco*
Oscar Beregi Jr. · *Joe Kulak*
Nehemiah Persoff · *Jake 'Greasy Thumb' Guzik*
Carl Milletaire · *Pete Konitz*
Walter Winchell · *Narrator*

Producers Quinn Martin, Jerry Thorpe, Leonard Freeman, Alan A. Armer (executive), Vincent McEveety, Del Reisman, Lloyd Richards (associate), Alvin Cooperman, Bert Granet, Paul Harrison, Roger Kay, Sidney Marshall, Del Reisman, Norman Retchin, Stuart Rosenberg, Charles Russell, Josef Shaftel **Writers** Various, including Jerome Ross, Robert C. Dennis, Joseph Petracca, Leonard Kantor, William Spier, David Z. Goodman, Harry Kronman, John Mantley, George Eckstein, Herman Groves, from the novel by Eliot Ness and Oscar Fraley **Theme Music** Nelson Riddle

In the time of prohibition, bootleggers and mobsters were rife; so was corruption within the law enforcement agencies. Only one small group of men seemed impervious to bribes and threats – the 'Untouchable' Eliot Ness and his men.

Although ostensibly based on the memoirs of the real Eliot Ness, this addictive and extremely violent crime series frequently exaggerated the man's success rate, crediting him with being responsible for the arrest of every big-shot gangster of the time. A fan favourite, though, was Frank Nitti, Al Capone's number two, who appeared in over a quarter of the episodes. *The Untouchables* TV series came out of an immensely popular two-part production for the Desilu Playhouse. It also marked the beginning of Quinn Martin's career as a producer of some of American TV's top-rated thrillers, including ***The Fugitive***, ***The Invaders*** and ***The Streets of San Francisco***.

Brian De Palma's lush film *The Untouchables* (1987) cast Kevin Costner as Eliot Ness, alongside Sean Connery, Andy Garcia and a scene-stealing Robert De Niro as Al Capone. Robert Stack played Ness once more for a 1991 TV movie, *The Return of Eliot Ness*, in which the stoical lawman joourneys back to Chicago to investigate the apparently mob-related murder of an old friend. A remake series ran for two seasons on American TV in 1993–4, with Tom Amandes starring as Eliot Ness.

Up Pompeii!

See pages 800–1

The Upper Hand

Sitcom | Central for ITV | episode duration 25–50 mins | broadcast 1 May 1990–7 Oct 1996

Regular Cast
Joe McGann · *Charlie Burrows*
Diana Weston · *Caroline Wheatley*
Honor Blackman · *Laura West*
Kellie Bright · *Joanna Burrows*
William Puttock · *Tom Wheatley*
David Atkins · *Pixie*
Lynda Baron · *Patricia Roberts*
Robert Beck · *Dan Thatcher*
Perry Benson · *Terry*
Patricia Brake · *Peggy Thatcher*
Roger Walker · *Jim Thatcher*
Tony O'Callaghan · *Paul Clark*

Creators Blake Hunter and Martin Cohan **Producers** Paul Spencer (executive), Christopher Walker **Writers** Various, including Blake Hunter, Colin Bostock-Smith, Robert Sternin, Prudence Fraser, Paul Robinson Hunter, Bud Wiser, Steve Curwick, Carrie Honigblum, Renee Phillips, Alan L. Gansberg, Seth Weisbrod, Renee Phillips, Carrie Honigblum, Robert Sternin,

Prudence Fraser, Ellen Guylas, Daniel Palladino, Gene Braunstein, Clay Graham, Claylene Jones, Michele J. Wolff, Richard Albrecht, Dawn Aldredge, Ken Cinnamon, Martin Cohan, John Donley, Phil Doran, Joe Fisch, Danny Kallis, Casey Keller, Sheldon Krasner, Adam Lapidus, David Lesser, Mona Marshall, Howard Meyers, Bob Rosenfarb, Mike Teverbaugh, Linda Va Salle, Barry Vigon, Karen Wengrod **Theme Music** Written by Debbie Wiseman, we'd not go so far as to say it actually was the theme from ***Knots Landing***, but compared side by side, the two are frighteningly similar.

Recycling plots form the American sitcom *Who's the Boss?* (which starred Tony Danza from ***Taxi***), *The Upper Hand* was a gender reversal comedy in which Caroline, a busy businesswoman, looks for a housekeeper but ends up with Charlie, a former football player, widowed and with a young daughter, Joanna. Putting aside her reservations about a male housekeeper, she's persuaded by her mother, Laura, to take on Charlie and allow him and Joanna to move in. Joanna and Caroline's son Tom don't always see eye to eye, but they soon notice what their parents seem to be avoiding – that despite their differences of opinion on almost everything, they're very much attracted to each other.

The plots weren't exactly groundbreaking in this very gentle of comedies, but what made it work was the genuinely likeable cast. Swapping his own Scouse accent for a London one, Joe McGann took on his first starring role (after a short stint in the ensemble cast of ***Rockliffe's Babies***) and won hearts as the perfect 'New Man', a perfectionist in the kitchen, a great dad and, as we later discover, an old romantic. Diana Weston faced a thankless task as the frosty Caroline, but viewers loved those moments when she thawed, especially when they added to the 'will-they, won't they?' ongoing story. The two juveniles were perfect moppets in the beginning (Kellie Bright had already had a taste of stardom in the final year of the children's comedy fantasy ***T-Bag***, and later appeared in prison drama ***Bad Girls*** as a lovelorn lesbian convicted of fraud), but the most experienced cast member was also its biggest scene-stealer – the divine Honor Blackman dominated every frame as the liberal swinger Laura and acted as a glorious reminder that women of a 'certain age' can be just as sexy as ever.

Upstairs, Downstairs

See pages 802–6

Lurcio (Frankie Howerd) gets an eye-full ...

Up Pompeii!

A sitcom written by one of the great masters of the quadruple entendre (for whom a mere *double* was never enough!) and starring the definitive instigator of the titter, *Up Pompeii!* was the closest thing that British TV had ever seen to a weekly *Carry On* movie. Frankie Howerd had already starred in one of Talbot Rothwell's groan-inducing movies, playing quack faith-healer Francis Bigger in *Carry On Doctor* (1968). Combining these two talents in a farcical frenzy was a gift sent from the Roman Gods themselves, creating a sitcom that not only tapped into the traditions of pantomime but also broke new ground in terms of blowing the conventions of TV comedy apart, Vesuvius style.

Frankie Howerd stars as Lurcio, sardonic slave to a wealthy Roman family living in the debauched city of Pompeii. Lurcio's master is the lecherous Senator Ludicrous Sextus, a man so used to playing away from home that he's forgotten where his own stadium is. Lurcio's wife Ammonia is similarly generous with her affections – a woman who'd have a reputation if it weren't for the fact that everyone else carries on in the same fashion. Completing the Sextus family is nubile young daughter Erotica and dopey son Nausius, a youth perpetually falling in love with yet another young beauty and setting down his feelings in an Ode. Constantly wandering in to predict death, destruction and disaster of all kinds, Senna the Soothsayer can be relied upon to throw an extra 'woe' or three into the mix. And all of the time, all Lurcio ever wants to do is to finish delivering 'the prologue' to the watching audience.

Comedy
BBC One/ITV
Episode Duration: 30–35 mins
Broadcast: 17 Sep 1969, 30 Mar–26 Oct 1970, 31 Mar 1975 (BBC), 14 Dec 1991 (ITV)

Regular Cast
Frankie Howerd · *Lurcio*
Max Adrian, Wallis Eaton, Mark Dignam · *Ludicrous Sextus*
Elizabeth Larner · *Ammonia*
Kerry Gardner · *Nausius*
Georgina Moon, Jennifer Lonsdale · *Erotica*
Jeanne Mockford · *Senna the Soothsayer*
Walter Horsbrugh, Willie Rushton · *Plautus*
Mollie Sugden · *Flavia*
Barbara Windsor · *Nymphia*
Lynda Baron · *Ambrosia*
Wendy Richard · *Soppia*
Lindsay Duncan · *Scrubba*

Creator Talbot Rothwell

Producers Michael Mills, David Croft, Sydney Lotterby (BBC), Paul Lewis (ITV)

Writers Talbot Rothwell, Sid Colin (BBC), Paul Minett, Brian Levenson (ITV)

Theme Music Alan Braden

Up Pompeii! was unique in so far as the audience watching the show – both at home and in the TV studio – were as much part of the programme as any of the other characters. Howerd's Lurcio talked directly to the audience throughout the episode, berating them for seeing double meanings in perfectly 'innocent' phrases and dragging them into his latest secret plan. This technique, known as 'breaking the fourth wall' of the studio, was later adopted by many other shows, from the hugely popular US drama series ***Moonlighting*** to the largely forgotten ***Sean's Show***. However, the technique actually owes a lot more to the traditions of pantomime, in which audience identification characters can often talk directly to the audience while other characters on stage remain completely oblivious to these discussions. Relishing his role as a Roman Widow Twankey, Frankie Howerd effortlessly held the audience in the palm of his hand – in short, there simply couldn't be an *Up Pompeii!* without Frankie's unique delivery (despite first appearances, all of the 'Ooohs', 'Aaahs' and 'Yes missus'es' were very carefully scripted in advance – again, in the grand tradition of pantos).

Following a successful pilot, only two short seasons of *Up Pompeii!* were broadcast – 14 episodes in total. Lurcio's adventures continued in one-off specials (both entitled *Further Up Pompeii!*) broadcast on BBC One in 1975, and then in December 1991 on ITV. Frankie Howerd also starred in two other *Pompeii*-style sitcoms for the BBC. In *Whoops Baghdad* (six episodes, shown in early 1973), Howerd once again addressed the audience as ever suffering Ali Oopla, servant to Derek Francis's Wazir. Then in 1982, Frankie recorded another six-part comedy called *Then Churchill Said to Me*, in which he played Private Potts, batman to the slightly incompetent Colonel Witherton (Nicholas Courtney). However, this series languished unseen in the BBC archives for more than ten years when the outbreak of the Falklands War meant it would be impossible to screen any kind of comedy based around war. *Then Churchill Said to Me* received its first screening on satellite channel UK Gold in 1993 before finally being screened on BBC Two in 2000 – eight years after Frankie Howerd's death.

Relishing his role as a Roman Widow Twankey, Frankie Howerd effortlessly held the audience in the palm of his hand.

Upstairs, Downstairs

Jean Marsh as house parlour-maid Rose Buck.

Upstairs, Downstairs was originally conceived by actresses Eileen Atkins and Jean Marsh as a possible comedy series about life among the servants in a Victorian country house, but they instead chose to turn their series into a drama, for which we should all be grateful. Going through a series of different potential titles (including *Behind the Green Baize Door, Below Stairs, Two Little Maids in Town, The Servants' Hall, That House in Eaton Square* and *165 Eaton Place*), the name *Upstairs, Downstairs* was finally coined during production of the first episode.

Events in the series revolve around the Bellamy family, who reside in a large house close to Buckingham Palace at 165 Eaton Place, in the heart of Belgravia. Upstairs live Conservative MP Richard Bellamy, his wife Lady Marjorie and their two children, the wilful and rebellious Elizabeth and the Bohemian playboy James. Downstairs are the family's servants – the dour Scottish butler Hudson, bullying cook Mrs Bridges, footman Alfred, kitchen maid Emily and parlour maids Rose and Sarah. Throughout five series, we follow the misadventures of both servants and masters as scandals and minor crises threaten to disturb the balance of life in Eaton Place. An early casualty of the harsh life suffered by working people in such houses is kitchen maid Emily, who commits suicide because she is forbidden to speak to her sweetheart. Replacing Emily is the 'nice but dim' Ruby, and, following the dismissal in disgrace of footman Alfred, the young and enthusiastic Edward joins the team.

Behind the scenes, the first series was made on a small budget and was not expected to be a major hit, scheduled at 10.30 p.m. on Sunday nights. Owing to an ITV strike, the first six episodes were taped in black and white. However, once the strike was over, the production team went back and re-recorded the first episode in colour to help boost sales of the programme to overseas markets. Two alternate versions of the end of the first episode exist – one leading into the next five black and white episodes, one linking directly to episode seven, the next colour instalment.

The most memorable servant in the first two seasons is Sarah, the rebellious part-time vaudeville performer whose life becomes intermingled with the family upstairs. Sarah falls in love with young rake James Bellamy and then (horror of horrors) finds herself pregnant by him. James is sent away to join the army in India throughout most of the second series, thereby avoiding much of the scandal that might have arisen with Sarah had he remained at home, though, in the event, the child dies soon after birth. Sarah eventually finds love in the form of the household's crafty new chauffeur Thomas, and when she falls pregnant again, the couple have to do some daring manipulation to financially secure their futures. Handing in his notice, Thomas reminds the Bellamys of all of the scandals he has helped to cover up for them (including a past indiscretion by Lady Bellamy), which Lord Bellamy deduces to be a veiled threat and offers to buy a car repair business – and the silence – for the wily pair in order to get them out of their lives forever. These characters – played by real-life husband and wife team Pauline Collins and John Alderton – would go on to star in their very own LWT series, *Thomas and Sarah*, which ran on ITV for 13 episodes from 14 January to 8 April 1979.

With Lord Bellamy in a prominent position in the government, Eaton Place would play a part in a number of the key historical events that marked the first years of the 20th century, reflecting, coping with and often bucking the strict and formal social mores that guided every facet of their lives. Lord and Lady Bellamy's daughter Elizabeth's wilful behaviour often shocked and scandalised her more conservative parents. Refusing to conform to their expectations, she falls in with a Bohemian crowd and, on a whim, marries fey artist Lawrence Kirkbridge, only to discover that his effete manner would mean their marriage would never be consummated. Instead, she allows herself to be seduced by her husband's friend, which results in the birth of a daughter. Trapped in a loveless marriage and unable to divorce lest she bring shame upon her whole family, Elizabeth never really settles down. She joins the suffragette movement (leading to a traumatic experience for Rose when she's wrongly sent to prison in her mistress's place) and takes another lover, only to find she is but one of the women he calls upon and has merely engaged her in romance to improve his political connections with her father. Tiring of English society and its ridiculously restrictive rules, Elizabeth emigrates to North America, a continent suitably large enough to contain her.

Times weren't always bad, however. In the most fondly remembered early episode of the series, the Bellamy household welcomes King Edward VII to dinner. While Lady Bellamy struggles to ensure the King is not cornered by some of her more boorish/boring guests, it's much more interesting to witness how delighted the 'Downstairs' staff were to put in huge amounts of extra work in honour of the King's visit. Seeing the servants exhausted but happy at the end of the dinner reveals more about the dynamic between the upper classes and their servants than any amount of documentaries ever could. Indeed, the one character in the series

Drama
Thames for ITV
Episode Duration: 50 mins
Broadcast: 10 Oct 1971–21 Dec 1975

Regular Cast
David Langton · *Richard Bellamy*
Rachel Gurney · *Lady Marjorie Bellamy*
Simon Williams · *James Bellamy*
Nicola Pagett · *Elizabeth Bellamy/Kirkbridge*
Gordon Jackson · *Angus Hudson*
Jean Marsh · *Rose Buck*
Angela Baddeley · *Mrs Kate Bridges*
Pauline Collins · *Sarah Moffat/Clémence/Clémence Délice*
Christopher Beeny · *Edward Barnes*
Evin Crowley · *Emily/Aoibhinn*
George Innes · *Alfred Harris*
John Alderton · *Thomas Watkins*
Jenny Tomasin · *Ruby Finch*
Patsy Smart · *Miss Maud Roberts*
Jacqueline Tong · *Daisy Peel/Barnes*
Meg Wynn Owen · *Hazel Forrest/Bellamy*
Lesley-Anne Down · *Georgina Worsley*
Hannah Gordon · *Virginia Hamilton/Bellamy*
Gareth Hunt · *Frederick Norton*
Karen Dotrice · *Lily Hawkins*
Ian Ogilvy · *Lawrence Kirkbridge*
Joan Benham · *Lady Prudence Fairfax*
Raymond Huntley · *Sir Geoffrey Dillon*
Celia Bannerman · *Lady Diana Newbury*
John Quayle · *Lord Bunny Newbury*
Keith Barron · *Gregory Wilmot*
Anne Yarker · *Alice Hamilton*
Jonathan Seeley · *William Hamilton*
Anthony Andrews · *Marquis of Stockbridge*

Creators Eileen Atkins, Jean Marsh

Producers John Hawkesworth, Rex Firkin

Writers John Hawkesworth, Alfred Shaughnessy, Jeremy Paul, Rosemary Anne Sisson, Fay Weldon, Anthony Skene, Terence Brady, Charlotte Bingham, Elizabeth Jane Howard

Theme Music The opening title waltz is called 'The Edwardians' by Alexander Faris. On some episodes, the closing music is called 'What are we Going to do with Uncle Arthur?' a music hall-style salso composed by Alexander Faris. Though it sounds very much of the period, the song was written especially for the series, with lyrics by Alfred Shaughnessy. The lyrics are hilarious and Pauline Collins gives it her all whenever required to blast it out.

that defends the structure of society more than any other is Hudson, a man who is proud to know his place and who is keen to ensure that everybody else knows theirs too. It's a testament to Gordon Jackson's portrayal of the uptight and authoritarian butler (which won him both a Royal Television Society and an Emmy award) that Hudson remains at heart still quite likeable. According to reports, Jackson himself had little time for the taciturn, class-obsessed authoritarian he portrayed.

The start of the third series saw the family reeling from tragedy when Lady Marjorie, on her way to visit Elizabeth in America, perishes on board the Titanic. Thrown into a period of shock and mourning, the household is kept together by the presence of Hazel Forrest, a young secretary working with Richard to help with the production of a family history book. Hazel's quiet efficiency and shy, middle-class demeanour appeals enormously to bored playboy James, and very quickly the couple fall in love and marry. The arrival of Hazel into the series neatly reflects the 'rise of the middle classes' being felt in British society at that time, and the discomfort felt in particular by the working classes about people getting 'above themselves'. One example of the way in which society was still able to stamp down on non conformist elements is shown in the episode when former footman Alfred makes a shock return to Eaton Place. Rose offers Alfred sanctuary in the house, unaware that Alfred is on the run, wanted by the police for the murder of his boyfriend. . . . Needless to say, Alfred's eventual fate is not hard to guess. Also confused about the changing nature of morality is Hazel, who discovers at an upper-crust country house weekend that the nobility has a very different set of morals from those adhered to by the 'lower' classes.

Halfway through the third series, two new characters joined *Upstairs, Downstairs*. Richard's ward Georgina Worsley arrives to live with the family, bringing a welcome air of enthusiastic youth and vitality to the stuffy household. Downstairs, new under-house parlour maid Daisy starts work, where her pretty face and nature soon attracts Edward's attention. Romance looms large in Rose's life too – for the first time she has an admirer, Australian sheep farmer Gregory Wilmot (***Duty Free*** actor Keith Barron delivering a great performance but a truly shocking Aussie accent!). Rose briefly considers emigrating to live on a vast Australian sheep farm, but she eventually decides not to join Gregory on his return voyage to Australia when she realises that she doesn't love him enough to abandon her life in London. Another relationship begins to sour when Hazel miscarries her first baby. James finds it impossible to express his feelings and heads out on the town with Georgina. Soon, James realises that he might have made a terrible mistake in marrying Hazel – not only is she 'beneath' him socially, but he begins to fall in love with Georgina too. As the third season draws to a close, Britain and its allies realise that war is brewing in Europe. Patriotic fervour sweeps the nation, and the Bellamy household is far from immune from its intoxicating spell.

With no love lost between himself and Hazel, James immediately re-enlists in the army and is quickly posted to the Front. As the

German armies move across Europe, thousands of ordinary families are displaced, and friend of the family Lady Pru (a marvellously fruity recurring performance from Joan Benham) persuades Hazel that they should temporarily look after a family of Belgian refugees. Hearing the story of German atrocities only hardens the hearts of the staff downstairs to do everything they can to support the war effort. Sick of being abused in the street for cowardice, Edward joins up. Rose eventually takes a part-time job as a 'clippy' on the omnibuses and even Ruby quits her job to work in a munitions factory (much to the dismay of Mrs Bridges, who bemoans the fact that she will have to undertake menial kitchen jobs herself). With the staff all gainfully employed in the war effort, Hudson tries to volunteer for armed service but is told that his age and poor eyesight make him unsuitable. Furious at being unable to do his bit, Hudson realises the best way to contribute is to become a special police constable, a role that still enables him to oversee the running of the house and ensure that the Master and his family are cared for. The Upstairs family do their bit too, with Georgina training to be an army nurse and Richard promoted to work at the Admiralty.

Gradually, enthusiasm for the war begins to ebb away as the true cost of battle begins to be felt. Rose's Australian beau is killed in action, Edward is invalided out of the army with shell-shock, and James is listed as missing presumed dead after the Battle of Passchendaele. The impact of these assorted incidents brings out the very best performances in the cast, especially in the astounding four consecutive episodes 'The Glorious Dead', 'Another Year', 'The Hero's Farewell' and 'Missing Believed Killed'. At a time when the world was still reeling from the aftermath of Vietnam, *Upstairs, Downstairs* managed to neatly convey to a modern audience the fact that they weren't the first generation to question the validity of war.

Some six years after the death of his wife, Richard finds love again in the form of beautiful widow Virginia Hamilton. As the war (and the fourth season) draws to a close, all appears well in the Bellamy household, with even James and Hazel now apparently reconciled to spending their lives together. However, happiness is short-lived when Hazel becomes ill and joins the ranks of the 'lost generation' as a victim of 'Spanish Flu' (which claimed the lives of 228,000 people in Britain in 1918–19). This drew to a close the magnificent fourth season of *Upstairs, Downstairs*, which is rightfully regarded by fans as the most consistent run of quality episodes in the programme's history.

When producer John Hawkesworth brought the programme back for a fifth season, he was determined that it should be the last. However, the management at London Weekend Television (LWT) were appalled at this decision; *Upstairs, Downstairs* was a huge international hit, both commercially and critically. It had won the BAFTA award for Best Drama Series in 1972 and 1974 (as well as being nominated in 1973), and had just been sold to the American Public Broadcasting Service network (leading to the programme winning a clutch of Emmy Awards for best Drama Series in 1976 and 1977, as well as nominations for Best Actress for Jean Marsh, Angela Baddeley and Jacqueline Tong). Curtailing a profitable and highly successful show seemed like madness to LWT bosses. However, Hawkesworth believed that it would be impossible to continue the story of a family and its servants into the economic depression of the 1930s. Hawkesworth made a concession to LWT and extended the fifth season to a whopping 16 episodes, which would cover the time period from 1919 through to 1930.

The final series begins with a period of great uncertainty for the household. With Hazel dead, James considers selling off the family home and moving on. It's only when Richard's new wife Virginia is persuaded to forget about the ghosts of unhappiness that taint 165 Eaton Place and make a home there for her and her children that the future of the servants is once again secured. Meanwhile, Georgina, along with many of her generation, is largely responsible for starting the 'Roaring Twenties' with her determination to forget about the horrors of war and simply party 'til she drops. In effect, the final series sums up the huge changes facing British society in the post-war years. Mrs Bridges finds it impossible to recruit subservient staff any more; Edward and Daisy temporarily find themselves living in poverty when there's no employment waiting for him back in Civvy Street. And, most notably, we follow James's search for a worthwhile career – something that previous generations of the young upper class would never have had to worry about. A brief dalliance with his father's chosen profession of politics ends in a noble failure, and his attempts to master the joys of aeroplane flight nearly lead to tragedy for both him and Virginia.

James finally confronts his infatuation with Georgina and proposes marriage, but when she rebuffs him, he petulantly rushes off to visit his sister Elizabeth in America (meanwhile Georgina falls in love with the handsome Marquis of Stockbridge and agrees to marry him). James finally returns from America in October 1929 a hugely wealthy man, having made a fortune on the stock market. He actively encourages Rose to invest the money she inherited after the death of her boyfriend in shares – a plan that disintegrates after the devastating Wall Street crash. Penniless, in debt to too many people and responsible for Rose being broke too, James commits suicide. For possibly the first time, our hearts go out to James, dying alone and off-screen in a boarding house, unwilling to leave the horrid task of cleaning up after him to anyone he knows. Typically, James' final act again results in his father having to pick up the pieces. Unable to pay his son's debts, Richard and Virginia are forced to sell 165 Eaton Place to satisfy the creditors.

Richard and Virginia move to a smaller house, with only Rose going with them to look after the children. Mr Hudson, Mrs Bridges and Ruby open a seaside boarding house, and Edward and Daisy go to work for Miss Georgina and her new husband. As the final items of the Bellamys' furniture are removed from 165 Eaton Place, Rose walks through the rooms, hearing the echoes of events long past before she shuts the door behind her and heads off to a new life.

Despite the period setting, *Upstairs, Downstairs* is not just a 'mums and aunties' programme – the 68 episodes are as hard-hitting, dramatic, funny and totally engrossing today as they have ever been.

TRIVIA

The part of Sarah was originally conceived and written with the intention that actress and series co-creator Eileen Atkins would play her, though when the programme finally came to be recorded, Atkins was unavailable on the necessary recording dates and the part went instead to Pauline Collins.

Angela Baddeley was heavily padded up to play the buxom Mrs Bridges – in reality she was quite a petite woman. Look carefully at her forearms and you'll notice that they are far skinnier than the rest of her appears to be!

A spin-off series about the adventures of Hudson, Mrs Bridges and Ruby in their boarding house was actively considered at the end of the run of *Upstairs, Downstairs*. The untimely death of Angela Baddeley meant the idea was never developed.

A US version of *Upstairs, Downstairs* was broadcast to American viewers in 1975. *Beacon Hill* told the story of a wealthy Boston family and their servants in the 1920s, but despite a quality cast and massive advance publicity, the series bombed and was pulled after just 13 episodes.

Jean Marsh and Eileen Atkins reunited to create another period drama, ***The House of Eliott***, which ran for three seasons from 1991.

V

Science Fiction | Warner Bros Television for NBC (shown on ITV) | episode duration 50 mins | broadcast 1–2 May 1983, 6–8 May 1984, 26 Oct 1984–22 Mar 1985 (USA)

Recurring Cast
Jane Badler · *'Diana'*
Marc Singer · *Mike Donovan*
Faye Grant · *Dr Juliet Parrish*
Michael Durrell · *Robert Maxwell*
Penelope Windust · *Kathleen Maxwell*
Blair Tefkin · *Robin Maxwell*
Viveka Davis · *Polly Maxwell*
Marin May · *Katie Maxwell*
Brandy Gold, Jenny Beck, Jennifer Cooke · *'Star Child' /Elizabeth Maxwell*
Jason Bernard · *Caleb Taylor*
Michael Wright · *Elias Taylor*
Richard Lawson · *Dr Ben Taylor*
Bonnie Bartlett · *Lynn Bernstein*
Leonardo Cimino · *Abraham Bernstein*
George Morfogen · *Stanley Bernstein*
David Packer · *Daniel Bernstein*
Neva Patterson · *Eleanor Dupres*
Hansford Rowe · *Arthur Dupres*
Jenny Sullivan · *Kristine Walsh*
Tommy Peterson · *Josh Brooks*
Richard Herd · *'John'*
Andrew Prine · *'Steven'*
Frank Ashmore · *'Martin'/'Philip'*
Peter Nelson · *'Brian'*
Rafael Campos · *Sancho Gomez*
Michael Alldredge · *Bill Graham*
Camila Ashland · *Ruby Engels*
Diane Civita · *Harmony Moore*
Robert Englund · *'Willie'*
Eric Johnston, Nicky Katt · *Sean Donovan*
Joanna Kerns · *Marjorie Donovan*
Thomas Hill · *Father Andrew Doyle*
Michael Ironside · *Ham Tyler*
Mickey Jones · *Chris Farber*
Dick Miller · *Dan Pascal*
Denise Galik-Furey · *Maggie Blodgett*
Sarah Douglas · *'Pamela'*
Jeff Yagher · *Kyle Bates*
Lane Smith · *Nathan Bates*
June Chadwick · *'Lydia'*
Duncan Regehr · *'Charles'*
Judson Scott · *Lieutenant James*
Marilyn Jones · *'Thelma'*
Frank Ashmore · *'Philip'*
Bruce Davison · *John Langley*
Aki Aleong · *Mr Chiang*

Producers Kenneth Johnson, Daniel H. Blatt, Robert Singer (executive), Patrick Boyriven, Michael Eliot (associate), Chuck Bowman, David J. Latt, Dean O'Brien, Ralph Riskin, Garner Simmons, Skip Ward, Steven E. De Souza **Writers** Kenneth Johnson, Brian Taggert, Peggy Goldman, Diane Frolov, Lillian Weezer, Diane Frolov, Peggy Goldman, Craig Buck, Paul Monash, Steven E. De Souza, David Braff, Garner Simmons, David Abramowitz, Paul F. Edwards, Chris Manheim, Carleton Eastlake, Mark Rosner, Donald R. Boyle **Theme Music** Each of the mini series had its own theme. The first, by Joe Harnell, deliberately mimicked Bernard Herrmann's score for Alfred Hitchcock's *North by Northwest* (1959), while Dennis McCarthy's music for *V: The Final Battle* is reminiscent of Gustav Holst's 'Mars' from *The Planets*. For *V: The Series*, McCarthy took a piece of incidental music from *The Final Battle*, a four-note synthesiser motif, and used it within a rather generic orchestral theme of the kind you'd hear on almost any American drama series.

When the first mother ships arrived, they blocked out the skies. They hung in the air above major cities across the globe, including Los Angeles. Their inhabitants, known as 'the Visitors', claimed to be on a peaceful mission to swap cures for deadly diseases in return for water, a commodity they claimed was in short supply on their planet. But they lied. Their human faces were merely latex skins hiding their true reptilian form, while their mission was not to drain water from Earth, but to harvest humans for food. To prevent their secret from being exposed, the Visitors spread propaganda against scientists and systematically detained any they find.

War journalist Mike Donovan, fresh from an assignment in El Salvador, is selected to film the Visitors' arrival, accompanied by his former lover, reporter Kristine Walsh. Though Kristine emerges as the Visitors' spokeswoman, personally selected by 'Diana', one of the Visitors' leaders, Mike stumbles across the truth and becomes a wanted man. Joining forces with scientist Juliet Parrish, the Maxwell family and an assorted band of other refugees, Mike coordinates humanity's last stand against the alien invaders. But then young Robin Maxwell is discovered to be pregnant with twins – the product of a one-night stand with one of the aliens. One of her children is a hideous reptilian creature that soon dies, while the other, seemingly human, rapidly grows into a young girl – the 'Star Child' – after only a few weeks. Catholic priest Father Andrew Doyle believes the girl might be a symbol for peace between the races, but he hasn't bargained for the ruthless ambition of Diana, who plots against even her own kind to become sole ruler of planet Earth. . .

While most of sport-obsessed Britain were watching the 1984 Olympics in Los Angeles, some viewers turned to ITV to see a mini series that had captivated American audiences for two years, a science fiction drama and World War Two allegory, transposing the Nazi domination of Europe with an alien occupation of the world as seen through the eyes of the people of LA. *V* began as a four-hour mini series created by writer-producer-director Kenneth Johnson. Such was the success of the programme that Warner Bros executives wanted to commission a full TV series, but Johnson resisted, eventually creating a second, six-hour mini series, *V: The Final Battle*. We Brits,

however, got both series shown in two-hour episodes across one week. Lucky us!

The parallel with the rise of the Nazis is sometimes a little obvious: the Visitors' symbol is a black disjointed 'S' shape that, when shown on the red flags and tunics, look startlingly swastika-like, while the recruitment of teens eager for a bit of power has obvious overtones of the Hitler Youth movement. In the first mini series, however, there were plenty of unexpectedly subtle and delicate touches. The cast included characters who had survived the Nazi holocaust only for their own grandson, the vain and bullying Daniel, to betray them to the invaders (it's the old Jewish man who introduces one of the other motifs of the series, a spray-painted 'V', standing not for 'Visitor' but for 'victory'), while an early scene in which a young boy watching the TV news reports notes with disappointment that their leader, John, doesn't even look like Mr Spock, nicely sets us up for the shock of what the Visitors really look like underneath their masks.

The matte paintings that create the intimidating mother ships are extremely effective in all but a very few shots, while the remaining special effects are what we'd expect from what was, at the time, one of the most expensive mini series ever made (and coming from Britain, we're hardly in a position to be sniffy about special effects in 1980s TV science fiction in any case). A scene that everyone vividly remembers comes when Mike Donovan, hiding in a ventilation shaft (that most enduring of science fiction clichés), sees Diana extending her jaws wider than humanly possibly to devour a guinea pig whole. It's a trick we see again in the series with a variety of small animals and birds, but that first example of alien cuisine is never bettered for sheer shock value.

Unfortunately, even by the time of the second mini series, *The Final Battle*, the cliché count began to soar far beyond mere ventilation shafts (although there continues to be extensive use of them). No longer is the allegory World War Two; it's more 'Cowboys and Indians'. Michael Ironside turns up as a hard-nosed mercenary and begins to chew the scenery (and someone must have known what they were letting themselves in for by calling his character 'Ham'), while Marc Singer as Mike Donovan displays the most suspicious body language during his many 'covert' break-ins to various Visitor installations (it's a wonder the alien troops don't shoot him just for looking so shifty). Still it was fun if only for Jane Badler's manic, power-hungry Diana and her various power struggles with other Visitors – including Sarah Douglas (one of the evil superbeings from *Superman 2*, 1980) as the purring arch-bitch 'Pamela'.

After two successful mini series came the series proper. With the virus that won the war now a pollutant in the earth's ecosystem, the fight is on to repair the damage. Meanwhile, the Visitor forces amass on the dark side of the moon. Led by Diana, they eventually return to Earth and try to reclaim the planet before concentrating on Los Angeles – one of the most highly polluted cities in the world. If that sounds dumb, the series features one hilarious twist that the writers really hadn't thought through: resistance-supporting alien 'Martin' is killed and replaced by his twin brother to act as a double agent for the Visitors. But why go to all that bother when the only physical similarities identifiable as Martin come from the latex human face he wore over his scales?

One of the highlights of the series was Diana's continuing political battles to reign supreme and her desperate attempts to impress the Visitors' great leader, whom she was once romantically involved with (though as one of her adversaries notes, they couldn't have been that close if he was willing to post her to the opposite side of the galaxy). Diana's main foil in the series is 'Charles' (yup – Charles and Diana), whose attempt to trick Diana into marriage results in his own death. Diana, meanwhile, only ever one step away from being Joan Collins in space, parades through a succession of increasingly glamorous gowns that in the end made her the only element of the series worth watching.

The final episode transmitted saw Star Child Elizabeth taken away by the oft-mentioned leader of the aliens, little realising that a bomb had been planted on board his ship. A stunning cliffhanger to finish on, it unfortunately failed to recapture the audience that either of the preceding mini series had done. In the UK, *V: The Series* was a victim of the erratic scheduling around the ITV regions typical of late-night television, with, for example, Yorkshire TV completing its run before Granada showed the first episode. When it finally was broadcast, it was in a timeslot just a little too late for the teen audience who would have undoubtedly loved the combination of high camp, all-out adventure and that one shot of the shuttle going through the tunnel in Griffith Park that they kept recycling. But the original mini series remains a hugely influential piece of drama, as we're sure the makers of *Independence Day* (1996) would be only too willing to admit.

Website
www.thevisitors.info

Van der Valk

Crime Drama | Euston Films/Thames/Elmgate for ITV | episode duration 50–120 mins | broadcast 13 Sep 1972–10 Oct 1973, 5 Sep–21 Nov 1977, 16 Jan 1991–19 Feb 1992

Regular Cast
Barry Foster · *Piet van der Valk*
Susan Travers, Joanna Dunham, Meg Davies · *Arlette van der Valk*
Martin Wyldeck, Nigel Stock, Ronald Hines · *Hof-Commisaris Samson*
Michael Latimer · *Inspector Johnny Kroon*
Alan Haines · *Brigadier Mertens*
Dave Carter · *Brigadier Stribos*
Richard Huw · *Wim van der Valk*

Creator Nicholas Freeling **Producers** Lloyd Shirley, George Taylor, Brian Walcroft (executive), Chris Burt, Mary Morgan (associate), Michael Chapman, Robert Love, Geoffrey Gilbert, Chris Burt **Writers** Various, including Michael Chapman, Geoffrey Gilbert, Philip Broadley, Arden Winch, Peter Yeldham, Jeremy Paul, David Butler, Paul Wheeler, Ted Childs, Leslie Sands, Robert Wales, Patrick O'Brien, Roger Marshall, Jonathan Hales, Don Shaw, Keith Dewhurst, Peter Buckman, Kenneth Ware, Stuart Hepburn **Theme Music** 'Eye Level', written by Jack Trombey (a pseudonym for Jan Stoeckhart), was the first TV theme to become a British No. 1 single, on 29 September 1973, thanks to the Simon Park Orchestra.

Inspired by the novels of Nicholas Freeling, *Van der Valk* slotted nicely into the Euston Films family album alongside *Special Branch* and ***The Sweeney***. Taking the gruff, cynical detective of old and placing him in the liberal Amsterdam, storylines exposed viewers to drugs, prostitution and other issues that the Great British public wouldn't want to think about existing on their own doorstep but were quite happy for someone else to deal with. Star Barry Foster had appeared in BBC soap ***The Troubleshooters*** and had enjoyed big screen success only a couple of months before *Van der Valk*'s launch when he'd played the brutal 'neck tie murderer' Bob Rusk in Alfred Hitchcock's *Frenzy*. This leant him a wonderful air of suspicion and distrust as Piet van der Valk, a seen-it-all detective in Amsterdam's CID. Aiming for promotion, he lacks much of the diplomacy and political attentiveness of his superior, Samson, but he's an intuitive copper with a knack for solving cases purely on the reliance on hunches.

Van der Valk enjoyed moderate success on first broadcast in 1972–3, and enjoyed two revivals, in 1977 and 1991, again starring Foster, though the actors playing his wife and boss changed each time. For his final small-screen appearance, van der Valk had finally made it to Commisaris, though promotion did little to soften his cynicism.

Entirely separately to Euston Films' production, West Germany were treated to their own van der Valk in the form of a TV movie, *Van der Valk und die Reichen*, showing on 26 December 1973 and starring Frank Finlay as the detective.

Vanity Fair

Drama | BBC/A&E for BBC One | episode duration 50 mins | broadcast 1 Nov–6 Dec 1998

Principal Cast

Natasha Little · *Becky Sharp*
Nathaniel Parker · *Rawdon Crawley*
Frances Grey · *Amelia Sedley*
Philip Glenister · *William Dobbin*
Miriam Margolyes · *Miss Crawley*
Tim Woodward · *Mr John Osborne*
Tom Ward · *George Osborne*
Jeremy Swift · *Joss Sedley*
Roger Ashton-Griffiths · *King George IV*
David Bradley · *Sir Pitt Crawley*
Eleanor Bron · *Lady Bareacres*
Zoe Chester · *Little Rose*
Carol Ann Crawford · *Mrs Blenkinsop*
Graham Crowden · *Lord Bareacres*
Sarah Crowden · *Lady Blanche*
Janet Dale · *Miss Briggs*
Windsor Davies · *General Tufto*
Felix Dexter · *Samuel*
Michele Dotrice · *Mrs Sedley*
Janine Duvitski · *Mrs Bute Crawley*
Stephen Frost · *Bute Crawley*
Pat Keen · *Miss Pinkerton*
Mark Lambert · *Major O'Dowd*
John Leeson · *Priest*
Anton Lesser · *Mr Pitt Crawley*
Sylvestra Le Touzel · *Lady Jane Crawley*
Gerard Murphy · *Lord Steyne*
Casey O'Connor · *Little Violet*
Sara Powell · *Miss Swartz*
Bryan Pringle · *Raggles*
Maurice Roëves · *Captain MacMurdo*
David Ross · *Mr Sedley*
Patsy Rowlands · *Mrs Tinker*

Producers Michael Wearing, Delia Fine, Suzan Harrison (executive), Gillian McNeill **Writer** Andrew Davies, from the novel by William Makepeace Thackery **Theme Music** Murray Gold

During the time of the Napoleonic Wars, two young ladies emerge from an academy run by the Misses Pinkerton: Miss Amelia Sedley, a young lady of good family and fortune, and her friend, Miss Becky Sharp, a poor but clever and beautiful temptress. It is a time in England when appearances are everything, the possession of money is of paramount importance and where bankruptcy loomed large for many. Only the clever opportunist can survive. For a young lady with no fortune or influential friends, Becky Sharp has only her wits and beauty to assist her in pursuit of a man – any man – with a large fortune. Cruel and conniving, yet superficially a good friend to Amelia, Becky sets Amelia's rich brother in her targets and sets about reeling him in for her husband. But Becky isn't the only one using Amelia for their own ends; her suitor George Osborne is an utter cad – though his premature death at Waterloo prevents her from discovering his true nature. And while Amelia and her family suffer, Becky shrugs and goes on to her next lucrative opportunity . . .

Vanity Fair is a novel that has enjoyed frequent outings on British television, first in 1956, then again a decade later for BBC Two, where Becky was played by Susan Hampshire (fresh from ***The Forsyte Saga*** earlier the same year), and then in 1987, a 16-part BBC One version cast Eve Matheson as the scheming Miss Sharp. Most recently, Andrew Davies's adaptation was treated to a sumptuous production, riding the wave of popularity for costume dramas post-***Pride and Prejudice***. Natasha Little plays

Becky Sharp to perfection, thoroughly relishing the chance for a romp through Georgian England, while Frances Gray is suitably piteous as Amelia Sedley.

A Very British Coup

Drama | Skreba Films for Channel 4 | episode duration 60 mins | broadcast 19 Jun–3 Jul 1988

Regular Cast

Ray McAnally · *Harry Perkins*
Majorie Yates · *Joan Cook*
Jim Carter · *Newsome*
Geoffrey Beevers · *Lawrence Wainwright*
Roger Brierley · *Andrews*
Hugh Martin · *Sampson*
Keith Allen · *Fred Thompson*
Oliver Ford Davies · *Horace Tweed*
Bernard Kay · *Inspector Page*
Alan MacNaughtan · *Sir Percy Browne*
Tim McInnerny · *Fiennes*
Christine Kavanagh · *Liz Fain*
David McKail · *Sir James Robertson*
Michael Godley · *Gibbon*
Oscar Quitak · *Sir Montague Kowalski*
Shane Rimmer · *Morgan, US Secretary of State*
Philip O'Brien · *President*
Erin Donovan · *Chambers*
Robert Arden · *Ambassador*
Dennis Creaghan · *Head of CIA*
Clive Merrison · *TV Interviewer*
Philip Madoc · *Sir George Fison*
Jeremy Young · *Alford*
Clive Panto · *Producer*
Zuleema Dene · *BBC Vision Mixer*
Stephanie Fayerman · *Editor*
Terry John, George Rossi · *Photographers*
Jessica Carney · *Maureen*
Caroline John · *Annette Newsome*
Harmage Singh Kalirai · *Patel*
Preston Lockwood · *Lord Fain*
Gabrielle Daye · *Mum*
Kika Markham · *Helen Jarvis*

Producers Ann Skinner and Sally Hibbin **Writer** Alan Plater, based on the novel by Chris Mullin **Theme Music** The Great Mass in C Minor by Mozart

When former steelworker Harry Perkins leads the Labour Party to a landslide victory in the general election, his far-left politics instantly create powerful enemies for him in influential circles. The press try to turn the public against him, the Americans withdraw financial support in retaliation for Perkins' orders to remove all US military personnel from British soil, the power unions are persuaded to strike, leaving the country plunged in darkness and civil servants within his own staff conspire to undermine him at every turn. Is Britain really prepared for a Prime Minister who insists on telling the truth? And can any politician really be as conscientious and scandal free as Perkins purports to be?

When *A Very British Coup* was first screened in 1988, the reality of Labour becoming electable still seemed a long way off. The three-day week of the 1970s, the miners' strike of 1985 and the internal battles with the 'Militant' faction were still fresh in voters' minds, while the Tories appeared to show a stronger united front, the victory of the Falklands war having won them a second term in office and their links with the United States of America offering us some comfort in the ever-growing threat of the Cold War becoming nuclear.

A Very British Coup is a 'What if' that appears more fanciful and so more desirable as the story unfolds. In the late 1980s it was enough to ask, 'What if Labour was an electable party?' though the broader question of, 'What if we found ourselves with a leader who was incorruptible and honest?' is just as valid.

Harry Perkins proves to be a witty, intelligent man. When asked if he intends to abolish First Class train carriages, he counters that he'd prefer to abolish Second Class, as he believes all people to be First Class; and his victory speech, where he quotes the press's criticism that he's a simple-minded fool only to agree with them, is a masterstroke of rhetoric that would have made Mark Antony an envious man. Having campaigned on a platform of disarmament, Harry makes good on his promises by organising the televised disarming of a nuclear warhead. When the Americans try to put pressure on him by withdrawing their financial support to Britain, Perkins responds by telling them to remove all US forces from the UK and instead getting a loan from a Soviet-backed bank.

It's the link to the Soviets that provides the drama's biggest red herring. We're waiting for the inevitable moment when Perkins hands the country over to the Russian, so she biggest surprise comes with the realisation that the coup of the title refers not to Perkins' government but to the constant campaign by the old guard establishment to overthrow Perkins. Their mistake is both to assume he was as corruptible as they are and then to think that he's susceptible to intimidation. They're wrong on both counts. Blackmailed through manufactured evidence into resigning, Perkins instead exposes the conspiracy live on television and announces that he will let the voters decide whether to trust him as he calls another General Election.

While comparisons with ***House of Cards*** are inevitable, *A Very British Coup* is a much more straightforward drama with few of the Machiavellian twists and turns of Francis Urquart's government. New Labour was still some years off when Ray McAnally gave us his own interpretation of the acceptable face of socialism, more in the spirit of John Smith than Tony Blair. In retrospect, it's terrifying to see just how wide of the mark this vision of a future Britain turned out to be.

A Very Peculiar Practice

Comedy/Drama | BBC Two | episode duration 50 mins | broadcast 21 May 1986–6 April 1988

Regular Cast
Peter Davison · *Stephen Daker*
Graham Crowden · *Jock McCannon*
Barbara Flynn · *Dr Rose Marie*
David Troughton · *Bob Buzzard*
Amanda Hillwood · *Lyn Turtle*
Joanna Kanska · *Grete Grotowska*
John Bird · *Ernest Hemmingway*
Michael J. Shannon · *Jack Daniels*
Lindy Whiteford · *Maureen Gahagan*
Toria Fuller · *Julie Daniels*
James Grout · *Professor George Bunn*
Colin Stinton · *Charlie Dusenberry*
Gillian Raine · *Mrs Kramer*
Joe Melia · *Ron Rust*
Takashi Kawahara · *Chen Sung Yau*
Hugh Grant · *Preacher Colin*
Timothy West · *Professor Furie*
Jean Haywood · *Lillian Hubbard*
Dominic Arnold · *Sammy Limb*
Kathy Burke · *Alice*
Sonia Hart, Elaine Turrell · *Nuns*

Creator/Writer Andrew Davies **Producers** Ken Riddington **Director** David Tucker **Theme Music** 'A Long Way from Anywhere', written by Dave Greenslade, was sung by chart star Elkie Brooks and featured a typically 1980s saxophone solo.

Subversive, sarcastic, sophisticated and downright hilarious, *A Very Peculiar Practice* marked the first major TV role for Peter Davison post-***Doctor Who***, and the first breakthrough hit for now-legendary screenwriter Andrew Davies. Never afraid to mix comedy with drama of near-heartbreaking proportions, *A Very Peculiar Practice* dealt with life on the campus of fictional Lowlands University. Recent divorcee Stephen Daker arrives to join the three other medics who are already part of the campus health centre: demented capitalist Bob Buzzard, who'd be perfectly happy if it wasn't for the patients; radical feminist Dr Rose Marie; and sozzled old Scot, Jock McCannon. Together with ever-suffering Irish nurse Maureen and snooty receptionist Mrs Kramer, the doctors of this very peculiar practice do their best to solve the physical and mental problems of the students and staff of this 'piss-ant swamp of fear and loathing'. Stephen soon finds himself falling in love with policewoman Lyn Turtle and unwittingly battling the insidious schemes of self-serving Vice Chancellor Ernest Hemmingway. In the second series, the university is taken over by American Jack Daniels, whose own vision of the future of Lowlands is an even darker one. With Lyn now at the police training college at Hendon, Steven's new paramour is 'rude, nasty Polish girl' Grete.

Created as the antithesis to traditional medical dramas featuring a wise old doctor nurturing an eager young buck, *A Very Peculiar Practice* only rarely allows you to sympathise with Stephen Daker – a man so damaged by his divorce that he has a phobia about getting close to a woman ever again. In addition, his colleagues are so completely incapable of providing anything approaching a professional healthcare service that you despair of anyone ever getting well at Lowlands. Very much a product of its time, this series taps into the fears and concerns prevalent in the mid-1980s in establishments like the NHS and institutes of higher education, where the pressures of the commercial marketplace began to be felt for the first time.

Blessed with scalpel-sharp scripts from Andrew Davies (later better known for his successful adaptations of classic novels, such as ***Pride and Prejudice***) and an ensemble of outstanding performances (with special praise going to Barbara Flynn and David Troughton for creating two of the most charismatic freaks ever seen on TV), *A Very Peculiar Practice* is one of the high points of 1980s TV drama, nominated for Best Drama in the 1987 BAFTA awards. Never repeated on terrestrial television – possibly due to its highly contentious political content – the second series represents none the less a particular high-water mark. Four years after the show finished a 90-minute sequel movie was screened on BBC One. In *A Very Polish Practice* (1992), the action moves to Grete's home country, where Stephen faces trouble from smuggler Alfred Molina.

The Vicar of Dibley

See pages 812–14

Victoria Wood: As Seen On TV

See pages 815–18

The Virginian/Men from Shiloh

Western | Revue Studios/Universal TV for NBC (shown on ITV) | episode duration 75 mins | broadcast 19 Sep 1962–24 Mar 1971

Regular Cast
James Drury · *The Virginian*
Doug McClure · *Trampas*
Lee J. Cobb · *Judge Henry Garth*
Roberta Shore · *Betsy Garth*
Frank Sully · *Danny the Bartender*
Gary Clarke · *Steve Hill*
Pippa Scott · *Molly Wood*
Russell Thorson · *Sheriff Stan Evans*
Jan Stine · *Eddie*
Randy Boone · *Randy Benton*
L. Q. Jones · *Belden*
Continued on page 819

The Vicar of Dibley

Dawn French as Geraldine Granger.

The residents of the sleepy English village of Dibley get a shock one day when their ancient vicar Mr Pottle drops dead in the middle of a service. They're even more shocked when his replacement arrives – larger-than-life, vivacious Geraldine Granger, one of the UK's first female Church of England vicars. Predictably, the local parish council are at first more than a little bit stunned by her arrival. In particular, the self-appointed spokesperson for the parish council, local landowner David Horton, is aghast that new, trendy ideas have caused a liberal-minded female vicar to be foisted upon his corner of 'little Britain'. Slowly but surely, Geraldine's good heart and popularity amongst the other parishioners of St Barnabas's Church win David around. Although he regularly disagrees with her on individual matters, he acknowledges the benefit she has brought to their village – specifically a massive increase in attendance at services.

Created and (largely) written by legendary Britcom author Richard Curtis (the man behind ***Mr Bean***, ***Blackadder*** and films like the 1993 smash hit *Four Weddings and a Funeral*), *The Vicar of Dibley* surprised many people when the public voted it the third-best

British sitcom of all time in the BBC's 2004 survey, ahead of more predictable choices like ***Fawlty Towers*** and ***Dad's Army***. If this placing proved one thing, it was that the popularity of the traditional, 'safe', middle-class sitcom can never be underestimated. By the time of the launch of *The Vicar of Dibley*, it more or less stood alone in the schedules as a family-friendly sitcom among edgier, more 'challenging' comedy. It's also ironic that with *Dibley*, Curtis and French completed their transformation from members of the anti-establishment 'alternative comedy' circuit into the very pillars of the comedy establishment themselves. Indeed, from having been the bane of 'old-fashioned' sitcoms like ***Mind your Language***, French and Curtis now found themselves on the receiving end of criticism that they too had become just too 'safe' and respectable. Although such a change in their circumstances is entirely understandable and appropriate (young turks will always challenge the old guard in every walk of life), the criticism that *Dibley* was safe and inoffensive is actually untrue – the BBC has continued to receive complaints from conservative Christians who vociferously objected to the portrayal of a liberal (and God forbid) female vicar and from people offended by the bad language.

The Vicar of Dibley was actually more worrying for blue-rinsed Middle England than many of its critics gave it credit for. Simply showing a female vicar on television wasn't enough for Curtis: his vicar Geraldine – a woman keen to find herself a boyfriend – has framed pictures of idols like Mel Gibson (and later Sean Bean and Robbie Williams) on the wall next to a picture of Jesus Christ. It's always been accepted that male Church of England vicars were permitted to find a wife for themselves; by showing a female vicar actively looking for a partner of her own, this little sitcom did more to challenge prejudice and promote public acceptance of this radical change to the Church of England than any number of official proclamations from the General Synod ever could.

Casting Dawn French in the lead role of Geraldine Granger was a masterstroke. With her comedy partner Jennifer Saunders kept busy by her series ***Absolutely Fabulous***, *Dibley* provided French with the opportunity to play an ongoing character of her own for the first time since appearing in sitcom ***Girls on Top*** in the mid-1980s. French turned Curtis's scripts into comedy gold, giving a warmth and humanity to the role that few other artists would have been able to match. The rest of the ensemble cast were utterly flawless too. With perhaps the most thankless part, Gary Waldhorn (previously seen playing a similar kind of role opposite Karl Howman in ***Brush Strokes***) produced a performance of subtlety and depth that turned the pig-headed conservative David from just being a pantomime villain into a fully rounded and believable character. Having a 'realistic' character like David was absolutely essential when surrounded so many outlandish freaks. Of particular note were Roger Lloyd Pack (in a part that was almost indistinguishable from his role as Trigger in ***Only Fools and Horses***) as the hygienically challenged farmer Owen Newitt, and Trevor Peacock as Jim Trott, the randy old man unable to separate his 'no . . . no . . . no . . . no's from his 'yes'es.

Sitcom
Tiger Aspect Productions for BBC One
Episode Duration: 30 mins, plus 40–60 min specials
Broadcast: 10 Nov 1994–1 Jan 2000, 25 Dec 2004, 1 Jan 2005

Regular Cast
Dawn French · *Geraldine Granger*
Gary Waldhorn · *David Horton*
Emma Chambers · *Alice Tinker/Horton*
James Fleet · *Hugo Horton*
John Bluthal · *Frank Pickle*
Roger Lloyd Pack · *Owen Newitt*
Trevor Peacock · *Jim Trott*
Liz Smith · *Letitia Cropley*
Simon McBurney · *Cecil the Choirmaster*
Clive Mantle · *Simon Horton*
Peter Capaldi · *Tristan Campbell*

Creator Richard Curtis

Producers Richard Curtis, Peter Bennett-Jones (executive), Jon Plowman, Sue Vertue, Margot Gavan Duffy, Rachel Salter

Writers Richard Curtis, Paul Mayhew-Archer, Kit Hesketh-Harvey

Theme Music Howard Goodall composed a 'traditional'-sounding piece of music to put the words of the 23rd Psalm to, performed by the Choir of Christ Church Cathedral in Oxford, with soloist George Humphreys taking the lead.

Ongoing continuity between episodes was a particular strength of *The Vicar of Dibley*, with storylines evolving over many months or even years. Who could have predicted that quiet, dull – no, *boring* – Frank Pickle could ever have held the secret of his homosexuality for so long? Utterly adorable as the equally dim Alice and Hugo were Emma Chambers and James Fleet. Their budding romance was one of the most delightful ongoing plotlines in the series: who can ever forget their bonkers wedding ceremony, complete with bridesmaids dressed as Teletubbies? And watching Geraldine's burgeoning romance with David's eligible brother Simon (played by ***Casualty***'s Clive Mantle) was another heart-warming treat. Even the writing-out of a regular character was done with tenderness and sensitivity. When, by mutual agreement, Liz Smith chose to quit the (somewhat supporting) role of Letitia Cropley, it was delivered in a poignant and memorable way that went beyond the bounds of what would normally be expected within a traditional sitcom format. Thankfully Liz's next role, playing batty grandma Norma in ***The Royle Family***, was just as well written and well received by viewers.

With *Only Fools and Horses* now finally consigned to the great bargain bin of TV history, in 2004 it fell to *The Vicar of Dibley* to spearhead the BBC One Christmas schedule. The two-part special, shown on Christmas Day and New Year's Day, topped the ratings and simultaneously launched the 'Make Poverty History' campaign. Richard Curtis had long been a pivotal player in the bi-annual ***Comic Relief*** events. As such, he had learned at first hand about many of the root causes behind Third World poverty. Realising that 2005 would see Britain taking the chair of many international organisations (such as the European Union), Curtis took his chance to launch the campaign in the New Year's Day episode. Although some people complained about using a sitcom for political ends, they had perhaps missed the entire point of *The Vicar of Dibley*. Whether you're a Christian, a Muslim or even an atheist, surely the whole message of the programme was simply to try to be as supportive and charitable as possible to each other – preferably with a smile on our faces at the same time. It's certainly what Geraldine Granger would do.

Casting Dawn French in the lead role of Geraldine Granger was a masterstroke. French turned Curtis's scripts into comedy gold, giving a warmth and humanity to the role that few other artists would have been able to match.

Victoria Wood: As Seen On TV

Victoria Wood as 'Miss Bertha' and Julie Walters as 'Mrs Overall' from Acorn Antiques.

Shy Lancashire lass Victoria Wood was born in May 1953 in Prestwich and later brought up in Bolton. Realising that she had some talent for the performing arts, Wood went to study drama and theatre at Birmingham University. Deciding to capitalise on her honed skills, Wood chose to enter the ITV talent show ***New Faces***, which she won in 1975 at the remarkably young age of 22. Known for her ability to write and sing her own songs at a piano, Wood's next major job was for BBC One's perennial consumer programme ***This Life***, which she joined the following year, providing a topical song per episode. However, Wood's skill as a comedy writer didn't really get much chance to flourish until Granada TV produced her first play, *Talent*, in August 1979. Co-starring her friend Julie Walters (whom she had first met in 1970 at Manchester Polytechnic, before crossing paths again when working in revue in London eight years later), the play won a number of writing awards for Wood and cemented a working relationship between the two women that remains to the present day.

Following the success of *Talent*, Granada quickly signed Wood and Walters up to appear in a sketch show of their own, called (surprisingly) *Wood and Walters*. A one-off episode in 1981 was followed by a full series in 1982 and consisted of a combination of sketches, stand-up comedy and self-penned songs. Three years later, the BBC poached Wood to come and produce a new show, a kind of upgraded and improved *Wood and Walters*. The show, *Victoria Wood: As Seen On TV*, would become one of the most beloved comedy programmes in the history of television, endlessly quoted and re-quoted by devotees across the land. Thankfully, Julie Walters was signed up at the same time. Although she no longer shared top

Comedy
BBC Two
Episode Duration: 35–40 mins
Broadcast: 11 Jan 1985–15 Dec 1986, 18 Dec 1987

Regular Cast
Victoria Wood, Julie Walters, Celia Imrie, Duncan Preston, Susie Blake, Patricia Routledge

Creator/Writer/Theme Music Victoria Wood

Producer Geoff Posner

billing with Wood, Walters' own career had taken off (thanks to her appearance in Oscar-nominated film *Educating Rita*, 1983) to such an extent that it only seemed fair for Wood not to be overshadowed by her friend's new-found fame.

Wood's unique talent was in creating memorable characters that never seemed to be just over-the-top grotesques. Grotesque they might be, but there was always a deep-rooted core of reality and truth in them. Especially memorable was the girl looking for her friend Kimberley – 'she's really really tall and really really wide' – a decrepit waitress dripping soup over the floor of a small café ('Two soups!'), and the immortal cast of freaks from the world's worst soap opera, *Acorn Antiques*. The ongoing exploits of Miss Babs, Miss Berta, Mr Clifford and Mrs Boadicea Overall proved to be a highlight of every episode – especially for people who were ***Crossroads*** fans, who watched and winced with recognition at every deliberately fluffed line of dialogue, every missed cue and every bit of wobbly scenery. The great fondness that the British public has for *Acorn Antiques* was demonstrated in early 2005 when a full-length West End musical (written by Victoria Wood) hit the stage to rave reviews.

Victoria Wood: As Seen On TV **would become one of the most beloved comedy programmes in the history of television, endlessly quoted and re-quoted by devotees across the land.**

In recent years, Ricky Gervais has received praise from critics for his innovative mock-documentary ***The Office***. Yet Victoria Wood was doing the very same thing 20 years earlier. Two of *As Seen On TV*'s 'mockumentaries' were about a chubby northern girl training to swim the English Channel, and an Elvis-obsessed pushy mother (guest star Stephanie Beacham) convinced that 'the King' fathered her two offspring. By recording these 'documentaries' on film (rather than on the videotape used for the rest of the show) and providing them with a portentous narrator, the 'reality' was enhanced to such an extent that many people watching during the show's first broadcast were momentarily nonplussed: was the Victoria Wood show over? Were they now watching a typically boring BBC Two documentary? The fact that it took a short while to twig what was going on made the resulting belly laugh all the greater.

Another regular guest on *Victoria Wood: As Seen On TV* was the redoubtable actress Patricia Routledge, still some five years away from taking on her most famous TV role of Hyacinth Bouquet in ***Keeping Up Appearances***. Here, Routledge played middle-class Kitty, a woman with equally high standards as Hyacinth but with a much baser desire to know all of the gossip in her town. The Kitty sketches were written in the form of a rambling Ronnie Corbett-style monologue delivered straight at the camera. She was always in a mad dash to get somewhere: 'I can't stop . . .' she'd bellow, as she headed off to yet another coffee morning.

Equally hilarious, but for a completely different reason, was Susie Blake's snobby TV continuity announcer. Yet again, Wood's scripts were achingly funny, showing on this occasion the pain, angst and frustration lurking just beneath this woman's veneer of professionalism. Viewers were treated to her views on romance, men and other completely inappropriate topics; as a result of Blake's portrayal and Wood's scripts, we wondered if all TV continuity announcers were just a hair's breadth away from letting rip and telling us all precisely what they thought. Wood shows us that people on TV are real people too, complete with the same prejudices and fallibilities as everyone else. If she didn't have such a strong grip on life, we imagine she'd be perpetually on the verge of a nervous breakdown. One of Wood's most iconic, memorable and endlessly repeatable lines of dialogue was delivered by Blake's posh southern announcer: 'We'd like to apologise to viewers in the North. It must be terrible for you.'

Like a quality repertory company in a regional theatre, the *As Seen On TV* gang could turn their hands to practically any role that was required of them.

Victoria Wood writes her comedy in a northern 'voice' that many people have compared to that of Alan Bennett (but without the angst). It's not that she can't do angst – her later work *Pat and Margaret* and ***dinnerladies*** have clearly shown that isn't so. Wood's comedy comes from the same source tapped into by Rob Wilton ('The Day War Broke Out') and ***Coronation Street*** – astutely accurate observation of the rhythm of northern speech. It's the form of speech that includes 'barmcakes' and the 'Whit Week Walk', and the accompanying mindset where someone can declare they're diabetic in order to jump the canteen queue, and where the ineptitude of the service industries is endearing rather than frustrating. Most of all, Wood's critiques of certain areas of life are offset by a cheery pragmatism. Wood's characters recognise that life is crap – but wallowing in introspection isn't how to get on: you've got to make the best of a bad lot.

Wood's comedy isn't innovative. Indeed, her best jokes come from the moments when she perpetuates the values of nostalgia. Her popularity, especially in the North, comes from the fact that she invites us to wallow in our heritage and not to be ashamed of it. In fact, she delights in pointing out the absurdities of modern British culture. In one of her stand-up routines, Wood explains how a young couple could quite easily make mad passionate love in the middle of a train carriage without anybody around them raising an eyebrow; it's only if they tried to light up a quick post-coital ciggy that somebody would curtly inform them: 'I think you'll find this is a no-smoking compartment!' Another of Wood's most famous *As Seen On TV* moments was her most famous self-penned song 'The Ballad of Freda and Barry' – better known by most people as 'Let's Do It'. Once again, Wood paints a perfect picture of a real relationship, combining the conventions of comic songs with naturalistic turns of phrase ('Come and melt the buttons on me flame-proof nightie' indeed!). We can't imagine that anyone who's ever heard the 'Ballad' will ever be able to look at a copy of *Woman's Weekly* in the same light again . . .

Perhaps the greatest strength of *Victoria Wood: As Seen On TV* came from the talented group of performers that Wood assembled around her. Like a quality repertory company in a regional theatre, the *As Seen On TV* gang could turn their hands to practically any role that was required of them. Duncan Preston's naturally lugubrious delivery contrasted neatly with Celia Imrie's ability to rattle off Wood's quick-fire dialogue with the speed of a sub-machine gun. It's testament to all concerned with this programme that every member of the team has chosen to reunite at regular intervals and work with each other time and again.

It's amazing to think that *As Seen On TV* lasted for just 13 episodes. The next time that Victoria Wood returned to television, she appeared in a series of six stand-alone comedy playlets in late 1989 (simply entitled *Victoria Wood*). Unfortunately these just didn't seem to sparkle as much as her previous BBC work, so when she returned to BBC One on Christmas Day 1992 the format was very much in the style of her last big success. *Victoria Wood's All Day Breakfast* was a triumphant return to form, taking the mickey out of daytime television shows like ITV's ***This Morning***. This one-off special even included an exclusive behind-the-scenes look at the making of an episode of *Acorn Antiques*, in which we discover that the actress playing broad Brummie Mrs Overall is in fact a horrific ego-maniac with received pronunciation and a large supply of haemorrhoid remedies. Wood then moved on to writing the poignant comedy-drama *Pat and Margaret* and the sublime sitcom *dinnerladies*. A unique voice within British comedy, Victoria Wood continues to delight audiences into the 21st century – we eagerly await her next TV work.

Wood's unique talent was in creating memorable characters that never seemed to be just over-the-top grotesques: there was always a deep-rooted core of reality and truth in them.

Roy Engel · *Barney Wingate*
Clu Gulager · *Deputy Emmett Ryker*
Harlan Warde · *Sheriff John Brannan*
Stuart Nisbet · *Bart the Bartender*
John Dehner · *Morgan Starr*
Diane Roter · *Jennifer Sommers*
Sara Lane · *Elizabeth Grainger*
Don Quine · *Stacey Grainger*
Charles Bickford · *John Grainger*
John McIntire · *Clay Grainger*
Jeanette Nolan · *Holly Grainger*
Harper Flaherty · *Harper*
Jean Peloquin · *Gene*
Dick Shane · *Dick*
David Hartman · *David Sutton*
Ken Swofford · *Seth Petit*
Tim Matheson · *Jim Horn*
Stewart Granger · *Colonel Alan MacKenzie*
Lee Majors · *Roy Tate*
John McLiam · *Parker*

Creator Owen Wister, from his novel *The Virginian* **Producers** Charles Marquis Warren, Roy Huggins, Frank Price, Norman MacDonnell, Leslie Stevens, Herbert Hirschman, Glen A. Larson (executive) **Writers** Various including Morton Fine, David Friedkin, John Hawkins, Ward Hawkins, Howard Browne, Harry Kleiner, Frank Fenton, Frank Chase, Dean Riesner, Carey Wilber, Herman Groves, True Boardman, Sy Salkowitz, Herman Miller, Leslie Stevens **Theme Music** Percy Faith's tune appeared for all bar the final 'Shiloh' year, which had a theme from king of western scores Ennio Morricone.

An unusual approach for television, *The Virginian* was a full-colour series of feature-length episodes (the story had already been adapted for cinema four times and transferred to the stage). The western genre was full of nameless heroes, but 'the Virginian' was an original, a decent, law-abiding man whose hard work ethic made him much respected. The setting was the Shiloh Ranch, near Medicine Bow, Wyoming, where the Virginian was the head of a bunch of ranch hands, reporting initially to Judge Henry Garth. Like *Wagon Train* and ***Bonanza***, the series was almost an anthology, with characters coming and going each week, bringing their stories and problems with them and hopefully leaving with the right solution. A slew of famous faces popped up over the years, including Ricardo Montalban, George C. Scott and Bette Davis, while regulars included respected stage and screen actor Lee J. Cobb and future bionic man Lee Majors. For the series' final year, it underwent a name-change to *The Men from Shiloh*.

Vision On

Children's Entertainment | BBC One | episode duration 30 mins | broadcast 6 Mar 1964–11 May 1976

Presenters

Tony Hart, Pat Keysell, Sylvester McCoy, David Cleveland (The Prof), Wilf Lunn, Ben Benison, Larry Parker

Creators Patrick Dowling, Ursula Eason **Producers** Patrick Dowling, Leonard Chase, Ursula Eason **Theme Music** 'Acroche-Toi Caroline' by the Paris Studio Group was the show's title music, with 'Java' by Al Hirt/Toussaint playing over the end credits. However, it's the music that played in the background during the Gallery sequence that is forever linked with *Vision On* – it was a little-known piece of stock music called 'Leftbank 2', written by Wayne Hill.

A programme targeted at children who were deaf and hard of hearing, but with plenty of appeal to anybody who happened to be watching at the same time, *Vision On* was a perfect combination of all three of the BBC's Reithian ideals – to inform, educate and entertain. *Vision On* was the follow-up programme to the earlier show *For Deaf Children*, which had begun broadcasting way back in 1952. This updated show provided a combination of painting projects and crafts (presented by talented artist Tony Hart), daffy sketches and jokes (the vast majority of which were performed without the need for any dialogue) and crazy inventions courtesy of madcap boffin Wilf Lunn (who would go on to perform a similar function on '80s kids show *Jigsaw*).

Each week, there would also be a section of the programme in which pieces of art composed by the viewers at home were put on display in 'The Gallery' – for many viewers, this was the highlight of the show, either watching and hoping that their own masterpiece might have been picked to appear on TV, or (as they grew up) laughing and chortling at other children's collages, finger paintings and attempts at pointillism portraits of the latest pop stars. Key to the entire proceedings was presenter Pat Keysell, who provided a full commentary to deaf and hard-of-hearing children at home through sign language. The programme's weird logo (which consisted of cursive handwriting of the words 'Vision On' mirrored) was nicknamed 'The Grog' by the production team, because apparently it looked like a cross between a grasshopper and a frog!

When *Vision On* finally came to an end in 1976, it was replaced by another programme presented by Tony Hart, a show that was aimed at a more mainstream audience and focused strictly on promoting artwork rather than combining it with entertainment or signing for the deaf. ***Take Hart*** once again featured The Gallery of viewers' artwork and ran for seven years from 1977 to 1983, before being replaced by the remarkably similar *Hartbeat*, which lasted for nine more years.

Website

www.its-prof-again.co.uk/vision_on.htm is a charming and affectionate tribute to this most unusual and memorable of children's shows.

The Voyage of the Dawntreader

See THE CHRONICLES OF NARNIA

Voyage to the Bottom of the Sea

Action-Adventure | 20th Century Fox/Cambridge Productions for ABC (shown on ITV) | episode duration 50 mins | broadcast 14 Sep 1964–24 Mar 1968

Regular Cast

Richard Basehart · *Admiral Harriman Nelson*
David Hedison · *Captain Lee B. Crane*
Del Monroe · *Kowalski*
Paul Trinka · *Patterson*
Richard Bull · *Doctor*
Arch Whiting · *Sparks*
Robert Dowdell · *Lieutenant Comdander Chip Morton*
Henry Kulky · *Chief Curley Jones*
Terry Becker · *Chief Francis Ethelbert Sharkey*
Allan Hunt · *Stuart Riley*

Creator Irwin Allen **Producers** Irwin Allen (executive), Allan Balter, Joseph Gantman, Frank La Tourette, William Welch **Writers** Various, including Irwin Allen, Harlan Ellison, William Welch, William Read Woodfield, Charles Bennett **Theme Music** Paul Sawtell

While everyone else was preparing for journeys among the stars, the crew of the *Seaview*, a nuclear-powered experimental submarine, were exploring the depths of the ocean. Another formulaic action adventure series from Irwin Allen – the king of disaster movies – like all of his series, *Voyage to the Bottom of the Sea* fitted the template perfectly: it had a 'Ronseal'-like title that explained its premise clearly, and it started out fairly serious but soon descended into silliness with unconvincing monsters and spurious character motivations for its villains.

The series came out of Irwin Allen's 1961 movie, which had starred Walter Pidgeon as the good Admiral Nelson, along with Joan Fontaine, Barbara Eden and Peter Lorre.

Wacky Races

Animation | Hanna-Barbera/Heatter-Quigley (shown on BBC One) | episode duration 25 mins | broadcast 14 Sep 1968–4 Jan 1969 (USA)

Regular Voice Cast
Paul Winchell · *Dick Dastardly, Clyde, Private Pinkley*
Don Messick · *Muttley, Professor Pat Pending, Sawtooth, Little Gruesome*
Daws Butler · *Peter Perfect, Rufus Ruffcut, The Slag Brothers, Sergeant Blast, Red Max, Big Gruesome*
Janet Waldo · *Penelope Pitstop*
John Stephenson · *Luke, Blubber Bear, The General*
Mel Blanc · *The Ant Hill Mob*
Dave Willock · *Narrator*

Creators Jerry Eisenberg and Iwao Takamoto (creators of the characters), William Hanna and Joseph Barbera **Producers** William Hanna, Joseph Barbera, Alex Lovy, Art Scott **Writers** Larz Bourne, Tom Dagenais, Dalton Sandifer, Michael Maltese **Theme Music** Joseph Barbera, William Hanna and Hoyt S. Curtin

Eleven driving teams battle it out to win the title of World's Wackiest Racer on a succession of death-inviting courses. In car No. 00 – prepare to boo – is the Mean Machine's Dick Dastardly with his co-driver Muttley; in car No. 1, the Boulder Mobile, we have Rock and Gravel Slag; the Gruesome Twosome are behind the wheel of No. 2, the Creepy Coupé; Professor Pat Pending's Ring-a-Ding Convert-a-Car is No. 3; while No. 4, Crimson Haybailer, is the pride and joy of the Red Max; No. 5 is the Compact Pussycat, owned by the luscious Penelope Pitstop; and No. 6,the Army Surplus Special, is steered by the General, Sergeant Blast and Private Pinkley; Clyde and the Ant Hill Mob are in No. 7,the Bulletproof Bomb; in No. 8, the Arkansas Chugabug are Luke and Blubber Bear; No. 9 is the Turbo Terrific, driven by Peter Perfect; and finally it's No. 10, Rufus Ruffcut and Sawtooth's Buzz Wagon.

It was Gore Vidal who once said that in any competition it's not enough to win – 'others must fail'. Never has this been more clearly demonstrated than in the classic Hanna-Barbera cartoon *Wacky Races*, and specifically with the villain we all love to hate, Dick Dastardly. Had he simply just got on with the race, he'd have blown the competition out of the water every single time. However, poor Dick (complete with ever-snickering canine sidekick Muttley) seemed obsessed with sabotaging all of his rivals' vehicles or laying traps for them to fall into. He never really wanted to win as much as he wanted to see others lose. Inevitably, as for Wile E. Coyote, such overly complicated schemes would rebound back on the moustachioed one, leaving him shaking his fist in impotent fury as the rest of the Wacky Racers shot past the finishing line ahead of him.

Introducing a massive cast of characters, many of whom would find life beyond the dusty racetracks, *Wacky Races* featured more or less the same plot each week, one that was a loving homage to Blake Edwards' movie *The Great Race* (1965). In a different location each time (usually in the USA, but sometimes abroad), the eleven cars would jostle for pole position, with pretty much all of the drivers (except for the nauseatingly nice Peter Perfect and Penelope Pitstop) doing their best to nobble each other on the way to the finishing line. More often than not there would have to be a photo finish to determine who had won each race, and the honours were shared pretty evenly between the contestants. And yes, even Dastardly and Muttley won at least one of the races, although they would be subsequently disallowed. The gadget-laden vehicles were a particular joy to behold for viewers of all ages, although we suspect that younger viewers may not have registered the phallic shape of Peter Perfect's extendable Turbo Terrific or the 'vibrator' setting clearly visible on Penelope Pitstop's dashboard.

Wacky Races proved to be so popular that two long-running and successful spin-off series soon emerged. The blonde Southern belle Penelope Pitstop and the 1930s-style gangsters of the Ant Hill Mob became the stars of *The Perils of Penelope Pitstop*, in which the heroine becomes even more of a damsel in distress when threatened by the evil plans of the Hooded Claw (who unbeknown to her is actually her guardian Sylvester Sneakley). Meanwhile, irrepressible villains Dick Dastardly and Muttley did their best to 'stop the pigeon' in *Dastardly and Muttley in their Flying Machines*. *Wacky Races* is still so familiar to TV audiences that the Vauxhall Corsa recently used the programme's title music and a group of 11 multi-coloured cars in a recent advertising campaign, while a cross-platform videogame was released in 2000.

Wait Till Your Father Gets Home

Animation | Hanna-Barbera/ Rhodes Productions (shown on ITV) | episode duration 25 mins | broadcast 12 Sep 1972–8 Oct 1974 (USA)

Regular Voice Cast
Tom Bosley · *Harry Boyle*
Joan Gerber · *Irma Boyle*
Kristina Holland · *Alice Boyle*
David Hayward · *Chet Boyle*
Jackie Haley · *Jamie Boyle*
Jack Burns · *Ralph*

Creators Harvey Bullock and R. S. Allen **Producers** William Hanna and Joseph Barbera **Writers** Various, including Jack Ellinson, Norman Paul **Theme Music** 'Every single time anything goes wrong/Mom starts to sing that familiar song'. Joan Gerber, David Hayward and Kristina Holland voiced the theme music in character, with Gerber delivering the title in her nasal twang: 'Wait Till Yer Faather Gets Home.'

A proto-***Simpsons***, *Wait Till Your Father Gets Home* was the third 'domestic animated sitcom' produced by Hanna-Barbera, following in the footsteps of ***The Flintstones*** and

The Jetsons. In fact, just as *The Flintstones* had been based upon *The Honeymooners* and ***Top Cat*** had drawn on *Bilko* (see **The Phil Silvers Show**), *Wait Till Your Father Gets Home* was inspired by the American series ***All in the Family*** (itself a reworking of our very own ***Till Death Us Do Part***). A pilot episode, 'Love and the Old-Fashioned Father', originally formed part of the line-up for *Love, American Style*, an anthology show with a view to finding prospective new series.

Harry Boyle runs his own restaurant supply company and is the very image of an all-American dad: slightly conservative and constantly frustrated by the behaviour of his layabout eldest son and freethinking daughter. Only his youngest son Jamie seems to be on the same wavelength as Harry, with wife Irma's ineffectual attempts at discipline providing the programme with its title (and marvellously memorable title song). Next-door neighbour Ralph is a hyper-paranoid anti-Commie vigilante type with a striking resemblance to disgraced US president Richard Nixon. Each episode features yet another challenge to Harry's stable happy family life, normally brought about by (what Ralph might call) 'hippy pinko' influences on his kids.

With a rather minimalist animation style (most of the backgrounds were just line drawings, with only important elements such as the characters themselves 'filled in'), *Wait Till Your Father Gets Home* is perhaps most memorable for its groovy theme tune and 'battle of the generations' theme. By establishing a contemporary domestic setting as a suitable concept for a cartoon series, *Wait Till Your Father Gets Home* paved the way for later, more successful shows like *The Simpsons* and *King of the Hill*.

Voice artist Tom Bosley next starred as another long-suffering dad, Mr Cunningham, in ***Happy Days***, which, like *Wait Till Your Father Gets Home*, began as an episode of *Love, American Style*, although with Harold Gould in the role that Bosley would make his own.

Waiting for God

Sitcom | BBC One | episode duration 30 mins | broadcast 28 Jun 1990–27 Oct 1994

Principal Cast
Stephanie Cole · *Diana Trent*
Graham Crowden · *Tom Ballard*
Daniel Hill · *Harvey Bains*
Janine Duvitski · *Jane Edwards*
Andrew Tourell · *Geoffrey Ballard*
Sandra Payne · *Marion Ballard*
Michael Bilton · *Basil*
Lucy Ashton · *Sarah*
Dawn Hope · *Jenny*
Chico Andrade · *Antonio*
Tim Preece · *Reverend Sparrow*

Creator/Writer Michael Aitkens **Producer** Gareth Gwenlan **Theme Music** The Nash Ensemble wrote and performed a lovely bit of elegant, refined and slightly old-fashioned music – quite appropriate for the series, really.

It's strange that two sitcoms about the onset of age hit BBC One screens at more or less the same time, but *Waiting for God* did indeed begin just six months after the start of ***One Foot in the Grave***. In fact, *Waiting for God* could perhaps best be described as a pre-watershed version of *One Foot in the Grave*, a comedy that addressed the concerns of the UK's ever-ageing population and showed that growing old disgracefully could be a jolly good thing.

Tom Ballard is deposited in Bayview Retirement Village by his wimpish son Geoffrey, primarily at the urging of his selfish and unpleasant wife Marion. A genial and decent chap, Tom is appalled to discover that most of the other 'inmates' in the home have more or less given up the fight, allowing themselves to suffer inedible food and patronising behaviour from the facility manager Harvey Bains. Tom's cheerful insolence brings him to the attention of Bayview's resident battleaxe, Diana Trent. An ex-journalist, Diana is a foul tempered and embittered woman who rails against the unfairness of being old. It's only when united with cheerful Tom that she begins to turn her frustration and intellect outwards, using her pent-up energy to start to have a bit of fun with the people who try and pigeonhole her as being decrepit and past it. Together, Diana and Tom become a pair of mischief-makers and rabble-rousers, bringing headaches to the youngsters like Harvey Bains who are, in fact, already old beyond their years.

A tour de force for two veteran TV performers Stephanie Cole and Graham Crowden, *Waiting for God* was a warm-hearted sitcom with a sensible message – being old doesn't mean your life is over. In particular, Stephanie Cole (perhaps best-known previously for her role as fearsome camp doctor Beatrice Mason in ***Tenko***) was exceptional as Diana, a woman ready with a lethal retort for anyone who dared cross her.

Walking with Dinosaurs

Documentary | BBC/Discovery/TV Asahi/ProSieben/France 3 for BBC One | episode duration 30 mins | broadcast 4 Oct 1999–23 Nov 2003

Cast
Kenneth Brannagh · *Narrator*
Robert Winston, Nigel Marvin · *Presenters*

Creator Tim Haines **Producers** John Lynch, Tim Haines (executive), Kate Bartlett, Nigel Patterson, Jasper James **Theme Music** Ben Bartlett

With Steven Spielberg's *Jurassic Park* (1993) showing how dinosaurs can be brought back to life thanks to computers, in the mid-1990s, the BBC commissioned a short pilot to prove that dinosaurs could be made realistically on a BBC-scale budget. Tim Haines and his team then spent a

year storyboarding their ideas with the help of 60 experts and specialists before setting out to film around the world in locations that would capture what current theories believe the Earth looked like 220 million years ago.

Using a combination of animatronic puppets and computer-generated images, the six-part *Walking with Dinosaurs* approached the subject as if it were a modern-day wildlife programme, including subtle tricks of the camera that made the footage look handheld. Captions would identify dense jungle or tropical islands as such glamorous locations as 'Oxfordshire'. Each episode told a basic story, following the journey of one group of animals but darting off occasionally to look at others. The stories drew in the audience as they told of a mother failing to protect her young from predators or of the many failures those predators would suffer before they managed to feed; in doing so, our loyalties were often torn between a small but rather pathetic early mammal and a resilient but ultimately advantaged dinosaur.

While some of the creatures are well known, many came as surprises. A memorable scene that opened the third episode, 'The Cruel Sea', showed a Tyrannosaurus Rex hunting for food near the shore only to be plucked from a rock by a Liopleurodon – at 25 metres long it put Jaws to shame. It was the largest carnivore the planet Earth ever gave a home to, and a terrifying sight to witness ploughing through the depths with its four powerful flippers.

A hugely popular and critically acclaimed series, *Walking with Dinosaurs* nevertheless drew criticism from some quarters about the necessary reliance on supposition and guesswork for many of its supposedly factual features. But like *Jurassic Park*, the series made real the immensely rich pre-human history of Earth for adults and children alike.

A special edition, *The Ballad of Big Al*, took centre-stage on Christmas Day 2000, focusing on the life cycle of an Allosaur, a predator whose near-complete fossil had been recently discovered in Wyoming. In 2001, a follow-up series, *Walking with Beasts*, looked at the animals that inhabited the Earth after the time of the dinosaurs, while in 2003, Robert Winston traced the evolution of our ancient ancestors in *Walking with Cavemen*. Most dramatic of all, though, was *Sea Monsters – A Walking with Dinosaurs Trilogy*. This was a journey back in time with naturalist Nigel Marven, who appeared in shot alongside some of the most terrifying aquatic creatures to have ever lived, including our friend the Liopleurodon.

Wallace and Gromit

Animation | Aardman Animations for BBC One | episode duration 20–30 mins | broadcast 15 Feb 1989 (*A Grand Day Out*), 26 Dec 1993 (*The Wrong Trousers*), 24 Dec 1995 (*A Close Shave*), 15 Oct 2002 (*Cracking Contraptions*)

Voice Cast
Peter Sallis · *Wallace*
Anne Reid · *Wendolene Ramsbottom*

Creator Nick Park **Producers** Peter Lord, Colin Rose, Peter Salmon, David Sproxton (executive), Rob Copeland, Soozy Mealing, Christopher Moll, Michael Rose, Carla Shelley **Writers** Nick Park, Steve Rushton, Bob Baker **Theme Music** Julian Nott

Cheese-obsessed Yorkshire-born inventor Wallace and his too-intelligent dog Gromit live in a world where a home-made rocket can take you on a trip to the moon and back in a day, where every domestic chore can be solved through a little lateral thinking and where penguins are not to be trusted. These award-winning modelling-clay heroes were the creations of Nick Park, who completed his student project *A Grand Day Out* while working at Aardman Animations. The result was the first of three Oscar nominations for best short animated film and an audience suddenly gripped by the quirky story and Northern brass-band charm. The film was crammed full of clever sight gags and witticisms, including Wallace's labour-saving devices that get him out of bed every morning, make his breakfast and cause disaster at every turn.

A sequel followed in 1993, *The Wrong Trousers*, in which Wallace's mechanical remote-controlled leg-wear causes mayhem, courtesy of Feathers McGraw, a sinister criminal penguin dressed as a chicken. A third short, *A Close Shave*, introduced a brief romance for Wallace when he falls for the divine wool-shop owner Wendolene only for Wendolene's dog, Preston, to frame poor Gromit for sheep rustling. Both *The Wrong Trousers* and *A Close Shave* won the Oscar that had slipped through *A Grand Day Out*'s clammy fingers.

Nick Park diverted his attention from the Wensleydale-eating duo to work on his first feature film, *Chicken Run* (2000) – a *Great Escape*-inspired adventure that starred chickens voiced by Mel Gibson, Julia Sawalha and Jane Horrocks. In 2002, a series of very short Wallace and Gromit cartoons called *Cracking Contraptions* introduced us to such barking inventions as the Snowmanotron, Autochef and the Turbo Diner. A 2005 feature film followed in *Chicken Run*'s footsteps to become one of the most eagerly anticipated movies of the year – *Wallace and Gromit: The Curse of the Were-Rabbit*. Not bad for a year that contained the final *Star Wars* film, the fourth *Harry Potter*, *The Hitchhiker's Guide to the Galaxy*, *The Lion, The Witch and the Wardrobe*, ***The League of Gentlemen*** and a new *Batman*.

Nick Park's other successes include *Creature Comforts*, the Oscar-winning shorts that took vox-pop interviews and turned them into animated masterpieces of anthropomorphic animal opinion. The *Creature Comfort* approach has since been used on a series of adverts for the *Heat Electric* campaign and the channel idents for BBC Three.

The Waltons

Drama | Lorimar Television for CBS (shown on BBC Two) | episode duration 50 mins | broadcast 14 Sep 1972–4 Jun 1981, 21 Nov 1993, 12 Feb 1995, 31 Mar 1997

Regular Cast

Ralph Waite · *John Walton*
Michael Learned · *Olivia Walton*
Richard Thomas, Robert Wightman · *John Boy Walton*
Will Geer · *Grandpa Zeb Walton*
Ellen Corby · *Grandma Esther Walton*
Judy Norton-Taylor · *Mary Ellen Walton/Willard*
Jon Walmsley · *Jason Walton*
Mary Elizabeth McDonough · *Erin Walton*
David W Harper · *Jim-Bob Walton*
Eric Scott · *Ben Walton*
Kami Cotler · *Elizabeth Walton*
Earl Hamner Jr · *Narrator*
Joe Conley · *Ike Godsey*
Ronnie Claire Edwards · *Corabeth Walton Godsey*
Mary Jackson · *'Miss Emily' Baldwin*
Helen Kleeb · *'Miss Mamie' Baldwin*
John Ritter · *Reverend Matthew Fordwick*
Mariclare Costello · *Rosemary Fordwick*
John Crawford · *Sheriff Ep Bridges*
Tom Bower · *Dr Curtis Willard*
Richard Gilliland · *Jonesy*
Lesley Winston · *Cindy Brunson/Walton*
Peggy Rae · *Rose Burton*

Creator Earl Hamner Jr **Producers** Lee Rich (executive), Robert L. Jacks, Andy White, Rod Peterson, Roger La Page, Claylene Jones **Writers** Various, including Earl Hamner Jr, John McGreevey, John Furia Jr, Claire Whittaker, Nancy Greenwald, Nigel McKeand, Carol Evan McKeand, Colby Chester, William Bast, Robert Malcom Young, Calvin Clements Jr, Joanna Lee, Robert Pirosh **Theme Music** Jerry Goldsmith

In the Blue Ridge Mountains of Virginia (cue Laurel and Hardy) lives the Walton family, a large brood of decent, hard-working, God-fearing Americans. Despite their strong family values and unbreakable ties, life isn't easy for the Waltons, living in poor Jefferson County in the middle of the Great Depression. However their borderline poverty never gets the family down for long, because each and every week the family manages to solve most of their problems, learn a valuable moral lesson and still have time to wish each other a 'good night' before turning the lights out.

A one-off movie called *The Homecoming* introduced American TV audiences to *The Waltons*, giving them a healthy dose of nostalgia and a benchmark of decent family living that hit home at a time when the country was reeling from a barrage of uncertainties ranging from the Vietnam War through to the Civil Rights movement. At the moral core of the family were Ada and Mum, John and Olivia, parents to a large brood of devoted siblings. Eldest was earnest John Boy, a wannabe writer and protagonist for most of the plotlines. Mary Ellen was the tomboy always getting into scrapes, whereas Erin was the more conventionally pretty one leaving a trail of broken hearts behind her. As the years went by, the younger Walton children began to get more and more screen time, with John Boy leaving the series at the end of the fifth season (only to return later with a different actor) and Mary Ellen settling down with nice doctor Curtis Willard.

Season seven's 'The Changeling', which aired just before Halloween 1978, is one of the most famous episodes. Elizabeth is approaching her 13th birthday, and is rather concerned about the prospect of having to face maturity. This concern begins to manifest itself in the form of a poltergeist, a malevolent spirit that moves things around and starts smashing items of furniture – a remarkable spin on the normal format for the series. Other traumas affected the family too – Grandma left the series when actress Ellen Corby suffered a stroke that left her partially paralysed. She returned to the series permanently when much-loved actor Will Geer (Grandpa Walton) died in between seasons.

The Waltons was based upon real-life incidents that occurred in series creator Earl Hamner Jr's life, with the character of John Boy loosely based upon his own experiences. Hamner himself narrated the events of each episode, told as a flashback by a grown-up John Boy. Many scenes were shot in the Virginia town of Schuyler (the location of regular *Waltons* conventions), but Frazier National Park in California often doubled for Virginia in order to save time and money. All in all, 221 episodes were produced over nine years, with six reunion movies detailing the later events in the lives of the Walton clan.

Watchdog

Consumer Affairs | BBC One | episode duration 30 mins | broadcast 1980–3, 14 Jul 1985–present

Cast

Hugh Scully, Nick Ross, Lynn Faulds Wood, John Stapleton, Alice Beer, Anne Robinson, Chris Choi, Simon Walton, Jonathan Maitland, Judith Hann, Nicky Campbell · *Presenters/Reporters*

Watchdog began as a weekly slot on the BBC's national news magazine programme *Nationwide*, presented by Hugh Scully. It began simply as a feature on how to complain but soon developed a particular knack for exposing misleading advertising, dodgy deals and some particularly corrupt business people. When it was spun off into its own series, it was hosted by Nick Ross and Lynn Faulds Wood for the first year, and when Ross left, Faulds Wood was joined by her husband John Stapleton. Throughout the 1990s, a certain fearsome red-headed presenter called Anne Robinson made mincemeat out of

dodgy company bosses – good solid training for her role as grand inquisitor on ***The Weakest Link***.

Watchdog Healthcheck arrived on 15 May 1995, focusing on medical matters and hosted by former ***Tomorrow's World*** presenter Judith Hann alongside Alice Beer, an assistant producer on the main show who gradually moved in front of the cameras.

Watching

Sitcom | Granada for ITV | episode duration 25 mins, 2 × 50-min specials | broadcast 5 Jul 1987–4 Apr 1993

Regular Cast

Emma Wray · *Brenda Wilson*
Paul Bown · *Malcolm Stoneway*
Liza Tarbuck · *Pamela Wilson/Lynch*
Patsy Byrne · *Mrs Stoneway*
John Bowler · *David Lynch*
Perry Fenwick · *Terry Milton*
Liz Crowther · *Susan Roberts*
Russell Boulter · *Chris*
Elizabeth Morton · *Lucinda Davis/Stoneway*
Al T Kossy · *Harold*
Bill Moores · *Cedric*
Noreen Kershaw · *Joyce Wilson*
Andrew Hilton · *Gerald Wilson*

Creator/Writer Jim Hitchmough **Producers** David Liddiment (executive), Les Chatfield **Theme Music** 'I'm not blessed with charm/I bring chaos where there was calm/So the question should be what does he . . . see in me?' sang Emma Wray, with series music from Richie Close.

Watching was a rare specimen, a breed only occasionally spotted by the most devoted of keen observers – a funny, successful, ITV sitcom from the late 1980s. Liverpudlian sisters Brenda and Pamela like nothing better than people-watching – making up imaginary life stories for the people they saw walking down the street or in their local pub. One day in The Grapes, they meet wimpy-looking Malcolm, and on Pamela's suggestion, Brenda goes to speak to him. Malcolm doesn't watch people though – he watches birds, being a keen ornithologist. Amazingly, Brenda agrees to go on a birdwatching trip with Malcolm, and against her better judgement, slowly but surely she begins to discover that there's a mutual attraction between them. Malcolm's mother, however, is less than impressed with Brenda – she feels that Brenda's far too common and 'Scouse' for her middle-class son. Pamela, meanwhile, is too wrapped up in her own romance with David Lynch to pass too many comments on her sister's new beau.

What could have been yet another dull comedy about a mismatched couple was instead a vibrant, witty series that shined out from the schedules with its warmth and humanity. With every single one of its 56 scripts written by the same author (ex-teacher Jim Hitchmough), believable characterisation was one of *Watching*'s great strengths. The other was its strong performances, in particular from Jimmy Tarbuck's daughter Liza (an early role for the future star of ***Linda Green***) and first-time actress Emma Wray as the two argumentative sisters. Watching was also a breeding ground for several actors who would go on to greater fame, including ***EastEnders*** star Perry Fenwick and ***The Bill***'s Russell Boulter and John Bowler.

We Are The Champions

Children's Game Show | BBC One | episode duration 25 mins | broadcast 13 Jun 1973–20 Aug 1987, plus one-off specials to 25 Jul 1995

Regular Cast

Ron Pickering, Donna Murray, Gary Lineker, Linford Christie · *Presenter*

Producers Alan Russell, Clive Doig, Peter Charlton

More like a televised (and slightly more fun) version of a school sports day than an episode of ***It's a Knockout*** or *Superstars, We Are The Champions* was, in fact, carefully designed to convince children that taking part in any kind of sporting activity was something to be enjoyed rather than loathed. Teams from three schools would compete against each other in several rounds of games played on a playing field before then relocating to a nearby swimming pool for a further two rounds of water-based relay races or challenges. A wide array of coloured tennis balls, quoits, hula hoops, crawling nets and seesaws were used to make these relay races far more interesting that your normal 100 metre run at school – each team would be adorned with T-shirts consisting of a primary colour and a bold shape like a triangle or a star, just so that the viewers at home who were still watching on black and white sets would be able to tell them apart.

Each week, a sports star would join presenter Ron Pickering to act as the referee – in between the field games and the water games, a few minutes of tedium would see a few of the child competitors interviewing the celebrity about their sporting career and what their greatest achievements were. Most people watching at home would gnash their teeth at these interviews, because a) sports stars are inherently very, very dull people, and b) the really exciting games in the swimming pool were about to start. In fact, when you're nine years old, *nothing* looked more fun than to obey Ron Pickering's closing shout – 'Away You Go!' – and jump into the swimming pool and muck about with the dinghys, inflatables and rafts. Special editions of *We Are The Champions* were produced each year for children with disabilities (called 'Handicapped' when they first began – love that '70s politically incorrect terminology) – in fact, these annual shows continued for eight years after the regular programme drew to a close in 1987, with Gary Lineker and Linford Christie presenting.

The Weakest Link

Quiz Show | BBC Two/One | episode duration 45 mins | broadcast 14 Aug 2000–present

Regular Cast

Anne Robinson · *Host*

Jon Briggs · *Announcer*

Creators Fintan Coyle, Cathy Dunning **Producers** Various, including James Baker, Lesley Katon, Alexandra McLeod, Jo Street, Andy Rowe **Theme Music** Paul Farrer

A show designed for anyone who's ever shouted at the TV in frustration because of the stupidity of a quiz show contestant, the key to *The Weakest Link*'s appeal is that it's possibly the only quiz show where even the winner is made to feel beneath contempt. Presenter Anne Robinson had left the cosiness of ***Points of View*** and the reassurances of ***Watchdog*** behind her when she agreed to present the self-styled nastiest show on television.

Initially, nine contestants face each other in an arc, Anne acting as the inquisitor in the middle. The objective is to complete a chain of answers and win the jackpot available for each round. Anne asks each contestant a question, and money is awarded for every correct answer. Each successive answer increases the money awards, but one wrong answer can empty the pot, so contestants can also choose to 'bank', which keeps the total for the round safe, but also sets the money for the next question to the lowest available value. Most of the questions are fairly basic pub-quiz fodder, but some of them are so easy as to leave players panicking that there must be a trick. At the end of each round, all the players nominate who they feel is the weakest link in the chain, then before that weakest link is sent packing, Anne will pick on a few of the contestants and humiliate them, about their hairstyle, their clothes, their tactical voting or just the complete lack of contribution they make to society. With one player summarily dismissed with the catchphrase 'You are the weakest link – goodbye' and forced to make the 'Walk of Shame' back to the Green Room, the strongest player from the previous round will then be the first player in the next. And so on, until just two players are left and a head-to-head decides which of them bags the money and which of them joins the other players to return home empty-handed.

Compassionless, yet compelling, this theatre of cruelty has been exported around the world (Anne presented the American version herself, leaving unprepared viewers horrified at how spiteful she could be). It first began as a daytime show on BBC Two, but was later given additional shows on BBC One. Since it really took off, there have been a number of themed editions to keep the format fresh. One show brought together top Drag Queens armed with their bitchiest come-backs for Anne, another involving former reality TV show participants and there was also a rematch for previous 'bad losers' of *The Weakest Link*. Celebrity editions have become a regular part of the Saturday night fixture list on BBC One, including an ***EastEnders*** special that saw Adam 'Ian Beale' Woodyat comfortably claim the strongest link title.

Despite the star status of the contestants, Anne can still be relied upon to decimate a celeb for their inability to answer basic questions, but occasionally they get their own back by making Annie laugh: Northern comic Johnny Vegas once confessed that Anne's strict demeanour reminded him of his mother, 'Except I'm sexually attracted t'ya', while in the 'TV Doctors' edition, former ***Doctor Who*** Colin Baker maintained his dignity with a little mild flirtation. Colin narrowly lost out on the grand charity prize that week to a psychologist from ***Big Brother***, which was a shame, considering Anne's customary comment that though the Strongest Link would leave with the prize money, the rest would 'go home with nothing'. It's a harsh world.

The West Wing

See pages 828–31

What's My Line?

Panel Game | BBC/Thames/Meridian for BBC One/ITV | episode duration 30 mins | broadcast 1951–1962, 1973–1974, 1984–1990, 1994

Regular Cast

Eamonn Andrews, Ron Randall, Derek Jacobs, Penelope Keith, Angela Rippon, Emma Forbes · *Hosts*

Creators Mark Goodson, Hal Schaffel and Bill Todman **Theme Music** 'Parisian Mode' by Woolf Phillips

'And will our next guest sign in please . . .', an invitation that would begin a round of one of the most enduring of panel games, originally an American show from 1950 but imported a year later for British consumption. A panel of celebrities (or at least vaguely familiar faces) would watch as a contestant would perform a mime that depicted an aspect of their occupation. The panel would then have to question the guest in ways that could be answered 'Yes' or 'No.' Each member of the panel would ask increasingly specific questions to pin down the person's job, with a 'no' answer moving control over to the next panellist. If all of the panellists had received a 'no' answer it would become a free-for-all, but if the guest answered 'no' ten times, they'd win the round. Things would be spiced up a little by the occasional famous guest, for which the panellists would don a blindfold and ascertain their identity through the usual questions and the hope of the guest's voice giving them a clue. Ha!

Whatever Happened to the Likely Lads?

See THE LIKELY LADS

Wheel of Fortune

Game Show | Scottish Television for ITV | episode duration 25 mins | broadcast 1988–2001

Cast

Nicky Campbell, Bradley Walsh, John Leslie, Paul Hendy · *Hosts*
Angela Ekeate, Carol Smillie, Jenny Powell, Terri Seymour · *Co-hosts*
Steve Hamilton · *Announcer*

Creator Merv Griffin **Theme Music** 'Spin to Win' by David Pringle and Bobbie Heatlie

An import of a popular American game show that first aired over there on 6 January 1975, our own version of *Wheel of Fortune* was originally hosted by Nicky Campbell, a former Radio 1 DJ, alongside Angela Ekeate, who swapped banter with Campbell while flipping the letters on for each of the puzzles. Other presenters followed, with Carol Smillie taking over from Angela Ekeate after just one year and launching her career in programmes like ***Changing Rooms*** as a result.

The format remained largely the same, with players competing against each other to light up the letters to a word or phrase. Points were amassed by spinning a wheel, trying to avoid the segments on the wheel that would miss them a turn or even bankrupt them for the round. Prizes were also modelled by male and female models (a departure from the female-only norm), one of whom was former *GMTV* weatherman and future TV presenter Simon Biagi.

When the Boat Comes In

Drama | BBC One | episode duration 50 mins | broadcast 8 Jan 1976–4 Feb 1977, 17 Feb–21 Apr 1981

Regular Cast

James Bolam · *Jack Ford*
Susan Jameson · *Jessie Seaton*
James Garbutt · *Bill Seaton*
Jean Heywood · *Bella May Seaton*
John Nightingale · *Tom Seaton*
Michelle Newell · *Mary Seaton*
Edward Wilson · *Billy Seaton*
Malcolm Terris · *Matt Headley*
Madelaine Newton · *Dolly*
Basil Henson · *Sir Horatio Manners*
Geoffrey Rose · *Arthur Ashton*
Lois Baxter/Isla Blair · *Lady Caroline*
Christopher Benjamin · *Channing*
Ian Cullen · *Geordie Watson*

Creator James Mitchell **Producers** Leonard Lewis **Writers** James Mitchell, Tom Hadaway, Alex Glasgow, Sid Chaplin **Theme Music** A traditional Northumbrian folk song arranged by David Fanshawe and sung by series writer Alex Glasgow. All together now: 'Dance for your daddy, sing for your mammy/Dance for your daddy when the boat comes in . . .'

A gritty and bleak (yet occasionally heartwarming, too) Northern saga from the creator of ***Callan***, *When the Boat Comes In* portrayed life in the post-Great War years to perfection. Having seen many of his friends and colleagues slaughtered on the battlefields of World War One, returning soldier Jack Ford is determined to make life as good as possible for his home community of Gallowshields, Tyneside. However, events conspire against his well-meaning ambitions – poverty is rife, corruption is rife among the bosses and the trade unions, and the spectre of unemployment looms over the entire area.

Jack discovers a kindred spirit in local teacher Jessie Seaton, and soon becomes friends with her and her parents Bill and Bella. As the series progressed, Jack became involved with the Union in the local shipyard, got Dolly (the maid of Sir Horatio Manners) pregnant and married her, romanced Lady Caroline, emigrated to the USA, returned back after the Great Depression and finally got caught up in the Spanish Civil War, where he was shot and killed trying to smuggle weapons to the anti-government rebels.

With his portrayal of angry young idealist Jack Ford, James Bolam managed to lay to rest any fears that he was just a comedy performer, wiping out completely the memory of ***The Likely Lads***' Terry Collier and instantly establishing himself as a credible leading man for TV dramas such as ***The Beiderbecke Affair*** and *Born and Bred*. *When the Boat Comes In* is notable for another reason too – Bolam's on-screen love interest Jessie was played by his real-life wife, actress Susan Jameson.

Whicker's World

Documentary | BBC One/ITV | episode duration 25–50 mins | broadcast 1957–present

Cast

Alan Whicker · *Presenter*

Today, we might think of Michael Palin as our most well-travelled TV personality. In Palin's previous incarnation as one-sixth of the ***Monty Python*** team he took part in a sketch set on an island populated by 'Alan Whickers'. It's an enduring idea (indeed, in 2005 the ***Dead Ringers*** team resurrected it for their own Bruce Forsyth farm), but such was the strength of Alan Whicker's public image in the

Continued on page 832

The West Wing

Martin Sheen, as President Jed Bartlet.

Any television programme that wins the Emmy Award for Outstanding Drama Series for each of its first four seasons (and only narrowly pipped by ***The Sopranos*** for its fifth) has to be something special indeed. *The West Wing* is more than just a great television programme – at times it becomes something almost Reithian in its ambitions to inform, educate and entertain its audience.

Democrat President Josiah 'Jed' Bartlet is a Nobel Prize-winning liberal intellectual from New England, whose policies and attitudes infuriate the conservatives and right-wingers in his country. Bartlet's America is one that's very similar (but not quite identical) to the present-day USA. For example, his government may have dealings with Israel and Russia, but the names of those countries' leaders will be changed, while foreign policy interventions into countries in the Middle East or Africa occasionally take place within newly created countries such as Qumar. The series begins with Bartlet about 18 months into his first term, with the harsh realities of political life beginning to filter through to him and his staff.

Bartlet's staff (based in the administrative offices of the West Wing of the White House) is a dedicated and driven bunch of quirky characters. Bartlet's best friend and right-hand man is the grumpy, stoic yet reliable chief of staff Leo McGarry, who at the start of the series has yet to admit to the electorate that he's a recovering alcoholic. Despite this, Leo is perhaps the second most important man in Bartlet's USA, able to persuade and encourage the president into making difficult decisions when need be.

Leo's deputy is the dynamic and inspirational Josh Lyman, a sharply intelligent man who aspires to be optimistic but lacks the patience to put up with the bureaucracy of Washington and the misplaced idealism of less well-informed people. Josh's assistant,

Donna Moss, often plays the Linus to Josh's Charlie Brown – she's the dreamer who likes to believe, and is the main conduit for the audience, who are often left scratching their heads over complex issues until she asks Josh to explain what's going on. Donna is nevertheless a highly intelligent woman, but one playing on a field of superstars. Against such odds she manages to hold her own and, despite Josh's constant teasing, is a vital member of the team.

Toby Ziegler is Bartlet's director of communications, ironic considering he's not exactly verbose. Few people would ever use the word joyful to describe Toby – a man who carries the weight of this world (and possibly many others) on his shoulders. Toby's wit is bitter and rarely sugared, but Bartlet chose him for the job because Toby's often the only one who has the courage to challenge him, and when he does so, he's rarely wrong. Toby works well with his assistant, Sam, the president's main speech writer, because if anything, Sam is more of an optimist than Josh, lacking the self-belief to be as sarcastic as the people around him (and also possibly the only person in Washington innocent enough to believe that a platonic relationship with a prostitute wouldn't get him into trouble). Together, Sam and Toby are the heart of Bartlet's administration.

Charlie is the president's personal assistant, elevated by chance after his attempt to work in the White House mailroom was sabotaged when his talent was spotted and he was quickly promoted to work next to the Oval Office. His only problem is that he fails to see his own ability. Charlie is dry witted and far too serious for a man of his age, but then few young men have had to deal with what he has so early in life; his police officer mother was shot and killed just prior to the start of the series.

Finally, we have 'CJ' Cregg, the woman dubbed by her FBI protection squad as the 'Flamingo'. CJ is the public face of Bartlet's presidency, spending most of her time deflecting awkward questions from the assembled media in the White House press room. As such, it's vital that she's kept up to date and informed about everything that's occurring, so occasionally it can seem as though she's playing catch-up with the rest of the staff. However, anyone who made the mistake of undervaluing her importance need only stand in her place for a single press briefing to see just how expertly she dodges press bullets on a day-to-day basis. CJ is the only female member of senior staff. She's able to talk directly to the most powerful man in the world, a man who also happens to be a father of three wilful daughters. This relationship is reciprocated, with Bartlet sometimes using her full first names – Claudia Jean – when he's playfully reprimanding her.

Outside of the president's staff is, of course, his family, who often influence his policies as much as his advisers, whether he'll admit it or not. The formidable First Lady is Dr Abbey Bartlet, a woman with beliefs and agendas just as strong as her husband's. As in the real-life Clinton household, there is the suggestion that the wife is the brighter of the two, which in no way undermines her husband – far from it. Fiercely loyal to her husband and her children, Abbey is headstrong and will occasionally try to lobby both the president and

Drama
John Wells Productions/Warner Bros for NBC (shown on Channel 4)
Episode Duration: 45 mins
Broadcast: 22 Sep 1999–present (USA)

Regular Cast
Martin Sheen · *President Jed Bartlet*
John Spencer · *Leo McGarry*
Richard Schiff · *Toby Ziegler*
Bradley Whitford · *Josh Lyman*
Rob Lowe · *Sam Seaborn*
Allison Janney · *'CJ' Cregg*
Janel Moloney · *Donna Moss*
Dulé Hill · *Charlie Young*
Stockard Channing · *First Lady Dr Abbey Bartlet*
Moira Kelly · *Mandy Hampton*
Joshua Malina · *Will Bailey*
John Amos · *Admiral Percy Fitzwallace*
Timothy Busfield · *Danny Concannon*
Kathryn Joosten · *Mrs Dolores Landingham*
NiCole Robinson · *Margaret*
Tim Matheson · *Vice President John Hoynes*
Marlee Matlin · *Joey Lucas*
Bill O'Brien · *Kenny Thurman*
Kim Webster · *Ginger*
Renée Estevez · *Nancy*
Melissa Fitzgerald · *Carol*
Bill Duffy · *Larry*
Peter James Smith · *Ed*
Elizabeth Moss · *Zoey Bartlet*
Roger Rees · *Lord John Marbury*
Edward James Olmos · *Roberto Mendoza*
Jorja Fox · *Agent Gina Toscano*
Ted McGinley · *Mark Gottfried*
Mary-Louise Parker · *Amy Gardner*
Clifford Calley · *Mark Feuerstein*
Oliver Platt · *Oliver Babish*
Emily Procter · *Ainsley Hayes*
Ron Silver · *Bruno Gianelli*
Anna Deavere Smith · *Security Adviser Nancy McNally*
Mark Harmon · *Agent Simon Donovan*
James Brolin · *Governor Robert Ritchie*
Lily Tomlin · *Debbie Fiderer*
Mary McCormack · *Kate Harper*
Nina Siemaszko · *Ellie Bartlet*
Annabeth Gish · *Elizabeth Bartlet Westin*
John Goodman · *Glenallen Walken*
William Devane · *Lewis Berryhill*
Matthew Perry · *Joe Quincy*
Gary Cole · *Vice President 'Bingo' Bob Russell*
Jay Mohr · *Taylor Reid*
Terry O'Quinn · *General Nicholas Alexander*
Milo O'Shea · *Chief Justice Roy Ashland*
Steven Eckholdt · *Doug Westin*
Glenn Close · *Chief Justice Evelyn Baker Lang*
Jason Isaacs · *Colin Ayres*

his staff to achieve her own ends. But she's no Lady Macbeth; Abbey finds no joy in power for power's sake and genuinely feels that she has to use her position to make the world a better place.

Of vital importance to Jed and Abbey are their three daughters. We first meet Zoey, the youngest of the clan, as she's about to head off to college. Her brief relationship with Charlie shows that she's uncomfortable with the level of press intrusion her father's work causes, but she puts up with it – until a terrible chain of events at the end of series four tests her and her father to the limit. Ellie is the difficult middle child who always felt that she never had much of a connection with her father and, as a consequence, is probably the most independent of the three. Finally, there's Liz, married with a child too young to understand why he never gets much time alone with his grandfather, and a husband eager for political office but not prepared to start even near the bottom of the ladder. What's the point of being the president's son-in-law if you can't use it to step up a few rungs?

Aside from the magnificent, fully rounded characterisation of its regular cast, one of the key strengths of *The West Wing* is that although it features self-contained episodes like any standard drama series, the ongoing plotlines and character developments lend this particular show an almost soap opera level of compulsiveness. Very early in the first series, viewers are given exclusive insight into a Barlet family secret – that the president has been suffering from multiple sclerosis for eight years, and that he, Abbey and his chief of staff Leo chose to hide this from the electorate when he stood for the presidency. When Bartlet is shot in an assassination attempt by a group of white supremacists determined to stop the relationship between Zoey and Charley, the truth about his MS slowly begins to leak out and the president and his staff face impeachment for lying to the American public about his health. More importantly, Bartlet nearly faces a rebellion by his own staff, most notably Toby, who is incandescent with rage about the deception, a deception that effectively left the USA operating under a secret coup d'état masterminded by Leo and Abbey during one of Bartlet's previous 'episodes'.

The West Wing is more than just a great television programme – at times it becomes something almost Reithian in its ambitions to inform, educate and entertain its audience.

As the seasons progress, the stakes for Bartlet's liberal administration become higher and higher. He chooses to authorise the assassination of a foreign leader when he learns of his involvement in terrorist activities on US soil. This event leads to a massive escalation in Middle East tensions and eventually to a horrific incident much closer to home, which brings the Bartlet family to the brink of destruction.

The West Wing artfully manages to weave plots that alternate between high comedy and edge-of-the-seat tension. Although there isn't a single bad performance among any of the cast, special praise has to be given to Alison Janney, who makes CJ into one of the most interesting female characters on American television. Janney, who at six feet in height towers over many of the rest of the cast, was once told by her agent that the only roles she would ever be cast in would be aliens or lesbians. The bold move of casting an unconventionally attractive actress for her intelligence and acting ability rather than for a stereotyped image of beauty has paid off in full, with Janney receiving award after award for her portrayal. Equally marvellous are Richard Schiff, putting in a performance full of subtlety and depth as Toby, and Bradley Whitford's scene-stealing turns as the cocky and charming Josh. The high quality of writing and acting in *The West Wing* has, in turn, attracted a stellar line-up of guest stars, few of whom seem to have been included for the sake of 'stunt casting'. Often the guest cast are invited to play Republicans, against their own reputations, with such noted real-life Democrats as James Brolin and Alan Alda stepping into the ring to spar with their fellow left-winger Sheen.

Originally developed to revolve around Rob Lowe's character, the show shifted in focus once Martin Sheen was cast. Though the show remains an ensemble piece, Sheen's skill in making Bartlet a totally convincing politician is the greatest asset *The West Wing* possesses. Many American critics and viewers have claimed that Jed Bartlet is the best president the USA never had (some have even ventured that Martin Sheen would be a shoo-in if he ever thought of standing for office). As Jed Bartlet, he is a man torn between his desire to change the world for the better and the awareness of his own restricted abilities. Bartlet is too bright for his own good and often reacts badly to anyone showing any sign of not being up to his intellectual level. Were it not for the fact that he clearly deserves it, the treatment that Bartlet doles out to his political opponent in his campaign for election might be considered the actions of a bully. But then, any politician who, like Governor Richie, reacts to the news that a member of staff has just been shot dead with, 'Boy, crime, I just don't know . . .' probably deserves to get his ass kicked.

Sometimes, the purpose of drama is to show us a situation we'll never be in. Sometimes it's to warn us against what might be. And sometimes it serves merely to offer us an alternative to reality. *The West Wing* is a curious example of all three. Some liberals hate it because it creates the illusion of American politics being 'right'. Republicans hate the fact that it's an hour of prime time each week that sets out to attack them and everything they believe in. But we love it for being the best drama to come out of the USA in at least the last decade. As the programme reaches its sixth season, the ticking clock spelling out the final days of the Bartlet presidency gathers pace. But how *The West Wing* will progress is still anybody's guess. Will the show come to a natural conclusion when Bartlet's eight years are up, or will it follow the effort to get a successor elected to the White House? With the casting of Jimmy Smits and Alan Alda as a potential presidential candidates, the story of *The West Wing* may not be over just yet. . . .

Armin Mueller-Stahl · *Prime Minister Eli Zahavy*
Kristin Chenoweth · *Annabeth Schott*
Jimmy Smits · *Matt Santos*
Alan Alda · *Senator Arnold Vinick*

Creator Aaron Sorkin

Producers Aaron Sorkin, Thomas Schlamme, John Wells, Andrew Stearn, Eli Attie, Kristin Harms, Lawrence O'Donnell Jr, Llewellyn Wells, Michael Hissrich, Neal Ahern Jr, Alexa Junge, Carol Flint, John Sacret Young, Paul Redford, Peter Noah

Writers Various, including Aaron Sorkin, Lawrence O'Donnell Jr, Patrick Caddell, Paul Redford, Rick Cleveland, Ron Osborn, Jeff Reno, Dee Dee Myers, Peter Parnell, Allison Abner, Kevin Falls, Laura Glasser, Felicia Willson, Eli Attie, Gene Sperling, Julia Dahl, Debora Cahn, Mark Goffman, William Sind, Michael Oates, David Gerken, David Handelman, Paula Yoo, Lauren Schmidt, Jon Robin Baitz, John Wells, Carol Flint, Peter Noah, John Sacret Young, Alexa Junge

Theme Music W. G. Snuffy Walden

1960s and '70s that he was synonymous with tropical beaches and foreign climes.

Whicker arrived on the scene via the news magazine programme *Tonight*, presenting filmed reports of locations around the world, a feature that eventually span off into *Whicker's World*. His presentation style was distinctive, a calm, easy purr of contentment and always immaculately turned out with his slicked-back hair and clipped moustache. His skill was in not only showing us what places looked like, but what the people were like too – and as often as not, how we Brits might behave there. In a time when only the rich could afford to holiday in such locations, it gave the common folk back home insights into all sorts of lives, indigenous and would-be colonial. It also presented Whicker with enough subjects who would speak for themselves – often damning themselves in the process.

He left the BBC in 1968 for the slightly more lucrative appeal of ITV, having helped to launch Yorkshire Television the previous year. He's been a familiar face in the revolving doors of both channels ever since, presenting special editions that look at specific figures, from John Paul Getty to Pavarotti. In the mid-1980s, Whicker declined an invitation to attempt a re-creation of Jules Verne's ***Around the World in 80 Days***; the job went to Michael Palin. Funny old world.

In recent years, Alan Whicker has supplemented his travelling by lending his tones to an advertising campaign for a holiday company, a rather clever way to inspire confidence in internet bookings among the over-forties.

Who Dares, Wins . . .

Comedy | Holmes Associates/Who Dares Wins Productions for Channel 4 | episode duration 35–45 mins | broadcast 4 Nov 1983, 12 May 1984–25 May 1988

Regular Cast
Julia Hills, Rory McGrath, Jimmy Mulville, Philip Pope, Tony Robinson

Producers Andy Hamilton, Denise O'Donoughue, Laurie Rowley **Writers** Andy Hamilton, Guy Jenkin, Colin Bostock-Smith, Rory McGrath, Jimmy Mulville, Tony Sarchent **Theme Music** Philip Pope

To celebrate the first birthday of Channel 4, a team of up-and-coming comedy stars was assembled to front a live sketch show. With the express aim of being as topical as possible, script elements were only finalised on the afternoon of transmission – a feature that co-writers Andy Hamilton and Guy Jenkin would re-use on their later sitcom success ***Drop the Dead Donkey***. The result was a critical and popular success, and the *Who Dares, Wins . . .* team were brought back the following summer for the first of four late-night comedy series that perpetually pushed back the boundaries for what was (and what wasn't) acceptable on TV.

Named after the slogan of the SAS, *Who Dares, Wins . . .* was essential viewing for anybody who enjoyed the alternative style of comedy shown in ***The Young Ones*** mixed with the traditional sketch format perfected by ***Morecambe and Wise*** and ***The Two Ronnies***. However, rather than quips about the vagaries of the English language or dance routines starring newsreaders, *Who Dares, Wins . . .* featured foul-mouthed pandas talking about their sex life (or lack of it) and their plans to break out of their prison-like zoo compound. Sketches veered from 'Some People Will Do Anything to Get on TV', in which the team played ordinary members of the public encouraged to eat 'live' frogs or shoot their husbands, to others in which star-struck young girls are taken away from their parents by the NSPCC in order to 'prevent another Bonnie Langford'. Satirical songs were performed by team member Philip Pope, Julia Hills regularly played a terrified and incompetent TV interviewer (before moving on to ***2 Point 4 Children***), and newly discovered Tony Robinson, having just made a name for himself on BBC One's ***The Black Adder***, took several available opportunities to appear stark naked. The two remaining team members, Rory McGrath and Jimmy Mulville, formed the independent production company Hat Trick. One of their first projects was *Chelmsford 123* (appearing in 13 episodes on Channel 4, 9 Mar 1988–20 Feb 1990), a sitcom set in Roman Britain, starring McGrath, Mulville, Pope and future *Drop the Dead Donkey* star Neil Pearson.

Who Pays the Ferryman?

Drama | BBC One | episode duration 50 mins | broadcast 7 Nov–26 Dec 1977

Principal Cast
Jack Hedley · *Alan Haldane/Leandros*
Betty Arvaniti · *Annika Zeferis*
Takis Emmanuel · *Matheos Noukakis*
Stefan Gryff · *Major*
Patience Collier · *Katharina Matakis*
Neil McCarthy · *Babis Spiradakis*
Alexis Sergis · *Alexis Vassikalis*
Maria Sokali · *Elena Vassilakis*
Nikos Verlekis · *Nikos Vassilakis*

Creator/Writer Michael J. Bird **Producer** William Slater **Theme Music** A No. 11 hit single in 1977 for its composer Yannis Markopoulos

Michael J. Bird returned to the islands of Greece for *Who Pays the Ferryman?*, the setting of his 1972–3 thriller ***The Lotus Eaters***. This time the location was Crete. It's possibly the best remembered of Bird's canon, perhaps due to the haunting, top twenty theme by Yannis Markopoulis. Jack Hedley stars as the former Greek resistance fighter returning to the island for a reunion but discovering that for some, World War Two had never

really ended. So popular was this series, that the BBC immediately asked Bird for another and, in 1979, the public got the eight-part ***The Aphrodite Inheritance***, featuring Peter McEnery on Cyprus, trying to investigate the mysterious death of his brother. As the story progressed, Bird poured over the more mythological aspects of the area, leaving little doubt that the characters played by Alexandra Bastedo, Brian Blessed and Stefan Gryff were, in fact, from the legendary pantheon of Grecian gods, sent to Earth to help McEnery on his voyage of discovery.

Website

An authorised tribute site to Michael J. Bird can be found at birdland2.netfirms.com.

Who Wants to be a Millionaire?

Quiz Show | Celador for ITV | episode duration 25–45 mins | broadcast 4 Sep 1998–present

Cast

Chris Tarrant · *Host*

Creator David Briggs **Producer** Paul Smith **Theme Music** Keith and Matthew Strachan, cleverly reworking the song from the 1953 Marilyn Monroe film *How to Marry a Millionaire*

When *Who Wants to be a Millionaire?* first hit the screens it was one of the biggest TV events in years. Twelve consecutive days were cleared to make way for the show, enabling the tension to be built up, creating a level of excitement that host Chris Tarrant was determined not to let go of. Sadly, no-one won the million that time, but it was so successful, with its combination of play-at-home fun, genuine edge-of-the-seat tension and a peak of 18 million viewers, that ITV would have been fools not to recommission it.

First of all, there's the qualifier, where the potential contestants have to place four items in ordinal or chronological order. The 'fastest finger' goes on to play the main game, in which 15 questions stand in the way between each contestant and the million. Each question is multiple choice and the value of prize money rises with each correct question. There are two 'guarantee points', where the player can afford to get a wrong answer and still walk home with something. These come after question five (for £1000) and question ten (for £32,000). At the start, the player carries three lifelines: a '50-50' choice that removes two of the wrong answers; 'Ask the Audience', where the audiences use their keypads to show what they think the answer is, which will hopefully offer a clue to the correct answer through consensus of opinion (though of course, this isn't at all guaranteed); and 'Phone a Friend', in which the player will be asked to choose from their bank of friends one contact who is most likely to know the answer to the question. One additional lifeline – the 'Flip' (in which a contestant could discard a question they really didn't like in exchange for one of their remaining lifelines) was quickly abandoned.

The names of the lifelines have become some of the many catchphrases from the show to leak into common parlance. Other phrases include: 'We don't wanna give you that', when the player is shown a cheque for their current winnings just as Tarrant moves on to the next stage of questions; 'Is that your final answer?'; and the dreaded 'We'll take a quick break', where Tarrant links to the obligatory adverts at a really tense moment. Such catchphrases have made Tarrant a figure of frustration as he teases the contestant and milks the situation for as much tension as he can with his stock phrases – but we love him for it. It's a far more respectable pursuit than lashing grown-ups with water like he used to do on ***TISWAS***.

It took 122 editions for anyone to get to the million. Answering the question 'Which king was married to Eleanor of Aquitaine?', Judith Keppel coolly answered 'B – Henry II' and entered the history books. She wasn't Britain's first game show millionaire, though – on Christmas Eve 1999, Chris Evans (ever the publicist) chose to steal Millionaire's thunder on his own programme ***TFI Friday*** by giving away a million pounds to a lucky contestant called Ian Woodley – beating Judith Keppel by 11 months. A *slightly* more controversial (cough) winner than the posh Judith Keppel was Major Charles Ingram who (cough) managed to correctly identify a one followed by 100 zeros as a 'Googol' (we often wondered where they got the name for that search engine from). Only later was it revealed that Ingram had won through a conspiracy of coughs, courtesy of college lecturer Tecwen Whittock. The pair were later found guilty of 'conspiracy to obtain a valuable security by deception'.

The series has now been exported around the world; you can even take part in a live version of the show in Disney-MGM Studios theme park in Orlando, Florida.

Whoops Apocalypse

Sitcom | LWT for ITV | episode duration 25 mins | broadcast 14 Mar–18 Apr 1982

Principal Cast

Barry Morse · *President Johnny Cyclops*
Richard Griffiths · *President Dubienkin*
Peter Jones · *Prime Minister Kevin Pork*
John Cleese · *Lacrobat*
David Kelly · *Abdab*
John Barron · *The Deacon*
Ed Bishop · *Jay Garrick*
Alexei Sayle · *Commissar Solzhenitsyn*
Geoffrey Palmer · *Foreign Secretary*
Richard Davies · *Chancellor of the Exchequer*
Bruce Montague · *Shah Mashiq Rassim*
Lou Hirsch · *Jeb Grodd*

Creator/Writers Andrew Marshall, David Renwick **Producer** Humphrey Barclay **Theme Music** Nigel Hess

Andrew Marshall and David Renwick are two of the most accomplished sitcom writers of the past 20 years, and in *Whoops Apocalypse* they scored one of their first big hits, one with a distinctly bleak sense of humour. Just as was the case in the real world at the start of the Eighties, the two great superpowers of the USA and USSR stand on the brink of annihilating each other and the rest of the planet. President Johnny Cyclops (a former actor) has lost a lot of his support back home in the States and decides that he needs to do something to restore his popularity. Unfortunately, Cyclops has recently had a lobotomy and takes most of his advice from religious fundamentalist nutter the Deacon, who honestly believes that he's able to speak directly to God. On the Soviet side, their arsenal of nuclear weapons is controlled by the antediluvian old duffer Premier Dubienkin. Trying to keep the peace between the two superpowers is the deeply dim and ineffectual British PM Kevin Pork. Between them all, the world teeters on the brink of Armageddon, with problems in the Middle East with the Shah of Iran fading into insignificance when a freelance terrorist called Lacrobat manages to steal a nuclear warhead . . .

It's difficult to recall just how much of a concern the prospect of nuclear war was for many people in the early 1980s. With both America and the USSR seemingly determined to keep escalating the arms race, and the UK suddenly thrown into the middle of the nuclear cold war thanks to the arrival of American Cruise Missiles at Greenham Common airbase, it's not especially surprising that comedy writers should turn their satirical gaze on the bewildering behaviour being exhibited by world leaders at the time. The witty and subversive scripts in *Whoops Apocalypse* are supported by an astounding international cast, including John Cleese (as the terrorist Lacrobat) in his one and only sitcom appearance aside from ***Fawlty Towers***. In 1987, a feature film of *Whoops Apocalypse* was produced – sadly, it wasn't a patch on the TV version, despite featuring an even more stellar cast (including *M*A*S*H**'s Loretta Swit, Peter Cook and Herbert Lom).

Four years after *Whoops Apocalypse*, writers Marshall and Renwick turned their satirical gaze onto the world of the tabloid newspaper with ***Hot Metal***, another outstanding series that made viewers laugh and think at the same time.

Whose Line is it Anyway?

Comedy | Hat Trick for Channel 4 | episode duration 25 mins | broadcast 23 Sep 1988–18 Jun 1998, plus compilations

Cast

Clive Anderson · *Host*

Josie Lawrence, Tony Slattery, Mike McShane, Paul Merton, John Sessions, Ryan Stiles, Greg Proops, Sandi Toksvig, Colin Mochrie, Jim Sweeney, Stephen Frost, Caroline Quentin, Brad Sherwood · *Contestants*

Richard Vranch, Laura Hall · *Piano and Keyboards*

Creators Dan Patterson and Mark Leveson **Producers** Denise O'Donoghue (executive), Anne Marie Thorogood, Ruth Wallace (associate), Dan Patterson **Theme Music** Philip Pope

Hosted by Clive Anderson, the drollest of dry wits, *Whose Line is it Anyway?* was yet another Radio 4 comedy that transferred to television. Celebrating the art form that is improvised comedy, it relied on quick wits, a strong imagination and often no shame. The panel would consist of four participants – usually, but not limited to, comedians – plus musical accompaniment that was just as improvised, from Richard Vranch (and later Laura Hall). Anderson would introduce the rounds and the panel would be told to participate solo, all together, in pairs or three at once, with points being totted up on a seemingly arbitrary basis. The decided winner of the game would be given the opportunity to read out the credits to the show in the style of Anderson's choosing – which might be a sex-talk line, an auction house, a rodeo or somesuch other style to create hilarity as the winner name-checks the crew.

Rounds consisted of a number of regular games. 'Party Quirks' involved one player acting as host to a party while the other three arrived one at a time, acting in the style of whatever was on their card; the host would then have to work out that one of them could only speak in the style of a Restoration comedy, another was a slippery politician and the third a children's TV presenter. 'World's Worst' required the players to deliver a one-liner in the style of the world's worst (for example) funeral director, babysitter or DIY expert. Often, they'd be divided into pairs to improvise around an object. 'Film and Theatre Styles' required Anderson to collate suggestions from the audience, which the participants would then have to switch between at the sound of Anderson's buzzer. That particular round was always fun to watch when it involved people who had no idea how to rap properly or who'd never really got the hang of Country rhythm. And 'Standing, Leaning, Sitting' was self-evidently a game that was harder than it looked, where one person must be standing, one leaning and, yes, one sitting, which improvising around a given conversation.

In among the regular performers were a few celebs who wanted to give the game a go. Such guests included Rory Bremner, Peter Cook, Stephen Fry, Jonathan Pryce, Jan Ravens, Griff Rhys Jones, Ron West, Steve Steen, Eddie Izzard, Ardal O'Hanlon and Catherine O'Hara. From 1998, we received the US version that starred Drew Carey as host, with some of our own regulars making the journey over the water.

Why Don't You . . .?

Children's Magazine | BBC One | episode duration 25 mins | broadcast 20 Aug 1973–21 Apr 1995

Creator Patrick Dowling **Producers** Patrick Dowling, Molly Cox, Peter Charlton, Catherine McFarlane, Hilary Murphy, Alan Cooke, David J. Evans, Brian Willis, John F. D. Northover, Kirstie Fisher, Trevor Long, Alex Lonsdale, Judy Merry, Richard Simkin

Spearheading 'user-generated content' long before anyone had a name for it, *Why Don't You . . .?* (or, to give it its full title as revealed in the various theme songs, *Why Don't you just Switch off your Television Set and Go Out and Do Something Less Boring Instead?*) invited kids to send in their ideas for how to fill those long, drawn-out summer holidays. As the producers soon discovered, kids' activities aren't really that interesting – the first edition had a film about collecting worms, while the recipe segments led to the production teams being inundated with yet more identical recipes for chocolate rice krispie cakes.

The show began in Bristol, but eventually *Why Don't You . . .?* gangs sprung up in Cardiff, Newcastle, Liverpool and Northern Ireland. In the mid-1980s, young assistant producer Russell Davies came up with the idea of introducing ongoing stories to the proceedings, a hint of where his future lay once he'd added the middle initial 'T' to his name and become one of Britain's top dramatists (he was responsible for ***Queer as Folk, The Second Coming, Casanova*** and the hugely successful 2005 ***Doctor Who*** revival).

Widows

Crime Drama | Euston Films/Thames for ITV | episode duration 50 mins | broadcast 16 Mar 1983–8 May 1985

Principal Cast

Ann Mitchell · *Dolly Rawlins*
Maureen O'Farrell · *Linda Perelli*
Fiona Hendley · *Shirley Miller*
Eva Mottley, Debby Bishop · *Bella O'Reilly*
David Calder · *DI George Resnick*
Thelma Whiteley · *Kathleen Resnick*
Maurice O'Connell · *Harry Rawlins*
Stanley Meadows · *Eddie Rawlins*
Kate Williams · *Audrey Withey*
Peter Lovstrom · *Greg Withey*
Dudley Sutton · *Boxer Davis*
George Costigan · *Charlie*
Terry Cowling · *Jimmy Nunn*
Christopher Ellison · *Tony Fisher*
Jeffrey Chiswick · *Arnie Fisher*
Irene Marot · *Gloria*
Terence Harvey · *Chief Inspector Saunders*
Paul Jesson · *DS/DI Alec Fuller*
Peter Machin · *DC Andrews*
David Fielder · *Donald Franks*
Carol Gillies · *Alice*
Anthony Heaton · *Bill Grant*
Geoffrey Hutchings · *Willy Daily*
James Lister · *Carlos Moreno*
Catherine Neilson · *Trudie Nunn*
Michael John Paliotti · *Joe Perelli*
John Rowe · *Brian Miller*
Judith Fellows · *Mother Superior*
Stephen Yardley · *Vic Morgan*
Peter Jonfield · *Jimmy Glazier*
Damien Thomas · *José Camarena*
Andrew Kazamia · *Micky Tesco*
Aran Bell · *Brian Fisk*
Jim Carter · *DI Frinton*
Ann Michelle · *Jackie Rawlins*
Catherine Neilson · *Trudie Nunn*
Winston Crooke · *Harvey Rintle*
Mike Felix · *Eddie Bates*
Ann Davies · *Mildred Soal*
Pavel Douglas · *DC Reynolds*
Alan Downer · *Colin Soal*
Patrick Durkin · *Kevin White*
Carole Hayman · *Marion Gordon*
Tristram Jellinek · *Mr Jarrow*

Creator/Writer Lynda La Plante **Producers** Verity Lambert, Linda Agran, Johnny Goodman (executive), Ron Purdie (associate), Irving Teitelbaum **Theme Music** The main *Widows* theme, which features a motif played on Spanish guitar, was written by Stanley Myers. For series two, the end theme was written and performed by Gerard Kenny, with lyrics by Michael Leeson. The end music to the final episode of each series was the aria 'Che farò senza Euridice' from the opera *Orfeo ed Euridice* by Christoph Willibald von Gluck, performed by the legendary Kathleen Ferrier.

When a gang of armed robbers led by gangster Harry Rawlins are killed during a raid on a security van, rival gangsters begin to search for Harry's infamous ledgers – detailed notes of possible jobs that Harry had spent years compiling. Only Harry's widow Dolly knows where the ledgers are hidden, and plans to complete the job that killed her husband, drafting in help from Shirley and Linda (widows of the gang members Terry Miller and Joe Perelli) and a stripper called Bella, whose partner recently died of a drugs overdose. As the day for the robbery draws close, Dolly learns that Harry might not be dead after all. . .

Created as a reaction to the generally male-centred shows Lynda La Plante had worked on while an actress (under her stage name Lynda Marchal), *Widows* began La Plante's career as one of Britain's premier TV writers. With a cast of largely unknown actors, the series had the characteristic look and feel of a Euston Films production, with washed-out film and realistic settings, but there was something about the lack of theatricality of this particular drama that raised it above the rest.

The series begins with the botched job on the security van, trapped between the gang's vehicles in the Waterloo Bridge–Kingsway underpass in central London (a shot that reveals just how much has changed on the South Bank in the last 20 years). As the vehicles collide, an explosion rips through the tunnel, killing all bar one of the gang members. Later episodes reveal how the operation was set up, giving viewers a chance to get to know the men the women lost, including Harry Rawlins himself. Clips of the men training for the job are intercut with the women mirroring their every move on the training ground in preparation for their own attempt. Only once we've become used to Harry's face do we gain a flashback to the robbery and see that the man who got away was actually Rawlins.

Each of the other widows proves to be both an asset and a liability to Dolly's plans: Linda is good with her hands, learning the intricacies of car maintenance. Unfortunately she's a soft touch where a handsome face is concerned and discovers almost too late that her new boyfriend is in the pocket of rival gang the Fisher brothers (Terry Fisher, a nasty bully, is played by Chris Ellison, who would later join the other side of the law for a long stretch in ***The Bill*** as Burnside). Shirley, meanwhile, is a timid but ambitious model whose fragility in the first series transforms into determination for the second. It's Linda who brings in the fourth member of the gang, a hard-as-nails stripper called Bella whose steadiness and common sense eventually win round an initially reluctant Dolly.

Like her husband, Dolly rules with a combination of ruthlessness and charm, one minute impassive and grim, the next flashing a winning smile that gets her the results she needs. Her role is the most difficult of all, especially when she becomes aware of Harry's deception (in the final scene of the first series, Dolly shows her associates just how much the fact of Harry's survival tears through her, a point she illustrates by raking her perfectly manicured nails down the underside of her forearm). For Dolly, the deception is made worse by the discovery that Harry has both a mistress and a child, something she was never able to provide him with. When her surrogate baby, a poodle, is accidentally killed during a break-in at her home, Dolly reveals just how hard she has to work to keep grief and sentimentality at bay so that she doesn't just fall apart. It's no wonder the character is still so highly regarded by the viewers – a breathtaking exercise in self-restraint by Ann Mitchell.

Working to piece together the legacy of Harry Rawlins is DI Resnick (the sublime David Calder), a man two steps behind Dolly's gang and just one step away from his first heart attack. Determined to prove that Rawlins is still alive, Resnick ends up alienating his superiors and colleagues in his relentless pursuit of ghosts. Unfortunately for him, Harry is anything but dead, as Resnick discovers when he suffers a savage beating while on a stakeout outside Dolly's house, an attack that effectively removes him from the investigation and invalids him out of the police service.

The 'widows' pull off the robbery, of course, and hotfoot it to Rio to start a new life. Originally, that was going to be that, but such was the success of the series that a sequel was in production a year later. Sadly, shortly into rehearsals, Eva Mottley, who'd played Bella, left the production after a row. She was found dead a few weeks later following a suspected drugs overdose. For the second series (often erroneously called *Widows 2*), her part was filled at short notice by Debby Bishop, a comedy actress best known at the time for her appearances on the Jasper Carrott show and making her 'straight' acting debut on the series. Mottley's was a tough act to follow and as a consequence Bishop's interpretation tends to be viewed in a more negative light than if the part had been played by her from the outset.

As the women realise they have less in common than they'd thought, and as Bella in particular tries to make a fresh start for herself, it's Linda who ends up feeling the most excluded. Dolly returns to the UK to set up appointments with a plastic surgeon while Shirley is happy never to see the women again as she begins to finally make progress as a model. But then Harry Rawlins comes looking for the money he believes should have been his, and Linda and Bella are forced to flee Rio and return home. Dolly hires a private detective to keep an eye on Harry while Shirley and Bella decide to rid themselves of Harry once and for all by offering him a share of the money from the security van job with the intention of informing the police and pinning the robbery on him. But of course it all goes wrong and Linda is left dead after being run over by Harry's car.

It was inevitable that Dolly would end up a) killing her husband and b) arrested for both the murder and the initial robbery. Sentenced to five years on a reduced sentence for helping the police recover the money, Dolly would have to wait a lot longer to be released. Her final story wasn't revealed until ***She's Out***, almost ten years later.

Trivia

A US remake of the series in 2002 starred Mercedes Ruehl as Dolly.

Will and Grace

Sitcom | Komut/3 Sisters Entertainment for NBC (shown on Living/Channel 4) | episode duration 25 mins plus 1 × 50-min special | broadcast 21 Sep 1998–present (USA)

Regular Cast

Eric McCormack · *Will Truman*
Debra Messing · *Grace Adler*
Sean Hayes · *Jack McFarland*
Megan Mullally · *Karen Walker*
Shelley Morrison · *Rosario*
Woody Harrelson · *Nathan*
Debbie Reynolds · *Grace's Mom*
Gregory Hines · *Ben*

Creators David Kohan, Matt Mutchnick **Producers** James Burrows, David Kohan, Matt Mutchnick (executive), Bruce Alden, Peter Chakos, Suzy Mamann Greenberg **Writer** Various, including David Kohan, Matt Mutchnick, Adam Barr, Jeff Greenstein, Karl Lizer, Sally Bradford, Bill Wrubel **Theme Music** Jonathan Wolff

Will Truman and Grace Adler are the ideal modern good-looking couple – they share each other's interests, live together in a gorgeous apartment and enjoy the fruits of two successful careers, Will as a lawyer, Grace running her own interior design agency. The only minor problem is that Will happens to be gay – if they could just get round that one tiny little issue, then they'd both be blissfully happy. As it happens, their friendship is about the only thing that keeps them both sane in their endless quest to find Mr Right. Will's best friend Jack is a flamboyantly out gay man, always ready with a sharply barbed retort or a bitchy little comment. Jack meets his match, though, in Grace's employee Karen, a hugely wealthy woman with a tongue even sharper than his and absolutely no sense of personal shame or embarrassment to limit her outrageous behaviour and comments. In particular, Karen treats her housemaid Rosario with a combination of utter contempt, disdain and out-and-out lust.

Will and Grace was a surprise smash hit success in the USA, considering that its basic set-up (a 'hom-rom-com') might have seemed likely to alienate a large section of the American viewing public. However, the non-threatening sexuality of lead character Will, combined with dynamically funny scripts and appealing performances from all four leads (especially Megan Mullally as the monstrous Karen) have ensured its longevity – at the time of writing, an eighth season had just been commissioned. The programme kind of crept in under the radar in the UK, however, with cable channel Living getting first transmission rights prior to their screenings on Channel 4. Gradually *Will and Grace* is building a devoted following in the UK (many of whom suspect the show should really be called *Jack and Karen*).

William

Comedy Drama | BBC TV | episode duration 30 mins | broadcast 26 May 1962–4 May 1963

Cast

Dennis Waterman, Denis Gilmore · *William Brown*
Christopher Witty · *Ginger*
Bobby Bannerman, Kaplan Kaye · *Henry*
Carlo Cura · *Douglas*
Gillian Gostling · *Violet Elizabeth Bott*
Patricia Marmont · *Mrs Brown*
Lockwood West · *Mr Brown*
Suzanne Neve · *Ethel Brown*
Marjorie Gresley · *Mrs Bott*

Producer Leonard Chase **Writer** C. E. Webber, from the novels by Richmal Crompton

For commentary, see JUST WILLIAM

Willo the Wisp

Animation | Spargo for BBC One | episode duration 5 mins | broadcast 14 Sep 1981

Voice Cast

Kenneth Williams

Creator/Producer/Writer Nicholas Spargo **Theme Music** Tony Kinsey

In the depths of Doyley Wood lives Willo the Wisp, a strange blue spirit of the forest with the habit of telling tales about his fellow wood-dwellers and a visage and voice suspiciously like that of *Carry On* star Kenneth Williams. Regular characters involved in Willo the Wisp's stories included Arthur the Caterpillar, fat fairy Mavis Cruet, stupid yet happy doggy the Moog, short-sighted cat Carwash, the Beast (formerly Prince Humbert the Handsome) and of course wicked witch Evil Edna (who for some reason had taken the shape of a knackered old television set).

Each of the 26 episodes of *Willo the Wisp* was broadcast right before the 6 o'clock *News* on BBC One, thereby granting it both a large cross-generation audience and increased longevity, thanks to mums and dads who found Williams' narration much more witty and entertaining than usual for a kids' TV show. Ron Murdoch's simple yet beautifully effective animation was devised by series maestro Nick Spargo. The latter had originally created the cartoon as in-house publicity film called *Supernatural* for British Gas in the late 1970s, and subsequently *Willo the Wisp* became the only British cartoon series with a credit thanking a utility company.

Winston Churchill: The Wilderness Years

Drama | Southern for ITV | episode duration 50 mins | broadcast 6 Sep–25 Oct 1981

Principal Cast

Robert Hardy · *Winston Churchill*
Siân Phillips · *Clementine Churchill*
Nigel Havers · *Randolph Churchill*
Chloe Salaman · *Sarah Churchill*
Tamsin Murray-Leach, Katherine Levy · *Mary Churchill*
Tim Pigott-Smith · *Brendan Bracken*
David Swift · *Professor Lindemann*
Sherrie Hewson · *Mrs Pearman*
Moray Watson · *Major Desmond Morton*
Paul Freeman · *Ralph Wigram*
Frank Middlemass · *Lord Derby*
David Quilter · *Wing Commander Torr Anderson*
Sam Wanamaker · *Bernard Baruch*
Peter Barkworth · *Stanley Baldwin*
Eric Porter · *Neville Chamberlain*

Edward Woodward · *Sir Samuel Hoare*
Peter Vaughan · *Sir Thomas Inskip*
Robert James · *Ramsay McDonald*
Tony Mathews · *Anthony Eden*
Ian Collier · *Harold Macmillan*
Norman Jones · *Clement Attlee*
Richard Murdoch · *Lord Halifax*
Walter Gotell · *Lord Swinton*
Clive Swift · *Sir Horace Wilson*
Marcella Markham · *Nancy Astor*
Phil Brown · *Lord Beaverbrook*
Stratford Johns · *Lord Rothermere*

Creators Martin Gilbert and Richard Broke **Producers** Mark Shivas (executive), Richard Broke **Writer** Ferdinand Fairfax **Theme Music** Carl Davis

After World War One, Winston Churchill found himself ousted by his own party in favour of Stanley Baldwin. A tour in America with his son helped him raise funds until the Wall Street crash wiped them out. Even after his return to England, he wasn't taken seriously, tricked by Baldwin into delivering a career-suicide speech, while his early warnings against Hitler were ignored even after Hitler moved his troops into the Rhineland. This series followed Churchill's fluctuating popularity as he convinced more and more of his peers to take note of the warnings coming from Germany but almost undermined it all by showing support for the King in his choice to abdicate.

The part of Churchill offered a superb opportunity for Robert Hardy, who at the time was more familiar to viewers as the avuncular Siegfried Farnon in the BBC's ***All Creatures Great and Small***. Robert Hardy left us in no doubt why Churchill had grown to be known as the greatest Briton of all time, with the highest approval rating of any prime minister of the 20th century. It was a glorious dramatic production too for Southern Television, who sadly lost their ITV franchise soon after.

Wipeout

Quiz Show | Action Time for BBC One | episode duration 30 mins | broadcast 25 May 1994–2003

Cast
Paul Daniels, Bob Monkhouse · *Quizmasters*

Creator Bob Fraser **Producers** Rick Gardner, Graham Owens

Imported to BBC One from America, this game show was all about winning as many points as possible without picking a wrong answer, which would wipe out your points for the round. Contestants faced a grid of 16 squares containing possible answers to a collection – films of a particular movie star, players for a specific team, words derived from Latin – with 11 right answers and five wrong answers that would 'wipe out' the player's points. Each player would have to make one pick from the grid, at which point they could choose to continue picking or, if they weren't feeling confident, they could pass over to the next player.

TV magician Paul Daniels had already made the move over to quizmaster thanks to ***Every Second Counts***, and continued here with a slightly condescending approach to the players. When the series was moved to the daytime schedule, legendary Bob Monkhouse took on the position of quizmaster. Despite clearly struggling under the pressure of churning out multiple editions of a daytime quiz, Bob still hadn't lost his spark. What he had lost, however, was the roar of a live audience – the cheers, applause and shots of the crowd were added afterwards. Sadly, *Wipeout* was Bob's final quiz show; he died in 2003 after a lengthy battle with prostate cancer.

Wish You Were Here. . .?

Documentary/Travel | Thames/Fremantle for ITV | episode duration 25 mins | broadcast Apr 1974–2004

Cast
Judith Chalmers, Chris Kelly, Anneka Rice, John Carter, Anthea Turner, Anna Walker, Mary Nightingale, Julia Bradbury, Ruth England, Russell Amerasekera, Rhodri Owen · *Presenters*

Creator Peter Hughes **Producers** Peter Hughes, Christopher Palmer **Theme Music** Gordon Giltrap's 'The Carnival'. Giltrap also wrote 'Heartsong', one of the theme tunes to the BBC's *Holiday*.

ITV's long-running travel show was created to rival the BBC's *Holiday*. The series took a critical look at package holidays and told viewers what to expect: are the beaches as golden as they look in the brochure (not if you're going to the Canary Islands, they're not . . .)? Will the hotel be built by the time you get there? How much can you expect to spend without going mad? Though other personalities hosted shows, Judith Chalmers was the series' main presenter from beginning to end, with the peak-time series coming to a close only when she decided to leave in 2004 (though it continued in the daytime schedules as *Wish You Were Here Today*). The BBC's show might have been on TV longer, but it's Judith people refer back to when talking about their continental holidays and heavy suntans.

Within These Walls

Drama | LWT for ITV | episode duration 50 mins | broadcast 4 Jan 1974–15 Apr 1978

Regular Cast
Googie Withers · *Governor Faye Boswell*
Mona Bruce · *Mrs Armitage*
Jerome Willis · *Charles Radley*
Denys Hawthorne · *Dr Peter Mayes*

Janet Lees Price · *Janet Harker*
Beth Harris · *Liz Clarke*
Sonia Graham · *Martha Parrish*
Audrey Muir · *Miss Flaxton*
Diana Rayworth · *Miss Berryman*
Raymond Adamson · *Bill Boswell*
Nigel Crewe · *Paul Boswell*
Sonia Graham · *Martha Parrish*
Diana Rayworth · *Officer Berryman*
Elaine Wells · *Officer Spencer*
Audrey Muir · *Officer Flaxton*
Crispin Gillbard · *Paul Boswell*
Katharine Blake · *Governor Helen Forrester*
Miranda Forbes · *Officer Parsons*
Floella Benjamin · *Barbara*
Sarah Lawson · *Governor Susan Marshall*

Creator David Butler **Producers** Rex Firkin (executive), Jack Williams **Writers** David Butler, Adele Rose, Tony Hoare, Terence Feely, Tony Parker, Rosemary Anne Sisson, Susan Pleat, P. J. Hammond, Felicity Douglas, Kathleen J. Smith, Peter Wildeblood, Victor Pemberton, Stuart Douglass, Julia Jones, Mona Bruce, Robert James, John Gorrie **Theme Music** Denis King

Faye Boswell has only recently taken up the post of governor of HM women's prison Stone Park. In her first month she has to tackle newspaper allegations of misconduct by prison staff, one prisoner's fears of racial abuse from warders and a new arrival on drugs charges who happens to be her son's girlfriend. As Faye struggles to improve the situation for the women in her care, she also has to beware of people likely to take advantage of her more liberal outlook on the penal system.

Pre-dating ***Bad Girls*** by more than 25 years, *Within These Walls* looked at the British prison system from the point of view of the prison staff, with a less sensationalist approach than those that followed it. Former star of the British film industry Googie Withers initially appeared as the well-meaning governor, Faye Boswell, replaced in later seasons by Helen Forrester and then Susan Marshall. The series might seem tame compared to other prison dramas that followed, but *Within These Walls* still pushed the boundaries by tackling subjects such as drugs, lesbianism and abuse of the system that would become standard elements of the Australian drama series it inspired, ***Prisoner: Cell Block H*** – notably the governor of Wentworth, Erica Davidson, who was almost a clone of our own Ms Boswell.

Considering the show's popularity at the time, it's strange that the fifth season was not fully networked across ITV; only LWT, Southern and Anglia showed it.

Wogan

Chat Show | BBC One | episode duration 35 mins | broadcast 15 Jan 1983–22 Dec 1984, 18 Feb 1985–3 Jul 1992

Cast

Terry Wogan · *Host*
Gloria Hunniford, Selina Scott, Joanna Lumley, Clive Anderson, Kenneth Williams, Anna Ford · *Guest Presenters*

Any description of Terry Wogan's approach to interviewing has to include the word 'amiable'. His style is not confrontational but generally well mannered and wanting to please. He came over to British broadcasting from Ireland's RTE, was one of a number of DJs to be present at the birth of Radio 1, and he presented a lunchtime chat show for ATV in the 1970s. His big TV breakthrough, however, came with the quiz show ***Blankety Blank***. From 1980, he hosted his own prime-time Saturday evening chat show, *What's on Wogan?*. It was on this show that Larry Hagman guested and shocked his legions of fans by announcing that he was still in discussion with the producers of ***Dallas*** as to whether or not he'd be returning to the series after the infamous 'Who Shot JR?' storyline; the public reaction was so strong at the thought of losing their favourite soap bastard that *Dallas*'s producers had little choice but to sign Hagman back up – at a much better salary, naturally. A point to Mr Hagman, and a great result for Wogan too. With Michael Parkinson's departure from the BBC to host *TV:AM*, Terry got his chance at Parky's much-coveted Saturday night slot, from January 1983. With the reshuffle of weekday evenings in 1985 to accommodate ***EastEnders***, *Wogan* went thrice weekly on Mondays, Wednesdays and Fridays at 7.00 p.m. When the usually graceful Terry slipped off a piano stool on the very first edition, the nation loved him for just laughing it off and getting on with the show.

All kinds of people sat on that sofa next to the man with the most-touched knee in television: ex-footballer George Best famously disgraced himself coming on steaming drunk (much to Terry's visible embarrassment); Robert De Niro, not known for being comfortable outside of a character, gave a very mono-syllabic interview, though apparently he later asked Terry if he could get a copy of the edition as he thought it had been the best he'd done; and Anne Bancroft was similarly phased by the experience, only discovering mere seconds before she came on that the show was live. But for every dodgy interview there were many classics, from James Stewart's tears as he read a poem about his dead dog to Kenneth Williams chewing the scenery in each and every one of his appearances (Williams even stood – or rather sat – in for Wogan on one of his brief breaks). On the 1000th edition on 22 July 1991, his big guest was Madonna. Two days later, Tel pre-recorded an edition for the following week that would mark the final ever broadcast from the BBC's TV theatre in Shepherds Bush.

Weekday *Wogan* came to an end on 3 July 1992 to make way for – of all things – ***Eldorado***. In recompense, Terry was given a Friday night slot – conveniently called *Terry Wogan's Friday Night* (2 Oct 1992–5 Mar 1993). He continues to be the BBC's voice of reason and sanity during the annual ***Eurovision Song Contest*** as well as hosting the *Children in*

Need appeals (which he's done since 1980) and since 1999 he's been the host of the viewers' letters slot *Points of View*. He also continues to broadcast on Radio 2, with his legion of 'TOGS' ('Terry's Old Geezers') tuning in every morning to *Wake up with Wogan*.

The Woman in Black

Drama | Central for ITV | episode duration 100 mins | broadcast 24 Dec 1989

Principal Cast

Adrian Rawlins · *Arthur Kidd*
Bernard Hepton · *Sam Toovey*
David Daker · *Josiah Freston*
Pauline Moran · *'Woman in Black'*
David Ryall · *Sweetman*
Clare Holman · *Stella Kidd*
John Cater · *Arnold Pepperell*
Fiona Walker · *Mrs Toovey*
William Simons · *John Keckwick*
Robin Weaver · *Bessie*
Caroline John · *Stella's Mother*
Joseph Upton · *Eddie Kidd*
Steven Mackintosh · *Rolfe*

Producers Ted Childs (executive), Chris Bur **Writer** Nigel Kneale, from the novel by Susan Hill **Theme Music** Rachel Portman

Arthur Kidd, a young solicitor, is sent by his employer to Eel Marsh House near the market town of Grythin Gifford to administer the affairs of the recently deceased client, Mrs Alice Drablow, and to attend her funeral. Curious as to why his boss is reluctant to attend to this final business himself, Arthur sets off during a heavy fog, anxious to get the business over as quickly as possible.

The young solicitor soon realises that there is more to the affairs of Eel Marsh House than he had been led to believe; the residents of Grythin Gifford refuse to either discuss Mrs Drablow or take Arthur anywhere near her house. Arthur reluctantly stays at the remote Eel Marsh House alone, with just enough provisions to see him through long enough to conclude his business. There, he finally realises the cause of the fear in the eyes of the locals when he begins to see a woman dressed head to foot in black. Her fearful aspect, which Arthur witnesses at Mrs Drablow's graveside and on the treacherous causeway that spans the nearby salt marshes, will bring unimaginable horror into Arthur's life.

Responsible for bringing scares to the screen since the early 1950s, Nigel Kneale had already approached the ghost story genre a number of times in his career: ***Quatermass and the Pit*** dealt with residual race memories from another world while ***The Stone Tape*** combined the supernatural with the technological. Kneale's adaptation of Susan Hill's 1983 novel was in the best tradition of the BBC's ***A Ghost Story for Christmas*** plays, with more than a couple of genuinely terrifying sequences.

Director Herbert Wise brought together an ensemble cast, many of whom worked on Wise's earlier production, ***I, Claudius***. In 1989, *The Woman in Black* came to the London stage (and, at the time of writing, is still there) and has since toured in America and Japan.

The Woman in White (1966)

Drama | BBC One | episode duration 55 mins | broadcast 2 Oct–6 Nov 1966, 14 Apr–12 May 1982, 1997

Cast

Alan Badel · *Count Fosco*
Georgine Anderson · *Countess Fosco*
Diana Quick · *Marian Halcombe*
Jenny Seagrove · *Laura Fairlie*
Ian Richardson · *Frederick Fairlie*
Deirdra Morris · *Ann Catherick*
Daniel Gerroll · *Walter Hartright*
Milo Sperber · *Pesca*
Ann Queensberry · *Mrs Hartright*
Clare Bonass · *Sarah Hertright*
Anna Lindup · *Fanny*
Gladis Robinson · *Mrs Vesey*
John Shrapnel · *Sir Percival Glyde*
Alan Dudley · *Dempster*
Russell Bowman · *Jacob Postlethwaite*
Anna Wing · *Mrs Clements*
Kenneth Keeling · *Mr Gilmore*
Andrew Carr · *Fletcher*
Jeannie Crowther · *Margaret Porcher*

Producer Jonathan Powell **Writer** Ray Jenkins, from the novel by Wilkie Collins **Theme Music** Patrick Gowers

Possibly the greatest Victorian novel, certainly one of the finest thrillers in literary history, Wilkie Collins' *The Woman in White* has been filmed a number of times (it's even been turned, loosely, into a stage musical by Andrew Lloyd Webber, starring ***Some Mothers Do 'Ave 'Em***'s Michael Crawford) but television is where it has fared best in this 1982 production directed by John Bruce. Turning the convoluted, experimental narrative of the book into a stunning, luscious and dramatic piece of television that remained faithful to the source but still suited the visual medium, was no mean feat. That Bruce's team achieved it so well is a testament to their work and it seems a shame that it remains an overlooked gem from an era of classic TV adaptations in the early Eighties.

Without a doubt, despite a relatively short amount of screen time, it is Alan Badel's truly malevolent Count Fosco, complete with pet mice, who steals the show, but he is ably supported by the likes of Diana Quick and Ian Richardson as the story of Walter Hartwright's search for the truth about the death of Ann Catherick and the mystery behind the enigmatic Laura Fairlie is played out.

It actually picked up a BAFTA, although only for Patrick Gowers' delightful music and not in any of the other craft categories it was nominated in. Shame.

It's sad to realise that this superb production has been overshadowed in recent years by the 1997 BBC remake which boasted a star-studded cast including Tara Fitzgerald, Andrew Lincoln and, as Fosco, a marvellous turn by Simon Callow. While looking sumptuous and gloriously made, the actual feat of trimming the book to just two hours, and spicing it up with more titillation than might otherwise have been relevant, proved too overwhelming a task and instead of a beguiling mystery and an exercise of character development, the 1997 version is just an average piece of period drama lacking any real depth or plot.

The Woman in White (1997)

Drama | BBC/Carlton/WGBH Boston for BBC One | duration 120 mins | broadcast 28–29 Dec 1997

Principal Cast
Tara Fitzgerald · *Marian Fairlie*
Simon Callow · *Count Fosco*
Justine Waddell · *Laura Fairlie*
Andrew Lincoln · *Walter Hartright*
Susan Vidler · *Anne Catherick*
John Standing · *Mr Gilmore*
Adie Allen · *Margaret Porcher*
Ian Richardson · *Mr Fairlie*
James Wilby · *Sir Percival Glyde*
Ann Bell · *Mrs Rideout*
Anne Etchells · *Liza*
Kika Markham · *Madame Fosco*

Producers Ted Childs, Rebecca Eaton, Jonathan Powell, David M. Thompson (executive), Margaret Mitchell (associate), Gareth Neame **Writer** David Pirie, based on the novel by Wilkie Collins **Theme Music** David Ferguson

For commentary, see THE WOMAN IN WHITE (1966)

A Woman of Substance

Drama | Portman Artemis for Channel 4 | episode duration 50 mins | broadcast 2–4 Jan 1985

Principal Cast
Deborah Kerr, Jenny Seagrove · *Emma Harte*
Liam Neeson · *Blackie O'Neill*
Barry Bostwick · *Major Paul McGill*
Barry Morse · *Murgatroyd*
Del Henney · *Jack Harte*
John Mills · *Henry Rossiter*
Miranda Richardson · *Paula McGill Amory*
Gayle Hunnicutt · *Olivia Wainwright*
John Duttine · *Joe Lowther*
Diane Baker · *Laura O'Neill*
George Baker · *Bruce McGill*
Peter Chelsom · *Edwin Fairley*
Peter Egan · *Adam Fairley*
Mick Ford · *Frank Harte*
Christopher Gable · *Arthur Ainsley*
Christopher Guard · *Gerald Fairley*
Dominic Guard · *Winston Harte*
Amanda Hillwood · *Daisy McGill*
Meg Wynn Owen · *Elizabeth Harte*
Nicola Pagett · *Adele Fairley*
Saskia Reeves · *Edwina*
Joris Stuyck · *David Kallinski*
Stephen Collins · *Shane O'Neill*
James Brolin · *Ross Nelson*
Claire Bloom · *Edwina, Lady Dunvale*
Paul Daneman · *David Amory*
Fiona Fullerton · *Sky Smith*
Suzanna Hamilton · *Emily Barkstone*
Nigel Havers · *Jim Fairley*
Pauline Yates · *Daisy Amory*
Valentine Pelka · *Winston Harte*
Sarah-Jane Varley · *Sally Harte*
Paul Geoffrey · *Anthony, the Earl of Dunvale*

Creator Barbara Taylor Bradford **Producers** Tom Donald, Ian Warren (executive), Dickie Bamber (associate), Diane Baker **Writers** Tom Blomquist, Lee Langley, from the novel by Barbara Taylor Bradford **Theme Music** Nigel Hess, with Elkie Brooks singing the theme to the sequel

Emma Harte is a successful businesswoman with a chain of department stores across the world. But she wasn't always a wealthy woman, as this mini series showed, tracking her life from 1905 as a poor servant girl, through to the first modest shop that leads to the birth of her huge business empire. But she is betrayed along the way, left as an unmarried mother and eventually persuaded to marry twice out of convenience while longing for the one man she can never have.

Glamorous melodramas are rarely as faithful to the time period as *A Woman of Substance* strives to be. So, aside from the usual motivations of love, hatred and revenge, we're treated to some well-researched glimpses into the past (not that anyone was watching hoping for a history lesson).

In the sequel, *Hold the Dream*, shown a year later, Emma has to settle her affairs and hand over to her heir, Paula (played by Miranda Richardson in the first series but Jenny Seagrove in the sequel), while taking advice from old friends Henry Rossiter and Blackie O'Neill.

The Wombles

See pages 842–3

The Wombles

From L–R Wellington, Orinoco, Bungo, Tomsk and Uncle Bulgaria.

Back in the early 1960s ***The Magic Roundabout*** established the weekday timeslot immediately before the 6 o'clock *News* on BBC One as an important one. The bridge between children's telly and the point when grown-ups can legitimately shush the kids into silence, that timeslot remained the domain of animated classics until the end of 1986, when the evening repeat of ***Neighbours*** brought the tradition to an untimely end.

Inheriting that slot from Dougal, Zebedee and the gang were a group of grey-furred, floppy-eared rodents housed deep within the hillocks of Wimbledon Common. *The Wombles* were created by Elisabeth Beresford in 1968 for what became a series of books. Beresford had been inspired by one of her young children's inability to pronounce the place name 'Wimbledon'. Margaret Gordon's illustrations depicted the creatures as small, brown, scruffy and bear-like – oh, and naked, though they later acquired clothing, presumably left behind by the careless humans whose litter they recycled into useful objects around the Womble burrow. For television, the little fellows received a dramatic restyling courtesy of Barry Leith, a designer and animator working for Ivor Wood. Animated by stop motion, as *The Magic Roundabout* characters had been (also by Ivor Wood), the new Wombles were still shaggy looking, but now with long, velvety snouts and huge floppy ears. Versatile character actor Bernard Cribbins provided the voices of them all: Great Uncle Bulgaria, the patriarchal head of the burrow and habitual *Times* reader; Tobermory, the DIY man who can make marvels from junk; Madame Cholet, whose presence in the burrow shows that Wombles come in both sexes and from all over the world (she's French); Bungo, who's stubborn and bossy (and with his Burberry cap would make a rather good Chav); bookish, timid, bespectacled Wellington; Tomsk, the 'jock', whose strength is useful even if his lack of brains doesn't; and finally Orinoco, fat, greedy and lazy, always trying to catch an extra '40 winks'. Despite his failings, Orinoco became the nation's favourite Womble, with his big floppy hat and woollen scarf making him look like a rather hirsute Tom Baker from his ***Doctor Who*** days.

Animation
FilmFair for BBC One
Episode Duration: 5 mins
Broadcast: 5 Feb 1973–24 Oct 1975

Voice Cast
Bernard Cribbins · *Narrator, Character Voices*

Creator/Writer Elisabeth Beresford

Producer Ivor Wood

Theme Music 'The Wombling Song' was composed and sung by Mike Batt ('Underground, overground, Wombling free'), although he was often mistaken for Bernard Cribbins.

Although the stories involved collecting rubbish from Wimbledon Common and putting it all to good use, the series wasn't really thought of as being about environmental issues. For the most part, the scavenging animals would simply try to collect as much useful stuff as possible without being seen by any 'human beans'; in one particularly memorable episode, Orinoco climbed up inside an abandoned mackintosh on a bench only for a human to sit down next to him. Thankfully his hat hid his face well enough for the human not to even notice.

The Wombles also became singing sensations akin to the Bay City Rollers. Orinoco sang lead vocals and played saxophone, Wellington was on guitar, with Madame Cholet on bass, Great Uncle Bulgaria played the violin and Bungo the drums (we're guessing that Tobermory and Tomsk were the band's roadies). The all-singing, all-shuffling Wombles made appearances on ***Crackerjack*** and other variety shows and even scored a fair few successes in the singles chart with the show's theme tune as well as songs like 'Remember You're a Womble' and 'Wombling Merry Christmas', also written by Mike Batt. In 1977, the versatile creatures attempted the next stage in their plans for global domination with the release of a feature film. *Wombling Free* was written and directed by Lionel Jeffries, and starred David Tomlinson, Frances de la Tour and Bonnie Langford, with Mike Batt providing the songs, as usual.

Ivor Wood made 60 episodes, but regular repeat runs have kept *The Wombles* on our screens for over 30 years now. A revival in 1990 eventually led to two new series of ten-minute episodes, courtesy of Canadian production company CINAR (transmission dates unavailable). This time, the subtle environmental themes of the original were hammered home in very conscious lessons on recycling and conservation. The addition of new characters such as extreme environmentalist Alderney (named after the Channel Island where Elizabeth Beresford now lives), the Asian Shansi and dreadlocked Stepney might have struck fans of the original series as extreme tokenism, but it at least showed that the Wombles' hearts were still in the right place. For those looking for a slightly less didactic Wombling experience, the original episodes are available on DVD.

WEBSITES

A search on the internet might leave you a little puzzled should you stumble across www.wombles.org.uk – a site for an anti-capitalist anarchist group. The official website (www.wombles.easyweb-solutions.co.uk) would appear to be still in the process of construction at the time of writing, so in the meantime we suggest you pay a visit to the official site of the wonderful Mike Batt (www.mikebatt.com), who as well as providing an insight into his battle with Sony Music to regain the rights to *The Wombles*' music, also discusses his other projects over the years, including his music for *Watership Down* (1978) – yes, he wrote 'Bright Eyes' (sniff) – and how he discovered the latest hot musical sensation Katie Melua. We did tell you he was wonderful.

Wonder Woman

Adventure | Douglas S. Cramer/Bruce Lansbury Productions for ABC/CBS (shown on BBC One) | episode duration 50 mins | broadcast 7 Nov 1975, 2 Apr 1976–11 Sep 1979 (USA)

Regular Cast

Lynda Carter · *Wonder Woman/Princess Diana/Diana Prince*
Lyle Waggoner · *Major Steve Trevor/Steve Trevor Jr*
Beatrice Colen · *Etta Candy*
Richard Eastham · *General Phil Blankenship*
Saundra Sharp · *Eve*
Norman Burton · *Joe Atkinson*
Tom Kratochvil · *Voice of I. R. A. C.*
Debra Winger · *Wonder Girl/Drusilla*
Cloris Leachman, Carolyn Jones, Beatrice Straight · *Queen Hippolyta*

Creator William Moulton Marston created the character of Wonder Woman for DC Comics back in December 1941 (in issue 8 of *All Star Comics*). Her first self-titled comic book appeared six months later. **Producers** Douglas S. Cramer (executive), Peter J. Elkington, Rod Holcomb, Arnold Turner (associate), Bruce Lansbury (supervising), Wilford Lloyd Baumes, Charles B. Fitzsimons, Mark Rodgers **Writers** Various, including Stanley Ralph Ross, Barbara Avedon, Barbara Corday, Elroy Schwartz, Glen Olson, Katharyn Powers, Ron Friedman, Jimmy Sangster (no, not the co-author of this book but the Hammer films screenplay writer) **Theme Music** There are few lyrics outside of a Village People song that are camper than the *Wonder Woman* theme: 'In your satin tights, fighting for your rights, and the old Red White and Blue ooooh!' Stand up and take a bow for your mighty work, Charles Fox.

In the middle of World War Two, an aeroplane piloted by US officer Steve Trevor crash lands near Paradise Island, the hidden home for the long-lost Amazonian race. The all-female islanders are shocked to discover the evil of the Nazis is spreading across the globe, and so Princess Diana volunteers to leave their hidden Utopia and journey to the outside world and aid humanity in its fight against the forces of oppression. When the time is right, Diana transforms from ordinary yeoman Diana Prince into the spandex-clad superhero Wonder Woman, complete with magic belt to give her strength, bullet-repelling bracelets, a boomerang-style tiara and a magic lasso that forces anyone caught within its loops to tell the truth. At the end of World War Two (and coincidentally, at the end of the first season), Diana returns home to Paradise Island, her work done.

For the second and third seasons, the action moved forward to contemporary stories set in the 1970s, Diana coming out of 'retirement' on Paradise Island when the son of her old friend Steve Trevor (played, of course, by the same actor Lyle Waggoner) called upon Wonder Woman's services once again.

Five-foot, nine-inch tall brunette beauty Lynda Carter was cast as the all-action heroine. Lynda had previously been Miss USA in 1973, entering (but not winning) the Miss World contest, a fact that was clear to anyone watching the skimpy outfit that Lynda had to endure as Wonder Woman. Lynda was joined by a range of big name stars in her show, including future Hollywood star Debra Winger as her younger sister, Wonder Girl.

The Wonder Years

Comedy Drama | New World Television/The Black/Marlens Company for ABC (shown on Channel 4) | episode duration 25 mins | broadcast 15 Mar 1988–1 Sep 1993

Principal Cast

Fred Savage · *Kevin Arnold*
Jason Hervey · *Wayne Arnold*
Olivia d'Abo · *Karen Arnold*
Alley Mills · *Norma Arnold*
Dan Lauria · *Jack Arnold*
Josh Saviano · *Paul Pfeiffer*
Danica McKellar · *Winnie Cooper*
Robert Picardo · *Coach Cutlip*

Creators Neal Marlens and Carol Black **Producers** Carol Black, Neal Marlens, Bob Brush, Bob Brush, Michael Dinner, Jill Gordon, Sy Rosen, Bob Stevens (executive) **Writers** Various, including Neal Marlens, Carol Black, David M. Stern, Bob Brush, Matthew Carlson, Todd W. Langen, Mark B. Perry, Jill Gordon, Mark Levin, Eric Gilliland, David Chambers, Craig Hoffman, David Greenwalt, Sy Rosen, Jon Harmon Feldman **Theme Music** 'With a Little Help from my Friends' by Lennon and McCartney, though it's the Joe Cocker version used on the show

Timing is everything. Had *The Wonder Years* not been commissioned for a mid-season replacement and been scheduled to run right after the all-important Superbowl, it might not have had the instant impact that it did. A heart-swellingly nostalgic look at the late 1960s and early '70s through the eyes of a 12-year-old boy, the series took in everything from the Vietnam War, the rise and fall of the hippy and the Apollo missions (all experienced from the point of view of an onlooker rather than a participant) to first love, friendships that are supposed to last forever but rarely do and the family's first colour TV. Over the period of six years we got to know Kevin's family – hard-working mom and dad, idealist sister and bratty elder brother – his best friend, the geeky Paul (a possible inspiration for ***The Simpsons***' Milhouse) and the love of Kevin's life, Winnie.

The Wonder Years boasted uniformly excellent performances – particularly from Fred Savage and the rest of the younger cast members, on whose shoulders the series rested. But a series that relies on kids remaining cute and chubby-faced is inevitably going to suffer when they begin to grow up. Rather than risk being canned by the network, the producers decided to bring the show to an end with a wonderfully bitter-sweet ending in which the adult Kevin (Daniel Stern, who had been our narrator through 114 episodes – not counting the pilot, which Ayre

Gross had voiced) tells us that his dad died of a heart attack, leaving the family businesses to Kevin's once-annoying older brother. Kevin and Winnie didn't get together, but they stay in touch, even after they find their own partners and settle down.

Even for those of us who weren't born in the 1960s, *The Wonder Years* made us wish we had done, or at least made us wish we could all remember the best years of our life so vividly and with such obvious affection.

Trivia

Rumours continue to circulate that shock rocker Marilyn Manson played Kevin's friend Paul. He didn't.

Wood and Walters

See VICTORIA WOOD: AS SEEN ON TV

The Woodentops

Children's Puppetry | Westerham Arts Films for BBC TV | episode duration 15 mins | broadcast 9 Sep 1955–c.21 Mar 1958

Voice Cast

Eileen Browne, Josephina Ray, Peter Hawkins · *Various Characters*

Creators Maria Bird, Freda Lingstrom **Producer** Freda Lingstrom **Writer** Maria Bird **Theme Music** Maria Bird

As the *Watch with Mother* slot expanded from Tuesday-through-Thursday to cover the full working week, the Friday slot was taken by *The Woodentops*. This weekly serial about a family of wooden string puppets lasted for 26 episodes but was repeated constantly throughout the remaining black-and-white era of telly (and four of those had to be remade, presumably because the original films had worn through). Mummy and Daddy Woodentop, their twins Willie and Jenny, and a little baby were frightfully middle-class, with their cleaner Mrs Scrubbit and farmhand Sam, but despite some rather cheery stories that were only slightly less dramatic than those of ***The Grove Family***, the only element the kids were watching for was the huge family pet, Spotty Dog.

The Woodentops came from the same production stable as *Watch with Mother*'s other stars, ***Andy Pandy, Flower Pot Men*** and ***Rag, Tag and Bobtail***. The puppets were operated by Audrey Atterbury, Molly Gibson and a young Gordon Murray, a man who would later jump over to stop motion animation for his clutch of stories set within Trumptonshire. Watching the episodes now, it's clear that there was a certain level of improvisation among the voice actors, padding out scenes to cover slight puppetry problems. They really must have been juggling cradles up there with three people controlling six or more characters at once, especially for the big wave goodbye at the end of each episode.

The Word

Magazine | 24 Hour/Planet 24 for Channel 4 | episode duration 50 mins | broadcast 1990–1995

Cast

Dani Behr, Terry Christian, Amanda de Cadenet, Mark Lamarr, Katie Puckrick, Hufty Rae, Alan Connor, Jasmine Dottiwala · *Presenters*

Fenella Fielding, Jennie Linden · *Narrators*

Creator Charlie Parsons **Producers** Charlie Parsons (executive), Sebastian Scott, Paul Ross, Duncan Grey (editors), Dele Onyia, Richard Godfrey, Tamsin Summers, Asif Zubairy **Theme Music** 'In Your Face' by 808 State, which got to No. 9 in the UK singles chart

A shameless, guilt-free examination of the excesses of youth, and the first prog to really expose the lurking desperation within most people to achieve fame and celebrity, *The Word* was a programme that shocked, repulsed and riveted viewers in equal measure – without *The Word*, there'd be no ***I'm A Celebrity . . . Get Me Out of Here***, no *Heat* magazine, and certainly nowhere near as much delight in downright unpleasantness sprawled across our TV screens. In many ways, the arrival of *The Word* marked the end for old-style television of the Sixties, Seventies and Eighties, in which scripted entertainment performed or presented by accomplished performers was just about the only style of programme you got. *The Word* blew that rulebook apart. From that moment on, reality became more important than fantasy, with the public themselves becoming even bigger audience draws than star names. Even though it was itself never watched by a large audience, it established the ground rules for subsequent, bigger-rated hits that dominated the schedules.

It crawled out of the wreckage of an earlier Channel 4 programme called *Club X*, which was a weekly attempt to make serious high-brow arts more accessible to a youth audience by mixing features on sculpture and opera with alternative comedians and rock music. When *The Word* began in 1990, it initially filled the 6.00 p.m. Fridays timeslot that had previously been inhabited by pop showcase *The Tube*, but its content soon saw it shifted to a post-pub slot. Unlike most other 'Yoof' programmes, it decided to ditch any pretence of culturally relevant programming, and instead featured items on porn stars, interviews with celebrities (some, like Oliver Reed and ***Coronation Street***'s Lynn Perrie, were invited on purely to show what they were like after abusing the green room's alcohol stash) and live bands in the studio (including, famously, a pre-success Oasis and a just-about-to-be-huge Nirvana). The presenters never looked as though they were entirely in control of proceedings, which was precisely what the show's producers wanted. One notable success, however, was when Mark Lamarr valiantly

Continued on page 848

Worzel Gummidge

The Crowman sits with Worzel and his friends Sue and John.

A move to the country changes the lives of children John and Sue Peters in more ways than one. In the nearby Ten Acre Field of Scatterbrooke Farm they meet a living scarecrow who goes by the name of Worzel Gummidge. Initially terrified of him, the children realise he's actually harmless, if a little prone to mischief. They discover that he was made by someone called the Crowman and that he has a choice of different heads – including a brave head and a clever head. As the children try in vain to prevent him from being noticed by the villagers, Worzel sets about finding himself a wife, for he's fallen in love with a fairground attraction called 'Aunt Sally'. Unfortunately, Sally is not at all impressed with Worzel, even when he has his handsome head on!

Most actors would pray for one great role that made them instantly identifiable with the public. Jon Pertwee achieved that with ***Doctor Who***, second only to his successor, Tom Baker, in terms of recognition but for many his was the definitive performance in the role. After leaving the TARDIS and the monsters behind in 1974, who would have thought that Pertwee would get a second bite of the cherry with a TV adaptation of *Worzel Gummidge*, the scarecrow who first appeared in print in 1941.

Not long after Barbara Euphan Todd's *Worzel Gummidge* books began to take hold of children's imaginations, BBC Radio began to dramatise them in their *Children's Hour* slot. Worzel's first TV appearance came in 1953 with *Worzel Gummidge Turns Detective*, starring Frank Atkinson as a rather stereotypical-looking scarecrow. In the 1970s, writers Keith Waterhouse and Willis Hall began work on adapting Barbara Euphan Todd's books for television, knowing that Jon Pertwee, at one time known as 'the Man of a Thousand Voices', would be perfect for the lead role. Pertwee threw himself enthusiastically into the part and even devised the idea of Worzel's removable heads, a gimmick that allowed him to make greater use of his vocal dexterity. Other additions for the TV series included the Crowman, the person responsible for building scarecrows and bringing them to life, and Aunt Sally, a painted wooden mannequin who replaced the books' Earthy Mangold as the object of Worzel's affections. The trio had hoped to mount a film based on their ideas, but their plans proved unsuccessful. By the time Southern Television agreed to produce a TV series instead, two years had gone by.

Cast as the authoritarian Crowman, Worzel's maker, was Geoffrey Bayldon, who'd played a similar character to Worzel as the star of ***Catweazle***. Una Stubbs joined the cast from the third episode as Aunt Sally, a wooden doll built as a fairground attraction where people would pay to throw things at her and knock her over. Though Worzel helps Sally escape, she rarely shows her gratitude to him, often conspiring to make Worzel take the blame for her actions. She thinks of Worzel as a disgusting, dirty creature (well, he is), but still feels a pang of jealousy whenever she sees him with another doll, such as the Saucy Nancy, a rather brassy ship's figurehead (played by the inimitable Barbara Windsor) and the very glamorous tailor's dummy Dolly Clothes-Peg (Lorraine Chase).

Pop singer Mike Berry (who also starred in ***Are You Being Served?*** and a series of catchy adverts for Blue Riband wafer biscuits) played Mr Peters, while Charlotte Colman was cast as one of the two children who befriend the mischievous scarecrow. Coleman later starred in the *Marmalade Atkins* series and drew critical acclaim for her role in ***Oranges Are Not the Only Fruit***; she tragically died in 2001 after a severe asthma attack.

Much hilarity came from Worzel's devil-may-care attitude. He had little respect for other people's property or possessions and his ignorance of social etiquette made him alarmingly blunt as he rarely considered that people might be offended by his opinions of them. Even though most episodes ended with some kind of rebuke from the Crowman that left Worzel acting contrite, we all knew that the next episode would see him stealing buns or throwing potatoes at passers by as always.

When Southern lost their ITV franchise, *Worzel Gummidge* was one of many casualties as new franchise holder TVS wanted to make a clean sweep and begin producing their own new programmes. A planned remount of the show set in Ireland never materialised and for a time it looked as if Worzel's adventures were over. Thanks to a producer from New Zealand called Grahame McLean, Worzel found a new home on Channel 4. *Worzel Gummidge Down Under*, set in McLean's home country and featuring a more sinister Crowman and elements of Maori culture (including the really creepy creation of a Maori 'Crowman'), came to TV screens in 1986 shortly after Channel 4 had completed repeats of the original series.

Children's Comedy Drama
Southern Television for ITV/Toti Productions for Channel 4
Episode Duration: 25 mins
Broadcast: 25 Feb 1979–16 Apr 1989, 4 Oct 1987–16 Apr 1989

Regular Cast
Jon Pertwee · *Worzel Gummidge*
Geoffrey Bayldon · *The Crowman*
Una Stubbs · *Aunt Sally*
Jeremy Austin · *John Peters*
Charlotte Coleman · *Sue Peters*
Mike Berry · *Mr Peters*
Norman Bird · *Mr Braithwaite*
Megs Jenkins · *Mrs Braithwaite*
Joan Sims · *Mrs Bloomsbury-Barton*
Lorraine Chase · *Dolly Clothes-Peg*
Denis Gilmore · *Harry*
Bill Maynard · *Sergeant Beetroot*
Michael Ripper · *Mr Shepherd*
Thorley Walters · *Colonel Bloodstock*
Barbara Windsor · *Saucy Nancy*
Frank Marlborough · *Dafthead*
Sarah Thomas · *Enid Simmons*
Bruce Phillips · *The New Zealand Crowman*
Jonathan Marks · *Mickey*
Olivia Ihimaera-Smiler · *Manu*
Michael Haigh · *Professor Pike*
Anne Chamberlain · *Deirdre*
Wi Kuki Kaa · *Travelling Scarecrow Maker*

Creator Barbara Euphan Todd

Producers Lewis Rudd (executive), David Pick (associate), James Hill, Grahame McLean

Writers Willis Hall, Keith Waterhouse, Jon Pertwee, James Hill, Anthony McCarten, Frances Walsh, from the novels by Barbara Euphan Todd

Theme Tune 'Worzel's Song', sung by Jon Pertwee, reached No. 33 in the British UK singles charts. The song is a basic lesson in 'Worzelese', which involves putting a 'wor' after 'W', and a 'wor' after 'O' and so on.

WEBSITE

www.scatterbrook.co.uk – a superb fansite containing background information on the series.

challenged reggae performer Shabba Ranks over his quite unpalatable homophobic comments – a rare moment of genuine political awareness and a refusal to allow an opinionated fool to get away with spouting offensive rubbish just because of his own perceived stardom.

Each advert break would be topped and tailed with a quiz question (something along the lines of 'What links these celebrities? Answer after the break'), a crafty way to ensure that post-pub viewers didn't just switch off as tiredness overcame them. Memorable segments of the programme included brief snatches from famous Hollywood actors' first early acting roles in soft porn films and, of course, 'The Hopefuls', the moment each week that caused most viewers' stomachs to lurch. Members of the public showed up, willing to 'do anything to be on TV' – these challenges included bathing in liquid manure, French kissing a granny for 30 seconds, chewing a sponge that had been wiped all over every crevice of a sweaty fat man and drinking a pint of their own vomit. Well, they did say they'd do anything to get on TV – the fools.

With a flurry of swearwords or a badly behaving drunken celebrity never more than a few minutes away, *The Word* made perfect viewing for young people just staggering back home from the pub on a Friday night. It was unmissable TV if you were the target demographic – unwatchable if you weren't.

The World at War

Documentary | Thames for ITV | episode duration 30 mins | broadcast 31 Oct 1973–8 May 1974

Cast
Laurence Olivier · *Narrator*

Producers Jeremy Isaacs (executive), Jerome Kuehl (associate), David Elstein, Peter Batty, Ted Childs, Martin Smith, Michael Darlow, John Pett, Phillip Whitehead, Hugh Raggett
Theme Music Carl Davis

It's a little unsettling to realise that we are now longer away from this groundbreaking documentary series than it was to its subject. Though it had been nearly 30 years since the end of World War Two, it was as much a part of British obsession as it arguably still is today. There's a greater fascination with both the war itself and the effect it had on the people than the politics behind it, but here Jeremy Isaacs' team looked at the times from all angles, using film footage, the available documentation (some of which had only recently become available) and diary extracts from Anne Frank and Charles Douglas Home. While some of the material has since been superseded to some extent by the colour film footage unearthed for ITV's 1999 series *The Second World War in Colour* and documents that have subsequently become available, *The World at War* still stands as a hugely impressive work. It was repeated in full by Channel 4 in the 1980s and on BBC Two in the 1990s.

Worzel Gummidge

See pages 846–7

The X Factor

Reality TV/Talent Show | ITV | episode duration 25–50 mins, plus extended final | broadcast 4 Sep 2004–present

Principal Cast
Kate Thornton · *X Factor Presenter*
Simon Cowell, Sharon Osbourne, Louis Walsh · *X Factor Judges*
Steve Brookstein · *X Factor Winner, 2004*

Creator Simon Cowell **Producers** Various, including Nigel Hall, Richard Holloway, Claire Horton (executive)

For commentary, see POPSTARS

The X Files

See pages 850–3

Xena: Warrior Princess

Action-Adventure | MCA/Universal/Renaissance (shown on Five) | episode duration 45 mins | broadcast 4 Sep 1995–18 Jun 2001 (USA)

Regular Cast
Lucy Lawless · *Xena*
Renee O'Connor · *Gabrielle*
Ted Raimi · *Joxer*
Bruce Campbell · *Autolycus*
Hudson Leick · *Callisto*
Adrienne Wilkinson · *Livia/Eve*
Kevin Smith · *Ares – God of War*
Karl Urban · *Julius Caesar*
Alexandra Tydings · *Aphrodite*

Creator Robert G. Tapert **Producers** Sam Raimi, Robert G. Tapert, R. J. Stewart (executive), Emily Skopov, Liz Friedman (supervising) **Writers** Various, including Robert G. Tapert, R. J. Stewart, Emily Skopov, Adam Armus, Alan Jay Glueckman, Chris Black, Chris Manheim, Melissa Good, Nora Kay Foster, Jeff Vlaming, Joel Metzger, Kevin Maynard, Paul Robert Coyle, Peter Allan Fields **Theme Music** Joseph LoDuca

A spin-off series from the earlier hit series *Hercules: The Legendary Journeys, Xena: Warrior Princess* soon became even more successful and popular than its parent show. Xena made her first appearance in a three-part story in ***Hercules***, at which point she was a distinctly unpleasant character. Realising the error of her ways, Xena teams up with a young bard called Gabrielle, and together the two of them travel around ancient Greece fighting monsters, defeating sorcerers and generally kicking lots and lots of male butt. Unlike many other heroes and heroines, Xena wasn't blessed with special or magical powers – she was simply a tough, no-nonsense woman who took no rubbish from anybody.

Unsurprisingly for a show with two attractive female leads, Xena soon garnered a vocal and enthusiastic lesbian following. What is much more surprising is that the programme-makers decided to actively capitalise on this, and turned the friendship/relationship between Xena and Gabrielle into a sophisticated and totally non-exploitative portrayal of a close friendship between two women. For many viewers, Xena and Gabrielle were the first 'out' lesbian couple in an adventure series – for others, their relationship was entirely platonic. Many other viewers, for whom Sapphic subtexts weren't really their kind of thing, preferred to revel in Xena's clever parodies and homages to other TV shows and movies, or to lap up the witty and post-modern dialogue. For younger viewers, it was simply a brilliant action-adventure series with groovy monsters – all shot on location in Auckland, New Zealand, years before Peter Jackson ever dreamt of combining hobbits with Kiwi vistas.

The X Files

David Duchovny and Gillian Anderson as Agents Mulder and Scully.

One day, back in the 1970s, a 12-year-old boy and his eight-year-old sister are at home alone, playing games and watching TV. Suddenly, a strange bright light envelops their house and the boy watches, unable to do anything, as his sister disappears from his life for ever. For Fox Mulder, the disappearance of his sister Samantha would become a lifelong search to discover the truth about the phenomenon of alien abduction – to find out if the Truth Is Out There . . . .

Beginning as a low-profile series on the rarely watched fourth American TV network, Fox, *The X Files* managed to do something that ***Star Trek*** and all of its sequel series never did – become an internationally successful science fiction series that appealed not only to a cult TV audience but also managed to be a crossover hit that was, for about three years, the absolute epitome of cool. Of course, *The X Files* had an advantage over most cult TV shows: two leading actors who were unconventionally attractive, in a just-sexy-enough-that-you-might-stand-a-chance kind of way. Gillian Anderson, although born in the USA, had been raised in London and had gained a reputation as a bit of a tomboy and a rebel before embarking on a career in acting. David Duchovny had made an impact in the cult TV drama ***Twin Peaks*** playing a transvestite FBI agent. Pairing the two together created an on-screen chemistry that launched a thousand magazine covers and led to the greatest will-they won't-they partnership seen on television since Maddie and David first traded insults in ***Moonlighting***.

Science Fiction
Ten-Thirteen Productions for Fox Network (shown on Sky One, BBC Two/One)
Episode Duration: 45 mins
Broadcast: 10 Sep 1993–19 May 2002 (USA)

Regular Cast
David Duchovny · *Special Agent Fox Mulder*
Gillian Anderson · *Special Agent Dana Scully*
Mitch Pileggi · *Assistant Director Walter Skinner*
William B. Davis · *'Cigarette-Smoking Man'/C. G. B. Spender*
Nicholas Lea · *Alex Krycek*
Chris Owens · *Jeffrey Spender*
Robert Patrick · *Agent John Doggett*
Annabeth Gish · *Agent Monica Reyes*
Charles Cioffi · *Section Chief Scott Blevins*
Jerry Hardin · *'Deep Throat'*
Tom Braidwood · *Melvin Frohike*
Dean Haglund · *Richard 'Ringo' Langly*
Bruce Harwood · *John Byers*
Don S. Davis · *Bill Scully*
Steven Williams · *'X'*
Melinda McGraw · *Melissa Scully*
Sheila Larken · *Margaret Scully*
Brian Thompson · *Alien Bounty Hunter*
Brendan Beiser · *Agent Pendrell*
Rebecca Toolan · *Teena Mulder*
Peter Donat · *William Mulder*
Floyd 'Red Crow' Westerman · *Albert Hosteen*
Don S. Williams · *The First Elder*
John Neville · *'Well-Manicured Man'*
Laurie Holden · *Marita Covarrubias*
Pat Skipper · *Bill Scully Jr*
John Finn · *Michael Kritschgau*
Jeff Gulka · *Gibson Praise*
Veronica Cartwright · *Cassandra Spender*
Mimi Rogers · *Agent Diana Fowley*
James Pickens Jr · *Assistant/Deputy Director Alvin Kersh*
Adam Baldwin · *Knowle Rohrer*
Cary Elwes · *Assistant Director Brad Follmer*
Laurie Holden · *Marita Covarrubias*

Already convinced of the existence of aliens and other extraordinary phenomena, FBI agent Fox Mulder has been assigned to work for a special division of the Bureau specifically set up to investigate cases that appear to involve weird occurrences. With an office tucked away in the FBI's basement, these 'X Files' (and Mulder in particular) are a bit of a joke among the other agents. Determined to discredit Mulder and his pet project, senior FBI staff (under the guidance of a mysterious, cigarette-smoking figure) assign sceptical medical doctor Dana Scully to work alongside Mulder and debunk his outlandish theories. However, despite her best intentions to dismiss them, Scully soon realises that there might be more to Mulder's bizarre theories than first meets the eye. Over the course of the first season, Mulder and Scully investigate everything from UFO sightings to strange parasites buried in the Antarctic ice, from a man who can squeeze through tiny openings to another who can create fire at will. Throughout all of these escapades, a mysterious government employee, nicknamed 'Deep Throat', gives them hints and advice. When Deep Throat's leaks become too blatant, he is assassinated and both Mulder and Scully are reassigned from their job on the X Files. But when Scully is herself apparently abducted by aliens (a clever plot twist designed to cover actress Gillian Anderson's pregnancy), Mulder discovers that he has more friends within the FBI and the government – another informant, nicknamed X, and more importantly Assistant Director Skinner, a man who becomes their greatest supporter and protector against those shadowy government forces. Other allies include three nerdy researchers who call themselves 'the Lone Gunmen', men with their finger on the pulse of the latest conspiracy theory.

The episodes of *The X Files* can largely be divided into two specific types. Most are 'monster of the week' stories, where a creature or person with supernatural/paranormal powers supplies the challenge for Mulder and Scully's investigative skills. The other types of episode were what became known as the 'Mythology' stories, where viewers discover, little by little, more facts about the abduction of Mulder's sister, about the government's involvement in a cover-up concerning the existence of aliens, and eventually the horrifying truth that aliens are not only here already, but actually in control of many people in positions of power. During the first few seasons of *The X Files*, the Mythology episodes tended to provide the most exciting plotlines; it became utterly enthralling to watch the next instalment of what seemed to be a long-term, ongoing storyline. However, as time went by, the Mythology started to become so convoluted that they were in danger of disappearing up their own Close Encounters. Indeed, by the fourth or fifth series, it was so difficult to keep up with these storylines (Who were the shape-changing aliens? What was the black oil? Why were the conspirators cultivating swarms of killer bees?) that audiences became increasingly disillusioned with the show. Instead, it was the one-off episodes that seemed more entertaining: in particular, the occasional storylines played totally for laughs proved to be a blessed relief from the po-faced seriousness of the Mythology episodes.

Creator Chris Carter

Producers Chris Carter, Vince Gilligan, R. W. Goodwin, Howard Gordon, David Greenwalt, Kim Manners, Michelle Maxwell MacLaren, Glen Morgan, John Shiban, Frank Spotnitz, Michael Watkins, James Wong (executive), Crawford Hawkins, Suzanne Holmes, Gina Lamar, Lori Jo Nemhauser, Denise Pleune (associate), Paul Barber, Larry Barber, Rob Bowman, David Amann, Harry V. Bring, Paul Brown, Bernadette Caulfield, Charles Grant Craig, Joseph Patrick Finn, Alex Gansa, Ken Horton, Lori Jo Nemhauser, David Nutter, Paul Rabwin, Paul Rabwin, Daniel Sackheim, Mark R. Schilz, Tim Silver, Tony Wharmby

Writers Various, including Chris Carter, Glen Morgan, James Wong, Howard Gordon, Alex Gansa, Darin Morgan, David Duchovny, Frank Spotnitz, Vince Gilligan, John Shiban, Tim Minear, Stephen King, William Gibson, David Amann, Jeffrey Bell, Steven Maeda, Greg Walker, Thomas Schnauz

Theme Music Mark Snow's theme music, although instantly recognisable, is perhaps a little bit 'obvious', relying as it did on creepy echoes and whistles, for a show that redefined a genre.

Many fans of *The X Files* (known as 'X-Philes') were looking forward to a few answers being forthcoming when a feature film, *The X Files: Fight the Future*, was released in 1998. However, instead of using the cinema film to wrap up some of the programme's ongoing plotlines, it actually did the reverse and threw extra elements into the whole on-going jigsaw puzzle. Although the feature film was a highly enjoyable piece of entertainment, it marked the moment when *The X Files* reached the peak of its popularity. The programme carried on for several more years, but it was no longer either as cool or as much of a zeitgeist-surfing phenomenon than it had been at the time of the movie, with even a song about the series' two lead characters reaching No. 3 in the charts ('Mulder and Scully' by Welsh band Catatonia).

Indeed, viewers weren't the only ones sensing that *The X Files*' time was drawing to a close. In the eighth season, star David Duchovny decided to phase out his involvement in the programme, with the result that Fox Mulder only appeared in about half of the episodes. Replacing Duchovny as Scully's new partner, Doggett, was actor Robert Patrick, someone already used to appearing in science fiction thanks to his earlier starring role as the morphing killer robot in *Terminator 2: Judgment Day* (1991). Of course, with many years of battling freaks, aliens and mutants under her belt, Scully by now was the 'believer' in the partnership, with a dumbfounded Agent Doggett slowly losing his scepticism. This unfortunately had the effect of changing the dynamic of the programme, reverting back to a traditional, more sexist way of presenting belief/non-belief. By having a female portrayed as the logical, methodical sceptic, the first few seasons of *The X Files* had gently subverted the gender roles audiences might have expected to see in such a series.

By the time the ninth and final series was aired, Duchovny had disappeared from the title sequence and another new agent had joined the team, folklore and mythology expert Monica Reyes. Although the introduction of new regulars (and an increased role for FBI boss Skinner) injected much-needed variety into the programme, it soon became clear to everyone concerned that it was time for *The X Files* to be closed down. Sadly, a spin-off series focusing on the slightly more humorous exploits of the Lone Gunmen (and entitled *The Lone Gunmen*) failed to take off and was canned after just 13 episodes. The last two-part episode of *The X Files* saw the return of Mulder, on trial for murder and now the victim of one of the government conspiracies he had done so much to uncover. Mulder and Scully finally discover the date for the full-scale alien invasion that has been brewing since the Roswell Incident in 1957 – the world as we know it will

By making science fiction cool and sexy, *The X Files* attracted a very different range of viewers compared to shows like *Star Trek* or *Doctor Who* – with just as many young women as men happy to be seen out and about wearing 'The Truth Is Out There' T-shirts.

apparently come to an end on 22 December 2012. Everything finishes on a fairly melancholy note, with Mulder realising that he hasn't actually achieved many of the things he'd set out to do: the alien conspiracy is still hidden, his sister is still missing, and everybody is still carrying on their lives in blissful ignorance of the threat facing humanity. In a way, this conclusion neatly mirrored many of the best episodes of *The X Files*, a programme that was rarely tempted to resort to neat conclusions with all of the loose ends of a plotline tidied up.

By making science fiction cool and sexy, as well as being an undeniable popular hit, *The X Files* did much for changing the perception of a genre of television that had fallen out of favour with many TV executives. Furthermore, it also attracted a very different range of viewers compared to shows like *Star Trek* or ***Doctor Who*** – with just as many young women as men happy to be seen out and about on the streets wearing 'The Truth Is Out There' T-shirts. Without *The X Files*, it's unlikely that shows like ***Buffy*** or ***Smallville*** would ever have been major successes, and for that at least *The X Files* deserves every little bit of praise that's been heaped on it. With the benefit of hindsight, it's perhaps hard to see precisely why *The X Files* became so huge, but for everyone who likes their TV to be just a tiny bit more imaginative than yet another programme about doctors or police officers, we really should be grateful to 'Spooky' Mulder and an FBI lady resembling Clarice Starling from *Silence of the Lambs* . . .

WEBSITES

The official site from Fox (www.foxhome.com/xfilesportal/) is a pretty soulless affair geared around the DVD releases, but one of our favourite X-Philes sites is Roadrunners (www.xfroadrunners.com), which contains lots of useful *X Files* info and displays a healthy sense of humour to boot.

A Year in Provence

Drama | BBC One | episode duration 30 mins | broadcast 28 Feb–16 May 1993

Cast
John Thaw · *Peter Mayle*
Lindsay Duncan · *Annie Mayle*
Jean-Pierre Delage · *Colombani*
Jo Doumerg · *Amedee Clement*
Marcel Champel · *Antoine Riviere*
Annie Sinigalia · *Madame Hermonville*
Bernard Spiegel · *Marcel*
Christian Luciani · *Raymond*
Francine Olivier · *Hugette Clément*
Susie Blake · *Susan Hopkins*
Jim Carter · *Ted Hopkins*
Geoffrey Hutchings · *Ralph Tompkins*
Maggie Steed · *Libby Tompkins*
Liz Crowther · *Georgina*
Frank Middlemass · *Clive Parrott*
Alfred Molina · *Tony Havers*
Catherine Rabett · *Marion Hart-Bowers*

Producers Barry Hanson (executive), Ian Brindle (associate), Ken Riddington **Writer** Michael Sadler, from the book by Peter Mayle **Theme Music** Carl Davis

An advertising executive and his accountant wife decide to up sticks and move to the south of France for a new beginning. Peter hopes to get a novel out of the experience, but the book he ends up writing bears more than a passing similarity to the real events around him.

This 12-part series, adapting month by month from the diaries of Peter Mayle was lauded as one of the big prestigious productions of the BBC in 1993, but a decidedly lukewarm response to the sight of two middle-class Brits living it up in France resulted in *A Year in Provence* becoming a by-phrase for tedious, self-indulgently uninvolving television for years after.

Yes – Honestly

Sitcom | LWT for ITV | episode duration 25 mins | broadcast 9 Jan 1976–23 Apr 1977

Principal Cast
Liza Goddard · *Lily Pond/Browne*
Donal Donnelly · *Matthew Browne*
Eve Pearce, Irene Hamilton · *Mrs Pond*
Beatrix Lehmann · *Littlema*
Dudley Jones · *Mr Krocski*
Georgina Melville · *Jun*

Creators/Writers Terence Brady, Charlotte Bingham **Producer** Humphrey Barclay **Theme Music** There were two theme tunes for *Yes – Honestly*, one per season. The first was written and performed by chart-topper Georgie Fame. Lynsey de Paul (who had composed the theme for the earlier parent show *No – Honestly*) returned for the second.

For commentary, see NO – HONESTLY

Yes, Minister

See pages 756–8

Yogi Bear

Animation | Hanna Barbera/Screen Gems (shown on ITV) | episode duration 25 mins | broadcast 30 Jan 1961–present (USA)

Voice Cast
Daws Butler · *Yogi Bear*
Don Messick · *Boo Boo Bear, Ranger John Smith, Snagglepuss*
Julie Bennett · *Cindy Bear*
Vance 'Pinto' Colvig · *Chopper*
Jimmy Weldon · *Yakky Doodle*

Creators/Producers Joseph Barbera and William Hanna **Writers** Warren Foster, Dan Gordon, Michael Maltese, Charles Shows **Theme Music** Joseph Barbera, William Hanna, Hoyt Curtin

Challenged in the UK by Paddington and Rupert as animation's biggest celebrity bear, Yogi's the worldwide winner. Yogi was named after New York Yankees pitcher Yogi Berra (famous for his malapropisms and hilariously ill-thought-out sayings), while his voice was inspired by Art Carney's character Ed Norton in the American sitcom *The Honeymooners* (which in turn inspired ***The Flintstones***).

Yogi Bear and his best buddy Boo Boo live in a cave inside Jellystone Park. Lazy, greedy and fond of stealing other people's picnic ('pic-a-nic') baskets, Yogi is the bane of Ranger Smith's life, despite being 'smarter than the average bear' (and considering he must be able to do up that green neck-tie of his, we don't doubt it).

Yogi first appeared on 2 October 1958 as a support player in *The Huckleberry Hound Show*. After three years, he finally got his own show, syndicated across America prior to a full network transmission on ABC later that year. As the series continued, Yogi gained a girlfriend in the form of Southern Belle bear Cindy ('Ah do declare!') while sharing the timeslot with Snagglepuss the theatrical pink mountain lion and Yakky Doodle, a little duck accompanied by a bulldog called Chopper.

From then on, Yogi has starred in numerous other shows, including *Yogi's Gang* (1973), *Yogi's Space Race* (1978), *Yogi's Treasure Hunt* (1985) (all about the SS *Jelly Roger*), and *The New Yogi Bear Show* (1988), where he was voiced by Greg Burson. He also starred in his own feature-length presentation, *Hey There, It's Yogi Bear* in 1964.

You Rang, M'Lord?

Sitcom | BBC One | episode duration 50 mins | broadcast 14 Jan 1990–24 Apr 1993

Cast
Paul Shane · *Alf Stokes*
Su Pollard · *Ivy Teasdale*
Jeffrey Holland · *James Twelvetrees*
Michael Knowles · *The Honourable Teddy Meldrum*
Donald Hewlett · *Lord George Meldrum*
Susie Brann · *Poppy Meldrum*
Catherine Rabett · *Cissy Meldrum*
Bill Pertwee · *PC Wilson*
Brenda Cowling · *Mrs Blanche Lipton*
Mavis Pugh · *Lady Lavender*
Perry Benson · *Henry Livingstone*
Barbara New · *Mabel Wheeler*
Angela Scoular · *Lady Agatha Shawcross*
Yvonne Marsh · *Madge Cartwright*
John D. Collins · *Jerry*
Felix Bowness · *Mr Pearson*

Creators/Writers Jimmy Perry and David Croft **Producer** David Croft **Theme Music** Composed by Jimmy Perry and Roy Moore, performed by Bob Monkhouse and Paul Shane

During World War One, Alf Stokes and James Twelvetrees had served together in the trenches in France. Ten years later, James is working for Lord Meldrum, whose brother Teddy was saved by James during the war. Lord Meldrum lives in the house with his two daughters, the flighty Poppy and the androgynously beautiful Cissy. James and Alf's paths cross again when Alf successfully applies for the post of butler at the Meldrum house. The downstairs staff welcomes another new arrival with Ivy, a maid with a secret–Alf is her father, and he's only working at the Meldum's place to fleece them of their money. Even though Teddy Meldrum is a bit of a letch, Ivy doesn't feel at all comfortable with her dad's plan. But what can she do to stop him?

Jimmy Perry and David Croft have been responsible for some of the very best British sitcoms. Together they came up with ***Dad's Army***, ***It Ain't Half Hot Mum*** and ***Hi-De-Hi!***, while with Jeremy Lloyd, Croft had produced ***Are You Being Served?*** and ***'Allo, 'Allo!***. At the end of the 1980s they reconvened their partnership to create a spoof of the hugely popular 1970s drama ***Upstairs, Downstairs***. While their wartime comedies weren't exactly topical, it did seem odd to target a series that had ceased production over a decade earlier. It was such a clever concept, but sadly it wasn't destined to join its predecessors as a classic. Audiences found it difficult to warm to a series that featured their former favourite Ted Bovis from *Hi-De-Hi!* (Paul Shane) as a self-serving crook–indeed, few of the lead characters were sympathetic enough to allow the audience to connect with. With so many of the leading roles taken by the 'usual suspects' from David Croft's previous successes, only Catherine Rabett, as the predatory lesbian daughter, was offering anything new.

You've Been Framed!

Reality TV | Granada for ITV | episode duration 25 mins | broadcast 1989–present

Cast
Jeremy Beadle, Lisa Riley, Jonathan Wilkes, Harry Hill · *Presenters*

Theme Music Ray Monk

While Dennis Norden's long-running ***It'll Be Alright On The Night*** made a feature out of mistakes happening to TV personalities, and *Beadle's About* involved hidden-camera pranks on members of the public, *You've Been Framed!* combined the two to give us a clips show involving everyday people doing extraordinary things. Viewers sent their clips in of aunties slipping over while dancing at weddings, children falling over, household pets running amok and other examples of home video hilarity. To tempt people out of their embarrassment at being captured on camera, prize money is offered for each clip shown, often with a bigger prize for the funniest clip (in early series it was £1000 and a new camcorder).

Richard Madeley starred in an unbroadcast pilot for the show, but for its first eight years, TV prankster Jeremy Beadle was its host. The show mirrors obsessions in other countries with the public laughing at itself, with *America's Funniest Home Videos* and *Australia's Funniest Home Video Show* being regular schedule fillers in their respective countries. With the rise in repeats filling out cable channels, the series has also been shown under the title *NEW You've Been Framed!*

Of course, not every clip is 100 per cent accidental. Aware that more and more tapes were being submitted with obviously faked situations, Jeremy Beadle hosted *Beadle's Hotshots*, a one-off special in 1994 in which viewers were asked to create their own comedy sketches. The special proved popular enough for ITV to commission a full series, which ran from 1996 to 1997. Perhaps realising that it's the clips that people want to see rather than a presenter, the decision was eventually made to abandon pre-filming of *You've Been Framed!* with a studio audience, instead relying solely on the vocal talents of Harry Hill to link each clip together. The result, unsurprisingly, was a much funnier programme.

The Young Ones

See pages 859–61

Yes, Minister

James Hacker (seated) with Sir Humphrey and Bernard at his side.

As we note in ***The West Wing***, if a leader is lacking in some way – intellectually, morally or politically – fiction has a habit of delivering something closer to the ideal (see also Palmer in the first three years of the thriller ***24***). Generally speaking, the reverse is also true. Whether or not we agree with their policies at the time, we Brits tend to elect people who at least look the part and as a consequence our fictional Prime Ministers are more likely to exist within the realm of comedy than drama (and one notable exception, ***A Very British Coup***, was more a critique of the Labour leadership than the Premier herself). In the late-1970s and early '80s we had no doubt whatsoever that Margaret Thatcher was in charge, to the extent where some might have worried that the country was being run by one woman rather than the collective government we elected. So, fiction once again stepped in and gave us the leader we really wanted, a man so easily influenced he never quite manages to make up his mind, and when he does make a firm decision he has trained advisers around him to undo any damage he might cause. In short, we wanted someone who would make us laugh.

Yes, Minister was Paul Eddington's first starring vehicle after years of playing supporting roles in series as diverse as ***Dixon of Dock Green***, ***The Adventures of Robin Hood*** and ***The Avengers***. A familiar face on TV since the mid-1950s, it was the part of next-door neighbour Jerry Leadbetter in ***The Good Life*** that made him a household name. He first stepped into the shoes of Jim Hacker in 1980. Appointed Minister for the Department of Administrative Affairs, Hacker was swept in on a mandate of open government and an end to the bureaucracy of Whitehall. It soon becomes apparent that Hacker will achieve neither, partly thanks to the intervention of others and partly because he's too like the character Roger McGough described in his poem 'The Leader' ('I'm the leader/OK what shall we do?'), a man ill-equipped to cope with responsibility or grasp the complexities of government. He's a comic Hamlet, caught between the determination to do what's right but paralysed by fear of self-sacrifice.

It's unfortunate for Hacker (but fortunate for the government) that his position comes with two aides, his private secretary Bernard, whose impossible task it is to arrange Hacker's diary and explain some of the less deliberately obtrusive comments made by his other aide, the department's permanent secretary Sir Humphrey Appleby. Sir Humphrey reveals the true nature of politics, that elected officials come and go, but the Civil Service really runs the country. While Jim Hacker seeks to change the system, Sir Humphrey's role is to keep things exactly as they are, the epitome of procrastination by proxy. (One other adviser who is usually forgotten is Frank Weisel, a man who represented the issues Hacker had originally stood for, but as Sir Humphrey's influence grows, Weisel is sidelined, eventually being persuaded to join a Quango set up to reduce the number of Quangos.)

The writers made sure that Hacker's party was never identified. Though Hacker himself was clearly a moderate, he could have easily been a member of Labour or the Tories (and surprisingly, considering his incompetence, politicians tend to assume he's in whichever party they themselves are in). In fact, *Yes Minister/Prime Minister*, never ventured into the arena of the House of Commons; as co-creator Jonathan Lynn has noted, the Commons may be where the theatrical events take place, but politics always works from behind closed doors. Politicians fall over themselves to convince us that the programme's depiction of politics was eerily accurate. Margaret Thatcher, Prime Minister for the duration of the series, was quoted as saying that 'Its closely observed portrayal of what goes on in the corridors of power has given me hours of pure joy,' though whether that was because she recognised some truth in it or because it was just well written we can't say. The brilliance of the series was simply that you could enjoy it even if the political discourses sounded like inventive politico-babble. For most of the audience, it didn't matter that Sir Humphrey's long and windingly evasive explanations to Hacker contained even the merest grain of political practice (even though we believe they did). We just loved Hacker's facial expressions as he tried to decipher them without it appearing as if Sir Humphrey had once again got one over on him (which, of course, he had). And if that was too much to handle, we could always enjoy those cringe-inducing moments

Sitcom
BBC Two
Episode Duration: 30 mins
Broadcast: 25 Feb 1980–28 Jan 1988

Regular Cast
Paul Eddington · *James Hacker*
Nigel Hawthorne · *Sir Humphrey Appleby*
Derek Fowlds · *Bernard Woolley*
John Nettleton · *Sir Arnold Robinson*
Diana Hoddinott · *Annie Hacker*
Neil Fitzwiliam · *Frank Weisel*
Arthur Cox · *George*
John Savident · *Sir Frederick 'Jumbo' Stewart*
Deborah Norton · *Dorothy Wainwright*
Peter Cellier · *Sir Frank Gordon*
Antony Carrick · *Bill Pritchard*
Ludovic Kennedy · *Himself*

Creators/Writers Anthony Jay and Jonathan Lynn

Producers Stuart Allen, Sydney Lotterby, Peter Whitmore

Theme Music Ronnie Hazlehurst, accompanied by some typically cruel caricatures courtesy of Gerald Scarf, plays with the familiar chimes of Big Ben.

Hacker could have easily been a member of Labour or the Tories (and surprisingly, considering his incompetence, politicians tend to assume he's in whichever party they themselves are in).

when the Minister found himself completely out of his depth on live TV (often in front of interviewer Ludovic Kennedy) or when he found himself lapsing into Winston Churchillisms.

The 1984 Christmas special, 'Party Games', brought an end to *Yes, Minister* after 22 episodes. Fortunately, it didn't bring an end to Jim Hacker's career. When the Home Secretary is arrested for drink driving, both he and the Prime Minister are forced to resign in disgrace. Jim Hacker suddenly finds himself heading to Number 10 as Britain's PM. Moving up the ladder with him are Bernard, continuing as his private secretary, and Sir Humphrey, now Cabinet Secretary with responsibility for the entire Civil Service. *Yes, Prime Minister* ran for another two years, and continued the tradition of ending each episode with 'Yes, Prime Minister'.

The brilliance of the series was simply that you could enjoy it even if the political discourses sounded like inventive politico-babble.

The pairing of writers Antony Jay and Jonathan Lynn was a productive one. Jay's experience as head of BBC Talks and Factual has taught him much about the slow grind of bureaucracy, while Lynn was an actor and writer (including episodes of ***Doctor in the House*** and its sequels). Introduced to each other by John Cleese (who'd been at Cambridge with Jay), the pair created *Yes, Minister* inspired by the never-ending battle for supremacy of ***Steptoe and Son*** and the Master-Servant relationship in P. G. Wodehouse's ***Jeeves and Wooster*** stories. The collaboration paid off with a successful series that won the BAFTA for Best Comedy Series three years on the run.

Paul Eddington died in 1991 after a long and courageous battle with skin cancer. Nigel Hawthorne, who won three BAFTAs for his portrayal of Sir Humphrey, became an Academy Award nominee for *The Madness of King George* (1994). Post-Minister, Derek Fowlds became head of a police station in the rural romantic drama ***Heartbeat***. In Autumn 1997, he played Bernard Woolley once again, voicing a Radio 4 production of Antony Jay's *How to Beat Sir Humphrey: Every Citizen's Guide to Fighting Officialdom*.

The Young Ones

From L–R: Rick, Vyvyan, Neil and Mike.

As ***Big Brother*** has shown us, the key to sharing a house with others is picking your housemates really carefully or else all hell will break out. How Rick, Neil, Vyvyan and Mike ever met is anyone's guess. They didn't exactly get on with each other and were clearly on different courses, and it was only their appearance on ***University Challenge*** that confirmed they even attended the same institution, Scumbag College.

Rick claims to be an anarchist, though this was really just a mask for his selfishness and unwillingness to do any actual work. Obsessed with Cliff Richard, he is the self-titled people's poet, but more famous for his screeching hysterics than his verses. With a punk hair style, metal stars stuck to his forehead and the slogan 'Very Metal' written on the back of his sleeveless denim jacket, Vyvyan made an instant impression. His favourite pastime is mindless violence – the more mindless the better. It's Vyv who comes up with the idea of demolishing their house in the first episode to prevent the council from evicting them, and over the course of two series he manages to destroy virtually every section of the new house, kicking in the struts on the banister, breaking every rickety wooden chair and even eating the TV set. He is also the owner of SPG – Special Patrol Group – a vicious punk hamster. Neil struggles to provide balance and a daily meal. A committed vegetarian, it's his fault that the guys are forced to live off lentil slop every day. His varied attempts to end it all are doomed to fail – he really should have listened to Dorothy Parker, who wrote: 'Guns aren't lawful; nooses give; gas smells awful. So you might as well live.' Finally there's Mike, whose diminutive frame doesn't diminish his determination to get his end away. Unflappable and enterprising, he's a pragmatist who always tries to exploit the potential of any situation: oil is discovered in the basement – he establishes himself

Comedy
BBC Two
Episode Duration: 35 mins
Broadcast: 9 Nov 1982–19 Jun 1984

Regular Cast
Adrian Edmondson · *Vyvyan Basterd*
Rik Mayall · *Rick*
Nigel Planer · *Neil Pye*
Christopher Ryan · *Mike TheCoolPerson*
Alexei Sayle · *Members of the Balowski Family*
Paul Bradley, Ben Elton, Andy de la Tour, Robbie Coltrane, Mark Arden, Stephen Frost, Michael Redfern, Roger Sloman, Gareth Hale, Norman Pace, David Rappaport, Cindy Shelley, Dawn French, Jennifer Saunders, Pauline Melville · *Various Characters*

Creators/Writers Ben Elton, Rik Mayall, Lise Mayer, with additional material from Alexei Sayle

Producer Paul Jackson

Theme Music The cast sung a version of Cliff Richard's 'The Young Ones' for the opening sequence, while the end theme was by Roy C. Bennett and Sid Tepper.

as leader of a totalitarian state; he's short of money – he rents out Neil's room as a roller disco; he finds Buddy Holly alive and well inside his chimney – he begins to calculate the royalties he'll earn as the dead star's manager. Mike chooses not to accept the idea of failure, even when failure presents itself in the form of a woman determined not to be seduced by his limited charms.

One other regular contributor was Alexei Sayle. A left-wing skinhead Liverpudlian stand-up comic and former compere at the Comic Strip, Sayle played various members of the Balowski family who owned the gang's rented house. A section of each episode would be put aside for Sayle's rants about noisy neighbours, Dr Marten's boots or the fact that so many biscuits are named after revolutionaries.

The supporting cast consisted mainly of performers from Michael White's now legendary Comic Strip club in London, with only Chris Ryan an outsider, having been drafted in after Peter Richardson left to set up ***The Comic Strip Presents*** for Channel 4. The series introduced us to several performers who would become familiar faces over the next decade or so: Steve Frost and Mark Arden, who starred in a series of mickey-taking adverts for Carling Black Label and a sitcom, *Lazarus and Dingwall*, as well as performing as the Oblivion Boys; Gareth Hale and Norman Pace, better known as thick-headed bouncers 'the Management' on ***Saturday Live*** before being installed as ITV's naughty princes of comedy well into the 1990s; Robbie Coltrane, star of *Tutti Frutti*, ***Cracker*** and, more recently, the *Harry Potter* films; and Dawn French and Jennifer Saunders, who made their TV debuts playing, respectively, a persistent Happy Clapper killed by a giant sandwich and a surly party-goer. Not all of the people recruited from the Comic Strip found fame, though; spare a thought for poor Arnold Brown, who in one episode informed us that he was both Scottish and Jewish, 'two stereotypes for the price of one', but whose only significant contribution to television was as a rather vague commentator in *Hello Mum*, whose catchphrase was '. . . and why not'.

The pecking order at the BBC was such that drama always got the biggest budgets and comedy the lowest. The glory of a sitcom is that it generally requires just one or two standing sets, domestic environments like a living room and a kitchen. But *The Young Ones* set out from the beginning to subvert the genre, and to do this it needed more money. The idea of having musical guests popping in elevated the show to 'Light Entertainment', a category that receives bigger budgets! The musical acts weren't exactly consistent, however. They played host to Madness (twice), Dexy's Midnight Runners and Motorhead (performing 'Ace of Spaces' – yes!), but also Rip Rig and Panic (whose only other claim to fame is that one of their members was Neneh Cherry), Nine Below Zero and John Otway, whose 'Yeah Baby, It's Really Free' made him an unlikely one-hit wonder.

The Young Ones was sadly five years too late to really be called 'punk comedy', although the chaotic approach to each episode summed up much of the punk ethos. It would be great if this had all been planned from the beginning, but it's almost certain that the way each episode was written – Mayall and Mayer working together, Elton on his own, before their material would be haphazardly thrown together – accounted for the rather appealingly disjointed feel to it all. In addition, there were segues to unrelated scenes, subliminal flash frames of leaping frogs and puppet sequences that were too sick to be played out with humans. Its anti-establishment approach also led to it openly attacking the public image of the police force, depicting officers as institutionally racist: smashing up a record player after just a few bars of the Human League because of complaints about the noise; one officer mistaking a white man for black because he's wearing sunglasses (telling him off for pressing a doorbell and using 'white man's' electricity); and when, in desperate need of money, Neil is forced to join the 'fascist' organisation he fears and despises, he naturally shouts out a warning prior to a raid: 'Open up, it's the Pigs').

It's almost certain that the way each episode was written – Mayall and Mayer working together, Elton on his own, before their material would be thrown together – accounted for the rather appealingly disjointed feel to it all.

Like many of the best sitcoms, *The Young Ones* stopped after only 12 episodes, but the legacy of that style of comedy continues. The series started out as iconoclastic, mocking the establishment and traditional comedy values: it reserves particular bile for ***The Good Life***, which Vyvyan dismisses as being 'so bloody nice'. But through *The Comic Strip Presents*, one series of *Happy Families*, ***Bottom***, ***Absolutely Fabulous*** and the biannual ***Comic Relief*** events, the talents from the Comic Strip have *become* the establishment. Worse, *The Young Ones* has dated far more than *The Good Life* ever will.

The final episode saw the boys fleeing from 'the Pigs' in a stolen double-decker bus only to crash through a billboard of Cliff Richard ('Cliff!') and over the edge of a cliff ('cliff!') to a fiery demise. Miraculously, the Young Ones somehow escaped death, first for a successful stage show and then in 1985 for *Comic Relief*'s first No. 1 single, a cover of 'Living Doll' with Cliff Richard and Shadows guitarist Hank Marvin.

Z Cars

Jeremy Kemp and James Ellis, original drivers of the Z Cars.

The police drama is a major part of British television – at least one regular police series has been in production somewhere in the world almost since television began. In Britain, ***Fabian of the Yard*** was one of the first off the blocks, adapted from the case files of Detective Superintendent Robert Fabian. George Dixon, the copper who bit the dust in the film *The Blue Lamp* (1949), found himself unexpectedly returned from the grave for a TV series that began in 1955, ***Dixon of Dock Green***, while one-armed detective Mark Saber (in the series of the same name) solved crime after crime from the mid-1950s until 1961, making actor Donald Gray both a star and horribly typecast (he later voiced Colonel White in Gerry Anderson's ***Captain Scarlet*** and had a bit part in ***Emmerdale Farm*** before his death in 1978). But none of these continue to influence the TV productions of today; that is an accolade reserved for a series created as a reaction against the cosiness of *Dixon*.

Undoubtedly, *Dixon of Dock Green* had involved a great deal of in-depth research into police procedure, but even from the outset the view this show offered of police work was very much a romanticised one. It was more a PR job for the Metropolitan Police than an accurate representation of the job, while its comforting, family approach to crime persisted well into the 1970s until the avuncular Dixon was finally pensioned off.

A book by Detective Sergeant Bill Prendergast of the Liverpool City Police provided the inspiration for the setting, a new town on the outskirts of Merseyside similar to the real-life Kirkby (the second 'k', incidentally, is silent). Not far from both the city centre and the docklands of Seaforth and Litherland, Kirkby was a rapidly expanding community, a catchment for the overspill from Liverpool, with little heritage of its own, brand new flats and tower blocks built over the remains of terraced houses bombed during the Blitz and awaiting redevelopment ever since. Setting the drama in the suburbs of Liverpool (here named 'Newtown') not only presented different storylines to the kind offered by *Dixon* but also a completely new voice. Still a year or so away from the rise of Merseybeat, spearheaded by the Beatles, the Liverpool accent that had only begun to form during the 20th century was harsh and aggressive sounding compared to the more traditional Lancastrian accent of areas just a few miles away.

Z Cars began as *The Blue Lamp* had ended (and, coincidentally, how ***The Sweeney*** would also begin), with policemen grieving over the death of one of their own, PC Farrow, who was 'shot while executing his duty' investigating a warehouse robbery. That was its point of departure, though from the first episode it was clear that this would be a different type of storytelling. There's no cheery narrator here; just a documentary-style attempt at a realistic portrayal of police duties. In line with inner-city police forces across the country, and as a response to the rise of violent crime brought home by the death of young Farrow, Newtown Police are given funding for two crime patrols. DI Charlie Barlow 'volunteers' DS John Watt to head the team and choose his men. The original band of brothers included PC Bert Lynch, a Northern Irishman with a happy-go-lucky attitude, brash 'Fancy' Smith, Jock Weir and Bob Steele. These men become the first of many officers to drive the two patrol cars, Z Victor One and Z Victor Two. In the second series they were joined by dog handler Dave Graham (Colin Welland), a local lad who would become a patrol driver himself, partnered with Lynch after the departure of Bob Steele.

The series helped change the kind of stories television told as well as the way they were produced. Episodes were initially broadcast live with minimal film inserts of location footage. Directors became adept at handling scenes involving two actors stuck inside a studio-bound prop Zephyr with its windows removed to avoid reflecting the cameras and crew. Though eventually the production moved towards pre-recording, in line with the majority of television in the mid-1960s, the cast often expressed a preference for the excitement of live TV, with each episode akin to a first night in the theatre.

Live performance was a rare theatrical element for this gritty, urban TV drama, influenced by the Free Cinema movement of the late 1950s and 'kitchen sink' writers like John Osborne. As the series grew in popularity and received increasing critical acclaim, it was able to attract top-drawer scripts from television's best writers, including Elwyn Jones, Alan Plater, P. J. Hammond and ***Callan*** creator James Mitchell. The issues the series touched on were also much more true to life and more aggressively handled than they would have been in *Dixon of Dock Green*. In the first episode, Steele's wife is seen sporting a shiner, though this is later revealed to have been her own fault – the bruising occurred when she attacked Bob and he defended himself. Bert Lynch was shown to like the odd flutter on the horses, while the kind of villains the squad faced inevitably entailed a much more violent response than audiences had been used to seeing in British police dramas. In the first few years alone, the series looked at arson ('Fire!'), drunk driving ('Friday Night'), vandalism ('The Best Days'), blackmail and homosexuality ('Somebody . . . Help'). Stories would also follow the officers into court, where they delivered evidence ('Appearance in Court'), and

Crime Drama
BBC TV/BBC One
Episode Duration: 25/50 mins
Broadcast: 2 Jan 1962–20 Sep 1978

Regular Cast
Stratford Johns · *DCI Charlie Barlow*
Frank Windsor · *DS John Watt*
James Ellis · *PC/DC/Sergeant/Inspector Bert Lynch*
Brian Blessed · *PC 'Fancy' Smith*
Joseph Brady · *PC 'Jock' Weir*
Jeremy Kemp · *PC Bob Steele*
Leonard Williams · *Sergeant Percy Twentyman*
Terence Edmond · *PC Ian Sweet*
James Cossins · *Sergeant Michaelson*
Lynne Furlong · *WPC Stacey*
Dudley Foster · *DI Dunn*
Michael Forrest · *DC Hicks*
Colin Welland · *PC David Graham*
Robert Keegan · *Sergeant Blackitt*
Diane Aubrey · *Sally Clarkson*
Leonard Rossiter · *DI Bamber*
John Philips · *PC Robbins*
Leslie Sands · *Inspector Millar*
Geoffrey Whitehead · *PC Ken Baker, DS Miller*
Edward Kelsey · *Arthur Boyle*
Donald Webster · *PC Foster*
Michael Grover · *PC Boland*
Marcus Hammond · *PC Taylor*
Donald Gee · *Ray Walker*
John Barrie · *DI Sam Hudson*
John Slater · *DS Tom Stone*
Sebastian Breaks · *PC Steve Tate*
Stephen Yardley · *PC Alec May*
David Daker · *PC Owen Culshaw*
Luanshya Greer · *WPC Jane Shepherd*
George Sewell · *Inspector Brogan*
Bernard Holley · *PC Newcombe*
Christopher Coll · *DC Kane*
Joss Ackland · *Inspector Todd*
John Wreford · *PC Jackson*
John Woodvine · *Inspector Witty*
Ron Davies · *PC Roach*
Paul Angelis · *PC Bannerman*
Derek Waring · *Inspector Goss*
Ian Cullen · *Joe Skinner*
Barry Lowe · *PC Horrocks*
Douglas Fielding · *PC/Sergeant Mick Quilley*
John Challis · *PC/Sergeant Culshaw*
Ray Lonnen · *Sergeant Moffat*
Stephanie Turner · *Jill Howarth*
Jack Carr · *PC Covill*
James Walsh · *PC Lindsay*
Geoffrey Hayes · *PC Scatliff*
Alan O'Keefe · *PC Render*
Godfrey James · *PC Hicks*
Kenton Moore · *PC Logie*

John Woodnutt · *PC Birch*
John Swindells · *PC/Sergeant Bowman*
John Collin · *DS Hagger*
Sharon Duce · *WPC Cameron*
Gary Watson · *DI Connor*
Nicholas Smith · *PC Yates*
Alison Steadman · *WPC Bayliss*
David Jackson · *DC Braithwaite*
John Dunn-Hill · *Sergeant Knell*
Michael Stirrup · *PC Preston*
Paul Stewart · *Sergeant Chubb*
Brian Grellis · *PC/DS Bowker*
Tommy Boyle · *Inspector Maddan*
Victoria Plucknett · *WPC Beck*

Creator Troy Kennedy Martin

Producers David E. Rose, Colin Morris, Ronald Travers, Richard Beynon, Ron Craddock, Roderick Graham

Writers Various, including Troy Kennedy Martin, Allan Prior, Robert Barr, John Hopkins, Ray Dunbobbin, John McGrath, James Doran, Leslie Sands, Keith Dewhurst, Geoffrey Tetlow, Elwyn Jones, Alan Plater, Joan Clark, Brian Hayles, Bill Barron, Eric Coltart, William Emms, Ray Jenkins, Donald Bull, Colin Morris, Cyril Abraham, David Ellis, Derek Ford, Donald Ford, Adele Rose, Ben Bassett, Leslie Duxbury, P. J. Hammond, Philip Martin, James Mitchell, Len Rush, Jack Gerson, Ron Craddock, Bill Lyons, John Foster, Bob Baker, Dave Martin, Anthony Read, Pip Baker, Jane Baker

Theme Music Johnny Keating took the theme tune to No. 8 in the British singles chart in 1962. Based on 'Johnny Todd', a traditional folk song ('Johnny Todd he took a notion/For to cross the ocean wide . . .'), the distinctive combination of flutes and drums was arranged by Bridget Fry and her then husband Fritz Spiegl. Born in a small town on the Austro-Hungarian border, Spiegl moved to England and eventually took up a post as principal flautist with the Liverpool Philharmonic Orchestra. His links with the city of Liverpool are many: his theme tune was adopted by Everton Football Club (just as Liverpool FC took ownership of 'You'll Never Walk Alone'); and, responsible for the 'Usage and Abusage' column in the *Daily Telegraph*, Spiegl also penned numerous books about his adoptive city, including the hilarious *Lern Yerself Scouse*.

the officers would occasionally come under suspicion of corruption ('I Know My Coppers', 'The Long Spoon').

After five series over a period of three years, *Z Cars* was cancelled, but its popularity had been underestimated and, after a 15-month break, it returned in a slightly different format. Only Bert Lynch (now promoted to desk sergeant) and Jock Weir remained from the original cast and the episodes were halved to 25-minute instalments, though the show now appeared twice a week. Stories moved from principally stand-alone ones to multi-part, with plots spread over two or four editions. Reflecting developments in the real world, Z Victor Two was retired and two new Ford Escort 'Panda' cars took its place.

DS Watt and DCI Barlow were siphoned off into their own series, *Softly, Softly* (later *Softly, Softly – Taskforce*), which ran from 1966 to 1970. Barlow also starred in his own series, *Barlow at Large* (1971–3) and *Barlow* (1974–6), by which time he'd risen to the rank of detective chief superintendent.

Facing competition from ITV cop shows like *Special Branch* and later *The Sweeney* (which was created by Ian Kennedy Martin, the brother of *Z Cars*' creator, Troy Kennedy Martin), the half-hour editions were phased out as colour broadcasts were phased in. But with the programme still made on videotape, it began to look a little cheap when compared with the home-grown and imported film series boasted by ITV. *Z Cars* finally closed its doors in 1978 with its 800th episode, 'Pressure', in which Newtown Station is fitted with a heavy security shutter following a series of violent attacks. The episode was written by Troy Kennedy Martin and featured cameos from Brian Blessed and Colin Welland, while the show finished with DS Watt one week away from retirement. In the final shot, the security shutter closes in front of Bert Lynch, now an inspector and the only original cast member still appearing as a regular in the series, contemplating the realisation that he's still five years short of his own golden handshake.

With the loss of *Z Cars* creating a brief cop show 'vacancy', the BBC developed a twist on the format with ***Juliet Bravo***, a series that retained the northern setting of *Z Cars* and told similar stories but from the point of view of a female senior officer.

The original lead actors had long become familiar faces elsewhere by the time the series ended. Brian Blessed had starred in the BBC's Roman epic ***I, Claudius***, made an appearance in the first series of *The Sweeney* and would later create a character even louder and brasher than 'Fancy' Smith – Prince Vultan, strident leader of the Hawkmen in the feature film *Flash Gordon* (1980), not to mention his role as the equally strident King Richard IV in the first ***Blackadder*** series. Colin Welland won a BAFTA for his performance as Mr Farthing in the film *Kes* (1969) and an Oscar for writing the screenplay for *Chariots of Fire* (1981) – a victory that prompted his famous, ultimately unfulfilled, declaration: 'The British are coming!' In the 1980s, James Ellis starred in the comedy drama ***One by One*** and the cult sitcom *Nightingales*, as well as becoming a poet and an author of short stories.

Z Cars

See pages 862–4

Zorro

Action-Adventure | Walt Disney Television for ABC (shown on BBC) | episode duration 30 mins, plus 4 × 50-min specials | broadcast 10 Oct 1957–2 Apr 1961 (USA)

Regular Cast

Guy Williams · *Don Diego de la Vega/Zorro*
Henry Calvin · *Sergeant Demetrio Lopez Garcia*
Gene Sheldon · *Bernardo*
George J. Lewis · *Don Alejandro de la Vega*
Jan Arvan · *Don Ignacio 'Nacho' Torres*
Jolene Brand · *Anna Maria Verdugo*
Romney Brent · *Padre Felipe*
Don Diamond · *Corporal Reyes*
Eduard Franz · *Gregorio Verdugo*
Vinton Haworth · *Magistrando Carlos Galindo*
John Litel · *The Governor*
Britt Lomond · *Captain Monastario*

Creator Johnston McCulley **Producers** Walt Disney, Bill Anderson, Ron Miller **Writers** Various, including Norman Foster, Antony Ellis, Jackson Gillis, John Meredyth Lucas, Lowell S. Hawley, Malcolm S. Boyland, Tim Minear, Robert Bloomfield, Gene L. Coon, Roy Edward Disney, Lewis R. Foster, Maury Hill, Joel Kane, David Lang, Robert B. Shaw, N. B. Stone Jr, Bob Wehling **Theme Music** George Bruns, lyrics by Norman Foster ('Zorro, Zorro, the fox so cunning and free/Zorro, Zorro, who makes the sign of the Z' – a rhyme that doesn't work in British-English, unfortunately). The theme was sing by four gentlemen, Ravenscroft, Bill Lee, Bob Stevens and Max Smith.

Zorro was American literature's reworking of the English Robin Hood character. He first appeared in 1919 in 'The Curse of Capistrano', a short story by Johnston McCulley published in *All-Star Weekly*. Instead of Robin of Loxley locking swords with the Sheriff of Nottingham, it was Don Diego de la Vega – aka Zorro – and the tyrannical Captain Monastario of Los Angeles, at a time when the City of Angels was under Spanish control. Gone were the Lincoln-green tights; in came an all-black suit with cape, hat and black mask, and instead of the Merry Men, Zorro relied upon occasional help from Bernardo and two proud steeds, Phantom and Tornado. The TV series came about through Walt Disney's attempts to raise capital for his new Californian theme park, Disneyland – although in reality it took so long to persuade any of the major networks to take Disney's idea that Disneyland had already opened before *Zorro* hit television screens. The 1940 film version was another obstacle to overcome – whoever played Zorro would have to be able to erase Tyrone Power's interpretation and make the part his own. Eventually unknown actor Guy Williams was given the star part, which was lucky for Williams, who was on the verge of quitting acting for good (he later led the cast of Irwin Allen's science fiction romp ***Lost in Space***).

Unusually, *Zorro* ended not because of poor ratings – far from it – but because of legal wrangling behind the scenes between Disney and the network, ABC. It took two years for the problems to be ironed out, during which time Disney retained Guy Williams on full pay. But by the time the two sides had been reconciled, Disney felt the moment was lost and decided not to resurrect its hero after all.

Selected Bibliography

Archer, Simon and Hearn, Marcus *What Made Thunderbirds Go* (BBC Worldwide, 2002)

Attenborough, David *Life On Air: Memoirs of a Broadcaster* (BBC Worldwide, London, 2002)

Attwood, Tony *Blake's 7: The Programme Guide* (Virgin Books, London, 1994)

Bacon, Matt *No Strings Attached: The Inside Story of Jim Henson's Creature Shop* (Virgin Books, London, 1997)

Bailey, David and Martyn, Warren *Goodnight Seattle: The Unauthorised Guide to the World of Frasier* (Virgin Books, London, 1998)

Bentley, Chris *The Complete Gerry Anderson: The Authorised Episode Guide* (Reynolds & Hearn, London, 2003)

Bentley, Chris *The Complete Book of Captain Scarlet* (Carlton Books, London, 2001)

Bentley, Chris *The Complete Book of Gerry Anderson's UFO* (Reynolds & Hearn, London, 2003)

Bishop, David *Bright Lights, Baked Ziti: The Sopranos, An Unofficial and Unauthorised Guide* (Virgin Books, London, 2001)

Bourke, Terry *Prisoner: Cell Block H – Behind the Scenes* (Angus & Robertson, London, 1990)

Clapham, Mark and Smith, Jim *Soul Searching: The Unofficial Guide to the Life and Trials of Ally McBeal* (Virgin Books, London, 2000)

Condon, Paul *Six Feet Under: The Unofficial Guide* (Contender Books, London, 2002)

Cornell, Paul; Day, Martin and Topping, Keith *The Avengers Dossier* (Virgin Books, London, 1997)

Cornell, Paul; Day, Martin and Topping, Keith *The Discontinuity Guide* (Monkeybrain Books, Austin, Texas, 2004)

Cornell, Paul; Day, Martin and Topping, Keith *The Guinness Book of Classic British TV*, 2nd edn (Guinness Publishing, Enfield, 1996)

Cornell, Paul; Day, Martin and Topping, Keith *The New Star Trek Programme Guide* (Virgin Books, London, 1995)

Cornell, Paul; Day, Martin and Topping, Keith *X-Treme Possibilities: A Paranoid Rummage Through The X-Files* (Virgin Books, London, 1997)

Cox, Stephen L. *The Addams Chronicles: Everything You Ever Wanted to Know about The Addams Family* (Harper Perennial, New York, 1991)

Creeber, Glen *Fifty Key Television Programmes* (Arnold Publishers, London, 2004)

Croft, David *You Have Been Watching . . . The Autobiography of David Croft* (BBC Worldwide, London, 2004)

Davies, Steven Paul *The Prisoner Companion: An Unauthorised Handbook* (Boxtree, London, 2002)

Evans, Jeff *The Guinness Television Encyclopaedia* (Guinness Publishing, London, 1995)

Evans, Jeff *The Penguin TV Companion*, 2nd edn (Penguin Books, London, 2003)

Fairclough, Robert and Kenwood, Mike *Sweeney! The Official Companion* (Reynolds & Hearn, London, 2002)

Fane-Saunders, Kilmeny *Radio Times Guide to Films* (BBC Worldwide, London, 2000)

Fiddy, Dick *Missing Believed Wiped: Searching for the Lost Treasures of British Television* (BFI Publishing, London, 2001)

Galton, Ray; Simpson, Alan and Ross, Robert *Steptoe and Son* (BBC Worldwide, London, 2002)

Gambaccini, Paul; Rice, Tim; Rice, Jonathan and Brown, Tony *The Complete Eurovision Song Contest Companion* (Pavillion, London, 1998)

Hancock, Freddie and Nathan, David *Hancock* (BBC Worldwide, London, 1997)

Hayward, Anthony and Rennert, Amy *Prime Suspect* (Carlton Books, London, 1996)

Howarth, Chris and Lyons, Steve *Red Dwarf Programme Guide*, 2nd revised edn (Virgin Books, London, 1997)

Howe, David J. and Walker, Stephen James *The Television Companion: The Unofficial and Unauthorised Guide to Doctor Who* (Telos Publishing, Tolworth, 2003)

Kingsley, Hilary *The Bill – The First Ten Years* (Boxtree, London, 1994)

Kingsley, Hilary *Casualty – The Inside Story* (BBC Worldwide, London, 1993)

Kingsley, Hilary *Prisoner: Cell Block H – The Inside Story* (Boxtree, London, 1990)

Lane, Andy *The Babylon Files* (Virgin Books, 1997)

Lewis, Jon E. and Stempel, Penny *Cult TV: The Essential Critical Guide* (Pavilion Books, London, 1993)

Lewis, Jon E. and Stempel, Penny *Cult TV: The . . . Detectives* (Pavilion Books, London, 1999)

Lewisohn, Mark *Radio Times Guide to TV Comedy* (BBC Worldwide, London, 2003)

Lewis-Smith, Victor *Inside the Magic Rectangle* (Victor Gollancz, London, 1995)

Little, Daran *40 Years of Coronation Street* (Granada, London, 2000)

Lynch, Tony *The Bill* (Boxtree, London, 1992)

Martyn, Warren and Wood, Adrian *I Can't Believe It's An Unofficial Simpsons Guide* (Virgin Books, London, 1997)

McCann, Graham *Dad's Army: The Story of a Classic Television Show* (4th Estate, London, 2001)

McGown, Alistair D. and Docherty, Mark J. *The Hill and Beyond: Children's Television Drama – An Encyclopaedia* (BFI Publishing, London, 2003)

Perry, Christopher and Down, Richard *British Television Drama Episode Guide 1950–1994* (Kaleidoscope Publishing, Dudley, 1994)

Richie, Jean *Big Brother – The Official Unseen Story* (Channel 4 Books, London, 2000)

Richie, Jean *Inside Big Brother – Getting In and Staying In* (Channel 4 Books, London, 2002)

Roberts, David *British Hit Singles and Albums*, 17th edn (Guinness World Records, London, 2004)

Rogers, Dave *The Complete Avengers* (Boxtree, London, 1992)

Ross, Robert *The Complete Goodies* (B. T. Batsford, London, 2000)

Sangster, Jim *24: The Unofficial Guide* (Contender Books, London, 2002)

Sangster, Jim and Bailey, David *Friends Like Us: The Unofficial Guide to Friends* (Virgin Books, London, 1997)

Sangster, Jim *The Press Gang Programme Guide* (Leomac Publishing, 1995)

Sangster, Jim *Spooks Confidential: The Official Handbook* (Contender Books, London, 2003)

Sheridan, Simon *The A-Z of Classic Children's Television* (Reynolds & Hearn, London, 2004)

Silver, Rachel *The Bill – The Inside Story* (HarperCollins, London, 1999)

Simpson, Paul *The Rough Guide to Cult TV: The Good, the Bad and the Strangely Compelling* (Rough Guides, London, 2002)

Smith, Jim *Manhattan Dating Game: An Unoffical and Unauthorised Guide to Sex and the City* (Virgin Books, London, 2002)

Stevens, Alan and Moore, Fiona *Liberation: The Unofficial and Unauthorised Guide to Blake's 7* (Telos Publishing, Tolworth, 2003)

Tibballs, Geoff *Phil Redmond's Brookside – Life in the Close* (Boxtree, London, 1994)

Tibballs, Geoff *Randall & Hopkirk Deceased* (Boxtree, London, 1994)

Tibballs, Geoff *Total Brookside* (Ebury Press, London, 1998)

Topping, Keith *Inside Bartlet's White House: An Unofficial and Unauthorised Guide to The West Wing* (Virgin Books, London, 2002)

Topping, Keith *Slayer: An Unofficial and Unauthorised Guide to Buffy The Vampire Slayer* (Virgin Books, London, 2002)

Turner, Chris *Planet Simpson* (Ebury Press, London, 2004)

Webber, Richard; Clement, Dick and La Frenais, Ian *Porridge: The Inside Story* (Headline Book Publishing, London, 2001)

Wild, David *Friends: The Official Companion* (Boxtree, London, 1995)

Periodicals

Cult TV (various issues; Future Publishing)
Doctor Who Magazine (various issues; Marvel/Panini)
Heat (various issues; Emap)
Radio Times (various issues; BBC Worldwide)
S.I.G. (various issues; Engale Marketing)
TV Times (various issues; IPC)

Websites

In addition to the many websites listed throughout this book, we'd like to recommend a few more:

Action TV – www.action-tv.org.uk/ – does what it says on the tin, covering action-based dramas and thrillers.

The **BBC** – bbc.co.uk – prides itself on being the biggest content website in Europe. Pages and pages of information pertinent to this book can be found in the comedy and cult sites, while h2g2 – www.bbc.co.uk/h2g2/ – the Guide to Life, the Universe and Everything, created by Douglas Adams as a real-life Hitchhiker's Guide to the Galaxy – is an ever-growing resource on all manner of topics, and is also available for mobiles and PDAs.

The **British Film Institute**'s website – www.screenonline.org.uk/ – contains loads of essays and data about hundreds of TV shows.

Epguides.com – epguides.com/ – and **TV.com** (formerly **TV Tome** – www.tv.com – are both excellent for episode listings and transmission dates.

The **Internet Movie DataBase** – www.imdb.com/ – relies on input from members of the public and so occasionally carries the odd mistake, but if you register it's easy to post amendments and additions and the site remains one of the absolute best resources on the internet.

Kaleidoscope – www.kaleidoscope.org.uk/ – is a group of TV enthusiasts whose work in archive research is simply phenomenal. These wonderful people spend their lives cataloguing every single broadcast of every single British programme ever made. They also organise events every year where enthusiasts can meet up and share info.

Little Gems – www.thechestnut.com/ – specialises in children's TV.

The Mausoleum Club – www.the-mausoleum-club.org.uk/ – promotes the perhaps understandable view that, with very few exceptions, nothing of merit has been produced in the last 15 years. This is the place to come if you miss the good old days when we had only three channels and they were wall-to-wall crammed with period dramas.

Off the Telly – www.offthetelly.co.uk/

SatKids – www.paulmorris.co.uk/satkids/ – the place to go for information about British Saturday morning TV.

TV Comedy Resources – www.phill.co.uk/ – offers an amazing amount of information about British comedy shows.

TV Cream – www.tv.cream.org/ – the original TV nostalgia site, which now includes downloadable theme tunes and retro adverts.

UK Gameshows – www.ukgameshows.com/

Whirlygig – www.whirligig-tv.co.uk/ – specialises in 1950s' nostalgia.

Wikipedia – www.wikipedia.com – the free encyclopaedia.

Glossary

405 line All television pictures are made up of a number of lines of definition – go up close to your own TV screen to see them. Until 1964, British television pictures consisted of 405 separate lines.

525 line The standard broadcast system in the USA and many other countries around the globe. 525-line pictures contain more sharpness of detail than the older British 405-line pictures, but less than the 625-line system currently used in the UK.

625 line Beginning with the launch of BBC Two on 20 April 1964, British television began phasing out the 405-line TV pictures and replacing them with higher-definition 625-line pictures for sharper quality. By 1969, all TV programmes in the UK were broadcast using the 625 system.

ABC (Australia) (Australian Broadcasting Company) The ABC is Australia's national public service broadcaster (similar to the BBC), producing national and local TV, radio and online services.

ABC (UK) (Associated-British Picture Corporation) One of the first ITV regional franchise holders, responsible for broadcasting on weekends to London and the Midlands of England.

ABC (USA) (American Broadcasting Company) One of the primary US TV networks. Nowadays owned by the Walt Disney Corporation, the ABC began regular TV broadcasts in 1948.

Action-Adventure A genre description that usually denotes swashbuckling, guns, car-chases and other such exciting fares, but not necessarily that much emotional depth.

Anglia One of the many companies that once held an ITV franchise, covering the East of England.

Anthology A series where there is little or no continuity between stories. Most anthologies would have a different cast and setting each time.

Associated-Rediffusion One of the first ITV regional franchise holders, responsible (until 1968) for broadcasting to London during weekdays.

ATV (Associated Television) One of the first ITV regional franchise holders, responsible for broadcasting to the Midlands of England (and in the early days, it also looked after London's weekend programming).

BARB Ratings (Broadcasters' Audience Research Board Ltd) BARB is the company responsible for producing the television ratings for the UK. As with every other system of generating ratings around the world, BARB bases its published figures upon an estimate – they don't have a special bit of magical equipment that works out the precise number of TVs around the country tuned in to a particular channel. Instead, BARB assembles a representative panel of UK residents that match the precise breakdown of the UK's population. They then attach a device to every TV set in the selected household, which monitors the viewing habits within that household (also taking into account such things as unexpected visitors) before feeding the information back automatically to BARB overnight. These 'Overnight' figures give an initial idea of the number of viewers – later, consolidated figures are published to take into account the additional number of viewers who might have watched a programme on video within the week following the broadcast.

BBC (British Broadcasting Corporation) The BBC is responsible for public service broadcasting in the United Kingdom, funded by a license fee payable by anyone who owns equipment capable of receiving television broadcasts. In 1964, BBC TV became BBC One with the arrival of BBC Two. At the time of writing, the BBC's television output is made up of BBC One, BBC Two, BBC Three, BBC Four, BBC News 24, BBC Parliament, CBBC and CBeebies, plus international channels BBC World and BBC Prime.

Border One of the many companies that once held an ITV franchise, covering Cumbria, the Scottish borders and the Isle of Man.

BSB (British Satellite Broadcasting) The only serious challenger to Sky for satellite television, it both arrived and collapsed in 1990, eventually merging with Sky to form British Sky Broadcasting.

Carlton An ITV franchise holder for the London region, taking over from Thames in 1991.

CBS (Columbia Broadcasting System) One of the primary American TV networks, CBS began life as a network of independent radio broadcasters before opening up its first TV station in New York (W2XAB) in 1931. Regular TV broadcasts began in 1946 – its logo is that of a stylised eye.

Central One of the many companies that once held an ITV franchise, covering the Midlands region during the 1980s and '90s.

CGI (Computer Generated Imagery) Often shortened nowadays to simply 'CG', the amazing effects achieved in this field have revolutionised many aspects of television broadcasting, enabling top-notch visual effects to be created in a fraction of the time and expense previously required.

Channel 4 Created in 1982 to cater for minority interests in England, Scotland and Northern Ireland. S4C covers Wales. Channel 4 currently offers an additional digital channel, E4.

Cliffhanger Used to describe a tense, unexpected or climactic scene that brings an episode to a nail-biting end. The term comes from the 1930s' serials where the hero would be literally hanging from a cliff and the audience would be left wondering how he'd escape. Now, it's used in soaps and serial dramas as a hook to entice viewers back for the next episode.

Closedown The time of day when TV used to stop broadcasting, play the national anthem and then fade to a test card for the rest of the night. Thanks to 24-hour programming, this no longer happens on terrestrial TV, though some cable/satellite channels run only in evenings or, on children's channels, up to a certain time.

Comedy A generic term for productions setting out to be funny. In this book, we use the term to describe a show that doesn't stick to the conventions of sitcom ?- for example, sketch-based shows.

CSO (Colour Separation Overlay) CSO is one of the technical terms used to describe the special effects process that most members of the public know as 'blue-screen' - the other industry name for it is Chromakey. The process replaces one specific colour in a TV picture with another image 'fed in' from another camera - you'll be familiar with the process if you've ever watched a news programme, weather forecast or any science fiction programme made in the UK in the 1970s or '80s. Any colour can be used as the colour to be replaced, although blue and green tend to be used most frequently.

Five Formerly Channel Five - the UK's fifth terrestrial channel.

Fox One of the main US TV networks, established in 1986 with the financial backing of international media magnate Rupert Murdoch, and trading upon the well-known entertainment brand name of 20th Century Fox.

Game Show A generic term for a production that involves some degree of physical participation. There may be quiz elements, but in this book we use the term to differentiate from the more sedate quiz show genre.

GM:TV The company currently in charge of ITV's breakfast service. It took over from TV AM in 1991.

Grampian One of the many companies that once held an ITV franchise, covering the Northern Highlands of Scotland.

Granada One of the first ITV regional franchise holders, responsible for broadcasting to the North of England.

HTV/HTV West/HTV Wales/ Cymru Harlech Television was one of the many companies that once held an ITV franchise, covering Wales and the southwest of England during the 1970s, '80s and '90s.

ITV (Independent Television in the United Kingdom) Until 2004, ITV was made up of smaller companies with responsibility for different regions across the UK. Now, ITV is one company and its television output is made up of ITV1, ITV2 and ITV3.

Lifestyle A generic term describing productions that try to show us how to lead our lives. DIY, gardening, heath and fashion shows would come under this banner.

Light Entertainment Traditionally used to describe programmes that are a bit light and fluffy, such as variety shows that combine comedy, music and dancing.

Live Broadcast As opposed to pre-recorded programming, we use this term to describe some of the big historical events mentioned in this book, such as *The Coronation of Queen Elizabeth II* and *Live Aid*.

LWT (London Weekend Television) LWT was one of the many companies that once held an ITV franchise, covering the London region from Friday evening until closedown on Sunday each weekend from 1968.

Magazine Describes programmes that are made up of smaller features. Presenters may come and go, but the formula for celebrity chat, light-hearted discussions, music and lifestyle tips remains generally constant.

NBC (National Broadcasting Company) One of the main American TV networks, created originally in 1926 as a chain of independent radio stations. Regular TV broadcasts began in 1946. Its logo is of a colourful peacock's tail.

Network While a TV service for a region or country might be run by one company, they might belong to an affiliated network that is responsible for providing programmes. In the UK, both the BBC and ITV channels have regional opt-outs but generally show the same programmes at the same time across the country. In the USA, the networks - including ABC, NBC and CBS - are the major players in the ratings wars.

Nielsen Ratings The company that produces the ratings for the US television networks. With an estimated 105 million households in the USA, a single Nielsen ratings point equates to approximately 1,055,000 viewers - therefore, a show that gets a Nielsen of 8.8 means that 9.63 million households in the USA were tuned in to the programme. So for stressed TV executives, the phrase 'the Nielsens were amazing!' can be one of the happiest that they can ever hear . . .

NTSC (National Television Systems Commission) NTSC is the television broadcasting system used in the USA, Canada, Japan and several other countries around the globe. It uses 525 lines of definition, shown at 60 half frames per second in order to create its images. This means that (in comparison to the UK's PAL system – see below) NTSC has a more stable, fluid image, but one with slightly less detail in the image as there are fewer lines of definition used to create the picture. One of the main criticisms levelled at NTSC is that the system fails to accurately recreate colour – indeed, the system has been nicknamed 'Never Twice the Same Colour' by technical wags.

PAL (Phase Alternating Line) PAL and is the television broadcasting system used in the UK, as well as many European countries and places like Australasia. It uses 625 lines of definition, shown at 50 half frames per second in order to create its images. This means that (in comparison to the American NTSC system) PAL has a sharper image, but one that appears to 'flicker' more as there are fewer individual frames shown per second. However PAL images have much more reliable colour signals than NTSC images. The different standards used in different countries around the globe to form their TV pictures mean that it's normally impossible to play back an American video tape on a British video recorder and television set, as the two systems use different numbers of lines and frame rates to compose their images. However, in recent years, many domestic video recorders and TVs in the UK have been fitted with on-board conversion equipment that allows the machines to replay NTSC tapes – if your machine is labelled 'NTSC playback', then the chances are you'll be able to watch American tapes in the UK. Unfortunately for our friends on the other side of the Atlantic, their VCRs don't normally boast a feature to replay PAL tapes.

Panel Game Similar to a quiz show but comprising either teams or simply a group of people answering questions, being flippant and focusing more on being entertaining than being right. Few panel games have a specific reward other than to be declared the winner of that edition.

PBS (Public Broadcasting Service) PBS is a real rarity in US broadcasting – a non profit-making network of small local TV stations whose philosophy is to carry the highest quality of programming rather than the shows that will attract the biggest audiences for their advertisers. Funded by donations from members of the public as well as corporate sponsors, the PBS network was established in 1969 and has provided a home for programmes such as *Sesame Street* and many British comedies and dramas (often under the banner *Masterpiece Theatre*) over the years. Although PBS can be received in more US homes than any other network, its educational or 'high-brow' remit means that few programmes receive more than minimal ratings.

Pre-School Shows directed at children aged five and under.

Quiz Show A programme that rewards knowledge over physical ability.

Ratings For most TV executives, the ratings that their programme receives are the difference between success and failure. In the highly competitive world of commercial television, a programme that fails to deliver a large enough audience (or an audience of the wrong type of viewer – advertisers prefer to attract younger, more affluent viewers than pensioners) will often find itself vanishing from the schedules quicker than you can say 'Celebrity Wrestling'.

Reality TV Also known as 'people shows', this term has come into favour to describe any programme that involves members of the public. It might follow them around their place of work or poke into their home life, or it might involve putting 'normal' people into an environment or situation they wouldn't usually experience. The phrase covers everything from *Driving School* to *Big Brother* and is often accompanied with a sneer by some critics.

Science Fiction H. G. Wells is usually credited with inventing the term, which loosely coves anything that uses situations or characters outside of normal human existence, often in an alien or space-related context.

Scottish Television One of the many companies that once held an ITV franchise, covering the central lowlands of Scotland.

Sitcom A comedy within a given situation – home, work, prison – using the same sets and characters.

Sky Although formally known as 'British Sky Broadcasting' after it merged with BSB, Britain's main satellite TV provider is commonly known as 'Sky'.

Soap Originally, this word was used to describe formulaic dramas that, in the USA, were sponsored by soap manufacturers like Lux. Now it's used as a generic term to cover any production that veers into melodrama. In the USA, soaps tend to be glossy and about extended wealthy families. In the UK, the longer lasting ones are more down to earth and involve working-class characters dealing with death, infidelity and anything else that might provide a decent cliffhanger to entice viewers back for the next edition. *The Grove Family* is credited with being the first British 'soap', though the similar *The Appleyards* pre-dated it but loses out to the title of 'First Soap' because it was made for children.

Southern One of the many companies that once held an ITV franchise, covering the south of England.

Stripped and stranded Describing how a channel schedules its programmes, this term effectively means that as a viewer, you can turn on a channel and know what to expect according to the day of the week and time of day. It was a major selling point of BBC Two and later Channel Five at launch, with each day of the week being themed (factual, lifestyle, drama, etc.), and with programmes slotted into 30-, 60- or 120-minute slots. It's a headache to maintain and most channels that adopt a 'stripped and stranded' policy tend to abandon it pretty sharpish.

Syndication In the USA, as well as the big national TV networks there are smaller, independent local stations. When TV shows come to the end of their lifespan, they're often sold on as a complete package to individual stations. Many TV shows that have been dropped from channels like NBC or CBS have later gained popularity in syndication, such as *Star Trek* and *The Addams Family*.

Telefantasy This is a generic term for the kind of TV show that steps outside of the boundaries of realism. Such programmes might include action-adventure serials like Ivanhoe, detective shows such as *Department S* or *Danger Man*, or science fiction like *Doctor Who*. The word is common among obsessive fans of archive television but not so much elsewhere.

Terrestrial Terrestrial channels can be received through analog receivers and TV aerials. The word 'terrestrial' is used to distinguish between channels that are available to all and those available only to cable/satellite subscribers.

Thames An ITV franchise holder, set up in 1968 to cover the London region during weekdays.

TV AM The original franchise holder for ITV's breakfast service. They were replaced in 1991 by GM:TV.

Tyne Tees One of the many companies that once held an ITV franchise, covering the northeast of England.

Ulster One of the many companies that once held an ITV franchise, covering Northern Ireland.

UPN (United Paramount Network) A late addition to the main US TV networks, UPN was established by Viacom (who also own the CBS network) in 1995.

VCR (Video Cassette Recorder) An acronym more common in the USA and among TV professionals than among most of the UK population, who seem much happier asking their family or friends, 'Did you set the video?'

WB The WB Television Network was founded in 1995 as a joint venture between the Warner Bros Film Studio and the Tribune Company. Its logo is a frog wearing a top hat – indeed, the network is occasionally referred to as 'The Frog'. Much of its programming is aimed at teen or ethnic minority audiences.

Yorkshire/YTV One of the many companies that once held an ITV franchise, covering the Yorkshire region.

Index of programmes

Index of programmes

The entries and page numbers in **bold** represent main entries in the A–Z of TV

D

E

Index of people

B

G

L

S

Picture Credits

pp. 24, 48, 76, 110, 117, 124, 168, 208, 220, 246, 254, 272, 290, 302, 306, 314, 340, 343, 350, 362, 428, 434, 438, 448, 490, 494, 498, 520, 534, 537, 542, 562, 568, 596, 646, 700, 718, 742, 768, 792, 800, 812, 815, 856, 859, 862 © BBC Photo Library;
p. 44 © Mark Lawrence/scopefeatures.com;
p. 62 © scopefeatures.com; p. 68 © UPPA/Photoshot;
p. 90 © Alan Olley/scopefeatures.com; p. 93 © uppa.co.uk;
p. 98 © TVTimes/scopefeatures.com; p. 140 © uppa.co.uk;
p. 148 © Band Photo/uppa.co.uk; p. 156 © uppa.co.uk;
p. 158 © scopefeatures.com; p. 164 © UPPA/Photoshot;
p. 196 © TVTimes/scopefeatures.com; p. 212 © TVTimes/scopefeatures.com; p. 225 © uppa.co.uk; p. 249 © TVTimes/scopefeatures.com; p. 266 © Band Photo/uppa.co.uk;
p. 282 © scopefeatures.com; p. 304 © TVTimes/scopefeatures.com;
p. 324 © Band Photo/uppa.co.uk; p. 400 © 2005 Oliver Postgate/Peter Firmin; p. 458 © Magic Rights Ltd/M Danot 2004;
p. 478 © Rollo Rights Ltd 2005; p. 486 © Python (Monty) Pictures Ltd; p. 501 © UPPA/Photoshot; p. 512 © FremantleMedia Stills;
p. 574 © Mark Bourdillon/scopefeatures.com;
p. 577 © scopefeatures.com; p. 581 reproduced courtesy of ITV plc(Granada Int'l)/LFI; p. 585 © FremantleMedia Stills;
p. 589 © scopefeatures.com; p. 602 © Paul Jones;
p. 610 © TVTimes/scopefeatures.com; p. 612 reproduced courtesy of ITV plc(Granada Int'l)/LFI; p. 616 © Chris Ridley/Grant Naylor Productions Ltd; p. 624 © Brian Moody/scopefeatures.com;
p. 652 © ITV Granada; p. 656 © UPPA/Photoshot;
p. 664 © Brian Moody/scopefeatures.com; p. 672 © uppa.co.uk;
p. 688 © scopefeatures.com; p. 690 © Band Photo/uppa.co.uk;
p. 704 © uppa.co.uk; p. 712 © CORBIS KIPA;
p. 730 © TVTimes/scopefeatures.com; p. 758 © uppa.co.uk;
p. 776 © 2005 Gordon Murray (Trumptonshire) Ltd/Licensed by Entertainment Rights Distribution Ltd; p. 782 © UPPA/Photoshot;
p. 784 © Rex Features; p. 789 © UPPA/Photoshot;
p. 802 © scopefeatures.com; p. 828 © UPPA/Photoshot;
p. 842 © TVTimes/scopefeatures.com; p. 846 © scopefeatures.com;
p. 850 © Band Photo/uppa.co.uk

Acknowledgements

We are indebted beyond imagining to Mark Wright, Dan Hogarth and Gary Russell, whose additional research proved life saving in the final run. Without their hard work this volume would have been considerably slimmer.

Paul Cornell made the book possible, firstly by being a pathfinder and mentor through the years, but mainly through being far too busy to write it himself, for which we also thank *Doctor Who* and the other projects that kept him from us.

Steve Berry, Louis Niebur and Alistair McGowan provided a constant stream of facts, credits and enthusiasm long after our own had been exhausted. Thanks for always being there and never refusing our begging emails. Huge thanks also to Ian Garrard, Mark Hodder, Tim Worthington and Colin Hunter for input and advice on their own areas of expertise.

We're hugely grateful for the research of many others who continue to educate, inform and entertain us all on the subject of TV history, including Richard Bignall, John Binns, John Brand, Gary Gillatt, Clayton Hickman, Chris Howarth, Robert Franks, Andy Lane, Steve Lyons, Andrew Martin, Richy Moosbally, Adrian Petford, Gareth Roberts, Jim Smith, Gary Wah.

Thanks to the busy beavers at Kaleidoscope, whose phone-book-sized reference guides are the single most valuable research work we've encountered.

Thanks to all the marvellous team at HarperCollins, in particular Helen Brocklehurst and Emma Callery for waiting and patience. Huge thanks also to Kate Parker for her eagle-eyes and to Julia Koppitz for unstinting work on tracking down the wonderful pictures you see in this book.

We'd also like to say a huge thanks to a number of very special individuals who've kept our spirits high throughout the whole process of writing this book: Neil Bastian, Andrew Webb, Jane Glennon, Caroline Clayton, Venus Speedwell, Richard Smith, Darren Sellars, Dan Judd, James Goss, Lisa and Ian Hodge (and Josh and Rose, of course!) and Wendy Leston.

A special mention for Natalie Johnson – for patience, encouragement, style, Pingu, cake and perspective.

And finally to our parents, Audrey & Mark Condon and Jim & Marge Sangster, without whom . . .

Contact us

If you'd like to drop us a line about anything in (or indeed not in) this book you can email us at tv@collins.co.uk with your comments.

We can't promise to reply to every email, but we look forward to hearing from you!